THE CONCISE FRENCH DICTIONARY

French-English, English-French

Wordsworth Editions

This edition published 1991 by Wordsworth Editions Ltd,
8b East Street, Ware, Hertfordshire, under licence
from the proprietor.

ISBN 1-85326-958-1

Printed and bound in Great Britain by Mackays of Chatham.

INTRODUCTION

L'usager qui désire comprendre l'anglais – qui déchiffre – trouvera dans ce dictionnaire un vocabulaire moderne et très complet, comprenant de nombreux composés et locutions appartenant à la langue contemporaine. Il trouvera aussi dans l'ordre alphabétique les principales formes irrégulières, avec un renvoi à la forme de base où figure la traduction, ainsi qu'abréviations, sigles et noms géographiques choisis parmi les plus courants.

L'usager qui veut s'exprimer – communiquer – dans la langue étrangère trouvera un traitement détaillé du vocabulaire fondamental, avec de nombreuses indications le guidant vers la traduction juste, et lui montrant comment l'utiliser correctement.

The user whose aim is to read and understand French will find in this dictionary a comprehensive and up-to-date wordlist including numerous phrases in current use. He will also find listed alphabetically the main irregular forms with a cross-reference to the basic form where a translation is given, as well as some of the most common abbreviations, acronyms and geographical names.

The user who wishes to communicate and to express himself in the foreign language will find clear and detailed treatment of all the basic words, with numerous indications pointing to the appropriate translation, and helping him to use it correctly.

CONTENTS

ABRÉVIATIONS		ABBREVIATIONS
adjectif, locution adjective	**a**	adjective, adjectival phrase
abréviation	**ab(b)r**	abbreviation
adverbe, locution adverbiale	**ad**	adverb, adverbial phrase
administration	**ADMIN**	administration
agriculture	**AGR**	agriculture
anatomie	**ANAT**	anatomy
architecture	**ARCHIT**	architecture
l'automobile	**AUT(O)**	the motor car and motoring
aviation, voyages aériens	**AVIAT**	flying, air travel
biologie	**BIO(L)**	biology
botanique	**BOT**	botany
anglais de Grande-Bretagne	**Brit**	British English
conjonction	**cj**	conjunction
langue familière (! emploi vulgaire)	**col (!)**	colloquial usage (! particularly offensive)
commerce, finance, banque	**COMM**	commerce, finance, banking
construction	**CONSTR**	building
nom utilisé comme adjectif, ne peut s'employer ni comme attribut, ni après le nom qualifié	**cpd**	compound element: noun used as an adjective and which cannot follow the noun it qualifies
cuisine, art culinaire	**CULIN**	cookery
déterminant: article, adjectif démonstratif ou indéfini etc	**dét, det**	determiner: article, demonstrative etc.
économie	**ECON**	economics
électricité, électronique	**ELEC**	electricity, electronics
exclamation, interjection	**excl**	exclamation, interjection
féminin	**f**	feminine
langue familière (! emploi vulgaire)	**fam (!)**	colloquial usage (! particularly offensive)
emploi figuré	**fig**	figurative use
(verbe anglais) dont la particule est inséparable du verbe	**fus**	(phrasal verb) where the particle cannot be separated from main verb
dans la plupart des sens; généralement	**gén, gen**	in most or all senses; generally
géographie, géologie	**GEO**	geography, geology
géométrie	**GEOM**	geometry
invariable	**inv**	invariable
irrégulier	**irg**	irregular
domaine juridique	**JUR**	law
grammaire, linguistique	**LING**	grammar, linguistics
masculin	**m**	masculine
mathématiques, algèbre	**MATH**	mathematics, calculus
médecine	**MED**	medical term, medicine
masculin ou féminin, suivant le sexe	**m/f**	either masculine or feminine depending on sex
domaine militaire, armée	**MIL**	military matters
musique	**MUS**	music
nom	**n**	noun
navigation, nautisme	**NAVIG, NAUT**	sailing, navigation
adjectif ou nom numérique	**num**	numeral adjective or noun
	o.s.	oneself
péjoratif	**péj, pej**	derogatory, pejorative
photographie	**PHOT(O)**	photography
physiologie	**PHYSIOL**	physiology
pluriel	**pl**	plural
politique	**POL**	politics
participe passé	**pp**	past participle
préposition	**prép, prep**	preposition
psychologie, psychiatrie	**PSYCH**	psychology, psychiatry

temps du passé	**pt**	past tense
nom non comptable: ne peut s'utiliser au pluriel	**q**	collective (uncountable) noun: is not used in the plural
quelque chose	**qch**	
quelqu'un	**qn**	
religions, domaine ecclésiastique	**REL**	religions, church service
	sb	somebody
enseignement, système scolaire et universitaire	**SCOL**	schooling, schools and universities
singulier	**sg**	singular
	sth	something
subjonctif	**sub**	subjunctive
sujet (grammatical)	**su(b)j**	(grammatical) subject
techniques, technologie	**TECH**	technical term, technology
télécommunications	**TEL**	telecommunications
télévision	**TV**	television
typographie	**TYP(O)**	typography, printing
anglais des USA	**US**	American English
verbe	**vb**	verb
verbe ou groupe verbal à fonction intransitive	**vi**	verb or phrasal verb used intransitively
verbe ou groupe verbal à fonction transitive	**vt**	verb or phrasal verb used transitively
zoologie	**ZOOL**	zoology
marque déposée	**®**	registered trademark
indique une équivalence culturelle	**≈**	introduces a cultural equivalent

FRANÇAIS-ANGLAIS
FRENCH-ENGLISH

A

a *vb voir* **avoir.**

à (*à* + *le* = **au**, *à* + *les* = **aux**) [a, o] *prép* (*situation*) at, in ; (*direction, attribution*) to ; (*provenance*) from ; (*moyen*) with, by ; **payé au mois** paid by the month ; **100 km/unités à l'heure** 100 km/units per hour ; **à 3 heures/minuit** at 3 o'clock/midnight ; **au mois de juin** in the month of June ; **se chauffer au gaz** to heat one's house with gas ; **à bicyclette** by bicycle *ou* on a bicycle ; **l'homme aux yeux bleus** the man with the blue eyes ; **à la semaine prochaine!** see you next week! ; **à la russe** the Russian way, in the Russian fashion.

abaisser [abese] *vt* to lower, bring down ; (*manette*) to pull down ; (*fig*) to debase ; to humiliate ; **s'~** *vi* to go down ; (*fig*) to demean o.s. ; **s'~ à faire/à qch** to stoop *ou* descend to doing/to sth.

abandon [abɑ̃dɔ̃] *nm* abandoning ; deserting ; giving up ; relinquishing ; (*SPORT*) withdrawal ; (*fig*) lack of constraint ; relaxed pose *ou* mood ; **être à l'~** to be in a state of neglect.

abandonné, e [abɑ̃dɔne] *a* (*solitaire*) deserted.

abandonner [abɑ̃dɔne] *vt* to leave, abandon, desert ; (*projet, activité*) to abandon, give up ; (*SPORT*) to retire *ou* withdraw from ; (*céder*) to surrender, relinquish ; **s'~** *vi* to let o.s. go ; **s'~ à** (*paresse, plaisirs*) to give o.s. up to.

abasourdir [abazuʀdiʀ] *vt* to stun, stagger.

abat-jour [abaʒuʀ] *nm inv* lampshade.

abats [aba] *nmpl* (*de bœuf, porc*) offal *sg* ; (*de volaille*) giblets.

abattage [abataʒ] *nm* cutting down, felling ; (*entrain*) go, dynamism.

abattement [abatmɑ̃] *nm* enfeeblement ; dejection, despondency ; (*déduction*) reduction ; **~ fiscal** ≈ tax allowance.

abattis [abati] *nmpl* giblets.

abattoir [abatwaʀ] *nm* abattoir, slaughterhouse.

abattre [abatʀ(ə)] *vt* (*arbre*) to cut down, fell ; (*mur, maison*) to pull down ; (*avion, personne*) to shoot down ; (*animal*) to shoot, kill ; (*fig*) to wear out, tire out ; to demoralize ; **s'~** *vi* to crash down ; **s'~ sur** to beat down on ; to rain down on.

abbaye [abei] *nf* abbey.

abbé [abe] *nm* priest ; (*d'une abbaye*) abbot ; **M. l'~** Father.

abc, ABC [abese] *nm* alphabet primer ; (*fig*) rudiments *pl*.

abcès [apsɛ] *nm* abscess.

abdication [abdikɑsjɔ̃] *nf* abdication.

abdiquer [abdike] *vi* to abdicate // *vt* to renounce, give up.

abdomen [abdɔmɛn] *nm* abdomen ; **abdominal, e, aux** *a* abdominal // *nmpl*: **faire des abdominaux** to do exercises for the stomach muscles.

abécédaire [abesedɛʀ] *nm* alphabet primer.

abeille [abɛj] *nf* bee.

aberrant, e [abɛʀɑ̃, -ɑ̃t] *a* absurd.

abêtir [abetiʀ] *vt* to turn into a half-wit.

abhorrer [abɔʀe] *vt* to abhor, loathe.

abîme [abim] *nm* abyss, gulf.

abîmer [abime] *vt* to spoil, damage ; **s'~** *vi* to get spoilt *ou* damaged ; (*tomber*) to sink, founder.

abject, e [abʒɛkt] *a* abject, despicable.

abjurer [abʒyʀe] *vt* to abjure, renounce.

ablation [ablɑsjɔ̃] *nf* removal.

ablutions [ablysjɔ̃] *nfpl*: **faire ses ~** to perform one's ablutions.

abnégation [abnegɑsjɔ̃] *nf* (self-) abnegation.

aboiement [abwamɑ̃] *nm* bark, barking *q*.

abois [abwa] *nmpl*: **aux ~** at bay.

abolir [abɔliʀ] *vt* to abolish ; **abolition** *nf* abolition.

abominable [abɔminabl(ə)] *a* abominable.

abondance [abɔ̃dɑ̃s] *nf* abundance ; (*richesse*) affluence.

abondant, e [abɔ̃dɑ̃, -ɑ̃t] *a* plentiful, abundant, copious.

abonder [abɔ̃de] *vi* to abound, be plentiful ; **~ en** to be full of, abound in ; **~ dans le sens de qn** to concur with sb.

abonné, e [abɔne] *nm/f* subscriber ; season ticket holder.

abonnement [abɔnmɑ̃] *nm* subscription ; (*pour transports en commun, concerts*) season ticket.

abonner [abɔne] *vt*: **s'~ à** to subscribe to, take out a subscription to.

abord [abɔʀ] *nm*: **être d'un ~ facile** to be approachable ; **~s** *nmpl* surroundings ; **au premier ~** at first sight, initially ; **d'~** *ad* first.

abordable [abɔʀdabl(ə)] *a* approachable ; reasonably priced.

abordage [abɔʀdaʒ] *nm* boarding.

aborder [abɔʀde] *vi* to land // *vt* (*sujet, difficulté*) to tackle ; (*personne*) to approach ; (*rivage etc*) to reach ; (*NAVIG*: *attaquer*) to board ; (: *heurter*) to collide with.

aborigène [abɔʀiʒɛn] *nm* aborigine, native.

aboulique [abulik] *a* totally lacking in willpower.

aboutir [abutiʀ] *vi* (*négociations etc*) to succeed ; **~ à/dans/sur** to end up at/in/on ; **aboutissants** *nmpl voir* **tenants.**

aboyer [abwaje] *vi* to bark.

abracadabrant, e [abʀakadabʀɑ̃, -ɑ̃t] *a* incredible, preposterous.

abrasif, ive [abʀazif, -iv] *a, nm* abrasive.

abrégé [abʀeʒe] *nm* summary.

abréger [abʀeʒe] *vt* (*texte*) to shorten, abridge ; (*mot*) to shorten, abbreviate ; (*réunion, voyage*) to cut short, shorten.

abreuver [abʀœve] *vt* to water; (*fig*): ~ **qn de** to shower *ou* swamp sb with; **s'**~ *vi* to drink; **abreuvoir** *nm* watering place.
abréviation [abʀevjɑsjɔ̃] *nf* abbreviation.
abri [abʀi] *nm* shelter; **à l'**~ under cover; **à l'**~ **de** sheltered from; (*fig*) safe from.
abricot [abʀiko] *nm* apricot; **abricotier** *nm* apricot tree.
abriter [abʀite] *vt* to shelter; (*loger*) to accommodate; **s'**~ to shelter, take cover.
abroger [abʀɔʒe] *vt* to repeal, abrogate.
abrupt, e [abʀypt] *a* sheer, steep; (*ton*) abrupt.
abruti, e [abʀyti] *nm/f* (*fam*) idiot, moron.
abrutir [abʀytiʀ] *vt* to daze; to exhaust; to stupefy.
abscisse [apsis] *nf* abscissa, X axis.
absence [apsɑ̃s] *nf* absence; (*MÉD*) blackout; mental blank.
absent, e [apsɑ̃, -ɑ̃t] *a* absent; (*chose*) missing, lacking; (*distrait*: *air*) vacant, faraway // *nm/f* absentee; **absentéisme** *nm* absenteeism; **s'absenter** *vi* to take time off work; (*sortir*) to leave, go out.
absinthe [apsɛ̃t] *nf* (*boisson*) absinth(e); (*BOT*) wormwood, absinth(e).
absolu, e [apsɔly] *a* absolute; (*caractère*) rigid, uncompromising; ~**ment** *ad* absolutely.
absolution [apsɔlysjɔ̃] *nf* absolution.
absolutisme [apsɔlytism(ə)] *nm* absolutism.
absolve *etc vb voir* **absoudre**.
absorbant, e [apsɔʀbɑ̃, -ɑ̃t] *a* absorbent.
absorbé, e [apsɔʀbe] *a* engrossed, absorbed.
absorber [apsɔʀbe] *vt* to absorb; (*gén MÉD*: *manger, boire*) to take.
absoudre [apsudʀ(ə)] *vt* to absolve.
abstenir [apstəniʀ]: **s'**~ *vi* (*POL*) to abstain; **s'**~ **de qch/de faire** to refrain from sth/from doing; **abstention** *nf* abstention; **abstentionnisme** *nm* abstentionism.
abstinence [apstinɑ̃s] *nf* abstinence.
abstraction [apstʀaksjɔ̃] *nf* abstraction; **faire** ~ **de** to set *ou* leave aside.
abstraire [apstʀɛʀ] *vt* to abstract; **abstrait, e** *a* abstract.
absurde [apsyʀd(ə)] *a* absurd // *nm* absurdity; absurd; **par l'**~ ad absurdio; **absurdité** *nf* absurdity.
abus [aby] *nm* (*excès*) abuse, misuse; (*injustice*) abuse; ~ **de confiance** breach of trust; embezzlement.
abuser [abyze] *vi* to go too far, overstep the mark // *vt* to deceive, mislead; ~ **de** *vt* (*force, droit*) to misuse; (*alcool*) to take to excess; (*violer, duper*) to take advantage of; **s'**~ (*se méprendre*) to be mistaken; **abusif, ive** *a* exorbitant; excessive; improper.
acabit [akabi] *nm*: **de cet** ~ of that type.
académicien, ne [akademisjɛ̃, -jɛn] *nm/f* academician.
académie [akademi] *nf* (*société*) learned society; (*école*: *d'art, de danse*) academy; (*ART*: *nu*) nude; (*SCOL*: *circonscription*) ≈ regional education authority; **l'A**~ **(française)** the French Academy; **académique** *a* academic.
acajou [akaʒu] *nm* mahogany.
acariâtre [akaʀjɑtʀ(ə)] *a* sour(-tempered).
accablement [akɑbləmɑ̃] *nm* despondency, depression.
accabler [akɑble] *vt* to overwhelm, overcome; (*suj*: *témoignage*) to condemn, damn; ~ **qn d'injures** to heap *ou* shower abuse on sb; ~ **qn de travail** to overburden sb with work; **accablé de dettes/soucis** weighed down with debts/cares.
accalmie [akalmi] *nf* lull.
accaparer [akapaʀe] *vt* to monopolize; (*sujet*: *travail etc*) to take up (all) the time *ou* attention of.
accéder [aksede]: ~ **à** *vt* (*lieu*) to reach; (*fig*: *pouvoir*) to accede to; (: *poste*) to attain; (*accorder*: *requête*) to grant, accede to.
accélérateur [akseleʀatœʀ] *nm* accelerator.
accélération [akseleʀɑsjɔ̃] *nf* speeding up; acceleration.
accélérer [akseleʀe] *vt* (*mouvement, travaux*) to speed up // *vi* (*AUTO*) to accelerate.
accent [aksɑ̃] *nm* accent; (*inflexions expressives*) tone (of voice); (*PHONÉTIQUE, fig*) stress; **aux** ~**s de** (*musique*) to the strains of; **mettre l'**~ **sur** (*fig*) to stress; ~ **aigu/grave** acute/grave accent.
accentuation [aksɑ̃tɥɑsjɔ̃] *nf* accenting; stressing.
accentuer [aksɑ̃tɥe] *vt* (*LING*: *orthographe*) to accent; (: *phonétique*) to stress, accent; (*fig*) to accentuate, emphasize; to increase; **s'**~ *vi* to become more marked *ou* pronounced.
acceptable [aksɛptabl(ə)] *a* satisfactory, acceptable.
acceptation [aksɛptɑsjɔ̃] *nf* acceptance.
accepter [aksɛpte] *vt* to accept; ~ **de faire** to agree to do; (*tolérer*): ~ **que qn fasse** to agree to sb doing, let sb do.
acception [aksɛpsjɔ̃] *nf* meaning, sense.
accès [aksɛ] *nm* (*à un lieu*) access; (*MÉD*) attack; fit, bout; outbreak // *nmpl* (*routes etc*) means of access, approaches; **d'**~ **facile** easily accessible; ~ **de colère** fit of anger; ~ **de joie** burst of joy; **donner** ~ **à** (*lieu*) to give access to; (*carrière*) to open the door to; **avoir** ~ **auprès de qn** to have access to sb.
accessible [aksesibl(ə)] *a* accessible; (*livre, sujet*): ~ **à qn** within the reach of sb; (*sensible*): ~ **à la pitié/l'amour** open to pity/love.
accession [aksɛsjɔ̃] *nf*: ~ **à** accession to; attainment of.
accessit [aksesit] *nm* (*SCOL*) ≈ certificate of merit.
accessoire [akseswaʀ] *a* secondary, of secondary importance; incidental // *nm* accessory; (*THÉÂTRE*) prop; **accessoiriste** *nm/f* (*TV, CINÉMA*) property man/girl.
accident [aksidɑ̃] *nm* accident; **par** ~ by chance; ~ **de la route** road accident; **accidenté e** *a* damaged *ou* injured (in an accident); (*relief, terrain*) uneven; hilly; **accidentel, le** *a* accidental.
acclamation [aklamɑsjɔ̃] *nf*: **par** ~

(*vote*) by acclamation ; ~**s** *nfpl* cheers, cheering *sg*.
acclamer [aklame] *vt* to cheer, acclaim.
acclimatation [aklimatɑsjɔ̃] *nf* acclimatization.
acclimater [aklimate] *vt* to acclimatize ; **s'**~ *vi* to become acclimatized.
accointances [akwɛ̃tɑ̃s] *nfpl*: **avoir des ~ avec** to have contacts with.
accolade [akɔlad] *nf* (*amicale*) embrace ; (*signe*) brace ; **donner l'~ à qn** to embrace sb.
accoler [akɔle] *vt* to place side by side.
accommodant, e [akɔmɔdɑ̃, -ɑ̃t] *a* accommodating.
accommodement [akɔmɔdmɑ̃] *nm* compromise.
accommoder [akɔmɔde] *vt* (*CULIN*) to prepare ; (*points de vue*) to reconcile ; **s'~ de** to put up with ; to make do with.
accompagnateur, trice [akɔ̃paɲatœʀ, -tʀis] *nm/f* (*MUS*) accompanist ; (*de voyage*: *guide*) guide ; (: *d'enfants*) accompanying adult ; (: *de voyage organisé*) courier.
accompagnement [akɔ̃paɲmɑ̃] *nm* (*MUS*) accompaniment.
accompagner [akɔ̃paɲe] *vt* to accompany, be *ou* go *ou* come with ; (*MUS*) to accompany.
accompli, e [akɔ̃pli] *a* accomplished.
accomplir [akɔ̃pliʀ] *vt* (*tâche, projet*) to carry out ; (*souhait*) to fulfil ; **s'~** *vi* to be fulfilled ; **accomplissement** *nm* carrying out ; fulfilment.
accord [akɔʀ] *nm* (*entente, convention, LING*) agreement ; (*entre des styles, tons etc*) harmony ; (*consentement*) agreement, consent ; (*MUS*) chord ; **se mettre d'~** to come to an agreement (with each other) ; **être d'~** to agree ; ~ **parfait** (*MUS*) tonic chord.
accordéon [akɔʀdeɔ̃] *nm* (*MUS*) accordion ; **accordéoniste** *nm/f* accordionist.
accorder [akɔʀde] *vt* (*faveur, délai*) to grant ; (*harmoniser*) to match ; (*MUS*) to tune ; **s'~** to get on together ; to agree ; (*LING*) to agree ; **accordeur** *nm* (*MUS*) tuner.
accoster [akɔste] *vt* (*NAVIG*) to draw alongside ; (*personne*) to accost // *vi* (*NAVIG*) to berth.
accotement [akɔtmɑ̃] *nm* (*de route*) verge, shoulder ; ~**s non stabilisés** soft verges.
accoter [akɔte] *vt*: ~ **qch contre/à** to lean *ou* rest sth against/on ; **s'~ contre/à** to lean against/on.
accouchement [akuʃmɑ̃] *nm* delivery, (child)birth ; labour.
accoucher [akuʃe] *vi* to give birth, have a baby ; (*être en travail*) to be in labour // *vt* to deliver ; ~ **d'un garçon** to give birth to a boy ; **accoucheur** *nm*: **(médecin) accoucheur** obstetrician ; **accoucheuse** *nf* midwife.
accouder [akude]: **s'~** *vi*: **s'~ à/contre** to rest one's elbows on/against ; **accoudoir** *nm* armrest.
accouplement [akupləmɑ̃] *nm* mating ; coupling.
accoupler [akuple] *vt* to couple ; (*pour la reproduction*) to mate ; **s'~** to mate.
accourir [akuʀiʀ] *vi* to rush *ou* run up.
accoutrement [akutʀəmɑ̃] *nm* (*péj*) getup, rig-out.
accoutumance [akutymɑ̃s] *nf* (*gén*) adaptation ; (*MÉD*) addiction.
accoutumé, e [akutyme] *a* (*habituel*) customary, usual.
accoutumer [akutyme] *vt*: ~ **qn à qch/faire** to accustom sb to sth/to doing ; **s'~ à** to get accustomed *ou* used to.
accréditer [akʀedite] *vt* (*nouvelle*) to substantiate ; ~ **qn (auprès de)** to accredit sb (to).
accroc [akʀo] *nm* (*déchirure*) tear ; (*fig*) hitch, snag.
accrochage [akʀɔʃaʒ] *nm* hanging (up) ; hitching (up) ; (*AUTO*) (minor) collision, bump ; (*MIL*) encounter, engagement ; (*dispute*) clash, brush.
accroche-cœur [akʀɔʃkœʀ] *nm* kiss-curl.
accrocher [akʀɔʃe] *vt* (*suspendre*): ~ **qch à** to hang sth (up) on ; (*attacher*: *remorque*): ~ **qch à** to hitch sth (up) to ; (*heurter*) to catch ; to catch on ; to hit ; (*déchirer*): ~ **qch (à)** to catch sth (on) ; (*MIL*) to engage ; (*fig*) to catch, attract ; **s'~** (*se disputer*) to have a clash *ou* brush ; **s'~ à** (*rester pris à*) to catch on ; (*agripper, fig*) to hang on *ou* cling to.
accroissement [akʀwasmɑ̃] *nm* increase.
accroître [akʀwatʀ(ə)] *vt* to increase ; **s'~** *vi* to increase.
accroupi, e [akʀupi] *a* squatting, crouching (down).
accroupir [akʀupiʀ]: **s'~** *vi* to squat, crouch (down).
accru, e [akʀy] *pp de* **accroître.**
accu [aky] *nm abr de* **accumulateur.**
accueil [akœj] *nm* welcome ; **comité d'~** reception committee.
accueillir [akœjiʀ] *vt* to welcome ; (*loger*) to accommodate.
acculer [akyle] *vt*: ~ **qn à** *ou* **contre** to drive sb back against ; ~ **qn dans** to corner sb in ; ~ **qn à** (*faillite*) to drive sb to the brink of.
accumulateur [akymylatœʀ] *nm* accumulator.
accumulation [akymylɑsjɔ̃] *nf* accumulation ; **chauffage/radiateur à ~** (night-)storage heating/heater.
accumuler [akymyle] *vt* to accumulate, amass ; **s'~** *vi* to accumulate ; to pile up.
accusateur, trice [akyzatœʀ, -tʀis] *nm/f* accuser // *a* accusing ; (*document, preuve*) incriminating.
accusatif [akyzatif] *nm* (*LING*) accusative.
accusation [akyzɑsjɔ̃] *nf* (*gén*) accusation ; (*JUR*) charge ; (*partie*): **l'~** the prosecution ; **mettre en ~** to indict.
accusé, e [akyze] *nm/f* accused ; defendant ; ~ **de réception** acknowledgement of receipt.
accuser [akyze] *vt* to accuse ; (*fig*) to emphasize, bring out ; to show ; ~ **qn de** to accuse sb of ; (*JUR*) to charge sb with ; ~ **qch de** (*rendre responsable*) to blame sth for ; ~ **réception de** to acknowledge receipt of.
acerbe [asɛʀb(ə)] *a* caustic, acid.

acéré, e [aseʀe] *a* sharp.
achalandé, e [aʃalɑ̃de] *a*: **bien ~** well-stocked; well-patronized.
acharné, e [aʃaʀne] *a* (*lutte, adversaire*) fierce, bitter; (*travail*) relentless, unremitting.
acharnement [aʃaʀnəmɑ̃] *nm* fierceness; relentlessness.
acharner [aʃaʀne]: **s'~** *vi*: **s'~ sur** to go at fiercely, hound; **s'~ contre** to set o.s. against; to dog, pursue; **s'~ à faire** to try doggedly to do; to persist in doing.
achat [aʃa] *nm* buying *q*; purchase; **faire l'~ de** to buy, purchase; **faire des ~s** to do some shopping, buy a few things.
acheminer [aʃmine] *vt* (*courrier*) to forward, dispatch; (*troupes*) to convey, transport; (*train*) to route; **s'~ vers** to head for.
acheter [aʃte] *vt* to buy, purchase; (*soudoyer*) to buy; **~ qch à** (*marchand*) to buy *ou* purchase sth from; (*ami etc*: *offrir*) to buy sth for; **acheteur, euse** *nm/f* buyer; shopper; (COMM) buyer; (JUR) vendee, purchaser.
achevé, e [aʃve] *a*: **d'un ridicule ~** thoroughly *ou* absolutely ridiculous.
achèvement [aʃɛvmɑ̃] *nm* completion; finishing.
achever [aʃve] *vt* to complete, finish; to end; (*blessé*) to finish off; **s'~** *vi* to end.
achoppement [aʃɔpmɑ̃] *nm*: **pierre d'~** stumbling block.
acide [asid] *a* acid, sharp; (CHIMIE) acid(ic) // *nm* (CHIMIE) acid; **acidifier** *vt* to acidify; **acidité** *nf* acidity; sharpness; **acidulé, e** *a* slightly acid; **bonbons acidulés** acid drops.
acier [asje] *nm* steel; **aciérie** *nf* steelworks *sg*.
acné [akne] *nf* acne.
acolyte [akɔlit] *nm* (*péj*) confederate.
acompte [akɔ̃t] *nm* deposit; (*versement régulier*) instalment; (*sur somme due*) payment on account; **un ~ de 100 F** 100 F on account.
acoquiner [akɔkine]: **s'~ avec** *vt* (*péj*) to team up with.
à-côté [akote] *nm* side-issue; (*argent*) extra.
à-coup [aku] *nm* (*du moteur*) (hic)cough; (*fig*) jolt; **sans ~s** smoothly; **par ~s** by fits and starts.
acoustique [akustik] *nf* (*d'une salle*) acoustics *pl*; (*science*) acoustics *sg* // *a* acoustic.
acquéreur [akeʀœʀ] *nm* buyer, purchaser.
acquérir [akeʀiʀ] *vt* to acquire; (*par achat*) to purchase, acquire; (*valeur*) to gain; **ce que ses efforts lui ont acquis** what his efforts have won *ou* gained (for) him.
acquiescer [akjese] *vi* (*opiner*) to agree; (*consentir*): **~ (à qch)** to acquiesce *ou* assent (to sth).
acquis, e [aki, -iz] *pp de* **acquérir** // *nm* (accumulated) experience; **être ~ à** (*plan, idée*) to fully agree with; **son aide nous est ~e** we can count on *ou* be sure of her help.
acquisition [akizisjɔ̃] *nf* acquisition; purchase; **faire l'~ de** to acquire; to purchase.
acquit [aki] *vb voir* **acquérir** // *nm* (*quittance*) receipt; **pour ~** received; **par ~ de conscience** to set one's mind at rest.
acquittement [akitmɑ̃] *nm* acquittal; payment, settlement.
acquitter [akite] *vt* (JUR) to acquit; (*facture*) to pay, settle; **s'~ de** to discharge; to fulfil, carry out.
âcre [ɑkʀ(ə)] *a* acrid, pungent.
acrobate [akʀɔbat] *nm/f* acrobat.
acrobatie [akʀɔbasi] *nf* (*art*) acrobatics *sg*; (*exercice*) acrobatic feat; **~ aérienne** aerobatics *sg*; **acrobatique** *a* acrobatic.
acte [akt(ə)] *nm* act, action; (THÉÂTRE) act; **~s** *nmpl* (*compte-rendu*) proceedings; **prendre ~ de** to note, take note of; **faire ~ de présence** to put in an appearance; **l'~ d'accusation** the charges; the bill of indictment; **~ de naissance** birth certificate.
acteur, trice [aktœʀ, -tʀis] *nm/f* actor/actress.
actif, ive [aktif, -iv] *a* active // *nm* (COMM) assets *pl*; (*fig*): **avoir à son ~** to have to one's credit; **mettre à son ~** to add to one's list of achievements.
action [aksjɔ̃] *nf* (*gén*) action; (COMM) share; **une bonne ~** a good deed; **~ en diffamation** libel action; **actionnaire** *nm/f* shareholder; **actionner** *vt* to work; to activate.
active [aktiv] *a voir* **actif**; **~ment** *ad* actively.
activer [aktive] *vt* to speed up; **s'~** *vi* to bustle about; to hurry up.
activiste [aktivist(ə)] *nm/f* activist.
activité [aktivite] *nf* activity; **volcan en ~** active volcano.
actrice [aktʀis] *nf voir* **acteur.**
actualiser [aktɥalize] *vt* to actualize; to bring up to date.
actualité [aktɥalite] *nf* (*d'un problème*) topicality; (*événements*): **l'~** current events; **les ~s** (CINÉMA, TV) the news.
actuel, le [aktɥɛl] *a* (*présent*) present; (*d'actualité*) topical; (*non virtuel*) actual; **~lement** *ad* at present; at the present time.
acuité [akɥite] *nf* acuteness.
acuponcteur, acupuncteur [akypɔ̃ktœʀ] *nm* acupuncturist.
acuponcture, acupuncture [akypɔ̃ktyʀ] *nf* acupuncture.
adage [adaʒ] *nm* adage.
adagio [adadʒjo] *nm* adagio.
adaptateur, trice [adaptatœʀ, -tʀis] *nm/f* adapter // *nm* (ÉLEC) adapter.
adaptation [adaptɑsjɔ̃] *nf* adaptation.
adapter [adapte] *vt* to adapt; **~ qch à** (*approprier*) to adapt sth to (fit); **~ qch sur/dans/à** (*fixer*) to fit sth on/into/to; **s'~ (à)** (*suj*: *personne*) to adapt (to).
additif [aditif] *nm* additional clause; (CHIMIE) additive.
addition [adisjɔ̃] *nf* addition; (*au café*) bill; **additionnel, le** *a* additional.
additionner [adisjɔne] *vt* to add (up); ~

un produit d'eau to add water to a product.
adepte [adɛpt(ə)] *nm/f* follower.
adéquat, e [adekwa, -at] *a* appropriate, suitable.
adhérence [adeʀɑ̃s] *nf* adhesion.
adhérent, e [adeʀɑ̃, -ɑ̃t] *nm/f* (*de club*) member.
adhérer [adeʀe] *vi* (*coller*) to adhere, stick; **~ à** *vt* (*coller*) to adhere *ou* stick to; (*se rallier à: parti, club*) to join; to be a member of; (: *opinion, mouvement*) to support; **adhésif, ive** *a* adhesive, sticky // *nm* adhesive; **adhésion** *nf* joining; membership; support.
ad hoc [adɔk] *a* ad hoc.
adieu, x [adjø] *excl* goodbye // *nm* farewell; **dire ~ à qn** to say goodbye *ou* farewell to sb.
adipeux, euse [adipø, -øz] *a* bloated, fat; (ANAT) adipose.
adjacent, e [adʒasɑ̃, -ɑ̃t] *a* adjacent.
adjectif [adʒɛktif] *nm* adjective; **~ attribut** adjectival complement; **~ épithète** attributive adjective.
adjoindre [adʒwɛ̃dʀ(ə)] *vt*: **~ qch à** to attach sth to; to add sth to; **~ qn à** (*personne*) to appoint sb as an assistant to; (*comité*) to appoint sb to, attach sb to; **s'~** (*collaborateur etc*) to take on, appoint; **adjoint, e** *nm/f* assistant; **adjoint au maire** deputy mayor; **directeur adjoint** assistant manager; **adjonction** *nf* attaching; addition; appointment.
adjudant [adʒydɑ̃] *nm* (MIL) warrant officer.
adjudicataire [adʒydikatɛʀ] *nm/f* successful bidder, purchaser; successful tenderer.
adjudication [adʒydikɑsjɔ̃] *nf* sale by auction; (*pour travaux*) invitation to tender.
adjuger [adʒyʒe] *vt* (*prix, récompense*) to award; (*lors d'une vente*) to auction (off); **s'~** *vt* to take for o.s.
adjurer [adʒyʀe] *vt*: **~ qn de faire** to implore *ou* beg sb to do.
adjuvant [adʒyvɑ̃] *nm* adjuvant; additive; stimulant.
admettre [admɛtʀ(ə)] *vt* (*visiteur, nouveau-venu*) to admit, let in; (*candidat*: SCOL) to pass; (TECH: *gaz, eau, air*) to admit; (*tolérer*) to allow, accept; (*reconnaître*) to admit, acknowledge.
administrateur, trice [administʀatœʀ, -tʀis] *nm/f* (COMM) director; (ADMIN) administrator.
administratif, ive [administʀatif, -iv] *a* administrative.
administration [administʀɑsjɔ̃] *nf* administration; **l'A~** ≈ the Civil Service.
administré, e [administʀe] *nm/f*: **ses ~s** the citizens in his care.
administrer [administʀe] *vt* (*firme*) to manage, run; (*biens, remède, sacrement etc*) to administer.
admirable [admiʀabl(ə)] *a* admirable, wonderful.
admirateur, trice [admiʀatœʀ, -tʀis] *nm/f* admirer.
admiratif, ive [admiʀatif, -iv] *a* admiring.
admiration [admiʀɑsjɔ̃] *nf* admiration.
admirer [admiʀe] *vt* to admire.
admis, e *pp de* **admettre**.
admissible [admisibl(ə)] *a* (*candidat*) eligible; (*comportement*) admissible, acceptable.
admission [admisjɔ̃] *nf* admission; acknowledgement; **tuyau d'~** intake pipe; **demande d'~** application for membership.
admonester [admɔnɛste] *vt* to admonish.
adolescence [adɔlesɑ̃s] *nf* adolescence.
adolescent, e [adɔlesɑ̃, -ɑ̃t] *nm/f* adolescent.
adonner [adɔne]: **s'~ à** *vt* (*sport*) to devote o.s. to; (*boisson*) to give o.s. over to.
adopter [adɔpte] *vt* to adopt; (*projet de loi etc*) to pass; **adoptif, ive** *a* (*parents*) adoptive; (*fils, patrie*) adopted; **adoption** *nf* adoption.
adoration [adɔʀɑsjɔ̃] *nf* adoration; worship.
adorer [adɔʀe] *vt* to adore; (REL) to worship, adore.
adosser [adose] *vt*: **~ qch à** *ou* **contre** to stand sth against; **s'~ à** *ou* **contre** to lean with one's back against.
adoucir [adusiʀ] *vt* (*goût, température*) to make milder; (*avec du sucre*) to sweeten; (*peau, voix*) to soften; (*caractère, personne*) to mellow; (*peine*) to soothe, allay; **s'~** *vi* to become milder; to soften; to mellow.
adresse [adʀɛs] *nf* (*voir adroit*) skill, dexterity; (*domicile*) address; **à l'~ de** (*pour*) for the benefit of.
adresser [adʀese] *vt* (*lettre: expédier*) to send; (: *écrire l'adresse sur*) to address; (*injure, compliments*) to address; **~ qn à un docteur/bureau** to refer *ou* send sb to a doctor/an office; **~ la parole à qn** to speak to *ou* address sb; **s'~ à** (*parler à*) to speak to, address; (*s'informer auprès de*) to go and see, go and speak to; (: *bureau*) to enquire at; (*suj: livre, conseil*) to be aimed at.
Adriatique [adʀiatik] *nf*: **l'~** the Adriatic.
adroit, e [adʀwa, -wat] *a* (*joueur, mécanicien*) skilful, dext(e)rous; (*politicien etc*) shrewd, skilled; **adroitement** *ad* skilfully; dext(e)rously.
aduler [adyle] *vt* to adulate.
adulte [adylt(ə)] *nm/f* adult, grown-up // *a* (*chien, arbre*) fully-grown, mature; (*attitude*) adult, grown-up; **l'âge ~** adulthood.
adultère [adyltɛʀ] *a* adulterous // *nm/f* adulterer/adulteress // *nm* (*acte*) adultery; **adultérin, e** *a* born of adultery.
advenir [advəniʀ] *vi* to happen; **qu'est-il advenu de** what has become of.
adverbe [advɛʀb(ə)] *nm* adverb.
adversaire [advɛʀsɛʀ] *nm/f* (SPORT, *gén*) opponent, adversary; (MIL) adversary, enemy; (*non partisan*): **~ de** opponent of.
adverse [advɛʀs(ə)] *a* opposing.
adversité [advɛʀsite] *nf* adversity.
aérateur [aeʀatœʀ] *nm* ventilator.
aération [aeʀɑsjɔ̃] *nf* airing; ventilation;

conduit d'~ ventilation shaft; **bouche d'~** air-vent.
aéré, e [aeʀe] *a* (*pièce, local*) airy, well-ventilated; (*tissu*) loose-woven.
aérer [aeʀe] *vt* to air; (*fig*) to lighten; **s'~** *vi* to get some (fresh) air.
aérien, ne [aeʀjɛ̃ -jɛn] *a* (AVIAT) air *cpd*, aerial; (*câble, métro*) overhead; (*fig*) light.
aéro... [aeʀɔ] *préfixe:* **~-club** *nm* flying club; **~drome** *nm* aerodrome; **~dynamique** *a* aerodynamic, streamlined // *nf* aerodynamics *sg*; **~gare** *nf* airport (buildings); (*en ville*) air terminal; **~glisseur** *nm* hovercraft; **~nautique** *a* aeronautical // *nf* aeronautics *sg*; **~naval, e** *a* air and sea *cpd* // *nf* the Fleet Air Arm; **~phagie** *nf* aerophagy; **~port** *nm* airport; **~porté, e** *a* airborne, airlifted; **~sol** *nm* aerosol; **~spatial, e, aux** *a* aerospace; **~train** *nm* hovertrain.
affable [afabl(ə)] *a* affable.
affadir [afadiʀ] *vt* to make insipid *ou* tasteless.
affaiblir [afebliʀ] *vt* to weaken; **s'~** *vi* to weaken, grow weaker; **affaiblissement** *nm* weakening.
affaire [afɛʀ] *nf* (*problème, question*) matter; (*criminelle, judiciaire*) case; (*scandaleuse etc*) affair; (*entreprise*) business; (*marché, transaction*) (business) deal; (piece of) business *q*; (*occasion intéressante*) good deal, bargain; **~s** *nfpl* affairs; (*activité commerciale*) business *sg*; (*effets personnels*) things, belongings; **ce sont mes ~s** (*cela me concerne*) that's my business; **ceci fera l'~** this will do (nicely); **avoir ~ à** to be faced with; to be dealing with; **les A~s étrangères** (POL) Foreign Affairs; **s'affairer** *vi* to busy o.s., bustle about; **affairisme** *nm* (political) racketeering.
affaisser [afese]: **s'~** *vi* (*terrain, immeuble*) to subside, sink; (*personne*) to collapse.
affaler [afale]: **s'~** *vi*: **s'~ dans/sur** to collapse *ou* slump into/onto.
affamer [afame] *vt* to starve.
affectation [afɛktɑsjɔ̃] *nf* allotment; appointment; posting; (*voir affecté*) affectedness.
affecté, e [afɛkte] *a* affected.
affecter [afɛkte] *vt* (*émouvoir*) to affect, move; (*feindre*) to affect, feign; (*telle ou telle forme etc*) to take on, assume; **~ qch à** to allocate *ou* allot sth to; **~ qn à** to appoint sb to; (*diplomate*) to post sb to; **~ qch d'un coefficient** *etc* to modify sth by a coefficient *etc*, tag a coefficient *etc* onto sth.
affectif, ive [afɛktif, -iv] *a* emotional, affective.
affection [afɛksjɔ̃] *nf* affection; (*mal*) ailment; **affectionner** *vt* to be fond of.
affectueux, euse [afɛktɥø, -øz] *a* affectionate.
afférent, e [aferɑ̃, -ɑ̃t] *a*: **~ à** pertaining *ou* relating to.
affermir [afɛʀmiʀ] *vt* to consolidate, strengthen.
affichage [afiʃaʒ] *nm* billposting; (*électronique*) display; **~ numérique** *ou* **digital** digital display.
affiche [afiʃ] *nf* poster; (*officielle*) (public) notice; (THÉÂTRE) bill.
afficher [afiʃe] *vt* (*affiche*) to put up, post up; (*réunion*) to announce by (means of) posters *ou* public notices; (*électroniquement*) to display; (*fig*) to exhibit, display; **s'~** (*péj*) to flaunt o.s.
affilée [afile]: **d'~** *ad* at a stretch.
affiler [afile] *vt* to sharpen.
affilier [afilje] *vt*: **s'~ à** to become affiliated to.
affiner [afine] *vt* to refine; **s'~** *vi* to become (more) refined.
affinité [afinite] *nf* affinity.
affirmatif, ive [afiʀmatif, -iv] *a* affirmative // *nf*: **répondre par l'affirmative** to reply yes *ou* in the affirmative; **dans l'affirmative** if (the answer is) yes, if he does (*ou* you do *etc*).
affirmation [afiʀmɑsjɔ̃] *nf* assertion.
affirmer [afiʀme] *vt* (*prétendre*) to maintain, assert; (*autorité etc*) to assert.
affleurer [aflœʀe] *vi* to show on the surface.
affliction [afliksjɔ̃] *nf* affliction.
affligé, e [afliʒe] *a* distressed, grieved; **~ de** (*maladie, tare*) afflicted with.
affliger [afliʒe] *vt* (*peiner*) to distress, grieve.
affluence [aflyɑ̃s] *nf* crowds *pl*; **heures d'~** rush hours; **jours d'~** busiest days.
affluent [aflyɑ̃] *nm* tributary.
affluer [aflye] *vi* (*secours, biens*) to flood in, pour in; (*sang*) to rush, flow; **afflux** *nm* flood, influx; rush.
affoler [afɔle] *vt* to throw into a panic; **s'~** *vi* to panic.
affranchir [afʀɑ̃ʃiʀ] *vt* to put a stamp *ou* stamps on; (*à la machine*) to frank; (*esclave*) to enfranchise, emancipate; (*fig*) to free, liberate; **affranchissement** *nm* franking; freeing; **tarifs d'affranchissement** postal rates; **affranchissement insuffisant** insufficient postage.
affres [afʀ(ə)] *nfpl*: **dans les ~ de** in the throes of.
affréter [afʀete] *vt* to charter.
affreux, euse [afʀø, -øz] *a* (*laid*) hideous, ghastly; (*épouvantable*) dreadful, awful.
affriolant, e [afʀijɔlɑ̃, -ɑ̃t] *a* tempting, arousing.
affront [afʀɔ̃] *nm* affront.
affronter [afʀɔ̃te] *vt* to confront, face.
affubler [afyble] *vt* (*péj*): **~ qn de** to rig *ou* deck sb out in; (*surnom*) to attach to sb.
affût [afy] *nm* (*de canon*) gun carriage; **à l'~ (de)** (*gibier*) lying in wait (for); (*fig*) on the look-out (for).
affûter [afyte] *vt* to sharpen, grind.
afin [afɛ̃]: **~ que** *cj* so that, in order that; **~ de faire** in order to do, so as to do.
a fortiori [afɔʀsjɔʀi] *ad* all the more, a fortiori.
A.F.P. *sigle f* = *Agence France Presse.*
africain, e [afʀikɛ̃, -ɛn] *a, nm/f* African.
Afrique [afʀik] *nf*: **l'~** Africa; **l'~ du Sud** South Africa.
agacer [agase] *vt* to pester, tease; (*involontairement*) to irritate, aggravate; (*aguicher*) to excite, lead on.

âge [ɑʒ] *nm* age; **quel ~ as-tu?** how old are you?; **prendre de l'~** to be getting on (in years), grow older; **l'~ ingrat** the awkward *ou* difficult age; **l'~ mûr** maturity, middle age; **âgé, e** *a* old, elderly; **âgé de 10 ans** 10 years old.

agence [aʒɑ̃s] *nf* agency, office; (*succursale*) branch; **~ immobilière** estate agent's (office); **~ matrimoniale** marriage bureau; **~ de voyages** travel agency.

agencer [aʒɑ̃se] *vt* to put together; to arrange, lay out.

agenda [aʒɛ̃da] *nm* diary.

agenouiller [aʒnuje]: **s'~** *vi* to kneel (down).

agent [aʒɑ̃] *nm* (*aussi*: **~ de police**) policeman; (ADMIN) official, officer; (*fig*: *élément, facteur*) agent; **~ d'assurances** insurance broker; **~ de change** stockbroker; **~ (secret)** (secret) agent.

agglomération [aglɔmeʀɑsjɔ̃] *nf* town; built-up area; **l'~ parisienne** the urban area of Paris.

aggloméré [aglɔmeʀe] *nm* (*bois*) chipboard; (*pierre*) conglomerate.

agglomérer [aglɔmeʀe] *vt* to pile up; (TECH: *bois, pierre*) to compress.

agglutiner [aglytine] *vt* to stick together; **s'~** *vi* to congregate.

aggraver [agʀave] *vt* to worsen, aggravate; (JUR: *peine*) to increase; **s'~** *vi* to worsen.

agile [aʒil] *a* agile, nimble; **agilité** *nf* agility, nimbleness.

agir [aʒiʀ] *vi* (*se comporter*) to behave, act; (*faire quelque chose*) to act, take action; (*avoir de l'effet*) to act; **il s'agit de** it's a matter *ou* question of; it is about; (*il importe que*): **il s'agit de faire** we (*ou* you *etc*) must do; **agissements** *nmpl* (*gén péj*) schemes, intrigues.

agitateur, trice [aʒitatœʀ, -tʀis] *nm/f* agitator.

agitation [aʒitɑsjɔ̃] *nf* (hustle and) bustle; agitation, excitement; (*politique*) unrest, agitation.

agité, e [aʒite] *a* fidgety, restless; agitated, perturbed; (*journée*) hectic; **une mer ~e** a rough *ou* choppy sea; **un sommeil ~** (a) disturbed *ou* broken sleep.

agiter [aʒite] *vt* (*bouteille, chiffon*) to shake; (*bras, mains*) to wave; (*préoccuper, exciter*) to trouble, perturb; **s'~** *vi* to bustle about; (*dormeur*) to toss and turn; (*enfant*) to fidget; (POL) to grow restless.

agneau, x [aɲo] *nm* lamb.

agonie [agɔni] *nf* mortal agony, pangs *pl* of death; (*fig*) death throes *pl*.

agonir [agɔniʀ] *vt*: **~ qn d'injures** to hurl abuse at sb.

agoniser [agɔnize] *vi* to be dying.

agrafe [agʀaf] *nf* (*de vêtement*) hook, fastener; (*de bureau*) staple; **agrafer** *vt* to fasten; to staple; **agrafeuse** *nf* stapler.

agraire [agʀɛʀ] *a* agrarian; (*mesure, surface*) land *cpd*.

agrandir [agʀɑ̃diʀ] *vt* (*magasin, domaine*) to extend, enlarge; (*trou*) to enlarge, make bigger; (PHOTO) to enlarge, blow up; **s'~** *vi* to be extended; to be enlarged; **agrandissement** *nm* extension; enlargement; **agrandisseur** *nm* (PHOTO) enlarger.

agréable [agʀeabl(ə)] *a* pleasant, nice.

agréé, e [agʀee] *a*: **concessionnaire ~** registered dealer.

agréer [agʀee] *vt* (*requête*) to accept; **~ à** *vt* to please, suit; **veuillez ~ ...** (*formule épistolaire*) yours faithfully.

agrégation [agʀegɑsjɔ̃] *nf highest teaching diploma in France (competitive examination)*; **agrégé, e** *nm/f* holder of the *agrégation*.

agréger [agʀeʒe]: **s'~** *vi* to aggregate.

agrément [agʀemɑ̃] *nm* (*accord*) consent, approval; (*attraits*) charm, attractiveness; (*plaisir*) pleasure.

agrémenter [agʀemɑ̃te] *vt* to embellish, adorn.

agrès [agʀɛ] *nmpl* (gymnastics) apparatus *sg*.

agresser [agʀese] *vt* to attack.

agresseur [agʀɛsœʀ] *nm* aggressor, attacker; (POL, MIL) aggressor.

agressif, ive [agʀɛsif, -iv] *a* aggressive.

agression [agʀɛsjɔ̃] *nf* attack; (POL, MIL, PSYCH) aggression.

agressivité [agʀesivite] *nf* aggressiveness.

agreste [agʀɛst(ə)] *a* rustic.

agricole [agʀikɔl] *a* agricultural, farm *cpd*.

agriculteur [agʀikyltœʀ] *nm* farmer.

agriculture [agʀikyltyʀ] *nf* agriculture, farming.

agripper [agʀipe] *vt* to grab, clutch; (*pour arracher*) to snatch, grab; **s'~ à** to cling (on) to, clutch, grip.

agronome [agʀɔnɔm] *nm/f* agronomist.

agronomie [agʀɔnɔmi] *nf* agronomy, agronomics *sg*.

agrumes [agʀym] *nmpl* citrus fruit(s).

aguerrir [ageʀiʀ] *vt* to harden.

aguets [agɛ]: **aux ~** *ad*: **être aux ~** to be on the look-out.

aguicher [agiʃe] *vt* to entice.

ahurissement [ayʀismɑ̃] *nm* stupefaction.

ai *vb voir* **avoir.**

aide [ɛd] *nm/f* assistant // *nf* assistance, help; (*secours financier*) aid; **à l'~ de** (*avec*) with the help *ou* aid of; **aller à l'~ de qn** to go to sb's aid *ou* to help sb; **venir en ~ à qn** to help sb, come to sb's assistance; **appeler (qn) à l'~** to call for help (from sb); **~ comptable** *nm* accountant's assistant; **~ électricien** *nm* electrician's mate; **~ familiale** *nf* mother's help, home help; **~ de laboratoire** *nm/f* laboratory assistant; **~ sociale** *nf* (*assistance*) ≈ social security; **~ soignant, e** *nm/f* auxiliary nurse; **~-mémoire** *nm inv* memoranda pages *pl*; (key facts) handbook.

aider [ede] *vt* to help; **~ à qch** (*faciliter*) to help (towards) sth; **s'~ de** (*se servir de*) to use, make use of.

aie *etc vb voir* **avoir.**

aïe [aj] *excl* ouch.

aïeul, e [ajœl] *nm/f* grandparent, grandfather/grandmother; forbear.

aïeux [ajø] *nmpl* grandparents; forbears, forefathers.

aigle [ɛgl(ə)] *nm* eagle.

aigre [ɛgʀ(ə)] *a* sour, sharp; (*fig*) sharp, cutting; **~-doux, douce** *a* bitter-sweet; **~let, te** *a* sourish, sharpish; **aigreur** *nf* sourness; sharpness; **aigreurs d'estomac** heartburn *sg*; **aigrir** *vt* (*personne*) to embitter; (*caractère*) to sour; **s'aigrir** *vi* to become embittered; to sour; (*lait etc*) to turn sour.

aigu, ë [egy] *a* (*objet, arête*) sharp, pointed; (*son, voix*) high-pitched, shrill; (*note*) high(-pitched); (*douleur, intelligence*) acute, sharp.

aigue-marine [ɛgmaʀin] *nf* aquamarine.

aiguillage [egɥijaʒ] *nm* (RAIL) points *pl*.

aiguille [egɥij] *nf* needle; (*de montre*) hand; **~ à tricoter** knitting needle.

aiguiller [egɥije] *vt* (*orienter*) to direct; (RAIL) to shunt; **aiguilleur** *nm* (RAIL) pointsman; **aiguilleur du ciel** air traffic controller.

aiguillon [egɥijɔ̃] *nm* (*d'abeille*) sting; (*fig*) spur, stimulus; **aiguillonner** *vt* to spur *ou* goad on.

aiguiser [egize] *vt* to sharpen, grind; (*fig*) to stimulate; to sharpen; to excite.

ail [aj] *nm* garlic.

aile [ɛl] *nf* wing; **ailé, e** *a* winged; **aileron** *nm* (*de requin*) fin; (*d'avion*) aileron; (*de voiture*) aerofoil; **ailette** *nf* (TECH) fin; blade; wing; **ailier** *nm* winger.

aille *etc vb voir* **aller.**

ailleurs [ajœʀ] *ad* elsewhere, somewhere else; **partout/nulle part ~** everywhere/nowhere else; **d'~** *ad* (*du reste*) moreover, besides; **par ~** *ad* (*d'autre part*) moreover, furthermore.

aimable [ɛmabl(ə)] *a* kind, nice; **~ment** *ad* kindly.

aimant [ɛmɑ̃] *nm* magnet.

aimant, e [ɛmɑ̃, -ɑ̃t] *a* loving, affectionate.

aimanter [ɛmɑ̃te] *vt* to magnetize.

aimer [eme] *vt* to love; (*d'amitié, affection, par goût*) to like; (*souhait*): **j'aimerais...** I would like...; **bien ~ qn/qch** to quite like sb/sth; **j'aime mieux** *ou* **autant vous dire que** I may as well tell you that; **j'aimerais autant y aller maintenant** I'd sooner *ou* rather go now; **j'aimerais mieux y aller maintenant** I'd much rather go now.

aine [ɛn] *nf* groin.

aîné, e [ene] *a* elder, older; (*le plus âgé*) eldest, oldest // *nm/f* oldest child *ou* one, oldest boy *ou* son/girl *ou* daughter; **il est mon ~ (de 2 ans)** (*rapports non familiaux*) he's (2 years) older than me, he's 2 years my senior; **~s** *nmpl* (*fig: anciens*) elders; **aînesse** *nf*: **droit d'aînesse** birthright.

ainsi [ɛ̃si] *ad* (*de cette façon*) like this, in this way, thus; (*ce faisant*) thus // *cj* thus, so; **~ que** (*comme*) (just) as; (*et aussi*) as well as; **pour ~ dire** so to speak, as it were; **et ~ de suite** and so on (and so forth).

air [ɛʀ] *nm* air; (*mélodie*) tune; (*expression*) look, air; **en l'~** (up) into the air; **tirer en l'~** to fire shots in the air; **prendre l'~** to get some (fresh) air; (*avion*) to take off; **avoir l'~** (*sembler*) to look, appear; **avoir l'~ de** to look like; **avoir l'~ de faire** to look as though one is doing, appear to be doing.

aire [ɛʀ] *nf* (*zone, fig,* MATH) area; (*nid*) eyrie; **~ d'atterrissage** landing strip; landing patch; **~ de jeu** play area; **~ de lancement** launching site; **~ de stationnement** parking area; (*d'autoroute*) lay-by.

aisance [ɛzɑ̃s] *nf* ease; (*richesse*) affluence; **être dans l'~** to be well-off, be affluent.

aise [ɛz] *nf* comfort // *a*: **être bien ~ que** to be delighted that; **~s** *nfpl*: **aimer ses ~s** to like one's (creature) comforts; **prendre ses ~s** to make o.s. comfortable; **frémir d'~** to shudder with pleasure; **être à l'~** *ou* **à son ~** to be comfortable; (*pas embarrassé*) to be at ease; (*financièrement*) to be comfortably off; **se mettre à l'~** to make o.s. comfortable; **être mal à l'~** *ou* **à son ~** to be uncomfortable; to be ill at ease; **mettre qn mal à l'~** to make sb feel ill at ease; **à votre ~** please yourself, just as you like; **en faire à son ~** to do as one likes; **aisé, e** *a* easy; (*assez riche*) well-to-do, well-off; **aisément** *ad* easily.

aisselle [ɛsɛl] *nf* armpit.

ait *vb voir* **avoir.**

ajonc [aʒɔ̃] *nm* gorse *q*.

ajouré, e [aʒuʀe] *a* openwork *cpd*.

ajournement [aʒuʀnəmɑ̃] *nm* adjournment; deferment; postponement.

ajourner [aʒuʀne] *vt* (*réunion*) to adjourn; (*décision*) to defer, postpone; (*candidat*) to refer; (*conscrit*) to defer.

ajout [aʒu] *nm* addition.

ajouter [aʒute] *vt* to add; **~ à** *vt* (*accroître*) to add to; **s'~ à** to add to; **~ foi à** to lend *ou* give credence to.

ajustage [aʒystaʒ] *nm* fitting.

ajusté, e [aʒyste] *a*: **bien ~** (*robe etc*) close-fitting.

ajustement [aʒystəmɑ̃] *nm* adjustment.

ajuster [aʒyste] *vt* (*régler*) to adjust; (*vêtement*) to alter; (*coup de fusil*) to aim; (*cible*) to aim at; (TECH, *gén: adapter*): **~ qch à** to fit sth to; **ajusteur** *nm* metal worker.

alambic [alɑ̃bik] *nm* still.

alanguir [alɑ̃giʀ]: **s'~** *vi* to grow languid.

alarme [alaʀm(ə)] *nf* alarm; **donner l'~** to give *ou* raise the alarm; **alarmer** *vt* to alarm; **s'alarmer** *vi* to become alarmed.

Albanie [albani] *nf*: **l'~** Albania.

albâtre [albɑtʀ(ə)] *nm* alabaster.

albatros [albatʀos] *nm* albatross.

albinos [albinos] *nm/f* albino.

album [albɔm] *nm* album.

albumen [albymɛn] *nm* albumen.

albumine [albymin] *nf* albumin; **avoir** *ou* **faire de l'~** to suffer from albuminuria.

alcalin, e [alkalɛ̃, -in] *a* alkaline.

alchimie [alʃimi] *nf* alchemy; **alchimiste** *nm* alchemist.

alcool [alkɔl] *nm*: **l'~** alcohol; **un ~** a spirit, a brandy; **~ à brûler** methylated spirits; **~ à 90°** surgical spirit; **~ique** *a, nm/f* alcoholic; **~isé, e** *a* alcoholic; **~isme** *nm* alcoholism; **alco(o)test** ® *nm* breathalyser; (*test*) breath-test.

alcôve [alkov] *nf* alcove, recess.

aléas [alea] *nmpl* hazards ; **aléatoire** *a* uncertain.
alentour [alɑ̃tuʀ] *ad* around (about) ; **~s** *nmpl* surroundings ; **aux ~s de** in the vicinity *ou* neighbourhood of, around about ; (*temps*) (a)round about.
alerte [alɛʀt(ə)] *a* agile, nimble ; brisk, lively // *nf* alert ; warning ; **donner l'~** to give the alert ; **alerter** *vt* to alert.
alèse [alɛz] *nf* (*drap*) undersheet, drawsheet.
aléser [aleze] *vt* to ream.
alevin [alvɛ̃] *nm* alevin, young fish.
algarade [algaʀad] *nf* row, dispute.
algèbre [alʒɛbʀ(ə)] *nf* algebra ; **algébrique** *a* algebraic.
Alger [alʒe] *n* Algiers.
Algérie [alʒeʀi] *nf* Algeria ; **algérien, ne** *a, nm/f* Algerian.
Algérois, e [alʒeʀwa, -waz] *nm/f* inhabitant *ou* native of Algiers // *nm*: **l'~** the Algiers region.
algorithme [algɔʀitm(ə)] *nm* algorithm.
algue [alg(ə)] *nf* (*gén*) seaweed *q* ; (BOT) alga (*pl* algae).
alibi [alibi] *nm* alibi.
aliénation [aljenɑsjɔ̃] *nf* alienation.
aliéné, e [aljene] *nm/f* insane person, lunatic (*péj*).
aliéner [aljene] *vt* to alienate ; (*bien, liberté*) to give up ; **s'~** *vt* to alienate.
alignement [aliɲmɑ̃] *nm* alignment ; lining up ; **à l'~** in line.
aligner [aliɲe] *vt* to align, line up ; (*idées, chiffres*) to string together ; (*adapter*): **~ qch sur** to bring sth into alignment with ; **s'~** (*soldats etc*) to line up ; **s'~ sur** (POL) to align o.s. on.
aliment [alimɑ̃] *nm* food ; **alimentaire** *a* food *cpd* ; (*péj*: *besogne*) done merely to earn a living, done as a potboiler ; **produits alimentaires** foodstuffs, foods.
alimentation [alimɑ̃tɑsjɔ̃] *nf* feeding ; supplying ; (*commerce*) food trade ; (*produits*) groceries *pl* ; (*régime*) diet.
alimenter [alimɑ̃te] *vt* to feed ; (TECH): **~ (en)** to supply (with) ; to feed (with) ; (*fig*) to sustain, keep going.
alinéa [alinea] *nm* paragraph ; **'nouvel ~'** new line.
aliter [alite]: **s'~** *vi* to take to one's bed.
alizé [alize] *a, nm*: **(vent) ~** trade wind.
allaiter [alete] *vt* to (breast-)feed, nurse ; (*suj*: *animal*) to suckle.
allant [alɑ̃] *nm* drive, go.
allécher [aleʃe] *vt*: **~ qn** to make sb's mouth water ; to tempt sb, entice sb.
allée [ale] *nf* (*de jardin*) path ; (*en ville*) avenue, drive. **~s et venues** *nfpl* comings and goings.
allégation [alegɑsjɔ̃] *nf* allegation.
alléger [aleʒe] *vt* (*voiture*) to make lighter ; (*chargement*) to lighten ; (*souffrance*) to alleviate, soothe.
allégorie [alegɔʀi] *nf* allegory.
allègre [alɛgʀ(ə)] *a* lively, jaunty ; gay, cheerful.
allégresse [alegʀɛs] *nf* (*joie*) elation, gaiety.
alléguer [alege] *vt* to put forward (as proof *ou* an excuse).
Allemagne [aləmaɲ] *nf*: **l'~** Germany ; **l'~ de l'Est/Ouest** East/West Germany ; **allemand, e** *a, nm/f, nm* (*langue*) German.
aller [ale] *nm* (*trajet*) outward journey ; (*billet*) single *ou* one-way ticket // *vi* (*gén*) to go ; **~ à** (*convenir*) to suit ; (*suj*: *forme, pointure etc*) to fit ; **~ avec** (*couleurs, style etc*) to go (well) with ; **je vais y aller/me fâcher** I'm going to go/to get angry ; **~ voir** to go and see, go to see ; **comment allez-vous** *ou* **ça va?** how are you? ; **comment ça va?** (*affaires etc*) how are things? ; **il va bien/mal** he's well/not well, he's fine/ill ; **ça va bien/mal** (*affaires etc*) it's going well/not going well ; **il y va de leur vie** their lives are at stake ; **s'en ~** *vi* (*partir*) to be off, go, leave ; (*disparaître*) to go away ; **~ et retour** *nm* (*trajet*) return trip *ou* journey ; (*billet*) return (ticket).
allergie [alɛʀʒi] *nf* allergy ; **allergique** *a* allergic ; **allergique à** allergic to.
alliage [aljaʒ] *nm* alloy.
alliance [aljɑ̃s] *nf* (MIL, POL) alliance ; (*mariage*) marriage ; (*bague*) wedding ring ; **neveu par ~** nephew by marriage.
allié, e [alje] *nm/f* ally ; **parents et ~s** relatives and relatives by marriage.
allier [alje] *vt* (*métaux*) to alloy ; (POL, *gén*) to ally ; (*fig*) to combine ; **s'~** to become allies ; (*éléments, caractéristiques*) to combine ; **s'~ à** to become allied to *ou* with.
allô [alo] *excl* hullo, hallo.
allocataire [alɔkatɛʀ] *nm/f* beneficiary.
allocation [alɔkɑsjɔ̃] *nf* allowance ; **~ (de) chômage** unemployment benefit ; **~ (de) logement** rent allowance *ou* subsidy ; **~s familiales** family allowance(s).
allocution [alɔkysjɔ̃] *nf* short speech.
allonger [alɔ̃ʒe] *vt* to lengthen, make longer ; (*étendre*: *bras, jambe*) to stretch (out) ; **s'~** *vi* to get longer ; (*se coucher*) to lie down, stretch out ; **~ le pas** to hasten one's step(s).
allouer [alwe] *vt*: **~ qch à** to allocate sth to, allot sth to.
allumage [alymaʒ] *nm* (AUTO) ignition.
allume... [alym] *préfixe*: **~-cigare** *nm inv* cigar lighter ; **~-gaz** *nm inv* gas lighter.
allumer [alyme] *vt* (*lampe, phare, radio*) to put *ou* switch on ; (*pièce*) to put *ou* switch the light(s) on in ; (*feu*) to light ; **s'~** *vi* (*lumière, lampe*) to come *ou* go on.
allumette [alymɛt] *nf* match.
allumeuse [alymøz] *nf* (*péj*) teaser, vamp.
allure [alyʀ] *nf* (*vitesse*) speed ; pace ; (*démarche*) walk ; (*maintien*) bearing ; (*aspect, air*) look ; **avoir de l'~** to have style *ou* a certain elegance ; **à toute ~** at top *ou* full speed.
allusion [alyzjɔ̃] *nf* allusion ; (*sous-entendu*) hint ; **faire ~ à** to allude ou refer to ; to hint at.
alluvions [alyvjɔ̃] *nfpl* alluvial deposits, alluvium *sg*.
almanach [almana] *nm* almanac.
aloi [alwa] *nm*: **de bon ~** of genuine worth *ou* quality.
alors [alɔʀ] *ad* then, at that time // *cj* then, so ; **~ que** *cj* (*au moment où*) when, as ; (*pendant que*) while, when ; (*tandis que*) whereas, while.

alouette [alwɛt] *nf* (sky)lark.
alourdir [aluʀdiʀ] *vt* to weigh down, make heavy.
aloyau [alwajo] *nm* sirloin.
alpage [alpaʒ] *nm* high mountain pasture.
Alpes [alp(ə)] *nfpl*: **les ~** the Alps; **alpestre** *a* alpine.
alphabet [alfabɛ] *nm* alphabet; (*livre*) ABC (book), primer; **alphabétique** *a* alphabetic(al); **alphabétiser** *vt* to teach to read and write; to eliminate illiteracy in.
alpin, e [alpɛ̃, -in] *a* alpine; **alpinisme** *nm* mountaineering, climbing; **alpiniste** *nm/f* mountaineer, climber.
Alsace [alzas] *nf* Alsace; **alsacien, ne** *a, nm/f* Alsatian.
altérer [alteʀe] *vt* to falsify; to distort; to debase; to impair; (*donner soif à*) to make thirsty; **s'~** *vi* to deteriorate; to spoil.
alternance [altɛʀnɑ̃s] *nf* alternation; **en ~** alternately.
alternateur [altɛʀnatœʀ] *nm* alternator.
alternatif, ive [altɛʀnatif, -iv] *a* alternating // *nf* (*choix*) alternative; **alternativement** *ad* alternately.
alterner [altɛʀne] *vt* to alternate // *vi*: **~ (avec)** to alternate (with); **(faire) ~ qch avec qch** to alternate sth with sth.
Altesse [altɛs] *nf* Highness.
altier, ière [altje, -jɛʀ] *a* haughty.
altimètre [altimɛtʀ(ə)] *nm* altimeter.
altiste [altist(ə)] *nm/f* viola player, violist.
altitude [altityd] *nf* altitude, height; **à 1000 m d'~** at a height *ou* an altitude of 1000 m; **en ~** at high altitudes.
alto [alto] *nm* (*instrument*) viola // *nf* (contr)alto.
altruisme [altʀɥism(ə)] *nm* altruism.
aluminium [alyminjɔm] *nm* aluminium.
alunir [alyniʀ] *vi* to land on the moon.
alvéole [alveɔl] *nf* (*de ruche*) alveolus; **alvéolé, e** *a* honeycombed.
amabilité [amabilite] *nf* kindness, amiability; **il a eu l'~ de** he was kind *ou* good enough to.
amadou [amadu] *nm* touchwood, amadou.
amadouer [amadwe] *vt* to coax, cajole; to mollify, soothe.
amaigrir [amegʀiʀ] *vt* to make thin *ou* thinner; **régime amaigrissant** slimming diet.
amalgamer [amalgame] *vt* to amalgamate.
amande [amɑ̃d] *nf* (*de l'amandier*) almond; (*de noyau de fruit*) kernel; **amandier** *nm* almond (tree).
amant [amɑ̃] *nm* lover.
amarre [amaʀ] *nf* (NAVIG) (mooring) rope *ou* line; **~s** moorings; **amarrer** *vt* (NAVIG) to moor; (*gén*) to make fast.
amas [amɑ] *nm* heap, pile.
amasser [amɑse] *vt* to amass; **s'~** *vi* to pile up; to accumulate; to gather.
amateur [amatœʀ] *nm* amateur; **en ~** (*péj*) amateurishly; **musicien/sportif ~** amateur musician/sportsman; **~ de musique/sport** *etc* music/sport *etc* lover; **~isme** *nm* amateurism; (*péj*) amateurishness.
amazone [amazon] *nf*: **en ~** sidesaddle.
ambages [ɑ̃baʒ]: **sans ~** *ad* without beating about the bush, plainly.
ambassade [ɑ̃basad] *nf* embassy; (*mission*): **en ~** on a mission; **ambassadeur, drice** *nm/f* ambassador/ambassadress.
ambiance [ɑ̃bjɑ̃s] *nf* atmosphere.
ambiant, e [ɑ̃bjɑ̃, -ɑ̃t] *a* (*air, milieu*) surrounding; (*température*) ambient.
ambidextre [ɑ̃bidɛkstʀ(ə)] *a* ambidextrous.
ambigu, ë [ɑ̃bigy] *a* ambiguous; **ambiguïté** *nf* ambiguousness *q*, ambiguity.
ambitieux, euse [ɑ̃bisjø, -øz] *a* ambitious.
ambition [ɑ̃bisjɔ̃] *nf* ambition; **ambitionner** *vt* to have as one's aim *ou* ambition.
ambivalent, e [ɑ̃bivalɑ̃, -ɑ̃t] *a* ambivalent.
ambre [ɑ̃bʀ(ə)] *nm*: **~ (jaune)** amber; **~ gris** ambergris.
ambulance [ɑ̃bylɑ̃s] *nf* ambulance; **ambulancier, ière** *nm/f* ambulance man/woman.
ambulant, e [ɑ̃bylɑ̃, -ɑ̃t] *a* travelling, itinerant.
âme [ɑm] *nf* soul; **~ sœur** kindred spirit.
améliorer [ameljɔʀe] *vt* to improve; **s'~** *vi* to improve, get better.
aménagement [amenaʒmɑ̃] *nm* fitting out; laying out; developing; **~s** *nmpl* developments; **l'~ du territoire** ≈ town and country planning; **~s fiscaux** tax adjustments.
aménager [amenaʒe] *vt* (*agencer, transformer*) to fit out; to lay out; (: *quartier, territoire*) to develop; (*installer*) to fix up, put in; **ferme aménagée** converted farmhouse.
amende [amɑ̃d] *nf* fine; **mettre à l'~** to penalize; **faire ~ honorable** to make amends.
amender [amɑ̃de] *vt* (*loi*) to amend; (*terre*) to enrich; **s'~** *vi* to mend one's ways.
amène [amɛn] *a* affable; **peu ~** unkind.
amener [amne] *vt* to bring; (*causer*) to bring about; (*baisser*: *drapeau, voiles*) to strike; **s'~** *vi* (*fam*) to show up, turn up.
amenuiser [amənɥize]: **s'~** *vi* to grow slimmer, lessen; to dwindle.
amer, amère [amɛʀ] *a* bitter.
américain, e [ameʀikɛ̃, -ɛn] *a, nm/f* American.
Amérique [ameʀik] *nf* America; **l'~ centrale** Central America; **l'~ latine** Latin America; **l'~ du Nord** North America; **l'~ du Sud** South America.
amerrir [ameʀiʀ] *vi* to land (on the sea).
amertume [amɛʀtym] *nf* bitterness.
améthyste [ametist(ə)] *nf* amethyst.
ameublement [amœbləmɑ̃] *nm* furnishing; (*meubles*) furniture; **articles d'~** furnishings; **tissus d'~** soft furnishings, fabrics.
ameuter [amøte] *vt* (*badauds*) to draw a crowd of; (*peuple*) to rouse, stir up.
ami, e [ami] *nm/f* friend; (*amant/maîtresse*) boyfriend/girlfriend // *a*: **pays/groupe ~** friendly country/group; **être (très) ~ avec qn** to be (very)

good friends with sb; **être ~ de l'ordre** to be a lover of order; **un ~ des arts** a patron of the arts; **un ~ des chiens** a dog lover.
amiable [amjabl(ə)]: **à l'~** *ad* (JUR) out of court; (*gén*) amicably.
amiante [amjɑ̃t] *nm* asbestos.
amibe [amib] *nf* amoeba (*pl* ae).
amical, e, aux [amikal, -o] *a* friendly // *nf* (*club*) association.
amidon [amidɔ̃] *nm* starch; **amidonner** *vt* to starch.
amincir [amɛ̃siʀ] *vt* (*objet*) to thin (down); **~ qn** to make sb thinner *ou* slimmer; **s'~** *vi* to get thinner; to get slimmer.
amiral, aux [amiʀal, -o] *nm* admiral; **amirauté** *nf* admiralty.
amitié [amitje] *nf* friendship; **prendre en ~** to take a liking to, befriend; **faire** *ou* **présenter ses ~s à qn** to send sb one's best wishes *ou* kind regards.
ammoniac [amɔnjak] *nm*: **(gaz) ~** ammonia.
ammoniaque [amɔnjak] *nf* ammonia (water).
amnésie [amnezi] *nf* amnesia; **amnésique** *a* amnesic.
amnistie [amnisti] *nf* amnesty; **amnistier** *vt* to amnesty.
amoindrir [amwɛ̃dʀiʀ] *vt* to reduce.
amollir [amɔliʀ] *vt* to soften.
amonceler [amɔ̃sle] *vt*, **s'~** *vi* to pile *ou* heap up; (*fig*) to accumulate.
amont [amɔ̃]: **en ~** *ad* upstream; (*sur une pente*) uphill; **en ~ de** *prép* upstream from; uphill from, above.
amorce [amɔʀs(ə)] *nf* (*sur un hameçon*) bait; (*explosif*) cap; primer; priming; (*fig: début*) beginning(s), start; **amorcer** *vt* to bait; to prime; to begin, start.
amorphe [amɔʀf(ə)] *a* passive, lifeless.
amortir [amɔʀtiʀ] *vt* (*atténuer: choc*) to absorb, cushion; (*bruit, douleur*) to deaden; (COMM: *dette*) to pay off, amortize; (: *mise de fonds*) to write off; (: *matériel*) to write off, depreciate; **~ un abonnement** to make a season ticket pay (for itself).
amour [amuʀ] *nm* love; (*liaison*) love affair, love; (*statuette etc*) cupid; **faire l'~** to make love; **s'~acher de** (*péj*) to become infatuated with; **~ette** *nf* passing fancy; **~eux, euse** *a* (*regard, tempérament*) amorous; (*vie, problèmes*) love *cpd*; (*personne*): **~eux (de qn)** in love (with sb) // *nm/f* lover // *nmpl* courting couple(s); **être ~eux de qch** to be passionately fond of sth; **un ~eux de la nature** a nature lover; **~-propre** *nm* self-esteem, pride.
amovible [amɔvibl(ə)] *a* removable, detachable.
ampère [ɑ̃pɛʀ] *nm* amp(ere); **~mètre** *nm* ammeter.
amphibie [ɑ̃fibi] *a* amphibious.
amphithéâtre [ɑ̃fiteɑtʀ(ə)] *nm* amphitheatre; (*d'université*) lecture hall *ou* theatre.
amphore [ɑ̃fɔʀ] *nf* amphora.
ample [ɑ̃pl(ə)] *a* (*vêtement*) roomy, ample; (*gestes, mouvement*) broad; (*ressources*) ample; **~ment** *ad* amply; **~ment suffisant** ample, more than enough; **ampleur** *nf* (*importance*) scale, size; extent, magnitude.
amplificateur [ɑ̃plifikatœʀ] *nm* amplifier.
amplifier [ɑ̃plifje] *vt* (*son, oscillation*) to amplify; (*fig*) to expand, increase.
amplitude [ɑ̃plityd] *nf* amplitude; (*des températures*) range.
ampoule [ɑ̃pul] *nf* (*électrique*) bulb; (*de médicament*) phial; (*aux mains, pieds*) blister.
ampoulé, e [ɑ̃pule] *a* (*péj*) turgid, pompous.
amputation [ɑ̃pytɑsjɔ̃] *nf* amputation.
amputer [ɑ̃pyte] *vt* (MÉD) to amputate; (*fig*) to cut *ou* reduce drastically; **~ qn d'un bras/pied** to amputate sb's arm/foot.
amulette [amylɛt] *nf* amulet.
amusant, e [amyzɑ̃, -ɑ̃t] *a* (*divertissant, spirituel*) entertaining, amusing; (*comique*) funny, amusing.
amusé, e [amyze] *a* amused.
amuse-gueule [amyzgœl] *nm inv* appetizer, snack.
amusement [amyzmɑ̃] *nm* (*voir amusé*) amusement; (*voir amuser*) entertaining, amusing; (*jeu etc*) pastime, diversion.
amuser [amyze] *vt* (*divertir*) to entertain, amuse; (*égayer, faire rire*) to amuse; (*détourner l'attention de*) to distract; **s'~** *vi* (*jouer*) to amuse o.s., play; (*se divertir*) to enjoy o.s., have fun; (*fig*) to mess about; **s'~ de qch** (*trouver comique*) to find sth amusing; **s'~ avec** *ou* **de qn** (*duper*) to make a fool of sb; **amusette** *nf* idle pleasure, trivial pastime; **amuseur** *nm* entertainer; (*péj*) clown.
amygdale [amidal] *nf* tonsil; **opérer qn des ~s** to take sb's tonsils out.
an [ɑ̃] *nm* year.
anachronique [anakʀɔnik] *a* anachronistic; **anachronisme** *nm* anachronism.
anagramme [anagʀam] *nf* anagram.
anal, e, aux [anal, -o] *a* anal.
analgésique [analʒezik] *nm* analgesic.
analogie [analɔʒi] *nf* analogy.
analogue [analɔg] *a*: **~ (à)** analogous (to), similar (to).
analphabète [analfabɛt] *nm/f* illiterate.
analyse [analiz] *nf* (*gén*) analysis; (MÉD) test; **faire l'~ de** to analyse; **~ grammaticale** grammatical analysis, parsing (SCOL); **analyser** *vt* to analyse; (MÉD) to test; **analyste** *nm/f* analyst; (*psychanalyste*) (psycho)analyst; **analytique** *a* analytical.
ananas [anana] *nm* pineapple.
anarchie [anaʀʃi] *nf* (*gén*, POL) anarchy; **anarchisme** *nm* anarchism; **anarchiste** *a* anarchistic // *nm/f* anarchist.
anathème [anatɛm] *nm*: **jeter l'~ sur, lancer l'~ contre** to anathematize, curse.
anatomie [anatɔmi] *nf* anatomy; **anatomique** *a* anatomical.
ancestral, e, aux [ɑ̃sɛstʀal, -o] *a* ancestral.
ancêtre [ɑ̃sɛtʀ(ə)] *nm/f* ancestor; (*fig*): **l'~ de** the forerunner of; **~s** *nmpl* (*aïeux*) ancestors, forefathers.

anche [ɑ̃ʃ] *nf* reed.
anchois [ɑ̃ʃwa] *nm* anchovy.
ancien, ne [ɑ̃sjɛ̃, -jɛn] *a* old ; (*de jadis, de l'antiquité*) ancient ; (*précédent, ex-*) former, old // *nm/f* (*dans une tribu*) elder ; **un ~ ministre** a former minister ; **être plus ~ que qn dans une maison** to have been in a firm longer than sb ; to be senior to sb (in a firm) ; **anciennement** *ad* formerly ; **ancienneté** *nf* oldness ; antiquity ; (*ADMIN*) (length of) service ; seniority.
ancrage [ɑ̃kʀaʒ] *nm* anchoring ; (*NAVIG*) anchorage ; (*CONSTR*) cramp(-iron), anchor.
ancre [ɑ̃kʀ(ə)] *nf* anchor ; **jeter/lever l'~** to cast/weigh anchor ; **à l'~** at anchor.
ancrer [ɑ̃kʀe] *vt* (*CONSTR: câble etc*) to anchor ; (*fig*) to fix firmly ; **s'~** *vi* (*NAVIG*) to (cast) anchor.
Andorre [ɑ̃dɔʀ] *n* Andorra.
andouille [ɑ̃duj] *nf* (*CULIN*) *sausage made of chitterlings* ; (*fam*) clot, nit.
âne [ɑn] *nm* donkey, ass ; (*péj*) dunce, fool.
anéantir [aneɑ̃tiʀ] *vt* to annihilate, wipe out ; (*fig*) to obliterate, destroy ; to overwhelm.
anecdote [anɛkdɔt] *nf* anecdote ; **anecdotique** *a* anecdotal.
anémie [anemi] *nf* anaemia ; **anémié, e** *a* anaemic ; (*fig*) enfeebled ; **anémique** *a* anaemic.
anémone [anemɔn] *nf* anemone ; **~ de mer** sea anemone.
ânerie [ɑnʀi] *nf* stupidity ; stupid *ou* idiotic comment *etc*.
ânesse [ɑnɛs] *nf* she-ass.
anesthésie [anɛstezi] *nf* anaesthesia ; **faire une ~ locale à qn** to give sb a local anaesthetic ; **anesthésier** *vt* to anaesthetize ; **anesthésique** *a* anaesthetic ; **anesthésiste** *nm/f* anaesthetist.
anfractuosité [ɑ̃fʀaktɥozite] *nf* crevice.
ange [ɑ̃ʒ] *nm* angel ; **être aux ~s** to be over the moon ; **~ gardien** guardian angel ; **angélique** *a* angelic(al).
angélus [ɑ̃ʒelys] *nm* angelus.
angine [ɑ̃ʒin] *nf* sore throat, throat infection (*tonsillitis or pharyngitis*) ; **~ de poitrine** angina (pectoris).
anglais, e [ɑ̃glɛ, -ɛz] *a* English // *nm/f*: **A~, e** Englishman/woman // *nm* (*langue*) English ; **les A~** the English ; **~es** *nfpl* (*cheveux*) ringlets ; **filer à l'~e** to take French leave.
angle [ɑ̃gl(ə)] *nm* angle ; (*coin*) corner ; **~ droit/obtus/aigu** right/obtuse/acute angle.
Angleterre [ɑ̃glətɛʀ] *nf*: **l'~** England.
anglican, e [ɑ̃glikɑ̃, -an] *a* Anglican.
anglicisme [ɑ̃glisism(ə)] *nm* anglicism.
angliciste [ɑ̃glisist(ə)] *nm/f* English scholar ; student of English.
anglo... [ɑ̃glɔ] *préfixe* Anglo-, anglo(-) ; **~phile** *a* anglophilic ; **~phobe** *a* anglophobic ; **~phone** *a* English-speaking ; **~-saxon, ne** *a* Anglo-Saxon.
angoisse [ɑ̃gwas] *nf*: **l'~** anguish *q* ; **angoisser** *vt* to harrow, cause anguish to.
anguille [ɑ̃gij] *nf* eel ; **~ de mer** conger (eel).
angulaire [ɑ̃gylɛʀ] *a* angular.
anguleux, euse [ɑ̃gylø, -øz] *a* angular.
anicroche [anikʀɔʃ] *nf* hitch, snag.
animal, e, aux [animal, -o] *a, nm* animal ; **~ier** *a*: **peintre ~ier** animal painter.
animateur, trice [animatœʀ, -tʀis] *nm/f* (*de télévision, music-hall*) compère ; (*de maison de jeunes*) leader, organizer.
animation [animɑsjɔ̃] *nf* (*voir animé*) business ['bɪzɪnɪs] ; liveliness ; (*CINÉMA: technique*) animation.
animé, e [anime] *a* (*rue, lieu*) busy, lively ; (*conversation, réunion*) lively, animated ; (*opposé à inanimé, aussi LING*) animate.
animer [anime] *vt* (*ville, soirée*) to liven up, enliven ; (*mettre en mouvement*) to drive ; (*stimuler*) to drive, impel ; **s'~** *vi* to liven up, come to life.
animosité [animozite] *nf* animosity.
anis [ani] *nm* (*CULIN*) aniseed ; (*BOT*) anise.
ankyloser [ɑ̃kiloze]: **s'~** *vi* to get stiff, to ankylose.
annales [anal] *nfpl* annals.
anneau, x [ano] *nm* (*de rideau, bague*) ring ; (*de chaîne*) link.
année [ane] *nf* year ; **l'~ scolaire/fiscale** the school/tax year ; **~-lumière** *nf* light year.
annexe [anɛks(ə)] *a* (*problème*) related ; (*document*) appended ; (*salle*) adjoining // *nf* (*bâtiment*) annex(e) ; (*de document, ouvrage*) annex, appendix ; (*jointe à une lettre, un dossier*) enclosure.
annexer [anɛkse] *vt* (*pays, biens*) to annex ; **~ qch à** (*joindre*) to append sth to ; **annexion** *nf* annexation.
annihiler [aniile] *vt* to annihilate.
anniversaire [anivɛʀsɛʀ] *nm* birthday ; (*d'un événement, bâtiment*) anniversary // *a*: **jour ~** anniversary.
annonce [anɔ̃s] *nf* announcement ; (*signe, indice*) sign ; (*aussi*: **~ publicitaire**) advertisement ; (*CARTES*) declaration ; **les petites ~s** the classified advertisements, the small ads.
annoncer [anɔ̃se] *vt* to announce ; (*être le signe de*) to herald ; **s'~ bien/difficile** to look promising/difficult ; **annonceur, euse** *nm/f* (*TV, RADIO: speaker*) announcer ; (*publicitaire*) advertiser ; **l'Annonciation** *nf* the Annunciation.
annotation [anɔtɑsjɔ̃] *nf* annotation.
annoter [anɔte] *vt* to annotate.
annuaire [anɥɛʀ] *nm* yearbook, annual ; **~ téléphonique** (telephone) directory, phone book.
annuel, le [anɥɛl] *a* annual, yearly ; **~lement** *ad* annually, yearly.
annuité [anɥite] *nf* annual instalment.
annulaire [anylɛʀ] *nm* ring *ou* third finger.
annulation [anylɑsjɔ̃] *nf* cancellation ; annulment ; quashing.
annuler [anyle] *vt* (*rendez-vous, voyage*) to cancel, call off ; (*mariage*) to annul ; (*jugement*) to quash ; (*résultats*) to declare void ; (*MATH, PHYSIQUE*) to cancel out.
anoblir [anɔbliʀ] *vt* to ennoble.
anode [anɔd] *nf* anode.
anodin, e [anɔdɛ̃, -in] *a* harmless ; insignificant, trivial.
anomalie [anɔmali] *nf* anomaly.

ânonner [ɑnɔne] *vi, vt* to read in a drone; to read in a fumbling manner.
anonymat [anɔnima] *nm* anonymity.
anonyme [anɔnim] *a* anonymous; (*fig*) impersonal.
anorak [anɔRak] *nm* anorak.
anormal, e, aux [anɔRmal, -o] *a* abnormal; (*insolite*) unusual, abnormal.
anse [ɑ̃s] *nf* (*de panier, tasse*) handle; (GÉO) cove.
antagoniste [ɑ̃tagɔnist(ə)] *a* antagonistic // *nm* antagonist.
antan [ɑ̃tɑ̃]: **d'~** *a* of yesteryear, of long ago.
antarctique [ɑ̃taRktik] *a* Antarctic // *nm*: **l'A~** the Antarctic.
antécédent [ɑ̃tesedɑ̃] *nm* (LING) antecedent; **~s** *nmpl* (MÉD *etc*) past history *sg*.
antédiluvien, ne [ɑ̃tedilyvjɛ̃, -jɛn] *a* (*fig*) ancient, antediluvian.
antenne [ɑ̃tɛn] *nf* (*de radio, télévision*) aerial; (*d'insecte*) antenna (*pl* ae), feeler; (*poste avancé*) outpost; (*petite succursale*) sub-branch; **passer à l'~** to go on the air; **prendre l'~** to tune in; **2 heures d'~** 2 hours' broadcasting time.
antépénultième [ɑ̃tepenyltjɛm] *a* antepenultimate, last but two.
antérieur, e [ɑ̃teRjœR] *a* (*d'avant*) previous, earlier; (*de devant*) front; **~ à** prior *ou* previous to; **passé/futur ~** (LING) past/future anterior; **~ement** *ad* earlier; previously; **~ement à** prior *ou* previous to; **antériorité** *nf* precedence (*in time*).
anthologie [ɑ̃tɔlɔʒi] *nf* anthology.
anthracite [ɑ̃tRasit] *nm* anthracite.
anthropo... [ɑ̃tRɔpɔ] *préfixe*: **~centrisme** *nm* anthropocentrism; **~logie** *nf* anthropology; **~logue** *nm/f* anthropologist; **~métrie** *nf* anthropometry; **~morphisme** *nm* anthropomorphism; **~phage** *a* cannibalistic, anthropophagous.
anti... [ɑ̃ti] *préfixe* anti...; **~aérien, ne** *a* anti-aircraft; **abri ~aérien** air-raid shelter; **~alcoolique** *a* against alcohol; **ligue ~alcoolique** temperance league; **~atomique** *a*: **abri ~atomique** fallout shelter; **~biotique** *nm* antibiotic; **~brouillard** *a*: **phare ~brouillard** fog lamp; **~cancéreux, euse** *a* cancer *cpd*.
antichambre [ɑ̃tiʃɑ̃bR(ə)] *nf* antechamber, anteroom; **faire ~** to wait (for an audience).
antichar [ɑ̃tiʃaR] *a* anti-tank.
anticipation [ɑ̃tisipɑsjɔ̃] *nf* anticipation; payment in advance; **livre/film d'~** science fiction book/film.
anticipé, e [ɑ̃tisipe] *a* (*règlement, paiement*) early, in advance; (*joie etc*) anticipated, early; **avec mes remerciements ~s** thanking you in advance *ou* anticipation.
anticiper [ɑ̃tisipe] *vt* (*événement, coup*) to anticipate, foresee; (*paiement*) to pay *ou* make in advance // *vi* to look *ou* think ahead; to jump ahead; to anticipate; **~ sur** to anticipate.
anticlérical, e, aux [ɑ̃tikleRikal, -o] *a* anticlerical.
anticonceptionnel, le [ɑ̃tikɔ̃sɛpsjɔnɛl] *a* contraceptive.
anticorps [ɑ̃tikɔR] *nm* antibody.
anticyclone [ɑ̃tisiklon] *nm* anticyclone.
antidater [ɑ̃tidate] *vt* to backdate, predate.
antidérapant, e [ɑ̃tideRapɑ̃, -ɑ̃t] *a* non-skid.
antidote [ɑ̃tidɔt] *nm* antidote.
antienne [ɑ̃tjɛn] *nf* (*fig*) chant, refrain.
antigel [ɑ̃tiʒɛl] *nm* antifreeze.
Antilles [ɑ̃tij] *nfpl*: **les ~** the West Indies.
antilope [ɑ̃tilɔp] *nf* antelope.
antimilitariste [ɑ̃timilitaRist(ə)] *a* antimilitarist.
antimite(s) [ɑ̃timit] *a, nm*: **(produit) ~** mothproofer; moth repellent.
antiparasite [ɑ̃tipaRazit] *a* (RADIO, TV) anti-interference; **dispositif ~** suppressor.
antipathie [ɑ̃tipati] *nf* antipathy; **antipathique** *a* unpleasant, disagreeable.
antiphrase [ɑ̃tifRɑz] *nf*: **par ~** ironically.
antipodes [ɑ̃tipɔd] *nmpl* (GÉO): **les ~** the antipodes; (*fig*): **être aux ~ de** to be the opposite extreme of.
antiquaire [ɑ̃tikɛR] *nm/f* antique dealer.
antique [ɑ̃tik] *a* antique; (*très vieux*) ancient, antiquated.
antiquité [ɑ̃tikite] *nf* (*objet*) antique; **l'A~** Antiquity; **magasin d'~s** antique shop.
antirabique [ɑ̃tiRabik] *a* rabies *cpd*.
antiraciste [ɑ̃tiRasist(ə)] *a* antiracist, antiracialist.
antirides [ɑ̃tiRid] *a* (*crème*) anti-wrinkle.
antirouille [ɑ̃tiRuj] *a inv*: **peinture ~** anti-rust paint; **traitement ~** rustproofing.
antisémite [ɑ̃tisemit] *a* anti-semitic; **antisémitisme** *nm* anti-semitism.
antiseptique [ɑ̃tisɛptik] *a, nm* antiseptic.
antitétanique [ɑ̃titetanik] *a* tetanus *cpd*.
antithèse [ɑ̃titɛz] *nf* antithesis.
antituberculeux, euse [ɑ̃titybɛRkylø, -øz] *a* tuberculosis *cpd*.
antivol [ɑ̃tivɔl] *a, nm*: **(dispositif) ~** anti-theft device.
antre [ɑ̃tR(ə)] *nm* den, lair.
anus [anys] *nm* anus.
anxiété [ɑ̃ksjete] *nf* anxiety.
anxieux, euse [ɑ̃ksjø, -øz] *a* anxious, worried.
aorte [aɔRt(ə)] *nf* aorta.
août [u] *nm* August.
apaisement [apɛzmɑ̃] *nm* calming; soothing; appeasement; **~s** *nmpl* soothing reassurances; pacifying words.
apaiser [apeze] *vt* (*colère*) to calm, quell, soothe; (*faim*) to appease, assuage; (*douleur*) to soothe; (*personne*) to calm (down), pacify; **s'~** *vi* (*tempête, bruit*) to die down, subside.
apanage [apanaʒ] *nm*: **être l'~ de** to be the privilege *ou* prerogative of.
aparté [apaRte] *nm* (THÉÂTRE) aside; (*entretien*) private conversation; **en ~** *ad* in an aside; in private.
apathie [apati] *nf* apathy; **apathique** *a* apathetic.
apatride [apatRid] *nm/f* stateless person.
apercevoir [apɛRsəvwaR] *vt* to see; **s'~ de** *vt* to notice; **s'~ que** to notice that.

aperçu [apɛʀsy] *nm* (*vue d'ensemble*) general survey ; (*intuition*) insight.
apéritif, ive [apeʀitif, -iv] *nm* (*boisson*) aperitif ; (*réunion*) pre-lunch (*ou* -dinner) drinks *pl* // *a* which stimulates the appetite ; **prendre l'~** to have drinks (before lunch *ou* dinner) *ou* an aperitif.
apesanteur [apəzɑ̃tœʀ] *nf* weightlessness.
à-peu-près [apøpʀɛ] *nm inv* (*péj*) vague approximation.
apeuré, e [apœʀe] *a* frightened, scared.
aphone [afɔn] *a* voiceless.
aphrodisiaque [afʀɔdizjak] *a, nm* aphrodisiac.
aphte [aft(ə)] *nm* mouth ulcer.
aphteuse [aftøz] *af*: **fièvre ~** foot-and-mouth disease.
apiculteur [apikyltœʀ] *nm* beekeeper.
apiculture [apikyltyʀ] *nf* beekeeping, apiculture.
apitoyer [apitwaje] *vt* to move to pity ; **~ qn sur** to move sb to pity for, make sb feel sorry for ; **s'~ (sur)** to feel pity *ou* compassion (for).
aplanir [aplaniʀ] *vt* to level ; (*fig*) to smooth away, iron out.
aplati, e [aplati] *a* flat, flattened.
aplatir [aplatiʀ] *vt* to flatten ; **s'~** *vi* to become flatter ; to be flattened ; (*fig*) to lie flat on the ground ; (: *fam*) to fall flat on one's face ; (: *péj*) to grovel.
aplomb [aplɔ̃] *nm* (*équilibre*) balance, equilibrium ; (*fig*) self-assurance ; nerve ; **d'~** *ad* steady ; (CONSTR) plumb.
apocalypse [apɔkalips(ə)] *nf* apocalypse.
apogée [apɔʒe] *nm* (*fig*) peak, apogee.
apolitique [apɔlitik] *a* apolitical.
apologie [apɔlɔʒi] *nf* vindication, praise.
apoplexie [apɔplɛksi] *nf* apoplexy.
a posteriori [apɔsteʀjɔʀi] *ad* after the event, with hindsight, a posteriori.
apostolat [apɔstɔla] *nm* (REL) apostolate, discipleship ; (*gén*) proselytism, preaching ; **apostolique** *a* apostolic.
apostrophe [apɔstʀɔf] *nf* (*signe*) apostrophe ; (*appel*) interpellation.
apostropher [apɔstʀɔfe] *vt* (*interpeller*) to shout at, address sharply.
apothéose [apɔteoz] *nf* pinnacle (of achievement) ; grand finale.
apôtre [apotʀ(ə)] *nm* apostle, disciple.
apparaître [apaʀɛtʀ(ə)] *vi* to appear // *vb avec attribut* to appear, seem ; **il apparaît que** it appears that.
apparat [apaʀa] *nm*: **tenue/dîner d'~** ceremonial dress/dinner ; **~ critique** (*d'un texte*) critical apparatus.
appareil [apaʀɛj] *nm* piece of apparatus, device ; appliance ; (*politique, syndical*) machinery ; (*avion*) (aero)plane, aircraft *inv* ; (*téléphonique*) phone ; (*dentier*) brace ; **~ digestif/reproducteur** digestive/reproductive system *ou* apparatus ; **qui est à l'~?** who's speaking? ; **dans le plus simple ~** in one's birthday suit ; **~ de photographie, ~(-photo)** *nm* camera ; **~ 24 x 36** *ou* **petit format** 35mm. camera.
appareillage [apaʀɛjaʒ] *nm* (*appareils*) equipment ; (NAVIG) casting off, getting under way.
appareiller [apaʀeje] *vi* (NAVIG) to cast off, get under way // *vt* (*assortir*) to match up.
apparemment [apaʀamɑ̃] *ad* apparently.
apparence [apaʀɑ̃s] *nf* appearance ; **en ~** apparently, seemingly.
apparent, e [apaʀɑ̃, -ɑ̃t] *a* visible ; obvious ; (*superficiel*) apparent ; **coutures ~es** topstitched seams ; **poutres ~es** exposed beams.
apparenté, e [apaʀɑ̃te] *a*: **~ à** related to ; (*fig*) similar to.
appariteur [apaʀitœʀ] *nm* attendant, porter (*in French universities*).
apparition [apaʀisjɔ̃] *nf* appearance ; (*surnaturelle*) apparition.
appartement [apaʀtəmɑ̃] *nm* flat.
appartenance [apaʀtənɑ̃s] *nf*: **~ à** belonging to, membership of.
appartenir [apaʀtəniʀ]: **~ à** *vt* to belong to ; (*faire partie de*) to belong to, be a member of ; **il lui appartient de** it is up to him to, it is his duty to.
apparu, e *pp de* **apparaître.**
appas [apɑ] *nmpl* (*d'une femme*) charms.
appât [apɑ] *nm* (PÊCHE) bait ; (*fig*) lure, bait ; **appâter** *vt* (*hameçon*) to bait ; (*poisson, fig*) to lure, entice.
appauvrir [apovʀiʀ] *vt* to impoverish ; **s'~** *vi* to grow poorer, become impoverished.
appel [apɛl] *nm* call ; (*nominal*) roll call ; (: SCOL) register ; (MIL: *recrutement*) call up ; (JUR) appeal ; **faire ~ à** (*invoquer*) to appeal to ; (*avoir recours à*) to call on ; (*nécessiter*) to call for, require ; **faire** *ou* **interjeter ~** (JUR) to appeal, lodge an appeal ; **faire l'~** to call the roll ; to call the register ; **sans ~** (*fig*) final, irrevocable ; **~ d'air** in-draught ; **~ d'offres** (COMM) invitation to tender ; **faire un ~ de phares** to flash one's headlights ; **~ (téléphonique)** (tele)phone call.
appelé [aple] *nm* (MIL) conscript.
appeler [aple] *vt* to call ; (*faire venir*: *médecin etc*) to call, send for ; (*fig*: *nécessiter*) to call for, demand ; **être appelé à** (*fig*) to be destined to ; **~ qn à comparaître** (JUR) to summon sb to appear ; **en ~ à** to appeal to ; **s'~**: **elle s'appelle Gabrielle** her name is Gabrielle, she's called Gabrielle ; **comment ça s'appelle?** what is it called?
appellation [apelɑsjɔ̃] *nf* designation, appellation.
appendice [apɛ̃dis] *nm* appendix ; **appendicite** *nf* appendicitis.
appentis [apɑ̃ti] *nm* lean-to.
appesantir [apzɑ̃tiʀ]: **s'~** *vi* to grow heavier ; **s'~ sur** (*fig*) to dwell at length on.
appétissant, e [apetisɑ̃, -ɑ̃t] *a* appetizing, mouth-watering.
appétit [apeti] *nm* appetite ; **avoir un gros/petit ~** to have a big/small appetite ; **bon ~!** enjoy your meal!
applaudir [aplodiʀ] *vt* to applaud // *vi* to applaud, clap ; **~ à** *vt* (*décision*) to applaud, commend ; **applaudissements** *nmpl* applause *sg*, clapping *sg*.
application [aplikɑsjɔ̃] *nf* application.

applique [aplik] *nf* wall lamp.

appliqué, e [aplike] *a* (*élève etc*) industrious, assiduous; (*science*) applied.

appliquer [aplike] *vt* to apply; (*loi*) to enforce; **s'~** *vi* (*élève etc*) to apply o.s.; **s'~ à faire qch** to apply o.s. to doing sth, take pains to do sth.

appoint [apwɛ̃] *nm* (extra) contribution *ou* help; **avoir/faire l'~** (*en payant*) to have/give the right change *ou* money; **chauffage d'~** extra heating.

appointements [apwɛ̃tmɑ̃] *nmpl* salary.

appontement [apɔ̃tmɑ̃] *nm* landing stage, wharf.

apport [apɔʀ] *nm* supply; contribution.

apporter [apɔʀte] *vt* to bring.

apposer [apoze] *vt* to append; to affix.

apposition [apozisjɔ̃] *nf* appending; affixing; (LING): **en ~** in apposition.

appréciable [apʀesjabl(ə)] *a* (*important*) appreciable, significant.

appréciation [apʀesjɑsjɔ̃] *nf* appreciation; estimation, assessment; **~s** (*avis*) assessment *sg*, appraisal *sg*.

apprécier [apʀesje] *vt* to appreciate; (*évaluer*) to estimate, assess.

appréhender [apʀeɑ̃de] *vt* (*craindre*) to dread; (*arrêter*) to apprehend; **~ que** to fear that; **~ de faire** to dread doing.

appréhension [apʀeɑ̃sjɔ̃] *nf* apprehension.

apprendre [apʀɑ̃dʀ(ə)] *vt* to learn; (*événement, résultats*) to learn of, hear of; **~ qch à qn** (*informer*) to tell sb (of) sth; (*enseigner*) to teach sb sth; **~ à faire qch** to learn to do sth; **~ à qn à faire qch** to teach sb to do sth; **apprenti, e** *nm/f* apprentice; (*fig*) novice, beginner; **apprentissage** *nm* learning; (COMM, SCOL: *période*) apprenticeship.

apprêt [apʀɛ] *nm* (*sur un cuir, une étoffe*) dressing; (*sur un mur*) size; (*sur un papier*) finish.

apprêté, e [apʀete] *a* (*fig*) affected.

apprêter [apʀete] *vt* to dress, finish.

appris, e *pp de* **apprendre**.

apprivoiser [apʀivwaze] *vt* to tame.

approbateur, trice [apʀɔbatœʀ, -tʀis] *a* approving.

approbation [apʀɔbɑsjɔ̃] *nf* approval.

approche [apʀɔʃ] *nf* approaching; approach; **à l'~ du bateau/de l'ennemi** as the ship/enemy approached *ou* drew near.

approché, e [apʀɔʃe] *a* approximate.

approcher [apʀɔʃe] *vi* to approach, come near // *vt* (*vedette, artiste*) to come close to, approach; (*rapprocher*): **~ qch (de qch)** to bring *ou* put *ou* move sth near (to sth); **~ de** *vt* to draw near to; (*quantité, moment*) to approach; **s'~ de** *vt* to approach, go *ou* come *ou* move near to.

approfondi, e [apʀɔfɔ̃di] *a* thorough, detailed.

approfondir [apʀɔfɔ̃diʀ] *vt* to deepen, make deeper; (*fig*) to go (deeper *ou* further) into.

approprié, e [apʀɔpʀije] *a*: **~ (à)** appropriate (to), suited to.

approprier [apʀɔpʀije]: **s'~** *vt* to appropriate, take over.

approuver [apʀuve] *vt* to agree with; (*autoriser: loi, projet*) to approve, pass; (*trouver louable*) to approve of.

approvisionnement [apʀɔvizjɔnmɑ̃] *nm* supplying; (*provisions*) supply, stock.

approvisionner [apʀɔvizjɔne] *vt* to supply; (*compte bancaire*) to pay funds into; **~ qn en** to supply sb with; **s'~ en** to stock up with.

approximatif, ive [apʀɔksimatif, -iv] *a* approximate, rough; vague; **approximativement** *ad* approximately, roughly; vaguely.

Appt *abr de* **appartement.**

appui [apɥi] *nm* support; **prendre ~ sur** to lean on; to rest on; **à l'~ de** (*pour prouver*) in support of; **l'~ de la fenêtre** the windowsill, the window ledge; **appui-tête** *nm*, **appuie-tête** *nm inv* headrest.

appuyer [apɥije] *vt* (*poser*): **~ qch sur/contre** to lean *ou* rest sth on/against; (*soutenir: personne, demande*) to support, back (up); **~ sur** (*bouton*) to press, push; (*frein*) to press on, push down; (*mot, détail*) to stress, emphasize; (*suj: chose: peser sur*) to rest (heavily) on, press against; **s'~ sur** *vt* to lean on; to rely on; **~ à droite** to bear (to the) right.

âpre [ɑpʀ(ə)] *a* acrid, pungent; (*fig*) harsh; bitter; **~ au gain** grasping, greedy.

après [apʀɛ] *prép* after // *ad* afterwards; **2 heures ~** 2 hours later; **~ qu'il est** *ou* **soit parti/avoir fait** after he left/having done; **d'~** *prép* (*selon*) according to; **~ coup** *ad* after the event, afterwards; **~ tout** *ad* (*au fond*) after all; **et (puis) ~?** so what?; **~-demain** *ad* the day after tomorrow; **~-guerre** *nm* postwar years *pl*; **~-midi** *nm ou nf inv* afternoon; **~-ski** *nm inv* (*chaussure*) snow boot; (*moment*) après-ski.

à-propos [apʀɔpo] *nm* (*d'une remarque*) aptness; **faire preuve d'~** to show presence of mind, do the right thing.

apte [apt(ə)] *a*: **~ à qch/faire qch** capable of sth/doing sth; **~ (au service)** (MIL) fit (for service); **aptitude** *nf* ability, aptitude.

aquarelle [akwaʀɛl] *nf* (*tableau*) watercolour; (*genre*) watercolours *pl*, aquarelle.

aquarium [akwaʀjɔm] *nm* aquarium.

aquatique [akwatik] *a* aquatic, water *cpd*.

aqueduc [akdyk] *nm* aqueduct.

aqueux, euse [akø, -øz] *a* aqueous.

arabe [aʀab] *a* Arabic; (*désert, cheval*) Arabian; (*nation, peuple*) Arab // *nm/f*: **A~** Arab // *nm* (*langue*) Arabic.

arabesque [aʀabɛsk(ə)] *nf* arabesque.

Arabie [aʀabi] *nf*: **l'~ (Séoudite)** Saudi Arabia.

arable [aʀabl(ə)] *a* arable.

arachide [aʀaʃid] *nf* (*plante*) groundnut (plant); (*graine*) peanut, groundnut.

araignée [aʀeɲe] *nf* spider; **~ de mer** spider crab.

araser [aʀɑze] *vt* to level; to plane (down).

aratoire [aʀatwaʀ] *a*: **instrument ~** ploughing implement.

arbalète [aʀbalɛt] *nf* crossbow.

arbitrage [aʀbitʀaʒ] *nm* refereeing; umpiring; arbitration.

arbitraire [aʀbitʀɛʀ] *a* arbitrary.
arbitre [aʀbitʀ(ə)] *nm* (SPORT) referee; (: TENNIS, CRICKET) umpire; (*fig*) arbiter, judge; (JUR) arbitrator; **arbitrer** *vt* to referee; to umpire; to arbitrate.
arborer [aʀbɔʀe] *vt* to bear, display; to sport.
arboriculture [aʀbɔʀikyltyʀ] *nf* arboriculture.
arbre [aʀbʀ(ə)] *nm* tree; (TECH) shaft; ~ **généalogique** family tree; ~ **de transmission** (AUTO) driveshaft; **arbrisseau, x** *nm* shrub.
arbuste [aʀbyst(ə)] *nm* small shrub, bush.
arc [aʀk] *nm* (*arme*) bow; (GÉOM) arc; (ARCHIT) arch; ~ **de cercle** arc of a circle; **en** ~ **de cercle** *a* semi-circular; **A**~ **de triomphe** Triumphal Arch.
arcade [aʀkad] *nf* arch(way); ~**s** arcade *sg*, arches; ~ **sourcilière** arch of the eyebrows.
arcanes [aʀkan] *nmpl* mysteries.
arc-boutant [aʀkbutɑ̃] *nm* flying buttress.
arc-bouter [aʀkbute]: **s'**~ *vi*: **s'**~ **contre** to lean *ou* press against.
arceau, x [aʀso] *nm* (*métallique etc*) hoop.
arc-en-ciel [aʀkɑ̃sjɛl] *nm* rainbow.
archaïque [aʀkaik] *a* archaic; **archaïsme** *nm* archaism.
arche [aʀʃ(ə)] *nf* arch; ~ **de Noé** Noah's Ark.
archéologie [aʀkeɔlɔʒi] *nf* archeology; **archéologique** *a* archeological; **archéologue** *nm/f* archeologist.
archer [aʀʃe] *nm* archer.
archet [aʀʃɛ] *nm* bow.
archevêché [aʀʃəveʃe] *nm* archbishopric; archbishop's palace.
archevêque [aʀʃəvɛk] *nm* archbishop.
archi... [aʀʃi] *préfixe* (*très*) dead, extra; ~**simple** dead simple; ~**bondé** chock-a-block, packed solid.
archipel [aʀʃipɛl] *nm* archipelago.
architecte [aʀʃitɛkt(ə)] *nm* architect.
architecture [aʀʃitɛktyʀ] *nf* architecture.
archives [aʀʃiv] *nfpl* archives; **archiviste** *nm/f* archivist.
arçon [aʀsɔ̃] *nm voir* **cheval**.
arctique [aʀktik] *a* Arctic // *nm*: **l'A**~ the Arctic; **l'océan A**~ the Arctic Ocean.
ardemment [aʀdamɑ̃] *ad* ardently, fervently.
ardent, e [aʀdɑ̃, -ɑ̃t] *a* (*soleil*) blazing; (*fièvre*) raging; (*amour*) ardent, passionate; (*prière*) fervent; **ardeur** *nf* blazing heat; fervour, ardour.
ardoise [aʀdwaz] *nf* slate.
Ardt *abr de* **arrondissement.**
ardu, e [aʀdy] *a* arduous, difficult.
are [aʀ] *nm* are, 100 square metres.
arène [aʀɛn] *nf* arena; ~**s** *nfpl* bull-ring *sg*.
arête [aʀɛt] *nf* (*de poisson*) bone; (*d'une montagne*) ridge; (GÉOM, *gén*) edge (*where two faces meet*).
argent [aʀʒɑ̃] *nm* (*métal*) silver; (*monnaie*) money; ~ **liquide** ready money, (ready) cash; ~ **de poche** pocket money; **argenté, e** *a* silver(y); (*métal*) silver-plated; **argenter** *vt* to silver(-plate); **argenterie** *nf* silverware; silver plate.
argentin, e [aʀʒɑ̃tɛ̃, -in] *a* (*son*) silvery; (*d'Argentine*) Argentinian, Argentine // *nm/f* Argentinian, Argentine.
Argentine [aʀʒɑ̃tin] *nf*: **l'**~ Argentina, the Argentine.
argile [aʀʒil] *nf* clay; **argileux, euse** *a* clayey.
argot [aʀgo] *nm* slang; **argotique** *a* slang *cpd*; slangy.
arguer [aʀgɥe]: ~ **de** *vt* to put forward as a pretext *ou* reason.
argument [aʀgymɑ̃] *nm* argument.
argumenter [aʀgymɑ̃te] *vi* to argue.
argus [aʀgys] *nm guide to second-hand car prices.*
arguties [aʀgysi] *nfpl* pettifoggery *sg*, quibbles.
aride [aʀid] *a* arid.
aristocrate [aʀistɔkʀat] *nm/f* aristocrat.
aristocratie [aʀistɔkʀasi] *nf* aristocracy; **aristocratique** *a* aristocratic.
arithmétique [aʀitmetik] *a* arithmetic(al) // *nf* arithmetic.
armateur [aʀmatœʀ] *nm* shipowner.
armature [aʀmatyʀ] *nf* framework; (*de tente etc*) frame; (*de soutien-gorge*) bone, wiring.
arme [aʀm(ə)] *nf* weapon; (*section de l'armée*) arm; ~**s** *nfpl* (*blason*) (coat of) arms; **les** ~**s** (*profession*) soldiering *sg*; **passer par les** ~**s** to execute (by firing squad); **en** ~**s** up in arms; **prendre/présenter les** ~**s** to take up/present arms; **se battre à l'**~ **blanche** to fight with blades; ~ **à feu** firearm.
armée [aʀme] *nf* army; ~ **de l'air** Air Force; **l'**~ **du Salut** the Salvation Army; ~ **de terre** Army.
armement [aʀməmɑ̃] *nm* (*matériel*) arms *pl*, weapons *pl*; (: *d'un pays*) arms *pl*, armament.
armer [aʀme] *vt* to arm; (*arme à feu*) to cock; (*appareil-photo*) to wind on; ~ **qch de** to fit sth with; to reinforce sth with; ~ **qn de** to arm *ou* equip sb with.
armistice [aʀmistis] *nm* armistice.
armoire [aʀmwaʀ] *nf* (tall) cupboard; (*penderie*) wardrobe.
armoiries [aʀmwaʀi] *nfpl* coat *sg* of arms.
armure [aʀmyʀ] *nf* armour *q*, suit of armour.
armurier [aʀmyʀje] *nm* gunsmith; armourer.
aromates [aʀɔmat] *nmpl* seasoning *sg*, herbs (and spices).
aromatisé, e [aʀɔmatize] *a* flavoured.
arôme [aʀom] *nm* aroma; fragrance.
arpège [aʀpɛʒ] *nm* arpeggio.
arpentage [aʀpɑ̃taʒ] *nm* (land) surveying.
arpenter [aʀpɑ̃te] *vt* (*salle, couloir*) to pace up and down.
arpenteur [aʀpɑ̃tœʀ] *nm* land surveyor.
arqué, e [aʀke] *a* bow, bandy; arched.
arrachage [aʀaʃaʒ] *nm*: ~ **des mauvaises herbes** weeding.
arrache-pied [aʀaʃpje]: **d'**~ *ad* relentlessly.
arracher [aʀaʃe] *vt* to pull out; (*page etc*) to tear off, tear out; (*déplanter*: *légume*) to lift; (: *herbe, souche*) to pull up; (*bras etc*: *par explosion*) to blow off; (: *par accident*)

to tear off ; ~ **qch à qn** to snatch sth from sb ; (*fig*) to wring sth out of sb, wrest sth from sb ; ~ **qn à** (*solitude, rêverie*) to drag sb out of ; (*famille etc*) to tear *ou* wrench sb away from ; **s'~** *vt* (*article très recherché*) to fight over.

arraisonner [aʀɛzɔne] *vt* (*bateau*) to board and search.

arrangeant, e [aʀɑ̃ʒɑ̃, -ɑ̃t] *a* accommodating, obliging.

arrangement [aʀɑ̃ʒmɑ̃] *nm* arrangement.

arranger [aʀɑ̃ʒe] *vt* (*gén*) to arrange ; (*réparer*) to fix, put right ; (*régler*) to settle, sort out ; (*convenir à*) to suit, be convenient for ; **s'~** (*se mettre d'accord*) to come to an agreement *ou* arrangement ; **je vais m'~** I'll try and manage ; **ça va s'~** it'll sort itself out ; **s'~ pour faire** to manage so that one can do ; **arrangeur** *nm* (*MUS*) arranger.

arrestation [aʀɛstɑsjɔ̃] *nf* arrest.

arrêt [aʀɛ] *nm* stopping ; (*de bus etc*) stop ; (*JUR*) judgment, decision ; (*FOOTBALL*) save ; **~s** *nmpl* (*MIL*) arrest *sg* ; **être à l'~** to be stopped, have come to a halt ; **rester** *ou* **tomber en ~ devant** to stop short in front of ; **sans ~** without stopping, non-stop ; continually ; **~ de travail** stoppage (of work).

arrêté [aʀete] *nm* order, decree.

arrêter [aʀete] *vt* to stop ; (*chauffage etc*) to turn off, switch off ; (*fixer: date etc*) to appoint, decide on ; (*criminel, suspect*) to arrest ; **~ de faire** to stop doing ; **s'~** *vi* to stop.

arrhes [aʀ] *nfpl* deposit *sg*.

arrière [aʀjɛʀ] *nm* back ; (*SPORT*) fullback // *a inv*: **siège/roue ~** back *ou* rear seat/wheel ; **à l'~** *ad* behind, at the back ; **en ~** *ad* behind ; (*regarder*) back, behind ; (*tomber, aller*) backwards ; **en ~ de** *prép* behind ; **arriéré, e** *a* (*péj*) backward // *nm* (*d'argent*) arrears *pl* ; **~-boutique** *nf* back shop ; **~-garde** *nf* rearguard ; **~-goût** *nm* aftertaste ; **~-grand-mère** *nf* great-grandmother ; *nm* great-grandfather ; **~-pays** *nm inv* hinterland ; **~-pensée** *nf* ulterior motive ; mental reservation ; **~-petits-enfants** *nmpl* great-grandchildren ; **~-plan** *nm* background ; **~-saison** *nf* late autumn ; **~-train** *nm* hindquarters *pl*.

arrimer [aʀime] *vt* to stow ; to secure, fasten securely.

arrivage [aʀivaʒ] *nm* arrival.

arrivée [aʀive] *nf* arrival ; (*ligne d'arrivée*) finish ; **~ d'air/de gaz** air/gas inlet ; **à mon ~** when I arrived.

arriver [aʀive] *vi* to arrive ; (*survenir*) to happen, occur ; **il arrive à Paris à 8h** he gets to *ou* arrives at Paris at 8 ; **~ à** (*atteindre*) to reach ; **~ à faire qch** to succeed in doing sth ; **il arrive que** it happens that ; **il lui arrive de faire** he sometimes does ; **arriviste** *nm/f* go-getter.

arrogance [aʀɔgɑ̃s] *nf* arrogance.

arrogant, e [aʀɔgɑ̃, -ɑ̃t] *a* arrogant.

arroger [aʀɔʒe]: **s'~** *vt* to assume (without right).

arrondi, e [aʀɔ̃di] *a* round // *nm* roundness.

arrondir [aʀɔ̃diʀ] *vt* (*forme, objet*) to round ; (*somme*) to round off ; **s'~** *vi* to become round(ed).

arrondissement [aʀɔ̃dismɑ̃] *nm* (*ADMIN*) ≈ district.

arrosage [aʀozaʒ] *nm* watering ; **tuyau d'~** hose(pipe).

arroser [aʀoze] *vt* to water ; (*victoire*) to celebrate (over a drink) ; (*CULIN*) to baste ; **arroseuse** *nf* water cart ; **arrosoir** *nm* watering can.

arsenal, aux [aʀsənal, -o] *nm* (*NAVIG*) naval dockyard ; (*MIL*) arsenal ; (*fig*) gear, paraphernalia.

arsenic [aʀsənik] *nm* arsenic.

art [aʀ] *nm* art ; **~s et métiers** applied arts and crafts ; **~s ménagers** homecraft *sg*, domestic science *sg*.

artère [aʀtɛʀ] *nf* (*ANAT*) artery ; (*rue*) main road ; **artériel, le** *a* arterial ; **artériosclérose** *nf* arteriosclerosis.

arthrite [aʀtʀit] *nf* arthritis.

arthrose [aʀtʀoz] *nf* (degenerative) osteoarthritis.

artichaut [aʀtiʃo] *nm* artichoke.

article [aʀtikl(ə)] *nm* article ; (*COMM*) item, article ; **à l'~ de la mort** at the point of death ; **~ de fond** (*PRESSE*) feature article.

articulaire [aʀtikylɛʀ] *a* of the joints, articular.

articulation [aʀtikylɑsjɔ̃] *nf* articulation ; (*ANAT*) joint.

articuler [aʀtikyle] *vt* to articulate ; **s'~ (sur)** (*ANAT, TECH*) to articulate (to).

artifice [aʀtifis] *nm* device, trick.

artificiel, le [aʀtifisjɛl] *a* artificial ; **~lement** *ad* artificially.

artificier [aʀtifisje] *nm* pyrotechnist.

artificieux, euse [aʀtifisjø, -øz] *a* guileful, deceitful.

artillerie [aʀtijʀi] *nf* artillery, ordnance ; **artilleur** *nm* artilleryman, gunner.

artisan [aʀtizɑ̃] *nm* artisan, (self-employed) craftsman ; **l'~ de la victoire** the architect of victory ; **artisanal, e, aux** *a* of *ou* made by craftsmen ; (*péj*) cottage industry *cpd*, unsophisticated ; **artisanat** *nm* arts and crafts *pl*.

artiste [aʀtist(ə)] *nm/f* artist ; (*de variétés*) entertainer ; performer ; singer ; actor/actress ; **artistique** *a* artistic.

aryen, ne [aʀjɛ̃, -jɛn] *a* Aryan.

as *vb* [a] *voir* **avoir** // *nm* [ɑs] ace.

ascendance [asɑ̃dɑ̃s] *nf* (*origine*) ancestry.

ascendant, e [asɑ̃dɑ̃, -ɑ̃t] *a* upward // *nm* ascendancy ; **~s** *nmpl* ascendants.

ascenseur [asɑ̃sœʀ] *nm* lift.

ascension [asɑ̃sjɔ̃] *nf* ascent ; climb ; **l'A~** (*REL*) the Ascension.

ascète [asɛt] *nm/f* ascetic ; **ascétique** *a* ascetic.

asepsie [asɛpsi] *nf* asepsis ; **aseptique** *a* aseptic ; **aseptiser** *vt* to sterilize ; to disinfect.

asiatique [azjatik] *a, nm/f* Asiatic, Asian.

Asie [azi] *nf* Asia.

asile [azil] *nm* (*refuge*) refuge, sanctuary ; (*POL*): **droit d'~** (political) asylum ; (*pour malades mentaux*) home, asylum ; (*pour vieillards*) home.

aspect [aspɛ] *nm* appearance, look; (*fig*) aspect, side; (LING) aspect; **à l'~ de** at the sight of.
asperge [aspɛʀʒ(ə)] *nf* asparagus *q*.
asperger [aspɛʀʒe] *vt* to spray, sprinkle.
aspérité [aspeʀite] *nf* excrescence, protruding bit (of rock *etc*).
aspersion [aspɛʀsjɔ̃] *nf* spraying, sprinkling.
asphalte [asfalt(ə)] *nm* asphalt; **asphalter** *vt* to asphalt.
asphyxie [asfiksi] *nf* suffocation, asphyxia, asphyxiation; **asphyxier** *vt* to suffocate, asphyxiate; (*fig*) to stifle.
aspic [aspik] *nm* (ZOOL) asp; (CULIN) aspic.
aspirant, e [aspiʀɑ̃, -ɑ̃t] *a*: **pompe ~e** suction pump // *nm* (NAVIG) midshipman.
aspirateur [aspiʀatœʀ] *nm* vacuum cleaner, hoover.
aspiration [aspiʀɑsjɔ̃] *nf* inhalation; sucking (up); drawing up; **~s** *nfpl* (*ambitions*) aspirations.
aspirer [aspiʀe] *vt* (*air*) to inhale; (*liquide*) to suck (up); (*suj*: *appareil*) to suck *ou* draw up; **~ à** *vt* to aspire to.
aspirine [aspiʀin] *nf* aspirin.
assagir [asaʒiʀ] *vt*, **s'~** *vi* to quieten down, sober down.
assaillant, e [asajɑ̃, -ɑ̃t] *nm/f* assailant, attacker.
assaillir [asajiʀ] *vt* to assail, attack; **~ qn de** (*questions*) to assail *ou* bombard sb with.
assainir [aseniʀ] *vt* to clean up; to purify.
assaisonnement [asɛzɔnmɑ̃] *nm* seasoning.
assaisonner [asɛzɔne] *vt* to season.
assassin [asasɛ̃] *nm* murderer; assassin.
assassinat [asasina] *nm* murder; assassination.
assassiner [asasine] *vt* to murder; to assassinate.
assaut [aso] *nm* assault, attack; **prendre d'~** to (take by) storm, assault; **donner l'~** to attack; **faire ~ de** (*rivaliser*) to vie with *ou* rival each other in.
assécher [aseʃe] *vt* to drain.
assemblage [asɑ̃blaʒ] *nm* assembling; (MENUISERIE) joint; **un ~ de** (*fig*) a collection of.
assemblée [asɑ̃ble] *nf* (*réunion*) meeting; (*public, assistance*) gathering; assembled people; (POL) assembly; **l'A~ Nationale** the (French) National Assembly.
assembler [asɑ̃ble] *vt* (*joindre, monter*) to assemble, put together; (*amasser*) to gather (together), collect (together); **s'~** *vi* to gather, collect.
assener, asséner [asene] *vt*: **~ un coup à qn** to deal sb a blow.
assentiment [asɑ̃timɑ̃] *nm* assent, consent; approval.
asseoir [aswaʀ] *vt* (*malade, bébé*) to sit up; to sit down; (*autorité, réputation*) to establish; **~ qch sur** to build sth on; to base sth on; **s'~** *vi* to sit (o.s.) down.
assermenté, e [asɛʀmɑ̃te] *a* sworn, on oath.
asservir [asɛʀviʀ] *vt* to subjugate, enslave.
assesseur [asesœʀ] *nm* (JUR) assessor.
asseye *etc vb voir* **asseoir.**
assez [ase] *ad* (*suffisamment*) enough, sufficiently; (*passablement*) rather, quite, fairly; **est-il ~ fort/rapide?** is he strong/fast enough *ou* sufficiently strong/fast?; **il est passé ~ vite** he went past rather *ou* quite *ou* fairly fast; **~ de pain/livres** enough *ou* sufficient bread/books; **travailler ~** to work sufficiently (hard), work (hard) enough.
assidu, e [asidy] *a* assiduous, painstaking; regular; **assiduités** *nfpl* assiduous attentions.
assied *etc vb voir* **asseoir.**
assiéger [asjeʒe] *vt* to besiege, lay siege to; (*suj*: *foule, touristes*) to mob, besiege.
assiérai *etc vb voir* **asseoir.**
assiette [asjɛt] *nf* plate; (*contenu*) plate(ful); (*équilibre*) seat; seating; trim; **~ anglaise** assorted cold meats; **~ creuse** (soup) dish, soup plate; **~ à dessert** dessert plate; **~ de l'impôt** basis of (tax) assessment; **~ plate** (dinner) plate.
assigner [asiɲe] *vt*: **~ qch à** (*poste, part, travail*) to assign *ou* allot sth to; (*limites*) to set *ou* fix sth to; (*cause, effet*) to ascribe *ou* attribute sth to; **~ qn à** (*affecter*) to assign sb to; **~ qn à résidence** (JUR) to assign a forced residence to sb.
assimiler [asimile] *vt* to assimilate, absorb; (*comparer*): **~ qch/qn à** to liken *ou* compare sth/sb to; **ils sont assimilés aux infirmières** (ADMIN) they are classed as nurses; **s'~** *vi* (*s'intégrer*) to be assimilated *ou* absorbed.
assis, e [asi, -iz] *pp de* **asseoir** // *a* sitting (down), seated // *nf* (CONSTR) course; (GÉO) stratum (*pl* a); (*fig*) basis (*pl* bases), foundation; **~es** *nfpl* (JUR) assizes; (*congrès*) (annual) conference.
assistance [asistɑ̃s] *nf* (*public*) audience; (*aide*) assistance; **porter ~ à qn** to give sb assistance; **l'A~ (publique)** (*-1953*) ≈ National Assistance; Child Care.
assistant, e [asistɑ̃, -ɑ̃t] *nm/f* assistant; (*d'université*) probationary lecturer; **les ~s** *nmpl* (*auditeurs etc*) those present; **~e sociale** social worker.
assisté, e [asiste] *a* (AUTO) power assisted.
assister [asiste] *vt* to assist; **~ à** *vt* (*scène, événement*) to witness; (*conférence, séminaire*) to attend, be (present) at; (*spectacle, match*) to be at, see.
association [asɔsjɑsjɔ̃] *nf* association.
associé, e [asɔsje] *nm/f* associate; partner.
associer [asɔsje] *vt* to associate; **~ qn à** (*profits*) to give sb a share of; (*affaire*) to make sb a partner in; (*joie, triomphe*) to include sb in; **~ qch à** (*joindre, allier*) to combine sth with; **s'~** (*suj pl*) to join together; (COMM) to form a partnership; **s'~** *vt* (*collaborateur*) to take on (as a partner); **s'~ à qn pour faire** to join (forces) *ou* join together with sb to do; **s'~ à** to be combined with; (*opinions, joie de qn*) to share in.
assoiffé, e [aswafe] *a* thirsty.
assolement [asɔlmɑ̃] *nm* (systematic) rotation of crops.

assombrir [asɔ̃bʀiʀ] *vt* to darken ; (*fig*) to fill with gloom ; **s'~** *vi* to darken ; to cloud over ; to become gloomy.
assommer [asɔme] *vt* to batter to death ; (*étourdir, abrutir*) to knock out ; to stun ; (*fam: ennuyer*) to bore stiff.
Assomption [asɔ̃psjɔ̃] *nf*: **l'~** the Assumption.
assorti, e [asɔʀti] *a* matched, matching ; **fromages/légumes ~s** assorted cheeses/vegetables ; **~ à** matching.
assortiment [asɔʀtimɑ̃] *nm* assortment, selection.
assortir [asɔʀtiʀ] *vt* to match ; **~ qch à** to match sth with ; **~ qch de** to accompany sth with ; **s'~ de** to be accompanied by.
assoupi, e [asupi] *a* dozing, sleeping ; (*fig*) (be)numbed ; dulled ; stilled.
assoupir [asupiʀ]: **s'~** *vi* to doze off.
assouplir [asupliʀ] *vt* to make supple ; (*fig*) to relax.
assourdir [asuʀdiʀ] *vt* (*bruit*) to deaden, muffle ; (*suj: bruit*) to deafen.
assouvir [asuviʀ] *vt* to satisfy, appease.
assujettir [asyʒetiʀ] *vt* to subject, subjugate ; **~ qn à** (*règle, impôt*) to subject sb to.
assumer [asyme] *vt* (*fonction, emploi*) to assume, take on.
assurance [asyʀɑ̃s] *nf* (*certitude*) assurance ; (*confiance en soi*) (self-)confidence ; (*contrat*) insurance (policy) ; (*secteur commercial*) insurance ; **~ maladie** health insurance ; **~ tous risques** (AUTO) comprehensive insurance ; **~s sociales** ≈ National Insurance ; **~-vie** *nf* life assurance *ou* insurance.
assuré, e [asyʀe] *a* (*victoire etc*) certain, sure ; (*démarche, voix*) assured, (self-)confident ; (*certain*): **~ de** confident of // *nm/f* insured (person) ; **~ social** ≈ member of the National Insurance scheme ; **~ment** *ad* assuredly, most certainly.
assurer [asyʀe] *vt* (COMM) to insure ; (*stabiliser*) to steady ; to stabilize ; (*victoire etc*) to ensure, make certain ; (*frontières, pouvoir*) to make secure ; (*service, garde*) to provide ; to operate ; (*garantir*): **~ qch à qn** to secure *ou* guarantee sth for sb ; (*certifier*) to assure sb of sth ; **~ à qn que** to assure sb that ; **~ qn de** to assure sb of ; **s'~ (contre)** (COMM) to insure o.s. (against) ; **s'~ de/que** (*vérifier*) to make sure of/that ; **s'~ (de)** (*aide de qn*) to secure (for o.s.) ; **assureur** *nm* insurance agent ; insurers *pl*.
astérisque [asteʀisk(ə)] *nm* asterisk.
asthmatique [asmatik] *a* asthmatic.
asthme [asm(ə)] *nm* asthma.
asticot [astiko] *nm* maggot.
astiquer [astike] *vt* to polish, shine.
astre [astʀ(ə)] *nm* star.
astreignant, e [astʀɛɲɑ̃, -ɑ̃t] *a* demanding.
astreindre [astʀɛ̃dʀ(ə)] *vt*: **~ qn à qch** to force sth upon sb ; **~ qn à faire** to compel *ou* force sb to do.
astringent, e [astʀɛ̃ʒɑ̃, -ɑ̃t] *a* astringent.
astrologie [astʀɔlɔʒi] *nf* astrology ; **astrologue** *nm/f* astrologer.
astronaute [astʀɔnot] *nm/f* astronaut.
astronautique [astʀɔnotik] *nf* astronautics *sg*.
astronome [astʀɔnɔm] *nm/f* astronomer.
astronomie [astʀɔnɔmi] *nf* astronomy ; **astronomique** *a* astronomic(al).
astuce [astys] *nf* shrewdness, astuteness ; (*truc*) trick, clever way ; (*plaisanterie*) wisecrack ; **astucieux, euse** *a* shrewd, clever, astute.
asymétrique [asimetʀik] *a* asymmetric(al).
atelier [atəlje] *nm* workshop ; (*de peintre*) studio.
athée [ate] *a* atheistic // *nm/f* atheist.
Athènes [atɛn] *n* Athens.
athlète [atlɛt] *nm/f* (SPORT) athlete ; (*costaud*) muscleman ; **athlétique** *a* athletic ; **athlétisme** *nm* athletics *sg*.
atlantique [atlɑ̃tik] *a* Atlantic // *nm*: **l'(océan) A~** the Atlantic (Ocean).
atlas [atlɑs] *nm* atlas.
atmosphère [atmɔsfɛʀ] *nf* atmosphere ; **atmosphérique** *a* atmospheric.
atome [atom] *nm* atom ; **atomique** *a* (*bombe, pile*) atomic, nuclear ; (*usine*) nuclear ; (*nombre, masse*) atomic.
atomiseur [atɔmizœʀ] *nm* atomiser.
atone [atɔn] *a* lifeless.
atours [atuʀ] *nmpl* attire *sg*, finery *sg*.
atout [atu] *nm* trump ; (*fig*) asset ; trump card ; **'~ pique/trèfle'** spades/clubs are trumps.
âtre [ɑtʀ(ə)] *nm* hearth.
atroce [atʀɔs] *a* atrocious ; dreadful ; **atrocité** *nf* atrocity.
atrophie [atʀɔfi] *nf* atrophy.
atrophier [atʀɔfje]: **s'~** *vi* to atrophy.
attabler [atable]: **s'~** *vi* to sit down at (the) table.
attachant, e [ataʃɑ̃, -ɑ̃t] *a* engaging, lovable, likeable.
attache [ataʃ] *nf* clip, fastener ; (*fig*) tie ; **à l'~** (*chien*) tied up.
attaché, e [ataʃe] *a*: **être ~ à** (*aimer*) to be attached to // *nm* (ADMIN) attaché ; **~-case** *nm inv* attaché case.
attachement [ataʃmɑ̃] *nm* attachment.
attacher [ataʃe] *vt* to tie up ; (*étiquette*) to attach, tie on ; (*souliers*) to do up // *vi* (*poêle, riz*) to stick ; **s'~ à** (*par affection*) to become attached to ; **s'~ à faire qch** to endeavour to do sth ; **~ qch à** to tie *ou* fasten *ou* attach sth to.
attaquant [atakɑ̃] *nm* (MIL) attacker ; (SPORT) striker, forward.
attaque [atak] *nf* attack ; (*cérébrale*) stroke ; (*d'épilepsie*) fit.
attaquer [atake] *vt* to attack ; (*en justice*) to bring an action against, sue ; (*travail*) to tackle, set about // *vi* to attack ; **s'~ à** to attack ; (*épidémie, misère*) to tackle, attack.
attardé, e [ataʀde] *a* (*passants*) late ; (*enfant*) backward ; (*conceptions*) old-fashioned.
attarder [ataʀde]: **s'~** *vi* to linger ; to stay on.

atteindre [atɛ̃dʀ(ə)] *vt* to reach ; (*blesser*) to hit ; (*contacter*) to reach, contact, get in touch with ; (*émouvoir*) to affect.

atteint, e [atɛ̃, -ɛ̃t] *a* (MÉD): **être ~ de** to be suffering from // *nf* attack ; **hors d'~e** out of reach ; **porter ~e à** to strike a blow at ; to undermine.

attelage [atlaʒ] *nm* (*de remorque etc*) coupling ; (*animaux*) team ; (*harnachement*) harness ; yoke.

atteler [atle] *vt* (*cheval, bœufs*) to hitch up ; (*wagons*) to couple ; **s'~ à** (*travail*) to buckle down to.

attelle [atɛl] *nf* splint.

attenant, e [atnɑ̃, -ɑ̃t] *a*: **~ (à)** adjoining.

attendre [atɑ̃dʀ(ə)] *vt* (*gén*) to wait for ; (*être destiné ou réservé à*) to await, be in store for // *vi* to wait ; **s'~ à (ce que)** (*escompter*) to expect (that) ; **~ un enfant** to be expecting (a baby) ; **~ de faire/d'être** to wait until one does/is ; **~ que** to wait until ; **~ qch de** to expect sth of ; **en attendant** *ad* meanwhile, in the meantime ; be that as it may.

attendri, e [atɑ̃dʀi] *a* tender.

attendrir [atɑ̃dʀiʀ] *vt* to move (to pity) ; (*viande*) to tenderize ; **s'~ (sur)** to be moved *ou* touched (by) ; **attendrissant, e** *a* moving, touching ; **attendrissement** *nm* emotion ; pity.

attendu [atɑ̃dy] *nm*: **~s** *reasons adduced for a judgment* ; **~ que** *cj* considering that, since.

attentat [atɑ̃ta] *nm* assassination attempt ; **~ à la bombe** bomb attack ; **~ à la pudeur** indecent exposure *q* ; indecent assault *q*.

attente [atɑ̃t] *nf* wait ; (*espérance*) expectation.

attenter [atɑ̃te]: **~ à** *vt* (*liberté*) to violate ; **~ à la vie de qn** to make an attempt on sb's life.

attentif, ive [atɑ̃tif, -iv] *a* (*auditeur*) attentive ; (*travail*) scrupulous ; careful ; **~ à** paying attention to ; mindful of ; careful to.

attention [atɑ̃sjɔ̃] *nf* attention ; (*prévenance*) attention, thoughtfulness *q* ; **à l'~ de** for the attention of ; **faire ~ (à)** to be careful (of) ; **faire ~ (à ce) que** to be *ou* make sure that ; **~!** careful!, watch *ou* mind (out)! ; **attentionné, e** *a* thoughtful, considerate.

attentisme [atɑ̃tism(ə)] *nm* wait-and-see policy.

attentivement [atɑ̃tivmɑ̃] *ad* attentively.

atténuer [atenɥe] *vt* to alleviate, ease ; to lessen ; to mitigate the effects of ; **s'~** *vi* to ease ; to abate.

atterrer [ateʀe] *vt* to dismay, appal.

atterrir [ateʀiʀ] *vi* to land ; **atterrissage** *nm* landing ; **atterrissage sur le ventre** belly landing.

attestation [atɛstɑsjɔ̃] *nf* certificate ; **~ médicale** doctor's certificate.

attester [atɛste] *vt* to testify to, vouch for ; (*démontrer*) to attest, testify to ; **~ que** to testify that.

attiédir [atjediʀ]: **s'~** *vi* to become lukewarm ; (*fig*) to cool down.

attifé, e [atife] *a* (*fam*) got up, rigged out.

attique [atik] *nm*: **appartement en ~** penthouse (flat).

attirail [atiʀaj] *nm* gear ; (*péj*) paraphernalia.

attirance [atiʀɑ̃s] *nf* attraction ; (*séduction*) lure.

attirant, e [atiʀɑ̃, -ɑ̃t] *a* attractive, appealing.

attirer [atiʀe] *vt* to attract ; (*appâter*) to lure, entice ; **~ qn dans un coin/vers soi** to draw sb into a corner/towards one ; **~ l'attention de qn (sur)** to attract sb's attention (to) ; to draw sb's attention (to) ; **s'~ des ennuis** to bring trouble upon o.s., get into trouble.

attiser [atize] *vt* (*feu*) to poke (up), stir up ; (*fig*) to fan the flame of, stir up.

attitré, e [atitʀe] *a* qualified ; accredited ; appointed.

attitude [atityd] *nf* attitude ; (*position du corps*) bearing.

attouchements [atuʃmɑ̃] *nmpl* touching *sg* ; (*sexuels*) fondling *sg*, stroking *sg*.

attraction [atʀaksjɔ̃] *nf* (*gén*) attraction ; (*de cabaret, cirque*) number.

attrait [atʀɛ] *nm* appeal, attraction ; lure ; **éprouver de l'~ pour** to be attracted to ; **~s** *nmpl* attractions.

attrape [atʀap] *nf voir* **farce** // *préfixe*: **~-nigaud** *nm* con.

attraper [atʀape] *vt* (*gén*) to catch ; (*habitude, amende*) to get, pick up ; (*fam: duper*) to take in.

attrayant, e [atʀɛjɑ̃, -ɑ̃t] *a* attractive.

attribuer [atʀibɥe] *vt* (*prix*) to award ; (*rôle, tâche*) to allocate, assign ; (*imputer*): **~ qch à** to attribute sth to, ascribe sth to, put sth down to ; **s'~** *vt* (*s'approprier*) to claim for o.s.

attribut [atʀiby] *nm* attribute ; (LING) complement.

attribution [atʀibysjɔ̃] *nf* awarding ; allocation, assignment ; attribution ; **~s** *nfpl* (*compétence*) attributions.

attrister [atʀiste] *vt* to sadden.

attroupement [atʀupmɑ̃] *nm* crowd, mob.

attrouper [atʀupe]: **s'~** *vi* to gather.

au [o] *prép + dét voir* **à**.

aubade [obad] *nf* dawn serenade.

aubaine [obɛn] *nf* godsend ; (*financière*) windfall.

aube [ob] *nf* dawn, daybreak ; **à l'~** at dawn *ou* daybreak ; **à l'~ de** (*fig*) at the dawn of.

aubépine [obepin] *nf* hawthorn.

auberge [obɛʀʒ(ə)] *nf* inn ; **~ de jeunesse** youth hostel.

aubergine [obɛʀʒin] *nf* aubergine.

aubergiste [obɛʀʒist(ə)] *nm/f* inn-keeper, hotel-keeper.

aucun, e [okœ̃, -yn] *dét* no, *tournure négative +* any ; (*positif*) any // *pronom* none, *tournure négative +* any ; any(one) ; **il n'y a ~ livre** there isn't any book, there is no book ; **je n'en vois ~ qui** I can't see any which, I (can) see none which ; **sans ~ doute** without any doubt ; **plus qu'~ autre** more than any other ; **~ des deux** neither of the two ; **~ d'entre eux** none of them ; **d'~s** (*certains*) some ;

aucunement *ad* in no way, not in the least.
audace [odas] *nf* daring, boldness; (*péj*) audacity; **audacieux, euse** *a* daring, bold.
au-delà [odla] *ad* beyond // *nm*: **l'~** the beyond; **~ de** *prép* beyond.
au-dessous [odsu] *ad* underneath; below; **~ de** *prép* under(neath), below; (*limite, somme etc*) below, under; (*dignité, condition*) below.
au-dessus [odsy] *ad* above; **~ de** *prép* above.
au-devant [odvɑ̃]: **~ de** *prép*: **aller ~ de** (*personne, danger*) to go (out) and meet; (*souhaits de qn*) to anticipate.
audience [odjɑ̃s] *nf* audience; (*JUR: séance*) hearing; **trouver ~ auprès de** to arouse much interest among, get the (interested) attention of.
audio-visuel, le [odjɔvizɥɛl] *a* audio-visual.
auditeur, trice [oditœʀ, -tʀis] *nm/f* (*à la radio*) listener; (*à une conférence*) member of the audience, listener; **~ libre** unregistered student (*attending lectures*).
audition [odisjɔ̃] *nf* (*ouïe, écoute*) hearing; (*JUR: de témoins*) examination; (*MUS, THÉÂTRE: épreuve*) audition; **auditionner** *vt, vi* to audition.
auditoire [oditwaʀ] *nm* audience.
auditorium [oditɔʀjɔm] *nm* (public) studio.
auge [oʒ] *nf* trough.
augmentation [ɔgmɑ̃tɑsjɔ̃] *nf* increasing; raising; increase; **~ (de salaire)** rise (in salary).
augmenter [ɔgmɑ̃te] *vt* (*gén*) to increase; (*salaire, prix*) to increase, raise, put up; (*employé*) to increase the salary of, give a (salary) rise to // *vi* to increase.
augure [ɔgyʀ] *nm* soothsayer, oracle; **de bon/mauvais ~** of good/ill omen.
augurer [ɔgyʀe] *vt*: **~ qch de** to foresee sth (coming) out of; **~ bien de** to augur well for.
auguste [ɔgyst(ə)] *a* august, noble, majestic.
aujourd'hui [oʒuʀdɥi] *ad* today.
aumône [ɔmon] *nf* alms *sg* (*pl inv*); **faire l'~ (à qn)** to give alms (to sb); **faire l'~ de qch à qn** (*fig*) to favour sb with sth.
aumônerie [ɔmonʀi] *nf* chaplaincy.
aumônier [ɔmonje] *nm* chaplain.
auparavant [opaʀavɑ̃] *ad* before(hand).
auprès [opʀɛ]: **~ de** *prép* next to, close to; (*recourir, s'adresser*) to; (*en comparaison de*) compared with, next to.
auquel [okɛl] *prép + pronom voir* **lequel.**
aurai *etc vb voir* **avoir**.
auréole [ɔʀeɔl] *nf* halo; (*tache*) ring.
auriculaire [ɔʀikylɛʀ] *nm* little finger.
aurons *etc vb voir* **avoir**.
aurore [ɔʀɔʀ] *nf* dawn, daybreak; **~ boréale** northern lights *pl*.
ausculter [ɔskylte] *vt* to auscultate.
auspices [ɔspis] *nmpl*: **sous les ~ de** under the patronage *ou* auspices of; **sous de bons/mauvais ~** under favourable/unfavourable auspices.
aussi [osi] *ad* (*également*) also, too; (*de comparaison*) as // *cj* therefore, consequently; **~ fort que** as strong as; **moi ~** me too, so do I; **~ bien que** (*de même que*) as well as.
aussitôt [osito] *ad* straight away, immediately; **~ que** as soon as; **~ envoyé** as soon as it is (*ou* was) sent.
austère [ɔstɛʀ] *a* austere; **austérité** *nf* austerity.
austral, e [ɔstʀal] *a* southern.
Australie [ɔstʀali] *nf* Australia; **australien, ne** *a, nm/f* Australian.
autant [otɑ̃] *ad* so much; (*comparatif*): **~ (que)** as much (as); (*nombre*) as many (as); **~ (de)** so much (*ou* many); as much (*ou* many); **~ partir** we (*ou* you *etc*) had better leave; **y en a-t-il ~ (qu'avant)?** are there as many (as before)?; is there as much (as before)?; **il n'est pas découragé pour ~** he isn't discouraged for all that; **pour ~ que** *cj* assuming, as long as; **d'~ plus/mieux (que)** all the more/the better (since).
autarcie [otaʀsi] *nf* autarchy.
autel [ɔtɛl] *nm* altar.
auteur [otœʀ] *nm* author; **l'~ de cette remarque** the person who said that; **~-compositeur** *nm* composer-songwriter.
authentifier [ɔtɑ̃tifje] *vt* to authenticate.
authentique [ɔtɑ̃tik] *a* authentic, genuine.
auto [ɔto] *nf* car.
auto... [ɔto] *préfixe* auto..., self-; **~biographie** *nf* autobiography.
autobus [ɔtɔbys] *nm* bus.
autocar [ɔtɔkaʀ] *nm* coach.
autochtone [ɔtɔktɔn] *nm/f* native.
auto-collant, e [ɔtɔkɔlɑ̃, -ɑ̃t] *a* self-adhesive; (*enveloppe*) self-seal // *nm* sticker.
auto-couchettes [ɔtɔkuʃɛt] *a*: **train ~** car sleeper train.
autocratique [ɔtɔkʀatik] *a* autocratic.
autocritique [ɔtɔkʀitik] *nf* self-criticism.
autodéfense [ɔtɔdefɑ̃s] *nf* self-defence; **groupe d'~** vigilance committee.
autodidacte [ɔtɔdidakt(ə)] *nm/f* self-taught person.
auto-école [ɔtɔekɔl] *nf* driving school.
autofinancement [ɔtɔfinɑ̃smɑ̃] *nm* self-financing.
autogestion [ɔtɔʒɛstjɔ̃] *nf* self-management.
autographe [ɔtɔgʀaf] *nm* autograph.
automate [ɔtɔmat] *nm* automaton.
automatique [ɔtɔmatik] *a* automatic // *nm*: **l'~** ≈ subscriber trunk dialling; **~ment** *ad* automatically; **automatiser** *vt* to automate; **automatisme** *nm* automatism.
automne [ɔtɔn] *nm* autumn.
automobile [ɔtɔmɔbil] *a* motor *cpd* // *nf* (motor) car; **l'~** motoring; the car industry; **automobiliste** *nm/f* motorist.
autonome [ɔtɔnɔm] *a* autonomous; **autonomie** *nf* autonomy; (*POL*) self-government, autonomy; **autonomie de vol** range.
autopsie [ɔtɔpsi] *nf* post mortem (examination), autopsy.
autorisation [ɔtɔʀizɑsjɔ̃] *nf* permission, authorization; (*papiers*) permit; **avoir l'~ de faire** to be allowed *ou* have permission to do, be authorized to do.

autorisé, e [ɔtɔʀize] *a* (*opinion, sources*) authoritative.
autoriser [ɔtɔʀize] *vt* to give permission for, authorize; (*fig*) to allow (of), sanction; ~ **qn à faire** to give permission to sb to do, authorize sb to do.
autoritaire [ɔtɔʀitɛʀ] *a* authoritarian.
autorité [ɔtɔʀite] *nf* authority; **faire** ~ to be authoritative.
autoroute [ɔtɔʀut] *nf* motorway.
auto-stop [ɔtɔstɔp] *nm*: **l'**~ hitch-hiking; **faire de l'**~ to hitch-hike; **prendre qn en** ~ to give sb a lift; ~**peur, euse** *nm/f* hitch-hiker, hitcher.
autour [otuʀ] *ad* around; ~ **de** *prép* around; (*environ*) around, about; **tout** ~ *ad* all around.
autre [otʀ(ə)] *a* other; **un** ~ **verre** (*supplémentaire*) one more glass, another glass; (*différent*) another glass, a different glass; **un** ~ another (one); **l'**~ the other (one); **les** ~**s** (*autrui*) others; **l'un et l'**~ both (of them); **se détester** *etc* **l'un l'**~**/les uns les** ~**s** to hate *etc* each other/one another; **se sentir** ~ to feel different; **d'une semaine à l'**~ from one week to the next; (*incessammant*) any week now; ~ **chose** something else; ~ **part** *ad* somewhere else; **d'**~ **part** *ad* on the other hand; **entre** ~**s** among others; among other things; **nous/vous** ~**s** us/you (lot).
autrefois [otʀəfwa] *ad* in the past.
autrement [otʀəmɑ̃] *ad* differently; in another way; (*sinon*) otherwise; ~ **dit** in other words.
Autriche [otʀiʃ] *nf* Austria; **autrichien, ne** *a, nm/f* Austrian.
autruche [otʀyʃ] *nf* ostrich.
autrui [otʀɥi] *pronom* others.
auvent [ovɑ̃] *nm* canopy.
aux [o] *prép* + *dét voir* **à**.
auxiliaire [ɔksiljɛʀ] *a, nm, nf* auxiliary.
auxquels, auxquelles [okɛl] *prép* + *pronom voir* **lequel**.
av. *abr de* **avenue**.
avachi, e [avaʃi] *a* limp, flabby.
aval [aval] *nm* (*accord*) endorsement, backing; (GÉO): **en** ~ downstream, downriver; (*sur une pente*) downhill; **en** ~ **de** downstream *ou* downriver from; downhill from.
avalanche [avalɑ̃ʃ] *nf* avalanche; ~ **poudreuse** powder snow avalanche.
avaler [avale] *vt* to swallow.
avance [avɑ̃s] *nf* (*de troupes etc*) advance; progress; (*d'argent*) advance; (*opposé à retard*) lead; being ahead of schedule; ~**s** *nfpl* overtures; (*amoureuses*) advances; **une** ~ **de 300 m/4 h** (SPORT) a 300 m/4 hour lead; **(être) en** ~ (to be) early; (*sur un programme*) (to be) ahead of schedule; **payer d'**~ to pay in advance; **à l'**~ in advance, beforehand.
avancé, e [avɑ̃se] *a* advanced; well on *ou* under way // *nf* projection; overhang; jutting part.
avancement [avɑ̃smɑ̃] *nm* (*professionnel*) promotion.
avancer [avɑ̃se] *vi* to move forward, advance; (*projet, travail*) to make progress; (*être en saillie*) to overhang; to project; to jut out; (*montre, réveil*) to be fast; to gain // *vt* to move forward, advance; (*argent*) to advance; **s'**~ *vi* to move forward, advance; (*fig*) to commit o.s.; to overhang; to project; to jut out; **j'avance (d'une heure)** I'm (an hour) fast.
avanies [avani] *nfpl* snubs.
avant [avɑ̃] *prép* before // *ad*: **trop/plus** ~ too far/further forward // *a inv*: **siège/roue** ~ front seat/wheel // *nm* (*d'un véhicule, bâtiment*) front; (SPORT: *joueur*) forward; ~ **qu'il parte/de faire** before he leaves/doing; ~ **tout** (*surtout*) above all; **à l'**~ (*dans un véhicule*) in (the) front; **en** ~ *ad* forward(s); **en** ~ **de** *prép* in front of.
avantage [avɑ̃taʒ] *nm* advantage; (TENNIS): ~ **service/dehors** advantage *ou* van in/out; ~**s sociaux** fringe benefits; **avantager** *vt* (*favoriser*) to favour; (*embellir*) to flatter; **avantageux, euse** *a* attractive; attractively priced.
avant-bras [avɑ̃bʀa] *nm inv* forearm.
avant-centre [avɑ̃sɑ̃tʀ(ə)] *nm* centre-forward.
avant-coureur [avɑ̃kuʀœʀ] *a*: **signe** ~ forerunner.
avant-dernier, ère [avɑ̃dɛʀnje, -jɛʀ] *a, nm/f* next to last, last but one.
avant-garde [avɑ̃gaʀd(ə)] *nf* (MIL) vanguard; (*fig*) avant-garde.
avant-goût [avɑ̃gu] *nm* foretaste.
avant-hier [avɑ̃tjɛʀ] *ad* the day before yesterday.
avant-poste [avɑ̃pɔst(ə)] *nm* outpost.
avant-première [avɑ̃pʀəmjɛʀ] *nf* (*de film*) preview.
avant-projet [avɑ̃pʀɔʒɛ] *nm* pilot study.
avant-propos [avɑ̃pʀɔpo] *nm* foreword.
avant-veille [avɑ̃vɛj] *nf*: **l'**~ two days before.
avare [avaʀ] *a* miserly, avaricious // *nm/f* miser; ~ **de** (*compliments etc*) sparing of; **avarice** *nf* avarice, miserliness; **avaricieux, euse** *a* miserly, niggardly.
avarié, e [avaʀje] *a* rotting, going off.
avaries [avaʀi] *nfpl* (NAVIG) damage *sg*.
avatar [avataʀ] *nm* misadventure; metamorphosis (*pl* phoses).
avec [avɛk] *prép* with; (*à l'égard de*) to(wards), with.
avenant, e [avnɑ̃, -ɑ̃t] *a* pleasant; **à l'**~ *ad* in keeping.
avènement [avɛnmɑ̃] *nm* (*d'un roi*) accession, succession; (*d'un changement*) advent, coming.
avenir [avniʀ] *nm* future; **à l'**~ in future; **politicien d'**~ politician with prospects *ou* a future.
Avent [avɑ̃] *nm*: **l'**~ Advent.
aventure [avɑ̃tyʀ] *nf* adventure; (*amoureuse*) affair; **s'aventurer** *vi* to venture; **aventureux, euse** *a* adventurous, venturesome; (*projet*) risky, chancy; **aventurier, ère** *nm/f* adventurer // *nf* (*péj*) adventuress.
avenu, e [avny] *a*: **nul et non** ~ null and void.
avenue [avny] *nf* avenue.
avérer [aveʀe]: **s'**~ *vb avec attribut* to prove (to be).

averse [avɛʀs(ə)] *nf* shower.
aversion [avɛʀsjɔ̃] *nf* aversion, loathing.
averti, e [avɛʀti] *a* (well-)informed.
avertir [avɛʀtiʀ] *vt*: ~ **qn (de qch/que)** to warn sb (of sth/that); (*renseigner*) to inform sb (of sth/that); **avertissement** *nm* warning; **avertisseur** *nm* horn, hooter.
aveu, x [avø] *nm* confession.
aveugle [avœgl(ə)] *a* blind; **~ment** *nm* blindness; **aveuglément** *ad* blindly; **aveugler** *vt* to blind; **à l'aveuglette** *ad* groping one's way along; (*fig*) in the dark, blindly.
aviateur, trice [avjatœʀ, -tʀis] *nm/f* aviator, pilot.
aviation [avjɑsjɔ̃] *nf* aviation; (*sport*) flying; (*MIL*) air force.
avide [avid] *a* eager; (*péj*) greedy, grasping; **avidité** *nf* eagerness; greed.
avilir [aviliʀ] *vt* to debase.
aviné, e [avine] *a* intoxicated, drunken.
avion [avjɔ̃] *nm* aeroplane; **aller (quelque part) en ~** to go (somewhere) by plane, fly (somewhere); **par ~** by airmail; **~ à réaction** jet (aeroplane).
aviron [aviʀɔ̃] *nm* oar; (*sport*): **l'~** rowing.
avis [avi] *nm* opinion; (*notification*) notice; **être d'~ que** to be of the opinion that; **changer d'~** to change one's mind; **jusqu'à nouvel ~** until further notice.
avisé, e [avize] *a* sensible, wise; **être bien/mal ~ de faire** to be well-/ill-advised to do.
aviser [avize] *vt* (*voir*) to notice, catch sight of; (*informer*): **~ qn de/que** to advise *ou* inform sb of/that // *vi* to think about things, assess the situation; **s'~ de qch/que** to become suddenly aware of sth/that; **s'~ de faire** to take it into one's head to do.
avocat, e [avɔka, -at] *nm/f* (*JUR*) barrister; (*fig*) advocate, champion // *nm* (*CULIN*) avocado (pear); **l'~ de la défense/partie civile** the counsel for the defence/plaintiff; **~ d'affaires** business lawyer; **~ général** assistant public prosecutor; **~-stagiaire** *nm* ≈ barrister doing his articles.
avoine [avwan] *nf* oats *pl*.
avoir [avwaʀ] *nm* assets *pl*, resources *pl* // *vt* (*gén*) to have; (*fam*: *duper*) to do // *vb auxiliaire* to have; **~ à faire qch** to have to do sth; **il a 3 ans** he is 3 (years old); *voir* **faim, peur** *etc*; **~ 3 mètres de haut** to be 3 metres high; **il y a** there is + *sg*, there are + *pl*; (*temporel*): **il y a 10 ans** 10 years ago; **il y a 10 ans/longtemps que je le sais** I've known it for 10 years/a long time; **il y a 10 ans qu'il est arrivé** it's 10 years since he arrived; **il ne peut y en ~ qu'un** there can only be one; **il n'y a qu'à** we (*ou* you *etc*) will just have to; **qu'est-ce qu'il y a?** what's the matter?, what is it?; **en ~ à** *ou* **contre qn** to have a down on sb.
avoisinant, e [avwazinɑ̃, -ɑ̃t] *a* neighbouring.
avoisiner [avwazine] *vt* to be near *ou* close to; (*fig*) to border *ou* verge on.
avortement [avɔʀtəmɑ̃] *nm* abortion.
avorter [avɔʀte] *vi* (*MÉD*) to have an abortion; (*fig*) to fail.
avorton [avɔʀtɔ̃] *nm* (*péj*) little runt.
avoué, e [avwe] *a* avowed // *nm* (*JUR*) ≈ solicitor.
avouer [avwe] *vt* (*crime, défaut*) to confess (to); **~ avoir fait/que** to admit *ou* confess to having done/that.
avril [avʀil] *nm* April.
axe [aks(ə)] *nm* axis (*pl* axes); (*de roue etc*) axle; (*fig*) main line; **~ routier** trunk road, main road; **~ de symétrie** symmetry axis; **axer** *vt*: **axer qch sur** to centre sth on.
ayant droit [ɛjɑ̃dʀwa] *nm* assignee; **~ à** (*pension etc*) person eligible for *ou* entitled to.
ayons *etc vb voir* **avoir**.
azalée [azale] *nf* azalea.
azimut [azimyt] *nm* azimuth; **tous ~s** *a* (*fig*) omnidirectional.
azote [azɔt] *nm* nitrogen; **azoté, e** *a* nitrogenous.
azur [azyʀ] *nm* (*couleur*) azure, sky blue; (*ciel*) sky, skies *pl*.
azyme [azim] *a*: **pain ~** unleavened bread.

B

B.A. *sigle f* (*= bonne action*) good deed (for the day).
babiller [babije] *vi* to prattle, chatter; (*bébé*) to babble.
babines [babin] *nfpl* chops.
babiole [babjɔl] *nf* (*bibelot*) trinket; (*vétille*) trifle.
bâbord [bɑbɔʀ] *nm*: **à** *ou* **par ~** to port, on the port side.
babouin [babwɛ̃] *nm* baboon.
bac [bak] *nm* (*SCOL*) *abr de* **baccalauréat**; (*bateau*) ferry; (*récipient*) tub; tray; tank; **~ à glace** ice-tray.
baccalauréat [bakalɔʀea] *nm* ≈ *GCE A-levels*.
bâche [bɑʃ] *nf* tarpaulin, canvas sheet.
bachelier, ère [baʃəlje, -ljɛʀ] *nm/f holder of the baccalauréat.*
bâcher [bɑʃe] *vt* to cover (with a canvas sheet *ou* a tarpaulin).
bachot [baʃo] *nm abr de* **baccalauréat**.
bacille [basil] *nm* bacillus (*pl* i).
bâcler [bɑkle] *vt* to botch (up).
bactérie [bakteʀi] *nf* bacterium (*pl* ia); **bactériologie** *nf* bacteriology.
badaud, e [bado, -od] *nm/f* idle onlooker, stroller.
baderne [badɛʀn(ə)] *nf* (*péj*): **(vieille) ~** old fossil.
badigeon [badiʒɔ̃] *nm* distemper; colourwash; **badigeonner** *vt* to distemper; to colourwash; (*barbouiller*) to daub.
badin, e [badɛ̃, -in] *a* light-hearted, playful.
badinage [badinaʒ] *nm* banter.
badine [badin] *nf* switch (*stick*).
badiner [badine] *vi*: **~ avec qch** to treat sth lightly.
badminton [badmintɔn] *nm* badminton.
baffe [baf] *nf* (*fam*) slap, clout.
bafouer [bafwe] *vt* to deride, ridicule.
bafouiller [bafuje] *vi, vt* to stammer.

bâfrer [bɑfʀe] *vi, vt* (*fam*) to guzzle, gobble.
bagage [bagaʒ] *nm*: **~s** luggage *sg*; **~ littéraire** (stock of) literary knowledge; **~s à main** hand-luggage.
bagarre [bagaʀ] *nf* fight, brawl; **il aime la ~** he loves a fight, he likes fighting; **se bagarrer** *vi* to have a fight *ou* scuffle, fight.
bagatelle [bagatɛl] *nf* trifle, trifling sum *ou* matter.
bagnard [baɲaʀ] *nm* convict.
bagne [baɲ] *nm* penal colony.
bagnole [baɲɔl] *nf* (*fam*) car, motor.
bagout [bagu] *nm* glibness; **avoir du ~** to have the gift of the gab.
bague [bag] *nf* ring; **~ de fiançailles** engagement ring; **~ de serrage** clip.
baguenauder [bagnode]: **se ~** *vi* to trail around, loaf around.
baguer [bage] *vt* to ring.
baguette [bagɛt] *nf* stick; (*cuisine chinoise*) chopstick; (*de chef d'orchestre*) baton; (*pain*) stick of (French) bread; **~ magique** magic wand; **~ de tambour** drumstick.
bahut [bay] *nm* chest.
baie [bɛ] *nf* (GÉO) bay; (*fruit*) berry; **~ (vitrée)** picture window.
baignade [bɛɲad] *nf* bathing.
baigné, e [beɲe] *a*: **~ de** bathed in; soaked with; flooded with.
baigner [beɲe] *vt* (*bébé*) to bath // *vi*: **~ dans son sang** to lie in a pool of blood; **~ dans la brume** to be shrouded in mist; **se ~** *vi* to have a swim, go swimming *ou* bathing; **baigneur, euse** *nm/f* bather; **baignoire** *nf* bath(tub).
bail, baux [baj, bo] *nm* lease.
bâillement [bɑjmɑ̃] *nm* yawn.
bâiller [bɑje] *vi* to yawn; (*être ouvert*) to gape.
bailleur [bajœʀ] *nm*: **~ de fonds** sponsor, backer.
bâillon [bɑjɔ̃] *nm* gag; **bâillonner** *vt* to gag.
bain [bɛ̃] *nm* bath; **prendre un ~** to have a bath; **~ de foule** walkabout; **~ de soleil** sunbathing *q*; **prendre un ~ de soleil** to sunbathe; **~s de mer** sea bathing *sg*; **~-marie** *nm* double boiler; **faire chauffer au ~-marie** (*boîte etc*) to immerse in boiling water.
baïonnette [bajɔnɛt] *nf* bayonet.
baisemain [bɛzmɛ̃] *nm* kissing a lady's hand.
baiser [beze] *nm* kiss // *vt* (*main, front*) to kiss; (*fam!*) to screw (!).
baisse [bɛs] *nf* fall, drop; **'~ sur la viande'** 'meat prices down'.
baisser [bese] *vt* to lower; (*radio, chauffage*) to turn down; (AUTO: *phares*) to dip // *vi* to fall, drop, go down; **se ~** *vi* to bend down.
bajoues [baʒu] *nfpl* chaps, chops.
bal [bal] *nm* dance; (*grande soirée*) ball; **~ costumé** fancy-dress ball; **~ musette** dance (*with accordion accompaniment*).
balade [balad] *nf* walk, stroll; (*en voiture*) drive.
balader [balade] *vt* (*traîner*) to trail round; **se ~** *vi* to go for a walk *ou* stroll; to go for a drive.
baladeuse [baladøz] *nf* inspection lamp.
baladin [baladɛ̃] *nm* wandering entertainer.
balafre [balafʀ(ə)] *nf* gash, slash; (*cicatrice*) scar; **balafrer** *vt* to gash, slash.
balai [balɛ] *nm* broom, brush; **~-brosse** *nm* deck scrubber.
balance [balɑ̃s] *nf* scales *pl*; (*de précision*) balance; (*signe*): **la B~** Libra, the Scales; **être de la B~** to be Libra; **~ des comptes/forces** balance of payments/power; **~ romaine** steelyard.
balancer [balɑ̃se] *vt* to swing; (*lancer*) to fling, chuck; (*renvoyer, jeter*) to chuck out // *vi* to swing; **se ~** *vi* to swing; to rock; to sway; **se ~ de** (*fam*) not to care about; **balancier** *nm* (*de pendule*) pendulum; (*de montre*) balance wheel; (*perche*) (balancing) pole; **balançoire** *nf* swing; (*sur pivot*) seesaw.
balayer [baleje] *vt* (*feuilles etc*) to sweep up, brush up; (*pièce*) to sweep; (*chasser*) to sweep away; to sweep aside; (*suj*: *radar*) to scan; (: *phares*) to sweep across; **balayeur, euse** *nm/f* roadsweeper // *nf* (*engin*) roadsweeper; **balayures** *nfpl* sweepings.
balbutier [balbysje] *vi, vt* to stammer.
balcon [balkɔ̃] *nm* balcony; (THÉÂTRE) dress circle.
baldaquin [baldakɛ̃] *nm* canopy.
baleine [balɛn] *nf* whale; (*de parapluie, corset*) rib; **baleinière** *nf* whaleboat.
balise [baliz] *nf* (NAVIG) beacon; (marker) buoy; (AVIAT) runway light, beacon; (AUTO, SKI) sign, marker; **baliser** *vt* to mark out (with beacons *ou* lights *etc*).
balistique [balistik] *nf* ballistics *sg*.
balivernes [balivɛʀn(ə)] *nfpl* twaddle *sg*, nonsense *sg*.
ballade [balad] *nf* ballad.
ballant, e [balɑ̃, -ɑ̃t] *a* dangling.
ballast [balast] *nm* ballast.
balle [bal] *nf* (*de fusil*) bullet; (*de sport*) ball; (*du blé*) chaff; (*paquet*) bale; **~ perdue** stray bullet.
ballerine [balʀin] *nf* ballet dancer; ballet shoe.
ballet [balɛ] *nm* ballet.
ballon [balɔ̃] *nm* (*de sport*) ball; (*jouet*, AVIAT) balloon; (*de vin*) glass; **~ de football** football.
ballonner [balɔne] *vt*: **j'ai le ventre ballonné** I feel bloated.
ballon-sonde [balɔ̃sɔ̃d] *nm* sounding balloon.
ballot [balo] *nm* bundle; (*péj*) nitwit.
ballottage [balɔtaʒ] *nm* (POL) second ballot.
ballotter [balɔte] *vi* to roll around; to toss // *vt* to shake *ou* throw about; to toss.
balluchon [balyʃɔ̃] *nm* bundle (of clothes).
balnéaire [balneɛʀ] *a* seaside *cpd*.
balourd, e [baluʀ, -uʀd(ə)] *a* clumsy, doltish; **balourdise** *nf* clumsiness, doltishness; blunder.
balte [balt] *a* Baltic.

Baltique [baltik] *nf*: **la (mer)** ~ the Baltic (Sea).
baluchon [balyʃɔ̃] *nm* = **balluchon.**
balustrade [balystʀad] *nf* railings *pl*, handrail.
bambin [bɑ̃bɛ̃] *nm* little child.
bambou [bɑ̃bu] *nm* bamboo.
ban [bɑ̃] *nm* round of applause, cheer ; **~s** *nmpl* (*de mariage*) banns ; **être/mettre au ~ de** to be outlawed/to outlaw from ; **le ~ et l'arrière-~ de sa famille** every last one of his relatives.
banal, e [banal] *a* banal, commonplace ; (*péj*) trite ; **four/moulin ~** village oven/mill ; **~ité** *nf* banality ; truism, trite remark.
banane [banan] *nf* banana ; **~raie** *nf* banana plantation ; **bananier** *nm* banana tree ; banana boat.
banc [bɑ̃] *nm* seat, bench ; (*de poissons*) shoal ; **~ des accusés** dock ; **~ d'essai** (*fig*) testing ground ; **~ de sable** sandbank ; **~ des témoins** witness box.
bancaire [bɑ̃kɛʀ] *a* banking, bank *cpd*.
bancal, e [bɑ̃kal] *a* wobbly ; bandy-legged.
bandage [bɑ̃daʒ] *nm* bandaging ; bandage ; **~ herniaire** truss.
bande [bɑ̃d] *nf* (*de tissu etc*) strip ; (MÉD) bandage ; (*motif*) stripe ; (*magnétique etc*) tape ; (*groupe*) band ; (*péj*): **~ de** bunch *ou* crowd of ; **par la ~** in a roundabout way ; **donner de la ~** to list ; **faire ~ à part** to keep to o.s. ; **~ dessinée** strip cartoon ; **~ perforée** punched tape ; **~ de roulement** (*de pneu*) tread ; **~ sonore** sound track.
bandeau, x [bɑ̃do] *nm* headband ; (*sur les yeux*) blindfold ; (MÉD) head bandage.
bander [bɑ̃de] *vt* (*blessure*) to bandage ; (*muscle*) to tense ; **~ les yeux à qn** to blindfold sb.
banderole [bɑ̃dʀɔl] *nf* banner, streamer.
bandit [bɑ̃di] *nm* bandit ; **banditisme** *nm* violent crime, armed robberies *pl*.
bandoulière [bɑ̃duljɛʀ] *nf*: **en ~** (slung *ou* worn) across the shoulder.
banjo [bɑ̃(d)ʒo] *nm* banjo.
banlieue [bɑ̃ljø] *nf* suburbs *pl* ; **lignes/quartiers de ~** suburban lines/areas ; **trains de ~** commuter trains.
bannière [banjɛʀ] *nf* banner.
bannir [baniʀ] *vt* to banish.
banque [bɑ̃k] *nf* bank ; (*activités*) banking ; **~ d'affaires** merchant bank.
banqueroute [bɑ̃kʀut] *nf* bankruptcy.
banquet [bɑ̃kɛ] *nm* dinner ; (*d'apparat*) banquet.
banquette [bɑ̃kɛt] *nf* seat.
banquier [bɑ̃kje] *nm* banker.
banquise [bɑ̃kiz] *nf* ice field.
baptême [batɛm] *nm* christening ; baptism ; **~ de l'air** first flight ; **baptiser** *vt* to christen.
baquet [bakɛ] *nm* tub, bucket.
bar [baʀ] *nm* bar.
baragouin [baʀagwɛ̃] *nm* gibberish.
baraque [baʀak] *nf* shed ; (*fam*) house ; **~ foraine** fairground stand.
baraqué, e [baʀake] *a* well-built, hefty.
baraquements [baʀakmɑ̃] *nmpl* huts (*for refugees, workers etc*).
baratin [baʀatɛ̃] *nm* (*fam*) smooth talk, patter ; **baratiner** *vt* to chat up.
barbare [baʀbaʀ] *a* barbaric // *nm/f* barbarian.
barbe [baʀb(ə)] *nf* beard ; **quelle ~** (*fam*) what a drag *ou* bore ; **~ à papa** candy-floss.
barbelé [baʀbəle] *nm* barbed wire *q*.
barbiche [baʀbiʃ] *nf* goatee.
barbiturique [baʀbityʀik] *nm* barbiturate.
barboter [baʀbɔte] *vi* to paddle, dabble // *vt* (*fam*) to filch.
barboteuse [baʀbɔtøz] *nf* rompers *pl*.
barbouiller [baʀbuje] *vt* to daub ; **avoir l'estomac barbouillé** to feel queasy *ou* sick.
barbu, e [baʀby] *a* bearded.
barda [baʀda] *nm* (*fam*) kit, gear.
barde [baʀd(ə)] *nf* (CULIN) sliver of fat bacon.
bardé, e [baʀde] *a*: **~ de médailles** *etc* bedecked with medals *etc*.
barder [baʀde] *vi* (*fam*): **ça va ~** sparks will fly, things are going to get hot.
barème [baʀɛm] *nm* scale ; table ; **~ des salaires** salary scale.
barguigner [baʀgiɲe] *vi*: **sans ~** without (any) humming and hawing *ou* shilly-shallying.
baril [baʀil] *nm* barrel ; keg.
barillet [baʀijɛ] *nm* (*de revolver*) cylinder.
bariolé, e [baʀjɔle] *a* many-coloured, rainbow-coloured.
baromètre [baʀɔmɛtʀ(ə)] *nm* barometer.
baron [baʀɔ̃] *nm* baron ; **baronne** *nf* baroness.
baroque [baʀɔk] *a* (ART) baroque ; (*fig*) weird.
baroud [baʀud] *nm*: **~ d'honneur** gallant last stand.
barque [baʀk(ə)] *nf* small boat.
barrage [baʀaʒ] *nm* dam ; (*sur route*) roadblock, barricade.
barre [baʀ] *nf* bar ; (NAVIG) helm ; (*écrite*) line, stroke ; (JUR): **comparaître à la ~** to appear as a witness ; **~ fixe** (GYM) horizontal bar ; **~ à mine** crowbar ; **~s parallèles** (GYM) parallel bars.
barreau, x [baʀo] *nm* bar ; (JUR): **le ~** the Bar.
barrer [baʀe] *vt* (*route etc*) to block ; (*mot*) to cross out ; (*chèque*) to cross ; (NAVIG) to steer ; **se ~** *vi* (*fam*) to clear off.
barrette [baʀɛt] *nf* (*pour cheveux*) (hair) slide.
barreur [baʀœʀ] *nm* helmsman ; (*aviron*) coxswain.
barricade [baʀikad] *nf* barricade ; **barricader** *vt* to barricade ; **se barricader chez soi** (*fig*) to lock o.s. in.
barrière [baʀjɛʀ] *nf* fence ; (*obstacle*) barrier.
barrique [baʀik] *nf* barrel, cask.
baryton [baʀitɔ̃] *nm* baritone.
bas, basse [bɑ, bɑs] *a* low // *nm* bottom, lower part ; (*chaussette*) stocking // *nf* (MUS) bass // *ad* low ; **plus ~** lower down ; (*dans un texte*) further on, below ; (*parler*) more softly ; **au ~ mot** at the lowest estimate ; **enfant en ~ âge** infant, young

child ; **en** ~ down below ; at (*ou* to) the bottom ; (*dans une maison*) downstairs ; **en** ~ **de** at the bottom of ; **mettre** ~ *vi* to give birth ; **à** ~ **...!** 'down with ...!' ; ~ **morceaux** *nmpl* (*viande*) cheap cuts.
basalte [bazalt(ə)] *nm* basalt.
basané, e [bazane] *a* tanned, bronzed.
bas-côté [bɑkote] *nm* (*de route*) verge ; (*d'église*) (side) aisle.
bascule [baskyl] *nf*: **(jeu de)** ~ seesaw ; **(balance à)** ~ scales *pl* ; **fauteuil à** ~ rocking chair ; **système à** ~ tip-over device ; rocker device.
basculer [baskyle] *vi* to fall over, topple (over) ; (*benne*) to tip up // *vt* (*gén*: **faire** ~) to topple over ; to tip out, tip up.
base [bɑz] *nf* base ; (POL) rank and file ; (*fondement, principe*) basis (*pl* bases) ; **de** ~ basic ; **à** ~ **de café** *etc* coffee *etc* -based ; **baser** *vt* to base ; **se baser sur** (*données, preuves*) to base one's argument on.
bas-fond [bɑfɔ̃] *nm* (NAVIG) shallow ; ~**s** (*fig*) dregs.
basilic [bazilik] *nm* (CULIN) basil.
basilique [bazilik] *nf* basilica.
basket(-ball) [baskɛt(bol)] *nm* basketball.
basque [bask(ə)] *a, nm/f* Basque.
bas-relief [bɑʀəljɛf] *nm* bas relief.
basse [bɑs] *a, nf voir* **bas** ; ~**-cour** *nf* farmyard.
bassin [basɛ̃] *nm* (*cuvette*) bowl ; (*pièce d'eau*) pond, pool ; (*de fontaine,* GÉO) basin ; (ANAT) pelvis ; (*portuaire*) dock.
bassiste [bɑsist(ə)] *nm/f* (double) bass player.
bastingage [bastɛ̃gaʒ] *nm* (ship's) rail.
bastion [bastjɔ̃] *nm* bastion.
bas-ventre [bɑvɑ̃tʀ(ə)] *nm* (lower part of the) stomach.
bat *vb voir* **battre**.
bât [bɑ] *nm* packsaddle.
bataille [batɑj] *nf* battle ; fight.
bataillon [batajɔ̃] *nm* battalion.
bâtard, e [bɑtaʀ, -aʀd(ə)] *nm/f* illegitimate child, bastard (*péj*).
bateau, x [bato] *nm* boat, ship.
batelier, -ière [batəlje, -jɛʀ] *nm/f* (*de bac*) ferryman.
bat-flanc [baflɑ̃] *nm inv raised boards for sleeping, in cells, army huts etc.*
bâti, e [bɑti] *a*: **bien** ~ well-built // *nm* (*armature*) frame.
batifoler [batifɔle] *vi* to frolic *ou* lark about.
bâtiment [bɑtimɑ̃] *nm* building ; (NAVIG) ship, vessel ; (*industrie*) building trade.
bâtir [bɑtiʀ] *vt* to build.
bâtisse [bɑtis] *nf* building.
bâton [bɑtɔ̃] *nm* stick ; **à** ~**s rompus** informally.
bâtonnier [bɑtɔnje] *nm* ≈ president of the Bar.
batraciens [batʀasjɛ̃] *nmpl* amphibians.
bats *vb voir* **battre**.
battage [bataʒ] *nm* (*publicité*) (hard) plugging.
battant [batɑ̃] *nm* (*de cloche*) clapper ; (*de volets*) shutter, flap ; (*de porte*) side ; **porte à double** ~ double door.
battement [batmɑ̃] *nm* (*de cœur*) beat ; (*intervalle*) interval (*between classes, trains etc*) ; ~ **de paupières** blinking *q* (of eyelids) ; **10 minutes de** ~ 10 minutes to spare.
batterie [batʀi] *nf* (MIL, ÉLEC) battery ; (MUS) drums *pl*, drum kit ; ~ **de cuisine** pots and pans *pl*, kitchen utensils *pl*.
batteur [batœʀ] *nm* (MUS) drummer ; (*appareil*) whisk ; **batteuse** *nf* (AGR) threshing machine.
battre [batʀ(ə)] *vt* to beat ; (*suj*: *pluie, vagues*) to beat *ou* lash against ; (*œufs etc*) to beat up, whisk ; (*blé*) to thresh ; (*passer au peigne fin*) to scour // *vi* (*cœur*) to beat ; (*volets etc*) to bang, rattle ; **se** ~ *vi* to fight ; ~ **la mesure** to beat time ; ~ **en brèche** to demolish ; ~ **son plein** to be at its height, be going full swing ; ~ **pavillon britannique** to fly the British flag ; ~ **des mains** to clap one's hands ; ~ **des ailes** to flap its wings ; ~ **en retraite** to beat a retreat.
battue [baty] *nf* (*chasse*) beat ; (*policière etc*) search, hunt.
baume [bom] *nm* balm.
bauxite [boksit] *nf* bauxite.
bavard, e [bavaʀ, -aʀd(ə)] *a* (very) talkative ; gossipy ; **bavardage** *nm* chatter *q* ; gossip *q* ; **bavarder** *vi* to chatter ; (*indiscrètement*) to gossip ; to blab.
bave [bav] *nf* dribble ; (*de chien etc*) slobber, slaver ; (*d'escargot*) slime ; **baver** *vi* to dribble ; to slobber, slaver ; **bavette** *nf* bib ; **baveux, euse** *a* dribbling ; (*omelette*) runny.
bavure [bavyʀ] *nf* smudge ; (*fig*) hitch, flaw.
bayer [baje] *vi*: ~ **aux corneilles** to stand gaping.
bazar [bazaʀ] *nm* general store ; (*fam*) jumble ; **bazarder** *vt* (*fam*) to chuck out.
B.C.G. *sigle m* (= *bacille Calmette-Guérin*) BCG.
bd. *abr de* **boulevard**.
B.D. *sigle f* = **bande dessinée**.
béant, e [beɑ̃, -ɑ̃t] *a* gaping.
béat, e [bea, -at] *a* showing open-eyed wonder ; blissful ; **béatitude** *nf* bliss.
beau(bel), belle, beaux [bo, bɛl] *a* beautiful, fine, lovely ; (*homme*) handsome // *nf* (SPORT) decider // *ad*: **il fait** ~ the weather's fine *ou* fair ; **un** ~ **jour** one (fine) day ; **de plus belle** more than ever, even more ; **on a** ~ **essayer** however hard *ou* no matter how hard we try ; **faire le** ~ (*chien*) to sit up and beg.
beaucoup [boku] *ad* a lot ; much (*gén en tournure négative*) ; **il ne boit pas** ~ he doesn't drink much *ou* a lot ; ~ **de** (*nombre*) many, a lot of ; (*quantité*) a lot of, much ; ~ **plus/trop** *etc* far *ou* much more/too much ; **de** ~ by far.
beau-fils [bofis] *nm* son-in-law ; (*remariage*) stepson.
beau-frère [bofʀɛʀ] *nm* brother-in-law.
beau-père [bopɛʀ] *nm* father-in-law ; stepfather.
beauté [bote] *nf* beauty ; **de toute** ~ beautiful ; **en** ~ with a flourish, brilliantly.
beaux-arts [bozaʀ] *nmpl* fine arts.

beaux-parents [bopaʀɑ̃] *nmpl* wife's/husband's family *sg ou pl*, in-laws.
bébé [bebe] *nm* baby.
bec [bɛk] *nm* beak, bill; (*de plume*) nib; (*de récipient*) spout; lip; (*fam*) mouth; ~ **de gaz** (street) gaslamp; ~ **verseur** pouring lip.
bécane [bekan] *nf* bike.
bécasse [bekas] *nf* (ZOOL) woodcock; (*fam*) silly goose.
bec-de-lièvre [bɛkdəljɛvʀ(ə)] *nm* harelip.
bêche [bɛʃ] *nf* spade; **bêcher** *vt* to dig.
bécoter [bekɔte]: **se** ~ *vi* to smooch.
becquée [beke] *nf*: **donner la** ~ **à** to feed.
becqueter [bɛkte] *vt* to peck (at).
bedaine [bədɛn] *nf* paunch.
bedeau, x [bədo] *nm* beadle.
bedonnant, e [bədɔnɑ̃, -ɑ̃t] *a* paunchy, potbellied.
bée [be] *a*: **bouche** ~ gaping.
beffroi [befʀwa] *nm* belfry.
bégayer [begeje] *vt, vi* to stammer.
bègue [bɛg] *nm/f*: **être** ~ to have a stammer.
bégueule [begœl] *a* prudish.
béguin [begɛ̃] *nm*: **avoir le** ~ **de** *ou* **pour** to have a crush on.
beige [bɛʒ] *a* beige.
beignet [bɛɲɛ] *nm* fritter.
bel [bɛl] *a voir* **beau.**
bêler [bele] *vi* to bleat.
belette [bəlɛt] *nf* weasel.
belge [bɛlʒ(ə)] *a, nm/f* Belgian.
Belgique [bɛlʒik] *nf* Belgium.
bélier [belje] *nm* ram; (*engin*) (battering) ram; (*signe*): **le B**~ Aries, the Ram; **être du B**~ to be Aries.
belle [bɛl] *af, nf voir* **beau**; ~**-fille** *nf* daughter-in-law; (*remariage*) stepdaughter; ~**-mère** *nf* mother-in-law; stepmother; ~**-sœur** *nf* sister-in-law.
belligérant, e [beliʒeʀɑ̃, -ɑ̃t] *a* belligerent.
belliqueux, euse [belikø, -øz] *a* aggressive, warlike.
belvédère [bɛlvedɛʀ] *nm* panoramic viewpoint (*or small building at such a place*).
bémol [bemɔl] *nm* (MUS) flat.
bénédiction [benediksjɔ̃] *nf* blessing.
bénéfice [benefis] *nm* (COMM) profit; (*avantage*) benefit; **bénéficiaire** *nm/f* beneficiary; **bénéficier de** *vt* to enjoy; to benefit by *ou* from; to get, be given; **bénéfique** *a* beneficial.
benêt [bənɛ] *nm* simpleton.
bénévole [benevɔl] *a* voluntary, unpaid.
bénin, igne [benɛ̃, -iɲ] *a* minor, mild; (*tumeur*) benign.
bénir [beniʀ] *vt* to bless; **bénit, e** *a* consecrated; **eau bénite** holy water; **bénitier** *nm* stoup, font (*for holy water*).
benjamin, e [bɛ̃ʒamɛ̃, -in] *nm/f* youngest child.
benne [bɛn] *nf* skip; (*de téléphérique*) (cable) car; ~ **basculante** tipper.
benzine [bɛ̃zin] *nf* benzine.
béotien, ne [beɔsjɛ̃, -jɛn] *nm/f* philistine.
B.E.P.C. *sigle m voir* **brevet**.
béquille [bekij] *nf* crutch; (*de bicyclette*) stand.
bercail [bɛʀkaj] *nm* fold.
berceau, x [bɛʀso] *nm* cradle, crib.
bercer [bɛʀse] *vt* to rock, cradle; (*suj: musique etc*) to lull; ~ **qn de** (*promesses etc*) to delude sb with; **berceuse** *nf* lullaby.
béret (basque) [beʀɛ(bask(ə))] *nm* beret.
berge [bɛʀʒ(ə)] *nf* bank.
berger, ère [bɛʀʒe, -ɛʀ] *nm/f* shepherd/shepherdess; **bergerie** *nf* sheep pen.
berline [bɛʀlin] *nf* (AUTO) saloon (car).
berlingot [bɛʀlɛ̃go] *nm* (*emballage*) carton (*pyramid shaped*).
berlue [bɛʀly] *nf*: **j'ai la** ~ I must be seeing things.
berne [bɛʀn(ə)] *nf*: **en** ~ at half-mast.
berner [bɛʀne] *vt* to fool.
besogne [bəzɔɲ] *nf* work *q*, job; **besogneux, euse** *a* hard-working.
besoin [bəzwɛ̃] *nm* need; (*pauvreté*): **le** ~ need, want; ~**s (naturels)** nature's needs; **faire ses** ~**s** to relieve o.s.; **avoir** ~ **de qch/faire qch** to need sth/to do sth; **au** ~ if need be; **pour les** ~**s de la cause** for the purpose in hand.
bestial, e, aux [bɛstjal, -o] *a* bestial, brutish.
bestiaux [bɛstjo] *nmpl* cattle.
bestiole [bɛstjɔl] *nf* (tiny) creature.
bétail [betaj] *nm* livestock, cattle *pl*.
bête [bɛt] *nf* animal; (*bestiole*) insect, creature // *a* stupid, silly; **il cherche la petite** ~ he's being pernickety *ou* over-fussy; ~ **noire** pet hate, bugbear; ~ **sauvage** wild beast; ~ **de somme** beast of burden.
bêtise [betiz] *nf* stupidity; stupid thing (to say *ou* do).
béton [betɔ̃] *nm* concrete; ~ **armé** reinforced concrete; **bétonner** *vt* to concrete (over); **bétonnière** *nf* cement mixer.
betterave [bɛtʀav] *nf* (*rouge*) beetroot; ~ **fourragère** mangel-wurzel; ~ **sucrière** sugar beet.
beugler [bøgle] *vi* to low; (*radio etc*) to blare // *vt* (*chanson etc*) to bawl out.
beurre [bœʀ] *nm* butter; **beurrer** *vt* to butter; **beurrier** *nm* butter dish.
beuverie [bœvʀi] *nf* drinking session.
bévue [bevy] *nf* blunder.
bi... [bi] *préfixe* bi..., two-.
biais [bjɛ] *nm* (*moyen*) device, expedient; (*aspect*) angle; **en** ~**, de** ~ (*obliquement*) at an angle; (*fig*) indirectly; **biaiser** *vi* (*fig*) to sidestep the issue.
bibelot [biblo] *nm* trinket, curio.
biberon [bibʀɔ̃] *nm* (feeding) bottle; **nourrir au** ~ to bottle-feed.
bible [bibl(ə)] *nf* bible.
biblio... [biblijɔ] *préfixe*: ~**bus** *nm* mobile library van; ~**graphie** *nf* bibliography; ~**phile** *nm/f* booklover; ~**thécaire** *nm/f* librarian; ~**thèque** *nf* library; (*meuble*) bookcase.
biblique [biblik] *a* biblical.
bicarbonate [bikaʀbɔnat] *nm*: ~ **(de soude)** bicarbonate of soda.
biceps [bisɛps] *nm* biceps.
biche [biʃ] *nf* doe.

bichonner [biʃɔne] *vt* to groom.
bicolore [bikɔlɔʀ] *a* two-coloured.
bicoque [bikɔk] *nf* (*péj*) shack.
bicorne [bikɔʀn(ə)] *nm* cocked hat.
bicyclette [bisiklɛt] *nf* bicycle.
bide [bid] *nm* (*fam*: *ventre*) belly ; (THÉÂTRE) flop.
bidet [bidɛ] *nm* bidet.
bidon [bidɔ̃] *nm* can // *a inv* (*fam*) phoney.
bidonville [bidɔ̃vil] *nm* shanty town.
bielle [bjɛl] *nf* connecting rod.
bien [bjɛ̃] *nm* good ; (*patrimoine*) property *q* ; **faire du ~ à qn** to do sb good ; **dire du ~ de** to speak well of ; **changer en ~** to turn to the good ; **~s de consommation** consumer goods // *ad* (*travailler*) well ; **~ jeune** rather young ; **~ assez** quite enough ; **~ mieux** very much better ; **~ du temps/ des gens** quite a time/a number of people ; **j'espère ~ y aller** I do hope to go ; **je veux ~ le faire** (*concession*) I'm (quite) willing to do it ; **il faut ~ le faire** it has to be done ; **~ sûr** certainly ; **c'est ~ fait** (*mérité*) it serves him (*ou* her *etc*) right ; **croyant ~ faire** thinking he was doing the right thing // *a inv* (*à l'aise*): **être ~** to be fine ; **ce n'est pas ~ de** it's not right to ; **cette maison est ~** this house is (very) good ; **elle est ~** (*jolie*) she's good-looking ; **des gens ~** (*parfois péj*) respectable people ; **être ~ avec qn** to be on good terms with sb ; **~ que** *cj* although ; **~-aimé, e** a, *nm/f* beloved ; **~-être** *nm* well-being ; **~faisance** *nf* charity ; **~faisant, e** *a* (*chose*) beneficial ; **~fait** *nm* act of generosity, benefaction ; (*de la science etc*) benefit ; **~faiteur, trice** *nm/f* benefactor/benefactress ; **~-fondé** *nm* soundness ; **~-fonds** *nm* property ; **~heureux, euse** *a* happy ; (REL) blessed, blest.
biennal, e, aux [bjenal, -o] *a* biennial.
bienséance [bjɛ̃seɑ̃s] *nf* propriety, decorum *q*.
bienséant, e [bjɛ̃seɑ̃, -ɑ̃t] *a* proper, seemly.
bientôt [bjɛ̃to] *ad* soon ; **à ~** see you soon.
bienveillance [bjɛ̃vɛjɑ̃s] *nf* kindness.
bienveillant, e [bjɛ̃vɛjɑ̃, -ɑ̃t] *a* kindly.
bienvenu, e [bjɛ̃vny] *a* welcome // *nm/f*: **être le ~/la ~e** to be welcome // *nf*: **souhaiter la ~e à** to welcome ; **~e à** welcome to.
bière [bjɛʀ] *nf* (*boisson*) beer ; (*cercueil*) bier ; **~ blonde** lager ; **~ brune** brown ale ; **~ (à la) pression** draught beer.
biffer [bife] *vt* to cross out.
bifteck [biftɛk] *nm* steak.
bifurcation [bifyʀkɑsjɔ̃] *nf* fork (*in road*).
bifurquer [bifyʀke] *vi* (*route*) to fork ; (*véhicule*) to turn off.
bigame [bigam] *a* bigamous ; **bigamie** *nf* bigamy.
bigarré, e [bigaʀe] *a* multicoloured ; (*disparate*) motley.
bigorneau, x [bigɔʀno] *nm* winkle.
bigot, e [bigo, -ɔt] (*péj*) *a* churchy // *nm/f* church fiend.
bigoudi [bigudi] *nm* curler.
bijou, x [biʒu] *nm* jewel ; **~terie** *nf* jeweller's (shop) ; jewellery ; **~tier, ière** *nm/f* jeweller.
bikini [bikini] *nm* bikini.
bilan [bilɑ̃] *nm* (COMM) balance sheet(s) ; end of year statement ; (*fig*) (net) outcome ; (: *de victimes*) toll ; **faire le ~ de** to assess ; to review ; **déposer son ~** to file a bankruptcy statement.
bilatéral, e, aux [bilateʀal, -o] *a* bilateral.
bile [bil] *nf* bile ; **se faire de la ~** (*fam*) to worry o.s. sick.
biliaire [biljɛʀ] *a* biliary.
bilieux, euse [biljø, -øz] *a* bilious ; (*fig*: *colérique*) testy.
bilingue [bilɛ̃g] *a* bilingual.
billard [bijaʀ] *nm* billiards *sg* ; billiard table.
bille [bij] *nf* (*gén*) ball ; (*du jeu de billes*) marble ; (*de bois*) log.
billet [bijɛ] *nm* (*aussi*: **~ de banque**) (bank)note ; (*de cinéma, de bus etc*) ticket ; (*courte lettre*) note ; **~ circulaire** round-trip ticket ; **~ de faveur** complimentary ticket ; **~ de loterie** lottery ticket ; **~ de quai** platform ticket.
billion [biljɔ̃] *nm* billion.
billot [bijo] *nm* block.
bimensuel, le [bimɑ̃sɥɛl] *a* bimonthly, two-monthly.
bimoteur [bimɔtœʀ] *a* twin-engined.
binaire [binɛʀ] *a* binary.
binocle [binɔkl(ə)] *nm* pince-nez.
binôme [binom] *nm* binomial.
bio... [bjɔ] *préfixe* bio... ; **~-dégradable** *a* biodegradable ; **~graphe** *nm/f* biographer ; **~graphie** *nf* biography ; **~graphique** *a* biographical ; **~logie** *nf* biology ; **~logique** *a* biological ; **~logiste** *nm/f* biologist.
bipède [bipɛd] *nm* biped, two-footed creature.
biplan [biplɑ̃] *nm* biplane.
biréacteur [biʀeaktœʀ] *nm* twin- engined jet.
bis, e [bi, biz] *a* (*couleur*) greyish brown // *ad* [bis]: **12 ~** 12a *ou* A // *excl, nm* [bis] encore // *nf* (*baiser*) kiss ; (*vent*) North wind.
bisannuel, le [bizanɥɛl] *a* biennial.
bisbille [bisbij] *nf*: **être en ~ avec qn** to be at loggerheads with sb.
biscornu, e [biskɔʀny] *a* crooked, weird(-looking).
biscotte [biskɔt] *nf* rusk.
biscuit [biskɥi] *nm* biscuit ; sponge cake.
bise [biz] *a, nf voir* **bis.**
biseau, x [bizo] *nm* bevelled edge ; **en ~** bevelled ; **~ter** *vt* to bevel.
bison [bizɔ̃] *nm* bison.
bisque [bisk(ə)] *nf*: **~ d'écrevisses** shrimp bisque.
bissectrice [bisɛktʀis] *nf* bisector.
bisser [bise] *vt* to encore.
bissextile [bisɛkstil] *a*: **année ~** leap year.
bissexué, e [bisɛksɥe] *a* bisexual.
bistouri [bisturi] *nm* lancet.
bistre [bistʀ(ə)] *a* bistre.
bistro(t) [bistʀo] *nm* bistrot, café.

bitte [bit] *nf*: ~ **d'amarrage** bollard (*NAUT*).
bitume [bitym] *nm* asphalt.
bivouac [bivwak] *nm* bivouac; **bivouaquer** *vi* to bivouac.
bizarre [bizaʀ] *a* strange, odd.
blafard, e [blafaʀ, -aʀd(ə)] *a* wan.
blague [blag] *nf* (*propos*) joke; (*farce*) trick; **sans ~!** no kidding!; ~ **à tabac** tobacco pouch.
blaguer [blage] *vi* to joke // *vt* to tease; **blagueur, euse** *a* teasing // *nm/f* joker.
blaireau, x [blɛʀo] *nm* (*ZOOL*) badger; (*brosse*) shaving brush.
blâmable [blɑmabl(ə)] *a* blameworthy.
blâme [blɑm] *nm* blame; (*sanction*) reprimand.
blâmer [blɑme] *vt* to blame.
blanc, blanche [blɑ̃, blɑ̃ʃ] *a* white; (*non imprimé*) blank; (*innocent*) pure // *nm/f* white, white man/woman // *nm* (*couleur*) white; (*linge*): **le ~** whites *pl*; (*espace non écrit*) blank; (*aussi*: ~ **d'œuf**) (egg-)white; (*aussi*: ~ **de poulet**) breast, white meat; (*aussi*: **vin ~**) white wine // *nf* (*MUS*) minim; **chèque en ~** blank cheque; **à ~** *ad* (*chauffer*) white-hot; (*tirer, charger*) with blanks; **~-bec** *nm* greenhorn; **blancheur** *nf* whiteness.
blanchir [blɑ̃ʃiʀ] *vt* (*gén*) to whiten; (*linge*) to launder; (*CULIN*) to blanch; (*fig: disculper*) to clear // *vi* to grow white; (*cheveux*) to go white; **blanchissage** *nm* (*du linge*) laundering; **blanchisserie** *nf* laundry; **blanchisseur, euse** *nm/f* launderer.
blanc-seing [blɑ̃sɛ̃] *nm* signed blank paper.
blaser [blɑze] *vt* to make blasé.
blason [blazɔ̃] *nm* coat of arms.
blasphème [blasfɛm] *nm* blasphemy; **blasphémer** *vi* to blaspheme // *vt* to blaspheme against.
blatte [blat] *nf* cockroach.
blazer [blazɛʀ] *nm* blazer.
blé [ble] *nm* wheat; ~ **en herbe** wheat on the ear.
bled [blɛd] *nm* (*péj*) hole; (*en Afrique du nord*): **le ~** the interior.
blême [blɛm] *a* pale.
blennoragie [blenɔʀaʒi] *nf* blennorrhoea.
blessant, e [blɛsɑ̃, -ɑ̃t] *a* hurtful.
blessé, e [blese] *a* injured // *nm/f* injured person; casualty.
blesser [blese] *vt* to injure; (*délibérément: MIL etc*) to wound; (*suj: souliers etc, offenser*) to hurt; **se ~** to injure o.s.; **se ~ au pied** *etc* to injure one's foot *etc*.
blessure [blesyʀ] *nf* injury; wound.
blet, te [blɛ, blɛt] *a* overripe.
bleu [blø] *a* blue; (*bifteck*) very rare // *nm* (*couleur*) blue; (*novice*) greenhorn; (*contusion*) bruise; (*vêtement: aussi*: **~s**) overalls *pl*; **au ~** (*CULIN*) au bleu.
bleuet [bløɛ] *nm* cornflower.
bleuir [bløiʀ] *vt, vi* to turn blue.
bleuté, e [bløte] *a* blue-shaded.
blindage [blɛ̃daʒ] *nm* armour-plating.
blinder [blɛ̃de] *vt* to armour; (*fig*) to harden.
blizzard [blizaʀ] *nm* blizzard.
bloc [blɔk] *nm* (*de pierre etc*) block; (*de papier à lettres*) pad; (*ensemble*) group, block; **serré à ~** tightened right down; **en ~** as a whole; wholesale; ~ **opératoire** operating theatre suite.
blocage [blɔkaʒ] *nm* blocking; jamming; freezing; (*PSYCH*) hang-up.
bloc-moteur [blɔkmɔtœʀ] *nm* engine block.
bloc-notes [blɔknɔt] *nm* note pad.
blocus [blɔkys] *nm* blockade.
blond, e [blɔ̃, -ɔ̃d] *a* fair, blond; (*sable, blés*) golden // *nm/f* fair-haired *ou* blond man/woman; ~ **cendré** ash blond; **blondeur** *nf* fairness.
bloquer [blɔke] *vt* (*passage*) to block; (*pièce mobile*) to jam; (*crédits, compte*) to freeze; (*regrouper*) to group; ~ **les freins** to jam on the brakes.
blottir [blɔtiʀ]: **se ~** *vi* to huddle up.
blouse [bluz] *nf* overall.
blouson [bluzɔ̃] *nm* lumber jacket; ~ **noir** (*fig*) ≈ teddy boy.
blues [bluz] *nm* blues *pl*.
bluet [blyɛ] *nm* = **bleuet.**
bluff [blœf] *nm* bluff; **~er** *vi, vt* to bluff.
boa [bɔa] *nm* boa.
bobard [bɔbaʀ] *nm* (*fam*) tall story.
bobèche [bɔbɛʃ] *nf* candle-ring.
bobine [bɔbin] *nf* reel; (*machine à coudre*) spool; (*ÉLEC*) coil.
bocage [bɔkaʒ] *nm* grove, copse.
bocal, aux [bɔkal, -o] *nm* jar.
bock [bɔk] *nm* (beer) glass; glass of beer.
bœuf [bœf, *pl* bø] *nm* ox (*pl* oxen), steer; (*CULIN*) beef.
bohème [bɔɛm] *a* happy-go-lucky, unconventional.
bohémien, ne [bɔemjɛ̃, -jɛn] *nm/f* gipsy.
boire [bwaʀ] *vt* to drink; (*s'imprégner de*) to soak up; ~ **un verre** to have a drink.
bois [bwa] *nm* wood; **de ~, en ~** wooden; ~ **de lit** bedstead.
boisé, e [bwaze] *a* wooded.
boiser [bwaze] *vt* (*galerie de mine*) to timber; (*chambre*) to panel; (*terrain*) to plant with trees.
boiseries [bwazʀi] *nfpl* panelling *sg*.
boisson [bwasɔ̃] *nf* drink; **pris de ~** drunk, intoxicated; **~s alcoolisées** alcoholic beverages *ou* drinks; **~s gazeuses** fizzy drinks.
boîte [bwat] *nf* box; **aliments en ~** canned *ou* tinned foods; ~ **de sardines/petits pois** can *ou* tin of sardines/peas; ~ **d'allumettes** box of matches; (*vide*) matchbox; ~ **de conserves** can *ou* tin (of food); ~ **crânienne** cranium, brainpan; ~ **à gants** glove compartment; ~ **aux lettres** letterbox; ~ **de nuit** night club; ~ **postale (B.P.)** P.O. Box; ~ **de vitesses** gear box.
boiter [bwate] *vi* to limp; (*fig*) to wobble; to be shaky; **boiteux, euse** *a* lame; wobbly; shaky.
boîtier [bwatje] *nm* case; ~ **de montre** watch case.
boive *etc vb voir* **boire**.
bol [bɔl] *nm* bowl; **un ~ d'air** a dose of fresh air.

bolet [bɔlɛ] *nm* boletus (mushroom).
bolide [bɔlid] *nm* racing car; **comme un ~** at top speed, like a rocket.
bombance [bɔ̃bɑ̃s] *nf*: **faire ~** to have a feast, revel.
bombardement [bɔ̃baʀdəmɑ̃] *nm* bombing.
bombarder [bɔ̃baʀde] *vt* to bomb; **~ qn de** (*cailloux, lettres*) to bombard sb with; **~ qn directeur** to thrust sb into the director's seat; **bombardier** *nm* bomber.
bombe [bɔ̃b] *nf* bomb; (*atomiseur*) (aerosol) spray; **faire la ~** (*fam*) to go on a binge.
bombé, e [bɔ̃be] *a* rounded; bulging; cambered.
bomber [bɔ̃be] *vi* to bulge; to camber // *vt*: **~ le torse** to swell out one's chest.
bon, bonne [bɔ̃, bɔn] *a* good; (*charitable*): **~ (envers)** good (to), kind (to); (*juste*): **le ~ numéro/moment** the right number/moment; (*approprié*): **~ à/pour** fit to/for // *nm* (*billet*) voucher; (*aussi*: **~ cadeau**) gift coupon *ou* voucher // *nf* (*domestique*) maid // *ad*: **il fait ~** it's *ou* the weather's fine; **sentir ~** to smell good; **tenir ~** to stand firm, hold out; **pour de ~** for good; **de bonne heure** early; **~ anniversaire!** happy birthday!; **~ voyage!** have a good journey!, enjoy your trip!; **bonne chance!** good luck!; **bonne année!** happy New Year!; **bonne nuit!** good night!; **~ enfant** *a inv* accommodating, easy-going; **~ d'essence** *nm* petrol coupon; **~ marché** *a inv, ad* cheap; **~ mot** *nm* witticism; **~ sens** *nm* common sense; **~ à tirer** *nm* pass for press; **~ du Trésor** *nm* Treasury bond; **~ vivant** *nm* jovial chap; **bonne d'enfant** *nf* nanny; **bonne femme** *nf* (*péj*) woman; female; **bonne à tout faire** *nf* general help; **bonnes œuvres** *nfpl* charitable works; charities.
bonasse [bɔnas] *a* soft, meek.
bonbon [bɔ̃bɔ̃] *nm* (boiled) sweet.
bonbonne [bɔ̃bɔn] *nf* demijohn; carboy.
bonbonnière [bɔ̃bɔnjɛʀ] *nf* sweet box, bonbonnière.
bond [bɔ̃] *nm* leap; **faire un ~** to leap in the air.
bonde [bɔ̃d] *nf* (*d'évier etc*) plug; (: *trou*) plughole; (*de tonneau*) bung; bunghole.
bondé, e [bɔ̃de] *a* packed (full).
bondir [bɔ̃diʀ] *vi* to leap.
bonheur [bɔnœʀ] *nm* happiness; **porter ~ (à qn)** to bring (sb) luck; **au petit ~** haphazardly; **par ~** fortunately.
bonhomie [bɔnɔmi] *nf* goodnaturedness.
bonhomme [bɔnɔm] *nm* (*pl* **bonshommes** [bɔ̃zɔm]) fellow // *a* good-natured; **aller son ~ de chemin** to carry on in one's own sweet way; **~ de neige** snowman.
boni [bɔni] *nm* profit.
bonification [bɔnifikɑsjɔ̃] *nf* bonus.
bonifier [bɔnifje] *vt* to improve.
boniment [bɔnimɑ̃] *nm* patter *q*.
bonjour [bɔ̃ʒuʀ] *excl, nm* good morning (*ou* afternoon); hello; **dire ~ à qn** to say hello *ou* good morning/afternoon to sb.
bonne [bɔn] *a, nf voir* **bon**; **~ment** *ad*: **tout ~ment** quite simply.
bonnet [bɔnɛ] *nm* bonnet, hat; (*de soutien-gorge*) cup; **~ d'âne** dunce's cap; **~ de bain** bathing cap; **~ de nuit** nightcap.
bonneterie [bɔnɛtʀi] *nf* hosiery.
bon-papa [bɔ̃papa] *nm* grandpa, grandad.
bonsoir [bɔ̃swaʀ] *excl* good evening.
bonté [bɔ̃te] *nf* kindness *q*; **avoir la ~ de** to be kind *ou* good enough to.
borborygme [bɔʀbɔʀigm] *nm* rumbling noise.
bord [bɔʀ] *nm* (*de table, verre, falaise*) edge; (*de rivière, lac*) bank; (*de route*) side; **(monter) à ~** (to go) on board; **jeter par-dessus ~** to throw overboard; **le commandant/les hommes du ~** the ship's master/crew; **au ~ de la mer** at the seaside; **être au ~ des larmes** to be on the verge of tears.
bordage [bɔʀdaʒ] *nm* planking *q*, plating *q*.
bordeaux [bɔʀdo] *nm* Bordeaux (wine) // *a inv* maroon.
bordée [bɔʀde] *nf* broadside; **une ~ d'injures** a volley of abuse.
bordel [bɔʀdɛl] *nm* brothel.
border [bɔʀde] *vt* (*être le long de*) to border; to line; (*garnir*): **~ qch de** to line sth with; to trim sth with; (*qn dans son lit*) to tuck up.
bordereau, x [bɔʀdəʀo] *nm* docket; slip; statement, invoice.
bordure [bɔʀdyʀ] *nf* border; (*sur un vêtement*) trim(ming), border; **en ~ de** on the edge of.
borgne [bɔʀɲ(ə)] *a* one-eyed; **hôtel ~** shady hotel.
borne [bɔʀn(ə)] *nf* boundary stone; (*gén*: **~ kilométrique**) kilometre-marker, ≈ milestone; **~s** *nfpl* (*fig*) limits; **dépasser les ~s** to go too far; **sans ~(s)** boundless.
borné, e [bɔʀne] *a* narrow; narrow-minded.
borner [bɔʀne] *vt* to limit; to confine; **se ~ à faire** to content o.s. with doing; to limit o.s. to doing.
bosquet [bɔskɛ] *nm* copse, grove.
bosse [bɔs] *nf* (*de terrain etc*) bump; (*enflure*) lump; (*du bossu, du chameau*) hump; **avoir la ~ des maths** *etc* to have a gift for maths *etc*; **il a roulé sa ~** he's been around.
bosseler [bɔsle] *vt* (*ouvrer*) to emboss; (*abîmer*) to dent.
bosser [bɔse] *vi* (*fam*) to work; to slog (hard).
bossu, e [bɔsy] *nm/f* hunchback.
bot [bo] *am*: **pied ~** club foot.
botanique [bɔtanik] *nf*: **la ~** botany // *a* botanic(al).
botaniste [bɔtanist(ə)] *nm/f* botanist.
botte [bɔt] *nf* (*soulier*) (high) boot; (ESCRIME) thrust; (*gerbe*): **~ de paille** bundle of straw; **~ de radis/d'asperges** bunch of radishes/asparagus; **~s de caoutchouc** wellington boots.
botter [bɔte] *vt* to put boots on; to kick; (*fam*): **ça me botte** I fancy that.

bottier [bɔtje] *nm* bootmaker.
bottin [bɔtɛ̃] *nm* directory.
bottine [bɔtin] *nf* ankle boot, bootee.
bouc [buk] *nm* goat; (*barbe*) goatee; ~ **émissaire** scapegoat.
boucan [bukɑ̃] *nm* din, racket.
bouche [buʃ] *nf* mouth; **faire le ~ à ~ à qn** to give sb the kiss of life, to practise mouth-to-mouth resuscitation on sb; **~ de chaleur** hot air vent; **~ d'égout** manhole; **~ d'incendie** fire hydrant; **~ de métro** métro entrance.
bouché, e [buʃe] *a* (*temps, ciel*) overcast; (*péj: personne*) thick; (*JAZZ: trompette*) muted; **avoir le nez ~** to have a blocked (-up) nose.
bouchée [buʃe] *nf* mouthful; **~s à la reine** chicken vol-au-vents.
boucher [buʃe] *nm* butcher // *vt* (*pour colmater*) to stop up; to fill up; (*obstruer*) to block (up); **se ~ le nez** to hold one's nose; **se ~** (*tuyau etc*) to block up, get blocked up.
bouchère [buʃɛʀ] *nf* (woman) butcher; butcher's wife.
boucherie [buʃʀi] *nf* butcher's (shop); butchery; (*fig*) slaughter.
bouche-trou [buʃtʀu] *nm* (*fig*) stop-gap.
bouchon [buʃɔ̃] *nm* (*en liège*) cork; (*autre matière*) stopper; (*fig: embouteillage*) holdup; (*PÊCHE*) float; **~ doseur** measuring cap.
bouchonner [buʃɔne] *vt* to rub down.
boucle [bukl(ə)] *nf* (*forme, figure*) loop; (*objet*) buckle; **~ (de cheveux)** curl; **~ d'oreilles** earring.
bouclé, e [bukle] *a* curly; (*tapis*) uncut.
boucler [bukle] *vt* (*fermer: ceinture etc*) to fasten up; (*: magasin*) to shut; (*terminer*) to finish off; to complete; (*: budget*) to balance; (*enfermer*) to shut away; to lock up; (*: quartier*) to seal off // *vi* to curl.
bouclier [buklije] *nm* shield.
bouddhiste [budist(ə)] *nm/f* Buddhist.
bouder [bude] *vi* to sulk // *vt* to turn one's nose up at; to refuse to have anything to do with; **bouderie** *nf* sulking *q*; **boudeur, euse** *a* sullen, sulky.
boudin [budɛ̃] *nm* (*CULIN*) black pudding; (*TECH*) roll.
boudoir [budwaʀ] *nm* boudoir.
boue [bu] *nf* mud.
bouée [bwe] *nf* buoy; **~ (de sauvetage)** lifebuoy.
boueux, euse [bwø, -øz] *a* muddy // *nm* refuse collector.
bouffe [buf] *nf* (*fam*) grub, food.
bouffée [bufe] *nf* puff; **~ de fièvre/de honte** flush of fever/shame; **~ d'orgueil** fit of pride.
bouffer [bufe] *vi* (*fam*) to eat; (*COUTURE*) to puff out // *vt* (*fam*) to eat.
bouffi, e [bufi] *a* swollen.
bouffon, ne [bufɔ̃, -ɔn] *a* farcical, comical // *nm* jester.
bouge [buʒ] *nm* (low) dive; hovel.
bougeoir [buʒwaʀ] *nm* candlestick.
bougeotte [buʒɔt] *nf*: **avoir la ~** to have the fidgets.
bouger [buʒe] *vi* to move; (*dent etc*) to be loose; (*changer*) to alter; (*agir*) to stir // *vt* to move.
bougie [buʒi] *nf* candle; (*AUTO*) sparking plug.
bougon, ne [bugɔ̃, -ɔn] *a* grumpy.
bougonner [bugɔne] *vi, vt* to grumble.
bougre [bugʀ(ə)] *nm* chap; (*fam*): **ce ~ de** that confounded.
bouillabaisse [bujabɛs] *nf* bouillabaisse.
bouillant, e [bujɑ̃, -ɑ̃t] *a* (*qui bout*) boiling; (*très chaud*) boiling (hot); (*fig: ardent*) hot-headed.
bouilleur de cru [bujœʀdəkʀy] *nm* (home) distiller.
bouillie [buji] *nf* gruel; (*de bébé*) cereal; **en ~** (*fig*) crushed.
bouillir [bujiʀ] *vi, vt* to boil; **~ de colère** *etc* to seethe with anger *etc*.
bouilloire [bujwaʀ] *nf* kettle.
bouillon [bujɔ̃] *nm* (*CULIN*) stock *q*; (*bulles, écume*) bubble; **~ de culture** culture medium.
bouillonner [bujɔne] *vi* to bubble; (*fig*) to bubble up; to foam.
bouillotte [bujɔt] *nf* hot-water bottle.
boulanger, ère [bulɑ̃ʒe, -ɛʀ] *nm/f* baker // *nf* (woman) baker; baker's wife.
boulangerie [bulɑ̃ʒʀi] *nf* bakery, baker's (shop); (*commerce*) bakery; **~ industrielle** bakery; **~-pâtisserie** *nf* baker's and confectioner's (shop).
boule [bul] *nf* (*gén*) ball; (*pour jouer*) bowl; **~ de neige** snowball; **faire ~ de neige** to snowball.
bouleau, x [bulo] *nm* (silver) birch.
bouledogue [buldɔg] *nm* bulldog.
boulet [bulɛ] *nm* (*aussi* : **~ de canon**) cannonball; (*de bagnard*) ball and chain; (*charbon*) (coal) nut.
boulette [bulɛt] *nf* ball.
boulevard [bulvaʀ] *nm* boulevard.
bouleversement [bulvɛʀsəmɑ̃] *nm* (*politique, social*) upheaval.
bouleverser [bulvɛʀse] *vt* (*émouvoir*) to overwhelm; (*causer du chagrin*) to distress; (*pays, vie*) to disrupt; (*papiers, objets*) to turn upside down, upset.
boulier [bulje] *nm* abacus; (*de jeu*) scoring board.
boulimie [bulimi] *nf* compulsive eating, bulimia.
boulon [bulɔ̃] *nm* bolt; **boulonner** *vt* to bolt.
boulot [bulo] *nm* (*fam: travail*) work.
boulot, te [bulo, -ɔt] *a* plump, tubby.
bouquet [bukɛ] *nm* (*de fleurs*) bunch (of flowers), bouquet; (*de persil etc*) bunch; (*parfum*) bouquet; (*fig*) crowning piece.
bouquetin [buktɛ̃] *nm* ibex.
bouquin [bukɛ̃] *nm* book; **bouquiner** *vi* to read; to browse around (in a bookshop); **bouquiniste** *nm/f* bookseller.
bourbeux, euse [buʀbø, -øz] *a* muddy.
bourbier [buʀbje] *nm* (quag)mire.
bourde [buʀd(ə)] *nf* (*erreur*) howler; (*gaffe*) blunder.
bourdon [buʀdɔ̃] *nm* bumblebee.
bourdonnement [buʀdɔnmɑ̃] *nm* buzzing.

bourdonner [buʀdɔne] *vi* to buzz.
bourg [buʀ] *nm* town.
bourgade [buʀgad] *nf* township.
bourgeois, e [buʀʒwa, -waz] *a* (*souvent péj*) ≈ (upper) middle class; bourgeois // *nm/f* (*autrefois*) burgher.
bourgeoisie [buʀʒwazi] *nf* ≈ upper middle classes *pl*; bourgeoisie; **petite ~** middle classes.
bourgeon [buʀʒɔ̃] *nm* bud; **bourgeonner** *vi* to bud.
Bourgogne [buʀgɔɲ] *nf*: **la ~** Burgundy // *nm*: **b~** burgundy (wine).
bourguignon, ne [buʀgiɲɔ̃, -ɔn] *a* of *ou* from Burgundy, Burgundian; **bœuf ~** bœuf bourguignon.
bourlinguer [buʀlɛ̃ge] *vi* to knock about a lot, get around a lot.
bourrade [buʀad] *nf* shove, thump.
bourrage [buʀaʒ] *nm*: **~ de crâne** brainwashing; (*SCOL*) cramming.
bourrasque [buʀask(ə)] *nf* squall.
bourratif, ive [buʀatif, -iv] *a* filling, stodgy.
bourreau, x [buʀo] *nm* executioner; (*fig*) torturer; **~ de travail** glutton for work.
bourreler [buʀle] *vt*: **être bourrelé de remords** to be racked by remorse.
bourrelet [buʀlɛ] *nm* draught excluder; (*de peau*) fold *ou* roll (of flesh).
bourrer [buʀe] *vt* (*pipe*) to fill; (*poêle*) to pack; (*valise*) to cram (full); **~ de** to cram (full) with; to stuff with; **~ de coups** to hammer blows on, pummel.
bourrique [buʀik] *nf* (*âne*) ass.
bourru, e [buʀy] *a* surly, gruff.
bourse [buʀs(ə)] *nf* (*subvention*) grant; (*porte-monnaie*) purse; **la B~** the Stock Exchange; **boursier, ière** *a* (*COMM*) Stock Market *cpd* // *nm/f* (*SCOL*) grant-holder.
boursouflé, e [buʀsufle] *a* swollen, puffy; (*fig*) bombastic, turgid.
boursoufler [buʀsufle] *vt* to puff up, bloat; **se ~** *vi* (*visage*) to swell *ou* puff up; (*peinture*) to blister.
bous *vb voir* **bouillir**.
bousculade [buskylad] *nf* rush; crush.
bousculer [buskyle] *vt* to knock over; to knock into; (*fig*) to push, rush.
bouse [buz] *nf*: **~ (de vache)** (cow) dung *q*.
bousiller [buzije] *vt* (*fam*) to wreck.
boussole [busɔl] *nf* compass.
bout [bu] *vb voir* **bouillir** // *nm* bit; (*extrémité*: *d'un bâton etc*) tip; (: *d'une ficelle, table, rue, période*) end; **au ~ de** (*après*) at the end of, after; **pousser qn à ~** to push sb to the limit (of his patience); **venir à ~ de** to manage to overcome *ou* finish (off); **à ~ portant** at point-blank range; **~ filtre** filter tip.
boutade [butad] *nf* quip, sally.
boute-en-train [butɑ̃tʀɛ̃] *nm inv* live wire.
bouteille [butɛj] *nf* bottle; (*de gaz butane*) cylinder.
boutique [butik] *nf* shop; **boutiquier, ière** *nm/f* shopkeeper.
bouton [butɔ̃] *nm* (*BOT*) bud; (*MÉD*) spot; (*électrique etc*) button; (*de porte*) knob; **~ de manchette** cuff-link; **~ d'or** buttercup; **boutonner** *vt* to button up, do up; **boutonneux, euse** *a* spotty; **boutonnière** *nf* buttonhole; **~-pression** *nm* press stud, snap fastener.
bouture [butyʀ] *nf* cutting.
bouvreuil [buvʀœj] *nm* bullfinch.
bovidé [bɔvide] *nm* bovine.
bovin, e [bɔvɛ̃, -in] *a* bovine; **~s** *nmpl* cattle.
bowling [bɔliŋ] *nm* (tenpin) bowling; (*salle*) bowling alley.
box [bɔks] *nm* lock-up (garage); cubicle; (*d'écurie*) loose-box; **le ~ des accusés** the dock.
boxe [bɔks(ə)] *nf* boxing; **boxer** *vi* to box; **boxeur** *nm* boxer.
boyau, x [bwajo] *nm* (*corde de raquette etc*) (cat) gut; (*galerie*) passage(way); (narrow) gallery; (*pneu de bicyclette*) tubeless tyre // *nmpl* (*viscères*) entrails, guts.
boycotter [bɔjkɔte] *vt* to boycott.
B.P. *sigle de* **boîte postale**.
bracelet [bʀaslɛ] *nm* bracelet; **~-montre** *nm* wristwatch.
braconner [bʀakɔne] *vi* to poach; **braconnier** *nm* poacher.
brader [bʀade] *vt* to sell off, sell cheaply.
braguette [bʀagɛt] *nf* fly, flies *pl*.
brailler [bʀɑje] *vi* to bawl, yell // *vt* to bawl out, yell out.
braire [bʀɛʀ] *vi* to bray.
braise [bʀɛz] *nf* embers *pl*.
braiser [bʀeze] *vt* to braise.
bramer [bʀɑme] *vi* to bell; (*fig*) to wail.
brancard [bʀɑ̃kaʀ] *nm* (*civière*) stretcher; (*bras, perche*) shaft; **brancardier** *nm* stretcher-bearer.
branchages [bʀɑ̃ʃaʒ] *nmpl* branches, boughs.
branche [bʀɑ̃ʃ] *nf* branch; (*de lunettes*) side-piece.
brancher [bʀɑ̃ʃe] *vt* to connect (up); (*en mettant la prise*) to plug in.
branchies [bʀɑ̃ʃi] *nfpl* gills.
brandir [bʀɑ̃diʀ] *vt* to brandish, wield.
brandon [bʀɑ̃dɔ̃] *nm* firebrand.
branle [bʀɑ̃l] *nm*: **donner le ~ à** to set in motion.
branle-bas [bʀɑ̃lbɑ] *nm inv* commotion.
branler [bʀɑ̃le] *vi* to be shaky, be loose // *vt*: **~ la tête** to shake one's head.
braquage [bʀakaʒ] *nm* (*fam*) stick-up; (*AUTO*): **rayon de ~** turning circle.
braquer [bʀake] *vi* (*AUTO*) to turn (the wheel) // *vt* (*revolver etc*): **~ qch sur** to aim sth at, point sth at; (*mettre en colère*): **~ qn** to antagonize sb, put sb's back up.
bras [bʀa] *nm* arm // *nmpl* (*fig*: *travailleurs*) labour *sg*, hands; **saisir qn à ~-le-corps** to take hold of sb (a)round the waist; **à ~ raccourcis** with fists flying; **~ droit** (*fig*) right-hand man; **~ de levier** lever arm; **~ de mer** arm of the sea, sound.
brasero [bʀɑzeʀo] *nm* brazier.
brasier [bʀɑzje] *nm* blaze, (blazing) inferno.
brassage [bʀasaʒ] *nm* mixing.
brassard [bʀasaʀ] *nm* armband.
brasse [bʀas] *nf* (*nage*) breast-stroke;

(*mesure*) fathom ; ~ **papillon** butterfly (-stroke).
brassée [bRase] *nf* armful.
brasser [bRase] *vt* to mix ; ~ **l'argent/les affaires** to handle a lot of money/business.
brasserie [bRasRi] *nf* (*restaurant*) brasserie ; (*usine*) brewery.
brasseur [bRasœR] *nm* (*de bière*) brewer ; ~ **d'affaires** big businessman.
brassière [bRasjɛR] *nf* (baby's) vest.
bravache [bRavaʃ] *nm* blusterer, braggart.
bravade [bRavad] *nf*: **par** ~ out of bravado.
brave [bRav] *a* (*courageux*) brave ; (*bon, gentil*) good, kind.
braver [bRave] *vt* to defy.
bravo [bRavo] *excl* bravo // *nm* cheer.
bravoure [bRavuR] *nf* bravery.
break [bRɛk] *nm* (AUTO) estate car.
brebis [bRəbi] *nf* ewe ; ~ **galeuse** black sheep.
brèche [bRɛʃ] *nf* breach, gap ; **être sur la** ~ (*fig*) to be on the go.
bredouille [bRəduj] *a* empty-handed.
bredouiller [bRəduje] *vi, vt* to mumble, stammer.
bref, brève [bRɛf, bRɛv] *a* short, brief // *ad* in short // *nf*: **(voyelle) brève** short vowel ; **d'un ton** ~ sharply, curtly ; **en** ~ in short, in brief.
brelan [bRəlɑ̃] *nm* three of a kind ; ~ **d'as** three aces.
brème [bRɛm] *nf* bream.
Brésil [bRezil] *nm* Brazil ; **b~ien, ne** *a, nm/f* Brazilian.
Bretagne [bRətaɲ] *nf* Brittany.
bretelle [bRətɛl] *nf* (*de fusil etc*) sling ; (*de combinaison, soutien-gorge*) strap ; (*autoroute*) slip road ; **~s** *nfpl* (*pour pantalon*) braces.
breton, ne [bRətɔ̃, -ɔn] *a, nm/f* Breton.
breuvage [bRœvaʒ] *nm* beverage, drink.
brève [bRɛv] *a, nf voir* **bref.**
brevet [bRəvɛ] *nm* diploma, certificate ; ~ **(d'invention)** patent ; ~ **d'apprentissage** certificate of apprenticeship ; ~ **d'études du premier cycle (B.E.P.C.)** ≈ O levels ; **breveté, e** *a* patented ; (*diplômé*) qualified ; **breveter** *vt* to patent.
bréviaire [bRevjɛR] *nm* breviary.
bribes [bRib] *nfpl* bits, scraps ; snatches ; **par** ~ piecemeal.
bric-à-brac [bRikabRak] *nm inv* bric-a-brac, jumble.
bricolage [bRikɔlaʒ] *nm*: **le** ~ do-it-yourself (jobs).
bricole [bRikɔl] *nf* trifle ; small job.
bricoler [bRikɔle] *vi* to do D.I.Y. jobs ; to potter about ; to do odd jobs // *vt* to fix up ; to tinker with ; **bricoleur, euse** *nm/f* handyman, D.I.Y. enthusiast.
bride [bRid] *nf* bridle ; (*d'un bonnet*) string, tie ; **à** ~ **abattue** flat out, hell for leather ; **tenir en** ~ to keep in check ; **lâcher la** ~ **à, laisser la** ~ **sur le cou à** to give free rein to.
bridé, e [bRide] *a*: **yeux ~s** slit eyes.
brider [bRide] *vt* (*réprimer*) to keep in check ; (*cheval*) to bridle ; (CULIN: *volaille*) to truss.
bridge [bRidʒ(ə)] *nm* bridge.
brièvement [bRijɛvmɑ̃] *ad* briefly.
brièveté [bRijɛvte] *nf* brevity.
brigade [bRigad] *nf* (POLICE) squad ; (MIL) brigade ; (*gén*) team.
brigand [bRigɑ̃] *nm* brigand.
brigandage [bRigɑ̃daʒ] *nm* robbery.
briguer [bRige] *vt* to aspire to.
brillamment [bRijamɑ̃] *ad* brilliantly.
brillant, e [bRijɑ̃, -ɑ̃t] *a* brilliant ; bright ; (*luisant*) shiny, shining // *nm* (*diamant*) brilliant.
briller [bRije] *vi* to shine.
brimade [bRimad] *nf* vexation, harassment *q* ; bullying *q*.
brimbaler [bRɛ̃bale] *vb* = **bringuebaler.**
brimer [bRime] *vt* to harass ; to bully.
brin [bRɛ̃] *nm* (*de laine, ficelle etc*) strand ; (*fig*): **un** ~ **de** a bit of ; ~ **d'herbe** blade of grass ; ~ **de muguet** sprig of lily of the valley ; ~ **de paille** wisp of straw.
brindille [bRɛ̃dij] *nf* twig.
bringuebaler [bRɛ̃gbale] *vi* to shake (about) // *vt* to cart about.
brio [bRijo] *nm* brilliance ; (MUS) brio ; **avec** ~ brilliantly, with panache.
brioche [bRijɔʃ] *nf* brioche (bun) ; (*fam: ventre*) paunch.
brique [bRik] *nf* brick // *a inv* brick red.
briquer [bRike] *vt* to polish up.
briquet [bRikɛ] *nm* (cigarette) lighter.
brisant [bRizɑ̃] *nm* reef ; (*vague*) breaker.
brise [bRiz] *nf* breeze.
brise-glace [bRizglas] *nm inv* icebreaker.
brise-jet [bRizʒɛ] *nm inv* tap swirl.
brise-lames [bRizlam] *nm inv* breakwater.
briser [bRize] *vt* to break ; **se** ~ *vi* to break ; **briseur, euse de grève** *nm/f* strike-breaker.
britannique [bRitanik] *a* British // *nm/f* British person ; **les B~s** the British.
broc [bRo] *nm* pitcher.
brocanteur, euse [bRɔkɑ̃tœR, -øz] *nm/f* junkshop owner ; junk dealer.
broche [bRɔʃ] *nf* brooch ; (CULIN) spit ; (*fiche*) spike, peg ; **à la** ~ spit-roast, roasted on a spit.
broché, e [bRɔʃe] *a* (*livre*) paper-backed.
brochet [bRɔʃɛ] *nm* pike *inv*.
brochette [bRɔʃɛt] *nf* skewer ; ~ **de décorations** row of medals.
brochure [bRɔʃyR] *nf* pamphlet, brochure, booklet.
broder [bRɔde] *vt* to embroider // *vi* to embroider the facts ; **broderie** *nf* embroidery.
bromure [bRɔmyR] *nm* bromide.
broncher [bRɔ̃ʃe] *vi*: **sans** ~ without flinching ; without turning a hair.
bronches [bRɔ̃ʃ] *nfpl* bronchial tubes ; **bronchite** *nf* bronchitis ; **broncho-pneumonie** [bRɔ̃kɔ-] *nf* bronco-pneumonia *q*.
bronze [bRɔ̃z] *nm* bronze.
bronzé, e [bRɔ̃ze] *a* tanned.
bronzer [bRɔ̃ze] *vt* to tan // *vi* to get a tan ; **se** ~ to sunbathe.
brosse [bRɔs] *nf* brush ; **donner un coup de** ~ **à qch** to give sth a brush ; **coiffé**

en ~ with a crewcut ; ~ **à cheveux** hairbrush ; ~ **à dents** toothbrush ; ~ **à habits** clothesbrush ; **brosser** *vt* (*nettoyer*) to brush ; (*fig*: *tableau etc*) to paint ; to draw.
brouette [bRuɛt] *nf* wheelbarrow.
brouhaha [bRuaa] *nm* hubbub.
brouillard [bRujaR] *nm* fog.
brouille [bRuj] *nf* quarrel.
brouiller [bRuje] *vt* to mix up ; to confuse ; (*RADIO*) to cause interference to ; to jam ; (*rendre trouble*) to cloud ; (*désunir*: *amis*) to set at odds ; **se** ~ *vi* (*ciel, vue*) to cloud over ; (*détails*) to become confused ; **se** ~ **(avec)** to fall out (with).
brouillon, ne [bRujɔ̃, -ɔn] *a* disorganised ; unmethodical // *nm* draft.
broussailles [bRusɑj] *nfpl* undergrowth *sg* ; **broussailleux, euse** *a* bushy.
brousse [bRus] *nf*: **la** ~ the bush.
brouter [bRute] *vt* to graze on // *vi* to graze ; (*AUTO*) to judder.
broutille [bRutij] *nf* trifle.
broyer [bRwaje] *vt* to crush ; ~ **du noir** to be down in the dumps.
bru [bRy] *nf* daughter-in-law.
brucelles [bRysɛl] *nfpl*: **(pinces)** ~ tweezers.
bruine [bRɥin] *nf* drizzle.
bruiner [bRɥine] *vb impersonnel*: **il bruine** it's drizzling, there's a drizzle.
bruire [bRɥiR] *vi* to murmur ; to rustle.
bruit [bRɥi] *nm*: **un** ~ a noise, a sound ; (*fig*: *rumeur*) a rumour ; **le** ~ noise ; **pas/trop de** ~ no/too much noise ; **sans** ~ without a sound, noiselessly ; ~ **de fond** background noise.
bruitage [bRɥitaʒ] *nm* sound effects *pl* ; **bruiteur, euse** *nm/f* sound-effects engineer.
brûlant, e [bRylɑ̃, -ɑ̃t] *a* burning (hot) ; (*liquide*) boiling (hot) ; (*regard*) fiery ; (*sujet*) red-hot.
brûlé, e [bRyle] *a* (*fig*: *démasqué*) blown // *nm*: **odeur de** ~ smell of burning.
brûle-pourpoint [bRylpuRpwɛ̃]: **à** ~ *ad* point-blank.
brûler [bRyle] *vt* to burn ; (*suj*: *eau bouillante*) to scald ; (*consommer*: *électricité, essence*) to use ; (*feu rouge, signal*) to go through (without stopping) // *vi* to burn ; (*jeu*) to be warm ; **se** ~ to burn o.s. ; to scald o.s. ; **se** ~ **la cervelle** to blow one's brains out ; ~ **(d'impatience) de faire qch** to burn with impatience *ou* be dying to do sth.
brûleur [bRylœR] *nm* burner.
brûlure [bRylyR] *nf* (*lésion*) burn ; (*sensation*) burning (sensation) ; ~**s d'estomac** heartburn *sg*.
brume [bRym] *nf* mist ; **brumeux, euse** *a* misty ; (*fig*) hazy.
brun, e [bRœ̃, -yn] *a* brown ; (*cheveux, personne*) dark // *nm* (*couleur*) brown ; **brunir** *vi* to get a tan // *vt* to tan.
brusque [bRysk(ə)] *a* (*soudain*) abrupt, sudden ; (*rude*) abrupt, brusque ; ~**ment** *ad* (*soudainement*) abruptly ; suddenly ; **brusquer** *vt* to rush ; **brusquerie** *nf* abruptness, brusqueness.
brut, e [bRyt] *a* raw, crude, rough ; (*COMM*) gross // *nf* brute ; **(champagne)** ~ brut champagne ; **(pétrole)** ~ crude (oil).
brutal, e, aux [bRytal, -o] *a* brutal ; ~**iser** *vt* to handle roughly, manhandle ; ~**ité** *nf* brutality *q*.
brute [bRyt] *a, nf voir* **brut.**
Bruxelles [bRysɛl] *n* Brussels.
bruyamment [bRɥijamɑ̃] *ad* noisily.
bruyant, e [bRɥijɑ̃, -ɑ̃t] *a* noisy.
bruyère [bRyjɛR] *nf* heather.
bu, e *pp de* **boire**.
buanderie [bɥɑ̃dRi] *nf* laundry.
buccal, e, aux [bykal, -o] *a*: **par voie** ~**e** orally.
bûche [byʃ] *nf* log ; **prendre une** ~ (*fig*) to come a cropper ; ~ **de Noël** Yule log.
bûcher [byʃe] *nm* pyre ; bonfire // *vb* (*fam*) *vi* to swot, slog away // *vt* to swot up.
bûcheron [byʃRɔ̃] *nm* woodcutter.
bucolique [bykɔlik] *a* bucolic, pastoral.
budget [bydʒɛ] *nm* budget ; **budgétaire** [bydʒetɛR] *a* budgetary, budget *cpd*.
buée [bɥe] *nf* (*sur une vitre*) mist ; (*de l'haleine*) steam.
buffet [byfɛ] *nm* (*meuble*) sideboard ; (*de réception*) buffet ; ~ **(de gare)** station buffet.
buffle [byfl(ə)] *nm* buffalo.
buis [bɥi] *nm* box tree ; (*bois*) box(wood).
buisson [bɥisɔ̃] *nm* bush.
buissonnière [bɥisɔnjɛR] *af*: **faire l'école** ~ to play truant.
bulbe [bylb(ə)] *nm* (*BOT, ANAT*) bulb ; (*coupole*) onion-shaped dome.
bulgare [bylgaR] *a, nm/f* Bulgarian.
Bulgarie [bylgaRi] *nf* Bulgaria.
bulldozer [buldozœR] *nm* bulldozer.
bulle [byl] *nf* bubble ; (*papale*) bull ; ~ **de savon** soap bubble.
bulletin [byltɛ̃] *nm* (*communiqué, journal*) bulletin ; (*papier*) form ; ticket ; (*SCOL*) report ; ~ **d'informations** news bulletin ; ~ **météorologique** weather report ; ~ **de santé** medical bulletin ; ~ **(de vote)** ballot paper.
buraliste [byRalist(ə)] *nm/f* tobacconist ; clerk.
bure [byR] *nf* homespun ; frock.
bureau, x [byRo] *nm* (*meuble*) desk ; (*pièce, service*) office ; ~ **de change** (foreign) exchange office *ou* bureau ; ~ **de location** box office ; ~ **de poste** post office ; ~ **de tabac** tobacconist's (shop) ; ~ **de vote** polling station ; ~**crate** *nm* bureaucrat ; ~**cratie** [-kRasi] *nf* bureaucracy ; ~**cratique** *a* bureaucratic.
burette [byRɛt] *nf* (*de mécanicien*) oilcan ; (*de chimiste*) burette.
burin [byRɛ̃] *nm* cold chisel ; (*ART*) burin.
buriné, e [byRine] *a* (*fig*: *visage*) craggy, seamed.
burlesque [byRlɛsk(ə)] *a* ridiculous ; (*LITTÉRATURE*) burlesque.
burnous [byRnu(s)] *nm* burnous.
bus *vb* [by] *voir* **boire** // *nm* [bys] bus.
buse [byz] *nf* buzzard.
busqué, e [byske] *a*: **nez** ~ hook(ed) nose.
buste [byst(e)] *nm* (*ANAT*) chest ; bust ; (*sculpture*) bust.

but [by] *vb voir* **boire** // *nm* [*parfois* byt] (*cible*) target; (*fig*) goal; aim; (*FOOTBALL etc*) goal; **de ~ en blanc** point-blank; **avoir pour ~ de faire** to aim to do; **dans le ~ de** with the intention of.
butane [bytan] *nm* butane; calor gas.
buté, e [byte] *a* stubborn, obstinate // *nf* (*TECH*) stop; (*ARCHIT*) abutment.
buter [byte] *vi*: **~ contre/sur** to bump into; to stumble against // *vt* to antagonize; **se ~** *vi* to get obstinate; to dig in one's heels.
buteur [bytœʀ] *nm* striker.
butin [bytɛ̃] *nm* booty, spoils *pl*; (*d'un vol*) loot.
butiner [bytine] *vi* to gather nectar.
butor [bytɔʀ] *nm* (*fig*) lout.
butte [byt] *nf* mound, hillock; **être en ~ à** to be exposed to.
buvais *etc vb voir* **boire**.
buvard [byvaʀ] *nm* blotter.
buvette [byvɛt] *nf* refreshment room; refreshment stall.
buveur, euse [byvœʀ, -øz] *nm/f* drinker.
byzantin, e [bizɑ̃tɛ̃, -in] *a* Byzantine.

C

c' [s] *dét voir* **ce**.
ça [sa] *pronom* (*pour désigner*) this; (*: plus loin*) that; (*comme sujet indéfini*) it; **~ m'étonne que** it surprises me that; **~ va?** how are you?; how are things?; (*d'accord?*) OK?, all right?; **c'est ~** that's right.
çà [sa] *ad*: **~ et là** here and there.
caban [kabɑ̃] *nm* reefer jacket, donkey jacket.
cabane [kaban] *nf* hut, cabin.
cabanon [kabanɔ̃] *nm* chalet; (country) cottage.
cabaret [kabaʀɛ] *nm* night club.
cabas [kabɑ] *nm* shopping bag.
cabestan [kabɛstɑ̃] *nm* capstan.
cabillaud [kabijo] *nm* cod *inv*.
cabine [kabin] *nf* (*de bateau*) cabin; (*de plage*) (beach) hut; (*de piscine etc*) cubicle; (*de camion, train*) cab; (*d'avion*) cockpit; **~ (d'ascenseur)** lift cage; **~ d'essayage** fitting room; **~ spatiale** space capsule; **~ (téléphonique)** call *ou* (tele)phone box, (tele)phone booth.
cabinet [kabinɛ] *nm* (*petite pièce*) closet; (*de médecin*) surgery; (*de notaire etc*) office; (*: clientèle*) practice; (*POL*) Cabinet; (*d'un ministre*) advisers *pl*; **~s** *nmpl* (*w.-c.*) toilet *sg*, loo *sg*; **~ d'affaires** business consultants' (bureau), business partnership; **~ de toilette** toilet; **~ de travail** study.
câble [kɑbl(ə)] *nm* cable.
câbler [kɑble] *vt* to cable.
cabosser [kabɔse] *vt* to dent.
cabotage [kabɔtaʒ] *nm* coastal navigation; **caboteur** *nm* coaster.
cabotinage [kabɔtinaʒ] *nm* playacting; third-rate acting, ham acting.
cabrer [kɑbʀe]: **se ~** *vi* (*cheval*) to rear up; (*avion*) to nose up; (*fig*) to revolt, rebel; to jib.
cabri [kabʀi] *nm* kid.
cabriole [kabʀijɔl] *nf* caper; somersault.
cabriolet [kabʀijɔlɛ] *nm* convertible.
cacahuète [kakaɥɛt] *nf* peanut.
cacao [kakao] *nm* cocoa (powder); (*boisson*) cocoa.
cachalot [kaʃalo] *nm* sperm whale.
cache [kaʃ] *nm* mask, card (for masking) // *nf* hiding place.
cache-cache [kaʃkaʃ] *nm*: **jouer à ~** to play hide-and-seek.
cachemire [kaʃmiʀ] *nm* cashmere // *a*: **dessin ~** paisley pattern.
cache-nez [kaʃne] *nm inv* scarf, muffler.
cache-pot [kaʃpo] *nm inv* flower-pot holder.
cacher [kaʃe] *vt* to hide, conceal; **~ qch à qn** to hide *ou* conceal sth from sb; **se ~** to hide; to be hidden *ou* concealed; **il ne s'en cache pas** he makes no secret of it.
cachet [kaʃɛ] *nm* (*comprimé*) tablet; (*sceau: du roi*) seal; (*: de la poste*) postmark; (*rétribution*) fee; (*fig*) style, character; **cacheter** *vt* to seal.
cachette [kaʃɛt] *nf* hiding place; **en ~** on the sly, secretly.
cachot [kaʃo] *nm* dungeon.
cachotterie [kaʃɔtʀi] *nf* mystery; **faire des ~s** to be secretive.
cactus [kaktys] *nm* cactus.
cadastre [kadastʀ(ə)] *nm* cadastre, land register.
cadavérique [kadɑveʀik] *a* deathly (pale), deadly pale.
cadavre [kadɑvʀ(ə)] *nm* corpse, (dead) body.
cadeau, x [kado] *nm* present, gift; **faire un ~ à qn** to give sb a present *ou* gift; **faire ~ de qch à qn** to make a present of sth to sb, give sb sth as a present.
cadenas [kadnɑ] *nm* padlock; **cadenasser** *vt* to padlock.
cadence [kadɑ̃s] *nf* (*MUS*) cadence; rhythm; (*de travail etc*) rate; **~s** *nfpl* (*en usine*) production rate *sg*; **en ~** rhythmically; in time; **cadencé, e** *a* rhythmic(al).
cadet, te [kadɛ, -ɛt] *a* younger; (*le plus jeune*) youngest // *nm/f* youngest child *ou* one, youngest boy *ou* son/girl *ou* daughter; **il est mon ~ (de deux ans)** (*rapports non familiaux*) he's (2 years) younger than me, he's 2 years my junior; **les ~s** (*SPORT*) the minors (*15 - 17 years*).
cadran [kadʀɑ̃] *nm* dial; **~ solaire** sundial.
cadre [kɑdʀ(ə)] *nm* frame; (*environnement*) surroundings *pl*; (*limites*) scope // *nm/f* (*ADMIN*) managerial employee, executive // *a*: **loi ~** outline *ou* blueprint law; **~ moyen/supérieur** (*ADMIN*) middle/senior management employee, junior/senior executive; **rayer qn des ~s** to discharge sb; to dismiss sb; **dans le ~ de** (*fig*) within the framework *ou* context of.
cadrer [kɑdʀe] *vi*: **~ avec** to tally *ou* correspond with // *vt* (*CINÉMA*) to centre.
caduc, uque [kadyk] *a* obsolete; (*BOT*) deciduous.

cafard [kafaʀ] *nm* cockroach ; **avoir le ~** to be down in the dumps, be feeling low.
café [kafe] *nm* coffee ; (*bistro*) café // *a inv* coffee-coloured ; **~ au lait** white coffee ; **~ noir** black coffee ; **~ tabac** *tobacconist's or newsagent's also serving coffee and spirits* ; **~ine** *nf* caffeine ; **cafetier, ière** *nm/f* café-owner // *nf* (*pot*) coffee-pot.
cafouiller [kafuje] *vi* to get in a shambles ; to work in fits and starts.
cage [kaʒ] *nf* cage ; **~ (des buts)** goal ; **en ~** in a cage, caged up *ou* in ; **~ d'ascenseur** lift shaft ; **~ d'escalier** (stair)well ; **~ thoracique** rib cage.
cageot [kaʒo] *nm* crate.
cagibi [kaʒibi] *nm* shed.
cagneux, euse [kaɲø, -øz] *a* knock-kneed.
cagnotte [kaɲɔt] *nf* kitty.
cagoule [kagul] *nf* cowl ; hood ; (SKI *etc*) cagoule.
cahier [kaje] *nm* notebook ; (TYPO) signature ; **~ de revendications/doléances** list of claims/grievances ; **~ de brouillons** roughbook, jotter ; **~ des charges** schedule (of conditions) ; **~ d'exercices** exercise book.
cahin-caha [kaɛ̃kaa] *ad*: **aller ~** to jog along ; (*fig*) to be so-so.
cahot [kao] *nm* jolt, bump ; **cahoter** *vi* to bump along, jog along.
cahute [kayt] *nf* shack, hut.
caïd [kaid] *nm* big chief, boss.
caille [kɑj] *nf* quail.
caillé, e [kɑje] *a*: **lait ~** curdled milk, curds *pl*.
cailler [kɑje] *vi* (*lait*) to curdle ; (*sang*) to clot.
caillot [kajo] *nm* (blood) clot.
caillou, x [kaju] *nm* (little) stone ; **~ter** *vt* (*chemin*) to metal ; **~teux, euse** *a* stony ; pebbly.
Caire [kɛʀ] *nm*: **le ~** Cairo.
caisse [kɛs] *nf* box ; (*où l'on met la recette*) cashbox ; till ; (*où l'on paye*) cash desk ; check-out ; (*de banque*) cashier's desk ; teller's desk ; (TECH) case, casing ; **~ enregistreuse** cash register ; **~ d'épargne** savings bank ; **~ de retraite** pension fund ; **caissier, ière** *nm/f* cashier.
caisson [kɛsɔ̃] *nm* box, case.
cajoler [kaʒɔle] *vt* to wheedle, coax ; to surround with love and care, make a fuss of.
cake [kɛk] *nm* fruit cake.
calaminé, e [kalamine] *a* (AUTO) coked up.
calamité [kalamite] *nf* calamity, disaster.
calandre [kalɑ̃dʀ(ə)] *nf* radiator grill ; (*machine*) calender, mangle.
calanque [kalɑ̃k] *nf* rocky inlet.
calcaire [kalkɛʀ] *nm* limestone // *a* (*eau*) hard ; (GÉO) limestone *cpd*.
calciné, e [kalsine] *a* burnt to ashes.
calcium [kalsjɔm] *nm* calcium.
calcul [kalkyl] *nm* calculation ; **le ~** (SCOL) arithmetic ; **~ différentiel/intégral** differential/integral calculus ; **~ (biliaire)** (gall)stone ; **~ (rénal)** (kidney) stone ; **~ateur** *nm*, **~atrice** *nf* calculator.
calculer [kalkyle] *vt* to calculate, work out, reckon ; (*combiner*) to calculate.
cale [kal] *nf* (*de bateau*) hold ; (*en bois*) wedge, chock ; **~ sèche** dry dock.
calé, e [kale] *a* (*fam*) clever, bright.
calebasse [kalbɑs] *nf* calabash, gourd.
caleçon [kalsɔ̃] *nm* pair of underpants, trunks *pl* ; **~ de bain** bathing trunks *pl*.
calembour [kalɑ̃buʀ] *nm* pun.
calendes [kalɑ̃d] *nfpl*: **renvoyer aux ~ grecques** to postpone indefinitely.
calendrier [kalɑ̃dʀije] *nm* calendar ; (*fig*) timetable.
cale-pied [kalpje] *nm inv* toe clip.
calepin [kalpɛ̃] *nm* notebook.
caler [kale] *vt* to wedge, chock up ; **~ (son moteur/véhicule)** to stall (one's engine/vehicle).
calfater [kalfate] *vt* to caulk.
calfeutrer [kalføtʀe] *vt* to (make) draughtproof ; **se ~** to make o.s. snug and comfortable.
calibre [kalibʀ(ə)] *nm* (*d'un fruit*) grade ; (*d'une arme*) bore, calibre ; (*fig*) calibre ; **calibrer** *vt* to grade.
calice [kalis] *nm* (REL) chalice ; (BOT) calyx.
califourchon [kalifuʀʃɔ̃]: **à ~** *ad* astride ; **à ~ sur** astride, straddling.
câlin, e [kɑlɛ̃, -in] *a* cuddly, cuddlesome ; tender.
câliner [kɑline] *vt* to fondle, cuddle.
calleux, euse [kalø, -øz] *a* horny, callous.
calligraphie [kaligʀafi] *nf* calligraphy.
calmant [kalmɑ̃] *nm* tranquillizer, sedative ; painkiller.
calme [kalm(ə)] *a* calm, quiet // *nm* calm(ness), quietness ; **~ plat** (NAVIG) dead calm.
calmer [kalme] *vt* to calm (down) ; (*douleur, inquiétude*) to ease, soothe ; **se ~** to calm down.
calomnie [kalɔmni] *nf* slander ; (*écrite*) libel ; **calomnier** *vt* to slander ; to libel ; **calomnieux, euse** *a* slanderous ; libellous.
calorie [kalɔʀi] *nf* calorie.
calorifère [kalɔʀifɛʀ] *nm* stove.
calorifique [kalɔʀifik] *a* calorific.
calorifuge [kalɔʀifyʒ] *a* (heat-)insulating, heat-retaining.
calot [kalo] *nm* forage cap.
calotte [kalɔt] *nf* (*coiffure*) skullcap ; (*gifle*) slap ; **~ glaciaire** icecap.
calque [kalk(ə)] *nm* (*dessin*) tracing ; (*fig*) carbon copy.
calquer [kalke] *vt* to trace ; (*fig*) to copy exactly.
calvaire [kalvɛʀ] *nm* (*croix*) wayside cross, calvary ; (*souffrances*) suffering, martyrdom.
calvitie [kalvisi] *nf* baldness.
camaïeu [kamajø] *nm*: **(motif en) ~** monochrome motif.
camarade [kamaʀad] *nm/f* friend, pal ; (POL) comrade ; **~rie** *nf* friendship.
cambouis [kɑ̃bwi] *nm* engine oil.
cambrer [kɑ̃bʀe] *vt* to arch ; **se ~** to arch one's back ; **pied très cambré** foot with high arches *ou* insteps.
cambriolage [kɑ̃bʀijɔlaʒ] *nm* burglary.
cambrioler [kɑ̃bʀijɔle] *vt* to burgle ; **cambrioleur, euse** *nm/f* burglar.

cambrure [kɑ̃bʀyʀ] *nf* (*de la route*) camber.
cambuse [kɑ̃byz] *nf* storeroom.
came [kam] *nf*: **arbre à ~s** camshaft; **arbre à ~s en tête** overhead camshaft.
camée [kame] *nm* cameo.
caméléon [kameleɔ̃] *nm* chameleon.
camelot [kamlo] *nm* street pedlar.
camelote [kamlɔt] *nf* rubbish, trash, junk.
caméra [kameʀa] *nf* camera; (*d'amateur*) cine-camera.
camion [kamjɔ̃] *nm* lorry, truck; (*plus petit, fermé*) van; **~-citerne** *nm* tanker; **camionnage** *nm* haulage; **camionnette** *nf* (small) van; **camionneur** *nm* (*entrepreneur*) haulage contractor; (*chauffeur*) lorry *ou* truck driver; van driver.
camisole [kamizɔl] *nf*: **~ (de force)** strait jacket.
camomille [kamɔmij] *nf* camomile; (*boisson*) camomile tea.
camouflage [kamuflaʒ] *nm* camouflage.
camoufler [kamufle] *vt* to camouflage; (*fig*) to conceal, cover up.
camouflet [kamuflɛ] *nm* snub.
camp [kɑ̃] *nm* camp; (*fig*) side; **~ de nudistes/vacances** nudist/holiday camp; **~ de concentration** concentration camp.
campagnard, e [kɑ̃paɲaʀ, -aʀd(ə)] *a* country *cpd* // *nm/f* countryman/woman.
campagne [kɑ̃paɲ] *nf* country, countryside; (*MIL, POL, COMM*) campaign; **à la ~** in the country; **faire ~ pour** to campaign for.
campement [kɑ̃pmɑ̃] *nm* camp, encampment.
camper [kɑ̃pe] *vi* to camp // *vt* to pull *ou* put on firmly; to sketch; **se ~ devant** to plant o.s. in front of; **campeur, euse** *nm/f* camper.
camphre [kɑ̃fʀ(ə)] *nm* camphor.
camping [kɑ̃piŋ] *nm* camping; **(terrain de) ~** campsite, camping site; **faire du ~** to go camping.
camus, e [kamy, -yz] *a*: **nez ~** pug nose.
Canada [kanada] *nm*: **le ~** Canada; **canadien, ne** *a, nm/f* Canadian // *nf* (*veste*) fur-lined jacket.
canaille [kanɑj] *nf* (*péj*) scoundrel // *a* raffish, rakish.
canal, aux [kanal, -o] *nm* canal; (*naturel*) channel; (*ADMIN*): **par le ~ de** through (the medium of), via.
canalisation [kanalizɑsjɔ̃] *nf* (*tuyau*) pipe.
canaliser [kanalize] *vt* to canalize; (*fig*) to channel.
canapé [kanape] *nm* settee, sofa; (*CULIN*) canapé, open sandwich.
canard [kanaʀ] *nm* duck.
canari [kanaʀi] *nm* canary.
cancans [kɑ̃kɑ̃] *nmpl* (malicious) gossip *sg*.
cancer [kɑ̃sɛʀ] *nm* cancer; (*signe*): **le C~** Cancer, the Crab; **être du C~** to be Cancer; **cancéreux, euse** *a* cancerous; suffering from cancer; **cancérigène** *a* carcinogenic.
cancre [kɑ̃kʀ(ə)] *nm* dunce.
cancrelat [kɑ̃kʀəla] *nm* cockroach.
candélabre [kɑ̃delɑbʀ(ə)] *nm* candelabrum; street lamp, lamppost.
candeur [kɑ̃dœʀ] *nf* ingenuousness, guilelessness.
candi [kɑ̃di] *a inv*: **sucre ~** (sugar-)candy.
candidat, e [kɑ̃dida, -at] *nm/f* candidate; (*à un poste*) applicant, candidate; **candidature** *nf* candidature; application; **poser sa candidature** to submit an application, apply.
candide [kɑ̃did] *a* ingenuous, guileless, naïve.
cane [kan] *nf* (female) duck.
caneton [kantɔ̃] *nm* duckling.
canette [kanɛt] *nf* (*de bière*) (flip-top) bottle; (*de machine à coudre*) spool.
canevas [kanva] *nm* (*COUTURE*) canvas (for tapestry work); (*fig*) framework, structure.
caniche [kaniʃ] *nm* poodle.
canicule [kanikyl] *nf* scorching heat; midsummer heat, dog days *pl*.
canif [kanif] *nm* penknife, pocket knife.
canin, e [kanɛ̃, -in] *a* canine // *nf* canine (tooth), eye tooth; **exposition ~e** dog show.
caniveau, x [kanivo] *nm* gutter.
canne [kan] *nf* (walking) stick; **~ à pêche** fishing rod; **~ à sucre** sugar cane.
canné, e [kane] *a* (*chaise*) cane *cpd*.
cannelle [kanɛl] *nf* cinnamon.
cannelure [kanlyʀ] *nf* flute, fluting *q*.
cannibale [kanibal] *nm/f* cannibal.
canoë [kanɔe] *nm* canoe; (*sport*) canoeing.
canon [kanɔ̃] *nm* (*arme*) gun; (*d'une arme: tube*) barrel; (*fig*) model; canon // *a*: **droit ~** canon law; **~ rayé** rifled barrel.
cañon [kaɲɔ̃] *nm* canyon.
canoniser [kanɔnize] *vt* to canonize.
canonnade [kanɔnad] *nf* cannonade.
canonnier [kanɔnje] *nm* gunner.
canonnière [kanɔnjɛʀ] *nf* gunboat.
canot [kano] *nm* boat, ding(h)y; **~ pneumatique** rubber *ou* inflatable ding(h)y; **~ de sauvetage** lifeboat; **canoter** *vi* to go rowing.
canotier [kanɔtje] *nm* boater.
cantate [kɑ̃tat] *nf* cantata.
cantatrice [kɑ̃tatʀis] *nf* (opera) singer.
cantine [kɑ̃tin] *nf* canteen.
cantique [kɑ̃tik] *nm* hymn.
canton [kɑ̃tɔ̃] *nm district regrouping several communes*; (*en Suisse*) canton.
cantonade [kɑ̃tɔnad]: **à la ~** *ad* to everyone in general; from the rooftops.
cantonner [kɑ̃tɔne] *vt* (*MIL*) to billet; to station; **se ~ dans** to confine o.s. to.
cantonnier [kɑ̃tɔnje] *nm* roadmender, roadman.
canular [kanylaʀ] *nm* hoax.
caoutchouc [kautʃu] *nm* rubber; **~ mousse** foam rubber; **caoutchouté, e** *a* rubberized; **caoutchouteux, euse** *a* rubbery.
cap [kap] *nm* (*GÉO*) cape; headland; (*fig*) hurdle; watershed; (*NAVIG*): **changer de ~** to change course; **mettre le ~ sur** to head *ou* steer for.

C.A.P. *sigle m* = *Certificat d'aptitude professionnelle* (*obtained after trade apprenticeship*).
capable [kapabl(ə)] *a* able, capable ; **~ de qch/faire** capable of sth/doing ; **livre ~ d'intéresser** book liable *ou* likely to be of interest.
capacité [kapasite] *nf* (*compétence*) ability ; (JUR, *contenance*) capacity ; **~ (en droit)** *basic legal qualification.*
cape [kap] *nf* cape, cloak ; **rire sous ~** to laugh up one's sleeve.
C.A.P.E.S. [kapɛs] *sigle m* = *Certificat d'aptitude au professorat de l'enseignement du second degré.*
capharnaüm [kafaʀnaɔm] *nm* shambles *sg.*
capillaire [kapilɛʀ] *a* (*soins, lotion*) hair *cpd* ; (*vaisseau etc*) capillary ; **capillarité** *nf* capillarity.
capilotade [kapilɔtad]: **en ~** *ad* crushed to a pulp ; smashed to pieces.
capitaine [kapitɛn] *nm* captain ; **~ des pompiers** fire chief, firemaster ; **~rie** *nf* (*du port*) harbour master's (office).
capital, e, aux [kapital -o] *a* major ; of paramount importance ; fundamental ; (JUR) capital // *nm* capital ; (*fig*) stock ; asset // *nf* (*ville*) capital ; (*lettre*) capital (letter) ; // *nmpl* (*fonds*) capital *sg*, money *sg* ; **~ (social)** authorized capital ; **~iser** *vt* to amass, build up ; (COMM) to capitalize ; **~isme** *nm* capitalism ; **~iste** *a, nm/f* capitalist.
capiteux, euse [kapitø, -øz] *a* heady ; sensuous, alluring.
capitonner [kapitɔne] *vt* to pad.
capitulation [kapitylɑsjɔ̃] *nf* capitulation.
capituler [kapityle] *vi* to capitulate.
caporal, aux [kapɔʀal, -o] *nm* lance corporal.
capot [kapo] *nm* (AUTO) bonnet.
capote [kapɔt] *nf* (*de voiture*) hood ; (*de soldat*) greatcoat.
capoter [kapɔte] *vi* to overturn.
câpre [kɑpʀ(ə)] *nf* caper.
caprice [kapʀis] *nm* whim, caprice ; passing fancy ; **~s** (*de la mode etc*) vagaries ; **capricieux, euse** *a* capricious ; whimsical ; temperamental.
Capricorne [kapʀikɔʀn] *nm*: **le ~** Capricorn, the Goat ; **être du ~** to be Capricorn.
capsule [kapsyl] *nf* (*de bouteille*) cap ; (*amorce*) primer ; cap ; (BOT *etc, spatiale*) capsule.
capter [kapte] *vt* (*ondes radio*) to pick up ; (*eau*) to harness ; (*fig*) to win, capture.
captieux, euse [kapsjø, -øz] *a* specious.
captif, ive [kaptif, -iv] *a* captive // *nm/f* captive, prisoner.
captiver [kaptive] *vt* to captivate.
captivité [kaptivite] *nf* captivity ; **en ~** in captivity.
capture [kaptyʀ] *nf* capture, catching *q* ; catch.
capturer [kaptyʀe] *vt* to capture, catch.
capuche [kapyʃ] *nf* hood.
capuchon [kapyʃɔ̃] *nm* hood ; (*de stylo*) cap, top.
capucin [kapysɛ̃] *nm* Capuchin monk.
capucine [kapysin] *nf* (BOT) nasturtium.
caquet [kakɛ] *nm*: **rabattre le ~ à qn** to bring sb down a peg or two.
caqueter [kakte] *vi* (*poule*) to cackle ; (*fig*) to prattle, blether.
car [kaʀ] *nm* coach // *cj* because, for ; **~ de reportage** broadcasting *ou* radio van.
carabine [kaʀabin] *nf* carbine, rifle.
caracoler [kaʀakɔle] *vi* to caracole, prance.
caractère [kaʀaktɛʀ] *nm* (*gén*) character ; **en ~s gras** in bold type ; **en petits ~s** in small print ; **avoir du ~** to have character ; **avoir bon/mauvais ~** to be good-/ill-natured *ou* -tempered ; **caractériel, le** *a* (of) character // *nm/f* emotionally disturbed child.
caractérisé, e [kaʀakteʀize] *a*: **c'est une grippe/de l'insubordination ~e** it is a clear(-cut) case of flu/insubordination.
caractériser [kaʀakteʀize] *vt* to characterize ; **se ~ par** to be characterized *ou* distinguished by.
caractéristique [kaʀakteʀistik] *a, nf* characteristic.
carafe [kaʀaf] *nf* decanter ; carafe.
carambolage [kaʀɑ̃bɔlaʒ] *nm* multiple crash, pileup.
caramel [kaʀamɛl] *nm* (*bonbon*) caramel, toffee ; (*substance*) caramel ; **caraméliser** *vt* to caramelize.
carapace [kaʀapas] *nf* shell.
carat [kaʀa] *nm* carat ; **or à 18 ~s** 18-carat gold.
caravane [kaʀavan] *nf* caravan ; **caravanier** *nm* caravanner ; **caravaning** *nm* caravanning ; (*emplacement*) caravan site.
carbone [kaʀbɔn] *nm* carbon ; (*feuille*) carbon, sheet of carbon paper ; (*double*) carbon (copy).
carbonique [kaʀbɔnik] *a*: **gaz ~** carbonic acid gas ; **neige ~** dry ice.
carbonisé, e [kaʀbɔnize] *a* charred.
carboniser [kaʀbɔnize] *vt* to carbonize ; to burn down, reduce to ashes.
carburant [kaʀbyʀɑ̃] *nm* (motor) fuel.
carburateur [kaʀbyʀatœʀ] *nm* carburettor.
carburation [kaʀbyʀɑsjɔ̃] *nf* carburation.
carcan [kaʀkɑ̃] *nm* (*fig*) yoke, shackles *pl.*
carcasse [kaʀkas] *nf* carcass ; (*de véhicule etc*) shell.
carder [kaʀde] *vt* to card.
cardiaque [kaʀdjak] *a* cardiac, heart *cpd* // *nm/f* heart patient.
cardigan [kaʀdigɑ̃] *nm* cardigan.
cardinal, e, aux [kaʀdinal, -o] *a* cardinal // *nm* (REL) cardinal.
cardiologie [kaʀdjɔlɔʒi] *nf* cardiology ; **cardiologue** *nm/f* cardiologist, heart specialist.
carême [kaʀɛm] *nm*: **le C~** Lent.
carence [kaʀɑ̃s] *nf* incompetence, inadequacy ; (*manque*) deficiency ; **~ vitaminique** vitamin deficiency.
carène [kaʀɛn] *nf* hull.
caréner [kaʀene] *vt* (NAVIG) to careen ; (*carrosserie*) to streamline.

caressant, e [karɛsɑ̃, -ɑ̃t] *a* affectionate; caressing, tender.
caresse [karɛs] *nf* caress.
caresser [karese] *vt* to caress, stroke, fondle; (*fig: projet, espoir*) to toy with.
cargaison [kargɛzɔ̃] *nf* cargo, freight.
cargo [kargo] *nm* cargo boat, freighter.
caricatural, e, aux [karikatyral, -o] *a* caricatural, caricature-like.
caricature [karikatyr] *nf* caricature; (*politique etc*) (satirical) cartoon; **caricaturiste** *nm/f* caricaturist; (satirical) cartoonist.
carie [kari] *nf*: **la ~ (dentaire)** tooth decay; **une ~** a hole (in a tooth); **carié, e** *a*: **dent cariée** bad *ou* decayed tooth.
carillon [karijɔ̃] *nm* (*d'église*) bells *pl*; (*pendule*) chimes *pl*; (*de porte*): **~ (électrique)** (electric) door chime *ou* bell; **carillonner** *vi* to ring, chime, peal.
carlingue [karlɛ̃g] *nf* cabin.
carnage [karnaʒ] *nm* carnage, slaughter.
carnassier, ière [karnasje, -jɛr] *a* carnivorous // *nm* carnivore.
carnation [karnɑsjɔ̃] *nf* complexion; **~s** (PEINTURE) flesh tones.
carnaval [karnaval] *nm* carnival.
carné, e [karne] *a* meat *cpd*, meat-based.
carnet [karnɛ] *nm* (*calepin*) notebook; (*de tickets, timbres etc*) book; (*d'école*) school report; (*journal intime*) diary; **~ de chèques** cheque book; **~ de commandes** order book; **~ à souches** counterfoil book.
carnier [karnje] *nm* gamebag.
carnivore [karnivɔr] *a* carnivorous // *nm* carnivore.
carotide [karɔtid] *nf* carotid (artery).
carotte [karɔt] *nf* carrot.
carpe [karp(ə)] *nf* carp.
carpette [karpɛt] *nf* rug.
carquois [karkwa] *nm* quiver.
carre [kar] *nf* (*de ski*) edge.
carré, e [kare] *a* square; (*fig: franc*) straightforward // *nm* (*de terrain, jardin*) patch, plot; (NAVIG: *salle*) wardroom; (MATH) square; **élever un nombre au ~** to square a number; **mètre/kilomètre ~** square metre/kilometre; (CARTES): **~ d'as/de rois** four aces/kings.
carreau, x [karo] *nm* (*en faïence etc*) (floor) tile; (wall) tile; (*de fenêtre*) (window) pane; (*motif*) check, square; (CARTES: *couleur*) diamonds *pl*; (: *carte*) diamond; **tissu à ~x** checked fabric.
carrefour [karfur] *nm* crossroads *sg*.
carrelage [karlaʒ] *nm* tiling.
carreler [karle] *vt* to tile.
carrelet [karlɛ] *nm* (*poisson*) plaice.
carreleur [karlœr] *nm* (floor) tiler.
carrément [karemɑ̃] *ad* straight out, bluntly; straight; definitely.
carrer [kare]: **se ~** *vi*: **se ~ dans un fauteuil** to settle o.s. comfortably *ou* ensconce o.s. in an armchair.
carrier [karje] *nm*: **(ouvrier) ~** quarryman, quarrier.
carrière [karjɛr] *nf* (*de roches*) quarry; (*métier*) career; **militaire de ~** professional soldier; **faire ~ dans** to make one's career in.
carriole [karjɔl] *nf* (*péj*) old cart.
carrossable [karɔsabl(ə)] *a* suitable for (motor) vehicles.
carrosse [karɔs] *nm* (horse-drawn) coach.
carrosserie [karɔsri] *nf* body, coachwork *q*; (*activité, commerce*) coachbuilding; **atelier de ~** coachbuilder's workshop; (*pour réparations*) body repairs shop, panel beaters' (yard); **carrossier** *nm* coachbuilder; (*dessinateur*) car designer.
carrousel [karuzɛl] *nm* (ÉQUITATION) carousel; (*fig*) merry-go-round.
carrure [karyr] *nf* build; (*fig*) stature, calibre.
cartable [kartabl(ə)] *nm* (*d'écolier*) satchel, (school)bag.
carte [kart(ə)] *nf* (*de géographie*) map; (*marine, du ciel*) chart; (*de fichier, d'abonnement etc, à jouer*) card; (*au restaurant*) menu; (*aussi*: **~ postale**) (post)card; (*aussi*: **~ de visite**) (visiting) card; **avoir/donner ~ blanche** to have/give carte blanche *ou* a free hand; **à la ~** (*au restaurant*) à la carte; **~ de crédit** credit card; **~ d'état-major** ≈ Ordnance Survey map; **la ~ grise** (AUTO) the (car) registration book; **~ d'identité** identity card; **~ perforée** punch(ed) card; **la ~ verte** (AUTO) the green card; **la ~ des vins** the wine list; **~-lettre** *nf* letter-card.
carter [kartɛr] *nm* (AUTO: *d'huile*) sump; (: *de la boîte de vitesses*) casing; (*de bicyclette*) chain guard.
cartilage [kartilaʒ] *nm* (ANAT) cartilage.
cartographe [kartɔgraf] *nm/f* cartographer.
cartographie [kartɔgrafi] *nf* cartography, map-making.
cartomancien, ne [kartɔmɑ̃sjɛ̃, -ɛn] *nm/f* fortune-teller (*with cards*).
carton [kartɔ̃] *nm* (*matériau*) cardboard; (*boîte*) (cardboard) box; (*d'invitation*) invitation card; (ART) sketch; cartoon; **faire un ~** (*au tir*) to have a go at the rifle range; to score a hit; **~ (à dessin)** portfolio; **cartonnage** *nm* cardboard (packing); **cartonné, e** *a* (*livre*) hardback, cased; **~-pâte** *nm* pasteboard; **de ~-pâte** (*fig*) cardboard *cpd*.
cartouche [kartuʃ] *nf* cartridge; (*de cigarettes*) carton; **cartouchière** *nf* cartridge belt.
cas [kɑ] *nm* case; **faire peu de ~/grand ~ de** to attach little/great importance to; **en aucun ~** on no account, under no circumstances (whatsoever); **au ~ où** in case; **en ~ de** in case of, in the event of; **en ~ de besoin** if need be; **en tout ~** in any case, at any rate; **~ de conscience** matter of conscience.
casanier, ière [kazanje, -jɛr] *a* stay-at-home.
casaque [kazak] *nf* (*de jockey*) blouse.
cascade [kaskad] *nf* waterfall, cascade; (*fig*) stream, torrent.
cascadeur, euse [kaskadœr, -øz] *nm/f* stuntman/girl.
case [kɑz] *nf* (*hutte*) hut; (*compartiment*) compartment; (*pour le courrier*)

pigeonhole; (*sur un formulaire, de mots croisés, d'échiquier*) square.
casemate [kazmat] *nf* blockhouse.
caser [kɑze] *vt* to put; to tuck; to put up; (*péj*) to find a job for; to find a husband for.
caserne [kazɛʀn(ə)] *nf* barracks *sg ou pl*; **~ment** *nm* barrack buildings *pl*.
cash [kaʃ] *ad*: **payer ~** to pay cash down.
casier [kɑzje] *nm* (*à journaux etc*) rack; (*de bureau*) filing cabinet; (: *à cases*) set of pigeonholes; (*case*) compartment; pigeonhole; (: *à clef*) locker; (PÊCHE) lobster pot; **~ à bouteilles** bottle rack; **~ judiciaire** police record.
casino [kazino] *nm* casino.
casque [kask(ə)] *nm* helmet; (*chez le coiffeur*) (hair-)drier; (*pour audition*) (head-)phones *pl*, headset.
casquette [kaskɛt] *nf* cap.
cassant, e [kɑsɑ̃, -ɑ̃t] *a* brittle; (*fig*) brusque, abrupt.
cassate [kasat] *nf*: **(glace) ~** cassata.
cassation [kɑsɑsjɔ̃] *nf*: **recours en ~** appeal to the Supreme Court.
casse [kɑs] *nf* (*pour voitures*): **mettre à la ~** to scrap, send to the breakers; (*dégâts*): **il y a eu de la ~** there were a lot of breakages.
casse... [kɑs] *préfixe*: **~-cou** *a inv* daredevil, reckless; **crier ~-cou à qn** to warn sb (*against a risky undertaking*); **~-croûte** *nm inv* snack; **~-noisette(s), ~-noix** *nm inv* nutcrackers *pl*; **~-pieds** *a, nm/f inv* (*fam*): **il est ~-pieds, c'est un ~-pieds** he's a pain (in the neck).
casser [kɑse] *vt* to break; (ADMIN: *gradé*) to demote; (JUR) to quash // *vi*, **se ~** to break.
casserole [kasʀɔl] *nf* saucepan; **à la ~** (CULIN) braised.
casse-tête [kɑstɛt] *nm inv* (*fig*) brain teaser; headache (*fig*).
cassette [kasɛt] *nf* (*bande magnétique*) cassette; (*coffret*) casket.
cassis [kasis] *nm* blackcurrant; (*de la route*) dip, bump.
cassonade [kasɔnad] *nf* brown sugar.
cassoulet [kasulɛ] *nm* cassoulet.
cassure [kɑsyʀ] *nf* break, crack.
castagnettes [kastaɲɛt] *nfpl* castanets.
caste [kast(ə)] *nf* caste.
castor [kastɔʀ] *nm* beaver.
castrer [kastʀe] *vt* to castrate; to geld; to doctor.
cataclysme [kataklism(ə)] *nm* cataclysm.
catacombes [katakɔ̃b] *nfpl* catacombs.
catadioptre [katadjɔptʀ(ə)] *nm* = **cataphote.**
catafalque [katafalk(ə)] *nm* catafalque.
catalogue [katalɔg] *nm* catalogue.
cataloguer [katalɔge] *vt* to catalogue, to list; (*péj*) to put a label on.
catalyse [kataliz] *nf* catalysis; **catalyseur** *nm* catalyst.
cataphote [katafɔt] *nm* reflector.
cataplasme [kataplasm(ə)] *nm* poultice.
catapulte [katapylt(ə)] *nf* catapult; **catapulter** *vt* to catapult.
cataracte [kataʀakt(ə)] *nf* cataract; **opérer qn de la ~** to operate on sb for (a) cataract.
catarrhe [kataʀ] *nm* catarrh.
catastrophe [katastʀɔf] *nf* catastrophe, disaster; **catastrophique** *a* catastrophic, disastrous.
catch [katʃ] *nm* (all-in) wrestling; **~eur, euse** *nm/f* (all-in) wrestler.
catéchiser [kateʃize] *vt* to catechize; to indoctrinate; to lecture; **catéchisme** *nm* catechism; **catéchumène** [katekymɛn] *nm/f* catechumen (*trainee convert*).
catégorie [kategɔʀi] *nf* category.
catégorique [kategɔʀik] *a* categorical.
cathédrale [katedʀal] *nf* cathedral.
cathode [katɔd] *nf* cathode.
catholicisme [katɔlisism(ə)] *nm* (Roman) Catholicism.
catholique [katɔlik] *a, nm/f* (Roman) Catholic; **pas très ~** a bit shady *ou* fishy.
catimini [katimini]: **en ~** *ad* on the sly, on the quiet.
cauchemar [kɔʃmaʀ] *nm* nightmare; **~desque** *a* nightmarish.
caudal, e, aux [kodal, -o] *a* caudal, tail *cpd*.
causal, e [kozal] *a* causal; **~ité** *nf* causality.
cause [koz] *nf* cause; (JUR) lawsuit, case; brief; **à ~ de** because of, owing to; **pour ~ de** on account of; owing to; **(et) pour ~** and for (a very) good reason; **être en ~** to be at stake; to be involved; to be in question; **mettre en ~** to implicate; to call into question; **remettre en ~** to challenge, call into question.
causer [koze] *vt* to cause // *vi* to chat, talk.
causerie [kozʀi] *nf* talk.
caustique [kostik] *a* caustic.
cauteleux, euse [kotlø, -øz] *a* wily.
cautériser [kɔteʀize] *vt* to cauterize.
caution [kosjɔ̃] *nf* guarantee, security; (JUR) bail (bond); (*fig*) backing, support; **payer la ~ de qn** to stand bail for sb; **libéré sous ~** released on bail.
cautionnement [kosjɔnmɑ̃] *nm* (*somme*) guarantee, security.
cautionner [kosjɔne] *vt* to guarantee; (*soutenir*) to support.
cavalcade [kavalkad] *nf* (*fig*) stampede.
cavalerie [kavalʀi] *nf* cavalry.
cavalier, ière [kavalje, -jɛʀ] *a* (*désinvolte*) offhand // *nm/f* rider; (*au bal*) partner // *nm* (ÉCHECS) knight; **faire ~ seul** to go it alone.
cave [kav] *nf* cellar; (*cabaret*) (cellar) nightclub // *a*: **yeux ~s** sunken eyes.
caveau, x [kavo] *nm* vault.
caverne [kavɛʀn(ə)] *nf* cave.
caverneux, euse [kavɛʀnø, -øz] *a* cavernous.
caviar [kavjaʀ] *nm* caviar(e).
cavité [kavite] *nf* cavity.
CC *sigle voir* **corps.**
C.C.P. *sigle m voir* **compte.**
CD *sigle voir* **corps.**
ce(c'), cet, cette, ces [sə, sɛt, se] *dét* (*gén*) this; these *pl*; (*non-proximité*) that; those *pl*; **cette nuit** (*qui vient*) tonight; (*passée*) last night // *pronom*: **~ qui, ~**

que what; (*chose qui* ...): **il est bête, ~ qui me chagrine** he's stupid, which saddens me; **tout ~ qui bouge** everything that *ou* which moves; **tout ~ que je sais** all I know; **~ dont j'ai parlé** what I talked about; **ce que c'est grand** how big it is!, what a size it is!; **c'est petit/grand** it's *ou* it is small/big; **c'est un peintre, ce sont des peintres** he's *ou* he is a painter, they are painters; **c'est le facteur** *etc* (*à la porte*) it's the postman *etc*; **c'est une voiture** it's a car; **qui est-ce?** who is it?; (*en désignant*) who is he/she?; **qu'est-ce?** what is it?; *voir aussi* **-ci, est-ce que, n'est-ce pas, c'est-à-dire.**

ceci [səsi] *pronom* this.

cécité [sesite] *nf* blindness.

céder [sede] *vt* to give up // *vi* (*pont, barrage*) to give way; (*personne*) to give in; **~ à** to yield to, give in to.

cédille [sedij] *nf* cedilla.

cèdre [sɛdʀ(ə)] *nm* cedar.

C.E.E. *sigle f* (= *Communauté économique européenne*) EEC (European Economic Community).

ceindre [sɛ̃dʀ(ə)] *vt* (*mettre*) to put on, don; (*entourer*): **~ qch de qch** to put sth round sth.

ceinture [sɛ̃tyʀ] *nf* belt; (*taille*) waist; (*fig*) ring; belt; circle; **~ de sécurité** safety *ou* seat belt; **~ (de sécurité) à enrouleur** inertia reel seat belt; **ceinturer** *vt* (*saisir*) to grasp (round the waist); (*entourer*) to surround; **ceinturon** *nm* belt.

cela [səla] *pronom* that; (*comme sujet indéfini*) it; **~ m'étonne que** it surprises me that; **quand/où ~?** when/where (was that)?

célèbre [selɛbʀ(ə)] *a* famous.

célébrer [selebʀe] *vt* to celebrate; (*louer*) to extol.

célébrité [selebʀite] *nf* fame; (*star*) celebrity.

céleri [sɛlʀi] *nm*: **~(-rave)** celeriac; **~ (en branche)** celery.

célérité [seleʀite] *nf* speed, swiftness.

céleste [selɛst(ə)] *a* celestial; heavenly.

célibat [seliba] *nm* celibacy; bachelor/spinsterhood.

célibataire [selibatɛʀ] *a* single, unmarried // *nm/f* bachelor/unmarried *ou* single woman.

celle, celles [sɛl] *pronom voir* **celui**.

cellier [selje] *nm* storeroom.

cellophane [selɔfan] *nf* cellophane.

cellulaire [selylɛʀ] *a* (*BIO*) cell *cpd*, cellular; **voiture** *ou* **fourgon ~** prison *ou* police van.

cellule [selyl] *nf* (*gén*) cell.

cellulite [selylit] *nf* excess fat, cellulitis.

cellulose [selyloz] *nf* cellulose.

celui, celle, ceux, celles [səlɥi, sɛl, sø] *pronom* the one; **~ qui bouge** the one which *ou* that moves; (*personne*) the one who moves; **~ que je vois** the one (which *ou* that) I see; the one (whom) I see; **~ dont je parle** the one I'm talking about; **~ qui veut** (*valeur indéfinie*) whoever wants, the man *ou* person who wants; **~ du salon/du dessous** the one in (*ou* from) the lounge/below; **~ de mon frère** my brother's; **celui-ci/-là, celle-ci/-là** this/that one; **ceux-ci, celles-ci** these ones; **ceux-là, celles-là** those (ones).

cénacle [senakl(ə)] *nm* (literary) coterie *ou* set.

cendre [sɑ̃dʀ(ə)] *nf* ash; **~s** (*d'un foyer*) ash(es), cinders; (*volcaniques*) ash *sg*; (*d'un défunt*) ashes; **sous la ~** (*CULIN*) in (the) embers; **cendré, e** *a* (*couleur*) ashen; (**piste**) **cendrée** cinder track; **cendrier** *nm* ashtray.

cène [sɛn] *nf*: **la ~** (Holy) Communion; (*ART*) the Last Supper.

censé, e [sɑ̃se] *a*: **être ~ faire** to be supposed to do.

censeur [sɑ̃sœʀ] *nm* (*SCOL*) vice-principal, deputy-head; (*CINÉMA, POL*) censor.

censure [sɑ̃syʀ] *nf* censorship.

censurer [sɑ̃syʀe] *vt* (*CINÉMA, PRESSE*) to censor; (*POL*) to censure.

cent [sɑ̃] *num* a hundred, one hundred; **centaine** *nf*: **une centaine (de)** about a hundred, a hundred or so; (*COMM*) a hundred; **plusieurs centaines (de)** several hundred; **des centaines (de)** hundreds (of); **centenaire** *a* hundred-year-old // *nm/f* centenarian // *nm* (*anniversaire*) centenary; **centième** *num* hundredth; **centigrade** *nm* centigrade; **centigramme** *nm* centigramme; **centilitre** *nm* centilitre; **centime** *nm* centime; **centimètre** *nm* centimetre; (*ruban*) tape measure, measuring tape.

central, e, aux [sɑ̃tʀal, -o] *a* central // *nm*: **~ (téléphonique)** (telephone) exchange // *nf*: **~e électrique/nucléaire** electric/nuclear power-station; **~e syndicale** group of affiliated trade unions.

centraliser [sɑ̃tʀalize] *vt* to centralize.

centre [sɑ̃tʀ(ə)] *nm* centre; **~ de gravité** centre of gravity; **~ de tri** (*POSTES*) sorting office; **le ~-ville** the town centre; **centrer** *vt* to centre // *vi* (*FOOTBALL*) to centre the ball.

centrifuge [sɑ̃tʀifyʒ] *a*: **force ~** centrifugal force; **centrifuger** *vt* to centrifuge.

centripète [sɑ̃tʀipɛt] *a*: **force ~** centripetal force.

centuple [sɑ̃typl(ə)] *nm*: **le ~ de qch** a hundred times sth; **au ~** a hundredfold; **centupler** *vi, vt* to increase a hundredfold.

cep [sɛp] *nm* (vine) stock; **cépage** *nm* (type of) vine.

cèpe [sɛp] *nm* (edible) boletus.

cependant [səpɑ̃dɑ̃] *ad* however, nevertheless.

céramique [seʀamik] *nf* ceramic; (*art*) ceramics *sg*.

cercle [sɛʀkl(ə)] *nm* circle; (*objet*) band, hoop; **~ vicieux** vicious circle.

cercueil [sɛʀkœj] *nm* coffin.

céréale [seʀeal] *nf* cereal.

cérébral, e, aux [seʀebʀal, -o] *a* (*ANAT*) cerebral, brain *cpd*; (*fig*) mental, cerebral.

cérémonial [seʀemɔnjal] *nm* ceremonial.

cérémonie [seʀemɔni] *nf* ceremony; **~s** (*péj*) fuss *sg*, to-do *sg*; **cérémonieux, euse** *a* ceremonious, formal.

cerf [sɛʀ] *nm* stag.

cerfeuil [sɛRfœj] *nm* chervil.
cerf-volant [sɛRvɔlɑ̃] *nm* kite.
cerise [səRiz] *nf* cherry; **cerisier** *nm* cherry (tree).
cerné, e [sɛRne] *a*: **les yeux ~s** with dark rings *ou* shadows under the eyes.
cerner [sɛRne] *vt* (*MIL etc*) to surround; (*fig: problème*) to delimit, define.
cernes [sɛRn(ə)] *nfpl* (dark) rings, shadows (under the eyes).
certain, e [sɛRtɛ̃, -ɛn] *a* certain; (*sûr*): **~ (de/que)** certain *ou* sure (of/ that) // *dét* certain; **d'un ~ âge** past one's prime, not so young; **un ~ temps** (quite) some time; **~s** *pronom* some; **certainement** *ad* (*probablement*) most probably *ou* likely; (*bien sûr*) certainly, of course.
certes [sɛRt(ə)] *ad* admittedly; of course; indeed (yes).
certificat [sɛRtifika] *nm* certificate; **le ~ d'études** the school leaving certificate.
certifié, e [sɛRtifje] *a*: **professeur ~** qualified teacher.
certifier [sɛRtifje] *vt* to certify, guarantee; **~ à qn que** to assure sb that, guarantee to sb that.
certitude [sɛRtityd] *nf* certainty.
cerveau, x [sɛRvo] *nm* brain.
cervelas [sɛRvəla] *nm* saveloy.
cervelle [sɛRvɛl] *nf* (*ANAT*) brain; (*CULIN*) brain(s).
cervical, e, aux [sɛRvikal, -o] *a* cervical.
ces [se] *dét voir* **ce**.
césarienne [sezaRjɛn] *nf* caesarean (section), section.
cessantes [sɛsɑ̃t] *afpl*: **toutes affaires ~** forthwith.
cessation [sɛsɑsjɔ̃] *nf*: **~ des hostilités** cessation of hostilities: **~ de paiements/commerce** suspension of payments/trading.
cesse [sɛs]: **sans ~** *ad* continually, constantly; continuously; **il n'avait de ~ que** he would not rest until.
cesser [sese] *vt* to stop // *vi* to stop, cease; **~ de faire** to stop doing.
cessez-le-feu [seselfø] *nm inv* ceasefire.
cession [sɛsjɔ̃] *nf* transfer.
c'est-à-dire [sɛtadiR] *ad* that is (to say).
cet [sɛt] *dét voir* **ce**.
cétacé [setase] *nm* cetacean.
cette [sɛt] *dét voir* **ce**.
ceux [sø] *pronom voir* **celui**.
C.F.D.T. *sigle f = Confédération française et démocratique du travail (a major association of French trade unions).*
C.G.C. *sigle f = Confédération générale des cadres (union of managerial employees).*
C.G.T. *sigle f = Confédération générale du travail (a major association of French trade unions).*
chacal [ʃakal] *nm* jackal.
chacun, e [ʃakœ̃, -yn] *pronom* each; (*indéfini*) everyone, everybody.
chagrin, e [ʃagRɛ̃, -gRin] *a* ill-humoured, morose // *nm* grief, sorrow; **avoir du ~** to be grieved *ou* sorrowful; **chagriner** *vt* to grieve, distress; (*contrarier*) to bother, worry.
chahut [ʃay] *nm* uproar; **chahuter** *vt* to rag, bait // *vi* to make an uproar; **chahuteur, euse** *nm/f* rowdy.
chai [ʃɛ] *nm* wine and spirit store(house).
chaîne [ʃɛn] *nf* chain; (*RADIO, TV: stations*) channel; **travail à la ~** production line work; **faire la ~** to form a (human) chain; **~ (haute-fidélité** *ou* **hi-fi)** hi-fi system; **~ (de montage** *ou* **de fabrication)** production *ou* assembly line; **~ (de montagnes)** (mountain) range; **chaînette** *nf* (small) chain; **chaînon** *nm* link.
chair [ʃɛR] *nf* flesh // *a*: **(couleur) ~** flesh-coloured; **avoir la ~ de poule** to have goosepimples *ou* gooseflesh; **bien en ~** plump, well-padded; **~ à saucisses** sausage meat.
chaire [ʃɛR] *nf* (*d'église*) pulpit; (*d'université*) chair.
chaise [ʃɛz] *nf* chair; **~ de bébé** high chair; **~ longue** deckchair.
chaland [ʃalɑ̃] *nm* (*bateau*) barge.
châle [ʃɑl] *nm* shawl.
chalet [ʃalɛ] *nm* chalet.
chaleur [ʃalœR] *nf* heat; (*fig*) warmth; fire, fervour; heat.
chaleureux, euse [ʃalœRø, -øz] *a* warm.
challenge [ʃalɑ̃ʒ] *nm* contest, tournament.
chaloupe [ʃalup] *nf* launch; (*de sauvetage*) lifeboat.
chalumeau, x [ʃalymo] *nm* blowlamp, blowtorch.
chalut [ʃaly] *nm* trawl (net); **chalutier** *nm* trawler; (*pêcheur*) trawlerman.
chamailler [ʃamɑje]: **se ~** *vi* to squabble, bicker.
chamarré, e [ʃamaRe] *a* richly coloured *ou* brocaded.
chambarder [ʃɑ̃baRde] *vt* to turn upside down, upset.
chambranle [ʃɑ̃bRɑ̃l] *nm* (door) frame.
chambre [ʃɑ̃bR(ə)] *nf* bedroom; (*TECH*) chamber; (*POL*) chamber, house; (*JUR*) court; (*COMM*) chamber; federation; **faire ~ à part** to sleep in separate rooms; **stratège en ~** armchair strategist; **~ à un lit/deux lits** (*à l'hôtel*) single-/double- *ou* twin-bedded room; **~ d'accusation** court of criminal appeal; **~ à air** (*de pneu*) (inner) tube; **~ d'amis** spare *ou* guest room; **~ à coucher** bedroom; **la C~ des députés** the Chamber of Deputies, ≈ the House (of Commons); **~ forte** strongroom; **~ froide** *ou* **frigorifique** cold room; **~ des machines** engine-room; **~ meublée** bed-sitter, furnished room; **~ noire** (*PHOTO*) dark room.
chambrée [ʃɑ̃bRe] *nf* room.
chambrer [ʃɑ̃bRe] *vt* (*vin*) to bring to room temperature.
chameau, x [ʃamo] *nm* camel.
chamois [ʃamwa] *nm* chamois // *a*: **(couleur) ~** fawn, buff (-coloured).
champ [ʃɑ̃] *nm* field; (*PHOTO*): **dans le ~** in the picture; **prendre du ~** to draw back; **~ de bataille** battlefield; **~ de courses** racecourse; **~ de mines** minefield.
champagne [ʃɑ̃paɲ] *nm* champagne.
champêtre [ʃɑ̃pɛtR(ə)] *a* country *cpd*, rural.

champignon [ʃɑ̃piɲɔ̃] *nm* mushroom; (*terme générique*) fungus (*pl* i); ~ **de couche** *ou* **de Paris** cultivated mushroom; ~ **vénéneux** toadstool, poisonous mushroom.
champion, ne [ʃɑ̃pjɔ̃, -jɔn] *a, nm/f* champion; **championnat** *nm* championship.
chance [ʃɑ̃s] *nf*: **la** ~ luck; **une** ~ a stroke *ou* piece of luck *ou* good fortune; (*occasion*) a lucky break; ~**s** *nfpl* (*probabilités*) chances; **avoir de la** ~ to be lucky; **il a des** ~**s de gagner** he has a chance of winning.
chanceler [ʃɑ̃sle] *vi* to totter.
chancelier [ʃɑ̃səlje] *nm* (*allemand*) chancellor; (*d'ambassade*) secretary.
chanceux, euse [ʃɑ̃sø, -øz] *a* lucky, fortunate.
chancre [ʃɑ̃kʀ(ə)] *nm* canker.
chandail [ʃɑ̃daj] *nm* (thick) jumper *ou* sweater.
Chandeleur [ʃɑ̃dlœʀ] *nf*: **la** ~ Candlemas.
chandelier [ʃɑ̃dəlje] *nm* candlestick; (*à plusieurs branches*) candelabra, candlestick.
chandelle [ʃɑ̃dɛl] *nf* (tallow) candle; **dîner aux** ~**s** candlelight dinner.
change [ʃɑ̃ʒ] *nm* (COMM) exchange; **opérations de** ~ (foreign) exchange transactions; **contrôle des** ~**s** exchange control.
changeant, e [ʃɑ̃ʒɑ̃, -ɑ̃t] *a* changeable, fickle.
changement [ʃɑ̃ʒmɑ̃] *nm* change; ~ **de vitesses** gears; gear change.
changer [ʃɑ̃ʒe] *vt* (*modifier*) to change, alter; (*remplacer*, COMM, *rhabiller*) to change // *vi* to change, alter; **se** ~ to change (o.s.); ~ **de** (*remplacer*: *adresse, nom, voiture etc*) to change one's; (*échanger, alterner*: *côté, place, train etc*) to change + *npl*; ~ **de couleur/direction** to change colour/direction; ~ **d'idée** to change one's mind; ~ **de place avec qn** to change places with sb; ~ **(de train** *etc***)** to change (trains *etc*); ~ **qch en** to change sth into.
changeur [ʃɑ̃ʒœʀ] *nm* (*personne*) moneychanger; ~ **automatique** change machine; ~ **de disques** record changer, autochange.
chanoine [ʃanwan] *nm* canon.
chanson [ʃɑ̃sɔ̃] *nf* song.
chansonnier [ʃɑ̃sɔnje] *nm* cabaret artist (*specializing in political satire*); song book.
chant [ʃɑ̃] *nm* song; (*art vocal*) singing; (*d'église*) hymn; (*de poème*) canto; (TECH): **de** ~ on edge.
chantage [ʃɑ̃taʒ] *nm* blackmail; **faire du** ~ to use blackmail; **soumettre qn à un** ~ to blackmail sb.
chanter [ʃɑ̃te] *vt, vi* to sing; **si cela lui chante** (*fam*) if he feels like it *ou* fancies it.
chanterelle [ʃɑ̃tʀɛl] *nf* chanterelle (*edible mushroom*).
chanteur, euse [ʃɑ̃tœʀ, -øz] *nm/f* singer.
chantier [ʃɑ̃tje] *nm* (building) site; (*sur une route*) roadworks *pl*; **mettre en** ~ to put in hand, start work on; ~ **naval** shipyard.
chantonner [ʃɑ̃tɔne] *vi, vt* to sing to oneself, hum.
chanvre [ʃɑ̃vʀ(ə)] *nm* hemp.
chaos [kao] *nm* chaos; **chaotique** *a* chaotic.
chaparder [ʃapaʀde] *vt* to pinch, pilfer.
chapeau, x [ʃapo] *nm* hat; ~ **mou** trilby; ~**x de roues** hub caps.
chapeauter [ʃapote] *vt* (ADMIN) to head, oversee.
chapelet [ʃaplɛ] *nm* (REL) rosary; (*fig*): **un** ~ **de** a string of; **dire son** ~ to tell one's beads.
chapelle [ʃapɛl] *nf* chapel; ~ **ardente** chapel of rest.
chapelure [ʃaplyʀ] *nf* (dried) bread-crumbs *pl*.
chaperon [ʃapʀɔ̃] *nm* chaperon; **chaperonner** *vt* to chaperon.
chapiteau, x [ʃapito] *nm* (ARCHIT) capital; (*de cirque*) marquee, big top.
chapitre [ʃapitʀ(ə)] *nm* chapter; (*fig*) subject, matter; **avoir voix au** ~ to have a say in the matter.
chapitrer [ʃapitʀe] *vt* to lecture.
chaque [ʃak] *dét* each, every; (*indéfini*) every.
char [ʃaʀ] *nm* (*à foin etc*) cart, waggon; (*de carnaval*) float; ~ **(d'assaut)** tank.
charabia [ʃaʀabja] *nm* (*péj*) gibberish, gobbledygook.
charade [ʃaʀad] *nf* riddle; (*mimée*) charade.
charbon [ʃaʀbɔ̃] *nm* coal; ~ **de bois** charcoal; **charbonnage** *nm*: **les charbonnages de France** the (French) Coal Board *sg*; **charbonnier** *nm* coalman.
charcuterie [ʃaʀkytʀi] *nf* (*magasin*) pork butcher's shop and delicatessen; (*produits*) cooked pork meats *pl*; **charcutier, ière** *nm/f* pork butcher.
chardon [ʃaʀdɔ̃] *nm* thistle.
charge [ʃaʀʒ(ə)] *nf* (*fardeau*) load, burden; (*explosif*, ÉLEC, MIL, JUR) charge; (*rôle, mission*) responsibility; ~**s** *nfpl* (*du loyer*) service charges; **à la** ~ **de** (*dépendant de*) dependent upon, supported by; (*aux frais de*) chargeable to, payable by; **j'accepte, à** ~ **de revanche** I accept, provided I can do the same for you (in return) one day; **prendre en** ~ to take charge of; (*suj: véhicule*) to take on; (*dépenses*) to take care of; ~ **utile** (AUTO) live load; ~**s sociales** social security contributions.
chargé [ʃaʀʒe] *nm*: ~ **d'affaires** chargé d'affaires; ~ **de cours** ≈ senior lecturer.
chargement [ʃaʀʒəmɑ̃] *nm* (*action*) loading; charging; (*objets*) load.
charger [ʃaʀʒe] *vt* (*voiture, fusil, caméra*) to load; (*batterie*) to charge // vi (MIL *etc*) to charge; **se** ~ **de** to see to, take care *ou* charge of; ~ **qn de qch/faire qch** to give sb the responsibility for sth/of doing sth; to put sb in charge of sth/doing sth.
chariot [ʃaʀjo] *nm* trolley; (*charrette*) waggon; (*de machine à écrire*) carriage; ~ **élévateur** fork-lift truck.
charitable [ʃaʀitabl(ə)] *a* charitable; kind.
charité [ʃaʀite] *nf* charity; **faire la** ~ to

give to charity; to do charitable works; **faire la ~ à** to give (something) to.
charlatan [ʃaRlatɑ̃] *nm* charlatan.
charmant, e [ʃaRmɑ̃, -ɑ̃t] *a* charming.
charme [ʃaRm(ə)] *nm* charm; **charmer** *vt* to charm; **je suis charmé de** I'm delighted to; **charmeur, euse** *nm/f* charmer; **charmeur de serpents** snake charmer.
charnel, le [ʃaRnɛl] *a* carnal.
charnier [ʃaRnje] *nm* mass grave.
charnière [ʃaRnjɛR] *nf* hinge; (*fig*) turning-point.
charnu, e [ʃaRny] *a* fleshy.
charogne [ʃaRɔɲ] *nf* carrion *q*; (*fam!*) bastard (!).
charpente [ʃaRpɑ̃t] *nf* frame(work); (*fig*) structure, framework; build, frame; **charpentier** *nm* carpenter.
charpie [ʃaRpi] *nf*: **en ~** (*fig*) in shreds *ou* ribbons.
charretier [ʃaRtje] *nm* carter.
charrette [ʃaRɛt] *nf* cart.
charrier [ʃaRje] *vt* to carry (along); to cart, carry.
charrue [ʃaRy] *nf* plough.
charte [ʃaRt(ə)] *nf* charter.
chas [ʃa] *nm* eye (*of needle*).
chasse [ʃas] *nf* hunting; (*au fusil*) shooting; (*poursuite*) chase; (*aussi*: **~ d'eau**) flush; **la ~ est ouverte** the hunting season is open; **~ gardée** private hunting grounds *pl*; **prendre en ~, donner la ~ à** to give chase to; **tirer la ~ (d'eau)** to flush the toilet, pull the chain; **~ à courre** hunting; **~ à l'homme** manhunt; **~ sous-marine** underwater fishing.
châsse [ʃɑs] *nf* reliquary, shrine.
chassé-croisé [ʃasekRwaze] *nm* (DANSE) chassé-croisé; (*fig*) *mix-up where people miss each other in turn.*
chasse-neige [ʃasnɛʒ] *nm inv* snowplough.
chasser [ʃase] *vt* to hunt; (*expulser*) to chase away *ou* out, drive away *ou* out; (*dissiper*) to chase *ou* sweep away; to dispel, drive away; **chasseur, euse** *nm/f* hunter // *nm* (*avion*) fighter; (*domestique*) page (boy), messenger (boy); **chasseurs alpins** mountain infantry *sg ou pl.*
chassieux, ieuse [ʃasjø, -øz] *a* sticky, gummy.
châssis [ʃɑsi] *nm* (AUTO) chassis; (*cadre*) frame; (*de jardin*) cold frame.
chaste [ʃast(ə)] *a* chaste; **~té** *nf* chastity.
chasuble [ʃazybl(ə)] *nf* chasuble.
chat [ʃa] *nm* cat; **~ sauvage** wildcat.
châtaigne [ʃɑtɛɲ] *nf* chestnut; **châtaignier** *nm* chestnut (tree).
châtain [ʃɑtɛ̃] *a inv* chestnut (brown); chestnut-haired.
château, x [ʃɑto] *nm* castle; **~ d'eau** water tower; **~ fort** stronghold, fortified castle; **~ de sable** sandcastle.
châtier [ʃɑtje] *vt* to punish, castigate; (*fig*: *style*) to polish, refine; **châtiment** *nm* punishment, castigation.
chatoiement [ʃatwamɑ̃] *nm* shimmer(ing).
chaton [ʃatɔ̃] *nm* (ZOOL) kitten; (BOT) catkin; (*de bague*) bezel; stone.
chatouiller [ʃatuje] *vt* to tickle; (*l'odorat, le palais*) to titillate; **chatouilleux, euse** *a* ticklish; (*fig*) touchy, over-sensitive.
chatoyer [ʃatwaje] *vi* to shimmer.
châtrer [ʃɑtRe] *vt* to castrate; to geld; to doctor.
chatte [ʃat] *nf* (she-)cat.
chaud, e [ʃo, -od] *a* (*gén*) warm; (*très chaud*) hot; (*fig*) hearty; keen; heated; **il fait ~** it's warm; it's hot; **manger ~** to have something hot to eat; **avoir ~** to be warm; to be hot; **ça me tient ~** it keeps me warm; **rester au ~** to stay in the warmth; **chaudement** *ad* warmly; (*fig*) hotly.
chaudière [ʃodjɛR] *nf* boiler.
chaudron [ʃodRɔ̃] *nm* cauldron.
chaudronnerie [ʃodRɔnRi] *nf* (*usine*) boilerworks; (*activité*) boilermaking; (*boutique*) coppersmith's workshop.
chauffage [ʃofaʒ] *nm* heating; **~ central** central heating.
chauffant, e [ʃofɑ̃, -ɑ̃t] *a*: **couverture ~e** electric blanket; **plaque ~e** hotplate.
chauffard [ʃofaR] *nm* (*péj*) reckless driver; roadhog; hit-and-run driver.
chauffe-bain [ʃofbɛ̃] *nm*, **chauffe-eau** [ʃofo] *nm inv* water-heater.
chauffer [ʃofe] *vt* to heat // *vi* to heat up, warm up; (*trop chauffer*: *moteur*) to overheat; **se ~** (*se mettre en train*) to warm up; (*au soleil*) to warm o.s.
chaufferie [ʃofRi] *nf* boiler room.
chauffeur [ʃofœR] *nm* driver; (*privé*) chauffeur.
chaume [ʃom] *nm* (*du toit*) thatch; (*tiges*) stubble.
chaumière [ʃomjɛR] *nf* (thatched) cottage.
chaussée [ʃose] *nf* road(way); (*digue*) causeway.
chausse-pied [ʃospje] *nm* shoe-horn.
chausser [ʃose] *vt* (*bottes, skis*) to put on; (*enfant*) to put shoes on; (*suj*: *soulier*) to fit; **~ du 38/42** to take size 38/42; **~ grand/bien** to be big-/well-fitting; **se ~** to put one's shoes on.
chaussette [ʃosɛt] *nf* sock.
chausseur [ʃosœR] *nm* (*marchand*) footwear specialist, shoemaker.
chausson [ʃosɔ̃] *nm* slipper; **~ (aux pommes)** (apple) turnover.
chaussure [ʃosyR] *nf* shoe; (*commerce*) shoe industry *ou* trade; **~s montantes** ankle boots; **~s de ski** ski boots.
chaut [ʃo] *vb*: **peu me ~** it matters little to me.
chauve [ʃov] *a* bald.
chauve-souris [ʃovsuRi] *nf* bat.
chauvin, e [ʃovɛ̃, -in] *a* chauvinistic, jingoistic; **chauvinisme** *nm* chauvinism; jingoism.
chaux [ʃo] *nf* lime; **blanchi à la ~** whitewashed.
chavirer [ʃaviRe] *vi* to capsize, overturn.
chef [ʃɛf] *nm* head, leader; (*de cuisine*) chef; **en ~** (MIL *etc*) in chief; **~ d'accusation** charge, count (of indictment); **~ d'atelier** (shop) foreman; **~ de bureau** head clerk; **~ de clinique** senior hospital lecturer; **~ d'entreprise**

company head; ~ **d'équipe** team leader; ~ **d'état** head of state; ~ **de famille** head of the family; ~ **de file** (*de parti etc*) leader; ~ **de gare** station master; ~ **d'orchestre** conductor; ~ **de rayon** department(al) supervisor; ~ **de service** departmental head.
chef-d'œuvre [ʃɛdœvʀ(ə)] *nm* masterpiece.
chef-lieu [ʃɛfljø] *nm* county town.
cheftaine [ʃɛftɛn] *nf* (guide) captain.
cheik [ʃɛk] *nm* sheik.
chemin [ʃəmɛ̃] *nm* path; (*itinéraire, direction, trajet*) way; **en** ~ on the way; ~ **de fer** railway; **par** ~ **de fer** by rail; **les** ~**s de fer** the railways.
cheminée [ʃəmine] *nf* chimney; (*à l'intérieur*) chimney piece, fireplace; (*de bateau*) funnel.
cheminement [ʃəminmɑ̃] *nm* progress; course.
cheminer [ʃəmine] *vi* to walk (along).
cheminot [ʃəmino] *nm* railwayman.
chemise [ʃəmiz] *nf* shirt; (*dossier*) folder; ~ **de nuit** nightdress; ~**rie** *nf* (gentlemen's) outfitters'; **chemisette** *nf* short-sleeved shirt.
chemisier [ʃəmizje] *nm* blouse.
chenal, aux [ʃənal, -o] *nm* channel.
chêne [ʃɛn] *nm* oak (tree); (*bois*) oak.
chenet [ʃənɛ] *nm* fire-dog, andiron.
chenil [ʃənil] *nm* kennels *pl.*
chenille [ʃənij] *nf* (ZOOL) caterpillar; (AUTO) caterpillar track; **véhicule à** ~**s** tracked vehicle, caterpillar; **chenillette** *nf* tracked vehicle.
cheptel [ʃɛptɛl] *nm* livestock.
chèque [ʃɛk] *nm* cheque; ~ **barré/sans provision** crossed/bad cheque; ~ **au porteur** cheque to bearer; **chéquier** *nm* cheque book.
cher, ère [ʃɛʀ] *a* (*aimé*) dear; (*coûteux*) expensive, dear // *ad*: **cela coûte** ~ it's expensive, it costs a lot of money // *nf*: **la bonne chère** good food; **mon** ~**, ma chère** my dear.
chercher [ʃɛʀʃe] *vt* to look for; (*gloire etc*) to seek; **aller** ~ to go for, go and fetch; ~ **à faire** to try to do.
chercheur, euse [ʃɛʀʃœʀ, -øz] *nm/f* researcher, research worker; ~ **de** seeker of; hunter of; ~ **d'or** gold digger.
chère [ʃɛʀ] *a,nf voir* **cher**.
chéri, e [ʃeʀi] *a* beloved, dear; **(mon)** ~ darling.
chérir [ʃeʀiʀ] *vt* to cherish.
cherté [ʃɛʀte] *nf*: **la** ~ **de la vie** the high cost of living.
chérubin [ʃeʀybɛ̃] *nm* cherub.
chétif, ive [ʃetif, -iv] *a* puny, stunted.
cheval, aux [ʃəval, -o] *nm* horse; (AUTO): ~ **(vapeur) (C.V.)** horsepower *q;* **50 chevaux (au frein)** 50 brake horsepower, 50 b.h.p.; **10 chevaux (fiscaux)** 10 horsepower (*for tax purposes*); **faire du** ~ to ride; **à** ~ on horseback; **à** ~ **sur** astride, straddling; (*fig*) overlapping; ~ **d'arçons** vaulting horse.
chevaleresque [ʃəvalʀɛsk(ə)] *a* chivalrous.
chevalerie [ʃəvalʀi] *nf* chivalry; knighthood.
chevalet [ʃəvalɛ] *nm* easel.
chevalier [ʃəvalje] *nm* knight; ~ **servant** escort.
chevalière [ʃəvaljɛʀ] *nf* signet ring.
chevalin, e [ʃəvalɛ̃, -in] *a* of horses, equine; (*péj*) horsy; **boucherie** ~**e** horse-meat butcher's.
cheval-vapeur [ʃəvalvapœʀ] *nm voir* **cheval.**
chevauchée [ʃəvoʃe] *nf* ride; cavalcade.
chevaucher [ʃəvoʃe] *vi* (*aussi:* **se** ~) to overlap (each other) // *vt* to be astride, straddle.
chevelu, e [ʃəvly] *a* with a good head of hair, hairy (*péj*).
chevelure [ʃəvlyʀ] *nf* hair *q.*
chevet [ʃəvɛ] *nm*: **au** ~ **de qn** at sb's bedside; **lampe de** ~ bedside lamp.
cheveu, x [ʃəvø] *nm* hair; // *nmpl* (*chevelure*) hair *sg*; **avoir les** ~**x courts** to have short hair.
cheville [ʃəvij] *nf* (ANAT) ankle; (*de bois*) peg; (*pour enfoncer un clou*) plug; ~ **ouvrière** (*fig*) kingpin.
chèvre [ʃɛvʀ(ə)] *nf* (she-)goat.
chevreau, x [ʃɛvʀo] *nm* kid.
chèvrefeuille [ʃɛvʀəfœj] *nm* honeysuckle.
chevreuil [ʃəvʀœj] *nm* roe deer *inv*; (CULIN) venison.
chevron [ʃəvʀɔ̃] *nm* (*poutre*) rafter; (*motif*) chevron, v(-shape); **à** ~**s** chevron-patterned; herringbone.
chevronné, e [ʃəvʀɔne] *a* seasoned, experienced.
chevrotant, e [ʃəvʀɔtɑ̃, -ɑ̃t] *a* quavering.
chevrotine [ʃəvʀɔtin] *nf* buckshot *q.*
chewing-gum [ʃwiŋgɔm] *nm* chewing gum.
chez [ʃe] *prép* (*à la demeure de*): ~ **qn** at (*ou* to) sb's house *ou* place; (*parmi*) among; ~ **moi** at home; (*avec direction*) home; ~ **le boulanger** (*à la boulangerie*) at the baker's; ~ **ce musicien** (*dans ses œuvres*) in this musician; ~**-soi** *nm inv* home.
chic [ʃik] *a inv* chic, smart; (*généreux*) nice, decent // *nm* stylishness; **avoir le** ~ **de** to have the knack of; **de** ~ *ad* off the cuff; ~**!** great!, terrific!
chicane [ʃikan] *nf* (*obstacle*) zigzag; (*querelle*) squabble.
chiche [ʃiʃ] *a* niggardly, mean // *excl* (*à un défi*) you're on!
chicorée [ʃikɔʀe] *nf* (*café*) chicory; (*salade*) endive.
chicot [ʃiko] *nm* stump.
chien [ʃjɛ̃] *nm* dog; (*de pistolet*) hammer; **en** ~ **de fusil** curled up; ~ **de garde** guard dog.
chiendent [ʃjɛ̃dɑ̃] *nm* couch grass.
chien-loup [ʃjɛ̃lu] *nm* wolfhound.
chienne [ʃjɛn] *nf* dog, bitch.
chier [ʃje] *vi* (*fam!*) to crap (!).
chiffe [ʃif] *nf*: **il est mou comme une** ~**, c'est une** ~ **molle** he's spineless *ou* wet.
chiffon [ʃifɔ̃] *nm* (*de ménage*) (piece of) rag.

chiffonner [ʃifɔne] *vt* to crumple, crease.
chiffonnier [ʃifɔnje] *nm* ragman, rag-and-bone man; (*meuble*) chiffonier.
chiffre [ʃifʀ(ə)] *nm* (*représentant un nombre*) figure; numeral; (*montant, total*) total, sum; (*d'un code*) code, cipher; **~s romains/arabes** roman/arabic figures *ou* numerals; **en ~s ronds** in round figures; **écrire un nombre en ~s** to write a number in figures; **~ d'affaires** turnover; **chiffrer** *vt* (*dépense*) to put a figure to, assess; (*message*) to (en)code, cipher.
chignole [ʃiɲɔl] *nf* drill.
chignon [ʃiɲɔ̃] *nm* chignon, bun.
Chili [ʃili] *nm*: **le ~** Chile; **chilien, ne** *a, nm/f* Chilean.
chimère [ʃimɛʀ] *nf* (wild) dream, chimera; pipe dream, idle fancy.
chimie [ʃimi] *nf*: **la ~** chemistry; **chimique** *a* chemical; **produits chimiques** chemicals; **chimiste** *nm/f* chemist.
Chine [ʃin] *nf*: **la ~** China.
chiné, e [ʃine] *a* flecked.
chinois, e [ʃinwa, -waz] *a* Chinese; (*fig: péj*) pernickety, fussy // *nm/f* Chinese // *nm* (*langue*): **le ~** Chinese.
chiot [ʃjo] *nm* pup(py).
chipoter [ʃipɔte] *vi* to nibble; to quibble; to haggle.
chips [ʃips] *nfpl* (*aussi*: **pommes ~**) crisps.
chique [ʃik] *nf* quid, chew.
chiquenaude [ʃiknod] *nf* flick, flip.
chiquer [ʃike] *vi* to chew tobacco.
chiromancien, ne [kiʀɔmɑ̃sjɛ̃, -ɛn] *nm/f* palmist.
chirurgical, e, aux [ʃiʀyʀʒikal, -o] *a* surgical.
chirurgie [ʃiʀyʀʒi] *nf* surgery; **~ esthétique** plastic surgery; **chirurgien, ne** *nm/f* surgeon.
chiure [ʃjyʀ] *nf*: **~s de mouche** fly specks.
chlore [klɔʀ] *nm* chlorine.
chloroforme [klɔʀɔfɔʀm(ə)] *nm* chloroform.
chlorophylle [klɔʀɔfil] *nf* chlorophyll.
choc [ʃɔk] *nm* impact; shock; crash; (*moral*) shock; (*affrontement*) clash; **~ opératoire/nerveux** post-operative/(nervous) shock.
chocolat [ʃɔkɔla] *nm* chocolate; (*boisson*) (hot) chocolate; **~ à croquer** plain chocolate; **~ au lait** milk chocolate.
chœur [kœʀ] *nm* (*chorale*) choir; (OPÉRA, THÉÂTRE) chorus; (ARCHIT) choir, chancel; **en ~** in chorus.
choir [ʃwaʀ] *vi* to fall.
choisi, e [ʃwazi] *a* (*de premier choix*) carefully chosen; select; **textes ~s** selected writings.
choisir [ʃwaziʀ] *vt* to choose, select.
choix [ʃwa] *nm* choice; selection; **avoir le ~** to have the choice; **premier ~** (COMM) class *ou* grade one; **de ~** choice, selected; **au ~** as you wish *ou* prefer.
choléra [kɔleʀa] *nm* cholera.
chômage [ʃomaʒ] *nm* unemployment; **mettre au ~** to make redundant, put out of work; **être au ~** to be unemployed *ou* out of work; **~ partiel** short-time working; **~ technique** lay-offs *pl*; **chômer** *vi* to be unemployed, be idle; **jour chômé** public holiday; **chômeur, euse** *nm/f* unemployed person, person out of work.
chope [ʃɔp] *nf* tankard.
choquer [ʃɔke] *vt* (*offenser*) to shock; (*commotionner*) to shake (up).
choral, e [kɔʀal] *a* choral // *nf* choral society, choir.
chorégraphe [kɔʀegʀaf] *nm/f* choreographer.
chorégraphie [kɔʀegʀafi] *nf* choreography.
choriste [kɔʀist(ə)] *nm/f* choir member; (OPÉRA) chorus member.
chorus [kɔʀys] *nm*: **faire ~ (avec)** to voice one's agreement (with).
chose [ʃoz] *nf* thing; **c'est peu de ~** it's nothing (really); it's not much.
chou, x [ʃu] *nm* cabbage // *a inv* cute; **mon petit ~** (my) sweetheart; **~ à la crème** cream bun (*made of choux pastry*).
choucas [ʃuka] *nm* jackdaw.
chouchou, te [ʃuʃu, -ut] *nm/f* (SCOL) teacher's pet.
choucroute [ʃukʀut] *nf* sauerkraut.
chouette [ʃwɛt] *nf* owl // *a* (*fam*) great, smashing.
chou-fleur [ʃuflœʀ] *nm* cauliflower.
chou-rave [ʃuʀav] *nm* kohlrabi.
choyer [ʃwaje] *vt* to cherish; to pamper.
chrétien, ne [kʀetjɛ̃, -ɛn] *a, nm/f* Christian; **chrétiennement** *ad* in a Christian way *ou* spirit; **chrétienté** *nf* Christendom.
Christ [kʀist] *nm*: **le ~** Christ; **c~** (*crucifix etc*) figure of Christ; **christianiser** *vt* to convert to Christianity; **christianisme** *nm* Christianity.
chromatique [kʀɔmatik] *a* chromatic.
chrome [kʀom] *nm* chromium; **chromé, e** *a* chromium-plated.
chromosome [kʀɔmozom] *nm* chromosome.
chronique [kʀɔnik] *a* chronic // *nf* (*de journal*) column, page; (*historique*) chronicle; (RADIO, TV): **la ~ sportive/théâtrale** the sports/theatre review; **la ~ locale** local news and gossip; **chroniqueur** *nm* columnist; chronicler.
chronologie [kʀɔnɔlɔʒi] *nf* chronology; **chronologique** a chronological.
chronomètre [kʀɔnɔmɛtʀ(ə)] *nm* stopwatch; **chronométrer** *vt* to time.
chrysalide [kʀizalid] *nf* chrysalis.
chrysanthème [kʀizɑ̃tɛm] *nm* chrysanthemum.
chu, e [ʃy] *pp de* **choir.**
chuchoter [ʃyʃɔte] *vt, vi* to whisper.
chuinter [ʃɥɛ̃te] *vi* to hiss.
chut [ʃyt] *excl* sh!
chute [ʃyt] *nf* fall; (*de bois, papier: déchet*) scrap; **la ~ des cheveux** hair loss; **faire une ~ (de 10 m)** to fall (10 m); **~s de pluie/neige** rain/snowfalls; **~ (d'eau)** waterfall; **~ libre** free fall.

Chypre [ʃipʀ] *n* Cyprus; **chypriote** *a, nm/f* = **cypriote.**
-ci, ci- [si] *ad voir* **par, ci-contre, ci-joint** *etc* // *dét*: **ce garçon-ci/-là** this/that boy; **ces femmes-ci/-là** these/those women.
ci-après [siapʀɛ] *ad* hereafter.
cible [sibl(ə)] *nf* target.
ciboire [sibwaʀ] *nm* ciborium (*vessel*).
ciboule [sibul] *nf* (large) chive; **ciboulette** *nf* (smaller) chive.
cicatrice [sikatʀis] *nf* scar.
cicatriser [sikatʀize] *vt* to heal; **se ~** to heal (up), form a scar.
ci-contre [sikɔ̃tʀ(ə)] *ad* opposite.
ci-dessous [sidəsu] *ad* below.
ci-dessus [sidəsy] *ad* above.
ci-devant [sidəvɑ̃] *nm/f aristocrat who lost his/her title in the French Revolution.*
cidre [sidʀ(ə)] *nm* cider.
Cie *abr de* **compagnie.**
ciel [sjɛl] *nm* sky; (REL) heaven; **~s** *nmpl* (PEINTURE *etc*) skies; **cieux** *nmpl* sky *sg*, skies; (REL) heaven *sg*; **à ~ ouvert** open-air; (*mine*) opencast; **~ de lit** canopy.
cierge [sjɛʀʒ(ə)] *nm* candle.
cigale [sigal] *nf* cicada.
cigare [sigaʀ] *nm* cigar.
cigarette [sigaʀɛt] *nf* cigarette.
ci-gît [siʒi] *ad + vb* here lies.
cigogne [sigɔɲ] *nf* stork.
ciguë [sigy] *nf* hemlock.
ci-inclus, e [siɛ̃kly, -yz] *a, ad* enclosed.
ci-joint, e [siʒwɛ̃, -ɛ̃t] *a, ad* enclosed.
cil [sil] *nm* (eye)lash.
ciller [sije] *vi* to blink.
cimaise [simɛz] *nf* picture rail.
cime [sim] *nf* top; (*montagne*) peak.
ciment [simɑ̃] *nm* cement; **~ armé** reinforced concrete; **cimenter** *vt* to cement; **cimenterie** *nf* cement works *sg*.
cimetière [simtjɛʀ] *nm* cemetery; (*d'église*) churchyard; **~ de voitures** scrapyard.
cinéaste [sineast(ə)] *nm/f* film-maker.
ciné-club [sineklœb] *nm* film club; film society.
cinéma [sinema] *nm* cinema; **~scope** *nm* cinemascope; **~thèque** *nf* film archives *pl ou* library; **~tographique** *a* film *cpd*, cinema *cpd*.
cinéphile [sinefil] *nm/f* film *ou* cinema enthusiast.
cinétique [sinetik] *a* kinetic.
cinglé, e [sɛ̃gle] *a* (*fam*) barmy.
cingler [sɛ̃gle] *vt* to lash; (*fig*) to sting // *vi* (NAVIG): **~ vers** to make *ou* head for.
cinq [sɛ̃k] *num* five.
cinquantaine [sɛ̃kɑ̃tɛn] *nf*: **une ~ (de)** about fifty.
cinquante [sɛ̃kɑ̃t] *num* fifty; **~naire** *a, nm/f* fifty-year-old; **cinquantième** *num* fiftieth.
cinquième [sɛ̃kjɛm] *num* fifth.
cintre [sɛ̃tʀ(ə)] *nm* coat-hanger; (ARCHIT) arch; **~s** *nmpl* (THÉÂTRE) flies.
cintré, e [sɛ̃tʀe] *a* curved; (*chemise*) fitted, slim-fitting.
cirage [siʀaʒ] *nm* (shoe) polish.
circoncision [siʀkɔ̃sizjɔ̃] *nf* circumcision.
circonférence [siʀkɔ̃feʀɑ̃s] *nf* circumference.
circonflexe [siʀkɔ̃flɛks(ə)] *a*: **accent ~** circumflex accent.
circonscription [siʀkɔ̃skʀipsjɔ̃] *nf* district; **~ électorale** (*d'un député*) constituency.
circonscrire [siʀkɔ̃skʀiʀ] *vt* to define, delimit; (*incendie*) to contain.
circonspect, e [siʀkɔ̃spɛkt] *a* circumspect, cautious.
circonstance [siʀkɔ̃stɑ̃s] *nf* circumstance; (*occasion*) occasion; **~s atténuantes** attenuating circumstances.
circonstancié, e [siʀkɔ̃stɑ̃sje] *a* detailed.
circonstanciel, le [siʀkɔ̃stɑ̃sjɛl] *a*: **complément/proposition ~(le)** adverbial phrase/clause.
circonvenir [siʀkɔ̃vniʀ] *vt* to circumvent.
circonvolutions [siʀkɔ̃vɔlysjɔ̃] *nfpl* twists, convolutions.
circuit [siʀkɥi] *nm* (*trajet*) tour, (round) trip; (ÉLEC, TECH) circuit; **~ automobile** motor circuit; **~ de distribution** distribution network.
circulaire [siʀkylɛʀ] *a, nf* circular.
circulation [siʀkylɑsjɔ̃] *nf* circulation; (AUTO): **la ~** (the) traffic; **mettre en ~** to put into circulation.
circuler [siʀkyle] *vi* to drive (along); to walk along; (*train etc*) to run; (*sang, devises*) to circulate; **faire ~** (*nouvelle*) to spread (about), circulate; (*badauds*) to move on.
cire [siʀ] *nf* wax.
ciré [siʀe] *nm* oilskin.
cirer [siʀe] *vt* to wax, polish; **cireur** *nm* shoeshine-boy; **cireuse** *nf* floor polisher.
cirque [siʀk(ə)] *nm* circus; (*arène*) amphitheatre; (GÉO) cirque; (*fig*) chaos, bedlam; carry-on.
cirrhose [siʀoz] *nf*: **~ du foie** cirrhosis of the liver.
cisaille(s) [sizɑj] *nf(pl)* (gardening) shears *pl*; **cisailler** *vt* to clip.
ciseau, x [sizo] *nm*: **~ (à bois)** chisel; // *nmpl* (pair of) scissors; **sauter en ~x** to do a scissors jump; **~ à froid** cold chisel.
ciseler [sizle] *vt* to chisel, carve.
citadelle [sitadɛl] *nf* citadel.
citadin, e [sitadɛ̃, -in] *nm/f* city dweller // *a* town *cpd*, city *cpd*, urban.
citation [sitɑsjɔ̃] *nf* (*d'auteur*) quotation; (JUR) summons *sg*; (MIL: *récompense*) mention.
cité [site] *nf* town; (*plus grande*) city; **~ ouvrière** (workers') housing estate; **~ universitaire** students' residences *pl*.
citer [site] *vt* (*un auteur*) to quote (from); (*nommer*) to name; (JUR) to summon.
citerne [sitɛʀn(ə)] *nf* tank.
cithare [sitaʀ] *nf* zither.
citoyen, ne [sitwajɛ̃, -ɛn] *nm/f* citizen; **citoyenneté** *nf* citizenship.
citron [sitʀɔ̃] *nm* lemon; **~ vert** lime; **citronnade** *nf* lemonade; **citronnier** *nm* lemon tree.
citrouille [sitʀuj] *nf* pumpkin.
civet [sivɛ] *nm* stew; **~ de lièvre** jugged hare.

civette [sivɛt] *nf* (BOT) chives *pl*; (ZOOL) civet (cat).
civière [sivjɛʀ] *nf* stretcher.
civil, e [sivil] *a* (JUR, ADMIN, *poli*) civil; (*non militaire*) civilian // *nm* civilian; **en ~** in civilian clothes; **dans le ~** in civilian life.
civilisation [sivilizɑsjɔ̃] *nf* civilization.
civiliser [sivilize] *vt* to civilize.
civique [sivik] *a* civic.
civisme [sivism(ə)] *nm* public-spiritedness.
claie [klɛ] *nf* grid, riddle.
clair, e [klɛʀ] *a* light; (*chambre*) light, bright; (*eau, son, fig*) clear // *ad*: **voir ~** to see clearly; **bleu ~** light blue; **tirer qch au ~** to clear sth up, clarify sth; **mettre au ~** (*notes etc*) to tidy up; **le plus ~ de son temps/argent** the better part of his time/money; **en ~** (*non codé*) in clear; **~ de lune** *nm* moonlight; **~ement** *ad* clearly.
claire-voie [klɛʀvwa]: **à ~** *ad* letting the light through; openwork *cpd*.
clairière [klɛʀjɛʀ] *nf* clearing.
clairon [klɛʀɔ̃] *nm* bugle; **claironner** *vt* (*fig*) to trumpet, shout from the rooftops.
clairsemé, e [klɛʀsəme] *a* sparse.
clairvoyant, e [klɛʀvwajɑ̃, -ɑ̃t] *a* perceptive, clear-sighted.
clameur [klamœʀ] *nf* clamour.
clandestin, e [klɑ̃dɛstɛ̃, -in] *a* clandestine; (POL) underground, clandestine.
clapier [klapje] *nm* (rabbit) hutch.
clapoter [klapɔte] *vi* to lap; **clapotis** *nm* lap(ping).
claquage [klakaʒ] *nm* pulled *ou* strained muscle.
claque [klak] *nf* (*gifle*) slap.
claquer [klake] *vi* (*drapeau*) to flap; (*porte*) to bang, slam; (*coup de feu*) to ring out // *vt* (*porte*) to slam, bang; (*doigts*) to snap; **se ~ un muscle** to pull *ou* strain a muscle.
claquettes [klakɛt] *nfpl* tap-dancing *sg*.
clarifier [klaʀifje] *vt* (*fig*) to clarify.
clarinette [klaʀinɛt] *nf* clarinet.
clarté [klaʀte] *nf* lightness; brightness; (*d'un son, de l'eau*) clearness; (*d'une explication*) clarity.
classe [klɑs] *nf* class; (SCOL: *local*) class(room); (: *leçon*) class; (: *élèves*) class, form; **~ touriste** economy class; **faire ses ~s** (MIL) to do one's (recruit's) training; **faire la ~** (SCOL) to be a *ou* the teacher; to teach; **aller en ~** to go to school.
classement [klɑsmɑ̃] *nm* classifying; filing; grading; closing; (*rang*: SCOL) place; (: SPORT) placing; (*liste*: SCOL) class list (in order of merit); (: SPORT) placings *pl*; **premier au ~ général** (SPORT) first overall.
classer [klɑse] *vt* (*idées, livres*) to classify; (*papiers*) to file; (*candidat, concurrent*) to grade; (JUR: *affaire*) to close; **se ~ premier/dernier** to come first/last; (SPORT) to finish first/last.
classeur [klɑsœʀ] *nm* (*cahier*) file; (*meuble*) filing cabinet.
classification [klasifikɑsjɔ̃] *nf* classification.
classifier [klɑsifje] *vt* to classify.
classique [klasik] *a* classical; (*sobre: coupe etc*) classic(al); (*habituel*) standard, classic // *nm* classic; classical author.
claudication [klodikɑsjɔ̃] *nf* limp.
clause [kloz] *nf* clause.
claustrer [klostʀe] *vt* to confine.
claustrophobie [klostʀɔfɔbi] *nf* claustrophobia.
clavecin [klavsɛ̃] *nm* harpsichord.
clavicule [klavikyl] *nf* clavicle, collarbone.
clavier [klavje] *nm* keyboard.
clé *ou* **clef** [kle] *nf* key; (MUS) clef; (*de mécanicien*) spanner // *a*: **problème ~** key problem; **~ de sol/de fa** treble/bass clef; **~ anglaise** (monkey) wrench; **~ de contact** ignition key; **~ à molette** adjustable spanner; **~ de voûte** keystone.
clémence [klemɑ̃s] *nf* mildness; leniency.
clément, e [klemɑ̃, -ɑ̃t] *a* (*temps*) mild; (*indulgent*) lenient.
cleptomane [klɛptɔman] *nm/f* = **kleptomane.**
clerc [klɛʀ] *nm*: **~ de notaire** solicitor's clerk.
clergé [klɛʀʒe] *nm* clergy.
clérical, e, aux [kleʀikal, -o] *a* clerical.
cliché [kliʃe] *nm* (PHOTO) negative; print; (TYPO) (printing) plate; (LING) cliché.
client, e [klijɑ̃, -ɑ̃t] *nm/f* (*acheteur*) customer, client; (*d'hôtel*) guest, patron; (*du docteur*) patient; (*de l'avocat*) client; **clientèle** *nf* (*du magasin*) customers *pl*, clientèle; (*du docteur, de l'avocat*) practice; **accorder sa clientèle à** to give one's custom to.
cligner [kliɲe] *vi*: **~ des yeux** to blink (one's eyes); **~ de l'œil** to wink.
clignotant [kliɲɔtɑ̃] *nm* (AUTO) indicator.
clignoter [kliɲɔte] *vi* (*étoiles etc*) to twinkle; (*lumière: à intervalles réguliers*) to flash; (: *vaciller*) to flicker.
climat [klima] *nm* climate; **climatique** *a* climatic.
climatisation [klimatizɑsjɔ̃] *nf* air conditioning; **climatisé, e** *a* air-conditioned.
clin d'œil [klɛ̃dœj] *nm* wink; **en un ~** in a flash.
clinique [klinik] *a* clinical // *nf* nursing home, (private) clinic.
clinquant, e [klɛ̃kɑ̃, -ɑ̃t] *a* flashy.
cliqueter [klikte] *vi* to clash; to jangle, jingle; to chink.
clitoris [klitɔʀis] *nm* clitoris.
clivage [klivaʒ] *nm* cleavage.
clochard, e [klɔʃaʀ, -aʀd(ə)] *nm/f* tramp.
cloche [klɔʃ] *nf* (*d'église*) bell; (*fam*) clot; **~ à fromage** cheese-cover.
cloche-pied [klɔʃpje]: **à ~** *ad* on one leg, hopping (along).
clocher [klɔʃe] *nm* church tower; (*en pointe*) steeple // *vi* (*fam*) to be *ou* go wrong; **de ~** (*péj*) parochial.
clocheton [klɔʃtɔ̃] *nm* pinnacle.
clochette [klɔʃɛt] *nf* bell.
cloison [klwazɔ̃] *nf* partition (wall); **cloisonner** *vt* to partition (off); to divide up; (*fig*) to compartmentalize.

cloître [klwatʀ(ə)] *nm* cloister.
cloîtrer [klwatʀe] *vt*: **se** ~ to shut o.s. up *ou* away; (*REL*) to enter a convent *ou* monastery.
clopin-clopant [klɔpɛ̃klɔpɑ̃] *ad* hobbling along; (*fig*) so-so.
cloporte [klɔpɔʀt(ə)] *nm* woodlouse (*pl* lice).
cloque [klɔk] *nf* blister.
clore [klɔʀ] *vt* to close; **clos, e** *a voir* **maison, huis, vase** // *nm* (enclosed) field.
clôture [klotyʀ] *nf* closure, closing; (*barrière*) enclosure, fence; **clôturer** *vt* (*terrain*) to enclose, close off; (*festival, débats*) to close.
clou [klu] *nm* nail; (*MÉD*) boil; ~**s** *nmpl* = **passage clouté**; **pneus à** ~**s** studded tyres; **le** ~ **du spectacle** the highlight of the show; ~ **de girofle** clove; ~**er** *vt* to nail down *ou* up; (*fig*): ~**er sur/contre** to pin to/against; ~**té, e** *a* studded.
clown [klun] *nm* clown; **faire le** ~ (*fig*) to clown (about), play the fool.
club [klœb] *nm* club.
C.N.R.S. *sigle m* = *Centre national de la recherche scientifique*.
coaguler [kɔagyle] *vi, vt*, **se** ~ to coagulate.
coaliser [kɔalize]: **se** ~ *vi* to unite, join forces.
coalition [kɔalisjɔ̃] *nf* coalition.
coasser [kɔase] *vi* to croak.
cobaye [kɔbaj] *nm* guinea-pig.
cocagne [kɔkaɲ] *nf*: **pays de** ~ land of plenty; **mât de** ~ greasy pole (*fig*).
cocaïne [kɔkain] *nf* cocaine.
cocarde [kɔkaʀd(ə)] *nf* rosette.
cocardier, ère [kɔkaʀdje, -ɛʀ] *a* jingoistic, chauvinistic.
cocasse [kɔkas] *a* comical, funny.
coccinelle [kɔksinɛl] *nf* ladybird.
coccyx [kɔksis] *nm* coccyx.
cocher [kɔʃe] *nm* coachman // *vt* to tick off; (*entailler*) to notch.
cochère [kɔʃɛʀ] *af*: **porte** ~ carriage entrance.
cochon, ne [kɔʃɔ̃, -ɔn] *nm* pig // *nm/f* (*péj*) (filthy) pig; beast; swine // *a* (*fam*) dirty, smutty; **cochonnerie** *nf* (*fam*) filth; rubbish, trash.
cochonnet [kɔʃɔnɛ] *nm* (*BOULES*) jack.
cocktail [kɔktɛl] *nm* cocktail; (*réception*) cocktail party.
coco [kɔko] *nm voir* **noix**; (*fam*) bloke, geezer.
cocon [kɔkɔ̃] *nm* cocoon.
cocorico [kɔkɔʀiko] *excl, nm* cock-a-doodle-do.
cocotier [kɔkɔtje] *nm* coconut palm.
cocotte [kɔkɔt] *nf* (*en fonte*) casserole; ~ **(minute)** pressure cooker; ~ **en papier** paper shape; **ma** ~ (*fam*) sweetie (pie).
cocu [kɔky] *nm* cuckold.
code [kɔd] *nm* code // *a*: **éclairage** ~, **phares** ~**s** dipped lights; **se mettre en** ~**(s)** to dip one's (head)lights; ~ **civil** Common Law; ~ **pénal** penal code; ~ **postal** (*numéro*) postal code; ~ **de la route** highway code; **coder** *vt* to (en)code; **codifier** *vt* to codify.
coefficient [kɔefisjɑ̃] *nm* coefficient.
coercition [kɔɛʀsisjɔ̃] *nf* coercion.
cœur [kœʀ] *nm* heart; (*CARTES: couleur*) hearts *pl*; (: *carte*) heart; **avoir bon** ~ to be kind-hearted; **avoir mal au** ~ to feel sick; ~ **de laitue/d'artichaut** lettuce/artichoke heart; **de tout son** ~ with all one's heart; **en avoir le** ~ **net** to be clear in one's own mind (about it); **par** ~ by heart; **de bon** ~ willingly; **avoir à** ~ **de faire** to make a point of doing; **cela lui tient à** ~ that's (very) close to his heart.
coffrage [kɔfʀaʒ] *nm* (*CONSTR: action*) coffering; (: *dispositif*) form(work).
coffre [kɔfʀ(ə)] *nm* (*meuble*) chest; (*d'auto*) boot; **avoir du** ~ (*fam*) to have a lot of puff; ~**(-fort)** *nm* safe.
coffrer [kɔfʀe] *vt* (*fam*) to put inside, lock up.
coffret [kɔfʀɛ] *nm* casket; ~ **à bijoux** jewel box.
cogner [kɔɲe] *vi* to knock.
cohabiter [kɔabite] *vi* to live together.
cohérent, e [kɔeʀɑ̃, -ɑ̃t] *a* coherent, consistent.
cohésion [kɔezjɔ̃] *nf* cohesion.
cohorte [kɔɔʀt(ə)] *nf* troop.
cohue [kɔy] *nf* crowd.
coi, coite [kwa, kwat] *a*: **rester** ~ to remain silent.
coiffe [kwaf] *nf* headdress.
coiffé, e [kwafe] *a*: **bien/mal** ~ with tidy/untidy hair; ~ **d'un béret** wearing a beret; ~ **en arrière** with one's hair brushed *ou* combed back.
coiffer [kwafe] *vt* (*fig*) to cover, top; ~ **qn** to do sb's hair; ~ **qn d'un béret** to put a beret on sb; **se** ~ to do one's hair; to put on a *ou* one's hat.
coiffeur, euse [kwafœʀ, -øz] *nm/f* hairdresser // *nf* (*table*) dressing table.
coiffure [kwafyʀ] *nf* (*cheveux*) hairstyle, hairdo; (*chapeau*) hat, headgear *q*; (*art*): **la** ~ hairdressing.
coin [kwɛ̃] *nm* corner; (*pour graver*) die; (*pour coincer*) wedge; (*poinçon*) hallmark; **l'épicerie du** ~ the local grocer; **dans le** ~ (*les alentours*) in the area, around about; locally; **au** ~ **du feu** by the fireside; **regard en** ~ side(ways) glance.
coincer [kwɛ̃se] *vt* to jam; (*fam*) to catch (out); to nab.
coïncidence [kɔɛ̃sidɑ̃s] *nf* coincidence.
coïncider [kɔɛ̃side] *vi*: ~ **(avec)** to coincide (with).
coing [kwɛ̃] *nm* quince.
coït [kɔit] *nm* coitus.
coite [kwat] *af voir* **coi**.
coke [kɔk] *nm* coke.
col [kɔl] *nm* (*de chemise*) collar; (*encolure, cou*) neck; (*de montagne*) pass; ~ **du fémur** neck of the thighbone; ~ **roulé** polo-neck; ~ **de l'utérus** cervix.
coléoptère [kɔleɔptɛʀ] *nm* beetle.
colère [kɔlɛʀ] *nf* anger; **une** ~ a fit of anger; **coléreux, euse** *a*, **colérique** *a* quick-tempered, irascible.
colifichet [kɔlifiʃɛ] *nm* trinket.
colimaçon [kɔlimasɔ̃] *nm*: **escalier en** ~ spiral staircase.

colin [kɔlɛ̃] *nm* hake.
colique [kɔlik] *nf* diarrhoea ; colic (pains).
colis [kɔli] *nm* parcel.
collaborateur, trice [kɔlabɔʀatœʀ, -tʀis] *nm/f* (*aussi* POL) collaborator ; (*d'une revue*) contributor.
collaboration [kɔlabɔʀɑsjɔ̃] *nf* collaboration.
collaborer [kɔlabɔʀe] *vi* to collaborate ; ~ **à** to collaborate on ; (*revue*) to contribute to.
collant, e [kɔlɑ̃, -ɑ̃t] *a* sticky ; (*robe etc*) clinging, skintight ; (*péj*) clinging // *nm* (*bas*) tights *pl* ; (*de danseur*) leotard.
collation [kɔlɑsjɔ̃] *nf* light meal.
colle [kɔl] *nf* glue ; (*à papiers peints*) (wallpaper) paste ; (*devinette*) teaser, poser.
collecte [kɔlɛkt(ə)] *nf* collection.
collecter [kɔlɛkte] *vt* to collect ; **collecteur** *nm* (*égout*) main sewer.
collectif, ive [kɔlɛktif, -iv] *a* collective ; (*visite, billet etc*) group *cpd*.
collection [kɔlɛksjɔ̃] *nf* collection ; (ÉDITION) series ; **pièce de** ~ collector's item ; **faire (la)** ~ **de** to collect ; **collectionner** *vt* (*tableaux, timbres*) to collect ; **collectionneur, euse** *nm/f* collector.
collectivité [kɔlɛktivite] *nf* group ; **la** ~ the community, the collectivity ; **les** ~**s locales** local communities.
collège [kɔlɛʒ] *nm* (*école*) (secondary) school ; (*assemblée*) body ; **collégial, e, aux** *a* collegiate ; **collégien, ne** *nm/f* schoolboy/girl.
collègue [kɔlɛg] *nm/f* colleague.
coller [kɔle] *vt* (*papier, timbre*) to stick (on) ; (*affiche*) to stick up ; (*enveloppe*) to stick down ; (*morceaux*) to stick *ou* glue together ; (*fam: mettre, fourrer*) to stick, shove ; (SCOL: *fam*) to keep in, give detention to // *vi* (*être collant*) to be sticky ; (*adhérer*) to stick ; ~ **qch sur** to stick (*ou* paste *ou* glue) sth on(to) ; ~ **à** to stick to ; (*fig*) to cling to.
collerette [kɔlʀɛt] *nf* ruff ; (TECH) flange.
collet [kɔlɛ] *nm* (*piège*) snare, noose ; (*cou*): **prendre qn au** ~ to grab sb by the throat ; ~ **monté** *a inv* straight-laced.
collier [kɔlje] *nm* (*bijou*) necklace ; (*de chien*, TECH) collar ; ~ **(de barbe), barbe en** ~ narrow beard along the line of the jaw.
colline [kɔlin] *nf* hill.
collision [kɔlizjɔ̃] *nf* collision, crash ; **entrer en** ~ **(avec)** to collide (with).
colloque [kɔlɔk] *nm* colloquium, symposium.
colmater [kɔlmate] *vt* (*fuite*) to seal off ; (*brèche*) to plug, fill in.
colombe [kɔlɔ̃b] *nf* dove.
colon [kɔlɔ̃] *nm* settler ; (*enfant*) boarder (*in children's holiday camp*).
côlon [kolɔ̃] *nm* colon.
colonel [kɔlɔnɛl] *nm* colonel ; (*armée de l'air*) group captain.
colonial, e, aux [kɔlɔnjal, -o] *a* colonial ; ~**isme** *nm* colonialism.
colonie [kɔlɔni] *nf* colony ; ~ **(de vacances)** holiday camp (*for children*).
colonisation [kɔlɔnizɑsjɔ̃] *nf* colonization.
coloniser [kɔlɔnize] *vt* to colonize.
colonne [kɔlɔn] *nf* column ; **se mettre en** ~ **par deux/quatre** to get into twos/fours ; **en** ~ **par deux** in double file ; ~ **de secours** rescue party ; ~ **(vertébrale)** spine, spinal column.
colophane [kɔlɔfan] *nf* rosin.
colorant [kɔlɔʀɑ̃] *nm* colouring.
coloration [kɔlɔʀɑsjɔ̃] *nf* colour(ing).
colorer [kɔlɔʀe] *vt* to colour.
colorier [kɔlɔʀje] *vt* to colour (in) ; **album à** ~ colouring book.
coloris [kɔlɔʀi] *nm* colour, shade.
colossal, e, aux [kɔlɔsal, -o] *a* colossal, huge.
colporter [kɔlpɔʀte] *vt* to hawk, peddle ; **colporteur, euse** *nm/f* hawker, pedlar.
colza [kɔlza] *nm* rape(seed).
coma [kɔma] *nm* coma ; **être dans le** ~ to be in a coma ; ~**teux, euse** *a* comatose.
combat [kɔ̃ba] *nm* fight ; fighting *q* ; ~ **de boxe** boxing match ; ~ **de rues** street fighting *q*.
combatif, ive [kɔ̃batif, -iv] *a* of a fighting spirit.
combattant [kɔ̃batɑ̃] *nm* combatant ; (*d'une rixe*) brawler ; **ancien** ~ war veteran.
combattre [kɔ̃batʀ(ə)] *vt* to fight ; (*épidémie, ignorance*) to combat, fight against.
combien [kɔ̃bjɛ̃] *ad* (*quantité*) how much ; (*nombre*) how many ; (*exclamatif*) how ; ~ **de** how much ; how many ; ~ **de temps** how long, how much time ; ~ **coûte/pèse ceci?** how much does this cost/weigh?
combinaison [kɔ̃binɛzɔ̃] *nf* combination ; (*astuce*) device, scheme ; (*de femme*) slip ; (*d'aviateur*) flying suit ; (*d'homme-grenouille*) wetsuit ; (*bleu de travail*) boilersuit.
combine [kɔ̃bin] *nf* trick ; (*péj*) scheme, fiddle.
combiné [kɔ̃bine] *nm* (*aussi*: ~ **téléphonique**) receiver.
combiner [kɔ̃bine] *vt* to combine ; (*plan, horaire*) to work out, devise.
comble [kɔ̃bl(ə)] *a* (*salle*) packed (full) // *nm* (*du bonheur, plaisir*) height ; ~**s** *nmpl* (CONSTR) attic *sg*, loft *sg* ; **c'est le** ~**!** that beats everything!, that takes the biscuit!
combler [kɔ̃ble] *vt* (*trou*) to fill in ; (*besoin, lacune*) to fill ; (*déficit*) to make good ; (*satisfaire*) to gratify, fulfil ; ~ **qn de joie** to fill sb with joy ; ~ **qn d'honneurs** to shower sb with honours.
combustible [kɔ̃bystibl(ə)] *a* combustible // *nm* fuel.
combustion [kɔ̃bystjɔ̃] *nf* combustion.
comédie [kɔmedi] *nf* comedy ; (*fig*) playacting *q* ; ~ **musicale** musical ; **comédien, ne** *nm/f* actor/actress ; (*comique*) comedy actor/actress, comedian/comedienne ; (*fig*) sham.
comestible [kɔmɛstibl(ə)] *a* edible.
comète [kɔmɛt] *nf* comet.
comique [kɔmik] *a* (*drôle*) comical ; (THÉÂTRE) comic // *nm* (*artiste*) comic,

comedian; **le ~ de qch** the funny *ou* comical side of sth.

comité [kɔmite] *nm* committee; **~ d'entreprise** work's council.

commandant [kɔmɑ̃dɑ̃] *nm* (*gén*) commander, commandant; (*MIL: grade*) major; (*armée de l'air*) squadron leader; (*NAVIG, AVIAT*) captain.

commande [kɔmɑ̃d] *nf* (*COMM*) order; **~s** *nfpl* (*AVIAT etc*) controls; **passer une ~ (de)** to put in an order (for); **sur ~** to order; **~ à distance** remote control.

commandement [kɔmɑ̃dmɑ̃] *nm* command; (*ordre*) command, order; (*REL*) commandment.

commander [kɔmɑ̃de] *vt* (*COMM*) to order; (*diriger, ordonner*) to command; **~ à** (*MIL*) to command; (*contrôler, maîtriser*) to have control over; **~ à qn de faire** to command *ou* order sb to do.

commanditaire [kɔmɑ̃ditɛʀ] *nm* sleeping partner.

commandite [kɔmɑ̃dit] *nf*: **(société en) ~** limited partnership.

commando [kɔmɑ̃do] *nm* commando (squad).

comme [kɔm] *prép* like; (*en tant que*) as // *cj* as; (*parce que, puisque*) as, since // *ad*: **~ il est fort/c'est bon!** how strong he is/good it is!; **faites-le ~ cela** *ou* **ça** do it like this *ou* this way; **~ ci ~ ça** so-so, middling; **joli ~ tout** ever so pretty.

commémoration [kɔmemɔʀɑsjɔ̃] *nf* commemoration.

commémorer [kɔmemɔʀe] *vt* to commemorate.

commencement [kɔmɑ̃smɑ̃] *nm* beginning; start; commencement; **~s** (*débuts*) beginnings.

commencer [kɔmɑ̃se] *vt* to begin, start, commence; (*être placé au début de*) to begin // *vi* to begin, start, commence; **~ à** *ou* **de faire** to begin *ou* start doing.

commensal, e, aux [kɔmɑ̃sal, -o] *nm/f* companion at table.

comment [kɔmɑ̃] *ad* how; **~?** (*que dites-vous*) (I beg your) pardon?

commentaire [kɔmɑ̃tɛʀ] *nm* comment; remark; **~ (de texte)** (*SCOL*) commentary.

commentateur, trice [kɔmɑ̃tatœʀ, -tʀis] *nm/f* commentator.

commenter [kɔmɑ̃te] *vt* (*jugement, événement*) to comment (up)on; (*RADIO, TV: match, manifestation*) to cover, give a commentary on.

commérages [kɔmeʀaʒ] *nmpl* gossip *sg*.

commerçant, e [kɔmɛʀsɑ̃, -ɑ̃t] *a* commercial; shopping; trading; commercially shrewd // *nm/f* shopkeeper, trader.

commerce [kɔmɛʀs(ə)] *nm* (*activité*) trade, commerce; (*boutique*) business; **le petit ~** small shopowners *pl*, small traders *pl*; **faire ~ de** to trade in; (*fig: péj*) to trade on; **vendu dans le ~** sold in the shops; **vendu hors-~** sold directly to the public; **commercial, e, aux** *a* commercial, trading; (*péj*) commercial; **commercialiser** *vt* to market.

commère [kɔmɛʀ] *nf* gossip.

commettre [kɔmɛtʀ(ə)] *vt* to commit.

commis [kɔmi] *nm* (*de magasin*) (shop) assistant; (*de banque*) clerk; **~ voyageur** commercial traveller.

commisération [kɔmizeʀɑsjɔ̃] *nf* commiseration.

commissaire [kɔmisɛʀ] *nm* (*de police*) ≈ (police) superintendent; (*de rencontre sportive etc*) steward; **~-priseur** *nm* auctioneer.

commissariat [kɔmisaʀja] *nm* police station; (*ADMIN*) commissionership.

commission [kɔmisjɔ̃] *nf* (*comité, pourcentage*) commission; (*message*) message; (*course*) errand; **~s** *nfpl (achats)* shopping *sg*; **commissionnaire** *nm* delivery boy (*ou* man); messenger.

commissure [kɔmisyʀ] *nf*: **les ~s des lèvres** the corners of the mouth.

commode [kɔmɔd] *a* (*pratique*) convenient, handy; (*facile*) easy; (*air, personne*) easy-going; (*personne*): **pas ~** awkward (to deal with) // *nf* chest of drawers; **commodité** *nf* convenience.

commotion [kɔmosjɔ̃] *nf*: **~ (cérébrale)** concussion; **commotionné, e** *a* shocked, shaken.

commuer [kɔmɥe] *vt* to commute.

commun, e [kɔmœ̃, -yn] *a* common; (*pièce*) communal, shared; (*réunion, effort*) joint // *nf* (*ADMIN*) commune, ≈ district; (*: urbaine*) ≈ borough; **~s** *nmpl* (*bâtiments*) outbuildings; **cela sort du ~** it's out of the ordinary; **le ~ des mortels** the common run of people; **en ~** (*faire*) jointly; **mettre en ~** to pool, share; **communal, e, aux** *a* (*ADMIN*) of the commune, ≈ (district *ou* borough) council *cpd*.

communauté [kɔmynote] *nf* community; (*JUR*): **régime de la ~** communal estate settlement.

commune [kɔmyn] *a, nf voir* **commun.**

communiant, e [kɔmynjɑ̃, -ɑ̃t] *nm/f* communicant; **premier ~** child taking his first communion.

communicatif, ive [kɔmynikatif, -iv] *a* (*personne*) communicative; (*rire*) infectious.

communication [kɔmynikɑsjɔ̃] *nf* communication; **~ (téléphonique)** (telephone) call; **vous avez la ~** this is your call, you're through; **donnez-moi la ~ avec** put me through to; **~ interurbaine** trunk call; **~ en PCV** reverse charge call.

communier [kɔmynje] *vi* (*REL*) to receive communion; (*fig*) to be united.

communion [kɔmynjɔ̃] *nf* communion.

communiqué [kɔmynike] *nm* communiqué.

communiquer [kɔmynike] *vt* (*nouvelle, dossier*) to pass on, convey; (*maladie*) to pass on; (*peur etc*) to communicate; (*chaleur, mouvement*) to transmit // *vi* to communicate; **se ~ à** (*se propager*) to spread to.

communisme [kɔmynism(ə)] *nm* communism; **communiste** *a, nm/f* communist.

commutateur [kɔmytatœʀ] *nm* (*ÉLEC*) (change-over) switch, commutator.

compact, e [kɔ̃pakt] *a* dense; compact.
compagne [kɔ̃paɲ] *nf* companion.
compagnie [kɔ̃paɲi] *nf* (*firme*, MIL) company; (*groupe*) gathering; (*présence*): **la ~ de qn** sb's company; **tenir ~ à qn** to keep sb company; **fausser ~ à** to give sb the slip, slip *ou* sneak away from sb; **en ~ de** in the company of; **Dupont et ~, Dupont et Cie** Dupont and Company, Dupont and Co.
compagnon [kɔ̃paɲɔ̃] *nm* companion; (*autrefois: ouvrier*) craftsman; journeyman.
comparable [kɔ̃paʀabl(ə)] *a*: **~ (à)** comparable (to).
comparaison [kɔ̃paʀɛzɔ̃] *nf* comparison; (*métaphore*) simile.
comparaître [kɔ̃paʀɛtʀ(ə)] *vi*: **~ (devant)** to appear (before).
comparatif, ive [kɔ̃paʀatif, -iv] *a* comparative.
comparé, e [kɔ̃paʀe] *a*: **littérature** *etc* **~e** comparative literature *etc*.
comparer [kɔ̃paʀe] *vt* to compare; **~ qch/qn à** *ou* **et** (*pour choisir*) to compare sth/sb with *ou* and; (*pour établir une similitude*) to compare sth/sb to.
comparse [kɔ̃paʀs(ə)] *nm/f* (*péj*) associate, stooge.
compartiment [kɔ̃paʀtimɑ̃] *nm* compartment; **compartimenté, e** *a* partitioned; (*fig*) compartmentalized.
comparution [kɔ̃paʀysjɔ̃] *nf* appearance.
compas [kɔ̃pa] *nm* (GÉOM) (pair of) compasses *pl*; (NAVIG) compass.
compassé, e [kɔ̃pɑse] *a* starchy, formal.
compassion [kɔ̃pɑsjɔ̃] *nf* compassion.
compatible [kɔ̃patibl(ə)] *a* compatible.
compatir [kɔ̃patiʀ] *vi*: **~ (à)** to sympathize (with).
compatriote [kɔ̃patʀijɔt] *nm/f* compatriot.
compensation [kɔ̃pɑ̃sɑsjɔ̃] *nf* compensation; (BANQUE) clearing.
compenser [kɔ̃pɑ̃se] *vt* to compensate for, make up for.
compère [kɔ̃pɛʀ] *nm* accomplice.
compétence [kɔ̃petɑ̃s] *nf* competence.
compétent, e [kɔ̃petɑ̃, -ɑ̃t] *a* (*apte*) competent, capable; (JUR) competent.
compétition [kɔ̃petisjɔ̃] *nf* (*gén*) competition; (SPORT: *épreuve*) event; **la ~** competitive sport; **la ~ automobile** motor racing.
compiler [kɔ̃pile] *vt* to compile.
complainte [kɔ̃plɛ̃t] *nf* lament.
complaire [kɔ̃plɛʀ]: **se ~** *vi*: **se ~ dans/parmi** to take pleasure in/in being among.
complaisance [kɔ̃plɛzɑ̃s] *nf* kindness; (*péj*) indulgence; **attestation de ~** *certificate produced to oblige a patient etc*; **pavillon de ~** flag of convenience.
complaisant, e [kɔ̃plɛzɑ̃, -ɑ̃t] *a* (*aimable*) kind; obliging; (*péj*) over-obliging, indulgent.
complément [kɔ̃plemɑ̃] *nm* complement; supplement; remainder; (LING) complement; **~ d'information** (ADMIN) supplementary *ou* further information; **~ d'agent** agent; **~ (d'objet) direct/indirect** direct/indirect object; **~ (circonstanciel) de lieu/temps** adverbial phrase of place/time; **~ de nom** possessive phrase; **complémentaire** *a* complementary; (*additionnel*) supplementary.
complet, ète [kɔ̃plɛ, -ɛt] *a* complete; (*plein: hôtel etc*) full // *nm* (*aussi*: **~-veston**) suit; **compléter** *vt* (*porter à la quantité voulue*) to complete; (*augmenter*) to complement, supplement; to add to; **se compléter** *vt réciproque* (*personnes*) to complement one another // *vi* (*collection etc*) to be building up.
complexe [kɔ̃plɛks(ə)] *a* complex // *nm* (PSYCH) complex, hang-up; (*bâtiments*): **~ hospitalier** hospital complex; **complexé, e** *a* mixed-up, hung-up; **complexité** *nf* complexity.
complication [kɔ̃plikɑsjɔ̃] *nf* complexity, intricacy; (*difficulté, ennui*) complication.
complice [kɔ̃plis] *nm* accomplice; **complicité** *nf* complicity.
compliment [kɔ̃plimɑ̃] *nm* (*louange*) compliment; **~s** *nmpl* (*félicitations*) congratulations; **complimenter qn (sur** *ou* **de)** to congratulate *ou* compliment sb (on).
compliqué, e [kɔ̃plike] *a* complicated, complex, intricate; (*personne*) complicated.
compliquer [kɔ̃plike] *vt* to complicate; **se ~** *vi* (*situation*) to become complicated; **se ~ la vie** to make life difficult *ou* complicated for o.s.
complot [kɔ̃plo] *nm* plot; **comploter** *vi, vt* to plot.
comportement [kɔ̃pɔʀtəmɑ̃] *nm* behaviour; (TECH: *d'une pièce, d'un véhicule*) behaviour, performance.
comporter [kɔ̃pɔʀte] *vt* to be composed of, consist of, comprise; (*être équipé de*) to have; (*impliquer*) to entail, involve; **se ~** *vi* to behave; (TECH) to behave, perform.
composant [kɔ̃pozɑ̃] *nm* component, constituent.
composante [kɔ̃pozɑ̃t] *nf* component.
composé, e [kɔ̃poze] *a* (*visage, air*) studied; (BIO, CHIMIE, LING) compound // *nm* (CHIMIE, LING) compound.
composer [kɔ̃poze] *vt* (*musique, texte*) to compose; (*mélange, équipe*) to make up; (*faire partie de*) to make up, form; (TYPO) to set // *vi* (SCOL) to sit *ou* do a test; (*transiger*) to come to terms; **se ~ de** to be composed of, be made up of; **~ un numéro** (*au téléphone*) to dial a number.
composite [kɔ̃pozit] *a* heterogeneous.
compositeur, trice [kɔ̃pozitœʀ, -tʀis] *nm/f* (MUS) composer; (TYPO) compositor, typesetter.
composition [kɔ̃pozisjɔ̃] *nf* composition; (SCOL) test; (TYPO) typesetting, composition; **de bonne ~** (*accommodant*) easy to deal with; **amener qn à ~** to get sb to come to terms.
composter [kɔ̃pɔste] *vt* to date stamp; to punch; **composteur** *nm* date stamp; punch; (TYPO) composing stick.
compote [kɔ̃pɔt] *nf* stewed fruit *q*; **~ de pommes** stewed apples; **compotier** *nm* fruit dish *ou* bowl.
compréhensible [kɔ̃pʀeɑ̃sibl(ə)] *a* comprehensible; (*attitude*) understandable.

compréhensif, ive [kɔ̃pReɑ̃sif, -iv] *a* understanding.
compréhension [kɔ̃pReɑ̃sjɔ̃] *nf* understanding; comprehension.
comprendre [kɔ̃pRɑ̃dR(ə)] *vt* to understand; (*se composer de*) to comprise, consist of.
compresse [kɔ̃pRɛs] *nf* compress.
compresseur [kɔ̃pRɛsœR] *am voir* **rouleau.**
compression [kɔ̃pRɛsjɔ̃] *nf* compression; reduction.
comprimé, e [kɔ̃pRime] *a*: **air ~** compressed air // *nm* tablet.
comprimer [kɔ̃pRime] *vt* to compress; (*fig*: *crédit etc*) to reduce, cut down.
compris, e [kɔ̃pRi, -iz] *pp de* **comprendre** // *a* (*inclus*) included; **~ entre** (*situé*) contained between; **la maison ~e/non ~e, y/non ~ la maison** including/excluding the house; **service ~** service (charge) included; **100 F tout ~** 100 F all inclusive *ou* all-in.
compromettre [kɔ̃pRɔmɛtR(ə)] *vt* to compromise.
compromis [kɔ̃pRɔmi] *nm* compromise.
compromission [kɔ̃pRɔmisjɔ̃] *nf* compromise, deal.
comptabilité [kɔ̃tabilite] *nf* (*activité, technique*) accounting, accountancy; (*d'une société*: *comptes*) accounts *pl*, books *pl*; (: *service*) accounts office *ou* department.
comptable [kɔ̃tabl(ə)] *nm/f* accountant // *a* accounts *cpd*, accounting.
comptant [kɔ̃tɑ̃] *ad*: **payer ~** to pay cash; **acheter ~** to buy for cash.
compte [kɔ̃t] *nm* count, counting; (*total, montant*) count, (right) number; (*bancaire, facture*) account; **~s** *nmpl* accounts, books; (*fig*) explanation *sg*; **faire le ~ de** to count up, make a count of; **en fin de ~** (*fig*) all things considered, weighing it all up; **à bon ~** at a favourable price; (*fig*) lightly; **avoir son ~** (*fig*: *fam*) to have had it; **pour le ~ de** on behalf of; **travailler à son ~** to work for oneself; **rendre ~ (à qn) de qch** to give (sb) an account of sth; **~ chèques postaux (C.C.P.)** ≈ (Post Office) Giro account; **~ courant** current account; **~ de dépôt** deposit account; **~ à rebours** countdown.
compte-gouttes [kɔ̃tgut] *nm inv* dropper.
compter [kɔ̃te] *vt* to count; (*facturer*) to charge for; (*avoir à son actif, comporter*) to have; (*prévoir*) to allow, reckon; (*espérer*): **~ réussir/revenir** to expect to succeed/return // *vi* to count; (*être économe*) to economize; (*être non négligeable*) to count, matter; (*valoir*): **~ pour** to count for; (*figurer*): **~ parmi** to be *ou* rank among; **~ sur** *vt* to count (up)on; **~ avec qch/qn** to reckon with *ou* take account of sth/sb; **sans ~ que** besides which; **à ~ du 10 janvier** (*COMM*) (as) from 10th January.
compte-rendu [kɔ̃tRɑ̃dy] *nm* account, report; (*de film, livre*) review.
compte-tours [kɔ̃ttuR] *nm inv* rev(olution) counter.
compteur [kɔ̃tœR] *nm* meter; **~ de vitesse** speedometer.
comptine [kɔ̃tin] *nf* nursery rhyme.
comptoir [kɔ̃twaR] *nm* (*de magasin*) counter; (*de café*) counter, bar; (*colonial*) trading post.
compulser [kɔ̃pylse] *vt* to consult.
comte, comtesse [kɔ̃t, kɔ̃tɛs] *nm/f* count/countess.
con, ne [kɔ̃, kɔn] *a* (*fam*!) bloody stupid (!).
concave [kɔ̃kav] *a* concave.
concéder [kɔ̃sede] *vt* to grant; (*défaite, point*) to concede; **~ que** to concede that.
concentration [kɔ̃sɑ̃tRɑsjɔ̃] *nf* concentration.
concentrationnaire [kɔ̃sɑ̃tRɑsjɔnɛR] *a* of *ou* in concentration camps.
concentré [kɔ̃sɑ̃tRe] *nm* concentrate.
concentrer [kɔ̃sɑ̃tRe] *vt* to concentrate; **se ~** to concentrate.
concentrique [kɔ̃sɑ̃tRik] *a* concentric.
concept [kɔ̃sɛpt] *nm* concept.
conception [kɔ̃sɛpsjɔ̃] *nf* conception.
concerner [kɔ̃sɛRne] *vt* to concern; **en ce qui me concerne** as far as I am concerned; **en ce qui concerne ceci** as far as this is concerned, with regard to this.
concert [kɔ̃sɛR] *nm* concert; **de ~** *ad* in unison; together.
concerter [kɔ̃sɛRte] *vt* to devise; **se ~** (*collaborateurs etc*) to put one's heads together, consult (each other).
concertiste [kɔ̃sɛRtist(ə)] *nm/f* concert artist.
concerto [kɔ̃sɛRto] *nm* concerto.
concession [kɔ̃sesjɔ̃] *nf* concession.
concessionnaire [kɔ̃sesjɔnɛR] *nm/f* agent, dealer.
concevoir [kɔ̃svwaR] *vt* (*idée, projet*) to conceive (of); (*méthode, plan d'appartement, décoration etc*) to plan, devise; (*enfant*) to conceive; **appartement bien/mal conçu** well-/badly-designed *ou* -planned flat.
concierge [kɔ̃sjɛRʒ(ə)] *nm/f* caretaker.
concile [kɔ̃sil] *nm* council, synod.
conciliabules [kɔ̃siljabyl] *nmpl* (private) discussions, confabulations.
conciliation [kɔ̃siljɑsjɔ̃] *nf* conciliation.
concilier [kɔ̃silje] *vt* to reconcile; **se ~ qn/l'appui de qn** to win sb over/sb's support.
concis, e [kɔ̃si, -iz] *a* concise; **concision** *nf* concision, conciseness.
concitoyen, ne [kɔ̃sitwajɛ̃, -jɛn] *nm/f* fellow citizen.
conclave [kɔ̃klav] *nm* conclave.
concluant, e [kɔ̃klyɑ̃, -ɑ̃t] *a* conclusive.
conclure [kɔ̃klyR] *vt* to conclude; **~ à l'acquittement** to decide in favour of an acquittal; **~ au suicide** to come to the conclusion (*ou* (*JUR*) to pronounce) that it is a case of suicide.
conclusion [kɔ̃klyzjɔ̃] *nf* conclusion; **~s** *nfpl* (*JUR*) submissions; findings.
conçois *etc vb voir* **concevoir**.
concombre [kɔ̃kɔ̃bR(ə)] *nm* cucumber.
concordance [kɔ̃kɔRdɑ̃s] *nf* concordance; **la ~ des temps** (*LING*) the sequence of tenses.
concorde [kɔ̃kɔRd(ə)] *nf* concord.

concorder [kɔ̃kɔʀde] *vi* to tally, agree.
concourir [kɔ̃kuʀiʀ] *vi* (SPORT) to compete; ~ **à** *vt* (*effet etc*) to work towards.
concours [kɔ̃kuʀ] *nm* competition; (SCOL) competitive examination; (*assistance*) aid, help; **recrutement par voie de** ~ recruitment by (competitive) examination; ~ **de circonstances** combination of circumstances; ~ **hippique** horse show.
concret, ète [kɔ̃kʀɛ, -ɛt] *a* concrete.
concrétiser [kɔ̃kʀetize] *vt* (*plan, projet*) to put in concrete form; **se** ~ *vi* to materialize.
conçu, e [kɔ̃sy] *pp de* **concevoir.**
concubinage [kɔ̃kybinaʒ] *nm* (JUR) cohabitation.
concupiscence [kɔ̃kypisɑ̃s] *nf* concupiscence.
concurremment [kɔ̃kyʀamɑ̃] *ad* concurrently; jointly.
concurrence [kɔ̃kyʀɑ̃s] *nf* competition; **jusqu'à** ~ **de** up to; ~ **déloyale** unfair competition.
concurrent, e [kɔ̃kyʀɑ̃, -ɑ̃t] *a* competing // *nm/f* (SPORT, ÉCON *etc*) competitor; (SCOL) candidate.
condamnation [kɔ̃dɑnɑsjɔ̃] *nf* condemnation; sentencing; sentence; conviction; ~ **à mort** death sentence.
condamner [kɔ̃dɑne] *vt* (*blâmer*) to condemn; (JUR) to sentence; (*porte, ouverture*) to fill in, block up; (*obliger*): ~ **qn à qch/faire** to condemn sb to sth/to do; ~ **qn à 2 ans de prison** to sentence sb to 2 years' imprisonment; ~ **qn à une amende** to impose a fine on sb, request sb to pay a fine.
condensateur [kɔ̃dɑ̃satœʀ] *nm* condenser.
condensation [kɔ̃dɑ̃sɑsjɔ̃] *nf* condensation.
condensé [kɔ̃dɑ̃se] *nm* digest.
condenser [kɔ̃dɑ̃se] *vt*, **se** ~ *vi* to condense.
condescendre [kɔ̃desɑ̃dʀ(ə)] *vi*: ~ **à** to condescend to.
condiment [kɔ̃dimɑ̃] *nm* condiment.
condisciple [kɔ̃disipl(ə)] *nm/f* school fellow, fellow student.
condition [kɔ̃disjɔ̃] *nf* condition; ~**s** *nfpl* (*tarif, prix*) terms; (*circonstances*) conditions; **sans** ~ *a* unconditional // *ad* unconditionally; **sous** ~ **que** on condition that; **à** ~ **de/que** provided that; **conditionnel, le** *a* conditional // *nm* conditional (tense); **conditionner** *vt* (*déterminer*) to determine; (COMM: *produit*) to package; (*fig*: *personne*) to condition; **air conditionné** air conditioning; **réflexe conditionné** conditioned reflex.
condoléances [kɔ̃dɔleɑ̃s] *nfpl* condolences.
conducteur, trice [kɔ̃dyktœʀ, -tʀis] *a* (ÉLEC) conducting // *nm/f* driver // *nm* (ÉLEC *etc*) conductor.
conduire [kɔ̃dɥiʀ] *vt* (*véhicule, passager*) to drive; (*délégation, troupeau*) to lead; **se** ~ *vi* to behave; ~ **vers/à** to lead towards/to; ~ **qn quelque part** to take sb somewhere; to drive sb somewhere.
conduit [kɔ̃dɥi] *nm* (TECH) conduit, pipe; (ANAT) duct, canal.
conduite [kɔ̃dɥit] *nf* (*en auto*) driving; (*comportement*) behaviour; (*d'eau, de gaz*) pipe; **sous la** ~ **de** led by; ~ **forcée** pressure pipe; ~ **à gauche** left-hand drive; ~ **intérieure** saloon (car).
cône [kon] *nm* cone.
confection [kɔ̃fɛksjɔ̃] *nf* (*fabrication*) making; (COUTURE): **la** ~ the clothing industry, the rag trade; **vêtement de** ~ ready-to-wear *ou* off-the-peg garment.
confectionner [kɔ̃fɛksjɔne] *vt* to make.
confédération [kɔ̃fedeʀɑsjɔ̃] *nf* confederation.
conférence [kɔ̃feʀɑ̃s] *nf* (*exposé*) lecture; (*pourparlers*) conference; ~ **de presse** press conference; **conférencier, ère** *nm/f* lecturer.
conférer [kɔ̃feʀe] *vt*: ~ **à qn** (*titre, grade*) to confer on sb; ~ **à qch/qn** (*aspect etc*) to endow sth/sb with, give (to) sth/sb.
confesser [kɔ̃fese] *vt* to confess; **se** ~ (REL) to go to confession; **confesseur** *nm* confessor.
confession [kɔ̃fɛsjɔ̃] *nf* confession; (*culte*: *catholique etc*) denomination; **confessionnal, aux** *nm* confessional; **confessionnel, le** *a* denominational.
confetti [kɔ̃feti] *nm* confetti *q*.
confiance [kɔ̃fjɑ̃s] *nf* confidence, trust; faith; **avoir** ~ **en** to have confidence *ou* faith in, trust; **mettre qn en** ~ to win sb's trust; ~ **en soi** self-confidence.
confiant, e [kɔ̃fjɑ̃, -ɑ̃t] *a* confident; trusting.
confidence [kɔ̃fidɑ̃s] *nf* confidence.
confident, e [kɔ̃fidɑ̃, -ɑ̃t] *nm/f* confidant/confidante.
confidentiel, le [kɔ̃fidɑ̃sjɛl] *a* confidential.
confier [kɔ̃fje] *vt*: ~ **à qn** (*objet en dépôt, travail etc*) to entrust to sb; (*secret, pensée*) to confide to sb; **se** ~ **à qn** to confide in sb.
configuration [kɔ̃figyʀɑsjɔ̃] *nf* configuration, layout.
confiné, e [kɔ̃fine] *a* enclosed; stale.
confiner [kɔ̃fine] *vt*: **se** ~ **dans** *ou* **à** to confine o.s. to; ~ **à** *vt* to confine to.
confins [kɔ̃fɛ̃] *nmpl*: **aux** ~ **de** on the borders of.
confirmation [kɔ̃fiʀmɑsjɔ̃] *nf* confirmation.
confirmer [kɔ̃fiʀme] *vt* to confirm.
confiscation [kɔ̃fiskɑsjɔ̃] *nf* confiscation.
confiserie [kɔ̃fizʀi] *nf* (*magasin*) confectioner's *ou* sweet shop; ~**s** *nfpl* (*bonbons*) confectionery *sg*, sweets; **confiseur, euse** *nm/f* confectioner.
confisquer [kɔ̃fiske] *vt* to confiscate.
confit, e [kɔ̃fi, -it] *a*: **fruits** ~**s** crystallized fruits // *nm*: ~ **d'oie** conserve of goose.
confiture [kɔ̃fityʀ] *nf* jam; ~ **d'oranges** (orange) marmalade.
conflit [kɔ̃fli] *nm* conflict.
confluent [kɔ̃flyɑ̃] *nm* confluence.
confondre [kɔ̃fɔ̃dʀ(ə)] *vt* (*jumeaux, faits*) to confuse, mix up; (*témoin, menteur*) to confound; **se** ~ *vi* to merge; **se** ~ **en**

excuses to offer profuse apologies, apologize profusely.
confondu, e [kɔ̃fɔ̃dy] *a* (*stupéfait*) speechless, overcome.
conformation [kɔ̃fɔʀmɑsjɔ̃] *nf* conformation.
conforme [kɔ̃fɔʀm(ə)] *a*: ~ **à** in accordance with; in keeping with; true to.
conformé, e [kɔ̃fɔʀme] *a*: **bien** ~ well-formed.
conformer [kɔ̃fɔʀme] *vt*: ~ **qch à** to model sth on; **se** ~ **à** to conform to; **conformisme** *nm* conformity; **conformiste** *a, nm/f* conformist.
conformité [kɔ̃fɔʀmite] *nf* conformity; agreement; **en** ~ **avec** in accordance with; in keeping with.
confort [kɔ̃fɔʀ] *nm* comfort; **tout** ~ (*COMM*) with all mod cons; **confortable** *a* comfortable.
confrère [kɔ̃fʀɛʀ] *nm* colleague; fellow member; **confrérie** *nf* brotherhood.
confrontation [kɔ̃fʀɔ̃tɑsjɔ̃] *nf* confrontation.
confronté, e [kɔ̃fʀɔ̃te] *a*: ~ **à** confronted by, facing.
confronter [kɔ̃fʀɔ̃te] *vt* to confront; (*textes*) to compare, collate.
confus, e [kɔ̃fy, -yz] *a* (*vague*) confused; (*embarrassé*) embarrassed.
confusion [kɔ̃fyzjɔ̃] *nf* (*voir confus*) confusion; embarrassment; (*voir confondre*) confusion; mixing up; (*erreur*) confusion.
congé [kɔ̃ʒe] *nm* (*vacances*) holiday; (*arrêt de travail*) time off *q*; leave *q*; (*MIL*) leave *q*; (*avis de départ*) notice; **en** ~ on holiday; off (work); on leave; **semaine/jour de** ~ week/day off; **prendre** ~ **de qn** to take one's leave of sb; **donner son** ~ **à** to hand *ou* give in one's notice to; ~ **de maladie** sick leave; ~**s payés** paid holiday.
congédier [kɔ̃ʒedje] *vt* to dismiss.
congélateur [kɔ̃ʒelatœʀ] *nm* freezer, deep freeze.
congeler [kɔ̃ʒle] *vt* to freeze.
congénère [kɔ̃ʒenɛʀ] *nm/f* fellow (bear *ou* lion *etc*), fellow creature.
congénital, e, aux [kɔ̃ʒenital, -o] *a* congenital.
congère [kɔ̃ʒɛʀ] *nf* snowdrift.
congestion [kɔ̃ʒɛstjɔ̃] *nf* congestion; ~ **cérébrale** stroke; ~ **pulmonaire** congestion of the lungs.
congestionner [kɔ̃ʒɛstjɔne] *vt* to congest; (*MED*) to flush.
congratuler [kɔ̃gʀatyle] *vt* to congratulate.
congre [kɔ̃gʀ(ə)] *nm* conger (eel).
congrégation [kɔ̃gʀegɑsjɔ̃] *nf* (*REL*) congregation; (*gén*) assembly; gathering.
congrès [kɔ̃gʀɛ] *nm* congress.
congru, e [kɔ̃gʀy] *a*: **la portion** ~**e** the smallest *ou* meanest share.
conifère [kɔnifɛʀ] *nm* conifer.
conique [kɔnik] *a* conical.
conjecture [kɔ̃ʒɛktyʀ] *nf* conjecture, speculation *q*.
conjecturer [kɔ̃ʒɛktyʀe] *vt, vi* to conjecture.
conjoint, e [kɔ̃ʒwɛ̃, -wɛ̃t] *a* joint // *nm/f* spouse.
conjonctif, ive [kɔ̃ʒɔ̃ktif, -iv] *a*: **tissu** ~ connective tissue.
conjonction [kɔ̃ʒɔ̃ksjɔ̃] *nf* (*LING*) conjunction.
conjonctivite [kɔ̃ʒɔ̃ktivit] *nf* conjunctivitis.
conjoncture [kɔ̃ʒɔ̃ktyʀ] *nf* circumstances *pl*; **la** ~ (**économique**) the economic climate *ou* circumstances.
conjugaison [kɔ̃ʒygɛzɔ̃] *nf* (*LING*) conjugation.
conjugal, e, aux [kɔ̃ʒygal, -o] *a* conjugal; married.
conjuguer [kɔ̃ʒyge] *vt* (*LING*) to conjugate; (*efforts etc*) to combine.
conjuration [kɔ̃ʒyʀɑsjɔ̃] *nf* conspiracy.
conjuré, e [kɔ̃ʒyʀe] *nm/f* conspirator.
conjurer [kɔ̃ʒyʀe] *vt* (*sort, maladie*) to avert; ~ **qn de faire qch** to beseech *ou* entreat sb to do sth.
connaissance [kɔnɛsɑ̃s] *nf* (*savoir*) knowledge *q*; (*personne connue*) acquaintance; (*conscience, perception*) consciousness; **être sans** ~ to be unconscious; **perdre** ~ to lose consciousness; **à ma/sa** ~ to (the best of) my/his knowledge; **avoir** ~ **de** to be aware of; **prendre** ~ **de** (*document etc*) to peruse; **en** ~ **de cause** with full knowledge of the facts.
connaisseur, euse [kɔnɛsœʀ, -øz] *nm/f* connoisseur // *a* expert.
connaître [kɔnɛtʀ(ə)] *vt* to know; (*éprouver*) to experience; (*avoir*) to have; to enjoy; ~ **de nom/vue** to know by name/sight; **ils se sont connus à Genève** they (first) met in Geneva.
connecter [kɔnɛkte] *vt* to connect.
connexe [kɔnɛks(ə)] *a* closely related.
connexion [kɔnɛksjɔ̃] *nf* connection.
connu, e [kɔny] *a* (*célèbre*) well-known.
conquérant, e [kɔ̃keʀɑ̃, -ɑ̃t] *nm/f* conqueror.
conquérir [kɔ̃keʀiʀ] *vt* to conquer, win; **conquête** *nf* conquest.
consacrer [kɔ̃sakʀe] *vt* (*REL*): ~ **qch** (**à**) to consecrate sth (to); (*fig: usage etc*) to sanction, establish; (*employer*): ~ **qch à** to devote *ou* dedicate sth to; **se** ~ **à qch/faire** to dedicate *ou* devote o.s. to/to doing.
consanguin, e [kɔ̃sɑ̃gɛ̃, -in] *a* between blood relations.
conscience [kɔ̃sjɑ̃s] *nf* conscience; (*perception*) consciousness; **avoir/prendre** ~ **de** to be/become aware of; **perdre** ~ to lose consciousness; **avoir bonne/mauvaise** ~ to have a clear/guilty conscience; ~ **professionnelle** professional conscience; **consciencieux, euse** *a* conscientious; **conscient, e** *a* conscious; **conscient de** aware *ou* conscious of.
conscription [kɔ̃skʀipsjɔ̃] *nf* conscription.
conscrit [kɔ̃skʀi] *nm* conscript.
consécration [kɔ̃sekʀɑsjɔ̃] *nf* consecration.

consécutif, ive [kɔ̃sekytif, -iv] *a* consecutive; ~ **à** following upon.
conseil [kɔ̃sɛj] *nm* (*avis*) piece of advice, advice *q*; (*assemblée*) council; (*expert*): ~ **en recrutement** recruitment consultant // *a*: **ingénieur-~** consulting engineer, engineering consultant; **tenir ~** to hold a meeting; to deliberate; **prendre ~ (auprès de qn)** to take advice (from sb); ~ **d'administration** board (of directors); ~ **de discipline** disciplinary committee; ~ **de guerre** court-martial; **le ~ des ministres** ≈ the Cabinet; ~ **municipal** town council.
conseiller [kɔ̃seje] *vt* (*personne*) to advise; (*méthode, action*) to recommend, advise.
conseiller, ère [kɔ̃seje, kɔ̃sɛjɛʀ] *nm/f* adviser; ~ **matrimonial** marriage guidance counsellor; ~ **municipal** town councillor.
consentement [kɔ̃sɑ̃tmɑ̃] *nm* consent.
consentir [kɔ̃sɑ̃tiʀ] *vt*: ~ **(à qch/faire)** to agree *ou* consent (to sth/to doing); ~ **qch à qn** to grant sb sth.
conséquence [kɔ̃sekɑ̃s] *nf* consequence, outcome; ~**s** *nfpl* consequences, repercussions; **en ~** (*donc*) consequently; (*de façon appropriée*) accordingly; **ne pas tirer à ~** to be unlikely to have any repercussions.
conséquent, e [kɔ̃sekɑ̃, -ɑ̃t] *a* logical, rational; **par ~** consequently.
conservateur, trice [kɔ̃sɛʀvatœʀ, -tʀis] *a* conservative // *nm/f* (POL) conservative; (*de musée*) curator.
conservation [kɔ̃sɛʀvɑsjɔ̃] *nf* preserving; preservation; retention; keeping.
conservatoire [kɔ̃sɛʀvatwaʀ] *nm* academy.
conserve [kɔ̃sɛʀv(ə)] *nf* (*gén pl*) canned *ou* tinned food; ~**s de poisson** canned *ou* tinned fish; **en ~** canned, tinned; **de ~** (*ensemble*) in convoy; in concert.
conserver [kɔ̃sɛʀve] *vt* (*faculté*) to retain, keep; (*amis, livres*) to keep; (*maintenir en bon état, aussi* CULIN) to preserve; **conserverie** *nf* canning factory.
considérable [kɔ̃sideʀabl(ə)] *a* considerable, significant, extensive.
considération [kɔ̃sideʀɑsjɔ̃] *nf* consideration; (*estime*) esteem, respect; ~**s** *nfpl* (*remarques*) reflections; **prendre en ~** to take into consideration *ou* account; **en ~ de** given, because of.
considéré, e [kɔ̃sideʀe] *a* respected.
considérer [kɔ̃sideʀe] *vt* to consider; (*regarder*) to consider, study; ~ **qch comme** to regard sth as.
consigne [kɔ̃siɲ] *nf* (COMM) deposit; (*de gare*) left luggage (office); (*punition*: SCOL) detention; (: MIL) confinement to barracks; (*ordre, instruction*) orders *pl*.
consigner [kɔ̃siɲe] *vt* (*note, pensée*) to record; (*punir*) to confine to barracks; to put in detention; (COMM) to put a deposit on.
consistance [kɔ̃sistɑ̃s] *nf* consistency.
consistant, e [kɔ̃sistɑ̃, -ɑ̃t] *a* thick; solid.
consister [kɔ̃siste] *vi*: ~ **en/dans/à faire** to consist of/in/in doing.
consœur [kɔ̃sœʀ] *nf* (lady) colleague; fellow member.
consolation [kɔ̃sɔlɑsjɔ̃] *nf* consolation *q*, comfort *q*.
console [kɔ̃sɔl] *nf* console.
consoler [kɔ̃sɔle] *vt* to console; **se ~ (de qch)** to console o.s. (for sth).
consolider [kɔ̃sɔlide] *vt* to strengthen, reinforce; (*fig*) to consolidate.
consommateur, trice [kɔ̃sɔmatœʀ, -tʀis] *nm/f* (ÉCON) consumer; (*dans un café*) customer.
consommation [kɔ̃sɔmɑsjɔ̃] *nf* consumption; (JUR) consummation; (*boisson*) drink; ~ **aux 100 km** (AUTO) (fuel) consumption per 100 km, ≈ miles per gallon (m.p.g.).
consommé, e [kɔ̃sɔme] *a* consummate // *nm* consommé.
consommer [kɔ̃sɔme] *vt* (*suj*: *personne*) to eat *ou* drink, consume; (*suj*: *voiture, usine, poêle*) to use (up), consume; (JUR) to consummate // *vi* (*dans un café*) to (have a) drink.
consonance [kɔ̃sɔnɑ̃s] *nf* consonance; **nom à ~ étrangère** foreign-sounding name.
consonne [kɔ̃sɔn] *nf* consonant.
consorts [kɔ̃sɔʀ] *nmpl*: **et ~** (*péj*) and company, and his bunch *ou* like.
conspirateur, trice [kɔ̃spiʀatœʀ, -tʀis] *nm/f* conspirator, plotter.
conspiration [kɔ̃spiʀɑsjɔ̃] *nf* conspiracy.
conspirer [kɔ̃spiʀe] *vi* to conspire, plot.
conspuer [kɔ̃spɥe] *vt* to boo, shout down.
constamment [kɔ̃stamɑ̃] *ad* constantly.
constant, e [kɔ̃stɑ̃, -ɑ̃t] *a* constant; (*personne*) steadfast.
constat [kɔ̃sta] *nm* (*d'huissier*) certified report (*by bailiff*); (*de police*) report.
constatation [kɔ̃statɑsjɔ̃] *nf* noticing; certifying; (*remarque*) observation.
constater [kɔ̃state] *vt* (*remarquer*) to note, notice; (ADMIN, JUR: *attester*) to certify; (*dégâts*) to note; ~ **que** (*dire*) to state that.
constellation [kɔ̃stelɑsjɔ̃] *nf* constellation.
constellé, e [kɔ̃stele] *a*: ~ **de** studded *ou* spangled with; spotted with.
consternation [kɔ̃stɛʀnɑsjɔ̃] *nf* consternation, dismay.
constipation [kɔ̃stipɑsjɔ̃] *nf* constipation.
constipé, e [kɔ̃stipe] *a* constipated; (*fig*) stiff.
constitué, e [kɔ̃stitɥe] *a*: ~ **de** made up *ou* composed of; **bien ~** of sound constitution; well-formed.
constituer [kɔ̃stitɥe] *vt* (*comité, équipe*) to set up, form; (*dossier, collection*) to put together, build up; (*suj*: *éléments, parties*: *composer*) to make up, constitute; (*représenter, être*) to constitute; **se ~ prisonnier** to give o.s. up.
constitution [kɔ̃stitysjɔ̃] *nf* setting up; building up; (*composition*) composition, make-up; (*santé*, POL) constitution; **constitutionnel, le** *a* constitutional.
constructeur [kɔ̃stʀyktœʀ] *nm* manufacturer, builder.
construction [kɔ̃stʀyksjɔ̃] *nf* construction, building.

construire [kɔ̃stʀɥiʀ] *vt* to build, construct.

consul [kɔ̃syl] *nm* consul; **~aire** *a* consular; **~at** *nm* consulate.

consultation [kɔ̃syltɑsjɔ̃] *nf* consultation; **~s** *nfpl* (*POL*) talks; **aller à la ~** (*MÉD*) to go to the surgery; **heures de ~** (*MÉD*) surgery hours.

consulter [kɔ̃sylte] *vt* to consult // *vi* (*médecin*) to hold surgery.

consumer [kɔ̃syme] *vt* to consume; **se ~** *vi* to burn; **se ~ de chagrin/douleur** to be consumed with sorrow/grief.

contact [kɔ̃takt] *nm* contact; **au ~ de** (*air, peau*) on contact with; (*gens*) through contact with; **mettre/couper le ~** (*AUTO*) to switch on/off the ignition; **entrer en ~** (*fils, objets*) to come into contact, make contact; **se mettre en ~ avec** (*RADIO*) to make contact with; **prendre ~ avec** (*relation d'affaires, connaissance*) to get in touch *ou* contact with; **~er** *vt* to contact, get in touch with.

contagieux, euse [kɔ̃taʒjø, -øz] *a* contagious, infectious.

contagion [kɔ̃taʒjɔ̃] *nf* contagion.

container [kɔ̃tɛnɛʀ] *nm* container.

contaminer [kɔ̃tamine] *vt* to contaminate.

conte [kɔ̃t] *nm* tale; **~ de fées** fairy tale.

contempler [kɔ̃tɑ̃ple] *vt* to contemplate, gaze at.

contemporain, e [kɔ̃tɑ̃pɔʀɛ̃, -ɛn] *a*, *nm/f* contemporary.

contenance [kɔ̃tnɑ̃s] *nf* (*d'un récipient*) capacity; (*attitude*) bearing, attitude; **perdre ~** to lose one's composure; **se donner une ~** to give the impression of composure.

contenir [kɔ̃tniʀ] *vt* to contain; (*avoir une capacité de*) to hold.

content, e [kɔ̃tɑ̃, -ɑ̃t] *a* pleased, glad; **~ de** pleased with; **contentement** *nm* contentment, satisfaction; **contenter** *vt* to satisfy, please; (*envie*) to satisfy; **se contenter de** to content o.s. with.

contentieux [kɔ̃tɑ̃sjø] *nm* (*COMM*) litigation; litigation department; (*POL etc*) contentious issues *pl*.

contenu [kɔ̃tny] *nm* (*d'un bol*) contents *pl*; (*d'un texte*) content.

conter [kɔ̃te] *vt* to recount, relate.

contestable [kɔ̃tɛstabl(ə)] *a* questionable.

contestation [kɔ̃tɛstɑsjɔ̃] *nf* questioning, contesting; (*POL*): **la ~** anti-establishment activity, protest.

conteste [kɔ̃tɛst(ə)]: **sans ~** *ad* unquestionably, indisputably.

contester [kɔ̃tɛste] *vt* to question, contest // *vi* (*POL, gén*) to protest, rebel (against established authority).

conteur, euse [kɔ̃tœʀ, -øz] *nm/f* storyteller.

contexte [kɔ̃tɛkst(ə)] *nm* context.

contigu, ë [kɔ̃tigy] *a*: **~ (à)** adjacent (to).

continent [kɔ̃tinɑ̃] *nm* continent; **continental, e, aux** *a* continental.

contingences [kɔ̃tɛ̃ʒɑ̃s] *nfpl* contingencies.

contingent [kɔ̃tɛ̃ʒɑ̃] *nm* (*MIL*) contingent; (*COMM*) quota; **contingenter** *vt* (*COMM*) to fix a quota on.

continu, e [kɔ̃tiny] *a* continuous; **(courant) ~** direct current, DC.

continuation [kɔ̃tinɥɑsjɔ̃] *nf* continuation.

continuel, le [kɔ̃tinɥɛl] *a* (*qui se répète*) constant, continual; (*continu*) continuous.

continuer [kɔ̃tinɥe] *vt* (*travail, voyage etc*) to continue (with), carry on (with), go on (with); (*prolonger: alignement, rue*) to continue // *vi* (*pluie, vie, bruit*) to continue, go on; (*voyageur*) to go on; **~ à** *ou* **de faire** to go on *ou* continue doing.

continuité [kɔ̃tinɥite] *nf* continuity; continuation.

contorsion [kɔ̃tɔʀsjɔ̃] *nf* contortion; **se contorsionner** *vi* to contort o.s., writhe about.

contour [kɔ̃tuʀ] *nm* outline, contour; **~s** *nmpl* (*d'une rivière etc*) windings.

contourner [kɔ̃tuʀne] *vt* to bypass, walk (*ou* drive) round.

contraceptif, ive [kɔ̃tʀasɛptif, -iv] *a*, *nm* contraceptive.

contraception [kɔ̃tʀasɛpsjɔ̃] *nf* contraception.

contracté, e [kɔ̃tʀakte] *a* (*muscle*) tense, contracted; (*personne: tendu*) tense, tensed up.

contracter [kɔ̃tʀakte] *vt* (*muscle etc*) to tense, contract; (*maladie, dette, obligation*) to contract; (*assurance*) to take out; **se ~** *vi* (*métal, muscles*) to contract; **contraction** *nf* contraction.

contractuel, le [kɔ̃tʀaktɥɛl] *a* contractual // *nm/f* (*agent*) traffic warden; (*employé*) contract employee.

contradiction [kɔ̃tʀadiksjɔ̃] *nf* contradiction; **contradictoire** *a* contradictory, conflicting; **débat contradictoire** (open) debate.

contraignant, e [kɔ̃tʀɛɲɑ̃, -ɑ̃t] *a* restricting.

contraindre [kɔ̃tʀɛ̃dʀ(ə)] *vt*: **~ qn à faire** to force *ou* compel sb to do.

contraint, e [kɔ̃tʀɛ̃, -ɛ̃t] *a* (*mine, air*) constrained, forced // *nf* constraint; **sans ~e** unrestrainedly, unconstrainedly.

contraire [kɔ̃tʀɛʀ] *a*, *nm* opposite; **~ à** contrary to; **au ~** *ad* on the contrary.

contrarier [kɔ̃tʀaʀje] *vt* (*personne*) to annoy, bother; (*fig*) to impede; to thwart, frustrate; **contrariété** *nf* annoyance.

contraste [kɔ̃tʀast(ə)] *nm* contrast; **contraster** *vi* to contrast.

contrat [kɔ̃tʀa] *nm* contract.

contravention [kɔ̃tʀavɑ̃sjɔ̃] *nf* (*infraction*): **~ à** contravention of; (*amende*) fine; (*P.V. pour stationnement interdit*) parking ticket; **dresser ~ à** (*automobiliste*) to book; to write out a parking ticket for.

contre [kɔ̃tʀ(ə)] *prép* against; (*en échange*) (in exchange) for // *préfixe*: **~-amiral, aux** *nm* rear admiral; **~-attaque** *nf* counter-attack; **~-attaquer** *vi* to counter-attack; **~-balancer** *vt* to counterbalance; (*fig*) to offset.

contrebande [kɔ̃tʀəbɑ̃d] *nf* (*trafic*) contraband, smuggling; (*marchandise*) contraband, smuggled goods *pl*; **faire la ~ de** to smuggle; **contrebandier** *nm* smuggler.

contrebas [kɔ̃tʀəbɑ]: **en** ~ *ad* (down) below.

contrebasse [kɔ̃tʀəbɑs] *nf* (double) bass; **contrebassiste** *nm/f* (double) bass player.

contrecarrer [kɔ̃tʀəkaʀe] *vt* to thwart.

contrecœur [kɔ̃tʀəkœʀ]: **à** ~ *ad* (be)grudgingly, reluctantly.

contrecoup [kɔ̃tʀəku] *nm* repercussions *pl*.

contre-courant [kɔ̃tʀəkuʀɑ̃]: **à** ~ *ad* against the current.

contredire [kɔ̃tʀədiʀ] *vt* (*personne*) to contradict; (*témoignage, assertion, faits*) to refute.

contrée [kɔ̃tʀe] *nf* region; land.

contre-écrou [kɔ̃tʀekʀu] *nm* lock nut.

contre-espionnage [kɔ̃tʀɛspjɔnaʒ] *nm* counter-espionage.

contre-expertise [kɔ̃tʀɛkspɛʀtiz] *nf* second (expert) assessment.

contrefaçon [kɔ̃tʀəfasɔ̃] *nf* forgery.

contrefaire [kɔ̃tʀəfɛʀ] *vt* (*document, signature*) to forge, counterfeit; (*personne, démarche*) to mimic; (*dénaturer: sa voix etc*) to disguise.

contrefait, e [kɔ̃tʀəfɛ, -ɛt] *a* misshapen, deformed.

contreforts [kɔ̃tʀəfɔʀ] *nmpl* foothills.

contre-indication [kɔ̃tʀɛ̃dikɑsjɔ̃] *nf* contra-indication.

contre-jour [kɔ̃tʀəʒuʀ]: **à** ~ *ad* against the sunlight.

contremaître [kɔ̃tʀəmɛtʀ(ə)] *nm* foreman.

contre-manifestation [kɔ̃tʀəmanifɛstɑsjɔ̃] *nf* counter-demonstration.

contremarque [kɔ̃tʀəmaʀk(ə)] *nf* (*ticket*) pass-out ticket.

contre-offensive [kɔ̃tʀɔfɑ̃siv] *nf* counter-offensive.

contrepartie [kɔ̃tʀəpaʀti] *nf* compensation; **en** ~ in compensation; in return.

contre-performance [kɔ̃tʀəpɛʀfɔʀmɑ̃s] *nf* below-average performance.

contrepèterie [kɔ̃tʀəpetʀi] *nf* spoonerism.

contre-pied [kɔ̃tʀəpje] *nm*: **prendre le** ~ **de** to take the opposing view of; to take the opposite course to; **prendre qn à** ~ (*SPORT*) to wrong-foot sb.

contre-plaqué [kɔ̃tʀəplake] *nm* plywood.

contre-plongée [kɔ̃tʀəplɔ̃ʒe] *nf* low-angle shot.

contrepoids [kɔ̃tʀəpwa] *nm* counterweight, counterbalance; **faire** ~ to act as a counterbalance.

contrepoint [kɔ̃tʀəpwɛ̃] *nm* counter point.

contrer [kɔ̃tʀe] *vt* to counter.

contresens [kɔ̃tʀəsɑ̃s] *nm* misinterpretation; mistranslation; nonsense *q*; **à** ~ *ad* the wrong way.

contresigner [kɔ̃tʀəsiɲe] *vt* to countersign.

contretemps [kɔ̃tʀətɑ̃] *nm* hitch, contretemps; **à** ~ *ad* (*MUS*) out of time; (*fig*) at an inopportune moment.

contre-terrorisme [kɔ̃tʀətɛʀɔʀism(ə)] *nm* counter-terrorism.

contre-torpilleur [kɔ̃tʀətɔʀpijœʀ] *nm* destroyer.

contrevenir [kɔ̃tʀəvniʀ]: ~ **à** *vt* to contravene.

contribuable [kɔ̃tʀibɥabl(ə)] *nm/f* taxpayer.

contribuer [kɔ̃tʀibɥe]: ~ **à** *vt* to contribute towards; **contribution** *nf* contribution; **les contributions** (*bureaux*) ≈ the Tax Office, the Inland Revenue; **contributions directes/indirectes** (*impôts*) direct/indirect taxation; **mettre à contribution** to call upon.

contrit, e [kɔ̃tʀi, -it] *a* contrite.

contrôle [kɔ̃tʀol] *nm* checking *q*, check; supervision; monitoring; **perdre le** ~ **de son véhicule** to lose control of one's vehicle; ~ **d'identité** identity check; ~ **des naissances** birth control.

contrôler [kɔ̃tʀole] *vt* (*vérifier*) to check; (*surveiller*) to supervise; to monitor, control; (*maîtriser, COMM: firme*) to control; **contrôleur, euse** *nm/f* (*de train*) (ticket) inspector; (*de bus*) (bus) conductor/tress.

contrordre [kɔ̃tʀɔʀdʀ(ə)] *nm* counter-order, countermand; **sauf** ~ unless otherwise directed.

controverse [kɔ̃tʀɔvɛʀs(ə)] *nf* controversy; **controversé, e** *a* much debated.

contumace [kɔ̃tymas]: **par** ~ *ad* in absentia.

contusion [kɔ̃tyzjɔ̃] *nf* bruise, contusion.

convaincre [kɔ̃vɛ̃kʀ(ə)] *vt*: ~ **qn (de qch)** to convince sb (of sth); ~ **qn (de faire)** to persuade sb (to do); ~ **qn de** (*JUR: délit*) to convict sb of.

convalescence [kɔ̃valesɑ̃s] *nf* convalescence; **maison de** ~ convalescent home.

convalescent, e [kɔ̃valesɑ̃, -ɑ̃t] *a, nm/f* convalescent.

convenable [kɔ̃vnabl(ə)] *a* (*décent*) acceptable, proper; (*assez bon*) decent, acceptable; adequate, passable.

convenance [kɔ̃vnɑ̃s] *nf*: **à ma/votre** ~ to my/your liking; ~**s** *nfpl* proprieties.

convenir [kɔ̃vniʀ] *vi* to be suitable; ~ **à** to suit; **il convient de** it is advisable to; (*bienséant*) it is right *ou* proper to; ~ **de** *vt* (*bien-fondé de qch*) to admit (to), acknowledge; (*date, somme etc*) to agree upon; ~ **que** (*admettre*) to admit that, acknowledge the fact that; ~ **de faire qch** to agree to do sth; **il a été convenu que** it has been agreed that; **comme convenu** as agreed.

convention [kɔ̃vɑ̃sjɔ̃] *nf* convention; ~**s** *nfpl* (*convenances*) convention *sg*, social conventions; **de** ~ conventional; ~ **collective** (*ÉCON*) collective agreement; **conventionné, e** *a* (*ADMIN*) ≈ National Health *cpd*; **conventionnel, le** *a* conventional.

conventuel, le [kɔ̃vɑ̃tɥɛl] *a* monastic; monastery *cpd*; conventual, convent *cpd*.

convenu, e *pp de* **convenir**.

convergent, e [kɔ̃vɛʀʒɑ̃, -ɑ̃t] *a* convergent.

converger [kɔ̃vɛʀʒe] *vi* to converge.

conversation [kɔ̃vɛʀsɑsjɔ̃] *nf* conversation; **avoir de la** ~ to be a good conversationalist.

converser [kɔ̃vɛʀse] *vi* to converse.
conversion [kɔ̃vɛʀsjɔ̃] *nf* conversion; (*SKI*) kick turn.
convertir [kɔ̃vɛʀtiʀ] *vt*: ~ **qn (à)** to convert sb (to); ~ **qch en** to convert sth into; **se** ~ **(à)** to be converted (to).
convexe [kɔ̃vɛks(ə)] *a* convex.
conviction [kɔ̃viksjɔ̃] *nf* conviction.
convienne *etc vb voir* **convenir.**
convier [kɔ̃vje] *vt*: ~ **qn à** (*dîner etc*) to (cordially) invite sb to; ~ **qn à faire** to urge sb to do.
convive [kɔ̃viv] *nm/f* guest (*at table*).
convocation [kɔ̃vɔkɑsjɔ̃] *nf* convening, convoking; invitation; summoning; (*document*) notification to attend; summons *sg*.
convoi [kɔ̃vwa] *nm* (*de voitures, prisonniers*) convoy; (*train*) train; ~ (**funèbre**) funeral procession.
convoiter [kɔ̃vwate] *vt* to covet; **convoitise** *nf* covetousness; (*sexuelle*) lust, desire.
convoler [kɔ̃vɔle] *vi*: ~ **(en justes noces)** to be wed.
convoquer [kɔ̃vɔke] *vt* (*assemblée*) to convene, convoke; (*subordonné, témoin*) to summon; ~ **qn (à)** (*réunion*) to invite sb (to attend).
convoyer [kɔ̃vwaje] *vt* to escort; **convoyeur** *nm* (*NAVIG*) escort ship; **convoyeur de fonds** security guard.
convulsions [kɔ̃vylsjɔ̃] *nfpl* convulsions.
coopératif, ive [kɔɔpeʀatif, -iv] *a, nf* co-operative.
coopération [kɔɔpeʀɑsjɔ̃] *nf* co-operation; (*ADMIN*): **la C~** ≈ Voluntary Service Overseas (*sometimes done in place of Military Service*).
coopérer [kɔɔpeʀe] *vi*: ~ **(à)** to cooperate (in).
coordination [kɔɔʀdinɑsjɔ̃] *nf* co-ordination.
coordonné, e [kɔɔʀdɔne] *a* coordinated // *nf* (*LING*) coordinate clause; ~**s** *nmpl* (*vêtements*) coordinates; ~**es** *nfpl* (*MATH*) coordinates.
coordonner [kɔɔʀdɔne] *vt* to coordinate.
copain, copine [kɔpɛ̃, kɔpin] *nm/f* mate, pal // *a*: **être** ~ **avec** to be pally with.
copeau, x [kɔpo] *nm* shaving; (*de métal*) turning.
copie [kɔpi] *nf* copy; (*SCOL*) script, paper; exercise.
copier [kɔpje] *vt* to copy; **copieuse** *nf* photo-copier.
copieux, euse [kɔpjø, -øz] *a* copious, hearty.
copilote [kɔpilɔt] *nm* (*AVIAT*) co-pilot; (*AUTO*) co-driver, navigator.
copine [kɔpin] *nf voir* **copain.**
copiste [kɔpist(ə)] *nm/f* copyist, transcriber.
coproduction [kɔpʀɔdyksjɔ̃] *nf* coproduction, joint production.
copropriété [kɔpʀɔpʀijete] *nf* co-ownership, joint ownership; **acheter en** ~ to buy on a co-ownership basis.
copulation [kɔpylɑsjɔ̃] *nf* copulation.
coq [kɔk] *nm* cock, rooster.
coq-à-l'âne [kɔkalɑn] *nm inv* abrupt change of subject.
coque [kɔk] *nf* (*de noix, mollusque*) shell; (*de bateau*) hull; **à la** ~ (*CULIN*) boiled.
coquelicot [kɔkliko] *nm* poppy.
coqueluche [kɔklyʃ] *nf* whooping-cough.
coquet, te [kɔkɛ, -ɛt] *a* flirtatious; appearance-conscious; pretty.
coquetier [kɔktje] *nm* egg-cup.
coquillage [kɔkijaʒ] *nm* (*mollusque*) shellfish *inv*; (*coquille*) shell.
coquille [kɔkij] *nf* shell; (*TYPO*) misprint; ~ **de beurre** shell of butter; ~ **de noix** nutshell; ~ **St Jacques** scallop.
coquin, e [kɔkɛ̃, -in] *a* mischievous, roguish; (*polisson*) naughty // *nm/f* (*péj*) rascal.
cor [kɔʀ] *nm* (*MUS*) horn; (*MÉD*): ~ **(au pied)** corn; **réclamer à** ~ **et à cri** (*fig*) to clamour for; ~ **anglais** cor anglais; ~ **de chasse** hunting horn.
corail, aux [kɔʀaj, -o] *nm* coral *q*.
Coran [kɔʀɑ̃] *nm*: **le** ~ the Koran.
corbeau, x [kɔʀbo] *nm* crow.
corbeille [kɔʀbɛj] *nf* basket; (*à la Bourse*): **la** ~ the stockbrokers' central enclosure; ~ **de mariage** (*fig*) wedding presents *pl*; ~ **à ouvrage** work-basket; ~ **à pain** bread-basket; ~ **à papier** waste paper basket *ou* bin.
corbillard [kɔʀbijaʀ] *nm* hearse.
cordage [kɔʀdaʒ] *nm* rope; ~**s** *nmpl* (*de voilure*) rigging *sg*.
corde [kɔʀd(ə)] *nf* rope; (*de violon, raquette, d'arc*) string; (*trame*): **la** ~ the thread; (*ATHLÉTISME, AUTO*): **la** ~ the rails *pl*; **semelles de** ~ rope soles; ~ **à linge** washing *ou* clothes line; ~ **lisse** (climbing) rope; ~ **à nœuds** knotted climbing rope; ~ **raide** tight-rope; ~ **à sauter** skipping rope; ~**s vocales** vocal cords.
cordeau, x [kɔʀdo] *nm* string, line; **tracé au** ~ as straight as a die.
cordée [kɔʀde] *nf* (*d'alpinistes*) rope, roped party.
cordial, e, aux [kɔʀdjal, -jo] *a* warm, cordial; ~**ité** *nf* warmth, cordiality.
cordon [kɔʀdɔ̃] *nm* cord, string; ~ **sanitaire/de police** sanitary/police cordon; ~ **bleu** cordon bleu; ~ **ombilical** umbilical cord.
cordonnerie [kɔʀdɔnʀi] *nf* shoe repairer's *ou* mender's (shop).
cordonnier [kɔʀdɔnje] *nm* shoe repairer *ou* mender, cobbler.
coreligionnaire [kɔʀəliʒjɔnɛʀ] *nm/f* (*d'un musulman, juif etc*) fellow Mahometan/Jew *etc*.
coriace [kɔʀjas] *a* tough.
cormoran [kɔʀmɔʀɑ̃] *nm* cormorant.
cornac [kɔʀnak] *nm* elephant driver.
corne [kɔʀn(ə)] *nf* horn; (*de cerf*) antler; ~ **d'abondance** horn of plenty; ~ **de brume** (*NAVIG*) foghorn.
cornée [kɔʀne] *nf* cornea.
corneille [kɔʀnɛj] *nf* crow.
cornélien, ne [kɔʀneljɛ̃, -jɛn] *a* (*débat etc*) where love and duty conflict.
cornemuse [kɔʀnəmyz] *nf* bagpipes *pl*.

corner *nm* [kɔʀnɛʀ] (*FOOTBALL*) corner (kick) // *vb* [kɔʀne] *vt* (*pages*) to make dog-eared // *vi* (*klaxonner*) to blare out.
cornet [kɔʀnɛ] *nm* (paper) cone ; (*de glace*) cornet, cone ; ~ **à piston** cornet.
cornette [kɔʀnɛt] *nf* cornet (*headgear*).
corniaud [kɔʀnjo] *nm* (*chien*) mongrel ; (*péj*) twit, clot.
corniche [kɔʀniʃ] *nf* cornice.
cornichon [kɔʀniʃɔ̃] *nm* gherkin.
cornue [kɔʀny] *nf* retort.
corollaire [kɔʀɔlɛʀ] *nm* corollary.
corolle [kɔʀɔl] *nf* corolla.
coron [kɔʀɔ̃] *nm* mining cottage ; mining village.
coronaire [kɔʀɔnɛʀ] *a* coronary.
corporation [kɔʀpɔʀɑsjɔ̃] *nf* corporate body ; (*au moyen-âge*) guild.
corporel, le [kɔʀpɔʀɛl] *a* bodily ; (*punition*) corporal ; **soins ~s** care *sg* of the body.
corps [kɔʀ] *nm* (*gén*) body ; (*cadavre*) (dead) body ; **à son ~ défendant** against one's will ; **à ~ perdu** headlong ; **perdu ~ et biens** lost with all hands ; **prendre ~** to take shape ; **faire ~ avec** to be joined to ; to form one body with ; **~ d'armée** army corps ; **~ de ballet** corps de ballet ; **le ~ consulaire (CC)** the consular corps ; **~ à ~** *ad* hand-to-hand // *nm* clinch ; **le ~ du délit** (*JUR*) corpus delicti ; **le ~ diplomatique (CD)** the diplomatic corps ; **le ~ électoral** the electorate ; **le ~ enseignant** the teaching profession ; **~ étranger** (*MÉD*) foreign body ; **~ de garde** guardroom.
corpulent, e [kɔʀpylɑ̃, -ɑ̃t] *a* stout, corpulent.
correct, e [kɔʀɛkt] *a* (*exact*) accurate, correct ; (*bienséant, honnête*) correct ; (*passable*) adequate ; **~ement** *ad* accurately ; correctly.
correcteur, trice [kɔʀɛktœʀ, -tʀis] *nm/f* (*SCOL*) examiner, marker ; (*TYPO*) proof-reader.
correction [kɔʀɛksjɔ̃] *nf* (*voir corriger*) correction ; marking ; (*voir correct*) correctness ; (*rature, surcharge*) correction, emendation ; (*coups*) thrashing ; **~ (des épreuves)** proofreading.
correctionnel, le [kɔʀɛksjɔnɛl] *a* (*JUR*): **chambre ~le** ≈ police magistrate's court.
corrélation [kɔʀelɑsjɔ̃] *nf* correlation.
correspondance [kɔʀɛspɔ̃dɑ̃s] *nf* correspondence ; (*de train, d'avion*) connection ; **ce train assure la ~ avec l'avion de 10 heures** this train connects with the 10 o'clock plane ; **cours par ~** correspondence course ; **vente par ~** mail-order business ; **correspondancier, ère** *nm/f* correspondence clerk.
correspondant, e [kɔʀɛspɔ̃dɑ̃, -ɑ̃t] *nm/f* correspondent.
correspondre [kɔʀɛspɔ̃dʀ(ə)] *vi* (*données, témoignages*) to correspond, tally ; (*chambres*) to communicate ; **~ à** to correspond to ; **~ avec qn** to correspond with sb.
corrida [kɔʀida] *nf* bullfight.
corridor [kɔʀidɔʀ] *nm* corridor, passage.
corrigé [kɔʀiʒe] *nm* (*SCOL*) correct version ; fair copy.
corriger [kɔʀiʒe] *vt* (*devoir*) to correct, mark ; (*texte*) to correct, emend ; (*erreur, défaut*) to correct, put right ; (*punir*) to thrash ; **~ qn de** (*défaut*) to cure sb of.
corroborer [kɔʀɔbɔʀe] *vt* to corroborate.
corroder [kɔʀɔde] *vt* to corrode.
corrompre [kɔʀɔ̃pʀ(ə)] *vt* (*soudoyer*) to bribe ; (*dépraver*) to corrupt.
corrosion [kɔʀozjɔ̃] *nf* corrosion.
corruption [kɔʀypsjɔ̃] *nf* bribery ; corruption.
corsage [kɔʀsaʒ] *nm* bodice ; blouse.
corsaire [kɔʀsɛʀ] *nm* pirate, corsair ; privateer.
corse [kɔʀs(ə)] *a, nm/f* Corsican // *nf*: **la C~** Corsica.
corsé, e [kɔʀse] *a* vigorous ; full-flavoured ; (*fig*) spicy ; tricky.
corselet [kɔʀsəlɛ] *nm* corselet.
corset [kɔʀsɛ] *nm* corset ; bodice.
corso [kɔʀso] *nm*: **~ fleuri** procession of floral floats.
cortège [kɔʀtɛʒ] *nm* procession.
corvée [kɔʀve] *nf* chore, drudgery *q* ; (*MIL*) fatigue (duty).
cosmétique [kɔsmetik] *nm* hair-oil ; beauty care product.
cosmique [kɔsmik] *a* cosmic.
cosmonaute [kɔsmɔnot] *nm/f* cosmonaut, astronaut.
cosmopolite [kɔsmɔpɔlit] *a* cosmopolitan.
cosmos [kɔsmɔs] *nm* outer space ; cosmos.
cosse [kɔs] *nf* (*BOT*) pod, hull.
cossu, e [kɔsy] *a* opulent-looking, well-to-do.
costaud, e [kɔsto, -od] *a* strong, sturdy.
costume [kɔstym] *nm* (*d'homme*) suit ; (*de théâtre*) costume ; **costumé, e** *a* dressed up.
cote [kɔt] *nf* (*en Bourse etc*) quotation ; quoted value ; (*d'un cheval*): **la ~ de** the odds *pl* on ; (*d'un candidat etc*) rating ; (*mesure: sur une carte*) spot height ; (: *sur un croquis*) dimension ; (*de classement*) (classification) mark ; reference number ; **inscrit à la ~** quoted on the Stock Exchange ; **~ d'alerte** danger *ou* flood level.
côte [kot] *nf* (*rivage*) coast(line) ; (*pente*) slope ; (: *sur une route*) hill ; (*ANAT*) rib ; (*d'un tricot, tissu*) rib, ribbing *q* ; **~ à ~** *ad* side by side ; **la C~ (d'Azur)** the (French) Riviera.
côté [kote] *nm* (*gén*) side ; (*direction*) way, direction ; **de tous les ~s** from all directions ; **de quel ~ est-il parti?** which way *ou* in which direction did he go? ; **de ce/de l'autre ~** this/the other way ; **du ~ de** (*provenance*) from ; (*direction*) towards ; **du ~ de Lyon** (*proximité*) the Lyons way, near Lyons ; **de ~** *ad* sideways ; on one side ; to one side ; aside ; **laisser de ~** to leave on one side ; **mettre de ~** to put on one side, put aside ; **à ~** *ad* (right) nearby ; beside ; next door ; (*d'autre part*) besides ; **à ~ de** beside, next to ; (*fig*) in comparison to ; **à ~ (de la cible)** off target, wide (of the mark) ; **être aux ~s de** to be by the side of.

coteau, x [kɔto] *nm* hill.
côtelé, e [kotle] *a* ribbed; **pantalon en velours ~** corduroy trousers *pl*.
côtelette [kotlɛt] *nf* chop.
coter [kɔte] *vt* (*en Bourse*) to quote.
coterie [kɔtʀi] *nf* set.
côtier, ière [kotje, -jɛʀ] *a* coastal.
cotisation [kɔtizɑsjɔ̃] *nf* subscription, dues *pl*; (*pour une pension*) contributions *pl*.
cotiser [kɔtize] *vi*: ~ (**à**) to pay contributions (to); **se** ~ to club together.
coton [kɔtɔ̃] *nm* cotton; ~ **hydrophile** (absorbent) cotton-wool.
côtoyer [kotwaje] *vt* to be close to; to rub shoulders with; to run alongside; to be bordering *ou* verging on.
cotte [kɔt] *nf*: ~ **de mailles** coat of mail.
cou [ku] *nm* neck.
couard, e [kwaʀ, -aʀd] *a* cowardly.
couchage [kuʃaʒ] *nm voir* **sac**.
couchant [kuʃɑ̃] *a*: **soleil** ~ setting sun.
couche [kuʃ] *nf* (*strate*: *gén*, GÉO) layer, stratum (*pl* a); (*de peinture, vernis*) coat; (*de poussière, crème*) layer; (*de bébé*) nappy, napkin; ~**s** *nfpl*, (MÉD) confinement *sg*; ~**s sociales** social levels *ou* strata; ~**-culotte** *nf* disposable nappy and waterproof pants in one.
coucher [kuʃe] *nm* (*du soleil*) setting // *vt* (*personne*) to put to bed; (: *loger*) to put up; (*objet*) to lay on its side; (*écrire*) to inscribe, couch // *vi* (*dormir*) to sleep, spend the night; (*fam*): ~ **avec qn** to sleep with sb, go to bed with sb; **se** ~ *vi* (*pour dormir*) to go to bed; (*pour se reposer*) to lie down; (*soleil*) to set, go down; **à prendre avant le** ~ (MÉD) take at night *ou* before going to bed; ~ **de soleil** sunset.
couchette [kuʃɛt] *nf* couchette; (*de marin*) bunk.
coucou [kuku] *nm* cuckoo // *excl* peek-a-boo.
coude [kud] *nm* (ANAT) elbow; (*de tuyau, de la route*) bend; ~ **à** ~ *ad* shoulder to shoulder, side by side.
cou-de-pied [kudpje] *nm* instep.
coudre [kudʀ(ə)] *vt* (*bouton*) to sew on; (*robe*) to sew (up) // *vi* to sew.
couenne [kwan] *nf* (*de lard*) rind.
couettes [kwɛt] *nfpl* bunches.
couffin [kufɛ̃] *nm* Moses basket; (straw) basket.
couiner [kwine] *vi* to squeal.
coulant, e [kulɑ̃, -ɑ̃t] *a* (*indulgent*) easy-going; (*fromage etc*) runny.
coulée [kule] *nf* (*de lave, métal en fusion*) flow; ~ **de neige** snowslide.
couler [kule] *vi* to flow, run; (*fuir*: *stylo, récipient*) to leak; (*sombrer*: *bateau*) to sink // *vt* (*cloche, sculpture*) to cast; (*bateau*) to sink; (*fig*) to ruin, bring down; **se** ~ **dans** (*interstice etc*) to slip into; **il a coulé une bielle** (AUTO) his big-end went.
couleur [kulœʀ] *nf* colour; (CARTES) suit.
couleuvre [kulœvʀ(ə)] *nf* grass snake.
coulisse [kulis] *nf* (TECH) runner; ~**s** *nfpl* (THÉÂTRE) wings; (*fig*): **dans les** ~**s** behind the scenes; **porte à** ~ sliding door; **coulisser** *vi* to slide, run.
couloir [kulwaʀ] *nm* corridor, passage; (*de bus*) gangway; (SPORT: *de piste*) lane; (GÉO) gully; ~ **de navigation** shipping lane.
coulpe [kulp(ə)] *nf*: **battre sa** ~ to repent openly.
coup [ku] *nm* (*heurt, choc*) knock; (*affectif*) blow, shock; (*agressif*) blow; (*avec arme à feu*) shot; (*de l'horloge*) chime; stroke; (SPORT) stroke; shot; blow; (ÉCHECS) move; ~ **de coude/genou** nudge (with the elbow)/with the knee; **à** ~**s de hache/marteau** (hitting) with an axe/a hammer; ~ **de tonnerre** clap of thunder; ~ **de sonnette** ring of the bell; ~ **de crayon/pinceau** stroke of the pencil/brush; **donner un** ~ **de balai** to sweep up, give the floor a sweep; **donner un** ~ **de chiffon** to go round with the duster; **avoir le** ~ (*fig*) to have the knack; **boire un** ~ to have a drink; **d'un seul** ~ (*subitement*) suddenly; (*à la fois*) at one go; in one blow; **du premier** ~ first time *ou* go, at the first attempt; **du même** ~ at the same time; **à** ~ **sûr** definitely, without fail; ~ **sur** ~ in quick succession; **sur le** ~ outright; **sous le** ~ **de** (*surprise etc*) under the influence of; **tomber sous le** ~ **de la loi** to constitute a statutory offence; ~ **de chance** stroke of luck; ~ **de couteau** stab (of a knife); ~ **dur** hard blow; ~ **d'envoi** kick-off; ~ **d'essai** first attempt; ~ **d'état** coup d'état; ~ **de feu** shot; ~ **de filet** (POLICE) haul; ~ **franc** free kick; ~ **de frein** (sharp) braking *q*; ~ **de fusil** rifle shot; ~ **de grâce** coup de grâce; ~ **de main**: **donner un** ~ **de main à qn** to give sb a (helping) hand; ~ **d'œil** glance; ~ **de pied** kick; ~ **de poing** punch; ~ **de soleil** sunburn; ~ **de téléphone** phone call; ~ **de tête** (*fig*) (sudden) impulse; ~ **de théâtre** (*fig*) dramatic turn of events; ~ **de vent** gust of wind.
coupable [kupabl(ə)] *a* guilty; (*pensée*) guilty, culpable // *nm/f* (*gén*) culprit; (JUR) guilty party; ~ **de** guilty of.
coupe [kup] *nf* (*verre*) goblet; (*à fruits*) dish; (SPORT) cup; (*de cheveux, de vêtement*) cut; (*graphique, plan*) (cross) section; **être sous la** ~ **de** to be under the control of; **faire des** ~**s sombres dans** to make drastic cuts in.
coupé [kupe] *nm* (AUTO) coupé.
coupe-circuit [kupsiʀkɥi] *nm inv* cutout, circuit breaker.
coupée [kupe] *nf* (NAVIG) gangway.
coupe-papier [kuppapje] *nm inv* paper knife.
couper [kupe] *vt* to cut; (*retrancher*) to cut (out), take out; (*route, courant*) to cut off; (*appétit*) to take away; (*fièvre*) to take down, reduce; (*vin, cidre*) to blend; (: *à table*) to dilute (with water) // *vi* to cut; (*prendre un raccourci*) to take a short-cut; (CARTES: *diviser le paquet*) to cut; (: *avec l'atout*) to trump; **se** ~ (*se blesser*) to cut o.s.; (*en témoignant etc*) to give o.s. away; ~ **la parole à qn** to cut sb short.
couperet [kupʀɛ] *nm* cleaver, chopper.
couperosé, e [kupʀoze] *a* blotchy.
couple [kupl(ə)] *nm* couple; ~ **de torsion** torque.

coupler [kuple] *vt* to couple (together).
couplet [kuplɛ] *nm* verse.
coupole [kupɔl] *nf* dome; cupola.
coupon [kupɔ̃] *nm* (*ticket*) coupon; (*de tissu*) remnant; roll; **~-réponse international** international reply coupon.
coupure [kupyʀ] *nf* cut; (*billet de banque*) note; (*de journal*) cutting; **~ de courant** power cut.
cour [kuʀ] *nf* (*de ferme, jardin*) (court)yard; (*d'immeuble*) back yard; (*JUR, royale*) court; **faire la ~ à qn** to court sb; **~ d'assises** court of assizes, ≈ Crown Court; **~ de cassation** Court of Cassation; **~ martiale** court-martial.
courage [kuʀaʒ] *nm* courage, bravery; **courageux, euse** *a* brave, courageous.
couramment [kuʀamɑ̃] *ad* commonly; (*avec aisance: parler*) fluently.
courant, e [kuʀɑ̃, -ɑ̃t] *a* (*fréquent*) common; (*COMM, gén: normal*) standard; (*en cours*) current // *nm* current; (*fig*) movement; trend; **être au ~ (de)** (*fait, nouvelle*) to know (about); **mettre qn au ~ (de)** (*fait, nouvelle*) to tell sb (about); (*nouveau travail etc*) to teach sb the basics (of); **se tenir au ~ (de)** (*techniques etc*) to keep o.s. up-to-date (on); **dans le ~ de** (*pendant*) in the course of; **le 10 ~** (*COMM*) the 10th inst; **~ d'air** draught; **~ électrique** (electric) current, power.
courbature [kuʀbatyʀ] *nf* ache; **courbaturé, e** *a* aching.
courbe [kuʀb(ə)] *a* curved // *nf* curve; **~ de niveau** contour line.
courber [kuʀbe] *vt* to bend; **~ la tête** to bow one's head; **se ~** *vi* (*branche etc*) to bend, curve; (*personne*) to bend (down).
courbette [kuʀbɛt] *nf* low bow.
coureur, euse [kuʀœʀ, -øz] *nm/f* (*SPORT*) runner (*ou* driver); (*péj*) womaniser/manhunter; **~ cycliste/automobile** racing cyclist/driver.
courge [kuʀʒ(ə)] *nf* (*BOT*) gourd; (*CULIN*) marrow.
courgette [kuʀʒɛt] *nf* courgette, zucchini.
courir [kuʀiʀ] *vi* (*gén*) to run; (*se dépêcher*) to rush; (*fig: rumeurs*) to go round; (*COMM: intérêt*) to accrue // *vt* (*SPORT: épreuve*) to compete in; (*risque*) to run; (*danger*) to face; **~ les cafés/bals** to do the rounds of the cafés/dances; **le bruit court que** the rumour is going round that; **~ après qn** to run after sb, chase (after) sb.
couronne [kuʀɔn] *nf* crown; (*de fleurs*) wreath, circlet.
couronnement [kuʀɔnmɑ̃] *nm* coronation, crowning; (*fig*) crowning achievement.
couronner [kuʀɔne] *vt* to crown.
courons *etc vb voir* **courir.**
courre [kuʀ] *vb voir* **chasse.**
courrier [kuʀje] *nm* mail, post; (*lettres à écrire*) letters *pl*; (*rubrique*) column; **long/moyen ~** *a* (*AVIAT*) long-/medium-haul; **~ du cœur** problem page.
courroie [kuʀwɑ] *nf* strap; (*TECH*) belt; **~ de transmission/de ventilateur** driving/fan belt.
courrons *etc vb voir* **courir.**
courroucé, e [kuʀuse] *a* wrathful.
cours [kuʀ] *nm* (*leçon*) lesson; class; (*série de leçons*) course; (*cheminement*) course; (*écoulement*) flow; (*avenue*) walk; (*COMM*) rate; price; **donner libre ~ à** to give free expression to; **avoir ~** (*monnaie*) to be legal tender; (*fig*) to be current; (*SCOL*) to have a class *ou* lecture; **en ~** (*année*) current; (*travaux*) in progress; **en ~ de route** on the way; **au ~ de** in the course of, during; **le ~ du change** the exchange rate; **~ d'eau** water course, *generic term for streams, rivers*; **~ du soir** night school.
course [kuʀs(ə)] *nf* running; (*SPORT: épreuve*) race; (*trajet: du soleil*) course; (*: d'un projectile*) flight; (*: d'une pièce mécanique*) travel; (*excursion*) outing; climb; (*d'un taxi, autocar*) journey, trip; (*petite mission*) errand; **~s** *nfpl* (*achats*) shopping *sg*; (*HIPPISME*) races.
court, e [kuʀ, kuʀt(ə)] *a* short // *ad* short // *nm*: **~ (de tennis)** (tennis) court; **tourner ~** to come to a sudden end; **à ~ de** short of; **prendre qn de ~** to catch sb unawares; **tirer à la ~e paille** to draw lots; **~-bouillon** *nm* court-bouillon; **~-circuit** *nm* short-circuit.
courtier, ère [kuʀtje, -jɛʀ] *nm/f* broker.
courtisan [kuʀtizɑ̃] *nm* courtier.
courtisane [kuʀtizan] *nf* courtesan.
courtiser [kuʀtize] *vt* to court, woo.
courtois, e [kuʀtwa, -waz] *a* courteous; **courtoisie** *nf* courtesy.
couru, e *pp de* **courir.**
cousais *etc vb voir* **coudre.**
cousin, e [kuzɛ̃, -in] *nm/f* cousin.
coussin [kusɛ̃] *nm* cushion.
cousu, e [kuzy] *pp de* **coudre** // *a*: **~ d'or** rolling in riches.
coût [ku] *nm* cost; **le ~ de la vie** the cost of living.
coûtant [kutɑ̃] *am*: **au prix ~** at cost price.
couteau, x [kuto] *nm* knife; **~ à cran d'arrêt** flick-knife; **~ de poche** pocket knife; **~-scie** *nm* serrated-edged knife.
coutellerie [kutɛlʀi] *nf* cutlery shop; cutlery.
coûter [kute] *vt, vi* to cost; **combien ça coûte?** how much is it?, what does it cost?; **coûte que coûte** at all costs; **coûteux, euse** *a* costly, expensive.
coutume [kutym] *nf* custom; **coutumier, ère** *a* customary.
couture [kutyʀ] *nf* sewing; dress-making; (*points*) seam.
couturier [kutyʀje] *nm* fashion designer, couturier.
couturière [kutyʀjɛʀ] *nf* dressmaker.
couvée [kuve] *nf* brood, clutch.
couvent [kuvɑ̃] *nm* (*de sœurs*) convent; (*de frères*) monastery; (*établissement scolaire*) convent (school).
couver [kuve] *vt* to hatch; (*maladie*) to be sickening for // *vi* (*feu*) to smoulder; (*révolte*) to be brewing; **~ qn/qch des yeux** to look lovingly at; to look longingly at.
couvercle [kuvɛʀkl(ə)] *nm* lid; (*de bombe aérosol etc, qui se visse*) cap, top.

couvert, e [kuvɛʀ, -ɛʀt(ə)] *pp de* **couvrir** // *a* (*ciel*) overcast; (*coiffé d'un chapeau*) wearing a hat // *nm* place setting; (*place à table*) place; (*au restaurant*) cover charge; **~s** *nmpl* place settings; cutlery *sg*; **~ de** covered with *ou* in; **bien ~** (*habillé*) well wrapped up; **mettre le ~** to lay the table; **à ~** under cover; **sous le ~ de** under the shelter of; (*fig*) under cover of.
couverture [kuvɛʀtyʀ] *nf* (*de lit*) blanket; (*de bâtiment*) roofing; (*de livre, fig: d'un espion etc*) cover.
couveuse [kuvøz] *nf* (*à poules*) sitter, brooder; (*de maternité*) incubator.
couvre... [kuvʀ(ə)] *préfixe*: **~-chef** *nm* hat; **~-feu** *nm* curfew; **~-lit** *nm* bedspread.
couvreur [kuvʀœʀ] *nm* roofer.
couvrir [kuvʀiʀ] *vt* to cover; **se ~** (*ciel*) to cloud over; (*s'habiller*) to cover up, wrap up; (*se coiffer*) to put on one's hat; (*par une assurance*) to cover o.s.; **se ~ de** (*fleurs, boutons*) to become covered in.
crabe [kʀɑb] *nm* crab.
crachat [kʀaʃa] *nm* spittle *q*, spit *q*.
cracher [kʀaʃe] *vi* to spit // *vt* to spit out; (*fig: lave etc*) to belch (out); **~ du sang** to spit blood.
crachin [kʀaʃɛ̃] *nm* drizzle.
crachoir [kʀaʃwaʀ] *nm* spittoon; (*de dentiste*) bowl.
craie [kʀɛ] *nf* chalk.
craindre [kʀɛ̃dʀ(ə)] *vt* to fear, be afraid of; (*être sensible à: chaleur, froid*) to be easily damaged by; **~ de/que** to be afraid of/that.
crainte [kʀɛ̃t] *nf* fear; **de ~ de/que** for fear of/that; **craintif, ive** *a* timid.
cramoisi, e [kʀamwazi] *a* crimson.
crampe [kʀɑ̃p] *nf* cramp; **~ d'estomac** stomach cramp.
crampon [kʀɑ̃pɔ̃] *nm* (*de semelle*) stud; (ALPINISME) crampon.
cramponner [kʀɑ̃pɔne]: **se ~** *vi*: **se ~ (à)** to hang *ou* cling on (to).
cran [kʀɑ̃] *nm* (*entaille*) notch; (*de courroie*) hole; (*courage*) guts *pl*; **~ d'arrêt** safety catch; **~ de mire** bead.
crâne [kʀɑn] *nm* skull.
crâner [kʀɑne] *vi* (*fam*) to swank, show off.
crânien, ne [kʀɑnjɛ̃, -jɛn] *a* cranial, skull *cpd*, brain *cpd*.
crapaud [kʀapo] *nm* toad.
crapule [kʀapyl] *nf* villain.
craquelure [kʀaklyʀ] *nf* crack; crackle *q*.
craquement [kʀakmɑ̃] *nm* crack, snap; (*du plancher*) creak, creaking *q*.
craquer [kʀake] *vi* (*bois, plancher*) to creak; (*fil, branche*) to snap; (*couture*) to come apart, burst; (*fig*) to break down // *vt*: **~ une allumette** to strike a match.
crasse [kʀas] *nf* grime, filth.
crassier [kʀasje] *nm* slag heap.
cratère [kʀatɛʀ] *nm* crater.
cravache [kʀavaʃ] *nf* (riding) crop; **cravacher** *vt* to use the crop on.
cravate [kʀavat] *nf* tie; **cravater** *vt* to put a tie on; (*fig*) to grab round the neck.
crawl [kʀol] *nm* crawl; **dos crawlé** backstroke.
crayeux, euse [kʀɛjø, -øz] *a* chalky.
crayon [kʀɛjɔ̃] *nm* pencil; (*de rouge à lèvres etc*) stick, pencil; **écrire au ~** to write in pencil; **~ à bille** ball-point pen; **~ de couleur** crayon, colouring pencil.
créance [kʀeɑ̃s] *nf* (COMM) (financial) claim, (recoverable) debt; **créancier, ière** *nm/f* creditor.
créateur, trice [kʀeatœʀ, -tʀis] *a* creative // *nm/f* creator.
création [kʀeɑsjɔ̃] *nf* creation.
créature [kʀeatyʀ] *nf* creature.
crécelle [kʀesɛl] *nf* rattle.
crèche [kʀɛʃ] *nf* (*de Noël*) crib; (*garderie*) crèche, day nursery.
crédence [kʀedɑ̃s] *nf* (small) sideboard.
crédit [kʀedi] *nm* (*gén*) credit; **~s** *nmpl* funds; **payer/acheter à ~** to pay/buy on credit *ou* on easy terms; **faire ~ à qn** to give sb credit; **créditer** *vt*: **créditer un compte (de)** to credit an account (with); **créditeur, trice** *a* in credit, credit *cpd* // *nm/f* customer in credit.
crédule [kʀedyl] *a* credulous, gullible; **crédulité** *nf* credulity, gullibility.
créer [kʀee] *vt* to create; (THÉÂTRE) to produce (for the first time).
crémaillère [kʀemajɛʀ] *nf* (RAIL) rack; (*tige crantée*) trammel; **direction à ~** (AUTO) rack and pinion steering; **pendre la ~** to have a house-warming party.
crémation [kʀemɑsjɔ̃] *nf* cremation.
crématoire [kʀematwaʀ] *a*: **four ~** crematorium.
crème [kʀɛm] *nf* cream; (*entremets*) cream dessert // *a inv* cream(-coloured); **un (café) ~** ≈ a white coffee; **~ fouettée** whipped cream; **~ à raser** shaving cream; **crémerie** *nf* dairy; (*tearoom*) teashop; **crémeux, euse** *a* creamy; **crémier, ière** *nm/f* dairyman/woman.
créneau, x [kʀeno] *nm* (*de fortification*) crenel(le); (*fig*) gap; slot; (AUTO): **faire un ~** to reverse into a parking space (*between cars alongside the kerb*).
créole [kʀeɔl] *a, nm, nf* Creole.
crêpe [kʀɛp] *nf* (*galette*) pancake // *nm* (*tissu*) crêpe; (*de deuil*) black mourning crêpe; black armband (*ou* hatband *ou* ribbon); **semelle (de) ~** crêpe sole; **crêpé, e** *a* (*cheveux*) backcombed; **~rie** *nf* pancake shop *ou* restaurant.
crépi [kʀepi] *nm* roughcast; **crépir** *vt* to roughcast.
crépiter [kʀepite] *vi* to sputter, splutter; to crackle; to rattle out; to patter.
crépon [kʀepɔ̃] *nm* seersucker.
crépu, e [kʀepy] *a* frizzy, fuzzy.
crépuscule [kʀepyskyl] *nm* twilight, dusk.
crescendo [kʀeʃɛndo] *nm, ad* (MUS) crescendo; **aller ~** (*fig*) to rise higher and higher, grow ever greater.
cresson [kʀesɔ̃] *nm* watercress.
crête [kʀɛt] *nf* (*de coq*) comb; (*de vague, montagne*) crest.
crétin, e [kʀetɛ̃, -in] *nm/f* cretin.
cretonne [kʀətɔn] *nf* cretonne.

creuser [kRøze] *vt* (*trou, tunnel*) to dig; (*sol*) to dig a hole in; (*bois*) to hollow out; (*fig*) to go (deeply) into; **cela creuse (l'estomac)** that gives you a real appetite; **se ~ (la cervelle)** to rack one's brains.
creuset [kRøzɛ] *nm* crucible; (*fig*) melting pot; (severe) test.
creux, euse [kRø, -øz] *a* hollow // *nm* hollow; (*fig: sur graphique etc*) trough; **heures creuses** slack periods; off-peak periods; **le ~ de l'estomac** the pit of the stomach.
crevaison [kRəvɛzɔ̃] *nf* puncture.
crevasse [kRəvas] *nf* (*dans le sol*) crack, fissure; (*de glacier*) crevasse; (*de la peau*) crack.
crevé, e [kRəve] *a* (*fatigué*) fagged out, worn out.
crève-cœur [kRɛvkœR] *nm inv* heartbreak.
crever [kRəve] *vt* (*papier*) to tear, break; (*tambour, ballon*) to burst // *vi* (*pneu*) to burst; (*automobiliste*) to have a puncture; (*abcès, outre, nuage*) to burst (open); (*fam*) to die; **cela lui a crevé un œil** it blinded him in one eye.
crevette [kRəvɛt] *nf*: **~ (rose)** prawn; **~ grise** shrimp.
cri [kRi] *nm* cry, shout; (*d'animal: spécifique*) cry, call; **c'est le dernier ~** (*fig*) it's the latest fashion.
criant, e [kRijɑ̃, -ɑ̃t] *a* (*injustice*) glaring.
criard, e [kRijaR, -aRd(ə)] *a* (*couleur*) garish, loud; yelling.
crible [kRibl(ə)] *nm* riddle; (*mécanique*) screen, jig; **passer qch au ~** to put sth through a riddle; (*fig*) to go over sth with a fine-tooth comb.
criblé, e [kRible] *a*: **~ de** riddled with.
cric [kRik] *nm* (AUTO) jack.
crier [kRije] *vi* (*pour appeler*) to shout, cry (out); (*de peur, de douleur etc*) to scream, yell; (*fig: grincer*) to squeal, screech // *vt* (*ordre, injure*) to shout (out), yell (out); **crieur de journaux** *nm* newspaper seller.
crime [kRim] *nm* crime; (*meurtre*) murder; **criminaliste** *nm/f* specialist in criminal law; **criminalité** *nf* criminality, crime; **criminel, le** *a* criminal // *nm/f* criminal; murderer; **criminel de guerre** war criminal; **criminologiste** *nm/f* criminologist.
crin [kRɛ̃] *nm* hair *q*; (*fibre*) horsehair; **à tous ~s, à tout ~** diehard, out-and-out.
crinière [kRinjɛR] *nf* mane.
crique [kRik] *nf* creek, inlet.
criquet [kRikɛ] *nm* locust; grasshopper.
crise [kRiz] *nf* crisis (*pl* crises); (MÉD) attack; fit; **~ cardiaque** heart attack; **~ de foi** crisis of belief; **~ de foie** bilious attack; **~ de nerfs** attack of nerves.
crispation [kRispɑsjɔ̃] *nf* twitch; contraction; tenseness.
crisper [kRispe] *vt* to tense; (*poings*) to clench; **se ~** to tense; to clench; (*personne*) to get tense.
crisser [kRise] *vi* (*neige*) to crunch; (*tissu*) to rustle; (*pneu*) to screech.
cristal, aux [kRistal, -o] *nm* crystal // *nmpl* (*objets*) crystal(ware) *sg*; **~ de plomb** (lead) crystal; **~ de roche** rock-crystal; **cristaux de soude** washing soda *sg*.
cristallin, e [kRistalɛ̃, -in] *a* crystal-clear // *nm* (ANAT) crystalline lens.
cristalliser [kRistalize] *vi, vt*, **se ~** *vi* to crystallize.
critère [kRitɛR] *nm* criterion (*pl* ia).
critique [kRitik] *a* critical // *nm/f* (*de théâtre, musique*) critic // *nf* criticism; (THÉÂTRE *etc: article*) review; **la ~** (*activité*) criticism; (*personnes*) the critics *pl*.
critiquer [kRitike] *vt* (*dénigrer*) to criticize; (*évaluer, juger*) to assess, examine (critically).
croasser [kRɔase] *vi* to caw.
croc [kRo] *nm* (*dent*) fang; (*de boucher*) hook.
croc-en-jambe [kRɔkɑ̃ʒɑ̃b] *nm*: **faire un ~ à qn** to trip sb up.
croche [kRɔʃ] *nf* (MUS) quaver; **double ~** semiquaver.
crochet [kRɔʃɛ] *nm* hook; (*clef*) picklock; (*détour*) detour; (BOXE): **~ du gauche** left hook; (TRICOT: *aiguille*) crochet-hook; (: *technique*) crochet; **~s** *nmpl* (TYPO) square brackets; **vivre aux ~s de qn** to live *ou* sponge off sb; **crocheter** *vt* (*serrure*) to pick.
crochu, e [kRɔʃy] *a* hooked; claw-like.
crocodile [kRɔkɔdil] *nm* crocodile.
crocus [kRɔkys] *nm* crocus.
croire [kRwaR] *vt* to believe; **~ qn honnête** to believe sb (to be) honest; **se ~ fort** to think one is strong; **~ que** to believe *ou* think that; **~ à, ~ en** to believe in.
croîs *vb voir* **croître.**
croisade [kRwazad] *nf* crusade.
croisé, e [kRwaze] *a* (*veston*) double-breasted // *nm* (*guerrier*) crusader // *nf* (*fenêtre*) window, casement; **~e d'ogives** intersecting ribs; **à la ~e des chemins** at the crossroads.
croisement [kRwazmɑ̃] *nm* (*carrefour*) crossroads *sg*; (BIO) crossing; crossbreed.
croiser [kRwaze] *vt* (*personne, voiture*) to pass; (*route*) to cross, cut across; (BIO) to cross // *vi* (NAVIG) to cruise; **~ les jambes/bras** to cross one's legs/fold one's arms; **se ~** (*personnes, véhicules*) to pass each other; (*routes*) to cross, intersect; (*lettres*) to cross (in the post); (*regards*) to meet.
croiseur [kRwazœR] *nm* cruiser (*warship*).
croisière [kRwazjɛR] *nf* cruise; **vitesse de ~** (AUTO *etc*) cruising speed.
croisillon [kRwazijɔ̃] *nm*: **motif/fenêtre à ~s** lattice pattern/window.
croissance [kRwasɑ̃s] *nf* growing, growth; **maladie de ~** growth disease; **~ économique** economic growth.
croissant, e [kRwasɑ̃, -ɑ̃t] *a* growing; rising // *nm* (*à manger*) croissant; (*motif*) crescent.
croître [kRwɑtR(ə)] *vi* to grow; (*lune*) to wax.
croix [kRwa] *nf* cross; **en ~** *a, ad* in the form of a cross; **la C~ Rouge** the Red Cross.
croquant, e [kRɔkɑ̃, -ɑ̃t] *a* crisp, crunchy // *nm/f* (*péj*) yokel, (country) bumpkin.

croque... [kRɔk] *préfixe*: **~-mitaine** *nm* bog(e)y-man ; **~-monsieur** *nm inv* toasted ham and cheese sandwich ; **~-mort** *nm* (*péj*) pallbearer.
croquer [kRɔke] *vt* (*manger*) to crunch ; to munch ; (*dessiner*) to sketch // *vi* to be crisp *ou* crunchy.
croquet [kRɔkɛ] *nm* croquet.
croquette [kRɔkɛt] *nf* croquette.
croquis [kRɔki] *nm* sketch.
cross(-country) [kRɔs(kuntRi)] *nm* cross-country race *ou* run ; cross-country racing *ou* running.
crosse [kRɔs] *nf* (*de fusil*) butt ; (*de revolver*) grip ; (*d'évêque*) crook, crosier ; (*de hockey*) hockey stick.
crotte [kRɔt] *nf* droppings *pl*.
crotté, e [kRɔte] *a* muddy, mucky.
crottin [kRɔtɛ̃] *nm*: **~ (de cheval)** (horse) dung *ou* manure.
crouler [kRule] *vi* (*s'effondrer*) to collapse ; (*être délabré*) to be crumbling.
croupe [kRup] *nf* croup, rump ; **en ~** pillion.
croupier [kRupje] *nm* croupier.
croupir [kRupiR] *vi* to stagnate.
croustillant, e [kRustijɑ̃, -ɑ̃t] *a* crisp ; (*fig*) spicy.
croustiller [kRustije] *vi* to be crisp *ou* crusty.
croûte [kRut] *nf* crust ; (*du fromage*) rind ; (*de vol-au-vent*) case ; (*MÉD*) scab ; **en ~** (*CULIN*) in pastry, in a pie ; **~ aux champignons** mushrooms on toast ; **~ au fromage** cheese on toast *q* ; **~ de pain** (*morceau*) crust (of bread) ; **~ terrestre** earth's crust.
croûton [kRutɔ̃] *nm* (*CULIN*) crouton ; (*bout du pain*) crust, heel.
croyance [kRwajɑ̃s] *nf* belief.
croyant, e [kRwajɑ̃, -ɑ̃t] *nm/f* believer.
C.R.S. *sigle fpl = Compagnies républicaines de sécurité* (*a state security police force*) // *sigle m member of the* C.R.S..
cru, e [kRy] *pp de* **croire** // *a* (*non cuit*) raw ; (*lumière, couleur*) harsh ; (*paroles, description*) crude // *nm* (*vignoble*) vineyard ; (*vin*) wine // *nf* (*d'un cours d'eau*) swelling, rising ; **de son (propre) ~** (*fig*) of his own devising ; **du ~** local ; **en ~e** in spate.
crû *pp de* **croître.**
cruauté [kRyote] *nf* cruelty.
cruche [kRyʃ] *nf* pitcher, (earthenware) jug.
crucial, e, aux [kRysjal, -o] *a* crucial.
crucifier [kRysifje] *vt* to crucify.
crucifix [kRysifi] *nm* crucifix.
cruciforme [kRysifɔRm(ə)] *a* cruciform, cross-shaped.
cruciverbiste [kRysivɛRbist(ə)] *nm/f* crossword puzzle enthusiast.
crudité [kRydite] *nf* crudeness *q* ; harshness *q* ; **~s** *nfpl* (*CULIN*) salads.
crue [kRy] *nf voir* **cru.**
cruel, le [kRyɛl] *a* cruel.
crus *etc*, **crûs** *etc vb voir* **croire**, **croître.**
crustacés [kRystase] *nmpl* shellfish.
crypte [kRipt(ə)] *nf* crypt.
cubage [kybaʒ] *nm* cubage, cubic content.
cube [kyb] *nm* cube ; (*jouet*) brick, building block ; **mètre ~** cubic metre ; **2 au ~ = 8** 2 cubed is 8 ; **élever au ~** to cube ; **cubique** *a* cubic.
cueillette [kœjɛt] *nf* picking, gathering ; harvest *ou* crop (of fruit).
cueillir [kœjiR] *vt* (*fruits, fleurs*) to pick, gather ; (*fig*) to catch.
cuiller *ou* **cuillère** [kɥijɛR] *nf* spoon ; **~ à café** coffee spoon ; (*CULIN*) ≈ teaspoonful ; **~ à soupe** soup-spoon ; (*CULIN*) ≈ tablespoonful ; **cuillerée** *nf* spoonful.
cuir [kɥiR] *nm* leather ; (*avant tannage*) hide ; **~ chevelu** scalp.
cuirasse [kɥiRas] *nf* breastplate ; **cuirassé** *nm* (*NAVIG*) battleship.
cuire [kɥiR] *vt* (*aliments*) to cook ; (*poterie*) to fire // *vi* to cook ; (*picoter*) to smart, sting, burn ; **bien cuit** (*viande*) well done ; **trop cuit** overdone.
cuisine [kɥizin] *nf* (*pièce*) kitchen ; (*art culinaire*) cookery, cooking ; (*nourriture*) cooking, food ; **faire la ~** to cook, make a *ou* the meal ; **cuisiner** *vt* to cook ; (*fam*) to grill // *vi* to cook ; **cuisinier, ière** *nm/f* cook // *nf* (*poêle*) cooker.
cuisse [kɥis] *nf* (*ANAT*) thigh ; (*CULIN*) leg.
cuisson [kɥisɔ̃] *nf* cooking ; firing.
cuistre [kɥistR(ə)] *nm* prig.
cuit, e *pp de* **cuire.**
cuivre [kɥivR(ə)] *nm* copper ; **les ~s** (*MUS*) the brass ; **cuivré, e** *a* coppery ; bronzed.
cul [ky] *nm* (*fam!*) arse (!), bum ; **~ de bouteille** bottom of a bottle.
culasse [kylas] *nf* (*AUTO*) cylinder-head ; (*de fusil*) breech.
culbute [kylbyt] *nf* somersault ; (*accidentelle*) tumble, fall ; **culbuter** *vi* to (take a) tumble, fall (head over heels) ; **culbuteur** *nm* (*AUTO*) rocker arm.
cul-de-jatte [kydʒat] *nm/f* legless cripple.
cul-de-sac [kydsak] *nm* cul-de-sac.
culinaire [kylinɛR] *a* culinary.
culminant, e [kylminɑ̃, -ɑ̃t] *a*: **point ~** highest point.
culminer [kylmine] *vi* to reach its highest point ; to tower.
culot [kylo] *nm* (*d'ampoule*) cap ; (*effronterie*) cheek, nerve.
culotte [kylɔt] *nf* (*pantalon*) pants *pl*, trousers *pl* ; (*de femme*): **(petite) ~** knickers *pl* ; **~ de cheval** riding breeches *pl*.
culotté, e [kylɔte] *a* (*pipe*) seasoned ; (*cuir*) mellowed ; (*effronté*) cheeky.
culpabilité [kylpabilite] *nf* guilt.
culte [kylt(ə)] *nm* (*religion*) religion ; (*hommage, vénération*) worship ; (*protestant*) service.
cultivateur, trice [kyltivatœR, -tRis] *nm/f* farmer.
cultivé, e [kyltive] *a* (*personne*) cultured, cultivated.
cultiver [kyltive] *vt* to cultivate ; (*légumes*) to grow, cultivate.
culture [kyltyR] *nf* cultivation ; growing ; (*connaissances etc*) culture ; **(champs de) ~s** land(s) under cultivation ; **~ physique** physical training ; **culturel, le** *a* cultural ; **culturisme** *nm* body-building.

cumin [kymɛ̃] *nm* (CULIN) caraway seeds *pl*, cumin.
cumul [kymyl] *nm* (*voir cumuler*) holding (*ou* drawing) concurrently; ~ **de peines** sentences to run consecutively.
cumuler [kymyle] *vt* (*emplois, honneurs*) to hold concurrently; (*salaires*) to draw concurrently; (JUR: *droits*) to accumulate.
cupide [kypid] *a* greedy, grasping.
curatif, ive [kyʀatif, -iv] *a* curative.
cure [kyʀ] *nf* (MÉD) course of treatment; (REL) cure, ≈ living; presbytery, ≈ vicarage; **faire une ~ de fruits** to go on a fruit cure *ou* diet; **n'avoir ~ de** to pay no attention to; ~ **de sommeil** sleep therapy *q*.
curé [kyʀe] *nm* parish priest; **M. le ~** ≈ Vicar.
cure-dent [kyʀdɑ̃] *nm* toothpick.
cure-pipe [kyʀpip] *nm* pipe cleaner.
curer [kyʀe] *vt* to clean out.
curieux, euse [kyʀjø, -øz] *a* (*étrange*) strange, curious; (*indiscret*) curious, inquisitive; (*intéressé*) inquiring, curious // *nmpl* (*badauds*) onlookers, bystanders; **curiosité** *nf* curiosity, inquisitiveness; (*objet*) curio(sity); (*site*) unusual feature *ou* sight.
curiste [kyʀist(ə)] *nm/f* person taking the waters at a spa.
curriculum vitae [kyʀikylɔmvite] *nm inv* (*abr* **C.V.**) curriculum vitae.
curry [kyʀi] *nm* curry; **poulet au ~** curried chicken, chicken curry.
curseur [kyʀsœʀ] *nm* (*de règle*) slide; (*de fermeture-éclair*) slider.
cursif, ive [kyʀsif, -iv] *a*: **écriture cursive** cursive script.
cutané, e [kytane] *a* cutaneous, skin *cpd*.
cuti-réaction [kytiʀeaksjɔ̃] *nf* (MÉD) skin-test.
cuve [kyv] *nf* vat; (*à mazout etc*) tank.
cuvée [kyve] *nf* vintage.
cuvette [kyvɛt] *nf* (*récipient*) bowl, basin; (*du lavabo*) (wash)basin; (*des w.-c.*) pan; (GÉO) basin.
C.V. *sigle m* (AUTO) *voir* **cheval;** (COMM) = **curriculum vitae.**
cyanure [sjanyʀ] *nm* cyanide.
cybernétique [sibɛʀnetik] *nf* cybernetics *sg*.
cyclable [siklabl(ə)] *a*: **piste ~** cycle track.
cyclamen [siklamɛn] *nm* cyclamen.
cycle [sikl(ə)] *nm* cycle.
cyclique [siklik] *a* cyclic(al).
cyclisme [siklism(ə)] *nm* cycling.
cycliste [siklist(ə)] *nm/f* cyclist // *a* cycle *cpd*.
cyclomoteur [siklɔmɔtœʀ] *nm* moped; **cyclomotoriste** *nm/f* moped-rider.
cyclone [siklon] *nm* hurricane.
cygne [siɲ] *nm* swan.
cylindre [silɛ̃dʀ(ə)] *nm* cylinder; **moteur à 4 ~s en ligne** straight-4 engine; **cylindrée** *nf* (AUTO) (cubic) capacity; **une (voiture de) grosse cylindrée** a big-engined car; **cylindrique** *a* cylindrical.
cymbale [sɛ̃bal] *nf* cymbal.
cynique [sinik] *a* cynical; **cynisme** *nm* cynicism.
cyprès [sipʀɛ] *nm* cypress.
cypriote [sipʀjɔt] *a, nm/f* Cypriot.
cyrillique [siʀilik] *a* Cyrillic.
cystite [sistit] *nf* cystitis.
cytise [sitiz] *nm* laburnum.

D

d' *prép, dét voir* **de**.
dactylo [daktilo] *nf* (*aussi*: **~graphe**) typist; (*aussi*: **~graphie**) typing, typewriting; **~graphier** *vt* to type (out).
dada [dada] *nm* hobby-horse.
daigner [deɲe] *vt* to deign.
daim [dɛ̃] *nm* (fallow) deer *inv*; (*peau*) buckskin; (*imitation*) suede.
dallage [dalaʒ] *nm* paving.
dalle [dal] *nf* paving stone, flag(stone); slab.
daltonien, ne [daltɔnjɛ̃, -jɛn] *a* colour-blind.
dam [dam] *nm*: **au grand ~ de** much to the detriment *ou* annoyance of.
dame [dam] *nf* lady; (CARTES, ÉCHECS) queen; **~s** *nfpl* (*jeu*) draughts *sg*.
damer [dame] *vt* to ram *ou* pack down; **~ le pion à** (*fig*) to get the better of.
damier [damje] *nm* draughtboard; (*dessin*) check (pattern).
damner [dɑne] *vt* to damn.
dancing [dɑ̃siŋ] *nm* dance hall.
dandiner [dɑ̃dine]: **se ~** *vi* to sway about; to waddle along.
Danemark [danmaʀk] *nm* Denmark.
danger [dɑ̃ʒe] *nm* danger; **mettre en ~** to endanger, put in danger; **dangereux, euse** *a* dangerous.
danois, e [danwa, -waz] *a* Danish // *nm/f*: **D~, e** Dane // *nm* (*langue*) Danish.
dans [dɑ̃] *prép* in; (*direction*) into, to; (*à l'intérieur de*) in, inside; **je l'ai pris ~ le tiroir/salon** I took it out of *ou* from the drawer/lounge; **boire ~ un verre** to drink out of *ou* from a glass; **~ 2 mois** in 2 months, in 2 months' time, 2 months from now; **~ les 20 F** about 20 F.
dansant, e [dɑ̃sɑ̃, -ɑ̃t] *a*: **soirée ~e** evening of dancing; dinner dance.
danse [dɑ̃s] *nf*: **la ~** dancing; (*classique*) (ballet) dancing; **une ~** a dance; **danser** *vi, vt* to dance; **danseur, euse** *nm/f* ballet dancer/ballerina; (*au bal etc*) dancer; partner; **en danseuse** (*à vélo*) standing on the pedals.
dard [daʀ] *nm* sting (*organ*).
darder [daʀde] *vt* to shoot, send forth.
date [dat] *nf* date; **faire ~** to mark a milestone; **~ de naissance** date of birth; **dater** *vt, vi* to date; **dater de** to date from, go back to; **à dater de** (as) from.
datif [datif] *nm* dative.
datte [dat] *nf* date; **dattier** *nm* date palm.
dauphin [dofɛ̃] *nm* (ZOOL) dolphin; (*du roi*) dauphin; (*fig*) heir apparent.
daurade [dɔʀad] *nf* gilt-head.
davantage [davɑ̃taʒ] *ad* more; (*plus longtemps*) longer; **~ de** more.
DCA [desea] *sigle f* (= *défense contre avions*): **la ~** anti-aircraft defence.

de (*de* + *le* = **du**, *de* + *les* = **des**) [də, dy, de] *prép* of; (*provenance*) from; (*moyen*) with; **la voiture d'Élisabeth/de mes parents** Elizabeth's/my parents' car; **un mur de brique/bureau d'acajou** a brick wall/mahogany desk; **augmenter** *etc* **de 10F** to increase by 10F; **une pièce de 2 m de large** *ou* **large de 2 m** a room 2 m wide *ou* in width, a 2 m wide room; **un bébé de 10 mois** a 10-month-old baby; **un séjour de 2 ans** a 2-year stay; **12 mois de crédit/travail** 12 months' credit/work // *dét*: **du vin, de l'eau, des pommes** (some) wine, (some) water, (some) apples; **des enfants sont venus** some children came; **a-t-il du vin?** has he got any wine?; **il ne veut pas de pommes** he doesn't want any apples; **il n'a pas d'enfants** he has no children, he hasn't got any children; **pendant des mois** for months.

dé [de] *nm* (*à jouer*) die *ou* dice (*pl* dice); (*aussi*: ~ **à coudre**) thimble; **~s** *nmpl* (*jeu*) (game of) dice; **un coup de ~s** a throw of the dice.

déambuler [deɑ̃byle] *vi* to stroll about.

débâcle [debɑkl(ə)] *nf* rout.

déballer [debale] *vt* to unpack.

débandade [debɑ̃dad] *nf* rout; scattering.

débarbouiller [debaʀbuje] *vt* to wash; **se** ~ to wash (one's face).

débarcadère [debaʀkadɛʀ] *nm* landing stage.

débardeur [debaʀdœʀ] *nm* docker, stevedore; (*maillot*) slipover, tank top.

débarquement [debaʀkəmɑ̃] *nm* unloading; landing; disembarcation; (MIL) landing.

débarquer [debaʀke] *vt* to unload, land // *vi* to disembark; (*fig*) to turn up.

débarras [debaʀa] *nm* lumber room; junk cupboard; outhouse; **bon ~!** good riddance!

débarrasser [debaʀase] *vt* to clear; ~ **qn de** (*vêtements, paquets*) to relieve sb of; (*habitude, ennemi*) to rid sb of; ~ **qch de** (*fouillis etc*) to clear sth of; **se ~ de** *vt* to get rid of; to rid o.s. of.

débat [deba] *nm* discussion, debate; **~s** (POL) proceedings, debates.

débattre [debatʀ(ə)] *vt* to discuss, debate; **se** ~ *vi* to struggle.

débauche [deboʃ] *nf* debauchery; **une ~ de** (*fig*) a profusion of; a riot of.

débaucher [deboʃe] *vt* (*licencier*) to lay off, dismiss; (*entraîner*) to lead astray, debauch.

débile [debil] *a* weak, feeble; ~ **mental, e** *nm/f* mental defective.

débit [debi] *nm* (*d'un liquide, fleuve*) (rate of) flow; (*d'un magasin*) turnover (of goods); (*élocution*) delivery; (*bancaire*) debit; **avoir un ~ de 10 F** to be 10 F in debit; ~ **de boissons** drinking establishment; ~ **de tabac** tobacconist's (shop); **débiter** *vt* (*compte*) to debit; (*liquide, gaz*) to yield, produce, give out; (*couper*: *bois, viande*) to cut up; (*vendre*) to retail; (*péj*: *paroles etc*) to come out with, churn out; **débiteur, trice** *nm/f* debtor // *a* in debit.

déblai [deblɛ] *nm* earth (*moved*).

déblaiement [deblɛmɑ̃] *nm* clearing; **travaux de** ~ earth moving *sg*.

déblayer [debleje] *vt* to clear.

débloquer [deblɔke] *vt* (*frein*) to release; (*prix, crédits*) to free.

déboires [debwaʀ] *nmpl* setbacks.

déboiser [debwaze] *vt* to clear of trees; to deforest.

déboîter [debwate] *vt* (AUTO) to pull out; **se ~ le genou** *etc* to dislocate one's knee *etc*.

débonnaire [debɔnɛʀ] *a* easy-going, good-natured.

débordé, e [debɔʀde] *a*: **être ~ de** (*travail, demandes*) to be snowed under with.

débordement [debɔʀdəmɑ̃] *nm* overflowing.

déborder [debɔʀde] *vi* to overflow; (*lait etc*) to boil over // *vt* (MIL, SPORT) to outflank; ~ **(de) qch** (*dépasser*) to extend beyond sth; ~ **de** (*joie, zèle*) to be brimming over with *ou* bursting with.

débouché [debuʃe] *nm* (*pour vendre*) outlet; (*perspective d'emploi*) opening; (*sortie*): **au ~ de la vallée** where the valley opens out (onto the plain); **au ~ de la rue Dupont (sur le boulevard)** where the rue Dupont meets the boulevard.

déboucher [debuʃe] *vt* (*évier, tuyau etc*) to unblock; (*bouteille*) to uncork, open // *vi*: ~ **de** to emerge from, come out of; ~ **sur** to come out onto; to open out onto; (*fig*) to arrive at, lead up to.

débourser [debuʀse] *vt* to pay out, lay out.

debout [dəbu] *ad*: **être ~** (*personne*) to be standing, stand; (: *levé, éveillé*) to be up (and about); (*chose*) to be upright; **être encore ~** (*fig*: *en état*) to be still going; to be still standing; **se mettre ~** to get up (on one's feet); **se tenir ~** to stand; **~!** stand up!; (*du lit*) get up!; **cette histoire ne tient pas ~** this story doesn't hold water.

déboutonner [debutɔne] *vt* to undo, unbutton; **se** ~ *vi* to come undone *ou* unbuttoned.

débraillé, e [debʀɑje] *a* slovenly, untidy.

débrayage [debʀɛjaʒ] *nm* (AUTO) clutch; (: *action*) disengaging the clutch; (*grève*) stoppage; **faire un double ~** to double-declutch.

débrayer [debʀeje] *vi* (AUTO) to declutch, disengage the clutch; (*cesser le travail*) to stop work.

débridé, e [debʀide] *a* unbridled, unrestrained.

débris [debʀi] *nm* (*fragment*) fragment // *nmpl* (*déchets*) pieces; rubbish *sg*; debris *sg*.

débrouillard, e [debʀujaʀ, -aʀd(ə)] *a* smart, resourceful.

débrouiller [debʀuje] *vt* to disentangle, untangle; (*fig*) to sort out, unravel; **se** ~ *vi* to manage.

débroussailler [debʀusɑje] *vt* to clear (of brushwood).

débusquer [debyske] *vt* to drive out (from cover).

début [deby] *nm* beginning, start ; **~s** *nmpl* beginnings ; début *sg*.
débutant, e [debytɑ̃, -ɑ̃t] *nm/f* beginner, novice.
débuter [debyte] *vi* to begin, start ; (*faire ses débuts*) to start out.
deçà [dəsa]: **en ~ de** *prép* this side of.
décacheter [dekaʃte] *vt* to unseal, open.
décade [dekad] *nf* (*10 jours*) (period of) ten days ; (*10 ans*) decade.
décadence [dekadɑ̃s] *nf* decadence ; decline.
décaféiné, e [dekafeine] *a* decaffeinated, caffeine-free.
décalage [dekalaʒ] *nm* gap ; discrepancy ; move forward *ou* back ; shift forward *ou* back ; **~ horaire** time difference (between time zones) ; time-lag.
décalcomanie [dekalkɔmani] *nf* transfer.
décaler [dekale] *vt* (*dans le temps*: *avancer*) to bring forward ; (: *retarder*) to put back ; (*changer de position*) to shift forward *ou* back ; **~ de 2 h** to bring *ou* move forward 2 hours ; to put back 2 hours.
décalquer [dekalke] *vt* to trace ; (*par pression*) to transfer.
décamper [dekɑ̃pe] *vi* to clear out *ou* off.
décanter [dekɑ̃te] *vt* to (allow to) settle (and decant) ; **se ~** to settle.
décapant [dekapɑ̃] *nm* acid solution ; scouring agent ; paint stripper.
décaper [dekape] *vt* to clean ; (*avec abrasif*) to scour ; (*avec papier de verre*) to sand.
décapiter [dekapite] *vt* to behead ; (*par accident*) to decapitate ; (*fig*) to cut the top off ; to remove the top men from.
décapotable [dekapɔtabl(ə)] *a* convertible.
décapoter [dekapɔte] *vt* to put down the top of.
décapsuler [dekapsyle] *vt* to take the cap *ou* top off ; **décapsuleur** *nm* bottle-opener.
décathlon [dekatlɔ̃] *nm* decathlon.
décédé, e [desede] *a* deceased.
décéder [desede] *vi* to die.
déceler [desle] *vt* to discover, detect ; to indicate, reveal.
décélération [deseleʀɑsjɔ̃] *nf* deceleration.
décembre [desɑ̃bʀ(ə)] *nm* December.
décemment [desamɑ̃] *ad* decently.
décence [desɑ̃s] *nf* decency.
décennie [desni] *nf* decade.
décent, e [desɑ̃, -ɑ̃t] *a* decent.
décentraliser [desɑ̃tʀalize] *vt* to decentralize.
décentrer [desɑ̃tʀe] *vt* to decentre ; **se ~** to move off-centre.
déception [desɛpsjɔ̃] *nf* disappointment.
décerner [desɛʀne] *vt* to award.
décès [desɛ] *nm* death, decease.
décevoir [dɛsvwaʀ] *vt* to disappoint.
déchaîner [deʃene] *vt* (*passions, colère*) to unleash ; (*rires etc*) to give rise to, arouse ; **se ~** *vi* to rage ; to burst out, explode ; (*se mettre en colère*) to fly into a rage, loose one's fury.
déchanter [deʃɑ̃te] *vi* to become disillusioned.
décharge [deʃaʀʒ(ə)] *nf* (*dépôt d'ordures*) rubbish tip *ou* dump ; (*électrique*) electrical discharge ; (*salve*) volley of shots ; **à la ~ de** in defence of.
déchargement [deʃaʀʒəmɑ̃] *nm* unloading.
décharger [deʃaʀʒe] *vt* (*marchandise, véhicule*) to unload ; (ÉLEC) to discharge ; (*arme: neutraliser*) to unload ; (: *faire feu*) to discharge, fire ; **~ qn de** (*responsabilité*) to relieve sb of, release sb from.
décharné, e [deʃaʀne] *a* bony, emaciated, fleshless.
déchausser [deʃose] *vt* (*personne*) to take the shoes off ; (*skis*) to take off ; **se ~** to take off one's shoes ; (*dent*) to come *ou* work loose.
déchéance [deʃeɑ̃s] *nf* degeneration ; decay, decline ; fall.
déchet [deʃɛ] *nm* (*de bois, tissu etc*) scrap ; (*perte: gén* COMM) wastage, waste ; **~s** *nmpl* (*ordures*) refuse *sg*, rubbish *sg*.
déchiffrer [deʃifʀe] *vt* to decipher.
déchiqueter [deʃikte] *vt* to tear *ou* pull to pieces.
déchirant, e [deʃiʀɑ̃, -ɑ̃t] *a* heart-breaking, heart-rending.
déchirement [deʃiʀmɑ̃] *nm* (*chagrin*) wrench, heartbreak ; (*gén pl*: *conflit*) rift, split.
déchirer [deʃiʀe] *vt* to tear ; (*mettre en morceaux*) to tear up ; (*pour ouvrir*) to tear off ; (*arracher*) to tear out ; (*fig*) to rack ; to tear ; to tear apart ; **se ~** *vi* to tear, rip ; **se ~ un muscle** to tear a muscle.
déchirure [deʃiʀyʀ] *nf* (*accroc*) tear, rip ; **~ musculaire** torn muscle.
déchoir [deʃwaʀ] *vi* (*personne*) to lower o.s., demean o.s.
déchu, e [deʃy] *a* fallen ; deposed.
décibel [desibɛl] *nm* decibel.
décidé, e [deside] *a* (*personne, air*) determined ; **c'est ~** it's decided ; **être ~ à faire** to be determined to do.
décidément [desidemɑ̃] *ad* undoubtedly ; really.
décider [deside] *vt*: **~ qch** to decide on sth ; **~ de faire/que** to decide to do/that ; **~ qn (à faire qch)** to persuade *ou* induce sb (to do sth) ; **~ de qch** to decide upon sth ; (*suj*: *chose*) to determine sth ; **se ~ (à faire)** to decide (to do), make up one's mind (to do) ; **se ~ pour** to decide on *ou* in favour of.
décilitre [desilitʀ(ə)] *nm* decilitre.
décimal, e, aux [desimal, -o] *a, nf* decimal.
décimer [desime] *vt* to decimate.
décimètre [desimɛtʀ(ə)] *nm* decimetre ; **double ~** (20 cm) ruler.
décisif, ive [desizif, -iv] *a* decisive ; (*qui l'emporte*): **le facteur/ l'argument ~** the deciding factor/ argument.
décision [desizjɔ̃] *nf* decision ; (*fermeté*) decisiveness, decision ; **emporter** *ou* **faire la ~** to be decisive.
déclamation [deklamɑsjɔ̃] *nf* declamation ; (*péj*) ranting, spouting.
déclaration [deklaʀɑsjɔ̃] *nf* declaration ; registration ; (*discours*: POL *etc*) statement ; **~ (d'amour)** declaration ; **~ de décès**

registration of death; ~ **de guerre** declaration of war; ~ **(d'impôts)** statement of income, tax declaration, ≈ tax return; ~ **(de sinistre)** (insurance) claim.

déclarer [deklaʀe] *vt* to declare, announce; (*revenus, marchandises*) to declare; (*décès, naissance*) to register; **se** ~ (*feu, maladie*) to break out; ~ **que** to declare that.

déclassement [deklɑsmɑ̃] *nm* (RAIL *etc*) change of class.

déclasser [deklɑse] *vt* to relegate; to downgrade; to lower in status.

déclenchement [deklɑ̃ʃmɑ̃] *nm* release; setting off.

déclencher [deklɑ̃ʃe] *vt* (*mécanisme etc*) to release; (*sonnerie*) to set off, activate; (*attaque, grève*) to launch; (*provoquer*) to trigger off; **se** ~ *vi* to release itself; to go off.

déclic [deklik] *nm* trigger mechanism; (*bruit*) click.

déclin [deklɛ̃] *nm* decline.

déclinaison [deklinɛzɔ̃] *nf* declension.

décliner [dekline] *vi* to decline // *vt* (*invitation*) to decline, refuse; (*responsabilité*) to refuse to accept; (*nom, adresse*) to state; (LING) to decline.

déclivité [deklivite] *nf* slope, incline; **en** ~ sloping, on the incline.

décocher [dekɔʃe] *vt* to throw; to shoot.

décoder [dekɔde] *vt* to decipher, decode.

décoiffer [dekwafe] *vt*: ~ **qn** to disarrange *ou* mess up sb's hair; to take sb's hat off; **se** ~ to take off one's hat.

décoincer [dekwɛ̃se] *vt* to unjam, loosen.

déçois *etc vb voir* **décevoir**.

décolérer [dekɔleʀe] *vi*: **il ne décolère pas** he's still angry, he hasn't calmed down.

décollage [dekɔlaʒ] *nm* (AVIAT) takeoff.

décoller [dekɔle] *vt* to unstick // *vi* (*avion*) to take off; **se** ~ to come unstuck.

décolletage [dekɔltaʒ] *nm* (TECH) cutting.

décolleté, e [dekɔlte] *a* low-necked, low-cut; wearing a low-cut dress // *nm* low neck(line); (bare) neck and shoulders; (*plongeant*) cleavage.

décolorant [dekɔlɔʀɑ̃] *nm* decolorant, bleaching agent.

décoloration [dekɔlɔʀɑsjɔ̃] *nf*: **se faire une** ~ (*chez le coiffeur*) to have one's hair bleached *ou* lightened.

décolorer [dekɔlɔʀe] *vt* (*tissu*) to fade; (*cheveux*) to bleach, lighten; **se** ~ *vi* to fade.

décombres [dekɔ̃bʀ(ə)] *nmpl* rubble *sg*, debris *sg*.

décommander [dekɔmɑ̃de] *vt* to cancel; (*invités*) to put off; **se** ~ to cancel one's appointment *etc*, cry off.

décomposé, e [dekɔ̃poze] *a* (*visage*) haggard, distorted.

décomposer [dekɔ̃poze] *vt* to break up; (CHIMIE) to decompose; (MATH) to factorize; **se** ~ *vi* (*pourrir*) to decompose; **décomposition** *nf* breaking up; decomposition; factorization; **en décomposition** (*organisme*) in a state of decay, decomposing.

décompression [dekɔ̃pʀɛsjɔ̃] *nf* decompression.

décompte [dekɔ̃t] *nm* deduction; (*facture*) breakdown (of an account), detailed account.

déconcentration [dekɔ̃sɑ̃tʀɑsjɔ̃] *nf* (*des industries etc*) dispersal.

déconcentré, e [dekɔ̃sɑ̃tʀe] *a* (*sportif etc*) who has lost (his/her) concentration.

déconcerter [dekɔ̃sɛʀte] *vt* to disconcert, confound.

déconfit, e [dekɔ̃fi, -it] *a* crestfallen, downcast.

déconfiture [dekɔ̃fityʀ] *nf* failure, defeat; collapse, ruin.

décongeler [dekɔ̃ʒle] *vt* to thaw (out).

décongestionner [dekɔ̃ʒɛstjɔne] *vt* (MÉD) to decongest; (*rues*) to relieve congestion in.

déconnecter [dekɔnɛkte] *vt* to disconnect.

déconseiller [dekɔ̃seje] *vt*: ~ **qch (à qn)** to advise (sb) against sth; ~ **à qn de faire** to advise sb against doing.

déconsidérer [dekɔ̃sideʀe] *vt* to discredit.

déconsigner [dekɔ̃siɲe] *vt* (*valise*) to collect (*from left luggage*); (*bouteille*) to return the deposit on.

décontenancer [dekɔ̃tnɑ̃se] *vt* to disconcert, discountenance.

décontracter [dekɔ̃tʀakte] *vt*, **se** ~ to relax.

déconvenue [dekɔ̃vny] *nf* disappointment.

décor [dekɔʀ] *nm* décor; (*paysage*) scenery; ~**s** *nmpl* (THÉÂTRE) scenery *sg*, décor *sg*; (CINÉMA) set *sg*.

décorateur [dekɔʀatœʀ] *nm* (interior) decorator; (CINÉMA) set designer.

décoratif, ive [dekɔʀatif, -iv] *a* decorative.

décoration [dekɔʀɑsjɔ̃] *nf* decoration.

décorer [dekɔʀe] *vt* to decorate.

décortiquer [dekɔʀtike] *vt* to shell; (*riz*) to hull; (*fig*) to dissect.

décorum [dekɔʀɔm] *nm* decorum; etiquette.

découcher [dekuʃe] *vi* to spend the night away from home.

découdre [dekudʀ(ə)] *vt* to unpick, take the stitching out of; **se** ~ to come unstitched; **en** ~ (*fig*) to fight, do battle.

découler [dekule] *vi*: ~ **de** to ensue *ou* follow from.

découpage [dekupaʒ] *nm* cutting up; carving; (*image*) cut-out (figure); ~ **électoral** division into constituencies.

découper [dekupe] *vt* (*papier, tissu etc*) to cut up; (*volaille, viande*) to carve; (*détacher*: *manche, article*) to cut out; **se** ~ **sur** (*ciel, fond*) to stand out against.

découplé, e [dekuple] *a*: **bien** ~ well-built, well-proportioned.

découpure [dekupyʀ] *nf*: ~**s** (*morceaux*) cut-out bits; (*d'une côte, arête*) indentations, jagged outline *sg*.

découragement [dekuʀaʒmɑ̃] *nm* discouragement, despondency.

décourager [dekuʀaʒe] *vt* to discourage, dishearten; (*dissuader*) to discourage, put off; **se** ~ to lose heart, become

discouraged; ~ **qn de faire/de qch** to discourage sb from doing/from sth, put sb off doing/sth.
décousu, e [dekuzy] *a* unstitched; (*fig*) disjointed, disconnected.
découvert, e [dekuvɛʀ, -ɛʀt(ə)] *a* (*tête*) bare, uncovered; (*lieu*) open, exposed // *nm* (*bancaire*) overdraft // *nf* discovery; **à** ~ *ad* (MIL) exposed, without cover; (*fig*) openly // *a* (COMM) overdrawn; **aller à la ~e de** to go in search of.
découvrir [dekuvʀiʀ] *vt* to discover; (*apercevoir*) to see; (*enlever ce qui couvre ou protège*) to uncover; (*montrer, dévoiler*) to reveal; **se** ~ to take off one's hat; to take off some clothes; (*au lit*) to uncover o.s.; (*ciel*) to clear; ~ **que** to discover that, find out that.
décrasser [dekʀase] *vt* to clean.
décrépi, e [dekʀepi] *a* peeling; with roughcast rendering removed.
décrépit, e [dekʀepi, -it] *a* decrepit; **décrépitude** *nf* decrepitude; decay.
decrescendo [dekʀeʃɛndo] *nm* (MUS) decrescendo; **aller** ~ (*fig*) to decline, be on the wane.
décret [dekʀɛ] *nm* decree; **décréter** *vt* to decree; to order; to declare; **~-loi** *nm* statutory order.
décrié, e [dekʀije] *a* disparaged.
décrire [dekʀiʀ] *vt* to describe; (*courbe, cercle*) to follow, describe.
décrochement [dekʀɔʃmɑ̃] *nm* (*d'un mur etc*) recess.
décrocher [dekʀɔʃe] *vt* (*dépendre*) to take down; (*téléphone*) to take off the hook; (: *pour répondre*): ~ **(le téléphone)** to pick up *ou* lift the receiver; (*fig: contrat etc*) to get, land // *vi* to drop out; to switch off.
décroître [dekʀwatʀ(ə)] *vi* to decrease, decline, diminish.
décrue [dekʀy] *nf* drop in level (of the waters).
décrypter [dekʀipte] *vt* to decipher.
déçu, e [desy] *pp de* **décevoir.**
déculotter [dekylɔte] *vt*: ~ **qn** to take off *ou* down sb's trousers.
décuple [dekypl(ə)] *nm*: **le** ~ **de** ten times; **au** ~ tenfold; **décupler** *vt, vi* to increase tenfold.
dédaigner [dedeɲe] *vt* to despise, scorn; (*négliger*) to disregard, spurn; ~ **de faire** to consider it beneath one to do; not to deign to do; **dédaigneux, euse** *a* scornful, disdainful.
dédain [dedɛ̃] *nm* scorn, disdain.
dédale [dedal] *nm* maze.
dedans [dədɑ̃] *ad* inside; (*pas en plein air*) indoors, inside // *nm* inside; **au** ~ on the inside; inside; **en** ~ (*vers l'intérieur*) inwards; *voir aussi* **là.**
dédicace [dedikas] *nf* dedication; (*manuscrite, sur une photo etc*) inscription.
dédicacer [dedikase] *vt*: ~ **(à qn)** to sign (for sb), autograph (for sb), inscribe (to sb).
dédier [dedje] *vt* to dedicate.
dédire [dediʀ]: **se** ~ *vi* to go back on one's word; to retract, recant.
dédit [dedi] *nm* (COMM) forfeit, penalty.
dédommagement [dedɔmaʒmɑ̃] *nm* compensation.
dédommager [dedɔmaʒe] *vt*: ~ **qn (de)** to compensate sb (for); (*fig*) to repay sb (for).
dédouaner [dedwane] *vt* to clear through customs.
dédoublement [dedubləmɑ̃] *nm* splitting; (PSYCH): ~ **de la personnalité** split *ou* dual personality.
dédoubler [deduble] *vt* (*classe, effectifs*) to split (into two); (*couverture etc*) to unfold; (*manteau*) to remove the lining of; ~ **un train/les trains** to run a relief train/additional trains.
déduction [dedyksjɔ̃] *nf* (*d'argent*) deduction; (*raisonnement*) deduction, inference.
déduire [dedɥiʀ] *vt*: ~ **qch (de)** (*ôter*) to deduct sth (from); (*conclure*) to deduce *ou* infer sth (from).
déesse [deɛs] *nf* goddess.
défaillance [defajɑ̃s] *nf* (*syncope*) blackout; (*fatigue*) (sudden) weakness *q*; (*technique*) fault, failure; (*morale etc*) weakness; ~ **cardiaque** heart failure.
défaillant, e [defajɑ̃, -ɑ̃t] *a* (JUR: *témoin*) defaulting.
défaillir [defajiʀ] *vi* to faint; to feel faint; (*mémoire etc*) to fail.
défaire [defɛʀ] *vt* (*installation, échafaudage*) to take down, dismantle; (*paquet etc, nœud, vêtement*) to undo; **se** ~ *vi* to come undone; **se** ~ **de** *vt* (*se débarrasser de*) to get rid of; (*se séparer de*) to part with.
défait, e [defɛ, -ɛt] *a* (*visage*) haggard, ravaged // *nf* defeat.
défaitiste [defetist(ə)] *a, nm/f* defeatist.
défalquer [defalke] *vt* to deduct.
défaut [defo] *nm* (*moral*) fault, failing, defect; (*d'étoffe, métal*) fault, flaw, defect; (*manque, carence*): ~ **de** lack of; shortage of; **en** ~ at fault; in the wrong; **faire** ~ (*manquer*) to be lacking; **à** ~ *ad* failing that; **à** ~ **de** for lack *ou* want of; **par** ~ (JUR) in his (*ou* her *etc*) absence.
défaveur [defavœʀ] *nf* disfavour.
défavorable [defavɔʀabl(ə)] *a* unfavourable.
défavoriser [defavɔʀize] *vt* to put at a disadvantage.
défectif, ive [defɛktif, -iv] *a*: **verbe** ~ defective verb.
défection [defɛksjɔ̃] *nf* defection, failure to give support *ou* assistance; failure to appear; **faire** ~ (*d'un parti etc*) to withdraw one's support, leave.
défectueux, euse [defɛktɥø, -øz] *a* faulty, defective; **défectuosité** *nf* defectiveness *q*; defect, fault.
défendre [defɑ̃dʀ(ə)] *vt* to defend; (*interdire*) to forbid; ~ **à qn qch/de faire** to forbid sb sth/to do; **se** ~ to defend o.s.; **il se défend** (*fig*) he can hold his own; **ça se défend** (*fig*) it holds together; **se** ~ **de/contre** (*se protéger*) to protect o.s. from/against; **se** ~ **de** (*se garder de*) to refrain from; (*nier*): **se** ~ **de vouloir** to deny wanting.
défense [defɑ̃s] *nf* defence; (*d'éléphant etc*) tusk; **'~ de fumer/cracher'** 'no

smoking/ spitting', 'smoking/spitting prohibited'; **défenseur** *nm* defender; (*JUR*) counsel for the defence; **défensif, ive** *a, nf* defensive.

déférent, e [defeʀɑ̃, -ɑ̃t] *a* (*poli*) deferential, deferent.

déférer [defeʀe] *vt* (*JUR*) to refer; ~ **à** *vt* (*requête, décision*) to defer to; ~ **qn à la justice** to hand sb over to justice.

déferlement [defɛʀləmɑ̃] *nm* breaking; surge.

déferler [defɛʀle] *vi* (*vagues*) to break; (*fig*) to surge.

défi [defi] *nm* (*provocation*) challenge; (*bravade*) defiance.

défiance [defjɑ̃s] *nf* mistrust, distrust.

déficience [defisjɑ̃s] *nf* deficiency.

déficit [defisit] *nm* (*COMM*) deficit; (*PSYCH etc: manque*) defect; **être en** ~ to be in deficit, be in the red.

défier [defje] *vt* (*provoquer*) to challenge; (*fig*) to defy, brave; **se** ~ **de** (*se méfier de*) to distrust, mistrust; ~ **qn de faire** to challenge *ou* defy sb to do; ~ **qn à** (*jeu etc*) to challenge sb to.

défigurer [defigyʀe] *vt* to disfigure; (*suj: boutons etc*) to mar *ou* spoil (the looks of); (*fig: œuvre*) to mutilate, deface.

défilé [defile] *nm* (*GÉO*) (narrow) gorge *ou* pass; (*soldats*) parade; (*manifestants*) procession, march; **un** ~ **de** (*voitures, visiteurs etc*) a stream of.

défiler [defile] *vi* (*troupes*) to march past; (*sportifs*) to parade; (*manifestants*) to march; (*visiteurs*) to pour, stream; **se** ~ *vi* (*se dérober*) to slip away, sneak off.

défini, e [defini] *a* definite.

définir [definiʀ] *vt* to define.

définitif, ive [definitif, -iv] *a* (*final*) final, definitive; (*pour longtemps*) permanent, definitive; (*sans appel*) final, definite // *nf*: **en définitive** eventually; (*somme toute*) when all is said and done.

définition [definisjɔ̃] *nf* definition; (*de mots croisés*) clue; (*TV*) (picture) resolution.

définitivement [definitivmɑ̃] *ad* definitively; permanently; definitely.

déflagration [deflagʀɑsjɔ̃] *nf* explosion.

déflation [deflɑsjɔ̃] *nf* deflation; **déflationniste** *a* deflationist, deflationary.

déflecteur [deflɛktœʀ] *nm* (*AUTO*) quarterlight.

déflorer [deflɔʀe] *vt* (*jeune fille*) to deflower; (*fig*) to spoil the charm of.

défoncer [defɔ̃se] *vt* (*caisse*) to stave in; (*porte*) to smash in *ou* down; (*lit, fauteuil*) to burst (the springs of); (*terrain, route*) to rip *ou* plough up.

déformant, e [defɔʀmɑ̃, -ɑ̃t] *a*: **glace** *ou* **miroir** ~**(e)** distorting mirror.

déformation [defɔʀmɑsjɔ̃] *nf* loss of shape; deformation; distortion; ~ **professionnelle** conditioning by one's job.

déformer [defɔʀme] *vt* to put out of shape; (*corps*) to deform; (*pensée, fait*) to distort; **se** ~ *vi* to lose its shape.

défouler [defule]: **se** ~ *vi* (*PSYCH*) to work off one's tensions, release one's pent-up feelings; (*gén*) to unwind, let off steam.

défraîchir [defʀeʃiʀ]: **se** ~ *vi* to fade; to become worn.

défrayer [defʀeje] *vt*: ~ **qn** to pay sb's expenses; ~ **la chronique** to be in the news, be the main topic of conversation.

défricher [defʀiʃe] *vt* to clear (for cultivation).

défroquer [defʀɔke] *vi* (*gén*: **se** ~) to give up the cloth, renounce one's vows.

défunt, e [defœ̃, -œ̃t] *a*: **son** ~ **père** his late father // *nm/f* deceased.

dégagé, e [degaʒe] *a* clear; (*ton, air*) casual, jaunty.

dégagement [degaʒmɑ̃] *nm* emission; freeing; clearing; (*espace libre*) clearing; passage; clearance; (*FOOTBALL*) clearance; **voie de** ~ slip road; **itinéraire de** ~ alternative route (*to relieve traffic congestion*).

dégager [degaʒe] *vt* (*exhaler*) to give off, emit; (*délivrer*) to free, extricate; (*MIL troupes*) to relieve; (*désencombrer*) to clear; (*isoler: idée, aspect*) to bring out; ~ **qn de** (*engagement, parole etc*) to release *ou* free sb from; **se** ~ *vi* (*odeur*) to emanate, be given off; (*passage, ciel*) to clear; **se** ~ **de** (*fig: engagement etc*) to get out of; to go back on.

dégainer [degene] *vt* to draw.

dégarnir [degaʀniʀ] *vt* (*vider*) to empty, clear; **se** ~ *vi* to empty; to be cleaned out *ou* cleared; (*tempes, crâne*) to go bald.

dégâts [degɑ] *nmpl* damage *sg*.

dégazer [degɑze] *vi* (*pétrolier*) to clean its tanks.

dégel [deʒɛl] *nm* thaw.

dégeler [deʒle] *vt* to thaw (out); (*fig*) to unfreeze // *vi* to thaw (out).

dégénéré, e [deʒeneʀe] *a, nm/f* degenerate.

dégénérer [deʒeneʀe] *vi* to degenerate; (*empirer*) to go from bad to worse.

dégingandé, e [deʒɛ̃gɑ̃de] *a* gangling, lanky.

dégivrage [deʒivʀaʒ] *nm* defrosting; de-icing.

dégivrer [deʒivʀe] *vt* (*frigo*) to defrost; (*vitres*) to de-ice; **dégivreur** *nm* defroster; de-icer.

déglutir [deglytiʀ] *vi* to swallow.

dégonflé, e [degɔ̃fle] *a* (*pneu*) flat.

dégonfler [degɔ̃fle] *vt* (*pneu, ballon*) to let down, deflate; **se** ~ *vi* (*fam*) to chicken out.

dégouliner [deguline] *vi* to trickle, drip; ~ **de** to be dripping with.

dégoupiller [degupije] *vt* (*grenade*) to take the pin out of.

dégourdi, e [deguʀdi] *a* smart, resourceful.

dégourdir [deguʀdiʀ] *vt* to warm (up); **se** ~ **(les jambes)** to stretch one's legs (*fig*).

dégoût [degu] *nm* disgust, distaste.

dégoûtant, e [degutɑ̃, -ɑ̃t] *a* disgusting.

dégoûter [degute] *vt* to disgust; **cela me dégoûte** I find this disgusting *ou* revolting; ~ **qn de qch** to put sb off sth.

dégoutter [degute] *vi* to drip; ~ **de** to be dripping with.

dégradé, e [degʀade] *a* (*couleur*) shaded off // *nm* (*PEINTURE*) gradation.

dégrader [degʀade] *vt* (*MIL: officier*) to degrade; (*abîmer*) to damage, deface;

(*avilir*) to degrade, debase ; **se ~** (*relations, situation*) to deteriorate.
dégrafer [degʀafe] *vt* to unclip, unhook, unfasten.
dégraissage [degʀɛsaʒ] *nm*: **~ et nettoyage à sec** dry cleaning.
dégraisser [degʀese] *vt* (*soupe*) to skim ; (*vêtement*) to take the grease marks out of.
degré [dəgʀe] *nm* degree ; (*d'escalier*) step ; **brûlure au 1er/2ème ~** 1st/2nd degree burn ; **équation du 1er/2ème ~** linear/quadratic equation ; **alcool à 90 ~s** 90% proof alcohol (*on Gay-Lussac scale*) ; **vin de 10 ~s** 10° wine (*on Gay-Lussac scale*) ; **par ~(s)** *ad* by degrees, gradually.
dégressif, ive [degʀesif, -iv] *a* on a decreasing sliding scale, degressive.
dégrever [degʀəve] *vt* to grant tax relief to ; to reduce the tax burden on.
dégringoler [degʀɛ̃gɔle] *vi* to tumble (down).
dégriser [degʀize] *vt* to sober up.
dégrossir [degʀosiʀ] *vt* (*bois*) to trim ; (*fig*) to work out roughly ; to knock the rough edges off.
déguenillé, e [degnije] *a* ragged, tattered.
déguerpir [degɛʀpiʀ] *vi* to clear off, scarper.
déguisement [degizmɑ̃] *nm* disguise.
déguiser [degize] *vt* to disguise ; **se ~** (*se costumer*) to dress up ; (*pour tromper*) to disguise o.s.
dégustation [degystɑsjɔ̃] *nf* tasting ; sampling ; savouring ; (*séance*): **~ de vin(s)** wine-tasting session.
déguster [degyste] *vt* (*vins*) to taste ; (*fromages etc*) to sample ; (*savourer*) to enjoy, savour.
déhancher [deɑ̃ʃe]: **se ~** *vi* to sway one's hips ; to lean (one's weight) on one hip.
dehors [dəɔʀ] *ad* outside ; (*en plein air*) outdoors, outside // *nm* outside // *nmpl* (*apparences*) appearances, exterior *sg* ; **mettre** *ou* **jeter ~** (*expulser*) to throw out ; **au ~** outside ; outwardly ; **au ~ de** outside ; **en ~** (*vers l'extérieur*) outside ; outwards ; **en ~ de** (*hormis*) apart from.
déjà [deʒa] *ad* already ; (*auparavant*) before, already ; **quel nom, ~?** what was the name again?
déjanter [deʒɑ̃te]: **se ~** *vi* (*pneu*) to come off the rim.
déjeté, e [dɛʒte] *a* lop-sided, crooked.
déjeuner [deʒœne] *vi* to (have) lunch ; (*le matin*) to have breakfast // *nm* lunch ; (*petit déjeuner*) breakfast.
déjouer [deʒwe] *vt* to elude ; to foil, thwart.
delà [dəla] *ad*: **par ~, en ~ (de), au ~ (de)** beyond.
délabrer [delɑbʀe]: **se ~** *vi* to fall into decay, become dilapidated.
délacer [delase] *vt* to unlace, undo.
délai [delɛ] *nm* (*attente*) waiting period ; (*sursis*) extension (of time) ; (*temps accordé*) time limit ; **sans ~** without delay ; **à bref ~** shortly, very soon ; at short notice ; **dans les ~s** within the time limit ; **comptez un ~ de livraison de 10 jours** allow 10 days for delivery.
délaisser [delese] *vt* to abandon, desert.
délasser [delɑse] *vt* (*reposer*) to relax ; (*divertir*) to divert, entertain ; **se ~** to relax.
délateur, trice [delatœʀ, -tʀis] *nm/f* informer.
délation [delɑsjɔ̃] *nf* denouncement, informing.
délavé, e [delave] *a* faded.
délayer [deleje] *vt* (CULIN) to mix (with water *etc*) ; (*peinture*) to thin down ; (*fig*) to pad out, spin out.
delco [dɛlko] *nm* (AUTO) distributor.
délecter [delɛkte]: **se ~** *vi*: **se ~ de** to revel *ou* delight in.
délégation [delegɑsjɔ̃] *nf* delegation.
délégué, e [delege] *a* delegated // *nm/f* delegate ; representative.
déléguer [delege] *vt* to delegate.
délester [delɛste] *vt* (*navire*) to unballast.
délibération [delibeʀɑsjɔ̃] *nf* deliberation.
délibéré, e [delibeʀe] *a* (*conscient*) deliberate ; (*déterminé*) determined, resolute.
délibérément [delibeʀemɑ̃] *ad* deliberately.
délibérer [delibeʀe] *vi* to deliberate.
délicat, e [delika, -at] *a* delicate ; (*plein de tact*) tactful ; (*attentionné*) thoughtful ; (*exigeant*) fussy, particular ; **procédés peu ~s** unscrupulous methods ; **délicatement** *ad* delicately ; (*avec douceur*) gently ; **délicatesse** *nf* delicacy, delicate nature ; tactfulness ; thoughtfulness ; **délicatesses** *nfpl* attentions, consideration *sg*.
délice [delis] *nm* delight.
délicieux, euse [delisjø, -jøz] *a* (*au goût*) delicious ; (*sensation, impression*) delightful.
délictueux, euse [deliktɥø, -ɥøz] *a* criminal.
délié, e [delje] *a* nimble, agile ; slender, fine // *nm*: **les ~s** the upstrokes (*in handwriting*).
délier [delje] *vt* to untie ; **~ qn de** (*serment etc*) to free *ou* release sb from.
délimitation [delimitɑsjɔ̃] *nf* delimitation, demarcation.
délimiter [delimite] *vt* to delimit, demarcate ; to determine ; to define.
délinquance [delɛ̃kɑ̃s] *nf* criminality ; **~ juvénile** juvenile delinquency.
délinquant, e [delɛ̃kɑ̃, -ɑ̃t] *a, nm/f* delinquent.
déliquescence [delikesɑ̃s] *nf*: **en ~** in a state of decay.
délire [deliʀ] *nm* (*fièvre*) delirium ; (*fig*) frenzy ; lunacy.
délirer [deliʀe] *vi* to be delirious ; (*fig*) to be raving, be going wild.
délit [deli] *nm* (criminal) offence ; **~ de droit commun** violation of common law ; **~ politique** political offence ; **~ de presse** violation of the press laws.
délivrance [delivʀɑ̃s] *nf* freeing, release ; (*sentiment*) relief.
délivrer [delivʀe] *vt* (*prisonnier*) to (set) free, release ; (*passeport, certificat*) to issue ; **~ qn de** (*ennemis*) to set sb free from, deliver *ou* free sb from ; (*fig*) to relieve sb of ; to rid sb of.
déloger [delɔʒe] *vt* (*locataire*) to turn out ; (*objet coincé, ennemi*) to dislodge.

déloyal, e, aux [delwajal, -o] *a* disloyal; unfair.
delta [dɛlta] *nm* (GÉO) delta.
déluge [delyʒ] *nm* (*biblique*) Flood, Deluge; (*grosse pluie*) downpour, deluge; (*grand nombre*): ~ **de** flood of.
déluré, e [delyʀe] *a* smart, resourceful; (*péj*) forward, pert.
démagnétiser [demaɲetize] *vt* to demagnetize.
démagogie [demagɔʒi] *nf* demagogy, demagoguery; **démagogique** *a* demagogic, popularity-seeking; vote-catching; **démagogue** *a* demagogic // *nm* demagogue.
démaillé, e [demɑje] *a* (*bas*) laddered, with a run, with runs.
demain [dəmɛ̃] *ad* tomorrow.
demande [dəmɑ̃d] *nf* (*requête*) request; (*revendication*) demand; (ADMIN, *formulaire*) application; (ÉCON): **la** ~ demand; **'~s d'emploi'** situations wanted; ~ **en mariage** (marriage) proposal; ~ **de naturalisation** application for naturalization; ~ **de poste** job application.
demandé, e [dəmɑ̃de] *a* (*article etc*): **très** ~ (very) much in demand.
demander [dəmɑ̃de] *vt* to ask for; (*question: date, heure etc*) to ask; (*requérir, nécessiter*) to require, demand; ~ **qch à qn** to ask sb for sth; to ask sb sth; ~ **à qn de faire** to ask sb to do; ~ **que/pourquoi** to ask that/why; **se** ~ **si/pourquoi** *etc* to wonder if/why *etc*; (*sens purement réfléchi*) to ask o.s. if/why *etc*; **on vous demande au téléphone** you're wanted on the phone, someone's asking for you on the phone.
demandeur, euse [dəmɑ̃dœʀ, -øz] *nm/f*: ~ **d'emploi** job-seeker; (job) applicant.
démangeaison [demɑ̃ʒɛzɔ̃] *nf* itching.
démanger [demɑ̃ʒe] *vi* to itch; **la main me démange** my hand is itching; **l'envie me démange de** I'm itching to.
démanteler [demɑ̃tle] *vt* to break up; to demolish.
démaquillant [demakijɑ̃] *nm* make-up remover.
démaquiller [demakije] *vt*: **se** ~ to remove one's make-up.
démarcage [demaʀkaʒ] *nm* = **démarquage.**
démarcation [demaʀkɑsjɔ̃] *nf* demarcation.
démarchage [demaʀʃaʒ] *nm* (COMM) door-to-door selling.
démarche [demaʀʃ(ə)] *nf* (*allure*) gait, walk; (*intervention*) step; approach; (*fig: intellectuelle*) thought processes *pl*; approach; **faire des ~s auprès de qn** to approach sb.
démarcheur, euse [demaʀʃœʀ, -øz] *nm/f* (COMM) door-to-door salesman/woman.
démarquage [demaʀkaʒ] *nm* mark-down.
démarqué, e [demaʀke] *a* (FOOTBALL) unmarked.
démarquer [demaʀke] *vt* (*prix*) to mark down; (*joueur*) to stop marking.
démarrage [demaʀaʒ] *nm* starting *q*, start; ~ **en côte** hill start.
démarrer [demaʀe] *vi* (*conducteur*) to start (up); (*véhicule*) to move off; (*travaux*) to get moving; (*coureur: accélérer*) to pull away; **démarreur** *nm* (AUTO) starter.
démasquer [demaske] *vt* to unmask.
démâter [demɑte] *vt* to dismast // *vi* to be dismasted.
démêler [demele] *vt* to untangle, disentangle.
démêlés [demele] *nmpl* problems.
démembrer [demɑ̃bʀe] *vt* to slice up, tear apart.
déménagement [demenaʒmɑ̃] *nm* (*du point de vue du locataire*) move; (: *du déménageur*) removal; **entreprise/camion de** ~ removal firm/van.
déménager [demenaʒe] *vt* (*meubles*) to (re)move // *vi* to move (house); **déménageur** *nm* removal man; (*entrepreneur*) furniture remover.
démence [demɑ̃s] *nf* dementia; madness, insanity.
démener [demne] : **se** ~ *vi* to thrash about; (*fig*) to exert o.s.
démenti [demɑ̃ti] *nm* denial, refutation.
démentiel, le [demɑ̃sjɛl] *a* insane.
démentir [demɑ̃tiʀ] *vt* (*nouvelle*) to refute; (*suj: faits etc*) to belie, refute; ~ **que** to deny that; **ne pas se** ~ not to fail; to keep up.
démériter [demeʀite] *vi*: ~ **auprès de qn** to come down in sb's esteem.
démesure [deməzyʀ] *nf* immoderation, immoderateness; **démesuré, e** *a* immoderate, disproportionate.
démettre [demɛtʀ(ə)] *vt*: ~ **qn de** (*fonction, poste*) to dismiss sb from; **se** ~ **(de ses fonctions)** to resign (from) one's duties; **se** ~ **l'épaule** *etc* to dislocate one's shoulder *etc.*
demeurant [dəmœʀɑ̃]: **au** ~ *ad* for all that.
demeure [dəmœʀ] *nf* residence; **mettre qn en** ~ **de faire** to enjoin *ou* order sb to do; **à** ~ *ad* permanently.
demeurer [dəmœʀe] *vi* (*habiter*) to live; (*séjourner*) to stay; (*rester*) to remain.
demi, e [dəmi] *a*: **et** ~: **trois heures/bouteilles et ~es** three and a half hours/bottles, three hours/bottles and a half; **il est 2 heures/midi et ~e** it's half past 2/12 // *nm* (*bière*) ≈ half-pint (.25 litre); (FOOTBALL) half-back; **à** ~ *ad* half-; **ouvrir à** ~ to half-open; **à** ~ **fini** half-completed; **à la ~e** (*heure*) on the half-hour.
demi... [dəmi] *préfixe* half-, semi..., demi-; **~-cercle** *nm* semicircle; **en ~-cercle** *a* semicircular // *ad* in a half circle; **~-douzaine** *nf* half-dozen, half a dozen; **~-finale** *nf* semifinal; **~-fond** *nm* (SPORT) medium-distance running; **~-frère** *nm* half-brother; **~-gros** *nm* wholesale trade; **~-heure** *nf* half-hour, half an hour; **~-jour** *nm* half-light; **~-journée** *nf* half-day, half a day.
démilitariser [demilitaʀize] *vt* to demilitarize.
demi-litre [dəmilitʀ(ə)] *nm* half-litre, half a litre.

demi-livre [dəmilivʀ(ə)] *nf* half-pound, half a pound.
demi-longueur [dəmilɔ̃gœʀ] *nf* (SPORT) half-length, half a length.
demi-lune [dəmilyn] *ad*: **en ~** semicircular.
demi-mesure [dəmimzyʀ] *nf* half-measure.
demi-mot [dəmimo]: **à ~** *ad* without having to spell things out.
déminer [demine] *vt* to clear of mines; **démineur** *nm* bomb disposal expert.
demi-pension [dəmipɑ̃sjɔ̃] *nf (à l'hôtel)* half-board.
demi-pensionnaire [dəmipɑ̃sjɔnɛʀ] *nm/f (au lycée)* half-boarder.
demi-place [dəmiplas] *nf* half-fare.
démis, e [demi, -iz] *a (épaule etc)* dislocated.
demi-saison [dəmisɛzɔ̃] *nf*: **vêtements de ~** spring *ou* autumn clothing.
demi-sel [dəmisɛl] *a inv (beurre, fromage)* slightly salted.
demi-sœur [dəmisœʀ] *nf* half-sister.
démission [demisjɔ̃] *nf* resignation; **donner sa ~** to give *ou* hand in one's notice, hand in one's resignation; **démissionner** *vi (de son poste)* to resign, give *ou* hand in one's notice.
demi-tarif [dəmitaʀif] *nm* half-price; (TRANSPORTS) half-fare.
demi-tour [dəmituʀ] *nm* about-turn; **faire un ~** (MIL *etc*) to make an about-turn; **faire ~** to turn (and go) back; (AUTO) to do a U-turn.
démobilisation [demɔbilizɑsjɔ̃] *nf* demobilization.
démocrate [demɔkʀat] *a* democratic // *nm/f* democrat.
démocratie [demɔkʀasi] *nf* democracy; **~ populaire/libérale** people's/liberal democracy.
démocratique [demɔkʀatik] *a* democratic.
démocratiser [demɔkʀatize] *vt* to democratize.
démodé, e [demɔde] *a* old-fashioned.
démographie [demɔgʀafi] *nf* demography.
démographique [demɔgʀafik] *a* demographic; **poussée ~** increase in population.
demoiselle [dəmwazɛl] *nf (jeune fille)* young lady; *(célibataire)* single lady, maiden lady; **~ d'honneur** bridesmaid.
démolir [demɔliʀ] *vt* to demolish.
démolisseur [demɔlisœʀ] *nm* demolition worker.
démolition [demɔlisjɔ̃] *nf* demolition.
démon [demɔ̃] *nm* demon, fiend; evil spirit; *(enfant turbulent)* devil, demon; **le D~** the Devil.
démoniaque [demɔnjak] *a* fiendish.
démonstrateur, trice [demɔ̃stʀatœʀ, -tʀis] *nm/f* demonstrator.
démonstratif, ive [demɔ̃stʀatif, -iv] *a (aussi* LING*)* demonstrative.
démonstration [demɔ̃stʀɑsjɔ̃] *nf* demonstration; *(aérienne, navale)* display.
démonté, e [demɔ̃te] *a (fig)* raging, wild.
démonter [demɔ̃te] *vt (machine etc)* to take down, dismantle; *(fig: personne)* to disconcert; **se ~** *vi (personne)* to lose countenance.
démontrer [demɔ̃tʀe] *vt* to demonstrate, show.
démoraliser [demɔʀalize] *vt* to demoralize.
démordre [demɔʀdʀ(ə)] *vi*: **ne pas ~ de** to refuse to give up, stick to.
démouler [demule] *vt (gâteau)* to turn out.
démoustiquer [demustike] *vt* to clear of mosquitoes.
démultiplication [demyltiplikɑsjɔ̃] *nf* reduction; reduction ratio.
démuni, e [demyni] *a (sans argent)* impoverished; **~ de** without, lacking in.
démunir [demyniʀ] *vt*: **~ qn de** to deprive sb of; **se ~ de** to part with, give up.
dénatalité [denatalite] *nf* fall in the birth rate.
dénaturer [denatyʀe] *vt (goût)* to alter (completely); *(pensée, fait)* to distort, misrepresent.
dénégations [denegɑsjɔ̃] *nfpl* denials.
dénicher [deniʃe] *vt* to unearth; to track *ou* hunt down.
dénier [denje] *vt* to deny.
dénigrer [denigʀe] *vt* to denigrate, run down.
dénivellation [denivɛlɑsjɔ̃] *nf*, **dénivellement** [denivɛlmɑ̃] *nm* ramp; dip; difference in level.
dénombrer [denɔ̃bʀe] *vt (compter)* to count; *(énumérer)* to enumerate, list.
dénominateur [denɔminatœʀ] *nm* denominator; **~ commun** common denominator.
dénomination [denɔminɑsjɔ̃] *nf* designation, appellation.
dénommer [denɔme] *vt* to name.
dénoncer [denɔ̃se] *vt* to denounce; **se ~** to give o.s. up, come forward; **dénonciation** *nf* denunciation.
dénoter [denɔte] *vt* to denote.
dénouement [denumɑ̃] *nm* outcome, conclusion; (THÉÂTRE) dénouement.
dénouer [denwe] *vt* to unknot, undo.
dénoyauter [denwajote] *vt* to stone; **appareil à ~, dénoyauteur** *nm* stoner.
denrée [dɑ̃ʀe] *nf* food(stuff); **~s alimentaires** foodstuffs.
dense [dɑ̃s] *a* dense.
densité [dɑ̃site] *nf* denseness; density; (PHYSIQUE) density.
dent [dɑ̃] *nf* tooth (*pl* teeth); **faire ses ~s** to teethe, cut (one's) teeth; **en ~s de scie** serrated; jagged; **~ de lait/sagesse** milk/wisdom tooth; **dentaire** *a* dental; **denté, e** *a*: **roue dentée** cog wheel.
dentelé, e [dɑ̃tle] *a* jagged, indented.
dentelle [dɑ̃tɛl] *nf* lace *q*.
dentier [dɑ̃tje] *nm* denture.
dentifrice [dɑ̃tifʀis] *nm*, *a*: **(pâte) ~** toothpaste.
dentiste [dɑ̃tist(ə)] *nm/f* dentist.
dentition [dɑ̃tisjɔ̃] *nf* teeth *pl*; dentition.
dénudé, e [denyde] *a* bare.
dénuder [denyde] *vt* to bare.

dénué, e [denɥe] *a*: ~ **de** devoid of; lacking in.
dénuement [denymɑ̃] *nm* destitution.
déodorant [deɔdɔʀɑ̃] *nm* deodorant.
dépannage [depanaʒ] *nm*: **service de** ~ (AUTO) breakdown service.
dépanner [depane] *vt* (*voiture, télévision*) to fix, repair; (*fig*) to bail out, help out; **dépanneuse** *nf* breakdown lorry.
déparer [depaʀe] *vt* to spoil, mar.
départ [depaʀ] *nm* leaving *q*, departure; (SPORT) start; (*sur un horaire*) departure; **à son** ~ when he left.
départager [depaʀtaʒe] *vt* to decide between.
département [depaʀtəmɑ̃] *nm* department.
départir [depaʀtiʀ]: **se** ~ **de** *vt* to abandon, depart from.
dépassé, e [depɑse] *a* superseded, outmoded.
dépassement [depɑsmɑ̃] *nm* (AUTO) overtaking *q*.
dépasser [depɑse] *vt* (*véhicule, concurrent*) to overtake; (*endroit*) to pass, go past; (*somme, limite*) to exceed; (*fig*: *en beauté etc*) to surpass, outshine; (*être en saillie sur*) to jut out above (*ou* in front of) // *vi* (AUTO) to overtake; (*jupon*) to show.
dépaysement [depeizmɑ̃] *nm* disorientation; change of scenery.
dépayser [depeize] *vt* to disorientate.
dépecer [depəse] *vt* to joint, cut up; to dismember.
dépêche [depɛʃ] *nf* dispatch; ~ **(télégraphique)** wire.
dépêcher [depeʃe] *vt* to dispatch; **se** ~ *vi* to hurry.
dépeindre [depɛ̃dʀ(ə)] *vt* to depict.
dépendance [depɑ̃dɑ̃s] *nf* dependence, dependency.
dépendre [depɑ̃dʀ(ə)] *vt* (*tableau*) to take down; ~ **de** *vt* to depend on; (*financièrement etc*) to be dependent on.
dépens [depɑ̃] *nmpl*: **aux** ~ **de** at the expense of.
dépense [depɑ̃s] *nf* spending *q*, expense, expenditure *q*; (*fig*) consumption; expenditure; **une** ~ **de 100 F** an outlay *ou* expenditure of 100 F; ~ **physique** (physical) exertion; ~**s publiques** public expenditure.
dépenser [depɑ̃se] *vt* to spend; (*gaz, eau*) to use; (*fig*) to expend, use up; **se** ~ (*se fatiguer*) to exert o.s.
dépensier, ière [depɑ̃sje, -jɛʀ] *a*: **il est** ~ he's a spendthrift.
déperdition [depɛʀdisjɔ̃] *nf* loss.
dépérir [depeʀiʀ] *vi* to waste away; to wither.
dépêtrer [depetʀe] *vt*: **se** ~ **de** to extricate o.s. from.
dépeupler [depœple] *vt* to depopulate; **se** ~ to be depopulated; (*rivière, forêt*) to empty of wildlife *etc*.
déphasé, e [defɑze] *a* (ÉLEC) out of phase; (*fig*) out of touch.
dépilatoire [depilatwaʀ] *a* depilatory, hair removing.
dépistage [depistaʒ] *nm* (MÉD) detection.
dépister [depiste] *vt* to detect; (*voleur*) to track down; (*poursuivants*) to throw off the scent.
dépit [depi] *nm* vexation, frustration; **en** ~ **de** *prép* in spite of; **en** ~ **du bon sens** contrary to all good sense; **dépité, e** *a* vexed, frustrated.
déplacé, e [deplase] *a* (*propos*) out of place, uncalled-for.
déplacement [deplasmɑ̃] *nm* moving; shifting; transfer; trip, travelling *q*; ~ **d'air** displacement of air; ~ **de vertèbre** slipped disc.
déplacer [deplase] *vt* (*table, voiture*) to move, shift; (*employé*) to transfer, move; **se** ~ *vi* to move; (*organe*) to be displaced; (*voyager*) to travel // *vt* (*vertèbre etc*) to displace.
déplaire [deplɛʀ] *vi*: **ceci me déplaît** I don't like this, I dislike this; **il cherche à nous** ~ he's trying to displease us *ou* be disagreeable to us; **se** ~ **quelque part** to dislike it somewhere; **déplaisant, e** *a* disagreeable, unpleasant.
déplaisir [deplezir] *nm* displeasure, annoyance.
dépliant [deplijɑ̃] *nm* leaflet.
déplier [deplije] *vt* to unfold.
déplisser [deplise] *vt* to smooth out.
déploiement [deplwamɑ̃] *nm* deployment; display.
déplorer [deplɔʀe] *vt* to deplore; to lament.
déployer [deplwaje] *vt* to open out, spread; to deploy; to display, exhibit.
dépoli, e [depɔli] *a*: **verre** ~ frosted glass.
déportation [depɔʀtɑsjɔ̃] *nf* deportation.
déporté, e [depɔʀte] *nm/f* deportee; (*39-45*) concentration camp prisoner.
déporter [depɔʀte] *vt* (POL) to deport; (*dévier*) to carry off course.
déposant, e [depozɑ̃, -ɑ̃t] *nm/f* (*épargnant*) depositor.
dépose [depoz] *nf* taking out; taking down.
déposer [depoze] *vt* (*gén*: *mettre, poser*) to lay down, put down, set down; (*à la banque, à la consigne*) to deposit; (*passager*) to drop (off), set down; (*démonter*: *serrure, moteur*) to take out; (: *rideau*) to take down; (*roi*) to depose; (ADMIN: *faire enregistrer*) to file; to lodge; to submit; to register // *vi* to form a sediment *ou* deposit; (JUR): ~ **(contre)** to testify *ou* give evidence (against); **se** ~ *vi* to settle; **dépositaire** *nm/f* (JUR) depository; (COMM) agent; **déposition** *nf* (JUR) deposition.
déposséder [depɔsede] *vt* to dispossess.
dépôt [depo] *nm* (*à la banque, sédiment*) deposit; (*entrepôt, réserve*) warehouse, store; (*gare*) depot; (*prison*) cells *pl*; ~ **légal** registration of copyright.
dépotoir [depɔtwaʀ] *nm* dumping ground, rubbish dump.
dépouille [depuj] *nf* (*d'animal*) skin, hide; (*humaine*): ~ **(mortelle)** mortal remains *pl*.
dépouillé, e [depuje] *a* (*fig*) bare, bald; ~ **de** stripped of; lacking in.
dépouiller [depuje] *vt* (*animal*) to skin; (*spolier*) to deprive of one's possessions; (*documents*) to go through, peruse; ~

qn/qch de to strip sb/sth of ; ~ le scrutin to count the votes.
dépourvu, e [depuRvy] *a*: ~ **de** lacking in, without ; **au** ~ *ad* unprepared.
dépoussiérer [depusjeRe] *vt* to remove dust from.
dépravation [depRavɑsjɔ̃] *nf* depravity.
dépraver [depRave] *vt* to deprave.
dépréciation [depResjɑsjɔ̃] *nf* depreciation.
déprécier [depResje] *vt*, **se** ~ *vi* to depreciate.
déprédations [depRedɑsjɔ̃] *nfpl* damage *sg*.
dépression [depRɛsjɔ̃] *nf* depression ; ~ **(nerveuse)** (nervous) breakdown.
déprimer [depRime] *vt* to depress.
dépuceler [depysle] *vt* (*fam*) to take the virginity of.
depuis [dəpɥi] *prép* (*temps: date*) since ; (: *période*) for ; (*espace*) since, from ; (*quantité, rang*: *à partir de*) from // *ad* (ever) since ; ~ **que** (ever) since ; ~ **quand le connaissez-vous?** how long have you known him? ; **je le connais** ~ **3 ans** I've known him for 3 years ; ~ **lors** since then.
députation [depytɑsjɔ̃] *nf* deputation ; (*fonction*) position of deputy, ≈ Parliamentary seat.
député, e [depyte] *nm/f* (POL) deputy, ≈ Member of Parliament.
députer [depyte] *vt* to delegate ; ~ **qn auprès de** to send sb (as a representative) to.
déraciner [deRasine] *vt* to uproot.
déraillement [deRɑjmɑ̃] *nm* derailment.
dérailler [deRɑje] *vi* (*train*) to be derailed ; **faire** ~ to derail.
dérailleur [deRɑjœR] *nm* (*de vélo*) dérailleur gears *pl*.
déraisonnable [deRɛzɔnabl(ə)] *a* unreasonable.
déraisonner [deRɛzɔne] *vi* to talk nonsense, rave.
dérangement [deRɑ̃ʒmɑ̃] *nm* (*gêne*) trouble ; (*gastrique etc*) disorder ; (*mécanique*) breakdown ; **en** ~ (*téléphone*) out of order.
déranger [deRɑ̃ʒe] *vt* (*personne*) to trouble, bother ; to disturb ; (*projets*) to disrupt, upset ; (*objets, vêtements*) to disarrange ; **se** ~ to put o.s. out ; to (take the trouble to) come *ou* go out ; **est-ce que cela vous dérange si** do you mind if.
dérapage [deRapaʒ] *nm* skid, skidding *q*.
déraper [deRape] *vi* (*voiture*) to skid ; (*personne, semelles, couteau*) to slip ; (*fig*) to go out of control.
dératiser [deRatize] *vt* to rid of rats.
déréglé, e [deRegle] *a* (*mœurs*) dissolute.
dérégler [deRegle] *vt* (*mécanisme*) to put out of order, cause to break down ; (*estomac*) to upset ; **se** ~ *vi* to break down, go wrong.
dérider [deRide] *vt*, **se** ~ *vi* to brighten up.
dérision [deRizjɔ̃] *nf*: **tourner en** ~ to deride.
dérisoire [deRizwaR] *a* derisory.
dérivatif [deRivatif] *nm* distraction.
dérivation [deRivɑsjɔ̃] *nf* derivation ; diversion.
dérive [deRiv] *nf* (*de dériveur*) centre-board ; **aller à la** ~ (NAVIG, *fig*) to drift.
dérivé, e [deRive] *a* derived // *nm* (LING) derivative ; (TECH) by-product // *nf* (MATH) derivative.
dériver [deRive] *vt* (MATH) to derive ; (*cours d'eau etc*) to divert // *vi* (*bateau*) to drift ; ~ **de** to derive from ; **dériveur** *nm* sailing dinghy.
dermatologie [dɛRmatɔlɔʒi] *nf* dermatology ; **dermatologue** *nm/f* dermatologist.
dernier, ière [dɛRnje, -jɛR] *a* last ; (*le plus récent*) latest, last ; **lundi/le mois** ~ last Monday/month ; **du** ~ **chic** extremely smart ; **les** ~**s honneurs** the last tribute ; **en** ~ *ad* last ; **ce** ~ the latter ; **dernièrement** *ad* recently ; ~**-né, dernière-née** *nm/f* (*enfant*) last-born.
dérobade [deRɔbad] *nf* side-stepping *q*.
dérobé, e [deRɔbe] *a* (*porte*) secret, hidden ; **à la** ~**e** surreptitiously.
dérober [deRɔbe] *vt* to steal ; ~ **qch à (la vue de) qn** to conceal *ou* hide sth from sb('s view) ; **se** ~ *vi* (*s'esquiver*) to slip away ; to shy away ; **se** ~ **sous** (*s'effondrer*) to give way beneath ; **se** ~ **à** (*justice, regards*) to hide from ; (*obligation*) to shirk.
dérogation [deRɔgɑsjɔ̃] *nf* (special) dispensation.
déroger [deRɔʒe]: ~ **à** *vt* to go against, depart from.
dérouiller [deRuje] *vt*: **se** ~ **les jambes** to stretch one's legs (*fig*).
déroulement [deRulmɑ̃] *nm* (*d'une opération etc*) progress.
dérouler [deRule] *vt* (*ficelle*) to unwind ; (*papier*) to unroll ; **se** ~ *vi* to unwind ; to unroll, come unrolled ; (*avoir lieu*) to take place ; (*se passer*) to go on ; to go (off) ; to unfold.
déroute [deRut] *nf* rout ; total collapse ; **mettre en** ~ to rout.
dérouter [deRute] *vt* (*avion, train*) to reroute, divert ; (*étonner*) to disconcert, throw (out).
derrière [dɛRjɛR] *ad* behind // *prép* behind // *nm* (*d'une maison*) back ; (*postérieur*) behind, bottom ; **les pattes de** ~ the back legs, the hind legs ; **par** ~ from behind ; (*fig*) in an underhand way, behind one's back.
des [de] *dét, prép* + *dét voir* **de.**
dès [dɛ] *prép* from ; ~ **que** *cj* as soon as ; ~ **son retour** as soon as he was (*ou* is) back ; ~ **lors** *ad* from then on ; ~ **lors que** *cj* from the moment (that).
D.E.S. *sigle m* = *diplôme d'études supérieures*.
désabusé, e [dezabyze] *a* disillusioned.
désaccord [dezakɔR] *nm* disagreement.
désaccordé, e [dezakɔRde] *a* (MUS) out of tune.
désaffecté, e [dezafɛkte] *a* disused.
désaffection [dezafɛksjɔ̃] *nf*: ~ **pour** estrangement from.

désagréable [dezagReable(ə)] *a* unpleasant, disagreeable.
désagréger [dezagReʒe]: **se ~** *vi* to disintegrate, break up.
désagrément [dezagRemɑ̃] *nm* annoyance, trouble *q*.
désaltérer [dezalteRe] *vt*: **se ~** to quench one's thirst; **ça désaltère** it's thirst-quenching, it takes your thirst away.
désamorcer [dezamɔRse] *vt* to remove the primer from; (*fig*) to defuse; to forestall.
désappointé, e [dezapwɛ̃te] *a* disappointed.
désapprobation [dezapRɔbɑsjɔ̃] *nf* disapproval.
désapprouver [dezapRuve] *vt* to disapprove of.
désarçonner [dezaRsɔne] *vt* to unseat, throw; (*fig*) to throw, nonplus.
désarmement [dezaRməmɑ̃] *nm* disarmament.
désarmer [dezaRme] *vt* (MIL, *aussi fig*) to disarm; (NAVIG) to lay up.
désarroi [dezaRwa] *nm* helplessness, disarray.
désarticulé, e [dezaRtikyle] *a* (*pantin, corps*) dislocated.
désarticuler [dezaRtikyle] *vt*: **se ~** (*acrobate*) to contort (o.s.).
désassorti, e [dezasɔRti] *a* unmatching, unmatched.
désastre [dezastR(ə)] *nm* disaster; **désastreux, euse** *a* disastrous.
désavantage [dezavɑ̃taʒ] *nm* disadvantage; (*inconvénient*) drawback, disadvantage; **désavantager** *vt* to put at a disadvantage; **désavantageux, euse** *a* unfavourable, disadvantageous.
désavouer [dezavwe] *vt* to disown, repudiate, disclaim.
désaxé, e [dezakse] *a* (*fig*) unbalanced.
désaxer [dezakse] *vt* (*roue*) to put out of true.
desceller [desele] *vt* (*pierre*) to pull free.
descendance [desɑ̃dɑ̃s] *nf* (*famille*) descendants *pl*, issue; (*origine*) descent.
descendant, e [desɑ̃dɑ̃, -ɑ̃t] *nm/f* descendant.
descendre [desɑ̃dR(ə)] *vt* (*escalier, montagne*) to go (*ou* come) down; (*valise, paquet*) to take *ou* get down; (*étagère etc*) to lower; (*fam*: *abattre*) to shoot down // *vi* to go (*ou* come) down; (*chemin*) to go down; (*passager*: *s'arrêter*) to get out, alight; (*niveau, température*) to go *ou* come down, fall, drop; **~ à pied/en voiture** to walk/drive down, to go down on foot/by car; **~ de** (*famille*) to be descended from; **~ du train** to get out of *ou* off the train; **~ d'un arbre** to climb down from a tree; **~ de cheval** to dismount, get off one's horse.
descente [desɑ̃t] *nf* descent, going down; (*chemin*) way down; (SKI) downhill (race); **au milieu de la ~** halfway down; **freinez dans les ~s** use the brakes going downhill; **~ de lit** bedside rug; **~ (de police)** (police) raid.
description [dɛskRipsjɔ̃] *nf* description.
désembuer [dezɑ̃bɥe] *vt* to demist.
désemparé, e [dezɑ̃paRe] *a* bewildered, distraught; (*véhicule*) crippled.
désemparer [dezɑ̃paRe] *vi*: **sans ~** without stopping.
désemplir [dezɑ̃pliR] *vi*: **ne pas ~** to be always full.
désenchantement [dezɑ̃ʃɑ̃tmɑ̃] *nm* disenchantment; disillusion.
désenfler [dezɑ̃fle] *vi* to become less swollen.
désengagement [dezɑ̃gaʒmɑ̃] *nm* (POL) disengagement.
désensibiliser [desɑ̃sibilize] *vt* (MÉD) to desensitize.
déséquilibre [dezekilibR(ə)] *nm* (*position*): **être en ~** to be unsteady; (*fig: des forces, du budget*) imbalance; (PSYCH) unbalance.
déséquilibré, e [dezekilibRe] *nm/f* (PSYCH) unbalanced person.
déséquilibrer [dezekilibRe] *vt* to throw off balance.
désert, e [dezɛR, -ɛRt(ə)] *a* deserted // *nm* desert.
déserter [dezɛRte] *vi, vt* to desert; **déserteur** *nm* deserter; **désertion** *nf* desertion.
désertique [dezɛRtik] *a* desert *cpd*; barren, empty.
désescalade [dezɛskalad] *nf* (MIL) de-escalation.
désespéré, e [dezɛspeRe] *a* desperate; **~ment** *ad* desperately.
désespérer [dezɛspeRe] *vt* to drive to despair // *vi*, **se ~** *vi* to despair; **~ de** to despair of.
désespoir [dezɛspwaR] *nm* despair; **faire le ~ de qn** to be the despair of sb; **en ~ de cause** in desperation.
déshabillé, e [dezabije] *a* undressed // *nm* négligée.
déshabiller [dezabije] *vt* to undress; **se ~** to undress (o.s.).
déshabituer [dezabitɥe] *vt*: **se ~ de** to get out of the habit of.
désherbant [dezɛRbɑ̃] *nm* weed-killer.
déshériter [dezeRite] *vt* to disinherit.
déshérités [dezeRite] *nmpl*: **les ~** the underprivileged.
déshonneur [dezɔnœR] *nm* dishonour, disgrace.
déshonorer [dezɔnɔRe] *vt* to dishonour, bring disgrace upon.
déshydraté, e [dezidRate] *a* dehydrated.
desiderata [dezideRata] *nmpl* requirements.
désignation [deziɲɑsjɔ̃] *nf* naming, appointment; (*signe, mot*) name, designat on.
désigner [deziɲe] *vt* (*montrer*) to point out, indicate; (*dénommer*) to denote, refer to; (*nommer: candidat etc*) to name, appoint.
désillusion [dezilyzjɔ̃] *nf* disillusion(ment).
désinence [dezinɑ̃s] *nf* ending, inflexion.
désinfectant, e [dezɛ̃fɛktɑ̃, -ɑ̃t] *a, nm* disinfectant.
désinfecter [dezɛ̃fɛkte] *vt* to disinfect.

désinfection [dezɛ̃fɛksjɔ̃] *nf* disinfection.
désintégrer [dezɛ̃tegʀe] *vt*, **se ~** *vi* to disintegrate.
désintéressé, e [dezɛ̃teʀese] *a* disinterested, unselfish.
désintéresser [dezɛ̃teʀese] *vt*: **se ~ (de)** to lose interest (in).
désintoxication [dezɛ̃tɔksikɑsjɔ̃] *nf* treatment for alcoholism.
désinvolte [dezɛ̃vɔlt(ə)] *a* casual, off-hand; **désinvolture** *nf* casualness.
désir [deziʀ] *nm* wish; (*fort, sensuel*) desire.
désirer [deziʀe] *vt* to want, wish for; (*sexuellement*) to desire; **je désire ...** (*formule de politesse*) I would like ...; **il désire que tu l'aides** he would like *ou* he wants you to help him; **~ faire** to want *ou* wish to do.
désireux, euse [deziʀø, -øz] *a*: **~ de faire** anxious to do.
désistement [dezistəmɑ̃] *nm* withdrawal.
désister [deziste] : **se ~** *vi* to stand down, withdraw.
désobéir [dezɔbeiʀ] *vi*: **~ (à qn/qch)** to disobey (sb/sth); **désobéissance** *nf* disobedience; **désobéissant, e** *a* disobedient.
désobligeant, e [dezɔbliʒɑ̃, -ɑ̃t] *a* disagreeable, unpleasant.
désodorisant [dezɔdɔʀizɑ̃] *nm* air freshener, deodorizer.
désœuvré, e [dezœvʀe] *a* idle; **désœuvrement** *nm* idleness.
désolation [dezɔlɑsjɔ̃] *nf* distress, grief; desolation, devastation.
désolé, e [dezɔle] *a* (*paysage*) desolate; **je suis ~** I'm sorry.
désoler [dezɔle] *vt* to distress, grieve.
désolidariser [desɔlidaʀize] *vt*: **se ~ de** *ou* **d'avec** to dissociate o.s. from.
désopilant, e [dezɔpilɑ̃, -ɑ̃t] *a* screamingly funny, hilarious.
désordonné, e [dezɔʀdɔne] *a* untidy, disorderly.
désordre [dezɔʀdʀ(ə)] *nm* disorder(liness), untidiness; (*anarchie*) disorder; **~s** *nmpl* (POL) disturbances, disorder *sg*; **en ~** in a mess, untidy.
désorganiser [dezɔʀganize] *vt* to disorganize.
désorienté, e [dezɔʀjɑ̃te] *a* disorientated; (*fig*) bewildered.
désormais [dezɔʀmɛ] *ad* in future, from now on.
désosser [dezɔse] *vt* to bone.
despote [dɛspɔt] *nm* despot; tyrant; **despotisme** *nm* despotism.
desquels, desquelles [dekɛl] *prép + pronom voir* **lequel**.
dessaisir [desezi ʀ]: **se ~ de** *vt* to give up, part with.
dessaler [desale] *vt* (*eau de mer*) to desalinate; (CULIN) to soak.
desséché, e [deseʃe] *a* dried up.
dessécher [deseʃe] *vt* to dry out, parch; **se ~** *vi* to dry out.
dessein [desɛ̃] *nm* design; **dans le ~ de** with the intention of; **à ~** intentionally, deliberately.
desserrer [deseʀe] *vt* to loosen; (*frein*) to release; (*poing, dents*) to unclench; (*objets alignés*) to space out.
dessert [desɛʀ] *nm* dessert, pudding.
desserte [desɛʀt(ə)] *nf* (*table*) sideboard table; (*transport*): **la ~ du village est assurée par autocar** there is a coach service to the village.
desservir [desɛʀviʀ] *vt* (*ville, quartier*) to serve; (*nuire à*) to go against, put at a disadvantage; **~ (la table)** to clear the table.
dessin [desɛ̃] *nm* (*œuvre, art*) drawing; (*motif*) pattern, design; (*contour*) (out)line; **~ animé** cartoon (film); **~ humoristique** cartoon.
dessinateur, trice [desinatœʀ, -tʀis] *nm/f* drawer; (*de bandes dessinées*) cartoonist; (*industriel*) draughtsman.
dessiner [desine] *vt* to draw; (*concevoir: carrosserie, maison*) to design.
dessoûler [desule] *vt, vi* to sober up.
dessous [dəsu] *ad* underneath, beneath // *nm* underside // *nmpl* (*sous-vêtements*) underwear *sg*; **en ~, par ~** underneath; below; **au-~** below; **de ~ le lit** from under the bed; **au-~ de** below; (*peu digne de*) beneath; **avoir le ~** to get the worst of it; **~-de-plat** *nm inv* tablemat.
dessus [dəsy] *ad* on top; (*collé, écrit*) on it // *nm* top; **en ~** above; **par ~** *ad* over it // *prép* over; **au-~** above; **au-~ de** above; **avoir le ~** to get the upper hand; **~-de-lit** *nm inv* bedspread.
destin [dɛstɛ̃] *nm* fate; (*avenir*) destiny.
destinataire [dɛstinatɛʀ] *nm/f* (POSTES) addressee; (*d'un colis*) consignee.
destination [dɛstinɑsjɔ̃] *nf* (*lieu*) destination; (*usage*) purpose; **à ~ de** bound for, travelling to.
destinée [dɛstine] *nf* fate; (*existence, avenir*) destiny.
destiner [dɛstine] *vt*: **~ qn à** (*poste, sort*) to destine sb for, intend sb to + *verbe*; **~ qn/qch à** (*prédestiner*) to mark sb/sth out for, destine sb/sth to + *verbe*; **~ qch à** (*envisager d'affecter*) to intend to use sth for; **~ qch à qn** (*envisager de donner*) to intend to give sth to sb, intend sb to have sth; (*adresser*) to intend sth for sb; to aim sth at sb; **se ~ à l'enseignement** to intend to become a teacher; **être destiné à** (*sort*) to be destined to + *verbe*; (*usage*) to be intended *ou* meant for; (*suj: sort*) to be in store for.
destituer [dɛstitɥe] *vt* to depose.
destructeur, trice [dɛstʀyktœʀ, -tʀis] *a* destructive.
destruction [dɛstʀyksjɔ̃] *nf* destruction.
désuet, ète [desɥɛ, -ɛt] *a* outdated, outmoded; **désuétude** *nf*: **tomber en désuétude** to fall into disuse, become obsolete.
désuni, e [dezyni] *a* divided, disunited.
détachant [detaʃɑ̃] *nm* stain remover.
détachement [detaʃmɑ̃] *nm* detachment.
détacher [detaʃe] *vt* (*enlever*) to detach, remove; (*délier*) to untie; (ADMIN): **~ qn (auprès de/à)** to send sb on secondment (to); (MIL) to detail; **se ~** *vi* (*tomber*) to come off; to come out; (*se défaire*) to come undone; (SPORT) to pull *ou* break away; **se**

~ sur to stand out against; **se ~ de** (*se désintéresser*) to grow away from.
détail [detaj] *nm* detail; (*COMM*): **le ~** retail; **au ~** *ad* (*COMM*) retail; separately; **donner le ~ de** to give a detailed account of; (*compte*) to give a breakdown of; **en ~** in detail.
détaillant [detajɑ̃] *nm* retailer.
détaillé, e [detaje] *a* (*récit*) detailed.
détailler [detaje] *vt* (*COMM*) to sell retail; to sell separately; (*expliquer*) to explain in detail; to detail; (*examiner*) to look over, examine.
détartrant [detaʀtʀɑ̃] *nm* descaling agent.
détaxer [detakse] *vt* to reduce the tax on; to remove the tax from.
détecter [detɛkte] *vt* to detect; **détecteur** *nm* detector; **détection** *nf* detection.
détective [detɛktiv] *nm* (*Brit*: *policier*) detective; **~ (privé)** private detective *ou* investigator.
déteindre [detɛ̃dʀ(ə)] *vi* (*tissu*) to lose its colour; (*fig*): **~ sur** to rub off on.
dételer [detle] *vt* to unharness; to unhitch.
détendre [detɑ̃dʀ(ə)] *vt* (*fil*) to slacken, loosen; (*relaxer*) to relax; **se ~** to lose its tension; to relax.
détenir [detniʀ] *vt* (*fortune, objet, secret*) to be in possession of, have (in one's possession); (*prisonnier*) to detain, hold; (*record*) to hold; **~ le pouvoir** to be in power.
détente [detɑ̃t] *nf* relaxation; (*POL*) détente; (*d'une arme*) trigger; (*d'un athlète qui saute*) spring.
détenteur, trice [detɑ̃tœʀ, -tʀis] *nm/f* holder.
détention [detɑ̃sjɔ̃] *nf* possession; detention; holding; **~ préventive** (pre-trial) custody.
détenu, e [detny] *nm/f* prisoner.
détergent [detɛʀʒɑ̃] *nm* detergent.
détérioration [deteʀjɔʀɑsjɔ̃] *nf* damaging; deterioration, worsening.
détériorer [deteʀjɔʀe] *vt* to damage; **se ~** *vi* to deteriorate.
déterminant [detɛʀminɑ̃] *nm* (*LING*) determiner.
détermination [detɛʀminɑsjɔ̃] *nf* determining; (*résolution*) determination.
déterminé, e [detɛʀmine] *a* (*résolu*) determined; (*précis*) specific, definite.
déterminer [detɛʀmine] *vt* (*fixer*) to determine; (*décider*): **~ qn à faire** to decide sb to do; **se ~ à faire** to make up one's mind to do.
déterrer [deteʀe] *vt* to dig up.
détersif [detɛʀsif] *nm* detergent.
détestable [detɛstabl(ə)] *a* foul, ghastly; detestable, odious.
détester [deteste] *vt* to hate, detest.
détonant, e [detɔnɑ̃, -ɑ̃t] *a*: **mélange ~** explosive mixture.
détonateur [detɔnatœʀ] *nm* detonator.
détonation [detɔnɑsjɔ̃] *nf* detonation, bang, report (of a gun).
détoner [detɔne] *vi* to detonate, explode.
détonner [detɔne] *vi* (*MUS*) to go out of tune; (*fig*) to clash.
détour [detuʀ] *nm* detour; (*tournant*) bend, curve; **sans ~** (*fig*) without beating about the bush, in a straightforward manner.
détourné, e [detuʀne] *a* (*moyen*) roundabout.
détournement [detuʀnəmɑ̃] *nm* diversion, rerouting; **~ d'avion** hijacking; **~ (de fonds)** embezzlement *ou* misappropriation (of funds); **~ de mineur** corruption of a minor.
détourner [detuʀne] *vt* to divert; (*avion*) to divert, reroute; (: *par la force*) to hijack; (*yeux, tête*) to turn away; (*de l'argent*) to embezzle, misappropriate; **se ~** to turn away.
détracteur, trice [detʀaktœʀ, -tʀis] *nm/f* disparager, critic.
détraquer [detʀake] *vt* to put out of order; (*estomac*) to upset; **se ~** *vi* to go wrong.
détrempe [detʀɑ̃p] *nf* (*ART*) tempera.
détrempé, e [detʀɑ̃pe] *a* (*sol*) sodden, waterlogged.
détresse [detʀɛs] *nf* distress.
détriment [detʀimɑ̃] *nm*: **au ~ de** to the detriment of.
détritus [detʀitys] *nmpl* rubbish *sg*, refuse *sg*.
détroit [detʀwa] *nm* strait.
détromper [detʀɔ̃pe] *vt* to disabuse.
détrôner [detʀone] *vt* to dethrone, depose; (*fig*) to oust, dethrone.
détrousser [detʀuse] *vt* to rob.
détruire [detʀɥiʀ] *vt* to destroy.
dette [dɛt] *nf* debt.
D.E.U.G. [døg] *sigle m* = *diplôme d'études universitaires générales*.
deuil [dœj] *nm* (*perte*) bereavement; (*période*) mourning; (*chagrin*) grief; **porter le/être en ~** to wear/be in mourning.
deux [dø] *num* two; **les ~** both; **ses ~ mains** both his hands, his two hands; **les ~ points** the colon *sg*; **deuxième** *num* second; **~-pièces** *nm inv* (*tailleur*) two-piece suit; (*de bain*) two-piece (swimsuit); (*appartement*) two-roomed flat; **~-roues** *nm inv* two-wheeled vehicle; **~-temps** *a* two-stroke.
devais *etc vb voir* **devoir**.
dévaler [devale] *vt* to hurtle down.
dévaliser [devalize] *vt* to rob, burgle.
dévaloriser [devalɔʀize] *vt*, **se ~** *vi* to depreciate.
dévaluation [devalɥɑsjɔ̃] *nf* depreciation; (*ECON*: *mesure*) devaluation.
dévaluer [devalɥe] *vt* to devalue.
devancer [dəvɑ̃se] *vt* to be ahead of; to get ahead of; to arrive before; (*prévenir*) to anticipate; **~ l'appel** (*MIL*) to enlist before call-up; **devancier, ière** *nm/f* precursor.
devant [dəvɑ̃] *ad* in front; (*à distance*: *en avant*) ahead // *prép* in front of; ahead of; (*avec mouvement*: *passer*) past; (*fig*) before, in front of; faced with, in the face of; in view of // *nm* front; **prendre les ~s** to make the first move; **les pattes de ~** the front legs, the forelegs; **par ~** (*boutonner*) at the front; (*entrer*) the front way; **aller au-~ de qn** to go out to meet

sb; **aller au-~ de** (*désirs de qn*) to anticipate.
devanture [dəvɑ̃tyʀ] *nf* (*façade*) (shop) front; (*étalage*) display; (shop) window.
dévastation [devastɑsjɔ̃] *nf* devastation.
dévaster [devaste] *vt* to devastate.
déveine [devɛn] *nf* rotten luck *q*.
développement [devlɔpmɑ̃] *nm* development.
développer [devlɔpe] *vt* to develop; **se ~** *vi* to develop.
devenir [dəvniʀ] *vb avec attribut* to become; **~ instituteur** to become a teacher; **que sont-ils devenus?** what has become of them?
dévergondé, e [devɛʀgɔ̃de] *a* wild, shameless.
devers [dəvɛʀ] *ad*: **par ~ soi** to oneself.
déverser [devɛʀse] *vt* (*liquide*) to pour (out); (*ordures*) to tip (out); **se ~ dans** (*fleuve, mer*) to flow into; **déversoir** *nm* overflow.
dévêtir [devetiʀ] *vt*, **se ~** to undress.
devez *etc vb voir* **devoir**.
déviation [devjɑsjɔ̃] *nf* (*aussi* AUTO) diversion; **~ de la colonne (vertébrale)** curvature of the spine.
dévider [devide] *vt* to unwind; **dévidoir** *nm* reel.
devienne *etc vb voir* **devenir**.
dévier [devje] *vt* (*fleuve, circulation*) to divert; (*coup*) to deflect // *vi* to veer (off course); **(faire) ~** (*projectile*) to deflect; (*véhicule*) to push off course.
devin [dəvɛ̃] *nm* soothsayer, seer.
deviner [dəvine] *vt* to guess; (*prévoir*) to foretell; to foresee; (*apercevoir*) to distinguish.
devinette [dəvinɛt] *nf* riddle.
devins *etc vb voir* **devenir**.
devis [dəvi] *nm* estimate, quotation.
dévisager [devizaʒe] *vt* to stare at.
devise [dəviz] *nf* (*formule*) motto, watchword; (ÉCON: *monnaie*) currency; **~s** *nfpl* (*argent*) currency *sg*.
deviser [dəvize] *vi* to converse.
dévisser [devise] *vt* to unscrew, undo; **se ~** *vi* to come unscrewed.
dévoiler [devwale] *vt* to unveil.
devoir [dəvwaʀ] *nm* duty; (SCOL) piece of homework, homework *q*; (: *en classe*) exercise // *vt* (*argent, respect*): **~ qch (à qn)** to owe (sb) sth; (*suivi de l'infinitif*: *obligation*): **il doit le faire** he has to do it, he must do it; (: *intention*): **il doit partir demain** he is (due) to leave tomorrow; (: *probabilité*): **il doit être tard** it must be late.
dévolu, e [devɔly] *a*: **~ à** allotted to // *nm*: **jeter son ~ sur** to fix one's choice on.
dévorant, e [devɔʀɑ̃, -ɑ̃t] *a* (*faim, passion*) raging.
dévorer [devɔʀe] *vt* to devour; (*suj*: *feu, soucis*) to consume.
dévot, e [devo, -ɔt] *a* devout, pious.
dévotion [devosjɔ̃] *nf* devoutness; **être à la ~ de qn** to be totally devoted to sb.
dévoué, e [devwe] *a* devoted.
dévouement [devumɑ̃] *nm* devotion, dedication.
dévouer [devwe]: **se ~** *vi* (*se sacrifier*): **se ~ (pour)** to sacrifice o.s. (for); (*se consacrer*): **se ~ à** to devote *ou* dedicate o.s. to.
dévoyé, e [devwaje] *a* delinquent.
devrai *etc vb voir* **devoir**.
dextérité [dɛksteʀite] *nf* skill, dexterity.
diabète [djabɛt] *nm* diabetes *sg*; **diabétique** *nm/f* diabetic.
diable [djɑbl(ə)] *nm* devil; **diabolique** *a* diabolical.
diabolo [djabɔlo] *nm* (*boisson*) lemonade and fruit (*ou* mint *etc*) cordial.
diacre [djakʀ(ə)] *nm* deacon.
diadème [djadɛm] *nm* diadem.
diagnostic [djagnɔstik] *nm* diagnosis *sg*; **diagnostiquer** *vt* to diagnose.
diagonal, e aux [djagɔnal, -o] *a, nf* diagonal; **en ~e** diagonally; **lire en ~e** to skim through.
diagramme [djagʀam] *nm* chart, graph.
dialecte [djalɛkt(ə)] *nm* dialect.
dialogue [djalɔg] *nm* dialogue; **dialoguer** *vi* to converse; (POL) to have a dialogue.
diamant [djamɑ̃] *nm* diamond; **diamantaire** *nm* diamond dealer.
diamètre [djamɛtʀ(ə)] *nm* diameter.
diapason [djapazɔ̃] *nm* tuning fork.
diaphragme [djafʀagm] *nm* (ANAT, PHOTO) diaphragm; (*contraceptif*) diaphragm, cap; **ouverture du ~** (PHOTO) aperture.
diapositive [djapozitiv] *nf* transparency, slide.
diapré, e [djapʀe] *a* many-coloured.
diarrhée [djaʀe] *nf* diarrhoea.
diatribe [djatʀib] *nf* diatribe.
dictaphone [diktafɔn] *nm* Dictaphone.
dictateur [diktatœʀ] *nm* dictator; **dictatorial, e, aux** *a* dictatorial; **dictature** *nf* dictatorship.
dictée [dikte] *nf* dictation; **prendre sous ~** to take down (*sth dictated*).
dicter [dikte] *vt* to dictate.
diction [diksjɔ̃] *nf* diction, delivery; **cours de ~** speech production lesson.
dictionnaire [diksjɔnɛʀ] *nm* dictionary; **~ bilingue/encyclopédique** bilingual/encyclopaedic dictionary.
dicton [diktɔ̃] *nm* saying, dictum.
didactique [didaktik] *a* technical; didactic.
dièse [djɛz] *nm* sharp.
diesel [djezɛl] *nm, a inv* diesel.
diète [djɛt] *nf* (*jeûne*) starvation diet; (*régime*) diet; **être à la ~** to be on a starvation diet.
diététicien, ne [djetetisjɛ̃, -jɛn] *nm/f* dietician.
diététique [djetetik] *nf* dietetics *sg*; **magasin ~** health food shop.
dieu, x [djø] *nm* god; **D~** God; **le bon D~** the good Lord.
diffamation [difamɑsjɔ̃] *nf* slander; (*écrite*) libel; **attaquer qn en ~** to sue sb for libel (*ou* slander).
diffamer [difame] *vt* to slander, defame; to libel.
différé [difeʀe] *nm* (TV): **en ~** (pre-)recorded.

différence [difeʀɑ̃s] *nf* difference ; **à la ~ de** unlike.
différencier [difeʀɑ̃sje] *vt* to differentiate ; **se ~** *vi* (*organisme*) to become differentiated ; **se ~ de** to differentiate o.s. from ; to differ from.
différend [difeʀɑ̃] *nm* difference (of opinion), disagreement.
différent, e [difeʀɑ̃, -ɑ̃t] *a*: **~ (de)** different (from) ; **~s objets** different *ou* various objects.
différentiel, le [difeʀɑ̃sjɛl] *a, nm* differential.
différer [difeʀe] *vt* to postpone, put off // *vi*: **~ (de)** to differ (from) ; **~ de faire** to delay doing.
difficile [difisil] *a* difficult ; (*exigeant*) hard to please, difficult (to please) ; **~ment** *ad* with difficulty ; **~ment lisible** difficult *ou* hard to read.
difficulté [difikylte] *nf* difficulty ; **en ~** (*bateau, alpiniste*) in trouble *ou* difficulties ; **avoir de la ~ à faire** to have difficulty (in) doing.
difforme [difɔʀm(ə)] *a* deformed, misshapen ; **difformité** *nf* deformity.
diffracter [difʀakte] *vt* to diffract.
diffus, e [dify, -yz] *a* diffuse.
diffuser [difyze] *vt* (*chaleur, bruit*) to diffuse ; (*émission, musique*) to broadcast ; (*nouvelle, idée*) to circulate ; (COMM) to distribute ; **diffuseur** *nm* diffuser ; distributor ; **diffusion** *nf* diffusion ; broadcast(ing) ; circulation ; distribution.
digérer [diʒeʀe] *vt* to digest ; (*fig: accepter*) to stomach, put up with ; **digestible** *a* digestible ; **digestif, ive** *a* digestive // *nm* (after-dinner) liqueur ; **digestion** *nf* digestion.
digital, e, aux [diʒital, -o] *a* digital.
digne [diɲ] *a* dignified ; **~ de** worthy of ; **~ de foi** trustworthy.
dignitaire [diɲitɛʀ] *nm* dignitary.
dignité [diɲite] *nf* dignity.
digue [dig] *nf* dike, dyke.
dilapider [dilapide] *vt* to squander, waste.
dilater [dilate] *vt* to dilate ; (*gaz, métal*) to cause to expand ; (*ballon*) to distend ; **se ~** *vi* to expand.
dilemme [dilɛm] *nm* dilemma.
diligence [diliʒɑ̃s] *nf* stagecoach, diligence ; (*empressement*) despatch.
diligent, e [diliʒɑ̃, -ɑ̃t] *a* prompt and efficient, diligent.
diluer [dilɥe] *vt* to dilute.
diluvien, ne [dilyvjɛ̃, -jɛn] *a*: **pluie ~ne** torrential rain.
dimanche [dimɑ̃ʃ] *nm* Sunday.
dimension [dimɑ̃sjɔ̃] *nf* (*grandeur*) size ; (*cote, de l'espace*) dimension.
diminuer [diminɥe] *vt* to reduce, decrease ; (*ardeur etc*) to lessen ; (*personne: physiquement*) to undermine ; (*dénigrer*) to belittle // *vi* to decrease, diminish, **diminutif** *nm* (LING) diminutive ; (*surnom*) pet name ; **diminution** *nf* decreasing, diminishing.
dinde [dɛ̃d] *nf* turkey.
dindon [dɛ̃dɔ̃] *nm* turkey.
dîner [dine] *nm* dinner // *vi* to have dinner.
dingue [dɛ̃g] *a* (*fam*) crazy.
diode [djɔd] *nf* diode.
diphtérie [difteʀi] *nf* diphtheria.
diphtongue [diftɔ̃g] *nf* diphthong.
diplomate [diplɔmat] *a* diplomatic // *nm* diplomat ; (*fig*) diplomatist.
diplomatie [diplɔmasi] *nf* diplomacy ; **diplomatique** *a* diplomatic.
diplôme [diplom] *nm* diploma, certificate ; (diploma) examination ; **diplômé, e** *a* qualified.
dire [diʀ] *nm*: **au ~ de** according to ; **leur ~s** what they say // *vt* to say ; (*secret, mensonge*) to tell ; **~ l'heure/la vérité** to tell the time/the truth ; **~ qch à qn** to tell sb sth ; **~ que** to say that ; **~ à qn que** to tell sb that ; **~ à qn qu'il fasse** *ou* **de faire** to tell sb to do ; **on dit que** they say that ; **si cela lui dit** (*plaire*) if he fancies it ; **que dites-vous de** (*penser*) what do you think of ; **on dirait que** it looks (*ou* sounds *etc*) as though.
direct, e [diʀɛkt] *a* direct // *nm* (TV): **en ~** live ; **~ement** *ad* directly.
directeur, trice [diʀɛktœʀ, -tʀis] *nm/f* (*d'entreprise*) director ; (*de service*) manager/eress ; (*d'école*) headmaster/mistress ; **~ de thèse** (SCOL) supervisor.
direction [diʀɛksjɔ̃] *nf* management ; conducting ; supervision ; (AUTO) steering ; (*sens*) direction ; **sous la ~ de** (MUS) conducted by.
directive [diʀɛktiv] *nf* directive, instruction.
dirent *vb voir* **dire**.
dirigeable [diʀiʒabl(ə)] *a, nm*: **(ballon) ~** dirigible.
dirigeant, e [diʀiʒɑ̃, -ɑ̃t] *a* managerial ; ruling // *nm/f* (*d'un parti etc*) leader ; (*d'entreprise*) manager, member of the management.
diriger [diʀiʒe] *vt* (*entreprise*) to manage, run ; (*véhicule*) to steer ; (*orchestre*) to conduct ; (*recherches, travaux*) to supervise, be in charge of ; (*braquer: regard, arme*): **~ sur** to point *ou* level *ou* aim at ; (*fig: critiques*): **~ contre** to aim at ; **se ~** (*s'orienter*) to find one's way ; **se ~ vers** *ou* **sur** to make *ou* head for.
dirigisme [diʀiʒism(ə)] *nm* (ÉCON) state intervention, interventionism.
dis *etc vb voir* **dire**.
discernement [disɛʀnəmɑ̃] *nm* discernment, judgment.
discerner [disɛʀne] *vt* to discern, make out.
disciple [disipl(ə)] *nm/f* disciple.
disciplinaire [disiplinɛʀ] *a* disciplinary.
discipline [disiplin] *nf* discipline ; **discipliné, e** *a* (well-)disciplined ; **discipliner** *vt* to discipline ; to control.
discontinu, e [diskɔ̃tiny] *a* intermittent.
discontinuer [diskɔ̃tinɥe] *vi*: **sans ~** without stopping, without a break.
disconvenir [diskɔ̃vniʀ] *vi*: **ne pas ~ de qch/que** not to deny sth/that.
discordance [diskɔʀdɑ̃s] *nf* discordance ; conflict.
discordant, e [diskɔʀdɑ̃, -ɑ̃t] *a* discordant ; conflicting.

discorde [diskɔʀd(ə)] *nf* discord, dissension.
discothèque [diskɔtɛk] *nf* (*disques*) record collection ; (: *dans une bibliothèque*) record library ; (*boîte de nuit*) disco(thèque).
discourir [diskuʀiʀ] *vi* to discourse, hold forth.
discours [diskuʀ] *nm* speech.
discréditer [diskʀedite] *vt* to discredit.
discret, ète [diskʀɛ, -ɛt] *a* discreet ; (*fig*) unobtrusive ; quiet ; **discrètement** *ad* discreetly.
discrétion [diskʀesjɔ̃] *nf* discretion ; **être à la ~ de qn** to be in sb's hands ; **à ~** unlimited ; as much as one wants.
discrimination [diskʀiminɑsjɔ̃] *nf* discrimination ; **sans ~** indiscriminately ; **discriminatoire** *a* discriminatory.
disculper [diskylpe] *vt* to exonerate.
discussion [diskysjɔ̃] *nf* discussion.
discuté, e [diskyte] *a* controversial.
discuter [diskyte] *vt* (*contester*) to question, dispute ; (*débattre*: *prix*) to discuss // *vi* to talk ; (*ergoter*) to argue ; **~ de** to discuss.
dise *etc vb voir* **dire**.
disert, e [dizɛʀ, -ɛʀt(ə)] *a* loquacious.
disette [dizɛt] *nf* food shortage.
diseuse [dizøz] *nf*: **~ de bonne aventure** fortuneteller.
disgrâce [disgʀɑs] *nf* disgrace.
disgracieux, euse [disgʀasjø, -jøz] *a* ungainly, awkward.
disjoindre [disʒwɛ̃dʀ(ə)] *vt* to take apart ; **se ~** *vi* to come apart.
disjoncteur [disʒɔ̃ktœʀ] *nm* (ÉLEC) circuit breaker, cutout.
dislocation [dislɔkɑsjɔ̃] *nf* dislocation.
disloquer [dislɔke] *vt* (*membre*) to dislocate ; (*chaise*) to dismantle ; (*troupe*) to disperse ; **se ~** *vi* (*parti, empire*) to break up ; **se ~ l'épaule** to dislocate one's shoulder.
disons *vb voir* **dire**.
disparaître [dispaʀɛtʀ(ə)] *vi* to disappear ; (*à la vue*) to vanish, disappear ; to be hidden *ou* concealed ; (*être manquant*) to go missing, disappear ; (*se perdre*: *traditions etc*) to die out ; **faire ~** to remove ; to get rid of.
disparate [dispaʀat] *a* disparate ; ill-assorted.
disparité [dispaʀite] *nf* disparity.
disparition [dispaʀisjɔ̃] *nf* disappearance.
disparu, e [dispaʀy] *nm/f* missing person ; (*défunt*) departed.
dispendieux, euse [dispɑ̃djø, -jøz] *a* extravagant, expensive.
dispensaire [dispɑ̃sɛʀ] *nm* community clinic.
dispense [dispɑ̃s] *nf* exemption ; **~ d'âge** special exemption from age limit.
dispenser [dispɑ̃se] *vt* (*donner*) to lavish, bestow ; (*exempter*): **~ qn de** to exempt sb from ; **se ~ de** to avoid ; to get out of.
disperser [dispɛʀse] *vt* to scatter ; (*fig*: *son attention*) to dissipate ; **se ~** *vi* to scatter ; (*fig*) to dissipate one's efforts.
disponibilité [disponibilite] *nf* availability ; (ADMIN): **être en ~** to be on leave of absence.
disponible [disponibl(ə)] *a* available.
dispos [dispo] *am*: **(frais et) ~** fresh (as a daisy).
disposé, e [dispoze] *a* (*d'une certaine manière*) arranged, laid-out ; **bien/mal ~** (*humeur*) in a good/bad mood ; **~ à** (*prêt à*) willing *ou* prepared to.
disposer [dispoze] *vt* (*arranger, placer*) to arrange ; (*inciter*): **~ qn à qch/faire qch** to dispose *ou* incline sb towards sth/to do sth // *vi*: **vous pouvez ~** you may leave ; **~ de** *vt* to have (at one's disposal) ; to use ; **se ~ à faire** to prepare to do, be about to do.
dispositif [dispozitif] *nm* device ; (*fig*) system, plan of action ; set-up.
disposition [dispozisjɔ̃] *nf* (*arrangement*) arrangement, layout ; (*humeur*) mood ; (*tendance*) tendency ; **~s** *nfpl* (*mesures*) steps, measures ; (*préparatifs*) arrangements ; (*testamentaires*) provisions ; (*aptitudes*) bent *sg*, aptitude *sg*; **à la ~ de qn** at sb's disposal.
disproportion [dispʀɔpɔʀsjɔ̃] *nf* disproportion ; **disproportionné, e** *a* disproportionate, out of all proportion.
dispute [dispyt] *nf* quarrel, argument.
disputer [dispyte] *vt* (*match*) to play ; (*combat*) to fight ; (*course*) to run, fight ; **se ~** *vi* to quarrel, have a quarrel ; **~ qch à qn** to fight with sb for *ou* over sth.
disquaire [diskɛʀ] *nm/f* record dealer.
disqualification [diskalifikɑsjɔ̃] *nf* disqualification.
disqualifier [diskalifje] *vt* to disqualify.
disque [disk(ə)] *nm* (MUS) record ; (*forme, pièce*) disc ; (SPORT) discus ; **~ d'embrayage** (AUTO) clutch plate.
dissection [disɛksjɔ̃] *nf* dissection.
dissemblable [disɑ̃blabl(ə)] *a* dissimilar.
disséminer [disemine] *vt* to scatter.
disséquer [diseke] *vt* to dissect.
dissertation [disɛʀtɑsjɔ̃] *nf* (SCOL) essay.
disserter [disɛʀte] *vi*: **~ sur** to discourse upon.
dissident, e [disidɑ̃, -ɑ̃t] *a, nm/f* dissident.
dissimulation [disimylɑsjɔ̃] *nf* concealing ; (*duplicité*) dissimulation.
dissimuler [disimyle] *vt* to conceal ; **se ~** to conceal o.s. ; to be concealed.
dissipation [disipɑsjɔ̃] *nf* squandering ; unruliness ; (*débauche*) dissipation.
dissiper [disipe] *vt* to dissipate ; (*fortune*) to squander, fritter away ; **se ~** *vi* (*brouillard*) to clear, disperse ; (*doutes*) to disappear, melt away ; (*élève*) to become undisciplined *ou* unruly.
dissolu, e [disɔly] *a* dissolute.
dissolution [disɔlysjɔ̃] *nf* dissolving ; (POL, JUR) dissolution.
dissolvant, e [disɔlvɑ̃, -ɑ̃t] *a* (*fig*) debilitating // *nm* (CHIMIE) solvent ; **~ (gras)** nail varnish remover.
dissonant, e [disɔnɑ̃, -ɑ̃t] *a* discordant.
dissoudre [disudʀ(ə)] *vt* to dissolve ; **se ~** *vi* to dissolve.
dissuader [disɥade] *vt*: **~ qn de faire/de qch** to dissuade sb from doing/from sth.

dissuasion [disɥɑzjɔ̃] *nf* dissuasion; **force de ~** deterrent power.
dissymétrique [disimetʀik] *a* dissymmetrical.
distance [distɑ̃s] *nf* distance; (*fig: écart*) gap; **à ~** at *ou* from a distance; **à une ~ de 10 km, à 10 km de ~** 10 km away, at a distance of 10 km; **à 2 ans de ~** with a gap of 2 years; **garder ses ~s** to keep one's distance; **tenir la ~** (SPORT) to cover the distance, last the course; **distancer** *vt* to outdistance, leave behind.
distant, e [distɑ̃, -ɑ̃t] *a* (*réservé*) distant, aloof; (*éloigné*) distant, far away; **~ de** (*lieu*) far away *ou* a long way from; **~ de 5 km (d'un lieu)** 5 km away (from a place).
distendre [distɑ̃dʀ(ə)] *vt*, **se ~** *vi* to distend.
distillation [distilɑsjɔ̃] *nf* distillation, distilling.
distillé, e [distile] *a*: **eau ~e** distilled water.
distiller [distile] *vt* to distil; (*fig*) to exude; to elaborate; **distillerie** *nf* distillery.
distinct, e [distɛ̃(kt), distɛ̃kt(ə)] *a* distinct; **distinctement** *ad* distinctly; **distinctif, ive** *a* distinctive.
distinction [distɛ̃ksjɔ̃] *nf* distinction.
distingué, e [distɛ̃ge] *a* distinguished.
distinguer [distɛ̃ge] *vt* to distinguish.
distraction [distʀaksjɔ̃] *nf* (*manque d'attention*) absent-mindedness; (*oubli*) lapse (in concentration *ou* attention); (*détente*) diversion, recreation; (*passe-temps*) distraction, entertainment.
distraire [distʀɛʀ] *vt* (*déranger*) to distract; (*divertir*) to entertain, divert; (*détourner: somme d'argent*) to divert, misappropriate; **se ~** to amuse *ou* enjoy o.s.
distrait, e [distʀɛ, -ɛt] *a* absent-minded.
distribuer [distʀibɥe] *vt* to distribute; to hand out; (CARTES) to deal (out); (*courrier*) to deliver; **distributeur** *nm* (COMM) distributor; (*automatique*) (vending *ou* slot) machine; **distribution** *nf* distribution; (*postale*) delivery; (*choix d'acteurs*) casting, cast; **distribution des prix** (SCOL) prize giving.
district [distʀik(t)] *nm* district.
dit, e [di, dit] *pp de* **dire** // *a* (*fixé*): **le jour ~** the arranged day; (*surnommé*): **X, ~ Pierrot** X, known as *ou* called Pierrot.
dites *vb voir* **dire**.
dithyrambique [ditiʀɑ̃bik] *a* eulogistic.
diurétique [djyʀetik] *a* diuretic.
diurne [djyʀn(ə)] *a* diurnal, daytime *cpd*.
divagations [divagɑsjɔ̃] *nfpl* wanderings, ramblings; ravings.
divaguer [divage] *vi* to ramble; to rave.
divan [divɑ̃] *nm* divan; **~-lit** *nm* divan (bed).
divergence [divɛʀʒɑ̃s] *nf* divergence.
divergent, e [divɛʀʒɑ̃, -ɑ̃t] *a* divergent.
diverger [divɛʀʒe] *vi* to diverge.
divers, e [divɛʀ, -ɛʀs(ə)] *a* (*varié*) diverse, varied; (*différent*) different, various, // *dét* (*plusieurs*) various, several; **(frais) ~** sundries, miscellaneous (expenses); **diversement** *ad* in various *ou* diverse ways; **diversifier** *vt* to diversify.
diversion [divɛʀsjɔ̃] *nf* diversion; **faire ~** to create a diversion.
diversité [divɛʀsite] *nf* diversity; variety.
divertir [divɛʀtiʀ] *vt* to amuse, entertain; **se ~** to amuse *ou* enjoy o.s.; **divertissement** *nm* entertainment; (MUS) divertimento, divertissement.
dividende [dividɑ̃d] *nm* (MATH, COMM) dividend.
divin, e [divɛ̃, -in] *a* divine; **diviniser** *vt* to deify; **divinité** *nf* divinity.
diviser [divize] *vt* (*gén*, MATH) to divide; (*morceler, subdiviser*) to divide (up), split (up); **diviseur** *nm* (MATH) divisor; **division** *nf* (*gén*) division.
divorce [divɔʀs(ə)] *nm* divorce; **divorcé, e** *nm/f* divorcee; **divorcer** *vi* to get a divorce, get divorced; **divorcer de** *ou* **d'avec qn** to divorce sb.
divulgation [divylgɑsjɔ̃] *nf* disclosure.
divulguer [divylge] *vt* to divulge, disclose.
dix [dis] *num* ten; **dixième** *num* tenth.
dizaine [dizɛn] *nf* (*10*) ten; (*environ 10*): **une ~ (de)** about ten, ten or so.
do [do] *nm* (*note*) C; (*en chantant la gamme*) do(h).
docile [dɔsil] *a* docile; **docilité** *nf* docility.
dock [dɔk] *nm* dock.
docker [dɔkɛʀ] *nm* docker.
docte [dɔkt(ə)] *a* learned.
docteur [dɔktœʀ] *nm* doctor.
doctoral, e, aux [dɔktɔʀal, -o] *a* pompous, bombastic.
doctorat [dɔktɔʀa] *nm*: **~ d'Université** ≈ Ph.D.; **~ d'état** ≈ Higher Doctorate.
doctoresse [dɔktɔʀɛs] *nf* lady doctor.
doctrinaire [dɔktʀinɛʀ] *a* doctrinaire; pompous, sententious.
doctrine [dɔktʀin] *nf* doctrine.
document [dɔkymɑ̃] *nm* document.
documentaire [dɔkymɑ̃tɛʀ] *a, nm* documentary.
documentaliste [dɔkymɑ̃talist(ə)] *nm/f* archivist; researcher.
documentation [dɔkymɑ̃tɑsjɔ̃] *nf* documentation, literature; (PRESSE, TV: *service*) research.
documenté, e [dɔkymɑ̃te] *a* well-informed, well-documented; well-researched.
documenter [dɔkymɑ̃te] *vt*: **se ~ (sur)** to gather information *ou* material (on *ou* about).
dodeliner [dɔdline] *vi*: **~ de la tête** to nod one's head gently.
dodo [dɔdo] *nm*: **aller faire ~** to go to bye-byes.
dodu, e [dɔdy] *a* plump.
dogmatique [dɔgmatik] *a* dogmatic.
dogme [dɔgm(ə)] *nm* dogma.
dogue [dɔg] *nm* mastiff.
doigt [dwa] *nm* finger; **à deux ~s de** within an ace *ou* an inch of; **un ~ de lait/whisky** a drop of milk/whisky; **~ de pied** toe.
doigté [dwate] *nm* (MUS) fingering; fingering technique; (*fig: habileté*) diplomacy, tact.

doigtier [dwatje] *nm* fingerstall.
doit *etc vb voir* **devoir**.
doléances [dɔleɑ̃s] *nfpl* complaints; grievances.
dolent, e [dɔlɑ̃, -ɑ̃t] *a* doleful, mournful.
dollar [dɔlaʀ] *nm* dollar.
D.O.M. [*parfois* dɔm] *sigle m ou mpl* = *département(s) d'outre-mer.*
domaine [dɔmɛn] *nm* estate, property; (*fig*) domain, field; **tomber dans le ~ public** (JUR) to be out of copyright.
domanial, e, aux [dɔmanjal, -jo] *a* (*forêt, biens*) national, state *cpd.*
dôme [dom] *nm* dome.
domesticité [dɔmɛstisite] *nf* (domestic) staff.
domestique [dɔmɛstik] *a* domestic // *nm/f* servant, domestic.
domestiquer [dɔmɛstike] *vt* to domesticate.
domicile [dɔmisil] *nm* home, place of residence; **à ~** at home; **domicilié, e** *a*: **être domicilié à** to have one's home in *ou* at.
dominant, e [dɔminɑ̃, -ɑ̃t] *a* dominant; predominant.
dominateur, trice [dɔminatœʀ, -tʀis] *a* dominating; domineering.
domination [dɔminɑsjɔ̃] *nf* domination.
dominer [dɔmine] *vt* to dominate; (*passions etc*) to control, master; (*surpasser*) to outclass, surpass; (*surplomber*) to tower above, dominate // *vi* to be in the dominant position; **se ~** to control o.s.
dominical, e, aux [dɔminikal, -o] *a* Sunday *cpd*, dominical.
domino [dɔmino] *nm* domino; **~s** *nmpl* (*jeu*) dominoes *sg.*
dommage [dɔmaʒ] *nm* (*préjudice*) harm, injury; (*dégâts, pertes*) damage *q*; **c'est ~ de faire/que** it's a shame *ou* pity to do/that; **~s-intérêts** *nmpl* damages.
dompter [dɔ̃te] *vt* to tame; **dompteur, euse** *nm/f* trainer; liontamer.
don [dɔ̃] *nm* (*cadeau*) gift; (*charité*) donation; (*aptitude*) gift, talent; **avoir des ~s pour** to have a gift *ou* talent for.
donateur, trice [dɔnatœʀ, -tʀis] *nm/f* donor.
donation [dɔnɑsjɔ̃] *nf* donation.
donc [dɔ̃k] *cj* therefore, so; (*après une digression*) so, then.
donjon [dɔ̃ʒɔ̃] *nm* keep, donjon.
donné, e [dɔne] *a* (*convenu*) given // *nf* (MATH, *gén*) datum (*pl* data); **étant ~ ...** given ... .
donner [dɔne] *vt* to give; (*vieux habits etc*) to give away; (*spectacle*) to show; to put on; **~ qch à qn** to give sb sth, give sth to sb; **~ sur** (*suj*: *fenêtre, chambre*) to look (out) onto; **~ dans** (*piège etc*) to fall into; **se ~ à fond (à son travail)** to give one's all (to one's work); **s'en ~ à cœur joie** (*fam*) to have a great time (of it).
donneur, euse [dɔnœʀ, -øz] *nm/f* (MÉD) donor; (CARTES) dealer; **~ de sang** blood donor.
dont [dɔ̃] *pronom relatif*: **la maison ~ je vois le toit** the house whose roof I can see, the house I can see the roof of; **la maison ~ le toit est rouge** the house whose roof is red *ou* the roof of which is red; **l'homme ~ je connais la sœur** the man whose sister I know; **10 blessés, ~ 2 grièvement** 10 injured, 2 of them seriously; **2 livres, ~ l'un est** 2 books, one of which is; **il y avait plusieurs personnes, ~ Gabrielle** there were several people, among whom was Gabrielle; **le fils ~ il est si fier** the son he's so proud of; **ce ~ je parle** what I'm talking about; *voir adjectifs et verbes à complément prépositionnel*: **responsable de, souffrir de** *etc.*
dorade [dɔʀad] *nf* = **daurade**.
doré, e [dɔʀe] *a* golden; (*avec dorure*) gilt, gilded.
dorénavant [dɔʀenavɑ̃] *ad* from now on, henceforth.
dorer [dɔʀe] *vt* (*cadre*) to gild; **(faire) ~** (CULIN) to brown (in the oven).
dorloter [dɔʀlɔte] *vt* to pamper, cosset.
dormant, e [dɔʀmɑ̃, -ɑ̃t] *a*: **eau ~e** still water.
dormeur, euse [dɔʀmœʀ, -øz] *nm/f* sleeper.
dormir [dɔʀmiʀ] *vi* to sleep; (*être endormi*) to be asleep.
dorsal, e, aux [dɔʀsal, -o] *a* dorsal.
dortoir [dɔʀtwaʀ] *nm* dormitory.
dorure [dɔʀyʀ] *nf* gilding.
doryphore [dɔʀifɔʀ] *nm* Colorado beetle.
dos [do] *nm* back; (*de livre*) spine; **'voir au ~'** 'see over'; **de ~** from the back, from behind; **à ~ de chameau** riding on a camel.
dosage [dozaʒ] *nm* mixture.
dos-d'âne [dodɑn] *nm* humpback.
dose [doz] *nf* dose.
doser [doze] *vt* to measure out; to mix in the correct proportions; (*fig*) to expend in the right amounts *ou* proportion; to strike a balance between; **doseur** *nm* measure.
dossard [dosaʀ] *nm* number (*worn by competitor*).
dossier [dosje] *nm* (*renseignements, fichier*) file; (*enveloppe*) folder, file; (*de chaise*) back.
dot [dɔt] *nf* dowry.
doter [dɔte] *vt*: **~ qn/qch de** to equip sb/sth with.
douairière [dwɛʀjɛʀ] *nf* dowager.
douane [dwan] *nf* (*poste, bureau*) customs *pl*; (*taxes*) (customs) duty; **passer la ~** to go through customs; **douanier, ière** *a* customs *cpd* // *nm* customs officer.
doublage [dublaʒ] *nm* (CINÉMA) dubbing.
double [dubl(e)] *a, ad* double // *nm* (*2 fois plus*): **le ~ (de)** twice as much (*ou* many) (as), double the amount (*ou* number) (of); (*autre exemplaire*) duplicate, copy; (*sosie*) double; **en ~ (exemplaire)** in duplicate; **faire ~ emploi** to be redundant; **~ carburateur** twin carburettor; **à ~s commandes** dual-control; **~ messieurs/mixte** men's/mixed doubles *sg*; **~ toit** (*de tente*) fly sheet.
doublé, e [duble] *a* (*vêtement*): **~ (de)** lined (with).
doublement [dubləmɑ̃] *nm* doubling;

twofold increase // *ad* doubly; in two ways, on two counts.

doubler [duble] *vt* (*multiplier par 2*) to double; (*vêtement*) to line; (*dépasser*) to overtake, pass; (*film*) to dub; (*acteur*) to stand in for // *vi* to double, increase twofold; ~ **(la classe)** (SCOL) to repeat a year.

doublure [dublyʀ] *nf* lining; (CINÉMA) stand-in.

douce [dus] *a voir* **doux**; **~âtre** *a* sickly sweet; **~ment** *ad* gently; slowly; **~reux, euse** *a* (*péj*) sugary, suave; **douceur** *nf* mildness; gentleness; softness; sweetness; **douceurs** *nfpl* (*friandises*) sweets.

douche [duʃ] *nf* shower; **~s** *nfpl* (*salle*) shower room *sg*; **se doucher** to have *ou* take a shower.

doué, e [dwe] *a* gifted, talented; ~ **de** endowed with.

douille [duj] *nf* (ÉLEC) socket; (*de projectile*) case.

douillet, te [dujɛ, -ɛt] *a* cosy; (*péj*) soft.

douleur [dulœʀ] *nf* pain; (*chagrin*) grief, distress; **il a eu la ~ de perdre son père** he suffered the grief of losing his father; **douloureux, euse** *a* painful.

doute [dut] *nm* doubt; **sans ~** *ad* no doubt.

douter [dute] *vt* to doubt; ~ **de** *vt* (*allié*) to doubt, have (one's) doubts about; (*résultat*) to be doubtful of; **se ~ de qch/que** to suspect sth/that; **je m'en doutais** I suspected as much.

douteux, euse [dutø, -øz] *a* (*incertain*) doubtful; (*discutable*) dubious, questionable; (*péj*) dubious-looking.

douve [duv] *nf* (*de château*) moat; (*de tonneau*) stave.

Douvres [duvʀ(ə)] *n* Dover.

doux, douce [du, dus] *a* (*lisse, moelleux, pas vif*: *couleur, non calcaire*: *eau*) soft; (*sucré, agréable*) sweet; (*peu fort*: *moutarde etc, clément*: *climat*) mild; (*pas brusque*) gentle.

douzaine [duzɛn] *nf* (*12*) dozen; (*environ 12*): **une ~ (de)** a dozen or so, twelve or so.

douze [duz] *num* twelve; **douzième** *num* twelfth.

doyen, ne [dwajɛ̃, -ɛn] *nm/f* (*en âge, ancienneté*) most senior member; (*de faculté*) dean.

draconien, ne [dʀakɔnjɛ̃, -jɛn] *a* draconian; stringent.

dragage [dʀagaʒ] *nm* dredging.

dragée [dʀaʒe] *nf* sugared almond; (MÉD) (sugar-coated) pill.

dragon [dʀagɔ̃] *nm* dragon.

drague [dʀag] *nf* (*filet*) dragnet; (*bateau*) dredger; **draguer** *vt* (*rivière*) to dredge; to drag // *vi* (*fam*) to try and pick up girls; to chat up birds; **dragueur de mines** *nm* minesweeper.

drainage [dʀɛnaʒ] *nm* drainage.

drainer [dʀene] *vt* to drain.

dramatique [dʀamatik] *a* dramatic; (*tragique*) tragic // *nf* (TV) (television) drama.

dramatiser [dʀamatize] *vt* to dramatize.

dramaturge [dʀamatyʀʒ(ə)] *nm* dramatist, playwright.

drame [dʀam] *nm* (THÉÂTRE) drama; (*catastrophe*) drama, tragedy.

drap [dʀa] *nm* (*de lit*) sheet; (*tissu*) woollen fabric.

drapeau, x [dʀapo] *nm* flag; **sous les ~x** with the colours, in the army.

draper [dʀape] *vt* to drape.

draperies [dʀapʀi] *nfpl* hangings.

drapier [dʀapje] *nm* (woollen) cloth manufacturer; (*marchand*) clothier.

dresser [dʀese] *vt* (*mettre vertical, monter*: *tente*) to put up, erect; (*fig*: *liste, bilan, contrat*) to draw up; (*animal*) to train; **se ~** *vi* (*falaise, obstacle*) to stand; to tower (up); (*personne*) to draw o.s. up; **~ qn contre qn d'autre** to set sb against sb else.

dresseur, euse [dʀɛsœʀ, -øz] *nm/f* trainer.

dressoir [dʀɛswaʀ] *nm* dresser.

dribbler [dʀible] *vt, vi* (SPORT) to dribble.

drogue [dʀɔg] *nf* drug; **la ~** drugs *pl*.

drogué, e [dʀɔge] *nm/f* drug addict.

droguer [dʀɔge] *vt* (*victime*) to drug; (*malade*) to give drugs to; **se ~** (*aux stupéfiants*) to take drugs; (*péj*: *de médicaments*) to dose o.s. up.

droguerie [dʀɔgʀi] *nf* hardware shop.

droguiste [dʀɔgist(ə)] *nm* keeper (*ou* owner) of a hardware shop.

droit, e [dʀwa, dʀwat] *a* (*non courbe*) straight; (*vertical*) upright, straight; (*fig*: *loyal, franc*) upright, straight(forward); (*opposé à gauche*) right, right-hand // *ad* straight // *nm* (*prérogative*) right; (*taxe*) duty, tax; (: *d'inscription*) fee; (*lois, branche*): **le ~** law // *nf* (*ligne*) straight line; **avoir le ~ de** to be allowed to; **avoir ~ à** to be entitled to; **être en ~ de** to have a *ou* the right to; **faire ~ à** to grant, accede to; **être dans son ~** to be within one's rights; **à ~e** on the right; (*direction*) (to the) right; **de ~e** (POL) right-wing; **~ d'auteur** copyright; **~s d'auteur** royalties; **le ~ de vote** the (right to) vote.

droitier, ière [dʀwatje, -jɛʀ] *nm/f* right-handed person.

droiture [dʀwatyʀ] *nf* uprightness, straightness.

drôle [dʀol] *a* (*amusant*) funny, amusing; (*bizarre*) funny, peculiar.

dromadaire [dʀɔmadɛʀ] *nm* dromedary.

dru, e [dʀy] *a* (*cheveux*) thick, bushy; (*pluie*) heavy.

drugstore [dʀœgstɔʀ] *nm* drugstore.

D.S.T. *sigle f* = *direction de la surveillance du territoire* (*the French internal security service*).

du [dy] *prép + dét, dét voir* **de**.

dû, due [dy] *vb voir* **devoir** // *a* (*somme*) owing, owed; (: *venant à échéance*) due; (*causé par*): **~ à** due to // *nm* due; (*somme*) dues *pl*.

dubitatif, ive [dybitatif, -iv] *a* doubtful, dubious.

duc [dyk] *nm* duke; **duché** *nm* dukedom; **duchesse** *nf* duchess.

duel [dɥɛl] *nm* duel.

dûment [dymɑ̃] *ad* duly.

dune [dyn] *nf* dune.
Dunkerque [dœ̃kɛʀk] *n* Dunkirk.
duo [dɥo] *nm* (MUS) duet ; (*fig*: *couple*) duo, pair.
dupe [dyp] *nf* dupe // *a*: **(ne pas) être ~ de** (not) to be taken in by.
duper [dype] *vt* to dupe, deceive.
duperie [dypʀi] *nf* deception, dupery.
duplex [dyplɛks] *nm* (*appartement*) split-level appartment, duplex.
duplicata [dyplikata] *nm* duplicate.
duplicateur [dyplikatœʀ] *nm* duplicator.
duplicité [dyplisite] *nf* duplicity.
duquel [dykɛl] *prép* + *pronom voir* **lequel**.
dur, e [dyʀ] *a* (*pierre, siège, travail, problème*) hard ; (*lumière, voix, climat*) harsh ; (*sévère*) hard, harsh ; (*cruel*) hard(-hearted) ; (*porte, col*) stiff ; (*viande*) tough // *ad* hard ; **~ d'oreille** hard of hearing.
durable [dyʀabl(ə)] *a* lasting.
durant [dyʀɑ̃] *prép* (*au cours de*) during ; (*pendant*) for ; **~ des mois, des mois ~** for months.
durcir [dyʀsiʀ] *vt*, *vi*, **se ~** *vi* to harden.
durcissement [dyʀsismɑ̃] *nm* hardening.
durée [dyʀe] *nf* length ; (*d'une pile etc*) life ; (*déroulement*: *des opérations etc*) duration ; **pour une ~ illimitée** for an unlimited length of time.
durement [dyʀmɑ̃] *ad* harshly.
durer [dyʀe] *vi* to last.
dureté [dyʀte] *nf* hardness ; harshness ; stiffness ; toughness.
durit [dyʀit] *nf* ® (radiator) hose (*for car*).
dus *etc vb voir* **devoir**.
duvet [dyvɛ] *nm* down ; **(sac de couchage en) ~** down-filled sleeping bag.
dynamique [dinamik] *a* dynamic.
dynamisme [dinamism(ə)] *nm* dynamism.
dynamite [dinamit] *nf* dynamite.
dynamiter [dinamite] *vt* to (blow up with) dynamite.
dynamo [dinamo] *nf* dynamo.
dynastie [dinasti] *nf* dynasty.
dysenterie [disɑ̃tʀi] *nf* dysentery.
dyslexie [dislɛksi] *nf* dyslexia, word-blindness.
dyspepsie [dispɛpsi] *nf* dyspepsia.

E

eau, x [o] *nf* water // *nfpl* waters ; **prendre l'~** to leak, let in water ; **faire ~** to leak ; **tomber à l'~** (*fig*) to fall through ; **~ de Cologne** Eau de Cologne ; **~ courante** running water ; **~ douce** fresh water ; **~ de Javel** bleach ; **~ minérale** mineral water ; **~ salée** salt water ; **~ de toilette** toilet water ; **les E~x et Forêts** (ADMIN) ≈ the National Forestry Commission ; **~-de-vie** *nf* brandy ; **~-forte** *nf* etching.
ébahi, e [ebai] *a* dumbfounded, flabbergasted.
ébats [eba] *nmpl* frolics, gambols.
ébattre [ebatʀ(ə)]: **s'~** *vi* to frolic.
ébauche [eboʃ] *nf* (rough) outline, sketch.
ébaucher [eboʃe] *vt* to sketch out, outline ; **s'~** *vi* to take shape.
ébène [ebɛn] *nf* ebony.
ébéniste [ebenist(ə)] *nm* cabinetmaker ; **ébénisterie** *nf* cabinetmaking ; (*bâti*) cabinetwork.
éberlué, e [ebɛʀlɥe] *a* astounded, flabbergasted.
éblouir [ebluiʀ] *vt* to dazzle.
éblouissement [ebluismɑ̃] *nm* dazzle ; (*faiblesse*) dizzy turn.
éborgner [ebɔʀɲe] *vt*: **~ qn** to blind sb in one eye.
éboueur [ebwœʀ] *nm* dustman.
ébouillanter [ebujɑ̃te] *vt* to scald ; (CULIN) to blanch.
éboulement [ebulmɑ̃] *nm* falling rocks *pl*, rock fall.
ébouler [ebule]: **s'~** *vi* to crumble, collapse.
éboulis [ebuli] *nmpl* fallen rocks.
ébouriffé, e [ebuʀife] *a* tousled, ruffled.
ébranler [ebʀɑ̃le] *vt* to shake ; (*rendre instable*: *mur*) to weaken ; **s'~** *vi* (*partir*) to move off.
ébrécher [ebʀeʃe] *vt* to chip.
ébriété [ebʀijete] *nf*: **en état d'~** in a state of intoxication.
ébrouer [ebʀue]: **s'~** *vi* to shake o.s. ; to snort.
ébruiter [ebʀɥite] *vt* to spread, disclose.
ébullition [ebylisjɔ̃] *nf* boiling point ; **en ~** boiling ; (*fig*) in an uproar.
écaille [ekɑj] *nf* (*de poisson*) scale ; (*de coquillage*) shell ; (*matière*) tortoiseshell ; (*de roc etc*) flake.
écailler [ekɑje] *vt* (*poisson*) to scale ; (*huître*) to open ; **s'~** *vi* to flake *ou* peel (off).
écarlate [ekaʀlat] *a* scarlet.
écarquiller [ekaʀkije] *vt*: **~ les yeux** to stare wide-eyed.
écart [ekaʀ] *nm* gap ; (*embardée*) swerve ; sideways leap ; (*fig*) departure, deviation ; **à l'~** *ad* out of the way ; **à l'~ de** *prép* away from ; (*fig*) out of ; **~ de conduite** misdemeanour.
écarté, e [ekaʀte] *a* (*maison, route*) out-of-the-way, remote ; (*ouvert*): **les jambes ~es** legs apart ; **les bras ~s** arms outstretched.
écarteler [ekaʀtəle] *vt* to quarter ; (*fig*) to tear.
écartement [ekaʀtəmɑ̃] *nm* space, gap ; (RAIL) gauge.
écarter [ekaʀte] *vt* (*séparer*) to move apart, separate ; (*éloigner*) to push back, move away ; (*ouvrir*: *bras, jambes*) to spread, open ; (: *rideau*) to draw (back) ; (*éliminer*: *candidat, possibilité*) to dismiss ; **s'~** *vi* to part ; to move away ; **s'~ de** to wander from.
ecchymose [ekimoz] *nf* bruise.
ecclésiastique [eklezjastik] *a* ecclesiastical // *nm* ecclesiastic.
écervelé, e [esɛʀvəle] *a* scatterbrained, featherbrained.
échafaud [eʃafo] *nm* scaffold.
échafaudage [eʃafodaʒ] *nm* scaffolding ; (*fig*) heap, pile.
échafauder [eʃafode] *vt* (*plan*) to construct.

échalas [eʃala] *nm* stake, pole.
échalote [eʃalɔt] *nf* shallot.
échancrure [eʃɑ̃kRyR] *nf* (*de robe*) scoop neckline; (*de côte, arête rocheuse*) indentation.
échange [eʃɑ̃ʒ] *nm* exchange; **en ~ de** in exchange *ou* return for.
échanger [eʃɑ̃ʒe] *vt*: **~ qch (contre)** to exchange sth (for); **échangeur** *nm* (AUTO) interchange.
échantillon [eʃɑ̃tijɔ̃] *nm* sample; **échantillonnage** *nm* selection of samples.
échappatoire [eʃapatwaR] *nf* way out.
échappée [eʃape] *nf* (*vue*) vista; (CYCLISME) breakaway.
échappement [eʃapmɑ̃] *nm* (AUTO) exhaust.
échapper [eʃape]: **~ à** *vt* (*gardien*) to escape (from); (*punition, péril*) to escape; **~ à qn** (*détail, sens*) to escape sb; (*objet qu'on tient*) to slip out of sb's hands; **s'~** *vi* to escape; **l'~ belle** to have a narrow escape.
écharde [eʃaRd(ə)] *nf* splinter (of wood).
écharpe [eʃaRp(ə)] *nf* scarf (*pl* scarves); (*de maire*) sash; **avoir un bras en ~** to have one's arm in a sling; **prendre en ~** (*dans une collision*) to hit sideways on.
écharper [eʃaRpe] *vt* to tear to pieces.
échasse [eʃɑs] *nf* stilt.
échassier [eʃɑsje] *nm* wader.
échauffement [eʃofmɑ̃] *nm* overheating.
échauffer [eʃofe] *vt* (*métal, moteur*) to overheat; (*fig: exciter*) to fire, excite; **s'~** (SPORT) to warm up; (*dans la discussion*) to become heated.
échauffourée [eʃofuRe] *nf* clash, brawl.
échéance [eʃeɑ̃s] *nf* (*d'un paiement: date*) settlement date; (*: somme due*) financial commitment(s); (*fig*) deadline; **à brève/longue ~** *a* short-/long-term // *ad* in the short/long run.
échéant [eʃeɑ̃]: **le cas ~** *ad* if the case arises.
échec [eʃɛk] *nm* failure; (ÉCHECS): **~ et mat/au roi** checkmate/check; **~s** *nmpl* (*jeu*) chess *sg*; **tenir en ~** to hold in check; **faire ~ à** to foil *ou* thwart.
échelle [eʃɛl] *nf* ladder; (*fig, d'une carte*) scale; **à l'~ de** on the scale of; **sur une grande ~** on a large scale; **faire la courte ~ à qn** to give sb a leg up.
échelon [eʃlɔ̃] *nm* (*d'échelle*) rung; (ADMIN) grade.
échelonner [eʃlɔne] *vt* to space out, spread out.
écheveau, x [ɛʃvo] *nm* skein, hank.
échevelé, e [eʃəvle] *a* tousled, dishevelled; wild, frenzied.
échine [eʃin] *nf* backbone, spine.
échiquier [eʃikje] *nm* chessboard.
écho [eko] *nm* echo; **~s** *nmpl* (*potins*) gossip *sg*, rumours.
échoir [eʃwaR] *vi* (*dette*) to fall due; (*délais*) to expire; **~ à** *vt* to fall to.
échoppe [eʃɔp] *nf* stall, booth.
échouer [eʃwe] *vi* to fail // *vt* (*bateau*) to ground; **s'~** *vi* to run aground.
échu, e [eʃy] *pp voir* **échoir.**
éclabousser [eklabuse] *vt* to splash.
éclair [eklɛR] *nm* (*d'orage*) flash of lightning, lightning *q*; (*fig*) flash, spark; (*gâteau*) éclair.
éclairage [eklɛRaʒ] *nm* lighting.
éclaircie [eklɛRsi] *nf* bright *ou* sunny interval.
éclaircir [eklɛRsiR] *vt* to lighten; (*fig*) to clear up; to clarify; (CULIN) to thin (down); **s'~ la voix** to clear one's throat; **éclaircissement** *nm* clearing up; clarification.
éclairer [ekleRe] *vt* (*lieu*) to light (up); (*personne: avec une lampe de poche etc*) to light the way for; (*fig*) to enlighten; to shed light on // *vi*: **~ mal/bien** to give a poor/good light; **s'~ à la bougie/l'électricité** to use candlelight/have electric lighting.
éclaireur, euse [eklɛRœR, -øz] *nm/f* (*scout*) (boy) scout/(girl) guide // *nm* (MIL) scout; **partir en ~** to go off to reconnoitre.
éclat [ekla] *nm* (*de bombe, de verre*) fragment; (*du soleil, d'une couleur etc*) brightness, brilliance; (*d'une cérémonie*) splendour; (*scandale*): **faire un ~** to cause a commotion; **des ~s de verre** broken glass; flying glass; **~ de rire** burst *ou* roar of laughter; **~ de voix** shout.
éclatant, e [eklatɑ̃, -ɑ̃t] *a* brilliant, bright.
éclater [eklate] *vi* (*pneu*) to burst; (*bombe*) to explode; (*guerre, épidémie*) to break out; (*groupe, parti*) to break up; **~ de rire** to burst out laughing.
éclipse [eklips(ə)] *nf* eclipse.
éclipser [eklipse] *vt* to eclipse; **s'~** *vi* to slip away.
éclopé, e [eklɔpe] *a* lame.
éclore [eklɔR] *vi* (*œuf*) to hatch; (*fleur*) to open (out).
écluse [eklyz] *nf* lock; **éclusier** *nm* lock keeper.
écœurer [ekœRe] *vt*: **~ qn** to make sb feel sick.
école [ekɔl] *nf* school; **aller à l'~** to go to school; **faire ~** to collect a following; **~ de dessin/danse** art/dancing school; **~ hôtelière** catering college; **~ normale (d'instituteurs)** teachers' training college; **~ de secrétariat** secretarial college; **écolier, ière** *nm/f* schoolboy/girl.
écologie [ekɔlɔʒi] *nf* ecology; environmental studies *pl*; **écologique** *a* ecological; environmental; **écologiste** *nm/f* ecologist; environmentalist.
éconduire [ekɔ̃dɥiR] *vt* to dismiss.
économat [ekɔnɔma] *nm* bursar's office.
économe [ekɔnɔm] *a* thrifty // *nm/f* (*de lycée etc*) bursar.
économie [ekɔnɔmi] *nf* (*vertu*) economy, thrift; (*gain: d'argent, de temps etc*) saving; (*science*) economics *sg*; (*situation économique*) economy; **~s** *nfpl* (*pécule*) savings; **économique** *a* (*avantageux*) economical; (ÉCON) economic.
économiser [ekɔnɔmize] *vt, vi* to save.
économiste [ekɔnɔmist(ə)] *nm/f* economist.
écoper [ekɔpe] *vi* to bale out; (*fig*) to cop it; **~ (de)** *vt* to get.
écorce [ekɔRs(ə)] *nf* bark; (*de fruit*) peel; **écorcer** *vt* to bark.

écorché [ekɔʀʃe] *nm* cut-away drawing.
écorcher [ekɔʀʃe] *vt* (*animal*) to skin; (*égratigner*) to graze; **écorchure** *nf* graze.
écossais, e [ekɔsɛ, -ɛz] *a* Scottish // *nm/f*: **E~, e** Scot.
Écosse [ekɔs] *nf* Scotland.
écosser [ekɔse] *vt* to shell.
écot [eko] *nm*: **payer son ~** to pay one's share.
écouler [ekule] *vt* to sell; to dispose of; **s'~** *vi* (*eau*) to flow (out); (*jours, temps*) to pass (by).
écourter [ekuʀte] *vt* to curtail, cut short.
écoute [ekut] *nf* (RADIO, TV): **temps/heure d'~** listening (*ou* viewing) time/hour; **prendre l'~** to tune in; **rester à l'~ (de)** to stay listening (to) *ou* tuned in (to); **~s téléphoniques** phone tapping *sg*.
écouter [ekute] *vt* to listen to; **écouteur** *nm* (TÉL) receiver; (RADIO) headphones *pl*, headset.
écoutille [ekutij] *nf* hatch.
écran [ekʀɑ̃] *nm* screen.
écrasant, e [ekʀɑzɑ̃, -ɑ̃t] *a* overwhelming.
écraser [ekʀɑze] *vt* to crush; (*piéton*) to run over; **s'~ (au sol)** to crash; **s'~ contre** to crash into.
écrémer [ekʀeme] *vt* to skim.
écrevisse [ekʀəvis] *nf* crayfish *inv*.
écrier [ekʀije]: **s'~** *vi* to exclaim.
écrin [ekʀɛ̃] *nm* case, box.
écrire [ekʀiʀ] *vt* to write; **ça s'écrit comment?** how is it spelt?, how do you write that?; **écrit** *nm* document; (*examen*) written paper; **par écrit** in writing.
écriteau, x [ekʀito] *nm* notice, sign.
écritoire [ekʀitwaʀ] *nf* writing case.
écriture [ekʀityʀ] *nf* writing; (COMM) entry; **~s** *nfpl* (COMM) accounts, books; **l'É~ (sainte), les É~s** the Scriptures.
écrivain [ekʀivɛ̃] *nm* writer.
écrou [ekʀu] *nm* nut.
écrouer [ekʀue] *vt* to imprison; to remand in custody.
écrouler [ekʀule]: **s'~** *vi* to collapse.
écru, e [ekʀy] *a* (*toile*) raw, unbleached.
écueil [ekœj] *nm* reef; (*fig*) pitfall; stumbling block.
écuelle [ekɥɛl] *nf* bowl.
éculé, e [ekyle] *a* (*chaussure*) down-at-heel; (*fig*: *péj*) hackneyed.
écume [ekym] *nf* foam; (CULIN) scum; **écumer** *vt* (CULIN) to skim; (*fig*) to plunder // *vi* (*mer*) to foam; (*fig*) to boil with rage; **écumoire** *nf* skimmer.
écureuil [ekyʀœj] *nm* squirrel.
écurie [ekyʀi] *nf* stable.
écusson [ekysɔ̃] *nm* badge.
écuyer, ère [ekɥije, -ɛʀ] *nm/f* rider.
eczéma [ɛgzema] *nm* eczema.
édenté, e [edɑ̃te] *a* toothless.
E.D.F. *sigle f* = *Électricité de France*, ≈ Electricity Board.
édifice [edifis] *nm* building, edifice.
édifier [edifje] *vt* to build, erect; (*fig*) to edify.
édiles [edil] *nmpl* city fathers.
édit [edi] *nm* edict.
éditer [edite] *vt* (*publier*) to publish; (: *disque*) to produce; (*préparer*: *texte*) to edit; **éditeur, trice** *nm/f* editor; publisher; **édition** *nf* editing *q*; edition; (*industrie du livre*) publishing.
éditorial, aux [editɔʀjal, -o] *nm* editorial, leader; **~iste** *nm/f* editorial *ou* leader writer.
édredon [edʀədɔ̃] *nm* eiderdown.
éducatif, ive [edykatif, -iv] *a* educational.
éducation [edykɑsjɔ̃] *nf* education; (*familiale*) upbringing; (*manières*) (good) manners *pl*; **l'É~ (Nationale)** ≈ The Department of Education; **~ physique** physical education.
édulcorer [edylkɔʀe] *vt* to sweeten; (*fig*) to tone down.
éduquer [edyke] *vt* to educate; (*élever*) to bring up; (*faculté*) to train.
effacer [efase] *vt* to erase, rub out; **s'~** *vi* (*inscription etc*) to wear off; (*pour laisser passer*) to step aside; **~ le ventre** to pull one's stomach in.
effarement [efaʀmɑ̃] *nm* alarm.
effarer [efaʀe] *vt* to alarm.
effaroucher [efaʀuʃe] *vt* to frighten *ou* scare away; to alarm.
effectif, ive [efɛktif, -iv] *a* real; effective // *nm* (MIL) strength; (SCOL) total number of pupils, size; **~s** *nmpl* numbers, strength *sg*; **effectivement** *ad* effectively; (*réellement*) actually, really; (*en effet*) indeed.
effectuer [efɛktɥe] *vt* (*opération, mission*) to carry out; (*déplacement, trajet*) to make, complete; (*mouvement*) to execute, make.
efféminé, e [efemine] *a* effeminate.
effervescent, e [efɛʀvesɑ̃, -ɑ̃t] *a* (*cachet, boisson*) effervescent; (*fig*) agitated, in a turmoil.
effet [efɛ] *nm* (*résultat, artifice*) effect; (*impression*) impression; **~s** *nmpl* (*vêtements etc*) things; **faire de l'~** (*médicament, menace*) to have an effect, be effective; **en ~** *ad* indeed.
effeuiller [efœje] *vt* to remove the leaves (*ou* petals) from.
efficace [efikas] *a* (*personne*) efficient; (*action, médicament*) effective; **efficacité** *nf* efficiency; effectiveness.
effigie [efiʒi] *nf* effigy.
effilé, e [efile] *a* slender; sharp; streamlined.
effiler [efile] *vt* (*cheveux*) to thin (out); (*tissu*) to fray.
effilocher [efilɔʃe]: **s'~** *vi* to fray.
efflanqué, e [eflɑ̃ke] *a* emaciated.
effleurer [eflœʀe] *vt* to brush (against); (*sujet, ideé*) to touch upon; (*suj*: *ideé, pensée*): **~ qn** to cross sb's mind.
effluves [eflyv] *nmpl* exhalation(s).
effondrement [efɔ̃dʀəmɑ̃] *nm* collapse.
effondrer [efɔ̃dʀe]: **s'~** *vi* to collapse.
efforcer [efɔʀse]: **s'~ de** *vt*: **s'~ de faire** to try hard to do.
effort [efɔʀ] *nm* effort; **faire un ~** to make an effort.
effraction [efʀaksjɔ̃] *nf* breaking-in; **s'introduire par ~ dans** to break into.
effrangé, e [efʀɑ̃ʒe] *a* fringed; (*effiloché*) frayed.
effrayant, e [efʀɛjɑ̃, -ɑ̃t] *a* frightening, fearsome; (*sens affaibli*) dreadful.

effrayer [efReje] *vt* to frighten, scare; (*rebuter*) to put off; **s'~ (de)** to be frightened *ou* scared (by).
effréné, e [efRene] *a* wild.
effriter [efRite]: **s'~** *vi* to crumble.
effroi [efRwɑ] *nm* terror, dread *q*.
effronté, e [efRɔ̃te] *a* insolent, brazen.
effroyable [efRwajabl(ə)] *a* horrifying, appalling.
effusion [efyzjɔ̃] *nf* effusion; **sans ~ de sang** without bloodshed.
égailler [egaje]: **s'~** *vi* to scatter, disperse.
égal, e, aux [egal, -o] *a* (*identique, ayant les mêmes droits*) equal; (*plan: surface*) even, level; (*constant: vitesse*) steady; (*équitable*) even // *nm/f* equal; **être ~ à** (*prix, nombre*) to be equal to; **ça lui est ~** it's all the same to him, it doesn't matter to him; he doesn't mind; **sans ~** matchless, unequalled; **à l'~ de** (*comme*) just like; **d'~ à ~** as equals; **~ement** *ad* equally; evenly; steadily; (*aussi*) too, as well; **~er** *vt* to equal; **~iser** *vt* (*sol, salaires*) to level (out); (*chances*) to equalize // *vi* (SPORT) to equalize; **~itaire** *a* egalitarian; **~ité** *nf* equality; evenness; steadiness; (MATH) identity; **être à ~ité (de points)** to be level; **~ité de droits** equality of rights; **~ité d'humeur** evenness of temper.
égard [egaR] *nm*: **~s** *nmpl* consideration *sg*; **à cet ~** in this respect; **eu ~ à** in view of; **par ~ pour** out of consideration for; **sans ~ pour** without regard for; **à l'~ de** *prép* towards; concerning.
égarement [egaRmɑ̃] *nm* distraction; aberration.
égarer [egaRe] *vt* (*objet*) to mislay; (*moralement*) to lead astray; **s'~** *vi* to get lost, lose one's way; (*objet*) to go astray; (*fig: dans une discussion*) to wander.
égayer [egeje] *vt* (*personne*) to amuse; to cheer up; (*récit, endroit*) to brighten up, liven up.
égide [eʒid] *nf*: **sous l'~ de** under the aegis of.
églantier [eglɑ̃tje] *nm* wild *ou* dog rose(-bush).
églantine [eglɑ̃tin] *nf* wild *ou* dog rose.
églefin [egləfɛ̃] *nm* haddock.
église [egliz] *nf* church; **aller à l'~** (*être pratiquant*) to go to church, be a churchgoer.
égocentrique [egɔsɑ̃tRik] *a* egocentric, self-centred.
égoïsme [egɔism(ə)] *nm* selfishness, egoism; **égoïste** *a* selfish, egoistic // *nm/f* egoist.
égorger [egɔRʒe] *vt* to cut the throat of.
égosiller [egozije]: **s'~** *vi* to shout o.s. hoarse.
égout [egu] *nm* sewer; **égoutier** *nm* sewer worker.
égoutter [egute] *vt* (*linge*) to wring out; (*vaisselle*) to drain // *vi*, **s'~** *vi* to drip; **égouttoir** *nm* draining board; (*mobile*) draining rack.
égratigner [egRatiɲe] *vt* to scratch; **égratignure** *nf* scratch.
égrener [egRəne] *vt*: **~ une grappe, ~ des raisins** to pick grapes off a bunch.
égrillard, e [egRijaR, -aRd(ə)] *a* ribald, bawdy.
Égypte [eʒipt(ə)] *nf* Egypt; **égyptien, ne** *a, nm/f* Egyptian; **égyptologie** *nf* Egyptology.
eh [e] *excl* hey!; **~ bien** well.
éhonté, e [eɔ̃te] *a* shameless, brazen.
éjaculation [eʒakylɑsjɔ̃] *nf* ejaculation.
éjaculer [eʒakyle] *vi* to ejaculate.
éjectable [eʒɛktabl(ə)] *a*: **siège ~** ejector seat.
éjecter [eʒɛkte] *vt* (TECH) to eject; (*fam*) to kick *ou* chuck out.
élaboration [elabɔRɑsjɔ̃] *nf* elaboration.
élaborer [elabɔRe] *vt* to elaborate.
élaguer [elage] *vt* to prune.
élan [elɑ̃] *nm* (ZOOL) elk, moose; (SPORT: *avant le saut*) run up; (*de véhicule ou objet en mouvement*) momentum; (*fig: de tendresse etc*) surge; **prendre son ~/de l'~** to take a run up/gather speed.
élancé, e [elɑ̃se] *a* slender.
élancement [elɑ̃smɑ̃] *nm* shooting pain.
élancer [elɑ̃se]: **s'~** *vi* to dash, hurl o.s.; (*fig: arbre, clocher*) to soar (upwards).
élargir [elaRʒiR] *vt* to widen; (*vêtement*) to let out; (JUR) to release; **s'~** *vi* to widen; (*vêtement*) to stretch.
élasticité [elastisite] *nf* (*aussi* ÉCON) elasticity.
élastique [elastik] *a* elastic // *nm* (*de bureau*) rubber band; (*pour la couture*) elastic *q*.
électeur, trice [elɛktœR, -tRis] *nm/f* elector, voter.
élection [elɛksjɔ̃] *nf* election; **~s** *nfpl* (POL) election(s); **~ partielle** ≈ by-election.
électoral, e, aux [elɛktɔRal, -o] *a* electoral, election *cpd*.
électorat [elɛktɔRa] *nm* electorate.
électricien, ne [elɛktRisjɛ̃, -jɛn] *nm/f* electrician.
électricité [elɛktRisite] *nf* electricity; **allumer/éteindre l'~** to put on/off the light; **~ statique** static electricity.
électrifier [elɛktRifje] *vt* (RAIL) to electrify.
électrique [elɛktRik] *a* electric(al).
électriser [elɛktRize] *vt* to electrify.
électro... [elɛktRɔ] *préfixe*: **~-aimant** *nm* electromagnet; **~cardiogramme** *nm* electrocardiogram; **~choc** *nm* electric shock treatment; **~cuter** *vt* to electrocute; **~cution** *nf* electrocution; **électrode** *nf* electrode; **~-encéphalogramme** *nm* electroencephalogram; **~gène** *a*: **groupe ~gène** generating set; **~lyse** *nf* electrolysis *sg*; **~magnétique** *a* electromagnetic; **~ménager** *a*: **appareils ~ménagers** domestic (electrical) appliances.
électron [elɛktRɔ̃] *nm* electron.
électronicien, ne [elɛktRɔnisjɛ̃, -jɛn] *nm/f* electronics engineer.
électronique [elɛktRɔnik] *a* electronic // *nf* electronics *sg*.
électrophone [elɛktRɔfɔn] *nm* record player.
élégance [elegɑ̃s] *nf* elegance.
élégant, e [elegɑ̃, -ɑ̃t] *a* elegant; (*solution*)

neat, elegant; (*attitude, procédé*) courteous, civilized.
élément [elemɑ̃] *nm* element; (*pièce*) component, part; **~s** *nmpl* (*aussi: rudiments*) elements; **élémentaire** *a* elementary; (CHIMIE) elemental.
éléphant [elefɑ̃] *nm* elephant.
élevage [ɛlvaʒ] *nm* breeding; (*de bovins*) cattle breeding *ou* rearing.
élévateur [elevatœʀ] *nm* elevator.
élévation [elevɑsjɔ̃] *nf* (*gén*) elevation; (*voir élever*) raising; (*voir s'élever*) rise.
élève [elɛv] *nm/f* pupil; **~ infirmière** *nf* student nurse.
élevé, e [ɛlve] *a* (*prix, sommet*) high; (*fig: noble*) elevated; **bien/mal ~** well-/ill-mannered.
élever [ɛlve] *vt* (*enfant*) to bring up, raise; (*bétail, volaille*) to breed; (*abeilles*) to keep; (*hausser: immeuble, taux, niveau*) to raise; (*fig: âme, esprit*) to elevate; (*édifier: monument*) to put up, erect; **s'~** *vi* (*avion, alpiniste*) to go up; (*niveau, température, aussi: cri etc*) to rise; *survenir: difficultés*) to arise; **s'~ à** (*suj: frais, dégâts*) to amount to, add up to; **s'~ contre qch** to rise up against sth; **~ une protestation/critique** to raise a protest/make a criticism; **~ la voix** to raise one's voice; **~ qn au rang de** to raise *ou* elevate sb to the rank of; **éleveur, euse** *nm/f* cattle breeder.
élidé, e [elide] *a* elided.
éligible [eliʒibl(ə)] *a* eligible.
élimé, e [elime] *a* worn (thin), threadbare.
élimination [eliminɑsjɔ̃] *nf* elimination.
éliminatoire [eliminatwaʀ] *a* eliminatory; disqualifying // *nf* (SPORT) heat.
éliminer [elimine] *vt* to eliminate.
élire [eliʀ] *vt* to elect; **~ domicile à** to take up residence in *ou* at.
élision [elizjɔ̃] *nf* elision.
élite [elit] *nf* elite.
elle [ɛl] *pronom* (*sujet*) she; (*: chose*) it; (*complément*) her; it; **~s** (*sujet*) they; (*complément*) them; **~-même** herself; itself; **~s-mêmes** themselves; *voir note sous* **il**.
ellipse [elips(ə)] *nf* ellipse; (LING) ellipsis *sg*; **elliptique** *a* elliptical.
élocution [elɔkysjɔ̃] *nf* delivery; **défaut d'~** speech impediment.
éloge [elɔʒ] *nm* praise (*gén q*); **faire l'~ de** to praise; **élogieux, euse** *a* laudatory, full of praise.
éloigné, e [elwaɲe] *a* distant, far-off.
éloignement [elwaɲmɑ̃] *nm* removal; putting off; estrangement; distance.
éloigner [elwaɲe] *vt* (*objet*): **~ qch (de)** to move *ou* take sth away (from); (*personne*): **~ qn (de)** to take sb away *ou* remove sb (from); (*échéance*) to put off, postpone; (*soupçons, danger*) to ward off; **s'~ (de)** (*personne*) to go away (from); (*véhicule*) to move away (from); (*affectivement*) to become estranged (from).
élongation [elɔ̃gɑsjɔ̃] *nf* strained muscle.
éloquence [elɔkɑ̃s] *nf* eloquence.
éloquent, e [elɔkɑ̃, -ɑ̃t] *a* eloquent.
élu, e [ely] *pp de* **élire** // *nm/f* (POL) elected representative.
élucider [elyside] *vt* to elucidate.
élucubrations [elykybʀɑsjɔ̃] *nfpl* wild imaginings.
éluder [elyde] *vt* to evade.
émacié, e [emasje] *a* emaciated.
émail, aux [emaj, -o] *nm* enamel.
émaillé, e [emaje] *a* enamelled; (*fig*): **~ de** dotted with.
émanation [emanɑsjɔ̃] *nf* emanation, exhalation.
émanciper [emɑ̃sipe] *vt* to emancipate; **s'~** (*fig*) to become emancipated *ou* liberated.
émaner [emane]: **~ de** *vt* to come from; (ADMIN) to proceed from.
émarger [emaʀʒe] *vt* to sign; **~ de 1000 F à un budget** to receive 1000 F out of a budget.
émasculer [emaskyle] *vt* to emasculate.
emballage [ɑ̃balaʒ] *nm* wrapping; packaging.
emballer [ɑ̃bale] *vt* to wrap (up); (*dans un carton*) to pack (up); (*fig: fam*) to thrill (to bits); **s'~** *vi* (*moteur*) to race; (*cheval*) to bolt; (*fig: personne*) to get carried away.
embarcadère [ɑ̃baʀkadɛʀ] *nm* landing stage, pier.
embarcation [ɑ̃baʀkɑsjɔ̃] *nf* (small) boat, (small) craft *inv*.
embardée [ɑ̃baʀde] *nf* swerve; **faire une ~** to swerve.
embargo [ɑ̃baʀgo] *nm* embargo; **mettre l'~ sur** to put an embargo on, embargo.
embarquement [ɑ̃baʀkəmɑ̃] *nm* embarkation; loading; boarding.
embarquer [ɑ̃baʀke] *vt* (*personne*) to embark; (*marchandise*) to load; (*fam*) to cart off; to nick // *vi* (*passager*) to board; (NAVIG) to ship water; **s'~** *vi* to board; **s'~ dans** (*affaire, aventure*) to embark upon.
embarras [ɑ̃baʀa] *nm* (*obstacle*) hindrance; (*confusion*) embarrassment; (*ennuis*): **être dans l'~** to be in a predicament *ou* an awkward position; **~ gastrique** stomach upset.
embarrasser [ɑ̃baʀase] *vt* (*encombrer*) to clutter (up); (*gêner*) to hinder, hamper; (*fig*) to cause embarrassment to; to put in an awkward position; **s'~ de** to burden o.s. with.
embauche [ɑ̃boʃ] *nf* hiring; **bureau d'~** labour office.
embaucher [ɑ̃boʃe] *vt* to take on, hire; **s'~** to get o.s. hired.
embauchoir [ɑ̃boʃwaʀ] *nm* shoetree.
embaumer [ɑ̃bome] *vt* to embalm; to fill with its fragrance; **~ la lavande** to be fragrant with (the scent of) lavender.
embellir [ɑ̃beliʀ] *vt* to make more attractive; (*une histoire*) to embellish // *vi* to grow lovelier *ou* more attractive.
embêtements [ɑ̃bɛtmɑ̃] *nmpl* trouble *sg*.
embêter [ɑ̃bete] *vt* to bother; **s'~** *vi* (*s'ennuyer*) to be bored; **il ne s'embête pas!** (*ironique*) he does all right for himself!
emblée [ɑ̃ble]: **d'~** *ad* straightaway.

emblème [ɑ̃blɛm] *nm* emblem.
emboîter [ɑ̃bwate] *vt* to fit together; **s'~ dans** to fit into; **s'~ (l'un dans l'autre)** to fit together; **~ le pas à qn** to follow in sb's footsteps.
embolie [ɑ̃bɔli] *nf* embolism.
embonpoint [ɑ̃bɔ̃pwɛ̃] *nm* stoutness.
embouché, e [ɑ̃buʃe] *a*: **mal ~** foul-mouthed.
embouchure [ɑ̃buʃyʀ] *nf* (GÉO) mouth; (MUS) mouthpiece.
embourber [ɑ̃buʀbe]: **s'~** *vi* to get stuck in the mud.
embourgeoiser [ɑ̃buʀʒwaze]: **s'~** *vi* to adopt a middle-class outlook.
embout [ɑ̃bu] *nm* (*de canne*) tip; (*de tuyau*) nozzle.
embouteillage [ɑ̃butɛjaʒ] *nm* traffic jam, (traffic) holdup.
emboutir [ɑ̃butiʀ] *vt* (TECH) to stamp; (*heurter*) to crash into, ram.
embranchement [ɑ̃bʀɑ̃ʃmɑ̃] *nm* (*routier*) junction; (*classification*) branch.
embraser [ɑ̃bʀɑze]: **s'~** *vi* to flare up.
embrassades [ɑ̃bʀasad] *nfpl* hugging and kissing *sg*.
embrasser [ɑ̃bʀase] *vt* to kiss; (*sujet, période*) to embrace, encompass; (*carrière, métier*) to take up, enter upon.
embrasure [ɑ̃bʀɑzyʀ] *nf*: **dans l'~ de la porte** in the door(way).
embrayage [ɑ̃bʀɛjaʒ] *nm* (*mécanisme*) clutch.
embrayer [ɑ̃bʀeje] *vi* (AUTO) to let in the clutch.
embrigader [ɑ̃bʀigade] *vt* to recruit.
embrocher [ɑ̃bʀɔʃe] *vt* to (put on a) spit.
embrouillamini [ɑ̃bʀujamini] *nm* (*fam*) muddle.
embrouiller [ɑ̃bʀuje] *vt* (*fils*) to tangle (up); (*fiches, idées, personne*) to muddle up; **s'~** *vi* (*personne*) to get in a muddle.
embroussaillé, e [ɑ̃bʀusɑje] *a* overgrown, bushy.
embruns [ɑ̃bʀœ̃] *nmpl* sea spray *sg*.
embryon [ɑ̃bʀijɔ̃] *nm* embryo; **embryonnaire** *a* embryonic.
embûches [ɑ̃byʃ] *nfpl* pitfalls, traps.
embué, e [ɑ̃bɥe] *a* misted up.
embuscade [ɑ̃byskad] *nf* ambush; **tendre une ~ à** to lay an ambush for.
embusquer [ɑ̃byske] *vt* to put in ambush; **s'~** *vi* to take up position (for an ambush).
éméché, e [emeʃe] *a* tipsy, merry.
émeraude [ɛmʀod] *nf* emerald // *a inv* emerald-green.
émerger [emɛʀʒe] *vi* to emerge; (*faire saillie, aussi fig*) to stand out.
émeri [ɛmʀi] *nm*: **toile** *ou* **papier ~** emery paper.
émérite [emeʀit] *a* highly skilled.
émerveiller [emɛʀveje] *vt* to fill with wonder; **s'~ de** to marvel at.
émetteur, trice [emɛtœʀ, -tʀis] *a* transmitting; **(poste) ~** transmitter.
émettre [emɛtʀ(ə)] *vt* (*son, lumière*) to give out, emit; (*message etc*: RADIO) to transmit; (*billet, timbre, emprunt*) to issue; (*hypothèse, avis*) to voice, put forward // *vi*: **~ sur ondes courtes** to broadcast on short wave.
émeus *etc vb voir* **émouvoir**.
émeute [emøt] *nf* riot; **émeutier, ère** *nm/f* rioter.
émietter [emjete] *vt* to crumble; (*fig*) to split up, to disperse.
émigrant, e [emigʀɑ̃, -ɑ̃t] *nm/f* emigrant.
émigré, e [emigʀe] *nm/f* expatriate.
émigrer [emigʀe] *vi* to emigrate.
éminemment [eminamɑ̃] *ad* eminently.
éminence [eminɑ̃s] *nf* distinction; (*colline*) knoll, hill; **Son É~** his (*ou* her) Eminence.
éminent, e [eminɑ̃, -ɑ̃t] *a* distinguished.
émir [emiʀ] *nm* emir; **~at** *nm* emirate.
émissaire [emisɛʀ] *nm* emissary.
émission [emisjɔ̃] *nf* emission; transmission; issue; (RADIO, TV) programme, broadcast.
emmagasiner [ɑ̃magazine] *vt* to (put into) store; (*fig*) to store up.
emmailloter [ɑ̃majɔte] *vt* to wrap up.
emmanchure [ɑ̃mɑ̃ʃyʀ] *nf* armhole.
emmêler [ɑ̃mele] *vt* to tangle (up); (*fig*) to muddle up; **s'~** to get into a tangle.
emménager [ɑ̃menaʒe] *vi* to move in; **~ dans** to move into.
emmener [ɑ̃mne] *vt* to take (with one); (*comme otage, capture*) to take away; (SPORT, MIL: *joueurs, soldats*) to lead; **~ qn au cinéma** to take sb to the cinema.
emmerder [ɑ̃mɛʀde] (*fam!*) *vt* to bug, bother; **s'~** (*s'ennuyer*) to be bored stiff.
emmitoufler [ɑ̃mitufle] *vt* to wrap up (warmly).
emmurer [ɑ̃myʀe] *vt* to wall up, immure.
émoi [emwa] *nm* (*agitation, effervescence*) commotion; (*trouble*) agitation.
émoluments [emɔlymɑ̃] *nmpl* remuneration *sg*, fee *sg*.
émonder [emɔ̃de] *vt* to prune.
émotif, ive [emɔtif, -iv] *a* emotional.
émotion [emosjɔ̃] *nf* emotion; **avoir des ~s** (*fig*) to get a fright; **émotionnel, le** *a* emotional.
émoulu, e [emuly] *a*: **frais ~ de** fresh from, just out of.
émousser [emuse] *vt* to blunt; (*fig*) to dull.
émouvoir [emuvwaʀ] *vt* (*troubler*) to stir, affect; (*toucher, attendrir*) to move; (*indigner*) to rouse; (*effrayer*) to disturb, worry; **s'~** *vi* to be affected; to be moved; to be roused; to be disturbed *ou* worried.
empailler [ɑ̃pɑje] *vt* to stuff.
empaler [ɑ̃pale] *vt* to impale.
empaqueter [ɑ̃pakte] *vt* to pack up.
emparer [ɑ̃paʀe]: **s'~ de** *vt* (*objet*) to seize, grab; (*comme otage*, MIL) to seize; (*suj*: *peur, doute*) to take hold of.
empâter [ɑ̃pɑte]: **s'~** *vi* to thicken out.
empattement [ɑ̃patmɑ̃] *nm* (AUTO) wheelbase; (TYPO) serif.
empêchement [ɑ̃pɛʃmɑ̃] *nm* (unexpected) obstacle, hitch.
empêcher [ɑ̃peʃe] *vt* to prevent; **~ qn de faire** to prevent *ou* stop sb (from) doing; **~ que qch (n')arrive/qn (ne)**

fasse to prevent sth from happening/sb from doing; **il n'empêche que** nevertheless, be that as it may; **il n'a pas pu s'~ de rire** he couldn't help laughing.
empêcheur [ɑ̃pɛʃœʀ] *nm*: **~ de danser en rond** spoilsport, killjoy.
empeigne [ɑ̃pɛɲ] *nf* upper(s).
empereur [ɑ̃pʀœʀ] *nm* emperor.
empesé, e [ɑ̃pəze] *a* (*fig*) stiff, starchy.
empeser [ɑ̃pəze] *vt* to starch.
empester [ɑ̃pɛste] *vt* (*lieu*) to stink out // *vi* to stink, reek; **~ le tabac/le vin** to stink *ou* reek of tobacco/wine.
empêtrer [ɑ̃petʀe] *vt*: **s'~ dans** (*fils etc*) to get tangled up in.
emphase [ɑ̃fɑz] *nf* pomposity, bombast.
empierrer [ɑ̃pjeʀe] *vt* (*route*) to metal.
empiéter [ɑ̃pjete]: **~ sur** *vt* to encroach upon.
empiffrer [ɑ̃pifʀe]: **s'~** *vi* (*péj*) to stuff o.s.
empiler [ɑ̃pile] *vt* to pile (up), stack (up).
empire [ɑ̃piʀ] *nm* empire; (*fig*) influence.
empirer [ɑ̃piʀe] *vi* to worsen, deteriorate.
empirique [ɑ̃piʀik] *a* empirical.
emplacement [ɑ̃plasmɑ̃] *nm* site.
emplâtre [ɑ̃plɑtʀ(ə)] *nm* plaster; (*fam*) twit.
emplette [ɑ̃plɛt] *nf*: **faire l'~ de** to purchase; **~s** *nfpl* shopping *sg*.
emplir [ɑ̃pliʀ] *vt* to fill; **s'~ (de)** to fill (with).
emploi [ɑ̃plwa] *nm* use; (COMM, ÉCON) employment; (*poste*) job, situation; **d'~ facile** easy to use; **~ du temps** timetable, schedule.
employé, e [ɑ̃plwaje] *nm/f* employee; **~ de bureau/banque** office/bank employee *ou* clerk.
employer [ɑ̃plwaje] *vt* (*outil, moyen, méthode, mot*) to use; (*ouvrier, main-d'œuvre*) to employ; **s'~ à faire** to apply *ou* devote o.s. to doing; **employeur, euse** *nm/f* employer.
empocher [ɑ̃pɔʃe] *vt* to pocket.
empoignade [ɑ̃pwaɲad] *nf* row, set-to.
empoigne [ɑ̃pwaɲ] *nf*: **foire d'~** free-for-all.
empoigner [ɑ̃pwaɲe] *vt* to grab; **s'~** (*fig*) to have a row *ou* set-to.
empoisonnement [ɑ̃pwazɔnmɑ̃] *nm* poisoning.
empoisonner [ɑ̃pwazɔne] *vt* to poison; (*empester: air, pièce*) to stink out; (*fam*): **~ qn** to drive sb mad.
emportement [ɑ̃pɔʀtəmɑ̃] *nm* fit of rage, anger *q*.
emporte-pièce [ɑ̃pɔʀtəpjɛs] *nm inv* (TECH) punch; **à l'~** *a* (*fig*) incisive.
emporter [ɑ̃pɔʀte] *vt* to take (with one); (*en dérobant ou enlevant, emmener: blessés, voyageurs*) to take away; (*entraîner*) to carry away *ou* along; (*arracher*) to tear off; to carry away; (MIL: *position*) to take; (*avantage, approbation*) to win; **s'~** *vi* (*de colère*) to fly into a rage, lose one's temper; **l'~ (sur)** to get the upper hand (of); (*méthode etc*) to prevail (over); **boissons à (l')~** take-away drinks.
empourpré, e [ɑ̃puʀpʀe] *a* crimson.
empreint, e [ɑ̃pʀɛ̃, -ɛ̃t] *a*: **~ de** marked with; tinged with // *nf* (*de pied, main*) print; (*fig*) stamp, mark; **~e (digitale)** fingerprint.
empressé, e [ɑ̃pʀese] *a* attentive; (*péj*) overanxious to please, overattentive.
empressement [ɑ̃pʀɛsmɑ̃] *nm* (*hâte*) eagerness.
empresser [ɑ̃pʀese]: **s'~** *vi* to bustle about; **s'~ auprès de qn** to surround sb with attentions; **s'~ de faire** (*se hâter*) to hasten to do.
emprise [ɑ̃pʀiz] *nf* hold, ascendancy; **sous l'~ de** under the influence of.
emprisonnement [ɑ̃pʀizɔnmɑ̃] *nm* imprisonment.
emprisonner [ɑ̃pʀizɔne] *vt* to imprison, jail.
emprunt [ɑ̃pʀœ̃] *nm* borrowing *q*, loan (*from debtor's point of view*); (LING *etc*) borrowing; **~ public à 5%** 5% public loan.
emprunté, e [ɑ̃pʀœ̃te] *a* (*fig*) ill-at-ease, awkward.
emprunter [ɑ̃pʀœ̃te] *vt* to borrow; (*itinéraire*) to take, follow; (*style, manière*) to adopt, assume; **emprunteur, euse** *nm/f* borrower.
empuantir [ɑ̃pɥɑ̃tiʀ] *vt* to stink out.
ému, e [emy] *pp de* **émouvoir** // *a* excited; touched; moved.
émulation [emylɑsjɔ̃] *nf* emulation.
émule [emyl] *nm/f* imitator.
émulsion [emylsjɔ̃] *nf* emulsion.
en [ɑ̃] *prép* in; (*avec direction*) to; (*moyen*): **~ avion/taxi** by plane/taxi; (*composition*): **~ verre** made of glass, glass *cpd*; **se casser ~ plusieurs morceaux** to break into several pieces; **~ dormant** while sleeping, as one sleeps; **~ sortant** on going out, as he went out; **~ réparation** being repaired, under repair; **~ T/étoile** T-/star-shaped; **~ chemise/chaussettes** in one's shirt/socks; **peindre qch ~ rouge** to paint sth red; **~ soldat** as a soldier; **le même ~ plus grand** the same only *ou* but bigger // *pronom* (*provenance*): **j'~ viens** I've come from there; (*cause*): **il ~ est malade** he's ill because of it; (*complément de nom*): **j'~ connais les dangers** I know its dangers; (*indéfini*): **j'~ ai/veux** I have/want some; **~ as-tu?** have you got any?; **je n'~ veux pas** I don't want any; **j'~ ai assez** I've got enough (of it *ou* them); (*fig*) I've had enough; **j'~ ai 2** I've got 2 (of them); **combien y ~ a-t-il?** how many (of them) are there?; **j'~ suis fier/ai besoin** I am proud of it/need it: *voir le verbe ou l'adjectif lorsque 'en' correspond à 'de' introduisant un complément prépositionnel.*
E.N.A. [ena] *sigle f* = École Nationale d'Administration: *one of the Grandes Écoles*; **énarque** *nm/f* former E.N.A. student.
encablure [ɑ̃kablyʀ] *nf* (NAVIG) cable's length.
encadrement [ɑ̃kɑdʀəmɑ̃] *nm* framing; training; (*de porte*) frame.
encadrer [ɑ̃kɑdʀe] *vt* (*tableau, image*) to frame; (*fig: entourer*) to surround; to

flank; (*personnel, soldats etc*) to train; **encadreur** *nm* (picture) framer.

encaisse [ɑ̃kɛs] *nf* cash in hand; ~ **or/métallique** gold/gold and silver reserves.

encaissé, e [ɑ̃kese] *a* steep-sided; with steep banks.

encaisser [ɑ̃kese] *vt* (*chèque*) to cash; (*argent*) to collect; (*fig: coup, défaite*) to take; **encaisseur** *nm* collector (*of debts etc*).

encan [ɑ̃kɑ̃]: **à l'~** *ad* by auction.

encanailler [ɑ̃kanɑje]: **s'~** *vi* to become vulgar *ou* common; to mix with the riff-raff.

encart [ɑ̃kaʀ] *nm* insert.

encastrer [ɑ̃kastʀe] *vt*: ~ **qch dans** (*mur*) to embed sth in(to); (*boîtier*) to fit sth into; **s'~ dans** to fit into; (*heurter*) to crash into.

encaustique [ɑ̃kɔstik] *nf* polish, wax; **encaustiquer** *vt* to polish, wax.

enceinte [ɑ̃sɛ̃t] *af*: ~ **(de 6 mois)** (6 months) pregnant // *nf* (*mur*) wall; (*espace*) enclosure; ~ **(acoustique)** speaker system.

encens [ɑ̃sɑ̃] *nm* incense; **encenser** *vt* to (in)cense; (*fig*) to praise to the skies; **encensoir** *nm* thurible.

encercler [ɑ̃sɛʀkle] *vt* to surround.

enchaîner [ɑ̃ʃene] *vt* to chain up; (*mouvements, séquences*) to link (together) // *vi* to carry on.

enchanté, e [ɑ̃ʃɑ̃te] *a* delighted; enchanted; ~ **(de faire votre connaissance)** pleased to meet you, how do you do?.

enchantement [ɑ̃ʃɑ̃tmɑ̃] *nm* delight; (*magie*) enchantment; **comme par** ~ as if by magic.

enchanter [ɑ̃ʃɑ̃te] *vt* to delight.

enchâsser [ɑ̃ʃɑse] *vt*: ~ **qch (dans)** to set sth (in).

enchère [ɑ̃ʃɛʀ] *nf* bid; **faire une** ~ to (make a) bid; **mettre/vendre aux ~s** to put up for (sale by)/sell by auction.

enchevêtrer [ɑ̃ʃvetʀe] *vt* to tangle (up).

enclave [ɑ̃klav] *nf* enclave; **enclaver** *vt* to enclose, hem in.

enclencher [ɑ̃klɑ̃ʃe] *vt* (*mécanisme*) to engage; **s'~** *vi* to engage.

enclin, e [ɑ̃klɛ̃, -in] *a*: ~ **à** inclined *ou* prone to.

enclore [ɑ̃klɔʀ] *vt* to enclose.

enclos [ɑ̃klo] *nm* enclosure.

enclume [ɑ̃klym] *nf* anvil.

encoche [ɑ̃kɔʃ] *nf* notch.

encoignure [ɑ̃kɔɲyʀ] *nf* corner.

encoller [ɑ̃kɔle] *vt* to paste.

encolure [ɑ̃kɔlyʀ] *nf* (*tour de cou*) collar size; (*col, cou*) neck.

encombrant, e [ɑ̃kɔ̃bʀɑ̃, -ɑ̃t] *a* cumbersome, bulky.

encombre [ɑ̃kɔ̃bʀ(ə)]: **sans** ~ *ad* without mishap *ou* incident.

encombrement [ɑ̃kɔ̃bʀəmɑ̃] *nm* (*d'un lieu*) cluttering (up); (*d'un objet: dimensions*) bulk.

encombrer [ɑ̃kɔ̃bʀe] *vt* to clutter (up); (*gêner*) to hamper; **s'~ de** (*bagages etc*) to load *ou* burden o.s. with; ~ **le passage** to block *ou* obstruct the way.

encontre [ɑ̃kɔ̃tʀ(ə)]: **à l'~ de** *prép* against, counter to.

encorbellement [ɑ̃kɔʀbɛlmɑ̃] *nm* corbelled construction; **fenêtre en~** oriel window.

encore [ɑ̃kɔʀ] *ad* (*continuation*) still; (*de nouveau*) again; (*restriction*) even then *ou* so; (*intensif*): ~ **plus fort/mieux** even louder/better; **pas** ~ not yet; ~ **une fois** (once) again; ~ **deux jours** still two days, two more days; **si** ~ if only.

encouragement [ɑ̃kuʀaʒmɑ̃] *nm* encouragement.

encourager [ɑ̃kuʀaʒe] *vt* to encourage.

encourir [ɑ̃kuʀiʀ] *vt* to incur.

encrasser [ɑ̃kʀase] *vt* to foul up; to soot up.

encre [ɑ̃kʀ(ə)] *nf* ink; ~ **de Chine** Indian ink; ~ **sympathique** invisible ink; **encrer** *vt* to ink; **encreur** *am*: **rouleau encreur** inking roller; **encrier** *nm* inkwell.

encroûter [ɑ̃kʀute]: **s'~** *vi* (*fig*) to get into a rut, get set in one's ways.

encyclique [ɑ̃siklik] *nf* encyclical.

encyclopédie [ɑ̃siklɔpedi] *nf* encyclopaedia; **encyclopédique** *a* encyclopaedic.

endémique [ɑ̃demik] *a* endemic.

endetter [ɑ̃dete] *vt*, **s'~** *vi* to get into debt.

endeuiller [ɑ̃dœje] *vt* to plunge into mourning; **manifestation endeuillée par** event over which a tragic shadow was cast by.

endiablé, e [ɑ̃djɑble] *a* furious; boisterous.

endiguer [ɑ̃dige] *vt* to dyke (up); (*fig*) to check, hold back.

endimancher [ɑ̃dimɑ̃ʃe] *vt*: **s'~** to put on one's Sunday best.

endive [ɑ̃div] *nf* chicory *q*.

endocrine [ɑ̃dɔkʀin] *af*: **glande** ~ endocrine (gland).

endoctriner [ɑ̃dɔktʀine] *vt* to indoctrinate.

endommager [ɑ̃dɔmaʒe] *vt* to damage.

endormi, e [ɑ̃dɔʀmi] *a* asleep; (*fig*) sleepy, drowsy; sluggish.

endormir [ɑ̃dɔʀmiʀ] *vt* to put to sleep; (MÉD: *dent, nerf*) to anaesthetize; (*fig: soupçons*) to allay; **s'~** *vi* to fall asleep, go to sleep.

endosser [ɑ̃dose] *vt* (*responsabilité*) to take, shoulder; (*chèque*) to endorse; (*uniforme, tenue*) to put on, don.

endroit [ɑ̃dʀwa] *nm* place; (*opposé à l'envers*) right side; **à l'~** right side out; the right way up; (*vêtement*) the right way out; **à l'~ de** *prép* regarding, with regard to.

enduire [ɑ̃dɥiʀ] *vt* to coat; ~ **qch de** to coat sth with; **enduit** *nm* coating.

endurance [ɑ̃dyʀɑ̃s] *nf* endurance.

endurant, e [ɑ̃dyʀɑ̃, -ɑ̃t] *a* tough, hardy.

endurcir [ɑ̃dyʀsiʀ] *vt* (*physiquement*) to toughen; (*moralement*) to harden; **s'~** *vi* to become tougher; to become hardened.

endurer [ɑ̃dyʀe] *vt* to endure, bear.

énergétique [enɛʀʒetik] *a* (*ressources etc*) energy *cpd*.

énergie [enɛʀʒi] *nf* (PHYSIQUE) energy; (TECH) power; (*fig: physique*) energy;

(: *morale*) vigour, spirit; **énergique** *a* energetic; vigorous; (*mesures*) drastic, stringent.
énergumène [enɛʀgymɛn] *nm* rowdy character *ou* customer.
énerver [enɛʀve] *vt* to irritate, annoy; **s'~** *vi* to get excited, get worked up.
enfance [ɑ̃fɑ̃s] *nf* (*âge*) childhood; (*fig*) infancy; (*enfants*) children *pl*; **petite ~** infancy.
enfant [ɑ̃fɑ̃] *nm/f* child (*pl* children); **~ de chœur** *nm* (REL) altar boy; **~ prodige** child prodigy; **enfanter** *vi* to give birth // *vt* to give birth to; **enfantillage** *nm* (*péj*) childish behaviour *q*; **enfantin, e** *a* childlike; child *cpd*.
enfer [ɑ̃fɛʀ] *nm* hell.
enfermer [ɑ̃fɛʀme] *vt* to shut up; (*à clef, interner*) to lock up.
enferrer [ɑ̃feʀe]: **s'~** *vi*: **s'~ dans** to tangle o.s. up in.
enfiévré, e [ɑ̃fjevʀe] *a* (*fig*) feverish.
enfilade [ɑ̃filad] *nf*: **une ~ de** a series *ou* line of (interconnecting).
enfiler [ɑ̃file] *vt* (*vêtement*): **~ qch** to slip sth on, slip into sth; (*insérer*): **~ qch dans** to stick sth into; (*rue, couloir*) to take; (*perles*) to string; (*aiguille*) to thread; **s'~ dans** to disappear into.
enfin [ɑ̃fɛ̃] *ad* at last; (*en énumérant*) lastly; (*de restriction, résignation*) still; well; (*pour conclure*) in a word.
enflammer [ɑ̃flame] *vt* to set fire to; (MÉD) to inflame; **s'~** to catch fire; to become inflamed.
enflé, e [ɑ̃fle] *a* swollen; (*péj*: *style*) bombastic, turgid.
enfler [ɑ̃fle] *vi* to swell (up); **s'~** *vi* to swell; **enflure** *nf* swelling.
enfoncer [ɑ̃fɔ̃se] *vt* (*clou*) to drive in; (*faire pénétrer*): **~ qch dans** to push *ou* knock *ou* drive sth into; (*forcer*: *porte*) to break open; (: *plancher*) to cause to cave in; (*fam*: *surpasser*) to lick // *vi* (*dans la vase etc*) to sink in; (*sol, surface porteuse*) to give way; **s'~** *vi* to sink; **s'~ dans** to sink into; (*forêt, ville*) to disappear into.
enfouir [ɑ̃fwiʀ] *vt* (*dans le sol*) to bury; (*dans un tiroir etc*) to tuck away; **s'~ dans/sous** to bury o.s. in/under.
enfourcher [ɑ̃fuʀʃe] *vt* to mount.
enfourner [ɑ̃fuʀne] *vt*: **~ qch dans** to shove *ou* stuff sth into.
enfreindre [ɑ̃fʀɛ̃dʀ(ə)] *vt* to infringe, break.
enfuir [ɑ̃fɥiʀ]: **s'~** *vi* to run away *ou* off.
enfumer [ɑ̃fyme] *vt* to smoke out.
engagé, e [ɑ̃gaʒe] *a* (*littérature etc*) engagé, committed.
engageant, e [ɑ̃gaʒɑ̃, -ɑ̃t] *a* attractive, appealing.
engagement [ɑ̃gaʒmɑ̃] *nm* taking on, engaging; starting; investing; (*d'un écrivain etc, professionnel, financier*) commitment; (*promesse*) agreement, promise; (MIL: *combat*) engagement; **prendre l'~ de faire** to undertake to do; **sans ~** (COMM) without obligation.
engager [ɑ̃gaʒe] *vt* (*embaucher*) to take on, engage; (*commencer*) to start; (*lier*) to bind, commit; (*impliquer, entraîner*) to involve; (*investir*) to invest, lay out; (*faire intervenir*) to engage; (*inciter*): **~ qn à faire** to urge sb to do; (*faire pénétrer*): **~ qch dans** to insert sth into; **s'~** (*s'embaucher*) to hire o.s., get taken on; (MIL) to enlist; (*promettre, politiquement*) to commit o.s.; (*débuter*) to start (up); **s'~ à faire** to undertake to do; **s'~ dans** (*rue, passage*) to enter, turn into; (*s'emboîter*) to engage *ou* fit into; (*fig*: *affaire, discussion*) to enter into, embark on.
engelures [ɑ̃ʒlyʀ] *nfpl* chilblains.
engendrer [ɑ̃ʒɑ̃dʀe] *vt* to father; (*fig*) to create, breed.
engin [ɑ̃ʒɛ̃] *nm* machine; instrument; vehicle; (AVIAT) aircraft *inv*; missile; **~ (explosif)** (explosive) device.
englober [ɑ̃glɔbe] *vt* to include.
engloutir [ɑ̃glutiʀ] *vt* to swallow up; **s'~** to be engulfed.
engoncé, e [ɑ̃gɔ̃se] *a*: **~ dans** cramped in.
engorger [ɑ̃gɔʀʒe] *vt* to obstruct, block; **s'~** *vi* to become blocked.
engouement [ɑ̃gumɑ] *nm* (sudden) passion.
engouffrer [ɑ̃gufʀe] *vt* to swallow up, devour; **s'~ dans** to rush into.
engourdi, e [ɑ̃guʀdi] *a* numb.
engourdir [ɑ̃guʀdiʀ] *vt* to numb; (*fig*) to dull, blunt; **s'~** *vi* to go numb.
engrais [ɑ̃gʀɛ] *nm* manure; **~ (chimique)** (chemical) fertilizer.
engraisser [ɑ̃gʀese] *vt* to fatten (up) // *vi* (*péj*) to get fat(ter).
engrenage [ɑ̃gʀənaʒ] *nm* gears *pl*, gearing; (*fig*) chain.
engueuler [ɑ̃gœle] *vt* (*fam*) to bawl out.
enhardir [ɑ̃aʀdiʀ]: **s'~** *vi* to grow bolder.
énigmatique [enigmatik] *a* enigmatic.
énigme [enigm(ə)] *nf* riddle.
enivrer [ɑ̃nivʀe] *vt*: **s'~** to get drunk; **s'~ de** (*fig*) to become intoxicated with.
enjambée [ɑ̃ʒɑ̃be] *nf* stride.
enjamber [ɑ̃ʒɑ̃be] *vt* to stride over; (*suj*: *pont etc*) to span, straddle.
enjeu, x [ɑ̃ʒø] *nm* stakes *pl*.
enjoindre [ɑ̃ʒwɛ̃dʀ(ə)] *vt*: **~ à qn de faire** to enjoin *ou* order sb to do.
enjôler [ɑ̃ʒole] *vt* to coax, wheedle.
enjoliver [ɑ̃ʒɔlive] *vt* to embellish; **enjoliveur** *nm* (AUTO) hub cap.
enjoué, e [ɑ̃ʒwe] *a* playful.
enlacer [ɑ̃lase] *vt* (*étreindre*) to embrace, hug; (*suj*: *lianes*) to wind round, entwine.
enlaidir [ɑ̃lediʀ] *vt* to make ugly // *vi* to become ugly.
enlèvement [ɑ̃lɛvmɑ̃] *nm* removal; abduction, kidnapping; **l'~ des ordures ménagères** refuse collection.
enlever [ɑ̃lve] *vt* (*ôter*: *gén*) to remove; (: *vêtement, lunettes*) to take off; (: MÉD: *organe*) to remove, take out; (*emporter*: *ordures etc*) to collect, take away; (*prendre*): **~ qch à qn** to take sth (away) from sb; (*kidnapper*) to abduct, kidnap; (*obtenir*: *prix, contrat*) to win; (MIL: *position*) to take; (*morceau de piano etc*) to execute with spirit *ou* brio.
enliser [ɑ̃lize]: **s'~** *vi* to sink, get stuck.

enluminure [ɑ̃lyminyʀ] *nf* illumination.
enneigé, e [ɑ̃neʒe] *a* snowy; snowed-up.
enneigement [ɑ̃nɛʒmɑ̃] *nm* depth of snow, snowfall; **bulletin d'~** snow report.
ennemi, e [ɛnmi] *a* hostile; (*MIL*) enemy *cpd* // *nm, nf* enemy; **être ~ de** to be strongly averse *ou* opposed to.
ennoblir [ɑ̃nɔbliʀ] *vt* to ennoble.
ennui [ɑ̃nɥi] *nm* (*lassitude*) boredom; (*difficulté*) trouble *q*; **avoir des ~s** to be in trouble; **ennuyer** *vt* to bother; (*lasser*) to bore; **s'ennuyer** to be bored; **s'ennuyer de** (*regretter*) to miss; **ennuyeux, euse** *a* boring, tedious; annoying.
énoncé [enɔ̃se] *nm* terms *pl*; wording; (*LING*) utterance.
énoncer [enɔ̃se] *vt* to say, express; (*conditions*) to set out, state.
enorgueillir [ɑ̃nɔʀgœjiʀ]: **s'~ de** *vt* to pride o.s. on; to boast.
énorme [enɔʀm(ə)] *a* enormous, huge; **énormément** *ad* enormously, tremendously; **énormément de neige/gens** an enormous amount of snow/number of people; **énormité** *nf* enormity, hugeness; outrageous remark.
enquérir [ɑ̃keʀiʀ]: **s'~ de** *vt* to inquire about.
enquête [ɑ̃kɛt] *nf* (*de journaliste, de police*) investigation; (*judiciaire, administrative*) inquiry; (*sondage d'opinion*) survey; **enquêter** *vi* to investigate; to hold an inquiry; to conduct a survey; **enquêteur, euse** *ou* **trice** *nm/f* officer in charge of the investigation; person conducting a survey.
enquiers *etc vb voir* **enquérir**.
enraciné, e [ɑ̃ʀasine] *a* deep-rooted.
enragé, e [ɑ̃ʀaʒe] *a* (*MÉD*) rabid, with rabies; (*fig*) fanatical.
enrageant, e [ɑ̃ʀaʒɑ̃, -ɑ̃t] *a* infuriating.
enrager [ɑ̃ʀaʒe] *vi* to be furious, be in a rage.
enrayer [ɑ̃ʀeje] *vt* to check, stop; **s'~** *vi* (*arme à feu*) to jam.
enregistrement [ɑ̃ʀʒistʀəmɑ̃] *nm* recording; (*ADMIN*) registration; **~ des bagages** (*à l'aéroport*) luggage check-in.
enregistrer [ɑ̃ʀʒistʀe] *vt* (*MUS etc*) to record; (*remarquer, noter*) to note, record; (*fig: mémoriser*) to make a mental note of; (*ADMIN*) to register; (*bagages: par train*) to register; (*: à l'aéroport*) to check in.
enrhumer [ɑ̃ʀyme]: **s'~** *vi* to catch a cold.
enrichir [ɑ̃ʀiʃiʀ] *vt* to make rich(er); (*fig*) to enrich; **s'~** to get rich(er).
enrober [ɑ̃ʀɔbe] *vt*: **~ qch de** to coat sth with; (*fig*) to wrap sth up in.
enrôler [ɑ̃ʀole] *vt* to enlist; **s'~ (dans)** to enlist (in).
enrouer [ɑ̃ʀwe]: **s'~** *vi* to go hoarse.
enrouler [ɑ̃ʀule] *vt* (*fil, corde*) to wind (up); **~ qch autour de** to wind sth (a)round; **s'~** to coil up; to wind; **enrouleur** *nm voir* **ceinture.**
enrubanné, e [ɑ̃ʀybane] *a* trimmed with ribbon.
ensabler [ɑ̃sɑble] *vt* (*port, canal*) to silt up, sand up; (*embarcation*) to strand (on a sandbank); **s'~** *vi* to silt up; to get stranded.
ensanglanté, e [ɑ̃sɑ̃glɑ̃te] *a* covered with blood.
enseignant, e [ɑ̃sɛɲɑ̃, -ɑ̃t] *a* teaching // *nm/f* teacher.
enseigne [ɑ̃sɛɲ] *nf* sign // *nm*: **~ de vaisseau** lieutenant; **à telle ~ que** so much so that; **~ lumineuse** neon sign.
enseignement [ɑ̃sɛɲmɑ̃] *nm* teaching; (*ADMIN*): **~ primaire/ secondaire** primary/secondary education.
enseigner [ɑ̃seɲe] *vt, vi* to teach; **~ qch à qn/à qn que** to teach sb sth/sb that.
ensemble [ɑ̃sɑ̃bl(ə)] *ad* together // *nm* (*assemblage, MATH*) set; (*totalité*): **l'~ du/de la** the whole *ou* entire; (*vêtement féminin*) ensemble, suit; (*unité, harmonie*) unity; (*résidentiel*) housing development; **impression/idée d'~** overall *ou* general impression/ idea; **dans l'~** (*en gros*) on the whole; **~ vocal/musical** vocal/musical ensemble.
ensemblier [ɑ̃sɑ̃blije] *nm* interior designer.
ensemencer [ɑ̃smɑ̃se] *vt* to sow.
enserrer [ɑ̃seʀe] *vt* to hug (tightly).
ensevelir [ɑ̃səvliʀ] *vt* to bury.
ensoleillé, e [ɑ̃sɔleje] *a* sunny.
ensoleillement [ɑ̃sɔlɛjmɑ̃] *nm* period *ou* hours of sunshine.
ensommeillé, e [ɑ̃sɔmeje] *a* sleepy, drowsy.
ensorceler [ɑ̃sɔʀsəle] *vt* to enchant, bewitch.
ensuite [ɑ̃sɥit] *ad* then, next; (*plus tard*) afterwards, later; **~ de quoi** after which.
ensuivre [ɑ̃sɥivʀ(ə)]: **s'~** *vi* to follow, ensue.
entaille [ɑ̃tɑj] *nf* (*encoche*) notch; (*blessure*) cut.
entailler [ɑ̃tɑje] *vt* to notch; to cut; **s'~ le doigt** to cut one's finger.
entamer [ɑ̃tame] *vt* (*pain, bouteille*) to start; (*hostilités, pourparlers*) to open; (*fig: altérer*) to make a dent in; to shake; to damage.
entartrer [ɑ̃taʀtʀe]: **s'~** *vi* to fur up; (*dents*) to scale.
entassement [ɑ̃tɑsmɑ̃] *nm* (*tas*) pile, heap.
entasser [ɑ̃tɑse] *vt* (*empiler*) to pile up, heap up; (*tenir à l'étroit*) to cram together; **s'~** *vi* to pile up; to cram.
entendement [ɑ̃tɑ̃dmɑ̃] *nm* understanding.
entendre [ɑ̃tɑ̃dʀ(ə)] *vt* to hear; (*comprendre*) to understand; (*vouloir dire*) to mean; (*vouloir*): **~ être obéi/que** to intend *ou* mean to be obeyed/that; **j'ai entendu dire que** I've heard (it said) that; **~ raison** to see sense; **s'~** *vi* (*sympathiser*) to get on; (*se mettre d'accord*) to agree; **s'~ à qch/à faire** (*être compétent*) to be good at sth/doing.
entendu, e [ɑ̃tɑ̃dy] *a* (*réglé*) agreed; (*au courant: air*) knowing; **(c'est) ~!** all right, agreed; **c'est ~** (*concession*) all right, granted; **bien ~!** of course!
entente [ɑ̃tɑ̃t] *nf* (*entre amis, pays*) understanding, harmony; (*accord, traité*) agreement, understanding; **à double ~** (*sens*) with a double meaning.

entériner [ɑ̃teʀine] *vt* to ratify, confirm.
entérite [ɑ̃teʀit] *nf* enteritis *q*.
enterrement [ɑ̃tɛʀmɑ̃] *nm* burying; (*cérémonie*) funeral, burial.
enterrer [ɑ̃teʀe] *vt* to bury.
entêtant, e [ɑ̃tɛtɑ̃, -ɑ̃t] *a* heady.
en-tête [ɑ̃tɛt] *nm* heading; **papier à ~** headed notepaper.
entêté, e [ɑ̃tete] *a* stubborn.
entêter [ɑ̃tete]: **s'~** *vi*: **s'~ (à faire)** to persist (in doing).
enthousiasme [ɑ̃tuzjasm(ə)] *nm* enthusiasm; **enthousiasmer** *vt* to fill with enthusiasm; **s'enthousiasmer (pour qch)** to get enthusiastic (about sth); **enthousiaste** *a* enthusiastic.
enticher [ɑ̃tiʃe]: **s'~ de** *vt* to become infatuated with.
entier, ère [ɑ̃tje, -jɛʀ] *a* (*non entamé, en totalité*) whole; (*total, complet*) complete; (*fig*: *caractère*) unbending, averse to compromise // *nm* (MATH) whole; **en ~** totally; in its entirety; **lait ~** full-cream milk; **pain ~** wholemeal bread; **entièrement** *ad* entirely, completely, wholly.
entité [ɑ̃tite] *nf* entity.
entonner [ɑ̃tɔne] *vt* (*chanson*) to strike up.
entonnoir [ɑ̃tɔnwaʀ] *nm* (*ustensile*) funnel; (*trou*) shell-hole, crater.
entorse [ɑ̃tɔʀs(ə)] *nf* (MÉD) sprain; (*fig*): **~ à la loi/au règlement** infringement of the law/rule.
entortiller [ɑ̃tɔʀtije] *vt* (*envelopper*): **~ qch dans/avec** to wrap sth in/with; (*enrouler*): **~ qch autour de** to twist *ou* wind sth (a)round; (*fam*): **~ qn** to get round sb; to hoodwink sb.
entourage [ɑ̃tuʀaʒ] *nm* circle; family (circle); entourage; (*ce qui enclôt*) surround.
entourer [ɑ̃tuʀe] *vt* to surround; (*apporter son soutien à*) to rally round; **~ de** to surround with; (*trait*) to encircle with.
entourloupettes [ɑ̃tuʀlupɛt] *nfpl* mean tricks.
entracte [ɑ̃tʀakt(ə)] *nm* interval.
entraide [ɑ̃tʀɛd] *nf* mutual aid *ou* assistance; **s'entraider** to help each other.
entrailles [ɑ̃tʀɑj] *nfpl* entrails; bowels.
entrain [ɑ̃tʀɛ̃] *nm* spirit; **avec/sans ~** spiritedly/half-heartedly.
entraînant, e [ɑ̃tʀɛnɑ̃, -ɑ̃t] *a* (*musique*) stirring, rousing.
entraînement [ɑ̃tʀɛnmɑ̃] *nm* training; (TECH): **~ à chaîne/galet** chain/wheel drive.
entraîner [ɑ̃tʀene] *vt* (*tirer*: *wagons*) to pull; (*charrier*) to carry *ou* drag along; (TECH) to drive; (*emmener*: *personne*) to take (off); (*mener à l'assaut, influencer*) to lead; (SPORT) to train; (*impliquer*) to entail; (*causer*) to lead to, bring about; **~ qn à faire** (*inciter*) to lead sb to do; **s'~** (SPORT) to train; **s'~ à qch/à faire** to train o.s. for sth/to do; **entraîneur, euse** *nm/f* (SPORT) coach, trainer // *nm* (HIPPISME) trainer // *nf* (*de bar*) hostess.
entrave [ɑ̃tʀav] *nf* hindrance.
entraver [ɑ̃tʀave] *vt* (*circulation*) to hold up; (*action, progrès*) to hinder, hamper.
entre [ɑ̃tʀ(ə)] *prép* between; (*parmi*) among(st); **l'un d'~ eux/nous** one of them/us; **ils se battent ~ eux** they are fighting among(st) themselves.
entrebâillé, e [ɑ̃tʀəbɑje] *a* half-open, ajar.
entrechoquer [ɑ̃tʀəʃɔke]: **s'~** *vi* to knock *ou* bang together.
entrecôte [ɑ̃tʀəkot] *nf* entrecôte *ou* rib steak.
entrecouper [ɑ̃tʀəkupe] *vt*: **~ qch de** to intersperse sth with.
entrecroiser [ɑ̃tʀəkʀwaze] *vt*, **s'~** *vi* intertwine.
entrée [ɑ̃tʀe] *nf* entrance; (*accès*: *au cinéma etc*) admission; (*billet*) (admission) ticket; (CULIN) first course; **d'~** *ad* from the outset; **'~ interdite'** 'no admittance *ou* entry'; **'~ libre'** 'admission free'; **~ des artistes** stage door; **~ en matière** introduction; **~ de service** service entrance.
entrefaites [ɑ̃tʀəfɛt]: **sur ces ~** *ad* at this juncture.
entrefilet [ɑ̃tʀəfilɛ] *nm* paragraph (*short article*).
entregent [ɑ̃tʀəʒɑ̃] *nm*: **avoir de l'~** to have an easy manner.
entrejambes [ɑ̃tʀəʒɑ̃b] *nm* crotch.
entrelacer [ɑ̃tʀəlase] *vt*, **s'~** *vi* to intertwine.
entrelarder [ɑ̃tʀəlaʀde] *vt* to lard.
entremêler [ɑ̃tʀəmele] *vt*: **~ qch de** to (inter)mingle sth with.
entremets [ɑ̃tʀəmɛ] *nm* cream dessert.
entremetteur, euse [ɑ̃tʀəmɛtœʀ, -øz] *nm/f* go-between.
entremettre [ɑ̃tʀəmɛtʀ(ə)]: **s'~** *vi* to intervene.
entremise [ɑ̃tʀəmiz] *nf* intervention; **par l'~ de** through.
entrepont [ɑ̃tʀəpɔ̃] *nm* steerage.
entreposer [ɑ̃tʀəpoze] *vt* to store, put into storage.
entrepôt [ɑ̃tʀəpo] *nm* warehouse.
entreprenant, e [ɑ̃tʀəpʀənɑ̃, -ɑ̃t] *a* (*actif*) enterprising; (*trop galant*) forward.
entreprendre [ɑ̃tʀəpʀɑ̃dʀ(ə)] *vt* (*se lancer dans*) to undertake; (*commencer*) to begin *ou* start (upon); (*personne*) to buttonhole; to tackle; **~ de faire** to undertake to do.
entrepreneur [ɑ̃tʀəpʀənœʀ] *nm*: **~ (en bâtiment)** (building) contractor; **~ de pompes funèbres** (funeral) undertaker.
entreprise [ɑ̃tʀəpʀiz] *nf* (*société*) firm, concern; (*action*) undertaking, venture.
entrer [ɑ̃tʀe] *vi* to go (*ou* come) in, enter; **(faire) ~ qch dans** to get sth into; **~ dans** (*gén*) to enter; (*pièce*) to go (*ou* come) into, enter; (*club*) to join; (*heurter*) to run into; (*partager*: *vues, craintes de qn*) to share; (*être une composante de*) to go into; to form part of; **~ à l'hôpital** to go into hospital; **laisser ~ qn/qch** to let sb/sth in; **faire ~** (*visiteur*) to show in.
entresol [ɑ̃tʀəsɔl] *nm* entresol, mezzanine.
entre-temps [ɑ̃tʀətɑ̃] *ad* meanwhile, (in the) meantime.
entretenir [ɑ̃tʀətniʀ] *vt* to maintain; (*amitié*) to keep alive; (*famille, maîtresse*) to support, keep; **~ qn (de)** to speak to sb (about); **s'~ (de)** to converse (about).

entretien [ɑ̃tʀətjɛ̃] *nm* maintenance; (*discussion*) discussion, talk; (*audience*) interview.
entrevoir [ɑ̃tʀəvwaʀ] *vt* (*à peine*) to make out; (*brièvement*) to catch a glimpse of.
entrevue [ɑ̃tʀəvy] *nf* meeting; (*audience*) interview.
entrouvert, e [ɑ̃tʀuvɛʀ, -ɛʀt(ə)] *a* half-open.
énumérer [enymeʀe] *vt* to list, enumerate.
envahir [ɑ̃vaiʀ] *vt* to invade; (*suj: inquiétude, peur*) to come over; **envahissant, e** *a* (*péj: personne*) interfering, intrusive; **envahisseur** *nm* (MIL) invader.
enveloppe [ɑ̃vlɔp] *nf* (*de lettre*) envelope; (TECH) casing; outer layer; **mettre sous ~** to put in an envelope.
envelopper [ɑ̃vlɔpe] *vt* to wrap; (*fig*) to envelop, shroud.
envenimer [ɑ̃vnime] *vt* to aggravate.
envergure [ɑ̃vɛʀgyʀ] *nf* (*d'un oiseau, avion*) wingspan; (*fig*) scope; calibre.
enverrai *etc vb voir* **envoyer**.
envers [ɑ̃vɛʀ] *prép* towards, to // *nm* other side; (*d'une étoffe*) wrong side; **à l'~** upside down; back to front; (*vêtement*) inside out.
envie [ɑ̃vi] *nf* (*sentiment*) envy; (*souhait*) desire, wish; (*tache sur la peau*) birthmark; (*filet de peau*) hangnail; **avoir ~ de** to feel like; (*désir plus fort*) to want; **avoir ~ de faire** to feel like doing; to want to do; **avoir ~ que** to wish that; **donner à qn l'~ de faire** to make sb want to do; **ça lui fait ~** he would like that; **envier** *vt* to envy; **envieux, euse** *a* envious.
environ [ɑ̃viʀɔ̃] *ad*: **~ 3 h/2 km, 3 h/2 km ~** (around) about 3 o'clock/2 km, 3 o'clock/2 km or so; **~s** *nmpl* surroundings; **aux ~s de** around.
environnement [ɑ̃viʀɔnmɑ̃] *nm* environment.
environner [ɑ̃viʀɔne] *vt* to surround.
envisager [ɑ̃vizaʒe] *vt* (*examiner, considérer*) to view, contemplate; (*avoir en vue*) to envisage; **~ de faire** to consider *ou* contemplate doing.
envoi [ɑ̃vwa] *nm* sending; (*paquet*) parcel, consignment.
envol [ɑ̃vɔl] *nm* takeoff.
envolée [ɑ̃vɔle] *nf* (*fig*) flight.
envoler [ɑ̃vɔle]: **s'~** *vi* (*oiseau*) to fly away *ou* off; (*avion*) to take off; (*papier, feuille*) to blow away; (*fig*) to vanish (into thin air).
envoûter [ɑ̃vute] *vt* to bewitch.
envoyé, e [ɑ̃vwaje] *nm/f* (POL) envoy; (PRESSE) correspondent.
envoyer [ɑ̃vwaje] *vt* to send; (*lancer*) to hurl, throw; **~ chercher** to send for; **envoyeur, euse** *nm/f* sender.
éolien, ne [eɔljɛ̃, -jɛn] *a* wind *cpd*.
épagneul, e [epaɲœl] *nm/f* spaniel.
épais, se [epɛ, -ɛs] *a* thick; **épaisseur** *nf* thickness; **épaissir** *vt*, **s'épaissir** *vi* to thicken.
épanchement [epɑ̃ʃmɑ̃] *nm*: **un ~ de sinovie** water on the knee; **~s** *nmpl* (*fig*) (sentimental) outpourings.
épancher [epɑ̃ʃe] *vt* to give vent to; **s'~** *vi* to open one's heart; (*liquide*) to pour out.
épandage [epɑ̃daʒ] *nm* manure spreading.
épanouir [epanwiʀ]: **s'~** *vi* (*fleur*) to bloom, open out; (*visage*) to light up; (*fig*) to blossom (out), bloom; to open up; **épanouissement** *nm* blossoming; opening up.
épargnant, e [epaʀɲɑ̃, -ɑ̃t] *nm/f* saver, investor.
épargne [epaʀɲ(ə)] *nf* saving.
épargner [epaʀɲe] *vt* to save; (*ne pas tuer ou endommager*) to spare // *vi* to save; **~ qch à qn** to spare sb sth.
éparpiller [epaʀpije] *vt* to scatter; (*pour répartir*) to disperse; (*fig: efforts*) to dissipate; **s'~** *vi* to scatter; (*fig*) to dissipate one's efforts.
épars, e [epaʀ, -aʀs(ə)] *a* scattered.
épatant, e [epatɑ̃, -ɑ̃t] *a* (*fam*) super, splendid.
épaté, e [epate] *a*: **nez ~** flat nose (with wide nostrils).
épater [epate] *vt* to amaze; to impress.
épaule [epol] *nf* shoulder.
épaulement [epolmɑ̃] *nm* escarpment; retaining wall.
épauler [epole] *vt* (*aider*) to back up, support; (*arme*) to raise (to one's shoulder) // *vi* to (take) aim.
épaulette [epolɛt] *nf* (MIL) epaulette; (*de combinaison*) shoulder strap.
épave [epav] *nf* wreck.
épée [epe] *nf* sword.
épeler [ɛple] *vt* to spell.
éperdu, e [epɛʀdy] *a* distraught, overcome; passionate; frantic.
éperon [epʀɔ̃] *nm* spur; **éperonner** *vt* to spur (on); (*navire*) to ram.
épervier [epɛʀvje] *nm* (ZOOL) sparrowhawk; (PÊCHE) casting net.
éphèbe [efɛb] *nm* beautiful young man.
éphémère [efemɛʀ] *a* ephemeral, fleeting.
éphéméride [efemeʀid] *nf* block *ou* tear-off calendar.
épi [epi] *nm* (*de blé, d'orge*) ear; **stationnement en ~** angled parking.
épice [epis] *nf* spice; **épicé, e** *a* highly spiced, spicy; (*fig*) spicy.
épicéa [episea] *nm* spruce.
épicer [epise] *vt* to spice; (*fig*) to add spice to.
épicerie [episʀi] *nf* (*magasin*) grocer's shop; (*denrées*) groceries *pl*; **~ fine** delicatessen (shop); **épicier, ière** *nm/f* grocer.
épidémie [epidemi] *nf* epidemic.
épiderme [epidɛʀm(ə)] *nm* skin, epidermis; **épidermique** *a* skin *cpd*, epidermic.
épier [epje] *vt* to spy on, watch closely; (*occasion*) to look out for.
épieu, x [epjø] *nm* (hunting-)spear.
épilatoire [epilatwaʀ] *a* depilatory, hair-removing.
épilepsie [epilɛpsi] *nf* epilepsy; **épileptique** *a*, *nm/f* epileptic.
épiler [epile] *vt* (*jambes*) to remove the hair from; (*sourcils*) to pluck; **se faire ~** to get unwanted hair removed.

épilogue [epilɔg] *nm* (*fig*) conclusion, dénouement.
épiloguer [epilɔge] *vi*: ~ **sur** to hold forth on.
épinard [epinaʀ] *nm* spinach *q*.
épine [epin] *nf* thorn, prickle; (*d'oursin etc*) spine, prickle; ~ **dorsale** backbone; **épineux, euse** *a* thorny, prickly.
épingle [epɛ̃gl(ə)] *nf* pin; **virage en ~ à cheveux** hairpin bend; ~ **de cravate** tie pin; ~ **de nourrice** *ou* **de sûreté** *ou* **double** safety pin.
épingler [epɛ̃gle] *vt* (*badge, décoration*): ~ **qch sur** to pin sth on(to); (*fam*) to catch, nick.
épinière [epinjɛʀ] *af voir* **moelle**.
Épiphanie [epifani] *nf* Epiphany.
épique [epik] *a* epic.
épiscopal, e, aux [episkɔpal, -o] *a* episcopal.
épiscopat [episkɔpa] *nm* bishopric, episcopate.
épisode [epizɔd] *nm* episode; **film/roman à ~s** serialized film/novel, serial; **épisodique** *a* occasional.
épissure [episyʀ] *nf* splice.
épistolaire [epistɔlɛʀ] *a* epistolary.
épitaphe [epitaf] *nf* epitaph.
épithète [epitɛt] *nf* (*nom, surnom*) epithet; **adjectif** ~ attributive adjective.
épître [epitʀ(ə)] *nf* epistle.
éploré, e [eplɔʀe] *a* in tears, tearful.
épluche-légumes [eplyʃlegym] *nm inv* potato peeler.
éplucher [eplyʃe] *vt* (*fruit, légumes*) to peel; (*comptes, dossier*) to go over with a fine-tooth comb; **éplucheur** *nm* (automatic) peeler; **épluchures** *nfpl* peelings.
épointer [epwɛ̃te] *vt* to blunt.
éponge [epɔ̃ʒ] *nf* sponge; **éponger** *vt* (*liquide*) to mop *ou* sponge up; (*surface*) to sponge; (*fig: déficit*) to soak up, absorb; **s' éponger le front** to mop one's brow.
épopée [epɔpe] *nf* epic.
époque [epɔk] *nf* (*de l'histoire*) age, era; (*de l'année, la vie*) time; **d'~** *a* (*meuble*) period *cpd*.
épouiller [epuje] *vt* to pick lice off; to delouse.
époumoner [epumɔne]: **s'~** *vi* to shout o.s. hoarse.
épouse [epuz] *nf* wife (*pl* wives).
épouser [epuze] *vt* to marry; (*fig: idées*) to espouse; (*: forme*) to fit.
épousseter [epuste] *vt* to dust.
époustouflant, e [epustuflɑ̃, -ɑ̃t] *a* staggering, mind-boggling.
épouvantable [epuvɑ̃tabl(ə)] *a* appalling, dreadful.
épouvantail [epuvɑ̃taj] *nm* (*à moineaux*) scarecrow; (*fig*) bog(e)y; bugbear.
épouvante [epuvɑ̃t] *nf* terror; **film d'~** horror film; **épouvanter** *vt* to terrify.
époux [epu] *nm* husband // *nmpl* (married) couple.
éprendre [epʀɑ̃dʀ(ə)]: **s'~ de** *vt* to fall in love with.
épreuve [epʀœv] *nf* (*d'examen*) test; (*malheur, difficulté*) trial, ordeal; (PHOTO) print; (*d'imprimerie*) proof; (SPORT) event; **à l'~ des balles** bulletproof; **à toute ~** unfailing; **mettre à l'~** to put to the test.
épris, e [epʀi, -iz] *vb voir* **éprendre**.
éprouver [epʀuve] *vt* (*tester*) to test; (*mettre à l'épreuve*) to put to the test; (*marquer, faire souffrir*) to afflict, distress; (*ressentir*) to feel.
éprouvette [epʀuvɛt] *nf* test tube.
épuisé, e [epɥize] *a* exhausted; (*livre*) out of print.
épuisement [epɥizmɑ̃] *nm* exhaustion; **jusqu'à ~ des stocks** while stocks last.
épuiser [epɥize] *vt* (*fatiguer*) to exhaust, wear *ou* tire out; (*stock, sujet*) to exhaust; **s'~** *vi* to wear *ou* tire o.s. out, exhaust o.s. (*stock*) to run out.
épuisette [epɥizɛt] *nf* landing net; shrimping net.
épurer [epyʀe] *vt* (*liquide*) to purify; (*parti, administration*) to purge; (*langue, texte*) to refine.
équarrir [ekaʀiʀ] *vt* (*pierre, arbre*) to square (off); (*animal*) to quarter.
équateur [ekwatœʀ] *nm* equator; **(la république de) l'É~** Ecuador.
équation [ekwasjɔ̃] *nf* equation; **mettre en ~** to equate.
équatorial, e, aux [ekwatɔʀjal, -o] *a* equatorial.
équerre [ekɛʀ] *nf* (*à dessin*) (set) square; (*pour fixer*) brace; **en ~** at right angles; **à l'~, d'~** straight.
équestre [ekɛstʀ(ə)] *a* equestrian.
équidistant, e [ekɥidistɑ̃, -ɑ̃t] *a*: ~ **(de)** equidistant (from).
équilatéral, e, aux [ekɥilateʀal, -o] *a* equilateral.
équilibrage [ekilibʀaʒ] *nm* (AUTO): ~ **des roues** wheel balancing.
équilibre [ekilibʀ(ə)] *nm* balance; (*d'une balance*) equilibrium; **garder/perdre l'~** to keep/lose one's balance; **être en ~** to be balanced; **équilibré, e a** (*fig*) well-balanced, stable; **équilibrer** *vt* to balance; **s'équilibrer** (*poids*) to balance; (*fig: défauts etc*) to balance each other out; **équilibriste** *nm/f* tightrope walker.
équinoxe [ekinɔks] *nm* equinox.
équipage [ekipaʒ] *nm* crew.
équipe [ekip] *nf* team; (*bande: parfois péj*) bunch.
équipée [ekipe] *nf* escapade.
équipement [ekipmɑ̃] *nm* equipment; **~s** *nmpl* amenities, facilities; installations.
équiper [ekipe] *vt* to equip; (*voiture, cuisine*) to equip, fit out; ~ **qn/qch de** to equip sb/sth with; **s'~** (*sportif*) to equip o.s., kit o.s. out.
équipier, ière [ekipje, -jɛʀ] *nm/f* team member.
équitable [ekitabl(ə)] *a* fair.
équitation [ekitasjɔ̃] *nf* (horse-)riding.
équité [ekite] *nf* equity.
équivalence [ekivalɑ̃s] *nf* equivalence.
équivalent, e [ekivalɑ̃, -ɑ̃t] *a, nm* equivalent.
équivaloir [ekivalwaʀ]: ~ **à** *vt* to be equivalent to; (*représenter*) to amount to.
équivoque [ekivɔk] *a* equivocal, ambiguous; (*louche*) dubious // *nf* ambiguity.

érable [eRabl(ə)] *nm* maple.
érafler [eRɑfle] *vt* to scratch ; **éraflure** *nf* scratch.
éraillé, e [eRɑje] *a* (*voix*) rasping, hoarse.
ère [ɛR] *nf* era ; **en l'an 1050 de notre ~** in the year 1050 A.D.
érection [eRɛksjɔ̃] *nf* erection.
éreinter [eRɛ̃te] *vt* to exhaust, wear out ; (*fig: critiquer*) to slate.
ergot [ɛRgo] *nm* (*de coq*) spur ; (TECH) lug.
ériger [eRiʒe] *vt* (*monument*) to erect ; **s'~ en critique** to set o.s. up as a critic.
ermitage [ɛRmitaʒ] *nm* retreat.
ermite [ɛRmit] *nm* hermit.
éroder [eRɔde] *vt* to erode ; **érosion** *nf* erosion.
érotique [eRɔtik] *a* erotic ; **érotisme** *nm* eroticism.
erratum, a [ɛRatɔm, -a] *nm* erratum (*pl* a).
errer [ɛRe] *vi* to wander.
erreur [ɛRœR] *nf* mistake, error ; (*morale*) error ; **être dans l'~** to be mistaken ; **par ~** by mistake ; **~ judiciaire** miscarriage of justice ; **~ de jugement** error of judgment.
erroné, e [ɛRɔne] *a* wrong, erroneous.
éructer [eRykte] *vt* belch, eructate.
érudit, e [eRydi, -it] *a* erudite, learned // *nm/f* scholar ; **érudition** *nf* erudition, scholarship.
éruptif, ive [eRyptif, -iv] *a* eruptive.
éruption [eRypsjɔ̃] *nf* eruption ; (*cutanée*) outbreak.
es *vb voir* **être**.
ès [ɛs] *prép*: **licencié ~ lettres/sciences** ≈ Bachelor of Arts/Science.
escabeau, x [ɛskabo] *nm* (*tabouret*) stool ; (*échelle*) stepladder.
escadre [ɛskadR(ə)] *nf* (NAVIG) squadron ; (AVIAT) wing.
escadrille [ɛskadRij] *nf* (AVIAT) flight.
escadron [ɛskadRɔ̃] *nm* squadron.
escalade [ɛskalad] *nf* climbing *q* ; (POL *etc*) escalation.
escalader [ɛskalade] *vt* to climb, scale.
escale [ɛskal] *nf* (NAVIG) call ; port of call ; (AVIAT) stop(over) ; **faire ~ à** to put in at, call in at ; to stop over at.
escalier [ɛskalje] *nm* stairs *pl* ; **dans l'~** *ou* **les ~s** on the stairs ; **~ roulant** escalator ; **~ de service** backstairs.
escalope [ɛskalɔp] *nf* escalope.
escamotable [ɛskamɔtabl(ə)] *a* retractable ; fold-away.
escamoter [ɛskamɔte] *vt* (*esquiver*) to get round, evade ; (*faire disparaître*) to conjure away.
escapade [ɛskapad] *nf*: **faire une ~** to go on a jaunt ; to run away *ou* off.
escargot [ɛskaRgo] *nm* snail.
escarmouche [ɛskaRmuʃ] *nf* skirmish.
escarpé, e [ɛskaRpe] *a* steep.
escarpement [ɛskaRpəmɑ̃] *nm* steep slope.
escarpin [ɛskaRpɛ̃] *nm* flat(-heeled) shoe.
escarre [ɛskaR] *nf* bedsore.
escient [esjɑ̃] *nm*: **à bon ~** advisedly.
esclaffer [ɛsklafe]: **s'~** *vi* to guffaw.
esclandre [ɛsklɑ̃dR(ə)] *nm* scene, fracas.
esclavage [ɛsklavaʒ] *nm* slavery.
esclave [ɛsklav] *nm/f* slave ; **être ~ de** (*fig*) to be a slave of.
escompte [ɛskɔ̃t] *nm* discount.
escompter [ɛskɔ̃te] *vt* (COMM) to discount ; (*espérer*) to expect, reckon upon ; **~ que** to reckon *ou* expect that.
escorte [ɛskɔRt(ə)] *nf* escort ; **escorter** *vt* to escort ; **escorteur** *nm* (NAVIG) escort (ship).
escouade [ɛskwad] *nf* squad.
escrime [ɛskRim] *nf* fencing ; **escrimeur, euse** *nm/f* fencer.
escrimer [ɛskRime]: **s'~** *vi*: **s'~ à faire** to wear o.s. out doing.
escroc [ɛskRo] *nm* swindler, conman.
escroquer [ɛskRɔke] *vt*: **~ qn (de qch)/qch (à qn)** to swindle sb (out of sth)/sth (out of sb) ; **escroquerie** *nf* swindle.
espace [ɛspas] *nm* space ; **~ vital** living space.
espacer [ɛspase] *vt* to space out ; **s'~** *vi* (*visites etc*) to become less frequent.
espadon [ɛspadɔ̃] *nm* swordfish *inv*.
espadrille [ɛspadRij] *nf* rope-soled sandal.
Espagne [ɛspaɲ(ə)] *nf*: **l'~** Spain ; **espagnol, e** *a* Spanish // *nm/f*: **Espagnol, e** Spaniard // *nm* (*langue*) Spanish.
espagnolette [ɛspaɲɔlɛt] *nf* (window) catch ; **fermé à l'~** resting on the catch.
espèce [ɛspɛs] *nf* (BIO, BOT, ZOOL) species *inv* ; (*gén: sorte*) sort, kind, type ; (*péj*): **~ de maladroit/de brute!** you clumsy oaf/brute! ; **~s** *nfpl* (COMM) cash *sg* ; (REL) species ; **en l'~** *ad* in the case in point.
espérance [ɛspeRɑ̃s] *nf* hope ; **~ de vie** (DÉMOGRAPHIE) life expectancy.
espérer [ɛspeRe] *vt* to hope for ; **j'espère (bien)** I hope so ; **~ que/faire** to hope that/to do ; **~ en** to trust in.
espiègle [ɛspjɛgl(ə)] *a* mischievous ; **~rie** *nf* mischievousness ; piece of mischief.
espion, ne [ɛspjɔ̃, -ɔn] *nm/f* spy ; **avion ~** spy plane.
espionnage [ɛspjɔnaʒ] *nm* espionage, spying.
espionner [ɛspjɔne] *vt* to spy (up)on.
esplanade [ɛsplanad] *nf* esplanade.
espoir [ɛspwaR] *nm* hope.
esprit [ɛspRi] *nm* (*pensée, intellect*) mind ; (*humour, ironie*) wit ; (*mentalité, d'une loi etc, fantôme etc*) spirit ; **l'~ d'équipe/de compétition** team/competitive spirit ; **faire de l'~** to try to be witty ; **reprendre ses ~s** to come to ; **perdre l'~** to lose one's mind ; **~s chagrins** faultfinders.
esquif [ɛskif] *nm* skiff.
esquimau, de, x [ɛskimo, -od] *a, nm/f* Eskimo.
esquinter [ɛskɛ̃te] *vt* (*fam*) to mess up.
esquisse [ɛskis] *nf* sketch ; **l'~ d'un sourire/changement** the suggestion of a smile/of change.
esquisser [ɛskise] *vt* to sketch ; **s'~** *vi* (*amélioration*) to begin to be detectable ; **~ un sourire** to give a vague smile.
esquive [ɛskiv] *nf* (BOXE) dodging ; (*fig*) side-stepping.

esquiver [ɛskive] *vt* to dodge; **s'~** *vi* to slip away.
essai [esɛ] *nm* testing; trying; (*tentative*) attempt, try, (RUGBY) try; (LITTÉRATURE) essay; **~s** (AUTO) trials; **~ gratuit** (COMM) free trial; **à l'~** on a trial basis.
essaim [esɛ̃] *nm* swarm; **essaimer** *vi* to swarm; (*fig*) to spread, expand.
essayage [esɛjaʒ] *nm* (*d'un vêtement*) trying on, fitting.
essayer [eseje] *vt* (*gén*) to try; (*vêtement, chaussures*) to try (on); (*tester*: *ski, voiture*) to test; (*restaurant, méthode*) to try (out) // *vi* to try; **~ de faire** to try *ou* attempt to do; **s'~ à faire** to try one's hand at doing.
essence [esɑ̃s] *nf* (*de voiture*) petrol; (*extrait de plante*, PHILOSOPHIE) essence; (*espèce*: *d'arbre*) species *inv*; **prendre de l'~** to get petrol; **~ de citron/rose** lemon/rose oil.
essentiel, le [esɑ̃sjɛl] *a* essential; **emporter l'~** to take the essentials; **c'est l'~** (*ce qui importe*) that's the main thing; **l'~ de** (*la majeure partie*) the main part of.
esseulé, e [esœle] *a* forlorn.
essieu, x [esjø] *nm* axle.
essor [esɔR] *nm* (*de l'économie etc*) rapid expansion; **prendre son ~** (*oiseau*) to fly off.
essorer [esɔRe] *vt* (*en tordant*) to wring (out); (*par la force centrifuge*) to spin-dry; **essoreuse** *nf* mangle, wringer; spin-dryer.
essouffler [esufle] *vt* to make breathless; **s'~** *vi* to get out of breath.
essuie-glace [esɥiglas] *nm inv* windscreen wiper.
essuie-mains [esɥimɛ̃] *nm inv* hand towel.
essuyer [esɥije] *vt* to wipe; (*fig*: *subir*) to suffer; **s'~** (*après le bain*) to dry o.s.; **~ la vaisselle** to dry up, dry the dishes.
est [ɛst] *vb* [ɛ] *voir* **être** // *nm*: **l'~** the east // *a* east; (*côte*) east(ern); **à l'~** in the east; (*direction*) to the east, east(wards); **à l'~ de** (to the) east of.
estafette [ɛstafɛt] *nf* (MIL) dispatch rider.
estafilade [ɛstafilad] *nf* gash, slash.
est-allemand, e [ɛstalmɑ̃, -ɑ̃d] *a* East German.
estaminet [ɛstaminɛ] *nm* tavern.
estampe [ɛstɑ̃p] *nf* print, engraving.
estampille [ɛstɑ̃pij] *nf* stamp.
est-ce que [ɛskə] *ad*: **~ c'est cher/c'était bon?** is it expensive/was it good?; **quand est-ce qu'il part?** when does he leave?, when is he leaving?; **qui est-ce qui le connaît/a fait ça?** who knows him/did that?; *voir aussi* **que**.
esthète [ɛstɛt] *nm/f* aesthete.
esthéticienne [ɛstetisjɛn] *nf* beautician.
esthétique [ɛstetik] *a* attractive; aesthetically pleasing // *nf* aesthetics *sg*.
estimation [ɛstimɑsjɔ̃] *nf* valuation; assessment.
estime [ɛstim] *nf* esteem, regard.
estimer [ɛstime] *vt* (*respecter*) to esteem, hold in high regard; (*expertiser*) to value; (*évaluer*) to assess, estimate; (*penser*): **~ que/être** to consider that/o.s. to be; **j'estime la distance à 10 km** I reckon the distance to be 10 km.
estival, e, aux [ɛstival, -o] *a* summer *cpd*.
estivant, e [ɛstivɑ̃, -ɑ̃t] *nm/f* (summer) holiday-maker.
estocade [ɛstɔkad] *nf* death-blow.
estomac [ɛstɔma] *nm* stomach.
estomaqué, e [ɛstɔmake] *a* flabbergasted.
estompe [ɛstɔ̃p] *nf* stump; stump-drawing.
estomper [ɛstɔ̃mpe] *vt* (ART) to shade off; (*fig*) to blur, dim; **s'~** *vi* to soften; to become blurred.
estrade [ɛstRad] *nf* platform, rostrum.
estragon [ɛstRagɔ̃] *nm* tarragon.
estropié, e [ɛstRɔpje] *nm/f* cripple.
estropier [ɛstRɔpje] *vt* to cripple, maim; (*fig*) to twist, distort.
estuaire [ɛstɥɛR] *nm* estuary.
estudiantin, e [ɛstydjɑ̃tɛ̃, -in] *a* student *cpd*.
esturgeon [ɛstyRʒɔ̃] *nm* sturgeon.
et [e] *cj* and; **~ lui?** what about him?; **~ alors!** so what!.
étable [etabl(ə)] *nf* cowshed.
établi [etabli] *nm* (work)bench.
établir [etabliR] *vt* (*papiers d'identité, facture*) to make out; (*liste, programme*) to draw up; (*gouvernement, artisan etc*: *aider à s'installer*) to set up, establish; (*entreprise, atelier, camp*) to set up; (*réputation, usage, fait, culpabilité*) to establish; **s'~** *vi* (*se faire*: *entente etc*) to be established; **s'~ (à son compte)** to set up one's own business; **s'~ à/près de** to settle in/near.
établissement [etablismɑ̃] *nm* making out; drawing up; setting up, establishing; (*entreprise, institution*) establishment; **~ de crédit** credit institution; **~ industriel** industrial plant, factory; **~ scolaire** school, educational establishment.
étage [etaʒ] *nm* (*d'immeuble*) storey, floor; (*de fusée*) stage; (GÉO: *de culture, végétation*) level; **au 2ème ~** on the 2nd floor; **de bas ~** *a* low; **étager** *vt* (*cultures*) to lay out in tiers; **s'étager** *vi* (*prix*) to range; (*zones, cultures*) to lie on different levels.
étagère [etaʒɛR] *nf* (*rayon*) shelf; (*meuble*) shelves *pl*, set of shelves.
étai [etɛ] *nm* stay, prop.
étain [etɛ̃] *nm* tin; (ORFÈVRERIE) pewter *q*.
étais *etc vb voir* **être**.
étal [etal] *nm* stall.
étalage [etalaʒ] *nm* display; display window; **faire ~ de** to show off, parade; **étalagiste** *nm/f* window-dresser.
étale [etal] *a* (*mer*) slack.
étalement [etalmɑ̃] *nm* spreading, staggering.
étaler [etale] *vt* (*carte, nappe*) to spread (out); (*peinture, liquide*) to spread; (*échelonner*: *paiements, dates, vacances*) to spread, stagger; (*exposer*: *marchandises*) to display; (*richesses, connaissances*) to parade; **s'~** *vi* (*liquide*) to spread out; (*fam*) to come a cropper; **s'~ sur** (*suj*: *paiements etc*) to be spread out over.
étalon [etalɔ̃] *nm* (*mesure*) standard; (*cheval*) stallion; **étalonner** *vt* to calibrate.

étamer [etame] *vt* (*casserole*) to tin(plate); (*glace*) to silver.
étamine [etamin] *nf* (BOT) stamen; (*tissu*) butter muslin.
étanche [etɑ̃ʃ] *a* (*récipient*) watertight; (*montre, vêtement*) waterproof.
étancher [etɑ̃ʃe] *vt* (*liquide*) to stop (flowing); **~ sa soif** to quench *ou* slake one's thirst.
étang [etɑ̃] *nm* pond.
étant [etɑ̃] *vb voir* **être, donné.**
étape [etap] *nf* stage; (*lieu d'arrivée*) stopping place; (: CYCLISME) staging point; **faire ~ à** to stop off at.
état [eta] *nm* (POL, *condition*) state; (*d'un article d'occasion etc*) condition, state; (*liste*) inventory, statement; (*condition professionnelle*) profession, trade; (: *sociale*) status; **en mauvais ~** in poor condition; **en ~ (de marche)** in (working) order; **remettre en ~** to repair; **hors d'~** out of order; **être en ~/hors d'~ de faire** to be in a/in no fit state to do; **en tout ~ de cause** in any event; **être dans tous ses ~s** to be in a state; **faire ~ de** (*alléguer*) to put forward; **en ~ d'arrestation** under arrest; **en ~ de grâce** (REL) in a state of grace; (*fig*) inspired; **~ civil** civil status; **~ des lieux** inventory of fixtures; **~ de santé** state of health; **~ de siège/d'urgence** state of siege/emergency; **~s d'âme** moods; **~s de service** service record *sg*; **étatiser** *vt* to bring under state control.
état-major [etamaʒɔʀ] *nm* (MIL) staff; (*d'un parti etc*) top advisers *pl*; top management.
États-Unis [etazyni] *nmpl*: **les ~ (d'Amérique)** the United States (of America).
étau, x [eto] *nm* vice.
étayer [eteje] *vt* to prop *ou* shore up; (*fig*) to back up.
et c(a)etera [ɛtseteʀa], **etc.** *ad* et cetera, and so on, etc.
été [ete] *pp de* **être** // *nm* summer.
éteignoir [etɛɲwaʀ] *nm* (candle) extinguisher; (*péj*) killjoy, wet blanket.
éteindre [etɛ̃dʀ(ə)] *vt* (*lampe, lumière, radio*) to turn *ou* switch off; (*cigarette, incendie, bougie*) to put out, extinguish; (JUR: *dette*) to extinguish; **s'~** *vi* to go out; to go off; (*mourir*) to pass away; **éteint, e** *a* (*fig*) lacklustre, dull; (*volcan*) extinct.
étendard [etɑ̃daʀ] *nm* standard.
étendre [etɑ̃dʀ(ə)] *vt* (*appliquer*: *pâte, liquide*) to spread; (*déployer*: *carte etc*) to spread out; (*sur un fil*: *lessive, linge*) to hang up *ou* out; (*bras, jambes, par terre*: *blessé*) to stretch out; (*diluer*) to dilute, thin; (*fig*: *agrandir*) to extend; (*fam*: *adversaire*) to floor; **s'~** *vi* (*augmenter, se propager*) to spread; (*terrain, forêt etc*): **s'~ jusqu'à/de ... à** to stretch as far as/from ... to; **s'~ (sur)** (*s'allonger*) to stretch out (upon); (*se reposer*) to lie down (on); (*fig*: *expliquer*) to elaborate *ou* enlarge (upon).
étendu, e [etɑ̃dy] *a* extensive // *nf* (*d'eau, de sable*) stretch, expanse; (*importance*) extent.
éternel, le [etɛʀnɛl] *a* eternal; **les neiges ~les** perpetual snow.
éterniser [etɛʀnize]: **s'~** *vi* to last for ages; to stay for ages.
éternité [etɛʀnite] *nf* eternity; **de toute ~** from time immemorial.
éternuer [etɛʀnɥe] *vi* to sneeze.
êtes *vb voir* **être.**
étêter [etete] *vt* (*arbre*) to poll(ard); (*clou, poisson*) to cut the head off.
éther [etɛʀ] *nm* ether.
éthique [etik] *a* ethical // *nf* ethics *sg*.
ethnie [ɛtni] *nf* ethnic group.
ethnographie [ɛtnɔgʀafi] *nf* ethnography.
ethnologie [ɛtnɔlɔʒi] *nf* ethnology; **ethnologue** *nm/f* ethnologist.
éthylisme [etilism(ə)] *nm* alcoholism.
étiage [etjaʒ] *nm* low water.
étiez *vb voir* **être.**
étinceler [etɛ̃sle] *vi* to sparkle.
étincelle [etɛ̃sɛl] *nf* spark.
étioler [etjɔle]: **s'~** *vi* to wilt.
étique [etik] *a* skinny, bony.
étiqueter [etikte] *vt* to label.
étiquette [etikɛt] *nf* label; (*protocole*): **l'~** etiquette.
étirer [etiʀe] *vt* to stretch; (*ressort*) to stretch out; **s'~** *vi* (*personne*) to stretch; (*convoi, route*): **s'~ sur** to stretch out over.
étoffe [etɔf] *nf* material, fabric.
étoffer [etɔfe] *vt*, **s'~** *vi* to fill out.
étoile [etwal] *nf* star; **à la belle ~** in the open; **~ filante** shooting star; **~ de mer** starfish; **étoilé, e** *a* starry.
étole [etɔl] *nf* stole.
étonnant, e [etɔnɑ̃, -ɑ̃t] *a* amazing.
étonnement [etɔnmɑ̃] *nm* surprise, amazement.
étonner [etɔne] *vt* to surprise, amaze; **s'~ que/de** to be amazed that/at; **cela m'étonnerait (que)** (*j'en doute*) I'd be very surprised (if).
étouffant, e [etufɑ̃, -ɑ̃t] *a* stifling.
étouffée [etufe]: **à l'~** *ad* (CULIN) steamed; braised.
étouffer [etufe] *vt* to suffocate; (*bruit*) to muffle; (*scandale*) to hush up // *vi* to suffocate; (*avoir trop chaud*) to feel stifled; **s'~** *vi* (*en mangeant etc*) to choke.
étourderie [etuʀdəʀi] *nf* heedlessness; thoughtless blunder.
étourdi, e [etuʀdi] *a* (*distrait*) scatterbrained, heedless.
étourdir [etuʀdiʀ] *vt* (*assommer*) to stun, daze; (*griser*) to make dizzy *ou* giddy; **étourdissant, e** *a* staggering; **étourdissement** *nm* dizzy spell.
étourneau, x [etuʀno] *nm* starling.
étrange [etʀɑ̃ʒ] *a* strange.
étranger, ère [etʀɑ̃ʒe, -ɛʀ] *a* foreign; (*pas de la famille, non familier*) strange // *nm/f* foreigner; stranger // *nm*: **à l'~** abroad; **de l'~** from abroad; **~ à** (*fig*) unfamiliar to; irrelevant to.
étranglement [etʀɑ̃gləmɑ̃] *nm* (*d'une vallée etc*) constriction, narrow passage.
étrangler [etʀɑ̃gle] *vt* to strangle; **s'~** *vi* (*en mangeant etc*) to choke; (*se resserrer*) to make a bottleneck.

étrave [etʀav] *nf* stem.
être [ɛtʀ(ə)] *nm* being // *vb avec attribut, vi* to be // *vb auxiliaire* to have (*ou parfois* be); **il est instituteur** he is a teacher; ~ **à qn** (*appartenir*) to be sb's, to belong to sb; **c'est à moi/eux** it is *ou* it's mine/theirs; **c'est à lui de le faire** it's up to him to do it; ~ **de** (*provenance, origine*) to be from; (*appartenance*) to belong to; **nous sommes le 10 janvier** it's the 10th of January (today); **il est 10 heures, c'est 10 heures** it is *ou* it's 10 o'clock; **c'est à réparer** it needs repairing; **c'est à essayer** it should be tried; ~ **humain** human being; *voir aussi* **est-ce que, n'est-ce pas, c'est-à-dire, ce.**
étreindre [etʀɛ̃dʀ(ə)] *vt* to clutch, grip; (*amoureusement, amicalement*) to embrace; **s'**~ to embrace; **étreinte** *nf* clutch, grip; embrace.
étrenner [etʀene] *vt* to use (*ou* wear) for the first time.
étrennes [etʀɛn] *nfpl* Christmas box *sg* (*fig*).
étrier [etʀije] *nm* stirrup.
étriller [etʀije] *vt* (*cheval*) to curry; (*fam: battre*) to trounce.
étriper [etʀipe] *vt* to gut; (*fam*): ~ **qn** to tear sb's guts out.
étriqué, e [etʀike] *a* skimpy.
étroit, e [etʀwa, -wat] *a* narrow; (*vêtement*) tight; (*fig: serré*) close, tight; **à l'**~ *ad* cramped; ~ **d'esprit** narrow-minded; **étroitesse** *nf* narrowness.
étude [etyd] *nf* studying; (*ouvrage, rapport*) study; (*de notaire: bureau*) office; (: *charge*) practice; (SCOL: *salle de travail*) study room; ~**s** *nfpl* (SCOL) studies; **être à l'**~ (*projet etc*) to be under consideration; **faires des ~s de droit/médecine** to study *ou* read law/medicine.
étudiant, e [etydjɑ̃, -ɑ̃t] *nm/f* student.
étudié, e [etydje] *a* (*démarche*) studied; (*système*) carefully designed.
étudier [etydje] *vt, vi* to study.
étui [etɥi] *nm* case.
étuve [etyv] *nf* steamroom; (*appareil*) sterilizer.
étuvée [etyve]: **à l'**~ *ad* braised.
étymologie [etimɔlɔʒi] *nf* etymology; **étymologique** *a* etymological.
eu, eue [y] *pp voir* **avoir.**
eucalyptus [økaliptys] *nm* eucalyptus.
eugénique [øʒenik] *a* eugenic // *nf* eugenics *sg*.
euh [ø] *excl* er.
eunuque [ønyk] *nm* eunuch.
euphémisme [øfemism(ə)] *nm* euphemism.
euphonie [øfɔni] *nf* euphony.
euphorie [øfɔʀi] *nf* euphoria; **euphorique** *a* euphoric.
eurasien, ne [øʀazjɛ̃, -ɛn] *a, nm/f* Eurasian.
Europe [øʀɔp] *nf* Europe; **européen, ne** *a, nm/f* European.
eus *etc vb voir* **avoir.**
euthanasie [øtanazi] *nf* euthanasia.
eux [ø] *pronom* (*sujet*) they; (*objet*) them.
évacuation [evakɥɑsjɔ̃] *nf* evacuation.
évacuer [evakɥe] *vt* (*salle, région*) to evacuate, clear; (*occupants, population*) to evacuate; (*toxine etc*) to evacuate, discharge.
évadé, e [evade] *a* escaped // *nm/f* escapee.
évader [evade]: **s'**~ *vi* to escape.
évaluation [evalɥɑsjɔ̃] *nf* assessment, evaluation.
évaluer [evalɥe] *vt* to assess, evaluate.
évangélique [evɑ̃ʒelik] *a* evangelical.
évangéliser [evɑ̃ʒelize] *vt* to evangelize.
évangile [evɑ̃ʒil] *nm* gospel.
évanouir [evanwiʀ]: **s'**~ *vi* to faint, pass out; (*disparaître*) to vanish, disappear.
évanouissement [evanwismɑ̃] *nm* (*syncope*) fainting fit; (*dans un accident*) loss of consciousness.
évaporation [evapɔʀɑsjɔ̃] *nf* evaporation.
évaporé, e [evapɔʀe] *a* giddy, scatterbrained.
évaporer [evapɔʀe]: **s'**~ *vi* to evaporate.
évaser [evɑze] *vt* (*tuyau*) to widen, open out; (*jupe, pantalon*) to flare; **s'**~ *vi* to widen, open out.
évasif, ive [evazif, -iv] *a* evasive.
évasion [evazjɔ̃] *nf* escape; **littérature d'**~ escapist literature.
évêché [eveʃe] *nm* bishopric; bishop's palace.
éveil [evɛj] *nm* awakening; **être en** ~ to be alert.
éveillé, e [eveje] *a* awake; (*vif*) alert, sharp.
éveiller [eveje] *vt* to (a)waken; **s'**~ *vi* to (a)waken; (*fig*) to be aroused.
événement [evɛnmɑ̃] *nm* event.
éventail [evɑ̃taj] *nm* fan; (*choix*) range; **en** ~ fanned out; fan-shaped.
éventaire [evɑ̃tɛʀ] *nm* stall, stand.
éventer [evɑ̃te] *vt* (*secret*) to discover, lay open; (*avec un éventail*) to fan; **s'**~ *vi* (*parfum*) to go stale.
éventrer [evɑ̃tʀe] *vt* to disembowel; (*fig*) to tear *ou* rip open.
éventualité [evɑ̃tɥalite] *nf* eventuality; possibility; **dans l'**~ **de** in the event of.
éventuel, le [evɑ̃tɥɛl] *a* possible; ~**lement** *ad* possibly.
évêque [evɛk] *nm* bishop.
évertuer [evɛʀtɥe]: **s'**~ *vi*: **s'**~ **à faire** to try very hard to do.
éviction [eviksjɔ̃] *nf* ousting, supplanting; (*de locataire*) eviction.
évidemment [evidamɑ̃] *ad* obviously.
évidence [evidɑ̃s] *nf* obviousness; obvious fact; **de toute** ~ quite obviously *ou* evidently; **en** ~ conspicuous; **mettre en** ~ to highlight; to bring to the fore.
évident, e [evidɑ̃, -ɑ̃t] *a* obvious, evident.
évider [evide] *vt* to scoop out.
évier [evje] *nm* (kitchen) sink.
évincer [evɛ̃se] *vt* to oust, supplant.
évitement [evitmɑ̃] *nm*: **place d'**~ (AUTO) passing place.
éviter [evite] *vt* to avoid; ~ **de faire/que qch ne se passe** to avoid doing/sth happening; ~ **qch à qn** to spare sb sth.

évocateur, trice [evɔkatœʀ, -tʀis] *a* evocative, suggestive.
évocation [evɔkɑsjɔ̃] *nf* evocation.
évolué, e [evɔlɥe] *a* advanced.
évoluer [evɔlɥe] *vi* (*enfant, maladie*) to develop; (*situation, moralement*) to evolve, develop; (*aller et venir: danseur etc*) to move about, circle; **évolution** *nf* development; evolution; **évolutions** *nfpl* movements.
évoquer [evɔke] *vt* to call to mind, evoke; (*mentionner*) to mention.
ex... [ɛks] *préfixe* ex-.
exacerber [ɛgzasɛʀbe] *vt* to exacerbate.
exact, e [ɛgzakt] *a* (*précis*) exact, accurate, precise; (*correct*) correct; (*ponctuel*) punctual; **l'heure ~e** the right *ou* exact time; **~ement** *ad* exactly, accurately, precisely; correctly; (*c'est cela même*) exactly.
exactions [ɛgzaksjɔ̃] *nfpl* exactions.
exactitude [ɛgzaktityd] *nf* exactitude, accurateness, precision.
ex aequo [ɛgzeko] *a* equally placed; **classé 1er ~** placed equal first.
exagération [ɛgzaʒeʀɑsjɔ̃] *nf* exaggeration.
exagéré, e [ɛgzaʒeʀe] *a* (*prix etc*) excessive.
exagérer [ɛgzaʒeʀe] *vt* to exaggerate // *vi* (*abuser*) to go too far; overstep the mark; (*déformer les faits*) to exaggerate.
exaltation [ɛgzaltɑsjɔ̃] *nf* exaltation.
exalté, e [ɛgzalte] *a* (over)excited // *nm/f* (*péj*) fanatic.
exalter [ɛgzalte] *vt* (*enthousiasmer*) to excite, elate; (*glorifier*) to exalt.
examen [ɛgzamɛ̃] *nm* examination; (*SCOL*) exam, examination; **à l'~** under consideration; (*COMM*) on approval; **~ blanc** mock exam(ination); **~ de la vue** sight test.
examinateur, trice [ɛgzaminatœʀ, -tʀis] *nm/f* examiner.
examiner [ɛgzamine] *vt* to examine.
exaspération [ɛgzaspeʀɑsjɔ̃] *nf* exasperation.
exaspérer [ɛgzaspeʀe] *vt* to exasperate; to exacerbate.
exaucer [ɛgzose] *vt* (*vœu*) to grant, fulfil; **~ qn** to grant sb's wishes.
excavateur [ɛkskavatœʀ] *nm* excavator, mechanical digger.
excavation [ɛkskavɑsjɔ̃] *nf* excavation.
excavatrice [ɛkskavatʀis] *nf* = **excavateur.**
excédent [ɛksedɑ̃] *nm* surplus; **en ~** surplus; **~ de bagages** excess luggage; **excédentaire** *a* surplus, excess.
excéder [ɛksede] *vt* (*dépasser*) to exceed; (*agacer*) to exasperate.
excellence [ɛksɛlɑ̃s] *nf* excellence; (*titre*) Excellency.
excellent, e [ɛksɛlɑ̃, -ɑ̃t] *a* excellent.
exceller [ɛksele] *vi*: **~ (dans)** to excel (in).
excentricité [ɛksɑ̃tʀisite] *nf* eccentricity; **excentrique** *a* eccentric; (*quartier*) outlying.
excepté, e [ɛksɛpte] *a*, *prép*: **les élèves ~s, ~ les élèves** except for *ou* apart from the pupils; **~ si** except if.
excepter [ɛksɛpte] *vt* to except.
exception [ɛksɛpsjɔ̃] *nf* exception; **à l'~ de** except for, with the exception of; **d'~** (*mesure, loi*) special, exceptional; **exceptionnel, le** *a* exceptional.
excès [ɛksɛ] *nm* surplus // *nmpl* excesses; **à l'~** (*méticuleux, généreux*) to excess; **~ de vitesse** speeding *q*, exceeding the speed limit; **~ de zèle** overzealousness *q*; **excessif, ive** *a* excessive.
exciper [ɛksipe]: **~ de** *vt* to plead.
excitant [ɛksitɑ̃] *nm* stimulant.
excitation [ɛksitɑsjɔ̃] *nf* (*état*) excitement.
exciter [ɛksite] *vt* to excite; (*suj: café etc*) to stimulate; **s'~** *vi* to get excited; **~ qn à** (*révolte etc*) to incite sb to.
exclamation [ɛksklamɑsjɔ̃] *nf* exclamation.
exclamer [ɛksklame]: **s'~** *vi* to exclaim.
exclure [ɛksklyʀ] *vt* (*faire sortir*) to expel; (*ne pas compter*) to exclude, leave out; (*rendre impossible*) to exclude, rule out; **exclusif, ive** *a* exclusive; **exclusion** *nf* expulsion; **à l'exclusion de** with the exclusion *ou* exception of; **exclusivement** *ad* exclusively; **exclusivité** *nf* exclusiveness; (*COMM*) exclusive rights *pl*; **film passant en exclusivité à** film showing only at.
excommunier [ɛkskɔmynje] *vt* to excommunicate.
excréments [ɛkskʀemɑ̃] *nmpl* excrement *sg*, faeces.
excroissance [ɛkskʀwasɑ̃s] *nf* excrescence, outgrowth.
excursion [ɛkskyʀsjɔ̃] *nf* (*en autocar*) excursion, trip; (*à pied*) walk, hike; **faire une ~** to go on an excursion *ou* a trip; to go on a walk *ou* hike; **excursionniste** *nm/f* tripper; hiker.
excuse [ɛkskyz] *nf* excuse; **~s** *nfpl* apology *sg*, apologies.
excuser [ɛkskyze] *vt* to excuse; **s'~ (de)** to apologize (for); **'excusez-moi'** 'I'm sorry'; (*pour attirer l'attention*) 'excuse me'.
exécrable [ɛgzekʀabl(ə)] *a* atrocious.
exécrer [ɛgzekʀe] *vt* to loathe, abhor.
exécutant, e [ɛgzekytɑ̃, -ɑ̃t] *nm/f* performer.
exécuter [ɛgzekyte] *vt* (*prisonnier*) to execute; (*tâche etc*) to execute, carry out; (*MUS: jouer*) to perform, execute; **s'~** *vi* to comply; **exécuteur, trice** *nm/f* (*testamentaire*) executor // *nm* (*bourreau*) executioner; **exécutif, ive** *a*, *nm* (*POL*) executive; **exécution** *nf* execution; carrying out; **mettre à exécution** to carry out.
exégèse [ɛgzeʒɛz] *nf* exegesis.
exemplaire [ɛgzɑ̃plɛʀ] *a* exemplary // *nm* copy.
exemple [ɛgzɑ̃pl(ə)] *nm* example; **par ~** for instance, for example; **donner l'~** to set an example; **prendre ~ sur** to take as a model; **à l'~ de** just like.
exempt, e [ɛgzɑ̃, -ɑ̃t] *a*: **~ de** (*dispensé de*) exempt from; (*ne comportant pas de*) free from.
exempter [ɛgzɑ̃te] *vt*: **~ de** to exempt from.

exercé, e [ɛgzɛʀse] *a* trained.
exercer [ɛgzɛʀse] *vt* (*pratiquer*) to exercise, practise; (*faire usage de: prérogative*) to exercise; (*effectuer: influence, contrôle, pression*) to exert; (*former*) to exercise, train // *vi* (*médecin*) to be in practice; **s'~** (*sportif, musicien*) to practise; (*se faire sentir: pression etc*) to be exerted.
exercice [ɛgzɛʀsis] *nm* practice; exercising; (*tâche, travail*) exercise; (*activité, sportive, physique*): **l'~** exercise; (MIL): **l'~** drill; (COMM, ADMIN: *période*) accounting period; **en ~** (*juge*) in office; (*médecin*) practising; **dans l'~ de ses fonctions** in the discharge of his duties.
exhaler [ɛgzale] *vt* to exhale; to utter, breathe; **s'~** *vi* to rise (up).
exhaustif, ive [ɛgzostif, -iv] *a* exhaustive.
exhiber [ɛgzibe] *vt* (*montrer: papiers, certificat*) to present, produce; (*péj*) to display, flaunt **s'~** to parade; (*suj: exhibitionniste*) to expose o.s; **exhibitionnisme** *nm* exhibitionism.
exhorter [ɛgzɔʀte] *vt*: **~ qn à faire** to urge sb to do.
exhumer [ɛgzyme] *vt* to exhume.
exigeant, e [ɛgziʒɑ̃, -ɑ̃t] *a* demanding; (*péj*) hard to please.
exigence [ɛgziʒɑ̃s] *nf* demand, requirement.
exiger [ɛgziʒe] *vt* to demand, require.
exigu, ë [ɛgzigy] *a* (*lieu*) cramped, tiny.
exil [ɛgzil] *nm* exile; **en ~** in exile; **~é, e** *nm/f* exile; **~er** *vt* to exile; **s'~er** to go into exile.
existence [ɛgzistɑ̃s] *nf* existence.
exister [ɛgziste] *vi* to exist; **il existe un/des** there is a/are (some).
exode [ɛgzɔd] *nm* exodus.
exonérer [ɛgzɔneʀe] *vt*: **~ de** to exempt from.
exorbitant, e [ɛgzɔʀbitɑ̃, -ɑ̃t] *a* exorbitant.
exorbité, e [ɛgzɔʀbite] *a*: **yeux ~s** bulging eyes.
exorciser [ɛgzɔʀsize] *vt* to exorcize.
exotique [ɛgzɔtik] *a* exotic; **exotisme** *nm* exoticism; exotic flavour *ou* atmosphere.
expansif, ive [ɛkspɑ̃sif, -iv] *a* expansive, communicative.
expansion [ɛkspɑ̃sjɔ̃] *nf* expansion.
expatrier [ɛkspatʀije] *vt*: **s'~** to leave one's country, expatriate o.s.
expectative [ɛkspɛktativ] *nf*: **être dans l'~** to be still waiting.
expectorer [ɛkspɛktɔʀe] *vi* to expectorate.
expédient [ɛkspedjɑ̃] *nm* (*péj*) expedient; **vivre d'~s** to live by one's wits.
expédier [ɛkspedje] *vt* (*lettre, paquet*) to send; (*troupes*) to dispatch; (*péj: travail etc*) to dispose of, dispatch; **expéditeur, trice** *nm/f* sender.
expéditif, ive [ɛkspeditif, -iv] *a* quick, expeditious.
expédition [ɛkspedisjɔ̃] *nf* sending; (*scientifique, sportive,* MIL) expedition.
expéditionnaire [ɛkspedisjɔnɛʀ] *a*: **corps ~** task force.
expérience [ɛkspeʀjɑ̃s] *nf* (*de la vie*) experience; (*scientifique*) experiment; **avoir de l'~** to have experience, be experienced; **avoir l'~ de** to have experience of.
expérimental, e, aux [ɛkspeʀimɑ̃tal, -o] *a* experimental.
expérimenté, e [ɛkspeʀimɑ̃te] *a* experienced.
expérimenter [ɛkspeʀimɑ̃te] *vt* (*technique*) to test out, experiment with.
expert, e [ɛkspɛʀ, -ɛʀt(ə)] *a, nm* expert; **~ en assurances** insurance valuer; **~-comptable** *nm* ≈ chartered accountant.
expertise [ɛkspɛʀtiz] *nf* valuation; assessment; valuer's (*ou* assessor's) report; (JUR) (forensic) examination.
expertiser [ɛkspɛʀtize] *vt* (*objet de valeur*) to value; (*voiture accidentée etc*) to assess damage to.
expier [ɛkspje] *vt* to expiate, atone for.
expiration [ɛkspiʀɑsjɔ̃] *nf* expiry; breathing out *q*.
expirer [ɛkspiʀe] *vi* (*venir à échéance, mourir*) to expire; (*respirer*) to breathe out.
explétif, ive [ɛkspletif, -iv] *a* expletive.
explicatif, ive [ɛksplikatif, -iv] *a* explanatory.
explication [ɛksplikɑsjɔ̃] *nf* explanation; (*discussion*) discussion; argument; **~ de texte** (SCOL) critical analysis (of a text).
explicite [ɛksplisit] *a* explicit; **expliciter** *vt* to make explicit.
expliquer [ɛksplike] *vt* to explain; **s'~** (*discuter*) to discuss things; to have it out; **son erreur s'explique** one can understand his mistake.
exploit [ɛksplwa] *nm* exploit, feat.
exploitant [ɛksplwatɑ̃] *nm* farmer.
exploitation [ɛksplwatɑsjɔ̃] *nf* exploitation; running; **~ agricole** farming concern.
exploiter [ɛksplwate] *vt* (*mine*) to exploit, work; (*entreprise, ferme*) to run, operate; (*clients, ouvriers, erreur, don*) to exploit; **exploiteur, euse** *nm/f* exploiter.
explorateur, trice [ɛksplɔʀatœʀ, -tʀis] *nm/f* explorer.
exploration [ɛksplɔʀɑsjɔ̃] *nf* exploration.
explorer [ɛksplɔʀe] *vt* to explore.
exploser [ɛksploze] *vi* to explode, blow up; (*engin explosif*) to go off; (*fig: joie, colère*) to burst out, explode; (*personne: de colère*) to explode, flare up; **explosif, ive** *a, nm* explosive; **explosion** *nf* explosion.
exportateur, trice [ɛkspɔʀtatœʀ, -tʀis] *a* export *cpd*, exporting // *nm* exporter.
exportation [ɛkspɔʀtɑsjɔ̃] *nf* exportation; export.
exporter [ɛkspɔʀte] *vt* to export.
exposant [ɛkspozɑ̃] *nm* exhibitor; (MATH) exponent.
exposé, e [ɛkspoze] *nm* talk // *a*: **~ au sud** facing south, with a southern aspect; **bien ~** well situated; **très ~** very exposed.
exposer [ɛkspoze] *vt* (*marchandise*) to display; (*peinture*) to exhibit, show; (*parler de: problème, situation*) to explain, set out; (*mettre en danger, orienter,* PHOTO) to expose; **~ qn/qch à** to expose sb/sth

to; **exposition** *nf* displaying; exhibiting; setting out; (*voir exposé*) aspect, situation; (*manifestation*) exhibition; (*PHOTO*) exposure.
exprès [ɛksprɛ] *ad* (*délibérément*) on purpose; (*spécialement*) specially; **faire ~ de faire qch** to do sth on purpose.
exprès, esse [ɛksprɛs] *a* (*ordre, défense*) express, formal // *a inv, ad* (*PTT*) express.
express [ɛksprɛs] *a, nm*: **(café) ~** espresso; **(train) ~** fast train.
expressément [ɛksprɛsemɑ̃] *ad* expressly; specifically.
expressif, ive [ɛkspresif, -iv] *a* expressive.
expression [ɛksprɛsjɔ̃] *nf* expression.
exprimer [ɛksprime] *vt* (*sentiment, idée*) to express; (*jus, liquide*) to press out; **s'~** *vi* (*personne*) to express o.s.
expropriation [ɛksprɔprijɑsjɔ̃] *nf* expropriation; **frapper d'~** to put a compulsory purchase order on.
exproprier [ɛksprɔprije] *vt* to buy up (*ou* buy the property of) by compulsory purchase, expropriate.
expulser [ɛkspylse] *vt* to expel; (*locataire*) to evict; (*FOOTBALL*) to send off; **expulsion** *nf* expulsion; eviction; sending off.
expurger [ɛkspyrʒe] *vt* to expurgate, bowdlerize.
exquis, e [ɛkski, -iz] *a* exquisite; delightful.
exsangue [ɛksɑ̃g] *a* bloodless, drained of blood.
extase [ɛkstɑz] *nf* ecstasy; **s'extasier sur** to go into ecstasies *ou* raptures over.
extenseur [ɛkstɑ̃sœr] *nm* (*SPORT*) chest expander.
extensible [ɛkstɑ̃sibl(ə)] *a* extensible.
extensif, ive [ɛkstɑ̃sif, -iv] *a* extensive.
extension [ɛkstɑ̃sjɔ̃] *nf* (*d'un muscle, ressort*) stretching; (*MÉD*) **à l'~** in traction; (*fig*) extension; expansion.
exténuer [ɛkstenɥe] *vt* to exhaust.
extérieur, e [ɛksterjœr] *a* (*porte, mur etc*) outer, outside; (*au dehors: escalier, w.-c.*) outside; (*commerce*) foreign; (*influences*) external; (*apparent: calme, gaieté etc*) surface *cpd* // *nm* (*d'une maison, d'un récipient etc*) outside, exterior; (*d'une personne: apparence*) exterior; (*d'un groupe social*): **l'~** the outside world; **à l'~** outside; (*à l'étranger*) abroad; **~ement** *ad* on the outside; (*en apparence*) on the surface; **extérioriser** *vt* to show; to exteriorize.
exterminer [ɛkstɛrmine] *vt* to exterminate, wipe out.
externat [ɛkstɛrna] *nm* day school.
externe [ɛkstɛrn(ə)] *a* external, outer // *nm/f* (*MÉD*) non-resident medical student; (*SCOL*) day pupil.
extincteur [ɛkstɛ̃ktœr] *nm* (fire) extinguisher.
extinction [ɛkstɛ̃ksjɔ̃] *nf* extinction; (*JUR: d'une dette*) extinguishment; **~ de voix** loss of voice.
extirper [ɛkstirpe] *vt* (*tumeur*) to extirpate; (*plante*) to root out, pull up.
extorquer [ɛkstɔrke] *vt*: **~ qch à qn** to extort sth from sb.
extra [ɛkstra] *a inv* first-rate; top-quality // *nm inv* extra help.
extraction [ɛkstraksjɔ̃] *nf* extraction.
extrader [ɛkstrade] *vt* to extradite; **extradition** *nf* extradition.
extraire [ɛkstrɛr] *vt* to extract; **extrait** *nm* (*de plante*) extract; (*de film, livre*) extract, excerpt.
extra-lucide [ɛkstralysid] *a*: **voyante ~** clairvoyant.
extraordinaire [ɛkstraɔrdinɛr] *a* extraordinary; (*POL: mesures*) special; **ambassadeur ~** ambassador extraordinary.
extravagance [ɛkstravagɑ̃s] *nf* extravagance *q*; extravagant behaviour *q*.
extravagant, e [ɛkstravagɑ̃, -ɑ̃t] *a* extravagant; wild.
extraverti, e [ɛkstravɛrti] *a* extrovert.
extrême [ɛkstrɛm] *a, nm* extreme; **~ment** *ad* extremely; **~-onction** *nf* last rites *pl*, Extreme Unction; **E~-Orient** *nm* Far East; **extrémiste** *a, nm/f* extremist.
extrémité [ɛkstremite] *nf* end; (*situation*) straits *pl*, plight; (*geste désespéré*) extreme action; **~s** *nfpl* (*pieds et mains*) extremities; **à la dernière ~** (*à l'agonie*) on the point of death.
exubérant, e [ɛgzyberɑ̃, -ɑ̃t] *a* exuberant.
exulter [ɛgzylte] *vi* to exult.
exutoire [ɛgzytwar] *nm* outlet, release.
ex-voto [ɛksvɔto] *nm inv* ex-voto.

F

F *abr de* **franc.**
fa [fɑ] *nm inv* (*MUS*) F; (*en chantant la gamme*) fa.
fable [fɑbl(ə)] *nf* fable; (*mensonge*) story, tale.
fabricant [fabrikɑ̃] *nm* manufacturer, maker.
fabrication [fabrikɑsjɔ̃] *nf* manufacture, making.
fabrique [fabrik] *nf* factory.
fabriquer [fabrike] *vt* to make; (*industriellement*) to manufacture, make; (*fig*): **qu'est-ce qu'il fabrique?** what is he doing?
fabulation [fabylɑsjɔ̃] *nf* fantasizing.
fabuleux, euse [fabylø, -øz] *a* fabulous, fantastic.
façade [fasad] *nf* front, façade; (*fig*) façade.
face [fas] *nf* face; (*fig: aspect*) side // *a*: **le côté ~** heads; **perdre la ~** to lose face; **en ~ de** *prép* opposite; (*fig*) in front of; **de ~** *ad* from the front; face on; **~ à** *prép* facing; (*fig*) faced with, in the face of; **faire ~ à** to face; **~ à ~** *ad* facing each other // *nm inv* encounter; **~-à-main** *nm* lorgnette.
facéties [fasesi] *nfpl* jokes, pranks.
facétieux, euse [fasesjø, -øz] *a* mischievous.
facette [fasɛt] *nf* facet.
fâché, e [fɑʃe] *a* angry; (*désolé*) sorry.
fâcher [fɑʃe] *vt* to anger; **se ~** *vi* to get angry; **se ~ avec** (*se brouiller*) to fall out with.

fâcheux, euse [fɑʃø, -øz] *a* unfortunate, regrettable.
facial, e, aux [fasjal, -o] *a* facial.
faciès [fasjɛs] *nm* features *pl*, facies.
facile [fasil] *a* easy ; (*accommodant*) easy-going ; **~ment** *ad* easily ; **facilité** *nf* easiness ; (*disposition, don*) aptitude ; **facilités** *nfpl* facilities ; **facilités de paiement** easy terms ; **faciliter** *vt* to make easier.
façon [fasɔ̃] *nf* (*manière*) way ; (*d'une robe etc*) making-up ; cut ; **~s** *nfpl* (*péj*) fuss *sg* ; **de quelle ~?** (in) what way? ; **de ~ à** so as to ; **de ~ à ce que** so that ; **de toute ~** anyway, in any case.
faconde [fakɔ̃d] *nf* loquaciousness, volubility.
façonner [fasɔne] *vt* (*fabriquer*) to manufacture ; (*travailler*: *matière*) to shape, fashion ; (*fig*) to mould, shape.
fac-similé [faksimile] *nm* facsimile.
facteur, trice [faktœʀ, -tʀis] *nm/f* postman/woman // *nm* (MATH, *fig*: *élément*) factor ; **~ d'orgues** organ builder ; **~ de pianos** piano maker.
factice [faktis] *a* artificial.
faction [faksjɔ̃] *nf* (*groupe*) faction ; (*surveillance*) guard *ou* sentry (duty) ; watch ; **en ~** on guard ; standing watch ; **factionnaire** *nm* guard, sentry.
factoriel, le [faktɔʀjɛl] *a* factorial.
factotum [faktɔtɔm] *nm* odd-job man, dogsbody.
facture [faktyʀ] *nf* (*à payer*: *gén*) bill ; (: COMM) invoice ; (*d'un artisan, artiste*) technique, workmanship ; **facturer** *vt* to invoice.
facultatif, ive [fakyltatif, -iv] *a* optional ; (*arrêt de bus*) request *cpd*.
faculté [fakylte] *nf* (*intellectuelle, d'université*) faculty ; (*pouvoir, possibilité*) power.
fadaises [fadɛz] *nfpl* twaddle *sg*.
fade [fad] *a* insipid.
fading [fadiŋ] *nm* (RADIO) fading.
fagot [fago] *nm* (*de bois*) bundle of sticks.
fagoté, e [fagɔte] *a* (*fam*): **drôlement ~** in a peculiar getup.
faible [fɛbl(ə)] *a* weak ; (*voix, lumière, vent*) faint ; (*rendement, intensité, revenu etc*) low // *nm* weak point ; weakness, soft spot ; **~ d'esprit** feeble-minded ; **faiblesse** *nf* weakness ; **faiblir** *vi* to weaken ; (*lumière*) to dim ; (*vent*) to drop.
faïence [fajɑ̃s] *nf* earthenware *q* ; piece of earthenware.
faignant, e [fɛɲɑ̃, -ɑ̃t] *nm/f* = **fainéant, e**.
faille [faj] *vb voir* **falloir** // *nf* (GÉO) fault ; (*fig*) flaw, weakness.
faillible [fajibl(ə)] *a* fallible.
faim [fɛ̃] *nf* hunger ; **avoir ~** to be hungry ; **rester sur sa ~** (*aussi fig*) to be left wanting more.
fainéant, e [fɛneɑ̃, -ɑ̃t] *nm/f* idler, loafer.
faire [fɛʀ] *vt* to make ; (*effectuer*: *travail, opération*) to do ; **vraiment? fit-il** really? he said ; **fait à la main/machine** hand-/machine-made ; **~ du bruit/des taches** to make a noise/marks ; **~ du rugby/piano** to play rugby/play the piano ; **~ le malade/l'ignorant** to act the invalid/the fool ; **~ de qn un frustré/avocat** to make sb a frustrated person/a lawyer ; **cela ne me fait rien** (*m'est égal*) I don't care *ou* mind ; (*me laisse froid*) it has no effect on me ; **cela ne fait rien** it doesn't matter ; **je vous le fais 10 F** (*j'en demande 10 F*) I'll let you have it for 10 F ; **que faites-vous?** (*quel métier etc*) what do you do? ; (*quelle activité: au moment de la question*) what are you doing? ; **comment a-t-il fait pour** how did he manage to ; **qu'a-t-il fait de sa valise?** what has he done with his case? ; **2 et 2 font 4** 2 and 2 are *ou* make 4 // *vb avec attribut*: **ça fait 10 m/15 F** it's 10 m/15 F // *vb substitut*: **ne le casse pas comme je l'ai fait** don't break it as I did // *vb impersonnel voir* **jour, froid** *etc* ; **ça fait 2 ans qu'il est parti** it's 2 years since he left ; **ça fait 2 ans qu'il y est** he's been there for 2 years ; **faites!** please do! ; **il ne fait que critiquer** (*sans cesse*) all he (ever) does is criticize ; (*seulement*) he's only criticizing ; **~ vieux/démodé** to look old/old-fashioned // **~ faire**: **~ réparer qch** to get *ou* have sth repaired ; **~ tomber/bouger qch** to make sth fall/move ; **cela fait dormir** it makes you sleep ; **~ travailler les enfants** to make the children work, get the children to work ; **~ punir les enfants** to have the children punished ; **~ démarrer un moteur/chauffer de l'eau** to start up an engine/heat some water ; **se ~ examiner la vue/opérer** to have one's eyes tested/have an operation ; **il s'est fait aider (par qn)** he got sb to help him ; **il va se ~ tuer/punir** he's going to get himself killed/get (himself) punished ; **se ~ faire un vêtement** to get a garment made for o.s. // **se ~** *vi* (*fromage, vin*) to mature ; **se ~ à** (*s'habituer*) to get used to ; **cela se fait beaucoup/ne se fait pas** it's done a lot/not done ; **comment se fait-il/faisait-il que** how is it/was it that ; **se ~ vieux** to be getting old ; **se ~ des amis** to make friends ; **il ne s'en fait pas** he doesn't worry.
faisable [fəzabl(ə)] *a* feasible.
faisan, e [fəzɑ̃, -an] *nm/f* pheasant.
faisandé, e [fəzɑ̃de] *a* high.
faisceau, x [fɛso] *nm* (*de lumière etc*) beam ; (*de branches etc*) bundle.
faiseur, euse [fəzœʀ, -øz] *nm/f* (*gén:péj*): **~ de** maker of // *nm* (bespoke) tailor.
faisons *vb voir* **faire.**
fait [fɛ] *nm* (*événement*) event, occurrence ; (*réalité, donnée: s'oppose à hypothèse*) fact ; **le ~ que/de manger** the fact that/of eating ; **être le ~ de** (*causé par*) to be the work of ; **être au ~ (de)** to be informed (of) ; **au ~** (*à propos*) by the way ; **en venir au ~** to get to the point ; **de ~** *a* (*opposé à: de droit*) de facto // *ad* in fact ; **du ~ de ceci/qu'il a menti** because of *ou* on account of this/his having lied ; **de ce ~** therefore, for this reason ; **en ~** in fact ; **en ~ de repas** by way of a meal ; **prendre ~ et cause pour qn** to support sb, side with sb ; **prendre qn sur le ~** to catch sb in the act ; **~ d'armes** feat of arms ; **~ divers** (short) news item ; **les ~s et gestes de qn** sb's actions *ou* doings.

fait, e [fɛ, fɛt] *a* (*mûr*: *fromage, melon*) ripe ; **un homme** ~ a grown man ; **c'en est** ~ **de notre tranquillité** that's the end of our peace.
faîte [fɛt] *nm* top ; (*fig*) pinnacle, height.
faites *vb voir* **faire.**
faîtière [fɛtjɛʀ] *nf* (*de tente*) ridge pole.
fait-tout *nm inv*, **faitout** *nm* [fɛtu] stewpot.
fakir [fakiʀ] *nm* wizard.
falaise [falɛz] *nf* cliff.
fallacieux, euse [falasjø, -øz] *a* fallacious ; deceptive ; illusory.
falloir [falwaʀ] *vb impersonnel*: **il va** ~ **100 F** we'll (*ou* I'll) need 100 F ; **il doit** ~ **du temps** that must take time ; **il me faudrait 100 F** I would need 100 F ; **il vous faut tourner à gauche après l'église** you have to *ou* want to turn left past the church ; **nous avons ce qu'il (nous) faut** we have what we need ; **il faut qu'il parte/a fallu qu'il parte** (*obligation*) he has to *ou* must leave/had to leave ; **il a fallu le faire** it had to be done // **s'en** ~: **il s'en est fallu de 100 F/5 minutes** we (*ou* they) were 100 F short/5 minutes late (*ou* early) ; **il s'en faut de beaucoup qu'il soit** he is far from being ; **il s'en est fallu de peu que cela n'arrive** it very nearly happened.
falot, e [falo, -ɔt] *a* dreary, colourless // *nm* lantern.
falsifier [falsifje] *vt* to falsify ; to doctor.
famé, e [fame] *a*: **mal** ~ disreputable, of ill repute.
famélique [famelik] *a* half-starved.
fameux, euse [famø, -øz] *a* (*illustre*) famous ; (*bon*: *repas, plat etc*) first-rate, first-class.
familial, e, aux [familjal, -o] *a* family *cpd* // *nf* (AUTO) estate car.
familiariser [familjaʀize] *vt*: ~ **qn avec** to familiarize sb with.
familiarité [familjaʀite] *nf* informality ; familiarity ; ~ **avec** (*sujet, science*) familiarity with ; ~**s** *nfpl* familiarities.
familier, ière [familje, -jɛʀ] *a* (*connu, impertinent*) familiar ; (*dénotant une certaine intimité*) informal, friendly ; (LING) informal, colloquial // *nm* regular (visitor).
famille [famij] *nf* family ; **il a de la** ~ **à Paris** he has relatives in Paris.
famine [famin] *nf* famine.
fan [fan] *nm/f* fan.
fanal, aux [fanal, -o] *nm* beacon ; lantern.
fanatique [fanatik] *a* fanatical // *nm/f* fanatic ; **fanatisme** *nm* fanaticism.
faner [fane]: **se** ~ *vi* to fade.
faneur, euse [fanœʀ, -øz] *nm/f* haymaker.
fanfare [fɑ̃faʀ] *nf* (*orchestre*) brass band ; (*musique*) fanfare.
fanfaron, ne [fɑ̃faʀɔ̃, -ɔn] *nm/f* braggart.
fange [fɑ̃ʒ] *nf* mire.
fanion [fanjɔ̃] *nm* pennant.
fanon [fanɔ̃] *nm* (*de baleine*) plate of baleen ; (*repli de peau*) dewlap, wattle.
fantaisie [fɑ̃tezi] *nf* (*spontanéité*) fancy, imagination ; (*caprice*) whim ; extravagance ; (MUS) fantasia // *a*: **bijou/pain** ~ fancy jewellery/bread ;
fantaisiste *a* (*péj*) unorthodox, eccentric // *nm/f* (*de music-hall*) variety artist *ou* entertainer.
fantasme [fɑ̃tasm(ə)] *nm* fantasy.
fantasque [fɑ̃task(ə)] *a* whimsical, capricious ; fantastic.
fantassin [fɑ̃tasɛ̃] *nm* infantryman.
fantastique [fɑ̃tastik] *a* fantastic.
fantoche [fɑ̃tɔʃ] *nm* (*péj*) puppet.
fantomatique [fɑ̃tɔmatik] *a* ghostly.
fantôme [fɑ̃tom] *nm* ghost, phantom.
faon [fɑ̃] *nm* fawn.
farce [faʀs(ə)] *nf* (*viande*) stuffing ; (*blague*) (practical) joke ; (THÉÂTRE) farce ; ~**s et attrapes** jokes and novelties ; **farceur, euse** *nm/f* practical joker ; **farcir** *vt* (*viande*) to stuff ; (*fig*): **farcir qch de** to stuff sth with.
fard [faʀ] *nm* make-up.
fardeau, x [faʀdo] *nm* burden.
farder [faʀde] *vt* to make up.
farfelu, e [faʀfəly] *a* cranky, hare-brained.
farfouiller [faʀfuje] *vi* (*péj*) to rummage around.
farine [faʀin] *nf* flour ; **farineux, euse** *a* (*sauce, pomme*) floury // *nmpl* (*aliments*) starchy foods.
farouche [faʀuʃ] *a* shy, timid ; savage, wild ; fierce.
fart [faʀ(t)] *nm* (ski) wax ; **farter** *vt* to wax.
fascicule [fasikyl] *nm* volume.
fascination [fasinɑsjɔ̃] *nf* fascination.
fasciner [fasine] *vt* to fascinate.
fascisme [fasism(ə)] *nm* fascism ; **fasciste** *a, nm/f* fascist.
fasse *etc vb voir* **faire.**
faste [fast(ə)] *nm* splendour // *a*: **c'est un jour** ~ it's his (*ou* our) lucky day.
fastidieux, euse [fastidjø, -øz] *a* tedious, tiresome.
fastueux, euse [fastɥø, -øz] *a* sumptuous, luxurious.
fat [fa] *am* conceited, smug.
fatal, e [fatal] *a* fatal ; (*inévitable*) inevitable ; ~**isme** *nm* fatalism ; fatalistic outlook ; ~**ité** *nf* fate ; fateful coincidence ; inevitability.
fatidique [fatidik] *a* fateful.
fatigant, e [fatigɑ̃, -ɑ̃t] *a* tiring ; (*agaçant*) tiresome.
fatigue [fatig] *nf* tiredness, fatigue.
fatiguer [fatige] *vt* to tire, make tired ; (TECH) to put a strain on, strain ; (*fig*: *importuner*) to wear out // *vi* (*moteur*) to labour, strain ; **se** ~ to get tired ; to tire o.s. (out).
fatras [fatʀa] *nm* jumble, hotchpotch.
fatuité [fatɥite] *nf* conceitedness, smugness.
faubourg [fobuʀ] *nm* suburb.
fauché, e [foʃe] *a* (*fam*) broke.
faucher [foʃe] *vt* (*herbe*) to cut ; (*champs, blés*) to reap ; (*fig*) to cut down ; to mow down ; **faucheur, euse** *nm/f, nf* (*machine*) reaper, mower.
faucille [fosij] *nf* sickle.
faucon [fokɔ̃] *nm* falcon, hawk.
faudra *vb voir* **falloir.**
faufiler [fofile] *vt* to tack, baste ; **se** ~ *vi*: **se** ~ **dans** to edge one's way into ; **se** ~

parmi/entre to thread one's way among/between.
faune [fon] *nf* (*ZOOL*) wildlife, fauna // *nm* faun.
faussaire [fosɛʀ] *nm* forger.
fausse [fos] *a voir* **faux**.
faussement [fosmɑ̃] *ad* (*accuser*) wrongly, wrongfully; (*croire*) falsely, erroneously.
fausser [fose] *vt* (*objet*) to bend, buckle; (*fig*) to distort.
fausset [fosɛ] *nm*: **voix de ~** falsetto voice.
faussete [foste] *nf* wrongness; falseness.
faut *vb voir* **falloir.**
faute [fot] *nf* (*erreur*) mistake, error; (*péché, manquement*) misdemeanour; (*FOOTBALL etc*) offence; (*TENNIS*) fault; (*responsabilité*): **par la ~ de** through the fault of, because of; **c'est de sa/ma ~** it's his/my fault; **être en ~** to be in the wrong; **~ de** (*temps, argent*) for *ou* through lack of; **sans ~** *ad* without fail; **~ de frappe** typing error; **~ d'orthographe** spelling mistake; **~ professionnelle** professional misconduct *q*.
fauteuil [fotœj] *nm* armchair; **~ club** (big) easy chair; **~ d'orchestre** seat in the front stalls; **~ roulant** wheelchair.
fauteur [fotœʀ] *nm*: **~ de troubles** trouble-maker.
fautif, ive [fotif, -iv] *a* (*incorrect*) incorrect, inaccurate; (*responsable*) at fault, in the wrong; guilty // *nm/f* culprit.
fauve [fov] *nm* wildcat // *a* (*couleur*) fawn.
faux [fo] *nf* scythe.
faux, fausse [fo, fos] *a* (*inexact*) wrong; (*falsifié*) fake; forged; (*sournois, postiche*) false // *ad* (*MUS*) out of tune // *nm* (*copie*) fake, forgery; (*opposé au vrai*): **le ~** falsehood; **le ~ numéro/la fausse clef** the wrong number/key; **faire ~ bond à qn** to stand sb up; **~ col** detachable collar; **~ frais** *nmpl* extras, incidental expenses; **~ mouvement** awkward movement; **~ nez** funny nose; **~ pas** tripping *q*; (*fig*) faux pas; **~ témoignage** (*délit*) perjury; **fausse alerte** false alarm; **fausse couche** miscarriage; **~-filet** *nm* sirloin; **~-fuyant** *nm* equivocation; **~-monnayeur** *nm* counterfeiter, forger.
faveur [favœʀ] *nf* favour; (*ruban*) ribbon; **traitement de ~** preferential treatment; **à la ~ de** under cover of; thanks to; **en ~ de** in favour of.
favorable [favɔʀabl(ə)] *a* favourable.
favori, te [favɔʀi, -it] *a, nm/f* favourite; **~s** *nmpl* (*barbe*) sideboards, sideburns.
favoriser [favɔʀize] *vt* to favour.
favoritisme [favɔʀitism(ə)] *nm* (*péj*) favouritism.
FB *sigle* = *franc belge*.
fébrile [febʀil] *a* feverish, febrile.
fécal, e, aux [fekal, -o] *a voir* **matière.**
fécond, e [fekɔ̃, -ɔ̃d] *a* fertile; **féconder** *vt* to fertilize; **fécondité** *nf* fertility.
fécule [fekyl] *nf* potato flour.
fédéral, e, aux [fedeʀal, -o] *a* federal; **fédéralisme** *nm* federalism.
fédération [fedeʀɑsjɔ̃] *nf* federation.
fée [fe] *nf* fairy; **~rie** *nf* enchantment; **~rique** *a* magical, fairytale *cpd*.
feignant, e [fɛɲɑ̃, -ɑ̃t] *nm/f* = **fainéant, e**.
feindre [fɛ̃dʀ(ə)] *vt* to feign // *vi* to dissemble; **~ de faire** to pretend to do.
feinte [fɛ̃t] *nf* (*SPORT*) dummy.
fêler [fele] *vt* to crack.
félicitations [felisitɑsjɔ̃] *nfpl* congratulations.
félicité [felisite] *nf* bliss.
féliciter [felisite] *vt*: **~ qn (de)** to congratulate sb (on).
félin, e [felɛ̃, -in] *a* feline // *nm* (big) cat.
félon, ne [felɔ̃, -ɔn] *a* perfidious, treacherous.
fêlure [felyʀ] *nf* crack.
femelle [fəmɛl] *a* (*aussi ÉLEC, TECH*) female // *nf* female; **souris ~** female mouse, she-mouse.
féminin, e [feminɛ̃, -in] *a* feminine; (*sexe*) female; (*équipe, vêtements etc*) women's // *nm* feminine; **féministe** *a* feminist; **féminité** *nf* femininity.
femme [fam] *nf* woman; (*épouse*) wife (*pl* wives); **devenir ~** to attain womanhood; **~ de chambre** cleaning lady; **~ de ménage** domestic help, cleaning lady.
fémur [femyʀ] *nm* femur, thighbone.
fenaison [fənɛzɔ̃] *nf* haymaking.
fendre [fɑ̃dʀ(ə)] *vt* (*couper en deux*) to split; (*fissurer*) to crack; (*fig: traverser*) to cut through; to cleave through; **se ~** *vi* to crack; **fendu, e** *a* (*sol, mur*) cracked; (*jupe*) slit.
fenêtre [fənɛtʀ(ə)] *nf* window.
fenouil [fənuj] *nm* fennel.
fente [fɑ̃t] *nf* (*fissure*) crack; (*de boîte à lettres etc*) slit.
féodal, e, aux [feɔdal, -o] *a* feudal; **féodalité** *nf* feudality.
fer [fɛʀ] *nm* iron; (*de cheval*) shoe; **au ~ rouge** with a red-hot iron; **~ à cheval** horseshoe; **~ forgé** wrought iron; **~ de lance** spearhead; **~ (à repasser)** iron; **~ à souder** soldering iron.
ferai *etc vb voir* **faire.**
fer-blanc [fɛʀblɑ̃] *nm* tin(plate); **ferblanterie** *nf* tinplate making; tinware; **ferblantier** *nm* tinsmith.
férié, e [feʀje] *a*: **jour ~** public holiday.
ferions *etc vb voir* **faire.**
férir [feʀiʀ]: **sans coup ~** *ad* without meeting any opposition.
ferme [fɛʀm(ə)] *a* firm // *ad* (*travailler etc*) hard // *nf* (*exploitation*) farm; (*maison*) farmhouse.
fermé, e [fɛʀme] *a* closed, shut; (*gaz, eau etc*) off; (*fig: personne*) uncommunicative; (*: milieu*) exclusive.
ferment [fɛʀmɑ̃] *nm* ferment.
fermentation [fɛʀmɑ̃tɑsjɔ̃] *nf* fermentation.
fermenter [fɛʀmɑ̃te] *vi* to ferment.
fermer [fɛʀme] *vt* to close, shut; (*cesser l'exploitation de*) to close down, shut down; (*eau, lumière, électricité, robinet*) to put off, turn off; (*aéroport, route*) to close // *vi* to close, shut; to close down, shut down; **se**

~ *vi* (*yeux*) to close, shut; (*fleur, blessure*) to close up.
fermeté [fɛʀməte] *nf* firmness.
fermeture [fɛʀmətyʀ] *nf* closing; shutting; closing *ou* shutting down; putting *ou* turning off; (*dispositif*) catch; fastening, fastener; **heure de ~** (COMM) closing time; **jour de ~** (COMM) day on which the shop (*etc*) is closed; **~ éclair** ® *ou* **à glissière** zip (fastener), zipper.
fermier, ière [fɛʀmje, -jɛʀ] *nm* farmer // *nf* woman farmer; farmer's wife // *a*: **beurre/cidre ~** farm butter/cider.
fermoir [fɛʀmwaʀ] *nm* clasp.
féroce [feʀɔs] *a* ferocious, fierce.
ferons *vb voir* **faire.**
ferraille [fɛʀɑj] *nf* scrap iron; **mettre à la ~** to scrap; **ferrailleur** *nm* scrap merchant.
ferré, e [fɛʀe] *a* hobnailed; steel-tipped; (*fam*): **~ en** well up on, hot at.
ferrer [fɛʀe] *vt* (*cheval*) to shoe; (*chaussure*) to nail; (*canne*) to tip; (*poisson*) to strike.
ferreux, euse [fɛʀø, -øz] *a* ferrous.
ferronnerie [fɛʀɔnʀi] *nf* ironwork; **~ d'art** wrought iron work; **ferronnier** *nm* craftsman in wrought iron; ironware merchant.
ferroviaire [fɛʀɔvjɛʀ] *a* rail(way) *cpd.*
ferrure [fɛʀyʀ] *nf* (ornamental) hinge.
ferry-boat [fɛʀebot] *nm* ferry.
fertile [fɛʀtil] *a* fertile; **~ en incidents** eventful, packed with incidents; **fertiliser** *vt* to fertilize; **fertilité** *nf* fertility.
féru, e [feʀy] *a*: **~ de** with a keen interest in.
férule [feʀyl] *nf*: **être sous la ~ de qn** to be under sb's (iron) rule.
fervent, e [fɛʀvɑ̃, -ɑ̃t] *a* fervent.
ferveur [fɛʀvœʀ] *nf* fervour.
fesse [fɛs] *nf* buttock; **fessée** *nf* spanking.
festin [fɛstɛ̃] *nm* feast.
festival [fɛstival] *nm* festival; **~ier** *nm* festival-goer.
festivités [fɛstivite] *nfpl* festivities, merry-making *sg.*
feston [fɛstɔ̃] *nm* (ARCHIT) festoon; (COUTURE) scallop.
festoyer [fɛstwaje] *vi* to feast.
fêtard [fɛtaʀ] *nm* (*péj*) high liver, merry-maker.
fête [fɛt] *nf* (*religieuse*) feast; (*publique*) holiday; (*en famille etc*) celebration; (*kermesse*) fête, fair, festival; (*du nom*) feast day, name day; **faire la ~** to live it up; **faire ~ à qn** to give sb a warm welcome; **les ~s (de fin d'année)** the Christmas and New Year holidays, the festive season; **la salle/le comité des ~s** the village hall/ festival committee; **~ foraine** (fun) fair; **~ mobile** movable feast (day); **la F~ Nationale** the national holiday; **la Fête-Dieu** Corpus Christi; **fêter** *vt* to celebrate; (*personne*) to have a celebration for.
fétiche [fetiʃ] *nm* fetish; **fétichisme** *nm* fetishism.
fétide [fetid] *a* fetid.
fétu [fety] *nm*: **~ de paille** wisp of straw.
feu [fø] *a inv*: **~ son père** his late father.
feu, x [fø] *nm* (*gén*) fire; (*signal lumineux*) light; (*de cuisinière*) ring; (*sensation de brûlure*) burning (sensation) // *nmpl* (*éclat, lumière*) fire *sg*; (AUTO) (traffic) lights; **à ~ doux/vif** over a slow/brisk heat; **à petit ~** (CULIN) over a gentle heat; **faire ~** to fire; **tué au ~** killed in action; **mettre à ~** (*fusée*) to fire off; **prendre ~** to catch fire; **mettre le ~ à** to set fire to, set on fire; **faire du ~** to make a fire; **avez-vous du ~?** (*pour cigarette*) have you (got) a light?; **~ rouge/vert/orange** red/green/ amber light; **~ arrière** rear light; **~ d'artifice** firework; (*spectacle*) fireworks *pl*; **~ de camp** campfire; **~ de cheminée** chimney fire; **~ de joie** bonfire; **~ de paille** (*fig*) flash in the pan; **~x de brouillard** fog-lamps; **~x de croisement** dipped headlights; **~x de position** sidelights; **~x de route** headlights, headlamps.
feuillage [fœjaʒ] *nm* foliage, leaves *pl.*
feuille [fœj] *nf* (*d'arbre*) leaf (*pl* leaves); **~ (de papier)** sheet (of paper); **~ d'or/de métal** gold/metal leaf; **~ d'impôts** tax form; **~ morte** dead leaf; **~ de température** temperature chart; **~ de vigne** (BOT) vine leaf; (*sur statue*) fig leaf; **~ volante** loose sheet.
feuillet [fœjɛ] *nm* leaf (*pl* leaves), page.
feuilleté, e [fœjte] *a* (CULIN) flaky.
feuilleter [fœjte] *vt* (*livre*) to leaf through.
feuilleton [fœjtɔ̃] *nm* serial.
feuillu, e [fœjy] *a* leafy; **~s** *nmpl* (BOT) broad-leaved trees.
feulement [følmɑ̃] *nm* growl.
feutre [føtʀ(ə)] *nm* felt; (*chapeau*) felt hat; **feutré, e** *a* feltlike; (*pas, voix*) muffled; **feutrer** *vt* to felt; (*fig*) to muffle // *vi*, **se feutrer** *vi* to felt; **feutrine** *nf* (lightweight) felt.
fève [fɛv] *nf* broad bean.
février [fevʀije] *nm* February.
FF *sigle* = *franc français.*
F.F.I. *sigle fpl* = *Forces françaises de l'intérieur* (*1942-45*) // *sigle m member of the F.F.I.*
fi [fi] *excl*: **faire ~ de** to snap one's fingers at.
fiacre [fjakʀ(ə)] *nm* (hackney) cab *ou* carriage.
fiançailles [fjɑ̃saj] *nfpl* engagement *sg.*
fiancé, e [fjɑ̃se] *nm/f* fiancé/fiancée // *a*: **être ~ (à)** to be engaged (to).
fiancer [fjɑ̃se]: **se ~** *vi*: **se ~(avec)** to become engaged (to).
fibre [fibʀ(ə)] *nf* fibre; **~ de verre** fibre-glass, glass fibre; **fibreux, euse** *a* fibrous; (*viande*) stringy.
ficeler [fisle] *vt* to tie up.
ficelle [fisɛl] *nf* string *q*; piece *ou* length of string.
fiche [fiʃ] *nf* (*pour fichier*) (index) card; (*formulaire*) form; (ÉLEC) plug.
ficher [fiʃe] *vt* (*pour un fichier*) to file; (POLICE) to put on file; (*planter*): **~ qch dans** to stick *ou* drive sth into; (*fam*) to do; to give; to stick *ou* shove; **fiche(-moi) le camp** (*fam*) clear off; **fiche-moi la paix** (*fam*) leave me alone; **se ~ dans** (*s'enfoncer*) to get stuck in, embed itself

in; **se ~ de** (*fam*) to make fun of; not to care about.
fichier [fiʃje] *nm* file; card index.
fichu, e [fiʃy] *pp de* **ficher** (*fam*) // *a* (*fam*: *fini, inutilisable*) bust, done for; (: *intensif*) wretched, darned // *nm* (*foulard*) (head)scarf (*pl* scarves); **mal ~** (*fam*) feeling lousy; useless.
fictif, ive [fiktif, -iv] *a* fictitious.
fiction [fiksjɔ̃] *nf* fiction; (*fait imaginé*) invention.
fidèle [fidɛl] *a*: **~ (à)** faithful (to) // *nm/f* (REL): **les ~s** the faithful; (*à l'église*) the congregation; **fidélité** *nf* faithfulness; **fidélité conjugale** marital fidelity.
fief [fjɛf] *nm* fief; (*fig*) preserve; stronghold.
fiel [fjɛl] *nm* gall.
fiente [fjɑ̃t] *nf* (bird) droppings *pl*.
fier [fje]: **se ~ à** *vt* to trust.
fier, fière [fjɛʀ] *a* proud; **~ de** proud of; **avoir fière allure** to cut a fine figure; **~té** *nf* pride.
fièvre [fjɛvʀ(ə)] *nf* fever; **avoir de la ~/39 de ~** to have a high temperature/a temperature of 39°C; **~ typhoïde** typhoid fever; **fiévreux, euse** *a* feverish.
fifre [fifʀ(ə)] *nm* fife; fife-player.
figer [fiʒe] *vt* to congeal; (*fig*: *personne*) to freeze, root to the spot; **se ~** *vi* to congeal; to freeze; (*institutions etc*) to become set, stop evolving.
figue [fig] *nf* fig; **figuier** *nm* fig tree.
figurant, e [figyʀɑ̃, -ɑ̃t] *nm/f*; (THÉÂTRE) walk-on; (CINÉMA) extra.
figuratif, ive [figyʀatif, -iv] *a* representational, figurative.
figuration [figyʀɑsjɔ̃] *nf* walk-on parts *pl*; extras *pl*.
figure [figyʀ] *nf* (*visage*) face; (*image, tracé, forme, personnage*) figure; (*illustration*) picture, diagram; **faire ~ de** to look like.
figuré, e [figyʀe] *a* (*sens*) figurative.
figurer [figyʀe] *vi* to appear // *vt* to represent; **se ~ que** to imagine that.
figurine [figyʀin] *nf* figurine.
fil [fil] *nm* (*brin, fig*: *d'une histoire*) thread; (*du téléphone*) cable, wire; (*textile de lin*) linen; (*d'un couteau*: *tranchant*) edge; **au ~ des années** with the passing of the years; **au ~ de l'eau** with the stream *ou* current; **donner/recevoir un coup de ~** to make/get a phone call; **~ à coudre** (sewing) thread *ou* yarn; **~ électrique** electric wire; **~ de fer** wire; **~ de fer barbelé** barbed wire; **~ à pêche** fishing line; **~ à plomb** plumbline; **~ à souder** soldering wire.
filament [filamɑ̃] *nm* (ÉLEC) filament; (*de liquide*) trickle, thread.
filandreux, euse [filɑ̃dʀø, -øz] *a* stringy.
filasse [filas] *a inv* white blond.
filature [filatyʀ] *nf* (*fabrique*) mill; (*policière*) shadowing *q*, tailing *q*.
file [fil] *nf* line; **~ (d'attente)** queue; **prendre la ~** to join the (end of the) queue; **prendre la ~ de droite** (AUTO) to move into the right-hand lane; **se mettre en ~** to form a line; (AUTO) to get into lane; **en ~ indienne** in single file; **à la ~** *ad* (*d'affilée*) in succession.
filer [file] *vt* (*tissu, toile, verre*) to spin; (*dérouler*: *câble etc*) to pay *ou* let out; to veer out; (*prendre en filature*) to shadow, tail; (*fam*: *donner*): **~ qch à qn** to slip sb sth // *vi* (*bas, maille, liquide, pâte*) to run; (*aller vite*) to fly past *ou* by; (*fam*: *partir*) to make off; **~ doux** to behave o.s., toe the line.
filet [filɛ] *nm* net; (CULIN) fillet; (*d'eau, de sang*) trickle; **~ (à provisions)** string bag.
filetage [filtaʒ] *nm* threading; thread.
fileter [filte] *vt* to thread.
filial, e, aux [filjal, -o] *a* filial // *nf* (COMM) subsidiary.
filiation [filjɑsjɔ̃] *nf* filiation.
filière [filjɛʀ] *nf*: **passer par la ~** to go through the (administrative) channels; **suivre la ~** (*dans sa carrière*) to work one's way up (through the hierarchy).
filiforme [filifɔʀm(ə)] *a* spindly; thread-like.
filigrane [filigʀan] *nm* (*d'un billet, timbre*) watermark; **en ~** (*fig*) showing just beneath the surface.
filin [filɛ̃] *nm* rope.
fille [fij] *nf* girl; (*opposé à fils*) daughter; **~ de joie** prostitute; **~ de salle** waitress; **~-mère** (*péj*) unmarried mother; **fillette** *nf* (little) girl.
filleul, e [fijœl] *nm/f* godchild, godson/daughter.
film [film] *nm* (*pour photo*) (roll of) film; (*œuvre*) film, picture, movie; (*couche*) film; **~ muet/parlant** silent/talking picture *ou* movie; **~ d'animation** animated film; **filmer** *vt* to film.
filon [filɔ̃] *nm* vein, lode; (*fig*) lucrative line, money spinner.
fils [fis] *nm* son; **~ de famille** moneyed young man.
filtre [filtʀ(ə)] *nm* filter; **'~ ou sans ~?'** 'tipped or plain?'; **~ à air** (AUTO) air filter; **filtrer** *vt* to filter; (*fig*: *candidats, visiteurs*) to screen // *vi* to filter (through).
fin [fɛ̃] *nf* end; **~s** *nfpl* (*but*) ends; **à (la) ~ mai** at the end of May; **en ~ de semaine** at the end of the week; **prendre ~** to come to an end; **mettre ~ à** to put an end to; **à la ~** *ad* in the end, eventually; **sans ~** *a* endless // *ad* endlessly.
fin, e [fɛ̃, fin] *a* (*papier, couche, fil*) thin; (*cheveux, poudre, pointe, visage*) fine; (*taille*) neat, slim; (*esprit, remarque*) subtle; shrewd // *ad* (*moudre, couper*) finely // *nf* (*alcool*) liqueur brandy; **~ prêt/soûl** quite ready/drunk; **un ~ tireur** a crack shot; **avoir la vue/l'ouïe ~e** to have sharp eyes/ears, have keen eyesight/hearing; **or/linge/vin ~** fine gold/linen/wine; **repas ~** gourmet meal; **une ~e mouche** (*fig*) a sharp customer; **~es herbes** mixed herbs.
final, e [final] *a, nf* final; **quarts de ~e** quarter finals; **8èmes/16èmes de ~e** 2nd/1st round (*in 5 round knock-out competition*); **~ement** *ad* finally, in the end; (*après tout*) after all; **~iste** *nm/f* finalist.

finance [finɑ̃s] *nf* finance; **~s** *nfpl* (*situation financière*) finances; (*activités financières*) finance *sg*; **moyennant ~** for a fee *ou* consideration; **financer** *vt* to finance; **financier, ière** *a* financial // *nm* financier.
finaud, e [fino, -od] *a* wily.
finesse [finɛs] *nf* thinness; fineness; neatness, slimness; subtlety; shrewdness; **~s** *nfpl* (*subtilités*) niceties; finer points.
fini, e [fini] *a* finished; (*MATH*) finite; (*intensif*): **un égoïste ~** an egotist through and through // *nm* (*d'un objet manufacturé*) finish.
finir [finiʀ] *vt* to finish // *vi* to finish, end; **~ quelque part** to end *ou* finish up somewhere; **~ de faire** to finish doing; (*cesser*) to stop doing; **~ par faire** to end *ou* finish up doing; **il finit par m'agacer** he's beginning to get on my nerves; **~ en pointe/tragédie** to end in a point/in tragedy; **en ~ avec** to be *ou* have done with; **il va mal ~** he will come to a bad end.
finish [finiʃ] *nm* (*SPORT*) finish.
finissage [finisaʒ] *nm* finishing.
finition [finisjɔ̃] *nf* finishing; finish.
finlandais, e [fɛ̃lɑ̃dɛ, -ɛz] *a* Finnish // *nm/f* Finn.
Finlande [fɛ̃lɑ̃d] *nf*: **la ~** Finland; **finnois** *nm* Finnish.
fiole [fjɔl] *nf* phial.
fiord [fjɔʀ(d)] *nm* = **fjord**.
fioriture [fjɔʀityʀ] *nf* embellishment, flourish.
firmament [fiʀmamɑ̃] *nm* firmament, skies *pl*.
firme [fiʀm(ə)] *nf* firm.
fis *vb voir* **faire**.
fisc [fisk] *nm* tax authorities *pl*, ≈ Inland Revenue; **~al, e, aux** *a* tax *cpd*, fiscal; **~alité** *nf* tax system; (*charges*) taxation.
fission [fisjɔ̃] *nf* fission.
fissure [fisyʀ] *nf* crack.
fissurer [fisyʀe] *vt*, **se ~** *vi* to crack.
fiston [fistɔ̃] *nm* (*fam*) son, lad.
fit *vb voir* **faire**.
fixateur [fiksatœʀ] *nm* (*PHOTO*) fixer; (*pour cheveux*) hair cream.
fixatif [fiksatif] *nm* fixative.
fixation [fiksɑsjɔ̃] *nf* fixing; fastening; setting; (*de ski*) binding; (*PSYCH*) fixation.
fixe [fiks(ə)] *a* fixed; (*emploi*) steady, regular // *nm* (*salaire*) basic salary; **à heure ~** at a set time; **menu à prix ~** set menu.
fixé, e [fikse] *a*: **être ~ (sur)** (*savoir à quoi s'en tenir*) to have made up one's mind (about); to know for certain (about).
fixement [fiksəmɑ̃] *ad* (*regarder*) fixedly, steadily.
fixer [fikse] *vt* (*attacher*): **~ qch (à/sur)** to fix *ou* fasten sth (to/onto); (*déterminer*) to fix, set; (*CHIMIE, PHOTO*) to fix; (*poser son regard sur*) to look hard at, stare at; **se ~** (*s'établir*) to settle down; **se ~ sur** (*suj: attention*) to focus on.
fjord [fjɔʀ(d)] *nm* fjord, fiord.
flacon [flakɔ̃] *nm* bottle.
flageller [flaʒele] *vt* to flog, scourge.
flageoler [flaʒɔle] *vi* (*jambes*) to sag.
flageolet [flaʒɔlɛ] *nm* (*MUS*) flageolet; (*CULIN*) dwarf kidney bean.
flagorneur, euse [flagɔʀnœʀ, -øz] *nm/f* toady, fawner.
flagrant, e [flagʀɑ̃, -ɑ̃t] *a* flagrant, blatant; **en ~ délit** in the act, in flagrante delicto.
flair [flɛʀ] *nm* sense of smell; (*fig*) intuition; **flairer** *vt* (*humer*) to sniff (at); (*détecter*) to scent.
flamand, e [flamɑ̃, -ɑ̃d] *a, nm* (*langue*) Flemish // *nm/f* Fleming; **les F~s** the Flemish.
flamant [flamɑ̃] *nm* flamingo.
flambant [flɑ̃bɑ̃] *ad*: **~ neuf** brand new.
flambé, e [flɑ̃be] *a* (*CULIN*) flambé // *nf* blaze; (*fig*) flaring-up, explosion.
flambeau, x [flɑ̃bo] *nm* (flaming) torch.
flamber [flɑ̃be] *vi* to blaze (up) // *vt* (*poulet*) to singe; (*aiguille*) to sterilize.
flamboyant, e [flɑ̃bwajɑ̃, -ɑ̃t] *a* flashing, blazing; flaming.
flamboyer [flɑ̃bwaje] *vi* to blaze (up); to flame.
flamingant, e [flamɛ̃gɑ̃, -ɑ̃t] *a* Flemish-speaking.
flamme [flam] *nf* flame; (*fig*) fire, fervour; **en ~s** on fire, ablaze.
flammèche [flamɛʃ] *nf* (flying) spark.
flan [flɑ̃] *nm* (*CULIN*) custard tart *ou* pie.
flanc [flɑ̃] *nm* side; (*MIL*) flank; **à ~ de colline** on the hillside; **prêter le ~ à** (*fig*) to lay o.s. open to.
flancher [flɑ̃ʃe] *vi* to fail, pack up.
flanelle [flanɛl] *nf* flannel.
flâner [flɑne] *vi* to stroll; **flânerie** *nf* stroll.
flanquer [flɑ̃ke] *vt* to flank; (*fam: mettre*): **~ qch sur/dans** to bung *ou* shove sth on/into; (*: jeter*): **~ par terre/à la porte** to fling to the ground/chuck out.
flapi, e [flapi] *a* dog-tired.
flaque [flak] *nf* (*d'eau*) puddle; (*d'huile, de sang etc*) pool.
flash, *pl* **flashes** [flaʃ] *nm* (*PHOTO*) flash; **~ (d'information)** newsflash.
flasque [flask(ə)] *a* flabby.
flatter [flate] *vt* to flatter; (*caresser*) to stroke; **se ~ de qch** to pride o.s. on sth; **flatterie** *nf* flattery *q*; **flatteur, euse** *a* flattering // *nm/f* flatterer.
fléau, x [fleo] *nm* scourge, curse; (*de balance*) beam; (*pour le blé*) flail.
flèche [flɛʃ] *nf* arrow; (*de clocher*) spire; (*de grue*) jib; **monter en ~** (*fig*) to soar, rocket; **flécher** *vt* to arrow, mark with arrows; **fléchette** *nf* dart; **fléchettes** *nfpl* (*jeu*) darts *sg*.
fléchir [fleʃiʀ] *vt* (*corps, genou*) to bend; (*fig*) to sway, weaken // *vi* (*poutre*) to sag, bend; (*fig*) to weaken, flag; **fléchissement** *nm* bending; sagging; flagging.
flegmatique [flɛgmatik] *a* phlegmatic.
flegme [flɛgm(ə)] *nm* composure.
flemmard, e [flemaʀ, -aʀd(ə)] *nm/f* lazybones *sg*, loafer.
flétrir [fletʀiʀ] *vt* to wither; (*stigmatiser*) to condemn (in the most severe terms); **se ~** *vi* to wither.

fleur [flœʀ] *nf* flower ; (*d'un arbre*) blossom, bloom ; **être en ~** (*arbre*) to be in blossom *ou* bloom ; **tissu à ~s** flowered *ou* flowery fabric ; **à ~ de terre** just above the ground ; **~ de lis** fleur-de-lis.
fleurer [flœʀe] *vt*: **~ la lavande** to be fragrant with the scent of lavender.
fleuret [flœʀɛ] *nm* (*arme*) foil ; (*sport*) fencing.
fleuri, e [flœʀi] *a* in flower *ou* bloom ; surrounded by flowers ; (*fig*) flowery ; florid.
fleurir [flœʀiʀ] *vi* (*rose*) to flower ; (*arbre*) to blossom ; (*fig*) to flourish // *vt* (*tombe*) to put flowers on ; (*chambre*) to decorate with flowers.
fleuriste [flœʀist(ə)] *nm/f* florist.
fleuron [flœʀɔ̃] *nm* jewel (*fig*).
fleuve [flœv] *nm* river.
flexible [flɛksibl(ə)] *a* flexible.
flexion [flɛksjɔ̃] *nf* flexing, bending ; (LING) inflection.
flibustier [flibystje] *nm* buccaneer.
flic [flik] *nm* (*fam*: *péj*) cop.
flirter [flœʀte] *vi* to flirt.
F.L.N. *sigle m* = *Front de libération nationale* (*during the Algerian war*).
flocon [flɔkɔ̃] *nm* flake ; (*de laine etc*: *boulette*) flock ; **~s d'avoine** oatflakes.
flonflons [flɔ̃flɔ̃] *nmpl* blare *sg*.
floraison [flɔʀɛzɔ̃] *nf* flowering ; blossoming ; flourishing.
floral, e, aux [flɔʀal, -o] *a* floral, flower *cpd*.
floralies [flɔʀali] *nfpl* flower show *sg*.
flore [flɔʀ] *nf* flora.
florissant, e [flɔʀisɑ̃, -ɑ̃t] *vb voir* **fleurir** // *a* flourishing.
flot [flo] *nm* flood, stream ; (*marée*) flood tide ; **~s** *nmpl* (*de la mer*) waves ; **être à ~** (NAVIG) to be afloat ; (*fig*) to be on an even keel ; **entrer à ~s** to be streaming *ou* pouring in.
flottage [flɔtaʒ] *nm* (*du bois*) floating.
flottaison [flɔtɛzɔ̃] *nf*: **ligne de ~** waterline.
flottant, e [flɔtɑ̃, -ɑ̃t] *a* (*vêtement*) loose (-fitting) ; (*cours, barème*) floating.
flotte [flɔt] *nf* (NAVIG) fleet ; (*fam*) water ; rain.
flottement [flɔtmɑ̃] *nm* (*fig*) wavering, hesitation.
flotter [flɔte] *vi* to float ; (*nuage, odeur*) to drift ; (*drapeau*) to fly ; (*vêtements*) to hang loose ; (*monnaie*) to float // *vt* to float ; **faire ~** to float ; **flotteur** *nm* float.
flottille [flɔtij] *nf* flotilla.
flou, e [flu] *a* fuzzy, blurred ; (*fig*) woolly, vague.
flouer [flue] *vt* to swindle.
fluctuation [flyktɥasjɔ̃] *nf* fluctuation.
fluet, te [flyɛ, -ɛt] *a* thin, slight.
fluide [flɥid] *a* fluid ; (*circulation etc*) flowing freely // *nm* fluid ; (*force*) (mysterious) power ; **fluidité** *nf* fluidity ; free flow.
fluor [flyɔʀ] *nm* fluorine.
fluorescent, e [flyɔʀesɑ̃, -ɑ̃t] *a* fluorescent.
flûte [flyt] *nf* flute ; (*verre*) flute glass ; (*pain*) long loaf (*pl* loaves) ; **~!** drat it! ; **petite ~** piccolo (*pl* s) ; **~ à bec** recorder ; **~ de Pan** panpipes *pl*; **flûtiste** *nm/f* flautist, flute player.
fluvial, e, aux [flyvjal, -o] *a* river *cpd*, fluvial.
flux [fly] *nm* incoming tide ; (*écoulement*) flow ; **le ~ et le reflux** the ebb and flow.
fluxion [flyksjɔ̃] *nf*: **~ de poitrine** pneumonia.
FM *sigle voir* **modulation**.
F.M.I. *sigle m voir* **fonds**.
foc [fɔk] *nm* jib.
focal, e, aux [fɔkal, -o] *a* focal // *nf* focal length.
fœtal, e, aux [fetal, -o] *a* foetal, fetal.
fœtus [fetys] *nm* foetus, fetus.
foi [fwa] *nf* faith ; **sous la ~ du serment** under *ou* on oath ; **ajouter ~ à** to lend credence to ; **digne de ~** reliable ; **sur la ~ de** on the word *ou* strength of ; **être de bonne/mauvaise ~** to be sincere/insincere.
foie [fwa] *nm* liver ; **~ gras** foie gras.
foin [fwɛ̃] *nm* hay ; **faire les ~s** to make hay ; **faire du ~** (*fig*: *fam*) to kick up a row.
foire [fwaʀ] *nf* fair ; (*fête foraine*) (fun) fair ; **faire la ~** (*fig*: *fam*) to whoop it up ; **~ (exposition)** trade fair.
fois [fwa] *nf*: **une/deux ~** once/twice ; **trois/vingt ~** three/twenty times ; **2 ~ 2** twice 2, 2 times 2 ; **deux/quatre ~ plus grand (que)** twice/four times as large (as) ; **une ~** (*dans le passé*) once ; (*dans le futur*) sometime ; **une ~ pour toutes** once and for all ; **une ~ que c'est fait** once it's done ; **une ~ parti** once he had left ; **des ~** (*parfois*) sometimes ; **cette ~** this (*ou* that) time ; **à la ~** (*ensemble*) (all) at once ; **à la ~ grand et beau** both tall and handsome.
foison [fwazɔ̃] *nf*: **une ~ de** an abundance of ; **à ~** *ad* in plenty.
foisonner [fwazɔne] *vi* to abound ; **~ en** *ou* **de** to abound in.
fol [fɔl] *a voir* **fou**.
folâtre [fɔlɑtʀ(ə)] *a* playful.
folâtrer [fɔlɑtʀe] *vi* to frolic (about).
folie [fɔli] *nf* (*d'une décision, d'un acte*) madness, folly ; (*état*) madness, insanity ; (*acte*) folly ; **la ~ des grandeurs** delusions of grandeur ; **faire des ~s** (*en dépenses*) to be extravagant.
folklore [fɔlklɔʀ] *nm* folklore ; **folklorique** *a* folk *cpd* ; (*fam*) weird.
folle [fɔl] *a, nf voir* **fou** ; **~ment** *ad* (*très*) madly, wildly.
follet [fɔlɛ] *am*: **feu ~** will-o'-the-wisp.
fomenter [fɔmɑ̃te] *vt* to stir up, foment.
foncé, e [fɔ̃se] *a* dark ; **bleu ~** dark blue.
foncer [fɔ̃se] *vt* to make darker // *vi* to go darker ; (*fam*: *aller vite*) to tear *ou* belt along ; **~ sur** to charge at.
foncier, ière [fɔ̃sje, -jɛʀ] *a* (*honnêteté etc*) basic, fundamental ; (*malhonnêteté*) deep-rooted, (COMM) real estate *cpd* ; **foncièrement** *ad* basically ; thoroughly.
fonction [fɔ̃ksjɔ̃] *nf* (*rôle*, MATH, LING) function ; (*emploi, poste*) post, position ; **~s** (*professionnelles*) duties ; **entrer en ~s** to take up one's post *ou* duties ; to take

up office; **voiture de ~** car provided with the post; **être ~ de** (*dépendre de*) to depend on; **en ~ de** (*par rapport à*) according to; **faire ~ de** to serve as; **la ~ publique** the public *ou* state service.
fonctionnaire [fɔ̃ksjɔnɛʀ] *nm/f* state employee, local authority employee; (*dans l'administration*) ≈ civil servant.
fonctionnel, le [fɔ̃ksjɔnɛl] *a* functional.
fonctionnement [fɔ̃ksjɔnmɑ̃] *nm* functioning.
fonctionner [fɔ̃ksjɔne] *vi* to work, function; (*entreprise*) to operate, function; **faire ~** to work, operate.
fond [fɔ̃] *nm voir aussi* **fonds**; (*d'un récipient, trou*) bottom; (*d'une salle, scène*) back; (*d'un tableau, décor*) background; (*opposé à la forme*) content; (SPORT): **le ~** long distance (running); **au ~ de** at the bottom of; at the back of; **à ~** *ad* (*connaître, soutenir*) thoroughly; (*appuyer, visser*) right down *ou* home; **à ~ (de train)** *ad* (*fam*) full tilt; **dans le ~, au ~** *ad* (*en somme*) basically, really; **de ~ en comble** *ad* from top to bottom; **~ sonore** background noise; **~ de teint** make-up base.
fondamental, e, aux [fɔ̃damɑ̃tal, -o] *a* fundamental.
fondant, e [fɔ̃dɑ̃, -ɑ̃t] *a* (*neige*) melting; (*poire*) that melts in the mouth; (*chocolat*) fondant.
fondateur, trice [fɔ̃datœʀ, -tʀis] *nm/f* founder; **membre ~** founder member.
fondation [fɔ̃dɑsjɔ̃] *nf* founding; (*établissement*) foundation; **~s** *nfpl* (*d'une maison*) foundations; **travaux de ~** foundation works.
fondé, e [fɔ̃de] *a* (*accusation etc*) well-founded; **mal ~** unfounded; **être ~ à croire** to have grounds for believing *ou* good reason to believe; **~ de pouvoir** *nm* authorized representative; (banking) executive (*having the signature*).
fondement [fɔ̃dmɑ̃] *nm* (*derrière*) behind; **~s** *nmpl* foundations; **sans ~** *a* (*rumeur etc*) groundless, unfounded.
fonder [fɔ̃de] *vt* to found; (*fig*): **~ qch sur** to base sth on; **se ~ sur** (*suj*: *personne*) to base o.s. on.
fonderie [fɔ̃dʀi] *nf* smelting works *sg*.
fondeur [fɔ̃dœʀ] *nm*: **(ouvrier) ~** caster.
fondre [fɔ̃dʀ(ə)] *vt* to melt; (*dans l'eau*: *sucre, sel*) to dissolve; (*fig*: *mélanger*) to merge, blend // *vi* to melt; to dissolve; (*fig*) to melt away; (*se précipiter*): **~ sur** to swoop down on; **faire ~** to melt; to dissolve; **~ en larmes** to burst into tears.
fondrière [fɔ̃dʀijɛʀ] *nf* rut.
fonds [fɔ̃] *nm* (*de bibliothèque*) collection; (COMM): **~ (de commerce)** business; (*fig*): **~ de probité** *etc* fund of integrity *etc* // *nmpl* (*argent*) funds; **à ~ perdus** *ad* with little or no hope of getting the money back; **F~ Monétaire International (FMI)** International Monetary Fund (IMF); **~ de roulement** *nm* float.
fondu, e [fɔ̃dy] *a* (*beurre, neige*) melted; (*métal*) molten // *nm* (CINÉMA): **~ (enchaîné)** dissolve // *nf* (CULIN) fondue.
font *vb voir* **faire**.
fontaine [fɔ̃tɛn] *nf* fountain; (*source*) spring.
fonte [fɔ̃t] *nf* melting; (*métal*) cast iron; **la ~ des neiges** the (spring) thaw.
fonts baptismaux [fɔ̃batismo] *nmpl* (baptismal) font *sg*.
football [futbol] *nm* football, soccer; **~ de table** table football; **~eur** *nm* footballer, football *ou* soccer player.
footing [futiŋ] *nm* jogging.
for [fɔʀ] *nm*: **dans son ~ intérieur** in one's heart of hearts.
forage [fɔʀaʒ] *nm* drilling, boring.
forain, e [fɔʀɛ̃, -ɛn] *a* fairground *cpd* // *nm* stallholder; fairground entertainer.
forçat [fɔʀsa] *nm* convict.
force [fɔʀ(ə)] *nf* strength; (*puissance*: *surnaturelle etc*) power; (PHYSIQUE, MÉCANIQUE) force; **~s** *nfpl* (*physiques*) strength *sg*; (MIL) forces; (*effectifs*): **d'importantes ~s de police** big contingents of police; **à ~ d'insister** by dint of insisting; as he (*ou* I) kept on insisting; **de ~** *ad* forcibly, by force; **par la ~** using force; **faire ~ de rames/voiles** to ply the oars/cram on sail; **être de ~ à faire** to be up to doing; **de première ~** first class; **~ d'âme** fortitude; **~ de frappe** strike force; **~ d'inertie** force of inertia; **la ~ publique** the authorities responsible for public order; **~s d'intervention** peace-keeping force *sg*; **les ~s de l'ordre** the police.
forcé, e [fɔʀse] *a* forced; unintended; inevitable.
forcément [fɔʀsemɑ̃] *ad* necessarily; inevitably; (*bien sûr*) of course.
forcené, e [fɔʀsəne] *a* frenzied // *nm/f* maniac.
forceps [fɔʀsɛps] *nm* forceps *pl*.
forcer [fɔʀse] *vt* (*contraindre*): **~ qn à faire** to force sb to do; (*porte, serrure, plante*) to force; (*moteur, voix*) to strain // *vi* (SPORT) to overtax o.s.; **~ la dose/l'allure** to overdo it/increase the pace; **~ l'attention/le respect** to command attention/respect.
forcing [fɔʀsiŋ] *nm*: **faire le ~** to pile on the pressure.
forcir [fɔʀsiʀ] *vi* (*grossir*) to broaden out; (*vent*) to freshen.
forer [fɔʀe] *vt* to drill, bore.
forestier, ière [fɔʀɛstje, -jɛʀ] *a* forest *cpd*.
foret [fɔʀɛ] *nm* drill.
forêt [fɔʀɛ] *nf* forest.
foreuse [fɔʀøz] *nf* (electric) drill.
forfait [fɔʀfɛ] *nm* (COMM) fixed *ou* set price; all-in deal *ou* price; (*crime*) infamy; **déclarer ~** to withdraw; **gagner par ~** to win by a walkover; **travailler à ~** to work for a lump sum; **forfaitaire** *a* inclusive; set; **~-vacances** *nm* (all-inclusive) holiday package.
forfanterie [fɔʀfɑ̃tʀi] *nf* boastfulness *q*.
forge [fɔʀʒ(ə)] *nf* forge, smithy.
forger [fɔʀʒe] *vt* to forge; (*fig*: *personnalité*) to form; (: *prétexte*) to contrive, make up; **être forgé de toutes pièces** to be a complete fabrication.
forgeron [fɔʀʒəʀɔ̃] *nm* (black)smith.

formaliser [fɔʀmalize]: **se ~** *vi*: **se ~ (de)** to take offence (at).
formalité [fɔʀmalite] *nf* formality.
format [fɔʀma] *nm* size; **petit ~** small size; (PHOTO) 35 mm (film).
formation [fɔʀmɑsjɔ̃] *nf* forming; training; (MUS) group; (MIL, AVIAT, GÉO) formation; **la ~ professionnelle** professional training.
forme [fɔʀm(ə)] *nf* (*gén*) form; (*d'un objet*) shape, form; **~s** *nfpl* (*bonnes manières*) proprieties; (*d'une femme*) figure *sg*; **en ~ de poire** pear-shaped, in the shape of a pear; **être en ~** (SPORT *etc*) to be on form; **en bonne et due ~** in due form; **prendre ~** to take shape.
formel, le [fɔʀmɛl] *a* (*preuve, décision*) definite, positive; (*logique*) formal; **~lement** *ad* (*absolument*) positively.
former [fɔʀme] *vt* (*gén*) to form; (*éduquer*: *soldat, ingénieur etc*) to train; **se ~** *vi* to form.
formidable [fɔʀmidabl(ə)] *a* tremendous.
formol [fɔʀmɔl] *nm* formalin, formol.
formulaire [fɔʀmylɛʀ] *nm* form.
formule [fɔʀmyl] *nf* (*gén*) formula; (*formulaire*) form; **~ de politesse** polite phrase; letter ending.
formuler [fɔʀmyle] *vt* (*émettre*: *réponse, vœux*) to formulate; (*expliciter*: *sa pensée*) to express.
fort, e [fɔʀ, fɔʀt(ə)] *a* strong; (*intensité, rendement*) high, great; (*corpulent*) stout // *ad* (*serrer, frapper*) hard; (*sonner*) loud(ly); (*beaucoup*) greatly, very much; (*très*) most // *nm* (*édifice*) fort; (*point fort*) strong point, forte; **c'est un peu ~!** it's a bit much!; **avoir ~ à faire pour faire** to have a hard job doing; **se faire ~ de ...** to claim one can ...; **~ bien/peu** very well/few; **au plus ~ de** (*au milieu de*) in the thick of, at the height of.
forteresse [fɔʀtəʀɛs] *nf* fortress.
fortifiant [fɔʀtifjɑ̃] *nm* tonic.
fortifications [fɔʀtifikɑsjɔ̃] *nfpl* fortifications.
fortifier [fɔʀtifje] *vt* to strengthen, fortify; (MIL) to fortify.
fortin [fɔʀtɛ̃] *nm* (small) fort.
fortiori [fɔʀtjɔʀi]: **à ~** *ad* all the more so.
fortuit, e [fɔʀtɥi, -it] *a* fortuitous, chance *cpd*.
fortune [fɔʀtyn] *nf* fortune; **faire ~** to make one's fortune; **de ~** *a* makeshift; chance *cpd*.
fortuné, e [fɔʀtyne] *a* wealthy, well-off.
forum [fɔʀɔm] *nm* forum.
fosse [fos] *nf* (*grand trou*) pit; (*tombe*) grave; **la ~ aux lions/ours** the lions' den/bear pit; **~ commune** common *ou* communal grave; **~ (d'orchestre)** (orchestra) pit; **~ à purin** cesspit; **~s nasales** nasal fossae *pl*.
fossé [fose] *nm* ditch; (*fig*) gulf, gap.
fossette [fosɛt] *nf* dimple.
fossile [fosil] *nm* fossil // *a* fossilized, fossil.
fossoyeur [foswajœʀ] *nm* gravedigger.
fou(fol), folle [fu, fɔl] *a* mad; (*déréglé etc*) wild, erratic; (*fam*: *extrême, très grand*) terrific, tremendous // *nm/f* madman/woman // *nm* (*du roi*) jester, fool; (ÉCHECS) bishop; **être ~ de** to be mad *ou* crazy about; **faire le ~** (*enfant etc*) to play *ou* act the fool; **avoir le ~ rire** to have the giggles.
foudre [fudʀ(ə)] *nf* lightning; **~s** *nfpl* (*colère*) wrath *sg*.
foudroyant, e [fudʀwajɑ̃, -ɑ̃t] *a* lightning *cpd*, stunning.
foudroyer [fudʀwaje] *vt* to strike down; **il a été foudroyé** he was struck by lightning.
fouet [fwɛ] *nm* whip; (CULIN) whisk; **de plein ~** *ad* (*se heurter*) head on; **~ter** *vt* to whip; to whisk.
fougère [fuʒɛʀ] *nf* fern.
fougue [fug] *nf* ardour, spirit; **fougueux, euse** *a* fiery, ardent.
fouille [fuj] *nf* search; **~s** *nfpl* (*archéologiques*) excavations; **passer à la ~** to be searched.
fouiller [fuje] *vt* to search; (*creuser*) to dig // *vi*: **~ dans/parmi** to rummage in/among.
fouillis [fuji] *nm* jumble, muddle.
fouine [fwin] *nf* stone marten.
fouiner [fwine] *vi* (*péj*): **~ dans** to nose around *ou* about in.
fouisseur, euse [fwisœʀ, -øz] *a* burrowing.
foulante [fulɑ̃t] *af*: **pompe ~** force pump.
foulard [fulaʀ] *nm* scarf (*pl* scarves).
foule [ful] *nf* crowd; **la ~** crowds *pl*; **les ~s** the masses; **une ~ de** masses of.
foulée [fule] *nf* stride.
fouler [fule] *vt* to press; (*sol*) to tread upon; **se ~** (*fam*) to overexert o.s.; **se ~ la cheville** to sprain one's ankle; **~ aux pieds** to trample underfoot.
foulure [fulyʀ] *nf* sprain.
four [fuʀ] *nm* oven; (*de potier*) kiln; (THÉÂTRE: *échec*) flop.
fourbe [fuʀb(ə)] *a* deceitful; **~rie** *nf* deceitfulness; deceit.
fourbi [fuʀbi] *nm* (*fam*) gear, clobber.
fourbir [fuʀbiʀ] *vt*: **~ ses armes** (*fig*) to get ready for the fray.
fourbu, e [fuʀby] *a* exhausted.
fourche [fuʀʃ(ə)] *nf* pitchfork; (*de bicyclette*) fork.
fourchette [fuʀʃɛt] *nf* fork; (STATISTIQUE) bracket, margin.
fourchu, e [fuʀʃy] *a* split; forked.
fourgon [fuʀgɔ̃] *nm* van; (RAIL) wag(g)on; **~ mortuaire** hearse.
fourgonnette [fuʀgɔnɛt] *nf* (delivery) van.
fourmi [fuʀmi] *nf* ant; **~s** *nfpl* (*fig*) pins and needles; **~lière** *nf* ant-hill.
fourmiller [fuʀmije] *vi* to swarm; **~ de** to be teeming with; to be swarming with.
fournaise [fuʀnɛz] *nf* blaze; (*fig*) furnace, oven.
fourneau, x [fuʀno] *nm* stove.
fournée [fuʀne] *nf* batch.
fourni, e [fuʀni] *a* (*barbe, cheveux*) thick; (*magasin*): **bien ~ (en)** well stocked (with).
fournir [fuʀniʀ] *vt* to supply; (*preuve, exemple*) to provide, supply; (*effort*) to put in; **~ qch à qn** to supply sth to sb, to supply *ou* provide sb with sth; **~ qn en**

(*COMM*) to supply sb with; **fournisseur, euse** *nm/f* supplier.
fourniture [fuRnityR] *nf* supply(ing); **~s** *nfpl* supplies; **~s de bureau** office supplies, stationery; **~s scolaires** school stationery.
fourrage [fuRaʒ] *nm* fodder, forage.
fourrager [fuRaʒe] *vi*: **~ dans/ parmi** to rummage through/among.
fourrager, ère [fuRaʒe, -ɛR] *a* fodder *cpd.*
fourré, e [fuRe] *a* (*bonbon, chocolat*) filled; (*manteau, botte*) fur-lined // *nm* thicket.
fourreau, x [fuRo] *nm* sheath; (*de parapluie*) cover.
fourrer [fuRe] *vt* (*fam*): **~ qch dans** to stick *ou* shove sth into; **se ~ dans/sous** to get into/under.
fourre-tout [fuRtu] *nm inv* (*sac*) holdall; (*péj*) junk room *ou* cupboard; (*fig*) rag-bag.
fourreur [fuRœR] *nm* furrier.
fourrière [fuRjɛR] *nf* pound.
fourrure [fuRyR] *nf* fur; (*sur l'animal*) coat; **manteau/col de ~** fur coat/collar.
fourvoyer [fuRvwaje]: **se ~** *vi* to go astray, stray; **se ~ dans** to stray into.
foutre [futR(ə)] *vt* (*fam!*) = **ficher** (*fam*); **foutu, e** *a* (*fam!*) = **fichu, e** *a.*
foyer [fwaje] *nm* (*de cheminée*) hearth; (*fig*) seat, centre; family; home; (social) club; hostel; (*salon*) foyer; (*OPTIQUE, PHOTO*) focus *sg*; **lunettes à double ~** bi-focal glasses.
fracas [fRaka] *nm* din; crash; roar.
fracassant, e [fRakasɑ̃, -ɑ̃t] *a* sensational, staggering.
fracasser [fRakase] *vt* to smash.
fraction [fRaksjɔ̃] *nf* fraction; **fractionner** *vt* to divide (up), split (up).
fracture [fRaktyR] *nf* fracture; **~ du crâne** fractured skull; **~ de la jambe** broken leg.
fracturer [fRaktyRe] *vt* (*coffre, serrure*) to break open; (*os, membre*) to fracture.
fragile [fRaʒil] *a* fragile, delicate; (*fig*) frail; **fragilité** *nf* fragility.
fragment [fRagmɑ̃] *nm* (*d'un objet*) fragment, piece; (*d'un texte*) passage, extract; **fragmentaire** *a* sketchy; **fragmenter** *vt* to split up.
frai [fRɛ] *nm* spawn; spawning.
fraîche [fRɛʃ] *a voir* **frais**; **~ment** *ad* coolly; freshly, newly; **fraîcheur** *nf* coolness; freshness; **fraîchir** *vi* to get cooler; (*vent*) to freshen.
frais, fraîche [fRɛ, fRɛʃ] *a* (*air, eau, accueil*) cool; (*petit pois, œufs, souvenir, couleur, troupes*) fresh // *ad* (*récemment*) newly, fresh(ly); **il fait ~** it's cool; **servir ~** chill before serving, serve chilled // *nm*: **mettre au ~** to put in a cool place; **prendre le ~** to take a breath of cool air // *nmpl* (*débours*) expenses; (*COMM*) costs; charges; **faire des ~** to spend; to go to a lot of expense; **~ de déplacement** travel(ling) expenses; **~généraux** overheads; **~ de scolarité** school fees.
fraise [fRɛz] *nf* strawberry; (*TECH*) countersink (bit); (*de dentiste*) drill; **~ des bois** wild strawberry; **fraiser** *vt* to countersink; **fraisier** *nm* strawberry plant.
framboise [fRɑ̃bwaz] *nf* raspberry; **framboisier** *nm* raspberry bush.
franc, franche [fRɑ̃, fRɑ̃ʃ] *a* (*personne*) frank, straightforward; (*visage, rire*) open; (*net: refus, couleur*) clear; (*: coupure*) clean; (*intensif*) downright; (*exempt*): **~ de port** post free, postage paid, carriage paid // *ad*: **parler ~** to be frank *ou* candid // *nm* franc.
français, e [fRɑ̃sɛ, -ɛz] *a* French // *nm/f*: **F~, e** Frenchman/woman // *nm* (*langue*) French; **les F~** the French.
France [fRɑ̃s] *nf*: **la ~** France.
franche [fRɑ̃ʃ] *a voir* **franc**; **~ment** *ad* frankly; clearly; (*tout à fait*) downright.
franchir [fRɑ̃ʃiR] *vt* (*obstacle*) to clear, get over; (*seuil, ligne, rivière*) to cross; (*distance*) to cover.
franchise [fRɑ̃ʃiz] *nf* frankness; (*douanière, d'impôt*) exemption; (*ASSURANCES*) excess.
franciser [fRɑ̃size] *vt* to gallicize, Frenchify.
franc-maçon [fRɑ̃masɔ̃] *nm* freemason; **franc-maçonnerie** *nf* freemasonry.
franco [fRɑ̃ko] *ad* (*COMM*) carriage paid, postage paid.
franco... [fRɑ̃ko] *préfixe*: **~phile** *a* francophile; **~phone** *a* French-speaking // *nm/f* French speaker; **~phonie** *nf* French-speaking communities.
franc-parler [fRɑ̃paRle] *nm inv* outspokenness.
franc-tireur [fRɑ̃tiRœR] *nm* (*MIL*) irregular; (*fig*) freelance.
frange [fRɑ̃ʒ] *nf* fringe.
frangipane [fRɑ̃ʒipan] *nf* almond paste.
franquette [fRɑ̃kɛt]: **à la bonne ~** *ad* without (any) fuss.
frappe [fRap] *nf* (*d'une dactylo, pianiste, machine à écrire*) touch; (*BOXE*) punch; (*péj*) hood, thug.
frappé, e [fRape] *a* iced.
frapper [fRape] *vt* to hit, strike; (*étonner*) to strike; (*monnaie*) to strike, stamp; **se ~** (*s'inquiéter*) to get worked up; **~ à la porte** to knock (at) the door; **~ dans ses mains** to clap one's hands; **~ du poing sur** to bang one's fist on; **frappé de stupeur** dumbfounded.
frasques [fRask(ə)] *nfpl* escapades.
fraternel, le [fRatɛRnɛl] *a* brotherly, fraternal.
fraterniser [fRatɛRnize] *vi* to fraternize.
fraternité [fRatɛRnite] *nf* brotherhood.
fratricide [fRatRisid] *a* fratricidal.
fraude [fRod] *nf* fraud; (*SCOL*) cheating; **passer qch en ~** to smuggle sth in (*ou* out); **~ fiscale** tax evasion; **frauder** *vi, vt* to cheat; **fraudeur, euse** *nm/f* person guilty of fraud; candidate who cheats; tax evader; **frauduleux, euse** *a* fraudulent.
frayer [fReje] *vt* to open up, clear // *vi* to spawn; (*fréquenter*): **~ avec** to mix *ou* associate with; **se ~ un passage dans** to clear o.s. a path through, force one's way through.
frayeur [fRɛjœR] *nf* fright.
fredaines [fRədɛn] *nfpl* mischief *sg,* escapades.

fredonner [fʀədɔne] *vt* to hum.
freezer [fʀizœʀ] *nm* freezing compartment.
frégate [fʀegat] *nf* frigate.
frein [fʀɛ̃] *nm* brake ; **mettre un ~ à** (*fig*) to put a brake on, check ; **~ à main** handbrake ; **~ moteur** engine braking ; **~s à disques** disc brakes ; **~s à tambour** drum brakes.
freinage [fʀɛnaʒ] *nm* braking ; **distance de ~** braking distance ; **traces de ~** tyre marks.
freiner [fʀene] *vi* to brake // *vt* (*progrès etc*) to check.
frelaté, e [fʀəlate] *a* adulterated ; (*fig*) tainted.
frêle [fʀɛl] *a* frail, fragile.
frelon [fʀəlɔ̃] *nm* hornet.
frémir [fʀemiʀ] *vi* to tremble, shudder ; to shiver ; to quiver.
frêne [fʀɛn] *nm* ash.
frénénsie [fʀenezi] *nf* frenzy ; **frénétique** *a* frenzied, frenetic.
fréquemment [fʀekamɑ̃] *ad* frequently.
fréquence [fʀekɑ̃s] *nf* frequency.
fréquent, e [fʀekɑ̃, -ɑ̃t] *a* frequent.
fréquentation [fʀekɑ̃tɑsjɔ̃] *nf* frequenting ; seeing ; **~s** *nfpl* company *sg.*
fréquenté, e [fʀekɑ̃te] *a*: **très ~** (very) busy ; **mal ~** patronized by disreputable elements.
fréquenter [fʀekɑ̃te] *vt* (*lieu*) to frequent ; (*personne*) to see (frequently).
frère [fʀɛʀ] *nm* brother.
fresque [fʀɛsk(ə)] *nf* (ART) fresco.
fret [fʀɛ] *nm* freight.
fréter [fʀete] *vt* to charter.
frétiller [fʀetije] *vi* to wriggle.
fretin [fʀətɛ̃] *nm*: **le menu ~** the small fry.
friable [fʀijabl(ə)] *a* crumbly, friable.
friand, e [fʀijɑ̃, -ɑ̃d] *a*: **~ de** very fond of.
friandise [fʀijɑ̃diz] *nf* sweet.
fric [fʀik] *nm* (*fam*) cash.
fric-frac [fʀikfʀak] *nm* break-in.
friche [fʀiʃ]: **en ~** *a, ad* (lying) fallow.
friction [fʀiksjɔ̃] *nf* (*massage*) rub, rub-down ; (*chez le coiffeur*) scalp massage ; (*TECH*, fig) friction ; **frictionner** *vt* to rub (down) ; to massage.
frigidaire [fʀiʒidɛʀ] *nm* ® refrigerator.
frigide [fʀiʒid] *a* frigid ; **frigidité** *nf* frigidity.
frigo [fʀigo] *nm* fridge.
frigorifier [fʀigɔʀifje] *vt* to refrigerate ; **frigorifique** *a* refrigerating.
frileux, euse [fʀilø, -øz] *a* sensitive to (the) cold.
frimas [fʀimɑ] *nmpl* wintry weather *sg.*
frimousse [fʀimus] *nf* (sweet) little face.
fringale [fʀɛ̃gal] *nf*: **avoir la ~** to be ravenous.
fringant, e [fʀɛ̃gɑ̃, -ɑ̃t] *a* dashing.
fripé, e [fʀipe] *a* crumpled.
fripier, ère [fʀipje, -jɛʀ] *nm/f* secondhand clothes dealer.
fripon, ne [fʀipɔ̃, -ɔn] *a* roguish, mischievous // *nm/f* rascal, rogue.
fripouille [fʀipuj] *nf* scoundrel.
frire [fʀiʀ] *vt, vi,* **faire ~** to fry.
frise [fʀiz] *nf* frieze.
frisé, e [fʀize] *a* curly, curly-haired ; **(chicorée) ~e** curly endive.
friser [fʀize] *vt, vi* to curl ; **se faire ~** to have one's hair curled.
frisson [fʀisɔ̃] *nm* shudder, shiver ; quiver ; **frissonner** *vi* to shudder, shiver ; to quiver.
frit, e [fʀi, fʀit] *pp de* **frire** // *a* fried // *nf*: **(pommes) ~es** chips, French fried potatoes ; **friteuse** *nf* chip pan ; **friture** *nf* (*huile*) (deep) fat ; (*plat*): **friture (de poissons)** fried fish ; (*RADIO*) crackle, crackling *q.*
frivole [fʀivɔl] *a* frivolous.
froid, e [fʀwa, fʀwad] *a, nm* cold ; **il fait ~** it's cold ; **avoir ~** to be cold ; **prendre ~** to catch a chill *ou* cold ; **jeter un ~** (*fig*) to cast a chill ; **être en ~ avec** to be on bad terms with ; **froidement** *ad* (*accueillir*) coldly ; (*décider*) coolly.
froisser [fʀwase] *vt* to crumple (up), crease ; (*fig*) to hurt, offend ; **se ~** *vi* to crumple, crease ; to take offence *ou* umbrage ; **se ~ un muscle** to strain a muscle.
frôler [fʀole] *vt* to brush against ; (*suj: projectile*) to skim past ; (*fig*) to come within a hair's breadth of ; to come very close to.
fromage [fʀɔmaʒ] *nm* cheese ; **~ blanc** soft white cheese ; **~ de tête** pork brawn ; **fromager, ère** *nm/f* cheesemonger ; **fromagerie** *nf* cheese dairy.
froment [fʀɔmɑ̃] *nm* wheat.
froncer [fʀɔ̃se] *vt* to gather ; **~ les sourcils** to frown.
frondaisons [fʀɔ̃dɛzɔ̃] *nfpl* foliage *sg.*
fronde [fʀɔ̃d] *nf* sling ; (*fig*) rebellion, rebelliousness.
front [fʀɔ̃] *nm* forehead, brow ; (*MIL*) front ; **avoir le ~ de faire** to have the effrontery *ou* front to do ; **de ~** *ad* (*se heurter*) head-on ; (*rouler*) together (*i.e. 2 or 3 abreast*) ; (*simultanément*) at once ; **faire ~ à** to face up to ; **~ de mer** (sea) front ; **frontal, e, aux** *a* frontal.
frontalier, ière [fʀɔ̃talje, -jɛʀ] *a* border *cpd,* frontier *cpd* // *nm/f*: **(travailleurs) ~s** workers who cross the border to go to work, commuters from across the border.
frontière [fʀɔ̃tjɛʀ] *nf* (*GÉO, POL*) frontier, border ; (*fig*) frontier, boundary.
frontispice [fʀɔ̃tispis] *nm* frontispiece.
fronton [fʀɔ̃tɔ̃] *nm* pediment ; (*de pelote basque*) (front) wall.
frottement [fʀɔtmɑ̃] *nm* rubbing, scraping ; rubbing *ou* scraping noise.
frotter [fʀɔte] *vi* to rub, scrape // *vt* to rub ; (*pour nettoyer*) to rub (up) ; to scrub ; **~ une allumette** to strike a match.
frottoir [fʀɔtwaʀ] *nm* (*d'allumettes*) friction strip ; (*pour encaustiquer*) (long-handled) brush.
fructifier [fʀyktifje] *vi* to yield a profit ; **faire ~** to turn to good account.
fructueux, euse [fʀyktɥø, -øz] *a* fruitful ; profitable.

frugal, e, aux [fRygal, -o] *a* frugal.
fruit [fRɥi] *nm* fruit (*gén q*); **~s de mer** seafood(s); **~s secs** dried fruit *sg*; **fruité, e** *a* fruity; **fruitier, ière** *a*: **arbre fruitier** fruit tree // *nm/f* fruiterer, greengrocer.
fruste [fRyst(ə)] *a* unpolished, uncultivated.
frustration [fRystRɑsjɔ̃] *nf* frustration.
frustrer [fRystRe] *vt* to frustrate.
FS *sigle* = *franc suisse*.
fugace [fygas] *a* fleeting.
fugitif, ive [fyʒitif, -iv] *a* (*lueur, amour*) fleeting; (*prisonnier etc*) fugitive, runaway // *nm/f* fugitive.
fugue [fyg] *nf* (*d'un enfant*) running away *q*; (MUS) fugue; **faire une ~** to run away, abscond.
fuir [fɥiR] *vt* to flee from; (*éviter*) to shun // *vi* to run away; (*gaz, robinet*) to leak.
fuite [fɥit] *nf* flight; (*écoulement*) leak, leakage; (*divulgation*) leak; **être en ~** to be on the run; **mettre en ~** to put to flight; **prendre la ~** to take flight.
fulgurant, e [fylgyRɑ̃, -ɑ̃t] *a* lightning *cpd*, dazzling.
fulminer [fylmine] *vi*: **~ (contre)** to thunder forth (against).
fume-cigarette [fymsigaRɛt] *nm inv* cigarette holder.
fumé, e [fyme] *a* (CULIN) smoked; (*verres*) (grey-)tinted // *nf* smoke.
fumer [fyme] *vi* to smoke; (*soupe*) to steam // *vt* to smoke; (*terre, champ*) to manure.
fumerie [fymRi] *nf*: **~ d'opium** opium den.
fumerolles [fymRɔl] *nfpl* gas and smoke (*from volcano*).
fûmes *vb voir* **être**.
fumet [fymɛ] *nm* aroma.
fumeur, euse [fymœR, -øz] *nm/f* smoker.
fumeux, euse [fymø, -øz] *a* (*péj*) woolly.
fumier [fymje] *nm* manure.
fumigation [fymigɑsjɔ̃] *nf* fumigation.
fumigène [fymiʒɛn] *a* smoke *cpd*.
fumiste [fymist(ə)] *nm* (*ramoneur*) chimney sweep // *nm/f* (*péj*) shirker; phoney.
fumisterie [fymistəRi] *nf* (*péj*) fraud, con.
fumoir [fymwaR] *nm* smoking room.
funambule [fynɑ̃byl] *nm* tightrope walker.
funèbre [fynɛbR(ə)] *a* funeral *cpd*; (*fig*) doleful; funereal.
funérailles [fyneRɑj] *nfpl* funeral *sg*.
funéraire [fyneRɛR] *a* funeral *cpd*, funerary.
funeste [fynɛst(ə)] *a* disastrous; deathly.
funiculaire [fynikylɛR] *nm* funicular (railway).
fur [fyR]: **au ~ et à mesure** *ad* as one goes along; **au ~ et à mesure que** as, as soon as; **au ~ et à mesure de leur progression** as they advance (*ou* advanced).
furet [fyRɛ] *nm* ferret.
fureter [fyRte] *vi* (*péj*) to nose about.
fureur [fyRœR] *nf* fury; (*passion*): **~ de** passion for; **faire ~** to be all the rage.
furibond, e [fyRibɔ̃, -ɔ̃d] *a* furious.
furie [fyRi] *nf* fury; (*femme*) shrew, vixen; **en ~** (*mer*) raging; **furieux, euse** *a* furious.
furoncle [fyRɔ̃kl(ə)] *nm* boil, furuncle.
furtif, ive [fyRtif, -iv] *a* furtive.
fus *vb voir* **être**.
fusain [fyzɛ̃] *nm* (BOT) spindle-tree; (ART) charcoal.
fuseau, x [fyzo] *nm* (*pour filer*) spindle; **~ horaire** time zone.
fusée [fyze] *nf* rocket; **~ éclairante** flare.
fuselage [fyzlaʒ] *nm* fuselage.
fuselé, e [fyzle] *a* slender; tapering.
fuser [fyze] *vi* (*rires etc*) to burst forth.
fusible [fyzibl(ə)] *nm* (ÉLEC: *fil*) fuse wire; (: *fiche*) fuse.
fusil [fyzi] *nm* (*de guerre, à canon rayé*) rifle, gun; (*de chasse, à canon lisse*) shotgun, gun; **fusilier** [-lje] *nm* rifleman; **fusillade** [-jad] *nf* gunfire *q*, shooting *q*; shooting battle; **fusiller** *vt* to shoot; **~-mitrailleur** *nm* machine gun.
fusion [fyzjɔ̃] *nf* fusion, melting; (*fig*) merging; (COMM) merger; **en ~** (*métal, roches*) molten; **fusionner** *vi* to merge.
fustiger [fystiʒe] *vt* to denounce.
fut *vb voir* **être**.
fût [fy] *nm* (*tonneau*) barrel, cask; (*de canon*) stock; (*d'arbre*) bole, trunk; (*de colonne*) shaft.
futaie [fytɛ] *nf* forest, plantation.
futile [fytil] *a* futile; frivolous.
futur, e [fytyR] *a, nm* future; **au ~** (LING) in the future; **~iste** *a* futuristic.
fuyant, e [fɥijɑ̃, -ɑ̃t] *vb voir* **fuir** // *a* (*regard etc*) evasive; (*lignes etc*) receding; (*perspective*) vanishing.
fuyard, e [fɥijaR, -aRd(ə)] *nm/f* runaway.

G

gabardine [gabaRdin] *nf* gabardine.
gabarit [gabaRi] *nm* (*fig*) size; calibre; (TECH) template.
gabegie [gabʒi] *nf* (*péj*) chaos.
gâcher [gɑʃe] *vt* (*gâter*) to spoil, ruin; (*gaspiller*) to waste; (*plâtre*) to temper; (*mortier*) to mix.
gâchette [gɑʃɛt] *nf* trigger.
gâchis [gɑʃi] *nm* waste *q*.
gadoue [gadu] *nf* sludge.
gaffe [gaf] *nf* (*instrument*) boat hook; (*erreur*) blunder; **faire ~** (*fam*) to be careful; **gaffer** *vi* to blunder.
gag [gag] *nm* gag.
gage [gaʒ] *nm* (*dans un jeu*) forfeit; (*fig*: *de fidélité*) token; **~s** *nmpl* (*salaire*) wages; (*garantie*) guarantee *sg*; **mettre en ~** to pawn; **laisser en ~** to leave as a security.
gager [gaʒe] *vt*: **~ que** to bet *ou* wager that.
gageure [gaʒyR] *nf*: **c'est une ~** it's attempting the impossible.
gagnant, e [gaɲɑ̃, -ɑ̃t] *a*: **billet/numéro ~** winning ticket/number // *nm/f* winner.
gagne-pain [gaɲpɛ̃] *nm inv* job.
gagner [gaɲe] *vt* to win; (*somme d'argent, revenu*) to earn; (*aller vers, atteindre*) to

reach // *vi* to win; (*fig*) to gain; ~ **du temps/de la place** to gain time/save space; ~ **sa vie** to earn one's living; ~ **du terrain** to gain ground; ~ **à faire** (*s'en trouver bien*) to be better off doing.
gai, e [ge] *a* gay, cheerful; (*un peu ivre*) merry.
gaieté [gete] *nf* cheerfulness; ~**s** *nfpl* (*souvent ironique*) delights; **de ~ de cœur** with a light heart.
gaillard, e [gajaR, -aRd(ə)] *a* (*robuste*) sprightly; (*grivois*) bawdy, ribald // *nm/f* (strapping) fellow/wench.
gain [gɛ̃] *nm* (*revenu*) earnings *pl*; (*bénéfice*: *gén pl*) profits *pl*; (*au jeu*: *gén pl*) winnings *pl*; (*fig*: *de temps, place*) saving; **avoir ~ de cause** to win the case; (*fig*) to be proved right.
gaine [gɛn] *nf* (*corset*) girdle; (*fourreau*) sheath; (*de fil électrique etc*) outer covering; ~**-culotte** *nf* pantie girdle; **gainer** *vt* to cover.
gala [gala] *nm* official reception; **soirée de ~** gala evening.
galant, e [galɑ̃, -ɑ̃t] *a* (*courtois*) courteous, gentlemanly; (*entreprenant*) flirtatious, gallant; (*aventure, poésie*) amorous; **en ~e compagnie** with a lady friend/gentleman friend.
galaxie [galaksi] *nf* galaxy.
galbe [galb(ə)] *nm* curve(s); shapeliness.
gale [gal] *nf* scabies *sg*.
galéjade [galeʒad] *nf* tall story.
galère [galɛR] *nf* galley.
galerie [galRi] *nf* gallery; (THÉÂTRE) circle; (*de voiture*) roof rack; (*fig*: *spectateurs*) audience; ~ **marchande** shopping arcade; ~ **de peinture** (private) art gallery.
galérien [galeRjɛ̃] *nm* galley slave.
galet [galɛ] *nm* pebble; (TECH) wheel; ~**s** *nmpl* pebbles, shingle *sg*.
galette [galɛt] *nf* flat cake.
galeux, euse [galø, -øz] *a*: **un chien ~** a mangy dog.
galimatias [galimatja] *nm* (*péj*) gibberish.
Galles [gal] *n*: **le pays de ~** Wales.
gallicisme [galisism(ə)] *nm* French idiom; (*tournure fautive*) gallicism.
gallois, e [galwa, -waz] *a, nm* (*langue*) Welsh // *nm/f*: **G~, e** Welshman/woman.
galon [galɔ̃] *nm* (MIL) stripe; (*décoratif*) piece of braid.
galop [galo] *nm* gallop; **au ~** at a gallop.
galopade [galɔpad] *nf* stampede.
galoper [galɔpe] *vi* to gallop.
galopin [galɔpɛ̃] *nm* urchin, ragamuffin.
galvaniser [galvanize] *vt* to galvanize.
galvauder [galvode] *vt* to debase.
gambader [gɑ̃bade] *vi* (*animal, enfant*) to leap about.
gamelle [gamɛl] *nf* mess tin; billy can; (*fam*): **ramasser une ~** to come a cropper.
gamin, e [gamɛ̃, -in] *nm/f* kid // *a* mischievous, playful.
gamme [gam] *nf* (MUS) scale; (*fig*) range.
gammé, e [game] *a*: **croix ~e** swastika.
gang [gɑ̃g] *nm* gang.
ganglion [gɑ̃glijɔ̃] *nm* ganglion.
gangrène [gɑ̃gRɛn] *nf* gangrene.
gangue [gɑ̃g] *nf* coating.
ganse [gɑ̃s] *nf* braid.
gant [gɑ̃] *nm* glove; ~ **de toilette** (face) flannel; ~**s de boxe** boxing gloves; **ganté, e** *a*: **ganté de blanc** wearing white gloves; **ganterie** *nf* glove trade; glove shop.
garage [gaRaʒ] *nm* garage; ~ **à vélos** bicycle shed; **garagiste** *nm/f* garage owner; garage mechanic *ou* man.
garant, e [gaRɑ̃, -ɑ̃t] *nm/f* guarantor // *nm* guarantee; **se porter ~ de** to vouch for; to be answerable for.
garantie [gaRɑ̃ti] *nf* guarantee; (*gage*) security, surety; **(bon de) ~** guarantee *ou* warranty slip.
garantir [gaRɑ̃tiR] *vt* to guarantee; (*protéger*): ~ **de** to protect from; **je vous garantis que** I can assure you that; **garanti 2 ans/pure laine** guaranteed for 2 years/pure wool.
garçon [gaRsɔ̃] *nm* boy; (*célibataire*) bachelor; (*jeune homme*) boy, lad; ~ **boucher/ coiffeur** butcher's/hairdresser's assistant; ~ **de courses** messenger; ~ **d'écurie** stable lad; **garçonnet** *nm* small boy; **garçonnière** *nf* bachelor flat.
garde [gaRd(ə)] *nm* (*de prisonnier*) guard; (*de domaine etc*) warden; (*soldat, sentinelle*) guardsman // *nf* guarding; looking after; (*soldats*, BOXE, ESCRIME) guard; (*faction*) watch; (*d'une arme*) hilt; (TYPO): **(page de) ~** endpaper; flyleaf; **de ~** *a, ad* on duty; **monter la ~** to stand guard; **être sur ses ~s** to be on one's guard; **mettre en ~** to warn; **prendre ~ (à)** to be careful (of); ~ **champêtre** *nm* rural policeman; ~ **du corps** *nm* bodyguard; ~ **d'enfants** *nf* child minder; ~ **des enfants** *nf* (*après divorce*) custody of the children; ~ **forestier** *nm* forest warden; ~ **mobile** *nm, nf* mobile guard; ~ **des Sceaux** *nm* ≈ Lord Chancellor; ~ **à vue** *nf* (JUR) ≈ police custody; ~**-à-vous** *nm inv*: **être/se mettre au ~-à-vous** to be at/stand to attention.
garde... [gaRd(ə)] *préfixe*: ~**-barrière** *nm/f* level-crossing keeper; ~**-boue** *nm inv* mudguard; ~**-chasse** *nm* gamekeeper; ~**-fou** *nm* railing, parapet; ~**-malade** *nf* home nurse; ~**-manger** *nm inv* meat safe; pantry, larder; ~**-meuble** *nm* furniture depository; ~**-pêche** *nm inv* water bailiff; fisheries protection ship.
garder [gaRde] *vt* (*conserver*) to keep; (*surveiller*: *prisonnier, enfants*) to look after; (: *immeuble, lieu*) to guard; ~ **le lit/la chambre** to stay in bed/indoors; **se ~** (*aliment*: *se conserver*) to keep; **se ~ de faire** to be careful not to do; **pêche/chasse gardée** private fishing/hunting (ground).
garderie [gaRdəRi] *nf* day nursery, crèche.
garde-robe [gaRdəRɔb] *nf* wardrobe.
gardeur, euse [gaRdœR, -øz] *nm/f* (*d'animaux*) cowherd; goatherd.
gardien, ne [gaRdjɛ̃, -jɛn] *nm/f* (*garde*) guard; (*de prison*) warder; (*de domaine, réserve*) warden; (*de musée etc*) attendant; (*de phare, cimetière*) keeper; (*d'immeuble*) caretaker; (*fig*) guardian; ~ **de but**

goalkeeper ; ~ **de nuit** night watchman ; ~ **de la paix** policeman.
gare [gaR] *nf* (railway) station // *excl* watch out! ; ~ **à ne pas ...** mind you don't ... ; ~ **maritime** harbour station ; ~ **routière** coach station.
garenne [gaRɛn] *nf voir* **lapin.**
garer [gaRe] *vt* to park ; **se** ~ to park ; (*pour laisser passer*) to draw into the side.
gargariser [gaRgaRize]: **se** ~ *vi* to gargle ; **gargarisme** *nm* gargling *q* ; gargle.
gargote [gaRgɔt] *nf* cheap restaurant.
gargouille [gaRguj] *nf* gargoyle.
gargouiller [gaRguje] *vi* to gurgle.
garnement [gaRnəmɑ̃] *nm* tearaway, scallywag.
garni, e [gaRni] *a* (*plat*) served with vegetables (and chips or pasta or rice) // *nm* furnished accommodation *q*.
garnir [gaRniR] *vt* to decorate ; to fill ; to cover ; ~ **qch de** (*orner*) to decorate sth with ; to trim sth with ; (*approvisionner*) to fill *ou* stock sth with ; (*protéger*) to fit sth with ; (*CULIN*) to garnish sth with.
garnison [gaRnizɔ̃] *nf* garrison.
garniture [gaRnityR] *nf* (*CULIN*) vegetables *pl* ; trimmings *pl* ; filling ; (*décoration*) trimming ; (*protection*) fittings *pl* ; ~ **de frein** brake lining ; ~ **intérieure** (*AUTO*) interior trim.
garrot [gaRo] *nm* (*MÉD*) tourniquet ; (*torture*) garrotte.
garrotter [gaRɔte] *vt* to tie up ; (*fig*) to muzzle.
gars [gɑ] *nm* lad ; guy.
gas-oil [gɑzɔjl] *nm* diesel oil.
gaspillage [gaspijaʒ] *nm* waste.
gaspiller [gaspije] *vt* to waste.
gastrique [gastRik] *a* gastric, stomach *cpd*.
gastronome [gastRɔnɔm] *nm/f* gourmet.
gastronomie [gastRɔnɔmi] *nf* gastronomy.
gâteau, x [gɑto] *nm* cake ; ~ **sec** biscuit.
gâter [gɑte] *vt* to spoil ; **se** ~ *vi* (*dent, fruit*) to go bad ; (*temps, situation*) to change for the worse.
gâterie [gɑtRi] *nf* little treat.
gâteux, euse [gɑtø, -øz] *a* senile.
gauche [goʃ] *a* left, left-hand ; (*maladroit*) awkward, clumsy // *nf* (*POL*) left (wing) ; **à** ~ on the left ; (*direction*) (to the) left ; **à** ~ **de** (on *ou* to the) left of ; **à la** ~ **de** to the left of ; **gaucher, ère** *a* left-handed ; ~**rie** *nf* awkwardness, clumsiness ; **gauchir** *vt* to warp ; **gauchisant, e** *a* with left-wing tendencies ; **gauchiste** *nm/f* leftist.
gaufre [gofR(ə)] *nf* waffle.
gaufrer [gofRe] *vt* (*papier*) to emboss ; (*tissu*) to goffer.
gaufrette [gofRɛt] *nf* wafer.
gaule [gol] *nf* (long) pole.
gaulois, e [golwa, -waz] *a* Gallic ; (*grivois*) bawdy // *nm/f*: **G**~, **e** Gaul.
gausser [gose]: **se** ~ **de** *vt* to deride.
gaver [gave] *vt* to force-feed ; (*fig*): ~ **de** to cram with, fill up with.
gaz [gɑz] *nm inv* gas ; **mettre les** ~ (*AUTO*) to put one's foot down ; ~ **lacrymogène** tear gas ; ~ **de ville** town gas.
gaze [gɑz] *nf* gauze.
gazéifié, e [gazeifje] *a* aerated.
gazelle [gazɛl] *nf* gazelle.
gazer [gɑze] *vt* to gas // *vi* (*fam*) to be going *ou* working well.
gazette [gazɛt] *nf* news sheet.
gazeux, euse [gɑzø, -øz] *a* gaseous ; **eau gazeuse** soda water.
gazoduc [gɑzɔdyk] *nm* gas pipeline.
gazomètre [gɑzɔmɛtR(ə)] *nm* gasometer.
gazon [gɑzɔ̃] *nm* (*herbe*) turf ; grass ; (*pelouse*) lawn.
gazouiller [gazuje] *vi* to chirp ; (*enfant*) to babble.
geai [ʒɛ] *nm* jay.
géant, e [ʒeɑ̃, -ɑ̃t] *a* gigantic, giant ; (*COMM*) giant-size // *nm/f* giant.
geindre [ʒɛ̃dR(ə)] *vi* to groan, moan.
gel [ʒɛl] *nm* frost ; freezing.
gélatine [ʒelatin] *nf* gelatine ; **gélatineux, euse** *a* jelly-like, gelatinous.
gelé, e [ʒəle] *a* frozen.
gelée [ʒəle] *nf* jelly ; (*gel*) frost ; ~ **blanche** hoarfrost, white frost.
geler [ʒəle] *vt, vi* to freeze ; **il gèle** it's freezing ; **gelures** *nfpl* frostbite *sg*.
Gémeaux [ʒemo] *nmpl*: **les** ~ Gemini, the Twins ; **être des** ~ to be Gemini.
gémir [ʒemiR] *vi* to groan, moan ; **gémissement** *nm* groan, moan.
gemme [ʒɛm] *nf* gem(stone).
gênant, e [ʒɛnɑ̃, -ɑ̃t] *a* annoying ; embarrassing.
gencive [ʒɑ̃siv] *nf* gum.
gendarme [ʒɑ̃daRm(ə)] *nm* gendarme ; ~**rie** *nf military police force in countryside and small towns*; *their police station or barracks.*
gendre [ʒɑ̃dR(ə)] *nm* son-in-law.
gêne [ʒɛn] *nf* (*à respirer, bouger*) discomfort, difficulty ; (*dérangement*) bother, trouble ; (*manque d'argent*) financial difficulties *pl ou* straits *pl* ; (*confusion*) embarrassment.
gêné, e [ʒene] *a* embarrassed.
généalogie [ʒenealɔʒi] *nf* genealogy ; **généalogique** *a* genealogical.
gêner [ʒene] *vt* (*incommoder*) to bother ; (*encombrer*) to hamper ; to be in the way ; (*déranger*) to bother ; (*embarrasser*): ~ **qn** to make sb feel ill-at-ease ; **se** ~ to put o.s. out.
général, e, aux [ʒeneRal, -o] *a, nm* general // *nf*: **(répétition)** ~**e** final dress rehearsal ; **en** ~ usually, in general ; ~**ement** *ad* generally.
généralisation [ʒeneRalizɑsjɔ̃] *nf* generalization.
généralisé, e [ʒeneRalize] *a* general.
généraliser [ʒeneRalize] *vt, vi* to generalize ; **se** ~ *vi* to become widespread.
généraliste [ʒeneRalist(ə)] *nm/f* general practitioner, G.P.
généralités [ʒeneRalite] *nfpl* generalities ; (*introduction*) general points.
générateur, trice [ʒeneRatœR, -tRis] *a*: ~ **de** which causes *ou* brings about // *nf* generator.
génération [ʒeneRɑsjɔ̃] *nf* generation.

généreusement [ʒeneʀøzmɑ̃] *ad* generously.
généreux, euse [ʒeneʀø, -øz] *a* generous.
générique [ʒeneʀik] *a* generic // *nm* (CINÉMA) credits *pl*, credit titles *pl*.
générosité [ʒeneʀozite] *nf* generosity.
genèse [ʒənɛz] *nf* genesis.
genêt [ʒənɛ] *nm* broom *q*.
génétique [ʒenetik] *a* genetic // *nf* genetics *sg*.
Genève [ʒənɛv] *n* Geneva; **genevois, e** *a*, *nm/f* Genevan.
génial, e, aux [ʒenjal, -o] *a* of genius.
génie [ʒeni] *nm* genius; (MIL): **le** ~ the Engineers *pl*; ~ **civil** civil engineering.
genièvre [ʒənjɛvʀ(ə)] *nm* juniper (tree); (*boisson*) geneva; **grain de** ~ juniper berry.
génisse [ʒenis] *nf* heifer.
génital, e, aux [ʒenital, -o] *a* genital.
génitif [ʒenitif] *nm* genitive.
genou, x [ʒnu] *nm* knee; **à** ~**x** on one's knees; **se mettre à** ~**x** to kneel down; **genouillère** *nf* (SPORT) kneepad.
genre [ʒɑ̃ʀ] *nm* kind, type, sort; (*allure*) manner; (LING) gender; (ART) genre; (ZOOL etc) genus.
gens [ʒɑ̃] *nmpl* (*f in some phrases*) people *pl*.
gentil, le [ʒɑ̃ti, -ij] *a* kind; (*enfant: sage*) good; (*sympa: endroit etc*) nice; **gentillesse** *nf* kindness; **gentiment** *ad* kindly.
génuflexion [ʒenyflɛksjɔ̃] *nf* genuflexion.
géographe [ʒeɔgʀaf] *nm/f* geographer.
géographie [ʒeɔgʀafi] *nf* geography; **géographique** *a* geographical.
geôlier [ʒolje] *nm* jailer.
géologie [ʒeɔlɔʒi] *nf* geology; **géologique** *a* geological; **géologue** *nm/f* geologist.
géomètre [ʒeɔmɛtʀ(ə)] *nm/f*: **(arpenteur-)**~ (land) surveyor.
géométrie [ʒeɔmetʀi] *nf* geometry; **à** ~ **variable** (AVIAT) swing-wing; **géométrique** *a* geometric.
gérance [ʒeʀɑ̃s] *nf* management; **mettre en** ~ to appoint a manager for.
géranium [ʒeʀanjɔm] *nm* geranium.
gérant, e [ʒeʀɑ̃, -ɑ̃t] *nm/f* manager/manageress; ~ **d'immeuble** managing agent.
gerbe [ʒɛʀb(ə)] *nf* (*de fleurs*) spray; (*de blé*) sheaf (*pl* sheaves); (*fig*) shower, burst.
gercé, e [ʒɛʀse] *a* chapped.
gerçure [ʒɛʀsyʀ] *nf* crack.
gérer [ʒeʀe] *vt* to manage.
gériatrie [ʒeʀjatʀi] *nf* geriatrics *sg*; **gériatrique** *a* geriatric.
germain, e [ʒɛʀmɛ̃, -ɛn] *a*: **cousin** ~ first cousin.
germanique [ʒɛʀmanik] *a* Germanic.
germe [ʒɛʀm(ə)] *nm* germ.
germer [ʒɛʀme] *vi* to sprout; to germinate.
gésier [ʒezje] *nm* gizzard.
gésir [ʒeziʀ] *vi* to be lying (down); *voir aussi* **ci-gît**.
gestation [ʒɛstɑsjɔ̃] *nf* gestation.
geste [ʒɛst(ə)] *nm* gesture; move; motion.
gesticuler [ʒɛstikyle] *vi* to gesticulate.
gestion [ʒɛstjɔ̃] *nf* management.
gibecière [ʒibsjɛʀ] *nf* gamebag.
gibet [ʒibɛ] *nm* gallows *pl*.
gibier [ʒibje] *nm* (*animaux*) game; (*fig*) prey.
giboulée [ʒibule] *nf* sudden shower.
giboyeux, euse [ʒibwajø, -øz] *a* well-stocked with game.
gicler [ʒikle] *vi* to spurt, squirt.
gicleur [ʒiklœʀ] *nm* (AUTO) jet.
gifle [ʒifl(ə)] *nf* slap (in the face); **gifler** *vt* to slap (in the face).
gigantesque [ʒigɑ̃tɛsk(ə)] *a* gigantic.
gigogne [ʒigɔɲ] *a*: **lits** ~**s** pull-out *ou* stowaway beds; **tables/poupées** ~**s** nest of tables/dolls.
gigot [ʒigo] *nm* leg (of mutton *ou* lamb).
gigoter [ʒigɔte] *vi* to wriggle (about).
gilet [ʒilɛ] *nm* waistcoat; (*pull*) cardigan; (*de corps*) vest; ~ **pare-balles** bulletproof jacket; ~ **de sauvetage** life jacket.
gin [dʒin] *nm* gin.
gingembre [ʒɛ̃ʒɑ̃bʀ(ə)] *nm* ginger.
girafe [ʒiʀaf] *nf* giraffe.
giratoire [ʒiʀatwaʀ] *a*: **sens** ~ roundabout.
girofle [ʒiʀɔfl(ə)] *nm*: **clou de** ~ clove.
girouette [ʒiʀwɛt] *nf* weather vane *ou* cock.
gisait *etc vb voir* **gésir**.
gisement [ʒizmɑ̃] *nm* deposit.
gît *vb voir* **gésir**.
gitan, e [ʒitɑ̃, -an] *nm/f* gipsy.
gîte [ʒit] *nm* home; shelter; ~ **rural** farmhouse accommodation *q* (for tourists).
givrage [ʒivʀaʒ] *nm* icing.
givre [ʒivʀ(ə)] *nm* (hoar) frost.
glabre [glɑbʀ(ə)] *a* hairless; clean-shaven.
glace [glas] *nf* ice; (*crème glacée*) ice cream; (*verre*) sheet of glass; (*miroir*) mirror; (*de voiture*) window; ~**s** *nfpl* (GÉO) ice sheets, ice *sg*.
glacé, e [glase] *a* icy; (*boisson*) iced.
glacer [glase] *vt* to freeze; (*boisson*) to chill, ice; (*gâteau*) to ice; (*papier, tissu*) to glaze; (*fig*): ~ **qn** to chill sb; to make sb's blood run cold.
glaciaire [glasjɛʀ] *a* ice *cpd*; glacial.
glacial, e [glasjal] *a* icy.
glacier [glasje] *nm* (GÉO) glacier; (*marchand*) ice-cream maker.
glacière [glasjɛʀ] *nf* icebox.
glaçon [glasɔ̃] *nm* icicle; (*pour boisson*) ice cube.
glaïeul [glajœl] *nm* gladiola.
glaire [glɛʀ] *nf* (MÉD) phlegm *q*.
glaise [glɛz] *nf* clay.
gland [glɑ̃] *nm* acorn; (*décoration*) tassel; (ANAT) glans.
glande [glɑ̃d] *nf* gland.
glaner [glane] *vt, vi* to glean.
glapir [glapiʀ] *vi* to yelp.
glas [glɑ] *nm* knell, toll.
glauque [glok] *a* dull blue-green.
glissade [glisad] *nf* (*par jeu*) slide; (*chute*) slip; (*dérapage*) skid.
glissant, e [glisɑ̃, -ɑ̃t] *a* slippery.
glissement [glismɑ̃] *nm* sliding; (*fig*) shift; ~ **de terrain** landslide.

glisser [glise] *vi* (*avancer*) to glide *ou* slide along; (*coulisser, tomber*) to slide; (*déraper*) to slip; (*être glissant*) to be slippery // *vt*: ~ **qch sous/dans/à** to slip sth under/into/to; ~ **sur** (*fig*: *détail etc*) to skate over; **se ~ dans/entre** to slip into/between; **glissière** *nf* slide channel; **à glissière** sliding; **glissoire** *nf* slide.
global, e, aux [glɔbal, -o] *a* overall.
globe [glɔb] *nm* globe; **sous ~** under glass; ~ **oculaire** eyeball; **le ~ terrestre** the globe.
globule [glɔbyl] *nm* (*du sang*): ~ **blanc/rouge** white/red corpuscle.
globuleux, euse [glɔbylø, -øz] *a*: **yeux ~** protruding eyes.
gloire [glwaʀ] *nf* glory; (*mérite*) distinction, credit; (*personne*) celebrity; **glorieux, euse** *a* glorious; **glorifier** *vt* to glorify, extol.
glossaire [glɔsɛʀ] *nm* glossary.
glousser [gluse] *vi* to cluck; (*rire*) to chuckle.
glouton, ne [glutɔ̃, -ɔn] *a* gluttonous, greedy.
glu [gly] *nf* birdlime.
gluant, e [glyɑ̃, -ɑ̃t] *a* sticky, gummy.
glycine [glisin] *nf* wisteria.
go [go]: **tout de ~** *ad* straight out.
G.O. *sigle = grandes ondes.*
gobelet [gɔblɛ] *nm* tumbler; beaker; (*à dés*) cup.
gober [gɔbe] *vt* to swallow.
godet [gɔdɛ] *nm* pot.
godiller [gɔdije] *vi* to scull.
goéland [gɔelɑ̃] *nm* (sea)gull.
goélette [gɔelɛt] *nf* schooner.
goémon [gɔemɔ̃] *nm* wrack.
gogo [gɔgo] *nm* (*péj*) mug, sucker; **à ~** *ad* galore.
goguenard, e [gɔgnaʀ, -aʀd(ə)] *a* mocking.
goguette [gɔgɛt] *nf*: **en ~** on the binge.
goinfre [gwɛ̃fʀ(ə)] *nm* glutton; **se goinfrer** *vi* to make a pig of o.s.; **se goinfrer de** to guzzle.
goitre [gwatʀ(ə)] *nm* goitre.
golf [gɔlf] *nm* golf; golf course; ~ **miniature** crazy *ou* miniature golf.
golfe [gɔlf(ə)] *nm* gulf; bay.
gomme [gɔm] *nf* (*à effacer*) rubber, eraser; (*résine*) gum; **gommer** *vt* to erase; to gum.
gond [gɔ̃] *nm* hinge; **sortir de ses ~s** (*fig*) to fly off the handle.
gondole [gɔ̃dɔl] *nf* gondola.
gondoler [gɔ̃dɔle] *vi*, **se ~** *vi* to warp; to buckle.
gondolier [gɔ̃dɔlje] *nm* gondolier.
gonflage [gɔ̃flaʒ] *nm* inflating, blowing up.
gonflé, e [gɔ̃fle] *a* swollen; bloated.
gonfler [gɔ̃fle] *vt* (*pneu, ballon*) to inflate, blow up; (*nombre, importance*) to inflate // *vi* to swell (up); (CULIN: pâte) to rise; **gonfleur** *nm* air pump.
gong [gɔ̃g] *nm* gong.
goret [gɔʀɛ] *nm* piglet.
gorge [gɔʀʒ(ə)] *nf* (ANAT) throat; (*poitrine*) breast; (GÉO) gorge; (*rainure*) groove.
gorgé, e [gɔʀʒe] *a*: ~ **de** filled with; (*eau*) saturated with // *nf* mouthful; sip; gulp.
gorille [gɔʀij] *nm* gorilla; (*fam*) bodyguard.
gosier [gozje] *nm* throat.
gosse [gɔs] *nm/f* kid.
gothique [gɔtik] *a* gothic.
goudron [gudʀɔ̃] *nm* tar; **goudronner** *vt* to tarmac.
gouffre [gufʀ(ə)] *nm* abyss, gulf.
goujat [guʒa] *nm* boor.
goujon [guʒɔ̃] *nm* gudgeon.
goulée [gule] *nf* gulp.
goulet [gulɛ] *nm* bottleneck.
goulot [gulo] *nm* neck; **boire au ~** to drink from the bottle.
goulu, e [guly] *a* greedy.
goupillon [gupijɔ̃] *nm* (REL) sprinkler.
gourd, e [guʀ, guʀd(ə)] *a* numb (with cold).
gourde [guʀd(ə)] *nf* (*récipient*) flask.
gourdin [guʀdɛ̃] *nm* club, bludgeon.
gourmand, e [guʀmɑ̃, -ɑ̃d] *a* greedy; **gourmandise** *nf* greed; (*bonbon*) sweet.
gourmet [guʀmɛ] *nm* epicure.
gourmette [guʀmɛt] *nf* chain bracelet.
gousse [gus] *nf*: ~ **d'ail** clove of garlic.
gousset [gusɛ] *nm* (*de gilet*) fob.
goût [gu] *nm* taste; **prendre ~ à** to develop a taste *ou* a liking for.
goûter [gute] *vt* (*essayer*) to taste; (*apprécier*) to enjoy // *vi* to have (afternoon) tea // *nm* (afternoon) tea; ~ **à** to taste, sample; ~ **de** to have a taste of.
goutte [gut] *nf* drop; (MÉD) gout; (*alcool*) brandy; **~s** *nfpl* (MÉD) (nose) drops.
goutte-à-goutte [gutagut] *nm* (MÉD) drip; **alimenter au ~** to drip-feed.
gouttelette [gutlɛt] *nf* droplet.
gouttière [gutjɛʀ] *nf* gutter.
gouvernail [guvɛʀnaj] *nm* rudder; (*barre*) helm, tiller.
gouvernante [guvɛʀnɑ̃t] *nf* governess.
gouverne [guvɛʀn(ə)] *nf*: **pour sa ~** for his guidance.
gouvernement [guvɛʀnəmɑ̃] *nm* government; **membre du ~** ≈ Cabinet member; **gouvernemental, e, aux** *a* government *cpd*; pro-government.
gouverner [guvɛʀne] *vt* to govern; **gouverneur** *nm* governor; commanding officer.
grâce [gʀɑs] *nf* grace; favour; (JUR) pardon; **~s** *nfpl* (REL) grace *sg*; **dans les bonnes ~s de qn** in favour with sb; **faire ~ à qn de qch** to spare sb sth; **rendre ~(s) à** to give thanks to; **demander ~** to beg for mercy; **droit de ~** right of reprieve; ~ **à** *prép* thanks to; **gracier** *vt* to pardon; **gracieux, euse** *a* graceful.
gracile [gʀasil] *a* slender.
gradation [gʀadɑsjɔ̃] *nf* gradation.
grade [gʀad] *nm* rank; **monter en ~** to be promoted.
gradé [gʀade] *nm* officer.
gradin [gʀadɛ̃] *nm* tier; step; **~s** *nmpl* (*de stade*) terracing *sg*.
graduation [gʀadɥɑsjɔ̃] *nf* graduation.
graduel, le [gʀadɥɛl] *a* gradual; progressive.

graduer [gʀadɥe] *vt* (*effort etc*) to increase gradually; (*règle, verre*) to graduate; **exercices gradués** exercises graded for difficulty.

graffiti [gʀafiti] *nmpl* graffiti.

grain [gʀɛ̃] *nm* (*gén*) grain; (NAVIG) squall; ~ **de beauté** beauty spot; ~ **de café** coffee bean; ~ **de poivre** peppercorn; ~ **de poussière** speck of dust; ~ **de raisin** grape.

graine [gʀɛn] *nf* seed; ~**tier** *nm* seed merchant.

graissage [gʀɛsaʒ] *nm* lubrication, greasing.

graisse [gʀɛs] *nf* fat; (*lubrifiant*) grease; **graisser** *vt* to lubricate, grease; (*tacher*) to make greasy; **graisseux, euse** *a* greasy; (ANAT) fatty.

grammaire [gʀamɛʀ] *nf* grammar; **grammatical, e, aux** *a* grammatical.

gramme [gʀam] *nm* gramme.

grand, e [gʀɑ̃, gʀɑ̃d] *a* (*haut*) tall; (*gros, vaste, large*) big, large; (*long*) long; (*sens abstraits*) great // *ad*: ~ **ouvert** wide open; **son** ~ **frère** his older brother; **il est assez** ~ **pour** he's old enough to; **au** ~ **air** in the open (air); ~**s blessés/brûlés** casualties with severe injuries/burns; ~ **angle** *nm* (PHOTO) wide-angle lens *sg*; ~ **écart** splits *pl*; ~ **ensemble** housing scheme; ~ **magasin** department store; ~**e personne** grown-up; ~**es écoles** *prestige schools of university level, with competitive entrance examination*; ~**es lignes** (RAIL) main lines; ~**es vacances** summer holidays; **grand-chose** *nm/f inv*: **pas grand-chose** not much; **Grande-Bretagne** *nf*: **la Grande-Bretagne** (Great) Britain; **grandeur** *nf* (*dimension*) size; magnitude; (*fig*) greatness; **grandeur nature** life-size; **grandir** *vi* (*enfant, arbre*) to grow; (*bruit, hostilité*) to increase, grow // *vt*: **grandir qn** (*suj*: *vêtement, chaussure*) to make sb look taller; (*fig*) to make sb grow in stature; ~**-mère** *nf* grandmother; ~**-messe** *nf* high mass; ~**-père** *nm* grandfather; ~**-route** *nf* main road; ~**-rue** *nf* high street; ~**s-parents** *nmpl* grandparents.

grange [gʀɑ̃ʒ] *nf* barn.

granit [gʀanit] *nm* granite.

granulé [gʀanyle] *nm* granule.

granuleux, euse [gʀanylø, -øz] *a* granular.

graphie [gʀafi] *nf* written form.

graphique [gʀafik] *a* graphic // *nm* graph.

graphisme [gʀafism(ə)] *nm* graphic arts *pl*; graphics *sg*.

graphologie [gʀafɔlɔʒi] *nf* graphology; **graphologue** *nm/f* graphologist.

grappe [gʀap] *nf* cluster; ~ **de raisin** bunch of grapes.

grappiller [gʀapije] *vt* to glean.

grappin [gʀapɛ̃] *nm* grapnel; **mettre le** ~ **sur** (*fig*) to get one's claws on.

gras, se [gʀɑ, gʀɑs] *a* (*viande, soupe*) fatty; (*personne*) fat; (*surface, main*) greasy; (*toux*) loose, phlegmy; (*rire*) throaty; (*plaisanterie*) coarse; (*crayon*) soft-lead; (TYPO) bold // *nm* (CULIN) fat; **faire la** ~**se matinée** to have a lie-in; ~**sement** *ad*: ~**sement payé** handsomely paid; ~**souillet, te** *a* podgy, plump.

gratification [gʀatifikɑsjɔ̃] *nf* bonus.

gratifier [gʀatifje] *vt*: ~ **qn de** to favour sb with, reward sb with; (*sourire etc*) to favour sb with.

gratin [gʀatɛ̃] *nm* (CULIN) cheese-topped dish; cheese topping.

gratiné, e [gʀatine] *a* (CULIN) au gratin; (*fam*) hellish.

gratis [gʀatis] *ad* free.

gratitude [gʀatityd] *nf* gratitude.

gratte-ciel [gʀatsjɛl] *nm inv* skyscraper.

grattement [gʀatmɑ̃] *nm* (*bruit*) scratching (noise).

gratte-papier [gʀatpapje] *nm inv* (*péj*) penpusher.

gratter [gʀate] *vt* (*frotter*) to scrape; (*enlever*) to scrape off; (*bras, bouton*) to scratch; **grattoir** *nm* scraper.

gratuit, e [gʀatɥi, -ɥit] *a* (*entrée, billet*) free; (*fig*) gratuitous.

gratuitement [gʀatɥitmɑ̃] *ad* free.

gravats [gʀavɑ] *nmpl* rubble *sg*.

grave [gʀav] *a* (*maladie, accident*) serious, bad; (*sujet, problème*) serious, grave; (*air*) grave, solemn; (*voix, son*) deep, low-pitched // *nm* (MUS) low register; **blessé** ~ seriously injured person; ~**ment** *ad* seriously; gravely.

graver [gʀave] *vt* to engrave; **graveur** *nm* engraver.

gravier [gʀavje] *nm* gravel *q*; **gravillons** *nmpl* gravel *sg*, loose chippings *ou* gravel.

gravir [gʀaviʀ] *vt* to climb (up).

gravitation [gʀavitɑsjɔ̃] *nf* gravitation.

gravité [gʀavite] *nf* seriousness; gravity; (PHYSIQUE) gravity.

graviter [gʀavite] *vi*: ~ **autour de** to revolve around.

gravure [gʀavyʀ] *nf* engraving; (*reproduction*) print; plate.

gré [gʀe] *nm*: **à son** ~ to his liking; as he pleases; **au** ~ **de** according to, following; **contre le** ~ **de qn** against sb's will; **de son (plein)** ~ of one's own free will; **de** ~ **ou de force** whether one likes it or not; **de bon** ~ willingly; **de** ~ **à** ~ (COMM) by mutual agreement; **savoir** ~ **à qn de qch** to be grateful to sb for sth.

grec, grecque [gʀɛk] *a* Greek; (*classique*: *vase etc*) Grecian // *nm/f* Greek.

Grèce [gʀɛs] *nf*: **la** ~ Greece.

gréement [gʀemɑ̃] *nm* rigging.

greffe [gʀɛf] *nf* grafting *q*, graft; transplanting *q*, transplant // *nm* (JUR) office.

greffer [gʀefe] *vt* (BOT, MÉD: *tissu*) to graft; (MÉD: *organe*) to transplant.

greffier [gʀefje] *nm* clerk of the court.

grégaire [gʀegɛʀ] *a* gregarious.

grège [gʀɛʒ] *a*: **soie** ~ raw silk.

grêle [gʀɛl] *a* (very) thin // *nf* hail.

grêlé, e [gʀele] *a* pockmarked.

grêler [gʀele] *vb impersonnel*: **il grêle** it's hailing.

grêlon [gʀəlɔ̃] *nm* hailstone.

grelot [gʀəlo] *nm* little bell.

grelotter [gʀəlɔte] *vi* (*trembler*) to shiver.

grenade [gRənad] *nf* (*explosive*) grenade; (*BOT*) pomegranate; ~ **lacrymogène** teargas grenade.
grenadier [gRənadje] *nm* (*MIL*) grenadier; (*BOT*) pomegranate tree.
grenat [gRəna] *a inv* dark red.
grenier [gRənje] *nm* attic; (*de ferme*) loft.
grenouille [gRənuj] *nf* frog.
grenu, e [gRəny] *a* grainy, grained.
grès [gRɛ] *nm* sandstone; (*poterie*) stoneware.
grésiller [gRezije] *vi* to sizzle; (*RADIO*) to crackle.
grève [gRɛv] *nf* (*d'ouvriers*) strike; (*plage*) shore; **se mettre en/faire** ~ to go on/be on strike; ~ **de la faim** hunger strike; ~ **sauvage** wildcat strike; ~ **sur le tas** sit down strike; ~ **tournante** strike by rota; ~ **du zèle** work-to-rule *q*.
grever [gRəve] *vt* to put a strain on; **grevé d'impôts** crippled by taxes.
gréviste [grevist(ə)] *nm/f* striker.
gribouiller [gRibuje] *vt* to scribble, scrawl // *vi* to doodle.
grief [gRijɛf] *nm* grievance; **faire ~ à qn de** to reproach sb for.
grièvement [gRijɛvmɑ̃] *ad* seriously.
griffe [gRif] *nf* claw; (*fig*) signature.
griffer [gRife] *vt* to scratch.
griffonner [gRifɔne] *vt* to scribble.
grignoter [gRiɲɔte] *vt* to nibble *ou* gnaw at.
gril [gRil] *nm* steak *ou* grill pan.
grillade [gRijad] *nf* grill.
grillage [gRijaʒ] *nm* (*treillis*) wire netting; wire fencing.
grille [gRij] *nf* (*portail*) (metal) gate; (*d'égout*) (metal) grate; (*fig*) grid.
grille-pain [gRijpɛ̃] *nm inv* toaster.
griller [gRije] *vt* (*aussi*: **faire** ~: *pain*) to toast; (: *viande*) to grill; (*fig*: *ampoule etc*) to burn out, blow.
grillon [gRijɔ̃] *nm* cricket.
grimace [gRimas] *nf* grimace; (*pour faire rire*): **faire des ~s** to pull *ou* make faces.
grimer [gRime] *vt* to make up.
grimper [gRɛ̃pe] *vi, vt* to climb.
grincement [gRɛ̃smɑ̃] *nm* grating (noise); creaking (noise).
grincer [gRɛ̃se] *vi* (*porte, roue*) to grate; (*plancher*) to creak; ~ **des dents** to grind one's teeth.
grincheux, euse [gRɛ̃ʃø, -øz] *a* grumpy.
grippe [gRip] *nf* flu, influenza; **grippé, e** *a*: **être grippé** to have flu.
gripper [gRipe] *vt, vi* to jam.
gris, e [gRi, gRiz] *a* grey; (*ivre*) tipsy.
grisaille [gRizɑj] *nf* greyness, dullness.
grisant, e [gRizɑ̃, -ɑ̃t] *a* intoxicating, exhilarating.
griser [gRize] *vt* to intoxicate.
grisonner [gRizɔne] *vi* to be going grey.
grisou [gRizu] *nm* firedamp.
grive [gRiv] *nf* thrush.
grivois, e [gRivwa, -waz] *a* saucy.
grog [gRɔg] *nm* grog.
grogner [gRɔɲe] *vi* to growl; (*fig*) to grumble.
groin [gRwɛ̃] *nm* snout.
grommeler [gRɔmle] *vi* to mutter to o.s.
grondement [gRɔ̃dmɑ̃] *nm* rumble.
gronder [gRɔ̃de] *vi* to rumble; (*fig*: *révolte*) to be brewing // *vt* to scold.
gros, se [gRo, gRos] *a* big, large; (*obèse*) fat; (*travaux, dégâts*) extensive; (*large*: *trait, fil*) thick, heavy // *ad*: **risquer/gagner** ~ to risk/win a lot // *nm* (*COMM*): **le** ~ the wholesale business; **prix de** ~ wholesale price; **par ~ temps/~se mer** in rough weather/heavy seas; **le ~ de** the main body of; the bulk of; **en** ~ roughly; (*COMM*) wholesale; ~ **intestin** large intestine; ~ **lot** jackpot; ~ **mot** coarse word, vulgarity; ~ **plan** (*PHOTO*) close-up; ~ **sel** cooking salt; **~se caisse** big drum.
groseille [gRozɛj] *nf*: ~ **(rouge)/(blanche)** red/white currant; ~ **à maquereau** gooseberry; **groseillier** *nm* red *ou* white currant bush; gooseberry bush.
grosse [gRos] *a voir* **gros.**
grossesse [gRosɛs] *nf* pregnancy.
grosseur [gRosœR] *nf* size; fatness; (*tumeur*) lump.
grossier, ière [gRosje, -jɛR] *a* coarse; (*travail*) rough; crude; (*évident*: *erreur*) gross; **grossièrement** *ad* coarsely; roughly; crudely; (*en gros*) roughly.
grossir [gRosiR] *vi* (*personne*) to put on weight; (*fig*) to grow, get bigger; (*rivière*) to swell // *vt* to increase; to exaggerate; (*au microscope*) to magnify; (*suj*: *vêtement*): ~ **qn** to make sb look fatter; **grossissement** *nm* (*optique*) magnification.
grossiste [gRosist(ə)] *nm/f* wholesaler.
grosso modo [gRɔsomɔdo] *ad* roughly.
grotte [gRɔt] *nf* cave.
grouiller [gRuje] *vi* to mill about; to swarm about; ~ **de** to be swarming with.
groupe [gRup] *nm* group; ~ **sanguin** blood group.
groupement [gRupmɑ̃] *nm* grouping; group.
grouper [gRupe] *vt* to group; **se** ~ to get together.
gruau [gRyo] *nm*: **pain de** ~ wheaten bread.
grue [gRy] *nf* crane.
grumeaux [gRymo] *nmpl* lumps.
grutier [gRytje] *nm* crane driver.
Guadeloupe [gwadlup] *nf*: **la** ~ Guadeloupe.
gué [ge] *nm* ford; **passer à** ~ to ford.
guenilles [gənij] *nfpl* rags.
guenon [gənɔ̃] *nf* female monkey.
guépard [gepaR] *nm* cheetah.
guêpe [gɛp] *nf* wasp.
guêpier [gepje] *nm* (*fig*) trap.
guère [gɛR] *ad* (*avec adjectif, adverbe*): **ne ...** ~ hardly; (*avec verbe*): **ne ...** ~ *tournure négative* + much; hardly ever; *tournure négative* + (very) long; **il n'y a ~ que/de** there's hardly anybody (*ou* anything) but/hardly any.
guéridon [geRidɔ̃] *nm* pedestal table.
guérilla [geRija] *nf* guerrilla warfare.
guérillero [geRijeRo] *nm* guerrilla.
guérir [geRiR] *vt* (*personne, maladie*) to cure; (*membre, plaie*) to heal // *vi*

(*personne*) to recover, be cured; (*plaie, chagrin*) to heal; ~ **de** to be cured of, recover from; ~ **qn de** to cure sb of; **guérison** *nf* curing; healing; recovery; **guérissable** *a* curable; **guérisseur, euse** *nm/f* healer.
guérite [geʀit] *nf* sentry box.
guerre [gɛʀ] *nf* war; (*méthode*): ~ **atomique/de tranchées** atomic/ trench warfare *q*; **en** ~ at war; **faire la** ~ **à** to wage war against; **de** ~ **lasse** finally; ~ **civile/ mondiale** civil/world war; ~ **d'usure** war of attrition; **guerrier, ière** *a* warlike // *nm/f* warrior; **guerroyer** *vi* to wage war.
guet [gɛ] *nm*: **faire le** ~ to be on the watch *ou* look-out.
guet-apens [gɛtapɑ̃] *nm* ambush.
guêtre [gɛtʀ(ə)] *nf* gaiter.
guetter [gete] *vt* (*épier*) to watch (intently); (*attendre*) to watch (out) for; to be lying in wait for; **guetteur** *nm* look-out.
gueule [gœl] *nf* mouth; (*fam*) face; mouth; ~ **de bois** (*fam*) hangover.
gueuler [gœle] *vi* (*fam*) to bawl.
gueux [gø] *nm* beggar; rogue.
gui [gi] *nm* mistletoe.
guichet [giʃɛ] *nm* (*de bureau, banque*) counter, window; (*d'une porte*) wicket, hatch; **les** ~**s** (*à la gare, au théâtre*) the ticket office; **guichetier, ière** *nm/f* counter clerk.
guide [gid] *nm* guide.
guider [gide] *vt* to guide.
guidon [gidɔ̃] *nm* handlebars *pl.*
guignol [giɲɔl] *nm* ≈ Punch and Judy show; (*fig*) clown.
guillemets [gijmɛ] *nmpl*: **entre** ~ in inverted commas *ou* quotation marks; ~ **de répétition** ditto marks.
guilleret, te [gijʀɛ, -ɛt] *a* perky, bright.
guillotine [gijɔtin] *nf* guillotine; **guillotiner** *vt* to guillotine.
guindé, e [gɛ̃de] *a* stiff, starchy.
guirlande [giʀlɑ̃d] *nf* garland; (*de papier*) paper chain.
guise [giz] *nf*: **à votre** ~ as you wish *ou* please; **en** ~ **de** by way of.
guitare [gitaʀ] *nf* guitar; **guitariste** *nm/f* guitarist, guitar player.
gustatif, ive [gystatif, -iv] *a* gustatory; *voir* **papille.**
guttural, e, aux [gytyʀal, -o] *a* guttural.
Guyane [gɥijan] *n*: **la** ~ Guiana.
gymkhana [ʒimkana] *nm* rally.
gymnase [ʒimnɑz] *nm* gym(nasium).
gymnaste [ʒimnast(ə)] *nm/f* gymnast.
gymnastique [ʒimnastik] *nf* gymnastics *sg*; (*au réveil etc*) keep fit exercises *pl.*
gynécologie [ʒinekɔlɔʒi] *nf* gynaecology; **gynécologue** *nm/f* gynaecologist.
gypse [ʒips(ə)] *nm* gypsum.

H

h. *abr de* **heure.**
habile [abil] *a* skilful; (*malin*) clever; ~**té** *nf* skill, skilfulness; cleverness.
habilité, e [abilite] *a*: ~ **à faire** entitled to do, empowered to do.
habillé, e [abije] *a* dressed; (*chic*) dressy; (*TECH*): ~ **de** covered with; encased in.
habillement [abijmɑ̃] *nm* clothes *pl;* (*profession*) clothing industry.
habiller [abije] *vt* to dress; (*fournir en vêtements*) to clothe; **s'**~ to dress (o.s.); (*se déguiser, mettre des vêtements chic*) to dress up; **s'**~ **de/en** to dress in/dress up as; **s'**~ **chez/à** to buy one's clothes from/at.
habit [abi] *nm* outfit; ~**s** *nmpl* (*vêtements*) clothes; ~ **(de soirée)** tails *pl;* evening dress.
habitable [abitabl(ə)] *a* (in)habitable.
habitacle [abitakl(ə)] *nm* cockpit; (*AUTO*) passenger cell.
habitant, e [abitɑ̃, -ɑ̃t] *nm/f* inhabitant; (*d'une maison*) occupant, occupier; **loger chez l'**~ to stay with the locals.
habitat [abita] *nm* housing conditions *pl;* (*BOT, ZOOL*) habitat.
habitation [abitɑsjɔ̃] *nf* living; residence, home; house; ~**s à loyer modéré (HLM)** low-rent housing *sg*, ≈ council flats.
habité, e [abite] *a* inhabited; lived in.
habiter [abite] *vt* to live in; (*suj: sentiment*) to dwell in // *vi*: ~ **à/dans** to live in *ou* at/in.
habitude [abityd] *nf* habit; **avoir l'**~ **de faire** to be in the habit of doing; (*expérience*) to be used to doing; **d'**~ usually; **comme d'**~ as usual.
habitué, e [abitɥe] *a*: **être** ~ **à** to be used *ou* accustomed to // *nm/f* regular visitor; regular (customer).
habituel, le [abitɥɛl] *a* usual.
habituer [abitɥe] *vt*: ~ **qn à** to get sb used to; **s'**~ **à** to get used to.
***hâbleur, euse** ['ɑblœʀ, -øz] *a* boastful.
***hache** ['aʃ] *nf* axe.
***haché, e** ['aʃe] *a* minced; (*fig*) jerky.
***hacher** ['aʃe] *vt* (*viande*) to mince; (*persil*) to chop.
***hachis** ['aʃi] *nm* mince *q.*
***hachisch** ['aʃiʃ] *nm* hashish.
***hachoir** ['aʃwaʀ] *nm* chopper; (meat) mincer; chopping board.
***hachures** ['aʃyʀ] *nfpl* hatching *sg.*
***hagard, e** ['agaʀ, -aʀd(ə)] *a* wild, distraught.
***haie** ['ɛ] *nf* hedge; (*SPORT*) hurdle; (*fig: rang*) line, row; **200 m** ~**s** 200 m hurdles; ~ **d'honneur** guard of honour.
***haillons** ['ɑjɔ̃] *nmpl* rags.
***haine** ['ɛn] *nf* hatred; **haineux, euse** *a* full of hatred.
***haïr** ['aiʀ] *vt* to detest, hate.
***halage** ['alaʒ] *nm*: **chemin de** ~ towpath.
***hâle** ['ɑl] *nm* (sun)tan; ***hâlé, e** *a* (sun)tanned, sunburnt.
haleine [alɛn] *nf* breath; **hors d'**~ out of breath; **tenir en** ~ to hold spellbound; to keep in suspense; **de longue** ~ *a* long-term.
***haleter** ['alte] *vi* to pant.
***hall** ['ol] *nm* hall.
hallali [alali] *nm* kill.
***halle** ['al] *nf* (covered) market; ~**s** *nfpl* central food market *sg.*

hallucinant, e [alysinɑ̃, -ɑ̃t] *a* staggering.
hallucination [alysinɑsjɔ̃] *nf* hallucination.
halluciné, e [alysine] *nm/f* person suffering from hallucinations; (raving) lunatic.
***halo** ['alo] *nm* halo.
***halte** ['alt(ə)] *nf* stop, break; stopping place; (RAIL) halt // *excl* stop!; **faire ~** to stop.
haltère [altɛʀ] *nm* dumbbell, barbell; **~s** *nmpl* (*activité*) weight lifting *sg*; **haltérophile** *nm/f* weight lifter.
***hamac** ['amak] *nm* hammock.
***hameau, x** ['amo] *nm* hamlet.
hameçon [amsɔ̃] *nm* (fish) hook.
***hampe** ['ɑ̃p] *nf* shaft.
***hamster** ['amstɛʀ] *nm* hamster.
***hanche** ['ɑ̃ʃ] *nf* hip.
***hand-ball** ['ɑ̃dbal] *nm* handball.
***handicap** ['ɑ̃dikap] *nm* handicap; ***~é, e** *a* handicapped // *nm/f* physically (*ou* mentally) handicapped person; **~é moteur** spastic; ***~er** *vt* to handicap.
***hangar** ['ɑ̃gaʀ] *nm* shed.
***hanneton** ['antɔ̃] *nm* cockchafer.
***hanter** ['ɑ̃te] *vt* to haunt.
***hantise** ['ɑ̃tiz] *nf* obsessive fear.
***happer** ['ape] *vt* to snatch; (*suj: train etc*) to hit.
***haranguer** ['aʀɑ̃ge] *vt* to harangue.
***haras** ['aʀɑ] *nm* stud farm.
harassant, e ['aʀasɑ̃, -ɑ̃t] *a* exhausting.
***harceler** ['aʀsəle] *vt* (MIL, CHASSE) to harass, harry; (*importuner*) to plague.
***hardes** ['aʀd(ə)] *nfpl* rags.
***hardi, e** ['aʀdi] *a* bold, daring.
***hareng** ['aʀɑ̃] *nm* herring.
***hargne** ['aʀɲ(ə)] *nf* aggressiveness.
***haricot** ['aʀiko] *nm* bean; **~ vert/blanc** French/haricot bean.
harmonica [aʀmɔnika] *nm* mouth organ.
harmonie [aʀmɔni] *nf* harmony; **harmonieux, euse** *a* harmonious; **harmonique** *nm ou nf* harmonic; **harmoniser** *vt* to harmonize.
***harnaché, e** ['aʀnaʃe] *a* (*fig*) rigged out.
***harnacher** ['aʀnaʃe] *vt* to harness.
***harnais** ['aʀnɛ] *nm* harness.
***harpe** ['aʀp(ə)] *nf* harp; ***harpiste** *nm/f* harpist.
***harpon** ['aʀpɔ̃] *nm* harpoon; ***harponner** *vt* to harpoon; (*fam*) to collar.
***hasard** ['azaʀ] *nm*: **le ~** chance, fate; **un ~** a coincidence; a stroke of luck; **au ~** aimlessly; at random; haphazardly; **par ~** by chance; **à tout ~** just in case; on the off chance.
***hasarder** ['azaʀde] *vt* (*mot*) to venture; (*fortune*) to risk; **se ~ à faire** to risk doing, venture to do.
***hasardeux, euse** ['azaʀdø, -øz] *a* hazardous, risky; (*hypothèse*) rash.
***haschisch** ['aʃiʃ] *nm* hashish.
***hâte** ['ɑt] *nf* haste; **à la ~** hurriedly, hastily; **en ~** posthaste, with all possible speed; **avoir ~ de** to be eager *ou* anxious to; ***hâter** *vt* to hasten; **se hâter** to hurry; **se hâter de** to hurry *ou* hasten to.
***hâtif, ive** ['ɑtif, -iv] *a* hurried; hasty; (*légume*) early.
***hausse** ['os] *nf* rise, increase; (*de fusil*) backsight adjuster; **en ~** rising.
***hausser** ['ose] *vt* to raise; **~ les épaules** to shrug (one's shoulders).
***haut, e** ['o, 'ot] *a* high; (*grand*) tall; (*son, voix*) high(-pitched) // *ad* high // *nm* top (part); **de 3 m de ~** 3 m high, 3 m in height; **des ~s et des bas** ups and downs; **en ~ lieu** in high places; **à ~e voix** aloud, out loud; **du ~ de** from the top of; **de ~ en bas** up and down; downwards; **plus ~** higher up, further up; (*dans un texte*) above; (*parler*) louder; **en ~** up above; at (*ou* tc) the top; (*dans une maison*) upstairs; **en ~ de** at the top of; **la ~e couture/coiffure** haute couture/coiffure; **~e fidélité** hi-fi, high fidelity.
***hautain, e** ['otɛ̃, -ɛn] *a* (*personne, regard*) haughty.
***hautbois** ['obwɑ] *nm* oboe.
***haut-de-forme** ['odfɔʀm(ə)] *nm* top hat.
***hautement** ['otmɑ̃] *ad* highly.
***hauteur** ['otœʀ] *nf* height; (GÉO) height, hill; (*fig*) loftiness; haughtiness; **à ~ des yeux** at eye level; **à la ~ de** (*sur la même ligne*) level with; by; (*fig*) equal to; **à la ~** (*fig*) up to it, equal to the task.
***haut-fond** ['ofɔ̃] *nm* shallow, shoal.
***haut-fourneau** ['ofuʀno] *nm* blast *ou* smelting furnace.
***haut-le-cœur** ['olkœʀ] *nm inv* retch, heave.
***haut-parleur** ['opaʀlœʀ] *nm* (loud)speaker.
***hâve** ['ɑv] *a* gaunt.
***havre** ['ɑvʀ(ə)] *nm* haven.
***Haye** ['ɛ] *n*: **la ~** the Hague.
***hayon** ['ɛjɔ̃] *nm* tailgate.
hebdomadaire [ɛbdɔmadɛʀ] *a, nm* weekly.
héberger [ebɛʀʒe] *vt* to accommodate, lodge; (*réfugiés*) to take in.
hébété, e [ebete] *a* dazed.
hébraïque [ebʀaik] *a* Hebrew, Hebraic.
hébreu, x [ebʀø] *am, nm* Hebrew.
H.E.C. *sigle fpl* = *Hautes études commerciales*.
hécatombe [ekatɔ̃b] *nf* slaughter.
hectare [ɛktaʀ] *nm* hectare, 10,000 square metres.
hectolitre [ɛktolitʀ] *nm* hectolitre.
hégémonie [eʒemɔni] *nf* hegemony.
***hein** ['ɛ̃] *excl* eh?
hélas ['elɑs] *excl* alas! // *ad* unfortunately.
***héler** ['ele] *vt* to hail.
hélice [elis] *nf* propeller.
hélicoïdal, e, aux [elikɔidal, -o] *a* helical; helicoid.
hélicoptère [elikɔptɛʀ] *nm* helicopter.
héliogravure [eljɔgʀavyʀ] *nf* heliogravure.
héliport [elipɔʀ] *nm* heliport.
héliporté, e [elipɔʀte] *a* transported by helicopter.
hellénique [elenik] *a* Hellenic.
helvétique [ɛlvetik] *a* Swiss.

hématome [ematom] *nm* haematoma.
hémicycle [emisikl(ə)] *nm* semicircle; (*POL*): **l'~** ≈ the benches (of the Commons).
hémiplégie [emipleʒi] *nf* paralysis of one side, hemiplegia.
hémisphère [emisfɛʀ] *nf*: ~ **nord/sud** northern/southern hemisphere.
hémophile [emɔfil] *a* haemophiliac.
hémorragie [emɔʀaʒi] *nf* bleeding *q*, haemorrhage.
hémorroïdes [emɔʀɔid] *nfpl* piles, haemorrhoids.
***hennir** ['eniʀ] *vi* to neigh, whinny.
hépatite [epatit] *nf* hepatitis, liver infection.
herbe [ɛʀb(ə)] *nf* grass; (*CULIN, MÉD*) herb; **en** ~ unripe; (*fig*) budding; **herbeux, euse** *a* grassy; **herbicide** *nm* weed-killer; **herbier** *nm* herbarium; **herboriser** *vi* to collect plants, botanize; **herboriste** *nm/f* herbalist; **herboristerie** *nf* herbalist's shop; herb trade.
***hère** ['ɛʀ] *nm*: **pauvre** ~ poor wretch.
héréditaire [eʀeditɛʀ] *a* hereditary.
hérédité [eʀedite] *nf* heredity.
hérésie [eʀezi] *nf* heresy; **hérétique** *nm/f* heretic.
***hérissé, e** ['eʀise] *a* bristling; ~ **de** spiked with; (*fig*) bristling with.
***hérisser** ['eʀise] *vt*: ~ **qn** (*fig*) to ruffle sb; **se** ~ *vi* to bristle, bristle up.
***hérisson** ['eʀisɔ̃] *nm* hedgehog.
héritage [eʀitaʒ] *nm* inheritance; (*fig*) heritage; legacy; **faire un (petit)** ~ to come into (a little) money.
hériter [eʀite] *vi*: ~ **de qch (de qn)** to inherit sth (from sb); ~ **de qn** to inherit sb's property; **héritier, ière** *nm/f* heir/heiress.
hermétique [ɛʀmetik] *a* airtight; watertight; (*fig*) abstruse; impenetrable; **~ment** *ad* tightly, hermetically.
hermine [ɛʀmin] *nf* ermine.
***hernie** ['ɛʀni] *nf* hernia.
héroïne [eʀɔin] *nf* heroine; (*drogue*) heroin.
héroïque [eʀɔik] *a* heroic.
héroïsme [eʀɔism(ə)] *nm* heroism.
***héron** ['eʀɔ̃] *nm* heron.
***héros** ['eʀo] *nm* hero.
***herse** ['ɛʀs(ə)] *nf* harrow; (*de château*) portcullis.
hésitant, e [ezitɑ̃, -ɑ̃t] *a* hesitant.
hésitation [ezitɑsjɔ̃] *nf* hesitation.
hésiter [ezite] *vi*: ~ **(à faire)** to hesitate (to do).
hétéroclite [eteʀɔklit] *a* heterogeneous; (*objets*) sundry.
***hêtre** ['ɛtʀ(ə)] *nm* beech.
heure [œʀ] *nf* hour; (*SCOL*) period; (*moment, moment fixé*) time; **c'est l'~** it's time; **quelle ~ est-il?** what time is it?; **être à l'~** to be on time; (*montre*) to be right; **mettre à l'~** to set right; **à toute ~** at any time; **24 ~s sur 24** round the clock, 24 hours a day; **à l'~ qu'il est** at this time (of day); by now; **sur l'~** at once; ~ **locale/d'été** local/summer time; **~s de bureau** office hours; **~s supplémentaires** overtime *sg*.
heureusement [œʀøzmɑ̃] *ad* (*par bonheur*) fortunately, luckily.
heureux, euse [œʀø, -øz] *a* happy; (*chanceux*) lucky, fortunate; (*judicieux*) felicitous, fortunate.
***heurt** ['œʀ] *nm* (*choc*) collision; **~s** *nmpl* (*fig*) clashes.
***heurté, e** ['œʀte] *a* (*fig*) jerky, uneven.
***heurter** ['œʀte] *vt* (*mur*) to strike, hit; (*personne*) to collide with; (*fig*) to go against, upset; **se** ~ **à** *vt* to collide with; (*fig*) to come up against; **heurtoir** *nm* door knocker.
hexagone [ɛgzagɔn] *nm* hexagon.
***hiatus** ['jatys] *nm* hiatus.
hiberner [ibɛʀne] *vi* to hibernate.
***hibou, x** ['ibu] *nm* owl.
***hideux, euse** ['idø, -øz] *a* hideous.
hier [jɛʀ] *ad* yesterday; ~ **matin/soir** yesterday morning/ evening; **toute la journée d'~** all day yesterday; **toute la matinée d'~** all yesterday morning.
***hiérarchie** ['jeʀaʀʃi] *nf* hierarchy; ***hiérarchique** *a* hierarchic; ***hiérarchiser** *vt* to organize into a hierarchy.
hiéroglyphe [jeʀɔglif] *nm* hieroglyphic.
hilare [ilaʀ] *a* mirthful; **hilarité** *nf* hilarity, mirth.
hindou, e [ɛ̃du] *a, nm/f* Hindu; Indian.
hippique [ipik] *a* equestrian, horse *cpd*.
hippisme [ipism(ə)] *nm* (horse) riding.
hippodrome [ipɔdʀom] *nm* racecourse.
hippopotame [ipɔpɔtam] *nm* hippopotamus.
hirondelle [iʀɔ̃dɛl] *nf* swallow.
hirsute [iʀsyt] *a* hairy; shaggy; tousled.
hispanique [ispanik] *a* Hispanic.
***hisser** ['ise] *vt* to hoist, haul up; **se** ~ **sur** to haul o.s. up onto.
histoire [istwaʀ] *nf* (*science, événements*) history; (*anecdote, récit, mensonge*) story; (*affaire*) business *q*; (*chichis*: *gén pl*) fuss *q*; **~s** *nfpl* (*ennuis*) trouble *sg*; **historien, ne** *nm/f* historian; **historique** *a* historic.
hiver [ivɛʀ] *nm* winter; **~nal, e, aux** *a* winter *cpd*; wintry; **~ner** *vi* to winter.
H.L.M. *sigle m ou f voir* **habitation.**
***hocher** ['ɔʃe] *vt*: ~ **la tête** to nod; (*signe négatif ou dubitatif*) to shake one's head.
***hochet** ['ɔʃɛ] *nm* rattle.
***hockey** ['ɔkɛ] *nm*: ~ **(sur glace/gazon)** (ice/field) hockey; ***hockeyeur** *nm* hockey player.
holding ['ɔldiŋ] *nm* holding company.
hold-up ['ɔldœp] *nm inv* hold-up.
***hollandais, e** ['ɔlɑ̃dɛ, -ɛz] *a, nm* (*langue*) Dutch // *nm/f*: **H~, e** Dutchman/woman; **les H~** the Dutch.
***Hollande** ['ɔlɑ̃d] *nf* Holland.
***homard** ['ɔmaʀ] *nm* lobster.
homéopathie [ɔmeɔpati] *nf* homoeopathy; **homéopathique** *a* homoeopathic.
homérique [ɔmeʀik] *a* Homeric.
homicide [ɔmisid] *nm* murder // *nm/f* murderer/eress; ~ **involontaire** manslaughter.
hommage [ɔmaʒ] *nm* tribute; **~s** *nmpl*: **présenter ses ~s** to pay one's respects;

rendre ~ à to pay tribute *ou* homage to; **faire ~ de qch à qn** to present sb with sth.
homme [ɔm] *nm* man; **~ d'affaires** businessman; **~ d'État** statesman; **~ de main** hired man; **~ de paille** stooge; **~-grenouille** *nm* frogman; **~-orchestre** *nm* one-man band.
homogène [ɔmɔʒɛn] *a* homogeneous; **homogénéité** *nf* homogeneity.
homologue [ɔmɔlɔg] *nm/f* counterpart, opposite number.
homologué, e [ɔmɔlɔge] *a* (*SPORT*) officially recognized, ratified; (*tarif*) authorized.
homonyme [ɔmɔnim] *nm* (*LING*) homonym; (*d'une personne*) namesake.
homosexualité [ɔmɔsɛksɥalite] *nf* homosexuality.
homosexuel, le [ɔmɔsɛksɥɛl] *a* homosexual.
***Hongrie** ['ɔ̃gʀi] *nf*: **la ~** Hungary; ***hongrois, e** *a, nm/f, nm* (*langue*) Hungarian.
honnête [ɔnɛt] *a* (*intègre*) honest; (*juste, satisfaisant*) fair; **~ment** *ad* honestly; **~té** *nf* honesty.
honneur [ɔnœʀ] *nm* honour; (*mérite*): **l'~ lui revient** the credit is his; **en l'~ de** in honour of; (*événement*) on the occasion of; **faire ~ à** (*engagements*) to honour; (*famille*) to be a credit to; (*fig: repas etc*) to do justice to; **être à l'~** to be in the place of honour; **être en ~** to be in favour; **membre d'~** honorary member; **table d'~** top table.
honorable [ɔnɔʀabl(ə)] *a* worthy, honourable; (*suffisant*) decent; **~ment** *ad* honorably; decently.
honoraire [ɔnɔʀɛʀ] *a* honorary; **~s** *nmpl* fees *pl*; **professeur ~** professor emeritus.
honorer [ɔnɔʀe] *vt* to honour; (*estimer*) to hold in high regard; (*faire honneur à*) to do credit to; **s'~ de** to pride o.s. upon; **honorifique** *a* honorary.
***honte** ['ɔ̃t] *nf* shame; **avoir ~ de** to be ashamed of; **faire ~ à qn** to make sb (feel) ashamed; ***honteux, euse** *a* ashamed; (*conduite, acte*) shameful, disgraceful.
hôpital, aux [ɔpital, -o] *nm* hospital.
***hoquet** ['ɔkɛ] *nm* hiccough; **avoir le ~** to have (the) hiccoughs; **hoqueter** *vi* to hiccough.
horaire [ɔʀɛʀ] *a* hourly // *nm* timetable, schedule.
***horions** ['ɔʀjɔ̃] *nmpl* blows.
horizon [ɔʀizɔ̃] *nm* horizon; (*paysage*) landscape, view; **sur l'~** on the skyline *ou* horizon.
horizontal, e, aux [ɔʀizɔ̃tal, -o] *a* horizontal; **~ement** *ad* horizontally.
horloge [ɔʀlɔʒ] *nf* clock; **l'~ parlante** the speaking clock; **horloger, ère** *nm/f* watchmaker; clockmaker; **~rie** *nf* watchmaking; watchmaker's (shop); clockmaker's (shop); **pièces d'~rie** watch parts *ou* components.
***hormis** ['ɔʀmi] *prép* save.
hormonal, e, aux [ɔʀmɔnal, -o] *a* hormonal.
hormone [ɔʀmɔn] *nf* hormone.
horoscope [ɔʀɔskɔp] *nm* horoscope.
horreur [ɔʀœʀ] *nf* horror; **avoir ~ de** to loathe *ou* detest; **horrible** *a* horrible; **horrifier** *vt* to horrify.
horripiler [ɔʀipile] *vt* to exasperate.
***hors** ['ɔʀ] *prép* except (for); **~ de** out of; **~ pair** outstanding; **~ de propos** inopportune; **être ~ de soi** to be beside o.s.; **~-bord** *nm inv* speedboat (with outboard motor); **~-concours** *a* ineligible to compete; (*fig*) in a class of one's own; **~-d'œuvre** *nm inv* hors d'œuvre; **~-jeu** *nm inv* offside; **~-la-loi** *nm inv* outlaw; **~-taxe** *a* duty-free; **~-texte** *nm inv* plate.
hortensia [ɔʀtɑ̃sja] *nm* hydrangea.
horticulteur, trice [ɔʀtikyltœʀ, -tʀis] *nm/f* horticulturalist.
horticulture [ɔʀtikyltyʀ] *nf* horticulture.
hospice [ɔspis] *nm* (*de vieillards*) home.
hospitalier, ière [ɔspitalje, -jɛʀ] *a* (*accueillant*) hospitable; (*MÉD: service, centre*) hospital *cpd*.
hospitaliser [ɔspitalize] *vt* to take (*ou* send) to hospital, hospitalize.
hospitalité [ɔspitalite] *nf* hospitality.
hostie [ɔsti] *nf* host.
hostile [ɔstil] *a* hostile; **hostilité** *nf* hostility; **hostilités** *nfpl* hostilities.
hôte [ot] *nm* (*maître de maison*) host; (*invité*) guest; (*client*) patron; (*fig*) inhabitant, occupant.
hôtel [otɛl] *nm* hotel; **aller à l'~** to stay in a hotel; **~ (particulier)** (private) mansion; **~ de ville** town hall; **hôtelier, ière** *a* hotel *cpd* // *nm/f* hotelier, hotel-keeper; **~lerie** *nf* hotel business; (*auberge*) inn.
hôtesse [otɛs] *nf* hostess; **~ de l'air** air hostess *ou* stewardess.
***hotte** ['ɔt] *nf* (*panier*) basket (*carried on the back*); (*de cheminée*) hood; **~ aspirante** cooker hood.
***houblon** ['ublɔ̃] *nm* (*BOT*) hop; (*pour la bière*) hops *pl*.
***houille** ['uj] *nf* coal; **~ blanche** hydroelectric power; ***houiller, ère** *a* coal *cpd*; coal-bearing.
***houle** ['ul] *nf* swell.
***houlette** ['ulɛt] *nf*: **sous la ~ de** under the guidance of.
***houleux, euse** ['ulø, -øz] *a* heavy, swelling; (*fig*) stormy, turbulent.
***houppe** ['up] *nf*, ***houppette** ['upɛt] *nf* powder puff.
***hourra** ['uʀa] *nm* cheer // *excl* hurrah!
***houspiller** ['uspije] *vt* to scold.
***housse** ['us] *nf* cover; dust cover; loose *ou* stretch cover; **~ (penderie)** hanging wardrobe.
***houx** ['u] *nm* holly.
***hublot** ['yblo] *nm* porthole.
***huche** ['yʃ] *nf*: **~ à pain** bread bin.
***huées** ['ɥe] *nfpl* boos.
***huer** ['ɥe] *vt* to boo.
huile [ɥil] *nf* oil; (*ART*) oil painting; (*fam*) bigwig; **~ de foie de morue** cod-liver oil; **~ de table** salad oil; **huiler** *vt* to oil; **huileux, euse** *a* oily.
huis [ɥi] *nm*: **à ~ clos** in camera.

huissier [ɥisje] *nm* usher ; (JUR) ≈ bailiff.
***huit** ['ɥit] *num* eight ; **samedi en** ~ a week on Saturday ; **dans** ~ **jours** in a week('s time) ; **une huitaine de jours** a week or so ; ***huitième** *num* eighth.
huître [ɥitʀ(ə)] *nf* oyster.
humain, e [ymɛ̃, -ɛn] *a* human ; (*compatissant*) humane // *nm* human (being) ; **humaniser** *vt* to humanize ; **humanitaire** *a* humanitarian ; **humanité** *nf* humanity.
humble [œ̃bl(ə)] *a* humble.
humecter [ymɛkte] *vt* to dampen ; **s'**~ **les lèvres** to moisten one's lips.
***humer** ['yme] *vt* to smell ; to inhale.
humeur [ymœʀ] *nf* mood ; (*tempérament*) temper ; (*irritation*) bad temper ; **de bonne/mauvaise** ~ in a good/bad mood.
humide [ymid] *a* damp ; (*main, yeux*) moist ; (*climat, chaleur*) humid ; (*route*) wet ; **humidificateur** *nm* humidifier ; **humidifier** *vt* to humidify ; **humidité** *nf* humidity ; dampness ; **traces d'humidité** traces of moisture *ou* damp.
humiliation [ymiljɑsjɔ̃] *nf* humiliation.
humilier [ymilje] *vt* to humiliate.
humilité [ymilite] *nf* humility, humbleness.
humoriste [ymɔʀist(ə)] *nm/f* humorist.
humoristique [ymɔʀistik] *a* humorous ; humoristic.
humour [ymuʀ] *nm* humour ; **avoir de l'**~ to have a sense of humour ; ~ **noir** sick humour.
***huppé, e** ['ype] *a* crested ; (*fam*) posh.
***hurlement** ['yʀləmɑ̃] *nm* howling *q*, howl, yelling *q*, yell.
***hurler** ['yʀle] *vi* to howl, yell.
hurluberlu [yʀlybɛʀly] *nm* (*péj*) crank.
***hutte** ['yt] *nf* hut.
hybride [ibʀid] *a* hybrid.
hydratant, e [idʀatɑ̃, -ɑ̃t] *a* (*crème*) moisturizing.
hydrate [idʀat] *nm*: ~**s de carbone** carbohydrates.
hydraulique [idʀolik] *a* hydraulic.
hydravion [idʀavjɔ̃] *nm* seaplane, hydroplane.
hydro... [idʀɔ] *préfixe*: ~**carbures** *nmpl* hydrocarbon oils ; ~**cution** *nf* immersion syncope ; ~**-électrique** *a* hydroelectric ; ~**gène** *nm* hydrogen ; ~**glisseur** *nm* hydroplane ; ~**graphie** *nf* (*fleuves*) hydrography ; ~**phile** *a voir* **coton.**
hyène [jɛn] *nf* hyena.
hygiène [iʒjɛn] *nf* hygiene ; ~ **intime** personal hygiene ; **hygiénique** *a* hygienic.
hymne [imn(ə)] *nm* hymn ; ~ **national** national anthem.
hypermarché [ipɛʀmaʀʃe] *nm* hypermarket.
hypermétrope [ipɛʀmetʀɔp] *a* long-sighted, hypermetropic.
hypertension [ipɛʀtɑ̃sjɔ̃] *nf* high blood pressure, hypertension.
hypnose [ipnoz] *nf* hypnosis ; **hypnotique** *a* hypnotic ; **hypnotiser** *vt* to hypnotize.
hypocrisie [ipɔkʀizi] *nf* hypocrisy.
hypocrite [ipɔkʀit] *a* hypocritical // *nm/f* hypocrite.
hypotension [ipɔtɑ̃sjɔ̃] *nf* low blood pressure, hypotension.
hypothécaire [ipɔtekɛʀ] *a* hypothecary ; **garantie/prêt** ~ mortgage security/loan.
hypothèque [ipɔtɛk] *nf* mortgage ; **hypothéquer** *vt* to mortgage.
hypothèse [ipɔtɛz] *nf* hypothesis ; **hypothétique** *a* hypothetical.
hystérie [isteʀi] *nf* hysteria ; **hystérique** *a* hysterical.

I

ibérique [ibeʀik] *a*: **la péninsule** ~ the Iberian peninsula.
iceberg [isbɛʀg] *nm* iceberg.
ici [isi] *ad* here ; **jusqu'**~ as far as this ; until now ; **d'**~ **là** by then ; in the meantime ; **d'**~ **peu** before long.
icône [ikon] *nf* icon.
iconographie [ikɔnɔgʀafi] *nf* iconography ; (collection of) illustrations.
idéal, e, aux [ideal, -o] *a* ideal // *nm* ideal ; ideals *pl* ; ~**iser** *vt* to idealize ; ~**iste** *a* idealistic // *nm/f* idealist.
idée [ide] *nf* idea ; **avoir dans l'**~ **que** to have an idea that ; ~ **fixe** idée fixe, obsession ; ~**s noires** black *ou* dark thoughts ; ~**s reçues** accepted ideas.
identification [idɑ̃tifikɑsjɔ̃] *nf* identification.
identifier [idɑ̃tifje] *vt* to identify ; ~ **qch/qn à** to identify sth/sb with ; **s'**~ **à** (*héros etc*) to identify with.
identique [idɑ̃tik] *a*: ~ **(à)** identical (to).
identité [idɑ̃tite] *nf* identity.
idéologie [ideɔlɔʒi] *nf* ideology.
idiomatique [idjɔmatik] *a*: **expression** ~ idiom, idiomatic expression.
idiot, e [idjo, idjɔt] *a* idiotic // *nm/f* idiot ; **idiotie** [-si] *nf* idiocy ; idiotic remark *etc.*
idiotisme [idjɔtism(ə)] *nm* idiom, idiomatic phrase.
idolâtrer [idɔlɑtʀe] *vt* to idolize.
idole [idɔl] *nf* idol.
idylle [idil] *nf* idyll ; **idyllique** *a* idyllic.
if [if] *nm* yew.
I.F.O.P. [ifɔp] *sigle m* = *Institut français d'opinion publique.*
igloo [iglu] *nm* igloo.
ignare [iɲaʀ] *a* ignorant.
ignifugé, e [ignifyʒe] *a* fireproof(ed).
ignoble [iɲɔbl(ə)] *a* vile.
ignominie [iɲɔmini] *nf* ignominy ; ignominious *ou* base act.
ignorance [iɲɔʀɑ̃s] *nf* ignorance.
ignorant, e [iɲɔʀɑ̃, -ɑ̃t] *a* ignorant.
ignorer [iɲɔʀe] *vt* (*ne pas connaître*) not to know, be unaware *ou* ignorant of ; (*être sans expérience de: plaisir, guerre etc*) not to know about, have no experience of ; (*bouder: personne*) to ignore ; **j'ignore comment/si** I do not know how/if ; ~ **que** to be unaware that, not to know that.
il [il] *pronom* he ; (*animal, chose, en tournure impersonnelle*) it ; NB: *en anglais les navires et les pays sont en général assimilés aux femelles, et les bébés aux choses, si le sexe n'est pas spécifié* ; ~**s** they ; **il neige** it's snowing ; *voir aussi* **avoir**.

île [il] *nf* island ; **les ~s anglo-normandes** the Channel Islands ; **les ~s Britanniques** the British Isles.

illégal, e, aux [ilegal, -o] *a* illegal, unlawful ; **~ité** *nf* illegality, unlawfulness ; **être dans l'~ité** to be outside the law.

illégitime [ileʒitim] *a* illegitimate ; (*optimisme, sévérité*) unjustified ; unwarranted ; **illégitimité** *nf* illegitimacy ; **gouverner dans l'illégitimité** to rule illegally.

illettré, e [iletʀe] *a, nm/f* illiterate.

illicite [ilisit] *a* illicit.

illimité, e [ilimite] *a* (*immense*) boundless, unlimited ; (*congé, durée*) indefinite, unlimited.

illisible [ilizibl(ə)] *a* illegible ; (*roman*) unreadable.

illogique [ilɔʒik] *a* illogical.

illumination [ilyminɑsjɔ̃] *nf* illumination, floodlighting ; flash of inspiration ; **~s** *nfpl* illuminations, lights.

illuminer [ilymine] *vt* to light up ; (*monument, rue: pour une fête*) to illuminate, floodlight ; **s'~** *vi* to light up.

illusion [ilyzjɔ̃] *nf* illusion ; **se faire des ~s** to delude o.s. ; **faire ~** to delude *ou* fool people ; **~ d'optique** optical illusion ; **illusionniste** *nm/f* conjuror ; **illusoire** *a* illusory, illusive.

illustrateur [ilystʀatœʀ] *nm* illustrator.

illustration [ilystʀɑsjɔ̃] *nf* illustration ; (*d'un ouvrage: photos*) illustrations *pl*.

illustre [ilystʀ(ə)] *a* illustrious, renowned.

illustré, e [ilystʀe] *a* illustrated // *nm* illustrated magazine ; comic.

illustrer [ilystʀe] *vt* to illustrate ; **s'~** to become famous, win fame.

îlot [ilo] *nm* small island, islet ; (*de maisons*) block.

image [imaʒ] *nf* (*gén*) picture ; (*comparaison, ressemblance,* OPTIQUE) image ; **~ de marque** brand image ; (*d'un politicien*) public image ; **~ pieuse** holy picture ; **imagé, e** *a* full of imagery.

imaginaire [imaʒinɛʀ] *a* imaginary.

imagination [imaʒinɑsjɔ̃] *nf* imagination ; (*chimère*) fancy ; **avoir de l'~** to be imaginative, have a good imagination.

imaginer [imaʒine] *vt* to imagine ; (*inventer: expédient, mesure*) to devise, think up ; **s'~** *vt* (*se figurer: scène etc*) to imagine, picture ; **s'~ que** to imagine that ; **~ de faire** (*se mettre dans l'idée de*) to dream up the idea of doing.

imbattable [ɛ̃batabl(ə)] *a* unbeatable.

imbécile [ɛ̃besil] *a* idiotic // *nm/f* idiot ; (MÉD) imbecile ; **imbécillité** *nf* idiocy ; imbecility ; idiotic action (*ou* remark *etc*).

imberbe [ɛ̃bɛʀb(ə)] *a* beardless.

imbiber [ɛ̃bibe] *vt*: **~ qch de** to moisten *ou* wet sth with ; **s'~ de** to become saturated with.

imbriquer [ɛ̃bʀike]: **s'~** *vi* to overlap (each other) ; (*fig*) to become interlinked *ou* interwoven.

imbu, e [ɛ̃by] *a*: **~ de** full of.

imbuvable [ɛ̃byvabl(ə)] *a* undrinkable.

imitateur, trice [imitatœʀ, -tʀis] *nm/f* (*gén*) imitator ; (MUSIC-HALL: *d'une personnalité*) impersonator.

imitation [imitɑsjɔ̃] *nf* imitation ; (*sketch*) imitation, impression ; impersonation ; **sac ~ cuir** bag in imitation *ou* simulated leather.

imiter [imite] *vt* to imitate ; (*contrefaire: signature, document*) to forge, copy ; (*avoir l'aspect de*) to look like ; **il se leva et je l'imitai** he got up and I did likewise.

immaculé, e [imakyle] *a* spotless ; immaculate.

immangeable [ɛ̃mɑ̃ʒabl(ə)] *a* inedible, uneatable.

immanquable [ɛ̃mɑ̃kabl(ə)] *a* (*cible*) impossible to miss.

immatriculation [imatʀikylɑsjɔ̃] *nf* registration.

immatriculer [imatʀikyle] *vt* to register ; **faire/se faire ~** to register ; **voiture immatriculée dans la Seine** car with a Seine registration (number).

immédiat, e [imedja, -at] *a* immediate // *nm*: **dans l'~** for the time being ; **immédiatement** *ad* immediately.

immense [imɑ̃s] *a* immense.

immergé, e [imɛʀʒe] *a* submerged.

immerger [imɛʀʒe] *vt* to immerse, submerge ; to lay under water ; **s'~** *vi* (*sous-marin*) to dive, submerge.

immérité, e [imeʀite] *a* undeserved.

immeuble [imœbl(ə)] *nm* building // *a* (JUR) immovable, real ; **~ locatif** block of rented flats.

immigrant, e [imigʀɑ̃, -ɑ̃t] *nm/f* immigrant.

immigration [imigʀɑsjɔ̃] *nf* immigration.

immigré, e [imigʀe] *nm/f* immigrant.

immigrer [imigʀe] *vi* to immigrate.

imminent, e [iminɑ̃, -ɑ̃t] *a* imminent, impending.

immiscer [imise]: **s'~** *vi*: **s'~ dans** to interfere in *ou* with.

immobile [imɔbil] *a* still, motionless ; (*pièce de machine*) fixed ; (*fig*) unchanging.

immobilier, ière [imɔbilje, -jɛʀ] *a* property *cpd*, in real property // *nm*: **l'~** the property *ou* the real estate business.

immobilisation [imɔbilizɑsjɔ̃] *nf* immobilization ; **~s** *nfpl* (COMM) fixed assets.

immobiliser [imɔbilize] *vt* (*gén*) to immobilize ; (*circulation, véhicule, affaires*) to bring to a standstill ; **s'~** (*personne*) to stand still ; (*machine, véhicule*) to come to a halt *ou* standstill.

immobilité [imɔbilite] *nf* stillness ; immobility.

immodéré, e [imɔdeʀe] *a* immoderate, inordinate.

immoler [imɔle] *vt* to immolate, sacrifice.

immonde [imɔ̃d] *a* foul.

immondices [imɔ̃dis] *nmpl* refuse *sg* ; filth *sg*.

immoral, e, aux [imɔʀal, -o] *a* immoral.

immortaliser [imɔʀtalize] *vt* to immortalize.

immortel, le [imɔʀtɛl] a immortal.

immuable [imɥabl(ə)] *a* immutable ; unchanging.

immunisé, e [imynize] *a*: ~ **contre** immune to.
immuniser [imynize] *vt* to immunize.
immunité [imynite] *nf* immunity; ~ **diplomatique** diplomatic immunity; ~ **parlementaire** parliamentary privilege.
impact [ɛ̃pakt] *nm* impact.
impair, e [ɛ̃pɛʀ] *a* odd // *nm* faux pas, blunder.
imparable [ɛ̃paʀabl(ə)] *a* unstoppable.
impardonnable [ɛ̃paʀdɔnabl(ə)] *a* unpardonable, unforgivable.
imparfait, e [ɛ̃paʀfɛ, -ɛt] *a* imperfect // *nm* imperfect (tense).
impartial, e, aux [ɛ̃paʀsjal, -o] *a* impartial, unbiased; ~**ité** *nf* impartiality.
impartir [ɛ̃paʀtiʀ] *vt*: ~ **qch à qn** to assign sth to sb; to bestow sth upon sb.
impasse [ɛ̃pɑs] *nf* dead-end, cul-de-sac; (*fig*) deadlock.
impassible [ɛ̃pasibl(ə)] *a* impassive.
impatience [ɛ̃pasjɑ̃s] *nf* impatience.
impatient, e [ɛ̃pasjɑ̃, -ɑ̃t] *a* impatient; **impatienter** *vt* to irritate, annoy; **s'impatienter** to get impatient; **s'impatienter de/contre** to lose patience at/with, grow impatient at/with.
impayable [ɛ̃pɛjabl(ə)] *a* (*drôle*) priceless.
impayé, e [ɛ̃peje] *a* unpaid.
impeccable [ɛ̃pekabl(ə)] *a* faultless, impeccable; spotlessly clean; impeccably dressed; (*fam*) smashing.
impénétrable [ɛ̃penetʀabl(ə)] *a* impenetrable.
impénitent, e [ɛ̃penitɑ̃, -ɑ̃t] *a* unrepentant.
impensable [ɛ̃pɑ̃sabl(ə)] *a* unthinkable; unbelievable.
impératif, ive [ɛ̃peʀatif, -iv] *a* imperative; (JUR) mandatory // *nm* (LING) imperative; ~**s** *nmpl* requirements; demands.
impératrice [ɛ̃peʀatʀis] *nf* empress.
imperceptible [ɛ̃pɛʀsɛptibl(ə)] *a* imperceptible.
imperfection [ɛ̃pɛʀfɛksjɔ̃] *nf* imperfection.
impérial, e, aux [ɛ̃peʀjal, -o] *a* imperial // *nf* upper deck; **autobus à** ~**e** double-decker bus.
impérialiste [ɛ̃peʀjalist(ə)] *a* imperialist.
impérieux, euse [ɛ̃peʀjø, -øz] *a* (*caractère, ton*) imperious; (*obligation, besoin*) pressing, urgent.
impérissable [ɛ̃peʀisabl(ə)] *a* undying; imperishable.
imperméabiliser [ɛ̃pɛʀmeabilize] *vt* to waterproof.
imperméable [ɛ̃pɛʀmeabl(ə)] *a* waterproof; (GÉO) impermeable; (*fig*): ~ **à** impervious to // *nm* raincoat; ~ **à l'air** airtight.
impersonnel, le [ɛ̃pɛʀsɔnɛl] *a* impersonal.
impertinence [ɛ̃pɛʀtinɑ̃s] *nf* impertinence.
impertinent, e [ɛ̃pɛʀtinɑ̃, -ɑ̃t] *a* impertinent.
imperturbable [ɛ̃pɛʀtyʀbabl(ə)] *a* imperturbable; unruffled; unshakeable.
impétrant, e [ɛ̃petʀɑ̃, -ɑ̃t] *nm/f* (JUR) applicant.
impétueux, euse [ɛ̃petɥø, -øz] *a* fiery.
impie [ɛ̃pi] *a* impious, ungodly; **impiété** *nf* impiety.
impitoyable [ɛ̃pitwajabl(ə)] *a* pitiless, merciless.
implacable [ɛ̃plakabl(ə)] *a* implacable.
implanter [ɛ̃plɑ̃te] *vt* (*usine, industrie, usage*) to establish; (*colons etc*) to settle; (*idée, préjugé*) to implant; **s'**~ **dans** to be established in; to settle in; to become implanted in.
implication [ɛ̃plikɑsjɔ̃] *nf* implication.
implicite [ɛ̃plisit] *a* implicit.
impliquer [ɛ̃plike] *vt* to imply; ~ **qn (dans)** to implicate sb (in).
implorer [ɛ̃plɔʀe] *vt* to implore.
implosion [ɛ̃plosjɔ̃] *nf* implosion.
impoli, e [ɛ̃pɔli] *a* impolite, rude; ~**tesse** *nf* impoliteness, rudeness; impolite *ou* rude remark.
impondérable [ɛ̃pɔ̃deʀabl(ə)] *nm* imponderable.
impopulaire [ɛ̃pɔpylɛʀ] *a* unpopular.
importance [ɛ̃pɔʀtɑ̃s] *nf* importance; **avoir de l'**~ to be important; **sans** ~ unimportant.
important, e [ɛ̃pɔʀtɑ̃, -ɑ̃t] *a* important; (*en quantité*) considerable, sizeable; extensive; (*péj*: *airs, ton*) self-important // *nm*: **l'**~ the important thing.
importateur, trice [ɛ̃pɔʀtatœʀ, -tʀis] *a* importing // *nm* importer; **pays** ~ **de blé** wheat-importing country.
importation [ɛ̃pɔʀtɑsjɔ̃] *nf* importation; introduction; (*produit*) import.
importer [ɛ̃pɔʀte] *vt* (COMM) to import; (*maladies, plantes*) to introduce // *vi* (*être important*) to matter; ~ **à qn** to matter to sb; **il importe qu'il fasse** he must do, it is important that he should do; **peu m'importe** I don't mind; I don't care; **peu importe (que)** it doesn't matter (if); *voir aussi* **n'importe.**
import-export [ɛ̃pɔʀɛkspɔʀ] *nm* import-export business.
importun, e [ɛ̃pɔʀtœ̃, -yn] *a* irksome, importunate; (*arrivée, visite*) inopportune, ill-timed // *nm* intruder; **importuner** *vt* to bother.
imposable [ɛ̃pozabl(ə)] *a* taxable.
imposant, e [ɛ̃pozɑ̃, -ɑ̃t] *a* imposing.
imposer [ɛ̃poze] *vt* (*taxer*) to tax; ~ **qch à qn** to impose sth on sb; **s'**~ (*être nécessaire*) to be imperative; (*montrer sa prominence*) to stand out, emerge; (*artiste: se faire connaître*) to win recognition, come to the fore; **en** ~ **à** to impress.
imposition [ɛ̃pozisjɔ̃] *nf* (ADMIN) taxation.
impossibilité [ɛ̃pɔsibilite] *nf* impossibility; **être dans l'**~ **de faire** to be unable to do, find it impossible to do.
impossible [ɛ̃pɔsibl(ə)] *a* impossible; **il m'est** ~ **de le faire** it is impossible for me to do it, I can't possibly do it; **faire l'**~ **(pour que)** to do one's utmost (so that).
imposteur [ɛ̃pɔstœʀ] *nm* impostor.
imposture [ɛ̃pɔstyʀ] *nf* imposture, deception.

impôt [ɛ̃po] *nm* tax; (*taxes*) taxation; taxes *pl*; **~s** *nmpl* (*contributions*) (income) tax *sg*; **payer 1000 F d'~s** to pay 1,000 F in tax; **~ sur le chiffre d'affaires** corporation tax; **~ foncier** land tax; **~ sur les plus-values** capital gains tax; **~ sur le revenu** income tax.
impotent, e [ɛ̃pɔtɑ̃, -ɑ̃t] *a* disabled.
impraticable [ɛ̃pRatikabl(ə)] *a* (*projet*) impracticable, unworkable; (*piste*) impassable.
imprécation [ɛ̃pRekɑsjɔ̃] *nf* imprecation.
imprécis, e [ɛ̃pResi, -iz] *a* (*contours, souvenir*) imprecise, vague; (*tir*) inaccurate, imprecise.
imprégner [ɛ̃pReɲe] *vt* (*tissu, tampon*): **~ (de)** to soak *ou* impregnate (with); (*lieu, air*): **~ (de)** to fill (with); (*suj*: *amertume, ironie*) to pervade; **s'~ de** to become impregnated with; to be filled with; (*fig*) to absorb.
imprenable [ɛ̃pRənabl(ə)] *a* (*forteresse*) impregnable; **vue ~** unimpeded outlook.
impresario [ɛ̃pResaRjo] *nm* manager, impresario.
impression [ɛ̃pResjɔ̃] *nf* impression; (*d'un ouvrage, tissu*) printing; (PHOTO) exposure; **faire bonne ~** to make a good impression.
impressionnant, e [ɛ̃pResjɔnɑ̃, -ɑ̃t] *a* impressive; upsetting.
impressionner [ɛ̃pResjɔne] *vt* (*frapper*) to impress; (*troubler*) to upset; (PHOTO) to expose.
impressionnisme [ɛ̃pResjɔnism(ə)] *nm* impressionism.
imprévisible [ɛ̃pRevizibl(ə)] *a* unforeseeable.
imprévoyant, e [ɛ̃pRevwajɑ̃, -ɑ̃t] *a* lacking in foresight; (*en matière d'argent*) improvident.
imprévu, e [ɛ̃pRevy] *a* unforeseen, unexpected // *nm* unexpected incident; **en cas d'~** if anything unexpected happens.
imprimé [ɛ̃pRime] *nm* (*formulaire*) printed form; (POSTES) printed matter *q*; (*tissu*) printed fabric.
imprimer [ɛ̃pRime] *vt* to print; (*apposer*: *visa, cachet*) to stamp; (*empreinte etc*) to imprint; (*publier*) to publish; (*communiquer*: *mouvement, impulsion*) to impart, transmit; **imprimerie** *nf* printing; (*établissement*) printing works *sg*; (*atelier*) printing house, printery; **imprimeur** *nm* printer; **imprimeur-éditeur/-libraire** printer and publisher/bookseller.
improbable [ɛ̃pRɔbabl(ə)] *a* unlikely, improbable.
improductif, ive [ɛ̃pRɔdyktif, -iv] *a* unproductive.
impromptu, e [ɛ̃pRɔ̃pty] *a* impromptu; sudden.
impropre [ɛ̃pRɔpR(ə)] *a* inappropriate; **~ à** unsuitable for; **impropriété** *nf* **(de langage)** incorrect usage *q*.
improvisé, e [ɛ̃pRɔvize] *a* makeshift, improvised; (*jeu etc*) scratch, improvised.
improviser [ɛ̃pRɔvize] *vt, vi* to improvise; **s'~** (*secours, réunion*) to be improvised; **s'~ cuisinier** to (decide to) act as cook.
improviste [ɛ̃pRɔvist(ə)]: **à l'~** *ad* unexpectedly, without warning.
imprudemment [ɛ̃pRydamɑ̃] *ad* carelessly; unwisely, imprudently.
imprudence [ɛ̃pRydɑ̃s] *nf* carelessness; imprudence; act of carelessness; foolish *ou* unwise action.
imprudent, e [ɛ̃pRydɑ̃, -ɑ̃t] *a* (*conducteur, geste, action*) careless; (*remarque*) unwise, imprudent; (*projet*) foolhardy.
impubère [ɛ̃pybɛR] *a* below the age of puberty.
impudent, e [ɛ̃pydɑ̃, -ɑ̃t] *a* impudent; brazen.
impudique [ɛ̃pydik] *a* shameless.
impuissance [ɛ̃pɥisɑ̃s] *nf* helplessness; ineffectiveness; impotence.
impuissant, e [ɛ̃pɥisɑ̃, -ɑ̃t] *a* helpless; (*sans effet*) ineffectual; (*sexuellement*) impotent // *nm* impotent man; **~ à faire** powerless to do.
impulsif, ive [ɛ̃pylsif, -iv] *a* impulsive.
impulsion [ɛ̃pylsjɔ̃] *nf* (ÉLEC, *instinct*) impulse; (*élan, influence*) impetus.
impunément [ɛ̃pynemɑ̃] *ad* with impunity.
impur, e [ɛ̃pyR] *a* impure; **~eté** *nf* impurity.
imputation [ɛ̃pytɑsjɔ̃] *nf* imputation, charge.
imputer [ɛ̃pyte] *vt* (*attribuer*): **~ qch à** to ascribe *ou* impute sth to; (COMM): **~ à** *ou* **sur** to charge to.
imputrescible [ɛ̃pytResibl(ə)] *a* which does not rot.
inabordable [inabɔRdabl(ə)] *a* (*lieu*) inaccessible; (*cher*) prohibitive.
inaccentué, e [inaksɑ̃tɥe] *a* (LING) unstressed.
inacceptable [inaksɛptabl(ə)] *a* unacceptable; inadmissible.
inaccessible [inaksesibl(ə)] *a* inaccessible; unattainable; (*insensible*): **~ à** impervious to.
inaccoutumé, e [inakutyme] *a* unaccustomed.
inachevé, e [inaʃve] *a* unfinished.
inactif, ive [inaktif, -iv] *a* inactive, idle.
inaction [inaksjɔ̃] *nf* inactivity.
inactivité [inaktivite] *nf* (ADMIN): **en ~** out of active service.
inadapté, e [inadapte] *a* (*gén*): **~ à** not adapted to, unsuited to; (PSYCH) maladjusted.
inadmissible [inadmisibl(ə)] *a* inadmissible.
inadvertance [inadvɛRtɑ̃s]: **par ~** *ad* inadvertently.
inaliénable [inaljenabl(ə)] *a* inalienable.
inaltérable [inalteRabl(ə)] *a* (*matière*) stable; (*fig*) unchanging; **~ à** unaffected by; **couleur ~ (au lavage/à la lumière)** fast colour/fade-resistant colour.
inamovible [inamɔvibl(ə)] *a* fixed; (JUR) irremovable.
inanimé, e [inanime] *a* (*matière*) inanimate; (*évanoui*) unconscious; (*sans vie*) lifeless.
inanité [inanite] *nf* futility.
inanition [inanisjɔ̃] *nf*: **tomber d'~** to faint with hunger (and exhaustion).

inaperçu, e [inapɛʀsy] *a*: **passer ~** to go unnoticed.
inappliqué, e [inaplike] *a* lacking in application.
inappréciable [inapʀesjabl(ə)] *a* (*service*) invaluable; (*différence, nuance*) inappreciable.
inapte [inapt(ə)] *a*: **~ à** incapable of; (MIL) unfit for.
inattaquable [inatakabl(ə)] *a* (MIL) unassailable; (*texte, preuve*) irrefutable.
inattendu, e [inatɑ̃dy] *a* unexpected.
inattentif, ive [inatɑ̃tif, -iv] *a* inattentive; **~ à** (*dangers, détails*) heedless of; **inattention** *nf* inattention; **faute d'inattention** careless mistake.
inaugural, e, aux [inɔgyʀal, -o] *a* (*cérémonie*) inaugural, opening; (*vol, voyage*) maiden.
inauguration [inɔgyʀɑsjɔ̃] *nf* opening; unveiling.
inaugurer [inɔgyʀe] *vt* (*monument*) to unveil; (*exposition, usine*) to open; (*fig*) to inaugurate.
inavouable [inavwabl(ə)] *a* shameful; undisclosable.
inavoué, e [inavwe] *a* unavowed.
incalculable [ɛ̃kalkylabl(ə)] *a* incalculable.
incandescence [ɛ̃kɑ̃desɑ̃s] *nf* incandescence; **porter à ~** to heat white-hot.
incantation [ɛ̃kɑ̃tɑsjɔ̃] *nf* incantation.
incapable [ɛ̃kapabl(ə)] *a* incapable; **~ de faire** incapable of doing; (*empêché*) unable to do.
incapacité [ɛ̃kapasite] *nf* incapability; (JUR) incapacity; **être dans l'~ de faire** to be unable to do; **~ permantente/de travail** permanent/industrial disablement; **~ électorale** ineligibility to vote.
incarcérer [ɛ̃kaʀseʀe] *vt* to incarcerate.
incarnation [ɛ̃kaʀnɑsjɔ̃] *nf* incarnation.
incarné, e [ɛ̃kaʀne] *a* incarnate; (*ongle*) ingrown.
incarner [ɛ̃kaʀne] *vt* to embody, personify; (THÉÂTRE) to play; (REL) to incarnate.
incartade [ɛ̃kaʀtad] *nf* prank, escapade.
incassable [ɛ̃kɑsabl(ə)] *a* unbreakable.
incendiaire [ɛ̃sɑ̃djɛʀ] *a* incendiary; (*fig: discours*) inflammatory // *nm/f* fire-raiser, arsonist.
incendie [ɛ̃sɑ̃di] *nm* fire; **~ criminel** arson *q*; **~ de forêt** forest fire.
incendier [ɛ̃sɑ̃dje] *vt* (*mettre le feu à*) to set fire to, set alight; (*brûler complètement*) to burn down.
incertain, e [ɛ̃sɛʀtɛ̃, -ɛn] *a* uncertain; (*temps*) uncertain, unsettled; (*imprécis: contours*) indistinct, blurred; **incertitude** *nf* uncertainty.
incessamment [ɛ̃sɛsamɑ̃] *a* very shortly.
incessant, e [ɛ̃sɛsɑ̃, -ɑ̃t] *a* incessant, unceasing.
inceste [ɛ̃sɛst(ə)] *nm* incest.
inchangé, e [ɛ̃ʃɑ̃ʒe] *a* unchanged, unaltered.
incidemment [ɛ̃sidamɑ̃] *ad* in passing.
incidence [ɛ̃sidɑ̃s] *nf* (*effet, influence*) effect; (PHYSIQUE) incidence.
incident [ɛ̃sidɑ̃] *nm* incident; **~ de parcours** minor hitch *ou* setback; **~ technique** technical difficulties *pl*.
incinérateur [ɛ̃sineʀatœʀ] *nm* incinerator.
incinérer [ɛ̃sineʀe] *vt* (*ordures*) to incinerate; (*mort*) to cremate.
incise [ɛ̃siz] *nf* (LING) interpolated clause.
incisif, ive [ɛ̃sizif, -iv] *a* incisive, cutting // *nf* incisor.
incision [ɛ̃sizjɔ̃] *nf* incision; (*d'un abcès*) lancing.
inciter [ɛ̃site] *vt*: **~ qn à faire** to incite *ou* prompt sb to do.
inclinaison [ɛ̃klinɛzɔ̃] *nf* (*déclivité: d'une route etc*) incline; (*: d'un toit*) slope; (*état penché: d'un mur*) lean; (*: de la tête*) tilt; (*: d'un navire*) list.
inclination [ɛ̃klinɑsjɔ̃] *nf* (*penchant*) inclination, tendency; **~ de (la) tête** nod (of the head); **~ (de buste)** bow.
incliner [ɛ̃kline] *vt* (*tête, bouteille*) to tilt; (*inciter*): **~ qn à qch/à faire** to encourage sb towards sth/to do // *vi*: **~ à qch/à faire** to incline towards sth/doing; to tend towards sth/to do; **s'~** (*route*) to slope; **s'~ (devant)** to bow (before); (*céder*) to give in *ou* yield (to); **~ la tête *ou* le front** to give a slight bow.
inclure [ɛ̃klyʀ] *vt* to include; (*joindre à un envoi*) to enclose; **jusqu'au 10 mars inclus** until 10th March inclusive.
incoercible [ɛ̃kɔɛʀsibl(ə)] *a* uncontrollable.
incognito [ɛ̃kɔɲito] *ad* incognito.
incohérence [ɛ̃kɔeʀɑ̃s] *nf* inconsistency.
incohérent, e [ɛ̃kɔeʀɑ̃, -ɑ̃t] *a* inconsistent; incoherent.
incollable [ɛ̃kɔlabl(ə)] *a*: **il est ~** he's got all the answers.
incolore [ɛ̃kɔlɔʀ] *a* colourless.
incomber [ɛ̃kɔ̃be]: **~ à** *vt* (*suj: devoirs, responsabilité*) to rest *ou* be incumbent upon; (*: frais, travail*) to be the responsibility of.
incombustible [ɛ̃kɔ̃bystibl(ə)] *a* incombustible.
incommensurable [ɛ̃kɔmɑ̃syʀabl(ə)] *a* immeasurable.
incommode [ɛ̃kɔmɔd] *a* inconvenient; (*posture, siège*) uncomfortable.
incommoder [ɛ̃kɔmɔde] *vt*: **~ qn** to bother *ou* inconvenience sb; (*embarrasser*) to make sb feel uncomfortable *ou* ill at ease.
incomparable [ɛ̃kɔ̃paʀabl(ə)] *a* not comparable; (*inégalable*) incomparable, matchless.
incompatibilité [ɛ̃kɔ̃patibilite] *nf* incompatibility; **~ d'humeur** (mutual) incompatibility.
incompatible [ɛ̃kɔ̃patibl(ə)] *a* incompatible.
incompétent, e [ɛ̃kɔ̃petɑ̃, -ɑ̃t] *a* (*ignorant*) inexpert; (JUR) incompetent, not competent.
incomplet, ète [ɛ̃kɔ̃plɛ, -ɛt] *a* incomplete.
incompréhensible [ɛ̃kɔ̃pʀeɑ̃sibl(ə)] *a* incomprehensible.

incompréhensif, ive [ɛ̃kɔ̃pReɑ̃sif, -iv] *a* lacking in understanding ; unsympathetic.
incompris, e [ɛ̃kɔ̃pRi, -iz] *a* misunderstood.
inconcevable [ɛ̃kɔ̃svabl(ə)] *a* inconceivable.
inconciliable [ɛ̃kɔ̃siljabl(ə)] *a* irreconcilable.
inconditionnel, le [ɛ̃kɔ̃disjɔnɛl] *a* unconditional ; (*partisan*) unquestioning.
inconduite [ɛ̃kɔ̃dɥit] *nf* wild behaviour *q*.
inconfortable [ɛ̃kɔ̃fɔRtabl(ə)] *a* uncomfortable.
incongru, e [ɛ̃kɔ̃gRy] *a* unseemly.
inconnu, e [ɛ̃kɔny] *a* unknown ; new, strange // *nm/f* stranger ; unknown person (*ou* artist *etc*) // *nm*: **l'~** the unknown // *nf* (MATH) unknown ; (*fig*) unknown factor.
inconsciemment [ɛ̃kɔ̃sjamɑ̃] *ad* unconsciously ; thoughtlessly.
inconscience [ɛ̃kɔ̃sjɑ̃s] *nf* unconsciousness ; thoughtlessness, recklessness.
inconscient, e [ɛ̃kɔ̃sjɑ̃, -ɑ̃t] *a* unconscious ; (*irréfléchi*) thoughtless, reckless // *nm* (PSYCH): **l'~** the subconscious, the unconscious ; **~ de** unaware of.
inconsidéré, e [ɛ̃kɔ̃sideRe] *a* ill-considered.
inconsistant, e [ɛ̃kɔ̃sistɑ̃, -ɑ̃t] *a* flimsy, weak ; runny.
inconstant, e [ɛ̃kɔ̃stɑ̃, -ɑ̃t] *a* inconstant, fickle.
incontestable [ɛ̃kɔ̃tɛstabl(ə)] *a* indisputable.
incontesté, e [ɛ̃kɔ̃tɛste] *a* undisputed.
incontinence [ɛ̃kɔ̃tinɑ̃s] *nf* incontinence.
incontinent, e [ɛ̃kɔ̃tinɑ̃, -ɑ̃t] *a* incontinent // *ad* forthwith.
incontrôlable [ɛ̃kɔ̃tRolabl(ə)] *a* unverifiable.
inconvenant, e [ɛ̃kɔ̃vnɑ̃, -ɑ̃t] *a* unseemly, improper.
inconvénient [ɛ̃kɔ̃venjɑ̃] *nm* (*d'une situation, d'un projet*) disadvantage, drawback ; (*d'un remède, changement etc*) risk, inconvenience ; **si vous n'y voyez pas d'~** if you have no objections.
incorporation [ɛ̃kɔRpɔRɑsjɔ̃] *nf* (MIL) call-up.
incorporer [ɛ̃kɔRpɔRe] *vt* **~ (à)** to mix in (with) ; (*paragraphe etc*): **~ (dans)** to incorporate (in) ; (*territoire, immigrants*): **~ (à)** to incorporate (into) ; (MIL: *appeler*) to recruit, call up ; (: *affecter*): **~ qn dans** to enlist sb into.
incorrect, e [ɛ̃kɔRɛkt] *a* (*impropre, inconvenant*) improper ; (*défectueux*) faulty ; (*inexact*) incorrect ; (*impoli*) impolite ; (*déloyal*) underhand.
incorrigible [ɛ̃kɔRiʒibl(ə)] *a* incorrigible.
incorruptible [ɛ̃kɔRyptibl(ə)] *a* incorruptible.
incrédule [ɛ̃kRedyl] *a* incredulous ; (REL) unbelieving.
increvable [ɛ̃kRəvabl(ə)] *a* (*pneu*) puncture-proof ; (*fam*) tireless.
incriminer [ɛ̃kRimine] *vt* (*personne*) to incriminate ; (*action, conduite*) to bring under attack ; (*bonne foi, honnêteté*) to call into question.
incroyable [ɛ̃kRwajabl(ə)] *a* incredible ; unbelievable.
incroyant, e [ɛ̃kRwajɑ̃, -ɑ̃t] *nm/f* non-believer.
incrustation [ɛ̃kRystɑsjɔ̃] *nf* inlaying *q* ; inlay ; (*dans une chaudière etc*) fur *q*, scale *q*.
incruster [ɛ̃kRyste] *vt* (ART): **~ qch dans/qch de** to inlay sth into/sth with ; (*radiateur etc*) to coat with scale *ou* fur ; **s'~** *vi* (*invité*) to take root ; (*radiateur etc*) to become coated with fur *ou* scale ; **s'~ dans** (*suj*: *corps étranger, caillou*) to become embedded in.
incubateur [ɛ̃kybatœR] *nm* incubator.
incubation [ɛ̃kybɑsjɔ̃] *nf* incubation.
inculpation [ɛ̃kylpɑsjɔ̃] *nf* charging *q* ; charge.
inculpé, e [ɛ̃kylpe] *nm/f* accused.
inculper [ɛ̃kylpe] *vt*: **~ (de)** to charge (with).
inculquer [ɛ̃kylke] *vt*: **~ qch à** to inculcate sth in *ou* instil sth into.
inculte [ɛ̃kylt(ə)] *a* uncultivated ; (*esprit, peuple*) uncultured ; (*barbe*) unkempt.
incurable [ɛ̃kyRabl(ə)] *a* incurable.
incurie [ɛ̃kyRi] *nf* carelessness.
incursion [ɛ̃kyRsjɔ̃] *nf* incursion, foray.
incurvé, e [ɛ̃kyRve] *a* curved.
Inde [ɛ̃d] *nf*: **l'~** India.
indécence [ɛ̃desɑ̃s] *nf* indecency ; indecent remark (*ou* act *etc*).
indécent, e [ɛ̃desɑ̃, -ɑ̃t] *a* indecent.
indéchiffrable [ɛ̃deʃifRabl(ə)] *a* indecipherable.
indécis, e [ɛ̃desi, -iz] *a* indecisive ; (*perplexe*) undecided ; **indécision** *nf* indecision ; indecisiveness.
indéfendable [ɛ̃defɑ̃dabl(ə)] *a* indefensible.
indéfini, e [ɛ̃defini] *a* (*imprécis, incertain*) undefined ; (*illimité*, LING) indefinite ; **~ment** *ad* indefinitely ; **~ssable** *a* indefinable.
indéformable [ɛ̃defɔRmabl(ə)] *a* that keeps its shape.
indélébile [ɛ̃delebil] *a* indelible.
indélicat, e [ɛ̃delika, -at] *a* tactless ; dishonest.
indémaillable [ɛ̃demɑjabl(ə)] *a* run-resist.
indemne [ɛ̃dɛmn(ə)] *a* unharmed.
indemniser [ɛ̃dɛmnize] *vt*: **~ qn (de)** to compensate sb (for).
indemnité [ɛ̃dɛmnite] *nf* (*dédommagement*) compensation *q* ; (*allocation*) allowance ; **~ de licenciement** redundancy payment ; **~ de logement** housing allowance ; **~ parlementaire** ≈ M.P.'s salary.
indéniable [ɛ̃denjabl(ə)] *a* undeniable, indisputable.
indépendamment [ɛ̃depɑ̃damɑ̃] *ad* independently ; **~ de** (*abstraction faite de*) irrespective of ; (*en plus de*) over and above.
indépendance [ɛ̃depɑ̃dɑ̃s] *nf* independence.
indépendant, e [ɛ̃depɑ̃dɑ̃, -ɑ̃t] *a* independent ; **~ de** independent of ;

chambre ~e room with private entrance.
indescriptible [ɛ̃dɛskʀiptibl(ə)] *a* indescribable.
indésirable [ɛ̃deziʀabl(ə)] *a* undesirable.
indestructible [ɛ̃dɛstʀyktibl(ə)] *a* indestructible; (*marque, impression*) indelible.
indétermination [ɛ̃detɛʀminɑsjɔ̃] *nf* indecision; indecisiveness.
indéterminé, e [ɛ̃detɛʀmine] *a* unspecified; indeterminate; indeterminable.
index [ɛ̃dɛks] *nm* (*doigt*) index finger; (*d'un livre etc*) index; **mettre à l'~** to blacklist.
indexé, e [ɛ̃dɛkse] *a* (*ÉCON*): **~ (sur)** index-linked (to).
indicateur [ɛ̃dikatœʀ] *nm* (*POLICE*) informer; (*livre*) guide; directory; (*TECH*) gauge; indicator; **~ des chemins de fer** railway timetable; **~ de direction** (*AUTO*) indicator; **~ immobilier** property gazette; **~ de rues** street directory; **~ de vitesse** speedometer.
indicatif, ive [ɛ̃dikatif, -iv] *a*: **à titre ~** for (your) information // *nm* (*LING*) indicative; (*d'une émission*) theme *ou* signature tune; (*téléphonique*) dialling code; **~ d'appel** (*RADIO*) call sign.
indication [ɛ̃dikɑsjɔ̃] *nf* indication; (*renseignement*) information *q*; **~s** *nfpl* (*directives*) instructions.
indice [ɛ̃dis] *nm* (*marque, signe*) indication, sign; (*POLICE*: *lors d'une enquête*) clue; (*JUR*: *présomption*) piece of evidence; (*SCIENCE, TECH*) index; (*ADMIN*) grading; rating; **~ d'octane** octane rating; **~ des prix** price index; **~ de traitement** salary grading.
indicible [ɛ̃disibl(ə)] *a* inexpressible.
indien, ne [ɛ̃djɛ̃, -jɛn] *a* Indian // *nm/f*: **I~, ne** (*d'Amérique*) Red Indian; (*d'Inde*) Indian.
indifféremment [ɛ̃difeʀamɑ̃] *ad* (*sans distinction*) equally (well); indiscriminately.
indifférence [ɛ̃difeʀɑ̃s] *nf* indifference.
indifférent, e [ɛ̃difeʀɑ̃, -ɑ̃t] *a* (*peu intéressé*) indifferent; **~ à** (*insensible à*) indifferent to, unconcerned about; (*peu intéressant pour*) indifferent to; immaterial to.
indigence [ɛ̃diʒɑ̃s] *nf* poverty.
indigène [ɛ̃diʒɛn] *a* native, indigenous; local // *nm/f* native.
indigent, e [ɛ̃diʒɑ̃, -ɑ̃t] *a* destitute, poverty-stricken; (*fig*) poor.
indigeste [ɛ̃diʒɛst(ə)] *a* indigestible.
indigestion [ɛ̃diʒɛstjɔ̃] *nf* indigestion *q*.
indignation [ɛ̃diɲɑsjɔ̃] *nf* indignation.
indigne [ɛ̃diɲ] *a* unworthy.
indigner [ɛ̃diɲe] *vt* to make indignant; **s'~ (de/contre)** to be (*ou* become) indignant (at).
indignité [ɛ̃diɲite] *nf* unworthiness *q*; shameful act.
indiqué, e [ɛ̃dike] *a* (*adéquat*) appropriate, suitable; (*conseillé*) suitable, advisable.
indiquer [ɛ̃dike] *vt* (*désigner*): **~ qch/qn à qn** to point sth/sb out to sb; (*suj*: *pendule, aiguille*) to show; (*suj*: *étiquette, plan*) to show, indicate; (*faire connaître*: *médecin, restaurant*): **~ qch/qn à qn** to tell sb of sth/sb; (*renseigner sur*) to point out, tell; (*déterminer*: *date, lieu*) to give, state; (*dénoter*) to indicate, point to; **pourriez-vous m'~ les toilettes/l'heure?** could you direct me to the toilets/tell me the time?
indirect, e [ɛ̃diʀɛkt] *a* indirect.
indiscipline [ɛ̃disiplin] *nf* lack of discipline; **indiscipliné, e** *a* undisciplined; (*fig*) unmanageable.
indiscret, ète [ɛ̃diskʀɛ, -ɛt] *a* indiscreet; **indiscrétion** *nf* indiscretion.
indiscutable [ɛ̃diskytabl(ə)] *a* indisputable.
indispensable [ɛ̃dispɑ̃sabl(ə)] *a* indispensable; essential.
indisponible [ɛ̃dispɔnibl(ə)] *a* unavailable.
indisposé, e [ɛ̃dispoze] *a* indisposed, unwell.
indisposer [ɛ̃dispoze] *vt* (*incommoder*) to upset; (*déplaire à*) to antagonize.
indistinct, e [ɛ̃distɛ̃, -ɛ̃kt(ə)] *a* indistinct; **indistinctement** *ad* (*voir, prononcer*) indistinctly; (*sans distinction*) without distinction, indiscriminately.
individu [ɛ̃dividy] *nm* individual; **~aliser** *vt* to individualize; (*personnaliser*) to tailor to individual requirements; **~aliste** *nm/f* individualist.
individuel, le [ɛ̃dividɥɛl] *a* (*gén*) individual; (*opinion, livret, contrôle, avantages*) personal; **chambre ~le** single room; **maison ~le** detached house; **propriété ~le** personal *ou* private property.
indocile [ɛ̃dɔsil] *a* unruly.
indolent, e [ɛ̃dɔlɑ̃, -ɑ̃t] *a* indolent.
indolore [ɛ̃dɔlɔʀ] *a* painless.
indomptable [ɛ̃dɔ̃tabl(ə)] *a* untameable; (*fig*) invincible, indomitable.
Indonésie [ɛ̃donezi] *nf* Indonesia; **indonésien, ne** *a, nm/f* Indonesian.
indu, e [ɛ̃dy] *a*: **à des heures ~es** at some ungodly hour.
indubitable [ɛ̃dybitabl(ə)] *a* indubitable.
induire [ɛ̃dɥiʀ] *vt*: **~ qch de** to induce sth from; **~ qn en erreur** to lead sb astray, mislead sb.
indulgence [ɛ̃dylʒɑ̃s] *nf* indulgence; leniency.
indulgent, e [ɛ̃dylʒɑ̃, -ɑ̃t] *a* (*parent, regard*) indulgent; (*juge, examinateur*) lenient.
indûment [ɛ̃dymɑ̃] *ad* wrongfully; without due cause.
industrialiser [ɛ̃dystʀijalize] *vt* to industrialize; **s'~** to become industrialized.
industrie [ɛ̃dystʀi] *nf* industry; **~ du spectacle** entertainment business; **industriel, le** *a* industrial // *nm* industrialist; manufacturer.
industrieux, euse [ɛ̃dystʀijø, -øz] *a* industrious.
inébranlable [inebʀɑ̃labl(ə)] *a* (*masse, colonne*) solid; (*personne, certitude, foi*) steadfast, unwavering.
inédit, e [inedi, -it] *a* (*correspondance etc*)

hitherto unpublished; (*spectacle, moyen*) novel, original.
ineffable [inefabl(ə)] *a* inexpressible, ineffable.
ineffaçable [inefasabl(ə)] *a* indelible.
inefficace [inefikas] *a* (*remède, moyen*) ineffective; (*machine, employé*) inefficient; **inefficacité** *nf* ineffectiveness; inefficiency.
inégal, e, aux [inegal, -o] *a* unequal; uneven.
inégalable [inegalabl(e)] *a* matchless.
inégalé, e [inegale] *a* unmatched, unequalled.
inégalité [inegalite] *nf* inequality; unevenness *q*; ~ **de 2 hauteurs** difference *ou* disparity between 2 heights.
inélégant, e [inelegɑ̃, -ɑ̃t] *a* inelegant; (*indélicat*) discourteous.
inéligible [ineliʒibl(ə)] *a* ineligible.
inéluctable [inelyktabl(ə)] *a* inescapable, ineluctable.
inemployé, e [inɑ̃plwaje] *a* unused.
inénarrable [inenaʀabl(ə)] *a* hilarious.
inepte [inɛpt(ə)] *a* inept; **ineptie** [-si] *nf* ineptitude; nonsense *q*.
inépuisable [inepɥizabl(ə)] *a* inexhaustible.
inerte [inɛʀt(ə)] *a* lifeless; (*apathique*) passive, inert; (PHYSIQUE, CHIMIE) inert.
inertie [inɛʀsi] *nf* inertia.
inespéré, e [inɛspeʀe] *a* unhoped-for.
inesthétique [inɛstetik] *a* unsightly.
inestimable [inɛstimabl(e)] *a* priceless; (*fig: bienfait*) invaluable.
inévitable [inevitabl(ə)] *a* unavoidable; (*fatal, habituel*) inevitable.
inexact, e [inɛgzakt] *a* inaccurate, inexact; unpunctual; **~itude** *nf* inaccuracy.
inexcusable [inɛkskyzabl(ə)] *a* inexcusable, unforgivable.
inexécutable [inɛgzekytabl(ə)] *a* impracticable, unworkable; (MUS) unplayable.
inexistant, e [inɛgzistɑ̃, -ɑ̃t] *a* non-existent.
inexorable [inɛgzɔʀabl(ə)] *a* inexorable.
inexpérience [inɛkspeʀjɑ̃s] *nf* inexperience, lack of experience.
inexplicable [inɛksplikabl(ə) *a* inexplicable.
inexpliqué, e [inɛksplike] *a* unexplained.
inexploité, e [inɛksplwate] *a* unexploited, untapped.
inexpressif, ive [inɛkspʀesif, -iv] *a* inexpressive; expressionless.
inexprimable [inɛkspʀimabl(ə)] *a* inexpressible.
inexprimé, e [inɛkspʀime] *a* unspoken, unexpressed.
inextensible [inɛkstɑ̃sibl(ə)] *a* (*tissu*) non-stretch.
in extenso [inɛkstɛ̃so] *ad* in full.
inextricable [inɛkstʀikabl(ə] *a* inextricable.
in extremis [inɛkstʀemis] *ad* at the last minute // *a* last-minute; (*testament*) death bed *cpd*.

infaillibilité [ɛ̃fajibilite] *nf* infallibility.
infaillible [ɛ̃fajibl(ə)] *a* infallible; (*instinct*) infallible, unerring.
infâme [ɛ̃fɑm] *a* vile.
infanterie [ɛ̃fɑ̃tʀi] *nf* infantry.
infanticide [ɛ̃fɑ̃tisid] *nm/f* child-murderer/eress // *nm* (*meurtre*) infanticide.
infantile [ɛ̃fɑ̃til] *a* (MÉD) infantile, child *cpd*; (*ton, réaction, péj*) infantile, childish.
infarctus [ɛ̃faʀktys] *nm*: ~ **(du myocarde)** coronary (thrombosis).
infatigable [ɛ̃fatigabl(ə)] *a* tireless, indefatigable.
infatué, e [ɛ̃fatɥe] *a* conceited; ~ **de** full of.
infécond, e [ɛ̃fekɔ̃, -ɔ̃d] *a* infertile, barren.
infect, e [ɛ̃fɛkt] *a* vile, foul; (*repas, vin*) revolting, foul.
infecter [ɛ̃fɛkte] *vt* (*atmosphère, eau*) to contaminate; (MÉD) to infect; **s'~** to become infected *ou* septic; **infectieux, euse** [-sjø, -øz] *a* infectious; **infection** [-sjɔ̃] *nf* infection.
inféoder [ɛ̃feɔde] *vt*: **s'~ à** to pledge allegiance to.
inférer [ɛ̃feʀe] *vt*: ~ **qch de** to infer sth from.
inférieur, e [ɛ̃feʀjœʀ] *a* lower; (*en qualité, intelligence*) inferior // *nm/f* inferior; ~ **à** (*somme, quantité*) less *ou* smaller than; (*moins bon que*) inferior to; (*tâche: pas à la hauteur de*) unequal to; **infériorité** *nf* inferiority.
infernal, e, aux [ɛ̃fɛʀnal, -o] *a* (*chaleur, rythme*) infernal; (*méchanceté, complot*) diabolical.
infester [ɛ̃fɛste] *vt* to infest; **infesté de moustiques** infested with mosquitoes, mosquito-ridden.
infidèle [ɛ̃fidɛl] *a* unfaithful; (REL) infidel; **infidélité** *nf* unfaithfulness *q*.
infiltration [ɛ̃filtʀɑsjɔ̃] *nf* infiltration.
infiltrer [ɛ̃filtʀe]: **s'~** *vi*: **s'~ dans** to penetrate into; (*liquide*) to seep into; (*fig: noyauter*) to infiltrate.
infime [ɛ̃fim] *a* minute, tiny; (*inférieur*) lowly.
infini, e [ɛ̃fini] *a* infinite // *nm* infinity; **à l'~** (MATH) to infinity; (*discourir*) ad infinitum, endlessly; (*agrandir, varier*) infinitely; (*à perte de vue*) endlessly (into the distance); **~ment** *ad* infinitely; **infinité** *nf*: **une infinité de** an infinite number of.
infinitif, ive [ɛ̃finitif, -iv] *a, nm* infinitive.
infirme [ɛ̃fiʀm(ə)] *a* disabled // *nm/f* disabled person; ~ **de guerre** war cripple; ~ **du travail** industrially disabled person.
infirmer [ɛ̃fiʀme] *vt* to invalidate.
infirmerie [ɛ̃fiʀməʀi] *nf* sick bay.
infirmier, ière [ɛ̃fiʀmje, -jɛʀ] *nm/f* nurse; **infirmière chef** sister; **infirmière diplômée** registered nurse; **infirmière visiteuse** ≈ district nurse.
infirmité [ɛ̃fiʀmite] *nf* disability.
inflammable [ɛ̃flamabl(ə)] *a* (in)flammable.
inflammation [ɛ̃flamɑsjɔ̃] *nf* inflammation.

inflation [ɛ̃flɑsjɔ̃] *nf* inflation; **inflationniste** *a* inflationist.
infléchir [ɛ̃fleʃiʀ] *vt* (*fig: politique*) to reorientate, redirect.
inflexible [ɛ̃flɛksibl(ə)] *a* inflexible.
inflexion [ɛ̃flɛksjɔ̃] *nf* inflexion; **~ de la tête** slight nod (of the head).
infliger [ɛ̃fliʒe] *vt*: **~ qch (à qn)** to inflict sth (on sb); (*amende, sanction*) to impose sth (on sb).
influençable [ɛ̃flyɑ̃sabl(ə)] *a* easily influenced.
influence [ɛ̃flyɑ̃s] *nf* influence; (*d'un médicament*) effect; **influencer** *vt* to influence; **influent, e** *a* influential.
influer [ɛ̃flye]: **~ sur** *vt* to have an influence upon.
influx [ɛ̃fly] *nm*: **~ nerveux** (nervous) impulse.
informaticien, ne [ɛ̃fɔʀmatisjɛ̃, -jɛn] *nm/f* computer scientist.
information [ɛ̃fɔʀmɑsjɔ̃] *nf* (*renseignement*) piece of information; (PRESSE, TV: *nouvelle*) news *sg*; (*diffusion de renseignements,* INFORMATIQUE) information; (JUR) inquiry, investigation; **voyage d'~** fact-finding trip; **agence d'~** news agency; **journal d'~** quality newspaper.
informatique [ɛ̃fɔʀmatik] *nf* (*techniques*) data processing; (*science*) computer science; **informatiser** *vt* to computerize.
informe [ɛ̃fɔʀm(ə)] *a* shapeless.
informer [ɛ̃fɔʀme] *vt*: **~ qn (de)** to inform sb (of) // *vi* (JUR): **~ contre/sur** to initiate inquiries about; **s'~ (sur)** to inform o.s. (about); **s'~ (de/si)** to inquire *ou* find out (about/whether *ou* if).
infortune [ɛ̃fɔʀtyn] *nf* misfortune.
infraction [ɛ̃fʀaksjɔ̃] *nf* offence; **~ à** violation *ou* breach of; **être en ~** to be in breach of the law.
infranchissable [ɛ̃fʀɑ̃ʃisabl(ə)] *a* impassable; (*fig*) insuperable.
infrarouge [ɛ̃fʀaʀuʒ] *a, nm* infrared.
infrastructure [ɛ̃fʀastʀyktyʀ] *nf* (*d'une route etc*) substructure; (AVIAT, MIL) ground installations *pl*; (ÉCON: *touristique etc*) infrastructure.
infroissable [ɛ̃fʀwasabl(ə)] *a* crease-resistant.
infructueux, euse [ɛ̃fʀyktɥø, -øz] *a* fruitless, unfruitful.
infus, e [ɛ̃fy, -yz] *a*: **avoir la science ~e** to have innate knowledge.
infuser [ɛ̃fyze] *vt* (*thé*) to brew; (*tisane*) to infuse // *vi* to brew; to infuse; **infusion** *nf* (*tisane*) infusion, herb tea.
ingambe [ɛ̃gɑ̃b] *a* spry, nimble.
ingénier [ɛ̃ʒenje]: **s'~** *vi*: **s'~ à faire** to strive to do.
ingénieur [ɛ̃ʒenjœʀ] *nm* engineer; **~ agronome/chimiste** agricultural/chemical engineer; **~ du son** sound engineer.
ingénieux, euse [ɛ̃ʒenjø, -øz] *a* ingenious, clever; **ingéniosité** *nf* ingenuity.
ingénu, e [ɛ̃ʒeny] *a* ingenuous, artless // *nf* (THÉÂTRE) ingénue.
ingérer [ɛ̃ʒeʀe]: **s'~** *vi*: **s'~ dans** to interfere in.
ingrat, e [ɛ̃gʀa, -at] *a* (*personne*) ungrateful; (*sol*) barren, arid; (*travail, sujet*) arid, thankless; (*visage*) unprepossessing; **ingratitude** *nf* ingratitude.
ingrédient [ɛ̃gʀedjɑ̃] *nm* ingredient.
inguérissable [ɛ̃geʀisabl(ə)] *a* incurable.
ingurgiter [ɛ̃gyʀʒite] *vt* to swallow.
inhabile [inabil] *a* clumsy; (*fig*) inept.
inhabitable [inabitabl(ə)] *a* uninhabitable.
inhabité, e [inabite] *a* (*régions*) uninhabited; (*maison*) unoccupied.
inhabituel, le [inabitɥɛl] *a* unusual.
inhalateur [inalatœʀ] *nm* inhaler; **~ d'oxygène** oxygen mask.
inhalation [inalɑsjɔ̃] *nf* (MÉD) inhalation; **faire des ~s** to use an inhalation bath.
inhérent, e [ineʀɑ̃, -ɑ̃t] *a*: **~ à** inherent in.
inhibition [inibisjɔ̃] *nf* inhibition.
inhospitalier, ière [inɔspitalje, -jɛʀ] *a* inhospitable.
inhumain, e [inymɛ̃, -ɛn] *a* inhuman.
inhumation [inymɑsjɔ̃] *nf* interment, burial.
inhumer [inyme] *vt* to inter, bury.
inimaginable [inimaʒinabl(ə)] *a* unimaginable.
inimitable [inimitabl(ə)] *a* inimitable.
inimitié [inimitje] *nf* enmity.
ininflammable [inɛ̃flamabl(ə)] *a* non-flammable.
inintelligent, e [inɛ̃teliʒɑ̃, -ɑ̃t] *a* unintelligent.
inintelligible [inɛ̃teliʒibl(ə)] *a* unintelligible.
inintéressant, e [inɛ̃teʀɛsɑ̃, -ɑ̃t] *a* uninteresting.
ininterrompu, e [inɛ̃tɛʀɔ̃py] *a* (*file, série*) unbroken; (*flot, vacarme*) uninterrupted, non-stop; (*effort*) unremitting, continuous.
iniquité [inikite] *nf* iniquity.
initial, e, aux [inisjal, -o] *a, nf* initial.
initiateur, trice [inisjatœʀ, -tʀis] *nm/f* initiator; (*d'une mode, technique*) innovator, pioneer.
initiative [inisjativ] *nf* initiative; **prendre l'~ de qch/de faire** to take the initiative for sth/of *ou* in doing; **avoir de l'~** to have initiative, show enterprise.
initier [inisje] *vt*: **~ qn à** to initiate sb into; (*faire découvrir: art, jeu*) to introduce sb to.
injecté, e [ɛ̃ʒɛkte] *a*: **yeux ~s de sang** bloodshot eyes.
injecter [ɛ̃ʒɛkte] *vt* to inject; **injection** [-sjɔ̃] *nf* injection; **à injection** *a* (AUTO) fuel injection *cpd*.
injonction [ɛ̃ʒɔ̃ksjɔ̃] *nf* injunction, order.
injure [ɛ̃ʒyʀ] *nf* insult, abuse *q*.
injurier [ɛ̃ʒyʀje] *vt* to insult, abuse; **injurieux, euse** *a* abusive, insulting.
injuste [ɛ̃ʒyst(ə)] *a* unjust, unfair; **injustice** *nf* injustice.
inlassable [ɛ̃lɑsabl(ə)] *a* tireless, indefatigable.
inné, e [ine] *a* innate, inborn.
innocence [inɔsɑ̃s] *nf* innocence.
innocent, e [inɔsɑ̃, -ɑ̃t] *a* innocent // *nm/f*

innocent person; **innocenter** *vt* to clear, prove innocent.
innombrable [inɔ̃bRabl(ə)] *a* innumerable.
innommable [inɔmabl(ə)] *a* unspeakable.
innover [inɔve] *vi* to break new ground.
inobservation [inɔpsɛRvɑsjɔ̃] *nf* non-observation, inobservance.
inoccupé, e [inɔkype] *a* unoccupied.
inoculer [inɔkyle] *vt*: ~ **qch à qn** (*volontairement*) to inoculate sb with sth; (*accidentellement*) to infect sb with sth; ~ **qn contre** to inoculate sb against.
inodore [inɔdɔR] *a* (*gaz*) odourless; (*fleur*) scentless.
inoffensif, ive [inɔfɑ̃sif, -iv] *a* harmless, innocuous.
inondation [inɔ̃dɑsjɔ̃] *nf* flooding *q*; flood.
inonder [inɔ̃de] *vt* to flood; (*fig*) to inundate, overrun; ~ **de** (*fig*) to flood *ou* swamp with.
inopérable [inɔpeRabl(ə)] *a* inoperable.
inopérant, e [inɔpeRɑ̃, -ɑ̃t] *a* inoperative, ineffective.
inopiné, e [inɔpine] *a* unexpected, sudden.
inopportun, e [inɔpɔRtœ̃, -yn] *a* ill-timed, untimely; inappropriate; (*moment*) inopportune.
inoubliable [inublijabl(ə)] *a* unforgettable.
inouï, e [inwi] *a* unheard-of, extraordinary.
inoxydable [inɔksidabl(ə)] *a* stainless; (*couverts*) stainless steel *cpd.*
inqualifiable [ɛ̃kalifjabl(ə)] *a* unspeakable.
inquiet, ète [ɛ̃kjɛ, -ɛt] *a* (*par nature*) anxious; (*momentanément*) worried.
inquiétant, e [ɛ̃kjetɑ̃, -ɑ̃t] *a* worrying, disturbing.
inquiéter [ɛ̃kjete] *vt* to worry, disturb; (*harceler*) to harass; **s'~** to worry, become anxious; **s'~ de** to worry about; (*s'enquérir de*) to inquire about.
inquiétude [ɛ̃kjetyd] *nf* anxiety; **donner de l'~** *ou* **des ~s à** to worry; **avoir de l'~** *ou* **des ~s au sujet de** to feel anxious *ou* worried about.
inquisition [ɛ̃kizisjɔ̃] *nf* inquisition.
insaisissable [ɛ̃sezisabl(ə)] *a* elusive.
insalubre [ɛ̃salybR(ə)] *a* insalubrious, unhealthy.
insanité [ɛ̃sanite] *nf* madness *q*, insanity *q*.
insatiable [ɛ̃sasjabl(ə)] *a* insatiable.
insatisfait, e [ɛ̃satisfɛ, -ɛt] *a* (*non comblé*) unsatisfied; unfulfilled; (*mécontent*) dissatisfied.
inscription [ɛ̃skRipsjɔ̃] *nf* (*sur un mur, écriteau etc*) inscription; (*à une institution: voir s'inscrire*) enrolment; registration.
inscrire [ɛ̃skRiR] *vt* (*marquer: sur son calepin etc*) to note *ou* write down; (*: sur un mur, une affiche etc*) to write; (*: dans la pierre, le métal*) to inscribe; (*mettre: sur une liste, un budget etc*) to put down; ~ **qn à** (*club, école etc*) to enrol sb at; **s'~** (*pour une excursion etc*) to put one's name down; **s'~ (à)** (*club, parti*) to join; (*université*) to register *ou* enrol (at); (*examen, concours*) to register *ou* enter (for); **s'~ en faux contre** to challenge.
insecte [ɛ̃sɛkt(ə)] *nm* insect; **insecticide** *nm* insecticide.
insécurité [ɛ̃sekyRite] *nf* insecurity, lack of security.
I.N.S.E.E. [inse] *sigle m* = *Institut national de la statistique et des études économiques.*
insémination [ɛ̃seminɑsjɔ̃] *nf* insemination.
insensé, e [ɛ̃sɑ̃se] *a* insane.
insensibiliser [ɛ̃sɑ̃sibilize] *vt* to anaesthetize.
insensible [ɛ̃sɑ̃sibl(ə)] *a* (*nerf, membre*) numb; (*dur, indifférent*) insensitive; (*imperceptible*) imperceptible.
inséparable [ɛ̃sepaRabl(ə)] *a* inseparable.
insérer [ɛ̃seRe] *vt* to insert; **s'~ dans** to fit into; to come within.
insidieux, euse [ɛ̃sidjø, -øz] *a* insidious.
insigne [ɛ̃siɲ] *nm* (*d'un parti, club*) badge // *a* distinguished; **~s** *nmpl* (*d'une fonction*) insignia *pl.*
insignifiant, e [ɛ̃siɲifjɑ̃, -ɑ̃t] *a* insignificant; trivial.
insinuation [ɛ̃sinɥɑsjɔ̃] *nf* innuendo, insinuation.
insinuer [ɛ̃sinɥe] *vt* to insinuate, imply; **s'~ dans** to seep into; (*fig*) to worm one's way into; to creep into.
insipide [ɛ̃sipid] *a* insipid.
insistance [ɛ̃sistɑ̃s] *nf* insistence; **avec ~** insistently.
insister [ɛ̃siste] *vi* to insist; (*s'obstiner*) to keep trying; ~ **sur** (*détail, note*) to stress.
insociable [ɛ̃sɔsjabl(ə)] *a* unsociable.
insolation [ɛ̃sɔlɑsjɔ̃] *nf* (MÉD) sunstroke *q*; (*ensoleillement*) period of sunshine.
insolence [ɛ̃sɔlɑ̃s] *nf* insolence *q*.
insolent, e [ɛ̃sɔlɑ̃, -ɑ̃t] *a* insolent.
insolite [ɛ̃sɔlit] *a* strange, unusual.
insoluble [ɛ̃sɔlybl(ə)] *a* insoluble.
insolvable [ɛ̃sɔlvabl(ə)] *a* insolvent.
insomnie [ɛ̃sɔmni] *nf* insomnia *q*, sleeplessness *q*.
insondable [ɛ̃sɔ̃dabl(ə)] *a* unfathomable.
insonore [ɛ̃sɔnɔR] *a* soundproof; **insonoriser** *vt* to soundproof.
insouciance [ɛ̃susjɑ̃s] *nf* carefree attitude; heedless attitude.
insouciant, e [ɛ̃susjɑ̃, -ɑ̃t] *a* carefree; (*imprévoyant*) heedless.
insoumis, e [ɛ̃sumi, -iz] *a* (*caractère, enfant*) rebellious, refractory; (*contrée, tribu*) unsubdued.
insoumission [ɛ̃sumisjɔ̃] *nf* rebelliousness; (MIL) absence without leave.
insoupçonnable [ɛ̃supsɔnabl(ə)] *a* above suspicion.
insoupçonné, e [ɛ̃supsɔne] *a* unsuspected.
insoutenable [ɛ̃sutnabl(ə)] *a* (*argument*) untenable; (*chaleur*) unbearable.
inspecter [ɛ̃spɛkte] *vt* to inspect.
inspecteur, trice [ɛ̃spɛktœR, -tRis] *nm/f* inspector; ~ **d'Académie** ≈ Chief Education Officer; ~ **des finances** ≈ Treasury Inspector.
inspection [ɛ̃spɛksjɔ̃] *nf* inspection.
inspiration [ɛ̃spiRɑsjɔ̃] *nf* inspiration; breathing in *q*; **sous l'~ de** prompted by.

inspirer [ɛ̃spiʀe] *vt* (*gén*) to inspire // *vi* (*aspirer*) to breathe in ; **s'~ de** (*suj: artiste*) to draw one's inspiration from ; (*suj: tableau*) to be inspired by ; **~ à qn** (*œuvre, action*) to inspire sb with ; (*dégoût, crainte*) to fill sb with ; **ça ne m'inspire pas** I'm not keen on the idea.

instable [ɛ̃stabl(ə)] *a* (*meuble, équilibre*) unsteady ; (*population, temps*) unsettled ; (*paix, régime, caractère*) unstable.

installation [ɛ̃stalɑsjɔ̃] *nf* installation ; putting in *ou* up ; fitting out ; settling in ; (*appareils etc*) fittings *pl*, installations *pl* ; **~s** *nfpl* installations, plant *sg* ; facilities.

installer [ɛ̃stale] *vt* (*loger*): **~ qn** to get sb settled, install sb ; (*placer*) to put, place ; (*meuble*) to put in ; (*rideau, étagère, tente*) to put up ; (*gaz, électricité etc*) to put in, install ; (*appartement*) to fit out ; **s'~** (*s'établir: artisan, dentiste etc*) to set o.s. up ; (*se loger*) to settle (o.s.) ; (*emménager*) to settle in ; (*sur un siège, à un emplacement*) to settle (down) ; (*fig: maladie, grève*) to take a firm hold *ou* grip.

instamment [ɛ̃stamɑ̃] *ad* urgently.

instance [ɛ̃stɑ̃s] *nf* (JUR: *procédure*) (legal) proceedings *pl* ; (ADMIN: *autorité*) authority ; **~s** *nfpl* (*prières*) entreaties ; **affaire en ~** matter pending ; **être en ~ de divorce** to be awaiting a divorce ; **en seconde ~** on appeal.

instant [ɛ̃stɑ̃] *nm* moment, instant ; **dans un ~** in a moment ; **à l'~** this instant ; **à tout ~** at any moment ; constantly ; **pour l'~** for the moment, for the time being ; **par ~s** at times ; **de tous les ~s** perpetual.

instantané, e [ɛ̃stɑ̃tane] *a* (*lait, café*) instant ; (*explosion, mort*) instantaneous // *nm* snapshot.

instar [ɛ̃staʀ]: **à l'~ de** *prép* following the example of, like.

instaurer [ɛ̃stɔʀe] *vt* to institute.

instigateur, trice [ɛ̃stigatœʀ, -tʀis] *nm/f* instigator.

instigation [ɛ̃stigɑsjɔ̃] *nf*: **à l'~ de qn** at sb's instigation.

instinct [ɛ̃stɛ̃] *nm* instinct ; **~ de conservation** instinct of self-preservation ; **instinctif, ive** *a* instinctive.

instituer [ɛ̃stitɥe] *vt* to institute, set up.

institut [ɛ̃stity] *nm* institute ; **~ de beauté** beauty salon ; **I~ Universitaire de Technologie (IUT)** ≈ Polytechnic.

instituteur, trice [ɛ̃stitytœʀ, -tʀis] *nm/f* (primary school) teacher.

institution [ɛ̃stitysjɔ̃] *nf* institution ; (*collège*) private school.

instructeur, trice [ɛ̃stʀyktœʀ, -tʀis] *a* (MIL): **sergent ~** drill sergeant ; (JUR): **juge ~** examining magistrate // *nm/f* instructor.

instructif, ive [ɛ̃stʀyktif, -iv] *a* instructive.

instruction [ɛ̃stʀyksjɔ̃] *nf* (*enseignement, savoir*) education ; (JUR) (preliminary) investigation and hearing ; (*directive*) instruction ; **~s** *nfpl* (*mode d'emploi*) directions, instructions ; **~ civique** civics *sg* ; **~ religieuse** religious instruction ; **~ professionnelle** vocational training.

instruire [ɛ̃stʀɥiʀ] *vt* (*élèves*) to teach ; (*recrues*) to train ; (JUR: *affaire*) to conduct the investigation for ; **s'~** to educate o.s. ; **~ qn de qch** (*informer*) to inform *ou* advise sb of sth ; **instruit, e** *a* educated.

instrument [ɛ̃stʀymɑ̃] *nm* instrument ; **~ à cordes/vent** stringed/wind instrument ; **~ de mesure** measuring instrument ; **~ de musique** musical instrument ; **~ de travail** (working) tool.

insu [ɛ̃sy] *nm*: **à l'~ de qn** without sb knowing (it).

insubmersible [ɛ̃sybmɛʀsibl(ə)] *a* unsinkable.

insubordination [ɛ̃sybɔʀdinɑsjɔ̃] *nf* rebelliousness ; (MIL) insubordination.

insuccès [ɛ̃syksɛ] *nm* failure.

insuffisance [ɛ̃syfizɑ̃s] *nf* insufficiency ; inadequacy ; **~s** *nfpl* (*lacunes*) inadequacies ; **~ cardiaque** cardiac insufficiency *q*.

insuffisant, e [ɛ̃syfizɑ̃, -ɑ̃t] *a* insufficient ; (*élève, travail*) inadequate.

insuffler [ɛ̃syfle] *vt*: **~ qch dans** to blow sth into ; **~ qch à qn** to inspire sb with sth.

insulaire [ɛ̃sylɛʀ] *a* island *cpd* ; (*attitude*) insular.

insulte [ɛ̃sylt(ə)] *nf* insult ; **insulter** *vt* to insult.

insupportable [ɛ̃sypɔʀtabl(ə)] *a* unbearable.

insurgé, e [ɛ̃syʀʒe] *a, nm/f* insurgent, rebel.

insurger [ɛ̃syʀʒe]: **s'~** *vi*: **s'~ (contre)** to rise up *ou* rebel (against).

insurmontable [ɛ̃syʀmɔ̃tabl(ə)] *a* (*difficulté*) insuperable ; (*aversion*) unconquerable.

insurrection [ɛ̃syʀɛksjɔ̃] *nf* insurrection, revolt.

intact, e [ɛ̃takt] *a* intact.

intangible [ɛ̃tɑ̃ʒibl(ə)] *a* intangible ; (*principe*) inviolable.

intarissable [ɛ̃taʀisabl(ə)] *a* inexhaustible.

intégral, e, aux [ɛ̃tegʀal, -o] *a* complete // *nf* (MATH) integral ; **~ement** *ad* in full.

intégrant, e [ɛ̃tegʀɑ̃, -ɑ̃t] *a*: **faire partie ~e de** to be an integral part of, be part and parcel of.

intègre [ɛ̃tɛgʀ(ə)] *a* upright.

intégrer [ɛ̃tegʀe] *vt*: **~ qch à/dans** to integrate sth into ; **s'~ à/dans** to become integrated into.

intégrité [ɛ̃tegʀite] *nf* integrity.

intellect [ɛ̃telɛkt] *nm* intellect.

intellectuel, le [ɛ̃telɛktɥɛl] *a* intellectual // *nm/f* intellectual ; (*péj*) highbrow.

intelligence [ɛ̃teliʒɑ̃s] *nf* intelligence ; (*compréhension*): **l'~ de** the understanding of ; (*complicité*): **regard d'~** glance of complicity ; (*accord*): **vivre en bonne ~ avec qn** to be on good terms with sb ; **~s** *nfpl* (MIL, *fig*) secret contacts.

intelligent, e [ɛ̃teliʒɑ̃, -ɑ̃t] *a* intelligent.

intelligible [ɛ̃teliʒibl(ə)] *a* intelligible.

intempérance [ɛ̃tɑ̃peʀɑ̃s] *nf* intemperance *q* ; overindulgence *q*.

intempéries [ɛ̃tɑ̃peʀi] *nfpl* bad weather *sg*.

intempestif, ive [ɛ̃tɑ̃pɛstif, -iv] *a* untimely.

intenable [ɛ̃tnabl(ə)] *a* (*chaleur*) unbearable.

intendance [ɛ̃tɑ̃dɑ̃s] *nf* (MIL) supply corps; supplies office; (SCOL: *bureau*) bursar's office.

intendant, e [ɛ̃tɑ̃dɑ̃, -ɑ̃t] *nm/f* (MIL) quartermaster; (SCOL) bursar; (*d'une propriété*) steward.

intense [ɛ̃tɑ̃s] *a* intense; **intensif, ive** *a* intensive; **intensifier** *vt*, **s'intensifier** to intensify; **intensité** *nf* intensity.

intenter [ɛ̃tɑ̃te] *vt*: ~ **un procès contre** *ou* **à** to start proceedings against.

intention [ɛ̃tɑ̃sjɔ̃] *nf* intention; (JUR) intent; **avoir l'~ de faire** to intend to do, have the intention of doing; **à l'~ de** *prép* for; (*renseignement*) for the benefit *ou* information of; (*film, ouvrage*) aimed at; **à cette** ~ with this aim in view; **intentionné, e** *a*: **bien intentionné** well-meaning *ou* -intentioned; **mal intentionné** ill-intentioned; **intentionnel, le** *a* intentional, deliberate.

inter [ɛ̃tɛʀ] *nm* (TÉL) *abr de* **interurbain**; (SPORT): **~-gauche/ -droit** inside-left/-right.

intercalaire [ɛ̃tɛʀkalɛʀ] *a*: **feuillet** ~ insert; **fiche** ~ divider.

intercaler [ɛ̃tɛʀkale] *vt* to insert; **s'~ entre** to come in between; to slip in between.

intercéder [ɛ̃tɛʀsede] *vi*: ~ **(pour qn)** to intercede (on behalf of sb).

intercepter [ɛ̃tɛʀsɛpte] *vt* to intercept; (*lumière, chaleur*) to cut off; **interception** [-sjɔ̃] *nf* interception; **avion d'interception** interceptor.

interchangeable [ɛ̃tɛʀʃɑ̃ʒabl(ə)] *a* interchangeable.

interclasse [ɛ̃tɛʀklɑs] *nm* (SCOL) break (between classes).

interdiction [ɛ̃tɛʀdiksjɔ̃] *nf* ban; ~ **de séjour** (JUR) *order banning ex-prisoner from frequenting specified places.*

interdire [ɛ̃tɛʀdiʀ] *vt* to forbid; (ADMIN: *stationnement, meeting, passage*) to ban, prohibit; (: *journal, livre*) to ban; ~ **qch à qn** to forbid sb sth; ~ **à qn de faire** to forbid sb to do, prohibit sb from doing; (*suj: empêchement*) to prevent *ou* preclude sb from doing.

interdit, e [ɛ̃tɛʀdi, -it] *a* (*stupéfait*) taken aback // *nm* interdict, prohibition.

intéressant, e [ɛ̃teʀɛsɑ̃, -ɑ̃t] *a* interesting.

intéressé, e [ɛ̃teʀese] *a* (*parties*) involved, concerned; (*amitié, motifs*) self-interested; **les ~s** those concerned *ou* involved.

intéressement [ɛ̃teʀɛsmɑ̃] *nm* (COMM) profit-sharing.

intéresser [ɛ̃teʀese] *vt* (*captiver*) to interest; (*toucher*) to be of interest *ou* concern to; (ADMIN: *concerner*) to affect, concern; (COMM: *travailleur*) to give a share in the profits to; (: *partenaire*) to interest (in the business); **s'~ à** to take an interest in, be interested in.

intérêt [ɛ̃teʀɛ] *nm* (*gén, aussi* COMM) interest; (*égoïsme*) self-interest; **avoir des ~s dans** (COMM) to have a financial interest *ou* a stake in; **avoir ~ à faire** to be well-advised to do.

interférer [ɛ̃tɛʀfeʀe] *vi*: ~ **(avec)** to interfere (with).

intérieur, e [ɛ̃teʀjœʀ] *a* (*mur, escalier, poche*) inside; (*commerce, politique*) domestic; (*cour, calme, vie*) inner; (*navigation*) inland // *nm* (*d'une maison, d'un récipient etc*) inside; (*d'un pays, aussi: décor, mobilier*) interior; (POL): **l'I~** the Interior, ≈ the Home Office; **à l'~ (de)** inside; (*fig*) within; **en** ~ (CINÉMA) in the studio; **vêtement d'~** indoor garment.

intérim [ɛ̃teʀim] *nm* interim period; **assurer l'~ (de)** to deputize (for); **par** ~ *a* interim // *ad* in a temporary capacity; **~aire** *a* temporary, interim.

intérioriser [ɛ̃teʀjɔʀize] *vt* to internalize.

interjection [ɛ̃tɛʀʒɛksjɔ̃] *nf* interjection.

interligne [ɛ̃tɛʀliɲ] *nm* space between the lines // *nf* lead; **simple/double** ~ single/double spacing.

interlocuteur, trice [ɛ̃tɛʀlɔkytœʀ, -tʀis] *nm/f* speaker; **son** ~ the person he was speaking to.

interlope [ɛ̃tɛʀlɔp] *a* shady.

interloquer [ɛ̃tɛʀlɔke] *vt* to take aback.

interlude [ɛ̃tɛʀlyd] *nm* interlude.

intermède [ɛ̃tɛʀmɛd] *nm* interlude.

intermédiaire [ɛ̃tɛʀmedjɛʀ] *a* intermediate; middle; half-way // *nm/f* intermediary; (COMM) middleman; **sans** ~ directly; **par l'~ de** through.

interminable [ɛ̃tɛʀminabl(ə)] *a* never-ending.

intermittence [ɛ̃tɛʀmitɑ̃s] *nf*: **par** ~ sporadically, intermittently.

intermittent, e [ɛ̃tɛʀmitɑ̃, -ɑ̃t] *a* intermittent.

internat [ɛ̃tɛʀna] *nm* (SCOL) boarding school.

international, e, aux [ɛ̃tɛʀnasjɔnal, -o] *a* international // *nm/f* (SPORT) international player.

interne [ɛ̃tɛʀn(ə)] *a* internal // *nm/f* (SCOL) boarder; (MÉD) houseman.

interner [ɛ̃tɛʀne] *vt* (POL) to intern; (MÉD) to confine to a mental institution.

interpellation [ɛ̃tɛʀpelasjɔ̃] *nf* interpellation; (POL) question.

interpeller [ɛ̃tɛʀpele] *vt* (*appeler*) to call out to; (*apostropher*) to shout at; (POLICE) to take in for questioning; (POL) to question.

interphone [ɛ̃tɛʀfɔn] *nm* intercom.

interposer [ɛ̃tɛʀpoze] *vt* to interpose; **s'~** *vi* to intervene; **par personnes interposées** through a third party.

interprétariat [ɛ̃tɛʀpʀetaʀja] *nm* interpreting.

interprétation [ɛ̃tɛʀpʀetɑsjɔ̃] *nf* interpretation.

interprète [ɛ̃tɛʀpʀɛt] *nm/f* interpreter; (*porte-parole*) spokesman.

interpréter [ɛ̃tɛʀpʀete] *vt* to interpret.

interrogateur, trice [ɛ̃teʀɔgatœʀ, -tʀis] *a* questioning, inquiring // *nm/f* (SCOL) (oral) examiner.

interrogatif, ive [ɛ̃teʀɔgatif, -iv] *a* (LING) interrogative.

interrogation [ɛ̃teʀɔgɑsjɔ̃] *nf* question; (*SCOL*) (written *ou* oral) test.
interrogatoire [ɛ̃teʀɔgatwaʀ] *nm* (*POLICE*) questioning *q*; (*JUR*) cross-examination.
interroger [ɛ̃teʀɔʒe] *vt* to question; (*données, ordinateur*) to consult; (*SCOL*) to test.
interrompre [ɛ̃teʀɔ̃pʀ(ə)] *vt* (*gén*) to interrupt; (*travail, voyage*) to break off, interrupt; **s'~** to break off.
interrupteur [ɛ̃teʀyptœʀ] *nm* switch.
interruption [ɛ̃teʀypsjɔ̃] *nf* interruption; **sans ~** without a break; **~ de grossesse** termination of pregnancy.
intersection [ɛ̃tɛʀsɛksjɔ̃] *nf* intersection.
interstice [ɛ̃tɛʀstis] *nm* crack; slit.
interurbain [ɛ̃teʀyʀbɛ̃] *nm* (*TÉL*) trunk call service.
intervalle [ɛ̃tɛʀval] *nm* (*espace*) space; (*de temps*) interval; **dans l'~** in the meantime.
intervenir [ɛ̃tɛʀvəniʀ] *vi* (*gén*) to intervene; (*survenir*) to take place; **~ auprès de** to intervene with; **la police a dû ~** police had to be called in; **les médecins ont dû ~** the doctors had to operate.
intervention [ɛ̃tɛʀvɑ̃sjɔ̃] *nf* intervention; **~ chirurgicale** (surgical) operation.
intervertir [ɛ̃tɛʀvɛʀtiʀ] *vt* to invert (the order of), reverse.
interview [ɛ̃tɛʀvju] *nf* interview; **interviewer** *vt* [-ve] to interview.
intestin, e [ɛ̃tɛstɛ̃, -in] *a* internal // *nm* intestine; **~ grêle** small intestine; **intestinal, e, aux** *a* intestinal.
intime [ɛ̃tim] *a* intimate; (*vie, journal*) private; (*conviction*) inmost; (*dîner, cérémonie*) held among friends, quiet // *nm/f* close friend.
intimer [ɛ̃time] *vt* (*JUR*) to notify; **~ à qn l'ordre de faire** to order sb to do.
intimider [ɛ̃timide] *vt* to intimidate.
intimité [ɛ̃timite] *nf* intimacy; privacy; private life; **dans l'~** in private; (*sans formalités*) with only a few friends, quietly.
intitulé [ɛ̃tityle] *nm* title.
intituler [ɛ̃tityle] *vt*: **comment a-t-il intitulé son livre?** what title did he give his book?; **s'~** to be entitled; (*personne*) to call o.s.
intolérable [ɛ̃tɔleʀabl(ə)] *a* intolerable.
intolérance [ɛ̃tɔleʀɑ̃s] *nf* intolerance.
intolérant, e [ɛ̃tɔleʀɑ̃, -ɑ̃t] *a* intolerant.
intonation [ɛ̃tɔnɑsjɔ̃] *nf* intonation.
intouchable [ɛ̃tuʃabl(ə)] *a* (*fig*) above the law, sacrosanct; (*REL*) untouchable.
intoxication [ɛ̃tɔksikɑsjɔ̃] *nf* poisoning *q*; (*fig*) brainwashing; **~ alimentaire** food poisoning.
intoxiquer [ɛ̃tɔksike] *vt* to poison; (*fig*) to brainwash.
intraduisible [ɛ̃tʀadɥizibl(ə)] *a* untranslatable; (*fig*) impossible to render.
intraitable [ɛ̃tʀɛtabl(ə)] *a* inflexible, uncompromising.
intransigeance [ɛ̃tʀɑ̃ziʒɑ̃s] *nf* intransigence.
intransigeant, e [ɛ̃tʀɑ̃ziʒɑ̃, -ɑ̃t] *a* intransigent; (*morale, passion*) uncompromising.
intransitif, ive [ɛ̃tʀɑ̃zitif, -iv] *a* (*LING*) intransitive.
intransportable [ɛ̃tʀɑ̃spɔʀtabl(ə)] *a* (*blessé*) unable to travel.
intraveineux, euse [ɛ̃tʀavɛnø, -øz] *a* intravenous.
intrépide [ɛ̃tʀepid] *a* dauntless.
intrigant, e [ɛ̃tʀigɑ̃, -ɑ̃t] *nm/f* schemer.
intrigue [ɛ̃tʀig] *nf* intrigue.
intriguer [ɛ̃tʀige] *vi* to scheme // *vt* to puzzle, intrigue.
intrinsèque [ɛ̃tʀɛ̃sɛk] *a* intrinsic.
introduction [ɛ̃tʀɔdyksjɔ̃] *nf* introduction.
introduire [ɛ̃tʀɔdɥiʀ] *vt* to introduce; (*visiteur*) to show in; (*aiguille, clef*): **~ qch dans** to insert *ou* introduce sth into; **s'~** (*techniques, usages*) to be introduced; **s'~ dans** to gain entry into; to get o.s. accepted into; (*eau, fumée*) to get into.
introniser [ɛ̃tʀɔnize] *vt* to enthrone.
introspection [ɛ̃tʀɔspɛksjɔ̃] *nf* introspection.
introuvable [ɛ̃tʀuvabl(ə)] *a* which cannot be found; (*COMM*) unobtainable.
introverti, e [ɛ̃tʀɔvɛʀti] *nm/f* introvert.
intrus, e [ɛ̃tʀy, -yz] *nm/f* intruder.
intrusion [ɛ̃tʀyzjɔ̃] *nf* intrusion; interference.
intuitif, ive [ɛ̃tɥitif, -iv] *a* intuitive.
intuition [ɛ̃tɥisjɔ̃] *nf* intuition.
inusable [inyzabl(ə)] *a* hard-wearing.
inusité, e [inyzite] *a* not in common use; unaccustomed.
inutile [inytil] *a* useless; (*superflu*) unnecessary; **inutilisable** *a* unusable; **inutilité** *nf* uselessness.
invaincu, e [ɛ̃vɛ̃ky] *a* unbeaten; unconquered.
invalide [ɛ̃valid] *a* disabled; **~ de guerre** disabled ex-serviceman; **~ du travail** industrially disabled person.
invalider [ɛ̃valide] *vt* to invalidate.
invalidité [ɛ̃validite] *nf* disability.
invariable [ɛ̃vaʀjabl(ə)] *a* invariable.
invasion [ɛ̃vɑzjɔ̃] *nf* invasion.
invectiver [ɛ̃vɛktive] *vt* to hurl abuse at // *vi*: **~ contre** to rail against.
invendable [ɛ̃vɑ̃dabl(ə)] *a* unsaleable; unmarketable; **invendus** *nmpl* unsold goods.
inventaire [ɛ̃vɑ̃tɛʀ] *nm* inventory; (*COMM: liste*) stocklist; (*: opération*) stocktaking *q*; (*fig*) survey.
inventer [ɛ̃vɑ̃te] *vt* to invent; (*subterfuge*) to devise, invent; (*histoire, excuse*) to make up, invent; **~ de faire** to hit on the idea of doing; **inventeur** *nm* inventor; **inventif, ive** *a* inventive; **invention** [-sjɔ̃] *nf* invention.
inventorier [ɛ̃vɑ̃tɔʀje] *vt* to make an inventory of.
inverse [ɛ̃vɛʀs(ə)] *a* reverse; opposite; inverse // *nm* inverse, reverse; **en proportion ~** in inverse proportion; **dans l'ordre ~** in the reverse order; **en sens ~** in (*ou* from) the opposite direction; **~ment** *ad* conversely; **inverser** *vt* to invert, reverse; (*ÉLEC*) to reverse; **inversion** *nf* inversion; reversal.

inverti, e [ɛ̃vɛʀti] *nm f* homosexual.
investigation [ɛ̃vɛstigɑsjɔ̃] *nf* investigation, inquiry.
investir [ɛ̃vɛstiʀ] *vt* to invest; **investissement** *nm* investment; **investiture** *nf* investiture; (*à une élection*) nomination.
invétéré, e [ɛ̃veteʀe] *a* (*habitude*) ingrained; (*bavard, buveur*) inveterate.
invincible [ɛ̃vɛ̃sibl(ə)] *a* invincible, unconquerable.
invisible [ɛ̃vizibl(ə)] *a* invisible.
invitation [ɛ̃vitɑsjɔ̃] *nf* invitation.
invité, e [ɛ̃vite] *nm/f* guest.
inviter [ɛ̃vite] *vt* to invite; ~ **qn à faire** to invite sb to do, (*suj: chose*) to induce *ou* tempt sb to do.
involontaire [ɛ̃vɔlɔ̃tɛʀ] *a* (*mouvement*) involuntary; (*insulte*) unintentional; (*complice*) unwitting.
invoquer [ɛ̃vɔke] *vt* (*Dieu, muse*) to call upon, invoke; (*prétexte*) to put forward (as an excuse); (*témoignage*) to call upon; (*loi, texte*) to refer to; ~ **la clémence de qn** to beg sb *ou* appeal to sb for clemency.
invraisemblable [ɛ̃vʀɛsɑ̃blabl(ə)] *a* unlikely, improbable; incredible.
invulnérable [ɛ̃vylneʀabl(ə)] *a* invulnerable.
iode [jɔd] *nm* iodine.
ion [jɔ̃] *nm* ion.
ionique [jɔnik] *a* (ARCHIT) Ionic; (SCIENCE) ionic.
irai *etc vb voir* **aller.**
Irak [iʀɑk] *nm* Iraq; **irakien, ne** *a, nm/f* Iraqi.
Iran [iʀɑ̃] *nm* Iran; **iranien, ne** *nm/f* Iranian.
irascible [iʀasibl(ə)] *a* short-tempered, irascible.
irions *etc vb voir* **aller.**
iris [iʀis] *nm* iris.
irisé, e [iʀize] *a* iridescent.
irlandais, e [iʀlɑ̃dɛ, -ɛz] *a, nm (langue)* Irish // *nm/f*: **I~, e** Irishman/woman; **les I~** the Irish.
Irlande [iʀlɑ̃d] *nf* Ireland; ~ **du Nord** Northern Ireland.
ironie [iʀɔni] *nf* irony; **ironique** *a* ironical; **ironiser** *vi* to be ironical.
irons *etc vb voir* **aller.**
irradier [iʀadje] *vi* to radiate // *vt* to irradiate.
irraisonné, e [iʀɛzɔne] *a* irrational, unreasoned.
irrationnel, le [iʀasjɔnɛl] *a* irrational.
irréalisable [iʀealizabl(ə)] *a* unrealizable; impracticable.
irréconciliable [iʀekɔ̃siljabl(ə)] *a* irreconcilable.
irrécupérable [iʀekypeʀabl(ə)] *a* unreclaimable, beyond repair; (*personne*) beyond redemption *ou* recall.
irrécusable [iʀekyzabl(ə)] *a* unimpeachable.
irréductible [iʀedyktibl(ə)] *a* indomitable, implacable; (MATH) irreducible.
irréel, le [iʀeɛl] *a* unreal.
irréfléchi, e [iʀefleʃi] *a* thoughtless.
irréfutable [iʀefytabl(ə)] *a* irrefutable.
irrégularité [iʀegylaʀite] *nf* irregularity; unevenness *q*.
irrégulier, ière [iʀegylje, -jɛʀ] *a* irregular; uneven; (*élève, athlète*) erratic.
irrémédiable [iʀemedjabl(ə)] *a* irreparable.
irremplaçable [iʀɑ̃plasabl(ə)] *a* irreplaceable.
irréparable [iʀepaʀabl(ə)] *a* beyond repair; (*fig*) irreparable.
irrépressible [iʀepʀesibl(ə)] *a* irrepressible, uncontrollable.
irréprochable [iʀepʀɔʃabl(ə)] *a* irreproachable, beyond reproach; (*tenue, toilette*) impeccable.
irrésistible [iʀezistibl(ə)] *a* irresistible; (*preuve, logique*) compelling.
irrésolu, e [iʀezɔly] *a* irresolute.
irrespectueux, euse [iʀɛspɛktɥø, -øz] *a* disrespectful.
irrespirable [iʀɛspiʀabl(ə)] *a* unbreathable; (*fig*) oppressive, stifling.
irresponsable [iʀɛspɔ̃sabl(ə)] *a* irresponsible.
irrévérencieux, euse [iʀeveʀɑ̃sjø, -øz] *a* irreverent.
irréversible [iʀevɛʀsibl(ə)] *a* irreversible.
irrévocable [iʀevɔkabl(ə)] *a* irrevocable.
irrigation [iʀigɑsjɔ̃] *nf* irrigation.
irriguer [iʀige] *vt* to irrigate.
irritable [iʀitabl(ə)] *a* irritable.
irritation [iʀitɑsjɔ̃] *nf* irritation.
irriter [iʀite] *vt* (*agacer*) to irritate, annoy; (MÉD: *enflammer*) to irritate; **s'~ contre/de** to get annoyed *ou* irritated at/with.
irruption [iʀypsjɔ̃] *nf* irruption *q*; **faire ~ dans** to burst into.
Islam [islam] *nm* Islam; **islamique** *a* Islamic.
islandais, e [islɑ̃dɛ, -ɛz] *a, nm (langue)* Icelandic // *nm/f* Icelander.
Islande [islɑ̃d] *nf* Iceland.
isocèle [izɔsɛl] *a* isoceles.
isolant, e [izɔlɑ̃, -ɑ̃t] *a* insulating; (*insonorisant*) soundproofing.
isolation [izɔlɑsjɔ̃] *nf* insulation.
isolé, e [izɔle] *a* isolated; insulated.
isolement [izɔlmɑ̃] *nm* isolation; solitary confinement.
isoler [izɔle] *vt* to isolate; (*prisonnier*) to put in solitary confinement; (*ville*) to cut off, isolate; (ELEC) to insulate; **isoloir** *nm* polling booth.
Israël [isʀaɛl] *nm* Israel; **israélien, ne** *a, nm/f* Israeli; **israélite** *a* Jewish // *nm/f* Jew/Jewess.
issu, e [isy] *a*: ~ **de** descended from; (*fig*) stemming from // *nf* (*ouverture, sortie*) exit; (*solution*) way out, solution; (*dénouement*) outcome; **à l'~e de** at the conclusion *ou* close of; **rue sans ~e** dead end, no through road.
isthme [ism(ə)] *nm* isthmus.
Italie [itali] *nf* Italy; **italien, ne** *a, nm, nf* Italian.
italique [italik] *nm*: **en ~** in italics.
itinéraire [itineʀɛʀ] *nm* itinerary, route.

itinérant, e [itineʀɑ̃, -ɑ̃t] *a* itinerant, travelling.
I.U.T. *sigle m voir* **institut**.
ivoire [ivwaʀ] *nm* ivory.
ivre [ivʀ(ə)] *a* drunk; ~ **de** (*colère, bonheur*) wild with; **ivresse** *nf* drunkenness; **ivrogne** *nm/f* drunkard.

J

j' [ʒ] *pronom voir* **je**.
jabot [ʒabo] *nm* (ZOOL) crop; (*de vêtement*) jabot.
jacasser [ʒakase] *vi* to chatter.
jachère [ʒaʃɛʀ] *nf*: **(être) en** ~ (to lie) fallow.
jacinthe [ʒasɛ̃t] *nf* hyacinth.
jade [ʒad] *nm* jade.
jadis [ʒadis] *ad* in times past, formerly.
jaillir [ʒajiʀ] *vi* (*liquide*) to spurt out, gush out; (*fig*) to rear up; to burst out; to flood out.
jais [ʒɛ] *nm* jet; **(d'un noir) de** ~ jet-black.
jalon [ʒalɔ̃] *nm* range pole; (*fig*) milestone; **jalonner** *vt* to mark out; (*fig*) to mark, punctuate.
jalouser [ʒaluze] *vt* to be jealous of.
jalousie [ʒaluzi] *nf* jealousy; (*store*) (venetian) blind.
jaloux, se [ʒalu, -uz] *a* jealous.
jamais [ʒamɛ] *ad* never; (*sans négation*) ever; **ne ...** ~ never.
jambage [ʒɑ̃baʒ] *nm* (*de lettre*) downstroke; (*de porte*) jamb.
jambe [ʒɑ̃b] *nf* leg; **jambières** *nfpl* leggings; (SPORT) shin pads.
jambon [ʒɑ̃bɔ̃] *nm* ham.
jante [ʒɑ̃t] *nf* (wheel) rim.
janvier [ʒɑ̃vje] *nm* January.
Japon [ʒapɔ̃] *nm* Japan; **japonais, e** *a, nm, nf* Japanese.
japper [ʒape] *vi* to yap, yelp.
jaquette [ʒakɛt] *nf* (*de cérémonie*) morning coat; (*de livre*) dust cover, dust jacket.
jardin [ʒaʀdɛ̃] *nm* garden; ~ **d'acclimatation** zoological gardens *pl*; ~ **d'enfants** nursery school; ~ **public** (public) park, public gardens *pl*; **jardinage** *nm* gardening; **jardinier, ière** *nm/f* gardener // *nf* (*de fenêtre*) window box; **jardinière d'enfants** nursery school teacher.
jargon [ʒaʀgɔ̃] *nm* jargon.
jarre [ʒaʀ] *nf* (earthenware) jar.
jarret [ʒaʀɛ] *nm* back of knee, ham; (CULIN) knuckle, shin.
jarretelle [ʒaʀtɛl] *nf* suspender.
jarretière [ʒaʀtjɛʀ] *nf* garter.
jaser [ʒaze] *vi* to chatter, prattle; (*indiscrètement*) to gossip.
jasmin [ʒasmɛ̃] *nm* jasmin.
jaspe [ʒasp(ə)] *nm* jasper.
jatte [ʒat] *nf* basin, bowl.
jauge [ʒoʒ] *nf* (*capacité*) capacity, tonnage; (*instrument*) gauge; **jauger** *vt* to gauge the capacity of; (*fig*) to size up; **jauger 3000 tonneaux** to measure 3,000 tons.
jaune [ʒon] *a, nm* yellow // *nm/f* Asiatic // *ad* (*fam*): **rire** ~ to laugh on the other side of one's face; ~ **d'œuf** (egg) yolk; **jaunir** *vi, vt* to turn yellow.
jaunisse [ʒonis] *nf* jaundice.
javel [ʒavɛl] *nf voir* **eau.**
javelot [ʒavlo] *nm* javelin.
jazz [dʒaz] *nm* jazz.
J.-C. *sigle voir* **Jésus-Christ.**
je, j' [ʒ(ə)] *pronom* I.
jean [dʒin] *nm* jeans *pl.*
jérémiades [ʒeʀemjad] *nfpl* moaning *sg.*
jerrycan [ʒeʀikan] *nm* jerrycan.
jersey [ʒɛʀzɛ] *nm* jersey.
Jésus-Christ [ʒezykʀi(st)] *n* Jesus Christ; **600 avant/après** ~ *ou* **J.-C.** 600 B.C./A.D.
jet [ʒɛ] *nm* (*lancer*) throwing *q*, throw; (*jaillissement*) jet; spurt; (*de tuyau*) nozzle; (*avion*) [dʒɛt] jet; **arroser au** ~ to hose; **du premier** ~ at the first attempt *or* shot; ~ **d'eau** fountain; spray.
jetée [ʒəte] *nf* jetty; pier.
jeter [ʒəte] *vt* (*gén*) to throw; (*se défaire de*) to throw away *ou* out; (*son, lueur etc*) to give out; ~ **qch à qn** to throw sth to sb; (*de façon agressive*) to throw *ou* hurl sth at sb; ~ **un coup d'œil (à)** to take a look (at); ~ **l'effroi parmi** to spread fear among; ~ **un sort à qn** to cast a spell on sb; **se** ~ **dans** (*fleuve*) to flow into.
jeton [ʒətɔ̃] *nm* (*au jeu*) counter; (*de téléphone*) token; **~s de présence** (director's) fees.
jette *etc vb voir* **jeter.**
jeu, x [ʒø] *nm* (*divertissement,* TECH: *d'une pièce*) play; (*défini par des règles,* TENNIS: *partie,* FOOTBALL *etc*: *façon de jouer*) game; (THÉÂTRE *etc*) acting; (*au casino*): **le** ~ gambling; (*fonctionnement*) working, interplay; (*série d'objets, jouet*) set; (CARTES) hand; **en** ~ at stake; at work; (FOOTBALL) in play; **remettre en** ~ to throw in; **entrer/mettre en** ~ to come/bring into play; ~ **de boules** game of bowls; (*endroit*) bowling pitch; (*boules*) set of bowls; ~ **de cartes** card game; (*paquet*) pack of cards; ~ **de construction** building set; ~ **d'échecs** chess set; ~ **de hasard** game of chance; ~ **de mots** pun; **le** ~ **de l'oie** snakes and ladders *sg*; ~ **d'orgue(s)** organ stop; ~ **de société** parlour game; **J~x olympiques (J.O.)** Olympic Games.
jeudi [ʒødi] *nm* Thursday.
jeûn [ʒœ̃]: **à** ~ *ad* on an empty stomach.
jeune [ʒœn] *a* young; **les** ~**s** young people, the young; ~ **fille** *nf* girl; ~ **homme** *nm* young man; ~ **premier** leading man; ~**s gens** *nmpl* young people.
jeûne [ʒøn] *nm* fast.
jeunesse [ʒœnɛs] *nf* youth; (*aspect*) youthfulness; youngness; (*jeunes*) young people *pl*, youth.
J. O. *sigle mpl voir* **jeu**.
joaillerie [ʒɔajʀi] *nf* jewel trade; jewellery; **joaillier, ière** *nm/f* jeweller.
jobard [ʒɔbaʀ] *nm* (*péj*) sucker, mug.
jockey [ʒɔkɛ] *nm* jockey.

joie [ʒwa] *nf* joy.
joindre [ʒwɛ̃dʀ(ə)] *vt* to join; (*à une lettre*): ~ **qch à** to enclose sth with; (*contacter*) to contact, get in touch with; ~ **les mains/talons** to put one's hands/heels together; **se** ~ **à** to join.
joint [ʒwɛ̃] *nm* joint; (*ligne*) join; (*de ciment etc*) pointing *q*; ~ **de cardan** cardan joint; ~ **de culasse** cylinder head gasket; ~ **de robinet** washer.
joli [ʒɔli] *a* pretty, attractive; **c'est du** ~! (*ironique*) that's very nice!; ~**ment** *ad* prettily, attractively; (*fam: très*) pretty.
jonc [ʒɔ̃] *nm* (bul)rush.
joncher [ʒɔ̃ʃe] *vt* (*suj: choses*) to be strewed on; **jonché de** strewn with.
jonction [ʒɔ̃ksjɔ̃] *nf* joining; **(point de)** ~ junction; **opérer une** ~ (*MIL etc*) to rendez-vous.
jongler [ʒɔ̃gle] *vi* to juggle; **jongleur, euse** *nm/f* juggler.
jonquille [ʒɔ̃kij] *nf* daffodil.
Jordanie [ʒɔʀdani] *nf*: **la** ~ Jordan.
joue [ʒu] *nf* cheek; **mettre en** ~ to take aim at.
jouer [ʒwe] *vt* (*partie, carte, coup, MUS: morceau*) to play; (*somme d'argent, réputation*) to stake, wager; (*pièce, rôle*) to perform; (*film*) to show; (*simuler: sentiment*) to affect, feign // *vi* to play; (*THÉÂTRE, CINÉMA*) to act, perform; (*bois, porte: se voiler*) to warp; (*clef, pièce: avoir du jeu*) to be loose; ~ **sur** (*miser*) to gamble on; ~ **de** (*MUS*) to play; ~ **du couteau/des coudes** to use knives/one's elbows; ~ **à** (*jeu, sport, roulette*) to play; ~ **au héros** to play the hero; ~ **avec** (*risquer*) to gamble with; **se** ~ **de** (*difficultés*) to make light of; **se** ~ **de qn** to deceive *ou* dupe sb; ~ **un tour à qn** to play a trick on sb; ~ **serré** to play a close game; ~ **de malchance** to be dogged with ill-luck.
jouet [ʒwɛ] *nm* toy; **être le** ~ **de** (*illusion etc*) to be the victim of.
joueur, euse [ʒwœʀ, -øz] *nm/f* player; **être beau/mauvais** ~ to be a good/bad loser.
joufflu, e [ʒufly] *a* chubby-cheeked, chubby.
joug [ʒu] *nm* yoke.
jouir [ʒwiʀ]: ~ **de** *vt* to enjoy; **jouissance** *nf* pleasure; (*JUR*) use; **jouisseur, euse** *nm/f* sensualist.
joujou [ʒuʒu] *nm* (*fam*) toy.
jour [ʒuʀ] *nm* day; (*opposé à la nuit*) day, daytime; (*clarté*) daylight; (*fig: aspect*) light; (*ouverture*) opening; openwork *q*; **au** ~ **le** ~ from day to day; **de nos** ~**s** these days, nowadays; **il fait** ~ it's daylight; **au** ~ in daylight; **au grand** ~ (*fig*) in the open; **mettre au** ~ to uncover, disclose; **mettre à** ~ to bring up to date, update; **donner le** ~ **à** to give birth to; **voir le** ~ to be born; **se faire** ~ to become clear.
journal, aux [ʒuʀnal, -o] *nm* (news)paper; (*personnel*) journal, diary; ~ **parlé/télévisé** radio/ television news *sg*; ~ **de bord** log.
journalier, ière [ʒuʀnalje, -jɛʀ] *a* daily; (*banal*) everyday // *nm* day labourer.
journalisme [ʒuʀnalism(ə)] *nm* journalism; **journaliste** *nm/f* journalist.
journée [ʒuʀne] *nf* day; **la** ~ **continue** the 9 to 5 working day (with short lunch break).
journellement [ʒuʀnɛlmɑ̃] *ad* daily.
joute [ʒut] *nf* duel.
jouvence [ʒuvɑ̃s] *nf*: **bain de** ~ rejuvenating experience.
jovial [ʒɔvjal] *a* jovial, jolly.
joyau, x [ʒwajo] *nm* gem, jewel.
joyeux, euse [ʒwajø, -øz] *a* joyful, merry; ~ **Noël!** merry *ou* happy Christmas!; ~ **anniversaire!** many happy returns!
jubilé [ʒybile] *nm* jubilee.
jubiler [ʒybile] *vi* to be jubilant, exult.
jucher [ʒyʃe] *vt*: ~ **qch sur** to perch sth (up)on // *vi* (*oiseau*): ~ **sur** to perch (up)on; **se** ~ **sur** to perch o.s. (up)on.
judaïque [ʒydaik] *a* (*loi*) Judaic; (*religion*) Jewish.
judaïsme [ʒydaism(ə)] *nm* Judaism.
judas [ʒyda] *nm* (*trou*) spy-hole.
judiciaire [ʒydisjɛʀ] *a* judicial.
judicieux, euse [ʒydisjø, -øz] *a* judicious.
judo [ʒydo] *nm* judo; ~**ka** *nm/f* judoka.
juge [ʒyʒ] *nm* judge; ~ **d'instruction** examining magis-trate; ~ **de paix** justice of the peace; ~ **de touche** linesman.
jugé [ʒyʒe]: **au** ~ *ad* by guesswork.
jugement [ʒyʒmɑ̃] *nm* judgment; (*JUR: au criminel*) sentence; (*: au civil*) decision; ~ **de valeur** value judgment.
jugeote [ʒyʒɔt] *nf* (*fam*) gumption.
juger [ʒyʒe] *vt* to judge; ~ **qn/qch satisfaisant** to consider sb/sth (to be) satisfactory; ~ **que** to think *ou* consider that; ~ **bon de faire** to consider it a good idea to do, see fit to do; ~ **de** *vt* to appreciate.
jugulaire [ʒygylɛʀ] *a* jugular // *nf* (*MIL*) chinstrap.
juif, ive [ʒɥif, -iv] *a* Jewish // *nm/f* Jew/Jewess.
juillet [ʒɥijɛ] *nm* July.
juin [ʒɥɛ̃] *nm* June.
jumeau, elle, x [ʒymo, -ɛl] *a, nm/f* twin; **jumelles** *nfpl* binoculars.
jumeler [ʒymle] *vt* to twin; **roues jumelées** double wheels.
jumelle [ʒymɛl] *a, nf voir* **jumeau**.
jument [ʒymɑ̃] *nf* mare.
jungle [ʒɔ̃gl(ə)] *nf* jungle.
jupe [ʒyp] *nf* skirt; ~**-culotte** *nf* divided skirt, culotte(s).
jupon [ʒypɔ̃] *nm* waist slip *ou* petticoat.
juré, e [ʒyʀe] *nm/f* juror, juryman/wo-man // *a*: **ennemi** ~ sworn enemy.
jurer [ʒyʀe] *vt* (*obéissance etc*) to swear, vow // *vi* (*dire des jurons*) to swear, curse; (*dissoner*): ~ **(avec)** to clash (with); (*s'engager*): ~ **de faire/que** to swear *ou* vow to do/that; (*affirmer*): ~ **que** to swear *ou* vouch that; ~ **de qch** (*s'en porter garant*) to swear to sth.
juridiction [ʒyʀidiksjɔ̃] *nf* jurisdiction; court(s) of law.
juridique [ʒyʀidik] *a* legal.

juriste [ʒyʀist(ə)] *nm/f* jurist ; lawyer.
juron [ʒyʀɔ̃] *nm* curse, swearword.
jury [ʒyʀi] *nm* (JUR) jury ; (SCOL) board (of examiners), jury.
jus [ʒy] *nm* juice ; (*de viande*) gravy, (meat) juice ; ~ **de fruits** fruit juice ; ~ **de raisin/tomates** grape/tomato juice.
jusant [ʒyzɑ̃] *nm* ebb (tide).
jusque [ʒysk(ə)]: **jusqu'à** *prép* (*endroit*) as far as, (up) to ; (*moment*) until, till ; (*limite*) up to ; ~ **sur/dans** up to, as far as ; (*y compris*) even on/in ; **jusqu'à présent** until now, so far.
juste [ʒyst(ə)] *a* (*équitable*) just, fair ; (*légitime*) just, justified ; (*exact, vrai*) right ; (*étroit, insuffisant*) tight // *ad* right ; tight ; (*chanter*) in tune ; (*seulement*) just ; ~ **assez/au-dessus** just enough/above ; **pouvoir tout ~ faire** to be only just able to do ; **au ~** exactly, actually ; **le ~ milieu** the happy medium ; **~ment** *ad* rightly ; justly ; (*précisément*): **c'est ~ment ce que** that's just *ou* precisely what ; **justesse** *nf* (*précision*) accuracy ; (*d'une remarque*) aptness ; (*d'une opinion*) soundness ; **de justesse** just, by a narrow margin.
justice [ʒystis] *nf* (*équité*) fairness, justice ; (ADMIN) justice ; **rendre la ~** to dispense justice ; **obtenir ~** to obtain justice ; **rendre ~ à qn** to do sb justice ; **se faire ~** to take the law into one's own hands ; (*se suicider*) to take one's life.
justiciable [ʒystisjabl(ə)] *a*: ~ **de** (JUR) answerable to.
justicier, ière [ʒystisje, -jɛʀ] *nm/f* judge, righter of wrongs.
justifiable [ʒystifjabl(ə)] *a* justifiable.
justification [ʒystifikɑsjɔ̃] *nf* justification.
justifier [ʒystifje] *vt* to justify ; ~ **de** *vt* to prove.
jute [ʒyt] *nm* jute.
juteux, euse [ʒytø, -øz] *a* juicy.
juvénile [ʒyvenil] *a* young, youthful.
juxtaposer [ʒykstapoze] *vt* to juxtapose.

K

kaki [kaki] *a inv* khaki.
kaléidoscope [kaleidɔskɔp] *nm* kaleidoscope.
kangourou [kɑ̃guʀu] *nm* kangaroo.
karaté [kaʀate] *nm* karate.
karting [kaʀtiŋ] *nm* go-carting, karting.
kayac, kayak [kajak] *nm* kayak.
képi [kepi] *nm* kepi.
kermesse [kɛʀmɛs] *nf* bazaar, (charity) fête ; village fair.
kérosène [keʀozɛn] *nm* jet fuel ; rocket fuel.
kibboutz [kibuts] *nm* kibbutz.
kidnapper [kidnape] *vt* to kidnap.
kilogramme [kilɔgʀam] *nm*, **kilo** *nm* kilogramme.
kilométrage [kilɔmetʀaʒ] *nm* number of kilometres travelled, ≈ mileage.
kilomètre [kilɔmɛtʀ(ə)] *nm* kilometre.
kilométrique [kilɔmetʀik] *a* (*distance*) in kilometres ; **compteur ~** ≈ mileage indicator.
kilowatt [kilɔwat] *nm* kilowatt.
kinésithérapeute [kineziteʀapøt] *nm/f* physiotherapist.
kiosque [kjɔsk(ə)] *nm* kiosk, stall.
kirsch [kiʀʃ] *nm* kirsch.
klaxon [klaksɔn] *nm* horn ; **klaxonner** *vi, vt* to hoot.
kleptomane [klɛptɔman] *nm/f* kleptomaniac.
km. *abr de* **kilomètre** ; **km./h** (= *kilomètres-heure*) ≈ m.p.h. (miles per hour).
knock-out [nɔkawt] *nm* knock-out.
K.-O. [kao] *a inv* (knocked) out, out for the count.
kolkhoze [kɔlkoz] *nm* kolkhoz.
kyrielle [kiʀjɛl] *nf*: **une ~ de** a stream of.
kyste [kist(ə)] *nm* cyst.

L

l' [l] *dét voir* **le.**
la [la] *nm* (MUS) A : (*en chantant la gamme*) la.
la [la] *dét voir* **le.**
là [la] (*voir aussi* **-ci, celui**) *ad* there ; (*ici*) here ; (*dans le temps*) then ; **est-ce que Catherine est ~?** is Catherine there *ou* in? ; **elle n'est pas ~** she isn't in *ou* here ; **c'est ~ que** this is where ; ~ **où** where ; **de ~** (*fig*) hence ; **par ~** (*fig*) by that ; **tout est~** (*fig*) that's what it's all about ; **~-bas** *ad* there.
label [labɛl] *nm* stamp, seal.
labeur [labœʀ] *nm* toil *q*, toiling *q*.
labo [labo] *nm* (*abr de* **laboratoire**) lab.
laborantin, e [labɔʀɑ̃tɛ̃, -in] *nm/f* laboratory assistant.
laboratoire [labɔʀatwaʀ] *nm* laboratory ; ~ **de langues/ d'analyses** language/(medical) analysis laboratory.
laborieux, euse [labɔʀjø, -øz] *a* (*tâche*) laborious ; (*personne*) hard-working, industrious.
labour [labuʀ] *nm* ploughing *q* ; **~s** *nmpl* ploughed fields ; **cheval de ~** plough- *ou* cart-horse ; **bœuf de ~** ox (*pl* oxen).
labourer [labuʀe] *vt* to plough ; (*fig*) to make deep gashes *ou* furrows in ; **laboureur** *nm* ploughman.
labyrinthe [labiʀɛ̃t] *nm* labyrinth, maze.
lac [lak] *nm* lake.
lacer [lɑse] *vt* to lace *ou* do up.
lacérer [laseʀe] *vt* to tear to shreds, lacerate.
lacet [lɑsɛ] *nm* (*de chaussure*) lace ; (*de route*) sharp bend ; (*piège*) snare.
lâche [lɑʃ] *a* (*poltron*) cowardly ; (*desserré*) loose, slack // *nm/f* coward.
lâcher [lɑʃe] *nm* (*de ballons, oiseaux*) release // *vt* to let go of ; (*ce qui tombe, abandonner*) to drop ; (*oiseau, animal: libérer*) to release, set free ; (*fig: mot, remarque*) to let slip, come out with ; (SPORT *distancer*) to leave behind // *vi* (*fil, amarres*) to break, give way ; (*freins*) to fail ; ~ **les amarres** (NAVIG) to cast off (the moorings) ; ~ **les chiens** to unleash the dogs ; ~ **prise** to let go.

lâcheté [lɑʃte] *nf* cowardice ; lowness.
lacis [lɑsi] *nm* maze.
laconique [lakɔnik] *a* laconic.
lacrymogène [lakʀimɔʒɛn] *a voir* **gaz, grenade**.
lacté, e [lakte] *a* (*produit, régime*) milk *cpd*.
lacune [lakyn] *nf* gap.
lacustre [lakystʀ(ə)] *a* lake *cpd*, lakeside *cpd*.
lad [lad] *nm* stable-lad.
là-dedans [ladədɑ̃] *ad* inside (there), in it ; (*fig*) in that ; **là-dehors** *ad* out there ; **là-derrière** *ad* behind there ; (*fig*) behind that ; **là-dessous** *ad* underneath, under there ; (*fig*) behind that ; **là-dessus** *ad* on there ; (*fig*) at that point ; about that ; **là-devant** *ad* there (in front).
ladite [ladit] *dét voir* **ledit.**
ladre [lɑdʀ(ə)] *a* miserly.
lagon [lagɔ̃] *nm* lagoon.
lagune [lagyn] *nf* lagoon.
là-haut [la'o] *ad* up there.
laïc [laik] *a, nm/f* = **laïque.**
laïciser [laisize] *vt* to secularize.
laid, e [lɛ, lɛd] *a* ugly ; (*fig: acte*) mean, cheap ; **laideron** *nm* ugly girl ; **laideur** *nf* ugliness *q* ; meanness *q*.
laie [lɛ] *nf* wild sow.
lainage [lɛnaʒ] *nm* woollen garment ; woollen material.
laine [lɛn] *nf* wool ; **~ de verre** glass wool ; **laineux, euse** *a* woolly.
laïque [laik] *a* lay, civil ; (*SCOL*) state *cpd* (*as opposed to private and Roman Catholic*) // *nm/f* layman/woman.
laisse [lɛs] *nf* (*de chien*) lead, leash ; **tenir en ~** to keep on a lead.
laisser [lese] *vt* to leave // *vb auxiliaire:* **~ qn faire** to let sb do ; **se ~ exploiter** to let o.s. be exploited ; **se ~ aller** to let o.s. go ; **laisse-toi faire** let me (*ou* him) do it ; **cela ne laisse pas de surprendre** nonetheless it is surprising ; **~- aller** *nm* carelessness, slovenliness ; **laissez-passer** *nm inv* pass.
lait [lɛ] *nm* milk ; **frère/sœur de ~** foster brother/sister ; **~ écrémé/ concentré** skimmed/evaporated milk ; **~ démaquillant/de beauté** cleansing/beauty lotion ; **laitage** *nm* milk food ; **laiterie** *nf* dairy ; **laiteux, euse** *a* milky ; **laitier, ière** *a* milk *cpd* // *nm/f* milkman/dairywoman.
laiton [lɛtɔ̃] *nm* brass.
laitue [lety] *nf* lettuce.
laïus [lajys] *nm* (*péj*) spiel.
lambeau, x [lɑ̃bo] *nm* scrap ; **en ~x** in tatters, tattered.
lambin, e [lɑ̃bɛ̃, -in] *a* (*péj*) slow.
lambris [lɑ̃bʀi] *nm* panelling *q* ; **lambrissé, e** *a* panelled.
lame [lam] *nf* blade ; (*vague*) wave ; (*lamelle*) strip ; **~ de fond** ground swell *q* ; **~ de rasoir** razor blade.
lamé [lame] *nm* lamé.
lamelle [lamɛl] *nf* thin strip *ou* blade ; (*de champignon*) gill.
lamentable [lamɑ̃tabl(ə)] *a* appalling ; pitiful.
lamentation [lamɑ̃tɑsjɔ̃] *nf* wailing *q*, lamentation ; moaning *q*.
lamenter [lamɑ̃te]: **se ~** *vi*: **se ~ (sur)** to moan (over).
laminer [lamine] *vt* to laminate ; **laminoir** *nm* rolling mill.
lampadaire [lɑ̃padɛʀ] *nm* (*de salon*) standard lamp.
lampe [lɑ̃p(ə)] *nf* lamp ; (*TECH*) valve ; **~ à pétrole** paraffin lamp ; **~ de poche** torch ; **~ à souder** blowlamp.
lampée [lɑ̃pe] *nf* gulp, swig.
lampe-tempête [lɑ̃ptɑ̃pɛt] *nf* storm lantern.
lampion [lɑ̃pjɔ̃] *nm* Chinese lantern.
lampiste [lɑ̃pist(ə)] *nm* light (maintenance) man ; (*fig*) underling.
lance [lɑ̃s] *nf* spear ; **~ d'incendie** fire hose.
lancée [lɑ̃se] *nf*: **être/continuer sur sa ~** to be under way/keep going.
lance-flammes [lɑ̃sflam] *nm inv* flamethrower.
lance-grenades [lɑ̃sgʀənad] *nm inv* grenade launcher.
lancement [lɑ̃smɑ̃] *nm* launching.
lance-pierres [lɑ̃spjɛʀ] *nm inv* catapult.
lancer [lɑ̃se] *nm* (*SPORT*) throwing *q*, throw ; (*PÊCHE*) rod and reel fishing // *vt* to throw ; (*émettre, projeter*) to throw out, send out ; (*produit, fusée, bateau, artiste*) to launch ; (*injure*) to hurl, fling ; (*proclamation, mandat d'arrêt*) to issue ; (*moteur*) to send roaring away ; **~ qch à qn** to throw sth to sb ; (*de façon aggressive*) to throw *ou* hurl sth at sb ; **se ~** *vi* (*prendre de l'élan*) to build up speed ; (*se précipiter*): **se ~ sur/contre** to rush at ; **se ~ dans** (*discussion*) to launch into ; (*aventure*) to embark on ; **~ du poids** *nm* putting the shot ; **lance-roquettes** *nm inv* rocket launcher ; **lance-torpilles** *nm inv* torpedo tube.
lancinant, e [lɑ̃sinɑ̃, -ɑ̃t] *a* (*regrets etc*) haunting ; (*douleur*) shooting, throbbing.
landau [lɑ̃do] *nm* pram.
lande [lɑ̃d] *nf* moor.
langage [lɑ̃gaʒ] *nm* language.
lange [lɑ̃ʒ] *nm* flannel blanket ; **~s** swaddling clothes.
langer [lɑ̃ʒe] *vt* to change (the nappy of) ; **table à ~** changing table.
langoureux, euse [lɑ̃guʀø, -øz] *a* languorous.
langouste [lɑ̃gust(ə)] *nf* crayfish *inv* ; **langoustine** *nf* Dublin Bay prawn.
langue [lɑ̃g] *nf* (*ANAT, CULIN*) tongue ; (*LING*) language ; (*bande*): **~ de terre** spit of land ; **tirer la ~ (à)** to stick out one's tongue (at) ; **de ~ française** French-speaking ; **~ maternelle** native language ; mother tongue ; **~ verte** slang ; **~ vivante** living language ; **~-de-chat** *nf* finger biscuit, sponge finger.
languette [lɑ̃gɛt] *nf* tongue.
langueur [lɑ̃gœʀ] *nf* languidness.
languir [lɑ̃giʀ] *vi* to languish, (*conversation*) to flag: **faire ~ qn** to keep sb waiting.
lanière [lanjɛʀ] *nf* (*de fouet*) lash ; (*de valise, bretelle*) strap.
lanterne [lɑ̃tɛʀn(ə)] *nf* (*portable*) lantern ;

(*électrique*) light, lamp; (*de voiture*) (side)light; ~ **rouge** (*fig*) tail-ender.
lapalissade [lapalisad] *nf* statement of the obvious.
laper [lape] *vt* to lap up.
lapereau, x [lapʀo] *nm* young rabbit.
lapidaire [lapidɛʀ] *a* (*fig*) terse.
lapider [lapide] *vt* to stone.
lapin [lapɛ̃] *nm* rabbit; (*peau*) rabbitskin; ~ **de garenne** wild rabbit.
laps [laps] *nm*: ~ **de temps** space of time, time *q*.
lapsus [lapsys] *nm* slip.
laquais [lakɛ] *nm* lackey.
laque [lak] *nf* lacquer; (*brute*) lac, shellac // *nm* lacquer; piece of lacquer ware; **laqué, e** *a* lacquered; with lacquer finish.
laquelle [lakɛl] *pronom voir* **lequel.**
larbin [laʀbɛ̃] *nm* (*péj*) flunkey.
larcin [laʀsɛ̃] *nm* theft.
lard [laʀ] *nm* (*graisse*) fat; (*bacon*) (streaky) bacon.
larder [laʀde] *vt* (CULIN) to lard.
lardon [laʀdɔ̃] *nm* (CULIN) lardon.
large [laʀʒ(ə)] *a* wide; broad; (*fig*) generous // *ad*: **calculer/voir** ~ to allow extra/think big // *nm* (*largeur*): **5 m de** ~ 5 m wide *ou* in width; (*mer*): **le** ~ the open sea; **en** ~ *ad* sideways; **au** ~ **de** off; ~ **d'esprit** broad-minded; ~**ment** *ad* widely; greatly; easily; amply; generously; **largesse** *nf* generosity; **largesses** liberalities; **largeur** *nf* (*qu'on mesure*) width; (*impression visuelle*) wideness, width; breadth; broadness.
larguer [laʀge] *vt* to drop: ~ **les amarres** to cast off (the moorings).
larme [laʀm(ə)] *nf* tear; (*fig*): **une** ~ **de** a drop of; **en** ~**s** in tears; **larmoyant, e** *a* tearful; **larmoyer** *vi* (*yeux*) to water; (*se plaindre*) to whimper.
larron [laʀɔ̃] *nm* thief (*pl* thieves).
larve [laʀv(ə)] *nf* (ZOOL) larva (*pl* ae); (*fig*) worm.
larvé, e [laʀve] *a* (*fig*) latent.
laryngite [laʀɛ̃ʒit] *nf* laryngitis.
laryngologiste [laʀɛ̃gɔlɔʒist(ə)] *nm/f* throat specialist.
larynx [laʀɛ̃ks] *nm* larynx.
las, lasse [lɑ, lɑs] *a* weary.
lascar [laskaʀ] *nm* character; rogue.
lascif, ive [lasif, -iv] *a* lascivious.
laser [lazɛʀ] *a, nm*: **(rayon)** ~ laser (beam).
lasse [lɑs] *af voir* **las.**
lasser [lɑse] *vt* to weary, tire; **se** ~ **de** to grow weary *ou* tired of.
lassitude [lɑsityd] *nf* lassitude, weariness.
lasso [laso] *nm* lasso.
latent, e [latɑ̃, -ɑ̃t] *a* latent.
latéral, e, aux [lateʀal, -o] *a* side *cpd*, lateral.
latex [latɛks] *nm* latex.
latin, e [latɛ̃, -in] *a, nm, nf* Latin; **latiniste** *nm/f* Latin scholar (*ou* student); **latino-américain, e** *a* Latin-American.
latitude [latityd] *nf* latitude; (*fig*): **avoir la** ~ **de faire** to be left free *ou* be at liberty to do; **à 48° de** ~ **Nord** at latitude 48° North.
latrines [latʀin] *nfpl* latrines.
latte [lat] *nf* lath, slat; (*de plancher*) board.
lattis [lati] *nm* lathwork.
lauréat, e [lɔʀea, -at] *nm/f* winner.
laurier [lɔʀje] *nm* (BOT) laurel; (CULIN) bay leaves *pl*; ~**s** *nmpl* (*fig*) laurels.
lavable [lavabl(ə)] *a* washable.
lavabo [lavabo] *nm* (*de salle de bains*) washbasin; ~**s** *nmpl* toilet *sg*.
lavage [lavaʒ] *nm* washing *q*, wash; ~ **d'estomac/d'intestin** stomach/intestinal wash; ~ **de cerveau** brainwashing *q*.
lavande [lavɑ̃d] *nf* lavender.
lavandière [lavɑ̃djɛʀ] *nf* washerwoman.
lave [lav] *nf* lava *q*.
lave-glace [lavglas] *nm* (AUTO) windscreen washer.
lavement [lavmɑ̃] *nm* (MÉD) enema.
laver [lave] *vt* to wash; (*tache*) to wash off; (*fig*: *affront*) to avenge; **se** ~ to have a wash, wash; **se** ~ **les mains/dents** to wash one's hands/clean one's teeth; ~ **qn de** (*accusation*) to clear sb of; **laverie** *nf*: **laverie (automatique)** launderette.
lavette [lavɛt] *nf* dish cloth.
laveur, euse [lavœʀ, -øz] *nm/f* cleaner.
lave-vaisselle [lavvɛsɛl] *nm inv* dishwasher.
lavis [lavi] *nm* (*technique*) washing; (*dessin*) wash drawing.
lavoir [lavwaʀ] *nm* wash house; washtub.
laxatif, ive [laksatif, -iv] *a, nm* laxative.
laxisme [laksism(ə)] *nm* laxity.
layette [lɛjɛt] *nf* layette.
le(l'), la, les [l(ə), la, le] *dét* the // *pronom* (*personne*: *mâle*) him; (: *femelle*) her; (*animal, chose*) it; (*remplaçant une phrase*) it *ou non traduit*; (*indique la possession*): **se casser la jambe** *etc* to break one's leg *etc*; *voir note sous* **il**; **les** them; **je ne le savais pas** I didn't know (about it); **il était riche et ne l'est plus** he was once rich but no longer is; **levez la main** put your hand up; **avoir les yeux gris/le nez rouge** to have grey eyes/a red nose; **le jeudi** *etc ad* (*d'habitude*) on Thursdays *etc*; (*ce jeudi-là*) on the Thursday *etc*; **le matin/soir** *ad* in the morning/evening; mornings/evenings; **10 F le mètre/kilo** 10 F a *ou* per metre/kilo; **le tiers/quart de** a third/quarter of.
lécher [leʃe] *vt* to lick; (*laper*: *lait, eau*) to lick *ou* lap up; ~ **les vitrines** to go window-shopping.
leçon [ləsɔ̃] *nf* lesson; **faire la** ~ to teach; **faire la** ~ **à** (*fig*) to give a lecture to; ~**s de conduite** driving lessons; ~**s particulières** private lessons *ou* tuition *sg*.
lecteur, trice [lɛktœʀ, -tʀis] *nm/f* reader; (*d'université*) foreign language assistant // *nm* (TECH): ~ **de cassettes** cassette player.
lecture [lɛktyʀ] *nf* reading.
ledit [lədi], **ladite** [ladit], *mpl* **lesdits** [ledi], *fpl* **lesdites** [ledit] *dét* the aforesaid.
légal, e, aux [legal, -o] *a* legal; ~**ement** *ad* legally; ~**iser** *vt* to legalize; ~**ité** *nf* legality, lawfulness; **être dans/sortir de la** ~**ité** to be within/step outside the law.
légataire [legatɛʀ] *nm*: ~ **universel** sole legatee.

légation [legɑsjɔ̃] *nf* legation.
légendaire [leʒɑ̃dɛʀ] *a* legendary.
légende [leʒɑ̃d] *nf* (*mythe*) legend; (*de carte, plan*) key, legend; (*de dessin*) caption, legend.
léger, ère [leʒe, -ɛʀ] *a* light; (*bruit, retard*) slight; (*superficiel*) thoughtless; (*volage*) free and easy; flighty; **blessé ~** slightly injured person; **à la légère** *ad* (*parler, agir*) rashly, thoughtlessly; **légèrement** *ad* lightly; thoughtlessly, rashly; **légèrement plus grand** slightly bigger; **légèreté** *nf* lightness; thoughtlessness.
légiférer [leʒifeʀe] *vi* to legislate.
légion [leʒjɔ̃] *nf* legion; **~ étrangère** foreign legion; **~ d'honneur** Legion of Honour; **légionnaire** *nm* legionnaire.
législateur [leʒislatœʀ] *nm* legislator, lawmaker.
législatif, ive [leʒislatif, -iv] *a* legislative.
législation [leʒislɑsjɔ̃] *nf* legislation.
législature [leʒislatyʀ] *nf* legislature; term (of office).
légiste [leʒist(ə)] *a*: **médecin ~** forensic surgeon.
légitime [leʒitim] *a* (JUR) lawful, legitimate; (*fig*) justified, rightful, legitimate; **en état de ~ défense** in self-defence; **~ment** *ad* justifiably, rightfully; **légitimité** *nf* (JUR) legitimacy.
legs [lɛg] *nm* legacy.
léguer [lege] *vt*: **~ qch à qn** (JUR) to bequeath sth to sb; (*fig*) to hand sth down *ou* pass sth on to sb.
légume [legym] *nm* vegetable.
lendemain [lɑ̃dmɛ̃] *nm*: **le ~** the next *ou* following day; **le ~ matin/soir** the next *ou* following morning/evening; **le ~ de** the day after; **au ~ de** in the days following; in the wake of; **penser au ~** to think of the future; **sans ~** short-lived; **de beaux ~s** bright prospects.
lénifiant, e [lenifjɑ̃, -ɑ̃t] *a* soothing.
lent, e [lɑ̃, lɑ̃t] *a* slow; **lentement** *ad* slowly; **lenteur** *nf* slowness *q*.
lentille [lɑ̃tij] *nf* (OPTIQUE) lens *sg*; (BOT) lentil.
léopard [leɔpaʀ] *nm* leopard.
lèpre [lɛpʀ(ə)] *nf* leprosy; **lépreux, euse** *nm/f* leper // *a* (*fig*) flaking, peeling.
lequel [ləkɛl], **laquelle** [lakɛl], *mpl* **lesquels,** *fpl* **lesquelles** [lekɛl] (*avec à, de*: **auquel, duquel** *etc*) *pronom* (*interrogatif*) which, which one; (*relatif*: *personne*: *sujet*) who; (: *objet, après préposition*) whom; (: *chose*) which // *a*: **auquel cas** in which case.
les [le] *dét voir* **le.**
lesbienne [lɛsbjɛn] *nf* lesbian.
lesdits [ledi], **lesdites** [ledit] *dét voir* **ledit**.
léser [leze] *vt* to wrong.
lésiner [lezine] *vt*: **~ (sur)** to skimp (on).
lésion [lezjɔ̃] *nf* lesion, damage *q*; **~s cérébrales** brain damage.
lesquels, lesquelles [lekɛl] *pronom voir* **lequel.**
lessive [lesiv] *nf* (*poudre*) washing powder; (*linge*) washing *q*, wash; (*opération*) washing *q*; **faire la ~** to do the washing.
lessivé, e [lesive] *a* (*fam*) washed out; cleaned out.
lessiver [lesive] *vt* to wash.
lessiveuse [lesivøz] *nf* (*récipient*) (laundry) boiler.
lest [lɛst] *nm* ballast.
leste [lɛst(ə)] *a* sprightly, nimble.
lester [lɛste] *vt* to ballast.
léthargie [letaʀʒi] *nf* lethargy.
léthargique [letaʀʒik] *a* lethargic.
lettre [lɛtʀ(ə)] *nf* letter; **~s** *nfpl* literature *sg*; (SCOL) arts (subjects); **à la ~** literally; **en toutes ~s** in words, in full; **~ de change** bili of exchange.
lettré, e [letʀe] *a* well-read, scholarly.
leu [lø] *voir* **queue**.
leucémie [løsemi] *nf* leukaemia.
leur [lœʀ] *dét* their // *pronom* them; **le(la) ~, les ~s** theirs; **à ~ approche** as they came near; **à ~ vue** at the sight of them.
leurre [lœʀ] *nm* (*appât*) lure; (*fig*) delusion; snare.
leurrer [lœʀe] *vt* to delude, deceive.
levain [ləvɛ̃] *nm* leaven.
levant, e [ləvɑ̃, -ɑ̃t] *a*: **soleil ~** rising sun // *nm*: **le L~** the Levant.
levé, e [ləve] *a*: **être ~** to be up.
levée [ləve] *nf* (POSTES) collection; (CARTES) trick; **~ de boucliers** general outcry; **~ du corps** *collection of the body from house of the deceased, before funeral*; **~ d'écrou** release from custody; **~ de terre** levee; **~ de troupes** levy.
lever [ləve] *vt* (*vitre, bras etc*) to raise; (*soulever de terre, supprimer*: *interdiction, siège*) to lift; (*séance*) to close; (*impôts, armée*) to levy; (CHASSE) to start; to flush; (*fam*: *fille*) to pick up // *vi* (CULIN) to rise // *nm*: **au ~** on getting up; **se ~** *vi* to get up; (*soleil*) to rise; (*jour*) to break; (*brouillard*) to lift; **ça va se ~** the weather will clear; **~ du jour** daybreak; **~ du rideau** curtain; **~ de rideau** curtain raiser; **~ de soleil** sunrise.
levier [ləvje] *nm* lever; **faire ~ sur** to lever up (*ou* off); **~ de changement de vitesse** gear lever.
lèvre [lɛvʀ(ə)] *nf* lip; **petites/grandes ~s** (ANAT) labia minora/majora.
lévrier [levʀije] *nm* greyhound.
levure [ləvyʀ] *nf* yeast.
lexicographie [lɛksikɔgʀafi] *nf* lexicography, dictionary writing.
lexique [lɛksik] *nm* vocabulary; lexicon.
lézard [lezaʀ] *nm* lizard.
lézarde [lezaʀd(ə)] *nf* crack; **lézarder**: **se lézarder** *vi* to crack.
liaison [ljɛzɔ̃] *nf* (*rapport*) connection, link; (RAIL, AVIAT *etc*) link; (*amoureuse*) affair; (PHONÉTIQUE) liaison; **entrer/être en ~ avec** to get/be in contact with; **~ radio** radio contact.
liane [ljan] *nf* creeper.
liant, e [ljɑ̃, -ɑ̃t] *a* sociable.
liasse [ljas] *nf* wad, bundle.
Liban [libɑ̃] *nm*: **le ~** (the) Lebanon; **libanais, e** *a, nm/f* Lebanese.
libations [libɑsjɔ̃] *nfpl* libations.
libelle [libɛl] *nm* lampoon.
libeller [libele] *vt* (*chèque, mandat*): **~ (au nom de)** to make out (to); (*lettre*) to word.

libellule [libelyl] *nf* dragonfly.
libéral, e, aux [libeʀal, -o] *a, nm/f* liberal ; **~iser** *vt* to liberalize ; **~isme** *nm* liberalism.
libéralité [libeʀalite] *nf* liberality *q*, generosity *q*.
libérateur, trice [libeʀatœʀ, -tʀis] *a* liberating // *nm/f* liberator.
libération [libeʀɑsjɔ̃] *nf* liberation, freeing ; release ; discharge.
libérer [libeʀe] *vt* (*délivrer*) to free, liberate ; (: *moralement*, PSYCH) to liberate ; (*relâcher*) to release ; to discharge ; (*dégager*: *gaz, cran d'arrêt*) to release ; **se ~** (*de rendez-vous*) to try and be free, get out of previous engagements ; **~ qn de** to free sb from ; (*promesse*) to release sb from.
libertaire [libɛʀtɛʀ] *a* libertarian.
liberté [libɛʀte] *nf* freedom ; (*loisir*) free time ; **~s** *nfpl* (*privautés*) liberties ; **mettre/être en ~** to set/be free ; **en ~ provisoire/surveillée/conditionnelle** on bail/ probation/parole ; **~ d'esprit** independence of mind ; **~ d'opinion** freedom of thought ; **~ de réunion** right to hold meetings ; **~s individuelles** personal freedom *sg*.
libertin, e [libɛʀtɛ̃, -in] *a* libertine, licentious ; **libertinage** *nm* licentiousness.
libidineux, euse [libidinø, -øz] *a* libidinous, lustful.
libido [libido] *nf* libido.
libraire [libʀɛʀ] *nm/f* bookseller.
librairie [libʀeʀi] *nf* bookshop.
libre [libʀ(ə)] *a* free ; (*route*) clear ; (*pas pris ou occupé*: *place etc*) vacant ; empty ; not engaged ; not taken ; (SCOL) private and Roman Catholic (*as opposed to 'laïque'*) ; **~ de qch/de faire** free from sth/ to do ; **~-échange** *nm* free trade ; **~ment** *ad* freely ; **~-service** *nm* self-service store.
librettiste [libʀetist(ə)] *nm/f* librettist.
Libye [libi] *nf*: **la ~** Libya ; **libyen, ne** *a, nm/f* Libyan.
licence [lisɑ̃s] *nf* (*permis*) permit ; (*diplôme*) (first) degree ; (*liberté*) liberty ; licence ; licentiousness ; **licencié, e** *nm/f* (SCOL): **licencié ès lettres/en droit** ≈ Bachelor of Arts/Law ; (SPORT) *member of a sports federation.*
licenciement [lisɑ̃simɑ̃] *nm* dismissal ; laying off *q* ; redundancy.
licencier [lisɑ̃sje] *vt* (*renvoyer*) to dismiss ; (*débaucher*) to make redundant ; to lay off.
licencieux, euse [lisɑ̃sjø, -øz] *a* licentious.
lichen [likɛn] *nm* lichen.
licite [lisit] *a* lawful.
licorne [likɔʀn(ə)] *nf* unicorn.
licou [liku] *nm* halter.
lie [li] *nf* dregs *pl*, sediment.
lié, e [lje] *a*: **très ~ avec** very friendly with *ou* close to ; **~ par** (*serment*) bound by.
liège [ljɛʒ] *nm* cork.
lien [ljɛ̃] *nm* (*corde, fig*: *affectif*) bond ; (*rapport*) link, connection ; **~ de parenté** family tie.
lier [lje] *vt* (*attacher*) to tie up ; (*joindre*) to link up ; (*fig*: *unir, engager*) to bind ; (CULIN) to thicken ; **~ qch à** to tie sth to ; to link sth to ; **~ conversation avec** to strike up a conversation with ; **se ~ avec** to make friends with.
lierre [ljɛʀ] *nm* ivy.
liesse [ljɛs] *nf*: **être en ~** to be celebrating *ou* jubilant.
lieu, x [ljø] *nm* place // *nmpl* (*habitation*) premises ; (*endroit*: *d'un accident etc*) scene *sg* ; **en ~ sûr** in a safe place ; **en premier ~** in the first place ; **en dernier ~** lastly ; **avoir ~** to take place ; **avoir ~ de faire** to have grounds *ou* good reason for doing ; **tenir ~ de** to take the place of ; to serve as ; **donner ~ à** to give rise to, give cause for ; **au ~ de** instead of ; **au ~ qu'il y aille** instead of him going ; **~ commun** commonplace ; **~ géométrique** locus.
lieu-dit *nm, pl* **lieux-dits** [ljødi] locality.
lieue [ljø] *nf* league.
lieutenant [ljøtnɑ̃] *nm* lieutenant.
lièvre [ljɛvʀ(ə)] *nm* hare.
liftier [liftje] *nm* lift boy.
ligament [ligamɑ̃] *nm* ligament.
ligature [ligatyʀ] *nf* ligature ; **ligaturer** *vt* to ligature.
lige [liʒ] *a*: **homme ~** (*péj*) henchman.
ligne [liɲ] *nf* (*gén*) line ; (TRANSPORTS: *liaison*) service ; (: *trajet*) route ; (*silhouette féminine*): **garder la ~** to keep one's figure ; **'à la ~'** 'new paragraph' ; **entrer en ~ de compte** to be taken into account ; to come into it ; **~ de but/médiane** goal/halfway line ; **~ d'horizon** skyline.
lignée [liɲe] *nf* line ; lineage ; descendants *pl*.
ligneux, euse [liɲø, -øz] *a* ligneous, woody.
lignite [liɲit] *nm* lignite.
ligoter [ligɔte] *vt* to tie up.
ligue [lig] *nf* league ; **liguer**: **se liguer** *vi* to form a league ; **se liguer contre** (*fig*) to combine against.
lilas [lilɑ] *nm* lilac.
limace [limas] *nf* slug.
limaille [limɑj] *nf*: **~ de fer** iron filings *pl*.
limande [limɑ̃d] *nf* dab.
lime [lim] *nf* file ; **~ à ongles** nail file ; **limer** *vt* to file (down) ; (*ongles*) to file ; (*fig*: *prix*) to pare down, trim.
limier [limje] *nm* bloodhound ; (*détective*) sleuth.
liminaire [liminɛʀ] *a* (*propos*) introductory.
limitation [limitɑsjɔ̃] *nf* limitation, restriction.
limite [limit] *nf* (*de terrain*) boundary ; (*partie ou point extrême*) limit ; **charge/vitesse ~** maximum speed/load ; **cas ~** borderline case ; **date ~** deadline.
limiter [limite] *vt* (*restreindre*) to limit, restrict ; (*délimiter*) to border, form the boundary of.
limitrophe [limitʀɔf] *a* border *cpd* ; **~ de** bordering on.
limoger [limɔʒe] *vt* to dismiss.
limon [limɔ̃] *nm* silt.
limonade [limɔnad] *nf* (fizzy) lemonade.
limpide [lɛ̃pid] *a* limpid.
lin [lɛ̃] *nm* flax.

linceul [lɛ̃sœl] *nm* shroud.
linéaire [lineɛʀ] *a* linear.
linge [lɛ̃ʒ] *nm* (*serviettes etc*) linen; (*pièce de tissu*) cloth; (*aussi*: ~ **de corps**) underwear; (*aussi*: ~ **de toilette**) towel; (*lessive*) washing; ~ **sale** dirty linen.
lingerie [lɛ̃ʒʀi] *nf* lingerie, underwear.
lingot [lɛ̃go] *nm* ingot.
linguiste [lɛ̃gɥist(ə)] *nm/f* linguist.
linguistique [lɛ̃gɥistik] *a* linguistic // *nf* linguistics *sg*.
lino(léum) [linɔ(leɔm)] *nm* lino(leum).
lion, ne [ljɔ̃, ljɔn] *nm/f* lion/lioness; (*signe*): **le L~** Leo, the Lion; **être du L~** to be Leo; **lionceau, x** *nm* lion cub.
lippu, e [lipy] *a* thick-lipped.
liquéfier [likefje] *vt*, **se** ~ *vi* to liquefy.
liqueur [likœʀ] *nf* liqueur.
liquidation [likidɑsjɔ̃] *nf* liquidation; (COMM) clearance (sale).
liquide [likid] *a* liquid // *nm* liquid; (COMM): **en** ~ in ready money *ou* cash.
liquider [likide] *vt* (*société, biens, témoin gênant*) to liquidate; (*compte, problème*) to settle; (COMM: articles) to clear, sell off.
liquidités [likidite] *nfpl* (COMM) liquid assets.
liquoreux, euse [likɔʀø, -øz] *a* syrupy.
lire [liʀ] *nf* (*monnaie*) lira // *vt, vi* to read; ~ **qch à qn** to read sth (out) to sb.
lis *vb* [li] *voir* **lire** // *nm* [lis] = **lys**.
liseré [lizʀe] *nm* border, edging.
liseron [lizʀɔ̃] *nm* bindweed.
liseuse [lizøz] *nf* book-cover.
lisible [lizibl(ə)] *a* legible.
lisière [lizjɛʀ] *nf* (*de forêt*) edge; (*de tissu*) selvage.
lisons *vb voir* **lire**.
lisse [lis] *a* smooth; **lisser** *vt* to smooth.
liste [list(ə)] *nf* list; **faire la** ~ **de** to list, make out a list of; ~ **électorale** electoral roll.
lit [li] *nm* (*gén*) bed; **faire son** ~ to make one's bed; **aller/se mettre au** ~ to go to/get into bed; **prendre le** ~ to take to one's bed; **d'un premier** ~ (JUR) of a first marriage; ~ **de camp** campbed.
litanie [litani] *nf* litany.
literie [litʀi] *nf* bedding; bedclothes *pl*.
lithographie [litɔgʀafi] *nf* lithography; (*épreuve*) lithograph.
litière [litjɛʀ] *nf* litter.
litige [litiʒ] *nm* dispute; **litigieux, euse** *a* litigious, contentious.
litre [litʀ(ə)] *nm* litre; (*récipient*) litre measure.
littéraire [liteʀɛʀ] *a* literary.
littéral, e, aux [liteʀal, -o] *a* literal.
littérature [liteʀatyʀ] *nf* literature.
littoral, e, aux [litɔʀal, -o] *a* coastal // *nm* coast.
liturgie [lityʀʒi] *nf* liturgy; **liturgique** *a* liturgical.
livide [livid] *a* livid, pallid.
livraison [livʀɛzɔ̃] *nf* delivery.
livre [livʀ(ə)] *nm* book // *nf* (*poids, monnaie*) pound; ~ **de bord** logbook; ~ **d'or** visitors' book; ~ **de poche** paperback (*cheap and pocket size*).
livré, e [livʀe] *a*: ~ **à soi-même** left to o.s. *ou* one's own devices // *nf* livery.
livrer [livʀe] *vt* (COMM) to deliver; (*otage, coupable*) to hand over; (*secret, information*) to give away; **se** ~ **à** (*se confier*) to confide in; (*se rendre*) to give o.s. up to; (*s'abandonner à*: *débauche etc*) to give o.s. up *ou* over to; (*faire*: *pratiques, actes*) to indulge in; (: *travail*) to be engaged in, engage in; (: *sport*) to practise; (: *enquête*) to carry out; ~ **bataille** to give battle.
livresque [livʀɛsk(ə)] *a* bookish.
livret [livʀɛ] *nm* booklet; (*d'opéra*) libretto (*pl* s); ~ **de caisse d'épargne** (savings) bank-book; ~ **de famille** (official) family record book; ~ **scolaire** (school) report book.
livreur, euse [livʀœʀ, -øz] *nm/f* delivery boy *ou* man/girl *ou* woman.
lobe [lɔb] *nm*: ~ **de l'oreille** ear lobe.
lobé, e [lɔbe] *a* (ARCHIT) foiled.
lober [lɔbe] *vt* to lob.
local, e, aux [lɔkal, -o] *a* local // *nm* (*salle*) premises *pl* // *nmpl* premises.
localiser [lɔkalize] *vt* (*repérer*) to locate, place; (*limiter*) to localize, confine.
localité [lɔkalite] *nf* locality.
locataire [lɔkatɛʀ] *nm/f* tenant; (*de chambre*) lodger.
locatif, ive [lɔkatif, -iv] *a* (*charges, réparations*) incumbent upon the tenant; (*valeur*) rental; (*immeuble*) with rented flats, used as a letting concern.
location [lɔkɑsjɔ̃] *nf* (*par le locataire*) renting; (*par l'usager*: *de voiture etc*) hiring; (*par le propriétaire*) renting out, letting; hiring out; '~ **de voitures**' 'car hire *ou* rental'; ~**-vente** *nf form of hire purchase for housing*.
lock-out [lɔkawt] *nm inv* lockout.
locomotion [lɔkɔmosjɔ̃] *nf* locomotion.
locomotive [lɔkɔmɔtiv] *nf* locomotive, engine; (*fig*) pacesetter, pacemaker.
locution [lɔkysjɔ̃] *nf* phrase, locution.
logarithme [lɔgaʀitm(ə)] *nm* logarithm.
loge [lɔʒ] *nf* (THÉÂTRE: *d'artiste*) dressing room; (: *de spectateurs*) box; (*de concierge, franc-maçon*) lodge.
logement [lɔʒmɑ̃] *nm* accommodation *q*, flat; housing *q*; **chercher un** ~ to look for a flat *ou* for accommodation; **construire des** ~**s bon marché** to build cheap housing *sg ou* flats; **crise du** ~ housing shortage.
loger [lɔʒe] *vt* to accommodate // *vi* to live; **se** ~: **trouver à se** ~ to find accommodation; **se** ~ **dans** (*suj*: *balle, flèche*) to lodge itself in; **logeur, euse** *nm/f* landlord/landlady.
loggia [lɔdʒja] *nf* loggia.
logiciel [lɔʒisjɛl] *nm* software.
logique [lɔʒik] *a* logical // *nf* logic; ~**ment** *ad* logically.
logis [lɔʒi] *nm* home; abode, dwelling.
logistique [lɔʒistik] *nf* logistics *sg*.
loi [lwa] *nf* law; **faire la** ~ to lay down the law.
loin [lwɛ̃] *ad* far; (*dans le temps*) a long way off; a long time ago; **plus** ~ further; **moins** ~ **(que)** not as far (as); ~ **de** far

from ; **pas ~ de 1000 F** not far off a 1000 F ; **au ~** far off ; **de ~** *ad* from a distance ; (*fig*: *de beaucoup*) by far ; **il vient de ~** he's come a long way ; he comes from a long way away.
lointain, e [lwɛ̃tɛ̃, -ɛn] *a* faraway, distant ; (*dans le futur, passé*) distant, far-off ; (*cause, parent*) remote, distant // *nm*: **dans le ~** in the distance.
loir [lwaʀ] *nm* dormouse (*pl* mice).
loisir [lwaziʀ] *nm*: **heures de ~** spare time ; **~s** *nmpl* leisure *sg*; leisure activities ; **avoir le ~ de faire** to have the time *ou* opportunity to do ; **à ~** at leisure ; at one's pleasure.
londonien, ne [lɔ̃dɔnjɛ̃, -jɛn] *a* London *cpd*, of London // *nm/f*: **L~, ne** Londoner.
Londres [lɔ̃dʀ(ə)] *n* London.
long, longue [lɔ̃, lɔ̃g] *a* long // *ad*: **en savoir ~** to know a great deal // *nm*: **de 3 m de ~** 3 m long, 3 m in length // *nf*: **à la longue** in the end ; **faire ~ feu** to fizzle out ; **ne pas faire ~ feu** not to last long ; **du ~ cours** (NAVIG) ocean *cpd*, ocean-going ; **être ~ à faire** to take a long time to do ; **en ~** *ad* lengthwise ; **(tout) le ~ de** (all) along ; **tout au ~ de** (*année, vie*) throughout ; **de ~ en large** (*marcher*) to and fro, up and down.
longanimité [lɔ̃ganimite] *nf* forbearance.
longe [lɔ̃ʒ] *nf* (*corde*) tether ; lead ; (CULIN) loin.
longer [lɔ̃ʒe] *vt* to go (*ou* walk *ou* drive) along(side) ; (*suj*: *mur, route*) to border.
longévité [lɔ̃ʒevite] *nf* longevity.
longiligne [lɔ̃ʒiliɲ] *a* long-limbed.
longitude [lɔ̃ʒityd] *nf* longitude ; **à 45° de ~ ouest** at 45° longitude west.
longitudinal, e, aux [lɔ̃ʒitydinal, -o] *a* longitudinal, lengthways ; running lengthways.
longtemps [lɔ̃tɑ̃] *ad* (for) a long time, (for) long ; **avant ~** before long ; **pour/pendant ~** for a long time/long ; **mettre ~ à faire** to take a long time to do.
longue [lɔ̃g] *af voir* **long** ; **~ment** *ad* for a long time, at length.
longueur [lɔ̃gœʀ] *nf* length ; **~s** *nfpl* (*fig*: *d'un film etc*) lengthy *ou* drawn-out parts ; **sur une ~ de 10 km** for *ou* over 10 km ; **en ~** *ad* lengthwise ; **tirer en ~** to drag on ; **à ~ de journée** all day long ; **~ d'onde** wavelength.
longue-vue [lɔ̃gvy] *nf* telescope.
lopin [lɔpɛ̃] *nm*: **~ de terre** patch of land.
loquace [lɔkas] *a* loquacious, talkative.
loque [lɔk] *nf* (*personne*) wreck ; **~s** *nfpl* (*habits*) rags.
loquet [lɔkɛ] *nm* latch.
lorgner [lɔʀɲe] *vt* to eye ; to have one's eye on.
lorgnon [lɔʀɲɔ̃] *nm* lorgnette.
loriot [lɔʀjo] *nm* (golden) oriole.
lors [lɔʀ]: **~ de** *prép* at the time of ; during ; **~ même que** even though.
lorsque [lɔʀsk(ə)] *cj* when, as.
losange [lɔzɑ̃ʒ] *nm* diamond ; (GÉOM) lozenge ; **en ~** diamond-shaped.
lot [lo] *nm* (*part*) share ; (*de loterie*) prize ; (*fig*: *destin*) fate, lot.
loterie [lɔtʀi] *nf* lottery ; raffle.
loti, e [lɔti] *a*: **bien/mal ~** well-/badly off (*as regards luck, circumstances*).
lotion [losjɔ̃] *nf* lotion.
lotir [lɔtiʀ] *vt* (*terrain*) to divide into plots ; to sell by lots ; **lotissement** *nm* housing development ; plot, lot.
loto [lɔto] *nm* lotto ; numerical lottery.
louable [lwabl(ə)] *a* praiseworthy, commendable.
louage [lwaʒ] *nm*: **voiture de ~** hired car ; hire car.
louange [lwɑ̃ʒ] *nf*: **à la ~ de** in praise of ; **~s** *nfpl* praise *sg*.
louche [luʃ] *a* shady, fishy, dubious // *nf* ladle.
loucher [luʃe] *vi* to squint ; (*fig*): **~ sur** to have one's eye on.
louer [lwe] *vt* (*maison*: *suj*: *propriétaire*) to let, rent (out) ; (: *locataire*) to rent ; (*voiture etc*) to hire out, rent (out) ; to hire, rent ; (*réserver*) to book ; (*faire l'éloge de*) to praise ; **'à louer'** 'to let' ; **~ qn de** to praise sb for ; **se ~ de** to congratulate o.s. on.
loufoque [lufɔk] *a* crazy, zany.
loulou [lulu] *nm* (*chien*) spitz.
loup [lu] *nm* wolf (*pl* wolves) ; **~ de mer** (*marin*) old seadog.
loupe [lup] *nf* magnifying glass ; **~ de noyer** burr walnut.
louper [lupe] *vt* (*manquer*) to miss ; (*gâcher*) to mess up, bungle.
lourd, e [luʀ, luʀd(ə)] *a, ad* heavy ; **~ de** (*conséquences, menaces*) charged *ou* fraught with ; **lourdaud, e** *a* (*péj*) clumsy ; oafish ; **lourdement** *ad* heavily ; **lourdeur** *nf* heaviness ; **lourdeur d'estomac** indigestion *q*.
loutre [lutʀ(ə)] *nf* otter.
louve [luv] *nf* she-wolf.
louveteau, x [luvto] *nm* wolf-cub ; (*scout*) cub.
louvoyer [luvwaje] *vi* (NAVIG) to tack ; (*fig*) to hedge, evade the issue.
lover [lɔve]: **se ~** *vi* to coil up.
loyal, e, aux [lwajal, -o] *a* (*fidèle*) loyal, faithful ; (*fair-play*) fair ; **loyauté** *nf* loyalty, faithfulness ; fairness.
loyer [lwaje] *nm* rent.
lu, e [ly] *pp de* **lire**.
lubie [lybi] *nf* whim, craze.
lubrifiant [lybʀifjɑ̃] *nm* lubricant.
lubrifier [lybʀifje] *vt* to lubricate.
lubrique [lybʀik] *a* lecherous.
lucarne [lykaʀn(ə)] *nf* skylight.
lucide [lysid] *a* (*conscient*) lucid, conscious ; (*perspicace*) clear-headed ; lucid ; **lucidité** *nf* lucidity.
luciole [lysjɔl] *nf* firefly.
lucratif, ive [lykʀatif, -iv] *a* lucrative ; profitable ; **à but non ~** non profit-making.
luette [lɥɛt] *nf* uvula.
lueur [lɥœʀ] *nf* (*chatoyante*) glimmer *q* ; (*métallique, mouillée*) gleam *q* ; (*rougeoyante, chaude*) glow *q* ; (*pâle*) (faint) light ; (*fig*) glimmer ; gleam.
luge [lyʒ] *nf* sledge.
lugubre [lygybʀ(ə)] *a* gloomy ; dismal.

lui [lɥi] *pronom* (*chose, animal*) it; (*personne*: *mâle*) him; (: *en sujet*) he; (: *femelle*) her; *voir note sous* **il**; **~-même** himself; itself.
luire [lɥiʀ] *vi* to shine; to glow; to gleam.
lumbago [lɔ̃bago] *nm* lumbago.
lumière [lymjɛʀ] *nf* light; **~s** *nfpl* (*d'une personne*) knowledge *sg*, wisdom *sg*; **à la ~ de** by the light of; (*fig*) in the light of; **fais de la ~** let's have some light, give us some light; **mettre en ~** (*fig*) to bring out *ou* to light; **~ du jour/soleil** day/sunlight.
luminaire [lyminɛʀ] *nm* lamp, light.
lumineux, euse [lyminø, -øz] *a* (*émettant de la lumière*) luminous; (*éclairé*) illuminated; (*ciel, journée, couleur*) bright; (*relatif à la lumière*: *rayon etc*) of light, light *cpd*; (*fig*: *regard*) radiant; **luminosité** *nf* (TECH) luminosity.
lunaire [lynɛʀ] *a* lunar, moon *cpd*.
lunatique [lynatik] *a* whimsical, temperamental.
lunch [lœntʃ] *nm* (*réception*) buffet lunch.
lundi [lœ̃di] *nm* Monday; **~ de Pâques** Easter Monday.
lune [lyn] *nf* moon; **~ de miel** honeymoon.
luné, e [lyne] *a*: **bien/mal ~** in a good/bad mood.
lunette [lynɛt] *nf*: **~s** *nfpl* glasses, spectacles; (*protectrices*) goggles; **~ d'approche** telescope; **~ arrière** (AUTO) rear window; **~s noires** dark glasses; **~s de soleil** sunglasses.
lurette [lyʀɛt] *nf*: **il y a belle ~** ages ago.
luron, ne [lyʀɔ̃, -ɔn] *nm/f* lad/lass; **joyeux** *ou* **gai ~** gay dog.
lus *etc vb voir* **lire**.
lustre [lystʀ(ə)] *nm* (*de plafond*) chandelier; (*fig*: *éclat*) lustre.
lustrer [lystʀe] *vt* (*faire briller*) to lustre; (*poil d'un animal*) to put a sheen on; (*user*) to make shiny.
lut *vb voir* **lire**.
luth [lyt] *nm* lute; **luthier** *nm* (stringed-)instrument maker.
lutin [lytɛ̃] *nm* imp, goblin.
lutrin [lytʀɛ̃] *nm* lectern.
lutte [lyt] *nf* (*conflit*) struggle; (*sport*) wrestling; **lutter** *vi* to fight, struggle; to wrestle; **lutteur** *nm* wrestler; (*fig*) battler, fighter.
luxation [lyksɑsjɔ̃] *nf* dislocation.
luxe [lyks(ə)] *nm* luxury; **de ~** *a* luxury *cpd*.
Luxembourg [lyksɑ̃buʀ] *nm*: **le ~** Luxemburg.
luxer [lykse] *vt*: **se ~ l'épaule** to dislocate one's shoulder.
luxueux, euse [lyksɥø, -øz] *a* luxurious.
luxure [lyksyʀ] *nf* lust.
luxuriant, e [lyksyʀjɑ̃, -ɑ̃t] *a* luxuriant, lush.
luzerne [lyzɛʀn(ə)] *nf* lucerne, alfalfa.
lycée [lise] *nm* (state) secondary school; **lycéen, ne** *nm/f* secondary school pupil.
lymphatique [lɛ̃fatik] *a* (*fig*) lethargic, sluggish.
lymphe [lɛ̃f] *nf* lymph.
lyncher [lɛ̃ʃe] *vt* to lynch.
lynx [lɛ̃ks] *nm* lynx.
lyophilisé, e [ljɔfilize] *a* freeze-dried.
lyre [liʀ] *nf* lyre.
lyrique [liʀik] *a* lyrical; (OPÉRA) lyric; **comédie ~** comic opera; **théâtre ~** opera house (*for light opera*); **lyrisme** *nm* lyricism.
lys [lis] *nm* lily.

M

m' [m] *pronom voir* **me.**
M. [ɛm] *abr de* **Monsieur.**
ma [ma] *dét voir* **mon.**
maboul, e [mabul] *a* (*fam*) loony.
macabre [makɑbʀ(ə)] *a* macabre, gruesome.
macadam [makadam] *nm* tarmac.
macaron [makaʀɔ̃] *nm* (*gâteau*) macaroon; (*insigne*) (round) badge.
macaronis [makaʀɔni] *nmpl* macaroni *sg*.
macédoine [masedwan] *nf*: **~ de fruits** fruit salad.
macérer [maseʀe] *vi, vt* to macerate; (*dans du vinaigre*) to pickle.
mâchefer [mɑʃfɛʀ] *nm* clinker, cinders *pl*.
mâcher [mɑʃe] *vt* to chew; **ne pas ~ ses mots** not to mince one's words.
machin [maʃɛ̃] *nm* (*fam*) thingummy, whatsit; contraption, thing.
machinal, e, aux [maʃinal, -o] *a* mechanical, automatic.
machination [maʃinɑsjɔ̃] *nf* scheming, frame-up.
machine [maʃin] *nf* machine; (*locomotive*) engine; (*fig*: *rouages*) machinery; **faire ~ arrière** (NAVIG) to go astern; **~ à laver/coudre/ tricoter** washing/sewing/knitting machine; **~ à écrire** typewriter; **~ à sous** fruit machine; **~ à vapeur** steam engine; **~-outil** *nf* machine tool; **~rie** *nf* machinery, plant; (*d'un navire*) engine room; **machinisme** *nm* mechanization; **machiniste** *nm* (THÉÂTRE) scene shifter; (*de bus, métro*) driver.
mâchoire [mɑʃwaʀ] *nf* jaw; **~ de frein** brake shoe.
mâchonner [mɑʃɔne] *vt* to chew (at).
maçon [masɔ̃] *nm* bricklayer; builder.
maçonner [masɔne] *vt* (*revêtir*) to face, render (with cement); (*boucher*) to brick up.
maçonnerie [masɔnʀi] *nf* (*murs*) brickwork; masonry, stonework; (*activité*) bricklaying; building.
maçonnique [masɔnik] *a* masonic.
maculer [makyle] *vt* to stain; (TYPO) to mackle.
Madame [madam], *pl* **Mesdames** [medam] *nf*: **~ X** Mrs ['mɪsɪz] X; **occupez-vous de ~/Monsieur/ Mademoiselle** please serve this lady/gentleman/(young) lady; **bonjour ~/Monsieur/Mademoiselle** good morning; (*ton déférent*) good morning Madam/Sir/Madam; (*le nom est connu*) good morning Mrs/Mr/Miss X; **~/Monsieur/ Mademoiselle!** (*pour appeler*) Madam/Sir/Miss!; **~/Monsieur/Mademoiselle** (*sur lettre*) Dear Madam/Sir/Madam; **chère ~/cher**

Monsieur/chère Mademoiselle Dear Mrs/Mr/Miss X.
Mademoiselle [madmwazɛl], *pl* **Mesdemoiselles** [medmwazɛl] *nf* Miss; *voir aussi* **Madame.**
madère [madɛʀ] *nm* Madeira (wine).
madone [madɔn] *nf* madonna.
madré, e [madʀe] *a* crafty, wily.
madrier [madʀije] *nm* beam.
madrilène [madʀilɛn] *a* of *ou* from Madrid.
maestria [maɛstʀija] *nf* (masterly) skill.
maf(f)ia [mafja] *nf* Maf(f)ia.
magasin [magazɛ̃] *nm* (*boutique*) shop; (*entrepôt*) warehouse; (*d'une arme*) magazine; **en** ~ (*COMM*) in stock; **magasinier** *nm* warehouseman.
magazine [magazin] *nm* magazine.
mage [maʒ] *nm*: **les Rois M~s** the Magi, the (Three) Wise Men.
magicien, ne [maʒisjɛ̃, -jɛn] *nm/f* magician.
magie [maʒi] *nf* magic; **magique** *a* magic; (*enchanteur*) magical.
magistral, e, aux [maʒistʀal, -o] *a* (*œuvre, addresse*) masterly; (*ton*) authoritative; (*gifle etc*) sound, resounding; (*ex cathedra*): **enseignement** ~ lecturing, lectures *pl.*
magistrat [maʒistʀa] *nm* magistrate.
magistrature [maʒistʀatyʀ] *nf* magistracy, magistrature.
magma [magma] *nm* (*GÉO*) magma; (*fig*) jumble.
magnanerie [maɲanʀi] *nf* silk farm.
magnanime [maɲanim] *a* magnanimous.
magnat [magna] *nm* tycoon, magnate.
magnésie [maɲezi] *nf* magnesia.
magnésium [maɲezjɔm] *nm* magnesium.
magnétique [maɲetik] *a* magnetic.
magnétiser [maɲetize] *vt* to magnetize; (*fig*) to mesmerize, hypnotize.
magnétisme [maɲetism(ə)] *nm* magnetism.
magnéto [maɲeto] *nf* (*ÉLEC*) magneto.
magnétophone [maɲetɔfɔn] *nm* tape recorder; ~ **à cassettes** cassette recorder.
magnétoscope [maɲetɔskɔp] *nm* video-tape recorder.
magnificence [maɲifisɑ̃s] *nf* (*faste*) magnificence, splendour.
magnifique [maɲifik] *a* magnificent.
magnolia [maɲɔlja] *nm* magnolia.
magnum [magnɔm] *nm* magnum.
magot [mago] *nm* (*argent*) pile (of money); nest egg.
mahométan, e [maɔmetɑ̃, -an] *a* Mohammedan, Mahometan.
mai [mɛ] *nm* May.
maigre [mɛgʀ(ə)] *a* (very) thin, skinny; (*viande*) lean; (*fromage*) low-fat; (*végétation*) thin, sparse; (*fig*) poor, meagre, skimpy // *ad*: **faire** ~ not to eat meat; **jours** ~**s** days of abstinence, fish days; **maigreur** *nf* thinness; **maigrir** *vi* to get thinner, lose weight.
maille [mɑj] *nf* stitch; **avoir** ~ **à partir avec qn** to have a brush with sb.
maillet [majɛ] *nm* mallet.
maillon [mɑjɔ̃] *nm* link.
maillot [majo] *nm* (*aussi*: ~ **de corps**) vest; (*de danseur*) leotard; (*de sportif*) jersey; ~ **de bain** bathing costume, swimsuit; (*d'homme*) bathing trunks *pl.*
main [mɛ̃] *nf* hand; **à la** ~ in one's hand; **se donner la** ~ to hold hands; **donner** *ou* **tendre la** ~ **à qn** to hold out one's hand to sb; **se serrer la** ~ to shake hands; **serrer la** ~ **à qn** to shake hands with sb; **sous la** ~ to *ou* at hand; **à** ~ **levée** (*ART*) freehand; **à** ~**s levées** (*voter*) with a show of hands; **attaque à** ~ **armée** armed attack; **à** ~ **droite/gauche** to the right/left; **à remettre en** ~**s propres** to be delivered personally; **de première** ~ (*renseignement*) first-hand; (*COMM*: *voiture etc*) second-hand with only one previous owner; **faire** ~ **basse sur** to help o.s. to; **mettre la dernière** ~ **à** to put the finishing touches to; **se faire/perdre la** ~ to get one's hand in/lose one's touch; ~ **courante** handrail.
mainate [mɛnat] *nm* myna(h) bird.
main-d'œuvre [mɛ̃dœvʀ(ə)] *nf* manpower, labour.
main-forte [mɛ̃fɔʀt(ə)] *nf*: **prêter** ~ **à qn** to come to sb's assistance.
mainmise [mɛ̃miz] *nf* seizure; (*fig*): ~ **sur** complete hold on.
maint, e [mɛ̃, mɛ̃t] *a* many a; ~**s** many; **à** ~**es reprises** time and (time) again.
maintenant [mɛ̃tnɑ̃] *ad* now; (*actuellement*) nowadays.
maintenir [mɛ̃tniʀ] *vt* (*retenir, soutenir*) to support; (*contenir*: *foule etc*) to keep in check, hold back; (*conserver*) to maintain, uphold; (*affirmer*) to maintain; **se** ~ *vi* to hold; to keep steady; to persist.
maintien [mɛ̃tjɛ̃] *nm* maintaining, upholding; (*attitude*) bearing.
maire [mɛʀ] *nm* mayor.
mairie [meʀi] *nf* (*résidence*) town hall; (*administration*) town council.
mais [mɛ] *cj* but; ~ **non!** of course not!; ~ **enfin** but after all; (*indignation*) look here!
maïs [mais] *nm* maize.
maison [mɛzɔ̃] *nf* house; (*chez-soi*) home; (*COMM*) firm // *a inv* (*CULIN*) home-made; made by the chef; (*fig*) in-house, own; (*fam*) first-rate; **à la** ~ at home; (*direction*) home; ~ **d'arrêt** ≈ remand home; ~ **close** brothel; ~ **de correction** reformatory; ~ **des jeunes** ≈ youth club; ~ **mère** parent company; ~ **de repos** convalescent home; ~ **de retraite** old people's home; ~ **de santé** mental home; **maisonnée** *nf* household, family; **maisonnette** *nf* small house, cottage.
maître, esse [mɛtʀ(ə), mɛtʀɛs] *nm/f* master/mistress; (*SCOL*) teacher, schoolmaster/mistress // *nm* (*peintre etc*) master; (*titre*): **M~ (Me)** Maître, *term of address gen for a barrister* // *nf* (*amante*) mistress // *a* (*principal, essentiel*) main; **être** ~ **de** (*soi-même, situation*) to be in control of; **se rendre** ~ **de** (*pays, ville*) to gain control of; (*situation, incendie*) to bring under control; **une maîtresse femme** a managing woman; ~ **d'armes** fencing master; ~ **chanteur** blackmailer;

~ **de chapelle** choirmaster; ~ **de conférences** ≈ senior lecturer; ~**/maîtresse d'école** teacher, schoolmaster/ mistress; ~ **d'hôtel** (*domestique*) butler; (*d'hôtel*) head waiter; ~ **de maison** host; ~ **nageur** lifeguard; ~ **à penser** intellectual leader; ~ **queux** chef; **maîtresse de maison** hostess; housewife (*pl* wives); ~**-autel** *nm* high altar.

maîtrise [metʀiz] *nf* (*aussi*: ~ **de soi**) self-control, self-possession; (*habileté*) skill, mastery; (*suprématie*) mastery, command; (*diplôme*) ≈ master's degree.

maîtriser [metʀize] *vt* (*cheval, incendie*) to (bring under) control; (*sujet*) to master; (*émotion*) to control, master; **se** ~ *vt réfléchi* to control o.s.

majesté [maʒɛste] *nf* majesty.

majestueux, euse [maʒɛstɥø, -øz] *a* majestic.

majeur, e [maʒœʀ] *a* (*important*) major; (JUR) of age; (*fig*) adult // *nm/f* person who has come of age *ou* attained his/her majority // *nm* (*doigt*) middle finger; **en** ~**e partie** for the most part.

major [maʒɔʀ] *nm* (SCOL): ~ **de la promotion** first of one's year.

majordome [maʒɔʀdɔm] *nm* majordomo.

majorer [maʒɔʀe] *vt* to increase.

majorette [maʒɔʀɛt] *nf* majorette.

majoritaire [maʒɔʀitɛʀ] *a* majority *cpd*: **système/scrutin** ~ majority system/ ballot.

majorité [maʒɔʀite] *nf* (*gén*) majority; (*parti*) party in power; **en** ~ mainly.

majuscule [maʒyskyl] *a*, *nf*: **(lettre)** ~ capital (letter).

mal, maux [mal, mo] *nm* (*opposé au bien*) evil; (*tort, dommage*) harm; (*douleur physique*) pain, ache; (*maladie*) illness, sickness *q* // *ad* badly // *a*: **c'est** ~ **(de faire)** it's bad *ou* wrong (to do); **être** ~ to be uncomfortable; **être** ~ **avec qn** to be on bad terms with sb; **il comprend** ~ he has difficulty in understanding; **il a** ~ **compris** he misunderstood; **dire du** ~ **de** to speak ill of; **ne voir aucun** ~ **à** to see no harm in, see nothing wrong in; **craignant** ~ **faire** fearing he was doing the wrong thing; **faire du** ~ **à qn** to hurt sb; to harm sb; **se faire** ~ to hurt o.s.; **se faire** ~ **au pied** to hurt one's foot; **ça fait** ~ it hurts; **j'ai** ~ **(ici)** it hurts (here); **j'ai** ~ **au dos** my back aches, I've got a pain in my back; **avoir** ~ **à la tête/aux dents/au cœur** to have a headache/have toothache/feel sick; **avoir le** ~ **de l'air** to be airsick; **avoir le** ~ **du pays** to be homesick; **prendre** ~ to be taken ill, feel unwell; ~ **de mer** seasickness; ~ **en point** *a inv* in a bad state; **maux de ventre** stomach ache *sg*.

malade [malad] *a* ill, sick; (*poitrine, jambe*) bad; (*plante*) diseased // *nm/f* invalid, sick person; (*à l'hôpital etc*) patient; **tomber** ~ to fall ill; **être** ~ **du cœur** to have heart trouble *ou* a bad heart; ~ **mental** mentally sick *ou* ill person.

maladie [maladi] *nf* (*spécifique*) disease, illness; (*mauvaise santé*) illness, sickness; (*fig*: *manie*) mania; ~ **de peau** skin disease; **maladif, ive** *a* sickly; (*curiosité, besoin*) pathological.

maladresse [maladʀɛs] *nf* clumsiness *q*; (*gaffe*) blunder.

maladroit, e [maladʀwa, -wat] *a* clumsy.

malaise [malɛz] *nm* (MÉD) feeling of faintness; feeling of discomfort; (*fig*) uneasiness, malaise.

malaisé, e [maleze] *a* difficult.

malappris, e [malapʀi, -iz] *nm/f* ill-mannered *ou* boorish person.

malaria [malaʀja] *nf* malaria.

malavisé, e [malavize] *a* ill-advised, unwise.

malaxer [malakse] *vt* to knead; to mix.

malchance [malʃɑ̃s] *nf* misfortune, ill luck *q*; **par** ~ unfortunately; **malchanceux, euse** *a* unlucky.

malcommode [malkɔmɔd] *a* impractical, inconvenient.

maldonne [maldɔn] *nf* (CARTES) misdeal; **il y a** ~ (*fig*) there's been a misunderstanding.

mâle [mɑl] *a* (*aussi* ÉLEC, TECH) male; (*viril*: *voix, traits*) manly // *nm* male; **souris** ~ male mouse, he-mouse.

malédiction [malediksjɔ̃] *nf* curse.

maléfice [malefis] *nm* evil spell.

maléfique [malefik] *a* evil, baleful.

malencontreux, euse [malɑ̃kɔ̃tʀø, -øz] *a* unfortunate, untoward.

malentendu [malɑ̃tɑ̃dy] *nm* misunderstanding.

malfaçon [malfasɔ̃] *nf* fault.

malfaisant, e [malfəzɑ̃, -ɑ̃t] *a* evil, harmful.

malfaiteur [malfɛtœʀ] *nm* lawbreaker, criminal; burglar, thief (*pl* thieves).

malfamé, e [malfame] *a* disreputable, of ill repute.

malformation [malfɔʀmɑsjɔ̃] *nf* malformation.

malfrat [malfʀɑ] *nm* villain, crook.

malgache [malgaʃ] *a*, *nm/f* Madagascan, Malagasy // *nm* (*langue*) Malagasy.

malgré [malgʀe] *prép* in spite of, despite; ~ **tout** *ad* all the same.

malhabile [malabil] *a* clumsy.

malheur [malœʀ] *nm* (*situation*) adversity, misfortune; (*événement*) misfortune; disaster, tragedy; **malheureux, euse** *a* (*triste*) unhappy, miserable; (*infortuné, regrettable*) unfortunate; (*malchanceux*) unlucky; (*insignifiant*) wretched // *nm/f* poor soul; unfortunate creature; **les malheureux** the destitute.

malhonnête [malɔnɛt] *a* dishonest; (*impoli*) rude; ~**té** *nf* dishonesty; rudeness *q*.

malice [malis] *nf* mischievousness; (*méchanceté*): **par** ~ out of malice *ou* spite; **sans** ~ guileless; **malicieux, euse** *a* mischievous.

malin, igne [malɛ̃, -iɲ] *a* (*futé*: *f gén*: **maline**) smart, shrewd; (MÉD) malignant; **faire le** ~ to show off; **éprouver un** ~ **plaisir à** to take malicious pleasure in.

malingre [malɛ̃gʀ(ə)] *a* puny.

malle [mal] *nf* trunk.

malléable [maleabl(ə)] *a* malleable.

malle-poste [malpɔst(ə)] *nf* mail coach.
mallette [malɛt] *nf* (small) suitcase; overnight case; attaché case.
malmener [malməne] *vt* to manhandle; (*fig*) to give a rough handling to.
malodorant, e [malɔdɔʀɑ̃, -ɑ̃t] *a* foul- *ou* ill-smelling.
malotru [malɔtʀy] *nm* lout, boor.
malpoli, e [malpɔli] *nm/f* rude individual.
malpropre [malpʀɔpʀ(ə)] *a* dirty.
malsain, e [malsɛ̃, -ɛn] *a* unhealthy.
malséant, e [malseɑ̃, -ɑ̃t] *a* unseemly, unbecoming.
malsonnant, e [malsɔnɑ̃, -ɑ̃t] *a* offensive.
malt [malt] *nm* malt.
maltais, e [maltɛ, -ɛz] *a, nm/f* Maltese.
Malte [malt(ə)] *nf* Malta.
maltraiter [maltʀete] *vt* (*brutaliser*) to manhandle, ill-treat.
malveillance [malvɛjɑ̃s] *nf* (*animosité*) ill will; (*intention de nuire*) malevolence; (*JUR*) malicious intent *q*.
malveillant, e [malvɛjɑ̃, -ɑ̃t] *a* malevolent, malicious.
malversation [malvɛʀsɑsjɔ̃] *nf* embezzlement, misappropriation (of funds).
maman [mamɑ̃] *nf* mum, mother.
mamelle [mamɛl] *nf* teat.
mamelon [mamlɔ̃] *nm* (*ANAT*) nipple; (*colline*) knoll, hillock.
mammifère [mamifɛʀ] *nm* mammal.
mammouth [mamut] *nm* mammoth.
manche [mɑ̃ʃ] *nf* (*de vêtement*) sleeve; (*d'un jeu, tournoi*) round; (*GÉO*): **la M ~** the Channel // *nm* (*d'outil, casserole*) handle; (*de pelle, pioche etc*) shaft; (*de violon, guitare*) neck; (*fam*) clumsy oaf; **~ à air** *nf* (*AVIAT*) wind-sock; **~ à balai** *nm* broomstick; (*AVIAT*) joystick.
manchette [mɑ̃ʃɛt] *nf* (*de chemise*) cuff; (*coup*) forearm blow; (*titre*) headline.
manchon [mɑ̃ʃɔ̃] *nm* (*de fourrure*) muff; **~ à incandescence** incandescent (gas) mantle.
manchot [mɑ̃ʃo] *nm* one-armed man; armless man; (*ZOOL*) penguin.
mandarine [mɑ̃daʀin] *nf* mandarin (orange), tangerine.
mandat [mɑ̃da] *nm* (*postal*) postal *ou* money order; (*d'un député etc*) mandate; (*procuration*) power of attorney, proxy; (*POLICE*) warrant; **~ d'amener** summons *sg*; **~ d'arrêt** warrant for arrest; **~ de dépôt** committal order; **mandataire** *nm/f* representative; proxy.
mander [mɑ̃de] *vt* to summon.
mandibule [mɑ̃dibyl] *nf* mandible.
mandoline [mɑ̃dɔlin] *nf* mandolin(e).
manège [manɛʒ] *nm* riding school; (*à la foire*) roundabout, merry-go-round; (*fig*) game, ploy.
manette [manɛt] *nf* lever, tap.
manganèse [mɑ̃ganɛz] *nm* manganese.
mangeable [mɑ̃ʒabl(ə)] a edible, eatable.
mangeaille [mɑ̃ʒɑj] *nf* (*péj*) grub.
mangeoire [mɑ̃ʒwaʀ] *nf* trough, manger.
manger [mɑ̃ʒe] *vt* to eat; (*ronger*: *suj*: *rouille etc*) to eat into *ou* away // *vi* to eat; **mangeur, euse** *nm/f* eater.
mangouste [mɑ̃gust(ə)] *nf* mongoose.
mangue [mɑ̃g] *nf* mango.
maniable [manjabl(ə)] *a* (*outil*) handy; (*voiture, voilier*) easy to handle.
maniaque [manjak] *a* finicky, fussy; suffering from a mania // *nm/f* maniac.
manie [mani] *nf* mania; (*tic*) odd habit.
maniement [manimɑ̃] *nm* handling; **~ d'armes** arms drill.
manier [manje] *vt* to handle.
manière [manjɛʀ] *nf* (*façon*) way, manner; **~s** *nfpl* (*attitude*) manners; (*chichis*) fuss *sg*; **de ~ à** so as to; **de telle ~ que** in such a way that; **de cette ~** in this way *ou* manner; **d'une ~ générale** generally speaking, as a general rule; **de toute ~** in any case; **adverbe de ~** adverb of manner.
maniéré, e [manjeʀe] *a* affected.
manif [manif] *nf* demo (*pl* s).
manifestant, e [manifɛstɑ̃, -ɑ̃t] *nm/f* demonstrator.
manifestation [manifɛstɑsjɔ̃] *nf* (*de joie, mécontentement*) expression, demonstration; (*symptôme*) outward sign; (*fête etc*) event; (*POL*) demonstration.
manifeste [manifɛst(ə)] *a* obvious, evident // *nm* manifesto (*pl* s).
manifester [manifɛste] *vt* (*volonté, intentions*) to show, indicate; (*joie, peur*) to express, show // *vi* to demonstrate; **se ~** *vi* (*émotion*) to show *ou* express itself; (*difficultés*) to arise; (*symptômes*) to appear; (*témoin etc*) to come forward.
manigance [manigɑ̃s] *nf* scheme.
manigancer [manigɑ̃se] *vt* to plot, devise.
manioc [manjɔk] *nm* cassava, manioc.
manipuler [manipyle] *vt* to handle; (*fig*) to manipulate.
manivelle [manivɛl] *nf* crank.
manne [man] *nf* (*REL*) manna; (*fig*) godsend.
mannequin [mankɛ̃] *nm* (*COUTURE*) dummy; (*MODE*) model.
manœuvre [manœvʀ(ə)] *nf* (*gén*) manœuvre // *nm* labourer.
manœuvrer [manœvʀe] *vt* to manœuvre; (*levier, machine*) to operate // *vi* to manœuvre.
manoir [manwaʀ] *nm* manor *ou* country house.
manomètre [manɔmɛtʀ(ə)] *nm* gauge, manometer.
manquant, e [mɑ̃kɑ̃, -ɑ̃t] *a* missing.
manque [mɑ̃k] *nm* (*insuffisance*): **~ de** lack of; (*vide*) emptiness, gap; (*MÉD*) withdrawal; **~s** *nmpl* (*lacunes*) faults, defects; **~ à gagner** loss of profit *ou* earnings.
manqué, e [mɑ̃ke] *a* failed; **garçon ~** tomboy.
manquement [mɑ̃kmɑ̃] *nm*: **~ à** (*discipline, règle*) breach of.
manquer [mɑ̃ke] *vi* (*faire défaut*) to be lacking; (*être absent*) to be missing; (*échouer*) to fail // *vt* to miss // *vb impersonnel*: **il (nous) manque encore 100 F** we are still 100 F short; **il manque des pages (au livre)** there are some pages missing *ou* some pages are missing (from the book); **l'argent qui leur manque** the

money they need *ou* are short of; **le pied/la voix lui manqua** he missed his footing/his voice failed him; **~ à qn** (*absent etc*): **il/cela me manque** I miss him/this; **~ à** *vt* (*règles etc*) to be in breach of, fail to observe; **~ de** *vt* to lack; **ne pas ~ de faire: il n'a pas manqué de le dire** he sure enough said it, he didn't fail to say it; **~ (de) faire: il a manqué (de) se tuer** he very nearly got killed.

mansarde [mɑ̃saʀd(ə)] *nf* attic; **mansardé, e** *a* attic *cpd*.

mansuétude [mɑ̃sɥetyd] *nf* leniency.

mante [mɑ̃t] *nf*: **~ religieuse** praying mantis.

manteau, x [mɑ̃to] *nm* coat; **~ de cheminée** mantelpiece.

mantille [mɑ̃tij] *nf* mantilla.

manucure [manykyʀ] *nf* manicurist.

manuel, le [manɥɛl] *a* manual // *nm/f* manually gifted pupil *etc* (*as opposed to intellectually gifted*) // *nm* (*ouvrage*) manual, handbook.

manufacture [manyfaktyʀ] *nf* factory.

manufacturé, e [manyfaktyʀe] *a* manufactured.

manuscrit, e [manyskʀi, -it] *a* handwritten // *nm* manuscript.

manutention [manytɑ̃sjɔ̃] *nf* (COMM) handling; **manutentionnaire** *nm/f* warehouseman/woman, packer.

mappemonde [mapmɔ̃d] *nf* (*plane*) map of the world; (*sphère*) globe.

maquereau, x [makʀo] *nm* (ZOOL) mackerel *inv*; (*fam*) pimp.

maquerelle [makʀɛl] *nf* (*fam*) madam.

maquette [makɛt] *nf* (*d'un décor, bâtiment, véhicule*) (scale) model; (*d'une page illustrée*) paste-up.

maquignon [makiɲɔ̃] *nm* horse-dealer.

maquillage [makijaʒ] *nm* making up; faking; (*crème etc*) make-up.

maquiller [makije] *vt* (*personne, visage*) to make up; (*truquer: passeport, statistique*) to fake; (: *voiture volée*) to do over (*respray etc*); **se ~** to make up (one's face).

maquis [maki] *nm* (GÉO) scrub; (*fig*) tangle; (MIL) maquis, underground fighting *q*.

marabout [maʀabu] *nm* (ZOOL) marabou(t).

maraîcher, ère [maʀeʃe, maʀɛʃɛʀ] *a*: **cultures maraîchères** market gardening *sg* // *nm/f* market gardener.

marais [maʀɛ] *nm* marsh, swamp; **~ salant** salt pen, saltern.

marasme [maʀasm(ə)] *nm* stagnation, slump.

marathon [maʀatɔ̃] *nm* marathon.

marâtre [maʀɑtʀ(ə)] *nf* cruel mother.

maraude [maʀod] *nf* pilfering, thieving (*of poultry, crops*); (*dans un verger*) scrumping; (*vagabondage*) prowling; **en ~** on the prowl; (*taxi*) cruising.

marbre [maʀbʀ(ə)] *nm* (*pierre, statue*) marble; (*d'une table, commode*) marble top; (TYPO) stone, bed; **rester de ~** to remain stonily indifferent; **marbrer** *vt* to mottle, blotch; (TECH: *papier*) to marble; **~rie** *nf* monumental mason's yard; **marbrier** *nm* monumental mason.

marc [maʀ] *nm* (*de raisin, pommes*) marc; **~ de café** coffee grounds *pl ou* dregs *pl*.

marcassin [maʀkasɛ̃] *nm* young wild boar.

marchand, e [maʀʃɑ̃, -ɑ̃d] *nm/f* shopkeeper, tradesman/woman; (*au marché*) stallholder; (*spécifique*): **~ de cycles/tapis** bicycle/carpet dealer; **~ de charbon/vins** coal/wine merchant // *a*: **prix/valeur ~(e)** market price/value; **~ de biens** real estate agent; **~ de couleurs** ironmonger; **~/e de fruits** fruiterer, fruit merchant; **~/e de journaux** newsagent; **~/e de légumes** greengrocer; **~/e de poisson** fishmonger, fish merchant; **~e de quatre saisons** costermonger; **~ de tableaux** art dealer.

marchander [maʀʃɑ̃de] *vt* (*article*) to bargain *ou* haggle over; (*éloges*) to be sparing with // *vi* to bargain, haggle.

marchandise [maʀʃɑ̃diz] *nf* goods *pl*, merchandise *q*.

marche [maʀʃ(ə)] *nf* (*d'escalier*) step; (*activité*) walking; (*promenade, trajet, allure*) walk; (*démarche*) walk, gait; (MIL *etc*, MUS) march; (*fonctionnement*) running; (*progression*) progress; course; **ouvrir/fermer la ~** to lead the way/bring up the rear; **dans le sens de la ~** (RAIL) facing the engine; **en ~** (*monter etc*) while the vehicle is moving *ou* in motion; **mettre en ~** to start; **remettre qch en ~** to set *ou* start sth going again; **se mettre en ~** (*personne*) to get moving; (*machine*) to start; **~ arrière** reverse (gear); **faire ~ arrière** to reverse; (*fig*) to backtrack, back-pedal; **~ à suivre** (correct) procedure; (*sur notice*) (step by step) instructions *pl*.

marché [maʀʃe] *nm* (*lieu*, COMM, ÉCON) market; (*ville*) trading centre; (*transaction*) bargain, deal; **M~ commun** Common Market; **~ aux fleurs** flower market; **~ noir** black market; **faire du ~ noir** to buy and sell on the black market; **~ aux puces** flea market.

marchepied [maʀʃəpje] *nm* (RAIL) step; (AUTO) running board; (*fig*) stepping stone.

marcher [maʀʃe] *vi* to walk; (MIL) to march; (*aller: voiture, train, affaires*) to go; (*prospérer*) to go well; (*fonctionner*) to work, run; (*fam*) to go along, agree; to be taken in; **~ sur** to walk on; (*mettre le pied sur*) to step on *ou* in; (MIL) to march upon; **~ dans** (*herbe etc*) to walk in *ou* on; (*flaque*) to step in; **faire ~ qn** to pull sb's leg; to lead sb up the garden path; **marcheur, euse** *nm/f* walker.

mardi [maʀdi] *nm* Tuesday; **M~ gras** Shrove Tuesday.

mare [maʀ] *nf* pond; **~ de sang** pool of blood.

marécage [maʀekaʒ] *nm* marsh, swamp; **marécageux, euse** *a* marshy, swampy.

maréchal, aux [maʀeʃal, -o] *nm* marshal; **~ des logis** (MIL) sergeant.

maréchal-ferrant [maʀeʃalfɛʀɑ̃] *nm* blacksmith, farrier.

maréchaussée [maʀeʃose] *nf* constabulary.

marée [maʀe] *nf* tide; (*poissons*) fresh (sea) fish; **~ haute/basse** high/low tide;

~ **montante/ descendante** rising/ebb tide.
marelle [maʀɛl] *nf*: **(jouer à) la** ~ (to play) hopscotch.
marémotrice [maʀemɔtʀis] *af* tidal.
mareyeur, euse [maʀɛjœʀ, -øz] *nm/f* wholesale (sea) fish merchant.
margarine [maʀgaʀin] *nf* margarine.
marge [maʀʒ(ə)] *nf* margin; **en** ~ in the margin; **en** ~ **de** (*fig*) on the fringe of; cut off from; connected with; ~ **bénéficiaire** profit margin.
margelle [maʀʒɛl] *nf* coping.
margeur [maʀʒœʀ] *nm* margin stop.
marginal, e, aux [maʀʒinal, -o] *a* marginal.
marguerite [maʀgəʀit] *nf* marguerite, (oxeye) daisy.
marguillier [maʀgije] *nm* churchwarden.
mari [maʀi] *nm* husband.
mariage [maʀjaʒ] *nm* (*union, état, fig*) marriage; (*noce*) wedding; ~ **civil/religieux** civil *ou* registry office/church wedding; **un** ~ **de raison/d'amour** a marriage of convenience/love match; ~ **blanc** unconsummated marriage; ~ **en blanc** white wedding.
marié, e [maʀje] *a* married // *nm/f* (bride)groom/bride; **les** ~**s** the bride and groom; **les (jeunes)** ~**s** the newly-weds.
marier [maʀje] *vt* to marry; (*fig*) to blend; **se** ~ **(avec)** to marry, get married (to); (*fig*) to blend (with).
marin, e [maʀɛ̃, -in] *a* sea *cpd*, marine // *nm* sailor // *nf* navy; (ART) seascape; ~**e de guerre** navy; ~**e marchande** merchant navy; ~**e à voiles** sailing ships *pl*.
marinade [maʀinad] *nf* marinade.
marine [maʀin] *af, nf voir* **marin** // *a inv* navy (blue) // *nm* (MIL) marine.
mariner [maʀine] *vi, vt* to marinate, marinade.
marinier [maʀinje] *nm* bargee.
marinière [maʀinjɛʀ] *nf* smock // *a inv*: **moules** ~ mussels in white wine.
marionnette [maʀjɔnɛt] *nf* puppet.
marital, e, aux [maʀital, -o] *a* marital, husband's; ~**ement** *ad* as husband and wife.
maritime [maʀitim] *a* sea *cpd*, maritime.
marjolaine [maʀʒɔlɛn] *nf* marjoram.
mark [maʀk] *nm* mark.
marmaille [maʀmaj] *nf* (*péj*) (gang of) brats *pl*.
marmelade [maʀməlad] *nf* stewed fruit, compote; **en** ~ (*fig*) crushed (to a pulp).
marmite [maʀmit] *nf* (cooking-)pot.
marmiton [maʀmitɔ̃] *nm* kitchen boy.
marmonner [maʀmɔne] *vt, vi* to mumble, mutter.
marmot [maʀmo] *nm* brat.
marmotte [maʀmɔt] *nf* marmot.
marmotter [maʀmɔte] *vt* (*prière*) to mumble, mutter.
marne [maʀn(ə)] *nf* marl.
Maroc [maʀɔk] *nm*: **le** ~ Morocco; **marocain, e** *a, nm/f* Moroccan.
maroquin [maʀɔkɛ̃] *nm* morocco (leather); (*fig*) (minister's) portfolio.
maroquinerie [maʀɔkinʀi] *nf* leather craft; fine leather goods *pl*.
marotte [maʀɔt] *nf* fad.
marquant, e [maʀkɑ̃, -ɑ̃t] *a* outstanding.
marque [maʀk(ə)] *nf* mark; (SPORT, JEU: *décompte des points*) score; (COMM: *de produits*) brand; make; (: *de disques*) label; **à vos** ~**s!** (SPORT) on your marks!; **de** ~ *a* (COMM) brand-name *cpd*; proprietary; (*fig*) high-class; distinguished; ~ **déposée** registered trademark; ~ **de fabrique** trademark.
marqué, e [maʀke] *a* marked.
marquer [maʀke] *vt* to mark; (*inscrire*) to write down; (*bétail*) to brand; (SPORT: *but etc*) to score; (: *joueur*) to mark; (*accentuer*: *taille etc*) to emphasize; (*manifester*: *refus, intérêt*) to show // *vi* (*événement, personnalité*) to stand out, be outstanding; (SPORT) to score; ~ **les points** (*tenir la marque*) to keep the score.
marqueterie [maʀkətʀi] *nf* inlaid work, marquetry.
marquis, e [maʀki, -iz] *nm/f* marquis *ou* marquess/marchioness // *nf* (*auvent*) glass canopy *ou* awning.
marraine [maʀɛn] *nf* godmother.
marrant, e [maʀɑ̃, -ɑ̃t] *a* (*fam*) funny.
marre [maʀ] *ad* (*fam*): **en avoir** ~ **de** to be fed up with.
marrer [maʀe]: **se** ~ *vi* (*fam*) to have a (good) laugh.
marron [maʀɔ̃] *nm* (*fruit*) chestnut // *a inv* brown // *am* (*péj*) crooked; bogus; ~**s glacés** marrons glacés; **marronnier** *nm* chestnut (tree).
mars [maʀs] *nm* March.
Mars [maʀs] *nf ou m* Mars.
marsouin [maʀswɛ̃] *nm* porpoise.
marsupiaux [maʀsypjo] *nmpl* marsupials.
marteau, x [maʀto] *nm* hammer; (*de porte*) knocker; ~**-piqueur** *nm* pneumatic drill.
martel [maʀtɛl] *nm*: **se mettre** ~ **en tête** to worry o.s.
marteler [maʀtəle] *vt* to hammer.
martial, e, aux [maʀsjal, -o] *a* martial.
martien, ne [maʀsjɛ̃, -jɛn] *a* Martian, of *ou* from Mars.
martinet [maʀtinɛ] *nm* (*fouet*) small whip; (ZOOL) swift.
martingale [maʀtɛ̃gal] *nf* (COUTURE) half-belt; (JEU) winning formula.
Martinique [maʀtinik] *nf*: **la** ~ Martinique.
martin-pêcheur [maʀtɛ̃pɛʃœʀ] *nm* kingfisher.
martre [maʀtʀ(ə)] *nf* marten.
martyr, e [maʀtiʀ] *nm/f* martyr // *a* martyred; **enfants** ~**s** battered children.
martyre [maʀtiʀ] *nm* martyrdom; (*fig*: *sens affaibli*) agony, torture.
martyriser [maʀtiʀize] *vt* (REL) to martyr; (*fig*) to bully; to batter.
marxisme [maʀksism(ə)] *nm* Marxism.
mascarade [maskaʀad] *nf* masquerade.
mascotte [maskɔt] *nf* mascot.
masculin, e [maskylɛ̃, -in] *a* masculine; (*sexe, population*) male; (*équipe, vêtements*) men's; (*viril*) manly // *nm* masculine.

masochisme [mazɔʃism(ə)] *nm* masochism.
masque [mask(ə)] *nm* mask; ~ **à gaz** gas mask.
masqué, e [maske] *a* masked.
masquer [maske] *vt* (*cacher*: *paysage, porte*) to hide, conceal; (*dissimuler*: *vérité, projet*) to mask, obscure.
massacrant, e [masakʀɑ̃, -ɑ̃t] *a*: **humeur ~e** foul temper.
massacre [masakʀ(ə)] *nm* massacre, slaughter.
massacrer [masakʀe] *vt* to massacre, slaughter; (*fig*: *texte etc*) to murder.
massage [masaʒ] *nm* massage.
masse [mas] *nf* mass; (*péj*): **la ~** the masses *pl*; (ÉLEC) earth; (*maillet*) sledgehammer; **~s** *nfpl* masses; **une ~ de, des ~s de** (*fam*) masses *ou* loads of; **en ~** *ad* (*en bloc*) in bulk; (*en foule*) en masse // *a* (*exécutions, production*) mass *cpd*; **~ salariale** aggregate remuneration (of employees).
massepain [maspɛ̃] *nm* marzipan.
masser [mase] *vt* (*assembler*) to gather; (*pétrir*) to massage; **se ~** *vi* to gather; **masseur, euse** *nm/f* masseur/masseuse.
massicot [masiko] *nm* guillotine.
massif, ive [masif, -iv] *a* (*porte*) solid, massive; (*visage*) heavy, large; (*bois, or*) solid; (*dose*) massive; (*déportations etc*) mass *cpd* // *nm* (*montagneux*) massif; (*de fleurs*) clump, bank.
massue [masy] *nf* club, bludgeon.
mastic [mastik] *nm* (*pour vitres*) putty; (*pour fentes*) filler.
mastiquer [mastike] *vt* (*aliment*) to chew, masticate; (*fente*) to fill; (*vitre*) to putty.
masturbation [mastyʀbɑsjɔ̃] *nf* masturbation.
masure [mɑzyʀ] *nf* tumbledown cottage.
mat, e [mat] *a* (*couleur, métal*) mat(t); (*bruit, son*) dull // *a inv* (ÉCHECS): **être ~** to be checkmate.
mât [mɑ] *nm* (NAVIG) mast; (*poteau*) pole, post.
match [matʃ] *nm* match; **~ nul** draw; **faire ~ nul** to draw.
matelas [matla] *nm* mattress; **~ pneumatique** air bed *ou* mattress; **~ à ressorts** spring *ou* interior-sprung mattress.
matelasser [matlase] *vt* to pad; to quilt.
matelot [matlo] *nm* sailor, seaman.
mater [mate] *vt* (*personne*) to bring to heel, subdue; (*révolte*) to put down.
matérialiser [mateʀjalize]: **se ~** *vi* to materialize.
matérialiste [mateʀjalist(ə)] *a* materialistic.
matériau, x [mateʀjo] *nm* material // *nmpl* material(s).
matériel, le [mateʀjɛl] *a* material // *nm* equipment *q*; (*de camping etc*) gear *q*; **~ d'exploitation** (COMM) plant.
maternel, le [matɛʀnɛl] *a* (*amour, geste*) motherly, maternal; (*grand-père, oncle*) maternal // *nf* (*aussi*: **école ~le**) (state) nursery school.
maternité [matɛʀnite] *nf* (*établissement*) maternity hospital; (*état de mère*) motherhood, maternity; (*grossesse*) pregnancy.
mathématicien, ne [matematisjɛ̃, -jɛn] *nm/f* mathematician.
mathématique [matematik] *a* mathematical; **~s** *nfpl* (*science*) mathematics *sg*.
matière [matjɛʀ] *nf* (PHYSIQUE) matter; (COMM, TECH) material, matter *q*; (*fig*: *d'un livre etc*) subject matter, material; (SCOL) subject; **en ~ de** as regards; **donner ~ à** to give cause to; **~ plastique** plastic; **~s fécales** faeces; **~s grasses** fat content *sg*; **~s premières** raw materials.
matin [matɛ̃] *nm, ad* morning; **matinal, e, aux** *a* (*toilette, gymnastique*) morning *cpd*; (*de bonne heure*) early; **être matinal** (*personne*) to be up early; to be an early riser.
matinée [matine] *nf* morning; (*spectacle*) matinée, afternoon performance.
mâtiner [mɑtine] *vt* to cross.
matois, e [matwa, -waz] *a* wily.
matou [matu] *nm* tom(cat).
matraque [matʀak] *nf* cosh; (*de policier*) truncheon; **matraquer** *vt* to beat up (with a truncheon); to cosh; (*fig*: *disque*) to plug.
matriarcal, e, aux [matʀijaʀkal, -o] *a* matriarchal.
matrice [matʀis] *nf* (ANAT) womb; (TECH) mould; (MATH *etc*) matrix.
matricule [matʀikyl] *nf* (*aussi*: **registre ~**) roll, register // *nm* (*aussi*: **numéro ~**) (MIL) regimental number; (ADMIN) reference number.
matrimonial, e, aux [matʀimɔnjal, -o] *a* marital, marriage *cpd*.
mâture [mɑtyʀ] *nf* masts *pl*.
maturité [matyʀite] *nf* maturity; (*d'un fruit*) ripeness, maturity.
maudire [modiʀ] *vt* to curse.
maudit, e [modi, -it] *a* (*fam*: *satané*) blasted, confounded.
maugréer [mogʀee] *vi* to grumble.
Mauresque [mɔʀɛsk] *a* Moorish.
mausolée [mozɔle] *nm* mausoleum.
maussade [mosad] *a* sullen.
mauvais, e [mɔvɛ, -ɛz] *a* bad; (*faux*): **le ~ numéro/moment** the wrong number/moment; (*méchant, malveillant*) malicious, spiteful // *ad*: **il fait ~** the weather is bad; **sentir ~** to have a nasty smell, smell bad *ou* nasty; **la mer est ~e** the sea is rough; **~ coup** (*fig*) criminal venture; **~ garçon** tough; **~ plaisant** hoaxer; **~ traitements** ill treatment *sg*; **~e herbe** weed; **~e langue** gossip, scandalmonger; **~e passe** difficult situation; bad patch; **~e tête** rebellious *ou* headstrong customer.
mauve [mov] *a* mauve // *nf* mallow.
mauviette [movjɛt] *nf* (*péj*) weakling.
maux [mo] *nmpl voir* **mal.**
maximal, e, aux [maksimal, -o] *a* maximal.
maxime [maksim] *nf* maxim.
maximum [maksimɔm] *a, nm* maximum; **au ~** *ad* (*le plus possible*) to the full; as much as one can; (*tout au plus*) at the (very) most *ou* maximum.

mayonnaise [majɔnɛz] *nf* mayonnaise.
mazout [mazut] *nm* (fuel) oil.
me, m' [m(ə)] *pronom* me ; (*réfléchi*) myself.
Me *abr de* **Maître.**
méandres [meɑ̃dʀ(ə)] *nmpl* meanderings.
mec [mɛk] *nm* (*fam*) bloke.
mécanicien, ne [mekanisjɛ̃, -jɛn] *nm/f* mechanic ; (*RAIL*) (train *ou* engine) driver ; **~-dentiste** *nm/f* dental technician.
mécanique [mekanik] *a* mechanical // *nf* (*science*) mechanics *sg* ; (*technologie*) mechanical engineering ; (*AUTO*): **s'y connaître en ~** to be mechanically minded ; (*mécanisme*) mechanism ; engineering ; works *pl* ; **ennui ~** engine trouble *q* ; **mécaniser** *vt* to mechanize.
mécanisme [mekanism(ə)] *nm* mechanism.
mécanographie [mekanɔgʀafi] *nf* (mechanical) data processing.
mécène [mesɛn] *nm* patron.
méchanceté [meʃɑ̃ste] *nf* nastiness, maliciousness ; nasty *ou* spiteful *ou* malicious remark (*ou* action).
méchant, e [meʃɑ̃, -ɑ̃t] *a* nasty, malicious, spiteful ; (*enfant*: *pas sage*) naughty ; (*animal*) vicious ; (*avant le nom*: *valeur péjorative*) nasty ; miserable ; (: *intensive*) terrific.
mèche [mɛʃ] *nf* (*de lampe, bougie*) wick ; (*d'un explosif*) fuse ; (*de vilebrequin, perceuse*) bit ; (*de fouet*) lash ; (*de cheveux*) lock ; **vendre la ~** to give the game away ; **de ~ avec** in league with.
méchoui [meʃwi] *nm whole sheep barbecue.*
mécompte [mekɔ̃t] *nm* miscalculation ; (*déception*) disappointment.
méconnaissable [mekɔnɛsabl(ə)] *a* unrecognizable.
méconnaissance [mekɔnɛsɑ̃s] *nf* ignorance.
méconnaître [mekɔnɛtʀ(ə)] *vt* (*ignorer*) to be unaware of ; (*mésestimer*) to misjudge.
mécontent, e [mekɔ̃tɑ̃, -ɑ̃t] *a*: **~ (de)** discontented *ou* dissatisfied *ou* displeased (with) ; (*contrarié*) annoyed (at) ; **mécontentement** *nm* dissatisfaction, discontent, displeasure ; annoyance ; **mécontenter** *vt* to displease.
médaille [medaj] *nf* medal ; **médaillé, e** *nm/f* (*SPORT*) medal-holder.
médaillon [medajɔ̃] *nm* (*portrait*) medallion ; (*bijou*) locket ; (*CULIN*) médaillon ; **en ~** *a* (*carte etc*) inset.
médecin [mɛdsɛ̃] *nm* doctor ; **~ généraliste** general practitioner, G.P.
médecine [mɛdsin] *nf* medicine ; **~ légale** forensic medicine ; **~ du travail** occupational *ou* industrial medicine.
médian, e [medjɑ̃, -an] *a* (*MATH*) median.
médiateur, trice [medjatœʀ, -tʀis] *nm/f* mediator ; arbitrator.
médiation [medjɑsjɔ̃] *nf* mediation ; (*dans conflit social etc*) arbitration.
médical, e, aux [medikal, -o] *a* medical.
médicament [medikamɑ̃] *nm* medicine, drug.
médicinal, e, aux [medisinal, -o] *a* medicinal.
médico-légal, e, aux [medikɔlegal, -o] *a* forensic.
médiéval, e, aux [medjeval, -o] *a* medieval.
médiocre [medjɔkʀ(ə)] *a* mediocre, poor ; **médiocrité** *nf* mediocrity.
médire [mediʀ] *vi*: **~ de** to speak ill of ; **médisance** *nf* scandalmongering ; piece of scandal *ou* of malicious gossip.
méditatif, ive [meditatif, -iv] *a* thoughtful.
méditation [meditɑsjɔ̃] *nf* meditation.
méditer [medite] *vt* (*approfondir*) to meditate on, ponder (over) ; (*combiner*) to meditate // *vi* to meditate ; **~ de faire** to contemplate doing, plan to do.
Méditerranée [meditɛʀane] *nf*: **la (mer) ~** the Mediterranean (Sea) ; **méditerranéen, ne** *a, nm/f* Mediterranean.
médium [medjɔm] *nm* medium (*person*).
médius [medjys] *nm* middle finger.
méduse [medyz] *nf* jellyfish.
méduser [medyze] *vt* to dumbfound.
meeting [mitiŋ] *nm* (*POL, SPORT*) rally ; **~ d'aviation** air show.
méfait [mefɛ] *nm* (*faute*) misdemeanour, wrongdoing ; **~s** *nmpl* (*ravages*) ravages, damage *sg.*
méfiance [mefjɑ̃s] *nf* mistrust, distrust.
méfiant, e [mefjɑ̃, -ɑ̃t] *a* mistrustful, distrustful.
méfier [mefje]: **se ~** *vi* to be wary ; to be careful ; **se ~ de** *vt* to mistrust, distrust, be wary of ; (*faire attention*) to be careful about.
mégarde [megaʀd(ə)] *nf*: **par ~** accidentally ; by mistake.
mégère [meʒɛʀ] *nf* shrew.
mégot [mego] *nm* cigarette end.
meilleur, e [mɛjœʀ] *a, ad* better ; (*valeur superlative*) best // *nm*: **le ~** (*celui qui ...*) the best (one) ; (*ce qui ...*) the best // *nf*: **la ~e** the best (one) ; **le ~ des deux** the better of the two ; **~ marché** cheaper.
mélancolie [melɑ̃kɔli] *nf* melancholy, gloom ; **mélancolique** *a* melancholic, melancholy.
mélange [melɑ̃ʒ] *nm* mixture.
mélanger [melɑ̃ʒe] *vt* (*substances*) to mix ; (*vins, couleurs*) to blend ; (*mettre en désordre*) to mix up, muddle (up).
mélasse [melas] *nf* treacle, molasses *sg.*
mêlée [mele] *nf* mêlée, scramble ; (*RUGBY*) scrum(mage).
mêler [mele] *vt* (*substances, odeurs, races*) to mix ; (*embrouiller*) to muddle (up), mix up ; **se ~** to mix ; to mingle ; **se ~ à** (*suj*: *personne*) to join ; to mix with ; (: *odeurs etc*) to mingle with ; **se ~ de** (*suj*: *personne*) to meddle with, interfere in ; **~ qn à** (*affaire*) to get sb mixed up *ou* involved in.
mélodie [melɔdi] *nf* melody ; **mélodieux, euse** *a* melodious, tuneful ; **mélodique** *a* melodic.
mélodrame [melɔdʀam] *nm* melodrama.
mélomane [melɔman] *nm/f* music lover.
melon [məlɔ̃] *nm* (*BOT*) (honeydew) melon ; (*aussi*: **chapeau ~**) bowler (hat) ; **~ d'eau** watermelon.

mélopée [melɔpe] *nf* monotonous chant.
membrane [mɑ̃bʀan] *nf* membrane.
membre [mɑ̃bʀ(ə)] *nm* (ANAT) limb; (*personne, pays, élément*) member // *a* member; ~ **(viril)** (male) organ.
même [mɛm] *a* same // *pronom*: **le(la)** ~ the same (one) // *ad* even; **en ~ temps** at the same time; **ce sont ses paroles/celles-là ~s** they are his very words/the very ones; **il n'a ~ pas pleuré** he didn't even cry; **ici ~** at this very place; **à ~ la bouteille** straight from the bottle; **à ~ la peau** next to the skin; **être à ~ de faire** to be in a position *ou* be able to do; **mettre qn à ~ de faire** to enable sb to do; **faire de ~** to do likewise; **lui de ~** so does (*ou* did *ou* is) he; **de ~ que** just as; **il en va/est allé de ~ pour** the same goes/happened for.
mémento [memɛ̃to] *nm* (*agenda*) engagement diary; (*ouvrage*) summary.
mémoire [memwaʀ] *nf* memory // *nm* (ADMIN, JUR) memorandum (*pl* a); (SCOL) dissertation, paper; **~s** *nmpl* memoirs; **avoir la ~ des chiffres** to have a good memory for figures; **à la ~ de** to the *ou* in memory of; **pour ~** *ad* for the record; **de ~ d'homme** in living memory; **de ~** *ad* from memory.
mémorable [memɔʀabl(ə)] *a* memorable.
mémorandum [memɔʀɑ̃dɔm] *nm* memorandum (*pl* a).
mémorial, aux [memɔʀjal, -o] *nm* memorial.
menaçant, e [mənasɑ̃, -ɑ̃t] *a* threatening, menacing.
menace [mənas] *nf* threat.
menacer [mənase] *vt* to threaten.
ménage [menaʒ] *nm* (*travail*) housekeeping, housework; (*couple*) (married) couple; (*famille,* ADMIN) household; **faire le ~** to do the housework; **faire des ~s** to go out charring; **monter son ~** to set up house; **se mettre en ~ (avec)** to set up house (with); **heureux en ~** happily married; **faire bon ~ avec** to get on well with; **~ de poupée** doll's kitchen set; **~ à trois** love triangle.
ménagement [menaʒmɑ̃] *nm* care and attention; **~s** *nmpl* (*égards*) consideration *sg*, attention *sg*.
ménager [menaʒe] *vt* (*traiter*) to handle with tact; to treat considerately; (*utiliser*) to use sparingly; to use with care; (*prendre soin de*) to take (great) care of, look after; (*organiser*) to arrange; (*installer*) to put in; to make; **~ qch à qn** (*réserver*) to have sth in store for sb.
ménager, ère [menaʒe, -ɛʀ] *a* household *cpd*, domestic // *nf* housewife (*pl* wives).
ménagerie [menaʒʀi] *nf* menagerie.
mendiant, e [mɑ̃djɑ̃, -ɑ̃t] *nm/f* beggar.
mendicité [mɑ̃disite] *nf* begging.
mendier [mɑ̃dje] *vi* to beg // *vt* to beg (for).
menées [məne] *nfpl* intrigues, manœuvres.
mener [məne] *vt* to lead; (*enquête*) to conduct; (*affaires*) to manage // *vi*: **~ (à la marque)** to lead, be in the lead; **~ à/dans** (*emmener*) to take to/into; **~ qch à terme** *ou* **à bien** to see sth through (to a successful conclusion), complete sth successfully.
meneur, euse [mənœʀ, -øz] *nm/f* leader; (*péj*) agitator; **~ d'hommes** born leader; **~ de jeu** compère; quizmaster.
méningite [menɛ̃ʒit] *nf* meningitis *q*.
ménopause [menɔpoz] *nf* menopause.
menotte [mənɔt] *nf* (*main*) mitt, tiny hand; **~s** *nfpl* handcuffs; **passer les ~s à** to handcuff.
mensonge [mɑ̃sɔ̃ʒ] *nm* lie; lying *q*; **mensonger, ère** *a* false.
mensualité [mɑ̃sɥalite] *nf* monthly payment; monthly salary.
mensuel, le [mɑ̃sɥɛl] *a* monthly.
mensurations [mɑ̃syʀɑsjɔ̃] *nfpl* measurements.
mental, e, aux [mɑ̃tal, -o] *a* mental.
mentalité [mɑ̃talite] *nf* mentality.
menteur, euse [mɑ̃tœʀ, -øz] *nm/f* liar.
menthe [mɑ̃t] *nf* mint; **~ (à l'eau)** peppermint cordial.
mention [mɑ̃sjɔ̃] *nf* (*note*) note, comment; (SCOL): **~ bien** *etc* ≈ grade B *etc* (*ou* upper 2nd class *etc*) pass; **faire ~ de** to mention; **mentionner** *vt* to mention.
mentir [mɑ̃tiʀ] *vi* to lie; to be lying.
menton [mɑ̃tɔ̃] *nm* chin.
menu, e [məny] *a* slim, slight; tiny; (*frais, difficulté*) minor // *ad* (*couper, hacher*) very fine // *nm* menu; **par le ~** (*raconter*) in minute detail; **~e monnaie** small change.
menuet [mənɥɛ] *nm* minuet.
menuiserie [mənɥizʀi] *nf* (*travail*) joinery, carpentry; woodwork; (*local*) joiner's workshop; (*ouvrage*) woodwork *q*.
menuisier [mənɥizje] *nm* joiner, carpenter.
méprendre [mepʀɑ̃dʀ(ə)]: **se ~** *vi*: **se ~ sur** to be mistaken (about).
mépris [mepʀi] *nm* (*dédain*) contempt, scorn; (*indifférence*): **le ~ de** contempt *ou* disregard for; **au ~ de** regardless of, in defiance of.
méprisable [mepʀizabl(ə)] *a* contemptible, despicable.
méprisant, e [mepʀizɑ̃, -ɑ̃t] *a* contemptuous, scornful.
méprise [mepʀiz] *nf* mistake, error; misunderstanding.
mépriser [mepʀize] *vt* to scorn, despise; (*gloire, danger*) to scorn, spurn.
mer [mɛʀ] *nf* sea; (*marée*) tide; **en ~** at sea; **prendre la ~** to put out to sea; **en haute ~** off shore, on the open sea; **la ~ du Nord/Rouge** the North/Red Sea.
mercantile [mɛʀkɑ̃til] *a* (*péj*) mercenary.
mercenaire [mɛʀsənɛʀ] *nm* mercenary, hired soldier.
mercerie [mɛʀsəʀi] *nf* haberdashery; haberdasher's shop.
merci [mɛʀsi] *excl* thank you // *nf*: **à la ~ de qn/qch** at sb's mercy/the mercy of sth; **~ beaucoup** thank you very much; **~ de** thank you for; **sans ~** merciless.
mercier, ière [mɛʀsje, -jɛʀ] *nm/f* haberdasher.
mercredi [mɛʀkʀədi] *nm* Wednesday; **~ des Cendres** Ash Wednesday.
mercure [mɛʀkyʀ] *nm* mercury.

merde [mɛʀd(ə)] (*fam!*) *nf* shit (!) // *excl* bloody hell (!).
mère [mɛʀ] *nf* mother; ~ **célibataire** unmarried mother.
méridien [meʀidjɛ̃] *nm* meridian.
méridional, e, aux [meʀidjɔnal, -o] *a* southern // *nm/f* Southerner.
meringue [məʀɛ̃g] *nf* meringue.
merisier [məʀizje] *nm* wild cherry (tree).
méritant, e [meʀitɑ̃, -ɑ̃t] *a* deserving.
mérite [meʀit] *nm* merit; **le ~ (de ceci) lui revient** the credit (for this) is his.
mériter [meʀite] *vt* to deserve.
méritoire [meʀitwaʀ] *a* praiseworthy, commendable.
merlan [mɛʀlɑ̃] *nm* whiting.
merle [mɛʀl(ə)] *nm* blackbird.
merveille [mɛʀvɛj] *nf* marvel, wonder; **faire ~** to work wonders; **à ~** perfectly, wonderfully.
merveilleux, euse [mɛʀvɛjø, -øz] *a* marvellous, wonderful.
mes [me] *dét voir* **mon**.
mésalliance [mezaljɑ̃s] *nf* misalliance, mismatch.
mésange [mezɑ̃ʒ] *nf* tit(mouse) (*pl* mice); ~ **bleue** blue tit.
mésaventure [mezavɑ̃tyʀ] *nf* misadventure, misfortune.
Mesdames [medam] *nfpl voir* **Madame**.
Mesdemoiselles [medmwazɛl] *nfpl voir* **Mademoiselle**.
mésentente [mezɑ̃tɑ̃t] *nf* dissension, disagreement.
mésestimer [mezɛstime] *vt* to underestimate, underrate; to have low regard for.
mesquin, e [mɛskɛ̃, -in] *a* mean, petty; **mesquinerie** *nf* pettiness *q*, meanness *q*.
mess [mɛs] *nm* mess.
message [mesaʒ] *nm* message; ~ **téléphoné** telegram dictated by telephone; **messager, ère** *nm/f* messenger; **messageries** *nfpl* parcels service *sg*; distribution service *sg*.
messe [mɛs] *nf* mass; **aller à la ~** to go to mass; ~ **de minuit** midnight mass.
messie [mesi] *nm*: **le M~** the Messiah.
Messieurs [mesjø] *nmpl* (*abr* **Messrs**) *voir* **Monsieur**.
mesure [məzyʀ] *nf* (*évaluation, dimension*) measurement; (*étalon, récipient, contenu*) measure; (*MUS*: *cadence*) time, tempo; (: *division*) bar; (*retenue*) moderation; (*disposition*) measure, step; **sur ~** (*costume*) made-to-measure; **à la ~ de** (*fig*) worthy of; on the same scale as; **dans la ~ où** insofar as, inasmuch as; **à ~ que** as; **en ~** (*MUS*) in time *ou* tempo; **être en ~ de** to be in a position to; **dépasser la ~** (*fig*) to overstep the mark.
mesurer [məzyʀe] *vt* to measure; (*juger*) to weigh up, assess; (*limiter*) to limit, ration; (*modérer*) to moderate; (*proportionner*): ~ **qch à** to match sth to, gear sth to; **se ~ avec** to have a confrontation with; to tackle; **il mesure 1 m 80** he's 1 m 80 tall.
met *vb voir* **mettre**.
métairie [meteʀi] *nf* smallholding.
métal, aux [metal, -o] *nm* metal; **~lique** *a* metallic; **~lisé, e** *a* (*peinture*) metallic; **~lurgie** *nf* metallurgy; **~lurgiste** *nm/f* steel *ou* metal worker; metallurgist.
métamorphose [metamɔʀfoz] *nf* metamorphosis (*pl* oses).
métaphore [metafɔʀ] *nf* metaphor.
métaphysique [metafizik] *nf* metaphysics *sg* // *a* metaphysical.
métayer, ère [meteje, metɛjɛʀ] *nm/f* (tenant) farmer.
météo [meteo] *nf* weather report; ≈ Met Office.
météore [meteɔʀ] *nm* meteor.
météorologie [meteɔʀɔlɔʒi] *nf* meteorology; **météorologique** *a* meteorological, weather *cpd*.
métèque [metɛk] *nm* (*péj*) wop.
méthode [metɔd] *nf* method; (*livre, ouvrage*) manual, tutor; **méthodique** *a* methodical.
méticuleux, euse [metikylø, -øz] *a* meticulous.
métier [metje] *nm* (*profession*: *gén*) job; (: *manuel*) trade; (: *artisanal*) craft; (*technique, expérience*) (acquired) skill *ou* technique; (*aussi*: ~ **à tisser**) (weaving) loom; **être du ~** to be in the trade *ou* profession.
métis, se [metis] *a, nm/f* half-caste, half-breed.
métisser [metise] *vt* to cross.
métrage [metʀaʒ] *nm* (*de tissu*) length, ≈ yardage; (*CINÉMA*) footage, length; **long/moyen/court ~** full-length/medium-length/short film.
mètre [mɛtʀ(ə)] *nm* metre; (*règle*) (metre) rule; (*ruban*) tape measure; **métrique** *a* metric // *nf* metrics *sg*.
métro [metʀo] *nm* underground, subway.
métropole [metʀɔpɔl] *nf* (*capitale*) metropolis; (*pays*) home country; **métropolitain, e** *a* metropolitan.
mets [mɛ] *nm* dish.
metteur [mɛtœʀ] *nm*: ~ **en scène** (*THÉÂTRE*) producer; (*CINÉMA*) director; ~ **en ondes** producer.
mettre [mɛtʀ(ə)] *vt* (*placer*) to put; (*vêtement*: *revêtir*) to put on; (: *porter*) to wear; (*installer*: *gaz, l'électricité*) to put in; (*faire fonctionner*: *chauffage, électricité*) to put on; (*noter, écrire*) to say, put down; **mettons que** let's suppose *ou* say that; ~ **en bouteille/en sac** to bottle/put in bags *ou* sacks; **y ~ du sien** to pull one's weight; ~ **du temps/2 heures à faire** to take time/2 hours doing; **se ~**: **n'avoir rien à se ~** to have nothing to wear; **se ~ de l'encre sur les doigts** to get ink on one's fingers; **se ~ au lit** to get into bed; **se ~ au piano** (*s'asseoir*) to sit down at the piano; (*apprendre*) to start learning the piano; **se ~ à faire** to begin *ou* start doing *ou* to do; **se ~ au travail/à l'étude** to get down to work/one's studies.
meublant, e [mœblɑ̃, -ɑ̃t] *a* (*tissus etc*) effective (in the room), decorative.
meuble [mœbl(ə)] *nm* piece of furniture; furniture *q* // *a* (*terre*) loose, friable; (*JUR*): **biens ~s** movables; **meublé** *nm* furnished room (*ou* flatlet); **meubler** *vt* to furnish;

(*fig*): **meubler qch (de)** to fill sth (with); **se meubler** to furnish one's house.
meugler [møgle] *vi* to low, moo.
meule [møl] *nf* (*à broyer*) millstone; (*à aiguiser*) grindstone; (*à polir*) buffwheel; (*de foin, blé*) stack; (*de fromage*) round.
meunerie [mønʀi] *nf* flour trade; milling; **meunier, ière** *nm* miller // *nf* miller's wife // *af inv* (CULIN) meunière.
meure *etc vb voir* **mourir**.
meurtre [mœʀtʀ(ə)] *nm* murder; **meurtrier, ière** *a* (*arme etc*) deadly; (*fureur, instincts*) murderous // *nm/f* murderer/eress // *nf* (*ouverture*) loophole.
meurtrir [mœʀtʀiʀ] *vt* to bruise; (*fig*) to wound; **meurtrissure** *nf* bruise; (*fig*) scar.
meus *etc vb voir* **mouvoir**.
meute [møt] *nf* pack.
mexicain, e [mɛksikɛ̃, -ɛn] *a, nm/f* Mexican.
Mexico [mɛksiko] *n* Mexico City.
Mexique [mɛksik] *nm*: **le** ~ Mexico.
MF *sigle f voir* **modulation**.
Mgr *abr de* **Monseigneur**.
mi [mi] *nm* (MUS) E; (*en chantant la gamme*) mi.
mi... [mi] *préfixe* half(-); mid-; **à la ~-janvier** in mid-January; **~-bureau, ~-chambre** half office, half bedroom; **à ~-jambes/-corps** (up *ou* down) to the knees/waist; **à ~-hauteur/-pente** halfway up *ou* down/up *ou* down the hill.
miauler [mijole] *vi* to mew.
mica [mika] *nm* mica.
mi-carême [mikaʀɛm] *nf*: **la** ~ the third Thursday in Lent.
miche [miʃ] *nf* round *ou* cob loaf.
mi-chemin [miʃmɛ̃]: **à** ~ *ad* halfway, midway.
mi-clos, e [miklo, -kloz] *a* half-closed.
micmac [mikmak] *nm* (*péj*) carry-on.
micro [mikʀo] *nm* mike, microphone.
microbe [mikʀɔb] *nm* germ, microbe.
microfiche [mikʀɔfiʃ] *nf* microfiche.
microfilm [mikʀɔfilm] *nm* microfilm.
microphone [mikʀɔfɔn] *nm* microphone.
microscope [mikʀɔskɔp] *nm* microscope; **au** ~ under *ou* through the microscope.
midi [midi] *nm* midday, noon; (*moment du déjeuner*) lunchtime; **à** ~ at 12 (o'clock) *ou* midday *ou* noon; (*sud*) south; **en plein** ~ (right) in the middle of the day; facing south.
mie [mi] *nf* crumb (of the loaf).
miel [mjɛl] *nm* honey.
mielleux, euse [mjɛlø, -øz] *a* (*péj*) sugary, honeyed.
mien, ne [mjɛ̃, mjɛn] *pronom*: **le(la) ~(ne), les ~s** mine; **les ~s** my family.
miette [mjɛt] *nf* (*de pain, gâteau*) crumb; (*fig: de la conversation etc*) scrap; **en ~s** (*fig*) in pieces *ou* bits.
mieux [mjø] *ad* better // *a* better; (*plus joli*) better-looking // *nm* (*progrès*) improvement; **le** ~ the best (thing); **le(la) ~, les** ~ the best; **le ~ des deux** the better of the two; **les livres les ~ faits** the best made books; **de mon/ton** ~ as best I/you can (*ou* could); **de ~ en** ~ better and better; **pour le** ~ for the best; **au** ~ at best; **au ~ avec** on the best of terms with.
mièvre [mjɛvʀ(ə)] *a* mawkish, sickly sentimental.
mignon, ne [miɲɔ̃, -ɔn] *a* sweet, cute.
migraine [migʀɛn] *nf* headache; migraine.
migrateur, trice [migʀatœʀ, -tʀis] *a* migratory.
migration [migʀɑsjɔ̃] *nf* migration.
mijaurée [miʒɔʀe] *nf* pretentious girl.
mijoter [miʒɔte] *vt* to simmer; (*préparer avec soin*) to cook lovingly; (*affaire, projet*) to plot, cook up // *vi* to simmer.
mil [mil] *num* = **mille**.
mildiou [mildju] *nm* mildew.
milice [milis] *nf* militia; **milicien, ne** *nm/f* militia man/woman.
milieu, x [miljø] *nm* (*centre*) middle; (*fig*) middle course *ou* way; happy medium; (BIO, GÉO) environment; (*entourage social*) milieu; background; circle; (*pègre*): **le** ~ the underworld; **au ~ de** in the middle of.
militaire [militɛʀ] *a* military, army *cpd* // *nm* serviceman.
militant, e [militɑ̃, -ɑ̃t] *a, nm/f* militant.
militer [milite] *vi* to be a militant; **~ pour/contre** (*suj: faits, raisons etc*) to militate in favour of/against.
mille [mil] *num* a *ou* one thousand // *nm* (*mesure*): ~ **(marin)** nautical mile; **mettre dans le** ~ to hit the bull's-eye; to be bang on target; **~feuille** *nm* cream *ou* vanilla slice; **millénaire** *nm* millennium // *a* thousand-year-old; (*fig*) ancient; **~-pattes** *nm inv* centipede.
millésime [milezim] *nm* year; **millésimé, e** *a* vintage *cpd*.
millet [mijɛ] *nm* millet.
milliard [miljaʀ] *nm* milliard, thousand million; **milliardaire** *nm/f* multimillionaire.
millier [milje] *nm* thousand; **un ~ (de)** a thousand or so, about a thousand; **par ~s** in (their) thousands, by the thousand.
milligramme [miligʀam] *nm* milligramme.
millimètre [milimɛtʀ(ə)] *nm* millimetre; **millimétré, e** *a*: **papier millimétré** graph paper.
million [miljɔ̃] *nm* million; **deux ~s de** two million; **toucher cinq ~s** to get five million; **riche à ~s** worth millions; **millionnaire** *nm/f* millionaire.
mime [mim] *nm/f* (*acteur*) mime(r) // *nm* (*art*) mime, miming.
mimer [mime] *vt* to mime; (*singer*) to mimic, take off.
mimétisme [mimetism(ə)] *nm* (BIO) mimicry.
mimique [mimik] *nf* (funny) face; (*signes*) gesticulations *pl*, sign language *q*.
mimosa [mimoza] *nm* mimosa.
minable [minabl(ə)] *a* shabby (-looking); pathetic.
minauder [minode] *vi* to mince, simper.
mince [mɛ̃s] *a* thin; (*personne, taille*) slim, slender; (*fig: profit, connaissances*) slight, small // *excl* drat it!; **minceur** *nf* thinness; slimness, slenderness.

mine [min] *nf* (*physionomie*) expression, look; (*extérieur*) exterior, appearance; (*de crayon*) lead; (*gisement, exploitation, explosif*) mine; **~s** *nfpl* (*péj*) simpering airs; **avoir bonne ~** (*personne*) to look well; (*ironique*) to look an utter idiot; **avoir mauvaise ~** to look unwell *ou* poorly; **faire ~ de faire** to make a pretence of doing; to make as if to do; **~ de rien** *ad* with a casual air; although you wouldn't think so; **~ de charbon** coalmine; **~ à ciel ouvert** opencast mine.
miner [mine] *vt* (*saper*) to undermine, erode; (MIL) to mine.
minerai [minʀɛ] *nm* ore.
minéral, e, aux [mineʀal, -o] *a* mineral; (CHIMIE) inorganic // *nm* mineral.
minéralogie [mineʀalɔʒi] *nf* mineralogy.
minéralogique [mineʀalɔʒik] *a* mineralogical; **plaque ~** number plate; **numéro ~** registration number.
minet, te [minɛ, -ɛt] *nm/f* (*chat*) pussy-cat; (*péj*) young trendy/dollybird.
mineur, e [minœʀ] *a* minor // *nm/f* (JUR) minor, person under age // *nm* (*travailleur*) miner; **~ de fond** face worker.
miniature [minjatyʀ] *a, nf* miniature; **miniaturiser** *vt* to miniaturize.
minibus [minibys] *nm* minibus.
mini-cassette [minikasɛt] *nf* cassette (recorder).
minier, ière [minje, -jɛʀ] *a* mining.
mini-jupe [miniʒyp] *nf* mini-skirt.
minimal, e, aux [minimal, -o] *a* minimum.
minime [minim] *a* minor, minimal // *nm/f* (SPORT) junior.
minimiser [minimize] *vt* to minimize; (*fig*) to play down.
minimum [minimɔm] *a, nm* minimum; **au ~** (*au moins*) at the very least; **~ vital** living wage; subsistance level.
ministère [ministɛʀ] *nm* (*aussi* REL) ministry; (*cabinet*) government; **~ public** (JUR) Prosecution, State Prosecutor; **ministériel, le** *a* cabinet *cpd*; ministerial.
ministre [ministʀ(ə)] *nm* (*aussi* REL) minister; **~ d'État** senior minister (*of the Interior or of Justice*).
minium [minjɔm] *nm* red lead paint.
minois [minwa] *nm* little face.
minoritaire [minɔʀitɛʀ] *a* minority *cpd*.
minorité [minɔʀite] *nf* minority; **être en ~** to be in the *ou* a minority; **mettre en ~** (POL) to defeat.
minoterie [minɔtʀi] *nf* flour-mill.
minuit [minɥi] *nm* midnight.
minuscule [minyskyl] *a* minute, tiny // *nf*: **(lettre) ~** small letter.
minute [minyt] *nf* minute; (JUR: *original*) minute, draft; **à la ~** (just) this instant; there and then; **steak ~** minute steak; **minuter** *vt* to time; **minuterie** *nf* time switch.
minutieux, euse [minysjø, -øz] *a* meticulous; minutely detailed; requiring painstaking attention to detail.
mioche [mjɔʃ] *nm* (*fam*) nipper, brat.
mirabelle [miʀabɛl] *nf* (cherry) plum; (*eau-de-vie*) plum brandy.
miracle [miʀɑkl(ə)] *nm* miracle; **miraculé, e** *a* who has been miraculously cured (*ou* rescued); **miraculeux, euse** *a* miraculous.
mirador [miʀadɔʀ] *nm* (MIL) watchtower.
mirage [miʀaʒ] *nm* mirage.
mire [miʀ] *nf*: **point de ~** target; (*fig*) focal point; **ligne de ~** line of sight.
mirer [miʀe] *vt* (*œufs*) to candle; **se ~** *vi*: **se ~ dans** to gaze at one's reflection in; to be mirrored in.
mirifique [miʀifik] *a* wonderful.
mirobolant, e [miʀɔbɔlɑ̃, -ɑ̃t] *a* fantastic.
miroir [miʀwaʀ] *nm* mirror.
miroiter [miʀwate] *vi* to sparkle, shimmer; **faire ~ qch à qn** to paint sth in glowing colours for sb, dangle sth in front of sb's eyes.
miroiterie [miʀwatʀi] *nf* mirror factory; mirror dealer's (shop).
mis, e [mi, miz] *pp de* **mettre** // *a*: **bien ~** well dressed // *nf* (*argent*: *au jeu*) stake; (*tenue*) clothing; attire; **être de ~e** to be acceptable *ou* in season; **~e de fonds** capital outlay; **~e à mort** kill; **~e en plis** set; **~e au point** (*fig*) clarification (*voir aussi* **point**); **~e en scène** production.
misaine [mizɛn] *nf*: **mât de ~** foremast.
misanthrope [mizɑ̃tʀɔp] *nm/f* misanthropist.
mise [miz] *a, nf voir* **mis**.
miser [mize] *vt* (*enjeu*) to stake, bet; **~ sur** *vt* (*cheval, numéro*) to bet on; (*fig*) to bank *ou* count on.
misérable [mizeʀabl(ə)] *a* (*lamentable, malheureux*) pitiful, wretched; (*pauvre*) poverty-stricken; (*insignifiant, mesquin*) miserable // *nm/f* wretch; (*miséreux*) poor wretch.
misère [mizɛʀ] *nf* (extreme) poverty, destitution; **~s** *nfpl* woes, miseries; little troubles; **être dans la ~** to be destitute *ou* poverty-stricken; **salaire de ~** starvation wage; **miséreux, euse** *nm/f* down-and-out.
miséricorde [mizeʀikɔʀd(ə)] *nf* mercy, forgiveness; **miséricordieux, euse** *a* merciful, forgiving.
misogyne [mizɔʒin] *a* misogynous // *nm/f* misogynist.
missel [misɛl] *nm* missal.
missile [misil] *nm* missile.
mission [misjɔ̃] *nf* mission; **partir en ~** (ADMIN, POL) to go on an assignment; **missionnaire** *nm/f* missionary.
missive [misiv] *nf* missive.
mit *vb voir* **mettre**.
mitaine [mitɛn] *nf* mitt(en).
mite [mit] *nf* clothes moth; **mité, e** *a* moth-eaten.
mi-temps [mitɑ̃] *nf inv* (SPORT: *période*) half (*pl* halves); (: *pause*) half-time; **à ~** *a, ad* part-time.
miteux, euse [mitø, -øz] *a* seedy, shabby.
mitigé, e [mitiʒe] *a* lukewarm; mixed.
mitonner [mitɔne] *vt* to cook with loving care; (*fig*) to cook up quietly.
mitoyen, ne [mitwajɛ̃, -ɛn] *a* common, party *cpd*; **maisons ~nes** semi-detached houses; (*plus de deux*) terraced houses.

mitraille [mitʀɑj] *nf* grapeshot; shellfire.
mitrailler [mitʀɑje] *vt* to machine-gun; (*fig*: *photographier*) to take shot after shot of; ~ **qn de** to pelt sb with, bombard sb with; **mitraillette** *nf* submachine gun; **mitrailleur** *nm* machine gunner; **mitrailleuse** *nf* machine gun.
mitre [mitʀ(ə)] *nf* mitre.
mitron [mitʀɔ̃] *nm* baker's boy.
mi-voix [mivwa]: **à** ~ *ad* in a low *ou* hushed voice.
mixage [miksaʒ] *nm* (*CINÉMA*) (sound) mixing.
mixer [miksœʀ] *nm* (food) mixer.
mixité [miksite] *nf* (*SCOL*) coeducation.
mixte [mikst(ə)] *a* (*gén*) mixed; (*SCOL*) mixed, coeducational; **à usage** ~ dual-purpose; **cuisinière** ~ gas and electric cooker; **équipe** ~ combined team.
mixture [mikstyʀ] *nf* mixture; (*fig*) concoction.
M.L.F. *sigle m = mouvement de libération de la femme*, ≈ Women's Lib.
Mlle, *pl* **Mlles** *abr de* **Mademoiselle.**
MM *abr de* **Messieurs.**
Mme, *pl* **Mmes** *abr de* **Madame.**
mnémotechnique [mnemɔtɛknik] *a* mnemonic.
Mo *abr de* **métro.**
mobile [mɔbil] *a* mobile; (*pièce de machine*) moving; (*élément de meuble etc*) movable // *nm (motif)* motive; (*œuvre d'art*) mobile; (*PHYSIQUE*) moving object *ou* body.
mobilier, ière [mɔbilje, -jɛʀ] *a* (*JUR*) personal // *nm* furniture; **valeurs mobilières** transferable securities; **vente mobilière** sale of personal property *ou* chattels.
mobilisation [mɔbilizɑsjɔ̃] *nf* mobilization.
mobiliser [mɔbilize] *vt* (*MIL*, *gén*) to mobilize.
mobilité [mɔbilite] *nf* mobility.
mocassin [mɔkasɛ̃] *nm* moccasin.
moche [mɔʃ] *a* (*fam*) ugly; rotten.
modalité [mɔdalite] *nf* form, mode; ~**s** *nfpl* (*d'un accord etc*) clauses, terms.
mode [mɔd] *nf* fashion; (*commerce*) fashion trade *ou* industry // *nm* (*manière*) form, mode; (*LING*) mood; (*MUS*) mode; **à la** ~ fashionable, in fashion; ~ **d'emploi** directions *pl* (for use); ~ **de vie** way of life.
modèle [mɔdɛl] *a*, *nm* model; (*qui pose*: *de peintre*) sitter; ~ **déposé** registered design; ~ **réduit** small-scale model; ~ **de série** production model.
modelé [mɔdle] *nm* relief; contours *pl*.
modeler [mɔdle] *vt* (*ART*) to model, mould; (*suj*: *vêtement*, *érosion*) to mould, shape; ~ **qch sur/d'après** to model sth on.
modérateur, trice [mɔdeʀatœʀ, -tʀis] *a* moderating // *nm/f* moderator.
modération [mɔdeʀɑsjɔ̃] *nf* moderation.
modéré, e [mɔdeʀe] *a*, *nm/f* moderate.
modérer [mɔdeʀe] *vt* to moderate; **se** ~ *vi* to restrain o.s.
moderne [mɔdɛʀn(ə)] *a* modern // *nm* modern style; modern furniture; **moderniser** *vt* to modernize.
modeste [mɔdɛst(ə)] *a* modest; **modestie** *nf* modesty.
modicité [mɔdisite] *nf*: **la** ~ **des prix** *etc* the low prices *etc*.
modification [mɔdifikɑsjɔ̃] *nf* modification.
modifier [mɔdifje] *vt* to modify, alter; (*LING*) to modify; **se** ~ *vi* to alter.
modique [mɔdik] *a* modest.
modiste [mɔdist(ə)] *nf* milliner.
modulation [mɔdylɑsjɔ̃] *nf* modulation; ~ **de fréquence (FM** *ou* **MF)** frequency modulation.
module [mɔdyl] *nm* module.
moduler [mɔdyle] *vt* to modulate; (*air*) to warble.
moelle [mwal] *nf* marrow; (*fig*) pith, core; ~ **épinière** spinal chord.
moelleux, euse [mwalø, -øz] *a* soft; (*au goût, à l'ouïe*) mellow.
moellon [mwalɔ̃] *nm* rubble stone.
mœurs [mœʀ] *nfpl* (*conduite*) morals; (*manières*) manners; (*pratiques sociales, mode de vie*) habits; **passer dans les** ~ to become the custom; **contraire aux bonnes** ~ contrary to proprieties.
mohair [mɔɛʀ] *nm* mohair.
moi [mwa] *pronom* me; (*emphatique*): ~, **je** for my part, I, I myself.
moignon [mwaɲɔ̃] *nm* stump.
moi-même [mwamɛm] *pronom* myself; (*emphatique*) I myself.
moindre [mwɛ̃dʀ(ə)] *a* lesser; lower; **le(la)** ~, **les** ~**s** the least, the slightest.
moine [mwan] *nm* monk, friar.
moineau, x [mwano] *nm* sparrow.
moins [mwɛ̃] *ad* less // *cj*: ~ **2** minus 2; ~ **je travaille, mieux je me porte** the less I work the better I feel; ~ **grand que** not as tall as, less tall than; **le(la)** ~ **doué(e)** the least gifted; **le** ~ the least; ~ **de** (*sable, eau*) less; (*livres, gens*) fewer; ~ **de 2 ans/100 F** less than 2 years/100 F; ~ **de midi** not yet midday; **100 F/3 jours de** ~ 100 F/3 days less; **3 livres en** ~ 3 books fewer; 3 books too few; **de l'argent en** ~ less money; **le soleil en** ~ but for the sun, minus the sun; **à** ~ **que** *cj* unless; **à** ~ **de faire** unless we do (*ou* he does); **à** ~ **de** (*imprévu, accident*) barring any; **au** ~ at least; **de** ~ **en** ~ less and less; **pour le** ~ at the very least; **du** ~ at least; **il est** ~ **cinq** it's five to; **il fait** ~ **cinq** it's five below (freezing) *ou* minus five.
moiré, e [mwaʀe] *a* (*tissu, papier*) moiré, watered; (*reflets*) shimmering.
mois [mwa] *nm* month; ~ **double** (*COMM*) extra month's salary.
moïse [mɔiz] *nm* Moses basket.
moisi, e [mwazi] *a* mouldy, mildewed // *nm* mould, mildew; **odeur de** ~ musty smell.
moisir [mwaziʀ] *vi* to go mouldy; (*fig*) to rot; to hang about.
moisissure [mwazisyʀ] *nf* mould *q*.
moisson [mwasɔ̃] *nf* harvest; (*fig*): **faire une** ~ **de** to gather a wealth of; **moissonner** *vt* to harvest, reap; (*fig*) to collect; **moissonneur, euse** *nm/f* harvester, reaper // *nf* (*machine*)

harvester; **moissonneuse-batteuse** *nf* combine harvester.
moite [mwat] *a* sweaty, sticky.
moitié [mwatje] *nf* half (*pl* halves); (*épouse*): **sa ~** his loving wife, his better half; **la ~** half; **la ~ de** half (of), half the amount (*ou* number) of; **la ~ du temps/des gens** half the time/the people; **à la ~ de** halfway through; **~ moins grand** half as tall; **~ plus long** half as long again, longer by half; **à ~** half (*avant le verbe*); half- (*avant l'adjectif*); **de ~** by half; **~ ~** half-and-half.
moka [mɔka] *nm* mocha coffee; mocha cake.
mol [mɔl] *a voir* **mou**.
molaire [mɔlɛʀ] *nf* molar.
molécule [mɔlekyl] *nf* molecule.
moleskine [mɔlɛskin] *nf* imitation leather.
molester [mɔlɛste] *vt* to manhandle, maul (about).
molette [mɔlɛt] *nf* toothed *ou* cutting wheel.
molle [mɔl] *af voir* **mou**; **~ment** *ad* softly; (*péj*) sluggishly; (*protester*) feebly; **mollesse** *nf* softness; flabbiness; limpness; sluggishness.
mollet [mɔlɛ] *nm* calf (*pl* calves) // *am*: **œuf ~** soft-boiled egg; **molletière** *af*: **bande molletière** puttee.
molletonné, e [mɔltɔne] *a* fleece-lined, flannelette-lined.
mollir [mɔliʀ] *vi* to give way; to relent; to go soft.
mollusque [mɔlysk(ə)] *nm* (ZOOL) mollusc.
molosse [mɔlɔs] *nm* big ferocious dog.
môme [mom] *nm/f* (*fam*: *enfant*) brat; (: *fille*) bird.
moment [mɔmɑ̃] *nm* moment; **ce n'est pas le ~** this is not the (right) time; **à un certain ~** at some point; **pour un bon ~** for a good while; **pour le ~** for the moment, for the time being; **au ~ de** at the time of; **au ~ où** as; at a time when; **à tout ~** at any time *ou* moment; constantly, continually; **en ce ~** at the moment; at present; **sur le ~** at the time; **par ~s** now and then, at times; **du ~ où** *ou* **que** seeing that, since; **momentané, e** *a* temporary, momentary.
momie [mɔmi] *nf* mummy.
mon [mɔ̃], **ma** [ma], *pl* **mes** [me] *dét* my.
monacal, e, aux [mɔnakal, -o] *a* monastic.
monarchie [mɔnaʀʃi] *nf* monarchy; **monarchiste** *a, nm/f* monarchist.
monarque [mɔnaʀk(ə)] *nm* monarch.
monastère [mɔnastɛʀ] *nm* monastery.
monastique [mɔnastik] *a* monastic.
monceau, x [mɔ̃so] *nm* heap.
mondain, e [mɔ̃dɛ̃, -ɛn] *a* society *cpd*; social; fashionable // *nm/f* society man/woman, socialite // *nf*: **la M~e, la police ~e** ≈ the vice squad; **mondanités** *nfpl* society life *sg*; (society) small talk *sg*; (society) gossip column *sg*.
monde [mɔ̃d] *nm* world; (*haute société*): **le ~** (high) society; (*milieu*): **être du même ~** to move in the same circles; (*gens*): **il y a du ~** (*beaucoup de gens*) there are many people; (*quelques personnes*) there are some people; **y a-t-il du ~ dans le salon?** is there anybody in the lounge?; **beaucoup/peu de ~** many/few people; **le meilleur** *etc* **du ~** the best *etc* in the world *ou* on earth; **mettre au ~** to bring into the world; **pas le moins du ~** not in the least; **se faire un ~ de qch** to make a great deal of fuss about sth; **mondial, e, aux** *a* (*population*) world *cpd*; (*influence*) world-wide; **mondialement** *ad* throughout the world; **mondovision** *nf* world coverage by satellite.
monégasque [mɔnegask(ə)] *a* Monegasque, of *ou* from Monaco.
monétaire [mɔnetɛʀ] *a* monetary.
mongolien, ne [mɔ̃gɔljɛ̃, -jɛn] *a, nm/f* mongol.
mongolisme [mɔ̃gɔlism(ə)] *nm* mongolism.
moniteur, trice [mɔnitœʀ, -tʀis] *nm/f* (SPORT) instructor/instructress; (*de colonie de vacances*) supervisor // *nm*: **~ cardiaque** cardiac monitor; **~ d'auto-école** driving instructor.
monnaie [mɔnɛ] *nf* (*pièce*) coin; (ÉCON, *gén*: *moyen d'échange*) currency; (*petites pièces*): **avoir de la ~** to have (some) change; **faire de la ~** to get (some) change; **avoir/faire la ~ de 20 F** to have change of/get change for 20 F; **faire à qn la ~ de 20 F** to give sb change for 20 F, change 20 F for sb; **rendre à qn la ~ (sur 20 F)** to give sb the change (out of *ou* from 20 F); **c'est ~ courante** it's a common occurrence; **monnayer** *vt* to convert into cash; (*talent*) to capitalize on; **monnayeur** *nm voir* **faux**.
monocle [mɔnɔkl(ə)] *nm* monocle, eyeglass.
monocorde [mɔnɔkɔʀd(ə)] *a* monotonous.
monoculture [mɔnɔkyltyʀ] *nf* single-crop farming, monoculture.
monogramme [mɔnɔgʀam] *nm* monogram.
monolingue [mɔnɔlɛ̃g] *a* monolingual.
monologue [mɔnɔlɔg] *nm* monologue, soliloquy; **monologuer** *vi* to soliloquize.
monôme [mɔnom] *nm* (MATH) monomial; (*d'étudiants*) students' rag procession.
monoplace [mɔnɔplas] *a, nm, nf* single-seater, one-seater.
monopole [mɔnɔpɔl] *nm* monopoly; **monopoliser** *vt* to monopolize.
monorail [mɔnɔʀɑj] *nm* monorail, monorail train.
monosyllabe [mɔnɔsilab] *nm* monosyllable, word of one syllable.
monotone [mɔnɔtɔn] *a* monotonous; **monotonie** *nf* monotony.
monseigneur [mɔ̃sɛɲœʀ] *nm* (*archevêque, évêque*) Your (*ou* His) Grace; (*cardinal*) Your (*ou* His) Eminence; **Mgr Thomas** Bishop Thomas; Cardinal Thomas.
Monsieur [məsjø], *pl* **Messieurs** [mesjø] *titre* Mr ['mɪstə*] // *nm* (*homme quelconque*): **un/le m~** a/the gentleman; *voir aussi* **Madame**.
monstre [mɔ̃stʀ(ə)] *nm* monster // *a*: **un travail ~** a fantastic amount of work; an enormous job; **monstrueux, euse** *a* monstrous; **monstruosité** *nf* monstrosity.

mont [mɔ̃] *nm*: **par ~s et par vaux** up hill and down dale; **le M~ Blanc** Mont Blanc; **le ~ de Vénus** mons veneris.
montage [mɔ̃taʒ] *nm* putting up; mounting, setting; assembly; (PHOTO) photomontage; (CINÉMA) editing; **~ sonore** sound editing.
montagnard, e [mɔ̃taɲaʀ, -aʀd(ə)] *a* mountain *cpd* // *nm/f* mountain-dweller.
montagne [mɔ̃taɲ] *nf* (*cime*) mountain; (*région*): **la ~** the mountains *pl*; **~s russes** big dipper *sg*, switchback *sg*.
montant, e [mɔ̃tɑ̃, -ɑ̃t] *a* rising; (*robe, corsage*) high-necked // *nm* (*somme, total*), (sum) total, (total) amount; (*de fenêtre*) upright; (*de lit*) post.
mont-de-piété [mɔ̃dpjete] *nm* pawnshop.
monte-charge [mɔ̃tʃaʀʒ(ə)] *nm inv* goods lift, hoist.
montée [mɔ̃te] *nf* rising, rise; ascent, climb; (*chemin*) way up; (*côte*) hill; **au milieu de la ~** halfway up; **le moteur chauffe dans les ~s** the engine overheats going uphill.
monte-plats [mɔ̃tpla] *nm inv* service lift.
monter [mɔ̃te] *vt* (*escalier, côte*) to go (*ou* come) up; (*valise, paquet*) to take (*ou* bring) up; (*cheval*) to mount; (*femelle*) to cover, serve; (*étagère*) to raise; (*tente, échafaudage*) to put up; (*machine*) to assemble; (*bijou*) to mount, set; (COUTURE) to set in; to sew on; (CINÉMA) to edit; (THÉÂTRE) to put on, stage; (*société etc*) to set up // *vi* to go (*ou* come) up; (*avion etc*) to climb, go up; (*chemin, niveau, température*) to go up, rise; (*passager*) to get on; (*à cheval*): **~ bien/mal** to ride well/badly; **~ à pied/en voiture** to walk/drive up, go up on foot/by car; **~ dans le train/l'avion** to get into the train/plane, board the train/plane; **~ sur** to climb up onto; **~ à cheval** to get on *ou* mount a horse; **se ~** (*s'équiper*) to equip o.s., get kitted up; **se ~ à** (*frais etc*) to add up to, come to; **~ qn contre qn** to set sb against sb; **~ la tête à qn** to give sb ideas; **monteur, euse** *nm/f* (TECH) fitter; (CINÉMA) (film) editor.
monticule [mɔ̃tikyl] *nm* mound.
montre [mɔ̃tʀ(ə)] *nf* watch; (*ostentation*): **pour la ~** for show; **faire ~ de** to show, display; **contre la ~** (SPORT) against the clock; **~-bracelet** *nf* wrist watch.
montrer [mɔ̃tʀe] *vt* to show; **~ qch à qn** to show sb sth; **montreur de marionnettes** *nm* puppeteer.
monture [mɔ̃tyʀ] *nf* (*bête*) mount; (*d'une bague*) setting; (*de lunettes*) frame.
monument [mɔnymɑ̃] *nm* monument; **~ aux morts** war memorial; **monumental, e, aux** *a* monumental.
moquer [mɔke]: **se ~ de** *vt* to make fun of, laugh at; (*fam: se désintéresser de*) not to care about; (*tromper*): **se ~ de qn** to take sb for a ride.
moquerie [mɔkʀi] *nf* mockery *q*.
moquette [mɔkɛt] *nf* fitted carpet, wall-to-wall carpeting *q*.
moqueur, euse [mɔkœʀ, -øz] *a* mocking.
moral, e, aux [mɔʀal, -o] *a* moral // *nm* morale // *nf* (*conduite*) morals *pl*; (*règles*) moral code, ethic; (*valeurs*) moral standards *pl*, morality; (*science*) ethics *sg*, moral philosophy; (*conclusion: d'une fable etc*) moral; **au ~, sur le plan ~** morally; **faire la ~e à** to lecture, preach at; **~isateur, trice** *a* moralizing, sanctimonious; **~iser** *vt* (*sermonner*) to lecture, preach at; **~iste** *nm/f* moralist // *a* moralistic; **~ité** *nf* morality; (*conduite*) morals *pl*; (*conclusion, enseignement*) moral.
morbide [mɔʀbid] *a* morbid.
morceau, x [mɔʀso] *nm* piece, bit; (*d'une œuvre*) passage, extract; (MUS) piece; (CULIN: *de viande*) cut; **mettre en ~x** to pull to pieces *ou* bits.
morceler [mɔʀsəle] *vt* to break up, divide up.
mordant, e [mɔʀdɑ̃, -ɑ̃t] *a* scathing, cutting; biting // *nm* spirit; bite, punch.
mordicus [mɔʀdikys] *ad* (*affirmer etc*) obstinately, stubbornly.
mordiller [mɔʀdije] *vt* to nibble at, chew at.
mordoré, e [mɔʀdɔʀe] *a* lustrous bronze.
mordre [mɔʀdʀ(ə)] *vt* to bite; (*suj: lime, vis*) to bite into // *vi* (*poisson*) to bite; **~ dans** (*fruit*) to bite into; **~ sur** (*fig*) to go over into, overlap into; **~ à l'hameçon** to bite, rise to the bait.
mordu, e [mɔʀdy] *pp de* **mordre** // *a* (*amoureux*) smitten // *nm/f*: **un ~ du jazz/de la voile** a jazz/sailing fanatic *ou* buff.
morfondre [mɔʀfɔ̃dʀ(ə)]: **se ~** *vi* to fret.
morgue [mɔʀg(ə)] *nf* (*arrogance*) haughtiness; (*lieu: de la police*) morgue; (*: à l'hôpital*) mortuary.
moribond, e [mɔʀibɔ̃, -ɔ̃d] *a* dying, moribund.
morille [mɔʀij] *nf* morel.
morne [mɔʀn(ə)] *a* dismal, dreary.
morose [mɔʀoz] *a* sullen, morose.
morphine [mɔʀfin] *nf* morphine; **morphinomane** *nm/f* morphine addict.
morphologie [mɔʀfɔlɔʒi] *nf* morphology.
mors [mɔʀ] *nm* bit.
morse [mɔʀs(ə)] *nm* (ZOOL) walrus; (TEL) Morse (code).
morsure [mɔʀsyʀ] *nf* bite.
mort [mɔʀ] *nf* death; **se donner la ~** to take one's life.
mort, e [mɔʀ, mɔʀt(ə)] *pp de* **mourir** // *a* dead // *nm/f* (*défunt*) dead man/woman; (*victime*): **il y a eu plusieurs ~s** several people were killed, there were several killed // *nm* (CARTES) dummy; **~ ou vif** dead or alive; **~ de peur/fatigue** frightened to death/dead tired.
mortadelle [mɔʀtadɛl] *nf* mortadella (*type of luncheon meat*).
mortalité [mɔʀtalite] *nf* mortality, death rate.
mortel, le [mɔʀtɛl] *a* (*poison etc*) deadly, lethal; (*accident, blessure*) fatal; (REL) mortal; (*fig*) deathly; deadly boring // *nm/f* mortal.
morte-saison [mɔʀtəsɛzɔ̃] *nf* slack *ou* off season.
mortier [mɔʀtje] *nm* (*gén*) mortar.

mortifier [mɔʀtifje] *vt* to mortify.
mort-né, e [mɔʀne] *a* (*enfant*) stillborn; (*fig*) abortive.
mortuaire [mɔʀtɥɛʀ] *a* funeral *cpd*; **avis ~s** death announcements, intimations; **chapelle ~** mortuary chapel; **couronne ~** (funeral) wreath; **domicile ~** house of the deceased; **drap ~** pall.
morue [mɔʀy] *nf* (ZOOL) cod *inv*; (CULIN: *salée*) salt-cod; **morutier** *nm* cod fisherman; cod fishing boat.
morveux, euse [mɔʀvø, -øz] *a* (*fam*) snotty-nosed.
mosaïque [mɔzaik] *nf* (ART) mosaic; (*fig*) patchwork.
Moscou [mɔsku] *n* Moscow; **moscovite** *a* of *ou* from Moscow // *nm/f* Muscovite.
mosquée [mɔske] *nf* mosque.
mot [mo] *nm* word; (*message*) line, note; (*bon mot etc*) saying; sally; **~ à ~** *a, ad* word for word; **~ pour ~** word for word, verbatim; **prendre qn au ~** to take sb at his word; **avoir son ~ à dire** to have a say; **~s croisés** crossword (puzzle) *sg*; **~ d'ordre** watchword; **~ de passe** password.
motard [mɔtaʀ] *nm* motorcycle cop.
motel [mɔtɛl] *nm* motel.
moteur, trice [mɔtœʀ, -tʀis] *a* (ANAT, PHYSIOL) motor; (*troubles*) motory; (TECH) driving; (AUTO): **à 4 roues motrices** 4-wheel drive // *nm* engine, motor; (*fig*) mover, mainspring; **à ~** power-driven, motor *cpd*; **~ à deux temps** two-stroke engine; **~ à explosion** internal combustion engine.
motif [mɔtif] *nm* (*cause*) motive; (*décoratif*) design, pattern, motif; (*d'un tableau*) subject, motif; (MUS) figure, motif; **~s** *nmpl* (JUR) grounds *pl*; **sans ~** *a* groundless.
motion [mosjɔ̃] *nf* motion; **~ de censure** motion of censure, vote of no confidence.
motivation [mɔtivɑsjɔ̃] *nf* motivation.
motivé, e [mɔtive] *a* (*acte*) justified; (*personne*) motivated.
motiver [mɔtive] *vt* (*justifier*) to justify, account for; (ADMIN, JUR, PSYCH) to motivate.
moto [mɔto] *nf* (motor)bike; **~-cross** *nm* motocross; **~cyclette** *nf* motorbike, motorcycle; **~cyclisme** *nm* motorcycle racing; **~cycliste** *nm/f* motorcyclist.
motorisé, e [mɔtɔʀize] *a* (*troupe*) motorized; (*personne*) having transport *ou* a car.
motrice [mɔtʀis] *a voir* **moteur**; **motricité** *nf* motor functions.
motte [mɔt] *nf*: **~ de terre** lump of earth, clod (of earth); **~ de gazon** turf, sod; **~ de beurre** lump of butter.
motus [mɔtys] *excl*: **~ (et bouche cousue)!** mum's the word!
mou(mol), molle [mu, mɔl] *a* soft; (*péj*) flabby; limp; sluggish; feeble // *nm* (*abats*) lights *pl*, lungs *pl*; (*de la corde*): **avoir du ~** to be slack.
mouchard, e [muʃaʀ, -aʀd(ə)] *nm/f* grass // *nm* (*appareil*) control device.
mouche [muʃ] *nf* fly; (ESCRIME) button; (*de taffetas*) patch; **prendre la ~** to take the huff; **faire ~** to score a bull's-eye.
moucher [muʃe] *vt* (*enfant*) to blow the nose of; (*chandelle*) to snuff (out); **se ~** *vi* to blow one's nose.
moucheron [muʃʀɔ̃] *nm* midge.
moucheté, e [muʃte] *a* dappled; flecked; (ESCRIME) buttoned.
mouchoir [muʃwaʀ] *nm* handkerchief, hanky; **~ en papier** tissue, paper hanky.
moudre [mudʀ(ə)] *vt* to grind.
moue [mu] *nf* pout; **faire la ~** to pout; (*fig*) to pull a face.
mouette [mwɛt] *nf* (sea)gull.
moufle [mufl(ə)] *nf* (*gant*) mitt(en); (TECH) pulley block.
mouflon [muflɔ̃] *nm* mouf(f)lon.
mouillage [mujaʒ] *nm* (NAVIG: *lieu*) anchorage, moorings *pl*.
mouillé, e [muje] *a* wet.
mouiller [muje] *vt* (*humecter*) to wet, moisten; (*tremper*): **~ qn/qch** to make sb/sth wet; (*couper, diluer*) to water down; (*mine etc*) to lay // *vi* (NAVIG) to lie *ou* be at anchor; **se ~** to get wet; (*fam*) to commit o.s.; to get o.s. involved; **~ l'ancre** to drop *ou* cast anchor; **mouillure** *nf* wet *q*; wet patch.
moulage [mulaʒ] *nm* moulding, casting; (*objet*) cast.
moule [mul] *nf* mussel // *nm* (*creux*, CULIN) mould; (*modèle plein*) cast; **~ à gâteaux** *nm* cake tin.
moulent *vb voir aussi* **moudre**.
mouler [mule] *vt* (*brique*) to mould; (*statue*) to cast; (*visage, bas-relief*) to make a cast of; (*lettre*) to shape with care; (*suj: vêtement*) to hug, fit closely round; **~ qch sur** (*fig*) to model sth on.
moulin [mulɛ̃] *nm* mill; (*fam*) engine; **~ à café/à poivre** coffee/pepper mill; **~ à légumes** (vegetable) shredder; **~ à paroles** (*fig*) chatterbox; **~ à prières** prayer wheel; **~ à vent** windmill.
moulinet [mulinɛ] *nm* (*de treuil*) winch; (*de canne à pêche*) reel; (*mouvement*): **faire des ~s avec qch** to whirl sth around.
moulinette [mulinɛt] *nf* (vegetable) shredder.
moulu, e [muly] *pp de* **moudre.**
moulure [mulyʀ] *nf* (*ornement*) moulding.
mourant, e [muʀɑ̃, -ɑ̃t] *a* dying // *nm/f* dying man/woman.
mourir [muʀiʀ] *vi* to die; (*civilisation*) to die out; **~ de froid/faim** to die of exposure/hunger; **~ de faim/d'ennui** (*fig*) to be starving/be bored to death; **~ d'envie de faire** to be dying to do.
mousquetaire [muskətɛʀ] *nm* musketeer.
mousqueton [muskətɔ̃] *nm* (*fusil*) carbine; (*anneau*) snap-link, karabiner.
mousse [mus] *nf* (BOT) moss; (*écume*: *sur eau, bière*) froth, foam; (: *shampooing*) lather; (CULIN) mousse // *nm* (NAVIG) ship's boy; **bain de ~** bubble bath; **bas ~** stretch stockings; **balle ~** rubber ball; **~ carbonique** (fire-fighting) foam; **~ de nylon** stretch nylon; foam; **~ à raser** shaving foam.
mousseline [muslin] *nf* muslin; chiffon; **pommes ~** creamed potatoes.
mousser [muse] *vi* to foam; to lather.

mousseux, euse [musø, -øz] *a* frothy // *nm*: **(vin)** ~ sparkling wine.
mousson [musɔ̃] *nf* monsoon.
moussu, e [musy] *a* mossy.
moustache [mustaʃ] *nf* moustache; ~**s** *nfpl* (*du chat*) whiskers *pl*; **moustachu, e** *a* wearing a moustache.
moustiquaire [mustikɛʀ] *nf* mosquito net (*ou* screen).
moustique [mustik] *nm* mosquito.
moutarde [mutaʀd(ə)] *nf* mustard.
mouton [mutɔ̃] *nm* (*ZOOL*, *péj*) sheep *inv*; (*peau*) sheepskin; (*CULIN*) mutton; ~**s** *nmpl* (*fig*) white horses; fluffy *ou* fleecy clouds; bits of fluff.
mouture [mutyʀ] *nf* grinding; (*péj*) rehash.
mouvant, e [muvɑ̃, -ɑ̃t] *a* unsettled; changing; shifting.
mouvement [muvmɑ̃] *nm* (*gén, aussi: mécanisme*) movement; (*fig*) activity; impulse; reaction; gesture; (*MUS: rythme*) tempo (*pl* s); **en** ~ in motion; on the move; **mettre qch en** ~ to set sth in motion, set sth going; ~ **d'humeur** fit *ou* burst of temper; ~ **d'opinion** trend of (public) opinion; **le** ~ **perpétuel** perpetual motion; **mouvementé, e** *a* (*vie, poursuite*) eventful; (*réunion*) turbulent.
mouvoir [muvwaʀ] *vt* (*levier, membre*) to move; (*machine*) to drive; **se** ~ to move.
moyen, ne [mwajɛ̃, -ɛn] *a* average; (*tailles, prix*) medium; (*de grandeur moyenne*) medium-sized // *nm* (*façon*) means *sg*, way // *nf* average; (*MATH*) mean; (*SCOL: à l'examen*) pass mark; (*AUTO*) average speed; ~**s** *nmpl* (*capacités*) means; **au** ~ **de** by means of; **y a-t-il** ~ **de ...?** is it possible to ...?, can one ...?; **par quel** ~**?** how?, which way?, by which means?; **par tous les** ~**s** by every possible means, every possible way; **employer les grands** ~**s** to resort to drastic measures; **par ses propres** ~**s** all by oneself; **en** ~**ne** on (an) average; ~ **de locomotion/d'expression** means of transport/expression; ~ **âge** Middle Ages; ~**ne d'âge** average age.
moyennant [mwajɛnɑ̃] *prép* (*somme*) for; (*service, conditions*) in return for; (*travail, effort*) with.
Moyen-Orient [mwajɛnɔʀjɑ̃] *nm*: **le** ~ the Middle East.
moyeu, x [mwajø] *nm* hub.
mû, mue [my] *pp de* **mouvoir.**
mucosité [mykozite] *nf* mucus *q*.
mucus [mykys] *nm* mucus *q*.
mue [my] *pp voir* **mouvoir** // *nf* moulting; sloughing; breaking of the voice.
muer [mɥe] *vi* (*oiseau, mammifère*) to moult; (*serpent*) to slough; (*jeune garçon*): **il mue** his voice is breaking; **se** ~ **en** to transform into.
muet, te [mɥɛ, -ɛt] *a* dumb; (*fig*): ~ **d'admiration** *etc* speechless with admiration *etc*; (*joie, douleur, CINÉMA*) silent; (*LING: lettre*) silent, mute; (*carte*) blank // *nm/f* mute.
mufle [myfl(ə)] *nm* muzzle; (*goujat*) boor // *a* boorish.
mugir [myʒiʀ] *vi* to bellow; to low; (*fig*) to howl.
muguet [mygɛ] *nm* lily of the valley.
mulâtre, tresse [mylɑtʀ(ə), -tʀɛs] *nm/f* mulatto.
mule [myl] *nf* (*ZOOL*) (she-)mule; ~**s** *nfpl* (*pantoufles*) mules.
mulet [mylɛ] *nm* (*ZOOL*) (he-)mule; **muletier, ière** *a*: **chemin muletier** mule track.
mulot [mylo] *nm* field mouse (*pl* mice).
multicolore [myltikɔlɔʀ] *a* multicoloured.
multinational, e, aux [myltinasjɔnal, -o] *a* multinational.
multiple [myltipl(ə)] *a* multiple, numerous; (*varié*) many, manifold // *nm* (*MATH*) multiple.
multiplicateur [myltiplikatœʀ] *nm* multiplier.
multiplication [myltiplikɑsjɔ̃] *nf* multiplication.
multiplicité [myltiplisite] *nf* multiplicity.
multiplier [myltiplije] *vt* to multiply; **se** ~ *vi* to multiply; to increase in number.
multitude [myltityd] *nf* multitude; mass; **une** ~ **de** a vast number of, a multitude of.
municipal, e, aux [mynisipal, -o] *a* municipal; town *cpd*, ≈ borough *cpd*.
municipalité [mynisipalite] *nf* (*corps municipal*) town council, corporation; (*commune*) town, municipality.
munir [myniʀ] *vt*: ~ **qn/qch de** to equip sb/sth with.
munitions [mynisjɔ̃] *nfpl* ammunition *sg*.
muqueuse [mykøz] *nf* mucous membrane.
mur [myʀ] *nm* wall; ~ **du son** sound barrier.
mûr, e [myʀ] *a* ripe; (*personne*) mature // *nf* blackberry; mulberry.
muraille [myʀɑj] *nf* (high) wall.
mural, e, aux [myʀal, -o] *a* wall *cpd*; mural.
mûrement [myʀmɑ̃] *ad*: **ayant** ~ **réfléchi** having given the matter much thought.
murène [myʀɛn] *nf* moray (eel).
murer [myʀe] *vt* (*enclos*) to wall (in); (*porte, issue*) to wall up; (*personne*) to wall up *ou* in.
muret [myʀɛ] *nm* low wall.
mûrier [myʀje] *nm* blackberry bush; mulberry tree.
mûrir [myʀiʀ] *vi* (*fruit, blé*) to ripen; (*abcès, furoncle*) to come to a head; (*fig: idée, personne*) to mature // *vt* to ripen; to (make) mature.
murmure [myʀmyʀ] *nm* murmur; ~**s** *nmpl* (*plaintes*) murmurings, mutterings; **murmurer** *vi* to murmur; (*se plaindre*) to mutter, grumble.
musaraigne [myzaʀɛɲ] *nf* shrew.
musarder [myzaʀde] *vi* to dawdle (along); to idle (about).
musc [mysk] *nm* musk.
muscade [myskad] *nf* nutmeg.
muscat [myska] *nm* muscat grape; muscatel (wine).
muscle [myskl(ə)] *nm* muscle; **musclé, e** *a* muscular; **musculation** *nf*: **exercices de musculation** muscle-developing exercises; **musculature** *nf* muscle structure, muscles *pl*.

museau, x [myzo] *nm* muzzle.
musée [myze] *nm* museum ; art gallery.
museler [myzle] *vt* to muzzle ; **muselière** *nf* muzzle.
musette [myzɛt] *nf* (*sac*) lunchbag // *a inv* (*orchestre etc*) accordion *cpd.*
muséum [myzeɔm] *nm* museum.
musical, e, aux [myzikal, -o] *a* musical.
music-hall [myzikol] *nm* variety theatre ; (*genre*) variety.
musicien, ne [myzisjɛ̃, -jɛn] *nm/f* musician.
musique [myzik] *nf* music ; (*fanfare*) band ; **faire de la ~** to make some music ; to play an instrument ; **~ de chambre** chamber music ; **~ de fond** background music.
musqué, e [myske] *a* musky.
musulman, e [myzylmɑ̃, -an] *a, nm/f* Moslem, Muslim.
mutation [mytɑsjɔ̃] *nf* (ADMIN) transfer ; (BIO) mutation.
muter [myte] *vt* (ADMIN) to transfer.
mutilation [mytilɑsjɔ̃] *nf* mutilation.
mutilé, e [mytile] *nm/f* disabled person (*through loss of limbs*).
mutiler [mytile] *vt* to mutilate, maim ; (*fig*) to mutilate, deface.
mutin, e [mytɛ̃, -in] *a* (*air, ton*) mischievous, impish // *nm/f* (MIL, NAVIG) mutineer.
mutiner [mytine]: **se ~** *vi* to mutiny ; **mutinerie** *nf* mutiny.
mutisme [mytism(ə)] *nm* silence.
mutuel, le [mytɥɛl] *a* mutual // *nf* mutual benefit society.
myocarde [mjɔkaʀd(ə)] *nm voir* **infarctus.**
myope [mjɔp] *a* short-sighted ; **myopie** *nf* short-sightedness, myopia.
myosotis [mjozɔtis] *nm* forget-me-not.
myriade [miʀjad] *nf* myriad.
myrtille [miʀtij] *nf* bilberry, whortleberry.
mystère [mistɛʀ] *nm* mystery ; **mystérieux, euse** *a* mysterious.
mysticisme [mistisism(ə)] *nm* mysticism.
mystification [mistifikɑsjɔ̃] *nf* hoax ; mystification.
mystifier [mistifje] *vt* to fool ; to mystify.
mystique [mistik] *a* mystic, mystical // *nm/f* mystic.
mythe [mit] *nm* myth ; **mythique** *a* mythical.
mythologie [mitɔlɔʒi] *nf* mythology ; **mythologique** *a* mythological.
mythomane [mitɔman] *nm/f* mythomaniac.

N

n' [n] *ad voir* **ne.**
nacelle [nasɛl] *nf* (*de ballon*) basket.
nacre [nakʀ(ə)] *nf* mother of pearl ; **nacré, e** *a* pearly.
nage [naʒ] *nf* swimming ; style of swimming, stroke ; **tra-verser/s'éloigner à la ~** to swim across/away ; **en ~** bathed in perspiration.
nageoire [naʒwaʀ] *nf* fin.
nager [naʒe] *vi* to swim ; **nageur, euse** *nm/f* swimmer.
naguère [nagɛʀ] *ad* formerly.
naïf, ïve [naif, naiv] *a* naïve.
nain, e [nɛ̃, nɛn] *nm/f* dwarf.
naissance [nɛsɑ̃s] *nf* birth ; **donner ~ à** to give birth to ; (*fig*) to give rise to ; **aveugle de ~** born blind ; **Français de ~** French by birth ; **à la ~ des cheveux** at the roots of the hair.
naissant, e [nɛsɑ̃, -ɑ̃t] *a* budding, incipient ; dawning.
naître [nɛtʀ(ə)] *vi* to be born ; (*conflit, complications*): **~ de** to arise from, be born out of ; **~ à** (*amour, poésie*) to awaken to ; **il est né en 1960** he was born in 1960 ; **il naît plus de filles que de garçons** there are more girls born than boys ; **faire ~** (*fig*) to give rise to, arouse.
naïveté [naivte] *nf* naïvety.
nantir [nɑ̃tiʀ] *vt*: **~ qn de** to provide sb with ; **les nantis** (*péj*) the well-to-do.
napalm [napalm] *nm* napalm.
nappe [nap] *nf* tablecloth ; (*fig*) sheet ; layer ; **~ron** *nm* table-mat.
naquit *etc vb voir* **naître.**
narcisse [naʀsis] *nm* narcissus.
narcissisme [naʀsisism(ə)] narcissism.
narcotique [naʀkɔtik] *a, nm* narcotic.
narguer [naʀge] *vt* to taunt.
narine [naʀin] *nf* nostril.
narquois, e [naʀkwa, -waz] *a* derisive, mocking.
narrateur, trice [naʀatœʀ, -tʀis] *nm/f* narrator.
narrer [naʀe] *vt* to tell the story of, recount.
nasal, e, aux [nazal, -o] *a* nasal.
naseau, x [nazo] *nm* nostril.
nasiller [nazije] *vi* to speak with a (nasal) twang.
nasse [nas] *nf* fish-trap.
natal, e [natal] *a* native.
nataliste [natalist(ə)] *a* supporting a rising birth rate.
natalité [natalite] *nf* birth rate.
natation [natɑsjɔ̃] *nf* swimming.
natif, ive [natif, -iv] *a* native.
nation [nɑsjɔ̃] *nf* nation ; **les N~s Unies** the United Nations.
national, e, aux [nasjɔnal, -o] *a* national // *nf*: **(route) ~e** trunk road, ≈ A road ; **obsèques ~es** state funeral ; **~iser** *vt* to nationalize ; **~isme** *nm* nationalism ; **~ité** *nf* nationality.
natte [nat] *nf* (*tapis*) mat ; (*cheveux*) plait.
naturaliser [natyʀalize] *vt* to naturalize.
naturaliste [natyʀalist(ə)] *nm/f* naturalist.
nature [natyʀ] *nf* nature // *a, ad* (CULIN) plain, without seasoning or sweetening ; (*café, thé*) black, without sugar ; **payer en ~** to pay in kind ; **peint d'après ~** painted from life ; **~ morte** still-life ; **naturel, le** *a* (*gén, aussi*: *enfant*) natural // *nm* naturalness ; disposition, nature ; (*autochtone*) native ; **naturellement** *ad* naturally ; (*bien sûr*) of course ; **naturisme** *nm* naturism ; **naturiste** *nm/f* naturist.
naufrage [nofʀaʒ] *nm* (ship)wreck ; (*fig*) wreck ; **faire ~** to be shipwrecked ;

naufragé, e *nm/f* shipwreck victim, castaway.
nauséabond, e [nozeabɔ̃, -ɔ̃d] *a* foul, nauseous.
nausée [noze] *nf* nausea.
nautique [notik] *a* nautical, water *cpd*.
nautisme [notism] *nm* water sports.
naval, e [naval] *a* naval.
navet [navɛ] *nm* turnip; (*péj*) third-rate film.
navette [navɛt] *nf* shuttle; (*en car etc*) shuttle (service); **faire la ~ (entre)** to go to and fro *ou* shuttle (between).
navigable [navigabl(ə)] *a* navigable.
navigateur [navigatœʀ] *nm* (NAVIG) seafarer, sailor; (AVIAT) navigator.
navigation [navigɑsjɔ̃] *nf* navigation, sailing; shipping.
naviguer [navige] *vi* to navigate, sail.
navire [naviʀ] *nm* ship.
navrer [navʀe] *vt* to upset, distress; **je suis navré** I'm so sorry.
N.B. *sigle* (= *nota bene*) NB.
ne, n' [n(ə)] *ad voir* **pas, plus, jamais** *etc*; (*explétif*) *non traduit*.
né, e [ne] *pp* (*voir* **naître**): **~ en 1960** born in 1960; **~e Scott** née Scott // *a*: **un comédien ~** a born comedian.
néanmoins [neɑ̃mwɛ̃] *ad* nevertheless, yet.
néant [neɑ̃] *nm* nothingness; **réduire à ~** to bring to nought; to dash.
nébuleux, euse [nebylø, -øz] *a* nebulous.
nébulosité [nebylozite] *nf* cloud cover; **~ variable** cloudy *ou* some cloud in places.
nécessaire [nesesɛʀ] *a* necessary // *nm* necessary; (*sac*) kit; **~ de couture** sewing kit; **~ de toilette** toilet bag; **nécessité** *nf* necessity; **nécessiter** *vt* to require; **nécessiteux, euse** *a* needy.
nec plus ultra [nekplysyltʀa] *nm*: **le ~ de** the last word in.
nécrologique [nekʀɔlɔʒik] *a*: **article ~** obituary; **rubrique ~** obituary column.
nécromancien, ne [nekʀɔmɑ̃sjɛ̃, -jɛn] *nm/f* necromancer.
nécrose [nekʀoz] *nf* necrosis.
néerlandais, e [neɛʀlɑ̃dɛ, -ɛz] *a* Dutch.
nef [nɛf] *nf* (*d'église*) nave.
néfaste [nefast(ə)] *a* baneful; ill-fated.
négatif, ive [negatif, iv] *a* negative // *nm* (PHOTO) negative.
négligé, e [negliʒe] *a* (*en désordre*) slovenly // *nm* (*tenue*) negligee.
négligence [negliʒɑ̃s] *nf* carelessness *q*; careless omission.
négligent, e [negliʒɑ̃, -ɑ̃t] *a* careless.
négliger [negliʒe] *vt* (*épouse, jardin*) to neglect; (*tenue*) to be careless about; (*avis, précautions*) to disregard; **~ de faire** to fail to do, not bother to do; **se ~** to neglect o.s.
négoce [negɔs] *nm* trade.
négociant [negɔsjɑ̃] *nm* merchant.
négociateur [negɔsjatœʀ] *nm* negotiator.
négociation [negɔsjɑsjɔ̃] *nf* negotiation.
négocier [negɔsje] *vi, vt* to negotiate.
nègre [nɛgʀ(ə)] *nm* Negro; hack(writer) // *a* Negro.
négresse [negʀɛs] *nf* Negro woman.
neige [nɛʒ] *nf* snow; **~ carbonique** dry ice; **neiger** *vi* to snow; **neigeux, euse** *a* snowy, snow-covered.
nénuphar [nenyfaʀ] *nm* water-lily.
néologisme [neɔlɔʒism(ə)] *nm* neologism.
néon [neɔ̃] *nm* neon.
néophyte [neɔfit] *nm/f* novice.
néo-zélandais, e [neɔzelɑ̃dɛ, -ɛz] *a* New Zealand *cpd* // *nm/f* New Zealander.
nerf [nɛʀ] *nm* nerve; (*fig*) vim, stamina; **nerveux, euse** *a* nervous; (*voiture*) nippy, responsive; (*tendineux*) sinewy; **nervosité** *nf* excitability; state of agitation; nervousness.
nervure [nɛʀvyʀ] *nf* vein; (ARCHIT, TECH) rib.
n'est-ce pas [nɛspɑ] *ad* isn't it?, won't you? *etc, selon le verbe qui précède*; **~ que c'est bon?** it's good, don't you think?
net, nette [nɛt] *a* (*sans équivoque, distinct*) clear; (*évident*) definite; (*propre*) neat, clean; (COMM: *prix, salaire*) net // *ad* (*refuser*) flatly; **s'arrêter ~** to stop dead; **la lame a cassé ~** the blade snapped clean through; **mettre au ~** to copy out, tidy up; **~teté** *nf* clearness.
nettoyage [nɛtwajaʒ] *nm* cleaning; **~ à sec** dry cleaning.
nettoyer [nɛtwaje] *vi* to clean; (*fig*) to clean out.
neuf [nœf] *num* nine.
neuf, neuve [nœf, nœv] *a* new // *nm*: **repeindre à ~** to redecorate; **remettre à ~** to do up (as good as new), refurbish.
neurasthénique [nøʀastenik] *a* neurasthenic.
neurologie [nøʀɔlɔʒi] *nf* neurology.
neutraliser [nøtʀalize] *vt* to neutralize.
neutralité [nøtʀalite] *nf* neutrality.
neutre [nøtʀ(ə)] *a* neutral; (LING) neuter // *nm* (LING) neuter.
neutron [nøtʀɔ̃] *nm* neutron.
neuve [nœv] *a voir* **neuf.**
neuvième [nœvjɛm] *num* ninth.
névé [neve] *nm* permanent snowpatch.
neveu, x [nəvø] *nm* nephew.
névralgie [nevʀalʒi] *nf* neuralgia.
névrite [nevʀit] *nf* neuritis.
névrose [nevʀoz] *nf* neurosis; **névrosé, e** *a, nm/f* neurotic.
nez [ne] *nm* nose; **~ à ~ avec** face to face with.
ni [ni] *cj*: **~ l'un ~ l'autre ne sont** neither one nor the other are; **il n'a rien dit ~ fait** he hasn't said or done anything.
niais, e [njɛ, -ɛz] *a* silly, thick.
niche [niʃ] *nf* (*du chien*) kennel; (*de mur*) recess, niche.
nichée [niʃe] *nf* brood, nest.
nicher [niʃe] *vi* to nest; **se ~ dans** to lodge o.s. in; to hide in.
nickel [nikɛl] *nm* nickel.
nicotine [nikɔtin] *nf* nicotine.
nid [ni] *nm* nest; **~ de poule** pothole.
nièce [njɛs] *nf* niece.
nième [ɛnjɛm] *a*: **la ~ fois** the nth time.
nier [nje] *vt* to deny.
nigaud, e [nigo, -od] *nm/f* booby, fool.

n'importe [nɛ̃pɔʀt(ə)] *ad*: ~ **qui/quoi/où** anybody/anything/ anywhere; ~ **quand** any time; ~ **quel** any; ~ **lequel/laquelle** any (one); ~ **comment** (*sans soin*) carelessly.
nippes [nip] *nfpl* togs.
nippon, e [nipõ, -on] *a* Japanese.
nique [nik] *nf*: **faire la ~ à** to thumb one's nose at (*fig*).
nitouche [nituʃ] *nf* (*péj*): **c'est une sainte ~** she looks as if butter wouldn't melt in her mouth, she's a little hypocrite.
nitrate [nitʀat] *nm* nitrate.
nitroglycérine [nitʀogliseʀin] *nf* nitroglycerin(e).
niveau, x [nivo] *nm* level; (*des élèves, études*) standard; **de ~ (avec)** level (with); **~ (à bulle)** spirit level; **le ~ de la mer** sea level; **~ de vie** standard of living.
niveler [nivle] *vt* to level; **nivellement** *nm* levelling.
nobiliaire [nɔbiljɛʀ] *a voir* **particule.**
noble [nɔbl(ə)] *a* noble // *nm/f* noble (man/woman); **noblesse** *nf* nobility; (*d'une action etc*) nobleness.
noce [nɔs] *nf* wedding; (*gens*) wedding party (*ou* guests *pl*); **faire la ~** (*fam*) to go on a binge; **~s d'or/d'argent** golden/silver wedding.
nocif, ive [nɔsif, -iv] *a* harmful, noxious.
noctambule [nɔktɑ̃byl] *nm* night-bird, late-nighter.
nocturne [nɔktyʀn(ə)] *a* nocturnal // *nf* (SPORT) floodlit fixture.
Noël [nɔɛl] *nm* Christmas.
nœud [nø] *nm* (*de corde, du bois,* NAVIG) knot; (*ruban*) bow; (*fig: liens*) bond, tie; **~ coulant** noose; **~ papillon** bow tie.
noir, e [nwaʀ] *a* black; (*obscur, sombre*) dark // *nm/f* black man/woman, Negro/Negro woman // *nm*: **dans le ~** in the dark // *nf* (MUS) crotchet; **~ceur** *nf* blackness; darkness; **~cir** *vt, vi* to blacken.
noise [nwaz] *nf*: **chercher ~ à** to try and pick a quarrel with.
noisetier [nwaztje] *nm* hazel.
noisette [nwazɛt] *nf* hazelnut.
noix [nwa] *nf* walnut; (*fam*) twit; (CULIN): **une ~ de beurre** a knob of butter; **à la ~** (*fam*) worthless; **~ de cajou** cashew nut; **~ de coco** coconut; **~ muscade** nutmeg.
nom [nɔ̃] *nm* name; (LING) noun; **~ commun/propre** common/proper noun; **~ d'emprunt** assumed name; **~ de famille** surname; **~ de jeune fille** maiden name.
nomade [nɔmad] *a* nomadic // *nm/f* nomad.
nombre [nɔ̃bʀ(ə)] *nm* number; **venir en ~** to come in large numbers; **depuis ~ d'années** for many years; **ils sont au ~ de 3** there are 3 of them; **au ~ de mes amis** among my friends; **~ premier/entier** prime/whole number.
nombreux, euse [nɔ̃bʀø, -øz] *a* many, numerous; (*avec nom sg: foule etc*) large; **peu ~** few; small.
nombril [nɔ̃bʀi] *nm* navel.
nomenclature [nɔmɑ̃klatyʀ] *nf* wordlist; list of items.
nominal, e, aux [nɔminal, -o] *a* nominal.
nominatif [nɔminatif] *nm* nominative.
nomination [nɔminɑsjɔ̃] *nf* nomination.
nommément [nɔmemɑ̃] *ad* (*désigner*) by name.
nommer [nɔme] *vt* (*baptiser*) to name, give a name to; (*qualifier*) to call; (*mentionner*) to name, give the name of; (*élire*) to appoint, nominate; **se ~** : **il se nomme Pascal** his name's Pascal, he's called Pascal.
non [nɔ̃] *ad* (*réponse*) no; (*avec loin, sans, seulement*) not; **~ que** not that; **~ plus : moi ~ plus** neither do I, I don't either.
nonagénaire [nɔnaʒenɛʀ] *nm/f* man/woman in his/her nineties.
non-alcoolisé, e [nɔnalkɔlize] *a* non-alcoholic.
nonchalance [nɔ̃ʃalɑ̃s] *nf* nonchalance, casualness.
non-fumeur [nɔ̃fymœʀ] *nm* non-smoker.
non-lieu [nɔ̃ljø] *nm*: **il y a eu ~** the case was dismissed.
nonne [nɔn] *nf* nun.
nonobstant [nɔnɔpstɑ̃] *prép* notwithstanding.
non-sens [nɔ̃sɑ̃s] *nm* absurdity.
nord [nɔʀ] *nm* North // *a* northern; north; **~-africain, e** *a, nm/f* North-African; **~-est** *nm* North-East; **nordique** *a* nordic, northern European; **~-ouest** *nm* North-West.
normal, e, aux [nɔʀmal, -o] *a* normal // *nf*: **la ~e** the norm, the average; **~ement** *ad* normally; **~iser** *vi* (COMM, TECH) to standardize; (POL) to normalize.
normand, e [nɔʀmɑ̃, -ɑ̃d] *a* of Normandy.
Normandie [nɔʀmɑ̃di] *nf* Normandy.
norme [nɔʀm(ə)] *nf* norm; (TECH) standard.
Norvège [nɔʀvɛʒ] *nf* Norway; **norvégien, ne** *a, nm, nf* Norwegian.
nos [no] *dét voir* **notre.**
nostalgie [nɔstalʒi] *nf* nostalgia.
notable [nɔtabl(ə)] *a* notable, noteworthy; (*marqué*) noticeable, marked // *nm* prominent citizen.
notaire [nɔtɛʀ] *nm* notary; solicitor.
notamment [nɔtamɑ̃] *ad* in particular, among others.
notarié, e [nɔtaʀje] *a*: **acte ~** deed drawn up by a notary.
note [nɔt] *nf* (*écrite,* MUS) note; (SCOL) mark; (*facture*) bill; **prendre ~ de** to write down; to note; **~ de service** memorandum.
noté, e [nɔte] *a*: **être bien/mal ~** (*employé etc*) to have a good/bad record.
noter [nɔte] *vt* (*écrire*) to write down; (*remarquer*) to note, notice.
notice [nɔtis] *nf* summary, short article; (*brochure*) leaflet, instruction book.
notifier [nɔtifje] *vt*: **~ qch à qn** to notify sb of sth, notify sth to sb.
notion [nosjɔ̃] *nf* notion, idea.
notoire [nɔtwaʀ] *a* widely known; (*en mal*) notorious; **le fait est ~** *ou* **de notoriété publique** the fact is common knowledge.

notre, nos [nɔtʀ(ə), no] *dét* our.
nôtre [notʀ(ə)] *pronom*: **le/la ~** ours; **les ~s** ours; (*alliés etc*) our own people; **soyez des ~s** join us // *a* ours.
nouer [nwe] *vt* to tie, knot; (*fig: alliance etc*) to strike up; **sa gorge se noua** a lump came to her throat.
noueux, euse [nwø, -øz] *a* gnarled.
nougat [nuga] *nm* nougat.
nouilles [nuj] *nfpl* noodles; pasta *sg*.
nourri, e [nuʀi] *a* (*feu etc*) sustained.
nourrice [nuʀis] *nf* wet-nurse.
nourrir [nuʀiʀ] *vt* to feed; (*fig: espoir*) to harbour, nurse; **logé nourri** with board and lodging; **~ au sein** to breast-feed; **nourrissant, e** *a* nourishing, nutritious.
nourrisson [nuʀisɔ̃] *nm* (unweaned) infant.
nourriture [nuʀityʀ] *nf* food.
nous [nu] *pronom* (*sujet*) we; (*objet*) us; **~-mêmes** ourselves.
nouveau(nouvel), elle, x [nuvo, -ɛl] *a* new // *nm/f* new pupil (*ou* employee) // *nf* (piece of) news *sg*; (LITTÉRATURE) short story; **de ~, à ~** again; **je suis sans nouvelles de lui** I haven't heard from him; **~ venu, nouvelle venue** *nm/f* newcomer; **Nouvel An** New Year; **~-né, e** *nm/f* newborn baby; **Nouvelle-Zélande** *nf* New Zealand; **~té** *nf* novelty; (COMM) new film (*ou* book *ou* creation *etc*).
nouvel *am*, **nouvelle** *af*, *nf* [nuvɛl] *voir* **nouveau.**
novateur, trice [nɔvatœʀ, -tʀis] *nm/f* innovator.
novembre [nɔvɑ̃bʀ(ə)] *nm* November.
novice [nɔvis] *a* inexperienced // *nm/f* novice.
noyade [nwajad] *nf* drowning *q*.
noyau, x [nwajo] *nm* (*de fruit*) stone; (BIO, PHYSIQUE) nucleus; (ÉLEC, GÉO, *fig: centre*) core; **~ter** *vt* (POL) to infiltrate
noyé, e [nwaje] *nm/f* drowning (*ou* drowned) man/woman.
noyer [nwaje] *nm* walnut (tree); (*bois*) walnut // *vt* to drown; (*fig*) to flood; to submerge; **se ~** to be drowned, drown; (*suicide*) to drown o.s.
nu, e [ny] *a* naked; (*membres*) naked, bare; (*chambre, fil, plaine*) bare // *nm* (ART) nude; **le ~ intégral** total nudity; **~-pieds** barefoot; **~-tête,** bareheaded; **à mains ~es** with one's bare hands; **se mettre ~** to strip; **mettre à ~** to bare.
nuage [nɥaʒ] *nm* cloud; **nuageux, euse** *a* cloudy.
nuance [nɥɑ̃s] *nf* (*de couleur, sens*) shade; **il y a une ~ (entre)** there's a slight difference (between); **une ~ de tristesse** a tinge of sadness; **nuancer** *vt* (*opinion*) to bring some reservations *ou* qualifications to.
nubile [nybil] *a* nubile.
nucléaire [nykleɛʀ] *a* nuclear.
nudisme [nydism] *nm* nudism; **nudiste** *nm/f* nudist.
nudité [nydite] *nf* nudity, nakedness; bareness.
nuée [nɥe] *nf*: **une ~ de** a cloud *ou* host *ou* swarm of.
nues [ny] *nfpl*: **tomber des ~** to be taken aback; **porter qn aux ~** to praise sb to the skies.
nuire [nɥiʀ] *vi* to be harmful; **~ à** to harm, do damage to; **nuisible** *a* harmful; **animal nuisible** pest.
nuit [nɥi] *nf* night; **il fait ~** it's dark; **cette ~** last night; tonight; **~ blanche** sleepless night; **~ de noces** wedding night; **nuitamment** *ad* by night; **nuitées** *nfpl* overnight stays, beds occupied (*in statistics*).
nul, nulle [nyl] *a* (*aucun*) no; (*minime*) nil, non-existent; (*non valable*) null; (*péj*) useless, hopeless // *pronom* none, no one; **résultat ~, match ~** draw; **~le part** *ad* nowhere; **~lement** *ad* by no means; **~lité** *nf* nullity; hopelessness; hopeless individual, nonentity.
numéraire [nymeʀɛʀ] *nm* cash; metal currency.
numération [nymeʀɑsjɔ̃] *nf*: **~ décimale/binaire** decimal/binary notation.
numérique [nymeʀik] *a* numerical.
numéro [nymeʀo] *nm* number; (*spectacle*) act, turn; **~ter** *vt* to number.
numismate [nymismat] *nm/f* numismatist, coin collector.
nuptial, e, aux [nypsjal, -o] *a* nuptial; wedding *cpd*.
nuque [nyk] *nf* nape of the neck.
nutritif, ive [nytʀitif, -iv] *a* nutritional; (*aliment*) nutritious.
nylon [nilɔ̃] *nm* nylon.
nymphomane [nɛ̃fɔman] *nf* nymphomaniac.

O

oasis [ɔazis] *nf* oasis (*pl* oases).
obédience [ɔbedjɑ̃s] *nf* allegiance.
obéir [ɔbeiʀ] *vi* to obey; **~ à** to obey; (*suj: moteur, véhicule*) to respond to; **obéissance** *nf* obedience; **obéissant, e** *a* obedient.
obélisque [ɔbelisk(ə)] *nm* obelisk.
obèse [ɔbɛz] *a* obese; **obésité** *nf* obesity.
objecter [ɔbʒɛkte] *vt* (*prétexter*) to plead, put forward as an excuse; **~ qch à** (*argument*) to put forward sth against; **~ (à qn) que** to object (to sb) that.
objecteur [ɔbʒɛktœʀ] *nm*: **~ de conscience** conscientious objector.
objectif, ive [ɔbʒɛktif, -iv] *a* objective // *nm* (OPTIQUE, PHOTO) lens *sg*, objective; (MIL, *fig*) objective; **~ à focale variable** zoom lens.
objection [ɔbʒɛksjɔ̃] *nf* objection; **~ de conscience** conscientious objection.
objectivité [ɔbʒɛktivite] *nf* objectivity.
objet [ɔbʒɛ] *nm* object; (*d'une discussion, recherche*) subject; **être** *ou* **faire l'~ de** (*discussion*) to be the subject of; (*soins*) to be given *ou* shown; **sans ~** *a* purposeless; groundless; **~ d'art** objet d'art; **~s personnels** personal items; **~s de toilette** toilet requisites; **~s trouvés** lost property *sg*.
objurgations [ɔbʒyʀgɑsjɔ̃] *nfpl* objurgations; entreaties.
obligation [ɔbligɑsjɔ̃] *nf* obligation; (COMM) bond, debenture; **être dans l'~ de**

faire to be obliged to do; **avoir l'~ de faire** to be under an obligation to do; **obligatoire** *a* compulsory, obligatory.
obligé, e [ɔbliʒe] *a* (*redevable*): **être très ~ à qn** to be most obliged to sb; **obligeance** *nf*: **avoir l'obligeance de** to be kind *ou* good enough to; **obligeant, e** *a* obliging; kind.
obliger [ɔbliʒe] *vt* (*contraindre*): **~ qn à faire** to force *ou* oblige sb to do; (*JUR*: *engager*) to bind; (*rendre service à*) to oblige; **je suis bien obligé** I have to.
oblique [ɔblik] *a* oblique; **regard ~** sidelong glance; **en ~** *ad* diagonally; **obliquer** *vi*: **obliquer vers** to turn off towards.
oblitération [ɔbliteʀɑsjɔ̃] *nf* cancelling *q*, cancellation.
oblitérer [ɔbliteʀe] *vt* (*timbre-poste*) to cancel.
oblong, oblongue [ɔblɔ̃, -ɔ̃g] *a* oblong.
obnubiler [ɔbnybile] *vt* to obsess.
obole [ɔbɔl] *nf* offering.
obscène [ɔpsɛn] *a* obscene; **obscénité** *nf* obscenity.
obscur, e [ɔpskyʀ] *a* dark; (*fig*) obscure; vague; humble, lowly; **~cir** *vt* to darken; (*fig*) to obscure; **s'~cir** *vi* to grow dark; **~ité** *nf* darkness; **dans l'~ité** in the dark, in darkness.
obsédé, e [ɔpsede] *nm/f*: **~(e) sexuel(le)** sex maniac.
obséder [ɔpsede] *vt* to obsess, haunt.
obsèques [ɔpsɛk] *nfpl* funeral *sg*.
obséquieux, euse [ɔpsekjø, -øz] *a* obsequious.
observateur, trice [ɔpsɛʀvatœʀ, -tʀis] *a* observant, perceptive // *nm/f* observer.
observation [ɔpsɛʀvɑsjɔ̃] *nf* observation; (*d'un règlement etc*) observance; (*commentaire*) observation, remark; (*reproche*) reproof; **en ~** (*MÉD*) under observation.
observatoire [ɔpsɛʀvatwaʀ] *nm* observatory; (*lieu élevé*) observation post, vantage point.
observer [ɔpsɛʀve] *vt* (*regarder*) to observe, watch; (*examiner*) to examine; (*scientifiquement, aussi: règlement, jeûne etc*) to observe; (*surveiller*) to watch; (*remarquer*) to observe, notice; **faire ~ qch à qn** (*dire*) to point out sth to sb.
obsession [ɔpsesjɔ̃] *nf* obsession; **avoir l'~ de** to have an obsession with.
obstacle [ɔpstakl(ə)] *nm* obstacle; (*ÉQUITATION*) jump, hurdle; **faire ~ à** (*lumière*) to block out; (*projet*) to hinder, put obstacles in the path of; **~s antichars** tank defences.
obstétrique [ɔpstetʀik] *nf* obstetrics *sg*.
obstination [ɔpstinɑsjɔ̃] *nf* obstinacy.
obstiné, e [ɔpstine] *a* obstinate.
obstiner [ɔpstine]: **s'~** *vi* to insist, dig one's heels in; **s'~ à faire** to persist (obstinately) in doing; **s'~ sur qch** to keep working at sth, labour away at sth.
obstruction [ɔpstʀyksjɔ̃] *nf* obstruction, blockage; (*SPORT*) obstruction; **faire de l'~** (*fig*) to be obstructive.
obstruer [ɔpstʀye] *vt* to block, obstruct; **s'~** *vi* to become blocked.
obtempérer [ɔptɑ̃peʀe] *vi* to obey; **~ à** to obey, comply with.
obtenir [ɔptəniʀ] *vt* to obtain, get; (*total, résultat*) to arrive at, reach; to achieve, obtain; **~ de pouvoir faire** to obtain permission to do; **~ de qn qu'il fasse** to get sb to agree to do; **obtention** *nf* obtaining.
obturateur [ɔptyʀatœʀ] *nm* (*PHOTO*) shutter; **~ à rideau** focal plane shutter.
obturation [ɔptyʀɑsjɔ̃] *nf* closing (up); **~ (dentaire)** filling; **vitesse d'~** (*PHOTO*) shutter speed.
obturer [ɔptyʀe] *vt* to close (up); (*dent*) to fill.
obtus, e [ɔpty, -yz] *a* obtuse.
obus [ɔby] *nm* shell.
obvier [ɔbvje]: **~ à** *vt* to obviate.
O.C. *sigle voir* **onde**.
occasion [ɔkɑzjɔ̃] *nf* (*aubaine, possibilité*) opportunity; (*circonstance*) occasion; (*COMM*: *article non neuf*) secondhand buy; (: *acquisition avantageuse*) bargain; **à plusieurs ~s** on several occasions; **avoir l'~ de faire** to have the opportunity to do; **être l'~ de** to occasion, give rise to; **à l'~** *ad* sometimes, on occasions; some time; **d'~** *a, ad* secondhand; **occasionnel, le** *a* (*fortuit*) chance *cpd*: (*non régulier*) occasional; casual.
occasionner [ɔkazjɔne] *vt* to cause, bring about; **~ qch à qn** to cause sb sth.
occident [ɔksidɑ̃] *nm*: **l'~** the west; **occidental, e, aux** western; (*POL*) Western // *nm/f* Westerner.
occiput [ɔksipyt] *nm* back of the head, occiput.
occire [ɔksiʀ] *vt* to slay.
occitan, e [ɔksitɑ̃, -an] *a* of the langue d'oc, of Provençal French.
occlusion [ɔklyzjɔ̃] *nf*: **~ intestinale** obstruction of the bowels.
occulte [ɔkylt(ə)] *a* occult, supernatural.
occulter [ɔkylte] *vt* (*fig*) to overshadow.
occupant, e [ɔkypɑ̃, -ɑ̃t] *a* occupying // *nm/f* (*d'un appartement*) occupier, occupant // *nm* (*MIL*) occupying forces *pl*; (*POL*: *d'usine etc*) occupier.
occupation [ɔkypɑsjɔ̃] *nf* occupation.
occupé, e [ɔkype] *a* (*MIL, POL*) occupied; (*personne*: *affairé, pris*) busy; (*place, sièges*) taken; (*toilettes, ligne*) engaged.
occuper [ɔkype] *vt* to occupy; (*main-d'œuvre*) to employ; **s'~** to occupy o.s., keep o.s. busy; **s'~ de** (*être responsable de*) to be in charge of; (*se charger de*: *affaire*) to take charge of, deal with; (: *clients etc*) to attend to; (*s'intéresser à, pratiquer*) to be involved in; **ça occupe trop de place** it takes up too much room.
occurrence [ɔkyʀɑ̃s] *nf*: **en l'~** in this case.
océan [ɔseɑ̃] *nm* ocean; **l'~ Indien** the Indian Ocean; **l'Océanie** *nf* Oceania; **océanique** *a* oceanic; **océanographie** *nf* oceanography.
ocelot [ɔslo] *nm* ocelot; (*fourrure*) ocelot fur.
ocre [ɔkʀ(ə)] *a inv* ochre.
octane [ɔktan] *nm* octane.

octave [ɔktav] *nf* octave.
octobre [ɔktɔbʀ(ə)] *nm* October.
octogénaire [ɔktɔʒenɛʀ] *a, nm/f* octogenarian.
octogone [ɔktɔgɔn] *nm* octagon.
octroi [ɔktʀwa] *nm* granting.
octroyer [ɔktʀwaje] *vt*: ~ **qch à qn** to grant sth to sb, grant sb sth.
oculaire [ɔkylɛʀ] *a* ocular, eye *cpd* // *nm* (*de microscope*) eyepiece.
oculiste [ɔkylist(ə)] *nm/f* eye specialist, oculist.
ode [ɔd] *nf* ode.
odeur [ɔdœʀ] *nf* smell.
odieux, euse [ɔdjø, -øz] *a* odious, hateful.
odorant, e [ɔdɔʀɑ̃, -ɑ̃t] *a* sweet-smelling, fragrant.
odorat [ɔdɔʀa] *nm* (sense of) smell.
odoriférant, e [ɔdɔʀifeʀɑ̃, -ɑ̃t] *a* sweet-smelling, fragrant.
odyssée [ɔdise] *nf* odyssey.
œcuménique [ekymenik] *a* oecumenical.
œil [œj], *pl* **yeux** [jø] *nm* eye; **à l'~** (*fam*) for free; **à l'~ nu** with the naked eye; **tenir qn à l'~** to keep an eye *ou* a watch on sb; **avoir l'~ à** to keep an eye on; **faire de l'~ à qn** to make eyes at sb; **à l'~ vif** with a lively expression; **fermer les yeux (sur)** (*fig*) to turn a blind eye (to); **fermer l'~** to get a moment's sleep; ~ **de verre** glass eye.
œillade [œjad] *nf*: **lancer une ~ à qn** to wink at sb, give sb a wink; **faire des ~s à** to make eyes at.
œillères [œjɛʀ] *nfpl* blinkers.
œillet [œjɛ] *nm* (BOT) carnation; (*trou*) eyelet.
œnologue [enɔlɔg] *nm/f* oenologist, wine expert.
œsophage [ezɔfaʒ] *nm* oesophagus.
œuf [œf, *pl* ø] *nm* egg; **étouffer dans l'~** to nip in the bud; ~ **à la coque/dur** boiled/hard-boiled egg; ~ **au plat** fried egg; ~**s brouillés** scrambled eggs; ~ **de Pâques** Easter egg; ~ **à repriser** darning egg.
œuvre [œvʀ(ə)] *nf* (*tâche*) task, undertaking; (*ouvrage achevé, livre, tableau etc*) work; (*ensemble de la production artistique*) works *pl*; (*organisation charitable*) charity // *nm* (*d'un artiste*) works *pl*; (CONSTR): **le gros ~** the shell; **être à l'~** to be at work; **mettre en ~** (*moyens*) to make use of; ~ **d'art** work of art.
offense [ɔfɑ̃s] *nf* insult; (REL: *péché*) transgression, trespass.
offenser [ɔfɑ̃se] *vt* to offend, hurt; (*principes, Dieu*) to offend against; **s'~ de** to take offence at.
offensif, ive [ɔfɑ̃sif, -iv] *a, nf* offensive; **passer à l'offensive** to go into the attack *ou* offensive.
offert, e [ɔfɛʀ, -ɛʀt(ə)] *pp de* **offrir**.
offertoire [ɔfɛʀtwaʀ] *nm* offertory.
office [ɔfis] *nm* (*charge*) office; (*agence*) bureau, agency; (REL) service // *nm ou nf* (*pièce*) pantry; **faire ~ de** to act as; to do duty as; **d'~** *ad* automatically; **bons ~s** (POL) good offices; ~ **du tourisme** tourist bureau.
officialiser [ɔfisjalize] *vt* to make official.
officiel, le [ɔfisjɛl] *a, nm/f* official.
officier [ɔfisje] *nm* officer // *vi* to officiate; ~ **de l'état-civil** registrar; ~ **ministériel** member of the legal profession; ~ **de police** ≈ police officer.
officieux, euse [ɔfisjø, -øz] *a* unofficial.
officinal, e, aux [ɔfisinal, -o] *a*: **plantes ~es** medicinal plants.
officine [ɔfisin] *nf* (*de pharmacie*) dispensary; (*pharmacie*) pharmacy; (*gén péj*: *bureau*) agency, office.
offrande [ɔfʀɑ̃d] *nf* offering.
offrant [ɔfʀɑ̃] *nm*: **au plus ~** to the highest bidder.
offre [ɔfʀ(ə)] *nf* offer; (*aux enchères*) bid; (ADMIN: *soumission*) tender; (ÉCON): **l'~** supply; ~ **d'emploi** job advertised; **'~s d'emploi'** situations vacant; ~ **publique d'achat (O.P.A.)** takeover bid; ~**s de service** offer of service.
offrir [ɔfʀiʀ] *vt* to offer; (*faire cadeau de*): ~ **(à qn)** to give (to sb); **s'~** *vi* (*occasion, paysage*) to present itself // *vt* (*vacances, voiture*) to treat o.s. to; ~ **(à qn) de faire qch** to offer to do sth (for sb); ~ **à boire à qn** to offer sb a drink; **s'~ comme guide/en otage** to offer one's services as (a) guide/offer o.s. as hostage; **s'~ aux regards** (*suj*: *personne*) to expose o.s. to the public gaze.
offset [ɔfsɛt] *nm* offset (printing).
offusquer [ɔfyske] *vt* to offend; **s'~ de** to take offence at, be offended by.
ogive [ɔʒiv] *nf* (ARCHIT) diagonal rib; (*d'obus, de missile*) nose cone; **voûte en ~** rib vault; **arc en ~** lancet arch; ~ **nucléaire** nuclear warhead.
ogre [ɔgʀ(ə)] *nm* ogre.
oie [wa] *nf* (ZOOL) goose (*pl* geese).
oignon [ɔɲɔ̃] *nm* (BOT, CULIN) onion; (*de tulipe etc*: *bulbe*) bulb; (MÉD) bunion; **petits ~s** pickling onions.
oindre [wɛ̃dʀ(ə)] *vt* to anoint.
oiseau, x [wazo] *nm* bird; ~ **de proie** bird of prey; ~**-mouche** *nm* hummingbird.
oisellerie [wazɛlʀi] *nf* bird shop.
oiseux, euse [wazø, -øz] *a* pointless; trivial.
oisif, ive [wazif, -iv] *a* idle // *nm/f* (*péj*) man/woman of leisure; **oisiveté** *nf* idleness.
O.K. [okɛ] *excl* O.K., all right.
oléagineux, euse [ɔleaʒinø, -øz] *a* oleaginous, oil-producing.
oléoduc [ɔleɔdyk] *nm* (oil) pipeline.
olfactif, ive [ɔlfaktif, -iv] *a* olfactory.
oligarchie [ɔligaʀʃi] *nf* oligarchy.
olivâtre [ɔlivɑtʀ(ə)] *a* olive-greenish; (*teint*) sallow.
olive [ɔliv] *nf* (BOT) olive // *a inv* olive(-green); ~**raie** *nf* olive grove; **olivier** *nm* olive tree; (*bois*) olive wood.
olympiade [ɔlɛ̃pjad] *nf* (*période*) Olympiad; **les ~s** (*jeux*) the Olympiad *sg*.
olympien, ne [ɔlɛ̃pjɛ̃, -jɛn] *a* Olympian, of Olympian aloofness.
olympique [ɔlɛ̃pik] *a* Olympic.
ombilical, e, aux [ɔ̃bilikal, -o] *a* umbilical.

ombrage [ɔ̃bʀaʒ] *nm* (*ombre*) (leafy) shade; (*fig*): **prendre ~ de** to take umbrage *ou* offence at; **ombragé, e** *a* shaded, shady; **ombrageux, euse** *a* (*cheval*) skittish, nervous; (*personne*) touchy, easily offended.

ombre [ɔ̃bʀ(ə)] *nf* (*espace non ensoleillé*) shade; (*ombre portée, tache*) shadow; **à l'~** in the shade; (*fam*) behind bars; **à l'~ de** in the shade of; (*tout près de, fig*) in the shadow of; **tu me fais de l'~** you're in my light; **ça nous donne de l'~** it gives us (some) shade; **vivre dans l'~** (*fig*) to live in obscurity; **laisser dans l'~** (*fig*) to leave in the dark; **~ à paupières** eyeshadow; **~ portée** shadow; **~s chinoises** (*spectacle*) shadow show *sg*.

ombrelle [ɔ̃bʀɛl] *nf* parasol, sunshade.

omelette [ɔmlɛt] *nf* omelette; **~ au fromage/au jambon** cheese/ham omelette; **~ aux herbes** omelette with herbs.

omettre [ɔmɛtʀ(ə)] *vt* to omit, leave out; **~ de faire** to fail *ou* omit to do; **omission** *nf* omission.

omni... [ɔmni] *préfixe*: **~bus** *nm* slow *ou* stopping train; **~potent, e** *a* omnipotent; **~scient, e** *a* omniscient; **~vore** *a* omnivorous.

omoplate [ɔmɔplat] *nf* shoulder blade.

O.M.S. *sigle f voir* **organisation**.

on [ɔ̃] *pronom* (*indéterminé*): **~ peut le faire ainsi** you *ou* one can do it like this, it can be done like this; (*quelqu'un*): **~ les a attaqués** they were attacked; (*nous*): **~ va y aller demain** we're going tomorrow; (*les gens*): **autrefois, ~ croyait aux fantômes** they used to believe in ghosts years ago; **~ vous demande au téléphone** there's a phone call for you, there's somebody on the phone for you; **~ ne peut plus** *ad*: **~ ne peut plus stupide** as stupid as can be.

oncle [ɔ̃kl(ə)] *nm* uncle.

onctueux, euse [ɔ̃ktɥø, -øz] *a* creamy, smooth; (*fig*) smooth, unctuous.

onde [ɔ̃d] *nf* (PHYSIQUE) wave; **sur l'~** on the waters; **sur les ~s** on the radio; **mettre en ~s** to produce for the radio; **sur ~s courtes (o.c.)** on short wave *sg*; **moyennes/ longues ~s** medium/long wave *sg*.

ondée [ɔ̃de] *nf* shower.

on-dit [ɔ̃di] *nm inv* rumour.

ondoyer [ɔ̃dwaje] *vi* to ripple, wave.

ondulant, e [ɔ̃dylɑ̃, -ɑ̃t] *a* swaying; undulating.

ondulation [ɔ̃dylɑsjɔ̃] *nf* undulation.

onduler [ɔ̃dyle] *vi* to undulate; (*cheveux*) to wave.

onéreux, euse [ɔneʀø, -øz] *a* costly; **à titre ~** in return for payment.

ongle [ɔ̃gl(ə)] *nm* (ANAT) nail; **se faire les ~s** to do one's nails.

onglet [ɔ̃glɛ] *nm* (*rainure*) (thumbnail) groove; (*bande de papier*) tab.

onguent [ɔ̃gɑ̃] *nm* ointment.

onomatopée [ɔnɔmatɔpe] *nf* onomatopoeia.

ont *vb voir* **avoir**.

O.N.U. [ony] *sigle f voir* **organisation**.

onyx [ɔniks] *nm* onyx.

onze [ɔ̃z] *num* eleven; **onzième** *num* eleventh.

O.P.A. *sigle f voir* **offre**.

opacité [ɔpasite] *nf* opaqueness.

opale [ɔpal] *nf* opal.

opalin, e [ɔpalɛ̃, -in] *a, nf* opaline.

opaque [ɔpak] *a* opaque.

O.P.E.P. [ɔpɛp] *sigle f* (= *organisation des pays exportateurs de pétrole*) O.P.E.C. (organization of petroleum exporting countries).

opéra [ɔpeʀa] *nm* opera; (*édifice*) opera house; **~-comique** *nm* light opera, opéra comique.

opérateur, trice [ɔpeʀatœʀ, -tʀis] *nm/f* operator; **~ (de prise de vues)** cameraman.

opération [ɔpeʀɑsjɔ̃] *nf* operation; (COMM) dealing.

opératoire [ɔpeʀatwaʀ] *a* operating; (*choc etc*) post-operative.

opéré, e [ɔpeʀe] *nm/f* patient (*having undergone an operation*).

opérer [ɔpeʀe] *vt* (MÉD) to operate on; (*faire, exécuter*) to carry out, make // *vi* (*remède: faire effet*) to act, work; (*procéder*) to proceed; (MÉD) to operate; **s'~** *vi* (*avoir lieu*) to occur, take place; **se faire ~** to have an operation; **se faire ~ des amygdales/du cœur** to have one's tonsils out/have a heart operation.

opérette [ɔpeʀɛt] *nf* operetta, light opera.

ophtalmologie [ɔftalmɔlɔʒi] *nf* ophthalmology; **ophtalmologue** *nm/f* ophthalmologist.

opiner [ɔpine] *vi*: **~ de la tête** to nod assent.

opiniâtre [ɔpinjɑtʀ(ə)] *a* stubborn.

opinion [ɔpinjɔ̃] *nf* opinion; **l'~ (publique)** public opinion.

opium [ɔpjɔm] *nm* opium.

opportun, e [ɔpɔʀtœ̃, -yn] *a* timely, opportune; **en temps ~** at the appropriate time; **opportunisme** *nm* opportunism; **opportuniste** *a, nm/f* opportunist; **opportunité** *nf* timeliness, opportuneness.

opposant, e [ɔpozɑ̃, -ɑ̃t] *a* opposing; **~s** *nmpl* opponents.

opposé, e [ɔpoze] *a* (*direction, rive*) opposite; (*faction*) opposing; (*couleurs*) contrasting; (*opinions, intérêts*) conflicting; (*contre*): **~ à** opposed to, against // *nm*: **l'~** the other *ou* opposite side (*ou* direction); (*contraire*) the opposite; **à l'~** (*fig*) on the other hand; **à l'~ de** on the other *ou* opposite side from; (*fig*) contrary to, unlike.

opposer [ɔpoze] *vt* (*meubles, objets*) to place opposite each other; (*personnes, armées, équipes*) to oppose; (*couleurs, termes, tons*) to contrast; **~ qch à** (*comme obstacle, défense*) to set sth against; (*comme objection*) to put sth forward against; to put up sth to; (*en contraste*) to set sth opposite; to match sth with; **s'~** (*sens réciproque*) to conflict; to clash; to face each other; to contrast; **s'~ à** (*interdire, empêcher*) to oppose; (*tenir tête à*) to rebel against; **sa religion s'y oppose**

it's against his religion; **s'~ à ce que qn fasse** to be opposed to sb's doing.
opposition [ɔpozisjɔ̃] *nf* opposition; **par ~ à** as opposed to, in contrast with; **entrer en ~ avec** to come into conflict with; **être en ~ avec** (*idées, conduite*) to be at variance with; **faire ~ à un chèque** to stop a cheque.
oppresser [ɔpʀese] *vt* to oppress; **oppresseur** *nm* oppressor; **oppressif, ive** *a* oppressive; **oppression** *nf* oppression; (*malaise*) feeling of suffocation.
opprimer [ɔpʀime] *vt* to oppress; (*liberté, opinion*) to suppress, stifle; (*suj: chaleur etc*) to suffocate, oppress.
opprobre [ɔpʀɔbʀ(ə)] *nm* disgrace.
opter [ɔpte] *vi*: **~ pour** to opt for; **~ entre** to choose between.
opticien, ne [ɔptisjɛ̃, -ɛn] *nm/f* optician.
optimal, e, aux [ɔptimal, -o] *a* optimal.
optimisme [ɔptimism(ə)] *nm* optimism; **optimiste** *nm/f* optimist.
optimum [ɔptimɔm] *a* optimum.
option [ɔpsjɔ̃] *nf* option; **matière à ~** (*SCOL*) optional subject; **prendre une ~ sur** to take (out) an option on.
optique [ɔptik] *a* (*nerf*) optic; (*verres*) optical // *nf* (*PHOTO: lentilles etc*) optics *pl*; (*science, industrie*) optics *sg*; (*fig: manière de voir*) perspective.
opulence [ɔpylɑ̃s] *nf* wealth, opulence.
opulent, e [ɔpylɑ̃, -ɑ̃t] *a* wealthy, opulent; (*formes, poitrine*) ample, generous.
or [ɔʀ] *nm* gold // *cj* now, but; **en ~** gold *cpd*; (*fig*) golden, marvellous; **d'~** (*fig*) golden.
oracle [ɔʀɑkl(ə)] *nm* oracle.
orage [ɔʀaʒ] *nm* (thunder)storm; **orageux, euse** *a* stormy.
oraison [ɔʀɛzɔ̃] *nf* orison, prayer; **~ funèbre** funeral oration.
oral, e, aux [ɔʀal, -o] *a, nm* oral; **~ement** *ad* orally.
orange [ɔʀɑ̃ʒ] *nf, a inv* orange; **orangé, e** *a* orangey, orange-coloured; **orangeade** *nf* orangeade; **oranger** *nm* orange tree; **~raie** *nf* orange grove; **~rie** *nf* orangery.
orateur [ɔʀatœʀ] *nm* speaker; orator.
oratoire [ɔʀatwaʀ] *nm* oratory; wayside shrine // *a* oratorical.
orbital, e, aux [ɔʀbital, -o] *a* orbital.
orbite [ɔʀbit] *nf* (*ANAT*) (eye-)socket; (*PHYSIQUE*) orbit; **mettre sur ~** to put into orbit; (*fig*) to launch; **dans l'~ de** (*fig*) within the sphere of influence of.
orchestration [ɔʀkɛstʀɑsjɔ̃] *nf* orchestration.
orchestre [ɔʀkɛstʀ(ə)] *nm* orchestra; (*de jazz, danse*) band; (*places*) stalls *pl*; **orchestrer** *vt* (*MUS*) to orchestrate; (*fig*) to mount, stage-manage.
orchidée [ɔʀkide] *nf* orchid.
ordinaire [ɔʀdinɛʀ] *a* ordinary; everyday; standard // *nm* ordinary; (*menus*) everyday fare // *nf* (*essence*) ≈ two-star (petrol); **d'~** usually, normally; **à l'~** usually, ordinarily.
ordinal, e, aux [ɔʀdinal, -o] *a* ordinal.
ordinateur [ɔʀdinatœʀ] *nm* computer.
ordination [ɔʀdinɑsjɔ̃] *nf* ordination.
ordonnance [ɔʀdɔnɑ̃s] *nf* organization; layout; (*MÉD*) prescription; (*JUR*) order; (*MIL*) orderly, batman; **d'~** (*MIL*) regulation *cpd*.
ordonné, e [ɔʀdɔne] *a* tidy, orderly; (*MATH*) ordered // *nf* (*MATH*) ordinate, Y-axis.
ordonner [ɔʀdɔne] *vt* (*agencer*) to organize, arrange; (: *meubles, appartement*) to lay out, arrange; (*donner un ordre*): **~ à qn de faire** to order sb to do; (*MATH*) to (arrange in) order; (*REL*) to ordain; (*MÉD*) to prescribe; (*JUR*) to order.
ordre [ɔʀdʀ(ə)] *nm* (*gén*) order; (*propreté et soin*) orderliness, tidiness; (*nature*): **d'~ pratique** of a practical nature; **~s** *nmpl* (*REL*) holy orders; **mettre en ~** to tidy (up), put in order; **avoir de l'~** to be tidy *ou* orderly; **mettre bon ~ à** to put to rights, sort out; **être aux ~s de qn/sous les ~s de qn** to be at sb's disposal/under sb's command; **jusqu'à nouvel ~** until further notice; **dans le même ~ d'idées** in this connection; **donnez-nous un ~ de grandeur** give us some idea as regards size (*ou* the amount); **de premier ~** first-rate; **~ du jour** (*d'une réunion*) agenda; (*MIL*) order of the day; **à l'~ du jour** on the agenda; (*fig*) topical; (*MIL: citer*) in dispatches; **~ de route** marching orders *pl*.
ordure [ɔʀdyʀ] *nf* filth *q*; **~s** (*balayures, déchets*) rubbish *sg*, refuse *sg*; **~s ménagères** household refuse; **ordurier, ière** *a* lewd, filthy.
oreille [ɔʀɛj] *nf* (*ANAT*) ear; (*de marmite, tasse*) handle; **avoir de l'~** to have a good ear (for music).
oreiller [ɔʀeje] *nm* pillow.
oreillette [ɔʀɛjɛt] *nf* (*ANAT*) auricle.
oreillons [ɔʀɛjɔ̃] *nmpl* mumps *sg*.
ores [ɔʀ]: **d'~ et déjà** *ad* already.
orfèvre [ɔʀfɛvʀ(ə)] *nm* goldsmith; silversmith; **orfèvrerie** *nf* goldsmith's (*ou* silversmith's) trade; (*ouvrage*) gold (*ou* silver) plate.
orfraie [ɔʀfʀɛ] *nm* white-tailed eagle; **pousser des cris d'~** to yell at the top of one's voice.
organe [ɔʀgan] *nm* organ; (*porte-parole*) representative, mouthpiece; **~s de commande** (*TECH*) controls; **~s de transmission** (*TECH*) transmission system *sg*.
organigramme [ɔʀganigʀam] *nm* organization chart; flow chart.
organique [ɔʀganik] *a* organic.
organisateur, trice [ɔʀganizatœʀ, -tʀis] *nm/f* organizer.
organisation [ɔʀganizɑsjɔ̃] *nf* organization; **O~ des Nations Unies (O.N.U.)** United Nations (Organization) (U.N., U.N.O.); **O~ mondiale de la santé (O.M.S.)** World Health Organization (W.H.O.); **O~ du traité de l'Atlantique Nord (O.T.A.N.)** North Atlantic Treaty Organization (N.A.T.O.).
organiser [ɔʀganize] *vt* to organize; (*mettre sur pied: service etc*) to set up; **s'~** to get organized.
organisme [ɔʀganism(ə)] *nm* (*BIO*)

organism; (*corps humain*) body; (ADMIN, POL *etc*) body, organism.
organiste [ɔʀganist(ə)] *nm/f* organist.
orgasme [ɔʀgasm(ə)] *nm* orgasm, climax.
orge [ɔʀʒ(ə)] *nf* barley.
orgelet [ɔʀʒəlɛ] *nm* sty(e).
orgie [ɔʀʒi] *nf* orgy.
orgue [ɔʀg(ə)] *nm* organ; **~s** *nfpl* organ *sg*; **~ de Barbarie** barrel *ou* street organ.
orgueil [ɔʀgœj] *nm* pride; **orgueilleux, euse** *a* proud.
Orient [ɔʀjɑ̃] *nm*: **l'~** the East, the Orient.
orientable [ɔʀjɑ̃tabl(ə)] *a* adjustable.
oriental, e, aux [ɔʀjɑ̃tal, -o] *a* oriental, eastern; (*frontière*) eastern // *nm/f*: **O~, e** Oriental.
orientation [ɔʀjɑ̃tɑsjɔ̃] *nf* positioning; adjustment; orientation; direction; (*d'un journal*) leanings *pl*; **avoir le sens de l'~** to have a (good) sense of direction; **~ professionnelle** careers advising; careers advisory service.
orienté, e [ɔʀjɑ̃te] *a* (*fig*: *article, journal*) slanted; **bien/mal ~** (*appartement*) well/badly positioned; **~ au sud** facing south *ou* with a southern aspect.
orienter [ɔʀjɑ̃te] *vt* (*situer*) to position; (*placer, disposer*: *pièce mobile*) to adjust, position; (*tourner*) to direct, turn; (*voyageur, touriste, recherches*) to direct; (*fig*: *élève*) to orientate; **s'~** (*se repérer*) to find one's bearings; **s'~ vers** (*fig*) to turn towards; **orienteur** *nm* (SCOL) careers adviser.
orifice [ɔʀifis] *nm* opening, orifice.
oriflamme [ɔʀiflam] *nf* banner, standard.
origan [ɔʀigɑ̃] *nm* (CULIN) oregano.
originaire [ɔʀiʒinɛʀ] *a* original; **être ~ de** to be a native of; (*provenir de*) to originate from; to be native to.
original, e, aux [ɔʀiʒinal, -o] *a* original; (*bizarre*) eccentric // *nm/f* eccentric // *nm* (*document etc*, ART) original; (*dactylographie*) top copy; **~ité** *nf* originality *q*; eccentricity.
origine [ɔʀiʒin] *nf* origin; **d'~** of origin; (*pneus etc*) original; (*bureau postal*) dispatching; **dès l'~** at *ou* from the outset; **à l'~** originally; **avoir son ~ dans** to have its origins in, originate in; **originel, le** *a* original.
oripeaux [ɔʀipo] *nmpl* rags.
O.R.L. *nm/f ou titre* = **oto-rhino-laryngologiste**.
orme [ɔʀm(ə)] *nm* elm.
orné, e [ɔʀne] *a* ornate.
ornement [ɔʀnəmɑ̃] *nm* ornament; (*fig*) embellishment, adornment; **~s sacerdotaux** vestments; **ornemental, e, aux** *a* ornamental; **ornementer** *vt* to ornament.
orner [ɔʀne] *vt* to decorate, adorn; **~ qch de** to decorate sth with.
ornière [ɔʀnjɛʀ] *nf* rut.
ornithologie [ɔʀnitɔlɔʒi] *nf* ornithology.
orphelin, e [ɔʀfəlɛ̃, -in] *a* orphan(ed) // *nm/f* orphan; **~ de père/mère** fatherless/motherless; **orphelinat** *nm* orphanage.
O.R.S.E.C. [ɔʀsɛk] *sigle* (= *organisation des secours*): **le plan ~** *disaster contingency plan.*
orteil [ɔʀtɛj] *nm* toe; **gros ~** big toe.
O.R.T.F. *sigle m = Office de la radiodiffusion et télévision française (the French broadcasting corporation).*
orthodoxe [ɔʀtɔdɔks(ə)] *a* orthodox; **orthodoxie** *nf* orthodoxy.
orthographe [ɔʀtɔgʀaf] *nf* spelling; **orthographier** *vt* to spell; **mal orthographié** misspelt.
orthopédie [ɔʀtɔpedi] *nf* orthopaedics *sg*; **orthopédique** *a* orthopaedic; **orthopédiste** *nm/f* orthopaedic specialist.
ortie [ɔʀti] *nf* (stinging) nettle.
os [ɔs, *pl* o] *nm* bone; **sans ~** (BOUCHERIE) off the bone, boned; **~ à moelle** marrowbone.
O.S. *sigle m voir* **ouvrier**.
oscillation [ɔsilɑsjɔ̃] *nf* oscillation; **~s** *nfpl* (*fig*) fluctuations.
osciller [ɔsile] *vi* (*pendule*) to swing; (*au vent etc*) to rock; (TECH) to oscillate; (*fig*): **~ entre** to waver *ou* fluctuate between.
osé, e [oze] *a* daring, bold.
oseille [ozɛj] *nf* sorrel.
oser [oze] *vi, vt* to dare; **~ faire** to dare (to) do.
osier [ozje] *nm* willow; **d'~, en ~** wicker(work).
ossature [ɔsatyʀ] *nf* (ANAT) frame, skeletal structure; (: *du visage*) bone structure; (*fig*) framework.
osselet [ɔslɛ] *nm* (ANAT) ossicle; **jouer aux ~s** to play knucklebones.
ossements [ɔsmɑ̃] *nmpl* bones.
osseux, euse [ɔsø, -øz] *a* bony; (*tissu, maladie, greffe*) bone *cpd*.
ossifier [ɔsifje]: **s'~** *vi* to ossify.
ossuaire [ɔsɥɛʀ] *nm* ossuary.
ostensible [ɔstɑ̃sibl(ə)] *a* conspicuous.
ostensoir [ɔstɑ̃swaʀ] *nm* monstrance.
ostentation [ɔstɑ̃tɑsjɔ̃] *nf* ostentation; **faire ~ de** to parade, make a display of.
ostracisme [ɔstʀasism(ə)] *nm* ostracism; **frapper d'~** to ostracize.
ostréiculture [ɔstʀeikyltyʀ] *nf* oyster-farming.
otage [ɔtaʒ] *nm* hostage; **prendre qn comme ~** to take sb hostage.
O.T.A.N. [ɔtɑ̃] *sigle f voir* **organisation**.
otarie [ɔtaʀi] *nf* sea-lion.
ôter [ote] *vt* to remove; (*soustraire*) to take away; **~ qch à qn** to take sth (away) from sb; **~ qch de** to remove sth from.
otite [ɔtit] *nf* ear infection.
oto-rhino(-laryngologiste) [ɔtɔʀinɔ-(laʀɛ̃gɔlɔʒist(ə)] *nm/f* ear nose and throat specialist.
ou [u] *cj* or; **~ ... ~** either ... or; **~ bien** or (else).
où [u] *ad, pronom* where; (*dans lequel*) in which, into which; from which, out of which; (*sur lequel*) on which; (*sens de 'que'*): **au train ~ ça va/prix ~ c'est** at the rate it's going/price it is; **le jour ~ il est parti** the day (that) he left; **par ~ passer?** which way should we go?; **les villes par ~ il est passé** the towns he went through; **le village d'~ je viens** the village I come from; **la chambre ~ il était**

the room he was in ; **d'~ vient qu'il est parti?** how come he left?
ouate [wat] *nf* cotton wool ; (*bourre*) padding, wadding ; **ouaté, e** *a* cotton-wool ; (*doublé*) quilted ; (*fig*) cocoon-like ; muffled.
oubli [ubli] *nm* (*acte*): **l'~ de** forgetting ; (*étourderie*) forgetfulness *q* ; (*négligence*) omission, oversight ; (*absence de souvenirs*) oblivion ; **~ de soi** self-effacement, self-negation.
oublier [ublije] *vt* (*gén*) to forget ; (*ne pas voir*: *erreurs etc*) to miss ; (*ne pas mettre*: *virgule, nom*) to leave out ; (*laisser quelque part*: *chapeau etc*) to leave behind ; **s'~** to forget o.s.
oubliettes [ublijɛt] *nfpl* dungeon *sg*.
oublieux, euse [ublijø, -øz] *a* forgetful.
oued [wɛd] *nm* wadi.
ouest [wɛst] *nm* west // *a inv* west ; (*région*) western ; **à l'~** in the west ; (to the) west, westwards ; **à l'~ de** (to the) west of ; **vent d'~** westerly wind ; **~-allemand, e** *a, nm/f* West German.
ouf [uf] *excl* phew!
oui [wi] *ad* yes ; **répondre (par) ~** to answer yes.
ouï-dire [widiʀ] *nm inv*: **par ~** by hearsay.
ouïe [wi] *nf* hearing ; **~s** *nfpl* (*de poisson*) gills ; (*de violon*) sound-hole.
ouïr [wiʀ] *vt* to hear ; **avoir ouï dire que** to have heard it said that.
ouistiti [wistiti] *nm* marmoset.
ouragan [uʀagɑ̃] *nm* hurricane ; (*fig*) storm.
ourlé, e [uʀle] *a* hemmed ; (*fig*) rimmed.
ourler [uʀle] *vt* to hem.
ourlet [uʀlɛ] *nm* hem ; (*de l'oreille*) rim.
ours [uʀs] *nm* bear ; **~ brun/blanc** brown/polar bear ; **~ mal léché** uncouth fellow ; **~ (en peluche)** teddy (bear).
ourse [uʀs(ə)] *nf* (ZOOL) she-bear ; **la Grande/Petite O~** the Great/Little Bear, Ursa Major/ Minor.
oursin [uʀsɛ̃] *nm* sea urchin.
ourson [uʀsɔ̃] *nm* (bear-)cub.
ouste [ust(ə)] *excl* hop it!
outil [uti] *nm* tool.
outillage [utijaʒ] *nm* set of tools ; (*d'atelier*) equipment *q*.
outiller [utije] *vt* (*ouvrier, usine*) to equip.
outrage [utʀaʒ] *nm* insult ; **faire subir les derniers ~s à** (*femme*) to ravish ; **~ aux bonnes mœurs** outrage to public decency ; **~ à magistrat** contempt of court ; **~ à la pudeur** indecent behaviour *q*.
outrageant, e [utʀaʒɑ̃, -ɑ̃t] *a* offensive.
outrager [utʀaʒe] *vt* to offend gravely ; (*fig*: *contrevenir à*) to outrage, insult.
outrance [utʀɑ̃s] *nf* excessiveness *q*, excess ; **à ~** *ad* excessively, to excess ; **outrancier, ière** *a* extreme.
outre [utʀ(ə)] *nf* goatskin, water skin // *prép* besides // *ad*: **passer ~ à** to disregard, take no notice of ; **en ~** besides, moreover ; **~ que** apart from the fact that ; **~ mesure** immoderately ; unduly.
outré, e [utʀe] *a* excessive, exaggerated ; outraged.
outre-Atlantique [utʀəatlɑ̃tik] *ad* across the Atlantic.
outrecuidance [utʀəkɥidɑ̃s] *nf* presumptuousness *q*.
outre-Manche [utʀəmɑ̃ʃ] *ad* across the Channel.
outremer [utʀəmɛʀ] *a* ultramarine.
outre-mer [utʀəmɛʀ] *ad* overseas.
outrepasser [utʀəpɑse] *vt* to go beyond, exceed.
outrer [utʀe] *vt* to exaggerate ; to outrage.
outsider [awtsajdœʀ] *nm* outsider.
ouvert, e [uvɛʀ, -ɛʀt(ə)] *pp de* **ouvrir** // *a* open ; (*robinet, gaz etc*) on ; **ouvertement** *ad* openly.
ouverture [uvɛʀtyʀ] *nf* opening ; (MUS) overture ; (POL): **l'~** the widening of the political spectrum ; (PHOTO): **~ (du diaphragme)** aperture ; **~s** *nfpl* (*propositions*) overtures ; **~ d'esprit** open-mindedness ; **heures d'~** (COMM) opening hours ; **jours d'~** (COMM) days of opening.
ouvrable [uvʀabl(ə)] *a*: **jour ~** working day, weekday.
ouvrage [uvʀaʒ] *nm* (*tâche, de tricot etc*, MIL) work *q* ; (*texte, livre*) work ; **corbeille à ~** work basket ; **~ d'art** (GÉNIE CIVIL) *bridge or tunnel etc*.
ouvragé, e [uvʀaʒe] *a* finely embroidered (*ou* worked *ou* carved).
ouvrant, e [uvʀɑ̃, -ɑ̃t] *a*: **toit ~** (AUTO) sunshine roof.
ouvre-boîte(s) [uvʀəbwat] *nm inv* tin *ou* can opener.
ouvre-bouteille(s) [uvʀəbutɛj] *nm inv* bottle-opener.
ouvreuse [uvʀøz] *nf* usherette.
ouvrier, ière [uvʀije, -jɛʀ] *nm/f* worker // *nf* (ZOOL) worker (bee) // *a* working-class ; industrial, labour *cpd* ; workers' ; **classe ouvrière** working class ; **~ qualifié** skilled worker ; **~ spécialisé (O.S.)** semiskilled worker ; **~ d'usine** factory worker.
ouvrir [uvʀiʀ] *vt* (*gén*) to open ; (*brèche, passage*) to open up ; (*commencer l'exploitation de, créer*) to open (up) ; (*eau, électricité, chauffage, robinet*) to turn on ; (MÉD: *abcès*) to open up, cut open // *vi* to open ; to open up ; **s'~** *vi* to open ; **s'~ à** (*art etc*) to open one's mind to ; **s'~ à qn (de qch)** to open one's heart to sb (about sth) ; **s'~ les veines** to slash *ou* cut one's wrists ; **~ l'appétit à qn** to whet sb's appetite.
ouvroir [uvʀwaʀ] *nm* workroom ; sewing room.
ovaire [ɔvɛʀ] *nm* ovary.
ovale [ɔval] *a* oval.
ovation [ɔvɑsjɔ̃] *nf* ovation ; **ovationner** *vt*: **ovationner qn** to give sb an ovation.
O.V.N.I. [ɔvni] *sigle m* (= *objet volant non identifié*) U.F.O. (unidentified flying object).
ovule [ɔvyl] *nm* (PHYSIOL) ovum (*pl* ova) ; (MÉD) pessary.
oxydable [ɔksidabl(ə)] *a* liable to rust.
oxyde [ɔksid] *nm* oxide ; **~ de carbone** carbon monoxide.
oxyder [ɔkside]: **s'~** *vi* to become oxidized.

oxygène [ɔksiʒɛn] *nm* oxygen; (*fig*): **cure d'~** fresh air cure.
oxygéné, e [ɔksiʒene] *a*: **eau ~e** hydrogen peroxide.
ozone [ozɔn] *nm* ozone.

P

pacage [pakaʒ] *nm* grazing, pasture.
pachyderme [paʃidɛʀm(ə)] *nm* pachyderm; elephant.
pacifier [pasifje] *vt* to pacify.
pacifique [pasifik] *a* (*personne*) peaceable; (*intentions, coexistence*) peaceful // *nm*: **le P~, l'océan P~** the Pacific (Ocean).
pacotille [pakɔtij] *nf* (*péj*) cheap goods *pl*; **de ~** cheap.
pacte [pakt(ə)] *nm* pact, treaty.
pactiser [paktize] *vi*: **~ avec** to come to terms with.
pagaie [pagɛ] *nf* paddle.
pagaille [pagaj] *nf* mess, shambles *sg*.
pagayer [pageje] *vi* to paddle.
page [paʒ] *nf* page // *nm* page; **mettre en ~s** to make up (into pages); **à la ~** (*fig*) up-to-date.
pagne [paɲ] *nm* loincloth.
pagode [pagɔd] *nf* pagoda.
paie [pɛ] *nf* = **paye**.
paiement [pɛmɑ̃] *nm* = **payement**.
païen, ne [pajɛ̃, -jɛn] *a, nm/f* pagan, heathen.
paillard, e [pajaʀ, -aʀd(ə)] *a* bawdy.
paillasse [pajas] *nf* straw mattress.
paillasson [pɑjasɔ̃] *nm* doormat.
paille [pɑj] *nf* straw; (*défaut*) flaw; **~ de fer** steel wool.
pailleté, e [pajte] *a* sequined.
paillette [pajɛt] *nf* speck, flake; **~s** *nfpl* (*décoratives*) sequins, spangles; **lessive en ~s** soapflakes *pl*.
pain [pɛ̃] *nm* (*substance*) bread; (*unité*) loaf (*pl* loaves) (of bread); (*morceau*): **~ de cire** *etc* bar of wax *etc*; **~ bis/complet** brown/ wholemeal bread; **~ d'épice** gingerbread; **~ grillé** toast; **~ de mie** sandwich loaf; **~ de seigle** rye bread; **~ de sucre** sugar loaf.
pair, e [pɛʀ] *a* (*nombre*) even // *nm* peer; **aller de ~ (avec)** to go hand in hand *ou* together (with); **au ~** (FINANCE) at par; **jeune fille au ~** au pair girl.
paire [pɛʀ] *nf* pair; **une ~ de lunettes/tenailles** a pair of glasses/pincers.
paisible [pezibl(ə)] *a* peaceful, quiet.
paître [pɛtʀ(ə)] *vi* to graze.
paix [pɛ] *nf* peace; (*fig*) peacefulness; peace; **faire la ~ avec** to make peace with; **avoir la ~** to have peace (and quiet).
palabrer [palabʀe] *vi* to argue endlessly.
palace [palas] *nm* luxury hotel.
palais [palɛ] *nm* palace; (ANAT) palate; **le P~ Bourbon** *the National Assembly buildings*; **~ des expositions** exhibition hall; **le P~ de Justice** the Law Courts *pl*.
palan [palɑ̃] *nm* hoist.
pale [pal] *nf* (*d'hélice, de rame*) blade; (*de roue*) paddle.
pâle [pɑl] *a* pale; **bleu ~** pale blue.
paléontologie [paleɔ̃tɔlɔʒi] *nf* paleontology.
Palestine [palɛstin] *nf*: **la ~** Palestine; **palestinien, ne** *a, nm/f* Palestinian.
palet [palɛ] *nm* disc; (HOCKEY) puck.
paletot [palto] *nm* (short) coat.
palette [palɛt] *nf* (*de peintre*) palette.
palétuvier [paletyvje] *nm* mangrove.
pâleur [pɑlœʀ] *nf* paleness.
palier [palje] *nm* (*d'escalier*) landing; (*fig*) level, plateau; (TECH) bearing; **nos voisins de ~** our neighbours across the landing; **en ~** *ad* level; **par ~s** in stages; **palière** *af* landing *cpd*.
pâlir [pɑliʀ] *vi* to turn *ou* go pale; (*couleur*) to fade.
palissade [palisad] *nf* fence.
palissandre [palisɑ̃dʀ(ə)] *nm* rosewood.
palliatif [paljatif] *nm* palliative; (*expédient*) stopgap measure.
pallier [palje] *vt*, **~ à** *vt* to offset, make up for.
palmarès [palmaʀɛs] *nm* record (of achievements); (SCOL) prize list; (SPORT) list of winners.
palme [palm(ə)] *nf* (BOT) palm leaf (*pl* leaves); (*symbole*) palm; (*en caoutchouc*) flipper; **~s (académiques)** *decoration for services to education*; **palmé, e** *a* (*pattes*) webbed.
palmeraie [palməʀɛ] *nf* palm grove.
palmier [palmje] *nm* palm tree.
palmipède [palmipɛd] *nm* palmiped, webfooted bird.
palombe [palɔ̃b] *nf* woodpigeon, ringdove.
pâlot, te [pɑlo, -ɔt] *a* pale, peaky.
palourde [paluʀd(ə)] *nf* clam.
palper [palpe] *vt* to feel, finger.
palpitant, e [palpitɑ̃, -ɑ̃t] *a* thrilling.
palpitation [palpitɑsjɔ̃] *nf* palpitation.
palpiter [palpite] *vi* (*cœur, pouls*) to beat; (*: plus fort*) to pound, throb; (*narines, chair*) to quiver.
paludisme [palydism(ə)] *nm* paludism, malaria.
pâmer [pɑme]: **se ~** *vi* to swoon; (*fig*): **se ~ devant** to go into raptures over; **pâmoison** *nf*: **tomber en pâmoison** to swoon.
pampa [pɑ̃pa] *nf* pampas *pl*.
pamphlet [pɑ̃flɛ] *nm* lampoon, satirical tract.
pamplemousse [pɑ̃pləmus] *nm* grapefruit.
pan [pɑ̃] *nm* section, piece // *excl* bang!; **~ de chemise** shirt tail.
panacée [panase] *nf* panacea.
panachage [panaʃaʒ] *nm* blend, mix.
panache [panaʃ] *nm* plume; (*fig*) spirit, panache.
panaché, e [panaʃe] *a*: **œillet ~** variegated carnation; **glace ~e** mixed-flavour ice cream; **salade ~e** mixed salad; **bière ~e** shandy.
panaris [panaʀi] *nm* whitlow.
pancarte [pɑ̃kaʀt(ə)] *nf* sign, notice; (*dans un défilé*) placard.

pancréas [pɑ̃kʀeɑs] *nm* pancreas.
pané, e [pane] *a* fried in breadcrumbs.
panier [panje] *nm* basket ; **mettre au ~** to chuck away ; **~ à provisions** shopping basket ; **~ à salade** Black Maria, police van ; **~-repas** *nm* packed lunch.
panification [panifikɑsjɔ̃] *nf* bread-making.
panique [panik] *nf, a* panic ; **paniquer** *vi* to panic.
panne [pan] *nf* (*d'un mécanisme, moteur*) breakdown ; **être/tomber en ~** to have broken down/break down ; **être en ~ d'essence** *ou* **sèche** to have run out of petrol ; **~ d'électricité** *ou* **de courant** power *ou* electrical failure.
panneau, x [pano] *nm* (*écriteau*) sign, notice ; (*de boiserie, de tapisserie etc*) panel ; **tomber dans le ~** (*fig*) to walk into the trap ; **~ d'affichage** notice board ; **~ de signalisation** roadsign ; **~-réclame** *nm* hoarding.
panonceau, x [panɔ̃so] *nm* sign.
panoplie [panɔpli] *nf* (*jouet*) outfit ; (*d'armes*) display ; (*fig*) array.
panorama [panɔʀama] *nm* panorama ; **panoramique** *a* panoramic ; (*carrosserie*) with panoramic windows.
panse [pɑ̃s] *nf* paunch.
pansement [pɑ̃smɑ̃] *nm* dressing, bandage ; **~ adhésif** sticking plaster.
panser [pɑ̃se] *vt* (*plaie*) to dress, bandage ; (*bras*) to put a dressing on, bandage ; (*cheval*) to groom.
pantalon [pɑ̃talɔ̃] *nm* (*aussi*: **~s, paire de ~s**) trousers *pl*, pair of trousers ; **~ de ski** ski pants *pl*.
pantelant, e [pɑ̃tlɑ̃, -ɑ̃t] *a* gasping for breath, panting.
panthère [pɑ̃tɛʀ] *nf* panther.
pantin [pɑ̃tɛ̃] *nm* jumping jack ; (*péj*) puppet.
pantois [pɑ̃twa] *am*: **rester ~** to be flabbergasted.
pantomime [pɑ̃tɔmim] *nf* mime ; (*pièce*) mime show.
pantouflard, e [pɑ̃tuflaʀ, -aʀd(ə)] *a* (*péj*) stay-at-home.
pantoufle [pɑ̃tufl(ə)] *nf* slipper.
panure [panyʀ] *nf* breadcrumbs *pl*.
paon [pɑ̃] *nm* peacock.
papa [papa] *nm* dad(dy).
papauté [papote] *nf* papacy.
pape [pap] *nm* pope.
paperasse [papʀas] *nf* (*péj*) bumf *q*, papers *pl* ; forms *pl* ; **~rie** *nf* (*péj*) red tape *q* ; paperwork *q*.
papeterie [papetʀi] *nf* (*usine*) paper mill ; (*magasin*) stationer's (shop).
papetier, ière [paptje, -jɛʀ] *nm/f* paper-maker ; stationer ; **~-libraire** *nm* bookseller and stationer.
papier [papje] *nm* paper ; (*article*) article ; **~s** *nmpl* (*aussi*: **~s d'identité**) (identity) papers ; **~ couché/glacé** art/glazed paper ; **~ (d')aluminium** aluminium foil, tinfoil ; **~ d'Arménie** incense paper ; **~ bible** India *ou* bible paper ; **~ buvard** blotting paper ; **~ calque** tracing paper ; **~ carbone** carbon paper ; **~ collant** sellotape ®, sticky tape ; **~ hygiénique** toilet paper ; **~ journal** newsprint ; (*pour emballer*) newspaper ; **~ à lettres** writing paper, notepaper ; **~ mâché** papier-mâché ; **~ machine** typing paper ; **~ peint** wallpaper ; **~ pelure** India paper ; **~ de soie** tissue paper ; **~ de tournesol** litmus paper ; **~ de verre** sandpaper.
papille [papij] *nf*: **~s gustatives** taste buds.
papillon [papijɔ̃] *nm* butterfly ; (*fam*: *contravention*) (parking) ticket ; (TECH: *écrou*) wing *ou* butterfly nut ; **~ de nuit** moth.
papillote [papijɔt] *nf* curlpaper.
papilloter [papijɔte] *vi* to blink, flicker.
papoter [papɔte] *vi* to chatter.
paprika [papʀika] *nm* paprika.
paquebot [pakbo] *nm* liner.
pâquerette [pɑkʀɛt] *nf* daisy.
Pâques [pɑk] *nm, nfpl* Easter ; **faire ses ~** to do one's Easter duties.
paquet [pakɛ] *nm* packet ; (*colis*) parcel ; (*fig*: *tas*): **~ de** pile *ou* heap of ; **mettre le ~** (*fam*) to give one's all ; **~ de mer** big wave ; **paquetage** *nm* (MIL) kit, pack ; **~-cadeau** *nm* gift-wrapped parcel.
par [paʀ] *prép* by ; **finir** *etc* **~** to end *etc* with ; **~ amour** out of love ; **passer ~ Lyon/la côte** to go via *ou* through Lyons/along by the coast ; **~ la fenêtre** (*jeter, regarder*) out of the window ; **3 ~ jour/personne** 3 a *ou* per day/head ; **2 ~ 2** two at a time ; in twos ; **~ où?** which way? ; **~ ici** this way ; (*dans le coin*) round here ; **~-ci, ~-là** here and there.
para [paʀa] *nm* (*abr de* **parachutiste**) para.
parabole [paʀabɔl] *nf* (REL) parable ; (GÉOM) parabola ; **parabolique** *a* parabolic.
parachever [paʀaʃve] *vt* to perfect.
parachute [paʀaʃyt] *nm* parachute.
parachutiste [paʀaʃytist(ə)] *nm/f* parachutist ; (MIL) paratrooper.
parade [paʀad] *nf* (*spectacle, défilé*) parade ; (ESCRIME, BOXE) parry ; (*ostentation*): **faire ~ de** to display, show off.
paradis [paʀadi] *nm* heaven, paradise.
paradoxal, e, aux [paʀadɔksal, -o] *a* paradoxical.
paradoxe [paʀadɔks(ə)] *nm* paradox.
parafe [paʀaf] *nm*, **parafer** [paʀafe] *vt* voir **paraphe, parapher.**
paraffine [paʀafin] *nf* paraffin ; paraffin wax.
parages [paʀaʒ] *nmpl*: **dans les ~ (de)** in the area *ou* vicinity (of).
paragraphe [paʀagʀaf] *nm* paragraph.
paraître [paʀɛtʀ(ə)] *vb avec attribut* to seem, look, appear // *vi* to appear ; (*être visible*) to show ; (PRESSE, ÉDITION) to be published, come out, appear ; (*briller*) to show off // *vb impersonnel*: **il paraît que** it seems *ou* appears that, they say that ; **il me paraît que** it seems to me that.
parallèle [paʀalɛl] *a* parallel ; (*police, marché*) unofficial // *nm* (*comparaison*): **faire un ~ entre** to draw a parallel between ; (GÉO) parallel // *nf* parallel (line) ; **parallélisme** *nm* parallelism ; (AUTO) wheel alignment ; **parallélogramme** *nm* parallelogram.

paralyser [paʀalize] *vt* to paralyze.
paralysie [paʀalizi] *nf* paralysis.
paralytique [paʀalitik] *a, nm/f* paralytic.
paramédical, e, aux [paʀamedikal, -o] *a* paramedical.
paranoïaque [paʀanɔjak] *nm/f* paranoiac.
parapet [paʀapɛ] *nm* parapet.
paraphe [paʀaf] *nm* flourish; initials *pl*; signature; **parapher** *vt* to initial; to sign.
paraphrase [paʀafʀɑz] *nf* paraphrase.
parapluie [paʀaplɥi] *nm* umbrella; ~ **pliant** telescopic umbrella.
parasite [paʀazit] *nm* parasite // *a* (BOT, BIO) parasitic(al); ~**s** (TÉL) interference *sg*.
parasol [paʀasɔl] *nm* parasol, sunshade.
paratonnerre [paʀatɔnɛʀ] *nm* lightning conductor.
paravent [paʀavɑ̃] *nm* folding screen.
parc [paʀk] *nm* (public) park, gardens *pl*; (*de château etc*) grounds *pl*; (*pour le bétail*) pen, enclosure; (*d'enfant*) playpen; (MIL: *entrepôt*) depot; (*ensemble d'unités*) stock; fleet; ~ **automobile** (*d'un pays*) number of cars on the roads; (*d'une société*) car fleet; ~ **à huîtres** oyster bed; ~ **national** national park; ~ **de stationnement** car park.
parcelle [paʀsɛl] *nf* fragment, scrap; (*de terrain*) plot, parcel.
parce que [paʀsk(ə)] *cj* because.
parchemin [paʀʃəmɛ̃] *nm* parchment.
parcimonie [paʀsimɔni] *nf* parsimony, parsimoniousness.
parc(o)mètre [paʀk(ɔ)mɛtʀ(ə)] *nm* parking meter.
parcourir [paʀkuʀiʀ] *vt* (*trajet, distance*) to cover; (*article, livre*) to skim *ou* glance through; (*lieu*) to go all over, travel up and down; (*suj: frisson, vibration*) to run through; ~ **des yeux** to run one's eye over.
parcours [paʀkuʀ] *nm* (*trajet*) journey; (*itinéraire*) route; (SPORT: *de golf etc*) course; (: *accompli par un concurrent*) round; run; lap.
par-delà [paʀdəla] *prép* beyond.
par-dessous [paʀdəsu] *prép, ad* under(neath).
pardessus [paʀdəsy] *nm* overcoat.
par-dessus [paʀdəsy] *prép* over (the top of) // *ad* over (the top); ~ **le marché** on top of all that.
par-devant [paʀdəvɑ̃] *prép* in the presence of, before // *ad* at the front; round the front.
pardon [paʀdɔ̃] *nm* forgiveness *q* // *excl* sorry; (*pour interpeller etc*) excuse me; **demander ~ à qn (de)** to apologize to sb (for); **je vous demande ~** I'm sorry; excuse me.
pardonner [paʀdɔne] *vt* to forgive; ~ **qch à qn** to forgive sb for sth.
paré, e [paʀe] *a* ready, prepared.
pare-balles [paʀbal] *a inv* bulletproof.
pare-boue [paʀbu] *nm inv* mudguard.
pare-brise [paʀbʀiz] *nm inv* windscreen.
pare-chocs [paʀʃɔk] *nm inv* bumper.
pareil, le [paʀɛj] *a* (*identique*) the same, alike; (*similaire*) similar; (*tel*): **un courage/livre ~** such courage/a book, courage/a book like this; **de ~s livres** such books; **j'en veux un ~** I'd like one just like it; **rien de ~** no (*ou* any) such thing, nothing (*ou* anything) like it; **ses ~s** one's fellow men; one's peers; **ne pas avoir son(sa) ~(le)** to be second to none; ~ **à** the same as; similar to; **sans ~** unparalleled, unequalled; ~**lement** *ad* the same, alike; in such a way; (*également*) likewise.
parement [paʀmɑ̃] *nm* (CONSTR) facing; (REL): ~ **d'autel** antependium.
parent, e [paʀɑ̃, -ɑ̃t] *nm/f*: **un/une ~/e** a relative *ou* relation // *a*: **être ~ de** to be related to; ~**s** *nmpl* (*père et mère*) parents; **parenté** *nf* (*lien*) relationship; (*personnes*) relatives *pl*, relations *pl*.
parenthèse [paʀɑ̃tɛz] *nf* (*ponctuation*) bracket, parenthesis; (MATH) bracket; (*digression*) parenthesis, digression; **ouvrir/ fermer la ~** to open/close the brackets; **entre ~s** in brackets; (*fig*) incidentally.
parer [paʀe] *vt* to adorn; (CULIN) to dress, trim; (*éviter*) to ward off; ~ **à** (*danger*) to ward off; (*inconvénient*) to deal with; ~ **au plus pressé** to attend to what's most urgent.
pare-soleil [paʀsɔlɛj] *nm inv* sun visor.
paresse [paʀɛs] *nf* laziness; **paresser** *vi* to laze around; **paresseux, euse** *a* lazy; (*fig*) slow, sluggish // *nm* (ZOOL) sloth.
parfaire [paʀfɛʀ] *vt* to perfect; to complete.
parfait, e [paʀfɛ, -ɛt] *a* perfect // *nm* (LING) perfect (tense); (CULIN) parfait // *excl* fine, excellent; **parfaitement** *ad* perfectly // *excl* (most) certainly.
parfois [paʀfwa] *ad* sometimes.
parfum [paʀfœ̃] *nm* (*produit*) perfume, scent; (*odeur: de fleur*) scent, fragrance; (: *de tabac, vin*) aroma; (*à choisir: de glace, milk-shake*) flavour; **parfumé, e** *a* (*fleur, fruit*) fragrant; (*papier à lettres etc*) scented; (*femme*) wearing perfume *ou* scent, perfumed; **parfumé au café** coffee-flavoured, flavoured with coffee; **parfumer** *vt* (*suj: odeur, bouquet*) to perfume; (*mouchoir*) to put scent *ou* perfume on; (*crème, gâteau*) to flavour; **se parfumer** to put on (some) perfume *ou* scent; to use perfume *ou* scent; **parfumerie** *nf* (*commerce*) perfumery; (*produits*) perfumes *pl*; (*boutique*) perfume shop.
pari [paʀi] *nm* bet, wager; (SPORT) bet; **P~ Mutuel urbain (P.M.U.)** (*State-controlled*) *organisation for forecast betting on horse-racing*.
paria [paʀja] *nm* outcast.
parier [paʀje] *vt* to bet; **parieur** *nm* (*turfiste etc*) punter.
Paris [paʀi] *n* Paris; **parisien, ne** *a* Parisian; (GÉO, ADMIN) Paris *cpd* // *nm/f*: **Parisien, ne** Parisian.
paritaire [paʀitɛʀ] *a*: **commission ~** joint commission.
parité [paʀite] *nf* parity.
parjure [paʀʒyʀ] *nm* (*acte*) false oath, perjury; breach of oath, perjury // *nm/f* perjurer; **se parjurer** to forswear *ou* perjure o.s.

parking [parkiŋ] *nm* (*lieu*) car park.
parlant, e [parlɑ̃, -ɑ̃t] *a* (*fig*) graphic, vivid; eloquent; (CINÉMA) talking // *ad*: **généralement ~** generally speaking.
parlement [parləmɑ̃] *nm* parliament; **parlementaire** *a* parliamentary // *nm/f* member of parliament; parliamentarian; negotiator, mediator.
parlementer [parləmɑ̃te] *vi* to negotiate, parley.
parler [parle] *nm* speech; dialect // *vi* to speak, talk; (*avouer*) to talk; **~ (à qn) de** to talk *ou* speak (to sb) about; **~ pour qn** (*intercéder*) to speak for sb; **~ le/en français** to speak French/in French; **~ affaires** to talk business; **~ en dormant/du nez** to talk in one's sleep/through one's nose; **sans ~ de** (*fig*) not to mention, to say nothing of; **tu parles!** you must be joking!
parloir [parlwar] *nm* (*d'une prison, d'un hôpital*) visiting room; (REL) parlour.
parmi [parmi] *prép* among(st).
parodie [parɔdi] *nf* parody; **parodier** *vt* (*œuvre, auteur*) to parody.
paroi [parwa] *nf* wall; (*cloison*) partition; **~ rocheuse** rock face.
paroisse [parwas] *nf* parish; **paroissial, e, aux** *a* parish *cpd*; **paroissien, ne** *nm/f* parishioner // *nm* prayer book.
parole [parɔl] *nf* (*faculté*): **la ~** speech; (*mot, promesse*) word; **~s** *nfpl* (MUS) words, lyrics; **tenir ~** to keep one's word; **prendre la ~** to speak; **demander la ~** to ask for permission to speak; **je le crois sur ~** I'll take his word for it.
paroxysme [parɔksism(ə)] *nm* height, paroxysm.
parpaing [parpɛ̃] *nm* bond-stone, parpen.
parquer [parke] *vt* (*voiture, matériel*) to park; (*bestiaux*) to pen (in *ou* up); (*prisonniers*) to pack in.
parquet [parkɛ] *nm* (parquet) floor; (JUR): **le ~** the Public Prosecutor's department; **parqueter** *vt* to lay a parquet floor in.
parrain [parɛ̃] *nm* godfather; (*d'un nouvel adhérent*) sponsor, proposer; **parrainer** *vt* (*nouvel adhérent*) to sponsor, propose; (*entreprise*) to promote, sponsor.
parricide [parisid] *nm, nf* parricide.
pars *vb voir* **partir**.
parsemer [parsəme] *vt* (*suj: feuilles, papiers*) to be scattered over; **~ qch de** to scatter sth with.
part [par] *nf* (*qui revient à qn*) share; (*fraction, partie*) part; (FINANCE) (non-voting) share; **prendre ~ à** (*débat etc*) to take part in; (*soucis, douleur de qn*) to share in; **faire ~ de qch à qn** to announce sth to sb, inform sb of sth; **pour ma ~** as for me, as far as I'm concerned; **à ~ entière** *a* full; **de la ~ de** (*au nom de*) on behalf of; (*donné par*) from; **de toute(s) ~(s)** from all sides *ou* quarters; **de ~ et d'autre** on both sides, on either side; **de ~ en ~** right through; **d'une ~ ... d'autre ~** on the one hand ... on the other hand; **à ~** *ad* separately; (*de côté*) aside // *prép* apart from, except for // *a* exceptional, special; **faire la ~ des choses** to make allowances.
partage [partaʒ] *nm* dividing up; sharing (out) *q*, share-out; sharing; **recevoir qch en ~** to receive sth as one's share (*ou* lot); **sans ~** undivided.
partagé, e [partaʒe] *a* (*opinions etc*) divided.
partager [partaʒe] *vt* to share; (*distribuer, répartir*) to share (out); (*morceler, diviser*) to divide (up); **se ~** *vt* (*héritage etc*) to share between themselves (*ou* ourselves).
partance [partɑ̃s]: **en ~** *ad* outbound, due to leave; **en ~ pour** (bound) for.
partant [partɑ̃] *vb voir* **partir** // *nm* (SPORT) starter; (HIPPISME) runner.
partenaire [partənɛr] *nm/f* partner.
parterre [partɛr] *nm* (*de fleurs*) (flower) bed, border; (THÉÂTRE) stalls *pl*.
parti [parti] *nm* (POL) party; (*décision*) course of action; (*personne à marier*) match; **tirer ~ de** to take advantage of, turn to good account; **prendre le ~ de faire** to make up one's mind to do, resolve to do; **prendre le ~ de qn** to stand up for sb, side with sb; **prendre ~ (pour/contre)** to take sides *ou* a stand (for/against); **prendre son ~ de** to come to terms with; **~ pris** bias.
partial, e, aux [parsjal, -o] *a* biased, partial.
participant, e [partisipɑ̃, -ɑ̃t] *nm/f* participant; (*à un concours*) entrant; (*d'une société*) member.
participation [partisipɑsjɔ̃] *nf* participation; sharing; (COMM) interest; **la ~ aux bénéfices** profit-sharing; **la ~ ouvrière** worker participation.
participe [partisip] *nm* participle; **~ passé/présent** past/present participle.
participer [partisipe]: **~ à** *vt* (*course, réunion*) to take part in; (*profits etc*) to share in; (*frais etc*) to contribute to; (*entreprise: financièrement*) to cooperate in; (*chagrin, succès de qn*) to share (in); **~ de** *vt* to partake of.
particularisme [partikylarism(ə)] *nm* sense of identity; specific characteristic.
particularité [partikylarite] *nf* particularity; (*distinctive*) characteristic, feature.
particule [partikyl] *nf* particle; **~ (nobiliaire)** nobiliary particle.
particulier, ière [partikylje, -jɛr] *a* (*personnel, privé*) private; (*spécial*) special, particular; (*caractéristique*) characteristic, distinctive; (*spécifique*) particular // *nm* (*individu*: ADMIN) private individual; **'~ vend ...'** (COMM) 'for sale privately ...'; **~ à** peculiar to; **en ~** *ad* (*surtout*) in particular, particularly; (*en privé*) in private; **particulièrement** *ad* particularly.
partie [parti] *nf* (*gén*) part; (*profession, spécialité*) field, subject; (JUR *etc: protagonistes*) party; (*de cartes, tennis etc*) game; **une ~ de campagne/de pêche** an outing in the country/a fishing party *ou* trip; **en ~** *ad* partly, in part; **faire ~ de** to belong to; (*suj: chose*) to be part of; **prendre qn à ~** to take sb to task; (*malmener*) to set on sb; **en grande ~** largely, in the main; **~ civile** (JUR) *private*

party associating in action with public prosecutor.

partiel, le [paRsjɛl] *a* partial // *nm* (*SCOL*) class exam.

partir [paRtiR] *vi* (*gén*) to go; (*quitter*) to go, leave; (*s'éloigner*) to go (*ou* drive *etc*) away *ou* off; (*moteur*) to start; (*pétard*) to go off; **~ de** (*lieu*: *quitter*) to leave; (: *commencer à*) to start from; (*date*) to run *ou* start from; **à ~ de** from.

partisan, e [paRtizɑ̃, -an] *nm/f* partisan // *a*: **être ~ de qch/faire** to be in favour of sth/doing.

partitif, ive [paRtitif, -iv] *a*: **article ~** article used in the partitive genitive.

partition [paRtisjɔ̃] *nf* (*MUS*) score.

partout [paRtu] *ad* everywhere; **~ où il allait** everywhere *ou* wherever he went; **trente ~** (*TENNIS*) thirty all.

paru, e *pp de* **paraître**.

parure [paRyR] *nf* (*toilette, bijoux*) finery *q*; jewellery *q*; (*assortiment*) set.

parution [paRysjɔ̃] *nf* publication, appearance.

parvenir [paRvəniR]: **~ à** *vt* (*atteindre*) to reach; (*réussir*): **~ à faire** to manage to do, succeed in doing; **faire ~ qch à qn** to have sth sent to sb.

parvenu, e [paRvəny] *nm/f* (*péj*) parvenu, upstart.

parvis [paRvi] *nm* square (*in front of a church*).

pas [pɑ] *nm voir le mot suivant* // *ad* not; **~ de** no; **ne ... ~**: **il ne le voit ~/ne l'a ~ vu/ne le verra ~** he doesn't see it/hasn't seen it *ou* didn't see it/won't see it; **ils n'ont ~ de voiture/d'enfants** they haven't got a car/any children, they have no car/children; **il m'a dit de ne ~ le faire** he told me not to do it; **il n'est ~ plus grand** he isn't bigger, he's no bigger; **... lui ~** *ou* **~ lui** he doesn't (*ou* isn't *etc*); **non ~ que ...** not that ...; **une pomme ~ mûre** an apple which isn't ripe; **~ du tout** not at all; **~ plus tard qu'hier** only yesterday; **~ mal** *a* not bad, quite good (*ou* pretty *ou* nice) // *ad* quite well; (*beaucoup*) quite a lot; **~ mal de** quite a lot of.

pas [pɑ] *ad voir le mot précédent* // *nm* (*allure, mesure*) pace; (*démarche*) tread; (*enjambée, DANSE*) step; (*bruit*) (foot)step; (*trace*) footprint; (*TECH*: *de vis, d'écrou*) thread; **~ à ~** step by step; **au ~** at walking pace; **mettre qn au ~** to bring sb to heel; **au ~ de gymnastique/de course** at a jog trot/at a run; **à ~ de loup** stealthily; **faire les cent ~** to pace up and down; **faire les premiers ~** to make the first move; **sur le ~ de la porte** on the doorstep; **le ~ de Calais** (*détroit*) the Straits of Dover; **~ de porte** (*COMM*) key money.

pascal, e, aux [paskal, -o] *a* Easter *cpd*.

passable [pɑsabl(ə)] *a* (*travail*) passable, tolerable.

passage [pɑsaʒ] *nm* (*fait de passer*) *voir* **passer**; (*lieu, prix de la traversée, extrait de livre etc*) passage; (*chemin*) way; **de ~** (*touristes*) passing through; (*amants etc*) casual; **~ clouté** pedestrian crossing; **'~ interdit'** 'no entry'; **~ à niveau** level crossing; **'~ protégé'** *right of way over secondary road(s) on your right*; **~ souterrain** subway, underground passage; **~ à tabac** beating-up.

passager, ère [pɑsaʒe, -ɛR] *a* passing // *nm/f* passenger; **~ clandestin** stowaway.

passant, e [pɑsɑ̃, -ɑ̃t] *a* (*rue, endroit*) busy // *nm/f* passer-by // *nm* (*pour ceinture etc*) loop.

passe [pɑs] *nf* (*SPORT, magnétique, NAVIG*) pass // *nm* (*passe-partout*) master *ou* skeleton key; **être en ~ de faire** to be on the way to doing.

passé, e [pɑse] *a* (*événement, temps*) past; (*couleur, tapisserie*) faded // *prép* after // *nm* past; (*LING*) past (tense); **il est ~ midi** *ou* **midi ~** it's gone twelve; **~ de mode** out of fashion; **~ composé** perfect (tense); **~ simple** past historic.

passe-droit [pɑsdRwa] *nm* special privilege.

passéiste [pɑseist] *a* backward-looking.

passementerie [pɑsmɑ̃tRi] *nf* trimmings *pl*.

passe-montagne [pɑsmɔ̃taɲ] *nm* balaclava.

passe-partout [pɑspaRtu] *nm inv* master *ou* skeleton key // *a inv* all-purpose.

passe-passe [pɑspɑs] *nm*: **tour de ~** trick, sleight of hand *q*.

passe-plats [pɑspla] *nm inv* serving hatch.

passeport [pɑspɔR] *nm* passport.

passer [pɑse] *vi* (*se rendre, aller*) to go; (*voiture, piétons*: *défiler*) to pass (by), go by; (*faire une halte rapide*: *facteur, laitier etc*) to come, call; (: *pour rendre visite*) to call *ou* drop in; (*courant, air, lumière, franchir un obstacle etc*) to get through; (*accusé, projet de loi*): **~ devant** to come before; (*film, émission*) to be on; (*temps, jours*) to pass, go by; (*couleur, papier*) to fade; (*douleur*) to pass, go away; (*CARTES*) to pass; (*SCOL*) to go up (to the next class) // *vt* (*frontière, rivière etc*) to cross; (*douane*) to go through; (*examen*) to sit, take; (*visite médicale etc*) to have; (*journée, temps*) to spend; (*donner*): **~ qch à qn** to pass sth to sb; to give sb sth; (*transmettre*): **~ qch à qn** to pass sth on to sb; (*enfiler*: *vêtement*) to slip on; (*faire entrer, mettre*): **(faire) ~ qch dans/par** to get sth into/through; (*café*) to pour the water on; (*thé, soupe*) to strain; (*film, pièce*) to show, put on; (*disque*) to play, put on; (*marché, accord*) to agree on; (*tolérer*): **~ qch à qn** to let sb get away with sth; **se ~** *vi* (*avoir lieu*: *scène, action*) to take place; (*se dérouler*: *entretien etc*) to go; (*arriver*): **que s'est-il passé?** what happened?; (*s'écouler*: *semaine etc*) to pass, go by; **se ~ de** *vt* to go *ou* do without; **se ~ les mains sous l'eau/de l'eau sur le visage** to put one's hands under the tap/run water over one's face; **~ par** to go through; **passe devant/par ici** go in front/this way; **~ sur** *vt* (*faute, détail inutile*) to pass over; **~ avant qch/qn** (*fig*) to come before sth/sb; **laisser ~** (*air, lumière, personne*) to let through; (*occasion*) to let slip, miss; (*erreur*) to overlook; **~ à la radio/fouille** to be

X-rayed/searched; ~ **à la radio/télévision** to be on the radio/on television; ~ **pour riche** to be taken for a rich man; **il passait pour avoir** he was said to have; ~ **à l'opposition** to go over to the opposition; **passons!** let's say no more (about it); ~ **en seconde,** ~ **la seconde** (*AUTO*) to change into second; ~ **qch en fraude** to smuggle sth in (*ou* out); ~ **la main par la portière** to stick one's hand out of the door; ~ **le balai/l'aspirateur** to sweep up/hoover; **je vous passe M. X** (*je vous mets en communication avec lui*) I'm putting you through to Mr X; (*je lui passe l'appareil*) here is Mr X, I'll hand you over to Mr X.
passerelle [pɑsʀɛl] *nf* footbridge; (*de navire, avion*) gangway.
passe-temps [pɑstɑ̃] *nm inv* pastime.
passeur, euse [pɑsœʀ, -øz] *nm/f* smuggler.
passible [pasibl(ə)] *a*: ~ **de** liable to.
passif, ive [pasif, -iv] *a* passive // *nm* (*LING*) passive; (*COMM*) liabilities *pl*.
passion [pɑsjɔ̃] *nf* passion; **avoir la** ~ **de** to have a passion for; **passionné, e** *a* passionate; impassioned; **passionnel, le** *a* of passion; **passionner** *vt* (*personne*) to fascinate, grip; **se passionner pour** to take an avid interest in; to have a passion for.
passoire [pɑswaʀ] *nf* sieve; (*à légumes*) colander; (*à thé*) strainer.
pastel [pastɛl] *nm, a inv* (*ART*) pastel.
pastèque [pastɛk] *nf* watermelon.
pasteur [pastœʀ] *nm* (*protestant*) minister, pastor.
pasteuriser [pastœʀize] *vt* to pasteurize.
pastiche [pastiʃ] *nm* pastiche.
pastille [pastij] *nf* (*à sucer*) lozenge, pastille; (*de papier etc*) (small) disc; ~**s pour la toux** throat lozenges.
pastis [pastis] *nm* pastis.
patate [patat] *nf* spud; ~ **douce** sweet potato.
patauger [patoʒe] *vi* (*pour s'amuser*) to splash about; (*avec effort*) to wade about; ~ **dans** (*en marchant*) to wade through.
pâte [pɑt] *nf* (*à tarte*) pastry; (*à pain*) dough; (*à frire*) batter; (*substance molle*) paste; cream; ~**s** *nfpl* (*macaroni etc*) pasta *sg*; **fromage à** ~ **dure/molle** hard/soft cheese; ~ **d'amandes** almond paste; ~ **brisée** shortcrust pastry; ~ **de fruits** crystallized fruit *q*; ~ **à modeler** modelling clay, Plasticine ®; ~ **à papier** paper pulp.
pâté [pɑte] *nm* (*charcuterie*) pâté; (*tache*) ink blot; (*de sable*) sandcastle, sandpie; ~ **en croûte** ≈ pork pie; ~ **de maisons** block (of houses).
pâtée [pɑte] *nf* mash, feed.
patente [patɑ̃t] *nf* (*COMM*) trading licence.
patère [patɛʀ] *nf* (coat-)peg.
paternel, le [patɛʀnɛl] *a* (*amour, soins*) fatherly; (*ligne, autorité*) paternal.
paternité [patɛʀnite] *nf* paternity, fatherhood.
pâteux, euse [pɑtø, -øz] *a* thick; pasty.
pathétique [patetik] *a* moving, pathetic.
pathologie [patɔlɔʒi] *nf* pathology.
patibulaire [patibylɛʀ] *a* sinister.
patience [pasjɑ̃s] *nf* patience.
patient, e [pasjɑ̃, -ɑ̃t] *a, nm/f* patient.
patienter [pasjɑ̃te] *vi* to wait.
patin [patɛ̃] *nm* skate; (*sport*) skating; (*de traîneau, luge*) runner; (*pièce de tissu*) cloth pad (*used as slippers to protect polished floor*); ~**s (à glace)** (ice) skates; ~**s à roulettes** roller skates.
patinage [patinaʒ] *nm* skating; ~ **artistique/de vitesse** figure/speed skating.
patine [patin] *nf* sheen.
patiner [patine] *vi* to skate; (*embrayage*) to slip; (*roue, voiture*) to spin; **se** ~ *vi* (*meuble, cuir*) to acquire a sheen, become polished; **patineur, euse** *nm/f* skater; **patinoire** *nf* skating rink, (ice) rink.
pâtir [pɑtiʀ]: ~ **de** *vt* to suffer because of.
pâtisserie [pɑtisʀi] *nf* (*boutique*) cake shop; (*métier*) confectionery; (*à la maison*) pastry- *ou* cake-making, baking; ~**s** *nfpl* (*gâteaux*) pastries, cakes; **pâtissier, ière** *nm/f* pastrycook; confectioner.
patois [patwa] *nm* dialect, patois.
patriarche [patʀijaʀʃ(ə)] *nm* patriarch.
patrie [patʀi] *nf* homeland.
patrimoine [patʀimwan] *nm* inheritance, patrimony.
patriote [patʀijɔt] *a* patriotic // *nm/f* patriot; **patriotique** *a* patriotic.
patron, ne [patʀɔ̃, -ɔn] *nm/f* (*chef*) boss, manager/eress; (*propriétaire*) owner, proprietor/tress; (*employeur*) employer; (*MÉD*) ≈ senior consultant; (*REL*) patron saint // *nm* (*COUTURE*) pattern; ~ **de thèse** supervisor (of postgraduate thesis); **patronal, e, aux** *a* (*syndicat, intérêts*) employers'.
patronage [patʀɔnaʒ] *nm* patronage; (parish) youth club.
patronat [patʀɔna] *nm* employers *pl*.
patronner [patʀɔne] *vt* to sponsor, support.
patrouille [patʀuj] *nf* patrol; **patrouiller** *vi* to patrol, be on patrol.
patte [pat] *nf* (*jambe*) leg; (*pied: de chien, chat*) paw; (*: d'oiseau*) foot; (*languette*) strap; (*: de poche*) flap; **à** ~**s d'éléphant** *a* bell-bottomed; ~**s d'oie** (*fig*) crow's feet.
pattemouille [patmuj] *nf* damp cloth (*for ironing*).
pâturage [pɑtyʀaʒ] *nm* pasture.
pâture [pɑtyʀ] *nf* food.
paume [pom] *nf* palm.
paumer [pome] *vt* (*fam*) to lose.
paupière [popjɛʀ] *nf* eyelid.
paupiette [popjɛt] *nf*: ~**s de veau** veal olives.
pause [poz] *nf* (*arrêt*) break; (*en parlant, MUS*) pause.
pauvre [povʀ(ə)] *a* poor // *nm/f* poor man/woman; **les** ~**s** the poor; ~ **en calcium** with a low calcium content; ~**té** *nf* (*état*) poverty.
pavaner [pavane]: **se** ~ *vi* to strut about.
pavé, e [pave] *a* paved; cobbled // *nm* (*bloc*) paving stone; cobblestone; (*pavage*) paving.

pavillon [pavijɔ̃] *nm* (*de banlieue*) small (detached) house; (*kiosque*) lodge; pavilion; (*d'hôpital*) ward; (*MUS*: *de cor etc*) bell; (*ANAT*: *de l'oreille*) pavilion, pinna; (*drapeau*) flag; ~ **de complaisance** flag of convenience.
pavoiser [pavwaze] *vt* to deck with flags // *vi* to put out flags; (*fig*) to rejoice, exult.
pavot [pavo] *nm* poppy.
payant, e [pɛjɑ̃, -ɑ̃t] *a* (*spectateurs etc*) paying; (*fig*: *entreprise*) profitable; **c'est** ~ you have to pay, there is a charge.
paye [pɛj] *nf* pay, wages *pl*.
payement [pɛjmɑ̃] *nm* payment.
payer [peje] *vt* (*créancier, employé, loyer*) to pay; (*achat, réparations, fig*: *faute*) to pay for // *vi* to pay; (*métier*) to be well-paid; (*tactique etc*) to pay off; **il me l'a fait** ~ **10 F** he charged me 10 F for it; ~ **qch à qn** to buy sth for sb, buy sb sth; **ils nous ont payé le voyage** they paid for our trip; ~ **de sa personne** to give of o.s.; ~ **d'audace** to act with great daring; **cela ne paie pas de mine** it doesn't look much; **se** ~ **la tête de qn** to take the mickey out of sb; to take sb for a ride.
pays [pei] *nm* country; land; region; village; **du** ~ *a* local.
paysage [peizaʒ] *nm* landscape; **paysagiste** *nm/f* landscape gardener; landscape painter.
paysan, ne [peizɑ̃, -an] *nm/f* countryman/woman; farmer; (*péj*) peasant // *a* country *cpd*; farming, farmers'.
Pays-Bas [peiba] *nmpl*: **les** ~ the Netherlands.
P.C.V. *sigle voir* **communication**.
P.D.G. *sigle m voir* **président**.
péage [peaʒ] *nm* toll; (*endroit*) tollgate; **pont à** ~ toll bridge.
peau, x [po] *nf* skin; **gants de** ~ fine leather gloves; ~ **de chamois** (*chiffon*) chamois leather, shammy; **P~-Rouge** *nm/f* Red Indian, redskin.
peccadille [pekadij] *nf* trifle; peccadillo.
pêche [pɛʃ] *nf* (*sport, activité*) fishing; (*poissons pêchés*) catch; (*fruit*) peach; ~ **à la ligne** (*en rivière*) angling.
péché [peʃe] *nm* sin; ~ **mignon** weakness.
pêche-abricot [pɛʃabʀiko] *nf* yellow peach.
pécher [peʃe] *vi* (*REL*) to sin; (*fig*) to err; to be flawed.
pêcher [peʃe] *nm* peach tree // *vi* to go fishing; (*en rivière*) to go angling // *vt* to catch, land; to fish for; ~ **au chalut** to trawl.
pécheur, eresse [peʃœʀ, peʃʀɛs] *nm/f* sinner.
pêcheur [pɛʃœʀ] *nm* fisherman; angler; ~ **de perles** pearl diver.
pectoraux [pɛktɔʀo] *nmpl* pectoral muscles.
pécule [pekyl] *nm* savings *pl*, nest egg; (*d'un détenu*) earnings *pl* (*paid on release*).
pécuniaire [pekynjɛʀ] *a* financial.
pédagogie [pedagɔʒi] *nf* educational methods *pl*, pedagogy; **pédagogique** *a* educational; **formation pédagogique** teacher training; **pédagogue** *nm/f* teacher; educationalist.
pédale [pedal] *nf* pedal; **pédaler** *vi* to pedal; **pédalier** *nm* pedal and gear mechanism.
pédalo [pedalo] *nm* pedalo, pedal-boat.
pédant, e [pedɑ̃, -ɑ̃t] *a* (*péj*) pedantic.
pédéraste [pedeʀast(ə)] *nm* homosexual, pederast.
pédestre [pedɛstʀ(ə)] *a*: **tourisme** ~ hiking.
pédiatre [pedjatʀ(ə)] *nm/f* paediatrician, child specialist.
pédiatrie [pedjatʀi] *nf* paediatrics *sg*.
pédicure [pedikyʀ] *nm/f* chiropodist.
pègre [pɛgʀ(ə)] *nf* underworld.
peignais *etc vb voir* **peindre**.
peigne [pɛɲ] *nm* comb.
peigné, e [peɲe] *a*: **laine** ~**e** wool worsted; combed wool.
peigner [peɲe] *vt* to comb (the hair of); **se** ~ to comb one's hair.
peignis *etc vb voir* **peindre**.
peignoir [pɛɲwaʀ] *nm* dressing gown; ~ **de bain** bathrobe.
peindre [pɛ̃dʀ(ə)] *vt* to paint; (*fig*) to portray, depict.
peine [pɛn] *nf* (*affliction*) sorrow, sadness *q*; (*mal, effort*) trouble *q*, effort; (*difficulté*) difficulty; (*punition, châtiment*) punishment; (*JUR*) sentence; **faire de la** ~ **à qn** to distress *ou* upset sb; **prendre la** ~ **de faire** to go to the trouble of doing; **se donner de la** ~ to make an effort; **ce n'est pas la** ~ **de faire** there's no point in doing, it's not worth doing; **avoir de la** ~ **à faire** to have difficulty doing; **à** ~ *ad* scarcely, hardly, barely; **à** ~ **... que** hardly ... than; **sous** ~: **sous** ~ **d'être puni** for fear of being punished; **défense d'afficher sous** ~ **d'amende** billposters will be fined; **peiner** *vi* to work hard; to struggle; (*moteur, voiture*) to labour // *vt* to grieve, sadden.
peintre [pɛ̃tʀ(ə)] *nm* painter; ~ **en bâtiment** house painter, painter and decorator; ~ **d'enseignes** signwriter.
peinture [pɛ̃tyʀ] *nf* painting; (*couche de couleur, couleur*) paint; (*surfaces peintes*: *aussi*: ~**s**) paintwork; ~ **mate/brillante** matt/gloss paint; '~ **fraîche**' 'wet paint'.
péjoratif, ive [peʒɔʀatif, -iv] *a* pejorative, derogatory.
pelage [pəlaʒ] *nm* coat, fur.
pêle-mêle [pɛlmɛl] *ad* higgledy-piggledy.
peler [pəle] *vt, vi* to peel.
pèlerin [pɛlʀɛ̃] *nm* pilgrim; **pèlerinage** *nm* pilgrimage; place of pilgrimage, shrine.
pélican [pelikɑ̃] *nm* pelican.
pelle [pɛl] *nf* shovel; (*d'enfant, de terrassier*) spade; ~ **à gâteau** cake slice; ~ **mécanique** mechanical digger; ~**ter** *vt* to shovel (up).
pelletier [pɛltje] *nm* furrier.
pellicule [pelikyl] *nf* film; ~**s** *nfpl* (*MÉD*) dandruff *sg*.
pelote [pəlɔt] *nf* (*de fil, laine*) ball; (*d'épingles*) pin cushion; ~ **basque** pelota.
peloter [pəlɔte] *vt* (*fam*) to feel (up); **se** ~ to pet.

peloton [pəlɔtɔ̃] *nm* group, squad; (*CYCLISME*) pack; ~ **d'exécution** firing squad.
pelotonner [pəlɔtɔne]: **se** ~ *vi* to curl (o.s.) up.
pelouse [pəluz] *nf* lawn.
peluche [pəlyʃ] *nf*: **animal en** ~ fluffy animal, soft toy; **pelucher** *vi* to become fluffy, fluff up.
pelure [pəlyʀ] *nf* peeling, peel *q*; ~ **d'oignon** onion skin.
pénal, e, aux [penal, -o] *a* penal.
pénaliser [penalize] *vt* to penalize.
pénalité [penalite] *nf* penalty.
penalty, ies [penalti, -z] *nm* (*SPORT*) penalty (kick).
penaud, e [pəno, -od] *a* sheepish, contrite.
penchant [pɑ̃ʃɑ̃] *nm* tendency, propensity; liking, fondness.
penché, e [pɑ̃ʃe] *a* slanting.
pencher [pɑ̃ʃe] *vi* to tilt, lean over // *vt* to tilt; **se** ~ *vi* to lean over; (*se baisser*) to bend down; **se** ~ **sur** to bend over; (*fig*: *problème*) to look into; **se** ~ **au dehors** to lean out; ~ **pour** to be inclined to favour.
pendaison [pɑ̃dɛzɔ̃] *nf* hanging.
pendant, e [pɑ̃dɑ̃, -ɑ̃t] *a* hanging (out); (*ADMIN, JUR*) pending // *nm* counterpart; matching piece // *prép* during; **faire** ~ **à** to match; to be the counterpart of; ~**s d'oreilles** drop *ou* pendant earrings.
pendeloque [pɑ̃dlɔk] *nf* pendant.
pendentif [pɑ̃dɑ̃tif] *nm* pendant.
penderie [pɑ̃dʀi] *nf* wardrobe; (*placard*) walk-in cupboard.
pendre [pɑ̃dʀ(ə)] *vt, vi* to hang; **se** ~ **(à)** (*se suicider*) to hang o.s. (on); **se** ~ **à** (*se suspendre*) to hang from; ~ **à** to hang (down) from; ~ **qch à** (*mur*) to hang sth (up) on; (*plafond*) to hang sth (up) from.
pendule [pɑ̃dyl] *nf* clock // *nm* pendulum.
pendulette [pɑ̃dylɛt] *nf* small clock.
pêne [pɛn] *nm* bolt.
pénétrer [penetʀe] *vi* to come *ou* get in // *vt* to penetrate; ~ **dans** to enter; (*suj*: *projectile*) to penetrate; (: *air, eau*) to come into, get into; **se** ~ **de qch** to get sth firmly set in one's mind.
pénible [penibl(ə)] *a* (*astreignant*) hard; (*affligeant*) painful; (*personne, caractère*) tiresome; ~**ment** *ad* with difficulty.
péniche [peniʃ] *nf* barge; ~ **de débarquement** landing craft *inv*.
pénicilline [penisilin] *nf* penicillin.
péninsule [penɛ̃syl] *nf* peninsula.
pénis [penis] *nm* penis.
pénitence [penitɑ̃s] *nf* (*repentir*) penitence; (*peine*) penance.
pénitencier [penitɑ̃sje] *nm* penitentiary.
pénombre [penɔ̃bʀ(ə)] *nf* half-light; darkness.
pense-bête [pɑ̃sbɛt] *nm* aide-mémoire.
pensée [pɑ̃se] *nf* thought; (*démarche, doctrine*) thinking *q*; (*BOT*) pansy; **en** ~ in one's mind.
penser [pɑ̃se] *vi* to think // *vt* to think; (*concevoir*: *problème, machine*) to think out; ~ **à** to think of; (*songer à*: *ami, vacances*) to think of *ou* about; (*réfléchir à*: *problème, offre*): ~ **à qch** to think about sth *ou* sth over; ~ **à faire qch** to think of doing sth; ~ **faire qch** to be thinking of doing sth, intend to do sth; **penseur** *nm* thinker; **pensif, ive** *a* pensive, thoughtful.
pension [pɑ̃sjɔ̃] *nf* (*allocation*) pension; (*prix du logement*) board and lodgings, bed and board; (*maison particulière*) boarding house; (*hôtel*) guesthouse, hotel; (*école*) boarding school; **prendre** ~ **chez** to take board and lodging at; **prendre qn en** ~ to take sb (in) as a lodger; **mettre en** ~ to send to boarding school; ~ **alimentaire** (*d'étudiant*) living allowance; (*de divorcée*) maintenance allowance; alimony; ~ **complète** full board; ~ **de famille** boarding house, guesthouse; **pensionnaire** *nm/f* boarder; guest; **pensionnat** *nm* boarding school.
pentagone [pɛ̃tagɔn] *nm* pentagon.
pente [pɑ̃t] *nf* slope; **en** ~ *a* sloping.
Pentecôte [pɑ̃tkot] *nf*: **la** ~ Whitsun; (*dimanche*) Whitsunday; **lundi de** ~ Whit Monday.
pénurie [penyʀi] *nf* shortage.
pépier [pepje] *vi* to chirp, tweet.
pépin [pepɛ̃] *nm* (*BOT*: *graine*) pip; (*ennui*) snag, hitch; (*fam*) brolly.
pépinière [pepinjɛʀ] *nf* tree nursery; (*fig*) nest, breeding-ground.
pépite [pepit] *nf* nugget.
perçant, e [pɛʀsɑ̃, -ɑ̃t] *a* sharp, keen; piercing, shrill.
percée [pɛʀse] *nf* (*trouée*) opening; (*MIL*) breakthrough; (*SPORT*) break.
perce-neige [pɛʀsənɛʒ] *nf inv* snowdrop.
percepteur [pɛʀsɛptœʀ] *nm* tax collector.
perceptible [pɛʀsɛptibl(ə)] *a* perceptible.
perception [pɛʀsɛpsjɔ̃] *nf* perception; (*d'impôts etc*) collection.
percer [pɛʀse] *vt* to pierce; (*ouverture etc*) to make; (*mystère, énigme*) to penetrate // *vi* to come through; to break through; ~ **une dent** to cut a tooth.
perceuse [pɛʀsøz] *nf* drill.
percevoir [pɛʀsəvwaʀ] *vt* (*distinguer*) to perceive, detect; (*taxe, impôt*) to collect; (*revenu, indemnité*) to receive.
perche [pɛʀʃ(ə)] *nf* (*ZOOL*) perch; (*bâton*) pole.
percher [pɛʀʃe] *vt*: ~ **qch sur** to perch sth on // *vi*, **se** ~ *vi* (*oiseau*) to perch; **perchoir** *nm* perch.
perclus, e [pɛʀkly, -yz] *a*: ~ **de** (*rhumatismes*) crippled with.
perçois *etc vb voir* **percevoir**.
percolateur [pɛʀkɔlatœʀ] *nm* percolator.
perçu, e *pp de* **percevoir**.
percussion [pɛʀkysjɔ̃] *nf* percussion.
percuter [pɛʀkyte] *vt* to strike; (*suj*: *véhicule*) to crash into.
perdant, e [pɛʀdɑ̃, -ɑ̃t] *nm/f* loser.
perdition [pɛʀdisjɔ̃] *nf*: **en** ~ (*NAVIG*) in distress; **lieu de** ~ den of vice.
perdre [pɛʀdʀ(ə)] *vt* to lose; (*gaspiller*: *temps, argent*) to waste; (*personne*: *moralement etc*) to ruin // *vi* to lose; (*sur une vente etc*) to lose out; (*récipient*) to leak; **se** ~ *vi* (*s'égarer*) to get lost, lose one's way; (*fig*) to go to waste; to disappear, vanish.

perdreau, x [pɛʀdʀo] *nm* (young) partridge.
perdrix [pɛʀdʀi] *nf* partridge.
perdu, e [pɛʀdy] *pp de* **perdre** // *a* (*isolé*) out-of-the-way, godforsaken; (COMM: *emballage*) non-returnable; (*malade*): **il est ~** there's no hope left for him; **à vos moments ~s** in your spare time.
père [pɛʀ] *nm* father; **~s** *nmpl* (*ancêtres*) forefathers; **de ~ en fils** from father to son; **~ de famille** man with a family; family man; **le ~ Noël** Father Christmas.
péremptoire [peʀɑ̃ptwaʀ] *a* peremptory.
perfection [pɛʀfɛksjɔ̃] *nf* perfection.
perfectionné, e [pɛʀfɛksjɔne] *a* sophisticated.
perfectionnement [pɛʀfɛksjɔnmɑ̃] *nm* improvement.
perfectionner [pɛʀfɛksjɔne] *vt* to improve, perfect; **se ~ en anglais** to improve one's English.
perfide [pɛʀfid] *a* perfidious, treacherous.
perforant, e [pɛʀfɔʀɑ̃, -ɑ̃t] *a* (*balle*) armour-piercing.
perforateur, trice [pɛʀfɔʀatœʀ, -tʀis] *nm/f* punch-card operator // *nm* (*perceuse*) borer; drill // *nf* (*perceuse*) borer; drill; (*pour cartes*) card-punch; (*de bureau*) punch.
perforation [pɛʀfɔʀɑsjɔ̃] *nf* perforation; punching; (*trou*) hole.
perforatrice [pɛʀfɔʀatʀis] *nf voir* **perforateur**.
perforer [pɛʀfɔʀe] *vt* to perforate; to punch a hole (*ou* holes) in; (*ticket, bande, carte*) to punch.
performance [pɛʀfɔʀmɑ̃s] *nf* performance.
perfusion [pɛʀfyzjɔ̃] *nf* perfusion; **faire une ~ à qn** to put sb on a drip.
péricliter [peʀiklite] *vi* to go downhill.
péril [peʀil] *nm* peril; **périlleux, euse** [-jø, -øz] *a* perilous.
périmé, e [peʀime] *a* (out)dated; (ADMIN) out-of-date, expired.
périmètre [peʀimɛtʀ(ə)] *nm* perimeter.
période [peʀjɔd] *nf* period; **périodique** *a* (*phases*) periodic; (*publication*) periodical; (MATH: *fraction*) recurring // *nm* periodical; **garniture** *ou* **serviette périodique** sanitary towel.
péripéties [peʀipesi] *nfpl* events, episodes.
périphérie [peʀifeʀi] *nf* periphery; (*d'une ville*) outskirts *pl*; **périphérique** *a* (*quartiers*) outlying; (ANAT, TECH) peripheral; (*station de radio*) *operating from outside France* // *nm* (AUTO) ring road.
périphrase [peʀifʀɑz] *nf* circumlocution.
périple [peʀipl(ə)] *nm* journey.
périr [peʀiʀ] *vi* to die, perish.
périscope [peʀiskɔp] *nm* periscope.
périssable [peʀisabl(ə)] *a* perishable.
péritonite [peʀitɔnit] *nf* peritonitis.
perle [pɛʀl(ə)] *nf* pearl; (*de plastique, métal, sueur*) bead.
perlé, e [pɛʀle] *a*: **grève ~e** go-slow.
perler [pɛʀle] *vi* to form in droplets.
perlier, ière [pɛʀlje, -jɛʀ] *a* pearl *cpd*.
permanence [pɛʀmanɑ̃s] *nf* permanence; (*local*) (duty) office; strike headquarters; emergency service; **assurer une ~** (*service public, bureaux*) to operate *ou* maintain a basic service; **être de ~** to be on call *ou* duty; **en ~** *ad* permanently; continuously.
permanent, e [pɛʀmanɑ̃, -ɑ̃t] *a* permanent; (*spectacle*) continuous // *nf* perm, permanent wave.
perméable [pɛʀmeabl(ə)] *a* (*terrain*) permeable; **~ à** (*fig*) receptive *ou* open to.
permettre [pɛʀmɛtʀ(ə)] *vt* to allow, permit; **~ à qn de faire/qch** to allow sb to do/sth.
permis [pɛʀmi] *nm* permit, licence; **~ de chasse** hunting permit; **~ (de conduire)** (driving) licence; **~ de construire** planning permission; **~ d'inhumer** burial certificate; **~ poids lourds** HGV (driving) licence; **~ de séjour** residence permit.
permission [pɛʀmisjɔ̃] *nf* permission; (MIL) leave; (: *papier*) pass; **en ~** on leave; **avoir la ~ de faire** to have permission to do, be allowed to do; **permissionnaire** *nm* soldier on leave.
permuter [pɛʀmyte] *vt* to change around, permutate // *vi* to change, swap.
pernicieux, euse [pɛʀnisjø, -øz] *a* pernicious.
pérorer [peʀɔʀe] *vi* to hold forth.
perpendiculaire [pɛʀpɑ̃dikylɛʀ] *a, nf* perpendicular.
perpétrer [pɛʀpetʀe] *vt* to perpetrate.
perpétuel, le [pɛʀpetɥɛl] *a* perpetual; (ADMIN *etc*) permanent; for life.
perpétuer [pɛʀpetɥe] *vt* to perpetuate.
perpétuité [pɛʀpetɥite] *nf*: **à ~** *a, ad* for life; **être condamné à ~** to be sentenced to life imprisonment, receive a life sentence.
perplexe [pɛʀplɛks(ə)] *a* perplexed, puzzled.
perquisition [pɛʀkizisjɔ̃] *nf* (police) search; **perquisitionner** *vi* to carry out a search.
perron [peʀɔ̃] *nm* steps *pl* (*in front of mansion etc*).
perroquet [peʀɔkɛ] *nm* parrot.
perruche [peʀyʃ] *nf* budgerigar, budgie.
perruque [peʀyk] *nf* wig.
persan, e [pɛʀsɑ̃, -an] *a* Persian.
persécuter [pɛʀsekyte] *vt* to persecute; **persécution** *nf* persecution.
persévérant, e [pɛʀseveʀɑ̃, -ɑ̃t] *a* persevering.
persévérer [pɛʀseveʀe] *vi* to persevere.
persiennes [pɛʀsjɛn] *nfpl* (metal) shutters.
persiflage [pɛʀsiflaʒ] *nm* mockery *q*.
persil [pɛʀsi] *nm* parsley.
Persique [pɛʀsik] *a*: **le golfe ~** the (Persian) Gulf.
persistant, e [pɛʀsistɑ̃, -ɑ̃t] *a* persistent; (*feuilles*) evergreen; **à feuillage ~** evergreen.
persister [pɛʀsiste] *vi* to persist; **~ à faire qch** to persist in doing sth.
personnage [pɛʀsɔnaʒ] *nm* (*notable*) personality; figure; (*individu*) character, individual; (THÉÂTRE) character; (PEINTURE) figure.

personnaliser [pɛRsɔnalize] *vt* to personalize.
personnalité [pɛRsɔnalite] *nf* personality.
personne [pɛRsɔn] *nf* person // *pronom* nobody, no one; (*quelqu'un*) anybody, anyone; **~s** people *pl*; **il n'y a ~** there's nobody in, there isn't anybody in; **10 F par ~** 10 F per person *ou* a head; **~ âgée** elderly person; **personnel, le** *a* personal // *nm* staff; personnel; **personnellement** *ad* personally; **personnifier** *vt* to personify; to typify.
perspective [pɛRspɛktiv] *nf* (ART) perspective; (*vue, coup d'œil*) view; (*point de vue*) viewpoint, angle; (*chose escomptée, envisagée*) prospect; **en ~** in prospect; in the offing.
perspicace [pɛRspikas] *a* clear-sighted, gifted with (*ou* showing) insight.
persuader [pɛRsɥade] *vt*: **~ qn (de/de faire)** to persuade sb (of/to do); **persuasif, ive** *a* persuasive; **persuasion** *nf* persuasion.
perte [pɛRt(ə)] *nf* loss; (*de temps*) waste; (*fig*: *morale*) ruin; **à ~** (COMM) at a loss; **à ~ de vue** as far as the eye can (*ou* could) see; (*fig*) interminably; **~ sèche** dead loss; **~s blanches** (vaginal) discharge *sg*.
pertinent, e [pɛRtinɑ̃, -ɑ̃t] *a* apt, pertinent; discerning, judicious.
perturbation [pɛRtyRbɑsjɔ̃] *nf* disruption; perturbation; **~ (atmosphérique)** atmospheric disturbance.
perturber [pɛRtyRbe] *vt* to disrupt; (PSYCH) to perturb, disturb.
pervenche [pɛRvɑ̃ʃ] *nf* periwinkle.
pervers, e [pɛRvɛR, -ɛRs(ə)] *a* perverted, depraved; perverse.
perversion [pɛRvɛRsjɔ̃] *nf* perversion.
perverti, e [pɛRvɛRti] *nm/f* pervert.
pervertir [pɛRvɛRtiR] *vt* to pervert.
pesage [pəzaʒ] *nm* weighing; (HIPPISME) weigh-in; weighing room; enclosure.
pesamment [pəzamɑ̃] *ad* heavily.
pesant, e [pəzɑ̃, -ɑ̃t] *a* heavy; (*fig*) burdensome // *nm*: **valoir son ~ de** to be worth one's weight in.
pesanteur [pəzɑ̃tœR] *nf* gravity.
pèse-bébé [pɛzbebe] *nm* (baby) scales *pl*.
pesée [pəze] *nf* weighing; (BOXE) weigh-in; (*pression*) pressure.
pèse-lettre [pɛzlɛtR(ə)] *nm* letter scales *pl*.
pèse-personne [pɛzpɛRsɔn] *nm* (bathroom) scales *pl*.
peser [pəze] *vt, vb avec attribut* to weigh // *vi* to be heavy; (*fig*) to carry weight; **~ sur** (*levier, bouton*) to press, push; (*fig*) to lie heavy on; to influence; **~ à qn** to weigh heavy on sb.
pessaire [pɛsɛR] *nm* pessary.
pessimisme [pesimism(ə)] *nm* pessimism; **pessimiste** *a* pessimistic // *nm/f* pessimist.
peste [pɛst(ə)] *nf* plague.
pester [pɛste] *vi*: **~ contre** to curse.
pestiféré, e [pɛstifeRe] *nm/f* plague victim.
pestilentiel, le [pɛstilɑ̃sjɛl] *a* foul.
pet [pɛ] *nm* (*fam!*) fart (!).
pétale [petal] *nm* petal.
pétanque [petɑ̃k] *nf* petanque (bowls).
pétarader [petaRade] *vi* to backfire.
pétard [petaR] *nm* banger; cracker; (RAIL) detonator.
péter [pete] *vi* (*fam*: *casser, sauter*) to burst; to bust; (*fam!*) to fart (!).
pétiller [petije] *vi* (*flamme, bois*) to crackle; (*mousse, champagne*) to bubble; (*yeux*) to sparkle.
petit, e [pəti, -it] *a* (*gén*) small; (*main, objet, colline, en âge*: *enfant*) small, little (*avant le nom*); (*voyage*) short, little; (*bruit etc*) faint, slight; (*mesquin*) mean // *nm* (*d'un animal*) young *pl*; **faire des ~s** to have kittens (*ou* puppies *etc*); **en ~** in miniature; **mon ~** son; little one; **ma ~e** dear; little one; **pauvre ~** poor little thing; **la classe des ~s** the infant class; **pour ~s et grands** for children and adults; **les tout-petits** the little ones, the tiny tots; **~ à ~** bit by bit, gradually; **~/e ami/e** boyfriend/girlfriend; **~ déjeuner** breakfast; **~ doigt** little finger, pinkie; **~ four** petit four; **~e vérole** smallpox; **~s pois** petit pois *pl*, garden pea(s); **~-bourgeois, ~e-bourgeoise** *a* (*péj*) petit-bourgeois(e), middle-class; **~e-fille** *nf* granddaughter; **~-fils** *nm* grandson.
pétition [petisjɔ̃] *nf* petition.
petit-lait [pətilɛ] *nm* whey.
petit-nègre [ptinɛgR(ə)] *nm* (*péj*) pidgin French.
petits-enfants [pətizɑ̃fɑ̃] *nmpl* grandchildren.
pétrifier [petRifje] *vt* to petrify; (*fig*) to paralyze, transfix.
pétrin [petRɛ̃] *nm* kneading-trough; (*fig*): **dans le ~** in a jam *ou* fix.
pétrir [petRiR] *vt* to knead.
pétrole [petRɔl] *nm* oil; (*pour lampe, réchaud etc*) paraffin (oil); **pétrolier, ière** *a* oil *cpd* // *nm* oil tanker; **pétrolifère** *a* oil(-bearing).
peu [pø] *ad* little, *tournure négative* + much; (*avec adjectif*) *tournure négative* + very // *pronom* few // *nm* little; **~ avant/après** shortly before/afterwards; **~ de** (*nombre*) few, *négation* + (very) many; (*quantité*) little, *négation* + (very) much; **pour ~ de temps** for (only) a short while; **le ~ de gens qui** the few people who; **le ~ de sable qui** what little sand, the little sand which; **un (petit) ~** a little (bit); **un ~ de** a little; **un ~ plus/moins de** slightly more/less (*ou* fewer); **de ~** (only) just; **~ à ~** little by little; **à ~ près** *ad* just about, more or less; **à ~ près 10 kg/10 F** approximately 10 kg/10 F; **avant ~** before long.
peuplade [pœplad] *nf* (*horde, tribu*) tribe, people.
peuple [pœpl(ə)] *nm* people.
peupler [pœple] *vt* (*pays, région*) to populate; (*étang*) to stock; (*suj*: *hommes, poissons*) to inhabit; (*fig*: *imagination, rêves*) to fill.
peuplier [pøplije] *nm* poplar (tree).
peur [pœR] *nf* fear; **avoir ~ (de/de faire/que)** to be frightened *ou* afraid (of/of doing/that); **faire ~ à** to frighten;

de ~ de/que for fear of/that; ~eux, euse *a* fearful, timorous.

peut *vb voir* **pouvoir**.

peut-être [pøtɛtʀ(ə)] *ad* perhaps, maybe; ~ **que** perhaps, maybe; ~ **bien qu'il fera/est** he may well do/be.

peux *etc vb voir* **pouvoir**.

phalange [falɑ̃ʒ] *nf* (ANAT) phalanx (*pl* phalanges); (MIL) phalanx (*pl* es).

phallocrate [falɔkʀat] *nm* male chauvinist.

phallus [falys] *nm* phallus.

phare [faʀ] *nm* (*en mer*) lighthouse; (*d'aéroport*) beacon; (*de véhicule*) headlamp; **mettre ses ~s** to put on the full beam; **~s de recul** reversing lights.

pharmaceutique [faʀmasøtik] *a* pharmaceutic(al).

pharmacie [faʀmasi] *nf* (*science*) pharmacology; (*magasin*) chemist's, pharmacy; (*officine*) dispensary; (*produits*) pharmaceuticals *pl*; **pharmacien, ne** *nm/f* pharmacist, chemist.

pharyngite [faʀɛ̃ʒit] *nf* pharyngitis *q*.

pharynx [faʀɛ̃ks] *nm* pharynx.

phase [fɑz] *nf* phase.

phénomène [fenɔmɛn] *nm* phenomenon (*pl* a); (*monstre*) freak.

philanthrope [filɑ̃tʀɔp] *nm/f* philanthropist.

philanthropie [filɑ̃tʀɔpi] *nf* philanthropy.

philatélie [filateli] *nf* philately, stamp collecting; **philatéliste** *nm/f* philatelist, stamp collector.

philharmonique [filaʀmɔnik] *a* philharmonic.

philo [filo] *nf abr de* **philosophie**.

philosophe [filɔzɔf] *nm/f* philosopher // *a* philosophical.

philosophie [filɔzɔfi] *nf* philosophy; **philosophique** *a* philosophical.

phobie [fɔbi] *nf* phobia.

phonétique [fɔnetik] *a* phonetic // *nf* phonetics *sg*.

phonographe [fɔnɔgʀaf] *nm* (wind-up) gramophone.

phoque [fɔk] *nm* seal; (*fourrure*) sealskin.

phosphate [fɔsfat] *nm* phosphate.

phosphore [fɔsfɔʀ] *nm* phosphorus.

phosphorescent, e [fɔsfɔʀesɑ̃, -ɑ̃t] *a* luminous.

photo [fɔtɔ] *nf* photo(graph); **en ~** in *ou* on a photograph; **prendre en ~** to take a photo of; **aimer la/faire de la ~** to like taking/take photos; **~ d'identité** passport photograph.

photo... [fɔtɔ] *préfixe*: **~copie** *nf* photocopying, photostatting; photocopy, photostat (copy); **~copier** *vt* to photocopy, photostat; **~-électrique** *a* photoelectric; **~génique** *a* photogenic; **~graphe** *nm/f* photographer; **~graphie** *nf* (*procédé, technique*) photography; (*cliché*) photograph; **faire de la ~graphie** to have photography as a hobby; to be a photographer; **~graphier** *vt* to photograph, take; **~graphique** *a* photographic; **~maton** *nm* photo-booth, photomat; **~-robot** *nf* identikit (picture).

phrase [fʀɑz] *nf* (LING) sentence; (*propos*, MUS) phrase; **~s** (*péj*) flowery language *sg*.

phtisie [ftizi] *nf* consumption.

physicien, ne [fizisjɛ̃, -ɛn] *nm/f* physicist.

physiologie [fizjɔlɔʒi] *nf* physiology; **physiologique** *a* physiological.

physionomie [fizjɔnɔmi] *nf* face; **physionomiste** *nm/f* good judge of faces; person who has a good memory for faces.

physique [fizik] *a* physical // *nm* physique // *nf* physics *sg*; **au ~** physically; **~ment** *ad* physically.

piaffer [pjafe] *vi* to stamp.

piailler [pjɑje] *vi* to squawk.

pianiste [pjanist(ə)] *nm/f* pianist.

piano [pjano] *nm* piano.

pianoter [pjanɔte] *vi* to tinkle away (at the piano); (*tapoter*): **~ sur** to drum one's fingers on.

piaule [pjol] *nf* (*fam*) pad.

piauler [pjole] *vi* to whimper; to cheep.

pic [pik] *nm* (*instrument*) pick(axe); (*montagne*) peak; (ZOOL) woodpecker; **à ~** *ad* vertically; (*fig*) just at the right time.

pichenette [piʃnɛt] *nf* flick.

pichet [piʃɛ] *nm* jug.

pickpocket [pikpɔkɛt] *nm* pickpocket.

pick-up [pikœp] *nm* record player.

picorer [pikɔʀe] *vt* to peck.

picotement [pikɔtmɑ̃] *nm* tickle *q*; smarting *q*; prickling *q*.

picoter [pikɔte] *vt* (*suj*: *oiseau*) to peck // *vi* (*irriter*) to smart, prickle.

pie [pi] *nf* magpie; (*fig*) chatterbox.

pièce [pjɛs] *nf* (*d'un logement*) room; (THÉÂTRE) play; (*de mécanisme, machine*) part; (*de monnaie*) coin; (COUTURE) patch; (*document*) document; (*de drap, fragment, de bétail, de collection*) piece; **dix francs ~** ten francs each; **vendre à la ~** to sell separately *ou* individually; **travailler/payer à la ~** to do piecework/pay piece rate; **un maillot une ~** a one-piece swimsuit; **un deux-~s cuisine** a two-room(ed) flat with kitchen; **~ à conviction** exhibit; **~ d'eau** ornamental lake *ou* pond; **~ d'identité**: **avez-vous une ~ d'identité?** have you got any (means of) identification?; **~ montée** tiered cake; **~s détachées** spares, (spare) parts; **en ~s détachées** (*à monter*) in kit form.

pied [pje] *nm* foot (*pl* feet); (*de verre*) stem; (*de table*) leg; (*de lampe*) base; **~s nus** barefoot; **à ~** on foot; **à ~ sec** without getting one's feet wet; **au ~ de la lettre** literally; **au ~ levé** at a moment's notice; **de ~ en cap** from head to foot; **en ~** (*portrait*) full-length; **avoir ~** to be able to touch the bottom, not to be out of one's depth; **avoir le ~ marin** to be a good sailor; **perdre ~** to lose one's footing; **sur ~** (AGR) on the stalk, uncut; (*debout, rétabli*) up and about; **mettre sur ~** (*entreprise*) to set up; **mettre à ~** to dismiss; to lay off; **sur le ~ de guerre** ready for action; **sur ~ d'intervention** on stand-by; **faire du ~ à qn** to give sb a (warning) kick; to play footsy with sb; **~ de lit** footboard; **~ de nez**: **faire un ~ de nez à** to thumb one's nose at; **~ de salade** lettuce plant; **~ de vigne** vine;

~-à-terre *nm inv* pied-à-terre ; ~-de-biche *nm* claw ; (COUTURE) presser foot ; ~-de-poule *a inv* hound's-tooth.

piédestal, aux [pjedɛstal, -o] *nm* pedestal.

pied-noir [pjenwaʀ] *nm Algerian-born Frenchman.*

piège [pjɛʒ] *nm* trap ; **prendre au ~** to trap ; **piéger** *vt* (*avec une mine*) to booby-trap ; **lettre/voiture piégée** letter-/car-bomb.

pierraille [pjɛʀɑj] *nf* loose stones *pl*.

pierre [pjɛʀ] *nf* stone ; **~ à briquet** flint ; **~ fine** semiprecious stone ; **~ de taille** freestone *q* ; **~ de touche** touchstone ; **mur de ~s sèches** drystone wall.

pierreries [pjɛʀʀi] *nfpl* gems, precious stones.

piété [pjete] *nf* piety.

piétiner [pjetine] *vi* (*trépigner*) to stamp (one's foot) ; (*marquer le pas*) to stand about ; (*fig*) to be at a standstill // *vt* to trample on.

piéton, ne [pjetɔ̃, -ɔn] *nm/f* pedestrian ; **piétonnier, ière** *a* pedestrian *cpd*.

piètre [pjɛtʀ(ə)] *a* poor, mediocre.

pieu, x [pjø] *nm* post ; (*pointu*) stake.

pieuvre [pjœvʀ(ə)] *nf* octopus.

pieux, euse [pjø, -øz] *a* pious.

pigeon [piʒɔ̃] *nm* pigeon ; **~ voyageur** homing pigeon ; **pigeonnier** *nm* pigeon house.

piger [piʒe] *vi, vt* (*fam*) to understand.

pigment [pigmɑ̃] *nm* pigment.

pignon [piɲɔ̃] *nm* (*de mur*) gable ; (*d'engrenage*) cog(wheel), gearwheel ; (*graine*) pine kernel ; **avoir ~ sur rue** (*fig*) to have a prosperous business.

pile [pil] *nf* (*tas*) pile ; (ÉLEC) battery // *a*: **le côté ~** tails // *ad* (*s'arrêter etc*) dead ; **à deux heures ~** at two on the dot ; **jouer à ~ ou face** to toss up (for it) ; **~ ou face?** heads or tails?

piler [pile] *vt* to crush, pound.

pileux, euse [pilø, -øz] *a*: **système ~** (body) hair.

pilier [pilje] *nm* pillar.

pillard, e [pijaʀ, -aʀd(ə)] *nm/f* looter ; plunderer.

piller [pije] *vt* to pillage, plunder, loot.

pilon [pilɔ̃] *nm* pestle.

pilonner [pilɔne] *vt* to pound.

pilori [pilɔʀi] *nm*: **mettre** *ou* **clouer au ~** to pillory.

pilotage [pilɔtaʒ] *nm* piloting ; flying ; **~ sans visibilité** blind flying.

pilote [pilɔt] *nm* pilot ; (*de char, voiture*) driver // *a* pilot *cpd* ; **~ de ligne/d'essai/de chasse** airline/test/fighter pilot.

piloter [pilɔte] *vt* to pilot ; to fly ; to drive ; (*fig*): **~ qn** to guide sb round.

pilotis [pilɔti] *nm* pile ; stilt.

pilule [pilyl] *nf* pill ; **prendre la ~** to be on the pill.

pimbêche [pɛ̃bɛʃ] *nf* (*péj*) stuck-up girl.

piment [pimɑ̃] *nm* (BOT) pepper, capsicum ; (*fig*) spice, piquancy ; **~ rouge** (CULIN) chilli.

pimpant, e [pɛ̃pɑ̃, -ɑ̃t] *a* trim and fresh-looking.

pin [pɛ̃] *nm* pine (tree) ; (*bois*) pine(wood).

pince [pɛ̃s] *nf* (*outil*) pliers *pl* ; (*de homard, crabe*) pincer, claw ; (COUTURE: *pli*) dart ; **~ à sucre/glace** sugar/ice tongs *pl* ; **~ à épiler** tweezers *pl* ; **~ à linge** clothes peg ; **~s de cycliste** bicycle clips.

pinceau, x [pɛ̃so] *nm* (paint)brush.

pincé, e [pɛ̃se] *a* (*air*) stiff // *nf*: **une ~e de** a pinch of.

pincer [pɛ̃se] *vt* to pinch ; (MUS: *cordes*) to pluck ; (COUTURE) to dart, put darts in ; (*fam*) to nab ; **se ~ le nez** to hold one's nose.

pince-sans-rire [pɛ̃ssɑ̃ʀiʀ] *a inv* deadpan.

pincettes [pɛ̃sɛt] *nfpl* (*pour le feu*) (fire) tongs.

pinède [pinɛd] *nf* pinewood, pine forest.

pingouin [pɛ̃gwɛ̃] *nm* penguin.

ping-pong [piŋpɔ̃g] *nm* table tennis.

pingre [pɛ̃gʀ(ə)] *a* niggardly.

pinson [pɛ̃sɔ̃] *nm* chaffinch.

pintade [pɛ̃tad] *nf* guinea-fowl.

pin-up [pinœp] *nf inv* pinup (girl).

pioche [pjɔʃ] *nf* pickaxe ; **piocher** *vt* to dig up (with a pickaxe) ; (*fam*) to swot at ; **piocher dans** to dig into.

piolet [pjɔlɛ] *nm* ice axe.

pion, ne [pjɔ̃, pjɔn] *nm/f* (SCOL: *péj*) *student paid to supervise schoolchildren* // *nm* (ÉCHECS) pawn ; (DAMES) piece, draught.

pionnier [pjɔnje] *nm* pioneer.

pipe [pip] *nf* pipe ; **~ de bruyère** briar pipe.

pipeau, x [pipo] *nm* (reed-)pipe.

pipe-line [pajplajn] *nm* pipeline.

pipi [pipi] *nm* (*fam*): **faire ~** to have a wee.

piquant, e [pikɑ̃, -ɑ̃t] *a* (*barbe, rosier etc*) prickly ; (*saveur, sauce*) hot, pungent ; (*fig*) racy ; biting // *nm* (*épine*) thorn, prickle ; (*de hérisson*) quill, spine ; (*fig*) spiciness, spice.

pique [pik] *nf* pike ; (*fig*) cutting remark // *nm* (CARTES: *couleur*) spades *pl* ; (: *carte*) spade.

piqué, e [pike] *a* (COUTURE) (machine-)stitched ; quilted ; (*fam*) barmy // *nm* (AVIAT) dive ; (TEXTILE) piqué.

pique-assiette [pikasjɛt] *nm/f inv* (*péj*) scrounger, sponger.

pique-nique [piknik] *nm* picnic.

piquer [pike] *vt* (*percer*) to prick ; (*planter*): **~ qch dans** to stick sth into ; (*fixer*): **~ qch à/sur** to pin sth onto ; (MÉD) to give a jab to ; (: *animal blessé*) to put to sleep ; (*suj*: *insecte, fumée, ortie*) to sting ; (*suj*: *poivre*) to burn ; (: *froid*) to bite ; (COUTURE) to machine (stitch) ; (*intérêt etc*) to arouse ; (*fam*) to pick up ; to pinch ; to nab // *vi* (*avion*) to go into a dive ; (*saveur*) to be pungent ; to be sour ; **~ sur** to swoop down on ; to head straight for ; **se ~ de faire** to pride o.s. on one's ability to do ; **~ du nez** (*avion*) to go into a nose-dive ; **~ un galop/un cent mètres** to break into a gallop/put on a sprint ; **~ une crise** to throw a fit.

piquet [pikɛ] *nm* (*pieu*) post, stake ; (*de tente*) peg ; **mettre un élève au ~** to make a pupil stand in the corner ; **~ de grève** (strike-)picket ; **~ d'incendie** fire-fighting squad.

piqueté, e [pikte] *a*: ~ **de** dotted with.
piqûre [pikyR] *nf* (*d'épingle*) prick; (*d'ortie*) sting; (*de moustique*) bite; (*MÉD*) injection; (*COUTURE*) (straight) stitch; straight stitching; **faire une** ~ **à qn** to give sb an injection.
pirate [piRat] *nm*, *a* pirate; ~ **de l'air** hijacker.
pire [piR] *a* worse; (*superlatif*): **le(la)** ~ ... the worst ... // *nm*: **le** ~ **(de)** the worst (of).
pirogue [piRɔg] *nf* dugout canoe.
pirouette [piRwɛt] *nf* pirouette.
pis [pi] *nm* (*de vache*) udder; (*pire*): **le** ~ the worst // *a*, *ad* worse; **pis-aller** *nm inv* stopgap.
pisciculture [pisikyltyR] *nf* fish farming.
piscine [pisin] *nf* (swimming) pool; ~ **couverte** indoor (swimming) pool.
pissenlit [pisɑ̃li] *nm* dandelion.
pisser [pise] *vi* (*fam!*) to pee (!); **pissotière** *nf* (*fam*) public urinal.
pistache [pistaʃ] *nf* pistachio (nut).
piste [pist(ə)] *nf* (*d'un animal, sentier*) track, trail; (*indice*) lead; (*de stade, de magnétophone*) track; (*de cirque*) ring; (*de danse*) floor; (*de patinage*) rink; (*de ski*) run; (*AVIAT*) runway.
pistil [pistil] *nm* pistil.
pistolet [pistɔlɛ] *nm* (*arme*) pistol, gun; (*à peinture*) spray gun; ~ **à bouchon/air comprimé** popgun/ airgun; ~-**mitrailleur** *nm* submachine gun.
piston [pistɔ̃] *nm* (*TECH*) piston; (*MUS*) valve; (*fig*) string-pulling; **pistonner** *vt* (*candidat*) to pull strings for.
pitance [pitɑ̃s] *nf* (*péj*) (means of) sustenance.
piteux, euse [pitø, -øz] *a* pitiful, sorry (*avant le nom*).
pitié [pitje] *nf* pity; **sans** ~ *a* pitiless, merciless; **faire** ~ to inspire pity; **il me fait** ~ I pity him, I feel sorry for him; **avoir** ~ **de** (*compassion*) to pity, feel sorry for; (*merci*) to have pity *ou* mercy on.
piton [pitɔ̃] *nm* (*clou*) peg, bolt; ~ **rocheux** rocky outcrop.
pitoyable [pitwajabl(ə)] *a* pitiful.
pitre [pitR(ə)] *nm* clown; **pitrerie** *nf* tomfoolery *q*.
pittoresque [pitɔRɛsk(ə)] *a* picturesque.
pivot [pivo] *nm* pivot; **pivoter** *vi* to swivel; to revolve.
pizza [pidza] *nf* pizza.
P.J. *sigle f voir* **police**.
Pl. *abr de* **place**.
placage [plakaʒ] *nm* (*bois*) veneer.
placard [plakaR] *nm* (*armoire*) cupboard; (*affiche*) poster, notice; (*TYPO*) galley; ~ **publicitaire** display advertisement; **placarder** *vt* (*affiche*) to put up.
place [plas] *nf* (*emplacement, situation, classement*) place; (*de ville, village*) square; (*espace libre*) room, space; (*de parking*) space; (*siège*: *de train, cinéma, voiture*) seat; (*emploi*) job; **en** ~ (*mettre*) in its place; **sur** ~ on the spot; **faire** ~ **à** to give way to; **faire de la** ~ **à** to make room for; **ça prend de la** ~ it takes up a lot of room *ou* space; **à la** ~ **de** in place of, instead of; **une quatre** ~**s** (*AUTO*) a four-seater; **il y a 20** ~**s assises/debout** there are 20 seats/is standing room for 20; ~ **forte** fortified town.
placé, e [plase] *a* (*HIPPISME*) placed; **haut** ~ (*fig*) high-ranking.
placement [plasmɑ̃] *nm* placing; investment; **bureau de** ~ employment agency.
placenta [plasɑ̃ta] *nm* placenta.
placer [plase] *vt* to place; (*convive, spectateur*) to seat; (*capital, argent*) to place, invest; (*dans la conversation*) to put *ou* get in; ~ **qn chez** to get sb a job at (*ou* with); **se** ~ **au premier rang** to go and stand (*ou* sit) in the first row.
placide [plasid] *a* placid.
plafond [plafɔ̃] *nm* ceiling.
plafonner [plafɔne] *vi* to reach one's (*ou* a) ceiling.
plage [plaʒ] *nf* beach; (*station*) (seaside) resort; (*fig*) band, bracket; (*de disque*) track, band; ~ **arrière** (*AUTO*) parcel *ou* back shelf.
plagiat [plaʒja] *nm* plagiarism.
plagier [plaʒje] *vt* to plagiarize.
plaider [plede] *vi* (*avocat*) to plead; (*plaignant*) to go to court, litigate // *vt* to plead; ~ **pour** (*fig*) to speak for; **plaideur, euse** *nm/f* litigant; **plaidoirie** *nf* (*JUR*) speech for the defence; **plaidoyer** *nm* (*JUR*) speech for the defence; (*fig*) plea.
plaie [plɛ] *nf* wound.
plaignant, e [plɛɲɑ̃, -ɑ̃t] *nm/f* plaintiff.
plaindre [plɛ̃dR(ə)] *vt* to pity, feel sorry for; **se** ~ (*gémir*) to moan; (*protester, rouspéter*): **se** ~ **(à qn) (de)** to complain (to sb) (about); (*souffrir*): **se** ~ **de** to complain of.
plaine [plɛn] *nf* plain.
plain-pied [plɛ̃pje]: **de** ~ *ad* at street-level; (*fig*) straight; **de** ~ **avec** on the same level as.
plainte [plɛ̃t] *nf* (*gémissement*) moan, groan; (*doléance*) complaint; **porter** ~ to lodge a complaint; **plaintif, ive** *a* plaintive.
plaire [plɛR] *vi* to be a success, be successful; to please; ~ **à**: **cela me plaît** I like it; **essayer de** ~ **à qn** (*en étant serviable etc*) to try and please sb; **elle plaît aux hommes** she's a success with men, men like her; **se** ~ **quelque part** to like being somewhere *ou* like it somewhere; **se** ~ **à faire** to take pleasure in doing; **ce qu'il vous plaira** what(ever) you like *ou* wish; **s'il vous plaît** please.
plaisamment [plɛzamɑ̃] *ad* pleasantly.
plaisance [plɛzɑ̃s] *nf* (*aussi*: **navigation de** ~) (pleasure) sailing, yachting; **plaisancier** *nm* amateur sailor, yachting enthusiast.
plaisant, e [plɛzɑ̃, -ɑ̃t] *a* pleasant; (*histoire, anecdote*) amusing.
plaisanter [plɛzɑ̃te] *vi* to joke; **pour** ~ for a joke; **on ne plaisante pas avec cela** that's no joking matter; **plaisanterie** *nf* joke; joking *q*; **plaisantin** *nm* joker.
plaise *etc vb voir* **plaire**.
plaisir [pleziR] *nm* pleasure; **faire** ~ **à qn** (*délibérément*) to be nice to sb, please sb; (*suj*: *cadeau, nouvelle etc*): **ceci me fait** ~ I'm delighted *ou* very pleased with this; **prendre** ~ **à/faire** to take pleasure in/in

doing; à ~ freely; for the sake of it; **au ~ (de vous revoir)** (I hope to) see you again; **pour le** *ou* **par** ~ for pleasure.
plan, e [plɑ̃, -an] *a* flat // *nm* plan; (GÉOM) plane; (*fig*) level, plane; (CINÉMA) shot; **au premier/second** ~ in the foreground/middle distance; **à l'arrière** ~ in the background; **mettre qch au premier** ~ (*fig*) to consider sth to be of primary importance; **sur le** ~ **sexuel** sexually, as far as sex is concerned; ~ **d'eau** stretch of water; ~ **de travail** work programme *ou* schedule.
planche [plɑ̃ʃ] *nf* (*pièce de bois*) plank, (wooden) board; (*illustration*) plate; **les ~s** (THÉÂTRE) the stage *sg*, the boards; **faire la** ~ (*dans l'eau*) to float on one's back; ~ **à dessin** drawing board; ~ **à pain** breadboard; ~ **à repasser** ironing board; ~ **de salut** (*fig*) sheet anchor.
plancher [plɑ̃ʃe] *nm* floor; floorboards *pl*; (*fig*) minimum level.
plancton [plɑ̃ktɔ̃] *nm* plankton.
planer [plane] *vi* to glide; ~ **sur** (*fig*) to hang over; to hover above.
planétaire [planetɛʀ] *a* planetary.
planète [planɛt] *nf* planet.
planeur [planœʀ] *nm* glider.
planification [planifikɑsjɔ̃] *nf* (economic) planning.
planifier [planifje] *vt* to plan.
planning [planiŋ] *nm* programme, schedule; ~ **familial** family planning.
planque [plɑ̃k] *nf* (*fam*) cushy number; hideout; stash.
plant [plɑ̃] *nm* seedling, young plant.
plantaire [plɑ̃tɛʀ] *a voir* **voûte**.
plantation [plɑ̃tɑsjɔ̃] *nf* plantation.
plante [plɑ̃t] *nf* plant; ~ **d'appartement** house *ou* pot plant; ~ **du pied** sole (of the foot).
planter [plɑ̃te] *vt* (*plante*) to plant; (*enfoncer*) to hammer *ou* drive in; (*tente*) to put up, pitch; (*fam*) to dump; to ditch; ~ **qch dans** to hammer *ou* drive sth into; to stick sth into; **se** ~ **dans** to sink into; to get stuck in; **se** ~ **devant** to plant o.s. in front of; **planteur** *nm* planter.
planton [plɑ̃tɔ̃] *nm* orderly.
plantureux, euse [plɑ̃tyʀø, -øz] *a* copious, lavish; buxom.
plaquage [plakaʒ] *nm* (RUGBY) tackle.
plaque [plak] *nf* plate; (*de verglas, d'eczéma*) patch; (*avec inscription*) plaque; **~s (minéralogiques** *ou* **de police** *ou* **d'immatriculation)** number plates; ~ **de beurre** tablet of butter; ~ **chauffante** hotplate; ~ **de chocolat** bar of chocolate; ~ **d'identité** identity disc; ~ **tournante** (*fig*) centre.
plaqué, e [plake] *a*: ~ **or/argent** gold-/silver-plated; ~ **acajou** veneered in mahogany.
plaquer [plake] *vt* (*bijou*) to plate; (*bois*) to veneer; (*aplatir*): ~ **qch sur/contre** to make sth stick *ou* cling to; (RUGBY) to bring down; (*fam*) to ditch; **se** ~ **contre** to flatten o.s. against; ~ **qn contre** to pin sb to.
plaquette [plakɛt] *nf* tablet; bar; (*livre*) small volume.
plasma [plasma] *nm* plasma.
plastic [plastik] *nm* plastic explosive.
plastifié, e [plastifje] *a* plastic-coated.
plastique [plastik] *a* plastic // *nm* plastic // *nf* plastic arts *pl*; modelling.
plastiquer [plastike] *vt* to blow up (*with a plastic bomb*).
plastron [plastʀɔ̃] *nm* shirt front.
plastronner [plastʀɔne] *vi* to swagger.
plat, e [pla, -at] *a* flat; (*cheveux*) straight; (*personne, livre*) dull // *nm* (*récipient*, CULIN) dish; (*d'un repas*): **le premier** ~ the first course; (*partie plate*): **le** ~ **de la main** the flat of the hand; **à** ~ **ventre** *ad* face down; (*tomber*) flat on one's face; **à** ~ *ad, a* (*aussi*: *pneu, batterie*) flat; ~ **du jour** day's special (menu); ~ **de résistance** main course.
platane [platan] *nm* plane tree.
plateau, x [plato] *nm* (*support*) tray; (GÉO) plateau; (*de tourne-disques*) turntable; (CINÉMA) set; ~ **à fromages** cheeseboard.
plate-bande [platbɑ̃d] *nf* flower bed.
platée [plate] *nf* dish(ful).
plate-forme [platfɔʀm(ə)] *nf* platform; ~ **de forage/pétrolière** drilling/oil rig.
platine [platin] *nm* platinum // *nf* (*d'un tourne-disque*) turntable.
plâtras [plɑtʀa] *nm* rubble *q*.
plâtre [plɑtʀ(ə)] *nm* (*matériau*) plaster; (*statue*) plaster statue; (MÉD) (plaster) cast; **avoir un bras dans le** ~ to have an arm in plaster; **plâtrer** *vt* to plaster; (MÉD) to set *ou* put in a (plaster) cast.
plausible [plozibl(ə)] *a* plausible.
plébiscite [plebisit] *nm* plebiscite.
plein, e [plɛ̃, -ɛn] *a* full; (*porte, roue*) solid; (*chienne, jument*) big (with young) // *nm*: **faire le** ~ **(d'essence)** to fill up (with petrol); **les ~s** the downstrokes (*in handwriting*); ~ **de** full of; **à ~es mains** (*ramasser*) in handfuls; (*empoigner*) firmly; **à** ~ **régime** at maximum revs; (*fig*) full steam; **à** ~ **temps** full-time; **en** ~ **air/~e mer** in the open air/on the open sea; **en** ~ **soleil** right out in the sun; **en ~e nuit/rue** in the middle of the night/street; **en** ~ **milieu** right in the middle; **en** ~ **jour** in broad daylight; **en** ~ **sur** right on; **~-emploi** *nm* full employment.
plénière [plenjɛʀ] *af*: **assemblée** ~ plenary assembly.
plénitude [plenityd] *nf* fullness.
pléthore [pletɔʀ] *nf*: ~ **de** overabundance *ou* plethora of.
pleurer [plœʀe] *vi* to cry; (*yeux*) to water // *vt* to mourn (for); ~ **sur** *vt* to lament (over), to bemoan.
pleurésie [plœʀezi] *nf* pleurisy.
pleurnicher [plœʀniʃe] *vi* to grizzle, whine.
pleurs [plœʀ] *nmpl*: **en** ~ in tears.
pleutre [pløtʀ(ə)] *a* cowardly.
pleuvoir [pløvwaʀ] *vb impersonnel* to rain // *vi* (*fig*): ~ **(sur)** to shower down (upon); to be showered upon.
plexiglas [plɛksiglɑs] *nm* plexiglass.
pli [pli] *nm* fold; (*de jupe*) pleat; (*de pantalon*) crease; (*aussi*: **faux** ~) crease; (*enveloppe*) envelope; (*lettre*) letter;

(*CARTES*) trick ; **prendre le ~ de faire** to get into the habit of doing ; **~ d'aisance** inverted pleat.
pliage [plijaʒ] *nm* folding ; (*ART*) origami.
pliant, e [plijɑ̃, -ɑ̃t] *a* folding // *nm* folding stool, campstool.
plier [plije] *vt* to fold ; (*pour ranger*) to fold up ; (*table pliante*) to fold down ; (*genou, bras*) to bend // *vi* to bend ; (*fig*) to yield ; **se ~ à** to submit to ; **~ bagages** to pack up (and go).
plinthe [plɛ̃t] *nf* skirting board.
plissé, e [plise] *a* (*GÉO*) folded // *nm* (*COUTURE*) pleats *pl*.
plissement [plismɑ̃] *nm* (*GÉO*) fold.
plisser [plise] *vt* (*rider, chiffonner*) to crease ; (*jupe*) to put pleats in.
plomb [plɔ̃] *nm* (*métal*) lead ; (*d'une cartouche*) (lead) shot ; (*PÊCHE*) sinker ; (*sceau*) (lead) seal ; (*ÉLEC*) fuse ; **mettre à ~** to plumb.
plombage [plɔ̃baʒ] *nm* (*de dent*) filling.
plomber [plɔ̃be] *vt* (*canne, ligne*) to weight (with lead) ; (*colis, wagon*) to put a lead seal on ; (*dent*) to fill.
plomberie [plɔ̃bʀi] *nf* plumbing.
plombier [plɔ̃bje] *nm* plumber.
plonge [plɔ̃ʒ] *nf*: **faire la ~** to be a washer-up.
plongeant, e [plɔ̃ʒɑ̃, -ɑ̃t] *a* (*vue*) from above ; (*tir, décolleté*) plunging.
plongée [plɔ̃ʒe] *nf* diving *q* ; (*de sous-marin*) submersion, dive ; **en ~** (*sous-marin*) submerged ; (*prise de vue*) high angle.
plongeoir [plɔ̃ʒwaʀ] *nm* diving board.
plongeon [plɔ̃ʒɔ̃] *nm* dive.
plonger [plɔ̃ʒe] *vi* to dive // *vt*: **~ qch dans** (*immerger*) to plunge *ou* dip sth into ; (*planter*) to thrust sth into ; (*fig*) to plunge sth into ; **plongeur, euse** *nm/f* diver ; (*de café*) washer-up.
ployer [plwaje] *vt* to bend // *vi* to sag ; to bend.
plu *pp de* **plaire, pleuvoir**.
pluie [plɥi] *nf* rain ; (*fig*): **~ de** shower of ; **retomber en ~** to shower down ; **sous la ~** in the rain.
plume [plym] *nf* feather ; (*pour écrire*) (pen) nib ; (*fig*) pen.
plumeau, x [plymo] *nm* feather duster.
plumer [plyme] *vt* to pluck.
plumet [plymɛ] *nm* plume.
plumier [plymje] *nm* pencil box.
plupart [plypaʀ]: **la ~** *pronom* the majority, most (of them) ; **la ~ des** most, the majority of ; **la ~ du temps/d'entre nous** most of the time/of us ; **pour la ~** *ad* for the most part, mostly.
pluriel [plyʀjɛl] *nm* plural ; **au ~** in the plural.
plus *vb* [ply] *voir* **plaire** // *ad* [ply, plyz + *voyelle*] (*comparatif*) more, *adjectif court* + ...er ; (*davantage*) [plys] more ; (*négatif*): **ne ... ~** no more, *tournure négative* + any more ; no longer // *cj* [plys]: **~ 2** plus 2 ; **~ que** more than ; **~ grand que** bigger than ; **~ de 10 personnes** more than 10 people, over 10 people ; **~ de pain** more bread ; **~ il travaille, ~ il est heureux** the more he works, the happier he is ; **le ~ intelligent/grand** the most intelligent/biggest ; **3 heures/kilos de ~ que** 3 hours/kilos more than ; **de ~** what's more, moreover ; **3 kilos en ~** 3 kilos more, 3 extra kilos ; **en ~ de** in addition to ; **de ~ en ~** more and more ; **(tout) au ~** at the (very) most ; **~ ou moins** more or less ; **ni ~ ni moins** no more, no less.
plusieurs [plyzjœʀ] *dét, pronom* several ; **ils sont ~** there are several of them.
plus-que-parfait [plyskəpaʀfɛ] *nm* pluperfect, past perfect.
plus-value [plyvaly] *nf* appreciation ; capital gain ; surplus.
plut *vb voir* **plaire**.
plûtot [plyto] *ad* rather ; **je ferais ~ ceci** I'd rather *ou* sooner do this ; **fais ~ comme ça** try this way instead, you'd better try this way ; **~ que (de) faire** rather than *ou* instead of doing.
pluvieux, euse [plyvjø, -øz] *a* rainy, wet.
P.M.U. *sigle m voir* **pari**.
pneu, x [pnø] *nm* tyre ; letter sent by pneumatic tube.
pneumatique [pnømatik] *a* pneumatic ; rubber *cpd* // *nm* tyre.
pneumonie [pnømɔni] *nf* pneumonia.
P.O. *sigle* = *petites ondes*.
poche [pɔʃ] *nf* pocket ; (*déformation*): **faire une/des ~(s)** to bag ; (*sous les yeux*) bag, pouch // *nm* (*abr de* **livre de ~**) (pocket-size) paperback ; **de ~** pocket *cpd*.
poché, e [pɔʃe] *a*: **œuf ~** poached egg ; **œil ~** black eye.
poche-revolver [pɔʃʀevɔlvɛʀ] *nf* hip pocket.
pochette [pɔʃɛt] *nf* (*de timbres*) wallet, envelope ; (*d'aiguilles etc*) case ; (*sur veston*) breast pocket ; (*mouchoir*) breast pocket handkerchief ; **~ d'allumettes** book of matches ; **~ de disque** record sleeve.
pochoir [pɔʃwaʀ] *nm* (*ART*) stencil ; transfer.
podium [pɔdjɔm] *nm* podium (*pl* ia).
poêle [pwɑl] *nm* stove // *nf*: **~ (à frire)** frying pan.
poêlon [pwɑlɔ̃] *nm* casserole.
poème [pɔɛm] *nm* poem.
poésie [pɔezi] *nf* (*poème*) poem ; (*art*): **la ~** poetry.
poète [pɔɛt] *nm* poet.
poétique [pɔetik] *a* poetic.
pognon [pɔɲɔ̃] *nm* (*fam*) dough.
poids [pwa] *nm* weight ; (*SPORT*) shot ; **vendre au ~** to sell by weight ; **prendre du ~** to put on weight ; **~ plume/mouche/coq/ moyen** (*BOXE*) feather/fly/bantam/ middleweight ; **~ et haltères** *nmpl* weight lifting *sg* ; **~ lourd** (*BOXE*) heavyweight ; (*camion*) (big) lorry ; (: *ADMIN*) heavy goods vehicle (HGV) ; **~ mort** dead load.
poignant, e [pwaɲɑ̃, -ɑ̃t] *a* poignant, harrowing.
poignard [pwaɲaʀ] *nm* dagger ; **poignarder** *vt* to stab, knife.
poigne [pwaɲ] *nf* grip ; (*fig*) firm-handedness.

poignée [pwaɲe] *nf* (*de sel etc, fig*) handful ; (*de couvercle, porte*) handle ; ~ **de main** handshake.
poignet [pwaɲɛ] *nm* (ANAT) wrist ; (*de chemise*) cuff.
poil [pwal] *nm* (ANAT) hair ; (*de pinceau, brosse*) bristle ; (*de tapis*) strand ; (*pelage*) coat ; (*ensemble des poils*): **avoir du ~ sur la poitrine** to have hair(s) on one's chest, have a hairy chest ; **à ~** *a* (*fam*) starkers ; **au ~** *a* (*fam*) hunky-dory ; **poilu, e** *a* hairy.
poinçon [pwɛ̃sɔ̃] *nm* awl ; bodkin ; style ; die ; (*marque*) hallmark ; **poinçonner** *vt* to stamp ; to hallmark ; (*billet, ticket*) to clip, punch ; **poinçonneuse** *nf* (*outil*) punch.
poing [pwɛ̃] *nm* fist.
point [pwɛ̃] *nm* (*marque, signe*) dot ; (: *de ponctuation*) full stop ; (*moment, de score etc, fig: question*) point ; (*endroit*) spot ; (COUTURE, TRICOT) stitch // *ad* = **pas** ; **faire le ~** (NAVIG) to take a bearing ; (*fig*) to take stock (of the situation) ; **en tout ~** in every respect ; **sur le ~ de faire** (just) about to do ; **à tel ~ que** so much so that ; **mettre au ~** (*mécanisme, procédé*) to perfect ; (*appareil-photo*) to focus ; (*affaire*) to settle ; **à ~** (CULIN) medium ; just right ; **à ~ (nommé)** just at the right time ; **~ (de côté)** stitch (*pain*) ; **~ culminant** summit ; (*fig*) height, climax ; **~ d'eau** spring ; water point ; **~ d'exclamation** exclamation mark ; **~ faible** weak point ; **~ final** full stop, period ; **~ d'interrogation** question mark ; **~ mort** (AUTO): **au ~ mort** in neutral ; **~ noir** (*sur le visage*) blackhead ; (AUTO) accident spot ; **~ de repère** landmark ; (*dans le temps*) point of reference ; **~ de vente** retail outlet ; **~ de vue** viewpoint ; (*fig: opinion*) point of view ; **du ~ de vue de** from the point of view of ; **~s cardinaux** points of the compass, cardinal points ; **~s de suspension** suspension points.
pointe [pwɛ̃t] *nf* point ; (*d'une île*) headland ; (*allusion*) dig ; sally ; (*fig*): **une ~ d'ail/d'accent** a touch *ou* hint of garlic/of an accent ; **être à la ~ de** (*fig*) to be in the forefront of ; **sur la ~ des pieds** on tip-toe ; **en ~** *ad* (*tailler*) into a point // *a* pointed, tapered ; **de ~** *a* (*technique etc*) leading ; **heures/jours de ~** peak hours/days ; **faire du 180 en ~** (AUTO) to have a top *ou* maximum speed of 180 ; **faire des ~s** (DANSE) to dance on points ; **~ de vitesse** burst of speed.
pointer [pwɛ̃te] *vt* (*cocher*) to tick off ; (*employés etc*) to check in (*ou* out) ; (*diriger: canon, longue-vue, doigt*): **~ vers qch** to point at sth // *vi* (*employé*) to clock in (*ou* out) ; **pointeuse** *nf* timeclock.
pointillé [pwɛ̃tije] *nm* (*trait*) dotted line ; (ART) stippling *q*.
pointilleux, euse [pwɛ̃tijø, -øz] *a* particular, pernickety.
pointu, e [pwɛ̃ty] *a* pointed ; (*clou*) sharp ; (*voix*) shrill.
pointure [pwɛ̃tyʀ] *nf* size.
point-virgule [pwɛ̃viʀgyl] *nm* semi-colon.
poire [pwaʀ] *nf* pear ; (*fam: péj*) mug ; **~ à injections** syringe.
poireau, x [pwaʀo] *nm* leek.
poirier [pwaʀje] *nm* pear tree.
pois [pwa] *nm* (BOT) pea ; (*sur une étoffe*) dot, spot ; **à ~** (*cravate etc*) dotted, polka-dot *cpd* ; **~ chiche** chickpea ; **~ de senteur** sweet pea.
poison [pwazɔ̃] *nm* poison.
poisse [pwas] *nf* rotten luck.
poisseux, euse [pwasø, -øz] *a* sticky.
poisson [pwasɔ̃] *nm* fish *gén inv* ; **les P~s** (*signe*) Pisces, the Fishes ; **être des P~s** to be Pisces ; **~ d'avril!** April fool! ; **poissonnerie** *nf* fish-shop ; **poissonneux, euse** *a* abounding in fish ; **poissonnier, ière** *nm/f* fishmonger.
poitrail [pwatʀaj] *nm* breast.
poitrine [pwatʀin] *nf* chest ; (*seins*) bust, bosom ; (CULIN) breast ; **~ de bœuf** brisket.
poivre [pwavʀ(ə)] *nm* pepper ; **~ en grains/moulu** whole/ground pepper ; **poivré, e** *a* peppery ; **poivrier** *nm* (BOT) pepper plant ; (*ustensile*) pepperpot.
poivron [pwavʀɔ̃] *nm* pepper, capsicum ; **~ vert/rouge** green/red pepper.
poker [pɔkɛʀ] *nm*: **le ~** poker ; **~ d'as** four aces.
polaire [pɔlɛʀ] *a* polar.
polariser [pɔlaʀize] *vt* to polarize ; (*fig*) to attract ; to focus.
pôle [pol] *nm* (GÉO, ÉLEC) pole ; **le ~ Nord/Sud** the North/South Pole.
polémique [pɔlemik] *a* controversial, polemic(al) // *nf* controversy ; **polémiste** *nm/f* polemist, polemicist.
poli, e [pɔli] *a* polite ; (*lisse*) smooth ; polished.
police [pɔlis] *nf* police ; (*discipline*): **assurer la ~ de** *ou* **dans** to keep order in ; **peine de simple ~** *sentence imposed by a magistrates' ou police court* ; **~ d'assurance** insurance policy ; **~ judiciaire, P.J.** ≈ Criminal Investigation Department, C.I.D. ; **~ des mœurs** ≈ vice squad ; **~ secours** ≈ emergency services *pl*.
polichinelle [pɔliʃinɛl] *nm* Punch ; (*péj*) buffoon.
policier, ière [pɔlisje, -jɛʀ] *a* police *cpd* // *nm* policeman ; (*aussi*: **roman ~**) detective novel.
policlinique [pɔliklinik] *nf* ≈ outpatients (department).
polio(myélite) [pɔljɔ(mjelit)] *nf* polio(myelitis) ; **poliomyélitique** *nm/f* polio patient *ou* case.
polir [pɔliʀ] *vt* to polish.
polisson, ne [pɔlisɔ̃, -ɔn] *a* naughty.
politesse [pɔlitɛs] *nf* politeness ; **~s** (exchange of) courtesies, polite gestures ; **rendre une ~ à qn** to return sb's favour.
politicien, ne [pɔlitisjɛ̃, -ɛn] *nm/f* politician.
politique [pɔlitik] *a* political // *nf* (*science, pratique, activité*) politics *sg* ; (*mesures, méthode*) policies *pl* ; **politiser** *vt* to politicize ; **politiser qn** to make sb politically aware.
pollen [pɔlɛn] *nm* pollen.
polluer [pɔlɥe] *vt* to pollute ; **pollution** *nf* pollution.
polo [pɔlo] *nm* (*sport*) polo ; (*tricot*) sweat shirt.

Pologne [pɔlɔɲ] *nf*: **la ~** Poland; **polonais, e** *a, nm (langue)* Polish // *nm/f* Pole.

poltron, ne [pɔltʀɔ̃, -ɔn] *a* cowardly.

poly... [pɔli] *préfixe*: **~clinique** *nf* polyclinic; **~copier** *vt* to duplicate; **~gamie** *nf* polygamy; **~glotte** *a* polyglot; **~gone** *nm* polygon.

Polynésie [pɔlinezi] *nf*: **la ~** Polynesia.

polytechnicien, ne [pɔlitɛknisjɛ̃, -ɛn] *nm/f student (or former student) of the École Polytechnique.*

polyvalent, e [pɔlivalɑ̃, -ɑ̃t] *a* polyvalent; versatile, multi-purpose // *nm* ≈ tax inspector.

pommade [pɔmad] *nf* ointment, cream.

pomme [pɔm] *nf* (BOT) apple; (*boule décorative*) knob; (*pomme de terre*): **steak ~s (frites)** steak and chips; **tomber dans les ~s** (*fam*) to pass out; **~ d'Adam** Adam's apple; **~ d'arrosoir** (sprinkler) rose; **~ de pin** pine *ou* fir cone; **~ de terre** potato; **~s vapeur** boiled potatoes.

pommé, e [pɔme] *a* (*chou etc*) firm, with a good heart.

pommeau, x [pɔmo] *nm* (*boule*) knob; (*de selle*) pommel.

pommette [pɔmɛt] *nf* cheekbone.

pommier [pɔmje] *nm* apple tree.

pompe [pɔ̃p] *nf* pump; (*faste*) pomp (and ceremony); **~ de bicyclette** bicycle pump; **~ à essence** petrol pump; **~ à incendie** fire engine (*apparatus*); **~s funèbres** funeral parlour *sg*, undertaker's *sg*.

pomper [pɔ̃pe] *vt* to pump; (*évacuer*) to pump out; (*aspirer*) to pump up; (*absorber*) to soak up // *vi* to pump.

pompeux, euse [pɔ̃pø, -øz] *a* pompous.

pompier [pɔ̃pje] *nm* fireman // *am* (*style*) pretentious, pompous.

pompon [pɔ̃pɔ̃] *nm* pompom, bobble.

pomponner [pɔ̃pɔne] *vt* to titivate, dress up.

ponce [pɔ̃s] *nf*: **pierre ~** pumice stone.

poncer [pɔ̃se] *vt* to sand (down); **ponceuse** *nf* sander.

poncif [pɔ̃sif] *nm* cliché.

ponction [pɔ̃ksjɔ̃] *nf*: **~ lombaire** lumbar puncture.

ponctualité [pɔ̃ktɥalite] *nf* punctuality.

ponctuation [pɔ̃ktɥɑsjɔ̃] *nf* punctuation.

ponctuel, le [pɔ̃ktɥɛl] *a* (*à l'heure, aussi* TECH) punctual; (*fig: opération etc*) one-off, single; (*scrupuleux*) punctilious, meticulous.

ponctuer [pɔ̃ktɥe] *vt* to punctuate; (MUS) to phrase.

pondéré, e [pɔ̃deʀe] *a* level-headed, composed.

pondre [pɔ̃dʀ(ə)] *vt* to lay; (*fig*) to produce // *vi* to lay.

poney [pɔnɛ] *nm* pony.

pongiste [pɔ̃ʒist] *nm/f* table tennis player.

pont [pɔ̃] *nm* bridge; (AUTO): **~ arrière/avant** rear/front axle; (NAVIG) deck; **faire le ~** to take the extra day off; **~ aérien** airlift; **~ d'envol** flight deck; **~ de graissage** ramp (*in garage*); **~ roulant** travelling crane; **~ suspendu** suspension bridge; **~ tournant** swing bridge; **P~s et Chaussées** highways department.

ponte [pɔ̃t] *nf* laying // *nm* (*fam*) big shot.

pontife [pɔ̃tif] *nm* pontiff.

pontifier [pɔ̃tifje] *vi* to pontificate.

pont-levis [pɔ̃lvi] *nm* drawbridge.

pop [pɔp] *a inv* pop.

populace [pɔpylas] *nf* (*péj*) rabble.

populaire [pɔpylɛʀ] *a* popular; (*manifestation*) mass *cpd*, of the people; (*milieux, clientèle*) working-class; **populariser** *vt* to popularize; **popularité** *nf* popularity.

population [pɔpylɑsjɔ̃] *nf* population.

populeux, euse [pɔpylø, -øz] *a* densely populated.

porc [pɔʀ] *nm* (ZOOL) pig; (CULIN) pork; (*peau*) pigskin.

porcelaine [pɔʀsəlɛn] *nf* porcelain, china; piece of china(ware).

porcelet [pɔʀsəlɛ] *nm* piglet.

porc-épic [pɔʀkepik] *nm* porcupine.

porche [pɔʀʃ(ə)] *nm* porch.

porcherie [pɔʀʃəʀi] *nf* pigsty.

porcin, e [pɔʀsɛ̃, -in] *a* porcine; (*fig*) piglike.

pore [pɔʀ] *nm* pore; **poreux, euse** *a* porous.

pornographie [pɔʀnɔgʀafi] *nf* pornography; **pornographique** *a* (*abr* **porno**) pornographic.

port [pɔʀ] *nm* (NAVIG) harbour, port; (*ville*) port; (*de l'uniforme etc*) wearing; (*pour lettre*) postage; (*pour colis, aussi: posture*) carriage; **~ d'arme** (JUR) carrying of a firearm; **~ d'attache** (NAVIG) port of registry; **~ franc** free port.

portail [pɔʀtaj] *nm* gate; (*de cathédrale*) portal.

portant, e [pɔʀtɑ̃, -ɑ̃t] *a* (*murs*) structural, weight-bearing; **bien/ mal ~** in good/poor health.

portatif, ive [pɔʀtatif, -iv] *a* portable.

porte [pɔʀt(ə)] *nf* door; (*de ville, forteresse,* SKI) gate; **mettre à la ~** to throw out; **~ d'entrée** front door; **~ à ~** *nm* door-to-door selling.

porte... [pɔʀt(ə)] *préfixe*: **~-à-faux** *nm*: **en ~-à-faux** cantilevered; precariously balanced; **~-avions** *nm inv* aircraft carrier; **~-bagages** *nm inv* luggage rack; **~-bonheur** *nm inv* lucky charm; **~-cartes** *nm inv* card holder; map wallet; **~-cigarettes** *nm inv* cigarette case; **~-clefs** *nm inv* keyring; **~-crayon** *nm* pencil holder; **~-documents** *nm inv* attaché *ou* document case.

portée [pɔʀte] *nf* (*d'une arme*) range; (*fig*) impact, import; scope, capability; (*de chatte etc*) litter; (MUS) stave, staff (*pl* staves); **à/hors de ~ (de)** within/out of reach (of); **à ~ de (la) main** within (arm's) reach; **à ~ de voix** within earshot; **à la ~ de qn** (*fig*) at sb's level, within sb's capabilities.

porte-fenêtre [pɔʀtfənɛtʀ(ə)] *nf* French window.

portefeuille [pɔʀtəfœj] *nm* wallet; (POL, BOURSE) portfolio.

porte-jarretelles [pɔʀtʒaʀtɛl] *nm inv* suspender belt.

portemanteau, x [pɔʀtmɑ̃to] *nm* coat hanger; coat rack.
porte-mine [pɔʀtəmin] *nm* propelling pencil.
porte-monnaie [pɔʀtmɔnɛ] *nm inv* purse.
porte-parole [pɔʀtpaʀɔl] *nm inv* spokesman.
porte-plume [pɔʀtəplym] *nm inv* penholder.
porter [pɔʀte] *vt* (*charge ou sac etc, aussi*: *fœtus*) to carry; (*sur soi*: *vêtement, barbe, bague*) to wear; (*fig*: *responsabilité etc*) to bear, carry; (*inscription, marque, titre, patronyme, suj*: *arbre*: *fruits, fleurs*) to bear; (*apporter*): ~ **qch quelque part/à qn** to take sth somewhere/to sb; (*inscrire*): ~ **qch sur** to put sth down on; to enter sth in // *vi* (*voix, regard, canon*) to carry; (*coup, argument*) to hit home; ~ **sur** (*peser*) to rest on; (*accent*) to fall on; (*conférence etc*) to concern; (*heurter*) to strike; **se** ~ *vi* (*se sentir*): **se** ~ **bien/mal** to be well/unwell; (*aller*): **se** ~ **vers** to go towards; **être porté à faire** to be apt *ou* inclined to do; **elle portait le nom de Rosalie** she was called Rosalie; ~ **qn au pouvoir** to bring sb to power; ~ **son âge** to look one's age; **se faire** ~ **malade** to report sick; ~ **la main à son chapeau** to raise one's hand to one's hat; ~ **son effort sur** to direct one's efforts towards.
porte-savon [pɔʀtsavɔ̃] *nm* soapdish.
porte-serviettes [pɔʀtsɛʀvjɛt] *nm inv* towel rail.
porteur, euse [pɔʀtœʀ, -øz] *a*: **être** ~ **de** (*nouvelle*) to be the bearer of // *nm* (*de bagages*) porter; (*COMM*: *de chèque*) bearer.
porte-voix [pɔʀtəvwa] *nm inv* loudhailer.
portier [pɔʀtje] *nm* commissionnaire, porter.
portière [pɔʀtjɛʀ] *nf* door.
portillon [pɔʀtijɔ̃] *nm* gate.
portion [pɔʀsjɔ̃] *nf* (*part*) portion, share; (*partie*) portion, section.
portique [pɔʀtik] *nm* (*GYM*) crossbar; (*ARCHIT*) portico; (*RAIL*) gantry.
porto [pɔʀto] *nm* port (wine).
portrait [pɔʀtʀɛ] *nm* portrait; photograph; **portraitiste** *nm/f* portrait painter; ~**-robot** *nm* Identikit *ou* photo-fit picture.
portuaire [pɔʀtɥɛʀ] *a* port *cpd*, harbour *cpd*.
portugais, e [pɔʀtygɛ, -ɛz] *a, nm, nf* Portuguese.
Portugal [pɔʀtygal] *nm*: **le** ~ Portugal.
pose [poz] *nf* laying; hanging; (*attitude, d'un modèle*) pose; (*PHOTO*) exposure.
posé, e [poze] *a* serious.
posemètre [pozmɛtʀ(ə)] *nm* exposure meter.
poser [poze] *vt* (*déposer*): ~ **qch (sur)/qn à** to put sth down (on)/drop sb at; (*placer*): ~ **qch sur/quelque part** to put sth on/somewhere; (*installer*: *moquette, carrelage*) to lay; (: *rideaux, papier peint*) to hang; (*question*) to ask; (*principe, conditions*) to lay *ou* set down; (*problème*) to formulate; (*difficulté*) to pose // *vi* (*modèle*) to pose; to sit; **se** ~ (*oiseau, avion*) to land; (*question*) to arise.
poseur, euse [pozœʀ, -øz] *nm/f* (*péj*) show-off, poseur; ~ **de parquets/carrelages** floor/tile layer.
positif, ive [pozitif, -iv] *a* positive.
position [pozisjɔ̃] *nf* position; **prendre** ~ (*fig*) to take a stand.
posologie [pɔsɔlɔʒi] *nf* directions *pl* for use, dosage.
posséder [pɔsede] *vt* to own, possess; (*qualité, talent*) to have, possess; (*bien connaître*: *métier, langue*) to master, have a thorough knowledge of; (*sexuellement, aussi*: *suj*: *colère etc*) to possess; (*fam*: *duper*) to take in; **possesseur** *nm* owner; **possessif, ive** *a, nm* possessive; **possession** *nf* ownership *q*; possession; **être/entrer en possession de qch** to be in/take possession of sth.
possibilité [pɔsibilite] *nf* possibility; ~**s** *nfpl* (*moyens*) means; (*potentiel*) potential *sg*; **avoir la** ~ **de faire** to be in a position to do; to have the opportunity to do.
possible [pɔsibl(ə)] *a* possible; (*projet, entreprise*) feasible // *nm*: **faire son** ~ to do all one can, do one's utmost; **le plus/moins de livres** ~ as many/few books as possible; **le plus/moins d'eau** ~ as much/little water as possible; **dès que** ~ as soon as possible; **gentil** *etc* **au** ~ as nice *etc* as it is possible to be.
postal, e, aux [pɔstal, -o] *a* postal, post office *cpd*; **sac** ~ mailbag, postbag.
poste [pɔst(ə)] *nf* (*service*) post, postal service; (*administration, bureau*) post office // *nm* (*fonction, MIL*) post; (*de radio etc*) set; (*de budget*) item; ~**s** *nfpl* post office *sg*; **P**~**s et Télécommunications (P.T.T.**: *abr de Postes, Télégraphes, Téléphones*) ≈ General Post Office (G.P.O.); ~ **(de radio/télévision)** *nm* (radio/television) set; ~ **émetteur** *nm* transmitting set; ~ **d'essence** *nm* petrol *ou* filling station; ~ **d'incendie** *nm* fire point; ~ **de péage** *nm* tollgate; ~ **de pilotage** *nm* cockpit; ~ **(de police)** *nm* police station; ~ **restante** *nf* poste restante; ~ **de secours** *nm* first-aid post.
poster *vt* [pɔste] to post // *nm* [pɔstɛʀ] poster.
postérieur, e [pɔsteʀjœʀ] *a* (*date*) later; (*partie*) back // *nm* (*fam*) behind.
posteriori [pɔsteʀjɔʀi]: **a** ~ *ad* with hindsight, a posteriori.
postérité [pɔsteʀite] *nf* posterity.
posthume [pɔstym] *a* posthumous.
postiche [pɔstiʃ] *a* false // *nm* hairpiece.
postillonner [pɔstijɔne] *vi* to sp(l)utter.
post-scriptum [pɔstskʀiptɔm] *nm inv* postscript.
postulant, e [pɔstylɑ̃, -ɑ̃t] *nm/f* applicant.
postulat [pɔstyla] *nm* postulate.
postuler [pɔstyle] *vt* (*emploi*) to apply for, put in for.
posture [pɔstyʀ] *nf* posture, position; (*fig*) position.
pot [po] *nm* jar, pot; carton; (*en métal*) tin; **boire un** ~ (*fam*) to have a drink; ~ **(de chambre)** (chamber)pot; ~ **d'échappement** exhaust pipe; ~ **de fleurs** plant pot, flowerpot; (*fleurs*) pot plant; ~ **à tabac** tobacco jar.

potable [pɔtabl(ə)] *a* (*fig*) drinkable; decent; **eau ~** drinking water.
potache [pɔtaʃ] *nm* schoolboy.
potage [pɔtaʒ] *nm* soup; soup course.
potager, ère [pɔtaʒe, -ɛʀ] *a* (*plante*) edible, vegetable *cpd*; **(jardin) ~** kitchen *ou* vegetable garden.
potasse [pɔtas] *nf* potassium hydroxide; (*engrais*) potash.
potasser [pɔtase] *vt* (*fam*) to swot up.
pot-au-feu [pɔtofø] *nm inv* (beef) stew; (*viande*) stewing beef.
pot-de-vin [podvɛ̃] *nm* bribe.
poteau, x [pɔto] *nm* post; **~ (d'exécution)** execution post, stake; **~ indicateur** signpost; **~ télégraphique** telegraph pole; **~x (de but)** goal-posts.
potelé, e [pɔtle] *a* plump, chubby.
potence [pɔtɑ̃s] *nf* gallows *sg.*
potentiel, le [pɔtɑ̃sjɛl] *a, nm* potential.
poterie [pɔtʀi] *nf* pottery; piece of pottery.
potiche [pɔtiʃ] *nf* large vase.
potier [pɔtje] *nm* potter.
potins [pɔtɛ̃] *nmpl* gossip *sg.*
potion [posjɔ̃] *nf* potion.
potiron [pɔtiʀɔ̃] *nm* pumpkin.
pot-pourri [popuʀi] *nm* potpourri, medley.
pou, x [pu] *nm* louse (*pl* lice).
poubelle [pubɛl] *nf* (dust)bin.
pouce [pus] *nm* thumb.
poudre [pudʀ(ə)] *nf* powder; (*fard*) (face) powder; (*explosif*) gunpowder; **en ~**: **café en ~** instant coffee; **savon en ~** soap powder; **lait en ~** dried *ou* powdered milk; **poudrer** *vt* to powder; **~rie** *nf* gunpowder factory; **poudreux, euse** *a* dusty; powdery; **neige poudreuse** powder snow; **poudrier** *nm* (powder) compact; **poudrière** *nf* powder magazine; (*fig*) powder keg.
poudroyer [pudʀwaje] *vi* to rise in clouds *ou* a flurry.
pouf [puf] *nm* pouffe.
pouffer [pufe] *vi*: **~ (de rire)** to snigger; to giggle.
pouilleux, euse [pujø, -øz] *a* flea-ridden; (*fig*) grubby; seedy.
poulailler [pulɑje] *nm* henhouse; (*THÉÂTRE*): **le ~** the gods *sg.*
poulain [pulɛ̃] *nm* foal; (*fig*) protégé.
poularde [pulaʀd(ə)] *nf* fatted chicken.
poule [pul] *nf* (*ZOOL*) hen; (*CULIN*) (boiling) fowl; (*fam*) tart; broad; **~ d'eau** moorhen; **~ mouillée** coward; **~ pondeuse** layer; **~ au riz** chicken and rice.
poulet [pulɛ] *nm* chicken; (*fam*) cop.
pouliche [puliʃ] *nf* filly.
poulie [puli] *nf* pulley; block.
poulpe [pulp(ə)] *nm* octopus.
pouls [pu] *nm* pulse; **prendre le ~ de qn** to feel sb's pulse.
poumon [pumɔ̃] *nm* lung; **~ d'acier** iron lung.
poupe [pup] *nf* stern; **en ~** astern.
poupée [pupe] *nf* doll; **jouer à la ~** to play with one's doll *ou* dolls.
poupon [pupɔ̃] *nm* babe-in-arms; **pouponnière** *nf* crèche, day nursery.
pour [puʀ] *prép* for; **~ faire** (so as) to do, in order to do; **~ avoir fait** for having done; **~ que** so that, in order that; **~ riche qu'il soit** rich though he may be; **~ 10 F d'essence** 10 francs' worth of petrol; **~ cent** per cent; **~ ce qui est de** as for; **le ~ et le contre** the pros and cons.
pourboire [puʀbwaʀ] *nm* tip.
pourcentage [puʀsɑ̃taʒ] *nm* percentage.
pourchasser [puʀʃase] *vt* to pursue.
pourlécher [puʀleʃe]: **se ~** *vi* to lick one's lips.
pourparlers [puʀpaʀle] *nmpl* talks, negotiations; **être en ~ avec** to be having talks with.
pourpre [puʀpʀ(ə)] *a* crimson.
pourquoi [puʀkwa] *ad, cj* why // *nm inv*: **le ~ (de)** the reason (for).
pourrai *etc vb voir* **pouvoir**.
pourri, e [puʀi] *a* rotten.
pourrir [puʀiʀ] *vi* to rot; (*fruit*) to go rotten *ou* bad // *vt* to rot; (*fig*) to corrupt; to spoil thoroughly; **pourriture** *nf* rot.
pourrons *etc vb voir* **pouvoir**.
poursuite [puʀsɥit] *nf* pursuit, chase; **~s** *nfpl* (*JUR*) legal proceedings; **(course) ~** track race; (*fig*) chase.
poursuivant, e [puʀsɥivɑ̃, -ɑ̃t] *nm/f* pursuer.
poursuivre [puʀsɥivʀ(ə)] *vt* to pursue, chase (after); (*relancer*) to hound, harry; (*obséder*) to haunt; (*JUR*) to bring proceedings against, prosecute; (: *au civil*) to sue; (*but*) to strive towards; (*voyage, études*) to carry on with, continue // *vi* to carry on, go on; **se ~** *vi* to go on, continue.
pourtant [puʀtɑ̃] *ad* yet; **c'est ~ facile** (and) yet it's easy.
pourtour [puʀtuʀ] *nm* perimeter.
pourvoi [puʀvwa] *nm* appeal.
pourvoir [puʀvwaʀ] *vt*: **~ qch/qn de** to equip sth/sb with // *vi*: **~ à** to provide for; (*emploi*) to fill; **se ~** (*JUR*): **se ~ en cassation** to take one's case to the Court of Appeal.
pourvu, e [puʀvy] *a*: **~ de** equipped with; **~ que** *cj* (*si*) provided that, so long as; (*espérons que*) let's hope (that).
pousse [pus] *nf* growth; (*bourgeon*) shoot.
poussé, e [puse] *a* sophisticated, advanced; (*moteur*) souped-up.
pousse-café [puskafe] *nm inv* (after-dinner) liqueur.
poussée [puse] *nf* thrust; (*coup*) push; (*MÉD*) eruption; (*fig*) upsurge.
pousse-pousse [puspus] *nm inv* rickshaw.
pousser [puse] *vt* to push; (*inciter*): **~ qn à** to urge *ou* press sb to + *infinitif*; (*acculer*): **~ qn à** to drive sb to; (*émettre*: *cri etc*) to give; (*stimuler*) to urge on; to drive hard; (*poursuivre*) to carry on (further) // *vi* to push; (*croître*) to grow; (*aller*): **~ plus loin** to push on a bit further; **se ~** *vi* to move over; **faire ~** (*plante*) to grow.
poussette [pusɛt] *nf* (*voiture d'enfant*) push chair.

poussière [pusjɛʀ] *nf* dust ; (*grain*) speck of dust ; **et des ~s** (*fig*) and a bit ; **~ de charbon** coaldust ; **poussiéreux, euse** *a* dusty.

poussif, ive [pusif, -iv] *a* wheezy, wheezing.

poussin [pusɛ̃] *nm* chick.

poutre [putʀ(ə)] *nf* beam ; (*en fer, ciment armé*) girder ; **poutrelle** *nf* girder.

pouvoir [puvwaʀ] *nm* power ; (POL: *dirigeants*): **le ~** those in power, the government // *vb* + *infinitif* can ; (*suj: personne*) can, to be able to ; (*permission*) can, may ; (*probabilité, hypothèse*) may ; **il peut arriver que** it may happen that ; **il pourrait pleuvoir** it might rain ; **déçu de ne pas ~ le faire** disappointed not to be able to do it *ou* that he couldn't do it ; **il aurait pu le dire!** he could *ou* might have said! ; **il se peut que** it may be that ; **je n'en peux plus** I'm exhausted ; I can't take any more ; **~ d'achat** purchasing power ; **les ~s publics** the authorities.

prairie [pʀeʀi] *nf* meadow.

praliné, e [pʀaline] *a* sugared ; praline-flavoured.

praticable [pʀatikabl(ə)] *a* passable, practicable.

praticien, ne [pʀatisjɛ̃, -jɛn] *nm/f* practitioner.

pratiquant, e [pʀatikɑ̃, -ɑ̃t] *a* practising.

pratique [pʀatik] *nf* practice // *a* practical ; **dans la ~** in (actual) practice ; **mettre en ~** to put into practice.

pratiquement [pʀatikmɑ̃] *ad* (*pour ainsi dire*) practically, virtually.

pratiquer [pʀatike] *vt* to practise ; (*intervention, opération*) to carry out ; (*ouverture, abri*) to make // *vi* (REL) to be a churchgoer.

pré [pʀe] *nm* meadow.

préalable [pʀealabl(ə)] *a* preliminary ; **condition ~ (de)** precondition (for), prerequisite (for) ; **sans avis ~** without prior *ou* previous notice ; **au ~** first, beforehand.

préambule [pʀeɑ̃byl] *nm* preamble ; (*fig*) prelude ; **sans ~** straight away.

préau, x [pʀeo] *nm* playground ; inner courtyard.

préavis [pʀeavi] *nm* notice ; **~ de congé** notice ; **communication avec ~** (TÉL) personal *ou* person to person call.

précaire [pʀekɛʀ] *a* precarious.

précaution [pʀekosjɔ̃] *nf* precaution ; **avec ~** cautiously ; **par ~** as a precaution.

précédemment [pʀesedamɑ̃] *ad* before, previously.

précédent, e [pʀesedɑ̃, -ɑ̃t] *a* previous // *nm* precedent ; **sans ~** unprecedented ; **le jour ~** the day before, the previous day.

précéder [pʀesede] *vt* to precede ; (*marcher ou rouler devant*) to be in front of ; (*arriver avant*) to get ahead of.

précepte [pʀesɛpt(ə)] *nm* precept.

précepteur, trice [pʀesɛptœʀ, tʀis] *nm/f* (private) tutor.

prêcher [pʀeʃe] *vt* to preach.

précieux, euse [pʀesjø, -øz] *a* precious ; invaluable ; (*style, écrivain*) précieux, precious.

précipice [pʀesipis] *nm* drop, chasm ; (*fig*) abyss ; **au bord du ~** at the edge of the precipice.

précipitamment [pʀesipitamɑ̃] *ad* hurriedly, hastily.

précipitation [pʀesipitɑsjɔ̃] *nf* (*hâte*) haste ; **~s (atmosphériques)** (atmospheric) precipitation *sg*.

précipité, e [pʀesipite] *a* fast ; hurried ; hasty.

précipiter [pʀesipite] *vt* (*faire tomber*): **~ qn/qch du haut de** to throw *or* hurl sb/sth off *ou* from ; (*hâter: marche*) to quicken ; (: *depart* (*événements*) to move faster ; **se ~ sur/vers** to rush at/towards.

précis, e [pʀesi, -iz] *a* precise ; (*tir, mesures*) accurate, precise // *nm* handbook ; **précisément** *ad* precisely ; **préciser** *vt* (*expliquer*) to be more specific about, clarify ; (*spécifier*) to state, specify ; **se préciser** *vi* to become clear(er) ; **précision** *nf* precision ; accuracy ; point *ou* detail (*made clear or to be clarified*) ; **précisions** *nfpl* further details.

précoce [pʀekɔs] *a* early ; (*enfant*) precocious ; (*calvitie*) premature.

préconçu, e [pʀekɔ̃sy] *a* preconceived.

préconiser [pʀekɔnize] *vt* to advocate.

précurseur [pʀekyʀsœʀ] *am* precursory // *nm* forerunner, precursor.

prédécesseur [pʀedesesœʀ] *nm* predecessor.

prédestiner [pʀedɛstine] *vt*: **~ qn à qch/faire** to predestine sb for sth/to do.

prédicateur [pʀedikatœʀ] *nm* preacher.

prédiction [pʀediksjɔ̃] *nf* prediction.

prédilection [pʀedilɛksjɔ̃] *nf*: **avoir une ~ pour** to be partial to ; **de ~** favourite.

prédire [pʀediʀ] *vt* to predict.

prédisposer [pʀedispoze] *vt*: **~ qn à qch/faire** to predispose sb to sth/to do.

prédominer [pʀedɔmine] *vi* to predominate ; (*avis*) to prevail.

préfabriqué, e [pʀefabʀike] *a* prefabricated // *nm* prefabricated material.

préface [pʀefas] *nf* preface ; **préfacer** *vt* to write a preface for.

préfectoral, e, aux [pʀefɛktɔʀal, -o] *a* prefectorial.

préfecture [pʀefɛktyʀ] *nf* prefecture ; **~ de police** police headquarters.

préférable [pʀefeʀabl(ə)] *a* preferable.

préféré, e [pʀefeʀe] *a, nm/f* favourite.

préférence [pʀefeʀɑ̃s] *nf* preference ; **de ~** preferably ; **de ~ à** in preference to, rather than ; **obtenir la ~ sur** to have preference over ; **préférentiel, le** *a* preferential.

préférer [pʀefeʀe] *vt*: **~ qn/qch (à)** to prefer sb/sth (to), like sb/sth better (than) ; **~ faire** to prefer to do ; **je préférerais du thé** I would rather have tea, I'd prefer tea.

préfet [pʀefɛ] *nm* prefect ; **~ de police** prefect of police, ≈ Metropolitan Commissioner.

préfixe [pʀefiks(ə)] *nm* prefix.

préhistoire [pʀeistwaʀ] *nf* prehistory ; **préhistorique** *a* prehistoric.

préjudice [pʀeʒydis] *nm* (*matériel*) loss; (*moral*) harm *q*; **porter ~ à** to harm, be detrimental to; **au ~ de** at the expense of.
préjugé [pʀeʒyʒe] *nm* prejudice; **avoir un ~ contre** to be prejudiced *ou* biased against.
préjuger [pʀeʒyʒe]: **~ de** *vt* to prejudge.
prélasser [pʀelɑse]: **se ~** *vi* to lounge.
prélat [pʀela] *nm* prelate.
prélavage [pʀelavaʒ] *nm* pre-wash.
prélèvement [pʀelɛvmɑ̃] *nm* deduction; withdrawal; **faire un ~ de sang** to take a blood sample.
prélever [pʀɛlve] *vt* (*échantillon*) to take; (*argent*): **~ (sur)** to deduct (from); (: *sur son compte*): **~ (sur)** to withdraw (from).
préliminaire [pʀeliminɛʀ] *a* preliminary; **~s** *nmpl* preliminary talks; preliminaries.
prélude [pʀelyd] *nm* prelude; (*avant le concert*) warm-up.
prématuré, e [pʀematyʀe] *a* premature; (*retraite*) early // *nm* premature baby.
préméditation [pʀemeditɑsjɔ̃] *nf*: **avec ~** *a* premeditated // *ad* with intent; **préméditer** *vt* to premeditate, plan.
premier, ière [pʀəmje, -jɛʀ] *a* first; (*branche, marche, grade*) bottom; (*fig*) basic; prime; initial // *nf* (THÉÂTRE) first night; (CINÉMA) première; (*exploit*) first; **le ~ venu** the first person to come along; **P~ Ministre** Prime Minister; **premièrement** *ad* firstly.
prémisse [pʀemis] *nf* premise.
prémonition [pʀemɔnisjɔ̃] *nf* premonition; **prémonitoire** *a* premonitory.
prémunir [pʀemyniʀ]: **se ~** *vi*: **se ~ contre** to protect o.s. from, guard o.s. against.
prénatal, e [pʀenatal] *a* (MÉD) antenatal.
prendre [pʀɑ̃dʀ(ə)] *vt* to take; (*ôter*): **~ qch à** to take sth from; (*aller chercher*) to get, fetch; (*se procurer*) to get; (*malfaiteur, poisson*) to catch; (*passager*) to pick up; (*personnel, aussi*: *couleur, goût*) to take on; (*locataire*) to take in; (*élève etc*: *traiter*) to handle; (*voix, ton*) to put on; (*coincer*): **se ~ les doigts dans** to get one's fingers caught in // *vi* (*liquide, ciment*) to set; (*greffe, vaccin*) to take; (*mensonge*) to be successful; (*feu*: *foyer*) to go; (: *incendie*) to start; (*allumette*) to light; (*se diriger*): **~ à gauche** to turn (to the) left; **~ qn pour** to take sb for; **se ~ pour** to think one is; **s'en ~ à** (*agresser*) to set about; (*critiquer*) to attack; **se ~ d'amitié/d'affection pour** to befriend/become fond of; **s'y ~** (*procéder*) to set about it; **s'y ~ à l'avance** to see to it in advance; **s'y ~ à deux fois** to try twice, make two attemps.
preneur [pʀənœʀ] *nm*: **être/trouver ~** to be willing to buy/find a buyer.
preniez, prenne *etc vb voir* **prendre**.
prénom [pʀenɔ̃] *nm* first *ou* Christian name; **prénommer** *vt*: **elle se prénomme Claude** her (first) name is Claude.
prénuptial, e, aux [pʀenypsjal, -o] *a* premarital.
préoccupation [pʀeɔkypɑsjɔ̃] *nf* (*souci*) worry, anxiety; (*idée fixe*) preoccupation.
préoccuper [pʀeɔkype] *vt* to worry; to preoccupy; **se ~ de qch** to be concerned about sth; to show concern about sth.
préparatifs [pʀepaʀatif] *nmpl* preparations.
préparation [pʀepaʀɑsjɔ̃] *nf* preparation; (SCOL) piece of homework.
préparatoire [pʀepaʀatwaʀ] *a* preparatory.
préparer [pʀepaʀe] *vt* to prepare; (*café*) to make; (*examen*) to prepare for; (*voyage, entreprise*) to plan; **se ~** *vi* (*orage, tragédie*) to brew, be in the air; **se ~ (à qch/faire)** to prepare (o.s.) *ou* get ready (for sth/to do); **~ qch à qn** (*surprise etc*) to have sth in store for sb.
prépondérant, e [pʀepɔ̃deʀɑ̃, -ɑ̃t] *a* major, dominating.
préposé, e [pʀepoze] *a*: **~ à** in charge of // *nm/f* employee; official; attendant; postman/ woman.
préposition [pʀepozisjɔ̃] *nf* preposition.
prérogative [pʀeʀɔgativ] *nf* prerogative.
près [pʀɛ] *ad* near, close; **~ de** *prép* near (to), close to; (*environ*) nearly, almost; **de ~** *ad* closely; **à 5 kg ~** to within about 5 kg; **à cela ~ que** apart from the fact that.
présage [pʀezaʒ] *nm* omen.
présager [pʀezaʒe] *vt* to foresee.
presbyte [pʀɛsbit] *a* long-sighted.
presbytère [pʀɛsbitɛʀ] *nm* presbytery.
presbytérien, ne [pʀɛsbiteʀjɛ̃, -jɛn] *a, nm/f* Presbyterian.
prescription [pʀɛskʀipsjɔ̃] *nf* (*instruction*) order, instruction; (MÉD, JUR) prescription.
prescrire [pʀɛskʀiʀ] *vt* to prescribe; **se ~** *vi* (JUR) to lapse; **prescrit, e** *a* (*date etc*) stipulated.
préséance [pʀeseɑ̃s] *nf* precedence *q*.
présence [pʀezɑ̃s] *nf* presence; (*au bureau etc*) attendance; **en ~ de** in (the) presence of; (*fig*) in the face of; **~ d'esprit** presence of mind.
présent, e [pʀezɑ̃, -ɑ̃t] *a, nm* present; **à ~ (que)** now (that).
présentateur, trice [pʀezɑ̃tatœʀ, -tʀis] *nm/f* presenter.
présentation [pʀezɑ̃tɑsjɔ̃] *nf* introduction; presentation; (*allure*) appearance.
présenter [pʀezɑ̃te] *vt* to present; (*soumettre*) to submit; (*invité, conférencier*): **~ qn (à)** to introduce sb (to) // *vi*: **~ mal/bien** to have an unattractive/a pleasing appearance; **se ~** *vi* (*sur convocation*) to report, come; (*à une élection*) to stand; (*occasion*) to arise; **se ~ bien/mal** to look good/not too good; **présentoir** *nm* display shelf (*pl* shelves).
préservatif [pʀezɛʀvatif] *nm* sheath, condom.
préserver [pʀezɛʀve] *vt*: **~ de** to protect from; to save from.
présidence [pʀezidɑ̃s] *nf* presidency; office of President; chairmanship.
président [pʀezidɑ̃] *nm* (POL) president; (*d'une assemblée*, COMM) chairman; **~ directeur général (P.D.G.)** chairman and managing director; **~ du jury** (JUR)

foreman of the jury; (*d'examen*) chief examiner; **présidente** *nf* president; president's wife; chairwoman; **présidentiel, le** [-sjɛl] *a* presidential.
présider [pʀezide] *vt* to preside over; (*dîner*) to be the guest of honour at; ~ **à** *vt* to direct; to govern.
présomption [pʀezɔ̃psjɔ̃] *nf* presumption.
présomptueux, euse [pʀezɔ̃ptɥø, -øz] *a* presumptuous.
presque [pʀɛsk(ə)] *ad* almost, nearly; ~ **rien** hardly anything; ~ **pas** hardly (at all).
presqu'île [pʀɛskil] *nf* peninsula.
pressant, e [pʀɛsɑ̃, -ɑ̃t] *a* urgent.
presse [pʀɛs] *nf* press; (*affluence*): **heures de** ~ busy times; **sous** ~ *a* in press, being printed; ~ **féminine** women's magazines *pl*; ~ **d'information** quality newspapers *pl*.
pressé, e [pʀese] *a* in a hurry; (*air*) hurried; (*besogne*) urgent; **orange** ~**e** fresh orange juice.
presse-citron [pʀɛssitʀɔ̃] *nm inv* lemon squeezer.
pressentiment [pʀesɑ̃timɑ̃] *nm* foreboding, premonition.
pressentir [pʀesɑ̃tiʀ] *vt* to sense; (*prendre contact avec*) to approach.
presse-papiers [pʀɛspapje] *nm inv* paperweight.
presser [pʀese] *vt* (*fruit, éponge*) to squeeze; (*interrupteur, bouton*) to press, push; (*allure, affaire*) to speed up; (*débiteur etc*) to press; (*inciter*): ~ **qn de faire** to urge *ou* press sb to do // *vi* to be urgent; **rien ne presse** there's no hurry; **se** ~ (*se hâter*) to hurry (up); (*se grouper*) to crowd; **se** ~ **contre qn** to squeeze up against sb; ~ **qn entre ses bras** to hug sb (tight).
pressing [pʀesiŋ] *nm* steam-pressing; (*magasin*) dry-cleaner's.
pression [pʀɛsjɔ̃] *nf* pressure; **faire** ~ **sur** to put pressure on; **sous** ~ pressurized, under pressure; (*fig*) keyed up; ~ **artérielle** blood pressure.
pressoir [pʀɛswaʀ] *nm* (wine *ou* oil *etc*) press.
pressurer [pʀesyʀe] *vt* (*fig*) to squeeze.
pressurisé, e [pʀesyʀize] *a* pressurized.
prestance [pʀɛstɑ̃s] *nf* presence, imposing bearing.
prestataire [pʀɛstatɛʀ] *nm/f* person receiving benefits.
prestation [pʀɛstɑsjɔ̃] *nf* (*allocation*) benefit; (*d'une assurance*) cover *q*; (*d'une entreprise*) service provided; (*d'un joueur, artiste*) performance; ~ **de serment** taking the oath; ~ **de service** provision of a service.
preste [pʀɛst(ə)] *a* nimble; swift; ~**ment** *ad* swiftly.
prestidigitateur, trice [pʀɛstidiʒitatœʀ, -tʀis] *nm/f* conjurer.
prestidigitation [pʀɛstidiʒitɑsjɔ̃] *nf* conjuring.
prestige [pʀɛstiʒ] *nm* prestige; **prestigieux, euse** *a* prestigious.
présumer [pʀezyme] *vt*: ~ **que** to presume *ou* assume that; ~ **de** to overrate; ~ **qn coupable** to presume sb guilty.
prêt, e [pʀɛ, pʀɛt] *a* ready // *nm* lending *q*; loan; ~ **sur gages** pawnbroking *q*; **prêt-à-porter** *nm* ready-to-wear *ou* off-the-peg clothes *pl*.
prétendant [pʀetɑ̃dɑ̃] *nm* pretender; (*d'une femme*) suitor.
prétendre [pʀetɑ̃dʀ(ə)] *vt* (*affirmer*): ~ **que** to claim that; (*avoir l'intention de*): ~ **faire qch** to mean *ou* intend to do sth; ~ **à** *vt* (*droit, titre*) to lay claim to; **prétendu, e** *a* (*supposé*) so-called.
prête-nom [pʀɛtnɔ̃] *nm* (*péj*) figurehead.
prétentieux, euse [pʀetɑ̃sjø, -øz] *a* pretentious.
prétention [pʀetɑ̃sjɔ̃] *nf* claim; pretentiousness.
prêter [pʀete] *vt* (*livres, argent*): ~ **qch (à)** to lend sth (to); (*supposer*): ~ **à qn** (*caractère, propos*) to attribute to sb // *vi* (*aussi*: **se** ~: *tissu, cuir*) to give; ~ **à** (*commentaires etc*) to be open to, give rise to; **se** ~ **à** to lend o.s. (*ou* itself) to; (*manigances etc*) to go along with; ~ **assistance à** to give help to; ~ **serment** to take the oath; ~ **l'oreille** to listen; **prêteur** *nm* moneylender; **prêteur sur gages** pawnbroker.
prétexte [pʀetɛkst(ə)] *nm* pretext, excuse; **sous aucun** ~ on no account; **prétexter** *vt* to give as a pretext *ou* an excuse.
prêtre [pʀɛtʀ(ə)] *nm* priest; **prêtrise** *nf* priesthood.
preuve [pʀœv] *nf* proof; (*indice*) proof, evidence *q*; **faire** ~ **de** to show; **faire ses** ~**s** to prove o.s. (*ou* itself).
prévaloir [pʀevalwaʀ] *vi* to prevail; **se** ~ **de** *vt* to take advantage of; to pride o.s. on.
prévenances [pʀɛvnɑ̃s] *nfpl* thoughtfulness *sg*, kindness *sg*.
prévenant, e [pʀɛvnɑ̃, -ɑ̃t] *a* thoughtful, kind.
prévenir [pʀɛvniʀ] *vt* (*avertir*): ~ **qn (de)** to warn sb (about); (*informer*): ~ **qn (de)** to tell *ou* inform sb (about); (*éviter*) to avoid, prevent; (*anticiper*) to forestall; to anticipate; (*influencer*): ~ **qn contre** to prejudice sb against.
préventif, ive [pʀɛvɑ̃tif, -iv] *a* preventive.
prévention [pʀevɑ̃sjɔ̃] *nf* prevention; ~ **routière** road safety.
prévenu, e [pʀɛvny] *nm/f* (JUR) defendant, accused.
prévision [pʀevizjɔ̃] *nf*: ~**s** predictions; forecast *sg*; **en** ~ **de** in anticipation of; ~**s météorologiques** *ou* **du temps** weather forecast *sg*.
prévoir [pʀevwaʀ] *vt* (*deviner*) to foresee; (*s'attendre à*) to expect, reckon on; (*prévenir*) to anticipate; (*organiser*) to plan; (*préparer, réserver*) to allow; **prévu pour 4 personnes** designed for 4 people; **prévu pour 10h** scheduled for 10 o'clock.
prévoyance [pʀevwajɑ̃s] *nf* foresight; **une société/caisse de** ~ a provident society/contingency fund.
prévoyant, e [pʀevwajɑ̃, -ɑ̃t] *a* gifted with (*ou* showing) foresight.

prier [pRije] *vi* to pray // *vt* (*Dieu*) to pray to; (*implorer*) to beg; (*demander*): ~ **qn de faire** to ask sb to do; **se faire** ~ to need coaxing *ou* persuading; **je vous en prie** please do; don't mention it.
prière [pRijɛR] *nf* prayer; '~ **de faire** ...' 'please do ...'.
primaire [pRimɛR] *a* primary; (*péj*) simple-minded; simplistic // *nm* (SCOL) primary education.
primauté [pRimote] *nf* (*fig*) primacy.
prime [pRim] *nf* (*bonification*) bonus; (*subside*) premium; allowance; (COMM: *cadeau*) free gift; (ASSURANCES, BOURSE) premium // *a*: **de** ~ **abord** at first glance; ~ **de risque** danger money *q*.
primer [pRime] *vt* (*l'emporter sur*) to prevail over; (*récompenser*) to award a prize to // *vi* to dominate; to prevail.
primesautier, ère [pRimsotje, -jɛR] *a* impulsive.
primeur [pRimœR] *nf*: **avoir la** ~ **de** to be the first to hear (*ou* see *etc*); ~**s** *nfpl* (*fruits, légumes*) early fruits and vegetables; **marchand de** ~**s** greengrocer.
primevère [pRimvɛR] *nf* primrose.
primitif, ive [pRimitif, -iv] *a* primitive; (*originel*) original // *nm/f* primitive.
primordial, e, aux [pRimɔRdjal, -o] *a* essential, primordial.
prince, esse [pRɛ̃s, pRɛ̃sɛs] *nm/f* prince/princess; ~ **de Galles** *nm inv* check cloth; ~ **héritier** crown prince; **princier, ière** *a* princely.
principal, e, aux [pRɛ̃sipal, -o] *a* principal, main // *nm* (SCOL) principal, head(master) // *nf*: **(proposition)** ~**e** main clause.
principauté [pRɛ̃sipote] *nf* Principality.
principe [pRɛ̃sip] *nm* principle; **partir du** ~ **que** to work on the principle *ou* assumption that; **pour le** ~ on principle, for the sake of it; **de** ~ *a* (*accord, hostilité*) automatic; **par** ~ on principle; **en** ~ (*habituellement*) as a rule; (*théoriquement*) in principle.
printanier, ère [pRɛ̃tanje, -jɛR] *a* spring *cpd*; spring-like.
printemps [pRɛ̃tɑ̃] *nm* spring.
priori [pRijɔRi]: **a** ~ *ad* without the benefit of hindsight; a priori; initially.
prioritaire [pRijɔRitɛR] *a* having priority; (AUTO) having right of way.
priorité [pRijɔRite] *nf* (AUTO): **avoir la** ~ **(sur)** to have right of way (over); ~ **à droite** right of way to vehicles coming from the right; **en** ~ as a (matter of) priority.
pris, e [pRi, pRiz] *pp de* **prendre** // *a* (*place*) taken; (*journée, mains*) full; (*billets*) sold; (*personne*) busy; (MÉD: *enflammé*): **avoir le nez/la gorge** ~**(e)** to have a stuffy nose/a hoarse throat; (*saisi*): **être** ~ **de peur/de fatigue** to be stricken with fear/overcome with fatigue.
prise [pRiz] *nf* (*d'une ville*) capture; (PÊCHE, CHASSE) catch; (*de judo ou catch, point d'appui ou pour empoigner*) hold; (ÉLEC: *fiche*) plug; (: *femelle*) socket; (: *au mur*) point; **en** ~ (AUTO) in gear; **être aux** ~**s avec** to be grappling with; to be battling with; **lâcher** ~ to let go; ~ **en charge** (*taxe*) pick-up charge; ~ **de courant** power point; ~ **d'eau** water (supply) point; tap; ~ **multiple** adaptor; ~ **de sang** blood test; ~ **de son** sound recording; ~ **de tabac** pinch of snuff; ~ **de terre** earth; ~ **de vue** (*photo*) shot; (*action*): ~ **de vue(s)** filming, shooting.
priser [pRize] *vt* (*tabac, héroïne*) to take; (*estimer*) to prize, value // *vi* to take snuff.
prisme [pRism(ə)] *nm* prism.
prison [pRizɔ̃] *nf* prison; **aller/être en** ~ to go to/be in prison *ou* jail; **faire de la** ~ to serve time; **prisonnier, ière** *nm/f* prisoner // *a* captive; **faire qn prisonnier** to take sb prisoner.
prit *vb voir* **prendre**.
privations [pRivɑsjɔ̃] *nfpl* privations, hardships.
privé, e [pRive] *a* private; (*dépourvu*): ~ **de** without, lacking; **en** ~ in private.
priver [pRive] *vt*: ~ **qn de** to deprive sb of; **se** ~ **de** to go *ou* do without; **ne pas se** ~ **de faire** not to refrain from doing.
privilège [pRivilɛʒ] *nm* privilege; **privilégié, e** *a* privileged.
prix [pRi] *nm* (*valeur*) price; (*récompense*, SCOL) prize; **hors de** ~ exorbitantly priced; **à aucun** ~ not at any price; **à tout** ~ at all costs; ~ **d'achat/de vente** purchasing/selling price.
probabilité [pRɔbabilite] *nf* probability.
probable [pRɔbabl(ə)] *a* likely, probable; ~**ment** *ad* probably.
probant, e [pRɔbɑ̃, -ɑ̃t] *a* convincing.
probité [pRɔbite] *nf* integrity, probity.
problème [pRɔblɛm] *nm* problem.
procédé [pRɔsede] *nm* (*méthode*) process; (*comportement*) behaviour *q*.
procéder [pRɔsede] *vi* to proceed; to behave; ~ **à** *vt* to carry out.
procédure [pRɔsedyR] *nf* (ADMIN, JUR) procedure.
procès [pRɔsɛ] *nm* trial; (*poursuites*) proceedings *pl*; **être en** ~ **avec** to be involved in a lawsuit with.
procession [pRɔsesjɔ̃] *nf* procession.
processus [pRɔsesys] *nm* process.
procès-verbal, aux [pRɔsɛvɛRbal, -o] *nm* (*constat*) statement; (*aussi*: **P.V.**): **avoir un** ~ to get a parking ticket; to be booked; (*de réunion*) minutes *pl*.
prochain, e [pRɔʃɛ̃, -ɛn] *a* next; (*proche*) impending; near // *nm* fellow man; **la** ~**e fois/semaine** ~**e** next time/week; **prochainement** *ad* soon, shortly.
proche [pRɔʃ] *a* nearby; (*dans le temps*) imminent; close at hand; (*parent, ami*) close; ~**s** *nmpl* close relatives, next of kin; **être** ~ **(de)** to be near, be close (to); **de** ~ **en** ~ gradually; **le P**~ **Orient** the Middle East, the Near East.
proclamation [pRɔklamɑsjɔ̃] *nf* proclamation.
proclamer [pRɔklame] *vt* to proclaim.
procréer [pRɔkRee] *vt* to procreate.
procuration [pRɔkyRɑsjɔ̃] *nf* proxy; power of attorney.
procurer [pRɔkyRe] *vt* (*fournir*): ~ **qch à qn** to get *ou* obtain sth for sb; (*causer*:

plaisir etc): ~ **qch à qn** to bring *ou* give sb sth; **se** ~ *vt* to get.
procureur [pRɔkyRœR] *nm* public prosecutor.
prodige [pRɔdiʒ] *nm* marvel, wonder; (*personne*) prodigy; **prodigieux, euse** *a* prodigious; phenomenal.
prodigue [pRɔdig] *a* generous; extravagant, wasteful; **fils** ~ prodigal son.
prodiguer [pRɔdige] *vt* (*argent, biens*) to be lavish with; (*soins, attentions*): ~ **qch à qn** to give sb sth; to lavish sth on sb.
producteur, trice [pRɔdyktœR, -tRis] *a*: ~ **de blé** wheat-producing // *nm/f* producer.
productif, ive [pRɔdyktif, -iv] *a* productive.
production [pRɔdyksjɔ̃] *nf* (*gén*) production; (*rendement*) output; (*produits*) products *pl*, goods *pl*.
productivité [pRɔdyktivite] *nf* productivity.
produire [pRɔdɥiR] *vt* to produce; **se** ~ *vi* (*acteur*) to perform, appear; (*événement*) to happen, occur.
produit [pRɔdɥi] *nm* (*gén*) product; ~**s agricoles** farm produce *sg*; ~ **d'entretien** cleaning product.
proéminent, e [pRɔeminɑ̃, -ɑ̃t] *a* prominent.
profane [pRɔfan] *a* (*REL*) secular // *nm/f* layman.
profaner [pRɔfane] *vt* to desecrate.
proférer [pRɔfeRe] *vt* to utter.
professer [pRɔfese] *vt* (*déclarer*) to profess // *vi* to teach.
professeur [pRɔfɛsœR] *nm* teacher; (*titulaire d'une chaire*) professor; ~ **(de faculté)** (university) lecturer.
profession [pRɔfɛsjɔ̃] *nf* profession; **sans** ~ unemployed; **professionnel, le** *a*, *nm/f* professional.
professorat [pRɔfɛsɔRa] *nm*: **le** ~ the teaching profession.
profil [pRɔfil] *nm* profile; (*d'une voiture*) line, contour; **de** ~ in profile; ~**er** *vt* to streamline; **se** ~**er** *vi* (*arbre, tour*) to stand out, be silhouetted.
profit [pRɔfi] *nm* (*avantage*) benefit, advantage; (*COMM, FINANCE*) profit; **au** ~ **de** in aid of; **tirer** ~ **de** to profit from; **mettre à** ~ to take advantage of; to turn to good account.
profitable [pRɔfitabl(ə)] *a* beneficial; profitable.
profiter [pRɔfite] *vi*: ~ **de** to take advantage of; to make the most of; ~ **à** to be of benefit to, benefit; to be profitable to.
profond, e [pRɔfɔ̃, -ɔ̃d] *a* deep; (*méditation, mépris*) profound; **profondeur** *nf* depth.
profusion [pRɔfyzjɔ̃] *nf* profusion; **à** ~ in plenty.
progéniture [pRɔʒenityR] *nf* offspring *inv*.
programmation [pRɔgRamɑsjɔ̃] *nf* programming.
programme [pRɔgRam] *nm* programme; (*TV, RADIO*) programmes *pl*; (*SCOL*) syllabus, curriculum; (*INFORMATIQUE*) program; **au** ~ **de ce soir** (*TV*) among tonight's programmes; **programmer** *vt* (*TV, RADIO*) to put on, show; (*INFORMATIQUE*) to program; **programmeur, euse** *nm/f* computer programmer.
progrès [pRɔgRɛ] *nm* progress *q*; **faire des/être en** ~ to make/be making progress.
progresser [pRɔgRese] *vi* to progress; (*troupes etc*) to make headway *ou* progress; **progressif, ive** *a* progressive; **progression** *nf* progression; (*d'une troupe etc*) advance, progress.
prohiber [pRɔibe] *vt* to prohibit, ban.
proie [pRwa] *nf* prey *q*; **être la** ~ **de** to fall prey to; **être en** ~ **à** to be prey to; to be suffering.
projecteur [pRɔʒɛktœR] *nm* projector; (*de théâtre, cirque*) spotlight.
projectile [pRɔʒɛktil] *nm* missile; (*d'arme*) projectile, bullet (*ou* shell *etc*).
projection [pRɔʒɛksjɔ̃] *nf* projection; showing; **conférence avec** ~**s** lecture with slides (*ou* a film).
projet [pRɔʒɛ] *nm* plan; (*ébauche*) draft; **faire des** ~**s** to make plans; ~ **de loi** bill.
projeter [pRɔʒte] *vt* (*envisager*) to plan; (*film, photos*) to project; (*: passer*) to show; (*ombre, lueur*) to throw, cast, project; (*jeter*) to throw up (*ou* off *ou* out).
prolétaire [pRɔletɛR] *nm* proletarian; **prolétariat** *nm* proletariat.
proliférer [pRɔlifeRe] *vi* to proliferate.
prolifique [pRɔlifik] *a* prolific.
prolixe [pRɔliks(ə)] *a* verbose.
prologue [pRɔlɔg] *nm* prologue.
prolongation [pRɔlɔ̃gɑsjɔ̃] *nf* prolongation; extension; ~**s** *nfpl* (*FOOTBALL*) extra time *sg*.
prolongement [pRɔlɔ̃ʒmɑ̃] *nm* extension; ~**s** *nmpl* (*fig*) repercussions, effects; **dans le** ~ **de** running on from.
prolonger [pRɔlɔ̃ʒe] *vt* (*débat, séjour*) to prolong; (*délai, billet, rue*) to extend; (*suj: chose*) to be a continuation *ou* an extension of; **se** ~ *vi* to go on.
promenade [pRɔmnad] *nf* walk (*ou* drive *ou* ride); **faire une** ~ to go for a walk; **une** ~ **en voiture/à vélo** a drive/(bicycle) ride.
promener [pRɔmne] *vt* (*chien*) to take out for a walk; (*fig*) to carry around; to trail round; (*doigts, regard*): ~ **qch sur** to run sth over; **se** ~ *vi* to go for (*ou* be out for) a walk; (*fig*): **se** ~ **sur** to wander over; **promeneur, euse** *nm/f* walker, stroller.
promesse [pRɔmɛs] *nf* promise; ~ **d'achat** commitment to buy.
prometteur, euse [pRɔmɛtœR, -øz] *a* promising.
promettre [pRɔmɛtR(ə)] *vt* to promise // *vi* to be *ou* look promising; **se** ~ **de faire** to resolve *ou* mean to do; ~ **à qn de faire** to promise sb that one will do.
promiscuité [pRɔmiskɥite] *nf* crowding; lack of privacy.
promontoire [pRɔmɔ̃twaR] *nm* headland.
promoteur, trice [pRɔmɔtœR, -tRis] *nm/f* (*instigateur*) instigator, promoter; ~ **(immobilier)** property developer.

promotion [pRɔmosjɔ̃] *nf* promotion.
promouvoir [pRɔmuvwaR] *vt* to promote.
prompt, e [pRɔ̃, pRɔ̃t] *a* swift, rapid.
promulguer [pRɔmylge] *vt* to promulgate.
prôner [pRone] *vt* (*louer*) to laud, extol; (*préconiser*) to advocate, commend.
pronom [pRɔnɔ̃] *nm* pronoun; **pronominal, e, aux** *a* pronominal; reflexive.
prononcé, e [pRɔnɔ̃se] *a* pronounced, marked.
prononcer [pRɔnɔ̃se] *vt* (*son, mot, jugement*) to pronounce; (*dire*) to utter; (*allocution*) to deliver // *vi*: ~ **bien/mal** to have a good/poor pronunciation; **se** ~ *vi* to reach a decision, give a verdict; **se** ~ **sur** to give an opinion on; **se** ~ **contre** to come down against; **prononciation** *nf* pronunciation.
pronostic [pRɔnɔstik] *nm* (MÉD) prognosis (*pl* oses); (*fig*: *aussi*: ~**s**) forecast.
propagande [pRɔpagɑ̃d] *nf* propaganda.
propager [pRɔpaʒe] *vt* to spread; **se** ~ *vi* to spread; (PHYSIQUE) to be propagated.
prophète [pRɔfɛt] *nm* prophet.
prophétie [pRɔfesi] *nf* prophecy; **prophétiser** *vt* to prophesy.
propice [pRɔpis] *a* favourable.
proportion [pRɔpɔRsjɔ̃] *nf* proportion; **en** ~ **de** in proportion to; **toute(s)** ~**(s) gardée(s)** making due allowance(s); **proportionnel, le** *a* proportional; **proportionner** *vt*: **proportionner qch à** to proportion *ou* adjust sth to.
propos [pRɔpo] *nm* (*paroles*) talk *q*, remark; (*intention*) intention, aim; (*sujet*): **à quel** ~**?** what about?; **à** ~ **de** about, regarding; **à tout** ~ for no reason at all; **à** ~ *ad* by the way; (*opportunément*) (just) at the right moment.
proposer [pRɔpoze] *vt* (*suggérer*): ~ **qch (à qn)/de faire** to suggest sth (to sb)/doing, propose to do; (*offrir*): ~ **qch à qn/de faire** to offer sb sth/to do; (*candidat*) to nominate, put forward; (*loi, motion*) to propose; **se** ~ **(pour faire)** to offer one's services (to do); **se** ~ **de faire** to intend *ou* propose to do; **proposition** *nf* suggestion; proposal; offer; (LING) clause.
propre [pRɔpR(ə)] *a* clean; (*net*) neat, tidy; (*possessif*) own; (*sens*) literal; (*particulier*): ~ **à** peculiar to, characteristic of; (*approprié*): ~ **à** suitable *ou* appropriate for; (*de nature à*): ~ **à faire** likely to do, that will do // *nm*: **recopier au** ~ to make a fair copy of; ~**ment** *ad* cleanly; neatly, tidily; **à** ~**ment parler** strictly speaking; ~**té** *nf* cleanliness, cleanness; neatness; tidiness.
propriétaire [pRɔpRijetɛR] *nm/f* owner; (*d'hôtel etc*) proprietor/ tress, owner; (*pour le locataire*) landlord/lady; ~ **(immobilier)** house-owner; householder; ~ **récoltant** grower; ~ **(terrien)** landowner.
propriété [pRɔpRijete] *nf* (*droit*) ownership; (*objet, immeuble etc*) property *gén q*: (*villa*) residence, property; (*terres*) property *gén q*, land *gén q*; (*qualité*, CHIMIE, MATH) property; (*correction*) appropriateness, suitability.
propulser [pRɔpylse] *vt* (*missile*) to propel; (*projeter*) to hurl, fling.
prorata [pRɔRata] *nm inv*: **au** ~ **de** in proportion to, on the basis of.
proroger [pRɔRɔʒe] *vt* to put back, defer; (*assemblée*) to adjourn, prorogue.
prosaïque [pRozaik] *a* mundane, prosaic.
proscrire [pRɔskRiR] *vt* (*bannir*) to banish; (*interdire*) to ban, prohibit.
prose [pRoz] *nf* prose (*style*).
prospecter [pRɔspɛkte] *vt* to prospect; (COMM) to canvass.
prospectus [pRɔspɛktys] *nm* (*feuille*) leaflet; (*dépliant*) brochure, leaflet.
prospère [pRɔspɛR] *a* prosperous; (*entreprise*) thriving, flourishing; **prospérer** *vi* to thrive; **prospérité** *nf* prosperity.
prosterner [pRɔstɛRne]: **se** ~ *vi* to bow low, prostrate o.s.
prostituée [pRɔstitɥe] *nf* prostitute.
prostitution [pRɔstitysjɔ̃] *nf* prostitution.
prostré, e [pRɔstRe] *a* prostrate.
protagoniste [pRɔtagɔnist(ə)] *nm* protagonist.
protecteur, trice [pRɔtɛktœR, -tRis] *a* protective; (*air, ton*: *péj*) patronizing // *nm/f* protector.
protection [pRɔtɛksjɔ̃] *nf* protection; (*d'un personnage influent*: *aide*) patronage.
protégé, e [pRɔteʒe] *nm/f* protégé/e.
protège-cahier [pRɔtɛʒkaje] *nm* exercise-book cover.
protéger [pRɔteʒe] *vt* to protect; **se** ~ **de/contre** to protect o.s. from.
protéine [pRɔtein] *nf* protein.
protestant, e [pRɔtɛstɑ̃, -ɑ̃t] *a, nm/f* Protestant; **protestantisme** *nm* Protestantism.
protestation [pRɔtɛstɑsjɔ̃] *nf* (*plainte*) protest; (*déclaration*) protestation, profession.
protester [pRɔtɛste] *vi*: ~ **(contre)** to protest (against *ou* about); ~ **de** (*son innocence, sa loyauté*) to protest.
prothèse [pRɔtɛz] *nf* artificial limb, prosthesis; ~ **dentaire** denture; dental engineering.
protocolaire [pRɔtɔkɔlɛR] *a* formal; of protocol.
protocole [pRɔtɔkɔl] *nm* protocol; (*fig*) etiquette; ~ **d'accord** draft treaty.
prototype [pRɔtɔtip] *nm* prototype.
protubérance [pRɔtybeRɑ̃s] *nf* bulge, protuberance; **protubérant, e** *a* protruding, bulging, protuberant.
proue [pRu] *nf* bow(s *pl*), prow.
prouesse [pRuɛs] *nf* feat.
prouver [pRuve] *vt* to prove.
provenance [pRɔvnɑ̃s] *nf* origin; (*de mot, coutume*) source; **avion en** ~ **de** plane (arriving) from.
provenir [pRɔvniR]: ~ **de** *vt* to come from; (*résulter de*) to be due to, be the result of.
proverbe [pRɔvɛRb(ə)] *nm* proverb; **proverbial, e, aux** *a* proverbial.
providence [pRɔvidɑ̃s] *nf*: **la** ~ providence; **providentiel, le** *a* providential.

province [pRɔvɛ̃s] *nf* province; **provincial, e, aux** *a* provincial.
proviseur [pRɔvizœR] *nm* ≈ head(master).
provision [pRɔvizjɔ̃] *nf* (*réserve*) stock, supply; (*avance: à un avocat, avoué*) retainer, retaining fee; (COMM) funds *pl* (in account); reserve; **~s** *nfpl* (*vivres*) provisions, food *q*; **faire ~ de** to stock up with; **armoire à ~s** food cupboard.
provisoire [pRɔvizwaR] *a* temporary; (JUR) provisional; **~ment** *ad* temporarily, for the time being.
provocant, e [pRɔvɔkɑ̃, -ɑ̃t] *a* provocative.
provocation [pRɔvɔkɑsjɔ̃] *nf* provocation.
provoquer [pRɔvɔke] *vt* (*défier*) to provoke; (*causer*) to cause, bring about; (: *curiosité*) to arouse, give rise to; (: *aveux*) to prompt, elicit.
proxénète [pRɔksenɛt] *nm* procurer.
proximité [pRɔksimite] *nf* nearness, closeness, proximity; (*dans le temps*) imminence, closeness; **à ~** near *ou* close by; **à ~ de** near (to), close to.
prude [pRyd] *a* prudish.
prudence [pRydɑ̃s] *nf* carefulness; caution; prudence; **avec ~** carefully; cautiously; wisely; **par (mesure de) ~** as a precaution.
prudent, e [pRydɑ̃, -ɑ̃t] *a* (*pas téméraire*) careful, cautious, prudent; (: *en général*) safety-conscious; (*sage, conseillé*) wise, sensible; (*réservé*) cautious; **ce n'est pas ~** it's risky; it's not sensible; **soyez ~** take care, be careful.
prune [pRyn] *nf* plum.
pruneau, x [pRyno] *nm* prune.
prunelle [pRynɛl] *nf* pupil; eye.
prunier [pRynje] *nm* plum tree.
psalmodier [psalmɔdje] *vt* to chant; (*fig*) to drone out.
psaume [psom] *nm* psalm.
pseudonyme [psødɔnim] *nm* (*gén*) fictitious name; (*d'écrivain*) pseudonym, pen name; (*de comédien*) stage name.
psychanalyse [psikanaliz] *nf* psychoanalysis; **psychanalyser** *vt* to psychoanalyze; **se faire psychanalyser** to undergo (psycho)analysis; **psychanalyste** *nm/f* psychoanalyst.
psychiatre [psikjatR(ə)] *nm/f* psychiatrist.
psychiatrie [psikjatRi] *nf* psychiatry; **psychiatrique** *a* psychiatric; (*hôpital*) mental, psychiatric.
psychique [psiʃik] *a* psychological.
psychologie [psikɔlɔʒi] *nf* psychology; **psychologique** *a* psychological; **psychologue** *nm/f* psychologist; **être psychologue** (*fig*) to be a good psychologist.
psychose [psikoz] *nf* psychosis; obsessive fear.
Pte *abr de* **porte**.
P.T.T. *sigle fpl voir* **poste**.
pu *pp de* **pouvoir**.
puanteur [pɥɑ̃tœR] *nf* stink, stench.
pubère [pybɛR] *a* pubescent; **puberté** *nf* puberty.
pubis [pybis] *nm* (*bas-ventre*) pubes *pl*; (*os*) pubis.
public, ique [pyblik] *a* public; (*école, instruction*) state *cpd* // *nm* public; (*assistance*) audience; **en ~** in public.
publication [pyblikɑsjɔ̃] *nf* publication.
publiciste [pyblisist(ə)] *nm/f* adman.
publicitaire [pyblisitɛR] *a* advertising *cpd*; (*film, voiture*) publicity *cpd*.
publicité [pyblisite] *nf* (*méthode, profession*) advertising; (*annonce*) advertisement; (*révélations*) publicity.
publier [pyblije] *vt* to publish.
publique [pyblik] *af voir* **public**.
puce [pys] *nf* flea; **~s** *nfpl* (*marché*) flea market *sg*.
puceau, x [pyso] *am*: **être ~** to be a virgin.
pucelle [pysɛl] *af*: **être ~** to be a virgin.
pudeur [pydœR] *nf* modesty.
pudibond, e [pydibɔ̃, -ɔ̃d] *a* prudish.
pudique [pydik] *a* (*chaste*) modest; (*discret*) discreet.
puer [pɥe] (*péj*) *vi* to stink // *vt* to stink of, reek of.
puéricultrice [pɥeRikyltRis] *nf* paediatric nurse.
puériculture [pɥeRikyltyR] *nf* paediatric nursing; infant care.
puéril, e [pɥeRil] *a* childish.
pugilat [pyʒila] *nm* (fist) fight.
puis [pɥi] *vb voir* **pouvoir** // *ad* then; **et ~** and (then).
puiser [pɥize] *vt* (*eau*): **~ (dans)** to draw (from); **~ dans qch** to dip into sth.
puisque [pɥisk(ə)] *cj* since.
puissance [pɥisɑ̃s] *nf* power; **en ~** *a* potential; **2 (à la) ~ 5** 2 to the power of 5.
puissant, e [pɥisɑ̃, -ɑ̃t] *a* powerful.
puisse *etc vb voir* **pouvoir**.
puits [pɥi] *nm* well; **~ de mine** mine shaft.
pull(-over) [pul(ɔvœR)] *nm* sweater, jumper.
pulluler [pylyle] *vi* to swarm.
pulmonaire [pylmɔnɛR] *a* lung *cpd*; (*artère*) pulmonary.
pulpe [pylp(ə)] *nf* pulp.
pulsation [pylsɑsjɔ̃] *nf* beat.
pulsion [pylsjɔ̃] *nf* drive, urge.
pulvérisateur [pylveRizatœR] *nm* spray.
pulvériser [pylveRize] *vt* (*solide*) to pulverize; (*liquide*) to spray; (*fig*) to pulverize; to smash.
punaise [pynɛz] *nf* (ZOOL) bug; (*clou*) drawing pin.
punch [pɔ̃ʃ] *nm* (*boisson*) punch; [pœnʃ] (BOXE) punching ability; (*fig*) punch; **punching-ball** *nm* punchball.
punir [pyniR] *vt* to punish; **punition** *nf* punishment.
pupille [pypij] *nf* (ANAT) pupil // *nm/f* (*enfant*) ward; **~ de l'État** child in care; **~ de la Nation** war orphan.
pupitre [pypitR(ə)] *nm* (SCOL) desk; (REL) lectern; (*de chef d'orchestre*) rostrum; **~ de commande** panel.
pur, e [pyR] *a* pure; (*vin*) undiluted; (*whisky*) neat; **en ~e perte** fruitlessly, to no avail.

purée [pyʀe] *nf*: ~ **(de pommes de terre)** mashed potatoes *pl*; ~ **de marrons** chestnut purée.
pureté [pyʀte] *nf* purity.
purgatif [pyʀgatif] *nm* purgative, purge.
purgatoire [pyʀgatwaʀ] *nm* purgatory.
purge [pyʀʒ(ə)] *nf* (POL) purge; (MÉD) purging *q*; purge.
purger [pyʀʒe] *vt* (*radiateur*) to flush (out), drain; (*circuit hydraulique*) to bleed; (MÉD, POL) to purge; (JUR: *peine*) to serve.
purifier [pyʀifje] *vt* to purify; (TECH: *métal*) to refine.
purin [pyʀɛ̃] *nm* liquid manure.
puritain, e [pyʀitɛ̃, -ɛn] *a, nm/f* Puritan; **puritanisme** *nm* Puritanism.
pur-sang [pyʀsɑ̃] *nm inv* thoroughbred, purebred.
purulent, e [pyʀylɑ̃, -ɑ̃t] *a* purulent.
pus [py] *nm* pus.
pusillanime [pyzilanim] *a* fainthearted.
putain [pytɛ̃] *nf* (*fam!*) whore(!); **ce/cette ~ de ...** this bloody ...(!).
putréfier [pytʀefje] *vt*, **se ~** *vi* to putrefy, rot.
puzzle [pœzl(ə)] *nm* jigsaw (puzzle).
P.V. *sigle m* = **procès-verbal**.
pygmée [pigme] *nm* pygmy.
pyjama [piʒama] *nm* pyjamas *pl*, pair of pyjamas.
pylône [pilon] *nm* pylon.
pyramide [piʀamid] *nf* pyramid.
pyromane [piʀɔman] *nm/f* fire bug, arsonist.
python [pitɔ̃] *nm* python.

Q

QG [kyʒe] *voir* **quartier**.
QI [kyi] *voir* **quotient**.
quadragénaire [kadʀaʒenɛʀ] *nm/f* man/woman in his/her forties.
quadrangulaire [kwadʀɑ̃gylɛʀ] *a* quadrangular.
quadrilatère [k(w)adʀilatɛʀ] *nm* quadrilateral; four-sided area.
quadrillage [kadʀijaʒ] *nm* (*lignes etc*) square pattern, criss-cross pattern.
quadrillé, e [kadʀije] *a* (*papier*) squared.
quadriller [kadʀije] *vt* (*papier*) to mark out in squares; (POLICE) to keep under tight control, be positioned throughout.
quadrimoteur [k(w)adʀimɔtœʀ] *nm* four-engined plane.
quadripartite [kwadʀipaʀtit] *a* four-power; four-party.
quadriphonie [kadʀifɔni] *nf* quadraphony.
quadriréacteur [k(w)adʀiʀeaktœʀ] *nm* four-engined jet.
quadrupède [k(w)adʀypɛd] *nm* quadruped.
quadruple [k(w)adʀypl(ə)] *nm*: **le ~ de** four times as much as; **quadrupler** *vt, vi* to increase fourfold; **quadruplés, ées** *nm/fpl* quadruplets, quads.
quai [ke] *nm* (*de port*) quay; (*de gare*) platform; (*de cours d'eau, canal*) embankment; **être à ~** (*navire*) to be alongside; (*train*) to be in the station.
qualificatif, ive [kalifikatif, -iv] *a* (LING) qualifying // *nm* (*terme*) term; (LING) qualifier.
qualification [kalifikɑsjɔ̃] *nf* qualification.
qualifier [kalifje] *vt* to qualify; (*appeler*): **~ qch/qn de** to describe sth/sb as; **se ~** *vi* (SPORT) to qualify; **être qualifié pour** to be qualified for.
qualité [kalite] *nf* quality; (*titre, fonction*) position; **en ~ de** in one's capacity as; **avoir ~ pour** to have authority to.
quand [kɑ̃] *cj, ad* when; **~ je serai riche** when I'm rich; **~ même** nevertheless; all the same; really; **~ bien même** even though.
quant [kɑ̃]: **~ à** *prép* as for, as to; regarding.
quant-à-soi [kɑ̃taswa] *nm*: **rester sur son ~** to remain aloof.
quantième [kɑ̃tjɛm] *nm* day (of the month).
quantifier [kɑ̃tifje] *vt* to quantify.
quantitatif, ive [kɑ̃titatif, -iv] *a* quantitative.
quantité [kɑ̃tite] *nf* quantity, amount; (SCIENCE) quantity; (*grand nombre*): **une** *ou* **des ~(s) de** a great deal of; a lot of; **en grande ~** in large quantities; **du travail en ~** a great deal of work; **~ de** many.
quarantaine [kaʀɑ̃tɛn] *nf* (MÉD) quarantine; **la ~** forty, the forty mark; (*âge*) forty, the forties *pl*; **une ~ (de)** forty or so, about forty; **mettre en ~** to put into quarantine; (*fig*) to send to Coventry.
quarante [kaʀɑ̃t] *num* forty.
quart [kaʀ] *nm* (*fraction*) quarter; (*surveillance*) watch; (*partie*): **un ~ de poulet/fromage** a chicken quarter/a quarter of a cheese; **un ~ de beurre** a quarter kilo of butter, ≈ a half pound of butter; **un ~ de vin** a quarter litre of wine; **une livre un ~** *ou* **et ~** one and a quarter pounds; **le ~ de** a quarter of; **~ d'heure** quarter of an hour; **être de/prendre le ~** to keep/take the watch; **~ de tour** quarter turn.
quarteron [kaʀtəʀɔ̃] *nm* (*péj*) small bunch, handful.
quartette [kwaʀtɛt] *nm* quartet(te).
quartier [kaʀtje] *nm* (*de ville*) district, area; (*de bœuf*) quarter; (*de fruit, fromage*) piece; **~s** *nmpl* (MIL, BLASON) quarters; **cinéma de ~** local cinema; **avoir ~ libre** (MIL) to have leave from barracks; **ne pas faire de ~** to spare no-one, give no quarter; **~ général (QG)** headquarters (HQ).
quartier-maître [kaʀtjemɛtʀ(ə)] *nm* ≈ leading seaman.
quartz [kwaʀts] *nm* quartz.
quasi [kazi] *ad* almost, nearly // *préfixe*: **~-certitude** near certainty; **~ment** *ad* almost, nearly.
quatorze [katɔʀz(ə)] *num* fourteen.
quatrain [katʀɛ̃] *nm* quatrain.
quatre [katʀ(ə)] *num* four; **à ~ pattes** on all fours; **tiré à ~ épingles** dressed up to the nines; **faire les ~ cent coups** to get a bit wild; **se mettre en ~ pour qn** to go out of one's way for sb; **~ à ~** (*monter, descendre*) four at a time; **~-**

vingt-dix *num* ninety; ~-**vingts** *num* eighty; **quatrième** *num* fourth.

quatuor [kwatɥɔʀ] *nm* quartet(te).

que [kə] *cj* (*gén*) that; (*après comparatif*) than; as: *voir* **plus, autant** *etc*; **il sait ~ tu es là** he knows (that) you're here; **je veux ~ tu acceptes** I want you to accept; **il a dit ~ oui** he said he would (*ou* it was *etc, suivant le contexte*); **si vous y allez ou ~ vous lui téléphoniez** if you go there or (if you) phone him; **quand il rentrera et qu'il aura mangé** when he gets back and (when he) has eaten; **qu'il le veuille ou non** whether he likes it or not; **tenez-le qu'il ne tombe pas** hold it so (that) it doesn't fall; **qu'il fasse ce qu'il voudra** let him do as he pleases; *voir* **avant, pour, tel** *etc* // *ad*: **qu'il** *ou* **qu'est-ce qu'il est bête/court vite** he is so silly/runs so fast; **~ de** what a lot of // *pronom*: **l'homme ~ je vois** the man (whom) I see; **le livre ~ tu vois** the book (that *ou* which) you see; **un jour ~ j'étais** a day when I was; **c'est une erreur ~ de croire** it's a mistake to believe; **~ fais-tu?, qu'est-ce que tu fais?** what are you doing?; **~ préfères-tu, celui-ci ou celui-là?** which do you prefer, this one or that one?

Québec [kebɛk] *nm*: **le ~** Quebec.

quel, quelle [kɛl] *a*: **~ livre/ homme?** what book/man?; (*parmi un certain choix*) which book/man?; **~ est cet homme/ce livre?** who/what is this man/ book?; **~ est le plus grand?** which is the tallest (*ou* biggest *etc*)?; **~s acteurs préférez-vous?** which actors do you prefer?; **dans ~s pays êtes-vous allé?** which *ou* what countries did you go to?; **~le surprise!** what a surprise!; **~ que soit le coupable** whoever is guilty; **~ que soit votre avis** whatever your opinion; whichever is your opinion.

quelconque [kɛlkɔ̃k] *a* (*médiocre*) indifferent, poor; (*sans attrait*) ordinary, plain; (*indéfini*): **un ami/ prétexte ~** some friend/pretext or other; **un livre ~ suffira** any book will do.

quelque [kɛlk(ə)] *dét* some; **~s** a few, some, *tournure interrogative* + any; **les ~s livres qui** the few books which // *ad* (*environ*): **~ 100 mètres** some 100 metres; **~ livre qu'il choisisse** whatever (*ou* whichever) book he chooses; **20 kg et ~(s)** a bit over 20 kg; **~ chose** something, *tournure interrogative* + anything; **~ chose d'autre** something else; anything else; **~ part** somewhere; **~ peu** rather, somewhat; **en ~ sorte** as it were; **quelquefois** *ad* sometimes; **quelques-uns, -unes** [-zœ̃] *pronom* some, a few.

quelqu'un, une [kɛlkœ̃, -yn] *pronom* someone, somebody, *tournure interrogative* + anyone *ou* anybody; **~ d'autre** someone *ou* somebody else; anybody else.

quémander [kemɑ̃de] *vt* to beg for.

qu'en dira-t-on [kɑ̃diʀatɔ̃] *nm inv*: **le ~** gossip, what people say.

quenelle [kənɛl] *nf* quenelle.

quenouille [kənuj] *nf* distaff.

querelle [kəʀɛl] *nf* quarrel.

quereller [kəʀele]: **se ~** *vi* to quarrel; **querelleur, euse** *a* quarrelsome.

qu'est-ce que (*ou* **qui**) [kɛskə(ki)] *voir* **que, qui**.

question [kəstjɔ̃] *nf* (*gén*) question; (*fig*) matter; issue; **il a été ~ de** we (*ou* they) spoke about; **il est ~ de les emprisonner** there's talk of them being jailed; **de quoi est-il ~?** what is it about?; **il n'en est pas ~** there's no question of it; **en ~** in question; **hors de ~** out of the question; **remettre en ~** to question; **poser la ~ de confiance** (POL) to ask for a vote of confidence.

questionnaire [kɛstjɔnɛʀ] *nm* questionnaire; **questionner** *vt* to question.

quête [kɛt] *nf* collection; (*recherche*) quest, search; **faire la ~** (*à l'église*) to take the collection; (*artiste*) to pass the hat round; **en ~ de qch** in search of sth; **quêter** *vi* (*à l'église*) to take the collection; (*dans la rue*) to collect money (for charity) // *vt* to seek.

quetsche [kwɛtʃ(ə)] *nf* damson.

queue [kø] *nf* tail; (*fig: du classement*) bottom; (*: de poêle*) handle; (*: de fruit, feuille*) stalk; (*: de train, colonne, file*) rear; **en ~ (de train)** at the rear (of the train); **faire la ~** to queue (up); **se mettre à la ~** to join the queue; **à la ~ leu leu** in single file; (*fig*) one after the other; **~ de cheval** ponytail; **~ de poisson**: **faire une ~ de poisson à qn** (AUTO) to cut in front of sb; **~-de-pie** *nf* (*habit*) tails *pl*, tail coat.

queux [kø] *am voir* **maître**.

qui [ki] *pronom* (*personne*) who, *prép* + whom; (*chose, animal*) which, that; **qu'est-ce ~ est sur la table?** what is on the table?; **à ~ est ce sac?** whose bag is this?; **à ~ parlais-tu?** who were you talking to?, to whom were you talking?; **amenez ~ vous voulez** bring who you like; **~ que ce soit** whoever it may be.

quiche [kiʃ] *nf*: **~ lorraine** quiche Lorraine.

quiconque [kikɔ̃k] *pronom* (*celui qui*) whoever, anyone who; (*personne*) anyone, anybody.

quidam [kɥidam] *nm* fellow.

quiétude [kjetyd] *nf* (*d'un lieu*) quiet, tranquillity; **en toute ~** in complete peace; (*mentale*) with complete peace of mind.

quignon [kiɲɔ̃] *nm*: **~ de pain** crust of bread; hunk of bread.

quille [kij] *nf* skittle; **(jeu de) ~s** ninepins *sg*, skittles *sg*.

quincaillerie [kɛ̃kajʀi] *nf* (*ustensiles*) hardware, ironmongery; (*magasin*) hardware shop, ironmonger's; **quincaillier, ère** *nm/f* ironmonger.

quinconce [kɛ̃kɔ̃s] *nm*: **en ~** in staggered rows.

quinine [kinin] *nf* quinine.

quinquagénaire [kɛ̃kaʒenɛʀ] *nm/f* man/woman in his/her fifties.

quinquennal, e, aux [kɛ̃kenal, -o] *a* five-year, quinquennial.

quintal, aux [kɛ̃tal, -o] *nm* quintal (*100 kg*).

quinte [kɛ̃t] *nf*: **~ (de toux)** coughing fit.

quintette [kɛ̃tɛt] *nm* quintet(te).
quintuple [kɛ̃typl(ə)] *nm*: **le ~ de** five times as much as; **quintupler** *vt, vi* to increase fivefold; **quintuplés, ées** *nm/fpl* quintuplets, quins.
quinzaine [kɛ̃zɛn] *nf*: **une ~ (de)** about fifteen, fifteen or so; **une ~ (de jours)** a fortnight, two weeks.
quinze [kɛ̃z] *num* fifteen; **demain en ~** a fortnight *ou* two weeks tomorrow; **dans ~ jours** in a fortnight('s time), in two weeks(' time).
quiproquo [kipRɔko] *nm* misunderstanding; (THÉÂTRE) (case of) mistaken identity.
quittance [kitɑ̃s] *nf* (*reçu*) receipt; (*facture*) bill.
quitte [kit] *a*: **être ~ envers qn** to be no longer in sb's debt; (*fig*) to be quits with sb; **être ~ de** (*obligation*) to be clear of; **en être ~ à bon compte** to get off lightly; **~ à faire** even if it means doing; **~ ou double** (*jeu*) double your money.
quitter [kite] *vt* to leave; (*espoir, illusion*) to give up; (*vêtement*) to take off; **se ~** (*couples, interlocuteurs*) to part; **ne quittez pas** (*au téléphone*) hold the line.
qui-vive [kiviv] *nm*: **être sur le ~** to be on the alert.
quoi [kwa] *pronom* (*interrogatif*) what; **~ de neuf?** what's the news?; **as-tu de ~ écrire?** have you anything to write with?; **il n'a pas de ~ se l'acheter** he can't afford it, he hasn't got the money to buy it; **~ qu'il arrive** whatever happens; **~ qu'il en soit** be that as it may; **~ que ce soit** anything at all; **'il n'y a pas de ~'** '(please) don't mention it'; **en ~ puis-je vous aider?** how can I help you?
quoique [kwak(ə)] *cj* (al)though.
quolibet [kɔlibɛ] *nm* gibe, jeer.
quorum [kɔRɔm] *nm* quorum.
quota [kwɔta] *nm* quota.
quote-part [kɔtpaR] *nf* share.
quotidien, ne [kɔtidjɛ̃, -ɛn] *a* daily; (*banal*) everyday // *nm* (*journal*) daily (paper).
quotient [kɔsjɑ̃] *nm* (MATH) quotient; **~ intellectuel (QI)** intelligence quotient (IQ).
quotité [kɔtite] *nf* (FINANCE) quota.

R

r. *abr de* **route, rue**.
rabâcher [Rabɑʃe] *vt* to harp on, keep on repeating.
rabais [Rabɛ] *nm* reduction, discount; **au ~** at a reduction *ou* discount.
rabaisser [Rabese] *vt* (*rabattre*) to reduce; (*dénigrer*) to belittle.
rabat [Raba] *nm* flap.
rabat-joie [Rabaʒwa] *nm/f inv* killjoy, spoilsport.
rabatteur, euse [RabatœR, -øz] *nm/f* (*de gibier*) beater; (*péj*) tout.
rabattre [RabatR(ə)] *vt* (*couvercle, siège*) to pull *ou* close down; (*col*) to turn down; (*gibier*) to drive; (*somme d'un prix*) to deduct, take off; **se ~** *vi* (*bords, couvercle*) to fall shut; (*véhicule, coureur*) to cut in; **se ~ sur** *vt* to fall back on.
rabbin [Rabɛ̃] *nm* rabbi.
rabique [Rabik] *a* rabies *cpd*.
râble [Rɑbl(ə)] *nm* back; (CULIN) saddle.
râblé, e [Rɑble] *a* broad-backed, stocky.
rabot [Rabo] *nm* plane; **raboter** *vt* to plane (down).
raboteux, euse [Rabɔtø, -øz] *a* uneven, rough.
rabougri, e [RabugRi] *a* stunted.
rabrouer [RabRue] *vt* to snub, rebuff.
racaille [Rakɑj] *nf* (*péj*) rabble, riffraff.
raccommodage [Rakɔmɔdaʒ] *nm* mending *q*, repairing *q*; darning *q*.
raccommoder [Rakɔmɔde] *vt* to mend, repair; (*chaussette*) to darn.
raccompagner [Rakɔ̃paɲe] *vt* to take *ou* see back.
raccord [RakɔR] *nm* link; **~ de maçonnerie** pointing *q*; **~ de peinture** join; touch up.
raccordement [RakɔRdəmɑ̃] *nm* joining up.
raccorder [RakɔRde] *vt* to join (up), link up; (*suj: pont etc*) to connect, link; **~ au réseau du téléphone** to connect to the telephone service.
raccourci [RakuRsi] *nm* short cut.
raccourcir [RakuRsiR] *vt* to shorten // *vi* (*vêtement*) to shrink.
raccroc [RakRo]: **par ~** *ad* by chance.
raccrocher [RakRɔʃe] *vt* (*tableau, vêtement*) to hang back up; (*récepteur*) to put down // *vi* (TÉL) to hang up, ring off; **se ~ à** *vt* to cling to, hang on to.
race [Ras] *nf* race; (*d'animaux, fig: espèce*) breed; (*ascendance, origine*) stock, race; **de ~** *a* purebred, pedigree; **racé, e** *a* thoroughbred.
rachat [Raʃa] *nm* buying; buying back; redemption; atonement.
racheter [Raʃte] *vt* (*article perdu*) to buy another; (*davantage*): **~ du lait/3 œufs** to buy more milk/another 3 eggs *ou* 3 more eggs; (*après avoir vendu*) to buy back; (*d'occasion*) to buy; (COMM: *part, firme*) to buy up; (: *pension, rente*) to redeem; (REL: *pécheur*) to redeem; (: *péché*) to atone for, expiate; (*mauvaise conduite, oubli, défaut*) to make up for; **se ~** (REL) to redeem o.s.; (*gén*) to make amends, make up for it.
rachitique [Raʃitik] *a* suffering from rickets; (*fig*) scraggy, scrawny.
racial, e, aux [Rasjal, -o] *a* racial.
racine [Rasin] *nf* root; **~ carrée/cubique** square/cube root; **prendre ~** (*fig*) to take root; to put down roots.
racisme [Rasism(ə)] *nm* racism, racialism; **raciste** *a, nm/f* racist, racialist.
racket [Rakɛt] *nm* racketeering *q*.
raclée [Rɑkle] *nf* (*fam*) hiding, thrashing.
racler [Rɑkle] *vt* (*os, plat*) to scrape; (*tache, boue*) to scrape off; (*suj: chose: frotter contre*) to scrape (against).
raclette [Rɑklɛt] *nf* (CULIN) raclette (*Swiss cheese dish*).
racoler [Rakɔle] *vt* (*attirer: suj: prostituée*) to solicit; (: *parti, marchand*) to tout for; (*attraper*) to pick up; **racoleur, euse** *a* (*péj: publicité*) cheap and alluring // *nf* streetwalker.

racontars [Rakɔ̃taR] *nmpl* stories, gossip *sg*.
raconter [Rakɔ̃te] *vt*: ~ **(à qn)** (*décrire*) to relate (to sb), tell (sb) about; (*dire*) to tell (sb).
racorni, e [RakɔRni] *a* hard(ened).
radar [RadaR] *nm* radar.
rade [Rad] *nf* (natural) harbour; **en** ~ **de Toulon** in Toulon harbour; **rester en** ~ (*fig*) to be left stranded.
radeau, x [Rado] *nm* raft.
radial, e, aux [Radjal, -o] *a* radial; **pneu à carcasse** ~**e** radial tyre.
radiateur [RadjatœR] *nm* radiator, heater; (AUTO) radiator; ~ **électrique/à gaz** electric/gas heater *ou* fire.
radiation [Radjɑsjɔ̃] *nf* (*voir radier*) striking off *q*; (PHYSIQUE) radiation.
radical, e, aux [Radikal, -o] *a* radical // *nm* (LING) stem.
radier [Radje] *vt* to strike off.
radieux, euse [Radjø, -øz] *a* radiant; brilliant, glorious.
radin, e [Radɛ̃, -in] *a* (*fam*) stingy.
radio [Radjo] *nf* radio; (MÉD) X-ray // *nm* radiogram, radiotelegram; radio operator; **à la** ~ on the radio; **se faire faire une** ~ **(des poumons)** to have an X-ray taken (of one's lungs).
radio... [Radjo] *préfixe*: ~**actif, ive** *a* radioactive; ~**activité** *nf* radioactivity; **radiodiffuser** *vt* to broadcast (by radio); ~**graphie** *nf* radiography; (*photo*) X-ray photograph, radiograph; ~**graphier** *vt* to X-ray; ~**logue** *nm/f* radiologist; ~**phonique** *a* radio *cpd*; ~**reportage** *nm* radio report; ~**scopie** *nf* radioscopy; ~**télégraphie** *nf* radiotelegraphy; ~**télévisé, e** *a* broadcast on radio and television.
radis [Radi] *nm* radish; ~ **noir** horseradish *q*.
radium [Radjɔm] *nm* radium.
radoter [Radɔte] *vi* to ramble on.
radoub [Radu] *nm*: **bassin de** ~ dry dock.
radoucir [RadusiR]: **se** ~ *vi* (*se réchauffer*) to become milder; (*se calmer*) to calm down; to soften.
rafale [Rafal] *nf* (*vent*) gust (of wind); (*tir*) burst of gunfire; ~ **de mitrailleuse** burst of machine-gun fire.
raffermir [RafɛRmiR] *vt*, **se** ~ *vi* (*tissus, muscle*) to firm up; (*fig*) to strengthen.
raffinage [Rafinaʒ] *nm* refining.
raffiné, e [Rafine] *a* refined.
raffinement [Rafinmɑ̃] *nm* refinement.
raffiner [Rafine] *vt* to refine; **raffinerie** *nf* refinery.
raffoler [Rafɔle]: ~ **de** *vt* to be very keen on.
raffut [Rafy] *nm* (*fam*) row, racket.
rafistoler [Rafistɔle] *vt* (*fam*) to patch up.
rafle [Rɑfl(ə)] *nf* (*de police*) roundup, raid.
rafler [Rɑfle] *vt* (*fam*) to swipe, run off with.
rafraîchir [RafReʃiR] *vt* (*atmosphère, température*) to cool (down); (*aussi*: **mettre à** ~) to chill; (*suj*: *air, eau*) to freshen up; (: *boisson*) to refresh; (*fig*: *rénover*) to brighten up; **se** ~ to grow cooler; to freshen up; to refresh o.s.; **rafraîchissant, e** *a* refreshing; **rafraîchissement** *nm* cooling; (*boisson etc*) cool drink, refreshment.
ragaillardir [RagajaRdiR] *vt* (*fam*) to perk *ou* buck up.
rage [Raʒ] *nf* (MÉD): **la** ~ rabies; (*fureur*) rage, fury; **faire** ~ to rage; ~ **de dents** (raging) toothache; **rager** *vi* to fume (with rage); **rageur, euse** *a* snarling; ill-tempered.
raglan [Raglɑ̃] *a inv* raglan.
ragot [Rago] *nm* (*fam*) malicious gossip *q*.
ragoût [Ragu] *nm* (*plat*) stew.
rai [Rɛ] *nm*: **un** ~ **de soleil/lumière** a sunray/ray of light.
raid [Rɛd] *nm* (MIL) raid; (SPORT) long-distance trek.
raide [Rɛd] *a* (*tendu*) taut, tight; (*escarpé*) steep; (*droit: cheveux*) straight; (*ankylosé, dur, guindé*) stiff; (*fam*) steep, stiff; stony broke // *ad* (*en pente*) steeply; ~ **mort** stone dead; **raideur** *nf* steepness; stiffness; **raidir** *vt* (*muscles*) to stiffen; (*câble*) to pull taut, tighten; **se raidir** *vi* to stiffen; to become taut; (*personne*) to tense up; to brace o.s.; to harden.
raie [Rɛ] *nf* (ZOOL) skate, ray; (*rayure*) stripe; (*des cheveux*) parting.
raifort [RɛfɔR] *nm* horseradish.
rail [Rɑj] *nm* (*barre d'acier*) rail; (*chemins de fer*) railways *pl*; **les** ~**s** (*la voie ferrée*) the rails, the track *sg*; **par** ~ by rail; ~ **conducteur** live *ou* conductor rail.
railler [Rɑje] *vt* to scoff at, jeer at.
rainure [RenyR] *nf* groove; slot.
rais [Rɛ] *nm* = **rai**.
raisin [Rɛzɛ̃] *nm* (*aussi*: ~**s**) grapes *pl*; (*variété*): ~ **muscat** muscat grape; ~**s secs** raisins, currants.
raison [Rɛzɔ̃] *nf* reason; **avoir** ~ to be right; **donner** ~ **à qn** to agree with sb; to prove sb right; **avoir** ~ **de qn/qch** to get the better of sb/sth; **se faire une** ~ to learn to live with it; **perdre la** ~ to become insane; to take leave of one's senses; **demander** ~ **à qn de** (*affront etc*) to demand satisfaction from sb for; ~ **de plus** all the more reason; **à plus forte** ~ all the more so; **en** ~ **de** because of; according to; in proportion to; **à** ~ **de** at the rate of; ~ **sociale** corporate name; **raisonnable** *a* reasonable, sensible.
raisonnement [Rɛzɔnmɑ̃] *nm* reasoning; arguing; argument.
raisonner [Rɛzɔne] *vi* (*penser*) to reason; (*argumenter, discuter*) to argue // *vt* (*personne*) to reason with; (*attitude: justifier*) to reason out.
rajeunir [RaʒœniR] *vt* (*suj: coiffure, robe*): ~ **qn** to make sb look younger; (*suj: cure etc*) to rejuvenate; (*fig*) to brighten up; to give a new look to; to inject new blood into // *vi* to become (*ou* look) younger.
rajouter [Raʒute] *vt*: ~ **du sel/un œuf** to add some more salt/another egg; ~ **que** to add that.
rajuster [Raʒyste] *vt* (*vêtement*) to straighten, tidy; (*salaires*) to adjust; (*machine*) to readjust; **se** ~ to tidy *ou* straighten o.s. up.
râle [Rɑl] *nm* groan; ~ **d'agonie** death rattle.

ralenti [ralɑ̃ti] *nm*: **au ~** (AUTO): **tourner au ~** to tick over, idle; (CINÉMA) in slow motion; (*fig*) at a slower pace.
ralentir [ralɑ̃tiʀ] *vt, vi*, **se ~** *vi* to slow down.
râler [ʀɑle] *vi* to groan; (*fam*) to grouse, moan (and groan).
ralliement [ʀalimɑ̃] *nm* rallying.
rallier [ʀalje] *vt* (*rassembler*) to rally; (*rejoindre*) to rejoin; (*gagner à sa cause*) to win over; **se ~ à** (*avis*) to come over *ou* round to.
rallonge [ʀalɔ̃ʒ] *nf* (*de table*) (extra) leaf (*pl* leaves); (*de vêtement etc*) extra piece.
rallonger [ʀalɔ̃ʒe] *vt* to lengthen.
rallumer [ʀalyme] *vt* to light up again; (*fig*) to revive; **se ~** *vi* (*lumière*) to come on again.
rallye [ʀali] *nm* rally; (POL) march.
ramages [ʀamaʒ] *nmpl* leaf pattern *sg*; songs.
ramassage [ʀamɑsaʒ] *nm*: **~ scolaire** school bus service.
ramassé, e [ʀamɑse] *a* (*trapu*) squat, stocky.
ramasse-miettes [ʀamɑsmjɛt] *nm inv* table-tidy.
ramasse-monnaie [ʀamɑsmɔnɛ] *nm inv* change-tray.
ramasser [ʀamɑse] *vt* (*objet tombé ou par terre, fam*) to pick up; (*recueillir*) to collect; (*récolter*) to gather; (*: pommes de terre*) to lift; **se ~** *vi* (*sur soi-même*) to huddle up; to crouch; **ramasseur, euse de balles** *nm/f* ballboy/girl; **ramassis** *nm* (*péj*) bunch; jumble.
rambarde [ʀɑ̃baʀd(ə)] *nf* guardrail.
rame [ʀam] *nf* (*aviron*) oar; (*de métro*) train; (*de papier*) ream; **~ de haricots** bean support.
rameau, x [ʀamo] *nm* (small) branch; **les R~x** (REL) Palm Sunday *sg*.
ramener [ʀamne] *vt* to bring back; (*reconduire*) to take back; (*rabattre: couverture, visière*): **~ qch sur** to pull sth back over; **~ qch à** (*réduire à, aussi* MATH) to reduce sth to; **se ~** *vi* (*fam*) to roll *ou* turn up; **se ~ à** (*se réduire à*) to come *ou* boil down to.
ramer [ʀame] *vi* to row; **rameur, euse** *nm/f* rower.
ramier [ʀamje] *nm*: **(pigeon) ~** wood-pigeon.
ramification [ʀamifikɑsjɔ̃] *nf* ramification.
ramifier [ʀamifje]: **se ~** *vi* (*tige, secte, réseau*): **se ~ (en)** to branch out (into); (*veines, nerfs*) to ramify.
ramollir [ʀamɔliʀ] *vt* to soften; **se ~** *vi* to go soft.
ramoner [ʀamɔne] *vt* to sweep; **ramoneur** *nm* (chimney) sweep.
rampe [ʀɑ̃p] *nf* (*d'escalier*) banister(s *pl*); (*dans un garage, d'un terrain*) ramp; (THÉÂTRE): **la ~** the footlights *pl*; **~ de lancement** launching pad.
ramper [ʀɑ̃pe] *vi* to crawl.
rancard [ʀɑ̃kaʀ] *nm* (*fam*) date; tip.
rancart [ʀɑ̃kaʀ] *nm*: **mettre au ~** to scrap.
rance [ʀɑ̃s] *a* rancid.
rancœur [ʀɑ̃kœʀ] *nf* rancour, resentment.
rançon [ʀɑ̃sɔ̃] *nf* ransom; (*fig*) price.
rancune [ʀɑ̃kyn] *nf* grudge, rancour; **garder ~ à qn (de qch)** to bear sb a grudge (for sth); **sans ~!** no hard feelings!; **rancunier, ière** *a* vindictive, spiteful.
randonnée [ʀɑ̃dɔne] *nf* ride; (*à pied*) walk, ramble; hike, hiking *q*.
rang [ʀɑ̃] *nm* (*rangée*) row; (*grade, condition sociale, classement*) rank; **~s** (MIL) ranks; **se mettre en ~s/sur un ~** to get into *ou* form rows/a line; **sur 3 ~s** (lined up) 3 deep; **se mettre en ~s par 4** to form fours *ou* rows of 4; **se mettre sur les ~s** (*fig*) to get into the running; **au premier ~** in the first row; (*fig*) ranking first; **avoir ~ de** to hold the rank of.
rangé, e [ʀɑ̃ʒe] *a* (*sérieux*) orderly, steady.
rangée [ʀɑ̃ʒe] *nf* row.
ranger [ʀɑ̃ʒe] *vt* (*classer, grouper*) to order, arrange; (*mettre à sa place*) to put away; (*mettre de l'ordre dans*) to tidy up; (*arranger, disposer: en cercle etc*) to arrange; (*fig: classer*): **~ qn/qch parmi** to rank sb/sth among; **se ~** *vi* (*véhicule, conducteur: s'écarter*) to pull over; (*: s'arrêter*) to pull in; (*piéton*) to step aside; (*s'assagir*) to settle down; **se ~ à** (*avis*) to come round to, fall in with.
ranimer [ʀanime] *vt* (*personne évanouie*) to bring round; (*revigorer: forces, courage*) to restore; (*réconforter: troupes etc*) to kindle new life in; (*douleur, souvenir*) to revive; (*feu*) to rekindle.
rapace [ʀapas] *nm* bird of prey // *a* (*péj*) rapacious, grasping.
rapatrier [ʀapatʀije] *vt* to repatriate; (*capitaux*) to bring (back) home.
râpe [ʀɑp] *nf* (CULIN) grater; (*à bois*) rasp.
râpé, e [ʀɑpe] *a* (*tissu*) threadbare; (CULIN) grated.
râper [ʀɑpe] *vt* (CULIN) to grate; (*gratter, râcler*) to rasp.
rapetasser [ʀaptase] *vt* (*fam*) to patch up.
rapetisser [ʀaptise] *vt*: **~ qch** to shorten sth; to make sth look smaller // *vi*, **se ~** *vi* to shrink.
rapide [ʀapid] *a* fast; (*prompt*) quick // *nm* express (train); (*de cours d'eau*) rapid; **~ment** *ad* fast; quickly; **rapidité** *nf* speed; quickness.
rapiécer [ʀapjese] *vt* to patch.
rappel [ʀapɛl] *nm* (*d'un ambassadeur*, MIL) recall; (THÉÂTRE) curtain call; (MÉD: *vaccination*) booster; (ADMIN: *de salaire*) back pay *q*; (*d'une aventure, d'un nom*) reminder; (TECH) return; (NAVIG) sitting out; (ALPINISME: *aussi*: **~ de corde**) abseiling *q*, roping down *q*, abseil; **~ à l'ordre** call to order.
rappeler [ʀaple] *vt* (*pour faire revenir, retéléphoner*) to call back; (*ambassadeur*, MIL) to recall; (*faire se souvenir*): **~ qch à qn** to remind sb of sth; **se ~** *vt* (*se souvenir de*) to remember, recall; **~ qn à la vie** to bring sb back to life; **ça rappelle la Provence** it's reminiscent of Provence, it reminds you of Provence.
rappliquer [ʀaplike] *vi* (*fam*) to turn up.

rapport [Rapɔr] *nm* (*compte rendu*) report ; (*profit*) yield, return ; revenue ; (*lien, analogie*) relationship ; (*proportion*: MATH, TECH) ratio (*pl* s) ; **~s** *nmpl* (*entre personnes, pays*) relations ; **avoir ~ à** to have something to do with, concern ; **être en ~ avec** (*idée de corrélation*) to be in keeping with ; **être/se mettre en ~ avec qn** to have dealings with sb/get in touch with sb ; **par ~ à** in relation to ; with regard to ; **sous le ~ de** from the point of view of ; **~s (sexuels)** (sexual) intercourse *sg*.

rapporter [Rapɔrte] *vt* (*rendre, ramener*) to bring back ; (*apporter davantage*) to bring more ; (COUTURE) to sew on ; (*suj: investissement*) to yield ; (: *activité*) to bring in ; (*relater*) to report ; (JUR: *annuler*) to revoke // *vi* (*investissement*) to give a good return *ou* yield ; (: *activité*) to be very profitable ; **~ qch à** (*fig: rattacher*) to relate sth to ; **se ~ à** (*correspondre à*) to relate to ; **s'en ~ à** to rely on ; **rapporteur, euse** *nm/f* (*de procès, commission*) reporter ; (*péj*) telltale // *nm* (GÉOM) protractor.

rapproché, e [RapRɔʃe] *a* (*proche*) near, close at hand ; **~s** (*l'un de l'autre*) at close intervals.

rapprochement [RapRɔʃmɑ̃] *nm* (*reconciliation: de nations, familles*) reconciliation ; (*analogie, rapport*) parallel.

rapprocher [RapRɔʃe] *vt* (*chaise d'une table*): **~ qch (de)** to bring sth closer (to) ; (*deux tuyaux*) to bring closer together ; (*réunir*) to bring together ; (*établir une analogie entre*) to establish a parallel between ; **se ~** *vi* to draw closer *ou* nearer ; (*fig: familles, pays*) to come together ; to come closer together ; **se ~ de** to come closer to ; (*présenter une analogie avec*) to be close to.

rapt [Rapt] *nm* abduction.

raquette [Rakɛt] *nf* (*de tennis*) racket ; (*de ping-pong*) bat ; (*à neige*) snowshoe.

rare [RaR] *a* rare ; (*main-d'œuvre, denrées*) scarce ; (*cheveux, herbe*) sparse.

raréfier [RaRefje]: **se ~** *vi* to grow scarce ; (*air*) to rarefy.

rarement [RaRmɑ̃] *ad* rarely, seldom.

rareté [RaRte] *nf* rarity ; scarcity.

ras, e [Rɑ, Rɑz] *a* (*tête, cheveux*) close-cropped ; (*poil, herbe*) short // *ad* short ; **en ~e campagne** in open country ; **à ~ bords** to the brim ; **au ~ de** level with ; **en avoir ~ le bol** (*fam*) to be fed up ; **~ du cou** *a* (*pull, robe*) crew-neck.

rasade [Razad] *nf* glassful.

rasé, e [Rɑze] *a*: **~ de frais** freshly shaven ; **~ de près** close-shaven.

rase-mottes [Rɑzmɔt] *nm inv*: **faire du ~** to hedgehop.

raser [Rɑze] *vt* (*barbe, cheveux*) to shave off ; (*menton, personne*) to shave ; (*fam: ennuyer*) to bore ; (*démolir*) to raze (to the ground) ; (*frôler*) to graze ; to skim ; **se ~** to shave ; (*fam*) to be bored (to tears) ; **rasoir** *nm* razor ; **rasoir électrique** electric shaver *ou* razor ; **rasoir de sûreté** safety razor.

rassasier [Rasazje] *vt* to satisfy ; **être rassasié** (*dégoûté*) to be sated ; to have had more than enough.

rassemblement [Rasɑ̃bləmɑ̃] *nm* (*groupe*) gathering ; (POL) union ; association ; (MIL): **le ~** parade.

rassembler [Rasɑ̃ble] *vt* (*réunir*) to assemble, gather ; (*regrouper, amasser*) to gather together, collect ; **se ~** *vi* to gather.

rasseoir [RaswaR]: **se ~** *vi* to sit down again.

rasséréner [RaseRene]: **se ~** *vi* to recover one's serenity.

rassis, e [Rasi, -iz] *a* (*pain*) stale.

rassurer [RasyRe] *vt* to reassure ; **se ~** to feel reassured ; **rassure-toi** put your mind at rest *ou* at ease.

rat [Ra] *nm* rat ; **~ d'hôtel** hotel thief (*pl* thieves) ; **~ musqué** muskrat.

ratatiné, e [Ratatine] *a* shrivelled (up), wrinkled.

rate [Rat] *nf* spleen.

raté, e [Rate] *a* (*tentative*) unsuccessful, failed // *nm/f* failure // *nm* misfiring *q*.

râteau, x [Rɑto] *nm* rake.

râtelier [Rɑtəlje] *nm* rack ; (*fam*) false teeth *pl*.

rater [Rate] *vi* (*affaire, projet etc*) to go wrong, fail // *vt* (*cible, train, occasion*) to miss ; (*démonstration, plat*) to spoil ; (*examen*) to fail.

ratifier [Ratifje] *vt* to ratify.

ration [Rɑsjɔ̃] *nf* ration ; (*fig*) share.

rationnel, le [Rasjɔnɛl] *a* rational.

rationnement [Rasjɔnmɑ̃] *nm* rationing ; **ticket de ~** ration coupon.

rationner [Rasjɔne] *vt* to ration.

ratisser [Ratise] *vt* (*allée*) to rake ; (*feuiller*) to rake up ; (*suj: armée, police*) to comb.

raton [Ratɔ̃] *nm*: **~ laveur** raccoon.

R.A.T.P. *sigle f* (= *Régie autonome des transports parisiens*) *Paris transport authority*.

rattacher [Rataʃe] *vt* (*animal, cheveux*) to tie up again ; (*incorporer*: ADMIN *etc*): **~ qch à** to join sth to, unite sth with ; (*fig: relier*): **~ qch à** to link sth with, relate sth to ; (: *lier*): **~ qn à** to bind *ou* tie sb to.

rattrapage [RatRapaʒ] *nm* (SCOL) remedial classes *pl*.

rattraper [RatRape] *vt* (*fugitif*) to recapture ; (*retenir, empêcher de tomber*) to catch (hold of) ; (*atteindre, rejoindre*) to catch up with ; (*réparer: imprudence, erreur*) to make up for ; **se ~** *vi* to make up for lost time ; to make good one's losses ; to make up for it ; **se ~ (à)** (*se raccrocher*) to stop o.s. falling (by catching hold of).

rature [RatyR] *nf* deletion, erasure ; **raturer** *vt* to cross out, delete, erase.

rauque [Rok] *a* raucous ; hoarse.

ravagé, e [Ravaʒe] *a* (*visage*) harrowed.

ravager [Ravaʒe] *vt* to devastate, ravage.

ravages [Ravaʒ] *nmpl* ravages ; **faire des ~** to wreak havoc.

ravaler [Ravale] *vt* (*mur, façade*) to restore ; (*déprécier*) to lower ; **~ sa colère/son dégoût** to stifle one's anger/distaste.

ravauder [Ravode] *vt* to repair, mend.

rave [Rav] *nf* (BOT) rape.

ravi, e [Ravi] *a* delighted ; **être ~ de/que** to be delighted with/that.

ravier [ʀavje] *nm* hors d'œuvre dish.
ravigote [ʀavigɔt] a: **sauce** ~ *oil and vinegar dressing with shallots.*
ravigoter [ʀavigɔte] *vt* (*fam*) to buck up.
ravin [ʀavɛ̃] *nm* gully, ravine.
raviner [ʀavine] *vt* to furrow, gully.
ravir [ʀaviʀ] *vt* (*enchanter*) to delight; (*enlever*): ~ **qch à qn** to rob sb of sth; **à** ~ *ad* beautifully.
raviser [ʀavize]: **se** ~ *vi* to change one's mind.
ravissant, e [ʀavisɑ̃, -ɑ̃t] *a* delightful; ravishing.
ravisseur, euse [ʀavisœʀ, -øz] *nm/f* abductor.
ravitaillement [ʀavitɑjmɑ̃] *nm* resupplying; refuelling; (*provisions*) supplies *pl*; **aller au** ~ to go for fresh supplies.
ravitailler [ʀavitɑje] *vt* to resupply; (*véhicule*) to refuel; **se** ~ *vi* to get fresh supplies.
raviver [ʀavive] *vt* (*feu, douleur*) to revive; (*couleurs*) to brighten up.
ravoir [ʀavwaʀ] *vt* to get back.
rayé, e [ʀeje] *a* (*à rayures*) striped; (*éraflé*) scratched.
rayer [ʀeje] *vt* (*érafler*) to scratch; (*barrer*) to cross *ou* score out; (*d'une liste: radier*) to cross *ou* strike off.
rayon [ʀɛjɔ̃] *nm* (*de soleil etc*) ray; (GÉOM) radius; (*de roue*) spoke; (*étagère*) shelf (*pl* shelves); (*de grand magasin*) department; (*de ruche*) (honey)comb; **dans un** ~ **de** within a radius of; ~ **d'action** range; ~ **de soleil** sunbeam, ray of sunlight; ~**s X** X-rays.
rayonnage [ʀɛjɔnaʒ] *nm* set of shelves.
rayonnement [ʀɛjɔnmɑ̃] *nm* radiation; (*fig*) radiance; influence.
rayonner [ʀɛjɔne] *vi* (*chaleur, énergie*) to radiate; (*fig*) to shine forth; to be radiant; (*avenues, axes etc*) to radiate; (*touriste*) to go touring (*from one base*).
rayure [ʀejyʀ] *nf* (*motif*) stripe; (*éraflure*) scratch; (*rainure, d'un fusil*) groove; **à** ~**s** striped.
raz-de-marée [ʀɑdmaʀe] *nm inv* tidal wave.
razzia [ʀazja] *nf* raid, foray.
ré [ʀe] *nm* (MUS) D; (*en chantant la gamme*) re.
réacteur [ʀeaktœʀ] *nm* jet engine.
réaction [ʀeaksjɔ̃] *nf* reaction; **moteur à** ~ jet engine; ~ **en chaîne** chain reaction; **réactionnaire** *a* reactionary.
réadapter [ʀeadapte] *vt* to readjust; (MÉD) to rehabilitate; **se** ~ **(à)** to readjust (to).
réaffirmer [ʀeafiʀme] *vt* to reaffirm, reassert.
réagir [ʀeaʒiʀ] *vi* to react.
réalisateur, trice [ʀealizatœʀ, -tʀis] *nm/f* (TV, CINÉMA) director.
réalisation [ʀealizɑsjɔ̃] *nf* carrying out; realization; fulfilment; achievement; production; (*œuvre*) production; creation; work.
réaliser [ʀealize] *vt* (*projet, opération*) to carry out, realize; (*rêve, souhait*) to realize, fulfil; (*exploit*) to achieve; (*achat, vente*) to make; (*film*) to produce; (*se rendre compte de,* COMM: *bien, capital*) to realize; **se** ~ *vi* to be realized.
réaliste [ʀealist(ə)] *a* realistic; (*peintre, roman*) realist // *nm/f* realist.
réalité [ʀealite] *nf* reality; **en** ~ in (actual) fact; **dans la** ~ in reality.
réanimation [ʀeanimasjɔ̃] *nf* resuscitation; **service de** ~ intensive care unit.
réarmer [ʀeaʀme] *vt* (*arme*) to reload // *vi* (*état*) to rearm.
réassurance [ʀeasyʀɑ̃s] *nf* reinsurance.
rébarbatif, ive [ʀebaʀbatif, -iv] *a* forbidding, off-putting.
rebattre [ʀəbatʀ(ə)] *vt*: ~ **les oreilles à qn de qch** to keep harping on to sb about sth; **rebattu, e** *a* hackneyed.
rebelle [ʀəbɛl] *nm/f* rebel // *a* (*troupes*) rebel; (*enfant*) rebellious; (*mèche etc*) unruly; ~ **à** unamenable to; unwilling to + *verbe.*
rebeller [ʀəbele]: **se** ~ *vi* to rebel.
rébellion [ʀebeljɔ̃] *nf* rebellion; (*rebelles*) rebel forces *pl.*
reboiser [ʀəbwaze] *vt* to replant with trees, reafforest.
rebondi, e [ʀəbɔ̃di] *a* rounded; chubby, well-rounded.
rebondir [ʀəbɔ̃diʀ] *vi* (*ballon: au sol*) to bounce; (*: contre un mur*) to rebound; (*fig: procès, action, conversation*) to get moving again, be suddenly revived; **rebondissements** *nmpl* (*fig*) twists and turns, sudden revivals.
rebord [ʀəbɔʀ] *nm* edge.
rebours [ʀəbuʀ]: **à** ~ *ad* the wrong way.
rebouteux, euse [ʀəbutø, -øz] *nm/f* (*péj*) bonesetter.
rebrousse-poil [ʀbʀuspwal]: **à** ~ *ad* the wrong way.
rebrousser [ʀəbʀuse] *vt*: ~ **chemin** to turn back.
rebuffade [ʀəbyfad] *nf* rebuff.
rébus [ʀebys] *nm inv* rebus.
rebut [ʀəby] *nm*: **mettre au** ~ to scrap, discard.
rebuter [ʀəbyte] *vt* to put off.
récalcitrant, e [ʀekalsitʀɑ̃, -ɑ̃t] *a* refractory.
recaler [ʀəkale] *vt* (SCOL) to fail.
récapituler [ʀekapityle] *vt* to recapitulate; to sum up.
recel [ʀəsɛl] *nm* receiving (stolen goods).
receler [ʀəsəle] *vt* (*produit d'un vol*) to receive; (*malfaiteur*) to harbour; (*fig*) to conceal; **receleur, euse** *nm/f* receiver.
récemment [ʀesamɑ̃] *ad* recently.
recensement [ʀəsɑ̃smɑ̃] *nm* census; inventory.
recenser [ʀəsɑ̃se] *vt* (*population*) to take a census of; (*inventorier*) to make an inventory of; (*dénombrer*) to list.
récent, e [ʀesɑ̃, -ɑ̃t] *a* recent.
récépissé [ʀesepise] *nm* receipt.
récepteur, trice [ʀesɛptœʀ, -tʀis] *a* receiving // *nm* receiver; ~ **(de radio)** radio set *ou* receiver.
réception [ʀesɛpsjɔ̃] *nf* receiving *q*; (*accueil*) reception, welcome; (*bureau*) reception desk; (*réunion mondaine*)

reception, party; (*pièces*) reception rooms *pl*; (*SPORT: après un saut*) landing; (: *du ballon*) catching *q*; **jour/heures de ~** day/hours for receiving visitors (*ou* students *etc*); (*MÉD*) surgery day/hours; **réceptionnaire** *nm/f* receiving clerk; **réceptionner** *vt* (*COMM*) to take delivery of; (*SPORT: ballon*) to catch (and control); **réceptionniste** *nm/f* receptionist.

récession [ʀesesjɔ̃] *nf* recession.

recette [ʀəsɛt] *nf* (*CULIN*) recipe; (*fig*) formula, recipe; (*COMM*) takings *pl*; (*ADMIN: bureau*) tax *ou* revenue office; **~s** *nfpl* (*COMM: rentrées*) receipts.

receveur, euse [ʀəsvœʀ, -øz] *nm/f* (*des contributions*) tax collector; (*des postes*) postmaster/mistress; (*d'autobus*) conductor/conductress.

recevoir [ʀəsvwaʀ] *vt* to receive; (*lettre, prime*) to receive, get; (*client, patient, représentant*) to see; (*SCOL: candidat*) to pass // *vi* to receive visitors; to give parties; to see patients *etc*; **se ~** *vi* (*athlète*) to land; **être reçu** (*à un examen*) to pass.

rechange [ʀəʃɑ̃ʒ]: **de ~** *a* (*pièces, roue*) spare; (*fig: plan*) alternative; **des vêtements de ~** a change of clothes.

rechaper [ʀəʃape] *vt* to remould, retread.

réchapper [ʀeʃape]: **~ de** *ou* **à** *vt* (*accident, maladie*) to come through.

recharge [ʀəʃaʀʒ(ə)] *nf* refill.

recharger [ʀəʃaʀʒe] *vt* (*camion, fusil, appareil-photo*) to reload; (*briquet, stylo*) to refill; (*batterie*) to recharge.

réchaud [ʀeʃo] *nm* (portable) stove; plate-warmer.

réchauffer [ʀeʃofe] *vt* (*plat*) to reheat; (*mains, personne*) to warm; **se ~** *vi* (*température*) to get warmer.

rêche [ʀɛʃ] *a* rough.

recherche [ʀəʃɛʀʃ(ə)] *nf* (*action*): **la ~ de** the search for; (*raffinement*) affectedness, studied elegance; (*scientifique etc*): **la ~** research; **~s** *nfpl* (*de la police*) investigations; (*scientifiques*) research *sg*; **être/se mettre à la ~ de** to be/go in search of.

recherché, e [ʀəʃɛʀʃe] *a* (*rare, demandé*) much sought-after; (*raffiné*) studied, affected.

rechercher [ʀəʃɛʀʃe] *vt* (*objet égaré, fugitif*) to look for, search for; (*témoins, main-d'œuvre*) to look for; (*causes d'un phénomène, nouveau procédé*) to try to find; (*bonheur etc, l'amitié de qn*) to seek.

rechigner [ʀəʃiɲe] *vi*: **~ (à)** to balk (at).

rechute [ʀəʃyt] *nf* (*MÉD*) relapse; (*dans le péché, le vice*) lapse; **faire une ~** to have a relapse.

récidiver [ʀesidive] *vi* to commit a second (*ou* subsequent) offence; (*fig*) to do it again; **récidiviste** *nm/f* second (*ou* habitual) offender, recidivist.

récif [ʀesif] *nm* reef.

récipient [ʀesipjɑ̃] *nm* container.

réciproque [ʀesipʀɔk] *a* reciprocal; **~ment** *ad* reciprocally; **et ~ment** and vice versa.

récit [ʀesi] *nm* story.

récital [ʀesital] *nm* recital.

récitation [ʀesitɑsjɔ̃] *nf* recitation.

réciter [ʀesite] *vt* to recite.

réclamation [ʀeklamɑsjɔ̃] *nf* complaint; **~s** (*bureau*) complaints department *sg*.

réclame [ʀeklam] *nf*: **la ~** advertising; **une ~** an advert(isement); **article en ~** special offer.

réclamer [ʀeklame] *vt* (*aide, nourriture etc*) to ask for; (*revendiquer: dû, part, indemnité*) to claim, demand; (*nécessiter*) to demand, require // *vi* to complain; **se ~ de** to give as one's authority; to claim filiation with.

reclasser [ʀəklɑse] *vt* (*fig: fonctionnaire etc*) to regrade.

reclus, e [ʀəkly, -yz] *nm/f* recluse.

réclusion [ʀeklyzjɔ̃] *nf* imprisonment.

recoin [ʀəkwɛ̃] *nm* nook, corner; (*fig*) hidden recess.

reçois *etc vb voir* **recevoir**.

récolte [ʀekɔlt(ə)] *nf* harvesting; gathering; (*produits*) harvest, crop; (*fig*) crop, collection.

récolter [ʀekɔlte] *vt* to harvest, gather (in); (*fig*) to collect; to get.

recommandable [ʀəkɔmɑ̃dabl(ə)] *a* commendable.

recommandation [ʀəkɔmɑ̃dɑsjɔ̃] *nf* recommendation.

recommandé [ʀəkɔmɑ̃de] *nm* (*POSTES*): **en ~** by registered mail.

recommander [ʀəkɔmɑ̃de] *vt* to recommend; (*suj: qualités etc*) to commend; (*POSTES*) to register; **~ à qn de faire** to recommend sb to do; **se ~ à qn** to commend o.s. to sb; **se ~ de qn** to give sb's name as a reference.

recommencer [ʀəkɔmɑ̃se] *vt* (*reprendre: lutte, séance*) to resume, start again; (*refaire: travail, explications*) to start afresh, start (over) again; (*récidiver: erreur*) to make again // *vi* to start again; (*récidiver*) to do it again.

récompense [ʀekɔ̃pɑ̃s] *nf* reward; (*prix*) award; **récompenser** *vt*: **récompenser qn (de** *ou* **pour)** to reward sb for.

réconciliation [ʀekɔ̃siljɑsjɔ̃] *nf* reconciliation.

réconcilier [ʀekɔ̃silje] *vt* to reconcile; **~ qn avec qch** to reconcile sb to sth; **se ~ (avec)** to be reconciled (with).

reconduction [ʀəkɔ̃dyksjɔ̃] *nf* renewal.

reconduire [ʀəkɔ̃dɥiʀ] *vt* (*raccompagner*) to take *ou* see back; (*JUR, POL: renouveler*) to renew.

réconfort [ʀekɔ̃fɔʀ] *nm* comfort.

réconforter [ʀekɔ̃fɔʀte] *vt* (*consoler*) to comfort; (*revigorer*) to fortify.

reconnaissance [ʀəkɔnɛsɑ̃s] *nf* recognition; acknowledgement; (*gratitude*) gratitude, gratefulness; (*MIL*) reconnaissance, recce; **~ de dette** acknowledgement of a debt, IOU.

reconnaissant, e [ʀəkɔnɛsɑ̃, -ɑ̃t] *a* grateful; **je vous serais ~ de bien vouloir** I should be most grateful if you would (kindly).

reconnaître [ʀəkɔnɛtʀ(ə)] *vt* to recognize; (*MIL: lieu*) to reconnoitre; (*JUR: enfant, dette, droit*) to acknowledge; **~ que** to admit *ou* acknowledge that; **~ qn/qch**

à (*l'identifier grâce à*) to recognize sb/sth by.

reconstituant, e [Rəkɔ̃stitɥɑ̃, -ɑ̃t] *a* (*régime*) strength-building // *nm* tonic, pick-me-up.

reconstituer [Rəkɔ̃stitɥe] *vt* (*monument ancien*) to recreate, build a replica of; (*fresque, vase brisé*) to piece together, reconstitute; (*événement, accident*) to reconstruct; (*fortune, patrimoine*) to rebuild; (*BIO: tissus etc*) to regenerate; **reconstitution** *nf* (*JUR: d'accident etc*) reconstruction.

reconstruire [Rəkɔ̃stRɥiR] *vt* to rebuild.

record [RəkɔR] *nm, a* record.

recoupement [Rəkupmɑ̃] *nm*: **par ~** by cross-checking.

recouper [Rəkupe]: **se ~** *vi* (*témoignages*) to tie *ou* match up.

recourbé, e [RəkuRbe] *a* curved; hooked; bent.

recourir [RəkuRiR]: **~ à** *vt* (*ami, agence*) to turn *ou* appeal to; (*force, ruse, emprunt*) to resort *ou* have recourse to.

recours [RəkuR] *nm* (*JUR*) appeal; **avoir ~ à = recourir à**; **en dernier ~** as a last resort; **sans ~** final; with no way out; **~ en grâce** plea for clemency (*ou* pardon).

recouvrer [RəkuvRe] *vt* (*vue, santé etc*) to recover, regain; (*impôts*) to collect; (*créance*) to recover.

recouvrir [RəkuvRiR] *vt* (*couvrir à nouveau*) to re-cover; (*couvrir entièrement, aussi fig*) to cover; (*cacher, masquer*) to conceal, hide; **se ~** (*se superposer*) to overlap.

recracher [RəkRaʃe[*vt* to spit out.

récréatif, ive [RekReatif, -iv] *a* of entertainment; recreational.

récréation [RekReɑsjɔ̃] *nf* recreation, entertainment; (*SCOL*) break.

récrier [RekRije]: **se ~** *vi* to exclaim.

récriminations [RekRiminɑsjɔ̃] *nfpl* remonstrations, complaints.

recroqueviller [RəkRɔkvije]: **se ~** *vi* (*feuilles*) to curl *ou* shrivel up; (*personne*) to huddle up.

recru, e [RəkRy] *a*: **~ de fatigue** exhausted // *nf* recruit.

recrudescence [RəkRydesɑ̃s] *nf* fresh outbreak.

recrue [RəkRy] *a, nf voir* **recru**.

recruter [RəkRyte] *vt* to recruit.

rectal, e, aux [Rɛktal, -o] *a*: **par voie ~e** rectally.

rectangle [Rɛktɑ̃gl(ə)] *nm* rectangle; **rectangulaire** *a* rectangular.

recteur [RɛktœR] *nm* ≈ (regional) director of education.

rectificatif, ive [Rɛktifikatif, -iv] *a* corrected // *nm* correction.

rectification [Rɛktifikɑsjɔ̃] *nf* correction.

rectifier [Rɛktifje] *vt* (*tracé, virage*) to straighten; (*calcul, adresse*) to correct; (*erreur, faute*) to rectify, put right.

rectiligne [Rɛktiliɲ] *a* straight; (*GÉOM*) rectilinear.

rectitude [Rɛktityd] *nf* rectitude, uprightness.

reçu, e [Rəsy] *pp de* **recevoir** // *a* (*admis, consacré*) accepted // *nm* (*COMM*) receipt.

recueil [Rəkœj] *nm* collection.

recueillement [Rəkœjmɑ̃] *nm* meditation, contemplation.

recueillir [RəkœjiR] *vt* to collect; (*voix, suffrages*) to win; (*accueillir: réfugiés, chat*) to take in; **se ~** *vi* to gather one's thoughts; to meditate.

recul [Rəkyl] *nm* retreat; recession; decline; (*d'arme à feu*) recoil, kick; **avoir un mouvement de ~** to recoil, start back; **prendre du ~** to stand back; **avec le ~** with the passing of time, in retrospect.

reculade [Rəkylad] *nf* (*péj*) climb-down.

reculé, e [Rəkyle] *a* remote.

reculer [Rəkyle] *vi* to move back, back away; (*AUTO*) to reverse, back (up); (*fig*) to (be on the) decline; to be losing ground; (*: se dérober*) to shrink back // *vt* to move back; to reverse, back (up); (*fig: possibilités, limites*) to extend; (*: date, décision*) to postpone.

reculons [Rəkylɔ̃]: **à ~** *ad* backwards.

récupérer [RekypeRe] *vt* (*rentrer en possession de*) to recover, get back; (*recueillir: ferraille etc*) to salvage (for reprocessing); (*délinquant etc*) to rehabilitate // *vi* to recover.

récurer [RekyRe] *vt* to scour.

récuser [Rekyze] *vt* to challenge; **se ~** to decline to give an opinion.

reçut *vb voir* **recevoir**.

recycler [Rəsikle] *vt* (*SCOL*) to reorientate; (*employés*) to retrain.

rédacteur, trice [RedaktœR, -tRis] *nm/f* (*journaliste*) writer; subeditor; (*d'ouvrage de référence*) editor, compiler; **~ en chef** chief editor; **~ publicitaire** copywriter.

rédaction [Redaksjɔ̃] *nf* writing; (*rédacteurs*) editorial staff; (*bureau*) editorial office(s); (*SCOL: devoir*) essay, composition.

reddition [Redisjɔ̃] *nf* surrender.

rédemption [Redɑ̃psjɔ̃] *nf* redemption.

redescendre [Rədesɑ̃dR(ə)] *vi* (*à nouveau*) to go back down; (*après la montée*) to go down (again) // *vt* (*pente etc*) to go down.

redevable [Rədvable(ə)] *a*: **être ~ de qch à qn** (*somme*) to owe sb sth; (*fig*) to be indebted to sb for sth.

redevance [Rədvɑ̃s] *nf* (*téléphonique*) rental charge; (*radiophonique*) licence fee.

rédhibitoire [RedibitwaR] *a*: **vice ~** (*fig*) irretrievable flaw.

rédiger [Rediʒe] *vt* to write; (*contrat*) to draw up.

redire [RədiR] *vt* to repeat; **trouver à ~ à** to find fault with; **redite** *nf* (needless) repetition.

redondance [Rədɔ̃dɑ̃s] *nf* redundancy.

redoublé, e [Rəduble] *a*: **à coups ~s** even harder, twice as hard.

redoubler [Rəduble] *vi* (*tempête, violence*) to intensify, get even stronger *ou* fiercer etc; (*SCOL*) to repeat a year; **~ de** *vt* to be twice as + *adjectif*; **le vent redouble de violence** the wind is blowing twice as hard.

redoutable [Rədutabl(ə)] *a* formidable, fearsome.
redouter [Rədute] *vt* to fear; (*appréhender*) to dread.
redressement [RədRɛsmɑ̃] *nm*: **maison de ~** reformatory.
redresser [RədRese] *vt* (*arbre, mât*) to set upright, right; (*pièce tordue*) to straighten out; (AVIAT, AUTO) to straighten up; (*situation, économie*) to put right; **se ~** *vi* (*objet penché*) to right itself; to straighten up; (*personne*) to sit (*ou* stand) up; to sit (*ou* stand) up straight.
redresseur [RədRɛsœR] *nm*: **~ de torts** righter of wrongs.
réduction [Redyksjɔ̃] *nf* reduction.
réduire [RedɥiR] *vt* (*gén, aussi* CULIN, MATH) to reduce; (*prix, dépenses*) to cut, reduce; (*carte*) to scale down, reduce; (MÉD: *fracture*) to set; (*rebelles*) to put down; **se ~ à** (*revenir à*) to boil down to; **se ~ en** (*se transformer en*) to be reduced to.
réduit [Redɥi] *nm* tiny room, recess.
rééducation [Reedykɑsjɔ̃] *nf* (*d'un membre*) re-education; (*de délinquants, d'un blessé*) rehabilitation; **~ de la parole** speech therapy.
réel, le [Reɛl] *a* real // *nm*: **le ~** reality.
réélection [Reelɛksjɔ̃] *nf* re-election.
réélire [ReeliR] *vt* to re-elect.
réellement [Reɛlmɑ̃] *ad* really.
réemploi [Reɑ̃plwa] *nm* = **remploi**.
réescompte [Reɛskɔ̃t] *nm* rediscount.
réévaluation [Reevalɥɑsjɔ̃] *nf* revaluation.
réévaluer [Reevalɥe] *vt* to revalue.
réexpédier [Reɛkspedje] *vt* (*à l'envoyeur*) to return, send back; (*au destinataire*) to send on, forward.
ref. *abr de* **référence**.
refaire [RəfɛR] *vt* (*faire de nouveau, recommencer*) to do again; (*réparer, restaurer*) to do up; **se ~** *vi* (*en santé*) to recover; (*en argent*) to make up one's losses; **être refait** (*fam*: *dupé*) to be had.
réfection [Refɛksjɔ̃] *nf* repair.
réfectoire [RefɛktwaR] *nm* (*de collège, couvent, caserne*) refectory.
référence [RefeRɑ̃s] *nf* reference; **~s** *nfpl* (*recommandations*) reference *sg*; **faire ~ à** to refer to; **ouvrage de ~** reference work.
référendum [RefeRɑ̃dɔm] *nm* referendum.
référer [RefeRe]: **se ~ à** *vt* to refer to; **en ~ à qn** to refer the matter to sb.
refiler [Rəfile] *vt* (*fam*): **~ qch à qn** to palm sth off on sb; to pass sth on to sb.
réfléchi, e [Refleʃi] *a* (*caractère*) thoughtful; (*action*) well-thought-out; (LING) reflexive.
réfléchir [RefleʃiR] *vt* to reflect // *vi* to think; **~ à** *ou* **sur** to think about.
reflet [Rəflɛ] *nm* reflection; (*sur l'eau etc*) sheen *q*, glint.
refléter [Rəflete] *vt* to reflect; **se ~** *vi* to be reflected.
réflex [Reflɛks] *a inv* (PHOTO) reflex.
réflexe [Reflɛks(ə)] *nm, a* reflex; **avoir de bons ~s** to have good reactions *ou* reflexes.
réflexion [Reflɛksjɔ̃] *nf* (*de la lumière etc, pensée*) reflection; (*fait de penser*) thought; (*remarque*) remark; **~s** *nfpl* (*méditations*) thought *sg*, reflection *sg*; **sans ~** without thinking; **~ faite, à la ~** on reflection.
refluer [Rəflye] *vi* to flow back; (*foule*) to surge back.
reflux [Rəfly] *nm* (*de la mer*) ebb.
refondre [Rəfɔ̃dR(ə)] *vt* (*texte*) to recast.
réformateur, trice [RefɔRmatœR, -tRis] *nm/f* reformer.
Réformation [RefɔRmɑsjɔ̃] *nf*: **la ~** the Reformation.
réforme [RefɔRm(ə)] *nf* reform; (MIL) declaration of unfitness for service; discharge (*on health grounds*); (REL): **la R~** the Reformation.
réformé, e [RefɔRme] *a, nm/f* (REL) Protestant.
réformer [RefɔRme] *vt* to reform; (MIL: *recrue*) to declare unfit for service; (: *soldat*) to discharge, invalid out.
réformisme [RefɔRmism(ə)] *nm* reformism, policy of reform.
refoulé, e [Rəfule] *a* (PSYCH) frustrated, repressed.
refoulement [Rəfulmɑ̃] *nm* (PSYCH) repression.
refouler [Rəfule] *vt* (*envahisseurs*) to drive back, repulse; (*liquide*) to force back; (*fig*) to suppress; (PSYCH) to repress.
réfractaire [RefRaktɛR] *a* (*minerai*) refractory; (*brique*) fire *cpd*; (*prêtre*) non-juring; **soldat ~** draft evader; **être ~ à** to resist.
réfracter [RefRakte] *vt* to refract.
refrain [RəfRɛ̃] *nm* (MUS) refrain, chorus; (*air, fig*) tune.
refréner, réfréner [RəfRene, RefRene] *vt* to curb, check.
réfrigérant, e [RefRiʒeRɑ̃, -ɑ̃t] *a* refrigerant, cooling.
réfrigérer [RefRiʒeRe] *vt* to refrigerate.
refroidir [RəfRwadiR] *vt* to cool; (*fig*) to have a cooling effect on // *vi* to cool (down); **se ~** *vi* (*prendre froid*) to catch a chill; (*temps*) to get cooler *ou* colder; (*fig*) to cool (off); **refroidissement** *nm* cooling; (*grippe etc*) chill.
refuge [Rəfyʒ] *nm* refuge; (*pour piétons*) (traffic) island.
réfugié, e [Refyʒje] *a, nm/f* refugee.
réfugier [Refyʒje]: **se ~** *vi* to take refuge.
refus [Rəfy] *nm* refusal; **ce n'est pas de ~** I won't say no, it's welcome.
refuser [Rəfyze] *vt* to refuse; (SCOL: *candidat*) to fail; **~ qch à qn/de faire** to refuse sb sth/to do; **~ du monde** to have to turn customers away; **se ~ à qch/à faire** to refuse to do.
réfuter [Refyte] *vt* to refute.
regagner [Rəgaɲe] *vt* (*argent, faveur*) to win back; (*lieu*) to get back to; **~ le temps perdu** to make up (for) lost time; **~ du terrain** to regain ground.
regain [Rəgɛ̃] *nm* (*herbe*) second crop of hay; (*renouveau*): **un ~ de** renewed + *nom*.
régal [Regal] *nm* treat.
régalade [Regalad] *ad*: **à la ~** from the bottle (held away from the lips).

régaler [Regale] *vt*: ~ **qn** to treat sb to a delicious meal; ~ **qn de** to treat sb to; **se** ~ *vi* to have a delicious meal; (*fig*) to enjoy o.s.

regard [Rəgar] *nm* (*coup d'œil*) look, glance; (*expression*) look (in one's eye); **parcourir/menacer du** ~ to cast an eye over/look threateningly at; **au** ~ **de** (*loi, morale*) from the point of view of; **en** ~ (*vis à vis*) opposite; **en** ~ **de** in comparison with.

regardant, e [Rəgardɑ̃, -ɑ̃t] *a*: **très/peu** ~ **(sur)** quite fussy/very free (about); (*économe*) very tight-fisted/quite generous (with).

regarder [Rəgarde] *vt* (*examiner, observer, lire*) to look at; (*film, télévision, match*) to watch; (*envisager: situation, avenir*) to view; (*considérer: son intérêt etc*) to be concerned with; (*être orienté vers*): ~ **(vers)** to face; (*concerner*) to concern // *vi* to look; ~ **à** *vt* (*dépense, qualité, détails*) to be fussy with *ou* over; ~ **à faire** to hesitate to do; **dépenser sans** ~ to spend freely; ~ **qn/qch comme** to regard sb/sth as; ~ **(qch) dans le dictionnaire/l'annuaire** to look (sth up) in the dictionary/directory; **cela me regarde** it concerns me, it's my business.

régate(s) [Regat] *nf(pl)* regatta.

régénérer [Reʒenere] *vt* to regenerate; (*fig*) to revive.

régent [Reʒɑ̃] *nm* regent.

régenter [Reʒɑ̃te] *vt* to rule over; to dictate to.

régie [Reʒi] *nf* (COMM, INDUSTRIE) state-owned company; (THÉÂTRE, CINÉMA) production; **la** ~ **de l'État** state control.

regimber [Rəʒɛ̃be] *vi* to balk, jib.

régime [Reʒim] *nm* (POL) régime; (ADMIN: *des prisons, fiscal etc*) system; (MÉD) diet; (GÉO) régime; (TECH) (engine) speed; (*fig*) rate, pace; (*de bananes, dattes*) bunch; **se mettre au/suivre un** ~ to go on/be on a diet; ~ **sans sel** salt-free diet; **à bas/haut** ~ (AUTO) at low/high revs; ~ **matrimonial** marriage settlement.

régiment [Reʒimɑ̃] *nm* (MIL: *unité*) regiment; (*fig: fam*): **un** ~ **de** an army of; **un copain de** ~ a pal from military service *ou* (one's) army days.

région [Reʒjɔ̃] *nf* region; **la** ~ **parisienne** the Paris area; **régional, e, aux** *a* regional; **régionalisme** *nm* regionalism.

régir [ReʒiR] *vt* to govern.

régisseur [Reʒisœr] *nm* (*d'un domaine*) steward; (CINÉMA, TV) assistant director; (THÉÂTRE) stage manager.

registre [Rəʒistr(ə)] *nm* (*livre*) register; logbook; ledger; (MUS, LING) register; (*d'orgue*) stop.

réglage [Reglaʒ] *nm* adjustment; tuning.

règle [Rɛgl(ə)] *nf* (*instrument*) ruler; (*loi, prescription*) rule; ~**s** *nfpl* (PHYSIOL) period *sg*; **en** ~ (*papiers d'identité*) in order; **être/se mettre en** ~ to be/put o.s. straight with the authorities; **en** ~ **générale** as a (general) rule; ~ **à calcul** slide rule.

réglé, e [Regle] *a* well-ordered; stable, steady; (*papier*) ruled; (*femme*): **bien** ~**e** whose periods are regular.

règlement [Rɛgləmɑ̃] *nm* settling; (*arrêté*) regulation; (*règles, statuts*) regulations *pl*, rules *pl*; ~ **de compte(s)** settling of scores; **réglementaire** *a* conforming to the regulations; (*tenue, uniforme*) regulation *cpd*.

réglementation [Rɛgləmɑ̃tɑsjɔ̃] *nf* regulation, control; regulations *pl*.

réglementer [Rɛgləmɑ̃te] *vt* to regulate, control.

régler [Regle] *vt* (*mécanisme, machine*) to regulate, adjust; (*moteur*) to tune; (*thermostat etc*) to set, adjust; (*emploi du temps etc*) to organize, plan; (*question, conflit, facture, dette*) to settle; (*fournisseur*) to settle up with, pay; (*papier*) to rule; ~ **son compte à qn** to sort sb out, settle sb; ~ **un compte avec qn** to settle a score with sb.

réglisse [Reglis] *nf* liquorice.

règne [Rɛɲ] *nm* (*d'un roi etc, fig*) reign; (BIO): **le** ~ **végétal/animal** the vegetable/animal kingdom.

régner [Reɲe] *vi* (*roi*) to rule, reign; (*fig*) to reign.

regorger [RəgɔRʒe] *vi* to overflow; ~ **de** to overflow with, be bursting with.

régression [RegResjɔ̃] *nf* regression, decline.

regret [RəgRɛ] *nm* regret; **à** ~ with regret; **avec** ~ regretfully; **être au** ~ **de devoir faire** to regret having to do.

regrettable [RəgRɛtabl(ə)] *a* regrettable.

regretter [RəgRete] *vt* to regret; (*personne*) to miss; ~ **que** to regret that, be sorry that; **je regrette** I'm sorry.

regrouper [RəgRupe] *vt* (*grouper*) to group together; (*contenir*) to include, comprise; **se** ~ *vi* to gather (together).

régulariser [RegylaRize] *vt* (*fonctionnement, trafic*) to regulate; (*passeport, papiers*) to put in order; (*sa situation*) to straighten out, regularize.

régularité [RegylaRite] *nf* regularity.

régulateur, trice [RegylatœR, -tRis] *a* regulating.

régulier, ière [Regylje, -jɛR] *a* (*gén*) regular; (*vitesse, qualité*) steady; (*répartition, pression, paysage*) even; (TRANSPORTS: *ligne, service*) scheduled, regular; (*légal, réglementaire*) lawful, in order; (*fam: correct*) straight, on the level; **régulièrement** *ad* regularly; steadily; evenly; normally.

réhabiliter [Reabilite] *vt* to rehabilitate; (*fig*) to restore to favour.

rehausser [Rəose] *vt* to heighten, raise; (*fig*) to set off, enhance.

rein [Rɛ̃] *nm* kidney; ~**s** *nmpl* (*dos*) back *sg*; **avoir mal aux** ~**s** to have backache.

reine [Rɛn] *nf* queen.

reine-claude [Rɛnklod] *nf* greengage.

reinette [Rɛnɛt] *nf* rennet, pippin.

réintégrer [Reɛ̃tegRe] *vt* (*lieu*) to return to; (*fonctionnaire*) to reinstate.

réitérer [ReiteRe] *vt* to repeat, reiterate.

rejaillir [RəʒajiR] *vi* to splash up; ~ **sur** to splash up onto; (*fig*) to rebound on; to fall upon.

rejet [Rəʒɛ] *nm* (*action, aussi* MÉD)

rejection; (*POÉSIE*) enjambement, rejet; (*BOT*) shoot.

rejeter [rəʒte] *vt* (*relancer*) to throw back; (*vomir*) to bring *ou* throw up; (*écarter*) to reject; (*déverser*) to throw out, discharge; ~ **la tête/les épaules en arrière** to throw one's head/pull one's shoulders back; ~ **la responsabilité de qch sur qn** to lay the responsibility for sth at sb's door.

rejeton [Rəʒtɔ̃] *nm* offspring.

rejoindre [Rəʒwɛ̃dR(ə)] *vt* (*famille, régiment*) to rejoin, return to; (*lieu*) to get (back) to; (*suj*: *route etc*) to meet, join; (*rattraper*) to catch up (with); **se** ~ *vi* to meet; **je te rejoins au café** I'll see *ou* meet you at the café.

réjoui, e [Reʒwi] *a* (*mine*) joyous.

réjouir [ReʒwiR] *vt* to delight; **se** ~ *vi* to be delighted; to rejoice; **se** ~ **de qch/faire** to be delighted about sth/to do; **réjouissances** *nfpl* (*joie*) rejoicing *sg*; (*fête*) festivities, merry-making *sg*.

relâche [Rəlɑʃ]: **faire** ~ *vi* (*navire*) to put into port; (*CINÉMA*) to be closed; **sans** ~ *ad* without respite *ou* a break.

relâché, e [Rəlɑʃe] *a* loose, lax.

relâcher [Rəlɑʃe] *vt* (*ressort, prisonnier*) to release; (*étreinte, cordes*) to loosen // *vi* (*NAVIG*) to put into port; **se** ~ *vi* to loosen; (*discipline*) to become slack *ou* lax; (*élève etc*) to slacken off.

relais [Rəlɛ] *nm* (*SPORT*): **(course de)** ~ relay (race); (*RADIO, TV*) relay; **équipe de** ~ shift team; relay team; **prendre le** ~ **(de)** to take over (from); ~ **de poste** post house, coaching inn; ~ **routier** ≈ transport café.

relance [Rəlɑ̃s] *nf* boosting, revival.

relancer [Rəlɑ̃se] *vt* (*balle*) to throw back (again); (*moteur*) to restart; (*fig*) to boost, revive; (*personne*): ~ **qn** to pester sb; to get on to sb again.

relater [Rəlate] *vt* to relate, recount.

relatif, ive [Rəlatif, -iv] *a* relative.

relation [Rəlɑsjɔ̃] *nf* (*récit*) account, report; (*rapport*) relation(ship); ~**s** *nfpl* (*rapports*) relations; relationship *sg*; (*connaissances*) connections; **être/entrer en** ~**(s) avec** to be in contact *ou* be dealing/get in contact with; ~**s publiques** public relations.

relativement [Rəlativmɑ̃] *ad* relatively; ~ **à** in relation to.

relativité [Rəlativite] *nf* relativity.

relax [Rəlaks] *a inv*, **relaxe** [Rəlaks(ə)] *a* informal, casual; easy-going.

relaxer [Rəlakse] *vt* to relax; (*JUR*) to discharge; **se** ~ *vi* to relax.

relayer [Rəleje] *vt* (*collaborateur, coureur etc*) to relieve, take over from; (*RADIO, TV*) to relay; **se** ~ (*dans une activité*) to take it in turns.

relégation [Rəlegɑsjɔ̃] *nf* (*SPORT*) relegation.

reléguer [Rəlege] *vt* to relegate.

relent(s) [Rəlɑ̃] *nm(pl)* (foul) smell.

relève [Rəlɛv] *nf* relief; relief team (*ou* troops *pl*); **prendre la** ~ to take over.

relevé, e [Rəlve] *a* (*bord de chapeau*) turned-up; (*manches*) rolled-up; (*virage*) banked; (*fig*: *style*) elevated; (: *sauce*) highly-seasoned // *nm* (*lecture*) reading; (*de cotes*) plotting; (*liste*) statement; list; (*facture*) account; ~ **de compte** bank statement.

relever [Rəlve] *vt* (*statue, meuble*) to stand up again; (*personne tombée*) to help up; (*vitre, plafond, niveau de vie*) to raise; (*col*) to turn up; (*style, conversation*) to elevate; (*plat, sauce*) to season; (*sentinelle, équipe*) to relieve; (*souligner*: *fautes, points*) to pick out; (*constater*: *traces etc*) to find, pick up; (*répliquer à*: *remarque*) to react to, reply to; (: *défi*) to accept, take up; (*noter*: *adresse etc*) to take down, note; (: *plan*) to sketch; (: *cotes etc*) to plot; (*compteur*) to read; (*ramasser*: *cahiers, copies*) to collect, take in; ~ **de** *vt* (*maladie*) to be recovering from; (*être du ressort de*) to be a matter for; (*ADMIN*: *dépendre de*) to come under; (*fig*) to pertain to; **se** ~ *vi* (*se remettre debout*) to get up; ~ **qn de** (*vœux*) to release sb from; (*fonctions*) to relieve sb of; ~ **la tête** to look up; to hold up one's head.

relief [Rəljɛf] *nm* relief; (*de pneu*) tread pattern; ~**s** *nmpl* (*restes*) remains; **en** ~ in relief; (*photographie*) three-dimensional; **mettre en** ~ (*fig*) to bring out, highlight.

relier [Rəlje] *vt* to link up; (*livre*) to bind; ~ **qch à** to link sth to; **livre relié cuir** leather-bound book; **relieur, euse** *nm/f* (book)binder.

religieux, euse [Rəliʒjø, -øz] *a* religious // *nm* monk // *nf* nun; (*gâteau*) cream bun.

religion [Rəliʒjɔ̃] *nf* religion; (*piété, dévotion*) faith; **entrer en** ~ to take one's vows.

reliquaire [RəlikɛR] *nm* reliquary.

reliquat [Rəlika] *nm* balance; remainder.

relique [Rəlik] *nf* relic.

relire [RəliR] *vt* (*à nouveau*) to reread, read again; (*vérifier*) to read over.

reliure [RəljyR] *nf* binding.

reluire [RəlɥiR] *vi* to gleam; **reluisant, e** *a* gleaming; **peu reluisant** (*fig*) unattractive; unsavoury.

remâcher [Rəmɑʃe] *vt* to chew or ruminate over.

remailler [Rəmɑje] *vt* to darn; to mend.

remaniement [Rəmanimɑ̃] *nm*: ~ **ministériel** Cabinet reshuffle.

remanier [Rəmanje] *vt* to reshape, recast; (*POL*) to reshuffle.

remarquable [RəmaRkabl(ə)] *a* remarkable.

remarque [RəmaRk(ə)] *nf* remark; (*écrite*) note.

remarquer [RəmaRke] *vt* (*voir*) to notice; (*dire*): ~ **que** to remark that; **se** ~ to be noticeable; **se faire** ~ to draw attention to o.s.; **faire** ~ **(à qn) que** to point out (to sb) that; **faire** ~ **qch (à qn)** to point sth out (to sb); **remarquez que** mark you, mind you.

rembarrer [Rɑ̃baRe] *vt*: ~ **qn** to rebuff sb; to put sb in his/her place.

remblai [Rɑ̃blɛ] *nm* embankment.

remblayer [Rɑ̃bleje] *vt* to bank up; (*fossé*) to fill in.

rembourrage [Rɑ̃buRaʒ] *nm* stuffing; padding.

rembourré, e [Rɑ̃buRe] *a* padded.
rembourrer [Rɑ̃buRe] *vt* to stuff; (*dossier, vêtement, souliers*) to pad.
remboursement [Rɑ̃buRsəmɑ̃] *nm* repayment; **envoi contre ~** cash on delivery.
rembourser [Rɑ̃buRse] *vt* to pay back, repay.
rembrunir [Rɑ̃bRyniR]: **se ~** *vi* to darken; to grow sombre.
remède [Rəmɛd] nm (*médicament*) medicine; (*traitement, fig*) remedy, cure.
remédier [Rəmedje]: **~ à** *vt* to remedy.
remembrement [Rəmɑ̃bRəmɑ̃] *nm* (AGR) regrouping of lands.
remémorer [RəmemɔRe]: **se ~** *vt* to recall, recollect.
remerciements [RəmɛRsimɑ̃] *nmpl* thanks.
remercier [RəmɛRsje] *vt* to thank; (*congédier*) to dismiss; **~ qn de/d'avoir fait** to thank sb for/for having done; **non, je vous remercie** no thank you.
remettre [RəmɛtR(ə)] *vt* (*vêtement*): **~ qch** to put sth back on, put sth on again; (*replacer*): **~ qch quelque part** to put sth back somewhere; (*ajouter*): **~ du sel/un sucre** to add more salt/another lump of sugar; (*rétablir*: *personne*): **~ qn** to set sb back on his/her feet; (*rendre, restituer*): **~ qch à qn** to give sth back to sb, return sth to sb; (*donner, confier*: *paquet, argent*): **~ qch à qn** to hand over sth to sb, deliver sth to sb; (*prix, décoration*): **~ qch à qn** to present sb with sth; (*ajourner*): **~ qch (à)** to postpone sth *ou* put sth off (until); **se ~** *vi* to get better, recover; **se ~ de** to recover from, get over; **s'en ~ à** to leave it (up) to.
remise [Rəmiz] *nf* delivery; presentation; (*rabais*) discount; (*local*) shed; **~ en jeu** (FOOTBALL) throw-in; **~ de peine** reduction of sentence.
rémission [Remisjɔ̃]: **sans ~** *a* irremediable // *ad* unremittingly.
remontant [Rəmɔ̃tɑ̃] *nm* tonic, pick-me-up.
remontée [Rəmɔ̃te] *nf* rising; ascent; **~s mécaniques** (SKI) towing equipment *sg ou* facilities.
remonte-pente [Rəmɔ̃tpɑ̃t] *nm* skilift, (ski) tow.
remonter [Rəmɔ̃te] *vi* (*à nouveau*) to go back up; (*après une descente*) to go up (again); (*jupe*) to pull *ou* ride up // *vt* (*pente*) to go up; (*fleuve*) to sail (*ou* swim *etc*) up; (*manches, pantalon*) to roll up; (*col*) to turn up; (*rayon, limite*) to raise; (*fig*: *personne*) to buck up; (*moteur, meuble*) to put back together, reassemble; (*garde-robe etc*) to renew, replenish; (*montre, mécanisme*) to wind up; **~ à** (*dater de*) to date *ou* go back to; **~ en voiture** to get back into the car.
remontoir [Rəmɔ̃twaR] *nm* winding mechanism, winder.
remontrance [Rəmɔ̃tRɑ̃s] *nf* reproof, reprimand.
remontrer [Rəmɔ̃tRe] *vt* (*fig*): **en ~ à** to prove one's superiority over.
remords [RəmɔR] *nm* remorse *q*; **avoir des ~** to feel remorse, be conscience-stricken.
remorque [RəmɔRk(ə)] *nf* trailer; **prendre/être en ~** to tow/be on tow; **remorquer** *vt* to tow; **remorqueur** *nm* tug(boat).
rémoulade [Remulad] *nf dressing with mustard and herbs.*
rémouleur [RemulœR] *nm* (knife- *ou* scissor-)grinder.
remous [Rəmu] *nm* (*d'un navire*) (back)wash *q*; (*de rivière*) swirl, eddy // *nmpl* (*fig*) stir *sg*.
rempailler [Rɑ̃pɑje] *vt* to reseat (*with straw*).
remparts [Rɑ̃paR] *nmpl* walls, ramparts.
rempiler [Rɑ̃pile] *vi* (MIL: *fam*) to join up again.
remplaçant, e [Rɑ̃plasɑ̃, -ɑ̃t] *nm/f* replacement, substitute, stand-in; (THÉÂTRE) understudy; (SCOL) supply teacher.
remplacement [Rɑ̃plasmɑ̃] *nm* replacement; (*job*) replacement work *q*; **assurer le ~ de qn** (*suj*: *remplaçant*) to stand in *ou* substitute for sb.
remplacer [Rɑ̃plase] *vt* to replace; (*prendre temporairement la place de*) to stand in for; (*tenir lieu de*) to take the place of, act as a substitute for; **~ qch/qn par** to replace sth/sb with.
rempli, e [Rɑ̃pli] *a* (*emploi du temps*) full, busy; **~ de** full of, filled with.
remplir [Rɑ̃pliR] *vt* to fill (up); (*questionnaire*) to fill out *ou* up; (*obligations, fonction, condition*) to fulfil; **se ~** *vi* to fill up.
remplissage [Rɑ̃plisaʒ] *nm* (*fig*: *péj*) padding.
remploi [Rɑ̃plwa] *nm* re-use.
remporter [Rɑ̃pɔRte] *vt* (*marchandise*) to take away; (*fig*) to win, achieve.
remuant, e [Rəmɥɑ̃, -ɑ̃t] *a* restless.
remue-ménage [Rəmymenaʒ] *nm inv* commotion.
remuer [Rəmɥe] *vt* to move; (*café, sauce*) to stir // *vi* to move; (*fig*: *opposants*) to show signs of unrest; **se ~** *vi* to move; (*se démener*) to stir o.s.; (*fam*) to get a move on.
rémunération [RemyneRɑsjɔ̃] *nf* remuneration.
rémunérer [RemyneRe] *vt* to remunerate, pay.
renâcler [Rənɑkle] *vi* to snort; (*fig*) to grumble, balk.
renaissance [Rənɛsɑ̃s] *nf* rebirth, revival; **la R~** the Renaissance.
renaître [RənɛtR(ə)] *vi* to be revived.
rénal, e, aux [Renal, -o] *a* renal, kidney *cpd*.
renard [RənaR] *nm* fox.
rencard [Rɑ̃kaR] *nm* = **rancard**.
rencart [Rɑ̃kaR] *nm* = **rancart**.
renchérir [Rɑ̃ʃeRiR] *vi* to become more expensive; (*fig*): **~ (sur)** to add something (to).
rencontre [Rɑ̃kɔ̃tR(ə)] *nf* (*entrevue, congrès, match etc*) meeting; (*imprévue*) encounter; **faire la ~ de qn** to meet sb;

aller à la ~ de qn to go and meet sb; **amours de ~** casual love affairs.

rencontrer [Rɑ̃kɔ̃tRe] *vt* to meet; (*mot, expression*) to come across; (*difficultés*) to meet with; **se ~** *vi* to meet; (*véhicules*) to collide.

rendement [Rɑ̃dmɑ̃] *nm* (*d'un travailleur, d'une machine*) output; (*d'une culture*) yield; (*d'un investissement*) return; **à plein ~** at full capacity.

rendez-vous [Rɑ̃devu] *nm* (*rencontre*) appointment; (*: d'amoureux*) date; (*lieu*) meeting place; **donner ~ à qn** to arrange to meet sb; **fixer un ~ à qn** to give sb an appointment; **avoir/prendre ~ (avec)** to have/make an appointment (with).

rendre [Rɑ̃dR(ə)] *vt* (*livre, argent etc*) to give back, return; (*otages, visite etc*) to return; (*sang, aliments*) to bring up; (*sons: suj: instrument*) to produce, make; (*exprimer, traduire*) to render; (*faire devenir*): **~ qn célèbre/qch possible** to make sb famous/sth possible; **se ~** *vi* (*capituler*) to surrender, give o.s. up; (*aller*): **se ~ quelque part** to go somewhere; **se ~ à** (*arguments etc*) to bow to; (*ordres*) to comply with; **~ la vue/la santé à qn** to restore sb's sight/health; **~ la liberté à qn** to set sb free.

renégat, e [Rənega, -at] *nm/f* renegade.

rênes [Rɛn] *nfpl* reins.

renfermé, e [Rɑ̃fɛRme] *a* (*fig*) withdrawn // *nm*: **sentir le ~** to smell stuffy.

renfermer [Rɑ̃fɛRme] *vt* to contain; **se ~ (sur soi-même)** to withdraw into o.s.

renflé, e [Rɑ̃fle] *a* bulging, bulbous.

renflement [Rɑ̃fləmɑ̃] *nm* bulge.

renflouer [Rɑ̃flue] *vt* to refloat; (*fig*) to set back on its (*ou* his/her) feet (again).

renfoncement [Rɑ̃fɔ̃smɑ̃] *nm* recess.

renforcer [Rɑ̃fɔRse] *vt* to reinforce.

renfort [Rɑ̃fɔR]: **~s** *nmpl* reinforcements; **en ~** as a back-up; **à grand ~ de** with a great deal of.

renfrogner [Rɑ̃fRɔɲe]: **se ~** *vi* to scowl.

rengaine [Rɑ̃gɛn] *nf* (*péj*) old tune.

rengainer [Rɑ̃gene] *vt* (*revolver*) to put back in its holster.

rengorger [Rɑ̃gɔRʒe]: **se ~** *vi* (*fig*) to puff o.s. up.

renier [Rənje] *vt* (*parents*) to disown, repudiate; (*foi*) to renounce.

renifler [Rənifle] *vi* to sniff // *vt* (*tabac*) to sniff up; (*odeur*) to sniff.

renne [Rɛn] *nm* reindeer *inv*.

renom [Rənɔ̃] *nm* reputation; renown; **renommé, e** *a* celebrated, renowned // *nf* fame.

renoncement [Rənɔ̃smɑ̃] *nm* abnegation, renunciation.

renoncer [Rənɔ̃se] *vi*: **~ à** *vt* to give up; **~ à faire** to give up all idea of doing; to give up trying to do.

renouer [Rənwe] *vt* (*cravate etc*) to retie; **~ avec** (*tradition*) to revive; (*habitude*) to take up again; **~ avec qn** to take up with sb again.

renouveau, x [Rənuvo] *nm*: **~ de succès** renewed success; **le ~ printanier** springtide.

renouveler [Rənuvle] *vt* to renew; (*exploit, méfait*) to repeat; **se ~** *vi* (*incident*) to recur, happen again, be repeated; (*cellules etc*) to be renewed *ou* replaced; **renouvellement** *nm* renewal; recurrence.

rénovation [Renɔvɑsjɔ̃] *nf* renovation; restoration.

rénover [Renɔve] *vt* (*immeuble*) to renovate, do up; (*meuble*) to restore; (*enseignement*) to reform.

renseignement [Rɑ̃sɛɲmɑ̃] *nm* information *q*, piece of information; **prendre des ~s sur** to make inquiries about, ask for information about; **(guichet des) ~s** information desk.

renseigner [Rɑ̃seɲe] *vt*: **~ qn (sur)** to give information to sb (about); **se ~** *vi* to ask for information, make inquiries.

rentable [Rɑ̃table(ə)] *a* profitable.

rente [Rɑ̃t] *nf* income; pension; government stock *ou* bond; **~ viagère** life annuity; **rentier, ière** *nm/f* person of private means.

rentrée [Rɑ̃tRe] *nf*: **~ (d'argent)** cash *q* coming in; **la ~ (des classes)** the start of the new school year; **la ~ (parlementaire)** the reopening *ou* reassembly of parliament; **faire sa ~** (*artiste, acteur*) to make a comeback.

rentrer [Rɑ̃tRe] *vi* (*entrer de nouveau*) to go (*ou* come) back in; (*entrer*) to go (*ou* come) in; (*revenir chez soi*) to go (*ou* come) (back) home; (*air, clou: pénétrer*) to go in; (*revenu, argent*) to come in // *vt* (*foins*) to bring in; (*véhicule*) to put away; (*chemise dans pantalon etc*) to tuck in; (*griffes*) to draw in; (*train d'atterrissage*) to raise; (*fig: larmes, colère etc*) to hold back; **~ le ventre** to pull in one's stomach; **~ dans** to go (*ou* come) back into; to go (*ou* come) into; (*famille, patrie*) to go back *ou* return to; (*heurter*) to crash into; **~ dans l'ordre** to be back to normal; **~ dans ses frais** to recover one's expenses (*ou* initial outlay).

renversant, e [Rɑ̃vɛRsɑ̃, -ɑ̃t] *a* amazing.

renverse [Rɑ̃vɛRs(ə)]: **à la ~** *ad* backwards.

renverser [Rɑ̃vɛRse] *vt* (*faire tomber: chaise, verre*) to knock over, overturn; (*piéton*) to knock down; (*liquide, contenu*) to spill, upset; (*retourner: verre, image*) to turn upside down, invert; (*: ordre des mots etc*) to reverse; (*fig: gouvernement etc*) to overthrow; (*stupéfier*) to bowl over, stagger; **se ~** *vi* to fall over; to overturn; to spill; **~ la tête/le corps (en arrière)** to tip one's head back/throw one's body back.

renvoi [Rɑ̃vwa] *nm* dismissal; return; reflection; postponement; (*référence*) cross-reference; (*éructation*) belch.

renvoyer [Rɑ̃vwaje] *vt* to send back; (*congédier*) to dismiss; (*lumière*) to reflect; (*son*) to echo; (*ajourner*): **~ qch (à)** to put sth off *ou* postpone sth (until); **~ qn à** (*fig*) to refer sb to.

réorganiser [ReɔRganize] *vt* to reorganize.

réouverture [RéuvɛRtyR] *nf* reopening.

repaire [RəpɛR] *nm* den.
repaître [RəpɛtR(ə)] *vt* to feast ; to feed ; **se ~ de** *vt* to feed on ; to wallow *ou* revel in.
répandre [Repɑ̃dR(ə)] *vt* (*renverser*) to spill ; (*étaler, diffuser*) to spread ; (*lumière*) to shed ; (*chaleur, odeur*) to give off ; **se ~** *vi* to spill ; to spread ; **se ~ en** (*injures etc*) to pour out ; **répandu, e** *a* (*opinion, usage*) widespread.
réparation [RepaRɑsjɔ̃] *nf* repairing *q*, repair.
réparer [RepaRe] *vt* to repair ; (*fig: offense*) to make up for, atone for ; (: *oubli, erreur*) to put right.
repartie [RəpaRti] *nf* retort ; **avoir de la ~** to be quick at repartee.
repartir [RəpaRtiR] *vi* to set off again ; to leave again ; (*fig*) to get going again, pick up again ; **~ à zéro** to start from scratch (again).
répartir [RepaRtiR] *vt* (*pour attribuer*) to share out ; (*pour disperser, disposer*) to divide up ; (*poids, chaleur*) to distribute ; **se ~** *vt* (*travail, rôles*) to share out between themselves ; **répartition** *nf* sharing out ; dividing up ; distribution.
repas [Rəpɑ] *nm* meal.
repasser [Rəpɑse] *vi* to come (*ou* go) back // *vt* (*vêtement, tissu*) to iron ; to retake, resit ; to show again ; (*leçon, rôle: revoir*) to go over (again).
repêchage [Rəpɛʃaʒ] *nm* (*SCOL*): **question de ~** question to give candidates a second chance.
repêcher [Rəpeʃe] *vt* (*noyé*) to recover the body of, fish out.
repentir [Rəpɑ̃tiR] *nm* repentance ; **se ~** *vi* to repent ; **se ~ de** to repent (of).
répercussions [RepɛRkysjɔ̃] *nfpl* repercussions.
répercuter [RepɛRkyte]: **se ~** *vi* (*bruit*) to reverberate ; (*fig*): **se ~ sur** to have repercussions on.
repère [RəpɛR] *nm* mark ; (*monument etc*) landmark.
repérer [RəpeRe] *vt* (*erreur, connaissance*) to spot ; (*abri, ennemi*) to locate ; **se ~** *vi* to find one's way about ; **se faire ~** to be spotted.
répertoire [RepɛRtwaR] *nm* (*liste*) (alphabetical) list ; (*carnet*) index notebook ; (*de carnet*) thumb index ; (*indicateur*) directory, index ; (*d'un théâtre, artiste*) repertoire ; **répertorier** *vt* to itemize, list.
répéter [Repete] *vt* to repeat ; (*préparer: leçon: aussi vi*) to learn, go over ; (*THÉÂTRE*) to rehearse ; **se ~** (*redire*) to repeat o.s. ; (*se reproduire*) to be repeated, recur.
répétition [Repetisjɔ̃] *nf* repetition ; rehearsal ; **~s** *nfpl* (*leçons*) private coaching *sg* ; **armes à ~** repeater weapons ; **~ générale** final dress rehearsal.
repeupler [Rəpœple] *vt* to repopulate ; to restock.
répit [Repi] *nm* respite ; **sans ~** without letting up.
replet, ète [Rəplɛ, -ɛt] *a* chubby, fat.
repli [Rəpli] *nm* (*d'une étoffe*) fold ; (*MIL. fig*) withdrawal.
replier [Rəplije] *vt* (*rabattre*) to fold down *ou* over ; **se ~** *vi* (*troupes, armée*) to withdraw, fall back.
réplique [Replik] *nf* (*repartie, fig*) reply ; (*THÉÂTRE*) line ; (*copie*) replica ; **donner la ~ à** to play opposite ; to match ; **sans ~** no-nonsense ; irrefutable.
répliquer [Replike] *vi* to reply ; (*riposter*) to retaliate.
répondre [Repɔ̃dR(ə)] *vi* to answer, reply ; (*freins, mécanisme*) to respond ; **~ à** *vt* to reply to, answer ; (*avec impertinence*): **~ à qn** to answer sb back ; (*invitation, convocation*) to reply to ; (*affection, salut*) to return ; (*provocation, suj: mécanisme etc*) to respond to ; (*correspondre à: besoin*) to answer ; (: *conditions*) to meet ; (: *description*) to match ; **~ que** to answer *ou* reply that ; **~ de** to answer for.
réponse [Repɔ̃s] *nf* answer, reply ; **avec ~ payée** (*POSTES*) reply-paid ; **en ~ à** in reply to.
report [RəpɔR] *nm* transfer ; postponement.
reportage [RəpɔRtaʒ] *nm* (*bref*) report ; (*écrit: documentaire*) story ; article ; (*en direct*) commentary ; (*genre, activité*): **le ~** reporting.
reporter *nm* [RəpɔRtɛR] reporter // *vt* [RəpɔRte] (*total*): **~ qch sur** to carry sth forward *ou* over to ; (*ajourner*): **~ qch (à)** to postpone sth (until) ; (*transférer*): **~ qch sur** to transfer sth to ; **se ~ à** (*époque*) to think back to ; (*document*) to refer to.
repos [Rəpo] *nm* rest ; (*fig*) peace (and quiet) ; peace of mind ; (*MIL*): **~!** stand at ease! ; **en ~** at rest ; **de tout ~** safe.
repose [Rəpoz] *nf* refitting.
reposé, e [Rəpoze] *a* fresh, rested.
reposer [Rəpoze] *vt* (*verre, livre*) to put down ; (*délasser*) to rest ; (*problème*) to reformulate // *vi* (*liquide, pâte*) to settle, rest ; **~ sur** to be built on ; (*fig*) to rest on ; **se ~** *vi* to rest ; **se ~ sur qn** to rely on sb.
repoussant, e [Rəpusɑ̃, -ɑ̃t] *a* repulsive.
repoussé, e [Rəpuse] *a* (*cuir*) embossed (by hand).
repousser [Rəpuse] *vi* to grow again // *vt* to repel, repulse ; (*offre*) to turn down, reject ; (*tiroir, personne*) to push back ; (*différer*) to put back.
répréhensible [RəpReɑ̃sibl(ə)] *a* reprehensible.
reprendre [RəpRɑ̃dR(ə)] *vt* (*prisonnier, ville*) to recapture ; (*objet prêté, donné*) to take back ; (*chercher*): **je viendrai te ~ à 4h** I'll come and fetch you *ou* I'll come back for you at 4 ; (*se resservir de*): **~ du pain/un œuf** to take (*ou* eat) more bread/another egg ; (*COMM: article usagé*) to take back ; to take in part exchange ; (*firme, entreprise*) to take over ; (*travail, promenade*) to resume ; (*emprunter: argument, idée*) to take up, use ; (*refaire: article etc*) to go over again ; (*jupe etc*) to alter ; to take in (*ou* up) ; to let out (*ou* down) ; (*émission, pièce*) to put on again ; (*réprimander*) to tell off ; (*corriger*) to correct // *vi* (*classes, pluie*) to start (up) again ; (*activités, travaux, combats*) to resume, start (up) again ; (*affaires,*

industrie) to pick up; (*dire*): **reprit-il** he went on; **se ~** (*se ressaisir*) to recover, pull o.s. together; **s'y ~** to make another attempt; **~ des forces** to recover one's strength; **~ courage** to take new heart; **~ ses habitudes/sa liberté** to get back into one's old habits/regain one's freedom; **~ la route** to resume one's journey, set off again; **~ haleine** *ou* **son souffle** to get one's breath back.

représailles [RəpRezɑj] *nfpl* reprisals, retaliation *sg*.

représentant, e [RəpRezɑ̃tɑ̃, -ɑ̃t] *nm/f* representative.

représentatif, ive [RəpRezɑ̃tatif, -iv] *a* representative.

représentation [RəpRezɑ̃tɑsjɔ̃] *nf* representation; performing; (*symbole, image*) representation; (*spectacle*) performance; (*COMM*): **la ~** commercial travelling; sales representation; **frais de ~** (*d'un diplomate*) entertainment allowance.

représenter [RəpRezɑ̃te] *vt* to represent; (*donner: pièce, opéra*) to perform; **se ~** *vt* (*se figurer*) to imagine; to visualize.

répression [RepResjɔ̃] *nf* suppression; repression; (*POL*): **la ~** repression.

réprimande [RepRimɑ̃d] *nf* reprimand, rebuke; **réprimander** *vt* to reprimand, rebuke.

réprimer [RepRime] *vt* to suppress, repress.

repris [RəpRi] *nm*: **~ de justice** ex-prisoner, ex-convict.

reprise [RəpRiz] *nf* (*TV*) repeat; (*CINÉMA*) rerun; (*AUTO*) acceleration *q*; (*COMM*) trade-in, part exchange; (*de location*) *sum asked for any extras or improvements made to the property*; (*raccommodage*) darn; mend; **à plusieurs ~s** on several occasions, several times.

repriser [RəpRize] *vt* to darn; to mend.

réprobateur, trice [RepRɔbatœR, -tRis] *a* reproving.

réprobation [RepRɔbɑsjɔ̃] *nf* reprobation.

reproche [RəpRɔʃ] *nm* (*remontrance*) reproach; **faire des ~s à qn** to reproach sb; **sans ~(s)** beyond *ou* above reproach.

reprocher [RəpRɔʃe] *vt*: **~ qch à qn** to reproach *ou* blame sb for sth; **~ qch à** (*machine, théorie*) to have sth against.

reproducteur, trice [RəpRɔdyktœR, -tRis] *a* reproductive.

reproduction [RəpRɔdyksjɔ̃] *nf* reproduction; **~ interdite** all rights (of reproduction) reserved.

reproduire [RəpRɔdɥiR] *vt* to reproduce; **se ~** *vi* (*BIO*) to reproduce; (*recommencer*) to recur, re-occur.

réprouvé, e [RepRuve] *nm/f* reprobate.

réprouver [RepRuve] *vt* to reprove.

reptation [Rɛptɑsjɔ̃] *nf* crawling.

reptile [Rɛptil] *nm* reptile.

repu, e [Rəpy] *a* satisfied, sated.

républicain, e [Repyblikɛ̃, -ɛn] *a, nm/f* republican.

république [Repyblik] *nf* republic; **la R~ fédérale allemande** the Federal Republic of Germany.

répudier [Repydje] *vt* (*femme*) to repudiate; (*doctrine*) to renounce.

répugnance [Repyɲɑ̃s] *nf* repugnance, loathing.

répugnant, e [Repyɲɑ̃, -ɑ̃t] *a* repulsive; loathsome.

répugner [Repyɲe]: **~ à** *vt*: **~ à qn** to repel *ou* disgust sb; **~ à faire** to be loath *ou* reluctant to do.

répulsion [Repylsjɔ̃] *nf* repulsion.

réputation [Repytɑsjɔ̃] *nf* reputation; **réputé, e** *a* renowned.

requérir [RəkeRiR] *vt* (*nécessiter*) to require, call for; (*au nom de la loi*) to call upon; (*JUR: peine*) to call for, demand.

requête [Rəkɛt] *nf* request, petition; (*JUR*) petition.

requiem [Rekɥijɛm] *nm* requiem.

requin [Rəkɛ̃] *nm* shark.

requis, e [Rəki, -iz] *pp de* **requérir** // *a* required.

réquisition [Rekizisjɔ̃] *nf* requisition; **réquisitionner** *vt* to requisition.

réquisitoire [RekizitwaR] *nm* (*JUR*) closing speech for the prosecution; (*fig*): **~ contre** indictment of.

R.E.R. *sigle m* (= *réseau express régional*) *Greater Paris high speed commuter train.*

rescapé, e [Rɛskape] *nm/f* survivor.

rescousse [Rɛskus] *nf*: **aller à la ~ de qn** to go to sb's aid *ou* rescue; **appeler qn à la ~** to call on sb for help.

réseau, x [Rezo] *nm* network.

réservation [RezɛRvɑsjɔ̃] *nf* booking, reservation.

réserve [RezɛRv(ə)] *nf* (*gén*) reserve; (*entrepôt*) storeroom; (*restriction, aussi: d'Indiens*) reservation; (*de pêche, chasse*) preserve; **sous ~ de** subject to; **sans ~** *ad* unreservedly; **de ~** (*provisions etc*) in reserve.

réservé, e [RezɛRve] *a* (*discret*) reserved; (*chasse, pêche*) private; **~ à/pour** reserved for.

réserver [RezɛRve] *vt* (*gén*) to reserve; (*retenir: par une agence, au guichet*) to book, reserve; (*mettre de côté, garder*): **~ qch pour/à** to keep *ou* save sth for; **~ qch à qn** to reserve (*ou* book) sth for sb; (*fig: destiner*) to have sth in store for sb; **se ~ le droit de faire** to reserve the right to do.

réserviste [RezɛRvist(ə)] *nm* reservist.

réservoir [RezɛRvwaR] *nm* tank; (*plan d'eau*) reservoir.

résidence [Rezidɑ̃s] *nf* residence; **~ secondaire** second home; **(en) ~ surveillée** (under) house arrest; **résidentiel, le** *a* residential.

résider [Rezide] *vi*: **~ à/dans/en** to reside in; **~ dans** (*fig*) to lie in.

résidu [Rezidy] *nm* residue *q*.

résignation [Reziɲɑsjɔ̃] *nf* resignation.

résigner [Reziɲe] *vt* to relinquish, resign; **se ~** *vi*: **se ~ (à qch/faire)** to resign o.s. (to sth/to doing).

résilier [Rezilje] *vt* to terminate.

résille [Rezij] *nf* (hair)net.

résine [Rezin] *nf* resin; **résiné, e** *a*: **vin résiné** retsina; **résineux, euse** *a* resinous // *nm* coniferous tree.

résistance [Rezistɑ̃s] *nf* resistance; (*de réchaud, bouilloire*: *fil*) element.
résistant, e [Rezistɑ̃, -ɑ̃t] *a* (*personne*) robust, tough; (*matériau*) strong, hard-wearing // *nm/f* (*patriote*) Resistance worker *ou* fighter.
résister [Reziste] *vi* to resist; ~ **à** *vt* (*assaut, tentation*) to resist; (*effort, souffrance*) to withstand; (*suj*: *matériau, plante*) to stand up to, withstand; (*personne*: *désobéir à*) to stand up to, oppose.
résolu, e [Rezɔly] *pp de* **résoudre** // *a* (*ferme*) resolute; **être ~ à qch/faire** to be set upon sth/doing.
résolution [Rezɔlysjɔ̃] *nf* solving; (*fermeté, décision*) resolution.
résolve *etc vb voir* **résoudre**.
résonance [Rezɔnɑ̃s] *nf* resonance.
résonner [Rezɔne] *vi* (*cloche, pas*) to reverberate, resound; (*salle*) to be resonant; ~ **de** to resound with.
résorber [RezɔRbe]: **se** ~ *vi* (*MÉD*) to be resorbed; (*fig*) to be reduced; to be absorbed.
résoudre [RezudR(ə)] *vt* to solve; ~ **de faire** to resolve to do; **se ~ à faire** to bring o.s. to do.
respect [Rɛspɛ] *nm* respect; **tenir en ~** to keep at bay.
respectable [Rɛspɛktabl(ə)] *a* respectable.
respecter [Rɛspɛkte] *vt* to respect; **le lexicographe qui se respecte** (*fig*) any self-respecting lexicographer.
respectif, ive [Rɛspɛktif, -iv] *a* respective; **respectivement** *ad* respectively.
respectueux, euse [Rɛspɛktɥø, -øz] *a* respectful; ~ **de** respectful of.
respiration [RɛspiRɑsjɔ̃] *nf* breathing *q*; **faire une ~ complète** to breathe in and out; ~ **artificielle** artificial respiration.
respirer [RɛspiRe] *vi* to breathe; (*fig*) to get one's breath, have a break; to breathe again // *vt* to breathe (in), inhale; (*manifester*: *santé, calme etc*) to exude.
resplendir [Rɛsplɑ̃diR] *vi* to shine; (*fig*): ~ **(de)** to be radiant (with).
responsabilité [Rɛspɔ̃sabilite] *nf* responsibility; (*légale*) liability; **refuser la ~ de** to deny responsibility (*ou* liability) for; **prendre ses ~s** to assume responsibility for one's actions.
responsable [Rɛspɔ̃sabl(ə)] *a* responsible // *nm/f* (*du ravitaillement etc*) person in charge; (*de parti, syndicat*) official; ~ **de** responsible for; (*légalement*: *de dégâts etc*) liable for; (*chargé de*) in charge of, responsible for.
resquiller [Rɛskije] *vi* (*au cinéma, au stade*) to get in on the sly; (*dans le train*) to fiddle a free ride; **resquilleur, euse** *nm/f* gatecrasher; fare dodger.
ressac [Rəsak] *nm* backwash.
ressaisir [RəseziR]: **se** ~ *vi* to regain one's self-control; (*équipe sportive*) to rally.
ressasser [Rəsɑse] *vt* (*remâcher*) to keep turning over; (*redire*) to keep trotting out.
ressemblance [Rəsɑ̃blɑ̃s] *nf* (*visuelle*) resemblance, similarity, likeness; (: *ART*) likeness; (*analogie, trait commun*) similarity.
ressemblant, e [Rəsɑ̃blɑ̃, -ɑ̃t] *a* (*portrait*) lifelike, true to life.
ressembler [Rəsɑ̃ble]: ~ **à** *vt* to be like; to resemble; (*visuellement*) to look like; **se ~** to be (*ou* look) alike.
ressemeler [Rəsəmle] *vt* to (re)sole.
ressentiment [Rəsɑ̃timɑ̃] *nm* resentment.
ressentir [Rəsɑ̃tiR] *vt* to feel; **se ~ de** to feel (*ou* show) the effects of.
resserre [RəsɛR] *nf* shed.
resserrer [RəseRe] *vt* (*pores*) to close; (*nœud, boulon*) to tighten (up); (*fig*: liens) to strengthen; **se** ~ *vi* (*route, vallée*) to narrow; (*liens*) to strengthen; **se ~ (autour de)** to draw closer (around); to close in (on).
resservir [RəsɛRviR] *vi* to do *ou* serve again // *vt*: ~ **qch (à qn)** to serve sth up again (to sb); ~ **de qch (à qn)** to give (sb) a second helping of sth; ~ **qn (d'un plat)** to give sb a second helping (of a dish).
ressort [RəsɔR] *nm* (*pièce*) spring; (*force morale*) spirit; (*recours*): **en dernier ~** as a last resort; (*compétence*): **être du ~ de** to fall within the competence of.
ressortir [RəsɔRtiR] *vi* to go (*ou* come) out (again); (*contraster*) to stand out; ~ **de** (*résulter de*): **il ressort de ceci que** it emerges from this that; ~ **à** (*JUR*) to come under the jurisdiction of; (*ADMIN*) to be the concern of; **faire ~** (*fig*: *souligner*) to bring out.
ressortissant, e [RəsɔRtisɑ̃, -ɑ̃t] *nm/f* national.
ressource [RəsuRs(ə)] *nf*: **avoir la ~ de** to have the possibility of; **leur seule ~ était de** the only course open to them was to; ~**s** *nfpl* resources; (*fig*) possibilities.
réssusciter [Resysite] *vt* to resuscitate, restore to life; (*fig*) to revive, bring back // *vi* to rise (from the dead).
restant, e [Rɛstɑ̃, -ɑ̃t] *a* remaining // *nm*: **le ~ (de)** the remainder (of); **un ~ de** (*de trop*) some left-over; (*fig*: *vestige*) a remnant *ou* last trace of.
restaurant [RɛstɔRɑ̃] *nm* restaurant; **manger au ~** to eat out; ~ **d'entreprise** staff canteen; ~ **universitaire** university refectory.
restaurateur, trice [RɛstɔRatœR, -tRis] *nm/f* restaurant owner, restaurateur; (*de tableaux*) restorer.
restauration [RɛstɔRɑsjɔ̃] *nf* restoration; (*hôtellerie*) catering.
restaurer [RɛstɔRe] *vt* to restore; **se** ~ *vi* to have something to eat.
restauroute [RɛstɔRut] *nm* = **restoroute.**
reste [Rɛst(ə)] *nm* (*restant*): **le ~ (de)** the rest (of); (*de trop*): **un ~ (de)** some left-over; (*vestige*): **un ~ de** a remnant *ou* last trace of; (*MATH*) remainder; ~**s** *nmpl* left-overs; (*d'une cité etc, dépouille mortelle*) remains; **avoir du temps de ~** to have time to spare; **ne voulant pas être en ~** not wishing to be outdone; **sans demander son ~** without waiting to hear more; **du ~, au ~** *ad* besides, moreover.
rester [Rɛste] *vi* (*dans un lieu, un état, une position*) to stay, remain; (*subsister*) to remain, be left; (*durer*) to last, live on //

vb impersonnel: **il reste du pain/2 œufs** there's some bread/there are 2 eggs left (over); **il reste du temps/10 minutes** there's some time/there are 10 minutes left; **il me reste assez de temps** I have enough time left; **ce qui reste à faire** what remains to be done; **ce qui me reste à faire** what remains for me to do; **en ~ à** (*stade, menaces*) to go no further than, only go as far as; **restons-en là** let's leave it at that; **y ~**: **il a failli y ~** he nearly met his end.

restituer [ʀɛstitɥe] *vt* (*objet, somme*): **~ qch (à qn)** to return sth (to sb); (TECH) to release; to reproduce.

restoroute [ʀɛstɔʀut] *nm* motorway restaurant.

restreindre [ʀɛstʀɛ̃dʀ(ə)] *vt* to restrict, limit; **se ~** *vi* (*champ de recherches*) to narrow.

restriction [ʀɛstʀiksjɔ̃] *nf* restriction; **~s** (*mentales*) reservations.

résultat [ʀezylta] *nm* result; (*conséquence*) outcome *q*, result; (*d'élection etc*) results *pl*; **~s sportifs** sports results.

résulter [ʀezylte]: **~ de** *vt* to result from, be the result of.

résumé [ʀezyme] *nm* summary, résumé; **en ~** *ad* in brief; to sum up.

résumer [ʀezyme] *vt* (*texte*) to summarize; (*récapituler*) to sum up; (*fig*) to epitomize, typify; **se ~ à** to come down to.

résurrection [ʀezyʀɛksjɔ̃] *nf* resurrection; (*fig*) revival.

rétablir [ʀetabliʀ] *vt* to restore, re-establish; (*personne*: *suj*: *traitement*): **~ qn** to restore sb to health, help sb recover; (ADMIN): **~ qn dans son emploi** to reinstate sb in his post; **se ~** *vi* (*guérir*) to recover; (*silence, calme*) to return, be restored; (GYM *etc*): **se ~ (sur)** to pull o.s. up (onto); **rétablissement** *nm* restoring; recovery; pull-up.

rétamer [ʀetame] *vt* to re-coat, re-tin.

retaper [ʀətape] *vt* (*maison, voiture etc*) to do up; (*fam*: *revigorer*) to buck up; (*redactylographier*) to retype.

retard [ʀətaʀ] *nm* (*d'une personne attendue*) lateness *q*; (*sur l'horaire, un programme, une échéance*) delay; (*fig*: *scolaire, mental etc*) backwardness; **en ~ (de 2 heures)** (2 hours) late; **avoir un ~ de 2 km** (SPORT) to be 2 km behind; **avoir du ~** to be late; (*sur un programme*) to be behind (schedule); **prendre du ~** (*train, avion*) to be delayed; (*montre*) to lose (time); **sans ~** *ad* without delay; **~ à l'allumage** (AUTO) retarded spark.

retardataire [ʀətaʀdatɛʀ] *nm/f* latecomer.

retardement [ʀətaʀdəmɑ̃]: **à ~** *a* delayed action *cpd*; **bombe à ~** time bomb.

retarder [ʀətaʀde] *vt* (*sur un horaire*): **~ qn (d'une heure)** to delay sb (an hour); (*sur un programme*): **~ qn (de 3 mois)** to set sb back *ou* delay sb (3 months); (*départ, date*): **~ qch (de 2 jours)** to put sth back (2 days), delay sth (for *ou* by 2 days) // *vi* (*montre*) to be slow; to lose (time); **je retarde (d'une heure)** I'm (an hour) slow.

retenir [ʀətniʀ] *vt* (*garder, retarder*) to keep, detain; (*maintenir*: *objet qui glisse, fig*: *colère, larmes*) to hold back; (: *objet suspendu*) to hold; (: *chaleur, odeur*) to retain; (*fig*: *empêcher d'agir*): **~ qn (de faire)** to hold sb back (from doing); (*se rappeler*) to remember; (*réserver*) to reserve; (*accepter*) to accept; (*prélever*): **~ qch (sur)** to deduct sth (from); **se ~** (*se raccrocher*): **se ~ à** to hold onto; (*se contenir*): **se ~ de faire** to restrain o.s. from doing; **~ son souffle** *ou* **haleine** to hold one's breath; **je pose 3 et je retiens 2** put down 3 and carry 2.

retentir [ʀətɑ̃tiʀ] *vi* to ring out; (*salle*): **~ de** to ring *ou* resound with; **~ sur** *vt* (*fig*) to have an effect upon.

retentissant, e [ʀətɑ̃tisɑ̃, -ɑ̃t] *a* resounding; (*fig*) impact-making.

retentissement [ʀətɑ̃tismɑ̃] *nm* repercussion; effect, impact; stir.

retenue [ʀətny] *nf* (*prélèvement*) deduction; (SCOL) detention; (*modération*) (self-)restraint; (*réserve*) reserve, reticence.

réticence [ʀetisɑ̃s] *nf* hesitation, reluctance *q*.

rétif, ive [ʀetif, -iv] *a* restive.

rétine [ʀetin] *nf* retina.

retiré, e [ʀətiʀe] *a* secluded.

retirer [ʀətiʀe] *vt* to withdraw; (*vêtement, lunettes*) to take off, remove; (*extraire*): **~ qch de** to take sth out of, remove sth from; (*reprendre*: *bagages, billets*) to collect, pick up; **~ des avantages de** to derive advantages from; **se ~** *vi* (*partir, reculer*) to withdraw; (*prendre sa retraite*) to retire; **se ~ de** to withraw from; to retire from.

retombées [ʀətɔ̃be] *nfpl* (*radioactives*) fallout *sg*; (*fig*) fallout; spin-offs.

retomber [ʀətɔ̃be] *vi* (*à nouveau*) to fall again; (*atterrir*: *après un saut etc*) to land; (*tomber, redescendre*) to fall back; (*pendre*) to fall, hang (down); (*échoir*): **~ sur qn** to fall on sb.

rétorquer [ʀetɔʀke] *vt*: **~ (à qn) que** to retort (to sb) that.

retors, e [ʀətɔʀ, -ɔʀs(ə)] *a* wily.

rétorsion [ʀetɔʀsjɔ̃] *nf*: **mesures de ~** reprisals.

retouche [ʀətuʃ] *nf* touching up *q*; alteration.

retoucher [ʀətuʃe] *vt* (*photographie, tableau*) to touch up; (*texte, vêtement*) to alter.

retour [ʀətuʀ] *nm* return; **au ~** when we (*ou* they *etc*) get (*ou* got) back; on the way back; **être de ~ (de)** to be back (from); **par ~ du courrier** by return of post; **~ en arrière** (CINÉMA) flashback; (*mesure*) backward step; **~ offensif** renewed attack.

retourner [ʀətuʀne] *vt* (*dans l'autre sens*: *matelas, crêpe*) to turn (over); (: *caisse*) to turn upside down; (: *sac, vêtement*) to turn inside out; (*fig*: *argument*) to turn back; (*e remuant*: *terre, sol, foin*) to turn over; (*émouvoir*: *personne*) to shake; (*renvoyer, restituer*): **~ qch à qn** to return sth to sb // *vi* (*aller, revenir*): **~ quelque part/à** to go back *ou* return somewhere/to; **~ à**

(*état, activite*) to return to, go back to; **se ~** *vi* to turn over; (*tourner la tête*) to turn round; **se ~ contre** (*fig*) to turn against; **savoir de quoi il retourne** to know what it is all about; **~ en arrière** *ou* **sur ses pas** to turn back, retrace one's steps.

retracer [RətRase] *vt* to relate, recount.

rétracter [RetRakte] *vt*, **se ~** *vi* to retract.

retraduire [RətRadɥiR] *vt* to translate again; (*dans la langue de départ*) to translate back.

retrait [RətRɛ] *nm* (*voir retirer*) withdrawal; collection; redemption; (*voir se retirer*) withdrawal; (*rétrécissement*) shrinkage; **en ~** *a* set back; **~ du permis (de conduire)** disqualification from driving.

retraite [RətRɛt] *nf* (*d'une armée,* REL, *refuge*) retreat; (*d'un employé*) retirement; (retirement) pension; **être/mettre à la ~** to be retired *ou* in retirement/pension off *ou* retire; **prendre sa ~** to retire; **~ anticipée** early retirement; **~ aux flambeaux** torchlight tattoo; **retraité, e** *a* retired // *nm/f* (old age) pensioner.

retranchement [RətRɑ̃ʃmɑ̃] *nm* entrenchment.

retrancher [RətRɑ̃ʃe] *vt* (*passage, détails*) to take out, remove; (*nombre, somme*): **~ qch de** to take *ou* deduct sth from; (*couper*) to cut off; **se ~ derrière/dans** to entrench o.s. behind/in; (*fig*) to take refuge behind/in.

retransmettre [RətRɑ̃smɛtR(ə)] *vt* (RADIO) to broadcast, relay; (TV) to show; **retransmission** *nf* broadcast; showing.

retraverser [RətRavɛRse] *vt* (*dans l'autre sens*) to cross back over.

rétrécir [RetResiR] *vt* (*vêtement*) to take in // *vi* to shrink; **se ~** *vi* to narrow.

retremper [RətRɑ̃pe] *vt*: **se ~ dans** (*fig*) to reimmerse o.s. in.

rétribuer [RetRibɥe] *vt* (*travail*) to pay for; (*personne*) to pay; **rétribution** *nf* payment.

rétro [RetRo] *a inv*: **la mode ~** the nostalgia vogue.

rétroactif, ive [RetRɔaktif, -iv] *a* retroactive.

rétrograde [RetRɔgRad] *a* reactionary, backward-looking.

rétrograder [RetRɔgRade] *vi* (*élève*) to fall back; (*économie*) to regress; (AUTO) to change down.

rétrospective [RetRɔspɛktiv] *nf* retrospective exhibition; season showing old films; **~ment** *ad* in retrospect.

retrousser [RətRuse] *vt* to roll up.

retrouvailles [RətRuvɑj] *nfpl* reunion *sg.*

retrouver [RətRuve] *vt* (*fugitif, objet perdu*) to find; (*occasion*) to find again; (*calme, santé*) to regain; (*revoir*) to see again; (*rejoindre*) to meet (again), join; **se ~** *vi* to meet; (*s'orienter*) to find one's way; **se ~ quelque part** to find o.s. somewhere; to end up somewhere; **s'y ~** (*rentrer dans ses frais*) to break even.

rétroviseur [RetRɔvizœR] *nm* (rear-view *ou* driving) mirror.

réunion [Reynjɔ̃] *nf* bringing together; joining; (*séance*) meeting; **l'île de la R~, la R~** Réunion.

réunir [ReyniR] *vt* (*convoquer*) to call together; (*rassembler*) to gather together; (*cumuler*) to combine; (*rapprocher*) to bring together (again), reunite; (*rattacher*) to join (together); **se ~** *vi* (*se rencontrer*) to meet; (*s'allier*) to unite.

réussi, e [Reysi] *a* successful.

réussir [ReysiR] *vi* to succeed, be successful; (*à un examen*) to pass; (*plante, culture*) to thrive, do well // *vt* to make a success of; to bring off; **~ à faire** to succeed in doing; **~ à qn** to go right for sb; to agree with sb.

réussite [Reysit] *nf* success; (CARTES) patience.

revaloir [RəvalwaR] *vt*: **je vous revaudrai cela** I'll repay you some day; (*en mal*) I'll pay you back for this.

revaloriser [RəvalɔRize] *vt* (*monnaie*) to revalue; (*salaires, pensions*) to raise the level of; (*institution, tradition*) to reassert the value of.

revanche [Rəvɑ̃ʃ] *nf* revenge; **prendre sa ~ (sur)** to take one's revenge (on); **en ~** on the other hand.

rêvasser [Rɛvase] *vi* to daydream.

rêve [Rɛv] *nm* dream; (*activité psychique*): **le ~** dreaming; **~ éveillé** daydreaming *q*, daydream.

revêche [Rəvɛʃ] *a* surly, sour-tempered.

réveil [Revɛj] *nm* (*d'un dormeur*) waking up *q*; (*fig*) awakening; (*pendule*) alarm (clock); **au ~** when I (*ou* he) woke up, on waking (up); **sonner le ~** (MIL) to sound the reveille.

réveille-matin [Revɛjmatɛ̃] *nm inv* alarm clock.

réveiller [Reveje] *vt* (*personne*) to wake up; (*fig*) to awaken, revive; **se ~** *vi* to wake up; (*fig*) to be revived, reawaken.

réveillon [Revɛjɔ̃] *nm* Christmas Eve; (*de la Saint-Sylvestre*) New Year's Eve; Christmas Eve (*ou* New Year's Eve) party *ou* dinner; **réveillonner** *vi* to celebrate Christmas Eve (*ou* New Year's Eve).

révélateur, trice [RevelatœR, -tRis] *a*: **~ (de qch)** revealing (sth) // *nm* (PHOTO) developer.

révélation [Revelɑsjɔ̃] *nf* revelation.

révéler [Revele] *vt* (*gén*) to reveal; (*divulguer*) to disclose, reveal; (*dénoter*) to reveal, show; (*faire connaître au public*): **~ qn/qch** to make sb/ sth widely known, bring sb/sth to the public's notice; **se ~** *vi* to be revealed, reveal itself // *vb avec attribut* to prove (to be).

revenant, e [Rəvnɑ̃, -ɑ̃t] *nm/f* ghost.

revendeur, euse [Rəvɑ̃dœR, -øz] *nm/f* (*détaillant*) retailer; (*d'occasions*) secondhand dealer.

revendication [Rəvɑ̃dikɑsjɔ̃] *nf* claim, demand; **journée de ~** day of action (in support of one's claims).

revendiquer [Rəvɑ̃dike] *vt* to claim, demand; (*responsabilité*) to claim // *vi* to agitate in favour of one's claims.

revendre [Rəvɑ̃dR(ə)] *vt* (*d'occasion*) to resell; (*détailler*) to sell; (*vendre davantage de*): **~ du sucre/un foulard/deux bagues** to sell more sugar/another scarf/ another two rings; **à ~** *ad* (*en abondance*) to spare, aplenty.

revenir [Rəvnir] *vi* to come back; (*CULIN*): **faire ~** to brown; (*coûter*): **~ cher/à 100 F (à qn)** to cost (sb) a lot/100 F; **~ à** (*études, projet*) to return to, go back to; (*équivaloir à*) to amount to; **~ à qn** (*rumeur, nouvelle*) to get back to sb, reach sb's ears; (*part, honneur*) to go to sb, be sb's; (*souvenir, nom*) to come back to sb; **~ de** (*fig: maladie, étonnement*) to recover from; **~ sur** (*question, sujet*) to go back over; (*engagement*) to go back on; **~ à la charge** to return to the attack; **~ à soi** to come round; **n'en pas ~: je n'en reviens pas** I can't get over it; **~ sur ses pas** to retrace one's steps; **cela revient à dire que** it amounts to saying that.

revente [Rəvɑ̃t] *nf* resale.

revenu [Rəvny] *nm* income; (*de l'État*) revenue; (*d'un capital*) yield; **~s** *nmpl* income *sg*.

rêver [Reve] *vi, vt* to dream; **~ de qch/faire** to dream of sth/doing; **~ à** to dream of.

réverbération [RevɛRbeRɑsjɔ̃] *nf* reflection.

réverbère [RevɛRbɛR] *nm* street lamp *ou* light.

réverbérer [RevɛRbeRe] *vt* to reflect.

révérence [ReveRɑ̃s] *nf* (*vénération*) reverence; (*salut*) bow; curtsey.

révérend, e [ReveRɑ̃, -ɑ̃d] *a*: **le ~ père Pascal** the Reverend Father Pascal.

révérer [ReveRe] *vt* to revere.

rêverie [RɛvRi] *nf* daydreaming *q*, daydream.

revers [RəvɛR] *nm* (*de feuille, main*) back; (*d'étoffe*) wrong side; (*de pièce, médaille*) back, reverse; (*TENNIS, PING-PONG*) backhand; (*de veston*) lapel; (*de pantalon*) turn-up; (*fig: échec*) setback; **le ~ de la médaille** (*fig*) the other side of the coin; **prendre à ~** (*MIL*) to take from the rear.

réversible [RevɛRsibl(ə)] *a* reversible.

revêtement [Rəvɛtmɑ̃] *nm* (*de paroi*) facing; (*des sols*) flooring; (*de chaussée*) surface; (*de tuyau etc: enduit*) coating.

revêtir [RəvetiR] *vt* (*habit*) to don, put on; (*fig*) to take on; **~ qn de** to dress sb in; (*fig*) to endow *ou* invest sb with; **~ qch de** to cover sth with; (*fig*) to cloak sth in; **~ d'un visa** to append a visa to.

rêveur, euse [RɛvœR, -øz] *a* dreamy // *nm/f* dreamer.

revient [Rəvjɛ̃] *vb voir* **revenir** // *nm*: **prix de ~** cost price.

revigorer [RəvigɔRe] *vt* to invigorate, brace up; to revive, buck up.

revirement [RəviRmɑ̃] *nm* change of mind; (*d'une situation*) reversal.

réviser [Revize] *vt* (*texte, SCOL: matière*) to revise; (*comptes*) to audit; (*machine, installation, moteur*) to overhaul, service; (*JUR: procès*) to review.

révision [Revizjɔ̃] *nf* revision; auditing *q*; overhaul; servicing *q*; review; **conseil de ~** (*MIL*) recruiting board; **faire ses ~s** (*SCOL*) to do one's revision, revise; **la ~ des 10000 km** (*AUTO*) the 10,000 km service.

revisser [Rəvise] *vt* to screw back again.

revivifier [Rəvivifje] *vt* to revitalize.

revivre [RəvivR(ə)] *vi* (*reprendre des forces*) to come alive again; (*traditions*) to be revived // *vt* (*épreuve, moment*) to relive.

révocation [Revɔkɑsjɔ̃] *nf* dismissal; revocation.

revoir [RəvwaR] *vt* to see again; (*réviser*) to revise // *nm*: **au ~** goodbye; **dire au ~ à qn** to say goodbye to sb.

révolte [Revɔlt(ə)] *nf* rebellion, revolt.

révolter [Revɔlte] *vt* to revolt; to outrage, appal; **se ~** *vi*: **se ~ (contre)** to rebel (against); **se ~ (à)** to be outraged (by).

révolu, e [Revɔly] *a* past; (*ADMIN*): **âgé de 18 ans ~s** over 18 years of age; **après 3 ans ~s** when 3 full years have passed.

révolution [Revɔlysjɔ̃] *nf* revolution; **révolutionnaire** *a, nm/f* revolutionary; **révolutionner** *vt* to revolutionize; (*fig*) to stir up.

revolver [RevɔlvɛR] *nm* gun; (*à barillet*) revolver.

révoquer [Revɔke] *vt* (*fonctionnaire*) to dismiss, remove from office; (*arrêt, contrat*) to revoke.

revue [Rəvy] *nf* (*inventaire, examen*) review; (*MIL: défilé*) review, march-past; (*: inspection*) inspection, review; (*périodique*) review, magazine; (*pièce satirique*) revue; (*de music-hall*) variety show; **passer en ~** to review, inspect; (*fig*) to review, survey; to go through.

révulsé, e [Revylse] *a* (*yeux*) rolled upwards; (*visage*) contorted.

rez-de-chaussée [Redʃose] *nm inv* ground floor.

RF *sigle* = *République Française.*

rhabiller [Rabije] *vt*: **se ~** to get dressed again, put one's clothes on again.

rhapsodie [Rapsɔdi] *nf* rhapsody.

rhénan, e [Renɑ̃, -an] *a* Rhine *cpd.*

Rhénanie [Renani] *nf*: **la ~** the Rhineland.

rhésus [Rezys] *a, nm* rhesus.

rhétorique [RetɔRik] *nf* rhetoric.

rhéto-roman, e [RetɔRɔmɑ̃, -an] *a* Rhaeto-Romanic.

Rhin [Rɛ̃] *nm*: **le ~** the Rhine.

rhinocéros [RinɔseRɔs] *nm* rhinoceros.

rhodanien, ne [Rɔdanjɛ̃, -jɛn] *a* Rhone *cpd.*

Rhodésie [Rɔdezi] *nf*: **la ~** Rhodesia; **rhodésien, ne** *a* Rhodesian.

rhododendron [Rɔdɔdɛ̃dRɔ̃] *nm* rhododendron.

Rhône [Ron] *nm*: **le ~** the Rhone.

rhubarbe [RybaRb(ə)] *nf* rhubarb.

rhum [Rɔm] *nm* rum.

rhumatisant, e [Rymatizɑ̃, -ɑ̃t] *nm/f* rheumatic.

rhumatismal, e, aux [Rymatismal, -o] *a* rheumatic.

rhumatisme [Rymatism(ə)] *nm* rheumatism *q*.

rhume [Rym] *nm* cold; **~ de cerveau** head cold; **le ~ des foins** hay fever.

ri [Ri] *pp de* **rire**.

riant, e [Rjɑ̃, -ɑ̃t] *a* smiling, cheerful.

ribambelle [Ribɑ̃bɛl] *nf*: **une ~ de** a herd *ou* swarm of.

ricaner [Rikane] *vi* (*avec méchanceté*) to snigger; (*bêtement, avec gêne*) to giggle.

riche [ʀiʃ] *a* (*gén*) rich; (*personne, pays*) rich, wealthy; ~ **en** rich in; ~ **de** full of; rich in; **richesse** *nf* wealth; (*fig*) richness; **richesses** *nfpl* wealth *sg*; treasures; **richesse en vitamines** high vitamin content.
ricin [ʀisɛ̃] *nm*: **huile de** ~ castor oil.
ricocher [ʀikɔʃe] *vi*: ~ **(sur)** to rebound (off); (*sur l'eau*) to bounce (on *ou* off); **faire** ~ (*galet*) to skim.
ricochet [ʀikɔʃɛ] *nm* rebound; bounce; **faire des** ~**s** to skim pebbles; **par** ~ *ad* on the rebound; (*fig*) as an indirect result.
rictus [ʀiktys] *nm* grin; (snarling) grimace.
ride [ʀid] *nf* wrinkle; (*fig*) ripple.
ridé, e [ʀide] *a* wrinkled.
rideau, x [ʀido] *nm* curtain; ~ **de fer** metal shutter; (POL): **le** ~ **de fer** the Iron Curtain.
ridelle [ʀidɛl] *nf* slatted side.
rider [ʀide] *vt* to wrinkle; (*fig*) to ripple; to ruffle the surface of; **se** ~ *vi* (*avec l'âge*) to become wrinkled; (*de contrariété*) to wrinkle.
ridicule [ʀidikyl] *a* ridiculous // *nm* ridiculousness *q*; **le** ~ ridicule; **tourner en** ~ to ridicule; **ridiculiser** *vt* to ridicule; **se ridiculiser** to make a fool of o.s.
rie *vb voir* **rire**.
rien [ʀjɛ̃] *pronom* nothing; (*quelque chose*) anything; **ne ...** ~ nothing, *tournure négative* + anything // *nm* nothing; ~ **d'autre** nothing else; ~ **du tout** nothing at all; ~ **que** just, only; nothing but; **il n'a** ~ (*n'est pas blessé*) he's all right; **un petit** ~ (*cadeau*) a little something; **des** ~**s** trivia *pl*.
rieur, euse [ʀjœʀ, -øz] *a* cheerful, merry.
rigide [ʀiʒid] *a* stiff; (*fig*) rigid; strict; **rigidité** *nf* stiffness; **la rigidité cadavérique** rigor mortis.
rigolade [ʀigɔlad] *nf*: **la** ~ fun; (*fig*): **c'est de la** ~ it's a cinch; it's a big farce.
rigole [ʀigɔl] *nf* (*conduit*) channel; (*filet d'eau*) rivulet.
rigoler [ʀigɔle] *vi* (*rire*) to laugh; (*s'amuser*) to have (some) fun; (*plaisanter*) to be joking *ou* kidding.
rigolo, ote [ʀigɔlo, -ɔt] *a* (*fam*) funny // *nm/f* comic; (*péj*) fraud, phoney.
rigoureux, euse [ʀiguʀø, -øz] *a* (*morale*) rigorous, strict; (*personne*) stern, strict; (*climat, châtiment*) rigorous, harsh, severe; (*interdiction, neutralité*) strict; (*preuves, analyse, méthode*) rigorous.
rigueur [ʀigœʀ] *nf* rigour; strictness; harshness; **'tenue de soirée de** ~**'** 'evening dress (to be worn)'; **être de** ~ to be the usual thing *ou* be the rule; **à la** ~ at a pinch; possibly; **tenir** ~ **à qn de qch** to hold sth against sb.
rillettes [ʀijɛt] *nfpl* potted meat *sg*.
rime [ʀim] *nf* rhyme; **rimer** *vi*: **rimer (avec)** to rhyme (with); **ne rimer à rien** not to make sense.
rinçage [ʀɛ̃saʒ] *nm* rinsing (out); (*opération*) rinse.
rince-doigts [ʀɛ̃sdwa] *nm inv* finger-bowl.
rincer [ʀɛ̃se] *vt* to rinse; (*récipient*) to rinse out.
ring [ʀiŋ] *nm* (boxing) ring.
rions *vb voir* **rire**.
ripaille [ʀipɑj] *nf*: **faire** ~ to feast.
ripoliné, e [ʀipɔline] *a* enamel-painted.
riposte [ʀipɔst(ə)] *nf* retort, riposte; (*fig*) counter-attack, reprisal.
riposter [ʀipɔste] *vi* to retaliate // *vt*: ~ **que** to retort that; ~ **à** *vt* to counter; to reply to.
rire [ʀiʀ] *vi* to laugh; (*se divertir*) to have fun // *nm* laugh; **le** ~ laughter; ~ **de** *vt* to laugh at; **se** ~ **de** to make light of; **pour** ~ (*pas sérieusement*) for a joke *ou* a laugh.
ris [ʀi] *vb voir* **rire** // *nm*: ~ **de veau** (calf) sweetbread.
risée [ʀize] *nf*: **être la** ~ **de** to be the laughing stock of.
risette [ʀizɛt] *nf*: **faire** ~ **(à)** to give a nice little smile (to).
risible [ʀizibl(ə)] *a* laughable, ridiculous.
risque [ʀisk(ə)] *nm* risk; **le** ~ danger; **prendre des** ~**s** to take risks; **à ses** ~**s et périls** at his own risk; **au** ~ **de** at the risk of.
risqué, e [ʀiske] *a* risky; (*plaisanterie*) risqué, daring.
risquer [ʀiske] *vt* to risk; (*allusion, question*) to venture, hazard; **tu risques qu'on te renvoie** you risk being dismissed; **ça ne risque rien** it's quite safe; ~ **de**: **il risque de se tuer** he could get *ou* risks getting himself killed; **il a risqué de se tuer** he almost got himself killed; **ce qui risque de se produire** what might *ou* could well happen; **il ne risque pas de recommencer** there's no chance of him doing that again; **se** ~ **dans** (*s'aventurer*) to venture into; **se** ~ **à faire** (*tenter*) to venture *ou* dare to do; **risque-tout** *nm/f inv* daredevil.
rissoler [ʀisɔle] *vi, vt*: **(faire)** ~ to brown.
ristourne [ʀistuʀn(ə)] *nf* rebate.
rite [ʀit] *nm* rite; (*fig*) ritual.
ritournelle [ʀituʀnɛl] *nf* (*fig*) tune.
rituel, le [ʀitɥɛl] *a, nm* ritual.
rivage [ʀivaʒ] *nm* shore.
rival, e, aux [ʀival, -o] *a, nm/f* rival.
rivaliser [ʀivalize] *vi*: ~ **avec** to rival, vie with; (*être comparable*) to hold its own against, compare with; ~ **avec qn de** (*élégance etc*) to vie with *ou* rival sb in.
rivalité [ʀivalite] *nf* rivalry.
rive [ʀiv] *nf* shore; (*de fleuve*) bank.
river [ʀive] *vt* (*clou, pointe*) to clinch; (*plaques*) to rivet together; **être rivé sur/à** to be riveted on/to.
riverain, e [ʀivʀɛ̃, -ɛn] *a* riverside *cpd*; lakeside *cpd*; roadside *cpd* // *nm/f* riverside (*ou* lakeside) resident; local *ou* roadside resident.
rivet [ʀivɛ] *nm* rivet; **riveter** *vt* to rivet (together).
rivière [ʀivjɛʀ] *nf* river; ~ **de diamants** diamond rivière.
rixe [ʀiks(ə)] *nf* brawl, scuffle.
riz [ʀi] *nm* rice; ~ **au lait** rice pudding; **rizière** *nf* paddy-field.
R.N. *sigle f* = *route nationale, voir* **national**.

robe [Rɔb] *nf* dress; (*de juge, d'ecclésiastique*) robe; (*de professeur*) gown; (*pelage*) coat; ~ **de soirée/de mariée** evening/ wedding dress; ~ **de baptême** christening robe; ~ **de chambre** dressing gown; ~ **de grossesse** maternity dress.
robinet [Rɔbinɛ] *nm* tap; ~ **du gaz** gas tap; ~ **mélangeur** mixer tap; **robinetterie** *nf* taps *pl*, plumbing.
roboratif, ive [RɔbɔRatif, -iv] *a* bracing, invigorating.
robot [Rɔbo] nm robot.
robuste [Rɔbyst(ə)] *a* robust, sturdy.
roc [Rɔk] *nm* rock.
rocade [Rɔkad] *nf* (AUTO) by-road, bypass.
rocaille [Rɔkɑj] *nf* loose stones *pl*; rocky *ou* stony ground; (*jardin*) rockery, rock garden // *a* (*style*) rocaille; **rocailleux, euse** *a* rocky, stony; (*voix*) harsh.
rocambolesque [Rɔkɑ̃bɔlɛsk(ə)] *a* fantastic, incredible.
roche [Rɔʃ] *nf* rock.
rocher [Rɔʃe] *nm* rock; (ANAT) petrosal bone.
rochet [Rɔʃɛ] *nm*: **roue à** ~ rachet wheel.
rocheux, euse [Rɔʃø, -øz] *a* rocky.
rock (and roll) [Rɔk(ɛnRɔl)] *nm* (*musique*) rock(-'n'-roll); (*danse*) jive.
rodage [Rɔdaʒ] *nm* running in; **en** ~ (AUTO) running in.
rodéo [Rɔdeo] *nm* rodeo (*pl* s).
roder [Rɔde] *vt* (*moteur, voiture*) to run in.
rôder [Rode] *vi* to roam *ou* wander about; (*de façon suspecte*) to lurk *ou* loiter (about *ou* around); **rôdeur, euse** *nm/f* prowler.
rodomontades [Rɔdɔmɔ̃tad] *nfpl* bragging *sg*; sabre rattling *sg*.
rogatoire [Rɔgatwar] *a*: **commission** ~ letters rogatory.
rogne [Rɔɲ] *nf*: **être en** ~ to be ratty *ou* in a temper.
rogner [Rɔɲe] *vt* to trim; to clip; (*fig*) to whittle down; ~ **sur** (*fig*) to cut down *ou* back on.
rognons [Rɔɲɔ̃] *nmpl* kidneys.
rognures [RɔɲyR] *nfpl* trimmings; clippings.
rogue [Rɔg] *a* arrogant.
roi [Rwa] *nm* king; **le jour** *ou* **la fête des R~s, les ~s** Twelfth Night.
roitelet [Rwatlɛ] *nm* wren; (*péj*) kinglet.
rôle [Rol] *nm* role; (*contribution*) part.
rollmops [Rɔlmɔps] *nm* rollmop.
romain, e [Rɔmɛ̃, -ɛn] *a, nm/f* Roman // *nf* (BOT) cos (lettuce).
roman, e [Rɔmɑ̃, -an] *a* (ARCHIT) Romanesque; (LING) Romance, Romanic // *nm* novel; ~ **d'espionnage** spy novel *ou* story; ~ **photo** romantic picture story.
romance [Rɔmɑ̃s] *nf* ballad.
romancer [Rɔmɑ̃se] *vt* to make into a novel; to romanticize.
romanche [Rɔmɑ̃ʃ] *a, nm* Romansh.
romancier, ière [Rɔmɑ̃sje, -jɛR] *nm/f* novelist.
romand, e [Rɔmɑ̃, -ɑ̃d] *a* of *ou* from French-speaking Switzerland.
romanesque [Rɔmanɛsk(ə)] *a* (*fantastique*) fantastic; storybook *cpd*; (*sentimental*) romantic; (LITTÉRATURE) novelistic.
roman-feuilleton [Rɔmɑ̃fœjtɔ̃] *nm* serialized novel.
romanichel, le [Rɔmaniʃɛl] *nm/f* gipsy.
romantique [Rɔmɑ̃tik] *a* romantic.
romantisme [Rɔmɑ̃tism(ə)] *nm* romanticism.
romarin [RɔmaRɛ̃] *nm* rosemary.
Rome [Rɔm] *nf* Rome.
rompre [Rɔ̃pR(ə)] *vt* to break; (*entretien, fiançailles*) to break off // *vi* (*fiancés*) to break it off; **se** ~ *vi* to break; (MÉD) to burst, rupture; **se** ~ **les os** *ou* **le cou** to break one's neck; ~ **avec** to break with; **rompez (les rangs)!** (MIL) dismiss!, fall out!
rompu, e [Rɔ̃py] *a* (*fourbu*) exhausted, worn out; ~ **à** with wide experience of; inured to.
romsteak [Rɔ̃mstɛk] *nm* rumpsteak *q*.
ronce [Rɔ̃s] *nf* (BOT) bramble branch; (MENUISERIE): ~ **de noyer** burr walnut; **~s** *nfpl* brambles, thorns.
ronchonner [Rɔ̃ʃɔne] *vi* (*fam*) to grouse, grouch.
rond, e [Rɔ̃, Rɔ̃d] *a* round; (*joues, mollets*) well-rounded; (*fam*: *ivre*) tight // *nm* (*cercle*) ring; (*fam*: *sou*) **je n'ai plus un** ~ I haven't a penny left // *nf* (*gén*: *de surveillance*) rounds *pl*, patrol; (*danse*) round (dance); (MUS) semibreve; **en** ~ (*s'asseoir, danser*) in a ring; **à la ~e** (*alentour*): **à 10 km à la ~e** for 10 km round; (*à chacun son tour*): **passer qch à la ~e** to pass sth (a)round; **faire des ~s de jambe** to bow and scrape; ~ **de serviette** serviette ring; **~-de-cuir** *nm* (*péj*) penpusher; **rondelet, te** *a* plump.
rondelle [Rɔ̃dɛl] *nf* (TECH) washer; (*tranche*) slice, round.
rondement [Rɔ̃dmɑ̃] *ad* briskly; frankly.
rondeur [Rɔ̃dœR] *nf* (*d'un bras, des formes*) plumpness; (*bonhomie*) friendly straightforwardness; **~s** *nfpl* (*d'une femme*) curves.
rondin [Rɔ̃dɛ̃] *nm* log.
rond-point [Rɔ̃pwɛ̃] *nm* roundabout.
ronéotyper [Rɔneɔtipe] *vt* to duplicate, roneo.
ronflant, e [Rɔ̃flɑ̃, -ɑ̃t] *a* (*péj*) high-flown, grand.
ronflement [Rɔ̃fləmɑ̃] *nm* snore, snoring *q*.
ronfler [Rɔ̃fle] *vi* to snore; (*moteur, poêle*) to hum; to roar.
ronger [Rɔ̃ʒe] *vt* to gnaw (at); (*suj*: *vers, rouille*) to eat into; ~ **son frein** to champ (at) the bit; **se** ~ **de souci, se** ~ **les sangs** to worry o.s. sick, fret; **se** ~ **les ongles** to bite one's nails; **rongeur, euse** *nm/f* rodent.
ronronner [Rɔ̃Rɔne] *vi* to purr.
roque [Rɔk] *nm* (ÉCHECS) castling; **roquer** *vi* to castle.
roquet [Rɔkɛ] *nm* nasty little lap-dog.
roquette [Rɔkɛt] *nf* rocket.
rosace [Rozas] *nf* (*vitrail*) rose window, rosace; (*motif*: *de plafond etc*) rose.
rosaire [RozɛR] *nm* rosary.
rosbif [Rɔsbif] *nm*: **du** ~ roasting beef; (*cuit*) roast beef; **un** ~ a joint of beef.

rose [ROz] *nf* rose; (*vitrail*) rose window // *a* pink; ~ **bonbon** *a inv* candy pink; ~ **des vents** compass card.

rosé, e [Roze] *a* pinkish; **(vin)** ~ rosé (wine).

roseau, x [Rozo] *nm* reed.

rosée [Roze] *nf* dew; **goutte de** ~ dewdrop.

roseraie [RozRɛ] *nf* rose garden; (*plantation*) rose nursery.

rosette [Rozɛt] *nf* rosette (*gen of the Légion d'honneur*).

rosier [Rozje] *nm* rosebush, rose tree.

rosir [RoziR] *vi* to go pink.

rosse [Rɔs] *nf* (*péj*: *cheval*) nag // *a* nasty, vicious.

rosser [Rɔse] *vt* (*fam*) to thrash.

rossignol [Rɔsiɲɔl] *nm* (*ZOOL*) nightingale; (*crochet*) picklock.

rot [Ro] *nm* belch; (*de bébé*) burp.

rotatif, ive [Rɔtatif, -iv] *a* rotary // *nf* rotary press.

rotation [Rɔtɑsjɔ̃] *nf* rotation; (*fig*) rotation, swap-around; turnover; **par** ~ on a rota basis; ~ **des cultures** rotation of crops; ~ **des stocks** stock turnover.

roter [Rɔte] *vi* (*fam*) to burp, belch.

rôti [Roti] *nm*: **du** ~ roasting meat; (*cuit*) roast meat; **un** ~ **de bœuf/porc** a joint of beef/pork.

rotin [Rɔtɛ̃] *nm* rattan (cane); **fauteuil en** ~ cane (arm)chair.

rôtir [RotiR] *vt* (*aussi*: **faire** ~**)** to roast // *vi* to roast; **se** ~ **au soleil** to bask in the sun; **rôtisserie** *nf* steakhouse; roast meat counter (*ou* shop); **rôtissoire** *nf* (roasting) spit.

rotonde [Rɔtɔ̃d] *nf* (*ARCHIT*) rotunda; (*RAIL*) engine shed.

rotondité [Rɔtɔ̃dite] *nf* roundness.

rotor [RɔtɔR] *nm* rotor.

rotule [Rɔtyl] *nf* kneecap, patella.

roturier, ière [RɔtyRje, -jɛR] *nm/f* commoner.

rouage [Rwaʒ] *nm* cog(wheel), gearwheel; (*de montre*) part; (*fig*) cog; ~**s** (*fig*) internal structure *sg*.

roublard, e [RublaR, -aRd(ə)] *a* (*péj*) crafty, wily.

rouble [Rubl(ə)] *nm* rouble.

roucouler [Rukule] *vi* to coo; (*fig*: *péj*) to warble.

roue [Ru] *nf* wheel; **faire la** ~ (*paon*) to spread *ou* fan its tail; (*GYM*) to do a cartwheel; **descendre en** ~ **libre** to freewheel *ou* coast down; ~ **à aubes** paddle wheel; ~ **dentée** cogwheel; ~ **de secours** spare wheel.

roué, e [Rwe] *a* wily.

rouer [Rwe] *vt*: ~ **qn de coups** to give sb a thrashing.

rouet [Rwɛ] *nm* spinning wheel.

rouge [Ruʒ] *a, nm/f* red // *nm* red; (*fard*) rouge; **(vin)** ~ red wine; **passer au** ~ (*signal*) to go red; (*automobiliste*) to go through the red lights; **porter au** ~ (*métal*) to bring to red heat; ~ **(à lèvres)** lipstick; **rougeâtre** *a* reddish; ~**-gorge** *nm* robin (redbreast).

rougeole [Ruʒɔl] *nf* measles *sg*.

rougeoyer [Ruʒwaje] *vi* to glow red.

rouget [Ruʒɛ] *nm* mullet.

rougeur [RuʒœR] *nf* redness; (*du visage*) red face; ~**s** *nfpl* (*MÉD*) red blotches.

rougir [RuʒiR] *vi* (*de honte, timidité*) to blush, flush; (*de plaisir, colère*) to flush; (*fraise, tomate*) to go *ou* turn red; (*ciel*) to redden.

rouille [Ruj] *nf* rust // *a inv* rust-coloured, rusty.

rouillé, e [Ruje] *a* rusty.

rouiller [Ruje] *vt* to rust // *vi* to rust, go rusty; **se** ~ *vi* to rust; (*fig*) to become rusty; to grow stiff.

roulade [Rulad] *nf* (*GYM*) roll; (*CULIN*) rolled meat *q*; (*MUS*) roulade, run.

roulant, e [Rulɑ̃, -ɑ̃t] *a* (*meuble*) on wheels; (*surface, trottoir*) moving; **matériel** ~ (*RAIL*) rolling stock; **personnel** ~ (*RAIL*) train crews *pl*.

rouleau, x [Rulo] *nm* (*de papier, tissu, pièces de monnaie, SPORT*) roll; (*de machine à écrire*) roller, platen; (*à mise en plis, à peinture, vague*) roller; ~ **compresseur** steamroller; ~ **à pâtisserie** rolling pin; ~ **de pellicule** roll of film.

roulement [Rulmɑ̃] *nm* (*bruit*) rumbling *q*, rumble; (*rotation*) rotation; turnover; **par** ~ on a rota basis; ~ **(à billes)** ball bearings *pl*; ~ **de tambour** drum roll.

rouler [Rule] *vt* to roll; (*papier, tapis*) to roll up; (*CULIN*: *pâte*) to roll out; (*fam*) to do, con // *vi* (*bille, boule*) to roll; (*voiture, train*) to go, run; (*automobiliste*) to drive; (*cycliste*) to ride; (*bateau*) to roll; (*tonnerre*) to rumble, roll; (*dégringoler*): ~ **en bas de** to roll down; ~ **sur** (*suj*: *conversation*) to turn on; **se** ~ **dans** (*boue*) to roll in; (*couverture*) to roll o.s. (up) in; ~ **les épaules/hanches** to sway one's shoulders/wiggle one's hips.

roulette [Rulɛt] *nf* (*de table, fauteuil*) castor; (*de pâtissier*) pastry wheel; (*jeu*): **la** ~ roulette; **à** ~**s** on castors.

roulis [Ruli] *nm* roll(ing).

roulotte [Rulɔt] *nf* caravan.

roumain, e [Rumɛ̃, -ɛn] *a, nm/f* Romanian.

Roumanie [Rumani] *nf* Romania.

roupiller [Rupije] *vi* (*fam*) to sleep.

rouquin, e [Rukɛ̃, -in] *nm/f* (*péj*) redhead.

rouspéter [Ruspete] *vi* (*fam*) to moan, grouse.

rousse [Rus] *a voir* **roux**.

rousseur [RusœR] *nf*: **tache de** ~ freckle.

roussi [Rusi] *nm*: **ça sent le** ~ there's a smell of burning; (*fig*) I can smell trouble.

roussir [RusiR] *vt* to scorch // *vi* (*feuilles*) to go *ou* turn brown; (*CULIN*): **faire** ~ to brown.

route [Rut] *nf* road; (*fig*: *chemin*) way; (*itinéraire, parcours*) route; (*fig*: *voie*) road, path; **par (la)** ~ by road; **il y a 3h de** ~ it's a 3-hour ride *ou* journey; **en** ~ *ad* on the way; **mettre en** ~ to start up; **se mettre en** ~ to set off; **faire** ~ **vers** to head towards; **routier, ière** *a* road *cpd* // *nm* (*camionneur*) (long-distance) lorry *ou* truck driver; (*restaurant*) ≈ transport café; (*scout*) ≈ rover // *nf* (*voiture*) touring car.

routine [Rutin] *nf* routine ; **routinier, ière** *a* (*péj*) humdrum ; addicted to routine.
rouvrir [RuvRiR] *vt, vi* to reopen, open again ; **se ~** *vi* (*blessure*) to open up again.
roux, rousse [Ru, Rus] *a* red ; (*personne*) red-haired // *nm/f* redhead // *nm* (CULIN) roux.
royal, e, aux [Rwajal, -o] *a* royal ; (*fig*) fit for a king, princely ; blissful ; thorough.
royaliste [Rwajalist(ə)] *a, nm/f* royalist.
royaume [Rwajom] *nm* kingdom ; (*fig*) realm ; **le R~ Uni** the United Kingdom.
royauté [Rwajote] *nf* (*dignité*) kingship ; (*régime*) monarchy.
R.S.V.P. *sigle* (= *répondez s'il vous plaît*) R.S.V.P.
Rte *abr de* **route**.
ruade [Ryad] *nf* kick.
ruban [Rybɑ̃] *nm* (*gén*) ribbon ; (*pour ourlet, couture*) binding ; (*de téléscripteur etc*) tape ; (*d'acier*) strip ; **~ adhésif** adhesive tape.
rubéole [Rybeɔl] *nf* German measles *sg*, rubella.
rubicond, e [Rybikɔ̃, -ɔ̃d] *a* rubicund, ruddy.
rubis [Rybi] *nm* ruby ; (HORLOGERIE) jewel.
rubrique [RybRik] *nf* (*titre, catégorie*) heading, rubric ; (PRESSE: *article*) column.
ruche [Ryʃ] *nf* hive.
rude [Ryd] *a* (*barbe, toile*) rough ; (*métier, tâche*) hard, tough ; (*climat*) severe, harsh ; (*bourru*) harsh, rough ; (*fruste*) rugged, tough ; (*fam*) jolly good ; **~ment** *ad* (*tomber, frapper*) hard ; (*traiter, reprocher*) harshly ; (*fam: très*) terribly, jolly ; (: *beaucoup*) jolly hard.
rudimentaire [Rydimɑ̃tɛR] *a* rudimentary, basic.
rudiments [Rydimɑ̃] *nmpl* rudiments ; basic knowledge *sg* ; basic principles.
rudoyer [Rydwaje] *vt* to treat harshly.
rue [Ry] *nf* street.
ruée [Rɥe] *nf* rush.
ruelle [Rɥɛl] *nf* alley(-way).
ruer [Rɥe] *vi* (*cheval*) to kick out ; **se ~** *vi*: **se ~ sur** to pounce on ; **se ~ vers/dans/hors de** to rush *ou* dash towards/into/out of ; **~ dans les brancards** to become rebellious.
rugby [Rygbi] *nm* Rugby (football) ; **~ à treize/quinze** Rugby League/Union.
rugir [RyʒiR] *vi* to roar ; **rugissement** *nm* roar, roaring *q*.
rugosité [Rygozite] *nf* roughness ; (*aspérité*) rough patch.
rugueux, euse [Rygø, -øz] *a* rough.
ruine [Rɥin] *nf* ruin ; **~s** *nfpl* ruins.
ruiner [Rɥine] *vt* to ruin ; **ruineux, euse** *a* terribly expensive to buy (*ou* run), ruinous ; extravagant.
ruisseau, x [Rɥiso] *nm* stream, brook ; (*caniveau*) gutter ; (*fig*): **~x de** floods of, streams of.
ruisseler [Rɥisle] *vi* to stream ; **~ (d'eau)** to be streaming (with water).
rumeur [RymœR] *nf* (*bruit confus*) rumbling ; hubbub *q* ; murmur(ing) ; (*nouvelle*) rumour.
ruminer [Rymine] *vt* (*herbe*) to ruminate ; (*fig*) to ruminate on *ou* over, chew over // *vi* (*vache*) to chew the cud, ruminate.
rumsteak [Rɔ̃mstɛk] *nm* = **romsteak.**
rupture [RyptyR] *nf* (*de câble, digue*) breaking ; (*de tendon*) rupture, tearing ; (*de négociations etc*) breakdown ; (*de contrat*) breach ; (*séparation, désunion*) break-up, split ; **en ~ de ban** at odds with authority.
rural, e, aux [RyRal, -o] *a* rural, country *cpd* // *nmpl*: **les ruraux** country people.
ruse [Ryz] *nf*: **la ~** cunning, craftiness ; trickery ; **une ~** a trick, a ruse ; **rusé, e** *a* cunning, crafty.
russe [Rys] *a, nm, nf* Russian.
Russie [Rysi] *nf*: **la ~** Russia.
rustique [Rystik] *a* rustic.
rustre [RystR(ə)] *nm* boor.
rut [Ryt] *nm*: **être en ~** to be in *ou* on heat, be rutting.
rutabaga [Rytabaga] *nm* swede.
rutilant, e [Rytilɑ̃, -ɑ̃t] *a* gleaming.
rythme [Ritm(ə)] *nm* rhythm ; (*vitesse*) rate ; (: *de la vie*) pace, tempo ; **au ~ de 10 par jour** at the rate of 10 a day ; **rythmé, e** *a* rhythmic(al) ; **rythmique** *a* rhythmic(al) // *nf* rhythmics *sg*.

S

s' [s] *pronom voir* **se**.
sa [sa] *dét voir* **son**.
S.A. *sigle voir* **société**.
sable [sɑbl(ə)] *nm* sand ; **~s mouvants** quicksand(s).
sablé [sɑble] *nm* shortbread biscuit.
sabler [sɑble] *vt* to sand ; (*contre le verglas*) to grit ; **~ le champagne** to drink champagne.
sableux, euse [sɑblø, -øz] *a* sandy.
sablier [sɑblije] *nm* hourglass ; (*de cuisine*) egg timer.
sablière [sɑblijɛR] *nf* sand quarry.
sablonneux, euse [sɑblɔnø, -øz] *a* sandy.
saborder [sabɔRde] *vt* (*navire*) to scuttle ; (*fig*) to wind up, shut down.
sabot [sabo] *nm* clog ; (*de cheval, bœuf*) hoof , **~ de frein** brake shoe.
sabotage [sabɔtaʒ] *nm* sabotage.
saboter [sabɔte] *vt* to sabotage ; **saboteur, euse** *nm/f* saboteur.
sabre [sɑbR(ə)] *nm* sabre.
sac [sak] *nm* bag ; (*à charbon etc*) sack ; (*pillage*) sack(ing) ; **mettre à ~** to sack ; **~ à provisions/de voyage** shopping/travelling bag ; **~ de couchage** sleeping bag ; **~ à dos** rucksack ; **~ à main** handbag.
saccade [sakad] *nf* jerk ; **par ~s** jerkily ; haltingly.
saccager [sakaʒe] *vt* (*piller*) to sack, lay waste ; (*dévaster*) to create havoc in, wreck.
saccharine [sakaRin] *nf* saccharin(e).
sacerdoce [sasɛRdɔs] *nm* priesthood ; (*fig*) calling, vocation ; **sacerdotal, e, aux** *a* priestly, sacerdotal.
sache *etc vb voir* **savoir**.
sachet [saʃɛ] *nm* (small) bag ; (*de lavande, poudre, shampooing*) sachet ; **~ de thé** tea bag.

sacoche [sakɔʃ] *nf* (*gén*) bag; (*de bicyclette*) saddlebag; (*du facteur*) (post-)bag; (*d'outils*) toolbag.
sacre [sakʀ(ə)] *nm* coronation; consecration.
sacré, e [sakʀe] *a* sacred; (*fam*: *satané*) blasted; (: *fameux*): **un ~ ...** a heck of a ...; (ANAT) sacral.
sacrement [sakʀəmɑ̃] *nm* sacrament; **les derniers ~s** the last rites.
sacrer [sakʀe] *vt* (*roi*) to crown; (*évêque*) to consecrate // *vi* to curse, swear.
sacrifice [sakʀifis] *nm* sacrifice.
sacrifier [sakʀifje] *vt* to sacrifice; **~ à** *vt* to conform to; **articles sacrifiés** (COMM) items given away at knock-down prices.
sacrilège [sakʀilɛʒ] *nm* sacrilege // *a* sacrilegious.
sacristain [sakʀistɛ̃] *nm* sexton; sacristan.
sacristie [sakʀisti] *nf* sacristy; (*culte protestant*) vestry.
sacro-saint, e [sakʀɔsɛ̃, -sɛ̃t] *a* sacrosanct.
sadique [sadik] *a* sadistic // *nm/f* sadist.
sadisme [sadism(ə)] *nm* sadism.
safari [safaʀi] *nm* safari; **faire un ~** to go on safari; **~-photo** *nm* photographic safari.
safran [safʀɑ̃] *nm* saffron.
sagace [sagas] *a* sagacious, shrewd.
sagaie [sagɛ] *nf* assegai.
sage [saʒ] *a* wise; (*enfant*) good // *nm* wise man; sage.
sage-femme [saʒfam] *nf* midwife (*pl* wives).
sagesse [saʒɛs] *nf* wisdom.
Sagittaire [saʒitɛʀ] *nm*: **le ~** Sagittarius, the Archer; **être du ~** to be Sagittarius.
Sahara [saaʀa] *nm*: **le ~** the Sahara (desert).
saharienne [saaʀjɛn] *nf* safari jacket.
saignant, e [sɛɲɑ̃, -ɑ̃t] *a* (*viande*) rare; (*blessure, plaie*) bleeding.
saignée [seɲe] *nf* (MÉD) bleeding *q*, bloodletting *q*; (ANAT): **la ~ du bras** the bend of the arm; (*fig*) heavy losses *pl*; savage cut.
saignement [sɛɲmɑ̃] *nm* bleeding; **~ de nez** nosebleed.
saigner [seɲe] *vi* to bleed // *vt* to bleed; (*animal*) to kill (by bleeding); **~ du nez** to have a nosebleed.
saillant, e [sajɑ̃, -ɑ̃t] *a* (*pommettes, menton*) prominent; (*corniche etc*) projecting; (*fig*) salient, outstanding.
saillie [saji] *nf* (*sur un mur etc*) projection; (*trait d'esprit*) witticism; (*accouplement*) covering, serving; **faire ~** to project, stick out.
saillir [sajiʀ] *vi* to project, stick out; (*veine, muscle*) to bulge // *vt* (ÉLEVAGE) to cover, serve.
sain, e [sɛ̃, sɛn] *a* healthy; (*dents, constitution*) healthy, sound; (*lectures*) wholesome; **~ et sauf** safe and sound, unharmed; **~ d'esprit** sound in mind, sane.
saindoux [sɛ̃du] *nm* lard.
saint, e [sɛ̃, sɛ̃t] *a* holy; (*fig*) saintly // *nm/f* saint; **le S~ Esprit** the Holy Spirit *ou* Ghost; **la S~e Vierge** the Blessed Virgin; **sainteté** *nf* holiness; **le S~-Père** the Holy Father, the Pontiff; **le S~-Siège** the Holy See; **la S~-Sylvestre** New Year's Eve.
sais *etc vb voir* **savoir**.
saisie [sezi] *nf* seizure.
saisir [seziʀ] *vt* to take hold of, grab; (*fig*: *occasion*) to seize; (*comprendre*) to grasp; (*entendre*) to get, catch; (*suj: émotions*) to take hold of, come over; (CULIN) to fry quickly; (JUR: *biens, publication*) to seize; (: *juridiction*): **~ un tribunal d'une affaire** to submit *ou* refer a case to a court; **se ~ de** *vt* to seize; **saisissant, e** *a* startling, striking; **saisissement** *nm* emotion.
saison [sɛzɔ̃] *nf* season; **la belle ~** the summer months; **en/hors ~** in/out of season; **haute/morte ~** high/slack season; **la ~ des pluies/des amours** the rainy/ mating season; **saisonnier, ière** *a* seasonal // *nm* (*travailleur*) seasonal worker.
sait *vb voir* **savoir**.
salace [salas] *a* salacious.
salade [salad] *nf* (BOT) lettuce *etc* (*generic term*); (CULIN) (green) salad; (*fam*) tangle, muddle; **haricots en ~** bean salad; **~ de concombres** cucumber salad; **~ de fruits** fruit salad; **~ russe** Russian salad; **saladier** *nm* salad bowl.
salaire [salɛʀ] *nm* (*annuel, mensuel*) salary; (*hebdomadaire, journalier*) pay, wages *pl*; (*fig*) reward; **~ de base** basic salary/wage; **~ minimum interprofessionnel garanti (SMIG)/de croissance (SMIC)** *index-linked guaranteed minimum wage*.
salaison [salɛzɔ̃] *nf* salting; **~s** *nfpl* salt meat *sg*.
salami [salami] *nm* salami *q*, salami sausage.
salant [salɑ̃] *am*: **marais ~** salt pan.
salarial, e, aux [salaʀjal, -o] *a* salary *cpd*, wage(s) *cpd*.
salarié, e [salaʀje] *a* salaried; wage-earning // *nm/f* salaried employee; wage-earner.
salaud [salo] *nm* (*fam!*) sod (!), bastard (!).
sale [sal] *a* dirty, filthy.
salé, e [sale] *a* (*liquide, saveur*) salty; (CULIN) salted, salt *cpd*; (*fig*) spicy, juicy; steep, stiff.
saler [sale] *vt* to salt.
saleté [salte] *nf* (*état*) dirtiness; (*crasse*) dirt, filth; (*tache etc*) dirt *q*, something dirty; (*fig*) filthy trick; rubbish *q*; filth *q*; infection, bug.
salière [saljɛʀ] *nf* saltcellar.
saligaud [saligo] *nm* (*fam!*) sod (!).
salin, e [salɛ̃, -in] *a* saline // *nf* saltworks *sg*; salt marsh.
salinité [salinite] *nf* salinity, salt-content.
salir [saliʀ] *vt* to (make) dirty; (*fig*) to soil the reputation of; **se ~** to get dirty; **salissant, e** *a* (*tissu*) which shows the dirt; (*métier*) dirty, messy.
salive [saliv] *nf* saliva; **saliver** *vi* to salivate.
salle [sal] *nf* room; (*d'hôpital*) ward; (*de restaurant*) dining room; (*d'un cinéma*) auditorium; (: *public*) audience; **faire ~**

comble to have a full house ; ~ **d'attente** waiting room ; ~ **de bain(s)** bathroom ; ~ **de bal** ballroom ; ~ **de cinéma** cinema ; ~ **de classe** classroom ; ~ **commune** (*d'hôpital*) ward ; ~ **de concert** concert hall ; ~ **de douches** shower-room ; ~ **d'eau** shower-room ; ~ **d'embarquement** (*à l'aéroport*) departure lounge ; ~ **des machines** engine room ; ~ **à manger** dining room ; ~ **d'opération** (*d'hôpital*) operating theatre ; ~ **de projection** film theatre ; ~ **de séjour** living room ; ~ **de spectacle** theatre ; cinema ; ~ **des ventes** saleroom.

salon [salɔ̃] *nm* lounge, sitting room ; (*mobilier*) lounge suite ; (*exposition*) exhibition, show ; (*mondain, littéraire*) salon ; ~ **de coiffure** hairdressing salon ; ~ **de thé** tearoom.

salopard [salɔpaʀ] *nm* (*fam!*) bastard (!).

salope [salɔp] *nf* (*fam!*) bitch(!).

saloperie [salɔpʀi] *nf* (*fam!*) filth *q* ; dirty trick ; rubbish *q*.

salopette [salɔpɛt] *nf* overall(s).

salpêtre [salpɛtʀ(ə)] *nm* saltpetre.

salsifis [salsifi] *nm* salsify, oyster-plant.

saltimbanque [saltɛ̃bɑ̃k] *nm/f* (travelling) acrobat.

salubre [salybʀ(ə)] *a* healthy, salubrious ; **salubrité** *nf* healthiness, salubrity ; **salubrité publique** public health.

saluer [salɥe] *vt* (*pour dire bonjour, fig*) to greet ; (*pour dire au revoir*) to take one's leave ; (MIL) to salute.

salut [saly] *nm* (*sauvegarde*) safety ; (REL) salvation ; (*geste*) wave ; (*parole*) greeting ; (MIL) salute // *excl* (*fam*) hi (there) ; (*style relevé*) (all) hail.

salutaire [salytɛʀ] *a* beneficial ; salutary.

salutations [salytɑsjɔ̃] *nfpl* greetings ; **recevez mes** ~ **distinguées** *ou* **respectueuses** yours faithfully.

salutiste [salytist(ə)] *nm/f* Salvationist.

salve [salv(ə)] *nf* salvo ; volley of shots.

samaritain [samaʀitɛ̃] *nm*: **le bon S~** the Good Samaritan.

samedi [samdi] *nm* Saturday.

sanatorium [sanatɔʀjɔm] *nm* sanatorium (*pl* a).

sanctifier [sɑ̃ktifje] *vt* to sanctify.

sanction [sɑ̃ksjɔ̃] *nf* sanction ; (*fig*) penalty ; **prendre des ~s contre** to impose sanctions on ; **sanctionner** *vt* (*loi, usage*) to sanction ; (*punir*) to punish.

sanctuaire [sɑ̃ktɥɛʀ] *nm* sanctuary.

sandale [sɑ̃dal] *nf* sandal.

sandalette [sɑ̃dalɛt] *nf* sandal.

sandwich [sɑ̃dwitʃ] *nm* sandwich ; **pris en** ~ sandwiched.

sang [sɑ̃] *nm* blood ; **en** ~ covered in blood ; **se faire du mauvais** ~ to fret, get in a state.

sang-froid [sɑ̃fʀwa] *nm* calm, sangfroid ; **de** ~ in cold blood.

sanglant, e [sɑ̃glɑ̃, -ɑ̃t] *a* bloody, covered in blood ; (*combat*) bloody.

sangle [sɑ̃gl(ə)] *nf* strap ; **~s** (*pour lit etc*) webbing *sg* ; **sangler** *vt* to strap up ; (*animal*) to girth.

sanglier [sɑ̃glije] *nm* (wild) boar.

sanglot [sɑ̃glo] *nm* sob ; **sangloter** *vi* to sob.

sangsue [sɑ̃sy] *nf* leech.

sanguin, e [sɑ̃gɛ̃, -in] *a* blood *cpd* ; (*fig*) fiery // *nf* blood orange ; (ART) red pencil drawing.

sanguinaire [sɑ̃ginɛʀ] *a* bloodthirsty ; bloody.

sanguinolent, e [sɑ̃ginɔlɑ̃, -ɑ̃t] *a* streaked with blood.

sanitaire [sanitɛʀ] *a* health *cpd* ; **installation/appareil** ~ bathroom plumbing/appliance ; **~s** *nmpl* (*salle de bain et w.-c.*) bathroom *sg*.

sans [sɑ̃] *prép* without ; ~ **qu'il s'en aperçoive** without him *ou* his noticing ; ~ **scrupules** unscrupulous ; ~ **manches** sleeveless ; **~-abri** *nmpl* homeless (*after a flood etc*) ; **~-emploi** *nmpl* jobless ; **~-façon** *a inv* fuss-free ; free and easy ; **~-gêne** *a inv* inconsiderate ; **~-logis** *nmpl* homeless (*through poverty*) ; **~-travail** *nmpl* unemployed, jobless.

santal [sɑ̃tal] *nm* sandal(wood).

santé [sɑ̃te] *nf* health ; **en bonne** ~ in good health ; **boire à la** ~ **de qn** to drink (to) sb's health ; **'à la** ~ **de'** 'here's to' ; **à ta/votre** ~**!** cheers!

santon [sɑ̃tɔ̃] *nm ornamental figure at a Christmas crib.*

saoul, e [su, sul] *a* = **soûl, e.**

sape [sap] *nf*: **travail de** ~ (MIL) sap ; (*fig*) insidious undermining process *ou* work.

saper [sape] *vt* to undermine, sap.

sapeur [sapœʀ] *nm* sapper ; **~-pompier** *nm* fireman.

saphir [safiʀ] *nm* sapphire.

sapin [sapɛ̃] *nm* fir (tree) ; (*bois*) fir ; ~ **de Noël** Christmas tree ; **sapinière** *nf* fir plantation *ou* forest.

sarabande [saʀabɑ̃d] *nf* saraband ; (*fig*) hullabaloo ; whirl.

sarbacane [saʀbakan] *nf* blowpipe, blowgun ; (*jouet*) peashooter.

sarcasme [saʀkasm(ə)] *nm* sarcasm *q* ; piece of sarcasm ; **sarcastique** *a* sarcastic.

sarcler [saʀcle] *vt* to weed ; **sarcloir** *nm* (weeding) hoe, spud.

sarcophage [saʀkɔfaʒ] *nm* sarcophagus (*pl* i).

Sardaigne [saʀdɛɲ] *nf*: **la** ~ Sardinia ; **sarde** *a, nm/f* Sardinian.

sardine [saʀdin] *nf* sardine ; **~s à l'huile** sardines in oil.

sardonique [saʀdɔnik] *a* sardonic.

S.A.R.L. *sigle voir* **société**.

sarment [saʀmɑ̃] *nm*: ~ **(de vigne)** vine shoot.

sarrasin [saʀazɛ̃] *nm* buckwheat.

sarrau [saʀo] *nm* smock.

Sarre [saʀ] *nf*: **la** ~ the Saar.

sarriette [saʀjɛt] *nf* savory.

sarrois, e [saʀwa, -waz] *a* Saar *cpd* // *nm/f*: **S~, e** inhabitant *ou* native of the Saar.

sas [sɑ] *nm* (*de sous-marin, d'engin spatial*) airlock ; (*d'écluse*) lock.

satané, e [satane] *a* confounded.

satanique [satanik] *a* satanic, fiendish.

satelliser [satelize] *vt* (*fusée*) to put into orbit ; (*fig: pays*) to make into a satellite.

satellite [satelit] *nm* satellite; **pays ~** satellite country; **~-espion** *nm* spy satellite.
satiété [sasjete]: **à ~** *ad* to satiety *ou* satiation; (*répéter*) ad nauseam.
satin [satɛ̃] *nm* satin; **satiné, e** *a* satiny; (*peau*) satin-smooth.
satire [satiʀ] *nf* satire; **satirique** *a* satirical; **satiriser** *vt* to satirize.
satisfaction [satisfaksjɔ̃] *nf* satisfaction.
satisfaire [satisfɛʀ] *vt* to satisfy; **~ à** *vt* (*engagement*) to fulfil; (*revendications, conditions*) to satisfy, meet; to comply with; **satisfaisant, e** *a* satisfactory; (*qui fait plaisir*) satisfying; **satisfait, e** *a* satisfied; **satisfait de** happy *ou* satisfied with; pleased with.
saturation [satyʀɑsjɔ̃] *nf* saturation.
saturer [satyʀe] *vt* to saturate.
satyre [satiʀ] *nm* satyr; (*péj*) lecher.
sauce [sos] *nf* sauce; (*avec un rôti*) gravy; **~ tomate** tomato sauce; **saucière** *nf* sauceboat; gravy boat.
saucisse [sosis] *nf* sausage.
saucisson [sosisɔ̃] *nm* (slicing) sausage; **~ à l'ail** garlic sausage.
sauf [sof] *prép* except; **~ si** (*à moins que*) unless; **~ erreur** if I'm not mistaken; **~ avis contraire** unless you hear to the contrary.
sauf, sauve [sof, sov] *a* unharmed, unhurt; (*fig*: *honneur*) intact, saved; **laisser la vie sauve à qn** to spare sb's life.
sauf-conduit [sofkɔ̃dɥi] *nm* safe-conduct.
sauge [soʒ] *nf* sage.
saugrenu, e [sogʀəny] *a* preposterous, ludicrous.
saule [sol] *nm* willow (tree); **~ pleureur** weeping willow.
saumâtre [somɑtʀ(ə)] *a* briny.
saumon [somɔ̃] *nm* salmon *inv* // *a inv* salmon (pink); **saumoné, e** *a*: **truite saumonée** salmon trout.
saumure [somyʀ] *nf* brine.
sauna [sona] *nm* sauna.
saupoudrer [sopudʀe] *vt*: **~ qch de** to sprinkle sth with.
saur [sɔʀ] *am*: **hareng ~** smoked *ou* red herring, kipper.
saurai *etc vb voir* **savoir**.
saut [so] *nm* jump; (*discipline sportive*) jumping; **faire un ~** to (make a) jump *ou* leap; **faire un ~ chez qn** to pop over to sb's (place); **au ~ du lit** on getting out of bed; **~ en hauteur/longueur** high/long jump; **~ à la corde** skipping; **~ à la perche** pole vaulting; **~ périlleux** somersault.
saute [sot] *nf*: **~ de vent/température** sudden change of wind direction/in the temperature.
sauté, e [sote] *a* (CULIN) sauté // *nm*: **~ de veau** sauté of veal.
saute-mouton [sotmutɔ̃] *nm*: **jouer à ~** to play leapfrog.
sauter [sote] *vi* to jump, leap; (*exploser*) to blow up, explode; (: *fusibles*) to blow; (*se rompre*) to snap, burst; (*se détacher*) to pop out (*ou* off) // *vt* to jump (over), leap (over); (*fig*: *omettre*) to skip, miss (out); **faire ~** to blow up; to burst open; (CULIN) to sauté; **~ à pieds joints** to make a standing jump; **~ en parachute** to make a parachute jump; **~ au cou de qn** to fly into sb's arms; **~ aux yeux** to be quite obvious.
sauterelle [sotʀɛl] *nf* grasshopper.
sauteur, euse [sotœʀ, -øz] *nm/f* (*athlète*) jumper // *nf* (*casserole*) shallow casserole; **~ à la perche** pole vaulter; **~ à skis** skijumper.
sautiller [sotije] *vi* to hop; to skip.
sautoir [sotwaʀ] *nm* chain; **~ (de perles)** string of pearls.
sauvage [sovaʒ] *a* (*gén*) wild; (*peuplade*) savage; (*farouche*) unsociable; (*barbare*) wild, savage; (*non officiel*) unauthorized, unofficial // *nm/f* savage; (*timide*) unsociable type, recluse; **~rie** *nf* wildness; savagery; unsociability.
sauve [sov] *af voir* **sauf**.
sauvegarde [sovgaʀd(ə)] *nf* safeguard; **sous la ~ de** under the protection of; **sauvegarder** *vt* to safeguard.
sauve-qui-peut [sovkipø] *nm inv* stampede, mad rush // *excl* run for your life!
sauver [sove] *vt* to save; (*porter secours à*) to rescue; (*récupérer*) to salvage, rescue; (*fig*: *racheter*) to save, redeem; **se ~** *vi* (*s'enfuir*) to run away; (*fam*: *partir*) to be off; **~ la vie à qn** to save sb's life; **sauvetage** *nm* rescue; **sauveteur** *nm* rescuer; **sauvette**: **à la sauvette** *ad* (*vendre*) without authorization; (*se marier etc*) hastily, hurriedly; **sauveur** *nm* saviour.
savais *etc vb voir* **savoir**.
savamment [savamɑ̃] *ad* (*avec érudition*) learnedly; (*habilement*) skilfully, cleverly.
savane [savan] *nf* savannah.
savant, e [savɑ̃, -ɑ̃t] *a* scholarly, learned; (*calé*) clever // *nm* scientist.
saveur [savœʀ] *nf* flavour; (*fig*) savour.
savoir [savwaʀ] *vt* to know; (*être capable de*): **il sait nager** he knows how to swim, he can swim // *nm* knowledge; **se ~** (*être connu*) to be known; **à ~** *ad* that is, namely; **faire ~ qch à qn** to inform sb about sth, to let sb know sth; **pas que je sache** not as far as I know; **~-faire** *nm inv* savoir-faire, know-how.
savon [savɔ̃] *nm* (*produit*) soap; (*morceau*) bar *ou* tablet of soap; (*fam*): **passer un ~ à qn** to give sb a good dressing-down; **savonner** *vt* to soap; **savonnette** *nf* bar *ou* tablet of soap; **savonneux, euse** *a* soapy.
savons *vb voir* **savoir**.
savourer [savuʀe] *vt* to savour.
savoureux, euse [savuʀø, -øz] *a* tasty; (*fig*) spicy, juicy.
saxo(phone) [saksɔ(fɔn)] *nm* sax(ophone); **saxophoniste** *nm/f* saxophonist, sax(ophone) player.
saynète [sɛnɛt] *nf* playlet.
sbire [sbiʀ] *nm* (*péj*) henchman.
scabreux, euse [skabʀø, -øz] *a* risky; (*indécent*) improper, shocking.
scalpel [skalpɛl] *nm* scalpel.

scalper [skalpe] *vt* to scalp.
scandale [skɑ̃dal] *nm* scandal; (*tapage*): **faire du ~** to make a scene, create a disturbance; **faire ~** to scandalize people; **scandaleux, euse** *a* scandalous, outrageous; **scandaliser** *vt* to scandalize; **se scandaliser (de)** to be scandalized (by).
scander [skɑ̃de] *vt* (*vers*) to scan; (*slogans*) to chant; **en scandant les mots** stressing each word.
scandinave [skɑ̃dinav] *a, nm/f* Scandinavian.
Scandinavie [skɑ̃dinavi] *nf* Scandinavia.
scaphandre [skafɑ̃dʀ(ə)] *nm* (*de plongeur*) diving suit; (*de cosmonaute*) space-suit; **~ autonome** aqualung.
scarabée [skaʀabe] *nm* beetle.
scarlatine [skaʀlatin] *nf* scarlet fever.
scarole [skaʀɔl] *nf* endive.
scatologique [skatɔlɔʒik] *a* scatological, lavatorial.
sceau, x [so] *nm* seal; (*fig*) stamp, mark.
scélérat, e [seleʀa, -at] *nm/f* villain, blackguard.
sceller [sele] *vt* to seal.
scellés [sele] *nmpl* seals.
scénario [senaʀjo] *nm* (CINÉMA) scenario; screenplay, script; (*fig*) pattern; scenario; **scénariste** *nm/f* scriptwriter.
scène [sɛn] *nf* (*gén*) scene; (*estrade, fig*: *théâtre*) stage; **entrer en ~** to come on stage; **mettre en ~** (THÉÂTRE) to stage; (CINÉMA) to direct; (*fig*) to present, introduce; **porter à la ~** to adapt for the stage; **faire une ~ (à qn)** to make a scene (with sb); **~ de ménage** domestic fight *ou* scene; **scénique** *a* theatrical; scenic.
scepticisme [sɛptisism(ə)] *nm* scepticism.
sceptique [sɛptik] *a* sceptical // *nm/f* sceptic.
sceptre [sɛptʀ(ə)] *nm* sceptre.
schéma [ʃema] *nm* (*diagramme*) diagram, sketch; (*fig*) outline; pattern; **schématique** *a* diagrammatic(al), schematic; (*fig*) oversimplified.
schisme [ʃism(ə)] *nm* schism; rift, split.
schiste [ʃist(ə)] *nm* schist.
schizophrène [skizɔfʀɛn] *nm/f* schizophrenic.
schizophrénie [skizɔfʀeni] *nf* schizophrenia.
sciatique [sjatik] *a*: **nerf ~** sciatic nerve // *nf* sciatica.
scie [si] *nf* saw; (*fam*) catch-tune; **~ à bois** wood saw; **~ circulaire** circular saw; **~ à découper** fretsaw; **~ à métaux** hacksaw.
sciemment [sjamɑ̃] *ad* knowingly, wittingly.
science [sjɑ̃s] *nf* science; (*savoir*) knowledge; (*savoir-faire*) art, skill; **~s naturelles** (SCOL) natural science *sg*, biology *sg*; **~-fiction** *nf* science fiction; **scientifique** *a* scientific // *nm/f* scientist; science student.
scier [sje] *vt* to saw; (*retrancher*) to saw off; **scierie** *nf* sawmill; **scieur de long** *nm* pit sawyer.
scinder [sɛ̃de] *vt*, **se ~** *vi* to split (up).
scintillement [sɛ̃tijmɑ̃] *nm* sparkling *q*.
scintiller [sɛ̃tije] *vi* to sparkle.
scission [sisjɔ̃] *nf* split.
sciure [sjyʀ] *nf*: **~ (de bois)** sawdust.
sclérose [skleʀoz] *nf* sclerosis; (*fig*) ossification; **~ en plaques** multiple sclerosis; **sclérosé, e** *a* sclerosed, sclerotic; ossified.
scolaire [skɔlɛʀ] *a* school *cpd*; (*péj*) schoolish; **scolariser** *vt* to provide with schooling (*ou* schools); **scolarité** *nf* schooling; **frais de scolarité** school fees.
scooter [skutœʀ] *nm* (motor) scooter.
scorbut [skɔʀbyt] *nm* scurvy.
score [skɔʀ] *nm* score.
scories [skɔʀi] *nfpl* scoria *pl*.
scorpion [skɔʀpjɔ̃] *nm* (*signe*): **le S~** Scorpio, the Scorpion; **être du S~** to be Scorpio.
scout, e [skut] *a, nm* scout; **scoutisme** *nm* (boy) scout movement; (*activités*) scouting.
scribe [skʀib] *nm* scribe; (*péj*) penpusher.
script [skʀipt] *nm* printing; (CINÉMA) (shooting) script; **~-girl** [-gœʀl] *nf* continuity girl.
scrupule [skʀypyl] *nm* scruple; **scrupuleux, euse** *a* scrupulous.
scrutateur, trice [skʀytatœʀ, -tʀis] *a* searching.
scruter [skʀyte] *vt* to search, scrutinize; (*l'obscurité*) to peer into; (*motifs, comportement*) to examine, scrutinize.
scrutin [skʀytɛ̃] *nm* (*vote*) ballot; (*ensemble des opérations*) poll; **~ à deux tours** poll with two ballots *ou* rounds; **~ de liste** list system.
sculpter [skylte] *vt* to sculpt; (*suj*: *érosion*) to carve; **sculpteur** *nm* sculptor.
sculptural, e, aux [skyltyʀal, -o] *a* sculptural; (*fig*) statuesque.
sculpture [skyltyʀ] *nf* sculpture; **~ sur bois** wood carving.
S.D.E.C.E. [zdɛk] *sigle m = service de documentation extérieure et de contre-espionnage*, ≈ *Intelligence Service*.
se, s' [s(ə)] *pronom* (*emploi réfléchi*) oneself, *m* himself, *f* herself, *sujet non humain* itself; *pl* themselves; (: *réciproque*) one another, each other; (: *passif*): **cela se répare facilement** it is easily repaired; (: *possessif*): **~ casser la jambe/laver les mains** to break one's leg/wash one's hands; *autres emplois pronominaux*: *voir le verbe en question*.
séance [seɑ̃s] *nf* (*d'assemblée, récréative*) meeting, session; (*de tribunal*) sitting, session; (*musicale*, CINÉMA, THÉÂTRE) performance; **~ tenante** forthwith.
séant, e [seɑ̃, -ɑ̃t] *a* seemly, fitting // *nm* posterior.
seau, x [so] *nm* bucket, pail; **~ à glace** ice-bucket.
sec, sèche [sɛk, sɛʃ] *a* dry; (*raisins, figues*) dried; (*cœur, personne*: *insensible*) hard, cold // *nm*: **tenir au ~** to keep in a dry place // *ad* hard; **je le bois ~** I drink it straight *ou* neat; **à ~** *a* dried up.
sécateur [sekatœʀ] *nm* secateurs *pl*, shears *pl*, pair of shears *ou* secateurs.
sécession [sesesjɔ̃] *nf*: **faire ~** to secede; **la guerre de S~** the American Civil War.

séchage [seʃaʒ] *nm* drying ; seasoning.
sèche [sɛʃ] *af voir* **sec**.
sèche-cheveux [sɛʃʃəvø] *nm inv* hair-drier.
sécher [seʃe] *vt* to dry ; (*dessécher*: *peau, blé*) to dry (out) ; (: *étang*) to dry up ; (*bois*) to season ; (*fam*: *classe, cours*) to skip // *vi* to dry ; to dry out ; to dry up ; (*fam*: *candidat*) to be stumped ; **se ~** (*après le bain*) to dry o.s.
sécheresse [sɛʃʀɛs] *nf* dryness ; (*absence de pluie*) drought.
séchoir [seʃwaʀ] *nm* drier.
second, e [səgɔ̃, -ɔ̃d] *a* second // *nm* (*assistant*) second in command ; (*NAVIG*) first mate // *nf* second ; **voyager en ~e** to travel second-class ; **de ~e main** second-hand ; **secondaire** *a* secondary ; **seconder** *vt* to assist.
secouer [səkwe] *vt* to shake ; (*passagers*) to rock ; (*traumatiser*) to shake (up) ; **se ~** (*chien*) to shake itself ; (*fam*: *se démener*) to shake o.s. up ; **~ la poussière d'un tapis** to shake off the dust from a carpet.
secourable [səkuʀabl(ə)] *a* helpful.
secourir [səkuʀiʀ] *vt* (*aller sauver*) to (go and) rescue ; (*prodiguer des soins à*) to help, assist ; (*venir en aide à*) to assist, aid ; **secourisme** *nm* first aid ; life saving ; **secouriste** *nm/f* first-aid worker.
secours [səkuʀ] *nm* help, aid, assistance // *nmpl* aid *sg* ; **cela lui a été d'un grand ~** this was a great help to him ; **au ~!** help! **appeler au ~** to shout *ou* call for help ; **appeler qn à son ~** to call sb to one's assistance ; **porter ~ à qn** to give sb assistance, help sb ; **les premiers ~** first aid *sg* ; **le ~ en montagne** mountain rescue.
secousse [səkus] *nf* jolt, bump ; (*électrique*) shock ; (*fig*: *psychologique*) jolt, shock ; **~ sismique** *ou* **tellurique** earth tremor.
secret, ète [səkʀɛ, -ɛt] *a* secret ; (*fig*: *renfermé*) reticent, reserved // *nm* secret ; (*discrétion absolue*): **le ~** secrecy ; **en ~** in secret, secretly ; **au ~** in solitary confinement ; **~ de fabrication** trade secret ; **~ professionnel** professional secrecy.
secrétaire [səkʀetɛʀ] *nm/f* secretary // *nm* (*meuble*) writing desk, secretaire ; **~ d'ambassade** embassy secretary ; **~ de direction** private *ou* personal secretary ; **~ d'État** Secretary of State ; **~ général** Secretary-General ; **~ de mairie** town clerk ; **~ de rédaction** sub-editor ; **secrétariat** *nm* (*profession*) secretarial work ; (*bureau*: *d'entreprise, d'école*) (secretary's) office ; (: *d'organisation internationale*) secretariat ; (*POL etc*: *fonction*) secretaryship, office of Secretary.
sécréter [sekʀete] *vt* to secrete ; **sécrétion** [-sjɔ̃] *nf* secretion.
sectaire [sɛktɛʀ] *a* sectarian, bigoted.
secte [sɛkt(ə)] *nf* sect.
secteur [sɛktœʀ] *nm* sector ; (*ADMIN*) district ; (*ÉLEC*): **branché sur le ~** plugged into the mains (supply) ; **fonctionne sur pile et ~** battery or mains operated ; **le ~ privé** the private sector ; **le ~ primaire/tertiaire** primary/tertiary industry.
section [sɛksjɔ̃] *nf* section ; (*de parcours d'autobus*) fare stage ; (*MIL*: *unité*) platoon ; **tube de ~ 6,5 mm** tube with a 6.5 mm bore ; **~ rythmique** rhythm section ; **sectionner** *vt* to sever.
sectoriel, le [sɛktɔʀjɛl] *a* sector-based.
séculaire [sekylɛʀ] *a* secular ; (*très vieux*) age-old.
séculier, ière [sekylje, -jɛʀ] *a* secular.
sécuriser [sekyʀize] *vt* to give (a feeling of) security to.
sécurité [sekyʀite] *nf* safety ; security ; **impression de ~** sense of security ; **la ~ internationale** international security ; **système de ~** safety system ; **être en ~** to be safe ; **la ~ de l'emploi** job security ; **la ~ routière** road safety ; **la ~ sociale** ≈ (the) Social Security.
sédatif, ive [sedatif, -iv] *a, nm* sedative.
sédentaire [sedɑ̃tɛʀ] *a* sedentary.
sédiment [sedimɑ̃] *nm* sediment ; **~s** *nmpl* (*alluvions*) sediment *sg*.
séditieux, euse [sedisjø, -øz] *a* insurgent ; seditious.
sédition [sedisjɔ̃] *nf* insurrection ; sedition.
séducteur, trice [sedyktœʀ, -tʀis] *a* seductive // *nm/f* seducer/seductress.
séduction [sedyksjɔ̃] *nf* seduction ; (*charme, attrait*) appeal, charm.
séduire [sedɥiʀ] *vt* to charm ; (*femme*: *abuser de*) to seduce ; **séduisant, e** *a* (*femme*) seductive ; (*homme, offre*) very attractive.
segment [sɛgmɑ̃] *nm* segment ; (*AUTO*): **~ (de piston)** piston ring ; **segmenter** *vt* to segment.
ségrégation [segʀegɑsjɔ̃] *nf* segregation.
seiche [sɛʃ] *nf* cuttlefish.
séide [seid] *nm* (*péj*) henchman.
seigle [sɛgl(ə)] *nm* rye.
seigneur [sɛɲœʀ] *nm* lord ; **le S~** the Lord ; **~ial, e, aux** *a* lordly, stately.
sein [sɛ̃] *nm* breast ; (*entrailles*) womb ; **au ~ de** *prép* (*équipe, institution*) within ; (*flots, bonheur*) in the midst of ; **donner le ~ à** (*bébé*) to feed (at the breast) ; to breast-feed.
séisme [seism(ə)] *nm* earthquake.
séismique [seismik] *etc voir* **sismique** *etc*.
seize [sɛz] *num* sixteen ; **seizième** *num* sixteenth.
séjour [seʒuʀ] *nm* stay ; (*pièce*) living room ; **~ner** *vi* to stay.
sel [sɛl] *nm* salt ; (*fig*) wit ; spice ; **~ de cuisine/de table** cooking/table salt ; **~ gemme** rock salt.
sélection [selɛksjɔ̃] *nf* selection ; **~ professionnelle** professional recruitment ; **sélectionner** *vt* to select.
self-service [sɛlfsɛʀvis] *a, nm* self-service.
selle [sɛl] *nf* saddle ; **~s** *nfpl* (*MÉD*) stools ; **aller à la ~** (*MÉD*) to pass a motion ; **se mettre en ~** to mount, get into the saddle ; **seller** *vt* to saddle.
sellette [sɛlɛt] *nf*: **être sur la ~** to be on the carpet.
sellier [selje] *nm* saddler.

selon [səlɔ̃] *prép* according to; (*en se conformant à*) in accordance with.
semailles [səmɑj] *nfpl* sowing *sg*.
semaine [səmɛn] *nf* week; **en ~** during the week, on weekdays.
sémantique [semɑ̃tik] *a* semantic // *nf* semantics *sg*.
sémaphore [semafɔʀ] *nm* semaphore signal.
semblable [sɑ̃blabl(ə)] *a* similar; (*de ce genre*): **de ~s mésaventures** such mishaps // *nm* fellow creature *ou* man; **~ à** similar to, like.
semblant [sɑ̃blɑ̃] *nm*: **un ~ de vérité** a semblance of truth; **faire ~ (de faire)** to pretend (to do).
sembler [sɑ̃ble] *vb avec attribut* to seem // *vb impersonnel*: **il semble que/inutile de** it seems *ou* appears that/useless to; **il me semble que** it seems to me that; I think (that); **~ être** to seem to be; **comme bon lui semble** as he sees fit.
semelle [səmɛl] *nf* sole; (*intérieure*) insole, inner sole; **~s compensées** platform soles.
semence [səmɑ̃s] *nf* (*graine*) seed; (*clou*) tack.
semer [səme] *vt* to sow; (*fig*: *éparpiller*) to scatter; (: *poursuivants*) to lose, shake off; **semé de** (*difficultés*) riddled with.
semestre [səmɛstʀ(ə)] *nm* half-year; (SCOL) semester; **semestriel, le** *a* half-yearly; semestral.
semeur, euse [səmœʀ, -øz] *nm/f* sower.
sémillant, e [semijɑ̃, -ɑ̃t] *a* vivacious; dashing.
séminaire [seminɛʀ] *nm* seminar; (REL) seminary; **séminariste** *nm* seminarist.
semi-remorque [səmiʀəmɔʀk(ə)] *nf* trailer // *nm* articulated lorry.
semis [səmi] *nm* (*terrain*) seedbed, seed plot; (*plante*) seedling.
sémite [semit] *a* Semitic.
sémitique [semitik] *a* Semitic.
semoir [səmwaʀ] *nm* seed-bag; seeder.
semonce [səmɔ̃s] *nf* reprimand; **coup de ~** warning shot across the bows.
semoule [səmul] *nf* semolina.
sempiternel, le [sɛ̃pitɛʀnɛl] *a* eternal, never-ending.
sénat [sena] *nm* Senate; **sénateur** *nm* Senator.
sénile [senil] *a* senile; **sénilité** *nf* senility.
sens [sɑ̃s] *nm* (PHYSIOL, *instinct*) sense; (*signification*) meaning, sense; (*direction*) direction // *nmpl* (*sensualité*) senses; **reprendre ses ~** to regain consciousness; **avoir le ~ des affaires/de la mesure** to have business sense/a sense of moderation; **ça n'a pas de ~** that doesn't make (any) sense; **dans le ~ des aiguilles d'une montre** clockwise; **~ commun** common sense; **~ dessus dessous** upside down; **~ interdit, ~ unique** one-way street.
sensation [sɑ̃sɑsjɔ̃] *nf* sensation; **faire ~** to cause a sensation, create a stir; **à ~** (*péj*) sensational; **sensationnel, le** *a* sensational; (*fig*) terrific.
sensé, e [sɑ̃se] *a* sensible.
sensibiliser [sɑ̃sibilize] *vt*: **~ qn à** to make sb sensitive to.
sensibilité [sɑ̃sibilite] *nf* sensitivity; (*affectivité, émotivité*) sensitivity, sensibility.
sensible [sɑ̃sibl(ə)] *a* sensitive; (*aux sens*) perceptible; (*appréciable*: *différence, progrès*) appreciable, noticeable; **~ à** sensitive to; **~ment** *ad* (*notablement*) appreciably, noticeably; (*à peu près*): **ils ont ~ment le même poids** they weigh approximately the same; **~rie** *nf* sentimentality, mawkishness; squeamishness.
sensitif, ive [sɑ̃sitif, -iv] *a* (*nerf*) sensory; (*personne*) oversensitive.
sensoriel, le [sɑ̃sɔʀjɛl] *a* sensory, sensorial.
sensualité [sɑ̃sɥalite] *nf* sensuality; sensuousness.
sensuel, le [sɑ̃sɥɛl] *a* sensual; sensuous.
sente [sɑ̃t] *nf* path.
sentence [sɑ̃tɑ̃s] *nf* (*jugement*) sentence; (*adage*) maxim; **sentencieux, euse** *a* sententious.
senteur [sɑ̃tœʀ] *nf* scent, perfume.
sentier [sɑ̃tje] *nm* path.
sentiment [sɑ̃timɑ̃] *nm* feeling; **recevez mes ~s respectueux** yours faithfully; **faire du ~** (*péj*) to be sentimental; **sentimental, e, aux** *a* sentimental; (*vie, aventure*) love *cpd*.
sentinelle [sɑ̃tinɛl] *nf* sentry; **en ~** on sentry duty; standing guard.
sentir [sɑ̃tiʀ] *vt* (*par l'odorat*) to smell; (*par le goût*) to taste; (*au toucher, fig*) to feel; (*répandre une odeur de*) to smell of; (: *ressemblance*) to smell like; (*avoir la saveur de*) to taste of; to taste like; (*fig*: *dénoter, annoncer*) to be indicative of; to smack of; to foreshadow // *vi* to smell; **~ mauvais** to smell bad; **se ~ bien** to feel good; **se ~ mal** (*être indisposé*) to feel unwell *ou* ill; **se ~ le courage/la force de faire** to feel brave/strong enough to do; **ne plus se ~ de joie** to be beside o.s. with joy; **il ne peut pas le ~** (*fam*) he can't stand him.
seoir [swaʀ]: **~ à** *vt* to become.
séparation [sepaʀɑsjɔ̃] *nf* separation; (*cloison*) division, partition; **~ de biens** division of property (*in marriage settlement*); **~ de corps** legal separation.
séparatisme [sepaʀatism(ə)] *nm* separatism.
séparé, e [sepaʀe] *a* (*appartements, pouvoirs*) separate; (*époux*) separated; **~ de** separate from; separated from; **~ment** *ad* separately.
séparer [sepaʀe] *vt* (*gén*) to separate; (*suj*: *divergences etc*) to divide; to drive apart; (: *différences, obstacles*) to stand between; (*détacher*): **~ qch de** to pull sth (off) from; (*dissocier*) to distinguish between; (*diviser*): **~ qch par** to divide sth (up) with; **~ une pièce en deux** to divide a room into two; **se ~** (*époux*) to separate, part; (*prendre congé*: *amis etc*) to part, leave each other; (*adversaires*) to separate; (*se diviser*: *route, tige etc*) to divide; (*se détacher*): **se ~ (de)** to split off (from); to come off; **se ~ de** (*époux*)

to separate *ou* part from; (*employé, objet personnel*) to part with.
sept [sɛt] *num* seven.
septembre [sɛptɑ̃bʀ(ə)] *nm* September.
septennat [sɛpetena] *nm* seven-year term (of office); seven-year reign.
septentrional, e, aux [sɛptɑ̃tʀijɔnal, -o] *a* northern.
septicémie [sɛptisemi] *nf* blood poisoning, septicaemia.
septième [sɛtjɛm] *num* seventh.
septique [sɛptik] *a*: **fosse ~** septic tank.
septuagénaire [sɛptɥaʒenɛʀ] *a, nm/f* septuagenarian.
sépulcre [sepylkʀ(ə)] *nm* sepulchre.
sépulture [sepyltyʀ] *nf* burial; burial place, grave.
séquelles [sekɛl] *nfpl* after-effects; (*fig*) aftermath *sg*; consequences.
séquence [sekɑ̃s] *nf* sequence.
séquestre [sekɛstʀ(ə)] *nm* impoundment; **mettre sous ~** to impound.
séquestrer [sekɛstʀe] *vt* (*personne*) to confine illegally; (*biens*) to impound.
serai *etc vb voir* **être**.
serein, e [səʀɛ̃, -ɛn] *a* serene; (*jugement*) dispassionate.
sérénade [seʀenad] *nf* serenade; (*fam*) hullabaloo.
sérénité [seʀenite] *nf* serenity.
serez *vb voir* **être**.
serf, serve [sɛʀ, sɛʀv(ə)] *nm/f* serf.
serge [sɛʀʒ(ə)] *nf* serge.
sergent [sɛʀʒɑ̃] *nm* sergeant; **~-chef** *nm* staff sergeant; **~-major** *nm* ≈ quartermaster sergeant.
sériciculture [seʀisikyltyʀ] *nf* silkworm breeding, sericulture.
série [seʀi] *nf* (*de questions, d'accidents*) series *inv*; (*de clés, casseroles, outils*) set; (*catégorie*: SPORT) rank; class; **en ~** in quick succession; (COMM) mass *cpd*; **de ~** *a* standard; **hors ~** (COMM) custom-built; (*fig*) outstanding; **~ noire** *nm* (crime) thriller; **sérier** *vt* to classify, sort out.
sérieusement [seʀjøzmɑ̃] *ad* seriously; reliably; responsibly; **~?** do you mean it?, are you talking in earnest?
sérieux, euse [seʀjø, -øz] *a* serious; (*élève, employé*) reliable, responsible; (*client, maison*) reliable, dependable; (*offre, proposition*) genuine, serious; (*grave, sévère*) serious, solemn; (*maladie, situation*) serious, grave // *nm* seriousness; reliability; **garder son ~** to keep a straight face; **manquer de ~** not to be very responsible (*ou* reliable); **prendre qch/qn au ~** to take sth/sb seriously.
serin [səʀɛ̃] *nm* canary.
seriner [səʀine] *vt*: **~ qch à qn** to drum sth into sb.
seringue [səʀɛ̃g] *nf* syringe.
serions *vb voir* **être**.
serment [sɛʀmɑ̃] *nm* (*juré*) oath; (*promesse*) pledge, vow; **faire le ~ de** to take a vow to, swear to; **sous ~** on *ou* under oath.
sermon [sɛʀmɔ̃] *nm* sermon; (*péj*) sermon, lecture.
serpe [sɛʀp(ə)] *nf* billhook.
serpent [sɛʀpɑ̃] *nm* snake; **~ à sonnettes** rattlesnake.
serpenter [sɛʀpɑ̃te] *vi* to wind.
serpentin [sɛʀpɑ̃tɛ̃] *nm* (*tube*) coil; (*ruban*) streamer.
serpillière [sɛʀpijɛʀ] *nf* floorcloth.
serrage [sɛʀaʒ] *nm* tightening; **collier de ~** clamp.
serre [sɛʀ] *nf* (AGR) greenhouse; **~s** *nfpl* (*griffes*) claws, talons; **~ chaude** hothouse.
serré, e [seʀe] *a* (*tissu*) closely woven; (*réseau*) dense; (*écriture*) close; (*habits*) tight; (*fig*: *lutte, match*) tight, close-fought; (*passagers etc*) (tightly) packed.
serre-livres [sɛʀlivʀ(ə)] *nm inv* book ends *pl*.
serrement [sɛʀmɑ̃] *nm*: **~ de main** handshake; **~ de cœur** pang of anguish.
serrer [seʀe] *vt* (*tenir*) to grip *ou* hold tight; (*comprimer, coincer*) to squeeze; (*poings, mâchoires*) to clench; (*suj*: *vêtement*) to be too tight for; to fit tightly; (*rapprocher*) to close up, move closer together; (*ceinture, nœud, frein, vis*) to tighten // *vi*: **~ à droite** to keep to the right; to move into the right-hand lane; **se ~** (*se rapprocher*) to squeeze up; **se ~ contre qn** to huddle up to sb; **se ~ les coudes** to stick together, back one another up; **~ la main à qn** to shake sb's hand; **~ qn dans ses bras** to hug sb, clasp sb in one's arms; **~ la gorge à qn** (*suj*: *chagrin*) to bring a lump to sb's throat; **~ qn de près** to follow close behind sb; **~ le trottoir** to hug the kerb; **~ sa droite** to keep well to the right; **~ la vis à qn** to crack down harder on sb.
serre-tête [sɛʀtɛt] *nm inv* (*bandeau*) headband; (*bonnet*) skullcap.
serrure [seʀyʀ] *nf* lock.
serrurerie [seʀyʀʀi] *nf* (*métier*) locksmith's trade; **~ d'art** ornamental ironwork.
serrurier [seʀyʀje] *nm* locksmith.
sert *etc vb voir* **servir**.
sertir [sɛʀtiʀ] *vt* (*pierre*) to set; (*pièces métalliques*) to crimp.
sérum [seʀɔm] *nm* serum; **~ antivenimeux** snakebite serum; **~ sanguin** (blood) serum; **~ de vérité** truth drug.
servage [sɛʀvaʒ] *nm* serfdom.
servant [sɛʀvɑ̃] *nm* server.
servante [sɛʀvɑ̃t] *nf* (maid)servant.
serve [sɛʀv] *nf voir* **serf**.
serveur, euse [sɛʀvœʀ, -øz] *nm/f* waiter/waitress.
serviable [sɛʀvjabl(ə)] *a* obliging, willing to help.
service [sɛʀvis] *nm* (*gén*) service; (*série de repas*): **premier ~** first sitting; (*pourboire*) service (charge); (*assortiment de vaisselle*) set, service; (*bureau*: *de la vente etc*) department, section; (*travail*): **pendant le ~** on duty; **~s** *nmpl* (*travail*, ÉCON) services; **faire le ~** to serve; **être en ~ chez qn** (*domestique*) to be in sb's service; **être au ~ de** (*patron, patrie*) to be in the service of; **être au ~ de qn** (*collaborateur, voiture*) to be at sb's service; **rendre ~**

à to help; **il aime rendre ~** he likes to help; **rendre un ~ à qn** to do sb a favour; **heures de ~** hours of duty; **être de ~** to be on duty; **avoir 25 ans de ~** to have completed 25 years' service; **être/mettre en ~** to be in/put into service *ou* operation; **~ à thé/café** tea/coffee set *ou* service; **~ après vente** after-sales service; **en ~ commandé** on an official assignment; **~ funèbre** funeral service; **~ militaire** military service; **~ d'ordre** police (*ou* stewards) in charge of maintaining order; **~s secrets** secret service *sg*.

serviette [sɛʀvjɛt] *nf* (*de table*) (table) napkin, serviette; (*de toilette*) towel; (*porte-documents*) briefcase; **~ hygiénique** sanitary towel *ou* pad; **~-éponge** *nf* terry towel.

servile [sɛʀvil] *a* servile.

servir [sɛʀviʀ] *vt* (*gén*) to serve; (*dîneur: au restaurant*) to wait on; (*client: au magasin*) to serve, attend to; (*fig: aider*): **~ qn** to aid sb; to serve sb's interests; to stand sb in good stead; (*COMM: rente*) to pay // *vi* (*TENNIS*) to serve; (*CARTES*) to deal; **se ~** (*prendre d'un plat*) to help o.s.; **se ~ de** (*plat*) to help o.s. to; (*voiture, outil, relations*) to use; **~ à qn** (*diplôme, livre*) to be of use to sb; **ça m'a servi pour faire** it was useful to me when I did; I used it to do; **~ à qch/faire** (*outil etc*) to be used for sth/doing; **ça peut ~** it may come in handy; **ça peut encore ~** it can still be used (*ou* of use); **à quoi cela sert-il (de faire)?** what's the use (of doing)?; **cela ne sert à rien** it's no use; **~ (à qn) de** to serve as (for sb); **~ la messe** to serve Mass; **~ à dîner (à qn)** to serve dinner (to sb).

serviteur [sɛʀvitœʀ] *nm* servant.

servitude [sɛʀvityd] *nf* servitude; (*fig*) constraint; (*JUR*) easement.

servo... [sɛʀvo] *préfixe*: **~frein** servo (-assisted) brake.

ses [se] *dét voir* **son**.

session [sesjɔ̃] *nf* session.

set [sɛt] *nm* set.

seuil [sœj] *nm* doorstep; (*fig*) threshold; **sur le ~ de sa maison** in the doorway of his house, on his doorstep; **au ~ de** (*fig*) on the threshold *ou* brink *ou* edge of.

seul, e [sœl] *a* (*sans compagnie, en isolation*) alone; (*avec nuance affective: isolé*) lonely; (*unique*): **un ~ livre** only one book, a single book; **le ~ livre** the only book; **~ ce livre, ce livre ~** this book alone, only this book // *ad* (*vivre*) alone, on one's own; **parler tout ~** to talk to oneself; **faire qch (tout) ~** to do sth (all) on one's own *ou* (all) by oneself // *nm, nf* **il en reste un(e) ~(e)** there's only one left; **à lui (tout) ~** single-handed, on his own.

seulement [sœlmɑ̃] *ad* (*pas davantage*): **~ 5, 5 ~** only 5; (*exclusivement*): **~ eux** only them, them alone; (*pas avant*): **~ hier/à 10h** only yesterday/at 10 o'clock; **non ~ ... mais aussi** *ou* **encore** not only ... but also.

sève [sɛv] *nf* sap.

sévère [sevɛʀ] *a* severe; **sévérité** *nf* severity.

sévices [sevis] *nmpl* (physical) cruelty *sg*, ill treatment *sg*.

sévir [seviʀ] *vi* (*punir*) to use harsh measures, crack down; (*suj: fléau*) to rage, be rampant; **~ contre** (*abus*) to deal ruthlessly with, crack down on.

sevrer [səvʀe] *vt* to wean; (*fig*): **~ qn de** to deprive sb of.

sexagénaire [sɛgzaʒenɛʀ] *a, nm/f* sexagenarian.

sexe [sɛks(ə)] *nm* sex; (*organe mâle*) member; **sexologue** *nm/f* sexologist, sex specialist.

sextant [sɛkstɑ̃] *nm* sextant.

sexualité [sɛksɥalite] *nf* sexuality.

sexué, e [sɛksɥe] *a* sexual.

sexuel, le [sɛksɥɛl] *a* sexual; **acte ~** sex act.

seyait *vb voir* **seoir**.

seyant, e [sɛjɑ̃, -ɑ̃t] *a* becoming.

shampooing [ʃɑ̃pwɛ̃] *nm* shampoo; **se faire un ~** to shampoo one's hair; **~ colorant** (colour) rinse.

short [ʃɔʀt] *nm* (pair of) shorts *pl*.

si [si] *nm* (*MUS*) B; (*en chantant la gamme*) si, se // *ad* (*oui*) yes; (*tellement*) so // *cj* if; **~ seulement** if only; **(tant et) ~ bien que** so much so that; **~ rapide qu'il soit** however fast he may be, fast though he is; **je me demande ~** I wonder if *ou* whether.

siamois, e [sjamwa, -waz] *a* Siamese; **frères/sœurs siamois/es** Siamese twins.

Sicile [sisil] *nf*: **la ~** Sicily; **sicilien, ne** *a* Sicilian.

sidéré, e [sideʀe] *a* staggered.

sidérurgie [sideʀyʀʒi] *nf* iron and steel industry.

siècle [sjɛkl(ə)] *nm* century; (*époque*) age; (*REL*): **le ~** the world.

sied [sje] *vb voir* **seoir**.

siège [sjɛʒ] *nm* seat; (*d'entreprise*) head office; (*d'organisation*) headquarters *pl*; (*MIL*) siege; **mettre le ~ devant** to besiege; **présentation par le ~** (*MÉD*) breech presentation; **~ baquet** bucket seat; **~ social** registered office.

siéger [sjeʒe] *vi* to sit.

sien, ne [sjɛ̃, sjɛn] *pronom*: **le(la) ~(ne), les ~s(~nes)** his; hers; its; **faire des ~nes** (*fam*) to be up to one's (usual) tricks; **les ~s** (*sa famille*) one's family.

siérait *etc vb voir* **seoir**.

sieste [sjɛst(ə)] *nf* (afternoon) snooze *ou* nap, siesta; **faire la ~** to have a snooze *ou* nap.

sieur [sjœʀ] *nm*: **le ~ Thomas** Mr Thomas; (*en plaisantant*) Master Thomas.

sifflant, e [siflɑ̃, -ɑ̃t] *a* (*bruit*) whistling; (*toux*) wheezing; **(consonne) ~e** sibilant.

sifflement [sifləmɑ̃] *nm* whistle, whistling *q*; hissing noise; whistling noise.

siffler [sifle] *vi* (*gén*) to whistle; (*avec un sifflet*) to blow (on) one's whistle; (*en parlant, dormant*) to wheeze; (*serpent, vapeur*) to hiss // *vt* (*chanson*) to whistle; (*chien etc*) to whistle for; (*fille*) to whistle at; (*pièce, orateur*) to hiss, boo; (*faute*) to blow one's whistle at; (*fin du match, départ*) to blow one's whistle for; (*fam: verre, bouteille*) to guzzle, knock back.

sifflet [siflɛ] *nm* whistle; **~s** *nmpl* (*de mécontentement*) whistles, boos; **coup de ~** whistle.
siffloter [siflɔte] *vi, vt* to whistle.
sigle [sigl(ə)] *nm* acronym, (set of) initials *pl.*
signal, aux [siɲal, -o] *nm* (*signe convenu, appareil*) signal; (*indice, écriteau*) sign; **donner le ~ de** to give the signal for; **~ d'alarme** alarm signal; **~ horaire** time signal; **signaux (lumineux)** (AUTO) traffic signals.
signalement [siɲalmɑ̃] *nm* description, particulars *pl.*
signaler [siɲale] *vt* to indicate; to announce; to report; (*faire remarquer*): **~ qch à qn/à qn que** to point out sth to sb/to sb that; **se ~ par** to distinguish o.s. by; **se ~ à l'attention de qn** to attract sb's attention.
signalétique [siɲaletik] *a*: **fiche ~** identification sheet.
signalisation [siɲalizɑsjɔ̃] *nf* signalling, signposting; signals *pl*, roadsigns *pl*; **panneau de ~** roadsign.
signaliser [siɲalize] *vt* to put up roadsigns on; to put signals on.
signataire [siɲatɛʀ] *nm/f* signatory.
signature [siɲatyʀ] *nf* signing; signature.
signe [siɲ] *nm* sign; (TYPO) mark; **c'est bon ~** it's a good sign; **faire un ~ de la main** to give a sign with one's hand; **faire ~ à qn** (*fig*) to get in touch with sb; **faire ~ à qn d'entrer** to motion (to) sb to come in; **en ~ de** as a sign *ou* mark of; **le ~ de la croix** the sign of the Cross; **~ de ponctuation** punctuation mark; **~ du zodiaque** sign of the zodiac.
signer [siɲe] *vt* to sign, **se ~** *vi* to cross o.s.
signet [siɲɛ] *nm* bookmark.
significatif, ive [siɲifikatif, -iv] *a* significant.
signification [siɲifikɑsjɔ̃] *nf* meaning.
signifier [siɲifje] *vt* (*vouloir dire*) to mean, signify; (*faire connaître*): **~ qch (à qn)** to make sth known (to sb); (JUR): **~ qch à qn** to serve notice of sth on sb.
silence [silɑ̃s] *nm* silence; (MUS) rest; **garder le ~** to keep silent, say nothing; **passer sous ~** to pass over (in silence); **réduire au ~** to silence; **silencieux, euse** *a* quiet, silent // *nm* silencer.
silex [silɛks] *nm* flint.
silhouette [silwɛt] *nf* outline, silhouette; (*lignes, contour*) outline; (*figure*) figure.
silicium [silisjɔm] *nm* silicon.
silicone [silikon] *nf* silicone.
silicose [silikoz] *nf* silicosis, dust disease.
sillage [sijaʒ] *nm* wake; (*fig*) trail.
sillon [sijɔ̃] *nm* furrow; (*de disque*) groove; **sillonner** *vt* to furrow; to cross, criss-cross.
silo [silo] *nm* silo.
simagrées [simagʀe] *nfpl* fuss *sg*; airs and graces.
simiesque [simjɛsk(ə)] *a* monkey-like, ape-like.
similaire [similɛʀ] *a* similar; **similarité** *nf* similarity; **simili...** *préfixe* imitation *cpd*, artificial; **similicuir** *nm* imitation leather; **similitude** *nf* similarity.
simple [sɛ̃pl(ə)] *a* (*gén*) simple; (*non multiple*) single; **~s** *nmpl* (MÉD) medicinal plants; **~ messieurs** (TENNIS) men's singles *sg*; **un ~ particulier** an ordinary citizen; **cela varie du ~ au double** it can double, it can be double the price *etc*; **~ course** *a* single; **~ d'esprit** *nm/f* simpleton; **~ soldat** private; **simplicité** *nf* simplicity; **simplifier** *vt* to simplify; **simpliste** *a* simplistic.
simulacre [simylakʀ(ə)] *nm* enactement; (*péj*): **un ~ de** a pretence of, a sham.
simulateur, trice [simylatœʀ, -tʀis] *nm/f* shammer, pretender; (*qui se prétend malade*) malingerer // *nm*: **~ de vol** flight simulator.
simulation [simylɑsjɔ̃] *nf* shamming, simulation; malingering.
simuler [simyle] *vt* to sham, simulate; (*suj: substance, revêtement*) to simulate.
simultané, e [simyltane] *a* simultaneous; **~ment** *ad* simultaneously.
sincère [sɛ̃sɛʀ] *a* sincere; genuine; heartfelt; **sincérité** *nf* sincerity.
sinécure [sinekyʀ] *nf* sinecure.
sine die [sinedje] *ad* sine die, indefinitely.
sine qua non [sinekwanɔn] *a*: **condition ~** indispensable condition.
singe [sɛ̃ʒ] *nm* monkey; (*de grande taille*) ape.
singer [sɛ̃ʒe] *vt* to ape, mimic.
singeries [sɛ̃ʒʀi] *nfpl* antics; (*simagrées*) airs and graces.
singulariser [sɛ̃gylaʀize] *vt* to mark out; **se ~** to call attention to o.s.
singularité [sɛ̃gylaʀite] *nf* peculiarity.
singulier, ière [sɛgylje, -jɛʀ] *a* remarkable, singular; (LING) singular // *nm* singular.
sinistre [sinistʀ(ə)] *a* sinister // *nm* (*incendie*) blaze; (*catastrophe*) disaster; (ASSURANCES) accident (*giving rise to a claim*); **sinistré, e** *a* disaster-stricken // *nm/f* disaster victim.
sino... [sino] *préfixe*: **~-indien** Sino-Indian, Chinese-Indian.
sinon [sinɔ̃] *cj* (*autrement, sans quoi*) otherwise, or else; (*sauf*) except, other than; (*si ce n'est*) if not.
sinueux, euse [sinɥø, -øz] *a* winding; (*fig*) tortuous; **sinuosités** *nfpl* winding *sg*, curves.
sinus [sinys] *nm* (ANAT) sinus; (GÉOM) sine; **sinusite** *nf* sinusitis, sinus infection.
sionisme [sjɔnism(ə)] *nm* Zionism.
siphon [sifɔ̃] *nm* (*tube, d'eau gazeuse*) siphon; (*d'évier etc*) U-bend; **siphonner** *vt* to siphon.
sire [siʀ] *nm* (*titre*): **S~** Sire; **un triste ~** an unsavoury individual.
sirène [siʀɛn] *nf* siren; **~ d'alarme** air-raid siren; fire alarm.
sirop [siʀo] *nm* (*à diluer: de fruit etc*) syrup, cordial; (*boisson*) cordial; (*pharmaceutique*) syrup, mixture; **~ de menthe** mint syrup *ou* cordial; **~ contre la toux** cough syrup *ou* mixture.
siroter [siʀɔte] *vt* to sip.

sis, e [si, siz] *a*: ~ **rue de la Paix** located in the rue de la Paix.
sismique [sismik] *a* seismic.
sismographe [sismɔgʀaf] *nm* seismograph.
sismologie [sismɔlɔʒi] *nf* seismology.
site [sit] *nm* (*paysage, environnement*) setting; (*d'une ville etc: emplacement*) site; ~ **(pittoresque)** beauty spot; ~**s touristiques** places of interest; ~**s naturels/historiques** natural/ historic sites.
sitôt [sito] *ad*: ~ **parti** as soon as he had left; **pas de** ~ not for a long time.
situation [sitɥasjɔ̃] *nf* (*gén*) situation; (*d'un édifice, d'une ville*) situation, position; location.
situé, e [sitɥe] *a*: **bien** ~ well situated, in a good location; ~ **à/près de** situated at/near.
situer [sitɥe] *vt* to site, situate; (*en pensée*) to set, place; **se** ~ *vi*: **se** ~ **à/près de** to be situated at/near.
six [sis] *num* six; **sixième** *num* sixth.
sketch [skɛtʃ] *nm* (variety) sketch.
ski [ski] *nm* (*objet*) ski; (*sport*) skiing; **faire du** ~ to ski; ~ **de fond** lang-lauf; ~ **nautique** water-skiing; ~ **de piste** downhill skiing; ~ **de randonnée** cross-country skiing; **skier** *vi* to ski; **skieur, euse** *nm/f* skier.
slalom [slalɔm] *nm* slalom; **faire du** ~ **entre** to slalom between; ~ **géant/spécial** giant/special slalom.
slave [slav] *a* Slav(onic), Slavic.
slip [slip] *nm* (*sous-vêtement*) pants *pl*, briefs *pl*; (*de bain: d'homme*) (bathing *ou* swimming) trunks *pl*; (: *du bikini*) (bikini) briefs *pl*.
slogan [slɔgɑ̃] *nm* slogan.
S.M.I.C., S.M.I.G. [smik, smig] *sigle m voir* **salaire**.
smoking [smɔkiŋ] *nm* dinner *ou* evening suit.
snack [snak] *nm* snack bar.
S.N.C.F. *sigle f = société nationale des chemins de fer français*, ≈ British Rail.
snob [snɔb] *a* snobbish // *nm/f* snob; ~**isme** *nm* snobbery.
sobre [sɔbʀ(ə)] *a* temperate, abstemious; (*élégance, style*) sober; ~ **de** (*gestes, compliments*) sparing of; **sobriété** *nf* temperance, abstemiousness; sobriety.
sobriquet [sɔbʀikɛ] *nm* nickname.
soc [sɔk] *nm* ploughshare.
sociable [sɔsjabl(ə)] *a* sociable.
social, e, aux [sɔsjal, -o] *a* social.
socialisme [sɔsjalism(ə)] *nm* socialism; **socialiste** *nm/f* socialist.
sociétaire [sɔsjetɛʀ] *nm/f* member.
société [sɔsjete] *nf* society; (*sportive*) club; (*COMM*) company; **la bonne** ~ polite society; **la** ~ **d'abondance/de consommation** the affluent/consumer society; ~ **anonyme (S.A.)** ≈ limited company; ~ **à responsabilité limitée (S.A.R.L.)** *type of limited liability company (with non negotiable shares)*.
sociologie [sɔsjɔlɔʒi] *nf* sociology; **sociologue** *nm/f* sociologist.
socle [sɔkl(ə)] *nm* (*de colonne, statue*) plinth, pedestal; (*de lampe*) base.
socquette [sɔkɛt] *nf* ankle sock.
sodium [sɔdjɔm] *nm* sodium.
sœur [sœʀ] *nf* sister; (*religieuse*) nun, sister; ~ **Élisabeth** (*REL*) Sister Elizabeth.
soi [swa] *pronom* oneself; **cela va de** ~ that *ou* it goes without saying, it stands to reason; ~**-disant** *a inv* so-called // *ad* supposedly.
soie [swa] *nf* silk; (*de porc, sanglier: poil*) bristle; ~**rie** *nf* (*industrie*) silk trade; (*tissu*) silk.
soif [swaf] *nf* thirst; (*fig*): ~ **de** thirst *ou* craving for; **avoir** ~ to be thirsty; **donner** ~ **à qn** to make sb thirsty.
soigné, e [swaɲe] *a* (*tenue*) well-groomed, neat; (*travail*) careful, meticulous; (*fam*) whopping; stiff.
soigner [swaɲe] *vt* (*malade, maladie: suj: docteur*) to treat; (*suj: infirmière, mère*) to nurse, look after; (*blessé*) to tend; (*travail, détails*) to take care over; (*jardin, chevelure, invités*) to look after; **soigneur** *nm* (*CYCLISME, FOOTBALL*) trainer; (*BOXE*) second.
soigneusement [swaɲøzmɑ̃] *ad* carefully.
soigneux, euse [swaɲø, -øz] *a* (*propre*) tidy, neat; (*méticuleux*) painstaking, careful; ~ **de** careful with.
soi-même [swamɛm] *pronom* oneself.
soin [swɛ̃] *nm* (*application*) care; (*propreté, ordre*) tidiness, neatness; (*responsabilité*): **le** ~ **de qch** the care of sth; ~**s** *nmpl* (*à un malade, blessé*) treatment *sg*, medical attention *sg*; (*attentions, prévenance*) care and attention *sg*; (*hygiène*) care *sg*; ~**s de la chevelure/de beauté** hair-/beauty care; **les** ~**s du ménage** the care of the home; **avoir** *ou* **prendre** ~ **de** to take care of, look after; **avoir** *ou* **prendre** ~ **de faire** to take care to do; **sans** ~ *a* careless; untidy; **les premiers** ~**s** first aid *sg*; **aux bons** ~**s de** c/o, care of.
soir [swaʀ] *nm, ad* evening; **ce** ~ this evening, tonight; **demain** ~ tomorrow evening, tomorrow night.
soirée [swaʀe] *nf* evening; (*réception*) party; **donner en** ~ (*film, pièce*) to give an evening performance of.
soit [swa] *vb voir* **être**; ~ **un triangle ABC** let ABC be a triangle // *cj* (*à savoir*) namely, to wit; (*ou*): ~ **...** ~ either ... or // *ad* so be it, very well; ~ **que ...** ~ **que** *ou* **ou que** whether ... or whether.
soixantaine [swasɑ̃tɛn] *nf*: **une** ~ **(de)** sixty or so, about sixty.
soixante [swasɑ̃t] *num* sixty.
soja [sɔʒa] *nm* soya; (*graines*) soya beans *pl*; **germes de** ~ beansprouts.
sol [sɔl] *nm* ground; (*de logement*) floor; (*revêtement*) flooring *q*; (*territoire, AGR, GÉO*) soil; (*MUS*) G; (*en chantant la gamme*) so(h).
solaire [sɔlɛʀ] *a* solar, sun *cpd*.
solarium [sɔlaʀjɔm] *nm* solarium.
soldat [sɔlda] *nm* soldier; **S**~ **inconnu** Unknown Warrior *ou* Soldier; ~ **de plomb** tin *ou* toy soldier.
solde [sɔld(ə)] *nf* pay // *nm* (*COMM*) balance; ~**s** *nmpl ou nfpl* (*COMM*) sale goods; sales; **à la** ~ **de qn** (*péj*) in sb's

pay ; ~ **à payer** balance outstanding ; **en** ~ at sale price ; **aux** ~**s** at the sales.
solder [sɔlde] *vt* (*compte*) to settle ; (*marchandise*) to sell at sale price, sell off ; **se** ~ **par** (*fig*) to end in ; **article soldé (à) 10 F** item reduced to 10 F.
sole [sɔl] *nf* sole *inv.*
soleil [sɔlɛj] *nm* sun ; (*lumière*) sun(light) ; (*temps ensoleillé*) sun(shine) ; (*feu d'artifice*) Catherine wheel ; (*acrobatie*) grand circle ; (BOT) sunflower ; **il y a** *ou* **il fait du** ~ it's sunny ; **au** ~ in the sun ; **le** ~ **de minuit** the midnight sun.
solennel, le [sɔlanɛl] *a* solemn ; ceremonial ; **solenniser** *vt* to solemnize ; **solennité** *nf* (*d'une fête*) solemnity ; (*fête*) grand occasion.
solfège [sɔlfɛʒ] *nm* rudiments *pl* of music.
soli [sɔli] *pl de* **solo**.
solidaire [sɔlidɛʀ] *a* (*personnes*) who stand together, who show solidarity ; (*pièces mécaniques*) interdependent ; **être** ~ **de** (*collègues*) to stand by ; (*mécanisme*) to be bound up with, be dependent on ; **se solidariser avec** to show solidarity with ; **solidarité** *nf* solidarity ; interdependence ; **par solidarité (avec)** (*cesser le travail etc*) in sympathy (with).
solide [sɔlid] *a* solid ; (*mur, maison, meuble*) solid, sturdy ; (*connaissances, argument*) sound ; (*personne, estomac*) robust, sturdy // *nm* solid ; **solidifier** *vt*, **se solidifier** *vi* to solidify ; **solidité** *nf* solidity ; sturdiness.
soliloque [sɔlilɔk] *nm* soliloquy.
soliste [sɔlist(ə)] *nm/f* soloist.
solitaire [sɔlitɛʀ] *a* (*sans compagnie*) solitary, lonely ; (*isolé*) solitary, isolated, lone ; (*désert*) lonely // *nm/f* recluse ; loner // *nm* (*diamant, jeu*) solitaire.
solitude [sɔlityd] *nf* loneliness ; (*paix*) solitude.
solive [sɔliv] *nf* joist.
sollicitations [sɔlisitɑsjɔ̃] *nfpl* entreaties, appeals ; enticements ; promptings.
solliciter [sɔlisite] *vt* (*personne*) to appeal to ; (*emploi, faveur*) to seek ; (*moteur*) to prompt ; (*suj*: *occupations, attractions etc*): ~ **qn** to appeal to sb's curiosity *etc* ; to entice sb ; to make demands on sb's time ; ~ **qn de faire** to appeal to *ou* request sb to do.
sollicitude [sɔlisityd] *nf* concern.
solo [sɔlo] *nm, pl* **soli** [sɔli] (MUS) solo (*pl* s *or* soli).
solstice [sɔlstis] *nm* solstice.
soluble [sɔlybl(ə)] *a* soluble.
solution [sɔlysjɔ̃] *nf* solution ; ~ **de continuité** solution of continuity, gap ; ~ **de facilité** easy way out.
solvabilité [sɔlvabilite] *nf* solvency.
solvable [sɔlvabl(ə)] *a* solvent.
solvant [sɔlvɑ̃] *nm* solvent.
sombre [sɔ̃bʀ(ə)] *a* dark ; (*fig*) sombre, gloomy.
sombrer [sɔ̃bʀe] *vi* (*bateau*) to sink, go down ; ~ **dans** (*misère, désespoir*) to sink into.
sommaire [sɔmɛʀ] *a* (*simple*) basic ; (*expéditif*) summary // *nm* summary.
sommation [sɔmɑsjɔ̃] *nf* (JUR) summons *sg* ; (*avant de faire feu*) warning.
somme [sɔm] *nf* (MATH) sum ; (*fig*) amount ; (*argent*) sum, amount // *nm*: **faire un** ~ to have a (short) nap ; **faire la** ~ **de** to add up ; **en** ~ *ad* all in all ; ~ **toute** *ad* when all's said and done.
sommeil [sɔmɛj] *nm* sleep ; **avoir** ~ to be sleepy ; **avoir le** ~ **léger** to be a light sleeper ; **en** ~ (*fig*) dormant ; **sommeiller** *vi* to doze ; (*fig*) to lie dormant.
sommelier [sɔməlje] *nm* wine waiter.
sommer [sɔme] *vt*: ~ **qn de faire** to command *ou* order sb to do ; (JUR) to summon sb to do.
sommes *vb voir aussi* **être**.
sommet [sɔmɛ] *nm* top ; (*d'une montagne*) summit, top ; (*fig*: *de la perfection, gloire*) height ; (GÉOM: *d'angle*) vertex (*pl* vertices).
sommier [sɔmje] *nm*: ~ **(à ressorts)** springing *q* ; (interior-sprung) divan base ; ~ **métallique** mesh-springing ; mesh-sprung divan base.
sommité [sɔmite] *nf* prominent person, leading light.
somnambule [sɔmnɑ̃byl] *nm/f* sleepwalker.
somnifère [sɔmnifɛʀ] *nm* sleeping drug (*ou* pill).
somnolent, e [sɔmnɔlɑ̃, -ɑ̃t] *a* sleepy, drowsy.
somnoler [sɔmnɔle] *vi* to doze.
somptuaire [sɔ̃ptɥɛʀ] *a*: **lois** ~**s** sumptuary laws ; **dépenses** ~**s** extravagant expenditure *sg*.
somptueux, euse [sɔ̃ptɥø, -øz] *a* sumptuous ; lavish.
son [sɔ̃], **sa** [sa], *pl* **ses** [se] *dét* (*antécédent humain mâle*) his ; (: *femelle*) her ; (: *valeur indéfinie*) one's, his/her ; (: *non humain*) its ; *voir note sous* **il**.
son [sɔ̃] *nm* sound ; (*résidu*) bran.
sonate [sɔnat] *nf* sonata.
sondage [sɔ̃daʒ] *nm* (*de terrain*) boring, drilling ; (*mer, atmosphère*) sounding ; probe ; (*enquête*) survey, sounding out of opinion ; ~ **(d'opinion)** (opinion) poll.
sonde [sɔ̃d] *nf* (NAVIG) lead *ou* sounding line ; (MÉTÉOROLOGIE) sonde ; (MÉD) probe ; catheter ; feeding tube ; (TECH) borer, driller ; (*pour fouiller etc*) probe ; ~ **à avalanche** pole (*for probing snow and locating victims*) ; ~ **spatiale** probe.
sonder [sɔ̃de] *vt* (NAVIG) to sound ; (*atmosphère, plaie, bagages etc*) to probe ; (TECH) to bore, drill ; (*fig*) to sound out ; to probe.
songe [sɔ̃ʒ] *nm* dream.
songer [sɔ̃ʒe] *vi* to dream ; ~ **à** (*rêver à*) to muse over, think over ; (*penser à*) to think of ; (*envisager*) to contemplate, think of ; to consider ; ~ **que** to consider that ; to think that ; **songerie** *nf* reverie ; **songeur, euse** *a* pensive.
sonnailles [sɔnɑj] *nfpl* jingle of bells.
sonnant, e [sɔnɑ̃, -ɑ̃t] *a*: **en espèces** ~**es et trébuchantes** in coin of the realm ; **à 8 heures** ~**es** on the stroke of 8.
sonné, e [sɔne] *a* (*fam*) cracked ; **il est midi** ~ it's gone twelve ; **il a quarante ans bien** ~**s** he's well into his forties.
sonner [sɔne] *vi* to ring // *vt* (*cloche*) to ring ; (*glas, tocsin*) to sound ; (*portier,*

infirmière) to ring for; (*messe*) to ring the bell for; (*fam*: *suj*: *choc, coup*) to knock out; ~ **du clairon** to sound the bugle; ~ **faux** (*instrument*) to sound out of tune; (*rire*) to ring false; ~ **les heures** to strike the hours; **minuit vient de** ~ midnight has just struck; ~ **chez qn** to ring sb's doorbell, ring at sb's door.

sonnerie [sɔnʀi] *nf* (*son*) ringing; (*sonnette*) bell; (*mécanisme d'horloge*) striking mechanism; ~ **d'alarme** alarm bell; ~ **de clairon** bugle call.

sonnet [sɔnɛ] *nm* sonnet.

sonnette [sɔnɛt] *nf* bell; ~ **d'alarme** alarm bell; ~ **de nuit** night-bell.

sono [sɔno] *nf abr de* **sonorisation**.

sonore [sɔnɔʀ] *a* (*voix*) sonorous, ringing; (*salle, métal*) resonant; (*ondes, film, signal*) sound *cpd*; (LING) voiced.

sonorisation [sɔnɔʀizɑsjɔ̃] *nf* (*installations*) public address system, P.A. system.

sonoriser [sɔnɔʀize] *vt* (*film, spectacle*) to add the sound track to; (*salle*) to fit with a public address system.

sonorité [sɔnɔʀite] *nf* (*de piano, violon*) tone; (*de voix, mot*) sonority; (*d'une salle*) resonance; acoustics *pl*.

sont *vb voir* **être**.

sophistiqué, e [sɔfistike] *a* sophisticated.

soporifique [sɔpɔʀifik] *a* soporific.

sorbet [sɔʀbɛ] *nm* water ice, sorbet.

sorcellerie [sɔʀsɛlʀi] *nf* witchcraft *q*, sorcery *q*.

sorcier, ière [sɔʀsje, -jɛʀ] *nm/f* sorcerer/witch *ou* sorceress.

sordide [sɔʀdid] *a* sordid; squalid.

sornettes [sɔʀnɛt] *nfpl* twaddle *sg*.

sort [sɔʀ] *nm* (*fortune, destinée*) fate; (*condition, situation*) lot; (*magique*) curse, spell; **le** ~ **en est jeté** the die is cast; **tirer au** ~ to draw lots; **tirer qch au** ~ to draw lots for sth.

sorte [sɔʀt(ə)] *nf* sort, kind; **de la** ~ *ad* in that way; **de** ~ **à** so as to, in order to; **de (telle)** ~ **que, en** ~ **que** so that; so much so that.

sortie [sɔʀti] *nf* (*issue*) way out, exit; (MIL) sortie; (*fig*: *verbale*) outburst; sally; (*promenade*) outing; (*le soir*: *au restaurant etc*) night out; (COMM: *somme*): ~**s** items of expenditure; outgoings *sans sg*; **à sa** ~ as he went out *ou* left; **à la** ~ **de l'école/l'usine** (*moment*) after school/work; when school/the factory comes out; (*lieu*) at the school/factory gates; **à la** ~ **de ce nouveau modèle** when this new model comes out, when they bring out this new model; ~ **de bain** (*vêtement*) bathrobe; **'**~ **de camions'** 'vehicle exit', 'lorries turning', ~ **de secours** emergency exit.

sortilège [sɔʀtilɛʒ] *nm* (magic) spell.

sortir [sɔʀtiʀ] *vi* (*gén*) to come out; (*partir, se promener, aller au spectacle etc*) to go out; (*numéro gagnant*) to come up // *vt* (*gén*) to take out; (*produit, ouvrage, modèle*) to bring out; (*boniments, incongruités*) to come out with; (*fam*: *expulser*) to throw out; ~ **qch de** to take sth out of; ~ **de** (*gén*) to leave; (*endroit*) to go (*ou* come) out of, leave; (*rainure etc*) to come out of; (*cadre, compétence*) to be outside; (*provenir de*: *famille etc*) to come from; **se** ~ **de** (*affaire, situation*) to get out of; **s'en** ~ (*malade*) to pull through; (*d'une difficulté etc*) to come through all right; to get through, be able to manage.

S.O.S. *sigle m* mayday, SOS.

sosie [sɔzi] *nm* double.

sot, sotte [so, sɔt] *a* silly, foolish // *nm/f* fool; **sottise** *nf* silliness, foolishness; silly *ou* foolish thing (to do *ou* say).

sou [su] *nm*: **près de ses** ~**s** tight-fisted; **sans le** ~ penniless; **pas un** ~ **de bon sens** not a scrap *ou* an ounce of good sense.

soubassement [subɑsmɑ̃] *nm* base.

soubresaut [subʀəso] *nm* start; jolt.

soubrette [subʀɛt] *nf* soubrette, maidservant.

souche [suʃ] *nf* (*d'arbre*) stump; (*de carnet*) counterfoil, stub; **de vieille** ~ of old stock.

souci [susi] *nm* (*inquiétude*) worry; (*préoccupation*) concern; (BOT) marigold; **se faire du** ~ to worry; **avoir (le)** ~ **de** to have concern for.

soucier [susje]: **se** ~ **de** *vt* to care about.

soucieux, euse [susjø, -øz] *a* concerned, worried; ~ **de** concerned about; **peu** ~ **de/que** caring little about/whether.

soucoupe [sukup] *nf* saucer; ~ **volante** flying saucer.

soudain, e [sudɛ̃, -ɛn] *a* (*douleur, mort*) sudden // *ad* suddenly, all of a sudden; **soudainement** *ad* suddenly; **soudaineté** *nf* suddenness.

soude [sud] *nf* soda.

soudé, e [sude] *a* (*fig*: *pétales, organes*) joined (together).

souder [sude] *vt* (*avec fil à souder*) to solder; (*par soudure autogène*) to weld; (*fig*) to bind *ou* knit together; to fuse (together).

soudoyer [sudwaje] *vt* (*péj*) to bribe, buy over.

soudure [sudyʀ] *nf* soldering; welding; (*joint*) soldered joint; weld.

souffert, e [sufɛʀ, -ɛʀt(ə)] *pp de* **souffrir**.

souffle [sufl(ə)] *nm* (*en expirant*) breath; (*en soufflant*) puff, blow; (*respiration*) breathing; (*d'explosion, de ventilateur*) blast; (*du vent*) blowing; (*fig*) inspiration; **avoir du/manquer de** ~ to have a lot of/be short of breath; **être à bout de** ~ to be out of breath; **avoir le** ~ **court** to be short-winded; **un** ~ **d'air** *ou* **de vent** a breath of air, a puff of wind.

soufflé, e [sufle] *a* (CULIN) soufflé; (*fam*: *ahuri, stupéfié*) staggered // *nm* (CULIN) soufflé.

souffler [sufle] *vi* (*gén*) to blow; (*haleter*) to puff (and blow) // *vt* (*feu, bougie*) to blow out; (*chasser*: *poussière etc*) to blow away; (TECH: *verre*) to blow; (*suj*: *explosion*) to destroy (with its blast); (*dire*): ~ **qch à qn** to whisper sth to sb; (*fam*: *voler*): ~ **qch à qn** to nick sth from sb; ~ **son rôle à qn** to prompt sb; **laisser** ~ **qn** (*fig*) to give sb a breather.

soufflet [suflɛ] *nm* (*instrument*) bellows *pl*; (*entre wagons*) vestibule; (*gifle*) slap (in the face).

souffleur, euse [suflœʀ, -øz] *nm/f* (THÉÂTRE) prompter.
souffrance [sufʀɑ̃s] *nf* suffering; **en ~** (*marchandise*) awaiting delivery; (*affaire*) pending.
souffrant, e [sufʀɑ̃, -ɑ̃t] *a* unwell.
souffre-douleur [sufʀədulœʀ] *nm inv* whipping boy, underdog.
souffreteux, euse [sufʀətø, -øz] *a* sickly.
souffrir [sufʀiʀ] *vi* to suffer; to be in pain // *vt* to suffer, endure; (*supporter*) to bear, stand; (*admettre*: *exception etc*) to allow *ou* admit of; **~ de** (*maladie, froid*) to suffer from; **~ des dents** to have trouble with one's teeth; **faire ~ qn** (*suj*: *personne*) to make sb suffer; (: *dents, blessure etc*) to hurt sb.
soufre [sufʀ(ə)] *nm* sulphur.
souhait [swɛ] *nm* wish; **tous nos ~s de** good wishes *ou* our best wishes for; **riche** *etc* **à ~** as rich *etc* as one could wish; **à vos ~s!** bless you!
souhaitable [swɛtabl(ə)] *a* desirable.
souhaiter [swete] *vt* to wish for; **~ le bonjour à qn** to bid sb good day; **~ la bonne année à qn** to wish sb a happy New Year.
souiller [suje] *vt* to dirty, soil; (*fig*) to sully, tarnish; **souillure** *nf* stain.
soûl, e [su, sul] *a* drunk // *nm*: **boire tout son ~** to drink one's fill.
soulagement [sulaʒmɑ̃] *nm* relief.
soulager [sulaʒe] *vt* to relieve.
soûler [sule] *vt*: **~ qn** to get sb drunk; (*suj*: *boisson*) to make sb drunk; (*fig*) to make sb's head spin *ou* reel; **se ~** to get drunk; **se ~ de** (*fig*) to intoxicate o.s. with; **soûlerie** *nf* (*péj*) drunken binge.
soulèvement [sulɛvmɑ̃] *nm* uprising; (GÉO) upthrust.
soulever [sulve] *vt* to lift; (*vagues, poussière*) to send up; (*peuple*) to stir up (to revolt); (*enthousiasme*) to arouse; (*question, débat*) to raise; **se ~** *vi* (*peuple*) to rise up; (*personne couchée*) to lift o.s. up; **cela me soulève le cœur** it makes me feel sick.
soulier [sulje] *nm* shoe; **~s plats/à talons** flat/heeled shoes.
souligner [suliɲe] *vt* to underline; (*fig*) to emphasize; to stress.
soumettre [sumɛtʀ] *vt* (*pays*) to subject, subjugate; (*rebelle*) to put down, subdue; **~ qn/qch à** to subject sb/sth to; **~ qch à qn** (*projet etc*) to submit sth to sb; **se ~ (à)** (*se rendre, obéir*) to submit (to); **se ~ à** (*formalités etc*) to submit to; (*régime etc*) to submit o.s. to.
soumis, e [sumi, -iz] *a* submissive; **revenus ~ à l'impôt** taxable income.
soumission [sumisjɔ̃] *nf* (*voir se soumettre*) submission; (*docilité*) submissiveness; (COMM) tender.
soupape [supap] *nf* valve; **~ de sûreté** safety valve.
soupçon [supsɔ̃] *nm* suspicion; (*petite quantité*): **un ~ de** a hint *ou* touch of; **soupçonner** *vt* to suspect; **soupçonneux, euse** *a* suspicious.
soupe [sup] *nf* soup; **~ au lait** *a inv* quick-tempered; **~ à l'oignon/de poisson** onion/fish soup; **~ populaire** soup kitchen.
soupente [supɑ̃t] *nf* cupboard under the stairs.
souper [supe] *vi* to have supper // *nm* supper; **avoir soupé de** (*fam*) to be sick and tired of.
soupeser [supəze] *vt* to weigh in one's hand(s), feel the weight of; (*fig*) to weigh up.
soupière [supjɛʀ] *nf* (soup) tureen.
soupir [supiʀ] *nm* sigh; (MUS) crotchet rest; **rendre le dernier ~** to breathe one's last.
soupirail, aux [supiʀaj, -o] *nm* (small) basement window.
soupirant [supiʀɑ̃] *nm* (*péj*) suitor, wooer.
soupirer [supiʀe] *vi* to sigh; **~ après qch** to yearn for sth.
souple [supl(ə)] *a* supple; (*fig*: *règlement, caractère*) flexible; (: *démarche, taille*) lithe, supple; **souplesse** *nf* suppleness; flexibility.
source [suʀs(ə)] *nf* (*point d'eau*) spring; (*d'un cours d'eau, fig*) source; **prendre sa ~ à/dans** (*suj*: *cours d'eau*) to have its source at/in; **tenir qch de bonne ~/de ~ sûre** to have sth on good authority/from a reliable source; **~ thermale/d'eau minérale** hot *ou* thermal/mineral spring.
sourcier [suʀsje] *nm* water diviner.
sourcil [suʀsij] *nm* (eye)brow; **sourcilière** *af voir* **arcade**.
sourciller [suʀsije] *vi*: **sans ~** without turning a hair *ou* batting an eyelid.
sourcilleux, euse [suʀsijø, -øz] *a* pernickety.
sourd, e [suʀ, suʀd(ə)] *a* deaf; (*bruit, voix*) muffled; (*couleur*) muted; (*douleur*) dull; (*lutte*) silent, hidden; (LING) voiceless // *nm/f* deaf person.
sourdait *etc vb voir* **sourdre**.
sourdine [suʀdin] *nf* (MUS) mute; **en ~** *ad* softly, quietly; **mettre une ~ à** (*fig*) to tone down.
sourd-muet, sourde-muette [suʀmyɛ, suʀdmyɛt] *a* deaf-and-dumb // *nm/f* deaf-mute.
sourdre [suʀdʀ(ə)] *vi* to rise.
souriant, e [suʀjɑ̃, -ɑ̃t] *a* cheerful.
souricière [suʀisjɛʀ] *nf* mousetrap; (*fig*) trap.
sourire [suʀiʀ] *nm* smile // *vi* to smile; **~ à qn** to smile at sb; (*fig*) to appeal to sb; to smile on sb; **faire un ~ à qn** to give sb a smile; **garder le ~** to keep smiling.
souris [suʀi] *nf* mouse (*pl* mice).
sournois, e [suʀnwa, -waz] *a* deceitful, underhand.
sous [su] *prép* (*gén*) under; **~ la pluie/le soleil** in the rain/sunshine; **~ terre** *a, ad* underground; **~ peu** *ad* shortly, before long.
sous... [su, suz + *vowel*] *préfixe* sub-; under...; **~-catégorie** sub-category; **~-alimenté/-équipé/ -développé** undernourished/equipped/developed.
sous-bois [subwa] *nm inv* undergrowth.

sous-chef [suʃɛf] *nm* deputy chief clerk.
souscription [suskʀipsjɔ̃] *nf* subscription; **offert en ~** available on subscription.
souscrire [suskʀiʀ]: **~ à** *vt* to subscribe to.
sous-directeur, trice [sudiʀɛktœʀ, -tʀis] *nm/f* assistant manager/manageress, sub-manager/manageress.
sous-emploi [suzɑ̃plwa] *nm* underemployment.
sous-entendre [suzɑ̃tɑ̃dʀ(ə)] *vt* to imply, infer; **sous-entendu, e** *a* implied; (*verbe, complément*) understood // *nm* innuendo, insinuation.
sous-estimer [suzɛstime] *vt* to underestimate.
sous-exposer [suzɛkspoze] *vt* to underexpose.
sous-fifre [sufifʀ] *nm* (*péj*) underling.
sous-jacent, e [suʒasɑ̃, -ɑ̃t] *a* underlying.
sous-lieutenant [suljøtnɑ̃] *nm* sub-lieutenant.
sous-locataire [sulɔkatɛʀ] *nm/f* subtenant.
sous-louer [sulwe] *vt* to sublet.
sous-main [sumɛ̃] *nm inv* desk blotter; **en ~** *ad* secretly.
sous-marin, e [sumaʀɛ̃, -in] *a* (*flore, volcan*) submarine; (*navigation, pêche, explosif*) underwater // *nm* submarine.
sous-officier [suzɔfisje] *nm* ≈ non-comissioned officer (N.C.O.).
sous-préfecture [supʀefɛktyʀ] *nf* sub-prefecture.
sous-préfet [supʀefɛ] *nm* sub-prefect.
sous-produit [supʀɔdɥi] *nm* by-product; (*fig: péj*) pale imitation.
sous-secrétaire [susəkʀetɛʀ] *nm*: **~ d'État** Under-Secretary of State.
soussigné, e [susiɲe] *a*: **je ~** I the undersigned.
sous-sol [susɔl] *nm* basement; (GÉO) subsoil.
sous-titre [sutitʀ(ə)] *nm* subtitle; **sous-titré, e** *a* with subtitles.
soustraction [sustʀaksjɔ̃] *nf* subtraction.
soustraire [sustʀɛʀ] *vt* to subtract, take away; (*dérober*): **~ qch à qn** to remove sth from sb; **~ qn à** (*danger*) to shield sb from; **se ~ à** (*autorité etc*) to elude, escape from.
sous-traitance [sutʀɛtɑ̃s(ə)] *nf* subcontracting.
sous-verre [suvɛʀ] *nm inv* glass mount.
sous-vêtement [suvɛtmɑ̃] *nm* undergarment, item of underwear; **~s** *nmpl* underwear *sg*.
soutane [sutan] *nf* cassock, soutane.
soute [sut] *nf* hold; **~ à bagages** baggage hold.
soutenable [sutnabl(ə)] *a* (*opinion*) tenable, defensible.
soutenance [sutnɑ̃s] *nf*: **~ de thèse** ≈ viva voce (examination).
soutènement [sutɛnmɑ̃] *nm*: **mur de ~** retaining wall.
souteneur [sutnœʀ] *nm* procurer.
soutenir [sutniʀ] *vt* to support; (*assaut, choc*) to stand up to, withstand; (*intérêt, effort*) to keep up; (*assurer*): **~ que** to maintain that; **se ~** (*dans l'eau etc*) to hold o.s. up; **~ la comparaison avec** to bear *ou* stand comparison with; **soutenu, e** *a* (*efforts*) sustained, unflagging; (*style*) elevated.
souterrain, e [sutɛʀɛ̃, -ɛn] *a* underground // *nm* underground passage.
soutien [sutjɛ̃] *nm* support; **~ de famille** breadwinner.
soutien-gorge [sutjɛ̃gɔʀʒ(ə)] *nm* bra.
soutirer [sutiʀe] *vt*: **~ qch à qn** to squeeze *ou* get sth out of sb.
souvenance [suvnɑ̃s] *nf*: **avoir ~ de** to recollect.
souvenir [suvniʀ] *nm* (*réminiscence*) memory; (*cadeau*) souvenir, keepsake; (*de voyage*) souvenir // *vb*: **se ~ de** *vt* to remember; **se ~ que** to remember that; **en ~ de** in memory *ou* remembrance of.
souvent [suvɑ̃] *ad* often; **peu ~** seldom, infrequently.
souverain, e [suvʀɛ̃, -ɛn] *a* sovereign; (*fig: mépris*) supreme // *nm/f* sovereign, monarch; **souveraineté** *nf* sovereignty.
soviétique [sɔvjetik] *a* Soviet // *nm/f*: **S~** Soviet citizen.
soyeux, euse [swajø, øz] *a* silky.
soyons *etc vb voir* **être**.
S.P.A. *sigle f* (= *société protectrice des animaux*) ≈ R.S.P.C.A.
spacieux, euse [spasjø, -øz] *a* spacious; roomy.
spaghettis [spageti] *nmpl* spaghetti *sg*.
sparadrap [spaʀadʀa] *nm* adhesive *ou* sticking plaster.
spartiate [spaʀsjat] *a* Spartan; **~s** *nfpl* (*sandales*) Roman sandals.
spasme [spazm(ə)] *nm* spasm.
spasmodique [spazmɔdik] *a* spasmodic.
spatial, e, aux [spasjal, -o] *a* (AVIAT) space *cpd*; (PSYCH) spatial.
spatule [spatyl] *nf* (*ustensile*) slice; spatula; (*bout*) tip.
speaker, ine [spikœʀ, -kʀin] *nm/f* announcer.
spécial, e, aux [spesjal, -o] *a* special; (*bizarre*) peculiar; **~ement** *ad* especially, particularly; (*tout exprès*) specially.
spécialisé, e [spesjalize] *a* specialised.
spécialiser [spesjalize] *vt*: **se ~** to specialize.
spécialiste [spesjalist(ə)] *nm/f* specialist.
spécialité [spesjalite] *nf* speciality; (SCOL) special field; **~ pharmaceutique** patent medicine.
spécieux, euse [spesjø, -øz] *a* specious.
spécification [spesifikɑsjɔ̃] *nf* specification.
spécifier [spesifje] *vt* to specify, state.
spécifique [spesifik] *a* specific.
spécimen [spesimɛn] *nm* specimen; (*revue etc*) specimen *ou* sample copy.
spectacle [spɛktakl(ə)] *nm* (*tableau, scène*) sight; (*représentation*) show; (*industrie*) show business, entertainment; **se donner en ~** (*péj*) to make a spectacle *ou* an exhibition of o.s.; **spectaculaire** *a* spectacular.
spectateur, trice [spɛktatœʀ, -tʀis] *nm/f* (CINÉMA *etc*) member of the audience;

(*SPORT*) spectator; (*d'un événement*) onlooker, witness.
spectre [spɛktʀ(ə)] *nm* (*fantôme, fig*) spectre; (*PHYSIQUE*) spectrum (*pl* a); ~ **solaire** solar spectrum.
spéculateur, trice [spekylatœʀ, -tʀis] *nm/f* speculator.
spéculation [spekylɑsjɔ̃] *nf* speculation.
spéculer [spekyle] *vi* to speculate; ~ **sur** (*COMM*) to speculate in; (*réfléchir*) to speculate on; (*tabler sur*) to bank *ou* rely on.
spéléologie [speleɔlɔʒi] *nf* (*étude*) speleology; (*activité*) potholing; **spéléologue** *nm/f* speleologist; potholer.
spermatozoïde [spɛʀmatozɔid] *nm* sperm, spermatozoon (*pl* zoa).
sperme [spɛʀm(ə)] *nm* semen, sperm.
sphère [sfɛʀ] *nf* sphere; **sphérique** *a* spherical.
sphincter [sfɛ̃ktɛʀ] *nm* sphincter.
spiral, aux [spiʀal, -o] *nm* hairspring.
spirale [spiʀal] *nf* spiral; **en** ~ in a spiral.
spire [spiʀ] *nm* (single) turn; whorl.
spiritisme [spiʀitism(ə)] *nm* spiritualism, spiritism.
spirituel, le [spiʀitɥɛl] *a* spiritual; (*fin, piquant*) witty; **musique** ~**le** sacred music; **concert** ~ concert of sacred music.
spiritueux [spiʀitɥø] *nm* spirit.
splendeur [splɑ̃dœʀ] *nf* splendour.
splendide [splɑ̃did] *a* splendid; magnificent.
spolier [spɔlje] *vt*: ~ **qn (de)** to despoil sb (of).
spongieux, euse [spɔ̃ʒjø, -øz] *a* spongy.
spontané, e [spɔ̃tane] *a* spontaneous.
sporadique [spɔʀadik] *a* sporadic.
sport [spɔʀ] *nm* sport // *a inv* (*vêtement*) casual; **faire du** ~ to do sport; ~**s d'équipe/d'hiver** team/winter sports; **sportif, ive** *a* (*journal, association, épreuve*) sports *cpd*; (*allure, démarche*) athletic; (*attitude, esprit*) sporting.
spot [spɔt] *nm* (*lampe*) spot(light); (*annonce*): ~ **(publicitaire)** commercial (break).
sprint [spʀint] *nm* sprint.
square [skwaʀ] *nm* public garden(s).
squelette [skəlɛt] *nm* skeleton; **squelettique** *a* scrawny; (*fig*) skimpy.
stabilisateur, trice [stabilizatœʀ, -tʀis] *a* stabilizing // *nm* stabilizer; anti-roll device; tailplane.
stabiliser [stabilize] *vt* to stabilize; (*terrain*) to consolidate.
stabilité [stabilite] *nf* stability.
stable [stabl(ə)] *a* stable, steady.
stade [stad] *nm* (*SPORT*) stadium; (*phase, niveau*) stage.
stage [staʒ] *nm* training period; training course; (*d'avocat stagiaire*) articles *pl*; **stagiaire** *nm/f, a* trainee.
stagnant, e [stagnɑ̃, -ɑ̃t] *a* stagnant.
stalactite [stalaktit] *nf* stalactite.
stalagmite [stalagmit] *nf* stalagmite.
stalle [stal] *nf* stall, box.
stand [stɑ̃d] *nm* (*d'exposition*) stand; (*de foire*) stall; ~ **de tir** (*MIL*) firing range; (*à la foire, SPORT*) shooting range; ~ **de ravitaillement** pit.
standard [stɑ̃daʀ] *a inv* standard // *nm* switchboard; **standardiser** *vt* to standardize; **standardiste** *nm/f* switchboard operator.
standing [stɑ̃diŋ] *nm* standing; **immeuble de grand** ~ block of luxury flats.
star [staʀ] *nf* star.
starter [staʀtɛʀ] *nm* (*AUTO*) choke.
station [stɑsjɔ̃] *nf* station; (*de bus*) stop; (*de villégiature*) resort; (*posture*): **la** ~ **debout** standing, an upright posture; ~ **de ski** ski resort; ~ **de taxis** taxi rank.
stationnaire [stasjɔnɛʀ] *a* stationary.
stationnement [stasjɔnmɑ̃] *nm* parking; **zone de** ~ **interdit** no parking area; ~ **alterné** parking on alternate sides.
stationner [stasjɔne] *vi* to park.
station-service [stasjɔ̃sɛʀvis] *nf* service station.
statique [statik] *a* static.
statisticien, ne [statistisjɛ̃, -jɛn] *nm/f* statistician.
statistique [statistik] *nf* (*science*) statistics *sg*; (*rapport, étude*) statistic // *a* statistical; ~**s** (*données*) statistics *pl*.
statue [staty] *nf* statue.
statuer [statɥe] *vi*: ~ **sur** to rule on, give a ruling on.
statuette [statɥɛt] *nf* statuette.
statu quo [statykwo] *nm* status quo.
stature [statyʀ] *nf* stature.
statut [staty] *nm* status; ~**s** *nmpl* (*JUR, ADMIN*) statutes; **statutaire** *a* statutory.
Sté *abr de* **société**.
steak [stɛk] *nm* steak.
stèle [stɛl] *nf* stela, stele.
stellaire [stelɛʀ] *a* stellar.
stencil [stɛnsil] *nm* stencil.
sténo... [stenɔ] *préfixe*: ~**(dactylo)** *nf* shorthand typist; ~**(graphie)** *nf* shorthand; ~**graphier** *vt* to take down in shorthand.
stentor [stɑ̃tɔʀ] *nm*: **voix de** ~ stentorian voice.
steppe [stɛp] *nf* steppe.
stère [stɛʀ] *nm* stere.
stéréo(phonie) [steʀeɔ(fɔni)] *nf* stereo(phony); **stéréo(phonique)** *a* stereo(phonic).
stéréotype [steʀeɔtip] *nm* stereotype; **stéréotypé, e** *a* stereotyped.
stérile [steʀil] *a* sterile; (*terre*) barren; (*fig*) fruitless, futile.
stérilet [steʀilɛ] *nm* coil, loop.
stériliser [steʀilize] *vt* to sterilize.
stérilité [steʀilite] *nf* sterility.
sternum [stɛʀnɔm] *nm* breastbone, sternum.
stéthoscope [stetɔskɔp] *nm* stethoscope.
stigmates [stigmat] *nmpl* scars, marks; (*REL*) stigmata *pl*.
stigmatiser [stigmatize] *vt* to denounce, stigmatize.
stimulant, e [stimylɑ̃, -ɑ̃t] *a* stimulating // *nm* (*MÉD*) stimulant; (*fig*) stimulus (*pl* i), incentive.

stimulation [stimylɑsjɔ̃] *nf* stimulation.
stimuler [stimyle] *vt* to stimulate.
stimulus, i [stimylys, -i] *nm* stimulus (*pl* i).
stipulation [stipylɑsjɔ̃] *nf* stipulation.
stipuler [stipyle] *vt* to stipulate, specify.
stock [stɔk] *nm* stock; ~ **d'or** (FINANCE) gold reserves *pl*; ~**er** *vt* to stock; ~**iste** *nm* stockist.
stoïque [stɔik] *a* stoic, stoical.
stomacal, e, aux [stɔmakal, -o] *a* gastric, stomach *cpd*.
stop [stɔp] *nm* (AUTO: *écriteau*) stop sign; (: *signal*) brake-light; (*dans un télégramme*) stop // *excl* stop.
stoppage [stɔpaʒ] *nm* invisible mending.
stopper [stɔpe] *vt* to stop, halt; (COUTURE) to mend // *vi* to stop, halt.
store [stɔʀ] *nm* blind; (*de magasin*) shade, awning.
strabisme [stʀabism(ə)] *nm* squinting.
strangulation [stʀɑ̃gylɑsjɔ̃] *nf* strangulation.
strapontin [stʀapɔ̃tɛ̃] *nm* jump *ou* foldaway seat.
strass [stʀas] *nm* paste, strass.
stratagème [stʀataʒɛm] *nm* stratagem.
stratège [stʀatɛʒ] *nm* strategist.
stratégie [stʀateʒi] *nf* strategy; **stratégique** *a* strategic.
stratifié, e [stʀatifje] *a* (GÉO) stratified; (TECH) laminated.
stratosphère [stʀatɔsfɛʀ] *nf* stratosphere.
strict, e [stʀikt(ə)] *a* strict; (*tenue, décor*) severe, plain; **son droit le plus** ~ his most basic right; **dans la plus** ~**e intimité** strictly in private; **le** ~ **nécessaire/minimum** the bare essentials/minimum.
strident, e [stʀidɑ̃, -ɑ̃t] *a* shrill, strident.
stridulations [stʀidylɑsjɔ̃] *nfpl* stridulations, chirrings.
strie [stʀi] *nf* streak; (ANAT, GÉO) stria (*pl* ae).
strier [stʀije] *vt* to streak; to striate.
strip-tease [stʀiptiz] *nm* striptease; **strip-teaseuse** *nf* stripper, striptease artist.
striures [stʀijyʀ] *nfpl* streaking *sg*.
strophe [stʀɔf] *nf* verse, stanza.
structure [stʀyktyʀ] *nf* structure; ~**s d'accueil/touristiques** reception/tourist facilities; **structurer** *vt* to structure.
stuc [styk] *nm* stucco.
studieux, euse [stydjø, -øz] *a* studious; devoted to study.
studio [stydjo] *nm* (*logement*) (one-roomed) flatlet; (*d'artiste*, TV *etc*) studio (*pl* s).
stupéfaction [stypefaksjɔ̃] *nf* stupefaction, amazement.
stupéfait, e [stypefɛ, -ɛt] *a* amazed.
stupéfiant, e [stypefjɑ̃, -ɑ̃t] *a* stunning, astounding // *nm* (MÉD) drug, narcotic.
stupéfier [stypefje] *vt* to stupefy; (*étonner*) to stun, astonish.
stupeur [stypœʀ] *nf* (*inertie, insensibilité*) stupor; (*étonnement*) astonishment, amazement.
stupide [stypid] *a* stupid; **stupidité** *nf* stupidity; stupid thing (to do *ou* say).
style [stil] *nm* style; **meuble de** ~ period piece of furniture.
stylé, e [stile] *a* well-trained.
stylet [stilɛ] *nm* stiletto, stylet.
stylisé, e [stilize] *a* stylized.
styliste [stilist(ə)] *nm/f* designer; stylist.
stylistique [stilistik] *nf* stylistics *sg*.
stylo [stilo] *nm*: ~ **(à encre)** (fountain) pen; ~ **(à) bille** ball-point pen; ~**-feutre** *nm* felt-tip pen.
su, e [sy] *pp de* **savoir** // *nm*: **au** ~ **de** with the knowledge of.
suaire [sɥɛʀ] *nm* shroud.
suave [sɥav] *a* sweet; suave, smooth; mellow.
subalterne [sybaltɛʀn(ə)] *a* (*employé, officier*) junior; (*rôle*) subordinate, subsidiary // *nm/f* subordinate, inferior.
subconscient [sypkɔ̃sjɑ̃] *nm* subconscious.
subdiviser [sybdivize] *vt* to subdivide; **subdivision** *nf* subdivision.
subir [sybiʀ] *vt* (*affront, dégâts, mauvais traitements*) to suffer; (*influence, charme*) to be under, be subjected to; (*traitement, opération, châtiment*) to undergo.
subit, e [sybi, -it] *a* sudden; **subitement** *ad* suddenly, all of a sudden.
subjectif, ive [sybʒɛktif, -iv] *a* subjective.
subjonctif [sybʒɔ̃ktif] *nm* subjunctive.
subjuguer [sybʒyge] *vt* to subjugate.
sublime [syblim] *a* sublime.
sublimer [syblime] *vt* to sublimate.
submergé, e [sybmɛʀʒe] *a* submerged; (*fig*): ~ **de** snowed under with; overwhelmed with.
submerger [sybmɛʀʒe] *vt* to submerge; (*suj*: *foule*) to engulf; (*fig*) to overwhelm.
submersible [sybmɛʀsibl(ə)] *nm* submarine.
subordination [sybɔʀdinɑsjɔ̃] *nf* subordination.
subordonné, e [sybɔʀdɔne] *a, nm/f* subordinate; ~ **à** subordinate to; subject to, depending on.
subordonner [sybɔʀdɔne] *vt*: ~ **qn/qch à** to subordinate sb/sth to.
subornation [sybɔʀnɑsjɔ̃] *nf* bribing.
subrepticement [sybʀɛptismɑ̃] *ad* surreptitiously.
subside [sypsid] *nm* grant.
subsidiaire [sypsidjɛʀ] *a*: **question** ~ deciding question.
subsistance [sybzistɑ̃s] *nf* subsistence; **pourvoir à la** ~ **de qn** to keep sb, provide for sb's subsistence *ou* keep.
subsister [sybziste] *vi* (*rester*) to remain, subsist; (*vivre*) to live; (*survivre*) to live on.
substance [sypstɑ̃s] *nf* substance.
substantiel, le [sypstɑ̃sjɛl] *a* substantial.
substantif [sypstɑ̃tif] *nm* noun, substantive; **substantiver** *vt* to nominalize.
substituer [sypstitɥe] *vt*: ~ **qn/qch à** to substitute sb/sth for; **se** ~ **à qn** (*représenter*) to substitute for sb; (*évincer*) to substitute o.s. for sb.

substitut [sypstity] *nm* (*JUR*) deputy public prosecutor; (*succédané*) substitute.
substitution [sypstitysjɔ̃] *nf* substitution.
subterfuge [syptɛʀfyʒ] *nm* subterfuge.
subtil, e [syptil] *a* subtle.
subtiliser [syptilize] *vt*: ~ **qch (à qn)** to spirit sth away (from sb).
subtilité [syptilite] *nf* subtlety.
subvenir [sybvəniʀ]: ~ **à** *vt* to meet.
subvention [sybvɑ̃sjɔ̃] *nf* subsidy, grant; **subventionner** *vt* to subsidize.
subversif, ive [sybvɛʀsif, -iv] *a* subversive; **subversion** *nf* subversion.
suc [syk] *nm* (*BOT*) sap; (*de viande, fruit*) juice; ~**s gastriques** gastric *ou* stomach juices.
succédané [syksedane] *nm* substitute.
succéder [syksede]: ~ **à** *vt* (*directeur, roi etc*) to succeed; (*venir après: dans une série*) to follow, succeed; **se** ~ *vi* (*accidents, années*) to follow one another.
succès [syksɛ] *nm* success; **avoir du** ~ to be a success, be successful; ~ **de librairie** bestseller; ~ **(féminins)** conquests.
successeur [syksesœʀ] *nm* successor.
successif, ive [syksesif, -iv] *a* successive.
succession [syksesjɔ̃] *nf* (*série, POL*) succession; (*JUR: patrimoine*) estate, inheritance; **prendre la** ~ **de** (*directeur*) to succeed, take over from; (*entreprise*) to take over.
succinct, e [syksɛ̃, -ɛ̃t] *a* succinct.
succion [syksjɔ̃] *nf*: **bruit de** ~ sucking noise.
succomber [sykɔ̃be] *vi* to die, succumb; (*fig*): ~ **à** to give way to, succumb to.
succulent, e [sykylɑ̃, -ɑ̃t] *a* succulent.
succursale [sykyʀsal] *nf* branch; **magasin à** ~**s multiples** chain *ou* multiple store.
sucer [syse] *vt* to suck.
sucette [sysɛt] *nf* (*bonbon*) lollipop.
sucre [sykʀ(ə)] *nm* (*substance*) sugar; (*morceau*) lump of sugar, sugar lump *ou* cube; ~ **de canne/betterave** cane/beet sugar; ~ **en morceaux/cristallisé/en poudre** lump/coarse-grained/ granulated sugar; ~ **d'orge** barley sugar; **sucré, e** *a* (*produit alimentaire*) sweetened; (*au goût*) sweet; (*péj*) sugary, honeyed; **sucrer** *vt* (*thé, café*) to sweeten, put sugar in; **sucrer qn** to put sugar in sb's tea (*ou* coffee *etc*); **se sucrer** to help o.s. to sugar, have some sugar; (*fam*) to line one's pocket(s); **sucrerie** *nf* (*usine*) sugar refinery; **sucreries** *nfpl* (*bonbons*) sweets, sweet things; **sucrier, ière** *a* sugar *cpd*; sugar-producing // *nm* (*fabricant*) sugar producer; (*récipient*) sugar bowl *ou* basin.
sud [syd] *nm*: **le** ~ the south // *a inv* south; (*côte*) south, southern; **au** ~ (*situation*) in the south; (*direction*) to the south; **au** ~ **de** (to the) south of; ~**-africain, e** *a, nm/f* South African; ~**-américain, e** *a, nm/f* South American.
sudation [sydɑsjɔ̃] *nf* sweating, sudation.
sud-est [sydɛst] *nm, a inv* south-east.
sud-ouest [sydwɛst] *nm, a inv* south-west.
Suède [sɥɛd] *nf*: **la** ~ Sweden; **suédois, e** *a* Swedish // *nm/f*: **Suédois, e** Swede // *nm* (*langue*) Swedish.
suer [sɥe] *vi* to sweat; (*suinter*) to ooze // *vt* (*fig*) to exude; ~ **à grosses gouttes** to sweat profusely.
sueur [sɥœʀ] *nf* sweat; **en** ~ sweating, in a sweat; **avoir des** ~**s froides** to be in a cold sweat.
suffire [syfiʀ] *vi* (*être assez*): ~ **(à qn/pour qch/pour faire)** to be enough *ou* sufficient (for sb/for sth/to do); (*satisfaire*): **cela lui suffit** he's content with this, this is enough for him; **se** ~ to be self-sufficient; **cela suffit pour les irriter/qu'ils se fâchent** it's enough to annoy them/for them to get angry; **il suffit d'une négligence/qu'on oublie pour que ...** it only takes one act of carelessness/one only needs to forget for ...
suffisamment [syfizamɑ̃] *ad* sufficiently, enough; ~ **de** sufficient, enough.
suffisance [syfizɑ̃s] *nf* (*vanité*) self-importance, bumptiousness; (*quantité*): **en** ~ in plenty.
suffisant, e [syfizɑ̃, -ɑ̃t] *a* (*temps, ressources*) sufficient; (*résultats*) satisfactory; (*vaniteux*) self-important, bumptious.
suffixe [syfiks(ə)] *nm* suffix.
suffocation [syfɔkɑsjɔ̃] *nf* suffocation.
suffoquer [syfɔke] *vt* to choke, suffocate; (*stupéfier*) to stagger, astound // *vi* to choke, suffocate.
suffrage [syfʀaʒ] *nm* (*POL: voix*) vote; (*: méthode*): ~ **indirect** indirect suffrage; (*du public etc*) approval *q*; ~**s exprimés** valid votes.
suggérer [sygʒeʀe] *vt* to suggest; **suggestif, ive** *a* suggestive; **suggestion** *nf* suggestion.
suicidaire [sɥisidɛʀ] *a* suicidal.
suicide [sɥisid] *nm* suicide.
suicidé, e [sɥiside] *nm/f* suicide.
suicider [sɥiside]: **se** ~ *vi* to commit suicide.
suie [sɥi] *nf* soot.
suif [sɥif] *nm* tallow.
suinter [sɥɛ̃te] *vi* to ooze.
suis *vb voir* **être**.
suisse [sɥis] *a, nm/f* Swiss // *nm* (*bedeau*) ≈ verger // *nf*: **la S**~ Switzerland; **la S**~ **romande/allemande** French-speaking/ German-speaking Switzerland ~ **romand, e** *a, nm/f* Swiss French; ~**-allemand, e** *a, nm/f* Swiss German; **Suissesse** *nf* Swiss (woman *ou* girl).
suite [sɥit] *nf* (*continuation: d'énumération etc*) rest, remainder; (*: de feuilleton*) continuation; (*: second film etc sur le même thème*) sequel; (*série: de maisons, succès*): **une** ~ **de** a series *ou* succession of; (*MATH*) series *sg*; (*conséquence*) result; (*ordre, liaison logique*) coherence; (*appartement, MUS*) suite; (*escorte*) retinue, suite; ~**s** *nfpl* (*d'une maladie etc*) effects; **prendre la** ~ **de** (*directeur etc*) to succeed, take over from; **donner** ~ **à** (*requête, projet*) to follow up; **faire** ~ **à** to follow; **(faisant)** ~ **à votre lettre du** further to your letter of the; **de** ~ *ad* (*d'affilée*) in succession; (*immédiatement*) at once; **par la** ~

afterwards, subsequently; **à la ~** *ad* one after the other; **à la ~ de** (*derrière*) behind; (*en conséquence de*) following; **par ~ de** owing to, as a result of; **avoir de la ~ dans les idées** to show great singleness of purpose; **attendre la ~** to wait and see what comes next.

suivant, e [sɥivɑ̃, -ɑ̃t] *a* next, following; (*ci-après*): **l'exercice ~** the following exercise // *prép* (*selon*) according to; **au ~!** next!

suiveur [sɥivœʀ] *nm* (CYCLISME) (official) follower.

suivi, e [sɥivi] *a* (*régulier*) regular; (COMM: *article*) in general production; (*cohérent*) consistent; coherent; **très/peu ~** (*cours*) well-/poorly-attended; (*feuilleton etc*) widely/not widely followed.

suivre [sɥivʀ(ə)] *vt* (*gén*) to follow; (SCOL: *cours*) to attend; (: *leçon*) to follow, attend to; (: *programme*) to keep up with; (COMM: *article*) to continue to stock // *vi* to follow; (*élève*) to attend, pay attention; to keep up, follow; **se ~** (*accidents etc*) to follow one after the other; (*raisonnement*) to be coherent; **faire ~** (*lettre*) to forward; **~ son cours** (*suj*: *enquête etc*) to run *ou* take its course; **'à ~'** 'to be continued'.

sujet, te [syʒɛ, -ɛt] *a*: **être ~ à** (*vertige etc*) to be liable *ou* subject to // *nm/f* (*d'un souverain*) subject // *nm* subject; (*raison*: *d'une dispute etc*) cause; **avoir ~ de se plaindre** to have cause for complaint; **au ~ de** *prép* about; **~ à caution** *a* questionable; **~ de conversation** topic *ou* subject of conversation; **~ d'examen** (SCOL) examination question; examination paper; **~ d'expérience** (BIO *etc*) experimental subject.

sujétion [syʒesjɔ̃] *nf* subjection; (*fig*) constraint.

sulfater [sylfate] *vt* to spray with copper sulphate.

sulfureux, euse [sylfyʀø, -øz] *a* sulphurous.

sulfurique [sylfyʀik] *a*: **acide ~** sulphuric acid.

summum [sɔmɔm] *nm*: **le ~ de** the height of.

superbe [sypɛʀb(ə)] *a* magnificent, superb.

super(carburant) [sypɛʀ(kaʀbyʀɑ̃)] *nm* high-octane petrol.

supercherie [sypɛʀʃəʀi] *nf* trick.

superfétatoire [sypɛʀfetatwaʀ] *a* superfluous.

superficie [sypɛʀfisi] *nf* (surface) area; (*fig*) surface.

superficiel, le [sypɛʀfisjɛl] *a* superficial.

superflu, e [sypɛʀfly] *a* superfluous.

supérieur, e [sypeʀjœʀ] *a* (*lèvre, étages, classes*) upper; (*plus élevé*: *température, niveau*): **~ (à)** higher (than); (*meilleur*: *qualité, produit*): **~ (à)** superior (to); (*excellent, hautain*) superior // *nm, nf* superior; **Mère ~e** Mother Superior; **à l'étage ~** on the next floor up; **~ en nombre** superior in number; **supériorité** *nf* superiority.

superlatif [sypɛʀlatif] *nm* superlative.

supermarché [sypɛʀmaʀʃe] *nm* supermarket.

superposer [sypɛʀpoze] *vt* to superpose; (*faire chevaucher*) to superimpose; **se ~** *vi* (*images, souvenirs*) to be superimposed; **lits superposés** bunk beds.

superpréfet [sypɛʀpʀefɛ] *nm prefect in charge of a region.*

superproduction [sypɛʀpʀɔdyksjɔ̃] *nf* (*film*) spectacular.

superpuissance [sypɛʀpɥisɑ̃s] *nf* superpower.

supersonique [sypɛʀsɔnik] *a* supersonic.

superstitieux, euse [sypɛʀstisjø, -øz] *a* superstitious.

superstition [sypɛʀstisjɔ̃] *nf* superstition.

superstructure [sypɛʀstʀyktyʀ] *nf* superstructure.

superviser [sypɛʀvize] *vt* to supervise.

supplanter [syplɑ̃te] *vt* to supplant.

suppléance [sypleɑ̃s] *nf* supply post.

suppléant, e [sypleɑ̃, -ɑ̃t] *a* (*juge, fonctionnaire*) deputy *cpd*; (*professeur*) supply *cpd* // *nm/f* deputy; supply teacher; **médecin ~** locum.

suppléer [syplee] *vt* (*ajouter*: *mot manquant etc*) to supply, provide; (*compenser*: *lacune*) to fill in; (: *défaut*) to make up for; (*remplacer*: *professeur*) to stand in for; (: *juge*) to deputize for; **~ à** *vt* to make up for; to substitute for.

supplément [syplemɑ̃] *nm* supplement; **un ~ de travail** extra *ou* additional work; **un ~ de frites** *etc* an extra portion of chips *etc*; **un ~ de 100 F** a supplement of 100 F, an extra *ou* additional 100 F; **ceci est en ~** (*au menu etc*) this is extra, there is an extra charge for this; **supplémentaire** *a* additional, further; (*train, bus*) relief *cpd*, extra.

supplétif, ive [sypletif, -iv] *a* (MIL) auxiliary.

supplication [syplikɑsjɔ̃] *nf* (REL) supplication; **~s** *nfpl* (*adjurations*) pleas, entreaties.

supplice [syplis] *nm* (*peine corporelle*) torture *q*; form of torture; (*douleur physique, morale*) torture, agony.

supplier [syplije] *vt* to implore, beseech.

supplique [syplik] *nf* petition.

support [sypɔʀ] *nm* support; (*pour livre, outils*) stand; **~ audio-visuel** audio-visual aid; **~ publicitaire** advertising medium.

supportable [sypɔʀtabl(ə)] *a* (*douleur*) bearable.

supporter *nm* [sypɔʀtɛʀ] supporter, fan // *vt* [sypɔʀte] (*poids, poussée*) to support; (*conséquences, épreuve*) to bear, endure; (*défauts, personne*) to tolerate, put up with; (*suj*: *chose*: *chaleur etc*) to withstand; (*suj*: *personne*: *chaleur, vin*) to take.

supposé, e [sypoze] *a* (*nombre*) estimated; (*auteur*) supposed.

supposer [sypoze] *vt* to suppose; (*impliquer*) to presuppose; **à ~ que** supposing (that); **supposition** *nf* supposition.

suppositoire [sypozitwaʀ] *nm* suppository.

suppôt [sypo] *nm* (*péj*) henchman.

suppression [sypʀesjɔ̃] *nf* removal; deletion; cancellation; suppression.

supprimer [sypRime] *vt* (*cloison, cause, anxiété*) to remove ; (*clause, mot*) to delete ; (*congés, service d'autobus etc*) to cancel ; (*publication, article*) to suppress ; (*emplois, privilèges, témoin gênant*) to do away with.
suppurer [sypyRe] *vi* to suppurate.
supputations [sypytasjɔ̃] *nfpl* calculations, reckonings.
supputer [sypyte] *vt* to calculate, reckon.
suprématie [sypRemasi] *nf* supremacy.
suprême [sypRɛm] *a* supreme.
sur [syR] *prép* (*gén*) on ; (*par-dessus*) over ; (*au-dessus*) above ; (*direction*) towards ; (*à propos de*) about, on ; **un ~ 10** one out of 10 ; **4m ~ 2** 4m by 2 ; **je n'ai pas d'argent ~ moi** I haven't got any money with *ou* on me ; **~ ce** *ad* hereupon.
sur, e [syR] *a* sour.
sûr, e [syR] *a* sure, certain ; (*digne de confiance*) reliable ; (*sans danger*) safe ; **peu ~** unreliable ; **~ de qch** sure *ou* certain of sth ; **être ~ de qn** to be sure of sb ; **~ de soi** self-assured, self-confident ; **le plus ~ est de** the safest thing is to.
surabonder [syRabɔ̃de] *vi* to be overabundant.
suraigu, uë [syRegy] *a* very shrill.
surajouter [syRaʒute] *vt*: **~ qch à** to add sth to.
suralimenté, e [syRalimɑ̃te] *a* overfed.
suranné, e [syRane] *a* outdated, outmoded.
surbaissé, e [syRbese] *a* lowered, low.
surcharge [syRʃaRʒ(ə)] *nf* (*de passagers, marchandises*) excess load ; (*correction*) alteration ; (PHILATÉLIE) surcharge ; **prendre des passagers en ~** to take on excess *ou* extra passengers ; **~ de bagages** excess luggage ; **~ de travail** extra work.
surcharger [syRʃaRʒe] *vt* to overload ; (*timbre-poste*) to surcharge.
surchauffé, e [syRʃofe] *a* overheated.
surchoix [syRʃwa] *a inv* top-quality.
surclasser [syRklɑse] *vt* to outclass.
surcouper [syRkupe] *vt* to overtrump.
surcroît [syRkRwa] *nm*: **un ~ de** additional + *nom* ; **par** *ou* **de ~** moreover ; **en ~** in addition.
surdi-mutité [syRdimytite] *nf*: **atteint de ~** deaf and dumb.
surdité [syRdite] *nf* deafness.
sureau, x [syRo] *nm* elder (tree).
surélever [syRɛlve] *vt* to raise, heighten.
sûrement [syRmɑ̃] *ad* reliably ; safely, securely ; (*certainement*) certainly.
surenchère [syRɑ̃ʃɛR] *nf* (*aux enchères*) higher bid ; (*sur prix fixe*) overbid ; (*fig*) overstatement ; outbidding tactics *pl* ; **surenchérir** *vi* to bid higher ; to raise one's bid ; (*fig*) to try and outbid each other.
surent *vb voir* **savoir**.
surestimer [syRɛstime] *vt* to overestimate.
sûreté [syRte] *nf* (*voir* *sûr*) reliability ; safety ; (JUR) guaranty ; surety ; **mettre en ~** to put in a safe place ; **pour plus de ~** as an extra precaution ; to be on the safe side ; **la S~ (nationale)** *division of the Ministère de l'Intérieur heading all police forces except the gendarmerie and the Paris préfecture de police.*
surexcité, e [syRɛksite] *a* overexcited.
surexposer [syRɛkspoze] *vt* to overexpose.
surf [syRf] *nm* surfing.
surface [syRfas] *nf* surface ; (*superficie*) surface area ; **faire ~** to surface ; **en ~** *ad* near the surface ; (*fig*) superficially ; **la pièce fait 100m² de ~** the room has a surface area of 100m² ; **~ de réparation** penalty area.
surfait, e [syRfɛ, -ɛt] *a* overrated.
surfin, e [syRfɛ̃, -in] *a* superfine.
surgelé, e [syRʒəle] *a* (deep-)frozen.
surgir [syRʒiR] *vi* (*personne, véhicule*) to appear suddenly ; (*geyser etc: de terre*) to shoot up ; (*fig: problème, conflit*) to arise.
surhomme [syRɔm] *nm* superman.
surhumain, e [syRymɛ̃, -ɛn] *a* superhuman.
surimposer [syRɛ̃poze] *vt* to overtax.
surimpression [syRɛ̃pResjɔ̃] *nf* (PHOTO) double exposure ; **en ~** superimposed.
sur-le-champ [syRləʃɑ̃] *ad* immediately.
surlendemain [syRlɑ̃dmɛ̃] *nm*: **le ~ (soir)** two days later (in the evening) ; **le ~ de** two days after.
surmenage [syRmənaʒ] *nm* overwork ; **le ~ intellectuel** mental fatigue.
surmené, e [syRməne] *a* overworked.
surmener [syRməne] *vt*, **se ~** *vi* to overwork.
surmonter [syRmɔ̃te] *vt* (*suj: coupole etc*) to surmount, top ; (*vaincre*) to overcome, surmount.
surmultiplié, e [syRmyltiplije] *a, nf*: **(vitesse) ~e** overdrive.
surnager [syRnaʒe] *vi* to float.
surnaturel, le [syRnatyRɛl] *a, nm* supernatural.
surnom [syRnɔ̃] *nm* nickname.
surnombre [syRnɔ̃bR(ə)] *nm*: **être en ~** to be too many (*ou* one too many).
surnommer [syRnɔme] *vt* to nickname.
surnuméraire [syRnymeRɛR] *nm/f* supernumerary.
suroît [syRwa] *nm* sou'wester.
surpasser [syRpɑse] *vt* to surpass.
surpeuplé, e [syRpœple] *a* overpopulated.
surplis [syRpli] *nm* surplice.
surplomb [syRplɔ̃] *nm* overhang ; **en ~** overhanging.
surplomber [syRplɔ̃be] *vi* to be overhanging // *vt* to overhang ; to tower above.
surplus [syRply] *nm* (COMM) surplus ; (*reste*): **~ de bois** wood left over ; **~ américains** American army surplus *sg*.
surprenant, e [syRpRənɑ̃, -ɑ̃t] *a* surprising.
surprendre [syRpRɑ̃dR(ə)] *vt* (*étonner, prendre à l'improviste*) to surprise ; (*tomber sur: intrus etc*) to catch ; (*fig*) to detect ; to chance *ou* happen upon ; to intercept ; to overhear ; **~ la vigilance/bonne foi de qn** to catch sb out/betray sb's good faith ; **se ~ à faire** to catch *ou* find o.s. doing.
surprime [syRpRim] *nf* additional premium.

surpris, e [syʀpʀi, -iz] *a*: ~ **(de/que)** surprised (at/that).
surprise [syʀpʀiz] *nf* surprise; **faire une ~ à qn** to give sb a surprise; **par ~** *ad* by surprise.
surprise-partie [syʀpʀizpaʀti] *nf* party.
surproduction [syʀpʀɔdyksjɔ̃] *nf* overproduction.
surréaliste [syʀʀealist(ə)] *a* surrealist.
sursaut [syʀso] *nm* start, jump; ~ **de** (*énergie, indignation*) sudden fit *ou* burst of; **en ~** *ad* with a start; **sursauter** *vi* to (give a) start, jump.
surseoir [syʀswaʀ]: ~ **à** *vt* to defer; (JUR) to stay.
sursis [syʀsi] *nm* (JUR: *gén*) suspended sentence; (*à l'exécution capitale, aussi fig*) reprieve; (MIL): ~ **(d'appel** *ou* **d'incorporation)** deferment; **condamné à 5 mois (de prison) avec ~** given a 5-month suspended (prison) sentence; **sursitaire** *nm* (MIL) deferred conscript.
sursois *etc vb voir* **surseoir.**
surtaxe [syʀtaks(ə)] *nf* surcharge.
surtout [syʀtu] *ad* (*avant tout, d'abord*) above all; (*spécialement, particulièrement*) especially; **il aime le sport, ~ le football** he likes sport, especially football; **cet été, il a ~ fait de la pêche** this summer he went fishing more than anything (else); ~, **ne dites rien!** whatever you do — don't say anything!; ~ **pas!** certainly *ou* definitely not!; ~ **que...** especially as ...

surveillance [syʀvɛjɑ̃s] *nf* watch; (POLICE, MIL) surveillance; **sous ~ médicale** under medical supervision; **la ~ du territoire** internal security (*voir aussi* **D.S.T.**).
surveillant, e [syʀvɛjɑ̃, -ɑ̃t] *nm/f* (*de prison*) warder; (SCOL) monitor; (*de travaux*) supervisor, overseer.
surveiller [syʀveje] *vt* (*enfant, élèves, bagages*) to watch, keep an eye on; (*malade*) to watch over; (*prisonnier, suspect*) to keep (a) watch on; (*territoire, bâtiment*) to (keep) watch over; (*travaux, cuisson*) to supervise; (SCOL: *examen*) to invigilate; **se ~** to keep a check *ou* watch on o.s.; ~ **son langage/sa ligne** to watch one's language/figure.
survenir [syʀvəniʀ] *vi* (*incident, retards*) to occur, arise; (*événement*) to take place; (*personne*) to appear, arrive.
survêtement [syʀvɛtmɑ̃] *nm* tracksuit.
survie [syʀvi] *nf* survival; (REL) afterlife; **une ~ de quelques mois** a few more months of life.
survivant, e [syʀvivɑ̃, -ɑ̃t] *nm/f* survivor.
survivre [syʀvivʀ(ə)] *vi* to survive; ~ **à** *vt* (*accident etc*) to survive; (*personne*) to outlive.
survol [syʀvɔl] *nm* flying over.
survoler [syʀvɔle] *vt* to fly over; (*fig*: *livre*) to skim through.
survolté, e [syʀvɔlte] *a* (ÉLEC) stepped up, boosted; (*fig*) worked up.
sus [sy(s)]: **en ~ de** *prép* in addition to, over and above; **en ~** *ad* in addition; ~ **à** *excl*: ~ **au tyran!** at the tyrant!
susceptibilité [sysɛptibilite] *nf* sensitiveness *q*.
susceptible [sysɛptibl(ə)] *a* touchy, sensitive; ~ **d'amélioration** *ou* **d'être amélioré** that can be improved, open to improvement; ~ **de faire** able to do; liable to do.
susciter [sysite] *vt* (*admiration*) to arouse; (*obstacles, ennuis*): ~ **(à qn)** to create (for sb).
susdit, e [sysdi, -dit] *a* foresaid.
susmentionné, e [sysmɑ̃sjɔne] *a* above-mentioned.
suspect, e [syspɛ(kt), -ɛkt(ə)] *a* suspicious; (*témoignage, opinions*) suspect // *nm/f* suspect; **peu ~ de** most unlikely to be suspected of.
suspecter [syspɛkte] *vt* to suspect; (*honnêteté de qn*) to question, have one's suspicions about; ~ **qn d'être** to suspect sb of being.
suspendre [syspɑ̃dʀ(ə)] *vt* (*accrocher*: *vêtement*): ~ **qch (à)** to hang sth up (on); (*fixer*: *lustre etc*): ~ **qch à** to hang sth from; (*interrompre, démettre*) to suspend; (*remettre*) to defer; **se ~ à** to hang from.
suspendu, e [syspɑ̃dy] *pp de* **suspendre** // *a* (*accroché*): ~ **à** hanging on (*ou* from); (*perché*): ~ **au-dessus de** suspended over; (AUTO): **bien/mal ~** with good/poor suspension.
suspens [syspɑ̃]: **en ~** *ad* (*affaire*) in abeyance; **tenir en ~** to keep in suspense.
suspense [syspɑ̃s] *nm* suspense.
suspension [syspɑ̃sjɔ̃] *nf* suspension; deferment; (AUTO) suspension; (*lustre*) pendent light fitting; **en ~** in suspension, suspended; ~ **d'audience** adjournment.
suspicion [syspisjɔ̃] *nf* suspicion.
sustenter [systɑ̃te]: **se ~** *vi* to take sustenance.
susurrer [sysyʀe] *vt* to whisper.
sut *vb voir* **savoir**.
suture [sytyʀ] *nf*: **point de ~** stitch; **suturer** *vt* to stitch up, suture.
svelte [svɛlt(ə)] *a* slender, svelte.
S.V.P. *sigle* (= *s'il vous plaît*) please.
syllabe [silab] *nf* syllable.
sylvestre [silvɛstʀ(ə)] *a*: **pin ~** Scots pine, Scotch fir.
sylviculture [silvikyltyʀ] *nf* forestry, sylviculture.
symbole [sɛ̃bɔl] *nm* symbol; **symbolique** *a* symbolic(al); (*geste, offrande*) token *cpd*; (*salaire, dommage-intérêts*) nominal; **symboliser** *vt* to symbolize.
symétrie [simetʀi] *nf* symmetry; **symétrique** *a* symmetrical.
sympa [sɛ̃pa] *a abr de* **sympathique.**
sympathie [sɛ̃pati] *nf* (*inclination*) liking; (*affinité*) fellow feeling; (*condoléances*) sympathy; **accueillir avec ~** (*projet*) to receive favourably; **avoir de la ~ pour qn** to like sb, have a liking for sb; **témoignages de ~** expressions of sympathy; **croyez à toute ma ~** you have my deepest sympathy.
sympathique [sɛ̃patik] *a* nice, friendly; likeable; pleasant.
sympathisant, e [sɛ̃patizɑ̃, -ɑ̃t] *nm/f* sympathizer.
sympathiser [sɛ̃patize] *vi* (*voisins etc*: *s'entendre*) to get on (well); (: *se fréquenter*)

to socialize, see each other; ~ **avec** to get on (well) with; to see, socialize with.
symphonie [sɛ̃fɔni] *nf* symphony; **symphonique** *a* (*orchestre, concert*) symphony *cpd*; (*musique*) symphonic.
symptomatique [sɛ̃ptɔmatik] *a* symptomatic.
symptôme [sɛ̃ptom] *nm* symptom.
synagogue [sinagɔg] *nf* synagogue.
synchronique [sɛ̃kʀɔnik] *a*: **tableau** ~ synchronic table of events.
synchroniser [sɛ̃kʀɔnize] *vt* to synchronize.
syncope [sɛ̃kɔp] *nf* (MÉD) blackout; (MUS) syncopation; **tomber en** ~ to faint, pass out; **syncopé, e** *a* syncopated.
syndic [sɛ̃dik] *nm* managing agent.
syndical, e, aux [sɛ̃dikal, -o] *a* (trade-)union *cpd*; **~isme** *nm* trade unionism; union(ist) activities *pl*; **~iste** *nm/f* trade unionist.
syndicat [sɛ̃dika] *nm* (*d'ouvriers, employés*) (trade) union; (*autre association d'intérêts*) union, association; ~ **d'initiative** tourist office *ou* bureau; ~ **patronal** employers' syndicate, federation of employers; ~ **de propriétaires** association of property owners.
syndiqué, e [sɛ̃dike] *a* belonging to a (trade) union; **non** ~ non-union.
syndiquer [sɛ̃dike]: **se** ~ *vi* to form a trade union; (*adhérer*) to join a trade union.
syndrome [sɛ̃dʀom] *nm* syndrome.
synode [sinɔd] *nm* synod.
synonyme [sinɔnim] *a* synonymous // *nm* synonym; ~ **de** synonymous with.
synoptique [sinɔptik] *a*: **tableau** ~ synoptic table.
synovie [sinɔvi] *nf* synovia.
syntaxe [sɛ̃taks(ə)] *nf* syntax.
synthèse [sɛ̃tɛz] *nf* synthesis (*pl* es); **faire la** ~ **de** to synthesize.
synthétique [sɛ̃tetik] *a* synthetic.
synthétiseur [sɛ̃tetizœʀ] *nm* (MUS) synthesizer.
syphilis [sifilis] *nf* syphilis.
Syrie [siʀi] *nf*: **la** ~ Syria; **syrien, ne** *a, nm/f* Syrian.
systématique [sistematik] *a* systematic.
systématiser [sistematize] *vt* to systematize.
système [sistɛm] *nm* system; **le** ~ **D** resourcefulness; **le** ~ **solaire** the solar system.

T

t' [t(ə)] *pronom voir* **te**.
ta [ta] *dét voir* **ton**.
tabac [taba] *nm* tobacco; tobacconist's (shop) // *a inv*: **(couleur)** ~ buff(-coloured); **passer qn à** ~ to beat sb up; ~ **blond/brun** light/dark tobacco; ~ **gris** shag; ~ **à priser** snuff; **tabagie** *nf* smoke den; **tabatière** *nf* snuffbox.
tabernacle [tabɛʀnakl(ə)] *nm* tabernacle.
table [tabl(ə)] *nf* table; **à ~!** dinner *etc* is ready!; **se mettre à** ~ to sit down to eat; (*fig*: *fam*) to come clean; **mettre la** ~ to lay the table; **faire** ~ **rase de** to make a clean sweep of; ~ **basse** coffee table; ~ **d'écoute** wire-tapping set; ~ **d'harmonie** sounding board; ~ **des matières** (table of) contents *pl*; ~ **de multiplication** multiplication table; ~ **de nuit** *ou* **de chevet** bedside table; ~ **ronde** (*débat*) round table; ~ **de toilette** washstand.
tableau, x [tablo] *nm* painting; (*reproduction, fig*) picture; (*panneau*) board; (*schéma*) table, chart; ~ **d'affichage** notice board; ~ **de bord** dashboard; (AVIAT) instrument panel; ~ **de chasse** tally; ~ **noir** blackboard.
tabler [table] *vi*: ~ **sur** to count *ou* bank on.
tablette [tablɛt] *nf* (*planche*) shelf (*pl* shelves); ~ **de chocolat** bar of chocolate.
tablier [tablije] *nm* apron; (*de pont*) roadway.
tabou [tabu] *nm, a* taboo.
tabouret [tabuʀɛ] *nm* stool.
tabulateur [tabylatœʀ] *nm* tabulator.
tac [tak] *nm*: **du** ~ **au** ~ tit for tat.
tache [taʃ] *nf* (*saleté*) stain, mark; (ART, *de couleur, lumière*) spot; splash, patch; **faire** ~ **d'huile** to spread, gain ground.
tâche [tɑʃ] *nf* task; **travailler à la** ~ to do general jobbing, work as a jobbing gardener/builder *etc*.
tacher [taʃe] *vt* to stain, mark; (*fig*) to sully, stain.
tâcher [tɑʃe] *vi*: ~ **de faire** to try *ou* endeavour to do.
tâcheron [tɑʃʀɔ̃] *nm* (*fig*) drudge.
tacite [tasit] *a* tacit.
taciturne [tasityʀn(ə)] *a* taciturn.
tacot [tako] *nm* (*péj*) banger.
tact [takt] *nm* tact; **avoir du** ~ to be tactful, have tact.
tactile [taktil] *a* tactile.
tactique [taktik] *a* tactical // *nf* (*technique*) tactics *sg*; (*plan*) tactic.
taie [tɛ] *nf*: ~ **(d'oreiller)** pillowslip, pillowcase.
taille [tɑj] *nf* cutting; pruning; (*milieu du corps*) waist; (*hauteur*) height; (*grandeur*) size; **de** ~ **à faire** capable of doing; **de** ~ *a* sizeable.
taille-crayon(s) [tɑjkʀɛjɔ̃] *nm* pencil sharpener.
tailler [tɑje] *vt* (*pierre, diamant*) to cut; (*arbre, plante*) to prune; (*vêtement*) to cut out; (*crayon*) to sharpen; **se** ~ *vt* (*ongles, barbe*) to trim, cut; (*fig*: *réputation*) to gain, win // *vi* (*fam*) to beat it; ~ **dans** (*chair, bois*) to cut into.
tailleur [tɑjœʀ] *nm* (*couturier*) tailor; (*vêtement*) suit, costume; **en** ~ (*assis*) cross-legged; ~ **de diamants** diamond-cutter.
taillis [taji] *nm* copse.
tain [tɛ̃] *nm* silvering; **glace sans** ~ two-way mirror.
taire [tɛʀ] *vt* to keep to o.s., conceal // *vi*: **faire** ~ **qn** to make sb be quiet; (*fig*) to silence sb; **se** ~ *vi* (*s'arrêter de parler*) to fall silent, stop talking; (*ne pas parler*) to be silent *ou* quiet; to keep quiet; **tais-toi!, taisez-vous!** be quiet!
talc [talk] *nm* talcum powder.

talé, e [tale] *a* (*fruit*) bruised.
talent [talɑ̃] *nm* talent; **talentueux, euse** *a* talented.
talion [taljɔ̃] *nm*: **la loi du ~** an eye for an eye.
talisman [talismɑ̃] *nm* talisman.
talon [talɔ̃] *nm* heel; (*de chèque, billet*) stub, counterfoil; **~s plats/aiguilles** flat/stiletto heels.
talonner [talɔne] *vt* to follow hard behind; (*fig*) to hound.
talonnette [talɔnɛt] *nf* heelpiece.
talquer [talke] *vt* to put talcum powder on.
talus [taly] *nm* embankment.
tambour [tɑ̃buʀ] *nm* (MUS, *aussi* TECH) drum; (*musicien*) drummer; (*porte*) revolving door(s *pl*).
tambourin [tɑ̃buʀɛ̃] *nm* tambourine.
tambouriner [tɑ̃buʀine] *vi*: **~ contre** to drum against *ou* on.
tambour-major [tɑ̃buʀmaʒɔʀ] *nm* drum major.
tamis [tami] *nm* sieve.
Tamise [tamiz] *nf*: **la ~** the Thames.
tamisé, e [tamize] *a* (*fig*) subdued, soft.
tamiser [tamize] *vt* to sieve, sift.
tampon [tɑ̃pɔ̃] *nm* (*de coton, d'ouate*) wad, pad; (*amortisseur*) buffer; (*bouchon*) plug, stopper; (*cachet, timbre*) stamp; **~ (hygiénique)** tampon; **tamponner** *vt* (*timbres*) to stamp; (*heurter*) to crash *ou* ram into; **tamponneuse** *a*: **autos tamponneuses** dodgems.
tam-tam [tamtam] *nm* tomtom.
tandem [tɑ̃dɛm] *nm* tandem; (*fig*) duo, pair.
tandis [tɑ̃di]: **~ que** *cj* while.
tangage [tɑ̃gaʒ] *nm* pitching (and tossing).
tangent, e [tɑ̃ʒɑ̃, -ɑ̃t] *a* (MATH): **~ à** tangential to; (*fam*) close // *nf* (MATH) tangent.
tangible [tɑ̃ʒibl(ə)] *a* tangible, concrete.
tango [tɑ̃go] *nm* tango.
tanguer [tɑ̃ge] *vi* to pitch (and toss).
tanière [tanjɛʀ] *nf* lair, den.
tanin [tanɛ̃] *nm* tannin.
tank [tɑ̃k] *nm* tank.
tanné, e [tane] *a* weather-beaten.
tanner [tane] *vt* to tan.
tannerie [tanʀi] *nf* tannery.
tanneur [tanœʀ] *nm* tanner.
tant [tɑ̃] *ad* so much; **~ de** (*sable, eau*) so much; (*gens, livres*) so many; **~ que** *cj* as long as; **~ que** (*comparatif*) as much as; **~ mieux** that's great; so much the better; **~ pis** never mind; too bad; **~ pis pour lui** too bad for him; **~ soit peu** a little bit; (even) remotely.
tante [tɑ̃t] *nf* aunt.
tantinet [tɑ̃tinɛ]: **un ~** *ad* a tiny bit.
tantôt [tɑ̃to] *ad* (*parfois*): **~ ... ~** now ... now; (*cet après-midi*) this afternoon.
taon [tɑ̃] *nm* horsefly, gadfly.
tapage [tapaʒ] *nm* uproar, din; **~ nocturne** (JUR) disturbance of the peace (at night).
tapageur, euse [tapaʒœʀ, -øz] *a* loud, flashy; noisy.
tape [tap] *nf* slap.
tape-à-l'œil [tapalœj] *a inv* flashy, showy.
taper [tape] *vt* (*porte*) to bang, slam; (*dactylographier*) to type (out); (*fam: emprunter*): **~ qn de 10 F** to touch sb for 10 F, cadge 10 F off sb // *vi* (*soleil*) to beat down; **~ sur qn** to thump sb; (*fig*) to run sb down; **~ sur qch** to hit sth; to bang on sth; **~ à** (*porte etc*) to knock on; **~ dans** *vt* (*se servir*) to dig into; **~ des mains/pieds** to clap one's hands/stamp one's feet; **~ (à la machine)** to type.
tapi, e [tapi] *a*: **~ dans/derrière** crouching *ou* cowering in/behind; hidden away in/behind.
tapioca [tapjɔka] *nm* tapioca.
tapis [tapi] *nm* carpet; (*de table*) cloth; **mettre sur le ~** (*fig*) to bring up for discussion; **~ roulant** conveyor belt; **~ de sol** (*de tente*) groundsheet; **~-brosse** *nm* doormat.
tapisser [tapise] *vt* (*avec du papier peint*) to paper; (*recouvrir*): **~ qch (de)** to cover sth (with).
tapisserie [tapisʀi] *nf* (*tenture, broderie*) tapestry; (*: travail*) tapestry-making; tapestry work; (*papier peint*) wallpaper; **faire ~** to sit out, be a wallflower.
tapissier, ière [tapisje, -jɛʀ] *nm/f*: **~ (-décorateur)** upholsterer (and decorator).
tapoter [tapɔte] *vt* to pat, tap.
taquet [takɛ] *nm* wedge; peg.
taquin, e [takɛ̃, -in] *a* teasing.
taquiner [takine] *vt* to tease.
tarabiscoté, e [taʀabiskɔte] *a* over-ornate, fussy.
tarabuster [taʀabyste] *vt* to bother, worry.
tarauder [taʀode] *vt* (TECH) to tap; to thread; (*fig*) to pierce.
tard [taʀ] *ad* late; **au plus ~** at the latest; **plus ~** later (on); **sur le ~** late in life.
tarder [taʀde] *vi* (*chose*) to be a long time coming; (*personne*): **~ à faire** to delay doing; **il me tarde d'être** I am longing to be; **sans (plus) ~** without (further) delay.
tardif, ive [taʀdif, -iv] *a* late; **tardivement** *ad* late.
tare [taʀ] *nf* (COMM) tare; (*fig*) defect; taint, blemish.
targuer [taʀge]: **se ~ de** *vt* to boast about.
tarif [taʀif] *nm* (*liste*) price list; tariff; (*barème*) rates *pl*; fares *pl*; tariff; (*prix*) rate; fare; **~aire** *a* tariff *cpd*; **~er** *vt* to fix the price *ou* rate for; **~é 10 F** priced 10 F.
tarir [taʀiʀ] *vi* to dry up, run dry // *vt* to dry up.
tarot(s) [taʀo] *nm(pl)* tarot cards.
tartare [taʀtaʀ] *a* (CULIN) tartar(e).
tarte [taʀt(ə)] *nf* tart; **~ aux pommes/à la crème** apple/custard tart; **~lette** *nf* tartlet.
tartine [taʀtin] *nf* slice of bread and butter (*ou* jam); **~ au miel** slice of bread and honey; **tartiner** *vt* to spread; **fromage à tartiner** cheese spread.
tartre [taʀtʀ(ə)] *nm* (*des dents*) tartar; (*de chaudière*) fur, scale.

tas [tɑ] *nm* heap, pile ; (*fig*): **un ~ de** heaps of, lots of ; **en ~** in a heap *ou* pile ; **dans le ~** (*fig*) in the crowd ; among them ; **formé sur le ~** trained on the job.
tasse [tɑs] *nf* cup.
tassé, e [tɑse] *a*: **bien ~** (*café etc*) strong.
tasser [tɑse] *vt* (*terre, neige*) to pack down ; (*entasser*): **~ qch dans** to cram sth into ; **se ~** *vi* (*terrain*) to settle ; (*fig*) to sort itself out, settle down.
tâter [tɑte] *vt* to feel ; (*fig*) to try out ; to test out ; **~ de** (*prison etc*) to have a taste of ; **se ~** (*hésiter*) to be in two minds ; **~ le terrain** (*fig*) to test the ground.
tatillon, ne [tatijɔ̃, -ɔn] *a* pernickety.
tâtonnement [tɑtɔnmɑ̃] *nm*: **par ~s** (*fig*) by trial and error.
tâtonner [tɑtɔne] *vi* to grope one's way along.
tâtons [tɑtɔ̃]: **à ~** *ad*: **chercher/avancer à ~** to grope around for/grope one's way forward.
tatouage [tatwaʒ] *nm* tattooing ; (*dessin*) tattoo.
tatouer [tatwe] *vt* to tattoo.
taudis [todi] *nm* hovel, slum.
taupe [top] *nf* mole ; **taupinière** *nf* molehill.
taureau, x [tɔʀo] *nm* bull ; (*signe*): **le T~** Taurus, the Bull ; **être du T~** to be Taurus.
tauromachie [tɔʀɔmaʃi] *nf* bullfighting.
taux [to] *nm* rate ; (*d'alcool*) level ; **~ d'intérêt** interest rate.
tavelé, e [tavle] *a* marbled.
taverne [tavɛʀn(ə)] *nf* inn, tavern.
taxe [taks] *nf* tax ; (*douanière*) duty ; **~ de séjour** tourist tax ; **~ à la valeur ajoutée (T.V.A.)** value added tax (V.A.T.).
taxer [takse] *vt* (*personne*) to tax ; (*produit*) to put a tax on, tax ; (*fig*): **~ qn de** to call sb + *attribut* ; to accuse sb of, tax sb with.
taxi [taksi] *nm* taxi.
taximètre [taksimɛtʀ(ə)] *nm* (taxi)meter.
taxiphone [taksifɔn] *nm* pay phone.
T.C.F. *sigle m* = *Touring Club de France*, ≈ AA *ou* RAC.
Tchécoslovaquie [tʃekɔslɔvaki] *nf* Czechoslovakia ; **tchèque** *a, nm, nf* Czech.
te, t' [t(ə)] *pronom* you ; (*réfléchi*) yourself.
té [te] *nm* T-square.
technicien, ne [tɛknisjɛ̃, -jɛn] *nm/f* technician.
technique [tɛknik] *a* technical // *nf* technique ; **~ment** *ad* technically.
technocrate [tɛknɔkʀat] *nm/f* technocrat.
technocratie [tɛknɔkʀasi] *nf* technocracy.
technologie [tɛknɔlɔʒi] *nf* technology ; **technologique** *a* technological.
teck [tɛk] *nm* teak.
teckel [tekɛl] *nm* dachshund.
teignais *etc vb voir* **teindre**.
teigne [tɛɲ] *nf* (ZOOL) moth ; (MÉD) ringworm.
teigneux, euse [tɛɲø, -øz] *a* (*péj*) nasty, scabby.
teindre [tɛ̃dʀ(ə)] *vt* to dye.
teint, e [tɛ̃, tɛ̃t] *a* dyed // *nm* (*du visage*) complexion, colouring ; colour // *nf* shade, colour ; **grand ~** *a inv* colourfast.
teinté, e [tɛ̃te] *a* (*verres*) tinted ; (*bois*) stained ; **~ acajou** mahogany-stained ; **~ de** (*fig*) tinged with.
teinter [tɛ̃te] *vt* to tint ; (*bois*) to stain ; **teinture** *nf* dyeing ; (*substance*) dye ; (MÉD): **teinture d'iode** tincture of iodine.
teinturerie [tɛ̃tyʀʀi] *nf* dry cleaner's.
teinturier [tɛ̃tyʀje] *nm* dry cleaner.
tel, telle [tɛl] *a* (*pareil*) such ; (*comme*): **~ un/des ...** like a/ like... ; (*indéfini*) such-and-such a, a given ; (*intensif*): **un ~/de ~s ...** such (a)/such ... ; **rien de ~** nothing like it, no such thing ; **~ que** *cj* like, such as ; **~ quel** as it is *ou* stands (*ou* was *etc*).
tél. *abr de* **téléphone**.
télé [tele] *nf* (*abr de* **télévision**) (*poste*) T.V. (set) ; **à la ~** on the telly, on T.V.
télé... [tele] *préfixe*: **~benne** *nf* (*benne*) telecabine, gondola // *nm* telecabine ; **~cabine** *nf* (*benne*) telecabine, gondola // *nm* telecabine ; **~commande** *nf* remote control ; **~commander** *vt* to operate by remote control ; **~communications** *nfpl* telecommunications ; **~férique** *nm* = **~phérique** ; **~gramme** *nm* telegram.
télégraphe [telegʀaf] *nm* telegraph ; **télégraphie** *nf* telegraphy ; **télégraphier** *vt* to telegraph, cable ; **télégraphique** *a* telegraph *cpd*, telegraphic ; (*fig*) telegraphic ; **télégraphiste** *nm/f* telegraphist.
téléguider [telegide] *vt* to operate by remote control, radio-control.
téléobjectif [teleɔbʒɛktif] *nm* telephoto lens *sg*.
télépathie [telepati] *nf* telepathy.
téléphérique [telefeʀik] *nm* cable-car.
téléphone [telefɔn] *nm* telephone ; (*appel*) (telephone) call ; telephone conversation ; **avoir le ~** to be on the (tele)phone ; **au ~** on the phone ; **les T~s** ≈ Post Office Telecommunications ; **~ arabe** bush telephone ; **~ manuel** manually-operated telephone system ; **téléphoner** *vt* to telephone // *vi* to telephone, ring ; to make a phone call ; **téléphoner à** to phone up, ring up, call up ; **téléphonique** *a* telephone *cpd*, phone *cpd* ; **téléphoniste** *nm/f* telephonist, telephone operator ; (*d'entreprise*) switchboard operator.
télescope [telɛskɔp] *nm* telescope.
télescoper [telɛskɔpe] *vt* to smash up ; **se ~** (*véhicules*) to concertina.
télescopique [telɛskɔpik] *a* telescopic.
téléscripteur [teleskʀiptœʀ] *nm* teleprinter.
télésiège [telesjɛʒ] *nm* chairlift.
téléski [teleski] *nm* ski-tow ; **~ à archets** T-bar tow ; **~ à perche** button lift.
téléspectateur, trice [telespɛktatœʀ, -tʀis] *nm/f* (television) viewer.
téléviser [televize] *vt* to televise.
téléviseur [televizœʀ] *nm* television set.
télévision [televizjɔ̃] *nf* television ; **avoir la ~** to have a television ; **à la ~** on television.
télex [telɛks] *nm* telex.
telle [tɛl] *a voir* **tel**.

tellement [tɛlmɑ̃] *ad* (*tant*) so much ; (*si*) so ; ~ **plus grand (que)** so much bigger (than) ; ~ **de** (*sable, eau*) so much ; (*gens, livres*) so many ; **il s'est endormi** ~ **il était fatigué** he was so tired (that) he fell asleep ; **pas** ~ not (all) that much ; not (all) that + *adjectif*.
tellurique [telyʀik] *a*: **secousse** ~ earth tremor.
téméraire [temeʀɛʀ] *a* reckless, rash ; **témérité** *nf* recklessness, rashness.
témoignage [temwaɲaʒ] *nm* (JUR: *déclaration*) testimony *q*, evidence *q* ; (: *faits*) evidence *q* ; (*rapport, récit*) account ; (*fig*: *d'affection etc*) token, mark ; expression.
témoigner [temwaɲe] *vt* (*intérêt, gratitude*) to show // *vi* (JUR) to testify, give evidence ; ~ **que** to testify that ; (*fig*) to reveal that, testify to the fact that ; ~ **de** *vt* to bear witness to, testify to.
témoin [temwɛ̃] *nm* witness ; (*fig*) testimony ; (SPORT) baton ; (CONSTR) telltale // *a* control *cpd*, test *cpd* ; **appartement** ~ show flat ; **être** ~ **de** to witness ; to vouch for ; **prendre à** ~ to call to witness ; ~ **de moralité** character reference ; ~ **oculaire** eyewitness.
tempe [tɑ̃p] *nf* temple.
tempérament [tɑ̃peʀamɑ̃] *nm* temperament, disposition ; (*santé*) constitution ; **à** ~ (*vente*) on deferred (payment) terms ; (*achat*) by instalments, hire purchase *cpd* ; **avoir du** ~ to be hot-blooded.
tempérance [tɑ̃peʀɑ̃s] *nf* temperance.
température [tɑ̃peʀatyʀ] *nf* temperature ; **prendre la** ~ **de** to take the temperature of ; (*fig*) to gauge the feeling of ; **avoir** *ou* **faire de la** ~ to have *ou* be running a temperature.
tempéré, e [tɑ̃peʀe] *a* temperate.
tempérer [tɑ̃peʀe] *vt* to temper.
tempête [tɑ̃pɛt] *nf* storm ; ~ **de sable/neige** sand/snowstorm.
tempêter [tɑ̃pete] *vi* to rant and rave.
temple [tɑ̃pl(ə)] *nm* temple ; (*protestant*) church.
tempo [tɛmpo] *nm* tempo (*pl* s).
temporaire [tɑ̃pɔʀɛʀ] *a* temporary ; ~**ment** *ad* temporarily.
temporel, le [tɑ̃pɔʀɛl] *a* temporal.
temporiser [tɑ̃pɔʀize] *vi* to temporize, play for time.
temps [tɑ̃] *nm* (*atmosphérique*) weather ; (*durée*) time ; (*époque*) time, times *pl* ; (LING) tense ; (MUS) beat ; (TECH) stroke ; **il fait beau/mauvais** ~ the weather is fine/bad ; **avoir le** ~**/tout le** ~**/juste le** ~ to have time/plenty of time/just enough time ; **avoir fait son** ~ (*fig*) to have had its (*ou* his *etc*) day ; **en** ~ **de paix/guerre** in peacetime/wartime ; **en** ~ **utile** *ou* **voulu** in due time *ou* course ; **de** ~ **en** ~**, de** ~ **à autre** from time to time, now and again ; **à** ~ (*partir, arriver*) in time ; **à** ~ **partiel** *ad, a* part-time ; **dans le** ~ at one time ; **de tout** ~ always ; **du** ~ **que** at the time when, in the days when ; ~ **d'arrêt** pause, halt ; ~ **mort** (COMM) slack period.
tenable [tənabl(ə)] *a* bearable.
tenace [tənas] *a* tenacious, persistent ; **ténacité** *nf* tenacity, persistence.
tenailler [tənɑje] (*fig*) *vt* to torment, torture.
tenailles [tənɑj] *nfpl* pincers.
tenais *etc vb voir* **tenir**.
tenancier, ière [tənɑ̃sje, -jɛʀ] *nm/f* manager/manageress.
tenant, e [tənɑ̃, -ɑ̃t] *a voir* **séance** // *nm/f* (SPORT): ~ **du titre** title-holder // *nm*: **d'un seul** ~ in one piece ; **les** ~**s et les aboutissants** the ins and outs.
tendance [tɑ̃dɑ̃s] *nf* (*opinions*) leanings *pl*, sympathies *pl* ; (*inclination*) tendency ; (*évolution*) trend ; ~ **à la hausse** upward trend ; **avoir** ~ **à** to have a tendency to, tend to ; **tendancieux, euse** *a* tendentious.
tendeur [tɑ̃dœʀ] *nm* (*de vélo*) chain-adjuster ; (*de câble*) wire-strainer ; (*de tente*) runner ; (*attache*) sandow, elastic strap.
tendon [tɑ̃dɔ̃] *nm* tendon, sinew ; ~ **d'Achille** Achilles' tendon.
tendre [tɑ̃dʀ(ə)] *a* (*viande, légumes*) tender ; (*bois, roche, couleur*) soft ; (*affectueux*) tender, loving // *vt* (*élastique, peau*) to stretch, draw tight ; (*muscle*) to tense ; (*donner*): ~ **qch à qn** to hold sth out to sb ; to offer sb sth ; (*fig*: *piège*) to set, lay ; (*tapisserie*): **tendu de soie** hung with silk, with silk hangings ; **se** ~ *vi* (*corde*) to tighten ; (*relations*) to become strained ; ~ **à qch/à faire** to tend towards sth/to do ; ~ **l'oreille** to prick up one's ears ; ~ **la main/le bras** to hold out one's hand/stretch out one's arm ; ~**ment** *ad* tenderly, lovingly ; **tendresse** *nf* tenderness.
tendu, e [tɑ̃dy] *pp de* **tendre** // *a* tight ; tensed ; strained.
ténèbres [tenɛbʀ(ə)] *nfpl* darkness *sg* ; **ténébreux, euse** *a* obscure, mysterious ; (*personne*) saturnine.
teneur [tənœʀ] *nf* content, substance ; (*d'une lettre*) terms *pl*, content ; ~ **en cuivre** copper content.
ténia [tenja] *nm* tapeworm.
tenir [təniʀ] *vt* to hold ; (*magasin, hôtel*) to run ; (*promesse*) to keep // *vi* to hold ; (*neige, gel*) to last ; **se** ~ *vi* (*avoir lieu*) to be held, take place ; (*être*: *personne*) to stand ; **se** ~ **droit** to stand up (*ou* sit up) straight ; **bien se** ~ to behave well ; **se** ~ **à qch** to hold on to sth ; **s'en** ~ **à qch** to confine o.s. to sth ; to stick to sth ; ~ **à** *vt* to be attached to ; to care about ; to depend on ; to stem from ; ~ **à faire** to want to do, be keen to do ; ~ **de** *vt* to partake of ; to take after ; **ça ne tient qu'à lui** it is entirely up to him ; ~ **qn pour** to take sb for ; ~ **qch de qn** (*histoire*) to have heard *ou* learnt sth from sb ; (*qualité, défaut*) to have inherited *ou* got sth from sb ; ~ **les comptes** to keep the books ; ~ **un rôle** to play a part ; ~ **l'alcool** to be able to hold a drink ; ~ **le coup** to hold out ; ~ **3 jours/2 mois** (*résister*) to hold out *ou* last 3 days/2 months ; ~ **au chaud/à l'abri** to keep hot/under shelter *ou* cover ; **tiens/tenez, voilà le stylo!**

there's the pen! ; **tiens, Alain!** look, here's Alain! ; **tiens?** (*surprise*) really?
tennis [tenis] *nm* tennis ; (*aussi*: **court de ~**) tennis court // *nm ou fpl* (*aussi*: **chaussures de ~**) tennis *ou* gym shoes ; **~ de table** table tennis ; **~man** *nm* tennis player.
ténor [tenɔʀ] *nm* tenor.
tension [tɑ̃sjɔ̃] *nf* tension ; (*fig*) tension ; strain ; (*MÉD*) blood pressure ; **faire** *ou* **avoir de la ~** to have high blood pressure.
tentaculaire [tɑ̃takylɛʀ] *a* (*fig*) sprawling.
tentacule [tɑ̃takyl] *nm* tentacle.
tentant, e [tɑ̃tɑ̃, -ɑ̃t] *a* tempting.
tentateur, trice [tɑ̃tatœʀ, -tʀis] *a* tempting // *nm* (*REL*) tempter.
tentation [tɑ̃tɑsjɔ̃] *nf* temptation.
tentative [tɑ̃tativ] *nf* attempt, bid ; **~ d'évasion** escape bid.
tente [tɑ̃t] *nf* tent ; **~ à oxygène** oxygen tent.
tenter [tɑ̃te] *vt* (*éprouver, attirer*) to tempt ; (*essayer*): **~ qch/de faire** to attempt *ou* try sth/to do ; **être tenté de** to be tempted to ; **~ sa chance** to try one's luck.
tenture [tɑ̃tyʀ] *nf* hanging.
tenu, e [təny] *pp de* **tenir** // *a* (*maison, comptes*): **bien ~** well-kept ; (*obligé*): **~ de faire** under an obligation to do // *nf* (*action de tenir*) running ; keeping ; holding ; (*vêtements*) clothes *pl*, gear ; (*allure*) dress *q*, appearance ; (*comportement*) manners *pl*, behaviour ; **en grande ~e** in full dress ; **en petite ~e** scantily dressed *ou* clad ; **avoir de la ~e** to have good manners ; (*journal*) to have a high standard ; **une ~e de voyage/sport** travelling/sports clothes *pl ou* gear *q* ; **~e de combat** combat gear *ou* dress ; **~e de route** (*AUTO*) road-holding ; **~e de soirée** evening dress.
ténu, e [teny] *a* (*indice, nuance*) tenuous, subtle ; (*fil, objet*) fine ; (*voix*) thin.
ter [tɛʀ] *a*: **16 ~** 16b *ou* B.
térébenthine [teʀebɑ̃tin] *nf*: **(essence de) ~** (oil of) turpentine.
tergiverser [tɛʀʒivɛʀse] *vi* to shilly-shally.
terme [tɛʀm(ə)] *nm* term ; (*fin*) end ; **vente/achat à ~** (*COMM*) forward sale/purchase ; **à court/long ~** *a* short-/long-term *ou* -range // *ad* in the short/long term ; **à ~** (*MÉD*) a full-term // *ad* at term ; **avant ~** (*MÉD*) *a* premature // *ad* prematurely ; **mettre un ~ à** to put an end *ou* a stop to.
terminaison [tɛʀminɛzɔ̃] *nf* (*LING*) ending.
terminal, e, aux [tɛʀminal, -o] *a* final // *nm* terminal // *nf* (*SCOL*) ≈ Upper Sixth.
terminer [tɛʀmine] *vt* to end ; (*nourriture, repas*) to finish ; **se ~** *vi* to end ; **se ~ par** to end with.
terminologie [tɛʀminɔlɔʒi] *nf* terminology.
terminus [tɛʀminys] *nm* terminus (*pl* i).
termite [tɛʀmit] *nm* termite, white ant.
terne [tɛʀn(ə)] *a* dull.
ternir [tɛʀniʀ] *vt* to dull ; (*fig*) to sully, tarnish ; **se ~** *vi* to become dull.
terrain [tɛʀɛ̃] *nm* (*sol, fig*) ground ; (*COMM*) land *q*, plot (of land) ; site ; **sur le ~** (*fig*) on the field ; **~ de football/rugby** football/rugby pitch ; **~ d'aviation** airfield ; **~ de camping** camping site ; **un ~ d'entente** an area of agreement ; **~ de golf** golf course ; **~ de jeu** games field ; playground ; **~ de sport** sports ground ; **~ vague** waste ground *q*.
terrasse [tɛʀas] *nf* terrace ; (*de café*) pavement area, terrasse ; **à la ~** (*café*) outside.
terrassement [tɛʀasmɑ̃] *nm* earth-moving, earthworks *pl* ; embankment.
terrasser [tɛʀase] *vt* (*adversaire*) to floor, bring down ; (*suj*: *maladie etc*) to lay low.
terrassier [tɛʀasje] *nm* navvy, roadworker.
terre [tɛʀ] *nf* (*gén, aussi ÉLEC*) earth ; (*substance*) soil, earth ; (*opposé à mer*) land *q* ; (*contrée*) land ; **~s** *nfpl* (*terrains*) lands, land *sg* ; **le travail de la ~** work on the land ; **en ~** (*pipe, poterie*) clay *cpd* ; **à ~** *ou* **par ~** (*mettre, être*) on the ground (*ou* floor) ; (*jeter, tomber*) to the ground, down ; **~ cuite** earthenware ; terracotta ; **la ~ ferme** dry land, terra firma ; **~ glaise** clay ; **la T~ Sainte** the Holy Land ; **~ à ~** *inv* down-to-earth, matter-of-fact.
terreau [tɛʀo] *nm* compost.
terre-plein [tɛʀplɛ̃] *nm* platform.
terrer [tɛʀe]: **se ~** *vi* to hide away ; to go to ground.
terrestre [tɛʀɛstʀ(ə)] *a* (*surface*) earth's, of the earth ; (*BOT, ZOOL, MIL*) land *cpd* ; (*REL*) earthly, worldly.
terreur [tɛʀœʀ] *nf* terror *q*, fear.
terrible [tɛʀibl(ə)] *a* terrible, dreadful ; (*fam*) terrific ; **~ment** *ad* (*très*) terribly, awfully.
terrien, ne [tɛʀjɛ̃, -jɛn] *nm/f* countryman/woman, man/woman of the soil ; (*non martien etc*) earthling.
terrier [tɛʀje] *nm* burrow, hole ; (*chien*) terrier.
terrifier [tɛʀifje] *vt* to terrify.
terril [tɛʀil] *nm* slag heap.
terrine [tɛʀin] *nf* (*récipient*) terrine ; (*CULIN*) pâté.
territoire [tɛʀitwaʀ] *nm* territory ; **territorial, e, aux** *a* territorial.
terroir [tɛʀwaʀ] *nm* (*AGR*) soil ; **accent du ~** country *ou* rural accent.
terroriser [tɛʀɔʀize] *vt* to terrorize ; **terrorisme** *nm* terrorism ; **terroriste** *nm/f* terrorist.
tertiaire [tɛʀsjɛʀ] *a* tertiary // *nm* (*ÉCON*) tertiary sector, service industries *pl*.
tertre [tɛʀtʀ(ə)] *nm* hillock, mound.
tes [te] *dét voir* **ton**.
tesson [tesɔ̃] *nm*: **~ de bouteille** piece of broken bottle.
test [tɛst] *nm* test.
testament [tɛstamɑ̃] *nm* (*JUR*) will ; (*REL*) Testament ; **faire son ~** to make out one's will ; **testamentaire** *a* of a will.
tester [tɛste] *vt* to test.
testicule [tɛstikyl] *nm* testicle.
tétanos [tetanos] *nm* tetanus, lockjaw.
têtard [tɛtaʀ] *nm* tadpole.
tête [tɛt] *nf* head ; (*cheveux*) hair *q* ; (*visage*) face ; (*FOOTBALL*) header ; **de ~** *a* (*wagon etc*) front *cpd* // *ad* (*calculer*) in one's head, mentally ; **perdre la ~** (*fig*) to lose one's

head; to go off one's head; **tenir ~ à qn** to stand up to *ou* defy sb; **la ~ en bas** with one's head down; **la ~ la première** (*tomber*) headfirst; **faire une ~** (FOOTBALL) to head the ball; **faire la ~** (*fig*) to sulk; **en ~** (SPORT) in the lead; at the front *ou* head; **en ~ à ~** in private, alone together; **de la ~ aux pieds** from head to toe; **~ d'affiche** (THÉÂTRE *etc*) top of the bill; **~ de bétail** head *inv* of cattle; **~ chercheuse** homing device; **~ de lecture** pickup head; **~ de liste** (POL) chief candidate; **~ de mort** skull and crossbones; **~ de série** (TENNIS) seeded player, seed; **~ de Turc** (*fig*) whipping boy; **~ de veau** (CULIN) calf's head; **~-à-queue** *nm inv*: **faire un ~-à-queue** to spin round; **~-à-~** *nm inv* tête-à-tête; **~-bêche** *ad* head to tail.

tétée [tete] *nf* (*action*) sucking; (*repas*) feed.

téter [tete] *vt*: **~ (sa mère)** to suck at one's mother's breast, feed.

tétine [tetin] *nf* teat; (*sucette*) dummy.

téton [tetɔ̃] *nm* (*fam*) breast.

têtu, e [tety] *a* stubborn, pigheaded.

texte [tɛkst(ə)] *nm* text; **apprendre son ~** (THÉÂTRE) to learn one's lines.

textile [tɛkstil] *a* textile *cpd* // *nm* textile; textile industry.

textuel, le [tɛkstɥɛl] *a* literal, word for word.

texture [tɛkstyʀ] *nf* texture.

thé [te] *nm* tea; **prendre le ~** to have tea; **faire le ~** to make the tea.

théâtral, e, aux [teɑtʀal, -o] *a* theatrical.

théâtre [teɑtʀ(ə)] *nm* theatre; (*techniques, genre*) drama, theatre; (*activité*) stage, theatre; (*œuvres*) plays *pl*, dramatic works *pl*; (*fig: lieu*): **le ~ de** the scene of; (*péj*) histrionics *pl*, playacting; **faire du ~** to be on the stage; to do some acting; **~ filmé** filmed stage productions *pl*.

théière [tejɛʀ] *nf* teapot.

thème [tɛm] *nm* theme; (SCOL: *traduction*) prose (composition).

théologie [teɔlɔʒi] *nf* theology; **théologien** *nm* theologian; **théologique** *a* theological.

théorème [teɔʀɛm] *nm* theorem.

théoricien, ne [teɔʀisjɛ̃, -jɛn] *nm/f* theoretician, theorist.

théorie [teɔʀi] *nf* theory; **théorique** *a* theoretical.

thérapeutique [teʀapøtik] *a* therapeutic // *nf* therapeutics *sg*.

thérapie [teʀapi] *nf* therapy.

thermal, e, aux [tɛʀmal, -o] *a* thermal; **station ~e** spa; **cure ~e** water cure.

thermes [tɛʀm(ə)] *nmpl* thermal baths; (*romains*) thermae *pl*.

thermique [tɛʀmik] *a* (*énergie*) thermic; (*unité*) thermal.

thermomètre [tɛʀmɔmɛtʀ(ə)] *nm* thermometer.

thermonucléaire [tɛʀmɔnykleɛʀ] *a* thermonuclear.

thermos ® [tɛʀmos] *nm ou nf*: **(bouteille) ~** vacuum *ou* Thermos ® flask.

thermostat [tɛʀmɔsta] *nm* thermostat.

thésauriser [tezɔʀize] *vi* to hoard money.

thèse [tɛz] *nf* thesis (*pl* theses).

thon [tɔ̃] *nm* tuna (fish).

thoracique [tɔʀasik] *a* thoracic.

thorax [tɔʀaks] *nm* thorax.

thrombose [tʀɔ̃boz] *nf* thrombosis.

thym [tɛ̃] *nm* thyme.

thyroïde [tiʀɔid] *nf* thyroid (gland).

tiare [tjaʀ] *nf* tiara.

tibia [tibja] *nm* shinbone, tibia; shin.

tic [tik] *nm* tic, (nervous) twitch; (*de langage etc*) mannerism.

ticket [tikɛ] *nm* ticket; **~ de quai** platform ticket.

tic-tac [tiktak] *nm inv* tick-tock; **tictaquer** *vi* to tick (away).

tiède [tjɛd] *a* lukewarm; tepid; (*vent, air*) mild, warm; **tiédir** *vi* to cool; to grow warmer.

tien, tienne [tjɛ̃, tjɛn] *pronom*: **le ~ (la tienne), les ~s (tiennes)** yours; **à la tienne!** cheers!

tiens [tjɛ̃] *vb, excl voir* **tenir**.

tierce [tjɛʀs(ə)] *a, nf voir* **tiers**.

tiercé [tjɛʀse] *nm system of forecast betting giving first 3 horses.*

tiers, tierce [tjɛʀ, tjɛʀs(ə)] *a* third // *nm* (JUR) third party; (*fraction*) third // *nf* (MUS) third; (CARTES) tierce; **une tierce personne** a third party; **~ provisionnel** *interim payment of tax.*

tige [tiʒ] *nf* stem; (*baguette*) rod.

tignasse [tiɲas] *nf* (*péj*) shock *ou* mop of hair.

tigre [tigʀ(ə)] *nm* tiger.

tigré, e [tigʀe] *a* striped; spotted.

tigresse [tigʀɛs] *nf* tigress.

tilleul [tijœl] *nm* lime (tree), linden (tree); (*boisson*) lime(-blossom) tea.

timbale [tɛ̃bal] *nf* (metal) tumbler; **~s** *nfpl* (MUS) timpani, kettledrums.

timbre [tɛ̃bʀ(ə)] *nm* (*tampon*) stamp; (*aussi*: **~-poste**) (postage) stamp; (*cachet de la poste*) postmark; (*sonnette*) bell; (MUS: *de voix, instrument*) timbre, tone.

timbrer [tɛ̃bʀe] *vt* to stamp.

timide [timid] *a* shy; timid; (*timoré*) timid, timorous; **timidité** *nf* shyness, timidity.

timonerie [timɔnʀi] *nf* wheelhouse.

timoré, e [timɔʀe] *a* timorous.

tins *etc vb voir* **tenir**.

tintamarre [tɛ̃tamaʀ] *nm* din, uproar.

tinter [tɛ̃te] *vi* to ring, chime; (*argent, clefs*) to jingle.

tir [tiʀ] *nm* (*sport*) shooting; (*fait ou manière de tirer*) firing *q*; (FOOTBALL) shot; (*stand*) shooting gallery; **~ d'obus/de mitraillette** shell/machine gun fire; **~ à l'arc** archery; **~ au pigeon** clay pigeon shooting.

tirade [tiʀad] *nf* tirade.

tirage [tiʀaʒ] *nm* (*action*) printing; (*de journal*) circulation; (*de livre*) (print-)run; edition; (*de cheminée*) draught; (*de loterie*) draw; (*désaccord*) friction; **~ au sort** drawing lots.

tirailler [tiʀɑje] *vt* to pull at, tug at // *vi* to fire at random; **tirailleur** *nm* skirmisher.

tirant [tiʀɑ̃] *nm*: ~ **d'eau** draught.
tire [tiʀ] *nf*: **vol à la** ~ pickpocketing.
tiré [tiʀe] *nm* (COMM) drawee; ~ **à part** off-print.
tire-au-flanc [tiʀoflɑ̃] *nm inv* (*péj*) skiver.
tire-bouchon [tiʀbuʃɔ̃] *nm* corkscrew.
tire-d'aile [tiʀdɛl]: **à** ~ *ad* swiftly.
tire-fesses [tiʀfɛs] *nm inv* ski-tow.
tirelire [tiʀliʀ] *nf* moneybox.
tirer [tiʀe] *vt* (*gén*) to pull; (*extraire*): ~ **qch de** to take *ou* pull sth out of; to get sth out of; to extract sth from; (*tracer*: *ligne, trait*) to draw, trace; (*fermer*: *volet, rideau*) to draw, close; (*choisir*: *carte, conclusion, aussi* COMM: *chèque*) to draw; (*en faisant feu*: *balle, coup*) to fire; (: *animal*) to shoot; (*journal, livre, photo*) to print; (FOOTBALL: *corner etc*) to take // *vi* (*faire feu*) to fire; (*faire du tir,* FOOTBALL) to shoot; (*cheminée*) to draw; **se** ~ *vi* (*fam*) to push off; **s'en** ~ to pull through, get off; ~ **sur** to pull on *ou* at; to shoot *ou* fire at; (*pipe*) to draw on; (*fig*: *avoisiner*) to verge *ou* border on; ~ **son nom de** to take *ou* get its name from; ~ **qn de** (*embarras etc*) to help *ou* get sb out of; ~ **à l'arc/la carabine** to shoot with a bow and arrow/with a rifle.
tiret [tiʀɛ] *nm* dash.
tireur, euse [tiʀœʀ, -øz] *nm/f* gunman; (COMM) drawer; **bon** ~ good shot; ~ **d'élite** marksman; ~**s débutants** beginners at shooting.
tiroir [tiʀwaʀ] *nm* drawer; ~**-caisse** *nm* till.
tisane [tizan] *nf* herb tea.
tison [tizɔ̃] *nm* brand; **tisonner** *vt* to poke; **tisonnier** *nm* poker.
tissage [tisaʒ] *nm* weaving *q*.
tisser [tise] *vt* to weave; **tisserand** *nm* weaver.
tissu [tisy] *nm* fabric, material, cloth *q*; (ANAT, BIO) tissue; ~ **de mensonges** web of lies.
tissu, e [tisy] *a*: ~ **de** woven through with.
tissu-éponge [tisyepɔ̃ʒ] *nm* (terry) towelling *q*.
titane [titan] *nm* titanium.
titanesque [titanɛsk(ə)] *a* titanic.
titre [titʀ(ə)] *nm* (*gén*) title; (*de journal*) headline; (*diplôme*) qualification; (COMM) security; (CHIMIE) titre; **en** ~ (*champion, responsable*) official, recognised; **à juste** ~ with just cause, rightly; **à quel** ~**?** on what grounds?; **à aucun** ~ on no account; **au même** ~ **(que)** in the same way (as); **à** ~ **d'exemple** as an *ou* by way of an example; **à** ~ **d'information** for (your) information; **à** ~ **gracieux** free of charge; **à** ~ **d'essai** on a trial basis; **à** ~ **privé** in a private capacity; ~ **de propriété** title deed; ~ **de transport** ticket.
titré, e [titʀe] *a* titled.
titrer [titʀe] *vt* (CHIMIE) to titrate; to assay; (PRESSE) to run as a headline; (*suj*: *vin*): ~ **10°** to be 10° proof.
tituber [titybe] *vi* to stagger *ou* reel (along).
titulaire [titylɛʀ] *a* (ADMIN) appointed, with tenure // *nm* (ADMIN) incumbent; **être** ~ **de** (*poste*) to hold; (*permis*) to be the holder of.
toast [tost] *nm* slice *ou* piece of toast; (*de bienvenue*) (welcoming) toast; **porter un** ~ **à qn** to propose *ou* drink a toast to sb.
toboggan [tɔbɔgɑ̃] *nm* toboggan.
toc [tɔk] *nm*: **en** ~ imitation *cpd*.
tocsin [tɔksɛ̃] *nm* alarm (bell).
toge [tɔʒ] *nf* toga; (*de juge*) gown.
tohu-bohu [tɔybɔy] *nm* confusion; commotion.
toi [twa] *pronom* you.
toile [twal] *nf* (*matériau*) cloth *q*; (*bâche*) piece of canvas; (*tableau*) canvas; **grosse** ~ canvas; **tisser sa** ~ (*araignée*) to spin its web; ~ **d'araignée** cobweb; ~ **cirée** oilcloth; ~ **de fond** (*fig*) backdrop; ~ **de jute** hessian; ~ **de lin** linen.
toilette [twalɛt] *nf* wash; (*s'habiller et se préparer*) getting ready, washing and dressing; (*habits*) outfit; dress *q*; ~**s** *nfpl* (*w.-c.*) toilet *sg*; **les** ~**s des dames/messieurs** the ladies'/gents' (toilets); **faire sa** ~ to have a wash, get washed; **articles de** ~ toiletries; ~ **intime** personal hygiene.
toi-même [twamɛm] *pronom* yourself.
toise [twaz] *nf*: **passer à la** ~ to have one's height measured.
toiser [twaze] *vt* to eye up and down.
toison [twazɔ̃] *nf* (*de mouton*) fleece; (*cheveux*) mane.
toit [twa] *nm* roof.
toiture [twatyʀ] *nf* roof.
tôle [tol] *nf* sheet metal *q*; (*plaque*) steel *ou* iron sheet; ~**s** (*carrosserie*) bodywork *sg*; panels; ~ **d'acier** sheet steel *q*; ~ **ondulée** corrugated iron.
tolérable [tɔleʀabl(ə)] *a* tolerable, bearable.
tolérance [tɔleʀɑ̃s] *nf* tolerance; (*hors taxe*) allowance.
tolérant, e [tɔleʀɑ̃, -ɑ̃t] *a* tolerant.
tolérer [tɔleʀe] *vt* to tolerate; (ADMIN: *hors taxe etc*) to allow.
tôlerie [tolʀi] *nf* sheet metal manufacture; sheet metal workshop.
tollé [tɔle] *nm*: **un** ~ **(de protestations)** a general outcry.
T.O.M. [*parfois*: tɔm] *sigle m(pl)* = *territoire(s) d'outre-mer.*
tomate [tɔmat] *nf* tomato.
tombal, e [tɔ̃bal] *a*: **pierre** ~**e** tombstone, gravestone.
tombant, e [tɔ̃bɑ̃, -ɑ̃t] *a* (*fig*) drooping, sloping.
tombe [tɔ̃b] *nf* (*sépulture*) grave; (*avec monument*) tomb.
tombeau, x [tɔ̃bo] *nm* tomb.
tombée [tɔ̃be] *nf*: **à la** ~ **du jour** *ou* **de la nuit** at the close of day, at nightfall.
tomber [tɔ̃be] *vi* to fall // *vt*: ~ **la veste** to slip off one's jacket; **laisser** ~ to drop; ~ **sur** *vt* (*rencontrer*) to come across; (*attaquer*) to set about; ~ **de fatigue/sommeil** to drop from exhaustion/be falling asleep on one's feet; **ça tombe bien** it comes at the right time; **il est bien tombé** he's been lucky.
tombereau, x [tɔ̃bʀo] *nm* tipcart.

tombeur [tɔ̃bœʀ] *nm* (*péj*) Casanova.
tombola [tɔ̃bɔla] *nf* tombola.
tome [tɔm] *nm* volume.
tommette [tɔmɛt] *nf* hexagonal floor tile.
ton, ta, *pl* **tes** [tɔ̃, ta, te] *dét* your.
ton [tɔ̃] *nm* (*gén*) tone ; (*MUS*) key ; (*couleur*) shade, tone ; **de bon ~** in good taste.
tonal, e [tɔnal] *a* tonal.
tonalité [tɔnalite] *nf* (*au téléphone*) dialling tone ; (*MUS*) tonality ; key ; (*fig*) tone.
tondeuse [tɔ̃døz] *nf* (*à gazon*) (lawn)-mower ; (*du coiffeur*) clippers *pl* ; (*pour la tonte*) shears *pl*.
tondre [tɔ̃dʀ(ə)] *vt* (*pelouse, herbe*) to mow ; (*haie*) to cut, clip ; (*mouton, toison*) to shear ; (*cheveux*) to crop.
tonifiant, e [tɔnifjɑ̃, -ɑ̃t] *a* invigorating, revivifying.
tonifier [tɔnifje] *vt* (*peau, organisme*) to tone up.
tonique [tɔnik] *a* fortifying // *nm, nf* tonic.
tonitruant, e [tɔnitʀyɑ̃, -ɑ̃t] *a*: **voix ~e** thundering voice.
tonnage [tɔnaʒ] *nm* tonnage.
tonne [tɔn] *nf* metric ton, tonne.
tonneau, x [tɔno] *nm* (*à vin, cidre*) barrel ; (*NAVIG*) ton ; **faire des ~x** (*voiture, avion*) to roll over.
tonnelier [tɔnəlje] *nm* cooper.
tonnelle [tɔnɛl] *nf* bower, arbour.
tonner [tɔne] *vi* to thunder ; **il tonne** it is thundering, there's some thunder.
tonnerre [tɔnɛʀ] *nm* thunder ; **~ d'applaudissements** thunderous applause ; **du ~** *a* (*fam*) terrific.
tonsure [tɔ̃syʀ] *nf* tonsure ; bald patch.
tonte [tɔ̃t] *nf* shearing.
tonus [tɔnys] *nm* tone.
top [tɔp] *nm*: **au 3ème ~** at the 3rd stroke // *a*: **~ secret** top secret.
topaze [tɔpɑz] *nf* topaz.
toper [tɔpe] *vi*: **tope-/topez-là**! it's a deal!, you're on!
topinambour [tɔpinɑ̃buʀ] *nm* Jerusalem artichoke.
topographie [tɔpɔgʀafi] *nf* topography ; **topographique** *a* topographical.
toponymie [tɔpɔnimi] *nf* study of place-names, toponymy.
toque [tɔk] *nf* (*de fourrure*) fur hat ; **~ de jockey/juge** jockey's/judge's cap ; **~ de cuisinier** chef's hat.
toqué, e [tɔke] *a* (*fam*) touched, cracked.
torche [tɔʀʃ(ə)] *nf* torch ; **se mettre en ~** (*parachute*) to candle.
torcher [tɔʀʃe] *vt* (*fam*) to wipe.
torchère [tɔʀʃɛʀ] *nf* flare.
torchon [tɔʀʃɔ̃] *nm* cloth, duster ; (*à vaisselle*) tea towel, dish towel.
tordre [tɔʀdʀ(ə)] *vt* (*chiffon*) to wring ; (*barre, fig: visage*) to twist ; **se ~** *vi* (*barre*) to bend ; (*roue*) to twist, buckle ; (*ver, serpent*) to writhe ; **se ~ le pied/bras** to twist *ou* sprain one's foot/arm ; **se ~ de douleur/rire** to writhe in pain/be doubled up with laughter.
tordu, e [tɔʀdy] *a* (*fig*) warped, twisted.
torero [tɔʀeʀo] *nm* bullfighter.
tornade [tɔʀnad] *nf* tornado.
torpeur [tɔʀpœʀ] *nf* torpor, drowsiness.
torpille [tɔʀpij] *nf* torpedo ; **torpiller** *vt* to torpedo.
torréfier [tɔʀefje] *vt* to roast.
torrent [tɔʀɑ̃] *nm* torrent, mountain stream ; (*fig*): **~ de** torrent *ou* flood of ; **il pleut à ~s** the rain is lashing down ; **torrentiel, le** *a* torrential.
torride [tɔʀid] *a* torrid.
torsade [tɔʀsad] *nf* twist ; (*ARCHIT*) cable moulding ; **torsader** *vt* to twist.
torse [tɔʀs(ə)] *nm* (*ANAT*) torso ; chest.
torsion [tɔʀsjɔ̃] *nf* twisting ; torsion.
tort [tɔʀ] *nm* (*défaut*) fault ; (*préjudice*) wrong *q* ; **~s** *nmpl* (*JUR*) fault *sg* ; **avoir ~** to be wrong ; **être dans son ~** to be in the wrong ; **donner ~ à qn** to lay the blame on sb ; (*fig*) to prove sb wrong ; **causer du ~ à** to harm ; to be harmful *ou* detrimental to ; **en ~** in the wrong, at fault ; **à ~** wrongly ; **à ~ et à travers** wildly.
torticolis [tɔʀtikɔli] *nm* stiff neck.
tortiller [tɔʀtije] *vt* to twist ; to twiddle ; **se ~** *vi* to wriggle, squirm.
tortionnaire [tɔʀsjɔnɛʀ] *nm* torturer.
tortue [tɔʀty] *nf* tortoise.
tortueux, euse [tɔʀtɥø, -øz] *a* (*rue*) twisting ; (*fig*) tortuous.
torture [tɔʀtyʀ] *nf* torture ; **torturer** *vt* to torture ; (*fig*) to torment.
torve [tɔʀv(ə)] *a*: **regard ~** menacing *ou* grim look.
tôt [to] *ad* early ; **~ ou tard** sooner or later ; **si ~** so early ; (*déjà*) so soon ; **au plus ~** at the earliest, as soon as possible ; **plus ~** earlier ; **il eut ~ fait de faire** he soon did.
total, e, aux [tɔtal, -o] *a, nm* total ; **au ~** in total *ou* all ; **faire le ~** to work out the total, add up ; **~ement** *ad* totally, completely ; **~iser** *vt* total (up).
totalitaire [tɔtalitɛʀ] *a* totalitarian.
totalité [tɔtalite] *nf*: **la ~ de** all of, the total amount (*ou* number) of ; the whole + *sg* ; **en ~** entirely.
totem [tɔtɛm] *nm* totem.
toubib [tubib] *nm* (*fam*) doctor.
touchant, e [tuʃɑ̃, -ɑ̃t] *a* touching.
touche [tuʃ] *nf* (*de piano, de machine à écrire*) key ; (*PEINTURE etc*) stroke, touch ; (*fig: de nostalgie*) touch, hint ; (*RUGBY*) line-out ; (*FOOTBALL: aussi*: **remise en ~**) throw-in ; (: **ligne de ~**) touch-line ; (*ESCRIME*) hit ; **en ~** in (*ou* into) touch ; **avoir une drôle de ~** to look a sight.
touche-à-tout [tuʃatu] *nm/f inv* (*péj*) meddler ; dabbler.
toucher [tuʃe] *nm* touch // *vt* to touch ; (*palper*) to feel ; (*atteindre: d'un coup de feu etc*) to hit ; (*affecter*) to touch, affect ; (*concerner*) to concern, affect ; (*contacter*) to reach, contact ; (*recevoir: récompense*) to receive, get ; (: *salaire*) to draw, get ; **au ~** to the touch ; **se ~** (*être en contact*) to touch ; **~ à** to touch ; (*modifier*) to touch, tamper *ou* meddle with ; (*traiter de, concerner*) to have to do with, concern ; **je vais lui en ~ un mot** I'll have a word with him about it ; **~ à sa fin** to be drawing to a close.

touffe [tuf] *nf* tuft.
touffu, e [tufy] *a* thick, dense; (*fig*) complex, involved.
toujours [tuʒuʀ] *ad* always; (*encore*) still; (*constamment*) forever; ~ **plus** more and more; **pour** ~ forever; ~ **est-il que** the fact remains that; **essaie** ~ (you can) try anyway.
toupie [tupi] *nf* (spinning) top.
tour [tuʀ] *nf* tower; (*immeuble*) high-rise block, tower block; (ÉCHECS) castle, rook // *nm* (*excursion*) stroll, walk; run, ride; trip; (SPORT: *aussi*: ~ **de piste**) lap; (*d'être servi ou de jouer etc, tournure, de vis ou clef*) turn; (*de roue etc*) revolution; (*circonférence*): **de 3 m de** ~ 3 m round, with a circumference *ou* girth of 3 m; (POL: *aussi*: ~ **de scrutin**) ballot; (*ruse, de prestidigitation*) trick; (*de potier*) wheel; (*à bois, métaux*) lathe; **faire le** ~ **de** to go round; (*à pied*) to walk round; **faire un** ~ to go for a walk; (*en voiture etc*) to go for a ride; **faire 2** ~**s** to go round twice; (*hélice etc*) to turn *ou* revolve twice; **fermer à double** ~ *vi* to double-lock the door; **c'est au** ~ **de Renée** it's Renée's turn; **à** ~ **de rôle,** ~ **à** ~ in turn; ~ **de taille/tête** waist/head measurement ~ **de chant** song recital; ~ **de contrôle** *nf* control tower; ~ **de garde** spell of duty; ~ **d'horizon** (*fig*) general survey; ~ **de lit** valance; ~ **de reins** sprained back.
tourbe [tuʀb(ə)] *nf* peat; **tourbière** *nf* peat-bog.
tourbillon [tuʀbijɔ̃] *nm* whirlwind; (*d'eau*) whirlpool; (*fig*) whirl, swirl; **tourbillonner** *vi* to whirl, swirl; to whirl *ou* swirl round.
tourelle [tuʀɛl] *nf* turret.
tourisme [turism(ə)] *nm* tourism; tourist industry; **agence de** ~ tourist agency; **faire du** ~ to do some sightseeing, go touring; **touriste** *nm/f* tourist; **touristique** *a* tourist *cpd*; (*région*) touristic, with tourist appeal.
tourment [tuʀmɑ̃] *nm* torment.
tourmente [tuʀmɑ̃t] *nf* storm.
tourmenté, e [tuʀmɑ̃te] *a* tormented, tortured.
tourmenter [tuʀmɑ̃te] *vt* to torment; **se** ~ *vi* to fret, worry o.s.
tournage [tuʀnaʒ] *nm* (*d'un film*) shooting.
tournant, e [tuʀnɑ̃, -ɑ̃t] *a*: *voir* **plaque, grève** // *nm* (*de route*) bend; (*fig*) turning point.
tournebroche [tuʀnəbʀɔʃ] *nm* roasting spit.
tourne-disque [tuʀnədisk(ə)] *nm* record player.
tournée [tuʀne] *nf* (*du facteur etc*) round; (*d'artiste, politicien*) tour; (*au café*) round (of drinks); ~ **musicale** concert tour.
tourner [tuʀne] *vt* to turn; (*contourner*) to get round; (CINÉMA) to shoot; to make // *vi* to turn; (*moteur*) to run; (*compteur*) to tick away; (*lait etc*) to turn (sour); **se** ~ *vi* to turn round; **se** ~ **vers** to turn to; to turn towards; **bien** ~ to turn out well; ~ **autour de** to go round; to revolve round; (*péj*) to hang round; ~ **à/en** to turn into; ~ **à la pluie/au rouge** to turn rainy/red; ~ **le dos à** to turn one's back on; to have one's back to; **se** ~ **les pouces** to twiddle one's thumbs; ~ **la tête** to look away; ~ **la tête à qn** (*fig*) to go to sb's head; ~ **de l'œil** to pass out.
tournesol [tuʀnəsɔl] *nm* sunflower.
tourneur [tuʀnœʀ] *nm* turner; lathe-operator.
tournevis [tuʀnəvis] *nm* screwdriver.
tourniquet [tuʀnikɛ] *nm* (*pour arroser*) sprinkler; (*portillon*) turnstile; (*présentoir*) revolving stand.
tournoi [tuʀnwa] *nm* tournament.
tournoyer [tuʀnwaje] *vi* to whirl round; to swirl round.
tournure [tuʀnyʀ] *nf* (LING) turn of phrase; form; phrasing; (*évolution*): **la** ~ **de qch** the way sth is developing; (*aspect*): **la** ~ **de** the look of; ~ **d'esprit** turn *ou* cast of mind; **la** ~ **des événements** the turn of events.
tourte [tuʀt(ə)] *nf* pie.
tourteau, x [tuʀto] *nm* (AGR) oilcake, cattle-cake; (ZOOL) edible crab.
tourterelle [tuʀtəʀɛl] *nf* turtledove.
tous *dét* [tu], *pronom* [tus] *voir* **tout.**
Toussaint [tusɛ̃] *nf*: **la** ~ All Saints' Day.
tousser [tuse] *vi* to cough; **toussoter** *vi* to have a slight cough; to cough a little; (*pour avertir*) to give a slight cough.
tout, e, *pl* **tous, toutes** [tu, tus, tut] *dét* all; ~ **le lait** all the milk, the whole of the milk; ~**e la nuit** all night, the whole night; ~ **le livre** the whole book; ~ **un pain** a whole loaf; **tous les livres** all the books; **toutes les nuits** every night; **à** ~ **âge** at any age; **toutes les fois** every time; **toutes les 3/2 semaines** every third/other *ou* second week; **tous les 2** both *ou* each of us (*ou* them); **toutes les 3** all 3 of us (*ou* them); ~ **le temps** *ad* all the time; the whole time; **c'est** ~ **le contraire** it's quite the opposite; **il avait pour** ~**e nourriture** his only food was // *pronom* everything, all; **tous, toutes** all (of them); **je les vois tous** I can see them all *ou* all of them; **nous y sommes tous allés** all of us went, we all went; **en** ~ in all // *ad* quite; very; ~ **en haut** right at the top; **le** ~ **premier** the very first; **le livre** ~ **entier** the whole book; ~ **seul** all alone; ~ **droit** straight ahead; ~ **en travaillant** while working, as *ou* while he *etc* works // *nm* whole; **le** ~ all of it (*ou* them), the whole lot; ~ **d'abord** first of all; ~ **à coup** suddenly; ~ **à fait** absolutely; ~ **à l'heure** a short while ago; in a short while, shortly; ~ **de même** all the same; ~ **le monde** everybody; ~ **de suite** immediately, straight away; ~ **terrain** *ou* **tous terrains** *a inv* general-purpose; ~**-à-l'égout** *nm inv* mains drainage.
toutefois [tutfwa] *ad* however.
toutou [tutu] *nm* (*fam*) doggie.
toux [tu] *nf* cough.
toxicomane [tɔksikɔman] *nm/f* drug addict.
toxine [tɔksin] *nf* toxin.
toxique [tɔksik] *a* toxic, poisonous.
trac [tʀak] *nm* nerves *pl*; (THÉÂTRE) stage

fright; **avoir le ~** to get an attack of nerves; to have stage fright.

tracas [tRaka] *nm* bother *q*, worry *q*; **tracasser** *vt* to worry, bother; to harass; **se tracasser** *vi* to worry o.s., fret; **tracasserie** *nf* annoyance *q*; harassment *q*; **tracassier, ière** *a* irksome.

trace [tRas] *nf* (*empreintes*) tracks *pl*; (*marques, aussi fig*) mark; (*restes, vestige*) trace; (*indice*) sign; **~s de pas** footprints.

tracé [tRase] *nm* line; layout.

tracer [tRase] *vt* to draw; (*mot*) to trace; (*piste*) to open up.

trachée(-artère) [tRaʃe(aRtɛR)] *nf* windpipe, trachea; **trachéite** [tRakeit] *nf* tracheitis.

tract [tRakt] *nm* tract, pamphlet.

tractations [tRaktɑsjɔ̃] *nfpl* dealings, bargaining *sg*.

tracteur [tRaktœR] *nm* tractor.

traction [tRaksjɔ̃] *nf* traction; (*GYM*) pull-up; **~ avant/arrière** front-wheel/rear-wheel drive; **~ électrique** electric(al) traction *ou* haulage.

tradition [tRadisjɔ̃] *nf* tradition; **traditionnel, le** *a* traditional.

traducteur, trice [tRadyktœR, -tRis] *nm/f* translator.

traduction [tRadyksjɔ̃] *nf* translation.

traduire [tRadɥiR] *vt* to translate; (*exprimer*) to render, convey; **~ en français** to translate into French; **~ en justice** to bring before the courts.

trafic [tRafik] *nm* traffic; **~ d'armes** arms dealing; **trafiquant, e** *nm/f* trafficker; dealer; **trafiquer** *vt* (*péj*) to doctor, tamper with // *vi* to traffic, be engaged in trafficking.

tragédie [tRaʒedi] *nf* tragedy; **tragédien, ne** *nm/f* tragedian/ tragedienne.

tragique [tRaʒik] *a* tragic; **~ment** *ad* tragically.

trahir [tRaiR] *vt* to betray; (*fig*) to give away, reveal; **trahison** *nf* betrayal; (*MIL*) treason.

train [tRɛ̃] *nm* (*RAIL*) train; (*allure*) pace; (*fig: ensemble*) set; **mettre qch en ~** to get sth under way; **mettre qn en ~** to put sb in good spirits; **se mettre en ~** to get started; to warm up; **se sentir en ~** to feel in good form; **~ avant/arrière** front-wheel/rear-wheel axle unit; **~ d'atterrissage** undercarriage; **~ autos-couchettes** car-sleeper train; **~ électrique** (*jouet*) (electric) train set; **~ de pneus** set of tyres; **~ de vie** style of living.

traînant, e [tRɛnɑ̃, -ɑ̃t] *a* (*voix, ton*) drawling.

traînard, e [tRɛnaR, -aRd(ə)] *nm/f* (*péj*) slowcoach.

traîne [tRɛn] *nf* (*de robe*) train; **être à la ~** to be in tow; to lag behind.

traîneau, x [tRɛno] *nm* sleigh, sledge.

traînée [tRene] *nf* streak, trail; (*péj*) slut.

traîner [tRene] (*remorque*) to pull; (*enfant, chien*) to drag *ou* trail along // *vi* (*être en désordre*) to lie around; (*marcher lentement*) to dawdle (along); (*vagabonder*) to hang about; (*agir lentement*) to idle about; (*durer*) to drag on; **se ~** *vi* to crawl along; to drag o.s. along; (*durer*) to drag on; **~ les pieds** to drag one's feet.

train-train [tRɛ̃tRɛ̃] *nm* humdrum routine.

traire [tRɛR] *vt* to milk.

trait [tRɛ] *nm* (*ligne*) line; (*de dessin*) stroke; (*caractéristique*) feature, trait; (*flèche*) dart, arrow; shaft; **~s** *nmpl* (*du visage*) features; **d'un ~** (*boire*) in one gulp; **de ~** *a* (*animal*) draught; **avoir ~ à** to concern; **~ de caractère** characteristic, trait; **~ d'esprit** flash of wit; **~ d'union** hyphen; (*fig*) link.

traitant [tRɛtɑ̃] *am*: **votre médecin ~** your usual *ou* family doctor; **shampooing ~** medicated shampoo.

traite [tRɛt] *nf* (*COMM*) draft; (*AGR*) milking; (*trajet*) stretch; **d'une (seule) ~** without stopping (once); **la ~ des noirs** the slave trade.

traité [tRete] *nm* treaty.

traitement [tRɛtmɑ̃] *nm* treatment; processing; (*salaire*) salary.

traiter [tRete] *vt* (*gén*) to treat; (*TECH: matériaux*) to process, treat; (*affaire*) to deal with, handle; (*qualifier*): **~ qn d'idiot** to call sb a fool // *vi* to deal; **~ de** *vt* to deal with; **bien/mal ~** to treat well/ill-treat.

traiteur [tRɛtœR] *nm* caterer.

traître, esse [tRɛtR(ə), -tRɛs] *a* (*dangereux*) treacherous // *nm* traitor; **prendre qn en ~** to make an insidious attack on sb; **traîtrise** *nf* treachery, treacherousness.

trajectoire [tRaʒɛktwaR] *nf* trajectory, path.

trajet [tRaʒɛ] *nm* journey; (*itinéraire*) route; (*fig*) path, course.

tralala [tRalala] *nm* (*péj*) fuss.

tram [tRam] *nm abr de* **tramway**.

trame [tRam] *nf* (*de tissu*) weft; (*fig*) framework; texture; (*TYPO*) screen.

tramer [tRame] *vt* to plot, hatch.

tramway [tRamwɛ] *nm* tram(way); tram(car).

tranchant, e [tRɑ̃ʃɑ̃, -ɑ̃t] *a* sharp; (*fig*) peremptory // *nm* (*d'un couteau*) cutting edge; (*de la main*) edge.

tranche [tRɑ̃ʃ] *nf* (*morceau*) slice; (*arête*) edge; (*partie*) section; (*série*) block; issue; bracket.

tranché, e [tRɑ̃ʃe] *a* (*couleurs*) distinct, sharply contrasted; (*opinions*) clear-cut, definite // *nf* trench.

trancher [tRɑ̃ʃe] *vt* to cut, sever; (*fig: résoudre*) to settle // *vi*: **~ avec** to contrast sharply with.

tranchet [tRɑ̃ʃɛ] *nm* knife.

tranchoir [tRɑ̃ʃwaR] *nm* chopper.

tranquille [tRɑ̃kil] *a* calm, quiet; (*enfant, élève*) quiet; (*rassuré*) easy in one's mind, with one's mind at rest; **se tenir ~** (*enfant*) to be quiet; **avoir la conscience ~** to have an easy conscience; **laisse-moi/laisse-ça ~!** leave me/it alone; **~ment** *ad* calmly; **tranquillisant** *nm* tranquillizer; **tranquilliser** *vt* to reassure; **tranquillité** *nf* quietness; peace (and quiet); **tranquillité (d'esprit)** peace of mind.

transaction [tRɑ̃zaksjɔ̃] *nf* (*COMM*) transaction, deal.
transat [tRɑ̃zat] *nm* deckchair.
transatlantique [tRɑ̃zatlɑ̃tik] *a* transatlantic // *nm* transatlantic liner.
transborder [tRɑ̃sbɔRde] *vt* to tran(s)ship.
transcendant, e [tRɑ̃sɑ̃dɑ̃, -ɑ̃t] *a* transcendent(al).
transcription [tRɑ̃skRipsjɔ̃] *nf* transcription.
transcrire [tRɑ̃skRiR] *vt* to transcribe.
transe [tRɑ̃s] *nf*: **entrer en ~** to go into a trance; **~s** agony *sg.*
transférer [tRɑ̃sfeRe] *vt* to transfer; **transfert** *nm* transfer.
transfigurer [tRɑ̃sfigyRe] *vt* to transform.
transformateur [tRɑ̃sfɔRmatœR] *nm* transformer.
transformation [tRɑ̃sfɔRmɑsjɔ̃] *nf* transformation; (*RUGBY*) conversion.
transformer [tRɑ̃sfɔRme] *vt* to transform, alter (*'alter' implique un changement moins radical*); (*matière première, appartement, RUGBY*) to convert; **~ en** to transform into; to turn into; to convert into; **se ~** *vi* to be transformed; to alter.
transfuge [tRɑ̃sfyʒ] *nm* renegade.
transfusion [tRɑ̃sfyzjɔ̃] *nf*: **~ sanguine** blood transfusion.
transgresser [tRɑ̃sgRese] *vt* to contravene, disobey.
transhumance [tRɑ̃zymɑ̃s] *nf* transhumance, seasonal move to new pastures.
transi, e [tRɑ̃zi] *a* numb (with cold), chilled to the bone.
transiger [tRɑ̃ziʒe] *vi* to compromise, come to an agreement.
transistor [tRɑ̃zistɔR] *nm* transistor.
transit [tRɑ̃zit] *nm* transit; **~er** *vi* to pass in transit.
transitif, ive [tRɑ̃zitif, -iv] *a* transitive.
transition [tRɑ̃zisjɔ̃] *nf* transition; **de ~** transitional; **transitoire** *a* transitional, provisional; transient.
translucide [tRɑ̃slysid] *a* translucent.
transmetteur [tRɑ̃smɛtœR] *nm* transmitter.
transmettre [tRɑ̃smɛtR(ə)] *vt* (*passer*): **~ qch à qn** to pass sth on to sb; (*TECH, TEL, MED*) to transmit; (*TV, RADIO*: *retransmettre*) to broadcast; **transmissible** *a* transmissible.
transmission [tRɑ̃smisjɔ̃] *nf* transmission, passing on; (*AUTO*) transmission; **~s** *nfpl* (*MIL*) ≈ signals corps; **~ de pensée** telepathy.
transparaître [tRɑ̃spaRɛtR(ə)] *vi* to show (through).
transparence [tRɑ̃spaRɑ̃s] *nf* transparence; **par ~** (*regarder*) against a source of light; (*voir*) showing through.
transparent, e [tRɑ̃spaRɑ̃, -ɑ̃t] *a* transparent.
transpercer [tRɑ̃spɛRse] *vt* to go through, pierce.
transpiration [tRɑ̃spiRɑsjɔ̃] *nf* perspiration.
transpirer [tRɑ̃spiRe] *vi* to perspire.
transplanter [tRɑ̃splɑ̃te] *vt* (*MÉD, BOT*) to transplant; (*personne*) to uproot, move.
transport [tRɑ̃spɔR] *nm* transport; **~s en commun** public transport *sg.*
transporter [tRɑ̃spɔRte] *vt* to carry, move; (*COMM*) to transport, convey; (*fig*) to send into raptures; **~ qn à l'hôpital** to take sb to hospital; **transporteur** *nm* haulier, haulage contractor.
transposer [tRɑ̃spoze] *vt* to transpose; **transposition** *nf* transposition.
transvaser [tRɑ̃svaze] *vt* to decant.
transversal, e, aux [tRɑ̃svɛRsal, -o] *a* transverse, cross(-); cross-country; running at right angles.
trapèze [tRapɛz] *nm* (*GÉOM*) trapezium; (*au cirque*) trapeze; **trapéziste** *nm/f* trapeze artist.
trappe [tRap] *nf* trap door.
trappeur [tRapœR] *nm* trapper, fur trader.
trapu, e [tRapy] *a* squat, stocky.
traquenard [tRaknaR] *nm* trap.
traquer [tRake] *vt* to track down; (*harceler*) to hound.
traumatiser [tRomatize] *vt* to traumatize.
traumatisme [tRomatism(ə)] *nm* traumatism.
travail, aux [tRavaj, -o] *nm* (*gén*) work; (*tâche, métier*) work *q*, job; (*ÉCON, MÉD*) labour // *nmpl* (*de réparation, agricoles etc*) work *sg*; (*sur route*) roadworks *pl*; (*de construction*) building (work); **être/entrer en ~** (*MÉD*) to be in/start labour; **être sans ~** (*employé*) to be out of work *ou* unemployed; **~ noir** moonlighting; **travaux des champs** farmwork *sg*; **travaux dirigés** (*SCOL*) supervised practical work *sg*; **travaux forcés** hard labour *sg*; **travaux manuels** (*SCOL*) handicrafts; **travaux ménagers** housework *sg*; **travaux publics** ≈ public works *sg.*
travaillé, e [tRavaje] *a* (*style*) polished.
travailler [tRavaje] *vi* to work; (*bois*) to warp // *vt* (*bois, métal*) to work; (*objet d'art, discipline, fig*: *influencer*) to work on; **cela le travaille** it is on his mind; **~ la terre** to till the land; **~ son piano** to do one's piano practice; **~ à** to work on; (*fig*: *contribuer à*) to work towards; **travailleur, euse** *a* hard-working // *nm/f* worker; **travailleur de force** labourer; **travailliste** *a* Labour.
travée [tRave] *nf* row; (*ARCHIT*) bay; span.
travelling [tRavliŋ] *nm* (*chariot*) dolly; (*technique*) tracking; **~ optique** zoom shots *pl.*
travers [tRavɛR] *nm* fault, failing; **en ~ (de)** across; **au ~ (de)** through; **de ~** *a* askew // *ad* sideways; (*fig*) the wrong way; **à ~** through; **regarder de ~** (*fig*) to look askance at.
traverse [tRavɛRs(ə)] *nf* (*RAIL*) sleeper; **chemin de ~** shortcut.
traversée [tRavɛRse] *nf* crossing.
traverser [tRavɛRse] *vt* (*gén*) to cross; (*ville, tunnel, aussi*: *percer, fig*) to go through; (*suj*: *ligne, trait*) to run across.
traversin [tRavɛRsɛ̃] *nm* bolster.

travesti [tʀavɛsti] *nm* (*costume*) fancy dress; (*artiste de cabaret*) female impersonator, drag artist; (*pervers*) transvestite.
travestir [tʀavɛstiʀ] *vt* (*vérité*) to misrepresent; **se ~** to dress up; to put on drag; to dress as a woman.
trébucher [tʀebyʃe] *vi*: **~ (sur)** to stumble (over), trip (against).
trèfle [tʀɛfl(ə)] *nm* (BOT) clover; (CARTES: *couleur*) clubs *pl*; (: *carte*) club; **~ à quatre feuilles** four-leaf clover.
treillage [tʀɛjaʒ] *nm* lattice work.
treille [tʀɛj] *nf* vine arbour; climbing vine.
treillis [tʀeji] *nm* (*métallique*) wire-mesh; (*toile*) canvas; (*uniforme*) battle-dress.
treize [tʀɛz] *num* thirteen; **treizième** *num* thirteenth.
tréma [tʀema] *nm* diaeresis.
tremble [tʀɑ̃bl(ə)] *nm* (BOT) aspen.
tremblement [tʀɑ̃bləmɑ̃] *nm* trembling *q*, shaking *q*, shivering *q*; **~ de terre** earthquake.
trembler [tʀɑ̃ble] *vi* to tremble, shake; **~ de** (*froid, fièvre*) to shiver *ou* tremble with; (*peur*) to shake *ou* tremble with; **~ pour qn** to fear for sb; **trembloter** *vi* to tremble *ou* shake slightly.
trémolo [tʀemɔlo] *nm* (*instrument*) tremolo; (*voix*) quaver.
trémousser [tʀemuse]: **se ~** *vi* to jig about, wriggle about.
trempe [tʀɑ̃p] *nf* (*fig*): **de cette/sa ~** of this/his calibre.
trempé, e [tʀɑ̃pe] *a* soaking (wet), drenched; (TECH) tempered.
tremper [tʀɑ̃pe] *vt* to soak, drench; (*aussi*: **faire ~, mettre à ~**) to soak; (*plonger*): **~ qch dans** to dip sth in(to) // *vi* to soak; (*fig*): **~ dans** to be involved *ou* have a hand in; **se ~** *vi* to have a quick dip; **se faire ~** to get soaked *ou* drenched; **trempette** *nf*: **faire trempette** to have a quick dip.
tremplin [tʀɑ̃plɛ̃] *nm* springboard; (SKI) ski-jump.
trentaine [tʀɑ̃tɛn] *nf*: **une ~ (de)** thirty or so, about thirty.
trente [tʀɑ̃t] *num* thirty; **trentième** *num* thirtieth.
trépaner [tʀepane] *vt* to trepan, trephine.
trépasser [tʀepase] *vi* to pass away.
trépider [tʀepide] *vi* to vibrate.
trépied [tʀepje] *nm* (*d'appareil*) tripod; (*meuble*) trivet.
trépigner [tʀepiɲe] *vi* to stamp (one's feet).
très [tʀɛ] *ad* very; much + *pp*, highly + *pp*; **~ critiqué** much criticized; **~ industrialisé** highly industrialized; **j'ai ~ faim** I'm very hungry.
trésor [tʀezɔʀ] *nm* treasure; (ADMIN) finances *pl*; funds *pl*; **T~ (public)** public revenue.
trésorerie [tʀezɔʀʀi] *nf* (*fonds*) funds *pl*; (*gestion*) accounts *pl*; (*bureaux*) accounts department; (*poste*) treasurership; **difficultés de ~** cash problems, shortage of cash *ou* funds.
trésorier, ière [tʀezɔʀje, -jɛʀ] *nm/f* treasurer; **~-payeur** *nm* paymaster.
tressaillir [tʀesajiʀ] *vi* to shiver, shudder; to quiver.
tressauter [tʀesote] *vi* to start, jump.
tresse [tʀɛs] *nf* braid, plait.
tresser [tʀese] *vt* (*cheveux*) to braid, plait; (*fil, jonc*) to plait; (*corbeille*) to weave; (*corde*) to twist.
tréteau, x [tʀeto] *nm* trestle; **les ~x** (*fig*) the stage.
treuil [tʀœj] *nm* winch; **treuiller** *vt* to winch up.
trêve [tʀɛv] *nf* (MIL, POL) truce; (*fig*) respite; **~ de ...** enough of this... .
tri [tʀi] *nm* sorting out *q*; selection; (POSTES) sorting; sorting office.
triage [tʀijaʒ] *nm* (RAIL) shunting; (*gare*) marshalling yard.
triangle [tʀijɑ̃gl(ə)] *nm* triangle; **~ rectangle** right-angled triangle.
tribal, e, aux [tʀibal, -o] *a* tribal.
tribord [tʀibɔʀ] *nm*: **à ~** to starboard, on the starboard side.
tribu [tʀiby] *nf* tribe.
tribulations [tʀibylusjɔ̃] *nfpl* tribulations, trials.
tribunal, aux [tʀibynal, -o] *nm* (JUR) court; (MIL) tribunal; **~ de police/pour enfants** police/juvenile court; **~ d'instance** ≈ magistrates' court; **~ de grande instance** ≈ high court.
tribune [tʀibyn] *nf* (*estrade*) platform, rostrum; (*débat*) forum; (*d'église, de tribunal*) gallery; (*de stade*) stand; **~ libre** (PRESSE) opinion column.
tribut [tʀiby] *nm* tribute.
tributaire [tʀibytɛʀ] *a*: **être ~ de** to be dependent on; (GÉO) to be a tributary of.
tricher [tʀiʃe] *vi* to cheat; **tricherie** *nf* cheating *q*; **tricheur, euse** *nm/f* cheat.
tricolore [tʀikɔlɔʀ] *a* three-coloured; (*français*) red, white and blue.
tricot [tʀiko] *nm* (*technique, ouvrage*) knitting *q*; (*tissu*) knitted fabric; (*vêtement*) jersey, sweater.
tricoter [tʀikɔte] *vt* to knit.
trictrac [tʀiktʀak] *nm* backgammon.
tricycle [tʀisikl(ə)] *nm* tricycle.
triennal, e, aux [tʀiɛnal, -o] *a* three-yearly; three-year.
trier [tʀije] *vt* to sort out; (POSTES, *fruits*) to sort.
trigonométrie [tʀigɔnɔmetʀi] *nf* trigonometry.
trimbaler [tʀɛ̃bale] *vt* to cart around, trail along.
trimer [tʀime] *vi* to slave away.
trimestre [tʀimɛstʀ(ə)] *nm* (SCOL) term; (COMM) quarter; **trimestriel, le** *a* quarterly; (SCOL) end-of-term.
tringle [tʀɛ̃gl(ə)] *nf* rod.
Trinité [tʀinite] *nf* Trinity.
trinquer [tʀɛ̃ke] *vi* to clink glasses; (*fam*) to cop it; **~ à qch/la santé de qn** to drink to sth/sb.
trio [tʀijo] *nm* trio.
triomphal, e, aux [tʀijɔ̃fal, -o] *a* triumphant, triumphal.
triomphant, e [tʀijɔ̃fɑ̃, -ɑ̃t] *a* triumphant.
triomphe [tʀijɔ̃f] *nm* triumph; **être reçu/porté en ~** to be given a triumphant

welcome/be carried shoulder-high in triumph.

triompher [tʀijɔ̃fe] *vi* to triumph, win; ~ **de** to triumph over, overcome.

tripes [tʀip] *nfpl* (CULIN) tripe *sg*; (*fam*) guts.

triple [tʀipl(ə)] *a* triple; treble // *nm*: **le ~ (de)** (*comparaison*) three times as much (as); **en ~ exemplaire** in triplicate; **~ment** *ad* three times over; in three ways, on three counts // *nm* trebling, threefold increase; **tripler** *vi, vt* to triple, treble, increase threefold.

tripot [tripo] *nm* (*péj*) dive.

tripotage [tʀipɔtaʒ] *nm* (*péj*) jiggery-pokery.

tripoter [tʀipɔte] *vt* to fiddle with, finger.

trique [tʀik] *nf* cudgel.

triste [tʀist(ə)] *a* sad; (*péj*): ~ **personnage/affaire** sorry individual/affair; **tristesse** *nf* sadness.

triturer [tʀityʀe] *vt* (*pâte*) to knead; (*objets*) to manipulate.

trivial, e, aux [tʀivjal, -o] *a* coarse, crude; (*commun*) mundane.

troc [tʀɔk] *nm* (ECON) barter; (*transaction*) exchange, swap.

troglodyte [tʀɔglɔdit] *nm/f* cave dweller, troglodyte.

trognon [tʀɔɲɔ̃] *nm* (*de fruit*) core; (*de légume*) stalk.

trois [tʀwɑ] *num* three; **troisième** *num* third; **troisièmement** *ad* thirdly; **~-quarts** *nmpl*: **les ~-quarts de** three-quarters of.

trolleybus [tʀɔlɛbys] *nm* trolley bus.

trombe [tʀɔ̃b] *nf* waterspout; **des ~s d'eau** a downpour; **en ~** (*arriver, passer*) like a whirlwind.

trombone [tʀɔ̃bɔn] *nm* (MUS) trombone; (*de bureau*) paper clip; **~ à coulisse** slide trombone; **tromboniste** *nm/f* trombonist.

trompe [tʀɔ̃p] *nf* (*d'éléphant*) trunk; (MUS) trumpet, horn; **~ d'Eustache** Eustachian tube; **~s utérines** Fallopian tubes.

trompe-l'œil [tʀɔ̃plœj] *nm*: **en ~** in trompe-l'œil style.

tromper [tʀɔ̃pe] *vt* to deceive; (*vigilance, poursuivants*) to elude; **se ~** *vi* to make a mistake, be mistaken; **se ~ de voiture/jour** to take the wrong car/get the day wrong; **se ~ de 3 cm/20 F** to be out by 3 cm/20 F; **tromperie** *nf* deception, trickery *q*.

trompette [tʀɔ̃pɛt] *nf* trumpet; **en ~** (*nez*) turned-up; **trompettiste** *nm/f* trumpet player.

trompeur, euse [tʀɔ̃pœʀ, -øz] *a* deceptive, misleading.

tronc [tʀɔ̃] *nm* (BOT, ANAT) trunk; (*d'église*) collection box; **~ d'arbre** tree trunk; **~ commun** (SCOL) common-core syllabus; **~ de cône** truncated cone.

tronche [tʀɔ̃ʃ] *nf* (*fam*) mug, face.

tronçon [tʀɔ̃sɔ̃] *nm* section.

tronçonner [tʀɔ̃sɔne] *vt* to saw up; **tronçonneuse** *nf* chain saw.

trône [tʀon] *nm* throne.

trôner [tʀone] *vi* (*fig*) to sit in the place of honour.

tronquer [tʀɔ̃ke] *vt* to truncate; (*fig*) to curtail.

trop [tʀo] *ad vb* + too much, too + *adjectif, adverbe*; **~ (nombreux)** too many; **~ peu (nombreux)** too few; **~ (souvent)** too often; **~ (longtemps)** (for) too long; **~ de** (*nombre*) too many; (*quantité*) too much; **de ~, en ~: des livres en ~** a few books too many, a few extra books; **du lait en ~** some milk over *ou* extra, too much milk; **3 livres/F de ~** 3 books too many/F too much.

trophée [tʀɔfe] *nm* trophy.

tropical, e, aux [tʀɔpikal, -o] *a* tropical.

tropique [tʀɔpik] *nm* tropic; **~s** *nmpl* tropics.

trop-plein [tʀɔplɛ̃] *nm* (*tuyau*) overflow *ou* outlet (pipe); (*liquide*) overflow.

troquer [tʀɔke] *vt*: **~ qch contre** to barter *ou* trade sth for; (*fig*) to swap sth for.

trot [tʀo] *nm* trot; **aller au ~** to trot along; **partir au ~** to set off at a trot.

trotter [tʀɔte] *vi* to trot; (*fig*) to scamper along (*ou* about).

trotteuse [tʀɔtøz] *nf* (*de montre*) second hand.

trottiner [tʀɔtine] *vi* (*fig*) to scamper along (*ou* about).

trottinette [tʀɔtinɛt] *nf* (child's) scooter.

trottoir [tʀɔtwaʀ] *nm* pavement; **faire le ~** (*péj*) to walk the streets; **~ roulant** moving walkway, travellator.

trou [tʀu] *nm* hole; (*fig*) gap; **~ d'air** air pocket; **~ de mémoire** blank, lapse of memory; **le ~ de la serrure** the keyhole.

troublant, e [tʀublɑ̃, -ɑ̃t] *a* disturbing.

trouble [tʀubl(ə)] *a* (*liquide*) cloudy; (*image, mémoire*) indistinct, hazy; (*affaire*) shady, murky // *nm* (*désarroi*) distress, agitation; (*émoi sensuel*) turmoil, agitation; (*embarras*) confusion; (*zizanie*) unrest, discord; **~s** *nmpl* (POL) disturbances, troubles, unrest *sg*; (MÉD) trouble *sg*, disorders.

trouble-fête [tʀubləfɛt] *nm/f inv* spoilsport.

troubler [tʀuble] *vt* (*embarrasser*) to confuse, disconcert; (*émouvoir*) to agitate; to disturb; to perturb; (*perturber: ordre etc*) to disrupt, disturb; (*liquide*) to make cloudy; **se ~** *vi* (*personne*) to become flustered *ou* confused; **~ l'ordre public** to cause a breach of the peace.

troué, e [tʀue] *a* with a hole (*ou* holes) in it // *nf* gap; (MIL) breach.

trouer [tʀue] *vt* to make a hole (*ou* holes) in; (*fig*) to pierce.

trouille [tʀuj] *nf* (*fam*): **avoir la ~** to have the jitters, be in a funk.

troupe [tʀup] *nf* (MIL) troop; (*groupe*) troop, group; **la ~** (MIL) the army; the troops *pl*; **~ (de théâtre)** (theatrical) company.

troupeau, x [tʀupo] *nm* (*de moutons*) flock; (*de vaches*) herd.

trousse [tʀus] *nf* case, kit; (*d'écolier*) pencil case; (*de docteur*) instrument case; **aux ~s de** (*fig*) on the heels *ou* tail of; **~ à outils** toolkit; **~ de toilette** toilet *ou* sponge bag.

trousseau, x [tʀuso] *nm* (*de jeune mariée*) trousseau; ~ **de clefs** bunch of keys.
trouvaille [tʀuvaj] *nf* find.
trouver [tʀuve] *vt* to find; (*rendre visite*): **aller/venir** ~ **qn** to go/come and see sb; **je trouve que** I find *ou* think that; ~ **à boire/critiquer** to find something to drink/criticize; **se** ~ *vi* (*être*) to be; (*être soudain*) to find o.s.; **se** ~ **être/avoir** to happen to be/have; **il se trouve que** it happens that, it turns out that; **se** ~ **bien** to feel well; **se** ~ **mal** to pass out.
truand [tʀyɑ̃] *nm* villain, crook.
truc [tʀyk] *nm* (*astuce*) way, device; (*de cinéma, prestidigitateur*) trick effect; (*chose*) thing; (*machin*) thingumajig, whatsit; **avoir le** ~ to have the knack.
truchement [tʀyʃmɑ̃] *nm*: **par le** ~ **de qn** through (the intervention of) sb.
truculent, e [tʀykylɑ̃, -ɑ̃t] *a* colourful.
truelle [tʀyɛl] *nf* trowel.
truffe [tʀyf] *nf* truffle; (*nez*) nose.
truffer [tʀyfe] *vt* (CULIN) to garnish with truffles; **truffé de** (*fig*) peppered with; bristling with.
truie [tʀɥi] *nf* sow.
truite [tʀɥit] *nf* trout *inv*.
truquage [tʀykaʒ] *nm* fixing; (CINÉMA) special effects *pl*.
truquer [tʀyke] *vt* (*élections, serrure, dés*) to fix; (CINÉMA) to use special effects in.
trust [tʀœst] *nm* (COMM) trust.
tsar [dzaʀ] *nm* tsar.
T.S.F. [teɛsɛf] *sigle f* (= *télégraphie sans fil*) wireless.
tsigane [tsigan] *a, nm/f* = **tzigane**.
T.S.V.P. *sigle* (= *tournez s.v.p.*) P.T.O. (please turn over).
T.T.C. *sigle* = *toutes taxes comprises*.
tu [ty] *pronom* you // *nm*: **employer le** ~ to use the 'tu' form.
tu, e [ty] *pp de* **taire**.
tuba [tyba] *nm* (MUS) tuba; (SPORT) snorkel.
tube [tyb] *nm* tube; pipe; (*chanson, disque*) hit song *ou* record; ~ **digestif** alimentary canal, digestive tract.
tuberculeux, euse [tybɛʀkylø, -øz] *a* tubercular // *nm/f* tuberculosis *ou* TB patient.
tuberculose [tybɛʀkyloz] *nf* tuberculosis.
tubulaire [tybylɛʀ] *a* tubular.
tubulure [tybylyʀ] *nf* pipe; piping *q*; (AUTO) manifold.
tué, e [tɥe] *nm/f*: **5** ~**s** 5 killed *ou* dead.
tuer [tɥe] *vt* to kill; **se** ~ *vi* to be killed; **se** ~ **au travail** (*fig*) to work o.s. to death; **tuerie** *nf* slaughter *q*.
tue-tête [tytɛt]: **à** ~ *ad* at the top of one's voice.
tueur [tɥœʀ] *nm* killer; ~ **à gages** hired killer.
tuile [tɥil] *nf* tile; (*fam*) spot of bad luck, blow.
tulipe [tylip] *nf* tulip.
tuméfié, e [tymefje] *a* puffy, swollen.
tumeur [tymœʀ] *nf* growth, tumour.
tumulte [tymylt(ə)] *nm* commotion, hubbub.
tumultueux, euse [tymyltɥø, -øz] *a* stormy, turbulent.
tunique [tynik] *nf* tunic; (*de femme*) smock, tunic.
Tunisie [tynizi] *nf*: **la** ~ Tunisia; **tunisien, ne** *a, nm/f* Tunisian.
tunnel [tynɛl] *nm* tunnel.
turban [tyʀbɑ̃] *nm* turban.
turbin [tyʀbɛ̃] *nm* (*fam*) work *q*.
turbine [tyʀbin] *nf* turbine.
turboréacteur [tyʀbɔʀeaktœʀ] *nm* turbojet.
turbulences [tyʀbylɑ̃s] *nfpl* (AVIAT) turbulence *sg*.
turbulent, e [tyʀbylɑ̃, -ɑ̃t] *a* boisterous, unruly.
turc, turque [tyʀk(ə)] *a* Turkish // *nm/f*: **T~, Turque** Turk/Turkish woman // *nm* (*langue*) Turkish; **à la turque** *ad* cross-legged // *a* (*w.-c.*) seatless.
turf [tyʀf] *nm* racing; ~**iste** *nm/f* racegoer.
turpitude [tyʀpityd] *nf* base act, baseness *q*.
turque [tyʀk(ə)] *a, nf voir* **turc**.
Turquie [tyʀki] *nf*: **la** ~ Turkey.
turquoise [tyʀkwaz] *nf, a inv* turquoise.
tus *etc vb voir* **taire**.
tutelle [tytɛl] *nf* (JUR) guardianship; (POL) trusteeship; **sous la** ~ **de** (*fig*) under the supervision of.
tuteur [tytœʀ] *nm* (JUR) guardian; (*de plante*) stake, support.
tutoyer [tytwaje] *vt*: ~ **qn** to address sb as 'tu'.
tuyau, x [tɥijo] *nm* pipe; (*flexible*) tube; (*fam*) tip; gen *q*; ~ **d'arrosage** hosepipe; ~ **d'échappement** exhaust pipe; ~**té, e** *a* fluted; ~**terie** *nf* piping *q*.
tuyère [tɥijɛʀ] *nf* nozzle.
T.V.A. *sigle f voir* **taxe**.
tympan [tɛ̃pɑ̃] *nm* (ANAT) eardrum.
type [tip] *nm* type; (*fam*) chap, bloke // *a* typical, standard; **avoir le** ~ **nordique** to be Nordic-looking.
typhoïde [tifɔid] *nf* typhoid (fever).
typhon [tifɔ̃] *nm* typhoon.
typhus [tifys] *nm* typhus (fever).
typique [tipik] *a* typical.
typographe [tipɔgʀaf] *nm/f* typographer.
typographie [tipɔgʀafi] *nf* typography; (*procédé*) letterpress (printing); **typographique** *a* typographical; letterpress *cpd*.
tyran [tiʀɑ̃] *nm* tyrant; **tyrannie** *nf* tyranny; **tyrannique** *a* tyrannical; **tyranniser** *vt* to tyrannize.
tzigane [dzigan] *a* gipsy, tzigane // *nm/f* (Hungarian) gipsy, Tzigane.

U

ubiquité [ybikɥite] *nf*: **avoir le don d'**~ to be everywhere at once *ou* be ubiquitous.
ulcère [ylsɛʀ] *nm* ulcer; ~ **à l'estomac** stomach ulcer.
ulcérer [ylseʀe] *vt* (MÉD) to ulcerate; (*fig*) to sicken, appal.
ultérieur, e [ylteʀjœʀ] *a* later, subsequent; **remis à une date** ~**e** postponed to a later date; ~**ement** *ad* later.

ultimatum [yltimatɔm] *nm* ultimatum.
ultime [yltim] *a* final.
ultra... [yltʀa] *préfixe*: **~moderne/-rapide** ultra-modern/-fast ; **~-sensible** *a* (PHOTO) high-speed ; **~-sons** *nmpl* ultrasonics ; **~-violet, te** *a* ultraviolet.
un, une [œ̃, yn] *dét* a, an + *voyelle // pronom, num, a* one ; **l'un l'autre, les ~s les autres** each other, one another ; **l'~ ..., l'autre** (the) one ..., the other ; **les ~s ..., les autres** some ..., others ; **l'~ et l'autre** both (of them) ; **l'~ ou l'autre** either (of them) ; **l'~ des meilleurs** one of the best.
unanime [ynanim] *a* unanimous ; **unanimité** *nf* unanimity ; **à l'unanimité** unanimously.
uni, e [yni] *a* (*ton, tissu*) plain ; (*surface*) smooth, even ; (*famille*) close(-knit) ; (*pays*) united.
unification [ynifikɑsjɔ̃] *nf* uniting ; unification ; standardization.
unifier [ynifje] *vt* to unite, unify ; (*systèmes*) to standardize, unify.
uniforme [ynifɔʀm(ə)] *a* (*mouvement*) regular, uniform ; (*surface, ton*) even ; (*objets, maisons*) uniform // *nm* uniform ; **être sous l'~** (MIL) to be serving ; **uniformiser** *vt* to make uniform ; (systèmes) to standardize ; **uniformité** *nf* regularity ; uniformity ; evenness.
unijambiste [ynizɑ̃bist(ə)] *nm/f* one-legged man/woman.
unilatéral, e, aux [ynilateʀal, -o] *a* unilateral ; **stationnement ~** parking on one side only.
union [ynjɔ̃] *nf* union ; **~ conjugale** union of marriage ; **~ de consommateurs** consumers' association ; **l'U~ soviétique** the Soviet Union.
unique [ynik] *a* (*seul*) only ; (*le même*): **un prix/système ~** a single price/system ; (*exceptionnel*) unique ; **ménage à salaire ~** one-salary family ; **route à voie ~** single-lane road ; **fils/fille ~** only son/daughter ; **~ en France** the only one of its kind in France ; **~ment** *ad* only, solely ; (*juste*) only, merely.
unir [yniʀ] *vt* (*nations*) to unite ; (*éléments, couleurs*) to combine ; (*en mariage*) to unite, join together ; **~ qch à** to unite sth with ; to combine sth with ; **s'~** to unite ; (*en mariage*) to be joined together.
unisson [ynisɔ̃]: **à l'~** *ad* in unison.
unitaire [ynitɛʀ] *a* unitary ; **prix ~** price per unit.
unité [ynite] *nf* (*harmonie, cohésion*) unity ; (COMM, MIL, *de mesure*, MATH) unit.
univers [ynivɛʀ] *nm* universe.
universel, le [ynivɛʀsɛl] *a* universal ; (*esprit*) all-embracing.
universitaire [ynivɛʀsitɛʀ] *a* university *cpd* ; (*diplôme, études*) academic, university *cpd // nm/f* academic.
université [ynivɛʀsite] *nf* university.
uranium [yʀanjɔm] *nm* uranium.
urbain, e [yʀbɛ̃, -ɛn] *a* urban, city *cpd*, town *cpd* ; (*poli*) urbane ; **urbaniser** *vt* to urbanize ; **urbanisme** *nm* town planning ; **urbaniste** *nm/f* town planner.
urgence [yʀʒɑ̃s] *nf* urgency ; (MÉD *etc*) emergency ; **d'~** *a* emergency *cpd // ad* as a matter of urgency.
urgent, e [yʀʒɑ̃, -ɑ̃t] *a* urgent.
urinal, aux [yʀinal, -o] *nm* (bed) urinal.
urine [yʀin] *nf* urine ; **uriner** *vi* to urinate ; **urinoir** *nm* (public) urinal.
urne [yʀn(ə)] *nf* (*électorale*) ballot box ; (*vase*) urn ; **aller aux ~s** (*voter*) to go to the polls.
URSS [*parfois*: yʀs] *sigle f*: **l'~** the USSR.
urticaire [yʀtikɛʀ] *nf* nettle rash.
us [ys] *nmpl*: **~ et coutumes** (habits and) customs.
U.S.A. *sigle mpl*: **les ~** the U.S.A.
usage [yzaʒ] *nm* (*emploi, utilisation*) use ; (*coutume*) custom ; (LING): **l'~** usage ; **faire ~ de** (*pouvoir, droit*) to exercise ; **avoir l'~ de** to have the use of ; **à l'~** *ad* with use ; **à l'~ de** (*pour*) for (use of) ; **en ~** in use ; **hors d'~** out of service ; wrecked ; **à ~ interne** to be taken ; **à ~ externe** for external use only.
usagé, e [yzaʒe] *a* (*usé*) worn ; (*d'occasion*) used.
usager, ère [yzaʒe, -ɛʀ] *nm/f* user.
usé, e [yze] *a* worn ; (*banal*) hackneyed.
user [yze] *vt* (*outil*) to wear down ; (*vêtement*) to wear out ; (*matière*) to wear away ; (*consommer: charbon etc*) to use ; **s'~** *vi* to wear ; to wear out ; (*fig*) to decline ; **s'~ à la tâche** to wear o.s. out with work ; **~ de** *vt* (*moyen, procédé*) to use, employ ; (*droit*) to exercise.
usine [yzin] *nf* factory ; **~ à gaz** gasworks *sg* ; **~ marémotrice** tidal power station.
usiner [yzine] *vt* (TECH) to machine.
usité, e [yzite] *a* in common use, common ; **peu ~** rarely used.
ustensile [ystɑ̃sil] *nm* implement ; **~ de cuisine** kitchen utensil.
usuel, le [yzɥɛl] *a* everyday, common.
usufruit [yzyfʀɥi] *nm* usufruct.
usuraire [yzyʀɛʀ] *a* usurious.
usure [yzyʀ] *nf* wear ; worn state ; (*de l'usurier*) usury ; **avoir qn à l'~** to wear sb down ; **usurier, ière** *nm/f* usurer.
usurper [yzyʀpe] *vt* to usurp.
ut [yt] *nm* (MUS) C.
utérin, e [yteʀɛ̃, -in] *a* uterine.
utérus [yteʀys] *nm* uterus, womb.
utile [ytil] *a* useful.
utilisation [ytilizɑsjɔ̃] *nf* use.
utiliser [ytilize] *vt* to use.
utilitaire [ytilitɛʀ] *a* utilitarian ; (*objets*) practical.
utilité [ytilite] *nf* usefulness *q* ; use ; **jouer les ~s** (THÉÂTRE) to play bit parts ; **reconnu d'~ publique** state-approved ; **c'est d'une grande ~** it's of great use.
utopie [ytɔpi] *nf* utopian idea *ou* view ; utopia ; **utopiste** *nm/f* utopian.
uvule [yvyl] *nf* uvula.

V

va *vb voir* **aller**.
vacance [vakɑ̃s] *nf* (ADMIN) vacancy ; **~s** *nfpl* holiday(s *pl*), vacation *sg* ; **prendre des/ses ~s** to take a holiday/one's holiday(s) ; **aller en ~s** to go on holiday ;

vacancier, ière *nm/f* holiday-maker.
vacant, e [vakɑ̃, -ɑ̃t] *a* vacant.
vacarme [vakaʀm(ə)] *nm* row, din.
vaccin [vaksɛ̃] *nm* vaccine; (*opération*) vaccination; **vaccination** *nf* vaccination; **vacciner** *vt* to vaccinate; (*fig*) to make immune.
vache [vaʃ] *nf* (ZOOL) cow; (*cuir*) cowhide // *a* (*fam*) rotten, mean; ~ **à eau** (canvas) water bag; ~ **à lait** (*péj*) mug, sucker; ~ **laitière** dairy cow; **vachement** *ad* (*fam*) damned, hellish; **vacher, ère** *nm/f* cowherd; **vacherie** *nf* (*fam*) meanness *q*; dirty trick; nasty remark.
vaciller [vasije] *vi* to sway, wobble; (*bougie, lumière*) to flicker; (*fig*) to be failing, falter.
vacuité [vakɥite] *nf* emptiness, vacuity.
vade-mecum [vademekɔm] *nm inv* pocketbook.
vadrouiller [vadʀuje] *vi* to rove around *ou* about.
va-et-vient [vaevjɛ̃] *nm inv* (*de pièce mobile*) to and fro (*ou* up and down) movement; (*de personnes, véhicules*) comings and goings *pl*, to-ings and fro-ings *pl*.
vagabond, e [vagabɔ̃, -ɔ̃d] *a* wandering; (*imagination*) roaming, roving // *nm* (*rôdeur*) tramp, vagrant; (*voyageur*) wanderer.
vagabondage [vagabɔ̃daʒ] *nm* roaming, wandering; (JUR) vagrancy.
vagabonder [vagabɔ̃de] *vi* to roam, wander.
vagin [vaʒɛ̃] *nm* vagina.
vagissement [vaʒismɑ̃] *nm* cry (*of newborn baby*).
vague [vag] *nf* wave // *a* vague; (*regard*) faraway; (*manteau, robe*) loose(-fitting); (*quelconque*): **un ~ bureau/cousin** some office/cousin or other // *nm*: **rester dans le ~** to keep things rather vague; **regarder dans le ~** to gaze into space; ~ **à l'âme** *nm* vague melancholy; ~ **d'assaut** *nf* (MIL) wave of assault; ~ **de chaleur** *nf* heatwave; ~ **de fond** *nf* ground swell; ~ **de froid** *nf* cold spell; ~**ment** *ad* vaguely.
vaillant, e [vajɑ̃, -ɑ̃t] *a* (*courageux*) brave, gallant; (*robuste*) vigorous, hale and hearty; **n'avoir plus un sou ~** to be penniless.
vaille *vb voir* **valoir**.
vain, e [vɛ̃, vɛn] *a* vain; **en ~** *ad* in vain.
vaincre [vɛ̃kʀ(ə)] *vt* to defeat; (*fig*) to conquer, overcome; **vaincu, e** *nm/f* defeated party; **vainqueur** *nm* victor; (SPORT) winner // *am* victorious.
vais *vb voir* **aller**.
vaisseau, x [vɛso] *nm* (ANAT) vessel; (NAVIG) ship, vessel; ~ **spatial** spaceship.
vaisselier [vɛsəlje] *nm* dresser.
vaisselle [vɛsɛl] *nf* (*service*) crockery; (*plats etc à laver*) (dirty) dishes *pl*; (*lavage*) washing-up; **faire la ~** to do the washing-up *ou* the dishes.
val, vaux *ou* **vals** [val, vo] *nm* valley.
valable [valabl(ə)] *a* valid; (*acceptable*) decent, worthwhile.
valent *etc vb voir* **valoir**.
valet [valɛ] *nm* valet; (CARTES) jack, knave; ~ **de chambre** manservant, valet; ~ **de ferme** farmhand; ~ **de pied** footman.
valeur [valœʀ] *nf* (*gén*) value; (*mérite*) worth, merit; (COMM: *titre*) security; **mettre en ~** (*bien*) to exploit; (*terrain, région*) to develop; (*fig*) to highlight; to show off to advantage; **avoir de la ~** to be valuable; **prendre de la ~** to go up *ou* gain in value.
valeureux, euse [valœʀø, -øz] *a* valorous.
valide [valid] *a* (*en bonne santé*) fit, well; (*indemne*) able-bodied, fit; (*valable*) valid; **valider** *vt* to validate; **validité** *nf* validity.
valions *vb voir* **valoir**.
valise [valiz] *nf* (suit)case; **la ~ (diplomatique)** the diplomatic bag.
vallée [vale] *nf* valley.
vallon [valɔ̃] *nm* small valley.
vallonné, e [valɔne] *n* undulating.
valoir [valwaʀ] *vi* (*être valable*) to hold, apply // *vt* (*prix, valeur, effort*) to be worth; (*causer*): ~ **qch à qn** to earn sb sth; **se ~** to be of equal merit; (*péj*) to be two of a kind; **faire ~** (*droits, prérogatives*) to assert; (*domaine, capitaux*) to exploit; **faire ~ que** to point out that; **à ~** on account; **à ~ sur** to be deducted from; **vaille que vaille** somehow or other; **cela ne me dit rien qui vaille** I don't like the look of it at all; **ce climat ne me vaut rien** this climate doesn't suit me; ~ **la peine** to be worth the trouble *ou* worth it; ~ **mieux: il vaut mieux se taire** it's better to say nothing; **ça ne vaut rien** it's worthless; **que vaut ce candidat?** how good is this applicant?
valoriser [valɔʀize] *vt* (ÉCON) to develop (the economy of); (PSYCH) to increase the standing of.
valse [vals(ə)] *nf* waltz; **valser** *vi* to waltz; (*fig*): **aller valser** to go flying.
valu, e [valy] *pp de* **valoir**.
valve [valv(ə)] *nf* valve.
vandale [vɑ̃dal] *nm/f* vandal; **vandalisme** *nm* vandalism.
vanille [vanij] *nf* vanilla.
vanité [vanite] *nf* vanity; **vaniteux, euse** *a* vain, conceited.
vanne [van] *nf* gate.
vanner [vane] *vt* to winnow.
vannerie [vanʀi] *nf* basketwork.
vantail, aux [vɑ̃taj, -o] *nm* door, leaf (*pl* leaves).
vantard, e [vɑ̃taʀ, -aʀd(ə)] *a* boastful; **vantardise** *nf* boastfulness *q*; boast.
vanter [vɑ̃te] *vt* to speak highly of, vaunt; **se ~** *vi* to boast, brag; **se ~ de** to boast of.
va-nu-pieds [vanypje] *nm/f inv* tramp, beggar.
vapeur [vapœʀ] *nf* steam; (*émanation*) vapour, fumes *pl*; ~**s** *nfpl* (*bouffées*) vapours; **à ~** steam-powered, steam *cpd*; **à toute ~** full steam ahead; (*fig*) at full tilt; **renverser la ~** to reverse engines; (*fig*) to backtrack, backpedal; **cuit à la ~** steamed.

vaporeux, euse [vapɔʀø, -øz] *a* (*flou*) hazy, misty; (*léger*) filmy, gossamer *cpd.*
vaporisateur [vapɔʀizatœʀ] *nm* spray.
vaporiser [vapɔʀize] *vt* (CHIMIE) to vaporize; (*parfum etc*) to spray.
vaquer [vake] *vi*: ~ **à ses occupations** to attend to one's affairs, go about one's business.
varappe [vaʀap] *nf* rock climbing; **varappeur, euse** *nm/f* (rock) climber.
varech [vaʀɛk] *nm* wrack, varec.
vareuse [vaʀøz] *nf* (*blouson*) pea jacket; (*d'uniforme*) tunic.
variable [vaʀjabl(ə)] *a* variable; (*temps, humeur*) changeable, variable; (TECH: *à plusieurs positions etc*) adaptable; (LING) inflectional; (*divers*: *résultats*) varied, various // *nf* (MATH) variable.
variante [vaʀjɑ̃t] *nf* variant.
variation [vaʀjɑsjɔ̃] *nf* variation; changing *q*, change.
varice [vaʀis] *nf* varicose vein.
varicelle [vaʀisɛl] *nf* chickenpox.
varié, e [vaʀje] *a* varied; (*divers*) various; **hors-d'œuvre ~s** selection of hors d'œuvres.
varier [vaʀje] *vi* to vary; (*temps, humeur*) to vary, change // *vt* to vary.
variété [vaʀjete] *nf* variety; **spectacle de ~s** variety show.
variole [vaʀjɔl] *nf* smallpox.
variqueux, euse [vaʀikø, -øz] *a* varicose.
vas *vb voir* **aller**.
vase [vɑz] *nm* vase // *nf* silt, mud; **en ~ clos** in isolation; **~ de nuit** chamberpot; **~s communicants** communicating vessels.
vaseline [vazlin] *nf* vaseline.
vaseux, euse [vɑzø, -øz] *a* silty, muddy; (*fig*: *confus*) woolly, hazy; (: *fatigué*) peaky; woozy.
vasistas [vazistɑs] *nm* fanlight.
vaste [vast(ə)] *a* vast, immense.
Vatican [vatikɑ̃] *nm*: **le ~** the Vatican.
vaticiner [vatisine] *vi* (*péj*) to make pompous predictions.
va-tout [vatu] *nm*: **jouer son ~** to stake one's all.
vaudeville [vodvil] *nm* vaudeville, light comedy.
vaudrai *etc vb voir* **valoir**.
vau-l'eau [volo]: **à ~** *ad* with the current; (*fig*) adrift.
vaurien, ne [voʀjɛ̃, -ɛn] *nm/f* good-for-nothing, guttersnipe.
vautour [votuʀ] *nm* vulture.
vautrer [votʀe]: **se ~** *vi*: **se ~ dans/sur** to wallow in/sprawl on.
vaux [vo] *pl de* **val** // *vb voir* **valoir**.
veau, x [vo] *nm* (ZOOL) calf (*pl* calves); (CULIN) veal; (*peau*) calfskin.
vecteur [vɛktœʀ] *nm* vector; (MIL) carrier.
vécu, e [veky] *pp de* **vivre** // *a* (*aventure*) real(-life).
vedette [vədɛt] *nf* (*artiste etc*) star; (*canot*) patrol boat; launch; **avoir la ~** to top the bill, get star billing.
végétal, e, aux [veʒetal, -o] *a* vegetable // *nm* vegetable, plant.
végétarien, ne [veʒetaʀjɛ̃, -ɛn] *a, nm/f* vegetarian.
végétarisme [veʒetaʀism(ə)] *nm* vegetarianism.
végétation [veʒetɑsjɔ̃] *nf* vegetation; **~s** *nfpl* (MÉD) adenoids.
végéter [veʒete] *vi* (*fig*) to vegetate; to stagnate.
véhément, e [veemɑ̃, -ɑ̃t] *a* vehement.
véhicule [veikyl] *nm* vehicle; **~ utilitaire** commercial vehicle.
veille [vɛj] *nf* (*garde*) watch; (PSYCH) wakefulness; (*jour*): **la ~** the day before, the previous day; **la ~ au soir** the previous evening; **la ~ de** the day before; **à la ~ de** on the eve of.
veillée [veje] *nf* (*soirée*) evening; (*réunion*) evening gathering; **~ d'armes** night before combat; **~ (mortuaire)** watch.
veiller [veje] *vi* to stay *ou* sit up; to be awake; to be on watch; to be watchful // *vt* (*malade, mort*) to watch over, sit up with; **~ à** *vt* to attend to, see to; **~ à ce que** to make sure that, see to it that; **~ sur** *vt* to keep a watch *ou* an eye on; **veilleur de nuit** *nm* night watchman.
veilleuse [vɛjøz] *nf* (*lampe*) night light; (AUTO) sidelight; (*flamme*) pilot light; **en ~** *a, ad* (*lampe*) dimmed.
veinard, e [vɛnaʀ, -aʀd(ə)] *nm/f* (*fam*) lucky devil.
veine [vɛn] *nf* (ANAT, *du bois etc*) vein; (*filon*) vein, seam; (*fam*: *chance*): **avoir de la ~** to be lucky; (*inspiration*) inspiration; **veiné, e** *a* veined; (*bois*) grained; **veineux, euse** *a* venous.
vêler [vele] *vi* to calve.
vélin [velɛ̃] *nm* vellum (paper).
velléitaire [veleitɛʀ] *a* irresolute, indecisive.
velléités [veleite] *nfpl* vague impulses.
vélo [velo] *nm* bike, cycle; **faire du ~** to go cycling.
véloce [velɔs] *a* swift.
vélodrome [velɔdʀɔm] *nm* velodrome.
vélomoteur [velɔmɔtœʀ] *nm* light motorcycle.
velours [vəluʀ] *nm* velvet; **~ côtelé** corduroy.
velouté, e [vəlute] *a* (*au toucher*) velvety; (*à la vue*) soft, mellow; (*au goût*) smooth, mellow // *nm*: **~ d'asperges/de tomates** cream of asparagus/tomato (soup).
velu, e [vəly] *a* hairy.
venais *etc vb voir* **venir**.
venaison [vənɛzɔ̃] *nf* venison.
vénal, e, aux [venal, -o] venal; **~ité** *nf* venality.
venant [vənɑ̃]: **à tout ~** *ad* to all and sundry.
vendange [vɑ̃dɑ̃ʒ] *nf* (*opération, période*: *aussi*: **~s**) grape harvest; (*raisins*) grape crop, grapes *pl.*
vendanger [vɑ̃dɑ̃ʒe] *vi* to harvest the grapes; **vendangeur, euse** *nm/f* grape-picker.
vendeur, euse [vɑ̃dœʀ, -øz] *nm/f* (*de magasin*) shop assistant; sales assistant; (COMM) salesman/ woman // *nm* (JUR) vendor, seller; **~ de journaux** newspaper seller.

vendre [vɑ̃dʀ(ə)] *vt* to sell ; ~ **qch à qn** to sell sb sth ; **cela se vend à la douzaine** these are sold by the dozen ; **cela se vend bien** it's selling well ; **'à ~'** 'for sale.'
vendredi [vɑ̃dʀədi] *nm* Friday ; **V~ saint** Good Friday.
vénéneux, euse [venenø, -øz] *a* poisonous.
vénérable [veneʀabl(ə)] *a* venerable.
vénération [veneʀɑsjɔ̃] *nf* veneration.
vénérer [veneʀe] *vt* to venerate.
vénérien, ne [veneʀjɛ̃, -ɛn] *a* venereal.
vengeance [vɑ̃ʒɑ̃s] *nf* vengeance *q*, revenge *q* ; act of vengeance *ou* revenge
venger [vɑ̃ʒe] *vt* to avenge ; **se ~** *vi* to avenge o.s. ; (*par rancune*) to take revenge ; **se ~ de qch** to avenge o.s. for sth ; to take one's revenge for sth ; **se ~ de qn** to take revenge on sb ; **se ~ sur** to wreak vengeance upon ; to take revenge on *ou* through ; to take it out on ; **vengeur, eresse** *a* vengeful // *nm/f* avenger.
véniel, le [venjɛl] *a* venial.
venimeux, euse [vənimø, -øz] *a* poisonous, venomous ; (*fig: haineux*) venomous, vicious.
venin [vənɛ̃] *nm* venom, poison.
venir [vəniʀ] *vi* to come ; ~ **de** to come from ; ~ **de faire**: **je viens d'y aller/de le voir** I've just been there/seen him ; **s'il vient à pleuvoir** if it should rain, if it happens to rain ; **j'en viens à croire que** I have come to believe that ; **il en est venu à mendier** he has been reduced to begging ; **faire ~** (*docteur, plombier*) to call (out).
vent [vɑ̃] *nm* wind ; **il y a du ~** it's windy ; **c'est du ~** it's all hot air ; **au ~** to windward ; **sous le ~** to leeward ; **avoir le ~ debout/arrière** to head into the wind/have the wind astern ; **dans le ~** (*fam*) trendy, with it ; **prendre le ~** (*fig*) to see which way the wind blows ; **avoir ~ de** to get wind of.
vente [vɑ̃t] *nf* sale ; **la ~** (*activité*) selling ; (*secteur*) sales *pl* ; **mettre en ~** to put on sale ; (*objets personnels*) to put up for sale ; ~ **de charité** sale in aid of charity ; ~ **aux enchères** auction sale.
venter [vɑ̃te] *vb impersonnel*: **il vente** the wind is blowing ; **venteux, euse** *a* windswept, windy.
ventilateur [vɑ̃tilatœʀ] *nm* fan.
ventilation [vɑ̃tilɑsjɔ̃] *nf* ventilation.
ventiler [vɑ̃tile] *vt* to ventilate ; (*total, statistiques*) to break down.
ventouse [vɑ̃tuz] *nf* (*ampoule*) cupping glass ; (*de caoutchouc*) suction pad ; (ZOOL) sucker.
ventre [vɑ̃tʀ(ə)] *nm* (ANAT) stomach ; (*fig*) belly ; **prendre du ~** to be getting a paunch ; **avoir mal au ~** to have stomach ache.
ventricule [vɑ̃tʀikyl] *nm* ventricle.
ventriloque [vɑ̃tʀilɔk] *nm/f* ventriloquist.
ventripotent, e [vɑ̃tʀipɔtɑ̃, -ɑ̃t] *a* potbellied.
ventru, e [vɑ̃tʀy] *a* potbellied.
venu, e [vəny] *pp de* **venir** // *a*: **être mal ~ à** *ou* **de faire** to have no grounds for doing, be in no position to do // *nf* coming.
vêpres [vɛpʀ(ə)] *nfpl* vespers.
ver [vɛʀ] *nm voir aussi* **vers** ; worm ; (*des fruits etc*) maggot ; (*du bois*) woodworm *q* ; ~ **luisant** glow-worm ; ~ **à soie** silkworm ; ~ **solitaire** tapeworm ; ~ **de terre** earthworm.
véracité [veʀasite] *nf* veracity.
véranda [veʀɑ̃da] *nf* veranda(h).
verbal, e, aux [vɛʀbal, -o] *a* verbal.
verbaliser [vɛʀbalize] *vi* (POLICE) to book *ou* report an offender.
verbe [vɛʀb(ə)] *nm* (LING) verb ; (*voix*): **avoir le ~ sonore** to have a sonorous tone (of voice) ; (*expression*): **la magie du ~** the magic of language *ou* the word ; (REL): **le V~** the Word.
verbeux, euse [vɛʀbø, -øz] *a* verbose, wordy.
verdâtre [vɛʀdɑtʀ(ə)] *a* greenish.
verdeur [vɛʀdœʀ] *nf* (*vigueur*) vigour, vitality ; (*crudité*) forthrightness ; (*défaut de maturité*) tartness, sharpness.
verdict [vɛʀdik(t)] *nm* verdict.
verdir [vɛʀdiʀ] *vi, vt* to turn green.
verdoyant, e [vɛʀdwajɑ̃, -ɑ̃t] *a* green, verdant.
verdure [vɛʀdyʀ] *nf* greenery, verdure.
véreux, euse [veʀø, -øz] *a* worm-eaten ; (*malhonnête*) shady, corrupt.
verge [vɛʀʒ(ə)] *nf* (ANAT) penis ; (*baguette*) stick, cane.
verger [vɛʀʒe] *nm* orchard.
verglacé, e [vɛʀglase] *a* icy, iced-over.
verglas [vɛʀgla] *nm* (black) ice.
vergogne [vɛʀgɔɲ]: **sans ~** *ad* shamelessly.
véridique [veʀidik] *a* truthful, veracious.
vérification [veʀifikɑsjɔ̃] *nf* checking *q*, check.
vérifier [veʀifje] *vt* to check ; (*corroborer*) to confirm, bear out.
vérin [veʀɛ̃] *nm* jack.
véritable [veʀitabl(ə)] *a* real ; (*ami, amour*) true ; **un ~ désastre** an absolute disaster.
vérité [veʀite] *nf* truth ; (*d'un portrait romanesque*) lifelikeness ; (*sincérité*) truthfulness, sincerity.
vermeil, le [vɛʀmɛj] *a* bright red, ruby-red // *nm* (*substance*) vermeil.
vermicelles [vɛʀmisɛl] *nmpl* vermicelli *sg*.
vermillon [vɛʀmijɔ̃] *a inv* vermilion, scarlet.
vermine [vɛʀmin] *nf* vermin *pl*.
vermoulu, e [vɛʀmuly] *a* worm-eaten, with woodworm.
vermout(h) [vɛʀmut] *nm* vermouth.
verni, e [vɛʀni] *a* (*fam*) lucky ; **cuir ~** patent leather.
vernir [vɛʀniʀ] *vt* (*bois, tableau, ongles*) to varnish ; (*poterie*) to glaze.
vernis [vɛʀni] *nm* (*enduit*) varnish ; glaze ; (*fig*) veneer ; ~ **à ongles** nail polish *ou* varnish.
vernissage [vɛʀnisaʒ] *nm* varnishing ; glazing ; (*d'une exposition*) preview.
vérole [veʀɔl] *nf* (*variole*) smallpox ; (*fam: syphilis*) pox.
verrai *etc vb voir* **voir**.
verre [vɛʀ] *nm* glass ; (*de lunettes*) lens *sg* ; **boire** *ou* **prendre un ~** to have a drink ;

~ **à vin/à liqueur** wine/liqueur glass; ~ **à dents** tooth mug; ~ **dépoli** frosted glass; ~ **de lampe** lamp glass *ou* chimney; ~ **de montre** watch glass; ~ **à pied** stemmed glass; ~**s de contact** contact lenses.
verrerie [vɛʀʀi] *nf* (*fabrique*) glassworks *sg*; (*activité*) glass-making; glass-working; (*objets*) glassware.
verrière [vɛʀjɛʀ] *nf* (*grand vitrage*) window; (*toit vitré*) glass roof.
verrons *etc vb voir* **voir**.
verroterie [vɛʀɔtʀi] *nf* glass beads *pl ou* jewellery.
verrou [vɛʀu] *nm* (*targette*) bolt; (*fig*) constriction; **mettre le** ~ to bolt the door; **mettre qn sous les** ~**s** to put sb behind bars; **verrouiller** *vt* to bolt; (*MIL: brèche*) to close.
verrue [vɛʀy] *nf* wart; (*fig*) eyesore.
vers [vɛʀ] *nm* line // *nmpl* (*poésie*) verse *sg* // *prép* (*en direction de*) toward(s); (*près de*) around (about); (*temporel*) about, around.
versant [vɛʀsɑ̃] *nm* slopes *pl*, side.
versatile [vɛʀsatil] *a* fickle, changeable.
verse [vɛʀs(ə)]: **à** ~ *ad*: **il pleut à** ~ it's pouring (with rain).
versé, e [vɛʀse] *a*: **être** ~ **dans** (*science*) to be (well-)versed in.
Verseau [vɛʀso] *nm*: **le** ~ Aquarius, the water-carrier; **être du** ~ to be Aquarius.
versement [vɛʀsəmɑ̃] *nm* payment; **en 3** ~**s** in 3 instalments.
verser [vɛʀse] *vt* (*liquide, grains*) to pour; (*larmes, sang*) to shed; (*argent*) to pay; (*soldat: affecter*): ~ **qn dans** to assign sb to // *vi* (*véhicule*) to overturn; (*fig*): ~ **dans** to lapse into.
verset [vɛʀsɛ] *nm* verse; versicle.
verseur [vɛʀsœʀ] *am voir* **bec**.
versifier [vɛʀsifje] *vt* to put into verse // *vi* to versify, write verse.
version [vɛʀsjɔ̃] *nf* version; (*SCOL*) translation (*into the mother tongue*).
verso [vɛʀso] *nm* back; **voir au** ~ see over(leaf).
vert, e [vɛʀ, vɛʀt(ə)] *a* green; (*vin*) young; (*vigoureux*) sprightly; (*cru*) forthright // *nm* green; ~ **d'eau** *a inv* sea-green; ~ **pomme** *a inv* apple-green; ~**-de-gris** *nm* verdigris // *a inv* grey(ish)-green.
vertébral, e, aux [vɛʀtebʀal, -o] *a voir* **colonne**.
vertèbre [vɛʀtɛbʀ(ə)] *nf* vertebra (*pl* ae); **vertébré, e** *a, nm/f* vertebrate.
vertement [vɛʀtəmɑ̃] *ad* (*réprimander*) sharply.
vertical, e, aux [vɛʀtikal, -o] *a, nf* vertical; **à la** ~**e** *ad*, ~**ement** *ad* vertically; ~**ité** *nf* verticalness, verticality.
vertige [vɛʀtiʒ] *nm* (*peur du vide*) vertigo; (*étourdissement*) dizzy spell; (*fig*) fever; **vertigineux, euse** *a* breathtaking; breathtakingly high (*ou* deep).
vertu [vɛʀty] *nf* virtue; **en** ~ **de** *prép* in accordance with; ~**eux, euse** *a* virtuous.
verve [vɛʀv(ə)] *nf* witty eloquence; **être en** ~ to be in brilliant form.
verveine [vɛʀvɛn] *nf* (*BOT*) verbena, vervain; (*infusion*) verbena tea.
vésicule [vezikyl] *nf* vesicle; ~ **biliaire** gall-bladder.
vespasienne [vɛspazjɛn] *nf* urinal.
vespéral, e, aux [vɛspeʀal, -o] *a* vespertine, evening *cpd*.
vessie [vesi] *nf* bladder.
veste [vɛst(ə)] *nf* jacket; ~ **droite/croisée** single-/double-breasted jacket.
vestiaire [vɛstjɛʀ] *nm* (*au théâtre etc*) cloakroom; (*de stade etc*) changing-room.
vestibule [vɛstibyl] *nm* hall.
vestige [vɛstiʒ] *nm* relic; trace; (*fig*) remnant, vestige; ~**s** *nmpl* remains; remnants, relics.
vestimentaire [vɛstimɑ̃tɛʀ] *a* (*dépenses*) clothing; (*détail*) of dress; (*élégance*) sartorial.
veston [vɛstɔ̃] *nm* jacket.
vêtement [vɛtmɑ̃] *nm* garment, item of clothing; (*COMM*): **le** ~ the clothing industry; ~**s** *nmpl* clothes; ~**s de sport** sportswear *sg*, sports clothes.
vétéran [veteʀɑ̃] *nm* veteran.
vétérinaire [veteʀinɛʀ] *a* veterinary // *nm/f* vet, veterinary surgeon.
vétille [vetij] *nf* trifle, triviality.
vétilleux, euse [vetijø, -øz] *a* punctilious.
vêtir [vetiʀ] *vt* to clothe, dress.
veto [veto] *nm* veto; **opposer un** ~ **à** to veto.
vêtu, e [vɛty] *pp de* **vêtir** // *a*: ~ **de** dressed in, wearing; **chaudement** ~ warmly dressed.
vétuste [vetyst(ə)] *a* ancient, timeworn.
veuf, veuve [vœf, vœv] *a* widowed // *nm* widower // *nf* widow.
veuille *etc vb voir* **vouloir**.
veule [vøl] *a* spineless.
veuvage [vœvaʒ] *nm* widowhood.
veuve [vœv] *a, nf voir* **veuf**.
veux *vb voir* **vouloir**.
vexations [vɛksɑsjɔ̃] *nfpl* humiliations.
vexatoire [vɛksatwaʀ] *a*: **mesures** ~**s** harassment *sg*.
vexer [vɛkse] *vt* to hurt, upset; **se** ~ *vi* to be hurt, get upset.
viabiliser [vjabilize] *vt* to provide with services (*water etc*).
viabilité [vjabilite] *nf* viability; (*d'un chemin*) practicability.
viable [vjabl(ə)] *a* viable.
viaduc [vjadyk] *nm* viaduct.
viager, ère [vjaʒe, -ɛʀ] *a*: **rente viagère** life annuity // *nm*: **mettre en** ~ to sell in return for a life annuity.
viande [vjɑ̃d] *nf* meat.
viatique [vjatik] *nm* (*REL*) viaticum; (*fig*) provisions *pl* (*ou* money) for the journey.
vibraphone [vibʀafɔn] *nm* vibraphone, vibes *pl*.
vibration [vibʀɑsjɔ̃] *nf* vibration.
vibrer [vibʀe] *vi* to vibrate; (*son, voix*) to be vibrant; (*fig*) to be stirred; **faire** ~ to (cause to) vibrate; to stir, thrill; **vibromasseur** *nm* vibrator.
vicaire [vikɛʀ] *nm* curate.
vice [vis] *nm* vice; (*défaut*) fault; ~ **de forme** legal flaw *ou* irregularity.

vice... [vis] *préfixe*: **~-consul** *nm* vice-consul ; **~-président, e** *nm/f* vice-president ; vice-chairman ; **~-roi** *nm* viceroy.

vice-versa [viseversa] *ad* vice versa.

vichy [viʃi] *nm* (*toile*) gingham ; (*eau*) Vichy water.

vicié, e [visje] *a* (*air*) polluted, tainted ; (*JUR*) invalidated.

vicieux, euse [visjø, -øz] *a* (*pervers*) dirty(-minded) ; nasty ; (*fautif*) incorrect, wrong.

vicinal, e, aux [visinal, -o] *a*: **chemin ~** by-road, byway.

vicissitudes [visisityd] *nfpl* (trials and) tribulations.

vicomte [vikɔ̃t] *nm* viscount.

victime [viktim] *nf* victim ; (*d'accident*) casualty ; **être (la) ~ de** to be the victim of ; **être ~ d'une attaque/d'un accident** to suffer a stroke/be involved in an accident.

victoire [viktwaʀ] *nf* victory ; **victorieux, euse** *a* victorious ; (*sourire, attitude*) triumphant.

victuailles [viktɥaj] *nfpl* provisions.

vidange [vidɑ̃ʒ] *nf* (*d'un fossé, réservoir*) emptying ; (*AUTO*) oil change ; (*de lavabo*: *bonde*) waste outlet ; **~s** *nfpl* (*matières*) sewage *sg* ; **faire la ~** (*AUTO*) to change the oil, do an oil change ; **vidanger** *vt* to empty.

vide [vid] *a* empty // *nm* (*PHYSIQUE*) vacuum ; (*solution de continuité*) (empty) space, gap ; (*sous soi*: *dans une falaise etc*) drop ; (*futilité, néant*) void ; **sous ~** *ad* in a vacuum ; **emballé sous ~** vacuum packed ; **à ~** *ad* (*sans occupants*) empty ; (*sans charge*) unladen ; (*TECH*) without gripping *ou* being in gear.

vide-ordures [vidɔʀdyʀ] *nm inv* (rubbish) chute.

vide-poches [vidpɔʃ] *nm inv* tidy ; (*AUTO*) glove compartment.

vider [vide] *vt* to empty ; (*CULIN*: *volaille, poisson*) to gut, clean out ; (*régler*: *querelle*) to settle ; (*fatiguer*) to wear out ; (*fam*: *expulser*) to throw out, chuck out ; **se ~** *vi* to empty ; **~ les lieux** to quit *ou* vacate the premises ; **videur** *nm* (*de boîte de nuit*) bouncer.

vie [vi] *nf* life (*pl* lives) ; **être en ~** to be alive ; **sans ~** lifeless ; **à ~** for life ; **avoir la ~ dure** to have nine lives ; to die hard ; **mener la ~ dure à qn** to make life a misery for sb.

vieil [vjɛj] *am voir* **vieux**.

vieillard [vjɛjaʀ] *nm* old man ; **les ~s** old people, the elderly.

vieille [vjɛj] *a, nf voir* **vieux**.

vieilleries [vjɛjʀi] *nfpl* old things *ou* stuff *sg*.

vieillesse [vjɛjɛs] *nf* old age ; (*vieillards*): **la ~** the old *pl*, the elderly *pl*.

vieillir [vjejiʀ] *vi* (*prendre de l'âge*) to grow old ; (*population, vin*) to age ; (*doctrine, auteur*) to become dated // *vt* to age ; **il a beaucoup vieilli** he has aged a lot ; **vieillissement** *nm* growing old ; ageing.

vieillot, te [vjɛjo, -ɔt] *a* antiquated, quaint.

vielle [vjɛl] *nf* hurdy-gurdy.

vienne, viens *etc vb voir* **venir**.

vierge [vjɛʀʒ(ə)] *a* virgin ; (*jeune fille*): **être ~** to be a virgin // *nf* virgin ; (*signe*): **la V~** Virgo, the Virgin ; **être de la V~** to be Virgo ; **~ de** (*sans*) free from, unsullied by.

vieux(vieil), vieille [vjø, vjɛj] *a* old // *nm/f* old man/woman // *nmpl* old people ; **un petit ~** a little old man ; **mon ~/ma vieille** (*fam*) old man/girl ; **prendre un coup de ~** to put years on ; **un ~ de la vieille** one of the old brigade ; **~ garçon** *nm* bachelor ; **~ jeu** *a inv* old-fashioned ; **~ rose** *a inv* old rose ; **vieil or** *a inv* old gold ; **vieille fille** *nf* spinster.

vif, vive [vif, viv] *a* (*animé*) lively ; (*alerte*) sharp, quick ; (*brusque*) sharp, brusque ; (*aigu*) sharp ; (*lumière, couleur*) brilliant ; (*air*) crisp ; (*vent*) keen ; (*émotion*) keen, sharp ; (*fort*: *regret, déception*) great, deep ; (*vivant*): **brûlé ~** burnt alive ; **de vive voix** personally ; **piquer qn au ~** to cut sb to the quick ; **tailler dans le ~** to cut into the living flesh ; **à ~** (*plaie*) open ; **avoir les nerfs à ~** to be on edge ; **sur le ~** (*ART*) from life ; **entrer dans le ~ du sujet** to get to the very heart of the matter.

vif-argent [vifaʀʒɑ̃] *nm inv* quicksilver.

vigie [viʒi] *nf* look-out ; look-out post, crow's nest.

vigilance [viʒilɑ̃s] *nf* vigilance.

vigilant, e [viʒilɑ̃, -ɑ̃t] *a* vigilant.

vigne [viɲ] *nf* (*plante*) vine ; (*plantation*) vineyard ; **~ vierge** Virginia creeper.

vigneron [viɲʀɔ̃] *nm* wine grower.

vignette [viɲɛt] *nf* (*motif*) vignette ; (*de marque*) manufacturer's label *ou* seal ; (*ADMIN*) ≈ (road) tax disc ; price label (*on medicines for reimbursement by Social Security*).

vignoble [viɲɔbl(ə)] *nm* (*plantation*) vineyard ; (*vignes d'une région*) vineyards *pl*.

vigoureux, euse [viguʀø, -øz] *a* vigorous, strong, robust.

vigueur [vigœʀ] *nf* vigour ; **être/entrer en ~** to be in/come into force ; **en ~** current.

vil, e [vil] *a* vile, base ; **à ~ prix** at a very low price.

vilain, e [vilɛ̃, -ɛn] *a* (*laid*) ugly ; (*affaire, blessure*) nasty ; (*pas sage*: *enfant*) naughty // *nm* (*paysan*) villein, villain ; **ça va tourner au ~** it's going to turn nasty.

vilebrequin [vilbʀəkɛ̃] *nm* (*outil*) (bit-)brace ; (*AUTO*) crankshaft.

vilenie [vilni] *nf* vileness *q*, baseness *q*.

vilipender [vilipɑ̃de] *vt* to revile, vilify.

villa [vila] *nf* (detached) house.

village [vilaʒ] *nm* village ; **~ de toile** tent village ; **villageois, e** *a* village *cpd* // *nm/f* villager.

ville [vil] *nf* town ; (*importante*) city ; (*administration*): **la ~** ≈ the Corporation ; ≈ the (town) council.

villégiature [vileʒjatyʀ] *nf* holiday ; (holiday) resort.

vin [vɛ̃] *nm* wine ; **avoir le ~ gai** to get happy after a few drinks ; **~ d'honneur** reception (*with wine and snacks*) ; **~ de**

messe mass wine ; ~ **ordinaire** table wine ; ~ **de pays** local wine.

vinaigre [vinɛgʀ(ə)] *nm* vinegar ; **tourner au** ~ (*fig*) to turn sour ; ~ **de vin/d'alcool** wine/spirit vinegar ; **vinaigrette** *nf* vinaigrette, French dressing ; **vinaigrier** *nm* (*fabricant*) vinegar-maker ; (*flacon*) vinegar cruet *ou* bottle.

vinasse [vinas] *nf* (*péj*) cheap wine.

vindicatif, ive [vɛ̃dikatif, -iv] *a* vindictive.

vindicte [vɛ̃dikt(ə)] *nf*: **désigner qn à la** ~ **publique** to expose sb to public condemnation.

vineux, euse [vinø, -øz] *a* win(e)y.

vingt [vɛ̃, vɛ̃t + *vowel and in 22 etc*] *num* twenty ; **vingtaine** *nf*: **une vingtaine (de)** around twenty, twenty or so ; **vingtième** *num* twentieth.

vinicole [vinikɔl] *a* wine *cpd*, wine-growing.

vins *etc vb voir* **venir**.

viol [vjɔl] *nm* (*d'une femme*) rape ; (*d'un lieu sacré*) violation.

violacé, e [vjɔlase] *a* purplish, mauvish.

violation [vjɔlɑsjɔ̃] *nf* desecration ; violation.

violemment [vjɔlamɑ̃] *ad* violently.

violence [vjɔlɑ̃s] *nf* violence ; ~**s** *nfpl* acts of violence ; **faire** ~ **à qn** to do violence to sb.

violent, e [vjɔlɑ̃, -ɑ̃t] *a* violent ; (*remède*) drastic ; (*besoin, désir*) intense, urgent.

violenter [vjɔlɑ̃te] *vt* to assault (sexually).

violer [vjɔle] *vt* (*femme*) to rape ; (*sépulture*) to desecrate, violate ; (*règlement, traité*) to violate.

violet, te [vjɔlɛ, -ɛt] *a, nm* purple, mauve // *nf* (*fleur*) violet.

violon [vjɔlɔ̃] *nm* violin ; (*fam*: *prison*) lock-up ; **premier** ~ (*MUS*) first violin *ou* fiddle ; ~ **d'Ingres** (artistic) hobby.

violoncelle [vjɔlɔ̃sɛl] *nm* cello ; **violoncelliste** *nm/f* cellist.

violoniste [vjɔlɔnist(ə)] *nm/f* violinist, violin-player.

vipère [vipɛʀ] *nf* viper, adder.

virage [viʀaʒ] *nm* (*d'un véhicule*) turn ; (*d'une route, piste*) bend ; (*CHIMIE*) change in colour ; (*de cuti-réaction*) positive reaction ; (*PHOTO*) toning ; (*fig*: *POL*) change in policy ; **prendre un** ~ to go into a bend, take a bend ; ~ **sans visibilité** blind bend.

viral, e, aux [viʀal, -o] *a* viral.

virée [viʀe] *nf* (*courte*) run ; (: *à pied*) walk ; (*longue*) trip ; hike, walking tour.

virement [viʀmɑ̃] *nm* (*COMM*) transfer ; ~ **bancaire/postal** (bank) credit/(National) Giro transfer.

virent *vb voir aussi* **voir**.

virer [viʀe] *vt* (*COMM*): ~ **qch (sur)** to transfer sth (into) ; (*PHOTO*) to tone // *vi* to turn ; (*CHIMIE*) to change colour ; (*cuti-réaction*) to come up positive ; (*PHOTO*) to tone ; ~ **au bleu** to turn blue ; ~ **de bord** to tack ; ~ **sur l'aile** to bank.

virevolte [viʀvɔlt(ə)] *nf* twirl ; **virevolter** *vi* to twirl around.

virginité [viʀʒinite] *nf* virginity.

virgule [viʀgyl] *nf* comma ; (*MATH*) point ; **4** ~ **2** 4 point 2 ; ~ **flottante** floating decimal.

viril, e [viʀil] *a* (*propre à l'homme*) masculine ; (*énergique, courageux*) manly, virile ; ~**ité** *nf* masculinity ; manliness ; (*sexuelle*) virility.

virtualité [viʀtɥalite] *nf* virtuality ; potentiality.

virtuel, le [viʀtɥɛl] *a* potential ; (*théorique*) virtual ; ~**lement** *a* potentially ; (*presque*) virtually.

virtuose [viʀtɥoz] *nm/f* (*MUS*) virtuoso ; (*gén*) master ; **virtuosité** *nf* virtuosity ; masterliness, masterful skills *pl*.

virulent, e [viʀylɑ̃, -ɑ̃t] *a* virulent.

virus [viʀys] *nm* virus.

vis *vb* [vi] *voir* **voir, vivre** // *nf* [vis] screw ; ~ **sans fin** worm, endless screw.

visa [viza] *nm* (*sceau*) stamp ; (*validation de passeport*) visa ; ~ **de censure** (censor's) certificate.

visage [vizaʒ] *nm* face ; **visagiste** *nm/f* beautician.

vis-à-vis [vizavi] *ad* face to face // *nm* person opposite ; house *etc* opposite ; ~ **de** *prép* opposite ; (*fig*) towards, vis-à-vis ; **en** ~ facing *ou* opposite each other, **sans** ~ (*immeuble*) with an open outlook.

viscéral, e, aux [viseʀal, -o] *a* (*fig*) deep-seated, deep-rooted.

viscères [visɛʀ] *nmpl* intestines, entrails.

viscosité [viskozite] *nf* viscosity.

visée [vize] *nf* (*avec une arme*) aiming ; (*ARPENTAGE*) sighting ; ~**s** *nfpl* (*intentions*) designs.

viser [vize] *vi* to aim // *vt* to aim at ; (*concerner*) to be aimed *ou* directed at ; (*apposer un visa sur*) to stamp, visa ; ~ **à qch/faire** to aim at sth/at doing *ou* to do.

viseur [vizœʀ] *nm* (*d'arme*) sights *pl* ; (*PHOTO*) viewfinder.

visibilité [vizibilite] *nf* visibility.

visible [vizibl(ə)] *a* visible ; (*disponible*): **est-il** ~? can he see me?, will he see visitors?

visière [vizjɛʀ] *nf* (*de casquette*) peak ; (*qui s'attache*) eyeshade.

vision [vizjɔ̃] *nf* vision ; (*sens*) (eye)sight, vision ; (*fait de voir*): **la** ~ **de** the sight of ; **première** ~ (*CINÉMA*) first showing ; **visionnaire** *a, nm/f* visionary ; **visionner** *vt* to view ; **visionneuse** *nf* viewer.

visite [vizit] *nf* visit ; (*personne qui rend visite*) visitor ; (*médicale, à domicile*) visit, call ; **la** ~ (*MÉD*) (medical) consultations *pl*, surgery ; (*MIL*: *d'entrée*) medicals *pl* ; (: *quotidienne*) sick parade ; **faire une** ~ **à qn** to call on sb, pay sb a visit ; **rendre** ~ **à qn** to visit sb, pay sb a visit ; **être en** ~ **(chez qn)** to be visiting (sb) ; **heures de** ~ (*hôpital, prison*) visiting hours ; **le droit de** ~ (*JUR*: *aux enfants*) right of access, access ; ~ **de douane** customs inspection *ou* examination.

visiter [vizite] *vt* to visit ; (*musée, ville*) to visit, go round ; **visiteur, euse** *nm/f* visitor ; **visiteur des douanes** customs inspector.

vison [vizɔ̃] *nm* mink.

visqueux, euse [viskø, -øz] *a* viscous ; (*péj*) gooey ; slimy.

visser [vise] *vt*: ~ **qch** (*fixer, serrer*) to screw sth on.
visu [vizy]: **de** ~ *ad* with one's own eyes.
visuel, le [vizɥɛl] *a* visual // *nm* (visual) display.
vit *vb voir* **voir, vivre**.
vital, e, aux [vital, -o] *a* vital.
vitalité [vitalite] *nf* vitality.
vitamine [vitamin] *nf* vitamin; **vitaminique** *a* vitamin *cpd*.
vite [vit] *ad* (*rapidement*) quickly, fast; (*sans délai*) quickly; soon; **faire** ~ to act quickly; to be quick; **viens** ~ come quick(ly).
vitesse [vitɛs] *nf* speed; (AUTO: *dispositif*) gear; **faire de la** ~ to drive fast *ou* at speed; **prendre qn de** ~ to outstrip sb; get ahead of sb; **prendre de la** ~ to pick up *ou* gather speed; **à toute** ~ at full *ou* top speed; ~ **acquise** momentum; ~ **du son** speed of sound.
viticole [vitikɔl] *a* wine *cpd*, wine-growing.
viticulteur [vitikyltœʀ] *nm* wine grower.
viticulture [vitikyltyʀ] *nf* wine growing.
vitrage [vitʀaʒ] *nm* (*cloison*) glass partition; (*toit*) glass roof; (*rideau*) net curtain.
vitrail, aux [vitʀaj, -o] *nm* stained-glass window.
vitre [vitʀ(ə)] *nf* (window) pane; (*de portière, voiture*) window.
vitré, e [vitʀe] *a* glass *cpd*.
vitrer [vitʀe] *vt* to glaze.
vitreux, euse [vitʀø, -øz] *a* vitreous; (*terne*) glassy.
vitrier [vitʀije] *nm* glazier.
vitrifier [vitʀifje] *vt* to vitrify; (*parquet*) to glaze.
vitrine [vitʀin] *nf* (*devanture*) (shop) window; (*étalage*) display; (*petite armoire*) display cabinet; **en** ~ in the window, on display; ~ **publicitaire** display case, showcase.
vitriol [vitʀijɔl] *nm* vitriol; **au** ~ (*fig*) vitriolic.
vitupérer [vitypeʀe] *vi* to rant and rave; ~ **contre** to rail against.
vivable [vivabl(ə)] *a* (*personne*) livable-with; (*endroit*) fit to live in.
vivace *a* [vivas] (*arbre, plante*) hardy; (*fig*) indestructible, inveterate // *ad* [vivatʃe] (MUS) vivace.
vivacité [vivasite] *nf* liveliness, vivacity; sharpness; brilliance.
vivant, e [vivɑ̃, -ɑ̃t] *a* (*qui vit*) living, alive; (*animé*) lively; (*preuve, exemple*) living // *nm*: **du** ~ **de qn** in sb's lifetime; **les** ~**s et les morts** the living and the dead.
vivats [viva] *nmpl* cheers.
vive [viv] *af voir* **vif** // *vb voir* **vivre** // *excl*: ~ **le roi!** long live the king!; ~ **les vacances!** hurrah for the holidays!; ~**ment** *ad* vivaciously; sharply // *excl*: ~**ment les vacances!** I can't wait for the holidays!, roll on the holidays!
viveur [vivœʀ] *nm* (*péj*) high liver, pleasure-seeker.
vivier [vivje] *nm* fish tank; fishpond.
vivifiant, e [vivifjɑ̃, -ɑ̃t] *a* invigorating.
vivions *vb voir* **vivre**.
vivisection [vivisɛksjɔ̃] *nf* vivisection.
vivoter [vivɔte] *vi* to rub along, struggle along.
vivre [vivʀ(ə)] *vi, vt* to live // *nm*: **le** ~ **et le logement** board and lodging; ~**s** *nmpl* provisions, food supplies; **il vit encore** he is still alive; **se laisser** ~ to take life as it comes; **ne plus** ~ (*être anxieux*) to live on one's nerves; **il a vécu** (*eu une vie aventureuse*) he has seen life; **ce régime a vécu** this regime has had its day; **être facile à** ~ to be easy to get on with; **faire** ~ **qn** (*pourvoir à sa subsistance*) to provide (a living) for sb; ~ **mal** (*chichement*) to have a meagre existence; ~ **de** (*salaire etc*) to live on.
vlan [vlɑ̃] *excl* wham!, bang!
vocable [vɔkabl(ə)] *nm* term.
vocabulaire [vɔkabylɛʀ] *nm* vocabulary.
vocal, e, aux [vɔkal, -o] *a* vocal.
vocalique [vɔkalik] *a* vocalic, vowel *cpd*.
vocalise [vɔkaliz] *nf* singing exercise.
vocation [vɔkɑsjɔ̃] *nf* vocation, calling.
vociférations [vɔsifeʀɑsjɔ̃] *nfpl* cries of rage, screams.
vociférer [vɔsifeʀe] *vi, vt* to scream.
vodka [vɔdka] *nf* vodka.
vœu, x [vø] *nm* wish; (*à Dieu*) vow; **faire** ~ **de** to take a vow of; ~**x de bonne année** best wishes for the New Year; **avec tous nos** ~**x** with every good wish *ou* our best wishes.
vogue [vɔg] *nf* fashion, vogue.
voguer [vɔge] *vi* to sail.
voici [vwasi] *prép* (*pour introduire, désigner*) here is + *sg*, here are + *pl*; **et** ~ **que...** and now it (*ou* he)...; *voir aussi* **voilà**.
voie [vwa] *nf* way; (RAIL) track, line; (AUTO) lane; **suivre la** ~ **hiérarchique** to go through official channels; **être en bonne** ~ to be shaping *ou* going well; **mettre qn sur la** ~ to put sb on the right track; **être en** ~ **d'achèvement/de rénovation** to be nearing completion/in the process of renovation; **à** ~ **étroite** narrow-gauge; **route à 2/3** ~**s** 2-/3-lane road; **par la** ~ **aérienne/maritime** by air/sea; ~ **d'eau** (NAVIG) leak; ~ **ferrée** track; railway line; **par** ~ **ferrée** by rail; ~ **de garage** (RAIL) siding; **la** ~ **lactée** the Milky Way; ~ **navigable** waterway; ~ **privée** private road; **la** ~ **publique** the public highway.
voilà [vwala] *prép* (*en désignant*) there is + *sg*, there are + *pl*; **les** ~ *ou* **voici** here *ou* there they are; **en** ~ *ou* **voici un** here's one, there's one; ~ *ou* **voici deux ans** two years ago; ~ *ou* **voici deux ans que** it's two years since; **et** ~! there we are!; ~ **tout** that's all; '~ *ou* **voici**' (*en offrant etc*) 'there *ou* here you are'.
voile [vwal] *nm* veil; (*tissu léger*) net // *nf* sail; (*sport*) sailing; **prendre le** ~ to take the veil; **mettre à la** ~ to make way under sail; ~ **du palais** *nm* soft palate, velum; ~ **au poumon** *nm* shadow on the lung.
voiler [vwale] *vt* to veil; (*fausser*: *roue*) to buckle; (: *bois*) to warp; **se** ~ *vi* (*lune, regard*) to mist over; (*ciel*) to grow hazy; (*voix*) to become husky; (*roue, disque*) to

buckle; (*planche*) to warp; **se ~ la face** to hide one's face.
voilette [vwalɛt] *nf* (hat) veil.
voilier [vwalje] *nm* sailing ship; (*de plaisance*) sailing boat.
voilure [vwalyʀ] *nf* (*de voilier*) sails *pl*; (*d'avion*) aerofoils *pl*; (*de parachute*) canopy.
voir [vwaʀ] *vi, vt* to see; **se ~**: **se ~ critiquer/transformer** to be criticized/transformed; **cela se voit** (*cela arrive*) it happens; (*c'est visible*) that's obvious, it shows; **~ venir** (*fig*) to wait and see; **faire ~ qch à qn** to show sb sth; **en faire ~ à qn** (*fig*) to give sb a hard time; **ne pas pouvoir ~ qn** (*fig*) not to be able to stand sb; **regardez ~** just look; **dites-~** tell me; **voyons!** let's see now; (*indignation etc*) come (along) now!; **avoir quelque chose à ~ avec** to have something to do with.
voire [vwaʀ] *ad* indeed; nay.
voirie [vwaʀi] *nf* highway maintenance; (*administration*) highways department; (*enlèvement des ordures*) refuse collection.
voisin, e [vwazɛ̃, -in] *a* (*proche*) neighbouring; (*contigu*) next; (*ressemblant*) connected // *nm/f* neighbour; **voisinage** *nm* (*proximité*) proximity; (*environs*) vicinity; (*quartier, voisins*) neighbourhood; **relations de bon voisinage** neighbourly terms; **voisiner** *vi*: **voisiner avec** to be side by side with.
voiture [vwatyʀ] *nf* car; (*wagon*) coach, carriage; **~ d'enfant** pram; **~ d'infirme** invalid carriage; **~ de sport** sports car; **~-lit** *nf* sleeper.
voix [vwa] *nf* voice; (POL) vote; **à haute ~** aloud; **à ~ basse** in a low voice; **à 2/4 ~** (MUS) in 2/4 parts; **avoir ~ au chapitre** to have a say in the matter; **mettre aux ~** to put to the vote.
vol [vɔl] *nm* (*mode de locomotion*) flying; (*trajet, voyage, groupe d'oiseaux*) flight; (*mode d'appropriation*) theft, stealing; (*larcin*) theft; **à ~ d'oiseau** as the crow flies; **au ~**: **attraper qch au ~** to catch sth as it flies past; **prendre son ~** to take flight; **en ~** in flight; **~ avec effraction** breaking and entering *q*, break-in; **~ libre** *ou* **sur aile delta** hang-gliding; **~ à main armée** armed robbery; **~ de nuit** night flight; **~ à voile** gliding.
volage [vɔlaʒ] *a* fickle.
volaille [vɔlaj] *nf* (*oiseaux*) poultry *pl*; (*viande*) poultry *q*; (*oiseau*) fowl; **volailler** *nm* poulterer.
volant, e [vɔlɑ̃, -ɑ̃t] *a voir* **feuille** *etc* // *nm* (*d'automobile*) (steering) wheel; (*de commande*) wheel; (*objet lancé*) shuttlecock; (*jeu*) battledore and shuttlecock; (*bande de tissu*) flounce; (*feuillet détachable*) tear-off portion; **les ~s** (AVIAT) the flight staff.
volatil, e [vɔlatil] *a* volatile.
volatile [vɔlatil] *nm* (*volaille*) bird; (*tout oiseau*) winged creature.
volatiliser [vɔlatilize]: **se ~** *vi* (CHIMIE) to volatilize; (*fig*) to vanish into thin air.
vol-au-vent [vɔlovɑ̃] *nm inv* vol-au-vent.
volcan [vɔlkɑ̃] *nm* volcano; **volcanique** *a* volcanic; **volcanologue** *nm/f* vulcanologist.
volée [vɔle] *nf* (*groupe d'oiseaux*) flight, flock; (TENNIS) volley; **~ de coups/de flèches** volley of blows/arrows; **à la ~**: **rattraper à la ~** to catch in mid air; **lancer à la ~** to fling about; **à toute ~** (*sonner les cloches*) vigorously; (*lancer un projectile*) with full force.
voler [vɔle] *vi* (*avion, oiseau, fig*) to fly; (*voleur*) to steal // *vt* (*objet*) to steal; (*personne*) to rob; **~ qch à qn** to steal sth from sb.
volet [vɔlɛ] *nm* (*de fenêtre*) shutter; (AVIAT) flap; (*de feuillet, document*) section; **trié sur le ~** hand-picked.
voleter [vɔlte] *vi* to flutter (about).
voleur, euse [vɔlœʀ, -øz] *nm/f* thief (*pl* thieves) // *a* thieving.
volière [vɔljɛʀ] *nf* aviary.
volontaire [vɔlɔ̃tɛʀ] *a* voluntary; (*caractère, personne: décidé*) self-willed // *nm/f* volunteer; **volontariat** *nm* voluntary service.
volonté [vɔlɔ̃te] *nf* (*faculté de vouloir*) will; (*énergie, fermeté*) will(power); (*souhait, désir*) wish; **se servir/boire à ~** to take/drink as much as one likes; **bonne ~** goodwill, willingness; **mauvaise ~** lack of goodwill, unwillingness.
volontiers [vɔlɔ̃tje] *ad* (*de bonne grâce*) willingly; (*avec plaisir*) willingly, gladly; (*habituellement, souvent*) readily, willingly; '~' 'with pleasure', 'I'd be glad to'.
volt [vɔlt] *nm* volt; **~age** *nm* voltage.
volte-face [vɔltəfas] *nf inv* about-turn.
voltige [vɔltiʒ] *nf* (EQUITATION) trick riding; (*au cirque*) acrobatic feat; (AVIAT) (aerial) acrobatics *sg*; **numéro de haute ~** acrobatic act.
voltiger [vɔltiʒe] *vi* to flutter (about).
voltigeur, euse [vɔltiʒœʀ, -øz] *nm/f* (*au cirque*) acrobat.
voltmètre [vɔltmɛtʀ(ə)] *nm* voltmeter.
volubile [vɔlybil] *a* voluble.
volume [vɔlym] *nm* volume; (GEOM: *solide*) solid; **volumineux, euse** *a* voluminous, bulky.
volupté [vɔlypte] *nf* sensual delight *ou* pleasure; **voluptueux, euse** *a* voluptuous.
volute [vɔlyt] *nf* (ARCHIT) volute; **~ de fumée** curl of smoke.
vomi [vɔmi] *nm* vomit.
vomir [vɔmiʀ] *vi* to vomit, be sick // *vt* to vomit, bring up; (*fig*) to belch out, spew out; (*exécrer*) to loathe, abhor; **vomissement** *nm* vomiting *q*; **vomissure** *nf* vomit *q*; **vomitif** *nm* emetic.
vont [vɔ̃] *vb voir* **aller.**
vorace [vɔʀas] *a* voracious.
vos [vo] *dét voir* **votre.**
votant, e [vɔtɑ̃, -ɑ̃t] *nm/f* voter.
vote [vɔt] *nm* vote; **~ par correspondance/procuration** postal/proxy vote.
voter [vɔte] *vi* to vote // *vt* (*loi, décision*) to vote for.
votre [vɔtʀ(ə)], *pl* **vos** [vo] *dét* your.
vôtre [votʀ(ə)] *pronom*: **le ~, la ~, les ~s** yours; **les ~s** (*fig*) your family *ou* folks; **à la ~** (*toast*) your (good) health!

voudrai *etc vb voir* **vouloir**.
voué, e [vwe] *a*: ~ **à** doomed to, destined for.
vouer [vwe] *vt*: ~ **qch à** (*Dieu/un saint*) to dedicate sth to; ~ **sa vie/son temps à** (*étude, cause etc*) to devote one's life/time to; ~ **une haine/amitié éternelle à qn** to vow undying hatred/love to sb.
vouloir [vulwaR] *vi* to show will, have willpower // *vt* to want // *nm*: **le bon ~ de qn** sb's goodwill; sb's pleasure; ~ **que qn fasse** to want sb to do; **je voudrais ceci** I would like this; **veuillez attendre** please wait; **je veux bien** (*bonne volonté*) I'll be happy to; (*concession*) fair enough, that's fine; **si on veut** (*en quelque sorte*) if you like; **que me veut-il?** what does he want with me?; ~ **dire (que)** (*signifier*) to mean (that); **sans le ~** (*involontairement*) without meaning to, unintentionally; **en ~ à qn** to bear sb a grudge; **en ~ à qch** (*avoir des visées sur*) to be after sth; **s'en ~ de** to be annoyed with o.s. for; ~ **de qch/qn** (*accepter*) to want sth/sb.
voulu, e [vuly] *a* (*requis*) required, requisite; (*délibéré*) deliberate, intentional.
vous [vu] *pronom* you; (*objet indirect*) (to) you; (*réfléchi*) yourself, *pl* yourselves; (*réciproque*) each other // *nm*: **employer le ~** (*vouvoyer*) to use the 'vous' form; **~-même** yourself; **~-mêmes** yourselves.
voûte [vut] *nf* vault; ~ **du palais** (ANAT) roof of the mouth; ~ **plantaire** arch (of the foot).
voûté, e [vute] *a* vaulted, arched; (*dos, personne*) bent, stooped.
voûter [vute] *vt* (ARCHIT) to arch, vault; **se~** *vi* (*dos, personne*) to become stooped.
vouvoyer [vuvwaje] *vt*: ~ **qn** to address sb as 'vous'.
voyage [vwajaʒ] *nm* journey, trip; (*fait de voyager*): **le ~** travel(ling); **partir/être en ~** to go off/be away on a journey *ou* trip; **faire un ~** to go on *ou* make a trip *ou* journey; **faire bon ~** to have a good journey; ~ **d'agrément/d'affaires** pleasure/business trip; ~ **de noces** honeymoon; ~ **organisé** package tour.
voyager [vwajaʒe] *vi* to travel; **voyageur, euse** *nm/f* traveller; (*passager*) passenger; **voyageur (de commerce)** commercial traveller.
voyant, e [vwajɑ̃, -ɑ̃t] *a* (*couleur*) loud, gaudy // *nm* (*signal*) (warning) light // *nf* clairvoyant.
voyelle [vwajɛl] *nf* vowel.
voyeur, euse [vwajœR, -øz] *nm/f* voyeur; peeping Tom.
voyou [vwaju] *nm* lout, hoodlum; (*enfant*) guttersnipe // *a* loutish.
vrac [vRak]: **en ~** *ad* higgledy-piggledy; (COMM) in bulk.
vrai, e [vRɛ] *a* (*véridique: récit, faits*) true; (*non factice, authentique*) real; **à ~ dire** to tell the truth; **être dans le ~** to be right.
vraiment [vRɛmɑ̃] *ad* really.
vraisemblable [vRɛsɑ̃blabl(ə)] *a* (*plausible*) likely, plausible; (*probable*) likely, probable; **~ment** *ad* in all likelihood, very likely.
vraisemblance [vRɛsɑ̃blɑ̃s] *nf* likelihood, plausibility; (*romanesque*) verisimilitude.
vrille [vRij] *nf* (*de plante*) tendril; (*outil*) gimlet; (*spirale*) spiral; (AVIAT) spin.
vriller [vRije] *vt* to bore into, pierce.
vrombir [vRɔ̃biR] *vi* to hum.
vu [vy] *prép* (*en raison de*) in view of; ~ **que** in view of the fact that.
vu, e [vy] *pp de* **voir** // *a*: **bien/mal ~** (*fig*) well/poorly thought of; good/bad form // *nm*: **au ~ et au su de tous** openly and publicly.
vue [vy] *nf* (*fait de voir*): **la ~ de** the sight of; (*sens, faculté*) (eye)sight; (*panorama, image, photo*) view; (*spectacle*) sight; **~s** *nfpl* (*idées*) views; (*dessein*) designs; **perdre la ~** to lose one's (eye)sight; **perdre de ~** to lose sight of; **à la ~ de tous** in full view of everybody; **hors de ~** out of sight; **à première ~** at first sight; **connaître de ~** to know by sight; **à ~** (COMM) at sight; **tirer à ~** to shoot on sight; **à ~ d'œil** *ad* visibly; at a quick glance; **en ~** (*visible*) in sight; (COMM) in the public eye; **avoir qch en ~** (*intentions*) to have one's sights on sth; **en ~ de** (*arriver, être*) within sight of; **en ~ de faire** with the intention of doing, with a view to doing; ~ **de l'esprit** theoretical view.
vulcaniser [vylkanize] *vt* to vulcanize.
vulgaire [vylgɛR] *a* (*grossier*) vulgar, coarse; (*trivial*) commonplace, mundane; (*péj: quelconque*): **de ~s touristes/chaises de cuisine** common tourists/kitchen chairs; (BOT, ZOOL: *non latin*) common; **~ment** *ad* vulgarly, coarsely; (*communément*) commonly; **vulgarisation** *nf*: **ouvrage de vulgarisation** popularizing work, popularization; **vulgariser** *vt* to popularize; to coarsen; **vulgarité** *nf* vulgarity, coarseness.
vulnérable [vylneRabl(ə)] *a* vulnerable.
vulve [vylv(ə)] *nf* vulva.

W X Y Z

wagon [vagɔ̃] *nm* (*de voyageurs*) carriage; (*de marchandises*) truck, wagon; **~-citerne** *nm* tanker; **~-lit** *nm* sleeper, sleeping car; **~-poste** *nm* mail van; **~-restaurant** *nm* restaurant *ou* dining car.
wallon, ne [valɔ̃, -ɔn] *a* Walloon.
waters [watɛR] *nmpl* toilet *sg*, loo *sg*.
watt [wat] *nm* watt.
w.-c. [vese] *nmpl* toilet *sg*, lavatory *sg*.
week-end [wikɛnd] *nm* weekend.
western [wɛstɛRn] *nm* western.
whisky, *pl* **whiskies** [wiski] *nm* whisky.

x [iks] *nm*: **plainte contre X** (JUR) action against person or persons unknown; **l'X** *the École Polytechnique*.
xénophobe [ksenɔfɔb] *nm/f* xenophobe.
xérès [gzeRɛs] *nm* sherry.
xylographie [ksilɔgRafi] *nf* xylography; (*image*) xylograph.
xylophone [ksilɔfɔn] *nm* xylophone.

y [i] *ad* (*à cet endroit*) there; (*dessus*) on it (*ou* them); (*dedans*) in it (*ou* them) // *pronom* (about *ou* on *ou* of) it: *vérifier la syntaxe du verbe employé*; **j'~ pense** I'm thinking about it; *voir aussi* **aller, avoir.**
yacht [jɔt] *nm* yacht.
yaourt [jauʀt] *nm* yoghourt.
yeux [jø] *pl de* **œil**.
yoga [jɔga] nm yoga.
yoghourt [jɔguʀt] *nm* = **yaourt**.
yole [jɔl] *nf* skiff.
yougoslave [jugɔslav] *a, nm/f* Yugoslav(ian).
Yougoslavie [jugɔslavi] *nf* Yugoslavia.
youyou [juju] *nm* dinghy.
yo-yo [jojo] *nm inv* yo-yo.

zèbre [zɛbʀ(ə)] *nm* (*ZOOL*) zebra.
zébré, e [zebʀe] *a* striped, streaked; **zébrure** *nf* stripe, streak.
zélateur, trice [zelatœʀ, -tʀis] *nm/f* partisan, zealot.
zèle [zɛl] *nm* zeal; **faire du ~** (*péj*) to be over-zealous; **zélé, e** *a* zealous.
zénith [zenit] *nm* zenith.
zéro [zeʀo] *nm* zero, nought; **au-dessous de ~** below zero (Centigrade) *ou* freezing; **partir de ~** to start from scratch; **trois (buts) à ~** 3 (goals to) nil.
zeste [zɛst(ə)] *nm* peel, zest; **un ~ de citron** a piece of lemon peel.
zézayer [zezeje] *vi* to have a lisp.
zibeline [ziblin] *nf* sable.
zigzag [zigzag] *nm* zigzag; **zigzaguer** *vi* to zigzag (along).
zinc [zɛ̃g] *nm* (*CHIMIE*) zinc; (*comptoir*) bar, counter.
zizanie [zizani] *nf*: **semer la ~** to stir up ill-feeling.
zizi [zizi] *nm* (*fam*) willy.
zodiaque [zɔdjak] *nm* zodiac.
zona [zona] *nm* shingles *sg*.
zone [zon] *nf* zone, area; (*quartiers*): **la ~** the slum belt; **~ bleue** ≈ restricted parking area.
zoo [zoo] *nm* zoo.
zoologie [zɔɔlɔʒi] *nf* zoology; **zoologique** *a* zoological; **zoologiste** *nm/f* zoologist.
Z.U.P. [zyp] *sigle f* = *zone à urbaniser en priorité*, ≈ (planned) housing scheme.
zut [zyt] *excl* dash (it)!

ENGLISH-FRENCH
ANGLAIS-FRANÇAIS

A

a, an [eɪ, ə, æn, ən, n] *det* un(e) ; **3 a day/week** 3 par jour/semaine ; **10 km an hour** 10 km à l'heure.

A [eɪ] *n* (MUS) la *m*.

A.A. *n abbr of Automobile Association* ; *Alcoholics Anonymous*.

aback [ə'bæk] *ad*: **to be taken ~** être stupéfait(e).

abacus, *pl* **abaci** ['æbəkəs, -saɪ] *n* boulier *m*.

abandon [ə'bændən] *vt* abandonner // *n* abandon *m*.

abashed [ə'bæʃt] *a* confus(e), embarrassé(e).

abate [ə'beɪt] *vi* s'apaiser, se calmer.

abattoir ['æbətwɑː*] *n* abattoir *m*.

abbey ['æbɪ] *n* abbaye *f*.

abbot ['æbət] *n* père supérieur.

abbreviate [ə'briːvɪeɪt] *vt* abréger ; **abbreviation** [-'eɪʃən] *n* abréviation *f*.

abdicate ['æbdɪkeɪt] *vt,vi* abdiquer ; **abdication** [-'keɪʃən] *n* abdication *f*.

abdomen ['æbdəmɛn] *n* abdomen *m* ; **abdominal** [æb'dɔmɪnl] *a* abdominal(e).

abduct [æb'dʌkt] *vt* enlever ; **abduction** [-ʃən] *n* enlèvement *m*.

abet [ə'bɛt] *vt* encourager ; aider.

abeyance [ə'beɪəns] *n*: **in ~** (*law*) en désuétude ; (*matter*) en suspens.

abhor [əb'hɔː*] *vt* abhorrer, exécrer ; **~rent** *a* odieux(euse), exécrable.

abide, *pt,pp* **abode** *or* **abided** [ə'baɪd, ə'bəud] *vt* souffrir, supporter ; **to ~ by** *vt fus* observer, respecter.

ability [ə'bɪlɪtɪ] *n* compétence *f* ; capacité *f* ; talent *m*.

ablaze [ə'bleɪz] *a* en feu, en flammes ; **~ with light** resplendissant de lumière.

able ['eɪbl] *a* compétent(e) ; **to be ~ to do sth** pouvoir faire qch, être capable de faire qch ; **~-bodied** *a* robuste ; **ably** *ad* avec compétence *or* talent, habilement.

abnormal [æb'nɔːməl] *a* anormal(e) ; **~ity** [-'mælɪtɪ] *n* anomalie *f*.

aboard [ə'bɔːd] *ad* à bord // *prep* à bord de.

abode [ə'bəud] *pt,pp of* **abide**.

abolish [ə'bɔlɪʃ] *vt* abolir.

abolition [æbəu'lɪʃən] *n* abolition *f*.

abominable [ə'bɔmɪnəbl] *a* abominable.

aborigine [æbə'rɪdʒɪnɪ] *n* aborigène *m/f*.

abort [ə'bɔːt] *vt* faire avorter ; **~ion** [ə'bɔːʃən] *n* avortement *m* ; **~ive** *a* manqué(e).

abound [ə'baund] *vi* abonder ; **to ~ in** abonder en, regorger de.

about [ə'baut] *prep* au sujet de, à propos de // *ad* environ ; (*here and there*) de côté et d'autre, çà et là ; **it takes ~ 10 hours** ça prend environ *or* à peu près 10 heures ; **at ~ 2 o'clock** vers 2 heures ; **it's ~ here** c'est par ici, c'est dans les parages ; **to walk ~ the town** se promener dans *or* à travers la ville ; **to be ~ to**: **he was ~ to cry** il allait pleurer, il était sur le point de pleurer ; **what** *or* **how ~ doing this?** et si nous faisions ceci? ; **~ turn** *n* demi-tour *m*.

above [ə'bʌv] *ad* au-dessus // *prep* au-dessus de ; **mentioned ~** mentionné ci-dessus ; **costing ~ £10** coûtant plus de 10 livres ; **~ all** par-dessus tout, surtout ; **~board** *a* franc(franche), loyal(e) ; honnête.

abrasion [ə'breɪʒən] *n* frottement *m* ; (*on skin*) écorchure *f*.

abrasive [ə'breɪzɪv] *a* abrasif(ive) ; (*fig*) caustique, agressif(ive).

abreast [ə'brɛst] *ad* de front ; **to keep ~ of** se tenir au courant de.

abridge [ə'brɪdʒ] *vt* abréger.

abroad [ə'brɔːd] *ad* à l'étranger.

abrupt [ə'brʌpt] *a* (*steep, blunt*) abrupt(e) ; (*sudden, gruff*) brusque.

abscess ['æbsɪs] *n* abcès *m*.

abscond [əb'skɔnd] *vi* disparaître, s'enfuir.

absence ['æbsəns] *n* absence *f*.

absent ['æbsənt] *a* absent(e) ; **~ee** [-'tiː] *n* absent/e ; **~eeism** [-'tiːɪzəm] *n* absentéisme *m* ; **~-minded** *a* distrait(e) ; **~-mindedness** *n* distraction *f*.

absolute ['æbsəluːt] *a* absolu(e) ; **~ly** [-'luːtlɪ] *ad* absolument.

absolve [əb'zɔlv] *vt*: **to ~ sb (from)** (*sin etc*) absoudre qn (de) ; **to ~ sb from** (*oath*) délier qn de.

absorb [əb'zɔːb] *vt* absorber ; **to be ~ed in a book** être plongé dans un livre ; **~ent** *a* absorbant(e) ; **~ent cotton** *n* (*US*) coton *m* hydrophile ; **~ing** *a* absorbant(e).

abstain [əb'steɪn] *vi*: **to ~ (from)** s'abstenir (de).

abstemious [əb'stiːmɪəs] *a* sobre, frugal(e).

abstention [əb'stɛnʃən] *n* abstention *f*.

abstinence ['æbstɪnəns] *n* abstinence *f*.

abstract *a and n* ['æbstrækt] *a* abstrait(e) // *n* (*summary*) résumé *m* // *vt* [æb'strækt] extraire.

absurd [əb'səːd] *a* absurde ; **~ity** *n* absurdité *f*.

abundance [ə'bʌndəns] *n* abondance *f* ; **abundant** *a* abondant(e).

abuse *n* [ə'bjuːs] abus *m* ; insultes *fpl*, injures *fpl* // *vt* [ə'bjuːz] abuser de ; **abusive** *a* grossier(ère), injurieux(euse).

abysmal [ə'bɪzməl] *a* exécrable ; (*ignorance etc*) sans bornes.

abyss [ə'bɪs] *n* abîme *m*, gouffre *m*.

academic [ækə'dɛmɪk] *a* universitaire ; (*pej*: *issue*) oiseux(euse), purement théorique // *n* universitaire *m/f* ; **~ freedom** *n* liberté *f* académique.

academy [ə'kædəmɪ] *n* (*learned body*) académie *f* ; (*school*) collège *m* ; **military/naval ~** école militaire/navale ; **~ of music** conservatoire *m*.

accede [æk'si:d] *vi*: **to ~ to** (*request, throne*) accéder à.
accelerate [æk'sɛləreɪt] *vt,vi* accélérer; **acceleration** [-'reɪʃən] *n* accélération *f*; **accelerator** *n* accélérateur *m*.
accent ['æksɛnt] *n* accent *m*.
accept [ək'sɛpt] *vt* accepter; **~able** *a* acceptable; **~ance** *n* acceptation *f*.
access ['æksɛs] *n* accès *m*; **to have ~ to** (*information, library etc*) avoir accès à, pouvoir utiliser *or* consulter; (*person*) avoir accès auprès de; **~ible** [æk'sɛsəbl] *a* accessible; **~ion** [æk'sɛʃən] *n* accession *f*.
accessory [æk'sɛsərɪ] *n* accessoire *m*; **toilet accessories** *npl* articles *mpl* de toilette.
accident ['æksɪdənt] *n* accident *m*; (*chance*) hasard *m*; **by ~** par hasard; accidentellement; **~al** [-'dɛntl] *a* accidentel(le); **~ally** [-'dɛntəlɪ] *ad* accidentellement; **~-prone** *a* sujet(te) aux accidents.
acclaim [ə'kleɪm] *vt* acclamer // *n* acclamation *f*.
acclimatize [ə'klaɪmətaɪz] *vt*: **to become ~d** s'acclimater.
accommodate [ə'kɔmədeɪt] *vt* loger, recevoir; (*oblige, help*) obliger; (*adapt*): **to ~ one's plans to** adapter ses projets à.
accommodating [ə'kɔmədeɪtɪŋ] *a* obligeant(e), arrangeant(e).
accommodation [əkɔmə'deɪʃən] *n* logement *m*; **he's found ~** il a trouvé à se loger; **they have ~ for 500** ils peuvent recevoir 500 personnes, il y a de la place pour 500 personnes.
accompaniment [ə'kʌmpənɪmənt] *n* accompagnement *m*.
accompanist [ə'kʌmpənɪst] *n* accompagnateur/trice.
accompany [ə'kʌmpənɪ] *vt* accompagner.
accomplice [ə'kʌmplɪs] *n* complice *m/f*.
accomplish [ə'kʌmplɪʃ] *vt* accomplir; **~ed** *a* accompli(e); **~ment** *n* accomplissement *m*; réussite *f*, résultat *m*; **~ments** *npl* talents *mpl*.
accord [ə'kɔ:d] *n* accord *m* // *vt* accorder; **of his own ~** de son plein gré; **~ance** *n*: **in ~ance with** conformément à; **~ing to** *prep* selon; **~ingly** *ad* en conséquence.
accordion [ə'kɔ:dɪən] *n* accordéon *m*.
accost [ə'kɔst] *vt* accoster, aborder.
account [ə'kaunt] *n* (COMM) compte *m*; (*report*) compte rendu; récit *m*; **by all ~s** au dire de tous; **of little ~** de peu d'importance; **on ~** en acompte; **on no ~** en aucun cas; **on ~ of** à cause de; **to take into ~, take ~ of** tenir compte de; **to ~ for** expliquer, rendre compte de; **~able** *a* responsable.
accountancy [ə'kauntənsɪ] *n* comptabilité *f*.
accountant [ə'kauntənt] *n* comptable *m/f*.
accredited [ə'krɛdɪtɪd] *a* accrédité(e); admis(e).
accretion [ə'kri:ʃən] *n* accroissement *m*.
accrue [ə'kru:] *vi* s'accroître; **~d interest** intérêt couru.
accumulate [ə'kju:mjuleɪt] *vt* accumuler, amasser // *vi* s'accumuler, s'amasser; **accumulation** [-'leɪʃən] *n* accumulation *f*.
accuracy ['ækjurəsɪ] *n* exactitude *f*, précision *f*.
accurate ['ækjurɪt] *a* exact(e), précis(e); **~ly** *ad* avec précision.
accusation [ækju'zeɪʃən] *n* accusation *f*.
accusative [ə'kju:zətɪv] *n* (LING) accusatif *m*.
accuse [ə'kju:z] *vt* accuser; **~d** *n* accusé/e.
accustom [ə'kʌstəm] *vt* accoutumer, habituer; **~ed** *a* (*usual*) habituel(le); **~ed to** habitué *or* accoutumé à.
ace [eɪs] *n* as *m*; **within an ~ of** à deux doigts *or* un cheveu de.
ache [eɪk] *n* mal *m*, douleur *f* // *vi* (*be sore*) faire mal, être douloureux(euse); **my head ~s** j'ai mal à la tête; **I'm aching all over** j'ai mal partout.
achieve [ə'tʃi:v] *vt* (*aim*) atteindre; (*victory, success*) remporter, obtenir; (*task*) accomplir; **~ment** *n* exploit *m*, réussite *f*.
acid ['æsɪd] *a,n* acide (*m*); **~ity** [ə'sɪdɪtɪ] *n* acidité *f*.
acknowledge [ək'nɔlɪdʒ] *vt* (*letter*) accuser réception de; (*fact*) reconnaître; **~ment** *n* accusé *m* de réception.
acne ['æknɪ] *n* acné *m*.
acorn ['eɪkɔ:n] *n* gland *m*.
acoustic [ə'ku:stɪk] *a* acoustique; **~s** *n,npl* acoustique *f*.
acquaint [ə'kweɪnt] *vt*: **to ~ sb with sth** mettre qn au courant de qch; **to be ~ed with** (*person*) connaître; **~ance** *n* connaissance *f*.
acquire [ə'kwaɪə*] *vt* acquérir.
acquisition [ækwɪ'zɪʃən] *n* acquisition *f*.
acquisitive [ə'kwɪzɪtɪv] *a* qui a l'instinct de possession *or* le goût de la propriété.
acquit [ə'kwɪt] *vt* acquitter; **to ~ o.s. well** bien se comporter, s'en tirer très honorablement; **~tal** *n* acquittement *m*.
acre ['eɪkə*] *n* acre *f* (= *4047* m^2); **~age** *n* superficie *f*.
acrimonious [ækrɪ'məunɪəs] *a* acrimonieux(euse), aigre.
acrobat ['ækrəbæt] *n* acrobate *m/f*.
acrobatics [ækrəu'bætɪks] *n,npl* acrobatie *f*.
across [ə'krɔs] *prep* (*on the other side*) de l'autre côté de; (*crosswise*) en travers de // *ad* de l'autre côté; en travers; **to walk ~ (the road)** traverser (la route); **to take sb ~ the road** faire traverser la route à qn; **a road ~ the wood** une route qui traverse le bois; **~ from** en face de.
act [ækt] *n* acte *m*, action *f*; (THEATRE) acte; (*in music-hall etc*) numéro *m*; (LAW) loi *f* // *vi* agir; (THEATRE) jouer; (*pretend*) jouer la comédie // *vt* (*part*) jouer, tenir; **to ~ Hamlet** tenir *or* jouer le rôle d'Hamlet; **to ~ the fool** faire l'idiot; **to ~ as** servir de; **~ing** *a* suppléant(e), par intérim // *n* (*of actor*) jeu *m*; (*activity*): **to do some ~ing** faire du théâtre (*or* du cinéma).
action ['ækʃən] *n* action *f*; (MIL) combat(s) *m(pl)*; (LAW) procès *m*, action en justice; **out of ~** hors de combat; hors d'usage; **to take ~** agir, prendre des mesures.
activate ['æktɪveɪt] *vt* (*mechanism*)

actionner, faire fonctionner; (*CHEM, PHYSICS*) activer.
active ['æktɪv] *a* actif(ive); (*volcano*) en activité; **~ly** *ad* activement.
activity [æk'tɪvɪtɪ] *n* activité *f*.
actor ['æktə*] *n* acteur *m*.
actress ['æktrɪs] *n* actrice *f*.
actual ['æktjuəl] *a* réel(le), véritable; **~ly** *ad* réellement, véritablement; en fait.
acumen ['ækjumən] *n* perspicacité *f*.
acupuncture ['ækjupʌŋktʃə*] *n* acupuncture *f*.
acute [ə'kju:t] *a* aigu(ë); (*mind, observer*) pénétrant(e).
ad [æd] *n abbr of* **advertisement**.
A.D. *ad* (*abbr of Anno Domini*) ap. J.-C.
Adam ['ædəm] *n* Adam *m*; **~'s apple** *n* pomme *f* d'Adam.
adamant ['ædəmənt] *a* inflexible.
adapt [ə'dæpt] *vt* adapter // *vi*: **to ~ (to)** s'adapter (à); **~able** *a* (*device*) adaptable; (*person*) qui s'adapte facilement; **~ation** [ædæp'teɪʃən] *n* adaptation *f*; **~er** *n* (*ELEC*) adapteur *m*.
add [æd] *vt* ajouter; (*figures*: *also*: **to ~ up**) additionner // *vi*: **to ~ to** (*increase*) ajouter à, accroître.
adder ['ædə*] *n* vipère *f*.
addict ['ædɪkt] *n* intoxiqué *m*; (*fig*) fanatique *m/f*; **~ed** [ə'dɪktɪd] *a*: **to be ~ed to** (*drink etc*) être adonné à; (*fig*: *football etc*) être un fanatique de; **~ion** [ə'dɪkʃən] *n* (*MED*) dépendance *f*.
adding machine ['ædɪŋməʃi:n] *n* machine *f* à calculer.
addition [ə'dɪʃən] *n* addition *f*; **in ~** de plus; de surcroît; **in ~ to** en plus de; **~al** *a* supplémentaire.
additive ['ædɪtɪv] *n* additif *m*.
addled ['ædld] *a* (*egg*) pourri(e).
address [ə'drɛs] *n* adresse *f*; (*talk*) discours *m*, allocution *f* //*vt* adresser; (*speak to*) s'adresser à.
adenoids ['ædɪnɔɪdz] *npl* végétations *fpl*.
adept ['ædɛpt] *a*: **~ at** expert(e) à *or* en.
adequate ['ædɪkwɪt] *a* adéquat(e); suffisant(e); compétent(e); **~ly** *ad* de façon adéquate.
adhere [əd'hɪə*] *vi*: **to ~ to** adhérer à; (*fig*: *rule, decision*) se tenir à.
adhesion [əd'hi:ʒən] *n* adhésion *f*.
adhesive [əd'hi:zɪv] *a* adhésif(ive) // *n* adhésif *m*.
adjacent [ə'dʒeɪsənt] *a* adjacent(e); **~ to** adjacent à.
adjective ['ædʒɛktɪv] *n* adjectif *m*.
adjoining [ə'dʒɔɪnɪŋ] *a* voisin(e), adjacent(e), attenant(e) // *prep* voisin de, adjacent à.
adjourn [ə'dʒə:n] *vt* ajourner // *vi* suspendre la séance; lever la séance; clore la session; (*go*) se retirer.
adjust [ə'dʒʌst] *vt* ajuster, régler; rajuster // *vi*: **to ~ (to)** s'adapter (à); **~able** *a* réglable; **~ment** *n* ajustage *m*, réglage *m*; (*of prices, wages*) rajustement *m*; (*of person*) adaptation *f*.
adjutant ['ædʒətənt] *n* adjudant *m*.
ad-lib [æd'lɪb] *vt,vi* improviser // *n* improvisation *f* // *ad*: **ad lib** à volonté, à discrétion.
administer [əd'mɪnɪstə*] *vt* administrer; (*justice*) rendre.
administration [ədmɪnɪs'treɪʃən] *n* administration *f*.
administrative [əd'mɪnɪstrətɪv] *a* administratif(ive).
administrator [əd'mɪnɪstreɪtə*] *n* administrateur/trice.
admirable ['ædmərəbl] *a* admirable.
admiral ['ædmərəl] *n* amiral *m*; **A~ty** *n* amirauté *f*; ministère *m* de la Marine.
admiration [ædmə'reɪʃən] *n* admiration *f*.
admire [əd'maɪə*] *vt* admirer; **~r** *n* admirateur/trice.
admission [əd'mɪʃən] *n* admission *f*; (*to exhibition, night club etc*) entrée *f*; (*confession*) aveu *m*.
admit [əd'mɪt] *vt* laisser entrer; admettre; (*agree*) reconnaître, admettre; **to ~ of** admettre, permettre; **to ~ to** reconnaître, avouer; **~tance** *n* admission *f*, (droit *m* d')entrée *f*; **~tedly** *ad* il faut en convenir.
admonish [əd'mɔnɪʃ] *vt* donner un avertissement à; réprimander.
ado [ə'du:] *n*: **without (any) more ~** sans plus de cérémonies.
adolescence [ædəu'lɛsns] *n* adolescence *f*.
adolescent [ædəu'lɛsnt] *a,n* adolescent(e).
adopt [ə'dɔpt] *vt* adopter; **~ed** *a* adoptif(ive), adopté(e); **~ion** [ə'dɔpʃən] *n* adoption *f*.
adore [ə'dɔ:*] *vt* adorer; **adoringly** *ad* avec adoration.
adorn [ə'dɔ:n] *vt* orner; **~ment** *n* ornement *m*.
adrenalin [ə'drɛnəlɪn] *n* adrénaline *f*.
Adriatic (Sea) [eɪdrɪ'ætɪk(si:)] *n* Adriatique *f*.
adrift [ə'drɪft] *ad* à la dérive.
adroit [ə'drɔɪt] *a* adroit(e), habile.
adult ['ædʌlt] *n* adulte *m/f*.
adulterate [ə'dʌltəreɪt] *vt* frelater, falsifier.
adultery [ə'dʌltərɪ] *n* adultère *m*.
advance [əd'vɑ:ns] *n* avance *f* // *vt* avancer // *vi* s'avancer; **in ~** en avance, d'avance; **~d** *a* avancé(e); (*SCOL*: *studies*) supérieur(e); **~ment** *n* avancement *m*.
advantage [əd'vɑ:ntɪdʒ] *n* (*also TENNIS*) avantage *m*; **to take ~ of** profiter de; **~ous** [ædvən'teɪdʒəs] *a* avantageux(euse).
advent ['ædvənt] *n* avènement *m*, venue *f*; **A~** Avent *m*.
adventure [əd'vɛntʃə*] *n* aventure *f*; **adventurous** [-tʃərəs] *a* aventureux(euse).
adverb ['ædvə:b] *n* adverbe *m*.
adversary ['ædvəsərɪ] *n* adversaire *m/f*.
adverse ['ædvə:s] *a* contraire, adverse; **in ~ circumstances** dans l'adversité; **~ to** hostile à.
adversity [əd'və:sɪtɪ] *n* adversité *f*.
advert ['ædvə:t] *n abbr of* **advertisement**.
advertise ['ædvətaɪz] *vi(vt)* faire de la publicité *or* de la réclame (pour); mettre une annonce (pour vendre).
advertisement [əd'və:tɪsmənt] *n* (*COMM*) réclame *f*, publicité *f*; (*in classified ads*) annonce *f*.

advertising ['ædvətaɪzɪŋ] *n* publicité *f*, réclame *f*.
advice [əd'vaɪs] *n* conseils *mpl*; (*notification*) avis *m*; **piece of ~** conseil.
advisable [əd'vaɪzəbl] *a* recommandable, indiqué(e).
advise [əd'vaɪz] *vt* conseiller; **to ~ sb of sth** aviser *or* informer qn de qch; **~r** *n* conseiller/ère; **advisory** [-ərɪ] *a* consultatif(ive).
advocate *vt* ['ædvəkeɪt] recommander, prôner.
aegis ['i:dʒɪs] *n*: **under the ~ of** sous l'égide de.
aerial ['ɛərɪəl] *n* antenne *f* // *a* aérien(ne).
aeroplane ['ɛərəpleɪn] *n* avion *m*.
aerosol ['ɛərəsɔl] *n* aérosol *m*.
aesthetic [ɪs'θɛtɪk] *a* esthétique.
afar [ə'fɑ:*] *ad*: **from ~** de loin.
affable ['æfəbl] *a* affable.
affair [ə'fɛə*] *n* affaire *f*; (*also*: **love ~**) liaison *f*; aventure *f*.
affect [ə'fɛkt] *vt* affecter; **~ation** [æfɛk'teɪʃən] *n* affectation *f*; **~ed** *a* affecté(e).
affection [ə'fɛkʃən] *n* affection *f*; **~ate** *a* affectueux(euse); **~ately** *ad* affectueusement.
affiliated [ə'fɪlɪeɪtɪd] *a* affilié(e).
affinity [ə'fɪnɪtɪ] *n* affinité *f*.
affirmation [æfə'meɪʃən] *n* affirmation *f*, assertion *f*.
affirmative [ə'fə:mətɪv] *a* affirmatif(ive) // *n*: **in the ~** dans *or* par l'affirmative.
affix [ə'fɪks] *vt* apposer, ajouter.
afflict [ə'flɪkt] *vt* affliger; **~ion** [ə'flɪkʃən] *n* affliction *f*, détresse *f*.
affluence ['æfluəns] *n* abondance *f*, opulence *f*.
affluent ['æfluənt] *a* abondant(e); opulent(e); (*person*) dans l'aisance, riche.
afford [ə'fɔ:d] *vt* se permettre; avoir les moyens d'acheter *or* d'entretenir; (*provide*) fournir, procurer; **I can't ~ the time** je n'ai vraiment pas le temps.
affray [ə'freɪ] *n* échauffourée *f*.
affront [ə'frʌnt] *n* affront *m*; **~ed** *a* insulté(e).
afield [ə'fi:ld] *ad*: **far ~** loin.
afloat [ə'fləut] *a* à flot // *ad*: **to stay ~** surnager; **to keep/get a business ~** maintenir à flot/lancer une affaire.
afoot [ə'fut] *ad*: **there is something ~** il se prépare quelque chose.
aforesaid [ə'fɔ:sɛd] *a* susdit(e), susmentionné(e).
afraid [ə'freɪd] *a* effrayé(e); **to be ~ of** *or* **to** avoir peur de; **I am ~ that** je crains que + *sub*.
afresh [ə'frɛʃ] *ad* de nouveau.
Africa ['æfrɪkə] *n* Afrique *f*; **~n** *a* africain(e) // *n* Africain/e.
aft [ɑ:ft] *ad* à l'arrière, vers l'arrière.
after ['ɑ:ftə*] *prep,ad* après // *cj* après que, après avoir *or* être + *pp*; **what/who are you ~?** que/qui cherchez-vous?; **ask ~ him** demandez de ses nouvelles; **~ all** après tout; **~-effects** *npl* répercussions *fpl*; (*of illness*) séquelles *fpl*, suites *fpl*; **~life** *n* vie future; **~math** *n* conséquences *fpl*; **in the ~math of** dans les mois *or* années *etc* qui suivirent, au lendemain de; **~noon** *n* après-midi *m or f*; **~-shave (lotion)** *n* after-shave *m*; **~thought** *n*: **I had an ~thought** il m'est venu une idée après coup; **~wards** *ad* après.
again [ə'gɛn] *ad* de nouveau; **to begin/see ~** recommencer/revoir; **not ... ~** ne ... plus; **~ and ~** à plusieurs reprises; **he's opened it ~** il l'a rouvert, il l'a de nouveau *or* l'a encore ouvert.
against [ə'gɛnst] *prep* contre; **~ a blue background** sur un fond bleu.
age [eɪdʒ] *n* âge *m* // *vt,vi* vieillir; **it's been ~s since** ça fait une éternité que; **to come of ~** atteindre sa majorité; **~d** *a* âgé(e); **~d 10** âgé de 10 ans; **the ~d** ['eɪdʒɪd] les personnes âgées; **~ group** *n* tranche *f* d'âge; **~less** *a* sans âge; **~ limit** *n* limite *f* d'âge.
agency ['eɪdʒənsɪ] *n* agence *f*; **through** *or* **by the ~ of** par l'entremise *or* l'action de.
agenda [ə'dʒɛndə] *n* ordre *m* du jour.
agent ['eɪdʒənt] *n* agent *m*.
aggravate ['ægrəveɪt] *vt* aggraver; (*annoy*) exaspérer.
aggravation [ægrə'veɪʃən] *n* (*of quarrel*) envenimement *m*.
aggregate ['ægrɪgeɪt] *n* ensemble *m*, total *m*; **on ~** (SPORT) au goal average.
aggression [ə'grɛʃən] *n* agression *f*.
aggressive [ə'grɛsɪv] *a* agressif(ive); **~ness** *n* agressivité *f*.
aggrieved [ə'gri:vd] *a* chagriné(e), affligé(e).
aghast [ə'gɑ:st] *a* consterné(e), atterré(e).
agile ['ædʒaɪl] *a* agile.
agitate ['ædʒɪteɪt] *vt* rendre inquiet(ète) *or* agité(e); agiter // *vi* faire de l'agitation (politique); **to ~ for** faire campagne pour; **agitator** *n* agitateur/trice (politique).
ago [ə'gəu] *ad*: **2 days ~** il y a deux jours; **not long ~** il n'y a pas longtemps.
agonizing ['ægənaɪzɪŋ] *a* angoissant(e); déchirant(e).
agony ['ægənɪ] *n* grande souffrance *or* angoisse; **to be in ~** souffrir le martyre.
agree [ə'gri:] *vt* (*price*) convenir de // *vi*: **to ~ (with)** (*person*) être d'accord (avec); (*statements etc*) concorder (avec); (LING) s'accorder (avec); **to ~ to do** accepter de *or* consentir à faire; **to ~ to sth** consentir à qch; **to ~ that** (*admit*) convenir *or* reconnaître que; **they ~ on this** ils sont d'accord sur ce point; **they ~d on going/a price** ils se mirent d'accord pour y aller/sur un prix; **garlic doesn't ~ with me** je ne supporte pas l'ail; **~able** *a* agréable; (*willing*) consentant(e), d'accord; **are you ~able to this?** est-ce que cela vous va *or* convient?; **~d** *a* (*time, place*) convenu(e); **to be ~d** être d'accord; **~ment** *n* accord *m*; **in ~ment** d'accord.
agricultural [ægrɪ'kʌltʃərəl] *a* agricole.
agriculture ['ægrɪkʌltʃə*] *n* agriculture *f*.
aground [ə'graund] *ad*: **to run ~** s'échouer.
ahead [ə'hɛd] *ad* en avant; devant; **~ of** devant; (*fig*: *schedule etc*) en avance sur; **~ of time** en avance; **go right** *or* **straight ~** allez tout droit; **they were (right) ~**

of us ils nous précédaient (de peu), ils étaient (juste) devant nous.

aid [eɪd] *n* aide *f* // *vt* aider ; **to ~ and abet** (LAW) se faire le complice de.

aide [eɪd] *n* (*person*) collaborateur/trice, assistant/e.

ailment ['eɪlmənt] *n* petite maladie, affection *f*.

aim [eɪm] *vt*: **to ~ sth at** (*such as gun, camera*) braquer *or* pointer qch sur, diriger qch contre ; (*missile*) lancer qch à *or* contre *or* en direction de ; (*remark, blow*) destiner *or* adresser qch à // *vi* (*also*: **to take ~**) viser // *n* but *m* ; **to ~ at** viser ; (*fig*) viser (à) ; avoir pour but *or* ambition ; **to ~ to do** avoir l'intention de faire ; **~less** *a* sans but ; **~lessly** *ad* sans but, à l'aventure.

air [ɛə*] *n* air *m* // *vt* aérer ; (*grievances, ideas*) exposer (librement) // *cpd* (*currents, attack etc*) aérien(ne) ; **~bed** *n* matelas *m* pneumatique ; **~borne** *a* en vol ; aeroporté(e) ; **~-conditioned** *a* climatisé(e), à air conditionné ; **~ conditioning** *n* climatisation *f* ; **~-cooled** *a* à refroidissement à air ; **~craft** *n,pl inv* avion *m* ; **~craft carrier** *n* porte-avions *m inv* ; **~ cushion** *n* coussin *m* d'air ; **A~ Force** *n* Armée *f* de l'air ; **~gun** *n* fusil *m* à air comprimé ; **~ hostess** *n* hôtesse *f* de l'air ; **~ily** *ad* d'un air dégagé ; **~ letter** *n* aérogramme *m* ; **~lift** *n* pont aérien ; **~line** *n* ligne aérienne ; compagnie *f* d'aviation ; **~liner** *n* avion *m* de ligne ; **~lock** *n* sas *m* ; **by ~mail** par avion ; **~port** *n* aéroport *m* ; **~ raid** *n* attaque aérienne ; **~sick** *a* qui a le mal de l'air ; **~strip** *n* terrain *m* d'atterrissage ; **~tight** *a* hermétique ; **~y** *a* bien aéré(e) ; (*manners*) dégagé(e).

aisle [aɪl] *n* (*of church*) allée centrale ; nef latérale.

ajar [ə'dʒɑ:*] *a* entrouvert(e).

alarm [ə'lɑ:m] *n* alarme *f* // *vt* alarmer ; **~ clock** *n* réveille-matin *m*, réveil *m* ; **~ist** *n* alarmiste *m/f*.

Albania [æl'beɪnɪə] *n* Albanie *f*.

album ['ælbəm] *n* album *m* ; (*L.P.*) 33 tours *m inv*.

albumen ['ælbjumɪn] *n* albumine *f* ; (*of egg*) albumen *m*.

alchemy ['ælkɪmɪ] *n* alchimie *f*.

alcohol ['ælkəhɔl] *n* alcool *m* ; **~ic** [-'hɔlɪk] *a,n* alcoolique (*m/f*) ; **~ism** *n* alcoolisme *m*.

alcove ['ælkəuv] *n* alcôve *f*.

alderman ['ɔ:ldəmən] *n* conseiller municipal (*en Angleterre*).

ale [eɪl] *n* bière *f*.

alert [ə'lə:t] *a* alerte, vif(vive) ; vigilant(e) // *n* alerte *f* ; **on the ~** sur le qui-vive ; (MIL) en état d'alerte.

algebra ['ældʒɪbrə] *n* algèbre *m*.

Algeria [æl'dʒɪərɪə] *n* Algérie *f* ; **~n** *a* algérien(ne) // *n* Algérien/ne.

Algiers [æl'dʒɪəz] *n* Alger.

alias ['eɪlɪæs] *ad* alias // *n* faux nom, nom d'emprunt.

alibi ['ælɪbaɪ] *n* alibi *m*.

alien ['eɪlɪən] *n* étranger/ère // *a*: **~ (to/from)** étranger(ère) (à) ; **~ate** *vt* aliéner ; s'aliéner ; **~ation** [-'neɪʃən] *n* aliénation *f*.

alight [ə'laɪt] *a,ad* en feu // *vi* mettre pied à terre ; (*passenger*) descendre ; (*bird*) se poser.

align [ə'laɪn] *vt* aligner ; **~ment** *n* alignement *m*.

alike [ə'laɪk] *a* semblable, pareil(le) // *ad* de même ; **to look ~** se ressembler.

alimony ['ælɪmənɪ] *n* (*payment*) pension *f* alimentaire.

alive [ə'laɪv] *a* vivant(e) ; (*active*) plein(e) de vie ; **~ with** grouillant(e) de ; **~ to** sensible à.

alkali ['ælkəlaɪ] *n* alcali *m*.

all [ɔ:l] *a* tout(e), tous(toutes) *pl* // *pronoun* tout *m* ; (*pl*) tous(toutes) // *ad* tout ; **~ wrong/alone** tout faux/seul ; **~ the time/his life** tout le temps/toute sa vie ; **~ five** (tous) les cinq ; **~ of them** tous, toutes ; **~ of it** tout ; **~ of us went** nous y sommes tous allés ; **not as hard** *etc* **as ~ that** pas si dur *etc* que ça ; **~ in ~** à tout prendre, l'un dans l'autre.

allay [ə'leɪ] *vt* (*fears*) apaiser, calmer.

allegation [ælɪ'geɪʃən] *n* allégation *f*.

allege [ə'lɛdʒ] *vt* alléguer, prétendre ; **~dly** [ə'lɛdʒɪdlɪ] *ad* à ce que l'on prétend, paraît-il.

allegiance [ə'li:dʒəns] *n* fidélité *f*, obéissance *f*.

allegory ['ælɪgərɪ] *n* allégorie *f*.

all-embracing ['ɔ:lɪm'breɪsɪŋ] *a* universel(le).

allergic [ə'lə:dʒɪk] *a*: **~ to** allergique à.

allergy ['ælədʒɪ] *n* allergie *f*.

alleviate [ə'li:vɪeɪt] *vt* soulager, adoucir.

alley ['ælɪ] *n* ruelle *f* ; (*in garden*) allée *f*.

alliance [ə'laɪəns] *n* alliance *f*.

allied ['ælaɪd] *a* allié(e).

alligator ['ælɪgeɪtə*] *n* alligator *m*.

all-important ['ɔ:lɪm'pɔ:tənt] *a* capital(e), crucial(e).

all-in ['ɔ:lɪn] *a* (*also ad*: *charge*) tout compris ; **~ wrestling** *n* catch *m*.

alliteration [əlɪtə'reɪʃən] *n* allitération *f*.

all-night ['ɔ:l'naɪt] *a* ouvert(e) *or* qui dure toute la nuit.

allocate ['æləkeɪt] *vt* (*share out*) répartir, distribuer ; (*duties*): **to ~ sth to** assigner *or* attribuer qch à ; (*sum, time*): **to ~ sth to** allouer qch à ; **to ~ sth for** affecter qch à.

allocation [æləu'keɪʃən] *n*: **~ (of money)** crédit(s) *m(pl)*, somme(s) allouée(s).

allot [ə'lɔt] *vt* (*share out*) répartir, distribuer ; (*time*): **to ~ sth to** allouer qch à ; (*duties*): **to ~ sth to** assigner qch à ; **~ment** *n* (*share*) part *f* ; (*garden*) lopin *m* de terre (*loué à la municipalité*).

all-out ['ɔ:laut] *a* (*effort etc*) total(e) // *ad*: **all out** à fond.

allow [ə'lau] *vt* (*practice, behaviour*) permettre, autoriser ; (*sum to spend etc*) accorder ; allouer ; (*sum, time estimated*) compter, prévoir ; (*concede*): **to ~ that** convenir que ; **to ~ sb to do** permettre à qn de faire, autoriser qn à faire ; **to ~ for** *vt fus* tenir compte de ; **~ance** *n* (*money received*) allocation *f* ; subside *m* ; indemnité *f* ; (TAX) somme *f* déductible du revenu imposable, abattement *m* ; **to make ~ances for** tenir compte de.

alloy ['ælɔɪ] *n* alliage *m*.
all right ['ɔ:l'raɪt] *ad* (*feel, work*) bien ; (*as answer*) d'accord.
all-round ['ɔ:l'raund] *a* compétent(e) dans tous les domaines ; (*athlete etc*) complet(ète).
all-time ['ɔ:l'taɪm] *a* (*record*) sans précédent, absolu(e).
allude [ə'lu:d] *vi*: **to ~ to** faire allusion à.
alluring [ə'ljuərɪŋ] *a* séduisant(e), alléchant(e).
allusion [ə'lu:ʒən] *n* allusion *f*.
alluvium [ə'lu:vɪəm] *n* alluvions *fpl*.
ally ['ælaɪ] *n* allié *m*.
almighty [ɔ:l'maɪtɪ] *a* tout-puissant.
almond ['ɑ:mənd] *n* amande *f*.
almost ['ɔ:lməust] *ad* presque.
alms [ɑ:mz] *n* aumône(s) *f(pl)*.
alone [ə'ləun] *a* seul(e) ; **to leave sb ~** laisser qn tranquille ; **to leave sth ~** ne pas toucher à qch.
along [ə'lɔŋ] *prep* le long de // *ad*: **is he coming ~?** vient-il avec nous? ; **he was hopping/limping ~** il venait *or* avançait en sautillant/boitant ; **~ with** en compagnie de ; avec, en plus de ; **~side** *prep* le long de ; au côté de // *ad* bord à bord ; côte à côte.
aloof [ə'lu:f] *a,ad* à distance, à l'écart ; **~ness** réserve (hautaine), attitude distante.
aloud [ə'laud] *ad* à haute voix.
alphabet ['ælfəbɛt] *n* alphabet *m* ; **~ical** [-'bɛtɪkəl] *a* alphabétique.
alpine ['ælpaɪn] *a* alpin(e), alpestre.
Alps [ælps] *npl*: **the ~** les Alpes *fpl*.
already [ɔ:l'rɛdɪ] *ad* déjà.
alright ['ɔ:l'raɪt] *ad* = **all right**.
also ['ɔ:lsəu] *ad* aussi.
altar ['ɔltə*] *n* autel *m*.
alter ['ɔltə*] *vt,vi* changer, modifier ; **~ation** [ɔltə'reɪʃən] *n* changement *m*, modification *f*.
alternate *a* [ɔl'tə:nɪt] alterné(e), alternant(e), alternatif(ive) // *vi* ['ɔltə:neɪt] alterner ; **on ~ days** un jour sur deux, tous les deux jours ; **~ly** *ad* alternativement, en alternant ; **alternating** *a* (*current*) alternatif(ive).
alternative [ɔl'tə:nətɪv] *a* (*solutions*) interchangeable, possible ; (*solution*) autre, de remplacement // *n* (*choice*) alternative *f*; (*other possibility*) solution *f* de remplacement *or* de rechange, autre possibilité *f*; **~ly** *ad*: **~ly one could** une autre *or* l'autre solution serait de.
alternator ['ɔltə:neɪtə*] *n* (AUT) alternateur *m*.
although [ɔ:l'ðəu] *cj* bien que + *sub*.
altitude ['æltɪtju:d] *n* altitude *f*.
alto ['æltəu] *n* (*female*) contralto *m* ; (*male*) haute-contre *f*.
altogether [ɔ:ltə'gɛðə*] *ad* entièrement, tout à fait ; (*on the whole*) tout compte fait ; (*in all*) en tout.
altruistic [æltru'ɪstɪk] *a* altruiste.
aluminium [ælju'mɪnɪəm], **aluminum** [ə'lu:mɪnəm] (*US*) *n* aluminium *m*.
always ['ɔ:lweɪz] *ad* toujours.
am [æm] *vb see* **be**.
a.m. *ad* (*abbr of ante meridiem*) du matin.
amalgamate [ə'mælgəmeɪt] *vt,vi* fusionner ; **amalgamation** [-'meɪʃən] *n* fusion *f*; (COMM) fusionnement *m* ; amalgame *m*.
amass [ə'mæs] *vt* amasser.
amateur ['æmətə*] *n* amateur *m* // *a* (SPORT) amateur *inv* ; **~ish** *a* (*pej*) d'amateur.
amaze [ə'meɪz] *vt* stupéfier ; **~ment** *n* stupéfaction *f*, stupeur *f*.
ambassador [æm'bæsədə*] *n* ambassadeur *m*.
amber ['æmbə*] *n* ambre *m* ; **at ~** (AUT) à l'orange.
ambidextrous [æmbɪ'dɛkstrəs] *a* ambidextre.
ambiguity [æmbɪ'gjuɪtɪ] *n* ambiguïté *f*.
ambiguous [æm'bɪgjuəs] *a* ambigu(ë).
ambition [æm'bɪʃən] *n* ambition *f*.
ambitious [æm'bɪʃəs] *a* ambitieux(euse).
ambivalent [æm'bɪvələnt] *a* (*attitude*) ambivalent(e).
amble ['æmbl] *vi* (*gen*: **to ~ along**) aller d'un pas tranquille.
ambulance ['æmbjuləns] *n* ambulance *f*.
ambush ['æmbuʃ] *n* embuscade *f* // *vt* tendre une embuscade à.
ameliorate [ə'mi:lɪəreɪt] *vt* améliorer.
amenable [ə'mi:nəbl] *a*: **~ to** (*advice etc*) disposé(e) à écouter *or* suivre ; **~ to the law** responsable devant la loi.
amend [ə'mɛnd] *vt* (*law*) amender ; (*text*) corriger ; (*habits*) réformer // *vi* s'amender, se corriger ; **to make ~s** réparer ses torts, faire amende honorable ; **~ment** *n* (*to law*) amendement *m* ; (*to text*) correction *f*.
amenities [ə'mi:nɪtɪz] *npl* aménagements *mpl* (*prévus pour le loisir des habitants*).
amenity [ə'mi:nɪtɪ] *n* charme *m*, agrément *m*.
America [ə'mɛrɪkə] *n* Amérique *f*; **~n** *a* américain(e) // *n* Américain/e ; **a~nize** *vt* américaniser.
amethyst ['æmɪθɪst] *n* améthyste *f*.
amiable ['eɪmɪəbl] *a* aimable, affable.
amicable ['æmɪkəbl] *a* amical(e).
amid(st) [ə'mɪd(st)] *prep* parmi, au milieu de.
amiss [ə'mɪs] *a,ad*: **there's something ~** il y a quelque chose qui ne va pas *or* qui cloche ; **to take sth ~** prendre qch mal *or* de travers.
ammunition [æmju'nɪʃən] *n* munitions *fpl*.
amnesia [æm'ni:zɪə] *n* amnésie *f*.
amnesty ['æmnɪstɪ] *n* amnistie *f*.
amok [ə'mɔk] *ad*: **to run ~** être pris(e) d'un accès de folie furieuse.
among(st) [ə'mʌŋ(st)] *prep* parmi, entre.
amoral [æ'mɔrəl] *a* amoral(e).
amorous ['æmərəs] *a* amoureux(euse).
amorphous [ə'mɔ:fəs] *a* amorphe.
amount [ə'maunt] *n* somme *f*; montant *m* ; quantité *f*; nombre *m* // *vi*: **to ~ to** (*total*) s'élever à ; (*be same as*) équivaloir à, revenir à.

amp(ère) ['æmp(ɛə*)] *n* ampère *m*.
amphibian [æm'fɪbɪən] *n* batracien *m*.
amphibious [æm'fɪbɪəs] *a* amphibie.
amphitheatre ['æmfɪθɪətə*] *n* amphithéâtre *m*.
ample ['æmpl] *a* ample; spacieux(euse); (*enough*): **this is ~** c'est largement suffisant; **to have ~ time/room** avoir bien assez de temps/place, avoir largement le temps/la place.
amplifier ['æmplɪfaɪə*] *n* amplificateur *m*.
amplify ['æmplɪfaɪ] *vt* amplifier.
amply ['æmplɪ] *ad* amplement, largement.
amputate ['æmpjuteɪt] *vt* amputer.
amuck [ə'mʌk] *ad* = **amok**.
amuse [ə'mju:z] *vt* amuser; **~ment** *n* amusement *m*.
an [æn, ən, n] *det see* **a**.
anaemia [ə'ni:mɪə] *n* anémie *f*.
anaemic [ə'ni:mɪk] *a* anémique.
anaesthetic [ænɪs'θɛtɪk] *a,n* anesthésique (*m*); **under the ~** sous anesthésie.
anaesthetist [æ'ni:sθɪtɪst] *n* anesthésiste *m/f*.
anagram ['ænəgræm] *n* anagramme *m*.
analgesic [ænæl'dʒi:sɪk] *a,n* analgésique (*m*).
analogy [ə'nælədʒɪ] *n* analogie *f*.
analyse ['ænəlaɪz] *vt* analyser.
analysis, *pl* **analyses** [ə'næləsɪs, -si:z] *n* analyse *f*.
analyst ['ænəlɪst] *n* (*US*) psychanalyste *m/f*.
analytic(al) [ænə'lɪtɪk(əl)] *a* analytique.
analyze ['ænəlaɪz] *vt* (*US*) = **analyse.**
anarchist ['ænəkɪst] *a,n* anarchiste (*m/f*).
anarchy ['ænəkɪ] *n* anarchie *f*.
anathema [ə'næθɪmə] *n*: **it is ~ to him** il a cela en abomination.
anatomical [ænə'tɔmɪkəl] *a* anatomique.
anatomy [ə'nætəmɪ] *n* anatomie *f*.
ancestor ['ænsɪstə*] *n* ancêtre *m*, aïeul *m*.
ancestral [æn'sɛstrəl] *a* ancestral(e).
ancestry ['ænsɪstrɪ] *n* ancêtres *mpl*; ascendance *f*.
anchor ['æŋkə*] *n* ancre *f* // *vi* (*also*: **to drop ~**) jeter l'ancre, mouiller // *vt* mettre à l'ancre; **~age** *n* mouillage *m*, ancrage *m*.
anchovy ['æntʃəvɪ] *n* anchois *m*.
ancient ['eɪnʃənt] *a* ancien(ne), antique; (*fig*) d'un âge vénérable, antique.
and [ænd] *cj* et; **~ so on** et ainsi de suite; **try ~ come** tâchez de venir; **come ~ sit here** viens t'asseoir ici; **better ~ better** de mieux en mieux; **more ~ more** de plus en plus.
Andes ['ændi:z] *npl*: **the ~** les Andes *fpl*.
anecdote ['ænɪkdəut] *n* anecdote *f*.
anemia [ə'ni:mɪə] *n* = **anaemia**.
anemic [ə'ni:mɪk] *a* = **anaemic**.
anesthetic [ænɪs'θɛtɪk] *a,n* = **anaesthetic**.
anesthetist [æ'ni:sθɪtɪst] *n* = **anaesthetist**.
anew [ə'nju:] *ad* à nouveau.
angel ['eɪndʒəl] *n* ange *m*.
anger ['æŋgə*] *n* colère *f* // *vt* mettre en colère, irriter.
angina [æn'dʒaɪnə] *n* angine *f* de poitrine.
angle ['æŋgl] *n* angle *m*; **from their ~** de leur point de vue // *vi*: **to ~ for** (*trout*) pêcher; (*compliments*) chercher, quêter; **~r** *n* pêcheur/euse à la ligne.
Anglican ['æŋglɪkən] *a,n* anglican(e).
anglicize ['æŋglɪsaɪz] *vt* angliciser.
angling ['æŋglɪŋ] *n* pêche *f* à la ligne.
Anglo- ['æŋgləu] *prefix* anglo(-); **~Saxon** *a,n* anglo-saxon(ne).
angrily ['æŋgrɪlɪ] *ad* avec colère.
angry ['æŋgrɪ] *a* en colère, furieux(euse); **to be ~ with sb/at sth** être furieux contre qn/de qch; **to get ~** se fâcher, se mettre en colère; **to make sb ~** mettre qn en colère.
anguish ['æŋgwɪʃ] *n* angoisse *f*.
angular ['æŋgjulə*] *a* anguleux(euse).
animal ['ænɪməl] *n* animal *m* // *a* animal(e); **~ spirits** *npl* entrain *m*, vivacité *f*.
animate *vt* ['ænɪmeɪt] animer // *a* ['ænɪmɪt] animé(e), vivant(e); **~d** *a* animé(e).
animosity [ænɪ'mɔsɪtɪ] *n* animosité *f*.
aniseed ['ænɪsi:d] *n* anis *m*.
ankle ['æŋkl] *n* cheville *f*.
annex *n* ['ænɛks] (*also*: **annexe**) annexe *f* // *vt* [ə'nɛks] annexer; **~ation** [-'eɪʃən] *n* annexion *f*.
annihilate [ə'naɪəleɪt] *vt* annihiler, anéantir.
anniversary [ænɪ'və:sərɪ] *n* anniversaire *m*; **~ dinner** *n* dîner commémoratif *or* anniversaire.
annotate ['ænəuteɪt] *vt* annoter.
announce [ə'nauns] *vt* annoncer; (*birth, death*) faire part de; **~ment** *n* annonce *f*; (*for births etc: in newspaper*) avis *m* de faire-part; (*:letter, card*) faire-part *m*; **~r** *n* (RADIO, TV) (*between programmes*) speaker/ine; (*in a programme*) présentateur/trice.
annoy [ə'nɔɪ] *vt* agacer, ennuyer, contrarier; **don't get ~ed!** ne vous fâchez pas!; **~ance** *n* mécontentement *m*, contrariété *f*; **~ing** *a* ennuyeux(euse), agaçant(e), contrariant(e).
annual ['ænjuəl] *a* annuel(le) // *n* (BOT) plante annuelle; (*book*) album *m*; **~ly** *ad* annuellement.
annuity [ə'nju:ɪtɪ] *n* rente *f*; **life ~** rente viagère.
annul [ə'nʌl] *vt* annuler; (*law*) abroger; **~ment** *n* annulation *f*; abrogation *f*.
annum ['ænəm] *n see* **per**.
anoint [ə'nɔɪnt] *vt* oindre.
anomalous [ə'nɔmələs] *a* anormal(e).
anomaly [ə'nɔməlɪ] *n* anomalie *f*.
anonymity [ænə'nɪmɪtɪ] *n* anonymat *m*.
anonymous [ə'nɔnɪməs] *a* anonyme.
anorak ['ænəræk] *n* anorak *m*.
another [ə'nʌðə*] *a*: **~ book** (*one more*) un autre livre, encore un livre, un livre de plus; (*a different one*) un autre livre // *pronoun* un(e) autre, encore un(e), un(e) de plus; *see also* **one.**
answer ['ɑ:nsə*] *n* réponse *f*; solution *f* // *vi* répondre // *vt* (*reply to*) répondre à; (*problem*) résoudre; (*prayer*) exaucer; **to ~ the phone** répondre (au téléphone);

in ~ to your letter suite à *or* en réponse à votre lettre ; **to ~ the bell** *or* **the door** aller *or* venir ouvrir (la porte) ; **to ~ back** *vi* répondre, répliquer ; **to ~ for** *vt fus* répondre de, se porter garant de ; être responsable de ; **to ~ to** *vt fus* (*description*) répondre *or* correspondre à ; **~able** *a*: **~able (to sb/for sth)** responsable (devant qn/de qch) ; **I am ~able to no-one** je n'ai de comptes à rendre à personne.

ant [ænt] *n* fourmi *f*.

antagonism [æn'tægənɪzəm] *n* antagonisme *m*.

antagonist [æn'tægənɪst] *n* antagoniste *m/f*, adversaire *m/f* ; **~ic** [æntægə'nɪstɪk] *a* opposé(e) ; antagoniste.

antagonize [æn'tægənaɪz] *vt* éveiller l'hostilité de, contrarier.

Antarctic [ænt'ɑ:ktɪk] *n* Antarctique *m* // *a* antarctique, austral(e).

anteater ['ænti:tə*] *n* fourmilier *m*, tamanoir *m*.

antecedent [æntɪ'si:dənt] *n* antécédent *m*.

antelope ['æntɪləup] *n* antilope *f*.

antenatal ['æntɪ'neɪtl] *a* prénatal(e) ; **~ clinic** *n* service *m* de consultation prénatale.

antenna, *pl* **~e** [æn'tɛnə, -ni:] *n* antenne *f*.

anthem ['ænθəm] *n* motet *m* ; **national ~** hymne national.

ant-hill ['ænthɪl] *n* fourmilière *f*.

anthology [æn'θɔlədʒɪ] *n* anthologie *f*.

anthropologist [ænθrə'pɔlədʒɪst] *n* anthropologue *m/f*.

anthropology [ænθrə'pɔlədʒɪ] *n* anthropologie *f*.

anti- ['æntɪ] *prefix* anti-.

anti-aircraft ['æntɪ'ɛəkrɑ:ft] *a* antiaérien(ne) ; **~ defence** *n* défense *f* contre avions, DCA *f*.

antibiotic ['æntɪbaɪ'ɔtɪk] *a,n* antibiotique (*m*).

anticipate [æn'tɪsɪpeɪt] *vt* s'attendre à ; prévoir ; (*wishes, request*) aller au devant de, devancer.

anticipation [æntɪsɪ'peɪʃən] *n* attente *f* ; **thanking you in ~** en vous remerciant d'avance, avec mes remerciements anticipés.

anticlimax ['æntɪ'klaɪmæks] *n réalisation décevante d'un événement que l'on escomptait important, intéressant etc.*

anticlockwise ['æntɪ'klɔkwaɪz] *a* dans le sens inverse des aiguilles d'une montre.

antics ['æntɪks] *npl* singeries *fpl*.

anticyclone ['æntɪ'saɪkləun] *n* anticyclone *m*.

antidote ['æntɪdəut] *n* antidote *m*, contrepoison *m*.

antifreeze ['æntɪ'fri:z] *n* antigel *m*.

antipathy [æn'tɪpəθɪ] *n* antipathie *f*.

antiquarian [æntɪ'kwɛərɪən] *a*: **~ bookshop** librairie *f* d'ouvrages anciens // *n* expert *m* en objets *or* livres anciens ; amateur *m* d'antiquités.

antiquated ['æntɪkweɪtɪd] *a* vieilli(e), suranné(e), vieillot(te).

antique [æn'ti:k] *n* objet *m* d'art ancien, meuble ancien *or* d'époque, antiquité *f* // *a* ancien(ne) ; (*pre-mediaeval*) antique ; **~ dealer** *n* antiquaire *m/f* ; **~ shop** *n* magasin *m* d'antiquités.

antiquity [æn'tɪkwɪtɪ] *n* antiquité *f*.

antiseptic [æntɪ'sɛptɪk] *a,n* antiseptique (*m*).

antisocial ['æntɪ'səuʃəl] *a* peu liant(e), sauvage, insociable ; (*against society*) antisocial(e).

antlers ['æntləz] *npl* bois *mpl*, ramure *f*.

anus ['eɪnəs] *n* anus *m*.

anvil ['ænvɪl] *n* enclume *f*.

anxiety [æŋ'zaɪətɪ] *n* anxiété *f* ; (*keenness*): **~ to do** grand désir *or* impatience *f* de faire.

anxious ['æŋkʃəs] *a* anxieux(euse), (très) inquiet(ète) ; (*keen*): **~ to do/that** qui tient beaucoup à faire/à ce que ; impatient(e) de faire/que ; **~ly** *ad* anxieusement.

any ['ɛnɪ] *a* (*in negative and interrogative sentences = some*) de, d' ; du, de l', de la, des ; (*no matter which*) n'importe quel(le), quelconque ; (*each and every*) tout(e), chaque ; **I haven't ~ money/books** je n'ai pas d'argent/de livres ; **have you ~ butter/children?** avez-vous du beurre/des enfants? ; **without ~ difficulty** sans la moindre difficulté ; **come (at) ~ time** venez à n'importe quelle heure ; **at ~ moment** à tout moment, d'un instant à l'autre ; **in ~ case** de toute façon ; en tout cas ; **at ~ rate** de toute façon // *pronoun* n'importe lequel(laquelle) ; (*anybody*) n'importe qui ; (*in negative and interrogative sentences*): **I haven't ~** je n'en ai pas, je n'en ai aucun ; **have you got ~?** en avez-vous? ; **can ~ of you sing?** est-ce que l'un d'entre vous *or* quelqu'un parmi vous sait chanter? // *ad* (*in negative sentences*) nullement, aucunement ; (*in interrogative and conditional constructions*) un peu ; tant soit peu ; **I can't hear him ~ more** je ne l'entends plus ; **are you feeling ~ better?** vous sentez-vous un peu mieux? ; **do you want ~ more soup?** voulez-vous encore un peu de soupe? ; **~body** *pronoun* n'importe qui ; (*in interrogative sentences*) quelqu'un ; (*in negative sentences*): **I don't see ~body** je ne vois personne ; **~how** *ad* quoi qu'il en soit ; **~one = ~body** ; **~thing** *pronoun* (*see* **anybody**) n'importe quoi ; quelque chose ; ne ... rien ; **~time** *ad* n'importe quand ; **~way** *ad* de toute façon ; **~where** *ad* (*see* **anybody**) n'importe où ; quelque part ; **I don't see him ~where** je ne le vois nulle part.

apart [ə'pɑ:t] *ad* (*to one side*) à part ; de côté ; à l'écart ; (*separately*) séparément ; **10 miles/a long way ~** à 10 milles/très éloignés l'un de l'autre ; **they are living ~** ils sont séparés ; **~ from** *prep* à part, excepté.

apartheid [ə'pɑ:teɪt] *n* apartheid *m*.

apartment [ə'pɑ:tmənt] *n* (*US*) appartement *m*, logement *m* ; **~s** *npl* appartement *m*.

apathetic [æpə'θɛtɪk] *a* apathique, indifférent(e).

apathy ['æpəθɪ] *n* apathie *f*, indifférence *f*.

ape [eɪp] *n* (grand) singe // *vt* singer.
aperitif [ə'pɛrɪtɪv] *n* apéritif *m*.
aperture ['æpətʃjuə*] *n* orifice *m*, ouverture *f*; (PHOT) ouverture (du diaphragme).
apex ['eɪpɛks] *n* sommet *m*.
aphrodisiac [æfrəu'dɪzɪæk] *a,n* aphrodisiaque (*m*).
apiece [ə'pi:s] *ad* (*for each person*) chacun(e), par tête; (*for each item*) chacun(e), (la) pièce.
aplomb [ə'plɔm] *n* sang-froid *m*, assurance *f*.
apocalypse [ə'pɔkəlɪps] *n* apocalypse *f*.
apolitical [eɪpə'lɪtɪkl] *a* apolitique.
apologetic [əpɔlə'dʒɛtɪk] *a* (*tone, letter*) d'excuse; **to be very ~ about** s'excuser vivement de.
apologize [ə'pɔlədʒaɪz] *vi*: **to ~ (for sth to sb)** s'excuser (de qch auprès de qn), présenter des excuses (à qn pour qch).
apology [ə'pɔlədʒɪ] *n* excuses *fpl*; **to send one's apologies** envoyer une lettre *or* un mot d'excuse, s'excuser (de ne pas pouvoir venir).
apoplexy ['æpəplɛksɪ] *n* apoplexie *f*.
apostle [ə'pɔsl] *n* apôtre *m*.
apostrophe [ə'pɔstrəfɪ] *n* apostrophe *f*.
appal [ə'pɔ:l] *vt* consterner, atterrer; horrifier; **~ling** *a* épouvantable; (*stupidity*) consternant(e).
apparatus [æpə'reɪtəs] *n* appareil *m*, dispositif *m*.
apparent [ə'pærənt] *a* apparent(e); **~ly** *ad* apparemment.
apparition [æpə'rɪʃən] *n* apparition *f*.
appeal [ə'pi:l] *vi* (LAW) faire *or* interjeter appel // *n* (LAW) appel *m*; (*request*) prière *f*; appel *m*; (*charm*) attrait *m*, charme *m*; **to ~ for** demander (instamment); implorer; **to ~ to** (*obj: person*) faire appel à; (*subj: thing*) plaire à; **to ~ to sb for mercy** implorer la pitié de qn, prier *or* adjurer qn d'avoir pitié; **it doesn't ~ to me** cela ne m'attire pas; **~ing** *a* (*nice*) attrayant(e); (*touching*) attendrissant(e).
appear [ə'pɪə*] *vi* apparaître, se montrer; (LAW) comparaître; (*publication*) paraître, sortir, être publié(e); (*seem*) paraître, sembler; **it would ~ that** il semble que; **to ~ in Hamlet** jouer dans Hamlet; **to ~ on TV** passer à la télé; **~ance** *n* apparition *f*; parution *f*; (*look, aspect*) apparence *f*, aspect *m*; **to put in** *or* **make an ~ance** faire acte de présence; (THEATRE): **by order of ~ance** par ordre d'entrée en scène.
appease [ə'pi:z] *vt* apaiser, calmer.
appendage [ə'pɛndɪdʒ] *n* appendice *m*.
appendicitis [əpɛndɪ'saɪtɪs] *n* appendicite *f*.
appendix, *pl* **appendices** [ə'pɛndɪks, -si:z] *n* appendice *m*.
appetite ['æpɪtaɪt] *n* appétit *m*.
appetizing ['æpɪtaɪzɪŋ] *a* appétissant(e).
applaud [ə'plɔ:d] *vt,vi* applaudir.
applause [ə'plɔ:z] *n* applaudissements *mpl*.
apple ['æpl] *n* pomme *f*; **it's the ~ of my eye** j'y tiens comme à la prunelle de mes yeux; **~ tree** *n* pommier *m*; **~ turnover** *n* chausson *m* aux pommes.
appliance [ə'plaɪəns] *n* appareil *m*.
applicable [ə'plɪkəbl] *a* applicable.
applicant ['æplɪkənt] *n* candidat/e (*for a post* à un poste).
application [æplɪ'keɪʃən] *n* application *f*; (*for a job, a grant etc*) demande *f*; candidature *f*; **on ~** sur demande.
applied [ə'plaɪd] *a* appliqué(e); **~ arts** *npl* arts décoratifs.
apply [ə'plaɪ] *vt* (*paint, ointment*): **to ~ (to)** appliquer (sur); (*theory, technique*): **to ~ (to)** appliquer (à) // *vi*: **to ~ to** (*ask*) s'adresser à; (*be suitable for, relevant to*) s'appliquer à; se rapporter à; être valable pour; **to ~ (for)** (*permit, grant*) faire une demande (en vue d'obtenir); (*job*) poser sa candidature (pour), faire une demande d'emploi (concernant); **to ~ the brakes** actionner les freins, freiner; **to ~ o.s. to** s'appliquer à.
appoint [ə'pɔɪnt] *vt* nommer, engager; (*date, place*) fixer, désigner; **~ment** *n* nomination *f*; rendez-vous *m*; **to make an ~ment (with)** prendre rendez-vous (avec).
apportion [ə'pɔ:ʃən] *vt* (*share out*) répartir, distribuer; **to ~ sth to sb** attribuer *or* assigner *or* allouer qch à qn.
appraisal [ə'preɪzl] *n* évaluation *f*.
appreciable [ə'pri:ʃəbl] *a* appréciable.
appreciate [ə'pri:ʃɪeɪt] *vt* (*like*) apprécier, faire cas de; être reconnaissant(e) de; (*assess*) évaluer; (*be aware of*) comprendre; se rendre compte de // *vi* (FINANCE) prendre de la valeur.
appreciation [əpri:ʃɪ'eɪʃən] *n* appréciation *f*; reconnaissance *f*; (COMM) hausse *f*, valorisation *f*.
appreciative [ə'pri:ʃɪətɪv] *a* (*person*) sensible; (*comment*) élogieux(euse).
apprehend [æprɪ'hɛnd] *vt* appréhender, arrêter; (*understand*) comprendre.
apprehension [æprɪ'hɛnʃən] *n* appréhension *f*, inquiétude *f*.
apprehensive [æprɪ'hɛnsɪv] *a* inquiet(ète), appréhensif(ive).
apprentice [ə'prɛntɪs] *n* apprenti *m*; **~ship** *n* apprentissage *m*.
approach [ə'prəutʃ] *vi* approcher // *vt* (*come near*) approcher de; (*ask, apply to*) s'adresser à; (*subject, passer-by*) aborder // *n* approche *f*; accès *m*, abord *m*; démarche *f* (*auprès de qn*); démarche (*intellectuelle*); **~able** *a* accessible.
approbation [æprə'beɪʃən] *n* approbation *f*.
appropriate *vt* [ə'prəuprɪeɪt] (*take*) s'approprier; (*allot*): **to ~ sth for** affecter qch à // *a* [ə'prəuprɪɪt] opportun(e); qui convient, approprié(e); **~ly** *ad* pertinemment, avec à-propos.
approval [ə'pru:vəl] *n* approbation *f*; **on ~** (COMM) à l'examen.
approve [ə'pru:v] *vt* approuver; **to ~ of** *vt fus* approuver; **~d school** *n* centre *m* d'éducation surveillée; **approvingly** *ad* d'un air approbateur.
approximate *a* [ə'prɔksɪmɪt] approximatif(ive) // *vt* [ə'prɔksɪmeɪt] se rapprocher de; être proche de;

approximation [-'meɪʃən] *n* approximation *f*.
apricot ['eɪprɪkɔt] *n* abricot *m*.
April ['eɪprəl] *n* avril *m*; ~ **fool!** poisson d'avril!
apron ['eɪprən] *n* tablier *m*.
apt [æpt] *a* (*suitable*) approprié(e); (*able*): ~ **(at)** doué(e) (pour); apte (à); (*likely*): ~ **to do** susceptible de faire; ayant tendance à faire.
aptitude ['æptɪtju:d] *n* aptitude *f*.
aqualung ['ækwəlʌŋ] *n* scaphandre *m* autonome.
aquarium [ə'kwɛərɪəm] *n* aquarium *m*.
Aquarius [ə'kwɛərɪəs] *n* le Verseau; **to be** ~ être du Verseau.
aquatic [ə'kwætɪk] *a* aquatique; (SPORT) nautique.
aqueduct ['ækwɪdʌkt] *n* aqueduc *m*.
Arab ['ærəb] *n* Arabe *m/f*.
Arabia [ə'reɪbɪə] *n* Arabie *f*; ~**n** *a* arabe.
Arabic ['ærəbɪk] *a,n* arabe (*m*).
arable ['ærəbl] *a* arable.
arbiter ['ɑ:bɪtə*] *n* arbitre *m*.
arbitrary ['ɑ:bɪtrərɪ] *a* arbitraire.
arbitrate ['ɑ:bɪtreɪt] *vi* arbitrer; trancher; **arbitration** [-'treɪʃən] *n* arbitrage *m*.
arbitrator ['ɑ:bɪtreɪtə*] *n* arbitre *m*, médiateur/trice.
arc [ɑ:k] *n* arc *m*.
arcade [ɑ:'keɪd] *n* arcade *f*; (*passage with shops*) passage *m*, galerie *f*.
arch [ɑ:tʃ] *n* arche *f*; (*of foot*) cambrure *f*, voûte *f* plantaire // *vt* arquer, cambrer // *a* malicieux(euse) // *prefix*: ~**(-)** achevé(e); par excellence; **pointed** ~ *n* ogive *f*.
archaeologist [ɑ:kɪ'ɔlədʒɪst] *n* archéologue *m/f*.
archaeology [ɑ:kɪ'ɔlədʒɪ] *n* archéologie *f*.
archaic [ɑ:'keɪɪk] *a* archaïque.
archbishop [ɑ:tʃ'bɪʃəp] *n* archevêque *m*.
arch-enemy ['ɑ:tʃ'ɛnɪmɪ] *n* ennemi *m* de toujours *or* par excellence.
archeologist [ɑ:kɪ'ɔlədʒɪst] *n* (*US*) = **archaeologist**.
archeology [ɑ:kɪ'ɔlədʒɪ] *n* (*US*) = **archaeology**.
archer ['ɑ:tʃə*] *n* archer *m*; ~**y** *n* tir *m* à l'arc.
archetype ['ɑ:kɪtaɪp] *n* prototype *m*, archétype *m*.
archipelago [ɑ:kɪ'pɛlɪgəu] *n* archipel *m*.
architect ['ɑ:kɪtɛkt] *n* architecte *m*; ~**ural** [ɑ:kɪ'tɛktʃərəl] *a* architectural(e); ~**ure** ['ɑ:kɪtɛktʃə*] *n* architecture *f*.
archives ['ɑ:kaɪvz] *npl* archives *fpl*; **archivist** ['ɑ:kɪvɪst] *n* archiviste *m/f*.
archway ['ɑ:tʃweɪ] *n* voûte *f*, porche voûté *or* cintré.
Arctic ['ɑ:ktɪk] *a* arctique // *n*: **the** ~ l'Arctique *m*.
ardent ['ɑ:dənt] *a* fervent(e).
arduous ['ɑ:djuəs] *a* ardu(e).
are [ɑ:*] *vb see* **be**.
area ['ɛərɪə] *n* (GEOM) superficie *f*; (*zone*) région *f*; (:*smaller*) secteur *m*; **dining** ~ *n* coin *m* salle à manger.
arena [ə'ri:nə] *n* arène *f*.
aren't [ɑ:nt] = **are not**.
Argentina [ɑ:dʒən'ti:nə] *n* Argentine *f*; **Argentinian** [-'tɪnɪən] *a* argentin(e) // *n* Argentin/e.
arguable ['ɑ:gjuəbl] *a* discutable.
argue ['ɑ:gju:] *vi* (*quarrel*) se disputer; (*reason*) argumenter; **to** ~ **that** objecter *or* alléguer que, donner comme argument que.
argument ['ɑ:gjumənt] *n* (*reasons*) argument *m*; (*quarrel*) dispute *f*, discussion *f*; (*debate*) discussion *f*, controverse *f*; ~**ative** [ɑ:gju'mɛntətɪv] *a* ergoteur(euse), raisonneur(euse).
arid ['ærɪd] *a* aride; ~**ity** [ə'rɪdɪtɪ] *n* aridité *f*.
Aries ['ɛərɪz] *n* le Bélier; **to be** ~ être du Bélier.
arise, *pt* **arose**, *pp* **arisen** [ə'raɪz, -'rəuz, -'rɪzn] *vi* survenir, se présenter; **to** ~ **from** résulter de.
aristocracy [ærɪs'tɔkrəsɪ] *n* aristocratie *f*.
aristocrat ['ærɪstəkræt] *n* aristocrate *m/f*; ~**ic** [-'krætɪk] *a* aristocratique.
arithmetic [ə'rɪθmətɪk] *n* arithmétique *f*.
ark [ɑ:k] *n*: **Noah's A**~ l'Arche *f* de Noé.
arm [ɑ:m] *n* bras *m*; (MIL: *branch*) arme *f* // *vt* armer; ~**s** *npl* (*weapons*, HERALDRY) armes *fpl*; ~ **in** ~ bras dessus bras dessous; ~**band** *n* brassard *m*; ~**chair** *n* fauteuil *m*; ~**ed** *a* armé(e); ~**ed robbery** *n* vol *m* à main armée; ~**ful** *n* brassée *f*.
armistice ['ɑ:mɪstɪs] *n* armistice *m*.
armour ['ɑ:mə*] *n* armure *f*; (*also*: ~**-plating**) blindage *m*; (MIL: *tanks*) blindés *mpl*; ~**ed car** *n* véhicule blindé; ~**y** *n* arsenal *m*.
armpit ['ɑ:mpɪt] *n* aisselle *f*.
army ['ɑ:mɪ] *n* armée *f*.
aroma [ə'rəumə] *n* arôme *m*; ~**tic** [ærə'mætɪk] *a* aromatique.
arose [ə'rəuz] *pt of* **arise**.
around [ə'raund] *ad* (tout) autour; dans les parages // *prep* autour de; (*fig*: *about*) environ; vers; **is he** ~**?** est-il dans les parages *or* là?
arouse [ə'rauz] *vt* (*sleeper*) éveiller; (*curiosity*, *passions*) éveiller, susciter; exciter.
arpeggio [ɑ:'pɛdʒɪəu] *n* arpège *m*.
arrange [ə'reɪndʒ] *vt* arranger; (*programme*) arrêter, convenir de; ~**ment** *n* arrangement *m*; (*plans etc*): ~**ments** dispositions *fpl*.
array [ə'reɪ] *n*: ~ **of** déploiement *m* *or* étalage *m* de.
arrears [ə'rɪəz] *npl* arriéré *m*; **to be in** ~ **with one's rent** devoir un arriéré de loyer, être en retard pour le paiement de son loyer.
arrest [ə'rɛst] *vt* arrêter; (*sb's attention*) retenir, attirer // *n* arrestation *f*; **under** ~ en état d'arrestation.
arrival [ə'raɪvəl] *n* arrivée *f*; (COMM) arrivage *m*; (*person*) arrivant/e.
arrive [ə'raɪv] *vi* arriver; **to** ~ **at** *vt fus* (*fig*) parvenir à.
arrogance ['ærəgəns] *n* arrogance *f*.
arrogant ['ærəgənt] *a* arrogant(e).

arrow ['ærəu] *n* flèche *f*.
arsenal ['ɑ:sɪnl] *n* arsenal *m*.
arsenic ['ɑ:snɪk] *n* arsenic *m*.
arson ['ɑ:sn] *n* incendie criminel.
art [ɑ:t] *n* art *m*; (*craft*) métier *m*; **A~s** *npl* (*SCOL*) les lettres *fpl*; **~ gallery** *n* musée *m* d'art; (*small and private*) galerie *f* de peinture.
artefact ['ɑ:tɪfækt] *n* objet fabriqué.
artery ['ɑ:tərɪ] *n* artère *f*.
artful ['ɑ:tful] *a* rusé(e).
arthritis [ɑ:'θraɪtɪs] *n* arthrite *f*.
artichoke ['ɑ:tɪtʃəuk] *n* artichaut *m*.
article ['ɑ:tɪkl] *n* article *m*; (*LAW*: *training*): **~s** *npl* ≈ stage *m*.
articulate *a* [ɑ:'tɪkjulɪt] (*person*) qui s'exprime clairement et aisément; (*speech*) bien articulé(e), prononcé(e) clairement // *vi* [ɑ:'tɪkjuleɪt] articuler, parler distinctement; **~d lorry** *n* (camion *m*) semi-remorque *m*.
artifice ['ɑ:tɪfɪs] *n* ruse *f*.
artificial [ɑ:tɪ'fɪʃəl] *a* artificiel(le); **~ respiration** *n* respiration artificielle.
artillery [ɑ:'tɪlərɪ] *n* artillerie *f*.
artisan ['ɑ:tɪzæn] *n* artisan/e.
artist ['ɑ:tɪst] *n* artiste *m/f*; **~ic** [ɑ:'tɪstɪk] *a* artistique; **~ry** *n* art *m*, talent *m*.
artless ['ɑ:tlɪs] *a* naïf(ïve), simple, ingénu(e).
as [æz, əz] *cj* (*cause*) comme, puisque; (*time*: *moment*) alors que, comme; (: *duration*) tandis que; (*manner*) comme; (*in the capacity of*) en tant que, en qualité de; **~ big ~** aussi grand que; **twice ~ big ~** deux fois plus grand que; **big ~ it is** si grand que ce soit; **~ she said** comme elle l'avait dit; **~ if** *or* **though** comme si; **~ for** *or* **to** en ce qui concerne, quant à; **~** *or* **so long ~** *cj* à condition que; si; **~ much/many (~)** autant (que); **~ soon ~** *cj* aussitôt que, dès que; **~ such** *ad* en tant que tel(le); **~ well** *ad* aussi; **~ well ~** *cj* en plus de, en même temps que; *see also* **so, such**.
asbestos [æz'bɛstəs] *n* asbeste *m*, amiante *m*.
ascend [ə'sɛnd] *vt* gravir; **~ancy** *n* ascendant *m*.
ascent [ə'sɛnt] *n* ascension *f*.
ascertain [æsə'teɪn] *vt* s'assurer de, vérifier; établir.
ascetic [ə'sɛtɪk] *a* ascétique.
ascribe [ə'skraɪb] *vt*: **to ~ sth to** attribuer qch à; (*blame*) imputer qch à.
ash [æʃ] *n* (*dust*) cendre *f*; **~ (tree)** frêne *m*.
ashamed [ə'ʃeɪmd] *a* honteux(euse), confus(e); **to be ~ of** avoir honte de; **to be ~ (of o.s.) for having done** avoir honte d'avoir fait.
ashen ['æʃn] *a* (*pale*) cendreux(euse), blême.
ashore [ə'ʃɔ:*] *ad* à terre; **to go ~** aller à terre, débarquer.
ashtray ['æʃtreɪ] *n* cendrier *m*.
Asia ['eɪʃə] *n* Asie *f*; **~ Minor** *n* Asie Mineure; **~n** *n* Asiatique *m/f* // *a* asiatique; **~tic** [eɪsɪ'ætɪk] *a* asiatique.
aside [ə'saɪd] *ad* de côté; à l'écart // *n* aparté *m*.
ask [ɑ:sk] *vt* demander; (*invite*) inviter; **to ~ sb sth/to do sth** demander à qn qch/de faire qch; **to ~ sb about sth** questionner qn au sujet de qch; se renseigner auprès de qn au sujet de qch; **to ~ about the price** s'informer du prix, se renseigner au sujet du prix; **to ~ (sb) a question** poser une question (à qn); **to ~ sb out to dinner** inviter qn au restaurant; **to ~ for** *vt fus* demander.
askance [ə'skɑ:ns] *ad*: **to look ~ at sb** regarder qn de travers *or* d'un œil désapprobateur.
askew [ə'skju:] *ad* de travers, de guinguois.
asleep [ə'sli:p] *a* endormi(e); **to be ~** dormir, être endormi; **to fall ~** s'endormir.
asp [æsp] *n* aspic *m*.
asparagus [əs'pærəgəs] *n* asperges *fpl*; **~ tips** *npl* pointes *fpl* d'asperges.
aspect ['æspɛkt] *n* aspect *m*; (*direction in which a building etc faces*) orientation *f*, exposition *f*.
aspersions [əs'pə:ʃənz] *npl* **to cast ~ on** dénigrer.
asphalt ['æsfælt] *n* asphalte *m*.
asphyxiate [æs'fɪksɪeɪt] *vt* asphyxier; **asphyxiation** [-'eɪʃən] *n* asphyxie *f*.
aspirate *vt* ['æspəreɪt] aspirer // *a* ['æspərɪt] aspiré(e).
aspiration [æspə'reɪʃən] *n* aspiration *f*.
aspire [əs'paɪə*] *vi*: **to ~ to** aspirer à.
aspirin ['æsprɪn] *n* aspirine *f*.
ass [æs] *n* âne *m*; (*col*) imbécile *m/f*.
assail [ə'seɪl] *vt* assaillir; **~ant** *n* agresseur *m*; assaillant *m*.
assassin [ə'sæsɪn] *n* assassin *m*; **~ate** *vt* assassiner; **~ation** [əsæsɪ'neɪʃən] *n* assassinat *m*.
assault [ə'sɔ:lt] *n* (*MIL*) assaut *m*; (*gen*: *attack*) agression *f*; (*LAW*): **~ (and battery)** voies *fpl* de fait, coups *mpl* et blessures *fpl* // *vt* attaquer; (*sexually*) violenter.
assemble [ə'sɛmbl] *vt* assembler // *vi* s'assembler, se rassembler.
assembly [ə'sɛmblɪ] *n* (*meeting*) rassemblement *m*; (*construction*) assemblage *m*; **~ line** *n* chaîne *f* de montage.
assent [ə'sɛnt] *n* assentiment *m*, consentement *m* // *vi* donner son assentiment, consentir.
assert [ə'sə:t] *vt* affirmer, déclarer; établir; **~ion** [ə'sə:ʃən] *n* assertion *f*, affirmation *f*; **~ive** *a* assuré(e), péremptoire.
assess [ə'sɛs] *vt* évaluer, estimer; (*tax, damages*) établir *or* fixer le montant de; (*property etc*: *for tax*) calculer la valeur imposable de; **~ment** *n* évaluation *f*, estimation *f*; **~or** *n* expert *m* (*en matière d'impôt et d'assurance*).
asset ['æsɛt] *n* avantage *m*, atout *m*; **~s** *npl* capital *m*; avoir(s) *m(pl)*; actif *m*.
assiduous [ə'sɪdjuəs] *a* assidu(e).
assign [ə'saɪn] *vt* (*date*) fixer, arrêter; (*task*): **to ~ sth to** assigner qch à; (*resources*): **to ~ sth to** affecter qch à; (*cause, meaning*): **to ~ sth to** attribuer qch à; **~ment** *n* tâche *f*, mission *f*.

assimilate [ə'sɪmɪleɪt] *vt* assimiler ; **assimilation** [-'leɪʃən] *n* assimilation *f*.

assist [ə'sɪst] *vt* aider, assister ; secourir ; **~ance** *n* aide *f*, assistance *f* ; secours *mpl* ; **~ant** *n* assistant/e, adjoint/e ; (*also*: **shop ~ant**) vendeur/euse.

assizes [ə'saɪzɪz] *npl* assises *fpl*.

associate *a,n* [ə'səuʃɪɪt] associé(e) // *vb* [ə'səuʃɪeɪt] *vt* associer // *vi*: **to ~ with sb** fréquenter qn.

association [əsəusɪ'eɪʃən] *n* association *f* ; **~ football** *n* football *m*.

assorted [ə'sɔ:tɪd] *a* assorti(e).

assortment [ə'sɔ:tmənt] *n* assortiment *m*.

assume [ə'sju:m] *vt* supposer ; (*responsibilities etc*) assumer ; (*attitude, name*) prendre, adopter ; **~d name** *n* nom *m* d'emprunt.

assumption [ə'sʌmpʃən] *n* supposition *f*, hypothèse *f*.

assurance [ə'ʃuərəns] *n* assurance *f*.

assure [ə'ʃuə*] *vt* assurer.

asterisk ['æstərɪsk] *n* astérisque *m*.

astern [ə'stə:n] *ad* à l'arrière.

asthma ['æsmə] *n* asthme *m* ; **~tic** [æs'mætɪk] *a,n* asthmatique (*m/f*).

astir [ə'stə:*] *ad* en émoi.

astonish [ə'stɔnɪʃ] *vt* étonner, stupéfier ; **~ment** *n* étonnement *m*.

astound [ə'staund] *vt* stupéfier, sidérer.

astray [ə'streɪ] *ad*: **to go ~** s'égarer ; (*fig*) quitter le droit chemin.

astride [ə'straɪd] *ad* à cheval // *prep* à cheval sur.

astringent [əs'trɪndʒənt] *a* astringent(e) // *n* astringent *m*.

astrologer [əs'trɔlədʒə*] *n* astrologue *m*.

astrology [əs'trɔlədʒɪ] *n* astrologie *f*.

astronaut ['æstrənɔ:t] *n* astronaute *m/f*.

astronomer [əs'trɔnəmə*] *n* astronome *m*.

astronomical [æstrə'nɔmɪkəl] *a* astronomique.

astronomy [əs'trɔnəmɪ] *n* astronomie *f*.

astute [əs'tju:t] *a* astucieux(euse), malin(igne).

asunder [ə'sʌndə*] *ad*: **to tear ~** déchirer.

asylum [ə'saɪləm] *n* asile *m*.

at [æt] *prep* à ; (*because of*: *following surprised, annoyed etc*) de ; par ; **~ Pierre's** chez Pierre ; **~ the baker's** chez le boulanger, à la boulangerie ; **~ times** parfois.

ate [eɪt] *pt of* **eat**.

atheism ['eɪθɪɪzəm] *n* athéisme *m*.

atheist ['eɪθɪɪst] *n* athée *m/f*.

Athens ['æθɪnz] *n* Athènes.

athlete ['æθli:t] *n* athlète *m/f*.

athletic [æθ'lɛtɪk] *a* athlétique ; **~s** *n* athlétisme *m*.

Atlantic [ət'læntɪk] *a* atlantique // *n*: **the ~ (Ocean)** l'Atlantique *m*, l'océan *m* Atlantique.

atlas ['ætləs] *n* atlas *m*.

atmosphere ['ætməsfɪə*] *n* atmosphère *f*.

atmospheric [ætməs'fɛrɪk] *a* atmosphérique ; **~s** *n* (RADIO) parasites *mpl*.

atoll ['ætɔl] *n* atoll *m*.

atom ['ætəm] *n* atome *m* ; **~ic** [ə'tɔmɪk] *a* atomique ; **~(ic) bomb** *n* bombe *f* atomique ; **~izer** ['ætəmaɪzə*] *n* atomiseur *m*.

atone [ə'təun] *vi*: **to ~ for** expier, racheter.

atrocious [ə'trəuʃəs] *a* (*very bad*) atroce, exécrable.

atrocity [ə'trɔsɪtɪ] *n* atrocité *f*.

atrophy ['ætrəfɪ] *n* atrophie *f* // *vt* atrophier // *vi* s'atrophier.

attach [ə'tætʃ] *vt* (*gen*) attacher ; (*document, letter*) joindre ; (MIL: *troops*) affecter ; **to be ~ed to sb/sth** (*to like*) être attaché à qn/qch ; **~é** [ə'tæʃeɪ] *n* attaché *m* ; **~é case** *n* mallette *f*, attaché-case *m* ; **~ment** *n* (*tool*) accessoire *m* ; (*love*): **~ment (to)** affection *f* (pour), attachement *m* (à).

attack [ə'tæk] *vt* attaquer ; (*task etc*) s'attaquer à // *n* attaque *f* ; (*also*: **heart ~**) crise *f* cardiaque ; **~er** *n* attaquant *m* ; agresseur *m*.

attain [ə'teɪn] *vt* (*also*: **to ~ to**) parvenir à, atteindre ; acquérir ; **~ments** *npl* connaissances *fpl*, résultats *mpl*.

attempt [ə'tɛmpt] *n* tentative *f* // *vt* essayer, tenter ; **~ed theft** *etc* (LAW) tentative de vol *etc* ; **to make an ~ on sb's life** attenter à la vie de qn.

attend [ə'tɛnd] *vt* (*course*) suivre ; (*meeting, talk*) assister à ; (*school, church*) aller à, fréquenter ; (*patient*) soigner, s'occuper de ; **to ~ (up)on** servir ; être au service de ; **to ~ to** *vt fus* (*needs, affairs etc*) s'occuper de ; (*customer*) s'occuper de, servir ; **~ance** *n* (*being present*) présence *f* ; (*people present*) assistance *f* ; **~ant** *n* employé/e ; gardien/ne // *a* concomitant(e), qui accompagne *or* s'ensuit.

attention [ə'tɛnʃən] *n* attention *f* ; **~s** attentions *fpl*, prévenances *fpl* ; **~!** (MIL) garde-à-vous! ; **at ~** (MIL) au garde-à-vous ; **for the ~ of** (ADMIN) à l'attention de.

attentive [ə'tɛntɪv] *a* attentif(ive) ; (*kind*) prévenant(e) ; **~ly** *ad* attentivement, avec attention.

attenuate [ə'tɛnjueɪt] *vt* atténuer // *vi* s'atténuer.

attest [ə'tɛst] *vi*: **to ~ to** témoigner de, attester (de).

attic ['ætɪk] *n* grenier *m*, combles *mpl*.

attire [ə'taɪə*] *n* habit *m*, atours *mpl*.

attitude ['ætɪtju:d] *n* attitude *f*, manière *f* ; pose *f*, maintien *m*.

attorney [ə'tə:nɪ] *n* (*lawyer*) avoué *m* ; (*having proxy*) mandataire *m* ; **A~ General** *n* (*Brit*) ≈ procureur général ; (*US*) ≈ garde *m* des Sceaux, ministre *m* de la Justice ; **power of ~** *n* procuration *f*.

attract [ə'trækt] *vt* attirer ; **~ion** [ə'trækʃən] *n* (*gen pl*: *pleasant things*) attraction *f*, attrait *m* ; (PHYSICS) attraction *f* ; (*fig*: *towards sth*) attirance *f* ; **~ive** *a* séduisant(e), attrayant(e).

attribute *n* ['ætrɪbju:t] attribut *m* // *vt* [ə'trɪbju:t]: **to ~ sth to** attribuer qch à.

attrition [ə'trɪʃən] *n*: **war of ~** guerre *f* d'usure.

aubergine ['əubəʒi:n] *n* aubergine *f*.

auburn ['ɔ:bən] *a* auburn *inv*, châtain roux *inv*.

auction ['ɔ:kʃən] *n* (*also*: **sale by ~**) vente *f* aux enchères // *vt* (*also*: **to sell by ~**) vendre aux enchères ; (*also*: **to put up for ~**) mettre aux enchères ; **~eer** [-'nɪə*] *n* commissaire-priseur *m*.
audacious [ɔ:'deɪʃəs] *a* impudent(e) ; audacieux(euse), intrépide.
audacity [ɔ:'dæsɪtɪ] *n* impudence *f*; audace *f*.
audible ['ɔ:dɪbl] *a* audible.
audience ['ɔ:dɪəns] *n* (*people*) assistance *f*, auditoire *m* ; auditeurs *mpl* ; spectateurs *mpl* ; (*interview*) audience *f*.
audio-visual [ɔ:dɪəu'vɪzjuəl] *a* audio-visuel(le).
audit ['ɔ:dɪt] *n* vérification *f* des comptes, apurement *m* // *vt* vérifier, apurer.
audition [ɔ:'dɪʃən] *n* audition *f*.
auditor ['ɔ:dɪtə*] *n* vérificateur *m* des comptes.
auditorium [ɔ:dɪ'tɔ:rɪəm] *n* auditorium *m*, salle *f* de concert *or* de spectacle.
augment [ɔ:g'mɛnt] *vt,vi* augmenter.
augur ['ɔ:gə*] *vt* (*be a sign of*) présager, annoncer // *vi*: **it ~s well** c'est bon signe *or* de bon augure, cela s'annonce bien.
August ['ɔ:gəst] *n* août *m*.
august [ɔ:'gʌst] *a* majestueux(euse), imposant(e).
aunt [ɑ:nt] *n* tante *f*; **~ie, ~y** *n diminutive of* **aunt**.
au pair ['əu'pɛə*] *n* (*also*: **~ girl**) jeune fille *f* au pair.
aura ['ɔ:rə] *n* atmosphère *f*.
auspices ['ɔ:spɪsɪz] *npl*: **under the ~ of** sous les auspices de.
auspicious [ɔ:s'pɪʃəs] *a* de bon augure, propice.
austere [ɔs'tɪə*] *a* austère.
Australia [ɔs'treɪlɪə] *n* Australie *f*; **~n** *a* australien(ne) // *n* Australien/ne.
Austria ['ɔstrɪə] *n* Autriche *f*; **~n** *a* autrichien(ne) // *n* Autrichien/ne.
authentic [ɔ:'θɛntɪk] *a* authentique ; **~ate** *vt* établir l'authenticité de.
author ['ɔ:θə*] *n* auteur *m*.
authoritarian [ɔ:θɔrɪ'tɛərɪən] *a* autoritaire.
authoritative [ɔ:'θɔrɪtətɪv] *a* (*account*) digne de foi ; (*study, treatise*) qui fait autorité ; (*manner*) autoritaire.
authority [ɔ:'θɔrɪtɪ] *n* autorité *f*; (*permission*) autorisation (formelle) ; **the authorities** *npl* les autorités *fpl*, l'administration *f*.
authorize ['ɔ:θəraɪz] *vt* autoriser.
authorship ['ɔ:θəʃɪp] *n* paternité *f* (*littéraire etc*).
autistic [ɔ:'tɪstɪk] *a* autistique.
auto ['ɔ:təu] *n* (*US*) auto *f*, voiture *f*.
autobiography [ɔ:təbaɪ'ɔgrəfɪ] *n* autobiographie *f*.
autocratic [ɔ:tə'krætɪk] *a* autocratique.
autograph ['ɔ:təgrɑ:f] *n* autographe *m* // *vt* signer, dédicacer.
automatic [ɔ:tə'mætɪk] *a* automatique // *n* (*gun*) automatique *m* ; **~ally** *ad* automatiquement.
automation [ɔ:tə'meɪʃən] *n* automatisation *f*.
automaton, *pl* **automata** [ɔ:'tɔmətən, -tə] *n* automate *m*.
automobile ['ɔ:təməbi:l] *n* (*US*) automobile *f*.
autonomous [ɔ:'tɔnəməs] *a* autonome.
autonomy [ɔ:'tɔnəmɪ] *n* autonomie *f*.
autopsy ['ɔ:tɔpsɪ] *n* autopsie *f*.
autumn ['ɔ:təm] *n* automne *m*.
auxiliary [ɔ:g'zɪlɪərɪ] *a* auxiliaire // *n* auxiliaire *m/f*.
Av. *abbr of* **avenue**.
avail [ə'veɪl] *vt*: **to ~ o.s. of** user de ; profiter de // *n*: **to no ~** sans résultat, en vain, en pure perte.
availability [əveɪlə'bɪlɪtɪ] *n* disponibilité *f*.
available [ə'veɪləbl] *a* disponible ; **every ~ means** tous les moyens possibles *or* à sa (*or* notre *etc*) disposition.
avalanche ['ævəlɑ:nʃ] *n* avalanche *f*.
avant-garde ['ævɑ̃ŋ'gɑ:d] *a* d'avant-garde.
avaricious [ævə'rɪʃəs] *a* avare.
Ave. *abbr of* **avenue**.
avenge [ə'vɛndʒ] *vt* venger.
avenue ['ævənju:] *n* avenue *f*.
average ['ævərɪdʒ] *n* moyenne *f* // *a* moyen(ne) // *vt* (*a certain figure*) atteindre *or* faire *etc* en moyenne ; **on ~** en moyenne ; **above/below (the) ~** au-dessus/en-dessous de la moyenne ; **to ~ out** *vi*: **to ~ out at** représenter en moyenne, donner une moyenne de.
averse [ə'və:s] *a*: **to be ~ to sth/doing** éprouver une forte répugnance envers qch/à faire ; **I wouldn't be ~ to a drink** un petit verre ne serait pas de refus, je ne dirais pas non à un petit verre.
aversion [ə'və:ʃən] *n* aversion *f*, répugnance *f*.
avert [ə'və:t] *vt* prévenir, écarter ; (*one's eyes*) détourner.
aviary ['eɪvɪərɪ] *n* volière *f*.
aviation [eɪvɪ'eɪʃən] *n* aviation *f*.
avid ['ævɪd] *a* avide ; **~ly** *ad* avidement, avec avidité.
avocado [ævə'kɑ:dəu] *n* (*also*: **~ pear**) avocat *m*.
avoid [ə'vɔɪd] *vt* éviter ; **~able** *a* évitable ; **~ance** *n le fait d'éviter*.
await [ə'weɪt] *vt* attendre ; **~ing attention/delivery** (COMM) en souffrance.
awake [ə'weɪk] *a* éveillé(e) ; (*fig*) en éveil // *vb* (*pt* **awoke** [ə'wəuk], *pp* **awoken** [ə'wəukən] *or* **awaked**) *vt* éveiller // *vi* s'éveiller ; **~ to** conscient de ; **he was still ~** il ne dormait pas encore ; **~ning** [ə'weɪknɪŋ] *n* réveil *m*.
award [ə'wɔ:d] *n* récompense *f*, prix *m* // *vt* (*prize*) décerner ; (LAW: *damages*) accorder.
aware [ə'wɛə*] *a*: **~ of** (*conscious*) conscient(e) de ; (*informed*) au courant de ; **to become ~ of** avoir conscience de, prendre conscience de ; se rendre compte de ; **politically/socially ~** sensibilisé aux *or* ayant pris conscience des problèmes politiques/sociaux ; **~ness** *n le fait d'être conscient, au courant etc*.
awash [ə'wɔʃ] *a* recouvert(e) (d'eau) ; **~ with** inondé(e) de.

away [ə'weɪ] *a,ad* (au) loin ; absent(e) ; **two kilometres** ~ à (une distance de) deux kilomètres, à deux kilomètres de distance ; **two hours** ~ **by car** à deux heures de voiture *or* de route ; **the holiday was two weeks** ~ il restait deux semaines jusqu'aux vacances ; ~ **from** loin de ; **he's** ~ **for a week** il est parti (pour) une semaine ; **to take** ~ *vt* emporter ; **to work/pedal/laugh** *etc* ~ *la particule indique la constance et l'énergie de l'action*: il pédalait *etc* tant qu'il pouvait ; **to fade/wither** *etc* ~ *la particule renforce l'idée de la disparition, l'éloignement* ; ~ **match** *n* (SPORT) match *m* à l'extérieur.

awe [ɔ:] *n* respect mêlé de crainte, effroi mêlé d'admiration ; **~-inspiring, ~some** *a* impressionnant(e) ; **~struck** *a* frappé(e) d'effroi.

awful ['ɔ:fəl] *a* affreux(euse) ; **~ly** *ad* (*very*) terriblement, vraiment.

awhile [ə'waɪl] *ad* un moment, quelque temps.

awkward ['ɔ:kwəd] *a* (*clumsy*) gauche, maladroit(e) ; (*inconvenient*) malaisé(e), d'emploi malaisé, peu pratique ; (*embarrassing*) gênant(e), délicat(e).

awl [ɔ:l] *n* alêne *f*.

awning ['ɔ:nɪŋ] *n* (*of tent*) auvent *m* ; (*of shop*) store *m* ;(*of hotel etc*) marquise *f* (de toile).

awoke, awoken [ə'wəuk, -kən] *pt,pp of* **awake**.

awry [ə'raɪ] *ad,a* de travers ; **to go** ~ mal tourner.

axe, ax (*US*) [æks] *n* hache *f* // *vt* (*employee*) renvoyer ; (*project etc*) abandonner ; (*jobs*) supprimer.

axiom ['æksɪəm] *n* axiome *m*.

axis, *pl* **axes** ['æksɪs, -si:z] *n* axe *m*.

axle ['æksl] *n* (*also*: **~-tree**) essieu *m*.

ay(e) [aɪ] *excl* (*yes*) oui ; **the ayes** *npl* les oui.

azure ['eɪʒə*] *a* azuré(e).

B

B [bi:] *n* (MUS) si *m*.

B.A. *abbr see* **bachelor**.

babble ['bæbl] *vi* babiller // *n* babillage *m*.

baboon [bə'bu:n] *n* babouin *m*.

baby ['beɪbɪ] *n* bébé *m* ; ~ **carriage** *n* (*US*) voiture *f* d'enfant ; **~hood** *n* petite enfance ; **~ish** *a* enfantin(e), de bébé ; **~-sit** *vi* garder les enfants ; **~-sitter** *n* baby-sitter *m/f*.

bachelor ['bætʃələ*] *n* célibataire *m* ; **B~ of Arts/Science (B.A./B.Sc.)** ≈ licencié/e ès *or* en lettres/sciences ; **B~ of Arts/Science degree (B.A./B.Sc.)** *n* ≈ licence *f* ès *or* en lettres/ sciences ; **~hood** *n* célibat *m*.

back [bæk] *n* (*of person, horse*) dos *m* ; (*of hand*) dos, revers *m* ; (*of house*) derrière *m* ; (*of car, train*) arrière *m* ; (*of chair*) dossier *m* ; (*of page*) verso *m* ; (FOOTBALL) arrière *m* // *vt* (*candidate*: *also*: ~ **up**) soutenir, appuyer ; (*horse*: *at races*) parier *or* miser sur ; (*car*) (faire) reculer // *vi* reculer ; (*car etc*) faire marche arrière // *a* (*in compounds*) de derrière, à l'arrière ; ~ **seats/wheels** (AUT) sièges *mpl*/roues *fpl* arrière ; ~ **payments/rent** arriéré *m* de paiements/loyer // *ad* (*not forward*) en arrière ; (*returned*): **he's** ~ il est rentré, il est de retour ; **he ran** ~ il est revenu en courant ; (*restitution*): **throw the ball** ~ renvoie la balle ; **can I have it** ~? puis-je le ravoir?, peux-tu me le rendre? ; (*again*): **he called** ~ il a rappelé ; **to** ~ **down** *vi* rabattre de ses prétentions ; **to** ~ **out** *vi* (*of promise*) se dédire ; **~ache** *n* maux *mpl* de reins ; **~bencher** *n membre du parlement sans portefeuille* ; **~biting** *n* médisance(s) *f(pl)* ; **~bone** *n* colonne vertébrale, épine dorsale ; **~-cloth** *n* toile *f* de fond ; **~date** *vt* (*letter*) antidater ; **~dated pay rise** augmentation *f* avec effet rétroactif ; **~er** *n* partisan *m* ; (COMM) commanditaire *m* ; **~fire** *vi* (AUT) pétarader ; (*plans*) mal tourner ; **~gammon** *n* trictrac *m* ; **~ground** *n* arrière-plan *m* ; (*of events*) situation *f*, conjoncture *f* ; (*basic knowledge*) éléments *mpl* de base ; (*experience*) formation *f* ; **family ~ground** milieu familial ; **~ground noise** *n* bruit *m* de fond ; **~hand** *n* (TENNIS: *also*: **~hand stroke**) revers *m* ; **~handed** *a* (*fig*) déloyal(e) ; équivoque ; **~hander** *n* (*bribe*) pot-de-vin *m* ; **~ing** *n* (*fig*) soutien *m*, appui *m* ; **~lash** *n* contre-coup *m*, répercussion *f* ; **~log** *n*: **~log of work** travail *m* en retard ; ~ **number** *n* (*of magazine etc*) vieux numéro ; ~ **pay** *n* rappel *m* de traitement ; **~side** *n* (*col*) derrière *m*, postérieur *m* ; **~stroke** *n* nage *f* sur le dos ; **~ward** *a* (*movement*) en arrière ; (*measure*) rétrograde ; (*person, country*) arriéré(e) ; attardé(e) ; (*shy*) hésitant(e) ; **~ward and forward movement** mouvement de va-et-vient ; **~wards** *ad* (*move, go*) en arrière ; (*read a list*) à l'envers, à rebours ; (*fall*) à la renverse ; (*walk*) à reculons ; (*in time*) en arrière, vers le passé ; **~water** *n* (*fig*) coin reculé ; bled perdu ; **~yard** *n* arrière-cour *f*.

bacon ['beɪkən] *n* bacon *m*, lard *m*.

bacteria [bæk'tɪərɪə] *npl* bactéries *fpl*.

bad [bæd] *a* mauvais(e) ; (*child*) vilain(e) ; (*meat, food*) gâté(e), avarié(e) ; **his** ~ **leg** sa jambe malade.

bade [bæd] *pt of* **bid**.

badge [bædʒ] *n* insigne *m* ; (*of policemen*) plaque *f*.

badger ['bædʒə*] *n* blaireau *m* // *vt* harceler.

badly ['bædlɪ] *ad* (*work, dress etc*) mal ; ~ **wounded** grièvement blessé ; **he needs it** ~ il en a absolument besoin ; ~ **off** *a,ad* dans la gêne.

badminton ['bædmɪntən] *n* badminton *m*.

bad-tempered ['bæd'tɛmpəd] *a* ayant mauvais caractère ; de mauvaise humeur.

baffle ['bæfl] *vt* (*puzzle*) déconcerter.

bag [bæg] *n* sac *m* ; (*of hunter*) gibecière *f* ; chasse *f* // *vt* (*col*: *take*) empocher ; s'approprier ; (TECH) mettre en sacs ; **~s under the eyes** poches *fpl* sous les yeux ; **~ful** *n* plein sac ; **~gage** *n* bagages *mpl* ; **~gy** *a* avachi(e), qui fait des poches ; **~pipes** *npl* cornemuse *f*.

Bahamas [bə'hɑ:məz] *npl*: **the** ~ les Bahamas *fpl*.

bail [beɪl] *n* caution *f* // *vt* (*prisoner*: *gen*: **to give ~ to**) mettre en liberté sous caution; (*boat*: *also*: **~ out**) écoper; *see* **bale**; **to ~ out** *vt* (*prisoner*) payer la caution de.

bailiff ['beɪlɪf] *n* huissier *m*.

bait [beɪt] *n* appât *m* // *vt* appâter; (*fig*) tourmenter.

bake [beɪk] *vt* (faire) cuire au four // *vi* cuire (au four); faire de la pâtisserie; **~d beans** *npl* haricots blancs à la sauce tomate; **~r** *n* boulanger *m*; **~ry** *n* boulangerie *f*; boulangerie industrielle; **baking** *n* cuisson *f*; **baking powder** *n* levure *f* (chimique).

balaclava [bælə'klɑːvə] *n* (*also*: **~ helmet**) passe-montagne *m*.

balance ['bæləns] *n* équilibre *m*; (COMM: *sum*) solde *m*; (*scales*) balance *f*; (ECON: *of trade etc*) balance // *vt* mettre *or* faire tenir en équilibre; (*pros and cons*) peser; (*budget*) équilibrer; (*account*) balancer; (*compensate*) compenser, contrebalancer; **~ of trade/payments** balance commerciale/des comptes *or* paiements; **~d** *a* (*personality, diet*) équilibré(e); **~ sheet** *n* bilan *m*; **~ wheel** *n* balancier *m*.

balcony ['bælkənɪ] *n* balcon *m*.

bald [bɔːld] *a* chauve; (*tree, hill*) dénudé(e); **~ness** *n* calvitie *f*.

bale [beɪl] *n* balle *f*, ballot *m*; **to ~ out** *vi* (*of a plane*) sauter en parachute.

baleful ['beɪlful] *a* funeste, maléfique.

balk [bɔːk] *vi*: **to ~ (at)** regimber (contre); (*horse*) se dérober (devant).

ball [bɔːl] *n* boule *f*; (*football*) ballon *m*; (*for tennis, golf*) balle *f*; (*dance*) bal *m*.

ballad ['bæləd] *n* ballade *f*.

ballast ['bæləst] *n* lest *m*.

ballerina [bælə'riːnə] *n* ballerine *f*.

ballet ['bæleɪ] *n* ballet *m*; (*art*) danse *f* (classique).

ballistics [bə'lɪstɪks] *n* balistique *f*.

balloon [bə'luːn] *n* ballon *m*; (*in comic strip*) bulle *f*; **~ist** *n* aéronaute *m/f*.

ballot ['bælət] *n* scrutin *m*; **~ box** *n* urne (électorale); **~ paper** *n* bulletin *m* de vote.

ball-point pen ['bɔːlpɔɪnt'pɛn] *n* stylo *m* à bille.

ballroom ['bɔːlrum] *n* salle *f* de bal.

balmy ['bɑːmɪ] *a* (*breeze, air*) doux(douce); (*col*) = **barmy**.

balsam ['bɔːlsəm] *n* baume *m*.

Baltic [bɔːltɪk] *a,n*: **the ~ (Sea)** la (mer) Baltique.

bamboo [bæm'buː] *n* bambou *m*.

bamboozle [bæm'buːzl] *vt* (*col*) embobiner.

ban [bæn] *n* interdiction *f* // *vt* interdire.

banal [bə'nɑːl] *a* banal(e).

banana [bə'nɑːnə] *n* banane *f*.

band [bænd] *n* bande *f*; (*at a dance*) orchestre *m*; (MIL) musique *f*, fanfare *f*; **to ~ together** *vi* se liguer.

bandage ['bændɪdʒ] *n* bandage *m*, pansement *m*.

bandit ['bændɪt] *n* bandit *m*.

bandwagon ['bændwægən] *n*: **to jump on the ~** (*fig*) monter dans *or* prendre le train en marche.

bandy ['bændɪ] *vt* (*jokes, insults*) échanger; **to ~ about** *vt* employer à tout bout de champ *or* à tort et à travers.

bandy-legged ['bændɪ'lɛgd] *a* aux jambes arquées.

bang [bæŋ] *n* détonation *f*; (*of door*) claquement *m*; (*blow*) coup (violent) // *vt* frapper (violemment); (*door*) claquer // *vi* détoner; claquer; **to ~ at the door** cogner à la porte.

banger ['bæŋə*] *n* (*car*: *gen*: **old ~**) (vieux) tacot.

bangle ['bæŋgl] *n* bracelet *m*.

banish ['bænɪʃ] *vt* bannir.

banister(s) ['bænɪstə(z)] *n*(*pl*) rampe *f* (d'escalier).

banjo, ~es *or* **~s** ['bændʒəu] *n* banjo *m*.

bank [bæŋk] *n* banque *f*; (*of river, lake*) bord *m*, rive *f*; (*of earth*) talus *m*, remblai *m* // *vi* (AVIAT) virer sur l'aile; (COMM): **they ~ with Pitt's** leur banque *or* banquier est Pitt's; **to ~ on** *vt fus* miser *or* tabler sur; **~ account** *n* compte *m* en banque; **~er** *n* banquier *m*; **B~ holiday** *n* jour férié (*où les banques sont fermées*); **~ing** *n* opérations *fpl* bancaires; profession *f* de banquier; **~ing hours** *npl* heures *fpl* d'ouverture des banques; **~note** *n* billet *m* de banque; **~ rate** *n* taux *m* de l'escompte.

bankrupt ['bæŋkrʌpt] *n* failli/e // *a* en faillite; **to go ~** faire faillite; **~cy** *n* faillite *f*.

banner ['bænə*] *n* bannière *f*.

bannister(s) ['bænɪstə(z)] *n*(*pl*) = **banister(s)**.

banns [bænz] *npl* bans *mpl* (de mariage).

banquet ['bæŋkwɪt] *n* banquet *m*, festin *m*.

bantam-weight ['bæntəmweɪt] *n* poids *m* coq *inv*.

banter ['bæntə*] *n* badinage *m*.

baptism ['bæptɪzəm] *n* baptême *m*.

Baptist ['bæptɪst] *n* baptiste *m/f*.

baptize [bæp'taɪz] *vt* baptiser.

bar [bɑː*] *n* barre *f*; (*of window etc*) barreau *m*; (*of chocolate*) tablette *f*, plaque *f*; (*fig*) obstacle *m*; mesure *f* d'exclusion; (*pub*) bar *m*; (*counter*: *in pub*) comptoir *m*, bar; (MUS) mesure *f* // *vt* (*road*) barrer; (*window*) munir de barreaux; (*person*) exclure; (*activity*) interdire; **~ of soap** savonnette *f*; **the B~** (LAW) le barreau; **~ none** sans exception.

Barbados [bɑː'beɪdɔs] *n* Barbade *f*.

barbaric [bɑː'bærɪk] *a* barbare.

barbarous ['bɑːbərəs] *a* barbare, cruel(le).

barbecue ['bɑːbɪkjuː] *n* barbecue *m*.

barbed wire ['bɑːbd'waɪə*] *n* fil *m* de fer barbelé.

barber ['bɑːbə*] *n* coiffeur *m* (pour hommes).

barbiturate [bɑː'bɪtjurɪt] *n* barbiturique *m*.

bare [bɛə*] *a* nu(e) // *vt* mettre à nu, dénuder; (*teeth*) montrer; **the ~ essentials** le strict nécessaire; **~back** *ad* à cru, sans selle; **~faced** *a* impudent(e), effronté(e); **~foot** *a,ad* nu-pieds, (les) pieds nus; **~headed** *a,ad* nu-tête, (la) tête nue; **~ly** *ad* à peine.

bargain ['bɑ:gɪn] *n* (*transaction*) marché *m*; (*good buy*) affaire *f*, occasion *f* // *vi* (*haggle*) marchander; (*trade*) négocier, traiter; **into the ~** par-dessus le marché.
barge [bɑ:dʒ] *n* péniche *f*; **to ~ in** *vi* (*walk in*) faire irruption; (*interrupt talk*) intervenir mal à propos; **to ~ into** *vt fus* rentrer dans.
baritone ['bærɪtəun] *n* baryton *m*.
bark [bɑ:k] *n* (*of tree*) écorce *f*; (*of dog*) aboiement *m* // *vi* aboyer.
barley ['bɑ:lɪ] *n* orge *f*.
barmaid ['bɑ:meɪd] *n* serveuse *f* (*de bar*), barmaid *f*.
barman ['bɑ:mən] *n* serveur *m* (*de bar*), barman *m*.
barmy ['bɑ:mɪ] *a* (*col*) timbré(e), cinglé(e).
barn [bɑ:n] *n* grange *f*.
barnacle ['bɑ:nəkl] *n* anatife *m*, bernache *f*.
barometer [bə'rɔmɪtə*] *n* baromètre *m*.
baron ['bærən] *n* baron *m*; **~ess** baronne *f*.
barracks ['bærəks] *npl* caserne *f*.
barrage ['bærɑ:ʒ] *n* (MIL) tir *m* de barrage; (*dam*) barrage *m*.
barrel ['bærəl] *n* tonneau *m*; (*of gun*) canon *m*; **~ organ** *n* orgue *m* de Barbarie.
barren ['bærən] *a* stérile; (*hills*) aride.
barricade [bærɪ'keɪd] *n* barricade *f* // *vt* barricader.
barrier ['bærɪə*] *n* barrière *f*.
barring ['bɑ:rɪŋ] *prep* sauf.
barrister ['bærɪstə*] *n* avocat (plaidant).
barrow ['bærəu] *n* (*cart*) charrette *f* à bras.
bartender ['bɑ:tɛndə*] *n* (*US*) barman *m*.
barter ['bɑ:tə*] *n* échange *m*, troc *m* // *vt*: **to ~ sth for** échanger qch contre.
base [beɪs] *n* base *f* // *vt*: **to ~ sth on** baser *or* fonder qch sur // *a* vil(e), bas(se); **coffee-~d** à base de café; **a Paris-~d firm** une maison opérant de Paris *or* dont le siège est à Paris; **~ball** *n* base-ball *m*; **~ment** *n* sous-sol *m*.
bases ['beɪsi:z] *npl of* **basis**; ['beɪsɪz] *npl of* **base**.
bash [bæʃ] *vt* (*col*) frapper, cogner; **~ed in** *a* enfoncé(e), défoncé(e).
bashful ['bæʃful] *a* timide; modeste.
bashing ['bæʃɪŋ] *n* (*col*) raclée *f*.
basic ['beɪsɪk] *a* fondamental(e), de base; réduit(e) au minimum, rudimentaire; **~ally** [-lɪ] *ad* fondamentalement, à la base; en fait, au fond.
basil ['bæzl] *n* basilic *m*.
basin ['beɪsn] *n* (*vessel, also* GEO) cuvette *f*, bassin *m*; (*for food*) bol *m*; (*also*: **wash~**) lavabo *m*.
basis, *pl* **bases** ['beɪsɪs, -si:z] *n* base *f*.
bask [bɑ:sk] *vi*: **to ~ in the sun** se chauffer au soleil.
basket ['bɑ:skɪt] *n* corbeille *f*; (*with handle*) panier *m*; **~ball** *n* basket-ball *m*.
bass [beɪs] *n* (MUS) basse *f*; **~ clef** *n* clé *f* de fa.
bassoon [bə'su:n] *n* basson *m*.
bastard ['bɑ:stəd] *n* enfant naturel(le), bâtard/e; (*col!*) salaud *m(!)*.
baste [beɪst] *vt* (CULIN) arroser; (SEWING) bâtir, faufiler.
bastion ['bæstɪən] *n* bastion *m*.
bat [bæt] *n* chauve-souris *f*; (*for baseball etc*) batte *f*; (*for table tennis*) raquette *f*; **off one's own ~** de sa propre initiative; **he didn't ~ an eyelid** il n'a pas sourcillé *or* bronché.
batch [bætʃ] *n* (*of bread*) fournée *f*; (*of papers*) liasse *f*.
bated ['beɪtɪd] *a*: **with ~ breath** en retenant son souffle.
bath [bɑ:θ, *pl* bɑ:ðz] *n see also* **baths**; bain *m*; (*bathtub*) baignoire *f* // *vt* baigner, donner un bain à; **to have a ~** prendre un bain; **~chair** *n* fauteuil roulant.
bathe [beɪð] *vi* se baigner // *vt* baigner; **~r** *n* baigneur/euse.
bathing ['beɪðɪŋ] *n* baignade *f*; **~ cap** *n* bonnet *m* de bain; **~ costume** *n* maillot *m* (de bain).
bath: **~mat** *n* tapis *m* de bain; **~room** *n* salle *f* de bains; **~s** *npl* établissement *m* de bains(-douches); **~ towel** *n* serviette *f* de bain.
batman ['bætmən] *n* (MIL) ordonnance *f*.
baton ['bætən] *n* bâton *m*; (MUS) baguette *f*; (*club*) matraque *f*.
battalion [bə'tælɪən] *n* bataillon *m*.
batter ['bætə*] *vt* battre // *n* pâte *f* à frire; **~ed** *a* (*hat, pan*) cabossé(e); **~ed wife/child** épouse/enfant maltraité(e) *or* martyr(e); **~ing ram** *n* bélier *m* (*fig*).
battery ['bætərɪ] *n* batterie *f*; (*of torch*) pile *f*.
battle ['bætl] *n* bataille *f*, combat *m* // *vi* se battre, lutter; **~ dress** *n* tenue *f* de campagne *or* d'assaut; **~field** *n* champ *m* de bataille; **~ments** *npl* remparts *mpl*; **~ship** *n* cuirassé *m*.
baulk [bɔ:lk] *vi* = **balk**.
bawdy ['bɔ:dɪ] *a* paillard(e).
bawl [bɔ:l] *vi* hurler, brailler.
bay [beɪ] *n* (*of sea*) baie *f*; **to hold sb at ~** tenir qn à distance *or* en échec.
bayonet ['beɪənɪt] *n* baïonnette *f*.
bay window ['beɪ'wɪndəu] *n* baie vitrée.
bazaar [bə'zɑ:*] *n* bazar *m*; vente *f* de charité.
bazooka [bə'zu:kə] *n* bazooka *m*.
b. & b., B. & B. *abbr see* **bed**.
BBC *n abbr of British Broadcasting Corporation* (*office de la radiodiffusion et télévision britannique*).
B.C. *ad* (*abbr of before Christ*) av. J.-C.
BCG *n* (*abbr of Bacillus Calmette-Guérin*) BCG.
be, *pt* **was, were,** *pp* **been** [bi:, wɔz, wə:*, bi:n] *vi* être; **how are you?** comment allez-vous?; **I am warm** j'ai chaud; **it is cold** il fait froid; **how much is it?** combien ça coûte?; **he is four (years old)** il a quatre ans; **2 and 2 are 4** 2 et 2 font 4; **where have you been?** où êtes-vous allé(s)?; où étiez-vous?.
beach [bi:tʃ] *n* plage *f* // *vt* échouer; **~wear** *n* tenues *fpl* de plage.
beacon ['bi:kən] *n* (*lighthouse*) fanal *m*; (*marker*) balise *f*.
bead [bi:d] *n* perle *f*.
beak [bi:k] *n* bec *m*.
beaker ['bi:kə*] *n* gobelet *m*.

beam [bi:m] *n* poutre *f*; (*of light*) rayon *m* // *vi* rayonner; **~ing** *a* (*sun, smile*) radieux(euse).
bean [bi:n] *n* haricot *m*; (*of coffee*) grain *m*.
bear [bɛə*] *n* ours *m* // *vb* (*pt* **bore,** *pp* **borne** [bɔ:*, bɔ:n]) *vt* porter; (*endure*) supporter // *vi*: **to ~ right/left** obliquer à droite/gauche, se diriger vers la droite/gauche; **to ~ the responsibility of** assumer la responsabilité de; **to ~ comparison with** soutenir la comparaison avec; **~able** *a* supportable.
beard [bɪəd] *n* barbe *f*; **~ed** *a* barbu(e).
bearer ['bɛərə*] *n* porteur *m*.
bearing ['bɛərɪŋ] *n* maintien *m*, allure *f*; (*connection*) rapport *m*; **(ball) ~s** *npl* roulements *mpl* (à billes); **to take a ~** faire le point; **to find one's ~s** s'orienter.
beast [bi:st] *n* bête *f*; (*col*): **he's a ~** c'est une brute; **~ly** *a* infect(e).
beat [bi:t] *n* battement *m*; (MUS) temps *m*; mesure *f*; (*of policeman*) ronde *f* // *vt* (*pt* **beat,** *pp* **beaten**) battre; **off the ~en track** hors des chemins *or* sentiers battus; **to ~ about the bush** tourner autour du pot; **to ~ time** battre la mesure; **to ~ off** *vt* repousser; **to ~ up** *vt* (*col: person*) tabasser; (*eggs*) battre; **~er** *n* (*for eggs, cream*) fouet *m*, batteur *m*; **~ing** *n* raclée *f*.
beautician [bju:'tɪʃən] *n* esthéticien/ne.
beautiful ['bju:tɪful] *a* beau(belle); **~ly** *ad* admirablement.
beautify ['bju:tɪfaɪ] *vt* embellir.
beauty ['bju:tɪ] *n* beauté *f*; **~ salon** *n* institut *m* de beauté; **~ spot** *n* grain *m* de beauté; (TOURISM) site naturel (d'une grande beauté).
beaver ['bi:və*] *n* castor *m*.
becalmed [bɪ'kɑ:md] *a* immobilisé(e) par le calme plat.
became [bɪ'keɪm] *pt of* **become**.
because [bɪ'kɔz] *cj* parce que; **~ of** *prep* à cause de.
beckon ['bɛkən] *vt* (*also*: **~ to**) faire signe (de venir) à.
become [bɪ'kʌm] *vt* (*irg*: *like* **come**) devenir; **to ~ fat/thin** grossir/maigrir; **what has ~ of him?** qu'est-il devenu?
becoming [bɪ'kʌmɪŋ] *a* (*behaviour*) convenable, bienséant(e); (*clothes*) seyant(e).
bed [bɛd] *n* lit *m*; (*of flowers*) parterre *m*; (*of coal, clay*) couche *f*; **to go to ~** aller se coucher; **~ and breakfast (b. & b.)** *n* (*terms*) chambre et petit déjeuner; **~clothes** *npl* couvertures *fpl* et draps *mpl*; **~cover** *n* couvre-lit *m*, dessus-de-lit *m*; **~ding** *n* literie *f*.
bedlam ['bɛdləm] *n* chahut *m*, cirque *m*.
bedpost ['bɛdpəust] *n* colonne *f* de lit.
bedraggled [bɪ'drægld] *a* dépenaillé(e), les vêtements en désordre.
bed: **~ridden** *a* cloué(e) au lit; **~room** *n* chambre *f* (à coucher); **~side** *n*: **at sb's ~side** au chevet de qn; **~side book** *n* livre *m* de chevet; **~sit(ter)** *n* chambre meublée, studio *m*; **~spread** *n* couvre-lit *m*, dessus-de-lit *m*.
bee [bi:] *n* abeille *f*.
beech [bi:tʃ] *n* hêtre *m*.
beef [bi:f] *n* bœuf *m*.
beehive ['bi:haɪv] *n* ruche *f*.
beeline ['bi:laɪn] *n*: **to make a ~ for** se diriger tout droit vers.
been [bi:n] *pp of* **be.**
beer [bɪə*] *n* bière *f*.
beetle ['bi:tl] *n* scarabée *m*; coléoptère *m*.
beetroot ['bi:tru:t] *n* betterave *f*.
befall [bɪ'fɔ:l] *vi(vt)* (*irg*: *like* **fall**) advenir (à).
befit [bɪ'fɪt] *vt* seoir à.
before [bɪ'fɔ:*] *prep* (*of time*) avant; (*of space*) devant // *cj* avant que + *sub*; avant de // *ad* avant; **the week ~** la semaine précédente *or* d'avant; **I've seen it ~** je l'ai déjà vu; **I've never seen it ~** c'est la première fois que je le vois; **~hand** *ad* au préalable, à l'avance.
befriend [bɪ'frɛnd] *vt* venir en aide à; traiter en ami.
beg [bɛg] *vi* mendier // *vt* mendier; (*favour*) quémander, solliciter; (*entreat*) supplier.
began [bɪ'gæn] *pt of* **begin**.
beggar ['bɛgə*] *n* (*also*: **~man, ~woman**) mendiant/e.
begin, *pt* **began,** *pp* **begun** [bɪ'gɪn, -'gæn, -'gʌn] *vt, vi* commencer; **~ner** *n* débutant/e; **~ning** *n* commencement *m*, début *m*.
begrudge [bɪ'grʌdʒ] *vt*: **to ~ sb sth** envier qch à qn; donner qch à contrecœur *or* à regret à qn; **I don't ~ doing it** je le fais volontiers.
begun [bɪ'gʌn] *pp of* **begin**.
behalf [bɪ'hɑ:f] *n*: **on ~ of** de la part de; au nom de; pour le compte de.
behave [bɪ'heɪv] *vi* se conduire, se comporter; (*well*: *also*: **~ o.s.**) se conduire bien *or* comme il faut.
behaviour, behavior (*US*) [bɪ'heɪvjə*] *n* comportement *m*, conduite *f* (*the latter often from a moral point of view, the former being more objective*).
beheld [bɪ'hɛld] *pt,pp of* **behold**.
behind [bɪ'haɪnd] *prep* derrière; (*time*) en retard sur // *ad* derrière; en retard // *n* derrière *m*; **~ the scenes** dans les coulisses.
behold [bɪ'həuld] *vt* (*irg*: *like* **hold**) apercevoir, voir.
beige [beɪʒ] *a* beige.
being ['bi:ɪŋ] *n* être *m*; **to come into ~** prendre naissance.
belated [bɪ'leɪtɪd] *a* tardif(ive).
belch [bɛltʃ] *vi* avoir un renvoi, roter // *vt* (*gen*: **~ out**: *smoke etc*) vomir, cracher.
belfry ['bɛlfrɪ] *n* beffroi *m*.
Belgian ['bɛldʒən] *a* belge, de Belgique // *n* Belge *m/f*.
Belgium ['bɛldʒəm] *n* Belgique *f*.
belie [bɪ'laɪ] *vt* démentir.
belief [bɪ'li:f] *n* (*opinion*) conviction *f*; (*trust, faith*) foi *f*; (*acceptance as true*) croyance *f*.
believable [bɪ'li:vəbl] *a* croyable.
believe [bɪ'li:v] *vt,vi* croire; **~r** *n* croyant/e.
belittle [bɪ'lɪtl] *vt* déprécier, rabaisser.

bell [bɛl] *n* cloche *f*; (*small*) clochette *f*, grelot *m*; (*on door*) sonnette *f*; (*electric*) sonnerie *f*; **~-bottomed trousers** *npl* pantalon *m* à pattes d'éléphant.
belligerent [bɪ'lɪdʒərənt] *a* (*at war*) belligérant(e); (*fig*) agressif(ive).
bellow ['bɛləu] *vi* mugir // *vt* (*orders*) hurler.
bellows ['bɛləuz] *npl* soufflet *m*.
belly ['bɛlɪ] *n* ventre *m*; **to ~ache** *vi* (*col*) ronchonner; **~button** *n* nombril *m*.
belong [bɪ'lɔŋ] *vi*: **to ~ to** appartenir à; (*club etc*) faire partie de; **this book ~s here** ce livre va ici, la place de ce livre est ici; **~ings** *npl* affaires *fpl*, possessions *fpl*.
beloved [bɪ'lʌvɪd] *a* (bien-)aimé(e), chéri(e) // *n* bien-aimé/e.
below [bɪ'ləu] *prep* sous, au-dessous de // *ad* en dessous; en contre-bas; **see ~** voir plus bas *or* plus loin *or* ci-dessous.
belt [bɛlt] *n* ceinture *f*; (TECH) courroie *f* // *vt* (*thrash*) donner une raclée à // *vi* (*col*) filer (à toutes jambes).
bench [bɛntʃ] *n* banc *m*; (*in workshop*) établi *m*; **the B~** (LAW) la magistrature, la Cour.
bend [bɛnd] *vb* (*pt,pp* **bent** [bɛnt]) *vt* courber; (*leg, arm*) plier // *vi* se courber // *n* (*in road*) virage *m*, tournant *m*; (*in pipe, river*) coude *m*; **to ~ down** *vi* se baisser; **to ~ over** *vi* se pencher.
beneath [bɪ'ni:θ] *prep* sous, au-dessous de; (*unworthy of*) indigne de // *ad* dessous, au-dessous, en bas.
benefactor ['bɛnɪfæktə*] *n* bienfaiteur *m*.
benefactress ['bɛnɪfæktrɪs] *n* bienfaitrice *f*.
beneficial [bɛnɪ'fɪʃəl] *a* salutaire; avantageux(euse).
benefit ['bɛnɪfɪt] *n* avantage *m*, profit *m*; (*allowance of money*) allocation *f* // *vt* faire du bien à, profiter à // *vi*: **he'll ~ from it** cela lui fera du bien, il y gagnera *or* s'en trouvera bien; **~ performance** *n* représentation *f or* gala *m* de bienfaisance.
Benelux ['bɛnɪlʌks] *n* Bénélux *m*.
benevolent [bɪ'nɛvələnt] *a* bienveillant(e).
bent [bɛnt] *pt,pp of* **bend** // *n* inclination *f*, penchant *m* // *a* (*dishonest*) véreux(euse); **to be ~ on** être résolu(e) à.
bequeath [bɪ'kwi:ð] *vt* léguer.
bequest [bɪ'kwɛst] *n* legs *m*.
bereaved [bɪ'ri:vd] *n*: **the ~** la famille du disparu.
bereavement [bɪ'ri:vmənt] *n* deuil *m*.
beret ['bɛreɪ] *n* béret *m*.
Bermuda [bə:'mju:də] *n* Bermudes *fpl*.
berry ['bɛrɪ] *n* baie *f*.
berserk [bə'sə:k] *a*: **to go ~** être pris(e) d'une rage incontrôlable; se déchaîner.
berth [bə:θ] *n* (*bed*) couchette *f*; (*for ship*) poste *m* d'amarrage; mouillage *m* // *vi* (*in harbour*) venir à quai; (*at anchor*) mouiller.
beseech, *pt,pp* **besought** [bɪ'si:tʃ, -'sɔ:t] *vt* implorer, supplier.
beset, *pt,pp* **beset** [bɪ'sɛt] *vt* assaillir.
beside [bɪ'saɪd] *prep* à côté de; **to be ~ o.s. (with anger)** être hors de soi.
besides [bɪ'saɪdz] *ad* en outre, de plus // *prep* en plus de; excepté.
besiege [bɪ'si:dʒ] *vt* (*town*) assiéger; (*fig*) assaillir.
besought [bɪ'sɔ:t] *pt,pp of* **beseech.**
bespectacled [bɪ'spɛktɪkld] *a* à lunettes.
best [bɛst] *a* meilleur(e) // *ad* le mieux; **the ~ part of** (*quantity*) le plus clair de, la plus grande partie de; **at ~** au mieux; **to make the ~ of sth** s'accommoder de qch (du mieux que l'on peut); **to the ~ of my knowledge** pour autant que je sache; **to the ~ of my ability** du mieux que je pourrai; **~ man** *n* garçon *m* d'honneur.
bestow [bɪ'stəu] *vt* accorder; (*title*) conférer.
bestseller ['bɛst'sɛlə*] *n* bestseller *m*, succès *m* de librairie.
bet [bɛt] *n* pari *m* // *vt,vi* (*pt,pp* **bet** *or* **betted**) parier.
betray [bɪ'treɪ] *vt* trahir; **~al** *n* trahison *f*.
better ['bɛtə*] *a* meilleur(e) // *ad* mieux // *vt* améliorer // *n*: **to get the ~ of** triompher de, l'emporter sur; **you had ~ do it** vous feriez mieux de le faire; **he thought ~ of it** il s'est ravisé; **to get ~** aller mieux; s'améliorer; **~ off** *a* plus à l'aise financièrement; (*fig*): **you'd be ~ off this way** vous vous en trouveriez mieux ainsi, ce serait mieux *or* plus pratique ainsi.
betting ['bɛtɪŋ] *n* paris *mpl*; **~ shop** *n* bureau *m* de paris.
between [bɪ'twi:n] *prep* entre // *ad* au milieu; dans l'intervalle.
bevel ['bɛvəl] *n* (*also*: **~ edge**) biseau *m*.
beverage ['bɛvərɪdʒ] *n* boisson *f* (*gén sans alcool*).
bevy ['bɛvɪ] *n*: **a ~ of** un essaim *or* une volée de.
beware [bɪ'wɛə*] *vt,vi*: **to ~ (of)** prendre garde (à).
bewildered [bɪ'wɪldəd] *a* dérouté(e), ahuri(e).
bewitching [bɪ'wɪtʃɪŋ] *a* enchanteur(teresse).
beyond [bɪ'jɔnd] *prep* (*in space*) au-delà de; (*exceeding*) au-dessus de // *ad* au-delà; **~ doubt** hors de doute; **~ repair** irréparable.
bias ['baɪəs] *n* (*prejudice*) préjugé *m*, parti pris; (*preference*) prévention *f*; **~(s)ed** *a* partial(e), montrant un parti pris.
bib [bɪb] *n* bavoir *m*, bavette *f*.
Bible ['baɪbl] *n* Bible *f*.
bibliography [bɪblɪ'ɔgrəfɪ] *n* bibliographie *f*.
bicker ['bɪkə*] *vi* se chamailler.
bicycle ['baɪsɪkl] *n* bicyclette *f*.
bid [bɪd] *n* offre *f*; (*at auction*) enchère *f*; (*attempt*) tentative *f* // *vb* (*pt* **bade** [bæd] *or* **bid,** *pp* **bidden** ['bɪdn] *or* **bid**) *vi* faire une enchère *or* offre // *vt* faire une enchère *or* offre de; **to ~ sb good day** souhaiter le bonjour à qn; **~der** *n*: **the highest ~der** le plus offrant; **~ding** *n* enchères *fpl*.
bide [baɪd] *vt*: **to ~ one's time** attendre son heure.

bier [bɪə*] *n* bière *f*.
big [bɪg] *a* grand(e) ; gros(se).
bigamy ['bɪgəmɪ] *n* bigamie *f*.
bigheaded ['bɪg'hɛdɪd] *a* prétentieux(euse).
big-hearted ['bɪg'hɑ:tɪd] *a* au grand cœur.
bigot ['bɪgət] *n* fanatique *m/f*, sectaire *m/f*; **~ed** *a* fanatique, sectaire ; **~ry** *n* fanatisme *m*, sectarisme *m*.
bigwig ['bɪgwɪg] *n* (*col*) grosse légume, huile *f*.
bike [baɪk] *n* vélo *m*, bécane *f*.
bikini [bɪ'ki:nɪ] *n* bikini *m*.
bile [baɪl] *n* bile *f*.
bilingual [baɪ'lɪŋgwəl] *a* bilingue.
bilious ['bɪlɪəs] *a* bilieux(euse) ; (*fig*) maussade, irritable.
bill [bɪl] *n* note *f*, facture *f*; (POL) projet *m* de loi ; (*US*: *banknote*) billet *m* (de banque) ; (*of bird*) bec *m* ; **to fit** *or* **fill the ~** (*fig*) faire l'affaire.
billet ['bɪlɪt] *n* cantonnement *m* (chez l'habitant).
billfold ['bɪlfəuld] *n* (*US*) portefeuille *m*.
billiards ['bɪlɪədz] *n* (jeu *m* de) billard *m*.
billion ['bɪlɪən] *n* (*Brit*) billion *m* (*million de millions*) ; (*US*) milliard *m*.
billy goat ['bɪlɪgəut] *n* bouc *m*.
bin [bɪn] *n* boîte *f*; (*also*: **dust~**) poubelle *f*; (*for coal*) coffre *m* ; **bread~** *n* boîte *f* *or* huche *f* à pain.
bind, *pt,pp* **bound** [baɪnd, baund] *vt* attacher ; (*book*) relier ; (*oblige*) obliger, contraindre ; **~ing** *n* (*of book*) reliure *f* // *a* (*contract*) constituant une obligation.
bingo ['bɪŋgəu] *n sorte de jeu de loto pratiqué dans des établissements publics et connaissant une grande vogue en Grande-Bretagne.*
binoculars [bɪ'nɔkjuləz] *npl* jumelles *fpl*.
bio... [baɪə'...] *prefix*: **~chemistry** *n* biochimie *f*; **~graphic(al)** *a* biographique ; **~graphy** [baɪ'ɔgrəfɪ] *n* biographie *f*; **~logical** *a* biologique ; **~logist** [baɪ'ɔlədʒɪst] *n* biologiste *m/f*; **~logy** [baɪ'ɔlədʒɪ] *n* biologie *f*.
birch [bə:tʃ] *n* bouleau *m*.
bird [bə:d] *n* oiseau *m* ; (*col*: *girl*) nana *f*; **~'s-eye view** *n* vue *f* à vol d'oiseau ; (*fig*) vue d'ensemble *or* générale ; **~ watcher** *n* ornithologue *m/f* amateur.
birth [bə:θ] *n* naissance *f*; **~ certificate** *n* acte *m* de naissance ; **~ control** *n* limitation *f* des naissances ; méthode(s) contraceptive(s) ; **~day** *n* anniversaire *m* ; **~place** *n* lieu *m* de naissance ; **~ rate** *n* (taux *m* de) natalité *f*.
biscuit ['bɪskɪt] *n* biscuit *m*.
bisect [baɪ'sɛkt] *vt* couper *or* diviser en deux.
bishop ['bɪʃəp] *n* évêque *m*.
bit [bɪt] *pt of* **bite** // *n* morceau *m* ; (*of tool*) mèche *f*; (*of horse*) mors *m* ; **a ~ of** un peu de ; **a ~ mad/dangerous** un peu fou/risqué.
bitch [bɪtʃ] *n* (*dog*) chienne *f*; (*col!*) salope *f* (!), garce *f*.
bite [baɪt] *vt,vi* (*pt* **bit** [bɪt], *pp* **bitten** ['bɪtn]) mordre // *n* morsure *f*; (*insect ~*) piqûre *f*; (*mouthful*) bouchée *f*; **let's have a ~ (to eat)** mangeons un morceau ; **to ~ one's nails** se ronger les ongles.
biting ['baɪtɪŋ] *a* mordant(e).
bitten ['bɪtn] *pp of* **bite**.
bitter ['bɪtə*] *a* amer(ère) ; (*wind, criticism*) cinglant(e) // *n* (*beer*) bière *f* (*à forte teneur en houblon*) ; **to the ~ end** jusqu'au bout ; **~ness** *n* amertume *f*; goût amer ; **~sweet** *a* aigre-doux(douce).
bivouac ['bɪvuæk] *n* bivouac *m*.
bizarre [bɪ'zɑ:*] *a* bizarre.
blab [blæb] *vi* jaser, trop parler // *vt* (*also*: **~ out**) laisser échapper, aller raconter.
black [blæk] *a* noir(e) // *n* noir *m* // *vt* (*shoes*) cirer ; (INDUSTRY) boycotter ; **to give sb a ~ eye** pocher l'œil à qn, faire un œil au beurre noir à qn ; **~ and blue** *a* couvert(e) de bleus ; **~berry** *n* mûre *f*; **~bird** *n* merle *m* ; **~board** *n* tableau noir ; **~currant** *n* cassis *m* ; **~en** *vt* noircir ; **~leg** *n* briseur *m* de grève, jaune *m* ; **~list** *n* liste noire ; **~mail** *n* chantage *m* // *vt* faire chanter, soumettre au chantage ; **~mailer** *n* maître-chanteur *m* ; **~ market** *n* marché noir ; **~out** *n* panne *f* d'électricité ; (*fainting*) syncope *f*; (*in wartime*) black-out *m* ; **the B~ Sea** *n* la mer Noire ; **~ sheep** *n* brebis galeuse ; **~smith** *n* forgeron *m*.
bladder ['blædə*] *n* vessie *f*.
blade [bleɪd] *n* lame *f*; (*of oar*) plat *m* ; **~ of grass** brin *m* d'herbe.
blame [bleɪm] *n* faute *f*, blâme *m* // *vt*: **to ~ sb/sth for sth** attribuer à qn/qch la responsabilité de qch ; reprocher qch à qn/qch ; **who's to ~?** qui est le fautif *or* coupable *or* responsable? ; **~less** *a* irréprochable.
bland [blænd] *a* affable ; (*taste*) doux(douce), fade.
blank [blæŋk] *a* blanc(blanche) ; (*look*) sans expression, dénué(e) d'expression // *n* espace *m* vide, blanc *m* ; (*cartridge*) cartouche *f* à blanc.
blanket ['blæŋkɪt] *n* couverture *f*.
blare [blɛə*] *vi* (*brass band, horns, radio*) beugler.
blarney ['blɑ:nɪ] *n* boniment *m*.
blasé ['blɑ:zeɪ] *a* blasé(e).
blasphemous ['blæsfɪməs] *a* (*words*) blasphématoire ; (*person*) blasphémateur(trice).
blasphemy ['blæsfɪmɪ] *n* blasphème *m*.
blast [blɑ:st] *n* souffle *m* ; explosion *f* // *vt* faire sauter *or* exploser ; **~-off** *n* (SPACE) lancement *m*.
blatant ['bleɪtənt] *a* flagrant(e), criant(e).
blaze [bleɪz] *n* (*fire*) incendie *m* ; (*fig*) flamboiement *m* // *vi* (*fire*) flamber ; (*fig*) flamboyer, resplendir // *vt*: **to ~ a trail** (*fig*) montrer la voie.
blazer ['bleɪzə*] *n* blazer *m*.
bleach [bli:tʃ] *n* (*also*: **household ~**) eau *f* de Javel // *vt* (*linen*) blanchir ; **~ed** *a* (*hair*) oxygéné(e), décoloré(e).
bleak [bli:k] *a* morne, désolé(e).
bleary-eyed ['blɪərɪ'aɪd] *a* aux yeux pleins de sommeil.
bleat [bli:t] *n* bêlement *m* // *vi* bêler.
bleed, *pt,pp* **bled** [bli:d, blɛd] *vt, vi*

saigner; **my nose is ~ing** je saigne du nez.

blemish ['blɛmɪʃ] *n* défaut *m*; (*on reputation*) tache *f*.

blend [blɛnd] *n* mélange *m* // *vt* mélanger // *vi* (*colours etc*) se mélanger, se fondre, s'allier.

bless, *pt,pp* **blessed** *or* **blest** [blɛs, blɛst] *vt* bénir; **to be ~ed with** avoir le bonheur de jouir de *or* d'avoir; **~ing** *n* bénédiction *f*; bienfait *m*.

blew [blu:] *pt of* **blow**.

blight [blaɪt] *n* (*of plants*) rouille *f* // *vt* (*hopes etc*) anéantir, briser.

blimey ['blaɪmɪ] *excl* (*col*) mince alors!

blind [blaɪnd] *a* aveugle // *n* (*for window*) store *m* // *vt* aveugler; **to turn a ~ eye (on** *or* **to)** fermer les yeux (sur); **~ alley** *n* impasse *f*; **~ corner** *n* virage *m* sans visibilité; **~fold** *n* bandeau *m* // *a,ad* les yeux bandés // *vt* bander les yeux à; **~ly** *ad* aveuglément; **~ness** *n* cécité *f*; (*fig*) aveuglement *m*; **~ spot** *n* (AUT *etc*) angle *m* aveugle; (*fig*) angle mort.

blink [blɪŋk] *vi* cligner des yeux; (*light*) clignoter; **~ers** *npl* œillères *fpl*.

blinking ['blɪŋkɪŋ] *a* (*col*): **this ~...** ce fichu *or* sacré ... .

bliss [blɪs] *n* félicité *f*, bonheur *m* sans mélange.

blister ['blɪstə*] *n* (*on skin*) ampoule *f*, cloque *f*; (*on paintwork*) boursouflure *f* // *vi* (*paint*) se boursoufler, se cloquer.

blithe [blaɪð] *a* joyeux(euse), allègre.

blithering ['blɪðərɪŋ] *a* (*col*): **this ~ idiot** cet espèce d'idiot.

blitz [blɪts] *n* bombardement (aérien).

blizzard ['blɪzəd] *n* blizzard *m*, tempête *f* de neige.

bloated ['bləutɪd] *a* (*face*) bouffi(e); (*stomach*) gonflé(e).

blob [blɔb] *n* (*drop*) goutte *f*; (*stain, spot*) tache *f*.

block [blɔk] *n* bloc *m*; (*in pipes*) obstruction *f*; (*toy*) cube *m*; (*of buildings*) pâté *m* (de maisons) // *vt* bloquer; **~ade** [-'keɪd] *n* blocus *m* // *vt* faire le blocus de; **~age** *n* obstruction *f*; **~head** *n* imbécile *m/f*; **~ of flats** *n* immeuble (locatif); **~ letters** *npl* majuscules *fpl*.

bloke [bləuk] *n* (*col*) type *m*.

blonde [blɔnd] *a,n* blond(e).

blood [blʌd] *n* sang *m*; **~ donor** *n* donneur/euse de sang; **~ group** *n* groupe sanguin; **~less** *a* (*victory*) sans effusion de sang; (*pale*) anémié(e); **~ poisoning** *n* empoisonnement *m* du sang; **~ pressure** *n* tension *f* (artérielle); **~shed** *n* effusion *f* de sang, carnage *m*; **~shot** *a*: **~shot eyes** yeux injectés de sang; **~stained** *a* taché(e) de sang; **~stream** *n* sang *m*, système sanguin; **~thirsty** *a* sanguinaire; **~ transfusion** *n* transfusion *f* de sang; **~y** *a* sanglant(e); (*col!*): **this ~y ...** ce foutu..., ce putain de... (!); **~y strong/good** (*col!*) vachement *or* sacrément fort/bon; **~y-minded** *a* (*col*) contrariant(e), obstiné(e).

bloom [blu:m] *n* fleur *f*; (*fig*) épanouissement *m* // *vi* être en fleur; (*fig*) s'épanouir; être florissant; **~ing** *a* (*col*): **this ~ing...** ce fichu *or* sacré... .

blossom ['blɔsəm] *n* fleur(s) *f(pl)* // *vi* être en fleurs; (*fig*) s'épanouir.

blot [blɔt] *n* tache *f* // *vt* tacher; (*ink*) sécher; **to ~ out** *vt* (*memories*) effacer; (*view*) cacher, masquer; (*nation, city*) annihiler.

blotchy ['blɔtʃɪ] *a* (*complexion*) couvert(e) de marbrures.

blotting paper ['blɔtɪŋpeɪpə*] *n* buvard *m*.

blouse [blauz] *n* (*feminine garment*) chemisier *m*, corsage *m*.

blow [bləu] *n* coup *m* // *vb* (*pt* **blew,** *pp* **blown** [blu:, bləun]) *vi* souffler // *vt* (*glass*) souffler; (*fuse*) faire sauter; **to ~ one's nose** se moucher; **to ~ a whistle** siffler; **to ~ away** *vt* chasser, faire s'envoler; **to ~ down** *vt* faire tomber, renverser; **to ~ off** *vt* emporter; **to ~ off course** faire dévier; **to ~ out** *vi* éclater, sauter; **to ~ over** *vi* s'apaiser; **to ~ up** *vi* exploser, sauter // *vt* faire sauter; (*tyre*) gonfler; (PHOT) agrandir; **~lamp** *n* chalumeau *m*; **~-out** *n* (*of tyre*) éclatement *m*.

blubber ['blʌbə*] *n* blanc *m* de baleine // *vi* (*pej*) pleurer comme un veau.

bludgeon ['blʌdʒən] *n* gourdin *m*, trique *f*.

blue [blu:] *a* bleu(e); **~ film/joke** film *m*/histoire *f* pornographique; **to have the ~s** avoir le cafard; **~bell** *n* jacinthe *f* des bois; **~bottle** *n* mouche *f* à viande; **~ jeans** *npl* blue-jeans *mpl*; **~print** *n* (*fig*) projet *m*, plan directeur.

bluff [blʌf] *vi* bluffer // *n* bluff *m* // *a* (*person*) bourru(e), brusque; **to call sb's ~** mettre qn au défi d'exécuter ses menaces.

blunder ['blʌndə*] *n* gaffe *f*, bévue *f* // *vi* faire une gaffe *or* une bévue.

blunt [blʌnt] *a* émoussé(e), peu tranchant(e); (*person*) brusque, ne mâchant pas ses mots // *vt* émousser; **~ly** *ad* carrément, sans prendre de gants; **~ness** *n* (*of person*) brusquerie *f*, franchise brutale.

blur [blə:*] *n* tache *or* masse floue *or* confuse // *vt* brouiller, rendre flou.

blurt [blə:t]: **to ~ out** *vt* (*reveal*) lâcher; (*say*) balbutier, dire d'une voix entrecoupée.

blush [blʌʃ] *vi* rougir // *n* rougeur *f*.

blustering ['blʌstərɪŋ] *a* fanfaron(ne).

blustery ['blʌstərɪ] *a* (*weather*) à bourrasques.

B.O. *n* (*abbr of body odour*) odeurs corporelles.

boar [bɔ:*] *n* sanglier *m*.

board [bɔ:d] *n* planche *f*; (*on wall*) panneau *m*; (*committee*) conseil *m*, comité *m*; (*in firm*) conseil d'administration // *vt* (*ship*) monter à bord de; (*train*) monter dans; **~ and lodging** *n* chambre *f* avec pension; **full ~** pension complète; **with ~ and lodging** (*job*) logé nourri; **to go by the ~** (*fig*): **which goes by the ~** (*fig*) qu'on laisse tomber, qu'on abandonne; **to ~ up** *vt* (*door*) condamner (*au moyen de planches, de tôle*); **~er** *n* pensionnaire *m/f*; (SCOL) interne *m/f*, pensionnaire *m/f*; **~ing house** *n* pension *f*; **~ing school** *n* internat *m*, pensionnat *m* ; ~ **room** *n* salle *f* du conseil d'administration (*souvent symbole de pouvoir décisionnaire*).

boast [bəust] *vi* se vanter // *vt* s'enorgueillir de // *n* vantardise *f*; sujet *m* d'orgueil *or* de fierté ; **~ful** *a* vantard(e) ; **~fulness** *n* vantardise *f*.

boat [bəut] *n* bateau *m* ; (*small*) canot *m* ; barque *f* ; **to be in the same ~** (*fig*) être logé à la même enseigne ; **~er** *n* (*hat*) canotier *m* ; **~ing** *n* canotage *m* ; **~swain** ['bəusn] *n* maître *m* d'équipage.

bob [bɔb] *vi* (*boat, cork on water*: *also*: **~ up and down**) danser, se balancer // *n* (*col*) = **shilling** ; **to ~ up** *vi* surgir *or* apparaître brusquement.

bobbin ['bɔbɪn] *n* bobine *f* ; (*of sewing machine*) navette *f*.

bobby ['bɔbɪ] *n* (*col*) ≈ agent *m* (de police).

bobsleigh ['bɔbsleɪ] *n* bob *m*.

bodice ['bɔdɪs] *n* corsage *m*.

bodily ['bɔdɪlɪ] *a* corporel(le) // *ad* physiquement ; dans son entier *or* ensemble ; en personne.

body ['bɔdɪ] *n* corps *m* ; (*of car*) carrosserie *f* ; (*of plane*) fuselage *m* ; (*fig*: *society*) organe *m*, organisme *m* ; (*fig*: *quantity*) ensemble *m*, masse *f* ; (*of wine*) corps *m* ; **in a ~** en masse, ensemble ; **~guard** *n* garde *m* du corps ; **~ repairs** *npl* travaux *mpl* de carrosserie ; **~work** *n* carrosserie *f*.

bog [bɔg] *n* tourbière *f* // *vt*: **to get ~ged down** (*fig*) s'enliser.

boggle ['bɔgl] *vi*: **the mind ~s** c'est incroyable, on en reste sidéré.

bogie ['bəugɪ] *n* bogie *m*.

bogus ['bəugəs] *a* bidon *inv* ; fantôme.

boil [bɔɪl] *vt* (faire) bouillir // *vi* bouillir // *n* (MED) furoncle *m* ; **to come to the ~** bouillir ; **to ~ down** *vi* (*fig*): **to ~ down to** se réduire *or* ramener à ; **~er** *n* chaudière *f* ; **~er suit** *n* bleu *m* de travail, combinaison *f* ; **~ing hot** *a* brûlant(e), bouillant(e) ; **~ing point** *n* point *m* d'ébullition.

boisterous ['bɔɪstərəs] *a* bruyant(e), tapageur(euse).

bold [bəuld] *a* hardi(e), audacieux(euse) ; (*pej*) effronté(e) ; (*outline, colour*) franc(franche), tranché(e), marqué(e) ; **~ness** *n* hardiesse *f*, audace *f* ; aplomb *m*, effronterie *f* ; **~ type** *n* caractères *mpl* gras.

Bolivia [bə'lɪvɪə] *n* Bolivie *f*.

bollard ['bɔləd] *n* (NAUT) bitte *f* d'amarrage ; (AUT) borne lumineuse *or* de signalisation.

bolster ['bəulstə*] *n* traversin *m* ; **to ~ up** *vt* soutenir.

bolt [bəult] *n* verrou *m* ; (*with nut*) boulon *m* // *vt* verrouiller ; (*food*) engloutir // *vi* se sauver, filer (comme une flèche) ; **a ~ from the blue** (*fig*) un coup de tonnerre dans un ciel bleu.

bomb [bɔm] *n* bombe *f* // *vt* bombarder ; **~ard** [bɔm'bɑ:d] *vt* bombarder ; **~ardment** [bɔm'bɑ:dmənt] *n* bombardement *m*.

bombastic [bɔm'bæstɪk] *a* grandiloquent(e), pompeux(euse).

bomb disposal ['bɔmdɪspəuzl] *n*: **~ unit** section *f* de déminage.

bomber ['bɔmə*] *n* caporal *m* d'artillerie ; (AVIAT) bombardier *m*.

bombing ['bɔmɪŋ] *n* bombardement *m*.

bombshell ['bɔmʃɛl] *n* obus *m* ; (*fig*) bombe *f*.

bona fide ['bəunə'faɪdɪ] *a* de bonne foi ; (*offer*) sérieux(euse).

bond [bɔnd] *n* lien *m* ; (*binding promise*) engagement *m*, obligation *f* ; (FINANCE) obligation *f*.

bone [bəun] *n* os *m* ; (*of fish*) arête *f* // *vt* désosser ; ôter les arêtes de ; **~-dry** *a* absolument sec(sèche) ; **~r** *n* (*US*) gaffe *f*, bourde *f*.

bonfire ['bɔnfaɪə*] *n* feu *m* (de joie) ; (*for rubbish*) feu *m*.

bonnet ['bɔnɪt] *n* bonnet *m* ; (*Brit*: *of car*) capot *m*.

bonus ['bəunəs] *n* prime *f*, gratification *f*.

bony ['bəunɪ] *a* (*arm, face,* MED: *tissue*) osseux(euse) ; (*meat*) plein(e) d'os ; (*fish*) plein d'arêtes.

boo [bu:] *excl* hou!, peuh! // *vt* huer // *n* huée *f*.

booby trap ['bu:bɪtræp] *n* engin piégé.

book [buk] *n* livre *m* ; (*of stamps etc*) carnet *m* ; (COMM): **~s** comptes *mpl*, comptabilité *f* // *vt* (*ticket*) prendre ; (*seat, room*) réserver ; (*driver*) dresser un procès-verbal à ; (*football player*) prendre le nom de ; **~able** *a*: **seats are ~able** on peut réserver ses places ; **~case** *n* bibliothèque *f* (*meuble*) ; **~ ends** *npl* serre-livres *m inv* ; **~ing office** *n* bureau *m* de location ; **~-keeping** *n* comptabilité *f* ; **~let** *n* brochure *f* ; **~maker** *n* bookmaker *m* ; **~seller** *n* libraire *m/f* ; **~shop** *n* librairie *f* ; **~stall** *n* kiosque *m* à journaux ; **~store** *n* = **~shop.**

boom [bu:m] *n* (*noise*) grondement *m* ; (*busy period*) boom *m*, vague *f* de prospérité // *vi* gronder ; prospérer.

boomerang ['bu:məræŋ] *n* boomerang *m*.

boon [bu:n] *n* bénédiction *f*, grand avantage.

boorish ['buərɪʃ] *a* grossier(ère), rustre.

boost [bu:st] *n* stimulant *m*, remontant *m* ; (MED: *vaccine*) rappel *m* // *vt* stimuler.

boot [bu:t] *n* botte *f* ; (*for hiking*) chaussure *f* (de marche) ; (*for football etc*) soulier *m* ; (*Brit*: *of car*) coffre *m* ; **to ~** (*in addition*) par-dessus le marché, en plus.

booth [bu:ð] *n* (*at fair*) baraque (foraine) ; (*of cinema, telephone etc*) cabine *f* ; (*also*: **voting ~**) isoloir *m*.

booty ['bu:tɪ] *n* butin *m*.

booze [bu:z] (*col*) *n* boissons *fpl* alcooliques, alcool *m* // *vi* boire, picoler.

border ['bɔ:də*] *n* bordure *f* ; bord *m* ; (*of a country*) frontière *f* ; **the B~** *la frontière entre l'Écosse et l'Angleterre* ; **the B~s** *la région frontière entre l'Écosse et l'Angleterre* ; **to ~ on** *vt fus* être voisin(e) de, toucher à ; **~line** *n* (*fig*) ligne *f* de démarcation ; **~line case** *n* cas *m* limite.

bore [bɔ:*] *pt of* **bear** // *vt* (*hole*) percer ; (*person*) ennuyer, raser // *n* (*person*) raseur/euse ; (*of gun*) calibre *m* ; **~dom** *n* ennui *m*.

boring ['bɔ:rɪŋ] *a* ennuyeux(euse).
born [bɔ:n] *a*: **to be ~** naître ; **I was ~ in 1960** je suis né en 1960 ; **~ blind** aveugle de naissance ; **a ~ comedian** un comédien-né.
borne [bɔ:n] *pp of* **bear**.
borough ['bʌrə] *n* municipalité *f*.
borrow ['bɔrəu] *vt*: **to ~ sth (from sb)** emprunter qch (à qn).
borstal ['bɔ:stl] *n* ≈ maison *f* de correction.
bosom ['buzəm] *n* poitrine *f*; (*fig*) sein *m*; **~ friend** *n* ami/e intime.
boss [bɔs] *n* patron/ne // *vt* commander ; **~y** *a* autoritaire.
bosun ['bəusn] *n* maître *m* d'équipage.
botanical [bə'tænɪkl] *a* botanique.
botanist ['bɔtənɪst] *n* botaniste *m/f*.
botany ['bɔtənɪ] *n* botanique *f*.
botch [bɔtʃ] *vt* (*also*: **~ up**) saboter, bâcler.
both [bəuθ] *a* les deux, l'un(e) et l'autre // *pronoun*: **~ (of them)** les deux, tous(toutes) (les) deux, l'un(e) et l'autre ; **~ of us went, we ~ went** nous y sommes allés (tous) les deux // *ad*: **they sell ~ the fabric and the finished curtains** ils vendent (et) le tissu et les rideaux (finis), ils vendent à la fois le tissu et les rideaux (finis).
bother ['bɔðə*] *vt* (*worry*) tracasser ; (*needle, bait*) importuner, ennuyer ; (*disturb*) déranger // *vi* (*gen*: **~ o.s.**) se tracasser, se faire du souci ; **to ~ doing** prendre la peine de faire // *n*: **it is a ~ to have to do** c'est vraiment ennuyeux d'avoir à faire ; **it was no ~ finding** il n'y a eu aucun problème pour *or* ç'a été très facile de trouver.
bottle ['bɔtl] *n* bouteille *f*; (*baby's*) biberon *m* // *vt* mettre en bouteille(s) ; **to ~ up** *vt* refouler, contenir ; **~neck** *n* étranglement *m*; **~-opener** *n* ouvre-bouteille *m*.
bottom ['bɔtəm] *n* (*of container, sea etc*) fond *m*; (*buttocks*) derrière *m*; (*of page, list*) bas *m*; (*of chair*) siège *m* // *a* du fond ; du bas ; **~less** *a* sans fond, insondable.
bough [bau] *n* branche *f*, rameau *m*.
bought [bɔ:t] *pt,pp of* **buy**.
boulder ['bəuldə*] *n* gros rocher (*gén lisse, arrondi*).
bounce [bauns] *vi* (*ball*) rebondir ; (*cheque*) être refusé (*étant sans provision*) ; (*gen*: **to ~ forward/out** *etc*) bondir, s'élancer // *vt* faire rebondir // *n* (*rebound*) rebond *m*.
bound [baund] *pt,pp of* **bind** // *n* (*gen pl*) limite *f*; (*leap*) bond *m* // *vt* (*leap*) bondir ; (*limit*) borner // *a*: **to be ~ to do sth** (*obliged*) être obligé(e) *or* avoir obligation de faire qch ; **out of ~s** dont l'accès est interdit ; **he's ~ to fail** (*likely*) il est sûr d'échouer, son échec est inévitable *or* assuré ; **~ for** à destination de.
boundary ['baundrɪ] *n* frontière *f*.
boundless ['baundlɪs] *a* illimité(e), sans bornes.
bout [baut] *n* période *f*; (*of malaria etc*) accès *m*, crise *f*, attaque *f*; (BOXING *etc*) combat *m*, match *m*.
bow *n* [bəu] nœud *m*; (*weapon*) arc *m*; (MUS) archet *m*; [bau] révérence *f*, inclination *f* (du buste *or* corps) // *vi* [bau] faire une révérence, s'incliner ; (*yield*): **to ~ to** *or* **before** s'incliner devant, se soumettre à.
bowels [bauəlz] *npl* intestins *mpl*; (*fig*) entrailles *fpl*.
bowl [bəul] *n* (*for eating*) bol *m*; (*for washing*) cuvette *f*; (*ball*) boule *f*; (*of pipe*) fourneau *m* // *vi* (CRICKET) lancer (la balle) ; **~s** *n* (jeu *m* de) boules *fpl*; **to ~ over** *vt* (*fig*) renverser (*fig*).
bow-legged ['bəulɛgɪd] *a* aux jambes arquées.
bowler ['bəulə*] *n* joueur *m* de boules ; (CRICKET) lanceur *m* (de la balle) ; (*also*: **~ hat**) (chapeau *m*) melon *m*.
bowling ['bəulɪŋ] *n* (*game*) jeu *m* de boules ; **~ alley** *n* bowling *m*; jeu *m* de quilles ; **~ green** *n* terrain *m* de boules (*gazonné et carré*).
bow tie ['bəu'taɪ] *n* nœud *m* papillon.
box [bɔks] *n* boîte *f*; (*also*: **cardboard ~**) carton *m*; (THEATRE) loge *f* // *vt* mettre en boîte ; (SPORT) boxer avec // *vi* boxer, faire de la boxe ; **~er** *n* (*person*) boxeur *m*; (*dog*) boxer *m*; **~ing** *n* (SPORT) boxe *f*; **B~ing Day** *n le lendemain de Noël* ; **~ing gloves** *npl* gants *mpl* de boxe ; **~ing ring** *n* ring *m*; **~ office** *n* bureau *m* de location ; **~ room** *n* débarras *m*; chambrette *f*.
boy [bɔɪ] *n* garçon *m*; (*servant*) boy *m*.
boycott ['bɔɪkɔt] *n* boycottage *m* // *vt* boycotter.
boyfriend ['bɔɪfrɛnd] *n* (petit) ami.
boyish ['bɔɪɪʃ] *a* d'enfant, de garçon.
B.R. *abbr of British Rail*.
bra [brɑ:] *n* soutien-gorge *m*.
brace [breɪs] *n* attache *f*, agrafe *f*; (*on teeth*) appareil *m* (dentaire) ; (*tool*) vilbrequin *m*; (TYP: *also*: **~ bracket**) accolade *f* // *vt* consolider, soutenir ; **~s** *npl* bretelles *fpl*; **to ~ o.s.** (*fig*) se préparer mentalement.
bracelet ['breɪslɪt] *n* bracelet *m*.
bracing ['breɪsɪŋ] *a* tonifiant(e), tonique.
bracken ['brækən] *n* fougère *f*.
bracket ['brækɪt] *n* (TECH) tasseau *m*, support *m*; (*group*) classe *f*, tranche *f*; (*also*: **brace ~**) accolade *f*; (*also*: **round ~**) parenthèse *f*; (*gen*: **square ~**) crochet *m* // *vt* mettre entre parenthèse(s).
brag [bræg] *vi* se vanter.
braid [breɪd] *n* (*trimming*) galon *m*; (*of hair*) tresse *f*, natte *f*.
Braille [breɪl] *n* braille *m*.
brain [breɪn] *n* cerveau *m*; **~s** *npl* cervelle *f*; **he's got ~s** il est intelligent ; **~less** *a* sans cervelle, stupide ; **~wash** *vt* faire subir un lavage de cerveau à ; **~wave** *n* idée géniale ; **~y** *a* intelligent(e), doué(e).
braise [breɪz] *vt* braiser.
brake [breɪk] *n* (*on vehicle*) frein *m* // *vt,vi* freiner.
bramble ['bræmbl] *n* ronces *fpl*.
bran [bræn] *n* son *m*.
branch [brɑ:ntʃ] *n* branche *f*; (COMM) succursale *f* // *vi* bifurquer.
brand [brænd] *n* marque (commerciale) // *vt* (*cattle*) marquer (au fer rouge) ; (*fig*:

pej): **to ~ sb a communist** *etc* traiter *or* qualifier qn de communiste *etc*.
brandish ['brændɪʃ] *vt* brandir.
brand-new ['brænd'nju:] *a* tout(e) neuf(neuve), flambant neuf(neuve).
brandy ['brændɪ] *n* cognac *m*, fine *f*.
brash [bræʃ] *a* effronté(e).
brass [brɑ:s] *n* cuivre *m* (jaune), laiton *m*; **the ~** (MUS) les cuivres; **~ band** *n* fanfare *f*.
brassière ['bræsɪə*] *n* soutien-gorge *m*.
brat [bræt] *n* (*pej*) mioche *m/f*, môme *m/f*.
bravado [brə'vɑ:dəu] *n* bravade *f*.
brave [breɪv] *a* courageux(euse), brave // *n* guerrier indien // *vt* braver, affronter; **~ry** *n* bravure *f*, courage *m*.
brawl [brɔ:l] *n* rixe *f*, bagarre *f* // *vi* se bagarrer.
brawn [brɔ:n] *n* muscle *m*; (*meat*) fromage *m* de tête; **~y** *a* musclé(e), costaud(e).
bray [breɪ] *n* braiement *m* // *vi* braire.
brazen ['breɪzn] *a* impudent(e), effronté(e) // *vt*: **to ~ it out** payer d'effronterie, crâner.
brazier ['breɪzɪə*] *n* brasero *m*.
Brazil [brə'zɪl] *n* Brésil *m*; **~ian** *a* brésilien(ne) // *n* Brésilien/ne; **~ nut** *n* noix *f* du Brésil.
breach [bri:tʃ] *vt* ouvrir une brèche dans // *n* (*gap*) brèche *f*; (*breaking*): **~ of confidence** abus *m* de confiance; **~ of contract** rupture *f* de contrat; **~ of the peace** attentat *m* à l'ordre public.
bread [brɛd] *n* pain *m*; **~ and butter** *n* tartines *fpl* (beurrées); (*fig*) subsistance *f*; **~crumbs** *npl* miettes *fpl* de pain; (CULIN) chapelure *f*, panure *f*; **~ line** *n*: **to be on the ~ line** être sans le sou *or* dans l'indigence.
breadth [brɛtθ] *n* largeur *f*.
breadwinner ['brɛdwɪnə*] *n* soutien *m* de famille.
break [breɪk] *vb* (*pt* **broke** [brəuk], *pp* **broken** ['brəukən]) *vt* casser, briser; (*promise*) rompre; (*law*) violer // *vi* (se) casser, se briser; (*weather*) tourner // *n* (*gap*) brèche *f*; (*fracture*) cassure *f*; (*rest*) interruption *f*, arrêt *m*; (:*short*) pause *f*; (:*at school*) récréation *f*; (*chance*) chance *f*, occasion *f* favorable; **to ~ one's leg** *etc* se casser la jambe *etc*; **to ~ a record** battre un record; **to ~ the news to sb** annoncer la nouvelle à qn; **to ~ down** *vt* (*figures, data*) décomposer, analyser // *vi* s'effondrer; (MED) faire une dépression (nerveuse); (AUT) tomber en panne; **to ~ even** *vi* rentrer dans ses frais; **to ~ free** *or* **loose** *vi* se dégager, s'échapper; **to ~ in** *vt* (*horse etc*) dresser // *vi* (*burglar*) entrer par effraction; **to ~ into** *vt fus* (*house*) s'introduire *or* pénétrer par effraction dans; **to ~ off** *vi* (*speaker*) s'interrompre; (*branch*) se rompre; **to ~ open** *vt* (*door etc*) forcer, fracturer; **to ~ out** *vi* éclater, se déclarer; **to ~ out in spots** se couvrir de boutons; **to ~ up** *vi* (*partnership*) cesser, prendre fin; (*friends*) se séparer // *vt* fracasser, casser; (*fight etc*) interrompre, faire cesser; **~able** *a* cassable, fragile; **~age** *n* casse *f*; **~down** *n* (AUT) panne *f*; (*in communications*) rupture *f*; (MED: *also*: **nervous ~down**) dépression (nerveuse); **~down lorry** *n* dépanneuse *f*; **~down service** *n* service *m* de dépannage; **~er** *n* brisant *m*.
breakfast ['brɛkfəst] *n* petit déjeuner *m*.
breakthrough ['breɪkθru:] *n* percée *f*.
breakwater ['breɪkwɔ:tə*] *n* brise-lames *m inv*, digue *f*.
breast [brɛst] *n* (*of woman*) sein *m*; (*chest*) poitrine *f*; **~-stroke** *n* brasse *f*.
breath [brɛθ] *n* haleine *f*, souffle *m*; **to go out for a ~ of air** sortir prendre l'air; **out of ~** à bout de souffle, essoufflé(e); **~alyser** *n* alcootest *m*.
breathe [bri:ð] *vt,vi* respirer; **~r** *n* moment *m* de repos *or* de répit.
breathless ['brɛθlɪs] *a* essoufflé(e), haletant(e); oppressé(e).
breath-taking ['brɛθteɪkɪŋ] *a* stupéfiant(e), à vous couper le souffle.
breed [bri:d] *vb* (*pt,pp* **bred** [brɛd]) *vt* élever, faire l'élevage de // *vi* se reproduire // *n* race *f*, variété *f*; **~er** *n* (*person*) éleveur *m*; **~ing** *n* reproduction *f*; élevage *m*.
breeze [bri:z] *n* brise *f*.
breezy ['bri:zɪ] *a* frais(fraîche); aéré(e); désinvolte, jovial(e).
brevity ['brɛvɪtɪ] *n* brièveté *f*.
brew [bru:] *vt* (*tea*) faire infuser; (*beer*) brasser; (*plot*) tramer, préparer // *vi* (*tea*) infuser; (*beer*) fermenter; (*fig*) se préparer, couver; **~er** *n* brasseur *m*; **~ery** *n* brasserie *f* (*fabrique*).
bribe [braɪb] *n* pot-de-vin *m* // *vt* acheter; soudoyer; **~ry** *n* corruption *f*.
brick [brɪk] *n* brique *f*; **~layer** *n* maçon *m*; **~work** *n* briquetage *m*, maçonnerie *f*; **~works** *n* briqueterie *f*.
bridal ['braɪdl] *a* nuptial(e); **~ party** *n* noce *f*.
bride [braɪd] *n* mariée *f*, épouse *f*; **~groom** *n* marié *m*, époux *m*; **~smaid** *n* demoiselle *f* d'honneur.
bridge [brɪdʒ] *n* pont *m*; (NAUT) passerelle *f* (de commandement); (*of nose*) arête *f*; (CARDS, DENTISTRY) bridge *m* // *vt* (*river*) construire un pont sur; (*gap*) combler; **bridging loan** *n* prêt *m* de raccord.
bridle ['braɪdl] *n* bride *f* // *vt* refréner, mettre la bride à; (*horse*) brider; **~ path** *n* piste *or* allée cavalière.
brief [bri:f] *a* bref(brève) // *n* (LAW) dossier *m*, cause *f* // *vt* donner des instructions à; **~s** *npl* slip *m*; **~case** *n* serviette *f*; porte-documents *m inv*; **~ing** *n* instructions *fpl*; **~ly** *ad* brièvement; **~ness** *n* brièveté *f*.
brigade [brɪ'geɪd] *n* (MIL) brigade *f*.
brigadier [brɪgə'dɪə*] *n* brigadier général.
bright [braɪt] *a* brillant(e); (*room, weather*) clair(e); (*person*) intelligent(e), doué(e); (*colour*) vif(vive); **~en** *vt* (*room*) éclaircir; égayer // *vi* s'éclaircir; (*person*: *gen*: **~en up**) retrouver un peu de sa gaieté; **~ly** *ad* brillamment.
brilliance ['brɪljəns] *n* éclat *m*.
brilliant ['brɪljənt] *a* brillant(e).
brim [brɪm] *n* bord *m*; **~ful** *a* plein(e) à ras bord; (*fig*) débordant(e).
brine [braɪn] *n* eau salée; (CULIN) saumure *f*.

bring, *pt,pp* **brought** [brɪŋ, brɔ:t] *vt* (*thing*) apporter ; (*person*) amener ; **to ~ about** *vt* provoquer, entraîner ; **to ~ back** *vt* rapporter ; ramener ; **to ~ down** *vt* abaisser ; faire s'effondrer ; **to ~ forward** *vt* avancer ; **to ~ off** *vt* (*task, plan*) réussir, mener à bien ; **to ~ out** *vt* (*meaning*) faire ressortir, mettre en relief ; **to ~ round** *or* **to** *vt* (*unconscious person*) ranimer ; **to ~ up** *vt* élever ; (*question*) soulever.
brink [brɪŋk] *n* bord *m*.
brisk [brɪsk] *a* vif(vive), alerte.
bristle ['brɪsl] *n* poil *m* // *vi* se hérisser ; **bristling with** hérissé(e) de.
Britain ['brɪtən] *n* Grande-Bretagne *f*.
British ['brɪtɪʃ] *a* britannique ; **the ~** *npl* les Britanniques *mpl* ; **the ~ Isles** *npl* les Îles *fpl* Britanniques.
Briton ['brɪtən] *n* Britannique *m/f*.
Brittany ['brɪtənɪ] *n* Bretagne *f*.
brittle ['brɪtl] *a* cassant(e), fragile.
broach [brəutʃ] *vt* (*subject*) aborder.
broad [brɔ:d] *a* large ; (*distinction*) général(e) ; (*accent*) prononcé(e) ; **in ~ daylight** en plein jour ; **~ hint** *n* allusion transparente ; **~cast** *n* émission *f* // *vb* (*pt,pp* **broadcast**) *vt* radiodiffuser ; téléviser // *vi* émettre ; **~casting** *n* radiodiffusion *f* ; télévision *f* ; **~en** *vt* élargir // *vi* s'élargir ; **~ly** *ad* en gros, généralement ; **~-minded** *a* large d'esprit.
brochure ['brəuʃjuə*] *n* prospectus *m*, dépliant *m*.
broil [brɔɪl] *vt* rôtir ; **~er** *n* (*fowl*) poulet *m* (*à rôtir*).
broke [brəuk] *pt of* **break** // *a* (*col*) fauché(e) ; **~n** *pp of* **break** // *a*: **~n leg** *etc* jambe *etc* cassée ; **in ~n French/English** dans un français/anglais approximatif *or* hésitant ; **~n-hearted** *a* (ayant) le cœur brisé.
broker ['brəukə*] *n* courtier *m*.
bronchitis [brɔŋ'kaɪtɪs] *n* bronchite *f*.
bronze [brɔnz] *n* bronze *m* ; **~d** *a* bronzé(e), hâlé(e).
brooch [brəutʃ] *n* broche *f*.
brood [bru:d] *n* couvée *f* // *vi* (*hen, storm*) couver ; (*person*) méditer (sombrement), ruminer ; **~y** *a* (*fig*) taciturne, mélancolique.
brook [bruk] *n* ruisseau *m*.
broom [brum] *n* balai *m* ; **~stick** *n* manche *m* à balai.
Bros. *abbr of Brothers*.
broth [brɔθ] *n* bouillon *m* de viande et de légumes.
brothel ['brɔθl] *n* maison close, bordel *m*.
brother ['brʌðə*] *n* frère *m* ; **~hood** *n* fraternité *f* ; **~-in-law** *n* beau-frère *m* ; **~ly** *a* fraternel(le).
brought [brɔ:t] *pt,pp of* **bring**.
brow [brau] *n* front *m* ; (*rare, gen*: **eye~**) sourcil *m* ; (*of hill*) sommet *m* ; **~beat** *vt* intimider, brusquer.
brown [braun] *a* brun(e) // *n* (*colour*) brun *m* // *vt* brunir ; (CULIN) faire dorer, faire roussir ; **~ie** *n* jeannette *f*, éclaireuse (cadette).
browse [brauz] *vi* (*among books*) bouquiner, feuilleter les livres.
bruise [bru:z] *n* bleu *m*, ecchymose *f*, contusion *f* // *vt* contusionner, meurtrir // *vi* (*fruit*) se taler, se meurtrir ; **to ~ one's arm** se faire un bleu au bras.
brunette [bru:'nɛt] *n* (femme) brune.
brunt [brʌnt] *n*: **the ~ of** (*attack, criticism etc*) le plus gros de.
brush [brʌʃ] *n* brosse *f* ; (*quarrel*) accrochage *m*, prise *f* de bec // *vt* brosser ; (*gen*: **~ past, ~ against**) effleurer, frôler ; **to ~ aside** *vt* écarter, balayer ; **to ~ up** *vt* (*knowledge*) rafraîchir, réviser ; **~-off** *n*: **to give sb the ~-off** envoyer qn promener ; **~wood** *n* broussailles *fpl*, taillis *m*.
Brussels ['brʌslz] *n* Bruxelles ; **~ sprout** *n* chou *m* de Bruxelles.
brutal ['bru:tl] *a* brutal(e) ; **~ity** [bru:'tælɪtɪ] *n* brutalité *f*.
brute [bru:t] *n* brute *f*.
brutish ['bru:tɪʃ] *a* grossier(ère), brutal(e).
B.Sc. *abbr see* **bachelor**.
bubble ['bʌbl] *n* bulle *f* // *vi* bouillonner, faire des bulles ; (*sparkle, fig*) pétiller.
buck [bʌk] *n* mâle *m* (*d'un lapin, lièvre, daim etc*) ; (*US: col*) dollar *m* // *vi* ruer, lancer une ruade ; **to pass the ~ (to sb)** se décharger de la responsabilité (sur qn) ; **to ~ up** *vi* (*cheer up*) reprendre du poil de la bête, se remonter.
bucket ['bʌkɪt] *n* seau *m*.
buckle ['bʌkl] *n* boucle *f* // *vt* boucler, attacher ; (*warp*) tordre, gauchir ; (: *wheel*) voiler.
bud [bʌd] *n* bourgeon *m* ; (*of flower*) bouton *m* // *vi* bourgeonner ; (*flower*) éclore.
Buddha ['budə] *n* Bouddha *m* ; **Buddhism** *n* bouddhisme *m* ; **Buddhist** *a* bouddhiste // *n* Bouddhiste *m/f*.
budding ['bʌdɪŋ] *a* (*flower*) en bouton ; (*poet etc*) en herbe ; (*passion etc*) naissant(e).
buddy ['bʌdɪ] *n* (*US*) copain *m*.
budge [bʌdʒ] *vt* faire bouger // *vi* bouger.
budgerigar ['bʌdʒərɪgɑ:*] *n* perruche *f*.
budget ['bʌdʒɪt] *n* budget *m* // *vi*: **to ~ for sth** inscrire qch au budget.
budgie ['bʌdʒɪ] *n* = **budgerigar**.
buff [bʌf] *a* (couleur *f*) chamois *m* // *n* (*enthusiast*) mordu/e.
buffalo, *pl* **~** *or* **~es** ['bʌfələu] *n* buffle *m* ; (*US*) bison *m*.
buffer ['bʌfə*] *n* tampon *m* ; **~ state** *n* état *m* tampon.
buffet *n* ['bufeɪ] (*bar, food*) buffet *m* // *vt* ['bʌfɪt] gifler, frapper ; secouer, ébranler.
buffoon [bə'fu:n] *n* buffon *m*, pitre *m*.
bug [bʌg] *n* (*insect*) punaise *f* ; (: *gen*) insecte *m*, bestiole *f* ; (: *fig*: *germ*) virus *m*, microbe *m* ; (*spy device*) dispositif *m* d'écoute (électronique), micro clandestin // *vt* garnir de dispositifs d'écoute ; **~bear** *n* cauchemar *m*, bête noire.
bugle ['bju:gl] *n* clairon *m*.
build [bɪld] *n* (*of person*) carrure *f*, charpente *f* // *vt* (*pt,pp* **built** [bɪlt]) construire, bâtir ; **~er** *n* entrepreneur *m* ; **~ing** *n* construction *f* ; bâtiment *m*, construction *f* ; (*habitation, offices*) immeuble *m* ; **~ing society** *n* société *f* de crédit immobilier ; **to ~ up** *vt* accumuler,

amasser ; accroître ; ~**-up** *n* (*of gas etc*) accumulation *f*.

built [bɪlt] *pt,pp of* **build** ; **well-~** *a* (*person*) bien bâti(e) ; ~**-in** *a* (*cupboard*) encastré(e) ; (*device*) incorporé(e) ; intégré(e) ; ~**-up area** *n* agglomération (urbaine) ; zone urbanisée.

bulb [bʌlb] *n* (BOT) bulbe *m*, oignon *m* ; (ELEC) ampoule *f* ; ~**ous** *a* bulbeux(euse).

Bulgaria [bʌl'gɛərɪə] *n* Bulgarie *f* ; ~**n** *a* bulgare // *n* Bulgare *m/f* ; (LING) bulgare *m*.

bulge [bʌldʒ] *n* renflement *m*, gonflement *m* // *vi* faire saillie ; présenter un renflement ; **to be bulging with** être plein(e) à craquer de.

bulk [bʌlk] *n* masse *f*, volume *m* ; **in** ~ (COMM) en vrac ; **the** ~ **of** la plus grande *or* grosse partie de ; ~**head** *n* cloison *f* (étanche) ; ~**y** *a* volumineux(euse), encombrant(e).

bull [bul] *n* taureau *m* ; ~**dog** *n* bouledogue *m*.

bulldoze ['buldəuz] *vt* passer *or* raser au bulldozer ; ~**r** *n* bulldozer *m*.

bullet ['bulɪt] *n* balle *f* (*de fusil etc*).

bulletin ['bulɪtɪn] *n* bulletin *m*, communiqué *m*.

bullfight ['bulfaɪt] *n* corrida *f*, course *f* de taureaux ; ~**er** *n* torero *m* ; ~**ing** *n* tauromachie *f*.

bullion ['buljən] *n* or *m* or argent *m* en lingots.

bullock ['bulək] *n* bœuf *m*.

bull's-eye ['bulzaɪ] *n* centre *m* (*de la cible*).

bully ['bulɪ] *n* brute *f*, tyran *m* // *vt* tyranniser, rudoyer ; (*frighten*) intimider ; ~**ing** *n* brimades *fpl*.

bum [bʌm] *n* (*col*: *backside*) derrière *m* ; (*tramp*) vagabond/e, traîne-savates *m/f inv* ; **to** ~ **around** *vi* vagabonder.

bumblebee ['bʌmblbi:] *n* (ZOOL) bourdon *m*.

bump [bʌmp] *n* (*blow*) coup *m*, choc *m* ; (*jolt*) cahot *m* ; (*on road etc, on head*) bosse *f* // *vt* heurter, cogner ; **to** ~ **along** *vi* avancer en cahotant ; **to** ~ **into** *vt fus* rentrer dans, tamponner ; ~**er** *n* (*Brit*) pare-chocs *m inv* // *a*: ~**er crop/harvest** récolte/moisson exceptionnelle.

bumptious ['bʌmpʃəs] *a* suffisant(e), prétentieux(euse).

bumpy ['bʌmpɪ] *a* cahoteux(euse).

bun [bʌn] *n* petit pain au lait ; (*of hair*) chignon *m*.

bunch [bʌntʃ] *n* (*of flowers*) bouquet *m* ; (*of keys*) trousseau *m* ; (*of bananas*) régime *m* ; (*of people*) groupe *m* ; ~ **of grapes** grappe *f* de raisin.

bundle ['bʌndl] *n* paquet *m* // *vt* (*also*: ~ **up**) faire un paquet de ; (*put*): **to** ~ **sth/sb into** fourrer *or* enfourner qch/qn dans ; **to** ~ **off** *vt* (*person*) faire sortir (en toute hâte) ; expédier ; **to** ~ **out** *vt* éjecter, sortir (sans ménagements).

bung [bʌŋ] *n* bonde *f*, bouchon *m* // *vt* (*throw*: *gen*: ~ **into**) flanquer.

bungalow ['bʌŋgələu] *n* bungalow *m*.

bungle ['bʌŋgl] *vt* bâcler, gâcher.

bunion ['bʌnjən] *n* oignon *m* (*au pied*).

bunk [bʌŋk] *n* couchette *f* ; ~ **beds** *npl* lits superposés.

bunker ['bʌŋkə*] *n* (*coal store*) soute *f* à charbon ; (MIL, GOLF) bunker *m*.

bunny ['bʌnɪ] *n* (*also*: ~ **rabbit**) Jeannot *m* lapin ; ~ **girl** *n hôtesse de cabaret*.

bunting ['bʌntɪŋ] *n* pavoisement *m*, drapeaux *mpl*.

buoy [bɔɪ] *n* bouée *f* ; **to** ~ **up** *vt* faire flotter ; (*fig*) soutenir, épauler ; ~**ancy** *n* (*of ship*) flottabilité *f* ; ~**ant** *a* gai(e), plein(e) d'entrain.

burden ['bə:dn] *n* fardeau *m*, charge *f* // *vt* charger ; (*oppress*) accabler, surcharger.

bureau, *pl* ~**x** [bjuə'rəu, -z] *n* (*furniture*) bureau *m*, secrétaire *m* ; (*office*) bureau *m*, office *m*.

bureaucracy [bjuə'rɔkrəsɪ] *n* bureaucratie *f*.

bureaucrat ['bjuərəkræt] *n* bureaucrate *m/f*, rond-de-cuir *m* ; ~**ic** [-'krætɪk] *a* bureaucratique.

burglar ['bə:glə*] *n* cambrioleur *m* ; ~ **alarm** *n* sonnerie *f* d'alarme ; ~**ize** *vt* (*US*) cambrioler ; ~**y** *n* cambriolage *m*.

burgle ['bə:gl] *vt* cambrioler.

Burgundy ['bə:gəndɪ] *n* Bourgogne *f*.

burial ['bɛrɪəl] *n* enterrement *m* ; ~ **ground** *n* cimetière *m*.

burlesque [bə:'lɛsk] *n* caricature *f*, parodie *f*.

burly ['bə:lɪ] *a* de forte carrure, costaud(e).

Burma ['bə:mə] *n* Birmanie *f* ; **Burmese** [-'mi:z] *a* birman(e), de Birmanie // *n, pl inv* Birman/e ; (LING) birman *m*.

burn [bə:n] *vt,vi* (*pt,pp* **burned** *or* **burnt** [bə:nt]) brûler // *n* brûlure *f* ; **to** ~ **down** *vt* incendier, détruire par le feu ; ~**er** *n* brûleur *m* ; ~**ing question** *n* question brûlante.

burnish ['bə:nɪʃ] *vt* polir.

burnt [bə:nt] *pt,pp of* **burn** ; ~ **sugar** *n* caramel *m*.

burp [bə:p] (*col*) *n* rot *m* // *vi* roter.

burrow ['bʌrəu] *n* terrier *m* // *vt* creuser.

bursar ['bə:sə*] *n* économe *m/f* ; (*student*) boursier/ère ; ~**y** *n* bourse *f* (d'études).

burst [bə:st] *vb* (*pt,pp* **burst**) *vt* crever ; faire éclater // *vi* éclater ; (*tyre*) crever // *n* explosion *f* ; (*also*: ~ **pipe**) rupture *f* ; fuite *f* ; ~ **of energy** déploiement soudain d'énergie, activité soudaine ; ~ **of laughter** éclat *m* de rire ; ~ **blood vessel** rupture *f* de vaisseau sanguin ; **to** ~ **into flames** s'enflammer soudainement ; **to** ~ **into laughter** éclater de rire ; **to** ~ **into tears** fondre en larmes ; **to be** ~**ing with** être plein (à craquer) de ; regorger de ; **to** ~ **into** *vt fus* (*room etc*) faire irruption dans ; **to** ~ **open** *vi* s'ouvrir violemment *or* soudainement ; **to** ~ **out of** *vt fus* sortir précipitamment de.

bury ['bɛrɪ] *vt* enterrer ; **to** ~ **one's face in one's hands** se couvrir le visage de ses mains ; **to** ~ **one's head in the sand** (*fig*) pratiquer la politique de l'autruche ; **to** ~ **the hatchet** enterrer la hache de guerre.

bus, ~**es** [bʌs, 'bʌsɪz] *n* autobus *m*.

bush [buʃ] *n* buisson *m* ; (*scrub land*) brousse *f*.

bushel ['buʃl] *n* boisseau *m*.
bushy ['buʃɪ] *a* broussailleux(euse), touffu(e).
busily ['bɪzɪlɪ] *ad* activement.
business ['bɪznɪs] *n* (*matter, firm*) affaire *f*; (*trading*) affaires *fpl*; (*job, duty*) travail *m*; **to be away on** ~ être en déplacement d'affaires; **it's none of my** ~ cela ne me regarde pas, ce ne sont pas mes affaires; **he means** ~ il ne plaisante pas, il est sérieux; ~**like** *a* sérieux(euse); efficace; ~**man** *n* homme *m* d'affaires.
bus-stop ['bʌsstɔp] *n* arrêt *m* d'autobus.
bust [bʌst] *n* buste *m* // *a* (*broken*) fichu(e), fini(e); **to go** ~ faire faillite.
bustle ['bʌsl] *n* remue-ménage *m*, affairement *m* // *vi* s'affairer, se démener; **bustling** *a* (*person*) affairé(e); (*town*) très animé(e).
bust-up ['bʌstʌp] *n* (*col*) engueulade *f*.
busy ['bɪzɪ] *a* occupé(e); (*shop, street*) très fréquenté(e) // *vt*: **to** ~ **o.s.** s'occuper; ~**body** *n* mouche *f* du coche, âme *f* charitable.
but [bʌt] *cj* mais // *prep* excepté, sauf; **nothing** ~ rien d'autre que; ~ **for** sans, si ce n'était pour; **all** ~ **finished** pratiquement fini; **anything** ~ **finished** tout sauf fini, très loin d'être fini.
butane ['bju:teɪn] *n* butane *m*.
butcher ['butʃə*] *n* boucher *m* // *vt* massacrer; (*cattle etc for meat*) tuer.
butler ['bʌtlə*] *n* maître *m* d'hôtel.
butt [bʌt] *n* (*cask*) gros tonneau; (*thick end*) (gros) bout; (*of gun*) crosse *f*; (*of cigarette*) mégot *m*; (*fig: target*) cible *f* // *vt* donner un coup de tête à.
butter ['bʌtə*] *n* beurre *m* // *vt* beurrer; ~ **dish** *n* beurrier *m*.
butterfly ['bʌtəflaɪ] *n* papillon *m*.
buttocks ['bʌtəks] *npl* fesses *fpl*.
button ['bʌtn] *n* bouton *m* // *vt* boutonner // *vi* se boutonner; ~**hole** *n* boutonnière *f* // *vt* accrocher, arrêter, retenir.
buttress ['bʌtrɪs] *n* contrefort *m*.
buxom ['bʌksəm] *a* aux formes avantageuses *or* épanouies, bien galbé(e).
buy [baɪ] *vb* (*pt,pp* **bought** [bɔ:t]) *vt* acheter; **to** ~ **sb sth/sth from sb** acheter qch à qn; **to** ~ **sb a drink** offrir un verre *or* à boire à qn; **to** ~ **up** *vt* acheter en bloc, rafler; ~**er** *n* acheteur/euse.
buzz [bʌz] *n* bourdonnement *m*; (*col: phone call*) coup *m* de fil // *vi* bourdonner.
buzzard ['bʌzəd] *n* buse *f*.
buzzer ['bʌzə*] *n* timbre *m* électrique.
by [baɪ] *prep* par; (*beside*) à côté de; au bord de; (*before*): ~ **4 o'clock** avant 4 heures, d'ici 4 heures // *ad see* **pass, go** *etc*; ~ **bus/car** en autobus/voiture; **paid** ~ **the hour** payé à l'heure; **to increase** *etc* ~ **the hour** augmenter *etc* d'heure en heure; **(all)** ~ **oneself** tout(e) seul(e); ~ **the way** à propos; ~ **and large** dans l'ensemble; ~ **and** ~ bientôt.
bye(-bye) ['baɪ('baɪ)] *excl* au revoir!, salut!
by(e)-law ['baɪlɔ:] *n* arrêté municipal.
by-election ['baɪɪlɛkʃən] *n* élection (législative) partielle.
bygone ['baɪgɔn] *a* passé(e) // *n*: **let** ~**s be** ~**s** passons l'éponge, oublions le passé.
bypass ['baɪpɑ:s] *n* (route *f* de) contournement *m* // *vt* éviter.
by-product ['baɪprɔdʌkt] *n* sous-produit *m*, dérivé *m*; (*fig*) conséquence *f* secondaire, retombée *f*.
byre ['baɪə*] *n* étable *f* (à vaches).
bystander ['baɪstændə*] *n* spectateur/-trice, badaud/e.
byword ['baɪwə:d] *n*: **to be a** ~ **for** être synonyme de (*fig*).

C

C [si:] *n* (MUS) do *m*.
C. *abbr of* **centigrade**.
C.A. *abbr of* **chartered accountant**.
cab [kæb] *n* taxi *m*; (*of train, truck*) cabine *f*; (*horse-drawn*) fiacre *m*.
cabaret ['kæbəreɪ] *n* attractions *fpl*, spectacle *m* de cabaret.
cabbage ['kæbɪdʒ] *n* chou *m*.
cabin ['kæbɪn] *n* cabane *f*, hutte *f*; (*on ship*) cabine *f*; ~ **cruiser** *n* yacht *m* (à moteur).
cabinet ['kæbɪnɪt] *n* (POL) cabinet *m*; (*furniture*) petit meuble à tiroirs et rayons; (*also*: **display** ~) vitrine *f*, petite armoire vitrée; **cocktail** ~ *n* meuble-bar *m*; **medicine** ~ *n* armoire *f* à pharmacie; ~-**maker** *n* ébéniste *m*.
cable ['keɪbl] *n* câble *m* // *vt* câbler, télégraphier; ~-**car** *n* téléphérique *m*; ~**gram** *n* câblogramme *m*; ~ **railway** *n* funiculaire *m*.
cache [kæʃ] *n* cachette *f*; **a** ~ **of food** *etc* un dépôt secret de provisions *etc*, une cachette contenant des provisions *etc*.
cackle ['kækl] *vi* caqueter.
cactus, *pl* **cacti** ['kæktəs, -taɪ] *n* cactus *m*.
caddie ['kædɪ] *n* caddie *m*.
cadet [kə'dɛt] *n* (MIL) élève *m* officier.
cadge [kædʒ] *vt* se faire donner; **to** ~ **a meal (off sb)** se faire inviter à manger (par qn); ~**r** *n* pique-assiette *m/f inv*, tapeur/euse.
Caesarean [si:'zɛərɪən] *a*: ~ **(section)** césarienne *f*.
café ['kæfeɪ] *n* ≈ café(-restaurant) *m* (*sans alcool*); **cafeteria** [kæfɪ'tɪərɪə] *n* cafeteria *f*.
caffein(e) ['kæfi:n] *n* caféine *f*.
cage [keɪdʒ] *n* cage *f* // *vt* mettre en cage.
cagey ['keɪdʒɪ] *a* (*col*) réticent(e); méfiant(e).
Cairo ['kaɪərəu] *n* le Caire.
cajole [kə'dʒəul] *vt* couvrir de flatteries *or* de gentillesses.
cake [keɪk] *n* gâteau *m*; ~ **of soap** savonnette *f*; ~**d** *a*: ~**d with** raidi(e) par, couvert(e) d'une croûte de.
calamitous [kə'læmɪtəs] *a* catastrophique, désastreux(euse).
calamity [kə'læmɪtɪ] *n* calamité *f*, désastre *m*.
calcium ['kælsɪəm] *n* calcium *m*.
calculate ['kælkjuleɪt] *vt* calculer; **calculating** *a* calculateur(trice); **calculation** [-'leɪʃən] *n* calcul *m*; **calculator** *n* machine *f* à calculer, calculatrice *f*.

calculus ['kælkjuləs] *n* analyse *f* (mathématique), calcul infinitésimal; **integral/differential** ~ calcul intégral/différentiel.
calendar ['kæləndə*] *n* calendrier *m*; ~ **month** *n* mois *m* (de calendrier); ~ **year** *n* année civile.
calf, calves [kɑ:f, kɑ:vz] *n* (*of cow*) veau *m*; (*of other animals*) petit *m*; (*also*: ~**skin**) veau *m*, vachette *f*; (ANAT) mollet *m*.
calibre, caliber (*US*) ['kælɪbə*] *n* calibre *m*.
call [kɔ:l] *vt* (*gen, also* TEL) appeler // *vi* appeler; (*visit*: *also*: ~ **in**, ~ **round**): **to** ~ **(for)** passer (prendre) // *n* (*shout*) appel *m*, cri *m*; (*visit*) visite *f*; (*also*: **telephone** ~) coup *m* de téléphone; communication *f*; **she's** ~**ed Suzanne** elle s'appelle Suzanne; **to be on** ~ être de permanence; **to** ~ **for** *vt fus* demander; **to** ~ **off** *vt* annuler; **to** ~ **on** *vt fus* (*visit*) rendre visite à, passer voir; (*request*): **to** ~ **on sb to do** inviter qn à faire; **to** ~ **up** *vt* (MIL) appeler, mobiliser; ~**box** *n* cabine *f* téléphonique; ~**er** *n* personne *f* qui appelle; visiteur *m*; ~ **girl** *n* call-girl *f*; ~**ing** *n* vocation *f*; (*trade, occupation*) état *m*; ~**ing card** *n* (*US*) carte *f* de visite.
callous ['kæləs] *a* dur(e), insensible; ~**ness** *n* dureté *f*, manque *m* de cœur, insensibilité *f*.
callow ['kæləu] *a* sans expérience (de la vie).
calm [kɑ:m] *n* calme *m* // *vt* calmer, apaiser // *a* calme; ~**ly** *ad* calmement, avec calme; ~**ness** *n* calme *m*; **to** ~ **down** *vi* se calmer, s'apaiser // *vt* calmer, apaiser.
calorie ['kælərɪ] *n* calorie *f*.
calve [kɑ:v] *vi* vêler, mettre bas.
calves [kɑ:vz] *npl of* **calf.**
camber ['kæmbə*] *n* (*of road*) bombement *m*.
Cambodia [kæm'bəudjə] *n* Cambodge *m*.
came [keɪm] *pt of* **come.**
camel ['kæməl] *n* chameau *m*.
cameo ['kæmɪəu] *n* camée *m*.
camera ['kæmərə] *n* appareil-photo *m*; (*also*: **cine-**~, **movie** ~) caméra *f*; **35mm** ~ appareil 24 x 36 *or* petit format; **in** ~ à huis clos, en privé; ~**man** *n* caméraman *m*.
camouflage ['kæməflɑ:ʒ] *n* camouflage *m* // *vt* camoufler.
camp [kæmp] *n* camp *m* //, *vi* camper.
campaign [kæm'peɪn] *n* (MIL, POL *etc*) campagne *f* // *vi* (*also fig*) faire campagne.
campbed ['kæmp'bɛd] *n* lit *m* de camp.
camper ['kæmpə*] *n* campeur/euse.
camping ['kæmpɪŋ] *n* camping *m*; ~ **site** *n* (terrain *m* de) camping.
campsite ['kæmpsaɪt] *n* campement *m*.
campus ['kæmpəs] *n* campus *m*.
can [kæn] *auxiliary vb* (*gen*) pouvoir; (*know how to*) savoir; **I** ~ **swim** *etc* je sais nager *etc*; **I** ~ **speak French** je parle français // *n* (*of milk, oil, water*) bidon *m*; (*US*: *tin*) boîte *f* (de conserve) // *vt* mettre en conserve.
Canada ['kænədə] *n* Canada *m*.
Canadian [kə'neɪdɪən] *a* canadien(ne) // *n* Canadien/ne.
canal [kə'næl] *n* canal *m*.
canary [kə'nɛərɪ] *n* canari *m*, serin *m*.
cancel ['kænsəl] *vt* annuler; (*train*) supprimer; (*party, appointment*) décommander; (*cross out*) barrer, rayer; (*stamp*) oblitérer; ~**lation** [-'leɪʃən] *n* annulation *f*; suppression *f*; oblitération *f*; (TOURISM) réservation annulée, client *etc* qui s'est décommandé.
cancer ['kænsə*] *n* cancer *m*; **C**~ (*sign*) le Cancer; **to be C**~ être du Cancer.
candid ['kændɪd] *a* (très) franc(franche), sincère.
candidate ['kændɪdeɪt] *n* candidat/e.
candle ['kændl] *n* bougie *f*; (*of tallow*) chandelle *f*; (*in church*) cierge *m*; **by** ~**light** à la lumière d'une bougie; (*dinner*) aux chandelles; ~**stick** *n* (*also*: ~ **holder**) bougeoir *m*; (*bigger, ornate*) chandelier *m*.
candour ['kændə*] *n* (grande) franchise *or* sincérité.
candy ['kændɪ] *n* sucre candi; (*US*) bonbon *m*; ~**-floss** *n* barbe *f* à papa.
cane [keɪn] *n* canne *f* // *vt* (SCOL) administrer des coups de bâton à.
canine ['kænaɪn] *a* canin(e).
canister ['kænɪstə*] *n* boîte *f* (*gén en métal*).
cannabis ['kænəbɪs] *n* (*drug*) cannabis *m*; (*also*: ~ **plant**) chanvre indien.
canned ['kænd] *a* (*food*) en boîte, en conserve.
cannibal ['kænɪbəl] *n* cannibale *m/f*, anthropophage *m/f*; ~**ism** *n* cannibalisme *m*, anthropophagie *f*.
cannon, *pl* ~ *or* ~**s** ['kænən] *n* (*gun*) canon *m*; ~**ball** *n* boulet *m* de canon.
cannot ['kænɔt] = **can not.**
canny ['kænɪ] *a* madré(e), finaud(e).
canoe [kə'nu:] *n* pirogue *f*; (SPORT) canoë *m*; ~**ing** *n* (SPORT) canoë *m*; ~**ist** *n* canoéiste *m/f*.
canon ['kænən] *n* (*clergyman*) chanoine *m*; (*standard*) canon *m*.
canonize ['kænənaɪz] *vt* canoniser.
can opener ['kænəupnə*] *n* ouvre-boîte *m*.
canopy ['kænəpɪ] *n* baldaquin *m*; dais *m*.
cant [kænt] *n* jargon *m* // *vt, vi* pencher.
can't [kænt] = **can not.**
cantankerous [kæn'tæŋkərəs] *a* querelleur(euse), acariâtre.
canteen [kæn'ti:n] *n* cantine *f*; (*of cutlery*) ménagère *f*.
canter ['kæntə*] *n* petit galop // *vi* aller au petit galop.
cantilever ['kæntɪli:və*] *n* porte-à-faux *m inv*.
canvas ['kænvəs] *n* (*gen*) toile *f*; **under** ~ (*camping*) sous la tente; (NAUT) toutes voiles dehors.
canvass ['kænvəs] *vt*: ~**ing** (POL) prospection électorale, démarchage électoral; (COMM) démarchage, prospection.
canyon ['kænjən] *n* cañon *m*, gorge (profonde).
cap [kæp] *n* casquette *f*; (*of pen*) capuchon *m*; (*of bottle*) capsule *f*; (*also*: **Dutch** ~)

diaphragme *m*; (FOOTBALL) sélection *f* pour l'équipe nationale // *vt* capsuler; (*outdo*) surpasser; **~ped with** coiffé(e) de.
capability [keɪpə'bɪlɪtɪ] *n* aptitude *f*, capacité *f*.
capable ['keɪpəbl] *a* capable; **~ of** capable de; susceptible de.
capacity [kə'pæsɪtɪ] *n* capacité *f*, contenance *f*; aptitude *f*; **in his ~ as** en sa qualité de; **to work at full ~** travailler à plein rendement.
cape [keɪp] *n* (*garment*) cape *f*; (GEO) cap *m*.
caper ['keɪpə*] *n* (CULIN: *gen*: **~s**) câpre *f*.
capital ['kæpɪtl] *n* (*also*: **~ city**) capitale *f*; (*money*) capital *m*; (*also*: **~ letter**) majuscule *f*; **~ gains** *npl* plus-values *fpl*; **~ism** *n* capitalisme *m*; **~ist** *a* capitaliste; **~ punishment** *n* peine capitale.
capitulate [kə'pɪtjuleɪt] *vi* capituler; **capitulation** [-'leɪʃən] *n* capitulation *f*.
capricious [kə'prɪʃəs] *a* capricieux(euse), fantasque.
Capricorn ['kæprɪkɔ:n] *n* le Capricorne; **to be ~** être du Capricorne.
capsize [kæp'saɪz] *vt* faire chavirer // *vi* chavirer.
capstan ['kæpstən] *n* cabestan *m*.
capsule ['kæpsju:l] *n* capsule *f*.
captain ['kæptɪn] *n* capitaine *m* // *vt* commander, être le capitaine de.
caption ['kæpʃən] *n* légende *f*.
captivate ['kæptɪveɪt] *vt* captiver, fasciner.
captive ['kæptɪv] *a*, *n* captif(ive).
captivity [kæp'tɪvɪtɪ] *n* captivité *f*.
capture ['kæptʃə*] *vt* capturer, prendre; (*attention*) capter // *n* capture *f*.
car [kɑ:*] *n* voiture *f*, auto *f*.
carafe [kə'ræf] *n* carafe *f*; (*in restaurant*: **~ wine**) ≈ vin ouvert.
caramel ['kærəməl] *n* caramel *m*.
carat ['kærət] *n* carat *m*.
caravan ['kærəvæn] *n* caravane *f*.
caraway ['kærəweɪ] *n*: **~ seed** graine *f* de cumin, cumin *m*.
carbohydrates [kɑ:bəu'haɪdreɪts] *npl* (*foods*) aliments *mpl* riches en hydrate de carbone.
carbon ['kɑ:bən] *n* carbone *m*; **~ copy** *n* carbone *m*; **~ paper** *n* papier *m* carbone.
carburettor [kɑ:bju'rɛtə*] *n* carburateur *m*.
carcass ['kɑ:kəs] *n* carcasse *f*.
card [kɑ:d] *n* carte *f*; **~board** *n* carton *m*; **~ game** *n* jeu *m* de cartes.
cardiac ['kɑ:dɪæk] *a* cardiaque.
cardigan ['kɑ:dɪgən] *n* cardigan *m*.
cardinal ['kɑ:dɪnl] *a* cardinal(e) // *n* cardinal *m*.
card index ['kɑ:dɪndɛks] *n* fichier *m* (alphabétique).
care [kɛə*] *n* soin *m*, attention *f*; (*worry*) souci *m* // *vi*: **to ~ about** se soucier de, s'intéresser à; **would you ~ to/for . . .?** voulez-vous ...?; **I wouldn't ~ to do it** je n'aimerais pas le faire; **in sb's ~** à la garde de qn, confié à qn; **to take ~** faire attention, prendre garde; **to take ~ of** *vt* s'occuper de, prendre soin de; **to ~ for** *vt fus* s'occuper de; (*like*) aimer; **I don't ~** ça m'est bien égal, peu m'importe; **I couldn't ~ less** cela m'est complètement égal, je m'en fiche complètement.
career [kə'rɪə*] *n* carrière *f* // *vi* (*also*: **~ along**) aller à toute allure.
carefree ['kɛəfri:] *a* sans souci, insouciant(e).
careful ['kɛəful] *a* soigneux(euse); (*cautious*) prudent(e); **(be) ~!** (fais) attention!; **~ly** *ad* avec soin, soigneusement; prudemment.
careless ['kɛəlɪs] *a* négligent(e); (*heedless*) insouciant(e); **~ly** *ad* négligemment; avec insouciance; **~ness** *n* manque *m* de soin, négligence *f*; insouciance *f*.
caress [kə'rɛs] *n* caresse *f* // *vt* caresser.
caretaker ['kɛəteɪkə*] *n* gardien/ne, concierge *m/f*.
car-ferry ['kɑ:fɛrɪ] *n* (*on sea*) ferry (-boat) *m*; (*on river*) bac *m*.
cargo, ~es ['kɑ:gəu] *n* cargaison *f*, chargement *m*.
Caribbean [kærɪ'bi:ən] *a*: **the ~ (Sea)** la mer des Antilles *or* Caraïbes.
caricature ['kærɪkətjuə*] *n* caricature *f*.
carnal ['kɑ:nl] *a* charnel(le).
carnation [kɑ:'neɪʃən] *n* œillet *m*.
carnival ['kɑ:nɪvəl] *n* (*public celebration*) carnaval *m*.
carol ['kærəl] *n*: **(Christmas) ~** chant *m* de Noël.
carp [kɑ:p] *n* (*fish*) carpe *f*; **to ~ at** *vt fus* critiquer.
car park ['kɑ:pɑ:k] *n* parking *m*, parc *m* de stationnement.
carpenter ['kɑ:pɪntə*] *n* charpentier *m*.
carpentry ['kɑ:pɪntrɪ] *n* charpenterie *f*, métier *m* de charpentier; (*woodwork*: *at school etc*) menuiserie *f*.
carpet ['kɑ:pɪt] *n* tapis *m* // *vt* recouvrir (d'un tapis).
carriage ['kærɪdʒ] *n* voiture *f*; (*of goods*) transport *m*; (: *taxe*) port *m*; (*of typewriter*) chariot *m*; (*bearing*) maintien *m*, port *m*; **~way** *n* (*part of road*) chaussée *f*.
carrier ['kærɪə*] *n* transporteur *m*, camionneur *m*; **~ bag** *n* sac *m* en papier *or* en plastique; **~ pigeon** *n* pigeon voyageur.
carrot ['kærət] *n* carotte *f*.
carry ['kærɪ] *vt* (*subj*: *person*) porter; (: *vehicle*) transporter; (*a motion, bill*) voter, adopter; (*involve*: *responsibilities etc*) comporter, impliquer // *vi* (*sound*) porter; **to be carried away** (*fig*) s'emballer, s'enthousiasmer; **to ~ on** *vi*: **to ~ on with sth/doing** continuer qch/à faire // *vt* entretenir, poursuivre; **to ~ out** *vt* (*orders*) exécuter; (*investigation*) effectuer; **~cot** *n* porte-bébé *m*.
cart [kɑ:t] *n* charrette *f* // *vt* transporter.
cartilage ['kɑ:tɪlɪdʒ] *n* cartilage *m*.
cartographer [kɑ:'tɔgrəfə*] *n* cartographe *m/f*.
carton ['kɑ:tən] *n* (*box*) carton *m*; (*of yogurt*) pot *m* (en carton); (*of cigarettes*) cartouche *f*.

cartoon [kɑ:'tu:n] *n* (PRESS) dessin *m* (humoristique); (*satirical*) caricature *f*; (*comic strip*) bande dessinée; (CINEMA) dessin animé; **~ist** *n* dessinateur/trice humoristique; caricaturiste *m/f*; auteur *m* de dessins animés; auteur de bandes dessinées.
cartridge ['kɑ:trɪdʒ] *n* (*for gun, pen*) cartouche *f*; (*for camera*) chargeur *m*; (*music tape*) cassette *f*; (*of record player*) cellule *f*.
carve [kɑ:v] *vt* (*meat*) découper; (*wood, stone*) tailler, sculpter; **carving** *n* (*in wood etc*) sculpture *f*; **carving knife** *n* couteau *m* à découper.
car wash ['kɑ:wɔʃ] *n* station *f* de lavage (de voitures).
cascade [kæs'keɪd] *n* cascade *f* // *vi* tomber en cascade.
case [keɪs] *n* cas *m*; (LAW) affaire *f*, procès *m*; (*box*) caisse *f*, boîte *f*, étui *m*; (*also*: **suit~**) valise *f*; **he hasn't put forward his ~ very well** ses arguments ne sont guère convaincants; **in ~ of** en cas de; **in ~ he** au cas où il; **just in ~** à tout hasard.
cash [kæʃ] *n* argent *m*; (COMM) argent liquide, numéraire *m*; liquidités *fpl*; (COMM: *in payment*) argent comptant, espèces *fpl* // *vt* encaisser; **to pay (in) ~** payer (en argent) comptant; **~ with order/ on delivery** (COMM) payable *or* paiement à la commande/livraison; **~book** *n* livre *m* de caisse; **~desk** *n* caisse *f*.
cashew [kæ'ʃu:] *n* (*also*: **~ nut**) noix *f* de cajou.
cashier [kæ'ʃɪə*] *n* caissier/ère.
cashmere [kæʃ'mɪə*] *n* cachemire *m*.
cash payment ['kæʃ'peɪmənt] *n* paiement comptant, versement *m* en espèces.
cash register ['kæʃrɛdʒɪstə*] *n* caisse enregistreuse.
casing ['keɪsɪŋ] *n* revêtement (protecteur), enveloppe (protectrice).
casino [kə'si:nəu] *n* casino *m*.
cask [kɑ:sk] *n* tonneau *m*.
casket ['kɑ:skɪt] *n* coffret *m*; (*US*: *coffin*) cercueil *m*.
casserole ['kæsərəul] *n* cocotte *f*; (*food*) ragoût *m* (en cocotte).
cassette [kæ'sɛt] *n* cassette *f*, musicassette *f*; **~player** lecteur *m* de cassettes; **~recorder** magnétophone *m* à cassettes.
cast [kɑ:st] *vt* (*pt, pp* **cast**) (*throw*) jeter; (*shed*) perdre; se dépouiller de; (*metal*) couler, fondre // *n* (THEATRE) distribution *f*; (*mould*) moule *m*; (*also*: **plaster ~**) plâtre *m*; (THEATRE): **to ~ sb as Hamlet** attribuer à qn le rôle d'Hamlet; **to ~ one's vote** voter, exprimer son suffrage; **to ~ off** *vi* (NAUT) larguer les amarres.
castanets [kæstə'nɛts] *npl* castagnettes *fpl*.
castaway ['kɑ:stəwəɪ] *n* naufragé/e.
caste [kɑ:st] *n* caste *f*, classe sociale.
casting ['kɑ:stɪŋ] *a*: **~ vote** voix prépondérante (*pour départager*).
cast iron ['kɑ:st'aɪən] *n* fonte *f*.
castle ['kɑ:sl] *n* château-fort *m*; (*manor*) château *m*.
castor ['kɑ:stə*] *n* (*wheel*) roulette *f*; **~ oil** *n* huile *f* de ricin; **~ sugar** *n* sucre *m* semoule.
castrate [kæs'treɪt] *vt* châtrer.
casual ['kæʒjul] *a* (*by chance*) de hasard, fait(e) au hasard, fortuit(e); (*irregular*: *work etc*) temporaire; (*unconcerned*) désinvolte; **~ wear** *n* vêtements *mpl* sport *inv*; **~ labour** *n* main-d'œuvre *f* temporaire; **~ly** *ad* avec désinvolture, négligemment; fortuitement.
casualty ['kæʒjultɪ] *n* accidenté/e, blessé/e; (*dead*) victime *f*, mort/e; **heavy casualties** *npl* lourdes pertes.
cat [kæt] *n* chat *m*.
catalogue, catalog (*US*) ['kætəlɔg] *n* catalogue *m* // *vt* cataloguer.
catalyst ['kætəlɪst] *n* catalyseur *m*.
catapult ['kætəpʌlt] *n* lance-pierres *m inv*, fronde *m*; (AVIAT, HISTORY) catapulte *f*.
cataract ['kætərækt] *n* (*also* MED) cataracte *f*.
catarrh [kə'tɑ:*] *n* rhume *m* chronique, catarrhe *f*.
catastrophe [kə'tæstrəfɪ] *n* catastrophe *f*; **catastrophic** [kætə'strɔfɪk] *a* catastrophique.
catch [kætʃ] *vb* (*pt,pp* **caught** [cɔ:t]) *vt* (*ball, train, thief, cold*) attraper; (*person*: *by surprise*) prendre, surprendre; (*understand*) saisir; (*get entangled*) accrocher // *vi* (*fire*) prendre // *n* (*fish etc caught*) prise *f*; (*thief etc caught*) capture *f*; (*trick*) attrape *f*; (TECH) loquet *m*; cliquet *m*; **to ~ sb's attention** *or* **eye** attirer l'attention de qn; **to ~ fire** prendre feu; **to ~ sight of** apercevoir; **to ~ up** *vi* se rattraper, combler son retard // *vt* (*also*: **~ up with**) rattraper.
catching ['kætʃɪŋ] *a* (MED) contagieux(euse).
catchment area ['kætʃmənt'ɛərɪə] *n* (SCOL) aire *f* de recrutement; (GEO) bassin *m* hydrographique.
catch phrase ['kætʃfreɪz] *n* slogan *m*; expression toute faite.
catchy ['kætʃɪ] *a* (*tune*) facile à retenir.
catechism ['kætɪkɪzəm] *n* (REL) catéchisme *m*.
categoric(al) [kætɪ'gɔrɪk(əl)] *a* catégorique.
categorize ['kætɪgəraɪz] *vt* classer par catégories.
category ['kætɪgərɪ] *n* catégorie *f*.
cater ['keɪtə*] *vi* (*gen*: **~ for sb**) préparer des repas, se charger de la restauration; **to ~ for** *vt fus* (*needs*) satisfaire, pourvoir à; (*readers, consumers*) s'adresser à, pourvoir aux besoins de; **~er** *n* traiteur *m*; fournisseur *m*; **~ing** *n* restauration *f*; approvisionnement *m*, ravitaillement *m*; **~ing (trade)** restauration *f*.
caterpillar ['kætəpɪlə*] *n* chenille *f*; **~ track** *n* chenille *f*; **~ vehicle** *n* véhicule *m* à chenille.
cathedral [kə'θi:drəl] *n* cathédrale *f*.
catholic ['kæθəlɪk] *a* éclectique; universel(le); libéral(e); **C~** *a,n* (REL) catholique (*m/f*).
cattle ['kætl] *npl* bétail *m*, bestiaux *mpl*.

catty ['kætı] *a* méchant(e).
Caucasus ['kɔ:kəsəs] *n* Caucase *m*.
caught [kɔ:t] *pt,pp of* **catch**.
cauliflower ['kɔlıflauə*] *n* chou-fleur *m*.
cause [kɔ:z] *n* cause *f* // *vt* causer ; **there is no ~ for concern** il n'y a pas lieu de s'inquiéter.
causeway ['kɔ:zweı] *n* chaussée (surélevée).
caustic ['kɔ:stık] *a* caustique.
caution ['kɔ:ʃən] *n* prudence *f*; (*warning*) avertissement *m* // *vt* avertir, donner un avertissement à.
cautious ['kɔ:ʃəs] *a* prudent(e) ; **~ly** *ad* prudemment, avec prudence ; **~ness** *n* prudence *f*.
cavalier [kævə'lıə*] *a* cavalier(ère), désinvolte.
cavalry ['kævəlrı] *n* cavalerie *f*.
cave [keıv] *n* caverne *f*, grotte *f*; **to ~ in** *vi* (*roof etc*) s'effondrer ; **~man** *n* homme *m* des cavernes.
cavern ['kævən] *n* caverne *f*.
caviar(e) ['kævıɑ:*] *n* caviar *m*.
cavity ['kævıtı] *n* cavité *f*.
cavort [kə'vɔ:t] *vi* cabrioler, faire des cabrioles.
CBI *n abbr of Confederation of British Industries* (*groupement du patronat*).
cc *abbr of cubic centimetres*; *carbon copy*.
cease [si:s] *vt,vi* cesser ; **~fire** *n* cessez-le-feu *m* ; **~less** *a* incessant(e), continuel(le).
cedar ['si:də*] *n* cèdre *m*.
cede [si:d] *vt* céder.
cedilla [sı'dılə] *n* cédille *f*.
ceiling ['si:lıŋ] *n* plafond *m*.
celebrate ['sɛlıbreıt] *vt,vi* célébrer ; **~d** *a* célèbre ; **celebration** [-'breıʃən] *n* célébration *f*.
celebrity [sı'lɛbrıtı] *n* célébrité *f*.
celery ['sɛlərı] *n* céleri *m* (en branches).
celestial [sı'lɛstıəl] *a* céleste.
celibacy ['sɛlıbəsı] *n* célibat *m*.
cell [sɛl] *n* (*gen*) cellule *f*; (ELEC) élément *m* (*de pile*).
cellar ['sɛlə*] *n* cave *f*.
'cellist ['tʃɛlıst] *n* violoncelliste *m/f*.
'cello ['tʃɛləu] *n* violoncelle *m*.
cellophane ['sɛləfeın] *n* ® cellophane *f* ®.
cellular ['sɛljulə*] *a* cellulaire.
cellulose ['sɛljuləus] *n* cellulose *f*.
Celtic ['kɛltık, 'sɛltık] *a* celte.
cement [sə'mɛnt] *n* ciment *m* // *vt* cimenter.
cemetery ['sɛmıtrı] *n* cimetière *m*.
cenotaph ['sɛnətɑ:f] *n* cénotaphe *m*.
censor ['sɛnsə*] *n* censeur *m* ; **~ship** *n* censure *f*.
censure ['sɛnʃə*] *vt* blâmer, critiquer.
census ['sɛnsəs] *n* recensement *m*.
cent [sɛnt] *n* (*US*: *coin*) cent *m*, = *1:100 du dollar*; *see also* **per**.
centenary [sɛn'ti:nərı] *n* centenaire *m*.
center ['sɛntə*] *n* (*US*) = **centre**.
centi... ['sɛntı] *prefix*: **~grade** *a* centigrade ; **~litre** *n* centilitre *m* ; **~metre** *n* centimètre *m*.
centipede ['sɛntıpi:d] *n* mille-pattes *m inv*.
central ['sɛntrəl] *a* central(e) ; **~ heating** *n* chauffage central ; **~ize** *vt* centraliser.
centre ['sɛntə*] *n* centre *m* ; **~-forward** *n* (SPORT) avant-centre *m* // *vt* centrer ; (PHOT) cadrer **~-half** *n* (SPORT) demi-centre *m*.
centrifugal [sɛn'trıfjugəl] *a* centrifuge.
century ['sɛntjurı] *n* siècle *m*.
ceramic [sı'ræmık] *a* céramique.
cereal ['si:rıəl] *n* céréale *f*.
ceremony ['sɛrıməni] *n* cérémonie *f*; **to stand on ~** faire des façons.
certain ['sə:tən] *a* certain(e) ; **to make ~ of** s'assurer de ; **for ~** certainement, sûrement ; **~ly** *ad* certainement ; **~ty** *n* certitude *f*.
certificate [sə'tıfıkıt] *n* certificat *m*.
certify ['sə:tıfaı] *vt* certifier // *vi*: **to ~ to** attester.
cervix ['sə:vıks] *n* col *m* de l'utérus.
cessation [sə'seıʃən] *n* cessation *f*, arrêt *m*.
cesspool ['sɛspu:l] *n* fosse *f* d'aisance.
Ceylon [sı'lɔn] *n* Ceylan *m*.
cf. (*abbr* = *compare*) cf., voir.
chafe [tʃeıf] *vt* irriter, frotter contre.
chaffinch ['tʃæfıntʃ] *n* pinson *m*.
chagrin ['ʃægrın] *n* contrariété *f*, déception *f*.
chain [tʃeın] *n* (*gen*) chaîne *f* // *vt* (*also*: **~ up**) enchaîner, attacher (avec une chaîne) ; **~ reaction** *n* réaction *f* en chaîne ; **to ~ smoke** *vi* fumer cigarette sur cigarette ; **~ store** *n* magasin *m* à succursales multiples.
chair [tʃɛə*] *n* chaise *f*; (*armchair*) fauteuil *m* ; (*of university*) chaire *f* // *vt* (*meeting*) présider ; **~lift** *n* télésiège *m* ; **~man** *n* président *m*.
chalet ['ʃæleı] *n* chalet *m*.
chalice ['tʃælıs] *n* calice *m*.
chalk [tʃɔ:k] *n* craie *f*.
challenge ['tʃælındʒ] *n* défi *m* // *vt* défier ; (*statement, right*) mettre en question, contester ; **to ~ sb to a fight/game** inviter qn à se battre/à jouer (*sous forme d'un défi*) ; **to ~ sb to do** mettre qn au défi de faire ; **~r** *n* (SPORT) challenger *m* ; **challenging** *a* de défi, provocateur(trice).
chamber ['tʃeımbə*] *n* chambre *f*; **~ of commerce** chambre *f* de commerce ; **~maid** *n* femme *f* de chambre ; **~ music** *n* musique *f* de chambre ; **~pot** *n* pot *m* de chambre.
chamois ['ʃæmwɑ:] *n* chamois *m* ; **~ leather** ['ʃæmılɛðə*] *n* peau *f* de chamois.
champagne [ʃæm'peın] *n* champagne *m*.
champion ['tʃæmpıən] *n* champion/ne ; **~ship** *n* championnat *m*.
chance [tʃɑ:ns] *n* hasard *m* ; (*opportunity*) occasion *f*, possibilité *f*; (*hope, likelihood*) chance *f* // *vt*: **to ~ it** risquer (le coup), essayer // *a* fortuit(e), de hasard ; **there is little ~ of his coming** il est peu probable *or* il y a peu de chances qu'il vienne ; **to take a ~** prendre un risque ; **by ~** par hasard.
chancel ['tʃɑ:nsəl] *n* chœur *m*.
chancellor ['tʃɑ:nsələ*] *n* chancelier *m* ;

C~ of the Exchequer *n* chancelier *m* de l'Échiquier.
chandelier [ʃændə'lɪə*] *n* lustre *m*.
change [tʃeɪndʒ] *vt* (*alter, replace,* COMM: *money*) changer; (*switch, substitute: gear, hands, trains, clothes, one's name etc*) changer de; (*transform*): **to ~ sb into** changer *or* transformer qn en // *vi* (*gen*) changer; (*change clothes*) se changer; (*be transformed*): **to ~ into** se changer *or* transformer en // *n* changement *m*; (*money*) monnaie *f*; **to ~ one's mind** changer d'avis; **a ~ of clothes** des vêtements de rechange; **for a ~** pour changer; **small ~** petite monnaie; **to give sb ~ for** *or* **of £10** faire à qn la monnaie de 10 livres; **~able** *a* (*weather*) variable; **~over** *n* (*to new system*) changement *m*, passage *m*.
changing ['tʃeɪndʒɪŋ] *a* changeant(e); **~ room** *n* (*in shop*) salon *m* d'essayage; (SPORT) vestiaire *m*.
channel ['tʃænl] *n* (TV) chaîne *f*; (*waveband, groove, fig: medium*) canal *m*; (*of river, sea*) chenal *m* // *vt* canaliser; **through the usual ~s** en suivant la filière habituelle; **the (English) C~** la Manche; **the C~ Islands** les îles de la Manche, les îles anglo-normandes.
chant [tʃɑ:nt] *n* chant *m*; mélopée *f*; psalmodie *f* // *vt* chanter, scander; psalmodier.
chaos ['keɪɔs] *n* chaos *m*.
chaotic [keɪ'ɔtɪk] a chaotique.
chap [tʃæp] *n* (*col: man*) type *m* // *vt* (*skin*) gercer, crevasser.
chapel ['tʃæpəl] *n* chapelle *f*.
chaperon ['ʃæpərəun] *n* chaperon *m* // *vt* chaperonner.
chaplain ['tʃæplɪn] *n* aumônier *m*.
chapter ['tʃæptə*] *n* chapitre *m*.
char [tʃɑ:*] *vt* (*burn*) carboniser // *vi* (*cleaner*) faire des ménages // *n* = **charlady**.
character ['kærɪktə*] *n* caractère *m*; (*in novel, film*) personnage *m*; (*eccentric*) numéro *m*, phénomène *m*; **~istic** [-'rɪstɪk] *a,n* caractéristique (*f*); **~ize** *vt* caractériser.
charade [ʃə'rɑ:d] *n* charade *f*.
charcoal ['tʃɑ:kəul] *n* charbon *m* de bois.
charge [tʃɑ:dʒ] *n* accusation f; (LAW) inculpation *f*; (*cost*) prix (demandé); (*of gun, battery,* MIL: *attack*) charge *f* // *vt* (LAW): **to ~sb (with)** inculper qn (de); (*gun, battery,* MIL: *enemy*) charger; (*customer, sum*) faire payer // *vi* (*gen with: up, along etc*) foncer; **~s** *npl*: **bank/labour ~s** frais *mpl* de banque/main -d'œuvre; **to ~ in/out** entrer/sortir en trombe; **to ~ down/up** dévaler/grimper à toute allure; **is there a ~?** doit-on payer?; **there's no ~** c'est gratuit, on ne fait pas payer; **to take ~ of** se charger de; **to be in ~ of** être responsable de, s'occuper de; **to have ~ of sb** avoir la charge de qn; **they ~d us £10 for the meal** ils nous ont fait payer le repas 10 livres, ils nous ont compté 10 livres pour le repas; **how much do you ~ for this repair?** combien demandez-vous pour cette réparation?; **to ~ an expense (up) to sb** mettre une dépense sur le compte de qn.
charitable ['tʃærɪtəbl] *a* charitable.
charity ['tʃærɪtɪ] *n* charité *f*; institution *f* charitable *or* de bienfaisance, œuvre *f* (de charité).
charlady ['tʃɑ:leɪdɪ] *n* femme *f* de ménage.
charm [tʃɑ:m] *n* charme *m* // *vt* charmer, enchanter; **~ing** *a* charmant(e).
chart [tʃɑ:t] *n* tableau *m*, diagramme *m*; graphique *m*; (*map*) carte marine // *vt* dresser *or* établir la carte de.
charter ['tʃɑ:tə*] *vt* (*plane*) affréter // *n* (*document*) charte *f*; **~ed accountant** *n* expert-comptable *m*; **~ flight** *n* charter *m*.
charwoman ['tʃɑ:wumən] *n* = **charlady.**
chase [tʃeɪs] *vt* poursuivre, pourchasser // *n* poursuite *f*, chasse *f*.
chasm ['kæzəm] *n* gouffre *m*, abîme *m*.
chassis ['ʃæsɪ] *n* châssis *m*.
chastity ['tʃæstɪtɪ] *n* chasteté *f*.
chat [tʃæt] *vi* (*also*: **have a ~**) bavarder, causer // *n* conversation *f*.
chatter ['tʃætə*] *vi* (*person*) bavarder, papoter // *n* bavardage *m*, papotage *m*; **my teeth are ~ing** je claque des dents; **~box** *n* moulin *m* à paroles, babillard/e.
chatty ['tʃætɪ] *a* (*style*) familier(ère); (*person*) enclin(e) à bavarder *or* au papotage.
chauffeur ['ʃəufə*] *n* chauffeur *m* (de maître).
cheap [tʃi:p] *a* bon marché *inv*, pas cher(chère); (*joke*) facile, d'un goût douteux; (*poor quality*) à bon marché, de qualité médiocre // *ad* à bon marché, pour pas cher; **~en** *vt* rabaisser, déprécier; **~ly** *ad* à bon marché, à bon compte.
cheat [tʃi:t] *vi* tricher // *vt* tromper, duper; (*rob*) escroquer // *n* tricheur/euse; escroc *m*; (*trick*) duperie *f*, tromperie *f*; **~ing** *n* tricherie *f*.
check [tʃɛk] *vt* vérifier; (*passport, ticket*) contrôler; (*halt*) enrayer; (*restrain*) maîtriser // *n* vérification *f*; contrôle *m*; (*curb*) frein *m*; (*bill*) addition *f*; (*pattern: gen pl*) carreaux *mpl*; (*US*) = **cheque; to ~ in** *vi* (*in hotel*) remplir sa fiche (d'hôtel); (*at airport*) se présenter à l'enregistrement // *vt* (*luggage*) (faire) enregistrer; **to ~ off** *vt* cocher; **to ~ out** *vi* (*in hotel*) régler sa note // *vt* (*luggage*) retirer; **to ~ up** *vi*: **to ~ up (on sth)** vérifier (qch); **to ~ up on sb** se renseigner sur le compte de qn; **~ers** *n* (*US*) jeu *m* de dames; **~mate** *n* échec et mat *m*; **~point** *n* contrôle *m*; **~up** *n* (MED) examen médical, check-up *m*.
cheek [tʃi:k] *n* joue *f*; (*impudence*) toupet *m*, culot *m*; **~bone** *n* pommette *f*; **~y** *a* effronté(e), culotté(e).
cheer [tʃɪə*] *vt* acclamer, applaudir; (*gladden*) réjouir, réconforter // *vi* applaudir // *n* (*gen pl*) acclamations *fpl*, applaudissements *mpl*; bravos *mpl*, hourras *mpl*; **~s!** (à votre) santé!; **to ~ up** *vi* se dérider, reprendre courage // *vt* remonter le moral à *or* de, dérider, égayer; **~ful** *a* gai(e), joyeux(euse); **~fulness** *n* gaieté *f*, bonne humeur; **~io** *excl* salut!, au revoir!; **~less** *a* sombre, triste.

cheese [tʃi:z] *n* fromage *m*; **~board** *n* plateau *m* à fromages.
chef [ʃɛf] *n* chef (cuisinier).
chemical ['kɛmɪkəl] *a* chimique // *n* produit *m* chimique.
chemist ['kɛmɪst] *n* pharmacien/ne; (*scientist*) chimiste *m/f*; **~ry** *n* chimie *f*; **~'s (shop)** *n* pharmacie *f*.
cheque [tʃɛk] *n* chèque *m*; **~book** *n* chéquier *m*, carnet *m* de chèques.
chequered ['tʃɛkəd] *a* (*fig*) varié(e).
cherish ['tʃɛrɪʃ] *vt* chérir; (*hope etc*) entretenir.
cheroot [ʃə'ru:t] *n* cigare *m* de Manille.
cherry ['tʃɛrɪ] *n* cerise *f*.
chess [tʃɛs] *n* échecs *mpl*; **~board** *n* échiquier *m*; **~man** *n* pièce *f* (de jeu d'échecs); **~player** *n* joueur/euse d'échecs.
chest [tʃɛst] *n* poitrine f; (*box*) coffre *m*, caisse *f*; **~ of drawers** *n* commode *f*.
chestnut ['tʃɛsnʌt] *n* châtaigne *f*; **~ (tree)** *n* châtaignier *m*.
chew [tʃu:] *vt* mâcher; **~ing gum** *n* chewing-gum *m*.
chic [ʃi:k] *a* chic *inv*, élégant(e).
chick [tʃɪk] *n* poussin *m*.
chicken ['tʃɪkɪn] *n* poulet *m*; **~ feed** *n* (*fig*) broutilles *fpl*, bagatelle *f*; **~ pox** *n* varicelle *f*.
chick pea ['tʃɪkpi:] *n* pois *m* chiche.
chicory ['tʃɪkərɪ] *n* (*for coffee*) chicorée *f*; (*salad*) endive *f*.
chief [tʃi:f] *n* chef *m* // *a* principal(e); **~ly** *ad* principalement, surtout.
chiffon ['ʃɪfɔn] *n* mousseline *f* de soie.
chilblain ['tʃɪlbleɪn] *n* engelure *f*.
child, *pl* **~ren** [tʃaɪld, 'tʃɪldrən] *n* enfant *m/f*; **~birth** *n* accouchement *m*; **~hood** *n* enfance *f*; **~ish** *a* puéril(e), enfantin(e); **~like** *a* innocent(e), pur(e); **~ minder** *n* garde *f* d'enfants.
Chile ['tʃɪlɪ] *n* Chili *m*; **~an** *a* chilien(ne) // *n* Chilien/ne.
chill [tʃɪl] *n* froid *m*; (MED) refroidissement *m*, coup *m* de froid // *a* froid(e), glacial(e) // *vt* faire frissonner; refroidir; (CULIN) mettre au frais, rafraîchir; **serve ~ed** à servir frais; **~y** *a* froid(e), glacé(e); (*sensitive to cold*) frileux(euse); **to feel ~y** avoir froid.
chime [tʃaɪm] *n* carillon *m* // *vi* carillonner, sonner.
chimney ['tʃɪmnɪ] *n* cheminée *f*.
chimpanzee [tʃɪmpæn'zi:] *n* chimpanzé *m*.
chin [tʃɪn] *n* menton *m*.
china ['tʃaɪnə] *n* porcelaine *f*; (vaisselle *f* en) porcelaine.
China ['tʃaɪnə] *n* Chine *f*.
Chinese [tʃaɪ'ni:z] *a* chinois(e) // *n* Chinois/e; (LING) chinois *m*.
chink [tʃɪŋk] *n* (*opening*) fente *f*, fissure *f*; (*noise*) tintement *m*.
chip [tʃɪp] *n* (*gen pl*: CULIN) frite *f*; (*of wood*) copeau *m*; (*of glass, stone*) éclat *m* // *vt* (*cup, plate*) ébrécher; **~board** *n* aggloméré *m*; **~pings** *npl*: **loose ~pings** gravillons *mpl*.
chiropodist [kɪ'rɔpədɪst] *n* pédicure *m/f*.
chirp [tʃə:p] *n* pépiement *m*, gazouillis *m* // *vi* pépier, gazouiller.
chisel ['tʃɪzl] *n* ciseau *m*.
chit [tʃɪt] *n* mot *m*, note *f*.
chitchat ['tʃɪttʃæt] *n* bavardage *m*, papotage *m*.
chivalrous ['ʃɪvəlrəs] *a* chevaleresque.
chivalry ['ʃɪvəlrɪ] *n* chevalerie *f*; esprit *m* chevaleresque.
chives [tʃaɪvz] *npl* ciboulette *f*, civette *f*.
chloride ['klɔ:raɪd] *n* chlorure *m*.
chlorine ['klɔ:ri:n] *n* chlore *m*.
chock [tʃɔk] *n* cale *f*; **~-a-block, ~-full** *a* plein(e) à craquer.
chocolate ['tʃɔklɪt] *n* chocolat *m*.
choice [tʃɔɪs] *n* choix *m* // *a* de choix.
choir ['kwaɪə*] *n* chœur *m*, chorale *f*; **~boy** *n* jeune choriste *m*, petit chanteur.
choke [tʃəuk] *vi* étouffer // *vt* étrangler; étouffer; (*block*) boucher, obstruer // *n* (AUT) starter *m*.
cholera ['kɔlərə] *n* choléra *m*.
choose, *pt* **chose,** *pp* **chosen** [tʃu:z, tʃəuz, 'tʃəuzn] *vt* choisir; **to ~ to do** décider de faire, juger bon de faire.
chop [tʃɔp] *vt* (*wood*) couper (à la hache); (CULIN: *also*: **~ up**) couper (fin), émincer, hacher (en morceaux) // *n* coup *m* (*de hache, du tranchant de la main*); (CULIN) côtelette *f*; **~s** *npl* (*jaws*) mâchoires *fpl*; babines *fpl*; **to ~ down** *vt* (*tree*) abattre; **~py** *a* (*sea*) un peu agité(e); **~sticks** *npl* baguettes *fpl*.
choral ['kɔ:rəl] *a* choral(e), chanté(e) en chœur.
chord [kɔ:d] *n* (MUS) accord *m*.
chore [tʃɔ:*] *n* travail *m* de routine; **household ~s** travaux *mpl* du ménage.
choreographer [kɔrɪ'ɔgrəfə*] *n* chorégraphe *m/f*.
chorister ['kɔrɪstə*] *n* choriste *m/f*.
chortle ['tʃɔ:tl] *vi* glousser.
chorus ['kɔ:rəs] *n* chœur *m*; (*repeated part of song, also fig*) refrain *m*.
chose [tʃəuz] *pt of* **choose**.
chosen ['tʃəuzn] *pp of* **choose**.
chow [tʃau] *n* (*dog*) chow-chow *m*.
Christ [kraɪst] *n* Christ *m*.
christen ['krɪsn] *vt* baptiser; **~ing** *n* baptême *m*.
Christian ['krɪstɪən] *a,n* chrétien(ne); **~ity** [-'ænɪtɪ] *n* christianisme *m*; chrétienté *f*; **~ name** *n* prénom *m*.
Christmas ['krɪsməs] *n* Noël *m or f*; **~ card** *n* carte *f* de Noël; **~ Eve** *n* la veille de Noël; la nuit de Noël; **~ tree** *n* arbre *m* de Noël.
chrome [krəum] *n* = **chromium.**
chromium ['krəumɪəm] *n* chrome *m*; (*also*: **~ plating**) chromage *m*.
chromosome ['krəuməsəum] *n* chromosome *m*.
chronic ['krɔnɪk] *a* chronique.
chronicle ['krɔnɪkl] *n* chronique *f*.
chronological [krɔnə'lɔdʒɪkəl] *a* chronologique.
chrysanthemum [krɪ'sænθəməm] *n* chrysanthème *m*.
chubby ['tʃʌbɪ] *a* potelé(e), rondelet(te).

chuck [tʃʌk] *vt* lancer, jeter ; **to ~ out** *vt* flanquer dehors *or* à la porte ; **to ~ (up)** *vt* lâcher, plaquer.
chuckle ['tʃʌkl] *vi* glousser.
chum [tʃʌm] *n* copain/copine.
chunk [tʃʌŋk] *n* gros morceau ; (*of bread*) quignon *m*.
church [tʃə:tʃ] *n* église *f*; **~yard** *n* cimetière *m*.
churlish ['tʃə:lɪʃ] *a* grossier(ère) ; hargneux(euse).
churn [tʃə:n] *n* (*for butter*) baratte *f*; (*for transport*: **milk ~**) (grand) bidon à lait.
chute [ʃu:t] *n* glissoire *f*; (*also*: **rubbish ~**) vide-ordures *m inv*; (*children's slide*) toboggan *m*.
chutney ['tʃʌtnɪ] *n* condiment *m à base de fruits*.
CID *n* (*abbr of Criminal Investigation Department*) ≈ Police *f* judiciaire (P.J.).
cider ['saɪdə*] *n* cidre *m*.
cigar [sɪ'gɑ:*] *n* cigare *m*.
cigarette [sɪgə'rɛt] *n* cigarette *f*; **~ case** *n* étui *m* à cigarettes ; **~ end** *n* mégot *m*; **~ holder** *n* fume-cigarettes *m inv*.
cinch [sɪntʃ] *n* (*col*): **it's a ~** c'est du gâteau, c'est l'enfance de l'art.
cinder ['sɪndə*] *n* cendre *f*.
cine ['sɪnɪ]: **~-camera** *n* caméra *f*; **~-film** *n* film *m*.
cinema ['sɪnəmə] *n* cinéma *m*.
cine-projector [sɪnɪprə'dʒɛktə*] *n* projecteur *m* de cinéma.
cinnamon ['sɪnəmən] *n* cannelle *f*.
cipher ['saɪfə*] *n* code secret ; (*fig*: *faceless employee etc*) numéro *m*.
circle ['sə:kl] *n* cercle *m*; (*in cinema*) balcon *m* // *vi* faire *or* décrire des cercles // *vt* (*surround*) entourer, encercler ; (*move round*) faire le tour de, tourner autour de.
circuit ['sə:kɪt] *n* circuit *m*; **~ous** [sə:'kjuɪtəs] *a* indirect(e), qui fait un détour.
circular ['sə:kjulə*] *a* circulaire // *n* circulaire *f*.
circulate ['sə:kjuleɪt] *vi* circuler // *vt* faire circuler ; **circulation** [-'leɪʃən] *n* circulation *f*; (*of newspaper*) tirage *m*.
circumcise ['sə:kəmsaɪz] *vt* circoncire.
circumference [sə'kʌmfərəns] *n* circonférence *f*.
circumspect ['sə:kəmspɛkt] *a* circonspect(e).
circumstances ['sə:kəmstənsɪz] *npl* circonstances *fpl*; (*financial condition*) moyens *mpl*, situation financière.
circus ['sə:kəs] *n* cirque *m*.
cistern ['sɪstən] *n* réservoir *m* (d'eau) ; (*in toilet*) réservoir de la chasse d'eau.
cite [saɪt] *vt* citer.
citizen ['sɪtɪzn] *n* (POL) citoyen/ne ; (*resident*): **the ~s of this town** les habitants de cette ville ; **~ship** *n* citoyenneté *f*.
citrus fruit ['sɪtrəs'fru:t] *n* agrume *m*.
city ['sɪtɪ] *n* ville *f*, cité *f*; **the C~** la Cité de Londres (*centre des affaires*).
civic ['sɪvɪk] *a* civique.
civil ['sɪvɪl] *a* civil(e) ; poli(e), civil ; **~ engineer** *n* ingénieur civil ; **~ engineering** *n* génie civil, travaux publics ; **~ian** [sɪ'vɪlɪən] *a,n* civil(e).
civilization [sɪvɪlaɪ'zeɪʃən] *n* civilisation *f*.
civilized ['sɪvɪlaɪzd] *a* civilisé(e) ; (*fig*) où règnent les bonnes manières, empreint(e) d'une courtoisie de bon ton.
civil: **~ law** *n* code civil ; (*study*) droit civil ; **~ servant** *n* fonctionnaire *m/f*; **C~ Service** *n* fonction publique, administration *f*; **~ war** *n* guerre civile.
claim [kleɪm] *vt* revendiquer ; demander, prétendre à ; déclarer, prétendre // *vi* (*for insurance*) faire une déclaration de sinistre // *n* revendication *f*; demande *f*; prétention *f*, déclaration *f*; (*right*) droit *m*, titre *m*; **(insurance) ~** demande *f* d'indemnisation, déclaration *f* de sinistre ; **~ant** *n* (ADMIN, LAW) requérant/e.
clam [klæm] *n* palourde *f*.
clamber ['klæmbə*] *vi* grimper, se hisser.
clammy ['klæmɪ] *a* humide et froid(e) (au toucher), moite.
clamp [klæmp] *n* étau *m* à main ; agrafe *f*, crampon *m* // *vt* serrer ; cramponner ; **to ~ down on** *vt fus* sévir contre, prendre des mesures draconiennes à l'égard de.
clan [klæn] *n* clan *m*.
clang [klæŋ] *n* bruit *m or* fracas *m* métallique.
clap [klæp] *vi* applaudir // *vt*: **to ~ (one's hands)** battre des mains // *n* claquement *m*; tape *f*; **~ping** *n* applaudissements *mpl*.
claret ['klærət] *n* (vin *m* de) bordeaux *m* (rouge).
clarification [klærɪfɪ'keɪʃən] *n* (*fig*) clarification *f*, éclaircissement *m*.
clarify ['klærɪfaɪ] *vt* clarifier.
clarinet [klærɪ'nɛt] *n* clarinette *f*.
clarity ['klærɪtɪ] *n* clarté *f*.
clash [klæʃ] *n* choc *m*; (*fig*) conflit *m* // *vi* se heurter ; être *or* entrer en conflit.
clasp [klɑ:sp] *n* fermoir *m* // *vt* serrer, étreindre.
class [klɑ:s] *n* (*gen*) classe *f* // *vt* classer, classifier.
classic ['klæsɪk] *a* classique // *n* (*author*) classique *m*; (*race etc*) classique *f*; **~al** *a* classique.
classification [klæsɪfɪ'keɪʃən] *n* classification *f*.
classified ['klæsɪfaɪd] *a* (*information*) secret(ète) ; **~ ads** petites annonces.
classify ['klæsɪfaɪ] *vt* classifier, classer.
classmate ['klɑ:smeɪt] *n* camarade *m/f* de classe.
classroom ['klɑ:srum] *n* (salle *f* de) classe *f*.
clatter ['klætə*] *n* cliquetis *m*; caquetage *m* // *vi* cliqueter ; (*talk*) caqueter, jacasser.
clause [klɔ:z] *n* clause *f*; (LING) proposition *f*.
claustrophobia [klɔ:strə'fəubɪə] *n* claustrophobie *f*.
claw [klɔ:] *n* griffe *f*; (*of bird of prey*) serre *f*; (*of lobster*) pince *f* // *vt* griffer ; déchirer.
clay [kleɪ] *n* argile *f*.
clean [kli:n] *a* propre ; (*clear, smooth*) net(te) // *vt* nettoyer ; **to ~ out** *vt* nettoyer (à fond) ; **to ~ up** *vt* nettoyer ; (*fig*) remettre de l'ordre dans ; **~er** *n* (*person*) nettoyeur/euse, femme *f* de ménage ; (*also*: **dry ~er**) teinturier/ière ; (*product*) détachant *m*; **~ing** *n* nettoyage

m; **~liness** ['klɛnlɪnɪs] *n* propreté *f*; **~ly** *ad* proprement; nettement.

cleanse [klɛnz] *vt* nettoyer; purifier; **~r** *n* détergent *m*; (*for face*) démaquillant *m*; **cleansing department** *n* service *m* de voirie.

clean-shaven ['kli:n'ʃeɪvn] *a* rasé(e) de près.

clean-up ['kli:n'ʌp] *n* nettoyage *m*.

clear [klɪə*] *a* clair(e); (*road, way*) libre, dégagé(e) // *vt* dégager, déblayer, débarrasser; faire évacuer; (COMM: *goods*) liquider; (LAW: *suspect*) innocenter; (*obstacle*) franchir *or* sauter sans heurter // *vi* (*weather*) s'éclaircir; (*fog*) se dissiper // *ad*: **~ of** à distance de, à l'écart de; **to ~ one's throat** s'éclaircir la gorge; **to ~ up** *vi* s'éclaircir, se dissiper // *vt* ranger, mettre en ordre; (*mystery*) éclaircir, résoudre; **~ance** *n* (*removal*) déblayage *m*; (*free space*) dégagement *m*; (*permission*) authorisation *f*; **~ance sale** *n* liquidation *f*; **~-cut** *a* précise(e), nettement défini(e); **~ing** *n* clairière *f*; (BANKING) compensation *f*, clearing *m*; **~ly** *ad* clairement; de toute évidence; **~way** *n* (*Brit*) route *f* à stationnement interdit.

cleavage ['kli:vɪdʒ] *n* (*of dress*) décolleté *m*.

clef [klɛf] *n* (MUS) clé *f*.

clench [klɛntʃ] *vt* serrer.

clergy ['klə:dʒɪ] *n* clergé *m*; **~man** *n* ecclésiastique *m*.

clerical ['klɛrɪkəl] *a* de bureau, d'employé de bureau; (REL) clérical(e), du clergé.

clerk [klɑ:k, (*US*) klə:rk] *n* employé/e de bureau; (*US*: *salesman/woman*) vendeur/-euse.

clever ['klɛvə*] *a* (*mentally*) intelligent(e); (*deft, crafty*) habile, adroit(e); (*device, arrangement*) ingénieux(euse), astucieux-(euse).

cliché ['kli:ʃeɪ] *n* cliché *m*.

click [klɪk] *vi* faire un bruit sec *or* un déclic.

client ['klaɪənt] *n* client/e; **~ele** [kli:ɑ̃:n'tɛl] *n* clientèle *f*.

cliff [klɪf] *n* falaise *f*.

climate ['klaɪmɪt] *n* climat *m*.

climax ['klaɪmæks] *n* apogée *m*, point culminant; (*sexual*) orgasme *m*.

climb [klaɪm] *vi* grimper, monter // *vt* gravir, escalader, monter sur // *n* montée *f*, escalade *f*; **to ~ down** *vi* (re)descendre; **~er** *n* (*also*: **rock ~er**) grimpeur/euse, varappeur/ euse; **~ing** *n* (*also*: **rock ~ing**) escalade *f*, varappe *f*.

clinch [klɪntʃ] *vt* (*deal*) conclure, sceller.

cling, *pt, pp* **clung** [klɪŋ, klʌŋ] *vi*: **to ~ (to)** se cramponner (à), s'accrocher (à); (*of clothes*) coller (à).

clinic ['klɪnɪk] *n* centre médical; **~al** *a* clinique.

clink [klɪŋk] *vi* tinter, cliqueter.

clip [klɪp] *n* (*for hair*) barrette *f*; (*also*: **paper ~**) trombone *m*; (*also*: **bulldog ~**) pince *f* de bureau; (*holding hose etc*) collier *m or* bague *f* (métallique) de serrage // *vt* (*also*: **~ together**: *papers*) attacher; (*hair, nails*) couper; (*hedge*) tailler; **~pers** *npl* tondeuse *f*; (*also*: **nail ~pers**) coupe-ongles *m inv*.

clique [kli:k] *n* clique *f*, coterie *f*.

cloak [kləuk] *n* grande cape; **~room** *n* (*for coats etc*) vestiaire *m*; (*W.C.*) toilettes *fpl*.

clock [klɔk] *n* (*large*) horloge *f*; (*small*) pendule *f*; **~wise** *ad* dans le sens des aiguilles d'une montre; **~work** *n* mouvement *m* (d'horlogerie); rouages *mpl*, mécanisme *m*.

clog [klɔg] *n* sabot *m* // *vt* boucher, encrasser // *vi* se boucher, s'encrasser.

cloister ['klɔɪstə*] *n* cloître *m*.

close *a, ad and derivatives* [kləus] *a* près, proche; (*writing, texture*) serré(e); (*watch*) étroit(e), strict(e); (*examination*) attentif(ive), minutieux(euse); (*weather*) lourd(e), étouffant(e); (*room*) mal aéré(e) // *ad* près, à proximité; **a ~ friend** un ami intime; **to have a ~ shave** (*fig*) l'échapper belle // *vb and derivatives* [kləuz] *vt* fermer // *vi* (*shop etc*) fermer; (*lid, door etc*) se fermer; (*end*) se terminer, se conclure // *n* (*end*) conclusion *f*; **to ~ down** *vt,vi* fermer (*définitivement*); **~d** *a* (*shop etc*) fermé(e); (*road*) fermé à la circulation; **~d shop** *n* organisation *f* qui n'admet que des travailleurs syndiqués; **~ly** *ad* (*examine, watch*) de près.

closet ['klɔzɪt] *n* (*cupboard*) placard *m*, réduit *m*.

close-up ['kləusʌp] *n* gros plan.

closure ['kləuʒə*] *n* fermeture *f*.

clot [klɔt] *n* (*gen*: **blood ~**) caillot *m* // *vi* (*blood*) former des caillots; (: *external bleeding*) se coaguler; **~ted cream** *n* crème caillée.

cloth [klɔθ] *n* (*material*) tissu *m*, étoffe *f*; (*also*: **tea~**) torchon *m*; lavette *f*.

clothe [kləuð] *vt* habiller, vêtir; **~s** *npl* vêtements *mpl*, habits *mpl*; **~s brush** *n* brosse *f* à habits; **~s line** *n* corde *f* (à linge); **~s peg** *n* pince *f* à linge.

clothing ['kləuðɪŋ] *n* = **clothes.**

cloud [klaud] *n* nuage *m*; **~burst** *n* violente averse; **~y** *a* nuageux(euse), couvert(e); (*liquid*) trouble.

clout [klaut] *n* (*blow*) taloche *f* // *vt* flanquer une taloche à.

clove [kləuv] *n* clou *m* de girofle; **~ of garlic** gousse *f* d'ail.

clover ['kləuvə*] *n* trèfle *m*; **~leaf** *n* feuille *f* de trèfle; **~leaf junction** (AUT) *n* croisement *m* en trèfle.

clown [klaun] *n* clown *m* // *vi* (*also*: **~ about, ~ around**) faire le clown.

club [klʌb] *n* (*society*) club *m*; (*weapon*) massue *f*, matraque *f*; (*also*: **golf ~**) club // *vt* matraquer // *vi*: **to ~ together** s'associer; **~s** *npl* (CARDS) trèfle *m*; **~house** *n* pavillon *m*.

cluck [klʌk] *vi* glousser.

clue [klu:] *n* indice *m*; (*in crosswords*) définition *f*; **I haven't a ~** je n'en ai pas la moindre idée.

clump [klʌmp] *n*: **~ of trees** bouquet *m* d'arbres.

clumsy ['klʌmzɪ] *a* (*person*) gauche, maladroit(e); (*object*) malcommode, peu maniable.

clung [klʌŋ] *pt, pp of* **cling.**

cluster ['klʌstə*] *n* (petit) groupe// *vi* se rassembler.

clutch [klʌtʃ] *n* (*grip, grasp*) étreinte *f*, prise *f*; (AUT) embrayage *m* // *vt* agripper, serrer fort; **to ~ at** se cramponner à.
clutter ['klʌtə*] *vt* encombrer.
Co. *abbr of* **county**; **company**.
c/o (*abbr of care of*) c/o, aux bons soins de.
coach [kəutʃ] *n* (*bus*) autocar *m*; (*horse-drawn*) diligence *f*; (*of train*) voiture *f*, wagon *m*; (SPORT: *trainer*) entraîneur/euse; (*school: tutor*) répétiteur/trice // *vt* entraîner; donner des leçons particulières à.
coagulate [kəu'ægjuleɪt] *vt* coaguler // *vi* se coaguler.
coal [kəul] *n* charbon *m*; **~ face** *n* front *m* de taille; **(~) face workers** *npl* mineurs *mpl* de fond; **~field** *n* bassin houiller.
coalition [kəuə'lɪʃən] *n* coalition *f*.
coalman, coal merchant ['kəulmən, 'kəulmə:tʃənt] *n* charbonnier *m*, marchand *m* de charbon.
coalmine ['kəulmaɪn] *n* mine *f* de charbon.
coarse [kɔ:s] *a* grossier(ère), rude.
coast [kəust] *n* côte *f* // *vi* (*with cycle etc*) descendre en roue libre; **~al** *a* côtier(ère); **~er** *n* caboteur *m*; **~guard** *n* garde-côte *m*; **~line** *n* côte *f*, littoral *m*.
coat [kəut] *n* manteau *m*; (*of animal*) pelage *m*, poil *m*; (*of paint*) couche *f* // *vt* couvrir, enduire; **~ of arms** *n* blason *m*, armoiries *fpl*; **~ hanger** *n* cintre *m*; **~ing** *n* couche *f*, enduit *m*.
coax [kəuks] *vt* persuader par des cajoleries.
cob [kɔb] *n see* **corn**.
cobbles, cobblestones ['kɔblz, 'kɔblstəunz] *npl* pavés (ronds).
cobra ['kəubrə] *n* cobra *m*.
cobweb ['kɔbwɛb] *n* toile *f* d'araignée.
cocaine [kɔ'keɪn] *n* cocaïne *f*.
cock [kɔk] *n* (*rooster*) coq *m*; (*male bird*) mâle *m* // *vt* (*gun*) armer; **to ~ one's ears** (*fig*) dresser l'oreille; **~erel** *n* jeune coq *m*; **~-eyed** *a* (*fig*) de travers; qui louche; qui ne tient pas debout (*fig*).
cockle ['kɔkl] *n* coque *f*.
cockney ['kɔknɪ] *n* cockney *m/f* (*habitant des quartiers populaires de l'East End de Londres*), ≈ faubourien/ne.
cockpit ['kɔkpɪt] *n* (*in aircraft*) poste *m* de pilotage, cockpit *m*.
cockroach ['kɔkrəutʃ] *n* cafard *m*, cancrelat *m*.
cocktail ['kɔkteɪl] *n* cocktail *m*; **~ cabinet** *n* (meuble-)bar *m*; **~ party** *n* cocktail *m*; **~ shaker** *n* shaker *m*.
cocoa ['kəukəu] *n* cacao *m*.
coconut ['kəukənʌt] *n* noix *f* de coco.
cocoon [kə'ku:n] *n* cocon *m*.
cod [kɔd] *n* morue (fraîche), cabillaud *m*.
code [kəud] *n* code *m*.
codify ['kəudɪfaɪ] *vt* codifier.
coeducational ['kəuɛdju'keɪʃənl] *a* mixte.
coerce [kəu'ə:s] *vt* contraindre; **coercion** [-'ə:ʃən] *n* contrainte *f*.
coexistence ['kəuɪg'zɪstəns] *n* coexistence *f*.
coffee ['kɔfɪ] *n* café *m*; **~ grounds** *npl* marc *m* de café; **~pot** *n* cafetière *f*; **~ table** *n* (petite) table basse.
coffin ['kɔfɪn] *n* cercueil *m*.
cog [kɔg] *n* dent *f* (d'engrenage); **~wheel** *n* roue dentée.
cogent ['kəudʒənt] *a* puissant(e), convaincant(e).
cognac ['kɔnjæk] *n* cognac *m*.
coherent [kəu'hɪərənt] *a* cohérent(e).
coil [kɔɪl] *n* rouleau *m*, bobine *f*; (*one loop*) anneau *m*, spire *f*; (*contraceptive*) stérilet *m* // *vt* enrouler.
coin [kɔɪn] *n* pièce *f* de monnaie // *vt* (*word*) inventer; **~age** *n* monnaie *f*, système *m* monétaire; **~-box** *n* cabine *f* téléphonique.
coincide [kəuɪn'saɪd] *vi* coïncider; **~nce** [kəu'ɪnsɪdəns] *n* coïncidence *f*.
coke [kəuk] *n* coke *m*.
colander ['kɔləndə*] *n* passoire *f* (à légumes).
cold [kəuld] *a* froid(e) // *n* froid *m*; (MED) rhume *m*; **it's ~** il fait froid; **to be ~** avoir froid; **to have ~ feet** avoir froid aux pieds; (*fig*) avoir la frousse *or* la trouille; **to give sb the ~ shoulder** battre froid à qn; **~ly** *a* froidement; **~ sore** *n* herpès *m*.
coleslaw ['kəulslɔ:] *n sorte de salade de chou cru*.
colic ['kɔlɪk] *n* colique(s) *f(pl)*.
collaborate [kə'læbəreɪt] *vi* collaborer; **collaboration** [-'reɪʃən] *n* collaboration *f*; **collaborator** *n* collaborateur/trice.
collage [kɔ'lɑ:ʒ] *n* (ART) collage *m*.
collapse [kə'læps] *vi* s'effondrer, s'écrouler // *n* effondrement *m*, écroulement *m*.
collapsible [kə'læpsəbl] *a* pliant(e); télescopique.
collar ['kɔlə*] *n* (*of coat, shirt*) col *m*; **~bone** *n* clavicule *f*.
collate [kɔ'leɪt] *vt* collationner.
colleague ['kɔli:g] *n* collègue *m/f*.
collect [kə'lɛkt] *vt* rassembler; ramasser; (*as a hobby*) collectionner; (*call and pick up*) (passer) prendre; (*mail*) faire la levée de, ramasser; (*money owed*) encaisser; (*donations, subscriptions*) recueillir // *vi* se rassembler; s'amasser; **~ed** *a*: **~ed works** œuvres complètes; **~ion** [kə'lɛkʃən] *n* collection *f*; levée *f*; (*for money*) collecte *f*, quête *f*.
collective [kə'lɛktɪv] *a* collectif(ive).
collector [kə'lɛktə*] *n* collectionneur *m*; (*of taxes*) percepteur *m*; (*of rent, cash*) encaisseur *m*.
college ['kɔlɪdʒ] *n* collège *m*; **~ of education** ≈ école normale.
collide [kə'laɪd] *vi*: **to ~ (with)** entrer en collision (avec); (*fig*) entrer en conflit (avec), se heurter (à).
colliery ['kɔlɪərɪ] *n* mine *f* de charbon, houillère *f*.
collision [kə'lɪʒən] *n* collision *f*, heurt *m*; (*fig*) conflit *m*.
colloquial [kə'ləukwɪəl] *a* familier(ère).
colon ['kəulən] *n* (*sign*) deux-points *mpl*; (MED) côlon *m*.
colonel ['kə:nl] *n* colonel *m*.
colonial [kə'ləunɪəl] *a* colonial(e).
colonize ['kɔlənaɪz] *vt* coloniser.

colony ['kɔlənı] *n* colonie *f*.
color ['kʌlə*] *n,vt* (*US*) = **colour.**
Colorado [kɔlə'rɑ:dəu]: ~ **beetle** *n* doryphore *m*.
colossal [kə'lɔsl] *a* colossal(e).
colour, color (*US*) ['kʌlə*] *n* couleur *f* // *vt* colorer ; peindre ; (*with crayons*) colorier ; (*news*) fausser, exagérer ; ~**s** *npl* (*of party, club*) couleurs *fpl* ; ~ **bar** *n* discrimination raciale (*dans un établissement etc*) ; ~**-blind** *a* daltonien(ne) ; ~**ed** *a* coloré(e) ; (*photo*) en couleur // *n*: ~**eds** personnes *fpl* de couleur ; ~ **film** *n* (*for camera*) pellicule *f* (en) couleur ; ~**ful** *a* coloré(e), vif(vive) ; (*personality*) pittoresque, haut(e) en couleurs ; ~ **scheme** *n* combinaison *f* de(s) couleurs ; ~ **television** *n* télévision *f* en couleur.
colt [kəult] *n* poulain *m*.
column ['kɔləm] *n* colonne *f*; ~**ist** ['kɔləmnıst] *n* rédacteur/trice d'une rubrique.
coma ['kəumə] *n* coma *m*.
comb [kəum] *n* peigne *m* // *vt* (*hair*) peigner ; (*area*) ratisser, passer au peigne fin.
combat ['kɔmbæt] *n* combat *m* // *vt* combattre, lutter contre.
combination [kɔmbı'neıʃən] *n* (*gen*) combinaison *f*.
combine *vb* [kəm'baın] *vt* combiner ; (*one quality with another*) joindre (à), allier (à) // *vi* s'associer ; (CHEM) se combiner // *n* ['kɔmbaın] association *f*; (ECON) trust *m* ; ~ **(harvester)** *n* moissonneuse-batteuse(-lieuse) *f*.
combustible [kəm'bʌstıbl] *a* combustible.
combustion [kəm'bʌstʃən] *n* combustion *f*.
come, *pt* **came,** *pp* **come** [kʌm, keım] *vi* venir ; arriver ; **to ~ into sight** *or* **view** apparaître ; **to ~ to** (*decision etc*) parvenir *or* arriver à ; **to ~ undone/loose** se défaire/desserrer ; **to ~ about** *vi* se produire, arriver ; **to ~ across** *vt fus* rencontrer par hasard, tomber sur ; **to ~ along** *vi* = **to come on** ; **to ~ apart** *vi* s'en aller en morceaux ; se détacher ; **to ~ away** *vi* partir, s'en aller ; se détacher ; **to ~ back** *vi* revenir ; **to ~ by** *vt fus* (*acquire*) obtenir, se procurer ; **to ~ down** *vi* descendre ; (*prices*) baisser ; (*buildings*) s'écrouler ; être démoli(e) ; **to ~ forward** *vi* s'avancer ; se présenter, s'annoncer ; **to ~ from** *vi* être originaire de ; venir de ; **to ~ in** *vi* entrer ; **to ~ in for** *vt fus* (*criticism etc*) être l'objet de ; **to ~ into** *vt fus* (*money*) hériter de ; **to ~ off** *vi* (*button*) se détacher ; (*stain*) s'enlever ; (*attempt*) réussir ; **to ~ on** *vi* (*pupil, undertaking*) faire des progrès, avancer ; ~ **on!** viens! ; allons!, allez! ; **to ~ out** *vi* sortir ; (*book*) paraître ; (*strike*) cesser le travail, se mettre en grève ; **to ~ to** *vi* revenir à soi ; **to ~ up** *vi* monter ; **to ~ up against** *vt fus* (*resistance, difficulties*) rencontrer ; **to ~ up with** *vt fus*: **he came up with an idea** il a eu une idée, il a proposé quelque chose ; **to ~ upon** *vt fus* tomber sur ; ~**back** *n* (THEATRE *etc*) rentrée *f*.

comedian [kə'mi:dıən] *n* (*in music hall etc*) comique *m* ; (THEATRE) comédien *m*.
comedienne [kəmi:dı'ɛn] *n* comédienne *f*.
comedown ['kʌmdaun] *n* déchéance *f*.
comedy ['kɔmıdı] *n* comédie *f*.
comet ['kɔmıt] *n* comète *f*.
comfort ['kʌmfət] *n* confort *m*, bien-être *m* ; (*solace*) consolation *f*, réconfort *m* // *vt* consoler, réconforter ; ~**s** *npl* aises *fpl* ; ~**able** *a* confortable ; ~ **station** *n* (*US*) toilettes *fpl*.
comic ['kɔmık] *a* (*also*: ~**al**) comique // *n* comique *m* ; (*magazine*) illustré *m* ; ~ **strip** *n* bande dessinée.
coming ['kʌmıŋ] *n* arrivée *f*; ~**(s) and going(s)** *n*(*pl*) va-et-vient *m inv*.
comma ['kɔmə] *n* virgule *f*.
command [kə'mɑ:nd] *n* ordre *m*, commandement *m* ; (MIL: *authority*) commandement ; (*mastery*) maîtrise *f* // *vt* (*troops*) commander ; (*be able to get*) (pouvoir) disposer de, avoir à sa disposition ; (*deserve*) avoir droit à ; **to ~ sb to do** donner l'ordre *or* commander à qn de faire ; ~**eer** [kɔmən'dıə*] *vt* réquisitionner (par la force) ; ~**er** *n* chef *m* ; (MIL) commandant *m* ; ~**ing officer** *n* commandant *m*.
commando [kə'mɑ:ndəu] *n* commando *m* ; membre *m* d'un commando.
commemorate [kə'mɛməreıt] *vt* commémorer ; **commemoration** [-'reıʃən] *n* commémoration *f*.
commemorative [kə'mɛmərətıv] *a* commémoratif(ive).
commence [kə'mɛns] *vt,vi* commencer.
commend [kə'mɛnd] *vt* louer ; recommander ; ~**able** *a* louable ; ~**ation** [kɔmɛn'deıʃən] *n* éloge *m* ; recommandation *f*.
commensurate [kə'mɛnʃərıt] *a*: ~ **with** en proportion de, proportionné(e) à.
comment ['kɔmɛnt] *n* commentaire *m* // *vi* faire des remarques *or* commentaires ; ~**ary** ['kɔməntərı] *n* commentaire *m* ; (SPORT) reportage *m* (en direct) ; ~**ator** ['kɔmənteıtə*] *n* commentateur *m* ; reporter *m*.
commerce ['kɔmə:s] *n* commerce *m*.
commercial [kə'mə:ʃəl] *a* commercial(e) // *n* (TV: *also*: ~ **break**) annonce *f* publicitaire, spot *m* (publicitaire) ; ~ **college** *n* école *f* de commerce ; ~**ize** *vt* commercialiser ; ~ **television** *n* la publicité à la télévision, les chaînes indépendantes ; ~ **traveller** *n* voyageur *m* de commerce ; ~ **vehicle** *n* véhicule *m* utilitaire.
commiserate [kə'mızəreıt] *vi*: **to ~ with** compatir à.
commission [kə'mıʃən] *n* (*committee, fee*) commission *f*; (*order for work of art etc*) commande *f* // *vt* (MIL) nommer (à un commandement) ; (*work of art*) commander, charger un artiste de l'exécution de ; **out of ~** (NAUT) hors de service ; ~**aire** [kəmıʃə'nɛə*] *n* (*at shop, cinema etc*) portier *m* (en uniforme) ; ~**er** *n* membre *m* d'une commission ; (POLICE) préfet *m* (de police).
commit [kə'mıt] *vt* (*act*) commettre ; (*to sb's care*) confier (à) ; **to ~ o.s. (to do)** s'engager (à faire) ; **to ~ suicide** se

suicider; **to ~ to writing** coucher par écrit; **~ment** *n* engagement *m*, responsabilité(s) *f(pl)*.

committee [kə'mɪtɪ] *n* comité *m*.

commodity [kə'mɔdɪtɪ] *n* produit *m*, marchandise *f*, article *m*; (*food*) denrée *f*.

common ['kɔmən] *a* (*gen, also pej*) commun(e); (*usual*) courant(e) // *n* terrain communal; **the C~s** *npl* la chambre des Communes; **in ~** en commun; **it's ~ knowledge that** il est bien connu *or* notoire que; **to the ~ good** pour le bien de tous, dans l'intérêt général; **~er** *n* roturier/ière; **~ ground** *n* (*fig*) terrain *m* d'entente; **~ law** *n* droit coutumier; **~ly** *ad* communément, généralement; couramment; **C~ Market** *n* Marché commun; **~place** *a* banal(e), ordinaire; **~room** *n* salle commune; (*SCOL*) salle des professeurs; **~ sense** *n* bon sens; **the C~wealth** *n* le Commonwealth.

commotion [kə'məuʃən] *n* désordre *m*, tumulte *m*.

communal ['kɔmju:nl] *a* (*life*) communautaire; (*for common use*) commun(e).

commune *n* ['kɔmju:n] (*group*) communauté *f* // *vi* [kə'mju:n]: **to ~ with** converser intimement avec; communier avec.

communicate [kə'mju:nɪkeɪt] *vt* communiquer, transmettre // *vi*: **to ~** (**with**) communiquer (avec).

communication [kəmju:nɪ'keɪʃən] *n* communication *f*; **~ cord** *n* sonnette *f* d'alarme.

communion [kə'mju:nɪən] *n* (*also*: **Holy C~**) communion *f*.

communiqué [kə'mju:nɪkeɪ] *n* communiqué *m*.

communism ['kɔmjunɪzəm] *n* communisme *m*; **communist** *a,n* communiste (*m/f*).

community [kə'mju:nɪtɪ] *n* communauté *f*; **~ centre** *n* foyer socio-éducatif, centre *m* de loisirs; **~ chest** *n* (*US*) fonds commun.

commutation ticket [kɔmju'teɪʃəntɪkɪt] *n* (*US*) carte *f* d'abonnement.

commute [kə'mju:t] *vi* faire le trajet journalier (de son domicile à un lieu de travail assez éloigné) // *vt* (*LAW*) commuer; (*MATH*: *terms etc*) opérer la commutation de; **~r** *n* banlieusard/e (qui ... *see vi*).

compact *a* [kəm'pækt] compact(e) // *n* ['kɔmpækt] contrat *m*, entente *f*; (*also*: **powder ~**) poudrier *m*.

companion [kəm'pænɪən] *n* compagnon/-compagne; **~ship** *n* camaraderie *f*.

company ['kʌmpənɪ] *n* (*also COMM, MIL, THEATRE*) compagnie *f*; **he's good ~** il est d'une compagnie agréable; **we have ~** nous avons de la visite; **to keep sb ~** tenir compagnie à qn; **to part ~ with** se séparer de; **~ secretary** *n* (*COMM*) secrétaire général (*d'une société*).

comparable ['kɔmpərəbl] *a* comparable.

comparative [kəm'pærətɪv] *a* comparatif(ive); (*relative*) relatif(ive).

compare [kəm'pɛə*] *vt*: **to ~ sth/sb with/to** comparer qch/qn avec *or* et/à // *vi*: **to ~ (with)** se comparer (à); être comparable (à); **comparison** [-'pærɪsn] *n* comparaison *f*; **in comparison (with)** en comparaison (de).

compartment [kəm'pɑ:tmənt] *n* (*also RAIL*) compartiment *m*.

compass ['kʌmpəs] *n* boussole *f*; **~es** *npl* compas *m*.

compassion [kəm'pæʃən] *n* compassion *f*, humanité *f*; **~ate** *a* accessible à la compassion, au cœur charitable et bienveillant; **on ~ate grounds** pour raisons personnelles *or* de famille.

compatible [kəm'pætɪbl] *a* compatible.

compel [kəm'pɛl] *vt* contraindre, obliger; **~ling** *a* (*fig*: *argument*) irrésistible.

compendium [kəm'pɛndɪəm] *n* abrégé *m*.

compensate ['kɔmpənseɪt] *vt* indemniser, dédommager // *vi*: **to ~ for** compenser; **compensation** [-'seɪʃən] *n* compensation *f*; (*money*) dédommagement *m*, indemnité *f*.

compère ['kɔmpɛə*] *n* présentateur/trice, animateur/trice.

compete [kəm'pi:t] *vi* (*take part*) concourir; (*vie*): **to ~ (with)** rivaliser (avec), faire concurrence (à).

competence ['kɔmpɪtəns] *n* compétence *f*, aptitude *f*.

competent ['kɔmpɪtənt] *a* compétent(e), capable.

competition [kɔmpɪ'tɪʃən] *n* compétition *f*, concours *m*; (*ECON*) concurrence *f*.

competitive [kəm'pɛtɪtɪv] *a* (*ECON*) concurrentiel(le); **~ examination** *n* (*SCOL*) concours *m*.

competitor [kəm'pɛtɪtə*] *n* concurrent/e.

compile [kəm'paɪl] *vt* compiler.

complacency [kəm'pleɪsnsɪ] *n* contentement *m* de soi, vaine complaisance.

complacent [kəm'pleɪsənt] *a* (trop) content(e) de soi; suffisant(e).

complain [kəm'pleɪn] *vi*: **to ~ (about)** se plaindre (de); (*in shop etc*) réclamer (au sujet de); **to ~ of** *vt fus* (*MED*) se plaindre de; **~t** *n* plainte *f*; réclamation *f*; (*MED*) affection *f*.

complement ['kɔmplɪmənt] *n* complément *m*; (*especially of ship's crew etc*) effectif complet; **~ary** [kɔmplɪ'mɛntərɪ] *a* complémentaire.

complete [kəm'pli:t] *a* complet(ète) // *vt* achever, parachever; (*a form*) remplir; **~ly** *ad* complètement; **completion** *n* achèvement *m*.

complex ['kɔmplɛks] *a* complexe // *n* (*PSYCH, buildings etc*) complexe *m*.

complexion [kəm'plɛkʃən] *n* (*of face*) teint *m*; (*of event etc*) aspect *m*, caractère *m*.

complexity [kəm'plɛksɪtɪ] *n* complexité *f*.

compliance [kəm'plaɪəns] *n* (*see compliant*) docilité *f*; (*see comply*): **~ with** le fait de se conformer à; **in ~ with** en conformité avec, conformément à.

compliant [kəm'plaɪənt] *a* docile, très accommodant(e).

complicate ['kɔmplɪkeɪt] *vt* compliquer;

~**d** *a* compliqué(e); **complication** [-'keɪʃən] *n* complication *f*.
compliment *n* ['kɔmplɪmənt] compliment *m* // *vt* ['kɔmplɪmɛnt] complimenter; ~**s** *npl* compliments *mpl*, hommages *mpl*; vœux *mpl*; ~**ary** [-'mɛntərɪ] *a* flatteur(euse); (*free*) à titre gracieux; ~**ary ticket** *n* billet *m* de faveur.
comply [kəm'plaɪ] *vi*: **to** ~ **with** se soumettre à, se conformer à.
component [kəm'pəunənt] *a* composant(e), constituant(e) // *n* composant *m*, élément *m*.
compose [kəm'pəuz] *vt* composer; **to** ~ **o.s.** se calmer, se maîtriser; prendre une contenance; ~**d** *a* calme, posé(e); ~**r** *n* (MUS) compositeur *m*.
composite ['kɔmpəzɪt] *a* composite; (BOT, MATH) composé(e).
composition [kɔmpə'zɪʃən] *n* composition *f*.
compost ['kɔmpɔst] *n* compost *m*.
composure [kəm'pəuʒə*] *n* calme *m*, maîtrise *f* de soi.
compound ['kɔmpaund] *n* (CHEM, LING) composé *m*; (*enclosure*) enclos *m*, enceinte *f* // *a* composé(e); ~ **fracture** *n* fracture compliquée; ~ **interest** *n* intérêt composé.
comprehend [kɔmprɪ'hɛnd] *vt* comprendre; **comprehension** [-'hɛnʃən] *n* compréhension *f*.
comprehensive [kɔmprɪ'hɛnsɪv] *a* (très) complet(ète); ~ **policy** *n* (INSURANCE) assurance *f* tous risques; ~ **(school)** *n* *école secondaire non sélective, avec libre circulation d'une section à l'autre,* ≈ C.E.S. *m*.
compress *vt* [kəm'prɛs] comprimer // *n* ['kɔmprɛs] (MED) compresse *f*; ~**ion** [-'prɛʃən] *n* compression *f*.
comprise [kəm'praɪz] *vt* (*also*: **be** ~**d of**) comprendre.
compromise ['kɔmprəmaɪz] *n* compromis *m* // *vt* compromettre // *vi* transiger, accepter un compromis.
compulsion [kəm'pʌlʃən] *n* contrainte *f*, force *f*.
compulsive [kəm'pʌlsɪv] *a* (*reason, demand*) coercitif(ive); (PSYCH) compulsif(ive); **he's a** ~ **smoker** c'est un fumeur invétéré.
compulsory [kəm'pʌlsərɪ] *a* obligatoire.
computer [kəm'pju:tə*] *n* ordinateur *m*; (*mechanical*) calculatrice *f*; ~**ize** *vt* traiter *or* automatiser par ordinateur; ~ **language** *n* langage *m* machine *or* de programmation; ~ **programming** *n* programmation *f*; ~ **science** *n* informatique *f*; ~ **scientist** *n* informaticien/ne.
comrade ['kɔmrɪd] *n* camarade *m/f*; ~**ship** *n* camaraderie *f*.
con [kɔn] *vt* duper; escroquer.
concave ['kɔn'keɪv] *a* concave.
conceal [kən'si:l] *vt* cacher, dissimuler.
concede [kən'si:d] *vt* concéder // *vi* céder.
conceit [kən'si:t] *n* vanité *f*, suffisance *f*, prétention *f*; ~**ed** *a* vaniteux(euse), suffisant(e).
conceivable [kən'si:vəbl] *a* concevable, imaginable.
conceive [kən'si:v] *vt* concevoir.
concentrate ['kɔnsəntreɪt] *vi* se concentrer // *vt* concentrer.
concentration [kɔnsən'treɪʃən] *n* concentration *f*; ~ **camp** *n* camp *m* de concentration.
concentric [kɔn'sɛntrɪk] *a* concentrique.
concept ['kɔnsɛpt] *n* concept *m*.
conception [kən'sɛpʃən] *n* conception *f*.
concern [kən'sə:n] *n* affaire *f*; (COMM) entreprise *f*, firme *f*; (*anxiety*) inquiétude *f*, souci *m* // *vt* concerner; **to be** ~**ed** (**about**) s'inquiéter (de), être inquiet (au sujet de); ~**ing** *prep* en ce qui concerne, à propos de.
concert ['kɔnsət] *n* concert *m*; **in** ~ à l'unisson, en chœur; ensemble; ~**ed** [kən'sə:tɪd] *a* concerté(e); ~ **hall** *n* salle *f* de concert.
concertina [kɔnsə'ti:nə] *n* concertina *m* // *vi* se télescoper, se caramboler.
concerto [kən'tʃə:təu] *n* concerto *m*.
concession [kən'sɛʃən] *n* concession *f*.
conciliation [kənsɪlɪ'eɪʃən] *n* conciliation *f*, apaisement *m*.
conciliatory [kən'sɪlɪətrɪ] *a* conciliateur(trice); conciliant(e).
concise [kən'saɪs] *a* concis(e).
conclave ['kɔnkleɪv] *n* assemblée secrète; (REL) conclave *m*.
conclude [kən'klu:d] *vt* conclure; **conclusion** [-'klu:ʒən] *n* conclusion *f*; **conclusive** [-'klu:sɪv] *a* concluant(e), définitif(ive).
concoct [kən'kɔkt] *vt* confectionner, composer.
concourse ['kɔŋkɔ:s] *n* (*hall*) hall *m*, salle *f* des pas perdus; (*crowd*) affluence *f*; multitude *f*.
concrete ['kɔŋkri:t] *n* béton *m* // *a* concret(ète); en béton.
concur [kən'kə:*] *vi* être d'accord.
concurrently [kən'kʌrntlɪ] *ad* simultanément.
concussion [kən'kʌʃən] *n* ébranlement *m*, secousse *f*; (MED) commotion (cérébrale).
condemn [kən'dɛm] *vt* condamner; ~**ation** [kɔndɛm'neɪʃən] *n* condamnation *f*.
condensation [kɔndɛn'seɪʃən] *n* condensation *f*.
condense [kən'dɛns] *vi* se condenser // *vt* condenser; ~**d milk** *n* lait condensé (sucré).
condescend [kɔndɪ'sɛnd] *vi* condescendre, s'abaisser; ~**ing** *a* condescendant(e).
condition [kən'dɪʃən] *n* condition *f* // *vt* déterminer, conditionner; **on** ~ **that** à condition que + *sub*, à condition de; ~**al** *a* conditionnel(le); **to be** ~**al upon** dépendre de.
condolences [kən'dəulənsɪz] *npl* condoléances *fpl*.
condone [kən'dəun] *vt* fermer les yeux sur, approuver (tacitement).
conducive [kən'dju:sɪv] *a*: ~ **to** favorable à, qui contribue à.
conduct *n* ['kɔndʌkt] conduite *f* // *vt* [kən'dʌkt] conduire; (*manage*) mener, diriger; (MUS) diriger; **to** ~ **o.s.** se

conduire, se comporter; **~ed tour** *n* voyage organisé, visite guidée; **~or** *n* (*of orchestra*) chef *m* d'orchestre; (*on bus*) receveur *m*; (ELEC) conducteur *m*; **~ress** *n* (*on bus*) receveuse *f*.

conduit ['kɔndɪt] *n* conduit *m*, tuyau *m*; tube *m*.

cone [kəun] *n* cône *m*; (*for ice-cream*) cornet *m*; (BOT) pomme *f* de pin, cône.

confectioner [kən'fɛkʃənə*] *n* (*of cakes*) pâtissier/ière; (*of sweets*) confiseur/euse; **~y** *n* pâtisserie *f*; confiserie *f*.

confederation [kənfɛdə'reɪʃən] *n* confédération *f*.

confer [kən'fə:*] *vt*: **to ~ sth on** conférer qch à // *vi* conférer, s'entretenir.

conference ['kɔnfərns] *n* conférence *f*.

confess [kən'fɛs] *vt* confesser, avouer // *vi* se confesser; **~ion** [-'fɛʃən] *n* confession *f*; **~ional** [-'fɛʃənl] *n* confessional *m*; **~or** *n* confesseur *m*.

confetti [kən'fɛtɪ] *n* confettis *mpl*.

confide [kən'faɪd] *vi*: **to ~ in** s'ouvrir à, se confier à.

confidence ['kɔnfɪdns] *n* confiance *f*; (*also*: **self-~**) assurance *f*, confiance en soi; (*secret*) confidence *f*; **~ trick** *n* escroquerie *f*; **confident** *a* sûr(e), assuré(e); **confidential** [kɔnfɪ'dɛnʃəl] *a* confidentiel(le).

confine [kən'faɪn] *vt* limiter, borner; (*shut up*) confiner, enfermer; **~s** ['kɔnfaɪnz] *npl* confins *mpl*, bornes *fpl*; **~d** *a* (*space*) restreint(e), réduit(e); **~ment** *n* emprisonnement *m*, détention *f*; (MIL) consigne *f* (au quartier); (MED) accouchement *m*.

confirm [kən'fə:m] *vt* (*report*) confirmer; (*appointment*) ratifier; **~ation** [kɔnfə'meɪʃən] *n* confirmation *f*; **~ed** *a* invétéré(e), incorrigible.

confiscate ['kɔnfɪskeɪt] *vt* confisquer; **confiscation** [-'keɪʃən] *n* confiscation *f*.

conflagration [kɔnflə'greɪʃən] *n* incendie *m*.

conflict *n* ['kɔnflɪkt] conflit *m*, lutte *f* // *vi* [kən'flɪkt] être *or* entrer en conflit; (*opinions*) s'opposer, se heurter; **~ing** *a* contradictoire.

conform [kən'fɔ:m] *vi*: **to ~ (to)** se conformer (à); **~ist** *n* conformiste *m/f*.

confound [kən'faund] *vt* confondre; **~ed** *a* maudit(e), sacré(e).

confront [kən'frʌnt] *vt* confronter, mettre en présence; (*enemy, danger*) affronter, faire face à; **~ation** [kɔnfrən'teɪʃən] *n* confrontation *f*.

confuse [kən'fju:z] *vt* embrouiller; (*one thing with another*) confondre; **confusing** *a* peu clair(e), déroutant(e); **confusion** [-'fju:ʒən] *n* confusion *f*.

congeal [kən'dʒi:l] *vi* (*oil*) se figer; (*blood*) se coaguler.

congenial [kən'dʒi:nɪəl] *a* sympathique, agréable.

congenital [kən'dʒɛnɪtl] *a* congénital(e).

conger eel ['kɔŋgəri:l] *n* congre *m*.

congested [kən'dʒɛstɪd] *a* (MED) congestionné(e); (*fig*) surpeuplé(e); congestionné; bloqué(e).

congestion [kən'dʒɛstʃən] *n* congestion *f*; (*fig*) encombrement *m*.

conglomeration [kənglɔmə'reɪʃən] *n* groupement *m*; agglomération *f*.

congratulate [kən'grætjuleɪt] *vt*: **to ~ sb (on)** féliciter qn (de); **congratulations** [-'leɪʃənz] *npl* félicitations *fpl*.

congregate [kɔŋgrɪgeɪt] *vi* se rassembler, se réunir.

congregation [kɔŋgrɪ'geɪʃən] *n* assemblée *f* (des fidèles).

congress ['kɔŋgrɛs] *n* congrès *m*; **~man** *n* (*US*) membre *m* du Congrès.

conical ['kɔnɪkl] *a* (de forme) conique.

conifer ['kɔnɪfə*] *n* conifère *m*; **~ous** [kə'nɪfərəs] *a* (*forest*) de conifères.

conjecture [kən'dʒɛktʃə*] *n* conjecture *f* // *vt, vi* conjecturer.

conjugal ['kɔndʒugl] *a* conjugal(e).

conjugate ['kɔndʒugeɪt] *vt* conjuguer; **conjugation** [-'geɪʃən] *n* conjugaison *f*.

conjunction [kən'dʒʌŋkʃən] *n* conjonction *f*.

conjunctivitis [kəndʒʌŋktɪ'vaɪtɪs] *n* conjonctivite *f*.

conjure ['kʌndʒə*] *vt* faire apparaître (par la prestidigitation); [kən'dʒuə*] conjurer, supplier; **to ~ up** *vt* (*ghost, spirit*) faire apparaître; (*memories*) évoquer; **~r** *n* prestidigitateur *m*, illusionniste *m/f*; **conjuring trick** *n* tour *m* de prestidigitation.

conk [kɔŋk]: **to ~ out** *vi* (*col*) tomber *or* rester en panne.

conman ['kɔnmæn] *n* escroc *m*.

connect [kə'nɛkt] *vt* joindre, relier; (ELEC) connecter; (*fig*) établir un rapport entre, faire un rapprochement entre // *vi* (*train*): **to ~ with** assurer la correspondance avec; **to be ~ed with** avoir un rapport avec; avoir des rapports avec, être en relation avec; **~ion** [-ʃən] *n* relation *f*, lien *m*; (ELEC) connexion *f*; (TEL) communication *f*; **in ~ion with** à propos de.

connexion [kə'nɛkʃən] *n* = **connection.**

conning tower ['kɔnɪŋtauə*] *n* kiosque *m* (*de sous-marin*).

connive [kə'naɪv] *vi*: **to ~ at** se faire le complice de.

connoisseur [kɔnɪ'sə*] *n* connaisseur *m*.

connotation [kɔnə'teɪʃən] *n* connotation *f*, implication *f*.

connubial [kɔ'nju:bɪəl] *a* conjugal(e).

conquer ['kɔŋkə*] *vt* conquérir; (*feelings*) vaincre, surmonter; **~or** *n* conquérant *m*, vainqueur *m*.

conquest ['kɔŋkwɛst] *n* conquête *f*.

cons [kɔnz] *npl see* **pro**, **convenience**.

conscience ['kɔnʃəns] *n* conscience *f*.

conscientious [kɔnʃɪ'ɛnʃəs] *a* consciencieux(euse); (*scruple, objection*) de conscience; **~ objector** *n* objecteur *m* de conscience.

conscious ['kɔnʃəs] *a* conscient(e); **~ness** *n* conscience *f*; (MED) connaissance *f*; **to lose/regain ~ness** perdre/reprendre connaissance.

conscript ['kɔnskrɪpt] *n* conscrit *m*; **~ion** [kən'skrɪpʃən] *n* conscription *f*.

consecrate ['kɔnsɪkreɪt] *vt* consacrer.
consecutive [kən'sɛkjutɪv] *a* consécutif(ive).
consensus [kən'sɛnsəs] *n* consensus *m*.
consent [kən'sɛnt] *n* consentement *m* // *vi*: **to ~ (to)** consentir (à) ; **age of ~** âge nubile (légal).
consequence ['kɔnsɪkwəns] *n* suites *fpl*, conséquence *f*; importance *f*.
consequently ['kɔnsɪkwəntlɪ] *ad* par conséquent, donc.
conservation [kɔnsə:'veɪʃən] *n* préservation *f*, protection *f*.
conservative [kən'sə:vətɪv] *a* conservateur(trice) ; (*cautious*) prudent(e) ; **C~** *a,n* conservateur(trice).
conservatory [kən'sə:vətrɪ] *n* (*greenhouse*) serre *f*.
conserve [kən'sə:v] *vt* conserver, préserver.
consider [kən'sɪdə*] *vt* considérer, réfléchir à ; (*take into account*) penser à, prendre en considération ; (*regard, judge*) considérer, estimer.
considerable [kən'sɪdərəbl] *a* considérable.
considerate [kən'sɪdərɪt] *a* prévenant(e), plein(e) d'égards.
consideration [kənsɪdə'reɪʃən] *n* considération *f*; (*reward*) rétribution *f*, rémunération *f*; **out of ~ for** par égard pour ; **under ~** à l'étude.
considering [kən'sɪdərɪŋ] *prep* étant donné.
consign [kən'saɪn] *vt* expédier, livrer ; **~ment** *n* arrivage *m*, envoi *m*.
consist [kən'sɪst] *vi*: **to ~ of** consister en, se composer de.
consistency [kən'sɪstənsɪ] *n* consistance *f*; (*fig*) cohérence *f*.
consistent [kən'sɪstənt] *a* logique, cohérent(e) ; **~ with** compatible avec, en accord avec.
consolation [kɔnsə'leɪʃən] *n* consolation *f*.
console *vt* [kən'səul] consoler // *n* ['kɔnsəul] console *f*.
consolidate [kən'sɔlɪdeɪt] *vt* consolider.
consommé [kən'sɔmeɪ] *n* consommé *m*.
consonant ['kɔnsənənt] *n* consonne *f*.
consortium [kən'sɔ:tɪəm] *n* consortium *m*, comptoir *m*.
conspicuous [kən'spɪkjuəs] *a* voyant(e), qui attire la vue *or* l'attention.
conspiracy [kən'spɪrəsɪ] *n* conspiration *f*, complot *m*.
conspire [kən'spaɪə*] *vi* conspirer, comploter.
constable ['kʌnstəbl] *n* ≈ agent *m* de police, gendarme *m* ; **chief ~** *n* ≈ préfet *m* de police.
constabulary [kən'stæbjulərɪ] *n* ≈ police *f*, gendarmerie *f*.
constant ['kɔnstənt] *a* constant(e) ; incessant(e) ; **~ly** *ad* constamment, sans cesse.
constellation [kɔnstə'leɪʃən] *n* constellation *f*.
consternation [kɔnstə'neɪʃən] *n* consternation *f*.
constipated ['kɔnstɪpeɪtəd] *a* constipé(e).
constipation [kɔnstɪ'peɪʃən] *n* constipation *f*.
constituency [kən'stɪtjuənsɪ] *n* circonscription électorale.
constituent [kən'stɪtjuənt] *n* électeur/-trice ; (*part*) élément constitutif, composant *m*.
constitute ['kɔnstɪtju:t] *vt* constituer.
constitution [kɔnstɪ'tju:ʃən] *n* constitution *f*; **~al** *a* constitutionnel(le).
constrain [kən'streɪn] *vt* contraindre, forcer ; **~ed** *a* contraint(e), gêné(e) ; **~t** *n* contrainte *f*.
constrict [kən'strɪkt] *vt* rétrécir, resserrer ; gêner, limiter.
construct [kən'strʌkt] *vt* construire ; **~ion** [-ʃən] *n* construction *f*; **~ive** *a* constructif(ive).
construe [kən'stru:] *vt* analyser, expliquer.
consul ['kɔnsl] *n* consul *m* ; **~ate** ['kɔnsjulɪt] *n* consulat *m*.
consult [kən'sʌlt] *vt* consulter ; **~ancy** *n*: **~ancy fee** honoraires *mpl* d'expert ; **~ant** *n* (MED) médecin consultant ; (*other specialist*) consultant *m*, (expert-)conseil *m* // *a*: **~ant engineer** ingénieur-conseil *m* ; **legal/management ~ant** conseiller *m* juridique/en gestion ; **~ation** [kɔnsəl'teɪʃən] *n* consultation *f*; **~ing room** *n* cabinet *m* de consultation.
consume [kən'sju:m] *vt* consommer ; **~r** *n* consommateur/ trice ; **consumerism** *n* mouvement *m* pour la protection des consommateurs ; **~r society** *n* société *f* de consommation.
consummate ['kɔnsʌmeɪt] *vt* consommer.
consumption [kən'sʌmpʃən] *n* consommation *f*; (MED) consomption *f* (pulmonaire).
cont. *abbr of continued.*
contact ['kɔntækt] *n* contact *m* ; (*person*) connaissance *f*, relation *f* // *vt* se mettre en contact *or* en rapport avec ; **~ lenses** *npl* verres *mpl* de contact.
contagious [kən'teɪdʒəs] *a* contagieux(euse).
contain [kən'teɪn] *vt* contenir ; **to ~ o.s.** se contenir, se maîtriser ; **~er** *n* récipient *m* ; (*for shipping etc*) container *m*.
contaminate [kən'tæmɪneɪt] *vt* contaminer ; **contamination** [-'neɪʃən] *n* contamination *f*.
cont'd *abbr of continued.*
contemplate ['kɔntəmpleɪt] *vt* contempler ; (*consider*) envisager ; **contemplation** [-'pleɪʃən] *n* contemplation *f*.
contemporary [kən'tɛmpərərɪ] *a* contemporain(e) ; (*design, wallpaper*) moderne // *n* contemporain/e.
contempt [kən'tɛmpt] *n* mépris *m*, dédain *m* ; **~ible** *a* méprisable, vil(e) ; **~uous** *a* dédaigneux(euse), méprisant(e).
contend [kən'tɛnd] *vt*: **to ~ that** soutenir *or* prétendre que // *vi*: **to ~ with** rivaliser avec, lutter avec ; **~er** *n* prétendant/e ; adversaire *m/f*.
content [kən'tɛnt] *a* content(e), satisfait(e) // *vt* contenter, satisfaire // *n* ['kɔntɛnt] contenu *m* ; teneur *f*; **~s** *npl*

contenu; (*of barrel etc*: *capacity*) contenance *f*; **(table of) ~s** table *f* des matières; **to be ~ with** se contenter de; **~ed** *a* content(e), satisfait(e).

contention [kən'tɛnʃən] *n* dispute *f*, contestation *f*; (*argument*) assertion *f*, affirmation *f*; **contentious** *a* querelleur(euse); litigieux(euse).

contentment [kən'tɛntmənt] *n* contentement *m*, satisfaction *f*.

contest *n* ['kɔntɛst] combat *m*, lutte *f*; (*competition*) concours *m* // *vt* [kən'tɛst] contester, discuter; (*compete for*) disputer; **~ant** [kən'tɛstənt] *n* concurrent/e; (*in fight*) adversaire *m/f*.

context ['kɔntɛkst] *n* contexte *m*.

continent ['kɔntɪnənt] *n* continent *m*; **the C~** l'Europe continentale; **~al** [-'nɛntl] *a* continental(e) // *n* Européen/ne (continental(e)).

contingency [kən'tɪndʒənsɪ] *n* éventualité *f*, événement imprévu; **~ plan** *n* plan *m* d'urgence.

contingent [kən'tɪndʒənt] *a* contingent(e) // *n* contingent *m*; **to be ~ upon** dépendre de.

continual [kən'tɪnjuəl] *a* continuel(le); **~ly** *ad* continuellement, sans cesse.

continuation [kəntɪnju'eɪʃən] *n* continuation *f*; (*after interruption*) reprise *f*; (*of story*) suite *f*.

continue [kən'tɪnju:] *vi* continuer // *vt* continuer; (*start again*) reprendre; **to be ~d** (*story*) à suivre.

continuity [kɔntɪ'njuɪtɪ] *n* continuité *f*; **~ girl** *n* (CINEMA) script-girl *f*.

continuous [kən'tɪnjuəs] *a* continu(e), permanent(e).

contort [kən'tɔ:t] *vt* tordre, crisper; **~ion** [-'tɔ:ʃən] *n* crispation *f*, torsion *f*; (*of acrobat*) contorsion *f*; **~ionist** [-'tɔ:ʃənɪst] *n* contorsionniste *m/f*.

contour ['kɔntuə*] *n* contour *m*, profil *m*; (*also*: **~ line**) courbe *f* de niveau.

contraband ['kɔntrəbænd] *n* contrebande *f*.

contraception [kɔntrə'sɛpʃən] *n* contraception *f*.

contraceptive [kɔntrə'sɛptɪv] *a* contraceptif(ive), anticonceptionnel(le) // *n* contraceptif *m*.

contract *n* ['kɔntrækt] contrat *m* // *vb* [kən'trækt] *vi* (COMM): **to ~ to do sth** s'engager (par contrat) à faire qch; (*become smaller*) se contracter, se resserrer // *vt* contracter; **~ion** [-ʃən] *n* contraction *f*; (LING) forme contractée; **~or** *n* entrepreneur *m*.

contradict [kɔntrə'dɪkt] *vt* contredire; (*be contrary to*) démentir, être en contradiction avec; **~ion** [-ʃən] *n* contradiction *f*.

contralto [kən'træltəu] *n* contralto *m*.

contraption [kən'træpʃən] *n* (*pej*) machin *m*, truc *m*.

contrary ['kɔntrərɪ] *a* contraire, opposé(e); [kən'trɛərɪ] (*perverse*) contrariant(e), entêté(e) // *n* contraire *m*; **on the ~** au contraire; **unless you hear to the ~** sauf avis contraire.

contrast *n* ['kɔntrɑ:st] contraste *m* // *vt* [kən'trɑ:st] mettre en contraste, contraster; **~ing** *a* opposé(e), contrasté(e).

contravene [kɔntrə'vi:n] *vt* enfreindre, violer, contrevenir à.

contribute [kən'trɪbju:t] *vi* contribuer // *vt*: **to ~ £10/an article to** donner 10 livres/un article à; **to ~ to** (*gen*) contribuer à; (*newspaper*) collaborer à; **contribution** [kɔntrɪ'bju:ʃən] *n* contribution *f*; **contributor** *n* (*to newspaper*) collaborateur/trice.

contrite ['kɔntraɪt] *a* contrit(e).

contrivance [kən'traɪvəns] *n* invention *f*, combinaison *f*; mécanisme *m*, dispositif *m*.

contrive [kən'traɪv] *vt* combiner, inventer // *vi*: **to ~ to do** s'arranger pour faire, trouver le moyen de faire.

control [kən'trəul] *vt* maîtriser; (*check*) contrôler // *n* contrôle *m*, autorité *f*; maîtrise *f*; **~s** *npl* commandes *fpl*; **to be in ~ of** être maître de, maîtriser; être responsable de; **circumstances beyond our ~** circonstances indépendantes de notre volonté; **~ point** *n* (poste *m* de) contrôle; **~ tower** *n* (AVIAT) tour *f* de contrôle.

controversial [kɔntrə'və:ʃl] *a* discutable, controversé(e).

controversy ['kɔntrəvə:sɪ] *n* controverse *f*, polémique *f*.

convalesce [kɔnvə'lɛs] *vi* relever de maladie, se remettre (d'une maladie).

convalescence [kɔnvə'lɛsns] *n* convalescence *f*.

convalescent [kɔnvə'lɛsnt] *a*, *n* convalescent(e).

convector [kən'vɛktə*] *n* radiateur *m* à convection, appareil *m* de chauffage par convection.

convene [kən'vi:n] *vt* convoquer, assembler // *vi* se réunir, s'assembler.

convenience [kən'vi:nɪəns] *n* commodité *f*; **at your ~** quand *or* comme cela vous convient; **all modern ~s, all mod cons** avec tout le confort moderne, tout confort.

convenient [kən'vi:nɪənt] *a* commode.

convent ['kɔnvənt] *n* couvent *m*; **~ school** *n* couvent *m*.

convention [kən'vɛnʃən] *n* convention *f*; **~al** *a* conventionnel(le).

converge [kən'və:dʒ] *vi* converger.

conversant [kən'və:snt] *a*: **to be ~ with** s'y connaître en; être au courant de.

conversation [kɔnvə'seɪʃən] *n* conversation *f*; **~al** *a* de la conversation; **~alist** *n* brillant/e causeur/euse.

converse *n* ['kɔnvə:s] contraire *m*, inverse *m*; **~ly** [-'və:slɪ] *ad* inversement, réciproquement.

conversion [kən'və:ʃən] *n* conversion *f*; **~ table** *n* table *f* de conversion.

convert *vt* [kən'və:t] (REL, COMM) convertir; (*alter*) transformer, aménager; (RUGBY) transformer // *n* ['kɔnvə:t] converti/e; **~ible** *n* (voiture *f*) décapotable *f*.

convex ['kɔn'vɛks] *a* convexe.

convey [kən'veɪ] *vt* transporter; (*thanks*) transmettre; (*idea*) communiquer; **~or belt** *n* convoyeur *m*, tapis roulant.

convict *vt* [kən'vɪkt] déclarer (*or* reconnaître) coupable // *n* ['kɔnvɪkt] forçat *m*, convict *m*; **~ion** [-ʃən] *n* condamnation *f*; (*belief*) conviction *f*.
convince [kən'vɪns] *vt* convaincre, persuader; **convincing** *a* persuasif(ive), convaincant(e).
convivial [kən'vɪvɪəl] *a* joyeux(euse), plein(e) d'entrain.
convoy ['kɔnvɔɪ] *n* convoi *m*.
convulse [kən'vʌls] *vt* ébranler; **to be ~d with laughter** se tordre de rire.
convulsion [kən'vʌlʃən] *n* convulsion *f*.
coo [ku:] *vi* roucouler.
cook [kuk] *vt* (faire) cuire // *vi* cuire; (*person*) faire la cuisine // *n* cuisinier/ière; **~book** *n* = **~ery book**; **~er** *n* cuisinière *f*; **~ery** *n* cuisine *f*; **~ery book** *n* livre *m* de cuisine; **~ie** *n* (*US*) biscuit *m*, petit gâteau sec; **~ing** *n* cuisine *f*.
cool [ku:l] *a* frais(fraîche); (*not afraid*) calme; (*unfriendly*) froid(e); (*impertinent*) effronté(e) // *vt*, *vi* rafraîchir, refroidir; **~ing tower** *n* refroidisseur *m*; **~ness** *n* fraîcheur *f*; sang-froid *m*, calme *m*.
coop [ku:p] *n* poulailler *m* // *vt*: **to ~ up** (*fig*) cloîtrer, enfermer.
co-op ['kəuɔp] *n abbr of Cooperative* (*Society*).
cooperate [kəu'ɔpəreɪt] *vi* coopérer, collaborer; **cooperation** [-'reɪʃən] *n* coopération *f*, collaboration *f*.
cooperative [kəu'ɔpərətɪv] *a* coopératif(ive) // *n* coopérative *f*.
coordinate [kəu'ɔ:dɪneɪt] *vt* coordonner; **coordination** [-'neɪʃən] coordination *f*.
coot [ku:t] *n* foulque *f*.
cop [kɔp] *n* (*col*) flic *m*.
cope [kəup] *vi* se débrouiller; **to ~ with** faire face à; s'occuper de.
co-pilot ['kəu'paɪlət] *n* copilote *m*.
copious ['kəupɪəs] *a* copieux(euse), abondant(e).
copper ['kɔpə*] *n* cuivre *m*; (*col: policeman*) flic *m*; **~s** *npl* petite monnaie.
coppice ['kɔpɪs] *n* taillis *m*.
copse [kɔps] *n* = **coppice**.
copulate ['kɔpjuleɪt] *vi* copuler.
copy ['kɔpɪ] *n* copie *f*; (*book etc*) exemplaire *m* // *vt* copier; **~cat** *n* (*pej*) copieur/euse; **~right** *n* droit *m* d'auteur, copyright *m*; **~right reserved** tous droits (de reproduction) réservés; **~writer** *n* rédacteur/trice publicitaire.
coral ['kɔrəl] *n* corail *m*; **~ reef** *n* récif *m* de corail.
cord [kɔ:d] *n* corde *f*; (*fabric*) velours côtelé; whipcord *m*; corde *f*.
cordial ['kɔ:dɪəl] *a* cordial(e), chaleureux(euse) // *n* sirop *m*; cordial *m*.
cordon ['kɔ:dn] *n* cordon *m*; **to ~ off** *vt* boucler (*par cordon de police*).
corduroy ['kɔ:dərɔɪ] *n* velours côtelé.
core [kɔ:*] *n* (*of fruit*) trognon *m*, cœur *m*; (*TECH*) noyau *m* // *vt* enlever le trognon *or* le cœur de.
coriander [kɔrɪ'ændə*] *n* coriandre *f*.
cork [kɔ:k] *n* liège *m*; (*of bottle*) bouchon *m*; **~age** *n droit payé par le client qui apporte sa propre bouteille de vin*; **~screw** *n* tire-bouchon *m*.
corm [kɔ:m] *n* bulbe *m*.
cormorant ['kɔ:mərnt] *n* cormorant *m*.
corn [kɔ:n] *n* blé *m*; (*US: maize*) maïs *m*; (*on foot*) cor *m*; **~ on the cob** (*CULIN*) épi *m* de maïs au naturel.
cornea ['kɔ:nɪə] *n* cornée *f*.
corned beef ['kɔ:nd'bi:f] *n* corned-beef *m*.
corner ['kɔ:nə*] *n* coin *m*; (*AUT*) tournant *m*, virage *m* // *vt* acculer, mettre au pied du mur; coincer; (*COMM: market*) accaparer // *vi* prendre un virage; **~ flag** *n* (*FOOTBALL*) piquet *m* de coin; **~ kick** *n* corner *m*; **~stone** *n* pierre *f* angulaire.
cornet ['kɔ:nɪt] *n* (*MUS*) cornet *m* à pistons; (*of ice-cream*) cornet (de glace).
cornflour ['kɔ:nflauə*] *n* farine *f* de maïs, maïzena *f*.
cornice ['kɔ:nɪs] *n* corniche *f*.
Cornish ['kɔ:nɪʃ] *a* de Cornouailles, cornouaillais(e).
cornucopia [kɔ:nju'kəupɪə] *n* corne *f* d'abondance.
Cornwall ['kɔ:nwəl] *n* Cornouailles *f*.
corny ['kɔ:nɪ] *a* (*col*) rebattu(e), galvaudé(e).
corollary [kə'rɔlərɪ] *n* corollaire *m*.
coronary ['kɔrənərɪ] *n*: **~ (thrombosis)** infarctus *m* (du myocarde), thrombose *f* coronaire.
coronation [kɔrə'neɪʃən] *n* couronnement *m*.
coroner ['kɔrənə*] *n* coroner *m*.
coronet ['kɔrənɪt] *n* couronne *f*.
corporal ['kɔ:pərl] *n* caporal *m*, brigadier *m* // *a*: **~ punishment** châtiment corporel.
corporate ['kɔ:pərɪt] *a* en commun; constitué(e) (en corporation).
corporation [kɔ:pə'reɪʃən] *n* (*of town*) municipalité *f*, conseil municipal; (*COMM*) société *f*; **~ tax** *n* ≈ impôt *m* sur les bénéfices.
corps [kɔ:*], *pl* **corps** [kɔ:z] *n* corps *m*.
corpse [kɔ:ps] *n* cadavre *m*.
corpuscle ['kɔ:pʌsl] *n* corpuscule *m*.
corral [kə'rɑ:l] *n* corral *m*.
correct [kə'rɛkt] *a* (*accurate*) correct(e), exact(e); (*proper*) correct(e), convenable // *vt* corriger; **~ion** [-ʃən] *n* correction *f*.
correlate ['kɔrɪleɪt] *vt* mettre en corrélation.
correspond [kɔrɪs'pɔnd] *vi* correspondre; **~ence** *n* correspondance *f*; **~ence course** *n* cours *m* par correspondance; **~ent** *n* correspondant/e.
corridor ['kɔrɪdɔ:*] *n* couloir *m*, corridor *m*.
corroborate [kə'rɔbəreɪt] *vt* corroborer, confirmer.
corrode [kə'rəud] *vt* corroder, ronger // *vi* se corroder; **corrosion** [-'rəuʒən] *n* corrosion *f*.
corrugated ['kɔrəgeɪtɪd] *a* plissé(e); cannelé(e); ondulé(e); **~ cardboard** *n* carton ondulé; **~ iron** *n* tôle ondulée.
corrupt [kə'rʌpt] *a* corrompu(e) // *vt* corrompre; **~ion** [-ʃən] *n* corruption *f*.

corset ['kɔ:sɪt] *n* corset *m*.
Corsica ['kɔ:sɪkə] *n* Corse *f*.
cortège [kɔ:'tɛ:ʒ] *n* cortège *m* (*gén funèbre*).
coruscating ['kɔrəskeɪtɪŋ] *a* scintillant(e).
cosh [kɔʃ] *n* matraque *f*.
cosignatory ['kəu'sɪgnətərɪ] *n* cosignataire *m/f*.
cosiness ['kəuzɪnɪs] *n* atmosphère douillette, confort *m*.
cos lettuce [kɔs'lɛtɪs] *n* (laitue *f*) romaine *f*.
cosmetic [kɔz'mɛtɪk] *n* produit *m* de beauté, cosmétique *m*.
cosmic ['kɔzmɪk] *a* cosmique.
cosmonaut ['kɔzmənɔ:t] *n* cosmonaute *m/f*.
cosmopolitan [kɔzmə'pɔlɪtn] *a* cosmopolite.
cosmos ['kɔzmɔs] *n* cosmos *m*.
cosset ['kɔsɪt] *vt* choyer, dorloter.
cost [kɔst] *n* coût *m* // *vb* (*pt, pp* **cost**) *vi* coûter // *vt* établir *or* calculer le prix de revient de; **it ~s £5/too much** cela coûte cinq livres/trop cher; **it ~ him his life/job** ça lui a coûté la vie/son emploi; **at all ~s** coûte que coûte, à tout prix.
co-star ['kəusta:*] *n* partenaire *m/f*.
costly ['kɔstlɪ] *a* coûteux(euse).
cost price ['kɔst'praɪs] *n* prix coûtant *or* de revient.
costume ['kɔstju:m] *n* costume *m*; (*lady's suit*) tailleur *m*; (*also*: **swimming ~**) maillot *m* (de bain); **~ jewellery** *n* bijoux *mpl* de fantaisie.
cosy ['kəuzɪ] *a* douillet(te).
cot [kɔt] *n* (*child's*) lit *m* d'enfant, petit lit.
cottage ['kɔtɪdʒ] *n* petite maison (à la campagne), cottage *m*; **~ cheese** *n* fromage blanc (*maigre*).
cotton ['kɔtn] *n* coton *m*; **~ dress** *etc* robe *etc* en *or* de coton; **~ wool** *n* ouate *f*, coton *m* hydrophile.
couch [kautʃ] *n* canapé *m*; divan *m* // *vt* formuler, exprimer.
cough [kɔf] *vi* tousser // *n* toux *f*; **~ drop** *n* pastille *f* pour *or* contre la toux.
could [kud] *pt of* **can**; **~n't = could not**.
council ['kaunsl] *n* conseil *m*; **city** *or* **town ~** conseil municipal; **~ estate** *n* (quartier *m or* zone *f* de) logements loués à/par la municipalité; **~ house** *n* maison *f* (à loyer modéré) louée par la municipalité; **~lor** *n* conseiller/ère.
counsel ['kaunsl] *n* avocat/e; consultation *f*, délibération *f*; **~lor** *n* conseiller/ère.
count [kaunt] *vt, vi* compter // *n* compte *m*; (*nobleman*) comte *m*; **to ~ on** *vt fus* compter sur; **to ~ up** *vt* compter, additionner; **~down** *n* compte *m* à rebours.
countenance ['kauntɪnəns] *n* expression *f* // *vt* approuver.
counter ['kauntə*] *n* comptoir *m*; (*machine*) compteur *m* // *vt* aller à l'encontre de, opposer; (*blow*) parer // *ad*: **~ to** à l'encontre de; contrairement à; **~act** *vt* neutraliser, contrebalancer; **~attack** *n* contre-attaque *f* // *vi* contre-attaquer; **~balance** *vt* contrebalancer, faire contrepoids à; **~-clockwise** *ad* en sens inverse des aiguilles d'une montre; **~-espionage** *n* contre-espionnage *m*.
counterfeit ['kauntəfɪt] *n* faux *m*, contrefaçon *f* // *vt* contrefaire // *a* faux(fausse).
counterfoil ['kauntəfɔɪl] *n* talon *m*, souche *f*.
counterpart ['kauntəpa:t] *n* (*of document etc*) double *m*; (*of person*) homologue *m/f*.
countersink ['kauntəsɪŋk] *vt* (*hole*) fraiser.
countess ['kauntɪs] *n* comtesse *f*.
countless ['kauntlɪs] *a* innombrable.
countrified ['kʌntrɪfaɪd] *a* rustique, à l'air campagnard.
country ['kʌntrɪ] *n* pays *m*; (*native land*) patrie *f*; (*as opposed to town*) campagne *f*; (*region*) région *f*, pays *m*; **~ dancing** *n* danse *f* folklorique; **~ house** *n* manoir *m*, (petit) château; **~man** *n* (*national*) compatriote *m*; (*rural*) habitant *m* de la campagne, campagnard *m*; **~side** *n* campagne *f*.
county ['kauntɪ] *n* comté *m*; **~ town** *n* chef-lieu *m*.
coup, ~s [ku:, -z] *n* beau coup *m*; (*also*: **~ d'état**) coup d'État.
coupé [ku:'peɪ] *n* coupé *m*.
couple ['kʌpl] *n* couple *m* // *vt* (*carriages*) atteler; (TECH) coupler; (*ideas, names*) associer; **a ~ of** deux.
couplet ['kʌplɪt] *n* distique *m*.
coupling ['kʌplɪŋ] *n* (RAIL) attelage *m*.
coupon ['ku:pɔn] *n* coupon *m*, bon-prime *m*, bon-réclame *m*; (COMM) coupon *m*.
courage ['kʌrɪdʒ] *n* courage *m*; **~ous** [kə'reɪdʒəs] *a* courageux (euse).
courier ['kurɪə*] *n* messager *m*, courrier *m*; (*for tourists*) accompagnateur/trice.
course [kɔ:s] *n* cours *m*; (*of ship*) route *f*; (CONSTR) assise *f*; (*for golf*) terrain *m*; (*part of meal*) plat *m*; **first ~** entrée *f*; **of ~** *ad* bien sûr; **in due ~** en temps utile *or* voulu; **~ of action** parti *m*, ligne *f* de conduite; **~ of lectures** série *f* de conférences; **~ of treatment** (MED) traitement *m*.
court [kɔ:t] *n* cour *f*; (LAW) cour, tribunal *m*; (TENNIS) court *m* // *vt* (*woman*) courtiser, faire la cour à; **out of ~** (LAW: *settle*) à l'amiable; **to take to ~** actionner *or* poursuivre en justice.
courteous ['kʌ:tɪəs] *a* courtois(e), poli(e).
courtesan [kɔ:tɪ'zæn] *n* courtisane *f*.
courtesy ['kə:təsɪ] *n* courtoisie *f*, politesse *f*.
court-house ['kɔ:thaus] *n* (*US*) palais *m* de justice.
courtier ['kɔ:tɪə*] *n* courtisan *m*, dame *f* de cour.
court-martial, *pl* **courts-martial** ['kɔ:t'ma:ʃəl] *n* cour martiale, conseil *m* de guerre.
courtroom ['kɔ:trum] *n* salle *f* de tribunal.
courtyard ['kɔ:tja:d] *n* cour *f*.
cousin ['kʌzn] *n* cousin/e.
cove [kəuv] *n* petite baie, anse *f*.
covenant ['kʌvənənt] *n* contrat *m*, engagement *m*.

cover ['kʌvə*] *vt* couvrir // *n* (*for bed, of book,* COMM) couverture *f*; (*of pan*) couvercle *m*; (*over furniture*) housse *f*; (*shelter*) abri *m*; **under ~** à l'abri; **~age** *n* reportage *m*; (INSURANCE) couverture *f*; **~ charge** *n* couvert *m* (*supplément à payer*); **~ing** *n* couverture *f*, enveloppe *f*; **~ing letter** *n* lettre explicative.

covet ['kʌvɪt] *vt* convoiter.

cow [kau] *n* vache *f* // *cpd* femelle.

coward ['kauəd] *n* lâche *m/f*; **~ice** [-ɪs] *n* lâcheté *f*; **~ly** *a* lâche.

cowboy ['kaubɔɪ] *n* cow-boy *m*.

cower ['kauə*] *vi* se recroqueviller; trembler.

cowshed ['kauʃɛd] *n* étable *f*.

coxswain ['kɔksn] *n* (*abbr*: **cox**) barreur *m*; (*of ship*) patron *m*.

coy [kɔɪ] *a* faussement effarouché(e) *or* timide.

coyote [kɔɪ'əutɪ] *n* coyote *m*.

crab [kræb] *n* crabe *m*; **~ apple** *n* pomme *f* sauvage.

crack [kræk] *n* fente *f*, fissure *f*; fêlure *f*; lézarde *f*; (*noise*) craquement *m*, coup (sec) // *vt* fendre, fissurer; fêler; lézarder; (*whip*) faire claquer; (*nut*) casser // *a* (*athlete*) de première classe, d'élite; **to ~ up** *vi* être au bout de son rouleau, flancher; **~ed** *a* (*col*) toqué(e), timbré(e); **~er** *n* pétard *m*; biscuit (salé), craquelin *m*.

crackle ['krækl] *vi* crépiter, grésiller // *n* (*of china*) craquelure *f*; **crackling** *n* crépitement *m*, grésillement *m*; (*of pork*) couenne *f*.

cradle ['kreɪdl] *n* berceau *m*.

craft [krɑ:ft] *n* métier (artisanal); (*cunning*) ruse *f*, astuce *f*; (*boat*) embarcation *f*, barque *f*; **~sman** *n* artisan *m*, ouvrier (qualifié); **~smanship** *n* métier *m*, habileté *f*; **~y** *a* rusé(e), malin(igne), astucieux(euse).

crag [kræg] *n* rocher escarpé; **~gy** *a* escarpé(e), rocheux(euse).

cram [kræm] *vt* (*fill*): **to ~ sth with** bourrer qch de; (*put*): **to ~ sth into** fourrer qch dans; **~ming** *n* (*fig*: *pej*) bachotage *m*.

cramp [kræmp] *n* crampe *f* // *vt* gêner, entraver; **~ed** *a* à l'étroit, très serré(e).

crampon [kræmpən] *n* crampon *m*.

cranberry ['krænbərɪ] *n* canneberge *f*.

crane [kreɪn] *n* grue *f*.

cranium, *pl* **crania** ['kreɪnɪəm, 'kreɪnɪə] *n* boîte crânienne.

crank [kræŋk] *n* manivelle *f*; (*person*) excentrique *m/f*; **~shaft** *n* vilebrequin *m*.

cranky ['kræŋkɪ] *a* excentrique, loufoque; (*bad-tempered*) grincheux(euse), revêche.

cranny ['krænɪ] *n see* **nook**.

crash [kræʃ] *n* fracas *m*; (*of car, plane*) collision *f* // *vt* (*plane*) écraser // *vi* (*plane*) s'écraser; (*two cars*) se percuter, s'emboutir; (*fig*) s'effondrer; **to ~ into** se jeter *or* se fracasser contre; **~ course** *n* cours intensif; **~ helmet** *n* casque (protecteur); **~ landing** *n* atterrissage forcé *or* en catastrophe.

crate [kreɪt] *n* cageot *m*.

crater ['kreɪtə*] *n* cratère *m*.

cravat(e) [krə'væt] *n* foulard (noué autour du cou).

crave [kreɪv] *vt*: **to ~ for** désirer violemment, avoir un besoin physiologique de, avoir une envie irrésistible de.

crawl [krɔ:l] *vi* ramper; (*vehicle*) avancer au pas // *n* (SWIMMING) crawl *m*.

crayfish ['kreɪfɪʃ] *n, pl inv* écrevisse *f*; langoustine *f*.

crayon ['kreɪən] *n* crayon *m* (de couleur).

craze [kreɪz] *n* engouement *m*.

crazy ['kreɪzɪ] *a* fou(folle); **~ paving** *n* dallage irrégulier (en pierres plates).

creak [kri:k] *vi* grincer; craquer.

cream [kri:m] *n* crème *f* // *a* (*colour*) crème *inv*; **~ cake** *n* (petit) gâteau à la crème; **~ cheese** *n* fromage *m* à la crème, fromage blanc; **~ery** *n* (*shop*) crémerie *f*; (*factory*) laiterie *f*; **~y** *a* crémeux(euse).

crease [kri:s] *n* pli *m* // *vt* froisser, chiffonner // *vi* se froisser, se chiffonner.

create [kri:'eɪt] *vt* créer; **creation** [-ʃən] *n* création *f*; **creative** *a* créateur(trice); **creator** *n* créateur/trice.

creature ['kri:tʃə*] *n* créature *f*.

credence ['kri:dns] *n* croyance *f*, foi *f*.

crèche, creche [krɛʃ] *n* garderie *f*, crèche *f*.

credentials [krɪ'dɛnʃlz] *npl* (*papers*) références *fpl*.

credibility [krɛdɪ'bɪlɪtɪ] *n* crédibilité *f*.

credible ['krɛdɪbl] *a* digne de foi, crédible.

credit ['krɛdɪt] *n* crédit *m* // *vt* (COMM) créditer; (*believe*: *also*: **give ~ to**) ajouter foi à, croire; **~s** *npl* (CINEMA) génerique *m*; **to ~ sb with** (*fig*) prêter *or* attribuer à qn; **to ~ £5 to sb** créditer (le compte de) qn de 5 livres; **to one's ~** à son honneur; à son actif; **to take the ~ for** s'attribuer le mérite de; **it does him ~** cela lui fait honneur; **~able** *a* honorable, estimable; **~ card** *n* carte *f* de crédit; **~or** *n* créancier/ière.

credulity [krɪ'dju:lɪtɪ] *n* crédulité *f*.

creed [kri:d] *n* croyance *f*; credo *m*, principes *mpl*.

creek [kri:k] *n* crique *f*, anse *f*; (*US*) ruisseau *m*, petit cours d'eau.

creep, *pt, pp* **crept** [kri:p, krɛpt] *vi* ramper; (*fig*) se faufiler, se glisser; (*plant*) grimper; **~er** *n* plante grimpante; **~y** *a* (*frightening*) qui fait frissonner, qui donne la chair de poule.

cremate [krɪ'meɪt] *vt* incinérer; **cremation** [-ʃən] *n* incinération *f*.

crematorium, *pl* **crematoria** [krɛmə'tɔ:rɪəm, -'tɔ:rɪə] *n* four *m* crématoire.

creosote ['krɪəsəut] *n* créosote *f*.

crêpe [kreɪp] *n* crêpe *m*; **~ bandage** *n* bande *f* Velpeau ®.

crept [krɛpt] *pt, pp of* **creep.**

crescendo [krɪ'ʃɛndəu] *n* crescendo *m*.

crescent ['krɛsnt] *n* croissant *m*; rue *f* (*en arc de cercle*).

cress [krɛs] *n* cresson *m*.

crest [krɛst] *n* crête *f*; (*of helmet*) cimier *m*; (*of coat of arms*) timbre *m*; **~fallen** *a* déconfit(e), découragé(e).

Crete ['kri:t] *n* Crète *f*.

crevasse [krɪ'væs] *n* crevasse *f*.
crevice ['krɛvɪs] *n* fissure *f*, lézarde *f*, fente *f*.
crew [kru:] *n* équipage *m*; **to have a ~-cut** avoir les cheveux en brosse; **~-neck** *n* col ras.
crib [krɪb] *n* lit *m* d'enfant // *vt* (*col*) copier.
cribbage ['krɪbɪdʒ] *n sorte de jeu de cartes.*
crick [krɪk] *n* crampe *f*.
cricket ['krɪkɪt] *n* (*insect*) grillon *m*, cri-cri *m inv*; (*game*) cricket *m*; **~er** *n* joueur *m* de cricket.
crime [kraɪm] *n* crime *m*; **criminal** ['krɪmɪnl] *a*, *n* criminel(le); **the Criminal Investigation Department (C.I.D.)** ≈ la police judiciaire (P.J.).
crimp [krɪmp] *vt* friser, frisotter.
crimson ['krɪmzn] *a* cramoisi(e).
cringe [krɪndʒ] *vi* avoir un mouvement de recul; (*fig*) s'humilier, ramper.
crinkle ['krɪŋkl] *vt* froisser, chiffonner.
cripple ['krɪpl] *n* boiteux/euse, infirme *m/f* // *vt* estropier, paralyser.
crisis, *pl* **crises** ['kraɪsɪs, -si:z] *n* crise *f*.
crisp [krɪsp] *a* croquant(e); (*fig*) vif(vive); brusque; **~s** *npl* (pommes) chips *fpl*.
criss-cross ['krɪskrɔs] *a* entrecroisé(e).
criterion, *pl* **criteria** [kraɪ'tɪərɪən, -'tɪərɪə] *n* critère *m*.
critic ['krɪtɪk] *n* critique *m/f*; **~al** *a* critique; **~ally** *ad* d'un œil critique; **~ally ill** gravement malade; **~ism** ['krɪtɪsɪzm] *n* critique *f*; **~ize** ['krɪtɪsaɪz] *vt* critiquer.
croak [krəuk] *vi* (*frog*) coasser; (*raven*) croasser.
crochet ['krəuʃeɪ] *n* travail *m* au crochet.
crockery ['krɔkərɪ] *n* vaisselle *f*.
crocodile ['krɔkədaɪl] *n* crocodile *m*.
crocus ['krəukəs] *n* crocus *m*.
croft [krɔft] *n* petite ferme; **~er** *n* fermier *m*.
crony ['krəunɪ] *n* copain/copine.
crook [kruk] *n* escroc *m*; (*of shepherd*) houlette *f*; **~ed** ['krukɪd] *a* courbé(e), tordu(e); (*action*) malhonnête.
crop [krɔp] *n* récolte *f*; culture *f*; **to ~ up** *vi* surgir, se présenter, survenir.
cropper ['krɔpə*] *n*: **to come a ~** (*col*) faire la culbute, s'étaler.
croquet ['krəukeɪ] *n* croquet *m*.
croquette [krə'kɛt] *n* croquette *f*.
cross [krɔs] *n* croix *f*; (BIOL) croisement *m* // *vt* (*street etc*) traverser; (*arms, legs,* BIOL) croiser; (*cheque*) barrer // *a* en colère, fâché(e); **to ~ out** *vt* barrer, biffer; **to ~ over** *vi* traverser; **~bar** *n* barre transversale; **~breed** *n* hybride *m*, métis/se; **~country (race)** *n* cross(-country) *m*; **~-examination** *n* examen *m* contradictoire (*d'un témoin*); **~-examine** *vt* (LAW) faire subir un examen contradictoire à; **~-eyed** *a* qui louche; **~ing** *n* croisement *m*, carrefour *m*; (*sea-passage*) traversée *f*; (*also*: **pedestrian ~ing**) passage clouté; **~-reference** *n* renvoi *m*, référence *f*; **~roads** *n* carrefour *m*; **~ section** *n* (BIOL) coupe transversale; (*in population*) échantillon *m*; **~wind** *n* vent *m* de travers; **~wise** *ad* en travers; **~word** *n* mots croisés *mpl*.
crotch [krɔtʃ] *n* (*of garment*) entre-jambes *m inv*.
crotchet ['krɔtʃɪt] *n* (MUS) noire *f*.
crotchety ['krɔtʃɪtɪ] *a* (*person*) grognon(ne), grincheux(euse).
crouch [krautʃ] *vi* s'accroupir; se tapir; se ramasser.
crouton ['kru:tɔn] *n* croûton *m*.
crow [krəu] (*bird*) corneille *f*; (*of cock*) chant *m* du coq, cocorico *m* // *vi* (*cock*) chanter; (*fig*) pavoiser, chanter victoire.
crowbar ['krəubɑ:*] *n* levier *m*.
crowd [kraud] *n* foule *f* // *vt* bourrer, remplir // *vi* affluer, s'attrouper, s'entasser; **~ed** *a* bondé(e), plein(e); **~ed with** plein(e) de.
crown [kraun] *n* couronne *f*; (*of head*) sommet *m* de la tête, calotte crânienne; (*of hat*) fond *m*; (*of hill*) sommet *m* // *vt* couronner; **C~ court** *n* ≈ Cour *f* d'assises; **~ jewels** *npl* joyaux *mpl* de la Couronne; **~ prince** *n* prince héritier.
crow's-nest ['krəuznɛst] (*on sailing-ship*) nid *m* de pie.
crucial ['kru:ʃl] *a* crucial(e), décisif(ive).
crucifix ['kru:sɪfɪks] *n* crucifix *m*; **~ion** [-'fɪkʃən] *n* crucifiement *m*, crucifixion *f*.
crucify ['kru:sɪfaɪ] *vt* crucifier, mettre en croix.
crude [kru:d] *a* (*materials*) brut(e); non raffiné(e); (*fig*: *basic*) rudimentaire, sommaire; (: *vulgar*) cru(e), grossier(ère); **~ (oil)** *n* (pétrole) brut *m*.
cruel ['kruəl] *a* cruel(le); **~ty** *n* cruauté *f*.
cruet ['kru:ɪt] huilier *m*; vinaigrier *m*.
cruise [kru:z] *n* croisière *f* // *vi* (*ship*) croiser; (*car*) rouler; (*aircraft*) voler; (*taxi*) être en maraude; **~r** *n* croiseur *m*; **cruising speed** *n* vitesse *f* de croisière.
crumb [krʌm] *n* miette *f*.
crumble ['krʌmbl] *vt* émietter // *vi* s'émietter; (*plaster etc*) s'effriter; (*land, earth*) s'ébouler; (*building*) s'écrouler, crouler; (*fig*) s'effondrer; **crumbly** *a* friable.
crumpet ['krʌmpɪt] *n* petite crêpe (épaisse).
crumple ['krʌmpl] *vt* froisser, friper.
crunch [krʌntʃ] *vt* croquer; (*underfoot*) faire craquer, écraser; faire crisser // *n* (*fig*) instant *m or* moment *m* critique, moment de vérité; **~y** *a* croquant(e), croustillant(e).
crusade [kru:'seɪd] *n* croisade *f*; **~r** *n* croisé *m*.
crush [krʌʃ] *n* foule *f*, cohue *f*; (*love*): **to have a ~ on sb** avoir le béguin pour qn; (*drink*): **lemon ~** citron pressé // *vt* écraser; (*crumple*) froisser; **~ing** *a* écrasant(e).
crust [krʌst] *n* croûte *f*.
crutch [krʌtʃ] *n* béquille *f*; (TECH) support *m*.
crux [krʌks] *n* point crucial.
cry [kraɪ] *vi* pleurer; (*shout*) crier // *n* cri *m*; **to ~ off** *vi* se dédire; se décommander; **~ing** *a* (*fig*) criant(e), flagrant(e).
crypt [krɪpt] *n* crypte *f*.

cryptic ['krɪptɪk] *a* énigmatique.
crystal ['krɪstl] *n* cristal *m*; **~-clear** *a* clair(e) comme de l'eau de roche; **crystallize** *vt* cristalliser // *vi* (se) cristalliser.
cu. *abbr*: **~ ft.** = *cubic feet*; **~ in.** = *cubic inches*.
cub [kʌb] *n* petit *m* (*d'un animal*).
Cuba ['kju:bə] *n* Cuba *m*; **~n** *a* cubain(e) // *n* Cubain/e.
cubbyhole ['kʌbɪhəul] *n* cagibi *m*.
cube [kju:b] *n* cube *m* // *vt* (MATH) élever au cube; **~ root** *n* racine *f* cubique; **cubic** *a* cubique; **cubic metre** *etc* mètre *m* cube *etc*.
cubicle ['kju:bɪkl] *n* box *m*, cabine *f*.
cuckoo ['kuku:] *n* coucou *m*; **~ clock** *n* (pendule *f* à) coucou *m*.
cucumber ['kju:kʌmbə*] *n* concombre *m*.
cud [kʌd] *n*: **to chew the ~** ruminer.
cuddle ['kʌdl] *vt* câliner, caresser // *vi* se blottir l'un contre l'autre; **cuddly** *a* câlin(e).
cudgel ['kʌdʒl] *n* gourdin *m*.
cue [kju:] *n* queue *f* de billard; (THEATRE *etc*) signal *m*.
cuff [kʌf] *n* (*of shirt, coat etc*) poignet *m*, manchette *f*; (*US*) = **turn-up**; **off the ~** *ad* de chic, à l'improviste; **~link** *n* bouton *m* de manchette.
cuisine [kwɪ'zi:n] *n* cuisine *f*, art *m* culinaire.
cul-de-sac ['kʌldəsæk] *n* cul-de-sac *m*, impasse *f*.
culinary ['kʌlɪnərɪ] *a* culinaire.
cull [kʌl] *vt* sélectionner.
culminate ['kʌlmɪneɪt] *vi* culminer; **culmination** [-'neɪʃən] *n* point culminant.
culpable ['kʌlpəbl] *a* coupable.
culprit ['kʌlprɪt] *n* coupable *m/f*.
cult [kʌlt] *n* culte *m*.
cultivate ['kʌltɪveɪt] *vt* (*also fig*) cultiver; **cultivation** [-'veɪʃən] *n* culture *f*.
cultural ['kʌltʃərəl] *a* culturel(le).
culture ['kʌltʃə*] *n* (*also fig*) culture *f*; **~d** *a* cultivé(e) (*fig*).
cumbersome ['kʌmbəsəm] *a* encombrant(e), embarrassant(e).
cumulative ['kju:mjulətɪv] *a* cumulatif(ive).
cunning ['kʌnɪŋ] *n* ruse *f*, astuce *f* // *a* rusé(e), malin(igne).
cup [kʌp] *n* tasse *f*; (*prize, event*) coupe *f*; (*of bra*) bonnet *m*.
cupboard ['kʌbəd] *n* placard *m*.
Cupid ['kju:pɪd] *n* Cupidon *m*; (*figurine*) amour *m*.
cupidity [kju:'pɪdɪtɪ] *n* cupidité *f*.
cupola ['kju:pələ] *n* coupole *f*.
cup-tie ['kʌptaɪ] *n* match *m* de coupe.
curable ['kjuərəbl] *a* guérissable, curable.
curate ['kju:rɪt] *n* vicaire *m*.
curator [kju'reɪtə*] *n* conservateur *m* (*d'un musée etc*).
curb [kə:b] *vt* refréner, mettre un frein à // *n* frein *m* (*fig*); (*US*) = **kerb.**
curdle ['kə:dl] *vi* (se) cailler.
curds [kə:ds] *npl* lait caillé.
cure [kjuə*] *vt* guérir; (CULIN) saler; fumer; sécher // *n* remède *m*.
curfew ['kə:fju:] *n* couvre-feu *m*.
curio ['kjuərɪəu] *n* bibelot *m*, curiosité *f*.
curiosity [kjuərɪ'ɔsɪtɪ] *n* curiosité *f*.
curious ['kjuərɪəs] *a* curieux(euse); **~ly** *ad* curieusement.
curl [kə:l] *n* boucle *f* (de cheveux) // *vt*, *vi* boucler; (*tightly*) friser; **to ~ up** *vi* s'enrouler; se pelotonner; **~er** *n* bigoudi *m*, rouleau *m*; (SPORT) joueur/euse de curling.
curling ['kə:lɪŋ] *n* (SPORT) curling *m*.
curly ['kə:lɪ] *a* bouclé(e); frisé(e).
currant ['kʌrnt] *n* raisin *m* de Corinthe, raisin sec.
currency ['kʌrnsɪ] *n* monnaie *f*; **foreign ~** devises étrangères, monnaie étrangère; **to gain ~** (*fig*) s'accréditer.
current ['kʌrnt] *n* courant *m* // *a* courant(e); **~ account** *n* compte courant; **~ affairs** *npl* (questions *fpl* d')actualité *f*; **~ly** *ad* actuellement.
curriculum, *pl* **~s** *or* **curricula** [kə'rɪkjuləm, -lə] *n* programme *m* d'études; **~ vitae** *n* curriculum vitae (C.V.) *m*.
curry ['kʌrɪ] *n* curry *m* // *vt*: **to ~ favour with** chercher à gagner la faveur *or* à s'attirer les bonnes grâces de; **chicken ~** curry de poulet, poulet *m* au curry; **~ powder** *n* poudre *f* de curry.
curse [kə:s] *vi* jurer, blasphémer // *vt* maudire // *n* malédiction *f*; fléau *m*; (*swearword*) juron *m*.
cursory ['kə:sərɪ] *a* superficiel(le), hâtif(ive).
curt [kə:t] *a* brusque, sec(sèche).
curtail [kə:'teɪl] *vt* (*visit etc*) écourter; (*expenses etc*) réduire.
curtain ['kə:tn] *n* rideau *m*.
curts(e)y ['kə:tsɪ] *n* révérence *f* // *vi* faire une révérence.
curve [kə:v] *n* courbe *f*; (*in the road*) tournant *m*, virage *m* // *vt* courber // *vi* se courber; (*road*) faire une courbe.
cushion ['kuʃən] *n* coussin *m* // *vt* (*seat*) rembourrer; (*shock*) amortir.
custard ['kʌstəd] *n* (*for pouring*) crème anglaise.
custodian [kʌs'təudɪən] *n* gardien/ne; (*of collection etc*) conservateur/trice.
custody ['kʌstədɪ] *n* (*of child*) garde *f*; (*for offenders*) détention préventive.
custom ['kʌstəm] *n* coutume *f*, usage *m*; (LAW) droit coutumier, coutume; (COMM) clientèle *f*; **~ary** *a* habituel(le).
customer ['kʌstəmə*] *n* client/e.
custom-made ['kʌstəm'meɪd] *a* (*clothes*) fait(e) sur mesure; (*other goods*) hors série, fait(e) sur commande.
customs ['kʌstəmz] *npl* douane *f*; **~ duty** *n* droits *mpl* de douane; **~ officer** *n* douanier *m*.
cut [kʌt] *vb* (*pt, pp* **cut**) *vt* couper; (*meat*) découper; (*shape, make*) tailler; couper; creuser; graver; (*reduce*) réduire // *vi* couper; (*intersect*) se couper // *n* (*gen*) coupure *f*; (*of clothes*) coupe *f*; (*of jewel*) taille *f*; (*in salary etc*) réduction *f*; (*of meat*) morceau *m*; **power ~** coupure de courant; **to ~ teeth** (*baby*) faire ses dents; **to ~ a tooth** percer une dent; **to ~ down (on)** *vt fus* réduire; **to ~ off** *vt*

couper; (*fig*) isoler; **to ~ out** *vt* ôter; découper; tailler; **~away** *a, n*: **~away (drawing)** écorché *m*; **~back** *n* réductions *fpl*.

cute [kju:t] *a* mignon(ne), adorable; (*clever*) rusé(e), astucieux(euse).

cut glass [kʌt'glɑ:s] *n* cristal taillé.

cuticle ['kju:tɪkl] *n* (*on nail*): **~ remover** *n* repousse-peaux *m inv*.

cutlery ['kʌtlərɪ] *n* couverts *mpl*; (*trade*) coutellerie *f*.

cutlet ['kʌtlɪt] *n* côtelette *f*.

cut: **~off switch** *n* interrupteur *m*; **~out** *n* coupe-circuit *m inv*; **~-price** *a* au rabais, à prix réduit; **~ throat** *n* assassin *m*.

cutting ['kʌtɪŋ] *a* tranchant(e), coupant(e); (*fig*) cinglant(e), mordant(e) // *n* (PRESS) coupure *f* (de journal); (RAIL) tranchée *f*.

cuttlefish ['kʌtlfɪʃ] *n* seiche *f*.

cut-up ['kʌtʌp] *a* affecté(e), démoralisé(e).

cwt *abbr of* **hundredweight(s)**.

cyanide ['saɪənaɪd] *n* cyanure *m*.

cybernetics [saɪbə'nɛtɪks] *n* cybernétique *f*.

cyclamen ['sɪkləmən] *n* cyclamen *m*.

cycle ['saɪkl] *n* cycle *m* // *vi* faire de la bicyclette.

cycling ['saɪklɪŋ] *n* cyclisme *m*.

cyclist ['saɪklɪst] *n* cycliste *m/f*.

cyclone ['saɪkləun] *n* cyclone *m*.

cygnet ['sɪgnɪt] *n* jeune cygne *m*.

cylinder ['sɪlɪndə*] *n* cylindre *m*; **~ block** *n* bloc-cylindres *m*; **~ capacity** *n* cylindrée *f*; **~ head** *n* culasse *f*; **~-head gasket** *n* joint *m* de culasse.

cymbals ['sɪmblz] *npl* cymbales *fpl*.

cynic ['sɪnɪk] *n* cynique *m/f*; **~al** *a* cynique; **~ism** ['sɪnɪsɪzəm] *n* cynisme *m*.

cypress ['saɪprɪs] *n* cyprès *m*.

Cypriot ['sɪprɪət] *a* cypriote, chypriote // *n* Cypriote *m/f*, Chypriote *m/f*.

Cyprus ['saɪprəs] *n* Chypre *f*.

cyst [sɪst] *n* kyste *m*.

cystitis [sɪs'taɪtɪs] cystite *f*.

czar [zɑ:*] *n* tsar *m*.

Czech [tʃɛk] *a* tchèque // *n* Tchèque *m/f*; (LING) tchèque *m*.

Czechoslovakia [tʃɛkəslə'vækɪə] *n* la Tchécoslovaquie; **~n** *a* tchécoslovaque // *n* Tchécoslovaque *m/f*.

D

D [di:] *n* (MUS) ré *m*; **~-day** *n* le jour J.

dab [dæb] *vt* (*eyes, wound*) tamponner; (*paint, cream*) appliquer (par petites touches *or* rapidement); **a ~ of paint** un petit coup de peinture.

dabble ['dæbl] *vi*: **to ~ in** faire *or* se mêler *or* s'occuper un peu de.

dad, daddy [dæd, 'dædɪ] *n* papa *m*; **daddy-long-legs** *n* tipule *f*; faucheux *m*.

daffodil ['dæfədɪl] *n* jonquille *f*.

daft [dɑ:ft] *a* idiot(e), stupide; **to be ~ about** être toqué *or* mordu de.

dagger ['dægə*] *n* poignard *m*; **to be at ~s drawn with sb** être à couteaux tirés avec qn; **to look ~s at sb** foudroyer qn du regard.

daily ['deɪlɪ] *a* quotidien(ne), journalier(ère) // *n* quotidien *m* // *ad* tous les jours.

dainty ['deɪntɪ] *a* délicat(e), mignon(ne).

dairy ['dɛərɪ] *n* (*shop*) crémerie *f*, laiterie *f*; (*on farm*) laiterie // *a* laitier(ère).

daisy ['deɪzɪ] *n* pâquerette *f*.

dale [deɪl] *n* vallon *m*.

dally ['dælɪ] *vi* musarder, flâner.

dam [dæm] *n* barrage *m* // *vt* endiguer.

damage ['dæmɪdʒ] *n* dégâts *mpl*, dommages *mpl*; (*fig*) tort *m* // *vt* endommager, abîmer; (*fig*) faire du tort à; **~s** *npl* (LAW) dommages-intérêts *mpl*.

damn [dæm] *vt* condamner; (*curse*) maudire // *n* (*col*): **I don't give a ~** je m'en fous // *a* (*col*): **this ~ ...** ce sacré *or* foutu ...; **~ (it)!** zut!; **~ing** *a* (*evidence*) accablant(e).

damp [dæmp] *a* humide // *n* humidité *f* // *vt* (*also*: **~en**) (*cloth, rag*) humecter; (*enthusiasm etc*) refroidir; **~ness** *n* humidité *f*.

damson ['dæmzən] *n* prune *f* de Damas.

dance [dɑ:ns] *n* danse *f*; (*ball*) bal *m* // *vi* danser; **~ hall** *n* salle *f* de bal, dancing *m*; **~r** *n* danseur/euse.

dancing ['dɑ:nsɪŋ] *n* danse *f*.

dandelion ['dændɪlaɪən] *n* pissenlit *m*.

dandruff ['dændrəf] *n* pellicules *fpl*.

Dane [deɪn] *n* Danois/e.

danger ['deɪndʒə*] *n* danger *m*; **there is a ~ of fire** il y a (un) risque d'incendie; **in ~** en danger; **he was in ~ of falling** il risquait de tomber; **~ous** *a* dangereux(euse); **~ously** *ad* dangereusement.

dangle ['dæŋgl] *vt* balancer; (*fig*) faire miroiter // *vi* pendre, se balancer.

Danish ['deɪnɪʃ] *a* danois(e) // *n* (LING) danois *m*.

dapper ['dæpə*] *a* pimpant(e).

dare [dɛə*] *vt*: **to ~ sb to do** défier qn *or* mettre qn au défi de faire // *vi*: **to ~ (to) do sth** oser faire qch; **~devil** *n* casse-cou *m inv*; **daring** *a* hardi(e), audacieux(euse).

dark [dɑ:k] *a* (*night, room*) obscur(e), sombre; (*colour, complexion*) foncé(e), sombre; (*fig*) sombre // *n*: **in the ~** dans le noir; **in the ~ about** (*fig*) ignorant tout de; **after ~** après la tombée de la nuit; **~en** *vt* obscurcir, assombrir // *vi* s'obscurcir, s'assombrir; **~ glasses** *npl* lunettes noires; **~ness** *n* obscurité *f*; **~ room** *n* chambre noire.

darling ['dɑ:lɪŋ] *a, n* chéri(e).

darn [dɑ:n] *vt* repriser.

dart [dɑ:t] *n* fléchette *f* // *vi*: **to ~ towards** (*also*: **make a ~ towards**) se précipiter *or* s'élancer vers; **to ~ away/along** partir/passer comme une flèche; **~s** *n* jeu *m* de fléchettes; **~board** *n* cible *f* (de jeu de fléchettes).

dash [dæʃ] *n* (*sign*) tiret *m* // *vt* (*missile*) jeter *or* lancer violemment; (*hopes*) anéantir // *vi*: **to ~ towards** (*also*: **make a ~ towards**) se précipiter *or* se ruer vers; **to ~ away** *vi* partir à toute allure;

~**board** *n* tableau *m* de bord ; ~**ing** *a* fringant(e).
data ['deɪtə] *npl* données *fpl* ; ~ **processing** *n* traitement *m* (électronique) de l'information.
date [deɪt] *n* date *f* ; rendez-vous *m* ; (*fruit*) datte *f* // *vt* dater ; **to** ~ *ad* à ce jour ; **out of** ~ périmé(e) ; **up to** ~ à la page ; mis(e) à jour ; moderne ; ~**d the 13th** daté du 13 ; ~**d** *a* démodé(e) ; ~**line** *n* ligne *f* de changement de date.
daub [dɔ:b] *vt* barbouiller.
daughter ['dɔ:tə*] *n* fille *f* ; ~**-in-law** *n* belle-fille *f*, bru *f*.
daunt [dɔ:nt] *vt* intimider, décourager ; ~**less** *a* intrépide.
dawdle ['dɔ:dl] *vi* traîner, lambiner.
dawn [dɔ:n] *n* aube *f*, aurore *f* // *vi* (*day*) se lever, poindre ; (*fig*) naître, se faire jour.
day [deɪ] *n* jour *m* ; (*as duration*) journée *f* ; (*period of time, age*) époque *f*, temps *m* ; **the** ~ **before** la veille, le jour précédent ; **the following** ~ le lendemain, le jour suivant ; **by** ~ de jour ; ~ **boy/girl** *n* (SCOL) externe *m/f* ; ~**break** *n* point *m* du jour ; ~**dream** *n* rêverie *f* // *vi* rêver (tout éveillé) ; ~**light** *n* (lumière *f* du) jour *m* ; ~**time** *n* jour *m*, journée *f*.
daze [deɪz] *vt* (*subject: drug*) hébéter ; (: *blow*) étourdir // *n*: **in a** ~ hébété(e) ; étourdi(e).
dazzle ['dæzl] *vt* éblouir, aveugler.
dead [dɛd] *a* mort(e) ; (*numb*) engourdi(e), insensible // *ad* absolument, complètement ; **he was shot** ~ il a été tué d'un coup de revolver ; ~ **on time** à l'heure pile ; ~ **tired** éreinté, complètement fourbu ; **to stop** ~ s'arrêter pile *or* net ; **the** ~ les morts ; ~**en** *vt* (*blow, sound*) amortir ; (*make numb*) endormir, rendre insensible ; ~ **end** *n* impasse *f* ; ~ **heat** *n* (SPORT): **to finish in a** ~ **heat** terminer ex-æquo ; ~**line** *n* date *f or* heure *f* limite ; ~**lock** *n* impasse *f* (*fig*) ; ~**ly** *a* mortel(le) ; (*weapon*) meurtrier(ère) ; ~**pan** *a* impassible ; (*humour*) pince-sans-rire *inv*.
deaf [dɛf] *a* sourd(e) ; ~**-aid** *n* appareil auditif ; ~**en** *vt* rendre sourd ; (*fig*) assourdir ; ~**ening** *a* assourdissant(e) ; ~**ness** *n* surdité *f* ; ~**-mute** *n* sourd/e-muet/te.
deal [di:l] *n* affaire *f*, marché *m* // *vt* (*pt, pp* **dealt** [dɛlt]) (*blow*) porter ; (*cards*) donner, distribuer ; **a great** ~ **(of)** beaucoup (de) ; **to** ~ **in** faire le commerce de ; **to** ~ **with** *vt fus* (COMM) traiter avec ; (*handle*) s'occuper *or* se charger de ; (*be about: book etc*) traiter de ; ~**er** *n* marchand *m* ; ~**ings** *npl* (COMM) transactions *fpl* ; (*relations*) relations *fpl*, rapports *mpl*.
dean [di:n] *n* (SCOL) doyen *m*.
dear [dɪə*] *a* cher(chère) ; (*expensive*) cher, coûteux(euse) // *n*: **my** ~ mon cher/ma chère ; ~ **me!** mon Dieu! ; **D**~ **Sir/Madam** (*in letter*) Monsieur/Madame ; **D**~ **Mr/Mrs X** Cher Monsieur/Chère Madame X ; ~**ly** *ad* (*love*) tendrement ; (*pay*) cher.
dearth [də:θ] *n* disette *f*, pénurie *f*.
death [dɛθ] *n* mort *f* ; (ADMIN) décès *m* ; ~**bed** *n* lit *m* de mort ; ~ **certificate** *n* acte *m* de décès ; ~ **duties** *npl* (*Brit*) droits *mpl* de succession ; ~**ly** *a* de mort ; ~ **penalty** *n* peine *f* de mort ; ~ **rate** *n* (taux *m* de) mortalité *f*.
debar [dɪ'bɑ:*] *vt*: **to** ~ **sb from a club** *etc* exclure qn d'un club *etc* ; **to** ~ **sb from doing** interdire à qn de faire.
debase [dɪ'beɪs] *vt* (*currency*) déprécier, dévaloriser ; (*person*) abaisser, avilir.
debatable [dɪ'beɪtəbl] *a* discutable, contestable.
debate [dɪ'beɪt] *n* discussion *f*, débat *m* // *vt* discuter, débattre // *vi* (*consider*): **to** ~ **whether** se demander si.
debauchery [dɪ'bɔ:tʃərɪ] *n* débauche *f*.
debit ['dɛbɪt] *n* débit *m* // *vt*: **to** ~ **a sum to sb** *or* **to sb's account** porter une somme au débit de qn, débiter qn d'une somme.
debris ['dɛbri:] *n* débris *mpl*, décombres *mpl*.
debt [dɛt] *n* dette *f* ; **to be in** ~ avoir des dettes, être endetté(e) ; ~**or** *n* débiteur/trice.
début ['deɪbju:] *n* début(s) *m(pl)*.
decade ['dɛkeɪd] *n* décennie *f*, décade *f*.
decadence ['dɛkədəns] *n* décadence *f*.
decanter [dɪ'kæntə*] *n* carafe *f*.
decarbonize [di:'kɑ:bənaɪz] *vt* (AUT) décalaminer.
decay [dɪ'keɪ] *n* décomposition *f*, pourrissement *m* ; (*fig*) déclin *m*, délabrement *m* ; (*also*: **tooth** ~) carie *f* (dentaire) // *vi* (*rot*) se décomposer, pourrir ; (*fig*) se délabrer ; décliner ; se détériorer.
decease [dɪ'si:s] *n* décès *m* ; ~**d** *n* défunt/e.
deceit [dɪ'si:t] *n* tromperie *f*, supercherie *f* ; ~**ful** *a* trompeur(euse).
deceive [dɪ'si:v] *vt* tromper ; **to** ~ **o.s.** s'abuser.
decelerate [di:'sɛləreɪt] *vt,vi* ralentir.
December [dɪ'sɛmbə*] *n* décembre *m*.
decency ['di:sənsɪ] *n* décence *f*.
decent ['di:sənt] *a* décent(e), convenable ; **they were very** ~ **about it** ils se sont montrés très chics.
decentralize [di:'sɛntrəlaɪz] *vt* décentraliser.
deception [dɪ'sɛpʃən] *n* tromperie *f*.
deceptive [dɪ'sɛptɪv] *a* trompeur(euse).
decibel ['dɛsɪbɛl] *n* décibel *m*.
decide [dɪ'saɪd] *vt* (*person*) décider ; (*question, argument*) trancher, régler // *vi* se décider, décider ; **to** ~ **to do/that** décider de faire/que ; **to** ~ **on** décider, se décider pour ; **to** ~ **on doing** décider de faire ; ~**d** *a* (*resolute*) résolu(e), décidé(e) ; (*clear, definite*) net(te), marqué(e) ; ~**dly** [-dɪdlɪ] *ad* résolument ; incontestablement, nettement.
deciduous [dɪ'sɪdjuəs] *a* à feuilles caduques.
decimal ['dɛsɪməl] *a* décimal(e) // *n* décimale *f* ; ~ **point** *n* ≈ virgule *f*.
decimate ['dɛsɪmeɪt] *vt* décimer.
decipher [dɪ'saɪfə*] *vt* déchiffrer.

decision [dɪ'sɪʒən] *n* décision *f*.
decisive [dɪ'saɪsɪv] *a* décisif(ive).
deck [dɛk] *n* (NAUT) pont *m*; (*of bus*): **top ~** impériale *f*; (*of cards*) jeu *m*; **~chair** *n* chaise longue; **~ hand** *n* matelot *m*.
declaration [dɛklə'reɪʃən] *n* déclaration *f*.
declare [dɪ'klɛə*] *vt* déclarer.
decline [dɪ'klaɪn] *n* (*decay*) déclin *m*; (*lessening*) baisse *f* // *vt* refuser, décliner // *vi* décliner; être en baisse, baisser.
declutch ['di:'klʌtʃ] *vi* débrayer.
decode ['di:'kəud] *vt* décoder.
decompose [di:kəm'pəuz] *vi* se décomposer; **decomposition** [di:kɔmpə'zɪʃən] *n* décomposition *f*.
decontaminate [di:kən'tæmɪneɪt] *vt* décontaminer.
décor ['deɪkɔ:*] *n* décor *m*.
decorate ['dɛkəreɪt] *vt* (*adorn, give a medal to*) décorer; (*paint and paper*) peindre et tapisser; **decoration** [-'reɪʃən] *n* (*medal etc, adornment*) décoration *f*; **decorative** ['dɛkərətɪv] *a* décoratif(ive); **decorator** *n* peintre *m* en bâtiment.
decoy ['di:kɔɪ] *n* piège *m*; **they used him as a ~ for the enemy** ils se sont servis de lui pour attirer l'ennemi.
decrease *n* ['di:kri:s] diminution *f* // *vt, vi* [di:'kri:s] diminuer.
decree [dɪ'kri:] *n* (POL, REL) décret *m*; (LAW: *of tribunal*) arrêt *m*, jugement *m*; **~ nisi** *n* jugement *m* provisoire de divorce.
decrepit [dɪ'krɛpɪt] *a* décrépit(e); délabré(e).
dedicate ['dɛdɪkeɪt] *vt* consacrer; (*book etc*) dédier.
dedication [dɛdɪ'keɪʃən] *n* (*devotion*) dévouement *m*.
deduce [dɪ'dju:s] *vt* déduire, conclure.
deduct [dɪ'dʌkt] *vt*: **to ~ sth (from)** déduire qch (de), retrancher qch (de); (*from wage etc*) prélever qch (sur), retenir qch (sur); **~ion** [dɪ'dʌkʃən] *n* (*deducting*) déduction *f*; (*from wage etc*) prélèvement *m*, retenue *f*; (*deducing*) déduction, conclusion *f*.
deed [di:d] *n* action *f*, acte *m*; (LAW) acte notarié, contrat *m*.
deep [di:p] *a* (*water, sigh, sorrow, thoughts*) profond(e); (*voice*) grave; **he took a ~ breath** il inspira profondément, il prit son souffle; **4 metres ~** de 4 mètres de profondeur // *ad*: **~ in snow** recouvert(e) d'une épaisse couche de neige; **spectators stood 20 ~** il y avait 20 rangs de spectateurs; **knee-~ in water** dans l'eau jusqu'aux genoux; **~en** *vt* (*hole*) approfondir // *vi* s'approfondir; (*darkness*) s'épaissir; **~-freeze** *n* congélateur *m* // *vt* surgeler; **~-fry** *vt* faire frire (en friteuse); **~-sea** *a*: **~-sea diving** *n* plongée sous-marine; **~-sea fishing** *n* pêche hauturière; **~-seated** *a* (*beliefs*) profondément enraciné(e); **~-set** *a* (*eyes*) enfoncé(e).
deer [dɪə*] *n, pl inv*: **the ~** les cervidés *mpl* (ZOOL); **(red) ~** cerf *m*; **(fallow) ~** daim *m*; **(roe) ~** chevreuil *m*; **~skin** *n* peau *f* de daim.
deface [dɪ'feɪs] *vt* dégrader; barbouiller; rendre illisible.
defamation [dɛfə'meɪʃən] *n* diffamation *f*.
default [dɪ'fɔ:lt] *vi* (LAW) faire défaut; (*gen*) manquer à ses engagements // *n*: **by ~** (LAW) par défaut, par contumace; (SPORT) par forfait; **~er** *n* (*in debt*) débiteur défaillant.
defeat [dɪ'fi:t] *n* défaite *f* // *vt* (*team, opponents*) battre; (*fig: plans, efforts*) faire échouer; **~ist** *a,n* défaitiste (*m/f*).
defect *n* ['di:fɛkt] défaut *m* // *vi* [dɪ'fɛkt]: **to ~ to the enemy/the West** passer à l'ennemi/l'Ouest; **~ive** [dɪ'fɛktɪv] *a* défectueux(euse).
defence [dɪ'fɛns] *n* défense *f*; **in ~ of** pour défendre; **~less** *a* sans défense.
defend [dɪ'fɛnd] *vt* défendre; **~ant** *n* défendeur/deresse; (*in criminal case*) accusé/e, prévenu/e; **~er** *n* défenseur *m*.
defense [dɪ'fɛns] *n* (*US*) = **defence.**
defensive [dɪ'fɛnsɪv] *a* défensif(ive).
defer [dɪ'fə:*] *vt* (*postpone*) différer, ajourner.
deference ['dɛfərəns] *n* déférence *f*; égards *mpl*.
defiance [dɪ'faɪəns] *n* défi *m*; **in ~ of** au mépris de.
defiant [dɪ'faɪənt] *a* provocant(e), de défi.
deficiency [dɪ'fɪʃənsɪ] *n* insuffisance *f*, déficience *f*; carence *f*; **~ disease** *n* maladie *f* de carence.
deficient [dɪ'fɪʃənt] *a* insuffisant(e); défectueux(euse); déficient(e); **~ in** manquant de.
deficit ['dɛfɪsɪt] *n* déficit *m*.
defile *vb* [dɪ'faɪl] *vt* souiller // *vi* défiler // *n* ['di:faɪl] défilé *m*.
define [dɪ'faɪn] *vt* définir.
definite ['dɛfɪnɪt] *a* (*fixed*) défini(e), (bien) déterminé(e); (*clear, obvious*) net(te), manifeste; (LING) défini(e); **he was ~ about it** il a été catégorique; il était sûr de son fait; **~ly** *ad* sans aucun doute.
definition [dɛfɪ'nɪʃən] *n* définition *f*.
definitive [dɪ'fɪnɪtɪv] *a* définitif(ive).
deflate [di:'fleɪt] *vt* dégonfler.
deflation [di:'fleɪʃən] *n* (COMM) déflation *f*.
deflect [dɪ'flɛkt] *vt* détourner, faire dévier.
deform [dɪ'fɔ:m] *vt* déformer; **~ed** *a* difforme; **~ity** *n* difformité *f*.
defraud [dɪ'frɔ:d] *vt* frauder; **to ~ sb of sth** soutirer qch malhonnêtement à qn; escroquer qch à qn; frustrer qn de qch.
defray [dɪ'freɪ] *vt*: **to ~ sb's expenses** défrayer qn (de ses frais), rembourser *or* payer à qn ses frais.
defrost [di:'frɔst] *vt* (*fridge*) dégivrer.
deft [dɛft] *a* adroit(e), preste.
defunct [dɪ'fʌŋkt] *a* défunt(e).
defuse [di:'fju:z] *vt* désamorcer.
defy [dɪ'faɪ] *vt* défier; (*efforts etc*) résister à.
degenerate *vi* [dɪ'dʒɛnəreɪt] dégénérer // *a* [dɪ'dʒɛnərɪt] dégénéré(e).
degradation [dɛgrə'deɪʃən] *n* dégradation *f*.
degrading [dɪ'greɪdɪŋ] *a* dégradant(e).
degree [dɪ'gri:] *n* degré *m*; grade *m* (universitaire); **a (first) ~ in maths** une licence en maths.
dehydrated [di:haɪ'dreɪtɪd] *a* déshydraté(e); (*milk, eggs*) en poudre.

de-ice [di:'aɪs] *vt* (*windscreen*) dégivrer.
deign [deɪn] *vi*: **to ~ to do** daigner faire.
deity ['di:ɪtɪ] *n* divinité *f*; dieu *m*, déesse *f*.
dejected [dɪ'dʒɛktɪd] *a* abattu(e), déprimé(e).
dejection [dɪ'dʒɛkʃən] *n* abattement *m*, découragement *m*.
delay [dɪ'leɪ] *vt* (*journey, operation*) retarder, différer; (*travellers, trains*) retarder // *n* délai *m*, retard *m*; **without ~** sans délai; sans tarder; **~ed-action** *a* à retardement.
delegate *n* ['dɛlɪgɪt] délégué/e // *vt* ['dɛlɪgeɪt] déléguer.
delegation [dɛlɪ'geɪʃən] *n* délégation *f*.
delete [dɪ'li:t] *vt* rayer, supprimer.
deliberate *a* [dɪ'lɪbərɪt] (*intentional*) délibéré(e); (*slow*) mesuré(e) // *vi* [dɪ'lɪbəreɪt] délibérer, réfléchir; **~ly** *ad* (*on purpose*) exprès, délibérément.
delicacy ['dɛlɪkəsɪ] *n* délicatesse *f*; (*choice food*) mets fin *or* délicat, friandise *f*.
delicate ['dɛlɪkɪt] *a* délicat(e).
delicatessen [dɛlɪkə'tɛsn] *n* épicerie fine.
delicious [dɪ'lɪʃəs] *a* délicieux(euse), exquis(e).
delight [dɪ'laɪt] *n* (grande) joie, grand plaisir // *vt* enchanter; **a ~ to the eyes** un régal *or* plaisir pour les yeux; **to take ~ in** prendre grand plaisir à; **to be the ~ of** faire les délices *or* la joie de; **~ful** *a* adorable; merveilleux(euse); délicieux(euse).
delinquency [dɪ'lɪŋkwənsɪ] *n* délinquance *f*.
delinquent [dɪ'lɪŋkwənt] *a,n* délinquant(e).
delirium [dɪ'lɪrɪəm] *n* délire *m*.
deliver [dɪ'lɪvə*] *vt* (*mail*) distribuer; (*goods*) livrer; (*message*) remettre; (*speech*) prononcer; (*warning, ultimatum*) lancer; (*free*) délivrer; (MED) accoucher; **to ~ the goods** (*fig*) tenir ses promesses; **~y** *n* distribution *f*; livraison *f*; (*of speaker*) élocution *f*; (MED) accouchement *m*; **to take ~y of** prendre livraison de.
delouse ['di:'laus] *vt* épouiller, débarrasser de sa (*or* leur *etc*) vermine.
delta ['dɛltə] *n* delta *m*.
delude [dɪ'lu:d] *vt* tromper, leurrer; **to ~ o.s.** se leurrer, se faire des illusions.
deluge ['dɛlju:dʒ] *n* déluge *m*.
delusion [dɪ'lu:ʒən] *n* illusion *f*.
delve [dɛlv] *vi*: **to ~ into** fouiller dans.
demagogue ['dɛməgɔg] *n* démagogue *m/f*.
demand [dɪ'mɑ:nd] *vt* réclamer, exiger // *n* exigence *f*; (*claim*) revendication *f*; (ECON) demande *f*; **in ~** demandé(e), recherché(e); **on ~** sur demande; **~ing** *a* (*boss*) exigeant(e); (*work*) astreignant(e).
demarcation [di:mɑ:'keɪʃən] *n* démarcation *f*.
demean [dɪ'mi:n] *vt*: **to ~ o.s.** s'abaisser.
demeanour [dɪ'mi:nə*] *n* comportement *m*; maintien *m*.
demented [dɪ'mɛntɪd] *a* dément(e), fou(folle).
demise [dɪ'maɪz] *n* décès *m*.
demister [di:'mɪstə*] *n* (AUT) dispositif *m* anti-buée *inv*.
demobilize [di:'məubɪlaɪz] *vt* démobiliser.
democracy [dɪ'mɔkrəsɪ] *n* démocratie *f*.
democrat ['dɛməkræt] *n* démocrate *m/f*; **~ic** [dɛmə'krætɪk] *a* démocratique.
demography [dɪ'mɔgrəfɪ] *n* démographie *f*.
demolish [dɪ'mɔlɪʃ] démolir.
demolition [dɛmə'lɪʃən] *n* démolition *f*.
demonstrate ['dɛmənstreɪt] *vt* démontrer, prouver.
demonstration [dɛmən'streɪʃən] *n* démonstration *f*, manifestation *f*.
demonstrative [dɪ'mɔnstrətɪv] *a* démonstratif(ive).
demonstrator ['dɛmənstreɪtə*] *n* (POL) manifestant/e.
demoralize [dɪ'mɔrəlaɪz] *vt* démoraliser.
demote [dɪ'məut] *vt* rétrograder.
demur [dɪ'mə:*] *vi* protester; hésiter.
demure [dɪ'mjuə*] *a* sage, réservé(e); d'une modestie affectée.
den [dɛn] *n* tanière *f*, antre *m*.
denial [dɪ'naɪəl] *n* démenti *m*; dénégation *f*.
denigrate ['dɛnɪgreɪt] *vt* dénigrer.
denim ['dɛnɪm] *n* coton émerisé; **~s** *npl* (blue-)jeans *mpl*.
Denmark ['dɛnmɑ:k] *n* Danemark *m*.
denomination [dɪnɔmɪ'neɪʃən] *n* (*money*) valeur *f*; (REL) confession *f*; culte *m*.
denominator [dɪ'nɔmɪneɪtə*] *n* dénominateur *m*.
denote [dɪ'nəut] *vt* dénoter.
denounce [dɪ'nauns] *vt* dénoncer.
dense [dɛns] *a* dense; (*stupid*) obtus(e), dur(e) *or* lent(e) à la comprenette; **~ly** *ad*: **~ly wooded** couvert d'épaisses forêts; **~ly populated** à forte densité (de population), très peuplé.
density ['dɛnsɪtɪ] *n* densité *f*.
dent [dɛnt] *n* bosse *f* // *vt* (*also*: **make a ~ in**) cabosser; **to make a ~ in** (*fig*) entamer.
dental ['dɛntl] *a* dentaire; **~ surgeon** *n* (chirurgien/ne) dentiste.
dentifrice ['dɛntɪfrɪs] *n* dentifrice *m*.
dentist ['dɛntɪst] *n* dentiste *m/f*; **~ry** *n* art *m* dentaire.
denture ['dɛntʃə*] *n* dentier *m*.
deny [dɪ'naɪ] *vt* nier; (*refuse*) refuser; (*disown*) renier.
deodorant [di:'əudərənt] *n* désodorisant *m*, déodorant *m*.
depart [dɪ'pɑ:t] *vi* partir; **to ~ from** (*leave*) quitter, partir de; (*fig*: *differ from*) s'écarter de.
department [dɪ'pɑ:tmənt] *n* (COMM) rayon *m*; (SCOL) section *f*; (POL) ministère *m*, département *m*; **~ store** *n* grand magasin.
departure [dɪ'pɑ:tʃə*] *n* départ *m*; (*fig*): **~ from** écart *m* par rapport à.
depend [dɪ'pɛnd] *vi*: **to ~ on** dépendre de; (*rely on*) compter sur; **it ~s** cela dépend; **~able** *a* sûr(e), digne de confiance; **~ence** *n* dépendance *f*; **~ant, ~ent** *n* personne *f* à charge.
depict [dɪ'pɪkt] *vt* (*in picture*) représenter; (*in words*) (dé)peindre, décrire.
depleted [dɪ'pli:tɪd] *a* (considérablement) réduit(e) *or* diminué(e).

deplorable [dɪ'plɔ:rəbl] *a* déplorable, lamentable.
deplore [dɪ'plɔ:*] *vt* déplorer.
deploy [dɪ'plɔɪ] *vt* déployer.
depopulation ['di:pɔpju'leɪʃən] *n* dépopulation *f*, dépeuplement *m*.
deport [dɪ'pɔ:t] *vt* déporter; expulser; **~ation** [di:pɔ:'teɪʃən] *n* déportation *f*, expulsion *f*; **~ment** *n* maintien *m*, tenue *f*.
depose [dɪ'pəuz] *vt* déposer.
deposit [dɪ'pɔzɪt] *n* (CHEM, COMM, GEO) dépôt *m*; (*of ore, oil*) gisement *m*; (*part payment*) arrhes *fpl*, acompte *m*; (*on bottle etc*) consigne *f*; (*for hired goods etc*) cautionnement *m*, garantie *f* // *vt* déposer; mettre *or* laisser en dépôt; fournir *or* donner en acompte; laisser en garantie; **~ account** *n* compte *m* de dépôt; **~or** *n* déposant/e.
depot ['dɛpəu] *n* dépôt *m*.
deprave [dɪ'preɪv] *vt* dépraver, corrompre, pervertir.
depravity [dɪ'prævɪtɪ] *n* dépravation *f*.
deprecate ['dɛprɪkeɪt] *vt* désapprouver.
depreciate [dɪ'pri:ʃɪeɪt] *vt* déprécier // *vi* se déprécier, se dévaloriser; **depreciation** [-'eɪʃən] *n* dépréciation *f*.
depress [dɪ'prɛs] *vt* déprimer; (*press down*) appuyer sur, abaisser; **~ed** *a* (*person*) déprimé(e), abattu(e); (*area*) en déclin, touché(e) par le sous-emploi; **~ing** *a* déprimant(e); **~ion** [dɪ'prɛʃən] *n* dépression *f*.
deprivation [dɛprɪ'veɪʃən] *n* privation *f*; (*loss*) perte *f*.
deprive [dɪ'praɪv] *vt*: **to ~ sb of** priver qn de; enlever à qn; **~d** *a* déshérité(e).
depth [dɛpθ] *n* profondeur *f*; **in the ~s of** au fond de; au cœur de; au plus profond de; **~ charge** *n* grenade sous-marine.
deputation [dɛpju'teɪʃən] *n* députation *f*, délégation *f*.
deputize ['dɛpjutaɪz] *vi*: **to ~ for** assurer l'intérim de.
deputy ['dɛpjutɪ] *a*: **~ chairman** vice-président *m*; **~ head** directeur adjoint, sous-directeur *m* // *n* (*replacement*) suppléant/e, intérimaire *m/f*; (*second in command*) adjoint/e.
derail [dɪ'reɪl] *vt* faire dérailler; **to be ~ed** dérailler; **~ment** *n* déraillement *m*.
deranged [dɪ'reɪndʒd] *a* (*machine*) déréglé(e); **to be (mentally) ~** avoir le cerveau dérangé.
derelict ['dɛrɪlɪkt] *a* abandonné(e), à l'abandon.
deride [dɪ'raɪd] *vt* railler.
derision [dɪ'rɪʒən] *n* dérision *f*.
derisive [dɪ'raɪsɪv] *a* moqueur (euse), railleur(euse).
derisory [dɪ'raɪsərɪ] *a* (*sum*) dérisoire; (*smile, person*) moqueur(euse), railleur(euse).
derivation [dɛrɪ'veɪʃən] *n* dérivation *f*.
derivative [dɪ'rɪvətɪv] *n* dérivé *m* // *a* dérivé(e).
derive [dɪ'raɪv] *vt*: **to ~ sth from** tirer qch de; trouver qch dans // *vi*: **to ~ from** provenir de, dériver de.
dermatology [də:mə'tɔlədʒɪ] *n* dermatologie *f*.
derogatory [dɪ'rɔgətərɪ] *a* désobligeant(e); péjoratif(ive).
derrick ['dɛrɪk] *n* mât *m* de charge; derrick *m*.
desalination [di:salɪ'neɪʃən] *n* dessalement *m*, dessalage *m*.
descend [dɪ'sɛnd] *vt, vi* descendre; **to ~ from** descendre de, être issu de; **~ant** *n* descendant/e.
descent [dɪ'sɛnt] *n* descente *f*; (*origin*) origine *f*.
describe [dɪs'kraɪb] *vt* décrire; **description** [-'krɪpʃən] *n* description *f*; (*sort*) sorte *f*, espèce *f*; **descriptive** [-'krɪptɪv] *a* descriptif(ive).
desecrate ['dɛsɪkreɪt] *vt* profaner.
desert *n* ['dɛzət] désert *m* // *vb* [dɪ'zə:t] *vt* déserter, abandonner // *vi* (MIL) déserter; **~er** *n* déserteur *m*; **~ion** [dɪ'zə:ʃən] *n* désertion *f*.
deserve [dɪ'zə:v] *vt* mériter; **deserving** *a* (*person*) méritant(e); (*action, cause*) méritoire.
design [dɪ'zaɪn] *n* (*sketch*) plan *m*, dessin *m*; (*layout, shape*) conception *f*, ligne *f*; (*pattern*) dessin *m*, motif(s) *m(pl)*; (COMM) esthétique industrielle; (*intention*) dessein *m* // *vt* dessiner; concevoir; **to have ~s on** avoir des visées sur; **well-~ed** *a* bien conçu(e).
designate *vt* ['dɛzɪgneɪt] désigner // *a* ['dɛzɪgnɪt] désigné(e); **designation** [-'neɪʃən] *n* désignation *f*.
designer [dɪ'zaɪnə*] *n* (ART, TECH) dessinateur/trice; (*fashion*) modéliste *m/f*.
desirability [dɪzaɪərə'bɪlɪtɪ] *n* avantage *m*; attrait *m*.
desirable [dɪ'zaɪərəbl] *a* désirable.
desire [dɪ'zaɪə*] *n* désir *m* // *vt* désirer, vouloir.
desirous [dɪ'zaɪərəs] *a*: **~ of** désireux(euse) de.
desk [dɛsk] *n* (*in office*) bureau *m*; (*for pupil*) pupitre *m*; (*in shop, restaurant*) caisse *f*; (*in hotel, at airport*) réception *f*.
desolate ['dɛsəlɪt] *a* désolé(e).
desolation [dɛsə'leɪʃən] *n* désolation *f*.
despair [dɪs'pɛə*] *n* désespoir *m* // *vi*: **to ~ of** désespérer de.
despatch [dɪs'pætʃ] *n,vt* = **dispatch**.
desperate ['dɛspərɪt] *a* désespéré(e); (*fugitive*) prêt(e) à tout; **~ly** *ad* désespérément; (*very*) terriblement, extrêmement.
desperation [dɛspə'reɪʃən] *n* désespoir *m*; **in ~** à bout de nerf; en désespoir de cause.
despicable [dɪs'pɪkəbl] *a* méprisable.
despise [dɪs'paɪz] *vt* mépriser, dédaigner.
despite [dɪs'paɪt] *prep* malgré, en dépit de.
despondent [dɪs'pɔndənt] *a* découragé(e), abattu(e).
dessert [dɪ'zə:t] *n* dessert *m*; **~spoon** *n* cuiller *f* à dessert.
destination [dɛstɪ'neɪʃən] *n* destination *f*.
destine ['dɛstɪn] *vt* destiner.
destiny ['dɛstɪnɪ] *n* destinée *f*, destin *m*.
destitute ['dɛstɪtju:t] *a* indigent(e), dans

le dénuement ; ~ **of** dépourvu *or* dénué de.
destroy [dɪs'trɔɪ] *vt* détruire ; **~er** *n* (*NAUT*) contre-torpilleur *m*.
destruction [dɪs'trʌkʃən] *n* destruction *f*.
destructive [dɪs'trʌktɪv] *a* destructeur(trice).
detach [dɪ'tætʃ] *vt* détacher ; **~able** *a* amovible, détachable ; **~ed** *a* (*attitude*) détaché(e) ; **~ed house** *n* pavillon *m*, maison(nette) (individuelle) ; **~ment** *n* (*MIL*) détachement *m* ; (*fig*) détachement *m*, indifférence *f*.
detail ['di:teɪl] *n* détail *m* // *vt* raconter en détail, énumérer ; (*MIL*): **to ~ sb (for)** affecter qn (à), détacher qn (pour) ; **in ~** en détail ; **~ed** *a* détaillé(e).
detain [dɪ'teɪn] *vt* retenir ; (*in captivity*) détenir ; (*in hospital*) hospitaliser.
detect [dɪ'tɛkt] *vt* déceler, percevoir ; (*MED, POLICE*) dépister ; (*MIL, RADAR, TECH*) détecter ; **~ion** [dɪ'tɛkʃən] *n* découverte *f* ; dépistage *m* ; détection *f* ; **to escape ~ion** échapper aux recherches, éviter d'être découvert ; **crime ~ion** le dépistage des criminels ; **~ive** *n* agent *m* de la sûreté, policier *m* ; **private ~ive** détective privé ; **~ive story** *n* roman policier ; **~or** *n* détecteur *m*.
detention [dɪ'tɛnʃən] *n* détention *f* ; (*SCOL*) retenue *f*, consigne *f*.
deter [dɪ'tə:*] *vt* dissuader.
detergent [dɪ'tə:dʒənt] *n* détersif *m*, détergent *m*.
deteriorate [dɪ'tɪərɪəreɪt] *vi* se détériorer, se dégrader ; **deterioration** [-'reɪʃən] *n* détérioration *f*.
determination [dɪtə:mɪ'neɪʃən] *n* détermination *f*.
determine [dɪ'tə:mɪn] *vt* déterminer ; **to ~ to do** résoudre de faire, se déterminer à faire ; **~d** *a* (*person*) déterminé(e), décidé(e) ; (*quantity*) déterminé, établi(e).
deterrent [dɪ'tɛrənt] *n* effet *m* de dissuasion ; force *f* de dissuasion.
detest [dɪ'tɛst] *vt* détester, avoir horreur de ; **~able** *a* détestable, odieux(euse).
detonate ['dɛtəneɪt] *vi* exploser ; détoner // *vt* faire exploser *or* détoner ; **detonator** *n* détonateur *m*.
detour ['di:tuə*] *n* détour *m*.
detract [dɪ'trækt] *vt*: **to ~ from** (*quality, pleasure*) diminuer ; (*reputation*) porter atteinte à.
detriment ['dɛtrɪmənt] *n*: **to the ~ of** au détriment de, au préjudice de ; **~al** [dɛtrɪ'mɛntl] *a*: **~al to** préjudiciable *or* nuisible à.
devaluation [dɪvælju'eɪʃən] *n* dévaluation *f*.
devalue ['di:'vælju:] *vt* dévaluer.
devastate ['dɛvəsteɪt] *vt* dévaster.
devastating ['dɛvəsteɪtɪŋ] *a* dévastateur(trice).
develop [dɪ'vɛləp] *vt* (*gen*) développer ; (*habit*) contracter ; (*resources*) mettre en valeur, exploiter // *vi* se développer ; (*situation, disease* ; *evolve*) évoluer ; (*facts, symptoms*: *appear*) se manifester, se produire ; **~er** *n* (*PHOT*) révélateur *m* ; (*of land*) promoteur *m* ; **~ing country** pays *m* en voie de développement ; **~ment** *n* développement *m* ; (*of affair, case*) rebondissement *m*, fait(s) nouveau(x).
deviate ['di:vɪeɪt] *vi* dévier.
deviation [di:vɪ'eɪʃən] *n* déviation *f*.
device [dɪ'vaɪs] *n* (*scheme*) moyen *m*, expédient *m* ; (*apparatus*) engin *m*, dispositif *m*.
devil ['dɛvl] *n* diable *m* ; démon *m* ; **~ish** *a* diabolique.
devious ['di:vɪəs] *a* (*means*) détourné(e) ; (*person*) sournois(e), dissimulé(e).
devise [dɪ'vaɪz] *vt* imaginer, concevoir.
devoid [dɪ'vɔɪd] *a*: **~ of** dépourvu(e) de, dénué(e) de.
devote [dɪ'vəut] *vt*: **to ~ sth to** consacrer qch à ; **~d** *a* dévoué(e) ; **to be ~d to** être dévoué *or* très attaché à ; **~e** [dɛvəu'ti:] *n* (*REL*) adepte *m/f* ; (*MUS, SPORT*) fervent/e.
devotion [dɪ'vəuʃən] *n* dévouement *m*, attachement *m* ; (*REL*) dévotion *f*, piété *f*.
devour [dɪ'vauə*] *vt* dévorer.
devout [dɪ'vaut] *a* pieux(euse), dévot(e).
dew [dju:] *n* rosée *f*.
dexterity [dɛks'tɛrɪtɪ] *n* dextérité *f*, adresse *f*.
diabetes [daɪə'bi:ti:z] *n* diabète *m* ; **diabetic** [-'bɛtɪk] *a, n* diabétique (*m/f*).
diaeresis [daɪ'ɛrɪsɪs] *n* tréma *m*.
diagnose [daɪəg'nəuz] *vt* diagnostiquer.
diagnosis, *pl* **diagnoses** [daɪəg'nəusɪs, -si:z] *n* diagnostic *m*.
diagonal [daɪ'ægənl] *a* diagonal(e) // *n* diagonale *f*.
diagram ['daɪəgræm] *n* diagramme *m*, schéma *m* ; graphique *m*.
dial ['daɪəl] *n* cadran *m* // *vt* (*number*) faire, composer ; **~ling tone** *n* tonalité *f*.
dialect ['daɪəlɛkt] *n* dialecte *m*.
dialogue ['daɪəlɔg] *n* dialogue *m*.
diameter [daɪ'æmɪtə*] *n* diamètre *m*.
diamond ['daɪəmənd] *n* diamant *m* ; (*shape*) losange *m* ; **~s** *npl* (*CARDS*) carreau *m*.
diaper ['daɪəpə*] *n* (*US*) couche *f*.
diaphragm ['daɪəfræm] *n* diaphragme *m*.
diarrhoea, diarrhea (*US*) [daɪə'ri:ə] *n* diarrhée *f*.
diary ['daɪərɪ] *n* (*daily account*) journal *m* ; (*book*) agenda *m*.
dice [daɪs] *n, pl inv* dé *m* // *vt* (*CULIN*) couper en dés *or* en cubes.
dictate *vt* [dɪk'teɪt] dicter // *n* ['dɪkteɪt] injonction *f*.
dictation [dɪk'teɪʃən] *n* dictée *f*.
dictator [dɪk'teɪtə*] *n* dictateur *m* ; **~ship** *n* dictature *f*.
diction ['dɪkʃən] *n* diction *f*, élocution *f*.
dictionary ['dɪkʃənrɪ] *n* dictionnaire *m*.
did [dɪd] *pt of* **do**.
die [daɪ] *n* (*pl*: **dice**) dé *m* ; (*pl*: **dies**) coin *m* ; matrice *f* ; étampe *f* // *vi* mourir ; **to ~ away** *vi* s'éteindre ; **to ~ down** *vi* se calmer, s'apaiser ; **to ~ out** *vi* disparaître, s'éteindre.
Diesel ['di:zəl]: **~ engine** *n* moteur *m* diesel.
diet ['daɪət] *n* alimentation *f* ; (*restricted food*) régime *m* // *vi* (*also*: **be on a ~**) suivre un régime.
differ ['dɪfə*] *vi*: **to ~ from sth** être différent de ; différer de ; **to ~ from sb**

over sth ne pas être d'accord avec qn au sujet de qch; **~ence** *n* différence *f*; (*quarrel*) différend *m*, désaccord *m*; **~ent** *a* différent(e); **~ential** [-'rɛnʃəl] *n* (AUT, *wages*) différentiel *m*; **~entiate** [-'rɛnʃɪeɪt] *vt* différencier // *vi* se différencier; **to ~entiate between** faire une différence entre; **~ently** *ad* différemment.

difficult ['dɪfɪkəlt] *a* difficile; **~y** *n* difficulté *f*.

diffidence ['dɪfɪdəns] *n* manque *m* de confiance en soi, manque d'assurance.

diffident ['dɪfɪdənt] *a* qui manque de confiance *or* d'assurance, peu sûr(e) de soi.

diffuse *a* [dɪ'fju:s] diffus(e) // *vt* [dɪ'fju:z] diffuser, répandre.

dig [dɪg] *vt* (*pt*, *pp* **dug** [dʌg]) (*hole*) creuser; (*garden*) bêcher // *n* (*prod*) coup *m* de coude; (*fig*) coup de griffe *or* de patte; **to ~ into** (*snow*, *soil*) creuser; **to ~ one's nails into** enfoncer ses ongles dans; **to ~ up** *vt* déterrer.

digest *vt* [daɪ'dʒɛst] digérer // *n* ['daɪdʒɛst] sommaire *m*, résumé *m*; **~ible** [dɪ'dʒɛstəbl] *a* digestible; **~ion** [dɪ'dʒɛstʃən] *n* digestion *f*.

digit ['dɪdʒɪt] *n* chiffre *m* (*de 0 à 9*); (*finger*) doigt *m*; **~al** *a* digital(e); à affichage numérique *or* digital.

dignified ['dɪgnɪfaɪd] *a* digne.

dignitary ['dɪgnɪtərɪ] *n* dignitaire *m*.

dignity ['dɪgnɪtɪ] *n* dignité *f*.

digress [daɪ'grɛs] *vi*: **to ~ from** s'écarter de, s'éloigner de; **~ion** [daɪ'grɛʃən] *n* digression *f*.

digs [dɪgz] *npl* (*Brit*: *col*) piaule *f*, chambre meublée.

dilapidated [dɪ'læpɪdeɪtɪd] *a* délabré(e).

dilate [daɪ'leɪt] *vt* dilater // *vi* se dilater.

dilatory ['dɪlətərɪ] *a* dilatoire.

dilemma [daɪ'lɛmə] *n* dilemme *m*.

diligent ['dɪlɪdʒənt] *a* appliqué(e), assidu(e).

dilute [daɪ'lu:t] *vt* diluer // *a* dilué(e).

dim [dɪm] *a* (*light*, *eyesight*) faible; (*memory*, *outline*) vague, indécis(e); (*stupid*) borné(e), obtus(e) // *vt* (*light*) réduire, baisser.

dime [daɪm] *n* (*US*) = *10 cents*.

dimension [dɪ'mɛnʃən] *n* dimension *f*.

diminish [dɪ'mɪnɪʃ] *vt*,*vi* diminuer.

diminutive [dɪ'mɪnjutɪv] *a* minuscule, tout(e) petit(e) // *n* (LING) diminutif *m*.

dimly ['dɪmlɪ] *ad* faiblement; vaguement.

dimple ['dɪmpl] *n* fossette *f*.

dim-witted ['dɪm'wɪtɪd] *a* (*col*) stupide, borné(e).

din [dɪn] *n* vacarme *m*.

dine [daɪn] *vi* dîner; **~r** *n* (*person*) dîneur/euse; (RAIL) = **dining car**.

dinghy ['dɪŋgɪ] *n* youyou *m*; canot *m* pneumatique; (*also*: **sailing ~**) voilier *m*, dériveur *m*.

dingy ['dɪndʒɪ] *a* miteux(euse), minable.

dining ['daɪnɪŋ] *cpd*: **~ car** *n* wagon-restaurant *m*; **~ room** *n* salle *f* à manger.

dinner ['dɪnə*] *n* dîner *m*; (*public*) banquet *m*; **~ jacket** *n* smoking *m*; **~ party** *n* dîner *m*; **~ time** *n* heure *f* du dîner.

diocese ['daɪəsɪs] *n* diocèse *m*.

dip [dɪp] *n* déclivité *f*; (*in sea*) baignade *f*, bain *m* // *vt* tremper, plonger; (AUT: *lights*) mettre en code, baisser // *vi* plonger.

diphtheria [dɪf'θɪərɪə] *n* diphtérie *f*.

diphthong ['dɪfθɔŋ] *n* diphtongue *f*.

diploma [dɪ'pləumə] *n* diplôme *m*.

diplomacy [dɪ'pləuməsɪ] *n* diplomatie *f*.

diplomat ['dɪpləmæt] *n* diplomate *m*; **~ic** [dɪplə'mætɪk] *a* diplomatique; **~ic corps** *n* corps *m* diplomatique.

dipstick ['dɪpstɪk] *n* (AUT) jauge *f* de niveau d'huile.

dire [daɪə*] *a* terrible, extrême, affreux(euse).

direct [daɪ'rɛkt] *a* direct(e) // *vt* diriger, orienter; **can you ~ me to...?** pouvez-vous m'indiquer le chemin de ...?; **~ current** *n* courant continu; **~ hit** *n* coup *m* au but, touché *m*.

direction [dɪ'rɛkʃən] *n* direction *f*; **sense of ~** sens *m* de l'orientation; **~s** *npl* (*advice*) indications *fpl*; **~s for use** mode *m* d'emploi.

directly [dɪ'rɛktlɪ] *ad* (*in straight line*) directement, tout droit; (*at once*) tout de suite, immédiatement.

director [dɪ'rɛktə*] *n* directeur *m*; administrateur *m*; (THEATRE) metteur *m* en scène; (CINEMA, TV) réalisateur/trice.

directory [dɪ'rɛktərɪ] *n* annuaire *m*.

dirt [də:t] *n* saleté *f*; crasse *f*; **~-cheap** *a* (ne) coûtant presque rien; **~ road** *n* (*US*) chemin non macadamisé *or* non revêtu; **~y** *a* sale // *vt* salir; **~y story** *n* histoire cochonne; **~y trick** *n* coup tordu.

disability [dɪsə'bɪlɪtɪ] *n* invalidité *f*, infirmité *f*.

disabled [dɪs'eɪbld] *a* infirme, invalide; (*maimed*) mutilé(e); (*through illness, old age*) impotent(e).

disadvantage [dɪsəd'vɑ:ntɪdʒ] *n* désavantage *m*, inconvénient *m*; **~ous** [dɪsædvɑ:n'teɪdʒəs] *a* désavantageux(euse).

disagree [dɪsə'gri:] *vi* (*differ*) ne pas concorder; (*be against, think otherwise*): **to ~ (with)** ne pas être d'accord (avec); **garlic ~s with me** l'ail ne me convient pas, je ne supporte pas l'ail; **~able** *a* désagréable; **~ment** *n* désaccord *m*, différend *m*.

disallow ['dɪsə'lau] *vt* rejeter, désavouer.

disappear [dɪsə'pɪə*] *vi* disparaître; **~ance** *n* disparition *f*.

disappoint [dɪsə'pɔɪnt] *vt* décevoir; **~ment** *n* déception *f*.

disapproval [dɪsə'pru:vəl] *n* désapprobation *f*.

disapprove [dɪsə'pru:v] *vi*: **to ~ of** désapprouver.

disarm [dɪs'ɑ:m] *vt* désarmer; **~ament** *n* désarmement *m*.

disarray [dɪsə'reɪ] *n* désordre *m*, confusion *f*.

disaster [dɪ'zɑ:stə*] *n* catastrophe *f*, désastre *m*; **disastrous** *a* désastreux(euse).

disband [dɪs'bænd] *vt* démobiliser ; disperser // *vi* se séparer ; se disperser.
disbelief ['dɪsbə'li:f] *n* incrédulité *f.*
disc [dɪsk] *n* disque *m.*
discard [dɪs'kɑ:d] *vt* (*old things*) se défaire de, mettre au rencart *or* au rebut ; (*fig*) écarter, renoncer à.
disc brake ['dɪskbreɪk] *n* frein *m* à disque.
discern [dɪ'sə:n] *vt* discerner, distinguer ; **~ing** *a* judicieux(euse), perspicace.
discharge *vt* [dɪs'tʃɑ:dʒ] (*duties*) s'acquitter de ; (*waste etc*) déverser ; décharger ; (*ELEC, MED*) émettre ; (*patient*) renvoyer (chez lui) ; (*employee, soldier*) congédier, licencier ; (*defendant*) relaxer, élargir // *n* ['dɪstʃɑ:dʒ] (*ELEC, MED*) émission *f* ; (*dismissal*) renvoi *m* ; licenciement *m* ; élargissement *m* ; **to ~ one's gun** faire feu.
disciple [dɪ'saɪpl] *n* disciple *m.*
disciplinary ['dɪsɪplɪnərɪ] *a* disciplinaire.
discipline ['dɪsɪplɪn] *n* discipline *f* // *vt* discipliner ; (*punish*) punir.
disc jockey ['dɪskdʒɔkɪ] *n* disque-jockey *m.*
disclaim [dɪs'kleɪm] *vt* désavouer, dénier.
disclose [dɪs'kləuz] *vt* révéler, divulguer ; **disclosure** [-'kləuʒə*] *n* révélation *f*, divulgation *f.*
disco ['dɪskəu] *n abbr of* **discothèque.**
discoloured [dɪs'kʌləd] *a* décoloré(e) ; jauni(e).
discomfort [dɪs'kʌmfət] *n* malaise *m*, gêne *f* ; (*lack of comfort*) manque *m* de confort.
disconcert [dɪskən'sə:t] *vt* déconcerter, décontenancer.
disconnect [dɪskə'nɛkt] *vt* détacher ; (*ELEC, RADIO*) débrancher ; (*gas, water*) couper ; **~ed** *a* (*speech, thought*) décousu(e), peu cohérent(e).
disconsolate [dɪs'kɔnsəlɪt] *a* inconsolable.
discontent [dɪskən'tɛnt] *n* mécontentement *m* ; **~ed** *a* mécontent(e).
discontinue [dɪskən'tɪnju:] *vt* cesser, interrompre ; **'~d'** (*COMM*) 'fin de série'.
discord ['dɪskɔ:d] *n* discorde *f*, dissension *f* ; (*MUS*) dissonance *f* ; **~ant** [dɪs'kɔ:dənt] *a* discordant(e), dissonant(e).
discothèque ['dɪskəutɛk] *n* discothèque *f.*
discount *n* ['dɪskaunt] remise *f*, rabais *m* // *vt* [dɪs'kaunt] ne pas tenir compte de.
discourage [dɪs'kʌrɪdʒ] *vt* décourager ; **discouraging** *a* décourageant(e).
discourteous [dɪs'kə:tɪəs] *a* incivil(e), discourtois(e).
discover [dɪs'kʌvə*] *vt* découvrir ; **~y** *n* découverte *f.*
discredit [dɪs'krɛdɪt] *vt* mettre en doute ; discréditer.
discreet [dɪ'skri:t] *a* discret(ète) ; **~ly** *ad* discrètement.
discrepancy [dɪ'skrɛpənsɪ] *n* divergence *f*, contradiction *f.*
discretion [dɪ'skrɛʃən] *n* discrétion *f.*
discriminate [dɪ'skrɪmɪneɪt] *vi*: **to ~ between** établir une distinction entre, faire la différence entre ; **to ~ against** pratiquer une discrimination contre ; **discriminating** *a* qui a du discernement ;
discrimination [-'neɪʃən] *n* discrimination *f* ; (*judgment*) discernement *m.*
discus ['dɪskəs] *n* disque *m.*
discuss [dɪ'skʌs] *vt* discuter de ; (*debate*) discuter ; **~ion** [dɪ'skʌʃən] *n* discussion *f.*
disdain [dɪs'deɪn] *n* dédain *m.*
disease [dɪ'zi:z] *n* maladie *f.*
disembark [dɪsɪm'bɑ:k] *vt,vi* débarquer.
disembodied [dɪsɪm'bɔdɪd] *a* désincarné(e).
disembowel [dɪsɪm'bauəl] *vt* éviscérer, étriper.
disenchanted [dɪsɪn'tʃɑ:ntɪd] *a* désenchanté(e), désabusé(e).
disengage [dɪsɪn'geɪdʒ] *vt* dégager ; (*TECH*) déclencher ; **to ~ the clutch** (*AUT*) débrayer ; **~ment** *n* (*POL*) désengagement *m.*
disentangle [dɪsɪn'tæŋgl] *vt* démêler.
disfavour [dɪs'feɪvə*] *n* défaveur *f* ; disgrâce *f* // *vt* voir d'un mauvais œil, désapprouver.
disfigure [dɪs'fɪgə*] *vt* défigurer.
disgorge [dɪs'gɔ:dʒ] *vt* déverser.
disgrace [dɪs'greɪs] *n* honte *f* ; (*disfavour*) disgrâce *f* // *vt* déshonorer, couvrir de honte ; **~ful** *a* scandaleux(euse), honteux(euse).
disgruntled [dɪs'grʌntld] *a* mécontent(e).
disguise [dɪs'gaɪz] *n* déguisement *m* // *vt* déguiser ; **in ~** déguisé(e).
disgust [dɪs'gʌst] *n* dégoût *m*, aversion *f* // *vt* dégoûter, écœurer ; **~ing** *a* dégoûtant(e) ; révoltant(e).
dish [dɪʃ] *n* plat *m* ; **to do** *or* **wash the ~es** faire la vaisselle ; **to ~ up** *vt* servir ; (*facts, statistics*) sortir, débiter ; **~cloth** *n* (*for drying*) torchon *m* ; (*for washing*) lavette *f.*
dishearten [dɪs'hɑ:tn] *vt* décourager.
dishevelled [dɪ'ʃɛvəld] *a* ébouriffé(e) ; décoiffé(e) ; débraillé(e).
dishonest [dɪs'ɔnɪst] *a* malhonnête ; **~y** *n* malhonnêteté *f.*
dishonour [dɪs'ɔnə*] *n* déshonneur *m* ; **~able** *a* déshonorant(e).
dishwasher ['dɪʃwɔʃə*] *n* lave-vaisselle *m* ; (*person*) plongeur/euse.
disillusion [dɪsɪ'lu:ʒən] *vt* désabuser, désenchanter // *n* désenchantement *m.*
disinfect [dɪsɪn'fɛkt] *vt* désinfecter ; **~ant** *n* désinfectant *m.*
disintegrate [dɪs'ɪntɪgreɪt] *vi* se désintégrer.
disinterested [dɪs'ɪntrəstɪd] *a* désintéressé(e).
disjointed [dɪs'dʒɔɪntɪd] *a* décousu(e), incohérent(e).
disk [dɪsk] *n* = **disc.**
dislike [dɪs'laɪk] *n* aversion *f*, antipathie *f* // *vt* ne pas aimer.
dislocate ['dɪsləkeɪt] *vt* disloquer ; déboiter ; désorganiser.
dislodge [dɪs'lɔdʒ] *vt* déplacer, faire bouger ; (*enemy*) déloger.
disloyal [dɪs'lɔɪəl] *a* déloyal(e).
dismal ['dɪzml] *a* lugubre, maussade.
dismantle [dɪs'mæntl] *vt* démonter ; (*fort, warship*) démanteler.
dismast [dɪs'mɑ:st] *vt* démâter.

dismay [dɪs'meɪ] *n* consternation *f* // *vt* consterner.
dismiss [dɪs'mɪs] *vt* congédier, renvoyer; (*idea*) écarter; (LAW) rejeter; **~al** *n* renvoi *m*.
dismount [dɪs'maunt] *vi* mettre pied à terre.
disobedience [dɪsə'bi:dɪəns] *n* désobéissance *f*; insoumission *f*.
disobedient [dɪsə'bi:dɪənt] *a* désobéissant(e); (*soldier*) indiscipliné(e).
disobey [dɪsə'beɪ] *vt* désobéir à.
disorder [dɪs'ɔ:də*] *n* désordre *m*; (*rioting*) désordres *mpl*; (MED) troubles *mpl*; **~ly** *a* en désordre; désordonné(e).
disorganize [dɪs'ɔ:gənaɪz] *vt* désorganiser.
disorientate [dɪs'ɔ:rɪɛnteɪt] *vt* désorienter.
disown [dɪs'əun] *vt* renier.
disparaging [dɪs'pærɪdʒɪŋ] *a* désobligeant(e).
disparity [dɪs'pærɪtɪ] *n* disparité *f*.
dispassionate [dɪs'pæʃənət] *a* calme, froid(e); impartial(e), objectif(ive).
dispatch [dɪs'pætʃ] *vt* expédier, envoyer // *n* envoi *m*, expédition *f*; (MIL, PRESS) dépêche *f*.
dispel [dɪs'pɛl] *vt* dissiper, chasser.
dispensary [dɪs'pɛnsərɪ] *n* pharmacie *f*; (*in chemist's*) officine *f*.
dispense [dɪs'pɛns] *vt* distribuer, administrer; **to ~ sb from** dispenser qn de; **to ~ with** *vt fus* se passer de; **~r** *n* (*container*) distributeur *m*; **dispensing chemist** *n* pharmacie *f*.
dispersal [dɪs'pə:sl] *n* dispersion *f*; (ADMIN) déconcentration *f*.
disperse [dɪs'pə:s] *vt* disperser; (*knowledge*) disséminer // *vi* se disperser.
dispirited [dɪs'pɪrɪtɪd] *a* découragé(e), déprimé(e).
displace [dɪs'pleɪs] *vt* déplacer; **~d person** *n* (POL) personne déplacée; **~ment** *n* déplacement *m*.
display [dɪs'pleɪ] *n* étalage *m*; déploiement *m*; affichage *m*; (*screen*) écran *m* de visualisation, visuel *m*; (*of feeling*) manifestation *f*; (*pej*) ostentation *f* // *vt* montrer; (*goods*) mettre à l'étalage, exposer; (*results, departure times*) afficher; (*troops*) déployer; (*pej*) faire étalage de.
displease [dɪs'pli:z] *vt* mécontenter contrarier; **~d with** mécontent(e) de; **displeasure** [-'plɛʒə*] *n* mécontentement *m*.
disposable [dɪs'pəuzəbl] *a* (*pack etc*) à jeter; (*income*) disponible.
disposal [dɪs'pəuzl] *n* (*availability, arrangement*) disposition *f*; (*of property*) disposition *f*, cession *f*; (*of rubbish*) évacuation *f*, destruction *f*; **at one's ~** à sa disposition.
dispose [dɪs'pəuz] *vt* disposer; **to ~ of** *vt* (*time, money*) disposer de; (*unwanted goods*) se débarrasser de, se défaire de; (*problem*) expédier; **~d** *a*: **~d to do** disposé(e) à faire; **disposition** [-'zɪʃən] *n* disposition *f*; (*temperament*) naturel *m*.
disproportionate [dɪsprə'pɔ:ʃənət] *a* disproportionné(e).
disprove [dɪs'pru:v] *vt* réfuter.
dispute [dɪs'pju:t] *n* discussion *f*; (*also*: **industrial ~**) conflit *m* // *vt* contester; (*matter*) discuter; (*victory*) disputer.
disqualification [dɪskwɔlɪfɪ'keɪʃən] *n* disqualification *f*; **~ (from driving)** retrait *m* du permis (de conduire).
disqualify [dɪs'kwɔlɪfaɪ] *vt* (SPORT) disqualifier; **to ~ sb for sth/from doing** rendre qn inapte à qch/à faire; signifier à qn l'interdiction de faire; mettre qn dans l'impossibilité de faire; **to ~ sb (from driving) for speeding** retirer à qn son permis (de conduire) pour excès de vitesse.
disquiet [dɪs'kwaɪət] *n* inquiétude *f*, trouble *m*.
disregard [dɪsrɪ'gɑ:d] *vt* ne pas tenir compte de.
disrepair [dɪsrɪ'pɛə*] *n* mauvais état.
disreputable [dɪs'rɛpjutəbl] *a* (*person*) de mauvaise réputation, peu recommandable; (*behaviour*) déshonorant(e).
disrespectful [dɪsrɪ'spɛktful] *a* irrespectueux(euse).
disrupt [dɪs'rʌpt] *vt* (*plans*) déranger; (*conversation*) interrompre; **~ion** [-'rʌpʃən] *n* dérangement *m*; interruption *f*.
dissatisfaction [dɪssætɪs'fækʃən] *n* mécontentement *m*, insatisfaction *f*.
dissatisfied [dɪs'sætɪsfaɪd] *a*: **~ (with)** mécontent(e) *or* insatisfait(e) (de).
dissect [dɪ'sɛkt] *vt* disséquer.
disseminate [dɪ'sɛmɪneɪt] *vt* disséminer.
dissent [dɪ'sɛnt] *n* dissentiment *m*, différence *f* d'opinion.
disservice [dɪs'sə:vɪs] *n*: **to do sb a ~** rendre un mauvais service à qn; desservir qn.
dissident ['dɪsɪdnt] *a* dissident(e).
dissimilar [dɪ'sɪmɪlə*] *a*: **~ (to)** dissemblable (à), différent(e) (de).
dissipate ['dɪsɪpeɪt] *vt* dissiper; (*energy, efforts*) disperser; **~d** *a* dissolu(e); débauché(e).
dissociate [dɪ'səuʃɪeɪt] *vt* dissocier.
dissolute ['dɪsəlu:t] *a* débauché(e), dissolu(e).
dissolve [dɪ'zɔlv] *vt* dissoudre // *vi* se dissoudre, fondre; (*fig*) disparaître.
dissuade [dɪ'sweɪd] *vt*: **to ~ sb (from)** dissuader qn (de).
distance ['dɪstns] *n* distance *f*; **in the ~** au loin.
distant ['dɪstnt] *a* lointain(e), éloigné(e); (*manner*) distant(e), froid(e).
distaste [dɪs'teɪst] *n* dégoût *m*; **~ful** *a* déplaisant(e), désagréable.
distemper [dɪs'tɛmpə*] *n* (*paint*) détrempe *f*, badigeon *m*.
distend [dɪs'tɛnd] *vt* distendre // *vi* se distendre, se ballonner.
distil [dɪs'tɪl] *vt* distiller; **~lery** *n* distillerie *f*.
distinct [dɪs'tɪŋkt] *a* distinct(e); (*preference, progress*) marqué(e); **~ion** [dɪs'tɪŋkʃən] *n* distinction *f*; (*in exam*) mention *f* très bien; **~ive** *a* distinctif(ive); **~ly** *ad* distinctement; expressément.

distinguish [dɪs'tɪŋgwɪʃ] *vt* distinguer ; différencier ; **~ed** *a* (*eminent*) distingué(e) ; **~ing** *a* (*feature*) distinctif(ive), caractéristique.
distort [dɪs'tɔ:t] *vt* déformer ; **~ion** [dɪs'tɔ:ʃən] *n* déformation *f*.
distract [dɪs'trækt] *vt* distraire, déranger ; **~ed** *a* éperdu(e), égaré(e) ; **~ion** [dɪs'trækʃən] *n* distraction *f*; égarement *m*; **to drive sb to ~ion** rendre qn fou(folle).
distraught [dɪs'trɔ:t] *a* éperdu(e).
distress [dɪs'trɛs] *n* détresse *f*; (*pain*) douleur *f* // *vt* affliger ; **~ed area** *n* zone sinistrée ; **~ing** *a* douloureux(euse), pénible ; **~ signal** *n* signal *m* de détresse.
distribute [dɪs'trɪbju:t] *vt* distribuer ; **distribution** [-'bju:ʃən] *n* distribution *f*; **distributor** *n* distributeur *m*.
district ['dɪstrɪkt] *n* (*of country*) région *f*; (*of town*) quartier *m*; (ADMIN) district *m*; **~ attorney** *n* (*US*) ≈ procureur *m* de la République ; **~ nurse** *n* (*Brit*) infirmière visiteuse.
distrust [dɪs'trʌst] *n* méfiance *f*, doute *m* // *vt* se méfier de.
disturb [dɪs'tə:b] *vt* troubler ; (*inconvenience*) déranger ; **~ance** *n* dérangement *m*; (*political etc*) troubles *mpl*; (*by drunks etc*) tapage *m*; **~ing** *a* troublant(e), inquiétant(e).
disuse [dɪs'ju:s] *n*: **to fall into ~** tomber en désuétude *f*.
disused [dɪs'ju:zd] *a* désaffecté(e).
ditch [dɪtʃ] *n* fossé *m* // *vt* (*col*) abandonner.
dither ['dɪðə*] *vi* hésiter.
ditto ['dɪtəu] *ad* idem.
divan [dɪ'væn] *n* divan *m*.
dive [daɪv] *n* plongeon *m*; (*of submarine*) plongée *f*; (AVIAT) piqué *m*; (*pej*) bouge *m* // *vi* plonger ; **~r** *n* plongeur *m*.
diverge [daɪ'və:dʒ] *vi* diverger.
diverse [daɪ'və:s] *a* divers(e).
diversify [daɪ'və:sɪfaɪ] *vt* diversifier.
diversion [daɪ'və:ʃən] *n* (AUT) déviation *f*; (*distraction*, MIL) diversion *f*.
diversity [daɪ'və:sɪtɪ] *n* diversité *f*, variété *f*.
divert [daɪ'və:t] *vt* (*traffic*) dévier ; (*river*) détourner ; (*amuse*) divertir.
divest [daɪ'vɛst] *vt*: **to ~ sb of** dépouiller qn de.
divide [dɪ'vaɪd] *vt* diviser ; (*separate*) séparer // *vi* se diviser ; **~d skirt** *n* jupe-culotte *f*.
dividend ['dɪvɪdɛnd] *n* dividende *m*.
divine [dɪ'vaɪn] *a* divin(e).
diving ['daɪvɪŋ] *n* plongée (sous-marine) ; **~ board** *n* plongeoir *m*; **~ suit** *n* scaphandre *m*.
divinity [dɪ'vɪnɪtɪ] *n* divinité *f*; théologie *f*.
division [dɪ'vɪʒən] *n* division *f*; séparation *f*; (*Brit* POL) vote *m*.
divorce [dɪ'vɔ:s] *n* divorce *m* // *vt* divorcer d'avec ; **~d** *a* divorcé(e) ; **~e** [-'si:] *n* divorcé/e.
divulge [daɪ'vʌldʒ] *vt* divulguer, révéler.
D.I.Y. *a,n abbr of* **do-it-yourself**.

dizziness ['dɪzɪnɪs] *n* vertige *m*, étourdissement *m*.
dizzy ['dɪzɪ] *a* (*height*) vertigineux(euse) ; **to make sb ~** donner le vertige à qn ; **to feel ~** avoir la tête qui tourne.
DJ *n abbr of* **disc jockey**.
do, *pt* **did**, *pp* **done** [du:, dɪd, dʌn] *vt, vi* faire ; **he didn't laugh** il n'a pas ri ; **~ you want any?** en voulez-vous?, est-ce que vous en voulez? ; **she swims better than I ~** elle nage mieux que moi ; **he laughed, didn't he?** il a ri, n'est-ce pas? ; **~ they?** ah oui?, vraiment? ; **who broke it? - I did** qui l'a cassé? - (c'est) moi ; **~ you agree? - I ~** êtes-vous d'accord? - oui ; **to ~ one's nails/teeth** se faire les ongles/brosser les dents ; **will it ~?** est-ce que ça ira? ; **to ~ without sth** se passer de qch ; **what did he ~ with the cat?** qu'a-t-il fait du chat? ; **to ~ away with** *vt fus* supprimer, abolir ; **to ~ up** *vt* remettre à neuf.
docile ['dəusaɪl] *a* docile.
dock [dɔk] *n* dock *m*; (LAW) banc *m* des accusés // *vi* se mettre à quai ; **~er** *n* docker *m*.
docket ['dɔkɪt] *n* bordereau *m*.
dockyard ['dɔkjɑ:d] *n* chantier *m* de construction navale.
doctor ['dɔktə*] *n* médecin *m*, docteur *m*; (*Ph.D. etc*) docteur // *vt* (*cat*) couper ; (*fig*) falsifier.
doctrine ['dɔktrɪn] *n* doctrine *f*.
document ['dɔkjumənt] *n* document *m*; **~ary** [-'mɛntərɪ] *a, n* documentaire (*m*) ; **~ation** [-'teɪʃən] *n* documentation *f*.
doddering ['dɔdərɪŋ] *a* (*senile*) gâteux(euse).
dodge [dɔdʒ] *n* truc *m*; combine *f* // *vt* esquiver, éviter.
dodgems ['dɔdʒəmz] *npl* autos tamponneuses.
dog [dɔg] *n* chien/ne ; **~ biscuits** *npl* biscuits *mpl* pour chien ; **~ collar** *n* collier *m* de chien ; (*fig*) faux-col *m* d'ecclésiastique ; **~-eared** *a* corné(e).
dogged ['dɔgɪd] *a* obstiné(e), opiniâtre.
dogma ['dɔgmə] *n* dogme *m*; **~tic** [-'mætɪk] *a* dogmatique.
doings ['duɪŋz] *npl* activités *fpl*.
do-it-yourself [du:ɪtjɔ:'sɛlf] *n* bricolage *m*.
doldrums ['dɔldrəmz] *npl*: **to be in the ~** avoir le cafard ; être dans le marasme.
dole [dəul] *n* (*Brit*) allocation *f* de chômage ; **on the ~** au chômage ; **to ~ out** *vt* donner au compte-goutte.
doleful ['dəulful] *a* triste, lugubre.
doll [dɔl] *n* poupée *f*; **to ~ o.s. up** se faire beau(belle).
dollar ['dɔlə*] *n* dollar *m*.
dolphin ['dɔlfɪn] *n* dauphin *m*.
domain [də'meɪn] *n* domaine *m*.
dome [dəum] *n* dôme *m*.
domestic [də'mɛstɪk] *a* (*duty, happiness*) familial(e) ; (*policy, affairs, flights*) intérieur(e) ; (*animal*) domestique ; **~ated** *a* domestiqué(e) ; (*pej*) d'intérieur.
domicile ['dɔmɪsaɪl] *n* domicile *m*.
dominant ['dɔmɪnənt] *a* dominant(e).
dominate ['dɔmɪneɪt] *vt* dominer ; **domination** [-'neɪʃən] *n* domination *f*;

domineering [-'nıərıŋ] *a* dominateur(trice), autoritaire.
dominion [də'mınıən] *n* domination *f*; territoire *m*; dominion *m*.
domino, ~es ['dɔmınəu] *n* domino *m*; **~es** *n* (*game*) dominos *mpl*.
don [dɔn] *n* professeur *m* d'université // *vt* revêtir.
donate [də'neıt] *vt* faire don de, donner; **donation** [də'neıʃən] *n* donation *f*, don *m*.
done [dʌn] *pp of* **do**.
donkey ['dɔŋkı] *n* âne *m*.
donor ['dəunə*] *n* (*of blood etc*) donneur/euse; (*to charity*) donateur/trice.
don't [dəunt] *vb* = **do not.**
doom [du:m] *n* destin *m*; ruine *f* // *vt*: **to be ~ed (to failure)** être voué(e) à l'échec; **~sday** *n* le Jugement dernier.
door [dɔ:*] *n* porte *f*; **~bell** *n* sonnette *f*; **~ handle** *n* poignée *f* de porte; **~man** *n* (*in hotel*) portier *m*; (*in block of flats*) concierge *m*; **~mat** *n* paillasson *m*; **~post** *n* montant *m* de porte; **~step** *n* pas *m* de (la) porte, seuil *m*.
dope [dəup] *n* (*col*) drogue *f* // *vt* (*horse etc*) doper.
dopey ['dəupı] *a* (*col*) à moitié endormi(e).
dormant ['dɔ:mənt] *a* assoupi(e), en veilleuse; (*rule, law*) inappliqué(e).
dormice ['dɔ:maıs] *npl of* **dormouse**.
dormitory ['dɔ:mıtrı] *n* dortoir *m*.
dormouse, *pl* **dormice** ['dɔ:maus, -maıs] *n* loir *m*.
dosage ['dəusıdʒ] *n* dose *f*; dosage *m*; (*on label*) posologie *f*.
dose [dəus] *n* dose *f*; (*bout*) attaque *f* // *vt*: **to ~ o.s.** se bourrer de médicaments.
doss house ['dɔshaus] *n* asile *m* de nuit.
dot [dɔt] *n* point *m* // *vt*: **~ted with** parsemé(e) de; **on the ~** à l'heure tapante.
dote [dəut]: **to ~ on** *vt fus* être fou(folle) de.
dotted line [dɔtıd'laın] *n* ligne pointillée; (AUT) ligne discontinue.
double ['dʌbl] *a* double // *ad* (*fold*) en deux; (*twice*): **to cost ~ (sth)** coûter le double (de qch) *or* deux fois plus (que qch) // *n* double *m*; (CINEMA) doublure *f* // *vt* doubler; (*fold*) plier en deux // *vi* doubler; **at the ~** au pas de course; **~s** *n* (TENNIS) double *m*; **~ bass** *n* contrebasse *f*; **~ bed** *n* grand lit; **~ bend** *n* virage *m* en S; **~-breasted** *a* croisé(e); **~cross** *vt* doubler, trahir; **~decker** *n* autobus *m* à impériale; **~ declutch** *vi* faire un double débrayage; **~ exposure** *n* surimpression *f*; **~ parking** *n* stationnement *m* en double file; **~ room** *n* chambre *f* pour deux; **doubly** *ad* doublement, deux fois plus.
doubt [daut] *n* doute *m* // *vt* douter de; **to ~ that** douter que; **~ful** *a* douteux(euse); (*person*) incertain(e); **~less** *ad* sans doute, sûrement.
dough [dəu] *n* pâte *f*; **~nut** *n* beignet *m*.
dour [duə*] *a* austère.
dove [dʌv] *n* colombe *f*.
Dover ['dəuvə*] *n* Douvres.
dovetail ['dʌvteıl] *n*: **~ joint** *n* assemblage *m* à queue d'aronde // *vi* (*fig*) concorder.
dowdy ['daudı] *a* démodé(e); mal fagoté(e).
down [daun] *n* (*fluff*) duvet *m* // *ad* en bas // *prep* en bas de // *vt* (*enemy*) abattre; (*col*: *drink*) vider; **the D~s** *collines crayeuses du S.-E. de l'Angleterre*; **~ with X!** à bas X!; **~-at-heel** *a* éculé(e); (*fig*) miteux(euse); **~cast** *a* démoralisé(e); **~fall** *n* chute *f*; ruine *f*; **~hearted** *a* découragé(e); **~hill** *ad*: **to go ~hill** descendre; **~ payment** *n* acompte *m*; **~pour** *n* pluie torrentielle, déluge *m*; **~right** *a* franc(franche); (*refusal*) catégorique; **~stairs** *ad* au rez-de-chaussée; à l'étage inférieur; **~stream** *ad* en aval; **~-to-earth** *a* terre à terre *inv*; **~town** *ad* en ville // *a* (*US*): **~town Chicago** le centre commerçant de Chicago; **~ward** ['daunwəd] *a,ad*, **~wards** ['daunwədz] *ad* vers le bas.
dowry ['daurı] *n* dot *f*.
doz. *abbr of* **dozen**.
doze [dəuz] *vi* sommeiller; **to ~ off** *vi* s'assoupir.
dozen ['dʌzn] *n* douzaine *f*; **a ~ books** une douzaine de livres.
Dr. *abbr of* **doctor**; **drive** (*n*).
drab [dræb] *a* terne, morne.
draft [drɑ:ft] *n* brouillon *m*; (COMM) traite *f*; (*US*: MIL) contingent *m*; (: *call-up*) conscription *f* // *vt* faire le brouillon de; *see also* **draught.**
drag [dræg] *vt* traîner; (*river*) draguer // *vi* traîner // *n* (*col*) raseur/euse; corvée *f*; **to ~ on** *vi* s'éterniser.
dragonfly ['drægənflaı] *n* libellule *f*.
drain [dreın] *n* égout *m*; (*on resources*) saignée *f* // *vt* (*land, marshes*) drainer, assécher; (*vegetables*) égoutter; (*reservoir etc*) vider // *vi* (*water*) s'écouler; **~age** *n* système *m* d'égouts; **~ing board, ~board** (*US*) *n* égouttoir *m*; **~pipe** *n* tuyau *m* d'écoulement.
dram [dræm] *n* petit verre.
drama ['drɑ:mə] *n* (*art*) théâtre *m*, art *m* dramatique; (*play*) pièce *f*; (*event*) drame *m*; **~tic** [drə'mætık] *a* dramatique; spectaculaire; **~tist** ['dræmətıst] *n* auteur *m* dramatique.
drank [dræŋk] *pt of* **drink**.
drape [dreıp] *vt* draper; **~s** *npl* (*US*) rideaux *mpl*; **~r** *n* marchand/e de nouveautés.
drastic ['dræstık] *a* sévère; énergique.
draught [drɑ:ft] *n* courant *m* d'air; (*of chimney*) tirage *m*; (NAUT) tirant *m* d'eau; **~s** *n* (jeu *m* de) dames *fpl*; **on ~** (*beer*) à la pression; **~board** *n* damier *m*.
draughtsman ['drɑ:ftsmən] *n* dessinateur/trice (industriel/le).
draw [drɔ:] *vb* (*pt* **drew,** *pp* **drawn** [dru:, drɔ:n]) *vt* tirer; (*attract*) attirer; (*picture*) dessiner; (*line, circle*) tracer; (*money*) retirer // *vi* (SPORT) faire match nul // *n* match nul; tirage *m* au sort; loterie *f*; **to ~ to a close** toucher à *or* tirer à sa fin; **to ~ near** *vi* s'approcher; approcher; **to ~ out** *vi* (*lengthen*) s'allonger // *vt* (*money*) retirer; **to ~ up** *vi* (*stop*) s'arrêter // *vt* (*document*) établir, dresser; **~back** *n* inconvénient *m*, désavantage *m*; **~bridge** *n* pont-levis *m*.

drawer [drɔ:*] *n* tiroir *m*.
drawing ['drɔ:ɪŋ] *n* dessin *m* ; ~ **board** *n* planche *f* à dessin ; ~ **pin** *n* punaise *f* ; ~ **room** *n* salon *m*.
drawl [drɔ:l] *n* accent traînant.
drawn [drɔ:n] *pp of* **draw.**
dread [drɛd] *n* épouvante *f*, effroi *m* // *vt* redouter, appréhender ; ~**ful** *a* épouvantable, affreux(euse).
dream [dri:m] *n* rêve *m* // *vt, vi* (*pt, pp* **dreamed** *or* **dreamt** [drɛmt]) rêver ; ~**er** *n* rêveur/euse ; ~ **world** *n* monde *m* imaginaire ; ~**y** *a* rêveur(euse).
dreary ['drɪərɪ] *a* triste ; monotone.
dredge [drɛdʒ] *vt* draguer ; ~**r** *n* (*ship*) dragueur *m* ; (*machine*) drague *f* ; (*also*: **sugar** ~**r**) saupoudreuse *f*.
dregs [drɛgz] *npl* lie *f*.
drench [drɛntʃ] *vt* tremper.
dress [drɛs] *n* robe *f* ; (*clothing*) habillement *m*, tenue *f* // *vt* habiller ; (*wound*) panser ; (*food*) préparer ; **to** ~ **up** *vi* s'habiller ; (*in fancy dress*) se déguiser ; ~ **circle** *n* premier balcon ; ~ **designer** *n* modéliste *m/f* ; ~**er** *n* (THEATRE) habilleur/euse ; (*also*: **window** ~**er**) étalagiste *m/f* ; (*furniture*) buffet *m* ; ~**ing** *n* (MED) pansement *m* ; (CULIN) sauce *f*, assaisonnement *m* ; ~**ing gown** *n* robe *f* de chambre ; ~**ing room** *n* (THEATRE) loge *f* ; (SPORT) vestiaire *m* ; ~**ing table** *n* coiffeuse *f* ; ~**maker** *n* couturière *f* ; ~**making** *n* couture *f* ; travaux *mpl* de couture ; ~ **rehearsal** *n* (répétition) générale ; ~ **shirt** *n* chemise *f* à plastron.
drew [dru:] *pt of* **draw.**
dribble ['drɪbl] *vi* tomber goutte à goutte ; (*baby*) baver // *vt* (*ball*) dribbler.
dried [draɪd] *a* (*fruit, beans*) sec(sèche) ; (*eggs, milk*) en poudre.
drift [drɪft] *n* (*of current etc*) force *f* ; direction *f* ; (*of sand etc*) amoncellement *m* ; (*of snow*) rafale *f* ; coulée *f* ; (: *on ground*) congère *f* ; (*general meaning*) sens général // *vi* (*boat*) aller à la dérive, dériver ; (*sand, snow*) s'amonceler, s'entasser ; ~**wood** *n* bois flotté.
drill [drɪl] *n* perceuse *f* ; (*bit*) foret *m* ; (*of dentist*) roulette *f*, fraise *f* ; (MIL) exercice *m* // *vt* percer // *vi* (*for oil*) faire un *or* des forage(s).
drink [drɪŋk] *n* boisson *f* // *vt, vi* (*pt* **drank,** *pp* **drunk** [dræŋk, drʌŋk]) boire ; **to have a** ~ boire quelque chose, boire un verre ; prendre l'apéritif ; ~**er** *n* buveur/euse ; ~**ing water** *n* eau *f* potable.
drip [drɪp] *n* bruit *m* d'égouttement ; goutte *f* ; (MED) goutte-à-goutte *m inv* ; perfusion *f* // *vi* tomber goutte à goutte ; (*washing*) s'égoutter ; (*wall*) suinter ; ~**-dry** *a* (*shirt*) sans repassage ; ~**-feed** *vt* alimenter au goutte-à-goutte *or* par perfusion ; ~**ping** *n* graisse *f* de rôti ; ~**ping wet** *a* trempé(e).
drive [draɪv] *n* promenade *f or* trajet *m* en voiture ; (*also*: ~**way**) allée *f* ; (*energy*) dynamisme *m*, énergie *f* ; (PSYCH) besoin *m* ; pulsion *f* ; (*push*) effort (concerté) ; campagne *f* ; (SPORT) drive *m* ; (TECH) entraînement *m* ; traction *f* ; transmission *f* // *vb* (*pt* **drove,** *pp* **driven** [drəuv, 'drɪvn]) *vt* conduire ; (*nail*) enfoncer ; (*push*) chasser, pousser ; (TECH: *motor*) actionner ; entraîner // *vi* (AUT: *at controls*) conduire ; (: *travel*) aller en voiture ; **left-/right-hand** ~ conduite *f* à gauche/droite.
driver ['draɪvə*] *n* conducteur/trice ; (*of taxi, bus*) chauffeur *m* ; ~**'s license** *n* (*US*) permis *m* de conduire.
driving ['draɪvɪŋ] *a*: ~ **rain** *n* pluie battante // *n* conduite *f* ; ~ **belt** *n* courroie *f* de transmission ; ~ **instructor** *n* moniteur *m* d'auto-école ; ~ **lesson** *n* leçon *f* de conduite ; ~ **licence** *n* (*Brit*) permis *m* de conduire ; ~ **school** *n* auto-école *f* ; ~ **test** *n* examen *m* du permis de conduire.
drizzle ['drɪzl] *n* bruine *f*, crachin *m* // *vi* bruiner.
droll [drəul] *a* drôle.
dromedary ['drɔmədərɪ] *n* dromadaire *m*.
drone [drəun] *n* bourdonnement *m* ; (*male bee*) faux-bourdon *m*.
drool [dru:l] *vi* baver.
droop [dru:p] *vi* s'affaisser ; tomber.
drop [drɔp] *n* goutte *f* ; (*fall*) baisse *f* ; (*also*: **parachute** ~) saut *m* ; (*of cliff*) dénivellation *f* ; à-pic *m* // *vt* laisser tomber ; (*voice, eyes, price*) baisser ; (*set down from car*) déposer // *vi* tomber ; **to** ~ **off** *vi* (*sleep*) s'assoupir ; **to** ~ **out** *vi* (*withdraw*) se retirer ; (*student etc*) abandonner, décrocher ; ~**pings** *npl* crottes *fpl*.
dross [drɔs] *n* déchets *mpl* ; rebut *m*.
drought [draut] *n* sécheresse *f*.
drove [drəuv] *pt of* **drive** // *n*: ~**s of people** une foule de gens.
drown [draun] *vt* noyer // *vi* se noyer.
drowsy ['drauzɪ] *a* somnolent(e).
drudge [drʌdʒ] *n* bête *f* de somme (*fig*) ; ~**ry** ['drʌdʒərɪ] *n* corvée *f*.
drug [drʌg] *n* médicament *m* ; (*narcotic*) drogue *f* // *vt* droguer ; ~ **addict** *n* toxicomane *m/f* ; ~**gist** *n* (*US*) pharmacien/ne-droguiste ; ~**store** *n* (*US*) pharmacie-droguerie *f*, drugstore *m*.
drum [drʌm] *n* tambour *m* ; (*for oil, petrol*) bidon *m* ; ~**mer** *n* (joueur *m* de) tambour *m* ; ~ **roll** *n* roulement *m* de tambour ; ~**stick** *n* (MUS) baguette *f* de tambour ; (*of chicken*) pilon *m*.
drunk [drʌŋk] *pp of* **drink** // *a* ivre, soûl(e) // *n* soûlard/e ; homme/femme soûl(e) ; ~**ard** ['drʌŋkəd] *n* ivrogne *m/f* ; ~**en** *a* ivre, soûl(e) ; ivrogne, d'ivrogne ; ~**enness** *n* ivresse *f* ; ivrognerie *f*.
dry [draɪ] *a* sec(sèche) ; (*day*) sans pluie // *vt* sécher ; (*clothes*) faire sécher // *vi* sécher ; **to** ~ **up** *vi* se tarir ; ~**-cleaner** *n* teinturier *m* ; ~**-cleaner's** *n* teinturerie *f* ; ~**-cleaning** *n* nettoyage *m* à sec ; ~**er** *n* séchoir *m* ; ~**ness** *n* sécheresse *f* ; ~ **rot** *n* pourriture sèche (*du bois*).
dual ['djuəl] *a* double ; ~ **carriageway** *n* route *f* à quatre voies ; ~**-control** *a* à doubles commandes ; ~ **nationality** *n* double nationalité *f* ; ~**-purpose** *a* à double emploi.
dubbed [dʌbd] *a* (CINEMA) doublé(e) ; (*nicknamed*) surnommé(e).
dubious ['dju:bɪəs] *a* hésitant(e), incertain(e) ; (*reputation, company*) douteux(euse).

duchess ['dʌtʃɪs] *n* duchesse *f.*
duck [dʌk] *n* canard *m* // *vi* se baisser vivement, baisser subitement la tête; **~ling** *n* caneton *m.*
duct [dʌkt] *n* conduite *f,* canalisation *f*; (ANAT) conduit *m.*
dud [dʌd] *n* (*shell*) obus non éclaté; (*object, tool*): **it's a ~** c'est de la camelote, ça ne marche pas // *a* (*cheque*) sans provision; (*note, coin*) faux(fausse).
due [dju:] *a* dû(due); (*expected*) attendu(e); (*fitting*) qui convient // *n* dû *m* // *ad*: **~ north** droit vers le nord; **~s** *npl* (*for club, union*) cotisation *f*; (*in harbour*) droits *mpl* (de port); **in ~ course** en temps utile *or* voulu; finalement; **~ to** dû(due) à; causé(e) par.
duel ['djuəl] *n* duel *m.*
duet [dju:'ɛt] *n* duo *m.*
dug [dʌg] *pt, pp of* **dig.**
duke [dju:k] *n* duc *m.*
dull [dʌl] *a* ennuyeux(euse); terne; (*sound, pain*) sourd(e); (*weather, day*) gris(e), maussade; (*blade*) émoussé(e) // *vt* (*pain, grief*) atténuer; (*mind, senses*) engourdir.
duly ['dju:lɪ] *ad* (*on time*) en temps voulu; (*as expected*) comme il se doit.
dumb [dʌm] *a* muet(te); (*stupid*) bête; **dumbfounded** [dʌm'faundɪd] *a* sidéré(e).
dummy ['dʌmɪ] *n* (*tailor's model*) mannequin *m*; (SPORT) feinte *f*; (*for baby*) tétine *f* // *a* faux(fausse), factice.
dump [dʌmp] *n* tas *m* d'ordures; (*place*) décharge (publique); (MIL) dépôt *m* // *vt* (*put down*) déposer; déverser; (*get rid of*) se débarrasser de; **~ing** *n* (ECON) dumping *m*; (*of rubbish*): **'no ~ing'** 'décharge interdite'.
dumpling ['dʌmplɪŋ] *n* boulette *f* (de pâte).
dunce [dʌns] *n* âne *m,* cancre *m.*
dune [dju:n] *n* dune *f.*
dung [dʌŋ] *n* fumier *m.*
dungarees [dʌŋgə'ri:z] *npl* bleu(s) *m(pl)*; salopette *f.*
dungeon ['dʌndʒən] *n* cachot *m.*
Dunkirk [dʌn'kə:k] *n* Dunkerque.
dupe [dju:p] *n* dupe *f* // *vt* duper, tromper.
duplicate *n* ['dju:plɪkət] double *m,* copie exacte // *vt* ['dju:plɪkeɪt] faire un double de; (*on machine*) polycopier; **in ~** en deux exemplaires, en double; **duplicator** *n* duplicateur *m.*
durable ['djuərəbl] *a* durable; (*clothes, metal*) résistant(e), solide.
duration [djuə'reɪʃən] *n* durée *f.*
duress [djuə'rɛs] *n*: **under ~** sous la contrainte.
during ['djuərɪŋ] *prep* pendant, au cours de.
dusk [dʌsk] *n* crépuscule *m*; **~y** *a* sombre.
dust [dʌst] *n* poussière *f* // *vt* (*furniture*) essuyer, épousseter; (*cake etc*): **to ~ with** saupoudrer de; **~bin** *n* (*Brit*) poubelle *f*; **~er** *n* chiffon *m*; **~ jacket** *n* jacquette *f*; **~man** *n* (*Brit*) boueux *m,* éboueur *m*; **~y** *a* poussiéreux(euse).
Dutch [dʌtʃ] *a* hollandais(e), néerlandais(e) // *n* (LING) hollandais *m*; **the ~** les Hollandais; **~man/woman** *n* Hollandais/e.
dutiable ['dju:tɪəbl] *a* taxable; soumis(e) à des droits de douane.
duty ['dju:tɪ] *n* devoir *m*; (*tax*) droit *m,* taxe *f*; **duties** *npl* fonctions *fpl*; **on ~** de service; (*at night etc*) de garde; **off ~** libre, pas de service *or* de garde; **~-free** *a* exempté(e) de douane, hors-taxe.
dwarf [dwɔ:f] *n* nain/e // *vt* écraser.
dwell, *pt, pp* **dwelt** [dwɛl, dwɛlt] *vi* demeurer; **to ~ on** *vt fus* s'étendre sur; **~ing** *n* habitation *f,* demeure *f.*
dwindle ['dwɪndl] *vi* diminuer, décroître.
dye [daɪ] *n* teinture *f* // *vt* teindre; **~stuffs** *npl* colorants *mpl.*
dying ['daɪɪŋ] *a* mourant(e), agonisant(e).
dyke [daɪk] *n* digue *f.*
dynamic [daɪ'næmɪk] *a* dynamique; **~s** *n or npl* dynamique *f.*
dynamite ['daɪnəmaɪt] *n* dynamite *f.*
dynamo ['daɪnəməu] *n* dynamo *f.*
dynasty ['dɪnəstɪ] *n* dynastie *f.*
dysentery ['dɪsntrɪ] *n* dysenterie *f.*

E

E [i:] *n* (MUS) mi *m.*
each [i:tʃ] *det* chaque // *pronoun* chacun(e); **~ one** chacun(e); **~ other** se (*or* nous *etc*); **they hate ~ other** ils se détestent (mutuellement); **you are jealous of ~ other** vous êtes jaloux l'un de l'autre.
eager [i:gə*] *a* impatient(e); avide; ardent(e), passionné(e); **to be ~ to do sth** être impatient de faire qch, brûler de faire qch; désirer vivement faire qch; **to be ~ for** désirer vivement, être avide de.
eagle ['i:gl] *n* aigle *m.*
ear [ɪə*] *n* oreille *f*; (*of corn*) épi *m*; **~ache** *n* douleurs *fpl* aux oreilles; **~drum** *n* tympan *m*; **~ nose and throat specialist** *n* oto-rhino-laryngologiste *m/f.*
earl [ə:l] *n* comte *m.*
earlier ['ə:ljə] *a* (*date etc*) plus rapproché(e); (*edition etc*) plus ancien(ne), antérieur(e) // *ad* plus tôt.
early ['ə:lɪ] *ad* tôt, de bonne heure; (*ahead of time*) en avance // *a* précoce; anticipé(e); qui se manifeste (*or* se fait) tôt *or* de bonne heure; **have an ~ night/start** couchez-vous/partez tôt *or* de bonne heure; **take the ~ train/plane** prenez le premier train/vol; **in the ~** *or* **~ in the spring/19th century** au début *or* commencement du printemps/ 19ème siècle; **~ retirement** *n* retraite anticipée.
earmark ['ɪəmɑ:k] *vt*: **to ~ sth for** réserver *or* destiner qch à.
earn [ə:n] *vt* gagner; (COMM: *yield*) rapporter; **this ~ed him much praise, he ~ed much praise for this** ceci lui a valu de nombreux éloges; **he's ~ed his rest/reward** il mérite *or* a bien mérité *or* a bien gagné son repos/sa récompense.
earnest ['ə:nɪst] *a* sérieux(euse); **in ~** *ad* sérieusement, pour de bon.
earnings ['ə:nɪŋz] *npl* salaire *m*; gains *mpl.*
earphones ['ɪəfəunz] *npl* écouteurs *mpl.*
earring ['ɪərɪŋ] *n* boucle *f* d'oreille.
earshot ['ɪəʃɔt] *n*: **out of/within ~** hors de portée/à portée de la voix.

earth [ə:θ] *n* (*gen, also* ELEC) terre *f*; (*of fox etc*) terrier *m* // *vt* (ELEC) relier à la terre; **~enware** *n* poterie *f*; faïence *f* // *a* de *or* en faïence; **~quake** *n* tremblement *m* de terre, séisme *m*; **~ tremor** *n* secousse *f* sismique; **~works** *npl* travaux *mpl* de terrassement; **~y** *a* (*fig*) terre à terre *inv*; truculent(e).
earwax ['ɪəwæks] *n* cérumen *m*.
earwig ['ɪəwɪg] *n* perce-oreille *m*.
ease [i:z] *n* facilité *f*, aisance *f* // *vt* (*soothe*) calmer; (*loosen*) relâcher, détendre; (*help pass*): **to ~ sth in/out** faire pénétrer/sortir qch délicatement *or* avec douceur; faciliter la pénétration/la sortie de qch; **life of ~** vie oisive; **at ~** à l'aise; (MIL) au repos; **to ~ off** *or* **up** *vi* diminuer; ralentir; se détendre.
easel ['i:zl] *n* chevalet *m*.
easily ['i:zɪlɪ] *ad* facilement.
east [i:st] *n* est *m* // *a* d'est // *ad* à l'est, vers l'est; **the E~** l'Orient *m*.
Easter ['i:stə*] *n* Pâques *fpl*.
easterly ['i:stəlɪ] *a* d'est.
eastern ['i:stən] *a* de l'est, oriental(e).
East Germany [i:st'dʒə:mənɪ] *n* Allemagne *f* de l'Est.
eastward(s) ['i:stwəd(z)] *ad* vers l'est, à l'est.
easy ['i:zɪ] *a* facile; (*manner*) aisé(e) // *ad*: **to take it** *or* **things ~** ne pas se fatiguer; ne pas (trop) s'en faire; **~ chair** *n* fauteuil *m*; **~ going** *a* accommodant(e), facile à vivre.
eat, *pt* **ate,** *pp* **eaten** [i:t, eɪt, 'i:tn] *vt* manger; **to ~ into, to ~ away at** *vt fus* ronger, attaquer; **~able** *a* mangeable; (*safe to eat*) comestible.
eaves [i:vz] *npl* avant-toit *m*.
eavesdrop ['i:vzdrɔp] *vi*: **to ~ (on a conversation)** écouter (une conversation) de façon indiscrète.
ebb [ɛb] *n* reflux *m* // *vi* refluer; (*fig*: *also*: **~ away**) décliner.
ebony ['ɛbənɪ] *n* ébène *f*.
ebullient [ɪ'bʌlɪənt] *a* exubérant(e).
eccentric [ɪk'sɛntrɪk] *a,n* excentrique (*m/f*).
ecclesiastic [ɪkli:zɪ'æstɪk] *n* ecclésiastique *m*; **~al** *a* ecclésiastique.
echo, ~es ['ɛkəu] *n* écho *m* // *vt* répéter; faire chorus avec // *vi* résonner; faire écho.
eclipse [ɪ'klɪps] *n* éclipse *f* // *vt* éclipser.
ecology [ɪ'kɔlədʒɪ] *n* écologie *f*.
economic [i:kə'nɔmɪk] *a* économique; (*business etc*) rentable; **~al** *a* économique; (*person*) économe; **~s** *n* économie *f* politique.
economist [ɪ'kɔnəmɪst] *n* économiste *m/f*.
economize [ɪ'kɔnəmaɪz] *vi* économiser, faire des économies.
economy [ɪ'kɔnəmɪ] *n* économie *f*.
ecstasy ['ɛkstəsɪ] *n* extase *f*; **to go into ecstasies over** s'extasier sur; **ecstatic** [-'tætɪk] *a* extatique, en extase.
ecumenical [i:kju'mɛnɪkl] *a* œcuménique.
eczema ['ɛksɪmə] *n* eczéma *m*.
eddy ['ɛdɪ] *n* tourbillon *m*.
edge [ɛdʒ] *n* bord *m*; (*of knife etc*) tranchant *m*, fil *m* // *vt* border; **on ~** (*fig*) = **edgy**; **to have the ~ on** l'emporter (de justesse) sur, être légèrement meilleur que; **to ~ away from** s'éloigner furtivement de; **~ways** *ad* latéralement; **he couldn't get a word in ~ways** il ne pouvait pas placer un mot; **edging** *n* bordure *f*.
edgy ['ɛdʒɪ] *a* crispé(e), tendu(e).
edible ['ɛdɪbl] *a* comestible; (*meal*) mangeable.
edict ['i:dɪkt] *n* décret *m*.
edifice ['ɛdɪfɪs] *n* édifice *m*.
edit ['ɛdɪt] *vt* éditer; **~ion** [ɪ'dɪʃən] *n* édition *f*; **~or** *n* (*in newspaper*) rédacteur/trice; rédacteur/trice en chef; (*of sb's work*) éditeur/trice; **~orial** [-'tɔ:rɪəl] *a* de la rédaction, éditorial(e) // *n* éditorial *m*.
educate ['ɛdjukeɪt] *vt* instruire; éduquer.
education [ɛdju'keɪʃən] *n* éducation *f*; (*schooling*) enseignement *m*, instruction *f*; **~al** *a* pédagogique; scolaire; instructif(ive).
EEC *n* (*abbr of European Economic Community*) C.E.E. (*Communauté économique européenne*).
eel [i:l] *n* anguille *f*.
eerie ['ɪərɪ] *a* inquiétant(e), spectral(e), surnaturel(le).
effect [ɪ'fɛkt] *n* effet *m* // *vt* effectuer; **~s** *npl* (THEATRE) effets *mpl*; **to take ~** (*law*) entrer en vigueur, prendre effet; (*drug*) agir, faire son effet; **in ~** en fait; **~ive** *a* efficace; **~iveness** *n* efficacité *f*.
effeminate [ɪ'fɛmɪnɪt] *a* efféminé(e).
effervescent [ɛfə'vɛsnt] *a* effervescent(e).
efficacy ['ɛfɪkəsɪ] *n* efficacité *f*.
efficiency [ɪ'fɪʃənsɪ] *n* efficacité *f*; rendement *m*.
efficient [ɪ'fɪʃənt] *a* efficace; **~ly** *ad* efficacement.
effigy ['ɛfɪdʒɪ] *n* effigie *f*.
effort ['ɛfət] *n* effort *m*; **~less** *a* sans effort, aisé(e).
effrontery [ɪ'frʌntərɪ] *n* effronterie *f*.
e.g. *ad* (*abbr of exempli gratia*) par exemple, p. ex.
egalitarian [ɪgælɪ'tɛərɪən] *a* égalitaire.
egg [ɛg] *n* œuf *m*; **to ~ on** *vt* pousser; **~cup** *n* coquetier *m*; **~plant** *n* aubergine *f*; **~shell** *n* coquille *f* d'œuf // *a* (*colour*) blanc cassé *inv*.
ego ['i:gəu] *n* moi *m*.
egoist ['ɛgəuɪst] *n* égoïste *m/f*.
egotist ['ɛgəutɪst] *n* égocentrique *m/f*.
Egypt ['i:dʒɪpt] *n* Égypte *f*; **~ian** [ɪ'dʒɪpʃən] *a* égyptien(ne) // *n* Égyptien/ne.
eiderdown ['aɪdədaun] *n* édredon *m*.
eight [eɪt] *num* huit; **~een** *num* dix-huit; **eighth** *num* huitième; **~y** *num* quatre-vingt(s).
Eire ['ɛərə] *n* République *f* d'Irlande.
either ['aɪðə*] *det* l'un ou l'autre; (*both, each*) chaque; **on ~ side** de chaque côté // *pronoun*: **~ (of them)** l'un ou l'autre; **I don't like ~** je n'aime ni l'un ni l'autre // *ad* non plus; **no, I don't ~** moi non plus // *cj*: **~ good or bad** ou bon ou mauvais, soit bon soit mauvais; **I haven't**

seen ~ one or the other je n'ai vu ni l'un ni l'autre.
ejaculation [ɪdʒækju'leɪʃən] *n* (PHYSIOL) éjaculation *f*.
eject [ɪ'dʒɛkt] *vt* expulser; éjecter; **~or seat** *n* siège *m* éjectable.
eke [i:k]: **to ~ out** *vt* faire durer; augmenter.
elaborate *a* [ɪ'læbərɪt] compliqué(e), recherché(e), minutieux (euse) // *vb* [ɪ'læbəreɪt] *vt* élaborer // *vi* entrer dans les détails.
elapse [ɪ'læps] *vi* s'écouler, passer.
elastic [ɪ'læstɪk] *a, n* élastique (*m*); **~ band** *n* élastique *m*; **~ity** [-'tɪsɪtɪ] *n* élasticité *f*.
elated [ɪ'leɪtɪd] *a* transporté(e) de joie.
elation [ɪ'leɪʃən] *n* (grande) joie, allégresse *f*.
elbow ['ɛlbəu] *n* coude *m*.
elder ['ɛldə*] *a* aîné(e) // *n* (*tree*) sureau *m*; **one's ~s** ses aînés; **~ly** *a* âgé(e) // *n*: **the ~ly** les personnes âgées.
eldest ['ɛldɪst] *a,n*: **the ~ (child)** l'aîné(e) (des enfants).
elect [ɪ'lɛkt] *vt* élire; **to ~ to do** choisir de faire // *a*: **the president ~** le président désigné; **~ion** [ɪ'lɛkʃən] *n* élection *f*; **~ioneering** [ɪlɛkʃə'nɪərɪŋ] *n* propagande électorale, manœuvres électorales; **~or** *n* électeur/trice; **~oral** *a* électoral(e); **~orate** *n* électorat *m*.
electric [ɪ'lɛktrɪk] *a* électrique; **~al** *a* électrique; **~ blanket** *n* couverture chauffante; **~ chair** *n* chaise *f* électrique; **~ cooker** *n* cuisinière *f* électrique; **~ current** *n* courant *m* électrique; **~ fire** *n* radiateur *m* électrique.
electrician [ɪlɛk'trɪʃən] *n* électricien *m*.
electricity [ɪlɛk'trɪsɪtɪ] *n* électricité *f*.
electrify [ɪ'lɛktrɪfaɪ] *vt* (RAIL) électrifier; (*audience*) électriser.
electro... [ɪ'lɛktrəu] *prefix*: **electrocute** [-kju:t] *vt* électrocuter; **electrode** [ɪ'lɛktrəud] *n* électrode *f*; **electrolysis** [ɪlɛk'trɔlɪsɪs] *n* électrolyse *f*.
electron [ɪ'lɛktrɔn] *n* électron *m*.
electronic [ɪlɛk'trɔnɪk] *a* électronique; **~s** *n* électronique *f*.
elegance ['ɛlɪgəns] *n* élégance *f*.
elegant ['ɛlɪgənt] *a* élégant(e).
element ['ɛlɪmənt] *n* (*gen*) élément *m*; (*of heater, kettle etc*) résistance *f*; **~ary** [-'mɛntərɪ] *a* élémentaire; (*school, education*) primaire.
elephant ['ɛlɪfənt] *n* éléphant *m*.
elevate ['ɛlɪveɪt] *vt* élever; **~d railway** *n* métro aérien.
elevation [ɛlɪ'veɪʃən] *n* élévation *f*; (*height*) altitude *f*.
elevator ['ɛlɪveɪtə*] *n* élévateur *m*, monte-charge *m inv*; (*US*: *lift*) ascenseur *m*.
eleven [ɪ'lɛvn] *num* onze; **~ses** *npl* ≈ pause-café *f*; **~th** *a* onzième.
elf, elves [ɛlf, ɛlvz] *n* lutin *m*.
elicit [ɪ'lɪsɪt] *vt*: **to ~ (from)** obtenir (de), arracher (à).
eligible ['ɛlɪdʒəbl] *a* éligible; (*for membership*) admissible; **~ for a pension** ayant droit à la retraite.
eliminate [ɪ'lɪmɪneɪt] *vt* éliminer; **elimination** *n* élimination *f*.
élite [eɪ'li:t] *n* élite *f*.
ellipse [ɪ'lɪps] *n* ellipse *f*.
elliptical [ɪ'lɪptɪkl] *a* elliptique.
elm [ɛlm] *n* orme *m*.
elocution [ɛlə'kju:ʃən] *n* élocution *f*.
elongated ['i:lɔŋgeɪtɪd] *a* étiré(e), allongé(e).
elope [ɪ'ləup] *vi* (*lovers*) s'enfuir (ensemble); **~ment** *n* fugue amoureuse.
eloquence ['ɛləkwəns] *n* éloquence *f*.
eloquent ['ɛləkwənt] *a* éloquent(e).
else [ɛls] *ad* d'autre; **something ~** quelque chose d'autre, autre chose; **somewhere ~** ailleurs, autre part; **everywhere ~** partout ailleurs; **where ~?** à quel autre endroit?; **little ~** pas grand-chose d'autre; **~where** *ad* ailleurs, autre part.
elucidate [ɪ'lu:sɪdeɪt] *vt* élucider.
elude [ɪ'lu:d] *vt* échapper à; (*question*) éluder.
elusive [ɪ'lu:sɪv] *a* insaisissable; (*answer*) évasif(ive).
elves [ɛlvz] *npl of* **elf**.
emaciated [ɪ'meɪsɪeɪtɪd] *a* émacié(e), décharnu(e).
emanate ['ɛməneɪt] *vi*: **to ~ from** émaner de.
emancipate [ɪ'mænsɪpeɪt] *vt* émanciper; **emancipation** [-'peɪʃən] *n* émancipation *f*.
embalm [ɪm'bɑ:m] *vt* embaumer.
embankment [ɪm'bæŋkmənt] *n* (*of road, railway*) remblai *m*, talus *m*; (*riverside*) berge *f*, quai *m*; (*dyke*) digue *f*.
embargo, ~es [ɪm'bɑ:gəu] *n* embargo *m* // *vt* frapper d'embargo, mettre l'embargo sur.
embark [ɪm'bɑ:k] *vi*: **to ~ (on)** (s')embarquer (à bord de *or* sur) // *vt* embarquer; **to ~ on** (*fig*) se lancer *or* s'embarquer dans; **~ation** [ɛmbɑ:'keɪʃən] *n* embarquement *m*.
embarrass [ɪm'bærəs] *vt* embarrasser, gêner; **~ing** *a* gênant(e), embarrassant(e); **~ment** *n* embarras *m*, gêne *f*.
embassy ['ɛmbəsɪ] *n* ambassade *f*.
embed [ɪm'bɛd] *vt* enfoncer, ficher, sceller.
embellish [ɪm'bɛlɪʃ] *vt* embellir; enjoliver.
embers ['ɛmbəz] *npl* braise *f*.
embezzle [ɪm'bɛzl] *vt* détourner; **~ment** *n* détournement *m* (de fonds).
embitter [ɪm'bɪtə*] *vt* aigrir; envenimer.
emblem ['ɛmbləm] *n* emblème *m*.
embodiment [ɪm'bɔdɪmənt] *n* personification *f*, incarnation *f*.
embody [ɪm'bɔdɪ] *vt* (*features*) réunir, comprendre; (*ideas*) formuler, exprimer.
embossed [ɪm'bɔst] *a* repoussé(e); gaufré(e); **~ with** où figure(nt) en relief.
embrace [ɪm'breɪs] *vt* embrasser, étreindre; (*include*) embrasser, couvrir // *n* étreinte *f*.
embroider [ɪm'brɔɪdə*] *vt* broder; (*fig*: *story*) enjoliver; **~y** *n* broderie *f*.
embryo ['ɛmbrɪəu] *n* (*also fig*) embryon *m*.
emerald ['ɛmərəld] *n* émeraude *f*.

emerge [ɪ'mə:dʒ] *vi* apparaître, surgir.
emergence [ɪ'mə:dʒəns] *n* apparition *f*.
emergency [ɪ'mə:dʒənsɪ] *n* urgence *f*; **in an ~** en cas d'urgence ; **state of ~** état *m* d'urgence ; **~ exit** *n* sortie *f* de secours.
emergent [ɪ'mə:dʒənt] *a*: **~ nation** pays *m* en voie de développement.
emery ['ɛmərɪ] *n*: **~ board** *n* lime *f* à ongles (*en carton émerisé*) ; **~ paper** *n* papier *m* (d')émeri.
emetic [ɪ'mɛtɪk] *n* vomitif *m*, émétique *m*.
emigrant ['ɛmɪgrənt] *n* émigrant/e.
emigrate ['ɛmɪgreɪt] *vi* émigrer ; **emigration**[-'greɪʃən] *n* émigration *f*.
eminence ['ɛmɪnəns] *n* éminence *f*.
eminent ['ɛmɪnənt] *a* éminent(e).
emission [ɪ'mɪʃən] *n* émission *f*.
emit [ɪ'mɪt] *vt* émettre.
emotion [ɪ'məuʃən] *n* émotion *f*; **~al** *a* (*person*) émotif(ive), très sensible ; (*scene*) émouvant(e) ; (*tone, speech*) qui fait appel aux sentiments ; **~ally** *ad*: **~ally disturbed** qui souffre de troubles de l'affectivité.
emotive [ɪ'məutɪv] *a* émotif(ive) ; **~ power** *n* capacité *f* d'émouvoir *or* de toucher.
emperor ['ɛmpərə*] *n* empereur *m*.
emphasis, *pl* **ases** ['ɛmfəsɪs, -si:z] *n* accent *m* ; force *f*, insistance *f*.
emphasize ['ɛmfəsaɪz] *vt* (*syllable, word, point*) appuyer *or* insister sur ; (*feature*) souligner, accentuer.
emphatic [ɛm'fætɪk] *a* (*strong*) énergique, vigoureux(euse) ; (*unambiguous, clear*) catégorique ; **~ally** *ad* avec vigueur *or* énergie ; catégoriquement.
empire ['ɛmpaɪə*] *n* empire *m*.
empirical [ɛm'pɪrɪkl] *a* empirique.
employ [ɪm'plɔɪ] *vt* employer ; **~ee** [-'i:] *n* employé/e ; **~er** *n* employeur/euse ; **~ment** *n* emploi *m* ; **~ment agency** *n* agence *f or* bureau *m* de placement ; **~ment exchange** *n* bourse *f* du travail.
empower [ɪm'pauə*] *vt*: **to ~ sb to do** autoriser *or* habiliter qn à faire.
empress ['ɛmprɪs] *n* impératrice *f*.
emptiness ['ɛmptɪnɪs] *n* vide *m*.
empty ['ɛmptɪ] *a* vide ; (*threat, promise*) en l'air, vain(e) // *vt* vider // *vi* se vider ; (*liquid*) s'écouler ; **on an ~ stomach** à jeun ; **~-handed** *a* les mains vides.
emulate ['ɛmjuleɪt] *vt* rivaliser avec, imiter.
emulsion [ɪ'mʌlʃən] *n* émulsion *f*; **~ (paint)** *n* peinture mate.
enable [ɪ'neɪbl] *vt*: **to ~ sb to do** permettre à qn de faire, donner à qn la possibilité de faire.
enamel [ɪ'næməl] *n* émail *m*.
enamoured [ɪ'næməd] *a*: **~ of** amoureux(euse) de ; (*idea*) enchanté(e) par.
encased [ɪn'keɪst] *a*: **~ in** enfermé(e) dans, recouvert(e) de.
enchant [ɪn'tʃɑ:nt] *vt* enchanter ; (*subject: magic spell*) ensorceler ; **~ing** *a* ravissant(e), enchanteur(eresse).
encircle [ɪn'sə:kl] *vt* entourer, encercler.
encl. (*abbr of enclosed*) annexe(s).
enclose [ɪn'kləuz] *vt* (*land*) clôturer ; (*letter etc*): **to ~ (with)** joindre (à) ; **please find ~d** veuillez trouver ci-joint.
enclosure [ɪn'kləuʒə*] *n* enceinte *f*; (COMM) annexe *f*.
encore [ɔŋ'kɔ:*] *excl*, *n* bis (*m*).
encounter [ɪn'kauntə*] *n* rencontre *f* // *vt* rencontrer.
encourage [ɪn'kʌrɪdʒ] *vt* encourager ; **~ment** *n* encouragement *m*.
encroach [ɪn'krəutʃ] *vi*: **to ~ (up)on** empiéter sur.
encyclop(a)edia [ɛnsaɪkləu'pi:dɪə] *n* encyclopédie *f*.
end [ɛnd] *n* (*gen, also: aim*) fin *f*; (*of table, street etc*) bout *m*, extrémité *f* // *vt* terminer ; (*also*: **bring to an ~, put an ~ to**) mettre fin à // *vi* se terminer, finir ; **to come to an ~** prendre fin ; **in the ~** finalement ; **on ~** (*object*) debout, dressé(e) ; **for 5 hours on ~** durant 5 heures d'affilée *or* de suite ; **for hours on ~** pendant des heures (et des heures) ; **to ~ up** *vi*: **to ~ up in** finir *or* se terminer par ; (*place*) finir *or* aboutir à.
endanger [ɪn'deɪndʒə*] *vt* mettre en danger.
endearing [ɪn'dɪərɪŋ] *a* attachant(e).
endeavour [ɪn'dɛvə*] *n* tentative *f*, effort *m* // *vi*: **to ~ to do** tenter *or* s'efforcer de faire.
ending ['ɛndɪŋ] *n* dénouement *m*, conclusion *f*; (LING) terminaison *f*.
endive ['ɛndaɪv] *n* chicorée *f*.
endless ['ɛndlɪs] *a* sans fin, interminable ; (*patience, resources*) inépuisable, sans limites.
endorse [ɪn'dɔ:s] *vt* (*cheque*) endosser ; (*approve*) appuyer, approuver, sanctionner ; **~ment** *n* (*on driving licence*) *contravention portée au permis de conduire*.
endow [ɪn'dau] *vt* (*provide with money*) faire une donation à, doter ; (*equip*): **to ~ with** gratifier de, doter de.
end product ['ɛndprɔdəkt] *n* produit fini ; (*fig*) résultat *m*.
endurable [ɪn'djuərəbl] *a* supportable.
endurance [ɪn'djuərəns] *n* endurance *f*, résistance *f*; patience *f*.
endure [ɪn'djuə*] *vt* supporter, endurer // *vi* durer.
enemy ['ɛnəmɪ] *a,n* ennemi(e).
energetic [ɛnə'dʒɛtɪk] *a* énergique ; actif(ive) ; qui fait se dispenser (physiquement).
energy ['ɛnədʒɪ] *n* énergie *f*.
enervating ['ɛnə:veɪtɪŋ] *a* débilitant(e), affaiblissant(e).
enforce [ɪn'fɔ:s] *vt* (LAW) appliquer, faire respecter ; **~d** *a* forcé(e).
engage [ɪn'geɪdʒ] *vt* engager ; (MIL) engager le combat avec // *vi* (TECH) s'enclencher, s'engrener ; **to ~ in** se lancer dans ; **~d** *a* (*busy, in use*) occupé(e) ; (*betrothed*) fiancé(e) ; **to get ~d** se fiancer ; **he is ~d in research/a survey** il fait de la recherche/une enquête ; **~ment** *n* obligation *f*, engagement *m* ; rendez-vous *m inv* ; (*to marry*) fiançailles *fpl* ; (MIL) combat *m* ; **~ment ring** *n* bague *f* de fiançailles.

engaging [ɪn'geɪdʒɪŋ] *a* engageant(e), attirant(e).
engender [ɪn'dʒɛndə*] *vt* produire, causer.
engine ['ɛndʒɪn] *n* (AUT) moteur *m*; (RAIL) locomotive *f*; ~ **failure** *n* panne *f*; ~ **trouble** *n* ennuis *mpl* mécaniques.
engineer [ɛndʒɪ'nɪə*] *n* ingénieur *m*; (*US*: RAIL) mécanicien *m*; ~**ing** *n* engineering *m*, ingénierie *f*; (*of bridges, ships*) génie *m*; (*of machine*) mécanique *f*.
England ['ɪŋglənd] *n* Angleterre *f*.
English ['ɪŋglɪʃ] *a* anglais(e) // *n* (LING) anglais *m*; **the** ~ les Anglais; ~**man/woman** *n* Anglais/e.
engrave [ɪn'greɪv] *vt* graver.
engraving [ɪn'greɪvɪŋ] *n* gravure *f*.
engrossed [ɪn'grəust] *a*: ~ **in** absorbé(e) par, plongé(e) dans.
engulf [ɪn'gʌlf] *vt* engloutir.
enhance [ɪn'hɑ:ns] *vt* rehausser, mettre en valeur.
enigma [ɪ'nɪgmə] *n* énigme *f*; ~**tic** [ɛnɪg'mætɪk] *a* énigmatique.
enjoy [ɪn'dʒɔɪ] *vt* aimer, prendre plaisir à; (*have: health, fortune*) jouir de; (*: success*) connaître; **to** ~ **oneself** s'amuser; ~**able** *a* agréable; ~**ment** *n* plaisir *m*.
enlarge [ɪn'lɑ:dʒ] *vt* accroître; (PHOT) agrandir // *vi*: **to** ~ **on** (*subject*) s'étendre sur; ~**ment** *n* (PHOT) agrandissement *m*.
enlighten [ɪn'laɪtn] *vt* éclairer; ~**ed** *a* éclairé(e); ~**ment** *n* édification *f*; vues éclairées; éclaircissements *mpl*; (HISTORY): **the E~ment** ≈ le Siècle des lumières.
enlist [ɪn'lɪst] *vt* recruter; (*support*) s'assurer // *vi* s'engager.
enmity ['ɛnmɪtɪ] *n* inimitié *f*.
enormity [ɪ'nɔ:mɪtɪ] *n* énormité *f*.
enormous [ɪ'nɔ:məs] *a* énorme.
enough [ɪ'nʌf] *a, n*: ~ **time/books** assez *or* suffisamment de temps/livres; **have you got** ~? (en) avez-vous assez? // *ad*: **big** ~ assez *or* suffisamment grand; **he has not worked** ~ il n'a pas assez *or* suffisamment travaillé, il n'a pas travaillé assez *or* suffisamment; ~! assez!, ça suffit!; **it's hot** ~ **(as it is)!** il fait assez chaud comme ça!; **... which, funnily** ~ ... qui, chose curieuse.
enquire [ɪn'kwaɪə*] *vt,vi* = **inquire**.
enrich [ɪn'rɪtʃ] *vt* enrichir.
enrol [ɪn'rəul] *vt* inscrire // *vi* s'inscrire; ~**ment** *n* inscription *f*.
ensconced [ɪn'skɔnst] *a*: ~ **in** bien calé(e) dans; plongé(e) dans.
ensign *n* (NAUT) ['ɛnsən] enseigne *f*, pavillon *m*; (MIL) ['ɛnsaɪn] porte- étendard *m*.
enslave [ɪn'sleɪv] *vt* asservir.
ensue [ɪn'sju:] *vi* s'ensuivre, résulter.
ensure [ɪn'ʃuə*] *vt* assurer; garantir; **to** ~ **that** s'assurer que.
entail [ɪn'teɪl] *vt* entraîner, nécessiter.
entangle [ɪn'tæŋgl] *vt* emmêler, embrouiller.
enter ['ɛntə*] *vt* (*room*) entrer dans, pénétrer dans; (*club, army*) entrer à; (*competition*) s'inscrire à *or* pour; (*sb for a competition*) (faire) inscrire; (*write down*) inscrire, noter; **to** ~ **for** *vt fus* s'inscrire à, se présenter pour *or* à; **to** ~ **into** *vt fus* (*exploration*) se lancer dans; (*debate*) prendre part à; (*agreement*) conclure; **to** ~ **up** *vt* inscrire; **to** ~ **(up)on** *vt fus* commencer.
enterprise ['ɛntəpraɪz] *n* entreprise *f*; (esprit *m* d')initiative *f*.
enterprising ['ɛntəpraɪzɪŋ] *a* entreprenant(e), dynamique.
entertain [ɛntə'teɪn] *vt* amuser, distraire; (*invite*) recevoir (à dîner); (*idea, plan*) envisager; ~**er** *n* artiste *m/f* de variétés; ~**ing** *a* amusant(e), distrayant(e); ~**ment** *n* (*amusement*) distraction *f*, divertissement *m*, amusement *m*; (*show*) spectacle *m*.
enthralled [ɪn'θrɔ:ld] *a* captivé(e).
enthusiasm [ɪn'θu:zɪæzəm] *n* enthousiasme *m*.
enthusiast [ɪn'θu:zɪæst] *n* enthousiaste *m/f*; **a jazz** *etc* ~ un fervent *or* passionné du jazz *etc*; ~**ic** [-'æstɪk] *a* enthousiaste.
entice [ɪn'taɪs] *vt* attirer, séduire.
entire [ɪn'taɪə*] *a* (tout) entier(ère); ~**ly** *ad* entièrement, complètement; ~**ty** [ɪn'taɪərətɪ] *n*: **in its** ~**ty** dans sa totalité.
entitle [ɪn'taɪtl] *vt* (*allow*): **to** ~ **sb to do** donner (le) droit à qn de faire; **to** ~ **sb to sth** donner droit à qch à qn; ~**d** *a* (*book*) intitulé(e); **to be** ~**d to do** avoir le droit de *or* être habilité à faire.
entrance *n* ['ɛntrns] entrée *f* // *vt* [ɪn'trɑ:ns] enchanter, ravir; **to gain** ~ **to** (*university etc*) être admis à; ~ **examination** *n* examen *m* d'entrée; ~ **fee** *n* droit *m* d'inscription; (*to museum etc*) prix *m* d'entrée.
entrant ['ɛntrnt] *n* participant/e; concurrent/e.
entreat [ɛn'tri:t] *vt* supplier; ~**y** *n* supplication *f*, prière *f*.
entrée ['ɔntreɪ] *n* (CULIN) entrée *f*.
entrenched [ɛn'trɛntʃd] *a* retranché(e).
entrust [ɪn'trʌst] *vt*: **to** ~ **sth to** confier qch à.
entry ['ɛntrɪ] *n* entrée *f*; (*in register*) inscription *f*; ~ **form** *n* feuille *f* d'inscription.
entwine [ɪn'twaɪn] *vt* entrelacer.
enumerate [ɪ'nju:məreɪt] *vt* énumérer.
enunciate [ɪ'nʌnsɪeɪt] *vt* énoncer; prononcer.
envelop [ɪn'vɛləp] *vt* envelopper.
envelope ['ɛnvələup] *n* enveloppe *f*.
envious ['ɛnvɪəs] *a* envieux(euse).
environment [ɪn'vaɪərnmənt] *n* milieu *m*; environnement *m*; ~**al** [-'mɛntl] *a* écologique; du milieu.
envisage [ɪn'vɪzɪdʒ] *vt* envisager; prévoir.
envoy ['ɛnvɔɪ] *n* envoyé/e.
envy ['ɛnvɪ] *n* envie *f* // *vt* envier.
enzyme ['ɛnzaɪm] *n* enzyme *m*.
ephemeral [ɪ'fɛmərl] *a* éphémère.
epic ['ɛpɪk] *n* épopée *f* // *a* épique.
epidemic [ɛpɪ'dɛmɪk] *n* épidémie *f*.
epilepsy ['ɛpɪlɛpsɪ] *n* épilepsie *f*; **epileptic** [-'lɛptɪk] *a,n* épileptique (*m/f*).
epilogue ['ɛpɪlɔg] *n* épilogue *m*.
episode ['ɛpɪsəud] *n* épisode *m*.
epistle [ɪ'pɪsl] *n* épître *f*.
epitaph ['ɛpɪtɑ:f] *n* épitaphe *f*.
epitome [ɪ'pɪtəmɪ] *n* résumé *m*;

quintessence *f*, type *m*; **epitomize** *vt* résumer; illustrer, incarner.
epoch ['i:pɔk] *n* époque *f*, ère *f*; **~-making** *a* qui fait époque.
equable ['ɛkwəbl] *a* égal(e); de tempérament égal.
equal ['i:kwl] *a* égal(e) // *n* égal/e // *vt* égaler; **~ to** (*task*) à la hauteur de; **~ to doing** de taille à *or* capable de faire; **~ity** [i:'kwɔlɪtɪ] *n* égalité *f*; **~ize** *vt,vi* égaliser; **~izer** *n* but égalisateur; **~ly** *ad* également; (*just as*) tout aussi; **~(s) sign** *n* signe *m* d'égalité.
equanimity [ɛkwə'nɪmɪtɪ] *n* égalité *f* d'humeur.
equate [ɪ'kweɪt] *vt*: **to ~ sth with** comparer qch à; assimiler qch à; **to ~ sth to** mettre qch en équation avec; égaler qch à; **equation** [ɪ'kweɪʃən] *n* (*MATH*) équation *f*.
equator [ɪ'kweɪtə*] *n* équateur *m*; **~ial** [ɛkwə'tɔ:rɪəl] *a* équatorial(e).
equilibrium [i:kwɪ'lɪbrɪəm] *n* équilibre *m*.
equinox ['i:kwɪnɔks] *n* équinoxe *m*.
equip [ɪ'kwɪp] *vt* équiper; **to ~ sb/sth with** équiper *or* munir qn/qch de; **~ment** *n* équipement *m*; (*electrical etc*) appareillage *m*, installation *f*.
equitable ['ɛkwɪtəbl] *a* équitable.
equity ['ɛkwɪtɪ] *n* équité *f*; **equities** *npl* (*COMM*) actions cotées en Bourse.
equivalent [ɪ'kwɪvəlnt] *a* équivalent(e) // *n* équivalent *m*.
equivocal [ɪ'kwɪvəkl] *a* équivoque; (*open to suspicion*) douteux(euse).
era ['ɪərə] *n* ère *f*, époque *f*.
eradicate [ɪ'rædɪkeɪt] *vt* éliminer.
erase [ɪ'reɪz] *vt* effacer; **~r** *n* gomme *f*.
erect [ɪ'rɛkt] *a* droit(e) // *vt* construire; (*monument*) ériger; élever; (*tent etc*) dresser.
erection [ɪ'rɛkʃən] *n* érection *f*.
ermine ['ə:mɪn] *n* hermine *f*.
erode [ɪ'rəud] *vt* éroder; (*metal*) ronger; **erosion** [ɪ'rəuʒən] *n* érosion *f*.
erotic [ɪ'rɔtɪk] *a* érotique; **~ism** [ɪ'rɔtɪsɪzm] *n* érotisme *m*.
err [ə:*] *vi* se tromper; (*REL*) pécher.
errand ['ɛrnd] *n* course *f*, commission *f*; **~ boy** *n* garçon *m* de courses.
erratic [ɪ'rætɪk] *a* irrégulier(ère); inconstant(e).
erroneous [ɪ'rəunɪəs] *a* erroné(e).
error ['ɛrə*] *n* erreur *f*.
erudite ['ɛrjudaɪt] *a* savant(e).
erupt [ɪ'rʌpt] *vi* entrer en éruption; (*fig*) éclater; **~ion** [ɪ'rʌpʃən] *n* éruption *f*.
escalate ['ɛskəleɪt] *vi* s'intensifier; **escalation** [-'leɪʃən] *n* escalade *f*.
escalator ['ɛskəleɪtə*] *n* escalier roulant.
escapade [ɛskə'peɪd] *n* fredaine *f*; équipée *f*.
escape [ɪ'skeɪp] *n* évasion *f*; fuite *f*; (*of gas etc*) échappement *m*; fuite // *vi* s'échapper, fuir; (*from jail*) s'évader; (*fig*) s'en tirer; (*leak*) s'échapper; fuir // *vt* échapper à; **to ~ from sb** échapper à qn; **to ~ from** (*place*) s'échapper de; (*fig*) fuir; **escapism** *n* évasion *f* (*fig*).
escort *n* ['ɛskɔ:t] escorte *f* // *vt* [ɪ'skɔ:t] escorter; **~ agency** *n* bureau *m* d'hôtesses.
Eskimo ['ɛskɪməu] *n* Esquimau/de.
especially [ɪ'spɛʃlɪ] *ad* particulièrement; surtout; exprès.
espionage ['ɛspɪənɑ:ʒ] *n* espionnage *m*.
esplanade [ɛsplə'neɪd] *n* esplanade *f*.
Esquire [ɪ'skwaɪə*] *n* (*abbr* **Esq.**): **J. Brown, ~** Monsieur J. Brown.
essay ['ɛseɪ] *n* (*SCOL*) dissertation *f*; (*LITERATURE*) essai *m*; (*attempt*) tentative *f*.
essence ['ɛsns] *n* essence *f*.
essential [ɪ'sɛnʃl] *a* essentiel(le); (*basic*) fondamental(e); **~ly** *ad* essentiellement.
establish [ɪ'stæblɪʃ] *vt* établir; (*business*) fonder, créer; (*one's power etc*) asseoir, affermir; **~ment** *n* établissement *m*; **the E~ment** les pouvoirs établis; l'ordre établi; les milieux dirigeants.
estate [ɪ'steɪt] *n* domaine *m*, propriété *f*; biens *mpl*, succession *f*; **~ agent** *n* agent immobilier; **~ car** *n* (*Brit*) break *m*.
esteem [ɪ'sti:m] *n* estime *f*.
esthetic [ɪs'θɛtɪk] *a* (*US*) = **aesthetic**.
estimate *n* ['ɛstɪmət] estimation *f*; (*COMM*) devis *m* // *vt* ['ɛstɪmeɪt] estimer; **estimation** [-'meɪʃən] *n* opinion *f*; estime *f*.
estuary ['ɛstjuərɪ] *n* estuaire *m*.
etching ['ɛtʃɪŋ] *n* eau-forte *f*.
eternal [ɪ'tə:nl] *a* éternel(le).
eternity [ɪ'tə:nɪtɪ] *n* éternité *f*.
ether ['i:θə*] *n* éther *m*.
ethical ['ɛθɪkl] *a* moral(e).
ethics ['ɛθɪks] *n* éthique *f* // *npl* moralité *f*.
ethnic ['ɛθnɪk] *a* ethnique.
ethnology [ɛθ'nɔlədʒɪ] *n* ethnologie *f*.
etiquette ['ɛtɪkɛt] *n* convenances *fpl*, étiquette *f*.
etymology [ɛtɪ'mɔlədʒɪ] *n* étymologie *f*.
eulogy ['ju:lədʒɪ] *n* éloge *m*.
euphemism ['ju:fəmɪzm] *n* euphémisme *m*.
euphoria [ju:'fɔ:rɪə] *n* euphorie *f*.
Europe ['juərəp] *n* Europe *f*; **~an** [-'pi:ən] *a* européen(ne) // *n* Européen/ne.
euthanasia [ju:θə'neɪzɪə] *n* euthanasie *f*.
evacuate [ɪ'vækjueɪt] *vt* évacuer; **evacuation** [-'eɪʃən] *n* évacuation *f*.
evade [ɪ'veɪd] *vt* échapper à; (*question etc*) éluder; (*duties*) se dérober à.
evaluate [ɪ'væljueɪt] *vt* évaluer.
evangelist [ɪ'vændʒəlɪst] *n* évangéliste *m*.
evangelize [ɪ'vændʒəlaɪz] *vt* évangéliser, prêcher l'Évangile à.
evaporate [ɪ'væpəreɪt] *vi* s'évaporer // *vt* faire évaporer; **~d milk** *n* lait concentré; **evaporation** [-'reɪʃən] *n* évaporation *f*.
evasion [ɪ'veɪʒən] *n* dérobade *f*; faux-fuyant *m*.
evasive [ɪ'veɪsɪv] *a* évasif(ive).
eve [i:v] *n*: **on the ~ of** à la veille de.
even ['i:vn] *a* régulier(ère), égal(e); (*number*) pair(e) // *ad* même; **~ more** encore plus; **~ so** quand même; **to ~ out** *vi* s'égaliser; **to get ~ with sb** prendre sa revanche sur qn.
evening ['i:vnɪŋ] *n* soir *m*; (*as duration, event*) soirée *f*; **in the ~** le soir; **~ class**

n cours *m* du soir ; ~ **dress** *n* (*man's*) habit *m* de soirée, smoking *m* ; (*woman's*) robe *f* de soirée.
evensong ['i:vnsɔŋ] *n* office *m* du soir.
event [ɪ'vɛnt] *n* événement *m* ; (SPORT) épreuve *f* ; **in the ~ of** en cas de ; **~ful** *a* mouvementé(e).
eventual [ɪ'vɛntʃuəl] *a* final(e) ; **~ity** [-'ælɪtɪ] *n* possibilité *f*, éventualité *f* ; **~ly** *ad* finalement.
ever ['ɛvə*] *ad* jamais ; (*at all times*) toujours ; **the best ~** le meilleur qu'on ait jamais vu ; **have you ~ seen it?** l'as-tu déjà vu?, as-tu eu l'occasion *or* t'est-il arrivé de le voir? ; **hardly ~** ne ... presque jamais ; **~ since** *ad* depuis // *cj* depuis que ; **~ so pretty** si joli ; **~green** *n* arbre *m* à feuilles persistantes ; **~lasting** *a* éternel(le).
every ['ɛvrɪ] *det* chaque ; **~ day** tous les jours, chaque jour ; **~ other/third day** tous les deux/trois jours ; **~ other car** une voiture sur deux ; **~ now and then** de temps en temps ; **~body** *pronoun* tout le monde, tous *pl* ; **~day** *a* quotidien(ne) ; de tous les jours ; **~one = ~body** ; **~thing** *pronoun* tout ; **~where** *ad* partout.
evict [ɪ'vɪkt] *vt* expulser ; **~ion** [ɪ'vɪkʃən] *n* expulsion *f*.
evidence ['ɛvɪdns] *n* (*proof*) preuve(s) *f(pl)* ; (*of witness*) témoignage *m* ; (*sign*): **to show ~ of** donner des signes de ; **to give ~** témoigner, déposer ; **in ~** (*obvious*) en évidence ; en vue.
evident ['ɛvɪdnt] *a* évident(e) ; **~ly** *ad* de toute évidence.
evil ['i:vl] *a* mauvais(e) // *n* mal *m*.
evocative [ɪ'vɔkətɪv] *a* évocateur(trice).
evoke [ɪ'vəuk] *vt* évoquer.
evolution [i:və'lu:ʃən] *n* évolution *f*.
evolve [ɪ'vɔlv] *vt* élaborer // *vi* évoluer, se transformer.
ewe [ju:] *n* brebis *f*.
ewer ['ju:ə*] *n* broc *m*.
ex- [ɛks] *prefix* ex-.
exact [ɪg'zækt] *a* exact(e) // *vt*: **to ~ sth (from)** extorquer qch (à) ; exiger qch (de) ; **~ing** *a* exigeant(e) ; (*work*) fatigant(e) ; **~itude** *n* exactitude *f*, précision *f* ; **~ly** *ad* exactement.
exaggerate [ɪg'zædʒəreɪt] *vt,vi* exagérer ; **exaggeration** [-'reɪʃən] *n* exagération *f*.
exalt [ɪg'zɔ:lt] *vt* exalter ; élever.
exam [ɪg'zæm] *n abbr of* **examination.**
examination [ɪgzæmɪ'neɪʃən] *n* (SCOL, MED) examen *m*.
examine [ɪg'zæmɪn] *vt* (*gen*) examiner ; (SCOL, LAW: *person*) interroger ; (*at customs*: *luggage*) inspecter ; **~r** *n* examinateur/trice.
example [ɪg'zɑ:mpl] *n* exemple *m* ; **for ~** par exemple.
exasperate [ɪg'zɑ:spəreɪt] *vt* exaspérer, agacer.
excavate ['ɛkskəveɪt] *vt* excaver ; (*object*) mettre au jour ; **excavation** [-'veɪʃən] *n* excavation *f* ; **excavator** *n* excavateur *m*, excavatrice *f*.
exceed [ɪk'si:d] *vt* dépasser ; (*one's powers*) outrepasser ; **~ingly** *ad* excessivement.
excel [ɪk'sɛl] *vi* exceller // *vt* surpasser.
excellence ['ɛksələns] *n* excellence *f*.
Excellency ['ɛksələnsɪ] *n*: **His ~** son Excellence *f*.
excellent ['ɛksələnt] *a* excellent(e).
except [ɪk'sɛpt] *prep* (*also*: **~ for, ~ing**) sauf, excepté, à l'exception de // *vt* excepter ; **~ if/when** sauf si/quand ; **~ that** excepté que, si ce n'est que ; **~ion** [ɪk'sɛpʃən] *n* exception *f* ; **to take ~ion to** s'offusquer de ; **~ional** [ɪk'sɛpʃənl] *a* exceptionnel(le).
excerpt ['ɛksə:pt] *n* extrait *m*.
excess [ɪk'sɛs] *n* excès *m* ; **~ fare** *n* supplément *m* ; **~ baggage** *n* excédent *m* de bagages ; **~ive** *a* excessif(ive).
exchange [ɪks'tʃeɪndʒ] *n* échange *m* ; (*also*: **telephone ~**) central *m* // *vt* échanger ; **~ market** *n* marché *m* des changes.
exchequer [ɪks'tʃɛkə*] *n* Échiquier *m*, ≈ ministère *m* des Finances.
excisable [ɪk'saɪzəbl] *a* taxable.
excise *n* ['ɛksaɪz] taxe *f* // *vt* [ɛk'saɪz] exciser ; **~ duties** *npl* impôts indirects.
excite [ɪk'saɪt] *vt* exciter ; **to get ~d** s'exciter ; **~ment** *n* excitation *f* ; **exciting** *a* passionnant(e).
exclaim [ɪk'skleɪm] *vi* s'exclamer ; **exclamation** [ɛksklə'meɪʃən] *n* exclamation *f* ; **exclamation mark** *n* point *m* d'exclamation.
exclude [ɪk'sklu:d] *vt* exclure ; **exclusion** [ɪk'sklu:ʒən] *n* exclusion *f*.
exclusive [ɪk'sklu:sɪv] *a* exclusif(ive) ; (*club, district*) sélect(e) ; (*item of news*) en exclusivité // *ad* (COMM) exclusivement, non inclus ; **~ of VAT** TVA non comprise ; **~ly** *ad* exclusivement ; **~ rights** *npl* (COMM) exclusivité *f*.
excommunicate [ɛkskə'mju:nɪkeɪt] *vt* excommunier.
excrement ['ɛkskrəmənt] *n* excrément *m*.
excruciating [ɪk'skru:ʃɪeɪtɪŋ] *a* atroce, déchirant(e).
excursion [ɪk'skə:ʃən] *n* excursion *f*.
excusable [ɪk'skju:zəbl] *a* excusable.
excuse *n* [ɪk'skju:s] excuse *f* // *vt* [ɪk'skju:z] excuser ; **to ~ sb from** (*activity*) dispenser qn de ; **~ me!** excusez-moi!, pardon!
execute ['ɛksɪkju:t] *vt* exécuter.
execution [ɛksɪ'kju:ʃən] *n* exécution *f* ; **~er** *n* bourreau *m*.
executive [ɪg'zɛkjutɪv] *n* (COMM) cadre *m* ; (POL) exécutif *m* // *a* exécutif(ive).
executor [ɪg'zɛkjutə*] *n* exécuteur/trice testamentaire.
exemplary [ɪg'zɛmplərɪ] *a* exemplaire.
exemplify [ɪg'zɛmplɪfaɪ] *vt* illustrer.
exempt [ɪg'zɛmpt] *a*: **~ from** exempté(e) *or* dispensé(e) de // *vt*: **to ~ sb from** exempter *or* dispenser qn de ; **~ion** [ɪg'zɛmpʃən] *n* exemption *f*, dispense *f*.
exercise ['ɛksəsaɪz] *n* exercice *m* // *vt* exercer ; (*patience, clemency*) faire preuve de ; (*dog*) promener ; **to take ~** prendre de l'exercice ; **~ book** *n* cahier *m*.
exert [ɪg'zə:t] *vt* exercer, employer ; **to ~ o.s.** se dépenser.

exhaust [ɪg'zɔ:st] *n* (*also*: ~ **fumes**) gaz *mpl* d'échappement ; (*also*: ~ **pipe**) tuyau *m* d'échappement // *vt* épuiser ; ~**ed** *a* épuisé(e) ; ~**ion** [ɪg'zɔ:stʃən] *n* épuisement *m* ; ~**ive** *a* très complet(ète).

exhibit [ɪg'zɪbɪt] *n* (ART) pièce *f* or objet *m* exposé(e) ; (LAW) pièce à conviction // *vt* exposer ; (*courage, skill*) faire preuve de ; ~**ion** [ɛksɪ'bɪʃən] *n* exposition *f* ; ~**ion of temper** *n* manifestation *f* de colère ; ~**ionist** [ɛksɪ'bɪʃənɪst] *n* exhibitionniste *m/f* ; ~**or** *n* exposant/e.

exhilarating [ɪg'zɪləreɪtɪŋ] *a* grisant(e) ; stimulant(e).

exhort [ɪg'zɔ:t] *vt* exhorter.

exile ['ɛksaɪl] *n* exil *m* ; exilé/e // *vt* exiler ; **in** ~ en exil.

exist [ɪg'zɪst] *vi* exister ; ~**ence** *n* existence *f* ; **to be in** ~**ence** exister.

exit ['ɛksɪt] *n* sortie *f*.

exonerate [ɪg'zɔnəreɪt] *vt*: **to** ~ **from** disculper de ; (*free*) exempter de.

exorcize ['ɛksɔ:saɪz] *vt* exorciser.

exotic [ɪg'zɔtɪk] *a* exotique.

expand [ɪk'spænd] *vt* agrandir ; accroître, étendre // *vi* (*trade etc*) se développer, s'accroître ; s'étendre ; (*gas, metal*) se dilater.

expanse [ɪk'spæns] *n* étendue *f*.

expansion [ɪk'spænʃən] *n* développement *m*, accroissement *m* ; dilatation *f*.

expatriate *n* [ɛks'pætrɪət] expatrié/e // *vt* [ɛks'pætrɪeɪt] expatrier, exiler.

expect [ɪk'spɛkt] *vt* (*anticipate*) s'attendre à, s'attendre à ce que + *sub* ; (*count on*) compter sur, escompter ; (*hope for*) espérer ; (*require*) demander, exiger ; (*suppose*) supposer ; (*await, also baby*) attendre // *vi*: **to be** ~**ing** être enceinte ; **to** ~ **sb to do** s'attendre à ce que qn fasse ; attendre de qn qu'il fasse ; ~**ant** *a* qui attend (quelque chose) ; ~**ant mother** *n* future maman ; ~**ation** [ɛkspɛk'teɪʃən] *n* attente *f*, prévisions *fpl* ; espérance(s) *f(pl)*.

expedience, expediency [ɛk'spi:dɪəns, ɛk'spi:dɪənsɪ] *n*: **for the sake of** ~ parce que c'est plus commode.

expedient [ɪk'spi:dɪənt] *a* indiqué(e), opportun(e) ; commode // *n* expédient *m*.

expedite ['ɛkspədaɪt] *vt* hâter ; expédier.

expedition [ɛkspə'dɪʃən] *n* expédition *f*.

expeditious [ɛkspə'dɪʃəs] *a* expéditif(ive), prompt(e).

expel [ɪk'spɛl] *vt* chasser, expulser ; (SCOL) renvoyer, exclure.

expend [ɪk'spɛnd] *vt* consacrer ; (*use up*) dépenser ; ~**able** *a* remplaçable ; ~**iture** [ɪk'spɛndɪtʃə*] *n* dépense *f* ; dépenses *fpl*.

expense [ɪk'spɛns] *n* dépense *f* ; frais *mpl* ; (*high cost*) coût *m* ; ~**s** *npl* (COMM) frais *mpl* ; **at great/little** ~ à grands/peu de frais ; **at the** ~ **of** aux dépens de ; ~ **account** *n* (note *f* de) frais *mpl*.

expensive [ɪk'spɛnsɪv] *a* cher(chère), coûteux(euse) ; **to be** ~ coûter cher ; ~ **tastes** *npl* goûts *mpl* de luxe.

experience [ɪk'spɪərɪəns] *n* expérience *f* // *vt* connaître ; éprouver ; ~**d** *a* expérimenté(e).

experiment [ɪk'spɛrɪmənt] *n* expérience *f* // *vi* faire une expérience ; **to** ~ **with** expérimenter ; ~**al** [-'mɛntl] *a* expérimental(e).

expert ['ɛkspə:t] *a* expert(e) // *n* expert *m* ; ~**ise** [-'ti:z] *n* (grande) compétence.

expire [ɪk'spaɪə*] *vi* expirer ; **expiry** *n* expiration *f*.

explain [ɪk'spleɪn] *vt* expliquer ; **explanation** [ɛksplə'neɪʃən] *n* explication *f* ; **explanatory** [ɪk'splænətrɪ] *a* explicatif(ive).

explicit [ɪk'splɪsɪt] *a* explicite ; (*definite*) formel(le).

explode [ɪk'spləud] *vi* exploser // *vt* faire exploser.

exploit *n* ['ɛksplɔɪt] exploit *m* // *vt* [ɪk'splɔɪt] exploiter ; ~**ation** [-'teɪʃən] *n* exploitation *f*.

exploration [ɛksplə'reɪʃən] *n* exploration *f*.

exploratory [ɪk'splɔrətrɪ] *a* (*fig*: *talks*) préliminaire.

explore [ɪk'splɔ:*] *vt* explorer ; (*possibilities*) étudier, examiner ; ~**r** *n* explorateur/trice.

explosion [ɪk'spləuʒən] *n* explosion *f*.

explosive [ɪk'spləusɪv] *a* explosif(ive) // *n* explosif *m*.

exponent [ɪk'spəunənt] *n* (*of school of thought etc*) interprète *m*, représentant *m* ; (MATH) exposant *m*.

export *vt* [ɛk'spɔ:t] exporter // *n* ['ɛkspɔ:t] exportation *f* // *cpd* d'exportation ; ~**ation** [-'teɪʃən] *n* exportation *f* ; ~**er** *n* exportateur *m*.

expose [ɪk'spəuz] *vt* exposer ; (*unmask*) démasquer, dévoiler ; **to** ~ **o.s.** (LAW) commettre un outrage à la pudeur.

exposure [ɪk'spəuʒə*] *n* exposition *f* ; (PHOT) (temps *m* de) pose *f* ; (: *shot*) pose *f* ; **suffering from** ~ (MED) souffrant des effets du froid et de l'épuisement ; ~ **meter** *n* posemètre *m*.

expound [ɪk'spaund] *vt* exposer, expliquer.

express [ɪk'sprɛs] *a* (*definite*) formel(le), exprès(esse) ; (*letter etc*) exprès *inv* // *n* (*train*) rapide *m* // *ad* (*send*) exprès // *vt* exprimer ; ~**ion** [ɪk'sprɛʃən] *n* expression *f* ; ~**ive** *a* expressif(ive) ; ~**ly** *ad* expressément, formellement.

expropriate [ɛks'prəuprɪeɪt] *vt* exproprier.

expulsion [ɪk'spʌlʃən] *n* expulsion *f* ; renvoi *m*.

exquisite [ɛk'skwɪzɪt] *a* exquis(e).

extend [ɪk'stɛnd] *vt* (*visit, street*) prolonger ; (*building*) agrandir ; (*offer*) présenter, offrir // *vi* (*land*) s'étendre.

extension [ɪk'stɛnʃən] *n* prolongation *f* ; agrandissement *m* ; (*building*) annexe *f* ; (*to wire, table*) rallonge *f* ; (*telephone*: *in offices*) poste *m* ; (: *in private house*) téléphone *m* supplémentaire.

extensive [ɪk'stɛnsɪv] *a* étendu(e), vaste ; (*damage, alterations*) considérable ; (*inquiries*) approfondi(e) ; (*use*) largement répandu(e) ; **he's travelled** ~**ly** il a beaucoup voyagé ; ~ **travelling** déplacements fréquents et prolongés.

extent [ɪk'stɛnt] *n* étendue *f*; **to some ~** dans une certaine mesure; **to what ~?** dans quelle mesure?, jusqu'à quel point?
exterior [ɛk'stɪərɪə*] *a* extérieur(e), du dehors // *n* extérieur *m*; dehors *m*.
exterminate [ɪk'stə:mɪneɪt] *vt* exterminer; **extermination** [-'neɪʃən] *n* extermination *f*.
external [ɛk'stə:nl] *a* externe; **~ly** *ad* extérieurement.
extinct [ɪk'stɪŋkt] *a* éteint(e); **~ion** [ɪk'stɪŋkʃən] *n* extinction *f*.
extinguish [ɪk'stɪŋgwɪʃ] *vt* éteindre; **~er** *n* extincteur *m*.
extol [ɪk'stəul] *vt* porter aux nues, chanter les louanges de.
extort [ɪk'stɔ:t] *vt*: **to ~ sth (from)** extorquer qch (à); **~ion** [ɪk'stɔ:ʃən] *n* extorsion *f*; **~ionate** [ɪk'stɔ:ʃnət] *a* exorbitant(e).
extra ['ɛkstrə] *a* supplémentaire, de plus // *ad* (*in addition*) en plus // *n* supplément *m*; (*THEATRE*) figurant/e.
extra... ['ɛkstrə] *prefix* extra... .
extract *vt* [ɪk'strækt] extraire; (*tooth*) arracher; (*money, promise*) soutirer // *n* ['ɛkstrækt] extrait *m*; **~ion** [ɪk'strækʃən] *n* (*also descent*) extraction *f*.
extradite ['ɛkstrədaɪt] *vt* extrader; **extradition** [-'dɪʃən] *n* extradition *f*.
extramarital [ɛkstrə'mærɪtl] *a* extra-conjugal(e).
extramural [ɛkstrə'mjuərl] *a* hors-faculté *inv*.
extraneous [ɛk'streɪnɪəs] *a*: **~ to** étranger(ère) à.
extraordinary [ɪk'strɔ:dnrɪ] *a* extraordinaire.
extra time [ɛkstrə'taɪm] *n* (*FOOTBALL*) prolongations *fpl*.
extravagant [ɪk'strævəgənt] *a* extravagant(e); (*in spending*) prodigue, dépensier(ère); dispendieux(euse).
extreme [ɪk'stri:m] *a,n* extrême (*m*); **~ly** *ad* extrêmement; **extremist** *a,n* extrémiste (*m/f*).
extremity [ɪk'strɛmətɪ] *n* extrémité *f*.
extricate ['ɛkstrɪkeɪt] *vt*: **to ~ sth (from)** dégager qch (de).
extrovert ['ɛkstrəvə:t] *n* extraverti/e.
exuberant [ɪg'zju:bərnt] *a* exubérant(e).
exude [ɪg'zju:d] *vt* exsuder; (*fig*) respirer; **the charm** *etc* **he ~s** le charme *etc* qui émane de lui.
exult [ɪg'zʌlt] *vi* exulter, jubiler.
eye [aɪ] *n* œil *m* (*pl* yeux); (*of needle*) trou *m*, chas *m* // *vt* examiner; **to keep an ~ on** surveiller; **in the public ~** en vue; **~ball** *n* globe *m* oculaire; **~bath** *n* œillère *f* (*pour bains d'œil*); **~brow** *n* sourcil *m*; **~-catching** *a* voyant(e), accrocheur(euse); **~drops** *npl* gouttes *fpl* pour les yeux; **~glass** *n* monocle *m*; **~lash** *n* cil *m*; **~let** ['aɪlɪt] *n* œillet *m*; **~lid** *n* paupière *f*; **~-opener** *n* révélation *f*; **~shadow** *n* ombre *f* à paupières; **~sight** *n* vue *f*; **~sore** *n* horreur *f*, chose *f* qui dépare *or* enlaidit; **~wash** *n* bain *m* d'œil; (*fig*) frime *f*; **~ witness** *n* témoin *m* oculaire.
eyrie ['ɪərɪ] *n* aire *f*.

F

F [ɛf] *n* (*MUS*) fa *m*.
F. *abbr of Fahrenheit*.
fable ['feɪbl] *n* fable *f*.
fabric ['fæbrɪk] *n* tissu *m*.
fabrication [fæbrɪ'keɪʃən] *n* invention(s) *f(pl)*, fabulation *f*; fait *m* (*or* preuve *f*) forgé(e) de toutes pièces.
fabulous ['fæbjuləs] *a* fabuleux(euse); (*col*: *super*) formidable, sensationnel(le).
façade [fə'sɑ:d] *n* façade *f*.
face [feɪs] *n* visage *m*, figure *f*; expression *f*; grimace *f*; (*of clock*) cadran *m*; (*of building*) façade *f*; (*side, surface*) face *f* // *vt* faire face à; **to lose ~** perdre la face; **to pull a ~** faire une grimace; **in the ~ of** (*difficulties etc*) face à, devant; **on the ~ of it** à première vue; **to ~ up to** *vt fus* faire face à, affronter; **~ cloth** *n* gant *m* de toilette; **~ cream** *n* crème *f* pour le visage; **~ lift** *n* lifting *m*; (*of façade etc*) ravalement *m*, retapage *m*; **~ powder** *n* poudre *f* (pour le visage).
facet ['fæsɪt] *n* facette *f*.
facetious [fə'si:ʃəs] *a* facétieux(euse).
face-to-face ['feɪstə'feɪs] *ad* face à face.
face value ['feɪs'vælju:] *n* (*of coin*) valeur nominale; **to take sth at ~** (*fig*) prendre qch pour argent comptant.
facia ['feɪʃə] *n* = **fascia**.
facial ['feɪʃəl] *a* facial(e).
facile ['fæsaɪl] *a* facile.
facilitate [fə'sɪlɪteɪt] *vt* faciliter.
facility [fə'sɪlɪtɪ] *n* facilité *f*; **facilities** *npl* installations *fpl*, équipement *m*.
facing ['feɪsɪŋ] *n* (*of wall etc*) revêtement *m*; (*SEWING*) revers *m*.
facsimile [fæk'sɪmɪlɪ] *n* fac-similé *m*.
fact [fækt] *n* fait *m*; **in ~** en fait.
faction ['fækʃən] *n* faction f.
factor ['fæktə*] *n* facteur *m*.
factory ['fæktərɪ] *n* usine *f*, fabrique *f*.
factual ['fæktjuəl] *a* basé(e) sur les faits.
faculty ['fækəltɪ] *n* faculté *f*; (*US*: *teaching staff*) corps enseignant.
fad [fæd] *n* manie *f*; engouement *m*.
fade [feɪd] *vi* se décolorer, passer; (*light, sound, hope*) s'affaiblir, disparaître; (*flower*) se faner.
fag [fæg] *n* (*col*: *cigarette*) sèche *f*; (: *chore*): **what a ~!** quelle corvée!; **~ end** *n* mégot *m*; **~ged out** *a* (*col*) crevé(e).
fail [feɪl] *vt* (*exam*) échouer à; (*candidate*) recaler; (*subj*: *courage, memory*) faire défaut à // *vi* échouer; (*supplies*) manquer; (*eyesight, health, light*) baisser, s'affaiblir; **to ~ to do sth** (*neglect*) négliger de faire qch; (*be unable*) ne pas arriver *or* parvenir à faire qch; **without ~** à coup sûr; sans faute; **~ing** *n* défaut *m* // *prep* faute de; **~ure** ['feɪljə*] *n* échec *m*; (*person*) raté/e; (*mechanical etc*) défaillance *f*.
faint [feɪnt] *a* faible; (*recollection*) vague; (*mark*) à peine visible // *n* évanouissement *m* // *vi* s'évanouir; **to feel ~** défaillir; **~-hearted** *a* pusillanime; **~ly** *ad*

faiblement; vaguement; **~ness** *n* faiblesse *f*.

fair [fɛə*] *a* blond(e); équitable, juste, impartial(e); (*skin, complexion*) pâle, blanc(blanche); (*weather*) beau(belle); (*good enough*) assez bon(ne); (*sizeable*) considérable // *ad* (*play*) franc-jeu // *n* foire *f*; **~ copy** *n* copie *f* au propre; corrigé *m*; **~ly** *ad* équitablement; (*quite*) assez; **~ness** *n* justice *f*, équité *f*, impartialité *f*.

fairy ['fɛərı] *n* fée *f*; **~ tale** *n* conte *m* de fées.

faith [feıθ] *n* foi *f*; (*trust*) confiance *f*; (*sect*) culte *m*, religion *f*; **~ful** *a* fidèle; **~fully** *ad* fidèlement.

fake [feık] *n* (*painting etc*) faux *m*; (*photo*) trucage *m*; (*person*) imposteur *m* // *a* faux(fausse); simulé(e) // *vt* simuler; (*photo*) truquer; (*story*) fabriquer; **his illness is a ~** sa maladie est une comédie *or* de la simulation.

falcon ['fɔ:lkən] *n* faucon *m*.

fall [fɔ:l] *n* chute *f*; (*US: autumn*) automne *m* // *vi* (*pt* **fell,** *pp* **fallen** [fɛl, 'fɔ:lən]) tomber; **~s** *npl* (*waterfall*) chute *f* d'eau, cascade *f*; **to ~ flat** *vi* (*on one's face*) tomber de tout son long, s'étaler; (*joke*) tomber à plat; (*plan*) échouer; **to ~ back on** *vt fus* se rabattre sur; **to ~ behind** *vi* prendre du retard; **to ~ down** *vi* (*person*) tomber; (*building, hopes*) s'effondrer, s'écrouler; **to ~ for** *vt fus* (*trick*) se laisser prendre à; (*person*) tomber amoureux de; **to ~ in** *vi* s'effondrer; (*MIL*) se mettre en rangs; **to ~ off** *vi* tomber; (*diminish*) baisser, diminuer; **to ~ out** *vi* (*friends etc*) se brouiller; **to ~ through** *vi* (*plan, project*) tomber à l'eau.

fallacy ['fæləsı] *n* erreur *f*, illusion *f*.

fallen ['fɔ:lən] *pp of* **fall**.

fallible ['fæləbl] *a* faillible.

fallout ['fɔ:laut] *n* retombées (radioactives).

fallow ['fæləu] *a* en jachère; en friche.

false [fɔ:ls] *a* faux(fausse); **under ~ pretences** sous un faux prétexte; **~ alarm** *n* fausse alerte; **~hood** *n* mensonge *m*; **~ly** *ad* (*accuse*) à tort; **~ teeth** *npl* fausses dents.

falter ['fɔ:ltə*] *vi* chanceler, vaciller.

fame [feım] *n* renommée *f*, renom *m*.

familiar [fə'mılıə*] *a* familier(ère); **to be ~ with** (*subject*) connaître; **~ity** [fəmılı'ærıtı] *n* familiarité *f*; **~ize** [fə'mılıəraız] *vt* familiariser.

family ['fæmılı] *n* famille *f*; **~ allowance** *n* allocations familiales; **~ business** *n* entreprise familiale; **~ doctor** *n* médecin *m* de famille; **~ life** *n* vie *f* de famille.

famine ['fæmın] *n* famine *f*.

famished ['fæmıʃt] *a* affamé(e).

famous ['feıməs] *a* célèbre; **~ly** *ad* (*get on*) fameusement, à merveille.

fan [fæn] *n* (*folding*) éventail *m*; (*ELEC*) ventilateur *m*; (*person*) fan *m*, admirateur/trice; supporter *m/f* // *vt* éventer; (*fire, quarrel*) attiser; **to ~ out** *vi* se déployer (en éventail).

fanatic [fə'nætık] *n* fanatique *m/f*; **~al** *a* fanatique.

fan belt ['fænbɛlt] *n* courroie *f* de ventilateur.

fancied ['fænsıd] *a* imaginaire.

fanciful ['fænsıful] *a* fantaisiste.

fancy ['fænsı] *n* fantaisie *f*, envie *f*; imagination *f* // *cpd* (de) fantaisie *inv* // *vt* (*feel like, want*) avoir envie de; **to take a ~ to** se prendre d'affection pour; s'enticher de; **it took** *or* **caught my ~** ça m'a plu; **to ~ that ...** se figurer *or* s'imaginer que ...; **he fancies her** elle lui plaît; **~ dress** *n* déguisement *m*, travesti *m*; **~-dress ball** *n* bal masqué *or* costumé.

fang [fæŋ] *n* croc *m*; (*of snake*) crochet *m*.

fanlight ['fænlaıt] *n* imposte *f*.

fantastic [fæn'tæstık] *a* fantastique.

fantasy ['fæntəzı] *n* imagination *f*, fantaisie *f*; fantasme *m*; chimère *f*.

far [fɑ:*] *a*: **the ~ side/end** l'autre côté/bout // *ad* loin; **~ away, ~ off** au loin, dans le lointain; **~ better** beaucoup mieux; **~ from** loin de; **by ~** de loin, de beaucoup; **go as ~ as the farm** allez jusqu'à la ferme; **as ~ as I know** pour autant que je sache; **as ~ as possible** dans la mesure du possible; **~away** *a* lointain(e).

farce [fɑ:s] *n* farce *f*.

farcical ['fɑ:sıkəl] *a* grotesque.

fare [fɛə*] *n* (*on trains, buses*) prix *m* du billet; (*in taxi*) prix de la course; (*passenger in taxi*) client *m*; (*food*) table *f*, chère *f* // *vi* se débrouiller.

Far East [fɑ:r'i:st] *n*: **the ~** l'Extrême-Orient *m*.

farewell [fɛə'wɛl] *excl, n* adieu *m*; **~ party** *n* soirée *f* d'adieux.

far-fetched ['fɑ:'fɛtʃt] *a* exagéré(e), poussé(e).

farm [fɑ:m] *n* ferme *f* // *vt* cultiver; **~er** *n* fermier/ère; cultivateur/trice; **~hand** *n* ouvrier/ère agricole; **~house** *n* (maison *f* de) ferme *f*; **~ing** *n* agriculture *f*; **intensive ~ing** culture intensive; **~land** *n* terres cultivées *or* arables; **~ worker** *n* = **~hand**; **~yard** *n* cour *f* de ferme.

far-reaching ['fɑ:'ri:tʃıŋ] *a* d'une grande portée.

far-sighted ['fɑ:'saıtıd] *a* presbyte; (*fig*) prévoyant(e), qui voit loin.

fart [fɑ:t] (*col!*) *n* pet *m* // *vi* péter.

farther ['fɑ:ðə*] *ad* plus loin.

farthest ['fɑ:ðıst] *superlative of* **far**.

fascia ['feıʃə] *n* (*AUT*) (garniture *f* du) tableau *m* de bord.

fascinate ['fæsıneıt] *vt* fasciner, captiver; **fascination** [-'neıʃən] *n* fascination *f*.

fascism ['fæʃızəm] *n* fascisme *m*.

fascist ['fæʃıst] *a,n* fasciste (*m/f*).

fashion ['fæʃən] *n* mode *f*; (*manner*) façon *f*, manière *f* // *vt* façonner; **in ~** à la mode; **out of ~** démodé(e); **~able** *a* à la mode; **~ show** *n* défilé *m* de mannequins *or* de mode.

fast [fɑ:st] *a* rapide; (*clock*): **to be ~** avancer; (*dye, colour*) grand *or* bon teint *inv* // *ad* vite, rapidement; (*stuck, held*) solidement // *n* jeûne *m* // *vi* jeûner; **~ asleep** profondément endormi.

fasten ['fɑ:sn] *vt* attacher, fixer; (*coat*) attacher, fermer // *vi* se fermer, s'attacher; **~er, ~ing** *n* fermeture *f*, attache *f*.
fastidious [fæs'tɪdɪəs] *a* exigeant(e), difficile.
fat [fæt] *a* gros(se) // *n* graisse *f*; (*on meat*) gras *m*.
fatal ['feɪtl] *a* mortel(le); fatal(e); désastreux(euse); **~ism** *n* fatalisme *m*; **~ity** [fə'tælɪtɪ] *n* (*road death etc*) victime *f*, décès *m*; **~ly** *ad* mortellement.
fate [feɪt] *n* destin *m*; (*of person*) sort *m*; **to meet one's ~** trouver la mort; **~ful** *a* fatidique.
father ['fɑ:ðə*] *n* père *m*; **~-in-law** *n* beau-père *m*; **~ly** *a* paternel(le).
fathom ['fæðəm] *n* brasse *f* (= *1828 mm*) // *vt* (*mystery*) sonder, pénétrer.
fatigue [fə'ti:g] *n* fatigue *f*; (MIL) corvée *f*.
fatness ['fætnɪs] *n* corpulence *f*, grosseur *f*.
fatten ['fætn] *vt,vi* engraisser.
fatty ['fætɪ] *a* (*food*) gras(se).
fatuous ['fætjuəs] *a* stupide.
faucet ['fɔ:sɪt] *n* (*US*) robinet *m*.
fault [fɔ:lt] *n* faute *f*; (*defect*) défaut *m*; (GEO) faille *f* // *vt* trouver des défauts à, prendre en défaut; **it's my ~** c'est de ma faute; **to find ~ with** trouver à redire *or* à critiquer à; **at ~** fautif(ive), coupable; **to a ~** à l'excès; **~less** *a* sans fautes; impeccable; irréprochable; **~y** *a* défectueux(euse).
fauna ['fɔ:nə] *n* faune *f*.
favour, favor (*US*) ['feɪvə*] *n* faveur *f*; (*help*) service *m* // *vt* (*proposition*) être en faveur de; (*pupil etc*) favoriser; (*team, horse*) donner gagnant; **to do sb a ~** rendre un service à qn; **in ~ of** en faveur de; **~able** *a* favorable; (*price*) avantageux(euse); **~ably** *ad* favorablement; **~ite** [-rɪt] *a,n* favori(te); **~itism** *n* favoritisme *m*.
fawn [fɔ:n] *n* faon *m* // *a* (*also*: **~-coloured**) fauve // *vi*: **to ~ (up)on** flatter servilement.
fear [fɪə*] *n* crainte *f*, peur *f* // *vt* craindre; **for ~ of** de peur que + *sub or* de + *infinitive*; **~ful** *a* craintif(ive); (*sight, noise*) affreux(euse), épouvantable; **~less** *a* intrépide, sans peur.
feasibility [fi:zə'bɪlɪtɪ] *n* (*of plan*) possibilité *f* de réalisation.
feasible ['fi:zəbl] *a* faisable, réalisable.
feast [fi:st] *n* festin *m*, banquet *m*; (REL: *also*: **~ day**) fête *f* // *vi* festoyer; **to ~ on** se régaler de.
feat [fi:t] *n* exploit *m*, prouesse *f*.
feather ['fɛðə*] *n* plume *f*; **~-weight** *n* poids *m* plume *inv*.
feature ['fi:tʃə*] *n* caractéristique *f*; (*article*) chronique *f*, rubrique *f* // *vt* (*subj*: *film*) avoir pour vedette(s) // *vi* figurer (en bonne place); **~s** *npl* (*of face*) traits *mpl*; **~ film** *n* film principal; **~less** *a* anonyme, sans traits distinctifs.
February ['fɛbruərɪ] *n* février *m*.
fed [fɛd] *pt,pp of* **feed**; **to be ~ up** en avoir marre *or* plein le dos.
federal ['fɛdərəl] *a* fédéral(e).
federation [fɛdə'reɪʃən] *n* fédération *f*.
fee [fi:] *n* rémunération *f*; (*of doctor, lawyer*) honoraires *mpl*; (*of school, college etc*) frais *mpl* de scolarité; (*for examination*) droits *mpl*.
feeble ['fi:bl] *a* faible; **~-minded** *a* faible d'esprit.
feed [fi:d] *n* (*of baby*) tétée *f* // *vt* (*pt, pp* **fed** [fɛd]) nourrir; (*horse etc*) donner à manger à; (*machine*) alimenter; (*data, information*): **to ~ into** fournir à; **to ~ on** *vt fus* se nourrir de; **~back** *n* feed-back *m*; **~ing bottle** *n* biberon *m*.
feel [fi:l] *n* sensation *f* // *vt* (*pt, pp* **felt** [fɛlt]) toucher; tâter, palper; (*cold, pain*) sentir; (*grief, anger*) ressentir, éprouver; (*think, believe*): **to ~ (that)** trouver que; **to ~ hungry/cold** avoir faim/froid; **to ~ lonely/better** se sentir seul/mieux; **to ~ sorry for** avoir pitié de; **it ~s soft** c'est doux au toucher; **it ~s like velvet** on dirait du velours, ça ressemble au velours; **to ~ like** (*want*) avoir envie de; **to ~ about** *or* **around** fouiller, tâtonner; **~er** *n* (*of insect*) antenne *f*; **to put out a ~er** tâter le terrain; **~ing** *n* sensation *f*; sentiment *m*; **my ~ing is that...** j'estime que... .
feet [fi:t] *npl of* **foot**.
feign [feɪn] *vt* feindre, simuler.
felicitous [fɪ'lɪsɪtəs] *a* heureux(euse).
fell [fɛl] *pt of* **fall** // *vt* (*tree*) abattre; (*person*) assommer; **~-walking** *n* randonnée *f* en montagne.
fellow ['fɛləu] *n* type *m*; compagnon *m*; (*of learned society*) membre *m*; **their ~ prisoners/students** leurs camarades prisonniers/étudiants; **~ citizen** *n* concitoyen/ne; **~ countryman** *n* compatriote *m*; **~ men** *npl* semblables *mpl*; **~ship** *n* association *f*; amitié *f*, camaraderie *f*; *sorte de bourse universitaire*.
felony ['fɛlənɪ] *n* crime *m*, forfait *m*.
felt [fɛlt] *pt, pp of* **feel** // *n* feutre *m*; **~-tip pen** *n* stylo-feutre *m*.
female ['fi:meɪl] *n* (ZOOL) femelle *f*; (*pej*: *woman*) bonne femme // *a* (BIOL, ELEC) femelle; (*sex, character*) féminin(e); (*vote etc*) des femmes; (*child etc*) du sexe féminin; **male and ~ students** étudiants et étudiantes; **~ impersonator** *n* travesti *m*.
feminine ['fɛmɪnɪn] *a* féminin(e) // *n* féminin *m*.
feminist ['fɛmɪnɪst] *n* féministe *m/f*.
fence [fɛns] *n* barrière *f*; (*col*: *person*) receleur/euse // *vt* (*also*: **~ in**) clôturer // *vi* faire de l'escrime; **fencing** *n* escrime *m*.
fend [fɛnd] *vi*: **to ~ for o.s.** se débrouiller (tout seul).
fender ['fɛndə*] *n* garde-feu *m inv*; (*US*) gardeboue *m inv*; pare-chocs *m inv*.
ferment *vi* [fə'mɛnt] fermenter // *n* ['fə:mɛnt] agitation *f*, effervescence *f*; **~ation** [-'teɪʃən] *n* fermentation *f*.
fern [fə:n] *n* fougère *f*.
ferocious [fə'rəuʃəs] *a* féroce.
ferocity [fə'rɔsɪtɪ] *n* férocité *f*.
ferry ['fɛrɪ] *n* (*small*) bac *m*; (*large*: *also*: **~boat**) ferry(-boat) *m* // *vt* transporter.

fertile ['fə:taɪl] *a* fertile ; (BIOL) fécond(e) ; ~ **period** *n* période *f* de fécondité ; **fertility** [fə'tɪlɪtɪ] *n* fertilité *f*; fécondité *f*; **fertilize** ['fə:tɪlaɪz] *vt* fertiliser ; féconder ; **fertilizer** *n* engrais *m*.
fervent ['fə:vənt] *a* fervent(e), ardent(e).
fester ['fɛstə*] *vi* suppurer.
festival ['fɛstɪvəl] *n* (REL) fête *f*; (ART, MUS) festival *m*.
festive ['fɛstɪv] *a* de fête ; **the ~ season** (*Christmas*) la période des fêtes.
festivities [fɛs'tɪvɪtɪz] *npl* réjouissances *fpl*.
fetch [fɛtʃ] *vt* aller chercher ; (*sell for*) se vendre.
fetching ['fɛtʃɪŋ] *a* charmant(e).
fête [feɪt] *n* fête *f*, kermesse *f*.
fetish ['fɛtɪʃ] *n* fétiche *m*.
fetters ['fɛtəz] *npl* chaînes *fpl*.
fetus ['fi:təs] *n* (*US*) = **foetus**.
feud [fju:d] *n* dispute *f*, dissension *f* // *vi* se disputer, se quereller ; **~al** *a* féodal(e) ; **~alism** *n* féodalité *f*.
fever ['fi:və*] *n* fièvre *f*; **~ish** *a* fiévreux(euse), fébrile.
few [fju:] *a* peu de ; **they were ~** ils étaient peu (nombreux) ; **a ~** *a* quelques // *pronoun* quelques-uns ; **~er** *a* moins de ; moins (nombreux) ; **~est** *a* le moins nombreux.
fiancé [fɪ'ɑ̃:ŋseɪ] *n* fiancé *m* ; **~e** *n* fiancée *f*.
fiasco [fɪ'æskəu] *n* fiasco *m*.
fib [fɪb] *n* bobard *m*.
fibre, fiber (*US*) ['faɪbə*] *n* fibre *f*; **~-glass** *n* fibre de verre.
fickle ['fɪkl] *a* inconstant(e), volage, capricieux(euse).
fiction ['fɪkʃən] *n* romans *mpl*, littérature *f* romanesque ; fiction *f*; **~al** *a* fictif(ive).
fictitious [fɪk'tɪʃəs] *a* fictif(ive), imaginaire.
fiddle ['fɪdl] *n* (MUS) violon *m* ; (*cheating*) combine *f*; escroquerie *f* // *vt* (*accounts*) falsifier, maquiller ; **to ~ with** *vt fus* tripoter ; **~r** *n* violoniste *m/f*.
fidelity [fɪ'dɛlɪtɪ] *n* fidélité *f*.
fidget ['fɪdʒɪt] *vi* se trémousser, remuer ; **~y** *a* agité(e), qui a la bougeotte.
field [fi:ld] *n* champ *m* ; (*fig*) domaine *m*, champ *m* ; (SPORT: *ground*) terrain *m* ; **~ glasses** *npl* jumelles *fpl* ; **~ marshal** *n* maréchal *m* ; **~work** *n* travaux *mpl* pratiques (sur le terrain).
fiend [fi:nd] *n* démon *m* ; **~ish** *a* diabolique.
fierce [fɪəs] *a* (*look*) féroce, sauvage ; (*wind, attack*) (très) violent(e) ; (*fighting, enemy*) acharné(e).
fiery ['faɪərɪ] *a* ardent(e), brûlant(e) ; fougueux(euse).
fifteen [fɪf'ti:n] *num* quinze.
fifth [fɪfθ] *num* cinquième.
fiftieth ['fɪftɪɪθ] *num* cinquantième.
fifty ['fɪftɪ] *num* cinquante.
fig [fɪg] *n* figue *f*.
fight [faɪt] *n* bagarre *f*; (MIL) combat *m* ; (*against cancer etc*) lutte *f* // *vb* (*pt, pp* **fought** [fɔ:t]) *vt* se battre contre ; (*cancer, alcoholism*) combattre, lutter contre // *vi* se battre ; **~er** *n* lutteur *m* (*fig*) ; (*plane*) chasseur *m* ; **~ing** *n* combats *mpl*.
figment ['fɪgmənt] *n*: **a ~ of the imagination** une invention.
figurative ['fɪgjurətɪv] *a* figuré(e).
figure ['fɪgə*] *n* (DRAWING, GEOM) figure *f*; (*number, cipher*) chiffre *m* ; (*body, outline*) silhouette *f*, ligne *f*, formes *fpl* // *vt* (*US*) supposer // *vi* (*appear*) figurer ; (*US*: *make sense*) s'expliquer ; **to ~ out** *vt* arriver à comprendre ; calculer ; **~head** *n* (NAUT) figure *f* de proue ; (*pej*) prête-nom *m* ; **figure skating** *n* figures imposées (*en patinage*).
filament ['fɪləmənt] *n* filament *m*.
file [faɪl] *n* (*tool*) lime *f*; (*dossier*) dossier *m* ; (*folder*) classeur *m* ; (*row*) file *f* // *vt* (*nails, wood*) limer ; (*papers*) classer ; (LAW: *claim*) faire enregistrer ; déposer ; **to ~ in/out** *vi* entrer/sortir l'un derrière l'autre ; **to ~ past** *vt fus* défiler devant.
filing ['faɪlɪŋ] *n* (travaux *mpl* de) classement *m* ; **~s** *npl* limaille *f*; **~ cabinet** *n* classeur *m* (*meuble*).
fill [fɪl] *vt* remplir // *n*: **to eat one's ~** manger à sa faim ; **to ~ in** *vt* (*hole*) boucher ; (*form*) remplir ; **to ~ up** *vt* remplir // *vi* (AUT) faire le plein ; **~ it up, please** (AUT) le plein, s'il vous plaît.
fillet ['fɪlɪt] *n* filet *m* // *vt* préparer en filets.
filling ['fɪlɪŋ] *n* (CULIN) garniture *f*, farce *f*; (*for tooth*) plombage *m* ; **~ station** *n* station *f* d'essence.
fillip ['fɪlɪp] *n* coup *m* de fouet (*fig*).
film [fɪlm] *n* film *m* ; (PHOT) pellicule *f*, film *m* // *vt* (*scene*) filmer ; **~ star** *n* vedette *f* de cinéma ; **~strip** *n* (film *m* pour) projection *f* fixe.
filter ['fɪltə*] *n* filtre *m* // *vt* filtrer ; **~ lane** *n* (AUT) voie *f* de sortie ; **~ tip** *n* bout *m* filtre.
filth [fɪlθ] *n* saleté *f*; **~y** *a* sale, dégoûtant(e) ; (*language*) ordurier (ère), grossier(ère).
fin [fɪn] *n* (*of fish*) nageoire *f*.
final ['faɪnl] *a* final(e), dernier(ère) ; définitif(ive) // *n* (SPORT) finale *f*; **~s** *npl* (SCOL) examens *mpl* de dernière année ; **~e** [fɪ'nɑ:lɪ] *n* finale *m* ; **~ist** *n* (SPORT) finaliste *m/f*; **~ize** *vt* mettre au point ; **~ly** *ad* (*lastly*) en dernier lieu ; (*eventually*) enfin, finalement ; (*irrevocably*) définitivement.
finance [faɪ'næns] *n* finance *f*; **~s** *npl* finances *fpl* // *vt* financer.
financial [faɪ'nænʃəl] *a* financier (ère) ; **~ly** *ad* financièrement ; **~ year** *n* année *f* budgétaire.
financier [faɪ'nænsɪə*] *n* financier *m*.
find [faɪnd] *vt* (*pt, pp* **found** [faund]) trouver ; (*lost object*) retrouver // *n* trouvaille *f*, découverte *f*; **to ~ sb guilty** (LAW) déclarer qn coupable ; **to ~ out** *vt* se renseigner sur ; (*truth, secret*) découvrir ; (*person*) démasquer ; **to ~ out about** se renseigner sur ; (*by chance*) apprendre ; **~ings** *npl* (LAW) conclusions *fpl*, verdict *m* ; (*of report*) constatations *fpl*.
fine [faɪn] *a* beau(belle) ; excellent(e) ; fin(e) // *ad* (*well*) très bien ; (*small*) fin, finement // *n* (LAW) amende *f*; contravention *f* // *vt* (LAW) condamner à

une amende ; donner une contravention à ; ~ **arts** *npl* beaux-arts *mpl*.
finery ['faınərı] *n* parure *f*.
finesse [fı'nɛs] *n* finesse *f*.
finger ['fıŋgə*] *n* doigt *m* // *vt* palper, toucher ; ~**nail** *n* ongle *m* (de la main) ; ~**print** *n* empreinte digitale ; ~**stall** *n* doigtier *m* ; ~**tip** *n* bout *m* du doigt.
finicky ['fınıkı] *a* tatillon(ne), méticuleux(euse) ; minutieux(euse).
finish ['fınıʃ] *n* fin *f*; (SPORT) arrivée *f*; (*polish etc*) finition *f* // *vt* finir, terminer // *vi* finir, se terminer ; (*session*) s'achever ; **to ~ off** *vt* finir, terminer ; (*kill*) achever ; **to ~ up** *vi,vt* finir ; ~**ing line** *n* ligne *f* d'arrivée ; ~**ing school** *n* institution privée (*pour jeunes filles*).
finite ['faınaıt] *a* fini(e) ; (*verb*) conjugué(e).
Finland ['fınlənd] *n* Finlande *f*.
Finn [fın] *n* Finnois/e ; Finlandais/e ; ~**ish** *a* finnois(e) ; finlandais(e) // *n* (LING) finnois *m*.
fiord [fjɔ:d] *n* fjord *m*.
fir [fə:*] *n* sapin *m*.
fire ['faıə*] *n* feu *m* ; incendie *m* // *vt* (*discharge*): **to ~ a gun** tirer un coup de feu ; (*fig*) enflammer, animer ; (*dismiss*) mettre à la porte, renvoyer // *vi* tirer, faire feu ; **on ~** en feu ; ~ **alarm** *n* avertisseur *m* d'incendie ; ~**arm** *n* arme *f* à feu ; ~ **brigade** *n* (régiment *m* de sapeurs-)pompiers *mpl* ; ~ **engine** *n* pompe *f* à incendie ; ~ **escape** *n* escalier *m* de secours ; ~ **extinguisher** *n* extincteur *m* ; ~**man** *n* pompier *m* ; ~ **master** *n* capitaine *m* des pompiers ; ~**place** *n* cheminée *f* ; ~**proof** *a* ignifuge ; ~**side** *n* foyer *m*, coin *m* du feu ; ~ **station** *n* caserne *f* de pompiers ; ~**wood** *n* bois *m* de chauffage ; ~**work** *n* feu *m* d'artifice ; ~**works** *npl* (*display*) feu(x) d'artifice.
firing ['faıərıŋ] *n* (MIL) feu *m*, tir *m* ; ~ **squad** *n* peloton *m* d'exécution.
firm [fə:m] *a* ferme // *n* compagnie *f*, firme *f*; ~**ly** *ad* fermement ; ~**ness** *n* fermeté *f*.
first [fə:st] *a* premier(ère) // *ad* (*before others*) le premier, la première ; (*before other things*) en premier, d'abord ; (*when listing reasons etc*) en premier lieu, premièrement // *n* (*person: in race*) premier/ère ; (SCOL) mention *f* très bien ; (AUT) première *f*; **at ~** au commencement, au début ; ~ **of all** tout d'abord, pour commencer ; ~ **aid** premiers secours *or* soins ; ~**-aid kit** *n* trousse *f* à pharmacie ; ~**-class** *a* de première classe ; ~**-hand** *a* de première main ; ~ **lady** *n* (*US*) femme *f* du président ; ~**ly** *ad* premièrement, en premier lieu ; ~ **name** *n* prénom *m* ; ~ **night** *n* (THEATRE) première *f*; ~**-rate** *a* excellent(e).
fir tree ['fə:tri:] *n* sapin *m*.
fiscal ['fıskəl] *a* fiscal(e).
fish [fıʃ] *n,pl inv* poisson *m* ; poissons *mpl* // *vt,vi* pêcher ; **to ~ a river** pêcher dans une rivière ; **to go ~ing** aller à la pêche ; ~**erman** *n* pêcheur *m* ; ~**ery** *n* pêcherie *f*; ~ **fingers** *npl* bâtonnets de poisson (congelés) ; ~ **hook** *n* hameçon *m* ; ~**ing boat** *n* barque *f* de pêche ; ~**ing line** *n* ligne *f* (de pêche) ; ~**ing rod** *n* canne *f* à pêche ; ~**ing tackle** *n* attirail *m* de pêche ; ~ **market** *n* marché *m* au poisson ; ~**monger** *n* marchand *m* de poisson ; ~ **slice** *n* pelle *f* à poisson ; ~**y** *a* (*fig*) suspect(e), louche.
fission ['fıʃən] *n* fission *f*.
fissure ['fıʃə*] *n* fissure *f*.
fist [fıst] *n* poing *m*.
fit [fıt] *a* (MED, SPORT) en (bonne) forme ; (*proper*) convenable ; approprié(e) // *vt* (*subj: clothes*) aller à ; (*adjust*) ajuster ; (*put in, attach*) installer, poser ; adapter ; (*equip*) équiper, garnir, munir // *vi* (*clothes*) aller ; (*parts*) s'adapter ; (*in space, gap*) entrer, s'adapter // *n* (MED) accès *m*, crise *f*; (*of coughing*) quinte *f*; ~ **to** en état de ; ~ **for** digne de ; apte à ; **this dress is a tight/good ~** cette robe est un peu juste/(me) va très bien ; **by ~s and starts** par à-coups ; **to ~ in** *vi* s'accorder ; s'adapter ; **to ~ out** (*also*: ~ **up**) *vt* équiper ; ~**ful** *a* intermittent(e) ; ~**ment** *n* meuble encastré, élément *m* ; ~**ness** *n* (MED) forme *f* physique ; (*of remark*) à-propos *m*, justesse *f*; ~**ter** *n* monteur *m* ; (DRESSMAKING) essayeur/euse ; ~**ting** *a* approprié(e) // *n* (*of dress*) essayage *m* ; (*of piece of equipment*) pose *f*, installation *f*; ~**tings** *npl* installations *fpl*.
five [faıv] *num* cinq ; ~**r** *n* (*Brit: col*) billet *m* de cinq livres.
fix [fıks] *vt* fixer ; arranger ; (*mend*) réparer // *n*: **to be in a ~** être dans le pétrin ; ~**ed** [fıkst] *a* (*prices etc*) fixe ; ~**ture** ['fıkstʃə*] *n* installation *f* (fixe) ; (SPORT) rencontre *f* (au programme).
fizz [fız] *vi* pétiller.
fizzle ['fızl] *vi* pétiller ; **to ~ out** *vi* rater.
fizzy ['fızı] *a* pétillant(e) ; gazeux(euse).
fjord [fjɔ:d] *n* = **fiord**.
flabbergasted ['flæbəgɑ:stıd] *a* sidéré(e), ahuri(e).
flabby ['flæbı] *a* mou(molle).
flag [flæg] *n* drapeau *m* ; (*also*: ~**stone**) dalle *f* // *vi* faiblir ; fléchir ; **to ~ down** *vt* héler, faire signe (de s'arrêter) à ; ~ **of convenience** *n* pavillon *m* de complaisance.
flagon ['flægən] *n* bonbonne *f*.
flagpole ['flægpəul] *n* mât *m*.
flagrant ['fleıgrənt] *a* flagrant(e).
flair [flɛə*] *n* flair *m*.
flake [fleık] *n* (*of rust, paint*) écaille *f*; (*of snow, soap powder*) flocon *m* // *vi* (*also*: ~ **off**) s'écailler.
flamboyant [flæm'bɔıənt] *a* flamboyant(e), éclatant(e) ; (*person*) haut(e) en couleur.
flame [fleım] *n* flamme *f*.
flamingo [flə'mıŋgəu] *n* flamant *m* (rose).
flammable ['flæməbl] *a* inflammable.
flan [flæn] *n* tarte *f*.
Flanders ['flɑ:ndəz] *n* Flandre(s) *f(pl)*.
flange [flændʒ] *n* boudin *m* ; collerette *f*.
flank [flæŋk] *n* flanc *m* // *vt* flanquer.
flannel ['flænl] *n* (*also*: **face ~**) gant *m* de toilette ; (*fabric*) flanelle *f*; (*col*) baratin *m* ; ~**s** *npl* pantalon *m* de flanelle.

flap [flæp] *n* (*of pocket, envelope*) rabat *m* // *vt* (*wings*) battre (de) // *vi* (*sail, flag*) claquer ; (*col*: *also*: **be in a ~**) paniquer.
flare [flεə*] *n* fusée éclairante ; (*in skirt etc*) évasement *m* ; **to ~ up** *vi* s'embraser ; (*fig*: *person*) se mettre en colère, s'emporter ; (: *revolt*) éclater ; **~d** *a* (*trousers*) à jambes évasées.
flash [flæʃ] *n* éclair *m* ; (*also*: **news ~**) flash *m* (d'information) ; (PHOT) flash *m* // *vt* (*switch on*) allumer (brièvement) ; (*direct*): **to ~ sth at** braquer qch sur ; (*display*) étaler, exhiber ; (*send*: *message*) câbler // *vi* briller ; jeter des éclairs ; (*light on ambulance etc*) clignoter ; **in a ~** en un clin d'œil ; **to ~ one's headlights** faire un appel de phares ; **he ~ed by** *or* **past** il passa (devant nous) comme un éclair ; **~back** *n* flashback *m*, retour *m* en arrière ; **~ bulb** *n* ampoule *f* de flash ; **~er** *n* (AUT) clignotant *m*.
flashy ['flæʃı] *a* (*pej*) tape-à-l'œil *inv*, tapageur(euse).
flask [flɑ:sk] *n* flacon *m*, bouteille *f* ; (CHEM) ballon *m* ; (*also*: **vacuum ~**) bouteille *f* thermos ®.
flat [flæt] *a* plat(e) ; (*tyre*) dégonflé(e), à plat ; (*denial*) catégorique ; (MUS) bémolisé(e) // *n* (*rooms*) appartement *m* ; (MUS) bémol *m* ; (AUT) crevaison *f*, pneu crevé ; **to be ~-footed** avoir les pieds plats ; **~ly** *ad* catégoriquement ; **~ness** *n* (*of land*) absence *f* de relief, aspect plat ; **~ten** *vt* (*also*: **~ten out**) aplatir.
flatter ['flætə*] *vt* flatter ; **~er** *n* flatteur *m* ; **~ing** *a* flatteur(euse) ; **~y** *n* flatterie *f*.
flatulence ['flætjuləns] *n* flatulence *f*.
flaunt [flɔ:nt] *vt* faire étalage de.
flavour, flavor (*US*) ['fleıvə*] *n* goût *m*, saveur *f* ; (*of ice cream etc*) parfum *m* // *vt* parfumer, aromatiser ; **vanilla~-ed** à l'arôme de vanille, vanillé(e) ; **to give** *or* **add ~ to** donner du goût à, relever ; **~ing** *n* arôme *m* (synthétique).
flaw [flɔ:] *n* défaut *m* ; **~less** *a* sans défaut.
flax [flæks] *n* lin *m* ; **~en** *a* blond(e).
flea [fli:] *n* puce *f*.
fledg(e)ling ['flεdʒlıŋ] *n* oisillon *m*.
flee, *pt, pp* **fled** [fli:, flεd] *vt* fuir, s'enfuir de // *vi* fuir, s'enfuir.
fleece [fli:s] *n* toison *f* // *vt* (*col*) voler, filouter.
fleet [fli:t] *n* flotte *f* ; (*of lorries etc*) parc *m* ; convoi *m*.
fleeting ['fli:tıŋ] *a* fugace, fugitif(ive) ; (*visit*) très bref(brève).
Flemish ['flεmıʃ] *a* flamand(e) // *n* (LING) flamand *m* ; **the ~** les Flamands.
flesh [flεʃ] *n* chair *f* ; **~ wound** *n* blessure superficielle.
flew [flu:] *pt of* **fly.**
flex [flεks] *n* fil *m or* câble *m* électrique (souple) // *vt* fléchir ; (*muscles*) tendre ; **~ibility** [-'bılıtı] *n* flexibilité *f* ; **~ible** *a* flexible.
flick [flık] *n* petite tape ; chiquenaude *f* ; sursaut *m* ; **~ knife** *n* couteau *m* à cran d'arrêt ; **to ~ through** *vt fus* feuilleter.
flicker ['flıkə*] *vi* vaciller // *n* vacillement *m* ; **a ~ of light** une brève lueur.
flier ['flaıə*] *n* aviateur *m*.
flight [flaıt] *n* vol *m* ; (*escape*) fuite *f* ; (*also*: **~ of steps**) escalier *m* ; **to take ~** prendre la fuite ; **to put to ~** mettre en fuite ; **~ deck** *n* (AVIAT) poste *m* de pilotage ; (NAUT) pont *m* d'envol.
flimsy ['flımzı] *a* (*partition, fabric*) peu solide, mince ; (*excuse*) pauvre, mince.
flinch [flıntʃ] *vi* tressaillir ; **to ~ from** se dérober à, reculer devant.
fling, *pt, pp* **flung** [flıŋ, flʌŋ] *vt* jeter, lancer.
flint [flınt] *n* silex *m* ; (*in lighter*) pierre *f* (à briquet).
flip [flıp] *n* chiquenaude *f*.
flippant ['flıpənt] *a* désinvolte, irrévérencieux(euse).
flirt [flə:t] *vi* flirter // *n* flirteuse *f* ; **~ation** [-'teıʃən] *n* flirt *m*.
flit [flıt] *vi* voleter.
float [fləut] *n* flotteur *m* ; (*in procession*) char *m* // *vi* flotter // *vt* faire flotter ; (*loan, business*) lancer ; **~ing** *a* flottant(e).
flock [flɔk] *n* troupeau *m* ; (*of people*) foule *f*.
flog [flɔg] *vt* fouetter.
flood [flʌd] *n* inondation *f* ; (*of words, tears etc*) flot *m*, torrent *m* // *vt* inonder ; **in ~** en crue ; **~ing** *n* inondation *f* ; **~light** *n* projecteur *m* // *vt* éclairer aux projecteurs, illuminer.
floor [flɔ:*] *n* sol *m* ; (*storey*) étage *m* ; (*fig*: *at meeting*): **the ~** l'assemblée *f*, les membres *mpl* de l'assemblée // *vt* terrasser ; **on the ~** par terre ; **ground ~** (*Brit*), **first ~** (*US*) rez-de-chaussée *m* ; **first ~** (*Brit*), **second ~** (*US*) premier étage ; **~board** *n* planche *f* (*du plancher*) ; **~ show** *n* spectacle *m* de variétés.
flop [flɔp] *n* fiasco *m* // *vi* (*fail*) faire fiasco.
floppy ['flɔpı] *a* lâche, flottant(e) ; **~ hat** *n* chapeau *m* à bords flottants.
flora ['flɔ:rə] *n* flore *f*.
floral ['flɔ:rl] *a* floral(e).
florid ['flɔrıd] *a* (*complexion*) fleuri(e) ; (*style*) plein(e) de fioritures.
florist ['flɔrıst] *n* fleuriste *m/f*.
flounce [flauns] *n* volant *m* ; **to ~ out** *vi* sortir dans un mouvement d'humeur.
flounder ['flaundə*] *vi* patauger.
flour ['flauə*] *n* farine *f*.
flourish ['flʌrıʃ] *vi* prospérer // *vt* brandir // *n* fioriture *f* ; (*of trumpets*) fanfare *f* ; **~ing** *a* prospère, florissant(e).
flout [flaut] *vt* se moquer de, faire fi de.
flow [fləu] *n* flot *m* ; courant *m* ; circulation *f* ; (*tide*) flux *m* // *vi* couler ; (*traffic*) s'écouler ; (*robes, hair*) flotter ; **~ chart** *n* organigramme *m*.
flower ['flauə*] *n* fleur *f* // *vi* fleurir ; **~ bed** *n* plate-bande *f* ; **~pot** *n* pot *m* (à fleurs) ; **~y** *a* fleuri(e).
flown [fləun] *pp of* **fly**.
flu [flu:] *n* grippe *f*.
fluctuate ['flʌktjueıt] *vi* varier, fluctuer ; **fluctuation** [-'eıʃən] *n* fluctuation *f*, variation *f*.
fluency ['flu:ənsı] *n* facilité *f*, aisance *f*.
fluent ['flu:ənt] *a* (*speech*) coulant(e), aisé(e) ; **he speaks ~ French, he's ~ in French** il parle le français couramment ;

~ly *ad* couramment; avec aisance *or* facilité.
fluff [flʌf] *n* duvet m; peluche *f*; **~y** *a* duveteux(euse); pelucheux (euse); **~y toy** *n* jouet *m* en peluche.
fluid ['flu:ɪd] *a,n* fluide (*m*); **~ ounce** *n* = *0.028 l; 0.05 pints.*
fluke [flu:k] *n* (*col*) coup *m* de veine *or* de chance.
flung [flʌŋ] *pt,pp of* **fling**.
fluorescent [fluə'rɛsnt] *a* fluorescent(e).
fluoride ['fluəraɪd] *n* fluor *m*.
fluorine ['fluəri:n] *n* fluor *m*.
flurry ['flʌrɪ] *n* (*of snow*) rafale *f*, bourrasque *f*; **~ of activity/excitement** affairement *m*/excitation *f* soudain(e).
flush [flʌʃ] *n* rougeur *f*; excitation *f* // *vt* nettoyer à grande eau // *vi* rougir // *a*: **~ with** au ras de, de niveau avec; **~ against** tout contre; **to ~ the toilet** tirer la chasse (d'eau); **~ed** *a* (tout(e)) rouge.
fluster ['flʌstə*] *n* agitation *f*, trouble *m*; **~ed** *a* énervé(e).
flute [flu:t] *n* flûte *f*.
fluted ['flu:tɪd] *a* cannelé(e).
flutter ['flʌtə*] *n* agitation *f*; (*of wings*) battement *m* // *vi* battre des ailes, voleter; (*person*) aller et venir dans une grande agitation.
flux [flʌks] *n*: **in a state of ~** fluctuant sans cesse.
fly [flaɪ] *n* (*insect*) mouche *f*; (*on trousers: also*: **flies**) braguette *f* // *vb* (*pt* **flew,** *pp* **flown** [flu:, fləun]) *vt* piloter; (*passengers, cargo*) transporter (par avion); (*distances*) parcourir // *vi* voler; (*passengers*) aller en avion; (*escape*) s'enfuir, fuir; (*flag*) se déployer; **to ~ open** *vi* s'ouvrir brusquement; **~ing** *n* (*activity*) aviation *f* // *a*: **~ing visit** visite *f* éclair *inv*; **with ~ing colours** haut la main; **~ing buttress** *n* arc-boutant *m*; **~ing saucer** *n* soucoupe volante; **~ing start** *n*: **to get off to a ~ing start** faire un excellent départ; **~over** *n* (*Brit*: *bridge*) saut-de-mouton *m*; **~past** *n* défilé aérien; **~sheet** *n* (*for tent*) double toit *m*; **~wheel** *n* volant *m* (de commande).
F.M. (*abbr of frequency modulation*) F.M., M.F. (modulation *f* de fréquence).
foal [fəul] *n* poulain *m*.
foam [fəum] *n* écume *f*; (*on beer*) mousse *f*; (*also*: **plastic ~**) mousse cellulaire *or* de plastique // *vi* écumer; (*soapy water*) mousser; **~ rubber** *n* caoutchouc *m* mousse.
fob [fɔb] *vt*: **to ~ sb off with** refiler à qn; se débarrasser de qn avec.
focal ['fəukəl] *a* focal(e).
focus ['fəukəs] *n* (*pl*: **~es**) foyer *m*; (*of interest*) centre *m* // *vt* (*field glasses etc*) mettre au point; (*light rays*) faire converger; **in ~** au point; **out of ~** pas au point.
fodder ['fɔdə*] *n* fourrage *m*.
foe [fəu] *n* ennemi *m*.
foetus ['fi:təs] *n* fœtus *m*.
fog [fɔg] *n* brouillard *m*; **~gy** *a*: **it's ~gy** il y a du brouillard.
foible ['fɔɪbl] *n* faiblesse *f*.
foil [fɔɪl] *vt* déjouer, contrecarrer // *n* feuille *f* de métal; (*also*: **kitchen ~**) papier *m* d'alu(minium); (FENCING) fleuret *m*; **to act as a ~ to** (*fig*) servir de repoussoir *or* de faire-valoir à.
fold [fəuld] *n* (*bend, crease*) pli *m*; (AGR) parc *m* à moutons; (*fig*) bercail *m* // *vt* plier; **to ~ up** *vi* (*map etc*) se plier, se replier; (*business*) fermer boutique // *vt* (*map etc*) plier, replier; **~er** *n* (*for papers*) chemise *f*; classeur *m*; (*brochure*) dépliant *m*; **~ing** *a* (*chair, bed*) pliant(e).
foliage ['fəulɪɪdʒ] *n* feuillage *m*.
folk [fəuk] *npl* gens *mpl* // *a* folklorique; **~s** *npl* famille *f*, parents *mpl*; **~lore** ['fəuklɔ:*] *n* folklore *m*; **~song** *n* chanson *f* folklorique (*gén de l'Ouest américain*).
follow ['fɔləu] *vt* suivre // *vi* suivre; (*result*) s'ensuivre; **he ~ed suit** il fit de même; **to ~ up** *vt* (*victory*) tirer parti de; (*letter, offer*) donner suite à; (*case*) suivre; **~er** *n* disciple *m/f*, partisan/e; **~ing** *a* suivant(e) // *n* partisans *mpl*, disciples *mpl*.
folly ['fɔlɪ] *n* inconscience *f*; sottise *f*; (*building*) folie *f*.
fond [fɔnd] *a* (*memory, look*) tendre, affectueux(euse); **to be ~ of** aimer beaucoup.
fondle ['fɔndl] *vt* caresser.
fondness ['fɔndnɪs] *n* (*for things*) attachement *m*; (*for people*) sentiments affectueux; **a special ~ for** une prédilection pour.
font [fɔnt] *n* fonts baptismaux.
food [fu:d] *n* nourriture *f*; **~ mixer** *n* mixeur *m*; **~ poisoning** *n* intoxication *f* alimentaire; **~stuffs** *npl* denrées *fpl* alimentaires.
fool [fu:l] *n* idiot/e; (HISTORY: *of king*) bouffon *m*, fou *m*; (CULIN) purée *f* de fruits à la crème // *vt* berner, duper // *vi* (*gen*: **~ around**) faire l'idiot *or* l'imbécile; **~hardy** *a* téméraire, imprudent(e); **~ish** *a* idiot(e), stupide; imprudent(e); écervelé(e); **~proof** *a* (*plan etc*) infaillible.
foot [fut] *n* (*pl*: **feet** [fi:t]) pied *m*; (*measure*) pied (= *304 mm*; *12 inches*); (*of animal*) patte *f* // *vt* (*bill*) casquer, payer; **on ~** à pied; **~ and mouth (disease)** *n* fièvre aphteuse; **~ball** *n* ballon *m* (de football); (*sport*) football *m*; **~baller** *n* footballeur *m*; **~brake** *n* frein *m* à pied; **~bridge** *n* passerelle *f*; **~hills** *npl* contreforts *mpl*; **~hold** *n* prise *f* (de pied); **~ing** *n* (*fig*) position *f*; **to lose one's ~ing** perdre pied; **on an equal ~ing** sur pied d'égalité; **~lights** *npl* rampe *f*; **~man** *n* laquais *m*; **~note** *n* note *f* (en bas de page); **~path** *n* sentier *m*; (*in street*) trottoir *m*; **~rest** *n* marchepied *m*; **~sore** *a* aux pieds endoloris; **~step** *n* pas *m*; **~wear** *n* chaussure(s) *f(pl)* (*terme générique en anglais*).
for [fɔ:*] *prep* pour; (*during*) pendant; (*in spite of*) malgré // *cj* car; **I haven't seen him ~ a week** je ne l'ai pas vu depuis une semaine, cela fait une semaine que je ne l'ai pas vu; **he went down ~ the paper** il est descendu chercher le journal; **~ sale** à vendre.
forage ['fɔrɪdʒ] *n* fourrage *m* // *vi* fourrager, fouiller; **~ cap** *n* calot *m*.

foray ['fɔreɪ] *n* incursion *f*.
forbad(e) [fə'bæd] *pt of* **forbid**.
forbearing [fɔ:'bɛərɪŋ] *a* patient(e), tolérant(e).
forbid, *pt* **forbad(e),** *pp* **forbidden** [fə'bɪd, -'bæd, -'bɪdn] *vt* défendre, interdire ; **~den** *a* défendu(e) ; **~ding** *a* d'aspect *or* d'allure sévère *or* sombre.
force [fɔ:s] *n* force *f* // *vt* forcer ; **the F~s** *npl* l'armée *f* ; **in ~** en force ; **to come into ~** entrer en vigueur ; **~d** [fɔ:st] *a* forcé(e) ; **~ful** *a* énergique, volontaire.
forceps ['fɔ:sɛps] *npl* forceps *m*.
forcibly ['fɔ:səblɪ] *ad* par la force, de force ; (*vigorously*) énergiquement.
ford [fɔ:d] *n* gué *m* // *vt* passer à gué.
fore [fɔ:*] *n*: **to the ~** en évidence.
forearm ['fɔ:rɑ:m] *n* avant-bras *m inv*.
foreboding [fɔ:'bəudɪŋ] *n* pressentiment *m* (néfaste).
forecast ['fɔ:kɑ:st] *n* prévision *f* // *vt* (*irg*: *like* **cast**) prévoir.
forecourt ['fɔ:kɔ:t] *n* (*of garage*) devant *m*.
forefathers ['fɔ:fɑ:ðəz] *npl* ancêtres *mpl*.
forefinger ['fɔ:fɪŋgə*] *n* index *m*.
forego, *pt* **forewent,** *pp* **foregone** [fɔ:'gəu, -'wɛnt, -'gɔn] *vt* = **forgo**.
foregone ['fɔ:gɔn] *a*: **it's a ~ conclusion** c'est à prévoir, c'est couru d'avance.
foreground ['fɔ:graund] *n* premier plan.
forehead ['fɔrɪd] *n* front *m*.
foreign ['fɔrɪn] *a* étranger(ère) ; (*trade*) extérieur(e) ; **~ body** *n* corps étranger ; **~er** *n* étranger/ère ; **~ exchange market** *n* marché *m* des devises ; **~ exchange rate** *n* cours *m* des devises ; **~ minister** *n* ministre *m* des Affaires étrangères.
foreleg ['fɔ:lɛg] *n* patte *f* de devant ; jambe antérieure.
foreman ['fɔ:mən] *n* contremaître *m*.
foremost ['fɔ:məust] *a* le(la) plus en vue ; premier(ère).
forensic [fə'rɛnsɪk] *a*: **~ medicine** médecine légale ; **~ expert** expert *m* de la police, expert légiste.
forerunner ['fɔ:rʌnə*] *n* précurseur *m*.
foresee, *pt* **foresaw,** *pp* **foreseen** [fɔ:'si:, -'sɔ:, -'si:n] *vt* prévoir ; **~able** *a* prévisible.
foresight ['fɔ:saɪt] *n* prévoyance *f*.
forest ['fɔrɪst] *n* forêt *f*.
forestall [fɔ:'stɔ:l] *vt* devancer.
forestry ['fɔrɪstrɪ] *n* sylviculture *f*.
foretaste ['fɔ:teɪst] *n* avant-goût *m*.
foretell, *pt,pp* **foretold** [fɔ:'tɛl, -'təuld] *vt* prédire.
forever [fə'rɛvə*] *ad* pour toujours ; (*fig*) continuellement.
forewent [fɔ:'wɛnt] *pt of* **forego**.
foreword ['fɔ:wə:d] *n* avant-propos *m inv*.
forfeit ['fɔ:fɪt] *n* prix *m*, rançon *f* // *vt* perdre ; (*one's life, health*) payer de.
forgave [fə'geɪv] *pt of* **forgive.**
forge [fɔ:dʒ] *n* forge *f* // *vt* (*signature*) contrefaire ; (*wrought iron*) forger ; **to ~ documents/a will** fabriquer des faux papiers/un faux testament ; **to ~ money** fabriquer de la fausse monnaie ; **to ~ ahead** *vi* pousser de l'avant, prendre de l'avance ; **~r** *n* faussaire *m* ; **~ry** *n* faux *m*, contrefaçon *f*.
forget, *pt* **forgot,** *pp* **forgotten** [fə'gɛt, -'gɔt, -'gɔtn] *vt,vi* oublier ; **~ful** *a* distrait(e), étourdi(e) ; **~ful of** oublieux(euse) de ; **~fulness** *n* tendance *f* aux oublis ; (*oblivion*) oubli *m*.
forgive, *pt* **forgave,** *pp* **forgiven** [fə'gɪv, -'geɪv, -'gɪvn] *vt* pardonner ; **~ness** *n* pardon *m*.
forgo, *pt* **forwent,** *pp* **forgone** [fɔ:'gəu, -'wɛnt, -'gɔn] *vt* renoncer à.
forgot [fə'gɔt] *pt of* **forget**.
forgotten [fə'gɔtn] *pp of* **forget**.
fork [fɔ:k] *n* (*for eating*) fourchette *f* ; (*for gardening*) fourche *f* ; (*of roads*) bifurcation *f* ; (*of railways*) embranchement *m* // *vi* (*road*) bifurquer ; **to ~ out** (*col*: *pay*) *vt* allonger, se fendre de // *vi* casquer ; **~ed** [fɔ:kt] *a* (*lightning*) en zigzags, ramifié(e) ; **~-lift truck** *n* chariot élévateur.
form [fɔ:m] *n* forme *f* ; (SCOL) classe *f* ; (*questionnaire*) formulaire *m* // *vt* former ; **in top ~** en pleine forme.
formal ['fɔ:məl] *a* (*offer, receipt*) en bonne et due forme ; (*person*) cérémonieux(euse), à cheval sur les convenances ; (*occasion, dinner*) officiel(le) ; (ART, PHILOSOPHY) formel(le) ; **~ly** *ad* officiellement ; formellement ; cérémonieusement.
format ['fɔ:mæt] *n* format *m*.
formation [fɔ:'meɪʃən] *n* formation *f*.
formative ['fɔ:mətɪv] *a*: **~ years** années *fpl* d'apprentissage (*fig*) *or* de formation (*d'un enfant, d'un adolescent*).
former ['fɔ:mə*] *a* ancien(ne) (*before n*), précédent(e) ; **the ~ ... the latter** le premier ... le second, celui-là ... celui-ci ; **~ly** *ad* autrefois.
formidable ['fɔ:mɪdəbl] *a* redoutable.
formula ['fɔ:mjulə] *n* formule *f*.
formulate ['fɔ:mjuleɪt] *vt* formuler.
forsake, *pt* **forsook,** *pp* **forsaken** [fə'seɪk, -'suk, -'seɪkən] *vt* abandonner.
fort [fɔ:t] *n* fort *m*.
forte ['fɔ:tɪ] *n* (point) fort *m*.
forth [fɔ:θ] *ad* en avant ; **to go back and ~** aller et venir ; **and so ~** et ainsi de suite ; **~coming** *a* qui va paraître *or* avoir lieu prochainement ; (*character*) ouvert(e), communicatif(ive) ; **~right** *a* franc(franche), direct(e).
fortieth ['fɔ:tɪɪθ] *num* quarantième.
fortification [fɔ:tɪfɪ'keɪʃən] *n* fortification *f*.
fortify ['fɔ:tɪfaɪ] *vt* fortifier ; **fortified wine** *n* vin liquoreux *or* de liqueur.
fortitude ['fɔ:tɪtju:d] *n* courage *m*, force *f* d'âme.
fortnight ['fɔ:tnaɪt] *n* quinzaine *f*, quinze jours *mpl* ; **~ly** *a* bimensuel(le) // *ad* tous les quinze jours.
fortress ['fɔ:trɪs] *n* forteresse *f*.
fortuitous [fɔ:'tju:ɪtəs] *a* fortuit(e).
fortunate ['fɔ:tʃənɪt] *a*: **to be ~** avoir de la chance ; **it is ~ that** c'est une chance que, il est heureux que ; **~ly** *ad* heureusement, par bonheur.
fortune ['fɔ:tʃən] *n* chance *f* ; (*wealth*) fortune *f* ; **~teller** *n* diseuse *f* de bonne aventure.

forty ['fɔ:tɪ] *num* quarante.
forum ['fɔ:rəm] *n* forum *m*, tribune *f*.
forward ['fɔ:wəd] *a* (*ahead of schedule*) en avance; (*movement, position*) en avant, vers l'avant; (*not shy*) ouvert(e); direct(e); effronté(e) // *ad* en avant // *n* (SPORT) avant *m* // *vt* (*letter*) faire suivre; (*parcel, goods*) expédier; (*fig*) promouvoir, contribuer au développement *or* à l'avancement de; **to move** ~ avancer; ~**s** *ad* en avant.
forwent [fɔ:'wɛnt] *pt of* **forgo**.
fossil ['fɔsl] *a,n* fossile (*m*).
foster ['fɔstə*] *vt* encourager, favoriser; ~ **brother** *n* frère adoptif; frère de lait; ~ **child** *n* enfant adopté; ~ **mother** *n* mère adoptive; mère nourricière.
fought [fɔ:t] *pt, pp of* **fight**.
foul [faul] *a* (*weather, smell, food*) infect(e); (*language*) ordurier(ère); (*deed*) infâme // *n* (FOOTBALL) faute *f* // *vt* salir, encrasser; (*football player*) commettre une faute sur; ~ **play** *n* (SPORT) jeu déloyal; ~ **play is not suspected** la mort (*or* l'incendie *etc*) n'a pas de causes suspectes, on écarte l'hypothèse d'un meurtre (*or* d'un acte criminel).
found [faund] *pt, pp of* **find** // *vt* (*establish*) fonder; ~**ation** [-'deɪʃən] *n* (*act*) fondation *f*; (*base*) fondement *m*; (*also*: ~**ation cream**) fond *m* de teint; ~**ations** *npl* (*of building*) fondations *fpl*.
founder ['faundə*] *n* fondateur *m* // *vi* couler, sombrer.
foundry ['faundrɪ] *n* fonderie *f*.
fount [faunt] *n* source *f*; ~**ain** ['fauntɪn] *n* fontaine *f*; ~**ain pen** *n* stylo *m* (à encre).
four [fɔ:*] *num* quatre; **on all** ~**s** à quatre pattes; ~**some** ['fɔ:səm] *n* partie *f* à quatre; sortie *f* à quatre; ~**teen** *num* quatorze; ~**teenth** *num* quatorzième; ~**th** *num* quatrième.
fowl [faul] *n* volaille *f*.
fox [fɔks] *n* renard *m* // *vt* mystifier.
foyer ['fɔɪeɪ] *n* vestibule *m*; (THEATRE) foyer *m*.
fraction ['frækʃən] *n* fraction *f*.
fracture ['fræktʃə*] *n* fracture *f* // *vt* fracturer.
fragile ['frædʒaɪl] *a* fragile.
fragment ['frægmənt] *n* fragment *m*; ~**ary** *a* fragmentaire.
fragrance ['freɪgrəns] *n* parfum *m*.
fragrant ['freɪgrənt] *a* parfumé(e), odorant(e).
frail [freɪl] *a* fragile, délicat(e).
frame [freɪm] *n* (*of building*) charpente *f*; (*of human, animal*) charpente, ossature *f*; (*of picture*) cadre *m*; (*of door, window*) encadrement *m*, chambranle *m*; (*of spectacles*: *also*: ~**s**) monture f // *vt* encadrer; (*theory, plan*) construire, élaborer; ~ **of mind** *n* disposition *f* d'esprit; ~**work** *n* structure *f*.
France [frɑ:ns] *n* France *f*.
franchise ['fræntʃaɪz] *n* (POL) droit *m* de vote.
frank [fræŋk] *a* franc(franche) // *vt* (*letter*) affranchir; ~**ly** *ad* franchement; ~**ness** *n* franchise *f*.
frantic ['fræntɪk] *a* frénétique; ~**ally** *ad* frénétiquement.
fraternal [frə'tə:nl] *a* fraternel(le).
fraternity [frə'tə:nɪtɪ] *n* (*club*) communauté *f*, confrérie *f*; (*spirit*) fraternité *f*.
fraternize ['frætənaɪz] *vi* fraterniser.
fraud [frɔ:d] *n* supercherie *f*, fraude *f*, tromperie *f*; imposteur *m*.
fraudulent ['frɔ:djulənt] *a* frauduleux(euse).
fraught [frɔ:t] *a*: ~ **with** chargé(e) de, plein(e) de.
fray [freɪ] *n* bagarre *f* // *vt* effilocher // *vi* s'effilocher; **tempers were** ~**ed** les gens commençaient à s'énerver *or* perdre patience; **her nerves were** ~**ed** elle était à bout de nerfs.
freak [fri:k] *n* (*also cpd*) phénomène *m*, *créature ou événement exceptionnel par sa rareté, son caractère d'anomalie.*
freckle ['frɛkl] *n* tache *f* de rousseur.
free [fri:] *a* libre; (*gratis*) gratuit(e); (*liberal*) généreux(euse), large // *vt* (*prisoner etc*) libérer; (*jammed object or person*) dégager; ~ (**of charge**) *ad* gratuitement; ~**dom** ['fri:dəm] *n* liberté *f*; ~**-for-all** *n* mêlée générale; ~ **kick** *n* coup franc; ~**lance** *a* indépendant(e); ~**ly** *ad* librement; (*liberally*) libéralement; ~**mason** *n* franc-maçon *m*; ~**masonry** *n* franc-maçonnerie *f*; ~ **trade** *n* libre-échange *m*; ~**way** *n* (*US*) autoroute *f*; ~**wheel** *vi* descendre en roue libre; ~ **will** *n* libre arbitre *m*; **of one's own** ~ **will** de son plein gré.
freeze [fri:z] *vb* (*pt* **froze**, *pp* **frozen** [frəuz, 'frəuzn]) *vi* geler // *vt* geler; (*food*) congeler; (*prices, salaries*) bloquer, geler // *n* gel *m*; blocage *m*; ~**-dried** *a* lyophilisé(e); ~**r** *n* congélateur *m*.
freezing ['fri:zɪŋ] *a*: ~ **cold** *a* glacial(e); ~ **point** *n* point *m* de congélation; **3 degrees below** ~ 3 degrés au-dessous de zéro.
freight [freɪt] *n* (*goods*) fret *m*, cargaison *f*; (*money charged*) fret, prix *m* du transport; ~ **car** *n* (*US*) wagon *m* de marchandises; ~**er** *n* (NAUT) cargo *m*.
French [frɛntʃ] *a* français(e) // *n* (LING) français *m*; **the** ~ les Français; ~ **fried (potatoes)** *npl* (pommes de terre *fpl*) frites *fpl*; ~**man** *n* Français *m*; ~ **window** *n* porte-fenêtre *f*; ~**woman** *n* Française *f*.
frenzy ['frɛnzɪ] *n* frénésie *f*.
frequency ['fri:kwənsɪ] *n* fréquence *f*.
frequent *a* ['fri:kwənt] fréquent(e) // *vt* [frɪ'kwɛnt] fréquenter; ~**ly** *ad* fréquemment.
fresco ['frɛskəu] *n* fresque *f*.
fresh [frɛʃ] *a* frais(fraîche); (*new*) nouveau(nouvelle); (*cheeky*) familier(ère), culotté(e); ~**en** *vi* (*wind, air*) fraîchir; **to** ~**en up** *vi* faire un brin de toilette; ~**ly** *ad* nouvellement, récemment; ~**ness** *n* fraîcheur *f*; ~**water** *a* (*fish*) d'eau douce.
fret [frɛt] *vi* s'agiter, se tracasser.
friar ['fraɪə*] *n* moine *m*, frère *m*.
friction ['frɪkʃən] *n* friction *f*, frottement *m*.
Friday ['fraɪdɪ] *n* vendredi *m*.

fridge [frɪdʒ] *n* frigo *m*, frigidaire *m* ®.
fried [fraɪd] *pt, pp of* **fry** // *a* frit(e).
friend [frɛnd] *n* ami/e ; **to make ~s with** se lier (d'amitié) avec ; **~liness** *n* attitude amicale ; **~ly** *a* amical(e) ; gentil(le) ; **to be ~ly with** être ami(e) avec ; **~ship** *n* amitié *f*.
frieze [fri:z] *n* frise *f*, bordure *f*.
frigate ['frɪgɪt] *n* (NAUT: *modern*) frégate *f*.
fright [fraɪt] *n* peur *f*, effroi *m* ; **she looks a ~** elle a l'air d'un épouvantail ; **~en** *vt* effrayer, faire peur à ; **~ened** *a*: **to be ~ened (of)** avoir peur (de) ; **~ening** *a* effrayant(e) ; **~ful** *a* affreux(euse) ; **~fully** *ad* affreusement.
frigid ['frɪdʒɪd] *a* (*woman*) frigide ; **~ity** [frɪ'dʒɪdɪtɪ] *n* frigidité *f*.
frill [frɪl] *n* (*of dress*) volant *m* ; (*of shirt*) jabot *m*.
fringe [frɪndʒ] *n* frange *f* ; (*edge*: *of forest etc*) bordure *f* ; (*fig*): **on the ~** en marge ; **~ benefits** *npl* avantages sociaux *or* en nature.
frisk [frɪsk] *vt* fouiller.
frisky ['frɪskɪ] *a* vif(vive), sémillant(e).
fritter ['frɪtə*] *n* beignet *m* ; **to ~ away** *vt* gaspiller.
frivolity [frɪ'vɔlɪtɪ] *n* frivolité *f*.
frivolous ['frɪvələs] *a* frivole.
frizzy ['frɪzɪ] *a* crépu(e).
fro [frəu] *see* **to**.
frock [frɔk] *n* robe *f*.
frog [frɔg] *n* grenouille *f* ; **~man** *n* homme-grenouille *m*.
frolic ['frɔlɪk] *n* ébats *mpl* // *vi* folâtrer, batifoler.
from [frɔm] *prep* de ; **~ a pound/January** à partir d'une livre/de janvier ; **~ what he says** d'après ce qu'il dit.
front [frʌnt] *n* (*of house, dress*) devant *m* ; (*of coach, train*) avant *m* ; (*of book*) couverture *f* ; (*promenade*: *also*: **sea ~**) bord *m* de mer ; (MIL, POL, METEOROLOGY) front *m* ; (*fig*: *appearances*) contenance *f*, façade *f* // *a* de devant ; premier(ère) ; **in ~ (of)** devant ; **~age** ['frʌntɪdʒ] *n* façade *f* ; **~al** *a* frontal(e) ; **~ door** *n* porte *f* d'entrée ; (*of car*) portière *f* avant ; **~ier** ['frʌntɪə*] *n* frontière *f* ; **~ page** *n* première page ; **~ room** *n* (*Brit*) pièce *f* de devant, salon *m* ; **~-wheel drive** *n* traction *f* avant.
frost [frɔst] *n* gel *m*, gelée *f* ; **~bite** *n* gelures *fpl* ; **~ed** *a* (*glass*) dépoli(e) ; **~y** *a* (*window*) couvert(e) de givre ; (*welcome*) glacial(e).
froth ['frɔθ] *n* mousse *f* ; écume *f*.
frown [fraun] *n* froncement *m* de sourcils // *vi* froncer les sourcils.
froze [frəuz] *pt of* **freeze** ; **~n** *pp of* **freeze** // *a* (*food*) congelé(e).
frugal ['fru:gəl] *a* frugal(e).
fruit [fru:t] *n, pl inv* fruit *m* ; **~erer** *n* fruitier *m*, marchand/e de fruits ; **~ful** *a* fructueux(euse) ; (*plant, soil*) fécond(e) ; **~ion** [fru:'ɪʃən] *n*: **to come to ~ion** se réaliser ; **~ machine** *n* machine *f* à sous ; **~ salad** *n* salade *f* de fruits.
frustrate [frʌs'treɪt] *vt* frustrer ; (*plot, plans*) faire échouer ; **~d** *a* frustré(e) ;
frustration [-'treɪʃən] *n* frustration *f*.

fry, *pt, pp* **fried** [fraɪ, -d] *vt* (faire) frire ; **the small ~** le menu fretin ; **~ing pan** *n* poêle *f* (à frire).
ft. *abbr of* **foot, feet**.
fuchsia ['fju:ʃə] *n* fuchsia *m*.
fuddy-duddy ['fʌdɪdʌdɪ] *n* (*pej*) vieux schnock.
fudge [fʌdʒ] *n* (CULIN) *sorte de confiserie à base de sucre, de beurre et de lait*.
fuel [fjuəl] *n* (*for heating*) combustible *m* ; (*for propelling*) carburant *m* ; **~ oil** *n* mazout *m* ; **~ tank** *n* cuve *f* à mazout, citerne *f* ; (*on vehicle*) réservoir *m* de *or* à carburant.
fugitive ['fju:dʒɪtɪv] *n* fugitif/ive.
fulfil [ful'fɪl] *vt* (*function*) remplir ; (*order*) exécuter ; (*wish, desire*) satisfaire, réaliser ; **~ment** *n* (*of wishes*) réalisation *f*.
full [ful] *a* plein(e) ; (*details, information*) complet(ète) ; (*skirt*) ample, large // *ad*: **to know ~ well that** savoir fort bien que ; **I'm ~** j'ai bien mangé ; **~ employment/fare** plein emploi/tarif ; **a ~ two hours** deux bonnes heures ; **at ~ speed** à toute vitesse ; **in ~** (*reproduce, quote*) intégralement ; (*write name etc*) en toutes lettres ; **~back** *n* (RUGBY, FOOTBALL) arrière *m* ; **~-length** *a* (*portrait*) en pied ; **~ moon** *n* pleine lune ; **~-sized** *a* (*portrait etc*) grandeur nature *inv* ; **~ stop** *n* point *m* ; **~-time** *a* (*work*) à plein temps // *n* (SPORT) fin *f* du match ; **~y** *ad* entièrement, complètement ; **~y-fledged** *a* (*teacher, barrister*) diplômé(e) ; (*citizen, member*) à part entière.
fumble ['fʌmbl] *vi* fouiller, tâtonner // *vt* (*ball*) mal réceptionner, cafouiller ; **to ~ with** *vt fus* tripoter.
fume [fju:m] *vi* rager ; **~s** *npl* vapeurs *fpl*, émanations *fpl*, gaz *mpl*.
fumigate ['fju:mɪgeɪt] *vt* désinfecter (par fumigation).
fun [fʌn] *n* amusement *m*, divertissement *m* ; **to have ~** s'amuser ; **for ~** pour rire ; **it's not much ~** ce n'est pas très drôle *or* amusant ; **to make ~ of** *vt fus* se moquer de.
function ['fʌŋkʃən] *n* fonction *f* ; cérémonie *f*, soirée officielle // *vi* fonctionner ; **~al** *a* fonctionnel(le).
fund [fʌnd] *n* caisse *f*, fonds *m* ; (*source, store*) source *f*, mine *f* ; **~s** *npl* fonds *mpl*.
fundamental [fʌndə'mɛntl] *a* fondamental(e) ; **~s** *npl* principes *mpl* de base ; **~ly** *ad* fondamentalement.
funeral ['fju:nərəl] *n* enterrement *m*, obsèques *fpl* (*more formal occasion*) ; **~ director** *n* entrepreneur *m* des pompes funèbres ; **~ service** *n* service *m* funèbre.
funereal [fju:'nɪərɪəl] *a* lugubre, funèbre.
fun fair ['fʌnfɛə*] *n* fête (foraine).
fungus, *pl* **fungi** ['fʌŋgəs, -gaɪ] *n* champignon *m* ; (*mould*) moisissure *f*.
funnel ['fʌnl] *n* entonnoir *m* ; (*of ship*) cheminée *f*.
funnily ['fʌnɪlɪ] *ad* drôlement ; curieusement.
funny ['fʌnɪ] *a* amusant(e), drôle ; (*strange*) curieux(euse), bizarre.
fur [fə:*] *n* fourrure *f* ; (*in kettle etc*) (dépôt *m* de) tartre *m* ; **~ coat** *n* manteau *m* de fourrure.

furious ['fjuərıəs] *a* furieux(euse); (*effort*) acharné(e); **~ly** *ad* furieusement; avec acharnement.
furl [fə:l] *vt* rouler; (*NAUT*) ferler.
furlong ['fə:lɔŋ] *n* = *201.17 m* (*terme d'hippisme*).
furlough ['fə:ləu] *n* (*US*) permission *f*, congé *m*.
furnace ['fə:nıs] *n* fourneau *m*.
furnish ['fə:nıʃ] *vt* meubler; (*supply*) fournir; **~ings** *npl* mobilier *m*, articles *mpl* d'ameublement.
furniture ['fə:nıtʃə*] *n* meubles *mpl*, mobilier *m*; **piece of ~** meuble *m*; **~ polish** *n* encaustique *f*.
furrier ['fʌrıə*] *n* fourreur *m*.
furrow ['fʌrəu] *n* sillon *m*.
furry ['fə:rı] *a* (*animal*) à fcurrure; (*toy*) en peluche.
further ['fə:ðə*] *a* supplémentaire, autre; nouveau(nouvelle); plus loin // *ad* plus loin; (*more*) davantage; (*moreover*) de plus // *vt* faire avancer *or* progresser, promouvoir; **until ~ notice** jusqu'à nouvel ordre *or* avis; **~ education** *n* enseignement *m* post-scolaire (*recyclage, formation professionnelle*); **~more** [fə:ðə'mɔ:*] *ad* de plus, en outre.
furthest ['fə:ðıst] *superlative of* **far**.
furtive ['fə:tıv] *a* furtif(ive); **~ly** *ad* furtivement.
fury ['fjuərı] *n* fureur *f*.
fuse, fuze (*US*) [fju:z] *n* fusible *m*; (*for bomb etc*) amorce *f*, détonateur *m* // *vt,vi* (*metal*) fondre; (*fig*) fusionner; (*ELEC*): **to ~ the lights** faire sauter les fusibles *or* les plombs; **~ box** *n* boîte *f* à fusibles.
fuselage ['fju:zəlɑ:ʒ] *n* fuselage *m*.
fusion ['fju:ʒən] *n* fusion *f*.
fuss [fʌs] *n* chichis *mpl*, façons *fpl*, embarras *mpl*; (*complaining*) histoire(s) *f(pl)*; **to make a ~** faire des façons *etc*; **~y** *a* (*person*) tatillon(ne), difficile; chichiteux(euse); (*dress, style*) tarabiscoté(e).
futile ['fju:taıl] *a* futile.
futility [fju:'tılıtı] *n* futilité *f*.
future ['fju:tʃə*] *a* futur(e) // *n* avenir *m*; (*LING*) futur *m*; **in (the) ~** à l'avenir; **futuristic** [-'rıstık] *a* futuriste.
fuze [fju:z] *n, vt, vi* (*US*) = **fuse**.
fuzzy ['fʌzı] *a* (*PHOT*) flou(e); (*hair*) crépu(e).

G

g. *abbr of* **gram(s)**.
G [dʒi:] *n* (*MUS*) sol *m*.
gabble ['gæbl] *vi* bredouiller; jacasser.
gable ['geıbl] *n* pignon *m*.
gadget ['gædʒıt] *n* gadget *m*.
Gaelic ['geılık] *n* (*LING*) gaélique *m*.
gag [gæg] *n* bâillon *m*; (*joke*) gag *m* // *vt* bâillonner.
gaiety ['geııtı] *n* gaieté *f*.
gaily ['geılı] *ad* gaiement.
gain [geın] *n* gain *m*, profit *m* // *vt* gagner // *vi* (*watch*) avancer; **to ~ in/by** gagner en/à; **to ~ 3lbs (in weight)** prendre 3 livres; **~ful** *a* profitable, lucratif(ive).
gainsay [geın'seı] *vt irg* (*like* **say**) contredire; nier.
gait [geıt] *n* démarche *f*.
gal. *abbr of* **gallon**.
gala ['gɑ:lə] *n* gala *m*.
galaxy ['gæləksı] *n* galaxie *f*.
gale [geıl] *n* rafale *f* de vent; coup *m* de vent.
gallant ['gælənt] *a* vaillant(e), brave; (*towards ladies*) empressé(e), galant(e); **~ry** *n* bravoure *f*, vaillance *f*; empressement *m*, galanterie *f*.
gall-bladder ['gɔ:lblædə*] *n* vésicule *f* biliaire.
gallery ['gælərı] *n* galerie *f*; (*also*: **art ~**) musée *m*; (: *private*) galerie.
galley ['gælı] *n* (*ship's kitchen*) cambuse *f*; (*ship*) galère *f*; (*TYP*) placard *m*, galée *f*.
gallon ['gæln] *n* gallon *m* (= *4.543 l*; *8 pints*).
gallop ['gæləp] *n* galop *m* // *vi* galoper.
gallows ['gæləuz] *n* potence *f*.
gallstone ['gɔ:lstəun] *n* calcul *m* (biliaire).
gambit ['gæmbıt] *n* (*fig*): **(opening) ~** manœuvre *f* stratégique.
gamble ['gæmbl] *n* pari *m*, risque calculé // *vt, vi* jouer; **to ~ on** (*fig*) miser sur; **~r** *n* joueur *m*; **gambling** *n* jeu *m*.
game [geım] *n* jeu *m*; (*event*) match *m*; (*HUNTING*) gibier *m* // *a* brave; (*ready*): **to be ~ (for sth/to do)** être prêt(e) (à qch/à faire), se sentir de taille (à faire); **a ~ of football/tennis** une partie de football/tennis; **big ~** *n* gros gibier; **~keeper** *n* garde-chasse *m*.
gammon ['gæmən] *n* (*bacon*) quartier *m* de lard fumé; (*ham*) jambon fumé.
gamut ['gæmət] *n* gamme *f*.
gang [gæŋ] *n* bande *f*, groupe *m* // *vi*: **to ~ up on sb** se liguer contre qn.
gangrene ['gæŋgri:n] *n* gangrène *f*.
gangster ['gæŋstə*] *n* gangster *m*, bandit *m*.
gangway ['gæŋweı] *n* passerelle *f*; (*of bus*) couloir central; (*THEATRE, CINEMA*) allée *f*.
gantry ['gæntrı] *n* portique *m*.
gaol [dʒeıl] *n, vt* = **jail**.
gap [gæp] *n* trou *m*; (*in time*) intervalle *f*; (*fig*) lacune *f*; vide *m*.
gape [geıp] *vi* être *or* rester bouche bée; **gaping** *a* (*hole*) béant(e).
garage ['gærɑ:ʒ] *n* garage *m*.
garb [gɑ:b] *n* tenue *f*, costume *m*.
garbage ['gɑ:bıdʒ] *n* ordures *fpl*, détritus *mpl*; **~ can** *n* (*US*) poubelle *f*, boîte *f* à ordures.
garbled ['gɑ:bld] *a* déformé(e); faussé(e).
garden ['gɑ:dn] *n* jardin *m* // *vi* jardiner; **~er** *n* jardinier *m*; **~ing** jardinage *m*.
gargle ['gɑ:gl] *vi* se gargariser // *n* gargarisme *m*.
gargoyle ['gɑ:gɔıl] *n* gargouille *f*.
garish ['gɛərıʃ] *a* criard(e), voyant(e).
garland ['gɑ:lənd] *n* guirlande *f*; couronne *f*.
garlic ['gɑ:lık] *n* ail *m*.
garment ['gɑ:mənt] *n* vêtement *m*.
garnish ['gɑ:nıʃ] *vt* garnir.
garret ['gærıt] *n* mansarde *f*.
garrison ['gærısn] *n* garnison *f* // *vt* mettre en garnison, stationner.

garrulous ['gærjuləs] *a* volubile, loquace.
garter ['gɑ:tə*] *n* jarretière *f*.
gas [gæs] *n* gaz *m*; (*used as anaesthetic*): **to be given ~** se faire endormir; (*US*: *gasoline*) essence *f* // *vt* asphyxier; (*MIL*) gazer; **~ cooker** *n* cuisinière *f* à gaz; **~ cylinder** *n* bouteille *f* de gaz; **~ fire** *n* radiateur *m* à gaz.
gash [gæʃ] *n* entaille *f*; (*on face*) balafre *f* // *vt* taillader; balafrer.
gasket ['gæskɪt] *n* (*AUT*) joint *m* de culasse.
gasmask ['gæsmɑ:sk] *n* masque *m* à gaz.
gas meter ['gæsmi:tə*] *n* compteur *m* à gaz.
gasoline ['gæsəli:n] *n* (*US*) essence *f*.
gasp [gɑ:sp] *vi* haleter; (*fig*) avoir le souffle coupé.
gas ring ['gæsrɪŋ] *n* brûleur *m*.
gas stove ['gæsstəuv] *n* réchaud *m* à gaz; (*cooker*) cuisinière *f* à gaz.
gassy ['gæsɪ] *a* gazeux(euse).
gastric ['gæstrɪk] *a* gastrique; **~ ulcer** *n* ulcère *m* de l'estomac.
gastronomy [gæs'trɔnəmɪ] *n* gastronomie *f*.
gasworks ['gæswə:ks] *n* usine *f* à gaz.
gate [geɪt] *n* (*of garden*) portail *m*; (*of farm*) barrière *f*; (*of building*) porte *f*; (*of lock*) vanne *f*; **~crash** *vt* s'introduire sans invitation dans; **~way** *n* porte *f*.
gather ['gæðə*] *vt* (*flowers, fruit*) cueillir; (*pick up*) ramasser; (*assemble*) rassembler, réunir; recueillir; (*understand*) comprendre // *vi* (*assemble*) se rassembler; **to ~ speed** prendre de la vitesse; **~ing** *n* rassemblement *m*.
gauche [gəuʃ] *a* gauche, maladroit(e).
gaudy ['gɔ:dɪ] *a* voyant(e).
gauge [geɪdʒ] *n* (*standard measure*) calibre *m*; (*RAIL*) écartement *m*; (*instrument*) jauge *f* // *vt* jauger.
gaunt [gɔ:nt] *a* décharné(e); (*grim, desolate*) désolé(e).
gauntlet ['gɔ:ntlɪt] *n* (*fig*): **to run the ~ through an angry crowd** se frayer un passage à travers une foule hostile *or* entre deux haies de manifestants *etc* hostiles.
gauze [gɔ:z] *n* gaze *f*.
gave [geɪv] *pt of* **give**.
gavel ['gævl] *n* marteau *m*.
gawp [gɔ:p] *vi*: **to ~ at** regarder bouche bée.
gay [geɪ] *a* (*person*) gai(e), réjoui(e); (*colour*) gai, vif(vive); (*col*) homosexuel(le).
gaze [geɪz] *n* regard *m* fixe; **to ~ at** *vt* fixer du regard.
gazelle [gə'zɛl] *n* gazelle *f*.
gazetteer [gæzə'tɪə*] *n* dictionnaire *m* géographique.
gazumping [gə'zʌmpɪŋ] *n le fait de revenir sur une promesse de vente pour accepter un prix plus élevé.*
G.B. *abbr of* **Great Britain**.
G.C.E. *n* (*abbr of General Certificate of Education*) ≈ baccalauréat *m*.
Gdns. *abbr of gardens*.
gear [gɪə*] *n* matériel *m*, équipement *m*; attirail *m*; (*TECH*) engrenage *m*; (*AUT*) vitesse *f*; **top/low/bottom ~** quatrième (*or* cinquième/deuxième/première vitesse; **in ~** en prise; **out of ~** au point mort; **~ box** *n* boîte *f* de vitesse; **~ lever, ~ shift** (*US*) *n* levier *m* de vitesse.
geese [gi:s] *npl of* **goose**.
gelatin(e) ['dʒɛləti:n] *n* gélatine *f*.
gelignite ['dʒɛlɪgnaɪt] *n* plastic *m*.
gem [dʒɛm] *n* pierre précieuse.
Gemini ['dʒɛmɪnaɪ] *n* les Gémeaux *mpl*; **to be ~** être des Gémeaux.
gender ['dʒɛndə*] *n* genre *m*.
general ['dʒɛnərl] *n* général *m* // *a* général(e); **in ~** en général; **~ election** *n* élection(s) législative(s); **~ization** [-'zeɪʃən] *n* généralisation *f*; **~ize** *vi* généraliser; **~ly** *ad* généralement; **G~ Post Office (GPO)** *n* Postes et Télécommunications *fpl* (PTT); **~ practitioner (G.P.)** *n* généraliste *m/f*; **who's your G.P.?** qui est votre médecin traitant?
generate ['dʒɛnəreɪt] *vt* engendrer; (*electricity*) produire.
generation [dʒɛnə'reɪʃən] *n* génération *f*.
generator ['dʒɛnəreɪtə*] *n* générateur *m*.
generosity [dʒɛnə'rɔsɪtɪ] *n* générosité *f*.
generous ['dʒɛnərəs] *a* généreux (euse); (*copious*) copieux(euse).
genetics [dʒɪ'nɛtɪks] *n* génétique *f*.
Geneva [dʒɪ'ni:və] *n* Genève.
genial ['dʒi:nɪəl] *a* cordial(e), chaleureux(euse); (*climate*) clément(e).
genitals ['dʒɛnɪtlz] *npl* organes génitaux.
genitive ['dʒɛnɪtɪv] *n* génitif *m*.
genius ['dʒi:nɪəs] *n* génie *m*.
gent [dʒɛnt] *n abbr of* **gentleman**.
genteel [dʒɛn'ti:l] *a* de bon ton, distingué(e).
gentle ['dʒɛntl] *a* doux(douce).
gentleman ['dʒɛntlmən] *n* monsieur *m*; (*well-bred man*) gentleman *m*.
gentleness ['dʒɛntlnɪs] *n* douceur *f*.
gently ['dʒɛntlɪ] *ad* doucement.
gentry ['dʒɛntrɪ] *n* petite noblesse.
gents [dʒɛnts] *n* W.-C. *mpl* (pour hommes).
genuine ['dʒɛnjuɪn] *a* véritable, authentique; sincère.
geographer [dʒɪ'ɔgrəfə*] *n* géographe *m/f*.
geographic(al) [dʒɪə'græfɪk(l)] *a* géographique.
geography [dʒɪ'ɔgrəfɪ] *n* géographie *f*.
geological [dʒɪə'lɔdʒɪkl] *a* géologique.
geologist [dʒɪ'ɔlədʒɪst] *n* géologue *m/f*.
geology [dʒɪ'ɔlədʒɪ] *n* géologie *f*.
geometric(al) [dʒɪə'mɛtrɪk(l)] *a* géométrique.
geometry [dʒɪ'ɔmətrɪ] *n* géométrie *f*.
geranium [dʒɪ'reɪnjəm] *n* géranium *m*.
germ [dʒə:m] *n* (*MED*) microbe *m*; (*BIO, fig*) germe *m*.
German ['dʒə:mən] *a* allemand(e) // *n* Allemand/e; (*LING*) allemand *m*; **~ measles** *n* rubéole *f*.
Germany ['dʒə:mənɪ] *n* Allemagne *f*.
germination [dʒə:mɪ'neɪʃən] *n* germination *f*.
gerrymandering ['dʒɛrɪmændərɪŋ] *n* tripotage *m* du découpage électoral.
gestation [dʒɛs'teɪʃən] *n* gestation *f*.

gesticulate [dʒɛs'tıkjuleıt] *vi* gesticuler.
gesture ['dʒɛstjə*] *n* geste *m*.
get, *pt, pp* **got,** *pp* **gotten** (*US*) [gɛt, gɔt, 'gɔtn] *vt* (*obtain*) avoir, obtenir; (*receive*) recevoir; (*find*) trouver, acheter; (*catch*) attraper; (*fetch*) aller chercher; (*understand*) comprendre, saisir; (*have*): **to have got** avoir; (*become*): **to ~ rich/old** s'enrichir/vieillir // *vi*: **to ~ to** (*place*) aller à; arriver à; parvenir à; **he got across the bridge/under the fence** il a traversé le pont/est passé par-dessous la barrière; **to ~ ready/washed/shaved** *etc* se préparer/laver/raser *etc*; **to ~ sb to do sth** faire faire qch à qn; **to ~ sth through/out of** faire passer qch par/sortir qch de; **to ~ about** *vi* se déplacer; (*news*) se répandre; **to ~ along** *vi* (*agree*) s'entendre; (*depart*) s'en aller; (*manage*) = **to get by**; **to ~ at** *vt fus* (*attack*) s'en prendre à; (*reach*) attraper, atteindre; **to ~ away** *vi* partir, s'en aller; (*escape*) s'échapper; **to ~ away with** *vt fus* en être quitte pour; se faire passer *or* pardonner; **to ~ back** *vi* (*return*) rentrer // *vt* récupérer, recouvrer; **to ~ by** *vi* (*pass*) passer; (*manage*) se débrouiller; **to ~ down** *vi, vt fus* descendre // *vt* descendre; (*depress*) déprimer; **to ~ down to** *vt fus* (*work*) se mettre à (faire); **to ~ in** *vi* entrer; (*train*) arriver; (*arrive home*) rentrer; **to ~ into** *vt fus* entrer dans; **to ~ into bed/a rage** se mettre au lit/en colère; **to ~ off** *vi* (*from train etc*) descendre; (*depart*: *person, car*) s'en aller; (*escape*) s'en tirer // *vt* (*remove*: *clothes, stain*) enlever // *vt fus* (*train, bus*) descendre de; **to ~ on** *vi* (*at exam etc*) se débrouiller; (*agree*): **to ~ on (with)** s'entendre (avec) // *vt fus* monter dans; (*horse*) monter sur; **to ~ out** *vi* sortir; (*of vehicle*) descendre // *vt* sortir; **to ~ out of** *vt fus* sortir de; (*duty etc*) échapper à, se soustraire à; **to ~ over** *vt fus* (*illness*) se remettre de; **to ~ round** *vt fus* contourner; (*fig*: *person*) entortiller; **to ~ through** *vi* (TEL) avoir la communication; **to ~ through to** *vt fus* (TEL) atteindre; **to ~ together** *vi* se réunir // *vt* assembler; **to ~ up** *vi* (*rise*) se lever // *vt fus* monter; **to ~ up to** *vt fus* (*reach*) arriver à; (*prank etc*) faire; **~away** *n* fuite *f*.
geyser ['gi:zə*] *n* chauffe-eau *m inv*; (GEO) geyser *m*.
Ghana ['gɑ:nə] *n* Ghana *m*; **~ian** [-'neıən] *a* ghanéen(ne) // *n* Ghanéen/ne.
ghastly ['gɑ:stlı] *a* atroce, horrible; (*pale*) livide, blême.
gherkin ['gə:kın] *n* cornichon *m*.
ghetto ['gɛtəu] *n* ghetto *m*.
ghost [gəust] *n* fantôme *m*, revenant *m*; **~ly** *a* fantomatique.
giant ['dʒaıənt] *n* géant/e // *a* géant(e), énorme.
gibberish ['dʒıbərıʃ] *n* charabia *m*.
gibe [dʒaıb] *n* sarcasme *m* // *vi*: **to ~ at** railler.
giblets ['dʒıblıts] *npl* abats *mpl*.
giddiness ['gıdınıs] *n* vertige *m*.
giddy ['gıdı] *a* (*dizzy*): **to be ~** avoir le vertige; (*height*) vertigineux(euse); (*thoughtless*) sot(te), étourdi(e).
gift [gıft] *n* cadeau *m*, présent *m*; (*donation, ability*) don *m*; **~ed** *a* doué(e).
gigantic [dʒaı'gæntık] *a* gigantesque.
giggle ['gıgl] *vi* pouffer, ricaner sottement // *n* petit rire sot, ricanement *m*.
gild [gıld] *vt* dorer.
gill *n* [dʒıl] (*measure*) = *0.14 l*; *0.25 pints*; **~s** [gılz] *npl* (*of fish*) ouïes *fpl*, branchies *fpl*.
gilt [gılt] *n* dorure *f* // *a* doré(e).
gimlet ['gımlıt] *n* vrille *f*.
gimmick ['gımık] *n* truc *m*.
gin [dʒın] *n* (*liquor*) gin *m*.
ginger ['dʒındʒə*] *n* gingembre *m*; **to ~ up** *vt* secouer; animer; **~ ale, ~ beer** *n* boisson gazeuse au gingembre; **~bread** *n* pain *m* d'épices; **~ group** *n* groupe *m* de pression; **~-haired** *a* roux(rousse).
gingerly ['dʒındʒəlı] *ad* avec précaution.
gingham ['gıŋəm] *n* vichy *m*.
gipsy ['dʒıpsı] *n* gitan/e, bohémien/ne.
giraffe [dʒı'rɑ:f] *n* girafe *f*.
girder ['gə:də*] *n* poutrelle *f*.
girdle ['gə:dl] *n* (*corset*) gaine *f* // *vt* ceindre.
girl [gə:l] *n* fille *f*, fillette *f*; (*young unmarried woman*) jeune fille; (*daughter*) fille; **an English ~** une jeune Anglaise; **a little English ~** une petite Anglaise; **~friend** *n* (*of girl*) amie *f*; (*of boy*) petite amie; **~ish** *a* de jeune fille.
Giro ['dʒaırəu] *n*: **the National ~** ≈ les comptes chèques postaux.
girth [gə:θ] *n* circonférence *f*; (*of horse*) sangle *f*.
gist [dʒıst] *n* essentiel *m*.
give [gıv] *n* (*of fabric*) élasticité *f* // *vb* (*pt* **gave,** *pp* **given** [geıv, 'gıvn]) *vt* donner // *vi* (*break*) céder; (*stretch*: *fabric*) se prêter; **to ~ sb sth, ~ sth to sb** donner qch à qn; **to ~ a cry/sigh** pousser un cri/un soupir; **to ~ away** *vt* donner; (*give free*) faire cadeau de; (*betray*) donner, trahir; (*disclose*) révéler; (*bride*) conduire à l'autel; **to ~ back** *vt* rendre; **to ~ in** *vi* céder // *vt* donner; **to ~ off** *vt* dégager; **to ~ out** *vt* distribuer; annoncer; **to ~ up** *vi* renoncer // *vt* renoncer à; **to ~ up smoking** arrêter de fumer; **to ~ o.s. up** se rendre; **to ~ way** *vi* céder; (AUT) donner la priorité.
glacier ['glæsıə*] *n* glacier *m*.
glad [glæd] *a* content(e); **~den** *vt* réjouir.
gladioli [glædı'əulaı] *npl* glaïeuls *mpl*.
gladly ['glædlı] *ad* volontiers.
glamorous ['glæmərəs] *a* séduisant(e).
glamour ['glæmə*] *n* éclat *m*, prestige *m*.
glance [glɑ:ns] *n* coup *m* d'œil // *vi*: **to ~ at** jeter un coup d'œil à; **to ~ off** (*bullet*) ricocher sur; **glancing** *a* (*blow*) oblique.
gland [glænd] *n* glande *f*.
glandular ['glændjulə*] *a*: **~ fever** *n* mononucléose infectieuse.
glare [glɛə*] *n* lumière éblouissante // *vi* briller d'un éclat aveuglant; **to ~ at** lancer un *or* des regard(s) furieux à; **glaring** *a* (*mistake*) criant(e), qui saute aux yeux.

glass [glɑ:s] *n* verre *m*; (*also*: **looking ~**) miroir *m*; **~es** *npl* lunettes *fpl*; **~house** *n* serre *f*; **~ware** *n* verrerie *f*; **~y** *a* (*eyes*) vitreux(euse).
glaze [gleɪz] *vt* (*door*) vitrer; (*pottery*) vernir // *n* vernis *m*; **~d** *a* (*eye*) vitreux(euse); (*pottery*) verni(e); (*tiles*) vitrifié(e).
glazier ['gleɪzɪə*] *n* vitrier *m*.
gleam [gli:m] *n* lueur *f*; rayon *m* // *vi* luire, briller; **~ing** *a* luisant(e).
glee [gli:] *n* joie *f*; **~ful** *a* joyeux(euse).
glen [glɛn] *n* vallée *f*.
glib [glɪb] *a* qui a du bagou; facile.
glide [glaɪd] *vi* glisser; (AVIAT, *birds*) planer // *n* glissement *m*; vol plané; **~r** *n* (AVIAT) planeur *m*; **gliding** *n* (AVIAT) vol *m* à voile.
glimmer ['glɪmə*] *vi* luire // *n* lueur *f*.
glimpse [glɪmps] *n* vision passagère, aperçu *m* // *vt* entrevoir, apercevoir.
glint [glɪnt] *n* éclair *m* // *vi* étinceler.
glisten ['glɪsn] *vi* briller, luire.
glitter ['glɪtə*] *vi* scintiller, briller // *n* scintillement *m*.
gloat [gləut] *vi*: **to ~ (over)** jubiler (à propos de).
global ['gləubl] *a* mondial(e).
globe [gləub] *n* globe *m*.
gloom [glu:m] *n* obscurité *f*; (*sadness*) tristesse *f*, mélancolie *f*; **~y** *a* sombre, triste, mélancolique.
glorification [glɔ:rɪfɪ'keɪʃən] *n* glorification *f*.
glorify ['glɔ:rɪfaɪ] *vt* glorifier.
glorious ['glɔ:rɪəs] *a* glorieux (euse); splendide.
glory ['glɔ:rɪ] *n* gloire *f*; splendeur *f*; **to ~ in** se glorifier de.
gloss [glɔs] *n* (*shine*) brillant *m*, vernis *m*; **to ~ over** *vt fus* glisser sur.
glossary ['glɔsərɪ] *n* glossaire *m*, lexique *m*.
gloss paint ['glɔspeɪnt] *n* peinture brillante.
glossy ['glɔsɪ] *a* brillant(e), luisant(e); **~ (magazine)** *n* revue *f* de luxe.
glove [glʌv] *n* gant *m*; **~ compartment** *n* (AUT) boîte *f* à gants, vide-poches *m inv*.
glow [gləu] *vi* rougeoyer; (*face*) rayonner // *n* rougeoiement *m*.
glower ['glauə*] *vi* lancer des regards mauvais.
glucose ['glu:kəus] *n* glucose *m*.
glue [glu:] *n* colle *f* // *vt* coller.
glum [glʌm] *a* maussade, morose.
glut [glʌt] *n* surabondance *f* // *vt* rassasier; (*market*) encombrer.
glutton ['glʌtn] *n* glouton/ne; **a ~ for work** un bourreau de travail; **~ous** *a* glouton(ne); **~y** *n* gloutonnerie *f*; (*sin*) gourmandise *f*.
glycerin(e) ['glɪsəri:n] *n* glycérine *f*.
gm, gms *abbr of* **gram(s)**.
gnarled [nɑ:ld] *a* noueux(euse).
gnat [næt] *n* moucheron *m*.
gnaw [nɔ:] *vt* ronger.
gnome [nəum] *n* gnome *m*, lutin *m*.
go [gəu] *vb* (*pt* **went**, *pp* **gone** [wɛnt, gɔn]) *vi* aller; (*depart*) partir, s'en aller; (*work*) marcher; (*be sold*): **to ~ for £10** se vendre 10 livres; (*fit, suit*): **to ~ with** aller avec; (*become*): **to ~ pale/mouldy** pâlir/moisir; (*break etc*) céder // *n* (*pl*: **~es**): **to have a ~ (at)** essayer (de faire); **to be on the ~** être en mouvement; **whose ~ is it?** à qui est-ce de jouer?; **he's going to do** il va faire, il est sur le point de faire; **to ~ for a walk** aller se promener; **to ~ dancing/shopping** aller danser/faire les courses; **how is it ~ing?** comment ça marche?; **how did it ~?** comment est-ce que ça s'est passé?; **to ~ round the back/by the shop** passer par derrière/devant le magasin; **to ~ about** *vi* (*rumour*) se répandre // *vt fus*: **how do I ~ about this?** comment dois-je m'y prendre (pour faire ceci)?; **to ~ ahead** *vi* (*make progress*) avancer; (*get going*) y aller; **to ~ along** *vi* aller, avancer // *vt fus* longer, parcourir; **as you ~ along (with your work)** au fur et à mesure (de votre travail); **to ~ away** *vi* partir, s'en aller; **to ~ back** *vi* rentrer; revenir; (*go again*) retourner; **to ~ back on** *vt fus* (*promise*) revenir sur; **to ~ by** *vi* (*years, time*) passer, s'écouler // *vt fus* s'en tenir à; en croire; **to ~ down** *vi* descendre; (*ship*) couler; (*sun*) se coucher // *vt fus* descendre; **to ~ for** *vt fus* (*fetch*) aller chercher; (*like*) aimer; (*attack*) s'en prendre à; attaquer; **to ~ in** *vi* entrer; **to ~ in for** *vt fus* (*competition*) se présenter à; (*like*) aimer; **to ~ into** *vt fus* entrer dans; (*investigate*) étudier, examiner; (*embark on*) se lancer dans; **to ~ off** *vi* partir, s'en aller; (*food*) se gâter; (*explode*) sauter; (*event*) se dérouler // *vt fus* ne plus aimer, ne plus avoir envie de; **the gun went off** le coup est parti; **to ~ off to sleep** s'endormir; **to ~ on** *vi* continuer; (*happen*) se passer; **to ~ on doing** continuer à faire; **to ~ on with** *vt fus* poursuivre, continuer; **to ~ out** *vi* sortir; (*fire, light*) s'éteindre; **to ~ over** *vi* (*ship*) chavirer // *vt fus* (*check*) revoir, vérifier; **to ~ through** *vt fus* (*town etc*) traverser; **to ~ up** *vi* monter; (*price*) augmenter // *vt fus* gravir; **to ~ without** *vt fus* se passer de.
goad [gəud] *vt* aiguillonner.
go-ahead ['gəuəhɛd] *a* dynamique, entreprenant(e) // *n* feu vert.
goal [gəul] *n* but *m*; **~keeper** *n* gardien *m* de but; **~-post** *n* poteau *m* de but.
goat [gəut] *n* chèvre *f*.
gobble ['gɔbl] *vt* (*also*: **~ down, ~ up**) engloutir.
go-between ['gəubɪtwi:n] *n* médiateur *m*.
goblet ['gɔblɪt] *n* goblet *m*.
goblin ['gɔblɪn] *n* lutin *m*.
go-cart ['gəukɑ:t] *n* kart *m*; **~ racing** *n* karting *m*.
god [gɔd] *n* dieu *m*; **G~** *n* Dieu *m*; **~child** *n* filleul/e; **~dess** *n* déesse *f*; **~father** *n* parrain *m*; **~-forsaken** *a* maudit(e); **~mother** *n* marraine *f*; **~send** *n* aubaine *f*; **~son** *n* filleul *m*.
goggle ['gɔgl] *vi*: **to ~ at** regarder avec des yeux ronds; **~s** *npl* lunettes *fpl* (protectrices: *de motocycliste etc*).
going ['gəuɪŋ] *n* (*conditions*) état *m* du terrain // *a*: **the ~ rate** le tarif (en

vigueur); **a ~ concern** une affaire prospère.
go-kart ['gəukɑ:t] *n* = **go-cart**.
gold [gəuld] *n* or *m* // *a* en or; **~en** *a* (*made of gold*) en or; (*gold in colour*) doré(e); **~en rule/age** règle/âge d'or; **~fish** *n* poisson *m* rouge; **~mine** *n* mine *f* d'or.
golf [gɔlf] *n* golf *m*; **~ club** *n* club *m* de golf; (*stick*) club *m*, crosse *f* de golf; **~ course** *n* terrain *m* de golf; **~er** *n* joueur/euse de golf.
gondola ['gɔndələ] *n* gondole *f*.
gone [gɔn] *pp of* **go** // *a* parti(e).
gong [gɔŋ] *n* gong *m*.
good [gud] *a* bon(ne); (*kind*) gentil(le); (*child*) sage // *n* bien *m*; **~s** *npl* marchandise *f*; articles *mpl*; **she is ~ with children/her hands** elle sait bien s'occuper des enfants/sait se servir de ses mains; **would you be ~ enough to ...?** auriez-vous la bonté *or* l'amabilité de ...?; **a ~ deal (of)** beaucoup (de); **a ~ many** beaucoup (de); **~ morning/afternoon!** bonjour!; **~ evening!** bonsoir!; **~ night!** bonsoir!; (*on going to bed*) bonne nuit!; **~bye!** au revoir!; **G~ Friday** *n* Vendredi saint; **~-looking** *a* bien *inv*; **~ness** *n* (*of person*) bonté *f*; **for ~ness sake!** je vous en prie!; **~ness gracious!** mon Dieu!; **~will** *n* bonne volonté; (COMM) réputation *f* (auprès de la clientèle).
goose, *pl* **geese** [gu:s, gi:s] *n* oie *f*.
gooseberry ['guzbərɪ] *n* groseille *f* à maquereau; **to play ~** tenir la chandelle.
gooseflesh ['gu:sflɛʃ] *n* chair *f* de poule.
gore [gɔ:*] *vt* encorner // *n* sang *m*.
gorge [gɔ:dʒ] *n* gorge *f* // *vt*: **to ~ o.s. (on)** se gorger (de).
gorgeous ['gɔ:dʒəs] *a* splendide, superbe.
gorilla [gə'rɪlə] *n* gorille *m*.
gorse [gɔ:s] *n* ajoncs *mpl*.
gory ['gɔ:rɪ] *a* sanglant(e).
go-slow ['gəu'sləu] *n* grève perlée.
gospel ['gɔspl] *n* évangile *m*.
gossamer ['gɔsəmə*] *n* (*cobweb*) fils *mpl* de la vierge; (*light fabric*) étoffe très légère.
gossip ['gɔsɪp] *n* bavardages *mpl*; commérage *m*, cancans *mpl*; (*person*) commère *f* // *vi* bavarder; (*maliciously*) cancaner, faire des commérages.
got [gɔt] *pt,pp of* **get**; **~ten** (*US*) *pp of* **get**.
gout [gaut] *n* goutte *f*.
govern ['gʌvən] *vt* (*gen*, LING) gouverner.
governess ['gʌvənɪs] *n* gouvernante *f*.
government ['gʌvnmənt] *n* gouvernement *m*; (*ministers*) ministère *m* // *cpd* de l'État; **~al** [-'mɛntl] *a* gouvernemental(e).
governor ['gʌvənə*] *n* (*of state, bank*) gouverneur *m*; (*of school, hospital*) administrateur *m*.
Govt *abbr of* **government**.
gown [gaun] *n* robe *f*; (*of teacher, judge*) toge *f*.
G.P. *n abbr see* **general**.
GPO *n abbr see* **general**.
grab [græb] *vt* saisir, empoigner; (*property, power*) se saisir de.
grace [greɪs] *n* grâce *f* // *vt* honorer; **5 days' ~** répit *m* de 5 jours; **to say ~** dire le bénédicité; (*after meal*) dire les grâces; **~ful** *a* gracieux(euse), élégant(e); **gracious** ['greɪʃəs] *a* bienveillant(e); de bonne grâce; miséricordieux(euse).
gradation [grə'deɪʃən] *n* gradation *f*.
grade [greɪd] *n* (COMM) qualité *f*; calibre *m*; catégorie *f*; (*in hierarchy*) grade *m*, échelon *m*; (*US*: SCOL) note *f*; classe *f* // *vt* classer; calibrer; graduer; **~ crossing** *n* (*US*) passage *m* à niveau.
gradient ['greɪdɪənt] *n* inclinaison *f*, pente *f*; (GEOM) gradient *m*.
gradual ['grædjuəl] *a* graduel(le), progressif(ive); **~ly** *ad* peu à peu, graduellement.
graduate *n* ['grædjuɪt] diplômé/e d'université // *vi* ['grædjueɪt] obtenir un diplôme d'université; **graduation** [-'eɪʃən] *n* cérémonie *f* de remise des diplômes.
graft [grɑ:ft] *n* (AGR, MED) greffe *f*; (*bribery*) corruption *f* // *vt* greffer; **hard ~** *n* (*col*) boulot acharné.
grain [greɪn] *n* grain *m*; **it goes against the ~** cela va à l'encontre de sa (*or* ma) nature.
gram [græm] *n* gramme *m*.
grammar ['græmə*] *n* grammaire *f*.
grammatical [grə'mætɪkl] *a* grammatical(e).
gramme [græm] *n* = **gram**.
gramophone ['græməfəun] *n* gramophone *m*.
granary ['grænərɪ] *n* grenier *m*.
grand [grænd] *a* magnifique, splendide; noble; **~children** *npl* petits-enfants *mpl*; **~dad** *n* grand-papa *m*; **~daughter** *n* petite-fille *f*; **~eur** ['grændjə*] *n* grandeur *f*, noblesse *f*; **~father** *n* grand-père *m*; **~iose** ['grændɪəuz] *a* grandiose; (*pej*) pompeux(euse); **~ma** *n* grand-maman *f*; **~mother** *n* grand-mère *f*; **~pa** *n* = **~dad**; **~ piano** *n* piano *m* à queue; **~son** *n* petit-fils *m*; **~stand** *n* (SPORT) tribune *f*.
granite ['grænɪt] *n* granit *m*.
granny ['grænɪ] *n* grand-maman *f*.
grant [grɑ:nt] *vt* accorder; (*a request*) accéder à; (*admit*) concéder // *n* (SCOL) bourse *f*; (ADMIN) subside *m*, subvention *f*; **to take sth for ~ed** considérer qch comme acquis *or* allant de soi.
granulated ['grænjuleɪtɪd] *a*: **~ sugar** *n* sucre *m* en poudre.
granule ['grænju:l] *n* granule *m*.
grape [greɪp] *n* raisin *m*.
grapefruit ['greɪpfru:t] *n* pamplemousse *m*.
graph [grɑ:f] *n* graphique *m*, courbe *f*; **~ic** *a* graphique; (*vivid*) vivant(e).
grapple ['græpl] *vi*: **to ~ with** être aux prises avec.
grasp [grɑ:sp] *vt* saisir, empoigner; (*understand*) saisir, comprendre // *n* (*grip*) prise *f*; (*fig*) emprise *f*, pouvoir *m*; compréhension *f*, connaissance *f*; **~ing** *a* avide.
grass [grɑ:s] *n* herbe *f*; gazon *m*; **~hopper** *n* sauterelle *f*; **~land** *n* prairie *f*; **~ snake** *n* couleuvre *f*; **~y** *a* herbeux(euse).
grate [greɪt] *n* grille *f* de cheminée // *vi* grincer // *vt* (CULIN) râper.

grateful ['greɪtful] *a* reconnaissant(e); **~ly** *ad* avec reconnaissance.
grater ['greɪtə*] *n* râpe *f*.
gratify ['grætɪfaɪ] *vt* faire plaisir à; (*whim*) satisfaire; **~ing** *a* agréable; satisfaisant(e).
grating ['greɪtɪŋ] *n* (*iron bars*) grille *f* // *a* (*noise*) grinçant(e).
gratitude ['grætɪtju:d] *n* gratitude *f*.
gratuitous [grə'tju:ɪtəs] *a* gratuit(e).
gratuity [grə'tju:ɪtɪ] *n* pourboire *m*.
grave [greɪv] *n* tombe *f* // *a* grave, sérieux(euse); **~digger** *n* fossoyeur *m*.
gravel ['grævl] *n* gravier *m*.
gravestone ['greɪvstəun] *n* pierre tombale.
graveyard ['greɪvjɑ:d] *n* cimetière *m*.
gravitate ['grævɪteɪt] *vi* graviter.
gravity ['grævɪtɪ] *n* (PHYSICS) gravité *f*; pesanteur *f*; (*seriousness*) gravité *f*, sérieux *m*.
gravy ['greɪvɪ] *n* jus *m* (de viande); sauce *f*.
gray [greɪ] *a* = **grey**.
graze [greɪz] *vi* paître, brouter // *vt* (*touch lightly*) frôler, effleurer; (*scrape*) écorcher // *n* (MED) écorchure *f*.
grease [gri:s] *n* (*fat*) graisse *f*; (*lubricant*) lubrifiant *m* // *vt* graisser; lubrifier; **~gun** *n* graisseur *m*; **~proof paper** *n* papier sulfurisé; **greasy** *a* gras(se), graisseux(euse).
great [greɪt] *a* grand(e); (*col*) formidable; **G~ Britain** *n* Grande-Bretagne *f*; **~-grandfather** *n* arrière-grand-père *m*; **~-grandmother** *n* arrière-grand-mère *f*; **~ly** *ad* très, grandement; (*with verbs*) beaucoup; **~ness** *n* grandeur *f*.
Grecian ['gri:ʃən] *a* grec(grecque).
Greece [gri:s] *n* Grèce *f*.
greed [gri:d] *n* (*also*: **~iness**) avidité *f*; (*for food*) gourmandise *f*; **~ily** *ad* avidement; avec gourmandise; **~y** *a* avide; gourmand(e).
Greek [gri:k] *a* grec(grecque) // *n* Grec/Grecque; (LING) grec *m*.
green [gri:n] *a* vert(e); (*inexperienced*) (bien) jeune, naïf(ïve) // *n* vert *m*; (*stretch of grass*) pelouse *f*; (*also*: **village ~**) ≈ place *f* du village; **~s** *npl* légumes verts; **~gage** *n* reine-claude *f*; **~grocer** *n* marchand *m* de fruits et légumes; **~house** *n* serre *f*; **~ish** *a* verdâtre.
Greenland ['gri:nlənd] *n* Groenland *m*.
greet [gri:t] *vt* accueillir; **~ing** *n* salutation *f*; **Christmas/birthday ~ings** souhaits *mpl* de Noël/de bon anniversaire; **~ing(s) card** *n* carte *f* de vœux.
gregarious [grə'gɛərɪəs] *a* grégaire; sociable.
grenade [grə'neɪd] *n* grenade *f*.
grew [gru:] *pt of* **grow**.
grey [greɪ] *a* gris(e); (*dismal*) sombre; **~-haired** *a* aux cheveux gris; **~hound** *n* lévrier *m*.
grid [grɪd] *n* grille *f*; (ELEC) réseau *m*; **~iron** *n* gril *m*.
grief [gri:f] *n* chagrin *m*, douleur *f*.
grievance ['gri:vəns] *n* doléance *f*, grief *m*.
grieve [gri:v] *vi* avoir du chagrin; se désoler // *vt* faire de la peine à, affliger; **to ~ at** se désoler de; pleurer.
grievous ['gri:vəs] *a* grave; cruel(le).
grill [grɪl] *n* (*on cooker*) gril *m* // *vt* griller; (*question*) interroger longuement, cuisiner.
grille [grɪl] *n* grillage *m*; (AUT) calandre *f*.
grill(room) ['grɪl(rum)] *n* rôtisserie *f*.
grim [grɪm] *a* sinistre, lugubre.
grimace [grɪ'meɪs] *n* grimace *f* // *vi* grimacer, faire une grimace.
grime [graɪm] *n* crasse *f*.
grimy ['graɪmɪ] *a* crasseux(euse).
grin [grɪn] *n* large sourire *m* // *vi* sourire.
grind [graɪnd] *vt* (*pt, pp* **ground** [graund]) écraser; (*coffee, pepper etc*) moudre; (*make sharp*) aiguiser // *n* (*work*) corvée *f*; **to ~ one's teeth** grincer des dents.
grip [grɪp] *n* étreinte *f*, poigne *f*; prise *f*; (*handle*) poignée *f*; (*holdall*) sac *m* de voyage // *vt* saisir, empoigner; étreindre; **to come to ~s with** en venir aux prises avec; **to ~ the road** (AUT) adhérer à la route.
gripe(s) [graɪp(s)] *n*(*pl*) coliques *fpl*.
gripping ['grɪpɪŋ] *a* prenant(e), palpitant(e).
grisly ['grɪzlɪ] *a* sinistre, macabre.
gristle ['grɪsl] *n* cartilage *m* (*de poulet etc*).
grit [grɪt] *n* gravillon *m*; (*courage*) cran *m* // *vt* (*road*) sabler; **to ~ one's teeth** serrer les dents.
grizzle ['grɪzl] *vi* pleurnicher.
groan [grəun] *n* gémissement *m*; grognement *m* // *vi* gémir; grogner.
grocer ['grəusə*] *n* épicier *m*; **at the ~'s** à l'épicerie, chez l'épicier; **~ies** *npl* provisions *fpl*.
grog [grɔg] *n* grog *m*.
groggy ['grɔgɪ] *a* groggy *inv*.
groin [grɔɪn] *n* aine *f*.
groom [gru:m] *n* palefrenier *m*; (*also*: **bride~**) marié *m* // *vt* (*horse*) panser; (*fig*): **to ~ sb for** former qn pour.
groove [gru:v] *n* sillon *m*, rainure *f*.
grope [grəup] *vi* tâtonner; **to ~ for** *vt fus* chercher à tâtons.
gross [grəus] *a* grossier(ère); (COMM) brut(e); **~ly** *ad* (*greatly*) très, grandement.
grotesque [grə'tɛsk] *a* grotesque.
grotto ['grɔtəu] *n* grotte *f*.
ground [graund] *pt, pp of* **grind** // *n* sol *m*, terre *f*; (*land*) terrain *m*, terres *fpl*; (SPORT) terrain; (*reason*: *gen pl*) raison *f* // *vt* (*plane*) empêcher de décoller, retenir au sol // *vi* (*ship*) s'échouer; **~s** *npl* (*of coffee etc*) marc *m*; (*gardens etc*) parc *m*, domaine *m*; **on the ~, to the ~** par terre; **~ floor** *n* rez-de-chaussée *m*; **~ing** *n* (*in education*) connaissances *fpl* de base; **~less** *a* sans fondement; **~sheet** *n* tapis *m* de sol; **~ staff** *n* équipage *m* au sol; **~work** *n* préparation *f*.
group [gru:p] *n* groupe *m* // *vt* (*also*: **~ together**) grouper // *vi* (*also*: **~ together**) se grouper.
grouse [graus] *n, pl inv* (*bird*) grouse *f* (*sorte de coq de bruyère*) // *vi* (*complain*) rouspéter, râler.
grove [grəuv] *n* bosquet *m*.

grovel ['grɔvl] *vi* (*fig*): **to ~ (before)** ramper (devant).
grow, *pt* **grew,** *pp* **grown** [grəu, gru:, grəun] *vi* (*plant*) pousser, croître; (*person*) grandir; (*increase*) augmenter, se développer; (*become*): **to ~ rich/weak** s'enrichir/s'affaiblir // *vt* cultiver, faire pousser; **to ~ up** *vi* grandir; **~er** *n* producteur *m*; **~ing** *a* (*fear, amount*) croissant(e), grandissant(e).
growl [graul] *vi* grogner.
grown [grəun] *pp of* **grow** // *a* adulte; **~-up** *n* adulte *m/f*, grande personne.
growth [grəuθ] *n* croissance *f*, développement *m*; (*what has grown*) pousse *f*; poussée *f*; (MED) grosseur *f*, tumeur *f*.
grub [grʌb] *n* larve *f*; (*col: food*) bouffe *f*.
grubby ['grʌbɪ] *a* crasseux(euse).
grudge [grʌdʒ] *n* rancune *f* // *vt*: **to ~ sb sth** donner qch à qn à contre-cœur; reprocher qch à qn; **to bear sb a ~ (for)** garder rancune *or* en vouloir à qn (de); **he ~s spending** il rechigne à dépenser; **grudgingly** *ad* à contre-cœur, de mauvaise grâce.
gruelling ['gruəlɪŋ] *a* exténuant(e).
gruesome ['gru:səm] *a* horrible.
gruff [grʌf] *a* bourru(e).
grumble ['grʌmbl] *vi* rouspéter, ronchonner.
grumpy ['grʌmpɪ] *a* grincheux (euse).
grunt [grʌnt] *vi* grogner // *n* grognement *m*.
G-string ['dʒi:strɪŋ] *n* (*garment*) cache-sexe *m inv*.
guarantee [gærən'ti:] *n* garantie *f* // *vt* garantir.
guarantor [gærən'tɔ:*] *n* garant/e.
guard [gɑ:d] *n* garde *f*, surveillance *f*; (*squad*, BOXING, FENCING) garde *f*; (*one man*) garde *m*; (RAIL) chef *m* de train // *vt* garder, surveiller; **~ed** *a* (*fig*) prudent(e); **~ian** *n* gardien/ne; (*of minor*) tuteur/trice; **~'s van** *n* (RAIL) fourgon *m*.
guerrilla [gə'rɪlə] *n* guérillero *m*; **~ warfare** *n* guérilla *f*.
guess [gɛs] *vi* deviner // *vt* deviner; (*US*) croire, penser // *n* supposition *f*, hypothèse *f*; **to take/have a ~** essayer de deviner; **~work** *n* hypothèse *f*.
guest [gɛst] *n* invité/e; (*in hotel*) client/e; **~-house** *n* pension *f*; **~ room** *n* chambre *f* d'amis.
guffaw [gʌ'fɔ:] *n* gros rire // *vi* pouffer de rire.
guidance ['gaɪdəns] *n* conseils *mpl*; **under the ~ of** conseillé(e) *or* encadré(e) par, sous la conduite de.
guide [gaɪd] *n* (*person, book etc*) guide *m* // *vt* guider; **(girl) ~** *n* guide *f*; **~book** *n* guide *m*; **~d missile** *n* missile téléguidé; **~ dog** *n* chien *m* d'aveugle; **~ lines** *npl* (*fig*) instructions générales, conseils *mpl*.
guild [gɪld] *n* corporation *f*; cercle *m*, association *f*; **~hall** *n* (*Brit*) hôtel *m* de ville.
guile [gaɪl] *n* astuce *f*; **~less** *a* candide.
guillotine ['gɪləti:n] *n* guillotine *f*; (*for paper*) massicot *m*.
guilt [gɪlt] *n* culpabilité *f*; **~y** *a* coupable.
guinea ['gɪnɪ] *n* (*Brit*) guinée *f* (= *21 shillings: cette monnaie de compte ne s'emploie plus*).
guinea pig ['gɪnɪpɪg] *n* cobaye *m*.
guise [gaɪz] *n* aspect *m*, apparence *f*.
guitar [gɪ'tɑ:*] *n* guitare *f*; **~ist** *n* guitariste *m/f*.
gulf [gʌlf] *n* golfe *m*; (*abyss*) gouffre *m*.
gull [gʌl] *n* mouette *f*.
gullet ['gʌlɪt] *n* gosier *m*.
gullible ['gʌlɪbl] *a* crédule.
gully ['gʌlɪ] *n* ravin *m*; ravine *f*; couloir *m*.
gulp [gʌlp] *vi* avaler sa salive; (*from emotion*) avoir la gorge serrée, s'étrangler // *vt* (*also*: **~ down**) avaler // *n*: **at one ~** d'un seul coup.
gum [gʌm] *n* (ANAT) gencive *f*; (*glue*) colle *f*; (*sweet*) boule *f* de gomme; (*also*: **chewing-~**) chewing-gum *m* // *vt* coller; **~boil** *n* abcès *m* dentaire; **~boots** *npl* bottes *fpl* en caoutchouc.
gumption ['gʌmpʃən] *n* bon sens, jugeote *f*.
gun [gʌn] *n* (*small*) revolver *m*, pistolet *m*; (*rifle*) fusil *m*, carabine *f*; (*cannon*) canon *m*; **~boat** *n* canonnière *f*; **~fire** *n* fusillade *f*; **~man** *n* bandit armé; **~ner** *n* artilleur *m*; **at ~point** sous la menace du pistolet (*or* fusil); **~powder** *n* poudre *f* à canon; **~shot** *n* coup *m* de feu; **within ~shot** à portée de fusil; **~smith** *n* armurier *m*.
gurgle ['gə:gl] *n* gargouillis *m* // *vi* gargouiller.
gush [gʌʃ] *n* jaillissement *m*, jet *m* // *vi* jaillir; (*fig*) se répandre en effusions.
gusset ['gʌsɪt] *n* gousset *m*, soufflet *m*.
gust [gʌst] *n* (*of wind*) rafale *f*; (*of smoke*) bouffée *f*.
gusto ['gʌstəu] *n* enthousiasme *m*.
gut [gʌt] *n* intestin *m*, boyau *m*; (MUS *etc*) boyau *m*; **~s** *npl* (*courage*) cran *m*.
gutter ['gʌtə*] *n* (*of roof*) gouttière *f*; (*in street*) caniveau *m*; (*fig*) ruisseau *m*.
guttural ['gʌtərl] *a* guttural(e).
guy [gaɪ] *n* (*also*: **~rope**) corde *f*; (*col: man*) type *m*; (*figure*) *effigie de Guy Fawkes*.
guzzle ['gʌzl] *vi* s'empiffrer // *vt* avaler gloutonnement.
gym [dʒɪm] *n* (*also*: **gymnasium**) gymnase *m*; (*also*: **gymnastics**) gym *f*; **~ shoes** *npl* chaussures *fpl* de gym(nastique); **~ slip** *n* tunique *f* (d'écolière).
gymnast ['dʒɪmnæst] *n* gymnaste *m/f*; **~ics** [-'næstɪks] *n, npl* gymnastique *f*.
gynaecologist, gynecologist (*US*) [gaɪnɪ'kɔlədʒɪst] *n* gynécologue *m/f*.
gynaecology, gynecology (*US*) [gaɪnə'kɔlədʒɪ] *n* gynécologie *f*.
gypsy ['dʒɪpsɪ] *n* = **gipsy**.
gyrate [dʒaɪ'reɪt] *vi* tournoyer.

H

haberdashery ['hæbə'dæʃərɪ] *n* mercerie *f*.
habit ['hæbɪt] *n* habitude *f*; (*costume*) habit *m*, tenue *f*.

habitable ['hæbɪtəbl] *a* habitable.
habitation [hæbɪ'teɪʃən] *n* habitation *f.*
habitual [hə'bɪtjuəl] *a* habituel(le); (*drinker, liar*) invétéré(e); **~ly** *ad* habituellement, d'habitude.
hack [hæk] *vt* hacher, tailler // *n* (*cut*) entaille *f*; (*blow*) coup *m*; (*pej: writer*) nègre *m.*
hackney cab ['hæknɪ'kæb] *n* fiacre *m.*
hackneyed ['hæknɪd] *a* usé(e), rebattu(e).
had [hæd] *pt, pp of* **have**.
haddock, *pl* **~** *or* **~s** ['hædək] *n* églefin *m*; **smoked ~** haddock *m.*
hadn't ['hædnt] = **had not**.
haemorrhage, hemorrhage (*US*) ['hɛmərɪdʒ] *n* hémorragie *f.*
haemorrhoids, hemorrhoids (*US*) ['hɛmərɔɪdz] *npl* hémorroïdes *fpl.*
haggard ['hægəd] *a* hagard(e), égaré(e).
haggle ['hægl] *vi* marchander; **to ~ over** chicaner sur; **haggling** *n* marchandage *m.*
Hague [heɪg] *n*: **The ~** La Haye.
hail [heɪl] *n* grêle *f* // *vt* (*call*) héler; (*greet*) acclamer // *vi* grêler; **~stone** *n* grêlon *m.*
hair [hɛə*] *n* cheveux *mpl*; (*single hair: on head*) cheveu *m*; (: *on body*) poil *m*; **to do one's ~** se coiffer; **~brush** *n* brosse *f* à cheveux; **~cut** *n* coupe *f* (de cheveux); **~do** ['hɛədu:] *n* coiffure *f*; **~dresser** *n* coiffeur/euse; **~-drier** *n* sèche-cheveux *m*; **~net** *n* résille *f*; **~ oil** *n* huile *f* capillaire; **~piece** *n* postiche *m*; **~pin** *n* épingle *f* à cheveux; **~pin bend** *n* virage *m* en épingle à cheveux; **~raising** *a* à (vous) faire dresser les cheveux sur la tête; **~ remover** *n* dépilateur *m*; **~ spray** *n* laque *f* (pour les cheveux); **~style** *n* coiffure *f*; **~y** *a* poilu(e); chevelu(e); (*fig*) effrayant(e).
hake [heɪk] *n* colin *m*, merlu *m.*
half [hɑ:f] *n* (*pl*: **halves** [hɑ:vz]) moitié *f* // *a* demi(e) // *ad* (à) moitié, à demi; **~-an-hour** une demi-heure; **two and a ~** deux et demi; **a week and a ~** une semaine et demie; **~ (of it)** la moitié; **~ (of)** la moitié de; **~ the amount of** la moitié de; **to cut sth in ~** couper qch en deux; **~-back** *n* (SPORT) demi *m*; **~-breed, ~-caste** *n* métis/se; **~-hearted** *a* tiède, sans enthousiasme; **~-hour** *n* demi-heure *f*; **~penny** ['heɪpnɪ] *n* demi-penny *m*; **(at) ~-price** à moitié prix; **~-time** *n* mi-temps *f*; **~way** *ad* à mi-chemin.
halibut ['hælɪbət] *n, pl inv* flétan *m.*
hall [hɔ:l] *n* salle *f*; (*entrance way*) hall *m*, entrée *f*; (*corridor*) couloir *m*; (*mansion*) château *m*, manoir *m*; **~ of residence** *n* pavillon *m or* résidence *f* universitaire.
hallmark ['hɔ:lmɑ:k] *n* poinçon *m*; (*fig*) marque *f.*
hallo [hə'ləu] *excl* = **hello**.
hallucination [həlu:sɪ'neɪʃən] *n* hallucination *f.*
halo ['heɪləu] *n* (*of saint etc*) auréole *f*; (*of sun*) halo *m.*
halt [hɔ:lt] *n* halte *f*, arrêt *m* // *vt* faire arrêter // *vi* faire halte, s'arrêter.
halve [hɑ:v] *vt* (*apple etc*) partager *or* diviser en deux; (*expense*) réduire de moitié.
halves [hɑ:vz] *npl of* **half**.
ham [hæm] *n* jambon *m.*
hamburger ['hæmbə:gə*] *n* hamburger *m.*
hamstring ['hæmstrɪŋ] *n* (ANAT) tendon *m* du jarret.
hamlet ['hæmlɪt] *n* hameau *m.*
hammer ['hæmə*] *n* marteau *m* // *vt* (*fig*) éreinter, démolir.
hammock ['hæmək] *n* hamac *m.*
hamper ['hæmpə*] *vt* gêner // *n* panier *m* (d'osier).
hand [hænd] *n* main *f*; (*of clock*) aiguille *f*; (*handwriting*) écriture *f*; (*at cards*) jeu *m*; (*worker*) ouvrier/ère // *vt* passer, donner; **to give sb a ~** donner un coup de main à qn; **at ~** à portée de la main; **in ~** en main; (*work*) en cours; **on the one ~ ..., on the other ~** d'une part ..., d'autre part; **to ~ in** *vt* remettre; **to ~ out** *vt* distribuer; **to ~ over** *vt* transmettre; céder; **~bag** *n* sac *m* à main; **~ball** *n* handball *m*; **~basin** *n* lavabo *m*; **~book** *n* manuel *m*; **~brake** *n* frein *m* à main; **~ cream** *n* crème *f* pour les mains; **~cuffs** *npl* menottes *fpl*; **~ful** *n* poignée *f.*
handicap ['hændɪkæp] *n* handicap *m* // *vt* handicaper.
handicraft ['hændɪkrɑ:ft] *n* travail *m* d'artisanat, technique artisanale.
handkerchief ['hæŋkətʃɪf] *n* mouchoir *m.*
handle ['hændl] *n* (*of door etc*) poignée *f*; (*of cup etc*) anse *f*; (*of knife etc*) manche *m*; (*of saucepan*) queue *f*; (*for winding*) manivelle *f* // *vt* toucher, manier; (*deal with*) s'occuper de; (*treat: people*) prendre; **'~ with care'** 'fragile'; **~bar(s)** *n(pl)* guidon *m.*
hand-luggage ['hændlʌgɪdʒ] *n* bagages *mpl* à main.
handmade ['hændmeɪd] *a* fait(e) à la main.
handout ['hændaut] *n* documentation *f*, prospectus *m.*
handshake ['hændʃeɪk] *n* poignée *f* de main.
handsome ['hænsəm] *a* beau(belle); généreux(euse); considérable.
handwriting ['hændraɪtɪŋ] *n* écriture *f.*
handwritten ['hændrɪtn] *a* manuscrit(e), écrit(e) à la main.
handy ['hændɪ] *a* (*person*) adroit(e); (*close at hand*) sous la main; (*convenient*) pratique; **handyman** *n* bricoleur *m*; (*servant*) homme *m* à tout faire.
hang, *pt, pp* **hung** [hæŋ, hʌŋ] *vt* accrocher; (*criminal: pt,pp* **hanged**) pendre // *vi* pendre; (*hair, drapery*) tomber; **to ~ about** *vi* flâner, traîner; **to ~ on** *vi* (*wait*) attendre; **to ~ up** *vi* (TEL) raccrocher // *vt* accrocher, suspendre.
hangar ['hæŋə*] *n* hangar *m.*
hanger ['hæŋə*] *n* cintre *m*, portemanteau *m.*
hanger-on [hæŋər'ɔn] *n* parasite *m.*
hang-gliding ['hæŋglaɪdɪŋ] *n* vol *m* libre *or* sur aile delta.
hangover ['hæŋəuvə*] *n* (*after drinking*) gueule *f* de bois.
hang-up ['hæŋʌp] *n* complexe *m.*

hank [hæŋk] *n* écheveau *m*.
hanker ['hæŋkə*] *vi*: **to ~ after** avoir envie de.
hankie, hanky ['hæŋkı] *n abbr of* **handkerchief.**
haphazard [hæp'hæzəd] *a* fait(e) au hasard, fait(e) au petit bonheur.
happen ['hæpən] *vi* arriver ; se passer, se produire ; **as it ~s** justement ; **~ing** *n* événement *m*.
happily ['hæpılı] *ad* heureusement.
happiness ['hæpınıs] *n* bonheur *m*.
happy ['hæpı] *a* heureux(euse) ; **~ with** (*arrangements etc*) satisfait(e) de ; **~-go-lucky** *a* insouciant(e).
harass ['hærəs] *vt* accabler, tourmenter ; **~ment** *n* tracasseries *fpl*.
harbour, harbor (*US*) ['hɑ:bə*] port *m* // *vt* héberger, abriter ; **~ master** *n* capitaine *m* du port.
hard [hɑ:d] *a* dur(e) // *ad* (*work*) dur ; (*think, try*) sérieusement ; **to drink ~** boire sec ; **~ luck!** pas de veine! ; **no ~ feelings!** sans rancune! ; **to be ~ of hearing** être dur(e) d'oreille ; **to be ~ done by** être traité(e) injustement ; **~back** *n* livre relié ; **~board** *n* Isorel *m* ® ; **~-boiled egg** *n* œuf dur ; **~ cash** *n* espèces *fpl* ; **~en** *vt* durcir ; (*fig*) endurcir // *vi* durcir ; **~ening** *n* durcissement *m* ; **~-headed** *a* réaliste ; décidé(e) ; **~ labour** *n* travaux forcés.
hardly ['hɑ:dlı] *ad* (*scarcely*) à peine ; **it's ~ the case** ce n'est guère le cas ; **~ anywhere** presque nulle part.
hardness ['hɑ:dnıs] *n* dureté *f*.
hard sell ['hɑ:d'sɛl] *n* (COMM) promotion de ventes agressive.
hardship ['hɑ:dʃıp] *n* épreuves *fpl* ; privations *fpl*.
hard-up [hɑ:d'ʌp] *a* (*col*) fauché(e).
hardware ['hɑ:dwɛə*] *n* quincaillerie *f* ; (COMPUTERS) matériel *m* ; **~ shop** *n* quincaillerie f.
hard-wearing [hɑ:d'wɛərıŋ] a solide.
hard-working [hɑ:d'wə:kıŋ] *a* travailleur(euse).
hardy ['hɑ:dı] *a* robuste ; (*plant*) résistant(e) au gel.
hare [hɛə*] *n* lièvre *m* ; **~-brained** *a* farfelu(e) ; écervelé(e) ; **~lip** *n* (MED) bec-de-lièvre *m*.
harem [hɑ:'ri:m] *n* harem *m*.
harm [hɑ:m] *n* mal *m* ; (*wrong*) tort *m* // *vt* (*person*) faire du mal *or* du tort à ; (*thing*) endommager ; **to mean no ~** ne pas avoir de mauvaises intentions ; **out of ~'s way** à l'abri du danger, en lieu sûr ; **~ful** *a* nuisible ; **~less** *a* inoffensif(ive) ; sans méchanceté.
harmonic [hɑ:'mɔnık] *a* harmonique.
harmonica [hɑ:'mɔnıkə] *n* harmonica *m*.
harmonics [hɑ:mɔnıks] *npl* harmoniques *mpl or fpl*.
harmonious [hɑ:'məunıəs] *a* harmonieux(euse).
harmonium [hɑ:'məunıəm] *n* harmonium *m*.
harmonize ['hɑ:mənaız] *vt* harmoniser // *vi* s'harmoniser.
harmony ['hɑ:mənı] *n* harmonie *f*.
harness ['hɑ:nıs] *n* harnais *m* // *vt* (*horse*) harnacher ; (*resources*) exploiter.
harp [hɑ:p] *n* harpe *f* // *vi*: **to ~ on about** parler tout le temps de ; **~ist** *n* harpiste *m/f*.
harpoon [hɑ:'pu:n] *n* harpon *m*.
harpsichord ['hɑ:psıkɔ:d] *n* clavecin *m*.
harrow ['hærəu] *n* (AGR) herse *f*.
harrowing ['hærəuıŋ] *a* déchirant(e).
harsh [hɑ:ʃ] *a* (*hard*) dur(e) ; (*severe*) sévère ; (*rough*: *surface*) rugueux(euse) ; (*unpleasant*: *sound*) discordant(e) ; (: *colour*) criard(e) ; cru(e) ; (: *wine*) âpre ; **~ly** *ad* durement ; sévèrement ; **~ness** *n* dureté *f* ; sévérité *f*.
harvest ['hɑ:vıst] *n* (*of corn*) moisson *f* ; (*of fruit*) récolte *f* ; (*of grapes*) vendange *f* // *vi* moissonner ; récolter ; vendanger ; **~er** *n* (*machine*) moissonneuse *f*.
has [hæz] *see* **have**.
hash [hæʃ] *n* (CULIN) hachis *m* ; (*fig*: *mess*) gâchis *m* ; *also abbr of* **hashish.**
hashish ['hæʃıʃ] *n* haschisch *m*.
hassle ['hæsl] *n* chamaillerie *f*.
haste [heıst] *n* hâte *f* ; précipitation *f* ; **~n** ['heısn] *vt* hâter, accélérer // *vi* se hâter, s'empresser ; **hastily** *ad* à la hâte ; précipitamment ; **hasty** *a* hâtif(ive) ; précipité(e).
hat [hæt] *n* chapeau *m* ; **~box** *n* carton *m* à chapeau.
hatch [hætʃ] *n* (NAUT: *also*: **~way**) écoutille *f* ; (*also*: **service ~**) passe-plats *m inv* // *vi* éclore // *vt* faire éclore ; (*plot*) tramer.
hatchback ['hætʃbæk] *n* (AUT) modèle *m* avec hayon arrière.
hatchet ['hætʃıt] *n* hachette *f*.
hate [heıt] *vt* haïr, détester // *n* haine *f* ; **to ~ to do** *or* **doing** détester faire ; **~ful** *a* odieux(euse), détestable.
hatred ['heıtrıd] *n* haine *f*.
hat trick ['hættrık] *n* (SPORT, *also fig*) triplé *m* (*3 buts réussis au cours du même match etc*).
haughty ['hɔ:tı] *a* hautain(e), arrogant(e).
haul [hɔ:l] *vt* traîner, tirer ; (*by lorry*) camionner ; (NAUT) haler // *n* (*of fish*) prise *f* ; (*of stolen goods etc*) butin *m* ; **~age** *n* halage *m* ; camionnage *m* ; **~ier** *n* transporteur (routier), camionneur *m*.
haunch [hɔ:ntʃ] *n* hanche *f* ; **~ of venison** *n* cuissot *m* de chevreuil.
haunt [hɔ:nt] *vt* (*subj*: *ghost, fear*) hanter ; (: *person*) fréquenter // *n* repaire *m*.
have *pt,pp* **had** [hæv, hæd] *vt* avoir ; (*meal, shower*) prendre ; **to ~ sth done** faire faire qch ; **he had a suit made** il s'est fait faire un costume ; **she has to do it** il faut qu'elle le fasse, elle doit le faire ; **I had better leave** je ferais mieux de partir ; **to ~ it out with sb** s'expliquer (franchement) avec qn ; **I won't ~ it** cela ne se passera pas ainsi ; **he's been had** (*col*) il s'est fait avoir *or* rouler.
haven ['heıvn] *n* port *m* ; (*fig*) havre *m*.
haversack ['hævəsæk] *n* sac *m* à dos.
havoc ['hævək] *n* ravages *mpl* ; **to play ~ with** (*fig*) désorganiser ; détraquer.

hawk [hɔ:k] *n* faucon *m*.
hawker ['hɔ:kə*] *n* colporteur *m*.
hay [heɪ] *n* foin *m*; ~ **fever** *n* rhume *m* des foins; ~**stack** *n* meule *f* de foin.
haywire ['heɪwaɪə*] *a* (*col*): **to go** ~ perdre la tête; mal tourner.
hazard ['hæzəd] *n* hasard *m*, chance *f*; danger *m*, risque *m* // *vt* risquer, hasarder; ~**ous** *a* hasardeux(euse), risqué(e).
haze [heɪz] *n* brume *f*.
hazelnut ['heɪzlnʌt] *n* noisette *f*.
hazy ['heɪzɪ] *a* brumeux(euse); (*idea*) vague; (*photograph*) flou(e).
he [hi:] *pronoun* il; **it is** ~ **who ...** c'est lui qui ...; **here** ~ **is** le voici; ~**-bear** *n* ours *m* mâle.
head [hɛd] *n* tête *f*; (*leader*) chef *m* // *vt* (*list*) être en tête de; (*group*) être à la tête de; ~**s** (*on coin*) (le côté) face; ~**s or tails** pile ou face; **to** ~ **the ball** faire une tête; **to** ~ **for** *vt fus* se diriger vers; ~**ache** *n* mal *m* de tête; ~ **cold** *n* rhume *m* de cerveau; ~**ing** *n* titre *m*; rubrique *f*; ~**lamp** *n* phare *m*; ~**land** *n* promontoire *m*, cap *m*; ~**light** = ~**lamp**; ~**line** *n* titre *m*; ~**long** *ad* (*fall*) la tête la première; (*rush*) tête baissée; ~**master** *n* directeur *m*, proviseur *m*; ~**mistress** *n* directrice *f*; ~ **office** *n* bureau central; ~**-on** *a* (*collision*) de plein fouet; ~**phones** *npl* casque *m* (à écouteurs); ~**quarters (HQ)** *npl* bureau *or* siège central; (MIL) quartier général; ~**-rest** *n* appui-tête *m*; ~**room** *n* (*in car*) hauteur *f* de plafond; (*under bridge*) hauteur limite; dégagement *m*; ~**scarf** *n* foulard *m*; ~**strong** *a* têtu(e), entêté(e); ~ **waiter** *n* maître *m* d'hôtel; ~**way** *n* avance *f*, progrès *m*; ~**wind** *n* vent *m* contraire; ~**y** *a* capiteux(euse); enivrant(e).
heal [hi:l] *vt,vi* guérir.
health [hɛlθ] *n* santé *f*; ~ **food shop** *n* magasin *m* diététique; **the H~ Service** ≈ la Sécurité Sociale; ~**y** *a* (*person*) en bonne santé; (*climate, food, attitude etc*) sain(e).
heap [hi:p] *n* tas *m*, monceau *m* // *vt* entasser, amonceler.
hear, *pt, pp* **heard** [hɪə*, hə:d] *vt* entendre; (*news*) apprendre; (*lecture*) assister à, écouter // *vi* entendre; **to** ~ **about** avoir des nouvelles de; entendre parler de; **did you** ~ **about the move?** tu es au courant du déménagement?; **to** ~ **from sb** recevoir des nouvelles de qn; ~**ing** *n* (*sense*) ouïe *f*; (*of witnesses*) audition *f*; (*of a case*) audience *f*; (*of committee*) séance *f*; ~**ing aid** *n* appareil *m* acoustique; **by** ~**say** *ad* par ouï-dire *m*.
hearse [hə:s] *n* corbillard *m*.
heart [hɑ:t] *n* cœur *m*; ~**s** *npl* (CARDS) cœur; **at** ~ au fond; **by** ~ (*learn, know*) par cœur; **to lose** ~ perdre courage, se décourager; ~ **attack** *n* crise *f* cardiaque; ~**beat** *n* battement *m* de cœur; ~**breaking** *a* navrant(e), déchirant(e); **to be** ~**broken** avoir beaucoup de chagrin; ~**burn** *n* brûlures *fpl* d'estomac; ~ **failure** *n* arrêt *m* du cœur; ~**felt** *a* sincère.
hearth [hɑ:θ] *n* foyer *m*, cheminée *f*.
heartily ['hɑ:tɪlɪ] *ad* chaleureusement; (*laugh*) de bon cœur; (*eat*) de bon appétit; **to agree** ~ être entièrement d'accord.
heartless ['hɑ:tlɪs] *a* sans cœur, insensible; cruel(le).
heartwarming ['hɑ:twɔ:mɪŋ] *a* réconfortant(e).
hearty ['hɑ:tɪ] *a* chaleureux(euse); robuste; vigoureux(euse).
heat [hi:t] *n* chaleur *f*; (*fig*) ardeur *f*; feu *m*; (SPORT: *also*: **qualifying** ~) éliminatoire *f* // *vt* chauffer; **to** ~ **up** *vi* (*liquids*) chauffer; (*room*) se réchauffer // *vt* réchauffer; ~**ed** *a* chauffé(e); (*fig*) passionné(e); échauffé(e), excité(e); ~**er** *n* appareil *m* de chauffage; radiateur *m*.
heath [hi:θ] *n* (*Brit*) lande *f*.
heathen ['hi:ðn] *a, n* païen(ne).
heather ['hɛðə*] *n* bruyère *f*.
heating ['hi:tɪŋ] *n* chauffage *m*.
heatstroke ['hi:tstrəuk] *n* coup *m* de chaleur.
heatwave ['hi:tweɪv] *n* vague *f* de chaleur.
heave [hi:v] *vt* soulever (avec effort) // *vi* se soulever // *n* nausée *f*, haut-le-cœur *m*; (*push*) poussée *f*.
heaven ['hɛvn] *n* ciel *m*, paradis *m*; ~ **forbid!** surtout pas!; ~**ly** *a* céleste, divin(e).
heavily ['hɛvɪlɪ] *ad* lourdement; (*drink, smoke*) beaucoup; (*sleep, sigh*) profondément.
heavy ['hɛvɪ] *a* lourd(e); (*work, sea, rain, eater*) gros(se); (*drinker, smoker*) grand(e); **it's** ~ **going** ça ne va pas tout seul, c'est pénible; ~**weight** *n* (SPORT) poids lourd.
Hebrew ['hi:bru:] *a* hébraïque // *n* (LING) hébreu *m*.
heckle ['hɛkl] *vt* interpeller (*un orateur*).
hectare ['hɛktɑ:*] *n* hectare *m*.
hectic ['hɛktɪk] *a* agité(e), trépidant(e).
he'd [hi:d] = **he would, he had**.
hedge [hɛdʒ] *n* haie *f* // *vi* se défiler; **to** ~ **one's bets** (*fig*) se couvrir; **to** ~ **in** *vt* entourer d'une haie.
hedgehog ['hɛdʒhɔg] *n* hérisson *m*.
heed [hi:d] *vt* (*also*: **take** ~ **of**) tenir compte de, prendre garde à; ~**less** *a* insouciant(e).
heel [hi:l] *n* talon *m* // *vt* (*shoe*) retalonner; **to bring sb to** ~ rappeler qn à l'ordre.
hefty ['hɛftɪ] *a* (*person*) costaud(e); (*parcel*) lourd(e); (*piece, price*) gros(se).
heifer ['hɛfə*] *n* génisse *f*.
height [haɪt] *n* (*of person*) taille *f*, grandeur *f*; (*of object*) hauteur *f*; (*of plane, mountain*) altitude *f*; (*high ground*) hauteur, éminence *f*; (*fig*: *of glory*) sommet *m*; (: *of stupidity*) comble *m*; ~**en** *vt* hausser, surélever; (*fig*) augmenter.
heir [ɛə*] *n* héritier *m*; ~**ess** *n* héritière *f*; ~**loom** *n* meuble *m* (*or* bijou *m or* tableau *m*) de famille.
held [hɛld] *pt, pp of* **hold**.
helicopter ['hɛlɪkɔptə*] *n* hélicoptère *m*.
helium ['hi:lɪəm] *n* hélium *m*.
hell [hɛl] *n* enfer *m*; **a** ~ **of a...** (*col*) un(e) sacré(e)... .
he'll [hi:l] = **he will, he shall**.

hellish ['hɛlɪʃ] *a* infernal(e).
hello [hə'ləu] *excl* bonjour! ; salut! (*to sb one addresses as 'tu'*) ; (*surprise*) tiens!
helm [hɛlm] *n* (NAUT) barre *f*.
helmet ['hɛlmɪt] *n* casque *m*.
helmsman ['hɛlmzmən] *n* timonier *m*.
help [hɛlp] *n* aide *f*; (*charwoman*) femme *f* de ménage ; (*assistant etc*) employé/e // *vt* aider ; **~!** au secours! ; **~ yourself (to bread)** servez-vous (de pain) ; **I can't ~ saying** je ne peux pas m'empêcher de dire ; **he can't ~ it** il n'y peut rien ; **~er** *n* aide *m/f*, assistant/e ; **~ful** *a* serviable, obligeant(e) ; (*useful*) utile ; **~ing** *n* portion *f*; **~less** *a* impuissant(e) ; faible.
hem [hɛm] *n* ourlet *m* // *vt* ourler ; **to ~ in** *vt* cerner.
hemisphere ['hɛmɪsfɪə*] *n* hémisphère *m*.
hemorrhage ['hɛmərɪdʒ] *n* (*US*) = **haemorrhage.**
hemorrhoids ['hɛmərɔɪdz] *npl* (*US*) = **haemorrhoids**.
hemp [hɛmp] *n* chanvre *m*.
hen [hɛn] *n* poule *f*.
hence [hɛns] *ad* (*therefore*) d'où, de là ; **2 years ~** d'ici 2 ans ; **~forth** *ad* dorénavant.
henchman ['hɛntʃmən] *n* (*pej*) acolyte *m*, séide *m*.
henpecked ['hɛnpɛkt] *a* dominé par sa femme.
her [hə:*] *pronoun* (*direct*) la, l' + *vowel or h mute*; (*indirect*) lui ; (*stressed, after prep*) elle ; *see note at* **she** // *a* son(sa), ses *pl*; **I see ~** je la vois ; **give ~ a book** donne-lui un livre ; **after ~** après elle.
herald ['hɛrəld] *n* héraut *m* // *vt* annoncer.
heraldry ['hɛrəldrɪ] *n* héraldique *f*.
herb [hə:b] *n* herbe *f*; **~s** *npl* (CULIN) fines herbes.
herd [hə:d] *n* troupeau *m* // *vt*: **~ed together** parqués (comme du bétail).
here [hɪə*] *ad* ici // *excl* tiens!, tenez! ; **~!** présent! ; **~'s my sister** voici ma sœur ; **~ she is** la voici ; **~ she comes** la voici qui vient ; **~after** *ad* après, plus tard ; ci-après // *n*: **the ~after** l'au-delà *m* ; **~by** *ad* (*in letter*) par la présente.
hereditary [hɪ'rɛdɪtrɪ] *a* héréditaire.
heredity [hɪ'rɛdɪtɪ] *n* hérédité *f*.
heresy ['hɛrəsɪ] *n* hérésie *f*.
heretic ['hɛrətɪk] *n* hérétique *m/f*; **~al** [hɪ'rɛtɪkl] *a* hérétique.
herewith [hɪə'wɪð] *ad* avec ceci, ci-joint.
heritage ['hɛrɪtɪdʒ] *n* héritage *m*.
hermetically [hə:'mɛtɪklɪ] *ad* hermétiquement.
hermit ['hə:mɪt] *n* ermite *m*.
hernia ['hə:nɪə] *n* hernie *f*.
hero, ~es ['hɪərəu] *n* héros *m* ; **~ic** [hɪ'rəuɪk] *a* héroïque.
heroin ['hɛrəuɪn] *n* héroïne *f*.
heroine ['hɛrəuɪn] *n* héroïne *f*.
heroism ['hɛrəuɪzm] *n* héroïsme *m*.
heron ['hɛrən] *n* héron *m*.
herring ['hɛrɪŋ] *n* hareng *m*.
hers [hə:z] *pronoun* le(la) sien(ne), les siens(siennes).
herself [hə:'sɛlf] *pronoun* (*reflexive*) se ; (*emphatic*) elle-même ; (*after prep*) elle.
he's [hi:z] = **he is, he has**.
hesitant ['hɛzɪtənt] *a* hésitant(e), indécis(e).
hesitate ['hɛzɪteɪt] *vi*: **to ~ (about/to do)** hésiter (sur/à faire) ; **hesitation** ['-teɪʃən] *n* hésitation *f*.
hessian ['hɛsɪən] *n* toile *f* de jute.
het up [hɛt'ʌp] *a* agité(e), excité(e).
hew [hju:] *vt* tailler (*à la hache*).
hexagon ['hɛksəgən] *n* hexagone *m* ; **~al** [-'sægənl] *a* hexagonal(e).
heyday ['heɪdeɪ] *n*: **the ~ of** l'âge *m* d'or de, les beaux jours de.
hi [haɪ] *excl* salut!
hibernate ['haɪbəneɪt] *vi* hiberner.
hiccough, hiccup ['hɪkʌp] *vi* hoqueter // *n* hoquet *m*; **to have (the) ~s** avoir le hoquet.
hid [hɪd] *pt of* **hide**.
hidden ['hɪdn] *pp of* **hide**.
hide [haɪd] *n* (*skin*) peau *f* // *vb* (*pt* **hid,** *pp* **hidden** [hɪd, 'hɪdn]) *vt*: **to ~ sth (from sb)** cacher qch (à qn) // *vi*: **to ~ (from sb)** se cacher de qn ; **~-and-seek** *n* cache-cache *m*; **~away** *n* cachette *f*.
hideous ['hɪdɪəs] *a* hideux(euse) ; atroce.
hiding ['haɪdɪŋ] *n* (*beating*) correction *f*, volée *f* de coups ; **to be in ~** (*concealed*) se tenir caché(e) ; **~ place** *n* cachette *f*.
hierarchy ['haɪərɑ:kɪ] *n* hiérarchie *f*.
high [haɪ] *a* haut(e) ; (*speed, respect, number*) grand(e) ; (*price*) élevé(e) ; (*wind*) fort(e), violent(e) ; (*voice*) aigu(aiguë) // *ad* haut, en haut ; **20 m ~** haut(e) de 20 m ; **~brow** *a,n* intellectuel(le) ; **~chair** *n* chaise haute (*pour enfant*) ; **~-flying** *a* (*fig*) ambitieux(euse) ; **~-handed** *a* très autoritaire ; très cavalier(ère) ; **~-heeled** *a* à hauts talons ; **~jack = hijack** ; **~ jump** *n* (SPORT) saut *m* en hauteur ; **~light** *n* (*fig: of event*) point culminant // *vt* faire ressortir, souligner ; **~ly** *ad* très, fort, hautement ; **~ly strung** *a* nerveux(euse), toujours tendu(e) ; **H~ Mass** *n* grand-messe *f*; **~ness** *n* hauteur *f*; **Her H~ness** son Altesse *f*; **~-pitched** *a* aigu(aiguë) ; **~-rise block** *n* tour *f* (d'habitation).
high school ['haɪsku:l] *n* lycée *m*; (*US*) établissement *m* d'enseignement supérieur.
high street ['haɪstri:t] *n* grand-rue *f*.
highway ['haɪweɪ] *n* grand'route *f*, route nationale.
hijack ['haɪdʒæk] *vt* détourner (*par la force*) ; **~er** *n* auteur *m* d'un détournement d'avion, pirate *m* de l'air.
hike [haɪk] *vi* aller à pied // *n* excursion *f* à pied, randonnée *f*; **~r** *n* promeneur/euse, excursionniste *m/f*; **hiking** *n* excursions *fpl* à pied, randonnée *f*.
hilarious [hɪ'lɛərɪəs] *a* (*behaviour, event*) désopilant(e).
hilarity [hɪ'lærɪtɪ] *n* hilarité *f*.
hill [hɪl] *n* colline *f*; (*fairly high*) montagne *f*; (*on road*) côte *f*; **~side** *n* (flanc *m* de) coteau *m* ; **~ start** *n* (AUT) démarrage *m* en côte ; **~y** *a* vallonné(e) ; montagneux (euse) ; (*road*) à fortes côtes.
hilt [hɪlt] *n* (*of sword*) garde *f*.
him [hɪm] *pronoun* (*direct*) le, l' + *vowel or h mute* ; (*stressed, indirect, after prep*) lui ;

I see ~ je le vois ; **give ~ a book** donne-lui un livre ; **after ~** après lui ; **~self** *pronoun* (*reflexive*) se ; (*emphatic*) lui-même ; (*after prep*) lui.

hind [haɪnd] *a* de derrière // *n* biche *f*.

hinder ['hɪndə*] *vt* gêner ; (*delay*) retarder ; (*prevent*): **to ~ sb from doing** empêcher qn de faire ; **hindrance** ['hɪndrəns] *n* gêne *f*, obstacle *m*.

Hindu ['hɪndu:] *n* Hindou/e.

hinge [hɪndʒ] *n* charnière *f* // *vi* (*fig*): **to ~ on** dépendre de.

hint [hɪnt] *n* allusion *f* ; (*advice*) conseil *m* // *vt*: **to ~ that** insinuer que // *vi*: **to ~ at** faire une allusion à.

hip [hɪp] *n* hanche *f* ; **~ pocket** *n* poche *f* revolver.

hippopotamus, *pl* **~es** *or* **hippopotami** [hɪpə'pɔtəməs, -'pɔtəmaɪ] *n* hippopotame *m*.

hire ['haɪə*] *vt* (*car, equipment*) louer ; (*worker*) embaucher, engager // *n* location *f* ; **for ~** à louer ; (*taxi*) libre ; **~ purchase (H.P.)** *n* achat *m* (*or* vente *f*) à tempérament *or* crédit.

his [hɪz] *pronoun* le(la) sien(ne), les siens(siennes) // *a* son(sa), ses *pl*.

hiss [hɪs] *vi* siffler // *n* sifflement *m*.

historian [hɪ'stɔ:rɪən] *n* historien/ne.

historic(al) [hɪ'stɔrɪk(l)] *a* historique.

history ['hɪstərɪ] *n* histoire *f*.

hit [hɪt] *vt* (*pt, pp* **hit**) frapper ; (*knock against*) cogner ; (*reach*: *target*) atteindre, toucher ; (*collide with*: *car*) entrer en collision avec, heurter ; (*fig*: *affect*) toucher ; (*find*) tomber sur // *n* coup *m* ; (*success*) coup réussi ; succès *m* ; (*song*) chanson *f* à succès, tube *m* ; **to ~ it off with sb** bien s'entendre avec qn ; **~-and-run driver** *n* chauffard *m* ; **~-or-miss** *a* fait(e) au petit bonheur.

hitch [hɪtʃ] *vt* (*fasten*) accrocher, attacher ; (*also*: **~ up**) remonter d'une saccade // *n* (*knot*) nœud *m* ; (*difficulty*) anicroche *f*, contretemps *m* ; **to ~ a lift** faire du stop.

hitch-hike ['hɪtʃhaɪk] *vi* faire de l'auto-stop ; **~r** *n* auto-stoppeur/ euse.

hive [haɪv] *n* ruche *f*.

H.M.S. *abbr of His*(*Her*) *Majesty's Ship.*

hoard [hɔ:d] *n* (*of food*) provisions *fpl*, réserves *fpl* ; (*of money*) trésor *m* // *vt* amasser.

hoarding ['hɔ:dɪŋ] *n* panneau *m* d'affichage *or* publicitaire.

hoarfrost ['hɔ:frɔst] *n* givre *m*.

hoarse [hɔ:s] *a* enroué(e).

hoax [həuks] *n* canular *m*.

hob [hɔb] *n* plaque chauffante.

hobble ['hɔbl] *vi* boitiller.

hobby ['hɔbɪ] *n* passe-temps favori ; **~-horse** *n* cheval *m* à bascule ; (*fig*) dada *m*.

hobo ['həubəu] *n* (*US*) vagabond *m*.

hock [hɔk] *n* vin *m* du Rhin.

hockey ['hɔkɪ] *n* hockey *m*.

hoe [həu] *n* houe *f*, binette *f* // *vt* biner, sarcler.

hog [hɔg] *n* sanglier *m* // *vt* (*fig*) accaparer ; **to go the whole ~** aller jusqu'au bout.

hoist [hɔɪst] *n* palan *m* // *vt* hisser.

hold [həuld] *vb* (*pt, pp* **held** [hɛld]) *vt* tenir ; (*contain*) contenir ; (*keep back*) retenir ; (*believe*) maintenir ; considérer ; (*possess*) avoir ; détenir // *vi* (*withstand pressure*) tenir (bon) ; (*be valid*) valoir // *n* prise *f* ; (*fig*) influence *f* ; (NAUT) cale *f* ; **~ the line!** (TEL) ne quittez pas! ; **to ~ one's own** (*fig*) (bien) se défendre ; **to catch** *or* **get (a) ~ of** saisir ; **to get ~ of** (*fig*) trouver ; **to get ~ of o.s.** se contrôler ; **to ~ back** *vt* retenir ; (*secret*) cacher ; **to ~ down** *vt* (*person*) maintenir à terre ; (*job*) occuper ; **to ~ off** *vt* tenir à distance ; **to ~ on** *vi* tenir bon ; (*wait*) attendre ; **~ on!** (TEL) ne quittez pas! ; **to ~ on to** *vt fus* se cramponner à ; (*keep*) conserver, garder ; **to ~ out** *vt* offrir // *vi* (*resist*) tenir bon ; **to ~ up** *vt* (*raise*) lever ; (*support*) soutenir ; (*delay*) retarder ; **~all** *n* fourre-tout *m inv* ; **~er** *n* (*of ticket, record*) détenteur/trice ; (*of office, title etc*) titulaire *m/f* ; **~ing** *n* (*share*) intérêts *mpl* ; (*farm*) ferme *f* ; **~ing company** *n* holding *m* ; **~up** *n* (*robbery*) hold-up *m* ; (*delay*) retard *m* ; (*in traffic*) embouteillage *m*.

hole [həul] *n* trou *m* // *vt* trouer, faire un trou dans.

holiday ['hɔlədɪ] *n* vacances *fpl* ; (*day off*) jour *m* de congé ; (*public*) jour férié ; **~-maker** *n* vacancier/ère ; **~ resort** *n* centre *m* de villégiature *or* de vacances.

holiness ['həulɪnɪs] *n* sainteté *f*.

Holland ['hɔlənd] *n* Hollande *f*.

hollow ['hɔləu] *a* creux(euse) ; (*fig*) faux(fausse) // *n* creux *m* ; (*in land*) dépression *f* (de terrain), cuvette *f* // *vt*: **to ~ out** creuser, évider.

holly ['hɔlɪ] *n* houx *m* ; **~hock** *n* rose trémière.

holster ['həulstə*] *n* étui *m* de revolver.

holy ['həulɪ] *a* saint(e) ; (*bread, water*) bénit(e) ; (*ground*) sacré(e) ; **H~ Ghost** *or* **Spirit** *n* Saint-Esprit *m* ; **~ orders** *npl* ordres (majeurs).

homage ['hɔmɪdʒ] *n* hommage *m* ; **to pay ~ to** rendre hommage à.

home [həum] *n* foyer *m*, maison *f* ; (*country*) pays natal, patrie *f* ; (*institution*) maison *f* // *a* de famille ; (ECON, POL) national(e), intérieur(e) // *ad* chez soi, à la maison ; au pays natal ; (*right in*: *nail etc*) à fond ; **at ~** chez soi, à la maison ; **to go** (*or* **come**) **~** rentrer (chez soi), rentrer à la maison (*or* au pays) ; **make yourself at ~** faites comme chez vous ; **near my ~** près de chez moi ; **~ address** *n* domicile permanent ; **~land** *n* patrie *f* ; **~less** *a* sans foyer ; sans abri ; **~ly** simple, sans prétention ; accueillant(e) ; **~-made** *a* fait(e) à la maison ; **~ rule** *n* autonomie *f* ; **H~ Secretary** *n* (*Brit*) ministre *m* de l'Intérieur ; **~sick** *a*: **to be ~sick** avoir le mal du pays ; s'ennuyer de sa famille ; **~ town** *n* ville natale ; **~ward** ['həumwəd] *a* (*journey*) du retour ; **~work** *n* devoirs *mpl*.

homicide ['hɔmɪsaɪd] *n* (*US*) homicide *m*.

homoeopathy [həumɪ'ɔpəθɪ] *n* homéopathie *f*.

homogeneous [hɔməu'dʒi:nɪəs] *a* homogène.

homosexual [hɔməu'sɛksjuəl] *a,n* homosexuel(le).
hone [həun] *n* pierre *f* à aiguiser // *vt* affûter, aiguiser.
honest ['ɔnɪst] *a* honnête; (*sincere*) franc(franche); **~ly** *ad* honnêtement; franchement; **~y** *n* honnêteté *f*.
honey ['hʌnɪ] *n* miel *m*; **~comb** *n* rayon *m* de miel; (*pattern*) nid *m* d'abeilles, motif alvéolé; **~moon** *n* lune *f* de miel; (*trip*) voyage *m* de noces.
honk [hɔŋk] *n* (AUT) coup *m* de klaxon // *vi* klaxonner.
honorary ['ɔnərərɪ] *a* honoraire; (*duty, title*) honorifique.
honour, honor (*US*) ['ɔnə*] *vt* honorer // *n* honneur *m*; **~able** *a* honorable; **~s degree** *n* (SCOL) *licence avec mention*.
hood [hud] *n* capuchon *m*; (*Brit*: AUT) capote *f*; (*US*: AUT) capot *m*; **~wink** *vt* tromper.
hoof, ~s *or* **hooves** [hu:f, hu:vz] *n* sabot *m*.
hook [huk] *n* crochet *m*; (*on dress*) agrafe *f*; (*for fishing*) hameçon *m* // *vt* accrocher; (*dress*) agrafer.
hooligan ['hu:lɪgən] *n* voyou *m*.
hoop [hu:p] *n* cerceau *m*; (*of barrel*) cercle *m*.
hoot [hu:t] *vi* (AUT) klaxonner; (*siren*) mugir // *vt* (*jeer at*) huer // *n* huée *f*; coup *m* de klaxon; mugissement *m*; **to ~ with laughter** rire aux éclats; **~er** *n* (AUT) klaxon *m*; (NAUT) sirène *f*.
hooves [hu:vz] *npl of* **hoof**.
hop [hɔp] *vi* sauter; (*on one foot*) sauter à cloche-pied // *n* saut *m*.
hope [həup] *vt,vi* espérer // *n* espoir *m*; **I ~ so** je l'espère; **I ~ not** j'espère que non; **~ful** *a* (*person*) plein(e) d'espoir; (*situation*) prometteur(euse), encourageant(e); **~fully** *ad* avec espoir, avec optimisme; **~less** *a* désespéré(e); (*useless*) nul(le).
hops [hɔps] *npl* houblon *m*.
horde [hɔ:d] *n* horde *f*.
horizon [hə'raɪzn] *n* horizon *m*; **~tal** [hɔrɪ'zɔntl] *a* horizontal(e).
hormone ['hɔ:məun] *n* hormone *f*.
horn [hɔ:n] *n* corne *f*; (MUS) cor *m*; (AUT) klaxon *m*; **~ed** *a* (*animal*) à cornes.
hornet ['hɔ:nɪt] *n* frelon *m*.
horny ['hɔ:nɪ] *a* corné(e); (*hands*) calleux(euse).
horoscope ['hɔrəskəup] *n* horoscope *m*.
horrible ['hɔrɪbl] *a* horrible, affreux(euse).
horrid ['hɔrɪd] *a* méchant(e), désagréable.
horrify ['hɔrɪfaɪ] *vt* horrifier.
horror ['hɔrə*] *n* horreur *f*; **~ film** *n* film *m* d'épouvante.
hors d'œuvre [ɔ:'də:vrə] *n* hors d'œuvre *m*.
horse [hɔ:s] *n* cheval *m*; **on ~back** à cheval; **~ chestnut** *n* marron *m* (d'Inde); **~-drawn** *a* tiré(e) par des chevaux; **~man** *n* cavalier *m*; **~power (h.p.)** *n* puissance *f* (en chevaux); **~-racing** *n* courses *fpl* de chevaux; **~radish** *n* raifort *m*; **~shoe** *n* fer *m* à cheval.
horsy ['hɔ:sɪ] *a* féru(e) d'équitation *or* de cheval; chevalin(e).
horticulture ['hɔ:tɪkʌltʃə*] *n* horticulture *f*.
hose [həuz] *n* (*also*: **~pipe**) tuyau *m*; (*also*: **garden ~**) tuyau d'arrosage.
hosiery ['həuzɪərɪ] *n* (*in shop*) (rayon *m* des) bas *mpl*.
hospitable ['hɔspɪtəbl] *a* hospitalier(ère).
hospital ['hɔspɪtl] *n* hôpital *m*; **in ~** à l'hôpital.
hospitality [hɔspɪ'tælɪtɪ] *n* hospitalité *f*.
host [həust] *n* hôte *m*; (*in hotel etc*) patron *m*; (*large number*): **a ~ of** une foule de; (REL) hostie *f*.
hostage ['hɔstɪdʒ] *n* otage *m*.
hostel ['hɔstl] *n* foyer *m*; (**youth**) **~** *n* auberge *f* de jeunesse.
hostess ['həustɪs] *n* hôtesse *f*.
hostile ['hɔstaɪl] *a* hostile.
hostility [hɔ'stɪlɪtɪ] *n* hostilité *f*.
hot [hɔt] *a* chaud(e); (*as opposed to only warm*) très chaud; (*spicy*) fort(e); (*fig*) acharné(e); brûlant(e); violent(e), passionné(e); **~ dog** *n* hot-dog *m*.
hotel [həu'tɛl] *n* hôtel *m*; **~ier** *n* hôtelier/ère.
hot: **~headed** *a* impétueux(euse); **~house** *n* serre chaude; **~ly** *ad* passionnément, violemment; **~-water bottle** *n* bouillotte *f*.
hound [haund] *vt* poursuivre avec acharnement // *n* chien courant; **the ~s** la meute.
hour ['auə*] *n* heure *f*; **~ly** *a* toutes les heures; **~ly paid** *a* payé(e) à l'heure.
house *n* [haus] (*pl*: **~s** ['hauzɪz]) (*also*: *firm*) maison *f*; (POL) chambre *f*; (THEATRE) salle *f*; auditoire *m* // *vt* [hauz] (*person*) loger, héberger; **the H~ (of Commons)** la Chambre des communes; **on the ~** (*fig*) aux frais de la maison; **~ arrest** *n* assignation *f* à domicile; **~boat** *n* bateau (aménagé en habitation); **~breaking** *n* cambriolage *m* (avec effraction); **~hold** *n* famille *f*, maisonnée *f*; ménage *m*; **~keeper** *n* gouvernante *f*; **~keeping** *n* (*work*) ménage *m*; **~-warming party** *n* pendaison *f* de crémaillère; **~wife** *n* ménagère *f*; **~work** *n* (travaux *mpl* du) ménage *m*.
housing ['hauzɪŋ] *n* logement *m*; **~ estate** *n* cité *f*, lotissement *m*; **~ shortage** *n* crise *f* du logement.
hovel ['hɔvl] *n* taudis *m*.
hover ['hɔvə*] *vi* planer; **to ~ round sb** rôder *or* tourner autour de qn; **~craft** *n* aéroglisseur *m*.
how [hau] *ad* comment; **~ are you?** comment allez-vous?; **~ long have you been here?** depuis combien de temps êtes-vous là?; **~ lovely!** que *or* comme c'est joli!; **~ many/much?** combien?; **~ many people/much milk** combien de gens/lait; **~ old are you?** quel âge avez-vous?; **~ is it that ...?** comment se fait-il que ...? *+ sub*; **~ever** *ad* de quelque façon *or* manière que *+ sub*; (*+ adjective*) quelque *or* si ... que *+ sub*; (*in questions*) comment // *cj* pourtant, cependant.
howl ['haul] *n* hurlement *m* // *vi* hurler.
howler ['haulə*] *n* gaffe *f*, bourde *f*.
h.p., H.P. *see* **hire**; **horse**.

HQ *abbr of* **headquarters**.
hr(s) *abbr of* **hour(s)**.
hub [hʌb] *n* (*of wheel*) moyeu *m* ; (*fig*) centre *m*, foyer *m*.
hubbub ['hʌbʌb] *n* brouhaha *m*.
hub cap ['hʌbkæp] *n* enjoliveur *m*.
huddle ['hʌdl] *vi*: **to ~ together** se blottir les uns contre les autres.
hue [hju:] *n* teinte *f*, nuance *f*; **~ and cry** *n* tollé (général), clameur *f*.
huff [hʌf] *n*: **in a ~** fâché(e) ; **to take the ~** prendre la mouche.
hug [hʌg] *vt* serrer dans ses bras ; (*shore, kerb*) serrer // *n* étreinte *f*; **to give sb a ~** serrer qn dans ses bras.
huge [hju:dʒ] *a* énorme, immense.
hulk [hʌlk] *n* (*ship*) vieux rafiot ; (*car etc*) carcasse *f*; **~ing** *a* balourd(e).
hull [hʌl] *n* (*of ship, nuts*) coque *f*; (*of peas*) cosse *f*.
hullo [hə'ləu] *excl* = **hello**.
hum [hʌm] *vt* (*tune*) fredonner // *vi* fredonner ; (*insect*) bourdonner ; (*plane, tool*) vrombir // *n* fredonnement *m* ; bourdonnement *m* ; vrombissement *m*.
human ['hju:mən] *a* humain(e) // *n* être humain.
humane [hju:'meɪn] *a* humain(e), humanitaire.
humanity [hju:'mænɪtɪ] *n* humanité *f*.
humble ['hʌmbl] *a* humble, modeste // *vt* humilier ; **humbly** *ad* humblement, modestement.
humbug ['hʌmbʌg] *n* fumisterie *f*; (*sweet*) *sorte de bonbon à la menthe*.
humdrum ['hʌmdrʌm] *a* monotone, routinier(ère).
humid ['hju:mɪd] *a* humide ; **~ity** [-'mɪdɪtɪ] *n* humidité *f*.
humiliate [hju:'mɪlɪeɪt] *vt* humilier ; **humiliation** [-'eɪʃən] *n* humiliation *f*.
humility [hju:'mɪlɪtɪ] *n* humilité *f*.
humorist ['hju:mərɪst] *n* humoriste *m/f*.
humorous ['hju:mərəs] *a* humoristique ; (*person*) plein(e) d'humour.
humour, humor (*US*) ['hju:mə*] *n* humour *m* ; (*mood*) humeur *f* // *vt* (*person*) faire plaisir à ; se prêter aux caprices de.
hump [hʌmp] *n* bosse *f*; **~back** *n* dos-d'âne *m*.
hunch [hʌntʃ] *n* bosse *f*; (*premonition*) intuition *f*; **~back** *n* bossu/e ; **~ed** *a* arrondi(e), voûté(e).
hundred ['hʌndrəd] *num* cent ; **~weight** *n* (*Brit*) = *50.8 kg*; *112 lb*; (*US*) = *45.3 kg*; *100 lb*.
hung [hʌŋ] *pt, pp of* **hang**.
Hungarian [hʌŋ'gɛərɪən] *a* hongrois(e) // *n* Hongrois/e ; (LING) hongrois *m*.
Hungary ['hʌŋgərɪ] *n* Hongrie *f*.
hunger ['hʌŋgə*] *n* faim *f* // *vi*: **to ~ for** avoir faim de, désirer ardemment.
hungrily ['hʌŋgrəlɪ] *ad* voracement ; (*fig*) avidement.
hungry ['hʌŋgrɪ] *a* affamé(e) ; **to be ~** avoir faim.
hunt [hʌnt] *vt* (*seek*) chercher ; (SPORT) chasser // *vi* chasser // *n* chasse *f*; **~er** *n* chasseur *m* ; **~ing** *n* chasse *f*.
hurdle ['hə:dl] *n* (*for fences*) claie *f*; (SPORT) haie *f*; (*fig*) obstacle *m*.
hurl [hə:l] *vt* lancer (avec violence).
hurrah, hurray [hu'rɑ:, hu'reɪ] *n* hourra *m*.
hurricane ['hʌrɪkən] *n* ouragan *m*.
hurried ['hʌrɪd] *a* pressé(e), précipité(e) ; (*work*) fait(e) à la hâte ; **~ly** *ad* précipitamment, à la hâte.
hurry ['hʌrɪ] *n* hâte *f*, précipitation *f* // *vi* se presser, se dépêcher // *vt* (*person*) faire presser, faire se dépêcher ; (*work*) presser ; **to be in a ~** être pressé(e) ; **to do sth in a ~** faire qch en vitesse ; **to ~ in/out** entrer/sortir précipitamment.
hurt [hə:t] *vb* (*pt, pp* **hurt**) *vt* (*cause pain to*) faire mal à ; (*injure, fig*) blesser // *vi* faire mal // *a* blessé(e) ; **~ful** *a* (*remark*) blessant(e).
hurtle ['hə:tl] *vt* lancer (de toutes ses forces) // *vi*: **to ~ past** passer en trombe ; **to ~ down** dégringoler.
husband ['hʌzbənd] *n* mari *m*.
hush [hʌʃ] *n* calme *m*, silence *m* // *vt* faire taire ; **~!** chut!
husk [hʌsk] *n* (*of wheat*) balle *f*; (*of rice, maize*) enveloppe *f*; (*of peas*) cosse *f*.
husky ['hʌskɪ] *a* rauque ; (*burly*) costaud(e) // *n* chien *m* esquimau *or* de traîneau.
hustle ['hʌsl] *vt* pousser, bousculer // *n* bousculade *f*; **~ and bustle** *n* tourbillon *m* (d'activité).
hut [hʌt] *n* hutte *f*; (*shed*) cabane *f*; (MIL) baraquement *m*.
hutch [hʌtʃ] *n* clapier *m*.
hyacinth ['haɪəsɪnθ] *n* jacinthe *f*.
hybrid ['haɪbrɪd] *a, n* hybride (*m*).
hydrant ['haɪdrənt] *n* prise *f* d'eau ; (*also*: **fire ~**) bouche *f* d'incendie.
hydraulic [haɪ'drɔ:lɪk] *a* hydraulique.
hydroelectric [haɪdrəuɪ'lɛktrɪk] *a* hydro-électrique.
hydrogen ['haɪdrədʒən] *n* hydrogène *m*.
hyena [haɪ'i:nə] *n* hyène *f*.
hygiene ['haɪdʒi:n] *n* hygiène *f*.
hygienic [haɪ'dʒi:nɪk] *a* hygiénique.
hymn [hɪm] *n* hymne *m*; cantique *m*.
hyphen ['haɪfn] *n* trait *m* d'union.
hypnosis [hɪp'nəusɪs] *n* hypnose *f*.
hypnotism ['hɪpnətɪzm] *n* hypnotisme *m*.
hypnotist ['hɪpnətɪst] *n* hypnotiseur/euse.
hypnotize ['hɪpnətaɪz] *vt* hypnotiser.
hypocrisy [hɪ'pɔkrɪsɪ] *n* hypocrisie *f*.
hypocrite ['hɪpəkrɪt] *n* hypocrite *m/f*; **hypocritical** [-'krɪtɪkl] *a* hypocrite.
hypothesis, *pl* **hypotheses** [haɪ'pɔθɪsɪs, -si:z] *n* hypothèse *f*.
hypothetic(al) [haɪpəu'θɛtɪk(l)] *a* hypothétique.
hysteria [hɪ'stɪərɪə] *n* hystérie *f*.
hysterical [hɪ'stɛrɪkl] *a* hystérique ; **to become ~** avoir une crise de nerfs.
hysterics [hɪ'stɛrɪks] *npl* (violente) crise de nerfs ; (*laughter*) crise de rire.

I

I [aɪ] *pronoun* je ; (*before vowel*) j' ; (*stressed*) moi.
ice [aɪs] *n* glace *f*; (*on road*) verglas *m* // *vt* (*cake*) glacer ; (*drink*) faire rafraîchir //

vi (*also*: ~ **over**) geler ; (*also*: ~ **up**) se givrer ; ~ **axe** *n* piolet *m* ; ~**berg** *n* iceberg *m* ; ~**box** *n* (*US*) réfrigérateur *m* ; (*Brit*) compartiment *m* à glace ; (*insulated box*) glacière *f* ; ~**-cold** *a* glacé(e) ; ~ **cream** *n* glace *f* ; ~ **cube** *n* glaçon *m* ; ~ **hockey** *n* hockey *m* sur glace.

Iceland ['aɪslənd] *n* Islande *f* ; ~**er** *n* Islandais/e ; ~**ic** [-'lændɪk] *a* islandais(e) // *n* (LING) islandais *m*.

ice rink ['aɪsrɪŋk] *n* patinoire *f*.

icicle ['aɪsɪkl] *n* glaçon *m* (*naturel*).

icing ['aɪsɪŋ] *n* (AVIAT *etc*) givrage *m* ; (CULIN) glaçage *m* ; ~ **sugar** *n* sucre *m* glace.

icon ['aɪkɔn] *n* icône *f*.

icy ['aɪsɪ] *a* glacé(e) ; (*road*) verglacé(e) ; (*weather, temperature*) glacial(e).

I'd [aɪd] = **I would, I had**.

idea [aɪ'dɪə] *n* idée *f*.

ideal [aɪ'dɪəl] *n* idéal *m* // *a* idéal(e) ; ~**ist** *n* idéaliste *m/f*.

identical [aɪ'dɛntɪkl] *a* identique.

identification [aɪdɛntɪfɪ'keɪʃən] *n* identification *f* ; **means of** ~ pièce *f* d'identité.

identify [aɪ'dɛntɪfaɪ] *vt* identifier.

identity [aɪ'dɛntɪtɪ] *n* identité *f*.

ideology [aɪdɪ'ɔlədʒɪ] *n* idéologie *f*.

idiocy ['ɪdɪəsɪ] *n* idiotie *f*, stupidité *f*.

idiom ['ɪdɪəm] *n* langue *f*, idiome *m* ; (*phrase*) expression *f* idiomatique.

idiosyncrasy [ɪdɪəu'sɪŋkrəsɪ] *n* particularité *f*, caractéristique *f*.

idiot ['ɪdɪət] *n* idiot/e, imbécile *m/f* ; ~**ic** [-'ɔtɪk] *a* idiot(e), bête, stupide.

idle ['aɪdl] *a* sans occupation, désœuvré(e) ; (*lazy*) oisif(ive), paresseux(euse) ; (*unemployed*) au chômage ; (*machinery*) au repos ; (*question, pleasures*) vain(e), futile ; **to lie** ~ être arrêté, ne pas fonctionner ; ~**ness** *n* désœuvrement *m* ; oisiveté *f* ; ~**r** *n* désœuvré/e ; oisif/ive.

idol ['aɪdl] *n* idole *f* ; ~**ize** *vt* idolâtrer, adorer.

idyllic [ɪ'dɪlɪk] *a* idyllique.

i.e. *ad* (*abbr of id est*) c'est-à-dire.

if [ɪf] *cj* si.

igloo ['ɪglu:] *n* igloo *m*.

ignite [ɪg'naɪt] *vt* mettre le feu à, enflammer // *vi* s'enflammer.

ignition [ɪg'nɪʃən] *n* (AUT) allumage *m* ; **to switch on/off the** ~ mettre/couper le contact ; ~ **key** *n* (AUT) clé *f* de contact.

ignoramus [ɪgnə'reɪməs] *n* personne *f* ignare.

ignorance ['ɪgnərəns] *n* ignorance *f*.

ignorant ['ɪgnərənt] *a* ignorant(e).

ignore [ɪg'nɔ:*] *vt* ne tenir aucun compte de, ne pas relever ; (*person*) faire semblant de ne pas reconnaître, ignorer ; (*fact*) méconnaître.

ikon ['aɪkɔn] *n* = **icon**.

I'll [aɪl] = **I will, I shall**.

ill [ɪl] *a* (*sick*) malade ; (*bad*) mauvais(e) // *n* mal *m* ; **to take** *or* **be taken** ~ tomber malade ; ~**-advised** *a* (*decision*) peu judicieux(euse) ; (*person*) malavisé(e) ; ~**-at-ease** *a* mal à l'aise.

illegal [ɪ'li:gl] *a* illégal(e) ; ~**ly** *ad* illégalement.

illegible [ɪ'lɛdʒɪbl] *a* illisible.

illegitimate [ɪlɪ'dʒɪtɪmət] *a* illégitime.

ill-fated [ɪl'feɪtɪd] *a* malheureux(euse) ; (*day*) néfaste.

ill feeling [ɪl'fi:lɪŋ] *n* ressentiment *m*, rancune *f*.

illicit [ɪ'lɪsɪt] *a* illicite.

illiterate [ɪ'lɪtərət] *a* illettré(e) ; (*letter*) plein(e) de fautes.

ill-mannered [ɪl'mænəd] *a* impoli(e), grossier(ère).

illness ['ɪlnɪs] *n* maladie *f*.

illogical [ɪ'lɔdʒɪkl] *a* illogique.

ill-treat [ɪl'tri:t] *vt* maltraiter.

illuminate [ɪ'lu:mɪneɪt] *vt* (*room, street*) éclairer ; (*building*) illuminer ; ~**d sign** *n* enseigne lumineuse ; **illumination** [-'neɪʃən] *n* éclairage *m* ; illumination *f*.

illusion [ɪ'lu:ʒən] *n* illusion *f* ; **to be under the** ~ **that** s'imaginer *or* croire que.

illusive, illusory [ɪ'lu:sɪv, ɪ'lu:sərɪ] *a* illusoire.

illustrate ['ɪləstreɪt] *vt* illustrer ; **illustration** [-'streɪʃən] *n* illustration *f*.

illustrious [ɪ'lʌstrɪəs] *a* illustre.

ill will [ɪl'wɪl] *n* malveillance *f*.

I'm [aɪm] = **I am**.

image ['ɪmɪdʒ] *n* image *f* ; (*public face*) image de marque ; ~**ry** *n* images *fpl*.

imaginary [ɪ'mædʒɪnərɪ] *a* imaginaire.

imagination [ɪmædʒɪ'neɪʃən] *n* imagination *f*.

imaginative [ɪ'mædʒɪnətɪv] *a* imaginatif(ive) ; plein(e) d'imagination.

imagine [ɪ'mædʒɪn] *vt* s'imaginer ; (*suppose*) imaginer, supposer.

imbalance [ɪm'bæləns] *n* déséquilibre *m*.

imbecile ['ɪmbəsi:l] *n* imbécile *m/f*.

imbue [ɪm'bju:] *vt*: **to** ~ **sth with** imprégner qch de.

imitate ['ɪmɪteɪt] *vt* imiter ; **imitation** [-'teɪʃən] *n* imitation *f* ; **imitator** *n* imitateur/trice.

immaculate [ɪ'mækjulət] *a* impeccable ; (REL) immaculé(e).

immaterial [ɪmə'tɪərɪəl] *a* sans importance, insignifiant(e).

immature [ɪmə'tjuə*] *a* (*fruit*) qui n'est pas mûr(e) ; (*person*) qui manque de maturité.

immediate [ɪ'mi:dɪət] *a* immédiat(e) ; ~**ly** *ad* (*at once*) immédiatement ; ~**ly next to** juste à côté de.

immense [ɪ'mɛns] *a* immense ; énorme.

immerse [ɪ'mə:s] *vt* immerger, plonger ; **to** ~ **sth in** plonger qch dans.

immersion heater [ɪ'mə:ʃnhi:tə*] *n* chauffe-eau *m* électrique.

immigrant ['ɪmɪgrənt] *n* immigrant/e ; immigré/e.

immigration [ɪmɪ'greɪʃən] *n* immigration *f*.

imminent ['ɪmɪnənt] *a* imminent(e).

immobilize [ɪ'məubɪlaɪz] *vt* immobiliser.

immoderate [ɪ'mɔdərət] *a* immodéré(e), démesuré(e).

immoral [ɪ'mɔrl] *a* immoral(e) ; ~**ity** [-'rælɪtɪ] *n* immoralité *f*.

immortal [ɪ'mɔ:tl] *a, n* immortel(le) ; ~**ize** *vt* immortaliser.

immune [ɪ'mju:n] *a*: ~ **(to)** immunisé(e) (contre).
immunization [ɪmjunaɪ'zeɪʃən] *n* immunisation *f*.
immunize ['ɪmjunaɪz] *vt* immuniser.
impact ['ɪmpækt] *n* choc *m*, impact *m*; (*fig*) impact.
impair [ɪm'pɛə*] *vt* détériorer, diminuer.
impale [ɪm'peɪl] *vt* empaler.
impartial [ɪm'pɑ:ʃl] *a* impartial(e); **~ity** [ɪmpɑ:ʃɪ'ælɪtɪ] *n* impartialité *f*.
impassable [ɪm'pɑ:səbl] *a* infranchissable; (*road*) impraticable.
impassioned [ɪm'pæʃənd] *a* passionné(e).
impatience [ɪm'peɪʃəns] *n* impatience *f*.
impatient [ɪm'peɪʃənt] *a* impatient(e).
impeach [ɪm'pi:tʃ] *vt* accuser, attaquer; (*public official*) mettre en accusation.
impeccable [ɪm'pɛkəbl] *a* impeccable, parfait(e).
impede [ɪm'pi:d] *vt* gêner.
impediment [ɪm'pɛdɪmənt] *n* obstacle *m*; (*also*: **speech** ~) défaut *m* d'élocution.
impending [ɪm'pɛndɪŋ] *a* imminent(e).
impenetrable [ɪm'pɛnɪtrəbl] *a* impénétrable.
imperative [ɪm'pɛrətɪv] *a* nécessaire; urgent(e), pressant(e); (*voice*) impérieux(euse) // *n* (LING) impératif *m*.
imperceptible [ɪmpə'sɛptɪbl] *a* imperceptible.
imperfect [ɪm'pə:fɪkt] *a* imparfait(e); (*goods etc*) défectueux(euse) // *n* (LING: *also*: ~ **tense**) imparfait *m*; **~ion** [-'fɛkʃən] *n* imperfection *f*, défectuosité *f*.
imperial [ɪm'pɪərɪəl] *a* impérial(e); (*measure*) légal(e); **~ism** *n* impérialisme *m*.
imperil [ɪm'pɛrɪl] *vt* mettre en péril.
impersonal [ɪm'pə:sənl] *a* impersonnel(le).
impersonate [ɪm'pə:səneɪt] *vt* se faire passer pour; (THEATRE) imiter; **impersonation** [-'neɪʃən] *n* (LAW) usurpation *f* d'identité; (THEATRE) imitation *f*.
impertinent [ɪm'pə:tɪnənt] *a* impertinent(e), insolent(e).
impervious [ɪm'pə:vɪəs] *a* imperméable; (*fig*): ~ **to** insensible à; inaccessible à.
impetuous [ɪm'pɛtjuəs] *a* impétueux(euse), fougueux(euse).
impetus ['ɪmpətəs] *n* impulsion *f*; (*of runner*) élan *m*.
impinge [ɪm'pɪndʒ]: **to ~ on** *vt fus* (*person*) affecter, toucher; (*rights*) empiéter sur.
implausible [ɪm'plɔ:zɪbl] *a* peu plausible.
implement *n* ['ɪmplɪmənt] outil *m*, instrument *m*; (*for cooking*) ustensile *m* // *vt* ['ɪmplɪmɛnt] exécuter, mettre à effet.
implicate ['ɪmplɪkeɪt] *vt* impliquer, compromettre; **implication** [-'keɪʃən] *n* implication *f*.
implicit [ɪm'plɪsɪt] *a* implicite; (*complete*) absolu(e), sans réserve.
implore [ɪm'plɔ:*] *vt* implorer, supplier.
imply [ɪm'plaɪ] *vt* suggérer, laisser entendre; indiquer, supposer.
impolite [ɪmpə'laɪt] *a* impoli(e).
imponderable [ɪm'pɔndərəbl] *a* impondérable.
import *vt* [ɪm'pɔ:t] importer // *n* ['ɪmpɔ:t] (COMM) importation *f*; (*meaning*) portée *f*, signification *f*.
importance [ɪm'pɔ:tns] *n* importance *f*.
important [ɪm'pɔ:tnt] *a* important(e).
importation [ɪmpɔ:'teɪʃən] *n* importation *f*.
imported [ɪm'pɔ:tɪd] *a* importé(e), d'importation.
importer [ɪm'pɔ:tə*] *n* importateur/trice.
impose [ɪm'pəuz] *vt* imposer // *vi*: **to ~ on sb** abuser de la gentillesse (*or* crédulité) de qn.
imposing [ɪm'pəuzɪŋ] *a* imposant(e), impressionnant(e).
impossibility [ɪmpɔsə'bɪlɪtɪ] *n* impossibilité *f*.
impossible [ɪm'pɔsɪbl] *a* impossible.
impostor [ɪm'pɔstə*] *n* imposteur *m*.
impotence ['ɪmpətns] *n* impuissance *f*.
impotent ['ɪmpətnt] *a* impuissant(e).
impound [ɪm'paund] *vt* confisquer, saisir.
impoverished [ɪm'pɔvərɪʃt] *a* pauvre, appauvri(e).
impracticable [ɪm'præktɪkəbl] *a* impraticable.
impractical [ɪm'præktɪkl] *a* pas pratique; (*person*) qui manque d'esprit pratique.
imprecise [ɪmprɪ'saɪs] *a* imprécis(e).
impregnable [ɪm'prɛgnəbl] *a* (*fortress*) imprenable; (*fig*) inattaquable; irréfutable.
impregnate ['ɪmprɛgneɪt] *vt* imprégner; (*fertilize*) féconder.
impresario [ɪmprɪ'sɑ:rɪəu] *n* impresario *m*.
impress [ɪm'prɛs] *vt* impressionner, faire impression sur; (*mark*) imprimer, marquer; **to ~ sth on sb** faire bien comprendre qch à qn.
impression [ɪm'prɛʃən] *n* impression *f*; (*of stamp, seal*) empreinte *f*; **to be under the ~ that** avoir l'impression que; **~able** *a* impressionnable, sensible; **~ist** *n* impressionniste *m/f*.
impressive [ɪm'prɛsɪv] *a* impressionnant(e).
imprinted [ɪm'prɪntɪd] *a*: ~ **on** imprimé(e) sur; (*fig*) imprimé(e) *or* gravé(e) dans.
imprison [ɪm'prɪzn] *vt* emprisonner, mettre en prison; **~ment** *n* emprisonnement *m*.
improbable [ɪm'prɔbəbl] *a* improbable; (*excuse*) peu plausible.
impromptu [ɪm'prɔmptju:] *a* impromptu(e).
improper [ɪm'prɔpə*] *a* incorrect(e); (*unsuitable*) déplacé(e), de mauvais goût; indécent(e); **impropriety** [ɪmprə'praɪətɪ] *n* inconvenance *f*; (*of expression*) impropriété *f*.
improve [ɪm'pru:v] *vt* améliorer // *vi* s'améliorer; (*pupil etc*) faire des progrès; **~ment** *n* amélioration *f*; progrès *m*.
improvisation [ɪmprəvaɪ'zeɪʃən] *n* improvisation *f*.
improvise ['ɪmprəvaɪz] *vt,vi* improviser.
imprudence [ɪm'pru:dns] *n* imprudence *f*.
imprudent [ɪm'pru:dnt] *a* imprudent(e).

impudent ['ɪmpjudnt] *a* impudent(e).
impulse ['ɪmpʌls] *n* impulsion *f*.
impulsive [ɪm'pʌlsɪv] *a* impulsif(ive).
impunity [ɪm'pju:nɪtɪ] *n* impunité *f*.
impure [ɪm'pjuə*] *a* impur(e).
impurity [ɪm'pjuərɪtɪ] *n* impureté *f*.
in [ɪn] *prep* dans ; (*with time*: *during, within*): ~ **May/2 days** en mai/2 jours ; (: *after*): ~ **2 weeks** dans 2 semaines ; (*with substance*) en ; (*with town*) à ; (*with country*): **it's ~ France/Portugal** c'est en France/au Portugal // *ad* dedans, à l'intérieur ; (*fashionable*) à la mode ; **is he ~?** est-il là? ; ~ **the country** à la campagne ; ~ **town** en ville ; ~ **the sun** au soleil ; ~ **the rain** sous la pluie ; ~ **French** en français ; **a man ~ 10** un homme sur 10 ; ~ **hundreds** par centaines ; **the best pupil ~ the class** le meilleur élève de la classe ; ~ **saying this** en disant ceci ; **their party is ~** leur parti est au pouvoir ; **to ask sb ~** inviter qn à entrer ; **to run/limp** *etc* ~ entrer en courant/boitant *etc* ; **the ~s and outs of** les tenants et aboutissants de.
in., ins *abbr of* **inch(es)**.
inability [ɪnə'bɪlɪtɪ] *n* incapacité *f*.
inaccessible [ɪnək'sɛsɪbl] *a* inaccessible.
inaccuracy [ɪn'ækjurəsɪ] *n* inexactitude *f*; manque *m* de précision.
inaccurate [ɪn'ækjurət] *a* inexact(e) ; (*person*) qui manque de précision.
inaction [ɪn'ækʃən] *n* inaction *f*, inactivité *f*.
inactivity [ɪnæk'tɪvɪtɪ] *n* inactivité *f*.
inadequacy [ɪn'ædɪkwəsɪ] *n* insuffisance *f*.
inadequate [ɪn'ædɪkwət] *a* insuffisant(e), inadéquat(e).
inadvertently [ɪnəd'və:tntlɪ] *ad* par mégarde.
inadvisable [ɪnəd'vaɪzəbl] *a* à déconseiller ; **it is ~ to** il est déconseillé de.
inane [ɪ'neɪn] *a* inepte, stupide.
inanimate [ɪn'ænɪmət] *a* inanimé(e).
inappropriate [ɪnə'prəuprɪət] *a* inopportun(e), mal à propos ; (*word, expression*) impropre.
inapt [ɪn'æpt] *a* inapte ; peu approprié(e) ; **~itude** *n* inaptitude *f*.
inarticulate [ɪnɑ:'tɪkjulət] *a* (*person*) qui s'exprime mal ; (*speech*) indistinct(e).
inasmuch as [ɪnəz'mʌtʃæz] *ad* dans la mesure où ; (*seeing that*) attendu que.
inattention [ɪnə'tɛnʃən] *n* manque *m* d'attention.
inattentive [ɪnə'tɛntɪv] *a* inattentif(ive), distrait(e) ; négligent(e).
inaudible [ɪn'ɔ:dɪbl] *a* inaudible.
inaugural [ɪ'nɔ:gjurəl] *a* inaugural(e).
inaugurate [ɪ'nɔ:gjureɪt] *vt* inaugurer ; (*president, official*) investir de ses fonctions ; **inauguration** [-'reɪʃən] *n* inauguration *f*; investiture *f*.
in-between [ɪnbɪ'twi:n] *a* entre les deux.
inborn [ɪn'bɔ:n] *a* (*feeling*) inné(e) ; (*defect*) congénital(e).
inbred [ɪn'brɛd] *a* inné(e), naturel(le) ; (*family*) consanguin(e).
inbreeding [ɪn'bri:dɪŋ] *n* croisement *m* d'animaux de même souche ; unions consanguines.
Inc. *abbr see* **incorporated**.
incalculable [ɪn'kælkjuləbl] *a* incalculable.
incapability [ɪnkeɪpə'bɪlɪtɪ] *n* incapacité *f*.
incapable [ɪn'keɪpəbl] *a* incapable.
incapacitate [ɪnkə'pæsɪteɪt] *vt*: **to ~ sb from doing** rendre qn incapable de faire ; **~d** *a* (LAW) frappé(e) d'incapacité.
incapacity [ɪnkə'pæsɪtɪ] *n* incapacité *f*.
incarcerate [ɪn'kɑ:səreɪt] *vt* incarcérer.
incarnate *a* [ɪn'kɑ:nɪt] incarné(e) // *vt* ['ɪnkɑ:neɪt] incarner ; **incarnation** [-'neɪʃən] *n* incarnation *f*.
incendiary [ɪn'sɛndɪərɪ] *a* incendiaire.
incense *n* ['ɪnsɛns] encens *m* // *vt* [ɪn'sɛns] (*anger*) mettre en colère ; ~ **burner** *n* encensoir *m*.
incentive [ɪn'sɛntɪv] *n* encouragement *m*, raison *f* de se donner de la peine ; ~ **bonus** *n* prime *f* d'encouragement.
incessant [ɪn'sɛsnt] *a* incessant(e) ; **~ly** *ad* sans cesse, constamment.
incest ['ɪnsɛst] *n* inceste *m*.
inch [ɪntʃ] *n* pouce *m* (= *25 mm*; *12 in a foot*) ; **within an ~ of** à deux doigts de ; ~ **tape** *n* centimètre *m* (de couturière).
incidence ['ɪnsɪdns] *n* (*of crime, disease*) fréquence *f*.
incident ['ɪnsɪdnt] *n* incident *m* ; (*in book*) péripétie *f*.
incidental [ɪnsɪ'dɛntl] *a* accessoire ; (*unplanned*) accidentel(le) ; ~ **to** qui accompagne ; ~ **expenses** *npl* faux frais *mpl*; **~ly** [-'dɛntəlɪ] *ad* (*by the way*) à propos.
incinerator [ɪn'sɪnəreɪtə*] *n* incinérateur *m*.
incipient [ɪn'sɪpɪənt] *a* naissant(e).
incision [ɪn'sɪʒən] *n* incision *f*.
incisive [ɪn'saɪsɪv] *a* incisif(ive) ; mordant(e).
incite [ɪn'saɪt] *vt* inciter, pousser.
inclement [ɪn'klɛmənt] *a* inclément(e), rigoureux(euse).
inclination [ɪnklɪ'neɪʃən] *n* inclination *f*.
incline *n* ['ɪnklaɪn] pente *f*, plan incliné // *vb* [ɪn'klaɪn] *vt* incliner // *vi*: **to ~ to** avoir tendance à ; **to be ~d to do** être enclin(e) à faire ; avoir tendance à faire ; **to be well ~d towards sb** être bien disposé(e) à l'égard de qn.
include [ɪn'klu:d] *vt* inclure, comprendre ; **including** *prep* y compris.
inclusion [ɪn'klu:ʒən] *n* inclusion *f*.
inclusive [ɪn'klu:sɪv] *a* inclus(e), compris(e) ; ~ **terms** *npl* prix tout compris.
incognito [ɪnkɔg'ni:təu] *ad* incognito.
incoherent [ɪnkəu'hɪərənt] *a* incohérent(e).
income ['ɪŋkʌm] *n* revenu *m* ; ~ **tax** *n* impôt *m* sur le revenu ; ~ **tax inspector** *n* inspecteur *m* des contributions directes ; ~ **tax return** *n* déclaration *f* des revenus.
incoming ['ɪnkʌmɪŋ] *a*: ~ **tide** *n* marée montante.
incompatible [ɪnkəm'pætɪbl] *a* incompatible.

incompetence [ɪn'kɔmpɪtns] *n* incompétence *f*, incapacité *f*.
incompetent [ɪn'kɔmpɪtnt] *a* incompétent(e), incapable.
incomplete [ɪnkəm'pli:t] *a* incomplet(ète).
incomprehensible [ɪnkɔmprɪ'hɛnsɪbl] *a* incompréhensible.
inconclusive [ɪnkən'klu:sɪv] *a* peu concluant(e) ; (*argument*) peu convaincant(e).
incongruous [ɪn'kɔŋgruəs] *a* peu approprié(e) ; (*remark, act*) incongru(e), déplacé(e).
inconsequential [ɪnkɔnsɪ'kwɛnʃl] *a* sans importance.
inconsiderate [ɪnkən'sɪdərət] *a* (*action*) inconsidéré(e) ; (*person*) qui manque d'égards.
inconsistent [ɪnkən'sɪstnt] *a* sans cohérence ; peu logique ; qui présente des contradictions ; ~ **with** en contradiction avec.
inconspicuous [ɪnkən'spɪkjuəs] *a* qui passe inaperçu(e) ; (*colour, dress*) discret(ète) ; **to make o.s.** ~ ne pas se faire remarquer.
inconstant [ɪn'kɔnstnt] *a* inconstant(e) ; variable.
incontinence [ɪn'kɔntɪnəns] *n* incontinence *f*.
incontinent [ɪn'kɔntɪnənt] *a* incontinent(e).
inconvenience [ɪnkən'vi:njəns] *n* inconvénient *m* ; (*trouble*) dérangement *m* // *vt* déranger.
inconvenient [ɪnkən'vi:njənt] *a* malcommode ; (*time, place*) mal choisi(e), qui ne convient pas.
incorporate [ɪn'kɔ:pəreɪt] *vt* incorporer ; (*contain*) contenir // *vi* fusionner ; (*two firms*) se constituer en société ; ~**d** *a*: ~**d company** (*US, abbr* **Inc.**) société *f* anonyme (S.A.).
incorrect [ɪnkə'rɛkt] *a* incorrect(e) ; (*opinion, statement*) inexact(e).
incorruptible [ɪnkə'rʌptɪbl] *a* incorruptible.
increase *n* ['ɪnkri:s] augmentation *f* // *vi, vt* [ɪn'kri:s] augmenter.
increasing [ɪn'kri:sɪŋ] *a* (*number*) croissant(e) ; ~**ly** *ad* de plus en plus.
incredible [ɪn'krɛdɪbl] *a* incroyable.
incredulous [ɪn'krɛdjuləs] *a* incrédule.
increment ['ɪnkrɪmənt] *n* augmentation *f*.
incriminate [ɪn'krɪmɪneɪt] *vt* incriminer, compromettre.
incubation [ɪnkju'beɪʃən] *n* incubation *f*.
incubator ['ɪnkjubeɪtə*] *n* incubateur *m* ; (*for babies*) couveuse *f*.
incur [ɪn'kə:*] *vt* (*expenses*) encourir ; (*anger, risk*) s'exposer à ; (*debt*) contracter ; (*loss*) subir.
incurable [ɪn'kjuərəbl] *a* incurable.
incursion [ɪn'kə:ʃən] *n* incursion *f*.
indebted [ɪn'dɛtɪd] *a*: **to be ~ to sb (for)** être redevable à qn (de).
indecent [ɪn'di:snt] *a* indécent(e), inconvenant(e) ; ~ **assault** *n* attentat *m* à la pudeur ; ~ **exposure** *n* outrage *m* (public) à la pudeur.
indecision [ɪndɪ'sɪʒən] *n* indécision *f*.
indecisive [ɪndɪ'saɪsɪv] *a* indécis(e) ; (*discussion*) peu concluant(e).
indeed [ɪn'di:d] *ad* en effet ; vraiment ; **yes** ~! certainement!
indefinable [ɪndɪ'faɪnəbl] *a* indéfinissable.
indefinite [ɪn'dɛfɪnɪt] *a* indéfini(e) ; (*answer*) vague ; (*period, number*) indéterminé(e) ; ~**ly** *ad* (*wait*) indéfiniment ; (*speak*) vaguement, avec imprécision.
indelible [ɪn'dɛlɪbl] *a* indélébile.
indemnify [ɪn'dɛmnɪfaɪ] *vt* indemniser, dédommager.
indentation [ɪndɛn'teɪʃən] *n* découpure *f* ; (TYP) alinéa *m* ; (*on metal*) bosse *f*.
independence [ɪndɪ'pɛndns] *n* indépendance *f*.
independent [ɪndɪ'pɛndnt] *a* indépendant(e) ; ~**ly** *ad* de façon indépendante ; ~**ly of** indépendamment de.
indescribable [ɪndɪ'skraɪbəbl] *a* indescriptible.
index ['ɪndɛks] *n* (*pl*: ~**es**: *in book*) index *m* ; (: *in library etc*) catalogue *m* ; (*pl*: **indices** ['ɪndɪsi:z]: *ratio, sign*) indice *m* ; ~ **card** *n* fiche *f* ; ~ **finger** *n* index *m* ; ~-**linked** *a* indexé(e) (sur le coût de la vie *etc*).
India ['ɪndɪə] *n* Inde *f* ; ~**n** *a* indien(ne) // *n* Indien/ne ; ~**n ink** *n* encre *f* de Chine ; ~**n Ocean** *n* océan Indien ; ~ **paper** *n* papier *m* bible.
indicate ['ɪndɪkeɪt] *vt* indiquer ; **indication** [-'keɪʃən] *n* indication *f*, signe *m*.
indicative [ɪn'dɪkətɪv] *a* indicatif(ive) // *n* (LING) indicatif *m*.
indicator ['ɪndɪkeɪtə*] *n* (*sign*) indicateur *m* ; (AUT) clignotant *m*.
indices ['ɪndɪsi:z] *npl of* **index**.
indict [ɪn'daɪt] *vt* accuser ; ~**able** *a* (*person*) passible de poursuites ; ~**able offence** *n* délit pénal ; ~**ment** *n* accusation *f*.
indifference [ɪn'dɪfrəns] *n* indifférence *f*.
indifferent [ɪn'dɪfrənt] *a* indifférent(e) ; (*poor*) médiocre, quelconque.
indigenous [ɪn'dɪdʒɪnəs] *a* indigène.
indigestible [ɪndɪ'dʒɛstɪbl] *a* indigeste.
indigestion [ɪndɪ'dʒɛstʃən] *n* indigestion *f*, mauvaise digestion.
indignant [ɪn'dɪgnənt] *a*: ~ **(at sth/with sb)** indigné(e) (de qch/contre qn).
indignation [ɪndɪg'neɪʃən] *n* indignation *f*.
indignity [ɪn'dɪgnɪtɪ] *n* indignité *f*, affront *m*.
indigo ['ɪndɪgəu] *a* indigo *inv* // *n* indigo *m*.
indirect [ɪndɪ'rɛkt] *a* indirect(e) ; ~**ly** *ad* indirectement.
indiscreet [ɪndɪ'skri:t] *a* indiscret(ète) ; (*rash*) imprudent(e).
indiscretion [ɪndɪ'skrɛʃən] *n* indiscrétion *f* ; imprudence *f*.
indiscriminate [ɪndɪ'skrɪmɪnət] *a* (*person*) qui manque de discernement ; (*admiration*) aveugle ; (*killings*) commis(e) au hasard.
indispensable [ɪndɪ'spɛnsəbl] *a* indispensable.
indisposed [ɪndɪ'spəuzd] *a* (*unwell*) indisposé(e), souffrant(e).

indisposition [ɪndɪspə'zɪʃən] *n* (*illness*) indisposition *f*, malaise *m*.
indisputable [ɪndɪ'spju:təbl] *a* incontestable, indiscutable.
indistinct [ɪndɪ'stɪŋkt] *a* indistinct(e) ; (*memory, noise*) vague.
individual [ɪndɪ'vɪdjuəl] *n* individu *m* // *a* individuel(le) ; (*characteristic*) particulier(ère), original(e) ; **~ist** *n* individualiste *m/f*; **~ity** [-'ælɪtɪ] *n* individualité *f*; **~ly** *ad* individuellement.
indoctrinate [ɪn'dɔktrɪneɪt] *vt* endoctriner ; **indoctrination** [-'neɪʃən] *n* endoctrinement *m*.
indolent ['ɪndələnt] *a* indolent(e), nonchalant(e).
indoor ['ɪndɔ:*] *a* d'intérieur ; (*plant*) d'appartement ; (*swimming-pool*) couvert(e) ; (*sport, games*) pratiqué(e) en salle ; **~s** [ɪn'dɔ:z] *ad* à l'intérieur ; (*at home*) à la maison.
indubitable [ɪn'dju:bɪtəbl] *a* indubitable, incontestable.
induce [ɪn'dju:s] *vt* persuader ; (*bring about*) provoquer ; **~ment** *n* incitation *f*; (*incentive*) but *m* ; (*pej*: *bribe*) pot-de-vin *m*.
induct [ɪn'dʌkt] *vt* établir dans ses fonctions ; (*fig*) initier.
induction [ɪn'dʌkʃən] *n* (MED: *of birth*) accouchement provoqué ; **~ course** *n* stage *m* de mise au courant.
indulge [ɪn'dʌldʒ] *vt* (*whim*) céder à, satisfaire ; (*child*) gâter // *vi*: **to ~ in sth** s'offrir qch, se permettre qch ; se livrer à qch ; **~nce** *n* fantaisie *f* (que l'on s'offre) ; (*leniency*) indulgence *f*; **~nt** *a* indulgent(e).
industrial [ɪn'dʌstrɪəl] *a* industriel(le) ; (*injury*) du travail ; (*dispute*) ouvrier(ère) ; **~ action** *n* action revendicative ; **~ estate** *n* zone industrielle ; **~ist** *n* industriel *m* ; **~ize** *vt* industrialiser.
industrious [ɪn'dʌstrɪəs] *a* travailleur(euse).
industry ['ɪndəstrɪ] *n* industrie *f*; (*diligence*) zèle *m*, application *f*.
inebriated [ɪ'ni:brɪeɪtɪd] *a* ivre.
inedible [ɪn'ɛdɪbl] *a* immangeable ; (*plant etc*) non comestible.
ineffective [ɪnɪ'fɛktɪv] *a* inefficace.
ineffectual [ɪnɪ'fɛktʃuəl] *a* inefficace ; incompétent(e).
inefficiency [ɪnɪ'fɪʃənsɪ] *n* inefficacité *f*.
inefficient [ɪnɪ'fɪʃənt] *a* inefficace.
inelegant [ɪn'ɛlɪgənt] *a* peu élégant(e).
ineligible [ɪn'ɛlɪdʒɪbl] *a* (*candidate*) inéligible ; **to be ~ for sth** ne pas avoir droit à qch.
inept [ɪ'nɛpt] *a* inepte.
inequality [ɪnɪ'kwɔlɪtɪ] *n* inégalité *f*.
ineradicable [ɪnɪ'rædɪkəbl] *a* indéracinable, tenace.
inert [ɪ'nə:t] *a* inerte.
inertia [ɪ'nə:ʃə] *n* inertie *f*; **~ reel seat belt** *n* ceinture *f* de sécurité à enrouleur.
inescapable [ɪnɪ'skeɪpəbl] *a* inéluctable, inévitable.
inessential [ɪnɪ'sɛnʃl] *a* superflu(e).
inestimable [ɪn'ɛstɪməbl] *a* inestimable, incalculable.
inevitable [ɪn'ɛvɪtəbl] *a* inévitable.
inexact [ɪnɪg'zækt] *a* inexact(e).
inexhaustible [ɪnɪg'zɔ:stɪbl] *a* inépuisable.
inexorable [ɪn'ɛksərəbl] *a* inexorable.
inexpensive [ɪnɪk'spɛnsɪv] *a* bon marché *inv*.
inexperience [ɪnɪk'spɪərɪəns] *n* inexpérience *f*, manque *m* d'expérience ; **~d** *a* inexpérimenté(e).
inexplicable [ɪnɪk'splɪkəbl] *a* inexplicable.
inexpressible [ɪnɪk'sprɛsɪbl] *a* inexprimable.
inextricable [ɪnɪk'strɪkəbl] *a* inextricable.
infallibility [ɪnfælə'bɪlɪtɪ] *n* infaillibilité *f*.
infallible [ɪn'fælɪbl] *a* infaillible.
infamous ['ɪnfəməs] *a* infâme, abominable.
infamy ['ɪnfəmɪ] *n* infamie *f*.
infancy ['ɪnfənsɪ] *n* petite enfance, bas âge ; (*fig*) enfance *f*, débuts *mpl*.
infant ['ɪnfənt] *n* (*baby*) nourrisson *m* ; (*young child*) petit(e) enfant ; **~ile** *a* infantile ; **~ school** *n* classes *fpl* préparatoires (*entre 5 et 7 ans*).
infantry ['ɪnfəntrɪ] *n* infanterie *f*; **~man** *n* fantassin *m*.
infatuated [ɪn'fætjueɪtɪd] *a*: **~ with** entiché(e) de.
infatuation [ɪnfætju'eɪʃən] *n* toquade *f*; engouement *m*.
infect [ɪn'fɛkt] *vt* infecter, contaminer ; (*fig*: *pej*) corrompre ; **~ed with** (*illness*) atteint(e) de ; **~ion** [ɪn'fɛkʃən] *n* infection *f*; contagion *f*; **~ious** [ɪn'fɛkʃəs] *a* infectieux(euse) ; (*also*: *fig*) contagieux(euse).
infer [ɪn'fə:*] *vt* conclure, déduire ; **~ence** ['ɪnfərəns] *n* conclusion *f*; déduction *f*.
inferior [ɪn'fɪərɪə*] *a* inférieur(e) ; (*goods*) de qualité inférieure // *n* inférieur/e ; (*in rank*) subalterne *m/f*; **~ity** [ɪnfɪərɪ'ɔrətɪ] *n* infériorité *f*; **~ity complex** *n* complexe *m* d'infériorité.
infernal [ɪn'fə:nl] *a* infernal(e) ; **~ly** *ad* abominablement.
inferno [ɪn'fə:nəu] *n* enfer *m* ; brasier *m*.
infertile [ɪn'fə:taɪl] *a* stérile ; **infertility** [-'tɪlɪtɪ] *n* infertilité *f*, stérilité *f*.
infested [ɪn'fɛstɪd] *a*: **~ (with)** infesté(e) (de).
infidelity [ɪnfɪ'dɛlɪtɪ] *n* infidélité *f*.
in-fighting ['ɪnfaɪtɪŋ] *n* querelles *fpl* internes.
infiltrate ['ɪnfɪltreɪt] *vt* (*troops etc*) faire s'infiltrer ; (*enemy line etc*) s'infiltrer dans // *vi* s'infiltrer.
infinite ['ɪnfɪnɪt] *a* infini(e).
infinitive [ɪn'fɪnɪtɪv] *n* infinitif *m*.
infinity [ɪn'fɪnɪtɪ] *n* infinité *f*; (*also* MATH) infini *m*.
infirm [ɪn'fə:m] *a* infirme.
infirmary [ɪn'fə:mərɪ] *n* hôpital *m* ; (*in school, factory*) infirmerie *f*.
infirmity [ɪn'fə:mɪtɪ] *n* infirmité *f*.
inflame [ɪn'fleɪm] *vt* enflammer.
inflammable [ɪn'flæməbl] *a* inflammable.
inflammation [ɪnflə'meɪʃən] *n* inflammation *f*.
inflate [ɪn'fleɪt] *vt* (*tyre, balloon*) gonfler ; (*fig*) grossir ; gonfler ; faire monter ; **to ~ the currency** avoir recours à l'inflation ;

~**d** *a* (*style*) enflé(e); (*value*) exagéré(e); **inflation** [ɪn'fleɪʃən] *n* (*ECON*) inflation *f*.
inflexible [ɪn'flɛksɪbl] *a* inflexible, rigide.
inflict [ɪn'flɪkt] *vt*: **to ~ on** infliger à; ~**ion** [ɪn'flɪkʃən] *n* infliction *f*; affliction *f*.
inflow ['ɪnfləu] *n* afflux *m*.
influence ['ɪnfluəns] *n* influence *f* // *vt* influencer; **under the ~ of** sous l'effet de; **under the ~ of drink** en état d'ébriété.
influential [ɪnflu'ɛnʃl] *a* influent(e).
influenza [ɪnflu'ɛnzə] *n* grippe *f*.
influx ['ɪnflʌks] *n* afflux *m*.
inform [ɪn'fɔ:m] *vt*: **to ~ sb (of)** informer *or* avertir qn (de); **to ~ sb about** renseigner qn sur, mettre qn au courant de.
informal [ɪn'fɔ:ml] *a* (*person, manner*) simple, sans façon; (*visit, discussion*) dénué(e) de formalités; (*announcement, invitation*) non-officiel(le); **'dress ~'** 'tenue de ville'; ~**ity** [-'mælɪtɪ] *n* simplicité *f*, absence *f* de cérémonie; caractère non-officiel; ~ **language** *n* langage *m* de la conversation.
information [ɪnfə'meɪʃən] *n* information *f*; renseignements *mpl*; (*knowledge*) connaissances *fpl*; **a piece of ~** un renseignement.
informative [ɪn'fɔ:mətɪv] *a* instructif(ive).
informer [ɪn'fɔ:mə*] *n* dénonciateur/-trice; (*also*: **police ~**) indicateur/trice.
infra-red [ɪnfrə'rɛd] *a* infrarouge.
infrequent [ɪn'fri:kwənt] *a* peu fréquent(e), rare.
infringe [ɪn'frɪndʒ] *vt* enfreindre // *vi*: **to ~ on** empiéter sur; ~**ment** *n*: ~**ment (of)** infraction *f* (à).
infuriate [ɪn'fjuərɪeɪt] *vt* mettre en fureur; **infuriating** *a* exaspérant(e).
ingenious [ɪn'dʒi:njəs] *a* ingénieux(euse).
ingenuity [ɪndʒɪ'nju:ɪtɪ] *n* ingéniosité *f*.
ingenuous [ɪn'dʒɛnjuəs] *a* naïf(ïve), ingénu(e).
ingot ['ɪŋgət] *n* lingot *m*.
ingrained [ɪn'greɪnd] *a* enraciné(e).
ingratiate [ɪn'greɪʃɪeɪt] *vt*: **to ~ o.s. with** s'insinuer dans les bonnes grâces de, se faire bien voir de.
ingratitude [ɪn'grætɪtju:d] *n* ingratitude *f*.
ingredient [ɪn'gri:dɪənt] *n* ingrédient *m*; élément *m*.
ingrown ['ɪngrəun] *a*: ~ **toenail** ougle incarné.
inhabit [ɪn'hæbɪt] *vt* habiter.
inhabitant [ɪn'hæbɪtnt] *n* habitant/e.
inhale [ɪn'heɪl] *vt* inhaler; (*perfume*) respirer // *vi* (*in smoking*) avaler la fumée.
inherent [ɪn'hɪərənt] *a*: ~ **(in** *or* **to)** inhérent(e) (à).
inherit [ɪn'hɛrɪt] *vt* hériter (de); ~**ance** *n* héritage *m*; **law of ~ance** *n* droit *m* de la succession.
inhibit [ɪn'hɪbɪt] *vt* (*PSYCH*) inhiber; **to ~ sb from doing** empêcher *or* retenir qn de faire; ~**ing** *a* gênant(e); ~**ion** [-'bɪʃən] *n* inhibition *f*.
inhospitable [ɪnhɔs'pɪtəbl] *a* inhospitalier(ère).
inhuman [ɪn'hju:mən] *a* inhumain(e).
inimitable [ɪ'nɪmɪtəbl] *a* inimitable.
iniquity [ɪ'nɪkwɪtɪ] *n* iniquité *f*.
initial [ɪ'nɪʃl] *a* initial(e) // *n* initiale *f* // *vt* parafer; ~**s** *npl* initiales *fpl*; (*as signature*) parafe *m*; ~**ly** *ad* initialement, au début.
initiate [ɪ'nɪʃɪeɪt] *vt* (*start*) entreprendre; amorcer; lancer; (*person*) initier; **to ~ sb into a secret** initier qn à un secret; **to ~ proceedings against sb** (*LAW*) intenter une action à qn; **initiation** [-'eɪʃən] *n* (*into secret etc*) initiation *f*.
initiative [ɪ'nɪʃətɪv] *n* initiative *f*.
inject [ɪn'dʒɛkt] *vt* (*liquid*) injecter; (*person*) faire une piqûre à; ~**ion** [ɪn'dʒɛkʃən] *n* injection *f*, piqûre *f*.
injure ['ɪndʒə*] *vt* blesser; (*wrong*) faire du tort à; (*damage*: *reputation etc*) compromettre.
injury ['ɪndʒərɪ] *n* blessure *f*; (*wrong*) tort *m*; ~ **time** *n* (*SPORT*) arrêts *mpl* de jeu.
injustice [ɪn'dʒʌstɪs] *n* injustice *f*.
ink [ɪŋk] *n* encre *f*.
inkling ['ɪŋklɪŋ] *n* soupçon *m*, vague idée *f*.
inky ['ɪŋkɪ] *a* taché(e) d'encre.
inlaid ['ɪnleɪd] *a* incrusté(e); (*table etc*) marqueté(e).
inland *a* ['ɪnlənd] intérieur(e) // *ad* [ɪn'lænd] à l'intérieur, dans les terres; **I~ Revenue** *n* (*Brit*) fisc *m*, contributions directes; ~ **waterways** *npl* canaux *mpl* et rivières *fpl*.
in-laws ['ɪnlɔ:z] *npl* beaux-parents *mpl*; belle famille.
inlet ['ɪnlɛt] *n* (*GEO*) crique *f*; ~ **pipe** *n* (*TECH*) tuyau *m* d'arrivée.
inmate ['ɪnmeɪt] *n* (*in prison*) détenu/e; (*in asylum*) interné/e.
inn [ɪn] *n* auberge *f*.
innate [ɪ'neɪt] *a* inné(e).
inner ['ɪnə*] *a* intérieur(e); ~ **city** *n* centre *m* de zone urbaine; ~ **tube** *n* (*of tyre*) chambre *f* à air.
innocence ['ɪnəsns] *n* innocence *f*.
innocent ['ɪnəsnt] *a* innocent(e).
innocuous [ɪ'nɔkjuəs] *a* inoffensif(ive).
innovation [ɪnəu'veɪʃən] *n* innovation *f*.
innuendo, ~es [ɪnju'ɛndəu] *n* insinuation *f*, allusion (malveillante).
innumerable [ɪ'nju:mrəbl] *a* innombrable.
inoculation [ɪnɔkju'leɪʃən] *n* inoculation *f*.
inopportune [ɪn'ɔpətju:n] *a* inopportun(e).
inordinately [ɪ'nɔ:dɪnətlɪ] *ad* démesurément.
inorganic [ɪnɔ:'gænɪk] *a* inorganique.
in-patient ['ɪnpeɪʃənt] *n* malade hospitalisé(e).
input ['ɪnput] *n* (*ELEC*) énergie *f*, puissance *f*; (*of machine*) consommation *f*; (*of computer*) information fournie.
inquest ['ɪnkwɛst] *n* enquête (criminelle).
inquire [ɪn'kwaɪə*] *vi* demander // *vt* demander, s'informer de; **to ~ about** *vt fus* s'informer de, se renseigner sur; **to ~ after** *vt fus* demander des nouvelles de; **to ~ into** *vt fus* faire une enquête sur; **inquiring** *a* (*mind*) curieux(euse), investigateur(trice); **inquiry** *n* demande *f* de renseignements; (*LAW*) enquête *f*,

investigation *f*; **inquiry office** *n* bureau *m* de renseignements.
inquisitive [ɪn'kwɪzɪtɪv] *a* curieux(euse).
inroad ['ɪnrəud] *n* incursion *f*.
insane [ɪn'seɪn] *a* fou(folle); (MED) aliéné(e).
insanitary [ɪn'sænɪtərɪ] *a* insalubre.
insanity [ɪn'sænɪtɪ] *n* folie *f*; (MED) aliénation (mentale).
insatiable [ɪn'seɪʃəbl] *a* insatiable.
inscribe [ɪn'skraɪb] *vt* inscrire; (*book etc*): **to ~ (to sb)** dédicacer (à qn).
inscription [ɪn'skrɪpʃən] *n* inscription *f*; dédicace *f*.
inscrutable [ɪn'skru:təbl] *a* impénétrable.
insect ['ɪnsɛkt] *n* insecte *m*; **~icide** [ɪn'sɛktɪsaɪd] *n* insecticide *m*.
insecure [ɪnsɪ'kjuə*] *a* peu solide; peu sûr(e); (*person*) anxieux (euse); **insecurity** *n* insécurité *f*.
insensible [ɪn'sɛnsɪbl] *a* insensible; (*unconscious*) sans connaissance.
insensitive [ɪn'sɛnsɪtɪv] *a* insensible.
inseparable [ɪn'sɛprəbl] *a* inséparable.
insert *vt* [ɪn'sə:t] insérer // *n* ['ɪnsə:t] insertion *f*; **~ion** [ɪn'sə:ʃən] *n* insertion *f*.
inshore [ɪn'ʃɔ:*] *a* côtier(ère) // *ad* près de la côte; vers la côte.
inside ['ɪn'saɪd] *n* intérieur *m* // *a* intérieur(e) // *ad* à l'intérieur, dedans // *prep* à l'intérieur de; (*of time*): **~ 10 minutes** en moins de 10 minutes; **~s** *npl* (*col*) intestins *mpl*; **~ forward** *n* (SPORT) intérieur *m*; **~ lane** *n* (AUT: *in Britain*) voie *f* de gauche; **~ out** *ad* à l'envers; (*know*) à fond; **to turn ~ out** retourner.
insidious [ɪn'sɪdɪəs] *a* insidieux(euse).
insight ['ɪnsaɪt] *n* perspicacité *f*; (*glimpse, idea*) aperçu *m*.
insignificant [ɪnsɪg'nɪfɪknt] *a* insignifiant(e).
insincere [ɪnsɪn'sɪə*] *a* hypocrite; **insincerity** [-'sɛrɪtɪ] *n* manque *m* de sincérité, hypocrisie *f*.
insinuate [ɪn'sɪnjueɪt] *vt* insinuer; **insinuation** [-'eɪʃən] *n* insinuation *f*.
insipid [ɪn'sɪpɪd] *a* insipide, fade.
insist [ɪn'sɪst] *vi* insister; **to ~ on doing** insister pour faire; **to ~ that** insister pour que; (*claim*) maintenir *or* soutenir que; **~ence** *n* insistance *f*; **~ent** *a* insistant(e), pressant(e).
insolence ['ɪnsələns] *n* insolence *f*.
insolent ['ɪnsələnt] *a* insolent(e).
insoluble [ɪn'sɔljubl] *a* insoluble.
insolvent [ɪn'sɔlvənt] *a* insolvable; en faillite.
insomnia [ɪn'sɔmnɪə] *n* insomnie *f*.
inspect [ɪn'spɛkt] *vt* inspecter; (*ticket*) contrôler; **~ion** [ɪn'spɛkʃən] *n* inspection *f*; contrôle *m*; **~or** *n* inspecteur/trice; contrôleur/euse.
inspiration [ɪnspə'reɪʃən] *n* inspiration *f*.
inspire [ɪn'spaɪə*] *vt* inspirer; **inspiring** *a* inspirant(e).
instability [ɪnstə'bɪlɪtɪ] *n* instabilité *f*.
install [ɪn'stɔ:l] *vt* installer; **~ation** [ɪnstə'leɪʃən] *n* installation *f*.
instalment, installment (*US*) [ɪn'stɔ:lmənt] *n* acompte *m*, versement partiel; (*of* TV *serial etc*) épisode *m*.
instance ['ɪnstəns] *n* exemple *m*; **for ~** par exemple; **in many ~s** dans bien des cas.
instant ['ɪnstənt] *n* instant *m* // *a* immédiat(e); urgent(e); (*coffee, food*) instantané(e), en poudre; **the 10th ~** le 10 courant; **~ly** *ad* immédiatement, tout de suite.
instead [ɪn'stɛd] *ad* au lieu de cela; **~ of** au lieu de; **~ of sb** à la place de qn.
instep ['ɪnstɛp] *n* cou-de-pied *m*; (*of shoe*) cambrure *f*.
instigation [ɪnstɪ'geɪʃən] *n* instigation *f*.
instil [ɪn'stɪl] *vt*: **to ~ (into)** inculquer (à); (*courage*) insuffler (à).
instinct ['ɪnstɪŋkt] *n* instinct *m*.
instinctive [ɪn'stɪŋktɪv] *a* instinctif(ive); **~ly** *ad* instinctivement.
institute ['ɪnstɪtju:t] *n* institut *m* // *vt* instituer, établir; (*inquiry*) ouvrir; (*proceedings*) entamer.
institution [ɪnstɪ'tju:ʃən] *n* institution *f*; établissement *m* (scolaire); établissement (psychiatrique).
instruct [ɪn'strʌkt] *vt* instruire, former; **to ~ sb in sth** enseigner qch à qn; **to ~ sb to do** charger qn *or* ordonner à qn de faire; **~ion** [ɪn'strʌkʃən] *n* instruction *f*; **~ions** *npl* directives *fpl*; **~ions (for use)** mode *m* d'emploi; **~ive** *a* instructif(ive); **~or** *n* professeur *m*; (*for skiing, driving*) moniteur *m*.
instrument ['ɪnstrumənt] *n* instrument *m*; **~al** [-'mɛntl] *a* (MUS) instrumental(e); **to be ~al in** contribuer à; **~alist** [-'mɛntəlɪst] *n* instrumentiste *m/f*; **~ panel** *n* tableau *m* de bord.
insubordinate [ɪnsə'bɔ:dənɪt] *a* insubordonné(e); **insubordination** [-'neɪʃən] *n* insubordination *f*.
insufferable [ɪn'sʌfrəbl] *a* insupportable.
insufficient [ɪnsə'fɪʃənt] *a* insuffisant(e); **~ly** *ad* insuffisamment.
insular ['ɪnsjulə*] *a* insulaire; (*outlook*) étroit(e); (*person*) aux vues étroites.
insulate ['ɪnsjuleɪt] *vt* isoler; (*against sound*) insonoriser; **insulating tape** *n* ruban isolant; **insulation** [-'leɪʃən] *n* isolation *f*; insonorisation *f*.
insulin ['ɪnsjulɪn] *n* insuline *f*.
insult *n* ['ɪnsʌlt] insulte *f*, affront *m* // *vt* [ɪn'sʌlt] insulter, faire un affront à; **~ing** *a* insultant(e), injurieux(euse).
insuperable [ɪn'sju:prəbl] *a* insurmontable.
insurance [ɪn'ʃuərəns] *n* assurance *f*; **fire/life ~** assurance-incendie/-vie; **~ agent** *n* agent *m* d'assurances; **~ policy** *n* police *f* d'assurance.
insure [ɪn'ʃuə*] *vt* assurer.
insurrection [ɪnsə'rɛkʃən] *n* insurrection *f*.
intact [ɪn'tækt] *a* intact(e).
intake ['ɪnteɪk] *n* (TECH) admission *f*; adduction *f*; (*of food*) consommation *f*; (SCOL): **an ~ of 200 a year** 200 admissions *fpl* par an.
intangible [ɪn'tændʒɪbl] *a* intangible; (*assets*) immatériel(le).
integral ['ɪntɪgrəl] *a* intégral(e); (*part*) intégrant(e).

integrate ['ɪntɪgreɪt] *vt* intégrer // *vi* s'intégrer.

integrity [ɪn'tɛgrɪtɪ] *n* intégrité *f*.

intellect ['ɪntəlɛkt] *n* intelligence *f*; **~ual** [-'lɛktjuəl] *a, n* intellectuel(le).

intelligence [ɪn'tɛlɪdʒəns] *n* intelligence *f*; (MIL *etc*) informations *fpl*, renseignements *mpl*; **I~ Service** *n* services *mpl* de renseignements.

intelligent [ɪn'tɛlɪdʒənt] *a* intelligent(e); **~ly** *ad* intelligemment.

intelligible [ɪn'tɛlɪdʒɪbl] *a* intelligible.

intemperate [ɪn'tɛmpərət] *a* immodéré(e); (*drinking too much*) adonné(e) à la boisson.

intend [ɪn'tɛnd] *vt* (*gift etc*): **to ~ sth for** destiner qch à; **to ~ to do** avoir l'intention de faire; **~ed** *a* (*insult*) intentionnel(le); (*journey*) projeté(e); (*effect*) voulu(e).

intense [ɪn'tɛns] *a* intense; (*person*) véhément(e); **~ly** *ad* intensément; profondément.

intensify [ɪn'tɛnsɪfaɪ] *vt* intensifier.

intensity [ɪn'tɛnsɪtɪ] *n* intensité *f*.

intensive [ɪn'tɛnsɪv] *a* intensif(ive); **~ care unit** *n* service *m* de réanimation.

intent [ɪn'tɛnt] *n* intention *f* // *a* attentif(ive), absorbé(e); **to all ~s and purposes** en fait, pratiquement; **to be ~ on doing sth** être (bien) décidé à faire qch.

intention [ɪn'tɛnʃən] *n* intention *f*; **~al** *a* intentionnel(le), délibéré(e).

intently [ɪn'tɛntlɪ] *ad* attentivement.

inter [ɪn'tə:*] *vt* enterrer.

interact [ɪntər'ækt] *vi* avoir une action réciproque; **~ion** [-'ækʃən] *n* interaction *f*.

intercede [ɪntə'si:d] *vi*: **to ~ (with)** intercéder (auprès de).

intercept [ɪntə'sɛpt] *vt* intercepter; (*person*) arrêter au passage; **~ion** [-'sɛpʃən] *n* interception *f*.

interchange *n* ['ɪntətʃeɪndʒ] (*exchange*) échange *m*; (*on motorway*) échangeur *m* // *vt* [ɪntə'tʃeɪndʒ] échanger; mettre à la place l'un(e) de l'autre; **~able** *a* interchangeable.

intercom ['ɪntəkɔm] *n* interphone *m*.

interconnect [ɪntəkə'nɛkt] *vi* (*rooms*) communiquer.

intercourse ['ɪntəkɔ:s] *n* rapports *mpl*.

interest ['ɪntrɪst] *n* intérêt *m*; (COMM: *stake, share*) intérêts *mpl* // *vt* intéresser; **~ed** *a* intéressé(e); **to be ~ed in** s'intéresser à; **~ing** *a* intéressant(e).

interfere [ɪntə'fɪə*] *vi*: **to ~ in** (*quarrel, other people's business*) se mêler à; **to ~ with** (*object*) tripoter, toucher à; (*plans*) contrecarrer; (*duty*) être en conflit avec; **don't ~** mêlez-vous de vos affaires.

interference [ɪntə'fɪərəns] *n* (*gen*) intrusion *f*; (PHYSICS) interférence *f*; (RADIO, TV) parasites *mpl*.

interim ['ɪntərɪm] *a* provisoire; (*post*) intérimaire // *n*: **in the ~** dans l'intérim.

interior [ɪn'tɪərɪə*] *n* intérieur *m* // *a* intérieur(e).

interjection [ɪntə'dʒɛkʃən] *n* interjection *f*.

interlock [ɪntə'lɔk] *vi* s'enclencher // *vt* enclencher.

interloper ['ɪntələupə*] *n* intrus/e.

interlude ['ɪntəlu:d] *n* intervalle *m*; (THEATRE) intermède *m*.

intermarry [ɪntə'mærɪ] *vi* former des alliances entre familles (*or* tribus); former des unions consanguines.

intermediary [ɪntə'mi:dɪərɪ] *n* intermédiaire *m/f*.

intermediate [ɪntə'mi:dɪət] *a* intermédiaire; (SCOL: *course, level*) moyen(ne).

intermission [ɪntə'mɪʃən] *n* pause *f*; (THEATRE, CINEMA) entracte *m*.

intermittent [ɪntə'mɪtnt] *a* intermittent(e); **~ly** *ad* par intermittence, par intervalles.

intern *vt* [ɪn'tə:n] interner // *n* ['ɪntə:n] (*US*) interne *m/f*.

internal [ɪn'tə:nl] *a* interne; (*dispute, reform etc*) intérieur(e); **~ly** *ad* intérieurement; **'not to be taken ~ly'** 'pour usage externe'; **~ revenue** *n* (*US*) fisc *m*.

international [ɪntə'næʃənl] *a* international(e) // *n* (SPORT) international *m*.

internment [ɪn'tə:nmənt] *n* internement *m*.

interplay ['ɪntəpleɪ] *n* effet *m* réciproque, jeu *m*.

interpret [ɪn'tə:prɪt] *vt* interpréter // *vi* servir d'interprète; **~ation** [-'teɪʃən] *n* interprétation *f*; **~er** *n* interprète *m/f*; **~ing** *n* (*profession*) interprétariat *m*.

interrelated [ɪntərɪ'leɪtɪd] *a* en corrélation, en rapport étroit.

interrogate [ɪn'tɛrəugeɪt] *vt* interroger; (*suspect etc*) soumettre à un interrogatoire; **interrogation** [-'geɪʃən] *n* interrogation *f*; interrogatoire *m*; **interrogative** [ɪntə'rɔgətɪv] *a* interrogateur(trice) // *n* (LING) interrogatif *m*; **interrogator** *n* interrogateur/trice.

interrupt [ɪntə'rʌpt] *vt* interrompre; **~ion** [-'rʌpʃən] *n* interruption *f*.

intersect [ɪntə'sɛkt] *vt* couper, croiser // *vi* (*roads*) se croiser, se couper; **~ion** [-'sɛkʃən] *n* intersection *f*; (*of roads*) croisement *m*.

intersperse [ɪntə'spə:s] *vt*: **to ~ with** parsemer de.

intertwine [ɪntə'twaɪn] *vt* entrelacer // *vi* s'entrelacer.

interval ['ɪntəvl] *n* intervalle *m*; (SCOL) récréation *f*; (THEATRE) entracte *m*; (SPORT) mi-temps *f*; **bright ~s** (*in weather*) éclaircies *fpl*; **at ~s** par intervalles.

intervene [ɪntə'vi:n] *vi* (*time*) s'écouler (entre-temps); (*event*) survenir; (*person*) intervenir; **intervention** [-'vɛnʃən] *n* intervention *f*.

interview ['ɪntəvju:] *n* (RADIO, TV *etc*) interview *f*; (*for job*) entrevue *f* // *vt* interviewer; avoir une entrevue avec; **~er** *n* interviewer *m*.

intestate [ɪn'tɛsteɪt] *a* intestat.

intestinal [ɪn'tɛstɪnl] *a* intestinal(e).

intestine [ɪn'tɛstɪn] *n* intestin *m*.

intimacy ['ɪntɪməsɪ] *n* intimité *f*.

intimate *a* ['ɪntɪmət] intime; (*knowledge*) approfondi(e) // *vt* ['ɪntɪmeɪt] suggérer,

laisser entendre ; (*announce*) faire savoir ; **~ly** *ad* intimement.
intimation [ɪntɪ'meɪʃən] *n* annonce *f*.
intimidate [ɪn'tɪmɪdeɪt] *vt* intimider ; **intimidation** [-'deɪʃən] *n* intimidation *f*.
into ['ɪntu] *prep* dans ; **~ 3 pieces/French** en 3 morceaux/français.
intolerable [ɪn'tɔlərəbl] *a* intolérable.
intolerance [ɪn'tɔlərns] *n* intolérance *f*.
intolerant [ɪn'tɔlərnt] *a* intolérant(e).
intonation [ɪntəu'neɪʃən] *n* intonation *f*.
intoxicate [ɪn'tɔksɪkeɪt] *vt* enivrer ; **~d** *a* ivre ; **intoxication** [-'keɪʃən] *n* ivresse *f*.
intractable [ɪn'træktəbl] *a* (*child, temper*) indocile, insoumis(e) ; (*problem*) insoluble.
intransigent [ɪn'trænsɪdʒənt] *a* intransigeant(e).
intransitive [ɪn'trænsɪtɪv] *a* intransitif(ive).
intra-uterine [ɪntrə'ju:təraɪn] *a* intra-utérin(e) ; **~ device (I.U.D.)** *n* moyen de contraception intra-utérin.
intravenous [ɪntrə'vi:nəs] *a* intraveineux(euse).
intrepid [ɪn'trɛpɪd] *a* intrépide.
intricacy ['ɪntrɪkəsɪ] *n* complexité *f*.
intricate ['ɪntrɪkət] *a* complexe, compliqué(e).
intrigue [ɪn'tri:g] *n* intrigue *f* // *vt* intriguer ; **intriguing** *a* fascinant(e).
intrinsic [ɪn'trɪnsɪk] *a* intrinsèque.
introduce [ɪntrə'dju:s] *vt* introduire ; **to ~ sb (to sb)** présenter qn (à qn) ; **to ~ sb to** (*pastime, technique*) initier qn à ; **introduction** [-'dʌkʃən] *n* introduction *f* ; (*of person*) présentation *f* ; **introductory** *a* préliminaire, d'introduction.
introspective [ɪntrəu'spɛktɪv] *a* introspectif(ive).
introvert ['ɪntrəuvə:t] *a,n* introverti(e).
intrude [ɪn'tru:d] *vi* (*person*) être importun(e) ; **to ~ on** *or* **into** s'immiscer dans ; **am I intruding?** est-ce que je vous dérange? ; **~r** *n* intrus/e ; **intrusion** [-ʒən] *n* intrusion *f* ; **intrusive** *a* importun(e), gênant(e).
intuition [ɪntju:'ɪʃən] *n* intuition *f*.
intuitive [ɪn'tju:ɪtɪv] *a* intuitif(ive).
inundate ['ɪnʌndeɪt] *vt*: **to ~ with** inonder de.
invade [ɪn'veɪd] *vt* envahir ; **~r** *n* envahisseur *m*.
invalid *n* ['ɪnvəlɪd] malade *m/f* ; (*with disability*) invalide *m/f* // *a* [ɪn'vælɪd] (*not valid*) invalide, non valide ; **~ate** [ɪn'vælɪdeɪt] *vt* invalider, annuler.
invaluable [ɪn'væljuəbl] *a* inestimable, inappréciable.
invariable [ɪn'vɛərɪəbl] *a* invariable ; (*fig*) immanquable.
invasion [ɪn'veɪʒən] *n* invasion *f*.
invective [ɪn'vɛktɪv] *n* invective *f*.
invent [ɪn'vɛnt] *vt* inventer ; **~ion** [ɪn'vɛnʃən] *n* invention *f* ; **~ive** *a* inventif(ive) ; **~iveness** *n* esprit inventif *or* d'invention ; **~or** *n* inventeur/trice.
inventory ['ɪnvəntrɪ] *n* inventaire *m*.
inverse [ɪn'və:s] *a* inverse // *n* inverse *m*, contraire *m* ; **~ly** *ad* inversement.
invert [ɪn'və:t] *vt* intervertir ; (*cup, object*) retourner ; **~ed commas** *npl* guillemets *mpl*.
invertebrate [ɪn'və:tɪbrət] *n* invertébré *m*.
invest [ɪn'vɛst] *vt* investir // *vi* faire un investissement.
investigate [ɪn'vɛstɪgeɪt] *vt* étudier, examiner ; (*crime*) faire une enquête sur ; **investigation** [-'geɪʃən] *n* examen *m* ; (*of crime*) enquête *f*, investigation *f* ; **investigator** *n* investigateur/trice.
investiture [ɪn'vɛstɪtʃə*] *n* investiture *f*.
investment [ɪn'vɛstmənt] *n* investissement *m*, placement *m*.
investor [ɪn'vɛstə*] *n* épargnant/e ; actionnaire *m/f*.
inveterate [ɪn'vɛtərət] *a* invétéré(e).
invidious [ɪn'vɪdɪəs] *a* injuste ; (*task*) déplaisant(e).
invigorating [ɪn'vɪgəreɪtɪŋ] *a* vivifiant(e) ; stimulant(e).
invincible [ɪn'vɪnsɪbl] *a* invincible.
inviolate [ɪn'vaɪələt] *a* inviolé(e).
invisible [ɪn'vɪzɪbl] *a* invisible ; **~ ink** *n* encre *f* sympathique ; **~ mending** *n* stoppage *m*.
invitation [ɪnvɪ'teɪʃən] *n* invitation *f*.
invite [ɪn'vaɪt] *vt* inviter ; (*opinions etc*) demander ; (*trouble*) chercher ; **inviting** *a* engageant(e), attrayant(e) ; (*gesture*) encourageant(e).
invoice ['ɪnvɔɪs] *n* facture *f* // *vt* facturer.
invoke [ɪn'vəuk] *vt* invoquer.
involuntary [ɪn'vɔləntrɪ] *a* involontaire.
involve [ɪn'vɔlv] *vt* (*entail*) entraîner, nécessiter ; (*associate*): **to ~ sb (in)** impliquer qn (dans), mêler qn à ; faire participer qn (à) ; **~d** *a* complexe ; **to feel ~d** se sentir concerné(e) ; **~ment** *n* mise *f* en jeu ; implication *f* ; **~ment (in)** participation *f* (à) ; rôle *m* (dans).
invulnerable [ɪn'vʌlnərəbl] *a* invulnérable.
inward ['ɪnwəd] *a* (*movement*) vers l'intérieur ; (*thought, feeling*) profond(e), intime ; **~ly** *ad* (*feel, think etc*) secrètement, en son for intérieur ; **~(s)** *ad* vers l'intérieur.
iodine ['aɪəudi:n] *n* iode *m*.
iota [aɪ'əutə] *n* (*fig*) brin *m*, grain *m*.
IOU *n* (*abbr of I owe you*) reconnaissance *f* de dette.
IQ *n* (*abbr of intelligence quotient*) Q.I. *m* (quotient intellectuel).
Iran [ɪ'rɑ:n] *n* Iran *m* ; **~ian** [ɪ'reɪnɪən] *a* iranien(ne) // *n* Iranien/ne ; (LING) iranien *m*.
Iraq [ɪ'rɑ:k] *n* Irak *m* ; **~i** *a* irakien(ne) // *n* Irakien/ne ; (LING) irakien *m*.
irascible [ɪ'ræsɪbl] *a* irascible.
irate [aɪ'reɪt] *a* courroucé(e).
Ireland ['aɪlənd] *n* Irlande *f*.
iris, ~es ['aɪrɪs, -ɪz] *n* iris *m*.
Irish ['aɪrɪʃ] *a* irlandais(e) // *npl*: **the ~** les Irlandais ; **~man** *n* Irlandais *m* ; **~ Sea** *n* mer *f* d'Irlande ; **~woman** *n* Irlandaise *f*.
irk [ə:k] *vt* ennuyer ; **~some** *a* ennuyeux(euse).
iron ['aɪən] *n* fer *m* ; (*for clothes*) fer *m* à repasser // *a* de *or* en fer // *vt* (*clothes*) repasser ; **~s** *npl* (*chains*) fers *mpl*, chaînes

fpl; **to ~ out** *vt* (*crease*) faire disparaître au fer ; (*fig*) aplanir ; faire disparaître ; **the ~ curtain** *n* le rideau de fer.
ironic(al) [aɪ'rɔnɪk(l)] *a* ironique.
ironing ['aɪənɪŋ] *n* repassage *m* ; **~ board** *n* planche *f* à repasser.
ironmonger ['aɪənmʌŋgə*] *n* quincailler *m*; **~'s (shop)** *n* quincaillerie *f*.
iron ore ['aɪən'ɔ:*] *n* minerai *m* de fer.
ironworks ['aɪənwə:ks] *n* usine *f* sidérurgique.
irony ['aɪrənɪ] *n* ironie *f*.
irrational [ɪ'ræʃənl] *a* irrationnel(le) ; déraisonnable ; qui manque de logique.
irreconcilable [ɪrɛkən'saɪləbl] *a* irréconciliable ; (*opinion*): **~ with** inconciliable avec.
irredeemable [ɪrɪ'di:məbl] *a* (COMM) non remboursable.
irrefutable [ɪrɪ'fju:təbl] *a* irréfutable.
irregular [ɪ'rɛgjulə*] *a* irrégulier(ère) ; **~ity** [-'lærɪtɪ] *n* irrégularité *f*.
irrelevance [ɪ'rɛləvəns] *n* manque *m* de rapport *or* d'à-propos.
irrelevant [ɪ'rɛləvənt] *a* sans rapport, hors de propos.
irreligious [ɪrɪ'lɪdʒəs] *a* irréligieux(euse).
irreparable [ɪ'rɛprəbl] *a* irréparable.
irreplaceable [ɪrɪ'pleɪsəbl] *a* irremplaçable.
irrepressible [ɪrɪ'prɛsəbl] *a* irrépressible.
irreproachable [ɪrɪ'prəutʃəbl] *a* irréprochable.
irresistible [ɪrɪ'zɪstɪbl] *a* irrésistible.
irresolute [ɪ'rɛzəlu:t] *a* irrésolu(e), indécis(e).
irrespective [ɪrɪ'spɛktɪv]: **~ of** *prep* sans tenir compte de.
irresponsible [ɪrɪ'spɔnsɪbl] *a* (*act*) irréfléchi(e) ; (*person*) qui n'a pas le sens des responsabilités.
irretrievable [ɪrɪ'tri:vəbl] *a* irréparable, irrémédiable.
irreverent [ɪ'rɛvərnt] *a* irrévérencieux(euse).
irrevocable [ɪ'rɛvəkəbl] *a* irrévocable.
irrigate ['ɪrɪgeɪt] *vt* irriguer ; **irrigation** [-'geɪʃən] *n* irrigation *f*.
irritable ['ɪrɪtəbl] *a* irritable.
irritate ['ɪrɪteɪt] *vt* irriter ; **irritation** [-'teɪʃən] *n* irritation *f*.
is [ɪz] *vb see* **be**.
Islam ['ɪzlɑ:m] *n* Islam *m*.
island ['aɪlənd] *n* île *f*; (*also*: **traffic ~**) refuge *m* (pour piétons) ; **~er** *n* habitant/e d'une île, insulaire *m/f*.
isle [aɪl] *n* île *f*.
isn't ['ɪznt] = **is not**.
isolate ['aɪsəleɪt] *vt* isoler ; **~d** *a* isolé(e) ; **isolation** [-'leɪʃən] *n* isolement *m*; **isolationism** [-'leɪʃənɪzm] *n* isolationnisme *m*.
isotope ['aɪsəutəup] *n* isotope *m*.
Israel ['ɪzreɪl] *n* Israël *m* ; **~i** [ɪz'reɪlɪ] *a* israélien(ne) // *n* Israélien/ne.
issue ['ɪsju:] *n* question *f*, problème *m* ; (*outcome*) résultat *m*, issue *f* ; (*of banknotes etc*) émission *f* ; (*of newspaper etc*) numéro *m* ; (*offspring*) descendance *f* // *vt* (*rations, equipment*) distribuer ; (*orders*) donner ; (*book*) faire paraître, publier ; (*banknotes, cheques, stamps*) émettre, mettre en circulation ; **at ~** en jeu, en cause.
isthmus ['ɪsməs] *n* isthme *m*.
it [ɪt] *pronoun* (*subject*) il(elle) ; (*direct object*) le(la), l' ; (*indirect object*) lui ; (*impersonal*) il ; ce, cela, ça ; **~'s raining** il pleut ; **I've come from ~** j'en viens ; **it's on ~** c'est dessus ; **he's proud of ~** il en est fier ; **he agreed to ~** il y a consenti.
Italian [ɪ'tæljən] *a* italien(ne) // *n* Italien/ne ; (LING) italien *m*.
italic [ɪ'tælɪk] *a* italique ; **~s** *npl* italique *m*.
Italy ['ɪtəlɪ] *n* Italie *f*.
itch [ɪtʃ] *n* démangeaison *f* // *vi* (*person*) éprouver des démangeaisons ; (*part of body*) démanger ; **I'm ~ing to do** l'envie me démange de faire ; **~ing** *n* démangeaison *f*; **~y** *a* qui démange.
it'd ['ɪtd] = **it would**; **it had**.
item ['aɪtəm] *n* (*gen*) article *m* ; (*on agenda*) question *f*, point *m* ; (*in programme*) numéro *m* ; (*also*: **news ~**) nouvelle *f* ; **~ize** *vt* détailler, spécifier.
itinerant [ɪ'tɪnərənt] *a* itinérant(e) ; (*musician*) ambulant(e).
itinerary [aɪ'tɪnərərɪ] *n* itinéraire *m*.
it'll ['ɪtl] = **it will, it shall**.
its [ɪts] *a* son(sa), ses *pl* // *pronoun* le(la) sien(ne), les siens(siennes).
it's [ɪts] = **it is**; **it has**.
itself [ɪt'sɛlf] *pronoun* (*emphatic*) lui-même(elle-même) ; (*reflexive*) se.
ITV *n abbr of Independent Television* (*chaîne fonctionnant en concurrence avec la BBC*).
I.U.D. *n abbr see* **intra-uterine**.
I've [aɪv] = **I have**.
ivory ['aɪvərɪ] *n* ivoire *m* ; **~ tower** *n* (*fig*) tour *f* d'ivoire.
ivy ['aɪvɪ] *n* lierre *m*.

J

jab [dʒæb] *vt*: **to ~ sth into** enfoncer *or* planter qch dans // *n* coup *m* ; (MED: *col*) piqûre *f*.
jabber ['dʒæbə*] *vt,vi* bredouiller, baragouiner.
jack [dʒæk] *n* (AUT) cric *m* ; (BOWLS) cochonnet *m* ; (CARDS) valet *m* ; **to ~ up** *vt* soulever (au cric).
jacket ['dʒækɪt] *n* veste *f*, veston *m* ; (*of boiler etc*) enveloppe *f* ; (*of book*) couverture *f*, jaquette *f* ; **potatoes in their ~s** pommes de terre en robe des champs.
jack-knife ['dʒæknaɪf] *n* couteau *m* de poche // *vi*: **the lorry ~d** la remorque (du camion) s'est mise en travers.
jackpot ['dʒækpɔt] *n* gros lot.
jade [dʒeɪd] *n* (*stone*) jade *m*.
jaded ['dʒeɪdɪd] *a* éreinté(e), fatigué(e).
jagged ['dʒægɪd] *a* dentelé(e).
jail [dʒeɪl] *n* prison *f* ; **~break** *n* évasion *f* ; **~er** *n* geôlier/ière.
jam [dʒæm] *n* confiture *f* ; (*of shoppers etc*) cohue *f* ; (*also*: **traffic ~**) embouteillage *m* // *vt* (*passage etc*) encombrer, obstruer ; (*mechanism, drawer etc*) bloquer, coincer ; (RADIO) brouiller // *vi* (*mechanism, sliding*

part) se coincer, se bloquer; (*gun*) s'enrayer; **to ~ sth into** entasser *or* comprimer qch dans; enfoncer qch dans.
Jamaica [dʒə'meɪkə] *n* Jamaïque *f*.
jangle ['dʒæŋgl] *vi* cliqueter.
janitor ['dʒænɪtə*] *n* (*caretaker*) huissier *m*; concierge *m*.
January ['dʒænjuərɪ] *n* janvier *m*.
Japan [dʒə'pæn] *n* Japon *m*; **~ese** [dʒæpə'ni:z] *a* japonais(e) // *n, pl inv* Japonais/e; (LING) japonais *m*.
jar [dʒɑ:*] *n* (*glass*) pot *m*, bocal *m* // *vi* (*sound*) produire un son grinçant *or* discordant; (*colours etc*) détonner, jurer // *vt* (*subject: shock*) ébranler, secouer.
jargon ['dʒɑ:gən] *n* jargon *m*.
jasmin(e) ['dʒæzmɪn] *n* jasmin *m*.
jaundice ['dʒɔ:ndɪs] *n* jaunisse *f*; **~d** *a* (*fig*) envieux(euse), désapprobateur(trice).
jaunt [dʒɔ:nt] *n* balade *f*; **~y** *a* enjoué(e); désinvolte.
javelin ['dʒævlɪn] *n* javelot *m*.
jaw [dʒɔ:] *n* mâchoire *f*.
jaywalker ['dʒeɪwɔ:kə*] *n* piéton indiscipliné.
jazz [dʒæz] *n* jazz *m*; **to ~ up** *vt* animer, égayer; **~ band** *n* orchestre *m or* groupe *m* de jazz; **~y** *a* bariolé(e), tapageur(euse).
jealous ['dʒɛləs] *a* jaloux(ouse); **~y** *n* jalousie *f*.
jeans [dʒi:nz] *npl* (blue-)jean *m*.
jeep [dʒi:p] *n* jeep *f*.
jeer [dʒɪə*] *vi*: **to ~ (at)** huer; se moquer cruellement (de), railler; **~s** *npl* huées *fpl*; sarcasmes *mpl*.
jelly ['dʒɛlɪ] *n* gelée *f*; **~fish** *n* méduse *f*.
jeopardize ['dʒɛpədaɪz] *vt* mettre en danger *or* péril.
jeopardy ['dʒɛpədɪ] *n*: **in ~** en danger *or* péril.
jerk [dʒə:k] *n* secousse *f*; saccade *f*; sursaut *m*, spasme *m* // *vt* donner une secousse à // *vi* (*vehicles*) cahoter.
jerkin ['dʒə:kɪn] *n* blouson *m*.
jerky ['dʒə:kɪ] *a* saccadé(e); cahotant(e).
jersey ['dʒə:zɪ] *n* tricot *m*.
jest [dʒɛst] *n* plaisanterie *f*; **in ~** en plaisantant.
jet [dʒɛt] *n* (*gas, liquid*) jet *m*; (AUT) gicleur *m*; (AVIAT) avion *m* à réaction, jet *m*; **~-black** *a* (d'un noir) de jais; **~ engine** *n* moteur *m* à réaction.
jetsam ['dʒɛtsəm] *n* objets jetés à la mer (et rejetés sur la côte).
jettison ['dʒɛtɪsn] *vt* jeter par-dessus bord.
jetty ['dʒɛtɪ] *n* jetée *f*, digue *f*.
Jew [dʒu:] *n* Juif *m*.
jewel ['dʒu:əl] *n* bijou *m*, joyau *m*; **~ler** *n* bijoutier/ère, joaillier *m*; **~ler's (shop)** *n* bijouterie *f*, joaillerie *f*; **~lery** *n* bijoux *mpl*.
Jewess ['dʒu:ɪs] *n* Juive *f*.
Jewish ['dʒu:ɪʃ] *a* juif(juive).
jib [dʒɪb] *n* (NAUT) foc *m*; (*of crane*) flèche *f* // *vi*: **to ~ (at)** renâcler *or* regimber (devant).
jibe [dʒaɪb] *n* sarcasme *m*.
jiffy ['dʒɪfɪ] *n* (*col*): **in a ~** en un clin d'œil.
jigsaw ['dʒɪgsɔ:] *n* (*also*: **~ puzzle**) puzzle *m*.
jilt [dʒɪlt] *vt* laisser tomber, plaquer.
jingle ['dʒɪŋgl] *n* (*advert*) couplet *m* publicitaire // *vi* cliqueter, tinter.
jinx [dʒɪŋks] *n* (*col*) (mauvais) sort.
jitters ['dʒɪtəz] *npl* (*col*): **to get the ~** avoir la trouille *or* la frousse.
jiujitsu [dʒu:'dʒɪtsu:] *n* jiu-jitsu *m*.
job [dʒɔb] *n* travail *m*; (*employment*) emploi *m*, poste *m*, place *f*; **~bing** *a* (*workman*) à la tâche, à la journée; **~less** *a* sans travail, au chômage.
jockey ['dʒɔkɪ] *n* jockey *m* // *vi*: **to ~ for position** manœuvrer pour être bien placé.
jocular ['dʒɔkjulə*] *a* jovial(e), enjoué(e); facétieux(euse).
jog [dʒɔg] *vt* secouer // *vi*: **to ~ along** cahoter; trotter; **to ~ sb's memory** rafraîchir la mémoire de qn.
join [dʒɔɪn] *vt* unir, assembler; (*become member of*) s'inscrire à; (*meet*) rejoindre, retrouver; se joindre à // *vi* (*roads, rivers*) se rejoindre, se rencontrer // *n* raccord *m*; **to ~ up** *vi* s'engager.
joiner ['dʒɔɪnə*] *n* menuisier *m*; **~y** *n* menuiserie *f*.
joint [dʒɔɪnt] *n* (TECH) jointure *f*; joint *m*; (ANAT) articulation *f*, jointure; (CULIN) rôti *m*; (*col: place*) boîte *f* // *a* commun(e); **~ly** *ad* ensemble, en commun.
joist [dʒɔɪst] *n* solive *f*.
joke [dʒəuk] *n* plaisanterie *f*; (*also*: **practical ~**) farce *f* // *vi* plaisanter; **to play a ~ on** jouer un tour à, faire une farce à; **~r** *n* plaisantin *m*, blagueur/euse; (CARDS) joker *m*.
jollity ['dʒɔlɪtɪ] *n* réjouissances *fpl*, gaieté *f*.
jolly ['dʒɔlɪ] *a* gai(e), enjoué(e) // *ad* (*col*) rudement, drôlement.
jolt [dʒəult] *n* cahot *m*, secousse *f* // *vt* cahoter, secouer.
Jordan [dʒɔ:dən] *n* Jordanie *f*.
jostle ['dʒɔsl] *vt* bousculer, pousser // *vi* jouer des coudes.
jot [dʒɔt] *n*: **not one ~** pas un brin; **to ~ down** *vt* inscrire rapidement, noter; **~ter** *n* cahier *m* (de brouillon); bloc-notes *m*.
journal ['dʒə:nl] *n* journal *m*; **~ese** [-'li:z] *n* (*pej*) style *m* journalistique; **~ism** *n* journalisme *m*; **~ist** *n* journaliste *m/f*.
journey ['dʒə:nɪ] *n* voyage *m*; (*distance covered*) trajet *m*.
jowl [dʒaul] *n* mâchoire *f* (*inférieure*); bajoue *f*.
joy [dʒɔɪ] *n* joie *f*; **~ful, ~ous** *a* joyeux(euse); **~ ride** *n* virée *f* (*gén avec une voiture volée*).
J.P. *n abbr see* **justice.**
Jr, Jun., Junr *abbr of* **junior.**
jubilant ['dʒu:bɪlnt] triomphant(e); réjoui(e).
jubilation [dʒu:bɪ'leɪʃən] *n* jubilation *f*.
jubilee ['dʒu:bɪli:] *n* jubilé *m*.
judge [dʒʌdʒ] *n* juge *m* // *vt* juger; **judg(e)ment** *n* jugement *m*; (*punishment*) châtiment *m*; **in my judg(e)ment** à mon avis, selon mon opinion.
judicial [dʒu:'dɪʃl] *a* judiciaire; (*fair*) impartial(e).

judicious [dʒuːˈdɪʃəs] *a* judicieux(euse).
judo [ˈdʒuːdəu] *n* judo *m*.
jug [dʒʌg] *n* pot *m*, cruche *f*.
juggernaut [ˈdʒʌgənɔːt] *n* (*huge truck*) mastodonte *m*.
juggle [ˈdʒʌgl] *vi* jongler ; **~r** *n* jongleur *m*.
Jugoslav [ˈjuːgəuˈslɑːv] *a,n* = **Yugoslav**.
juice [dʒuːs] *n* jus *m*.
juicy [ˈdʒuːsɪ] *a* juteux(euse).
jukebox [ˈdʒuːkbɔks] *n* juke-box *m*.
July [dʒuːˈlaɪ] *n* juillet *m*.
jumble [ˈdʒʌmbl] *n* fouillis *m* // *vt* (*also*: **~ up**) mélanger, brouiller ; **~ sale** *n* (*Brit*) vente *f* de charité.
jumbo [ˈdʒʌmbəu] *a*: **~ jet** avion géant, gros porteur (à réaction).
jump [dʒʌmp] *vi* sauter, bondir ; (*start*) sursauter ; (*increase*) monter en flèche // *vt* sauter, franchir // *n* saut *m*, bond *m* ; sursaut *m* ; **to ~ the queue** passer avant son tour.
jumper [ˈdʒʌmpə*] *n* pull-over *m*.
jumpy [ˈdʒʌmpɪ] *a* nerveux(euse), agité(e).
junction [ˈdʒʌŋkʃən] *n* (*of roads*) carrefour *m* ; (*of rails*) embranchement *n*.
juncture [ˈdʒʌŋktʃə*] *n*: **at this ~** à ce moment-là, sur ces entrefaites.
June [dʒuːn] *n* juin *m*.
jungle [ˈdʒʌŋgl] *n* jungle *f*.
junior [ˈdʒuːnɪə*] *a, n*: **he's ~ to me (by 2 years), he's my ~ (by 2 years)** il est mon cadet (de 2 ans), il est plus jeune que moi (de 2 ans) ; **he's ~ to me** (*seniority*) il est en dessous de moi (dans la hiérarchie), j'ai plus d'ancienneté que lui ; **~ executive** *n* jeune cadre *m* ; **~ minister** *n* ministre *m* sous tutelle ; **~ partner** *n* associé(-adjoint) *m* ; **~ school** *n* école *f* primaire, cours moyen ; **~ sizes** *npl* (COMM) tailles *fpl* fillettes/garçonnets.
juniper[ˈdʒuːnɪpə*] *n*: **~ berry** baie *f* de genièvre.
junk [dʒʌŋk] *n* (*rubbish*) bric-à-brac *m inv* ; (*ship*) jonque *f* ; **~shop** *n* (boutique *f* de) brocanteur *m*.
junta [ˈdʒʌntə] *n* junte *f*.
jurisdiction [dʒuərɪsˈdɪkʃən] *n* juridiction *f*.
jurisprudence [dʒuərɪsˈpruːdəns] *n* jurisprudence *f*.
juror [ˈdʒuərə*] *n* juré *m*.
jury [ˈdʒuərɪ] *n* jury *m* ; **~man** *n* = **juror**.
just [dʒʌst] *a* juste // *ad*: **he's ~ done it/left** il vient de le faire/partir ; **~ as I expected** exactement *or* précisément comme je m'y attendais ; **~ right/two o'clock** exactement *or* juste ce qu'il faut/deux heures ; **~ as he was leaving** au moment *or* à l'instant précis où il partait ; **~ before/enough/here** juste avant/assez/là ; **it's ~ me/a mistake** ce n'est que moi/(rien) qu'une erreur ; **~ missed/caught** manqué/attrapé de justesse ; **~ listen to this!** écoutez un peu ça!
justice [ˈdʒʌstɪs] *n* justice *f* ; **Lord Chief J~** premier président de la cour d'appel ; **J~ of the Peace (J.P.)** *n* juge *m* de paix.
justifiable [dʒʌstɪˈfaɪəbl] *a* justifiable.
justifiably [dʒʌstɪˈfaɪəblɪ] *ad* légitimement.
justification [dʒʌstɪfɪˈkeɪʃən] *n* justification *f*.
justify [ˈdʒʌstɪfaɪ] *vt* justifier.
justly [ˈdʒʌstlɪ] *ad* avec raison, justement.
justness [ˈdʒʌstnɪs] *n* justesse *f*.
jut [dʒʌt] *vi* (*also*: **~ out**) dépasser, faire saillie.
juvenile [ˈdʒuːvənaɪl] *a* juvénile ; (*court, books*) pour enfants // *n* adolescent/e.
juxtapose [ˈdʒʌkstəpəuz] *vt* juxtaposer.

K

kaleidoscope [kəˈlaɪdəskəup] *n* kaléidoscope *m*.
kangaroo [kæŋgəˈruː] *n* kangourou *m*.
keel [kiːl] *n* quille *f* ; **on an even ~** (*fig*) à flot.
keen [kiːn] *a* (*interest, desire*) vif(vive) ; (*eye, intelligence*) pénétrant(e) ; (*competition*) vif, âpre ; (*edge*) effilé(e) ; (*eager*) plein(e) d'enthousiasme ; **to be ~ to do** *or* **on doing sth** désirer vivement faire qch, tenir beaucoup à faire qch ; **to be ~ on sth/sb** aimer beaucoup qch/qn ; **~ness** *n* (*eagerness*) enthousiasme *m* ; **~ness to do** vif désir de faire.
keep [kiːp] *vb* (*pt,pp* **kept** [kɛpt]) *vt* (*retain, preserve*) garder ; (*hold back*) retenir ; (*a shop, the books, a diary*) tenir ; (*feed*: *one's family etc*) entretenir, assurer la subsistance de ; (*a promise*) tenir ; (*chickens, bees, pigs etc*) élever // *vi* (*food*) se conserver ; (*remain*: *in a certain state or place*) rester // *n* (*of castle*) donjon *m* ; (*food etc*): **enough for his ~** assez pour (assurer) sa subsistance ; **to ~ doing sth** continuer à faire qch ; faire qch continuellement ; **to ~ sb from doing/sth from happening** empêcher qn de faire *or* que qn (ne) fasse/que qch (n')arrive ; **to ~ sb happy/a place tidy** faire que qn soit content/qu'un endroit reste propre ; **to ~ sth to o.s.** garder qch pour soi, tenir qch secret ; **to ~ sth (back) from sb** cacher qch à qn ; **to ~ time** (*clock*) être à l'heure, ne pas retarder ; **to ~ on** *vi* continuer ; **to ~ on doing** continuer à faire ; **to ~ out** *vt* empêcher d'entrer ; **'~ out'** 'défense d'entrer' ; **to ~ up** *vi* se maintenir // *vt* continuer, maintenir ; **to ~ up with** se maintenir au niveau de ; **~er** *n* gardien/ne ; **~ing** *n* (*care*) garde *f* ; **in ~ing with** à l'avenant de ; en accord avec ; **~sake** *n* souvenir *m*.
keg [kɛg] *n* barrique *f*, tonnelet *m*.
kennel [ˈkɛnl] *n* niche *f* ; **~s** *npl* chenil *m*.
Kenya [ˈkɛnjə] *n* Kenya *m*.
kept [kɛpt] *pt,pp* of **keep**.
kerb [kəːb] *n* bordure *f* du trottoir.
kernel [ˈkəːnl] *n* amande *f* ; (*fig*) noyau *m*.
kerosene [ˈkɛrəsiːn] *n* kérosène *m*.
ketchup [ˈkɛtʃəp] *n* ketchup *m*.
kettle [ˈkɛtl] *n* bouilloire *f*.
kettle drums [ˈkɛtldrʌmz] *npl* timbales *fpl*.
key [kiː] *n* (*gen*, MUS) clé *f* ; (*of piano, typewriter*) touche *f* // *cpd* (-)clé ; **~board** *n* clavier *m* ; **~hole** *n* trou *m* de la serrure ;

~note *n* (MUS) tonique *f*; (*fig*) note dominante; **~ ring** *n* porte-clés *m*.
khaki ['kɑ:kɪ] *a,n* kaki (*m*).
kibbutz [kɪ'bu:ts] *n* kibboutz *m*.
kick [kɪk] *vt* donner un coup de pied à // *vi* (*horse*) ruer // *n* coup *m* de pied; (*of rifle*) recul *m*; (*thrill*): **he does it for ~s** il le fait parce que ça l'excite, il le fait pour le plaisir; **to ~ around** *vi* (*col*) traîner; **to ~ off** *vi* (SPORT) donner le coup d'envoi; **~-off** *n* (SPORT) coup *m* d'envoi.
kid [kɪd] *n* gamin/e, gosse *m/f*; (*animal, leather*) chevreau *m* // *vi* (*col*) plaisanter, blaguer.
kidnap ['kɪdnæp] *vt* enlever, kidnapper; **~per** *n* ravisseur/euse; **~ping** *n* enlèvement *m*.
kidney ['kɪdnɪ] *n* (ANAT) rein *m*; (CULIN) rognon *m*.
kill [kɪl] *vt* tuer; (*fig*) faire échouer; détruire; supprimer // *n* mise *f* à mort; **~er** *n* tueur/euse; meurtrier/ère; **~ing** *n* meurtre *m*; tuerie *f*, massacre *m*; (*col*): **to make a ~ing** se remplir les poches, réussir un beau coup // *a* (*col*) tordant(e).
kiln [kɪln] *n* four *m*.
kilo ['ki:ləu] *n* kilo *m*; **~gram(me)** ['kɪləugræm] *n* kilogramme *m*; **~metre, ~meter** (*US*) ['kɪləmi:tə*] *n* kilomètre *m*; **~watt** ['kɪləuwɔt] *n* kilowatt *m*.
kilt [kɪlt] *n* kilt *m*.
kimono [kɪ'məunəu] *n* kimono *m*.
kin [kɪn] *n see* **next, kith.**
kind [kaɪnd] *a* gentil(le), aimable // *n* sorte *f*, espèce *f*; (*species*) genre *m*; **in ~** (COMM) en nature; (*fig*): **to repay sb in ~** rendre la pareille à qn.
kindergarten ['kɪndəgɑ:tn] *n* jardin *m* d'enfants.
kind-hearted [kaɪnd'hɑ:tɪd] *a* bon (bonne).
kindle ['kɪndl] *vt* allumer, enflammer.
kindly ['kaɪndlɪ] *a* bienveillant(e), plein(e) de gentillesse // *ad* avec bonté; **will you ~...** auriez-vous la bonté *or* l'obligeance de...; **he didn't take it ~** il l'a mal pris.
kindness ['kaɪndnɪs] *n* bonté *f*, gentillesse *f*.
kindred ['kɪndrɪd] *a* apparenté(e); **~ spirit** *n* âme *f* sœur.
kinetic [kɪ'nɛtɪk] *a* cinétique.
king [kɪŋ] *n* roi *m*; **~dom** *n* royaume *m*; **~fisher** *n* martin-pêcheur *m*; **~pin** *n* cheville ouvrière; **~-size** *a* long format *inv*; format géant *inv*.
kink [kɪŋk] *n* (*of rope*) entortillement *m*.
kinky ['kɪŋkɪ] *a* (*fig*) excentrique; aux goûts spéciaux.
kiosk ['ki:ɔsk] *n* kiosque *m*; cabine *f* (téléphonique).
kipper ['kɪpə*] *n* hareng fumé et salé.
kiss [kɪs] *n* baiser *m* // *vt* embrasser; **to ~ (each other)** s'embrasser.
kit [kɪt] *n* équipement *m*, matériel *m*; (*set of tools etc*) trousse *f*; (*for assembly*) kit *m*; **~bag** *n* sac *m* de voyage *or* de marin.
kitchen ['kɪtʃɪn] *n* cuisine *f*; **~ garden** *n* jardin *m* potager; **~ sink** *n* évier *m*; **~ware** *n* vaisselle *f*; ustensiles *mpl* de cuisine.
kite [kaɪt] *n* (*toy*) cerf-volant *m*; (ZOOL) milan *m*.
kith [kɪθ] *n*: **~ and kin** parents et amis *mpl*.
kitten ['kɪtn] *n* petit chat, chaton *m*.
kitty ['kɪtɪ] *n* (*pool of money*) cagnotte *f*.
kleptomaniac [klɛptəu'meɪnɪæk] *n* kleptomane *m/f*.
knack [næk] *n*: **to have the ~ (for doing)** avoir le coup (pour faire); **there's a ~** il y a un coup à prendre *or* une combine.
knapsack ['næpsæk] *n* musette *f*.
knave [neɪv] *n* (CARDS) valet *m*.
knead [ni:d] *vt* pétrir.
knee [ni:] *n* genou *m*; **~cap** *n* rotule *f*.
kneel [ni:l] *vi* (*pt,pp* **knelt** [nɛlt]) s'agenouiller.
knell [nɛl] *n* glas *m*.
knelt [nɛlt] *pt,pp of* **kneel**.
knew [nju:] *pt of* **know**.
knickers ['nɪkəz] *npl* culotte *f* (de femme).
knife, knives [naɪf, naɪvz] *n* couteau *m* // *vt* poignarder, frapper d'un coup de couteau.
knight [naɪt] *n* chevalier *m*; (CHESS) cavalier *m*; **~hood** *n* chevalerie *f*; (*title*): **to get a ~hood** être fait chevalier.
knit [nɪt] *vt* tricoter; (*fig*): **to ~ together** unir // *vi* (*broken bones*) se ressouder; **~ting** *n* tricot *m*; **~ting machine** *n* machine *f* à tricoter; **~ting needle** *n* aiguille *f* à tricoter; **~wear** *n* tricots *mpl*, lainages *mpl*.
knives [naɪvz] *npl of* **knife**.
knob [nɔb] *n* bouton *m*; (*fig*): **a ~ of butter** une noix de beurre.
knock [nɔk] *vt* frapper; heurter; (*fig: col*) dénigrer // *vi* (*engine*) cogner; (*at door etc*): **to ~ at/on** frapper à/sur // *n* coup *m*; **to ~ down** *vt* renverser; **to ~ off** *vi* (*col: finish*) s'arrêter (de travailler); **to ~ out** *vt* assommer; (BOXING) mettre k.-o.; **~er** *n* (*on door*) heurtoir *m*; **~-kneed** *a* aux genoux cagneux; **~out** *n* (BOXING) knock-out *m*, K.-O. *m*; **~out competition** *n* compétition *f* avec épreuves éliminatoires.
knot [nɔt] *n* (*gen*) nœud *m* // *vt* nouer; **~ty** *a* (*fig*) épineux(euse).
know [nəu] *vt* (*pt* **knew**, *pp* **known** [nju:, nəun]) savoir; (*person, author, place*) connaître; **to ~ that...** savoir que...; **to ~ how to do** savoir comment faire; **~-how** *n* savoir-faire *m*, technique *f*, compétence *f*; **~ing** *a* (*look etc*) entendu(e); **~ingly** *ad* sciemment; d'un air entendu.
knowledge ['nɔlɪdʒ] *n* connaissance *f*; (*learning*) connaissances, savoir *m*; **~able** *a* bien informé(e).
known [nəun] *pp of* **know**.
knuckle ['nʌkl] *n* articulation *f* (des phalanges), jointure *f*.
K.O. *n* (*abbr of knockout*) K.-O. *m* // *vt* mettre K.-O.
Koran [kɔ'rɑ:n] *n* Coran *m*.
kudos ['kju:dɔs] *n* gloire *f*, lauriers *mpl*.
kw *abbr of* **kilowatt(s)**.

L

l. *abbr of* **litre**.
lab [læb] *n* (*abbr of* **laboratory**) labo *m*.
label ['leɪbl] *n* étiquette *f*; (*brand*: *of record*) marque *f* // *vt* étiqueter; **to ~ sb a...** qualifier qn de... .
laboratory [lə'bɔrətərɪ] *n* laboratoire *m*.
laborious [lə'bɔ:rɪəs] *a* laborieux(euse).
labour ['leɪbə*] *n* (*task*) travail *m*; (*workmen*) main-d'œuvre *f*; (MED) travail, accouchement *m* // *vi*: **to ~ (at)** travailler dur (à), peiner (sur); **in ~** (MED) en travail; **L~, the L~ party** le parti travailliste, les travaillistes *mpl*; **~ camp** *n* camp *m* de travaux forcés; **~ed** *a* lourd(e), laborieux(euse); **~er** *n* manœuvre *m*; (*on farm*) ouvrier *m* agricole; **~ force** *n* main-d'œuvre *f*; **~ pains** *npl* douleurs *fpl* de l'accouchement.
labyrinth ['læbɪrɪnθ] *n* labyrinthe *m*, dédale *m*.
lace [leɪs] *n* dentelle *f*; (*of shoe etc*) lacet *m* // *vt* (*shoe*) lacer.
lack [læk] *n* manque *m* // *vt* manquer de; **through** *or* **for ~ of** faute de, par manque de; **to be ~ing** manquer, faire défaut; **to be ~ing in** manquer de.
lackadaisical [lækə'deɪzɪkl] *a* nonchalant(e), indolent(e).
laconic [lə'kɔnɪk] *a* laconique.
lacquer ['lækə*] *n* laque *f*.
lad [læd] *n* garçon *m*, gars *m*.
ladder ['lædə*] *n* échelle *f*; (*in tights*) maille filée // *vt*, *vi* (*tights*) filer.
laden ['leɪdn] *a*: **~ (with)** chargé(e) (de).
ladle ['leɪdl] *n* louche *f*.
lady ['leɪdɪ] *n* dame *f*; dame (du monde); **L~ Smith** lady Smith; **the ladies' (toilets)** les toilettes *fpl* des dames; **~bird**, **~bug** (US) *n* coccinelle *f*; **~-in-waiting** *n* dame *f* d'honneur; **~like** *a* distingué(e).
lag [læg] *n* = **time ~** // *vi* (*also*: **~ behind**) rester en arrière, traîner // *vt* (*pipes*) calorifuger.
lager ['lɑ:gə*] *n* bière blonde.
lagging ['lægɪŋ] *n* enveloppe isolante, calorifuge *m*.
lagoon [lə'gu:n] *n* lagune *f*.
laid [leɪd] *pt*, *pp of* **lay**.
lain [leɪn] *pp of* **lie**.
lair [lɛə*] *n* tanière *f*, gîte *m*.
laity ['leɪətɪ] *n* laïques *mpl*.
lake [leɪk] *n* lac *m*.
lamb [læm] *n* agneau *m*; **~ chop** *n* côtelette *f* d'agneau; **~skin** *n* (peau *f* d')agneau *m*; **~swool** *n* laine *f* d'agneau.
lame [leɪm] *a* boiteux(euse).
lament [lə'mɛnt] *n* lamentation *f* // *vt* pleurer, se lamenter sur; **~able** ['læməntəbl] *a* déplorable, lamentable.
laminated ['læmɪneɪtɪd] *a* laminé(e); (*windscreen*) (en verre) feuilleté.
lamp [læmp] *n* lampe *f*.
lampoon [læm'pu:n] *n* pamphlet *m*.
lamp: **~post** *n* réverbère *m*; **~shade** *n* abat-jour *m inv*.
lance [lɑ:ns] *n* lance *f* // *vt* (MED) inciser; **~ corporal** *n* (soldat *m* de) première classe *m*.
lancet ['lɑ:nsɪt] *n* bistouri *m*.
land [lænd] *n* (*as opposed to sea*) terre *f* (ferme); (*country*) pays *m*; (*soil*) terre; terrain *m*; (*estate*) terre(s), domaine(s) *m(pl)* // *vi* (*from ship*) débarquer; (AVIAT) atterrir; (*fig*: *fall*) (re)tomber // *vt* (*obtain*) décrocher; (*passengers, goods*) débarquer; **to ~ up** *vi* atterrir, (finir par) se retrouver; **~ed gentry** *n* propriétaires terriens *or* fonciers; **~ing** *n* débarquement *m*; atterrissage *m*; (*of staircase*) palier *m*; **~ing craft** *n* chaland *m* de débarquement; **~ing stage** *n* débarcadère *m*, embarcadère *m*; **~ing strip** *n* piste *f* d'atterrissage; **~lady** *n* propriétaire *f*, logeuse *f*; **~locked** *a* entouré(e) de terre(s), sans accès à la mer; **~lord** *n* propriétaire *m*, logeur *m*; (*of pub etc*) patron *m*; **~lubber** *n* terrien/ne; **~mark** *n* (point *m* de) repère *m*; **~owner** *n* propriétaire foncier *or* terrien.
landscape ['lænskeɪp] *n* paysage *m*; **~d** *a* aménagé(e) (par un paysagiste).
landslide ['lændslaɪd] *n* (GEO) glissement *m* (de terrain); (*fig*: POL) raz-de-marée (électoral).
lane [leɪn] *n* (*in country*) chemin *m*; (*in town*) ruelle *f*; (AUT) voie *f*; file *f*; (*in race*) couloir *m*.
language ['læŋgwɪdʒ] *n* langue *f*; (*way one speaks*) langage *m*; **bad ~** grossièretés *fpl*, langage grossier.
languid ['læŋgwɪd] *a* languissant(e); langoureux(euse).
languish ['læŋgwɪʃ] *vi* languir.
lank [læŋk] *a* (*hair*) raide et terne.
lanky ['læŋkɪ] *a* grand(e) et maigre, efflanqué(e).
lantern ['læntn] *n* lanterne *f*.
lap [læp] *n* (*of track*) tour *m* (de piste); (*of body*): **in** *or* **on one's ~** sur les genoux // *vt* (*also*: **~ up**) laper // *vi* (*waves*) clapoter; **~dog** *n* chien *m* d'appartement.
lapel [lə'pɛl] *n* revers *m*.
Lapland ['læplænd] *n* Laponie *f*.
Lapp [læp] *a* lapon(ne) // *n* Lapon/ne; (LING) lapon *m*.
lapse [læps] *n* défaillance *f* // *vi* (LAW) cesser d'être en vigueur; se périmer; **to ~ into bad habits** prendre de mauvaises habitudes; **~ of time** laps *m* de temps, intervalle *m*.
larceny ['lɑ:sənɪ] *n* vol *m*.
lard [lɑ:d] *n* saindoux *m*.
larder ['lɑ:də*] *n* garde-manger *m inv*.
large [lɑ:dʒ] *a* grand(e); (*person, animal*) gros(grosse); **at ~** (*free*) en liberté; (*generally*) en général; pour la plupart; **~ly** *ad* en grande partie; **~-scale** *a* (*map*) à grande échelle; (*fig*) important(e).
lark [lɑ:k] *n* (*bird*) alouette *f*; (*joke*) blague *f*, farce *f*; **to ~ about** *vi* faire l'idiot, rigoler.
larva, *pl* **larvae** ['lɑ:və, -i:] *n* larve *f*.
laryngitis [lærɪn'dʒaɪtɪs] *n* laryngite *f*.
larynx ['lærɪŋks] *n* larynx *m*.
lascivious [lə'sɪvɪəs] *a* lascif(ive).
laser ['leɪzə*] *n* laser *m*.

lash [læʃ] *n* coup *m* de fouet ; (*gen*: **eyelash**) cil *m* // *vt* fouetter ; (*tie*) attacher ; **to ~ out** *vi*: **to ~ out (at** *or* **against sb/sth)** attaquer violemment (qn/qch) ; **to ~ out (on sth)** (*col*: *spend*) se fendre (de qch).

lass [læs] *n* (jeune) fille *f*.

lasso [læ'su:] *n* lasso *m* // *vt* prendre au lasso.

last [lɑ:st] *a* dernier(ère) // *ad* en dernier // *vi* durer ; **~ week** la semaine dernière ; **~ night** hier soir, la nuit dernière ; **at ~** enfin ; **~ but one** avant-dernier(ère) ; **~ing** *a* durable ; **~-minute** *a* de dernière minute.

latch [lætʃ] *n* loquet *m* ; **~key** *n* clé *f* (de la porte d'entrée).

late [leɪt] *a* (*not on time*) en retard ; (*far on in day etc*) dernier(ère) ; tardif(ive) ; (*recent*) récent(e), dernier ; (*former*) ancien(ne) ; (*dead*) défunt(e) // *ad* tard ; (*behind time, schedule*) en retard ; **of ~** dernièrement ; **in ~ May** vers la fin (du mois) de mai, fin mai ; **the ~ Mr X** feu M. X ; **~comer** *n* retardataire *m/f* ; **~ly** *ad* récemment ; **~ness** *n* (*of person*) retard *m* ; (*of event*) heure tardive.

latent ['leɪtnt] *a* latent(e).

later ['leɪtə*] *a* (*date etc*) ultérieur(e) ; (*version etc*) plus récent(e) // *ad* plus tard.

lateral ['lætərl] *a* latéral(e).

latest ['leɪtɪst] *a* tout(e) dernier(ère) : **at the ~** au plus tard.

latex ['leɪtɛks] *n* latex *m*.

lath, ~s [læθ, læðz] *n* latte *f*.

lathe [leɪð] *n* tour *m* ; **~ operator** *n* tourneur *m* (*en usine*).

lather ['lɑ:ðə*] *n* mousse *f* (de savon) // *vt* savonner // *vi* mousser.

Latin ['lætɪn] *n* latin *m* // *a* latin(e) ; **~ America** *n* Amérique latine ; **~-American** *a* d'Amérique latine.

latitude ['lætɪtju:d] *n* latitude *f*.

latrine [lə'tri:n] *n* latrines *fpl*.

latter ['lætə*] *a* deuxième, dernier(ère) // *n*: **the ~** ce dernier, celui-ci ; **~ly** *ad* dernièrement, récemment.

lattice ['lætɪs] *n* treillis *m* ; treillage *m*.

laudable ['lɔ:dəbl] *a* louable.

laudatory ['lɔ:dətrɪ] *a* élogieux(euse).

laugh [lɑ:f] *n* rire *m* // *vi* rire ; **to ~ at** *vt fus* se moquer de ; **to ~ off** *vt* écarter *or* rejeter par une plaisanterie *or* par une boutade ; **~able** *a* risible, ridicule ; **~ing** *a* (*face*) rieur(euse) ; **the ~ing stock of** la risée de ; **~ter** *n* rire *m* ; rires *mpl*.

launch [lɔ:ntʃ] *n* lancement *m* ; (*boat*) chaloupe *f* ; (*also*: **motor ~**) vedette *f* // *vt* (*ship, rocket, plan*) lancer ; **~ing** *n* lancement *m* ; **~(ing) pad** *n* rampe *f* de lancement.

launder ['lɔ:ndə*] *vt* blanchir.

launderette [lɔ:n'drɛt] *n* laverie *f* (automatique).

laundry ['lɔ:ndrɪ] *n* blanchisserie *f* ; (*clothes*) linge *m* ; **to do the ~** faire la lessive.

laureate ['lɔ:rɪət] *a see* **poet**.

laurel ['lɔrl] *n* laurier *m*.

lava ['lɑ:və] *n* lave *f*.

lavatory ['lævətərɪ] *n* toilettes *fpl*.

lavender ['lævəndə*] *n* lavande *f*.

lavish ['lævɪʃ] *a* copieux(euse) ; somptueux(euse) ; (*giving freely*): **~ with** prodigue de // *vt*: **to ~ on sb/sth** (*care*) prodiguer à qn/qch ; (*money*) dépenser sans compter pour qn/qch.

law [lɔ:] *n* loi *f* ; (*science*) droit *m* ; **~-abiding** *a* respectueux(euse) des lois ; **~ and order** *n* l'ordre public ; **~breaker** *n* personne *f* qui transgresse la loi ; **~ court** *n* tribunal *m*, cour *f* de justice ; **~ful** *a* légal(e) ; permis(e) ; **~fully** *ad* légalement ; **~less** *a* sans loi.

lawn [lɔ:n] *n* pelouse *f* ; **~mower** *n* tondeuse *f* à gazon ; **~ tennis** [-'tɛnɪs] *n* tennis *m*.

law: **~ school** *n* faculté *f* de droit ; **~ student** *n* étudiant/e en droit.

lawsuit ['lɔ:su:t] *n* procès *m*.

lawyer ['lɔ:jə*] *n* (*consultant, with company*) juriste *m* ; (*for sales, wills etc*) ≈ notaire *m* ; (*partner, in court*) ≈ avocat *m*.

lax [læks] *a* relâché(e).

laxative ['læksətɪv] *n* laxatif *m*.

laxity ['læksɪtɪ] *n* relâchement *m*.

lay [leɪ] *pt of* **lie** // *a* laïque ; profane // *vt* (*pt, pp* **laid** [leɪd]) poser, mettre ; (*eggs*) pondre ; (*trap*) tendre ; (*plans*) élaborer ; **to ~ the table** mettre la table ; **to ~ aside** *or* **by** *vt* mettre de côté ; **to ~ down** *vt* poser ; **to ~ down the law** faire la loi ; **to ~ off** *vt* (*workers*) licencier ; **to ~ on** *vt* (*water, gas*) mettre, installer ; (*provide*) fournir ; (*paint*) étaler ; **to ~ out** *vt* (*design*) dessiner, concevoir ; (*display*) disposer ; (*spend*) dépenser ; **to ~ up** *vt* (*to store*) amasser ; (*car*) remiser ; (*ship*) désarmer ; (*subj*: *illness*) forcer à s'aliter ; **~about** *n* fainéant/e ; **~-by** *n* aire *f* de stationnement (sur le bas-côté).

layer ['leɪə*] *n* couche *f*.

layette [leɪ'ɛt] *n* layette *f*.

layman ['leɪmən] *n* laïque *m* ; profane *m*.

layout ['leɪaut] *n* disposition *f*, plan *m*, agencement *m* ; (PRESS) mise *f* en page.

laze [leɪz] *vi* paresser.

laziness ['leɪzɪnɪs] *n* paresse *f*.

lazy ['leɪzɪ] *a* paresseux(euse).

lb. *abbr of* **pound** (*weight*).

lead [li:d] *see also next headword* ; n (*front position*) tête *f* ; (*distance, time ahead*) avance *f* ; (*clue*) piste *f* ; (*in battery*) raccord *m* ; (ELEC) fil *m* ; (*for dog*) laisse *f* ; (THEATRE) rôle principal // *vb* (*pt,pp* **led** [lɛd]) *vt* mener, conduire ; (*induce*) amener ; (*be leader of*) être à la tête de ; (SPORT) être en tête de // *vi* mener, être en tête ; **to ~ to** mener à ; conduire à ; aboutir à ; **to ~ astray** *vt* détourner du droit chemin ; **to ~ away** *vt* emmener ; **to ~ back to** ramener à ; **to ~ on** *vt* (*tease*) faire marcher ; **to ~ on to** *vt* (*induce*) amener à ; **to ~ up to** conduire à.

lead [lɛd] *see also previous headword* ; *n* plomb *m* ; (*in pencil*) mine *f* ; **~en** *a* de *or* en plomb.

leader ['li:də*] *n* chef *m* ; dirigeant/e, leader *m* ; (*of newspaper*) éditorial *m* ; **~ship** *n* direction *f* ; qualités *fpl* de chef.

leading ['li:dɪŋ] *a* de premier plan ; principal(e) ; **~ lady** *n* (THEATRE) vedette (féminine); ~ **light** *n* (*person*) vedette *f*, sommité *f*; ~ **man** *n* (*THEATRE*) vedette (masculine).

leaf, leaves [li:f, li:vz] *n* feuille *f*; (*of table*) rallonge *f*.

leaflet ['li:flıt] prospectus *m*, brochure *f*; (*POL. REL*) tract *m*.

leafy ['li:fı] *a* feuillu(e).

league [li:g] *n* ligue *f*; (*FOOTBALL*) championnat *m*; (*measure*) lieue *f*; **to be in ~ with** avoir partie liée avec, être de mèche avec.

leak [li:k] *n* (*out, also fig*) fuite *f*; (*in*) infiltration *f* // *vi* (*pipe, liquid etc*) fuir; (*shoes*) prendre l'eau // *vt* (*liquid*) répandre; (*information*) divulguer; **to ~ out** *vi* fuir; être divulgué(e).

lean [li:n] *a* maigre // *n* (*of meat*) maigre *m* // *vb* (*pt,pp* **leaned** *or* **leant** [lɛnt]) *vt*: **to ~ sth on** appuyer qch sur // *vi* (*slope*) pencher; (*rest*): **to ~ against** s'appuyer contre; être appuyé(e) contre; **to ~ on** s'appuyer sur; **to ~ back/forward** *vi* se pencher en arrière/avant; **to ~ over** *vi* se pencher; **~ing** *a* penché(e) // *n*: **~ing (towards)** penchant *m* (pour); **~-to** *n* appentis *m*.

leap [li:p] *n* bond *m*, saut *m* // *vi* (*pt,pp* **leaped** *or* **leapt** [lɛpt]) bondir, sauter; **~frog** *n* jeu *m* de saute-mouton; ~ **year** *n* année *f* bissextile.

learn, *pt,pp* **learned** *or* **learnt** [lə:n, -t] *vt,vi* apprendre; **~ed** ['lə:nıd] *a* érudit(e), savant(e); **~er** *n* débutant/e; **~ing** *n* savoir *m*.

lease [li:s] *n* bail *m* // *vt* louer à bail.

leash [li:ʃ] *n* laisse *f*.

least [li:st] *ad* le moins // *a*: **the ~** + *noun* le (la) plus petit(e), le (la) moindre; (*smallest amount of*) le moins de; **the ~** + *adjective* le moins; **the ~ money** le moins d'argent; **the ~ expensive** le moins cher; **at ~** au moins; **not in the ~** pas le moins du monde.

leather ['lɛðə*] *n* cuir *m* // *cpd* en *or* de cuir.

leave [li:v] *vb* (*pt,pp* **left** [lɛft]) *vt* laisser; (*go away from*) quitter // *vi* partir, s'en aller // *n* (*time off*) congé *m*; (*MIL, also: consent*) permission *f*; **to be left** rester; **there's some milk left over** il reste du lait; **on ~** en permission; **to take one's ~ of** prendre congé de; **to ~ out** *vt* oublier, omettre.

leaves [li:vz] *npl of* **leaf**.

Lebanon ['lɛbənən] *n* Liban.

lecherous ['lɛtʃərəs] *a* lubrique.

lectern ['lɛktə:n] *n* lutrin *m*, pupitre *m*.

lecture ['lɛktʃə*] *n* conférence *f*; (*SCOL*) cours (magistral) // *vi* donner des cours; enseigner; **to ~ on** faire un cours (*or* son cours) sur.

lecturer ['lɛktʃərə*] *n* (*speaker*) conférencier/ère; (*at university*) professeur *m* (d'université), ≈ maître assistant, ≈ maître de conférences; **assistant ~** *n* ≈ assistant/e; **senior ~** *n* ≈ chargé/e d'enseignement.

led [lɛd] *pt,pp of* **lead**.

ledge [lɛdʒ] *n* (*of window, on wall*) rebord *m*; (*of mountain*) saillie *f*, corniche *f*.

ledger ['lɛdʒə*] *n* registre *m*, grand livre.

lee [li:] *n* côté *m* sous le vent.

leech [li:tʃ] *n* sangsue *f*.

leek [li:k] *n* poireau *m*.

leer [lıə*] *vi*: **to ~ at sb** regarder qn d'un air mauvais *or* concupiscent, lorgner qn.

leeway ['li:weı] *n* (*fig*): **to make up ~** rattraper son retard; **to have some ~** avoir une certaine liberté d'action.

left [lɛft] *pt,pp of* **leave** // *a* gauche // *ad* à gauche // *n* gauche *f*; **the L~** (*POL*) la gauche; **~-handed** *a* gaucher(ère); **~-hand side** *n* gauche *f*, côté *m* gauche; **~-luggage (office)** *n* consigne *f*; **~-overs** *npl* restes *mpl*; ~ **wing** *n* (*MIL, SPORT*) aile *f* gauche; (*POL*) gauche *f*; **~-wing** *a* (*POL*) de gauche.

leg [lɛg] *n* jambe *f*; (*of animal*) patte *f*; (*of furniture*) pied *m*; (*CULIN: of chicken*) cuisse *f*; **lst/2nd ~** (*SPORT*) match *m* aller/retour; (*of journey*) lère/2ème étape; ~ **of lamb** *n* (*CULIN*) gigot *m* d'agneau.

legacy ['lɛgəsı] *n* héritage *m*, legs *m*.

legal ['li:gl] *a* légal(e); **~ize** *vt* légaliser; **~ly** *ad* légalement; ~ **tender** *n* monnaie légale.

legation [lı'geıʃən] *n* légation *f*.

legend ['lɛdʒənd] *n* légende *f*; **~ary** *a* légendaire.

-legged ['lɛgıd] *suffix*: **two~** à deux pattes (*or* jambes *or* pieds).

leggings ['lɛgıŋz] *npl* jambières *fpl*, guêtres *fpl*.

legibility [lɛdʒı'bılıtı] *n* lisibilité *f*.

legible ['lɛdʒəbl] *a* lisible.

legibly ['lɛdʒəblı] *ad* lisiblement.

legion ['li:dʒən] *n* légion *f*.

legislate ['lɛdʒısleıt] *vi* légiférer; **legislation** [-'leıʃən] *n* législation *f*; **legislative** ['lɛdʒıslətıv] *a* législatif(ive); **legislator** *n* législateur/trice; **legislature** ['lɛdʒıslətʃə*] *n* corps législatif.

legitimacy [lı'dʒıtıməsı] *n* légitimité *f*.

legitimate [lı'dʒıtımət] *a* légitime.

leg-room ['lɛgru:m] *n* place *f* pour les jambes.

leisure ['lɛʒə*] *n* loisir *m*, temps *m* libre; loisirs *mpl*; **at ~** (tout) à loisir; à tête reposée; ~ **centre** *n* centre *m* de loisirs; **~ly** *a* tranquille; fait(e) sans se presser.

lemon ['lɛmən] *n* citron *m*; **~ade** *n* [-'neıd] limonade *f*; ~ **squeezer** *n* presse-citron *m inv*.

lend, *pt,pp* **lent** [lɛnd, lɛnt] *vt*: **to ~ sth (to sb)** prêter qch (à qn); **~er** *n* prêteur/euse; **~ing library** *n* bibliothèque *f* de prêt.

length [lɛŋθ] *n* longueur *f*; (*section: of road, pipe etc*) morceau *m*, bout *m*; ~ **of time** durée *f*; **at ~** (*at last*) enfin, à la fin; (*lengthily*) longuement; **~en** *vt* allonger, prolonger // *vi* s'allonger; **~ways** *ad* dans le sens de la longueur, en long; **~y** *a* (très) long(longue).

leniency ['li:nıənsı] *n* indulgence *f*, clémence *f*.

lenient ['li:nıənt] *a* indulgent(e), clément(e); **~ly** *ad* avec indulgence *or* clémence.

lens [lɛnz] *n* lentille *f*; (*of spectacles*) verre *m*; (*of camera*) objectif *m*.
lent [lɛnt] *pt,pp of* **lend**.
Lent [lɛnt] *n* Carême *m*.
lentil ['lɛntl] *n* lentille *f*.
Leo ['li:əu] *n* le Lion ; **to be** ~ être du Lion.
leopard ['lɛpəd] *n* léopard *m*.
leotard ['li:ətɑ:d] *n* collant *m* (*de danseur etc*).
leper ['lɛpə*] *n* lépreux/euse.
leprosy ['lɛprəsɪ] *n* lèpre *f*.
lesbian ['lɛzbɪən] *n* lesbienne *f*.
less [lɛs] *det* moins de // *pronoun, ad* moins ; ~ **than that/you** moins que cela/vous ; ~ **than half** moins de la moitié ; ~ **and** ~ de moins en moins ; **the** ~ **he works...** moins il travaille... .
lessen ['lɛsn] *vi* diminuer, s'amoindrir, s'atténuer // *vt* diminuer, réduire, atténuer.
lesson ['lɛsn] *n* leçon *f*; **a maths** ~ une leçon *or* un cours de maths.
lest [lɛst] *cj* de peur de + *infinitive*, de peur que + *sub*.
let, *pt,pp* **let** [lɛt] *vt* laisser ; (*lease*) louer ; **he** ~ **me go** il m'a laissé partir ; ~ **the water boil and...** faites bouillir l'eau et... ; ~**'s go** allons-y ; ~ **him come** qu'il vienne ; **'to** ~**'** 'à louer' ; **to** ~ **down** *vt* (*lower*) baisser ; (*dress*) rallonger ; (*hair*) défaire ; (*disappoint*) décevoir ; **to** ~ **go** *vi* lâcher prise // *vt* lâcher ; **to** ~ **in** *vt* laisser entrer ; (*visitor etc*) faire entrer ; **to** ~ **off** *vt* laisser partir ; (*firework etc*) faire partir ; (*smell etc*) dégager ; **to** ~ **out** *vt* laisser sortir ; (*dress*) élargir ; (*scream*) laisser échapper ; **to** ~ **up** *vi* diminuer, s'arrêter.
lethal ['li:θl] *a* mortel(le), fatal(e).
lethargic [lɛ'θɑ:dʒɪk] *a* léthargique.
lethargy ['lɛθədʒɪ] *n* léthargie *f*.
letter ['lɛtə*] *n* lettre *f*; ~**s** *npl* (LITERATURE) lettres ; ~ **bomb** *n* lettre piégée ; ~**box** *n* boîte *f* aux *or* à lettres ; ~**ing** *n* lettres *fpl*; caractères *mpl*.
lettuce ['lɛtɪs] *n* laitue *f*, salade *f*.
let-up ['lɛtʌp] *n* répit *m*, détente *f*.
leukaemia, leukemia (*US*) [lu:'ki:mɪə] *n* leucémie *f*.
level ['lɛvl] *a* plat(e), plan(e), uni(e) ; horizontal(e) // *n* niveau *m*; (*flat place*) terrain plat ; (*also*: **spirit** ~) niveau à bulle // *vt* niveler, aplanir ; **to be** ~ **with** être au même niveau que ; **'A'** ~**s** *npl* ≈ baccalauréat *m*; **'O'** ~**s** *npl* ≈ B.E.P.C. ; **on the** ~ à l'horizontale ; (*fig*: *honest*) régulier(ère) ; **to** ~ **off** *or* **out** *vi* (*prices etc*) se stabiliser ; ~ **crossing** *n* passage *m* à niveau ; ~**-headed** *a* équilibré(e).
lever ['li:və*] *n* levier *m* // *vt*: **to** ~ **up/out** soulever/extraire au moyen d'un levier ; ~**age** *n*: ~**age (on** *or* **with)** prise *f* (sur).
levity ['lɛvɪtɪ] *n* manque *m* de sérieux, légèreté *f*.
levy ['lɛvɪ] *n* taxe *f*, impôt *m* // *vt* prélever, imposer ; percevoir.
lewd [lu:d] *a* obscène, lubrique.
liability [laɪə'bɪlətɪ] *n* responsabilité *f*; (*handicap*) handicap *m*; **liabilities** *npl* obligations *fpl*, engagements *mpl*; (*on balance sheet*) passif *m*.
liable ['laɪəbl] *a* (*subject*): ~ **to** sujet(te) à ; passible de ; (*responsible*): ~ **(for)** responsable (de) ; (*likely*): ~ **to do** susceptible de faire.
liaison [li:'eɪzɔn] *n* liaison *f*.
liar ['laɪə*] *n* menteur/euse.
libel ['laɪbl] *n* écrit *m* diffamatoire ; diffamation *f* // *vt* diffamer.
liberal ['lɪbərl] *a* libéral(e) ; (*generous*): ~ **with** prodigue de, généreux(euse) avec.
liberate ['lɪbəreɪt] *vt* libérer ; **liberation** [-'reɪʃən] *n* libération *f*.
liberty ['lɪbətɪ] *n* liberté *f*; **at** ~ **to do** libre de faire ; **to take the** ~ **of** prendre la liberté de, se permettre de.
Libra ['li:brə] *n* la Balance ; **to be** ~ être de la Balance.
librarian [laɪ'brɛərɪən] *n* bibliothécaire *m/f*.
library ['laɪbrərɪ] *n* bibliothèque *f*.
libretto [lɪ'brɛtəu] *n* livret *m*.
Libya ['lɪbɪə] *n* Lybie *f*; ~**n** *a* lybien(ne), de Lybie // *n* Lybien/ne.
lice [laɪs] *npl of* **louse**.
licence, license (*US*) ['laɪsns] *n* autorisation *f*, permis *m* ; (COMM) licence *f* ; (RADIO, TV) redevance *f*; (*also*: **driving** ~) permis *m* (de conduire) ; (*excessive freedom*) licence ; ~ **plate** *n* plaque *f* minéralogique.
license ['laɪsns] *n* (*US*) = **licence** // *vt* donner une licence à ; ~**d** *a* (*for alcohol*) patenté(e) pour la vente des spiritueux, qui a une patente de débit de boissons.
licensee [laɪsən'si:] *n* (*in a pub*) patron/ne, gérant/e.
licentious [laɪ'sɛnʃəs] *a* licentieux(euse).
lichen ['laɪkən] *n* lichen *m*.
lick [lɪk] *vt* lécher // *n* coup *m* de langue ; **a** ~ **of paint** un petit coup de peinture.
licorice ['lɪkərɪs] *n* = **liquorice**.
lid [lɪd] *n* couvercle *m*.
lido ['laɪdəu] *n* piscine *f* en plein air.
lie [laɪ] *n* mensonge *m* // *vi* mentir ; (*pt* **lay,** *pp* **lain** [leɪ, leɪn]) (*rest*) être étendu(e) *or* allongé(e) *or* couché(e) ; (*in grave*) être enterré(e), reposer ; (*of object*: *be situated*) se trouver, être ; **to** ~ **low** (*fig*) se cacher, rester caché(e) ; **to** ~ **about** *vi* traîner ; **to have a** ~**-down** s'allonger, se reposer ; **to have a** ~**-in** faire la grasse matinée.
lieu [lu:]: **in** ~ **of** *prep* au lieu de.
lieutenant [lɛf'tɛnənt] *n* lieutenant *m*.
life, lives [laɪf, laɪvz] *n* vie *f* // *cpd* de vie ; de la vie ; à vie ; ~ **assurance** *n* assurance-vie *f*; ~**belt** *n* bouée *f* de sauvetage ; ~**boat** *n* canot *m or* chaloupe *f* de sauvetage ; ~**buoy** *n* bouée *f* de sauvetage ; ~ **expectancy** *n* espérance *f* de vie ; ~**guard** *n* surveillant *m* de baignade ; ~ **jacket** *n* gilet *m or* ceinture *f* de sauvetage ; ~**less** *a* sans vie, inanimé(e) ; (*dull*) qui manque de vie *or* de vigueur ; ~**like** *a* qui semble vrai(e) *or* vivant(e) ; ressemblant(e) ; ~**line** *n* corde *f* de sauvetage ; ~**long** *a* de toute une vie, de toujours ; ~ **preserver** *n* (*US*) gilet *m or* ceinture *f* de sauvetage ; (*Brit*: *col*) matraque *f*; ~**-raft** *n* radeau *m* de sauvetage ; ~**-saver** *n* surveillant *m* de baignade ; ~ **sentence** *n* condamnation *f*

à vie *or* à perpétuité ; **~-sized** *a* grandeur nature *inv* ; **~ span** *n* (durée *f* de) vie *f* ; **~ support system** *n* (MED) respirateur artificiel ; **~time** *n*: **in his ~time** de son vivant ; **in a ~time** au cours d'une vie entière ; dans sa vie.

lift [lɪft] *vt* soulever, lever ; (*steal*) prendre, voler // *vi* (*fog*) se lever // *n* (*elevator*) ascenseur *m* ; **to give sb a ~** emmener *or* prendre qn en voiture ; **~-off** *n* décollage *m*.

ligament ['lɪgəmənt] *n* ligament *m*.

light [laɪt] *n* lumière *f* ; (*daylight*) lumière, jour *m* ; (*lamp*) lampe *f* ; (AUT: *traffic ~, rear ~*) feu *m* ; (: *headlamp*) phare *m* ; (*for cigarette etc*): **have you got a ~?** avez-vous du feu? // *vt* (*pt, pp* **lighted** *or* **lit** [lɪt]) (*candle, cigarette, fire*) allumer ; (*room*) éclairer // *a* (*room, colour*) clair(e) ; (*not heavy, also fig*) léger(ère) ; **to ~ up** *vi* s'allumer ; (*face*) s'éclairer // *vt* (*illuminate*) éclairer, illuminer ; **~ bulb** *n* ampoule *f* ; **~en** *vi* s'éclairer // *vt* (*give light to*) éclairer ; (*make lighter*) éclaircir ; (*make less heavy*) alléger ; **~er** *n* (*also*: **cigarette ~**) briquet *m* ; (: *in car*) allume-cigare *m inv* ; (*boat*) péniche *f* ; **~-headed** *a* étourdi(e), écervelé(e) ; **~-hearted** *a* gai(e), joyeux(euse), enjoué(e) ; **~house** *n* phare *m* ; **~ing** *n* (*on road*) éclairage *m* ; (*in theatre*) éclairages ; **~ing-up time** *n* *heure officielle de la tombée du jour* ; **~ly** *ad* légèrement ; **~ meter** *n* (PHOT) photomètre *m*, cellule *f* ; **~ness** *n* clarté *f* ; (*in weight*) légèreté *f*.

lightning ['laɪtnɪŋ] *n* éclair *m*, foudre *f* ; **~ conductor** *n* paratonnerre *m*.

lightship ['laɪtʃɪp] *n* bateau-phare *m*.

lightweight ['laɪtweɪt] *a* (*suit*) léger(ère) ; (*boxer*) poids léger *inv*.

light year ['laɪtjɪə*] *n* année-lumière *f*.

lignite ['lɪgnaɪt] *n* lignite *m*.

like [laɪk] *vt* aimer (bien) // *prep* comme // *a* semblable, pareil(le) // *n*: **the ~** un(e) pareil(le) *or* semblable ; le(la) pareil(le) ; (*pej*) (d')autres du même genre *or* acabit ; **his ~s and dislikes** ses goûts *mpl or* préférences *fpl* ; **I would ~, I'd ~** je voudrais, j'aimerais ; **to be/look ~ sb/sth** ressembler à qn/qch ; **that's just ~ him** c'est bien de lui, ça lui ressemble ; **nothing ~...** rien de tel que... ; **~able** *a* sympathique, agréable.

likelihood ['laɪklɪhud] *n* probabilité *f*.

likely ['laɪklɪ] *a* probable ; plausible ; **he's ~ to leave** il va sûrement partir, il risque fort de partir.

like-minded [laɪk'maɪndɪd] *a* de même opinion.

liken ['laɪkən] *vt*: **to ~ sth to** comparer qch à.

likewise ['laɪkwaɪz] *ad* de même, pareillement.

liking ['laɪkɪŋ] *n*: **~ (for)** affection *f* (pour), penchant *m* (pour) ; goût *m* (pour).

lilac ['laɪlək] *n* lilas *m* // *a* lilas *inv*.

lilting ['lɪltɪŋ] *a* aux cadences mélodieuses ; chantant(e).

lily ['lɪlɪ] *n* lis *m* ; **~ of the valley** *n* muguet *m*.

limb [lɪm] *n* membre *m*.

limber ['lɪmbə*]: **to ~ up** *vi* se dégourdir, se mettre en train.

limbo ['lɪmbəu] *n*: **to be in ~** (*fig*) être tombé(e) dans l'oubli.

lime [laɪm] *n* (*tree*) tilleul *m* ; (*fruit*) lime *f* ; (GEO) chaux *f* ; **~ juice** *n* jus *m* de citron vert.

limelight ['laɪmlaɪt] *n*: **in the ~** (*fig*) en vedette, au premier plan.

limerick ['lɪmərɪk] *n* poème *m* humoristique (de 5 vers).

limestone ['laɪmstəun] *n* pierre *f* à chaux ; (GEO) calcaire *m*.

limit ['lɪmɪt] *n* limite *f* // *vt* limiter ; **~ation** [-'teɪʃən] *n* limitation *f*, restriction *f* ; **~ed** *a* limité(e), restreint(e) ; **~ed (liability) company (Ltd)** *n* ≈ société *f* anonyme (S.A.).

limousine ['lɪməzi:n] *n* limousine *f*.

limp [lɪmp] *n*: **to have a ~** boiter // *vi* boiter // *a* mou(molle).

limpet ['lɪmpɪt] *n* patelle *f* ; **like a ~** (*fig*) comme une ventouse.

line [laɪn] *n* (*gen*) ligne *f* ; (*rope*) corde *f* ; (*wire*) fil *m* ; (*of poem*) vers *m* ; (*row, series*) rangée *f* ; file *f*, queue *f* ; (COMM: *series of goods*) article(s) *m(pl)* // *vt* (*clothes*): **to ~ (with)** doubler (de) ; (*box*): **to ~ (with)** garnir *or* tapisser (de) ; (*subj*: *trees, crowd*) border ; **in his ~ of business** dans sa partie, dans son rayon ; **in ~ with** en accord avec ; **to ~ up** *vi* s'aligner, se mettre en rang(s) // *vt* aligner.

linear ['lɪnɪə*] *a* linéaire.

linen ['lɪnɪn] *n* linge *m* (de corps *or* de maison) ; (*cloth*) lin *m*.

liner ['laɪnə*] *n* paquebot *m* de ligne.

linesman ['laɪnzmən] *n* (TENNIS) juge *m* de ligne ; (FOOTBALL) juge de touche.

line-up ['laɪnʌp] *n* file *f* ; (SPORT) (composition *f* de l')équipe *f*.

linger ['lɪŋgə*] *vi* s'attarder ; traîner ; (*smell, tradition*) persister ; **~ing** *a* persistant(e) ; qui subsiste ; (*death*) lent(e).

lingo, ~es ['lɪŋgəu] *n* (*pej*) jargon *m*.

linguist ['lɪŋgwɪst] *n* linguiste *m/f* ; personne douée pour les langues ; **~ic** *a* linguistique ; **~ics** *n* linguistique *f*.

lining ['laɪnɪŋ] *n* doublure *f*.

link [lɪŋk] *n* (*of a chain*) maillon *m* ; (*connection*) lien *m*, rapport *m* // *vt* relier, lier, unir ; **~s** *npl* (terrain *m* de) golf *m* ; **to ~ up** *vt* relier // *vi* se rejoindre ; s'associer ; **~-up** *n* liaison *f*.

linoleum [lɪ'nəulɪəm] *n* linoléum *m*.

linseed oil ['lɪnsi:d'ɔɪl] *n* huile *f* de lin.

lint [lɪnt] *n* tissu ouaté (*pour pansements*).

lintel ['lɪntl] *n* linteau *m*.

lion ['laɪən] *n* lion *m* ; **~ cub** lionceau *m* ; **~ess** *n* lionne *f*.

lip [lɪp] *n* lèvre *f* ; (*of cup etc*) rebord *m* ; (*insolence*) insolences *fpl* ; **~read** *vi* lire sur les lèvres ; **to pay ~ service to sth** ne reconnaître le mérite de qch que pour la forme *or* qu'en paroles ; **~stick** *n* rouge *m* à lèvres.

liquefy ['lɪkwɪfaɪ] *vt* liquéfier.

liqueur [lɪ'kjuə*] *n* liqueur *f*.

liquid ['lɪkwɪd] *n* liquide *m* // *a* liquide ; **~ assets** *npl* liquidités *fpl*, disponibilités *fpl*.

liquidate ['lɪkwɪdeɪt] *vt* liquider; **liquidation** [-'deɪʃən] *n* liquidation *f*; **liquidator** *n* liquidateur *m*.
liquidize ['lɪkwɪdaɪz] *vt* (CULIN) passer au mixeur.
liquor ['lɪkə*] *n* spiritueux *m*, alcool *m*.
liquorice ['lɪkərɪs] *n* réglisse *m*.
lisp [lɪsp] *n* zézaiement *m*.
list [lɪst] *n* liste *f*; (*of ship*) inclinaison *f* // *vt* (*write down*) inscrire; faire la liste de; (*enumerate*) énumérer // *vi* (*ship*) gîter, donner de la bande.
listen ['lɪsn] *vi* écouter; **to ~ to** écouter; **~er** *n* auditeur/trice.
listless ['lɪstlɪs] *a* indolent(e), apathique; **~ly** *ad* avec indolence *or* apathie.
lit [lɪt] *pt,pp of* **light**.
litany ['lɪtənɪ] *n* litanie *f*.
literacy ['lɪtərəsɪ] *n* degré *m* d'alphabétisation, fait *m* de savoir lire et écrire.
literal ['lɪtərl] *a* littéral(e); (*unimaginative*) prosaïque, sans imagination; **~ly** *ad* littéralement.
literary ['lɪtərərɪ] *a* littéraire.
literate ['lɪtərət] *a* qui sait lire et écrire, instruit(e).
literature ['lɪtərɪtʃə*] *n* littérature *f*; (*brochures etc*) copie *f* publicitaire, prospectus *mpl*.
lithe [laɪð] *a* agile, souple.
lithography [lɪ'θɔgrəfɪ] *n* lithographie *f*.
litigate ['lɪtɪgeɪt] *vt* mettre en litige // *vi* plaider; **litigation** [-'geɪʃən] *n* litige *m*; contentieux *m*.
litmus ['lɪtməs] *n*: **~ paper** papier *m* de tournesol.
litre, liter (*US*) ['li:tə*] *n* litre *m*.
litter ['lɪtə*] *n* (*rubbish*) détritus *mpl*, ordures *fpl*; (*young animals*) portée *f* // *vt* éparpiller; laisser des détritus dans // *vi* (ZOOL) mettre bas; **~ bin** *n* boîte *f* à ordures, poubelle *f*; **~ed with** jonché(e) de, couvert(e) de.
little ['lɪtl] *a* (*small*) petit(e); (*not much*): **it's ~** c'est peu; **~ milk** peu de lait // *ad* peu; **a ~** un peu (de); **a ~ milk** un peu de lait; **~ by ~** petit à petit, peu à peu; **to make ~ of** faire peu de cas de.
liturgy ['lɪtədʒɪ] *n* liturgie *f*.
live *vi* [lɪv] vivre; (*reside*) vivre, habiter // *a* [laɪv] (*animal*) vivant(e), en vie; (*wire*) sous tension; (*broadcast*) (transmis(e)) en direct; **to ~ down** *vt* faire oublier (avec le temps); **to ~ in** *vi* être logé(e) et nourri(e); être interne; **to ~ on** *vt fus* (*food*) vivre de // *vi* survivre, subsister; **to ~ up to** *vt fus* se montrer à la hauteur de.
livelihood ['laɪvlɪhud] *n* moyens *mpl* d'existence.
liveliness ['laɪvlɪnəs] *n* vivacité *f*, entrain *m*.
lively ['laɪvlɪ] *a* vif(vive), plein(e) d'entrain.
liver ['lɪvə*] *n* (ANAT) foie *m*; **~ish** *a* qui a mal au foie; (*fig*) grincheux(euse).
livery ['lɪvərɪ] *n* livrée *f*.
lives [laɪvz] *npl of* **life**.
livestock ['laɪvstɔk] *n* cheptel *m*, bétail *m*.
livid ['lɪvɪd] *a* livide, blafard(e); (*furious*) furieux(euse), furibond(e).
living ['lɪvɪŋ] *a* vivant(e), en vie // *n*: **to earn** *or* **make a ~** gagner sa vie; **~ room** *n* salle *f* de séjour; **~ standards** *npl* niveau *m* de vie; **~ wage** *n* salaire *m* permettant de vivre (décemment).
lizard ['lɪzəd] *n* lézard *m*.
llama ['lɑ:mə] *n* lama *m*.
load [ləud] *n* (*weight*) poids *m*; (*thing carried*) chargement *m*, charge *f*; (ELEC, TECH) charge // *vt*: **to ~ (with)** (*lorry, ship*) charger (de); (*gun, camera*) charger (avec); **a ~ of, ~s of** (*fig*) un *or* des tas de, des masses de; **~ed** *a* (*dice*) pipé(e); (*question, word*) insidieux(euse); (*col*: *rich*) bourré(e) de fric; (: *drunk*) bourré.
loaf, loaves [ləuf, ləuvz] *n* pain *m*, miche *f* // *vi* (*also*: **~ about, ~ around**) fainéanter, traîner.
loam [ləum] *n* terreau *m*.
loan [ləun] *n* prêt *m* // *vt* prêter; **on ~** prêté(e), en prêt; **public ~** emprunt public.
loath [ləuθ] *a*: **to be ~ to do** répugner à faire.
loathe [ləuð] *vt* détester, avoir en horreur; **loathing** *n* dégoût *m*, répugnance *f*.
loaves [ləuvz] *npl of* **loaf**.
lobby ['lɔbɪ] *n* hall *m*, entrée *f*; (POL: *pressure group*) groupe *m* de pression, lobby *m* // *vt* faire pression sur.
lobe [ləub] *n* lobe *m*.
lobster ['lɔbstə*] *n* homard *m*.
local ['ləukl] *a* local(e) // *n* (*pub*) pub *m* *or* café *m* du coin; **the ~s** *npl* les gens *mpl* du pays *or* du coin; **~ call** *n* communication urbaine; **~ government** *n* administration locale *or* municipale.
locality [ləu'kælɪtɪ] *n* région *f*, environs *mpl*; (*position*) lieu *m*.
locally ['ləukəlɪ] *ad* localement; dans les environs *or* la région.
locate [ləu'keɪt] *vt* (*find*) trouver, repérer; (*situate*) situer.
location [ləu'keɪʃən] *n* emplacement *m*; **on ~** (CINEMA) en extérieur.
loch [lɔx] *n* lac *m*, loch *m*.
lock [lɔk] *n* (*of door, box*) serrure *f*; (*of canal*) écluse *f*; (*of hair*) mèche *f*, boucle *f* // *vt* (*with key*) fermer à clé; (*immobilize*) bloquer // *vi* (*door etc*) fermer à clé; (*wheels*) se bloquer.
locker ['lɔkə*] *n* casier *m*.
locket ['lɔkɪt] *n* médaillon *m*.
lockjaw ['lɔkdʒɔ:] *n* tétanos *m*.
locomotive [ləukə'məutɪv] *n* locomotive *f*.
locust ['ləukəst] *n* locuste *f*, sauterelle *f*.
lodge [lɔdʒ] *n* pavillon *m* (de gardien); (FREEMASONRY) loge *f* // *vi* (*person*): **to ~ (with)** être logé(e) (chez), être en pension (chez) // *vt* (*appeal etc*) présenter; déposer; **to ~ a complaint** porter plainte; **to ~ (itself) in/between** se loger dans/entre; **~r** *n* locataire *m/f*; (*with room and meals*) pensionnaire *m/f*.
lodgings ['lɔdʒɪŋz] *npl* chambre *f*; meublé *m*.
loft [lɔft] *n* grenier *m*.
lofty ['lɔftɪ] *a* élevé(e); (*haughty*) hautain(e).
log [lɔg] *n* (*of wood*) bûche *f*; (*book*) = **logbook**.

logarithm ['lɔgərɪðəm] *n* logarithme *m*.
logbook ['lɔgbuk] *n* (NAUT) livre *m* *or* journal *m* de bord ; (AVIAT) carnet *m* de vol ; (*of lorry-driver*) carnet de route ; (*of events, movement of goods etc*) registre *m* ; (*of car*) ≈ carte grise.
loggerheads ['lɔgəhɛdz] *npl*: **at ~ (with)** à couteaux tirés (avec).
logic ['lɔdʒɪk] *n* logique *f* ; **~al** *a* logique ; **~ally** *ad* logiquement.
logistics [lɔ'dʒɪstɪks] *n* logistique *f*.
loin [lɔɪn] *n* (CULIN) filet *m*, longe *f* ; **~s** *npl* reins *mpl*.
loiter ['lɔɪtə*] *vi* s'attarder ; **to ~ (about)** traîner, musarder ; (*pej*) rôder.
loll [lɔl] *vi* (*also*: **~ about**) se prélasser, fainéanter.
lollipop ['lɔlɪpɔp] *n* sucette *f* ; **~ man/lady** *n* contractuel/le qui fait traverser la rue aux enfants.
London ['lʌndən] *n* Londres *m* ; **~er** *n* Londonien/ne.
lone [ləun] *a* solitaire.
loneliness ['ləunlɪnɪs] *n* solitude *f*, isolement *m*.
lonely ['ləunlɪ] *a* seul(e) ; solitaire, isolé(e) ; **to feel ~** se sentir seul.
loner ['ləunə*] *n* solitaire *m/f*.
long [lɔŋ] *a* long(longue) // *ad* longtemps // *vi*: **to ~ for sth/to do** avoir très envie de qch/de faire ; attendre qch avec impatience/impatience de faire ; **he had ~ understood that...** il avait compris depuis longtemps que... ; **how ~ is this river/course?** quelle est la longueur de ce fleuve/la durée de ce cours? ; **6 metres ~** (long) de 6 mètres ; **6 months ~** qui dure 6 mois, de 6 mois ; **all night ~** toute la nuit ; **~ before** longtemps avant ; **before ~** (+ *future*) avant peu, dans peu de temps ; (+ *past*) peu de temps après ; **at ~ last** enfin ; **no ~er, any ~er** ne...plus ; **~-distance** *a* (*race*) de fond ; (*call*) interurbain(e) ; **~-haired** *a* (*person*) aux cheveux longs ; (*animal*) aux longs poils ; **~hand** *n* écriture normale *or* courante ; **~ing** *n* désir *m*, envie *f*, nostalgie *f* // *a* plein(e) d'envie *or* de nostalgie.
longitude ['lɔŋgɪtju:d] *n* longitude *f*.
long: **~ jump** *n* saut *m* en longueur ; **~-lost** *a* perdu(e) depuis longtemps ; **~-playing** *a*: **~-playing record (L.P.)** *n* (disque *m*) 33 tours *m inv* ; **~-range** *a* à longue portée ; **~-sighted** *a* presbyte ; (*fig*) prévoyant(e) ; **~-standing** *a* de longue date ; **~-suffering** *a* empreint(e) d'une patience résignée ; extrêmement patient(e) ; **~-term** *a* à long terme ; **~ wave** *n* grandes ondes ; **~-winded** *a* intarissable, interminable.
loo [lu:] *n* (*col*) w.-c. *mpl*, petit coin.
loofah ['lu:fə] *n sorte d'éponge végétale.*
look [luk] *vi* regarder ; (*seem*) sembler, paraître, avoir l'air ; (*building etc*): **to ~ south/on to the sea** donner au sud/sur la mer // *n* regard *m* ; (*appearance*) air *m*, allure *f*, aspect *m* ; **~s** *npl* mine *f* ; physique *m* ; beauté *f* ; **to ~ like** ressembler à ; **it ~s like him** on dirait que c'est lui ; **to ~ after** *vt fus* s'occuper de, prendre soin de ; garder, surveiller ; **to ~ at** *vt fus* regarder ; **to ~ down on** *vt fus* (*fig*) regarder de haut, dédaigner ; **to ~ for** *vt fus* chercher ; **to ~ forward to** *vt fus* attendre avec impatience ; **to ~ on** *vi* regarder (en spectateur) ; **to ~ out** *vi* (*beware*): **to ~ out (for)** prendre garde (à), faire attention (à) ; **to ~ out for** *vt fus* être à la recherche de ; guetter ; **to ~ to** *vt fus* veiller à ; (*rely on*) compter sur ; **to ~ up** *vi* lever les yeux ; (*improve*) s'améliorer // *vt* (*word*) chercher ; (*friend*) passer voir ; **to ~ up to** *vt fus* avoir du respect pour ; **~-out** *n* poste *m* de guet ; guetteur *m* ; **to be on the ~-out (for)** guetter.
loom [lu:m] *n* métier *m* à tisser // *vi* surgir ; (*fig*) menacer, paraître imminent(e).
loop [lu:p] *n* boucle *f* ; (*contraceptive*) stérilet *m* ; **~hole** *n* porte *f* de sortie (*fig*) ; échappatoire *f*.
loose [lu:s] *a* (*knot, screw*) desserré(e) ; (*stone*) branlant(e) ; (*clothes*) vague, ample, lâche ; (*animal*) en liberté, échappé(e) ; (*life*) dissolu(e) ; (*morals, discipline*) relâché(e) ; (*thinking*) peu rigoureux(euse), vague ; (*translation*) approximatif(ive) ; **to be at a ~ end** ne pas trop savoir quoi faire ; **~ly** *ad* sans serrer ; approximativement ; **~n** *vt* desserrer, relâcher, défaire.
loot [lu:t] *n* butin *m* // *vt* piller ; **~ing** *n* pillage *m*.
lop [lɔp]: **to ~ off** *vt* couper, trancher.
lop-sided ['lɔp'saɪdɪd] *a* de travers, asymétrique.
lord [lɔ:d] *n* seigneur *m* ; **L~ Smith** lord Smith ; **the L~** le Seigneur ; **the (House of) L~s** la Chambre des Lords ; **~ly** *a* noble, majestueux(euse) ; (*arrogant*) hautain(e) ; **~ship** *n*: **your L~ship** Monsieur le comte (*or* le baron *or* le Juge).
lore [lɔ:*] *n* tradition(s) *f(pl)*.
lorry ['lɔrɪ] *n* camion *m* ; **~ driver** *n* camionneur *m*, routier *m*.
lose, *pt,pp* **lost** [lu:z, lɔst] *vt* perdre ; (*opportunity*) manquer, perdre ; (*pursuers*) distancer, semer // *vi* perdre ; **to ~ (time)** (*clock*) retarder ; **to get lost** *vi* se perdre ; **~r** *n* perdant/e.
loss [lɔs] *n* perte *f* ; **to be at a ~** être perplexe *or* embarrassé(e) ; **to be at a ~ to do** se trouver incapable de faire.
lost [lɔst] *pt,pp of* **lose** // *a* perdu(e) ; **~ property** *n* objets trouvés.
lot [lɔt] *n* (*at auctions*) lot *m* ; (*destiny*) sort *m*, destinée *f* ; **the ~** le tout ; tous *mpl*, toutes *fpl* ; **a ~** beaucoup ; **a ~ of** beaucoup de ; **~s of** des tas de ; **to draw ~s (for sth)** tirer (qch) au sort.
lotion ['ləuʃən] *n* lotion *f*.
lottery ['lɔtərɪ] *n* loterie *f*.
loud [laud] *a* bruyant(e), sonore, fort(e) ; (*gaudy*) voyant(e), tapageur(euse) // *ad* (*speak etc*) fort ; **~hailer** *n* porte-voix *m inv* ; **~ly** *ad* fort, bruyamment ; **~speaker** *n* haut-parleur *m*.
lounge [laundʒ] *n* salon *m* // *vi* se prélasser, paresser ; **~ suit** *n* complet *m* ; 'tenue de ville'.
louse, *pl* **lice** [laus, laɪs] *n* pou *m*.
lousy ['lauzɪ] *a* (*fig*) infect(e), moche.

lout [laut] *n* rustre *m*, butor *m*.
lovable ['lʌvəbl] *a* très sympathique; adorable.
love [lʌv] *n* amour *m* // *vt* aimer; aimer beaucoup; **to ~ to do** aimer beaucoup *or* adorer faire; **to be in ~ with** être amoureux(euse) de; **to make ~** faire l'amour; **'15 ~'** (*TENNIS*) '15 à rien *or* zéro'; **~ at first sight** le coup de foudre; **~ affair** *n* liaison (amoureuse); **~ letter** *n* lettre *f* d'amour; **~ life** *n* vie sentimentale.
lovely ['lʌvlı] *a* (très) joli(e); ravissant(e), charmant(e); agréable.
lover ['lʌvə*] *n* amant *m*; (*amateur*): **a ~ of** un(e) ami(e) de; un(e) amoureux(euse) de.
lovesong ['lʌvsɔŋ] *n* chanson *f* d'amour.
loving ['lʌvıŋ] *a* affectueux(euse), tendre, aimant(e).
low [ləu] *a* bas(basse) // *ad* bas // *n* (*METEOROLOGY*) dépression *f* // *vi* (*cow*) mugir; **to feel ~** se sentir déprimé(e); **he's very ~** (*ill*) il est bien bas *or* très affaibli; **to turn (down) ~** *vt* baisser; **~-cut** *a* (*dress*) décolleté(e); **~er** *vt* abaisser, baisser; **~ly** *a* humble, modeste; **~-lying** *a* à faible altitude; **~-paid** *a* mal payé(e), aux salaires bas.
loyal ['lɔıəl] *a* loyal(e), fidèle; **~ty** *n* loyauté *f*, fidélité *f*.
lozenge ['lɔzındʒ] *n* (*MED*) pastille *f*; (*GEOM*) losange *m*.
L.P. *n abbr see* **long-playing**.
L-plates ['ɛlpleıts] *npl* plaques *fpl* d'apprenti conducteur.
Ltd *abbr see* **limited**.
lubricant ['lu:brıkənt] *n* lubrifiant *m*.
lubricate ['lu:brıkeıt] *vt* lubrifier, graisser.
lucid ['lu:sıd] *a* lucide; **~ity** [-'sıdıtı] *n* lucidité *f*.
luck [lʌk] *n* chance *f*; **bad ~** malchance *f*, malheur *m*; **good ~!** bonne chance! **~ily** *ad* heureusement, par bonheur; **~y** *a* (*person*) qui a de la chance; (*coincidence*) heureux(euse); (*number etc*) qui porte bonheur.
lucrative ['lu:krətıv] *a* lucratif(ive), rentable, qui rapporte.
ludicrous ['lu:dıkrəs] *a* ridicule, absurde.
ludo ['lu:dəu] *n* jeu *m* des petits chevaux.
lug [lʌg] *vt* traîner, tirer.
luggage ['lʌgıdʒ] *n* bagages *mpl*; **~ rack** *n* (*in train*) porte-bagages *m inv*; (: *made of string*) filet *m* à bagages; (*on car*) galerie *f*.
lugubrious [lu'gu:brıəs] *a* lugubre.
lukewarm ['lu:kwɔ:m] *a* tiède.
lull [lʌl] *n* accalmie *f* // *vt* (*child*) bercer; (*person, fear*) apaiser, calmer.
lullaby ['lʌləbaı] *n* berceuse *f*.
lumbago [lʌm'beıgəu] *n* lumbago *m*.
lumber ['lʌmbə*] *n* bric-à-brac *m inv*; **~jack** *n* bûcheron *m*.
luminous ['lu:mınəs] *a* lumineux(euse).
lump [lʌmp] *n* morceau *m*; (*in sauce*) grumeau *m*; (*swelling*) grosseur *f* // *vt* (*also*: **~ together**) réunir, mettre en tas; **a ~ sum** une somme globale *or* forfaitaire; **~y** *a* (*sauce*) qui a des grumeaux.
lunacy ['lu:nəsı] *n* démence *f*, folie *f*.
lunar ['lu:nə*] *a* lunaire.
lunatic ['lu:nətık] *n* fou/folle, dément/e // *a* fou(folle), dément(e).
lunch [lʌntʃ] *n* déjeuner *m*; **it is his ~ hour** c'est l'heure où il déjeune; **it is ~time** c'est l'heure du déjeuner.
luncheon ['lʌntʃən] *n* déjeuner *m*; **~ meat** *n sorte de saucisson*; **~ voucher** *n* chèque-déjeuner *m*.
lung [lʌŋ] *n* poumon *m*; **~ cancer** *n* cancer *m* du poumon.
lunge [lʌndʒ] *vi* (*also*: **~ forward**) faire un mouvement brusque en avant.
lupin ['lu:pın] *n* lupin *m*.
lurch [lə:tʃ] *vi* vaciller, tituber // *n* écart *m* brusque, embardée *f*.
lure [luə*] *n* appât *m*, leurre *m* // *vt* attirer *or* persuader par la ruse.
lurid ['luərıd] *a* affreux(euse), atroce.
lurk [lə:k] *vi* se tapir, se cacher.
luscious ['lʌʃəs] *a* succulent(e); appétissant(e).
lush [lʌʃ] *a* luxuriant(e).
lust [lʌst] *n* luxure *f*; lubricité *f*; désir *m*; (*fig*): **~ for** soif *f* de; **to ~ after** *vt fus* convoiter, désirer; **~ful** *a* lascif(ive).
lustre, luster (*US*) ['lʌstə*] *n* lustre *m*, brillant *m*.
lusty ['lʌstı] *a* vigoureux(euse), robuste.
lute [lu:t] *n* luth *m*.
Luxembourg ['lʌksəmbə:g] *n* Luxembourg *m*.
luxuriant [lʌg'zjuərıənt] *a* luxuriant(e).
luxurious [lʌg'zjuərıəs] *a* luxueux(euse).
luxury ['lʌkʃərı] *n* luxe *m* // *cpd* de luxe.
lying ['laııŋ] *n* mensonge(s) *m(pl)*.
lynch [lıntʃ] *vt* lyncher.
lynx [lıŋks] *n* lynx *m inv*.
lyre ['laıə*] *n* lyre *f*.
lyric ['lırık] *a* lyrique; **~s** *npl* (*of song*) paroles *fpl*; **~al** *a* lyrique; **~ism** ['lırısızəm] *n* lyrisme *m*.

M

m. *abbr of* **metre, mile, million**.
M.A. *abbr see* **master**.
mac [mæk] *n* imper(méable) *m*.
macaroni [mækə'rəunı] *n* macaronis *mpl*.
macaroon [mækə'ru:n] *n* macaron *m*.
mace [meıs] *n* masse *f*; (*spice*) macis *m*.
machine [mə'ʃi:n] *n* machine *f* // *vt* (*dress etc*) coudre à la machine; **~ gun** *n* mitrailleuse *f*; **~ry** *n* machinerie *f*, machines *fpl*; (*fig*) mécanisme(s) *m(pl)*; **~ tool** *n* machine-outil *f*; **machinist** *n* machiniste *m/f*.
mackerel ['mækrl] *n, pl inv* maquereau *m*.
mackintosh ['mækıntɔʃ] *n* imperméable *m*.
mad [mæd] *a* fou(folle); (*foolish*) insensé(e); (*angry*) furieux(euse).
madam ['mædəm] *n* madame *f*; **yes ~** oui Madame.
madden ['mædn] *vt* exaspérer.
made [meıd] *pt, pp of* **make**; **~-to-measure** *a* fait(e) sur mesure.
madly ['mædlı] *ad* follement.

madman ['mædmən] *n* fou *m*, aliéné *m*.
madness ['mædnıs] *n* folie *f*.
magazine [mægə'zi:n] *n* (PRESS) magazine *m*, revue *f*; (MIL: *store*) dépôt *m*, arsenal *m*; (*of firearm*) magasin *m*.
maggot ['mægət] *n* ver *m*, asticot *m*.
magic ['mædʒık] *n* magie *f* // *a* magique; **~al** *a* magique; **~ian** [mə'dʒıʃən] *n* magicien/ne.
magistrate ['mædʒıstreıt] *n* magistrat *m*; juge *m*.
magnanimous [mæg'nænıməs] *a* magnanime.
magnate ['mægneıt] *n* magnat *m*.
magnesium [mæg'ni:zıəm] *n* magnésium *m*.
magnet ['mægnıt] *n* aimant *m*; **~ic** [-'nɛtık] *a* magnétique; **~ism** *n* magnétisme *m*.
magnification [mægnıfı'keıʃən] *n* grossissement *m*.
magnificence [mæg'nıfısns] *n* magnificence *f*.
magnificent [mæg'nıfısnt] *a* superbe, magnifique.
magnify ['mægnıfaı] *vt* grossir; (*sound*) amplifier; **~ing glass** *n* loupe *f*.
magnitude ['mægnıtju:d] *n* ampleur *f*.
magnolia [mæg'nəulıə] *n* magnolia *m*.
magpie ['mægpaı] *n* pie *f*.
mahogany [mə'hɔgənı] *n* acajou *m* // *cpd* en (bois d')acajou.
maid [meıd] *n* bonne *f*; **old ~** (*pej*) vieille fille.
maiden ['meıdn] *n* jeune fille *f* // *a* (*aunt etc*) non mariée; (*speech, voyage*) inaugural(e); **~ name** *n* nom *m* de jeune fille.
mail [meıl] *n* poste *f*; (*letters*) courrier *m* // *vt* envoyer (par la poste); **~box** *n* (*US*) boîte *f* aux lettres; **~ing list** *n* liste *f* d'adresses; **~-order** *n* vente *f* *or* achat *m* par correspondance.
maim [meım] *vt* mutiler.
main [meın] *a* principal(e) // *n* (*pipe*) conduite principale, canalisation *f*; **the ~s** (ELEC) le secteur; **in the ~** dans l'ensemble; **~land** *n* continent *m*; **~stay** *n* (*fig*) pilier *m*.
maintain [meın'teın] *vt* entretenir; (*continue*) maintenir, préserver; (*affirm*) soutenir; **maintenance** ['meıntənəns] *n* entretien *m*.
maisonette [meızə'nɛt] *n* appartement *m* en duplex.
maize [meız] *n* maïs *m*.
majestic [mə'dʒɛstık] *a* majestueux(euse).
majesty ['mædʒıstı] *n* majesté *f*.
major ['meıdʒə*] *n* (MIL) commandant *m* // *a* important(e), principal(e); (MUS) majeur(e).
majority [mə'dʒɔrıtı] *n* majorité *f*.
make [meık] *vt* (*pt, pp* **made** [meıd]) faire; (*manufacture*) faire, fabriquer; (*cause to be*): **to ~ sb sad** *etc* rendre qn triste *etc*; (*force*): **to ~ sb do sth** obliger qn à faire qch, faire faire qch à qn; (*equal*): **2 and 2 ~ 4** 2 et 2 font 4 // *n* fabrication *f*; (*brand*) marque *f*; **to ~ do with** se contenter de; se débrouiller avec; **to ~ for** *vt fus* (*place*) se diriger vers; **to ~ out** *vt* (*write out*) écrire; (*understand*) comprendre; (*see*) distinguer; **to ~ up** *vt* (*invent*) inventer, imaginer; (*parcel*) faire // *vi* se réconcilier; (*with cosmetics*) se maquiller, se farder; **to ~ up for** *vt fus* compenser; racheter; **~-believe** *a* feint(e), de fantaisie; **~r** *n* fabricant *m*; **~shift** *a* provisoire, improvisé(e); **~-up** *n* maquillage *m*.
making ['meıkıŋ] *n* (*fig*): **in the ~** en formation *or* gestation.
maladjusted [mælə'dʒʌstıd] *a* inadapté(e).
malaise [mæ'leız] *n* malaise *m*.
malaria [mə'lɛərıə] *n* malaria *f*, paludisme *m*.
Malay [mə'leı] *a* malais(e) // *n* (*person*) Malais/e; (*language*) malais *m*.
Malaysia [mə'leızıə] *n* Malaisie *f*.
male [meıl] *n* (BIOL, ELEC) mâle *m* // *a* (*sex, attitude*) masculin(e); mâle; (*child etc*) du sexe masculin; **~ and female students** étudiants et étudiantes.
malevolence [mə'lɛvələns] *n* malveillance *f*.
malevolent [mə'lɛvələnt] *a* malveillant(e).
malfunction [mæl'fʌŋkʃən] *n* fonctionnement défectueux.
malice ['mælıs] *n* méchanceté *f*, malveillance *f*; **malicious** [mə'lıʃəs] *a* méchant(e), malveillant(e); (LAW) avec intention criminelle.
malign [mə'laın] *vt* diffamer, calomnier.
malignant [mə'lıgnənt] *a* (MED) malin(igne).
malingerer [mə'lıŋgərə*] *n* simulateur/trice.
malleable ['mælıəbl] *a* malléable.
mallet ['mælıt] *n* maillet *m*.
malnutrition [mælnju:'trıʃən] *n* malnutrition *f*.
malpractice [mæl'præktıs] *n* faute professionnelle; négligence *f*.
malt [mɔ:lt] *n* malt *m* // *cpd* (*whisky*) pur malt.
Malta ['mɔ:ltə] *n* Malte *f*; **Maltese** [-'ti:z] *a* maltais(e) // *n, pl inv* Maltais/e.
maltreat [mæl'tri:t] *vt* maltraiter.
mammal ['mæml] *n* mammifère *m*.
mammoth ['mæməθ] *n* mammouth *m* // *a* géant(e), monstre.
man, *pl* **men** [mæn,mɛn] *n* homme *m*; (CHESS) pièce *f*; (DRAUGHTS) pion *m* // *vt* garnir d'hommes; servir, assurer le fonctionnement de; être de service à; **an old ~** un vieillard.
manage ['mænıdʒ] *vi* se débrouiller // *vt* (*be in charge of*) s'occuper de; gérer; **to ~ to do** se débrouiller pour faire; réussir à faire; **~able** *a* maniable; faisable; **~ment** *n* administration *f*, direction *f*; **~r** *n* directeur *m*; administrateur *m*; (*of hotel etc*) gérant *m*; (*of artist*) impresario *m*; **~ress** [-ə'rɛs] *n* directrice *f*; gérante *f*; **~rial** [-ə'dʒıerıəl] *a* directorial(e); **~rial staff** *n* cadres *mpl*; **managing** *a*: **managing director** directeur général.
mandarin ['mændərın] *n* (*also*: **~ orange**) mandarine *f*; (*person*) mandarin *m*.

mandate ['mændeɪt] *n* mandat *m*.
mandatory ['mændətərɪ] *a* obligatoire ; (*powers etc*) mandataire.
mandolin(e) ['mændəlɪn] *n* mandoline *f*.
mane [meɪn] *n* crinière *f*.
maneuver [mə'nu:və*] *etc* (*US*) = **manoeuvre** *etc*.
manful ['mænful] *a* courageux(euse), vaillant(e).
manganese [mæŋgə'ni:z] *n* manganèse *m*.
mangle ['mæŋgl] *vt* déchiqueter ; mutiler // *n* essoreuse *f*; calandre *f*.
mango, ~es ['mæŋgəu] *n* mangue *f*.
mangrove ['mæŋgrəuv] *n* palétuvier *m*.
mangy ['meɪndʒɪ] *a* galeux(euse).
manhandle ['mænhændl] *vt* malmener.
manhole ['mænhəul] *n* trou *m* d'homme.
manhood ['mænhud] *n* âge *m* d'homme ; virilité *f*.
manhunt ['mænhʌnt] *n* chasse *f* à l'homme.
mania ['meɪnɪə] *n* manie *f*; **~c** ['meɪnɪæk] *n* maniaque *m/f*.
manicure ['mænɪkjuə*] *n* manucure *f* // *vt* (*person*) faire les mains à ; **~ set** *n* trousse *f* à ongles.
manifest ['mænɪfɛst] *vt* manifester // *a* manifeste, évident(e) ; **~ation** [-'teɪʃən] *n* manifestation *f*.
manifesto [mænɪ'fɛstəu] *n* manifeste *m*.
manipulate [mə'nɪpjuleɪt] *vt* manipuler.
mankind [mæn'kaɪnd] *n* humanité *f*, genre humain.
manly ['mænlɪ] *a* viril(e) ; courageux(euse).
man-made ['mæn'meɪd] *a* artificiel(le).
manner ['mænə*] *n* manière *f*, façon *f*; **~s** *npl* manières ; **~ism** *n* particularité *f* de langage (*or* de comportement), tic *m*.
manoeuvre, maneuver (*US*) [mə'nu:və*] *vt,vi* manœuvrer // *n* manœuvre *f*.
manor ['mænə*] *n* (*also*: **~ house**) manoir *m*.
manpower ['mænpauə*] *n* main-d'œuvre *f*.
manservant, *pl* **menservants** ['mænsə:vənt, 'mɛn-] *n* domestique *m*.
mansion ['mænʃən] *n* château *m*, manoir *m*.
manslaughter ['mænslɔ:tə*] *n* homicide *m* involontaire.
mantelpiece ['mæntlpi:s] *n* cheminée *f*.
mantle ['mæntl] *n* cape *f*; (*fig*) manteau *m*.
manual ['mænjuəl] *a* manuel(le) // *n* manuel *m*.
manufacture [mænju'fæktʃə*] *vt* fabriquer // *n* fabrication *f*; **~r** *n* fabricant *m*.
manure [mə'njuə*] *n* fumier *m* ; (*artificial*) engrais *m*.
manuscript ['mænjuskrɪpt] *n* manuscrit *m*.
many ['mɛnɪ] *det* beaucoup de, de nombreux(euses) // *pronoun* beaucoup, un grand nombre ; **a great ~** un grand nombre (de) ; **~ a...** bien des... , plus d'un(e)... .
map [mæp] *n* carte *f* // *vt* dresser la carte de ; **to ~ out** *vt* tracer.
maple ['meɪpl] *n* érable *m*.
mar [mɑ:*] *vt* gâcher, gâter.
marathon ['mærəθən] *n* marathon *m*.
marauder [mə'rɔ:də*] *n* maraudeur/euse.
marble ['mɑ:bl] *n* marbre *m* ; (*toy*) bille *f*; **~s** *n* (*game*) billes.
March [mɑ:tʃ] *n* mars *m*.
march [mɑ:tʃ] *vi* marcher au pas ; défiler // *n* marche *f*; (*demonstration*) rallye *m* ; **~-past** *n* défilé *m*.
mare [mɛə*] *n* jument *f*.
margarine [mɑ:dʒə'ri:n] *n* margarine *f*.
margin ['mɑ:dʒɪn] *n* marge *f*; **~al** *a* marginal(e).
marigold ['mærɪgəuld] *n* souci *m*.
marijuana [mærɪ'wɑ:nə] *n* marijuana *f*.
marina [mə'ri:nə] *n* marina *f*.
marine [mə'ri:n] *a* marin(e) // *n* fusilier marin ; (*US*) marine *m*.
marital ['mærɪtl] *a* matrimonial(e).
maritime ['mærɪtaɪm] *a* maritime.
marjoram ['mɑ:dʒərəm] *n* marjolaine *f*.
mark [mɑ:k] *n* marque *f*; (*of skid etc*) trace *f*; (SCOL) note *f*; (SPORT) cible *f*; (*currency*) mark *m* // *vt* marquer ; (*stain*) tacher ; (SCOL) noter ; corriger ; **to ~ time** marquer le pas ; **to ~ out** *vt* désigner ; **~ed** *a* marqué(e), net(te) ; **~er** *n* (*sign*) jalon *m* ; (*bookmark*) signet *m*.
market ['mɑ:kɪt] *n* marché *m* // *vt* (COMM) commercialiser ; **~ day** *n* jour *m* de marché ; **~ garden** *n* (*Brit*) jardin maraîcher ; **~ing** *n* marketing *m* ; **~ place** *n* place *f* du marché.
marksman ['mɑ:ksmən] *n* tireur *m* d'élite ; **~ship** *n* adresse *f* au tir.
marmalade ['mɑ:məleɪd] *n* confiture *f* d'oranges.
maroon [mə'ru:n] *vt* (*fig*): **to be ~ed (in** *or* **at)** être bloqué(e) (à) // *a* bordeaux *inv*.
marquee [mɑ:'ki:] *n* chapiteau *m*.
marquess, marquis ['mɑ:kwɪs] *n* marquis *m*.
marriage ['mærɪdʒ] *n* mariage *m* ; **~ bureau** *n* agence matrimoniale.
married ['mærɪd] *a* marié(e) ; (*life, love*) conjugal(e).
marrow ['mærəu] *n* moelle *f*; (*vegetable*) courge *f*.
marry ['mærɪ] *vt* épouser, se marier avec ; (*subj: father, priest etc*) marier // *vi* (*also*: **get married**) se marier.
Mars [mɑ:z] *n* (*planet*) Mars *f*.
marsh [mɑ:ʃ] *n* marais *m*, marécage *m*.
marshal ['mɑ:ʃl] *n* maréchal *m* ; (*US*: *fire, police*) ≈ capitaine *m* // *vt* rassembler ; **~ing yard** *n* gare *f* de triage.
marshy ['mɑ:ʃɪ] *a* marécageux(euse).
martial ['mɑ:ʃl] *a* martial(e) ; **~ law** *n* loi martiale.
Martian ['mɑ:ʃɪən] Martien/ne.
martyr ['mɑ:tə*] *n* martyr/e // *vt* martyriser ; **~dom** *n* martyre *m*.
marvel ['mɑ:vl] *n* merveille *f* // *vi*: **to ~ (at)** s'émerveiller (de) ; **~lous, ~ous** (*US*) *a* merveilleux(euse).
Marxism ['mɑ:ksɪzəm] *n* marxisme *m*.

Marxist ['mɑ:ksɪst] *a,n* marxiste (*m/f*).
marzipan ['mɑ:zɪpæn] *n* pâte *f* d'amandes.
mascara [mæs'kɑ:rə] *n* mascara *m*.
mascot ['mæskət] *n* mascotte *f*.
masculine ['mæskjulɪn] *a* masculin(e) // *n* masculin *m*; **masculinity** [-'lɪnɪtɪ] *n* masculinité *f*.
mashed [mæʃt] *a*: ~ **potatoes** purée *f* de pommes de terre.
mask [mɑ:sk] *n* masque *m* // *vt* masquer.
masochist ['mæsəukɪst] *n* masochiste *m/f*.
mason ['meɪsn] *n* (*also*: **stone~**) maçon *m*; (*also*: **free~**) franc-maçon *m*; **~ic** [mə'sɔnɪk] *a* maçonnique; **~ry** *n* maçonnerie *f*.
masquerade [mæskə'reɪd] *n* bal masqué; (*fig*) mascarade *f* // *vi*: **to ~ as** se faire passer pour.
mass [mæs] *n* multitude *f*, masse *f*; (PHYSICS) masse; (REL) messe *f* // *vi* se masser; **the ~es** les masses.
massacre ['mæsəkə*] *n* massacre *m* // *vt* massacrer.
massage ['mæsɑ:ʒ] *n* massage *m* // *vt* masser.
masseur [mæ'sə:*] *n* masseur *m*; **masseuse** [-'sə:z] *n* masseuse *f*.
massive ['mæsɪv] *a* énorme, massif(ive).
mass media ['mæs'mi:dɪə] *npl* mass-media *mpl*.
mass-produce ['mæsprə'dju:s] *vt* fabriquer en série.
mast [mɑ:st] *n* mât *m*.
master ['mɑ:stə*] *n* maître *m*; (*in secondary school*) professeur *m*; (*title for boys*): **M~ X** Monsieur X // *vt* maîtriser; (*learn*) apprendre à fond; (*understand*) posséder parfaitement *or* à fond; **M~'s degree** *n* ≈ maîtrise *f*; **~ key** *n* passe-partout *m inv*; **~ly** *a* magistral(e); **~mind** *n* esprit supérieur // *vt* diriger, être le cerveau de; **M~ of Arts/Science (M.A./M.Sc.)** *n* ≈ titulaire *m/f* d'une maîtrise (en lettres/science); **M~ of Arts/Science degree (M.A./M.Sc.)** *n* ≈ maîtrise *f*; **~piece** *n* chef-d'œuvre *m*; **~ plan** *n* stratégie *f* d'ensemble; **~ stroke** *n* coup *m* de maître; **~y** *n* maîtrise *f*; connaissance parfaite.
masturbate ['mæstəbeɪt] *vi* se masturber; **masturbation** [-'beɪʃən] *n* masturbation *f*.
mat [mæt] *n* petit tapis; (*also*: **door~**) paillasson *m* // *a* = **matt.**
match [mætʃ] *n* allumette *f*; (*game*) match *m*, partie *f*; (*fig*) égal/e; mariage *m*; parti *m* // *vt* assortir; (*go well with*) aller bien avec, s'assortir à; (*equal*) égaler, valoir // *vi* être assorti(e); **to be a good ~** être bien assorti(e); **to ~ up** *vt* assortir; **~box** *n* boîte *f* d'allumettes; **~ing** *a* assorti(e); **~less** *a* sans égal.
mate [meɪt] *n* camarade *m/f* de travail; (*col*) copain/copine; (*animal*) partenaire *m/f*, mâle/femelle; (*in merchant navy*) second *m* // *vi* s'accoupler // *vt* accoupler.
material [mə'tɪərɪəl] *n* (*substance*) matière *f*, matériau *m*; (*cloth*) tissu *m*, étoffe *f* // *a* matériel(le); (*important*) essentiel(le); **~s** *npl* matériaux *mpl*; **~istic** [-ə'lɪstɪk] *a* matérialiste; **~ize** *vi* se matérialiser, se réaliser; **~ly** *ad* matériellement.
maternal [mə'tə:nl] *a* maternel(le).
maternity [mə'tə:nɪtɪ] *n* maternité *f* // *cpd* de maternité, de grossesse; **~ hospital** *n* maternité *f*.
matey ['meɪtɪ] *a* (*col*) copain-copain *inv*.
mathematical [mæθə'mætɪkl] *a* mathématique.
mathematician [mæθəmə'tɪʃən] *n* mathématicien/ne.
mathematics [mæθə'mætɪks] *n* mathématiques *fpl*.
maths [mæθs] *n* math(s) *fpl*.
matinée ['mætɪneɪ] *n* matinée *f*.
mating ['meɪtɪŋ] *n* accouplement *m*; **~ call** *n* appel *m* du mâle; **~ season** *n* saison *f* des amours.
matriarchal [meɪtrɪ'ɑ:kl] *a* matriarcal(e).
matrices ['meɪtrɪsi:z] *npl of* **matrix**.
matriculation [mətrɪkju'leɪʃən] *n* inscription *f*.
matrimonial [mætrɪ'məunɪəl] *a* matrimonial(e), conjugal(e).
matrimony ['mætrɪmənɪ] *n* mariage *m*.
matrix, *pl* **matrices** ['meɪtrɪks, 'meɪtrɪsi:z] *n* matrice *f*.
matron ['meɪtrən] *n* (*in hospital*) infirmière-chef *f*; (*in school*) infirmière; **~ly** *a* de matrone; imposant(e).
matt [mæt] *a* mat(e).
matted ['mætɪd] *a* emmêlé(e).
matter ['mætə*] *n* question *f*; (PHYSICS) matière *f*, substance *f*; (*content*) contenu *m*, fond *m*; (MED: *pus*) pus *m* // *vi* importer; **it doesn't ~** cela n'a pas d'importance; (*I don't mind*) cela ne fait rien; **what's the ~?** qu'est-ce qu'il y a?, qu'est-ce qui ne va pas?; **no ~ what** quoiqu'il arrive; **that's another ~** c'est une autre affaire; **as a ~ of course** tout naturellement; **as a ~ of fact** en fait; **it's a ~ of habit** c'est une question d'habitude; **~-of-fact** *a* terre à terre, neutre.
matting ['mætɪŋ] *n* natte *f*.
mattress ['mætrɪs] *n* matelas *m*.
mature [mə'tjuə*] *a* mûr(e); (*cheese*) fait(e) // *vi* mûrir; se faire; **maturity** *n* maturité *f*.
maudlin ['mɔ:dlɪn] *a* larmoyant(e).
maul [mɔ:l] *vt* lacérer.
Mauritius [mə'rɪʃəs] *n* l'île *f* Maurice.
mausoleum [mɔ:sə'lɪəm] *n* mausolée *m*.
mauve [məuv] *a* mauve.
mawkish ['mɔ:kɪʃ] *a* mièvre; fade.
max. *abbr of* **maximum**.
maxim ['mæksɪm] *n* maxime *f*.
maxima ['mæksɪmə] *npl of* **maximum.**
maximum ['mæksɪməm] *a* maximum // *n* (*pl* **maxima** ['mæksɪmə]) maximum *m*.
May [meɪ] *n* mai *m*.
may [meɪ] *vi* (*conditional*: **might**) (*indicating possibility*): **he ~ come** il se peut qu'il vienne; (*be allowed to*): **~ I smoke?** puis-je fumer?; (*wishes*): **~ God bless you!** (que) Dieu vous bénisse!; **he might be there** il pourrait bien y être, il se pourrait qu'il y soit; **I might as well go** je ferais aussi bien d'y aller, autant y

aller ; **you might like to try** vous pourriez (peut-être) essayer.
maybe ['meɪbi:] *ad* peut-être ; ~ **he'll...** peut-être qu'il... .
mayday ['meɪdeɪ] *n* S.O.S. *m.*
May Day ['meɪdeɪ] *n* le Premier mai.
mayhem ['meɪhɛm] *n* grabuge *m.*
mayonnaise [meɪə'neɪz] *n* mayonnaise *f.*
mayor [mɛə*] *n* maire *m* ; ~**ess** *n* maire *m* ; épouse *f* du maire.
maypole ['meɪpəul] *n* mât enrubanné (*autour duquel on danse*).
maze [meɪz] *n* labyrinthe *m,* dédale *m.*
M.D. *abbr* = *Doctor of Medicine.*
me [mi:] *pronoun* me, m' + *vowel* ; (*stressed, after prep*) moi.
meadow ['mɛdəu] *n* prairie *f,* pré *m.*
meagre, meager (*US*) ['mi:gə*] *a* maigre.
meal [mi:l] *n* repas *m* ; (*flour*) farine *f* ; ~**time** *n* l'heure *f* du repas ; ~**y-mouthed** *a* mielleux(euse).
mean [mi:n] *a* (*with money*) avare, radin(e) ; (*unkind*) mesquin(e), méchant(e) ; (*average*) moyen(ne) // *vt* (*pt, pp* **meant** [mɛnt]) (*signify*) signifier, vouloir dire ; (*intend*): **to ~ to do** avoir l'intention de faire // *n* moyenne *f* ; ~**s** *npl* moyens *mpl* ; **by ~s of** par l'intermédiaire de ; au moyen de ; **by all ~s** je vous en prie ; **to be meant for** être destiné(e) à ; **what do you ~?** que voulez-vous dire?
meander [mɪ'ændə*] *vi* faire des méandres ; (*fig*) flâner.
meaning ['mi:nɪŋ] *n* signification *f,* sens *m* ; ~**ful** *a* significatif(ive) ; ~**less** *a* dénué(e) de sens.
meanness ['mi:nnɪs] *n* avarice *f* ; mesquinerie *f.*
meant [mɛnt] *pt, pp of* **mean**.
meantime ['mi:ntaɪm] *ad,* **meanwhile** ['mi:nwaɪl] *ad* (*also*: **in the ~**) pendant ce temps.
measles ['mi:zlz] *n* rougeole *f.*
measly ['mi:zlɪ] *a* (*col*) minable.
measurable ['mɛʒərəbl] *a* mesurable.
measure ['mɛʒə*] *vt, vi* mesurer // *n* mesure *f* ; (*ruler*) règle (graduée) ; ~**d** *a* mesuré(e) ; ~**ments** *npl* mesures *fpl* ; **chest/hip ~ment** tour *m* de poitrine/hanches.
meat [mi:t] *n* viande *f* ; ~ **pie** *n* pâté *m* en croûte ; ~**y** *a* qui a le goût de la viande ; (*fig*) substantiel(le).
Mecca ['mɛkə] *n* la Mecque.
mechanic [mɪ'kænɪk] *n* mécanicien *m* ; ~**s** *n* mécanique *f* // *npl* mécanisme *m* ; ~**al** *a* mécanique.
mechanism ['mɛkənɪzəm] *n* mécanisme *m.*
mechanization [mɛkənaɪ'zeɪʃən] *n* mécanisation *f.*
medal ['mɛdl] *n* médaille *f* ; ~**lion** [mɪ'dælɪən] *n* médaillon *m* ; ~**list,** ~**ist** (*US*) *n* (SPORT) médaillé/e.
meddle ['mɛdl] *vi*: **to ~ in** se mêler de, s'occuper de ; **to ~ with** toucher à ; ~**some** *a* indiscret(ète).
media ['mi:dɪə] *npl* media *mpl.*
mediaeval [mɛdɪ'i:vl] *a* = **medieval**.
mediate ['mi:dɪeɪt] *vi* s'interposer ; servir d'intermédiaire ; **mediation** [-'eɪʃən] *n* médiation *f* ; **mediator** *n* médiateur/trice.
medical ['mɛdɪkl] *a* médical(e) ; ~ **student** *n* étudiant/e en médecine.
medicated ['mɛdɪkeɪtɪd] *a* traitant(e), médicamenteux(euse).
medicinal [mɛ'dɪsɪnl] *a* médicinal(e).
medicine ['mɛdsɪn] *n* médecine *f* ; (*drug*) médicament *m* ; ~ **chest** *n* pharmacie *f* (*murale ou portative*).
medieval [mɛdɪ'i:vl] *a* médiéval(e).
mediocre [mi:dɪ'əukə*] *a* médiocre ; **mediocrity** [-'ɔkrɪtɪ] *n* médiocrité *f.*
meditate ['mɛdɪteɪt] *vi*: **to ~ (on)** méditer (sur) ; **meditation** [-'teɪʃən] *n* méditation *f.*
Mediterranean [mɛdɪtə'reɪnɪən] *a* méditerranéen(ne) ; **the ~ (Sea)** la (mer) Méditerranée.
medium ['mi:dɪəm] *a* moyen(ne) // *n* (*pl* **media**: *means*) moyen *m* ; (*pl* **mediums**: *person*) médium *m* ; **the happy ~** le juste milieu.
medley ['mɛdlɪ] *n* mélange *m.*
meek [mi:k] *a* doux(douce), humble.
meet, *pt,pp* **met** [mi:t, mɛt] *vt* rencontrer ; (*by arrangement*) retrouver, rejoindre ; (*for the first time*) faire la connaissance de ; (*go and fetch*): **I'll ~ you at the station** j'irai te chercher à la gare ; (*fig*) faire face à ; satisfaire à ; se joindre à // *vi* se rencontrer ; se retrouver ; (*in session*) se réunir ; (*join*: *objects*) se joindre ; **to ~ with** *vt fus* rencontrer ; ~**ing** *n* rencontre *f* ; (*session*: *of club etc*) réunion *f* ; (*interview*) entrevue *f* ; **she's at a ~ing** (COMM) elle est en conférence.
megaphone ['mɛgəfəun] *n* porte-voix *m inv.*
melancholy ['mɛlənkəlɪ] *n* mélancolie *f* // *a* mélancolique.
mellow ['mɛləu] *a* velouté(e) ; doux(douce) ; (*colour*) riche et profond(e) ; (*fruit*) mûr(e) // *vi* (*person*) s'adoucir.
melodious [mɪ'ləudɪəs] *a* mélodieux(euse).
melodrama ['mɛləudrɑ:mə] *n* mélodrame *m.*
melody ['mɛlədɪ] *n* mélodie *f.*
melon ['mɛlən] *n* melon *m.*
melt [mɛlt] *vi* fondre ; (*become soft*) s'amollir ; (*fig*) s'attendrir // *vt* faire fondre ; (*person*) attendrir ; **to ~ away** *vi* fondre complètement ; **to ~ down** *vt* fondre ; ~**ing point** *n* point *m* de fusion ; ~**ing pot** *n* (*fig*) creuset *m.*
member ['mɛmbə*] *n* membre *m* ; ~ **country/state** *n* pays *m*/état *m* member ; **M~ of Parliament (M.P.)** député *m* ; ~**ship** *n* adhésion *f* ; statut *m* de membre ; (nombre *m* de) membres *mpl,* adhérents *mpl.*
membrane ['mɛmbreɪn] *n* membrane *f.*
memento [mə'mɛntəu] *n* souvenir *m.*
memo ['mɛməu] *n* note *f* (de service).
memoir ['mɛmwɑ:*] *n* mémoire *m,* étude *f* ; ~**s** *npl* mémoires.
memorable ['mɛmərəbl] *a* mémorable.
memorandum, *pl* **memoranda** [mɛmə'rændəm, -də] *n* note *f* (de service) ; (DIPLOMACY) mémorandum *m.*

memorial [mɪ'mɔ:rɪəl] *n* mémorial *m* // *a* commémoratif(ive).
memorize ['mɛməraɪz] *vt* apprendre *or* retenir par cœur.
memory ['mɛmərɪ] *n* mémoire *f*; (*recollection*) souvenir *m*; **in ~ of** à la mémoire de.
men [mɛn] *npl of* **man.**
menace ['mɛnəs] *n* menace *f* // *vt* menacer; **menacing** *a* menaçant(e).
menagerie [mɪ'nædʒərɪ] *n* ménagerie *f.*
mend [mɛnd] *vt* réparer; (*darn*) raccommoder, repriser // *n* reprise *f*; **on the ~** en voie de guérison; **~ing** *n* raccommodages *mpl.*
menial ['mi:nɪəl] *a* de domestique, inférieur(e); subalterne.
meningitis [mɛnɪn'dʒaɪtɪs] *n* méningite *f.*
menopause ['mɛnəupɔ:z] *n* ménopause *f.*
menservants *npl of* **manservant.**
menstruate ['mɛnstrueɪt] *vi* avoir ses règles; **menstruation** [-'eɪʃən] *n* menstruation *f.*
mental ['mɛntl] *a* mental(e).
mentality [mɛn'tælɪtɪ] *n* mentalité *f.*
mention ['mɛnʃən] *n* mention *f* // *vt* mentionner, faire mention de; **don't ~ it!** je vous en prie, il n'y a pas de quoi!
menu ['mɛnju:] *n* (*set ~*) menu *m*; (*printed*) carte *f.*
mercantile ['mə:kəntaɪl] *a* marchand(e); (*law*) commercial(e).
mercenary ['mə:sɪnərɪ] *a* mercantile // *n* mercenaire *m.*
merchandise ['mə:tʃəndaɪz] *n* marchandises *fpl.*
merchant ['mə:tʃənt] *n* négociant *m*, marchand *m*; **timber/wine ~** négociant en bois/vins, marchand de bois/vins; **~ bank** *n* banque *f* d'affaires; **~ navy** *n* marine marchande.
merciful ['mə:sɪful] *a* miséricordieux(euse), clément(e).
merciless ['mə:sɪlɪs] *a* impitoyable, sans pitié.
mercurial [mə:'kjuərɪəl] *a* changeant(e); (*lively*) vif(vive).
mercury ['mə:kjurɪ] *n* mercure *m.*
mercy ['mə:sɪ] *n* pitié *f*, merci *f*; (*REL*) miséricorde *f*; **to have ~ on sb** avoir pitié de qn; **at the ~ of** à la merci de.
mere [mɪə*] *a* simple; **~ly** *ad* simplement, purement.
merge [mə:dʒ] *vt* unir // *vi* se fondre; (*COMM*) fusionner; **~r** *n* (*COMM*) fusion *f.*
meridian [mə'rɪdɪən] *n* méridien *m.*
meringue [mə'ræŋ] *n* meringue *f.*
merit ['mɛrɪt] *n* mérite *m*, valeur *f* // *vt* mériter.
mermaid ['mə:meɪd] *n* sirène *f.*
merrily ['mɛrɪlɪ] *ad* joyeusement, gaiement.
merriment ['mɛrɪmənt] *n* gaieté *f.*
merry ['mɛrɪ] *a* gai(e); **~-go-round** *n* manège *m.*
mesh [mɛʃ] *n* maille *f*; filet *m* // *vi* (*gears*) s'engrener.
mesmerize ['mɛzməraɪz] *vt* hypnotiser; fasciner.
mess [mɛs] *n* désordre *m*, fouillis *m*, pagaille *f*; (*MIL*) mess *m*, cantine *f*; **to ~ about** *vi* (*col*) perdre son temps; **to ~ about with** *vt fus* (*col*) chambarder, tripoter; **to ~ up** *vt* salir; chambarder; gâcher.
message ['mɛsɪdʒ] *n* message *m.*
messenger ['mɛsɪndʒə*] *n* messager *m.*
messy ['mɛsɪ] *a* sale; en désordre.
met [mɛt] *pt, pp of* **meet.**
metabolism [mɛ'tæbəlɪzəm] *n* métabolisme *m.*
metal ['mɛtl] *n* métal *m* // *vt* empierrer; **~lic** [-'tælɪk] *a* métallique; **~lurgy** [-'tælədʒɪ] *n* métallurgie *f.*
metamorphosis, *pl* **phoses** [mɛtə'mɔ:fəsɪs, -i:z] *n* métamorphose *f.*
metaphor ['mɛtəfə*] *n* métaphore *f.*
metaphysics [mɛtə'fɪzɪks] *n* métaphysique *f.*
mete [mi:t]: **to ~ out** *vt fus* infliger.
meteor ['mi:tɪə*] *n* météore *m.*
meteorological [mi:tɪərə'lɔdʒɪkl] *a* météorologique.
meteorology [mi:tɪə'rɔlədʒɪ] *n* météorologie *f.*
meter ['mi:tə*] *n* (*instrument*) compteur *m*; (*US*) = **metre.**
method ['mɛθəd] *n* méthode *f*; **~ical** [mɪ'θɔdɪkl] *a* méthodique.
Methodist ['mɛθədɪst] *a,n* méthodiste (*m/f*).
methylated spirit ['mɛθɪleɪtɪd'spɪrɪt] *n* (*also*: **meths**) alcool *m* à brûler.
meticulous [mɛ'tɪkjuləs] *a* méticuleux(euse).
metre, meter (*US*) ['mi:tə*] *n* mètre *m.*
metric ['mɛtrɪk] *a* métrique; **~al** *a* métrique; **~ation** [-'keɪʃən] *n* conversion *f* au système métrique.
metronome ['mɛtrənəum] *n* métronome *m.*
metropolis [mɪ'trɔpəlɪs] *n* métropole *f.*
mettle ['mɛtl] *n* courage *m.*
mew [mju:] *vi* (*cat*) miauler.
mews [mju:z] *n*: **~ cottage** *maisonnette aménagée dans les anciennes écuries d'un hôtel particulier.*
Mexican ['mɛksɪkən] *a* mexicain(e) // *n* Mexicain/e.
Mexico ['mɛksɪkəu] *n* Mexique *m*; **~ City** Mexico.
mezzanine ['mɛtsəni:n] *n* mezzanine *f*; (*of shops, offices*) entresol *m.*
miaow [mi:'au] *vi* miauler.
mice [maɪs] *npl of* **mouse.**
microbe ['maɪkrəub] *n* microbe *m.*
microfilm ['maɪkrəufɪlm] *n* microfilm *m* // *vt* microfilmer.
microphone ['maɪkrəfəun] *n* microphone *m.*
microscope ['maɪkrəskəup] *n* microscope *m*; **microscopic** [-'skɔpɪk] *a* microscopique.
mid [mɪd] *a*: **~ May** la mi-mai; **~ afternoon** le milieu de l'après-midi; **in ~ air** en plein ciel; **~day** midi *m.*
middle ['mɪdl] *n* milieu *m*; (*waist*) ceinture *f*, taille *f* // *a* du milieu; **~-aged** *a* d'un certain âge; **the M~ Ages** *npl* le moyen âge; **~-class** *a* ≈ bourgeois(e); **the ~ class(es)** ≈ les classes moyennes; **M~ East** *n* Proche-Orient *m*, Moyen-Orient *m*;

~man *n* intermédiaire *m*; **~ name** *n* deuxième nom *m*.
middling ['mɪdlɪŋ] *a* moyen(ne).
midge [mɪdʒ] *n* moucheron *m*.
midget ['mɪdʒɪt] *n* nain/e // *a* minuscule.
Midlands ['mɪdləndz] *npl comtés du centre de l'Angleterre*.
midnight ['mɪdnaɪt] *n* minuit *m*.
midriff ['mɪdrɪf] *n* estomac *m*, taille *f*.
midst [mɪdst] *n*: **in the ~ of** au milieu de.
midsummer [mɪd'sʌmə*] *n* milieu *m* de l'été.
midway [mɪd'weɪ] *a, ad*: **~ (between)** à mi-chemin (entre).
midweek [mɪd'wi:k] *n* milieu *m* de la semaine.
midwife, midwives ['mɪdwaɪf, -vz] *n* sage-femme *f*; **~ry** [-wɪfərɪ] *n* obstétrique *f*.
midwinter [mɪd'wɪntə*] *n* milieu *m* de l'hiver.
might [maɪt] *vb see* **may** // *n* puissance *f*, force *f*; **~y** *a* puissant(e) // *ad* (*col*) rudement.
migraine ['mi:greɪn] *n* migraine *f*.
migrant ['maɪgrənt] *n* (*bird, animal*) migrateur *m*; (*person*) migrant/e; nomade *m/f* // *a* migrateur(trice); migrant(e); nomade; (*worker*) saisonnier(ère).
migrate [maɪ'greɪt] *vi* émigrer; **migration** [-'greɪʃən] *n* migration *f*.
mike [maɪk] *n* (*abbr of* **microphone**) micro *m*.
mild [maɪld] *a* doux(douce); (*reproach*) léger(ère); (*illness*) bénin(bénigne) // *n* bière légère.
mildew ['mɪldju:] *n* mildiou *m*.
mildly ['maɪldlɪ] *ad* doucement; légèrement.
mildness ['maɪldnɪs] *n* douceur *f*.
mile [maɪl] *n* mil(l)e *m* (= *1609 m*); **~age** *n* distance *f* en milles, ≈ kilométrage *m*; **~ometer** *n* = **milometer**; **~stone** *n* borne *f*; (*fig*) jalon *m*.
milieu ['mi:ljə:] *n* milieu *m*.
militant ['mɪlɪtnt] *a,n* militant(e).
military ['mɪlɪtərɪ] *a* militaire // *n*: **the ~** l'armée *f*, les militaires *mpl*.
militate ['mɪlɪteɪt] *vi*: **to ~ against** militer contre.
militia [mɪ'lɪʃə] *n* milice *f*.
milk [mɪlk] *n* lait *m* // *vt* (*cow*) traire; (*fig*) dépouiller, plumer; **~ chocolate** *n* chocolat *m* au lait; **~ing** *n* traite *f*; **~man** *n* laitier *m*; **~ shake** *n* milk-shake *m*; **~y** *a* lacté(e); (*colour*) laiteux(euse); **M~y Way** *n* Voie lactée.
mill [mɪl] *n* moulin *m*; (*factory*) usine *f*, fabrique *f*; (*spinning* ~) filature *f*; (*flour* ~) minoterie *f* // *vt* moudre, broyer // *vi* (*also*: **~ about**) grouiller.
millennium, *pl* **~s** *or* **millennia** [mɪ'lɛnɪəm, -'lɛnɪə] *n* millénaire *m*.
miller ['mɪlə*] *n* meunier *m*.
millet ['mɪlɪt] *n* millet *m*.
milli... ['mɪlɪ] *prefix*: **~gram(me)** *n* milligramme *m*; **~litre** *n* millilitre *m*; **~metre** *n* millimètre *m*.
milliner ['mɪlɪnə*] *n* modiste *f*; **~y** *n* modes *fpl*.
million ['mɪljən] *n* million *m*; **~aire** *n* millionnaire *m*.
millstone ['mɪlstəun] *n* meule *f*.
millwheel ['mɪlwi:l] *n* roue *f* de moulin.
milometer [maɪ'lɔmɪtə*] *n* ≈ compteur *m* kilométrique.
mime [maɪm] *n* mime *m* // *vt, vi* mimer.
mimic ['mɪmɪk] *n* imitateur/trice // *vt, vi* imiter, contrefaire; **~ry** *n* imitation *f*; (ZOOL) mimétisme *m*.
min. *abbr of* **minute(s), minimum**.
minaret [mɪnə'rɛt] *n* minaret *m*.
mince [mɪns] *vt* hacher // *vi* (*in walking*) marcher à petits pas maniérés // *n* (CULIN) viande hachée, hachis *m*; **he does not ~ (his) words** il ne mâche pas ses mots; **~meat** *n hachis de fruits secs utilisés en pâtisserie*; **~ pie** *n sorte de tarte aux fruits secs*; **~r** *n* hachoir *m*.
mincing ['mɪnsɪŋ] *a* affecté(e).
mind [maɪnd] *n* esprit *m* // *vt* (*attend to, look after*) s'occuper de; (*be careful*) faire attention à; (*object to*): **I don't ~ the noise** je ne crains pas le bruit, le bruit ne me dérange pas; **do you ~ if ...?** est-ce que cela vous gêne si ...?; **I don't ~** cela ne me dérange pas; **it is on my ~** cela me préoccupe; **to my ~** à mon avis *or* sens; **to be out of one's ~** ne plus avoir toute sa raison; **never ~** peu importe, ça ne fait rien; **to keep sth in ~** ne pas oublier qch; **to bear sth in ~** tenir compte de qch; **to make up one's ~** se décider; **'~ the step'** 'attention à la marche'; **to have in ~ to do** avoir l'intention de faire; **~ful** *a*: **~ful of** attentif(ive) à, soucieux(euse) de; **~less** *a* irréfléchi(e).
mine [maɪn] *pronoun* le(la) mien(ne), *pl* les miens(miennes) // *a*: **this book is ~** ce livre est à moi // *n* mine *f* // *vt* (*coal*) extraire; (*ship, beach*) miner; **~ detector** *n* détecteur *m* de mines; **~field** *n* champ *m* de mines; **~r** *n* mineur *m*.
mineral ['mɪnərəl] *a* minéral(e) // *n* minéral *m*; **~s** *npl* (*soft drinks*) boissons gazeuses (sucrées); **~ogy** [-'rælədʒɪ] *n* minéralogie *f*; **~ water** *n* eau minérale.
minesweeper ['maɪnswi:pə*] *n* dragueur *m* de mines.
mingle ['mɪŋgl] *vt* mêler, mélanger // *vi*: **to ~ with** se mêler à.
mingy ['mɪndʒɪ] *a* (*col*) radin(e).
miniature ['mɪnətʃə*] *a* (en) miniature // *n* miniature *f*.
minibus ['mɪnɪbʌs] *n* minibus *m*.
minicab ['mɪnɪkæb] *n* minitaxi *m*.
minim ['mɪnɪm] *n* (MUS) blanche *f*.
minima ['mɪnɪmə] *npl of* **minimum.**
minimal ['mɪnɪml] *a* minimal(e).
minimize ['mɪnɪmaɪz] *vt* minimiser.
minimum ['mɪnɪməm] *n* (*pl*: **minima** ['mɪnɪmə]) minimum *m* // *a* minimum.
mining ['maɪnɪŋ] *n* exploitation minière // *a* minier(ère); de mineurs.
minion ['mɪnjən] *n* (*pej*) laquais *m*; favori/te.
miniskirt ['mɪnɪskə:t] *n* mini-jupe *f*.
minister ['mɪnɪstə*] *n* (POL) ministre *m*; (REL) pasteur *m*; **~ial** [-'tɪərɪəl] *a* (POL) ministériel(le).

ministry ['mɪnɪstrɪ] *n* ministère *m*; (REL): **to go into the ~** devenir pasteur.
mink [mɪŋk] *n* vison *m*; **~ coat** *n* manteau *m* de vison.
minnow ['mɪnəu] *n* vairon *m*.
minor ['maɪnə*] *a* petit(e), de peu d'importance; (MUS) mineur(e) // *n* (LAW) mineur/e.
minority [maɪ'nɔrɪtɪ] *n* minorité *f*.
minster ['mɪnstə*] *n* église abbatiale.
minstrel ['mɪnstrəl] *n* trouvère *m*, ménestrel *m*.
mint [mɪnt] *n* (*plant*) menthe *f*; (*sweet*) bonbon *m* à la menthe // *vt* (*coins*) battre; **the (Royal) M~** ≈ l'hôtel *m* de la Monnaie; **in ~ condition** à l'état de neuf; **~ sauce** *n* sauce *f* à la menthe.
minuet [mɪnju'ɛt] *n* menuet *m*.
minus ['maɪnəs] *n* (*also*: **~ sign**) signe *m* moins // *prep* moins.
minute *a* [maɪ'nju:t] minuscule; (*detail*) minutieux(euse) // *n* ['mɪnɪt] minute *f*; (*official record*) procès-verbal *m*, compte rendu; **~s** *npl* procès-verbal.
miracle ['mɪrəkl] *n* miracle *m*; **miraculous** [mɪ'rækjuləs] *a* miraculeux(euse).
mirage ['mɪrɑ:ʒ] *n* mirage *m*.
mirror ['mɪrə*] *n* miroir *m*, glace *f* // *vt* refléter.
mirth [mə:θ] *n* gaieté *f*.
misadventure [mɪsəd'vɛntʃə*] *n* mésaventure *f*; **death by ~** décès accidentel.
misanthropist [mɪ'zænθrəpɪst] *n* misanthrope *m/f*.
misapprehension ['mɪsæprɪ'hɛnʃən] *n* malentendu *m*, méprise *f*.
misappropriate [mɪsə'prəuprɪeɪt] *vt* détourner.
misbehave [mɪsbɪ'heɪv] *vi* se conduire mal; **misbehaviour** *n* mauvaise conduite.
miscalculate [mɪs'kælkjuleɪt] *vt* mal calculer; **miscalculation** [-'leɪʃən] *n* erreur *f* de calcul.
miscarriage ['mɪskærɪdʒ] *n* (MED) fausse couche; **~ of justice** erreur *f* judiciaire.
miscellaneous [mɪsɪ'leɪnɪəs] *a* (*items*) divers(es); (*selection*) varié(e).
miscellany [mɪ'sɛlənɪ] *n* recueil *m*.
mischance [mɪs'tʃɑ:ns] *n* malchance *f*.
mischief ['mɪstʃɪf] *n* (*naughtiness*) sottises *fpl*; (*harm*) mal *m*, dommage *m*; (*maliciousness*) méchanceté *f*; **mischievous** *a* (*naughty*) coquin(e), espiègle; (*harmful*) méchant(e).
misconception ['mɪskən'sɛpʃən] *n* idée fausse.
misconduct [mɪs'kɔndʌkt] *n* inconduite *f*; **professional ~** faute professionnelle.
misconstrue [mɪskən'stru:] *vt* mal interpréter.
miscount [mɪs'kaunt] *vt,vi* mal compter.
misdemeanour, misdemeanor (*US*) [mɪsdɪ'mi:nə*] *n* écart *m* de conduite; infraction *f*.
misdirect [mɪsdɪ'rɛkt] *vt* (*person*) mal renseigner; (*letter*) mal adresser.
miser ['maɪzə*] *n* avare *m/f*.
miserable ['mɪzərəbl] *a* malheureux(euse); (*wretched*) misérable.
miserly ['maɪzəlɪ] *a* avare.
misery ['mɪzərɪ] *n* (*unhappiness*) tristesse *f*; (*pain*) souffrances *fpl*; (*wretchedness*) misère *f*.
misfire [mɪs'faɪə*] *vi* rater; (*car engine*) avoir des ratés.
misfit ['mɪsfɪt] *n* (*person*) inadapté/e.
misfortune [mɪs'fɔ:tʃən] *n* malchance *f*, malheur *m*.
misgiving(s) [mɪs'gɪvɪŋ(z)] *n(pl)* craintes *fpl*, soupçons *mpl*.
misguided [mɪs'gaɪdɪd] *a* malavisé(e).
mishandle [mɪs'hændl] *vt* (*treat roughly*) malmener; (*mismanage*) mal s'y prendre pour faire *or* résoudre *etc*.
mishap ['mɪshæp] *n* mésaventure *f*.
mishear [mɪs'hɪə*] *vt irg* mal entendre.
misinform [mɪsɪn'fɔ:m] *vt* mal renseigner.
misinterpret [mɪsɪn'tə:prɪt] *vt* mal interpréter; **~ation** [-'teɪʃən] *n* interprétation erronée, contresens *m*.
misjudge [mɪs'dʒʌdʒ] *vt* méjuger, se méprendre sur le compte de.
mislay [mɪs'leɪ] *vt irg* égarer.
mislead [mɪs'li:d] *vt irg* induire en erreur; **~ing** *a* trompeur(euse).
mismanage [mɪs'mænɪdʒ] *vt* mal gérer; mal s'y prendre pour faire *or* résoudre *etc*; **~ment** *n* mauvaise gestion.
misnomer [mɪs'nəumə*] *n* terme *or* qualificatif trompeur *or* peu approprié.
misogynist [mɪ'sɔdʒɪnɪst] *n* misogyne *m/f*.
misplace [mɪs'pleɪs] *vt* égarer.
misprint ['mɪsprɪnt] *n* faute *f* d'impression.
mispronounce [mɪsprə'nauns] *vt* mal prononcer.
misread [mɪs'ri:d] *vt irg* mal lire.
misrepresent [mɪsrɛprɪ'zɛnt] *vt* présenter sous un faux jour.
miss [mɪs] *vt* (*fail to get*) manquer, rater; (*regret the absence of*): **I ~ him/it** il/cela me manque // *vi* manquer // *n* (*shot*) coup manqué; (*fig*): **that was a near ~** il s'en est fallu de peu; **to ~ out** *vt* oublier.
Miss [mɪs] *n* Mademoiselle.
missal ['mɪsl] *n* missel *m*.
misshapen [mɪs'ʃeɪpən] *a* difforme.
missile ['mɪsaɪl] *n* (AVIAT) missile *m*; (*object thrown*) projectile *m*.
missing ['mɪsɪŋ] *a* manquant(e); (*after escape, disaster: person*) disparu(e); **to go ~** disparaître.
mission ['mɪʃən] *n* mission *f*; **~ary** *n* missionnaire *m/f*.
missive ['mɪsɪv] *n* missive *f*.
misspent ['mɪs'spɛnt] *a*: **his ~ youth** sa folle jeunesse.
mist [mɪst] *n* brume *f*, brouillard *m* // *vi* (*also*: **~ over, ~ up**) devenir brumeux(euse); (*windows*) s'embuer.
mistake [mɪs'teɪk] *n* erreur *f*, faute *f* // *vt* (*irg*: *like* **take**) mal comprendre; se méprendre sur; **to make a ~** se tromper, faire une erreur; **to ~ for** prendre pour; **~n** *a* (*idea etc*) erroné(e); **to be ~n** faire erreur, se tromper; **~n identity** *n* erreur *f* d'identité.
mister ['mɪstə*] *n* (*col*) Monsieur *m*; *see* **Mr**.

mistletoe ['mɪsltəu] *n* gui *m*.
mistook [mɪs'tuk] *pt of* **mistake**.
mistranslation [mɪstræns'leɪʃən] *n* erreur *f* de traduction, contresens *m*.
mistreat [mɪs'tri:t] *vt* maltraiter.
mistress ['mɪstrɪs] *n* (*also*: *lover*) maîtresse *f*; (*in primary school*) institutrice *f*; *see* **Mrs**.
mistrust [mɪs'trʌst] *vt* se méfier de.
misty ['mɪstɪ] *a* brumeux(euse).
misunderstand [mɪsʌndə'stænd] *vt*, *vi irg* mal comprendre; **~ing** *n* méprise *f*, malentendu *m*.
misuse *n* [mɪs'ju:s] mauvais emploi; (*of power*) abus *m* // *vt* [mɪs'ju:z] mal employer; abuser de.
mitigate ['mɪtɪgeɪt] *vt* atténuer.
mitre, miter (*US*) ['maɪtə*] *n* mitre *f*; (CARPENTRY) onglet *m*.
mitt(en) ['mɪt(n)] *n* mitaine *f*; moufle *f*.
mix [mɪks] *vt* mélanger // *vi* se mélanger // *n* mélange *m*; dosage *m*; **to ~ up** *vt* mélanger; (*confuse*) confondre; **~ed** *a* (*assorted*) assortis(ies); (*school etc*) mixte; **~ed grill** *n* assortiment *m* de grillades; **~ed-up** *a* (*confused*) désorienté(e), embrouillé(e); **~er** *n* (*for food*) batteur *m*, mixeur *m*; (*person*): **he is a good ~er** il est très liant; **~ture** *n* assortiment *m*, mélange *m*; (MED) préparation *f*; **~-up** *n* confusion *f*.
moan [məun] *n* gémissement *m* // *vi* gémir; (*col*: *complain*): **to ~ (about)** se plaindre (de); **~ing** *n* gémissements *mpl*.
moat [məut] *n* fossé *m*, douves *fpl*.
mob [mɔb] *n* foule *f*; (*disorderly*) cohue *f*; (*pej*): **the ~** la populace // *vt* assaillir.
mobile ['məubaɪl] *a* mobile // *n* mobile *m*; **~ home** *n* caravane *f*.
mobility [məu'bɪlɪtɪ] *n* mobilité *f*.
moccasin ['mɔkəsɪn] *n* mocassin *m*.
mock [mɔk] *vt* ridiculiser, se moquer de // *a* faux(fausse); **~ery** *n* moquerie *f*, raillerie *f*; **~ing** *a* moqueur(euse); **~ingbird** *n* moqueur *m*; **~-up** *n* maquette *f*.
mod [mɔd] *a see* **convenience**.
mode [məud] *n* mode *m*.
model ['mɔdl] *n* modèle *m*; (*person*: *for fashion*) mannequin *m*; (: *for artist*) modèle // *vt* modeler // *vi* travailler comme mannequin // *a* (*railway*: *toy*) modèle réduit *inv*; (*child, factory*) modèle; **to ~ clothes** présenter des vêtements; **~ler, ~er** (*US*) *n* modeleur *m*; (**~** *maker*) maquettiste *m/f*; fabricant *m* de modèles réduits.
moderate *a,n* ['mɔdərət] *a* modéré(e) // *n* (POL) modéré/e // *vb* ['mɔdəreɪt] *vi* se modérer, se calmer // *vt* modérer; **moderation** [-'reɪʃən] *n* modération *f*, mesure *f*; **in moderation** à dose raisonnable, pris(e) *or* pratiqué(e) modérément.
modern ['mɔdən] *a* moderne; **~ize** *vt* moderniser.
modest ['mɔdɪst] *a* modeste; **~y** *n* modestie *f*.
modicum ['mɔdɪkəm] *n*: **a ~ of** un minimum de.
modification [mɔdɪfɪ'keɪʃən] *n* modification *f*.
modify ['mɔdɪfaɪ] *vt* modifier.
modulation [mɔdju'leɪʃən] *n* modulation *f*.
module ['mɔdju:l] *n* module *m*.
mohair ['məuhɛə*] *n* mohair *m*.
moist [mɔɪst] *a* humide, moite; **~en** ['mɔɪsn] *vt* humecter, mouiller légèrement; **~ure** ['mɔɪstʃə*] *n* humidité *f*; (*on glass*) buée *f*; **~urizer** ['mɔɪstʃəraɪzə*] *n* produit hydratant.
molar ['məulə*] *n* molaire *f*.
molasses [məu'læsɪz] *n* mélasse *f*.
mold [məuld] *n*, *vt* (*US*) = **mould**.
mole [məul] *n* (*animal*) taupe *f*; (*spot*) grain *m* de beauté.
molecule ['mɔlɪkju:l] *n* molécule *f*.
molehill ['məulhɪl] *n* taupinière *f*.
molest [məu'lɛst] *vt* tracasser; molester.
mollusc ['mɔləsk] *n* mollusque *m*.
mollycoddle ['mɔlɪkɔdl] *vt* chouchouter, couver.
molt [meult] *vi* (*US*) = **moult**.
molten ['meultən] *a* fondu(e).
moment ['məumənt] *n* moment *m*, instant *m*; importance *f*; **~ary** *a* momentané(e), passager(ère); **~ous** [-'mɛntəs] *a* important(e), capital(e).
momentum [məu'mɛntəm] *n* élan *m*, vitesse acquise; **to gather ~** prendre de la vitesse.
monarch ['mɔnək] *n* monarque *m*; **~ist** *n* monarchiste *m/f*; **~y** *n* monarchie *f*.
monastery ['mɔnəstərɪ] *n* monastère *m*.
monastic [mə'næstɪk] *a* monastique.
Monday ['mʌndɪ] *n* lundi *m*.
monetary ['mʌnɪtərɪ] *a* monétaire.
money ['mʌnɪ] *n* argent *m*; **to make ~** gagner de l'argent; faire des bénéfices; rapporter; **danger ~** prime *f* de risque; **~ed** *a* riche; **~lender** *n* prêteur/euse; **~ order** *n* mandat *m*.
mongol ['mɔŋgəl] *a,n* (MED) mongolien(ne).
mongoose ['mɔŋgu:s] *n* mangouste *f*.
mongrel ['mʌŋgrəl] *n* (*dog*) bâtard *m*.
monitor ['mɔnɪtə*] *n* (SCOL) chef *m* de classe; (*also*: **television ~**) moniteur *m* // *vt* contrôler.
monk [mʌŋk] *n* moine *m*.
monkey ['mʌŋkɪ] *n* singe *m*; **~ nut** *n* cacahuète *f*; **~ wrench** *n* clé *f* à molette.
mono... ['mɔnəu] *prefix*: **~chrome** *a* monochrome.
monocle ['mɔnəkl] *n* monocle *m*.
monogram ['mɔnəgræm] *n* monogramme *m*.
monologue ['mɔnəlɔg] *n* monologue *m*.
monopolize [mə'nɔpəlaɪz] *vt* monopoliser.
monopoly [mə'nɔpəlɪ] *n* monopole *m*.
monorail ['mɔnəureɪl] *n* monorail *m*.
monosyllabic [mɔnəusɪ'læbɪk] *a* monosyllabique; (*person*) laconique.
monotone ['mɔnətəun] *n* ton *m* (*or* voix *f*) monocorde.
monotonous [mə'nɔtənəs] *a* monotone.
monotony [mə'nɔtənɪ] *n* monotonie *f*.
monsoon [mɔn'su:n] *n* mousson *f*.
monster ['mɔnstə*] *n* monstre *m*.

monstrosity [mɔns'trɔsɪtɪ] *n* monstruosité *f*, atrocité *f*.
monstrous ['mɔnstrəs] *a* (*huge*) gigantesque; (*atrocious*) monstrueux(euse), atroce.
montage [mɔn'tɑ:ʒ] *n* montage *m*.
month [mʌnθ] *n* mois *m*; **~ly** *a* mensuel(le) // *ad* mensuellement // *n* (*magazine*) mensuel *m*, publication mensuelle.
monument ['mɔnjumənt] *n* monument *m*; **~al** [-'mɛntl] *a* monumental(e); **~al mason** *n* marbrier *m*.
moo [mu:] *vi* meugler, beugler.
mood [mu:d] *n* humeur *f*, disposition *f*; **to be in a good/bad ~** être de bonne/mauvaise humeur; **to be in the ~ for** être d'humeur à, avoir envie de; **~y** *a* (*variable*) d'humeur changeante, lunatique; (*sullen*) morose, maussade.
moon [mu:n] *n* lune *f*; **~beam** *n* rayon *m* de lune; **~light** *n* clair *m* de lune; **~lit** *a* éclairé(e) par la lune.
moor [muə*] *n* lande *f* // *vt* (*ship*) amarrer // *vi* mouiller.
Moor [muə*] *n* Maure/Mauresque.
moorings ['muərɪŋz] *npl* (*chains*) amarres *fpl*; (*place*) mouillage *m*.
Moorish ['muərɪʃ] *a* maure (mauresque).
moorland ['muələnd] *n* lande *f*.
moose [mu:s] *n*, *pl inv* élan *m*.
moot [mu:t] *vt* soulever // *a*: **~ point** point *m* discutable.
mop [mɔp] *n* balai *m* à laver // *vt* éponger, essuyer; **to ~ up** *vt* éponger; **~ of hair** *n* tignasse *f*.
mope [məup] *vi* avoir le cafard, se morfondre.
moped ['məupɛd] *n* (*Brit*) cyclomoteur *m*.
moquette [mɔ'kɛt] *n* moquette *f*.
moral ['mɔrl] *a* moral(e) // *n* morale *f*; **~s** *npl* moralité *f*.
morale [mɔ'rɑ:l] *n* moral *m*.
morality [mə'rælɪtɪ] *n* moralité *f*.
morally ['mɔrəlɪ] *ad* moralement.
morass [mə'ræs] *n* marais *m*, marécage *m*.
morbid ['mɔ:bɪd] *a* morbide.
more [mɔ:*] *det* plus de, davantage de // *ad* plus; **~ people** plus de gens; **I want ~** j'en veux plus *or* davantage; **~ dangerous than** plus dangereux que; **~ or less** plus ou moins; **~ than ever** plus que jamais.
moreover [mɔ:'rəuvə*] *ad* de plus.
morgue [mɔ:g] *n* morgue *f*.
moribund ['mɔrɪbʌnd] *a* moribond(e).
morning ['mɔ:nɪŋ] *n* matin *m*; matinée *f*; **in the ~** le matin; **7 o'clock in the ~** 7 heures du matin; **~ sickness** *n* nausées matinales.
Moroccan [mə'rɔkən] *a* marocain(e) // *n* Marocain/e.
Morocco [mə'rɔkəu] *n* Maroc *m*.
moron ['mɔ:rɔn] *n* idiot/e, minus *m/f*; **~ic** [mə'rɔnɪk] *a* idiot(e), imbécile.
morose [mə'rəus] *a* morose, maussade.
morphine ['mɔ:fi:n] *n* morphine *f*.
Morse [mɔ:s] *n* (*also*: **~ code**) morse *m*.
morsel ['mɔ:sl] *n* bouchée *f*.
mortal ['mɔ:tl] *a*, *n* mortel(le); **~ity** [-'tælɪtɪ] *n* mortalité *f*.
mortar ['mɔ:tə*] *n* mortier *m*.
mortgage ['mɔ:gɪdʒ] *n* hypothèque *f*; (*loan*) prêt *m* (*or* crédit *m*) hypothécaire // *vt* hypothéquer.
mortified ['mɔ:tɪfaɪd] *a* mortifié(e).
mortuary ['mɔ:tjuərɪ] *n* morgue *f*.
mosaic [məu'zeɪɪk] *n* mosaïque *f*.
Moscow ['mɔskəu] *n* Moscou.
Moslem ['mɔzləm] *a*, *n* = **Muslim**.
mosque [mɔsk] *n* mosquée *f*.
mosquito, ~es [mɔs'ki:təu] *n* moustique *m*; **~ net** *n* moustiquaire *f*.
moss [mɔs] *n* mousse *f*; **~y** *a* moussu(e).
most [məust] *det* la plupart de; le plus de // *pronoun* la plupart // *ad* le plus; (*very*) très, extrêmement; **the ~** (*also*: + *adjective*) le plus; **~ fish** la plupart des poissons; **~ of** la plus grande partie de; **I saw ~** j'en ai vu la plupart; c'est moi qui en ai vu le plus; **at the (very) ~** au plus; **to make the ~ of** profiter au maximum de; **~ly** *ad* surtout, principalement.
MOT *n* (*abbr of Ministry of Transport*): **the ~ (test)** *la visite technique (annuelle) obligatoire des véhicules à moteur.*
motel [məu'tɛl] *n* motel *m*.
moth [mɔθ] *n* papillon *m* de nuit; mite *f*; **~ball** *n* boule *f* de naphtaline; **~-eaten** *a* mité(e).
mother ['mʌðə*] *n* mère *f* // *vt* (*care for*) dorloter; **~hood** *n* maternité *f*; **~-in-law** *n* belle-mère *f*; **~ly** *a* maternel(le); **~-of-pearl** *n* nacre *f*; **~-to-be** *n* future maman; **~ tongue** *n* langue maternelle.
mothproof ['mɔθpru:f] *a* traité(e) à l'antimite.
motif [məu'ti:f] *n* motif *m*.
motion ['məuʃən] *n* mouvement *m*; (*gesture*) geste *m*; (*at meeting*) motion *f* // *vt*, *vi*: **to ~ (to) sb to do** faire signe à qn de faire; **~less** *a* immobile, sans mouvement; **~ picture** *n* film *m*.
motivated ['məutɪveɪtɪd] *a* motivé(e).
motivation [məutɪ'veɪʃən] *n* motivation *f*.
motive ['məutɪv] *n* motif *m*, mobile *m* // *a* moteur(trice).
motley ['mɔtlɪ] *a* hétéroclite; bigarré(e), bariolé(e).
motor ['məutə*] *n* moteur *m*; (*col*: *vehicle*) auto *f* // *a* moteur(trice); **~bike** *n* moto *f*; **~boat** *n* bateau *m* à moteur; **~car** *n* automobile *f*; **~cycle** *n* vélomoteur *m*; **~cyclist** *n* motocycliste *m/f*; **~ing** *n* tourisme *m* automobile // *a*: **~ing accident** *n* accident *m* de voiture; **~ing holiday** *n* vacances *fpl* en voiture; **~ist** *n* automobiliste *m/f*; **~ oil** *n* huile *f* de graissage; **~ racing** *n* course *f* automobile; **~ scooter** *n* scooter *m*; **~ vehicle** *n* véhicule *m* automobile; **~way** *n* (*Brit*) autoroute *f*.
mottled ['mɔtld] *a* tacheté(e), marbré(e).
motto, ~es ['mɔtəu] *n* devise *f*.
mould, mold (*US*) [məuld] *n* moule *m*; (*mildew*) moisissure *f* // *vt* mouler, modeler; (*fig*) façonner; **~er** *vi* (*decay*) moisir; **~ing** *n* (*in plaster*) moulage *m*,

moulure *f*; (*in wood*) moulure; **~y** *a* moisi(e).
moult, molt (*US*) [məult] *vi* muer.
mound [maund] *n* monticule *m*, tertre *m*.
mount [maunt] *n* mont *m*, montagne *f*; (*horse*) monture *f*; (*for jewel etc*) monture // *vt* monter // *vi* (*also*: **~ up**) s'élever, monter.
mountain ['mauntın] *n* montagne *f* // *cpd* de (la) montagne; **~eer** [-'nıə*] *n* alpiniste *m/f*; **~eering** [-'nıərıŋ] *n* alpinisme *m*; **to go ~eering** faire de l'alpinisme; **~ous** *a* montagneux(euse); (*very big*) gigantesque; **~ side** *n* flanc *m or* versant *m* de la montagne.
mourn [mɔ:n] *vt* pleurer // *vi*: **to ~ (for)** se lamenter (sur); **~er** *n* parent/e *or* ami/e du défunt; personne *f* en deuil *or* venue rendre hommage au défunt; **~ful** *a* triste, lugubre; **~ing** *n* deuil *m* // *cpd* (*dress*) de deuil; **in ~ing** en deuil.
mouse, *pl* **mice** [maus, maıs] *n* souris *f*; **~trap** *n* souricière *f*.
moustache [məs'tɑ:ʃ] *n* moustache(s) *f*(*pl*).
mousy ['mausı] *a* (*person*) effacé(e); (*hair*) d'un châtain terne.
mouth, ~s [mauθ, -ðz] *n* bouche *f*; (*of dog, cat*) gueule *f*; (*of river*) embouchure *f*; (*of bottle*) goulot *m*; (*opening*) orifice *m*; **~ful** *n* bouchée *f*; **~ organ** *n* harmonica *m*; **~piece** *n* (*of musical instrument*) embouchure *f*; (*spokesman*) porte-parole *m inv*; **~wash** *n* bain *m* de bouche; **~-watering** *a* qui met l'eau à la bouche.
movable ['mu:vəbl] *a* mobile.
move [mu:v] *n* (*movement*) mouvement *m*; (*in game*) coup *m*; (: *turn to play*) tour *m*; (*change of house*) déménagement *m* // *vt* déplacer, bouger; (*emotionally*) émouvoir; (POL: *resolution etc*) proposer // *vi* (*gen*) bouger, remuer; (*traffic*) circuler; (*also*: **~ house**) déménager; **to ~ towards** se diriger vers; **to ~ sb to do sth** pousser *or* inciter qn à faire qch; **to get a ~ on** se dépêcher, se remuer; **to ~ about** *vi* (*fidget*) remuer; (*travel*) voyager, se déplacer; **to ~ along** *vi* se pousser; **to ~ away** *vi* s'en aller, s'éloigner; **to ~ back** *vi* revenir, retourner; **to ~ forward** *vi* avancer // *vt* avancer; (*people*) faire avancer; **to ~ in** *vi* (*to a house*) emménager; **to ~ on** *vi* se remettre en route // *vt* (*onlookers*) faire circuler; **to ~ out** *vi* (*of house*) déménager; **to ~ up** *vi* avancer; (*employee*) avoir de l'avancement.
movement ['mu:vmənt] *n* mouvement *m*.
movie ['mu:vı] *n* film *m*; **the ~s** le cinéma; **~ camera** *n* caméra *f*.
moving ['mu:vıŋ] *a* en mouvement; émouvant(e).
mow, *pt* **mowed,** *pp* **mowed** *or* **mown** [məu, -n] *vt* faucher; (*lawn*) tondre; **to ~ down** *vt* faucher; **~er** *n* faucheur/euse.
M.P. *n abbr see* **member**.
m.p.g. *abbr* = *miles per gallon* (*30 m.p.g.* = 29.5 l. aux 100 km).
m.p.h. *abbr* = *miles per hour* (*60 m.p.h.* = *96 km/h*).
Mr ['mıstə*] *n*: **~ X** Monsieur X, M. X.
Mrs ['mısız] *n*: **~ X** Madame X, Mme X.
Ms [mız] *n* (= *Miss or Mrs*): **~ X** ≈ Madame X, Mme X.
M.Sc. *abbr see* **master**.
much [mʌtʃ] *det* beaucoup de // *ad, n or pronoun* beaucoup; **~ milk** beaucoup de lait; **how ~ is it?** combien est-ce que ça coûte?; **it's not ~** ce n'est pas beaucoup.
muck [mʌk] *n* (*mud*) boue *f*; (*dirt*) ordures *fpl*; **to ~ about** *vi* (*col*) faire l'imbécile; (*waste time*) traînasser; **to ~ up** *vt* (*col*: *ruin*) gâcher, esquinter; **~y** *a* (*dirty*) boueux(euse), sale.
mucus ['mju:kəs] *n* mucus *m*.
mud [mʌd] *n* boue *f*.
muddle ['mʌdl] *n* pagaille *f*; désordre *m*, fouillis *m* // *vt* (*also*: **~ up**) brouiller, embrouiller; **to be in a ~** (*person*) ne plus savoir ou l'on en est; **to get in a ~** (*while explaining etc*) s'embrouiller; **to ~ through** *vi* se débrouiller.
mud: **~dy** *a* boueux(euse); **~ flats** *npl* plage *f* de vase; **~guard** *n* garde-boue *m inv*; **~pack** *n* masque *m* de beauté; **~-slinging** *n* médisance *f*, dénigrement *m*.
muff [mʌf] *n* manchon *m*.
muffin ['mʌfın] *n petit pain rond et plat*.
muffle ['mʌfl] *vt* (*sound*) assourdir, étouffer; (*against cold*) emmitoufler; **~d** *a* étouffé(e), voilé(e).
mufti ['mʌftı] *n*: **in ~** en civil.
mug [mʌg] *n* (*cup*) tasse *f* (*sans soucoupe*); (: *for beer*) chope *f*; (*col*: *face*) bouille *f*; (: *fool*) poire *f* // *vt* (*assault*) agresser; **~ging** *n* agression *f*.
muggy ['mʌgı] *a* lourd(e), moite.
mulatto, ~es [mju'lætəu] *n* mulâtre/sse.
mule [mju:l] *n* mule *f*.
mull [mʌl] : **to ~ over** *vt* réfléchir à, ruminer.
mulled [mʌld] *a*: **~ wine** vin chaud.
multi... ['mʌltı] *prefix* multi...; **~coloured, ~colored** (*US*) *a* multicolore.
multifarious [mʌltı'fɛərıəs] *a* divers(es); varié(e).
multiple ['mʌltıpl] *a, n* multiple (*m*); **~ crash** *n* carambolage *m*; **~ sclerosis** *n* sclérose *f* en plaques; **~ store** *n* grand magasin (à succursales multiples).
multiplication [mʌltıplı'keıʃən] *n* multiplication *f*.
multiply ['mʌltıplaı] *vt* multiplier // *vi* se multiplier.
multitude ['mʌltıtju:d] *n* multitude *f*.
mum [mʌm] *n* maman *f* // *a*: **to keep ~** ne pas souffler mot; **~'s the word!** motus et bouche cousue!
mumble ['mʌmbl] *vt, vi* marmotter, marmonner.
mummy ['mʌmı] *n* (*mother*) maman *f*; (*embalmed*) momie *f*.
mumps [mʌmps] *n* oreillons *mpl*.
munch [mʌntʃ] *vt,vi* mâcher.
mundane [mʌn'deın] *a* banal(e), terre à terre *inv*.
municipal [mju:'nısıpl] *a* municipal(e); **~ity** [-'pælıtı] *n* municipalité *f*.
munitions [mju:'nıʃənz] *npl* munitions *fpl*.
mural ['mjuərl] *n* peinture murale.
murder ['mə:də*] *n* meurtre *m*, assassinat *m* // *vt* assassiner; **~er** *n* meurtrier *m*,

assassin *m*; ~**ess** *n* meurtrière *f*; ~**ous** *a* meurtrier(ère).
murk [mə:k] *n* obscurité *f*; ~**y** *a* sombre, ténébreux(euse).
murmur ['mə:mə*] *n* murmure *m* // *vt, vi* murmurer.
muscle ['mʌsl] *n* muscle *m*; **to ~ in** *vi* s'imposer, s'immiscer.
muscular ['mʌskjulə*] *a* musculaire; (*person, arm*) musclé(e).
muse [mju:z] *vi* méditer, songer // *n* muse *f*.
museum [mju:'zɪəm] *n* musée *m*.
mushroom ['mʌʃrum] *n* champignon *m* // *vi* (*fig*) pousser comme un (*or* des) champignon(s).
mushy ['mʌʃɪ] *a* en bouillie; (*pej*) à l'eau de rose.
music ['mju:zɪk] *n* musique *f*; ~**al** *a* musical(e); (*person*) musicien(ne) // *n* (*show*) comédie musicale; ~**al box** *n* boîte *f* à musique; ~**al instrument** *n* instrument *m* de musique; ~ **hall** *n* music-hall *m*; ~**ian** [-'zɪʃən] *n* musicien/ne; ~ **stand** *n* pupitre *m* à musique.
musket ['mʌskɪt] *n* mousquet *m*.
Muslim ['mʌzlɪm] *a, n* musulman(e).
muslin ['mʌzlɪn] *n* mousseline *f*.
musquash ['mʌskwɔʃ] *n* loutre *f*.
mussel ['mʌsl] *n* moule *f*.
must [mʌst] *auxiliary vb* (*obligation*): **I ~ do it** je dois le faire, il faut que je le fasse; (*probability*): **he ~ be there by now** il doit y être maintenant, il y est probablement maintenant, **I ~ have made a mistake** j'ai dû me tromper // *n* nécessité *f*, impératif *m*.
mustard ['mʌstəd] *n* moutarde *f*.
muster ['mʌstə*] *vt* rassembler.
mustn't ['mʌsnt] = **must not**.
musty ['mʌstɪ] *a* qui sent le moisi *or* le renfermé.
mute [mju:t] *a,n* muet(te).
muted ['mju:tɪd] *a* assourdi(e); voilé(e); (MUS) en sourdine; (: *trumpet*) bouché(e).
mutilate ['mju:tɪleɪt] *vt* mutiler; **mutilation** [-'leɪʃən] *n* mutilation *f*.
mutinous ['mju:tɪnəs] *a* (*troops*) mutiné(e); (*attitude*) rebelle.
mutiny ['mju:tɪnɪ] *n* mutinerie *f* // *vi* se mutiner.
mutter ['mʌtə*] *vt,vi* marmonner, marmotter.
mutton ['mʌtn] *n* mouton *m*.
mutual ['mju:tʃuəl] *a* mutuel(le), réciproque; ~**ly** *ad* mutuellement, réciproquement.
muzzle ['mʌzl] *n* museau *m*; (*protective device*) muselière *f*; (*of gun*) gueule *f* // *vt* museler.
my [maɪ] *a* mon(ma), mes *pl*.
myopic [maɪ'ɔpɪk] *a* myope.
myself [maɪ'sɛlf] *pronoun* (*reflexive*) me; (*emphatic*) moi-même; (*after prep*) moi.
mysterious [mɪs'tɪərɪəs] *a* mystérieux(euse).
mystery ['mɪstərɪ] *n* mystère *m*; ~ **story** *n* roman *m* à suspense.
mystic ['mɪstɪk] *n* mystique *m/f* // *a* (*mysterious*) ésotérique; ~**al** *a* mystique.
mystify ['mɪstɪfaɪ] *vt* mystifier; (*puzzle*) ébahir.
mystique [mɪs'ti:k] *n* mystique *f*.
myth [mɪθ] *n* mythe *m*; ~**ical** *a* mythique; ~**ological** [mɪθə'lɔdʒɪkl] *a* mythologique; ~**ology** [mɪ'θɔlədʒɪ] *n* mythologie *f*.

N

nab [næb] *vt* pincer, attraper.
nag [næg] *n* (*pej*: *horse*) canasson *m* // *vt* (*person*) être toujours après, reprendre sans arrêt; ~**ging** *a* (*doubt, pain*) persistant(e) // *n* remarques continuelles.
nail [neɪl] *n* (*human*) ongle *m*; (*metal*) clou *m* // *vt* clouer; **to ~ sb down to a date/price** contraindre qn à accepter *or* donner une date/un prix; ~**brush** *n* brosse *f* à ongles; ~**file** *n* lime *f* à ongles; ~ **polish** *n* vernis *m* à ongles; ~ **scissors** *npl* ciseaux *mpl* à ongles.
naïve [naɪ'i:v] *a* naïf(ïve).
naked ['neɪkɪd] *a* nu(e); ~**ness** *n* nudité *f*.
name [neɪm] *n* nom *m*; réputation *f* // *vt* nommer; citer; (*price, date*) fixer, donner; **in the ~ of** au nom de; ~ **dropping** *n* *mention f (pour se faire valoir) du nom de personnalités qu'on connaît (ou prétend connaître)*; ~**less** *a* sans nom; (*witness, contributor*) anonyme; ~**ly** *ad* à savoir; ~**sake** *n* homonyme *m*.
nanny ['nænɪ] *n* bonne *f* d'enfants; ~ **goat** *n* chèvre *f*.
nap [næp] *n* (*sleep*) (petit) somme; **to be caught ~ping** être pris à l'improviste *or* en défaut.
napalm ['neɪpɑ:m] *n* napalm *m*.
nape [neɪp] *n*: ~ **of the neck** nuque *f*.
napkin ['næpkɪn] *n* serviette *f* (de table); (*Brit*: *for baby*) couche *f* (*gen pl*).
nappy ['næpɪ] *n* couche *f* (*gen pl*).
narcissus, *pl* narcissi [nɑ:'sɪsəs, -saɪ] *n* narcisse *m*.
narcotic [nɑ:'kɔtɪk] *n* (*drug*) stupéfiant *m*; (MED) narcotique *m*.
nark [nɑ:k] *vt* mettre en rogne.
narrate [nə'reɪt] *vt* raconter, narrer.
narrative ['nærətɪv] *n* récit *m* // *a* narratif(ive).
narrator [nə'reɪtə*] *n* narrateur/trice.
narrow ['nærəu] *a* étroit(e); (*fig*) restreint(e), limité(e) // *vi* devenir plus étroit, se rétrécir; **to have a ~ escape** l'échapper belle; **to ~ sth down to** réduire qch à; ~ **gauge** *a* à voie étroite; ~**ly** *ad*: **he ~ly missed injury/the tree** il a failli se blesser/rentrer dans l'arbre; **he only ~ly missed the target** il a manqué la cible de peu *or* de justesse; ~**-minded** *a* à l'esprit étroit, borné(e).
nasal ['neɪzl] *a* nasal(e).
nastily ['nɑ:stɪlɪ] *ad* (*say, act*) méchamment.
nastiness ['nɑ:stɪnɪs] *n* (*of remark*) méchanceté *f*.
nasty ['nɑ:stɪ] *a* (*person*) méchant(e); très désagréable; (*smell*) dégoûtant(e); (*wound, situation*) mauvais(e), vilain(e); **it's a ~ business** c'est une sale affaire.

nation ['neɪʃən] *n* nation *f*.
national ['næʃənl] *a* national(e) // *n* (*abroad*) ressortissant/e ; (*when home*) national/e ; ~ **dress** *n* costume national ; ~**ism** *n* nationalisme *m* ; ~**ist** *a,n* nationaliste (*m/f*) ; ~**ity** [-'nælɪtɪ] *n* nationalité *f* ; ~**ization** [-aɪ'zeɪʃən] *n* nationalisation *f* ; ~**ize** *vt* nationaliser ; ~**ly** *ad* du point de vue national ; dans le pays entier ; ~ **park** *n* parc national.
nation-wide ['neɪʃənwaɪd] *a* s'étendant à l'ensemble du pays ; (*problem*) à l'échelle du pays entier // *ad* à travers *or* dans tout le pays.
native ['neɪtɪv] *n* habitant/e du pays, autochtone *m/f* ; (*in colonies*) indigène *m/f* // *a* du pays, indigène ; (*country*) natal(e) ; (*language*) maternel(le) ; (*ability*) inné(e) ; **a ~ of Russia** une personne originaire de Russie ; **a ~ speaker of French** une personne de langue maternelle française.
NATO ['neɪtəu] *n* (*abbr of North Atlantic Treaty Organization*) O.T.A.N.
natter ['nætə*] *vi* bavarder.
natural ['nætʃrəl] *a* naturel(le) ; ~ **gas** *n* gaz naturel ; ~**ist** *n* naturaliste *m/f* ; ~**ize** *vt* naturaliser ; (*plant*) acclimater ; ~**ly** *ad* naturellement ; ~**ness** *n* naturel *m*.
nature ['neɪtʃə*] *n* nature *f* ; **by ~** par tempérament, de nature.
naught [nɔ:t] *n* zéro *m*.
naughty ['nɔ:tɪ] *a* (*child*) vilain(e), pas sage ; (*story, film*) polisson(ne).
nausea ['nɔ:sɪə] *n* nausée *f* ; ~**te** ['nɔ:sɪeɪt] *vt* écœurer, donner la nausée à.
nautical ['nɔ:tɪkl] *a* nautique ; ~ **mile** *n* mille marin (= *1853 m*).
naval ['neɪvl] *a* naval(e) ; ~ **officer** *n* officier *m* de marine.
nave [neɪv] *n* nef *f*.
navel ['neɪvl] *n* nombril m.
navigable ['nævɪgəbl] *a* navigable.
navigate ['nævɪgeɪt] *vt* diriger, piloter // *vi* naviguer ; **navigation** [-'geɪʃən] *n* navigation *f* ; **navigator** *n* navigateur *m*.
navvy ['nævɪ] *n* terrassier *m*.
navy ['neɪvɪ] *n* marine *f* ; ~-(**blue**) *a* bleu marine *inv*.
neap [ni:p] *n* (*also*: ~**tide**) mortes- eaux *fpl*.
near [nɪə*] *a* proche // *ad* près // *prep* (*also*: ~ **to**) près de // *vt* approcher de ; **to come ~** *vi* s'approcher ; ~**by** [nɪə'baɪ] *a* proche // *ad* tout près, à proximité ; **N~ East** *n* Proche-Orient *m* ; ~**er** *a* plus proche // *ad* plus près ; ~**ly** *ad* presque ; **I ~ly fell** j'ai failli tomber ; ~ **miss** *n* collision évitée de justesse ; (*when aiming*) coup manqué de peu *or* de justesse ; ~**ness** *n* proximité *f* ; ~**side** *n* (AUT: *right-hand drive*) côté *m* gauche ; ~-**sighted** *a* myope.
neat [ni:t] *a* (*person, work*) soigné(e) ; (*room etc*) bien tenu(e) *or* rangé(e) ; (*solution, plan*) habile ; (*spirits*) pur(e) ; **I drink it ~** je le bois sec *or* sans eau ; ~**ly** *ad* avec soin *or* ordre ; habilement.
nebulous ['nɛbjuləs] *a* nébuleux(euse).
necessarily ['nɛsɪsrɪlɪ] *ad* nécessairement.
necessary ['nɛsɪsrɪ] *a* nécessaire.
necessitate [nɪ'sɛsɪteɪt] *vt* nécessiter.
necessity [nɪ'sɛsɪtɪ] *n* nécessité *f* ; chose nécessaire *or* essentielle.
neck [nɛk] *n* cou *m* ; (*of horse, garment*) encolure *f* ; (*of bottle*) goulot *m* ; ~ **and ~** à égalité.
necklace ['nɛklɪs] *n* collier *m*.
neckline ['nɛklaɪn] *n* encolure *f*.
necktie ['nɛktaɪ] *n* cravate *f*.
née [neɪ] *a*: ~ **Scott** née Scott.
need [ni:d] *n* besoin *m* // *vt* avoir besoin de ; **to ~ to do** devoir faire ; avoir besoin de faire.
needle ['ni:dl] *n* aiguille *f* // *vt* asticoter, tourmenter ; ~**cord** *n* velours *m* milleraies.
needless ['ni:dlɪs] *a* inutile ; ~**ly** *ad* inutilement.
needlework ['ni:dlwə:k] *n* (*activity*) travaux *mpl* d'aiguille ; (*object*) ouvrage *m*.
needy ['ni:dɪ] *a* nécessiteux(euse) ; **in ~ circumstances** dans le besoin.
negation [nɪ'geɪʃən] *n* négation *f*.
negative ['nɛgətɪv] *n* (PHOT, ELEC) négatif *m* ; (LING) terme *m* de négation // *a* négatif(ive) ; **to answer in the ~** répondre par la négative.
neglect [nɪ'glɛkt] *vt* négliger // *n* (*of person, duty, garden*) le fait de négliger ; (**state of**) ~ abandon *m*.
negligee ['nɛglɪʒeɪ] *n* déshabillé *m*.
negligence ['nɛglɪdʒəns] *n* négligence *f*.
negligent ['nɛglɪdʒənt] *a* négligent(e) ; ~**ly** *ad* par négligence ; (*offhandedly*) négligemment.
negligible ['nɛglɪdʒɪbl] *a* négligeable.
negotiable [nɪ'gəuʃɪəbl] *a* négociable.
negotiate [nɪ'gəuʃɪeɪt] *vi* négocier // *vt* (COMM) négocier ; (*obstacle*) franchir, négocier ; **negotiation** [-'eɪʃən] *n* négociation *f*, pourparlers *mpl* ; **negotiator** négociateur/trice.
Negress ['ni:grɪs] *n* négresse *f*.
Negro ['ni:grəu] *a* (*gen*) noir(e) ; (*music, arts*) nègre, noir // *n* (*pl*: ~**es**) Noir/e.
neighbour, neighbor (*US*) ['neɪbə*] *n* voisin/e ; ~**hood** *n* quartier *m* ; voisinage *m* ; ~**ing** *a* voisin(e), avoisinant(e) ; ~**ly** *a* obligeant(e) ; (*relations*) de bon voisinage.
neither ['naɪðə*] *a, pronoun* aucun(e) (des deux), ni l'un(e) ni l'autre // *cj*: **I didn't move and ~ did Claude** je n'ai pas bougé, (et) Claude non plus ; **..., ~ did I refuse** ..., (et *or* mais) je n'ai pas non plus refusé // *ad*: ~ **good nor bad** ni bon ni mauvais.
neo... ['ni:əu] *prefix* néo-.
neon ['ni:ɔn] *n* néon *m* ; ~ **light** *n* lampe *f* au néon ; ~ **sign** *n* enseigne (lumineuse) au néon.
nephew ['nɛvju:] *n* neveu *m*.
nerve [nə:v] *n* nerf *m* ; (*fig*) sang-froid *m*, courage *m* ; aplomb *m*, toupet *m* ; **he gets on my ~s** il m'énerve ; ~-**racking** *a* éprouvant (pour les nerfs).
nervous ['nə:vəs] *a* nerveux(euse) ; inquiet(ète), plein(e) d'appréhension ; ~ **breakdown** *n* dépression nerveuse ; ~**ly** *ad* nerveusement ; ~**ness** *n* nervosité *f* ; inquiétude *f*, appréhension *f*.
nest [nɛst] *n* nid *m* ; ~ **of tables** *n* table *f* gigogne.

nestle ['nɛsl] *vi* se blottir.
net [nɛt] *n* filet *m* // *a* net(te) ; **~ball** *n* netball *m.*
Netherlands ['nɛðələndz] *npl*: **the ~** les Pays-Bas *mpl.*
nett [nɛt] *a* = **net**.
netting ['nɛtɪŋ] *n* (*for fence etc*) treillis *m*, grillage *m.*
nettle ['nɛtl] *n* ortie *f.*
network ['nɛtwə:k] *n* réseau *m.*
neurosis, *pl* **neuroses** [njuə'rəusɪs, -si:z] *n* névrose *f.*
neurotic [njuə'rɔtɪk] *a, n* névrosé(e).
neuter ['nju:tə*] *a, n* neutre (*m*) // *vt* (*cat etc*) châtrer, couper.
neutral ['nju:trəl] *a* neutre // *n* (AUT) point mort ; **~ity** [-'trælɪtɪ] *n* neutralité *f.*
never ['nɛvə*] *ad* (ne ...) jamais ; **~ again** plus jamais ; **~-ending** *a* interminable ; **~theless** [nɛvəðə'lɛs] *ad* néanmoins, malgré tout.
new [nju:] *a* nouveau(nouvelle) ; (*brand new*) neuf(neuve) ; **~born** *a* nouveau-né(e) ; **~comer** ['nju:kʌmə*] *n* nouveau venu/nouvelle venue ; **~ly** *ad* nouvellement, récemment ; **~ moon** *n* nouvelle lune ; **~ness** *n* nouveauté *f.*
news [nju:z] *n* nouvelle(s) *f(pl)* ; (RADIO, TV) informations *fpl* ; **a piece of ~** une nouvelle ; **~ agency** *n* agence *f* de presse ; **~agent** *n* marchand *m* de journaux ; **~ flash** *n* flash *m* d'information ; **~letter** *n* bulletin *m* ; **~paper** *n* journal *m* ; **~reel** *n* actualités (filmées) ; **~ stand** *n* kiosque *m* à journaux.
New Year ['nju:'jɪə*] *n* Nouvel An ; **~'s Day** *n* le jour de l'An ; **~'s Eve** *n* la Saint-Sylvestre.
New Zealand [nju:'zi:lənd] *n* la Nouvelle-Zélande.
next [nɛkst] *a* (*seat, room*) voisin(e), d'à côté ; (*meeting, bus stop*) suivant(e) ; prochain(e) // *ad* la fois suivante ; la prochaine fois ; (*afterwards*) ensuite ; **when do we meet ~?** quand nous revoyons-nous? ; **~ door** *ad* à côté ; **~-of-kin** *n* parent *m* le plus proche ; **~ time** *ad* la prochaine fois ; **~ to** *prep* à côté de ; **~ to nothing** presque rien.
N.H.S. *n abbr of National Health Service.*
nib [nɪb] *n* (*of pen*) (bec *m* de) plume *f.*
nibble ['nɪbl] *vt* grignoter.
nice [naɪs] *a* (*holiday, trip*) agréable ; (*flat, picture*) joli(e) ; (*person*) gentil(le) ; (*distinction, point*) subtil(e) ; **~-looking** *a* joli(e) ; **~ly** *ad* agréablement ; joliment ; gentiment ; subtilement.
niceties ['naɪsɪtɪz] *npl* subtilités *fpl.*
nick [nɪk] *n* encoche *f* // *vt* (*col*) faucher, piquer ; **in the ~ of time** juste à temps.
nickel ['nɪkl] *n* nickel *m* ; (*US*) pièce *f* de 5 cents.
nickname ['nɪkneɪm] *n* surnom *m* // *vt* surnommer.
nicotine ['nɪkəti:n] *n* nicotine *f.*
niece [ni:s] *n* nièce *f.*
Nigeria [naɪ'dʒɪərɪə] *n* Nigéria *m or f* ; **~n** *a* nigérien(ne) // *n* Nigérien/ne.
niggardly ['nɪgədlɪ] *a* pingre.
niggling ['nɪglɪŋ] *a* tatillon(ne).
night [naɪt] *n* nuit *f* ; (*evening*) soir *m* ; **at ~** la nuit ; **by ~** de nuit ; **~cap** *n boisson prise avant le coucher* ; **~ club** *n* boîte *f* de nuit ; **~dress** *n* chemise *f* de nuit ; **~fall** *n* tombée *f* de la nuit ; **~ie** ['naɪtɪ] *n* chemise *f* de nuit.
nightingale ['naɪtɪŋgeɪl] *n* rossignol *m.*
night life ['naɪtlaɪf] *n* vie *f* nocturne.
nightly ['naɪtlɪ] *a* de chaque nuit *or* soir ; (*by night*) nocturne // *ad* chaque nuit *or* soir ; nuitamment.
nightmare ['naɪtmɛə*] *n* cauchemar *m.*
night school ['naɪtsku:l] *n* cours *mpl* du soir.
night-time ['naɪttaɪm] *n* nuit *f.*
night watchman ['naɪt'wɔtʃmən] *n* veilleur *m* de nuit.
nil [nɪl] *n* rien *m* ; (SPORT) zéro *m.*
nimble ['nɪmbl] *a* agile.
nine [naɪn] *num* neuf ; **~teen** *num* dix-neuf ; **~ty** *num* quatre-vingt-dix.
ninth [naɪnθ] *a* neuvième.
nip [nɪp] *vt* pincer // *n* pincement *m.*
nipple ['nɪpl] *n* (ANAT) mamelon *m*, bout *m* du sein.
nippy ['nɪpɪ] *a* (*person*) alerte, leste.
nitrogen ['naɪtrədʒən] *n* azote *m.*
no [nəu] *det* pas de, aucun(e) + *sg* // *ad, n* non (*m*) ; **~ entry** défense d'entrer, entrée interdite ; **~ dogs** les chiens ne sont pas admis.
nobility [nəu'bɪlɪtɪ] *n* noblesse *f.*
noble ['nəubl] *a* noble ; **~man** *n* noble *m* ; **nobly** *ad* noblement.
nobody ['nəubədɪ] *pronoun* personne (*with negative*).
nod [nɔd] *vi* faire un signe de (la) tête (*affirmatif ou amical*) ; (*sleep*) somnoler // *n* signe *m* de (la) tête ; **to ~ off** *vi* s'assoupir.
noise [nɔɪz] *n* bruit *m* ; **~less** *a* silencieux(euse) ; **noisily** *ad* bruyamment ; **noisy** *a* bruyant(e).
nomad ['nəumæd] *n* nomade *m/f* ; **~ic** [-'mædɪk] *a* nomade.
no man's land ['nəumænzlænd] *n* no man's land *m.*
nominal ['nɔmɪnl] *a* (*rent, fee*) symbolique ; (*value*) nominal(e).
nominate ['nɔmɪneɪt] *vt* (*propose*) proposer ; (*elect*) nommer.
nomination [nɔmɪ'neɪʃən] *n* nomination *f.*
nominee [nɔmɪ'ni:] *n* candidat agréé ; personne nommée.
non... [nɔn] *prefix* non- ; **~-alcoholic** *a* non-alcoolisé(e) ; **~-breakable** *a* incassable ; **~-committal** ['nɔnkə'mɪtl] *a* évasif(ive) ; **~descript** ['nɔndɪskrɪpt] *a* quelconque, indéfinissable.
none [nʌn] *pronoun* aucun/e ; **he's ~ the worse for it** il ne s'en porte pas plus mal.
nonentity [nɔ'nɛntɪtɪ] *n* personne insignifiante.
non: **~-fiction** *n* littérature *f* non-romanesque ; **~-flammable** *a* ininflammable.
nonplussed [nɔn'plʌst] *a* perplexe.
nonsense ['nɔnsəns] *n* absurdités *fpl*, idioties *fpl.*
non: **~-smoker** *n* non-fumeur *m* ; **~-stick** *a* qui n'attache pas ; **~-stop** *a*

direct(e), sans arrêt (*or* escale) // *ad* sans arrêt.

noodles ['nu:dlz] *npl* nouilles *fpl.*

nook [nuk] *n*: **~s and crannies** recoins *mpl.*

noon [nu:n] *n* midi *m.*

no one ['nəuwʌn] *pronoun* = **nobody**.

nor [nɔ:*] *cj* = **neither** // *ad see* **neither.**

norm [nɔ:m] *n* norme *f.*

normal ['nɔ:ml] *a* normal(e); **~ly** *ad* normalement.

Normandy ['nɔ:məndı] *n* Normandie *f.*

north [nɔ:θ] *n* nord *m* // *a* du nord, nord (*inv*) // *ad* au *or* vers le nord; **N~ America** *n* Amérique *f* du Nord; **~-east** *n* nord-est *m*; **~ern** ['nɔ:ðən] *a* du nord, septentrional(e); **N~ern Ireland** *n* Irlande *f* du Nord; **N~ Pole** *n* pôle *m* Nord; **N~ Sea** *n* mer *f* du Nord; **~ward(s)** ['nɔ:θwəd(z)] *ad* vers le nord; **~-west** *n* nord-ouest *m.*

Norway ['nɔ:weı] *n* Norvège *f.*

Norwegian [nɔ:'wi:dʒən] *a* norvégien(ne) // *n* Norvégien/ne; (*LING*) norvégien *m.*

nose [nəuz] *n* nez *m*; (*fig*) flair *m*; **~bleed** *n* saignement *m* de nez; **~-dive** *n* (descente *f* en) piqué *m*; **~y** *a* curieux(euse).

nostalgia [nɔs'tældʒıə] *n* nostalgie *f*; **nostalgic** *a* nostalgique.

nostril ['nɔstrıl] *n* narine *f*; (*of horse*) naseau *m.*

nosy ['nəuzı] *a* = **nosey**.

not [nɔt] *ad* (ne ...) pas; **~ at all** pas du tout; **you must ~** *or* **mustn't do this** tu ne dois pas faire ça; **he isn't...** il n'est pas... .

notable ['nəutəbl] *a* notable.

notably ['nəutəblı] *ad* en particulier.

notch [nɔtʃ] *n* encoche *f.*

note [nəut] *n* note *f*; (*letter*) mot *m*; (*banknote*) billet *m* // *vt* (*also*: **~ down**) noter; (*notice*) constater; **~book** *n* carnet *m*; **~-case** *n* porte-feuille *m*; **~d** ['nəutıd] *a* réputé(e); **~paper** *n* papier *m* à lettres.

nothing ['nʌθıŋ] *n* rien *m*; **~ new** rien de nouveau; **for ~** (*free*) pour rien, gratuitement.

notice ['nəutıs] *n* avis *m*; (*of leaving*) congé *m* // *vt* remarquer, s'apercevoir de; **to take ~ of** prêter attention à; **to bring sth to sb's ~** porter qch à la connaissance de qn; **to avoid ~** éviter de se faire remarquer; **~able** *a* visible; **~ board** *n* (*Brit*) panneau *m* d'affichage.

notify ['nəutıfaı] *vt*: **to ~ sth to sb** notifier qch à qn; **to ~ sb of sth** avertir qn de qch.

notion ['nəuʃən] *n* idée *f*; (*concept*) notion *f.*

notorious [nəu'tɔ:rıəs] *a* notoire (*souvent en mal*).

notwithstanding [nɔtwıθ'stændıŋ] *ad* néanmoins // *prep* en dépit de.

nougat ['nu:gɑ:] *n* nougat *m.*

nought [nɔ:t] *n* zéro *m.*

noun [naun] *n* nom *m.*

nourish ['nʌrıʃ] *vt* nourrir; **~ing** *a* nourrissant(e); **~ment** *n* nourriture *f.*

novel ['nɔvl] *n* roman *m* // *a* nouveau(nouvelle), original(e); **~ist** *n* romancier *m*; **~ty** *n* nouveauté *f.*

November [nəu'vɛmbə*] *n* novembre *m.*

novice ['nɔvıs] *n* novice *m/f.*

now [nau] *ad* maintenant; **~ and then, ~ and again** de temps en temps; **from ~ on** dorénavant; **~adays** ['nauədeız] *ad* de nos jours.

nowhere ['nəuwɛə*] *ad* nulle part.

nozzle ['nɔzl] *n* (*of hose*) jet *m*, lance *f.*

nuance ['nju:ɑ̃:ns] *n* nuance *f.*

nuclear ['nju:klıə*] *a* nucléaire.

nucleus, *pl* **nuclei** ['nju:klıəs, 'nju:klıaı] *n* noyau *m.*

nude [nju:d] *a* nu(e) // *n* (*ART*) nu *m*; **in the ~** (tout(e)) nu(e).

nudge [nʌdʒ] *vt* donner un (petit) coup de coude à.

nudist ['nju:dıst] *n* nudiste *m/f.*

nudity ['nju:dıtı] *n* nudité *f.*

nuisance ['nju:sns] *n*: **it's a ~** c'est (très) ennuyeux *or* gênant; **he's a ~** il est assommant *or* casse-pieds.

null [nʌl] *a*: **~ and void** nul(le) et non avenu(e); **~ify** ['nʌlıfaı] *vt* invalider.

numb [nʌm] *a* engourdi(e) // *vt* engourdir.

number ['nʌmbə*] *n* nombre *m*; (*numeral*) chiffre *m*; (*of house, car, telephone, newspaper*) numéro *m* // *vt* numéroter; (*include*) compter; **a ~ of** un certain nombre de; **the staff ~s 20** le nombre d'employés s'élève à *or* est de 20; **~ plate** *n* plaque *f* minéralogique *or* d'immatriculation.

numbness ['nʌmnıs] *n* engourdissement *m.*

numeral ['nju:mərəl] *n* chiffre *m.*

numerical [nju:'mɛrıkl] *a* numérique.

numerous ['nju:mərəs] *a* nombreux(euse).

nun [nʌn] *n* religieuse *f*, sœur *f.*

nurse [nə:s] *n* infirmière *f* // *vt* (*patient, cold*) soigner; (*hope*) nourrir; **~(maid)** *n* bonne *f* d'enfants.

nursery ['nə:sərı] *n* (*room*) nursery *f*; (*institution*) pouponnière *f*; (*for plants*) pépinière *f*; **~ rhyme** *n* comptine *f*, chansonnette *f* pour enfants; **~ school** *n* école maternelle; **~ slope** *n* (*SKI*) piste *f* pour débutants.

nursing ['nə:sıŋ] *n* (*profession*) profession *f* d'infirmière; **~ home** *n* clinique *f*; maison *f* de convalescence.

nut [nʌt] *n* (*of metal*) écrou *m*; (*fruit*) noix *f*, noisette *f*, cacahuète *f* (*terme générique en anglais*); **he's ~s** (*col*) il est dingue; **~case** *n* (*col*) dingue *m/f*; **~crackers** *npl* casse-noix *m inv*, casse-noisette(s) *m*; **~meg** ['nʌtmɛg] *n* (noix *f*) muscade *f.*

nutrient ['nju:trıənt] *n* substance nutritive.

nutrition [nju:'trıʃən] *n* nutrition *f*, alimentation *f.*

nutritious [nju:'trıʃəs] *a* nutritif(ive), nourrissant(e).

nutshell ['nʌtʃɛl] *n* coquille *f* de noix; **in a ~** en un mot.

nylon ['naılɔn] *n* nylon *m*; **~s** *npl* bas *mpl* nylon.

O

oaf [əuf] *n* balourd *m.*

oak [əuk] *n* chêne *m*.
O.A.P. *abbr see* **old**.
oar [ɔ:*] *n* aviron *m*, rame *f*; ~**sman/woman** rameur/euse.
oasis, *pl* **oases** [əu'eɪsɪs, əu'eɪsi:z] *n* oasis *f*.
oath [əuθ] *n* serment *m*; (*swear word*) juron *m*; **to take the** ~ prêter serment; **on** ~ sous serment; assermenté(e).
oatmeal ['əutmi:l] *n* flocons *mpl* d'avoine.
oats [əuts] *n* avoine *f*.
obedience [ə'bi:dɪəns] *n* obéissance *f*; **in** ~ **to** conformément à.
obedient [ə'bi:dɪənt] *a* obéissant(e).
obelisk ['ɔbɪlɪsk] *n* obélisque *m*.
obesity [əu'bi:sɪtɪ] *n* obésité *f*.
obey [ə'beɪ] *vt* obéir à; (*instructions, regulations*) se conformer à // *vi* obéir.
obituary [ə'bɪtjuərɪ] *n* nécrologie *f*.
object *n* ['ɔbdʒɪkt] objet *m*; (*purpose*) but *m*, objet *m*; (LING) complément *m* d'objet // *vi* [əb'dʒɛkt]: **to** ~ **to** (*attitude*) désapprouver; (*proposal*) protester contre, élever une objection contre; **I** ~**!** je proteste!; **he** ~**ed that ...** il a fait valoir *or* a objecté que ...; ~**ion** [əb'dʒɛkʃən] *n* objection *f*; (*drawback*) inconvénient *m*; **if you have no** ~**ion** si vous n'y voyez pas d'inconvénient; ~**ionable** [əb'dʒɛkʃənəbl] *a* très désagréable; choquant(e); ~**ive** *n* objectif *m* // *a* objectif(ive); ~**ivity** [ɔbdʒɪk'tɪvɪtɪ] *n* objectivité *f*; ~**or** *n* opposant/e.
obligation [ɔblɪ'geɪʃən] *n* obligation *f*, devoir *m*; (*debt*) dette *f* (de reconnaissance).
obligatory [ə'blɪgətərɪ] *a* obligatoire.
oblige [ə'blaɪdʒ] *vt* (*force*): **to** ~ **sb to do** obliger *or* forcer qn à faire; (*do a favour*) rendre service à, obliger; **to be** ~**d to sb for sth** être obligé(e) à qn de qch; **obliging** *a* obligeant(e), serviable.
oblique [ə'bli:k] *a* oblique; (*allusion*) indirect(e).
obliterate [ə'blɪtəreɪt] *vt* effacer.
oblivion [ə'blɪvɪən] *n* oubli *m*.
oblivious [ə'blɪvɪəs] *a*: ~ **of** oublieux(euse) de.
oblong ['ɔblɔŋ] *a* oblong(ue) // *n* rectangle *m*.
obnoxious [əb'nɔkʃəs] *a* odieux (euse); (*smell*) nauséabond(e).
oboe ['əubəu] *n* hautbois *m*.
obscene [əb'si:n] *a* obscène.
obscenity [əb'sɛnɪtɪ] *n* obscénité *f*.
obscure [əb'skjuə*] *a* obscur(e) // *vt* obscurcir; (*hide: sun*) cacher; **obscurity** *n* obscurité *f*.
obsequious [əb'si:kwɪəs] *a* obséquieux(euse).
observable [əb'zə:vəbl] *a* observable; (*appreciable*) notable.
observance [əb'zə:vns] *n* observance *f*, observation *f*.
observant [əb'zə:vnt] *a* observateur(trice).
observation [ɔbzə'veɪʃən] *n* observation *f*; (*by police etc*) surveillance *f*.
observatory [əb'zə:vətrɪ] *n* observatoire *m*.
observe [əb'zə:v] *vt* observer; (*remark*) faire observer *or* remarquer; ~**r** *n* observateur/trice.
obsess [əb'sɛs] *vt* obséder; ~**ion** [əb'sɛʃən] *n* obsession *f*; ~**ive** *a* obsédant(e).
obsolescence [ɔbsə'lɛsns] *n* vieillissement *m*; **built-in** *or* **planned** ~ (COMM) désuétude calculée.
obsolete ['ɔbsəli:t] *a* dépassé(e); démodé(e).
obstacle ['ɔbstəkl] *n* obstacle *m*; ~ **race** *n* course *f* d'obstacles.
obstetrics [ɔb'stɛtrɪks] *n* obstétrique *f*.
obstinacy ['ɔbstɪnəsɪ] *n* obstination *f*.
obstinate ['ɔbstɪnɪt] *a* obstiné(e); (*pain, cold*) persistant(e).
obstreperous [əb'strɛpərəs] *a* turbulent(e).
obstruct [əb'strʌkt] *vt* (*block*) boucher, obstruer; (*halt*) arrêter; (*hinder*) entraver; ~**ion** [əb'strʌkʃən] *n* obstruction *f*; obstacle *m*; ~**ive** *a* obstructionniste.
obtain [əb'teɪn] *vt* obtenir // *vi* avoir cours; ~**able** *a* qu'on peut obtenir.
obtrusive [əb'tru:sɪv] *a* (*person*) importun(e); (*smell*) pénétrant(e); (*building etc*) trop en évidence.
obtuse [əb'tju:s] *a* obtus(e).
obviate ['ɔbvɪeɪt] *vt* parer à, obvier à.
obvious ['ɔbvɪəs] *a* évident(e), manifeste; ~**ly** *ad* manifestement; bien sûr.
occasion [ə'keɪʒən] *n* occasion *f*; (*event*) événement *m* // *vt* occasionner, causer; ~**al** *a* pris(e) *or* fait(e) *etc* de temps en temps; occasionnel(le); ~**al table** *n* table décorative.
occupation [ɔkju'peɪʃən] *n* occupation *f*; (*job*) métier *m*, profession *f*; **unfit for** ~ (*house*) impropre à l'habitation; ~**al disease** *n* maladie *f* du travail; ~**al hazard** *n* risque *m* du métier.
occupier ['ɔkjupaɪə*] *n* occupant/e.
occupy ['ɔkjupaɪ] *vt* occuper; **to** ~ **o.s. with** *or* **by doing** s'occuper à faire.
occur [ə'kə:*] *vi* se produire; (*difficulty, opportunity*) se présenter; (*phenomenon, error*) se rencontrer; **to** ~ **to sb** venir à l'esprit de qn; ~**rence** *n* présence *f*, existence *f*; cas *m*, fait *m*.
ocean ['əuʃən] *n* océan *m*; ~**-going** *a* de haute mer; ~ **liner** *n* paquebot *m*.
ochre ['əukə*] *a* ocre.
o'clock [ə'klɔk] *ad*: **it is 5** ~ il est 5 heures.
octagonal [ɔk'tægənl] *a* octogonal(e).
octane ['ɔkteɪn] *n* octane *m*.
octave ['ɔktɪv] *n* octave *f*.
October [ɔk'təubə*] *n* octobre *m*.
octopus ['ɔktəpəs] *n* pieuvre *f*.
odd [ɔd] *a* (*strange*) bizarre, curieux(euse); (*number*) impair(e); (*left over*) qui reste, en plus; (*not of a set*) dépareillé(e); **60-**~ 60 et quelques; **at** ~ **times** de temps en temps; **the** ~ **one out** l'exception *f*; ~**ity** *n* bizarrerie *f*; (*person*) excentrique *m/f*; ~**-job man** *n* homme *m* à tout faire; ~ **jobs** *npl* petits travaux divers; ~**ly** *ad* bizarrement, curieusement; ~**ments** *npl* (COMM) fins *fpl* de série; ~**s** *npl* (*in betting*) cote *f*; **the** ~**s are against his coming** il y a peu de chances qu'il vienne; **it**

makes no ~s cela n'a pas d'importance ; **at ~s** en désaccord.

ode [əud] *n* ode *f*.

odious ['əudɪəs] *a* odieux(euse), détestable.

odour, odor (*US*) ['əudə*] *n* odeur *f*; **~less** *a* inodore.

of [ɔv, əv] *prep* de ; **a friend ~ ours** un de nos amis ; **3 ~ them went** 3 d'entre eux y sont allés ; **the 5th ~ July** le 5 juillet ; **a boy ~ 10** un garçon de 10 ans.

off [ɔf] *a,ad* (*engine*) coupé(e) ; (*tap*) fermé(e) ; (*food: bad*) mauvais(e), avancé(e) ; (*milk*) tourné(e) ; (*absent*) absent(e) ; (*cancelled*) annulé(e) // *prep* de ; sur ; **to be ~** (*to leave*) partir, s'en aller ; **to be ~ sick** être absent(e) pour cause de maladie ; **a day ~** un jour de congé ; **to have an ~ day** n'être pas en forme ; **he had his coat ~** il avait enlevé son manteau ; **the hook is ~** le crochet s'est détaché ; le crochet n'est pas mis ; **10% ~** (COMM) 10% de rabais ; **5 km ~ (the road)** à 5 km (de la route) ; **~ the coast** au large de la côte ; **a house ~ the main road** une maison à l'écart de la grand-route ; **I'm ~ meat** je ne mange plus de viande ; je n'aime plus la viande ; **on the ~ chance** à tout hasard.

offal ['ɔfl] *n* (CULIN) abats *mpl*.

offbeat ['ɔfbi:t] *a* excentrique.

off-colour ['ɔf'kʌlə*] *a* (*ill*) malade, mal fichu(e).

offence, offense (*US*) [ə'fɛns] *n* (*crime*) délit *m*, infraction *f*; **to give ~ to** blesser, offenser ; **to take ~ at** se vexer de, s'offenser de.

offend [ə'fɛnd] *vt* (*person*) offenser, blesser ; **~er** *n* délinquant/e ; (*against regulations*) contrevenant/e.

offensive [ə'fɛnsɪv] *a* offensant(e), choquant(e) ; (*smell etc*) très déplaisant(e) ; (*weapon*) offensif(ive) // *n* (MIL) offensive *f*.

offer ['ɔfə*] *n* offre *f*, proposition *f* // *vt* offrir, proposer ; **'on ~'** (COMM) 'en promotion' ; **~ing** *n* offrande *f*.

offhand [ɔf'hænd] *a* désinvolte // *ad* spontanément.

office ['ɔfɪs] *n* (*place*) bureau *m* ; (*position*) charge *f*, fonction *f*; **to take ~** entrer en fonctions ; **~ block** *n* immeuble *m* de bureaux ; **~ boy** *n* garçon *m* de bureau ; **~r** *n* (MIL *etc*) officier *m* ; (*of organization*) membre *m* du bureau directeur ; (*also*: **police ~r**) agent *m* (de police) **~ work** *n* travail *m* de bureau ; **~ worker** *n* employé/e de bureau.

official [ə'fɪʃl] *a* (*authorized*) officiel(le) // *n* officiel *m* ; (*civil servant*) fonctionnaire *m/f*; employé/e ; **~ly** *ad* officiellement.

officious [ə'fɪʃəs] *a* trop empressé(e).

offing ['ɔfɪŋ] *n*: **in the ~** (*fig*) en perspective.

off: **~-licence** *n* (*Brit: shop*) débit *m* de vins et de spiritueux ; **~-peak** *a* aux heures creuses ; **~-putting** *a* rébarbatif(ive) ; rebutant(e), peu engageant(e) ; **~-season** *a, ad* hors-saison.

offset ['ɔfsɛt] *vt irg* (*counteract*) contrebalancer, compenser // *n* (*also*: **~ printing**) offset *m*.

offshore [ɔf'ʃɔ:*] *a* (*breeze*) de terre ; (*island*) proche du littoral ; (*fishing*) côtier(ère).

offside ['ɔf'saɪd] *a* (SPORT) hors jeu // *n* (AUT: *with right-hand drive*) côté droit.

offspring ['ɔfsprɪŋ] *n* progéniture *f*.

off: **~stage** *ad* dans les coulisses ; **~-the-cuff** *ad* au pied levé ; de chic ; **~-the-peg** *ad* en prêt-à-porter ; **~-white** *a* blanc cassé *inv*.

often ['ɔfn] *ad* souvent ; **as ~ as not** la plupart du temps.

ogle ['əugl] *vt* lorgner.

oil [ɔɪl] *n* huile *f*; (*petroleum*) pétrole *m* ; (*for central heating*) mazout *m* // *vt* (*machine*) graisser ; **~can** *n* burette *f* de graissage ; (*for storing*) bidon *m* à huile ; **~ change** *n* vidange *f*; **~field** *n* gisement *m* de pétrole ; **~-fired** *a* au mazout ; **~ level** *n* niveau *m* d'huile ; **~ painting** *n* peinture *f* à l'huile ; **~ refinery** *n* raffinerie *f* de pétrole ; **~ rig** *n* derrick *m* ; (*at sea*) plate-forme pétrolière ; **~skins** *npl* ciré *m* ; **~ slick** *n* nappe *f* de mazout ; **~ tanker** *n* pétrolier *m* ; **~ well** *n* puits *m* de pétrole ; **~y** *a* huileux(euse) ; (*food*) gras(se).

ointment ['ɔɪntmənt] *n* onguent *m*.

O.K., okay ['əu'keɪ] *excl* d'accord! // *a* bien ; en règle ; en bon état ; pas mal // *vt* approuver, donner son accord à ; **is it ~?, are you ~?** ça va?

old [əuld] *a* vieux(vieille) ; (*person*) vieux, âgé(e) ; (*former*) ancien(ne), vieux ; **how ~ are you?** quel âge avez-vous? ; **he's 10 years ~** il a 10 ans, il est âgé de 10 ans ; **~ age** *n* vieillesse *f*; **~-age pensioner (O.A.P.)** *n* retraité/e ; **~er brother/sister** frère/sœur aîné(e) ; **~-fashioned** *a* démodé(e) ; (*person*) vieux jeu *inv* ; **~ people's home** *n* maison *f* de retraite.

olive ['ɔlɪv] *n* (*fruit*) olive *f*; (*tree*) olivier *m* // *a* (*also*: **~-green**) (vert) olive *inv* ; **~ oil** *n* huile *f* d'olive.

Olympic [əu'lɪmpɪk] *a* olympique ; **the ~ Games, the ~s** les Jeux *mpl* olympiques.

omelet(te) ['ɔmlɪt] *n* omelette *f*; **ham/cheese ~** omelette au jambon/fromage.

omen ['əumən] *n* présage *m*.

ominous ['ɔmɪnəs] *a* menaçant(e), inquiétant(e) ; (*event*) de mauvais augure.

omission [əu'mɪʃən] *n* omission *f*.

omit [əu'mɪt] *vt* omettre.

on [ɔn] *prep* sur // *ad* (*machine*) en marche ; (*light, radio*) allumé(e) ; (*tap*) ouvert(e) ; **is the meeting still ~?** est-ce que la réunion a bien lieu? ; la réunion dure-t-elle encore? ; **when is this film ~?** quand passe *or* passe-t-on ce film? ; **~ the train** dans le train ; **~ the wall** sur le *or* au mur ; **~ television** à la télévision ; **~ learning this** en apprenant cela ; **~ arrival** à l'arrivée ; **~ the left** à gauche ; **~ Friday** vendredi ; **~ Fridays** le vendredi ; **a week ~ Friday** vendredi en huit ; **to have one's coat ~** avoir (mis) son manteau ; **to walk** *etc* **~** continuer à marcher *etc* ; **it's not ~!** pas question! ; **~ and off** de temps à autre.

once [wʌns] *ad* une fois ; (*formerly*) autrefois // *cj* une fois que ; **at ~** tout de suite, immédiatement ; (*simultaneously*) à la fois ;

all at ~ *ad* tout d'un coup ; ~ **a week** une fois par semaine ; ~ **more** encore une fois ; ~ **and for all** une fois pour toutes.

oncoming ['ɔnkʌmɪŋ] *a* (*traffic*) venant en sens inverse.

one [wʌn] *det, num* un(e) // *pronoun* un(e) ; (*impersonal*) on ; **this** ~ celui-ci/celle-ci ; **that** ~ celui-là/celle-là ; **the** ~ **book which...** l'unique livre que... ; ~ **by** ~ un(e) par un(e) ; ~ **never knows** on ne sait jamais ; ~ **another** l'un(e) l'autre ; ~**-man** *a* (*business*) dirigé(e) *etc* par un seul homme ; ~**-man band** *n* homme-orchestre *m* ; ~**self** *pronoun* se ; (*after prep, also emphatic*) soi-même ; ~**-way** *a* (*street, traffic*) à sens unique.

ongoing ['ɔngəuɪŋ] *a* en cours ; suivi(e).

onion ['ʌnjən] *n* oignon *m*.

onlooker ['ɔnlukə*] *n* spectateur/trice.

only ['əunlɪ] *ad* seulement // *a* seul(e), unique // *cj* seulement, mais ; **an** ~ **child** un enfant unique ; **not** ~ non seulement ; **I** ~ **took one** j'en ai seulement pris un, je n'en ai pris qu'un.

onset ['ɔnsɛt] *n* début *m* ; (*of winter, old age*) approche *f*.

onshore ['ɔnʃɔ:*] *a* (*wind*) du large.

onslaught ['ɔnslɔ:t] *n* attaque *f*, assaut *m*.

onto ['ɔntu] *prep* = **on to**.

onus ['əunəs] *n* responsabilité *f*.

onward(s) ['ɔnwəd(z)] *ad* (*move*) en avant ; **from this time** ~ dorénavant.

onyx ['ɔnɪks] *n* onyx *m*.

ooze [u:z] *vi* suinter.

opacity [əu'pæsɪtɪ] *n* (*of substance*) opacité *f*.

opal ['əupl] *n* opale *f*.

opaque [əu'peɪk] a opaque.

OPEC [əupɛk] *n* (*abbr of Organization of petroleum exporting countries*) O.P.E.P. (*Organisation des pays exportateurs de pétrole*).

open ['əupn] *a* ouvert(e) ; (*car*) découvert(e) ; (*road, view*) dégagé(e) ; (*meeting*) public(ique) ; (*admiration*) manifeste ; (*question*) non résolu(e) ; (*enemy*) déclaré(e) // *vt* ouvrir // *vi* (*flower, eyes, door, debate*) s'ouvrir ; (*shop, bank, museum*) ouvrir ;. (*book etc: commence*) commencer, débuter ; **to** ~ **on to** *vt fus* (*subj: room, door*) donner sur ; **to** ~ **out** *vt* ouvrir // *vi* s'ouvrir ; **to** ~ **up** *vt* ouvrir ; (*blocked road*) dégager // *vi* s'ouvrir ; **in the** ~ **(air)** en plein air ; ~**-air** *a* en plein air ; ~**ing** *n* ouverture *f* ; (*opportunity*) occasion *f* ; débouché *m* ; (*job*) poste vacant ; ~**ly** *ad* ouvertement ; ~**-minded** *a* à l'esprit ouvert ; ~**-necked** *a* à col ouvert ; ~ **sandwich** *n* canapé *m* ; **the** ~ **sea** *n* le large.

opera ['ɔpərə] *n* opéra *m* ; ~ **glasses** *npl* jumelles *fpl* de théâtre ; ~ **house** *n* opéra *m*.

operate ['ɔpəreɪt] *vt* (*machine*) faire marcher, faire fonctionner ; (*system*) pratiquer // *vi* fonctionner ; (*drug*) faire effet ; **to** ~ **on sb (for)** (MED) opérer qn (de).

operatic [ɔpə'rætɪk] a d'opéra.

operating ['ɔpəreɪtɪŋ] *a*: ~ **table/theatre** table *f*/salle *f* d'opération.

operation [ɔpə'reɪʃən] *n* opération *f* ; **to be in** ~ (*machine*) être en service ; (*system*) être en vigueur ; ~**al** *a* opérationnel(le).

operative ['ɔpərətɪv] *a* (*measure*) en vigueur // *n* (*in factory*) ouvrier/ère.

operator ['ɔpəreɪtə*] *n* (*of machine*) opérateur/trice ; (TEL) téléphoniste *m/f*.

operetta [ɔpə'rɛtə] *n* opérette *f*.

opinion [ə'pɪnɪən] *n* opinion *f*, avis *m* ; **in my** ~ à mon avis ; ~**ated** *a* aux idées bien arrêtées ; ~ **poll** *n* sondage *m* (d'opinion).

opium ['əupɪəm] *n* opium *m*.

opponent [ə'pəunənt] *n* adversaire *m/f*.

opportune ['ɔpətju:n] *a* opportun(e) ; **opportunist** [-'tju:nɪst] *n* opportuniste *m/f*.

opportunity [ɔpə'tju:nɪtɪ] *n* occasion *f* ; **to take the** ~ **of doing** profiter de l'occasion pour faire.

oppose [ə'pəuz] *vt* s'opposer à ; ~**d to** *a* opposé(e) à ; **as** ~**d to** par opposition à ; **opposing** *a* (*side*) opposé(e).

opposite ['ɔpəzɪt] *a* opposé(e) ; (*house etc*) d'en face // *ad* en face // *prep* en face de // *n* opposé *m*, contraire *m* ; (*of word*) contraire *m* ; **'see** ~ **page'** 'voir ci-contre' ; **his** ~ **number** son homologue *m/f*.

opposition [ɔpə'zɪʃən] *n* opposition *f*.

oppress [ə'prɛs] *vt* opprimer ; ~**ion** [ə'prɛʃən] *n* oppression *f* ; ~**ive** *a* oppressif(ive).

opt [ɔpt] *vi*: **to** ~ **for** opter pour ; **to** ~ **to do** choisir de faire ; **to** ~ **out of** choisir de quitter.

optical ['ɔptɪkl] *a* optique ; (*instrument*) d'optique.

optician [ɔp'tɪʃən] *n* opticien/ne.

optimism ['ɔptɪmɪzəm] *n* optimisme *m*.

optimist ['ɔptɪmɪst] *n* optimiste *m/f* ; ~**ic** [-'mɪstɪk] a optimiste.

optimum ['ɔptɪməm] a optimum.

option ['ɔpʃən] *n* choix *m*, option *f* ; (SCOL) matière *f* à option ; (COMM) option ; **to keep one's** ~**s open** (*fig*) ne pas s'engager ; ~**al** *a* facultatif(ive) ; (COMM) en option.

opulence ['ɔpjuləns] *n* opulence *f* ; abondance *f*.

opulent ['ɔpjulənt] *a* opulent(e) ; abondant(e).

or [ɔ:*] *cj* ou ; (*with negative*): **he hasn't seen** ~ **heard anything** il n'a rien vu ni entendu ; ~ **else** sinon ; ou bien.

oracle ['ɔrəkl] *n* oracle *m*.

oral ['ɔ:rəl] *a* oral(e) // *n* oral *m*.

orange ['ɔrɪndʒ] *n* (*fruit*) orange *f* // *a* orange *inv*.

oration [ɔ:'reɪʃən] *n* discours solennel.

orator ['ɔrətə*] *n* orateur/trice.

oratorio [ɔrə'tɔ:rɪəu] *n* oratorio *m*.

orb [ɔ:b] *n* orbe *m*.

orbit ['ɔ:bɪt] *n* orbite *f* // *vt* décrire une *or* des orbite(s) autour de.

orchard ['ɔ:tʃəd] *n* verger *m*.

orchestra ['ɔ:kɪstrə] *n* orchestre *m* ; ~**l** [-'kɛstrəl] *a* orchestral(e) ; (*concert*) symphonique.

orchid ['ɔ:kɪd] *n* orchidée *f*.

ordain [ɔ:'deɪn] *vt* (REL) ordonner ; (*decide*) décréter.

ordeal [ɔ:'di:l] *n* épreuve *f*.

order ['ɔ:də*] *n* ordre *m* ; (COMM) commande *f* // *vt* ordonner ; (COMM) commander ; **in** ~ en ordre ; (*of document*) en règle ; **in ~ of size** par ordre de grandeur ; **in ~ to do/that** pour faire/que + *sub*; **to ~ sb to do** ordonner à qn de faire ; **the lower ~s** (*pej*) les classes inférieures ; **~ form** *n* bon *m* de commande ; **~ly** *n* (*MIL*) ordonnance *f* // *a* (*room*) en ordre ; (*mind*) méthodique ; (*person*) qui a de l'ordre.

ordinal ['ɔ:dɪnl] *a* (*number*) ordinal(e).

ordinary ['ɔ:dnrɪ] *a* ordinaire, normal(e) ; (*pej*) ordinaire, quelconque.

ordination [ɔ:dɪ'neɪʃən] *n* ordination *f*.

ordnance ['ɔ:dnəns] *n* (*MIL*: *unit*) service *m* du matériel ; **O~ Survey map** *n* ≈ carte *f* d'État-major.

ore [ɔ:*] *n* minerai *m*.

organ ['ɔ:gən] *n* organe *m* ; (*MUS*) orgue *m*, orgues *fpl*; **~ic** [ɔ:'gænɪk] *a* organique.

organism ['ɔ:gənɪzəm] *n* organisme *m*.

organist ['ɔ:gənɪst] *n* organiste *m/f*.

organization [ɔ:gənaɪ'zeɪʃən] *n* organisation *f*.

organize ['ɔ:gənaɪz] *vt* organiser ; **~d labour** *n* main-d'œuvre syndiquée ; **~r** *n* organisateur/trice.

orgasm ['ɔ:gæzəm] *n* orgasme *m*.

orgy ['ɔ:dʒɪ] *n* orgie *f*.

Orient ['ɔ:rɪənt] *n*: **the ~** l'Orient *m* ; **oriental** [-'ɛntl] *a* oriental(e) // *n* Oriental/e.

orientate ['ɔ:rɪənteɪt] *vt* orienter.

orifice ['ɔrɪfɪs] *n* orifice *m*.

origin ['ɔrɪdʒɪn] *n* origine *f*.

original [ə'rɪdʒɪnl] *a* original(e) ; (*earliest*) originel(le) // *n* original *m* ; **~ity** [-'nælɪtɪ] *n* originalité *f*; **~ly** *ad* (*at first*) à l'origine.

originate [ə'rɪdʒɪneɪt] *vi*: **to ~ from** être originaire de ; (*suggestion*) provenir de ; **to ~ in** prendre naissance dans ; avoir son origine dans ; **originator** auteur *m*.

ornament ['ɔ:nəmənt] *n* ornement *m* ; (*trinket*) bibelot *m* ; **~al** [-'mɛntl] *a* décoratif(ive) ; (*garden*) d'agrément ; **~ation** [-'teɪʃən] *n* ornementation *f*.

ornate [ɔ:'neɪt] *a* très orné(e).

ornithologist [ɔ:nɪ'θɔlədʒɪst] *n* ornithologue *m/f*.

ornithology [ɔ:nɪ'θɔlədʒɪ] *n* ornithologie *f*.

orphan ['ɔ:fn] *n* orphelin/e // *vt*: **to be ~ed** devenir orphelin ; **~age** *n* orphelinat *m*.

orthodox ['ɔ:θədɔks] *a* orthodoxe.

orthopaedic, orthopedic (*US*) [ɔ:θə'pi:dɪk] *a* orthopédique.

oscillate ['ɔsɪleɪt] *vi* osciller.

ostensible [ɔs'tɛnsɪbl] *a* prétendu(e) ; apparent(e) ; **ostensibly** *ad* en apparence.

ostentation [ɔstɛn'teɪʃən] *n* ostentation *f*.

ostentatious [ɔstɛn'teɪʃəs] *a* prétentieux(euse) ; ostentatoire.

osteopath ['ɔstɪəpæθ] *n* ostéopathe *m/f*.

ostracize ['ɔstrəsaɪz] *vt* frapper d'ostracisme.

ostrich ['ɔstrɪtʃ] *n* autruche *f*.

other ['ʌðə*] *a* autre ; **~ than** autrement que ; à part ; **~wise** *ad,cj* autrement.

otter ['ɔtə*] *n* loutre *f*.

ought, *pt* **ought** [ɔ:t] *auxiliary vb*: **I ~ to do it** je devrais le faire, il faudrait que je le fasse ; **this ~ to have been corrected** cela aurait dû être corrigé ; **he ~ to win** il devrait gagner.

ounce [auns] *n* once *f* (= *28.35 g*; *16 in a pound*).

our ['auə*] *a* notre, *pl* nos ; **~s** *pronoun* le(la) nôtre, les nôtres ; **~selves** *pronoun pl* (*reflexive, after preposition*) nous ; (*emphatic*) nous-mêmes.

oust [aust] *vt* évincer.

out [aut] *ad* dehors ; (*published, not at home etc*) sorti(e) ; (*light, fire*) éteint(e) ; **~ here** ici ; **~ there** là-bas ; **he's ~** (*absent*), il est sorti ; (*unconscious*) il est sans connaissance ; **to be ~ in one's calculations** s'être trompé dans ses calculs ; **to run/back** *etc* **~** sortir en courant/en reculant *etc* ; **~ loud** *ad* à haute voix ; **~ of** (*outside*) en dehors de ; (*because of*: *anger etc*) par ; (*from among*): **~ of 10** sur 10 ; (*without*): **~ of petrol** sans essence, à court d'essence ; **made ~ of wood** en *or* de bois ; **~ of order** (*machine*) en panne ; (*TEL*: *line*) en dérangement ; **~-of-the-way** écarté(e) ; (*fig*) insolite.

outback ['autbæk] *n* campagne isolée ; (*in Australia*) intérieur *m*.

outboard ['autbɔ:d] *n*: **~ (motor)** (moteur *m*) hors-bord *m*.

outbreak ['autbreɪk] *n* accès *m* ; début *m* ; éruption *f*.

outbuilding ['autbɪldɪŋ] *n* dépendance *f*.

outburst ['autbə:st] *n* explosion *f*, accès *m*.

outcast ['autkɑ:st] *n* exilé/e ; (*socially*) paria *m*.

outclass [aut'klɑ:s] *vt* surclasser.

outcome ['autkʌm] *n* issue *f*, résultat *m*.

outcry ['autkraɪ] *n* tollé *m* (général).

outdated [aut'deɪtɪd] *a* démodé(e).

outdo [aut'du:] *vt irg* surpasser.

outdoor [aut'dɔ:*] *a* de *or* en plein air ; **~s** *ad* dehors ; au grand air.

outer ['autə*] *a* extérieur(e) ; **~ space** *n* espace *m* cosmique ; **~ suburbs** *npl* grande banlieue.

outfit ['autfɪt] *n* équipement *m* ; (*clothes*) tenue *f*; **'~ter's'** 'confection pour hommes'.

outgoings ['autgəuɪŋz] *npl* (*expenses*) dépenses *fpl*.

outgrow [aut'grəu] *vt irg* (*clothes*) devenir trop grand(e) pour.

outing ['autɪŋ] *n* sortie *f*; excursion *f*.

outlandish [aut'lændɪʃ] *a* étrange.

outlaw ['autlɔ:] *n* hors-la-loi *m inv* // *vt* (*person*) mettre hors la loi ; (*practice*) proscrire.

outlay ['autleɪ] *n* dépenses *fpl*; (*investment*) mise *f* de fonds.

outlet ['autlɛt] *n* (*for liquid etc*) issue *f*, sortie *f*; (*for emotion*) exutoire *m* ; (*for goods*) débouché *m* ; (*also*: **retail ~**) point *m* de vente.

outline ['autlaɪn] *n* (*shape*) contour *m* ; (*summary*) esquisse *f*, grandes lignes.

outlive [aut'lɪv] *vt* survivre à.

outlook ['autluk] *n* perspective *f*.

outlying ['autlaɪɪŋ] *a* écarté(e).

outmoded [aut'məudɪd] *a* démodé(e) ; dépassé(e).

outnumber [aut'nʌmbə*] *vt* surpasser en nombre.
outpatient ['autpeɪʃənt] *n* malade *m/f* en consultation externe.
outpost ['autpəust] *n* avant-poste *m*.
output ['autput] *n* rendement *m*, production *f*.
outrage ['autreɪdʒ] *n* atrocité *f*, acte *m* de violence ; scandale *m* // *vt* outrager ; **~ous** [-'reɪdʒəs] *a* atroce ; scandaleux(euse).
outrider ['autraɪdə*] *n* (*on motorcycle*) motard *m*.
outright *ad* [aut'raɪt] complètement ; catégoriquement ; carrément ; sur le coup // *a* ['autraɪt] complet(ète) ; catégorique.
outset ['autsɛt] *n* début *m*.
outside [aut'saɪd] *n* extérieur *m* // *a* extérieur(e) // *ad* (au) dehors, à l'extérieur // *prep* hors de, à l'extérieur de ; **at the ~** (*fig*) au plus *or* maximum ; **~ lane** *n* (AUT: *in Britain*) voie *f* de droite ; **~-left/-right** (FOOTBALL) ailier gauche/droit ; **~r** *n* (*in race etc*) outsider *m* ; (*stranger*) étranger/ère.
outsize ['autsaɪz] *a* énorme ; (*clothes*) grande taille *inv*.
outskirts ['autskə:ts] *npl* faubourgs *mpl*.
outspoken [aut'spəukən] *a* très franc(he).
outstanding [aut'stændɪŋ] *a* remarquable, exceptionnel(le) ; (*unfinished*) en suspens ; en souffrance ; non réglé(e).
outstay [aut'steɪ] *vt*: **to ~ one's welcome** abuser de l'hospitalité de son hôte.
outstretched [aut'strɛtʃt] *a* (*hand*) tendu(e) ; (*body*) étendu(e).
outward ['autwəd] *a* (*sign, appearances*) extérieur(e) ; (*journey*) (d')aller ; **~ly** *ad* extérieurement ; en apparence.
outweigh [aut'weɪ] *vt* l'emporter sur.
outwit [aut'wɪt] *vt* se montrer plus malin que.
oval ['əuvl] *a,n* ovale (*m*).
ovary ['əuvərɪ] *n* ovaire *m*.
ovation [əu'veɪʃən] *n* ovation *f*.
oven ['ʌvn] *n* four *m* ; **~proof** *a* allant au four.
over ['əuvə*] *ad* (par-)dessus // *a* (*or ad*) (*finished*) fini(e), terminé(e) ; (*too much*) en plus // *prep* sur ; par-dessus ; (*above*) au-dessus de ; (*on the other side of*) de l'autre côté de ; (*more than*) plus de ; (*during*) pendant ; **~ here** ici ; **~ there** là-bas ; **all ~** (*everywhere*) partout ; (*finished*) fini(e) ; **~ and ~ (again)** à plusieurs reprises ; **~ and above** en plus de ; **to ask sb ~** inviter qn (à passer) ; **to go ~ to sb's** passer chez qn.
over... ['əuvə*] *prefix*: **~abundant** surabondant(e).
overact [əuvər'ækt] *vi* (THEATRE) outrer son rôle.
overall *a,n* ['əuvərɔ:l] *a* (*length*) total(e) ; (*study*) d'ensemble // *n* (*Brit*) blouse *f* // *ad* [əuvər'ɔ:l] dans l'ensemble, en général // **~s** *npl* bleus *mpl* (de travail).
overawe [əuvər'ɔ:] *vt* impressionner.
overbalance [əuvə'bæləns] *vi* basculer.
overbearing [əuvə'bɛərɪŋ] *a* impérieux(euse), autoritaire.
overboard ['əuvəbɔ:d] *ad* (NAUT) pardessus bord.
overcast ['əuvəkɑ:st] *a* couvert(e).
overcharge [əuvə'tʃɑ:dʒ] *vt*: **to ~ sb for sth** faire payer qch trop cher à qn.
overcoat ['əuvəkəut] *n* pardessus *m*.
overcome [əuvə'kʌm] *vt irg* triompher de ; surmonter ; **to be ~ by** être saisi(e) de ; succomber à ; être victime de ; **~ with grief** accablé(e) de douleur.
overcrowded [əuvə'kraudɪd] *a* bondé(e).
overcrowding [əuvə'kraudɪŋ] *n* surpeuplement *m* ; (*in bus*) encombrement *m*.
overdo [əuvə'du:] *vt irg* exagérer ; (*overcook*) trop cuire.
overdose ['əuvədəus] *n* dose excessive.
overdraft ['əuvədrɑ:ft] *n* découvert *m*.
overdrawn [əuvə'drɔ:n] *a* (*account*) à découvert.
overdrive ['əuvədraɪv] *n* (AUT) (vitesse) surmultipliée *f*.
overdue [əuvə'dju:] *a* en retard ; (*recognition*) tardif(ive).
overestimate [əuvər'ɛstɪmeɪt] *vt* surestimer.
overexcited [əuvərɪk'saɪtɪd] *a* surexcité(e).
overexertion [əuvərɪg'zə:ʃən] *n* surmenage *m* (physique).
overexpose [əuvərɪk'spəuz] *vt* (PHOT) surexposer.
overflow *vi* [əuvə'fləu] déborder // *n* ['əuvəfləu] trop-plein *m* ; (*also*: **~ pipe**) tuyau *m* d'écoulement, trop-plein *m*.
overgrown [əuvə'grəun] *a* (*garden*) envahi(e) par la végétation.
overhaul *vt* [əuvə'hɔ:l] réviser // *n* ['əuvəhɔ:l] révision *f*.
overhead *ad* [əuvə'hɛd] au-dessus // *a* ['əuvəhɛd] aérien(ne) ; (*lighting*) vertical(e) ; **~s** *npl* frais généraux.
overhear [əuvə'hɪə*] *vt irg* entendre (par hasard).
overjoyed [əuvə'dʒɔɪd] *a* ravi(e), enchanté(e).
overland ['əuvəlænd] *a, ad* par voie de terre.
overlap *vi* [əuvə'læp] se chevaucher // *n* ['əuvəlæp] chevauchement *m*.
overleaf [əuvə'li:f] *ad* au verso.
overload [əuvə'ləud] *vt* surcharger.
overlook [əuvə'luk] *vt* (*have view on*) donner sur ; (*miss*) oublier, négliger ; (*forgive*) fermer les yeux sur.
overlord ['əuvəlɔ:d] *n* chef *m* suprême.
overnight [əuvə'naɪt] *ad* (*happen*) durant la nuit ; (*fig*) soudain // *a* d'une (*or* de) nuit ; soudain(e) ; **he stayed there ~** il y a passé la nuit ; **if you travel ~...** si tu fais le voyage de nuit... ; **he'll be away ~** il ne rentrera pas ce soir.
overpass ['əuvəpɑ:s] *n* pont autoroutier.
overpower [əuvə'pauə*] *vt* vaincre ; (*fig*) accabler ; **~ing** *a* irrésistible ; (*heat, stench*) suffocant(e).
overrate [əuvə'reɪt] *vt* surestimer.
overreact [əuvəri:'ækt] *vi* réagir de façon excessive.
override [əuvə'raɪd] *vt* (*irg*: *like* **ride**) (*order, objection*) passer outre à ; (*decision*)

annuler; **overriding** *a* prépondérant(e).
overrule [əuvə'ru:l] *vt* (*decision*) annuler; (*claim*) rejeter.
overseas [əuvə'si:z] *ad* outre-mer; (*abroad*) à l'étranger // *a* (*trade*) extérieur(e); (*visitor*) étranger(ère).
overseer ['əuvəsɪə*] *n* (*in factory*) contremaître *m*.
overshadow [əuvə'ʃædəu] *vt* (*fig*) éclipser.
overshoot [əuvə'ʃu:t] *vt irg* dépasser.
oversight ['əuvəsaɪt] *n* omission *f*, oubli *m*.
oversimplify [əuve'sɪmplɪfaɪ] *vt* simplifier à l'excès.
oversleep [əuvə'sli:p] *vi irg* se réveiller (trop) tard.
overspill ['əuvəspɪl] *n* excédent *m* de population.
overstate [əuvə'steɪt] *vt* exagérer; **~ment** *n* exagération *f*.
overt [əu'və:t] *a* non dissimulé(e).
overtake [əuvə'teɪk] *vt irg* dépasser; (AUT) dépasser, doubler; **overtaking** *n* (AUT) dépassement *m*.
overthrow [əuvə'θrəu] *vt irg* (*government*) renverser.
overtime ['əuvətaɪm] *n* heures *fpl* supplémentaires.
overtone ['əuvətəun] *n* (*also*: **~s**) note *f*, sous-entendus *mpl*.
overture ['əuvətʃuə*] *n* (MUS, *fig*) ouverture *f*.
overturn [əuvə'tə:n] *vt* renverser // *vi* se retourner.
overweight [əuvə'weɪt] *a* (*person*) trop gros(se); (*luggage*) trop lourd(e).
overwhelm [əuvə'wɛlm] *vt* accabler; submerger; écraser; **~ing** *a* (*victory, defeat*) écrasant(e); (*desire*) irrésistible.
overwork [əuvə'wə:k] *n* surmenage *m* // *vt* surmener // *vi* se surmener.
overwrought [əuvə'rɔ:t] *a* excédé(e).
owe [əu] *vt* devoir; **to ~ sb sth, to ~ sth to sb** devoir qch à qn.
owing to ['əuɪŋtu:] *prep* à cause de, en raison de.
owl [aul] *n* hibou *m*.
own [əun] *vt* posséder // *a* propre; **a room of my ~** une chambre à moi, ma propre chambre; **to get one's ~ back** prendre sa revanche; **on one's ~** tout(e) seul(e); **to ~ up** *vi* avouer; **~er** *n* propriétaire *m/f*; **~ership** *n* possession *f*.
ox, *pl* **oxen** [ɔks, 'ɔksn] *n* bœuf *m*.
oxide ['ɔksaɪd] *n* oxyde *m*.
oxtail ['ɔksteɪl] *n*: **~ soup** soupe *f* à la queue de bœuf.
oxygen ['ɔksɪdʒən] *n* oxygène *m*; **~ mask/tent** *n* masque *m*/tente *f* à oxygène.
oyster ['ɔɪstə*] *n* huître *f*.
oz. *abbr of* **ounce(s)**.
ozone ['əuzəun] *n* ozone *m*.

P

p [pi:] *abbr of* **penny, pence**.
p.a. *abbr of* **per annum**.
P.A. *see* **public, personal**.
pa [pɑ:] *n* (*col*) papa *m*.
pace [peɪs] *n* pas *m*; (*speed*) allure *f*; vitesse *f* // *vi*: **to ~ up and down** faire les cent pas; **to keep ~ with** aller à la même vitesse que; (*events*) se tenir au courant de; **~maker** *n* (MED) stimulateur *m* cardiaque.
pacification [pæsɪfɪ'keɪʃən] *n* pacification *f*.
pacific [pə'sɪfɪk] *a* pacifique // *n*: **the P~ (Ocean)** le Pacifique, l'océan *m* Pacifique.
pacifist ['pæsɪfɪst] *n* pacifiste *m/f*.
pacify ['pæsɪfaɪ] *vt* pacifier; (*soothe*) calmer.
pack [pæk] *n* paquet *m*; ballot *m*; (*of hounds*) meute *f*; (*of thieves etc*) bande *f*; (*of cards*) jeu *m* // *vt* (*goods*) empaqueter, emballer; (*in suitcase etc*) emballer; (*box*) remplir; (*cram*) entasser; (*press down*) tasser; damer; **to ~ (one's bags)** faire ses bagages; **to ~ one's case** faire sa valise.
package ['pækɪdʒ] *n* paquet *m*; ballot *m*; (*also*: **~ deal**) marché global; forfait *m*; **~ tour** *n* voyage organisé.
packet ['pækɪt] *n* paquet *m*.
pack ice [pækaɪs] *n* banquise *f*.
packing ['pækɪŋ] *n* emballage *m*; **~ case** *n* caisse *f* (d'emballage).
pact [pækt] *n* pacte *m*; traité *m*.
pad [pæd] *n* bloc(-notes) *m*; (*for inking*) tampon encreur; (*col*: *flat*) piaule *f* // *vt* rembourrer; **~ding** *n* rembourrage *m*; (*fig*) délayage *m*.
paddle ['pædl] *n* (*oar*) pagaie *f* // *vi* barboter, faire trempette; **~ steamer** *n* bateau *m* à aubes; **paddling pool** *n* petit bassin.
paddock ['pædək] *n* enclos *m*; paddock *m*.
paddy ['pædɪ] *n*: **~ field** *n* rizière *f*.
padlock ['pædlɔk] *n* cadenas *m* // *vt* cadenasser.
padre ['pɑ:drɪ] *n* aumônier *m*.
paediatrics, pediatrics (*US*) [pi:dɪ'ætrɪks] *n* pédiatrie *f*.
pagan ['peɪgən] *a,n* païen(ne).
page [peɪdʒ] *n* (*of book*) page *f*; (*also*: **~ boy**) groom *m*, chasseur *m*; (*at wedding*) garçon *m* d'honneur // *vt* (*in hotel etc*) (faire) appeler.
pageant ['pædʒənt] *n* spectacle *m* historique; grande cérémonie; **~ry** *n* apparat *m*, pompe *f*.
pagoda [pə'gəudə] *n* pagode *f*.
paid [peɪd] *pt, pp of* **pay** // *a* (*work, official*) rémunéré(e); **to put ~ to** mettre fin à, régler.
pail [peɪl] *n* seau *m*.
pain [peɪn] *n* douleur *f*; **to be in ~** souffrir, avoir mal; **to have a ~ in** avoir mal à *or* une douleur à *or* dans; **to take ~s to do** se donner du mal pour faire; **~ed** *a* peiné(e), chagrin(e); **~ful** *a* douloureux(euse); difficile, pénible; **~fully** *ad* (*fig*: *very*) terriblement; **~killer** *n* calmant *m*; **~less** *a* indolore; **~staking** ['peɪnzteɪkɪŋ] *a* (*person*) soigneux(euse); (*work*) soigné(e).
paint [peɪnt] *n* peinture *f* // *vt* peindre; (*fig*) dépeindre; **to ~ the door blue**

peindre la porte en bleu ; **to ~ in oils** faire de la peinture à l'huile ; **~brush** *n* pinceau *m* ; **~er** *n* peintre *m* ; **~ing** *n* peinture *f*; (*picture*) tableau *m* ; **~-stripper** *n* décapant *m*.

pair [pɛə*] *n* (*of shoes, gloves etc*) paire *f*; (*of people*) couple *m* ; duo *m* ; paire ; **~ of scissors** (paire de) ciseaux *mpl* ; **~ of trousers** pantalon *m*.

pajamas [pɪ'dʒɑ:məz] *npl* (*US*) pyjama(s) *m(pl)*.

Pakistan [pɑ:kɪ'stɑ:n] *n* Pakistan *m* ; **~i** *a* pakistanais(e) // *n* Pakistanais/e.

pal [pæl] *n* (*col*) copain/copine.

palace ['pæləs] *n* palais *m*.

palatable ['pælɪtəbl] *a* bon(bonne), agréable au goût.

palate ['pælɪt] *n* palais *m*.

palaver [pə'lɑ:və*] *n* palabres *fpl or mpl* ; histoire(s) *f(pl)*.

pale [peɪl] *a* pâle ; **to grow ~** pâlir ; **~ blue** *a* bleu pâle *inv* ; **~ness** *n* pâleur *f*.

Palestine ['pælɪstaɪn] *n* Palestine *f*; **Palestinian** [-'tɪnɪən] *a* palestinien(ne) // *n* Palestinien/ne.

palette ['pælɪt] *n* palette *f*.

palisade [pælɪ'seɪd] *n* palissade *f*.

pall [pɔ:l] *n* (*of smoke*) voile *m* // *vi*: **to ~ (on)** devenir lassant (pour).

pallid ['pælɪd] *a* blême.

pally ['pælɪ] *a* (*col*) copain(copine).

palm [pɑ:m] *n* (ANAT) paume *f*; (*also*: **~ tree**) palmier *m* ; (*leaf, symbol*) palme *f* // *vt*: **to ~ sth off on sb** (*col*) refiler qch à qn ; **~ist** *n* chiromancien/ne ; **P~ Sunday** *n* le dimanche des Rameaux.

palpable ['pælpəbl] *a* évident(e), manifeste.

palpitation [pælpɪ'teɪʃən] *n* palpitation(s) *f(pl)*.

paltry ['pɔ:ltrɪ] *a* dérisoire ; piètre.

pamper ['pæmpə*] *vt* gâter, dorloter.

pamphlet ['pæmflət] *n* brochure *f*.

pan [pæn] *n* (*also*: **sauce~**) casserole *f*; (*also*: **frying ~**) poêle *f*; (*of lavatory*) cuvette *f* // *vi* (CINEMA) faire un panoramique.

panacea [pænə'sɪə] *n* panacée *f*.

Panama ['pænəmɑ:] *n* Panama *m* ; **~ canal** *n* canal *m* de Panama.

pancake ['pænkeɪk] *n* crêpe *f*.

panda ['pændə] *n* panda *m* ; **~ car** *n* ≈ voiture *f* pie *inv*.

pandemonium [pændɪ'məunɪəm] *n* tohu-bohu *m*.

pander ['pændə*] *vi*: **to ~ to** flatter bassement ; obéir servilement à.

pane [peɪn] *n* carreau *m* (de fenêtre).

panel ['pænl] *n* (*of wood, cloth etc*) panneau *m* ; (RADIO, TV) panel *m* ; invités *mpl*, experts *mpl* ; **~ling, ~ing** (*US*) *n* boiseries *fpl*.

pang [pæŋ] *n*: **~s of remorse** pincements *mpl* de remords ; **~s of hunger/conscience** tiraillements *mpl* d'estomac/de la conscience.

panic ['pænɪk] *n* panique *f*, affolement *m* // *vi* s'affoler, paniquer ; **~ky** *a* (*person*) qui panique *or* s'affole facilement.

pannier ['pænɪə*] *n* (*on animal*) bât *m* ; (*on bicycle*) sacoche *f*.

panorama [pænə'rɑ:mə] *n* panorama *m* ; **panoramic** *a* panoramique.

pansy ['pænzɪ] *n* (BOT) pensée *f*; (*col*) tapette *f*, pédé *m*.

pant [pænt] *vi* haleter // *n*: *see* **pants**.

pantechnicon [pæn'tɛknɪkən] *n* (grand) camion de déménagement.

panther ['pænθə*] *n* panthère *f*.

panties ['pæntɪz] *npl* slip *m*, culotte *f*.

pantomime ['pæntəmaɪm] *n* spectacle *m* de Noël.

pantry ['pæntrɪ] *n* garde-manger *m inv* ; (*room*) office *f or m*.

pants [pænts] *n* (*woman's*) culotte *f*, slip *m* ; (*man's*) slip, caleçon *m* ; (*US*: *trousers*) pantalon *m*.

papacy ['peɪpəsɪ] *n* papauté *f*.

papal ['peɪpəl] *a* papal(e), pontifical(e).

paper ['peɪpə*] *n* papier *m* ; (*also*: **wall~**) papier peint ; (*also*: **news~**) journal *m* ; (*study, article*) article *m* ; (*exam*) épreuve écrite // *a* en *or* de papier // *vt* tapisser (de papier peint) ; **(identity) ~s** *npl* papiers (d'identité) ; **~back** *n* livre *m* de poche ; livre broché *or* non relié // *a*: **~back edition** édition brochée ; **~ bag** *n* sac *m* en papier ; **~ clip** *n* trombone *m* ; **~ hankie** *n* mouchoir *m* en papier ; **~ mill** *n* papeterie *f*; **~weight** *n* presse-papiers *m inv* ; **~work** *n* paperasserie *f*.

papier-mâché ['pæpɪeɪ'mæʃeɪ] *n* papier mâché.

paprika ['pæprɪkə] *n* paprika *m*.

par [pɑ:*] *n* pair *m* ; (GOLF) normale *f* du parcours ; **on a ~ with** à égalité avec, au même niveau que.

parable ['pærəbl] *n* parabole *f* (REL).

parabola [pə'ræbələ] *n* parabole *f* (MATH).

parachute ['pærəʃu:t] *n* parachute *m* // *vi* sauter en parachute ; **~ jump** *n* saut *m* en parachute.

parade [pə'reɪd] *n* défilé *m* ; (*inspection*) revue *f*; (*street*) boulevard *m* // *vt* (*fig*) faire étalage de // *vi* défiler.

paradise ['pærədaɪs] *n* paradis *m*.

paradox ['pærədɔks] *n* paradoxe *m* ; **~ical** [-'dɔksɪkl] *a* paradoxal(e).

paraffin ['pærəfɪn] *n*: **~ (oil)** pétrole (lampant) ; **liquid ~** huile *f* de paraffine.

paragraph ['pærəgrɑ:f] *n* paragraphe *m*.

parallel ['pærəlɛl] *a* parallèle ; (*fig*) analogue // *n* (*line*) parallèle *f*; (*fig*, GEO) parallèle *m*.

paralysis [pə'rælɪsɪs] *n* paralysie *f*.

paralytic [pærə'lɪtɪk] *a* paralysé(e) ; paralysant(e).

paralyze ['pærəlaɪz] *vt* paralyser.

paramount ['pærəmaunt] *a*: **of ~ importance** de la plus haute *or* grande importance.

paranoia [pærə'nɔɪə] *n* paranoïa *f*.

paraphernalia [pærəfə'neɪlɪə] *n* attirail *m*, affaires *fpl*.

paraphrase ['pærəfreɪz] *vt* paraphraser.

paraplegic [pærə'pli:dʒɪk] *n* paraplégique *m/f*.

parasite ['pærəsaɪt] *n* parasite *m*.

paratrooper ['pærətru:pə*] *n* parachutiste *m* (*soldat*).

parcel ['pɑ:sl] *n* paquet *m*, colis *m* // *vt*

(*also*: ~ **up**) empaqueter; ~ **post** *n* service *m* de colis postaux.

parch [pɑ:ʃ] *vt* dessécher; ~**ed** *a* (*person*) assoiffé(e).

parchment ['pɑ:tʃmənt] *n* parchemin *m*.

pardon ['pɑ:dn] *n* pardon *m*; grâce *f* // *vt* pardonner à; (LAW) gracier; ~! pardon!; ~ **me!** excusez-moi!; **I beg your ~!** pardon!, je suis désolé!; **I beg your ~?** pardon?

parent ['pεərənt] *n* père *m or* mère *f*; ~**s** *npl* parents *mpl*; ~**al** [pə'rεntl] *a* parental(e), des parents.

parenthesis, *pl* **parentheses** [pə'rεnθısıs, -si:z] *n* parenthèse *f*.

Paris ['pærıs] *n* Paris.

parish ['pærıʃ] *n* paroisse *f*; (*civil*) ≈ commune *f* // *a* paroissial(e); ~**ioner** [pə'rıʃənə*] *n* paroissien/ne.

Parisian [pə'rızıən] *a* parisien(ne) // *n* Parisien/ne.

parity ['pærıtı] *n* parité *f*.

park [pɑ:k] *n* parc *m*, jardin public // *vt* garer // *vi* se garer; ~**ing** *n* stationnement *m*; ~**ing lot** *n* (*US*) parking *m*, parc *m* de stationnement; ~**ing meter** *n* parcomètre *m*; ~**ing place** *n* place *f* de stationnement.

parliament ['pɑ:ləmənt] *n* parlement *m*; ~**ary** [-'mεntərı] parlementaire.

parlour, parlor (*US*) ['pɑ:lə*] *n* salon *m*.

parochial [pə'rəukıəl] *a* paroissial(e); (*pej*) à l'esprit de clocher.

parody [pærədı] *n* parodie *f*.

parole [pə'rəul] *n*: **on** ~ en liberté conditionnelle.

parquet ['pɑ:keı] *n*: ~ **floor(ing)** parquet *m*.

parrot ['pærət] *n* perroquet *m*; ~ **fashion** *ad* comme un perroquet.

parry ['pærı] *vt* esquiver, parer à.

parsimonious [pɑ:sı'məunıəs] *a* parcimonieux(euse).

parsley ['pɑ:slı] *n* persil *m*.

parsnip ['pɑ:snıp] *n* panais *m*.

parson ['pɑ:sn] *n* ecclésiastique *m*; (*Church of England*) pasteur *m*.

part [pɑ:t] *n* partie *f*; (*of machine*) pièce *f*; (THEATRE *etc*) rôle *m*; (MUS) voix *f*; partie // *a* partiel(le) // *ad* = **partly** // *vt* séparer // *vi* (*people*) se séparer; (*roads*) se diviser; **to take ~ in** participer à, prendre part à; **on his ~** de sa part; **for my ~** en ce qui me concerne; **for the most ~** en grande partie; dans la plupart des cas; **to ~ with** *vt fus* se séparer de; se défaire de; (*take leave*) quitter, prendre congé de; **in ~ exchange** en reprise.

partial ['pɑ:ʃl] *a* partiel(le); (*unjust*) partial(e); **to be ~ to** aimer, avoir un faible pour; ~**ly** *ad* en partie, partiellement; partialement.

participate [pɑ:'tısıpeıt] *vi*: **to ~ (in)** participer (à), prendre part (à); **participation** [-'peıʃən] *n* participation *f*.

participle ['pɑ:tısıpl] *n* participe *m*.

particle ['pɑ:tıkl] *n* particule *f*.

particular [pə'tıkjulə*] *a* particulier(ère); spécial(e); (*detailed*) détaillé(e); (*fussy*) difficile; méticuleux(euse); ~**s** *npl* détails *mpl*; (*information*) renseignements *mpl*; ~**ly** *ad* particulièrement; en particulier.

parting ['pɑ:tıŋ] *n* séparation *f*; (*in hair*) raie *f* // *a* d'adieu.

partisan [pɑ:tı'zæn] *n* partisan/e // *a* partisan(e); de parti.

partition [pɑ:'tıʃən] *n* (POL) partition *f*, division *f*; (*wall*) cloison *f*.

partly ['pɑ:tlı] *ad* en partie, partiellement.

partner ['pɑ:tnə*] *n* (COMM) associé/e; (SPORT) partenaire *m/f*; (*at dance*) cavalier/ère // *vt* être l'associé *or* le partenaire *or* le cavalier de; ~**ship** *n* association *f*.

partridge ['pɑ:trıdʒ] *n* perdrix *f*.

part-time ['pɑ:t'taım] *a,ad* à mi-temps, à temps partiel.

party ['pɑ:tı] *n* (POL) parti *m*; (*team*) équipe *f*; groupe *m*; (LAW) partie *f*; (*celebration*) réception *f*; soirée *f*; fête *f*.

pass [pɑ:s] *vt* (*time, object*) passer; (*place*) passer devant; (*car, friend*) croiser; (*exam*) être reçu(e) à, réussir; (*candidate*) admettre; (*overtake, surpass*) dépasser; (*approve*) approuver, accepter // *vi* passer; (SCOL) être reçu(e) *or* admis(e), réussir // *n* (*permit*) laissez-passer *m inv*; carte *f* d'accès *or* d'abonnement; (*in mountains*) col *m*; (SPORT) passe *f*; (SCOL: *also*: ~ **mark**): **to get a ~** être reçu(e) (sans mention); **to ~ sth through a ring** *etc* (faire) passer qch dans un anneau *etc*; **could you ~ the vegetables round?** pourriez-vous faire passer les légumes?; **to ~ away** *vi* mourir; **to ~ by** *vi* passer // *vt* négliger; **to ~ for** passer pour; **to ~ out** *vi* s'évanouir; ~**able** *a* (*road*) praticable; (*work*) acceptable.

passage ['pæsıdʒ] *n* (*also*: ~**way**) couloir *m*; (*gen, in book*) passage *m*; (*by boat*) traversée *f*.

passenger ['pæsındʒə*] *n* passager/ère.

passer-by [pɑ:sə'baı] *n* passant/e.

passing ['pɑ:sıŋ] *a* (*fig*) passager(ère); **in ~** en passant.

passion ['pæʃən] *n* passion *f*; amour *m*; **to have a ~ for sth** avoir la passion de qch; ~**ate** *a* passionné(e).

passive ['pæsıv] *a* (*also* LING) passif(ive).

Passover ['pɑ:səuvə*] *n* Pâque (*juive*).

passport ['pɑ:spɔ:t] *n* passeport *m*.

password ['pɑ:swə:d] *n* mot *m* de passe.

past [pɑ:st] *prep* (*further than*) au delà de, plus loin que; après; (*later than*) après // *a* passé(e); (*president etc*) ancien(ne) // *n* passé *m*; **he's ~ forty** il a dépassé la quarantaine, il a plus de *or* passé quarante ans; **it's ~ midnight** il est plus de minuit, il est passé minuit; **for the ~ few/3 days** depuis quelques/3 jours; ces derniers/3 derniers jours; **to run ~** passer en courant; **he ran ~ me** il m'a dépassé en courant; il a passé devant moi en courant.

pasta ['pæstə] *n* pâtes *fpl*.

paste [peıst] *n* (*glue*) colle *f* (de pâte); (*jewellery*) strass *m*; (CULIN) pâté *m* (à tartiner); pâte *f* // *vt* coller.

pastel ['pæstl] *a* pastel *inv*.

pasteurized ['pæstəraızd] *a* pasteurisé(e).

pastille ['pæstl] *n* pastille *f*.

pastime ['pɑ:staım] *n* passe-temps *m inv*, distraction *f*.

pastoral ['pɑ:stərl] *a* pastoral(e).
pastry ['peɪstrɪ] *n* pâte *f*; (*cake*) pâtisserie *f*.
pasture ['pɑ:stʃə*] *n* pâturage *m*.
pasty *n* ['pæstɪ] petit pâté (en croûte) // *a* ['peɪstɪ] pâteux(euse); (*complexion*) terreux(euse).
pat [pæt] *vt* donner une petite tape à // *n*: **a ~ of butter** une noisette de beurre.
patch [pætʃ] *n* (*of material*) pièce *f*; (*spot*) tache *f*; (*of land*) parcelle *f* // *vt* (*clothes*) rapiécer; **a bad ~** une période difficile; **to ~ up** *vt* réparer; **~work** *n* patchwork *m*; **~y** *a* inégal(e).
pate [peɪt] *n*: **a bald ~** un crâne chauve *or* dégarni.
pâté ['pæteɪ] *n* pâté *m*, terrine *f*.
patent ['peɪtnt] *n* brevet *m* (d'invention) // *vt* faire breveter // *a* patent(e), manifeste; **~ leather** *n* cuir verni; **~ medicine** *n* spécialité *f* pharmaceutique.
paternal [pə'tə:nl] *a* paternel(le).
paternity [pə'tə:nɪtɪ] *n* paternité *f*.
path [pɑ:θ] *n* chemin *m*, sentier *m*; allée *f*; (*of planet*) course *f*; (*of missile*) trajectoire *f*.
pathetic [pə'θɛtɪk] *a* (*pitiful*) pitoyable; (*very bad*) lamentable, minable; (*moving*) pathétique.
pathologist [pə'θɔlədʒɪst] *n* pathologiste *m/f*.
pathology [pə'θɔlədʒɪ] *n* pathologie *f*.
pathos ['peɪθɔs] *n* pathétique *m*.
pathway ['pɑ:θweɪ] *n* chemin *m*, sentier *m*.
patience ['peɪʃns] *n* patience *f*; (CARDS) réussite *f*.
patient ['peɪʃnt] *n* patient/e; malade *m/f* // *a* patient(e) // **~ly** *ad* patiemment.
patio ['pætɪəu] *n* patio *m*.
patriotic [pætrɪ'ɔtɪk] *a* patriotique; (*person*) patriote.
patrol [pə'trəul] *n* patrouille *f* // *vt* patrouiller dans; **~ car** *n* voiture *f* de police; **~man** *n* (*US*) agent *m* de police.
patron ['peɪtrən] *n* (*in shop*) client/e; (*of charity*) patron/ne; **~ of the arts** mécène *m*; **~age** ['pætrənɪdʒ] *n* patronage *m*, appui *m*; **~ize** ['pætrənaɪz] *vt* être (un) client *or* un habitué de; (*fig*) traiter avec condescendance; **~ saint** *n* saint(e) patron(ne).
patter ['pætə*] *n* crépitement *m*, tapotement *m*; (*sales talk*) boniment *m* // *vi* crépiter, tapoter.
pattern ['pætən] *n* modèle *m*; (SEWING) patron *m*; (*design*) motif *m*; (*sample*) échantillon *m*.
paunch [pɔ:ntʃ] *n* gros ventre, bedaine *f*.
pauper ['pɔ:pə*] *n* indigent/e; **~'s grave** *n* fosse commune.
pause [pɔ:z] *n* pause *f*, arrêt *m*; (MUS) silence *m* // *vi* faire une pause, s'arrêter.
pave [peɪv] *vt* paver, daller; **to ~ the way for** ouvrir la voie à.
pavement ['peɪvmənt] *n* (*Brit*) trottoir *m*.
pavilion [pə'vɪlɪən] *n* pavillon *m*; tente *f*.
paving ['peɪvɪŋ] *n* pavage *m*, dallage *m*; **~ stone** *n* pavé *m*.
paw [pɔ:] *n* patte *f* // *vt* donner un coup de patte à; (*subj*: *person*: *pej*) tripoter.
pawn [pɔ:n] *n* gage *m*; (CHESS, *also fig*) pion *m* // *vt* mettre en gage; **~broker** *n* prêteur *m* sur gages; **~shop** *n* mont-de-piété *m*.
pay [peɪ] *n* salaire *m*; paie *f* // *vb* (*pt,pp* **paid** [peɪd]) *vt* payer // *vi* payer; (*be profitable*) être rentable; **to ~ attention (to)** prêter attention (à); **to ~ back** *vt* rembourser; **to ~ for** *vt* payer; **to ~ in** *vt* verser; **to ~ up** *vt* régler; **~able** *a* payable; **~ day** *n* jour *m* de paie; **~ee** *n* bénéficiaire *m/f*; **~ing** *a* payant(e); **~ment** *n* paiement *m*; règlement *m*; versement *m*; **~ packet** *n* paie *f*; **~roll** *n* registre *m* du personnel; **~ slip** *n* bulletin *m* de paie.
p.c. *abbr of* **per cent**.
pea [pi:] *n* (petit) pois.
peace [pi:s] *n* paix *f*; (*calm*) calme *m*, tranquillité *f*; **~able** *a* paisible; **~ful** *a* paisible, calme; **~-keeping** *n* maintien *m* de la paix; **~ offering** *n* gage *m* de réconciliation.
peach [pi:tʃ] *n* pêche *f*.
peacock ['pi:kɔk] *n* paon *m*.
peak [pi:k] *n* (*mountain*) pic *m*, cime *f*; (*fig*: *highest level*) maximum *m*; (: *of career, fame*) apogée *m*; **~ period** *n* période *f* de pointe.
peal [pi:l] *n* (*of bells*) carillon *m*; **~s of laughter** éclats *mpl* de rire.
peanut ['pi:nʌt] *n* arachide *f*, cacahuète *f*; **~ butter** *n* beurre *m* de cacahuète.
pear [pɛə*] *n* poire *f*.
pearl [pə:l] *n* perle *f*.
peasant ['pɛznt] *n* paysan/ne.
peat [pi:t] *n* tourbe *f*.
pebble ['pɛbl] *n* galet *m*, caillou *m*.
peck [pɛk] *vt* (*also*: **~ at**) donner un coup de bec à; (*food*) picorer // *n* coup *m* de bec; (*kiss*) bécot *m*; **~ing order** *n* ordre *m* des préséances; **~ish** *a* (*col*): **I feel ~ish** je mangerais bien quelque chose, j'ai la dent.
peculiar [pɪ'kju:lɪə*] *a* étrange, bizarre, curieux(euse); particulier(ère); **~ to** particulier à; **~ity** [pɪkju:lɪ'ærɪtɪ] *n* particularité *f*; (*oddity*) bizarrerie *f*.
pecuniary [pɪ'kju:nɪərɪ] *a* pécuniaire.
pedal ['pɛdl] *n* pédale *f* // *vi* pédaler.
pedantic [pɪ'dæntɪk] *a* pédant(e).
peddle ['pɛdl] *vt* colporter.
pedestal ['pɛdəstl] *n* piédestal *m*.
pedestrian [pɪ'dɛstrɪən] *n* piéton *m* // *a* piétonnier(ère); (*fig*) prosaïque, terre à terre *inv*; **~ crossing** *n* passage clouté *m*.
pediatrics [pi:dɪ'ætrɪks] *n* (*US*) = **paediatrics.**
pedigree ['pɛdɪgri:] *n* ascendance *f*; (*of animal*) pedigree *m* // *cpd* (*animal*) de race.
peek [pi:k] *vi* jeter un coup d'œil (furtif).
peel [pi:l] *n* pelure *f*, épluchure *f*; (*of orange, lemon*) écorce *f* // *vt* peler, éplucher // *vi* (*paint etc*) s'écailler; (*wallpaper*) se décoller; **~ings** *npl* pelures *fpl*, épluchures *fpl*.
peep [pi:p] *n* (*look*) coup d'œil furtif; (*sound*) pépiement *m* // *vi* jeter un coup d'œil (furtif); **to ~ out** *vi* se montrer (furtivement); **~hole** *n* judas *m*.

peer [pɪə*] *vi*: **to ~ at** regarder attentivement, scruter // *n* (*noble*) pair *m*; (*equal*) pair *m*, égal/e; **~age** *n* pairie *f*; **~less** *n* incomparable, sans égal.
peeved [pi:vd] *a* irrité(e), ennuyé(e).
peevish ['pi:vɪʃ] *a* grincheux(euse), maussade.
peg [pɛg] *n* cheville *f*; (*for coat etc*) patère *f*; (*also*: **clothes ~**) pince *f* à linge; **off the ~** *ad* en prêt-à-porter.
pejorative [pɪ'dʒɔrətɪv] *a* péjoratif(ive).
pekingese [pi:kɪ'ni:z] *n* pékinois *m*.
pelican ['pɛlɪkən] *n* pélican *m*.
pellet ['pɛlɪt] *n* boulette *f*; (*of lead*) plomb *m*.
pelmet ['pɛlmɪt] *n* cantonnière *f*; lambrequin *m*.
pelt [pɛlt] *vt*: **to ~ sb (with)** bombarder qn (de) // *vi* (*rain*) tomber à seaux // *n* peau *f*.
pelvis ['pɛlvɪs] *n* bassin *m*.
pen [pɛn] *n* (*for writing*) stylo *m*; (*for sheep*) parc *m*.
penal ['pi:nl] *a* pénal(e); **~ize** *vt* pénaliser; (*fig*) désavantager; **~ servitude** *n* travaux forcés.
penalty ['pɛnltɪ] *n* pénalité *f*; sanction *f*; (*fine*) amende *f*; (SPORT) pénalisation *f*; **~ (kick)** *n* (FOOTBALL) penalty *m*.
penance ['pɛnəns] *n* pénitence *f*.
pence [pɛns] *npl of* **penny.**
pencil ['pɛnsl] *n* crayon *m* // *vt*: **to ~ sth in** noter qch au crayon; **~ sharpener** *n* taille-crayon(s) *m inv*.
pendant ['pɛndnt] *n* pendentif *m*.
pending ['pɛndɪŋ] *prep* en attendant // *a* en suspens.
pendulum ['pɛndjuləm] *n* pendule *m*; (*of clock*) balancier *m*.
penetrate ['pɛnɪtreɪt] *vt* pénétrer dans; pénétrer; **penetrating** *a* pénétrant(e); **penetration** [-'treɪʃən] *n* pénétration *f*.
penfriend ['pɛnfrɛnd] *n* correspondant/e.
penguin ['pɛŋgwɪn] *n* pingouin *m*.
penicillin [pɛnɪ'sɪlɪn] *n* pénicilline *f*.
peninsula [pə'nɪnsjulə] péninsule *f*.
penis ['pi:nɪs] *n* pénis *m*, verge *f*.
penitence ['pɛnɪtns] *n* repentir *m*.
penitent ['pɛnɪtnt] *a* repentant(e).
penitentiary [pɛnɪ'tɛnʃərɪ] *n* (*US*) prison *f*.
penknife ['pɛnnaɪf] *n* canif *m*.
pennant ['pɛnənt] *n* flamme *f*, banderole *f*.
penniless ['pɛnɪlɪs] *a* sans le sou.
penny, *pl* **pennies** *or* **pence** ['pɛnɪ, 'pɛnɪz, pɛns] *n* penny *m* (*pl* pennies) (*new: 100 in a pound; old: 12 in a shilling; on tend à employer 'pennies' ou 'two-pence piece' etc pour les pièces, 'pence' pour la valeur*).
pension ['pɛnʃən] *n* retraite *f*; (MIL) pension *f*; **~able** *a* qui a droit à une retraite; **~er** *n* retraité/e; **~ fund** *n* caisse *f* de retraite.
pensive ['pɛnsɪv] *a* pensif(ive).
pentagon ['pɛntəgən] *n* pentagone *m*.
Pentecost ['pɛntɪkɔst] *n* Pentecôte *f*.
penthouse ['pɛnthaus] *n* appartement *m* (de luxe) en attique.
pent-up ['pɛntʌp] *a* (*feelings*) refoulé(e).
penultimate [pɛ'nʌltɪmət] *a* pénultième, avant-dernier(ère).
people ['pi:pl] *npl* gens *mpl*; personnes *fpl*; (*citizens*) peuple *m* // *n* (*nation, race*) peuple *m* // *vt* peupler; **4/several ~ came** 4/plusieurs personnes sont venues; **the room was full of ~** la salle était pleine de monde *or* de gens; **~ say that...** on dit *or* les gens disent que.
pep [pɛp] *n* (*col*) entrain *m*, dynamisme *m*; **to ~ up** *vt* remonter.
pepper ['pɛpə*] *n* poivre *m*; (*vegetable*) poivron *m* // *vt* poivrer; **~mint** *n* (*plant*) menthe poivrée; (*sweet*) pastille *f* de menthe.
peptalk ['pɛptɔ:k] *n* (*col*) (petit) discours d'encouragement.
per [pə:*] *prep* par; **~ hour** (*miles etc*) à l'heure; (*fee*) (de) l'heure; **~ kilo** *etc* le kilo *etc*; **~ day/person** par jour/personne; **~ cent** pour cent; **~ annum** par an.
perceive [pə'si:v] *vt* percevoir; (*notice*) remarquer, s'apercevoir de.
percentage [pə'sɛntɪdʒ] *n* pourcentage *m*.
perceptible [pə'sɛptɪbl] *a* perceptible.
perception [pə'sɛpʃən] *n* perception *f*; sensibilité *f*; perspicacité *f*.
perceptive [pə'sɛptɪv] *a* pénétrant(e); perspicace.
perch [pə:tʃ] *n* (*fish*) perche *f*; (*for bird*) perchoir *m* // *vi* (se) percher.
percolator ['pə:kəleɪtə*] *n* percolateur *m*; cafetière *f* électrique.
percussion [pə'kʌʃən] *n* percussion *f*.
peremptory [pə'rɛmptərɪ] *a* péremptoire.
perennial [pə'rɛnɪəl] *a* perpétuel(le); (BOT) vivace // *n* plante *f* vivace.
perfect *a,n* ['pə:fɪkt] *a* parfait(e) // *n* (*also*: **~ tense**) parfait *m* // *vt* [pə'fɛkt] parfaire; mettre au point; **~ion** [-'fɛkʃən] *n* perfection *f*; **~ionist** *n* perfectionniste *m/f*; **~ly** *ad* parfaitement.
perforate ['pə:fəreɪt] *vt* perforer, percer; **perforation** [-'reɪʃən] *n* perforation *f*; (*line of holes*) pointillé *m*.
perform [pə'fɔ:m] *vt* (*carry out*) exécuter, remplir; (*concert etc*) jouer, donner // *vi* jouer; **~ance** *n* représentation *f*, spectacle *m*; (*of an artist*) interprétation *f*; (*of player etc*) prestation *f*; (*of car, engine*) performance *f*; **~er** *n* artiste *m/f*; **~ing** *a* (*animal*) savant(e).
perfume ['pə:fju:m] *n* parfum *m* // *vt* parfumer.
perfunctory [pə'fʌŋktərɪ] *a* négligent(e), pour la forme.
perhaps [pə'hæps] *ad* peut-être; **~ he'll...** peut-être qu'il... .
peril ['pɛrɪl] *n* péril *m*; **~ous** *a* périlleux(euse).
perimeter [pə'rɪmɪtə*] *n* périmètre *m*; **~ wall** *n* mur *m* d'enceinte.
period ['pɪərɪəd] *n* période *f*; (HISTORY) époque *f*; (SCOL) cours *m*; (*full stop*) point *m*; (MED) règles *fpl* // *a* (*costume, furniture*) d'époque; **~ic** [-'ɔdɪk] *a* périodique; **~ical** [-'ɔdɪkl] *a* périodique // *n* périodique *m*; **~ically** [-'ɔdɪklɪ] *ad* périodiquement.

peripheral [pə'rɪfərəl] *a* périphérique.
periphery [pə'rɪfərɪ] *n* périphérie *f.*
periscope ['pərɪskəup] *n* périscope *m.*
perish ['pɛrɪʃ] *vi* périr, mourir ; (*decay*) se détériorer ; **~able** *a* périssable ; **~ing** *a* (*col*: *cold*) glacial(e).
perjure ['pə:dʒə*] *vt*: **to ~ o.s.** se parjurer ; **perjury** *n* (LAW: *in court*) faux témoignage ; (*breach of oath*) parjure *m.*
perk [pə:k] *n* avantage *m,* à-côté *m* ; **to ~ up** *vi* (*cheer up*) se ragaillardir ; **~y** *a* (*cheerful*) guilleret(te), gai(e).
perm [pə:m] *n* (*for hair*) permanente *f.*
permanence ['pə:mənəns] *n* permanence *f.*
permanent ['pə:mənənt] *a* permanent(e) ; **~ly** *ad* de façon permanente.
permeable ['pə:mɪəbl] *a* perméable.
permeate ['pə:mɪeɪt] *vi* s'infiltrer // *vt* s'infiltrer dans ; pénétrer.
permissible [pə'mɪsɪbl] *a* permis(e), acceptable.
permission [pə'mɪʃən] *n* permission *f,* autorisation *f.*
permissive [pə'mɪsɪv] *a* tolérant(e) ; **the ~ society** la société de tolérance.
permit *n* ['pə:mɪt] permis *m* // *vt* [pə'mɪt] permettre ; **to ~ sb to do** autoriser qn à faire, permettre à qn de faire.
permutation [pə:mju'teɪʃən] *n* permutation *f.*
pernicious [pə:'nɪʃəs] *a* pernicieux(euse), nocif(ive).
pernickety [pə'nɪkɪtɪ] *a* pointilleux(euse), tatillon(ne).
perpendicular [pə:pən'dɪkjulə*] *a,n* perpendiculaire (*f*).
perpetrate ['pə:pɪtreɪt] *vt* perpétrer, commettre.
perpetual [pə'pɛtjuəl] *a* perpétuel(le).
perpetuate [pə'pɛtjueɪt] *vt* perpétuer.
perpetuity [pə:pɪ'tju:ɪtɪ] *n*: **in ~** à perpétuité.
perplex [pə'plɛks] *vt* rendre perplexe ; (*complicate*) embrouiller.
persecute ['pə:sɪkju:t] *vt* persécuter ; **persecution** [-'kju:ʃən] *n* persécution *f.*
persevere [pə:sɪ'vɪə*] *vi* persévérer.
Persian ['pə:ʃən] *a* persan(e) // *n* (LING) persan *m* ; **the (~) Gulf** *n* le golfe Persique.
persist [pə'sɪst] *vi*: **to ~ (in doing)** persister (à faire), s'obstiner (à faire) ; **~ence** *n* persistance *f,* obstination *f* ; opiniâtreté *f* ; **~ent** *a* persistant(e), tenace.
person ['pə:sn] personne *f* ; **~able** *a* de belle prestance, au physique attrayant ; **~al** *a* personnel(le) ; individuel(le) ; **~al assistant (P.A.)** *n* secrétaire privé/e ; **~al call** (TEL) communication *f* avec préavis ; **~ality** [-'nælɪtɪ] *n* personnalité *f* ; **~ally** *ad* personnellement ; **~ify** [-'sɔnɪfaɪ] *vt* personnifier.
personnel [pə:sə'nɛl] *n* personnel *m* ; **~ manager** *n* chef *m* du personnel.
perspective [pə'spɛktɪv] *n* perspective *f.*
perspex ['pə:spɛks] *n sorte de plexiglas.*
perspicacity [pə:spɪ'kæsɪtɪ] *n* perspicacité *f.*
perspiration [pə:spɪ'reɪʃən] *n* transpiration *f.*
perspire [pə'spaɪə*] *vi* transpirer.
persuade [pə'sweɪd] *vt* persuader.
persuasion [pə'sweɪʒən] *n* persuasion *f.*
persuasive [pə'sweɪsɪv] *a* persuasif(ive).
pert [pə:t] *a* (*brisk*) sec(sèche), brusque ; (*bold*) effronté(e), impertinent(e).
pertaining [pə:'teɪnɪŋ]: **~ to** *prep* relatif(ive) à.
pertinent ['pə:tɪnənt] *a* pertinent(e).
perturb [pə'tə:b] *vt* perturber ; inquiéter.
Peru [pə'ru:] *n* Pérou *m.*
perusal [pə'ru:zl] *n* lecture (attentive).
Peruvian [pə'ru:vjən] *a* péruvien(ne) // *n* Péruvien/ne.
pervade [pə'veɪd] *vt* se répandre dans, envahir.
perverse [pə'və:s] *a* pervers(e) ; (*stubborn*) entêté(e), contrariant(e).
perversion [pə'və:ʃn] *n* perversion *f.*
perversity [pə'və:sɪtɪ] *n* perversité *f.*
pervert *n* ['pə:və:t] perverti/e // *vt* [pə'və:t] pervertir.
pessimism ['pɛsɪmɪzəm] *n* pessimisme *m.*
pessimist ['pəsɪmɪst] *n* pessimiste *m/f* ; **~ic** [-'mɪstɪk] *a* pessimiste.
pest [pɛst] *n* animal *m* (*or* insecte *m*) nuisible ; (*fig*) fléau *m.*
pester ['pɛstə*] *vt* importuner, harceler.
pesticide ['pɛstɪsaɪd] *n* pesticide *m.*
pestle ['pɛsl] *n* pilon *m.*
pet [pɛt] *n* animal familier ; (*favourite*) chouchou *m* // *vt* choyer // *vi* (*col*) se peloter ; **~ lion** *n* lion apprivoisé.
petal ['pɛtl] *n* pétale *m.*
peter ['pi:tə*]: **to ~ out** *vi* s'épuiser ; s'affaiblir.
petite [pə'ti:t] *a* menu(e).
petition [pə'tɪʃən] *n* pétition *f* // *vt* adresser une pétition à.
petrified ['pɛtrɪfaɪd] *a* (*fig*) mort(e) de peur.
petrify ['pətrɪfaɪ] *vt* pétrifier.
petrol ['pɛtrəl] *n* (*Brit*) essence *f* ; **~ engine** *n* moteur *m* à essence.
petroleum [pə'trəulɪəm] *n* pétrole *m.*
petrol: **~ pump** *n* (*in car, at garage*) pompe *f* à essence ; **~ station** *n* station-service *f* ; **~ tank** *n* réservoir *m* d'essence.
petticoat ['pɛtɪkəut] *n* jupon *m.*
pettifogging ['pɛtɪfɔgɪŋ] *a* chicanier(ère).
pettiness ['pɛtɪnɪs] *n* mesquinerie *f.*
petty ['pɛtɪ] *a* (*mean*) mesquin(e) ; (*unimportant*) insignifiant(e), sans importance ; **~ cash** *n* menue monnaie ; **~ officer** *n* second-maître *m.*
petulant ['pɛtjulənt] *a* irritable.
pew [pju:] *n* banc *m* (d'église).
pewter ['pju:tə*] *n* étain *m.*
phallic ['fælɪk] *a* phallique.
phantom ['fæntəm] *n* fantôme *m* ; (*vision*) fantasme *m.*
Pharaoh ['fɛərəu] *n* pharaon *m.*
pharmacist ['fɑ:məsɪst] *n* pharmacien/ne.
pharmacy ['fɑ:məsɪ] *n* pharmacie *f.*
phase [feɪz] *n* phase *f,* période *f* // *vt*: **to ~ sth in/out** introduire/supprimer qch progressivement.
Ph.D. (*abbr = Doctor of Philosophy*) *title* ≈ Docteur *m* en Droit *or* Lettres *etc* // *n* ≈ doctorat *m* ; titulaire *m* d'un doctorat.

pheasant ['fɛznt] *n* faisan *m*.
phenomenon, *pl* **phenomena** [fə'nɔmɪnən, -nə] *n* phénomène *m*.
phew [fju:] *excl* ouf!
phial ['faɪəl] *n* fiole *f*.
philanderer [fɪ'lændərə*] *n* don Juan *m*.
philanthropic [fɪlən'θrɔpɪk] *a* philanthropique.
philanthropist [fɪ'lænθrəpɪst] *n* philanthrope *m/f*.
philatelist [fɪ'lætəlɪst] *n* philatéliste *m/f*.
philately [fɪ'lætəlɪ] *n* philatélie *f*.
Philippines ['fɪlɪpi:nz] *npl* (*also*: **Philippine Islands**) Philippines *fpl*.
philosopher [fɪ'lɔsəfə*] *n* philosophe *m*.
philosophical [fɪlə'sɔfɪkl] *a* philosophique.
philosophy [fɪ'lɔsəfɪ] *n* philosophie *f*.
phlegm [flɛm] *n* flegme *m*; **~atic** [flɛg'mætɪk] *a* flegmatique.
phobia ['fəubjə] *n* phobie *f*.
phone [fəun] *n* téléphone *m* // *vt* téléphoner; **to be on the ~** avoir le téléphone; (*be calling*) être au téléphone; **to ~ back** *vt,vi* rappeler.
phonetics [fə'nɛtɪks] *n* phonétique *f*.
phoney ['fəunɪ] *a* faux(fausse), factice // *n* (*person*) charlatan *m*; fumiste *m/f*.
phonograph ['fəunəgrɑ:f] *n* (*US*) électrophone *m*.
phony ['fəunɪ] *a,n* = **phoney**.
phosphate ['fɔsfeɪt] *n* phosphate *m*.
phosphorus ['fɔsfərəs] *n* phosphore *m*.
photo ['fəutəu] *n* photo *f*.
photo... ['fəutəu] *prefix*: **~copier** *n* machine *f* à photocopier; **~copy** *n* photocopie *f* // *vt* photocopier; **~electric** *a* photoélectrique; **~genic** [-'dʒɛnɪk] *a* photogénique; **~graph** *n* photographie *f* // *vt* photographier; **~grapher** [fə'tɔgrəfə*] *n* photographe *m/f*; **~graphic** [-'græfɪk] *a* photographique; **~graphy** [fə'tɔgrəfɪ] *n* photographie *f*; **~stat** ['fəutəustæt] *n* photocopie *f*, photostat *m*.
phrase [freɪz] *n* expression *f*; (LING) locution *f* // *vt* exprimer; **~book** *n* recueil *m* d'expressions (pour touristes).
physical ['fɪzɪkl] *a* physique; **~ly** *ad* physiquement.
physician [fɪ'zɪʃən] *n* médecin *m*.
physicist ['fɪzɪsɪst] *n* physicien/ne.
physics ['fɪzɪks] *n* physique *f*.
physiology [fɪzɪ'ɔlədʒɪ] *n* physiologie *f*.
physiotherapist [fɪzɪəu'θɛrəpɪst] *n* kinésithérapeute *m/f*.
physiotherapy [fɪzɪəu'θɛrəpɪ] *n* kinésithérapie *f*.
physique [fɪ'zi:k] *n* physique *m*; constitution *f*.
pianist ['pi:ənɪst] *n* pianiste *m/f*.
piano [pɪ'ænəu] *n* piano *m*.
piccolo ['pɪkələu] *n* piccolo *m*.
pick [pɪk] *n* (*tool*: *also*: **~-axe**) pic *m*, pioche *f* // *vt* choisir; (*gather*) cueillir; **take your ~** faites votre choix; **the ~ of** le(la) meilleur(e) de; **to ~ a bone** ronger un os; **to ~ one's teeth** se curer les dents; **to ~ pockets** pratiquer le vol à la tire; **to ~ on** *vt fus* (*person*) harceler; **to ~ out** *vt* choisir; (*distinguish*) distinguer; **to ~ up** *vi* (*improve*) remonter, s'améliorer // *vt* ramasser; (*telephone*) décrocher; (*collect*) passer prendre; (*learn*) apprendre; **to ~ up speed** prendre de la vitesse; **to ~ o.s. up** se relever.
picket ['pɪkɪt] *n* (*in strike*) gréviste *m/f* participant à un piquet de grève; piquet *m* de grève // *vt* mettre un piquet de grève devant; **~ line** *n* piquet *m* de grève.
pickle ['pɪkl] *n* (*also*: **~s**: *as condiment*) pickles *mpl* // *vt* conserver dans du vinaigre *or* dans de la saumure.
pick-me-up ['pɪkmi:ʌp] *n* remontant *m*.
pickpocket ['pɪkpɔkɪt] *n* pickpocket *m*.
pickup ['pɪkʌp] *n* (*on record player*) bras *m* pick-up; (*small truck*) pick-up *m inv*.
picnic ['pɪknɪk] *n* pique-nique *m* // *vi* pique-niquer; **~ker** *n* pique-niqueur/euse.
pictorial [pɪk'tɔ:rɪəl] *a* illustré(e).
picture ['pɪktʃə*] *n* image *f*; (*painting*) peinture *f*, tableau *m*; (*photograph*) photo(graphie) *f*; (*drawing*) dessin *m*; (*film*) film *m* // *vt* se représenter; (*describe*) dépeindre, représenter; **the ~s** le cinéma *m*; **~ book** *n* livre *m* d'images.
picturesque [pɪktʃə'rɛsk] *a* pittoresque.
picture window ['pɪktʃəwɪndəu] *n* baie vitrée, fenêtre *f* panoramique.
piddling ['pɪdlɪŋ] *a* (*col*) insignifiant(e).
pidgin ['pɪdʒɪn] *a*: **~ English** *n* pidgin *m*.
pie [paɪ] *n* tourte *f*; (*of meat*) pâté *m* en croûte.
piebald ['paɪbɔ:ld] *a* pie *inv*.
piece [pi:s] *n* morceau *m*; (*of land*) parcelle *f*; (*item*): **a ~ of furniture/advice** un meuble/conseil // *vt*: **to ~ together** rassembler; **in ~s** (*broken*) en morceaux, en miettes; (*not yet assembled*) en pièces détachées; **to take to ~s** démonter; **~meal** *ad* par bouts; **~work** *n* travail *m* aux pièces.
pier [pɪə*] *n* jetée *f*; (*of bridge etc*) pile *f*.
pierce [pɪəs] *vt* percer, transpercer.
piercing ['pɪəsɪŋ] *a* (*cry*) perçant(e).
piety ['paɪətɪ] *n* piété *f*.
piffling ['pɪflɪŋ] *a* insignifiant(e).
pig [pɪg] *n* cochon *m*, porc *m*.
pigeon ['pɪdʒən] *n* pigeon *m*; **~hole** *n* casier *m*; **~-toed** *a* marchant les pieds en dedans.
piggy bank ['pɪgɪbæŋk] *n* tirelire *f*.
pigheaded ['pɪg'hɛdɪd] *a* entêté(e), têtu(e).
piglet ['pɪglɪt] *n* petit cochon, porcelet *m*.
pigment ['pɪgmənt] *n* pigment *m*; **~ation** [-'teɪʃən] *n* pigmentation *f*.
pigmy ['pɪgmɪ] *n* = **pygmy**.
pigsty ['pɪgstaɪ] *n* porcherie *f*.
pigtail ['pɪgteɪl] *n* natte *f*, tresse *f*.
pike [paɪk] *n* (*spear*) pique *f*; (*fish*) brochet *m*.
pilchard ['pɪltʃəd] *n* pilchard *m* (*sorte de sardine*).
pile [paɪl] *n* (*pillar, of books*) pile *f*; (*heap*) tas *m*; (*of carpet*) épaisseur *f* // *vb* (*also*: **~ up**) *vt* empiler, entasser // *vi* s'entasser.
piles [paɪlz] *n* hémorroïdes *fpl*.
pileup ['paɪlʌp] *n* (AUT) télescopage *m*, collision *f* en série.
pilfer ['pɪlfə*] *vt* chaparder; **~ing** *n* chapardage *m*.

pilgrim ['pɪlgrɪm] *n* pèlerin *m*; **~age** *n* pèlerinage *m*.
pill [pɪl] *n* pilule *f*; **the ~** la pilule.
pillage ['pɪlɪdʒ] *vt* piller.
pillar ['pɪlə*] *n* pilier *m*; **~ box** *n* (*Brit*) boîte *f* aux lettres.
pillion ['pɪljən] *n* (*of motor cycle*) siège *m* arrière; **to ride ~** être derrière; (*on horse*) être en croupe.
pillory ['pɪlərɪ] *n* pilori *m* // *vt* mettre au pilori.
pillow ['pɪləu] *n* oreiller *m*; **~case** *n* taie *f* d'oreiller.
pilot ['paɪlət] *n* pilote *m* // *cpd* (*scheme etc*) pilote, expérimental(e) // *vt* piloter; **~ boat** *n* bateau-pilote *m*; **~ light** *n* veilleuse *f*.
pimp [pɪmp] *n* souteneur *m*, maquereau *m*.
pimple ['pɪmpl] *n* bouton *m*; **pimply** *a* boutonneux(euse).
pin [pɪn] *n* épingle *f*; (TECH) cheville *f* // *vt* épingler; **~s and needles** fourmis *fpl*; **to ~ sb against/to** clouer qn contre/à; **to ~ sb down** (*fig*) obliger qn à répondre.
pinafore ['pɪnəfɔ:*] *n* tablier *m*; **~ dress** *n* robe-chasuble *f*.
pincers ['pɪnsəz] *npl* tenailles *fpl*.
pinch [pɪntʃ] *n* pincement *m*; (*of salt etc*) pincée *f* // *vt* pincer; (*col: steal*) piquer, chiper // *vi* (*shoe*) serrer; **at a ~** à la rigueur.
pincushion ['pɪnkuʃən] *n* pelote *f* à épingles.
pine [paɪn] *n* (*also*: **~ tree**) pin *m* // *vi*: **to ~ for** aspirer à, désirer ardemment; **to ~ away** *vi* dépérir.
pineapple ['paɪnæpl] *n* ananas *m*.
ping [pɪŋ] *n* (*noise*) tintement *m*; **~-pong** *n* ® ping-pong *m* ®.
pink [pɪŋk] *a* rose // *n* (*colour*) rose *m*; (BOT) œillet *m*, mignardise *f*.
pin money ['pɪnmʌnɪ] *n* argent *m* de poche.
pinnacle ['pɪnəkl] *n* pinacle *m*.
pinpoint ['pɪnpɔɪnt] *n* pointe *f* d'épingle // *vt* indiquer (avec précision).
pinstripe ['pɪnstraɪp] *n* rayure très fine.
pint [paɪnt] *n* pinte *f* (= *0.56 l*).
pinup ['pɪnʌp] *n* pin-up *f inv*.
pioneer [paɪə'nɪə*] *n* explorateur/trice; (*early settler*) pionnier *m*; (*fig*) pionnier *m*, précurseur *m*.
pious ['paɪəs] *a* pieux(euse).
pip [pɪp] *n* (*seed*) pépin *m*; (*time signal on radio*) top *m*.
pipe [paɪp] *n* tuyau *m*, conduite *f*; (*for smoking*) pipe *f*; (MUS) pipeau *m* // *vt* amener par tuyau; **~s** *npl* (*also*: **bag~s**) cornemuse *f*; **to ~ down** *vi* (*col*) se taire; **~ dream** *n* chimère *f*, utopie *f*; **~line** *n* pipe-line *m*; **~r** *n* joueur/euse de pipeau (*or* de cornemuse); **~ tobacco** *n* tabac *m* pour la pipe.
piping ['paɪpɪŋ] *ad*: **~ hot** très chaud(e).
piquant ['pi:kənt] *a* piquant(e).
pique ['pi:k] *n* dépit *m*.
piracy ['paɪərəsɪ] *n* piraterie *f*.
pirate ['paɪərət] *n* pirate *m*; **~ radio** *n* radio *f* pirate.
pirouette [pɪru'ɛt] *n* pirouette *f* // *vi* faire une *or* des pirouette(s).
Pisces ['paɪsi:z] *n* les Poissons *mpl*; **to be ~** être des Poissons.
pistol ['pɪstl] *n* pistolet *m*.
piston ['pɪstən] *n* piston *m*.
pit [pɪt] *n* trou *m*, fosse *f*; (*also*: **coal ~**) puits *m* de mine; (*also*: **orchestra ~**) fosse *f* d'orchestre // *vt*: **to ~ sb against sb** opposer qn à qn; **~s** *npl* (AUT) aire *f* de service; **to ~ o.s. against** se mesurer à.
pitch [pɪtʃ] *n* (*throw*) lancement *m*; (MUS) ton *m*; (*of voice*) hauteur *f*; (SPORT) terrain *m*; (NAUT) tangage *m*; (*tar*) poix *f* // *vt* (*throw*) lancer // *vi* (*fall*) tomber; (NAUT) tanguer; **to ~ a tent** dresser une tente; **to be ~ed forward** être projeté en avant; **~-black** *a* noir(e) comme poix; **~ed battle** *n* bataille rangée.
pitcher ['pɪtʃə*] *n* cruche *f*.
pitchfork ['pɪtʃfɔ:k] *n* fourche *f*.
piteous ['pɪtɪəs] *a* pitoyable.
pitfall ['pɪtfɔ:l] *n* trappe *f*, piège *m*.
pith [pɪθ] *n* (*of plant*) moelle *f*; (*of orange*) intérieur *m* de l'écorce; (*fig*) essence *f*; vigueur *f*.
pithead ['pɪthɛd] *n* bouche *f* de puits.
pithy ['pɪθɪ] *a* piquant(e); vigoureux(euse).
pitiable ['pɪtɪəbl] *a* pitoyable.
pitiful ['pɪtɪful] *a* (*touching*) pitoyable; (*contemptible*) lamentable.
pitiless ['pɪtɪlɪs] *a* impitoyable.
pittance ['pɪtns] *n* salaire *m* de misère.
pity ['pɪtɪ] *n* pitié *f* // *vt* plaindre; **what a ~!** quel dommage!; **~ing** *a* compatissant(e).
pivot ['pɪvət] *n* pivot *m* // *vi* pivoter.
pixie ['pɪksɪ] *n* lutin *m*.
placard ['plækɑ:d] *n* affiche *f*.
placate [plə'keɪt] *vt* apaiser, calmer.
place [pleɪs] *n* endroit *m*, lieu *m*; (*proper position, rank, seat*) place *f*; (*house*) maison *f*, logement *m*; (*home*): **at/to his ~** chez lui // *vt* (*object*) placer, mettre; (*identify*) situer; reconnaître; **to take ~** avoir lieu; se passer; **to ~ an order** passer une commande; **to be ~d** (*in race, exam*) se placer; **out of ~** (*not suitable*) déplacé(e), inopportun(e); **in the first ~** d'abord, en premier; **~ mat** *n* set *m* de table.
placid ['plæsɪd] *a* placide; **~ity** [plə'sɪdɪtɪ] *n* placidité *f*.
plagiarism ['pleɪdʒjərɪzm] *n* plagiat *m*.
plagiarize ['pleɪdʒjəraɪz] *vt* plagier.
plague [pleɪg] *n* fléau *m*; (MED) peste *f*.
plaice [pleɪs] *n*, *pl inv* carrelet *m*.
plaid [plæd] *n* tissu écossais.
plain [pleɪn] *a* (*clear*) clair(e), évident(e); (*simple*) simple, ordinaire; (*frank*) franc(franche); (*not handsome*) quelconque, ordinaire; (*cigarette*) sans filtre; (*without seasoning etc*) nature *inv*; (*in one colour*) uni(e) // *ad* franchement, carrément // *n* plaine *f*; **in ~ clothes** (*police*) en civil; **~ly** *ad* clairement; (*frankly*) carrément, sans détours; **~ness** *n* simplicité *f*.
plaintiff ['pleɪntɪf] *n* plaignant/e.
plait [plæt] *n* tresse *f*, natte *f* // *vt* tresser, natter.
plan [plæn] *n* plan *m*; (*scheme*) projet *m* // *vt* (*think in advance*) projeter; (*prepare*)

organiser // *vi* faire des projets; **to ~ to do** projeter de faire.
plane [pleɪn] *n* (AVIAT) avion *m*; (*tree*) platane *m*; (*tool*) rabot *m*; (ART, MATH *etc*) plan *m* // *a* plan(e), plat(e) // *vt* (*with tool*) raboter.
planet ['plænɪt] *n* planète *f*.
planetarium [plænɪ'tɛərɪəm] *n* planétarium *m*.
plank [plæŋk] *n* planche *f*; (POL) point *m* d'un programme.
plankton ['plæŋktən] *n* plancton *m*.
planner ['plænə*] *n* planificateur/trice.
planning ['plænɪŋ] *n* planification *f*; **family ~** planning familial.
plant [plɑːnt] *n* plante *f*; (*machinery*) matériel *m*; (*factory*) usine *f* // *vt* planter; (*colony*) établir; (*bomb*) déposer, poser.
plantation [plæn'teɪʃən] *n* plantation *f*.
plant pot ['plɑːntpɔt] *n* pot *m* (de fleurs).
plaque [plæk] *n* plaque *f*.
plasma ['plæzmə] *n* plasma *m*.
plaster ['plɑːstə*] *n* plâtre *m*; (*also*: **sticking ~**) pansement adhésif // *vt* plâtrer; (*cover*): **to ~ with** couvrir de; **in ~** (*leg etc*) dans le plâtre; **~ed** *a* (*col*) soûl(e); **~er** *n* plâtrier *m*.
plastic ['plæstɪk] *n* plastique *m* // *a* (*made of plastic*) en plastique; (*flexible*) plastique, malléable; (*art*) plastique.
plasticine ['plæstɪsiːn] *n* ® pâte *f* à modeler.
plastic surgery ['plæstɪk'səːdʒərɪ] *n* chirurgie *f* esthétique.
plate [pleɪt] *n* (*dish*) assiette *f*; (*sheet of metal*, PHOT) plaque *f*; (*in book*) gravure *f*; **gold/silver ~** (*dishes*) vaisselle *f* d'or/d'argent.
plateau, ~s *or* **~x** ['plætəu, -z] *n* plateau *m*.
plateful ['pleɪtful] *n* assiette *f*, assiettée *f*.
plate glass [pleɪt'glɑːs] *n* verre *m* (de vitrine).
platelayer ['pleɪtleɪə*] *n* (RAIL) poseur *m* de rails.
platform ['plætfɔːm] *n* (*at meeting*) tribune *f*; (*stage*) estrade *f*; (RAIL) quai *m*; **~ ticket** *n* billet *m* de quai.
platinum ['plætɪnəm] *n* platine *m*.
platitude ['plætɪtjuːd] *n* platitude *f*, lieu commun.
platoon [plə'tuːn] *n* peloton *m*.
platter ['plætə*] *n* plat *m*.
plausible ['plɔːzɪbl] *a* plausible; (*person*) convaincant(e).
play [pleɪ] *n* jeu *m*; (THEATRE) pièce *f* (de théâtre) // *vt* (*game*) jouer à; (*team, opponent*) jouer contre; (*instrument*) jouer de; (*play, part, piece of music, note*) jouer // *vi* jouer; **to ~ down** *vt* minimiser; **to ~ up** *vi* (*cause trouble*) faire des siennes; **to ~act** *vi* jouer la comédie; **~ed-out** *a* épuisé(e); **~er** *n* joueur/euse; (THEATRE) acteur/trice; (MUS) musicien/ne; **~ful** *a* enjoué(e); **~goer** *n* amateur/trice de théâtre, habitué/e des théâtres; **~ground** *n* cour *f* de récréation; **~group** *n* garderie *f*; **~ing card** *n* carte *f* à jouer; **~ing field** *n* terrain *m* de sport; **~mate** *n* camarade *m/f*, copain/copine; **~-off** *n* (SPORT) belle *f*; **~ on words** *n* jeu *m* de mots; **~pen** *n* parc *m* (pour bébé); **~thing** *n* jouet *m*; **~wright** *n* dramaturge *m*.
plea [pliː] *n* (*request*) appel *m*; (*excuse*) excuse *f*; (LAW) défense *f*.
plead [pliːd] *vt* plaider; (*give as excuse*) invoquer // *vi* (LAW) plaider; (*beg*): **to ~ with sb** implorer qn.
pleasant ['plɛznt] *a* agréable; **~ly** *ad* agréablement; **~ness** *n* (*of person*) amabilité *f*; (*of place*) agrément *m*; **~ry** *n* (*joke*) plaisanterie *f*; **~ries** *npl* (*polite remarks*) civilités *fpl*.
please [pliːz] *vt* plaire à // *vi* (*think fit*): **do as you ~** faites comme il vous plaira; **~!** s'il te (*or* vous) plaît; **my bill, ~** l'addition, s'il vous plaît; **~ yourself!** à ta (*or* votre) guise!; **~d** *a*: **~d (with)** content(e) (de); **~d to meet you** enchanté (de faire votre connaissance); **pleasing** *a* plaisant(e), qui fait plaisir.
pleasurable ['plɛʒərəbl] *a* très agréable.
pleasure ['plɛʒə*] *n* plaisir *m*; **'it's a ~'** 'je vous en prie'; **~ steamer** *n* vapeur *m* de plaisance.
pleat [pliːt] *n* pli *m*.
plebiscite ['plɛbɪsɪt] *n* plébiscite *m*.
plebs [plɛbz] *npl* (*pej*) bas peuple.
plectrum ['plɛktrəm] *n* plectre *m*.
pledge [plɛdʒ] *n* gage *m*; (*promise*) promesse *f* // *vt* engager; promettre.
plentiful ['plɛntɪful] *a* abondant(e), copieux(euse).
plenty ['plɛntɪ] *n* abondance *f*; **~ of** beaucoup de; (bien) assez de.
pleurisy ['pluərɪsɪ] *n* pleurésie *f*.
pliable ['plaɪəbl] *a* flexible; (*person*) malléable.
pliers ['plaɪəz] *npl* pinces *fpl*.
plight [plaɪt] *n* situation *f* critique.
plimsolls ['plɪmsəlz] *npl* (chaussures *fpl*) tennis *fpl*.
plinth [plɪnθ] *n* socle *m*.
plod [plɔd] *vi* avancer péniblement; (*fig*) peiner; **~der** *n* bûcheur/euse; **~ding** *a* pesant(e).
plonk [plɔŋk] (*col*) *n* (*wine*) pinard *m*, piquette *f* // *vt*: **to ~ sth down** poser brusquement qch.
plot [plɔt] *n* complot *m*, conspiration *f*; (*of story, play*) intrigue *f*; (*of land*) lot *m* de terrain, lopin *m* // *vt* (*mark out*) pointer; relever; (*conspire*) comploter // *vi* comploter; **~ter** *n* conspirateur/trice.
plough, plow (*US*) [plau] *n* charrue *f* // *vt* (*earth*) labourer; **to ~ back** *vt* (COMM) réinvestir; **to ~ through** *vt fus* (*snow etc*) avancer péniblement dans; **~ing** *n* labourage *m*.
ploy [plɔɪ] *n* stratagème *m*.
pluck [plʌk] *vt* (*fruit*) cueillir; (*musical instrument*) pincer; (*bird*) plumer // *n* courage *m*, cran *m*; **to ~ one's eyebrows** s'épiler les sourcils; **to ~ up courage** prendre son courage à deux mains; **~y** *a* courageux(euse).
plug [plʌg] *n* bouchon *m*, bonde *f*; (ELEC) prise *f* de courant; (AUT: *also*: **sparking ~**) bougie *f* // *vt* (*hole*) boucher; (*col: advertise*) faire du battage pour, matraquer; **to ~ in** *vt* (ELEC) brancher.

plum [plʌm] *n* (*fruit*) prune *f* // *a*: ~ **job** *n* (*col*) travail *m* en or.
plumb [plʌm] *a* vertical(e) // *n* plomb *m* // *ad* (*exactly*) en plein // *vt* sonder.
plumber ['plʌmə*] *n* plombier *m*.
plumbing ['plʌmɪŋ] *n* (*trade*) plomberie *f*; (*piping*) tuyauterie *f*.
plumbline ['plʌmlaɪn] *n* fil *m* à plomb.
plume [plu:m] *n* plume *f*, plumet *m*.
plummet ['plʌmɪt] *vi* plonger, dégringoler.
plump [plʌmp] *a* rondelet(te), dodu(e), bien en chair // *vt*: **to ~ sth (down) on** laisser tomber qch lourdement sur; **to ~ for** (*col*: *choose*) se décider pour.
plunder ['plʌndə*] *n* pillage *m* // *vt* piller.
plunge [plʌndʒ] *n* plongeon *m* // *vt* plonger // *vi* (*fall*) tomber, dégringoler; **to take the ~** se jeter à l'eau; **plunging** *a* (*neckline*) plongeant(e).
pluperfect [plu:'pə:fɪkt] *n* plus-que-parfait *m*.
plural ['pluərl] *a* pluriel(le) // *n* pluriel *m*.
plus [plʌs] *n* (*also*: **~ sign**) signe *m* plus // *prep* plus; **ten/twenty ~** plus de dix/vingt; **it's a ~** c'est un atout; **~ fours** *npl* pantalon *m* (de) golf.
plush [plʌʃ] *a* somptueux(euse) // *n* peluche *f*.
ply [plaɪ] *n* (*of wool*) fil *m*; (*of wood*) feuille *f*, épaisseur *f* // *vt* (*tool*) manier; (*a trade*) exercer // *vi* (*ship*) faire la navette; **three ~ (wool)** *n* laine *f* trois fils; **to ~ sb with drink** donner continuellement à boire à qn; **~wood** *n* contre-plaqué *m*.
P.M. *abbr see* **prime**.
p.m. *ad* (*abbr of post meridiem*) de l'après-midi.
pneumatic [nju:'mætɪk] *a* pneumatique.
pneumonia [nju:'məunɪə] *n* pneumonie *f*.
P.O. *abbr see* **post office**.
poach [pəutʃ] *vt* (*cook*) pocher; (*steal*) pêcher (*or* chasser) sans permis // *vi* braconner; **~ed** *a* (*egg*) poché(e); **~er** *n* braconnier *m*; **~ ing** *n* braconnage *m*.
pocket ['pɔkɪt] *n* poche *f* // *vt* empocher; **to be out of ~** en être de sa poche; **~book** *n* (*wallet*) portefeuille *m*; (*notebook*) carnet *m*; **~ knife** *n* canif *m*; **~ money** *n* argent *m* de poche.
pockmarked ['pɔkmɑ:kt] *a* (*face*) grêlé(e).
pod [pɔd] *n* cosse *f* // *vt* écosser.
podgy ['pɔdʒɪ] *a* rondelet(te).
poem ['pəuɪm] *n* poème *m*.
poet ['pəuɪt] *n* poète *m*; **~ic** [-'ɛtɪk] *a* poétique; **~ laureate** *n* poète lauréat (*nommé et appointé par la Cour royale*); **~ry** *n* poésie *f*.
poignant ['pɔɪnjənt] *a* poignant(e); (*sharp*) vif(vive).
point [pɔɪnt] *n* (*tip*) pointe *f*; (*in time*) moment *m*; (*in space*) endroit *m*; (GEOM, SCOL, SPORT, *on scale*) point *m*; (*subject, idea*) point *m*, sujet *m*; (*also*: **decimal ~**): **2 ~ 3 (2.3)** 2 virgule 3 (2,3) // *vt* (*show*) indiquer; (*wall, window*) jointoyer; (*gun etc*): **to ~ sth at** braquer *or* diriger qch sur // *vi* montrer du doigt; **~s** *npl* (AUT) vis platinées; (RAIL) aiguillage *m*; **to make a ~** faire une remarque; **to make one's ~** se faire comprendre; **to get the ~** comprendre, saisir; **to come to the ~** en venir au fait; **there's no ~ (in doing)** cela ne sert à rien (de faire); **good ~s** qualités *fpl*; **to ~ out** *vt* faire remarquer, souligner; **to ~ to** montrer du doigt; (*fig*) signaler; **~-blank** *ad* (*also*: **at ~-blank range**) à bout portant; (*fig*) catégorique; **~ed** *a* (*shape*) pointu(e); (*remark*) plein(e) de sous-entendus; **~edly** *ad* d'une manière significative; **~er** *n* (*stick*) baguette *f*; (*needle*) aiguille *f*; (*dog*) chien *m* d'arrêt; **~less** *a* inutile, vain(e); **~ of view** *n* point *m* de vue.
poise [pɔɪz] *n* (*balance*) équilibre *m*; (*of head, body*) port *m*; (*calmness*) calme *m* // *vt* placer en équilibre; **to be ~d for** (*fig*) être prêt à.
poison ['pɔɪzn] *n* poison *m* // *vt* empoisonner; **~ing** *n* empoisonnement *m*; **~ous** *a* (*snake*) venimeux(euse); (*substance etc*) vénéneux(euse).
poke [pəuk] *vt* (*fire*) tisonner; (*jab with finger, stick etc*) piquer; pousser du doigt; (*put*): **to ~ sth in(to)** fourrer *or* enfoncer qch dans // *n* (*to fire*) coup *m* de tisonnier; **to ~ about** *vi* fureter.
poker ['pəukə*] *n* tisonnier *m*; (CARDS) poker *m*; **~-faced** *a* au visage impassible.
poky ['pəukɪ] *a* exigu(ë).
Poland ['pəulənd] *n* Pologne *f*.
polar ['pəulə*] *a* polaire; **~ bear** *n* ours blanc.
polarize ['pəuləraɪz] *vt* polariser.
pole [pəul] *n* (*of wood*) mât *m*, perche *f*; (ELEC) poteau *m*; (GEO) pôle *m*.
Pole [pəul] *n* Polonais/e.
polecat ['pəulkæt] *n* (*US*) putois *m*.
polemic [pɔ'lɛmɪk] *n* polémique *f*.
pole star ['pəulstɑ:*] *n* étoile polaire *f*.
pole vault ['pəulvɔ:lt] *n* saut *m* à la perche.
police [pə'li:s] *n* police *f*, (*man*: *pl inv*) policier *m*, homme *m*; // *vt* maintenir l'ordre dans; **~ car** *n* voiture *f* de police; **~man** *n* agent *m* de police, policier *m*; **~ record** *n* casier *m* judiciaire; **~ state** *n* état policier; **~ station** *n* commissariat *m* de police; **~woman** *n* femme-agent *f*.
policy ['pɔlɪsɪ] *n* politique *f*; (*also*: **insurance ~**) police *f* (d'assurance).
polio ['pəulɪəu] *n* polio *f*.
Polish ['pəulɪʃ] *a* polonais(e) // *n* (LING) polonais *m*.
polish ['pɔlɪʃ] *n* (*for shoes*) cirage *m*; (*for floor*) cire *f*, encaustique *f*; (*for nails*) vernis *m*; (*shine*) éclat *m*, poli *m*; (*fig*: *refinement*) raffinement *m* // *vt* (*put polish on shoes, wood*) cirer; (*make shiny*) astiquer, faire briller; (*fig*: *improve*) perfectionner; **to ~ off** *vt* (*work*) expédier; (*food*) liquider; **~ed** *a* (*fig*) raffiné(e).
polite [pə'laɪt] *a* poli(e); **~ly** *ad* poliment; **~ness** *n* politesse *f*.
politic ['pɔlɪtɪk] *a* diplomatique; **~al** [pə'lɪtɪkl] *a* politique; **~ian** [-'tɪʃən] *n* homme *m* politique, politicien *m*; **~s** *npl* politique *f*.
polka ['pɔlkə] *n* polka *f*; **~ dot** *n* pois *m*.
poll [pəul] *n* scrutin *m*, vote *m*; (*also*: **opinion ~**) sondage *m* (d'opinion) // *vt* obtenir.
pollen ['pɔlən] *n* pollen *m*; **~ count** *n* taux *m* de pollen.

pollination [pɔlɪ'neɪʃən] *n* pollinisation *f.*
polling booth ['pəulɪŋbu:ð] *n* isoloir *m.*
polling day ['pəulɪŋdeɪ] *n* jour *m* des élections.
polling station ['pəlɪŋsteɪʃən] *n* bureau *m* de vote.
pollute [pə'lu:t] *vt* polluer.
pollution [pə'lu:ʃən] *n* pollution *f.*
polo ['pəuləu] *n* polo *m*; **~-neck** *a* à col roulé.
polyester [pɔlɪ'ɛstə*] *n* polyester *m.*
polygamy [pə'lɪgəmɪ] *n* polygamie *f.*
Polynesia [pɔlɪ'ni:zɪə] *n* Polynésie *f.*
polytechnic [pɔlɪ'tɛknɪk] *n* (*college*) I.U.T. *m*, Institut *m* Universitaire de Technologie.
polythene ['pɔlɪθi:n] *n* polyéthylène *m*; **~ bag** *n* sac *m* en plastique.
pomegranate ['pɔmɪgrænɪt] *n* grenade *f.*
pommel ['pɔml] *n* pommeau *m.*
pomp [pɔmp] *n* pompe *f*, faste *f*, apparat *m.*
pompous ['pɔmpəs] *a* pompeux(euse).
pond [pɔnd] *n* étang *m*; mare *f.*
ponder ['pɔndə*] *vi* réfléchir // *vt* considérer, peser; **~ous** *a* pesant(e), lourd(e).
pontiff ['pɔntɪf] *n* pontife *m.*
pontificate [pɔn'tɪfɪkeɪt] *vi* (*fig*): **to ~ (about)** pontifier (sur).
pontoon [pɔn'tu:n] *n* ponton *m.*
pony ['pəunɪ] *n* poney *m*; **~tail** *n* queue *f* de cheval; **~ trekking** *n* randonnée *f* à cheval.
poodle ['pu:dl] *n* caniche *m.*
pooh-pooh [pu:pu:] *vt* dédaigner.
pool [pu:l] *n* (*of rain*) flaque *f*; (*pond*) mare *f*; (*artificial*) bassin *m*; (*also*: **swimming ~**) piscine *f*; (*sth shared*) fonds commun; (*money at cards*) cagnotte *f*; (*billiards*) poule *f* // *vt* mettre en commun.
poor [puə*] *a* pauvre; (*mediocre*) médiocre, faible, mauvais(e) // *npl*: **the ~** les pauvres *mpl*; **~ly** *ad* pauvrement; médiocrement // *a* souffrant(e), malade.
pop [pɔp] *n* (*noise*) bruit sec; (*MUS*) musique *f* pop; (*US*: *col*: *father*) papa *m* // *vt* (*put*) fourrer, mettre (rapidement) // *vi* éclater; (*cork*) sauter; **to ~ in** *vi* entrer en passant; **to ~ out** *vi* sortir; **to ~ up** *vi* apparaître, surgir; **~ concert** *n* concert *m* pop; **~corn** *n* pop-corn *m.*
pope [pəup] *n* pape *m.*
poplar ['pɔplə*] *n* peuplier *m.*
poplin ['pɔplɪn] *n* popeline *f.*
poppy ['pɔpɪ] *n* coquelicot *m*; pavot *m.*
populace ['pɔpjuləs] *n* peuple *m.*
popular ['pɔpjulə*] *a* populaire; (*fashionable*) à la mode; **~ity** [-'lærɪtɪ] *n* popularité *f*; **~ize** *vt* populariser; (*science*) vulgariser.
populate ['pɔpjuleɪt] *vt* peupler.
population [pɔpju'leɪʃən] *n* population *f.*
populous ['pɔpjuləs] *a* populeux(euse).
porcelain ['pɔ:slɪn] *n* porcelaine *f.*
porch [pɔ:tʃ] *n* porche *m.*
porcupine ['pɔ:kjupaɪn] *n* porc-épic *m.*
pore [pɔ:*] *n* pore *m* // *vi*: **to ~ over** s'absorber dans, être plongé(e) dans.
pork [pɔ:k] *n* porc *m.*
pornographic [pɔ:nə'græfɪk] *a* pornographique.
pornography [pɔ:'nɔgrəfɪ] *n* pornographie *f.*
porous ['pɔ:rəs] *a* poreux(euse).
porpoise ['pɔ:pəs] *n* marsouin *m.*
porridge ['pɔrɪdʒ] *n* porridge *m.*
port [pɔ:t] *n* (*harbour*) port *m*; (*opening in ship*) sabord *m*; (*NAUT*: *left side*) bâbord *m*; (*wine*) porto *m*; **to ~** (*NAUT*) à bâbord.
portable ['pɔ:təbl] *a* portatif(ive).
portal ['pɔ:tl] *n* portail *m.*
portcullis [pɔ:t'kʌlɪs] *n* herse *f.*
portend [pɔ:'tɛnd] *vt* présager, annoncer.
portent ['pɔ:tɛnt] *n* présage *m.*
porter ['pɔ:tə*] *n* (*for luggage*) porteur *m*; (*doorkeeper*) gardien/ne; portier *m.*
porthole ['pɔ:thəul] *n* hublot *m.*
portico ['pɔ:tɪkəu] *n* portique *m.*
portion ['pɔ:ʃən] *n* portion *f*, part *f.*
portly ['pɔ:tlɪ] *a* corpulent(e).
portrait ['pɔ:treɪt] *n* portrait *m.*
portray [pɔ:'treɪ] *vt* faire le portrait de; (*in writing*) dépeindre, représenter; **~al** *n* portrait *m*, représentation *f.*
Portugal ['pɔ:tjugl] *n* Portugal *m.*
Portuguese [pɔ:tju'gi:z] *a* portugais(e) // *n, pl inv* Portugais/e; (*LING*) portugais *m.*
pose [pəuz] *n* pose *f*; (*pej*) affectation *f* // *vi* poser; (*pretend*): **to ~ as** se poser en // *vt* poser, créer; **~r** *n* question embarrassante.
posh [pɔʃ] *a* (*col*) chic *inv.*
position [pə'zɪʃən] *n* position *f*; (*job*) situation *f* // *vt* mettre en place *or* en position.
positive ['pɔzɪtɪv] *a* positif(ive); (*certain*) sûr(e), certain(e); (*definite*) formel(le), catégorique; indéniable, réel(le).
posse ['pɔsɪ] *n* (*US*) détachement *m.*
possess [pə'zɛs] *vt* posséder; **~ion** [pə'zɛʃən] *n* possession *f*; **~ive** *a* possessif(ive); **~ively** *ad* d'une façon possessive; **~or** *n* possesseur *m.*
possibility [pɔsɪ'bɪlɪtɪ] *n* possibilité *f*; éventualité *f.*
possible ['pɔsɪbl] *a* possible; **if ~** si possible; **as big as ~** aussi gros que possible.
possibly ['pɔsɪblɪ] *ad* (*perhaps*) peut-être; **if you ~ can** si cela vous est possible; **I cannot ~ come** il m'est impossible de venir.
post [pəust] *n* poste *f*; (*collection*) levée *f*; (*letters, delivery*) courrier *m*; (*job, situation*) poste *m*; (*pole*) poteau *m* // *vt* (*send by post, MIL*) poster; (*appoint*): **to ~ to** affecter à; (*notice*) afficher; **~age** *n* affranchissement *m*; **~al** *a* postal(e); **~al order** *n* mandat(-poste) *m*; **~box** *n* boîte *f* aux lettres; **~card** *n* carte postale.
postdate [pəustdeɪt] *vt* (*cheque*) postdater.
poster ['pəustə*] *n* affiche *f.*
poste restante [pəust'rɛstɑ̃:nt] *n* poste restante.
posterior [pɔs'tɪərɪə*] *n* (*col*) postérieur *m*, derrière *m.*
posterity [pɔs'tɛrɪtɪ] *n* postérité *f.*
postgraduate ['pəust'grædjuət] *n* ≈ étudiant/e de troisième cycle.

posthumous ['pɔstjuməs] *a* posthume; **~ly** *ad* après la mort de l'auteur, à titre posthume.
postman ['pəustmən] *n* facteur *m*.
postmark ['pəustmɑːk] *n* cachet *m* (de la poste).
postmaster ['pəustmɑːstə*] *n* receveur *m* des postes.
post-mortem [pəust'mɔːtəm] *n* autopsie *f*.
post office ['pəustɔfɪs] *n* (*building*) poste *f*; (*organization*) postes *fpl*; **~ box (P.O. box)** *n* boîte postale (B.P.).
postpone [pəs'pəun] *vt* remettre (à plus tard), reculer; **~ment** *n* ajournement *m*, renvoi *m*.
postscript ['pəustskrɪpt] *n* post-scriptum *m*.
postulate ['pɔstjuleɪt] *vt* postuler.
posture ['pɔstʃə*] *n* posture *f*, attitude *f* // *vi* poser.
postwar [pəust'wɔː*] *a* d'après-guerre.
posy ['pəuzɪ] *n* petit bouquet.
pot [pɔt] *n* (*for cooking*) marmite *f*; casserole *f*; (*for plants, jam*) pot *m*; (*col*: *marijuana*) herbe *f* // *vt* (*plant*) mettre en pot; **to go to ~** aller à vau-l'eau.
potash ['pɔtæʃ] *n* potasse *f*.
potato, ~es [pə'teɪtəu] *n* pomme *f* de terre; **~ flour** *n* fécule *f*.
potency ['pəutnsɪ] *n* puissance *f*, force *f*; (*of drink*) degré *m* d'alcool.
potent ['pəutnt] *a* puissant(e); (*drink*) fort(e), très alcoolisé(e).
potentate ['pəutnteɪt] *n* potentat *m*.
potential [pə'tɛnʃl] *a* potentiel(le) // *n* potentiel *m*; **~ly** *ad* en puissance.
pothole ['pɔthəul] *n* (*in road*) nid *m* de poule; (*underground*) gouffre *m*, caverne *f*; **~r** *n* spéléologue *m/f*; **potholing** *n*: **to go potholing** faire de la spéléologie.
potion ['pəuʃən] *n* potion *f*.
potluck [pɔt'lʌk] *n*: **to take ~** tenter sa chance.
potpourri [pəu'puriː] *n* pot-pourri *m*.
potshot ['pɔtʃɔt] *n*: **to take ~s at** canarder.
potted ['pɔtɪd] *a* (*food*) en conserve; (*plant*) en pot.
potter ['pɔtə*] *n* potier *m* // *vt*: **to ~ around, ~ about** bricoler; **~y** *n* poterie *f*.
potty ['pɔtɪ] *a* (*col*: *mad*) dingue // *n* (*child's*) pot *m*; **~-training** *n* apprentissage *m* de la propreté.
pouch [pautʃ] *n* (ZOOL) poche *f*; (*for tobacco*) blague *f*.
pouf(fe) [puːf] *n* (*stool*) pouf *m*.
poultice ['pəultɪs] *n* cataplasme *m*.
poultry ['pəultrɪ] *n* volaille *f*; **~ farm** *n* élevage *m* de volaille.
pounce [pauns] *vi*: **to ~ (on)** bondir (sur), fondre sur // *n* bond *m*, attaque *f*.
pound [paund] *n* livre *f* (*weight = 453g, 16 ounces; money = 100 new pence, 20 shillings*); (*for dogs, cars*) fourrière *f* // *vt* (*beat*) bourrer de coups, marteler; (*crush*) piler, pulvériser; (*with guns*) pilonner // *vi* (*beat*) battre violemment, taper; **~ sterling** *n* livre *f* sterling.
pour [pɔː*] *vt* verser // *vi* couler à flots; (*rain*) pleuvoir à verse; **to ~ away** *or* **off** *vt* vider; **to ~ in** *vi* (*people*) affluer, se précipiter; **to ~ out** *vi* (*people*) sortir en masse // *vt* vider; déverser; (*serve*: *a drink*) verser; **~ing** *a*: **~ing rain** pluie torrentielle.
pout [paut] *n* moue *f* // *vi* faire la moue.
poverty ['pɔvətɪ] *n* pauvreté *f*, misère *f*; **~-stricken** *a* pauvre, déshérité(e).
powder ['paudə*] *n* poudre *f* // *vt* poudrer; **~ room** *n* toilettes *fpl* (pour dames); **~y** *a* poudreux(euse).
power ['pauə*] *n* (*strength*) puissance *f*, force *f*; (*ability*, POL: *of party, leader*) pouvoir *m*; (MATH) puissance *f*; (*mental*) facultés mentales; (ELEC) courant *m* // *vt* faire marcher; **~ cut** *n* coupure *f* de courant; **~ed** *a*: **~ed by** actionné(e) par, fonctionnant à; **~ful** *a* puissant(e); **~less** *a* impuissant(e); **~ line** *n* ligne *f* électrique; **~ point** *n* prise *f* de courant; **~ station** *n* centrale *f* électrique.
powwow ['pauwau] *n* assemblée *f*.
pox [pɔks] *n* see **chicken**.
p.p. *abbr* (= *per procurationem*): **~ J. Smith** pour M. J. Smith.
P.R. *abbr of* **public relations**.
practicability [præktɪkə'bɪlɪtɪ] *n* possibilité *f* de réalisation.
practicable ['præktɪkəbl] *a* (*scheme*) réalisable.
practical ['præktɪkl] *a* pratique; **~ joke** *n* farce *f*; **~ly** *ad* (*almost*) pratiquement.
practice ['præktɪs] *n* pratique *f*; (*of profession*) exercice *m*; (*at football etc*) entraînement *m*; (*business*) cabinet *m*; clientèle *f* // *vt,vi* (*US*) = **practise**; **in ~** (*in reality*) en pratique; **out of ~** rouillé(e); **2 hours' piano ~** 2 heures de travail *or* d'exercices au piano; **~ match** *n* match *m* d'entraînement.
practise, (US) practice ['præktɪs] *vt* (*work at*: *piano, one's backhand etc*) s'exercer à, travailler; (*train for*: *skiing, running etc*) s'entraîner à; (*a sport, religion, method*) pratiquer; (*profession*) exercer // *vi* s'exercer, travailler; (*train*) s'entraîner; **to ~ for a match** s'entraîner pour un match; **practising** *a* (*Christian etc*) pratiquant(e); (*lawyer*) en exercice.
practitioner [præk'tɪʃənə*] *n* praticien/ne.
pragmatic [præg'mætɪk] *a* pragmatique.
prairie ['prɛərɪ] *n* savane *f*; (*US*): **the ~s** la Prairie.
praise [preɪz] *n* éloge(s) *m(pl)*, louange(s) *f(pl)* // *vt* louer, faire l'éloge de; **~worthy** *a* digne de louanges.
pram [præm] *n* landau *m*, voiture *f* d'enfant.
prance [prɑːns] *vi* (*horse*) caracoler.
prank [præŋk] *n* farce *f*.
prattle ['prætl] *vi* jacasser.
prawn [prɔːn] *n* crevette *f* (rose).
pray [preɪ] *vi* prier.
prayer [prɛə*] *n* prière *f*; **~ book** *n* livre *m* de prières.
preach [priːtʃ] *vt,vi* prêcher; **to ~ at sb** faire la morale à qn; **~er** *n* prédicateur *m*.

preamble [prɪ'æmbl] *n* préambule *m.*
prearranged [pri:ə'reɪndʒd] *a* organisé(e) *or* fixé(e) à l'avance.
precarious [prɪ'kɛərɪəs] *a* précaire.
precaution [prɪ'kɔ:ʃən] *n* précaution *f*; **~ary** *a* (*measure*) de précaution.
precede [prɪ'si:d] *vt,vi* précéder.
precedence ['prɛsɪdəns] *n* préséance *f.*
precedent ['prɛsɪdənt] *n* précédent *m.*
preceding [prɪ'si:dɪŋ] *a* qui précède (*or* précédait).
precept ['pri:sɛpt] *n* précepte *m.*
precinct ['pri:sɪŋkt] *n* (*round cathedral*) pourtour *m*, enceinte *f*; **pedestrian ~** *n* zone piétonnière; **shopping ~** *n* centre commerical.
precious ['prɛʃəs] *a* précieux(euse).
precipice ['prɛsɪpɪs] *n* précipice *m.*
precipitate *a* [prɪ'sɪpɪtɪt] (*hasty*) précipité(e) // *vt* [prɪ'sɪpɪteɪt] précipiter; **precipitation** [-'teɪʃən] *n* précipitation *f.*
precipitous [prɪ'sɪpɪtəs] *a* (*steep*) abrupt(e), à pic.
précis, *pl* **précis** ['preɪsi:, -z] *n* résumé *m.*
precise [prɪ'saɪs] *a* précis(e); **~ly** *ad* précisément.
preclude [prɪ'klu:d] *vt* exclure, empêcher; **to ~ sb from doing** empêcher qn de faire.
precocious [prɪ'kəuʃəs] *a* précoce.
preconceived [pri:kən'si:vd] *a* (*idea*) préconçu(e).
precondition [pri:kən'dɪʃən] *n* condition *f* nécessaire.
precursor [pri:'kə:sə*] *n* précurseur *m.*
predator ['prɛdətə*] *n* prédateur *m*, rapace *m*; **~y** *a* rapace.
predecessor ['pri:dɪsɛsə*] *n* prédécesseur *m.*
predestination [pri:dɛstɪ'neɪʃən] *n* prédestination *f.*
predetermine [pri:dɪ'tə:mɪn] *vt* déterminer à l'avance.
predicament [prɪ'dɪkəmənt] *n* situation *f* difficile.
predicate ['prɛdɪkɪt] *n* (LING) prédicat *m.*
predict [prɪ'dɪkt] *vt* prédire; **~ion** [-'dɪkʃən] *n* prédiction *f.*
predominance [prɪ'dɔmɪnəns] *n* prédominance *f.*
predominant [prɪ'dɔmɪnənt] *a* prédominant(e); **~ly** *ad* en majeure partie; surtout.
predominate [prɪ'dɔmɪneɪt] *vi* prédominer.
pre-eminent [pri:'ɛmɪnənt] *a* prééminent(e).
pre-empt [pri:'ɛmt] *vt* acquérir par droit de préemption; (*fig*): **to ~ the issue** conclure avant même d'ouvrir les débats.
preen [pri:n] *vt*: **to ~ itself** (*bird*) se lisser les plumes; **to ~ o.s.** s'admirer.
prefab ['pri:fæb] *n* bâtiment préfabriqué.
prefabricated [pri:'fæbrikeɪtɪd] *a* préfabriqué(e).
preface ['prɛfəs] *n* préface *f.*
prefect ['pri:fɛkt] *n* (*Brit: in school*) *élève chargé(e) de certaines fonctions de discipline*; (*in France*) préfet *m.*
prefer [prɪ'fə:*] *vt* préférer; **~able** ['prɛfrəbl] *a* préférable; **~ably** ['prɛfrəblɪ] *ad* de préférence; **~ence** ['prɛfrəns] *n* préférence *f*; **~ential** [prɛfə'rɛnʃəl] *a* préférentiel(le) **~ential treatment** traitement *m* de faveur.
prefix ['pri:fɪks] *n* préfixe *m.*
pregnancy ['prɛgnənsɪ] *n* grossesse *f.*
pregnant ['prɛgnənt] *a* enceinte *af.*
prehistoric ['pri:hɪs'tɔrɪk] *a* préhistorique.
prehistory [pri:'hɪstərɪ] *n* préhistoire *f.*
prejudge [pri:'dʒʌdʒ] *vt* préjuger de.
prejudice ['prɛdʒudɪs] *n* préjugé *m*; (*harm*) tort *m*, préjudice *m* // *vt* porter préjudice à; **~d** *a* (*person*) plein(e) de préjugés; (*view*) préconçu(e), partial(e).
prelate ['prɛlət] *n* prélat *m.*
preliminary [prɪ'lɪmɪnərɪ] *a* préliminaire; **preliminaries** *npl* préliminaires *mpl.*
prelude ['prɛlju:d] *n* prélude *m.*
premarital ['pri:'mærɪtl] *a* avant le mariage.
premature ['prɛmətʃuə*] *a* prématuré(e).
premeditated [pri:'mɛdɪteɪtɪd] *a* prémédité(e).
premeditation [pri:mɛdɪ'teɪʃən] *n* préméditation *f.*
premier ['prɛmɪə*] *a* premier(ère), capital(e), primordial(e) // *n* (POL) premier ministre.
première ['prɛmɪɛə*] *n* première *f.*
premise ['prɛmɪs] *n* prémisse *f*; **~s** *npl* locaux *mpl*; **on the ~s** sur les lieux; sur place.
premium ['pri:mɪəm] *n* prime *f.*
premonition [prɛmə'nɪʃən] *n* prémonition *f.*
preoccupation [pri:ɔkju'peɪʃən] *n* préoccupation *f.*
preoccupied [pri:'ɔkjupaɪd] *a* préoccupé(e).
prep [prɛp] *n* (SCOL: *study*) étude *f*; **~ school** *n* = **preparatory school.**
prepackaged [pri:'pækɪdʒd] *a* préempaqueté(e).
prepaid [pri:'peɪd] *a* payé(e) d'avance.
preparation [prɛpə'reɪʃən] *n* préparation *f*; **~s** *npl* (*for trip, war*) préparatifs *mpl.*
preparatory [prɪ'pærətərɪ] *a* préparatoire; **~ school** *n* école primaire privée.
prepare [prɪ'pɛə*] *vt* préparer // *vi*: **to ~ for** se préparer à; **~d for** preparé(e) à; **~d to** prêt(e) à.
preponderance [prɪ'pɔndərns] *n* prépondérance *f.*
preposition [prɛpə'zɪʃən] *n* préposition *f.*
preposterous [prɪ'pɔstərəs] *a* absurde.
prerequisite [pri:'rɛkwɪzɪt] *n* condition *f* préalable.
prerogative [prɪ'rɔgətɪv] *n* prérogative *f.*
presbyterian [prɛzbɪ'tɪərɪən] *a,n* presbytérien(ne).
presbytery ['prɛzbɪtərɪ] *n* presbytère *m.*
preschool ['pri:'sku:l] *a* préscolaire.
prescribe [prɪ'skraɪb] *vt* prescrire.
prescription [prɪ'skrɪpʃən] *n* prescription *f*; (MED) ordonnance *f.*
prescriptive [prɪ'skrɪptɪv] *a* normatif(ive).
presence ['prɛzns] *n* présence *f*; **~ of mind** *n* présence d'esprit.
present ['prɛznt] *a* présent(e) // *n* cadeau *m*; (*also*: **~ tense**) présent *m* // *vt*

[prɪ'zɛnt] présenter ; (*give*): **to ~ sb with sth** offrir qch à qn ; **at ~** en ce moment ; **~able** [prɪ'zɛntəbl] *a* présentable ; **~ation** [-'teɪʃən] *n* présentation *f*; (*gift*) cadeau *m*, présent *m* ; (*ceremony*) remise *f* du cadeau ; **~-day** *a* contemporain(e), actuel(le) ; **~ly** *ad* (*soon*) tout à l'heure, bientôt ; (*at present*) en ce moment.

preservation [prɛzə'veɪʃən] *n* préservation *f*, conservation *f*.

preservative [prɪ'zə:vətɪv] *n* agent *m* de conservation.

preserve [prɪ'zə:v] *vt* (*keep safe*) préserver, protéger ; (*maintain*) conserver, garder ; (*food*) mettre en conserve // *n* (*for game, fish*) réserve *f*; (*often pl*: *jam*) confiture *f*; (: *fruit*) fruits *mpl* en conserve.

preside [prɪ'zaɪd] *vi* présider.

presidency ['prɛzɪdənsɪ] *n* présidence *f*.

president ['prɛzɪdənt] *n* président/e ; **~ial** ['dɛnʃl] *a* présidentiel(le).

press [prɛs] *n* (*tool, machine, newspapers*) presse *f*; (*for wine*) pressoir *m*; (*crowd*) cohue *f*, foule *f* // *vt* (*push*) appuyer sur ; (*squeeze*) presser, serrer ; (*clothes*: *iron*) repasser ; (*pursue*) talonner ; (*insist*): **to ~ sth on sb** presser qn d'accepter qch // *vi* appuyer, peser ; se presser ; **we are ~ed for time** le temps nous manque ; **to ~ for sth** faire pression pour obtenir qch ; **to ~ on** *vi* continuer ; **~ agency** *n* agence *f* de presse ; **~ conference** *n* conférence *f* de presse ; **~ cutting** *n* coupure *f* de presse ; **~-gang** *n recruteurs de la marine* (*jusqu'au 19ème siècle*) ; **~ing** *a* urgent(e), pressant(e) // *n* repassage *m* ; **~ stud** *n* bouton-pression *m*.

pressure ['prɛʃə*] *n* pression *f*; (*stress*) tension *f*; **~ cooker** *n* cocotte-minute *f*; **~ gauge** *n* manomètre *m* ; **~ group** *n* groupe *m* de pression ; **pressurized** *a* pressurisé(e).

prestige [prɛs'ti:ʒ] *n* prestige *m*.

prestigious [prɛs'tɪdʒəs] *a* prestigieux(euse).

presumably [prɪ'zju:məblɪ] *ad* vraisemblablement.

presume [prɪ'zju:m] *vt* présumer, supposer ; **to ~ to do** (*dare*) se permettre de faire.

presumption [prɪ'zʌmpʃən] *n* supposition *f*, présomption *f*; (*boldness*) audace *f*.

presumptuous [prɪ'zʌmpʃəs] *a* présomptueux(euse).

presuppose [pri:sə'pəuz] *vt* présupposer.

pretence, pretense (*US*) [prɪ'tɛns] *n* (*claim*) prétention *f*; **to make a ~ of doing** faire semblant de faire ; **on the ~ of** sous le prétexte de.

pretend [prɪ'tɛnd] *vt* (*feign*) feindre, simuler // *vi* (*feign*) faire semblant ; (*claim*): **to ~ to sth** prétendre à qch ; **to ~ to do** faire semblant de faire.

pretense [prɪ'tɛns] *n* (*US*) = **pretence.**

pretentious [prɪ'tɛnʃəs] *a* prétentieux(euse).

preterite ['prɛtərɪt] *n* prétérit *m*.

pretext ['pri:tɛkst] *n* prétexte *m*.

pretty ['prɪtɪ] *a* joli(e) // *ad* assez.

prevail [prɪ'veɪl] *vi* (*win*) l'emporter, prévaloir ; (*be usual*) avoir cours ; (*persuade*): **to ~ (up)on sb to do** persuader qn de faire ; **~ing** *a* dominant(e).

prevalent ['prɛvələnt] *a* répandu(e), courant(e).

prevarication [prɪværɪ'keɪʃən] *n* (usage *m* de) faux-fuyants *mpl*.

prevent [prɪ'vɛnt] *vt*: **to ~ (from doing)** empêcher (de faire) ; **~able** *a* évitable ; **~ative** *a* préventif(ive) ; **~ion** [-'vɛnʃən] *n* prévention *f*; **~ive** *a* préventif(ive).

preview ['pri:vju:] *n* (*of film*) avant-première *f*; (*fig*) aperçu *m*.

previous ['pri:vɪəs] *a* précédent(e) ; antérieur(e) ; **~ to doing** avant de faire ; **~ly** *ad* précédemment, auparavant.

prewar [pri:'wɔ:*] *a* d'avant-guerre.

prey [preɪ] *n* proie *f* // *vi*: **to ~ on** s'attaquer à ; **it was ~ing on his mind** ça le rongeait *or* minait.

price [praɪs] *n* prix *m* // *vt* (*goods*) fixer le prix de ; tarifer ; **~less** *a* sans prix, inestimable ; **~ list** *n* liste *f* des prix, tarif *m*.

prick [prɪk] *n* piqûre *f* // *vt* piquer ; **to ~ up one's ears** dresser *or* tendre l'oreille.

prickle ['prɪkl] *n* (*of plant*) épine *f*; (*sensation*) picotement *m*.

prickly ['prɪklɪ] *a* piquant(e), épineux(euse) ; (*fig*: *person*) irritable ; **~ heat** *n* fièvre *f* miliaire ; **~ pear** *n* figue *f* de Barbarie.

pride [praɪd] *n* orgueil *m* ; fierté *f* // *vt*: **to ~ o.s. on** se flatter de ; s'enorgueillir de.

priest [pri:st] *n* prêtre *m* ; **~ess** *n* prêtresse *f*; **~hood** *n* prêtrise *f*, sacerdoce *m*.

prig [prɪg] *n* poseur/euse, fat *m*.

prim [prɪm] *a* collet monté *inv*, guindé(e).

primarily ['praɪmərɪlɪ] *ad* principalement, essentiellement.

primary ['praɪmərɪ] *a* primaire ; (*first in importance*) premier(ère), primordial(e) ; **~ colour** *n* couleur fondamentale ; **~ school** *n* école primaire *f*.

primate *n* (REL) ['praɪmɪt] primat *m* ; (ZOOL) ['praɪmeɪt] primate *m*.

prime [praɪm] *a* primordial(e), fondamental(e) ; (*excellent*) excellent(e) // *vt* (*gun, pump*) amorcer ; (*fig*) mettre au courant ; **in the ~ of life** dans la fleur de l'âge ; **~ minister (P.M.)** *n* premier ministre ; **~r** *n* (*book*) premier livre, manuel *m* élémentaire ; (*paint*) apprêt *m* ; (*of gun*) amorce *f*.

primeval [praɪ'mi:vl] *a* primitif(ive).

primitive ['prɪmɪtɪv] *a* primitif(ive).

primrose ['prɪmrəuz] *n* primevère *f*.

primus (stove) ['praɪməs(stəuv)] *n* ® réchaud *m* de camping.

prince [prɪns] *n* prince *m*.

princess [prɪn'sɛs] *n* princesse *f*.

principal ['prɪnsɪpl] *a* principal(e) // *n* (*headmaster*) directeur *m*, principal *m* ; (*money*) capital *m*, principal *m*.

principality [prɪnsɪ'pælɪtɪ] *n* principauté *f*.

principally ['prɪnsɪplɪ] *ad* principalement.

principle ['prɪnsɪpl] *n* principe *m*.

print [prɪnt] *n* (*mark*) empreinte *f*; (*letters*) caractères *mpl* ; (*fabric*) imprimé *m* ; (ART) gravure *f*, estampe *f*; (PHOT) épreuve *f* // *vt* imprimer ; (*publish*) publier ; (*write in capitals*) écrire en majuscules ; **out of ~** épuisé(e) ; **~ed matter** *n* imprimés *mpl*; **~er** *n* imprimeur *m*; **~ing** *n* impression *f*; **~ing press** *n* presse *f* typographique ; **~-out** *n* listage *m*.

prior ['praɪə*] *a* antérieur(e), précédent(e) // *n* prieur *m* ; **~ to doing** avant de faire.

priority [praɪ'ɔrɪtɪ] *n* priorité *f*.

priory ['praɪərɪ] *n* prieuré *m*.

prise [praɪz] *vt*: **to ~ open** forcer.

prism ['prɪzəm] *n* prisme *m*.

prison ['prɪzn] *n* prison *f*; **~er** *n* prisonnier/ère.

prissy ['prɪsɪ] *a* bégueule.

pristine ['prɪsti:n] *a* virginal(e).

privacy ['prɪvəsɪ] *n* intimité *f*, solitude *f*.

private ['praɪvɪt] *a* privé(e) ; personnel(le) ; (*house, car, lesson*) particulier(ère) // *n* soldat *m* de deuxième classe ; **'~'** (*on envelope*) 'personnelle' ; **in ~** en privé ; **~ eye** *n* détective privé ; **~ly** *ad* en privé ; (*within oneself*) intérieurement.

privet ['prɪvɪt] *n* troène *m*.

privilege ['prɪvɪlɪdʒ] *n* privilège *m* ; **~d** *a* privilégié(e).

privy ['prɪvɪ] *a*: **to be ~ to** être au courant de ; **P~ council** *n* conseil privé.

prize [praɪz] *n* prix *m* // *a* (*example, idiot*) parfait(e) ; (*bull, novel*) primé(e) // *vt* priser, faire grand cas de ; **~ fight** *n* combat professionnel ; **~ giving** *n* distribution *f* des prix ; **~winner** *n* gagnant/e.

pro [prəu] *n* (SPORT) professionnel/le ; **the ~s and cons** le pour et le contre.

probability [prɔbə'bɪlɪtɪ] *n* probabilité *f*.

probable ['prɔbəbl] *a* probable ; **probably** *ad* probablement.

probation [prə'beɪʃən] *n* (*in employment*) essai *m*; (LAW) liberté surveillée ; (REL) noviciat *m*, probation *f*; **on ~** (*employee*) à l'essai ; (LAW) en liberté surveillée ; **~ary** *a* (*period*) d'essai.

probe [prəub] *n* (MED, SPACE) sonde *f*; (*enquiry*) enquête *f*, investigation *f* // *vt* sonder, explorer.

probity ['prəubɪtɪ] *n* probité *f*.

problem ['prɔbləm] *n* problème *m* ; **~atic** [-'mætɪk] *a* problématique.

procedure [prə'si:dʒə*] *n* (ADMIN, LAW) procédure *f*; (*method*) marche *f* à suivre, façon *f* de procéder.

proceed [prə'si:d] *vi* (*go forward*) avancer ; (*go about it*) procéder ; (*continue*): **to ~ (with)** continuer, poursuivre ; **to ~ to** aller à ; passer à ; **to ~ to do** se mettre à faire ; **~ing** *n* procédé *m*, façon d'agir *f*; **~ings** *npl* mesures *fpl* ; (LAW) poursuites *fpl* ; (*meeting*) réunion *f*, séance *f*; (*records*) compte rendu ; actes *mpl*; **~s** ['prəusi:dz] *npl* produit *m*, recette *f*.

process ['prəusɛs] *n* processus *m*; (*method*) procédé *m* // *vt* traiter ; **~ed cheese** fromage fondu ; **in ~** en cours ; **~ing** *n* traitement *m*.

procession [prə'sɛʃən] *n* défilé *m*, cortège *m*; (REL) procession *f*.

proclaim [prə'kleɪm] *vt* déclarer, proclamer.

proclamation [prɔklə'meɪʃən] *n* proclamation *f*.

proclivity [prə'klɪvɪtɪ] *n* inclination *f*.

procrastination [prəukræstɪ'neɪʃən] *n* procrastination *f*.

procreation [prəukrɪ'eɪʃən] *n* procréation *f*.

procure [prə'kjuə*] *vt* (*for o.s.*) se procurer ; (*for sb*) procurer.

prod [prɔd] *vt* pousser // *n* (*push, jab*) petit coup, poussée *f*.

prodigal ['prɔdɪgl] *a* prodigue.

prodigious ['prə'dɪdʒəs] *a* prodigieux(euse).

prodigy ['prɔdɪdʒɪ] *n* prodige *m*.

produce *n* ['prɔdju:s] (AGR) produits *mpl* // *vt* [prə'dju:s] produire ; (*to show*) présenter ; (*cause*) provoquer, causer ; (THEATRE) monter, mettre en scène ; **~r** *n* (THEATRE) metteur *m* en scène ; (AGR, CINEMA) producteur *m*.

product ['prɔdʌkt] *n* produit *m*.

production [prə'dʌkʃən] *n* production *f*; (THEATRE) mise *f* en scène ; **~ line** *n* chaîne *f* (de fabrication).

productive [prə'dʌktɪv] *a* productif(ive).

productivity [prɔdʌk'tɪvɪtɪ] *n* productivité *f*.

profane [prə'feɪn] *a* sacrilège ; (*lay*) profane.

profess [prə'fɛs] *vt* professer.

profession [prə'fɛʃən] *n* profession *f*; **~al** *n* (SPORT) professionnel/le // *a* professionnel(le) ; (*work*) de professionnel ; **he's a ~al man** il exerce une profession libérale ; **~alism** *n* professionnalisme *m*.

professor [prə'fɛsə*] *n* professeur *m* (*titulaire d'une chaire*).

proficiency [prə'fɪʃənsɪ] *n* compétence *f*, aptitude *f*.

proficient [prə'fɪʃənt] *a* compétent(e), capable.

profile ['prəufaɪl] *n* profil *m*.

profit ['prɔfɪt] *n* bénéfice *m*; profit *m* // *vi*: **to ~ (by** *or* **from)** profiter (de) ; **~ability** [-'bɪlɪtɪ] *n* rentabilité *f*; **~able** *a* lucratif(ive), rentable.

profiteering [prɔfɪ'tɪərɪŋ] *n* (*pej*) mercantilisme *m*.

profound [prə'faund] *a* profond(e).

profuse [prə'fju:s] *a* abondant(e) ; (*with money*) prodigue ; **~ly** *ad* en abondance, profusion ; **profusion** [-'fju:ʒən] *n* profusion *f*, abondance *f*.

progeny ['prɔdʒɪnɪ] *n* progéniture *f*; descendants *mpl*.

programme, program (*US*) ['prəugræm] *n* programme *m*; (RADIO, TV) émission *f* // *vt* programmer ; **programming, programing** (*US*) *n* programmation *f*.

progress *n* ['prəugrɛs] progrès *m* // *vi* [prə'grɛs] progresser, avancer ; **in ~** en cours ; **to make ~** progresser, faire des progrès, être en progrès ; **~ion** [-'grɛʃən] *n* progression *f*; **~ive** [-'grɛsɪv] *a* progressif(ive) ; (*person*) progressiste ; **~ively** [-'grɛsɪvlɪ] *ad* progressivement.

prohibit [prə'hıbıt] *vt* interdire, défendre; **to ~ sb from doing** défendre *or* interdire à qn de faire; **~ion** [prəuı'bıʃən] *n* (*US*) prohibition *f*; **~ive** *a* (*price etc*) prohibitif(ive).
project *n* ['prɔdʒɛkt] (*plan*) projet *m*, plan *m*; (*venture*) opération *f*, entreprise *f*; (*gen* SCOL: *research*) étude *f*, dossier *m* // *vb* [prə'dʒɛkt] *vt* projeter // *vi* (*stick out*) faire saillie, s'avancer.
projectile [prə'dʒɛktaıl] *n* projectile *m*.
projection [prə'dʒɛkʃən] *n* projection *f*; saillie *f*.
projector [prə'dʒɛktə*] *n* projecteur *m*.
proletarian [prəulı'tɛərıən] *a* prolétarien(ne) // *n* prolétaire *m/f*.
proletariat [prəulı'tɛərıət] *n* prolétariat *m*.
proliferate [prə'lıfəreıt] *vi* proliférer; **proliferation** [-'reıʃən] *n* prolifération *f*.
prolific [prə'lıfık] *a* prolifique.
prologue ['prəulɔg] *n* prologue *m*.
prolong [prə'lɔŋ] *vt* prolonger.
prom [prɔm] *n abbr of* **promenade**; (*US*: *ball*) bal *m* d'étudiants.
promenade [prɔmə'nɑ:d] *n* (*by sea*) esplanade *f*, promenade *f*; **~ concert** *n* concert *m* (de musique classique); **~ deck** *n* pont *m* promenade.
prominence ['prɔmınəns] *n* proéminence *f*; importance *f*.
prominent ['prɔmınənt] *a* (*standing out*) proéminent(e); (*important*) important(e).
promiscuity [prɔmıs'kju:ıtı] *n* (*sexual*) légèreté *f* de mœurs.
promiscuous [prə'mıskjuəs] *a* (*sexually*) de mœurs légères.
promise ['prɔmıs] *n* promesse *f* // *vt,vi* promettre; **promising** *a* prometteur(euse).
promontory ['prɔməntrı] *n* promontoire *m*.
promote [prə'məut] *vt* promouvoir; (*venture, event*) organiser, mettre sur pied; (*new product*) lancer; **~r** *n* (*of sporting event*) organisateur/trice; **promotion** [-'məuʃən] *n* promotion *f*.
prompt [prɔmpt] *a* rapide // *ad* (*punctually*) à l'heure // *vt* inciter; provoquer; (THEATRE) souffler (son rôle *or* ses répliques) à; **to ~ sb to do** inciter *or* pousser qn à faire; **~er** *n* (THEATRE) souffleur *m*; **~ly** *ad* rapidement, sans délai; ponctuellement; **~ness** *n* rapidité *f*; promptitude *f*; ponctualité *f*.
promulgate ['prɔməlgeıt] *vt* promulguer.
prone [prəun] *a* (*lying*) couché(e) (face contre terre); **~ to** enclin(e) à.
prong [prɔŋ] *n* pointe *f*; (*of fork*) dent *f*.
pronoun ['prəunaun] *n* pronom *m*.
pronounce [prə'nauns] *vt* prononcer // *vi*: **to ~ (up)on** se prononcer sur; **~d** *a* (*marked*) prononcé(e); **~ment** *n* déclaration *f*.
pronunciation [prənʌnsı'eıʃən] *n* prononciation *f*.
proof [pru:f] *n* preuve *f*; (*test, of book*, PHOT) épreuve *f*; (*of alcohol*) degré *m* // *a*: **~ against** à l'épreuve de; **to be 70° ~** ≈ titrer 40 degrés; **~reader** *n* correcteur/trice (d'épreuves).
prop [prɔp] *n* support *m*, étai *m* // *vt* (*also*: **~ up**) étayer, soutenir; (*lean*): **to ~ sth against** appuyer qch contre *or* à.
propaganda [prɔpə'gændə] *n* propagande *f*.
propagation [prɔpə'geıʃən] *n* propagation *f*.
propel [prə'pɛl] *vt* propulser, faire avancer; **~ler** *n* hélice *f*; **~ling pencil** *n* porte-mine *m inv*.
propensity [prə'pɛnsıtı] *n* propension *f*.
proper ['prɔpə*] *a* (*suited, right*) approprié(e), bon(bonne); (*seemly*) correct(e), convenable; (*authentic*) vrai(e), véritable; (*col*: *real*) *n* + fini(e), vrai(e); **~ly** *ad* correctement, convenablement; bel et bien; **~ noun** *n* nom *m* propre.
property ['prɔpətı] *n* (*things owned*) biens *mpl*; propriété(s) *f(pl)*; immeuble *m*; terres *fpl*, domaine *m*; (CHEM *etc*: *quality*) propriété *f*; **it's their ~** cela leur appartient, c'est leur propriété; **~ owner** *n* propriétaire *m*.
prophecy ['prɔfısı] *n* prophétie *f*.
prophesy ['prɔfısaı] *vt* prédire // *vi* prophétiser.
prophet ['prɔfıt] *n* prophète *m*; **~ic** [prə'fɛtık] *a* prophétique.
proportion [prə'pɔ:ʃən] *n* proportion *f*; (*share*) part *f*; partie *f* // *vt* proportionner; **~al**, **~ate** *a* proportionnel(le).
proposal [prə'pəuzl] *n* proposition *f*, offre *f*; (*plan*) projet *m*; (*of marriage*) demande *f* en mariage.
propose [prə'pəuz] *vt* proposer, suggérer // *vi* faire sa demande en mariage; **to ~ to do** avoir l'intention de faire; **~r** *n* (*of motion etc*) auteur *m*.
proposition [prɔpə'zıʃən] *n* proposition *f*.
propound [prə'paund] *vt* proposer, soumettre.
proprietary [prə'praıətərı] *a* de marque déposée.
proprietor [prə'praıətə*] *n* propriétaire *m/f*.
propulsion [prə'pʌlʃən] *n* propulsion *f*.
pro rata [prəu'rɑ:tə] *ad* au prorata.
prosaic [prəu'zeıık] *a* prosaïque.
prose [prəuz] *n* prose *f*; (SCOL: *translation*) thème *m*.
prosecute ['prɔsıkju:t] *vt* poursuivre; **prosecution** [-'kju:ʃən] *n* poursuites *fpl* judiciaires; (*accusing side*) accusation *f*; **prosecutor** *n* procureur *m*; (*also*: **public ~**) ministère public.
prospect *n* ['prɔspɛkt] perspective *f*; (*hope*) espoir *m*, chances *fpl* // *vt,vi* [prə'spɛkt] prospecter; **~s** *npl* (*for work etc*) possibilités *fpl* d'avenir, débouchés *mpl*; **prospecting** *n* prospection *f*; **prospective** *a* (*possible*) eventuel(le); (*certain*) futur(e); **prospector** *n* prospecteur *m*.
prospectus [prə'spɛktəs] *n* prospectus *m*.
prosper ['prɔspə*] *vi* prospérer; **~ity** [-'spɛrıtı] *n* prospérité *f*; **~ous** *a* prospère.
prostitute ['prɔstıtju:t] *n* prostituée *f*.
prostrate ['prɔstreıt] *a* prosterné(e); (*fig*) prostré(e).
protagonist [prə'tægənıst] *n* protagoniste *m*.

protect [prə'tɛkt] *vt* protéger; **~ion** *n* protection *f*; **~ive** *a* protecteur(trice); **~or** *n* protecteur/trice.
protégé ['prəutɛʒei] *n* protégé *m*; **~e** *n* protégée *f*.
protein ['prəuti:n] *n* protéine *f*.
protest *n* ['prəutɛst] protestation *f* // *vi* [prə'tɛst] protester.
Protestant ['prɔtıstənt] *a,n* protestant(e).
protocol ['prəutəkɔl] *n* protocole *m*.
prototype ['prəutətaıp] *n* prototype *m*.
protracted [prə'træktıd] *a* prolongé(e).
protractor [prə'træktə*] *n* rapporteur *m*.
protrude [prə'tru:d] *vi* avancer, dépasser.
protuberance [prə'tju:bərəns] *n* protubérance *f*.
proud [praud] *a* fier(ère); (*pej*) orgueilleux(euse); **~ly** *ad* fièrement.
prove [pru:v] *vt* prouver, démontrer // *vi*: **to ~ correct** *etc* s'avérer juste *etc*; **to ~ o.s.** montrer ce dont on est capable; **to ~ o.s./itself (to be) useful** *etc* se montrer *or* se révéler utile *etc*.
proverb ['prɔvə:b] *n* proverbe *m*; **~ial** [prə'və:bıəl] *a* proverbial(e).
provide [prə'vaıd] *vt* fournir; **to ~ sb with sth** fournir qch à qn; **to ~ for** *vt* (*person*) subvenir aux besoins de; (*emergency*) prévoir; **~d (that)** *cj* à condition que + *sub*.
Providence ['prɔvıdəns] *n* Providence *f*.
providing [prə'vaıdıŋ] *cj* à condition que + *sub*.
province ['prɔvıns] *n* province *f*; **provincial** [prə'vınʃəl] *a* provincial(e).
provision [prə'vıʒən] *n* (*supply*) provision *f*; (*supplying*) fourniture *f*; approvisionnement *m*; (*stipulation*) disposition *f*; **~s** *npl* (*food*) provisions *fpl*; **~al** *a* provisoire; **~ally** *ad* provisoirement.
proviso [prə'vaızəu] *n* condition *f*.
provocation [prɔvə'keıʃən] *n* provocation *f*.
provocative [prə'vɔkətıv] *a* provocateur(trice), provocant(e).
provoke [prə'vəuk] *vt* provoquer; inciter.
prow [prau] *n* proue *f*.
prowess ['prauıs] *n* prouesse *f*.
prowl [praul] *vi* (*also*: **~ about, ~ around**) rôder // *n*: **on the ~** à l'affût; **~er** *n* rôdeur/euse.
proximity [prɔk'sımıtı] *n* proximité *f*.
proxy ['prɔksı] *n* procuration *f*; **by ~** par procuration.
prudence ['pru:dns] *n* prudence *f*.
prudent ['pru:dnt] *a* prudent(e).
prudish ['pru:dıʃ] *a* prude, pudibond(e).
prune [pru:n] *n* pruneau *m* // *vt* élaguer.
pry [praı] *vi*: **to ~ into** fourrer son nez dans.
psalm [sɑ:m] *n* psaume *m*.
pseudo- ['sju:dəu] *prefix* pseudo-; **~nym** *n* pseudonyme *m*.
psyche ['saıkı] *n* psychisme *m*.
psychiatric [saık'ætrık] *a* psychiatrique.
psychiatrist [saı'kaıətrıst] *n* psychiatre *m/f*.
psychiatry [saı'kaıətrı] *n* psychiatrie *f*.
psychic ['saıkık] *a* (*also*: **~al**) (méta)psychique; (*person*) doué(e) de télépathie *or* d'un sixième sens.
psychoanalyse [saıkəu'ænəlaız] *vt* psychanalyser.
psychoanalysis, *pl* **lyses** [saıkəuə'nælısıs, -si:z] *n* psychanalyse *f*.
psychoanalyst [saıkəu'ænəlıst] *n* psychanalyste *m/f*.
psychological [saıkə'lɔdʒıkl] *a* psychologique.
psychologist [saı'kɔlədʒıst] *n* psychologue *m/f*.
psychology [saı'kɔlədʒı] *n* psychologie *f*.
psychopath ['saıkəupæθ] *n* psychopathe *m/f*.
psychosomatic ['saıkəusə'mætık] *a* psychosomatique.
psychotic [saı'kɔtık] *a,n* psychotique (*m/f*).
P.T.O. *abbr* (= *please turn over*) T.S.V.P. (tournez s'il vous plaît).
pub [pʌb] *n* (*abbr of* **public house**) pub *m*.
puberty ['pju:bətı] *n* puberté *f*.
public ['pʌblık] *a* public(ique) // *n* public *m*; **the general ~** le grand public; **~ address system (P.A.)** sonorisation *f*; hauts-parleurs *mpl*.
publican ['pʌblıkən] *n* patron *m* de pub.
publication [pʌblı'keıʃən] *n* publication *f*.
public: ~ company *n* société *f* anonyme (*cotée en bourse*); **~ convenience** *n* toilettes *fpl*; **~ house** *n* pub *m*.
publicity [pʌb'lısıtı] *n* publicité *f*.
publicly ['pʌblıklı] *ad* publiquement.
public: ~ opinion *n* opinion publique; **~ relations (PR)** *n* relations publiques; **~ school** *n* (*Brit*) école privée; **~-spirited** *a* qui fait preuve de civisme.
publish ['pʌblıʃ] *vt* publier; **~er** *n* éditeur *m*; **~ing** *n* (*industry*) édition *f*; (*of a book*) publication *f*.
puce [pju:s] *a* puce.
puck [pʌk] *n* (*elf*) lutin *m*; (ICE HOCKEY) palet *m*.
pucker ['pʌkə*] *vt* plisser.
pudding ['pudıŋ] *n* dessert *m*, entremets *m*; (*sausage*) boudin *m*.
puddle ['pʌdl] *n* flaque *f* d'eau.
puerile ['pjuəraıl] *a* puéril(e).
puff [pʌf] *n* bouffée *f*; (*also*: **powder ~**) houppette *f* // *vt*: **to ~ one's pipe** tirer sur sa pipe // *vi* sortir par bouffées; (*pant*) haleter; **to ~ out smoke** envoyer des bouffées de fumée; **~ed** *a* (*col*: *out of breath*) tout(e) essoufflé(e).
puffin ['pʌfın] *n* macareux *m*.
puff pastry ['pʌf'peıstrı] *n* pâte feuilletée.
puffy ['pʌfı] *a* bouffi(e), boursouflé(e).
pugnacious [pʌg'neıʃəs] *a* pugnace, batailleur(euse).
pull [pul] *n* (*tug*): **to give sth a ~** tirer sur qch; (*fig*) influence *f* // *vt* tirer; (*muscle*) se claquer // *vi* tirer; **to ~ a face** faire une grimace; **to ~ to pieces** mettre en morceaux; **to ~ one's punches** ménager son adversaire; **to ~ one's weight** y mettre du sien; **to ~ o.s. together** se ressaisir; **to ~ sb's leg** faire marcher qn; **to ~ apart** *vt* séparer; (*break*) mettre en pièces, démantibuler; **to**

~ **down** *vt* baisser, abaisser; (*house*) démolir; (*tree*) abattre; **to ~ in** *vi* (*AUT: at the kerb*) se ranger; (*RAIL*) entrer en gare; **to ~ off** *vt* enlever, ôter; (*deal etc*) conclure; **to ~ out** *vi* démarrer, partir; se retirer; (*AUT: come out of line*) déboîter // *vt* sortir; arracher; (*withdraw*) retirer; **to ~ round** *vi* (*unconscious person*) revenir à soi; (*sick person*) se rétablir; **to ~ through** *vi* s'en sortir; **to ~ up** *vi* (*stop*) s'arrêter // *vt* remonter; (*uproot*) déraciner, arracher; (*stop*) arrêter.

pulley ['pulɪ] *n* poulie *f*.

pull-in ['pulɪn] *n* (*AUT*) parking *m*.

pullover ['puləuvə*] *n* pull-over *m*, tricot *m*.

pulp [pʌlp] *n* (*of fruit*) pulpe *f*; (*for paper*) pâte *f* à papier.

pulpit ['pulpɪt] *n* chaire *f*.

pulsate [pʌl'seɪt] *vi* battre, palpiter; (*music*) vibrer.

pulse [pʌls] *n* (*of blood*) pouls *m*; (*of heart*) battement *m*; (*of music, engine*) vibrations *fpl*.

pulverize ['pʌlvəraɪz] *vt* pulvériser.

puma ['pju:mə] *n* puma *m*.

pummel ['pʌml] *vt* rouer de coups.

pump [pʌmp] *n* pompe *f*; (*shoe*) escarpin *m* // *vt* pomper; (*fig: col*) faire parler; **to ~ up** *vt* gonfler.

pumpkin ['pʌmpkɪn] *n* potiron *m*, citrouille *f*.

pun [pʌn] *n* jeu *m* de mots, calembour *m*.

punch [pʌntʃ] *n* (*blow*) coup *m* de poing; (*fig: force*) vivacité *f*, mordant *m*; (*tool*) poinçon *m*; (*drink*) punch *m* // *vt* (*hit*): **to ~ sb/sth** donner un coup de poing à qn/sur qch; (*make a hole*) poinçonner, perforer; **to ~ a hole (in)** faire un trou (dans); **~-drunk** *a* sonné(e); **~-up** *n* (*col*) bagarre *f*.

punctual ['pʌŋktjuəl] *a* ponctuel(le); **~ity** [-'ælɪtɪ] *n* ponctualité *f*.

punctuate ['pʌŋktjueɪt] *vt* ponctuer; **punctuation** [-'eɪʃən] *n* ponctuation *f*.

puncture ['pʌŋktʃə*] *n* crevaison *f* // *vt* crever.

pundit ['pʌndɪt] *n* individu *m* qui pontifie, pontife *m*.

pungent ['pʌndʒənt] *a* piquant(e); (*fig*) mordant(e), caustique.

punish ['pʌnɪʃ] *vt* punir; **~able** *a* punissable; **~ment** *n* punition *f*, châtiment *m*.

punt [pʌnt] *n* (*boat*) bachot *m*; (*FOOTBALL*) coup *m* de volée.

punter ['pʌntə*] *n* (*gambler*) parieur/euse.

puny ['pju:nɪ] *a* chétif(ive).

pup [pʌp] *n* chiot *m*.

pupil ['pju:pl] *n* élève *m/f*.

puppet ['pʌpɪt] *n* marionnette *f*, pantin *m*.

puppy ['pʌpɪ] *n* chiot *m*, petit chien.

purchase ['pə:tʃ] *n* achat *m* // *vt* acheter; **~r** *n* acheteur/euse.

pure [pjuə*] *a* pur(e).

purée ['pjuəreɪ] *n* purée *f*.

purge [pə:dʒ] *n* (*MED*) purge *f*; (*POL*) épuration *f*, purge // *vt* purger; (*fig*) épurer, purger.

purification [pjuərɪfɪ'keɪʃən] *n* purification *f*.

purify ['pjuərɪfaɪ] *vt* purifier, épurer.

purist ['pjuərɪst] *n* puriste *m/f*.

puritan ['pjuərɪtən] *n* puritain/e; **~ical** [-'tænɪkl] *a* puritain(e).

purity ['pjuərɪtɪ] *n* pureté *f*.

purl [pə:l] *n* maille *f* à l'envers // *vt* tricoter à l'envers.

purple ['pə:pl] *a* violet(te); cramoisi(e).

purport [pə:'pɔ:t] *vi*: **to ~ to be/do** prétendre être/faire.

purpose ['pə:pəs] *n* intention *f*, but *m*; **on ~** exprès; **~ful** *a* déterminé(e), résolu(e); **~ly** *ad* exprès.

purr [pə:*] *n* ronronnement *m* // *vi* ronronner.

purse [pə:s] *n* porte-monnaie *m inv*, bourse *f* // *vt* serrer, pincer.

purser ['pə:sə*] *n* (*NAUT*) commissaire *m* du bord.

pursue [pə'sju:] *vt* poursuivre; **~r** *n* pursuivant/e.

pursuit [pə'sju:t] *n* poursuite *f*; (*occupation*) occupation *f*, activité *f*; **scientific ~s** recherches *fpl* scientifiques.

purveyor [pə'veɪə*] *n* fournisseur *m*.

pus [pʌs] *n* pus *m*.

push [puʃ] *n* poussée *f*; (*effort*) gros effort; (*drive*) énergie *f* // *vt* pousser; (*button*) appuyer sur; (*thrust*): **to ~ sth (into)** enfoncer qch (dans); (*fig*) mettre en avant, faire de la publicité pour // *vi* pousser; appuyer; **to ~ aside** *vt* écarter; **to ~ off** *vi* (*col*) filer, ficher le camp; **to ~ on** *vi* (*continue*) continuer; **to ~ over** *vt* renverser; **to ~ through** *vt* (*measure*) faire voter; **to ~ up** *vt* (*total, prices*) faire monter; **~chair** *n* poussette *f*; **~ing** *a* dynamique; **~over** *n* (*col*): **it's a ~over** c'est un jeu d'enfant; **~y** *a* (*pej*) arriviste.

puss, pussy(-cat) [pus, 'pusɪ(kæt)] *n* minet *m*.

put, *pt, pp* **put** [put] *vt* mettre, poser, placer; (*say*) dire, exprimer; (*a question*) poser; (*estimate*) estimer; **to ~ about** *vi* (*NAUT*) virer de bord // *vt* (*rumour*) faire courir; **to ~ across** *vt* (*ideas etc*) communiquer; faire comprendre; **to ~ away** *vt* (*store*) ranger; **to ~ back** *vt* (*replace*) remettre, replacer; (*postpone*) remettre; (*delay*) retarder; **to ~ by** *vt* (*money*) mettre de côté, économiser; **to ~ down** *vt* (*parcel etc*) poser, déposer; (*pay*) verser; (*in writing*) mettre par écrit, inscrire; (*suppress: revolt etc*) réprimer, faire cesser; (*attribute*) attribuer; **to ~ forward** *vt* (*ideas*) avancer, proposer; (*date*) avancer; **to ~ in** *vt* (*gas, electricity*) installer; (*application, complaint*) soumettre; **to ~ off** *vt* (*light etc*) éteindre; (*postpone*) remettre à plus tard, ajourner; (*discourage*) dissuader; **to ~ on** *vt* (*clothes, lipstick etc*) mettre; (*light etc*) allumer; (*play etc*) monter; (*food, meal*) servir; (*airs, weight*) prendre; (*brake*) mettre; **to ~ on the brakes** freiner; **to ~ out** *vt* mettre dehors; (*one's hand*) tendre; (*news, rumour*) faire courir, répandre; (*light etc*) éteindre; (*person: inconvenience*) déranger, gêner; **to ~ up** *vt* (*raise*) lever, relever, remonter; (*pin up*) afficher; (*hang*) accrocher; (*build*) construire, ériger; (*a tent*) monter; (*increase*) augmenter;

(*accommodate*) loger ; **to ~ up with** *vt fus* supporter.

putrid ['pju:trɪd] *a* putride.

putt [pʌt] *vt* poter (la balle) // *n* coup roulé ; **~er** *n* (GOLF) putter *m* ; **~ing green** *n* green *m*.

putty ['pʌtɪ] *n* mastic *m*.

put-up ['putʌp] *a*: **~ job** *n* affaire montée.

puzzle ['pʌzl] *n* énigme *f*, mystère *m* ; (*jigsaw*) puzzle *m* ; (*also*: **crossword ~**) problème *m* de mots croisés // *vt* intriguer, rendre perplexe // *vi* se creuser la tête ; **puzzling** *a* déconcertant(e), inexplicable.

PVC *abbr of polyvinyl chloride.*

pygmy ['pɪgmɪ] *n* pygmée *m/f*.

pyjamas [pɪ'dʒɑ:məz] *npl* pyjama *m*.

pylon ['paɪlən] *n* pylône *m*.

pyramid ['pɪrəmɪd] *n* pyramide *f*.

python ['paɪθən] *n* python *m*.

Q

quack [kwæk] *n* (*of duck*) coin-coin *m inv* ; (*pej*: *doctor*) charlatan *m*.

quad [kwɔd] *abbr of* **quadrangle**, **quadruplet**.

quadrangle ['kwɔdræŋgl] *n* (MATH) quadrilatère *m* ; (*courtyard*: *abbr*: **quad**) cour *f*.

quadruped ['kwɔdrupɛd] *n* quadrupède *m*.

quadruple [kwɔ'drupl] *a,n* quadruple (*m*) // *vt*, *vi* quadrupler ; **~t** [-'dru:plɪt] *n* quadruplé/e.

quagmire ['kwægmaɪə*] *n* bourbier *m*.

quail [kweɪl] *n* (ZOOL) caille *f*.

quaint [kweɪnt] *a* bizarre ; (*old-fashioned*) désuet(ète) ; au charme vieillot, pittoresque.

quake [kweɪk] *vi* trembler // *n abbr of* **earthquake**.

Quaker ['kweɪkə*] *n* quaker/esse.

qualification [kwɔlɪfɪ'keɪʃən] *n* (*degree etc*) diplôme *m* ; (*ability*) compétence *f*, qualification *f* ; (*limitation*) réserve *f*, restriction *f*.

qualified ['kwɔlɪfaɪd] *a* diplômé(e) ; (*able*) compétent(e), qualifié(e) ; (*limited*) conditionnel(le).

qualify ['kwɔlɪfaɪ] *vt* qualifier ; (*limit*: *statement*) apporter des réserves à // *vi*: **to ~ (as)** obtenir son diplôme (de) ; **to ~ (for)** remplir les conditions requises (pour) ; (SPORT) se qualifier (pour).

qualitative ['kwɔlɪtətɪv] *a* qualitatif(ive).

quality ['kwɔlɪtɪ] *n* qualité *f* // *cpd* de qualité ; **the ~ papers** la presse d'information.

qualm [kwɑ:m] *n* doute *m* ; scrupule *m*.

quandary ['kwɔndrɪ] *n*: **in a ~** devant un dilemme, dans l'embarras.

quantitative ['kwɔntɪtətɪv] *a* quantitatif(ive).

quantity ['kwɔntɪtɪ] *n* quantité *f* ; **~ surveyor** *n* métreur *m* vérificateur.

quarantine ['kwɔrnti:n] *n* quarantaine *f*.

quarrel ['kwɔrl] *n* querelle *f*, dispute *f* // *vi* se disputer, se quereller ; **~some** *a* querelleur(euse).

quarry ['kwɔrɪ] *n* (*for stone*) carrière *f* ; (*animal*) proie *f*, gibier *m* // *vt* (*marble etc*) extraire.

quart [kwɔ:t] *n* ≈ litre *m* (= *2 pints*).

quarter ['kwɔ:tə*] *n* quart *m* ; (*of year*) trimestre *m* ; (*district*) quartier *m* // *vt* partager en quartiers *or* en quatre ; (MIL) caserner, cantonner ; **~s** *npl* logement *m* ; (MIL) quartiers *mpl*, cantonnement *m* ; **a ~ of an hour** un quart d'heure ; **~-deck** *n* (NAUT) plage *f* arrière ; **~ final** *n* quart *m* de finale ; **~ly** *a* trimestriel(le) // *ad* tous les trois mois ; **~master** *n* (MIL) intendant *m* militaire de troisième classe ; (NAUT) maître *m* de manœuvre.

quartet(te) [kwɔ:'tɛt] *n* quatuor *m* ; (*jazz players*) quartette *m*.

quartz [kwɔ:ts] *n* quartz *m* ; **~ watch** *n* montre *f* à quartz.

quash [kwɔʃ] *vt* (*verdict*) annuler, casser.

quasi- ['kweɪzaɪ] *prefix* quasi- + *noun* ; quasi, presque + *adjective*.

quaver ['kweɪvə*] *n* (MUS) croche *f* // *vi* trembler.

quay [ki:] *n* (*also*: **~side**) quai *m*.

queasy ['kwi:zɪ] *a* (*stomach*) délicat(e) ; **to feel ~** avoir mal au cœur.

queen [kwi:n] *n* (*gen*) reine *f* ; (CARDS *etc*) dame *f* ; **~ mother** *n* reine mère *f*.

queer [kwɪə*] *a* étrange, curieux(euse) ; (*suspicious*) louche ; (*sick*): **I feel ~** je ne me sens pas bien // *n* (*col*) homosexuel *m*.

quell [kwɛl] *vt* réprimer, étouffer.

quench [kwɛntʃ] *vt* (*flames*) éteindre ; **to ~ one's thirst** se désaltérer.

query ['kwɪərɪ] *n* question *f* ; (*doubt*) doute *m* ; (*question mark*) point *m* d'interrogation // *vt* mettre en question *or* en doute.

quest [kwɛst] *n* recherche *f*, quête *f*.

question ['kwɛstʃən] *n* question *f* // *vt* (*person*) interroger ; (*plan*, *idea*) mettre en question *or* en doute ; **it's a ~ of doing** il s'agit de faire ; **there's some ~ of doing** il est question de faire ; **beyond ~** *ad* sans aucun doute ; **out of the ~** hors de question ; **~able** *a* discutable ; **~ing** *a* interrogateur(trice) // *n* interrogatoire *m* ; **~ mark** *n* point *m* d'interrogation.

questionnaire [kwɛstʃə'nɛə*] *n* questionnaire *m*.

queue [kju:] *n* queue *f*, file *f* // *vi* faire la queue.

quibble ['kwɪbl] *vi* ergoter, chicaner.

quick [kwɪk] *a* rapide ; (*reply*) prompt(e), rapide ; (*mind*) vif(vive) // *ad* vite, rapidement // *n*: **cut to the ~** (*fig*) touché(e) au vif ; **be ~!** dépêche-toi! ; **~en** *vt* accélérer, presser ; (*rouse*) stimuler // *vi* s'accélérer, devenir plus rapide ; **~lime** *n* chaux vive ; **~ly** *ad* vite, rapidement ; **~ness** *n* rapidité *f* ; promptitude *f* ; vivacité *f* ; **~sand** *n* sables mouvants ; **~step** *n* (*dance*) fox-trot *m* ; **~-witted** *a* à l'esprit vif.

quid [kwɪd] *n*, *pl inv* (*Brit*: *col*) livre *f*.

quiet ['kwaɪət] *a* tranquille, calme ; (*ceremony*, *colour*) discret(ète) // *n* tranquillité *f*, calme *m* ; **keep ~!** tais-toi! ; **on the ~** en secret, en cachette ; **~en** (*also*: **~en down**) *vi* se calmer, s'apaiser // *vt* calmer, apaiser ; **~ly** *ad* tranquillement, calmement ;

discrètement; ~**ness** *n* tranquillité *f*, calme *m*; silence *m*.
quill [kwɪl] *n* plume *f* (d'oie).
quilt [kwɪlt] *n* édredon *m*; **(continental)** ~ *n* couverture *f* édredon; ~**ing** *n* ouatine *f*; molletonnage *m*.
quin [kwɪn] *abbr of* **quintuplet**.
quince [kwɪns] *n* coing *m*; (*tree*) cognassier *m*.
quinine [kwɪ'ni:n] *n* quinine *f*.
quintet(te) [kwɪn'tɛt] *n* quintette *m*.
quintuplet [kwɪn'tju:plɪt] *n* quintuplé/e.
quip [kwɪp] *n* remarque piquante *or* spirituelle, pointe *f* // *vt*: ... **he** ~**ped** ... lança-t-il.
quirk [kwə:k] *n* bizarrerie *f*.
quit, *pt*, *pp* **quit** *or* **quitted** [kwɪt] *vt* quitter // *vi* (*give up*) abandonner, renoncer; (*resign*) démissionner; **to** ~ **doing** arrêter de faire; **notice to** ~ congé *m* (*signifié au locataire*).
quite [kwaɪt] *ad* (*rather*) assez, plutôt; (*entirely*) complètement, tout à fait; **I** ~ **understand** je comprends très bien; ~ **a few of them** un assez grand nombre d'entre eux; ~ **(so)!** exactement!
quits [kwɪts] *a*: ~ **(with)** quitte (envers).
quiver ['kwɪvə*] *vi* trembler, frémir // *n* (*for arrows*) carquois *m*.
quiz [kwɪz] *n* (*game*) jeu-concours *m*; test *m* de connaissances // *vt* interroger; ~**zical** *a* narquois(e).
quoits [kwɔɪts] *npl* jeu *m* du palet.
quorum ['kwɔ:rəm] *n* quorum *m*.
quota ['kwəutə] *n* quota *m*.
quotation [kwəu'teɪʃən] *n* citation *f*; (*of shares etc*) cote *f*, cours *m*; (*estimate*) devis *m*; ~ **marks** *npl* guillemets *mpl*.
quote [kwəut] *n* citation *f* // *vt* (*sentence*) citer; (*price*) donner, fixer; (*shares*) coter // *vi*: **to** ~ **from** citer; **to** ~ **for a job** établir un devis pour des travaux.
quotient ['kwəuʃənt] *n* quotient *m*.

R

rabbi ['ræbaɪ] *n* rabbin *m*.
rabbit ['ræbɪt] *n* lapin *m*; ~ **hole** *n* terrier *m* (de lapin); ~ **hutch** *n* clapier *m*.
rabble ['ræbl] *n* (*pej*) populace *f*.
rabid ['ræbɪd] *a* enragé(e).
rabies ['reɪbi:z] *n* rage *f*.
RAC *n abbr of Royal Automobile Club*.
raccoon [rə'ku:n] *n* raton *m* laveur.
race [reɪs] *n* race *f*; (*competition, rush*) course *f* // *vt* (*person*) faire la course avec; (*horse*) faire courir; (*engine*) emballer // *vi* courir; ~**course** *n* champ *m* de courses; ~**horse** *n* cheval *m* de course; ~ **relations** *npl* rapports *mpl* entre les races; ~**track** *n* piste *f*.
racial ['reɪʃl] *a* racial(e); ~ **discrimination** *n* discrimination raciale; ~**ism** *n* racisme *m*; ~**ist** *a*, *n* raciste *m/f*.
racing ['reɪsɪŋ] *n* courses *fpl*; ~ **car** *n* voiture *f* de course; ~ **driver** *n* pilote *m* de course.
racist ['reɪsɪst] *a,n* (*pej*) raciste (*m/f*).
rack [ræk] *n* (*also*: **luggage** ~) filet *m* à bagages; (*also*: **roof** ~) galerie *f* // *vt* tourmenter; **magazine** ~ *n* porte-revues *m inv*; **shoe** ~ *n* étagère *f* à chaussures; **toast** ~ *n* porte-toast *m*.
racket ['rækɪt] *n* (*for tennis*) raquette *f*; (*noise*) tapage *m*; vacarme *m*; (*swindle*) escroquerie *f*; (*organized crime*) racket *m*.
racoon [rə'ku:n] *n* = **raccoon**.
racquet ['rækɪt] *n* raquette *f*.
racy ['reɪsɪ] *a* plein(e) de verve; osé(e).
radar ['reɪdɑ:*] *n* radar *m* // *cpd* radar *inv*.
radiance ['reɪdɪəns] *n* éclat *m*, rayonnement *m*.
radiant ['reɪdɪənt] *a* rayonnant(e); (PHYSICS) radiant(e).
radiate ['reɪdɪeɪt] *vt* (*heat*) émettre, dégager // *vi* (*lines*) rayonner.
radiation [reɪdɪ'eɪʃən] *n* rayonnement *m*; (*radioactive*) radiation *f*.
radiator ['reɪdɪeɪtə*] *n* radiateur *m*; ~ **cap** *n* bouchon *m* de radiateur.
radical ['rædɪkl] *a* radical(e).
radii ['reɪdɪaɪ] *npl of* **radius**.
radio ['reɪdɪəu] *n* radio *f*; **on the** ~ à la radio; ~ **station** station *f* de radio.
radio... ['reɪdɪəu] *prefix*: ~**active** *a* radioactif(ive); ~**activity** *n* radioactivité *f*; ~**grapher** [-'ɔgrəfə*] *n* radiologue *m/f* (*technicien*); ~**graphy** [-'ɔgrəfɪ] *n* radiographie *f*; ~**logy** [-'ɔlədʒɪ] *n* radiologie *f*; ~**therapist** *n* radiothérapeute *m/f*.
radish ['rædɪʃ] *n* radis *m*.
radium ['reɪdɪəm] *n* radium *m*.
radius, *pl* **radii** ['reɪdɪəs, -ɪaɪ] *n* rayon *m*; (ANAT) radius *m*.
raffia ['ræfɪə] *n* raphia *m*.
raffish ['ræfɪʃ] *a* dissolu(e); canaille.
raffle ['ræfl] *n* tombola *f*.
raft [rɑ:ft] *n* (*also*: **life** ~) radeau *m*; (*logs*) train *m* de flottage.
rafter ['rɑ:ftə*] *n* chevron *m*.
rag [ræg] *n* chiffon *m*; (*pej*: *newspaper*) feuille *f*, torchon *m*; (*for charity*) *attractions organisées par les étudiants au profit d'œuvres de charité* // *vt* chahuter, mettre en boîte; ~**s** *npl* haillons *mpl*; ~**-and-bone man** *n* chiffonnier *m*; ~**bag** *n* (*fig*) ramassis *m*.
rage [reɪdʒ] *n* (*fury*) rage *f*, fureur *f* // *vi* (*person*) être fou(folle) de rage; (*storm*) faire rage, être déchaîné(e); **it's all the** ~ cela fait fureur.
ragged ['rægɪd] *a* (*edge*) inégal(e), qui accroche; (*cuff*) effiloché(e); (*appearance*) déguenillé(e).
raid [reɪd] *n* (MIL) raid *m*; (*criminal*) hold-up *m inv*; (*by police*) descente *f*, rafle *f* // *vt* faire un raid sur *or* un hold-up dans *or* une descente dans; ~**er** *n* malfaiteur *m*; (*plane*) bombardier *m*.
rail [reɪl] *n* (*on stair*) rampe *f*; (*on bridge, balcony*) balustrade *f*; (*of ship*) bastingage *m*; (*for train*) rail *m*; ~**s** *npl* rails *mpl*, voie ferrée; **by** ~ par chemin de fer; ~**ing(s)** *n(pl)* grille *f*; ~**road** *n* (*US*), ~**way** *n* chemin *m* de fer; ~**wayman** *n* cheminot *m*; ~**way station** *n* gare *f*.
rain [reɪn] *n* pluie *f* // *vi* pleuvoir; **in the** ~ sous la pluie; ~**bow** *n* arc-en-ciel *m*; ~**coat** *n* imperméable *m*; ~**drop** *n* goutte *f* de pluie; ~**fall** *n* chute *f* de pluie; (*measurement*) hauteur *f* des précipitations;

~proof *a* imperméable ; **~storm** *n* pluie torrentielle ; **~y** *a* pluvieux(euse).
raise [reɪz] *n* augmentation *f* // *vt* (*lift*) lever ; hausser ; (*build*) ériger ; (*increase*) augmenter ; (*a protest, doubt*) provoquer, causer ; (*a question*) soulever ; (*cattle, family*) élever ; (*crop*) faire pousser ; (*army, funds*) rassembler ; (*loan*) obtenir ; **to ~ one's voice** élever la voix.
raisin ['reɪzn] *n* raisin sec.
raj [rɑːdʒ] *n* empire *m* (*aux Indes*).
rajah ['rɑːdʒə] *n* radja(h) *m*.
rake [reɪk] *n* (*tool*) râteau *m* ; (*person*) débauché *m* // *vt* (*garden*) ratisser ; (*fire*) tisonner ; (*with machine gun*) balayer ; **to ~ through** (*fig: search*) fouiller (dans).
rakish ['reɪkɪʃ] *a* dissolu(e) ; cavalier(ère).
rally ['rælɪ] *n* (POL *etc*) meeting *m*, rassemblement *m* ; (AUT) rallye *m* ; (TENNIS) échange *m* // *vt* rassembler, rallier // *vi* se rallier ; (*sick person*) aller mieux ; (*Stock Exchange*) reprendre ; **to ~ round** *vt fus* se rallier à ; venir en aide à.
ram [ræm] *n* bélier *m* // *vt* enfoncer ; (*soil*) tasser ; (*crash into*) emboutir ; percuter ; éperonner.
ramble ['ræmbl] *n* randonnée *f* // *vi* (*pej: also:* **~ on**) discourir, pérorer ; **~r** *n* promeneur/euse, randonneur/euse ; (BOT) rosier grimpant ; **rambling** *a* (*speech*) décousu(e) ; (BOT) grimpant(e).
ramification [ræmɪfɪ'keɪʃən] *n* ramification *f*.
ramp [ræmp] *n* (*incline*) rampe *f* ; dénivellation *f* ; (*in garage*) pont *m*.
rampage [ræm'peɪdʒ] *n*: **to be on the ~** se déchaîner // *vi*: **they went rampaging through the town** ils ont envahi les rues et ont tout saccagé sur leur passage.
rampant ['ræmpənt] *a* (*disease etc*) qui sévit.
rampart ['ræmpɑːt] *n* rempart *m*.
ramshackle ['ræmʃækl] *a* (*house*) délabré(e) ; (*car etc*) déglingué(e).
ran [ræn] *pt of* **run**.
ranch [rɑːntʃ] *n* ranch *m* ; **~er** *n* propriétaire *m* de ranch ; cowboy *m*.
rancid ['rænsɪd] *a* rance.
rancour, rancor (*US*) ['ræŋkə*] *n* rancune *f*.
random ['rændəm] *a* fait(e) *or* établi(e) au hasard // *n*: **at ~** au hasard.
randy ['rændɪ] *a* (*col*) excité(e) ; lubrique.
rang [ræŋ] *pt of* **ring**.
range [reɪndʒ] *n* (*of mountains*) chaîne *f* ; (*of missile, voice*) portée *f* ; (*of products*) choix *m*, gamme *f* ; (MIL: *also:* **shooting ~**) champ *m* de tir ; (*also:* **kitchen ~**) fourneau *m* (de cuisine) // *vt* (*place*) mettre en rang, placer ; (*roam*) parcourir // *vi*: **to ~ over** couvrir ; **to ~ from ... to** aller de ... à ; **~r** *n* garde *m* forestier.
rank [ræŋk] *n* rang *m* ; (MIL) grade *m* ; (*also:* **taxi ~**) station *f* de taxis // *vi*: **to ~ among** compter *or* se classer parmi // *a* (qui sent) fort(e) ; extrême ; **the ~s** (MIL) la troupe ; **the ~ and file** (*fig*) la masse, la base.
rankle ['ræŋkl] *vi* (*insult*) rester sur le cœur.
ransack ['rænsæk] *vt* fouiller (à fond) ; (*plunder*) piller.
ransom ['rænsəm] *n* rançon *f* ; **to hold sb to ~** (*fig*) exercer un chantage sur qn.
rant [rænt] *vi* fulminer ; **~ing** *n* invectives *fpl*.
rap [ræp] *n* petit coup sec ; tape *f* // *vt* frapper sur *or* à ; taper sur.
rape [reɪp] *n* viol *m* // *vt* violer.
rapid ['ræpɪd] *a* rapide ; **~s** *npl* (GEO) rapides *mpl* ; **~ity** [rə'pɪdɪtɪ] *n* rapidité *f*.
rapist ['reɪpɪst] *n* auteur *m* d'un viol.
rapport [ræ'pɔː*] *n* entente *f*.
rapture ['ræptʃə*] *n* extase *f*, ravissement *m* ; **to go into ~s over** s'extasier sur ; **rapturous** *a* extasié(e) ; frénétique.
rare [rɛə*] *a* rare ; (CULIN: *steak*) saignant(e).
rarebit ['rɛəbɪt] *n see* **Welsh**.
rarefied ['rɛərɪfaɪd] *a* (*air, atmosphere*) raréfié(e).
rarely ['rɛəlɪ] *ad* rarement.
rarity ['rɛərɪtɪ] *n* rareté *f*.
rascal ['rɑːskl] *n* vaurien *m*.
rash [ræʃ] *a* imprudent(e), irréfléchi(e) // *n* (MED) rougeur *f*, éruption *f*.
rasher ['ræʃə*] *n* fine tranche (de lard).
rasp [rɑːsp] *n* (*tool*) lime *f*.
raspberry ['rɑːzbərɪ] *n* framboise *f* ; **~ bush** *n* framboisier *m*.
rasping ['rɑːspɪŋ] *a*: **~ noise** grincement *m*.
rat [ræt] *n* rat *m*.
ratable ['reɪtəbl] *a* = **rateable**.
ratchet ['rætʃɪt] *n*: **~ wheel** roue *f* à rochet.
rate [reɪt] *n* (*ratio*) taux *m*, pourcentage *m* ; (*speed*) vitesse *f*, rythme *m* ; (*price*) tarif *m* // *vt* classer ; évaluer ; **to ~ sb/sth as** considérer qn/qch comme ; **to ~ sb/sth among** classer qn/qch parmi ; **~s** *npl* (*Brit*) impôts locaux ; (*fees*) tarifs *mpl* ; **~able value** *n* valeur locative imposable ; **~ of exchange** *n* taux *m or* cours *m* du change ; **~ of flow** *n* débit *m* ; **~payer** *n* contribuable *m/f* (*payant les impôts locaux*).
rather ['rɑːðə*] *ad* plutôt ; **it's ~ expensive** c'est assez cher ; (*too much*) c'est un peu cher ; **I would** *or* **I'd ~ go** j'aimerais mieux *or* je préférerais partir ; **I had ~ go** il vaudrait mieux que je parte.
ratification [rætɪfɪ'keɪʃən] *n* ratification *f*.
ratify ['rætɪfaɪ] *vt* ratifier.
rating ['reɪtɪŋ] *n* classement *m* ; cote *f* ; (NAUT: *category*) classe *f* ; (: *sailor*) matelot *m*.
ratio ['reɪʃɪəu] *n* proportion *f* ; **in the ~ of 100 to 1** dans la proportion de 100 contre 1.
ration ['ræʃən] *n* (*gen pl*) ration(s) *f(pl)* // *vt* rationner.
rational ['ræʃənl] *a* raisonnable, sensé(e) ; (*solution, reasoning*) logique ; (MED) lucide ; **~e** [-'nɑːl] *n* raisonnement *m* ; justification *f* ; **~ize** *vt* rationaliser ; (*conduct*) essayer d'expliquer *or* de motiver ; **~ly** *ad* raisonnablement ; logiquement.
rationing ['ræʃnɪŋ] *n* rationnement *m*.
rat poison ['rætpɔɪzn] *n* mort-aux-rats *f inv*.

rat race ['rætreɪs] *n* foire *f* d'empoigne.

rattle ['rætl] *n* cliquetis *m*; (*louder*) bruit *m* de ferraille; (*object: of baby*) hochet *m*; (*: of sports fan*) crécelle *f* // *vi* cliqueter; faire un bruit de ferraille *or* du bruit // *vt* agiter (bruyamment); **~snake** *n* serpent *m* à sonnettes.

raucous ['rɔːkəs] *a* rauque; **~ly** *ad* d'une voix rauque.

ravage ['rævɪdʒ] *vt* ravager; **~s** *npl* ravages *mpl*.

rave [reɪv] *vi* (*in anger*) s'emporter; (*with enthusiasm*) s'extasier; (MED) délirer.

raven ['reɪvən] *n* corbeau *m*.

ravenous ['rævənəs] *a* affamé(e).

ravine [rə'viːn] *n* ravin *m*.

raving ['reɪvɪŋ] *a*: **~ lunatic** *n* fou furieux/folle furieuse.

ravioli [rævɪ'əulɪ] *n* ravioli *mpl*.

ravish ['rævɪʃ] *vt* ravir; **~ing** *a* enchanteur(eresse).

raw [rɔː] *a* (*uncooked*) cru(e); (*not processed*) brut(e); (*sore*) à vif, irrité(e); (*inexperienced*) inexpérimenté(e); **~ material** *n* matière première.

ray [reɪ] *n* rayon *m*; **~ of hope** *n* lueur *f* d'espoir.

rayon ['reɪɔn] *n* rayonne *f*.

raze [reɪz] *vt* raser, détruire.

razor ['reɪzə*] *n* rasoir *m*; **~ blade** *n* lame *f* de rasoir.

Rd *abbr of* **road**.

re [riː] *prep* concernant.

reach [riːtʃ] *n* portée *f*, atteinte *f*; (*of river etc*) étendue *f* // *vt* atteindre; parvenir à // *vi* s'étendre; **out of/within ~** (*object*) hors de/à portée; **within easy ~ (of)** (*place*) à proximité (de), proche (de); **to ~ out** *vi*: **to ~ out for** allonger le bras pour prendre.

react [riː'ækt] *vi* réagir; **~ion** [-'ækʃən] *n* réaction *f*; **~ionary** [-'ækʃənrɪ] *a,n* réactionnaire (*m/f*).

reactor [riː'æktə*] *n* réacteur *m*.

read, *pt,pp* **read** [riːd, rɛd] *vi* lire // *vt* lire; (*understand*) comprendre, interpréter; (*study*) étudier; (*subj: instrument etc*) indiquer, marquer; **to ~ out** *vt* lire à haute voix; **~able** *a* facile *or* agréable à lire; **~er** *n* lecteur/trice; (*book*) livre *m* de lecture; (*at university*) maître *m* de conférences; **~ership** *n* (*of paper etc*) (nombre *m* de) lecteurs *mpl*.

readily ['rɛdɪlɪ] *ad* volontiers, avec empressement; (*easily*) facilement.

readiness ['rɛdɪnɪs] *n* empressement *m*; **in ~** (*prepared*) prêt(e).

reading ['riːdɪŋ] *n* lecture *f*; (*understanding*) interprétation *f*; (*on instrument*) indications *fpl*; **~ lamp** *n* lampe *f* de bureau; **~ room** *n* salle *f* de lecture.

readjust [riːə'dʒʌst] *vt* rajuster; (*instrument*) régler de nouveau // *vi* (*person*): **to ~ (to)** se réadapter (à).

ready ['rɛdɪ] *a* prêt(e); (*willing*) prêt, disposé(e); (*quick*) prompt(e); (*available*) disponible // *ad*: **~-cooked** tout(e) cuit(e) (d'avance) // *n*: **at the ~** (MIL) prêt à faire feu; (*fig*) tout(e) prêt(e); **~ cash** *n* (argent *m*) liquide *m*; **~-made** *a* tout(e) fait(e); **~-mix** *n* (*for cakes etc*) préparation *f* en sachet; **~ reckoner** *n* barème *m*; **~-to-wear** *a* en prêt-à-porter.

real [rɪəl] *a* réel(le); véritable; **in ~ terms** dans la réalité; **~ estate** *n* biens fonciers *or* immobiliers; **~ism** *n* (*also* ART) réalisme *m*; **~ist** *n* réaliste *m/f*; **~istic** [-'lɪstɪk] *a* réaliste.

reality [riː'ælɪtɪ] *n* réalité *f*; **in ~** en réalité, en fait.

realization [rɪəlaɪ'zeɪʃən] *n* prise *f* de conscience; réalisation *f*.

realize ['rɪəlaɪz] *vt* (*understand*) se rendre compte de; (*a project*, COMM: *asset*) réaliser.

really ['rɪəlɪ] *ad* vraiment.

realm [rɛlm] *n* royaume *m*.

ream [riːm] *n* rame *f* (*de papier*).

reap [riːp] *vt* moissonner; (*fig*) récolter; **~er** *n* (*machine*) moissonneuse *f*.

reappear [riːə'pɪə*] *vi* réapparaître, reparaître; **~ance** *n* réapparition *f*.

reapply [riːə'plaɪ] *vi*: **to ~ for** faire une nouvelle demande d'emploi concernant; reposer sa candidature à.

rear [rɪə*] *a* de derrière, arrière *inv*; (AUT: *wheel etc*) arrière // *n* arrière *m*, derrière *m* // *vt* (*cattle, family*) élever // *vi* (*also*: **~ up**) (*animal*) se cabrer; **~-engined** *a* (AUT) avec moteur à l'arrière; **~guard** *n* arrière-garde *f*.

rearm [riː'ɑːm] *vt, vi* réarmer; **~ament** *n* réarmement *m*.

rearrange [riːə'reɪndʒ] *vt* réarranger.

rear-view ['rɪəvjuː] *a*: **~ mirror** *n* (AUT) rétroviseur *m*.

reason ['riːzn] *n* raison *f* // *vi*: **to ~ with sb** raisonner qn, faire entendre raison à qn; **to have ~ to think** avoir lieu de penser; **it stands to ~ that** il va sans dire que; **~able** *a* raisonnable; (*not bad*) acceptable; **~ably** *ad* raisonnablement; **one can ~ably assume that ...** on est fondé à *or* il est permis de supposer que ...; **~ed** *a* (*argument*) raisonné(e); **~ing** *n* raisonnement *m*.

reassemble [riːə'sɛmbl] *vt* rassembler; (*machine*) remonter.

reassert [riːə'səːt] *vt* réaffirmer.

reassure [riːə'ʃuə*] *vt* rassurer; **to ~ sb of** donner à qn l'assurance répétée de; **reassuring** *a* rassurant(e).

reawakening [riːə'weɪknɪŋ] *n* réveil *m*.

rebate ['riːbeɪt] *n* (*on product*) rabais *m*; (*on tax etc*) dégrèvement *m*; (*repayment*) remboursement *m*.

rebel *n* ['rɛbl] rebelle *m/f* // *vi* [rɪ'bɛl] se rebeller, se révolter; **~lion** *n* rébellion *f*, révolte *f*; **~lious** *a* rebelle.

rebirth [riː'bəːθ] *n* renaissance *f*.

rebound *vi* [rɪ'baund] (*ball*) rebondir; (*bullet*) ricocher // *n* ['riːbaund] rebond *m*; ricochet *m*.

rebuff [rɪ'bʌf] *n* rebuffade *f* // *vt* repousser.

rebuild [riː'bɪld] *vt irg* reconstruire.

rebuke [rɪ'bjuːk] *n* réprimande *f*, reproche *m* // *vt* réprimander.

rebut [rɪ'bʌt] *vt* réfuter; **~tal** *n* réfutation *f*.

recall [rɪ'kɔːl] *vt* rappeler; (*remember*) se rappeler, se souvenir de // *n* rappel *m*; **beyond ~** *a* irrévocable.

recant [rɪ'kænt] *vi* se rétracter ; (*REL*) abjurer.
recap ['ri:kæp] *n* récapitulation *f* // *vt, vi* récapituler.
recapture [ri:'kæptʃə*] *vt* reprendre ; (*atmosphere*) recréer.
recede [rɪ'si:d] *vi* s'éloigner ; reculer ; redescendre ; **receding** *a* (*forehead, chin*) fuyant(e) ; **receding hairline** *n* front dégarni.
receipt [rɪ'si:t] *n* (*document*) reçu *m* ; (*for parcel etc*) accusé *m* de réception ; (*act of receiving*) réception *f* ; **~s** *npl* (*COMM*) recettes *fpl*.
receive [rɪ'si:v] *vt* recevoir ; (*guest*) recevoir, accueillir.
receiver [rɪ'si:və*] *n* (*TEL*) récepteur *m*, combiné *m* ; (*of stolen goods*) receleur *m* ; (*COMM*) administrateur *m* judiciaire.
recent ['ri:snt] *a* récent(e) ; **~ly** *ad* récemment ; **as ~ly as** pas plus tard que.
receptacle [rɪ'sɛptɪkl] *n* récipient *m*.
reception [rɪ'sɛpʃən] *n* réception *f* ; (*welcome*) accueil *m*, réception ; **~ desk** *n* réception ; **~ist** *n* réceptionniste *m/f*.
receptive [rɪ'sɛptɪv] *a* réceptif(ive).
recess [rɪ'sɛs] *n* (*in room*) renfoncement *m* ; (*for bed*) alcôve *f* ; (*secret place*) recoin *m* ; (*POL etc: holiday*) vacances *fpl*.
recharge [ri:'tʃɑ:dʒ] *vt* (*battery*) recharger.
recipe ['rɛsɪpɪ] *n* recette *f*.
recipient [rɪ'sɪpɪənt] *n* bénéficiaire *m/f* ; (*of letter*) destinataire *m/f*.
reciprocal [rɪ'sɪprəkl] *a* réciproque.
reciprocate [rɪ'sɪprəkeɪt] *vt* retourner, offrir en retour.
recital [rɪ'saɪtl] *n* récital *m*.
recite [rɪ'saɪt] *vt* (*poem*) réciter ; (*complaints etc*) énumérer.
reckless ['rɛkləs] *a* (*driver etc*) imprudent(e) ; (*spender etc*) insouciant(e) ; **~ly** *ad* imprudemment ; avec insouciance.
reckon ['rɛkən] *vt* (*count*) calculer, compter ; (*consider*) considérer, estimer ; (*think*): **I ~ that ...** je pense que ... ; **to ~ on** *vt fus* compter sur, s'attendre à ; **~ing** *n* compte *m*, calcul *m* ; estimation *f* ; **the day of ~ing** le jour du Jugement.
reclaim [rɪ'kleɪm] *vt* (*land*) amender ; (*: from sea*) assécher ; (*: from forest*) défricher ; (*demand back*) réclamer (le remboursement *or* la restitution de) ; **reclamation** [rɛklə'meɪʃən] *n* amendement *m* ; assèchement *m* ; défrichement *m*.
recline [rɪ'klaɪn] *vi* être allongé(e) *or* étendu(e) ; **reclining** *a* (*seat*) à dossier réglable.
recluse [rɪ'klu:s] *n* reclus/e, ermite *m*.
recognition [rɛkəg'nɪʃən] *n* reconnaissance *f* ; **to gain ~** être reconnu(e) ; **transformed beyond ~** méconnaissable.
recognizable ['rɛkəgnaɪzəbl] *a*: **~ (by)** reconnaissable (à).
recognize ['rɛkəgnaɪz] *vt*: **to ~ (by/as)** reconnaître (à/comme étant).
recoil [rɪ'kɔɪl] *vi* (*gun*) reculer ; (*spring*) se détendre ; (*person*): **to ~ (from)** reculer (devant) // *n* recul *m* ; détente *f*.
recollect [rɛkə'lɛkt] *vt* se rappeler, se souvenir de ; **~ion** [-'lɛkʃən] *n* souvenir *m*.
recommend [rɛkə'mɛnd] *vt* recommander ; **~ation** [-'deɪʃən] *n* recommandation *f*.
recompense ['rɛkəmpɛns] *vt* récompenser ; (*compensate*) dédommager.
reconcilable ['rɛkənsaɪləbl] *a* (*ideas*) conciliable.
reconcile ['rɛkənsaɪl] *vt* (*two people*) réconcilier ; (*two facts*) concilier, accorder ; **to ~ o.s. to** se résigner à ; **reconciliation** [-sɪlɪ'eɪʃən] *n* réconciliation *f* ; conciliation *f*.
recondition [ri:kən'dɪʃən] *vt* remettre à neuf ; réviser entièrement.
reconnaissance [rɪ'kɔnɪsns] *n* (*MIL*) reconnaissance *f*.
reconnoitre, reconnoiter (*US*) [rɛkə'nɔɪtə*] (*MIL*) *vt* reconnaître // *vi* faire une reconnaissance.
reconsider [ri:kən'sɪdə*] *vt* reconsidérer.
reconstitute [ri:'kɔnstɪtju:t] *vt* reconstituer.
reconstruct [ri:kən'strʌkt] *vt* (*building*) reconstruire ; (*crime*) reconstituer ; **~ion** [-kʃən] *n* reconstruction *f* ; reconstitution *f*.
record *n* ['rɛkɔ:d] rapport *m*, récit *m* ; (*of meeting etc*) procès-verbal *m* ; (*register*) registre *m* ; (*file*) dossier *m* ; (*also*: **police ~**) casier *m* judiciaire ; (*MUS: disc*) disque *m* ; (*SPORT*) record *m* // *vt* [rɪ'kɔ:d] (*set down*) noter ; (*relate*) rapporter ; (*MUS: song etc*) enregistrer ; **in ~ time** dans un temps record *inv* ; **to keep a ~ of** noter ; **off the ~** *a* officieux(euse) ; **to keep the ~ straight** (*fig*) mettre les choses au point ; **~ card** *n* (*in file*) fiche *f* ; **~er** *n* (LAW) *avocat nommé à la fonction de juge* ; (*MUS*) flûte *f* à bec ; **~ holder** *n* (*SPORT*) détenteur/trice du record ; **~ing** *n* (*MUS*) enregistrement *m* ; **~ library** *n* discothèque *f* ; **~ player** *n* électrophone *m*.
recount [rɪ'kaunt] *vt* raconter.
re-count *n* ['ri:kaunt] (*POL: of votes*) pointage *m* // *vt* [ri:'kaunt] recompter.
recoup [rɪ'ku:p] *vt*: **to ~ one's losses** récupérer ce qu'on a perdu, se refaire.
recourse [rɪ'kɔ:s] *n* recours *m* ; expédient *m* ; **to have ~ to** recourir à, avoir recours à.
recover [rɪ'kʌvə*] *vt* récupérer // *vi* (*from illness*) se rétablir ; (*from shock*) se remettre ; (*country*) se redresser.
re-cover [ri:'kʌvə*] *vt* (*chair etc*) recouvrir.
recovery [rɪ'kʌvərɪ] *n* récupération *f* ; rétablissement *m* ; redressement *m*.
recreate [ri:krɪ'eɪt] *vt* recréer.
recreation [rɛkrɪ'eɪʃən] *n* récréation *f* ; détente *f* ; **~al** *a* pour la détente, récréatif(ive).
recrimination [rɪkrɪmɪ'neɪʃən] *n* récrimination *f*.
recruit [rɪ'kru:t] *n* recrue *f* // *vt* recruter ; **~ing office** *n* bureau *m* de recrutement ; **~ment** *n* recrutement *m*.
rectangle ['rɛktæŋgl] *n* rectangle *m* ; **rectangular** [-'tæŋgjulə*] *a* rectangulaire.
rectify ['rɛktɪfaɪ] *vt* (*error*) rectifier, corriger ; (*omission*) réparer.
rector ['rɛktə*] *n* (*REL*) pasteur *m* ; **rectory** *n* presbytère *m*.

recuperate [rɪ'kju:pəreɪt] *vi* récupérer; (*from illness*) se rétablir.
recur [rɪ'kə:*] *vi* se reproduire; (*idea, opportunity*) se retrouver; (*symptoms*) réapparaître; **~rence** *n* répétition *f*; réapparition *f*; **~rent** *a* périodique, fréquent(e); **~ring** *a* (MATH) périodique.
red [rɛd] *n* rouge *m*; (POL: *pej*) rouge *m/f* // *a* rouge; **in the ~** (*account*) à découvert; (*business*) en déficit; **~ carpet treatment** *n* réception *f* en grande pompe; **R~ Cross** *n* Croix-Rouge *f*; **~ currant** *n* groseille *f* (rouge); **~den** *vt,vi* rougir; **~dish** *a* rougeâtre; (*hair*) plutôt roux(rousse).
redecorate [ri:'dɛkəreɪt] *vt* refaire à neuf, repeindre et retapisser; **redecoration** [-'reɪʃən] *n* remise *f* à neuf.
redeem [rɪ'di:m] *vt* (*debt*) rembourser; (*sth in pawn*) dégager; (*fig, also* REL) racheter; **~ing** *a* (*feature*) qui sauve, qui rachète (le reste).
redeploy [ri:dɪ'plɔɪ] *vt* (*resources*) réorganiser.
red-haired [rɛd'hɛəd] *a* roux(rousse).
red-handed [rɛd'hændɪd] *a*: **to be caught ~** être pris(e) en flagrant délit *or* la main dans le sac.
redhead ['rɛdhɛd] *n* roux/rousse.
red herring ['rɛd'hɛrɪŋ] *n* (*fig*) diversion *f*, fausse piste.
red-hot [rɛd'hɔt] *a* chauffé(e) au rouge, brûlant(e).
redirect [ri:daɪ'rɛkt] *vt* (*mail*) faire suivre.
redistribute [ri:dɪ'strɪbju:t] *vt* redistribuer.
red-letter day ['rɛdlɛtə'deɪ] *n* grand jour, jour mémorable.
red light ['rɛd'laɪt] *n*: **to go through a ~** (AUT) brûler un feu rouge; **red-light district** *n* quartier réservé.
redness ['rɛdnɪs] *n* rougeur *f*; (*of hair*) rousseur *f*.
redo [ri:'du:] *vt irg* refaire.
redolent ['rɛdəulnt] *a*: **~ of** qui sent; (*fig*) qui évoque.
redouble [ri:'dʌbl] *vt*: **to ~ one's efforts** redoubler d'efforts.
redress [rɪ'drɛs] *n* réparation *f*.
red tape ['rɛd'teɪp] *n* (*fig*) paperasserie *f* (administrative).
reduce [rɪ'dju:s] *vt* réduire; (*lower*) abaisser; **'~ speed now'** (AUT) 'ralentir'; **at a ~d price** (*of goods*) au rabais, en solde; (*of ticket etc*) à prix réduit; **reduction** [rɪ'dʌkʃən] *n* réduction *f*; (*of price*) baisse *f*; (*discount*) rabais *m*; réduction.
redundancy [rɪ'dʌndənsɪ] *n* licenciement *m*, mise *f* au chômage.
redundant [rɪ'dʌndnt] *a* (*worker*) mis(e) au chômage, licencié(e); (*detail, object*) superflu(e); **to make ~** licencier, mettre au chômage.
reed [ri:d] *n* (BOT) roseau *m*; (MUS: *of clarinet etc*) anche *f*.
reef [ri:f] *n* (*at sea*) récif *m*, écueil *m*.
reek [ri:k] *vi*: **to ~ (of)** puer, empester.
reel [ri:l] *n* bobine *f*; (TECH) dévidoir *m*; (FISHING) moulinet *m*; (CINEMA) bande *f* // *vt* (TECH) bobiner; (*also*: **~ up**) enrouler // *vi* (*sway*) chanceler.
re-election [ri:ɪ'lɛkʃən] *n* réélection *f*.
re-engage [ri:ɪn'geɪdʒ] *vt* (*worker*) réembaucher.
re-enter [ri:'ɛntə*] *vt* rentrer dans; **re-entry** *n* rentrée *f*.
ref [rɛf] *n* (*col: abbr of* **referee**) arbitre *m*.
refectory [rɪ'fɛktərɪ] *n* réfectoire *m*.
refer [rɪ'fə:*] *vt*: **to ~ sb (*or* sth) to** (*dispute, decision*) soumettre qch à; (*inquirer: for information*) adresser *or* envoyer qn à; (*reader: to text*) renvoyer qn à; **to ~ to** *vt fus* (*allude to*) parler de, faire allusion à; (*apply to*) s'appliquer à; (*consult*) se reporter à; **~ring to your letter** (COMM) en réponse à votre lettre.
referee [rɛfə'ri:] *n* arbitre *m*; (*for job application*) répondant/e // *vt* arbitrer.
reference ['rɛfrəns] *n* référence *f*, renvoi *m*; (*mention*) allusion *f*, mention *f*; (*for job application: letter*) références; lettre *f* de recommandation; (: *person*) répondant/e; **with ~ to** en ce qui concerne; (COMM: *in letter*) me référant à; **'please quote this ~'** (COMM) 'prière de rappeler cette référence'; **~ book** *n* ouvrage *m* de référence.
referendum, *pl* referenda [rɛfə'rɛndəm, -də] *n* référendum *m*.
refill *vt* [ri:'fɪl] remplir à nouveau; (*pen, lighter etc*) recharger // *n* ['ri:fɪl] (*for pen etc*) recharge *f*.
refine [rɪ'faɪn] *vt* (*sugar, oil*) raffiner; (*taste*) affiner; **~d** *a* (*person, taste*) raffiné(e); **~ment** *n* (*of person*) raffinement *m*; **~ry** *n* raffinerie *f*.
reflect [rɪ'flɛkt] *vt* (*light, image*) réfléchir, refléter; (*fig*) refléter // *vi* (*think*) réfléchir, méditer; **to ~ on** *vt fus* (*discredit*) porter atteinte à, faire tort à; **~ion** [-'flɛkʃən] *n* réflexion *f*; (*image*) reflet *m*; (*criticism*): **~ion on** critique *f* de; atteinte *f* à; **on ~ion** réflexion faite; **~or** *n* (*also* AUT) réflecteur *m*.
reflex ['ri:flɛks] *a, n* réflexe (*m*); **~ive** [rɪ'flɛksɪv] *a* (LING) réfléchi(e).
reform [rɪ'fɔ:m] *n* réforme *f* // *vt* réformer; **the R~ation** [rɛfə'meɪʃən] *n* la Réforme; **~ed** *a* amendé(e), assagi(e); **~er** *n* réformateur/trice.
refrain [rɪ'freɪn] *vi*: **to ~ from doing** s'abstenir de faire // *n* refrain *m*.
refresh [rɪ'frɛʃ] *vt* rafraîchir; (*subj: food*) redonner des forces à; (: *sleep*) reposer; **~er course** *n* cours *m* de recyclage; **~ment room** *n* buffet *m*; **~ments** *npl* rafraîchissements *mpl*.
refrigeration [rɪfrɪdʒə'reɪʃən] *n* réfrigération *f*.
refrigerator [rɪ'frɪdʒəreɪtə*] *n* réfrigérateur *m*, frigidaire *m*.
refuel [ri:'fjuəl] *vt* ravitailler en carburant // *vi* se ravitailler en carburant.
refuge ['rɛfju:dʒ] *n* refuge *m*; **to take ~ in** se réfugier dans.
refugee [rɛfju'dʒi:] *n* réfugié/e.
refund *n* ['ri:fʌnd] remboursement *m* // *vt* [rɪ'fʌnd] rembourser.
refurbish [ri:'fə:bɪʃ] *vt* remettre à neuf.
refurnish [ri:'fə:nɪʃ] *vt* remeubler.
refusal [rɪ'fju:zəl] *n* refus *m*.

refuse *n* ['rɛfju:s] ordures *fpl*, détritus *mpl* // *vt*, *vi* [rɪ'fju:z] refuser ; ~ **collection** *n* ramassage *m* d'ordures ; ~ **collector** *n* éboueur *m*.
refute [rɪ'fju:t] *vt* réfuter.
regain [rɪ'geɪn] *vt* regagner ; retrouver.
regal ['ri:gl] *a* royal(e) ; ~**ia** [rɪ'geɪlɪə] *n* insignes *mpl* de la royauté.
regard [rɪ'gɑ:d] *n* respect *m*, estime *f*, considération *f* // *vt* considérer ; **to give one's ~s to** faire ses amitiés à ; **'with kindest ~s'** 'bien amicalement' ; ~**ing, as ~s, with ~ to** en ce qui concerne ; ~**less** *ad* quand même ; ~**less of** sans se soucier de.
regatta [rɪ'gætə] *n* régate *f*.
regency ['ri:dʒənsɪ] *n* régence *f*.
regent ['ri:dʒənt] *n* régent/e.
régime [reɪ'ʒi:m] *n* régime *m*.
regiment ['rɛdʒɪmənt] *n* régiment *m* ; ~**al** [-'mɛntl] *a* d'un *or* du régiment ; ~**ation** [-'teɪʃən] *n* réglementation excessive.
region ['ri:dʒən] *n* région *f* ; **in the ~ of** (*fig*) aux alentours de ; ~**al** *a* régional(e) ; ~**al development** *n* aménagement *m* du territoire.
register ['rɛdʒɪstə*] *n* registre *m* ; (*also:* **electoral** ~) liste électorale // *vt* enregistrer, inscrire ; (*birth*) déclarer ; (*vehicle*) immatriculer ; (*luggage*) enregistrer ; (*letter*) envoyer en recommandé ; (*subj: instrument*) marquer // *vi* se faire inscrire ; (*at hotel*) signer le registre ; (*make impression*) être (bien) compris(e) ; ~**ed** *a* (*design*) déposé(e) ; (*letter*) recommandé(e).
registrar ['rɛdʒɪstrɑ:*] *n* officier *m* de l'état civil ; secrétaire (général).
registration [rɛdʒɪs'treɪʃən] *n* (*act*) enregistrement *m* ; inscription *f* ; (*AUT: also:* ~ **number**) numéro *m* d'immatriculation.
registry ['rɛdʒɪstrɪ] *n* bureau *m* de l'enregistrement ; ~ **office** *n* bureau *m* de l'état civil ; **to get married in a ~ office** ≈ se marier à la mairie.
regret [rɪ'grɛt] *n* regret *m* // *vt* regretter ; **to ~ that** regretter que + *sub* ; ~**fully** *ad* à *or* avec regret ; ~**table** *a* regrettable.
regroup [ri:'gru:p] *vt* regrouper // *vi* se regrouper.
regular ['rɛgjulə*] *a* régulier(ère) ; (*usual*) habituel(le), normal(e) ; (*soldier*) de métier ; (*COMM: size*) ordinaire // *n* (*client etc*) habitué/e ; ~**ity** [-'lærɪtɪ] *n* régularité *f* ; ~**ly** *ad* régulièrement.
regulate ['rɛgjuleɪt] *vt* régler ; **regulation** [-'leɪʃən] *n* (*rule*) règlement *m* ; (*adjustment*) réglage *m* // *cpd* réglementaire.
rehabilitation ['ri:həbɪlɪ'teɪʃən] *n* (*of offender*) réhabilitation *f* ; (*of disabled*) rééducation *f*, réadaptation *f*.
rehash [ri:'hæʃ] *vt* (*col*) remanier.
rehearsal [rɪ'hə:səl] *n* répétition *f*.
rehearse [rɪ'hə:s] *vt* répéter.
reign [reɪn] *n* règne *m* // *vi* régner ; ~**ing** *a* (*monarch*) régnant(e) ; (*champion*) actuel(le).
reimburse [ri:ɪm'bə:s] *vt* rembourser.
rein [reɪn] *n* (*for horse*) rêne *f*.
reincarnation [ri:ɪnkɑ:'neɪʃən] *n* réincarnation *f*.
reindeer ['reɪndɪə*] *n* (*pl inv*) renne *m*.
reinforce [ri:ɪn'fɔ:s] *vt* renforcer ; ~**d concrete** *n* béton armé ; ~**ment** *n* (*action*) renforcement *m* ; ~**ments** *npl* (*MIL*) renfort(s) *m(pl)*.
reinstate [ri:ɪn'steɪt] *vt* rétablir, réintégrer.
reissue [ri:'ɪʃju:] *vt* (*book*) rééditer ; (*film*) ressortir.
reiterate [ri:'ɪtəreɪt] *vt* réitérer, répéter.
reject *n* ['ri:dʒɛkt] (*COMM*) article *m* de rebut // *vt* [rɪ'dʒɛkt] refuser ; (*COMM: goods*) mettre au rebut ; (*idea*) rejeter ; ~**ion** [rɪ'dʒɛkʃən] *n* rejet *m*, refus *m*.
rejoice [rɪ'dʒɔɪs] *vi*: **to ~ (at** *or* **over)** se réjouir (de).
rejuvenate [rɪ'dʒu:vəneɪt] *vt* rajeunir.
rekindle [ri:'kɪndl] *vt* rallumer ; (*fig*) raviver.
relapse [rɪ'læps] *n* (*MED*) rechute *f*.
relate [rɪ'leɪt] *vt* (*tell*) raconter ; (*connect*) établir un rapport entre ; ~**d** *a* apparenté(e) ; ~**d to** apparenté à ; **relating: relating to** *prep* concernant.
relation [rɪ'leɪʃən] *n* (*person*) parent/e ; (*link*) rapport *m*, lien *m* ; ~**ship** *n* rapport *m*, lien *m* ; (*personal ties*) relations *fpl*, rapports ; (*also:* **family ~ship**) lien *m* de parenté ; (*affair*) liaison *f*.
relative ['rɛlətɪv] *n* parent/e // *a* relatif(ive) ; (*respective*) respectif(ive) ; **all her ~s** toute sa famille ; ~**ly** *ad* relativement.
relax [rɪ'læks] *vi* se relâcher ; (*person: unwind*) se détendre // *vt* relâcher ; (*mind, person*) détendre ; ~**ation** [ri:læk'seɪʃən] *n* relâchement *m* ; détente *f* ; (*entertainment*) distraction *f* ; ~**ed** *a* relâché(e) ; détendu(e) ; ~**ing** *a* délassant(e).
relay ['ri:leɪ] *n* (*SPORT*) course *f* de relais // *vt* (*message*) retransmettre, relayer.
release [rɪ'li:s] *n* (*from prison, obligation*) libération *f* ; (*of gas etc*) émission *f* ; (*of film etc*) sortie *f* ; (*record*) disque *m* ; (*device*) déclencheur *m* // *vt* (*prisoner*) libérer ; (*book, film*) sortir ; (*report, news*) rendre public, publier ; (*gas etc*) émettre, dégager ; (*free: from wreckage etc*) dégager ; (*TECH: catch, spring etc*) déclencher ; (*let go*) relâcher ; lâcher ; desserrer ; **to ~ one's grip** *or* **hold** lâcher prise ; **to ~ the clutch** (*AUT*) débrayer.
relegate ['rɛləgeɪt] *vt* reléguer.
relent [rɪ'lɛnt] *vi* se laisser fléchir ; ~**less** *a* implacable.
relevance ['rɛləvəns] *n* pertinence *f* ; ~ **of sth to sth** rapport *m* entre qch et qch.
relevant ['rɛləvənt] *a* approprié(e) ; (*fact*) significatif(ive) ; (*information*) utile, pertinent(e) ; ~ **to** ayant rapport à, approprié à.
reliability [rɪlaɪə'bɪlɪtɪ] *n* sérieux *m* ; solidité *f*.
reliable [rɪ'laɪəbl] *a* (*person, firm*) sérieux(euse) ; (*method*) sûr(e) ; (*machine*) solide ; **reliably** *ad*: **to be reliably informed** savoir de source sûre.
reliance [rɪ'laɪəns] *n*: ~ **(on)** confiance *f* (en) ; besoin *m* (de), dépendance *f* (de).
relic ['rɛlɪk] *n* (*REL*) relique *f* ; (*of the past*) vestige *m*.
relief [rɪ'li:f] *n* (*from pain, anxiety*) soulagement *m* ; (*help, supplies*) secours *m(pl)* ; (*of*

guard) relève *f* ; (ART. GEO) relief *m* ; ~ **road** *n* route *f* de délestage ; ~ **valve** *n* soupape *f* de sûreté.
relieve [rɪ'li:v] *vt* (*pain, patient*) soulager ; (*bring help*) secourir ; (*take over from*: *gen*) relayer ; (: *guard*) relever ; **to ~ sb of sth** débarrasser qn de qch.
religion [rɪ'lɪdʒən] *n* religion *f*; **religious** *a* religieux(euse) ; (*book*) de piété.
reline [ri:'laɪn] *vt* (*brakes*) refaire la garniture de.
relinquish [rɪ'lɪŋkwɪʃ] *vt* abandonner ; (*plan, habit*) renoncer à.
relish ['rɛlɪʃ] *n* (CULIN) condiment *m* ; (*enjoyment*) délectation *f* // *vt* (*food etc*) savourer ; **to ~ doing** se délecter à faire.
relive [ri:'lɪv] *vt* revivre.
reload [ri:'ləud] *vt* recharger.
reluctance [rɪ'lʌktəns] *n* répugnance *f*.
reluctant [rɪ'lʌktənt] *a* peu disposé(e), qui hésite ; **~ly** *ad* à contrecœur, sans enthousiasme.
rely [rɪ'laɪ]: **to ~ on** *vt fus* compter sur ; (*be dependent*) dépendre de.
remain [rɪ'meɪn] *vi* rester ; **~der** *n* reste *m* ; (COMM) fin *f* de série ; **~ing** *a* qui reste ; **~s** *npl* restes *mpl*.
remand [rɪ'mɑ:nd] *n*: **on ~** en détention préventive // *vt*: **to ~ in custody** écrouer ; renvoyer en détention provisoire ; ~ **home** *n* maison *f* d'arrêt.
remark [rɪ'mɑ:k] *n* remarque *f*, observation *f* // *vt* (faire) remarquer, dire ; (*notice*) remarquer ; **~able** *a* remarquable.
remarry [ri:'mærɪ] *vi* se remarier.
remedial [rɪ'mi:dɪəl] *a* (*tuition, classes*) de rattrapage.
remedy ['rɛmədɪ] *n*: ~ **(for)** remède *m* (contre *or* à) // *vt* remédier à.
remember [rɪ'mɛmbə*] *vt* se rappeler, se souvenir de ; ~ **me to** (*in letter*) rappelez-moi au bon souvenir de ; **remembrance** *n* souvenir *m* ; mémoire *f*.
remind [rɪ'maɪnd] *vt*: **to ~ sb of sth** rappeler qch à qn ; **to ~ sb to do** faire penser à qn à faire, rappeler à qn qu'il doit faire ; **~er** *n* rappel *m* ; (*note etc*) pense-bête *m*.
reminisce [rɛmɪ'nɪs] *vi*: **to ~ (about)** évoquer ses souvenirs (de).
reminiscences [rɛmɪ'nɪsnsɪz] *npl* réminiscences *fpl*, souvenirs *mpl*.
reminiscent [rɛmɪ'nɪsnt] *a*: ~ **of** qui rappelle, qui fait penser à.
remission [rɪ'mɪʃən] *n* rémission *f*; (*of debt, sentence*) remise *f* ; (*of fee*) exemption *f*.
remit [rɪ'mɪt] *vt* (*send: money*) envoyer ; **~tance** *n* envoi *m*, paiement *m*.
remnant ['rɛmnənt] *n* reste *m*, restant *m* ; **~s** *npl* (COMM) coupons *mpl* ; fins *fpl* de série.
remorse [rɪ'mɔ:s] *n* remords *m* ; **~ful** *a* plein(e) de remords ; **~less** *a* (*fig*) impitoyable.
remote [rɪ'məut] *a* éloigné(e), lointain(e) ; (*person*) distant(e) ; ~ **control** *n* télécommande *f*; **~ly** *ad* au loin ; (*slightly*) très vaguement ; **~ness** *n* éloignement *m*.
remould ['ri:məuld] *n* (*tyre*) pneu rechapé.
removable [rɪ'mu:vəbl] *a* (*detachable*) amovible.
removal [rɪ'mu:vəl] *n* (*taking away*) enlèvement *m*; suppression *f*; (*from house*) déménagement *m* ; (*from office: sacking*) renvoi *m* ; (MED) ablation *f*; ~ **man** *n* déménageur *m* ; ~ **van** *n* camion *m* de déménagement.
remove [rɪ'mu:v] *vt* enlever, retirer ; (*employee*) renvoyer ; (*stain*) faire partir ; (*doubt, abuse*) supprimer ; **~r** (*for paint*) décapant *m* ; (*for varnish*) dissolvant *m* ; **~rs** *npl* (*company*) entreprise *f* de déménagement.
remuneration [rɪmju:nə'reɪʃən] *n* rémunération *f*.
rename [ri:'neɪm] *vt* rebaptiser.
rend, *pt, pp* **rent** [rɛnd, rɛnt] *vt* déchirer.
render ['rɛndə*] *vt* rendre ; (CULIN: *fat*) clarifier ; **~ing** *n* (MUS *etc*) interprétation *f*.
rendez-vous ['rɔndɪvu:] *n* rendez-vous *m inv* // *vi* opérer une jonction, se rejoindre.
renegade ['rɛnɪgeɪd] *n* rénégat/e.
renew [rɪ'nju:] *vt* renouveler ; (*negotiations*) reprendre ; (*acquaintance*) renouer ; **~al** *n* renouvellement *m* ; reprise *f*.
renounce [rɪ'nauns] *vt* renoncer à ; (*disown*) renier.
renovate ['rɛnəveɪt] *vt* rénover ; (*art work*) restaurer ; **renovation** [-'veɪʃən] *n* rénovation *f*; restauration *f*.
renown [rɪ'naun] *n* renommée *f*; **~ed** *a* renommé(e).
rent [rɛnt] *pt, pp of* **rend** // *n* loyer *m* // *vt* louer ; **~al** *n* (*for television, car*) (prix *m* de) location *f*.
renunciation [rɪnʌnsɪ'eɪʃən] *n* renonciation *f*; (*self-denial*) renoncement *m*.
reopen [ri:'əupən] *vt* rouvrir ; **~ing** *n* réouverture *f*.
reorder [ri:'ɔ:də*] *vt* commander de nouveau ; (*rearrange*) réorganiser.
reorganize [ri:'ɔ:gənaɪz] *vt* réorganiser.
rep [rɛp] *n* (COMM: *abbr of* **representative**) représentant *m* (de commerce) ; (THEATRE: *abbr of* **repertory**) théâtre *m* de répertoire.
repair [rɪ'pɛə*] *n* réparation *f* // *vt* réparer ; **in good/bad ~** en bon/mauvais état ; ~ **kit** *n* trousse *f* de réparations ; ~ **man** *n* réparateur *m* ; ~ **shop** *n* (AUT *etc*) atelier *m* de réparations.
repartee [rɛpɑ:'ti:] *n* repartie *f*.
repay [ri:'peɪ] *vt irg* (*money, creditor*) rembourser ; (*sb's efforts*) récompenser ; **~ment** *n* remboursement *m* ; récompense *f*.
repeal [rɪ'pi:l] *n* (*of law*) abrogation *f*; (*of sentence*) annulation *f* // *vt* abroger ; annuler.
repeat [rɪ'pi:t] *n* (RADIO, TV) reprise *f* // *vt* répéter ; (*pattern*) reproduire ; (*promise, attack, also* COMM: *order*) renouveler ; (SCOL: *a class*) redoubler ; **~edly** *ad* souvent, à plusieurs reprises.
repel [rɪ'pɛl] *vt* (*lit, fig*) repousser ; **~lent** *a* repoussant(e) // *n*: **insect ~lent** insectifuge *m* ; **moth ~lent** produit *m* antimite(s).
repent [rɪ'pɛnt] *vi*: **to ~ (of)** se repentir (de) ; **~ance** *n* repentir *m*.
repercussion [ri:pə'kʌʃən] *n* (*consequence*) répercussion *f*.

repertoire ['rɛpətwɑ:*] *n* répertoire *m.*
repertory ['rɛpətərı] *n* (*also*: ~ **theatre**) théâtre *m* de répertoire.
repetition [rɛpı'tıʃən] *n* répétition *f*; (*of promise*, COMM: *order etc*) renouvellement *m.*
repetitive [rı'pɛtıtıv] *a* (*movement, work*) répétitif(ive); (*speech*) plein(e) de redites.
replace [rı'pleıs] *vt* (*put back*) remettre, replacer; (*take the place of*) remplacer; (TEL): '~ **the receiver**' 'raccrochez'; ~**ment** *n* replacement *m*; remplacement *m*; (*person*) remplaçant/e; ~**ment part** *n* pièce *f* de rechange.
replenish [rı'plɛnıʃ] *vt* (*glass*) remplir (de nouveau); (*stock etc*) réapprovisionner.
replete [rı'pli:t] *a* rempli(e); (*well-fed*) rassasié(e).
replica ['rɛplıkə] *n* réplique *f*, copie exacte.
reply [rı'plaı] *n* réponse *f* // *vi* répondre.
report [rı'pɔ:t] *n* rapport *m*; (PRESS *etc*) reportage *m*; (*also*: **school** ~) bulletin *m* (scolaire); (*of gun*) détonation *f* // *vt* rapporter, faire un compte rendu de; (PRESS *etc*) faire un reportage sur; (*bring to notice*: *occurrence*) signaler; (: *person*) dénoncer // *vi* (*make a report*) faire un rapport (*or* un reportage); (*present o.s.*): **to** ~ **(to sb)** se présenter (chez qn); **it is** ~**ed that** on dit *or* annonce que; ~**ed speech** *n* (LING) discours indirect; ~**er** *n* reporter *m.*
reprehensible [rɛprı'hɛnsıbl] *a* répréhensible.
represent [rɛprı'zɛnt] *vt* représenter; (*explain*): **to** ~ **to sb that** expliquer à qn que; ~**ation** [-'teıʃən] *n* représentation *f*; ~**ations** *npl* (*protest*) démarche *f*; ~**ative** *n* représentant/e; (US: POL) député *m* // *a* représentatif(ive), caractéristique.
repress [rı'prɛs] *vt* réprimer; ~**ion** [-'prɛʃən] *n* répression *f*; ~**ive** *a* répressif(ive).
reprieve [rı'pri:v] *n* (LAW) grâce *f*; (*fig*) sursis *m*, délai *m* // *vt* gracier; accorder un sursis *or* un délai à.
reprimand ['rɛprımɑ:nd] *n* réprimande *f* // *vt* réprimander.
reprint *n* ['ri:prınt] réimpression *f* // *vt* [ri:'prınt] réimprimer.
reprisal [rı'praızl] *n* représailles *fpl.*
reproach [rı'prəutʃ] *n* reproche *m* // *vt*: **to** ~ **sb with sth** reprocher qch à qn; **beyond** ~ irréprochable; ~**ful** *a* de reproche.
reproduce [ri:prə'dju:s] *vt* reproduire // *vi* se reproduire; **reproduction** [-'dʌkʃən] *n* reproduction *f*; **reproductive** [-'dʌktıv] *a* reproducteur(trice).
reprove [rı'pru:v] *vt* (*action*) réprouver; (*person*): **to** ~ **(for)** blâmer (de); **reproving** *a* réprobateur(trice).
reptile ['rɛptaıl] *n* reptile *m.*
republic [rı'pʌblık] *n* république *f*; ~**an** *a,n* républicain(e).
repudiate [rı'pju:dıeıt] *vt* (*wife, accusation*) répudier; (*friend*) renier.
repugnant [rı'pʌgnənt] *a* répugnant(e).
repulse [rı'pʌls] *vt* repousser.
repulsion [rı'pʌlʃən] *n* répulsion *f.*
repulsive [rı'pʌlsıv] *a* repoussant(e), répulsif(ive).
reputable ['rɛpjutəbl] *a* de bonne réputation; (*occupation*) honorable.
reputation [rɛpju'teıʃən] *n* réputation *f*; **to have a** ~ **for** être réputé(e) pour.
repute [rı'pju:t] *n* (bonne) réputation; ~**d** *a* réputé(e); ~**dly** *ad* d'après ce qu'on dit.
request [rı'kwɛst] *n* demande *f*; (*formal*) requête *f* // *vt*: **to** ~ **(of** *or* **from sb)** demander (à qn); ~ **stop** *n* (*for bus*) arrêt facultatif.
requiem ['rɛkwıəm] *n* requiem *m.*
require [rı'kwaıə*] *vt* (*need*: *subj*: *person*) avoir besoin de; (: *thing, situation*) demander; (*want*) vouloir; exiger; (*order*) obliger; ~**d** *a* requis(e), voulu(e); **if** ~**d** s'il le faut; ~**ment** *n* exigence *f*; besoin *m*; condition requise.
requisite ['rɛkwızıt] *n* chose nécessaire // *a* requis(e), nécessaire; **toilet** ~**s** accessoires *mpl* de toilette.
requisition [rɛkwı'zıʃən] *n*: ~ **(for)** demande *f* (de) // *vt* (MIL) réquisitionner.
reroute [ri:'ru:t] *vt* (*train etc*) dérouter.
resale ['ri:'seıl] *n* revente *f.*
rescind [rı'sınd] *vt* annuler; (*law*) abroger; (*judgment*) rescinder.
rescue ['rɛskju:] *n* sauvetage *m*; (*help*) secours *mpl* // *vt* sauver; ~ **party** *n* équipe *f* de sauvetage; ~**r** *n* sauveteur *m.*
research [rı'sə:tʃ] *n* recherche(s) *f(pl)* // *vt* faire des recherches sur; ~**er** *n* chercheur/euse; ~ **work** *n* recherches *fpl*; ~ **worker** *n* chercheur/euse.
resell [ri:'sɛl] *vt irg* revendre.
resemblance [rı'zɛmbləns] *n* ressemblance *f.*
resemble [rı'zɛmbl] *vt* ressembler à.
resent [rı'zɛnt] *vt* éprouver du ressentiment de, être contrarié(e) par; ~**ful** *a* irrité(e), plein(e) de ressentiment; ~**ment** *n* ressentiment *m.*
reservation [rɛzə'veıʃən] *n* (*booking*) réservation *f*; (*doubt*) réserve *f*; (*protected area*) réserve; (*on road*: *also*: **central** ~) bande *f* médiane; **to make a** ~ **(in an hotel/a restaurant/a plane)** réserver *or* retenir une chambre/une table/une place.
reserve [rı'zə:v] *n* réserve *f*; (SPORT) remplaçant/e // *vt* (*seats etc*) réserver, retenir; ~**s** *npl* (MIL) réservistes *mpl*; **in** ~ en réserve; ~**d** *a* réservé(e); **reservist** *n* (MIL) réserviste *m.*
reservoir ['rɛzəvwɑ:*] *n* réservoir *m.*
reshape [ri:'ʃeıp] *vt* (*policy*) réorganiser.
reshuffle [ri:'ʃʌfl] *n*: **Cabinet** ~ (POL) remaniement ministériel.
reside [rı'zaıd] *vi* résider.
residence ['rɛzıdəns] *n* résidence *f*; ~ **permit** *n* permis *m* de séjour.
resident ['rɛzıdənt] *n* résident/e // *a* résidant(e).
residential [rɛzı'dɛnʃəl] *a* de résidence; (*area*) résidentiel(le).
residue ['rɛzıdju:] *n* reste *m*; (CHEM, PHYSICS) résidu *m.*
resign [rı'zaın] *vt* (*one's post*) se démettre de // *vi* démissionner; **to** ~ **o.s. to** (*endure*) se résigner à; ~**ation** [rɛzıg'neıʃən] *n* démission *f*; résignation *f*; ~**ed** *a* résigné(e).

resilience [rɪ'zɪlɪəns] *n* (*of material*) élasticité *f*; (*of person*) ressort *m*.
resilient [rɪ'zɪlɪənt] *a* (*person*) qui réagit, qui a du ressort.
resin ['rɛzɪn] *n* résine *f*.
resist [rɪ'zɪst] *vt* résister à; **~ance** *n* résistance *f*.
resolute ['rɛzəlu:t] *a* résolu(e).
resolution [rɛzə'lu:ʃən] *n* résolution *f*.
resolve [rɪ'zɔlv] *n* résolution *f* // *vt* (*decide*): **to ~ to do** résoudre *or* décider de faire; (*problem*) résoudre; **~d** *a* résolu(e).
resonant ['rɛzənənt] *a* résonnant(e).
resort [rɪ'zɔ:t] *n* (*town*) station *f*; (*recourse*) recours *m* // *vi*: **to ~ to** avoir recours à; **in the last ~** en dernier ressort.
resound [rɪ'zaund] *vi*: **to ~ (with)** retentir (de); **~ing** *a* retentissant(e).
resource [rɪ'sɔ:s] *n* ressource *f*; **~s** *npl* ressources; **~ful** *a* plein(e) de ressource, débrouillard(e); **~fulness** *n* ressource *f*.
respect [rɪs'pɛkt] *n* respect *m* // *vt* respecter; **with ~ to** en ce qui concerne; **in ~ of** sous le rapport de, quant à; **in this ~** sous ce rapport, à cet égard; **~ability** [-ə'bɪlɪtɪ] *n* respectabilité *f*; **~able** *a* respectable; **~ful** *a* respectueux(euse).
respective [rɪs'pɛktɪv] *a* respectif(ive); **~ly** *ad* respectivement.
respiration [rɛspɪ'reɪʃən] *n* respiration *f*.
respirator ['rɛspɪreɪtə*] *n* respirateur *m*.
respiratory [rɛs'pɪrətərɪ] *a* respiratoire.
respite ['rɛspaɪt] *n* répit *m*.
resplendent [rɪs'plɛndənt] *a* resplendissant(e).
respond [rɪs'pɔnd] *vi* répondre; (*to treatment*) réagir.
response [rɪs'pɔns] *n* réponse *f*; (*to treatment*) réaction *f*.
responsibility [rɪspɔnsɪ'bɪlɪtɪ] *n* responsabilité *f*.
responsible [rɪs'pɔnsɪbl] *a* (*liable*): **~ (for)** responsable (de); (*character*) digne de confiance; (*job*) qui comporte des responsabilités; **responsibly** *ad* avec sérieux.
responsive [rɪs'pɔnsɪv] *a* qui n'est pas réservé(e) *or* indifférent(e).
rest [rɛst] *n* repos *m*; (*stop*) arrêt *m*, pause *f*; (MUS) silence *m*; (*support*) support *m*, appui *m*; (*remainder*) reste *m*, restant *m* // *vi* se reposer; (*be supported*): **to ~ on** appuyer *or* reposer sur; (*remain*) rester // *vt* (*lean*): **to ~ sth on/against** appuyer qch sur/contre; **the ~ of them** les autres; **it ~s with him to** c'est à lui de.
restart [ri:'stɑ:t] *vt* (*engine*) remettre en marche; (*work*) reprendre.
restaurant ['rɛstərɔŋ] *n* restaurant *m*; **~ car** *n* wagon-restaurant *m*.
rest cure ['rɛstkjuə*] *n* cure *f* de repos.
restful ['rɛstful] *a* reposant(e).
rest home ['rɛsthəum] *n* maison *f* de repos.
restitution [rɛstɪ'tju:ʃən] *n* (*act*) restitution *f*; (*reparation*) réparation *f*.
restive ['rɛstɪv] *a* agité(e), impatient(e); (*horse*) rétif(ive).
restless ['rɛstlɪs] *a* agité(e); **~ly** *ad* avec agitation.
restock [ri:'stɔk] *vt* réapprovisionner.
restoration [rɛstə'reɪʃən] *n* restauration *f*; restitution *f*.
restore [rɪ'stɔ:*] *vt* (*building*) restaurer; (*sth stolen*) restituer; (*peace, health*) rétablir.
restrain [rɪs'treɪn] *vt* (*feeling*) contenir; (*person*): **to ~ (from doing)** retenir (de faire); **~ed** *a* (*style*) sobre; (*manner*) mesuré(e); **~t** *n* (*restriction*) contrainte *f*; (*moderation*) retenue *f*; (*of style*) sobriété *f*.
restrict [rɪs'trɪkt] *vt* restreindre, limiter; **~ed area** *n* (AUT) zone *f* à vitesse limitée; **~ion** [-kʃən] *n* restriction *f*, limitation *f*; **~ive** *a* restrictif(ive).
rest room ['rɛstrum] *n* (*US*) toilettes *fpl*.
result [rɪ'zʌlt] *n* résultat *m* // *vi*: **to ~ in** aboutir à, se terminer par.
resume [rɪ'zju:m] *vt, vi* (*work, journey*) reprendre.
resumption [rɪ'zʌmpʃən] *n* reprise *f*.
resurgence [rɪ'sə:dʒəns] *n* réapparition *f*.
resurrection [rɛzə'rɛkʃən] *n* résurrection *f*.
resuscitate [rɪ'sʌsɪteɪt] *vt* (MED) réanimer; **resuscitation** [-'teɪʃn] *n* réanimation *f*.
retail ['ri:teɪl] *n* (vente *f* au) détail *m* // *cpd* de *or* au détail // *vt* vendre au détail; **~er** *n* détaillant/e; **~ price** *n* prix *m* de détail.
retain [rɪ'teɪn] *vt* (*keep*) garder, conserver; (*employ*) engager; **~er** *n* (*servant*) serviteur *m*; (*fee*) acompte *m*, provision *f*.
retaliate [rɪ'tælɪeɪt] *vi*: **to ~ (against)** se venger (de); **to ~ (on sb)** rendre la pareille (à qn); **retaliation** [-'eɪʃən] *n* représailles *fpl*, vengeance *f*.
retarded [rɪ'tɑ:dɪd] *a* retardé(e).
retch [rɛtʃ] *vi* avoir des haut-le-coeur.
retentive [rɪ'tɛntɪv] *a*: **~ memory** excellente mémoire.
rethink ['ri:'θɪŋk] *vt* repenser.
reticence ['rɛtɪsns] *n* réticence *f*.
reticent ['rɛtɪsnt] *a* réticent(e).
retina ['rɛtɪnə] *n* rétine *f*.
retinue ['rɛtɪnju:] *n* suite *f*, cortège *m*.
retire [rɪ'taɪə*] *vi* (*give up work*) prendre sa retraite; (*withdraw*) se retirer, partir; (*go to bed*) (aller) se coucher; **~d** *a* (*person*) retraité(e); **~ment** *n* retraite *f*; **retiring** *a* (*person*) réservé(e); **retiring age** *n* âge *m* de la retraite.
retort [rɪ'tɔ:t] *n* (*reply*) riposte *f*; (*container*) cornue *f* // *vi* riposter.
retrace [ri:'treɪs] *vt* reconstituer; **to ~ one's steps** revenir sur ses pas.
retract [rɪ'trækt] *vt* (*statement, claws*) rétracter; (*undercarriage, aerial*) rentrer, escamoter // *vi* se rétracter; rentrer; **~able** *a* escamotable.
retrain [ri:'treɪn] *vt* (*worker*) recycler; **~ing** *n* recyclage *m*.
retread [ri:'trɛd] *vt* (AUT: *tyre*) rechaper.
retreat [rɪ'tri:t] *n* retraite *f* // *vi* battre en retraite; (*flood*) reculer.
retrial [ri:'traɪəl] *n* nouveau procès.

retribution [rɛtrɪ'bju:ʃən] *n* châtiment *m*.
retrieval [rɪ'tri:vəl] *n* récupération *f*; réparation *f*; recherche *f* et extraction *f*.
retrieve [rɪ'tri:v] *vt* (*sth lost*) récupérer; (*situation, honour*) sauver; (*error, loss*) réparer; (COMPUTERS) rechercher; **~r** *n* chien *m* d'arrêt.
retrospect ['rɛtrəspɛkt] *n*: **in ~** rétrospectivement, après coup; **~ive** [-'spɛktɪv] *a* (*law*) rétroactif(ive).
return [rɪ'tə:n] *n* (*going or coming back*) retour *m*; (*of sth stolen etc*) restitution *f*; (*recompense*) récompense *f*; (FINANCE: *from land, shares*) rapport *m*; (*report*) relevé *m*, rapport // *cpd* (*journey*) de retour; (*ticket*) aller et retour; (*match*) retour // *vi* (*person etc: come back*) revenir; (: *go back*) retourner // *vt* rendre; (*bring back*) rapporter; (*send back*) renvoyer; (*put back*) remettre; (POL: *candidate*) élire; **~s** *npl* (COMM) recettes *fpl*; bénéfices *mpl*; **many happy ~s (of the day)!** bon anniversaire!; **~able** *a* (*bottle etc*) consigné(e).
reunion [ri:'ju:nɪən] *n* réunion *f*.
reunite [ri:ju:'naɪt] *vt* réunir.
rev [rɛv] *n* (*abbr of* **revolution**: AUT) tour *m* // *vb* (*also*: **~ up**) *vt* emballer // *vi* s'emballer.
revamp ['ri:'væmp] *vt* (*house*) retaper; (*firm*) réorganiser.
reveal [rɪ'vi:l] *vt* (*make known*) révéler; (*display*) laisser voir; **~ing** *a* révélateur(trice); (*dress*) au décolleté généreux *or* suggestif.
reveille [rɪ'vælɪ] *n* (MIL) réveil *m*.
revel ['rɛvl] *vi*: **to ~ in sth/in doing** se délecter de qch/à faire.
revelation [rɛvə'leɪʃən] *n* révélation *f*.
reveller ['rɛvlə*] *n* fêtard *m*.
revelry ['rɛvlrɪ] *n* festivités *fpl*.
revenge [rɪ'vɛndʒ] *n* vengeance *f*; (*in game etc*) revanche *f* // *vt* venger; **to take ~** se venger; **~ful** *a* vengeur(eresse); vindicatif(ive).
revenue ['rɛvənju:] *n* revenu *m*.
reverberate [rɪ'və:bəreɪt] *vi* (*sound*) retentir, se répercuter; (*light*) se réverbérer; **reverberation** [-'reɪʃən] *n* répercussion *f*; réverbération *f*.
revere [rɪ'vɪə*] *vt* vénérer, révérer.
reverence ['rɛvərəns] *n* vénération *f*, révérence *f*.
reverent ['rɛvərənt] *a* respectueux(euse).
reverie ['rɛvərɪ] *n* rêverie *f*.
reversal [rɪ'və:sl] *n* (*of opinion*) revirement *m*.
reverse [rɪ'və:s] *n* contraire *m*, opposé *m*; (*back*) dos *m*, envers *m*; (AUT: *also*: **~ gear**) marche *f* arrière // *a* (*order, direction*) opposé(e), inverse // *vt* (*turn*) renverser, retourner; (*change*) renverser, changer complètement; (LAW: *judgment*) réformer // *vi* (AUT) faire marche arrière; **~d charge call** *n* (TEL) communication *f* en PCV.
reversion [rɪ'və:ʃən] *n* retour *m*.
revert [rɪ'və:t] *vi*: **to ~ to** revenir à, retourner à.
review [rɪ'vju:] *n* revue *f*; (*of book, film*) critique *f* // *vt* passer en revue; faire la critique de; **~er** *n* critique *m*.
revise [rɪ'vaɪz] *vt* (*manuscript*) revoir, corriger; (*opinion*) réviser, modifier; (*study: subject, notes*) réviser; **revision** [rɪ'vɪʒən] *n* révision *f*.
revitalize [ri:'vaɪtəlaɪz] *vt* revitaliser.
revival [rɪ'vaɪvəl] *n* reprise *f*; rétablissement *m*; (*of faith*) renouveau *m*.
revive [rɪ'vaɪv] *vt* (*person*) ranimer; (*custom*) rétablir; (*hope, courage*) redonner; (*play, fashion*) reprendre // *vi* (*person*) reprendre connaissance; (*hope*) renaître; (*activity*) reprendre.
revoke [rɪ'vəuk] *vt* révoquer; (*promise, decision*) revenir sur.
revolt [rɪ'vəult] *n* révolte *f* // *vi* se révolter, se rebeller; **~ing** *a* dégoûtant(e).
revolution [rɛvə'lu:ʃən] *n* révolution *f*; (*of wheel etc*) tour *m*, révolution; **~ary** *a, n* révolutionnaire (*m/f*); **rev(olution) counter** *n* compte-tours *m inv*; **~ize** *vt* révolutionner.
revolve [rɪ'vɔlv] *vi* tourner.
revolver [rɪ'vɔlvə*] *n* revolver *m*.
revolving [rɪ'vɔlvɪŋ] *a* (*chair*) pivotant(e); (*light*) tournant(e); **~ door** *n* (porte *f* à) tambour *m*.
revue [rɪ'vju:] *n* (THEATRE) revue *f*.
revulsion [rɪ'vʌlʃən] *n* dégoût *m*, répugnance *f*.
reward [rɪ'wɔ:d] *n* récompense *f* // *vt*: **to ~ (for)** récompenser (de); **~ing** *a* (*fig*) qui (en) vaut la peine.
rewind [ri:'waɪnd] *vt irg* (*watch*) remonter; (*ribbon etc*) réembobiner.
rewire [ri:'waɪə*] *vt* (*house*) refaire l'installation électrique de.
reword [ri:'wə:d] *vt* formuler *or* exprimer différemment.
rewrite [ri:'raɪt] *vt irg* récrire.
rhapsody ['ræpsədɪ] *n* (MUS) rhapsodie *f*; (*fig*) éloge délirant.
rhetoric ['rɛtərɪk] *n* rhétorique *f*; **~al** [rɪ'tɔrɪkl] *a* rhétorique.
rheumatic [ru:'mætɪk] *a* rhumatismal(e).
rheumatism ['ru:mətɪzəm] *n* rhumatisme *m*.
Rhine [raɪn] *n*: **the ~** le Rhin.
rhinoceros [raɪ'nɔsərəs] *n* rhinocéros *m*.
Rhodesia [rəu'di:ʒə] *n* Rhodésie *f*; **~n** *a* rhodésien(ne) // *n* Rhodésien/ne.
rhododendron [rəudə'dɛndrn] *n* rhododendron *m*.
Rhone [rəun] *n*: **the ~** le Rhône.
rhubarb ['ru:bɑ:b] *n* rhubarbe *f*.
rhyme [raɪm] *n* rime *f*; (*verse*) vers *mpl*.
rhythm ['rɪðm] *n* rythme *m*; **~ic(al)** *a* rythmique; **~ically** *ad* avec rythme.
rib [rɪb] *n* (ANAT) côte *f* // *vt* (*mock*) taquiner.
ribald ['rɪbəld] *a* paillard(e).
ribbed [rɪbd] *a* (*knitting*) à côtes; (*shell*) strié(e).
ribbon ['rɪbən] *n* ruban *m*; **in ~s** (*torn*) en lambeaux.
rice [raɪs] *n* riz *m*; **~field** *n* rizière *f*; **~ pudding** *n* riz *m* au lait.
rich [rɪtʃ] *a* riche; (*gift, clothes*) somptueux(euse); **the ~** les riches *mpl*; **~es** *npl* richesses *fpl*; **~ness** *n* richesse *f*.
rickets ['rɪkɪts] *n* rachitisme *m*.

rickety ['rɪkɪtɪ] *a* branlant(e).
rickshaw ['rɪkʃɔ:] *n* pousse(-pousse) *m inv.*
ricochet ['rɪkəʃeɪ] *n* ricochet *m* // *vi* ricocher.
rid, *pt, pp* **rid** [rɪd] *vt*: **to ~ sb of** débarrasser qn de; **to get ~ of** se débarrasser de; **good riddance!** bon débarras!
ridden ['rɪdn] *pp of* **ride**.
riddle ['rɪdl] *n* (*puzzle*) énigme *f* // *vt*: **to be ~d with** être criblé(e) de.
ride [raɪd] *n* promenade *f*, tour *m*; (*distance covered*) trajet *m* // *vb* (*pt* **rode**, *pp* **ridden** [rəud, 'rɪdn]) *vi* (*as sport*) monter (à cheval), faire du cheval; (*go somewhere: on horse, bicycle*) aller (à cheval *or* bicyclette *etc*); (*journey: on bicycle, motor cycle, bus*) rouler // *vt* (*a certain horse*) monter; (*distance*) parcourir, faire; **we rode all day/all the way** nous sommes restés toute la journée en selle/avons fait tout le chemin en selle *or* à cheval; **to ~ a horse/bicycle/camel** monter à cheval/à bicyclette/à dos de chameau; **to ~ at anchor** (NAUT) être à l'ancre; **horse/car ~** promenade *or* tour à cheval/en voiture; **to take sb for a ~** (*fig*) faire marcher qn; rouler qn; **~r** *n* cavalier/ère; (*in race*) jockey *m*; (*on bicycle*) cycliste *m/f*; (*on motorcycle*) motocycliste *m/f*; (*in document*) annexe *f*, clause additionnelle.
ridge [rɪdʒ] *n* (*of hill*) faîte *m*; (*of roof, mountain*) arête *f*; (*on object*) strie *f*.
ridicule ['rɪdɪkju:l] *n* ridicule *m*; dérision *f* // *vt* ridiculiser, tourner en dérision.
ridiculous [rɪ'dɪkjuləs] *a* ridicule.
riding ['raɪdɪŋ] *n* équitation *f*; **~ school** *n* manège *m*, école *f* d'équitation.
rife [raɪf] *a* répandu(e); **~ with** abondant(e) en.
riffraff ['rɪfræf] *n* racaille *f*.
rifle ['raɪfl] *n* fusil *m* (à canon rayé) // *vt* vider, dévaliser; **~ range** *n* champ *m* de tir; (*indoor*) stand *m* de tir.
rift [rɪft] *n* fente *f*, fissure *f*; (*fig: disagreement*) désaccord *m*.
rig [rɪg] *n* (*also*: **oil ~**: *on land*) derrick *m*; (: *at sea*) plate-forme pétrolière // *vt* (*election etc*) truquer; **to ~ out** *vt* habiller; (*pej*) fringuer, attifer; **to ~ up** *vt* arranger, faire avec des moyens de fortune; **~ging** *n* (NAUT) gréement *m*.
right [raɪt] *a* (*true*) juste, exact(e); (*correctly chosen: answer, road etc*) bon(bonne); (*suitable*) approprié(e), convenable; (*just*) juste, équitable; (*morally good*) bien *inv*; (*not left*) droit(e) // *n* (*title, claim*) droit *m*; (*not left*) droite *f* // *ad* (*answer*) correctement; (*not on the left*) à droite // *vt* redresser // *excl* bon!; **to be ~** (*person*) avoir raison; (*answer*) être juste *or* correct(e); **~ now** en ce moment même; tout de suite; **~ against the wall** tout contre le mur; **~ ahead** tout droit; droit devant; **~ in the middle** en plein milieu; **~ away** immédiatement; **by ~s** en toute justice; **on the ~** à droite; **~ angle** *n* angle droit; **~eous** ['raɪtʃəs] *a* droit(e), vertueux(euse); (*anger*) justifié(e); **~eousness** ['raɪtʃəsnɪs] *n* droiture *f*, vertu *f*; **~ful** *a* (*heir*) légitime; **~fully** *ad* à juste titre, légitimement; **~-handed** *a* (*person*) droitier(ère); **~-hand man** *n* bras droit (*fig*); **the ~-hand side** le côté droit; **~ly** *ad* bien, correctement; (*with reason*) à juste titre; **~-minded** *a* sensé(e), sain(e) d'esprit; **~ of way** *n* droit *m* de passage; (AUT) priorité *f*; **~ wing** *n* (MIL, SPORT) aile droite; (POL) droite *f*; **~-wing** *a* (POL) de droite.
rigid ['rɪdʒɪd] *a* rigide; (*principle*) strict(e); **~ity** [rɪ'dʒɪdɪtɪ] *n* rigidité *f*; **~ly** *ad* rigidement; (*behave*) inflexiblement.
rigmarole ['rɪgmərəul] *n* galimatias *m*; comédie *f*.
rigor mortis ['rɪgə'mɔ:tɪs] *n* rigidité *f* cadavérique.
rigorous ['rɪgərəs] *a* rigoureux (euse); **~ly** *ad* rigoureusement.
rigour, rigor (*US*) ['rɪgə*] *n* rigueur *f*.
rig-out ['rɪgaut] *n* (*col*) tenue *f*.
rile [raɪl] *vt* agacer.
rim [rɪm] *n* bord *m*; (*of spectacles*) monture *f*; (*of wheel*) jante *f*; **~less** *a* (*spectacles*) à monture invisible; **~med** *a* bordé(e); janté(e).
rind [raɪnd] *n* (*of bacon*) couenne *f*; (*of lemon etc*) écorce *f*.
ring [rɪŋ] *n* anneau *m*; (*on finger*) bague *f*; (*also*: **wedding ~**) alliance *f*; (*for napkin*) rond *m*; (*of people, objects*) cercle *m*; (*of spies*) réseau *m*; (*of smoke etc*) rond; (*arena*) piste *f*, arène *f*; (*for boxing*) ring *m*; (*sound of bell*) sonnerie *f*; (*telephone call*) coup *m* de téléphone // *vb* (*pt* **rang**, *pp* **rung** [ræŋ, rʌŋ]) *vi* (*person, bell*) sonner; (*also*: **~ out**: *voice, words*) retentir; (TEL) téléphoner // *vt* (TEL: *also*: **~ up**) téléphoner à; **to ~ the bell** sonner; **to ~ back** *vt, vi* (TEL) rappeler; **to ~ off** *vi* (TEL) raccrocher; **~ binder** *n* classeur *m* à anneaux; **~leader** *n* (*of gang*) chef *m*, meneur *m*.
ringlets ['rɪŋlɪts] *npl* anglaises *fpl*.
ring road ['rɪŋrəud] *n* route *f* de ceinture.
rink [rɪŋk] *n* (*also*: **ice ~**) patinoire *f*.
rinse [rɪns] *n* rinçage *m* // *vt* rincer.
riot ['raɪət] *n* émeute *f*, bagarres *fpl* // *vi* faire une émeute, manifester avec violence; **a ~ of colours** une débauche *or* orgie de couleurs; **to run ~** se déchaîner; **~er** *n* émeutier/ère, manifestant/e; **~ous** *a* tapageur(euse); tordant(e); **~ously funny** tordant(e).
rip [rɪp] *n* déchirure *f* // *vt* déchirer // *vi* se déchirer; **~cord** *n* poignée *f* d'ouverture.
ripe [raɪp] *a* (*fruit*) mûr(e); (*cheese*) fait(e); **~n** *vt* mûrir // *vi* mûrir; se faire; **~ness** *n* maturité *f*.
riposte [rɪ'pɔst] *n* riposte *f*.
ripple ['rɪpl] *n* ride *f*, ondulation *f*; égrènement *m*, cascade *f* // *vi* se rider, onduler // *vt* rider, faire onduler.
rise [raɪz] *n* (*slope*) côte *f*, pente *f*; (*hill*) élévation *f*; (*increase: in wages*) augmentation *f*; (: *in prices, temperature*) hausse *f*, augmentation; (*fig: to power etc*) essor *m*, ascension *f* // *vi* (*pt* **rose**, *pp* **risen** [rəuz, 'rɪzn]) s'élever, monter; (*prices*) augmenter, monter; (*waters, river*) monter; (*sun, wind, person: from chair, bed*) se lever; (*also*: **~ up**: *rebel*) se révolter;

se rebeller ; **to give ~ to** donner lieu à ; **to ~ to the occasion** se montrer à la hauteur.

risk [rɪsk] *n* risque *m* ; danger *m* // *vt* risquer ; **to take** *or* **run the ~ of doing** courir le risque de faire ; **at ~** en danger ; **at one's own ~** à ses risques et périls ; **~y** *a* risqué(e).

risqué ['ri:skeɪ] *a* (*joke*) risqué(e).

rissole ['rɪsəul] *n* croquette *f*.

rite [raɪt] *n* rite *m*.

ritual ['rɪtjuəl] *a* rituel(le) // *n* rituel *m*.

rival ['raɪvl] *n* rival/e ; (*in business*) concurrent/e // *a* rival(e) ; qui fait concurrence // *vt* être en concurrence avec ; **to ~ sb/sth in** rivaliser avec qn/qch de ; **~ry** *n* rivalité *f*; concurrence *f*.

river ['rɪvə*] *n* rivière *f*; (*major, also fig*) fleuve *m* ; **~bank** *n* rive *f*, berge *f* ; **~bed** *n* lit *m* (de rivière *or* de fleuve) ; **~side** *n* bord *m* de la rivière *or* du fleuve // *cpd* (*port, traffic*) fluvial(e).

rivet ['rɪvɪt] *n* rivet *m* // *vt* riveter ; (*fig*) river, fixer.

Riviera [rɪvɪ'ɛərə] *n*: **the (French) ~** la Côte d'Azur.

RN *abbr of Royal Navy*.

road [rəud] *n* route *f*; (*small*) chemin *m* ; (*in town*) rue *f*; (*fig*) chemin, voie *f*; **'~ up'** 'attention travaux' ; **~block** *n* barrage routier ; **~hog** *n* chauffard *m* ; **~ map** *n* carte routière ; **~side** *n* bord *m* de la route, bas-côté *m* // *cpd* (situé(e) *etc*) au bord de la route ; **~sign** *n* panneau *m* de signalisation ; **~ user** *n* usager *m* de la route ; **~way** *n* chaussée *f*; **~worthy** *a* en bon état de marche.

roam [rəum] *vi* errer, vagabonder // *vt* parcourir, errer par.

roar [rɔ:*] *n* rugissement *m* ; (*of crowd*) hurlements *mpl* ; (*of vehicle, thunder, storm*) grondement *m* // *vi* rugir ; hurler ; gronder ; **to ~ with laughter** éclater de rire ; **a ~ing fire** une belle flambée ; **to do a ~ing trade** faire des affaires d'or.

roast [rəust] *n* rôti *m* // *vt* (*meat*) (faire) rôtir.

rob [rɔb] *vt* (*person*) voler ; (*bank*) dévaliser ; **to ~ sb of sth** voler *or* dérober qch à qn ; (*fig: deprive*) priver qn de qch ; **~ber** *n* bandit *m*, voleur *m* ; **~bery** *n* vol *m*.

robe [rəub] *n* (*for ceremony etc*) robe *f*; (*also*: **bath ~**) peignoir *m* // *vt* revêtir (d'une robe).

robin ['rɔbɪn] *n* rouge-gorge *m*.

robot ['rəubɔt] *n* robot *m*.

robust [rəu'bʌst] *a* robuste ; (*material, appetite*) solide.

rock [rɔk] *n* (*substance*) roche *f*, roc *m* ; (*boulder*) rocher *m* ; roche ; (*sweet*) ≈ sucre *m* d'orge // *vt* (*swing gently: cradle*) balancer ; (: *child*) bercer ; (*shake*) ébranler, secouer // *vi* (se) balancer ; être ébranlé(e) *or* secoué(e) ; **on the ~s** (*drink*) avec des glaçons ; (*ship*) sur les écueils ; (*marriage etc*) en train de craquer ; **to ~ the boat** (*fig*) jouer les trouble-fête ; **~-bottom** *n* (*fig*) niveau le plus bas ; **~ery** *n* (jardin *m* de) rocaille *f*.

rocket ['rɔkɪt] *n* fusée *f*; (*MIL*) fusée, roquette *f*.

rock face ['rɔkfeɪs] *n* paroi rocheuse.

rock fall ['rɔkfɔ:l] *n* chute *f* de pierres.

rocking chair ['rɔkɪŋtʃɛə*] *n* fauteuil *m* à bascule.

rocking horse ['rɔkɪŋhɔ:s] *n* cheval *m* à bascule.

rocky ['rɔkɪ] *a* (*hill*) rocheux(euse) ; (*path*) rocailleux(euse) ; (*unsteady: table*) branlant(e).

rod [rɔd] *n* (*metallic*) tringle *f*; (*TECH*) tige *f*; (*wooden*) baguette *f*; (*also*: **fishing ~**) canne *f* à pêche.

rode [rəud] *pt of* **ride**.

rodent ['rəudnt] *n* rongeur *m*.

rodeo ['rəudɪəu] *n* rodéo *m*.

roe [rəu] *n* (*species: also*: **~ deer**) chevreuil *m* ; (*of fish*) œufs *mpl* de poisson ; **soft ~** laitance *f*; **~ deer** *n* chevreuil *m* ; chevreuil femelle.

rogue [rəug] *n* coquin/e ; **roguish** *a* coquin(e).

role [rəul] *n* rôle *m*.

roll [rəul] *n* rouleau *m* ; (*of banknotes*) liasse *f*; (*also*: **bread ~**) petit pain ; (*register*) liste *f* ; (*sound: of drums etc*) roulement *m* ; (*movement: of ship*) roulis *m* // *vt* rouler ; (*also*: **~ up**: *string*) enrouler ; (*also*: **~ out**: *pastry*) étendre au rouleau // *vi* rouler ; (*wheel*) tourner ; (*sway: person*) se balancer ; **to ~ by** *vi* (*time*) s'écouler, passer ; **to ~ in** *vi* (*mail, cash*) affluer ; **to ~ over** *vi* se retourner ; **to ~ up** *vi* (*col*: *arrive*) arriver, s'amener // *vt* (*carpet*) rouler ; **~ call** *n* appel *m* ; **~ed gold** *a* plaqué or *inv* ; **~er** *n* rouleau *m* ; (*wheel*) roulette *f* ; **~er skates** *npl* patins *mpl* à roulettes.

rollicking ['rɔlɪkɪŋ] *a* bruyant(e) et joyeux(euse) ; (*play*) bouffon(ne) ; **to have a ~ time** s'amuser follement.

rolling ['rəulɪŋ] *a* (*landscape*) onduleux(euse) ; **~ pin** *n* rouleau *m* à pâtisserie ; **~ stock** *n* (*RAIL*) matériel roulant.

roll-on-roll-off ['rəulɔn'rəulɔf] *a* (*ferry*) transroulier(ère).

roly-poly ['rəulɪ'pəulɪ] *n* (*CULIN*) roulé *m* à la confiture.

Roman ['rəumən] *a* romain(e) // *n* Romain/e ; **~ Catholic** *a, n* catholique (*m/f*).

romance [rə'mæns] *n* histoire *f* (*or* film *m* *or* aventure *f*) romanesque ; (*charm*) poésie *f* ; (*love affair*) idylle *f* // *vi* enjoliver (à plaisir), exagérer.

Romanesque [rəumə'nɛsk] *a* roman(e).

Romania [rəu'meɪnɪə] *n* Roumanie *f* ; **~n** *a* roumain(e) // *n* Roumain/e.

romantic [rə'mæntɪk] *a* romantique ; sentimental(e).

romanticism [rə'mæntɪsɪzəm] *n* romantisme *m*.

romp [rɔmp] *n* jeux bruyants // *vi* (*also*: **~ about**) s'ébattre, jouer bruyamment.

rompers ['rɔmpəz] *npl* barboteuse *f*.

rondo ['rɔndəu] *n* (*MUS*) rondeau *m*.

roof [ru:f] *n* toit *m* ; (*of tunnel, cave*) plafond *m* // *vt* couvrir (d'un toit) ; **the ~ of the mouth** la voûte du palais ; **~ garden** *n* toit-terrasse *m* ; **~ing** *n* toiture *f* ; **~ rack** *n* (*AUT*) galerie *f*.

rook [ruk] *n* (*bird*) freux *m*; (CHESS) tour *f* // *vt* (*cheat*) rouler, escroquer.

room [ru:m] *n* (*in house*) pièce *f*; (*also*: **bed~**) chambre *f* (à coucher); (*in school etc*) salle *f*; (*space*) place *f*; **~s** *npl* (*lodging*) meublé *m*; **'~s to let'** 'chambres à louer'; **~ing house** *n* (*US*) maison *f* de rapport; **~mate** *n* camarade *m/f* de chambre; **~ service** *n* service *m* des chambres (*dans un hôtel*); **~y** *a* spacieux(euse); (*garment*) ample.

roost [ru:st] *n* juchoir *m* // *vi* se jucher.

rooster ['ru:stə*] *n* coq *m*.

root [ru:t] *n* (BOT. MATH) racine *f*; (*fig*: *of problem*) origine *f*, fond *m* // *vt* (*plant, belief*) enraciner; **to ~ about** *vi* (*fig*) fouiller; **to ~ for** *vt fus* applaudir; **to ~ out** *vt* extirper.

rope [rəup] *n* corde *f*; (NAUT) cordage *m* // *vt* (*box*) corder; (*climbers*) encorder; **to ~ sb in** (*fig*) embringuer qn; **to know the ~s** (*fig*) être au courant, connaître les ficelles; **~ ladder** *n* échelle *f* de corde.

rosary ['rəuzərı] *n* chapelet *m*; rosaire *m*.

rose [rəuz] *pt of* **rise** // *n* rose *f*; (*also*: **~bush**) rosier *m*; (*on watering can*) pomme *f* // *a* rose.

rosé ['rəuzeı] *n* rosé *m*.

rose: **~bed** *n* massif *m* de rosiers; **~bud** *n* bouton *m* de rose; **~bush** *n* rosier *m*.

rosemary ['rəuzmərı] *n* romarin *m*.

rosette [rəu'zɛt] *n* rosette *f*; (*larger*) cocarde *f*.

roster ['rɔstə*] *n*: **duty ~** tableau *m* de service.

rostrum ['rɔstrəm] *n* tribune *f* (*pour un orateur etc*).

rosy ['rəuzı] *a* rose; **a ~ future** un bel avenir.

rot [rɔt] *n* (*decay*) pourriture *f*; (*fig*: *pej*) idioties *fpl*, balivernes *fpl* // *vt, vi* pourrir.

rota ['rəutə] *n* liste *f*, tableau *m* de service; **on a ~ basis** par roulement.

rotary ['rəutərı] *a* rotatif(ive).

rotate [rəu'teıt] *vt* (*revolve*) faire tourner; (*change round: crops*) alterner; (*:jobs*) faire à tour de rôle // *vi* (*revolve*) tourner; **rotating** *a* (*movement*) tournant(e); **rotation** [-'teıʃən] *n* rotation *f*; **in rotation** à tour de rôle.

rotor ['rəutə*] *n* rotor *m*.

rotten ['rɔtn] *a* (*decayed*) pourri(e); (*dishonest*) corrompu(e); (*col: bad*) mauvais(e), moche; **to feel ~** (*ill*) être mal fichu(e).

rotting ['rɔtıŋ] *a* pourrissant(e).

rotund [rəu'tʌnd] *a* rondelet(te); arrondi(e).

rouble, ruble (*US*) ['ru:bl] *n* rouble *m*.

rouge [ru:ʒ] *n* rouge *m* (à joues).

rough [rʌf] *a* (*cloth, skin*) rêche, rugueux(euse); (*terrain*) accidenté(e); (*path*) rocailleux(euse); (*voice*) rauque, rude; (*person, manner*: *coarse*) rude, fruste; (: *violent*) brutal(e); (*district, weather*) mauvais(e); (*plan*) ébauché(e); (*guess*) approximatif(ive) // *n* (GOLF) rough *m*; (*person*) voyou *m*; **to ~ it** vivre à la dure; **to play ~** jouer avec brutalité; **to sleep ~** coucher à la dure; **to feel ~** être mal fichu(e); **to ~ out** *vt* (*draft*) ébaucher; **~en** *vt* (*a surface*) rendre rude or rugueux(euse); **~ justice** *n* justice *f* sommaire; **~ly** *ad* (*handle*) rudement, brutalement; (*make*) grossièrement; (*approximately*) à peu près, en gros; **~ness** *n* rugosité *f*; rudesse *f*; brutalité *f*; **~ work** *n* (*at school etc*) brouillon *m*.

roulette [ru:'lɛt] *n* roulette *f*.

Roumania [ru:'meınıə] *n* = **Romania**.

round [raund] *a* rond(e) // *n* rond *m*, cercle *m*; (*of toast*) tranche *f*; (*duty: of policeman, milkman etc*) tournée *f*; (: *of doctor*) visites *fpl*; (*game: of cards, in competition*) partie *f*; (BOXING) round *m*; (*of talks*) série *f* // *vt* (*corner*) tourner; (*bend*) prendre; (*cape*) doubler // *prep* autour de // *ad*: **right ~, all ~** tout autour; **the long way ~** (par) le chemin le plus long; **all the year ~** toute l'année; **it's just ~ the corner** c'est juste après le coin; (*fig*) c'est tout près; **to go ~** faire le tour *or* un détour; **to go ~ to sb's (house)** aller chez qn; **to go ~ an obstacle** contourner un obstacle; **go ~ the back** passe par derrière; **to go ~ a house** visiter une maison, faire le tour d'une maison; **to go the ~s** (*disease, story*) circuler; **to ~ off** *vt* (*speech etc*) terminer; **to ~ up** *vt* rassembler; (*criminals*) effectuer une rafle de; (*prices*) arrondir (au chiffre supérieur); **~about** *n* (AUT) rond-point *m* (à sens giratoire); (*at fair*) manège *m* (de chevaux de bois) // *a* (*route, means*) détourné(e); **~ of ammunition** *n* cartouche *f*; **~ of applause** *n* ban *m*, applaudissements *mpl*; **~ of drinks** *n* tournée *f*; **~ of sandwiches** *n* sandwich *m*; **~ed** *a* arrondi(e); (*style*) harmonieux(euse); **~ly** *ad* (*fig*) tout net, carrément; **~-shouldered** *a* au dos rond; **~sman** *n* livreur *m*; **~ trip** *n* (voyage *m*) aller et retour *m*; **~up** *n* rassemblement *m*; (*of criminals*) rafle *f*.

rouse [rauz] *vt* (*wake up*) réveiller; (*stir up*) susciter; provoquer; éveiller; **rousing** *a* (*welcome*) enthousiaste.

rout [raut] *n* (MIL) déroute *f* // *vt* mettre en déroute.

route [ru:t] *n* itinéraire *m*; (*of bus*) parcours *m*; (*of trade, shipping*) route *f*; **'all ~s'** (AUT) 'toutes directions'; **~ map** *n* (*for journey*) croquis *m* d'itinéraire; (*for trains etc*) carte *f* du réseau.

routine [ru:'ti:n] *a* (*work*) ordinaire, courant(e); (*procedure*) d'usage // *n* (*pej*) routine *f*; (THEATRE) numéro *m*; **daily ~** occupations journalières.

roving ['rəuvıŋ] *a* (*life*) vagabond(e); **~ reporter** *n* reporter volant.

row [rəu] *n* (*line*) rangée *f*; (*of people, seats,* KNITTING) rang *m*; (*behind one another: of cars, people*) file *f* // *vi* (*in boat*) ramer; (*as sport*) faire de l'aviron // *vt* (*boat*) faire aller à la rame *or* à l'aviron; **in a ~** (*fig*) d'affilée.

row [rau] *n* (*noise*) vacarme *m*; (*dispute*) dispute *f*, querelle *f*; (*scolding*) réprimande *f*, savon *m* // *vi* se disputer, se quereller.

rowdiness ['raudınıs] *n* tapage *m*, chahut *m*; (*fighting*) bagarre *f*.

rowdy ['raudı] *a* chahuteur(euse); bagarreur(euse) // *n* voyou *m*.

rowing ['rəuɪŋ] *n* canotage *m*; (*as sport*) aviron *m*; ~ **boat** *n* canot *m* (à rames).
rowlock ['rɔlək] *n* dame *f* de nage, tolet *m*.
royal ['rɔɪəl] *a* royal(e); ~**ist** *a*, *n* royaliste (*m/f*).
royalty ['rɔɪəltɪ] *n* (*royal persons*) (membres *mpl* de la) famille royale; (*payment: to author*) droits *mpl* d'auteur; (: *to inventor*) royalties *fpl*.
r.p.m. *abbr* (AUT: = *revs per minute*) tr/mn (tours/minute).
R.S.P.C.A. *n* (*abbr of Royal Society for the Prevention of Cruelty to Animals*), ≈ S.P.A..
R.S.V.P. *abbr* (= *répondez s'il vous plaît*) R.S.V.P.
Rt Hon. *abbr* (= *Right Honourable*) *titre donné aux députés de la Chambre des communes.*
rub [rʌb] *n* (*with cloth*) coup *m* de chiffon *or* de torchon; (*on person*) friction *f* // *vt* frotter; frictionner; **to ~ sb up the wrong way** prendre qn à rebrousse-poil; **to ~ off** *vi* partir; **to ~ off on** déteindre sur.
rubber ['rʌbə*] *n* caoutchouc *m*; (*Brit*: eraser) gomme *f* (à effacer); ~ **band** *n* élastique *m*; ~ **plant** *n* caoutchouc *m* (*plante verte*); ~ **stamp** *n* tampon *m*; ~-**stamp** *vt* (*fig*) approuver sans discussion; ~**y** *a* caoutchouteux(euse).
rubbish ['rʌbɪʃ] *n* (*from household*) ordures *fpl*; (*fig:pej*) choses *fpl* sans valeur; camelote *f*; bêtises *fpl*, idioties *fpl*; ~ **bin** *n* boîte *f* à ordures, poubelle *f*; ~ **dump** *n* (*in town*) décharge publique, dépotoir *m*.
rubble ['rʌbl] *n* décombres *mpl*; (*smaller*) gravats *mpl*.
ruble ['ru:bl] *n* (*US*) = **rouble**.
ruby ['ru:bɪ] *n* rubis *m*.
rucksack ['rʌksæk] *n* sac *m* à dos.
ructions ['rʌkʃənz] *npl* grabuge *m*.
rudder ['rʌdə*] *n* gouvernail *m*.
ruddy ['rʌdɪ] *a* (*face*) coloré(e); (*sky*) rougeoyant(e); (*col: damned*) sacré(e), fichu(e).
rude [ru:d] *a* (*impolite: person*) impoli(e); (: *word, manners*) grossier(ère); (*shocking*) indécent(e), inconvenant(e); ~**ly** *ad* impoliment; grossièrement; ~**ness** *n* impolitesse *f*; grossièreté *f*.
rudiment ['ru:dɪmənt] *n* rudiment *m*; ~**ary** [-'mɛntərɪ] *a* rudimentaire.
rueful ['ru:ful] *a* triste.
ruff [rʌf] *n* fraise *f*, collerette *f*.
ruffian ['rʌfɪən] *n* brute *f*, voyou *m*.
ruffle ['rʌfl] *vt* (*hair*) ébouriffer; (*clothes*) chiffonner; (*water*) agiter; (*fig: person*) émouvoir, faire perdre son flegme à.
rug [rʌg] *n* petit tapis; (*for knees*) couverture *f*.
rugby ['rʌgbɪ] *n* (*also*: ~ **football**) rugby *m*.
rugged ['rʌgɪd] *a* (*landscape*) accidenté(e); (*tree bark*) rugueux(euse); (*features, kindness, character*) rude; (*determination*) farouche.
rugger ['rʌgə*] *n* (*col*) rugby *m*.
ruin ['ru:ɪn] *n* ruine *f* // *vt* ruiner; (*spoil: clothes*) abîmer; ~**s** *npl* ruine(s); ~**ation** [-'neɪʃən] *n* ruine *f*; ~**ous** *a* ruineux(euse).
rule [ru:l] *n* règle *f*; (*regulation*) règlement *m*; (*government*) autorité *f*, gouvernement *m* // *vt* (*country*) gouverner; (*person*) dominer; (*decide*) décider; (*draw: lines*) tirer à la règle // *vi* commander; décider; (LAW) statuer; **as a ~** normalement, en règle générale; ~**d** *a* (*paper*) réglé(e); ~**r** *n* (*sovereign*) souverain/e; (*leader*) chef *m* (d'État); (*for measuring*) règle *f*; **ruling** *a* (*party*) au pouvoir; (*class*) dirigeant(e) // *n* (LAW) décision *f*.
rum [rʌm] *n* rhum *m* // *a* (*col*) bizarre.
Rumania [ru:'meɪnɪə] *n* = **Romania**.
rumble ['rʌmbl] *n* grondement *m*; gargouillement *m* // *vi* gronder; (*stomach, pipe*) gargouiller.
rummage ['rʌmɪdʒ] *vi* fouiller.
rumour, rumor (*US*) ['ru:mə*] *n* rumeur *f*, bruit *m* (qui court) // *vt*: **it is ~ed that** le bruit court que.
rump [rʌmp] *n* (*of animal*) croupe *f*; ~**steak** *n* rumsteck *m*.
rumpus ['rʌmpəs] *n* (*col*) tapage *m*, chahut *m*; (*quarrel*) prise *f* de bec.
run [rʌn] *n* (pas *m* de) course *f*; (*outing*) tour *m* *or* promenade *f* (en voiture); parcours *m*, trajet *m*; (*series*) suite *f*, série *f*; (THEATRE) série de représentations; (SKI) piste *f* // *vb* (*pt* **ran**, *pp* **run** [ræn, rʌn]) *vt* (*operate: business*) diriger; (: *competition, course*) organiser; (: *hotel, house*) tenir; (*force through: rope, pipe*): **to ~ sth through** faire passer qch à travers; (*to pass: hand, finger*): **to ~ sth over** promener *or* passer qch sur; (*water, bath*) faire couler // *vi* courir; (*pass: road etc*) passer; (*work: machine, factory*) marcher; (*bus, train: operate*) être en service; (: *travel*) circuler; (*continue: play*) se jouer; (: *contract*) être valide; (*slide: drawer etc*) glisser; (*flow: river, bath*) couler; (*colours, washing*) déteindre; (*in election*) être candidat, se présenter; **there was a ~ on** (*meat, tickets*) les gens se sont rués sur; **to break into a ~** se mettre à courir; **in the long ~** à longue échéance; à la longue; en fin de compte; **in the short ~** à brève échéance, à court terme; **on the ~** en fuite; **I'll ~ you to the station** je vais vous emmener *or* conduire à la gare; **to ~ a risk** courir un risque; **to ~ about** *vi* (*children*) courir çà et là; **to ~ across** *vt fus* (*find*) trouver par hasard; **to ~ away** *vi* s'enfuir; **to ~ down** *vi* (*clock*) s'arrêter (faute d'avoir été remonté) // *vt* (AUT) renverser; (*criticize*) critiquer, dénigrer; **to be ~ down** être fatigué(e) *or* à plat; **to ~ off** *vi* s'enfuir; **to ~ out** *vi* (*person*) sortir en courant; (*liquid*) couler; (*lease*) expirer; (*money*) être épuisé(e); **to ~ out of** *vt fus* se trouver à court de; **to ~ over** *vt sep* (AUT) écraser // *vt fus* (*revise*) revoir, reprendre; **to ~ through** *vt fus* (*instructions*) reprendre, revoir; **to ~ up** *vt* (*debt*) laisser accumuler; **to ~ up against** (*difficulties*) se heurter à; ~**away** *a* (*horse*) emballé(e); (*truck*) fou(folle); (*inflation*) galopant(e).
rung [rʌŋ] *pp of* **ring** // *n* (*of ladder*) barreau *m*.
runner ['rʌnə*] *n* (*in race: person*) coureur/euse; (: *horse*) partant *m*; (*on sledge*) patin *m*; (*on curtain*) suspendeur

m; (*for drawer etc*) coulisseau *m*; (*carpet: in hall etc*) chemin *m*; ~ **bean** *n* (BOT) haricot *m* (à rames); ~**-up** *n* second/e.

running ['rʌnɪŋ] *n* course *f*; direction *f*; organisation *f*; marche *f*, fonctionnement *m* // *a* (*water*) courant(e); (*commentary*) suivi(e); **6 days** ~ 6 jours de suite.

runny ['rʌnɪ] *a* qui coule.

run-of-the-mill ['rʌnəvðə'mɪl] *a* ordinaire, banal(e).

runt [rʌnt] *n* (*also*: *pej*) avorton *m*.

run-through ['rʌnθru:] *n* répétition *f*, essai *m*.

runway ['rʌnweɪ] *n* (AVIAT) piste *f* (d'envol *cu* d'atterrissage).

rupee [ru:'pi:] *n* roupie *f*.

rupture ['rʌptʃə*] *n* (MED) hernie *f* // *vt*: **to** ~ **o.s.** se donner une hernie.

rural ['ruərl] *a* rural(e).

ruse [ru:z] *n* ruse *f*.

rush [rʌʃ] *n* course précipitée; (*of crowd*) ruée *f*, bousculade *f*; (*hurry*) hâte *f*, bousculade; (*current*) flot *m* // *vt* transporter *or* envoyer d'urgence; (*attack: town etc*) prendre d'assaut; (*col: overcharge*) estamper; faire payer // *vi* se précipiter; **don't** ~ **me!** laissez-moi le temps de souffler!; ~**es** *npl* (BOT) jonc *m*; ~ **hour** *n* heures *fpl* de pointe *or* d'affluence.

rusk [rʌsk] *n* biscotte *f*.

Russia ['rʌʃə] *n* Russie *f*; ~**n** *a* russe // *n* Russe *m/f*; (LING) russe *m*.

rust [rʌst] *n* rouille *f* // *vi* rouiller.

rustic ['rʌstɪk] *a* rustique // *n* (*pej*) rustaud/e.

rustle ['rʌsl] *vi* bruire, produire un bruissement // *vt* (*paper*) froisser; (*US: cattle*) voler.

rustproof ['rʌstpru:f] *a* inoxydable; ~**ing** *n* traitement *m* antirouille.

rusty ['rʌstɪ] *a* rouillé(e).

rut [rʌt] *n* ornière *f*; (ZOOL) rut *m*.

ruthless ['ru:θlɪs] *a* sans pitié, impitoyable; ~**ness** *n* dureté *f*, cruauté *f*.

rye [raɪ] *n* seigle *m*; ~ **bread** *n* pain *m* de seigle.

S

sabbath ['sæbəθ] *n* sabbat *m*.

sabbatical [sə'bætɪkl] *a*: ~ **year** *n* année *f* sabbatique.

sabotage ['sæbəta:ʒ] *n* sabotage *m* // *vt* saboter.

saccharin(e) ['sækərɪn] *n* saccharine *f*.

sack [sæk] *n* (*bag*) sac *m* // *vt* (*dismiss*) renvoyer, mettre à la porte; (*plunder*) piller, mettre à sac; **to get the** ~ être renvoyé *or* mis à la porte; **a** ~**ful of** un (plein) sac de; ~**ing** *n* toile *f* à sac; renvoi *m*.

sacrament ['sækrəmənt] *n* sacrement *m*.

sacred ['seɪkrɪd] *a* sacré(e).

sacrifice ['sækrɪfaɪs] *n* sacrifice *m* // *vt* sacrifier.

sacrilege ['sækrɪlɪdʒ] *n* sacrilège *m*.

sacrosanct ['sækrəusæŋkt] *a* sacro-saint(e).

sad [sæd] *a* (*unhappy*) triste; (*deplorable*) triste, fâcheux(euse); ~**den** *vt* attrister, affliger.

saddle ['sædl] *n* selle *f* // *vt* (*horse*) seller; **to be** ~**d with sth** (*col*) avoir qch sur les bras; ~**bag** *n* sacoche *f*.

sadism ['seɪdɪzm] *n* sadisme *m*; **sadist** *n* sadique *m/f*; **sadistic** [sə'dɪstɪk] *a* sadique.

sadly ['sædlɪ] *ad* tristement; fâcheusement.

sadness ['sædnɪs] *n* tristesse *f*.

safari [sə'fa:rɪ] *n* safari *m*.

safe [seɪf] *a* (*out of danger*) hors de danger, en sécurité; (*not dangerous*) sans danger; (*cautious*) prudent(e); (*sure*: *bet etc*) assuré(e) // *n* coffre-fort *m*; ~ **from** à l'abri de; ~ **and sound** sain(e) et sauf(sauve); **(just) to be on the** ~ **side** pour plus de sûreté, par précaution; ~**guard** *n* sauvegarde *f*, protection *f* // *vt* sauvegarder, protéger; ~**keeping** *n* bonne garde; ~**ly** *ad* sans danger, sans risque; (*without mishap*) sans accident.

safety ['seɪftɪ] *n* sécurité *f*; ~ **belt** *n* ceinture *f* de sécurité; ~ **curtain** *n* rideau *m* de fer; ~ **first!** la sécurité d'abord!; ~ **pin** *n* épingle *f* de sûreté *or* de nourrice.

saffron ['sæfrən] *n* safran *m*.

sag [sæg] *vi* s'affaisser, fléchir; pendre.

sage [seɪdʒ] *n* (*herb*) sauge *f*; (*man*) sage *m*.

Sagittarius [sædʒɪ'tɛərɪəs] *n* le Sagittaire; **to be** ~ être du Sagittaire.

sago ['seɪgəu] *n* sagou *m*.

said [sɛd] *pt, pp of* **say**.

sail [seɪl] *n* (*on boat*) voile *f*; (*trip*): **to go for a** ~ faire un tour en bateau // *vt* (*boat*) manœuvrer, piloter // *vi* (*travel: ship*) avancer, naviguer; (: *passenger*) aller *or* se rendre (en bateau); (*set off*) partir, prendre la mer; (SPORT) faire de la voile; **they** ~**ed into Le Havre** ils sont entrés dans le port du Havre; **to** ~ **through** *vi, vt fus* (*fig*) réussir haut la main; ~**boat** *n* (*US*) bateau *m* à voiles, voilier *m*; ~**ing** *n* (SPORT) voile *f*; **to go** ~**ing** faire de la voile; ~**ing boat** *n* bateau *m* à voiles, voilier *m*; ~**ing ship** *n* grand voilier; ~**or** *n* marin *m*, matelot *m*.

saint [seɪnt] *n* saint/e; ~**ly** *a* saint(e), plein(e) de bonté.

sake [seɪk] *n*: **for the** ~ **of** pour (l'amour de), dans l'intérêt de; par égard pour; **for pity's** ~ par pitié.

salad ['sæləd] *n* salade *f*; ~ **bowl** *n* saladier *m*; ~ **cream** *n* (sorte *f* de) mayonnaise *f*; ~ **dressing** *n* vinaigrette *f*; ~ **oil** *n* huile *f* de table.

salaried ['sælərɪd] *a* (*staff*) salarié(e), qui touche un traitement.

salary ['sælərɪ] *n* salaire *m*, traitement *m*.

sale [seɪl] *n* vente *f*; (*at reduced prices*) soldes *mpl*; **'for** ~**'** 'à vendre'; **on** ~ en vente; **on** ~ **or return** vendu(e) avec faculté de retour; ~**room** *n* salle *f* des ventes; ~**sman** *n* vendeur *m*; (*representative*) représentant *m* de commerce; ~**smanship** *n* art *m* de la vente; ~**swoman** *n* vendeuse *f*.

salient ['seɪlɪənt] *a* saillant(e).

saliva [sə'laɪvə] *n* salive *f*.

sallow ['sæləu] *a* cireux(euse).

salmon ['sæmən] *n, pl inv* saumon *m*; ~ **trout** *n* truite saumonée.

saloon [sə'lu:n] *n* (*US*) bar *m*; (AUT) berline *f*; (*ship's lounge*) salon *m*.
salt [sɔlt] *n* sel *m* // *vt* saler // *cpd* de sel; (CULIN) salé(e); ~ **cellar** *n* salière *f*; ~**-free** *a* sans sel; ~**y** *a* salé.
salutary ['sæljutərɪ] *a* salutaire.
salute [sə'lu:t] *n* salut *m* // *vt* saluer.
salvage ['sælvɪdʒ] *n* (*saving*) sauvetage *m*; (*things saved*) biens sauvés *or* récupérés // *vt* sauver, récupérer.
salvation [sæl'veɪʃən] *n* salut *m*; **S~ Army** *n* Armée *f* du Salut.
salver ['sælvə*] *n* plateau *m* de métal.
salvo ['sælvəu] *n* salve *f*.
same [seɪm] *a* même // *pronoun*: **the ~** le(la) même, les mêmes; **the ~ book as** le même livre que; **all** *or* **just the ~** tout de même, quand même; **to do the ~** faire de même, en faire autant; **to do the ~ as sb** faire comme qn; **the ~ again!** (*in bar etc*) la même chose!
sample ['sɑ:mpl] *n* échantillon *m*; (MED) prélèvement *m* // *vt* (*food, wine*) goûter.
sanatorium, *pl* **sanatoria** [sænə'tɔ:rɪəm, -rɪə] *n* sanatorium *m*.
sanctify ['sæŋktɪfaɪ] *vt* sanctifier.
sanctimonious [sæŋktɪ'məunɪəs] *a* moralisateur(trice).
sanction ['sæŋkʃən] *n* sanction *f* // *vt* cautionner, sanctionner.
sanctity ['sæŋktɪtɪ] *n* sainteté *f*, caractère sacré.
sanctuary ['sæŋktjuərɪ] *n* (*holy place*) sanctuaire *m*; (*refuge*) asile *m*; (*for wild life*) réserve *f*.
sand [sænd] *n* sable *m* // *vt* sabler; **~s** *npl* plage *f* (de sable).
sandal ['sændl] *n* sandale *f*.
sandbag ['sændbæg] *n* sac *m* de sable.
sandcastle ['sændkɑ:sl] *n* château *m* de sable.
sand dune ['sænddju:n] *n* dune *f* de sable.
sandpaper ['sændpeɪpə*] *n* papier *m* de verre.
sandpit ['sændpɪt] *n* (*for children*) tas *m* de sable.
sandstone ['sændstəun] *n* grès *m*.
sandwich ['sændwɪtʃ] *n* sandwich *m* // *vt* (*also*: **~ in**) intercaler; **~ed between** pris en sandwich entre; **cheese/ham ~** sandwich au fromage/jambon; **~ course** *n* cours *m* de formation professionnelle.
sandy ['sændɪ] *a* sablonneux(euse); couvert(e) de sable; (*colour*) sable *inv*, blond roux *inv*.
sane [seɪn] *a* (*person*) sain(e) d'esprit; (*outlook*) sensé(e), sain(e).
sang [sæŋ] *pt of* **sing**.
sanguine ['sæŋgwɪn] *a* optimiste.
sanitarium, *pl* **sanitaria** [sænɪ'tɛərɪəm, -rɪə] *n* (*US*) = **sanatorium**.
sanitary ['sænɪtərɪ] *a* (*system, arrangements*) sanitaire; (*clean*) hygiénique; **~ towel, ~ napkin** (*US*) *n* serviette *f* hygiénique.
sanitation [sænɪ'teɪʃən] *n* (*in house*) installations *fpl* sanitaires; (*in town*) système *m* sanitaire.
sanity ['sænɪtɪ] *n* santé mentale; (*common sense*) bon sens.
sank [sæŋk] *pt of* **sink**.
Santa Claus [sæntə'klɔ:z] *n* le Père Noël.
sap [sæp] *n* (*of plants*) sève *f* // *vt* (*strength*) saper, miner.
sapling ['sæplɪŋ] *n* jeune arbre *m*.
sapphire ['sæfaɪə*] *n* saphir *m*.
sarcasm ['sɑ:kæzm] *n* sarcasme *m*, raillerie *f*.
sarcastic [sɑ:'kæstɪk] *a* sarcastique.
sarcophagus, *pl* **sarcophagi** [sɑ:'kɔfəgəs, -gaɪ] *n* sarcophage *m*.
sardine [sɑ:'di:n] *n* sardine *f*.
Sardinia [sɑ:'dɪnɪə] *n* Sardaigne *f*.
sardonic [sɑ:'dɔnɪk] *a* sardonique.
sartorial [sɑ:'tɔ:rɪəl] *a* vestimentaire.
sash [sæʃ] *n* écharpe *f*; **~ window** *n* fenêtre *f* à guillotine.
sat [sæt] *pt,pp of* **sit**.
satanic [sə'tænɪk] *a* satanique, démoniaque.
satchel ['sætʃl] *n* cartable *m*.
satellite ['sætəlaɪt] *a, n* satellite (*m*).
satin ['sætɪn] *n* satin *m* // *a* en *or* de satin, satiné(e).
satire ['sætaɪə*] *n* satire *f*; **satirical** [sə'tɪrɪkl] *a* satirique; **satirize** ['sætɪraɪz] *vt* faire la satire de, satiriser.
satisfaction [sætɪs'fækʃən] *n* satisfaction *f*.
satisfactory [sætɪs'fæktərɪ] *a* satisfaisant(e).
satisfy ['sætɪsfaɪ] *vt* satisfaire, contenter; (*convince*) convaincre, persuader; **~ing** *a* satisfaisant(e).
saturate ['sætʃəreɪt] *vt*: **to ~ (with)** saturer (de); **saturation** [-'reɪʃən] *n* saturation *f*.
Saturday ['sætədɪ] *n* samedi *m*.
sauce [sɔ:s] *n* sauce *f*; **~pan** *n* casserole *f*.
saucer ['sɔ:sə*] *n* soucoupe *f*.
saucy ['sɔ:sɪ] *a* impertinent(e).
sauna ['sɔ:nə] *n* sauna *m*.
saunter ['sɔ:ntə*] *vi*: **to ~ to** aller en flânant *or* se balader jusqu'à.
sausage ['sɔsɪdʒ] *n* saucisse *f*; **~ roll** *n* friand *m*.
savage ['sævɪdʒ] *a* (*cruel, fierce*) brutal(e), féroce; (*primitive*) primitif(ive), sauvage // *n* sauvage *m/f* // *vt* attaquer férocement; **~ry** *n* sauvagerie *f*, brutalité *f*, férocité *f*.
save [seɪv] *vt* (*person, belongings*) sauver; (*money*) mettre de côté, économiser; (*time*) (faire) gagner; (*food*) garder; (*avoid: trouble*) éviter // *vi* (*also*: **~ up**) mettre de l'argent de côté // *n* (SPORT) arrêt *m* (du ballon) // *prep* sauf, à l'exception de.
saving ['seɪvɪŋ] *n* économie *f* // *a*: **the ~ grace of** ce qui rachète; **~s** *npl* économies *fpl*; **~s bank** *n* caisse *f* d'épargne.
saviour ['seɪvjə*] *n* sauveur *m*.
savour, savor (*US*) ['seɪvə*] *n* saveur *f*, goût *m* // *vt* savourer; **~y** *a* savoureux(euse); (*dish: not sweet*) salé(e).
savvy ['sævɪ] *n* (*col*) jugeote *f*.
saw [sɔ:] *pt of* **see** // *n* (*tool*) scie *f* // *vt* (*pt* **sawed**, *pp* **sawed** *or* **sawn** [sɔ:n]) scier; **~dust** *n* sciure *f*; **~mill** *n* scierie *f*.

saxophone ['sæksəfəun] *n* saxophone *m.*

say [seɪ] *n*: **to have one's ~** dire ce qu'on a à dire ; **to have a ~** avoir voix au chapitre // *vt* (*pt, pp* **said** [sɛd]) dire ; **could you ~ that again?** pourriez-vous répéter ceci? ; **that is to ~** c'est-à-dire ; **to ~ nothing of** sans compter ; **~ that ...** mettons *or* disons que ... ; **that goes without ~ing** cela va sans dire, cela va de soi ; **~ing** *n* dicton *m,* proverbe *m.*

scab [skæb] *n* croûte *f*; (*pej*) jaune *m* ; **~by** *a* croûteux(euse).

scaffold ['skæfəuld] *n* échafaud *m* ; **~ing** *n* échafaudage *m.*

scald [skɔːld] *n* brûlure *f* // *vt* ébouillanter ; **~ing** *a* (*hot*) brûlant(e), bouillant(e).

scale [skeɪl] *n* (*of fish*) écaille *f* ; (MUS) gamme *f* ; (*of ruler, thermometer etc*) graduation *f,* échelle (graduée) ; (*of salaries, fees etc*) barème *m* ; (*of map, also size, extent*) échelle *f* // *vt* (*mountain*) escalader ; (*fish*) écailler ; **~s** *npl* balance *f,* (*larger*) bascule *f* ; **on a large ~** sur une grande échelle, en grand ; **~ drawing** *n* dessin *m* à l'échelle ; **~ model** *n* modèle *m* à l'échelle ; **small-~ model** modèle réduit.

scallop ['skɔləp] *n* coquille *f* Saint-Jacques.

scalp [skælp] *n* cuir chevelu // *vt* scalper.

scalpel ['skælpl] *n* scalpel *m.*

scamp [skæmp] *vt* bâcler.

scamper ['skæmpə*] *vi*: **to ~ away, ~ off** détaler.

scan [skæn] *vt* scruter, examiner ; (*glance at quickly*) parcourir ; (*poetry*) scander ; (TV, RADAR) balayer.

scandal ['skændl] *n* scandale *m* ; (*gossip*) ragots *mpl* ; **~ize** *vt* scandaliser, indigner ; **~ous** *a* scandaleux(euse).

Scandinavia [skændɪ'neɪvɪə] *n* Scandinavie *f* ; **~n** *a* scandinave // *n* Scandinave *m/f.*

scant [skænt] *a* insuffisant(e) ; **~y** *a* peu abondant(e), insuffisant(e), maigre.

scapegoat ['skeɪpgəut] *n* bouc *m* émissaire.

scar [skɑː] *n* cicatrice *f* // *vt* laisser une cicatrice *or* une marque à.

scarce [skɛəs] *a* rare, peu abondant(e) ; **~ly** *ad* à peine, presque pas ; **scarcity** *n* rareté *f,* manque *m,* pénurie *f.*

scare [skɛə*] *n* peur *f* ; panique *f* // *vt* effrayer, faire peur à ; **to ~ sb stiff** faire une peur bleue à qn ; **bomb ~** alerte *f* à la bombe ; **~crow** *n* épouvantail *m* ; **~d** *a*: **to be ~d** avoir peur ; **~monger** *n* alarmiste *m/f.*

scarf, scarves [skɑːf, skɑːvz] *n* (*long*) écharpe *f* ; (*square*) foulard *m.*

scarlet ['skɑːlɪt] *a* écarlate ; **~ fever** *n* scarlatine *f.*

scarves [skɑːvz] *npl of* **scarf.**

scary ['skɛərɪ] *a* (*col*) qui fiche la frousse.

scathing ['skeɪðɪŋ] *a* cinglant(e), acerbe.

scatter ['skætə*] *vt* éparpiller, répandre ; (*crowd*) disperser // *vi* se disperser ; **~brained** *a* écervelé(e), étourdi(e) ; **~ed** *a* épars(e), dispersé(e).

scatty ['skætɪ] *a* (*col*) loufoque.

scavenger ['skævəndʒə*] *n* éboueur *m.*

scene [siːn] *n* (THEATRE, *fig etc*) scène *f* ; (*of crime, accident*) lieu(x) *m(pl),* endroit *m* ; (*sight, view*) spectacle *m,* vue *f* ; **to appear on the ~** faire son apparition ; **~ry** *n* (THEATRE) décor(s) *m(pl)* ; (*landscape*) paysage *m* ; **scenic** *a* scénique ; offrant de beaux paysages *or* panoramas.

scent [sɛnt] *n* parfum *m,* odeur *f* ; (*fig: track*) piste *f* ; (*sense of smell*) odorat *m* // *vt* parfumer ; (*smell, also fig*) flairer.

sceptic, skeptic (*US*) ['skɛptɪk] *n* sceptique *m/f* ; **~al** *a* sceptique ; **~ism** ['skɛptɪsɪzm] *n* scepticisme *m.*

sceptre, scepter (*US*) ['sɛptə*] *n* sceptre *m.*

schedule ['ʃɛdjuːl] *n* programme *m,* plan *m* ; (*of trains*) horaire *m* ; (*of prices etc*) barème *m,* tarif *m* // *vt* prévoir ; **as ~d** comme prévu ; **on ~** à l'heure (prévue) ; à la date prévue ; **to be ahead of/behind ~** avoir de l'avance/du retard.

scheme [skiːm] *n* plan *m,* projet *m* ; (*method*) procédé *m* ; (*dishonest plan, plot*) complot *m,* combine *f* ; (*arrangement*) arrangement *m,* classification *f* // *vt,vi* comploter, manigancer ; **scheming** *a* rusé(e), intrigant(e) // *n* manigances *fpl,* intrigues *fpl.*

schism ['skɪzəm] *n* schisme *m.*

schizophrenic [skɪtsə'frɛnɪk] *a* schizophrène.

scholar ['skɔlə*] *n* érudit/e ; **~ly** *a* érudit(e), savant(e) ; **~ship** *n* érudition *f* ; (*grant*) bourse *f* (d'études).

school [skuːl] *n* (*gen*) école *f* ; (*in university*) faculté *f* ; (*secondary school*) collège *m,* lycée *m* // *cpd* scolaire // *vt* (*animal*) dresser ; **~book** *n* livre *m* scolaire *or* de classe ; **~boy** *n* écolier *m* ; collégien *m,* lycéen *m* ; **~days** *npl* années *fpl* de scolarité ; **~girl** *n* écolière *f* ; collégienne *f,* lycéenne *f* ; **~ing** *n* instruction *f,* études *fpl* ; **~-leaving age** *n* âge *m* de fin de scolarité ; **~master** *n* (*primary*) instituteur *m* ; (*secondary*) professeur *m* ; **~mistress** *n* institutrice *f* ; professeur *m* ; **~ report** *n* bulletin *m* (scolaire) ; **~room** *n* (salle *f* de) classe *f* ; **~teacher** *n* instituteur/trice ; professeur *m.*

schooner ['skuːnə*] *n* (*ship*) schooner *m,* goélette *f* ; (*glass*) grand verre (à xérès).

sciatica [saɪ'ætɪkə] *n* sciatique *f.*

science ['saɪəns] *n* science *f* ; **~ fiction** *n* science-fiction *f* ; **scientific** [-'tɪfɪk] *a* scientifique ; **scientist** *n* scientifique *m/f* ; (*eminent*) savant *m.*

scintillating ['sɪntɪleɪtɪŋ] *a* scintillant(e), étincelant(e).

scissors ['sɪzəz] *npl* ciseaux *mpl* ; **a pair of ~** une paire de ciseaux.

sclerosis [sklɪ'rəusɪs] *n* sclérose *f.*

scoff [skɔf] *vt* (*col: eat*) avaler, bouffer // *vi*: **to ~ (at)** (*mock*) se moquer (de).

scold [skəuld] *vt* gronder, attraper, réprimander.

scone [skɔn] *n sorte de petit pain rond au lait.*

scoop [skuːp] *n* pelle *f* (à main) ; (*for ice cream*) boule *f* à glace ; (PRESS) reportage exclusif *or* à sensation ; **to ~ out** *vt* évider, creuser ; **to ~ up** *vt* ramasser.

scooter ['skuːtə*] *n* (*motor cycle*) scooter *m* ; (*toy*) trottinette *f.*

scope [skəup] *n* (*capacity: of plan, undertaking*) portée *f*, envergure *f*; (: *of person*) compétence *f*, capacités *fpl*; (*opportunity*) possibilités *fpl*; **within the ~ of** dans les limites de.
scorch [skɔ:tʃ] *vt* (*clothes*) brûler (légèrement), roussir; (*earth, grass*) dessécher, brûler; **~ed earth policy** *n* politique *f* de la terre brûlée; **~er** *n* (*col: hot day*) journée *f* torride; **~ing** *a* torride, brûlant(e).
score [skɔ:*] *n* score *m*, décompte *m* des points; (MUS) partition *f*; (*twenty*) vingt // *vt* (*goal, point*) marquer; (*success*) remporter // *vi* marquer des points; (FOOTBALL) marquer un but; (*keep score*) compter les points; **on that ~** sur ce chapitre, à cet égard; **to ~ well/6 out of 10** obtenir un bon résultat/6 sur 10; **~board** *n* tableau *m*; **~card** *n* (SPORT) carton *m*; feuille *f* de marque; **~r** *n* auteur *m* du but; marqueur *m* de buts; (*keeping score*) marqueur *m*.
scorn [skɔ:n] *n* mépris *m*, dédain *m* // *vt* mépriser, dédaigner; **~ful** *a* méprisant(e), dédaigneux(euse).
Scorpio ['skɔ:pıəu] *n* le Scorpion; **to be ~** être du Scorpion.
scorpion ['skɔ:pıən] *n* scorpion *m*.
Scot [skɔt] *n* Écossais/e.
scotch [skɔtʃ] *vt* faire échouer; enrayer; étouffer; **S~** *n* whisky *m*, scotch *m*.
scot-free ['skɔt'fri:] *a* sans être puni(e); sans payer.
Scotland ['skɔtlənd] *n* Écosse *f*.
Scots [skɔts] *a* écossais(e); **~man/woman** Écossais/e.
Scottish ['skɔtıʃ] *a* écossais(e).
scoundrel ['skaundrl] *n* vaurien *m*; (*child*) coquin *m*.
scour ['skauə*] *vt* (*clean*) récurer; frotter; décaper; (*search*) battre, parcourir; **~er** *n* tampon abrasif *or* à récurer.
scourge [skə:dʒ] *n* fléau *m*.
scout [skaut] *n* (MIL) éclaireur *m*; (*also*: **boy ~**) scout *m*; **to ~ around** explorer, chercher.
scowl [skaul] *vi* se renfrogner, avoir l'air maussade; **to ~ at** regarder de travers.
scraggy ['skrægı] *a* décharné(e), efflanqué(e), famélique.
scram [skræm] *vi* (*col*) ficher le camp.
scramble ['skræmbl] *n* bousculade *f*, ruée *f* // *vi* avancer tant bien que mal (à quatre pattes *or* en grimpant); **to ~ for** se bousculer *or* se disputer pour (avoir); **~d eggs** *npl* œufs brouillés.
scrap [skræp] *n* bout *m*, morceau *m*; (*fight*) bagarre *f*; (*also*: **~ iron**) ferraille *f* // *vt* jeter, mettre au rebut; (*fig*) abandonner, laisser tomber; **~s** *npl* (*waste*) déchets *mpl*; **~book** *n* album *m*.
scrape [skreıp] *vt,vi* gratter, racler // *n*: **to get into a ~** s'attirer des ennuis; **~r** *n* grattoir *m*, racloir *m*.
scrap: **~ heap** *n* tas *m* de ferraille; (*fig*): **on the ~ heap** au rancart *or* rebut; **~ merchant** *n* marchand *m* de ferraille; **~ paper** *n* papier *m* brouillon; **~py** *a* fragmentaire, décousu(e).
scratch [skrætʃ] *n* égratignure *f*, rayure *f*; éraflure *f*; (*from claw*) coup *m* de griffe // *a*: **~ team** *n* équipe de fortune *or* improvisé(e) // *vt* (*record*) rayer; (*paint etc*) érafler; (*with claw, nail*) griffer // *vi* (se) gratter; **to start from ~** partir de zéro; **to be up to ~** être à la hauteur.
scrawl [skrɔ:l] *n* gribouillage *m* // *vi* gribouiller.
scrawny ['skrɔ:nı] *a* décharné(e).
scream [skri:m] *n* cri perçant, hurlement *m* // *vi* crier, hurler; **to be a ~** être impayable.
scree [skri:] *n* éboulis *m*.
screech [skri:tʃ] *n* cri strident, hurlement *m*; (*of tyres, brakes*) crissement *m*, grincement *m* // *vi* hurler; crisser, grincer.
screen [skri:n] *n* écran *m*, paravent *m*; (CINEMA, TV) écran; (*fig*) écran, rideau *m* // *vt* masquer, cacher; (*from the wind etc*) abriter, protéger; (*film*) projeter; (*book*) porter à l'écran; (*candidates etc*) filtrer; **~ing** *n* (MED) test *m* (*or* tests) de dépistage.
screw [skru:] *n* vis *f*; (*propeller*) hélice *f* // *vt* visser; **to have one's head ~ed on** avoir la tête sur les épaules; **~driver** *n* tournevis *m*; **~y** *a* (*col*) dingue, cinglé(e).
scribble ['skrıbl] *n* gribouillage *m* // *vt* gribouiller, griffonner.
scribe [skraıb] *n* scribe *m*.
script [skrıpt] *n* (CINEMA *etc*) scénario *m*, texte *m*; (*in exam*) copie *f*.
Scripture ['skrıptʃə*] *n* Écriture Sainte.
scriptwriter ['skrıptraıtə*] *n* scénariste *m/f*, dialoguiste *m/f*.
scroll [skrəul] *n* rouleau *m*.
scrounge [skraundʒ] *vt* (*col*): **to ~ sth (off *or* from sb)** se faire payer qch (par qn), emprunter qch (à qn) // *vi*: **to ~ on sb** vivre aux crochets de qn; **~r** *n* parasite *m*.
scrub [skrʌb] *n* (*clean*) nettoyage *m* (à la brosse); (*land*) broussailles *fpl* // *vt* (*floor*) nettoyer à la brosse; (*pan*) récurer; (*washing*) frotter; (*reject*) annuler.
scruff [skrʌf] *n*: **by the ~ of the neck** par la peau du cou.
scruffy ['skrʌfı] *a* débraillé(e).
scrum(mage) ['skrʌm(ıdʒ)] *n* mêlée *f*.
scruple ['skru:pl] *n* scrupule *m*.
scrupulous ['skru:pjuləs] *a* scrupuleux(euse).
scrutinize ['skru:tınaız] *vt* scruter, examiner minutieusement.
scrutiny ['skru:tını] *n* examen minutieux.
scuff [skʌf] *vt* érafler.
scuffle ['skʌfl] *n* échauffourée *f*, rixe *f*.
scull [skʌl] *n* aviron *m*.
scullery ['skʌlərı] *n* arrière-cuisine *f*.
sculptor ['skʌlptə*] *n* sculpteur *m*.
sculpture ['skʌlptʃə*] *n* sculpture *f*.
scum [skʌm] *n* écume *f*, mousse *f*; (*pej: people*) rebut *m*, lie *f*.
scurrilous ['skʌrıləs] *a* haineux(euse), virulent(e); calomnieux(euse).
scurry ['skʌrı] *vi* filer à toute allure.
scurvy ['skə:vı] *n* scorbut *m*.
scuttle ['skʌtl] *n* (NAUT) écoutille *f*; (*also*: **coal ~**) seau *m* (à charbon) // *vt* (*ship*) saborder // *vi* (*scamper*): **to ~ away, ~ off** détaler.
scythe [saıð] *n* faux *f*.
sea [si:] *n* mer *f* // *cpd* marin(e), de (la) mer, maritime; **on the ~** (*boat*) en mer;

(*town*) au bord de la mer ; **to be all at ~** (*fig*) nager complètement ; **~ bird** *n* oiseau *m* de mer ; **~board** *n* côte *f* ; **~ breeze** *n* brise *f* de mer ; **~farer** *n* marin *m* ; **~food** *n* fruits *mpl* de mer ; **~ front** *n* bord *m* de mer ; **~going** *a* (*ship*) de haute mer ; **~gull** *n* mouette *f*.

seal [si:l] *n* (*animal*) phoque *m* ; (*stamp*) sceau *m*, cachet *m* ; (*impression*) cachet, estampille *f* // *vt* sceller ; (*envelope*) coller ; (: *with seal*) cacheter.

sea level ['si:lɛvl] *n* niveau *m* de la mer.

sealing wax ['si:lɪŋwæks] *n* cire *f* à cacheter.

sea lion ['si:laɪən] *n* lion *m* de mer.

seam [si:m] *n* couture *f* ; (*of coal*) veine *f*, filon *m*.

seaman ['si:mən] *n* marin *m*.

seamless ['si:mlɪs] *a* sans couture(s).

seamy ['si:mɪ] *a* louche, mal famé(e).

seance ['seɪɔns] *n* séance *f* de spiritisme.

seaplane ['si:pleɪn] *n* hydravion *m*.

seaport ['si:pɔ:t] *n* port *m* de mer.

search [sə:tʃ] *n* (*for person, thing*) recherche(s) *f(pl)* ; (*of drawer, pockets*) fouille *f* ; (LAW: *at sb's home*) perquisition *f* // *vt* fouiller ; (*examine*) examiner minutieusement ; scruter // *vi*: **to ~ for** chercher ; **to ~ through** *vt fus* fouiller ; **in ~ of** à la recherche de ; **~ing** *a* pénétrant(e) ; minutieux(euse) ; **~light** *n* projecteur *m* ; **~ party** *n* expédition *f* de secours ; **~ warrant** *n* mandat *m* de perquisition.

seashore ['si:ʃɔ:*] *n* rivage *m*, plage *f*, bord *m* de (la) mer.

seasick ['si:sɪk] *a* qui a le mal de mer.

seaside ['si:saɪd] *n* bord *m* de la mer ; **~ resort** *n* station *f* balnéaire.

season ['si:zn] *n* saison *f* // *vt* assaisonner, relever ; **~al** *a* saisonnier(ère) ; **~ing** *n* assaisonnement *m* ; **~ ticket** *n* carte *f* d'abonnement.

seat [si:t] *n* siège *m* ; (*in bus, train: place*) place *f* ; (PARLIAMENT) siège ; (*buttocks*) postérieur *m* ; (*of trousers*) fond *m* // *vt* faire asseoir, placer ; (*have room for*) avoir des places assises pour, pouvoir accueillir ; **~ belt** *n* ceinture *f* de sécurité ; **~ing room** *n* places assises.

sea water ['si:wɔ:tə*] *n* eau *f* de mer.

seaweed ['si:wi:d] *n* algues *fpl*.

seaworthy ['si:wə:ðɪ] *a* en état de naviguer.

sec. *abbr of* **second(s)**.

secede [sɪ'si:d] *vi* faire sécession.

secluded [sɪ'klu:dɪd] *a* retiré(e), à l'écart.

seclusion [sɪ'klu:ʒən] *n* solitude *f*.

second ['sɛkənd] *num* deuxième, second(e) // *ad* (*in race etc*) en seconde position ; (RAIL) en seconde // *n* (*unit of time*) seconde *f* ; (*in series, position*) deuxième *m/f*, second/e ; (SCOL) ≈ licence *f* avec mention bien *or* assez bien ; (AUT: *also*: **~ gear**) seconde *f* ; (COMM: *imperfect*) article *m* de second choix // *vt* (*motion*) appuyer ; **~ary** *a* secondaire ; **~ary school** *n* collège *m*, lycée *m* ; **~-class** *a* de deuxième classe ; **~er** *n* personne *f* qui appuie une motion ; **~hand** *a* d'occasion ; de seconde main ; **~ hand** *n* (*on clock*) trotteuse *f* ; **~ly** *ad* deuxièmement ; **~ment** [sɪ'kɔndmənt] *n* détachement *m* ; **~-rate** *a* de deuxième ordre, de qualité inférieure ; **~ thoughts** *npl* doutes *mpl* ; **on ~ thoughts** à la réflexion.

secrecy ['si:krəsɪ] *n* secret *m* ; **in ~** en secret, dans le secret.

secret ['si:krɪt] *a* secret(ète) // *n* secret *m*.

secretarial [sɛkrɪ'tɛərɪəl] *a* de secrétaire, de secrétariat.

secretariat [sɛkrɪ'tɛərɪət] *n* secrétariat *m*.

secretary ['sɛkrətərɪ] *n* secrétaire *m/f* ; (COMM) secrétaire général ; **S~ of State (for)** (*Brit*: POL) ministre *m* (de).

secretive ['si:krətɪv] *a* réservé(e) ; (*pej*) cachottier(ère), dissimulé(e).

sect [sɛkt] *n* secte *f* ; **~arian** [-'tɛərɪən] *a* sectaire.

section ['sɛkʃən] *n* coupe *f*, section *f* ; (*department*) section ; (COMM) rayon *m* ; (*of document*) section, article *m*, paragraphe *m* // *vt* sectionner ; **~al** *a* (*drawing*) en coupe.

sector ['sɛktə*] *n* secteur *m*.

secular ['sɛkjulə*] *a* profane ; laïque ; séculier(ère).

secure [sɪ'kjuə*] *a* (*free from anxiety*) sans inquiétude, sécurisé(e) ; (*firmly fixed*) solide, bien attaché(e) (*or* fermé(e) *etc*) ; (*in safe place*) en lieu sûr, en sûreté // *vt* (*fix*) fixer, attacher ; (*get*) obtenir, se procurer.

security [sɪ'kjurɪtɪ] *n* sécurité *f* ; mesures *fpl* de sécurité ; (*for loan*) caution *f*, garantie *f*.

sedate [sɪ'deɪt] *a* calme ; posé(e) // *vt* donner des sédatifs à.

sedation [sɪ'deɪʃən] *n* (MED) sédation *f*.

sedative ['sɛdɪtɪv] *n* calmant *m*, sédatif *m*.

sedentary ['sɛdntrɪ] *a* sédentaire.

sediment ['sɛdɪmənt] *n* sédiment *m*, dépôt *m*.

seduce [sɪ'dju:s] *vt* (*gen*) séduire ; **seduction** [-'dʌkʃən] *n* séduction *f* ; **seductive** [-'dʌktɪv] *a* séduisant(e), séducteur(trice).

see [si:] *vb* (*pt* **saw**, *pp* **seen** [sɔ:, si:n]) *vt* (*gen*) voir ; (*accompany*): **to ~ sb to the door** reconduire *or* raccompagner qn jusqu'à la porte // *vi* voir // *n* évêché *m* ; **to ~ that** (*ensure*) veiller à ce que + *sub*, faire en sorte que + *sub*, s'assurer que ; **to ~ off** *vt* accompagner (à la gare *or* à l'aéroport *etc*) ; **to ~ through** *vt* mener à bonne fin // *vt fus* voir clair dans ; **to ~ to** *vt fus* s'occuper de, se charger de ; **~ you!** au revoir!, à bientôt!

seed [si:d] *n* graine *f* ; (*fig*) germe *m* ; (TENNIS) tête *f* de série ; **to go to ~** monter en graine ; (*fig*) se laisser aller ; **~ling** *n* jeune plant *m*, semis *m* ; **~y** *a* (*shabby*) minable, miteux(euse).

seeing ['si:ɪŋ] *cj*: **~ (that)** vu que, étant donné que.

seek, *pt,pp* **sought** [si:k, sɔ:t] *vt* chercher, rechercher.

seem [si:m] *vi* sembler, paraître ; **there seems to be ...** il semble qu'il y a ... ; on dirait qu'il y a ... ; **~ingly** *ad* apparemment.

seen [si:n] *pp of* **see**.

seep [si:p] *vi* suinter, filtrer.

seer [sɪə*] *n* prophète/prophétesse, voyant/e.
seersucker ['sɪəsʌkə*] *n* cloqué *m*, étoffe cloquée.
seesaw ['si:sɔ:] *n* (jeu *m* de) bascule *f*.
seethe [si:ð] *vi* être en effervescence; **to ~ with anger** bouillir de colère.
see-through ['si:θru:] *a* transparent(e).
segment ['sɛgmənt] *n* segment *m*.
segregate ['sɛgrɪgeɪt] *vt* séparer, isoler; **segregation** [-'geɪʃən] *n* ségrégation *f*.
seismic ['saɪzmɪk] *a* sismique.
seize [si:z] *vt* (*grasp*) saisir, attraper; (*take possession of*) s'emparer de; (LAW) saisir; **to ~ (up)on** *vt fus* saisir, sauter sur; **to ~ up** *vi* (TECH) se gripper.
seizure ['si:ʒə*] *n* (MED) crise *f*, attaque *f*; (LAW) saisie *f*.
seldom ['sɛldəm] *ad* rarement.
select [sɪ'lɛkt] *a* choisi(e), d'élite; select *inv* // *vt* sélectionner, choisir; **~ion** [-'lɛkʃən] *n* sélection *f*, choix *m*; **~ive** *a* sélectif(ive); (*school*) à recrutement sélectif; **~or** *n* (*person*) sélectionneur/euse; (TECH) sélecteur *m*.
self [sɛlf] *n* (*pl* **selves** [sɛlvz]): **the ~** le moi *inv* // *prefix* auto-; **~-adhesive** *a* auto-collant(e); **~-assertive** *a* autoritaire; **~-assured** *a* sûr(e) de soi, plein(e) d'assurace; **~-catering** *a* avec cuisine, où l'on peut faire sa cuisine; **~-centred** *a* égocentrique; **~-coloured** *a* uni(e); **~-confidence** *n* confiance *f* en soi; **~-conscious** *a* timide, qui manque d'assurance; **~-contained** *a* (*flat*) avec entrée particulière, indépendant(e); **~-control** *n* maîtrise *f* de soi; **~-defeating** *a* qui a un effet contraire à l'effet recherché; **~-defence** *n* légitime défense *f*; **~-discipline** *n* discipline personnelle; **~-employed** *a* qui travaille à son compte; **~-evident** *a* évident(e), qui va de soi; **~-explanatory** *a* qui se passe d'explication; **~-indulgent** *a* qui ne se refuse rien; **~-interest** *n* intérêt personnel; **~ish** *a* égoïste; **~ishness** *n* égoïsme *m*; **~lessly** *ad* sans penser à soi; **~-pity** *n* apitoiement *m* sur soi-même; **~-portrait** *n* autoportrait *m*; **~-possessed** *a* assuré(e); **~-preservation** *n* instinct *m* de conservation; **~-reliant** *a* indépendant(e); **~-respect** *n* respect *m* de soi, amour-propre *m*; **~-respecting** *a* qui se respecte; **~-righteous** *a* satisfait(e) de soi, pharisaïque; **~-sacrifice** *n* abnégation *f*; **~-satisfied** *a* content(e) de soi, suffisant(e); **~-seal** *a* (envelope) auto-collant(e); **~-service** *n* libre-service *m*, self-service *m*; **~-sufficient** *a* indépendant(e); **~-supporting** *a* financièrement indépendant(e); **~-taught** *a* autodidacte.
sell, *pt,pp* **sold** [sɛl, səuld] *vt* vendre // *vi* se vendre; **to ~ at** *or* **for 10F** se vendre 10F; **to ~ off** *vt* liquider; **~er** *n* vendeur/euse, marchand/e; **~ing price** *n* prix *m* de vente.
sellotape ['sɛləuteɪp] *n* ® papier collant, scotch *m* ®.
sellout ['sɛlaut] *n* trahison *f*, capitulation *f*; (*of tickets*): **it was a ~** tous les billets ont été vendus.
selves [sɛlvz] *npl of* **self**.
semantic [sɪ'mæntɪk] *a* sémantique; **~s** *n* sémantique *f*.
semaphore ['sɛməfɔ:*] *n* signaux *mpl* à bras; (RAIL) sémaphore *m*.
semen ['si:mən] *n* sperme *m*.
semi ['sɛmɪ] *prefix* semi-, demi-; à demi, à moitié; **~-breve** ronde *f*; **~circle** *n* demi-cercle *m*; **~colon** *n* point-virgule *m*; **~conscious** *a* à demi conscient(e); **~detached (house)** *n* maison jumelée *or* jumelle; **~final** *n* demi-finale *f*.
seminar ['sɛmɪnɑ:*] *n* séminaire *m*.
semiquaver ['sɛmɪkweɪvə*] *n* double croche *f*.
semiskilled ['sɛmɪ'skɪld] *a*: **~ worker** *n* ouvrier/ère spécialisé/e.
semitone ['sɛmɪtəun] *n* (MUS) demi-ton *m*.
semolina [sɛmə'li:nə] *n* semoule *f*.
senate ['sɛnɪt] *n* sénat *m*; **senator** *n* sénateur *m*.
send, *pt,pp* **sent** [sɛnd, sɛnt] *vt* envoyer; **to ~ sb to Coventry** mettre qn en quarantaine; **to ~ away** *vt* (*letter, goods*) envoyer, expédier; **to ~ away for** *vt fus* commander par correspondance, se faire envoyer; **to ~ back** *vt* renvoyer; **to ~ for** *vt fus* envoyer chercher; faire venir; **to ~ off** *vt* (*goods*) envoyer, expédier; (SPORT: *player*) expulser *or* renvoyer du terrain; **to ~ out** *vt* (*invitation*) envoyer (par la poste); **to ~ up** *vt* (*person, price*) faire monter; (*parody*) mettre en boîte, parodier; (*blow up*) faire sauter; **~er** *n* expéditeur/trice; **~-off** *n*: **a good ~-off** des adieux chaleureux.
senile ['si:naɪl] *a* sénile.
senility [sɪ'nɪlɪtɪ] *n* sénilité *f*.
senior ['si:nɪə*] *a* (*older*) aîné(e), plus âgé(e); (*of higher rank*) supérieur(e) // *n* aîné/e; (*in service*) personne *f* qui a plus d'ancienneté; **~ity** [-'ɔrɪtɪ] *n* priorité *f* d'âge, ancienneté *f*.
sensation [sɛn'seɪʃən] *n* sensation *f*; **to create a ~** faire sensation; **~al** *a* qui fait sensation; (*marvellous*) sensationnel(le).
sense [sɛns] *n* sens *m*; (*feeling*) sentiment *m*; (*meaning*) signification *f*; (*wisdom*) bon sens // *vt* sentir, pressentir; **it makes ~** c'est logique; **~s** *npl* raison *f*; **~less** *a* insensé(e), stupide; (*unconscious*) sans connaissance; **anyone in his ~s** tout homme sensé.
sensibility [sɛnsɪ'bɪlɪtɪ] *n* sensibilité *f*; **sensibilities** *npl* susceptibilité *f*.
sensible ['sɛnsɪbl] *a* sensé(e), raisonnable; sage; pratique.
sensitive ['sɛnsɪtɪv] *a*: **~ (to)** sensible (à); **sensitivity** [-'tɪvɪtɪ] *n* sensibilité *f*.
sensual ['sɛnsjuəl] *a* sensuel(le).
sensuous ['sɛnsjuəs] *a* voluptueux(euse), sensuel(le).
sent [sɛnt] *pt,pp of* **send**.
sentence ['sɛntns] *n* (LING) phrase *f*; (LAW: *judgment*) condamnation *f*, sentence *f*; (: *punishment*) peine *f* // *vt*: **to ~ sb to death/to 5 years** condamner qn à mort/à 5 ans.
sentiment ['sɛntɪmənt] *n* sentiment *m*; (*opinion*) opinion *f*, avis *m*; **~al** [-'mɛntl] *a* sentimental(e); **~ality** [-'tælɪtɪ] *n* sentimentalité *f*, sensiblerie *f*.

sentry ['sɛntrɪ] *n* sentinelle *f*, factionnaire *m*.
separable ['sɛprəbl] *a* séparable.
separate *a* ['sɛprɪt] séparé(e), indépendant(e), différent(e) // *vb* ['sɛpəreɪt] *vt* séparer // *vi* se séparer ; **~ly** *ad* séparément ; **~s** *npl* (*clothes*) coordonnés *mpl* ; **separation** [-'reɪʃən] *n* séparation *f*.
September [sɛp'tɛmbə*] *n* septembre *m*.
septic ['sɛptɪk] *a* septique ; (*wound*) infecté(e).
sequel ['si:kwl] *n* conséquence *f* ; séquelles *fpl* ; (*of story*) suite *f*.
sequence ['si:kwəns] *n* ordre *m*, suite *f* ; **~ of tenses** concordance *f* des temps.
sequin ['si:kwɪn] *n* paillette *f*.
serenade [sɛrə'neɪd] *n* sérénade *f* // *vt* donner une sérénade à.
serene [sɪ'ri:n] *a* serein(e), calme, paisible ; **serenity** [sə'rɛnɪtɪ] *n* sérénité *f*, calme *m*.
sergeant ['sa:dʒənt] *n* sergent *m* ; (POLICE) brigadier *m*.
serial ['sɪərɪəl] *n* feuilleton *m* // *a* (*number*) de série ; **~ize** *vt* publier (*or* adapter) en feuilleton.
series ['sɪəri:s] *n* série *f* ; (PUBLISHING) collection *f*.
serious ['sɪərɪəs] *a* sérieux(euse), réfléchi(e) ; grave ; **~ly** *ad* sérieusement, gravement ; **~ness** *n* sérieux *m*, gravité *f*.
sermon ['sə:mən] *n* sermon *m*.
serrated [sɪ'reɪtɪd] *a* en dents de scie.
serum ['sɪərəm] *n* sérum *m*.
servant ['sə:vənt] *n* domestique *m/f* ; (*fig*) serviteur/servante.
serve [sə:v] *vt* (*employer etc*) servir, être au service de ; (*purpose*) servir à ; (*customer, food, meal*) servir ; (*apprenticeship*) faire, accomplir ; (*prison term*) faire ; purger // *vi* (*also* TENNIS) servir ; (*be useful*): **to ~ as/for/to do** servir de/à/faire // *n* (TENNIS) service *m* ; **it ~s him right** c'est bien fait pour lui ; **to ~ out, ~ up** *vt* (*food*) servir.
service ['sə:vɪs] *n* (*gen*) service *m* ; (AUT: *maintenance*) révision *f* // *vt* (*car, washing machine*) réviser ; **the S~s** les forces armées ; **to be of ~ to sb, to do sb a ~** rendre service à qn ; **to put one's car in for (a) ~** donner sa voiture à réviser ; **dinner ~** *n* service *m* de table ; **~able** *a* pratique, commode ; **~ area** *n* (*on motorway*) aire *f* de services ; **~man** *n* militaire *m* ; **~ station** *n* station-service *f*.
serviette [sə:vɪ'ɛt] *n* serviette *f* (de table).
servile ['sə:vaɪl] *a* servile.
session ['sɛʃən] *n* (*sitting*) séance *f* ; (SCOL) année *f* scolaire (*or* universitaire) ; **to be in ~** siéger, être en session *or* en séance.
set [sɛt] *n* série *f*, assortiment *m* ; (*of tools etc*) jeu *m* ; (RADIO, TV) poste *m* ; (TENNIS) set *m* ; (*group of people*) cercle *m*, milieu *m* ; (CINEMA) plateau *m* ; (THEATRE: *stage*) scène *f* ; (: *scenery*) décor *m* ; (MATH) ensemble *m* ; (HAIRDRESSING) mise *f* en plis // *a* (*fixed*) fixe, déterminé(e) ; (*ready*) prêt(e) // *vb* (*pt, pp* **set**) (*place*) mettre, poser, placer ; (*fix*) fixer ; (*adjust*) régler ; (*decide*: *rules etc*) fixer, choisir ; (TYP) composer // *vi* (*sun*) se coucher ; (*jam, jelly, concrete*) prendre ; **to be ~ on doing** être résolu à faire ; **to be (dead) ~ against** être (totalement) opposé à ; **to ~ (to music)** mettre en musique ; **to ~ on fire** mettre le feu à ; **to ~ free** libérer ; **to ~ sth going** déclencher qch ; **to ~ sail** partir, prendre la mer ; **to ~ about** *vt fus* (*task*) entreprendre, se mettre à ; **to ~ aside** *vt* mettre de côté ; **to ~ back** *vt* (*in time*): **to ~ back (by)** retarder (de) ; **to ~ off** *vi* se mettre en route, partir //*vt* (*bomb*) faire exploser ; (*cause to start*) déclencher ; (*show up well*) mettre en valeur, faire valoir ; **to ~ out** *vi*: **to ~ out to do** entreprendre de ; avoir pour but *or* intention de // *vt* (*arrange*) disposer ; (*state*) présenter, exposer ; **to ~ up** *vt* (*organization*) fonder, constituer ; (*record*) établir ; (*monument*) ériger ; **to ~ up shop** (*fig*) s'établir, s'installer ; **~back** *n* (*hitch*) revers *m*, contretemps *m*.
settee [sɛ'ti:] *n* canapé *m*.
setting ['sɛtɪŋ] *n* cadre *m* ; (*of jewel*) monture *f*.
settle ['sɛtl] *vt* (*argument, matter*) régler ; (*problem*) résoudre ; (MED: *calm*) calmer // *vi* (*bird, dust etc*) se poser ; (*sediment*) se déposer ; (*also*: **~ down**) s'installer, se fixer ; se calmer ; se ranger ; **to ~ to sth** se mettre sérieusement à qch ; **to ~ for sth** accepter qch, se contenter de qch ; **to ~ in** *vi* s'installer ; **to ~ on sth** opter *or* se décider pour qch ; **to ~ up with sb** régler (ce que l'on doit à) qn ; **~ment** *n* (*payment*) règlement *m* ; (*agreement*) accord *m* ; (*colony*) colonie *f* ; (*village etc*) établissement *m* ; hameau *m* ; **~r** *n* colon *m*.
setup ['sɛtʌp] *n* (*arrangement*) manière *f* dont les choses sont organisées ; (*situation*) situation *f*, allure *f* des choses.
seven ['sɛvn] *num* sept ; **~teen** *num* dix-sept ; **~th** *num* septième ; **~ty** *num* soixante-dix.
sever ['sɛvə*] *vt* couper, trancher ; (*relations*) rompre.
several ['sɛvərl] *a,pronoun* plusieurs (*m/fpl*) ; **~ of us** plusieurs d'entre nous.
severance ['sɛvərəns] *n* (*of relations*) rupture *f* ; **~ pay** *n* indemnité *f* de licenciement.
severe [sɪ'vɪə*] *a* sévère, strict(e) ; (*serious*) grave, sérieux(euse) ; (*hard*) rigoureux(euse), dur(e) ; (*plain*) sévère, austère ; **severity** [sɪ'vɛrɪtɪ] *n* sévérité *f* ; gravité *f* ; rigueur *f*.
sew, *pt* **sewed,** *pp* **sewn** [səu, səud, səun] *vt,vi* coudre ; **to ~ up** *vt* (re)coudre ; **it is all sewn up** (*fig*) c'est dans le sac *or* dans la poche.
sewage ['su:ɪdʒ] *n* vidange(s) *f(pl)*.
sewer ['su:ə*] *n* égout *m*.
sewing ['səuɪŋ] *n* couture *f* ; **~ machine** *n* machine *f* à coudre.
sewn [səun] *pp of* **sew**.
sex [sɛks] *n* sexe *m* ; **to have ~ with** avoir des rapports (sexuels) avec ; **~ act** *n* acte sexuel.
sextet [sɛks'tɛt] *n* sextuor *m*.
sexual ['sɛksjuəl] *a* sexuel(le).
sexy ['sɛksɪ] *a* sexy *inv*.
shabby ['ʃæbɪ] *a* miteux(euse) ; (*behaviour*) mesquin(e), méprisable.

shack [ʃæk] *n* cabane *f*, hutte *f*.
shackles ['ʃæklz] *npl* chaînes *fpl*, entraves *fpl*.
shade [ʃeɪd] *n* ombre *f*; (*for lamp*) abat-jour *m inv*; (*of colour*) nuance *f*, ton *m*; (*small quantity*): **a ~ of** un soupçon de // *vt* abriter du soleil, ombrager; **in the ~** à l'ombre; **a ~ smaller** un tout petit peu plus petit.
shadow ['ʃædəu] *n* ombre *f* // *vt* (*follow*) filer; **~ cabinet** *n* (POL) *cabinet parallèle formé par le parti qui n'est pas au pouvoir*; **~y** *a* ombragé(e); (*dim*) vague, indistinct(e).
shady ['ʃeɪdɪ] *a* ombragé(e); (*fig*: *dishonest*) louche, véreux(euse).
shaft [ʃɑ:ft] *n* (*of arrow, spear*) hampe *f*; (AUT, TECH) arbre *m*; (*of mine*) puits *m*; (*of lift*) cage *f*; (*of light*) rayon *m*, trait *m*.
shaggy ['ʃægɪ] *a* hirsute; en broussaille.
shake [ʃeɪk] *vb* (*pt* **shook,** *pp* **shaken** [ʃuk, 'ʃeɪkn]) *vt* secouer; (*bottle, cocktail*) agiter; (*house, confidence*) ébranler // *vi* trembler // *n* secousse *f*; **to ~ hands with sb** serrer la main à qn; **to ~ off** *vt* secouer; (*fig*) se débarrasser de; **to ~ up** *vt* secouer; **~-up** *n* grand remaniement; **shaky** *a* (*hand, voice*) tremblant(e); (*building*) branlant(e), peu solide.
shale [ʃeɪl] *n* schiste argileux.
shall [ʃæl] *auxiliary vb*: **I ~ go** j'irai.
shallot [ʃə'lɔt] *n* échalote *f*.
shallow ['ʃæləu] *a* peu profond(e); (*fig*) superficiel(le), qui manque de profondeur.
sham [ʃæm] *n* frime *f*; (*jewellery, furniture*) imitation *f* // *a* feint(e), simulé(e) // *vt* feindre, simuler.
shambles ['ʃæmblz] *n* confusion *f*, pagaïe *f*, fouillis *m*.
shame [ʃeɪm] *n* honte *f* // *vt* faire honte à; **it is a ~ (that/to do)** c'est dommage (que + *sub*/de faire); **what a ~!** quel dommage!; **~faced** *a* honteux(euse), penaud(e); **~ful** *a* honteux(euse), scandaleux(euse); **~less** *a* éhonté(e), effronté(e); (*immodest*) impudique.
shampoo [ʃæm'pu:] *n* shampooing *m* // *vt* faire un shampooing à.
shamrock ['ʃæmrɔk] *n* trèfle *m* (*emblème national de l'Irlande*).
shandy ['ʃændɪ] *n* bière panachée.
shan't [ʃɑ:nt] = **shall not**.
shanty ['ʃæntɪ] *n* cabane *f*, baraque *f*; **~town** *n* bidonville *m*.
shape [ʃeɪp] *n* forme *f* // *vt* façonner, modeler; (*statement*) formuler; (*sb's ideas*) former; (*sb's life*) déterminer // *vi* (*also*: **~ up**) (*events*) prendre tournure; (*person*) faire des progrès, s'en sortir; **to take ~** prendre forme *or* tournure; **-shaped** *suffix*: **heart-shaped** en forme de cœur; **~less** *a* informe, sans forme; **~ly** *a* bien proportionné(e), beau(belle).
share [ʃɛə*] *n* (*thing received, contribution*) part *f*; (COMM) action *f* // *vt* partager; (*have in common*) avoir en commun; **to ~ out (among** *or* **between)** partager (entre); **~holder** *n* actionnaire *m/f*.
shark [ʃɑ:k] *n* requin *m*.
sharp [ʃɑ:p] *a* (*razor, knife*) tranchant(e), bien aiguisé(e); (*point*) aigu(guë); (*nose, chin*) pointu(e); (*outline*) net(te); (*cold, pain*) vif(vive); (MUS) dièse; (*voice*) coupant(e); (*person*: *quick-witted*) vif(vive), éveillé(e); (: *unscrupulous*) malhonnête // *n* (MUS) dièse *m* // *ad*: **at 2 o'clock ~** à 2 heures pile *or* tapantes; **look ~!** dépêche-toi!; **~en** *vt* aiguiser; (*pencil*) tailler; (*fig*) aviver; **~ener** *n* (*also*: **pencil ~ener)** taille-crayon(s) *m inv*; (*also:* **knife ~ener**) aiguisoir *m*; **~-eyed** *a* à qui rien n'échappe; **~-witted** *a* à l'esprit vif, malin(igne).
shatter ['ʃætə*] *vt* fracasser, briser, faire voler en éclats; (*fig*: *upset*) bouleverser; (: *ruin*) briser, ruiner // *vi* voler en éclats, se briser, se fracasser.
shave [ʃeɪv] *vt* raser // *vi* se raser // *n*: **to have a ~** se raser; **~n** *a* (*head*) rasé(e); **~r** *n* (*also*: **electric ~**) rasoir *m* électrique.
shaving ['ʃeɪvɪŋ] *n* (*action*) rasage *m*; **~s** *npl* (*of wood etc*) copeaux *mpl*; **~ brush** *n* blaireau *m*; **~ cream** *n* crème *f* à raser; **~ soap** *n* savon *m* à barbe.
shawl [ʃɔ:l] *n* châle *m*.
she [ʃi:] *pronoun* elle // *cpd*: **~-** femelle; **~-cat** *n* chatte *f*; **~-elephant** *n* éléphant *m* femelle; NB: *for ships, countries follow the gender of your translation.*
sheaf, sheaves [ʃi:f, ʃi:vz] *n* gerbe *f*.
shear [ʃɪə*] *vt* (*pt* **~ed,** *pp* **~ed** *or* **shorn** [ʃɔ:n]) (*sheep*) tondre; **to ~ off** *vt* tondre; (*branch*) élaguer; **~s** *npl* (*for hedge*) cisaille(s) *f(pl)*.
sheath [ʃi:θ] *n* gaine *f*, fourreau *m*, étui *m*; (*contraceptive*) préservatif *m*; **~e** [ʃi:ð] *vt* gainer; (*sword*) rengainer.
sheaves [ʃi:vz] *npl of* **sheaf**.
shed [ʃɛd] *n* remise *f*, resserre *f* // *vt* (*pt,pp* **shed**) (*leaves, fur etc*) perdre; (*tears*) verser, répandre.
she'd [ʃi:d] = **she had**; **she would**.
sheep [ʃi:p] *n, pl inv* mouton *m*; **~dog** *n* chien *m* de berger; **~ish** *a* penaud(e), timide; **~skin** *n* peau *f* de mouton.
sheer [ʃɪə*] *a* (*utter*) pur(e), pur et simple; (*steep*) à pic, abrupt(e); (*almost transparent*) extrêmement fin(e) // *ad* à pic, abruptement.
sheet [ʃi:t] *n* (*on bed*) drap *m*; (*of paper*) feuille *f*; (*of glass, metal*) feuille, plaque *f*; **~ lightning** *n* éclair *m* en nappe(s); **~ metal** *n* tôle *f*.
sheik(h) [ʃeɪk] *n* cheik *m*.
shelf, shelves [ʃɛlf, ʃɛlvz] *n* étagère *f*, rayon *m*; **set of shelves** rayonnage *m*.
shell [ʃɛl] *n* (*on beach*) coquillage *m*; (*of egg, nut etc*) coquille *f*; (*explosive*) obus *m*; (*of building*) carcasse *f* // *vt* (*crab, prawn etc*) décortiquer; (*peas*) écosser; (MIL) bombarder (d'obus).
she'll [ʃi:l] = **she will**; **she shall**.
shellfish ['ʃɛlfɪʃ] *n, pl inv* (*crab etc*) crustacé *m*; (*scallop etc*) coquillage *m*; (*pl*: *as food*) crustacés; coquillages.
shelter ['ʃɛltə*] *n* abri *m*, refuge *m* // *vt* abriter, protéger; (*give lodging to*) donner asile à // *vi* s'abriter, se mettre à l'abri; **~ed** *a* (*life*) retiré(e), à l'abri des soucis; (*spot*) abrité(e).
shelve [ʃɛlv] *vt* (*fig*) mettre en suspens *or* en sommeil; **~s** *npl of* **shelf**.

shepherd ['ʃɛpəd] *n* berger *m* // *vt* (*guide*) guider, escorter ; **~ess** *n* bergère *f*; **~'s pie** *n* ≈ hachis *m* Parmentier.
sheriff ['ʃɛrɪf] *n* shérif *m*.
sherry ['ʃɛrɪ] *n* xérès *m*, sherry *m*.
she's [ʃi:z] = **she is**; **she has**.
shield [ʃi:ld] *n* bouclier *m* // *vt*: **to ~ (from)** protéger (de *or* contre).
shift [ʃɪft] *n* (*change*) changement *m*; (*of workers*) équipe *f*, poste *m* // *vt* déplacer, changer de place ; (*remove*) enlever // *vi* changer de place, bouger ; **~ work** *n* travail *m* en équipe *or* par relais *or* par roulement ; **~y** *a* sournois(e) ; (*eyes*) fuyant(e).
shilling ['ʃɪlɪŋ] *n* shilling *m* (= *12 old pence*; *20 in a pound*).
shilly-shally ['ʃɪlɪʃælɪ] *vi* tergiverser, atermoyer.
shimmer ['ʃɪmə*] *n* miroitement *m*, chatoiement *m* // *vi* miroiter, chatoyer.
shin [ʃɪn] *n* tibia *m*.
shine [ʃaɪn] *n* éclat *m*, brillant *m* // *vb* (*pt,pp* **shone** [ʃɔn]) *vi* briller // *vt* faire briller *or* reluire ; (*torch*): **to ~ sth on** braquer qch sur.
shingle ['ʃɪŋgl] *n* (*on beach*) galets *mpl*; (*on roof*) bardeau *m*; **~s** *n* (MED) zona *m*.
shiny ['ʃaɪnɪ] *a* brillant(e).
ship [ʃɪp] *n* bateau *m*; (*large*) navire *m* // *vt* transporter (par mer) ; (*send*) expédier (par mer) ; (*load*) charger, embarquer ; **~building** *n* construction navale ; **~ canal** *n* canal *m* maritime *or* de navigation ; **~ment** *n* cargaison *f*; **~per** *n* affréteur *m*, expéditeur *m*; **~ping** *n* (*ships*) navires *mpl*; (*traffic*) navigation *f*; **~shape** *a* en ordre impeccable ; **~wreck** *n* épave *f*; (*event*) naufrage *m*; **~yard** *n* chantier naval.
shire ['ʃaɪə*] *n* comté *m*.
shirk [ʃə:k] *vt* esquiver, se dérober à.
shirt [ʃə:t] *n* (*man's*) chemise *f*; **in ~ sleeves** en bras de chemise ; **~y** *a* (*col*) de mauvais poil.
shiver ['ʃɪvə*] *n* frisson *m* // *vi* frissonner.
shoal [ʃəul] *n* (*of fish*) banc *m*.
shock [ʃɔk] *n* (*impact*) choc *m*, heurt *m*; (ELEC) secousse *f*; (*emotional*) choc, secousse *f*; (MED) commotion *f*, choc // *vt* choquer, scandaliser ; bouleverser ; **~ absorber** *n* amortisseur *m*; **~ing** *a* choquant(e), scandaleux(euse) ; épouvantable ; révoltant(e) ; **~proof** *a* anti-choc *inv*.
shod [ʃɔd] *pt*,pp of **shoe**; **well-~** *a* bien chaussé(e).
shoddy ['ʃɔdɪ] *a* de mauvaise qualité, mal fait(e).
shoe [ʃu:] *n* chaussure *f*, soulier *m*; (*also*: **horse~**) fer *m* à cheval // *vt* (*pt,pp* **shod** [ʃɔd]) (*horse*) ferrer ; **~brush** *n* brosse *f* à chaussures ; **~horn** *n* chausse-pied *m*; **~lace** *n* lacet *m* (de soulier) ; **~ polish** *n* cirage *m*; **~shop** *n* magasin *m* de chaussures ; **~tree** *n* embauchoir *m*.
shone [ʃɔn] *pt,pp of* **shine**.
shook [ʃuk] *pt of* **shake**.
shoot [ʃu:t] *n* (*on branch, seedling*) pousse *f* // *vb* (*pt,pp* **shot** [ʃɔt]) *vt* (*game*) chasser ; tirer ; abattre ; (*person*) blesser (*or* tuer) d'un coup de fusil (*or* de revolver) ; (*execute*) fusiller ; (*film*) tourner // *vi* (*with gun, bow*): **to ~ (at)** tirer (sur) ; (FOOTBALL) shooter, tirer ; **to ~ down** *vt* (*plane*) abattre ; **to ~ in/out** *vi* entrer/sortir comme une flèche ; **to ~ up** *vi* (*fig*) monter en flèche ; **~ing** *n* (*shots*) coups *mpl* de feu, fusillade *f*; (HUNTING) chasse *f*; **~ing range** *n* stand *m* de tir ; **~ing star** *n* étoile filante.
shop [ʃɔp] *n* magasin *m*; (*workshop*) atelier *m* // *vi* (*also*: **go ~ping**) faire ses courses *or* ses achats ; **~ assistant** *n* vendeur/euse ; **~ floor** *n* ateliers *mpl*; (*fig*) ouvriers *mpl*; **~keeper** *n* marchand/e, commerçant/e ; **~lifter** *n* voleur/euse à l'étalage ; **~lifting** *n* vol *m* à l'étalage ; **~per** *n* personne *f* qui fait ses courses, acheteur/euse ; **~ping** *n* (*goods*) achats *mpl*, provisions *fpl*; **~ping bag** *n* sac *m* (à provisions) ; **~ping centre, ~ping center** (*US*) *n* centre commercial ; **~-soiled** *a* défraîchi(e), qui a fait la vitrine ; **~ steward** *n* (INDUSTRY) délégué/e syndical(e) ; **~ window** *n* vitrine *f*.
shore [ʃɔ:*] *n* (*of sea, lake*) rivage *m*, rive *f* // *vt*: **to ~ (up)** étayer.
shorn [ʃɔ:n] *pp of* **shear**; **~ of** dépouillé(e) de.
short [ʃɔ:t] *a* (*not long*) court(e) ; (*soon finished*) court, bref(brève) ; (*person, step*) petit(e) ; (*curt*) brusque, sec(sèche) ; (*insufficient*) insuffisant(e) // *n* (*also*: **~ film**) court métrage ; **(a pair of) ~s** un short ; **to be ~ of sth** être à court de *or* manquer de qch ; **I'm 3 ~** il m'en manque 3 ; **in ~** bref ; en bref ; **~ of doing** à moins de faire ; **everything ~ of** tout sauf ; **it is ~ for** c'est l'abréviation *or* le diminutif de ; **to cut ~** (*speech, visit*) abréger, écourter ; (*person*) couper la parole à ; **to fall ~ of** ne pas être à la hauteur de ; **to stop ~** s'arrêter net ; **to stop ~ of** ne pas aller jusqu'à ; **~age** *n* manque *m*, pénurie *f*; **~bread** *n* ≈ sablé *m*; **~-circuit** *n* court-circuit *m* // *vt* court-circuiter // *vi* se mettre en court-circuit ; **~coming** *n* défaut *m*; **~(crust) pastry** pâte brisée ; **~cut** *n* raccourci *m*; **~en** *vt* raccourcir ; (*text, visit*) abréger ; **~ening** *n* (CULIN) matière grasse ; **~hand** *n* sténo(graphie) *f*; **~hand typist** *n* sténodactylo *m/f*; **~ list** *n* (*for job*) liste *f* des candidats sélectionnés ; **~-lived** *a* de courte durée ; **~ly** *ad* bientôt, sous peu ; **~ness** *n* brièveté *f*; **~-sighted** *a* myope ; (*fig*) qui manque de clairvoyance ; **~ story** *n* nouvelle *f*; **~-tempered** *a* qui s'emporte facilement ; **~-term** *a* (*effect*) à court terme ; **~wave** *n* (RADIO) ondes courtes.
shot [ʃɔt] *pt,pp of* **shoot** // *n* coup *m* (de feu) ; (*person*) tireur *m*; (*try*) coup, essai *m*; (*injection*) piqûre *f*; (PHOT) photo *f*; **like a ~** comme une flèche ; (*very readily*) sans hésiter ; **~gun** *n* fusil *m* de chasse.
should [ʃud] *auxiliary vb*: **I ~ go now** je devrais partir maintenant ; **he ~ be there now** il devrait être arrivé maintenant ; **I ~ go if I were you** si j'étais vous j'irais ; **I ~ like to** j'aimerais bien, volontiers.
shoulder ['ʃəuldə*] *n* épaule *f*; (*of road*): **hard ~** accotement *m* // *vt* (*fig*) endosser, se charger de ; **~ bag** *n* sac *m* à

bandoulière; ~ **blade** *n* omoplate *f*; ~ **strap** *n* bretelle *f*.

shouldn't ['ʃudnt] = **should not**.

shout [ʃaut] *n* cri *m* // *vt* crier // *vi* crier, pousser des cris; **to give sb a** ~ appeler qn; **to** ~ **down** *vt* huer; ~**ing** *n* cris *mpl*.

shove [ʃʌv] *vt* pousser; (*col*: *put*): **to** ~ **sth in** fourrer *or* ficher qch dans; **to** ~ **off** *vi* (NAUT) pousser au large; (*fig*: *col*) ficher le camp.

shovel ['ʃʌvl] *n* pelle *f* // *vt* pelleter, enlever (*or* enfourner) à la pelle.

show [ʃəu] *n* (*of emotion*) manifestation *f*, démonstration *f*; (*semblance*) semblant *m*, apparence *f*; (*exhibition*) exposition *f*; salon *m*; (THEATRE) spectacle *m*, représentation *f*; (CINEMA) séance *f* // *vb* (*pt* ~**ed,** *pp* **shown** [ʃəun]) *vt* montrer; (*courage etc*) faire preuve de, manifester; (*exhibit*) exposer // *vi* se voir, être visible; **to** ~ **sb in** faire entrer qn; **to** ~ **off** *vi* (*pej*) crâner // *vt* (*display*) faire valoir; (*pej*) faire étalage de; **to** ~ **sb out** reconduire qn (jusqu'à la porte); **to** ~ **up** *vi* (*stand out*) ressortir; (*col*: *turn up*) se montrer // *vt* démontrer; (*unmask*) démasquer, dénoncer; ~ **business** *n* le monde du spectacle; ~**down** *n* épreuve *f* de force.

shower ['ʃauə*] *n* (*rain*) averse *f*; (*of stones etc*) pluie *f*, grêle *f*; (*also*: ~**bath**) douche *f* // *vi* prendre une douche, se doucher // *vt*: **to** ~ **sb with** (*gifts etc*) combler qn de; (*abuse etc*) accabler qn de; (*missiles*) bombarder qn de; ~**proof** *a* imperméable; ~**y** *a* (*weather*) pluvieux(euse).

showground ['ʃəugraund] *n* champ *m* de foire.

showing ['ʃəuɪŋ] *n* (*of film*) projection *f*.

show jumping ['ʃəudʒʌmpɪŋ] *n* concours *m* hippique.

showmanship ['ʃəumənʃɪp] *n* art *m* de la mise en scène.

shown [ʃəun] *pp of* **show**.

show-off ['ʃəuɔf] *n* (*col*: *person*) crâneur/euse, m'as-tu-vu/e.

showpiece ['ʃəupi:s] *n* (*of exhibition etc*) joyau *m*, clou *m*.

showroom ['ʃəurum] *n* magasin *m or* salle *f* d'exposition.

shrank [ʃræŋk] *pt of* **shrink**.

shrapnel ['ʃræpnl] *n* éclats *mpl* d'obus.

shred [ʃrɛd] *n* (*gen pl*) lambeau *m*, petit morceau // *vt* mettre en lambeaux, déchirer; (CULIN) râper; couper en lanières.

shrewd [ʃru:d] *a* astucieux(euse), perspicace; ~**ness** *n* perspicacité *f*.

shriek [ʃri:k] *n* cri perçant *or* aigu, hurlement *m* // *vt,vi* hurler, crier.

shrift [ʃrɪft] *n*: **to give sb short** ~ expédier qn sans ménagements.

shrill [ʃrɪl] *a* perçant(e), aigu(guë), strident(e).

shrimp [ʃrɪmp] *n* crevette grise.

shrine [ʃraɪn] *n* châsse *f*; (*place*) lieu *m* de pèlerinage.

shrink, *pt* **shrank,** *pp* **shrunk** [ʃrɪŋk, ʃræŋk, ʃrʌŋk] *vi* rétrécir; (*fig*) se réduire; se contracter // *vt* (*wool*) (faire) rétrécir // *n* (*col*: *pej*) psychanalyste; ~**age** *n* rétrécissement *m*.

shrivel ['ʃrɪvl] (*also*: ~ **up**) *vt* ratatiner, flétrir // *vi* se ratatiner, se flétrir.

shroud [ʃraud] *n* linceul *m* // *vt*: ~**ed in mystery** enveloppé(e) de mystère.

Shrove Tuesday ['ʃrəuv'tju:zdɪ] *n* (le) Mardi gras.

shrub [ʃrʌb] *n* arbuste *m*; ~**bery** *n* massif *m* d'arbustes.

shrug [ʃrʌg] *n* haussement *m* d'épaules // *vt,vi*: **to** ~ **(one's shoulders)** hausser les épaules; **to** ~ **off** *vt* faire fi de.

shrunk [ʃrʌŋk] *pp of* **shrink;** ~**en** *a* ratatiné(e).

shudder ['ʃʌdə*] *n* frisson *m*, frémissement *m* // *vi* frissonner, frémir.

shuffle ['ʃʌfl] *vt* (*cards*) battre; **to** ~ **(one's feet)** traîner les pieds.

shun [ʃʌn] *vt* éviter, fuir.

shunt [ʃʌnt] *vt* (RAIL: *direct*) aiguiller; (: *divert*) détourner // *vi*: **to** ~ **(to and fro)** faire la navette; ~**ing** *n* (RAIL) triage *m*.

shush [ʃuʃ] *excl* chut!

shut, *pt, pp* **shut** [ʃʌt] *vt* fermer // *vi* (se) fermer; **to** ~ **down** *vt, vi* fermer définitivement; **to** ~ **off** *vt* couper, arrêter; **to** ~ **up** *vi* (*col*: *keep quiet*) se taire // *vt* (*close*) fermer; (*silence*) faire taire; ~**ter** *n* volet *m*; (PHOT) obturateur *m*.

shuttle ['ʃʌtl] *n* navette *f*; (*also*: ~ **service**) (service *m* de) navette *f*.

shuttlecock ['ʃʌtlkɔk] *n* volant *m* (*de badminton*).

shy [ʃaɪ] *a* timide; **to fight** ~ **of** se dérober devant; ~**ness** *n* timidité *f*.

Siamese [saɪə'mi:z] *a*: ~ **cat** chat siamois.

Sicily ['sɪsɪlɪ] *n* Sicile *f*.

sick [sɪk] *a* (*ill*) malade; (*vomiting*): **to be** ~ vomir; (*humour*) noir(e), macabre; **to feel** ~ avoir envie de vomir, avoir mal au cœur; **to be** ~ **of** (*fig*) en avoir assez de; ~ **bay** *n* infirmerie *f*; ~**en** *vt* écœurer; ~**ening** *a* (*fig*) écœurant(e), révoltant(e), répugnant(e).

sickle ['sɪkl] *n* faucille *f*.

sick: ~ **leave** *n* congé *m* de maladie; ~**ly** *a* maladif(ive), souffreteux(euse); (*causing nausea*) écœurant(e); ~**ness** *n* maladie *f*; (*vomiting*) vomissement(s) *m(pl)*; ~ **pay** *n* indemnité *f* de maladie.

side [saɪd] *n* côté *m*; (*of lake, road*) bord *m* // *cpd* (*door, entrance*) latéral(e) // *vi*: **to** ~ **with sb** prendre le parti de qn, se ranger du côté de qn; **by the** ~ **of** au bord de; ~ **by** ~ côte à côte; **from all** ~**s** de tous côtés; **to take** ~**s (with)** prendre parti (pour); ~**board** *n* buffet *m*; ~**boards,** ~**burns** *npl* (*whiskers*) pattes *fpl*; ~ **effect** *n* (MED) effet *m* secondaire; ~**light** *n* (AUT) veilleuse *f*; ~**line** *n* (SPORT) (ligne *f* de) touche *f*; (*fig*) activité *f* secondaire; ~**long** *a* oblique, de coin; ~**road** *n* petite route, route transversale; ~**saddle** *ad* en amazone; ~ **show** *n* attraction *f*; ~**track** *vt* (*fig*) faire dévier de son sujet; ~**walk** *n* (*US*) trottoir *m*; ~**ways** *ad* de côté.

siding ['saɪdɪŋ] *n* (RAIL) voie *f* de garage.

sidle ['saɪdl] *vi*: **to** ~ **up (to)** s'approcher furtivement (de).

siege [si:dʒ] *n* siège *m*.

sieve [sɪv] *n* tamis *m*, passoire *f* // *vt* tamiser, passer (au tamis).
sift [sɪft] *vt* passer au tamis *or* au crible; (*fig*) passer au crible.
sigh [saɪ] *n* soupir *m* // *vi* soupirer, pousser un soupir.
sight [saɪt] *n* (*faculty*) vue *f*; (*spectacle*) spectacle *m*; (*on gun*) mire *f* // *vt* apercevoir; **in ~** visible; (*fig*) en vue; **out of ~** hors de vue; **~seeing** *n* tourisme *m*; **to go ~seeing** faire du tourisme; **~seer** *n* touriste *m/f*.
sign [saɪn] *n* (*gen*) signe *m*; (*with hand etc*) signe, geste *m*; (*notice*) panneau *m*, écriteau *m* // *vt* signer; **to ~ in/out** signer le registre (en arrivant/partant); **to ~ up** (*MIL*) *vt* engager // *vi* s'engager.
signal ['sɪgnl] *n* signal *m* // *vt* (*person*) faire signe à; (*message*) communiquer par signaux.
signature ['sɪgnətʃə*] *n* signature *f*; **~ tune** *n* indicatif musical.
signet ring ['sɪgnətrɪŋ] *n* chevalière *f*.
significance [sɪg'nɪfɪkəns] *n* signification *f*; importance *f*.
significant [sɪg'nɪfɪkənt] *a* significatif(ive); (*important*) important(e), considérable.
signify ['sɪgnɪfaɪ] *vt* signifier.
sign language ['saɪnlæŋgwɪdʒ] *n* langage *m* par signes.
signpost ['saɪnpəust] *n* poteau indicateur.
silence ['saɪlns] *n* silence *m* // *vt* faire taire, réduire au silence; **~r** *n* (*on gun*, *AUT*) silencieux *m*.
silent ['saɪlnt] *a* silencieux(euse); (*film*) muet(te); **~ly** *ad* silencieusement.
silhouette [sɪlu:'ɛt] *n* silhouette *f* // *vt*: **~d against** se profilant sur, se découpant contre.
silicon chip ['sɪlɪkən'tʃɪp] *n* plaquette *f* de silicium.
silk [sɪlk] *n* soie *f* // *cpd* de *or* en soie; **~y** *a* soyeux(euse).
silly ['sɪlɪ] *a* stupide, sot(te), bête.
silt [sɪlt] *n* vase *f*; limon *m*.
silver ['sɪlvə*] *n* argent *m*; (*money*) monnaie *f* (en pièces d'argent); (*also*: **~ware**) argenterie *f* // *cpd* d'argent, en argent; **~ paper** *n* papier *m* d'argent *or* d'étain; **~-plated** *a* plaqué(e) argent; **~smith** *n* orfèvre *m/f*; **~y** *a* argenté(e).
similar ['sɪmɪlə*] *a*: **~ (to)** semblable (à); **~ity** [-'lærɪtɪ] *n* ressemblance *f*, similarité *f*; **~ly** *ad* de la même façon, de même.
simile ['sɪmɪlɪ] *n* comparaison *f*.
simmer ['sɪmə*] *vi* cuire à feu doux, mijoter.
simple ['sɪmpl] *a* simple; **~-minded** *a* simplet(te), simple d'esprit; **simplicity** [-'plɪsɪtɪ] *n* simplicité *f*; **simplification** [-'keɪʃən] *n* simplification *f*; **simplify** ['sɪmplɪfaɪ] *vt* simplifier; **simply** *ad* simplement; avec simplicité.
simulate ['sɪmjuleɪt] *vt* simuler, feindre; **simulation** [-'leɪʃən] *n* simulation *f*.
simultaneous [sɪməl'teɪnɪəs] *a* simultané(e); **~ly** *ad* simultanément.
sin [sɪn] *n* péché *m* // *vi* pécher.
since [sɪns] *ad,prep* depuis // *cj* (*time*) depuis que; (*because*) puisque, étant donné que, comme; **~ then** depuis ce moment-là.
sincere [sɪn'sɪə*] *a* sincère; **sincerity** [-'sɛrɪtɪ] *n* sincérité *f*.
sine [saɪn] *n* (*MATH*) sinus *m*.
sinew ['sɪnju:] *n* tendon *m*; **~s** *npl* muscles *mpl*.
sinful ['sɪnful] *a* coupable.
sing, *pt* **sang**, *pp* **sung** [sɪŋ, sæŋ, sʌŋ] *vt,vi* chanter.
singe [sɪndʒ] *vt* brûler légèrement; (*clothes*) roussir.
singer ['sɪŋə*] *n* chanteur/euse.
singing ['sɪŋɪŋ] *n* chant *m*.
single ['sɪŋgl] *a* seul(e), unique; (*unmarried*) célibataire; (*not double*) simple // *n* (*also*: **~ ticket**) aller *m* (simple); (*record*) 45 tours *m*; **~s** *npl* (*TENNIS*) simple *m*; **to ~ out** *vt* choisir; distinguer; **~ bed** *n* lit à une place; **~-breasted** *a* droit(e); **in ~ file** en file indienne; **~-handed** *ad* tout(e) seul(e), sans (aucune) aide; **~-minded** *a* résolu(e), tenace; **~ room** *n* chambre *f* à un lit *or* pour une personne.
singlet ['sɪŋglɪt] *n* tricot *m* de corps.
singly ['sɪŋglɪ] *ad* séparément.
singular ['sɪŋgjulə*] *a* singulier(ère), étrange; remarquable; (*LING*) (au) singulier, du singulier // *n* (*LING*) singulier *m*; **~ly** *ad* singulièrement; remarquablement; étrangement.
sinister ['sɪnɪstə*] *a* sinistre.
sink [sɪŋk] *n* évier *m* // *vb* (*pt* **sank**, *pp* **sunk** [sæŋk, sʌŋk]) *vt* (*ship*) (faire) couler, faire sombrer; (*foundations*) creuser; (*piles etc*): **to ~ sth into** enfoncer qch dans // *vi* couler, sombrer; (*ground etc*) s'affaisser; **to ~ in** *vi* s'enfoncer, pénétrer; **a ~ing feeling** un serrement de cœur.
sinner ['sɪnə*] *n* pécheur/eresse.
Sino- ['saɪnəu] *prefix* sino-.
sinuous ['sɪnjuəs] *a* sinueux(euse).
sinus ['saɪnəs] *n* (*ANAT*) sinus *m inv*.
sip [sɪp] *n* petite gorgée // *vt* boire à petites gorgées.
siphon ['saɪfən] *n* siphon *m*; **to ~ off** *vt* siphonner.
sir [sə*] *n* monsieur *m*; **S~ John Smith** sir John Smith; **yes ~** oui Monsieur.
siren ['saɪərn] *n* sirène *f*.
sirloin ['sə:lɔɪn] *n* aloyau *m*.
sirocco [sɪ'rɔkəu] *n* sirocco *m*.
sissy ['sɪsɪ] *n* (*col*: *coward*) poule mouillée.
sister ['sɪstə*] *n* sœur *f*; (*nun*) religieuse *f*, (bonne) sœur; (*nurse*) infirmière *f* en chef; **~-in-law** *n* belle-sœur *f*.
sit, *pt,pp* **sat** [sɪt, sæt] *vi* s'asseoir; (*assembly*) être en séance, siéger; (*for painter*) poser // *vt* (*exam*) passer, se présenter à; **to ~ tight** ne pas bouger; **to ~ down** *vi* s'asseoir; **to ~ up** *vi* s'asseoir; (*not go to bed*) rester debout, ne pas se coucher.
sitcom ['sɪtkɔm] *n* (*abbr of* **situation comedy**) comédie *f* de situation.
site [saɪt] *n* emplacement *m*, site *m*; (*also*: **building ~**) chantier *m* // *vt* placer.
sit-in ['sɪtɪn] *n* (*demonstration*) sit-in *m inv*, occupation *f* de locaux.

siting ['saɪtɪŋ] *n* (*location*) emplacement *m*.
sitter ['sɪtə] *n* (*for painter*) modèle *m*.
sitting ['sɪtɪŋ] *n* (*of assembly etc*) séance *f*; (*in canteen*) service *m*; ~ **room** *n* salon *m*.
situated ['sɪtjueɪtɪd] *a* situé(e).
situation [sɪtju'eɪʃən] *n* situation *f*; **'~s vacant/wanted'** 'offres/demandes d'emploi'.
six [sɪks] *num* six; ~**teen** *num* seize; ~**th** *a* sixième; ~**ty** *num* soixante.
size [saɪz] *n* taille *f*; dimensions *fpl*; (*of clothing*) taille; (*of shoes*) pointure *f*; (*glue*) colle *f*; **to ~ up** *vt* juger, jauger; ~**able** *a* assez grand(e) *or* gros(se); assez important(e).
sizzle ['sɪzl] *vi* grésiller.
skate [skeɪt] *n* patin *m*; (*fish*: *pl inv*) raie *f* // *vi* patiner; ~**board** *n* skateboard *m*, planche *f* à roulettes; ~**r** *n* patineur/euse; **skating** *n* patinage *m*; **skating rink** *n* patinoire *f*.
skeleton ['skɛlɪtn] *n* squelette *m*; (*outline*) schéma *m*; ~ **staff** *n* effectifs réduits.
skeptic ['skɛptɪk] *n* (*US*) = **sceptic**.
sketch [skɛtʃ] *n* (*drawing*) croquis *m*, esquisse *f*; (THEATRE) sketch *m*, saynète *f* // *vt* esquisser, faire un croquis *or* une esquisse de; ~ **book** *n* carnet *m* à dessin; ~ **pad** *n* bloc *m* à dessin; ~**y** *a* incomplet(ète), fragmentaire.
skew [skju:] *n*: **on the ~** de travers, en biais.
skewer ['skju:ə*] *n* brochette *f*.
ski [ski:] *n* ski *m* // *vi* skier, faire du ski; ~ **boot** *n* chaussure *f* de ski.
skid [skɪd] *n* dérapage *m* // *vi* déraper; ~**mark** *n* trace *f* de dérapage.
skier ['ski:ə*] *n* skieur/euse.
skiing ['ski:ɪŋ] *n* ski *m*.
ski jump ['ski:dʒʌmp] *n* saut *m* à skis.
skilful ['skɪlful] *a* habile, adroit(e).
ski lift ['ski:lɪft] *n* remonte-pente *m inv*.
skill [skɪl] *n* habileté *f*, adresse *f*, talent *m*; ~**ed** *a* habile, adroit(e); (*worker*) qualifié(e).
skim [skɪm] *vt* (*milk*) écrémer; (*soup*) écumer; (*glide over*) raser, effleurer // *vi*: **to ~ through** (*fig*) parcourir.
skimp [skɪmp] *vt* (*work*) bâcler, faire à la va-vite; (*cloth etc*) lésiner sur; ~**y** *a* étriqué(e); maigre.
skin [skɪn] *n* peau *f* // *vt* (*fruit etc*) éplucher; (*animal*) écorcher; ~**-deep** *a* superficiel(le); ~ **diving** *n* plongée sous-marine; ~ **graft** *n* greffe *f* de peau; ~**ny** *a* maigre, maigrichon(ne); ~ **test** *n* cuti(-réaction) *f*; ~**tight** *a* (*dress etc*) collant(e), ajusté(e).
skip [skɪp] *n* petit bond *or* saut; (*container*) benne *f* // *vi* gambader, sautiller; (*with rope*) sauter à la corde // *vt* (*pass over*) sauter.
ski pants ['ski:pænts] *npl* fuseau *m* (de ski).
skipper ['skɪpə*] *n* (NAUT, SPORT) capitaine *m* // *vt* (*boat*) commander; (*team*) être le chef de.
skipping rope ['skɪpɪŋrəup] *n* corde *f* à sauter.
skirmish ['skə:mɪʃ] *n* escarmouche *f*, accrochage *m*.
skirt [skə:t] *n* jupe *f* // *vt* longer, contourner; ~**ing board** *n* plinthe *f*.
skit [skɪt] *n* sketch *m* satirique.
ski tow ['ski:təu] *n* = **ski lift**.
skittle ['skɪtl] *n* quille *f*; ~**s** *n* (*game*) (jeu *m* de) quilles.
skive [skaɪv] (*Brit*) *vi* (*col*) tirer au flanc.
skulk [skʌlk] *vi* rôder furtivement.
skull [skʌl] *n* crâne *m*.
skunk [skʌŋk] *n* mouffette *f*; (*fur*) sconse *m*.
sky [skaɪ] *n* ciel *m*; ~**-blue** *a* bleu ciel *inv*; ~**light** *n* lucarne *f*; ~**scraper** *n* gratte-ciel *m inv*.
slab [slæb] *n* plaque *f*; dalle *f*.
slack [slæk] *a* (*loose*) lâche, desserré(e); (*slow*) stagnant(e); (*careless*) négligent(e), peu sérieux(euse) *or* consciencieux(euse) // *n* (*in rope etc*) mou *m*; ~**s** *npl* pantalon *m*; ~**en** (*also*: ~**en off**) *vi* ralentir, diminuer; (*in one's work, attention*) se relâcher // *vt* relâcher.
slag [slæg] *n* scories *fpl*; ~ **heap** *n* crassier *m*.
slam [slæm] *vt* (*door*) (faire) claquer; (*throw*) jeter violemment, flanquer; (*criticize*) éreinter, démolir // *vi* claquer.
slander ['slɑ:ndə*] *n* calomnie *f*; diffamation *f* // *vt* calomnier; diffamer; ~**ous** *a* calomnieux(euse); diffamatoire.
slang [slæŋ] *n* argot *m*.
slant [slɑ:nt] *n* inclinaison *f*; (*fig*) angle *m*, point *m* de vue; ~**ed** *a* tendancieux(euse); ~**ing** *a* en pente, incliné(e); couché(e).
slap [slæp] *n* claque *f*, gifle *f*; tape *f* // *vt* donner une claque *or* une gifle *or* une tape à // *ad* (*directly*) tout droit, en plein; ~**dash** *a* fait(e) sans soin *or* à la va-vite; ~**stick** *n* (*comedy*) grosse farce, style *m* tarte à la crème; **a ~-up meal** un repas extra *or* fameux.
slash [slæʃ] *vt* entailler, taillader; (*fig*: *prices*) casser.
slate [sleɪt] *n* ardoise *f* // *vt* (*fig*: *criticize*) éreinter, démolir.
slaughter ['slɔ:tə*] *n* carnage *m*, massacre *m* // *vt* (*animal*) abattre; (*people*) massacrer; ~**house** *n* abattoir *m*.
Slav [slɑ:v] *a* slave.
slave [sleɪv] *n* esclave *m/f* // *vi* (*also*: ~ **away**) trimer, travailler comme un forçat; ~**ry** *n* esclavage *m*.
Slavic ['slævɪk] *a* slave.
slavish ['sleɪvɪʃ] *a* servile.
Slavonic [slə'vɔnɪk] *a* slave.
sleazy ['sli:zɪ] *a* miteux(euse), minable.
sledge [slɛdʒ] *n* luge *f*; ~**hammer** *n* marteau *m* de forgeron.
sleek [sli:k] *a* (*hair, fur*) brillant(e), luisant(e); (*car, boat*) aux lignes pures *or* élégantes.
sleep [sli:p] *n* sommeil *m* // *vi* (*pt, pp* **slept** [slɛpt]) dormir; (*spend night*) dormir, coucher; **to go to ~** s'endormir; **to ~ in** *vi* (*lie late*) faire la grasse matinée; (*oversleep*) se réveiller trop tard; ~**er** *n* (*person*) dormeur/euse; (RAIL: *on track*) traverse *f*; (: *train*) train *m* de voitures-lits; ~**ily** *ad* d'un air endormi; ~**ing** *a*

qui dort, endormi(e) ; **~ing bag** *n* sac *m* de couchage ; **~ing car** *n* wagon-lits *m*, voiture-lits *f*; **~ing pill** *n* somnifère *m* ; **~lessness** *n* insomnie *f*; **a ~less night** une nuit blanche ; **~walker** *n* somnambule *m/f*; **~y** *a* qui a envie de dormir ; (*fig*) endormi(e).
sleet [sli:t] *n* neige fondue.
sleeve [sli:v] *n* manche *f*; **~less** *a* (*garment*) sans manches.
sleigh [sleɪ] *n* traîneau *m*.
sleight [slaɪt] *n*: **~ of hand** tour *m* de passe-passe.
slender ['slɛndə*] *a* svelte, mince ; faible, ténu(e).
slept [slɛpt] *pt,pp of* **sleep**.
slice [slaɪs] *n* tranche *f*; (*round*) rondelle *f* // *vt* couper en tranches (*or* en rondelles).
slick [slɪk] *a* brillant(e) en apparence ; mielleux(euse) // *n* (*also*: **oil ~**) nappe *f* de pétrole, marée noire.
slid [slɪd] *pt,pp of* **slide**.
slide [slaɪd] *n* (*in playground*) toboggan *m* ; (PHOT) diapositive *f* ; (*also*: **hair ~**) barrette *f*; (*in prices*) chute *f*, baisse *f* // *vb* (*pt,pp* **slid** [slɪd]) *vt* (faire) glisser // *vi* glisser ; **~ rule** *n* règle *f* à calcul ; **sliding** *a* (*door*) coulissant(e) ; **sliding scale** *n* échelle *f* mobile.
slight [slaɪt] *a* (*slim*) mince, menu(e) ; (*frail*) frêle ; (*trivial*) faible, insignifiant(e) ; (*small*) petit(e), léger(ère) (*before n*) // *n* offense *f*, affront *m* // *vt* (*offend*) blesser, offenser ; **the ~est** le (*or* la) moindre ; **not in the ~est** pas le moins du monde, pas du tout ; **~ly** *ad* légèrement, un peu.
slim [slɪm] *a* mince // *vi* maigrir, suivre un régime amaigrissant.
slime [slaɪm] *n* vase *f*; substance visqueuse ; **slimy** *a* visqueux(euse), gluant(e).
sling [slɪŋ] *n* (MED) écharpe *f* // *vt* (*pt,pp* **slung** [slʌŋ]) lancer, jeter.
slip [slɪp] *n* faux pas ; (*mistake*) erreur *f*; étourderie *f*; bévue *f*; (*underskirt*) combinaison *f*; (*of paper*) petite feuille, fiche *f* // *vt* (*slide*) glisser // *vi* (*slide*) glisser ; (*move smoothly*): **to ~ into/out of** se glisser *or* se faufiler dans/hors de ; (*decline*) baisser ; **to give sb the ~** fausser compagnie à qn ; **a ~ of the tongue** un lapsus ; **to ~ away** *vi* s'esquiver ; **to ~ in** *vt* glisser ; **to ~ out** *vi* sortir ; **~ped disc** *n* déplacement *m* de vertèbres.
slipper ['slɪpə*] *n* pantoufle *f*.
slippery ['slɪpərɪ] *a* glissant(e) ; insaisissable.
slip road ['slɪprəud] *n* (*to motorway*) bretelle *f* d'accès.
slipshod ['slɪpʃɔd] *a* négligé(e), peu soigné(e).
slip-up ['slɪpʌp] *n* bévue *f*.
slipway ['slɪpweɪ] *n* cale *f* (de construction *or* de lancement).
slit [slɪt] *n* fente *f*; (*cut*) incision *f*; (*tear*) déchirure *f* // *vt* (*pt,pp* **slit**) fendre ; couper ; inciser ; déchirer.
slither ['slɪðə*] *vi* glisser, déraper.
slob [slɔb] *n* (*col*) rustaud/e.
slog [slɔg] *n* gros effort ; tâche fastidieuse // *vi* travailler très dur.
slogan ['sləugən] *n* slogan *m*.
slop [slɔp] *vi* (*also*: **~ over**) se renverser ; déborder // *vt* répandre ; renverser.
slope [sləup] *n* pente *f*, côte *f*; (*side of mountain*) versant *m* ; (*slant*) inclinaison *f* // *vi*: **to ~ down** être *or* descendre en pente ; **to ~ up** monter ; **sloping** *a* en pente, incliné(e) ; (*handwriting*) penché(e).
sloppy ['slɔpɪ] *a* (*work*) peu soigné(e), bâclé(e) ; (*appearance*) négligé(e), débraillé(e) ; (*film etc*) sentimental(e).
slot [slɔt] *n* fente *f* // *vt*: **to ~ into** encastrer *or* insérer dans ; **~ machine** *n* distributeur *m* (automatique), machine *f* à sous.
slouch [slautʃ] *vi* avoir le dos rond, être voûté(e).
slovenly ['slʌvənlɪ] *a* sale, débraillé(e), négligé(e).
slow [sləu] *a* lent(e) ; (*watch*): **to be ~** retarder // *ad* lentement // *vt,vi* (*also*: **~ down, ~ up**) ralentir ; **'~'** (*road sign*) 'ralentir' ; **~ly** *ad* lentement ; **in ~ motion** au ralenti ; **~ness** *n* lenteur *f*.
sludge [slʌdʒ] *n* boue *f*.
slug [slʌg] *n* limace *f*; (*bullet*) balle *f*; **~gish** *a* mou(molle), lent(e).
sluice [slu:s] *n* vanne *f*; écluse *f*.
slum [slʌm] *n* taudis *m*.
slumber ['slʌmbə*] *n* sommeil *m*.
slump [slʌmp] *n* baisse soudaine, effondrement *m* ; crise *f* // *vi* s'effondrer, s'affaisser.
slung [slʌŋ] *pt,pp of* **sling**.
slur [slə:*] *n* bredouillement *m* ; (*smear*): **~ (on)** atteinte *f* (à) ; insinuation *f* (contre) ; (MUS) liaison *f* // *vt* mal articuler ; **to be a ~ on** porter atteinte à.
slush [slʌʃ] *n* neige fondue ; **~y** *a* (*snow*) fondu(e) ; (*street*) couvert(e) de neige fondue ; (*fig*) sentimental(e).
slut [slʌt] *n* souillon *f*.
sly [slaɪ] *a* rusé(e) ; sournois(e) ; **on the ~** en cachette.
smack [smæk] *n* (*slap*) tape *f*; (*on face*) gifle *f* // *vt* donner une tape à, gifler ; (*child*) donner la fessée à // *vi*: **to ~ of** avoir des relents de, sentir ; **to ~ one's lips** se lécher les babines.
small [smɔ:l] *a* petit(e) ; **~ ads** *npl* petites annonces ; **~holder** *n* petit cultivateur ; **in the ~ hours** au petit matin ; **~ish** *a* plutôt *or* assez petit ; **~pox** *n* variole *f*; **~ talk** *n* menus propos.
smarmy ['smɑ:mɪ] *a* (*col*) flagorneur(euse), lécheur(euse).
smart [smɑ:t] *a* élégant(e), chic *inv*; (*clever*) intelligent(e), astucieux(euse), futé(e) ; (*quick*) rapide, vif(vive), prompt(e) // *vi* faire mal, brûler ; **to ~en up** *vi* devenir plus élégant(e), se faire beau(belle) // *vt* rendre plus élégant(e).
smash [smæʃ] *n* (*also*: **~-up**) collision *f*, accident *m* // *vt* casser, briser, fracasser ; (*opponent*) écraser ; (*hopes*) ruiner, détruire ; (SPORT: *record*) pulvériser // *vi* se briser, se fracasser ; s'écraser ; **~ing** *a* (*col*) formidable.
smattering ['smætərɪŋ] *n*: **a ~ of** quelques notions de.

smear [smɪə*] *n* tache *f*, salissure *f*; trace *f*; (*MED*) frottis *m* // *vt* enduire ; (*fig*) porter atteinte à.

smell [smɛl] *n* odeur *f*; (*sense*) odorat *m* // *vb* (*pt,pp* **smelt** *or* **smelled** [smɛlt, smɛld]) *vt* sentir // *vi* (*food etc*): **to ~ (of)** sentir ; (*pej*) sentir mauvais ; **~y** *a* qui sent mauvais, malodorant(e).

smile [smaɪl] *n* sourire *m* // *vi* sourire ; **smiling** *a* souriant(e).

smirk [smə:k] *n* petit sourire suffisant *or* affecté.

smith [smɪθ] *n* maréchal-ferrant *m*; forgeron *m*; **~y** *n* forge *f*.

smitten ['smɪtn] *a*: **~ with** pris(e) de ; frappé(e) de.

smock [smɔk] *n* blouse *f*, sarrau *m*.

smog [smɔg] *n* brouillard mêlé de fumée.

smoke [sməuk] *n* fumée *f* // *vt, vi* fumer ; **to have a ~** fumer une cigarette ; **~d** *a* (*bacon, glass*) fumé(e) ; **~r** *n* (*person*) fumeur/euse ; (*RAIL*) wagon *m* fumeurs ; **smoking** *n*: **'no smoking'** (*sign*) 'défense de fumer' ; **smoking room** *n* fumoir *m*; **smoky** *a* enfumé(e) ; (*surface*) noirci(e) par la fumée.

smolder ['sməuldə*] *vi* (*US*) = **smoulder**.

smooth [smu:ð] *a* lisse ; (*sauce*) onctueux(euse) ; (*flavour, whisky*) moelleux(euse) ; (*movement*) régulier(ère), sans à-coups *or* heurts ; (*person*) doucereux(euse), mielleux(euse) // *vt* lisser, défroisser ; (*also*: **~ out**) (*creases, difficulties*) faire disparaître.

smother ['smʌðə*] *vt* étouffer.

smoulder ['sməuldə*] *vi* couver.

smudge [smʌdʒ] *n* tache *f*, bavure *f* // *vt* salir, maculer.

smug [smʌg] *a* suffisant(e), content(e) de soi.

smuggle ['smʌgl] *vt* passer en contrebande *or* en fraude ; **~r** *n* contrebandier/ère ; **smuggling** *n* contrebande *f*.

smutty ['smʌtɪ] *a* (*fig*) grossier(ère), obscène.

snack [snæk] *n* casse-croûte *m inv*; **~ bar** *n* snack(-bar) *m*.

snag [snæg] *n* inconvénient *m*, difficulté *f*.

snail [sneɪl] *n* escargot *m*.

snake [sneɪk] *n* serpent *m*.

snap [snæp] *n* (*sound*) claquement *m*, bruit sec ; (*photograph*) photo *f*, instantané *m*; (*game*) sorte *f* de jeu de bataille // *a* subit(e) ; fait(e) sans réfléchir // *vt* faire claquer ; (*break*) casser net ; (*photograph*) prendre un instantané de // *vi* se casser net *or* avec un bruit sec ; **to ~ open/shut** s'ouvrir/se refermer brusquement ; **to ~ at** *vt fus* (*subj*: *dog*) essayer de mordre ; **to ~ off** *vt* (*break*) casser net ; **to ~ up** *vt* sauter sur, saisir ; **~ fastener** *n* bouton-pression *m*; **~py** *a* prompt(e) ; **~shot** *n* photo *f*, instantané *m*.

snare [snɛə*] *n* piège *m* // *vt* attraper, prendre au piège.

snarl [snɑ:l] *n* grondement *m* *or* grognement *m* féroce // *vi* gronder.

snatch [snætʃ] *n* (*fig*) vol *m*; (*small amount*): **~es of** des fragments *mpl* *or* bribes *fpl* de // *vt* saisir (*d'un geste vif*) ; (*steal*) voler.

sneak [sni:k] *vi*: **to ~ in/out** entrer/sortir furtivement *or* à la dérobée ; **~y** *a* sournois(e).

sneer [snɪə*] *n* ricanement *m* // *vi* ricaner, sourire d'un air sarcastique.

sneeze [sni:z] *n* éternuement *m* // *vi* éternuer.

snide [snaɪd] *a* sarcastique, narquois(e).

sniff [snɪf] *n* reniflement *m* // *vi* renifler // *vt* renifler, flairer.

snigger ['snɪgə*] *n* ricanement *m* ; rire moqueur // *vi* ricaner ; pouffer de rire.

snip [snɪp] *n* petit bout ; (*bargain*) (bonne) occasion *or* affaire // *vt* couper.

sniper ['snaɪpə*] *n* (*marksman*) tireur embusqué.

snippet ['snɪpɪt] *n* bribes *fpl*.

snivelling ['snɪvlɪŋ] *a* (*whimpering*) larmoyant(e), pleurnicheur(euse).

snob [snɔb] *n* snob *m/f*; **~bery** *n* snobisme *m*; **~bish** *a* snob *inv*.

snooker ['snu:kə*] *n sorte de jeu de billard*.

snoop ['snu:p] *vi*: **to ~ on sb** espionner qn.

snooty ['snu:tɪ] *a* snob *inv*, prétentieux(euse).

snooze [snu:z] *n* petit somme // *vi* faire un petit somme.

snore [snɔ:*] *vi* ronfler ; **snoring** *n* ronflement(s) *m*(*pl*).

snorkel ['snɔ:kl] *n* (*of swimmer*) tuba *m*.

snort [snɔ:t] *n* grognement *m* // *vi* grogner ; (*horse*) renâcler.

snotty ['snɔtɪ] *a* morveux(euse).

snout [snaut] *n* museau *m*.

snow [snəu] *n* neige *f* // *vi* neiger ; **~ball** *n* boule *f* de neige ; **~bound** *a* enneigé(e), bloqué(e) par la neige ; **~drift** *n* congère *f*; **~drop** *n* perce-neige *m*; **~fall** *n* chute *f* de neige ; **~flake** *n* flocon *m* de neige ; **~man** *n* bonhomme *m* de neige ; **~plough, ~plow** (*US*) *n* chasse-neige *m inv*; **~storm** *n* tempête *f* de neige.

snub [snʌb] *vt* repousser, snober // *n* rebuffade *f*; **~-nosed** *a* au nez retroussé.

snuff [snʌf] *n* tabac *m* à priser.

snug [snʌg] *a* douillet(te), confortable.

so [səu] *ad* (*degree*) si, tellement ; (*manner*: *thus*) ainsi, de cette façon // *cj* donc, par conséquent ; **~ as to do** afin de *or* pour faire ; **~ that** (*purpose*) afin de + *infinitive*, pour que *or* afin que + *sub* ; (*result*) si bien que, de (telle) sorte que ; **~ do I, ~ am I** *etc* moi *etc* aussi ; **if ~** si oui ; **I hope ~** je l'espère ; **10 or ~** 10 à peu près *or* environ ; **~ far** jusqu'ici, jusqu'à maintenant ; (*in past*) jusque-là ; **~ long!** à bientôt!, au revoir! ; **~ many** tant de ; **~ much** *ad* tant // *det* tant de ; **~ and ~** *n* un tel(une telle).

soak [səuk] *vt* faire *or* laisser tremper // *vi* tremper ; **to be ~ed through** être trempé jusqu'aux os ; **to ~ in** *vi* pénétrer, être absorbé(e) ; **to ~ up** *vt* absorber.

soap [səup] *n* savon *m*; **~flakes** *npl* paillettes *fpl* de savon ; **~ powder** *n* lessive *f*, détergent *m*; **~y** *a* savonneux(euse).

soar [sɔ:*] *vi* monter (en flèche), s'élancer.
sob [sɔb] *n* sanglot *m* // *vi* sangloter.
sober ['səubə*] *a* qui n'est pas (*or* plus) ivre ; (*sedate*) sérieux(euse), sensé(e) ; (*moderate*) mesuré(e) ; (*colour, style*) sobre, discret(ète) ; **to ~ up** *vt* dégriser // *vi* se dégriser.
Soc. *abbr of* **society**.
so-called ['səu'kɔ:ld] *a* soi-disant *inv*.
soccer ['sɔkə*] *n* football *m*.
sociable ['səuʃəbl] *a* sociable.
social ['səuʃl] *a* social(e) // *n* (petite) fête ; **~ club** *n* amicale *f*, foyer *m* ; **~ism** *n* socialisme *m* ; **~ist** *a,n* socialiste (*m/f*) ; **~ly** *ad* socialement, en société ; **~ science** *n* sciences humaines ; **~ security** *n* aide sociale ; **~ welfare** *n* sécurité sociale ; **~ work** *n* assistance sociale ; **~ worker** *n* assistant/e social/e.
society [sə'saɪətɪ] *n* société *f*; (*club*) société, association *f*; (*also*: **high ~**) (haute) société, grand monde.
sociological [səusɪə'lɔdʒɪkl] *a* sociologique.
sociologist [səusɪ'ɔlədʒɪst] *n* sociologue *m/f*.
sociology [səusɪ'ɔlədʒɪ] *n* sociologie *f*.
sock [sɔk] *n* chaussette *f* // vt (*hit*) flanquer un coup à.
socket ['sɔkɪt] *n* cavité *f*; (ELEC: *also*: **wall ~**) prise *f* de courant ; (: *for light bulb*) douille *f*.
sod [sɔd] *n* (*of earth*) motte *f*; (*col!*) con *m* (!) ; salaud *m* (!).
soda ['səudə] *n* (CHEM) soude *f*; (*also*: **~ water**) eau *f* de Seltz.
sodden ['sɔdn] *a* trempé(e) ; détrempé(e).
sodium ['səudɪəm] *n* sodium *m*.
sofa ['səufə] *n* sofa *m*, canapé *m*.
soft [sɔft] *a* (*not rough*) doux/(douce) ; (*not hard*) doux ; mou(molle) ; (*not loud*) doux, léger(ère) ; (*kind*) doux, gentil(le) ; (*weak*) indulgent(e) ; (*stupid*) stupide, débile ; **~ drink** *n* boisson non alcoolisée ; **~en** ['sɔfn] *vt* (r)amollir ; adoucir ; atténuer // *vi* se ramollir ; s'adoucir ; s'atténuer ; **~-hearted** *a* au cœur tendre ; **~ly** *ad* doucement ; gentiment ; **~ness** *n* douceur *f*; **~ware** *n* logiciel *m*, software *m*.
soggy ['sɔgɪ] *a* trempé(e) ; détrempé(e).
soil [sɔɪl] *n* (*earth*) sol *m*, terre *f* // *vt* salir ; (*fig*) souiller ; **~ed** *a* sale ; (COMM) défraîchi(e).
solar ['səulə*] *a* solaire.
sold [səuld] *pt,pp of* **sell** ; **~ out** *a* (COMM) épuisé(e).
solder ['səuldə*] *vt* souder (*au fil à souder*) // *n* soudure *f*.
soldier ['səuldʒə*] *n* soldat *m*, militaire *m*.
sole [səul] *n* (*of foot*) plante *f*; (*of shoe*) semelle *f*; (*fish*: *pl inv*) sole *f* // *a* seul(e), unique ; **~ly** *ad* seulement, uniquement.
solemn ['sɔləm] *a* solennel(le) ; sérieux(euse), grave.
solicitor [sə'lɪsɪtə*] *n* (*for wills etc*) ≈ notaire *m*; (*in court*) ≈ avocat *m*.
solid ['sɔlɪd] *a* (*not hollow*) plein(e), compact(e), massif(ive) ; (*strong, sound, reliable, not liquid*) solide ; (*meal*) consistant(e), substantiel(le) // *n* solide *m*.
solidarity [sɔlɪ'dærɪtɪ] *n* solidarité *f*.
solidify [sə'lɪdɪfaɪ] *vi* se solidifier // *vt* solidifier.
solidity [sə'lɪdɪtɪ] *n* solidité *f*.
soliloquy [sə'lɪləkwɪ] *n* monologue *m*.
solitaire [sɔlɪ'tɛə*] *n* (*game, gem*) solitaire *m*.
solitary ['sɔlɪtərɪ] *a* solitaire ; **~ confinement** *n* (LAW) isolement *m*.
solitude ['sɔlɪtju:d] *n* solitude *f*.
solo ['səuləu] *n* solo *m* ; **~ist** *n* soliste *m/f*.
solstice ['sɔlstɪs] *n* solstice *m*.
soluble ['sɔljubl] *a* soluble.
solution [sə'lu:ʃən] *n* solution *f*.
solve [sɔlv] *vt* résoudre.
solvent ['sɔlvənt] *a* (COMM) solvable // *n* (CHEM) (dis)solvant *m*.
sombre, somber (*US*) ['sɔmbə*] *a* sombre, morne.
some [sʌm] *det* (*a few*) quelques ; (*certain*) certains(certaines) ; (*a certain number or amount*) *see phrases below* ; (*unspecified*) un(e)... (quelconque) // *pronoun* quelques uns(unes) ; un peu // *ad*: **~ 10 people** quelque 10 personnes, 10 personnes environ ; **~ children came** des enfants sont venus ; **have ~ tea/ice-cream/water** prends du thé/de la glace/de l'eau ; **there's ~ milk in the fridge** il y a un peu de lait *or* du lait dans le frigo ; **~ (of it) was left** il en est resté un peu ; **I've got ~** (*i.e. books etc*) j'en ai (quelques uns) ; (*i.e. milk, money etc*) j'en ai (un peu) ; **~body** *pronoun* quelqu'un ; **~ day** *ad* un de ces jours, un jour ou l'autre ; **~how** *ad* d'une façon ou d'une autre ; (*for some reason*) pour une raison ou une autre ; **~one** *pronoun* = **somebody** ; **~place** *ad* (*US*) = **somewhere**.
somersault ['sʌməsɔ:lt] *n* culbute *f*, saut périlleux // *vi* faire la culbute *or* un saut périlleux ; (*car*) faire un tonneau.
something ['sʌmθɪŋ] *pronoun* quelque chose *m* ; **~ interesting** quelque chose d'intéressant.
sometime ['sʌmtaɪm] *ad* (*in future*) un de ces jours, un jour ou l'autre ; (*in past*): **~ last month** au cours du mois dernier.
sometimes ['sʌmtaɪmz] *ad* quelquefois, parfois.
somewhat ['sʌmwɔt] *ad* quelque peu, un peu.
somewhere ['sʌmwɛə*] *ad* quelque part.
son [sʌn] *n* fils *m*.
sonata [sə'nɑ:tə] *n* sonate *f*.
song [sɔŋ] *n* chanson *f*; **~book** *n* chansonnier *m* ; **~writer** *n* auteur-compositeur *m*.
sonic ['sɔnɪk] *a* (*boom*) supersonique.
son-in-law ['sʌnɪnlɔ:] *n* gendre *m*, beau-fils *m*.
sonnet ['sɔnɪt] *n* sonnet *m*.
sonny ['sʌnɪ] *n* (*col*) fiston *m*.
soon [su:n] *ad* bientôt ; (*early*) tôt ; **~ afterwards** peu après ; *see also* **as** ; **~er** *ad* (*time*) plus tôt ; (*preference*): **I would ~er do** j'aimerais autant *or* je préférerais faire ; **~er or later** tôt ou tard.
soot [sut] *n* suie *f*.

soothe [su:ð] *vt* calmer, apaiser.
sop [sɔp] *n*: **that's only a ~** c'est pour nous (*or* les *etc*) amadouer.
sophisticated [sə'fɪstɪkeɪtɪd] *a* raffiné(e); sophistiqué(e); hautement perfectionné(e), très complexe.
sophomore ['sɔfəmɔ:*] *n* (*US*) étudiant/e de seconde année.
soporific [sɔpə'rɪfɪk] *a* soporifique // *n* somnifère *m*.
sopping ['sɔpɪŋ] *a* (*also*: **~ wet**) tout(e) trempé(e).
soppy ['sɔpɪ] *a* (*pej*) sentimental(e).
soprano [sə'prɑ:nəu] *n* (*voice*) soprano *m*; (*singer*) soprano *m/f*.
sorcerer ['sɔ:sərə*] *n* sorcier *m*.
sordid ['sɔ:dɪd] *a* sordide.
sore [sɔ:*] *a* (*painful*) douloureux(euse), sensible; (*offended*) contrarié(e), vexé(e) // *n* plaie *f*; **~ly** *ad* (*tempted*) fortement.
sorrel ['sɔrəl] *n* oseille *f*.
sorrow ['sɔrəu] *n* peine *f*, chagrin *m*; **~ful** *a* triste.
sorry ['sɔrɪ] *a* désolé(e); (*condition, excuse*) triste, déplorable; **~!** pardon!, excusez-moi!; **to feel ~ for sb** plaindre qn.
sort [sɔ:t] *n* genre *m*, espèce *f*, sorte *f* // *vt* (*also*: **~ out**: *papers*) trier; classer; ranger; (: *letters etc*) trier; (: *problems*) résoudre, régler; **~ing office** *n* bureau *m* de tri.
SOS *n* (*abbr of save our souls*) S.O.S. *m*.
so-so ['səusəu] *ad* comme ci comme ça.
soufflé ['su:fleɪ] *n* soufflé *m*.
sought [sɔ:t] *pt,pp of* **seek.**
soul [səul] *n* âme *f*; **~-destroying** *a* démoralisant(e); **~ful** *a* plein(e) de sentiment; **~less** *a* sans cœur, inhumain(e).
sound [saund] *a* (*healthy*) en bonne santé, sain(e); (*safe, not damaged*) solide, en bon état; (*reliable, not superficial*) sérieux(euse), solide; (*sensible*) sensé(e) // *ad*: **~ asleep** dormant d'un profond sommeil // *n* (*noise*) son *m*; bruit *m*; (GEO) détroit *m*, bras *m* de mer // *vt* (*alarm*) sonner; (*also*: **~ out**: *opinions*) sonder // *vi* sonner, retentir; (*fig*: *seem*) sembler (être); **to ~ one's horn** (AUT) actionner son avertisseur; **to ~ like** ressembler à; **~ barrier** *n* mur *m* du son; **~ effects** *npl* bruitage *m*; **~ing** *n* (NAUT *etc*) sondage *m*; **~ly** *ad* (*sleep*) profondément; (*beat*) complètement, à plate couture; **~proof** *vt* insonoriser // *a* insonorisé(e); **~track** *n* (*of film*) bande *f* sonore.
soup [su:p] *n* soupe *f*, potage *m*; **in the ~** (*fig*) dans le pétrin; **~ course** *n* potage *m*; **~spoon** *n* cuiller *f* à soupe.
sour ['sauə*] *a* aigre, acide; (*milk*) tourné(e), aigre; (*fig*) acerbe, aigre; revêche; **it's ~ grapes** c'est du dépit.
source [sɔ:s] *n* source *f*.
south [sauθ] *n* sud *m* // *a* sud *inv*, du sud // *ad* au sud, vers le sud; **S~ Africa** *n* Afrique *f* du Sud; **S~ African** *a* sud-africain(e) // *n* Sud-Africain/e; **S~ America** *n* Amérique *f* du Sud; **S~ American** *a* sud-américain(e) // *n* Sud-Américain/e; **~-east** *n* sud-est *m*; **~erly** ['sʌðəlɪ] *a* du sud; au sud; **~ern** ['sʌðən] *a* (du) sud; méridional(e); exposé(e) au sud; **S~ Pole** *n* Pôle *m* Sud; **~ward(s)** *ad* vers le sud; **~-west** *n* sud-ouest *m*.
souvenir [su:və'nɪə*] *n* souvenir *m* (*objet*).
sovereign ['sɔvrɪn] *a,n* souverain(e); **~ty** *n* souveraineté *f*.
soviet ['səuvɪət] *a* soviétique; **the S~ Union** l'Union *f* soviétique.
sow *n* [sau] truie *f* // *vt* [səu] (*pt* **~ed,** *pp* **sown** [səun]) semer.
soy [sɔɪ] *n* (*also*: **~ sauce**) sauce *f* de soja.
soya bean ['sɔɪəbi:n] *n* graine *f* de soja.
spa [spɑ:] *n* (*spring*) source minérale; (*town*) station thermale.
space [speɪs] *n* (*gen*) espace *m*; (*room*) place *f*; espace; (*length of time*) laps *m* de temps // *cpd* spatial(e) // *vt* (*also*: **~ out**) espacer; **~craft** *n* engin spatial; **~man/woman** *n* astronaute *m/f*, cosmonaute *m/f*; **spacing** *n* espacement *m*; **single/double spacing** interligne *m* simple/double.
spacious ['speɪʃəs] *a* spacieux(euse), grand(e).
spade [speɪd] *n* (*tool*) bêche *f*, pelle *f*; (*child's*) pelle; **~s** *npl* (CARDS) pique *m*; **~work** *n* (*fig*) gros *m* du travail.
spaghetti [spə'gɛtɪ] *n* spaghetti *mpl*.
Spain [speɪn] *n* Espagne *f*.
span [spæn] *pt of* **spin** // *n* (*of bird, plane*) envergure *f*; (*of arch*) portée *f*; (*in time*) espace *m* de temps, durée *f* // *vt* enjamber, franchir; (*fig*) couvrir, embrasser.
Spaniard ['spænjəd] *n* Espagnol/e.
spaniel ['spænjəl] *n* épagneul *m*.
Spanish ['spænɪʃ] *a* espagnol(e), d'Espagne // *n* (LING) espagnol *m*.
spank [spæŋk] *vt* donner une fessée à.
spanner ['spænə*] *n* clé *f* (de mécanicien).
spare [spɛə*] *a* de réserve, de rechange; (*surplus*) de *or* en trop, de reste // *n* (*part*) pièce *f* de rechange, pièce détachée // *vt* (*do without*) se passer de; (*afford to give*) donner, accorder, passer; (*refrain from hurting*) épargner; (*refrain from using*) ménager; **to ~** (*surplus*) en surplus, de trop; **~ part** *n* pièce *f* de rechange, pièce détachée; **~ time** *n* moments *mpl* de loisir.
sparing ['spɛərɪŋ] *a* modéré(e), restreint(e); **~ of** chiche de; **~ly** *ad* avec modération.
spark [spɑ:k] *n* étincelle *f*; (*fig*) étincelle, lueur *f*; **~(ing) plug** *n* bougie *f*.
sparkle ['spɑ:kl] *n* scintillement *m*, étincellement *m*, éclat *m* // *vi* étinceler, scintiller; (*bubble*) pétiller; **sparkling** *a* étincelant(e), scintillant(e); (*wine*) mousseux (euse), pétillant(e).
sparrow ['spærəu] *n* moineau *m*.
sparse [spɑ:s] *a* clairsemé(e).
spasm ['spæzəm] *n* (MED) spasme *m*; (*fig*) accès *m*; **~odic** [-'mɔdɪk] *a* spasmodique; (*fig*) intermittent(e).
spastic ['spæstɪk] *n* handicapé/e moteur.
spat [spæt] *pt,pp of* **spit.**
spate [speɪt] *n* (*fig*): **~ of** avalanche *f* *or* torrent *m* de; **in ~** (*river*) en crue.
spatter ['spætə*] *n* éclaboussure(s) *f*(*pl*) // *vt* éclabousser // *vi* gicler.
spatula ['spætjulə] *n* spatule *f*.
spawn [spɔ:n] *vt* pondre // *vi* frayer // *n* frai *m*.

speak, *pt* **spoke,** *pp* **spoken** [spi:k, spəuk, 'spəukn] *vt* (*language*) parler ; (*truth*) dire // *vi* parler ; (*make a speech*) prendre la parole ; **to ~ to sb/of** *or* **about sth** parler à qn/de qch ; **it ~s for itself** c'est évident ; **~ up!** parle plus fort ! ; **~er** *n (in public)* orateur *m* ; (*also*: **loud~er**) haut-parleur *m* ; (POL): **the S~er** *le président de la chambre des Communes* ; **to be on ~ing terms** se parler.

spear [spɪə*] *n* lance *f* // *vt* transpercer.

spec [spɛk] *n* (*col*): **on ~** à tout hasard.

special ['spɛʃl] *a* spécial(e) ; **take ~ care** soyez particulièrement prudents ; **today's ~** (*at restaurant*) le menu ; **~ist** *n* spécialiste *m/f* ; **~ity** [spɛʃɪ'ælɪtɪ] *n* spécialité *f* ; **~ize** *vi*: **to ~ize (in)** se spécialiser (dans) ; **~ly** *ad* spécialement, particulièrement.

species ['spi:ʃi:z] *n* espèce *f*.

specific [spə'sɪfɪk] *a* précis(e) ; particulier(ère) ; (BOT, CHEM *etc*) spécifique ; **~ally** *ad* expressément, explicitement ; **~ation** [spɛsɪfɪ'keɪʃn] *n* spécification *f* ; stipulation *f*.

specify ['spɛsɪfaɪ] *vt* spécifier, préciser.

specimen ['spɛsɪmən] *n* spécimen *m*, échantillon *m* ; (MED) prélèvement *m*.

speck [spɛk] *n* petite tache, petit point ; (*particle*) grain *m*.

speckled ['spɛkld] *a* tacheté(e), moucheté(e).

specs [spɛks] *npl* (*col*) lunettes *fpl*.

spectacle ['spɛktəkl] *n* spectacle *m* ; **~s** *npl* lunettes *fpl* ; **spectacular** [-'tækjulə*] *a* spectaculaire // *n* (CINEMA *etc*) superproduction *f*.

spectator [spɛk'teɪtə*] *n* spectateur/trice.

spectra ['spɛktrə] *npl of* **spectrum**.

spectre, specter (*US*) ['spɛktə*] *n* spectre *m*, fantôme *m*.

spectrum, *pl* **spectra** ['spɛktrəm, -rə] *n* spectre *m* ; (*fig*) gamme *f*.

speculate ['spɛkjuleɪt] *vi* spéculer ; (*try to guess*): **to ~ about** s'interroger sur ; **speculation** [-'leɪʃən] *n* spéculation *f* ; conjectures *fpl* ; **speculative** *a* spéculatif(ive).

speech [spi:tʃ] *n* (*faculty*) parole *f* ; (*talk*) discours *m*, allocution *f* ; (*manner of speaking*) façon *f* de parler, langage *m* ; (*enunciation*) élocution *f* ; **~ day** *n* (SCOL) distribution *f* des prix ; **~less** *a* muet(te) ; **~ therapy** *n* orthophonie *f*.

speed [spi:d] *n* vitesse *f* ; (*promptness*) rapidité *f* ; **at full** *or* **top ~** à toute vitesse *or* allure ; **to ~ up** *vi* aller plus vite, accélérer // *vt* accélérer ; **~boat** *n* vedette *f* ; hors-bord *m inv* ; **~ily** *ad* rapidement, promptement ; **~ing** *n* (AUT) excès *m* de vitesse ; **~ limit** *n* limitation *f* de vitesse, vitesse maximale permise ; **~ometer** [spɪ'dɔmɪtə*] *n* compteur *m* (de vitesse) ; **~way** *n* (SPORT) piste *f* de vitesse pour motos ; **~y** *a* rapide, prompt(e).

speleologist [spɛlɪ'ɔlədʒɪst] *n* spéléologue *m/f*.

spell [spɛl] *n* (*also*: **magic ~**) sortilège *m*, charme *m* ; (*period of time*) (courte) période // *vt* (*pt,pp* **spelt** *or* **~ed** [spɛlt, spɛld]) (*in writing*) écrire, orthographier ; (*aloud*) épeler ; (*fig*) signifier ; **to cast a ~ on sb** jeter un sort à qn ; **he can't ~** il fait des fautes d'orthographe ; **~bound** *a* envoûté(e), subjugué(e) ; **~ing** *n* orthographe *f*.

spelt [spɛlt] *pt,pp of* **spell**.

spend, *pt,pp* **spent** [spɛnd, spɛnt] *vt* (*money*) dépenser ; (*time, life*) passer ; consacrer ; **~ing money** *n* argent *m* de poche ; **~thrift** *n* dépensier/ère.

spent [spɛnt] *pt,pp of* **spend** // *a* (*patience*) épuisé(e), à bout.

sperm [spə:m] *n* spermatozoïde *m* ; (*semen*) sperme *m* ; **~ whale** *n* cachalot *m*.

spew [spju:] *vt* vomir.

sphere [sfɪə*] *n* sphère *f* ; (*fig*) sphère, domaine *m* ; **spherical** ['sfɛrɪkl] *a* sphérique.

sphinx [sfɪŋks] *n* sphinx *m*.

spice [spaɪs] *n* épice *f* // *vt* épicer.

spick-and-span ['spɪkən'spæn] *a* impeccable.

spicy ['spaɪsɪ] *a* épicé(e), relevé(e) ; (*fig*) piquant(e).

spider ['spaɪdə*] *n* araignée *f*.

spiel [spi:l] *n* laïus *m inv*.

spike [spaɪk] *n* pointe *f*.

spill, *pt,pp* **spilt** *or* **~ed** [spɪl, -t, -d] *vt* renverser ; répandre // *vi* se répandre.

spin [spɪn] *n* (*revolution of wheel*) tour *m* ; (AVIAT) (chute *f* en) vrille *f* ; (*trip in car*) petit tour, balade *f* // *vb* (*pt* **spun, span,** *pp* **spun** [spʌn, spæn]) *vt* (*wool etc*) filer ; (*wheel*) faire tourner // *vi* tourner, tournoyer ; **to ~ a yarn** débiter une longue histoire ; **to ~ a coin** jouer à pile ou face ; **to ~ out** *vt* faire durer.

spinach ['spɪnɪtʃ] *n* épinard *m* ; (*as food*) épinards.

spinal ['spaɪnl] *a* vertébral(e), spinal(e) ; **~ cord** *n* moelle épinière.

spindly ['spɪndlɪ] *a* grêle, filiforme.

spin-drier [spɪn'draɪə*] *n* essoreuse *f*.

spine [spaɪn] *n* colonne vertébrale ; (*thorn*) épine *f*, piquant *m* ; **~less** *a* invertébré(e) ; (*fig*) mou(molle), sans caractère.

spinner ['spɪnə*] *n* (*of thread*) fileur/euse.

spinning ['spɪnɪŋ] *n* (*of thread*) filage *m* ; (*by machine*) filature *f* ; **~ top** *n* toupie *f* ; **~ wheel** *n* rouet *m*.

spinster ['spɪnstə*] *n* célibataire *f* ; vieille fille.

spiral ['spaɪərl] *n* spirale *f* // *a* en spirale // *vi* (*fig*) monter en flèche ; **~ staircase** *n* escalier *m* en colimaçon.

spire ['spaɪə*] *n* flèche *f*, aiguille *f*.

spirit ['spɪrɪt] *n* (*soul*) esprit *m*, âme *f* ; (*ghost*) esprit, revenant *m* ; (*mood*) esprit, état *m* d'esprit ; (*courage*) courage *m*, énergie *f* ; **~s** *npl* (*drink*) spiritueux *mpl*, alcool *m* ; **in good ~s** de bonne humeur ; **in low ~s** démoralisé(e) ; **~ed** *a* vif(vive), fougueux(euse), plein(e) d'allant ; **~ level** *n* niveau *m* à bulle.

spiritual ['spɪrɪtjuəl] *a* spirituel(le) ; religieux(euse) // *n* (*also*: **Negro ~**) spiritual *m* ; **~ism** *n* spiritisme *m*.

spit [spɪt] *n* (*for roasting*) broche *f* // *vi* (*pt, pp* **spat** [spæt]) cracher ; (*sound*) crépiter.

spite [spaɪt] *n* rancune *f*, dépit *m* // *vt* contrarier, vexer ; **in ~ of** en dépit de, malgré ; **~ful** *a* malveillant(e), rancunier(ère).

spitroast ['spɪt'rəust] *vt* faire rôtir à la broche.

spittle ['spɪtl] *n* salive *f*; bave *f*; crachat *m*.

spiv [spɪv] *n* (*col*) chevalier *m* d'industrie, aigrefin *m*.

splash [splæʃ] *n* éclaboussement *m* ; (*sound*) plouf ; (*of colour*) tache *f* // *vt* éclabousser ; *vi* (*also*: **~ about**) barboter, patauger.

splay [spleɪ] *a*: **~footed** marchant les pieds en dehors.

spleen [spli:n] *n* (ANAT) rate *f*.

splendid ['splɛndɪd] *a* splendide, superbe, magnifique.

splendour, splendor (*US*) ['splɛndə*] *n* splendeur *f*, magnificence *f*.

splice [splaɪs] *vt* épisser.

splint [splɪnt] *n* attelle *f*, éclisse *f*.

splinter ['splɪntə*] *n* (*wood*) écharde *f*; (*metal*) éclat *m* // *vi* se fragmenter.

split [splɪt] *n* fente *f*, déchirure *f*; (*fig*: POL) scission *f* // *vb* (*pt*, *pp* **split**) *vt* fendre, déchirer ; (*party*) diviser ; (*work*, *profits*) partager, répartir // *vi* (*divide*) se diviser ; **to ~ up** *vi* (*couple*) se séparer, rompre ; (*meeting*) se disperser ; **~ting headache** *n* mal *m* de tête atroce.

splutter ['splʌtə*] *vi* bafouiller ; postillonner.

spoil, *pt,pp* **spoilt** *or* **~ed** [spɔɪl, -t, -d] *vt* (*damage*) abîmer ; (*mar*) gâcher ; (*child*) gâter ; **~s** *npl* butin *m* ; **~sport** *n* trouble-fête *m*, rabat-joie *m*.

spoke [spəuk] *pt of* **speak** // *n* rayon *m*.

spoken ['spəukn] *pp of* **speak**.

spokesman ['spəuksmən] *n* porteparole *m inv*.

sponge [spʌndʒ] *n* éponge *f* // *vt* éponger // *vi*: **to ~ on** vivre aux crochets de ; **~ bag** *n* sac *m* de toilette ; **~ cake** *n* ≈ gâteau *m* de Savoie ; **~r** *n* (*pej*) parasite *m*; **spongy** *a* spongieux(euse).

sponsor ['spɔnsə*] *n* (RADIO, TV) personne *f* (*or* organisme *m*) qui assure le patronage // *vt* patronner ; parrainer ; **~ship** *n* patronage *m* ; parrainage *m*.

spontaneity [spɔntə'neɪɪtɪ] *n* spontanéité *f*.

spontaneous [spɔn'teɪnɪəs] *a* spontané(e).

spooky ['spu:kɪ] *a* qui donne la chair de poule.

spool [spu:l] *n* bobine *f*.

spoon [spu:n] *n* cuiller *f*; **~-feed** *vt* nourrir à la cuiller ; (*fig*) mâcher le travail à ; **~ful** *n* cuillerée *f*.

sporadic [spə'rædɪk] *a* sporadique.

sport [spɔ:t] *n* sport *m* ; (*person*) chic type/chic fille // *vt* arborer ; **~ing** *a* sportif(ive) ; **to give sb a ~ing chance** donner sa chance à qn ; **~s car** *n* voiture *f* de sport ; **~s jacket** *n* veste *f* de sport ; **~sman** *n* sportif *m* ; **~smanship** *n* esprit sportif, sportivité *f*; **~s page** *n* page *f* des sports ; **~swear** *n* vêtements *mpl* de sport ; **~swoman** *n* sportive *f*; **~y** *a* sportif(ive).

spot [spɔt] *n* tache *f* ; (*dot*: *on pattern*) pois *m* ; (*pimple*) bouton *m* ; (*place*) endroit *m*, coin *m* ; (*small amount*): **a ~ of** un peu de // *vt* (*notice*) apercevoir, repérer ; **on the ~** sur place, sur les lieux ; **to come out in ~s** se couvrir de boutons, avoir une éruption de boutons ; **~ check** *n* sondage *m*, vérification ponctuelle ; **~less** *a* immaculé(e) ; **~light** *n* projecteur *m* ; (AUT) phare *m* auxiliaire ; **~ted** *a* tacheté(e), moucheté(e) ; à pois ; **~ted with** tacheté(e) de ; **~ty** *a* (*face*) boutonneux(euse).

spouse [spauz] *n* époux/épouse.

spout [spaut] *n* (*of jug*) bec *m* ; (*of liquid*) jet *m* // *vi* jaillir.

sprain [spreɪn] *n* entorse *f*, foulure *f* // *vt*: **to ~ one's ankle** se fouler *or* se tordre la cheville.

sprang [spræŋ] *pt of* **spring**.

sprawl [sprɔ:l] *vi* s'étaler.

spray [spreɪ] *n* jet *m* (en fines gouttelettes) ; (*container*) vaporisateur *m*, bombe *f*; (*of flowers*) petit bouquet // *vt* vaporiser, pulvériser ; (*crops*) traiter.

spread [sprɛd] *n* propagation *f*; (*distribution*) répartition *f*; (CULIN) pâte *f* à tartiner // *vb* (*pt,pp* **spread**) *vt* étendre, étaler ; répandre ; propager // *vi* s'étendre ; se répandre ; se propager.

spree [spri:] *n*: **to go on a ~** faire la fête.

sprig [sprɪg] *n* rameau *m*.

sprightly ['spraɪtlɪ] *a* alerte.

spring [sprɪŋ] *n* (*leap*) bond *m*, saut *m* ; (*coiled metal*) ressort *m*; (*season*) printemps *m* ; (*of water*) source *f* // *vi* (*pt* **sprang**, *pp* **sprung** [spræŋ, sprʌŋ]) bondir, sauter ; **to ~ from** provenir de ; **to ~ up** *vi* (*problem*) se présenter, surgir ; **~board** *n* tremplin *m*; **~-clean** *n* (*also*: **~-cleaning**) grand nettoyage de printemps ; **~time** *n* printemps *m*; **~y** *a* élastique, souple.

sprinkle ['sprɪŋkl] *vt* (*pour*) répandre ; verser ; **to ~ water** *etc* **on, ~ with water** *etc* asperger d'eau *etc* ; **to ~ sugar** *etc* **on, ~ with sugar** *etc* saupoudrer de sucre *etc* ; **~d with** (*fig*) parsemé(e) de.

sprint [sprɪnt] *n* sprint *m* // *vi* sprinter ; **~er** *n* sprinteur/euse.

sprite [spraɪt] *n* lutin *m*.

sprout [spraut] *vi* germer, pousser ; **(Brussels) ~s** *npl* choux *mpl* de Bruxelles.

spruce [spru:s] *n* épicéa *m* // *a* net(te), pimpant(e).

sprung [sprʌŋ] *pp of* **spring**.

spry [spraɪ] *a* alerte, vif(vive).

spud [spʌd] *n* (*col*: *potato*) patate *f*.

spun [spʌn] *pt*, *pp of* **spin**.

spur [spə:*] *n* éperon *m* ; (*fig*) aiguillon *m* // *vt* (*also*: **~ on**) éperonner ; aiguillonner ; **on the ~ of the moment** sous l'impulsion du moment.

spurious ['spjuərɪəs] *a* faux(fausse).

spurn [spə:n] *vt* repousser avec mépris.

spurt [spə:t] *n* jet *m* ; (*of energy*) sursaut *m* // *vi* jaillir, gicler.

spy [spaɪ] *n* espion/ne // *vi*: **to ~ on** espionner, épier // *vt* (*see*) apercevoir ; **~ing** *n* espionnage *m*.

sq. (MATH), **Sq.** (*in address*) *abbr of* **square**.
squabble ['skwɔbl] *n* querelle *f*, chamaillerie *f* // *vi* se chamailler.
squad [skwɔd] *n* (MIL, POLICE) escouade *f*, groupe *m*; (FOOTBALL) contingent *m*.
squadron ['skwɔdrn] *n* (MIL) escadron *m*; (AVIAT, NAUT) escadrille *f*.
squalid ['skwɔlɪd] *a* sordide, ignoble.
squall [skwɔ:l] *n* rafale *f*, bourrasque *f*.
squalor ['skwɔlə*] *n* conditions *fpl* sordides.
squander ['skwɔndə*] *vt* gaspiller, dilapider.
square [skwɛə*] *n* carré *m*; (*in town*) place *f*; (*instrument*) équerre *f* // *a* carré(e); (*honest*) honnête, régulier(ère); (*col*: *ideas, tastes*) vieux jeu *inv*, qui retarde // *vt* (*arrange*) régler; arranger; (MATH) élever au carré // *vi* (*agree*) cadrer, s'accorder; **all ~** quitte; à égalité; **a ~ meal** un repas convenable; **2 metres ~** (de) 2 mètres sur 2; **1 ~ metre** 1 mètre carré; **~ly** *ad* carrément.
squash [skwɔʃ] *n* (*drink*): **lemon/orange ~** citronnade *f*/ orangeade *f*; (SPORT) squash *m* // *vt* écraser.
squat [skwɔt] *a* petit(e) et épais(se), ramassé(e) // *vi* s'accroupir; **~ter** *n* squatter *m*.
squawk [skwɔ:k] *vi* pousser un *or* des gloussement(s).
squeak [skwi:k] *n* grincement *m*; petit cri // *vi* grincer, crier.
squeal [skwi:l] *vi* pousser un *or* des cri(s) aigu(s) *or* perçant(s).
squeamish ['skwi:mɪʃ] *a* facilement dégoûté(e); facilement scandalisé(e).
squeeze [skwi:z] *n* pression *f*; restrictions *fpl* de crédit // *vt* presser; (*hand, arm*) serrer; **to ~ out** *vt* exprimer; (*fig*) soutirer.
squelch [skwɛltʃ] *vi* faire un bruit de succion; patauger.
squib [skwɪb] *n* pétard *m*.
squid [skwɪd] *n* calmar *m*.
squint [skwɪnt] *vi* loucher // *n*: **he has a ~** il louche, il souffre de strabisme.
squire ['skwaɪə*] *n* propriétaire terrien.
squirm [skwə:m] *vi* se tortiller.
squirrel ['skwɪrəl] *n* écureuil *m*.
squirt [skwə:t] *n* jet *m* // *vi* jaillir, gicler.
Sr *abbr of* **senior**.
St *abbr of* **saint**, **street**.
stab [stæb] *n* (*with knife etc*) coup *m* (de couteau *etc*); (*col*: *try*): **to have a ~ at (doing) sth** s'essayer à (faire) qch // *vt* poignarder.
stability [stə'bɪlɪtɪ] *n* stabilité *f*.
stabilize ['steɪbəlaɪz] *vt* stabiliser; **~r** *n* stabilisateur *m*.
stable ['steɪbl] *n* écurie *f* // *a* stable.
stack [stæk] *n* tas *m*, pile *f* // *vt* empiler, entasser.
stadium ['steɪdɪəm] *n* stade *m*.
staff [stɑ:f] *n* (*work force*) personnel *m*; (: SCOL) professeurs *mpl*; (: *servants*) domestiques *mpl*; (MIL) état-major *m*; (*stick*) perche *f*, bâton *m* // *vt* pourvoir en personnel.
stag [stæg] *n* cerf *m*.
stage [steɪdʒ] *n* scène *f*; (*profession*): **the ~** le théâtre; (*point*) étape *f*, stade *m*; (*platform*) estrade *f* // *vt* (*play*) monter, mettre en scène; (*demonstration*) organiser; (*fig*: *perform*: *recovery etc*) effectuer; **in ~s** par étapes, par degrés; **~coach** *n* diligence *f*; **~ door** *n* entrée *f* des artistes; **~ fright** *n* trac *m*; **~ manager** *n* régisseur *m*.
stagger ['stægə*] *vi* chanceler, tituber // *vt* (*person*) stupéfier; bouleverser; (*hours, holidays*) étaler, échelonner; **~ing** *a* (*amazing*) stupéfiant(e), renversant(e).
stagnant ['stægnənt] *a* stagnant(e).
stagnate [stæg'neɪt] *vi* stagner, croupir.
stag party ['stægpɑ:tɪ] *n* enterrement *m* de vie de garçon.
staid [steɪd] *a* posé(e), rassis(e).
stain [steɪn] *n* tache *f*; (*colouring*) colorant *m* // *vt* tacher; (*wood*) teindre; **~ed glass window** *n* vitrail *m*; **~less** *a* (*steel*) inoxydable; **~ remover** *n* détachant *m*.
stair [stɛə*] *n* (*step*) marche *f*; **~s** *npl* escalier *m*; **on the ~s** dans l'escalier; **~case**, **~way** *n* escalier *m*.
stake [steɪk] *n* pieu *m*, poteau *m*; (BETTING) enjeu *m* // *vt* risquer, jouer; **to be at ~** être en jeu.
stalactite ['stæləktaɪt] *n* stalactite *f*.
stalagmite ['stæləgmaɪt] *n* stalagmite *m*.
stale [steɪl] *a* (*bread*) rassis(e); (*beer*) éventé(e); (*smell*) de renfermé.
stalemate ['steɪlmeɪt] *n* pat *m*; (*fig*) impasse *f*.
stalk [stɔ:k] *n* tige *f* // *vt* traquer // *vi* marcher avec raideur.
stall [stɔ:l] *n* éventaire *m*, étal *m*; (*in stable*) stalle *f* // *vt* (AUT) caler // *vi* (AUT) caler; (*fig*) essayer de gagner du temps; **~s** *npl* (*in cinema, theatre*) orchestre *m*.
stalwart ['stɔ:lwət] *n* partisan *m* fidèle.
stamina ['stæmɪnə] *n* vigueur *f*, endurance *f*.
stammer ['stæmə*] *n* bégaiement *m* // *vi* bégayer.
stamp [stæmp] *n* timbre *m*; (*mark, also fig*) empreinte *f*; (*on document*) cachet *m* // *vi* taper du pied // *vt* tamponner, estamper; (*letter*) timbrer; **~ album** *n* album *m* de timbres(-poste); **~ collecting** *n* philatélie *f*.
stampede [stæm'pi:d] *n* ruée *f*.
stance [stæns] *n* position *f*.
stand [stænd] *n* (*position*) position *f*; (MIL) résistance *f*; (*structure*) guéridon *m*; support *m*; (COMM) étalage *m*, stand *m*; (SPORT) tribune *f* // *vb* (*pt,pp* **stood** [stud]) *vi* être *or* se tenir (debout); (*rise*) se lever, se mettre debout; (*be placed*) se trouver // *vt* (*place*) mettre, poser; (*tolerate, withstand*) supporter; **to make a ~** prendre position; **to ~ for parliament** se présenter aux élections (*comme candidat à la députation*); **it ~s to reason** c'est logique; cela va de soi; **to ~ by** *vi* (*be ready*) se tenir prêt // *vt fus* (*opinion*) s'en tenir à; **to ~ for** *vt fus* (*defend*) défendre, être pour; (*signify*) représenter, signifier; (*tolerate*) supporter, tolérer; **to ~ in for** *vt fus* remplacer; **to ~ out** *vi* (*be prominent*) ressortir; **to ~ up** *vi* (*rise*) se lever, se mettre debout; **to ~ up for** *vt*

fus défendre ; **to ~ up to** *vt fus* tenir tête à, résister à.
standard ['stændəd] *n* niveau voulu ; (*flag*) étendard *m* // *a* (*size etc*) ordinaire, normal(e) ; courant(e) ; **~s** *npl* (*morals*) morale *f*, principes *mpl* ; **~ization** [-'zeɪʃən] *n* standardisation *f* ; **~ize** *vt* standardiser ; **~ lamp** *n* lampadaire *m* ; **~ of living** *n* niveau *m* de vie.
stand-by ['stændbaɪ] *n* remplaçant/e ; **~ ticket** *n* (AVIAT) billet *m* sans garantie.
stand-in ['stændɪn] *n* remplaçant/e ; (CINEMA) doublure *f*.
standing ['stændɪŋ] *a* debout *inv* // *n* réputation *f*, rang *m*, standing *m* ; **of many years'** ~ qui dure *or* existe depuis longtemps ; **~ committee** *n* commission permanente ; **~ order** *n* (*at bank*) virement *m* automatique, prélèvement *m* bancaire ; **~ orders** *npl* (MIL) règlement *m* ; **~ room** places *fpl* debout.
stand-offish [stænd'ɔfɪʃ] *a* distant(e), froid(e).
standpoint ['stændpɔɪnt] *n* point *m* de vue.
standstill ['stændstɪl] *n*: **at a ~** à l'arrêt ; (*fig*) au point mort ; **to come to a ~** s'immobiliser, s'arrêter.
stank [stæŋk] *pt of* **stink.**
stanza ['stænzə] *n* strophe *f* ; couplet *m*.
staple ['steɪpl] *n* (*for papers*) agrafe *f* // *a* (*food etc*) de base, principal(e) // *vt* agrafer ; **~r** *n* agrafeuse *f*.
star [stɑ:*] *n* étoile *f* ; (*celebrity*) vedette *f* // *vi*: **to ~ (in)** être la vedette (de) // *vt* (CINEMA) avoir pour vedette.
starboard ['stɑ:bəd] *n* tribord *m* ; **to ~** à tribord.
starch [stɑ:tʃ] *n* amidon *m* ; **~ed** *a* (*collar*) amidonné(e), empesé(e) ; **~y** *a* riche en féculents ; (*person*) guindé(e).
stardom ['stɑ:dəm] *n* célébrité *f*.
stare [stɛə*] *n* regard *m* fixe // *vt*: **to ~ at** regarder fixement.
starfish ['stɑ:fɪʃ] *n* étoile *f* de mer.
stark [stɑ:k] *a* (*bleak*) désolé(e), morne // *ad*: **~ naked** complètement nu(e).
starlight ['stɑ:laɪt] *n*: **by ~** à la lumière des étoiles.
starling ['stɑ:lɪŋ] *n* étourneau *m*.
starlit ['stɑ:lɪt] *a* étoilé(e) ; illuminé(e) par les étoiles.
starry ['stɑ:rɪ] *a* étoilé(e) ; **~-eyed** *a* (*innocent*) ingénu(e).
start [stɑ:t] *n* commencement *m*, début *m* ; (*of race*) départ *m* ; (*sudden movement*) sursaut *m* // *vt* commencer // *vi* partir, se mettre en route ; (*jump*) sursauter ; **to ~ doing sth** se mettre à faire qch ; **to ~ off** *vi* commencer ; (*leave*) partir ; **to ~ up** *vi* commencer ; (*car*) démarrer // *vt* déclencher ; (*car*) mettre en marche ; **~er** *n* (AUT) démarreur *m* ; (SPORT: *official*) starter *m* ; (: *runner, horse*) partant *m* ; (CULIN) entrée *f* ; **~ing handle** *n* manivelle *f* ; **~ing point** *n* point *m* de départ.
startle ['stɑ:tl] *vt* faire sursauter ; donner un choc à ; **startling** *a* surprenant(e), saisissant(e).
starvation [stɑ:'veɪʃən] *n* faim *f*, famine *f* ; **to die of ~** mourir de faim *or* d'inanition.
starve [stɑ:v] *vi* mourir de faim ; être affamé(e) // *vt* affamer ; **I'm starving** je meurs de faim.
state [steɪt] *n* état *m* // *vt* déclarer, affirmer ; formuler ; **the S~s** les États-Unis *mpl* ; **to be in a ~** être dans tous ses états ; **~ control** *n* contrôle *m* de l'État ; **~d** *a* fixé(e), prescrit(e) ; **~ly** *a* majestueux(euse), imposant(e) ; **~ment** *n* déclaration *f* ; (LAW) déposition *f* ; **~ secret** *n* secret *m* d'État ; **~sman** *n* homme *m* d'État.
static ['stætɪk] *n* (RADIO) parasites *mpl* // *a* statique ; **~ electricity** *n* électricité *f* statique.
station ['steɪʃən] *n* gare *f* ; poste *m* (militaire *or* de police *etc*) ; (*rank*) condition *f*, rang *m* // *vt* placer, poster.
stationary ['steɪʃnərɪ] *a* à l'arrêt, immobile.
stationer ['steɪʃənə*] *n* papetier/ère ; **~'s (shop)** *n* papeterie *f* ; **~y** *n* papier *m* à lettres, petit matériel de bureau.
station master ['steɪʃənmɑ:stə*] *n* (RAIL) chef *m* de gare.
station wagon ['steɪʃənwægən] *n* (*US*) break *m*.
statistic [stə'tɪstɪk] *n* statistique *f* ; **~s** *npl* (*science*) statistique *f* ; **~al** *a* statistique.
statue ['stætju:] *n* statue *f*; **statuesque** [-'ɛsk] *a* sculptural(e).
stature ['stætʃə*] *n* stature *f*; (*fig*) envergure *f*.
status ['steɪtəs] *n* position *f*, situation *f* ; prestige *m* ; statut *m* ; **the ~ quo** le statu quo ; **~ symbol** *n* marque *f* de standing, signe extérieur de richesse.
statute ['stætju:t] *n* loi *f* ; **~s** *npl* (*of club etc*) statuts *mpl* ; **statutory** *a* statutaire, prévu(e) par un article de loi.
staunch [stɔ:ntʃ] *a* sûr(e), loyal(e).
stave [steɪv] *n* (MUS) portée *f* // *vt*: **to ~ off** (*attack*) parer ; (*threat*) conjurer.
stay [steɪ] *n* (*period of time*) séjour *m* // *vi* rester ; (*reside*) loger ; (*spend some time*) séjourner ; **to ~ put** ne pas bouger ; **to ~ with friends** loger chez des amis ; **to ~ the night** passer la nuit ; **to ~ behind** *vi* rester en arrière ; **to ~ in** *vi* (*at home*) rester à la maison ; **to ~ on** *vi* rester ; **to ~ out** *vi* (*of house*) ne pas rentrer ; **to ~ up** *vi* (*at night*) ne pas se coucher.
STD *n* (*abbr of Subscriber Trunk Dialling*) l'automatique *m*.
steadfast ['stɛdfɑ:st] *a* ferme, résolu(e).
steadily ['stɛdɪlɪ] *ad* progressivement ; sans arrêt ; (*walk*) d'un pas ferme.
steady ['stɛdɪ] *a* stable, solide, ferme ; (*regular*) constant(e), régulier(ère) ; (*person*) calme, pondéré(e) // *vt* stabiliser ; assujettir ; calmer ; **to ~ oneself** reprendre son aplomb.
steak [steɪk] *n* (*meat*) bifteck *m*, steak *m* ; (*fish*) tranche *f* ; **~house** *n* ≈ grill-room *m*.
steal, *pt* **stole**, *pp* **stolen** [sti:l, stəul, 'stəuln] *vt,vi* voler.
stealth [stɛlθ] *n*: **by ~** furtivement ; **~y** *a* furtif(ive).
steam [sti:m] *n* vapeur *f* // *vt* passer à la vapeur ; (CULIN) cuire à la vapeur // *vi* fumer ; (*ship*): **to ~ along** filer ; **~ engine**

n locomotive *f* à vapeur ; **~er** *n* (bateau *m* à) vapeur *m*; **~roller** *n* rouleau compresseur ; **~y** *a* embué(e), humide.
steed [sti:d] n coursier *m*.
steel [sti:l] *n* acier *m* // *cpd* d'acier ; **~works** *n* aciérie *f*.
steep [sti:p] *a* raide, escarpé(e) ; (*price*) très élevé(e), excessif(ive) // *vt* (faire) tremper.
steeple ['sti:pl] *n* clocher *m* ; **~chase** *n* steeple(-chase) *m* ; **~jack** *n* réparateur *m* de clochers et de hautes cheminées.
steeply ['sti:plɪ] *ad* en pente raide.
steer [stɪə*] *n* bœuf *m* // *vt* diriger, gouverner ; guider // *vi* tenir le gouvernail ; **~ing** *n* (AUT) conduite *f* ; **~ing column** *n* colonne *f* de direction ; **~ing wheel** *n* volant *m*.
stellar ['stɛlə*] *a* stellaire.
stem [stɛm] *n* tige *f*; queue *f*; (NAUT) avant *m*, proue *f* // *vt* contenir, endiguer, juguler ; **to ~ from** *vt fus* provenir de, découler de.
stench [stɛntʃ] *n* puanteur *f*.
stencil ['stɛnsl] *n* stencil *m* ; pochoir *m* // *vt* polycopier.
step [stɛp] *n* pas *m* ; (*stair*) marche *f*; (*action*) mesure *f*, disposition *f* // *vi*: **to ~ forward** faire un pas en avant, avancer ; **~s** *npl* = **stepladder** ; **to ~ down** *vi* (*fig*) se retirer, se désister ; **to ~ off** *vt fus* descendre de ; **to ~ over** *vt fus* marcher sur ; **to ~ up** *vt* augmenter ; intensifier ; **~brother** *n* demi-frère *m* ; **~child** *n* beau-fils/belle-fille ; **~father** *n* beau-père *m* ; **~ladder** *n* escabeau *m* ; **~mother** *n* belle-mère *f* ; **stepping stone** *n* pierre *f* de gué ; (*fig*) tremplin *m* ; **~sister** *n* demi-sœur *f*.
stereo ['stɛrɪəu] *n* (*system*) stéréo *f*; (*record player*) chaine *f* stéréo // *a* (*also*: **~phonic**) *a* stéréophonique.
stereotype ['stɪərɪətaɪp] *n* stéréotype *m* // *vt* stéréotyper.
sterile ['stɛraɪl] *a* stérile ; **sterility** [-'rɪlɪtɪ] *n* stérilité *f*; **sterilization** [-'zeɪʃən] *n* stérilisation *f*; **sterilize** ['stɛrɪlaɪz] *vt* stériliser.
sterling ['stə:lɪŋ] *a* sterling *inv* ; (*silver*) de bon aloi, fin(e) ; (*fig*) à toute épreuve, excellent(e) ; **~ area** *n* zone *f* sterling *inv*.
stern [stə:n] *a* sévère // *n* (NAUT) arrière *m*, poupe *f*.
stethoscope ['stɛθəskəup] *n* stéthoscope *m*.
stevedore ['sti:vədɔ:*] *n* docker *m*, débardeur *m*.
stew [stju:] *n* ragoût *m* // *vt*, *vi* cuire à la casserole ; **~ed tea** thé trop infusé.
steward ['stju:əd] *n* (AVIAT, NAUT, RAIL) steward *m* ; (*in club etc*) intendant *m* ; **~ess** *n* hôtesse *f*.
stick [stɪk] *n* bâton *m* ; morceau *m* // *vb* (*pt, pp* **stuck** [stʌk]) *vt* (*glue*) coller ; (*thrust*): **to ~ sth into** piquer *or* planter *or* enfoncer qch dans ; (*col*: *put*) mettre, fourrer ; (*col*: *tolerate*) supporter // *vi* se planter ; tenir ; (*remain*) rester ; **to ~ out, to ~ up** *vi* dépasser, sortir ; **to ~ up for** *vt fus* défendre ; **~er** *n* auto-collant *m*.
stickleback ['stɪklbæk] *n* épinoche *f*.
stickler ['stɪklə*] *n*: **to be a ~ for** être pointilleux(euse) sur.
sticky ['stɪkɪ] *a* poisseux(euse) ; (*label*) adhésif(ive).
stiff [stɪf] *a* raide ; rigide ; dur(e) ; (*difficult*) difficile, ardu(e) ; (*cold*) froid(e), distant(e) ; (*strong, high*) fort(e), élevé(e) ; **~en** *vt* raidir, renforcer // *vi* se raidir ; se durcir ; **~ neck** *n* torticolis *m* ; **~ness** *n* raideur *f*.
stifle ['staɪfl] *vt* étouffer, réprimer ; **stifling** *a* (*heat*) suffocant(e).
stigma, *pl* (BOT, MED, REL) **~ta**, (*fig*) **~s** ['stɪgmə, stɪg'mɑ:tə] *n* stigmate *m*.
stile [staɪl] *n* échalier *m*.
stiletto [stɪ'lɛtəu] *n* (*also*: **~ heel**) talon *m* aiguille.
still [stɪl] *a* immobile ; calme, tranquille // *ad* (*up to this time*) encore, toujours ; (*even*) encore ; (*nonetheless*) quand même, tout de même ; **~born** *a* mort-né(e) ; **~ life** *n* nature morte.
stilt [stɪlt] *n* échasse *f*; (*pile*) pilotis *m*.
stilted ['stɪltɪd] *a* guindé(e), emprunté(e).
stimulant ['stɪmjulənt] *n* stimulant *m*.
stimulate ['stɪmjuleɪt] *vt* stimuler ; **stimulating** *a* stimulant(e) ; **stimulation** [-'leɪʃən] *n* stimulation *f*.
stimulus, *pl* **stimuli** ['stɪmjuləs, 'stɪmjulaɪ] *n* stimulant *m* ; (BIOL, PSYCH) stimulus *m*.
sting [stɪŋ] *n* piqûre *f*; (*organ*) dard *m* // *vt* (*pt,pp* **stung** [stʌŋ]) piquer.
stingy ['stɪndʒɪ] *a* avare, pingre, chiche.
stink [stɪŋk] *n* puanteur *f* // *vi* (*pt* **stank**, *pp* **stunk** [stæŋk, stʌŋk]) puer, empester ; **~er** *n* (*col*) vacherie *f*; dégueulasse *m/f* ; **~ing** *a* (*col*): **a ~ing...** un(e) vache de..., un(e) foutu(e)... .
stint [stɪnt] *n* part *f* de travail// *vi*: **to ~ on** lésiner sur, être chiche de.
stipend ['staɪpɛnd] *n* (*of vicar etc*) traitement *m*.
stipulate ['stɪpjuleɪt] *vt* stipuler ; **stipulation** [-'leɪʃən] *n* stipulation *f*, condition *f*.
stir [stə:*] *n* agitation *f*, sensation *f* // *vt* remuer // *vi* remuer, bouger ; **to ~ up** *vt* exciter ; **~ring** *a* excitant(e) ; émouvant(e).
stirrup ['stɪrəp] *n* étrier *m*.
stitch [stɪtʃ] *n* (SEWING) point *m* ; (KNITTING) maille *f*; (MED) point de suture ; (*pain*) point de côté // *vt* coudre, piquer ; suturer.
stoat [stəut] *n* hermine *f* (*avec son pelage d'été*).
stock [stɔk] *n* réserve *f*, provision *f*; (COMM) stock *m* ; (AGR) cheptel *m*, bétail *m* ; (CULIN) bouillon *m* ; (FINANCE) valeurs *fpl*, titres *mpl* // *a* (*fig*: *reply etc*) courant(e) ; classique // *vt* (*have in stock*) avoir, vendre ; **well-~ed** bien approvisionné(e) *or* fourni(e) ; **to take ~** (*fig*) faire le point ; **to ~ up** *vt* remplir, garnir // *vi*: **to ~ up (with)** s'approvisionner (en).
stockade [stɔ'keɪd] *n* palissade *f*.
stockbroker ['stɔkbrəukə*] *n* agent *m* de change.
stock exchange ['stɔkɪkstʃeɪndʒ] *n* Bourse *f* (des valeurs).
stocking ['stɔkɪŋ] *n* bas *m*.

stockist ['stɔkɪst] *n* stockiste *m*.
stock market ['stɔkmɑ:kɪt] *n* Bourse *f*, marché financier.
stock phrase ['stɔk'freɪz] *n* cliché *m*.
stockpile ['stɔkpaɪl] *n* stock *m*, réserve *f* // *vt* stocker, accumuler.
stocktaking ['stɔkteɪkɪŋ] *n* (COMM) inventaire *m*.
stocky ['stɔkɪ] *a* trapu(e), râblé(e).
stodgy ['stɔdʒɪ] *a* bourratif(ive), lourd(e).
stoic ['stəuɪk] *n* stoïque *m/f*; **~al** *a* stoïque.
stoke [stəuk] *vt* garnir, entretenir; chauffer; **~r** *n* chauffeur *m*.
stole [stəul] *pt of* **steal** // *n* étole *f*.
stolen ['stəuln] *pp of* **steal**.
stolid ['stɔlɪd] *a* impassible, flegmatique.
stomach ['stʌmək] *n* estomac *m*; (*abdomen*) ventre *m* // *vt* supporter, digérer; **~ ache** *n* mal *m* à l'estomac *or* au ventre.
stone [stəun] *n* pierre *f*; (*pebble*) caillou *m*, galet *m*; (*in fruit*) noyau *m*; (MED) calcul *m*; (*weight*) *mesure de poids = 6.348 kg.*; *14 pounds* // *cpd* de *or* en pierre // *vt* dénoyauter; **~-cold** *a* complètement froid(e); **~-deaf** *a* sourd(e) comme un pot; **~mason** *n* tailleur *m* de pierre(s); **~work** *n* maçonnerie *f*; **stony** *n* pierreux(euse), rocailleux(euse).
stood [stud] *pt,pp of* **stand.**
stool [stu:l] *n* tabouret *m*.
stoop [stu:p] *vi* (*also*: **have a ~**) être voûté(e); (*bend*) se baisser, se courber.
stop [stɔp] *n* arrêt *m*; halte *f*; (*in punctuation*) point *m* // *vt* arrêter; (*break off*) interrompre; (*also*: **put a ~ to**) mettre fin à // *vi* s'arrêter; (*rain, noise etc*) cesser, s'arrêter; **to ~ doing sth** cesser *or* arrêter de faire qch; **to ~ dead** *vi* s'arrêter net; **to ~ off** *vi* faire une courte halte; **to ~ up** *vt* (*hole*) boucher; **~lights** *npl* (AUT) signaux *mpl* de stop, feux *mpl* arrière; **~over** *n* halte *f*; (AVIAT) escale *f*.
stoppage ['stɔpɪdʒ] *n* arrêt *m*; (*of pay*) retenue *f*; (*strike*) arrêt de travail.
stopper ['stɔpə*] *n* bouchon *m*.
stop-press ['stɔp'prɛs] *n* nouvelles *fpl* de dernière heure.
stopwatch ['stɔpwɔtʃ] *n* chronomètre *m*.
storage ['stɔ:rɪdʒ] *n* emmagasinage *m*; (COMPUTERS) mise *f* en mémoire *or* réserve.
store [stɔ:*] *n* provision *f*, réserve *f*; (*depot*) entrepôt *m*; (*large shop*) grand magasin // *vt* emmagasiner; **to ~ up** *vt* mettre en réserve, emmagasiner; **~room** *n* réserve *f*, magasin *m*.
storey, story (*US*) ['stɔ:rɪ] *n* étage *m*.
stork [stɔ:k] *n* cigogne *f*.
storm [stɔ:m] *n* orage *m*, tempête *f*; ouragan *m* // *vi* (*fig*) fulminer // *vt* prendre d'assaut; **~ cloud** *n* nuage *m* d'orage; **~y** *a* orageux(euse).
story ['stɔ:rɪ] *n* histoire *f*; récit *m*; (*US*) = **storey**; **~book** *n* livre *m* d'histoires *or* de contes; **~teller** *n* conteur/euse.
stout [staut] *a* solide; (*brave*) intrépide; (*fat*) gros(se), corpulent(e) // *n* bière brune.
stove [stəuv] *n* (*for cooking*) fourneau *m*; (*: small*) réchaud *m*; (*for heating*) poêle *m*.
stow [stəu] *vt* ranger; cacher; **~away** *n* passager/ère clandestin(e).
straddle ['strædl] *vt* enjamber, être à cheval sur.
strafe [strɑ:f] *vt* mitrailler.
straggle ['strægl] *vi* être (*or* marcher) en désordre; **~d along the coast** disséminé(e) tout au long de la côte; **~r** *n* traînard/e; **straggling, straggly** *a* (*hair*) en désordre.
straight [streɪt] *a* droit(e); (*frank*) honnête, franc(he) // *ad* (tout) droit; (*drink*) sec, sans eau // *n*: **the ~** la ligne droite; **to put** *or* **get ~** mettre en ordre, mettre de l'ordre dans; **~ away, ~off** (*at once*) tout de suite; **~ off, ~ out** sans hésiter; **~en** *vt* (*also*: **~en out**) redresser; **~forward** *a* simple; honnête, direct(e).
strain [streɪn] *n* (TECH) tension *f*; pression *f*; (*physical*) effort *m*; (*mental*) tension (nerveuse); (MED) entorse *f*; (*streak, trace*) tendance *f*; élément *m* // *vt* tendre fortement; mettre à l'épreuve; (*filter*) passer, filtrer // *vi* peiner, fournir un gros effort; **~s** *npl* (MUS) accords *mpl*, accents *mpl*; **~ed** *a* (*laugh etc*) forcé(e), contraint(e); (*relations*) tendu(e); **~er** *n* passoire *f*.
strait [streɪt] *n* (GEO) détroit *m*; **~ jacket** *n* camisole *f* de force; **~-laced** *a* collet monté *inv*.
strand [strænd] *n* (*of thread*) fil *m*, brin *m* // *vt* (*boat*) échouer; **~ed** *a* en rade, en plan.
strange [streɪndʒ] *a* (*not known*) inconnu(e); (*odd*) étrange, bizarre; **~ly** *ad* étrangement, bizarrement; **~r** *n* inconnu/e; étranger/ère.
strangle ['stræŋgl] *vt* étrangler; **~hold** *n* (*fig*) emprise totale, mainmise *f*; **strangulation** [-'leɪʃən] *n* strangulation *f*.
strap [stræp] *n* lanière *f*, courroie *f*, sangle *f*; (*of slip, dress*) bretelle *f* // *vt* attacher (avec une courroie *etc*); (*child etc*) administrer une correction à.
strapping ['stræpɪŋ] *a* bien découplé(e), costaud(e).
strata ['strɑ:tə] *npl of* **stratum**.
stratagem ['strætɪdʒəm] *n* strategème *m*.
strategic [strə'ti:dʒɪk] *a* stratégique.
strategist ['strætɪdʒɪst] *n* stratège *m*.
strategy ['strætɪdʒɪ] *n* stratégie *f*.
stratosphere ['strætəsfɪə*] *n* stratosphère *f*.
stratum, *pl* **strata** ['strɑ:təm, 'strɑ:tə] *n* strate *f*, couche *f*.
straw [strɔ:] *n* paille *f*.
strawberry ['strɔ:bərɪ] *n* fraise *f*; (*plant*) fraisier *m*.
stray [streɪ] *a* (*animal*) perdu(e), errant(e) // *vi* s'égarer; **~ bullet** *n* balle perdue.
streak [stri:k] *n* raie *f*, bande *f*, filet *m*; (*fig: of madness etc*): **a ~ of** une *or* des tendance(s) à // *vt* zébrer, strier // *vi*: **to ~ past** passer à toute allure; **~y** *a* zébré(e), strié(e); **~y bacon** *n* ≈ lard *m* (maigre).
stream [stri:m] *n* ruisseau *m*; courant *m*, flot *m*; (*of people*) défilé ininterrompu, flot // *vt* (SCOL) répartir par niveau // *vi*

ruisseler ; **to ~ in/out** entrer/sortir à flots.

streamer ['stri:mə*] *n* serpentin *m*, banderole *f*.

streamlined ['stri:mlaɪnd] *a* (AVIAT) fuselé(e), profilé(e) ; (AUT) aérodynamique ; (*fig*) rationalisé(e).

street [stri:t] *n* rue *f*; **~car** *n* (*US*) tramway *m* ; **~ lamp** *n* réverbère *m*.

strength [strɛŋθ] *n* force *f* ; (*of girder, knot etc*) solidité *f* ; **~en** *vt* fortifier ; renforcer ; consolider.

strenuous ['strɛnjuəs] *a* vigoureux(euse), énergique ; (*tiring*) ardu(e), fatigant(e).

stress [strɛs] *n* (*force, pressure*) pression *f* ; (*mental strain*) tension (nerveuse) ; (*accent*) accent *m* // *vt* insister sur, souligner.

stretch [strɛtʃ] *n* (*of sand etc*) étendue *f* // *vi* s'étirer ; (*extend*): **to ~ to/as far as** s'étendre jusqu'à // *vt* tendre, étirer ; (*spread*) étendre ; (*fig*) pousser (au maximum) ; **at a ~** sans discontinuer, sans interruption ; **to ~ a muscle** se distendre un muscle ; **to ~ out** *vi* s'étendre // *vt* (*arm etc*) allonger, tendre ; (*to spread*) étendre ; **to ~ out for something** allonger la main pour prendre qch.

stretcher ['strɛtʃə*] *n* brancard *m*, civière *f*.

strewn [stru:n] *a*: **~ with** jonché(e) de.

stricken ['strɪkən] *a* très éprouvé(e) ; dévasté(e) ; **~ with** frappé(e) *or* atteint(e) de.

strict [strɪkt] *a* strict(e) ; **~ly** *ad* strictement ; **~ness** *n* sévérité *f*.

stride [straɪd] *n* grand pas, enjambée *f* // *vi* (*pt* **strode**, *pp* **stridden** [strəud, 'strɪdn]) marcher à grands pas.

strident ['straɪdnt] *a* strident(e).

strife [straɪf] *n* conflit *m*, dissensions *fpl*.

strike [straɪk] *n* grève *f* ; (*of oil etc*) découverte *f* ; (*attack*) raid *m* // *vb* (*pt,pp* **struck** [strʌk]) *vt* frapper ; (*oil etc*) trouver, découvrir // *vi* faire grève ; (*attack*) attaquer ; (*clock*) sonner ; **to ~ a match** frotter une allumette ; **to ~ down** *vt* (*fig*) terrasser ; **to ~ out** *vt* rayer ; **to ~ up** *vt* (MUS) se mettre à jouer ; **to ~ up a friendship with** se lier d'amitié avec ; **~breaker** *n* briseur *m* de grève ; **~r** *n* gréviste *m/f* ; (SPORT) buteur *m* ; **striking** *a* frappant(e), saisissant(e).

string [strɪŋ] *n* ficelle *f*, fil *m* ; (*row*) rang *m* ; chapelet *m* ; file *f* ; (MUS) corde *f* // *vt* (*pt,pp* **strung** [strʌŋ]): **to ~ out** échelonner ; **the ~s** *npl* (MUS) les instruments *mpl* à corde ; **~ bean** *n* haricot vert ; **~(ed) instrument** *n* (MUS) instrument *m* à cordes.

stringent ['strɪndʒənt] *a* rigoureux(euse) ; (*need*) impérieux(euse).

strip [strɪp] *n* bande *f* // *vt* déshabiller ; dégarnir, dépouiller ; (*also*: **~ down**: *machine*) démonter // *vi* se déshabiller ; **~ cartoon** *n* bande dessinée.

stripe [straɪp] *n* raie *f*, rayure *f* ; **~d** *a* rayé(e), à rayures.

strip light ['strɪplaɪt] *n* (tube *m* au) néon *m*.

stripper ['strɪpə*] *n* strip-teaseuse *f*.

striptease ['strɪpti:z] *n* strip-tease *m*.

strive, *pt* **strove**, *pp* **striven** [straɪv, strəuv, 'strɪvn] *vi*: **to ~ to do** s'efforcer de faire.

strode [strəud] *pt of* **stride**.

stroke [strəuk] *n* coup *m* ; (MED) attaque *f* ; (*caress*) caresse *f* // *vt* caresser ; **at a ~** d'un (seul) coup ; **on the ~ of 5** à 5 heures sonnantes ; **a 2-~ engine** un moteur à 2 temps.

stroll [strəul] *n* petite promenade // *vi* flâner, se promener nonchalamment.

strong [strɔŋ] *a* fort(e) ; vigoureux(euse) ; solide ; vif(vive) ; **they are 50 ~** ils sont au nombre de 50 ; **~hold** *n* bastion *m* ; **~ly** *ad* fortement, avec force ; vigoureusement ; solidement ; **~room** *n* chambre forte.

strove [strəuv] *pt of* **strive**.

struck [strʌk] *pt,pp of* **strike**.

structural ['strʌktʃərəl] *a* structural(e) ; (CONSTR) de construction ; affectant les parties portantes ; **~ly** *ad* du point de vue de la construction.

structure ['strʌktʃə*] *n* structure *f* ; (*building*) construction *f* ; édifice *m*.

struggle ['strʌgl] *n* lutte *f* // *vi* lutter, se battre.

strum [strʌm] *vt* (*guitar*) gratter de.

strung [strʌŋ] *pt,pp of* **string**.

strut [strʌt] *n* étai *m*, support *m* // *vi* se pavaner.

stub [stʌb] *n* bout *m* ; (*of ticket etc*) talon *m* ; **to ~ out** *vt* écraser.

stubble ['stʌbl] *n* chaume *m* ; (*on chin*) barbe *f* de plusieurs jours.

stubborn ['stʌbən] *a* têtu(e), obstiné(e), opiniâtre.

stubby ['stʌbɪ] *a* trapu(e) ; gros(se) et court(e).

stuck [stʌk] *pt,pp of* **stick** // *a* (*jammed*) bloqué(e), coincé(e) ; **~-up** *a* prétentieux(euse).

stud [stʌd] *n* clou *m* (à grosse tête) ; bouton *m* de col ; (*of horses*) écurie *f*, haras *m* ; (*also*: **~ horse**) étalon *m* // *vt* (*fig*): **~ded with** parsemé(e) *or* criblé(e) de.

student ['stju:dənt] *n* étudiant/e // *cpd* estudiantin(e) ; universitaire ; d'étudiant.

studied ['stʌdɪd] *a* étudié(e), calculé(e).

studio ['stju:dɪəu] *n* studio *m*, atelier *m*.

studious ['stju:dɪəs] *a* studieux(euse), appliqué(e) ; (*studied*) étudié(e) ; **~ly** *ad* (*carefully*) soigneusement.

study ['stʌdɪ] *n* étude *f* ; (*room*) bureau *m* // *vt* étudier ; examiner // *vi* étudier, faire ses études.

stuff [stʌf] *n* chose(s) *f(pl)*, truc *m* ; affaires *fpl* ; (*substance*) substance *f* // *vt* rembourrer ; (CULIN) farcir ; **~ing** *n* bourre *f*, rembourrage *m* ; (CULIN) farce *f* ; **~y** *a* (*room*) mal ventilé(e) *or* aéré(e) ; (*ideas*) vieux jeu *inv*.

stumble ['stʌmbl] *vi* trébucher ; **to ~ across** (*fig*) tomber sur ; **stumbling block** *n* pierre *f* d'achoppement.

stump [stʌmp] *n* souche *f* ; (*of limb*) moignon *m* // *vt*: **to be ~ed** sécher, ne pas savoir que répondre.

stun [stʌn] *vt* étourdir ; abasourdir.

stung [stʌŋ] *pt, pp of* **sting**.
stunk [stʌŋk] *pp of* **stink**.
stunning ['stʌnɪŋ] *a* étourdissant(e), stupéfiant(e).
stunt [stʌnt] *n* tour *m* de force; truc *m* publicitaire; (AVIAT) acrobatie *f* // *vt* retarder, arrêter; **~ed** *a* rabougri(e); **~man** *n* cascadeur *m*.
stupefy ['stju:pɪfaɪ] *vt* étourdir; abrutir; (*fig*) stupéfier.
stupendous [stju:'pɛndəs] *a* prodigieux(euse), fantastique.
stupid ['stju:pɪd] *a* stupide, bête; **~ity** [-'pɪdɪtɪ] *n* stupidité *f*, bêtise *f*; **~ly** *ad* stupidement, bêtement.
stupor ['stju:pə*] *n* stupeur *f*.
sturdy ['stə:dɪ] *a* robuste, vigoureux(euse); solide.
sturgeon ['stə:dʒən] *n* esturgeon *m*.
stutter ['stʌtə*] *n* bégaiement *m* // *vi* bégayer.
sty [staɪ] *n* (*of pigs*) porcherie *f*.
stye [staɪ] *n* (MED) orgelet *m*.
style [staɪl] *n* style *m*; (*distinction*) allure *f*, cachet *m*, style *m*; **stylish** *a* élégant(e), chic *inv*.
stylized ['staɪlaɪzd] *a* stylisé(e).
stylus ['staɪləs] *n* (*of record player*) pointe *f* de lecture.
suave [swɑ:v] *a* doucereux(euse), onctueux(euse).
sub... [sʌb] *prefix* sub..., sous-; **subconscious** *a* subconscient(e) // *n* subconscient *m*; **subdivide** *vt* subdiviser; **subdivision** *n* subdivision *f*.
subdue [səb'dju:] *vt* subjuguer, soumettre; **~d** *a* contenu(e), atténué(e); (*light*) tamisé(e); (*person*) qui a perdu de son entrain.
subject *n* ['sʌbdʒɪkt] sujet *m*; (SCOL) matière *f* // *vt* [səb'dʒɛkt]: **to ~ to** soumettre à; exposer à; **to be ~ to** (*law*) être soumis(e) à; (*disease*) être sujet(te) à; **~ion** [-'dʒɛkʃən] soumission *f*, sujétion *f*; **~ive** *a* subjectif(ive); (LING) sujet(te); **~ matter** *n* sujet *m*; contenu *m*.
sub judice [sʌb'dju:dɪsɪ] *a* devant les tribunaux.
subjunctive [səb'dʒʌŋktɪv] *a* subjonctif(ive) // *n* subjonctif *m*.
sublet [sʌb'lɛt] *vt* sous-louer.
sublime [sə'blaɪm] *a* sublime.
submachine gun ['sʌbmə'ʃi:ngʌn] *n* fusil-mitrailleur *m*.
submarine [sʌbmə'ri:n] *n* sous-marin *m*.
submerge [səb'mə:dʒ] *vt* submerger; immerger // *vi* plonger.
submission [səb'mɪʃən] *n* soumission *f*.
submissive [səb'mɪsɪv] *a* soumis(e).
submit [səb'mɪt] *vt* soumettre // *vi* se soumettre.
subordinate [sə'bɔ:dɪnət] *a,n* subordonné(e).
subpoena [səb'pi:nə] (LAW) *n* citation *f*, assignation *f* // *vt* citer *or* assigner (à comparaître).
subscribe [səb'skraɪb] *vi* cotiser; **to ~ to** (*opinion, fund*) souscrire à; (*newspaper*) s'abonner à; être abonné(e) à; **~r** *n* (*to periodical, telephone*) abonné/e.
subscription [səb'skrɪpʃən] *n* souscription *f*; abonnement *m*.
subsequent ['sʌbsɪkwənt] *a* ultérieur(e), suivant(e); consécutif(ive); **~ly** *ad* par la suite.
subside [səb'saɪd] *vi* s'affaisser; (*flood*) baisser; (*wind*) tomber; **~nce** [-'saɪdns] *n* affaissement *m*.
subsidiary [səb'sɪdɪərɪ] *a* subsidiaire; accessoire // *n* filiale *f*.
subsidize ['sʌbsɪdaɪz] *vt* subventionner.
subsidy ['sʌbsɪdɪ] *n* subvention *f*.
subsistence [səb'sɪstəns] *n* existence *f*, subsistance *f*.
substance ['sʌbstəns] *n* substance *f*; (*fig*) essentiel *m*; **a man of ~** un homme jouissant d'une certaine fortune.
substandard [sʌb'stændəd] *a* de qualité inférieure.
substantial [səb'stænʃl] *a* substantiel(le); (*fig*) important(e); **~ly** *ad* considérablement; en grande partie.
substantiate [səb'stænʃɪeɪt] *vt* étayer, fournir des preuves à l'appui de.
substitute ['sʌbstɪtju:t] *n* (*person*) remplaçant/e; (*thing*) succédané *m* // *vt*: **to ~ sth/sb for** substituer qch/qn à, remplacer par qch/qn; **substitution** [-'tju:ʃən] *n* substitution *f*.
subterfuge ['sʌbtəfju:dʒ] *n* subterfuge *m*.
subterranean [sʌbtə'reɪnɪən] *a* souterrain(e).
subtitle ['sʌbtaɪtl] *n* (CINEMA) sous-titre *m*.
subtle ['sʌtl] *a* subtil(e); **~ty** *n* subtilité *f*.
subtract [səb'trækt] *vt* soustraire, retrancher; **~ion** [-'trækʃən] *n* soustraction *f*.
subtropical [sʌb'trɔpɪkl] *a* subtropical(e).
suburb ['sʌbə:b] *n* faubourg *m*; **the ~s** la banlieue; **~an** [sə'bə:bən] *a* de banlieue, suburbain(e).
subvention [səb'vɛnʃən] *n* (*US*: *subsidy*) subvention *f*.
subversive [səb'və:sɪv] *a* subversif(ive).
subway ['sʌbweɪ] *n* (*US*) métro *m*; (*Brit*) passage souterrain.
sub-zero [sʌb'zɪərəu] *a* au-dessous de zéro.
succeed [sək'si:d] *vi* réussir; avoir du succès // *vt* succéder à; **to ~ in doing** réussir à faire; **~ing** *a* (*following*) suivant(e).
success [sək'sɛs] *n* succès *m*; réussite *f*; **~ful** *a* (*venture*) couronné(e) de succès; **to be ~ful (in doing)** réussir (à faire); **~fully** *ad* avec succès.
succession [sək'sɛʃən] *n* succession *f*.
successive [sək'sɛsɪv] *a* successif(ive); consécutif(ive).
successor [sək'sɛsə*] *n* successeur *m*.
succinct [sək'sɪŋkt] *a* succinct(e), bref(brève).
succulent ['sʌkjulənt] *a* succulent(e).
succumb [sə'kʌm] *vi* succomber.
such [sʌtʃ] *a, det* tel(telle); (*of that kind*): **~ a book** un livre de ce genre *or* pareil, un tel livre; **~ books** des livres de ce genre *or* pareils, de tels livres; (*so much*): **~ courage** un tel courage; **~ a long trip** un si long voyage; **~ good books** de si

bons livres ; ~ **a long trip that** un voyage si *or* tellement long que ; ~ **a lot of** tellement *or* tant de ; **making** ~ **a noise that** faisant un tel bruit que *or* tellement de bruit que ; ~ **as** (*like*) tel(telle) que, comme ; **a noise** ~ **as to** un bruit de nature à ; **as** ~ *ad* en tant que tel(telle), à proprement parler ; **~-and-~** *det* tel(telle) ou tel(telle).

suck [sʌk] *vt* sucer ; (*breast, bottle*) téter ; **~er** *n* (BOT, ZOOL, TECH) ventouse *f* ; (*col*) naïf/ïve, poire *f*.

suckle ['sʌkl] *vt* allaiter.

suction ['sʌkʃən] *n* succion *f*.

sudden ['sʌdn] *a* soudain(e), subit(e) ; **all of a** ~ soudain, tout à coup ; **~ly** *ad* brusquement, tout à coup, soudain.

suds [sʌdz] *npl* eau savonneuse.

sue [su:] *vt* poursuivre en justice, intenter un procès à.

suede [sweɪd] *n* daim *m*, cuir suédé // *cpd* de daim.

suet ['suɪt] *n* graisse *f* de rognon *or* de bœuf.

Suez Canal ['su:ɪzkə'næl] *n* canal *m* de Suez.

suffer ['sʌfə*] *vt* souffrir, subir ; (*bear*) tolérer, supporter // *vi* souffrir ; **~er** *n* malade *m/f* ; victime *m/f* ; **~ing** *n* souffrance(s) *f(pl)*.

suffice [sə'faɪs] *vi* suffire.

sufficient [sə'fɪʃənt] *a* suffisant(e) ; ~ **money** suffisamment d'argent ; **~ly** *ad* suffisamment, assez.

suffix ['sʌfɪks] *n* suffixe *m*.

suffocate ['sʌfəkeɪt] *vi* suffoquer ; étouffer ; **suffocation** [-'keɪʃən] *n* suffocation *f* ; (MED) asphyxie *f*.

sugar ['ʃugə*] *n* sucre *m* // *vt* sucrer ; ~ **beet** *n* betterave sucrière ; ~ **cane** *n* canne *f* à sucre ; **~y** *a* sucré(e).

suggest [sə'dʒɛst] *vt* suggérer, proposer ; dénoter ; **~ion** [-'dʒɛstʃən] *n* suggestion *f* ; **~ive** *a* suggestif(ive).

suicidal [suɪ'saɪdl] *a* suicidaire.

suicide ['suɪsaɪd] *n* suicide *m*.

suit [su:t] *n* (*man's*) costume *m*, complet *m* ; (*woman's*) tailleur *m*, ensemble *m* ; (CARDS) couleur *f* // *vt* aller à ; convenir à ; (*adapt*): **to** ~ **sth to** adapter *or* approprier qch à ; **~able** *a* qui convient ; approprié(e) ; **~ably** *ad* comme il se doit (*or* se devait *etc*), convenablement.

suitcase ['su:tkeɪs] *n* valise *f*.

suite [swi:t] *n* (*of rooms, also* MUS) suite *f* ; (*furniture*): **bedroom/dining room** ~ (ensemble *m* de) chambre *f* à coucher/salle *f* à manger.

sulfur ['sʌlfə*] *etc* (*US*) = **sulphur** *etc*.

sulk [sʌlk] *vi* bouder ; **~y** *a* boudeur(euse), maussade.

sullen ['sʌlən] *a* renfrogné(e), maussade ; morne.

sulphur, sulfur (*US*) ['sʌlfə*] *n* soufre *m* ; **~ic** [-'fjuərɪk] *a*: **~ic acid** acide *m* sulfurique.

sultan ['sʌltən] *n* sultan *m*.

sultana [sʌl'tɑ:nə] *n* (*fruit*) raisin sec de Smyrne.

sultry ['sʌltrɪ] *a* étouffant(e).

sum [sʌm] *n* somme *f* ; (SCOL *etc*) calcul *m* ; *f* ; **to** ~ **up** *vt,vi* résumer.

summarize ['sʌməraɪz] *vt* résumer.

summary ['sʌmərɪ] *n* résumé *m* // *a* (*justice*) sommaire.

summer ['sʌmə*] *n* été *m* // *cpd* d'été, estival(e) ; **~house** *n* (*in garden*) pavillon *m* ; **~time** *n* (*season*) été *m* ; ~ **time** *n* (*by clock*) heure *f* d'été.

summit ['sʌmɪt] *n* sommet *m* ; ~ **(conference)** *n* (conférence *f* au) sommet *m*.

summon ['sʌmən] *vt* appeler, convoquer ; **to** ~ **up** *vt* rassembler, faire appel à ; **~s** *n* citation *f*, assignation *f* // *vt* citer, assigner.

sump [sʌmp] *n* (AUT) carter *m*.

sumptuous ['sʌmptjuəs] *a* somptueux(euse).

sun [sʌn] *n* soleil *m* ; **in the** ~ au soleil ; **~bathe** *vi* prendre un bain de soleil ; **~burnt** *a* bronzé(e), hâlé(e) ; (*painfully*) brûlé(e) par le soleil ; ~ **cream** *n* crème *f* (anti-)solaire.

Sunday ['sʌndɪ] *n* dimanche *m*.

sundial ['sʌndaɪəl] *n* cadran *m* solaire.

sundry ['sʌndrɪ] *a* divers(e), différent(e) ; **all and** ~ tout le monde, n'importe qui ; **sundries** *npl* articles divers.

sunflower ['sʌnflauə*] *n* tournesol *m*.

sung [sʌŋ] *pp of* **sing**.

sunglasses ['sʌnglɑ:sɪz] *npl* lunettes *fpl* de soleil.

sunk [sʌŋk] *pp of* **sink** ; **~en** *a* submergé(e) ; creux(euse).

sun: **~light** *n* (lumière *f* du) soleil *m* ; **~lit** *a* ensoleillé(e) ; **~ny** *a* ensoleillé(e) ; (*fig*) épanoui(e), radieux(euse) ; **~rise** *n* lever *m* du soleil ; **~set** *n* coucher *m* du soleil ; **~shade** *n* (*over table*) parasol *m* ; **~shine** *n* (lumière *f* du) soleil *m* ; **~spot** *n* tache *f* solaire ; **~stroke** *n* insolation *f*, coup *m* de soleil ; **~tan** *n* bronzage *m* ; **~tan oil** *n* huile *f* solaire ; **~trap** *n* coin très ensoleillé.

super ['su:pə*] *a* (*col*) formidable.

superannuation [su:pərænju'eɪʃən] *n* cotisations *fpl* pour la pension.

superb [su:'pə:b] *a* superbe, magnifique.

supercilious [su:pə'sɪlɪəs] *a* hautain(e), dédaigneux(euse).

superficial [su:pə'fɪʃəl] *a* superficiel(le) ; **~ly** *ad* superficiellement.

superfluous [su'pə:fluəs] *a* superflu(e).

superhuman [su:pə'hju:mən] *a* surhumain(e).

superimpose ['su:pərɪm'pəuz] *vt* superposer.

superintendent [su:pərɪn'tɛndənt] *n* directeur/trice ; (POLICE) ≈ commissaire *m*.

superior [su'pɪərɪə*] *a,n* supérieur(e) ; **~ity** [-'ɔrɪtɪ] *n* supériorité *f*.

superlative [su'pə:lətɪv] *a* sans pareil(le), suprême // *n* (LING) superlatif *m*.

superman ['su:pəmæn] *n* surhomme *m*.

supermarket ['su:pəmɑ:kɪt] *n* supermarché *m*.

supernatural [su:pə'nætʃərəl] *a* surnaturel(le).

superpower ['su:pəpauə*] *n* (POL) grande puissance.

supersede [su:pə'si:d] *vt* remplacer, supplanter.

supersonic ['su:pə'sɔnɪk] *a* supersonique.
superstition [su:pə'stɪʃən] *n* superstition *f*.
superstitious [su:pə'stɪʃəs] *a* superstitieux(euse).
supertanker ['su:pətæŋkə*] *n* pétrolier géant, superpétrolier *m*.
supervise ['su:pəvaɪz] *vt* surveiller; diriger; **supervision** [-'vɪʒən] *n* surveillance *f*; contrôle *m*; **supervisor** *n* surveillant/e; (*in shop*) chef *m* de rayon; **supervisory** *a* de surveillance.
supper ['sʌpə*] *n* dîner *m*; (*late*) souper *m*.
supple ['sʌpl] *a* souple.
supplement *n* ['sʌplɪmənt] supplément *m* // *vt* [sʌplɪ'mɛnt] ajouter à, compléter; **~ary** [-'mɛntərɪ] *a* supplémentaire.
supplier [sə'plaɪə*] *n* fournisseur *m*.
supply [sə'plaɪ] *vt* (*provide*) fournir; (*equip*): **to ~ (with)** approvisionner *or* ravitailler (en); fournir (en); alimenter (en) // *n* provision *f*, réserve *f*; (*supplying*) approvisionnement *m*; (TECH) alimentation *f* // *cpd* (*teacher etc*) suppléant(e); **supplies** *npl* (*food*) vivres *mpl*; (MIL) subsistances *fpl*; **~ and demand** l'offre *f* et la demande.
support [sə'pɔ:t] *n* (*moral, financial etc*) soutien *m*, appui *m*; (TECH) support *m*, soutien // *vt* soutenir, supporter; (*financially*) subvenir aux besoins de; (*uphold*) être pour, être partisan de, appuyer; (*endure*) supporter, tolérer; **~er** *n* (POL *etc*) partisan/e; (SPORT) supporter *m*.
suppose [sə'pəuz] *vt, vi* supposer; imaginer; **to be ~d to do** être censé(e) faire; **~dly** [sə'pəuzɪdlɪ] *ad* soi-disant; **supposing** *cj* si, à supposer que + *sub*; **supposition** [sʌpə'zɪʃən] *n* supposition *f*, hypothèse *f*.
suppress [sə'prɛs] *vt* réprimer; supprimer; étouffer; refouler; **~ion** [sə'prɛʃən] *n* suppression *f*, répression *f*; **~or** *n* (ELEC *etc*) dispositif *m* antiparasite.
supremacy [su'prɛməsɪ] *n* suprématie *f*.
supreme [su'pri:m] *a* suprême.
surcharge ['sə:tʃɑ:dʒ] *n* surcharge *f*; (*extra tax*) surtaxe *f*.
sure [ʃuə*] *a* (*gen*) sûr(e); (*definite, convinced*) sûr(e), certain(e); **~!** (*of course*) bien sûr!; **~ enough** effectivement; **to make ~ of** s'assurer de; vérifier; **~-footed** *a* au pied sûr; **~ly** *ad* sûrement; certainement.
surety ['ʃuərətɪ] *n* caution *f*.
surf [sə:f] *n* ressac *m*.
surface ['sə:fɪs] *n* surface *f* // *vt* (*road*) poser le revêtement de // *vi* remonter à la surface; faire surface; **~ mail** *n* courrier *m* par voie de terre (*or* maritime).
surfboard ['sə:fbɔ:d] *n* planche *f* de surf.
surfeit ['sə:fɪt] *n*: **a ~ of** un excès de; une indigestion de.
surfing ['sə:fɪŋ] *n* surf *m*.
surge [sə:dʒ] *n* vague *f*, montée *f* // *vi* déferler.
surgeon ['sə:dʒən] *n* chirurgien *m*.
surgery ['sə:dʒərɪ] *n* chirurgie *f*; (*room*) cabinet *m* (de consultation); **to undergo ~** être opéré(e); **~ hours** *npl* heures *fpl* de consultation.
surgical ['sə:dʒɪkl] *a* chirurgical(e); **~ spirit** *n* alcool *m* à 90s.
surly ['sə:lɪ] *a* revêche, maussade.
surmise [sə:'maɪz] *vt* présumer, conjecturer.
surmount [sə:'maunt] *vt* surmonter.
surname ['sə:neɪm] *n* nom *m* de famille.
surpass [sə:'pɑ:s] *vt* surpasser, dépasser.
surplus ['sə:pləs] *n* surplus *m*, excédent *m* // *a* en surplus, de trop.
surprise [sə'praɪz] *n* (*gen*) surprise *f*; (*astonishment*) étonnement *m* // *vt* surprendre; étonner; **surprising** *a* surprenant(e), étonnant(e).
surrealist [sə'rɪəlɪst] *a* surréaliste.
surrender [sə'rɛndə*] *n* reddition *f*, capitulation *f* // *vi* se rendre, capituler.
surreptitious [sʌrəp'tɪʃəs] *a* subreptice, furtif(ive).
surround [sə'raund] *vt* entourer; (MIL *etc*) encercler; **~ing** *a* environnant(e); **~ings** *npl* environs *mpl*, alentours *mpl*.
surveillance [sə:'veɪləns] *n* surveillance *f*.
survey *n* ['sə:veɪ] enquête *f*, étude *f*; (*in housebuying etc*) inspection *f*, (rapport *m* d')expertise *f*; (*of land*) levé *m* // *vt* [sə:'veɪ] passer en revue; enquêter sur; inspecter; **~ing** *n* (*of land*) arpentage *m*; **~or** *n* expert *m*; (arpenteur *m*) géomètre *m*.
survival [sə'vaɪvl] *n* survie *f*; (*relic*) vestige *m*.
survive [sə'vaɪv] *vi* survivre; (*custom etc*) subsister // *vt* survivre à, réchapper de; (*person*) survivre à; **survivor** *n* survivant/e.
susceptible [sə'sɛptəbl] *a*: **~ (to)** sensible (à); (*disease*) prédisposé(e) (à).
suspect *a, n* ['sʌspɛkt] suspect(e) // *vt* [səs'pɛkt] soupçonner, suspecter.
suspend [səs'pɛnd] *vt* suspendre; **~ed sentence** *n* condamnation *f* avec sursis; **~er belt** *n* porte-jarretelles *m inv*; **~ers** *npl* jarretelles *fpl*; (*US*) bretelles *fpl*.
suspense [səs'pɛns] *n* attente *f*; (*in film etc*) suspense *m*.
suspension [səs'pɛnʃən] *n* (*gen* AUT) suspension *f*; (*of driving licence*) retrait *m* provisoire; **~ bridge** *n* pont suspendu.
suspicion [səs'pɪʃən] *n* soupçon(s) *m(pl)*.
suspicious [səs'pɪʃəs] *a* (*suspecting*) soupçonneux(euse), méfiant(e); (*causing suspicion*) suspect(e).
sustain [səs'teɪn] *vt* supporter; soutenir; corroborer; (*suffer*) subir; recevoir; **~ed** *a* (*effort*) soutenu(e), prolongé(e).
sustenance ['sʌstɪnəns] *n* nourriture *f*; moyens *mpl* de subsistance.
swab [swɔb] *n* (MED) tampon *m*; prélèvement *m*.
swagger ['swægə*] *vi* plastronner, parader.
swallow ['swɔləu] *n* (*bird*) hirondelle *f*; (*of food etc*) gorgée *f* // *vt* avaler; (*fig*) gober; **to ~ up** *vt* engloutir.
swam [swæm] *pt of* **swim**.
swamp [swɔmp] *n* marais *m*, marécage *m* // *vt* submerger; **~y** *a* marécageux(euse).

swan [swɔn] *n* cygne *m*.
swap [swɔp] *n* échange *m*, troc *m* // *vt*: **to ~ (for)** échanger (contre), troquer (contre).
swarm [swɔ:m] *n* essaim *m* // *vi* fourmiller, grouiller.
swarthy ['swɔ:ðɪ] *a* basané(e), bistré(e).
swastika ['swɔstɪkə] *n* croix gammée.
swat [swɔt] *vt* écraser.
sway [sweɪ] *vi* se balancer, osciller; tanguer // *vt* (*influence*) influencer.
swear, *pt* **swore,** *pp* **sworn** [swɛə*, swɔ:*, swɔ:n] *vi* jurer; **to ~ to sth** jurer de qch; **~word** *n* gros mot, juron *m*.
sweat [swɛt] *n* sueur *f*, transpiration *f* // *vi* suer; **in a ~** en sueur.
sweater ['swɛtə*] *n* tricot *m*, pull *m*.
sweaty ['swɛtɪ] *a* en sueur, moite *or* mouillé(e) de sueur.
swede [swi:d] *n* rutabaga *m*.
Swede [swi:d] *n* Suédois/e.
Sweden ['swi:dn] *n* Suède *f*.
Swedish ['swi:dɪʃ] *a* suédois(e) // *n* (LING) suédois *m*.
sweep [swi:p] *n* coup *m* de balai; (*curve*) grande courbe; (*range*) champ *m*; (*also*: **chimney ~**) ramoneur *m* // *vb* (*pt, pp* **swept** [swɛpt]) *vt* balayer // *vi* avancer majestueusement *or* rapidement; s'élancer; s'étendre; **to ~ away** *vt* balayer; entraîner; emporter; **to ~ past** *vi* passer majestueusement *or* rapidement; **to ~ up** *vt, vi* balayer; **~ing** *a* (*gesture*) large; circulaire; **a ~ing statement** une généralisation hâtive.
sweet [swi:t] *n* dessert *m*; (*candy*) bonbon *m* // *a* doux(douce); (*not savoury*) sucré(e); (*fresh*) frais(fraîche), pur(e); (*fig*) agréable, doux; gentil(le); mignon(ne); **~bread** *n* ris *m* de veau; **~corn** *n* maïs sucré; **~en** *vt* sucrer; adoucir; **~heart** *n* amoureux/euse; **~ly** *ad* gentiment; mélodieusement; **~ness** *n* goût sucré; douceur *f*; **~ pea** *n* pois *m* de senteur; **to have a ~ tooth** aimer les sucreries.
swell [swɛl] *n* (*of sea*) houle *f* // *a* (*col*: *excellent*) chouette // *vb* (*pt* **~ed,** *pp* **swollen, ~ed** ['swəulən]) *vt* augmenter; grossir // *vi* grossir, augmenter; (*sound*) s'enfler; (MED) enfler; **~ing** *n* (MED) enflure *f*; grosseur *f*.
sweltering ['swɛltərɪŋ] *a* étouffant(e), oppressant(e).
swept [swɛpt] *pt,pp of* **sweep**.
swerve [swə:v] *vi* faire une embardée *or* un écart; dévier.
swift [swɪft] *n* (*bird*) martinet *m* // *a* rapide, prompt(e); **~ness** *n* rapidité *f*.
swig [swɪg] *n* (*col*: *drink*) lampée *f*.
swill [swɪl] *n* pâtée *f* // *vt* (*also*: **~ out, ~ down**) laver à grande eau.
swim [swɪm] *n*: **to go for a ~** aller nager *or* se baigner // *vb* (*pt* **swam,** *pp* **swum** [swæm, swʌm]) *vi* nager; (SPORT) faire de la natation; (*head, room*) tourner // *vt* traverser (à la nage); faire (à la nage); **~mer** *n* nageur/euse; **~ming** *n* nage *f*, natation *f*; **~ming baths** *npl* piscine *f*; **~ming cap** *n* bonnet *m* de bain; **~ming costume** *n* maillot *m* (de bain); **~ming pool** *n* piscine *f*; **~suit** *n* maillot *m* (de bain).
swindle ['swɪndl] *n* escroquerie *f* // *vt* escroquer; **~r** *n* escroc *m*.
swine [swaɪn] *n, pl inv* pourceau *m*, porc *m*; (*col!*) salaud *m* (*!*).
swing [swɪŋ] *n* balançoire *f*; (*movement*) balancement *m*, oscillations *fpl*; (MUS) swing *m*; rythme *m* // *vb* (*pt, pp* **swung** [swʌŋ]) *vt* balancer, faire osciller; (*also*: **~ round**) tourner, faire virer // *vi* se balancer, osciller; (*also*: **~ round**) virer, tourner; **to be in full ~** battre son plein; **~ bridge** *n* pont tournant; **~ door** *n* porte battante.
swingeing ['swɪndʒɪŋ] *a* écrasant(e); considérable.
swinging ['swɪŋɪŋ] *a* rythmé(e); entraînant(e).
swipe [swaɪp] *n* grand coup; gifle *f* // *vt* (*hit*) frapper à toute volée; gifler; (*col*: *steal*) piquer.
swirl [swə:l] *n* tourbillon *m* // *vi* tourbillonner, tournoyer.
swish [swɪʃ] *a* (*col*: *smart*) rupin(e) // *vi* siffler.
Swiss [swɪs] *a* suisse // *n, pl inv* Suisse/esse; **~ German** *a* suisse-allemand(e).
switch [swɪtʃ] *n* (*for light, radio etc*) bouton *m*; (*change*) changement *m*, revirement *m* // *vt* (*change*) changer; intervertir; **to ~ off** *vt* éteindre; (*engine*) arrêter; **to ~ on** *vt* allumer; (*engine, machine*) mettre en marche; **~back** *n* montagnes *fpl* russes; **~board** *n* (TEL) standard *m*; **~board operator** standardiste *m/f*.
Switzerland ['swɪtsələnd] *n* Suisse *f*.
swivel ['swɪvl] *vi* (*also*: **~ round**) pivoter, tourner.
swollen ['swəulən] *pp of* **swell** // *a* (*ankle etc*) enflé(e).
swoon [swu:n] *vi* se pâmer.
swoop [swu:p] *n* (*by police etc*) rafle *f*, descente *f* // *vi* (*also*: **~ down**) descendre en piqué, piquer.
swop [swɔp] *n, vt* = **swap**.
sword [sɔ:d] *n* épée *f*; **~fish** *n* espadon *m*.
swore [swɔ:*] *pt of* **swear**.
sworn [swɔ:n] *pp of* **swear**.
swot [swɔt] *vt, vi* bûcher, potasser.
swum [swʌm] *pp of* **swim**.
swung [swʌŋ] *pt, pp of* **swing**.
sycamore ['sɪkəmɔ:*] *n* sycomore *m*.
sycophantic [sɪkə'fæntɪk] *a* flagorneur(euse).
syllable ['sɪləbl] *n* syllabe *f*.
syllabus ['sɪləbəs] *n* programme *m*.
symbol ['sɪmbl] *n* symbole *m*; **~ic(al)** [-'bɔlɪk(l)] *a* symbolique; **~ism** *n* symbolisme *m*; **~ize** *vt* symboliser.
symmetrical [sɪ'mɛtrɪkl] *a* symétrique.
symmetry ['sɪmɪtrɪ] *n* symétrie *f*.
sympathetic [sɪmpə'θɛtɪk] *a* compatissant(e); bienveillant(e), compréhensif(ive); **~ towards** bien disposé(e) envers; **~ally** *ad* avec compassion (*or* bienveillance).
sympathize ['sɪmpəθaɪz] *vi*: **to ~ with**

sb plaindre qn ; s'associer à la douleur de qn ; **~r** *n* (*POL*) sympathisant/e.
sympathy ['sɪmpəθɪ] *n* compassion *f*; **in ~ with** en accord avec ; (*strike*) en *or* par solidarité avec ; **with our deepest ~** en vous priant d'accepter nos sincères condoléances.
symphonic [sɪm'fɔnɪk] *a* symphonique.
symphony ['sɪmfənɪ] *n* symphonie *f*; **~ orchestra** *n* orchestre *m* symphonique.
symposium [sɪm'pəuzɪəm] *n* symposium *m*.
symptom ['sɪmptəm] *n* symptôme *m*; indice *m*; **~atic** [-'mætɪk] *a* symptomatique.
synagogue ['sɪnəgɔg] *n* synagogue *f*.
synchromesh [sɪŋkrəu'mɛʃ] *n* synchronisation *f*.
synchronize ['sɪŋkrənaɪz] *vt* synchroniser // *vi*: **to ~ with** se produire en même temps que.
syncopated ['sɪŋkəpeɪtɪd] *a* syncopé(e).
syndicate ['sɪndɪkɪt] *n* syndicat *m*, coopérative *f*.
syndrome ['sɪndrəum] *n* syndrome *m*.
synonym ['sɪnənɪm] *n* synonyme *m*; **~ous** [sɪ'nɔnɪməs] *a*: **~ous (with)** synonyme (de).
synopsis, *pl* **synopses** [sɪ'nɔpsɪs, -si:z] *n* résumé *m*, synopsis *m or f*.
syntax ['sɪntæks] *n* syntaxe *f*.
synthesis, *pl* **syntheses** ['sɪnθəsɪs, -si:z] *n* synthèse *f*.
synthetic [sɪn'θɛtɪk] *a* synthétique ; **~s** *npl* textiles artificiels.
syphilis ['sɪfɪlɪs] *n* syphilis *f*.
syphon ['saɪfən] *n*, *vb* = **siphon**.
Syria ['sɪrɪə] *n* Syrie *f*; **~n** *a* syrien(ne) // *n* Syrien/ne.
syringe [sɪ'rɪndʒ] *n* seringue *f*.
syrup ['sɪrəp] *n* sirop *m*; (*also*: **golden ~**) mélasse raffinée ; **~y** *a* sirupeux(euse).
system ['sɪstəm] *n* système *m*; (*order*) méthode *f*; (*ANAT*) organisme *m*; **~atic** [-'mætɪk] *a* systématique ; méthodique ; **~s analyst** *n* analyste-programmeur *m/f*.

T

ta [tɑ:] *excl* (*Brit*: *col*) merci!
tab [tæb] *n* (*loop on coat etc*) attache *f*; (*label*) étiquette *f*; **to keep ~s on** (*fig*) surveiller.
tabby ['tæbɪ] *n* (*also*: **~ cat**) chat/te tigré(e).
tabernacle ['tæbənækl] *n* tabernacle *m*.
table ['teɪbl] *n* table *f* // *vt* (*motion etc*) présenter ; **to lay** *or* **set the ~** mettre le couvert *or* la table ; **~ of contents** *n* table *f* des matières ; **~cloth** *n* nappe *f*; **~ d'hôte** [tɑ:bl'dəut] *a* (*meal*) à prix fixe ; **~ lamp** *n* lampe *f* décorative ; **~mat** *n* (*for plate*) napperon *m*, set *m*; (*for hot dish*) dessous-de-plat *m inv*; **~ salt** *n* sel fin *or* de table ; **~spoon** *n* cuiller *f* de service ; (*also*: **~spoonful**: *as measurement*) cuillerée *f* à soupe.
tablet ['tæblɪt] *n* (*MED*) comprimé *m*; (: *for sucking*) pastille *f*; (*for writing*) bloc *m*; (*of stone*) plaque *f*.
table: **~ tennis** *n* ping-pong *m*, tennis *m* de table ; **~ wine** *n* vin *m* de table.
taboo [tə'bu:] *a*, *n* tabou (*m*).
tabulate ['tæbjuleɪt] *vt* (*data, figures*) mettre sous forme de table(s) ; **tabulator** *n* tabulateur *m*.
tacit ['tæsɪt] *a* tacite.
taciturn ['tæsɪtə:n] *a* taciturne.
tack [tæk] *n* (*nail*) petit clou ; (*stitch*) point *m* de bâti ; (*NAUT*) bord *m*, bordée *f* // *vt* clouer ; bâtir // *vi* tirer un *or* des bord(s) ; **to change ~** virer de bord ; **on the wrong ~** (*fig*) sur la mauvaise voie.
tackle ['tækl] *n* matériel *m*, équipement *m*; (*for lifting*) appareil *m* de levage ; (*RUGBY*) plaquage *m* // *vt* (*difficulty*) s'attaquer à ; (*RUGBY*) plaquer.
tacky ['tækɪ] *a* collant(e) ; pas sec(sèche).
tact [tækt] *n* tact *m*; **~ful** *a* plein(e) de tact ; **~fully** *ad* avec tact.
tactical ['tæktɪkl] *a* tactique ; **~ error** *n* erreur *f* de tactique.
tactics ['tæktɪks] *n,npl* tactique *f*.
tactless ['tæktlɪs] *a* qui manque de tact ; **~ly** *ad* sans tact.
tadpole ['tædpəul] *n* têtard *m*.
taffy ['tæfɪ] *n* (*US*) (bonbon *m* au) caramel *m*.
tag [tæg] *n* étiquette *f*; **to ~ along** *vi* suivre.
tail [teɪl] *n* queue *f*; (*of shirt*) pan *m* // *vt* (*follow*) suivre, filer ; **~s** (*on coin*) (le côté) pile ; **to ~ away, ~ off** *vi* (*in size, quality etc*) baisser peu à peu ; **~back** *n* bouchon *m*; **~ coat** *n* habit *m*; **~ end** *n* bout *m*, fin *f*; **~gate** hayon *m* (arrière).
tailor ['teɪlə*] *n* tailleur *m* (*artisan*) ; **~ing** *n* (*cut*) coupe *f*; **~-made** *a* fait(e) sur mesure ; (*fig*) conçu(e) spécialement.
tailwind ['teɪlwɪnd] *n* vent *m* arrière *inv*.
tainted ['teɪntɪd] *a* (*food*) gâté(e) ; (*water, air*) infecté(e) ; (*fig*) souillé(e).
take, *pt* **took,** *pp* **taken** [teɪk, tuk, 'teɪkn] *vt* prendre ; (*gain*: *prize*) remporter ; (*require*: *effort, courage*) demander ; (*tolerate*) accepter, supporter ; (*hold*: *passengers etc*) contenir ; (*accompany*) emmener, accompagner ; (*bring, carry*) apporter, emporter ; (*exam*) passer, se présenter à ; **to ~ sth from** (*drawer etc*) prendre qch dans ; (*person*) prendre qch à ; **I ~ it that** je suppose que ; **to ~ for a walk** (*child, dog*) emmener promener ; **to ~ after** *vt fus* ressembler à ; **to ~ apart** *vt* démonter ; **to ~ away** *vt* emporter ; enlever ; **to ~ back** *vt* (*return*) rendre, rapporter ; (*one's words*) retirer ; **to ~ down** *vt* (*building*) démolir ; (*letter etc*) prendre, écrire ; **to ~ in** *vt* (*deceive*) tromper, rouler ; (*understand*) comprendre, saisir ; (*include*) couvrir, inclure ; (*lodger*) prendre ; **to ~ off** *vi* (*AVIAT*) décoller // *vt* (*remove*) enlever ; (*imitate*) imiter, pasticher ; **to ~ on** *vt* (*work*) accepter, se charger de ; (*employee*) prendre, embaucher ; (*opponent*) accepter de se battre contre ; **to ~ out** *vt* sortir ; (*remove*) enlever ; (*licence*) prendre, se procurer ; **to ~ sth out of** enlever qch de ; prendre qch dans ; **to ~ over** *vt* (*business*) reprendre // *vi*: **to ~ over from sb** prendre la relève de qn ; **to ~ to** *vt fus* (*person*) se prendre

d'amitié pour ; (*activity*) prendre goût à ; **to ~ up** *vt* (*one's story, a dress*) reprendre ; (*occupy*: *time, space*) prendre, occuper ; (*engage in*: *hobby etc*) se mettre à ; **~away** *a* (*food*) à emporter ; **~-home pay** *n* salaire net ; **~off** *n* (AVIAT) décollage *m* ; **~over** *n* (COMM) rachat *m* ; **~over bid** *n* offre publique d'achat.

takings ['teɪkɪŋz] *npl* (COMM) recette *f.*

talc [tælk] *n* (*also*: **~um powder**) talc *m.*

tale [teɪl] *n* (*story*) conte *m,* histoire *f* ; (*account*) récit *m* ; (*pej*) histoire.

talent ['tælnt] *n* talent *m,* don *m* ; **~ed** *a* doué(e), plein(e) de talent.

talk [tɔ:k] *n* propos *mpl* ; (*gossip*) racontars *mpl* (*pej*) ; (*conversation*) discussion *f* ; (*interview*) entretien *m* ; (*a speech*) causerie *f,* exposé *m* // *vi* (*chatter*) bavarder ; **to ~ about** parler de ; (*converse*) s'entretenir *or* parler de ; **to ~ sb out of/into doing** persuader qn de ne pas faire/de faire ; **to ~ shop** parler métier *or* affaires ; **to ~ over** *vt* discuter (de) ; **~ative** *a* bavard(e) ; **~er** *n* causeur/euse ; (*pej*) bavard/e.

tall [tɔ:l] *a* (*person*) grand(e) ; (*building, tree*) haut(e) ; **to be 6 feet ~** ≈ mesurer 1 mètre 80 ; **~boy** *n* grande commode ; **~ness** *n* grande taille ; hauteur *f* ; **~ story** *n* histoire *f* invraisemblable.

tally ['tælɪ] *n* compte *m* // *vi*: **to ~ (with)** correspondre (à).

tambourine [tæmbə'ri:n] *n* tambourin *m.*

tame [teɪm] *a* apprivoisé(e) ; (*fig*: *story, style*) insipide.

tamper ['tæmpə*] *vi*: **to ~ with** toucher à (*en cachette ou sans permission*).

tampon ['tæmpən] *n* tampon *m* hygiénique *or* périodique.

tan [tæn] *n* (*also*: **sun~**) bronzage *m* // *vt,vi* bronzer, brunir // *a* (*colour*) brun roux *inv.*

tandem ['tændəm] *n* tandem *m.*

tang [tæŋ] *n* odeur (*or* saveur) piquante.

tangent ['tændʒənt] *n* (MATH) tangente *f.*

tangerine [tændʒə'ri:n] *n* mandarine *f.*

tangible ['tændʒəbl] *a* tangible.

tangle ['tæŋgl] *n* enchevêtrement *m* // *vt* enchevêtrer ; **to get in(to) a ~** s'emmêler.

tango ['tæŋgəu] *n* tango *m.*

tank [tæŋk] *n* réservoir *m* ; (*for processing*) cuve *f* ; (*for fish*) aquarium *m* ; (MIL) char *m* d'assaut, tank *m.*

tankard ['tæŋkəd] *n* chope *f.*

tanker ['tæŋkə*] *n* (*ship*) pétrolier *m,* tanker *m* ; (*truck*) camion-citerne *m.*

tanned [tænd] *a* (*skin*) bronzé(e).

tantalizing ['tæntəlaɪzɪŋ] *a* (*smell*) extrêmement appétissant(e) ; (*offer*) terriblement tentant(e).

tantamount ['tæntəmaunt] *a*: **~ to** qui équivaut à.

tantrum ['tæntrəm] *n* accès *m* de colère.

tap [tæp] *n* (*on sink etc*) robinet *m* ; (*gentle blow*) petite tape // *vt* frapper *or* taper légèrement ; (*resources*) exploiter, utiliser ; **~-dancing** *n* claquettes *fpl.*

tape [teɪp] *n* ruban *m* ; (*also*: **magnetic ~**) bande *f* (magnétique) // *vt* (*record*) enregistrer (sur bande) ; **~ measure** *n* mètre *m* à ruban.

taper ['teɪpə*] *n* cierge *m* // *vi* s'effiler.

tape recorder ['teɪprɪkɔ:də*] *n* magnétophone *m.*

tapered ['teɪpəd], **tapering** ['teɪpərɪŋ] *a* fuselé(e), effilé(e).

tapestry ['tæpɪstrɪ] *n* tapisserie *f.*

tapioca [tæpɪ'əukə] *n* tapioca *m.*

tappet ['tæpɪt] *n* (AUT) poussoir *m* (de soupape).

tar [tɑ:] *n* goudron *m.*

tarantula [tə'ræntjulə] *n* tarentule *f.*

tardy ['tɑ:dɪ] *a* tardif(ive).

target ['tɑ:gɪt] *n* cible *f* ; (*fig*: *objective*) objectif *m* ; **~ practice** *n* exercices *mpl* de tir (à la cible).

tariff ['tærɪf] *n* (COMM) tarif *m* ; (*taxes*) tarif douanier.

tarmac ['tɑ:mæk] *n* macadam *m* ; (AVIAT) aire *f* d'envol // *vt* goudronner.

tarnish ['tɑ:nɪʃ] *vt* ternir.

tarpaulin [tɑ:'pɔ:lɪn] *n* bâche goudronnée.

tarragon ['tærəgən] *n* estragon *m.*

tart [tɑ:t] *n* (CULIN) tarte *f* ; (*col*: *pej*: *woman*) poule *f* // *a* (*flavour*) âpre, aigrelet(te).

tartan ['tɑ:tn] *n* tartan *m* // *a* écossais(e).

tartar ['tɑ:tə*] *n* (*on teeth*) tartre *m* ; **~ sauce** *n* sauce *f* tartare.

task [tɑ:sk] *n* tâche *f* ; **to take to ~** prendre à partie ; **~ force** *n* (MIL, POLICE) détachement spécial.

Tasmania [tæz'meɪnɪə] *n* Tasmanie *f.*

tassel ['tæsl] *n* gland *m* ; pompon *m.*

taste [teɪst] *n* goût *m* ; (*fig*: *glimpse, idea*) idée *f,* aperçu *m* // *vt* goûter // *vi*: **to ~ of** (*fish etc*) avoir le *or* un goût de ; **it ~s like fish** ça a un *or* le goût de poisson, on dirait du poisson ; **what does it ~ like?** quel goût ça a? ; **you can ~ the garlic (in it)** on sent bien l'ail ; **can I have a ~ of this wine?** puis-je goûter un peu de ce vin? ; **to have a ~ of sth** goûter (à) qch ; **to have a ~ for sth** aimer qch, avoir un penchant pour qch ; **~ful** *a* de bon goût ; **~fully** *ad* avec goût ; **~less** *a* (*food*) qui n'a aucun goût ; (*remark*) de mauvais goût ; **tasty** *a* savoureux(euse), délicieux(euse).

tattered ['tætəd] *a see* **tatters.**

tatters ['tætəz] *mpl*: **in ~** (*also*: **tattered**) en lambeaux.

tattoo [tə'tu:] *n* tatouage *m* ; (*spectacle*) parade *f* militaire // *vt* tatouer.

tatty ['tætɪ] *a* (*col*) défraîchi(e), en piteux état.

taught [tɔ:t] *pt,pp of* **teach.**

taunt [tɔ:nt] *n* raillerie *f* // *vt* railler.

Taurus ['tɔ:rəs] *n* le Taureau ; **to be ~** être du Taureau.

taut [tɔ:t] *a* tendu(e).

tavern ['tævən] *n* taverne *f.*

tawdry ['tɔ:drɪ] *a* (d'un mauvais goût) criard.

tawny ['tɔ:nɪ] *a* fauve (*couleur*).

tax [tæks] *n* (*on goods etc*) taxe *f* ; (*on income*) impôts *mpl,* contributions *fpl* // *vt* taxer ; imposer ; (*fig*: *strain*: *patience etc*) mettre à l'épreuve ; **~ation** [-'seɪʃən] *n* taxation *f* ; impôts *mpl,* contributions *fpl* ; **~ avoidance** *n* évasion fiscale ; **~ collector** *n* percepteur *m* ; **~ evasion** *n* fraude fiscale ; ~ **exile** *n personne qui s'expatrie pour fuir une fiscalité excessive* ; ~**-free** *a* exempt(e) d'impôts.

taxi ['tæksɪ] *n* taxi *m* // *vi* (AVIAT) rouler (lentement) au sol.

taxidermist ['tæksɪdə:mɪst] *n* empailleur/euse (*d'animaux*).

taxi: ~ **driver** *n* chauffeur *m* de taxi ; ~ **rank**, ~ **stand** *n* station *f* de taxis.

tax: ~ **payer** *n* contribuable *m/f*; ~ **return** *n* déclaration *f* d'impôts *or* de revenus.

TB *abbr of* **tuberculosis**.

tea [ti:] *n* thé *m* ; (*snack*: *for children*) goûter *m* ; **high** ~ *collation combinant goûter et dîner* ; ~ **bag** *n* sachet *m* de thé ; ~ **break** *n* pause-thé *f* ; ~**cake** *n* petit pain brioché.

teach, *pt, pp* **taught** [ti:tʃ, tɔ:t] *vt*: **to** ~ **sb sth,** ~ **sth to sb** apprendre qch à qn ; (*in school etc*) enseigner qch à qn // *vi* enseigner ; ~**er** *n* (*in secondary school*) professeur *m* ; (*in primary school*) instituteur/trice ; ~**ing** *n* enseignement *m* ; ~**ing staff** *n* enseignants *mpl.*

tea cosy ['ti:kəuzɪ] *n* couvre-théière *m.*

teacup ['ti:kʌp] *n* tasse *f* à thé.

teak [ti:k] *n* teck *m* // *a* en *or* de teck.

tea leaves ['ti:li:vz] *npl* feuilles *fpl* de thé.

team [ti:m] *n* équipe *f*; (*of animals*) attelage *m* ; ~ **games/work** jeux *mpl*/travail *m* d'équipe.

tea party ['ti:pɑ:tɪ] *n* thé *m* (*réception*).

teapot ['ti:pɔt] *n* théière *f.*

tear *n* [tɛə*] déchirure *f*; [tɪə*] larme *f* // *vb* [tɛə*] (*pt* **tore,** *pp* **torn** [tɔ:*, tɔ:n]) *vt* déchirer // *vi* se déchirer ; **in** ~**s** en larmes ; **to burst into** ~**s** fondre en larmes ; **to** ~ **along** *vi* (*rush*) aller à toute vitesse ; ~**ful** *a* larmoyant(e) ; ~ **gas** *n* gaz *m* lacrymogène.

tearoom ['ti:ru:m] *n* salon *m* de thé.

tease [ti:z] *n* taquin/e // *vt* taquiner ; (*unkindly*) tourmenter.

tea set ['ti:sɛt] *n* service *m* à thé.

teashop ['ti:ʃɔp] *n* pâtisserie-salon de thé *f.*

teaspoon ['ti:spu:n] *n* petite cuiller ; (*also*: ~**ful**: *as measurement*) ≈ cuillerée *f* à café.

tea strainer ['ti:streɪnə*] *n* passoire *f* (à thé).

teat [ti:t] *n* tétine *f.*

teatime ['ti:taɪm] *n* l'heure *f* du thé.

tea towel ['ti:tauəl] *n* torchon *m* (à vaisselle).

tea urn ['ti:ə:n] *n* fontaine *f* à thé.

technical ['tɛknɪkl] *a* technique ; ~**ity** [-'kælɪtɪ] *n* technicité *f*; (*detail*) détail *m* technique ; ~**ly** *ad* techniquement.

technician [tɛk'nɪʃn] *n* technicien/ne.

technique [tɛk'ni:k] *n* technique *f.*

technological [tɛknə'lɔdʒɪkl] *a* technologique.

technologist [tɛk'nɔlədʒɪst] *n* technologue *m/f.*

technology [tɛk'nɔlədʒɪ] *n* technologie *f.*

teddy (bear) ['tɛdɪ(bɛə*)] *n* ours *m* (en peluche).

tedious ['ti:dɪəs] *a* fastidieux(euse).

tedium ['ti:dɪəm] *n* ennui *m.*

tee [ti:] *n* (GOLF) tee *m.*

teem [ti:m] *vi* grouiller, abonder ; **to** ~ **with** grouiller de ; **it is** ~**ing (with rain)** il pleut à torrents.

teenage ['ti:neɪdʒ] *a* (*fashions etc*) pour jeunes, pour adolescents ; ~**r** *n* jeune *m/f*, adolescent/e.

teens [ti:nz] *npl*: **to be in one's** ~ être adolescent(e).

tee-shirt ['ti:ʃə:t] *n* = **T-shirt**.

teeter ['ti:tə*] *vi* chanceler, vaciller.

teeth [ti:θ] *npl of* **tooth**.

teethe [ti:ð] *vi* percer ses dents.

teething ['ti:ðɪŋ] *a*: ~ **ring** *n* anneau *m* (*pour bébé qui perce ses dents*) ; ~ **troubles** *npl* (*fig*) difficultés initiales.

teetotal ['ti:'təutl] *a* (*person*) qui ne boit jamais d'alcool.

telecommunications ['tɛlɪkəmju:nɪ'keɪʃənz] *n* télécommunications *fpl.*

telegram ['tɛlɪgræm] *n* télégramme *m.*

telegraph ['tɛlɪgrɑ:f] *n* télégraphe *m* ; ~**ic** [-'græfɪk] *a* télégraphique ; ~ **pole** *n* poteau *m* télégraphique.

telepathic [tɛlɪ'pæθɪk] *a* télépathique.

telepathy [tə'lɛpəθɪ] *n* télépathie *f.*

telephone ['tɛlɪfəun] *n* téléphone *m* // *vt* (*person*) téléphoner à ; (*message*) téléphoner ; ~ **booth,** ~ **box** *n* cabine *f* téléphonique ; ~ **call** *n* coup *m* de téléphone, appel *m* téléphonique ; communication *f* téléphonique ; ~ **directory** *n* annuaire *m* (du téléphone) ; ~ **exchange** *n* central *m* (téléphonique) ; ~ **number** *n* numéro *m* de téléphone ; ~ **operator** téléphoniste *m/f*, standardiste *m/f*; **telephonist** [tə'lɛfənɪst] *n* téléphoniste *m/f.*

telephoto ['tɛlɪ'fəutəu] *a*: ~ **lens** *n* téléobjectif *m.*

teleprinter ['tɛlɪprɪntə*] *n* téléscripteur *m.*

telescope ['tɛlɪskəup] *n* télescope *m* // *vt* télescoper ; **telescopic** [-'skɔpɪk] *a* télescopique.

televiewer ['tɛlɪvju:ə*] *n* téléspectateur/trice.

televise ['tɛlɪvaɪz] *vt* téléviser.

television ['tɛlɪvɪʒən] *n* télévision *f*; ~ **programme** *n* émission *f* de télévision ; ~ **set** *n* poste *m* de télévision.

tell, *pt, pp* **told** [tɛl, təuld] *vt* dire ; (*relate*: *story*) raconter ; (*distinguish*): **to** ~ **sth from** distinguer qch de // *vi* (*have effect*) se faire sentir, se voir ; **to** ~ **sb to do** dire à qn de faire ; **to** ~ **on** *vt fus* (*inform against*) dénoncer, rapporter contre ; **to** ~ **off** *vt* réprimander, gronder ; ~**er** *n* (*in bank*) caissier/ère ; ~**ing** *a* (*remark, detail*) révélateur(trice) ; ~**tale** *a* (*sign*) éloquent(e), révélateur(trice) // *n* (CONSTR) témoin *m.*

telly ['tɛlɪ] *n* (*col*: *abbr of* **television**) télé *f.*

temerity [tə'mɛrɪtɪ] *n* témérité *f.*

temp [tɛmp] *n* (*abbr of* **temporary**) (secrétaire *f*) intérimaire *f.*

temper ['tɛmpə*] *n* (*nature*) caractère *m* ; (*mood*) humeur *f*; (*fit of anger*) colère *f* // *vt* (*moderate*) tempérer, adoucir ; **to be in a** ~ être en colère ; **to lose one's** ~ se mettre en colère.

temperament ['tɛmprəmənt] *n* (*nature*) tempérament *m*; **~al** [-'mɛntl] *a* capricieux(euse).
temperance ['tɛmpərns] *n* modération *f*; (*in drinking*) tempérance *f*.
temperate ['tɛmprət] *a* modéré(e); (*climate*) tempéré(e).
temperature ['tɛmprətʃə*] *n* température *f*; **to have** *or* **run a ~** avoir de la fièvre; **~ chart** *n* (MED) feuille *f* de température.
tempered ['tɛmpəd] *a* (*steel*) trempé(e).
tempest ['tɛmpɪst] *n* tempête *f*.
tempi ['tɛmpi:] *npl of* **tempo.**
template ['tɛmplɪt] *n* patron *m*.
temple ['tɛmpl] *n* (*building*) temple *m*; (ANAT) tempe *f*.
tempo, ~s *or* **tempi** ['tɛmpəu, 'tɛmpi:] *n* tempo *m*; (*fig: of life etc*) rythme *m*.
temporal ['tɛmpərl] *a* temporel(le).
temporarily ['tɛmpərərɪlɪ] *ad* temporairement; provisoirement.
temporary ['tɛmpərərɪ] *a* temporaire, provisoire; (*job, worker*) temporaire; **~ secretary** *n* (secrétaire *f*) intérimaire *f*.
temporize ['tɛmpəraɪz] *vi* atermoyer; transiger.
tempt [tɛmpt] *vt* tenter; **to ~ sb into doing** induire qn à faire; **~ation** [-'teɪʃən] *n* tentation *f*; **~ing** *a* tentant(e).
ten [tɛn] *num* dix.
tenable ['tɛnəbl] *a* défendable.
tenacious [tə'neɪʃəs] *a* tenace.
tenacity [tə'næsɪtɪ] *n* ténacité *f*.
tenancy ['tɛnənsɪ] *n* location *f*; état *m* de locataire.
tenant ['tɛnənt] *n* locataire *m/f*.
tend [tɛnd] *vt* s'occuper de // *vi*: **to ~ to do** avoir tendance à faire; (*colour*): **to ~ to** tirer sur.
tendency ['tɛndənsɪ] *n* tendance *f*.
tender ['tɛndə*] *a* tendre; (*delicate*) délicat(e); (*sore*) sensible; (*affectionate*) tendre, doux(douce) // *n* (COMM: *offer*) soumission *f*; (*money*): **legal ~** cours légal // *vt* offrir; **~ize** *vt* (CULIN) attendrir; **~ly** *ad* tendrement; **~ness** *n* tendresse *f*; (*of meat*) tendreté *f*.
tendon ['tɛndən] *n* tendon *m*.
tenement ['tɛnəmənt] *n* immeuble *m* (de rapport).
tenet ['tɛnət] *n* principe *m*.
tennis ['tɛnɪs] *n* tennis *m*; **~ ball** *n* balle *f* de tennis; **~ court** *n* (court *m* de) tennis; **~ racket** *n* raquette *f* de tennis.
tenor ['tɛnə*] *n* (MUS) ténor *m*; (*of speech etc*) sens général.
tense [tɛns] *a* tendu(e); (*person*) tendu, crispé(e) // *n* (LING) temps *m*; **~ness** *n* tension *f*.
tension ['tɛnʃən] *n* tension *f*.
tent [tɛnt] *n* tente f.
tentacle ['tɛntəkl] *n* tentacule *m*.
tentative ['tɛntətɪv] *a* timide, hésitant(e); (*conclusion*) provisoire.
tenterhooks ['tɛntəhuks] *npl*: **on ~** sur des charbons ardents.
tenth [tɛnθ] *num* dixième.
tent: **~ peg** *n* piquet *m* de tente; **~ pole** *n* montant *m* de tente.
tenuous ['tɛnjuəs] *a* ténu(e).
tenure ['tɛnjuə*] *n* (*of property*) bail *m*; (*of job*) période *f* de jouissance; statut *m* de titulaire.
tepid ['tɛpɪd] *a* tiède.
term [tə:m] *n* (*limit*) terme *m*; (*word*) terme, mot *m*; (SCOL) trimestre *m*; (LAW) session *f* // *vt* appeler; **~s** *npl* (*conditions*) conditions *fpl*; (COMM) tarif *m*; **~ of imprisonment** peine *f* de prison; **in the short/long ~** à court/long terme; **'easy ~s'** (COMM) 'facilités de paiement'; **to be on good ~s with** bien s'entendre avec, être en bons termes avec; **to come to ~s with** (*person*) arriver à un accord avec; (*problem*) faire face à.
terminal ['tə:mɪnl] *a* terminal(e); (*disease*) dans sa phase terminale // *n* (ELEC) borne *f*; (*for oil, ore etc*) terminal *m*; (*also*: **air ~**) aérogare *f*; (*also*: **coach ~**) gare routière.
terminate ['tə:mɪneɪt] *vt* mettre fin à // *vi*: **to ~ in** finir en *or* par.
termination [tə:mɪ'neɪʃən] *n* fin *f*; (*of contract*) résiliation *f*; **~ of pregnancy** *n* (MED) interruption *f* de grossesse.
termini ['tə:mɪnaɪ] *npl of* **terminus**.
terminology [tə:mɪ'nɔlədʒɪ] *n* terminologie *f*.
terminus, *pl* **termini** ['tə:mɪnəs, 'tə:mɪnaɪ] *n* terminus *m inv*.
termite ['tə:maɪt] *n* termite *m*.
terrace ['tɛrəs] *n* terrasse *f*; (*row of houses*) rangée *f* de maisons (*attenantes les unes aux autres*); **the ~s** (SPORT) les gradins *mpl*; **~ed** *a* (*garden*) en terrasses.
terracotta ['tɛrə'kɔtə] *n* terre cuite.
terrain [tɛ'reɪn] *n* terrain *m* (*sol*).
terrible ['tɛrɪbl] *a* terrible, atroce; (*weather, work*) affreux(euse), épouvantable; **terribly** *ad* terriblement; (*very badly*) affreusement mal.
terrier ['tɛerɪə*] *n* terrier *m* (*chien*).
terrific [tə'rɪfɪk] *a* fantastique, incroyable, terrible; (*wonderful*) formidable, sensationnel(le).
terrify ['tɛrɪfaɪ] *vt* terrifier.
territorial [tɛrɪ'tɔ:rɪəl] *a* territorial(e).
territory ['tɛrɪtərɪ] *n* territoire *m*.
terror ['tɛrə*] *n* terreur *f*; **~ism** *n* terrorisme *m*; **~ist** *n* terroriste *m/f*; **~ize** *vt* terroriser.
terse [tə:s] *a* (*style*) concis(e); (*reply*) laconique.
test [tɛst] *n* (*trial, check*) essai *m*; (: *of goods in factory*) contrôle *m*; (*of courage etc*) épreuve *f*; (MED) examens *mpl*; (CHEM) analyses *fpl*; (*exam: of intelligence etc*) test *m* (d'aptitude); (: *in school*) interrogation *f* de contrôle; (*also*: **driving ~**) (examen du) permis *m* de conduire // *vt* essayer; contrôler; mettre à l'épreuve; examiner; analyser; tester; faire subir une interrogation (de contrôle) à.
testament ['tɛstəmənt] *n* testament *m*; **the Old/New T~** l'Ancien/le Nouveau Testament.
test: **~ case** *n* (LAW, *fig*) affaire-test *f*; **~ flight** *n* vol *m* d'essai.
testicle ['tɛstɪkl] *n* testicule *m*.

testify ['tɛstɪfaɪ] *vi* (*LAW*) témoigner, déposer.
testimonial [tɛstɪ'məunɪəl] *n* (*reference*) recommandation *f*; (*gift*) témoignage *m* d'estime.
testimony ['tɛstɪmənɪ] *n* (*LAW*) témoignage *m*, déposition *f*.
test: ~ **match** *n* (*CRICKET, RUGBY*) match international; ~ **paper** *n* (*SCOL*) interrogation écrite; ~ **pilot** *n* pilote *m* d'essai; ~ **tube** *n* éprouvette *f*.
testy ['tɛstɪ] *a* irritable.
tetanus ['tɛtənəs] *n* tétanos *m*.
tether ['tɛðə*] *vt* attacher // *n*: **at the end of one's** ~ à bout (de patience).
text [tɛkst] *n* texte *m*; ~**book** *n* manuel *m*.
textile ['tɛkstaɪl] *n* textile *m*.
texture ['tɛkstʃə*] *n* texture *f*; (*of skin, paper etc*) grain *m*.
Thai [taɪ] *a* thaïlandais(e) // *n* Thaïlandais/e; (*LING*) thai *m*; ~**land** *n* Thaïlande *f*.
Thames [tɛmz] *n*: **the** ~ la Tamise.
than [ðæn, ðən] *cj* que; (*with numerals*): **more** ~ **10/once** plus de 10/d'une fois; **I have more/less** ~ **you** j'en ai plus/moins que toi; **she has more apples** ~ **pears** elle a plus de pommes que de poires.
thank [θæŋk] *vt* remercier, dire merci à; ~ **you (very much)** merci (beaucoup); ~**s** *npl* remerciements *mpl* // *excl* merci!; ~**s to** *prep* grâce à; ~**ful** *a*: ~**ful (for)** reconnaissant(e) (de); ~**less** *a* ingrat(e); **T~sgiving (Day)** *n* jour *m* d'action de grâce.
that [ðæt, ðət] *cj* que // *det* ce(cet + *vowel or h mute*), *f* cette; (*not 'this'*): ~ **book** ce livre-là // *pronoun* ce; (*not 'this one'*) cela, ça; (*the one*) celui(celle); (*relative: subject*) qui; (: *object*) que, *prep* + lequel(laquelle); (*with time*): **on the day** ~ **he came** le jour où il est venu // *ad*: ~ **high** aussi haut; si haut; **it's about** ~ **high** c'est à peu près de cette hauteur; ~ **one** celui-là(celle-là); **what's** ~**?** qu'est-ce que c'est?; **who's** ~**?** qui est-ce?; **is** ~ **you?** c'est toi?; ~**'s what he said** c'est *or* voilà ce qu'il a dit; ~ **is...** c'est-à-dire..., à savoir...; **all** ~ tout cela, tout ça; **I can't work** ~ **much** je ne peux pas travailler autant que cela.
thatched [θætʃt] *a* (*roof*) de chaume; ~ **cottage** chaumière *f*.
thaw [θɔ:] *n* dégel *m* // *vi* (*ice*) fondre; (*food*) dégeler // *vt* (*food*) (faire) dégeler; **it's** ~**ing** (*weather*) il dégèle.
the [ði:, ðə] *det* le, *f* la, (l' + *vowel or h mute*), *pl* les ;(*NB*: *à* + *le(s)* = au(x); *de* + *le* = du; *de* + *les* = des).
theatre, theater (*US*) ['θɪətə*] *n* théâtre *m*; ~**-goer** *n* habitué/e du théâtre.
theatrical [θɪ'ætrɪkl] *a* théâtral(e); ~ **company** *n* troupe *f* de théâtre.
theft [θɛft] *n* vol *m* (*larcin*).
their [ðɛə*] *a* leur, *pl* leurs; ~**s** *pronoun* le(la) leur, les leurs; **it is** ~**s** c'est à eux; **a friend of** ~**s** un de leurs amis.
them [ðɛm, ðəm] *pronoun* (*direct*) les; (*indirect*) leur; (*stressed, after prep*) eux(elles); **I see** ~ je les vois; **give** ~ **the book** donne-leur le livre.
theme [θi:m] *n* thème *m*; ~ **song** *n* chanson principale.
themselves [ðəm'sɛlvz] *pl pronoun* (*reflexive*) se; (*emphatic*) eux-mêmes(elles-mêmes); **between** ~ entre eux(elles).
then [ðɛn] *ad* (*at that time*) alors, à ce moment-là; (*next*) puis, ensuite; (*and also*) et puis // *cj* (*therefore*) alors, dans ce cas // *a*: **the** ~ **president** le président d'alors *or* de l'époque; **from** ~ **on** dès lors.
theologian [θɪə'ləudʒən] *n* théologien/ne.
theological [θɪə'lɔdʒɪkl] *a* théologique.
theology [θɪ'ɔlədʒɪ] *n* théologie *f*.
theorem ['θɪərəm] *n* théorème *m*.
theoretical [θɪə'rɛtɪkl] *a* théorique.
theorize ['θɪəraɪz] *vi* élaborer une théorie; (*pej*) faire des théories.
theory ['θɪərɪ] *n* théorie *f*.
therapeutic(al) [θɛrə'pju:tɪk(l)] *a* thérapeutique.
therapist ['θɛrəpɪst] *n* thérapeute *m/f*.
therapy ['θɛrəpɪ] *n* thérapie *f*.
there [ðɛə*] *ad* là, là-bas; ~, ~! allons, allons!; **it's** ~ c'est là; **he went** ~ il y est allé; ~ **is,** ~ **are** il y a; ~ **he is** le voilà; ~ **has been** il y a eu; **on/in** ~ là-dessus/ -dedans; **to go** ~ **and back** faire l'aller et retour; ~**abouts** *ad* (*place*) par là, près de là; (*amount*) environ, à peu près; ~**after** *ad* par la suite; ~**fore** *ad* donc, par conséquent; ~**'s** = ~ **is**; ~ **has**.
thermal ['θə:ml] *a* thermique.
thermometer [θə'mɔmɪtə*] *n* thermomètre *m*.
thermonuclear ['θə:məu'nju:klɪə*] *a* thermonucléaire.
Thermos ['θə:məs] *n* ® (*also*: ~ **flask**) thermos *m or f inv* ®.
thermostat ['θə:məustæt] *n* thermostat *m*.
thesaurus [θɪ'sɔ:rəs] *n* dictionnaire *m* synonymique.
these [ði:z] *pl pronoun* ceux-ci(celles-ci) // *pl det* ces; (*not 'those'*): ~ **books** ces livres-ci.
thesis, *pl* **theses** ['θi:sɪs, 'θi:si:z] *n* thèse *f*.
they [ðeɪ] *pl pronoun* ils(elles); (*stressed*) eux(elles); ~ **say that...** (*it is said that*) on dit que...; ~**'d** = **they had**; **they would**; ~**'ll** = **they shall**; **they will**; ~**'re** = **they are**; ~**'ve** = **they have**.
thick [θɪk] *a* épais(se); (*crowd*) dense; (*stupid*) bête, borné(e) // *n*: **in the** ~ **of** au beau milieu de, en plein cœur de; **it's 20 cm** ~ ça a 20 cm d'épaisseur; ~**en** *vi* s'épaissir // *vt* (*sauce etc*) épaissir; ~**ness** *n* épaisseur *f*; ~**set** *a* trapu(e), costaud(e); ~**skinned** *a* (*fig*) peu sensible.
thief, thieves [θi:f, θi:vz] *n* voleur/euse.
thieving ['θi:vɪŋ] *n* vol *m* (*larcin*).
thigh [θaɪ] *n* cuisse *f*; ~**bone** *n* fémur *m*.
thimble ['θɪmbl] *n* dé *m* (à coudre).
thin [θɪn] *a* mince; (*person*) maigre; (*soup*) peu épais(se); (*hair, crowd*) clairsemé(e); (*fog*) léger(ère) // *vt* (*hair*) éclaircir; **to** ~ **(down)** (*sauce, paint*) délayer.

thing [θɪŋ] *n* chose *f*; (*object*) objet *m*; (*contraption*) truc *m*; **~s** *npl* (*belongings*) affaires *fpl*; **for one ~** d'abord; **the best ~ would be to** le mieux serait de; **how are ~s?** comment ça va?
think, *pt, pp* **thought** [θɪŋk, θɔ:t] *vi* penser, réfléchir // *vt* penser, croire; (*imagine*) s'imaginer; **to ~ of** penser à; **what did you ~ of them?** qu'as-tu pensé d'eux?; **to ~ about sth/sb** penser à qch/qn; **I'll ~ about it** je vais y réfléchir; **to ~ of doing** avoir l'idée de faire; **I ~ so** je crois *or* pense que oui; **to ~ well of** avoir une haute opinion de; **to ~ over** *vt* bien réfléchir à; **to ~ up** *vt* inventer, trouver.
thinly ['θɪnlɪ] *ad* (*cut*) en tranches fines; (*spread*) en couche mince.
thinness ['θɪnnɪs] *n* minceur *f*; maigreur *f*.
third [θə:d] *num* troisième // *n* troisième *m/f*; (*fraction*) tiers *m*; (SCOL: *degree*) ≈ licence *f* avec mention passable; **a ~ of** le tiers de; **~ly** *ad* troisièmement; **~ party insurance** *n* assurance *f* au tiers; **~-rate** *a* de qualité médiocre; **the T~ World** *n* le Tiers-Monde.
thirst [θə:st] *n* soif *f*; **~y** *a* (*person*) qui a soif, assoiffé(e).
thirteen ['θə:'ti:n] *num* treize.
thirty ['θə:tɪ] *num* trente.
this [ðɪs] *det* ce(cet + *vowel or h mute*), *f* cette; (*not 'that'*): **~ book** ce livre-ci // *pronoun* ce; ceci; (*not 'that one'*) celui-ci(celle-ci); **~ is what he said** voici ce qu'il a dit.
thistle ['θɪsl] *n* chardon *m*.
thong [θɔŋ] *n* lanière *f*.
thorn [θɔ:n] *n* épine *f*; **~ bush** *n* buisson *m* d'épines; **~y** *a* épineux(euse).
thorough ['θʌrə] *a* (*search*) minutieux(euse); (*knowledge, research*) approfondi(e); (*work*) consciencieux(euse); (*cleaning*) à fond; **~bred** *n* (*horse*) pur-sang *m inv*; **~fare** *n* rue *f*; **'no ~fare'** 'passage interdit'; **~ly** *ad* minutieusement; en profondeur; à fond; **he ~ly agreed** il était tout à fait d'accord.
those [ðəuz] *pl pronoun* ceux-là(celles-là) // *pl det* ces; (*not 'these'*): **~ books** ces livres-là.
though [ðəu] *cj* bien que + *sub*, quoique + *sub* // *ad* pourtant.
thought [θɔ:t] *pt, pp of* **think** // *n* pensée *f*; (*opinion*) avis *m*; (*intention*) intention *f*; **~ful** *a* pensif(ive); réfléchi(e); (*considerate*) prévenant(e); **~less** *a* étourdi(e); qui manque de considération.
thousand ['θauzənd] *num* mille; **~th** *num* millième; **one ~** mille; **~s of** des milliers de.
thrash [θræʃ] *vt* rouer de coups; donner une correction à; (*defeat*) battre à plate couture; **to ~ about** *vi* se débattre; **to ~ out** *vt* débattre de.
thread [θrɛd] *n* fil *m*; (*of screw*) pas *m*, filetage *m* // *vt* (*needle*) enfiler; **to ~ one's way between** se faufiler entre; **~bare** *a* râpé(e), élimé(e).
threat [θrɛt] *n* menace *f*; **~en** *vi* (*storm*) menacer // *vt*: **to ~en sb with sth/to do** menacer qn de qch/de faire.
three [θri:] *num* trois (*m inv*); **~-dimensional** *a* à trois dimensions; (*film*) en relief; **~fold** *ad*: **to increase ~fold** tripler; **~-piece suit** *n* complet *m* (avec gilet); **~-piece suite** *n* salon *m* comprenant un canapé et deux fauteuils assortis; **~-ply** *a* (*wood*) à trois épaisseurs; (*wool*) trois fils *inv*; **~-wheeler** *n* (*car*) voiture *f* à trois roues.
thresh [θrɛʃ] *vt* (AGR) battre; **~ing machine** *n* batteuse *f*.
threshold ['θrɛʃhəuld] *n* seuil *m*.
threw [θru:] *pt of* **throw**.
thrift [θrɪft] *n* économie *f*; **~y** *a* économe.
thrill [θrɪl] *n* frisson *m*, émotion *f* // *vi* tressaillir, frissonner // *vt* (*audience*) électriser; **to be ~ed** (*with gift etc*) être ravi; **~er** *n* film *m* (*or* roman *m or* pièce *f*) à suspense.
thrive, *pt* **thrived**, **throve** *pp* **thrived**, **thriven** [θraɪv, θrəuv, 'θrɪvn] *vi* pousser *or* se développer bien; (*business*) prospérer; **he ~s on it** cela lui réussit; **thriving** *a* vigoureux(euse); prospère.
throat [θrəut] *n* gorge *f*; **to have a sore ~** avoir mal à la gorge.
throb [θrɔb] *n* (*of heart*) pulsation *f*; (*of engine*) vibration *f*; (*of pain*) élancement *m* // *vi* (*heart*) palpiter; (*engine*) vibrer; (*pain*) lanciner; (*wound*) causer des élancements.
throes [θrəuz] *npl*: **in the ~ of** au beau milieu de; en proie à; **in the ~ of death** à l'agonie.
thrombosis [θrɔm'bəusɪs] *n* thrombose *f*.
throne [θrəun] *n* trône *m*.
throttle ['θrɔtl] *n* (AUT) accélérateur *m* // *vt* étrangler.
through [θru:] *prep* à travers; (*time*) pendant, durant; (*by means of*) par, par l'intermédiaire de; (*owing to*) à cause de // *a* (*ticket, train, passage*) direct(e) // *ad* à travers; **to put sb ~ to sb** (TEL) passer qn à qn; **to be ~** (TEL) avoir la communication; (*have finished*) avoir fini; **'no ~ way'** 'impasse'; **~out** *prep* (*place*) partout dans; (*time*) durant tout(e) le(la) // *ad* partout.
throve [θrəuv] *pt of* **thrive**.
throw [θrəu] *n* jet *m*; (SPORT) lancer *m* // *vt* (*pt* **threw,** *pp* **thrown** [θru:, θrəun]) lancer, jeter; (SPORT) lancer; (*rider*) désarçonner; (*fig*) décontenancer; (*pottery*) tourner; **to ~ a party** donner une réception; **to ~ away** *vt* jeter; **to ~ off** *vt* se débarrasser de; **to ~ out** *vt* jeter dehors; (*reject*) rejeter; **to ~ up** *vi* vomir; **~away** *a* à jeter; **~-in** *n* (SPORT) remise *f* en jeu.
thru [θru:] *prep, a, ad* (*US*) = **through.**
thrush [θrʌʃ] *n* grive *f*.
thrust [θrʌst] *n* (TECH) poussée *f* // *vt* (*pt, pp* **thrust**) pousser brusquement; (*push in*) enfoncer; **~ing** *a* dynamique; (*fig*) qui se met trop en avant.
thud [θʌd] *n* bruit sourd.
thug [θʌg] *n* voyou *m*.
thumb [θʌm] *n* (ANAT) pouce *m* // *vt* (*book*) feuilleter; **to ~ a lift** faire de l'auto-stop, arrêter une voiture; **~ index** *n* répertoire *m* (à onglets); **~nail** *n* ongle *m* du pouce; **~tack** *n* (*US*) punaise *f* (*clou*).

thump [θʌmp] *n* grand coup ; (*sound*) bruit sourd // *vt* cogner sur // *vi* cogner, frapper.

thunder ['θʌndə*] *n* tonnerre *m* // *vi* tonner ; (*train etc*): **to ~ past** passer dans un grondement *or* un bruit de tonnerre ; **~clap** *n* coup *m* de tonnerre ; **~ous** *a* étourdissant(e) ; **~storm** *n* orage *m* ; **~struck** *a* (*fig*) abasourdi(e) ; **~y** *a* orageux(euse).

Thursday ['θə:zdı] *n* jeudi *m*.

thus [ðʌs] *ad* ainsi.

thwart [θwɔ:t] *vt* contrecarrer.

thyme [taım] *n* thym *m*.

thyroid ['θaırɔıd] *n* thyroïde *f*.

tiara [tı'ɑ:rə] *n* (*woman's*) diadème *m*.

tic [tık] *n* tic (nerveux).

tick [tık] *n* (*sound*: *of clock*) tic-tac *m* ; (*mark*) coche *f* ; (ZOOL) tique *f* ; (*col*): **in a ~** dans un instant // *vi* faire tic-tac // *vt* cocher ; **to ~ off** *vt* cocher ; (*person*) réprimander, attraper.

ticket ['tıkıt] *n* billet *m* ; (*for bus, tube*) ticket *m* ; (*in shop*: *on goods*) étiquette *f* ; (: *from cash register*) reçu *m*, ticket ; (*for library*) carte *f* ; **~ collector** *n* contrôleur/euse ; **~ holder** *n* personne munie d'un billet ; **~ office** *n* guichet *m*, bureau *m* de vente des billets.

tickle ['tıkl] *n* chatouillement *m* // *vt* chatouiller ; (*fig*) plaire à ; faire rire ; **ticklish** *a* chatouilleux(euse).

tidal ['taıdl] *a* à marée ; **~ wave** *n* raz-de-marée *m inv*.

tiddlywinks ['tıdlıwıŋks] *n* jeu *m* de puce.

tide [taıd] *n* marée *f* ; (*fig*: *of events*) cours *m* // *vt*: **to ~ sb over** dépanner qn.

tidily ['taıdılı] *ad* avec soin, soigneusement.

tidiness ['taıdınıs] *n* bon ordre ; goût *m* de l'ordre.

tidy ['taıdı] *a* (*room*) bien rangé(e) ; (*dress, work*) net(nette), soigné(e) ; (*person*) ordonné(e), qui a de l'ordre // *vt* (*also*: **~ up**) ranger ; **to ~ o.s. up** s'arranger.

tie [taı] *n* (*string etc*) cordon *m* ; (*also*: **neck~**) cravate *f* ; (*fig*: *link*) lien *m* ; (SPORT: *draw*) égalité *f* de points ; match nul // *vt* (*parcel*) attacher ; (*ribbon*) nouer // *vi* (SPORT) faire match nul ; finir à égalité de points ; **'black/white ~'** 'smoking/habit de rigueur' ; **to ~ sth in a bow** faire un nœud à *or* avec qch ; **to ~ a knot in sth** faire un nœud à qch ; **to ~ down** *vt* attacher ; (*fig*): **to ~ sb down to** contraindre qn à accepter, fixer à qn ; **to ~ up** *vt* (*parcel*) ficeler ; (*dog, boat*) attacher ; (*arrangements*) conclure ; **to be ~d up** (*busy*) être pris *or* occupé.

tier [tıə*] *n* gradin *m* ; (*of cake*) étage *m*.

tiff [tıf] *n* petite querelle.

tiger ['taıgə*] *n* tigre *m*.

tight [taıt] *a* (*rope*) tendu(e), raide ; (*clothes*) étroit(e), très juste ; (*budget, programme, bend*) serré(e) ; (*control*) strict(e), sévère ; (*col*: *drunk*) ivre, rond(e) // *ad* (*squeeze*) très fort ; (*shut*) à bloc, hermétiquement ; **~s** *npl* collant *m* ; **~en** *vt* (*rope*) tendre ; (*screw*) resserrer ; (*control*) renforcer // *vi* se tendre, se resserrer ; **~-fisted** *a* avare ; **~ly** *ad* (*grasp*) bien, très fort ; **~-rope** *n* corde *f* raide.

tile [taıl] *n* (*on roof*) tuile *f* ; (*on wall or floor*) carreau *m* ; **~d** *a* en tuiles ; carrelé(e).

till [tıl] *n* caisse (enregistreuse) // *vt* (*land*) cultiver // *prep, cj* = **until**.

tiller ['tılə*] *n* (NAUT) barre *f* (du gouvernail).

tilt [tılt] *vt* pencher, incliner // *vi* pencher, être incliné(e).

timber [tımbə*] *n* (*material*) bois *m* de construction ; (*trees*) arbres *mpl*.

time [taım] *n* temps *m* ; (*epoch*: *often pl*) époque *f*, temps ; (*by clock*) heure *f* ; (*moment*) moment *m* ; (*occasion, also* MATH) fois *f* ; (MUS) mesure *f* // *vt* (*race*) chronométrer ; (*programme*) minuter ; (*remark etc*) choisir le moment de ; **a long ~** un long moment, longtemps ; **for the ~ being** pour le moment ; **from ~ to ~** de temps en temps ; **in ~** (*soon enough*) à temps ; (*after some time*) avec le temps, à la longue ; (MUS) en mesure ; **in a week's ~** dans une semaine ; **on ~** à l'heure ; **5 ~s 5** 5 fois 5 ; **what ~ is it?** quelle heure est-il? ; **to have a good ~** bien s'amuser ; **~'s up!** c'est l'heure! ; **I've no ~ for it** (*fig*) cela m'agace ; **~ bomb** *n* bombe *f* à retardement ; **~keeper** *n* (SPORT) chronomètre *m* ; **~ lag** *n* décalage *m* ; (*in travel*) décalage *m* horaire ; **~less** *a* éternel(le) ; **~ limit** *n* limite *f* de temps, délai *m* ; **~ly** *a* opportun(e) ; **~ off** *n* temps *m* libre ; **~r** *n* (*in kitchen*) compte-minutes *m inv* ; **~-saving** *a* qui fait gagner du temps ; **~ switch** *n* minuteur *m* ; (*for lighting*) minuterie *f* ; **~table** *n* (RAIL) (indicateur *m*) horaire *m* ; (SCOL) emploi *m* du temps ; **~ zone** *n* fuseau *m* horaire.

timid ['tımıd] *a* timide ; (*easily scared*) peureux(euse).

timing ['taımıŋ] *n* minutage *m* ; chronométrage *m* ; **the ~ of his resignation** le moment choisi pour sa démission ; **~ device** *n* mécanisme *m* de retardement.

timpani ['tımpənı] *npl* timbales *fpl*.

tin [tın] *n* étain *m* ; (*also*: **~ plate**) fer-blanc *m* ; (*can*) boîte *f* (de conserve) ; (*for baking*) moule *m* (à gâteau) ; **~ foil** *n* papier *m* d'étain.

tinge [tındʒ] *n* nuance *f* // *vt*: **~d with** teinté(e) de.

tingle ['tıŋgl] *n* picotement *m* ; frisson *m* // *vi* picoter.

tinker ['tıŋkə*] *n* rétameur ambulant ; (*gipsy*) romanichel *m* ; **to ~ with** *vt* bricoler, rafistoler.

tinkle ['kıŋkl] *vi* tinter // *n* (*col*): **to give sb a ~** passer un coup de fil à qn.

tinned [tınd] *a* (*food*) en boîte, en conserve.

tinny ['tını] *a* métallique.

tin opener ['tınəupnə*] *n* ouvre-boîte(s) *m*.

tinsel ['tınsl] *n* guirlandes *fpl* de Noël (*argentées*).

tint [tınt] *n* teinte *f* ; (*for hair*) shampooing colorant.

tiny ['taını] *a* minuscule.

tip [tıp] *n* (*end*) bout *m* ; (*protective*: *on umbrella etc*) embout *m* ; (*gratuity*) pourboire *m* ; (*for coal*) terril *m* ; (*for rubbish*) décharge *f* ; (*advice*) tuyau *m* // *vt* (*waiter*) donner un pourboire à ; (*tilt*) incliner ; (*overturn*: *also*: **~ over**) renverser ; (*empty*: *also*: ~ **out**) déverser ; ~**-off** *n* (*hint*) tuyau *m* ; ~**ped** *a* (*cigarette*) (à bout) filtre *inv*; **steel-**~**ped** à bout métallique, à embout de métal.

tipple ['tɪpl] *vi* picoler // *n*: **to have a** ~ boire un petit coup.

tipsy ['tɪpsɪ] *a* un peu ivre, éméché(e).

tiptoe ['tɪptəu] *n*: **on** ~ sur la pointe des pieds.

tiptop ['tɪp'tɔp] *a*: **in** ~ **condition** en excellent état.

tire ['taɪə*] *n* (*US*) = **tyre** // *vt* fatiguer // *vi* se fatiguer ; ~**d** *a* fatigué(e) ; **to be** ~**d of** en avoir assez de, être las(lasse) de ; ~**dness** *n* fatigue *f*; ~**less** *a* infatigable, inlassable ; ~**some** *a* ennuyeux(euse) ; **tiring** *a* fatigant(e).

tissue ['tɪʃu:] *n* tissu *m*; (*paper handkerchief*) mouchoir *m* en papier, kleenex *m* ® ; ~ **paper** *n* papier *m* de soie.

tit [tɪt] *n* (*bird*) mésange *f*; **to give** ~ **for tat** rendre coup pour coup.

titanium [tɪ'teɪnɪəm] *n* titane *m*.

titbit ['tɪtbɪt] *n* (*food*) friandise *f*; (*news*) potin *m*.

titillate ['tɪtɪleɪt] *vt* titiller, exciter.

titivate ['tɪtɪveɪt] *vt* pomponner.

title ['taɪtl] *n* titre *m* ; ~ **deed** *n* (LAW) titre (constitutif) de propriété ; ~ **role** *n* rôle principal.

titter ['tɪtə*] *vi* rire (bêtement).

tittle-tattle ['tɪtltætl] *n* bavardages *mpl*.

titular ['tɪtjulə*] *a* (*in name only*) nominal(e).

tizzy ['tɪzɪ] *n*: **to be in a** ~ être dans tous ses états.

to [tu:, tə] *prep* à ; (*towards*) vers ; envers ; **give it** ~ **me** donne-le-moi ; **the key** ~ **the front door** la clé de la porte d'entrée ; **the main thing is** ~... l'important est de... ; **to go** ~ **France/Portugal** aller en France/au Portugal ; **I went** ~ **Claude's** je suis allé chez Claude ; **to go** ~ **town/school** aller en ville/à l'école ; **pull/push the door** ~ tire/pousse la porte ; **to go** ~ **and fro** aller et venir.

toad [təud] *n* crapaud *m*; ~**stool** *n* champignon (vénéneux) ; ~**y** *vi* flatter bassement.

toast [təust] *n* (CULIN) pain grillé, toast *m* ; (*drink, speech*) toast // *vt* (CULIN) faire griller ; (*drink to*) porter un toast à ; **a piece** *or* **slice of** ~ un toast ; ~**er** *n* grille-pain *m inv* ; ~**master** *n* animateur *m* pour réceptions ; ~**rack** *n* porte-toast *m*.

tobacco [tə'bækəu] *n* tabac *m* ; ~**nist** *n* marchand/e de tabac ; ~**nist's (shop)** *n* (bureau *m* de) tabac *m*.

toboggan [tə'bɔgən] *n* toboggan *m* ; (*child's*) luge *f*.

today [tə'deɪ] *ad,n* (*also fig*) aujourd'hui (*m*).

toddler ['tɔdlə*] *n* enfant *m/f* qui commence à marcher, bambin *m*.

toddy ['tɔdɪ] *n* grog *m*.

to-do [tə'du:] *n* (*fuss*) histoire *f*, affaire *f*.

toe [təu] *n* doigt *m* de pied, orteil *m* ; (*of shoe*) bout *m* ; **to** ~ **the line** (*fig*) obéir, se conformer ; ~**hold** *n* prise *f*; ~**nail** *n* ongle *m* de l'orteil.

toffee ['tɔfɪ] *n* caramel *m* ; ~ **apple** *n* pomme caramélisée.

toga ['təugə] *n* toge *f*.

together [tə'gɛðə*] *ad* ensemble ; (*at same time*) en même temps ; ~ **with** *prep* avec ; ~**ness** *n* camaraderie *f*; intimité *f*.

toil [tɔɪl] *n* dur travail, labeur *m* // *vi* travailler dur ; peiner.

toilet ['tɔɪlət] *n* (*lavatory*) toilettes *fpl*, cabinets *mpl* // *cpd* (*bag, soap etc*) de toilette ; ~ **bowl** *n* cuvette *f* des W.-C. ; ~ **paper** *n* papier *m* hygiénique ; ~**ries** *npl* articles *mpl* de toilette ; ~ **roll** *n* rouleau *m* de papier hygiénique ; ~ **water** *n* eau *f* de toilette.

token ['təukən] *n* (*sign*) marque *f*, témoignage *m* ; (*voucher*) bon *m*, coupon *m* ; **book/record** ~ *n* chèque-livre/disque *m*.

told [təuld] *pt, pp of* **tell.**

tolerable ['tɔlərəbl] *a* (*bearable*) tolérable ; (*fairly good*) passable.

tolerance ['tɔlərns] *n* (*also*: TECH) tolérance *f*.

tolerant ['tɔlərnt] *a*: ~ **(of)** tolérant(e) (à l'égard de).

tolerate ['tɔləreɪt] *vt* supporter ; (MED, TECH) tolérer ; **toleration** [-'reɪʃən] *n* tolérance *f*.

toll [təul] *n* (*tax, charge*) péage *m* // *vi* (*bell*) sonner ; **the accident** ~ **on the roads** le nombre des victimes de la route ; ~**bridge** *n* pont *m* à péage.

tomato, ~es [tə'mɑ:təu] *n* tomate *f*.

tomb [tu:m] *n* tombe *f*.

tombola [tɔm'bəulə] *n* tombola *f*.

tomboy ['tɔmbɔɪ] *n* garçon manqué.

tombstone ['tu:mstəun] *n* pierre tombale.

tomcat ['tɔmkæt] *n* matou *m*.

tomorrow [tə'mɔrəu] *ad,n* (*also fig*) demain (*m*) ; **the day after** ~ après-demain ; ~ **morning** demain matin.

ton [tʌn] *n* tonne *f* (= *1016 kg* ; *20 cwt*) ; (NAUT: *also*: **register** ~) tonneau *m* (= *2.83 cu.m* ; *100 cu. ft*) ; ~**s of** (*col*) des tas de.

tonal ['təunl] *a* tonal(e).

tone [təun] *n* ton *m* ; (*of radio*) tonalité *f* // *vi* s'harmoniser ; **to** ~ **down** *vt* (*colour, criticism*) adoucir ; (*sound*) baisser ; **to** ~ **up** *vt* (*muscles*) tonifier ; ~**-deaf** *a* qui n'a pas d'oreille.

tongs [tɔŋz] *npl* pinces *fpl* ; (*for coal*) pincettes *fpl* ; (*for hair*) fer *m* à friser.

tongue [tʌŋ] *n* langue *f*; ~ **in cheek** *ad* ironiquement ; ~**-tied** *a* (*fig*) muet(te) ; ~**-twister** *n* phrase *f* très difficile à prononcer.

tonic ['tɔnɪk] *n* (MED) tonique *m* ; (MUS) tonique *f* ; (*also*: ~ **water**) tonic *m*.

tonight [tə'naɪt] *ad, n* cette nuit ; (*this evening*) ce soir.

tonnage ['tʌnɪdʒ] *n* (NAUT) tonnage *m*.

tonne [tʌn] *n* (*metric ton*) tonne *f*.

tonsil ['tɔnsl] *n* amygdale *f* ; ~**litis** [-'laɪtɪs] *n* amygdalite *f*.

too [tu:] *ad* (*excessively*) trop ; (*also*) aussi ; ~ **much** *ad* trop // *det* trop de ; ~ **many** *det* trop de ; ~ **bad!** tant pis!

took [tuk] *pt of* **take**.

tool [tu:l] *n* outil *m* // *vt* travailler,

ouvrager ; ~ **box/kit** *n* boîte *f*/trousse *f* à outils.

toot [tu:t] *n* coup *m* de sifflet (*or* de klaxon) // *vi* siffler ; (*with car-horn*) klaxonner.

tooth, *pl* **teeth** [tu:θ, ti:θ] *n* (ANAT, TECH) dent *f* ; ~**ache** *n* mal *m* de dents ; ~**brush** *n* brosse *f* à dents ; ~**paste** *n* (pâte *f*) dentifrice *m* ; ~**pick** *n* cure-dent *m* ; ~ **powder** *n* poudre *f* dentifrice.

top [tɔp] *n* (*of mountain, head*) sommet *m* ; (*of page, ladder*) haut *m* ; (*of box, cupboard, table*) dessus *m* ; (*lid: of box, jar*) couvercle *m* ; (*: of bottle*) bouchon *m* ; (*toy*) toupie *f* // *a* du haut ; (*in rank*) premier(ère) ; (*best*) meilleur(e) // *vt* (*exceed*) dépasser ; (*be first in*) être en tête de ; **on** ~ **of** sur ; (*in addition to*) en plus de ; **from** ~ **to toe** de la tête aux pieds ; **at the** ~ **of the list** en tête de liste ; **to** ~ **up** *vt* remplir ; ~**coat** *n* pardessus *m* ; ~ **floor** *n* dernier étage ; ~ **hat** *n* haut-de-forme *m* ; ~-**heavy** *a* (*object*) trop lourd(e) du haut.

topic ['tɔpɪk] *n* sujet *m*, thème *m* ; ~**al** *a* d'actualité.

top: ~**less** *a* (*bather etc*) aux seins nus ; ~**less swimsuit** *n* monokini *m* ; ~-**level** *a* (*talks*) à l'échelon le plus élevé ; ~**most** *a* le(la) plus haut(e).

topple ['tɔpl] *vt* renverser, faire tomber // *vi* basculer ; tomber.

topsy-turvy ['tɔp si'tə:vɪ] *a,ad* sens dessus-dessous.

torch [tɔ:tʃ] *n* torche *f* ; (*electric*) lampe *f* de poche.

tore [tɔ:*] *pt of* **tear.**

torment *n* ['tɔ:mɛnt] tourment *m* // *vt* [tɔ:'mɛnt] tourmenter ; (*fig: annoy*) agacer.

torn [tɔ:n] *pp of* **tear** // *a*: ~ **between** (*fig*) tiraillé(e) entre.

tornado, ~**es** [tɔ:'neɪdəu] *n* tornade *f*.

torpedo, ~**es** [tɔ:'pi:dəu] *n* torpille *f*.

torpor ['tɔ:pə*] *n* torpeur *f*.

torque [tɔ:k] *n* couple *m* de torsion.

torrent ['tɔrnt] *n* torrent *m* ; ~**ial** [-'rɛnʃl] *a* torrentiel(le).

torso ['tɔ:səu] *n* torse *m*.

tortoise ['tɔ:təs] *n* tortue *f* ; ~**shell** ['tɔ:təʃɛl] *a* en écaille.

tortuous ['tɔ:tjuəs] *a* tortueux(euse).

torture ['tɔ:tʃə*] *n* torture *f* // *vt* torturer.

Tory ['tɔ:rɪ] *a* tory (*pl* tories), conservateur(trice) // *n* tory *m/f*, conservateur/trice.

toss [tɔs] *vt* lancer, jeter ; (*pancake*) faire sauter ; (*head*) rejeter en arrière ; **to** ~ **a coin** jouer à pile ou face ; **to** ~ **up for sth** jouer qch à pile ou face ; **to** ~ **and turn** (*in bed*) se tourner et se retourner.

tot [tɔt] *n* (*drink*) petit verre ; (*child*) bambin *m*.

total ['təutl] *a* total(e) // *n* total *m* // *vt* (*add up*) faire le total de, totaliser ; (*amount to*) s'élever à.

totalitarian [təutælɪ'tɛərɪən] *a* totalitaire.

totality [təu'tælɪtɪ] *n* totalité *f*.

totem pole ['təutəmpəul] *n* mât *m* totémique.

totter ['tɔtə*] *vi* chanceler.

touch [tʌtʃ] *n* contact *m*, toucher *m* ; (*sense, also skill: of pianist etc*) toucher ; (*fig: note, also:* FOOTBALL) touche *f* // *vt* (*gen*) toucher ; (*tamper with*) toucher à ; **a** ~ **of** (*fig*) un petit peu de ; une touche de ; **in** ~ **with** en contact *or* rapport avec ; **to get in** ~ **with** prendre contact avec ; **to lose** ~ (*friends*) se perdre de vue ; **to** ~ **on** *vt fus* (*topic*) effleurer, toucher ; **to** ~ **up** *vt* (*paint*) retoucher ; ~-**and-go** *a* incertain(e) ; **it was** ~-**and-go whether we did it** nous avons failli ne pas le faire ; ~**down** *n* atterrissage *m* ; (*on sea*) amerrissage *m* ; ~**ed** *a* touché(e) ; (*col*) cinglé(e) ; ~**ing** *a* touchant(e), attendrissant(e) ; ~**line** *n* (SPORT) (ligne *f* de) touche *f* ; ~**y** *a* (*person*) susceptible.

tough [tʌf] *a* dur(e) ; (*resistant*) résistant(e), solide ; (*meat*) dur, coriace // *n* (*gangster etc*) dur *m* ; ~ **luck!** pas de chance! ; tant pis! ; ~**en** *vt* rendre plus dur(e) (*or* plus résistant(e) *or* plus solide) ; ~**ness** *n* dureté *f* ; résistance *f* ; solidité *f*.

toupee ['tu:peɪ] *n* postiche *m*.

tour ['tuə*] *n* voyage *m* ; (*also:* **package** ~) voyage organisé ; (*of town, museum*) tour *m*, visite *f* ; (*by artist*) tournée *f* // *vt* visiter ; ~**ing** *n* voyages *mpl* touristiques, tourisme *m*.

tourism ['tuərɪzm] *n* tourisme *m*.

tourist ['tuərɪst] *n* touriste *m/f* // *ad* (*travel*) en classe touriste // *cpd* touristique ; ~ **office** *n* syndicat *m* d'initiative.

tournament ['tuənəmənt] *n* tournoi *m*.

tour operator ['tuər'ɔpəreɪtə*] *n* organisateur *m* de voyages.

tousled ['tauzld] *a* (*hair*) ébouriffé(e).

tout [taut] *vi*: **to** ~ **for** essayer de raccrocher, racoler ; **to** ~ **sth (around)** essayer de placer *or* (re)vendre qch.

tow [təu] *vt* remorquer ; **'on** ~**'** (AUT) 'véhicule en remorque'.

toward(s) [tə'wɔ:d(z)] *prep* vers ; (*of attitude*) envers, à l'égard de ; (*of purpose*) pour.

towel ['tauəl] *n* serviette *f* (de toilette) ; (*also:* **tea** ~) torchon *m* ; ~**ling** *n* (*fabric*) tissu-éponge *m* ; ~ **rail** *n* porte-serviettes *m inv*.

tower ['tauə*] *n* tour *f* ; ~ **block** *n* tour *f* (d'habitation) ; ~**ing** *a* très haut(e), imposant(e).

towline ['təulaɪn] *n* (câble *m* de) remorque *f*.

town [taun] *n* ville *f* ; **to go to** ~ aller en ville ; (*fig*) y mettre le paquet ; ~ **clerk** *n* ≈ secrétaire *m/f* de mairie ; ~ **council** *n* conseil municipal ; ~ **hall** *n* ≈ mairie *f* ; ~ **planner** *n* urbaniste *m/f* ; ~ **planning** *n* urbanisme *m*.

towpath ['təupɑ:θ] *n* (chemin *m* de) halage *m*.

towrope ['təurəup] *n* (câble *m* de) remorque *f*.

toxic ['tɔksɪk] *a* toxique.

toy [tɔɪ] *n* jouet *m* ; **to** ~ **with** *vt fus* jouer avec ; (*idea*) caresser ; ~**shop** *m* magasin *m* de jouets.

trace [treɪs] *n* trace *f* // *vt* (*draw*) tracer, dessiner ; (*follow*) suivre la trace de ; (*locate*) retrouver ; **without** ~ (*disappear*) sans laisser de traces.

track [træk] *n* (*mark*) trace *f* ; (*path: gen*) chemin *m*, piste *f* ; (*: of bullet etc*) trajectoire *f*; (: *of suspect, animal*) piste; (RAIL) voie ferrée, rails *mpl*; (*on tape*, SPORT) piste // *vt* suivre la trace *or* la piste de; **to keep ~ of** suivre; **to ~ down** *vt* (*prey*) trouver et capturer; (*sth lost*) finir par retrouver; **~ed** *a* (AUT) à chenille; **~er dog** *n* chien policier; **~suit** *n* survêtement *m*.

tract [trækt] *n* (GEO) étendue *f*, zone *f*; (*pamphlet*) tract *m*; **respiratory ~** (ANAT) système *m* respiratoire.

tractor ['træktə*] *n* tracteur *m*.

trade [treɪd] *n* commerce *m*; (*skill, job*) métier *m* // *vi* faire du commerce; **to ~ with/in** faire du commerce avec/le commerce de; **to ~ in** *vt* (*old car etc*) faire reprendre; **~-in (value)** *n* reprise *f*; **~mark** *n* marque *f* de fabrique; **~name** *n* marque déposée; **~r** *n* commerçant/e, négociant/e; **~sman** *n* (*shopkeeper*) commerçant; **~ union** *n* syndicat *m*; **~ unionist** syndicaliste *m/f*; **trading** *n* affaires *fpl*, commerce *m*; **trading estate** *n* zone industrielle; **trading stamp** *n* timbre-prime *m*.

tradition [trə'dɪʃən] *n* tradition *f*; **~s** *npl* coutumes *fpl*, traditions; **~al** *a* traditionnel(le).

traffic ['træfɪk] *n* trafic *m*; (*cars*) circulation *f* // *vi*: **to ~ in** (*pej*: *liquor, drugs*) faire le trafic de; **~ circle** *n* (*US*) rond-point *m*; **~ jam** *n* embouteillage *m*; **~ lights** *npl* feux *mpl* (de signalisation); **~ sign** *n* panneau *m* de signalisation; **~ warden** *n* contractuel/le.

tragedy ['trædʒədɪ] *n* tragédie *f*.

tragic ['trædʒɪk] *a* tragique.

trail [treɪl] *n* (*tracks*) trace *f*, piste *f*; (*path*) chemin *m*, piste; (*of smoke etc*) traînée *f* // *vt* traîner, tirer; (*follow*) suivre // *vi* traîner; **to ~ behind** *vi* traîner, être à la traîne; **~er** *n* (AUT) remorque *f*; (*US*) caravane *f*; (CINEMA) court film de lancement; **~ing plant** *n* plante rampante.

train [treɪn] *n* train *m*; (*in underground*) rame *f*; (*of dress*) traîne *f* // *vt* (*apprentice, doctor etc*) former; (*sportsman*) entraîner; (*dog*) dresser; (*memory*) exercer; (*point*: *gun etc*): **to ~ sth on** braquer qch sur // *vi* recevoir sa formation; s'entraîner; **one's ~ of thought** le fil de sa pensée; **~ed** *a* qualifié(e), qui a reçu une formation; dressé(e); **~ee** [treɪ'ni:] *n* stagiaire *m/f*; (*in trade*) apprenti/e; **~er** *n* (SPORT) entraîneur/euse; (*of dogs etc*) dresseur/euse; **~ing** *n* formation *f*; entraînement *m*; dressage *m*; **in ~ing** (SPORT) à l'entraînement; (*fit*) en forme; **~ing college** *n* école professionnelle; (*for teachers*) ≈ école normale.

traipse [treɪps] *vi* (se) traîner, déambuler.

trait [treɪt] *n* trait *m* (de caractère).

traitor ['treɪtə*] *n* traître *m*.

tram [træm] *n* (*also*: **~car**) tram(way) *m*; **~line** *n* ligne *f* de tram(way).

tramp [træmp] *n* (*person*) vagabond/e, clochard/e // *vi* marcher d'un pas lourd // *vt* (*walk through*: *town, streets*) parcourir à pied.

trample ['træmpl] *vt*: **to ~ (underfoot)** piétiner; (*fig*) bafouer.

trampoline ['træmpəli:n] *n* trampolino *m*.

trance [trɑ:ns] *n* transe *f*; (MED) catalepsie *f*.

tranquil ['træŋkwɪl] *a* tranquille; **~lity** *n* tranquillité *f*; **~lizer** *n* (MED) tranquillisant *m*.

transact [træn'zækt] *vt* (*business*) traiter; **~ion** [-'zækʃən] *n* transaction *f*; **~ions** *npl* (*minutes*) actes *mpl*.

transatlantic ['trænzət'læntɪk] *a* transatlantique.

transcend [træn'sɛnd] *vt* transcender; (*excel over*) surpasser.

transcript ['trænskrɪpt] *n* transcription *f* (*texte*); **~ion** [-'skrɪpʃən] *n* transcription.

transept ['trænsɛpt] *n* transept *m*.

transfer *n* ['trænsfə*] (*gen, also* SPORT) transfert *m*; (POL: *of power*) passation *f*; (*picture, design*) décalcomanie *f*; (: *stick-on*) autocollant *m* // *vt* [træns'fə:*] transférer; passer; décalquer; **to ~ the charges** (TEL) téléphoner en P.C.V.; **~able** [-'fə:rəbl] *a* transmissible, transférable; **'not ~able'** 'personnel'.

transform [træns'fɔ:m] *vt* transformer; **~ation** [-'meɪʃən] *n* transformation *f*; **~er** *n* (ELEC) transformateur *m*.

transfusion [træns'fju:ʒən] *n* transfusion *f*.

transient ['trænzɪənt] *a* transitoire, éphémère.

transistor [træn'zɪstə*] *n* (ELEC, *also*: **~ radio**) transistor *m*.

transit ['trænzɪt] *n*: **in ~** en transit; **~ lounge** *n* salle *f* de transit.

transition [træn'zɪʃən] *n* transition *f*; **~al** *a* transitoire.

transitive ['trænzɪtɪv] *a* (LING) transitif(ive).

transitory ['trænzɪtərɪ] *a* transitoire.

translate [trænz'leɪt] *vt* traduire; **translation** [-'leɪʃən] *n* traduction *f*; (SCOL: *as opposed to prose*) version *f*; **translator** *n* traducteur/trice.

transmission [trænz'mɪʃən] *n* transmission *f*.

transmit [trænz'mɪt] *vt* transmettre; (RADIO, TV) émettre; **~ter** *m* émetteur *m*.

transparency [træns'pɛərnsɪ] *n* (PHOT) diapositive *f*.

transparent [træns'pærnt] *a* transparent(e).

transplant *vt* [træns'plɑ:nt] transplanter; (*seedlings*) repiquer // *n* ['trænsplɑ:nt] (MED) transplantation *f*.

transport *n* ['trænspɔ:t] transport *m* // *vt* [træns'pɔ:t] transporter; **~ation** [-'teɪʃən] *n* (moyen *m* de) transport *m*; (*of prisoners*) transportation *f*; **~ café** *n* ≈ restaurant *m* de routiers.

transverse ['trænzvə:s] *a* transversal(e).

transvestite [trænz'vɛstaɪt] *n* travesti/e.

trap [træp] *n* (*snare, trick*) piège *m*; (*carriage*) cabriolet *m* // *vt* prendre au piège; (*immobilize*) bloquer; (*jam*) coincer; **to shut one's ~** (*col*) la fermer; **~ door** *n* trappe *f*.

trapeze [trə'pi:z] *n* trapèze *m*.

trapper ['træpə*] *n* trappeur *m*.

trappings ['træpɪŋz] *npl* ornements *mpl*; attributs *mpl*.

trash [træʃ] *n* (*pej*: *goods*) camelote *f*; (: *nonsense*) sottises *fpl*; ~ **can** *n* (*US*) boîte *f* à ordures.

trauma ['trɔ:mə] *n* traumatisme *m*; ~**tic** [-'mætɪk] *a* traumatisant(e).

travel ['trævl] *n* voyage(s) *m(pl)* // *vi* voyager; (*move*) aller, se déplacer // *vt* (*distance*) parcourir; ~ **agent's** *n* agence *f* de voyages; ~**ler,** ~**er** (*US*) *n* voyageur/euse; ~**ler's cheque** *n* chèque *m* de voyage; ~**ling,** ~**ing** (*US*) *n* voyage(s) *m(pl)* // *cpd* (*bag, clock*) de voyage; (*expenses*) de déplacement; ~ **sickness** *n* mal *m* de la route (*or* de mer *or* de l'air).

traverse ['trævəs] *vt* traverser.

travesty ['trævəstɪ] *n* parodie *f*.

trawler ['trɔ:lə*] *n* chalutier *m*.

tray [treɪ] *n* (*for carrying*) plateau *m*; (*on desk*) corbeille *f*.

treacherous ['trɛtʃərəs] *a* traître(sse).

treachery ['trɛtʃərɪ] *n* traîtrise *f*.

treacle ['tri:kl] *n* mélasse *f*.

tread [trɛd] *n* pas *m*; (*sound*) bruit *m* de pas; (*of tyre*) chape *f*, bande *f* de roulement // *vi* (*pt* **trod,** *pp* **trodden** [trɔd, 'trɔdn]) marcher; **to** ~ **on** *vt fus* marcher sur.

treason ['tri:zn] *n* trahison *f*.

treasure ['trɛʒə*] *n* trésor *m* // *vt* (*value*) tenir beaucoup à; (*store*) conserver précieusement; ~ **hunt** *n* chasse *f* au trésor.

treasurer ['trɛʒərə*] *n* trésorier/ère.

treasury ['trɛʒərɪ] *n* trésorerie *f*; **the T**~ (POL) le ministère des Finances.

treat [tri:t] *n* petit cadeau, petite surprise // *vt* traiter; **it was a** ~ ça m'a (*or* nous a *etc*) vraiment fait plaisir; **to** ~ **sb to sth** offrir qch à qn.

treatise ['tri:tɪz] *n* traité *m* (*ouvrage*).

treatment ['tri:tmənt] *n* traitement *m*.

treaty ['tri:tɪ] *n* traité *m*.

treble ['trɛbl] *a* triple // *n* (MUS) soprano *m* // *vt, vi* tripler; ~ **clef** *n* clé *f* de sol.

tree [tri:] *n* arbre *m*; ~**-lined** *a* bordé(e) d'arbres; ~**top** *n* cime *f* d'un arbre; ~ **trunk** *n* tronc *m* d'arbre.

trek [trɛk] *n* voyage *m*; randonnée *f*; (*tiring walk*) tirée *f* // *vi* (*as holiday*) faire de la randonnée.

trellis ['trɛlɪs] *n* treillis *m*, treillage *m*.

tremble ['trɛmbl] *vi* trembler; (*machine*) vibrer; **trembling** tremblement *m*; vibrations *fpl* // *a* tremblant(e); vibrant(e).

tremendous [trɪ'mɛndəs] *a* (*enormous*) énorme, fantastique; (*excellent*) formidable.

tremor ['trɛmə*] *n* tremblement *m*; (*also*: **earth** ~) secousse *f* sismique.

trench [trɛntʃ] *n* tranchée *f*.

trend [trɛnd] *n* (*tendency*) tendance *f*; (*of events*) cours *m*; (*fashion*) mode *f*; ~**y** *a* (*idea*) dans le vent; (*clothes*) dernier cri *inv*.

trepidation [trɛpɪ'deɪʃən] *n* vive agitation.

trespass ['trɛspəs] *vi*: **to** ~ **on** s'introduire sans permission dans; (*fig*) empiéter sur; **'no** ~**ing'** 'propriété privée', 'défense d'entrer'.

tress [trɛs] *n* boucle *f* de cheveux.

trestle ['trɛsl] *n* tréteau *m*; ~ **table** *n* table *f* à tréteaux.

trial ['traɪəl] *n* (LAW) procès *m*, jugement *m*; (*test*: *of machine etc*) essai *m*; (*hardship*) épreuve *f*; (*worry*) souci *m*; **to be on** ~ passer en jugement; **by** ~ **and error** par tâtonnements.

triangle ['traɪæŋgl] *n* (MATH, MUS) triangle *m*; **triangular** [-'æŋgjulə*] *a* triangulaire.

tribal ['traɪbəl] *a* tribal(e).

tribe [traɪb] *n* tribu *f*; ~**sman** *n* membre *m* de la tribu.

tribulation [trɪbju'leɪʃən] *n* tribulation *f*, malheur *m*.

tribunal [traɪ'bju:nl] *n* tribunal *m*.

tributary ['trɪbju:tərɪ] *n* (*river*) affluent *m*.

tribute ['trɪbju:t] *n* tribut *m*, hommage *m*; **to pay** ~ **to** rendre hommage à.

trice [traɪs] *n*: **in a** ~ en un clin d'œil.

trick [trɪk] *n* ruse *f*; (*clever act*) astuce *f*; (*joke*) tour *m*; (CARDS) levée *f* // *vt* attraper, rouler; **to play a** ~ **on sb** jouer un tour à qn; ~**ery** *n* ruse *f*.

trickle ['trɪkl] *n* (*of water etc*) filet *m* // *vi* couler en un filet *or* goutte à goutte; **to** ~ **in/out** (*people*) entrer/sortir par petits groupes.

tricky ['trɪkɪ] *a* difficile, délicat(e).

tricycle ['traɪsɪkl] *n* tricycle *m*.

trifle ['traɪfl] *n* bagatelle *f*; (CULIN) ≈ diplomate *m* // *ad*: **a** ~ **long** un peu long; **trifling** *a* insignifiant(e).

trigger ['trɪgə*] *n* (*of gun*) gâchette *f*; **to** ~ **off** *vt* déclencher.

trigonometry [trɪgə'nɔmətrɪ] *n* trigonométrie *f*.

trilby ['trɪlbɪ] *n* (chapeau *m* en) feutre *m*.

trim [trɪm] *a* net(te); (*house, garden*) bien tenu(e); (*figure*) svelte // *n* (*haircut etc*) légère coupe; (*embellishment*) finitions *fpl*; (*on car*) garnitures *fpl* // *vt* couper légèrement; (*decorate*): **to** ~ **(with)** décorer (de); (NAUT: *a sail*) gréer; ~**mings** *npl* décorations *fpl*; (*extras*: *gen* CULIN) garniture *f*.

Trinity ['trɪnɪtɪ] *n*: **the** ~ la Trinité.

trinket ['trɪŋkɪt] *n* bibelot *m*; (*piece of jewellery*) colifichet *m*.

trio ['tri:əu] *n* trio *m*.

trip [trɪp] *n* voyage *m*; (*excursion*) excursion *f*; (*stumble*) faux pas // *vi* faire un faux pas, trébucher; (*go lightly*) marcher d'un pas léger; **on a** ~ en voyage; **to** ~ **up** *vi* trébucher // *vt* faire un croc-en-jambe à.

tripe [traɪp] *n* (CULIN) tripes *fpl*; (*pej*: *rubbish*) idioties *fpl*.

triple ['trɪpl] *a* triple.

triplets ['trɪplɪts] *npl* triplés/ées.

triplicate ['trɪplɪkət] *n*: **in** ~ en trois exemplaires.

tripod ['traɪpɔd] *n* trépied *m*.

tripper ['trɪpə*] *n* touriste *m/f*; excursionniste *m/f*.

trite [traɪt] *a* banal(e).

triumph ['traɪʌmf] *n* triomphe *m* // *vi*: **to** ~ **(over)** triompher (de); ~**al** [-'ʌmfl] *a* triomphal(e); ~**ant** [-'ʌmfənt] *a* triomphant(e).

trivia ['trɪvɪə] *npl* futilités *fpl*.

trivial ['trɪvɪəl] *a* insignifiant(e); (*commonplace*) banal(e); ~**ity** [-'ælɪtɪ] *n* caractère insignifiant; banalité *f*.

trod [trɔd] *pt of* **tread**; **~den** *pp of* **tread**.
trolley ['trɔlı] *n* chariot *m*; **~ bus** *n* trolleybus *m*.
trollop ['trɔləp] *n* prostituée *f*.
trombone [trɔm'bəun] *n* trombone *m*.
troop [tru:p] *n* bande *f*, groupe *m*; **~s** *npl* (MIL) troupes *fpl*; (: *men*) hommes *mpl*, soldats *mpl*; **to ~ in/out** *vi* entrer/sortir en groupe; **~er** *n* (MIL) soldat *m* de cavalerie; **~ing the colour** (*ceremony*) le salut au drapeau; **~ship** *n* (navire *m* de) transport *m*.
trophy ['trəufı] *n* trophée *m*.
tropic ['trɔpık] *n* tropique *m*; **in the ~s** sous les tropiques; **T~ of Cancer/Capricorn** *n* tropique du Cancer/Capricorne; **~al** *a* tropical(e).
trot [trɔt] *n* trot *m* // *vi* trotter; **on the ~** (*fig*: *col*) d'affilée.
trouble ['trʌbl] *n* difficulté(s) *f(pl)*, problème(s) *m(pl)*; (*worry*) ennuis *mpl*, soucis *mpl*; (*bother, effort*) peine *f*; (POL) conflits *mpl*, troubles *mpl*; (MED): **stomach** *etc* **~** troubles gastriques *etc* // *vt* déranger, gêner; (*worry*) inquiéter // *vi*: **to ~ to do** prendre la peine de faire; **~s** *npl* (POL *etc*) troubles *mpl*; **to be in ~** avoir des ennuis; (*ship, climber etc*) être en difficulté; **to go to the ~ of doing** se donner le mal de faire; **it's no ~!** je vous en prie!; **what's the ~?** qu'est-ce qui ne va pas?; **~d** *a* (*person*) inquiet(ète); (*epoch, life*) agité(e); **~-free** *a* sans problèmes *or* ennuis; **~maker** *n* élément perturbateur, fauteur *m* de troubles; **~shooter** *n* (*in conflict*) conciliateur *m*; **~some** *a* ennuyeux(euse), gênant(e).
trough [trɔf] *n* (*also*: **drinking ~**) abreuvoir *m*; (*also*: **feeding ~**) auge *f*; (*channel*) chenal *m*; **~ of low pressure** *n* (GEO) dépression *f*.
trounce [trauns] *vt* (*defeat*) battre à plates coutures.
troupe [tru:p] *n* troupe *f*.
trousers ['trauzəz] *npl* pantalon *m*; **short ~** *npl* culottes courtes.
trousseau, *pl* **~x** *or* **~s** ['tru:səu, -z] *n* trousseau *m*.
trout [traut] *n, pl inv* truite *f*.
trowel ['trauəl] *n* truelle *f*.
truant ['truənt] *n*: **to play ~** faire l'école buissonnière.
truce [tru:s] *n* trêve *f*.
truck [trʌk] *n* camion *m*; (RAIL) wagon *m* à plate-forme; (*for luggage*) chariot *m* (à bagages); **~ driver** *n* camionneur *m*; **~ farm** *n* (*US*) jardin maraîcher.
truculent ['trʌkjulənt] *a* agressif(ive).
trudge [trʌdʒ] *vi* marcher lourdement, se traîner.
true [tru:] *a* vrai(e); (*accurate*) exact(e); (*genuine*) vrai, véritable; (*faithful*) fidèle.
truffle ['trʌfl] *n* truffe *f*.
truly ['tru:lı] *ad* vraiment, réellement; (*truthfully*) sans mentir; (*faithfully*) fidèlement; **'yours ~'** (*in letter*) 'je vous prie d'agréer l'expression de mes sentiments respectueux.'
trump [trʌmp] *n* atout *m*; **~ed-up** *a* inventé(e) (de toutes pièces).
trumpet ['trʌmpıt] *n* trompette *f*; (*player*) trompettiste *m/f*.
truncated [trʌŋ'keıtıd] *a* tronqué(e).
truncheon ['trʌntʃən] *n* bâton *m* (d'agent de police); matraque *f*.
trundle ['trʌndl] *vt, vi*: **to ~ along** rouler bruyamment.
trunk [trʌŋk] *n* (*of tree, person*) tronc *m*; (*of elephant*) trompe *f*; (*case*) malle *f*; **~s** *npl* caleçon *m*; (*also*: **swimming ~s**) maillot *m or* slip *m* de bain; **~ call** *n* (TEL) communication interurbaine; **~ road** ≈ route nationale.
truss [trʌs] *n* (MED) bandage *m* herniaire; **to ~ (up)** *vt* (CULIN) brider.
trust [trʌst] *n* confiance *f*; (LAW) fidéicommis *m*; (COMM) trust *m* // *vt* (*rely on*) avoir confiance en; (*entrust*): **to ~ sth to sb** confier qch à qn; **~ed** *a* en qui l'on a confiance; **~ee** [trʌs'ti:] *n* (LAW) fidéicommissaire *m/f*; (*of school etc*) administrateur/trice; **~ful, ~ing** *a* confiant(e); **~worthy** *a* digne de confiance; **~y** *a* fidèle.
truth, ~s [tru:θ, tru:ðz] *n* vérité *f*; **~ful** *a* (*person*) qui dit la vérité; (*description*) exact(e), vrai(e); **~fully** *ad* sincèrement, sans mentir; **~fulness** *n* véracité *f*.
try [traı] *n* essai *m*, tentative *f*; (RUGBY) essai // *vt* (LAW) juger; (*test*: *sth new*) essayer, tester; (*strain*) éprouver // *vi* essayer; **to ~ to do** essayer de faire; (*seek*) chercher à faire; **to ~ on** *vt* (*clothes*) essayer; **to ~ it on** (*fig*) tenter le coup, bluffer; **to ~ out** *vt* essayer, mettre à l'essai; **~ing** *a* pénible.
tsar [zɑ:*] *n* tsar *m*.
T-shirt ['ti:ʃə:t] *n* tee-shirt *m*.
T-square ['ti:skwεə*] *n* équerre *f* en T.
tub [tʌb] *n* cuve *f*; baquet *m*; (*bath*) baignoire *f*.
tuba ['tju:bə] *n* tuba *m*.
tubby ['tʌbı] *a* rondelet(te).
tube [tju:b] *n* tube *m*; (*underground*) métro *m*; (*for tyre*) chambre *f* à air.
tuberculosis [tjubə:kju'ləusıs] *n* tuberculose *f*.
tube station ['tju:bsteıʃən] *n* station *f* de métro.
tubing ['tju:bıŋ] *n* tubes *mpl*; **a piece of ~** un tube.
tubular ['tju:bjulə*] *a* tubulaire.
TUC *n* (*abbr of Trades Union Congress*) confédération *f* des syndicats britanniques.
tuck [tʌk] *n* (SEWING) pli *m*, rempli *m* // *vt* (*put*) mettre; **to ~ away** *vt* cacher, ranger; **to ~ in** *vt* rentrer; (*child*) border // *vi* (*eat*) manger de bon appétit; attaquer le repas; **to ~ up** *vt* (*child*) border; **~ shop** *n* boutique *f* à provisions (*dans une école*).
Tuesday ['tju:zdı] *n* mardi *m*.
tuft [tʌft] *n* touffe *f*.
tug [tʌg] *n* (*ship*) remorqueur *m* // *vt* tirer (sur); **~-of-war** *n* lutte *f* à la corde.
tuition [tju:'ıʃən] *n* leçons *fpl*.
tulip ['tju:lıp] *n* tulipe *f*.
tumble ['tʌmbl] *n* (*fall*) chute *f*, culbute *f* // *vi* tomber, dégringoler; (*with somersault*) faire une *or* des culbute(s) // *vt* renverser, faire tomber; **~down** *a*

délabré(e) ; ~ **dryer** *n* séchoir *m* (à linge) à air chaud.
tumbler ['tʌmblə*] *n* verre (droit), gobelet *m* ; acrobate *m/f.*
tummy ['tʌmɪ] *n* (*col*) ventre *m.*
tumour ['tju:mə*] *n* tumeur *f.*
tumult ['tju:mʌlt] *n* tumulte *m* ; ~**uous** [-'mʌltjuəs] *a* tumultueux(euse).
tuna ['tju:nə] *n, pl inv* (*also*: ~ **fish**) thon *m.*
tune [tju:n] *n* (*melody*) air *m* // *vt* (MUS) accorder ; (RADIO, TV, AUT) régler, mettre au point ; **to be in/out of** ~ (*instrument*) être accordé/désaccordé ; (*singer*) chanter juste/faux ; **to be in/out of** ~ **with** (*fig*) être en accord/désaccord avec ; **to** ~ **in (to)** (RADIO, TV) se mettre à l'écoute (de) ; **to** ~ **up** *vi* (*musician*) accorder son instrument ; ~**ful** *a* mélodieux(euse) ; ~**r** *n* (*radio set*) radio-préamplificateur *m* ; **piano** ~**r** accordeur *m* de pianos ; ~**r amplifier** *n* radio-ampli *m.*
tungsten ['tʌŋstn] *n* tungstène *m.*
tunic ['tju:nɪk] *n* tunique *f.*
tuning ['tju:nɪŋ] *n* réglage *m* ; ~ **fork** *n* diapason *m.*
Tunisia [tju:'nɪzɪə] *n* Tunisie *f* ; ~**n** *a* tunisien(ne) // *n* Tunisien/ne.
tunnel ['tʌnl] *n* tunnel *m* ; (*in mine*) galerie *f* // *vi* creuser un tunnel (*or* une galerie).
tunny ['tʌnɪ] *n* thon *m.*
turban ['tə:bən] *n* turban *m.*
turbid ['tə:bɪd] *a* boueux(euse).
turbine ['tə:baɪn] *n* turbine *f.*
turbojet ['tə:bəu'dʒɛt] *n* turboréacteur *m.*
turbot ['tə:bət] *n, pl inv* turbot *m.*
turbulence ['tə:bjuləns] *n* (AVIAT) turbulence *f.*
turbulent ['tə:bjulənt] *a* turbulent(e) ; (*sea*) agité(e).
tureen [tə'ri:n] *n* soupière *f.*
turf [tə:f] *n* gazon *m* ; (*clod*) motte *f* (de gazon) // *vt* gazonner ; **the T**~ *n* le turf, les courses *fpl* ; **to** ~ **out** *vt* (*col*) jeter ; jeter dehors.
turgid ['tə:dʒɪd] *a* (*speech*) pompeux(euse).
Turk [tə:k] *n* Turc/Turque.
turkey ['tə:kɪ] *n* dindon *m*, dinde *f.*
Turkey ['tə:kɪ] *n* Turquie *f.*
Turkish ['tə:kɪʃ] *a* turc(turque) // *n* (LING) turc *m* ; ~ **bath** *n* bain turc ; ~ **delight** *n* loukoum *m.*
turmoil ['tə:mɔɪl] *n* trouble *m*, bouleversement *m.*
turn [tə:n] *n* tour *m* ; (*in road*) tournant *m* ; (*tendency*: *of mind, events*) tournure *f* ; (*performance*) numéro *m* ; (MED) crise *f*, attaque *f* // *vt* tourner ; (*collar, steak*) retourner ; (*milk*) faire tourner ; (*change*): **to** ~ **sth into** changer qch en // *vi* tourner ; (*person*: *look back*) se (re)tourner ; (*reverse direction*) faire demi-tour ; (*change*) changer ; (*become*) devenir ; **to** ~ **into** se changer en ; **a good** ~ un service ; **a bad** ~ un mauvais tour ; **it gave me quite a** ~ ça m'a fait un coup ; **'no left** ~**'** (AUT) 'défense de tourner à gauche' ; **it's your** ~ c'est (à) votre tour ; **in** ~ à son tour ; à tour de rôle ; **to take** ~**s** se relayer ; **to take** ~**s at** faire à tour de rôle ; **to** ~ **about** *vi* faire demi-tour ; faire un demi-tour ; **to** ~ **away** *vi* se détourner, tourner la tête ; **to** ~ **back** *vi* revenir, faire demi-tour ; **to** ~ **down** *vt* (*refuse*) rejeter, refuser ; (*reduce*) baisser ; (*fold*) rabattre ; **to** ~ **in** *vi* (*col*: *go to bed*) aller se coucher // *vt* (*fold*) rentrer ; **to** ~ **off** *vi* (*from road*) tourner // *vt* (*light, radio etc*) éteindre ; (*engine*) arrêter ; **to** ~ **on** *vt* (*light, radio etc*) allumer ; (*engine*) mettre en marche ; **to** ~ **out** *vt* (*light, gas*) éteindre // *vi*: **to** ~ **out to be...** s'avérer..., se révéler... ; **to** ~ **up** (*person*) arriver, se pointer ; (*lost object*) être retrouvé(e) // *vt* (*collar*) remonter ; (*increase*: *sound, volume etc*) mettre plus fort ; ~**around** *n* volte-face *f* ; ~**ed-up** *a* (*nose*) retroussé(e) ; ~**ing** *n* (*in road*) tournant *m* ; ~**ing circle** *n* rayon *m* de braquage ; ~**ing point** *n* (*fig*) tournant *m*, moment décisif.
turnip ['tə:nɪp] *n* navet *m.*
turnout ['tə:naut] *n* (nombre *m* de personnes dans l') assistance *f.*
turnover ['tə:nəuvə*] *n* (COMM: *amount of money*) chiffre *m* d'affaires ; (: *of goods*) roulement *m* ; (CULIN) *sorte de chausson.*
turnpike ['tə:npaɪk] *n* (*US*) autoroute *f* à péage.
turnstile ['tə:nstaɪl] *n* tourniquet *m* (*d'entrée*).
turntable ['tə:nteɪbl] *n* (*on record player*) platine *f.*
turn-up ['tə:nʌp] *n* (*on trousers*) revers *m.*
turpentine ['tə:pəntaɪn] *n* (*also*: **turps**) (essence *f* de) térébenthine *f.*
turquoise ['tə:kwɔɪz] *n* (*stone*) turquoise *f* // *a* turquoise *inv.*
turret ['tʌrɪt] *n* tourelle *f.*
turtle ['tə:tl] *n* tortue marine ; ~**neck (sweater)** *n* pullover *m* à col montant.
tusk [tʌsk] *n* défense *f.*
tussle ['tʌsl] *n* bagarre *f*, mêlée *f.*
tutor ['tju:tə*] *n* (*in college*) directeur/trice d'études ; (*private teacher*) précepteur/-trice ; ~**ial** [-'tɔ:rɪəl] (SCOL) (séance *f* de) travaux *mpl* pratiques.
tuxedo [tʌk'si:dəu] *n* (*US*) smoking *m.*
T.V. [ti:'vi:] *n* (*abbr of* **television**) télé *f.*
twaddle ['twɔdl] *n* balivernes *fpl.*
twang [twæŋ] *n* (*of instrument*) son vibrant ; (*of voice*) ton nasillard // *vi* vibrer // *vt* (*guitar*) pincer les cordes de.
tweed [twi:d] *n* tweed *m.*
tweezers ['twi:zəz] *npl* pince *f* à épiler.
twelfth [twɛlfθ] *num* douzième ; **T**~ **Night** *n* la fête des Rois.
twelve [twɛlv] *num* douze ; **at** ~ à midi ; (*midnight*) à minuit.
twentieth ['twɛntɪɪθ] *num* vingtième.
twenty ['twɛntɪ] *num* vingt.
twerp [twə:p] *n* (*col*) imbécile *m/f.*
twice [twaɪs] *ad* deux fois ; ~ **as much** deux fois plus.
twig [twɪg] *n* brindille *f* // *vt, vi* (*col*) piger.
twilight ['twaɪlaɪt] *n* crépuscule *m.*
twill [twɪl] *n* sergé *m.*
twin [twɪn] *a,n* jumeau(elle) // *vt* jumeler.
twine [twaɪn] *n* ficelle *f* // *vi* (*plant*) s'enrouler ; (*road*) serpenter.
twinge [twɪndʒ] *n* (*of pain*) élancement *m* ; (*of conscience*) remords *m.*

twinkle ['twɪŋkl] *n* scintillement *m*; pétillement *m* // *vi* scintiller; (*eyes*) pétiller.
twin town [twɪn'taun] *n* ville jumelée.
twirl [twə:l] *n* tournoiement *m* // *vt* faire tournoyer // *vi* tournoyer.
twist [twɪst] *n* torsion *f*, tour *m*; (*in wire, flex*) tortillon *m*; (*in story*) coup *m* de théâtre // *vt* tordre; (*weave*) entortiller; (*roll around*) enrouler; (*fig*) déformer // *vi* s'entortiller; s'enrouler; (*road*) serpenter.
twit [twɪt] *n* (*col*) crétin/e.
twitch [twɪtʃ] *n* saccade *f*; (*nervous*) tic *m* // *vi* se convulser; avoir un tic.
two [tu:] *num* deux; **to put ~ and ~ together** (*fig*) faire le rapport; **~-door** *a* (AUT) à deux portes; **~-faced** *a* (*pej*: *person*) faux(fausse); **~fold** *ad*: **to increase ~fold** doubler; **~-piece (suit)** *n* (costume *m*) deux-pièces *m inv*; **~-piece (swimsuit)** *n* (maillot *m* de bain) deux-pièces *m inv*; **~-seater** *n* (*plane*) (avion *m*) biplace *m*; (*car*) voiture *f* à deux places; **~some** *n* (*people*) couple *m*; **~-way** *a* (*traffic*) dans les deux sens.
tycoon [taɪ'ku:n] *n*: **(business) ~** gros homme d'affaires.
type [taɪp] *n* (*category*) genre *m*, espèce *f*; (*model*) modèle *m*; (*example*) type *m*; (TYP) type, caractère *m* // *vt* (*letter etc*) taper (à la machine); **~-cast** *a* (*actor*) condamné(e) à toujours jouer le même rôle; **~script** *n* texte dactylographié; **~writer** *n* machine *f* à écrire; **~written** *a* dactylographié(e).
typhoid ['taɪfɔɪd] *n* typhoïde *f*.
typhoon [taɪ'fu:n] *n* typhon *m*.
typhus ['taɪfəs] *n* typhus *m*.
typical ['tɪpɪkl] *a* typique, caractéristique.
typify ['tɪpɪfaɪ] *vt* être caractéristique de.
typing ['taɪpɪŋ] *n* dactylo(graphie) *f*; **~ error** *n* faute *f* de frappe; **~ paper** *n* papier *m* machine.
typist ['taɪpɪst] *n* dactylo *m/f*.
tyranny ['tɪrənɪ] *n* tyrannie *f*.
tyrant ['taɪərnt] *n* tyran *m*.
tyre, tire (*US*) ['taɪə*] *n* pneu *m*; **~ pressure** *n* pression *f* (de gonflage).
tzar [zɑ:*] *n* = **tsar**.

U

U-bend ['ju:'bɛnd] *n* (AUT) coude *m*, virage *m* en épingle à cheveux; (*in pipe*) coude.
ubiquitous [ju:'bɪkwɪtəs] *a* doué(e) d'ubiquité, omniprésent(e).
udder ['ʌdə*] *n* pis *m*, mamelle *f*.
UFO ['ju:fəu] *n* (*abbr of unidentified flying object*) O.V.N.I. (objet volant non identifié).
ugh [ə:h] *excl* pouah!
ugliness ['ʌglɪnɪs] *n* laideur *f*.
ugly ['ʌglɪ] *a* laid(e), vilain(e); (*fig*) répugnant(e).
UHF *abbr of ultra-high frequency.*
UHT *a* (*abbr of ultra-heat treated*): **~ milk** *n* lait upérisé *or* longue conservation.
U.K. *n abbr see* **united**.
ulcer ['ʌlsə*] *n* ulcère *m*; (*also*: **mouth ~**) aphte *f*.
Ulster ['ʌlstə*] *n* Ulster *m*.
ulterior [ʌl'tɪərɪə*] *a* ultérieur(e); **~ motive** *n* arrière-pensée *f*.
ultimate ['ʌltɪmət] *a* ultime, final(e); (*authority*) suprême; **~ly** *ad* en fin de compte; finalement; par la suite.
ultimatum [ʌltɪ'meɪtəm] *n* ultimatum *m*.
ultraviolet ['ʌltrə'vaɪəlɪt] *a* ultraviolet(te).
umbilical [ʌmbɪ'laɪkl] *a*: **~ cord** cordon ombilical.
umbrage ['ʌmbrɪdʒ] *n*: **to take ~** prendre ombrage, se froisser.
umbrella [ʌm'brɛlə] *n* parapluie *m*; (*fig*): **under the ~ of** sous les auspices de; chapeauté(e) par.
umpire ['ʌmpaɪə*] *n* arbitre *m* // *vt* arbitrer.
umpteen [ʌmp'ti:n] *a* je ne sais combien de; **for the ~th time** pour la nième fois.
UN, UNO *abbr see* **united**.
unabashed [ʌnə'bæʃt] *a* nullement intimidé(e).
unabated [ʌnə'beɪtɪd] *a* non diminué(e).
unable [ʌn'eɪbl] *a*: **to be ~ to** ne (pas) pouvoir, être dans l'impossibilité de; être incapable de.
unaccompanied [ʌnə'kʌmpənɪd] *a* (*child, lady*) non accompagné(e).
unaccountably [ʌnə'kauntəblɪ] *ad* inexplicablement.
unaccustomed [ʌnə'kʌstəmd] *a* inaccoutumé(e), inhabituel(le); **to be ~ to sth** ne pas avoir l'habitude de qch.
unadulterated [ʌnə'dʌltəreɪtɪd] *a* pur(e), naturel(le).
unaided [ʌn'eɪdɪd] *a* sans aide, tout(e) seul(e).
unanimity [ju:nə'nɪmɪtɪ] *n* unanimité *f*.
unanimous [ju:'nænɪməs] *a* unanime; **~ly** *ad* à l'unanimité.
unashamed [ʌnə'ʃeɪmd] *a* sans honte; impudent(e).
unassuming [ʌnə'sju:mɪŋ] *a* modeste, sans prétentions.
unattached [ʌnə'tætʃt] *a* libre, sans attaches.
unattended [ʌnə'tɛndɪd] *a* (*car, child, luggage*) sans surveillance.
unattractive [ʌnə'træktɪv] *a* peu attrayant(e).
unauthorized [ʌn'ɔ:θəraɪzd] *a* non autorisé(e), sans autorisation.
unavoidable [ʌnə'vɔɪdəbl] *a* inévitable.
unaware [ʌnə'wɛə*] *a*: **to be ~ of** ignorer, ne pas savoir, être inconscient(e) de; **~s** *ad* à l'improviste, au dépourvu.
unbalanced [ʌn'bælənst] *a* déséquilibré(e).
unbearable [ʌn'bɛərəbl] *a* insupportable.
unbeatable [ʌn'bi:təbl] *a* imbattable.
unbeaten [ʌn'bi:tn] *a* invaincu(e).
unbecoming [ʌnbɪ'kʌmɪŋ] *a* malséant(e), inconvenant(e).
unbeknown(st) [ʌnbɪ'nəun(st)] *ad*: **~ to** à l'insu de.
unbelief [ʌnbɪ'li:f] *n* incrédulité *f*.
unbelievable [ʌnbɪ'li:vəbl] *a* incroyable.
unbend [ʌn'bɛnd] *vb (irg) vi* se détendre // *vt* (*wire*) redresser, détordre.
unbounded [ʌn'baundɪd] *a* sans bornes, illimité(e).

unbreakable [ʌn'breɪkəbl] *a* incassable.
unbridled [ʌn'braɪdld] *a* débridé(e), déchaîné(e).
unbroken [ʌn'brəukən] *a* intact(e); continu(e).
unburden [ʌn'bə:dn] *vt*: **to ~ o.s.** s'épancher, se livrer.
unbutton [ʌn'bʌtn] *vt* déboutonner.
uncalled-for [ʌn'kɔ:ldfɔ:*] *a* déplacé(e), injustifié(e).
uncanny [ʌn'kænɪ] *a* étrange, troublant(e).
unceasing [ʌn'si:sɪŋ] *a* incessant(e), continu(e).
uncertain [ʌn'sə:tn] *a* incertain(e); mal assuré(e); **~ty** *n* incertitude *f*, doutes *mpl*.
unchanged [ʌn'tʃeɪndʒd] *a* inchangé(e).
uncharitable [ʌn'tʃærɪtəbl] *a* peu charitable.
uncharted [ʌn'tʃɑ:tɪd] *a* inexploré(e).
unchecked [ʌn'tʃɛkt] *a* non réprimé(e).
uncle ['ʌŋkl] *n* oncle *m*.
uncomfortable [ʌn'kʌmfətəbl] *a* inconfortable; (*uneasy*) mal à l'aise, gêné(e); désagréable.
uncommon [ʌn'kɔmən] *a* rare, singulier(ère), peu commun(e).
uncompromising [ʌn'kɔmprəmaɪzɪŋ] *a* intransigeant(e), inflexible.
unconditional [ʌnkən'dɪʃənl] *a* sans conditions.
uncongenial [ʌnkən'dʒi:nɪəl] *a* peu agréable.
unconscious [ʌn'kɔnʃəs] *a* sans connaissance, évanoui(e); (*unaware*) inconscient(e) // *n*: **the ~** l'inconscient *m*; **~ly** *ad* inconsciemment.
uncontrollable [ʌnkən'trəuləbl] *a* irrépressible; indiscipliné(e).
uncork [ʌn'kɔ:k] *vt* déboucher.
uncouth [ʌn'ku:θ] *a* grossier(ère), fruste.
uncover [ʌn'kʌvə*] *vt* découvrir.
unctuous ['ʌŋktjuəs] *a* onctueux(euse), mielleux(euse).
undaunted [ʌn'dɔ:ntɪd] *a* non intimidé(e), inébranlable.
undecided [ʌndɪ'saɪdɪd] *a* indécis(e), irrésolu(e).
undeniable [ʌndɪ'naɪəbl] *a* indéniable, incontestable.
under ['ʌndə*] *prep* sous; (*less than*) (de) moins de; au-dessous de; (*according to*) selon, en vertu de // *ad* au-dessous; en dessous; **from ~ sth** de dessous *or* de sous qch; **~ there** là-dessous; **~ repair** en (cours de) réparation.
under... ['ʌndə*] *prefix* sous-; **~-age** *a* qui n'a pas l'âge réglementaire; **~carriage, ~cart** *n* train *m* d'atterrissage; **~clothes** *npl* sous-vêtements *mpl*; (*women's only*) dessous *mpl*; **~coat** *n* (*paint*) couche *f* de fond; **~cover** *a* secret(ète), clandestin(e); **~current** *n* courant sous-jacent; **~cut** *n* (CULIN) (morceau *m* de) filet *m* // *vt irg* vendre moins cher que; **~developed** *a* sous-développé(e); **~dog** *n* opprimé *m*; **~done** *a* (CULIN) saignant(e); (*pej*) pas assez cuit(e); **~estimate** *vt* sous-estimer, mésestimer; **~exposed** *a* (PHOT) sous-exposé(e); **~fed** *a* sous-alimenté(e); **~foot** *ad* sous les pieds; **~go** *vt irg* subir; (*treatment*) suivre; **~graduate** *n* étudiant/e (qui prépare la licence); **~ground** *n* métro *m*; (POL) clandestinité *f*; **~growth** *n* broussailles *fpl*, sous-bois *m*; **~hand(ed)** *a* (*fig*) sournois(e), en dessous; **~lie** *vt irg* être à la base de; **~line** *vt* souligner; **~ling** ['ʌndəlɪŋ] *n* (*pej*) sous-fifre *m*, subalterne *m*; **~mine** *vt* saper, miner; **~neath** [ʌndə'ni:θ] *ad* (en) dessous // *prep* sous, au-dessous de; **~paid** *a* sous-payé(e); **~pants** *npl* (*Brit*) caleçon *m*, slip *m*; **~pass** *n* passage souterrain; (*on motorway*) passage inférieur; **~play** *vt* minimiser; **~price** *vt* vendre à un prix trop bas; **~privileged** *a* défavorisé(e), économiquement faible; **~rate** *vt* sous-estimer, mésestimer; **~shirt** *n* (*US*) tricot *m* de corps; **~shorts** *npl* (*US*) caleçon *m*, slip *m*; **~side** *n* dessous *m*; **~skirt** *n* jupon *m*.
understand [ʌndə'stænd] *vb* (*irg: like* **stand**) *vt, vi* comprendre; **I ~ that...** je me suis laissé dire que...; je crois comprendre que...; **~able** *a* compréhensible; **~ing** *a* compréhensif(ive) // *n* compréhension *f*; (*agreement*) accord *m*.
understatement [ʌndə'steɪtmənt] *n*: **that's an ~** c'est (bien) peu dire, le terme est faible.
understood [ʌndə'stud] *pt, pp of* **understand** // *a* entendu(e); (*implied*) sous-entendu(e).
understudy ['ʌndəstʌdɪ] *n* doublure *f*.
undertake [ʌndə'teɪk] *vt irg* entreprendre; se charger de.
undertaker ['ʌndəteɪkə*] *n* entrepreneur *m* des pompes funèbres, croque-mort *m*.
undertaking [ʌndə'teɪkɪŋ] *n* entreprise *f*; (*promise*) promesse *f*.
underwater [ʌndə'wɔ:tə*] *ad* sous l'eau // *a* sous-marin(e).
underwear ['ʌndəwɛə*] *n* sous-vêtements *mpl*; (*women's only*) dessous *mpl*.
underweight [ʌndə'weɪt] *a* d'un poids insuffisant; (*person*) (trop) maigre.
underworld ['ʌndəwə:ld] *n* (*of crime*) milieu *m*, pègre *f*.
underwriter ['ʌndəraɪtə*] *n* (INSURANCE) souscripteur *m*.
undesirable [ʌndɪ'zaɪərəbl] *a* peu souhaitable; indésirable.
undies ['ʌndɪz] *npl* (*col*) dessous *mpl*, lingerie *f*.
undisputed [ʌndɪ'spju:tɪd] *a* incontesté(e).
undistinguished [ʌndɪs'tɪŋgwɪʃt] *a* médiocre, quelconque.
undo [ʌn'du:] *vt irg* défaire; **~ing** *n* ruine *f*, perte *f*.
undoubted [ʌn'dautɪd] *a* indubitable, certain(e); **~ly** *ad* sans aucun doute.
undress [ʌn'drɛs] *vi* se déshabiller.
undue [ʌn'dju:] *a* indu(e), excessif(ive).
undulating ['ʌndjuleɪtɪŋ] *a* ondoyant(e), onduleux(euse).
unduly [ʌn'dju:lɪ] *ad* trop, excessivement.
unearth [ʌn'ə:θ] *vt* déterrer; (*fig*) dénicher.
unearthly [ʌn'ə:θlɪ] *a* surnaturel(le); (*hour*) indu(e), impossible.
uneasy [ʌn'i:zɪ] *a* mal à l'aise, gêné(e); (*worried*) inquiet(ète).

uneconomic(al) ['ʌni:kə'nɔmɪk(l)] *a* peu économique ; peu rentable.
uneducated [ʌn'ɛdjukeɪtɪd] *a* sans éducation.
unemployed [ʌnɪm'plɔɪd] *a* sans travail, en chômage // *n*: **the ~** les chômeurs *mpl.*
unemployment [ʌnɪm'plɔɪmənt] *n* chômage *m.*
unending [ʌn'ɛndɪŋ] *a* interminable.
unenviable [ʌn'ɛnvɪəbl] *a* peu enviable.
unerring [ʌn'ə:rɪŋ] *a* infaillible, sûr(e).
uneven [ʌn'i:vn] *a* inégal(e) ; irrégulier(ère).
unexpected [ʌnɪk'spɛktɪd] *a* inattendu(e), imprévu(e).
unexploded [ʌnɪk'spləudɪd] *a* non explosé(e) *or* éclaté(e).
unfailing [ʌn'feɪlɪŋ] *a* inépuisable ; infaillible.
unfair [ʌn'fɛə*] *a*: **~ (to)** injuste (envers) ; **~ly** *ad* injustement.
unfaithful [ʌn'feɪθful] *a* infidèle.
unfamiliar [ʌnfə'mɪlɪə*] *a* étrange, inconnu(e).
unfasten [ʌn'fɑ:sn] *vt* défaire ; détacher.
unfathomable [ʌn'fæðəməbl] *a* insondable.
unfavourable, unfavorable (*US*) [ʌn'feɪvərəbl] *a* défavorable.
unfeeling [ʌn'fi:lɪŋ] *a* insensible, dur(e).
unfinished [ʌn'fɪnɪʃt] *a* inachevé(e).
unfit [ʌn'fɪt] *a* en mauvaise santé ; pas en forme ; (*incompetent*): **~ (for)** impropre (à) ; (*work, service*) inapte (à).
unflagging [ʌn'flægɪŋ] *a* infatigable, inlassable.
unflappable [ʌn'flæpəbl] *a* imperturbable.
unflinching [ʌn'flɪntʃɪŋ] *a* stoïque.
unfold [ʌn'fəuld] *vt* déplier ; (*fig*) révéler, exposer // *vi* se dérouler.
unforeseen ['ʌnfɔ:'si:n] *a* imprévu(e).
unforgivable [ʌnfə'gɪvəbl] *a* impardonnable.
unfortunate [ʌn'fɔ:tʃnət] *a* malheureux(euse) ; (*event, remark*) malencontreux(euse) ; **~ly** *ad* malheureusement.
unfounded [ʌn'faundɪd] *a* sans fondement.
unfriendly [ʌn'frɛndlɪ] *a* froid(e), inamical(e).
unfurnished [ʌn'fə:nɪʃt] *a* non meublé(e).
ungainly [ʌn'geɪnlɪ] *a* gauche, dégingandé(e).
ungodly [ʌn'gɔdlɪ] *a* impie ; **at an ~ hour** à une heure indue.
unguarded [ʌn'gɑ:dɪd] *a*: **~ moment** *n* moment *m* d'inattention.
unhappiness [ʌn'hæpɪnɪs] *n* tristesse *f*, peine *f.*
unhappy [ʌn'hæpɪ] *a* triste, malheureux(euse) ; **~ with** (*arrangements etc*) mécontent(e) de, peu satisfait(e) de.
unharmed [ʌn'hɑ:md] *a* indemne, sain(e) et sauf(sauve).
unhealthy [ʌn'hɛlθɪ] *a* (*gen*) malsain(e) ; (*person*) maladif(ive).
unheard-of [ʌn'hə:dɔv] *a* inouï(e), sans précédent.
unhook [ʌn'huk] *vt* décrocher ; dégrafer.
unhurt [ʌn'hə:t] *a* indemne, sain(e) et sauf(sauve).
unicorn ['ju:nɪkɔ:n] *n* licorne *f.*
unidentified [ʌnaɪ'dɛntɪfaɪd] *a* non identifié(e).
uniform ['ju:nɪfɔ:m] *n* uniforme *m* // *a* uniforme ; **~ity** [-'fɔ:mɪtɪ] *n* uniformité *f.*
unify ['ju:nɪfaɪ] *vt* unifier.
unilateral [ju:nɪ'lætərəl] *a* unilatéral(e).
unimaginable [ʌnɪ'mædʒɪnəbl] *a* inimaginable, inconcevable.
unimpaired [ʌnɪm'pɛəd] *a* intact(e).
uninhibited [ʌnɪn'hɪbɪtɪd] *a* sans inhibitions ; sans retenue.
unintentional [ʌnɪn'tɛnʃənəl] *a* involontaire.
union ['ju:njən] *n* union *f*; (*also*: **trade ~**) syndicat *m* // *cpd* du syndicat, syndical(e) ; **U~ Jack** *n drapeau du Royaume-Uni.*
unique [ju:'ni:k] *a* unique.
unison ['ju:nɪsn] *n*: **in ~** à l'unisson, en chœur.
unit ['ju:nɪt] *n* unité *f*; (*section: of furniture etc*) élément *m*, bloc *m* ; (*team, squad*) groupe *m*, service *m.*
unite [ju:'naɪt] *vt* unir // *vi* s'unir ; **~d** *a* uni(e) ; unifié(e) ; (*efforts*) conjugué(e) ; **U~d Kingdom (U.K.)** *n* Royaume-Uni *m* ; **U~d Nations (Organization) (UN, UNO)** *n* (Organisation *f* des) Nations unies (O.N.U.) ; **U~d States (of America) (US, USA)** *n* États-Unis *mpl.*
unit trust ['ju:nɪttrʌst] *n* (*Brit*) société *f* d'investissement.
unity ['ju:nɪtɪ] *n* unité *f.*
universal [ju:nɪ'və:sl] *a* universel(le).
universe ['ju:nɪvə:s] *n* univers *m.*
university [ju:nɪ'və:sɪtɪ] *n* université *f.*
unjust [ʌn'dʒʌst] *a* injuste.
unkempt [ʌn'kɛmpt] *a* mal tenu(e), débraillé(e) ; mal peigné(e).
unkind [ʌn'kaɪnd] *a* peu gentil(le), méchant(e).
unknown [ʌn'nəun] *a* inconnu(e).
unladen [ʌn'leɪdn] *a* (*ship, weight*) à vide.
unlawful [ʌn'lɔ:ful] *a* illégal(e).
unleash [ʌn'li:ʃ] *vt* détacher ; (*fig*) déchaîner, déclencher.
unleavened [ʌn'lɛvnd] *a* sans levain.
unless [ʌn'lɛs] *cj*: **~ he leaves** à moins qu'il (ne) parte ; **~ we leave** à moins de partir, à moins que nous (ne) partions ; **~ otherwise stated** sauf indication contraire.
unlicensed [ʌn'laɪsənst] *a* non patenté(e) pour la vente des spiritueux.
unlike [ʌn'laɪk] *a* dissemblable, différent(e) // *prep* à la différence de, contrairement à.
unlikely [ʌn'laɪklɪ] *a* improbable ; invraisemblable.
unlimited [ʌn'lɪmɪtɪd] *a* illimité(e).
unload [ʌn'ləud] *vt* décharger.
unlock [ʌn'lɔk] *vt* ouvrir.
unlucky [ʌn'lʌkɪ] *a* malchanceux(euse) ; (*object, number*) qui porte malheur.
unmannerly [ʌn'mænəlɪ] *a* mal élevé(e), impoli(e).

unmarried [ʌn'mærɪd] *a* célibataire.
unmask [ʌn'mɑ:sk] *vt* démasquer.
unmistakable [ʌnmɪs'teɪkəbl] *a* indubitable ; qu'on ne peut pas ne pas reconnaître.
unmitigated [ʌn'mɪtɪgeɪtɪd] *a* non mitigé(e), absolu(e), pur(e).
unnatural [ʌn'nætʃrəl] *a* non naturel(le) ; contre nature.
unnecessary [ʌn'nɛsəsərɪ] *a* inutile, superflu(e).
unnerve [ʌn'nə:v] *vt* faire perdre son sang-froid à.
UNO [ju:nəu] *n see* **united**.
unobtainable [ʌnəb'teɪnəbl] *a* (TEL) impossible à obtenir.
unoccupied [ʌn'ɔkjupaɪd] *a* (*seat etc*) libre.
unofficial [ʌnə'fɪʃl] *a* non officiel(le) ; (*strike*) ≈ non sanctionné(e) par la centrale.
unorthodox [ʌn'ɔ:θədɔks] *a* peu orthodoxe.
unpack [ʌn'pæk] *vi* défaire sa valise, déballer ses affaires.
unpalatable [ʌn'pælətəbl] *a* (*truth*) désagréable (à entendre).
unparalleled [ʌn'pærəlɛld] *a* incomparable, sans égal.
unpleasant [ʌn'plɛznt] *a* déplaisant(e), désagréable.
unplug [ʌn'plʌg] *vt* débrancher.
unpopular [ʌn'pɔpjulə*] *a* impopulaire.
unprecedented [ʌn'prɛsɪdəntɪd] *a* sans précédent.
unpredictable [ʌnprɪ'dɪktəbl] *a* imprévisible.
unprepossessing ['ʌnpri:pə'zɛsɪŋ] *a* peu avenant(e).
unpretentious [ʌnprɪ'tɛnʃəs] *a* sans prétention(s).
unqualified [ʌn'kwɔlɪfaɪd] *a* (*teacher*) non diplômé(e), sans titres ; (*success*) sans réserve, total(e).
unravel [ʌn'rævl] *vt* démêler.
unreal [ʌn'rɪəl] *a* irréel(le).
unreasonable [ʌn'ri:znəbl] *a* qui n'est pas raisonnable.
unrelated [ʌnrɪ'leɪtɪd] *a* sans rapport ; sans lien de parenté.
unrelenting [ʌnrɪ'lɛntɪŋ] *a* implacable ; acharné(e).
unreliable [ʌnrɪ'laɪəbl] *a* sur qui (*or* quoi) on ne peut pas compter, peu fiable.
unrelieved [ʌnrɪ'li:vd] *a* (*monotony*) constant(e), uniforme.
unremitting [ʌnrɪ'mɪtɪŋ] *a* inlassable, infatigable, acharné(e).
unrepeatable [ʌnrɪ'pi:təbl] *a* (*offer*) unique, exceptionnel(le).
unrepentant [ʌnrɪ'pɛntənt] *a* impénitent(e).
unrest[ʌn'rest] *n* agitation *f*, troubles *mpl.*
unroll [ʌn'rəul] *vt* dérouler.
unruly [ʌn'ru:lɪ] *a* indiscipliné(e).
unsafe [ʌn'seɪf] *a* dangereux(euse), hasardeux(euse).
unsaid [ʌn'sɛd] *a*: **to leave sth ~** passer qch sous silence.
unsatisfactory ['ʌnsætɪs'fæktərɪ] *a* qui laisse à désirer.
unsavoury, unsavory (*US*) [ʌn'seɪvərɪ] *a* (*fig*) peu recommandable, répugnant(e).
unscathed [ʌn'skeɪðd] *a* indemne.
unscrew [ʌn'skru:] *vt* dévisser.
unscrupulous [ʌn'skru:pjuləs] *a* sans scrupules, indélicat(e).
unseemly [ʌn'si:mlɪ] *a* inconvenant(e).
unsettled [ʌn'sɛtld] *a* perturbé(e) ; instable ; incertain(e).
unshaven [ʌn'ʃeɪvn] *a* non *or* mal rasé(e).
unsightly [ʌn'saɪtlɪ] *a* disgracieux(euse), laid(e).
unskilled [ʌn'skɪld] *a*: **~ worker** *n* manœuvre *m.*
unsophisticated [ʌnsə'fɪstɪkeɪtɪd] *a* simple, naturel(le).
unspeakable [ʌn'spi:kəbl] *a* indicible ; (*bad*) innommable.
unsteady [ʌn'stɛdɪ] *a* mal assuré(e), chancelant(e), instable.
unstuck [ʌn'stʌk] *a*: **to come ~** se décoller ; (*fig*) faire fiasco.
unsuccessful [ʌnsək'sɛsful] *a* (*attempt*) infructueux(euse) ; (*writer, proposal*) qui n'a pas de succès ; (*marriage*) malheureux(euse), qui ne réussit pas ; **to be ~** (*in attempting sth*) ne pas réussir ; ne pas avoir de succès ; (*application*) ne pas être retenu(e) ; **~ly** *ad* en vain.
unsuitable [ʌn'su:təbl] *a* qui ne convient pas, peu approprié(e) ; inopportun(e).
unsuspecting [ʌnsə'spɛktɪŋ] *a* qui ne se méfie pas.
unswerving [ʌn'swə:vɪŋ] *a* inébranlable.
untangle [ʌn'tæŋgl] *vt* démêler, débrouiller.
untapped [ʌn'tæpt] *a* (*resources*) inexploité(e).
unthinkable [ʌn'θɪŋkəbl] *a* impensable, inconcevable.
untidy [ʌn'taɪdɪ] *a* (*room*) en désordre ; (*appearance*) désordonné(e), débraillé(e) ; (*person*) sans ordre, désordonné ; débraillé ; (*work*) peu soigné(e).
untie [ʌn'taɪ] *vt* (*knot, parcel*) défaire ; (*prisoner, dog*) détacher.
until [ən'tɪl] *prep* jusqu'à ; (*after negative*) avant // *cj* jusqu'à ce que + *sub*, en attendant que + *sub* ; (*in past, after negative*) avant que + *sub* ; **~ then** jusque-là.
untimely [ʌn'taɪmlɪ] *a* inopportun(e) ; (*death*) prématuré(e).
untold [ʌn'təuld] *a* incalculable ; indescriptible.
untoward [ʌntə'wɔ:d] *a* fâcheux (euse), malencontreux(euse).
untranslatable [ʌntrænz'leɪtəbl] *a* intraduisible.
unused [ʌn'ju:zd] *a* neuf(neuve).
unusual [ʌn'ju:ʒuəl] *a* insolite, exceptionnel(le), rare.
unveil [ʌn'veɪl] *vt* dévoiler.
unwavering [ʌn'weɪvərɪŋ] *a* inébranlable.
unwell [ʌn'wɛl] *a* indisposé(e), souffrant(e).
unwieldy [ʌn'wi:ldɪ] *a* difficile à manier.
unwilling [ʌn'wɪlɪŋ] *a*: **to be ~ to do** ne pas vouloir faire ; **~ly** *ad* à contrecœur, contre son gré.

unwind [ʌn'waınd] *vb* (*irg*) *vt* dérouler // *vi* (*relax*) se détendre.
unwitting [ʌn'wıtıŋ] *a* involontaire.
unworthy [ʌn'wə:ðı] *a* indigne.
unwrap [ʌn'ræp] *vt* défaire; ouvrir.
unwritten [ʌn'rıtn] *a* (*agreement*) tacite.
up [ʌp] *prep*: **to go/be ~ sth** monter/être sur qch // *ad* en haut; en l'air; **~ there** là-haut; **~ above** au-dessus; **~ to** jusqu'à; **to be ~** (*out of bed*) être levé(e), être debout *inv*; **it is ~ to you** c'est à vous de décider, ça ne tient qu'à vous; **what is he ~ to?** qu'est-ce qu'il peut bien faire?; **he is not ~ to it** il n'en est pas capable; **~-and-coming** *a* plein d'avenir *or* de promesses; **~s and downs** *npl* (*fig*) hauts *mpl* et bas *mpl*.
upbringing ['ʌpbrıŋıŋ] *n* éducation *f*.
update [ʌp'deıt] *vt* mettre à jour.
upend [ʌp'ɛnd] *vt* mettre debout.
upgrade [ʌp'greıd] *vt* promouvoir; (*job*) revaloriser.
upheaval [ʌp'hi:vl] *n* bouleversement *m*; branle-bas *m*; crise *f*.
uphill [ʌp'hıl] *a* qui monte; (*fig: task*) difficile, pénible // *ad*: **to go ~** monter.
uphold [ʌp'həuld] *vt irg* maintenir; soutenir.
upholstery [ʌp'həulstərı] *n* rembourrage *m*; (*of car*) garniture *f*.
upkeep ['ʌpki:p] *n* entretien *m*.
upon [ə'pɔn] *prep* sur.
upper ['ʌpə*] *a* supérieur(e); du dessus // *n* (*of shoe*) empeigne *f*; **the ~ class** ≈ la haute bourgeoisie; **~-class** *a* ≈ bourgeois(e); **~most** *a* le(la) plus haut(e); en dessus.
upright ['ʌpraıt] *a* droit(e); vertical(e); (*fig*) droit, honnête // *n* montant *m*.
uprising ['ʌpraızıŋ] *n* soulèvement *m*, insurrection *f*.
uproar ['ʌprɔ:*] *n* tumulte *m*, vacarme *m*.
uproot [ʌp'ru:t] *vt* déraciner.
upset *n* ['ʌpsɛt] dérangement *m* // *vt* [ʌp'sɛt] (*irg*: *like* **set**) (*glass etc*) renverser; (*plan*) déranger; (*person: offend*) contrarier; (*: grieve*) faire de la peine à; bouleverser // *a* [ʌp'sɛt] contrarié(e); peiné(e); (*stomach*) détraqué(e), dérangé(e).
upshot ['ʌpʃɔt] *n* résultat *m*.
upside ['ʌpsaıd]: **~-down** *ad* à l'envers.
upstairs [ʌp'stɛəz] *ad* en haut // *a* (*room*) du dessus, d'en haut // *n*: **there's no ~** il n'y a pas d'étage.
upstart ['ʌpstɑ:t] *n* parvenu/e.
upstream [ʌp'stri:m] *ad* en amont.
uptake ['ʌpteık] *n*: **he is quick/slow on the ~** il comprend vite/est lent à comprendre.
up-to-date ['ʌptə'deıt] *a* moderne; très récent(e).
upturn ['ʌptə:n] *n* (*in luck*) retournement *m*.
upward ['ʌpwəd] *a* ascendant(e); vers le haut; **~(s)** *ad* vers le haut; **and ~(s)** et plus, et au-dessus.
uranium [juə'reınıəm] *n* uranium *m*.
urban ['ə:bən] *a* urbain(e).
urbane [ə:'beın] *a* urbain(e), courtois(e).
urchin ['ə:tʃın] *n* gosse *m*, garnement *m*; **sea ~** *n* oursin *m*.
urge [ə:dʒ] *n* besoin *m*; envie *f*; forte envie, désir *m* // *vt*: **to ~ sb to do** exhorter qn à faire, pousser qn à faire; recommander vivement à qn de faire; **to ~ on** *vt* aiguillonner, talonner.
urgency ['ə:dʒənsı] *n* urgence *f*; (*of tone*) insistance *f*.
urgent ['ə:dʒənt] *a* urgent(e); **~ly** *ad* d'urgence, sans délai.
urinal ['juərınl] *n* urinoir *m*.
urinate ['juərıneıt] *vi* uriner.
urn [ə:n] *n* urne *f*; (*also*: **tea ~**) fontaine *f* à thé.
us [ʌs] *pronoun* nous.
US, USA *n abbr see* **united**.
usage ['ju:zıdʒ] *n* usage *m*.
use *n* [ju:s] emploi *m*, utilisation *f*; usage *m* // *vt* [ju:z] se servir de, utiliser, employer; **she ~d to do it** elle le faisait (autrefois), elle avait coutume de le faire; **in ~** en usage; **out of ~** hors d'usage; **it's no ~** ça ne sert à rien; **to have the ~ of** avoir l'usage de; **to be ~d to** avoir l'habitude de, être habitué(e) à; **to ~ up** *vt* finir, épuiser; consommer; **~d** *a* (*car*) d'occasion; **~ful** *a* utile; **~fulness** *n* utilité *f*; **~less** *a* inutile; **~r** *n* utilisateur/trice, usager *m*.
usher ['ʌʃə*] *n* placeur *m*; **~ette** [-'rɛt] *n* (*in cinema*) ouvreuse *f*.
USSR *n*: **the ~** l'URSS *f*.
usual ['ju:ʒuəl] *a* habituel(le); **as ~** comme d'habitude; **~ly** *ad* d'habitude, d'ordinaire.
usurer ['ju:ʒərə*] *n* usurier/ère.
usurp [ju:'zə:p] *vt* usurper.
utensil [ju:'tɛnsl] *n* ustensile *m*.
uterus ['ju:tərəs] *n* utérus *m*.
utilitarian [ju:tılı'tɛərıən] *a* utilitaire.
utility [ju:'tılıtı] *n* utilité *f*; (*also*: **public ~**) service public.
utilization [ju:tılaı'zeıʃn] *n* utilisation *f*.
utilize ['ju:tılaız] *vt* utiliser; exploiter.
utmost ['ʌtməust] *a* extrême, le(la) plus grand(e) // *n*: **to do one's ~** faire tout son possible.
utter ['ʌtə*] *a* total(e), complet(ète) // *vt* prononcer, proférer; émettre; **~ance** *n* paroles *fpl*; **~ly** *ad* complètement, totalement.
U-turn ['ju:'tə:n] *n* demi-tour *m*.

V

v. *abbr of* **verse**, **versus**, **volt**; (*abbr of vide*) voir.
vacancy ['veıkənsı] *n* (*job*) poste vacant; (*room*) chambre *f* disponible; **'no vacancies'** 'complet'.
vacant ['veıkənt] *a* (*post*) vacant(e); (*seat etc*) libre, disponible; (*expression*) distrait(e).
vacate [və'keıt] *vt* quitter.
vacation [və'keıʃən] *n* vacances *fpl*; **~ course** *n* cours *mpl* de vacances.
vaccinate ['væksıneıt] *vt* vacciner; **vaccination** [-'neıʃən] *n* vaccination *f*.
vaccine ['væksi:n] *n* vaccin *m*.

vacuum ['vækjum] *n* vide *m*; ~ **cleaner** *n* aspirateur *m*; ~ **flask** *n* bouteille *f* thermos ®.
vagary ['veɪgərɪ] *n* caprice *m*.
vagina [və'dʒaɪnə] *n* vagin *m*.
vagrant ['veɪgrnt] *n* vagabond/e, mendiant/e.
vague [veɪg] *a* vague, imprécis(e); (*blurred*: *photo, memory*) flou(e); ~**ly** *ad* vaguement.
vain [veɪn] *a* (*useless*) vain(e); (*conceited*) vaniteux(euse); **in** ~ en vain.
valance ['væləns] *n* (*of bed*) tour *m* de lit.
valentine ['væləntaɪn] *n* (*also*: ~ **card**) carte *f* de la Saint-Valentin.
valeting ['vælɪtɪŋ] *a*: ~ **service** *n* pressing *m*.
valiant ['vælɪənt] *a* vaillant(e), courageux(euse).
valid ['vælɪd] *a* valide, valable; (*excuse*) valable; ~**ity** [-'lɪdɪtɪ] *n* validité *f*.
valise [və'li:z] *n* sac *m* de voyage.
valley ['vælɪ] *n* vallée *f*.
valuable ['væljuəbl] *a* (*jewel*) de grande valeur; (*time*) précieux (euse); ~**s** *npl* objets *mpl* de valeur.
valuation [vælju'eɪʃən] *n* évaluation *f*, expertise *f*.
value ['vælju:] *n* valeur *f* // *vt* (*fix price*) évaluer, expertiser; (*cherish*) tenir à; ~ **added tax (VAT)** *n* taxe *f* à la valeur ajoutée (T.V.A.); ~**d** *a* (*appreciated*) estimé(e); ~**r** *n* expert *m* (en estimations).
valve [vælv] *n* (*in machine*) soupape *f*; (*on tyre*) valve *f*; (*in radio*) lampe *f*.
van [væn] *n* (AUT) camionnette *f*; (RAIL) fourgon *m*.
vandal ['vændl] *n* vandale *m*/*f*; ~**ism** *n* vandalisme *m*; ~**ize** *vt* saccager.
vanguard ['vængɑ:d] *n* avant-garde *m*.
vanilla [və'nɪlə] *n* vanille *f* // *cpd* (*ice cream*) à la vanille.
vanish ['vænɪʃ] *vi* disparaître.
vanity ['vænɪtɪ] *n* vanité *f*; ~ **case** *n* sac *m* de toilette.
vantage ['vɑ:ntɪdʒ] *n*: ~ **point** bonne position.
vapour, vapor (*US*) ['veɪpə*] *n* vapeur *f*; (*on window*) buée *f*.
variable ['vɛərɪəbl] *a* variable; (*mood*) changeant(e).
variance ['vɛərɪəns] *n*: **to be at** ~ **(with)** être en désaccord (avec); (*facts*) être en contradiction (avec).
variant ['vɛərɪənt] *n* variante *f*.
variation [vɛərɪ'eɪʃən] *n* variation *f*; (*in opinion*) changement *m*.
varicose ['værɪkəus] *a*: ~ **veins** *npl* varices *fpl*.
varied ['vɛərɪd] *a* varié(e), divers(e).
variety [və'raɪətɪ] *n* variété *f*; (*quantity*) nombre *m*, quantité *f*; ~ **show** *n* (spectacle *m* de) variétés *fpl*.
various ['vɛərɪəs] *a* divers(e), différent(e); (*several*) divers, plusieurs.
varnish ['vɑ:nɪʃ] *n* vernis *m* // *vt* vernir.
vary ['vɛərɪ] *vt, vi* varier, changer; ~**ing** *a* variable.
vase [vɑ:z] *n* vase *m*.
vast [vɑ:st] *a* vaste, immense; (*amount, success*) énorme; ~**ly** *ad* infiniment, extrêmement; ~**ness** *n* immensité *f*.
vat [væt] *n* cuve *f*.
VAT [væt] *n abbr see* **value**.
Vatican ['vætɪkən] *n*: **the** ~ le Vatican.
vault [vɔ:lt] *n* (*of roof*) voûte *f*; (*tomb*) caveau *m*; (*in bank*) salle *f* des coffres; chambre forte; (*jump*) saut *m* // *vt* (*also*: ~ **over**) sauter (d'un bond).
vaunted ['vɔ:ntɪd] *a*: **much**-~ tant célébré(e).
VD *n abbr see* **venereal**.
veal [vi:l] *n* veau *m*.
veer [vɪə*] *vi* tourner; virer.
vegetable ['vɛdʒtəbl] *n* légume *m* // *a* végétal(e); ~ **garden** *n* potager *m*.
vegetarian [vɛdʒɪ'tɛərɪən] *a, n* végétarien(ne).
vegetate ['vɛdʒɪteɪt] *vi* végéter.
vegetation [vɛdʒɪ'teɪʃən] *n* végétation *f*.
vehemence ['vi:ɪməns] *n* véhémence *f*, violence *f*.
vehicle ['vi:ɪkl] *n* véhicule *m*.
vehicular [vɪ'hɪkjulə*] *a*: **'no** ~ **traffic'** 'interdit à tout véhicule'.
veil [veɪl] *n* voile *m* // *vt* voiler.
vein [veɪn] *n* veine *f*; (*on leaf*) nervure *f*; (*fig*: *mood*) esprit *m*.
velocity [vɪ'lɔsɪtɪ] *n* vélocité *f*.
velvet ['vɛlvɪt] *n* velours *m*.
vending machine ['vɛndɪŋməʃi:n] *n* distributeur *m* automatique.
vendor ['vɛndə*] *n* vendeur/euse.
veneer [və'nɪə*] *n* placage *m* de bois; (*fig*) vernis *m*.
venerable ['vɛnərəbl] *a* vénérable.
venereal [vɪ'nɪərɪəl] *a*: ~ **disease (VD)** *n* maladie vénérienne.
Venetian [vɪ'ni:ʃən] *a*: ~ **blind** *n* store vénitien.
Venezuela [vɛnɛ'zweɪlə] *n* Venezuela *m*; ~**n** *a* vénézuélien(ne) // *n* Vénézuélien/ne.
vengeance ['vɛndʒəns] *n* vengeance *f*; **with a** ~ (*fig*) vraiment, pour de bon.
venison ['vɛnɪsn] *n* venaison *f*.
venom ['vɛnəm] *n* venin *m*; ~**ous** *a* venimeux(euse).
vent [vɛnt] *n* orifice *m*, conduit *m*; (*in dress, jacket*) fente *f* // *vt* (*fig*: *one's feelings*) donner libre cours à.
ventilate ['vɛntɪleɪt] *vt* (*room*) ventiler, aérer; **ventilation** [-'leɪʃən] *n* ventilation *f*, aération *f*; **ventilator** *n* ventilateur *m*.
ventriloquist [vɛn'trɪləkwɪst] *n* ventriloque *m*/*f*.
venture ['vɛntʃə*] *n* entreprise *f* // *vt* risquer, hasarder // *vi* s'aventurer, se risquer.
venue ['vɛnju:] *n* lieu *m* de rendez-vous *or* rencontre; (SPORT) lieu de la rencontre.
veranda(h) [və'rændə] *n* véranda *f*.
verb [və:b] *n* verbe *m*; ~**al** *a* verbal(e); (*translation*) littéral(e).
verbatim [və:'beɪtɪm] *a, ad* mot pour mot.
verbose [və:'bəus] *a* verbeux(euse).
verdict ['və:dɪkt] *n* verdict *m*.
verge [və:dʒ] *n* bord *m*; **'soft** ~**s'** 'accotements non stabilisés'; **on the** ~ **of doing** sur le point de faire; **to** ~ **on** *vt fus* approcher de.

verger ['vəːdʒə*] *n* (REL) bedeau *m*.
verification [vɛrɪfɪ'keɪʃən] *n* vérification *f*.
verify ['vɛrɪfaɪ] *vt* vérifier.
vermin ['vəːmɪn] *npl* animaux *mpl* nuisibles; (*insects*) vermine *f*.
vermouth ['vəːməθ] *n* vermouth *m*.
vernacular [və'nækjulə*] *n* langue *f* vernaculaire, dialecte *m*.
versatile ['vəːsətaɪl] *a* (*person*) aux talents variés; (*machine, tool etc*) aux usages variés; aux applications variées.
verse [vəːs] *n* vers *mpl*; (*stanza*) strophe *f*; (*in bible*) verset *m*.
versed [vəːst] *a*: **(well-)~ in** versé(e) dans.
version ['vəːʃən] *n* version *f*.
versus ['vəːsəs] *prep* contre.
vertebra, *pl* **~e** ['vəːtɪbrə, -briː] *n* vertèbre *f*.
vertebrate ['vəːtɪbrɪt] *n* vertébré *m*.
vertical ['vəːtɪkl] *a* vertical(e) // *n* verticale *f*; **~ly** *ad* verticalement.
vertigo ['vəːtɪgəu] *n* vertige *m*.
verve [vəːv] *n* brio *m*; enthousiasme *m*.
very ['vɛrɪ] *ad* très // *a*: **the ~ book which** le livre même que; **at the ~ end** tout à la fin; **the ~ last** le tout dernier; **at the ~ least** au moins; **~ much** beaucoup.
vespers ['vɛspəz] *npl* vêpres *fpl*.
vessel ['vɛsl] *n* (ANAT, NAUT) vaisseau *m*; (*container*) récipient *m*.
vest [vɛst] *n* tricot *m* de corps; (*US: waistcoat*) gilet *m* // *vt*: **to ~ sb with sth, to ~ sth in sb** investir qn de qch; **~ed interests** *npl* (COMM) droits acquis.
vestibule ['vɛstɪbjuːl] *n* vestibule *m*.
vestige ['vɛstɪdʒ] *n* vestige *m*.
vestry ['vɛstrɪ] *n* sacristie *f*.
vet [vɛt] *n* (*abbr of* **veterinary surgeon**) vétérinaire *m/f* // *vt* examiner minutieusement; (*text*) revoir.
veteran ['vɛtərn] *n* vétéran *m*; (*also*: **war ~**) ancien combattant; **~ car** *n* voiture *f* d'époque.
veterinary ['vɛtrɪnərɪ] *a* vétérinaire; **~ surgeon** *n* vétérinaire *m/f*.
veto ['viːtəu] *n, pl* **~es** veto *m* // *vt* opposer son veto à.
vex [vɛks] *vt* fâcher, contrarier; **~ed** *a* (*question*) controversé(e).
VHF *abbr of very high frequency*.
via ['vaɪə] *prep* par, via.
viable ['vaɪəbl] *a* viable.
viaduct ['vaɪədʌkt] *n* viaduc *m*.
vibrate [vaɪ'breɪt] *vi*: **to ~ (with)** vibrer (de); (*resound*) retentir (de); **vibration** [-'breɪʃən] *n* vibration *f*.
vicar ['vɪkə*] *n* pasteur *m* (*de l'Église anglicane*); **~age** *n* presbytère *m*.
vice [vaɪs] *n* (*evil*) vice *m*; (TECH) étau *m*.
vice- [vaɪs] *prefix* vice-; **~chairman** *n* vice-président/e.
vice squad ['vaɪsskwɔd] *n* ≈ brigade mondaine.
vice versa ['vaɪsɪ'vəːsə] *ad* vice versa.
vicinity [vɪ'sɪnɪtɪ] *n* environs *mpl*, alentours *mpl*.
vicious ['vɪʃəs] *a* (*remark*) cruel(le), méchant(e); (*blow*) brutal(e); **~ness** *n* méchanceté *f*, cruauté *f*; brutalité *f*.
vicissitudes [vɪ'sɪsɪtjuːdz] *npl* vicissitudes *fpl*.
victim ['vɪktɪm] *n* victime *f*; **~ization** [-'zeɪʃən] *n* brimades *fpl*; représailles *fpl*; **~ize** *vt* brimer; exercer des représailles sur.
victor ['vɪktə*] *n* vainqueur *m*.
Victorian [vɪk'tɔːrɪən] *a* victorien(ne).
victorious [vɪk'tɔːrɪəs] *a* victorieux(euse).
victory ['vɪktərɪ] *n* victoire *f*.
video ['vɪdɪəu] *cpd* vidéo *inv*; **~ (-tape) recorder** *n* magnétoscope *m*.
vie [vaɪ] *vi*: **to ~ with** lutter avec, rivaliser avec.
Vienna [vɪ'ɛnə] *n* Vienne.
view [vjuː] *n* vue *f*; (*opinion*) avis *m*, vue // *vt* (*situation*) considérer; (*house*) visiter; **on ~** (*in museum etc*) exposé(e); **in my ~** à mon avis; **in ~ of the fact that** étant donné que; **to have in ~** avoir en vue; **~er** *n* (*viewfinder*) viseur *m*; (*small projector*) visionneuse *f*; (TV) téléspectateur/trice; **~finder** *n* viseur *m*; **~point** *n* point *m* de vue.
vigil ['vɪdʒɪl] *n* veille *f*; **~ance** *n* vigilance *f*; **~ance committee** *n* comité *m* d'autodéfense; **~ant** *a* vigilant(e).
vigorous ['vɪgərəs] *a* vigoureux(euse).
vigour, vigor (*US*) ['vɪgə*] *n* vigueur *f*.
vile [vaɪl] *a* (*action*) vil(e); (*smell*) abominable; (*temper*) massacrant(e).
vilify ['vɪlɪfaɪ] *vt* calomnier.
villa ['vɪlə] *n* villa *f*.
village ['vɪlɪdʒ] *n* village *m*; **~r** *n* villageois/e.
villain ['vɪlən] *n* (*scoundrel*) scélérat *m*; (*criminal*) bandit *m*; (*in novel etc*) traître *m*.
vindicate ['vɪndɪkeɪt] *vt* défendre avec succès; justifier.
vindictive [vɪn'dɪktɪv] *a* vindicatif(ive), rancunier(ère).
vine [vaɪn] *n* vigne *f*; (*climbing plant*) plante grimpante; **~ grower** *n* viticulteur *m*.
vinegar ['vɪnɪgə*] *n* vinaigre *m*.
vineyard ['vɪnjɑːd] *n* vignoble *m*.
vintage ['vɪntɪdʒ] *n* (*year*) année *f*, millésime *m*; **~ wine** *n* vin *m* de grand cru.
vinyl ['vaɪnl] *n* vinyle *m*.
viola [vɪ'əulə] *n* alto *m*.
violate ['vaɪəleɪt] *vt* violer; **violation** [-'leɪʃən] *n* violation *f*.
violence ['vaɪələns] *n* violence *f*; (POL *etc*) incidents violents.
violent ['vaɪələnt] *a* violent(e); **~ly** *ad* violemment; extrêmement.
violet ['vaɪələt] *a* (*colour*) violet(te) // *n* (*plant*) violette *f*.
violin [vaɪə'lɪn] *n* violon *m*; **~ist** *n* violoniste *m/f*.
VIP *n* (*abbr of very important person*) V.I.P. *m*.
viper ['vaɪpə*] *n* vipère *f*.
virgin ['vəːdʒɪn] *n* vierge *f* // *a* vierge; **she is a ~** elle est vierge; **the Blessed V~**

la Sainte Vierge; **~ity** [-'dʒɪnɪtɪ] *n* virginité *f*.
Virgo ['və:gəu] *n* la Vierge; **to be ~** être de la Vierge.
virile ['vɪraɪl] *a* viril(e).
virility [vɪ'rɪlɪtɪ] *n* virilité *f*.
virtually ['və:tjuəlɪ] *ad* (*almost*) pratiquement.
virtue ['və:tju:] *n* vertu *f*; (*advantage*) mérite *m*, avantage *m*; **by ~ of** par le fait de.
virtuoso [və:tju'əuzəu] *n* virtuose *m/f*.
virtuous ['və:tjuəs] *a* vertueux(euse).
virulent ['vɪrulənt] *a* virulent(e).
virus ['vaɪərəs] *n* virus *m*.
visa ['vi:zə] *n* visa *m*.
vis-à-vis [vi:zə'vi:] *prep* vis-à-vis de.
viscount ['vaɪkaunt] *n* vicomte *m*.
visibility [vɪzɪ'bɪlɪtɪ] *n* visibilité *f*.
visible ['vɪzəbl] *a* visible; **visibly** *ad* visiblement.
vision ['vɪʒən] *n* (*sight*) vue *f*, vision *f*; (*foresight, in dream*) vision; **~ary** *n* visionnaire *m/f*.
visit ['vɪzɪt] *n* visite *f*; (*stay*) séjour *m* // *vt* (*person*) rendre visite à; (*place*) visiter; **~ing card** *n* carte *f* de visite; **~ing professor** *n* ≈ professeur associé; **~or** *n* visiteur/euse; (*in hotel*) client/e; **~ors' book** *n* livre *m* d'or; (*in hotel*) registre *m*.
visor ['vaɪzə*] *n* visière *f*.
vista ['vɪstə] *n* vue *f*, perspective *f*.
visual ['vɪzjuəl] *a* visuel(le); (*nerve*) optique; **~ aid** *n* support visuel (pour l'enseignement).
visualize ['vɪzjuəlaɪz] *vt* se représenter; (*foresee*) prévoir.
vital ['vaɪtl] *a* vital(e); **~ity** [-'tælɪtɪ] *n* vitalité *f*; **~ly** *ad* extrêmement; **~ statistics** *npl* (*fig*) mensurations *fpl*.
vitamin ['vɪtəmɪn] *n* vitamine *f*.
vitiate ['vɪʃɪeɪt] *vt* vicier.
vivacious [vɪ'veɪʃəs] *a* animé(e), qui a de la vivacité.
vivacity [vɪ'væsɪtɪ] *n* vivacité *f*.
vivid ['vɪvɪd] *a* (*account*) frappant(e); (*light, imagination*) vif(vive); **~ly** *ad* (*describe*) d'une manière vivante; (*remember*) de façon précise.
vivisection [vɪvɪ'sɛkʃən] *n* vivisection *f*.
V-neck ['vi:nɛk] *n* décolleté *m* en V.
vocabulary [vəu'kæbjulərɪ] *n* vocabulaire *m*.
vocal ['vəukl] *a* (MUS) vocal(e); (*communication*) verbal(e); (*noisy*) bruyant(e); **~ chords** *npl* cordes vocales; **~ist** *n* chanteur/euse.
vocation [vəu'keɪʃən] *n* vocation *f*; **~al** *a* professionnel(le).
vociferous [və'sɪfərəs] *a* bruyant(e).
vodka ['vɔdkə] *n* vodka *f*.
vogue [vəug] *n* mode *f*; (*popularity*) vogue *f*.
voice [vɔɪs] *n* voix *f*; (*opinion*) avis *m* // *vt* (*opinion*) exprimer, formuler.
void [vɔɪd] *n* vide *m* // *a*: **~ of** vide de, dépourvu(e) de.
voile [vɔɪl] *n* voile *m* (*tissu*).
volatile ['vɔlətaɪl] *a* volatil(e); (*fig*) versatile.
volcanic [vɔl'kænɪk] *a* volcanique.
volcano, ~es [vɔl'keɪnəu] *n* volcan *m*.
volition [və'lɪʃən] *n*: **of one's own ~** de son propre gré.
volley ['vɔlɪ] *n* (*of gunfire*) salve *f*; (*of stones etc*) pluie *f*, volée *f*; (TENNIS *etc*) volée *f*; **~ball** *n* volley(-ball) *m*.
volt [vəult] *n* volt *m*; **~age** *n* tension *f*, voltage *m*.
voluble ['vɔljubl] *a* volubile.
volume ['vɔlju:m] *n* volume *m*; **~ control** *n* (RADIO, TV) bouton *m* de réglage du volume.
voluntarily ['vɔləntrɪlɪ] *ad* volontairement; bénévolement.
voluntary ['vɔləntərɪ] *a* volontaire; (*unpaid*) bénévole.
volunteer [vɔlən'tɪə*] *n* volontaire *m/f* // *vi* (MIL) s'engager comme volontaire; **to ~ to do** se proposer pour faire.
voluptuous [və'lʌptjuəs] *a* voluptueux(euse).
vomit ['vɔmɪt] *n* vomissure *f* // *vt, vi* vomir.
vote [vəut] *n* vote *m*, suffrage *m*; (*cast*) voix *f*, vote; (*franchise*) droit *m* de vote // *vt* (*bill*) voter; (*chairman*) élire // *vi* voter; **~ of censure** *n* motion *f* de censure; **~ of thanks** *n* discours *m* de remerciement; **~r** *n* électeur/trice; **voting** *n* scrutin *m*.
vouch [vautʃ]: **to ~ for** *vt* se porter garant de.
voucher ['vautʃə*] *n* (*for meal, petrol*) bon *m*; (*receipt*) reçu *m*.
vow [vau] *n* vœu *m*, serment *m* // *vi* jurer.
vowel ['vauəl] *n* voyelle *f*.
voyage ['vɔɪɪdʒ] *n* voyage *m* par mer, traversée *f*.
vulgar ['vʌlgə*] *a* vulgaire; **~ity** [-'gærɪtɪ] *n* vulgarité *f*.
vulnerability [vʌlnərə'bɪlɪtɪ] *n* vulnérabilité *f*.
vulnerable ['vʌlnərəbl] *a* vulnérable.
vulture ['vʌltʃə*] *n* vautour *m*.

W

wad [wɔd] *n* (*of cotton wool, paper*) tampon *m*; (*of banknotes etc*) liasse *f*.
wade [weɪd] *vi*: **to ~ through** marcher dans, patauger dans // *vt* passer à gué.
wafer ['weɪfə*] *n* (CULIN) gaufrette *f*; (REL) pain *m* d'hostie *f*.
waffle ['wɔfl] *n* (CULIN) gaufre *f*; (*col*) rabâchage *m*; remplissage *m* // *vi* parler pour ne rien dire; faire du remplissage.
waft [wɔft] *vt* porter // *vi* flotter.
wag [wæg] *vt* agiter, remuer // *vi* remuer.
wage [weɪdʒ] *n* salaire *m*, paye *f* // *vt*: **to ~ war** faire la guerre; **~s** *npl* salaire, paye; **~ claim** *n* demande *f* d'augmentation de salaire; **~ earner** *n* salarié/e; (*breadwinner*) soutien *m* de famille; **~ freeze** *n* blocage *m* des salaires.
wager ['weɪdʒə*] *n* pari *m*.
waggle ['wægl] *vt, vi* remuer.
wag(g)on ['wægən] *n* (*horse-drawn*) chariot *m*; (*truck*) camion *m*; (RAIL) wagon *m* (de marchandises).
wail [weɪl] *n* gémissement *m*; (*of siren*) hurlement *m* // *vi* gémir; hurler.

waist [weɪst] *n* taille *f*, ceinture *f*; **~coat** *n* gilet *m*; **~line** *n* (tour *m* de) taille *f*.

wait [weɪt] *n* attente *f* // *vi* attendre; **to lie in ~ for** guetter; **I can't ~ to** (*fig*) je meurs d'envie de; **to ~ behind** *vi* rester (à attendre); **to ~ for** attendre; **to ~ on** *vt fus* servir; **~er** *n* garçon *m* (de café), serveur *m*; **'no ~ing'** (AUT) 'stationnement interdit'; **~ing list** *n* liste *f* d'attente; **~ing room** *n* salle *f* d'attente; **~ress** *n* serveuse *f*.

waive [weɪv] *vt* renoncer à, abandonner.

wake [weɪk] *vb* (*pt* **woke, ~d,** *pp* **woken, ~d** [wəuk, 'wəukn]) *vt* (*also*: **~ up**) réveiller // *vi* (*also*: **~ up**) se réveiller // *n* (*for dead person*) veillée *f* mortuaire; (NAUT) sillage *m*; **~n** *vt, vi* = **wake.**

Wales [weɪlz] *n* pays *m* de Galles.

walk [wɔ:k] *n* promenade *f*; (*short*) petit tour; (*gait*) démarche *f*; (*pace*): **at a quick ~** d'un pas rapide; (*path*) chemin *m*; (*in park etc*) allée *f* // *vi* marcher; (*for pleasure, exercise*) se promener // *vt* (*distance*) faire à pied; (*dog*) promener; **10 minutes' ~ from** à 10 minutes de marche de; **from all ~s of life** de toutes conditions sociales; **~er** *n* (*person*) marcheur/euse; **~ie-talkie** ['wɔ:kɪ'tɔ:kɪ] *n* talkie-walkie *m*; **~ing** *n* marche *f* à pied; **~ing holiday** *n* vacances passées à faire de la randonnée; **~ing shoes** *npl* chaussures *fpl* de marche; **~ing stick** *n* canne *f*; **~out** *n* (*of workers*) grève-surprise *f*; **~over** *n* (*col*) victoire *f or* examen *m etc* facile; **~way** *n* promenade *f*.

wall [wɔ:l] *n* mur *m*; (*of tunnel, cave*) paroi *m*; **~ cupboard** *n* placard mural; **~ed** *a* (*city*) fortifié(e).

wallet ['wɔlɪt] *n* portefeuille *m*.

wallflower ['wɔ:lflauə*] *n* giroflée *f*; **to be a ~** (*fig*) faire tapisserie.

wallop ['wɔləp] *vt* (*col*) taper sur, cogner.

wallow ['wɔləu] *vi* se vautrer.

wallpaper ['wɔ:lpeɪpə*] *n* papier peint.

walnut ['wɔ:lnʌt] *n* noix *f*; (*tree*) noyer *m*.

walrus, *pl* **~** *or* **~es** ['wɔ:lrəs] *n* morse *m*.

waltz [wɔ:lts] *n* valse *f* // *vi* valser.

wan [wɔn] *a* pâle; triste.

wand [wɔnd] *n* (*also*: **magic ~**) baguette *f* (magique).

wander ['wɔndə*] *vi* (*person*) errer, aller sans but; (*thoughts*) vagabonder; (*river*) serpenter; **~er** *n* vagabond/e.

wane [weɪn] *vi* (*moon*) décroître; (*reputation*) décliner.

wangle ['wæŋgl] *vt* (*col*) se débrouiller pour avoir; carotter.

want [wɔnt] *vt* vouloir; (*need*) avoir besoin de; (*lack*) manquer de // *n*: **for ~ of** par manque de, faute de; **~s** *npl* (*needs*) besoins *mpl*; **to ~ to do** vouloir faire; **to ~ sb to do** vouloir que qn fasse; **to be found ~ing** ne pas être à la hauteur.

wanton ['wɔntn] *a* capricieux(euse); dévergondé(e).

war [wɔ:*] *n* guerre *f*; **to go to ~** se mettre en guerre.

ward [wɔ:d] *n* (*in hospital*) salle *f*; (POL) section électorale; (LAW: *child*) pupille *m/f*; **to ~ off** *vt* parer, éviter.

warden ['wɔ:dn] *n* (*of institution*) directeur/trice; (*of park, game reserve*) gardien/ne; (*also*: **traffic ~**) contractuel/le.

warder ['wɔ:də*] *n* gardien *m* de prison.

wardrobe ['wɔ:drəub] *n* (*cupboard*) armoire *f*; (*clothes*) garde-robe *f*; (THEATRE) costumes *mpl*.

warehouse ['wɛəhaus] *n* entrepôt *m*.

wares [wɛəz] *npl* marchandises *fpl*.

warfare ['wɔ:fɛə*] *n* guerre *f*.

warhead ['wɔ:hɛd] *n* (MIL) ogive *f*.

warily ['wɛərɪlɪ] *ad* avec prudence, avec précaution.

warlike ['wɔ:laɪk] *a* guerrier(ère).

warm [wɔ:m] *a* chaud(e); (*thanks, welcome, applause*) chaleureux(euse); **it's ~** il fait chaud; **I'm ~** j'ai chaud; **to ~ up** *vi* (*person, room*) se réchauffer; (*water*) chauffer; (*athlete, discussion*) s'échauffer // *vt* réchauffer; chauffer; (*engine*) faire chauffer; **~-hearted** *a* affectueux(euse); **~ly** *ad* chaudement; vivement; chaleureusement; **~th** *n* chaleur *f*.

warn [wɔ:n] *vt* avertir, prévenir; **~ing** *n* avertissement *m*; (*notice*) avis *m*; **~ing light** *n* avertisseur lumineux.

warp [wɔ:p] *vi* travailler, se voiler // *vt* voiler; (*fig*) pervertir.

warrant ['wɔrnt] *n* (*guarantee*) garantie *f*; (LAW: *to arrest*) mandat *m* d'arrêt; (: *to search*) mandat de perquisition.

warranty ['wɔrəntɪ] *n* garantie *f*.

warrior ['wɔrɪə*] *n* guerrier/ère.

warship ['wɔ:ʃɪp] *n* navire *m* de guerre.

wart [wɔ:t] *n* verrue *f*.

wartime ['wɔ:taɪm] *n*: **in ~** en temps de guerre.

wary ['wɛərɪ] *a* prudent(e).

was [wɔz] *pt of* **be**.

wash [wɔʃ] *vt* laver // *vi* se laver // *n* (*paint*) badigeon *m*; (*washing programme*) lavage *m*; (*of ship*) sillage *m*; **to give sth a ~** laver qch; **to have a ~** se laver, faire sa toilette; **to ~ away** *vt* (*stain*) enlever au lavage; (*subj*: *river etc*) emporter; **to ~ down** *vt* laver; laver à grande eau; **to ~ off** *vi* partir au lavage; **to ~ up** *vi* faire la vaisselle; **~able** *a* lavable; **~basin** *n* lavabo *m*; **~er** *n* (TECH) rondelle *f*, joint *m*; **~ing** *n* (*linen etc*) lessive *f*; **~ing machine** *n* machine *f* à laver; **~ing powder** *n* lessive *f* (en poudre); **~ing-up** *n* vaisselle *f*; **~-out** *n* (*col*) désastre *m*; **~room** *n* toilettes *fpl*.

wasn't ['wɔznt] = **was not**.

wasp [wɔsp] *n* guêpe *f*.

wastage ['weɪstɪdʒ] *n* gaspillage *m*; (*in manufacturing, transport etc*) déchet *m*.

waste [weɪst] *n* gaspillage *m*; (*of time*) perte *f*; (*rubbish*) déchets *mpl*; (*also*: **household ~**) ordures *fpl* // *a* (*material*) de rebut; (*heat*) perdu(e); (*food*) inutilisé(e); (*land*) inculte; // *vt* gaspiller; (*time, opportunity*) perdre; **~s** *npl* étendue *f* désertique; **to ~ away** *vi* dépérir; **~bin** *n* corbeille *f* à papier; (*in kitchen*) boîte *f* à ordures; **~ disposal unit** *n* broyeur *m* d'ordures; **~ful** *a* gaspilleur(euse); (*process*) peu économique; **~ ground** *n* terrain *m* vague; **~paper basket** *n* corbeille *f* à papier.

watch [wɔtʃ] *n* montre *f*; (*act of watching*) surveillance *f*; guet *m*; (*guard*: MIL) sentinelle *f*; (: NAUT) homme *m* de quart; (NAUT: *spell of duty*) quart *m* // *vt* (*look at*) observer; (: *match, programme*) regarder; (*spy on, guard*) surveiller; (*be careful of*) faire attention à // *vi* regarder; (*keep guard*) monter la garde; **to ~ out** *vi* faire attention; **~dog** *n* chien *m* de garde; **~ful** *a* attentif(ive), vigilant(e); **~maker** *n* horloger/ère; **~man** *n* gardien *m*; (*also*: **night ~man**) veilleur *m* de nuit; **~ strap** *n* bracelet *m* de montre.

water ['wɔ:tə*] *n* eau *f* // *vt* (*plant*) arroser; **in British ~s** dans les eaux territoriales Britanniques; **to ~ down** *vt* (*milk*) couper d'eau; (*fig*: *story*) édulcorer; **~ closet** *n* w.-c. *mpl*, waters *mpl*; **~colour** *n* aquarelle *f*; **~colours** *npl* couleurs *fpl* pour aquarelle; **~cress** *n* cresson *m* (de fontaine); **~fall** *n* chute *f* d'eau; **~ hole** *n* mare *f*; **~ ice** *n* sorbet *m*; **~ing can** *n* arrosoir *m*; **~ level** *n* niveau *m* de l'eau; (*of flood*) niveau *m* des eaux; **~ lily** *n* nénuphar *m*; **~logged** *a* détrempé(e); imbibé(e) d'eau; **~line** *n* (NAUT) ligne *f* de flottaison; **~ main** *n* canalisation *f* d'eau; **~mark** *n* (*on paper*) filigrane *m*; **~melon** *n* pastèque *f*; **~ polo** *n* water-polo *m*; **~proof** *a* imperméable; **~shed** *n* (GEO) ligne *f* de partage des eaux; (*fig*) moment *m* critique, point décisif; **~-skiing** *n* ski *m* nautique; **~ softener** *n* adoucisseur *m* d'eau; **~ tank** *n* réservoir *m* d'eau; **~tight** *a* étanche; **~works** *npl* station *f* hydraulique; **~y** *a* (*colour*) délavé(e); (*coffee*) trop faible.

watt [wɔt] *n* watt *m*.

wave [weɪv] *n* vague *f*; (*of hand*) geste *m*, signe *m*; (RADIO) onde *f*; (*in hair*) ondulation *f* // *vi* faire signe de la main; (*flag*) flotter au vent // *vt* (*handkerchief*) agiter; (*stick*) brandir; (*hair*) onduler; **~length** *n* longueur *f* d'ondes.

waver ['weɪvə*] *vi* vaciller; (*voice*) trembler; (*person*) hésiter.

wavy ['weɪvɪ] *a* ondulé(e); onduleux(euse).

wax [wæks] *n* cire *f*; (*for skis*) fart *m* // *vt* cirer; (*car*) lustrer // *vi* (*moon*) croître; **~en** *a* cireux(euse); **~works** *npl* personnages *mpl* de cire; musée *m* de cire.

way [weɪ] *n* chemin *m*, voie *f*; (*path, access*) passage *m*; (*distance*) distance *f*; (*direction*) chemin, direction *f*; (*manner*) façon *f*, manière *f*; (*habit*) habitude *f*, façon; (*condition*) état *m*; **which ~? — this ~** par où *or* de quel côté? — par ici; **to be on one's ~** être en route; **to be in the ~** bloquer le passage; (*fig*) gêner; **to go out of one's ~ to do** (*fig*) se donner du mal pour faire; **in a ~** d'un côté; **in some ~s** à certains égards; d'un côté; **in the ~ of** en fait de, comme; **'~ in'** 'entrée'; **'~ out'** 'sortie'; **the ~ back** le chemin du retour; **this ~ and that** par-ci par-là; **'give ~'** (AUT) 'cédez la priorité'.

waylay [weɪ'leɪ] *vt irg* attaquer; (*fig*) **I got waylaid** quelqu'un m'a accroché.

wayward ['weɪwəd] *a* capricieux(euse), entêté(e).

W.C. ['dʌblju'si:] *n* w.-c. *mpl*, waters *mpl*.

we [wi:] *pl pronoun* nous.

weak [wi:k] *a* faible; (*health*) fragile; (*beam etc*) peu solide; **~en** *vi* faiblir // *vt* affaiblir; **~ling** *n* gringalet *m*; faible *m/f*; **~ness** *n* faiblesse *f*; (*fault*) point *m* faible.

wealth [wɛlθ] *n* (*money, resources*) richesse(s) *f(pl)*; (*of details*) profusion *f*; **~y** *a* riche.

wean [wi:n] *vt* sevrer.

weapon ['wɛpən] *n* arme *f*.

wear [wɛə*] *n* (*use*) usage *m*; (*deterioration through use*) usure *f*; (*clothing*): **sports/baby~** vêtements *mpl* de sport/pour bébés // *vb* (*pt* **wore**, *pp* **worn** [wɔ:*, wɔ:n]) *vt* (*clothes*) porter; mettre; (*beard etc*) avoir; (*damage*: *through use*) user // *vi* (*last*) faire de l'usage; (*rub etc through*) s'user; **town/evening ~** *n* tenue *f* de ville/de soirée; **~ and tear** *n* usure *f*; **to ~ away** *vt* user, ronger // *vi* s'user, être rongé(e); **to ~ down** *vt* user; (*strength*) épuiser; **to ~ off** *vi* disparaître; **to ~ on** *vi* se poursuivre; passer; **to ~ out** *vt* user; (*person, strength*) épuiser.

wearily ['wɪərɪlɪ] *ad* avec lassitude.

weariness ['wɪərɪnɪs] *n* épuisement *m*, lassitude *f*.

weary ['wɪərɪ] *a* (*tired*) épuisé(e); (*dispirited*) las(lasse); abattu(e) // *vt* lasser // *vi*: **to ~ of** se lasser de.

weasel ['wi:zl] *n* (ZOOL) belette *f*.

weather ['wɛðə*] *n* temps *m* // *vt* (*wood*) faire mûrir; (*tempest, crisis*) essuyer, être pris(e) dans; survivre à, tenir le coup durant; **~-beaten** *a* (*person*) hâlé(e); (*building*) dégradé(e) par les intempéries; **~ cock** *n* girouette *f*; **~ forecast** *n* prévisions *fpl* météorologiques, météo *f*; **~ vane** *n* = **~ cock**.

weave, *pt* **wove**, *pp* **woven** [wi:v, wəuv, 'wəuvn] *vt* (*cloth*) tisser; (*basket*) tresser; **~r** *n* tisserand/e; **weaving** *n* tissage *m*.

web [wɛb] *n* (*of spider*) toile *f*; (*on foot*) palmure *f*; (*fabric, also fig*) tissu *m*; **~bed** *a* (*foot*) palmé(e); **~bing** *n* (*on chair*) sangles *fpl*.

wed [wɛd] *vt* (*pt, pp* **wedded**) épouser // *n*: **the newly-~s** les jeunes mariés.

we'd [wi:d] = **we had, we would**.

wedded ['wɛdɪd] *pt,pp of* **wed**.

wedding [wɛdɪŋ] *n* mariage *m*; **silver/golden ~** *n* noces *fpl* d'argent/d'or; **~ day** *n* jour *m* du mariage; **~ dress** *n* robe *f* de mariage; **~ present** *n* cadeau *m* de mariage; **~ ring** *n* alliance *f*.

wedge [wɛdʒ] *n* (*of wood etc*) coin *m*; (*under door etc*) cale *f*; (*of cake*) part *f* // *vt* (*fix*) caler; (*push*) enfoncer, coincer; **~-heeled shoes** *npl* chaussures *fpl* à semelles compensées.

wedlock ['wɛdlɔk] *n* (union *f* du) mariage *m*.

Wednesday ['wɛdnzdɪ] *n* mercredi *m*.

wee [wi:] *a* (*Scottish*) petit(e); tout(e) petit(e).

weed [wi:d] *n* mauvaise herbe // *vt* désherber; **~-killer** *n* désherbant *m*.

week [wi:k] *n* semaine *f*; **~day** *n* jour *m* de semaine; (COMM) jour ouvrable; **~end** *n* week-end *m*; **~ly** *ad* une fois par

semaine, chaque semaine // *a,n* hebdomadaire (*m*).
weep, *pt, pp* **wept** [wi:p, wɛpt] *vi* (*person*) pleurer; **~ing willow** *n* saule pleureur.
weigh [weɪ] *vt,vi* peser; **to ~ anchor** lever l'ancre; **to ~ down** *vt* (*branch*) faire plier; (*fig*: *with worry*) accabler; **to ~ up** *vt* examiner; **~bridge** *n* pont-bascule *m*.
weight [weɪt] *n* poids *m*; **sold by ~** vendu(e) au poids; **~lessness** *n* apesanteur *f*; **~ lifter** *n* haltérophile *m*; **~y** *a* lourd(e).
weir [wɪə*] *n* barrage *m*.
weird [wɪəd] *a* bizarre; (*eerie*) surnaturel(le).
welcome ['wɛlkəm] *a* bienvenu(e) // *n* accueil *m* // *vt* accueillir; (*also*: **bid ~**) souhaiter la bienvenue à; (*be glad of*) se réjouir de; **to be ~** être le(la) bienvenu(e); **welcoming** *a* accueillant(e); (*speech*) d'accueil.
weld [wɛld] *n* soudure *f* // *vt* souder; **~er** *n* (*person*) soudeur *m*; **~ing** *n* soudure *f* (autogène).
welfare ['wɛlfɛə*] *n* bien-être *m*; **~ state** *n* État-providence *m*; **~ work** *n* travail social.
well [wɛl] *n* puits *m* // *ad* bien // *a*: **to be ~** aller bien // *excl* eh bien!; bon!; enfin!; **~ done!** bravo!; **get ~ soon!** remets-toi vite!; **to do ~ in sth** bien réussir en *or* dans qch.
we'll [wi:l] = **we will, we shall.**
well: **~-behaved** *a* sage, obéissant(e); **~-being** *n* bien-être *m*; **~-built** *a* (*building*) bien construit(e); (*person*) bien bâti(e); **~-developed** *a* (*girl*) bien fait(e); **~-earned** *a* (*rest*) bien mérité(e); **~-groomed** *a* très soigné(e) de sa personne; **~-heeled** *a* (*col*: *wealthy*) fortuné(e), riche.
wellingtons ['wɛlɪŋtənz] *npl* (*also*: **wellington boots**) bottes *fpl* de caoutchouc.
well: **~-known** *a* (*person*) bien connu(e); **~-meaning** *a* bien intentionné(e); **~-off** *a* aisé(e), assez riche; **~-read** *a* cultivé(e); **~-to-do** *a* aisé(e), assez riche; **~-wisher** *n*: **scores of ~-wishers had gathered** de nombreux amis et admirateurs s'étaient rassemblés; **letters from ~-wishers** des lettres d'encouragement.
Welsh [wɛlʃ] *a* gallois(e) // *n* (LING) gallois *m*; **~man/woman** *n* Gallois/e; **~ rarebit** *n* croûte *f* au fromage.
went [wɛnt] *pt of* **go.**
wept [wɛpt] *pt, pp of* **weep.**
were [wə:*] *pt of* **be.**
we're [wɪə*] = **we are.**
weren't [wə:nt] = **were not.**
west [wɛst] *n* ouest *m* // *a* ouest *inv*, de *or* à l'ouest // *ad* à *or* vers l'ouest; **the W~** *n* l'Occident *m*, l'Ouest; **the W~ Country** *n* le sud-ouest de l'Angleterre; **~erly** *a* (*situation*) à l'ouest; (*wind*) d'ouest; **~ern** *a* occidental(e), de *or* à l'ouest // *n* (CINEMA) western *m*; **W~ Germany** *n* Allemagne *f* de l'Ouest; **W~ Indies** *npl* Antilles *fpl*; **~ward(s)** *ad* vers l'ouest.
wet [wɛt] *a* mouillé(e); (*damp*) humide; (*soaked*) trempé(e); (*rainy*) pluvieux(euse); **to get ~** se mouiller; **~ blanket** *n* (*fig*) rabat-joie *m inv*; **~ness** *n* humidité *f*; '**~ paint**' 'attention peinture fraîche'; **~ suit** *n* combinaison *f* de plongée.
we've [wi:v] = **we have.**
whack [wæk] *vt* donner un grand coup à; **~ed** *a* (*col*: *tired*) crevé(e).
whale [weɪl] *n* (ZOOL) baleine *f*.
wharf, wharves [wɔ:f, wɔ:vz] *n* quai *m*.
what [wɔt] *excl* quoi!, comment! // *det* quel(le) // *pronoun* (*interrogative*) que, *prep* + quoi; (*relative, indirect*: *object*) ce que; (: *subject*) ce qui; **~ are you doing?** que fais-tu?, qu'est-ce que tu fais?; **~ has happened?** que s'est-il passé?, qu'est-ce qui s'est passé?; **~'s in there?** qu'y a-t-il là-dedans?, qu'est-ce qu'il y a là-dedans?; **I saw ~ you did/is on the table** j'ai vu ce que vous avez fait/ce qui est sur la table; **~ a mess!** quel désordre!; **~ is it called?** comment est-ce que ça s'appelle?; **~ about doing ...?** et si on faisait ...?; **~ about me?** et moi?; **~ever** *det*: **~ever book** quel que soit le livre que (*or* qui) + *sub*; n'importe quel livre // *pronoun*: **do ~ever is necessary/you want** faites (tout) ce qui est nécessaire/(tout) ce que vous voulez; **~ever happens** quoi qu'il arrive; **no reason ~ever** *or* **~soever** pas la moindre raison.
wheat [wi:t] *n* blé *m*, froment *m*.
wheel [wi:l] *n* roue *f*; (AUT: *also*: **steering ~**) volant *m*; (NAUT) gouvernail *m* // *vt* pousser, rouler // *vi* (*also*: **~ round**) tourner; **~barrow** *n* brouette *f*; **~chair** *n* fauteuil roulant.
wheeze [wi:z] *n* respiration bruyante (*d'asthmatique*) // *vi* respirer bruyamment.
when [wɛn] *ad* quand // *cj* quand, lorsque; (*whereas*) alors que; **on the day ~ I met him** le jour où je l'ai rencontré; **~ever** *ad* quand donc // *cj* quand; (*every time that*) chaque fois que.
where [wɛə*] *ad,cj* où; **this is ~** c'est là que; **~abouts** *ad* où donc // *n*: **sb's ~abouts** l'endroit où se trouve qn; **~as** *cj* alors que; **~ver** [-'ɛvə*] *ad* où donc // *cj* où que + *sub*.
whet [wɛt] *vt* aiguiser.
whether ['wɛðə*] *cj* si; **I don't know ~ to accept or not** je ne sais pas si je dois accepter ou non; **it's doubtful ~** il est peu probable que; **~ you go or not** que vous y alliez ou non.
which [wɪtʃ] *det* (*interrogative*) quel(le), *pl* quels(quelles); **~ one of you?** lequel(laquelle) d'entre vous?; **tell me ~ one you want** dis-moi lequel tu veux *or* celui que tu veux // *pronoun* (*interrogative*) lequel(laquelle), *pl* lesquels (lesquelles); (*indirect*) celui(celle) qui (*or* que); (*relative*: *subject*) qui; (: *object*) que, *prep* + lequel(laquelle) (NB: *à* + *lequel* = auquel; *de* + *lequel* = duquel); **I don't mind ~** peu importe lequel; **the apple ~ you ate/~ is on the table** la pomme que vous avez mangée/qui est sur la table; **the chair on ~** la chaise sur laquelle; **the book of ~** le livre dont *or* duquel; **he said he knew, ~ is true/I feared** il a dit qu'il le savait, ce qui est vrai/ce que je

craignais ; **after ~** après quoi ; **in ~ case** auquel cas ; **~ever** *det*: **take ~ever book you prefer** prenez le livre que vous préférez, peu importe lequel ; **~ever book you take** quel que soit le livre que vous preniez ; **~ever way you** de quelque façon que vous + *sub*.

whiff [wɪf] *n* bouffée *f*.

while [waɪl] *n* moment *m* // *cj* pendant que ; (*as long as*) tant que ; (*whereas*) alors que ; bien que + *sub* ; **for a ~** pendant quelque temps.

whim [wɪm] *n* caprice *m*.

whimper ['wɪmpə*] *n* geignement *m* // *vi* geindre.

whimsical ['wɪmzɪkl] *a* (*person*) capricieux(euse) ; (*look*) étrange.

whine [waɪn] *n* gémissement *m* // *vi* gémir, geindre ; pleurnicher.

whip [wɪp] *n* fouet *m* ; (*for riding*) cravache *f* ; (*Brit*: POL: *person*) chef *m* de file (*assurant la discipline dans son groupe parlementaire*) // *vt* fouetter ; (*snatch*) enlever (*or* sortir) brusquement ; **~ped cream** *n* crème fouettée ; **~-round** *n* collecte *f*.

whirl [wə:l] *n* tourbillon *m* // *vt* faire tourbillonner ; faire tournoyer // *vi* tourbillonner ; **~pool** *n* tourbillon *m* ; **~wind** *n* tornade *f*.

whirr [wə:*] *vi* bruire ; ronronner ; vrombir.

whisk [wɪsk] *n* (CULIN) fouet *m* // *vt* fouetter, battre ; **to ~ sb away** *or* **off** emmener qn rapidement.

whisker [wɪskə*] *n*: **~s** (*of animal*) moustaches *fpl* ; (*of man*) favoris *mpl*.

whisky, whiskey (*Irlande, US*) ['wɪskɪ] *n* whisky *m*.

whisper ['wɪspə*] *n* chuchotement *m* ; (*fig*: *of leaves*) bruissement *m* ; (*rumour*) rumeur *f* // *vt,vi* chuchoter.

whist [wɪst] *n* whist *m*.

whistle ['wɪsl] *n* (*sound*) sifflement *m* ; (*object*) sifflet *m* // *vi* siffler.

white [waɪt] *a* blanc(blanche) ; (*with fear*) blême // *n* blanc *m* ; (*person*) blanc/blanche ; **~bait** *n* blanchaille *f* ; **~-collar worker** *n* employé/e de bureau ; **~ elephant** *n* (*fig*) objet dispendieux et superflu ; **~ lie** *n* pieux mensonge ; **~ness** *n* blancheur *f* ; **~ paper** *n* (POL) livre blanc ; **~wash** *n* (*paint*) lait *m* de chaux // *vt* blanchir à la chaux ; (*fig*) blanchir.

whiting ['waɪtɪŋ] *n, pl inv* (*fish*) merlan *m*.

Whitsun ['wɪtsn] *n* la Pentecôte.

whittle ['wɪtl] *vt*: **to ~ away, ~ down** (*costs*) réduire, rogner.

whizz [wɪz] *vi* aller (*or* passer) à toute vitesse ; **~ kid** *n* (*col*) petit prodige.

WHO *n* (*abbr of World Health Organization*) O.M.S. *f* (Organisation mondiale de la Santé).

who [hu:] *pronoun* qui ; **~dunit** [hu:'dʌnɪt] *n* (*col*) roman policier ; **~ever** *pronoun*: **~ever finds it** celui(celle) qui le trouve, (qui que ce soit), quiconque le trouve ; **ask ~ever you like** demandez à qui vous voulez ; **~ever he marries** qui que ce soit *or* quelle que soit la personne qu'il épouse ; **~ever told you that?** qui a bien pu vous dire ça?, qui donc vous a dit ça?

whole [həul] *a* (*complete*) entier(ère), tout(e) ; (*not broken*) intact(e), complet(ète) // *n* (*total*) totalité *f* ; (*sth not broken*) tout *m* ; **the ~ of the time** tout le temps ; **the ~ of the town** la ville tout entière ; **on the ~, as a ~** dans l'ensemble ; **~hearted** *a* sans réserve(s), sincère ; **~sale** *n* (vente *f* en) gros *m* // *a* de gros ; (*destruction*) systématique ; **~saler** *n* grossiste *m/f* ; **~some** *a* sain(e) ; (*advice*) salutaire ; **wholly** *ad* entièrement, tout à fait.

whom [hu:m] *pronoun* que, *prep* + qui (*check syntax of French verb used*) ; (*interrogative*) qui.

whooping cough ['hu:pɪŋkɔf] *n* coqueluche *f*.

whopping ['wɔpɪŋ] *a* (*col*: *big*) énorme.

whore [hɔ:*] *n* (*col*: *pej*) putain *f*.

whose [hu:z] *det*: **~ book is this?** à qui est ce livre? ; **~ pencil have you taken?** à qui est le crayon que vous avez pris?, c'est le crayon de qui que vous avez pris? ; **the man ~ son you rescued** l'homme dont *or* de qui vous avez sauvé le fils ; **the girl ~ sister you were speaking to** la fille à la sœur de qui *or* laquelle vous parliez // *pronoun*: **~ is this?** à qui est ceci? ; **I know ~ it is** je sais à qui c'est.

Who's Who ['hu:z'hu:] *n* ≈ Bottin Mondain.

why [waɪ] *ad* pourquoi // *excl* eh bien!, tiens! ; **the reason ~** la raison pour laquelle ; **~ever** *ad* pourquoi donc, mais pourquoi.

wick [wɪk] *n* mèche *f* (*de bougie*).

wicked ['wɪkɪd] *a* mauvais(e), méchant(e) ; inique ; cruel(le) ; (*mischievous*) malicieux(euse).

wicker ['wɪkə*] *n* osier *m* ; (*also*: **~work**) vannerie *f*.

wicket ['wɪkɪt] *n* (CRICKET) guichet *m* ; espace compris entre les deux guichets.

wide [waɪd] *a* large ; (*region, knowledge*) vaste, très étendu(e) ; (*choice*) grand(e) // *ad*: **to open ~** ouvrir tout grand ; **to shoot ~** tirer à côté ; **~-angle lens** *n* objectif *m* grand-angulaire ; **~-awake** *a* bien éveillé(e) ; **~ly** *ad* (*different*) radicalement ; (*spaced*) sur une grande étendue ; (*believed*) généralement ; **~n** *vt* élargir ; **~ness** *n* largeur *f* ; **~ open** *a* grand(e) ouvert(e) ; **~spread** *a* (*belief etc*) très répandu(e).

widow ['wɪdəu] *n* veuve *f* ; **~ed** *a* (qui est devenu(e)) veuf(veuve) ; **~er** *n* veuf *m*.

width [wɪdθ] *n* largeur *f*.

wield [wi:ld] *vt* (*sword*) manier ; (*power*) exercer.

wife, wives [waɪf, waɪvz] *n* femme (mariée), épouse *f*.

wig [wɪg] *n* perruque *f*.

wiggle ['wɪgl] *vt* agiter remuer // *vi* (*loose screw etc*) branler ; (*worm*) se tortiller.

wild [waɪld] *a* sauvage ; (*sea*) déchaîné(e) ; (*idea, life*) fou(folle) ; extravagant(e) ; **~s** *npl* régions *fpl* sauvages ; **~erness** ['wɪldənɪs] *n* désert *m*, région *f* sauvage ; **~-goose chase** *n* (*fig*) fausse piste ; **~life** *n* faune *f* ; **~ly** *ad* (*applaud*) frénétiquement ; (*hit, guess*) au hasard ; (*happy*) follement.

wilful ['wɪlful] *a* (*person*) obstiné(e) ; (*action*) délibéré(e) ; (*crime*) prémédité(e).

will [wɪl] *auxiliary vb*: **he ~ come** il viendra // *vt* (*pt, pp* **~ed**): **to ~ sb to do** souhaiter ardemment que qn fasse ; **he ~ed himself to go on** par un suprême effort de volonté, il continua // *n* volonté *f* ; testament *m* ; **~ing** *a* de bonne volonté, serviable ; **he's ~ing to do it** il est disposé à le faire, il veut bien le faire ; **~ingly** *ad* volontiers ; **~ingness** *n* bonne volonté.

willow ['wɪləu] *n* saule *m*.

will power ['wɪlpauə*] *n* volonté *f*.

wilt [wɪlt] *vi* dépérir.

wily ['waɪlɪ] *a* rusé(e).

win [wɪn] *n* (*in sports etc*) victoire *f* // *vb* (*pt, pp* **won** [wʌn]) *vt* (*battle, money*) gagner ; (*prize*) remporter ; (*popularity*) acquérir // *vi* gagner ; **to ~ over, ~ round** *vt* gagner, se concilier.

wince [wɪns] *n* tressaillement *m* // *vi* tressaillir.

winch [wɪntʃ] *n* treuil *m*.

wind *n* [wɪnd] (*also* MED) vent *m* // *vb* [waɪnd] (*pt, pp* **wound** [waund]) *vt* enrouler ; (*wrap*) envelopper ; (*clock, toy*) remonter ; (*take breath away*: [wɪnd]) couper le souffle à // *vi* (*road, river*) serpenter ; **the ~(s)** (MUS) les instruments *mpl* à vent ; **to ~ up** *vt* (*clock*) remonter ; (*debate*) terminer, clôturer ; **~break** *n* brise-vent *m inv* ; **~fall** *n* coup *m* de chance ; **~ing** *a* (*road*) sinueux(euse) ; (*staircase*) tournant(e) ; **~ instrument** *n* (MUS) instrument *m* à vent ; **~mill** *n* moulin *m* à vent.

window ['wɪndəu] *n* fenêtre *f* ; (*in car, train, also*: **~ pane**) vitre *f* ; (*in shop etc*) vitrine *f* ; **~ box** *n* jardinière *f* ; **~ cleaner** *n* (*person*) laveur/euse de vitres ; **~ frame** *n* châssis *m* de fenêtre ; **~ ledge** *n* rebord *m* de la fenêtre ; **~ pane** *n* vitre *f*, carreau *m* ; **~sill** *n* (*inside*) appui *m* de la fenêtre ; (*outside*) rebord *m* de la fenêtre.

windpipe ['wɪndpaɪp] *n* gosier *m*.

windscreen, windshield (*US*) ['wɪndskri:n, 'wɪndʃi:ld] *n* pare-brise *m inv* ; **~ washer** *n* lave-glace *m inv* ; **~ wiper** *n* essuie-glace *m inv*.

windswept ['wɪndswɛpt] *a* balayé(e) par le vent.

windy ['wɪndɪ] *a* venté(e), venteux(euse) ; **it's ~** il y a du vent.

wine [waɪn] *n* vin *m* ; **~ cellar** *n* cave *f* à vins ; **~ glass** *n* verre *m* à vin ; **~ list** *n* carte *f* des vins ; **~ merchant** *n* marchand/e de vins ; **~ tasting** *n* dégustation *f* (de vins) ; **~ waiter** *n* sommelier *m*.

wing [wɪŋ] *n* aile *f* ; (*in air force*) groupe *m* d'escadrilles ; **~s** *npl* (THEATRE) coulisses *fpl* ; **~er** *n* (SPORT) ailier *m*.

wink [wɪŋk] *n* clin *m* d'œil // *vi* faire un clin d'œil ; (*blink*) cligner des yeux.

winner ['wɪnə*] *n* gagnant/e.

winning ['wɪnɪŋ] *a* (*team*) gagnant(e) ; (*goal*) décisif(ive) ; **~s** *npl* gains *mpl* ; **~ post** *n* poteau *m* d'arrivée.

winter ['wɪntə*] *n* hiver *m* // *vi* hiverner ; **~ sports** *npl* sports *mpl* d'hiver.

wintry ['wɪntrɪ] *a* hivernal(e).

wipe [waɪp] *n* coup *m* de torchon (*or* de chiffon *or* d'éponge) // *vt* essuyer ; **to ~ off** *vt* essuyer ; **to ~ out** *vt* (*debt*) régler ; (*memory*) oublier ; (*destroy*) anéantir ; **to ~ up** *vt* essuyer.

wire ['waɪə*] *n* fil *m* (de fer) ; (ELEC) fil électrique ; (TEL) télégramme *m* // *vt* (*fence*) grillager ; (*house*) faire l'installation électrique de ; (*also*: **~ up**) brancher ; **~ brush** *n* brosse *f* métallique.

wireless ['waɪəlɪs] *n* télégraphie *f* sans fil ; (*set*) T.S.F. *f*.

wiry ['waɪərɪ] *a* noueux(euse), nerveux(euse).

wisdom ['wɪzdəm] *n* sagesse *f* ; (*of action*) prudence *f* ; **~ tooth** *n* dent *f* de sagesse.

wise [waɪz] *a* sage, prudent(e), judicieux(euse).

...wise [waɪz] *suffix*: **time~** en ce qui concerne le temps, question temps.

wisecrack ['waɪzkræk] *n* sarcasme *m*.

wish [wɪʃ] *n* (*desire,*) désir *m* ; (*specific desire*) souhait *m*, vœu *m* // *vt* souhaiter, désirer, vouloir ; **best ~es** (*on birthday etc*) meilleurs vœux ; **with best ~es** (*in letter*) bien amicalement ; **give her my best ~es** faites-lui mes amitiés ; **to ~ sb goodbye** dire au revoir à qn ; **he ~ed me well** il me souhaitait de réussir ; **to ~ to do/sb to do** désirer *or* vouloir faire/que qn fasse ; **to ~ for** souhaiter ; **it's ~ful thinking** c'est prendre ses désirs pour des réalités.

wisp [wɪsp] *n* fine mèche (*de cheveux*) ; (*of smoke*) mince volute *f* ; **a ~ of straw** un fétu de paille.

wistful ['wɪstful] *a* mélancolique.

wit [wɪt] *n* (*gen pl*) intelligence *f*, esprit *m* ; présence *f* d'esprit ; (*wittiness*) esprit ; (*person*) homme/femme d'esprit ; **to be at one's ~s' end** (*fig*) ne plus savoir que faire ; **to ~** *ad* à savoir.

witch [wɪtʃ] *n* sorcière *f* ; **~craft** *n* sorcellerie *f*.

with [wɪð, wɪθ] *prep* avec ; **red ~ anger** rouge de colère ; **the man ~ the grey hat** l'homme au chapeau gris ; **to be ~ it** (*fig*) être dans le vent ; **I am ~ you** (*I understand*) je vous suis.

withdraw [wɪθ'drɔ:] *vb* (*irg*) *vt* retirer // *vi* se retirer ; (*go back on promise*) se rétracter ; **~al** *n* retrait *m* ; (MED) état *m* de manque.

wither ['wɪðə*] *vi* se faner ; **~ed** *a* fané(e), flétri(e) ; (*limb*) atrophié(e).

withhold [wɪθ'həuld] *vt irg* (*money*) retenir ; (*decision*) remettre ; (*permission*): **to ~ (from)** refuser (à) ; (*information*): **to ~ (from)** cacher (à).

within [wɪð'ɪn] *prep* à l'intérieur de // *ad* à l'intérieur ; **~ sight of** en vue de ; **~ a mile of** à moins d'un mille de ; **~ the week** avant la fin de la semaine.

without [wɪð'aut] *prep* sans.

withstand [wɪθ'stænd] *vt irg* résister à.

witness ['wɪtnɪs] *n* (*person*) témoin *m* ; (*evidence*) témoignage *m* // *vt* (*event*) être témoin de ; (*document*) attester l'authenticité de ; **to bear ~ to sth** témoigner de qch ; **~ box, ~ stand** (*US*) *n* barre *f* des témoins.

witticism ['wɪtɪsɪzm] *n* mot *m* d'esprit.
witty ['wɪtɪ] *a* spirituel(le), plein(e) d'esprit.
wives [waɪvz] *npl of* **wife**.
wizard ['wɪzəd] *n* magicien *m*.
wk *abbr of* **week**.
wobble ['wɔbl] *vi* trembler; (*chair*) branler.
woe [wəu] *n* malheur *m*.
woke [wəuk] *pt of* **wake**; **~n** *pp of* **wake**.
wolf, wolves [wulf, wulvz] *n* loup *m*.
woman, *pl* **women** ['wumən, 'wɪmɪn] *n* femme *f*; **~ doctor** *n* femme *f* médecin; **~ly** *a* féminin(e); **~ teacher** *n* professeur *m* femme *f*.
womb [wu:m] *n* (ANAT) utérus *m*.
women ['wɪmɪn] *npl of* **woman**.
won [wʌn] *pt,pp of* **win**.
wonder ['wʌndə*] *n* merveille *f*, miracle *m*; (*feeling*) émerveillement *m* // *vi*: **to ~ whether** se demander si; **to ~ at** s'étonner de; s'émerveiller de; **to ~ about** songer à; **it's no ~ that** il n'est pas étonnant que + *sub*; **~ful** *a* merveilleux(euse); **~fully** *ad* (+ *adjective*) merveilleusement; (+ *vb*) à merveille.
wonky ['wɔŋkɪ] *a* (*col*) qui ne va *or* ne marche pas très bien.
won't [wəunt] = **will not**.
woo [wu:] *vt* (*woman*) faire la cour à.
wood [wud] *n* (*timber, forest*) bois *m*; **~ carving** *n* sculpture *f* en *or* sur bois; **~ed** *a* boisé(e); **~en** *a* en bois; (*fig*) raide; inexpressif(ive); **~pecker** *n* pic *m* (*oiseau*); **~wind** *n* (MUS) bois *m*; **the ~wind** (MUS) les bois; **~work** *n* menuiserie *f*; **~worm** *n* ver *m* du bois.
wool [wul] *n* laine *f*; **to pull the ~ over sb's eyes** (*fig*) en faire accroire à qn; **~len, ~en** (*US*) *a* de laine; (*industry*) lainier(ère); **~lens** *npl* lainages *mpl*; **~ly, ~y** (*US*) *a* laineux(euse); (*fig*: *ideas*) confus(e).
word [wə:d] *n* mot *m*; (*spoken*) mot, parole *f*; (*promise*) parole; (*news*) nouvelles *fpl* // *vt* rédiger, formuler; **in other ~s** en d'autres termes; **to break/keep one's ~** manquer à/tenir sa parole; **I'll take your ~ for it** je vous crois sur parole; **to send ~ of** prévenir de; **~ing** *n* termes *mpl*, langage *m*; **~y** *a* verbeux(euse).
wore [wɔ:*] *pt of* **wear**.
work [wə:k] *n* travail *m*; (ART, LITERATURE) œuvre *f* // *vi* travailler; (*mechanism*) marcher, fonctionner; (*plan etc*) marcher; (*medicine*) faire son effet // *vt* (*clay, wood etc*) travailler; (*mine etc*) exploiter; (*machine*) faire marcher *or* fonctionner; **to be out of ~** être au chômage; **~s** *n* (*factory*) usine *f* // *npl* (*of clock, machine*) mécanisme *m*; **Minister/Ministry of W~s** ministre *m*/ministère *m* des Travaux publics; **to ~ loose** *vi* se défaire, se desserrer; **to ~ on** *vt fus* travailler à; (*principle*) se baser sur; **to ~ out** *vi* (*plans etc*) marcher // *vt* (*problem*) résoudre; (*plan*) élaborer; **it ~s out at £100** ça fait 100 livres; **to get ~ed up** se mettre dans tous ses états; **~able** *a* (*solution*) réalisable; **~er** *n* travailleur/euse, ouvrier/ère; **~ing class** *n* classe ouvrière; **~ing-class** *a* ouvrier(ère); **~ing man** *n* travailleur *m*; **in ~ing order** en état de marche; **~man** *n* ouvrier *m*; **~manship** *n* métier *m*, habileté *f*; facture *f*; **~shop** *n* atelier *m*; **~-to-rule** *n* grève *f* du zèle.
world [wə:ld] *n* monde *m* // *cpd* (*champion*) du monde; (*power, war*) mondial(e); **to think the ~ of sb** (*fig*) ne jurer que par qn; **out of this ~** *a* extraordinaire; **~ly** *a* de ce monde; **~-wide** *a* universel(le).
worm [wə:m] *n* ver *m*.
worn [wɔ:n] *pp of* **wear** // *a* usé(e); **~-out** *a* (*object*) complètement usé(e); (*person*) épuisé(e).
worried ['wʌrɪd] *a* inquiet(ète).
worrier ['wʌrɪə*] *n* inquiet/ète.
worry ['wʌrɪ] *n* souci *m* // *vt* inquiéter // *vi* s'inquiéter, se faire du souci; **~ing** *a* inquiétant(e).
worse [wə:s] *a* pire, plus mauvais(e) // *ad* plus mal // *n* pire *m*; **a change for the ~** une détérioration; **~n** *vt,vi* empirer; **~ off** *a* moins à l'aise financièrement; (*fig*): **you'll be ~ off this way** ça ira moins bien de cette façon.
worship ['wə:ʃɪp] *n* culte *m* // *vt* (*God*) rendre un culte à; (*person*) adorer; **Your W~** (*to mayor*) Monsieur le Maire; (*to judge*) Monsieur le Juge; **~per** *n* adorateur/trice; (*in church*) fidèle *m/f*.
worst [wə:st] *a* le(la) pire, le(la) plus mauvais(e) // *ad* le plus mal // *n* pire *m*; **at ~** au pis aller.
worsted ['wustɪd] *n*: **(wool) ~** laine peignée.
worth [wə:θ] *n* valeur *f* // *a*: **to be ~** valoir; **it's ~ it** cela en vaut la peine; **50 pence ~ of apples** (pour) 50 pence de pommes; **~less** *a* qui ne vaut rien; **~while** *a* (*activity*) qui en vaut la peine; (*cause*) louable; **a ~while book** un livre qui vaut la peine d'être lu.
worthy [wə:ðɪ] *a* (*person*) digne; (*motive*) louable; **~ of** digne de.
would [wud] *auxiliary vb*: **she ~ come** elle viendrait; **he ~ have come** il serait venu; **~ you like a biscuit?** voulez-vous *or* voudriez-vous un biscuit?; **he ~ go there on Mondays** il y allait le lundi; **~-be** *a* (*pej*) soi-disant.
wound *vb* [waund] *pt, pp of* **wind** // *n,vt* [wu:nd] *n* blessure *f* // *vt* blesser; **~ed in the leg** blessé à la jambe.
wove [wəuv] *pt of* **weave**; **~n** *pp of* **weave**.
wrangle ['ræŋgl] *n* dispute *f* // *vi* se disputer.
wrap [ræp] *n* (*stole*) écharpe *f*; (*cape*) pèlerine *f* // *vt* (*also*: **~ up**) envelopper; **~per** *n* (*of book*) couverture *f*; **~ping paper** *n* papier *m* d'emballage; (*for gift*) papier cadeau.
wrath [rɔθ] *n* courroux *m*.
wreath, ~s [ri:θ, ri:ðz] *n* couronne *f*.
wreck [rɛk] *n* (*sea disaster*) naufrage *m*; (*ship*) épave *f*; (*pej*: *person*) loque humaine // *vt* démolir; (*ship*) provoquer le naufrage de; (*fig*) briser, ruiner; **~age** *n* débris *mpl*; (*of building*) décombres *mpl*; (*of ship*) épave *f*.

wren [rɛn] *n* (*ZOOL*) roitelet *m*.
wrench [rɛntʃ] *n* (*TECH*) clé *f* (à écrous); (*tug*) violent mouvement de torsion; (*fig*) arrachement *m* // *vt* tirer violemment sur, tordre; **to ~ sth from** arracher qch (violemment) à *or* de.
wrestle ['rɛsl] *vi*: **to ~ (with sb)** lutter (avec qn); **to ~ with** (*fig*) se débattre avec, lutter contre; **~r** *n* lutteur/euse; **wrestling** *n* lutte *f*; (*also*: **all-in wrestling**) catch *m*; **wrestling match** *n* rencontre *f* de lutte (*or* de catch).
wretched ['rɛtʃɪd] *a* misérable; (*col*) maudit(e).
wriggle ['rɪgl] *n* tortillement *m* // *vi* se tortiller.
wring, *pt, pp* **wrung** [rɪŋ, rʌŋ] *vt* tordre; (*wet clothes*) essorer; (*fig*): **to ~ sth out of** arracher qch à.
wrinkle ['rɪŋkl] *n* (*on skin*) ride *f*; (*on paper etc*) pli *m* // *vt* rider, plisser // *vi* se plisser.
wrist [rɪst] *n* poignet *m*; **~ watch** *n* montre-bracelet *f*.
writ [rɪt] *n* acte *m* judiciaire; **to issue a ~ against sb** assigner qn en justice.
write, *pt* **wrote,** *pp* **written** [raɪt, rəut, 'rɪtn] *vt,vi* écrire; **to ~ down** *vt* noter; (*put in writing*) mettre par écrit; **to ~ off** *vt* (*debt*) passer aux profits et pertes; (*depreciate*) amortir; **to ~ out** *vt* écrire; (*copy*) recopier; **to ~ up** *vt* rédiger; **~-off** *n* perte totale; **the car is a ~-off** la voiture est bonne pour la casse; **~r** *n* auteur *m*, écrivain *m*.
writhe [raɪð] *vi* se tordre.
writing ['raɪtɪŋ] *n* écriture *f*; (*of author*) œuvres *fpl*; **in ~** par écrit; **~ paper** *n* papier *m* à lettres.
written ['rɪtn] *pp of* **write**.
wrong [rɔŋ] *a* faux(fausse); (*incorrectly chosen*: *number, road etc*) mauvais(e); (*not suitable*) qui ne convient pas; (*wicked*) mal; (*unfair*) injuste // *ad* faux // *n* tort *m* // *vt* faire du tort à, léser; **you are ~ to do it** tu as tort de le faire; **you are ~ about that, you've got it ~** tu te trompes; **to be in the ~** avoir tort; **what's ~?** qu'est-ce qui ne va pas?; **to go ~** (*person*) se tromper; (*plan*) mal tourner; (*machine*) tomber en panne; **~ful** *a* injustifié(e); **~ly** *ad* à tort; **~ side** *n* (*of cloth*) envers *m*.
wrote [rəut] *pt of* **write.**
wrought [rɔ:t] *a*: **~ iron** fer forgé.
wrung [rʌŋ] *pt, pp of* **wring.**
wry [raɪ] *a* désabusé(e).
wt. *abbr of* **weight**.

X Y Z

Xmas ['ɛksməs] *n abbr of* **Christmas.**
X-ray [ɛks'reɪ] *n* rayon *m* X; (*photograph*) radio(graphie) *f* // *vt* radiographier.
xylophone ['zaɪləfəun] *n* xylophone *m*.
yacht [jɔt] *n* yacht *m*; voilier *m*; **~ing** *n* yachting *m*, navigation *f* de plaisance; **~sman** *n* yacht(s)man *m*.
Yank [jæŋk] *n* (*pej*) Amerloque *m/f*.
yap [jæp] *vi* (*dog*) japper.
yard [jɑ:d] *n* (*of house etc*) cour *f*; (*measure*) yard *m* (= *914 mm*; *3 feet*); **~stick** *n* (*fig*) mesure *f*, critère *m*.
yarn [jɑ:n] *n* fil *m*; (*tale*) longue histoire.
yawn [jɔ:n] *n* bâillement *m* // *vi* bâiller; **~ing** *a* (*gap*) béant(e).
yd. *abbr of* **yard(s)**.
year [jɪə*] *n* an *m*, année *f*; **every ~** tous les ans, chaque année; **to be 8 ~s old** avoir 8 ans ; **~ly** *a* annuel(le) // *ad* annuellement.
yearn [jə:n] *vi*: **to ~ for sth/to do** aspirer à qch/à faire, languir après qch; **~ing** *n* désir ardent, envie *f*.
yeast [ji:st] *n* levure *f*.
yell [jɛl] *n* hurlement *m*, cri *m* // *vi* hurler.
yellow ['jɛləu] *a,n* jaune (*m*); **~ fever** *n* fièvre *f* jaune.
yelp [jɛlp] *n* jappement *m*; glapissement *m* // *vi* japper; glapir.
yeoman ['jəumən] *n*: **Y~ of the Guard** hallebardier *m* de la garde royale.
yes [jɛs] *ad* oui; (*answering negative question*) si // *n* oui *m*.
yesterday ['jɛstədɪ] *ad,n* hier (*m*).
yet [jɛt] *ad* encore; déjà // *cj* pourtant, néanmoins; **it is not finished ~** ce n'est pas encore fini *or* toujours pas fini; **must you go just ~?** dois-tu déjà partir?; **the best ~** le meilleur jusqu'ici *or* jusque-là ; **as ~** jusqu'ici, encore; **a few days ~** encore quelques jours.
yew [ju:] *n* if *m*.
Yiddish ['jɪdɪʃ] *n* yiddish *m*.
yield [ji:ld] *n* production *f*, rendement *m*; rapport *m* // *vt* produire, rendre, rapporter; (*surrender*) céder // *vi* céder.
yodel ['jəudl] *vi* faire des tyroliennes, jodler.
yoga ['jəugə] *n* yoga *m*.
yog(h)ourt, yog(h)urt ['jəugət] *n* yaourt *m*.
yoke [jəuk] *n* joug *m*.
yolk [jəuk] *n* jaune *m* (d'œuf).
yonder ['jɔndə*] *ad* là(-bas).
you [ju:] *pronoun* tu; (*polite form*) vous; (*pl*) vous; (*complement*) te, t' + *vowel*; vous; (*stressed*) toi; vous; (*one*): **fresh air does ~ good** l'air frais fait du bien; **~ never know** on ne sait jamais.
you'd [ju:d] = **you had**; **you would**.
you'll [ju:l] = **you will**; **you shall**.
young [jʌŋ] *a* jeune // *npl* (*of animal*) petits *mpl*; (*people*): **the ~** les jeunes, la jeunesse; **~ish** *a* assez jeune; **~ster** *n* jeune *m* (garçon *m*); (*child*) enfant *m/f*.
your [jɔ:*] *a* ton(ta), *pl* tes; votre, *pl* vos.
you're [juə*] = **you are**.
yours [jɔ:z] *pronoun* le(la) tien(ne), les tiens(tiennes); le(la) vôtre, les vôtres; **is it ~?** c'est à toi (*or* à vous)?; **yours sincerely/faithfully** je vous prie d'agréer l'expression de mes sentiments les meilleurs/mes sentiments respectueux *or* dévoués.
yourself [jɔ:'sɛlf] *pronoun* (*reflexive*) te; vous; (*after prep*) toi; vous; (*emphatic*) toi-même; vous-même; **yourselves** *pl pronoun* vous; (*emphatic*) vous mêmes.
youth [ju:θ] *n* jeunesse *f*; (*young man*: *pl* **~s** [ju:ðz]) jeune homme *m*; **~ful** *a*

jeune ; de jeunesse ; juvénile ; ~ **hostel** *n* auberge *f* de jeunesse.

you've [ju:v] = **you have**.

Yugoslav ['ju:gəu'slɑ:v] *a* yougoslave // *n* Yougoslave *m/f*.

Yugoslavia ['ju:gəu'sla:vɪə] *n* Yougoslavie *f*.

Yule [ju:l]: ~ **log** *n* bûche *f* de Noël.

zany ['zeɪnɪ] *a* farfelu(e), loufoque.

zeal [zi:l] *n* zèle *m*, ferveur *f*; empressement *m* ; ~**ous** ['zɛləs] *a* zélé(e) ; empressé(e).

zebra ['zi:brə] *n* zèbre *m* ; ~ **crossing** *n* passage *m* pour piétons.

zenith ['zɛnɪθ] *n* zénith *m*.

zero ['zɪərəu] *n* zéro *m* ; ~ **hour** *n* l'heure *f* H.

zest [zɛst] *n* entrain *m*, élan *m* ; zeste *m*.

zigzag ['zɪgzæg] *n* zigzag *m* // *vi* zigzaguer, faire des zigzags.

zinc [zɪŋk] *n* zinc *m*.

Zionism ['zaɪənɪzm] *n* sionisme *m*.

zip [zip] *n* (*also*: ~ **fastener,** ~**per**) fermeture *f* éclair ® // *vt* (*also*: ~ **up**) fermer avec une fermeture éclair ®.

zither ['zɪðə*] *n* cithare *f*.

zodiac ['zəudɪæk] *n* zodiaque *m*.

zombie ['zɔmbɪ] *n* (*fig*): **like a** ~ l'air complètement dans les vapes, avec l'air d'un mort vivant.

zone [zəun] *n* zone *f*; (*subdivision of town*) secteur *m*.

zoo [zu:] *n* zoo *m*.

zoological [zuə'lɔdʒɪkl] *a* zoologique.

zoologist [zu'ɔlədʒɪst] *n* zoologiste *m/f*.

zoology [zu:'ɔlədʒɪ] *n* zoologie *f*.

zoom [zu:m] *vi*: **to** ~ **past** passer en trombe ; ~ **lens** *n* zoom *m*, objectif *m* à focale variable.

NOTES TO THE USER OF THIS DICTIONARY

I. Using the dictionary

In using this book, you will either want to check the meaning of a French word you don't know, or find the French for an English word. These two operations are quite different, and so are the problems you may face when using one side of the dictionary or the other. In order to help you, we have tried to explain below the main features of this book.

The 'wordlist' is the alphabetical list of all the items in large bold type, ie. all the 'headwords'. Each 'entry', or article, is introduced by a headword, and may contain additional 'references' in smaller bold type, such as phrases, derivatives, and compound words. Section 1. below deals with the way references are listed.

The typography distinguishes between three broad categories of text within the dictionary. All items in bold type, large or smaller, are 'source language' references, for which an equivalence in the other language is provided. All items in standard type are translations. Items in italics are information about the words being translated, ie. either labels, or 'signposts' pinpointing the appropriate translation, or explanations.

1. *Where to look for a word*

1.1 Derivatives

In order to save space, a number of derivatives have been listed within entries, provided this does not break alphabetical order. Thus, **pensionnaire** and **pensionnat** are listed within the entry for **pension,** or **caller** and **calling** under **call.** You must remember this when looking for a word you don't find listed as a headword. These derivatives are always listed last within an entry (see also I.2 on entry layout).

1.2 Homographs

Homographs are words which are spelt in exactly the same way, like French **boucher** (to block) and **boucher** (butcher), or English **fine** (nice etc) and **fine** (penalty). As a rule, in order to save space, such words have been treated as one headword only. In the very few cases where this was not possible, either a cross-reference is given (see **pas,** in the French wordlist), or else the presence of a feminine form helps distinguish between two consecutive homograph entries (**boulot** vs **boulot,-te, vu** vs **vu,-e** vs **vue**).

1.3 Phrases

Because of the constraints of space, there can be only a limited number of idiomatic phrases in a pocket dictionary like this one. Particular emphasis is given to verbal phrases like **mettre au point, mettre à jour, prendre feu, faire feu, faire du feu,** etc, and also to basic constructions (see for instance the entries for **apply, agree, apprendre, moment**).

Verbal phrases with the ten or so basic verbs like *faire*, *mettre*, *prendre*, etc. are listed under the noun. Other phrases and idioms are listed under the first key word (ie. not a preposition), for instance **filer doux** under **filer, d'emblée** under **emblée.**

1.4 Abbreviations and proper names

For easier reference, abbreviations, acronyms and proper names have been listed alphabetically in the wordlist, as opposed to being relegated to the appendices. **M.O.T.** is used in every way like **certificate** or **permit, R.E.R.** like **métro,** and these words are treated like other nouns.

1.5 Compounds

Housewife, bicycle track, pare-chocs and **pomme de terre** are all compounds. One-word compounds like 'housewife' are no problem as regards consulting the dictionary, since they can appear only in one place and in strict alphabetical order. When it comes to other compounds, however – hyphenated compounds and compounds made up of separate words – each language presents its own peculiar problems.

1.5.1 French compounds

There are many compounds made up of two or more 'words'. When it comes to checking a French compound, you might not be aware that you are dealing with a compound and not a string of autonomous words, and there might inevitably be some toing and froing between entries.

As spelling is quite set in French, we have listed French compounds under the first word, and grouped them alphabetically within that entry. For instance, **cour martiale** is within the entry for **cour** and comes before the headword **courage. Fête mobile** is within the entry for **fête,** and comes before **Fête-Dieu** and **fêter** at the end of the same entry (see also section 2.). Remember that the meaning of a phrase or of a compound can be quite different from that of its elements taken separately, so be prepared to check through an entry thoroughly before giving up.

1.5.2 French 'verbes pronominaux'

Verbs like **se rappeler, se noyer, se promener, s'arroger** are called 'pronominaux' in French because they are used with a 'pronom personnel': je *me* rappelle, tu *te* promènes etc. They must be distinguished from truly reflexive or reciprocal uses like 'il *se* regarde dans la glace' (he is looking *at himself* in the mirror) and 'ils *se* regardaient sans rien dire' (they were looking *at each other* in silence). The 'verbes pronominaux' are intransitive or transitive verbs in their own right: 'se promener' is intransitive like 'flâner', and 's'arroger' transitive in the same way as 'prendre'.

There are no such verbs in English (which has another type of 'compound verb', the phrasal verb, see 1.5.4), where a verb used with 'oneself' is as a rule truly reflexive. Compare for instance the translations for **se noyer** (accidentellement) and **se noyer** (suicide). These verbs have been listed as phrases under the entry for the key word. See for instance the entries for **rappeler, rapporter, ingénier.**

1.5.3 English compounds

Here there is a problem of where to find a compound because of less predictable spelling than is the case with French: is it **airgun, air-gun** or **air gun**? This is why we choose to list them according to strict alphabetical order. Thus **tea set** comes between **tease** and **teashop.** The entries between **tax** and **technical** will provide a good illustration of the system of listing. It has drawbacks, for instance in that **tax-free** and **tax-payer** are separated by **taxi, taxidermist** and three 'taxi' compounds. However, in a short dictionary used by beginners, it has the merit of simplicity and consistency.

1.5.4 English 'phrasal verbs'

'Phrasal verbs' are verbs like **go off, blow up, cut down** etc. Here you have the advantage of knowing that these words belong together, whereas it will take the foreign user some time before he can identify these verbs immediately. They have been listed under the entry for the basic verb (eg. **go, blow, cut**), grouped alphabetically before any other derivative or compound – eg. **pull up** comes before **pulley.** For instance, look up **to back out, to look up** (a word), **to look out.**

1.6 Irregular forms

When looking up a French word, you may not immediately find the form you are looking for, although the word in question has been duly entered in the dictionary. This is possibly because you are looking up an irregular noun or verb form, and these are not always given as entries in their own right. Obviously we have assumed that you know the basics regarding French verb forms, noun plurals and feminine forms. Thus you will be expected to know that 'chantent' is a form of the verb **chanter,** chevaux the plural of **cheval,** and so on. However, in order to help you, we have included the main irregular forms as entries in their own right, with a cross-reference to the basic form.

Thus, if you come across the word 'buvais' and attempt to look up a verb 'buver', you won't find it but what you will find at that place in the wordlist, between **butte** and **buvard,** is the entry **buvais** *etc vb voir* **boire.**

Similarly, **fausse,** and **fasse** are cross-referred to *faux* and *faire* respectively. With past participles, it sometimes happens that in addition to the purely verbal form there is an adjectival or noun use, for instance **connu** or **meublé.** These usages are translated as autonomous words, but they are also cross-referred to the verb whenever appropriate (see for instance entries for **couvert** or **assis**).

2. *Entry layout*

All entries, however long or complex, are arranged in a very systematic manner. But it may be a little difficult at first to find one's way through an entry like **passer, back, round** or **run** because homographs are grouped together (see 1.2) and the text is run on without any breakdown into paragraphs, in order to save space. Ease of reference comes with practice, but the guidelines below will make it easier for you.

2.1 'Signposting'

If you look up a French word and find a string of quite different English translations, you are unlikely to have much trouble finding out which is the relevant one for the context, because you know what the English words mean, and the context will almost automatically rule out unsuitable translations.

It is quite a different matter when you want to find the French for, say, **lock,** in the context 'we got to the lock around lunchtime', and are faced with an entry that reads 'lock: serrure (f); écluse (f); mèche (f), boucle (f)'. Obviously you can then go to the other side and check what each translation means. But this is time-consuming, and it doesn't always work. This is why we have provided the user with signposts which pinpoint the relevant translation. For instance with **lock,** the entry reads: ... (*of door, box*) serrure *f*; (*of canal*) écluse *f*; (*of hair*) mèche *f*, boucle *f* ...

For the context suggested above, it is now clear that 'écluse' is the right word.

2.2 Grammatical categories and meaning categories

Complex entries are first broken down into grammatical categories, eg.: **lock** *n* // *vt* // *vi*. Be prepared to go through entries like **run** or **back** carefully, and you will find how useful all these 'signposts' are. Each grammatical category is then split where appropriate into the various meanings, eg.:

> **lock** *n* (*of door, box*) serrure *f*; (*of canal*) écluse *f*; (*of hair*) mèche *f*, boucle *f* // *vt* (*with key*) fermer à clé; (*immobilize*) bloquer // *vi* (*door etc*) fermer à clé; (*wheels*) se bloquer.

3. *Using the translations*

3.1 Gender

All feminine endings for French adjectives have been given on the English-French side. This may appear to duplicate information given on the other side, but we feel it is a useful reminder where and when it matters. The feminine version is given for words like **driver, teacher, research worker** etc. Remember that the French equivalents of **his, her, its** or **the** do not behave like their English counterparts: see section II for more information.

3.2 Plural

We have assumed knowledge on the part of the user of plural formation in French (see section II), including the plural of compounds. A form like 'yeux' is given (see entry for **eye**), but in the main, plural forms are not shown.

3.3 Verb forms

Irregular French verbs appearing as translations have not been marked as such, and the user should refer to the French verb tables when in doubt (pp. 507–514).

3.4 Colloquial language

You should as a rule proceed with great caution when handling foreign language which has a degree of informality. When an English word or phrase has been labelled (*col*), ie. colloquial, you must assume that the translation belongs to a similar level of informality. If the translation is followed by (!) you should handle it with extreme care, or best avoid it unless you are with close friends!

3.5 'Grammatical words'

It is exceedingly difficult to give adequate treatment for words like **for, away, whose, which, out, off** etc. in a short dictionary such as this one. We have tried to go some way towards providing as much relevant information as possible regarding the most frequent uses of these words. However, for further information use a good monolingual dictionary of French, especially one for foreign learners, and a good modern French grammar.

3.6 'Approximate' translations and cultural equivalents

It is not always possible to give a genuine translation, when for instance an English word denotes a thing or institution which either does not exist in France, or is quite different. Therefore, only an approximate equivalence can be given, or else an explanation. See for instance **whip, shadow cabinet, C.I.D.,** and on the French-English side **hémicycle, R.E.R., rosette.**

3.7 Alternative translations

As a rule, translations separated by commas can be regarded as broadly interchangeable for the meaning indicated. Translations separated by a semi-colon are not interchangeable and when in doubt you should consult either a larger bilingual dictionary such as the Collins-Robert French dictionary, or a good monolingual French dictionary. You will find however that there are very few cases of translations separated by a semi-colon without an intervening 'signpost'.

II. Notes on French grammar

When you are first confronted with French at school, or if you happen to be at a business meeting where you are the only one speaking little or no French, it may seem to you that French is very different from English. On the other hand, if you stand back and consider a wider range of related and unrelated languages, French can look very close to English.

We have tried here to show some of the main differences, especially with the beginner and the dictionary user in mind, without dwelling on subtleties or aspects of French that are broadly similar to English. Among the greatest obstacles for the beginner are gender, verb forms and tenses, the position of adjectives, the use of prepositions and of course the sounds of French.

1. *Nouns and 'satellite' words (articles, adjectives)*

1.1 Gender

One of the basic differences: 'the table and the knife', but '**la** table et **le** couteau'. Largely unpredictable, this business of gender must be learned as a feature to be remembered with each new word. It is most important to get the article right, and of course the agreement of adjectives and past participles: 'la **vieille** maison et le **vieux** chalet'. See also 1.4 (possessive adjectives).

1.2 Articles: le, la, un, du, des etc.

Apart from the problem of gender, there is the question of whether the article is used or not, and French does not always follow the English pattern. For instance you say 'I like wine' but the French say 'j'aime **le** vin'. Conversely, 'my father is **a** publisher' but 'mon père est éditeur'.

1.2.1 'le, la, les'

(a) In almost all cases where 'the' is not used in English, the article must be used in French. For instance:

apples are good for you   **les** pommes sont bonnes pour la santé
salmon is expensive   **le** saumon est cher
love is not enough   **l'**amour ne suffit pas
he won't stand laziness   il ne tolère pas **la** paresse
France is beautiful   **la** France est belle
he likes skiing   il aime **le** ski

NB. A few names of countries are used without the article in French, like Cuba or Madagascar, Chypre, Malte, Jersey.

(b) use of 'le/la' with parts of the body

Where the possessive is used in English, 'le/la' tends to be used in French (sometimes together with a pronoun):

I broke **my** leg   je **me** suis cassé **la** jambe
Put up **your** hand   levez **la** main
He trod on **my** foot   il **m'**a marché sur **le** pied

(c) à + le, de + le

Remember the contracted forms (shown in the dictionary under **à** and **de**): je vais **au** cinéma, le parapet **du** pont.

1.2.2 'un, une, des'

(a) In structures of the type 'with incredible courage', the article 'un/une' is used in French:

He showed incredible coolness il a fait preuve d'**un** sang-froid incroyable
A film in appallingly bad taste un film d'**un** mauvais goût désolant

(b) On the other hand, this article is not used in French in structures equivalent to 'my father is a teacher':

my sister is **a** nurse ma sœur est infirmière
he is **a** sailor's son il est fils de marin (or: c'est **un** fils de marin, c'est le fils d'un marin)

But this only applies with names of professions and crafts:

his brother is an idiot son frère est un imbécile

my sister is a very liberated young lady ma sœur est une jeune fille très émancipée

(c) 'without a pen', 'without bread': no article in French

Where the English uses the article with a so-called 'countable' noun (like 'hat' as opposed to 'milk' or 'water' or 'bread'), the French doesn't: 'sans plume, on ne peut pas écrire', 'un repas sans pain'.

(d) 'des'

Remember to use 'des' in the plural, although there may be no article in English:

friends from Paris have arrived **des** amis de Paris sont arrivés

1.2.3 'du, de la, des', 'de' = 'some', 'any'

Remember not to confuse 'du' as in 'le titre du livre' and 'du' as in 'j'aimerais du pain' (see entry **de**). Where you have 'some' or 'any' or sometimes nothing in English, the French use 'du' etc., as shown below:

je veux du pain I want some bread

veux-tu du pain/de la soupe/des cigarettes? Would you like any (*or* some) bread/soup/cigarettes?

je ne veux pas de pain/soupe/cigarettes   I don't want any bread/soup/cigarettes

1.3 Adjectives

Apart from the question of gender (subtil-subtile *but* utile, etc.), the main difficulty is the position of adjectives. As a general rule, they follow the noun (des plantes marines, un repas délicieux, des volets rouges). Some adjectives or types of adjectives will always go after the noun (une maison délabrée, des plantes marines, une robe rouge). Some can also come before the noun for stylistic effect, without any change in meaning (un délicieux repas). A few others will usually or always go before the noun.

Among adjectives usually found before the noun are 'petit, grand, haut, long, gros; vieux, jeune; bon, mauvais, joli; nouveau, ancien'. Some like 'premier' are not found after the noun (except maybe in the odd set phrase). Others like 'brave' or 'ancien' will be found in either position, but with different meanings. The dictionary makes these different meanings clear.

1.4 Possessives

1.4.1 Son/sa, mon/ma, ton/ta *vs* his/her/its, my, your

Contrary to what happens in English, the possessive varies according to the gender of the noun it qualifies. Whether the owner is male or female, it will be **sa** valise and **son** parapluie. There is no such difference in the plural: **ses** valises et **ses** parapluies.

1.4.2 Le mien, la mienne, les miens, les miennes etc. *vs* mine etc.

Here again, the form of the possessive depends on the gender and number of the qualified noun (ie. 'hers' will be **la sienne** if a car – la voiture – is being referred to, and **le sien** if it's a handbag – le sac). In the plural (ie. several owners) with a plural noun there is no gender distinction: les nôtres, les vôtres, les leurs.

1.5 Demonstratives: *ce*, *ce ...-ci*, *celui-ci*, *ceux-ci* etc.

1.5.1 The distinction 'this' vs 'that' is rendered in French by a demonstrative plus '-ci' or '-là', eg. **ce** garçon-**ci** – this boy; **ce** garçon-**là** – that boy. However, whereas English always draws the distinction between 'this' and 'that', the French demonstratives are often used without the '-ci' and '-là' additions, so that '**ce** garçon' may mean 'this boy' or 'that boy'. The main difference is again one of gender: remember to use 'cette', 'celle' or 'celles' with a feminine noun.

1.6 Comparative and superlative: *plus ... que* etc.

1.6.1 The comparative and superlative in French are formed by placing **plus** and **le plus** respectively in front of the adjective or adverb. Eg.: plus grand – bigger; le plus grand – the biggest; plus vite – more quickly; le plus vite – the most quickly.

2. *Verbs*

This is one of the main areas of difficulty for English-speaking learners. There are four major problems. First the variety of endings (je par*s*, nous part*ons* etc) and the number of irregular or 'semi-irregular' forms. Second, the difference in the formation of negative or interrogative phrases (no equivalent of 'do', 'did' etc. as in 'I didn't go, did you?'). Third, the difference in the use of tenses (eg. no real equivalent of our 'continuous' tense). Fourth the use of 'avoir' or 'être' as auxiliary verbs where English just uses 'to have'.

2.1 Verb forms

The verb tables on pp. 507 to 514 will give you ending patterns for the main regular verbs, plus a list of the most common irregular verbs. There is no substitute for practice on this, but try not to look at these forms as a vast number of separate items to be learnt: there are two basic combining patterns, one relating to the person (a 'nous' form vs a 'vous' form etc), and one relating to the tense. Also, don't learn and practise too many different tenses at once, parrot-fashion. The present, the imperfect, the future, the conditional and the perfect will cater for most of your needs when it comes to expressing yourself in French.

2.2 Negatives and questions

'**ne** (**n'**) + verb form + **pas** (+ past participle)' is the basic pattern of negative verb phrases. 'Je **ne** crois (vraiment) **pas** que ...', 'il **n'**est **pas** parti (tout de suite)', il **n'**a **pas** (tout de suite) répondu'. The one place where no adverb can fit is between 'ne' and the verb form. Otherwise, there are various possible combinations, depending on the adverb and the meaning of the whole sentence.

One easy way to form an interrogative phrase is to use the invariable question form **est-ce que/qu'...**, eg. 'il part demain': '**est-ce qu'**il part demain?'. Alternatively, use the inversion of verb and subject (but only when the subject is a pronoun), eg. 'il part demain': 'part-il demain?'. Very often in spoken French (and, whatever they say to the contrary, for most people), intonation only is used to indicate the question form: 'il part demain?' (voice raised on the last syllable).

2.3 Tenses

2.3.1 There is no equivalent in French of our 'progressive' -ing form (I am reading). When the English has the sense of 'to be in the process of doing ...' it can be translated with the structure 'être en train de' + infinitive. In other cases, the present tense or the imperfect will convey the same meaning: I was living at Rosalie's: j'habitais chez Rosalie; we are seeing him tomorrow: nous le voyons demain.

2.3.2 The two tenses of the past in English (I went there, he has taken it) do not correspond closely to the French. Of the imperfect (j'habitais), the perfect (j'ai répondu) and the past historic (je partis), the last is hardly ever used in spoken French. The perfect is used much more widely than its counterpart in English and it can be used in many cases when the English would use the preterite (*I went*, *he gave* etc.).

2.3.3 The perfect tense ('passé composé')

The use of 'avoir' as an auxiliary verb is by far the most common, hence it is convenient to concentrate on the few verbs which use 'être'. They are all intransitive and verbs expressing movement or becoming, like *aller*, *venir*; *partir*, *arriver*, *retourner*; *descendre*, *monter*, *entrer*, *sortir*; *naître*, *mourir*, *devenir*.

The second thing to remember is that the past participle will occasionally take the marks of gender and/or plural. Thick tomes have been written on the agreement of the past participle, but two basic rules should enable you to cope with most problems. The past participle remains in the form of the masculine singular (j'ai répondu, il a passé) unless: *a*. with a transitive verb, the object precedes the verb – '*les livres* que j'ai lu*s*'; *b*. the auxiliary 'être' is used: '*elle* est parti*e* hier'.

2.3.4 The imperfect ('imparfait')

This is used for an action or state without definite limits in time. Compare for instance 'he lived in London during the war: il habitait à Londres pendant la guerre', 'he stood near the window: il se tenait (il était) près de la fenêtre' and 'they lived here from '64 to '68: ils ont habité ici de 64 à 68', 'he stood up: il s'est levé (il se leva)'.

2.4 The subjunctive ('subjonctif'): je veux qu'il fasse ... *vs* je sais qu'il fait ...

Good command of the present tense of the subjunctive is necessary in order to speak reasonably good French. However, as far as basic communication is concerned, in only a very few cases is the use of the subjunctive essential in order to avoid a misunderstanding. In other words, the use of the subjunctive is a constraint which if ignored will identify you as a poor speaker of French without impairing communication in any significant way.

One instance where ignoring the subjunctive might lead to a misunderstanding is with the verb 'dire': 'dites-lui qu'il vienne' means 'tell him to come', but 'dites-lui qu'il vient' means 'tell him (or her) that he's coming'.

It is not possible to give a simple rule showing when the subjunctive should be used. This dictionary will occasionally show you when a particular construction requires the use of the subjunctive (see for instance English **lest**).

It usually follows a verb + *que* construction where the sentence expresses doubt, a hypothesis rather than a fact, a question (tu veux qu'on y aille?), an interdiction.

It is always used after 'vouloir que ...', 'il faut que ...'. There are also a few conjunctions which always take the subjunctive, usually those which express desire or intention (eg. 'afin que ...', 'de sorte que ...' – 'so that ...').

2.5 The passive

Broadly speaking, the passive voice is similar in French. 'He was dismissed' or 'he has been dismissed' can both be rendered by 'il a été renvoyé'. Note that impersonal uses such as 'I was told that ...' are often best rendered by the 'on' construction: 'on m'a dit que ...' (see entry for French **on**).

Constructions like 'the road is being repaired' are often best translated without using the passive: 'la route est en réparation', 'on est en train de réparer la route'. In cases like 'the book I was given' or 'the book I was given by my brother', where the subject ('I') would in fact be the indirect object in the active voice, the passive cannot be used in French: 'le livre qu'on m'a donné', 'le livre que m'a donné mon frère'.

3. *Personal pronouns*

I, me	**je** voyage, **je me** coiffe, il **me** parle, il **me** voit, il **m'**a vu, et **moi**?
we, us	**nous** voyageons, **nous nous** coiffons, il **nous** parle, il **nous** voit, il **nous** a vus(vues), et **nous**?
he, him	**il** voyage, **il se** coiffe, je **lui** parle, je **le** vois, je **l'**ai vu, et **lui**?
she, her	**elle** voyage, **elle se** coiffe, je **lui** parle, je **la** vois, je **l'**ai vue, et **elle**?

it	**il(elle)** est rouge, **il(elle) se** casse, je **le(la)** vois, je **l'**ai vu(e)
they, them	**ils(elles)** voyagent, **ils(elles) se** coiffent, je **leur** parle, je **les** vois, je **les** ai vus(vues), et **eux(elles)**?
you (*plural*)	**vous** voyagez, **vous vous** coiffez, coiffez-**vous**, je **vous** parle, je **vous** vois, je **vous** ai vus(vues), et **vous**?
you (*singular*)	*familiar form*: **tu** voyages, **tu te** coiffes, coiffe-**toi**, je **te** parle, je **te** vois, je **t'**ai vu(vue), et **toi**?
	polite form: **vous** voyagez, **vous vous** coiffez, coiffez-**vous**, je **vous** parle, je **vous** vois, et **vous**?

'Voyager' is an intransitive verb; 'se coiffer' is a reflexive verb ('verbe pronominal'); 'parler' is shown here with an indirect object ('parler à quelqu'un'); 'voir' is shown with a direct object ('voir quelqu'un'); the strong pronoun form is shown last, and is the one used after a preposition ('pour moi', 'après lui', 'devant nous' etc.); the imperative is shown for the 2nd person with the reflexive verb.

When there is a direct and an indirect object, personal pronouns are in the following order (indirect object shown in bold):

me	il **me** le(la) donne, il **me** l'a donné(donnée), il ne **me** l'a pas donné(donnée)
us	il **nous** le(la) donne, il **nous** l'a donné(donnée), il ne **nous** l'a pas donné(donnée)
him, her	je le(la) **lui** donne, je le(la) **lui** ai donné(donnée), je ne le(la) **lui** ai pas donné(donnée)
them	je le(la) **leur** donne, je le(la) **leur** ai donné(donnée), je ne le(la) **leur** ai pas donné(donnée)
you (*plural*)	je **vous** le(la) donne, je **vous** l'ai donné(donnée), je ne **vous** l'ai pas donné(donnée)
you (*singular*)	*familiar form*: je **te** le(la) donne, je **te** l'ai donné(donnée), je ne **te** l'ai pas donné(donnée)
	polite form: je **vous** le(la) donne, je **vous** l'ai donné(donnée), je ne **vous** l'ai pas donné(donnée)

III. **French verbs**

1. The following tables of irregular verbs are self-explanatory. Unless stated otherwise, if one form only is given, it is the first person singular; if two forms are given, they are the first person singular and the first person plural. If not shown, the second person singular is the same as the first; the second and third person plural are regularly formed on the root of the first person plural (ie. *part*ons, *part*ez, *part*ent).

2. For verbs in '-ir' not appearing in the list of irregular verbs, follow 'finir'. For verbs in '-duire', follow 'conduire'. For verbs in '-andre, -ondre, -perdre, -ordre', follow 'rendre'.

3. Do not forget to use the appropriate pronoun with pronominal verbs: je me rase, il se rase, vous vous êtes coupé.

4. 'Semi-irregular' verbs.

Some verbs are only 'irregular' in a few predictable ways:

4.1 A 'c' will change to a 'ç' before 'o' or 'a' (the corresponding sound remaining [s]): **placer,** nous plaçons, nous plaçâmes.

4.2 A 'g' will change to 'ge' before 'o' or 'a' (the corresponding sound remaining [ʒ]): **bouger,** nous bougeons, nous bougeâmes; **protéger,** nous protégeons, nous protégeâmes.

4.3 An 'l' or a 't' will change to 'll' or 'tt' before 'e(s)' or 'ent', and in the future and conditional tenses (ie. at the end of a syllable): **appeler,** j'appelle, ils appellent, ils appelleront (*but*: nous appelons, j'appelais); **jeter,** je jette, ils jettent, nous jetterons (*but*: nous jetons, je jetais).

4.4 An 'e' will change to 'è' if followed by a consonant sound within the syllable: **geler,** il gèle, ils gèlent, il gèlera (*but*: nous gelons, il gelait); **acheter,** j'achète, ils achètent, ils achèteront (*but*: nous achetons, j'achetais); also: **dépecer, protéger.**

4.5 A 'y' will change to 'i' before 'e(s)', 'ent', and in the future and conditional tenses (ie. at the end of a syllable): **nettoyer,** il nettoie, ils nettoient, ils nettoieront (*but*: vous nettoyez, je nettoyais); also for '-uyer' and '-ayer' verbs (ennuyer, balayer). **Payer** may either retain the 'y' or follow the above changes.

5. The 'temps composés' are formed as follows:

5.1 Perfect ('passé composé'): with 'être' je suis parti, tu es parti etc. (see 'être'); with 'avoir' j'ai couru, tu as couru etc. (see 'avoir')

5.2 Pluperfect ('plus-que-parfait'): j'étais parti etc.; j'avais couru etc.

5.3 Future anterior ('futur antérieur'): je serai parti etc.; j'aurai couru etc.

5.4 Past conditional ('conditionnel passé'): je serais parti etc.; j'aurais couru etc.

5.5 The past anterior ('passé antérieur') – j'eus couru etc. – and the pluperfect subjunctive ('plus-que-parfait du subjonctif') – j'eusse couru etc. – are rarely used.

6. The imperfect subjunctive ('imparfait du subjonctif') is practically obsolete in spoken French and rare in written French. It is recognizable by its 'ss' element – que je fusse, que nous fussions; que j'eusse, que nous eussions etc – and also by the circumflex in the 3rd person singular – qu'il fût, qu'il eût, qu'il allât.

A typical regular verb: 'parler' [paʀle]

PAST HISTORIC			
parl-	ai	[paʀl...	[e]
	as		[a]
	a		
	âmes		[ɑm]
	âtes		[ɑt]
	èrent		[ɛʀ]
IMPERFECT			
parl-	ais	[paʀl...	[ɛ]
	ais		
	ait		
	ions		[jɔ̃]
	iez		[je]
	aient		[ɛ]

PRESENT (+SUBJUNCTIVE)			
	e		not sounded or [ə]
	es		
	e		
parl-		[paʀl...	
	ons (ions)		[ɔ̃] ([jɔ̃])
	ez (iez)		[e] ([je])
	ent		not sounded or [ə]
FUTURE (+CONDITIONAL)			
	ai (ais)		[e] ([ɛ])
	as (ais)		[a] ([ɛ])
	a (ait)		[a] ([ɛ])
parl-e-r-		[paʀləʀ...	
	ons (ions)		[ɔ̃] ([jɔ̃])
	ez (iez)		[e] ([je])
	ont (aient)		[ɔ̃] ([ɛ])
IMPERATIVE	parle, parlez [paʀl(ə), paʀle]		
PAST PARTICIPLE	parlé (parlée) [paʀle]		
PERFECT	j'ai parlé, tu as parlé etc.		

VERB TABLES

VERB TABLES: 1 Participe présent 2 Participe passé 3 Présent 4 Subjonctif présent 5 Imparfait 6 Futur 7 Conditionnel 8 Passé simple

absoudre 1 absolvant 2 absout(absoute) 3 absous, absout, absolvons 4 absolve, absolvions 5 absolvais, absolvions 6 absoudrai, absoudrons 7 absoudrais, absoudrions 8 absolus, absolûmes

acquérir 1 acquérant 2 acquis(acquise) 3 acquiers, acquiert, acquérons, acquièrent 4 acquière, acquérions 5 acquérais, acquérions 6 acquerrai, acquerrons 7 acquerrais, acquerrions 8 acquis, acquîmes

aller 1 allant 2 allé(allée) 3 vais, vas, va, allons, allez, vont 4 aille, ailles, aille, allions, alliez, aillent 5 allais, allions 6 irai, irons 7 irais, irions 8 allai, allâmes

assaillir 1 assaillant 2 assailli(assaillie) 3 assaille, assaillons 4 assaille, assaillions 5 assaillais, assaillions 6 assaillirai, assaillirons 7 assaillirais, assaillirions 8 assaillis, assaillîmes

asseoir 1 asseyant 2 assis(assise) 3 assieds, assied, asseyons, asseyez, asseyent 4 asseye, asseyions 5 asseyais, asseyions 6 assiérai, assiérons 7 assiérais, assiérions 8 assis, assîmes

atteindre 1 atteignant 2 atteint(atteinte) 3 atteins, atteint, atteignons 4 atteigne, atteignions 5 atteignais, atteignions 6 atteindrai, atteindrons 7 atteindrais, atteindrions 8 atteignis, atteignîmes

avoir 1 ayant 2 eu(eue) 3 ai, as, a, avons, avez, ont 4 aie, aies, ait, ayons, ayez, aient 5 avais, avions 6 aurai, aurons 7 aurais, aurions 8 eus, eûmes

battre 1 battant 2 battu(battue) 3 bats, bats, bat, battons, battez, battent 4 batte, battions 5 battais, battions 6 battrai, battrons 7 battrais, battrions 8 battis, battîmes

boire 1 buvant 2 bu(bue) 3 bois, boit, buvons, buvez, boivent 4 boive, buvions, boivent 5 buvais, buvions 6 boirai, boirons 7 boirais, boirions 8 bus, bûmes

bouillir 1 bouillant 2 bouilli(bouillie) 3 bous, bout, bouillons, bouillent 4 bouille, bouillions 5 bouillais, bouillions 6 bouillirai, bouillirons 7 bouillirais, bouillirions 8 bouillis, bouillîmes

clore 2 clos(close) 3 clos, clôt, closent 4 close 6 clorai 7 clorais

conclure 1 concluant 2 conclu(conclue) 3 conclus, conclut, concluons, concluent 4 conclue, concluions, concluent 5 concluais, concluions 6 conclurai, conclurons 7 conclurais, conclurions 8 conclus, conclûmes

conduire 1 conduisant 2 conduit(conduite) 3 conduis, conduit, conduisons 4 conduise, conduisions 5 conduisais, conduisions 6 conduirai, conduirons 7 conduirais, conduirions 8 conduisis, conduisîmes

connaître 1 connaissant 2 connu(connue) 3 connais, connaît, connaissons 4 connaisse, connaissions 5 connaissais, connaissions 6 connaîtrai, connaîtrons 7 connaîtrais, connaîtrions 8 connus, connûmes

coudre 1 cousant 2 cousu(cousue) 3 couds, coud, cousons 4 couse, cousions 5 cousais, cousions 6 coudrai, coudrons 7 coudrais, coudrions 8 cousis, cousîmes

courir 1 courant 2 couru(courue) 3 cours, court, courons 4 coure, courions 5 courais, courions 6 courrai, courrons 7 courrais, courrions 8 courus, courûmes

couvrir 1 couvrant 2 couvert(couverte) 3 couvre, couvrons 4 couvre, couvrions 5 couvrais, couvrions 6 couvrirai, couvrirons 7 couvrirais, couvririons 8 couvris, couvrîmes

craindre 1 craignant 2 craint(crainte) 3 crains, craint, craignons, craignent 4 craigne, craignions 5 craignais, craignions 6 craindrai, craindrons 7 craindrais, craindrions 8 craignis, craignîmes

croire 1 croyant 2 cru(crue) 3 crois, croit, croyons, croient 4 croie, croyions 5 croyais, croyions 6 croirai, croirons 7 croirais, croirions 8 crus, crûmes

croître 1 croissant 2 crû(crue) 3 croîs, croît, croissons 4 croisse, croissions **5** croissais, croissions **6** croîtrai, croîtrons **7** croîtrais, croîtrions **8** crûs, crûmes

cueillir **1** cueillant **2** cueilli(cueillie) **3** cueille, cueillons, cueillent **4** cueille, cueillions **5** cueillais, cueillions **6** cueillerai, cueillerons **7** cueillerais, cueillerions **8** cueillis, cueillîmes

devoir **1** devant **2** dû(due) **3** dois, doit, devons, doivent **4** doive, devions, doivent **5** devais, devions **6** devrai, devrons **7** devrais, devrions **8** dus, dûmes

dire **1** disant **2** dit(dite) **3** dis, dit, disons, dites, disent **4** dise, disions **5** disais, disions **6** dirai, dirons **7** dirais, dirions **8** dis, dîmes.

dormir **1** dormant **2** dormi **3** dors, dort, dormons **4** dorme, dormions **5** dormais, dormions **6** dormirai, dormirons **7** dormirais, dormirions **8** dormis, dormîmes

écrire **1** écrivant **2** écrit(écrite) **3** écris, écrit, écrivons **4** écrive, écrivions **5** écrivais, écrivions **6** écrirai, écrirons **7** écrirais, écririons **8** écrivis, écrivîmes

être **1** étant **2** été **3** suis, es, est, sommes, êtes, sont **4** sois, sois, soit, soyons, soyez, soient **5** étais, étions **6** serai, serons **7** serais, serions **8** fus, fûmes

faire **1** faisant **2** fait(faite) **3** fais, fais, fait, faisons, faites, font **4** fasse, fassions, fassent **5** faisais, faisions **6** ferai, ferons **7** ferais, ferions **8** fis, fîmes

falloir **2** fallu **3** faut **4** faille **5** fallait **6** faudra **7** faudrait **8** fallut

finir **1** finissant **2** fini(finie) **3** finis, finis, finit, finissons, finissez, finissent **4** finisse, finissions **5** finissais, finissions **6** finirai, finirons **7** finirais, finirions **8** finis, finîmes

fuir **1** fuyant **2** fui **3** fuis, fuit, fuyons, fuient **4** fuie, fuyions, fuient **5** fuyais, fuyions **6** fuirai, fuirons **7** fuirais, fuirions **8** fuis, fuîmes

haïr **1** haïssant **2** haï(haïe) **3** hais, hait, haïssons **4** haïsse, haïssions **5** haïssais, haïssions **6** haïrai, haïrons **7** haïrais, haïrions

joindre **1** joignant **2** joint(jointe) **3** joins, joint, joignons, joignent **4** joigne, joignions **5** joignais, joignions **6** joindrai, joindrons **7** joindrais, joindrions **8** joignis, joignîmes

lire **1** lisant **2** lu(lue) **3** lis, lit, lisons **4** lise, lisions **5** lisais, lisions **6** lirai, lirons **7** lirais, lirions **8** lus, lûmes

luire **1** luisant **2** lui **3** luis, luit, luisons **4** luise, luisions **5** luisais, luisions **6** luirai, luirons **7** luirais, luirions

maudire **1** maudissant **2** maudit(maudite) **3** maudis, maudit, maudissons **4** maudisse, maudissions **5** maudissais, maudissions **6** maudirai, maudirons **7** maudirais, maudirions **8** maudis, maudîmes

mentir **1** mentant **2** menti **3** mens, ment, mentons **4** mente, mentions **5** mentais, mentions **6** mentirai, mentirons **7** mentirais, mentirions **8** mentis, mentîmes

mettre **1** mettant **2** mis(mise) **3** mets, met, mettons **4** mette, mettions **5** mettais, mettions **6** mettrai, mettrons **7** mettrais, mettrions **8** mis, mîmes

moudre **1** moulant **2** moulu(moulue) **3** mouds, moud, moulons

4 moule, moulions 5 moulais, moulions 6 moudrai, moudrons 7 moudrais, moudrions 8 moulus, moulûmes

mourir 1 mourant 2 mort(morte) 3 meurs, meurt, mourons, meurent 4 meure, mourions, meurent 5 mourais, mourions 6 mourrai, mourrons 7 mourrais, mourrions 8 mourus, mourûmes

mouvoir 1 mouvant 2 mû(mue) 3 meus, meut, mouvons, meuvent 4 meuve, mouvions, meuvent 5 mouvais, mouvions 6 mouvrai, mouvrons 7 mouvrais, mouvrions 8 mus, mûmes

naître 1 naissant 2 né(née) 3 nais, naît, naissons 4 naisse, naissions 5 naissais, naissions 6 naîtrai, naîtrons 7 naîtrais, naîtrions 8 naquis, naquîmes

nuire *voir* **luire**

offrir 1 offrant 2 offert(offerte) 3 offre, offrons 4 offre, offrions 5 offrais, offrions 6 offrirai, offrirons 7 offrirais, offririons 8 offris, offrîmes

partir 1 partant 2 parti(partie) 3 pars, part, partons 4 parte, partions 5 partais, partions 6 partirai, partirons 7 partirais, partirions 8 partis, partîmes

peindre 1 peignant 2 peint(peinte) 3 peins, peint, peignons 4 peigne, peignions 5 peignais, peignions 6 peindrai, peindrons 7 peindrais, peindrions 8 peignis, peignîmes

placer 'ç' before a vowel other than 'e' or 'i': 'nous plaçons' etc.

plaire 1 plaisant 2 plu 3 plais, plaît, plaisons 4 plaise, plaisions 5 plaisais, plaisions 6 plairai, plairons 7 plairais, plairions 8 plus, plûmes

pleuvoir 1 pleuvant 2 plu 3 pleut, pleuvent 4 pleuve, pleuvent 5 pleuvait, pleuvaient 6 pleuvra, pleuvront 7 pleuvrait, pleuvraient *NB. 3rd person only*

pourvoir 1 pourvoyant 2 pourvu(pourvue) 3 pourvois, pourvoit, pourvoyons, pourvoient 4 pourvoie, pourvoyions 5 pourvoyais, pourvoyions 6 pourvoirai, pourvoirons 7 pourvoirais, pourvoirions 8 pourvus, pourvûmes

pouvoir 1 pouvant 2 pu 3 peux, peut, pouvons, peuvent 4 puisse, puissions, puissent 5 pouvais, pouvions 6 pourrai, pourrons 7 pourrais, pourrions 8 pus, pûmes

prendre 1 prenant 2 pris(prise) 3 prends, prend, prenons, prennent 4 prenne, prenions, prennent 5 prenais, prenions 6 prendrai, prendrons 7 prendrais, prendrions 8 pris, prîmes

prévoir 1 prévoyant 2 prévu(prévue) 3 prévois, prévoit, prévoyons, prévoient 4 prévoie, prévoyions, prévoient 5 prévoyais, prévoyions 6 prévoirai, prévoirons 7 prévoirais, prévoirions 8 prévis, prévîmes

recevoir 1 recevant 2 reçu(reçue) 3 reçois, reçoit, recevons, reçoivent 4 reçoive, recevions 5 recevais, recevions 6 recevrai, recevrons 7 recevrais, recevrions 8 reçus, reçûmes

rendre 1 rendant 2 rendu(rendue) 3 rends, rend, rendons 4 rende, rendions 5 rendais, rendions 6 rendrai, rendrons 7 rendrais, rendrions 8 rendis, rendîmes

résoudre 1 résolvant 2 résolu(résolue) 3 résous, résout, résolvons 4 résolve, résolvions 5 résolvais, résolvions 6 résoudrai, résoudrons 7 résoudrais, résoudrions 8 résolus, résolûmes

rire 1 riant 2 ri 3 ris, rit, rions, rient 4 rie, riions, rient 5 riais, riions 6 rirai, rirons 7 rirais, ririons 8 ris, rîmes

rompre 1 rompant 2 rompu(rompue) 3 romps, rompt, rompons 4 rompe, rompions 5 rompais, rompions 6 romprai, romprons 7 romprais, romprions 8 rompis, rompîmes

savoir 1 sachant 2 su(sue) 3 sais, sait, savons, savent 4 sache, sachions 5 savais, savions 6 saurai, saurons 7 saurais, saurions 8 sus, sûmes

sentir 1 sentant 2 senti(sentie) 3 sens, sent, sentons 4 sente, sentions 5 sentais, sentions 6 sentirai, sentirons 7 sentirais, sentirions 8 sentis, sentîmes

servir 1 servant 2 servi(servie) 3 sers, sert, servons 4 serve, servions 5 servais, servions 6 servirai, servirons 7 servirais, servirions 8 servis, servîmes

sortir 1 sortant 2 sorti(sortie) 3 sors, sort, sortons 4 sorte, sortions 5 sortais, sortions 6 sortirai, sortirons 7 sortirais, sortirions 8 sortis, sortîmes

souffrir 1 souffrant 2 souffert(soufferte) 3 souffre, souffrons 4 souffre, souffrions 5 souffrais, souffrions 6 souffrirai, souffrirons 7 souffrirais, souffririons 8 souffris, souffrîmes

suffire 1 suffisant 2 suffi 3 suffis, suffit, suffisons 4 suffise, suffisions 5 suffisais, suffisions 6 suffirai, suffirons 7 suffirais, suffirions 8 suffis, suffîmes

suivre 1 suivant 2 suivi(suivie) 3 suis, suit, suivons 4 suive, suivions 5 suivais, suivions 6 suivrai, suivrons 7 suivrais, suivrions 8 suivis, suivîmes

taire 1 taisant 2 tu(tue) 3 tais, tait, taisons 4 taise, taisions 5 taisais, taisions 6 tairai, tairons 7 tairais, tairions 8 tus, tûmes

tenir 1 tenant 2 tenu(tenue) 3 tiens, tient, tenons, tiennent 4 tienne, tenions, tiennent 5 tenais, tenions 6 tiendrai, tiendrons 7 tiendrais, tiendrions 8 tins, tînmes

traire 1 trayant 2 trait(traite) 3 trais, trait, trayons, traient 4 traie, trayions, traient 5 trayais, trayions 6 trairai, trairons 7 trairais, trairions

vaincre 1 vainquant 2 vaincu(vaincue) 3 vaincs, vainc, vainquons, vainquent 4 vainque, vainquions, vainquent 5 vainquais, vainquions 6 vaincrai, vaincrons 7 vaincrais, vaincrions 8 vainquis, vainquîmes

valoir 1 valant 2 valu 3 vaux, vaut, valons 4 vaille, valions, vaillent 5 valais, valions 6 vaudrai, vaudrons 7 vaudrais, vaudrions 8 valus, valûmes

venir 1 venant 2 venu(venue) 3 viens, vient, venons, viennent 4 vienne, venions, viennent 5 venais, venions 6 viendrai, viendrons 7 viendrais, viendrions 8 vins, vînmes

vêtir 1 vêtant 2 vêtu(vêtue) 3 vêts, vêt, vêtons, vêtent 4 vête, vêtions 5 vêtais, vêtions 6 vêtirai, vêtirons 7 vêtirais, vêtirions 8 vêtis, vêtîmes

vivre 1 vivant 2 vécu(vécue) 3 vis, vit, vivons 4 vive, vivions 5 vivais, vivions 6 vivrai, vivrons 7 vivrais, vivrions 8 vécus, vécûmes
voir 1 voyant 2 vu(vue) 3 vois, voit, voyons, voient 4 voie, voyions, voient 5 voyais, voyions 6 verrai, verrons 7 verrais, verrions 8 vis, vîmes
vouloir 1 voulant 2 voulu(voulue) 3 veux, veut, voulons, veulent 4 veuille, voulions, veuillent 5 voulais, voulions 6 voudrai, voudrons 7 voudrais, voudrions 8 voulus, voulûmes *impératif:* veuille, veuillez

IV. The sounds of French

Learning to pronounce French well is, as with all foreign languages, largely a matter of adopting different 'speech habits' from those used in speaking English.

A 'foreign accent' results from using the sounds of one's own language to approximate the sounds of the foreign language. This is particularly tempting when the same letter or letters represent similar sounds in each language. For instance the letter 'i' is used in both French and English, but to represent slightly different sounds in each, and many French speakers are unable to pronounce it in the English manner. It is possible that many do not even realize that the English speaker uses a different sound from the French – hence the typical French pronunciation of 'it is' which sounds to the English speaker as if it were written 'eet eese'.

These are the main ways in which French 'speech habits' differ from the English:

1. Activity of the lips
The lips play a very important part in French. When a vowel is described as having 'rounded' lips, the lips are slightly drawn together and pursed, as when the English speaker expresses exaggerated surprise with the vowel 'ooh!'. Equally, if the lips are said to be 'spread', the corners are pulled firmly back towards the cheeks, tending to reveal the front teeth.

In English, lip position is not important, and vowel sounds tend to merge because of this. In French, the activity of the lips means that every vowel sound is clearly distinct from every other.

2. No diphthongs
A diphthong is a glide between two vowel sounds in the same syllable. In English, there are few 'pure' vowel sounds, but largely diphthongs instead. Although speakers of English may *think* they produce one vowel sound in the word 'day', in fact they use a diphthong, which in this instance is a glide between the vowels [e] and [ɪ]: [deɪ]. In French the

tension maintained in the lips, tongue and the mouth in general prevents diphthongs occurring, as the vowel sound is kept constant throughout. Hence the French word corresponding to the above example, 'dé', is pronounced with no final [ɪ] sound, but is phonetically represented thus: [de].

3. Consonants
Consonants in French are always given their full value. In English, consonants are often pronounced with a degree of laxness that can result in their practically disappearing altogether although not strictly 'silent'. In a relaxed pronunciation of a word such as 'hat', the 't' is often scarcely heard, or is replaced by a 'glottal stop' (a sort of jerk in the throat). Hence a Frenchman sounds unmistakeably foreign to an English speaker if he pronounces the 't' and 'l' in a word such as 'bottle' as energetically as he would in French.

4. Stress
In English, each word has its own particular stress pattern – for instance, the two different stress patterns for the word 'escort' produces two different words, one a noun and one a verb (*an* es*cort bureau, may I* es*cort you*). There is no possibility of this in French, since individual words have no characteristic stress pattern; syllables are stressed only when they occur at the end of the sentence or phrase:
eg. je les ai *vus*
je les ai vus *hier*
je les ai vus hier ma*tin*

The stressed syllable is in italics in each case, and all the other syllables are unstressed. This gives French a peculiarly 'staccato' effect, since all unstressed syllables tend to be of about the same length.

Pronunciation of the sounds of French

I. Vowels

as in:	Hints on pronunciation
[a] p*a*tte pl*at* *a*mour	Pronounced more or less as in English 'pat'.
[ɑ] b*as* p*â*te	Longer and further back in the mouth than [a]. This sound resembles the English exclamation of surprise: 'ah!'. Similar to the vowel in English 'car', without the r-sound, but a little shorter.
[ɛ] l*ait* jou*et* m*e*rci	Similar to the sound in English 'pet', but the lips are slightly further apart. Beware of substituting the English diphthong [eɪ] as in 'pay' when the sound [ɛ] comes at the end of a word

[e] *été* jou*er*	The tongue is held very tense and quite high in the mouth to pronounce a pure [e] sound. Again quite different from English [eɪ] of 'pay'
[ə] l*e* pr*e*mier	The lips are slightly rounded for this vowel, and this is what distinguishes it from the sound in 'butt*er*'
[i] *ici* v*ie* lyc*ée*	The lips are well spread towards the cheeks and held very tensely while uttering this sound. Try saying English 'see' with your lips in this position. The sound is however shorter in French than the corresponding English vowel
[ɔ] m*o*rt h*o*mme	The lips must be well rounded, and the sound is half-way between 'u' and 'o' in the English words 'c*u*t' and 'c*o*t'
[o] m*o*t d*ô*me *eau*	A 'pure' vowel with strongly rounded lips. Make sure this sound does not become the diphthong used in English 'bone' and 'low'
[u] gen*ou* r*ou*e	Again, a 'pure' vowel with strongly rounded lips. The lip position is like that used at the beginning of the consonant [w] in English
[y] r*ue* vêt*u*	This sound is often considered the most difficult for English speakers to produce. Round your lips to say [u] (see above), then try to say [i] instead. Easier for Scots: try this sound in 'muesli' or 'Zürich'. There is no [j] sound (as in English 'pure') before this vowel
[œ] s*œu*r b*eu*rre	Similar to the vowel sound in English 'f*i*r' or 'm*u*rmur', but without the 'r' sounded, and with greater lip-rounding
[ø] p*eu* d*eux*	To pronounce this vowel, try to say [e] (see above) with strongly rounded lips

Nasal vowels

These are always spelt with a vowel followed by a 'nasal' consonant – *n* or *m*. The production of nasal vowels can scarcely be explained without the help of a teacher or a recording of the sound quality. As a guide, however, the vowel is pronounced by allowing air to come partly down the nose and partly through the mouth, and the consonant disappears altogether. Best tip: ask a native French speaker to say and repeat for you the words 'mais*on*', 'jard*in*', 'ch*am*bre', 'br*un*', and try to copy what you hear.

[ɑ̃] l*en*t s*ang* d*ans*	In each case the vowel shown in the phonetic symbol is pronounced in the normal way, but air is allowed to come down the nose as well as through the mouth
[ɛ̃] mat*in* pl*ein*	
[ɔ̃] n*on* p*on*t	
[œ̃] br*un* *un*	

II. **Consonants**

Those consonants which are pronounced more or less as in English are represented phonetically as [b, f, g, k, m, p, v, w]. There is no aspiration with the production of [b, p, d, t, g, k] in French. Most other consonants are similar to their English counterparts but slight differences should be noted:

[d] *d*in*d*e	The tip of the tongue touches the upper teeth and not the roof of the mouth as in English
[t] *t*en*t*e	
[n] *n*on*n*e	
[l] *Lill*e	
[s] *ç*a tou*s*	As in English, but the tip of the tongue is held low, behind the bottom teeth
[z] *z*éro ro*s*e	
[ʃ] *ch*ose ta*che*	As in English '*sh*out'
[ʒ] *j*e *g*ilet bei*ge*	As in English 'mea*s*ure', 'bei*ge*'
[j] *y*eux pa*ille*	As in English '*y*es'

Three consonant sounds are not heard in English:

[ʀ] *r*a*r*e veni*r*	For many speakers of English, 'r' is often silent, eg. 'fa*r*m'. In French, the 'r' is always pronounced, unless it follows an 'e' at the end of a word (cherch*er*, berg*er*). Its pronunciation in French is similar to the final sound of the Scottish word 'lo*ch*'. If you find this difficult, try thinking of the sound made when gargling, since the French [ʀ] is produced at the back of the mouth in a similar way

[ɲ] vi*gn*e a*gn*eau	Very similar to [nj] as in 'Spa*ni*ard'
[ɥ] *hu*ile l*u*eur	Like a very rapid [y] (see above) followed by the next vowel sound in the word

There are two extra symbols used in this dictionary: * and '. See for instance the entry for *haie*. These symbols mean that no liaison is made before the following vowel:

cf. la haie *vs* l'habitation
les haies *vs* le*s* habitations.

From spelling to sounds

French spelling can be very confusing since one and the same sound can be represented in many different ways in the written word. Conversely, a given letter or group of letters can have different pronunciations depending on its position in the word. You may therefore be surprised to learn that these differences are governed by fairly precise 'rules' that are not difficult to assimilate.

The most important distinction to be drawn is whether the group of letters comes at the end of a word or syllable, or whether the letters are split between two syllables. Eg. in 'ma-tin' the dash represents the break between syllables and you can see that the word consists of two syllables of which the final one ends in 'in', one of the characteristic spellings of the nasal vowel [ɛ̃]. However in 'ma-ti-née', as the dashes show, the 'i' and the 'n' belong to different syllables, and they no longer constitute a single sound. The 'i' has its usual value (as in 'ici'), and the 'n' is pronounced as part of the next syllable.

This example illustrates how one of several French consonants is silent when it occurs at the end of the word or syllable, but is sounded when it begins a word or syllable.

Other consonants which regularly behave in this way at the end of words are:

t	éclat [ekla]	BUT	écla-ter [ekla*t*e]
d	chaud [ʃo]	BUT	chau-dement [ʃo*d*mɑ̃]
s	des [de]	BUT	dé-sir [deziʀ]
n	vain [vɛ̃]	BUT	vai-nement [vɛ*n*mɑ̃]
	matin [matɛ̃]	BUT	mati-née [mati*n*e]
m	parfum [paʀfœ̃]	BUT	parfu-mer [paʀfy*m*e]
x	aux [o]	BUT	au-xiliaire [ɔ*k*siljɛʀ]
z	nez [ne]	BUT	zé-zayer [zezeje]
r	aider [ede]	BUT	nous parle-rons [paʀlə*ʀ*ɔ̃]

'm' and 'n' at the end of syllables (but not necessarily at the end of words):

m im-perméable
[ɛ̃pɛʀmeɑbl] BUT i-magination [imaʒinɑsjɔ̃]
BUT im-mobile [imɔbil]

n in-cident [ɛ̃sidɑ̃] BUT i-nique [inik]

Typical pronunciation of some French spellings

There are several groups of vowels in French spelling which are regularly pronounced in the same way, and these can easily be learnt:

spelling	pronunciation	examples
ai	[ɛ] or [e]	maison, marchai (verb form), faire
au	[o]	auberge, landau
eau	[o]	eau, beau, tableau
ou	[u]	fou, oublier
eu	[œ] or [ø]	peur, feu, heureux, feuille
œu	[œ]	sœur, cœur
ue	[y]	rue
		BUT recueil [ʀəkœj]

Added to these are the many groups of letters occurring at the end of words, where their pronunciation is predictable, bearing in mind the tendency (see above) of final consonants to remain silent:

typical words	*pronunciation of final syllable*
pas, mât, chat	[ɑ] or [a]
marcher, marchez, marchais, marchait, baie, valet, mes, fumée	[e] or [ɛ]
nid	[i]
chaud, vaut, faux, sot, tôt, Pernod, dos, croc	[o]
bout, bijoux, sous, boue	[u]
fut, fût, crus, crûs	[y]
queue, heureux, bleus	[ø]
en, vend, vent, an, sang, grand, dans	[ɑ̃]
fin, feint, frein, vain	[ɛ̃]
on, pont, fond, avons	[ɔ̃]
brun, parfum	[œ̃]

V. The time

what time is it?	quelle heure est-il?
it is ...	il est ..., c'est ...
at what time?	à quelle heure?
at ...	à ...

00.00 minuit
00.10 minuit dix
00.15 minuit et quart
00.30 minuit et demie, minuit trente
00.45 une heure moins (le) quart

01.00 une heure du matin
01.10 une heure dix (du matin)
01.15 une heure et quart, une heure quinze
01.30 une heure et demie, une heure trente
01.45 deux heures moins (le) quart, une heure quarante-cinq, une heure trois quarts
01.50 deux heures moins dix, une heure cinquante
01.59 deux heures moins une, une heure cinquante-neuf

12.00 midi, douze heures
12.30 midi et demie, midi trente

13.00 une heure de l'après-midi, treize heures
01.30 une heure et demie (de l'après-midi), une heure trente, treize heures trente

19.00 sept heures du soir, dix-neuf heures
19.30 sept heures et demie (du soir), sept heures trente, dix-neuf heures trente

23.00 onze heures (du soir), vingt-trois heures
23.45 onze heures trois quarts, onze heures quarante-cinq, vingt-trois heures quarante-cinq, minuit moins quart

in 20 minutes	dans vingt minutes
20 minutes ago	il y a vingt minutes
wake me up at 7	réveillez-moi à sept heures
1 hour, 20', 45''	une heure, vingt minutes et quarante-cinq secondes

Dates and numbers

1. The date

what's the date today?	quelle est la date d'aujourd'hui?, quel jour sommes-nous?
it's the ...	nous sommes le ..., c'est le ...
1st of February	premier février
2nd of February	deux février
28th of February	vingt-huit février
he's coming on the 7th (of May)	il vient le sept (mai)

NB: use cardinal numbers except for the first day of the month

I was born in 1945
je suis né en dix-neuf cent quarante-cinq
I was born on the 15th of July 1945
je suis né le quinze juillet dix-neuf cent quarante-cinq

during the sixties	dans les années soixante
in the twentieth century	au vingtième siècle
in May	en mai
on Monday (the 15th)	lundi (quinze)
on Mondays	le lundi
next/last Monday	lundi prochain/dernier
in 10 days' time	dans dix jours

2. Telephone numbers
I would like Paris 334 22 15
j'aimerais Paris trois cent trente-quatre / vingt-deux / quinze
give me Paris 302 02 02
donnez-moi Paris trois cent deux / zéro deux / zéro deux
could you get me Dijon 22 00 79, extension 2233
pouvez-vous m'appeler Dijon vingt-deux / zéro zéro / soixante-dix-neuf, poste vingt-deux / trente-trois
the Geneva prefix is 022
l'indicatif de Genève est zéro / vingt-deux

3. Using numbers

he lives at number 10	il habite au dix
it's in chapter 7, on page 7	c'est au chapitre sept, à la page sept
he lives on the 7th floor	il habite au septième (étage)
he came in 7th	il est arrivé (le) septième
a share of one seventh	une part d'un septième
cale 1:25,000	échelle au vingt-cinq millième

Numbers

1	un(une)	**1st**	premier(première), 1er
2	deux	**2nd**	deuxième, 2e *or* 2ème
3	trois	**3rd**	troisième, 3e *or* 3ème
4	quatre	**4th**	quatrième
5	cinq	**5th**	cinquième
6	six	**6th**	sixième
7	sept	**7th**	septième
8	huit	**8th**	huitième
9	neuf	**9th**	neuvième
10	dix	**10th**	dixième
11	onze	**11th**	onzième
12	douze	**12th**	douzième
13	treize	**13th**	treizième
14	quatorze	**14th**	quatorzième
15	quinze	**15th**	quinzième
16	seize	**16th**	seizième
17	dix-sept	**17th**	dix-septième
18	dix-huit	**18th**	dix-huitième
19	dix-neuf	**19th**	dix-neuvième
20	vingt	**20th**	vingtième
21	vingt et un(une)	**21st**	vingt-et-unième
22	vingt-deux	**22nd**	vingt-deuxième
30	trente	**30th**	trentième
40	quarante	**100th**	centième
50	cinquante	**101st**	cent-unième
60	soixante	**1,000th**	millième
70	soixante-dix		
71	soixante et onze	**1/2**	un demi
72	soixante-douze	**1/3**	un tiers
80	quatre-vingts	**2/3**	deux tiers
81	quatre-vingt-un(-une)	**1/4**	un quart
90	quatre-vingt-dix	**1/5**	un cinquième
91	quatre-vingt-onze		
100	cent	**0.5**	zéro virgule cinq, 0,5
101	cent un(une)	**1.5**	un virgule cinq, 1,5
300	trois cents	**10%**	dix pour cent
301	trois cent un(une)		
1,000	mille, 1 000	**2 + 2**	deux plus deux
1,001	mille un(une)	**2 ÷ 2**	deux divisé par deux
5,000	cinq mille, 5 000	**2 × 2**	deux fois deux
1,000,000	un million	**2 − 2 =**	deux moins deux égale ...

6^2 six au carré, six à la puissance deux; **20 m**^{2} vingt mètres carrés
6^3 six au cube, six à la puissance trois; **20 m**^{3} vingt mètres cubes